CURRENT LAW YEAR BOOK 1987

AUSTRALIA AND NEW ZEALAND
The Law Book Company Ltd.
Sydney : Melbourne : Perth

CANADA AND U.S.A.
The Carswell Company Ltd.
Agincourt, Ontario

INDIA
N. M. Tripathi Private Ltd.
Bombay
and
Eastern Law House Private Ltd.
Calcutta and Delhi
M.P.P. House
Bangalore

ISRAEL
Steimatzky's Agency Ltd.
Jerusalem : Tel Aviv : Haifa

CURRENT LAW YEAR BOOK 1987

Being a Comprehensive Statement of the Law of 1987

Editor in Chief
PETER ALLSOP, C.B.E., M.A.
Barrister

General Editor
KEVAN NORRIS, LL.B.
Solicitor

Assistant General Editors
GILLIAN BRONZE, LL.B.
SUSAN SHUAIB, B.A.

Editors

English Cases:

NICHOLAS BAATZ, M.A., B.C.L., *Barrister*
STEPHEN BRANDON, B.A., LL.M., *Barrister*
REX BRETTEN, Q.C., M.A., LL.B., *Barrister*
CHRISTOPHER BUTLER, LL.B., *Barrister*
JOHN ELVIDGE, M.A., LL.B., *Barrister*
SHAUN FERRIS, B.A., *Barrister*
IAN GOLDSWORTHY, *Barrister*
OLIVER GOODWIN, LL.B., *Barrister*
DAVID GRANT, M.A., LL.B., *Barrister*
CHARLES JOSEPH, B.A., *Barrister*
SIMON LEVENE, M.A., *Barrister*
ANN McALLISTER, B.A., LL.M., *Barrister*
JULIE O'MALLEY, LL.B., *Barrister*
LIONEL PERSEY, LL.B., *Barrister*
ANTHONY PITTS, *Barrister*
CLARE RENTON, *Barrister*
CHARLES SCOTT, LL.B., *Barrister*
ISOBEL SINCLAIR, LL.B., *Solicitor*
JOHN STEPHENS, *Barrister*
PATRICK STEWART, *Barrister*
STEPHEN SUTTLE, M.A., *Barrister*
HELEN TATE, LL.B., *Barrister*
AVTAR VIRDI, *Solicitor*
ROBERT WEBB, LL.B, *Barrister*

European Communities:

ALISON GREEN, LL.M., *Barrister*

Delegated Legislation:

JOHN TATE, LL.B., *Barrister*

Northern Ireland:

FRED MARTIN, LL.B., *Barrister*

Damages Awards:

DAVID KEMP, B.A., *Barrister*
DERRICK TURRIFF, *Barrister*

Commonwealth Cases and Articles:

ANDREW BURR, M.A., *Barrister*

LONDON
SWEET & MAXWELL LTD. STEVENS & SONS LTD.
1988

The Mode of Citation

of the Current Law Year Book

is *e.g.*:

[1987] C.L.Y. 1282

ISBN: This volume only: 0 421 40160 5
with Citators : 0 421 40150 8

Published in 1988 by
Sweet & Maxwell Limited of
11 New Fetter Lane, London,
and printed in Great Britain
by The Eastern Press Limited
of London and Reading

PREFACE

This volume completes forty-one years of Current Law publishing. It supersedes the monthly issues of *Current Law* for 1987 and covers the law from January 1 to December 31 of that year.

Citators

The Case Citator and the Statute Citator are contained in separate volumes, issued with this volume.

The *Current Law Citators* cover cases during the years 1977–87 and statutes during the period 1972–87. There are permanent bound volumes covering cases during the period 1947–76 and statutes during 1947–71.

The present volume contains a table of cases digested and reported in 1987 and the usual tables covering 1987 Statutory Instruments and their effect on the orders of earlier years and a table of Northern Ireland Statutory Rules and Orders.

Books and Articles

Indices of the books and articles published in 1987 are included at the back of this volume. The full title, reference and the name of the author is given in each case and both indices are arranged under Current Law headings.

Index

The Subject-matter Index in this volume follows the new improved format introduced at the beginning of 1987 in the monthly digest. It will be cumulative from 1987 onwards. The thirty-year Index from 1947–76 may be found in the 1976 *Year Book*. The Index for the years 1972–86 may be found in the 1986 *Year Book*.

Statutes and Orders

Fifty-seven Acts received the Royal Assent during the year. A complete list of Statutes appears under the title Statutes and Orders.

Alphabetical and numerical lists of the Statutory Instruments of 1987 are contained in this volume, together with a table showing the affect of the 1987 Instruments on previous delegated legislation.

Cases

The number of cases digested exceeds 2,500. This figure does not include the short reports showing what damages have been awarded in cases of injury or death. These decisions have been collected and edited by Mr. David Kemp and Mr. Derrick Turriff. The Quantum of Damages Table at the front of this volume provides a guide to the personal injury decisions reported in 1987.

The *Year Book* again includes a selection of cases of persuasive force from the Scottish courts and the courts of the Commonwealth and from the

English county courts. It also includes a section on the law of the European Communities.

Court of Appeal

As a service to the profession *Current Law* continues the publication of brief notes of decisions of the Court of Appeal (Civil Division) which have not hitherto been reported but whose transcripts are available in the Supreme Court Library at the Royal Courts of Justice. These reports are to be found throughout the *Year Book* under the relevant subject heading. The abbreviation C.A.T. (Court of Appeal Transcript) at the end of the report identifies such case notes. *Current Law* is indebted to Mr. Avtar S. Virdi, *Solicitor*, who has prepared the notes of the details of the cases. Transcripts of these cases were previously available in the Bar Library.

Northern Ireland

All Northern Irish Acts and Orders and the cases reported from the courts of Northern Ireland have been digested together with a selection of the cases reported from the courts of the Republic of Ireland. This work has been carried out by our editor in Northern Ireland, Mr. S. F. R. Martin.

Cases "ex relatione"

We welcome short reports of cases submitted by members of both branches of the legal profession. They are noted as "*ex rel.* A.B., Barrister" or "*ex rel.* C.D., Solicitors," as the case may be. These reports, we believe, are of considerable value to the profession since the contributor can properly be regarded as having first hand knowledge of the facts. Unfortunately, occasional instances have recently been brought to our notice in which reports of this kind have been misleading or even incorrect. We are grateful to those who bring such matters to our attention and we seek to correct the report in a later issue or in the "*Current Law Year Book.*" We must stress, however, that we are entirely dependent on the contributor for the accuracy of his or her report. It is impracticable for us independently to check the facts stated to us.

The General Editor thanks those who have pointed out errors and have sent in notes of interesting cases.

May 1988. P. A.

CONTENTS

Preface 5

Digest Headings in Use 9

Table of Cases 11

Table of Damages for Personal Injuries or Death 47

Alphabetical Table of Statutory Instruments 1987 51

Numerical Table of Statutory Instruments 1986–87 81

Table of S.R. & O. and S.I. Affected in 1987 93

Alphabetical Table of Northern Ireland S.R. & O. 1987 105

Numerical Table of Northern Ireland S.R. & O. 1987 115

Table of Abbreviations 119

Dates of Commencement 123

The Law of 1987 Digested under Titles:

Administrative Law, § 1
Agency, § 55
Agriculture, § 71
Animals, § 102
Arbitration, § 119
Armed Forces, § 158
Atomic Energy, § 168
Aviation, § 171

Bailment, § 183
Banking, § 185
Bankruptcy, § 206
British Commonwealth, § 216
Building and Construction, § 222
Building Societies, § 246
Burial and Cremation, § 268

Capital Gains Tax, § 269
Capital Transfer Tax, § 283
Carriers, § 286
Charities, § 292
Civil Defence, § 301
Civil Liberties, § 304
Clubs and Associations, § 306
Commons, § 315
Company Law, § 317
Compulsory Purchase, § 386
Conflict of Laws, § 397
Constitutional Law, § 410
Consumer Credit, § 411
Contract, § 412
Conveyancing, § 458
Copyright, § 496
Coroners, § 532
Corporation Tax, § 541
Criminal Evidence and Procedure, § 556
Criminal Law, § 751
Criminal Sentencing, § 854
Customs and Excise, § 1101

Damages, § 1125

Easements and Prescriptions, § 1231
Ecclesiastical Law, § 1238
Education, § 1247
Election Law, § 1277
Electricity, § 1284
Emergency Laws, § 1289
Employment, § 1293
Equity and Trusts, § 1420
Estoppel, § 1441
European Communities, § 1451
Evidence (Civil), § 1668
Executors and Administrators, § 1689
Extradition, § 1693

Family, § 1707
Fire Service, § 1792
Firearms and Explosives, § 1794
Fish and Fisheries, § 1798
Food and Drugs, § 1806
Foreign Jurisdictions, § 1819
Forestry, § 1823
Fraud, Misrepresentation and Undue Influence, § 1825

CONTENTS

Gaming and Wagering, § 1831
Gas, § 1839
Guarantee and Indemnity, § 1840

Health and Safety at Work, § 1848
Housing, § 1862
Human Rights, § 1908

Immigration, § 1920
Income Tax, § 2000
Industrial and Friendly Societies, § 2041
Inheritance Tax, § 2045
Insurance, § 2050
International Law, § 2080

Juries, § 2099

Land Charges, § 2107
Landlord and Tenant, § 2112
Law Reform, § 2253
Legal Aid, § 2279
Libel and Slander, § 2296
Licensing, § 2307
Lien, § 2320
Limitation of Actions, § 2321
Literary and Scientific Institutions, § 2338
Local Government, § 2343
London, § 2393

Medicine, § 2397
Mental Health, § 2419
Mining Law, § 2427
Minors, § 2432
Mortgages, § 2537

National Health, § 2545
Negligence, § 2560
Northern Ireland, § 2622
Nuisance, § 2756

Parliament, § 2760
Partnership, § 2767
Patents and Designs, § 2769
Pensions and Superannuation, § 2816
Petroleum, § 2846
Police, § 2852
Practice, § 2872
Prisons, § 3138
Public Entertainments and Recreation, § 3145
Public Health, § 3149

Rating and Valuation, § 3156
Registration of Births, Deaths and Marriages, § 3199
Revenue and Finance, § 3205
Road Traffic, § 3227

Sale of Goods, § 3312
Sea and Seashore, § 3347
Shipping and Marine Insurance, § 3358
Shops, Markets and Fairs, § 3448
Social Security, § 3451
Solicitors, § 3545
Stamp Duties, § 3563
Statutes and Orders, § 3566
Stock Exchange, § 3569

Telecommunications, § 3571
Tort, § 3580
Town and Country Planning, § 3594
Trade and Industry, § 3729
Trade Marks and Trade Names, § 3741
Trade Unions, § 3759
Transport, § 3773
Trespass, § 3794

Value Added Tax, § 3797

Water and Waterworks, § 3865
Weights and Measures, § 3871
Wills and Succession, § 3877
Words and Phrases, § 3886

BOOKS AND ARTICLES:

Books ... ... [1]

Index of Articles ... ... [24]

INDEX ... ... [65]

DIGEST HEADINGS IN USE

Administrative Law
Agency
Agriculture
Aliens
Animals
Arbitration
Armed Forces
Atomic Energy
Aviation

Bailment (*England/U.K.*)
Banking
Bankruptcy
British Commonwealth
Building and Construction
Building Societies
Burial and Cremation

Capital Gains Tax (*Scotland: see Capital Taxation*)
Capital Taxation (*Scotland*)
Capital Transfer Tax (*England/U.K.*)
Carriers
Charities
Children and Young Persons (*Scotland*)
Civil Defence
Civil Liberties
Clubs and Associations
Commons (*England/U.K.*)
Company Law
Compulsory Purchase
Conflict of Laws
Constitutional Law
Consumer Credit
Contract
Conveyancing (*England/U.K.*)
Copyright
Coroners (*England/U.K.*)
Corporation Tax
Criminal Evidence and Procedure
Criminal Law
Criminal Sentencing
Customs and Excise

Damages
Divorce and Consistorial Causes (*Scotland*)
Donation (*Scotland*)

Easements and Prescription (*England/U.K.*)
Ecclesiastical Law
Education
Election Law
Electricity
Emergency Laws
Employment
Equity and Trusts (*England/U.K.*)
Estoppel (*England/U.K.*)
European Communities
Evidence (Civil)
Executors and Administrators
Expenses (*Scotland*)
Extradition

Family (*England/U.K.*)
Fire Service
Firearms and Explosives
Fish and Fisheries
Food and Drugs
Forestry
Foreign Jurisdictions
Fraud, Misrepresentation and Undue Influence

Gaming and Wagering
Gas
Guarantee and Indemnity

Health and Safety at Work
Heritable Property and Conveyancing (*Scotland*)
Highways and Bridges (*Scotland*)
Housing
Human Rights
Husband and Wife (*Scotland*)

Immigration
Income Tax
Industrial and Friendly Societies
Inheritance Tax (*Scotland: see Capital Taxation*)
Insurance
International Law
Intoxicating Liquors (*Scotland*)

Juries
Jurisdiction (*Scotland*)
Jurisprudence
Justices of the Peace (*Scotland*)

Land Charges (*England/U.K.*)
Landlord and Tenant
Law Reform
Legal Aid (*Scotland: see Expenses; Practice*)
Legal History
Libel and Slander
Licensing (*England/U.K.*)
Lien
Limitation of Actions
Literary and Scientific Institutions
Local Government
London

Medicine
Mental Health
Mining Law
Minors (*England/U.K.*)
Money (*Scotland*)
Mortgages (*England/U.K.*)

National Health
Negligence
Northern Ireland
Nuisance

Parent and Child (*Scotland*)
Parliament
Partnership
Patents and Designs
Peerages and Dignities (*Scotland*)
Pensions and Superannuation
Personal Bar (*Scotland*)
Petroleum
Police
Post Office
Practice (Civil)
Prescription (*Scotland*)
Press
Prisons
Private Legislation Procedure (*Scotland*)
Public Entertainments and Recreation
Public Health

Rating and Valuation
Registers and Records (*Scotland*)
Registration of Births, Deaths and Marriages
Revenue and Finance
Reparation (*Scotland*)
Rights in Security (*Scotland*)
Road Traffic

DIGEST OF HEADINGS IN USE

Sale of Goods
Sea and Seashore
Sheriff Court Practice (*Scotland*)
Shipping and Marine Insurance
Shops, Markets and Fairs
Small Landholder (*Scotland*)
Social Security
Solicitors
Stamp Duties
Statutes and Orders
Stock Exchange
Succession (*Scotland*)

Telecommunications
Time (*Scotland*)
Tort (*England/U.K.*)

Town and Country Planning
Trade and Industry
Trade Marks and Trade Names
Trade Unions
Transport
Trespass (*England/U.K.*)
Trusts (*Scotland*)

Value Added Tax

Water and Waterworks
Weights and Measures
Wills (*Scotland*)
Wills and Succession (*England/U.K.*)
Words and Phrases

TABLE OF CASES

PARA.

A. (A MINOR) (ADOPTION: PARENTAL CONSENT), *Re* ... 2447
A. (CHILD IN CARE: WARDSHIP), *Re* ... 2520
A. *v.* A ... 2486
A *v.* A.; A. (A MINOR), *Re* ... 2536
A. *v.* B ... 2974
A.E. REALISATIONS (1985), *Re* ... 381
A.G.A. ESTATE AGENCIES, *Re* ... 338
AMEV-UDC FINANCE *v.* AUSTIN ... 439
A.P.D. INSULATIONS (GROUP) *v.* CUSTOMS AND EXCISE COMMISSIONERS ... 3843
ABBAS *v.* RUDOLFER ... 3046
ABBEY HOMESTEADS (DEVELOPMENTS) *v.* NORTHAMPTONSHIRE COUNTY COUNCIL ... 386
ABELS *v.* ADMINISTRATIVE BOARD OF THE BEDRIJFSVERENIGING VOOR DE METAAL-INDUSTRIE EN DE ELECTROTECHNISCHE INDUSTRIE (No. 135/83) ... 1528
ABERDEEN CITY DISTRICT COUNCIL *v.* SECRETARY OF STATE FOR SCOTLAND ... 3622
ABRAMS *v.* COOK ... 1158
ACTION S.A. *v.* BRITANNIC SHIPPING CORP.; AEGIS BRITANNIC, THE ... 3445
ADAMS *v.* ROWCLIFFE ... 1188
ADAMS & ADAMS *v.* RILEY (M.G.) ... 2949
ADAMSON *v.* CHIEF ADJUDICATION OFFICER ... 3503
ADDIS *v.* CLEMENT (V.O.) ... 3185
ADDISON *v.* BABCOCK F.A.T.A. ... 1388
ADOLF LEONHARDT, THE. *See* PAGNAN (R) & FRATELLI *v.* FINAGRAIN COMPAGNIE COMMERCIALE AGRICOLE ET FINANCIERE S.A.; ADOLF LEONHARDT, THE
ADOPTION APPLICATION (PAYMENT FOR ADOPTION), *Re*, ... 2450
ADOPTION APPLICATION: SURROGACY AA212/86. *See* ADOPTION APPLICATION (PAYMENT FOR ADOPTION), *Re*
ADVANCE DRILLING & GROUTING *v.* BRIAN HAULAGE ... 69
ADVANCE PAYMENT OF BUDGET CONTRIBUTIONS, *Re*: E.C. COMMISSION *v.* U.K. (No. 93/185) ... 1477
AEGIS BRITANNIC, THE. *See* ACTION S.A. *v.* BRITANNIC SHIPPING CORP.; AEGIS BRITANNIC, THE
AGREEMENT BETWEEN AUSTIN ROVER GROUP & UNIPART GROUP, *Re* ... 1481
AGREEMENT BETWEEN GERMAN PASTA MANUFACTURERS, *Re*, (No. IV/31.682) ... 1482
AGREEMENTS OF ENTE NAZIONALE IDROCABURI (ENI) AND MONTEDISON SpA, *Re* ... 1483
AGRICOLA COMMERCIALE OLIO Srl *v.* E.C. COMMISSION (No. 232/81) ... 1464
AGRICULTURAL PRODUCER GROUPS, *Re*: E.C. COMMISSION *v.* ITALY (No. 272/83) ... 1461
AHMED *v.* KENDRICK ... 470
AINLEY *v.* SECRETARY OF STATE FOR THE ENVIRONMENT AND FYLDE BOROUGH COUNCIL ... 3644

PARA.

AINSBURY *v.* MILLINGTON ... 2886
AINSCOUGH *v.* AINSCOUGH (CEDAR HOLDINGS INTERVENING) ... 1781
AINSWORTH *v.* E.C. COMMISSION AND COUNCIL OF THE EUROPEAN COMMUNITIES (Nos. 271/83; 15, 36, 113, 158, 203/84 AND 13/85) ... 1613
AIR ECOSSE *v.* CIVIL AVIATION AUTHORITY ... 342
AKTION MARITIME CORP. OF LIBERIA *v.* KASMAS (S.) & BROTHERS; AKTION, THE ... 3426
AKTION, THE. *See* AKTION MARITIME CORP. OF LIBERIA *v.* KASMAS (S.) & BROTHERS; AKTION, THE
AKZO CHEMIE BV *v.* E.C. COMMISSION (No. 62/86R) ... 1611
AKZO CHEMIE BV *v.* E.C. COMMISSION (ENGINEERING & CHEMICAL SUPPLIES (EPSOM & GLOUCESTER) INTERVENING) (No. 53/85) ... 1509
AL BIDA, THE. *See* ARAB MARITIME PETROLEUM TRANSPORT CO. *v.* LUXOR TRADING CORP AND GEOGAS ENTERPRISE S.A.; AL BIDA, THE
ALDIS S.A. *v.* CHABRAND (ANDRE) ... 1589
ALDRED *v.* NACANCO ... 1367
ALEXION HOPE, THE. *See* SCHIFFSHYPOTHEKENBANK ZU LUEBECK A.G. *v.* COMPTON (NORMAN PHILIP); ALEXION HOPE, THE
AL-FAYED *v.* AL-TAJIR ... 2297
ALGAR *v.* SHAW ... 2331
ALGHUSSEIN ESTABLISHMENT *v.* ETON COLLEGE ... 433
AL-KANDARI *v.* BROWN (J. R.) & CO ... 3557
ALLEN *v.* AVON RUBBER CO ... 1333
ALLEN & HANBURY *v.* GENERICS (U.K.) AND GIST BROCADES; BROCADES (GREAT BRITAIN); BEECHAM GROUP; COMPTROLLER GENERAL OF PATENTS ... 2804
ALLEN & HANBURY'S (SALBUTAMOL) PATENT ... 2803
ALLETTE *v.* ALLETTE ... 2438
ALLIED ARAB BANK *v.* HAJJAR ... 3137
ALLIED CORP. *v.* E.C. COUNCIL (E.C. COMMISSION INTERVENING) (No. 53/83) ... 1467
ALPINE BULK TRANSPORT CO. INC. *v.* SAUDI EAGLE SHIPPING CO. INC.; SAUDI EAGLE, THE ... 3044
ALTON HOUSE HOLDINGS *v.* CALFLANE (MANAGEMENT) ... 2175
ALUWIHARE (V.O.) *v.* M.F.I. PROPERTIES (LVC/121/1986) ... 3163
AMERSHAM INTERNATIONAL *v.* CORNING ... 2793
AMOCO OIL CO. *v.* PARPADA SHIPPING CO.; GEORGE S., THE ... 3378
AMOS *v.* D.P.P ... 669
AMUSAN *v.* TAUSSIG ... 2251
AN BORD BAINNE CO-OPERATIVE *v.* MILK MARKETING BOARD ... 1473
ANCHOR BREWHOUSE DEVELOPMENTS *v.* BERKLEY HOUSE (DOCKLANDS) DEVELOPMENT ... 3794

TABLE OF CASES

PARA.

ANEMONE, THE. *See* CLIPPER MARITIME *v.* SHIRLSTAR CONTAINER TRANSPORT; ANEMONE, THE
ANNA CH., THE. *See* ISLAMIC REPUBLIC OF IRAN SHIPPING LINES *v.* ROYAL BANK OF SCOTLAND; ANNA OF CH., THE
ANNUAL REVIEW 1986–87 2973
ANSELL *v.* SWIFT 753
ANTARES, THE (Nos. 1 AND 2). *See* KENYA RAILWAYS *v.* ANTARES CO. PTE.; ANTARES, THE (Nos. 1 AND 2)
ANTARES, THE (No. 2). *See* KENYA RAILWAYS *v.* ANTARES CO. PTE; ANTARES, THE (No. 2)
ANTCLIZO, THE. *See* FOOD CORP. OF INDIA *v.* ANTCLIZO SHIPPING CORP.; ANTCLIZO, THE
ANTERIST *v.* CRÉDIT LYONNAIS (No. 22/83). 1550
ANTHONY *v.* ANTHONY 1744
ANTHONY McNICHOLL *v.* MINISTER FOR AGRICULTURE. *See* McNICHOLL (ANTHONY) *v.* MINISTER FOR AGRICULTURE
AOKI'S APPLICATION 2778
APOLLONIUS, THE. *See* MAFRACHT *v.* PARNES SHIPPING CO. S.A.; APOLLONIUS, THE
APPEAL OF MAUDSLEY (V.O.), *Re* (LVC/184/1982) 3164
APPLETON *v.* ASPIN 2189
APPLICATION DES GAZ'S APPLICATION 2776
APPLICATION OF THE IRISH BANKS' STANDING COMMITTEE, *Re* (No. IV/31.362) 1486
APPLICATION OF WÜNSCHE HANDELSGESELLSCHAFT, *Re* 1511
AQUILA DESIGN (GRP) PRODUCTS *v.* CORNHILL INSURANCE 2952
ARAB MARITIME PETROLEUM TRANSPORT CO. *v.* LUXOR TRADING CORP. AND GEOGAS ENTERPRISE S.A.; AL BIDA, THE 3433
ARADI *v.* IMMIGRATION OFFICER, HEATHROW 1954
ARAMIS, THE 3379
ARCHITAL LUXFER *v.* DUNNING (A.J.) & SON (WEYHILL) 3103
ARGYLL STORES *v.* ORKNEY AND SHETLAND ASSESSOR 3161
ARNOLD *v.* CENTRAL ELECTRICITY GENERATING BOARD 2337
ARRAS, THE AND HOEGH ROVER, THE. *See* FOOD CORP. OF INDIA *v.* MOSVOLDS REDERI A/S; ARRAS, THE AND HOEGH ROVER, THE
ARTHUR *v.* STRINGER 964
ARUN DISTRICT COUNCIL *v.* ARGYLE STORES 1810
ASHBURN ANSTALT *v.* ARNOLD & CO. 2247
ASHTON *v.* SOBELMAN 2193
ASHVILLE INVESTMENTS *v.* ELMER CONTRACTORS 140
ASHWORTH (INSPECTOR OF TAXES) *v.* MAINLAND CAR DELIVERIES 554
ASLAM *v.* SINGH 2928
ASOCIACÍON PROVINCIAL DE ARMADORES DE BUQUES DE PESCA DE GRAN SOL DE PONTEVEDRA (ARPOSOL) *v.* E.C. COUNCIL (No. 55/86R) 1609
ASPIN *v.* ESTILL (INSPECTOR OF TAXES) 2001

PARA.

ASSOCIATED NEWSPAPERS GROUP *v.* INSERT MEDIA; EXPRESS NEWSPAPERS *v.* ARNOLD 3034
ASSOCIATED NEWSPAPERS GROUP *v.* NEWS GROUP NEWSPAPERS 506
ASSOCIATION OF UNIVERSITY TEACHERS *v.* UNIVERSITY OF NEWCASTLE-UPON-TYNE 1357
ASSOCIAZIONE BANCARIA ITALIANA, *Re* (No. IV/31.356) 1487
ATARI IRELAND AND ATARI INC. *v.* VALADON (ALAIN) 521
ATKINS INTERNATIONAL H.A. OF VADUZ *v.* ISLAMIC REPUBLIC OF IRAN SHIPPING LINES 3387
ATKINSON *v.* FITZWALTER 3081
ATTIA *v.* BRITISH GAS 2608
ATT.-GEN. *v.* ARTHUR ANDERSEN & CO. 3095
ATT.-GEN. *v.* CHANNEL FOUR TELEVISION CO. 3026
ATT.-GEN. *v.* COCKE 2323
ATT.-GEN. *v.* GUARDIAN NEWSPAPERS; SAME *v.* OBSERVER; SAME *v.* TIMES NEWSPAPERS 3023
ATT.-GEN. *v.* HARTE (J. D.) 537
ATT.-GEN. *v.* INDEPENDENT, THE. *See* ATT.-GEN. *v.* NEWSPAPER PUBLISHING.
ATT.-GEN. *v.* NEWSPAPER PUBLISHING 2923
ATT.-GEN. *v.* OBSERVER, THE; ATT.-GEN *v* GUARDIAN NEWSPAPERS; APPLICATION BY DERBYSHIRE COUNTY COUNCIL, *Re* .. 2364
ATT.-GEN. OF HONG KONG *v.* CHAN NAI-KEUNG (DANIEL) 838
ATT.-GEN OF HONG KONG *v.* HUMPHREYS ESTATE (QUEEN'S GARDENS) 1443
ATT.-GEN. OF HONG KONG *v.* WONG MUK PING 622
ATT.-GEN. OF HONG KONG *v.* YIP KAI-FOON 579
AUSTRALIAN SAFEWAY STORES PTY *v.* ZALUZNA 2611
AVANT PETROLEUM INC. *v.* GATOIL OVERSEAS INC. 3071
AZIZ *v.* TRINITY STREET TAXIS 1348
AZO-MASCHINENFABRIK ADOLF ZIMMERMAN GmbH *v.* CUSTOMS AND EXCISE COMMISSIONERS 3827

B. (A MINOR), *Re* 2532
B. (A MINOR) (STERILISATION). *See* B. (A MINOR) (WARDSHIP: STERILISATION), *Re*
B. (A MINOR) (WARDSHIP: STERILISATION), *Re* 2533
B. (COURT OF PROTECTION: NOTICE OF PROCEEDINGS), *Re* 2422
B. (MINORS), *Re*, ... 2467
B.P. PETROLEUM DEVELOPMENT *v.* RYDER 2847
B.P. PROPERTIES *v.* BUCKLER 2324
B. & Q. (RETAIL) *v.* DUDLEY METROPOLITAN BOROUGH COUNCIL 3450
BABCOCK F.A.T.A. *v.* ADDISON. *See* ADDISON *v.* BABCOCK F.A.T.A.
BACON *v.* JACK TIGHE (OFFSHORE) AND CAPE SCAFFOLDING 2568
BADKIN *v.* CHIEF CONSTABLE OF SOUTH YORKSHIRE 3281
BALDWIN *v.* TAMESIDE TRAVEL 1148
BALJINDER SINGH *v.* HAMMOND 1959
BALL *v.* PICKEN (BT/65/1986) 2685

TABLE OF CASES

PARA.

BALSTON *v.* HEADLINE FILTERS 1293
BALTIC LEASING *v.* CUSTOMS AND EXCISE COMMISSIONERS 3854
BAMCELL, THE (NOTE). *See* CENTURY INSURANCE CO. OF CANADA *v.* CASE EXISTOLOGICAL LABORATORIES; BAMCELL, THE (NOTE)
BANK GUARANTEE, A, *Re* 1553
BANK OF BARODA *v.* PANESSAR 326
BANKERS TRUST CO. *v.* GALADARI; CHASE MANHATTAN BANK N.A. (INTERVENER) ... 3004
BANKING INSURANCE AND FINANCE UNION *v.* BARCLAYS BANK 1383
BANQUE KEYSER ULLMANN S.A. *v.* SKANDIA (U.K.) INSURANCE CO. 2052
BAPTIST UNION CORP. *v.* SECRETARY OF STATE FOR THE ENVIRONMENT AND ST. ALBANS DISTRICT COUNCIL 3649
BARBER *v.* BARBER 1729
BARCLAYS BANK *v.* ANDERSON 1673
BARCLAYS BANK *v.* FORRESTER 2537
BARCLAYS BANK *v.* GERDES (V.O.) 3165
BARCLAYS BANK *v.* WILLOWBROOK INTERNATIONAL 1423
BARDER *v.* BARDER (CALUORI INTERVENING) 1746
BARDER *v.* CALUORI. *See* BARDER *v.* BARDER (CALUORI INTERVENING)
BAREMEDA ENTERPRISES PTY. *v.* O'CONNOR (RONALD PATRICK) AND K.F.V. FISHERIES (OLD) PTY; TIRUNA AND PELORUS, THE 3392
BARLEE MARINE CORP. *v.* TREVOR REX MOUNTAIN; LEEGAS, THE 3406
BARNES *v.* NAYER 3795
BARNET *v.* CROZIER 2301
BARNETT *v.* FIELDHOUSE 3285
BARR *v.* SOUTHERN HEALTH AND SOCIAL SERVICES BOARD 2711
BARRETT *v.* INDEPENDENT NEWSPAPERS .. 2299
BARRETTS & BAIRD (WHOLESALE) *v.* INSTITUTION OF PROFESSIONAL CIVIL SERVANTS 3769
BARTON *v.* UNIGATE DAIRIES 1809
BASHAM, (DEC'D), *Re* 1444
BASS HOLDINGS *v.* MORTON MUSIC 2156
BASSET *v.* SOCIETE DES AUTEURS, COMPOSITEURS ET EDITEURS DE MUSIQUE (SACEM) (No. 402/85) 1505
BATCHELOR *v.* BRITISH RAILWAYS BOARD 1396
BATH PRESS *v.* ROSE 3101
BATTY *v.* SOUTHERN COUNTIES STORAGE . 1201
BAYLINER MARINE CORP. *v.* DORAL BOATS 503
BAYLIS (INSPECTOR OF TAXES) *v.* GREGORY 270
BEANEY *v.* BRANCHETT 2243
BEAUCHAMP (INSPECTOR OF TAXES) *v.* WOOLWORTH (F.W.) 548
BECKFORD *v.* THE QUEEN 825
BEETS-PROPER *v.* F. VAN LANSCHOT BANKIERS N.V. (No. 262/84) 1637
BELGIAN PROPERTY TAX ON COMMUNITY OFFICIALS, *Re*: E.C. COMMISSION *v.* BELGIUM (No. 85/85) 1510
BELL *v.* CANTERBURY CITY COUNCIL (Ref. No. 166/1985) 3724
BELL CONCORD EDUCATIONAL TRUST *v.* CUSTOMS AND EXCISE COMMISSIONERS 3828
BELTON *v.* BELTON 2492

PARA.

BENARTY, THE 3098
BENESCH *v.* NEWMAN. *See* NEWMAN *v.* BENESCH
BENNET *v.* GOWER-SMITH 1192
BENNETTS OF SHEFFIELD *v.* CUSTOMS AND EXCISE COMMISSIONERS 3846
BERG *v.* TRAFFORD BOROUGH COUNCIL 1897
BERKELEY JACKSON *v.* STEPHENS 2964
BERNSTEIN *v.* PAMSON MOTORS (GOLDERS GREEN) 3335
BERTINI *v.* REGIONE LAZIO (No. 98/85, 162/85, 258/85) 1534
BEST TRAVEL CO. *v.* PATTERSON 843
BESTWORTH *v.* WEARWELL 514
BESWICK *v.* THE QUEEN 688
BETTERWARE PRODUCTS *v.* CUSTOMS AND EXCISE COMMISSIONERS 3849
BHADRA *v.* ELLAM (INSPECTOR OF TAXES) 2030
BHOGAL *v.* PUNJAB NATIONAL BANK 199
BIBBY BULK CARRIERS *v.* CANSULEX 2996
BILKA-KAUFHAUS GmbH *v.* WEBER VON HARTZ (No. 170/84) 1633
BIOVILAC S.A. *v.* E.C. COMMISSION (No. 59/83) 1455
BIRD *v.* BIRDS EYE WALLS 2878
BIRD *v.* I.R.C. 2038
BIRD SEMPLE & CRAWFORD HERRON *v.* CUSTOMS AND EXCISE COMMISSIONERS 3847
BIRMINGHAM DISTRICT COUNCIL *v.* McMAHON 2758
BISSESSAR v. GHOSN 2190
BISSETT *v.* MARWIN SECURITIES 2205
BLISS *v.* SOUTH EAST THAMES REGIONAL HEALTH AUTHORITY 1303
BLOCK *v.* NICHOLSON (T/A LIMASCUE STUD) 3064
BLOMQUIST *v.* ATT.-GEN. OF THE COMMONWEALTH OF DOMINICA 1819
BLUE CIRCLE *v.* HOLLAND DREDGING CO. (U.K.) 132
BLUNDEN *v.* GRAVELLE 844
BLYTH *v.* BLOOMSBURY HEALTH AUTHORITY 1677
BOARD *v.* CHECKLAND 1731
BOBOLAS *v.* ECONOMIST NEWSPAPER 3091
BOGDAL *v.* HALL 701
BOLDMARK *v.* COHEN AND COHEN 2233
BOLHAH *v.* JIGWOOD SECURITIES CONTINUATION 2170
BOLTON BOROUGH COUNCIL *v.* SECRETARY OF STATE FOR THE ENVIRONMENT AND BARRATT'S (MANCHESTER) 3686
BOOT (HENRY) BUILDING *v.* CROYDON HOTEL AND LEISURE CO. 438
BOOTS CO. *v.* LEES-COLLIER 1411
BORDEN (U.K.) *v.* POTTER 1318
BORG-WARNER CORP'S PATENT 2812
BOSTOCK *v.* DE LA PAGERIE. *See* BOSTOCK *v.* TACHER DE LA PAGERIE
BOSTOCK *v.* TACHER DE LA PAGERIE 2191
BOTT (E) *v.* PRICE (INSPECTOR OF TAXES) .. 551
BOWEN *v.* BOWEN 2927
BOWERS (DUDLEY) AMUSEMENTS ENTERPRISES *v.* SECRETARY OF STATE FOR THE ENVIRONMENT 3604
BOZANO *v.* FRANCE (No. 5/985/91/138) 1911
BRADFORD METROPOLITAN CITY COUNCIL *v.* BROWN 3027

TABLE OF CASES

PARA.

BRADFORD METROPOLITAN CITY COUNCIL *v.* SECRETARY OF STATE FOR THE ENVIRONMENT 3676
BRADLEY *v.* PORTAS 1681
BRADSHAW *v.* UNIVERSITY COLLEGE OF WALES, ABERYSTWYTH 293
BRADY *v.* BRADY 337
BRADY (INSPECTOR OF TAXES) *v.* GROUP LOTUS CAR COMPANIES 541
BRAY (INSPECTOR OF TAXES) *v.* BEST 2031
BREDA-GEOMINERARIA *v.* E.C. COMMISSION (No. 231/86R) 1606
BREEZE *v.* ELDEN & HYDE 2120
BRENT LONDON BOROUGH COUNCIL AND ALLOYDE 3669
BRESLIN *v.* DU PONT (U.K.) 2671
BRETT *v.* BRETT ESSEX GOLF CLUB 2215
BRIAN COOPER & CO. *v.* FAIRVIEW ESTATES (INVESTMENTS). *See* COOPER (BRIAN) & CO. *v.* FAIRVIEW ESTATES (INVESTMENTS)
BRIDGEN *v.* LANCASHIRE COUNTY COUNCIL 1299
BRIDGETT *v.* GREEN (V.O.) (LVC/468/1985) 3166
BRINK'S-MAT *v.* ELCOMBE 3021
BRINNAND *v.* EWENS 1448
BRISTOL CITY COUNCIL *v.* SECRETARY OF STATE FOR THE ENVIRONMENT AND WILLIAMSON (H.M.) 3638
BRISTOW *v.* CITY PETROLEUM 1306
BRITISH AMERICAN TOBACCO CO. AND REYNOLDS (R.J.) INDUSTRIES INC. *v.* E.C. COMMISSION (PHILIP MORRIS INC. AND REMBRANDT GROUP INTERVENING) (Nos. 142/84 and 156/84) 1490
BRITISH AMUSEMENT CATERING TRADES ASSOCIATION *v.* WESTMINSTER CITY COUNCIL 2310
BRITISH ASSOCIATION OF ADVISERS AND LECTURERS IN PHYSICAL EDUCATION *v.* NATIONAL UNION OF TEACHERS 313
BRITISH CAR AUCTIONS *v.* JACKSON 2894
BRITISH LEYLAND *v.* E.C. COMMISSION (MERSON INTERVENING) (No. 226/84) 1480
BRITISH PUBLISHING CO. *v.* FRASER 1317
BRITISH RAIL PENSION TRUSTEE CO. *v.* CARDSHOPS 2226
BRITTON (VICTOR) *v.* CUSTOMS AND EXCISE COMMISSIONERS 3819
BRODERICK, *Re* 2644
BRODT *v.* WELLS GENERAL COMMISSIONERS AND I.R.C. 3224
BROMILLEY *v.* BROMILLEY 1759
BROMLEY *v.* QUICK (H. & J.) 1323
BROOKER SETTLED ESTATES *v.* AYERS 2159
BROOME *v.* PERKINS 3266
BROUGHTON PARK TEXTILES (SALFORD) *v.* COMMERCIAL UNION ASSURANCE CO. .. 2054
BROWN *v.* STOCKTON-ON-TEES BOROUGH COUNCIL 1409
BROWN (IAN KEITH) *v.* C.B.S. (CONTRACTORS) 120
BRUCE (ROBERT) & PARTNERS *v.* WINYARD DEVELOPMENTS 61
BRYANT *v.* BEST 2181
BRYCE *v.* SWAN HUNTER GROUP 2562
BUFFERY *v.* BUFFERY 1711

PARA.

BUGDAYCAY *v.* SECRETARY OF STATE FOR THE HOME DEPARTMENT; NELIDOW SANTIS *v.* SAME; NORMAN *v.* SAME; MUSISI, *Re* 1989
BULK TRANSPORT GROUP SHIPPING CO. *v.* SEACRYSTAL SHIPPING; KYZIKOS, THE 3405
BULLIVANT (ROGER) *v.* ELLIS 1294
BURCHELL *v.* ADJUDICATION OFFICER (No. 377/85) 1641
BURKE *v.* BURKE 1779
BURMAN (INSPECTOR OF TAXES) *v.* WESTMINSTER PRESS 276
BURNET *v.* FRANCIS INDUSTRIES 3002
BURTON *v.* BURTON 1752
BURTON *v.* TIMMIS 76
BUSH TRANSPORT *v.* NELSON 2157
BUSINESS COMPUTERS INTERNATIONAL *v.* REGISTRAR OF COMPANIES 2582
BUSINESS TRANSFER LEGISLATION, *Re*: E.C. COMMISSION *v.* ITALY (No. 235/84) .. 1520
BUTLER (EDWARD) VINTNERS *v.* GRANGE SEYMOUR INTERNATIONALE 3028
BUTT *v.* BUTT 3031
BUTTERWORTH & CO. *v.* NG SUI NAM 527
BYRNE *v.* BIRMINGHAM CITY DISTRICT COUNCIL 1392

C. (A MINOR) (ADOPTION BY PARENT), *Re* .. 2444
C. (A MINOR) (CARE AND CONTROL), *Re* 2519
C. (MINORS) (WARDSHIP: MEDICAL EVIDENCE), *Re* 2535
C. *v.* BERKSHIRE COUNTY COUNCIL 2434
C. *v.* C. (CHILD ABUSE: EVIDENCE) 2433
C. *v.* S. 2501
C.B.S. SONGS *v.* AMSTRAD CONSUMER ELECTRONICS 501
CBS/SONY HONG KONG *v.* TELEVISION BROADCASTS 519
C.C.R. FISHING *v.* TOMENSON INC., LA POINTE, THE 3410
C.H.Z. "ROLIMPEX" *v.* EFTAVRYSSES COMPANIA NAVIERA S.A.; PANAGHIA TINNOU, THE 3444
C.T. BOWRING REINSURANCE *v.* BAXTER 3422
CAISSE PRIMAIRE D'ASSURANCE MALADIE DE ROUEN *v.* GUYOT (ANTJE) (No. 128/83) 1644
CALDANA (GIACOMO), CRIMINAL PROCEEDINGS AGAINST (No. 187/84) 1615
CALEDONIAN MINING CO. *v.* BASSETT 1362
CALLAGHAN (MYLES J.) (IN RECEIVERSHIP) *v.* CITY OF GLASGOW DISTRICT COUNCIL 358
CAMDEN LONDON BOROUGH COUNCIL *v.* McINERNEY (THOMAS) AND SONS 237
CAMDEN LONDON BOROUGH COUNCIL *v.* SHINDER 2383
CAMDEN LONDON BOROUGH COUNCIL AND LATHYRUS INC. 3646
CAMDEN LONDON BOROUGH COUNCIL AND LAVERY & CO. 3610
CAMDEN LONDON BOROUGH COUNCIL AND SORACCHI 3673
CAMPBELL *v.* SECRETARY OF STATE FOR THE HOME DEPARTMENT. *See* R. *v.* OXFORD REGIONAL MENTAL HEALTH REVIEW TRIBUNAL, *ex p.* SECRETARY OF STATE FOR THE HOME DEPARTMENT
CAMPEY & SONS *v.* BELLWOOD 1405
CAMPION *v.* HAMWORTHY ENGINEERING .. 1310

TABLE OF CASES

PARA.

CANADA ENTERPRISES CORP. *v.* MacNAB DISTILLERIES........ 3003
CANTERBURY CITY COUNCIL AND MARTY.. 3611
CANTERBURY CITY COUNCIL *v.* QUINE........ 3643
CAPITAL & COUNTIES FREEHOLD EQUITY TRUST *v.* B.L........ 2232
CAPOCCI *v.* GOBLE........ 2129
CAPON *v.* EVANS........ 413
CAPTAIN PANAGOS D.P., THE. *See* CONTINENTAL ILLINOIS NATIONAL BANK & TRUST CO. OF CHICAGO AND XENOFON MARITIME S.A. *v.* ALLIANCE ASSURANCE CO.; CAPTAIN PANAGOS D.P., THE
CARDINAL VAUGHAN MEMORIAL SCHOOL GOVERNORS *v.* ALIE........ 1397
CARR *v.* ATKINS........ 631
CARRON *v.* GERMANY (No. 198/85)........ 1545
CARTER-FEA *v.* CARTER-FEA........ 1719
CASTELLI *v.* OFFICE NATIONAL DES PENSIONS POUR TRAVAILLEURS SALARIES (No. 261/83)........ 1618
CASTORINA *v.* CHIEF CONSTABLE OF SURREY........ 3588
CELSTEEL *v.* ALTON HOUSE HOLDINGS (No. 2)........ 2139
CENTRALE MARKETINGGESELLSCHAFT DER DEUTSCHEN AGRARWIRTSCHAFT mbH *v.* EEC (represented by the E.C. COMMISSION) (No. 251/84)........ 1624
CENTRE PUBLIC D'AIDE SOCIALE DE COURCELLES *v.* LEBON (No. 316/85)........ 1642
CENTURY INSURANCE CO. OF CANADA *v.* CASE EXISTOLOGICAL LABORATORIES; BAMCELL, THE (NOTE)........ 3408
CEREX JEWELS *v.* PEACHEY PROPERTY CORP........ 2112
CHAN MAN-SIN *v.* THE QUEEN........ 776
CHANCERY LANE DEVELOPMENTS *v.* WADES DEPARTMENTAL STORES........ 489
CHANDLER *v.* CHURCH........ 3059
CHANDLESS *v.* WHITTOME........ 2950
CHANDROUTIE *v.* GAJADHAR........ 2767
CHANNEL ISLAND FERRIES *v.* SEALINK U.K. 422
CHAPMAN *v.* CPS COMPUTER GROUP........ 1356
CHAPPELL (FRED) *v.* NATIONAL CAR PARKS 183
CHARALAMBOUS *v.* ISLINGTON HEALTH AUTHORITY........ 1171
CHARLES FOLLETT *v.* CABTELL INVESTMENTS *See* FOLLETT (CHARLES) *v.* CABTELL INVESTMENTS
CHARLTON *v.* TYNE SHIP REPAIRERS........ 1197
CHARM MARITIME INC. *v.* KYRIAKOU........ 1441
CHARNLEY DAVIES BUSINESS SERVICES, *Re*........ 341
CHARTERED TRUST *v.* PITCHER........ 3332
CHATBROWN *v.* ALFRED McALPINE (SOUTHERN)........ 244
CHAUDHRY *v.* CHAUDHRY........ 1762
CHEBARO *v.* CHEBARO........ 1733
CHELLIAH *v.* IMMIGRATION APPEAL TRIBUNAL........ 1928
CHELMSFORD BOROUGH COUNCIL AND HARRIS QUEENSWAY........ 3631
CHELSEA MAN MENSWEAR *v.* CHELSEA GIRL........ 3753
CHEMCO LEASING S.p.A. *v.* REDIFFUSION.. 440
CHESTERTONS *v.* COLLINS........ 3018
CHESTERTONS (A FIRM) *v.* BARONE........ 64

PARA.

CHICHESTER DIOCESAN FUND AND BOARD OF FINANCE (INCORPORATED) *v.* SECRETARY OF STATE FOR THE ENVIRONMENT AND WEALDEN DISTRICT COUNCIL........ 3692
CHIEF ADJUDICATION OFFICER *v.* BRUNT... 3537
CHIEF CONSTABLE OF AVON AND SOMERSET *v.* FLEMING *Sub nom.* CHIEF CONSTABLE OF AVON AND SOMERSET CONSTABULARY *v.* FLEMING........ 3295
CHIEF CONSTABLE OF AVON AND SOMERSET CONSTABULARY *v.* O'BRIEN........ 3245
CHIEF CONSTABLE OF AVON AND SOMERSET CONSTABULARY *v.* SHIMMEN........ 771
CHIEF CONSTABLE OF AVON AND SOMERSET CONSTABULARY *v.* SINGH........ 3248
CHIEF CONSTABLE OF HAMPSHIRE *v.* MACE........ 760
CHIEF CONSTABLE OF WEST MERCIA POLICE *v.* WILLIAMS........ 3284
CHILTON *v.* TELFORD DEVELOPMENT CORP........ 387
CHINA OCEAN SHIPPING CO. (OWNERS OF XING CHENG) *v.* ANDROS (OWNERS OF THE ANDROS)........ 291
CHINOIN'S APPLICATION........ 2773
CHIOS INVESTMENT PROPERTY CO. *v.* LOPEZ........ 2242
CHOKO STAR, THE. *See* INDUSTRIE CHIMICHE ITALIA CENTRALE *v.* TSAVLIRIS (ALEXANDER G.) & SONS MARITIME CO.; PANCRISTO SHIPPING CO. S.A. AND BULA SHIPPING CORP., CHOKO STAR, THE
CHRISDELL *v.* JOHNSON AND TICKNER........ 2122
CHRISTCHURCH DRAINAGE BOARD *v.* BROWN........ 2591
CHRISTIE *v.* COMMISSIONER OF VALUATION FOR NORTHERN IRELAND (VR/4/1987)........ 2729
CHRISTODOULIDOU *v.* SECRETARY OF STATE FOR THE HOME DEPARTMENT........ 1994
CHURCH COTTAGE INVESTMENTS *v.* HILLINGDON LONDON BOROUGH COUNCIL 3674
CHURCH OF SCIENTOLOGY OF CALIFORNIA *v.* MILLER........ 3036
CHURMS *v.* GRAYSTON PLANT........ 1203
CIBA-GEIGY A.G.'s PATENT........ 2802
CITIBANK TRUST *v.* AYIVOR........ 2541
CITY AND METROPOLITAN PROPERTIES *v.* GREYCROFT........ 2142
CITY OF LONDON BUILDING SOCIETY *v.* FLEGG........ 2540
CLARK (V.O.), *Re* (LVC/307/1985)........ 3167
CLARKE *v.* BRUCE LANCE & CO........ 3549
CLARKE *v.* CHIEF ADJUDICATION OFFICER (No. 384/85)........ 1635
CLARKE *v.* HEGARTY *See* R. *v.* BRENTFORD MAGISTRATES' COURT, *ex p.* CLARKE
CLARKE *v.* SECRETARY OF STATE FOR NORTHERN IRELAND........ 2650
CLARKSON *v.* BRANSFORD........ 1166
CLARKSON *v.* WINKLEY........ 2440
CLAUSS *v.* PIR........ 67
CLAYDON *v.* BRADLEY........ 192
CLEETHORPES BOROUGH COUNCIL AND TOTAL OIL GREAT BRITAIN........ 3677
CLIFFORD *v.* TANNER........ 3881
CLIPPER MARITIME *v.* SHIRLSTAR CONTAINER TRANSPORT; ANEMONE, THE........ 1846

	PARA.
CLOSE'S APPLICATION, *Re*	2703
CLOWES *v.* NATIONAL COAL BOARD	2565
CLOWES (C.W) (INVESTMENTS) *v.* DERBY CITY COUNCIL (Ref/197/1985)	391
COASTPLACE *v.* HARTLEY	2117
COCKERILL—SAMBRE S.A. *v.* E.C. COMMISSION (No. 42/85)	1544
COCOA MERCHANTS *v.* NORTH BORNEO PLANTATIONS SDN BHD	3132
CODDINGTON *v.* HERN	1212
CO-INSURANCE SERVICES, *Re*: E.C. COMMISSION (NETHERLANDS AND U.K. INTERVENING) *v.* IRELAND (BELGIUM, DENMARK AND FRANCE INTERVENING) (No. 206/84)	1570
CO-INSURANCE SERVICES, *Re*: E.C. COMMISSION (U.K. AND NETHERLANDS INTERVENING) *v.* FRANCE (ITALY, BELGIUM, GERMANY AND IRELAND INTERVENING) (No. 220/83)	1571
COLE	1189
COLE *v.* BOON	3238
COLLARD *v.* MINING AND INDUSTRIAL HOLDINGS	545
COLLECTIVE REDUNDANCIES (No. 2), *Re*: E.C. COMMISSION *v.* ITALY (No. 131/84)	1614
COLLIER *v.* BURKE	1143
COLLINS *v.* COLLINS	1740
COLLINS *v.* D.P.P.	741
COLONIAL BANK *v.* EUROPEAN GRAIN & SHIPPING; DOMINIQUE, THE	3441
COLTMAN *v.* BIBBY TANKERS; DERBYSHIRE, THE	1307
COLUMBUS DIXON *v.* DINGLE BELLES (ORMSKIRK)	2888
COMDEL COMMODITIES *v.* SIPOREX TRADE S.A.	154
COMER *v.* BOLTON	1159
COMEX HOULDER DIVING *v.* COLNE FISHING CO.	364
COMMISSIONERS OF CUSTOMS AND EXCISE. *See* CUSTOMS AND EXCISE COMMISSIONERS	
COMMITTEE OF INSPECTION OF P.X. NUCLEAR'S APPLICATION. *See* P.X. NUCLEAR, *Re*	
COMMODITY OCEAN TRANSPORT CORP. *v.* BASFORD UNICORN INDUSTRIES; MITO, THE	3063
COMMUNITY, THE *v.* ACCIAIERIE E FERRIERA DEL CALEOTTO S.p.A.	1653
COMPAGNIE EUROPEENE DE CEREALS S.A. *v.* TRADAX EXPORT S.A.	136
COMPANY, A, *Re*	3123
COMPANY, A (No. 007281 of 1981), *Re*	378
COMPANY, A (No. 00477 of 1986), *Re*	350
COMPANY, A (No. 00596 of 1986), *Re*	351
COMPANY, A (No. 001761 of 1986), *Re*	347
COMPANY, A (No. 004175 of 1986), *Re*	353
COMPANY, A (No. 004377 of 1986), *Re*	366
COMPANY, A (No. 005136 of 1986), *Re*	334
COMPANY, A (No. 007281 of 1986), *Re*	385
COMPANY, A (No. 007523 of 1986), *Re*	325
COMPANY, A (No. 00175 of 1987), *Re*	340
COMPANY, A (No. 00359 of 1987), *Re*	375
COMPANY, A (No. 003318 of 1987), *Re*	376
CONCORD TRADE MARK	3752
CONEGATE *v.* H.M. CUSTOMS AND EXCISE	1114
CONSORZIO COOPERATIVE D'ABBRUZZO *v.* E.C. COMMISSION (No. 15/85)	1452
CONTINENTAL ILLINOIS NATIONAL BANK AND TRUST CO. OF CHICAGO *v.* DAVIES (DANIEL) & CO.	3545
CONTINENTAL ILLINOIS NATIONAL BANK & TRUST CO. OF CHICAGO *v.* PAPANICOLAOU; FEDORA, TATIANA AND ERETREA II, THE	2911
CONTINENTAL ILLINOIS NATIONAL BANK & TRUST CO. OF CHICAGO AND XENOFON MARITIME S.A. *v.* ALLIANCE ASSURANCE CO.; CAPTAIN PANAGOS D.P., THE	3434
CONTROL DATA BELGIUM INC. *v.* E.C. COMMISSION (No. 13/84)	1582
COOK *v.* COOK	2578
COOK *v.* SOUTHEND BOROUGH COUNCIL	2939
COOKE & ARKWRIGHT (A FIRM) *v.* HAYDON	2071
COOKSON *v.* LEYLAND VEHICLES	1195
COOMBS *v.* PARRY	2179
COOPER (BRIAN) & CO. *v.* FAIRVIEW ESTATES (INVESTMENTS)	60
CO-OPERATIEVE MELKPRODUCTENBEDRIJVEN 'NOORD-NEDERLAND' BA *v.* PRODUKTSCHAP VOOR ZUIVEL (No. 275/84)	1558
CO-OPERATIVE CENTRALE RAIFFEISEN-BOERENLEEN-BANK B.A. *v.* SUMITOMO BANK, THE; ROYAN, ABUKIRK, BRETAGNE AND AUBERNE, THE	202
CO-OPERATIVE CO-FRUTTA SRL *v.* AMMINISTRAZIONE DELLE FINANZE DELLO STATO (No. 193/85)	1583
COPYRIGHT AND TRADE MARK RIGHTS IN "ASTERIX", *Re* (2 U 115/84)	498
CORDON BLEU FREEZER FOOD CENTRES *v.* MARBLEACE	2211
CORNELIUS *v.* UNIVERSITY COLLEGE OF SWANSEA	1372
CORNER *v.* MUNDY	479
CORNWALL COAST COUNTRY CLUB *v.* CARDGRANGE	2204
CORNWELL *v.* MYSKOW	2305
CORPORATION OF THE CITY OF ADELAIDE *v.* JENNINGS INDUSTRIES	225
COTGROVE *v.* COONEY	3246
COTSWOLD DISTRICT COUNCIL AND SPOOK ERECTION	3607
COUNTRYSIDE PROPERTIES *v.* MOORE	2955
COUNTY PERSONNEL (EMPLOYMENT AGENCY) *v.* PULVER (ALAN R.) & CO. (A FIRM)	3551
COURAGE GROUP'S PENSION SCHEMES, *Re*; RYAN *v.* IMPERIAL BREWING AND LEISURE	2822
COURAGE TAKE HOME TRADE *v.* KEYS	1403
COURTAULDS NORTHERN SPINNING *v.* SIBSON	1413
COVENTRY CITY COUNCIL *v.* T.	2435
COVENTRY SCAFFOLDING CO. (LONDON) *v.* PARKER (JOHN BRIAN)	3634
COWAN *v.* CHARLESWORTH	2833
COX T/A U-HAUL VEHICLES HIRE *v.* PYRKE (V.O.) (LVC/37 & 38/1985)	3168
COY *v.* KIME (INSPECTOR OF TAXES)	2028
COYLE *v.* SECRETARY OF STATE FOR NORTHERN IRELAND	2723
CRAGG *v.* LEWES DISTRICT COUNCIL	582
CRAMER *v.* CRAMER	1750

TABLE OF CASES

PARA.

CRAVEN *v.* WHITE; I.R.C. *v.* BOWATER PROPERTY DEVELOPMENTS; BAYLIS *v.* GREGORY; BAYLIS *v.* GREGORY AND WEARE 282
CRAVEN (INSPECTOR OF TAXES) *v.* WHITE (STEPHEN); SAME *v.* WHITE (BRIAN). *See* CRAVEN *v.* WHITE
CREDIT ANCILLARY SERVICES *v.* CUSTOMS AND EXCISE COMMISSIONERS........ 3817
CREST HOMES *v.* MARKS 2885
CRESTAR *v.* CARR........ 139
CRIMINAL PROCEEDINGS AGAINST A PERSON OR PERSONS UNKNOWN (No. 14/86) 1542
CRONIN *v.* REDBRIDGE LONDON BOROUGH COUNCIL........ 1167
CROSBY *v.* CROSBY........ 1712
CROSVILLE MOTOR SERVICES *v.* ASHFIELD 1406
CROTTY *v.* AN TAOISEACH........ 1512
CROWN ESTATE COMMISSIONERS *v.* CONNOR AND THE LONDON RENT ASSESSMENT PANEL 2115
CROYDON LONDON BOROUGH *v.* N........ 2464
CRYSTAL GLASS INDUSTRIES *v.* ALWINCO PRODUCTS........ 507
CUCKSON *v.* BUGG........ 1814
CUMMINGS AND SCOTT *v.* PERSONAL REPRESENTATIVES OF SHERRARD (BT/84/1985: BT/85/1985) 2686
CUMSHAW *v.* BOWEN........ 2231
CUNNINGHAM *v.* B.L. COMPONENTS........ 2965
CUNNINGHAM-REID *v.* BUCHANAN-JARDINE........ 414
CURRAN *v.* NORTHERN IRELAND CO-OWNERSHIP HOUSING ASSOCIATION 2709a
CURRIE *v.* BARTON........ 42
CUSTOMS AND EXCISE COMMISSIONERS *v.* CLAUS........ 1111
CUSTOMS AND EXCISE COMMISSIONERS *v.* FAITH CONSTRUCTION 3848
CUSTOMS AND EXCISE COMMISSIONERS *v.* GREAT SHELFORD FREE CHURCH (BAPTIST), ... 3858
CUSTOMS AND EXCISE COMMISSIONERS *v.* QUAKER OATS 3862
CUSTOMS AND EXCISE COMMISSIONERS *v.* SHINGLETON........ 3833
CUSTOMS AND EXCISE COMMISSIONERS *v.* TARMAC ROADSTONE HOLDINGS........ 3841
CUSTOMS AND EXCISE COMMISSIONERS *v.* TEKNEQUIP........ 3842
CUSTOMS AND EXCISE COMMISSIONERS *v.* WILLMOTT (JOHN) HOUSING 3860
CUSTOMS AND EXCISE COMMISSIONERS *v.* ZINN 3808
CYNON VALLEY BOROUGH COUNCIL *v.* SECRETARY OF STATE FOR WALES AND OI MEE LAM........ 3710
CYPRUS POPULAR BANK *v.* MICHAEL........ 3078
CZARNIKOW (C.) *v.* BUNGE & CO.; SAME *v.* CARGILL B.V.; BUNGE & CO. *v.* KROHN & CO; IMPORT-EXPORT G.m.b.H. & Co. K.G........ 3339

D. (A MINOR), *Re* 2437
D. (A MINOR), *Re* 2456
D. (A MINOR), *Re* 2521

PARA.

D.M. (A MINOR) (WARDSHIP: JURISDICTION), *Re* 2518
D.S.Q. PROPERTY CO. *v.* LOTUS CARS........ 2953
D. & F. ESTATES *v.* CHURCH COMMISSIONERS FOR ENGLAND 3582
DACKHAM *v.* DACKHAM 1714
DALY *v.* LIME STREET UNDERWRITING AGENCIES........ 2078
DANECROFT JERSEY MILLS *v.* CRIEGEE...... 3341
DASTUR *v.* LAING (JOHN) CONSTRUCTION. *See* LAING (JOHN) CONSTRUCTION *v.* DASTUR
DATA EXPRESS, *Re*........ 360
DAVEY *v.* CHIEF CONSTABLE OF THE ROYAL ULSTER CONSTABULARY 2742
DAVID JAMES FAIRBAIRN *v.* VENNOOTSCHAP G VER VRIES ZN; PERGO, THE. *See* FAIRBAIRN (DAVID JAMES) *v.* VENNOOTSCHAP G VER VRIES ZN; PERGO, THE
DAVIES (JOSEPH OWEN) *v.* ELI LILLY & CO. 2942
DAVIES (JOSEPH OWEN) *v.* ELI LILLY & CO. 2991
DAVIES (JOSEPH OWEN) *v.* ELI LILLY & CO. 3056
DAVIS *v.* DEPARTMENT OF THE ENVIRONMENT FOR NORTHERN IRELAND (R/2/1986) 2643
DAVIS *v.* D.P.P. 3234
DAWKINS (DEC'D.), *Re*; DAWKINS *v.* JUDD . 3884
DAWSON *v.* I.R.C. 2029
DAWSON *v.* THOMPSON........ 1176
DAWSON PRINT GROUP, *Re*........ 332
DAY *v.* DAY 1736
DE DAMPIERRE *v.* DE DAMPIERRE........ 399
DE FRANCO *v.* COMMISSIONER OF POLICE OF THE METROPOLIS 3042
DE L'ISLE *v.* TIMES NEWSPAPERS. *See* VISCOUNT DE L'ISLE *v.* TIMES NEWSPAPERS
DE ROTHSCHILD (EVELYN) AND ERANDA HERDS *v.* SECRETARY OF STATE FOR TRANSPORT 388
DEAN *v.* AINLEY 452
DEAN *v.* DEAN........ 2937
DEAR *v.* D.P.P........ 3235
DEAR *v.* NEWHAM LONDON BOROUGH COUNCIL........ 3153
DEBENHAMS *v.* WESTMINSTER CITY COUNCIL 3195
DECOUVREUR *v.* JORDAN 1842
DEF LEPP MUSIC *v.* STUART-BROWN........ 517
DEFENDANT, A, *Re*........ 723
DEFOREIT'S PATENT........ 2788
DEGAN 1170
DEGAZON *v.* BARCLAYS BANK INTERNATIONAL........ 1691
DELAHAY *v.* MATLODGE........ 2158
DELLNEED *v.* CHIN 2176
DELTA NEWSAGENTS *v.* CUSTOMS AND EXCISE COMMISSIONERS 3855
DENARD *v.* ABBAS........ 849
DENKAVIT FRANCE Sàrl *v.* FONDS D'ORIENTATION ET DE REGULARISATION DES MARCHES AGRICOLES (No. 266/84)........ 1460
DENNEHY *v.* SEALINK U.K........ 1330
DENNIS AND ROBINSON *v.* KIOSSOS ESTABLISHMENT 2217
DENVER *v.* McILWAINE 2901
DEPARTMENT OF THE ENVIRONMENT *v.* ROYAL INSURANCE 2134

PARA.
DERBYSHIRE, THE. *See* COLTMAN *v.* BIBBY TANKERS; DERBYSHIRE, THE
DESIGN 5 *v.* KENISTON HOUSING ASSOCIATION 1142
DEUFIL GmbH & CO. KG *v.* E.C. COMMISSION (No. 310/85R) 1607
DEUTSCHE SCHACHTBAU-UND TIEFBOHRGESELLSCHAFT MbH *v.* THE R'AS AL KHAIMAH NATIONAL OIL CO. AND SHELL INTERNATIONAL PETROLEUM CO. 126
DEUTSCHE SCHACHTBAU- UND- TIEFBOHRGESELLSCHAFT mbH *v.* THE R'AS AL KHAIMAH NATIONAL OIL CO. AND SHELL INTERNATIONAL PETROLEUM CO. 3013
DEVON AND CORNWALL HOUSING ASSOCIATION *v.* ACLAND THORMAN AND MILLER-WILLIAMS 3126
DEW *v.* DEW 1741
DEWS *v.* NATIONAL COAL BOARD 1220
DHILLON, *Re* 3051
DIAMOND SHAMROCK TECHNOLOGIES S.A.'s PATENT 2801
DIDYMI CORP. *v.* ATLANTIC LINES AND NAVIGATION CO. INC. 3432
DIETMAN *v.* BRENT LONDON BOROUGH COUNCIL; WAHLSTROM *v.* SAME 1401
DIETMAN *v.* BRENT LONDON BOROUGH COUNCIL 1419
DILLINGHAM CANADA INTERNATIONAL *v.* MANA CONSTRUCTION 156
DINCH v. DINCH 1745
DINEFWR BOROUGH COUNCIL *v.* JONES 2237
DINERS CLUB *v.* CUSTOMS AND EXCISE COMMISSIONERS: CARDHOLDERS *v.* SAME 3807
D.P.P. *v.* BILLINGTON, CHAPPELL, RUMBLE AND EAST 3250
D.P.P. *v.* BUGG 603
D.P.P. *v.* EVANS AND HEWDEN STUART HEAVY CRANES 3290
D.P.P. *v.* FOUNTAIN 3236
D.P.P. *v.* WEBB 3267
DIXON *v.* ALLGOOD 2171
DODD *v.* BRITISH TELECOMMUNICATIONS. 1338
DOMINIQUE, THE. *See* COLONIAL BANK *v.* EUROPEAN GRAIN & SHIPPING: DOMINIQUE, THE
DONALD FISHER (EALING) *v.* SPENCER (INSPECTOR OF TAXES) *See* FISHER (DONALD) (EALING) *v.* SPENCER (INSPECTOR OF TAXES)
DONCASTER METROPOLITAN BOROUGH COUNCIL *v.* LOCKWOOD 1765
DONHUYSEN *v.* Pvba BUILDING MATERIALS VAN DEN BROECK 1546
DONOVAN *v.* SECRETARY OF STATE FOR THE ENVIRONMENT 3637
DORAN *v.* SECRETARY OF STATE FOR NORTHERN IRELAND 2649
DOUGHTY *v.* GENERAL DENTAL COUNCIL ... 2400
DOUGLAS *v.* DOUGLAS 2503
DOVER DISTRICT COUNCIL AND HUTCHINGS 3704
DOWNEY *v.* LOUGHRAN (BT/87/1986) 2687
DOWUONA *v.* JOHN LEWIS PARTNERSHIP.. 1344
DRAFT INSIDER TRADING DIRECTIVE 1519
DRAFT REGULATION ON KNOW-HOW LICENCES 1498

PARA.
DRAFT STOCK EXCHANGE LISTING PARTICULARS (MUTUAL RECOGNITION) DIRECTIVE 1654
DRAKE 1191
DRESDEN ESTATES *v.* COLLINSON 2252
DRISTAN TRADE MARK 3756
DU PONT DE NEMOURS (E.I.) & Co. *v.* ENKA A.G. 2771
DUDLEY BOWERS AMUSEMENTS ENTERPRISES *v.* SECRETARY OF STATE FOR THE ENVIRONMENT. *See* BOWERS (DUDLEY) AMUSEMENTS ENTERPRISES *v.* SECRETARY OF STATE FOR THE ENVIRONMENT
DUKE *v.* RELIANCE SYSTEMS 3084
DUKE AND DUKE *v.* PORTER 2245
DUKE OF WESTMINSTER *v.* JOHNSTON 2165
DUNDALK WATER SCHEME, *Re*: E.C. COMMISSION *v.* IRELAND (No. 45/87R) 1603
DUNDALK WATER SCHEME (No. 2), *Re*: E.C. COMMISSION *v.* IRELAND (No. 45/87R) 1604
DUNNING (A.J.) & SONS (SHOPFITTERS) *v.* SYKES & SON (POOLE) 473
DUNSTAN (INSPECTOR OF TAXES) *v.* YOUNG, AUSTEN & YOUNG 273
DUXBURY *v.* DUXBURY 1755
DYE *v.* MANNS 3229

E. (A MINOR) (CHILD ABUSE: EVIDENCE), *Re* 2471
EVTR, *Re* 345
E.I. DU PONT DE NEMOURS & Co. *v.* ENKA A.G. *See* DU PONT DE NEMOURS (E.I.) Co. *v.* ENKA A.G.
ELS WHOLESALE (WOLVERHAMPTON) *v.* SECRETARY OF STATE FOR THE ENVIRONMENT 2898
ETS SOULES ET COMPAGNIE *v.* HANDGATE CO. S.A.; HANDGATE, THE 3130
EAST *v.* BLADEN 2067
EAST HAMPSHIRE DISTRICT COUNCIL AND NASSINGTON PROPERTIES 3667
EASTGLEN INTERNATIONAL CORP. *v.* MONPARE S.A. 3068
EASTWOOD *v.* LOUGHRAN (BT/130/1986).... 2688
EGGAR FORESTER OFFSHORE *v.* HONG KONG UNITED DOCKYARDS; ENERGY SEARCHER, THE 68
ELECTRIC FURNACE CO. *v.* SELAS CORP. OF AMERICA 3131
ELECTRIC TOOL REPAIR *v.* CUSTOMS AND EXCISE COMMISSIONERS 3824
ELITE INVESTMENTS *v.* T.I. BAINBRIDGE SILENCERS (No. 2) 1230
ELLIOT *v.* STUMP (RICHARD) 1410
ELLIS *v.* BIGGINS 1179
ELLIS (INSPECTOR OF TAXES) *v.* B.P. NORTHERN IRELAND REFINERY; ELLIS (INSPECTOR OF TAXES) *v.* B.P. TYNE TANKER CO. 543
ENERGY SEARCHER, THE. *See* EGGAR FORRESTER OFFSHORE *v.* HONG KONG UNITED DOCKYARDS; ENERGY SEARCHER, THE
ENFIELD LONDON BOROUGH COUNCIL AND B. AND Q. (RETAIL) 3663
ENFIELD LONDON BOROUGH COUNCIL *v.* F. 1264

TABLE OF CASES

PARA.

ENGLISH AND AMERICAN INSURANCE CO. *v.* SMITH (HERBERT) & CO. (A FIRM) 3086
ENVIRO-SPRAY SYSTEM INC.'s PATENTS 2785
EPAPHUS, THE. *See* EURICO S.p.A *v.* PHILIPP BROTHERS: EPAPHUS, THE
EPIKHIRISEON METALLEFTIKON VIOMIKHANIKON KAI NAFTILIAKON A.E. *v.* E.C. COUNCIL AND COMMISSION (No. 121/86R) 1610
EPIKHIRISEON METALLEFTIKON VIOMIKHANIKON KAI NAFTILIAKON A.E. *v.* E.C. COUNCIL AND COMMISSION (No. 2) (No. 121–122/86R) 1541
EPPING FOREST DISTRICT COUNCIL *v.* MATTHEWS 3613
EPPING FOREST DISTRICT COUNCIL *v.* SCOTT 3630
EPPING FOREST DISTRICT COUNCIL and LEE VALLEY REGIONAL PARK AUTHORITY 3668
EPSOM & EWELL BOROUGH COUNCIL AND JAMES LONGLEY PROPERTIES; WELLCOME FOUNDATION INVESTMENT CO. AND MANUFACTURERS HANOVER FINANCE 3608
EQUITY & LAW LIFE ASSURANCE SOCIETY *v.* BODFIELD 2220
ESSEX COUNTY COUNCIL *v.* ELLAM (INSPECTOR OF TAXES) 2012
ETRI FANS *v.* NMB (U.K.) 157
ETTRIDGE *v.* MORRELL 2378
EURICO S.p.A. *v.* LEROS SHIPPING CO. AND SEABOARD MARITIME INC.; OMEGA LEROS, THE 3128
EURICO S.p.A. *v.* PHILIPP BROTHERS; EPAPHUS, THE 455
EURO-ACADEMY *v.* CUSTOMS AND EXCISE COMMISSIONERS 1662
EURO-DIAM *v.* BATHURST 2051
EUROPEAN BROADCASTING UNION, *Re* 1489
E.C. COMMISSION *v.* COUNCIL OF THE EUROPEAN COMMUNITIES (No. 45/86) 1627
E.C. COMMISSION *v.* DENMARK (No. 252/83) *See* INSURANCE SERVICES, *Re*: E.C. COMMISSION (NETHERLANDS AND U.K. INTERVENING) *v.* DENMARK (BELGIUM AND IRELAND INTERVENING)
E.C. COMMISSION *v.* DENMARK (No. 106/84) *See* TAXATION OF WINE, *Re*: E.C. COMMISSION *v.* DENMARK
E.C. COMMISSION *v.* FEDERAL REPUBLIC OF GERMANY (No. 178/84) 1594
E.C. COMMISSION (SUPPORTED BY THE NETHERLANDS AND THE U.K., INTERVENERS) *v.* FEDERAL REPUBLIC OF GERMANY (SUPPORTED BY BELGIUM, DENMARK, FRANCE, IRELAND AND ITALY, INTERVENERS) (205/84) 1631
E.C. COMMISSION *v.* FRANCE (No. 220/83) *See* CO-INSURANCE SERVICES, *Re*: E.C. COMMISSION (U.K. AND NETHERLANDS INTERVENING) *v.* FRANCE (ITALY, BELGIUM, GERMANY AND IRELAND INTERVENING)
E.C. COMMISSION *v.* GERMANY (No 303/84) *See* SUGAR TAX, *Re*; E.C. COMMISSION *v.* GERMANY

PARA.

E.C. COMMISSION *v.* IRELAND (No. 206/84) *See* CO-INSURANCE SERVICES, *Re*: E.C. COMMISSION (NETHERLANDS AND U.K. INTERVENING) *v.* IRELAND (BELGIUM, DENMARK AND FRANCE INTERVENING)
E.C. COMMISSION *v.* IRELAND (No. 45/87R), *See* DUNDALK WATER SCHEME, *Re*: E.C. COMMISSION *v.* IRELAND (No. 45/87R)
E.C. COMMISSION *v.* ITALY (No. 272/83). *See* AGRICULTURAL PRODUCER GROUPS, *Re*: E.C. COMMISSION *v.* ITALY
E.C. COMMISSION *v.* ITALY (No. 103/84) *See* SUBSIDY FOR ITALIAN MOTOR VEHICLES, *Re*: E.C. COMMISSION *v.* ITALY
E.C. COMMISSION *v.* ITALY (No. 235/84). *See* BUSINESS TRANSFER LEGISLATION, *Re*: E.C. COMMISSION *v.* ITALY
E.C. COMMISSION *v.* ITALY (No. 309/84). *See* VINEYARD REDUCTIONS, *Re*: E.C. COMMISSION *v.* ITALY
E.C. COMMISSION *v.* ITALY (No. 363/85) 1522
E.C. COMMISSION *v.* U.K. (No. 93/85). *See* ADVANCE PAYMENT OF BUDGET CONTRIBUTIONS, *Re*, E.C. COMMISSION *v.* U.K. (No. 93/85)
E.C. COMMISSION (SUPPORTED BY FRANCE, INTERVENER) *v.* U.K. (No. 23/84). *See* MILK MARKETING BOARDS, *Re*: E.C. COMMISSION (SUPPORTED BY FRANCE, INTERVENER) *v.* U.K. (No. 23/84)
EUROPEAN FEDERATION OF ASSOCIATIONS OF COFFEE ROASTERS *v.* INSTITUTO BRASILEIRO DO CAFÉ 1506
EUROPEAN SCHOOL IN BRUSSELS, *Re*: D. *v.* BELGIUM AND THE EUROPEAN COMMUNITIES 1913
EUROSTEM MARITIME, *Re* 330
EUROTRADER, THE. *See* IRISH AGRICULTURAL WHOLESALE SOCIETY *v.* PARTENREEDEREI: M.S. EUROTRADER; EUROTRADER, THE
EVANS *v.* CLAYHOPE PROPERTIES 2194
EVANS *v.* CLIFTON INNS 3876
EVELYN DE ROTHSCHILD AND ERANDA HERDS *v.* SECRETARY OF STATE FOR TRANSPORT. *See* DE ROTHSCHILD (EVELYN) AND ERANDA HERDS *v.* SECRETARY OF STATE FOR TRANSPORT
EVENING STANDARD CO. *v.* HENDERSON... 1296
EXCHANGE SECURITIES AND COMMODITIES (IN LIQUIDATION), *Re*; EXCHANGE SECURITIES FINANCIAL SERVICES (IN LIQUIDATION), *Re* 362
EXCOMM *v.* GUAN GUAN SHIPPING (PTE); GOLDEN BEAR, THE 147
EXPRESS & STAR *v.* BUNDAY 1404
EXXATE TRADE MARK 3743
EYRE *v.* HALL 2187

F.E.O.G.A. ACCOUNTS, *Re*: GREECE *v.* E.C. COMMISSION (No. 214/86R) 1605
FABIKUN *v.* AMUCHIENWA 3058
FACTORY HOLDINGS GROUP *v.* LEBOFF INTERNATIONAL 2212
FAETHON, THE 3389
FAIRBAIRN (DAVID JAMES) *v.* VENNOOTSCHAP G VER VRIES ZN; PERGO, THE..... 3427

TABLE OF CASES

PARA.

FAIRFAX (DENTAL) EQUIPMENT *v.* FILHOL (S.J.) 2799
FALCON (R.J.) DEVELOPMENTS, *Re* 383
FALCONER *v.* A.S.L.E.F. AND N.U.R. 3765
FALCONER & SONS *v.* REA (BT/117/1986) 2689
FAMOUS *v.* GE IM EX ITALIA SRL 194
FANNON *v.* BACKHOUSE 2334
FARLEY HEALTH PRODUCTS *v.* BABYLON TRADING CO. 1126
FARRELL *v.* STENNING 2872
FARRINGTON *v.* LEIGH 2300
FARROW (DEC'D.), *Re* 1737
FEDERAL REPUBLIC OF GERMANY, FRANCE, THE NETHERLANDS, DENMARK AND U.K. *v.* E.C. COMMISSION (SUPPORTED BY THE EUROPEAN PARLIAMENT, INTERVENER) (Nos. 281, 283, 284, 285 and 287/85) 1640
FEDORA, TATIANA AND ERETREA II, THE. *See* CONTINENTAL ILLINOIS NATIONAL BANK & TRUST CO. OF CHICAGO *v.* PAPANICOLAOU; FEDORA, TATIANA AND ERETREA II, THE
FELIXSTOWE DOCK AND RAILWAY CO. *v.* U.S. LINES INC.; FREIGHTLINERS *v.* SAME; B.V. *v.* SAME 3062
FEOGA ACCOUNTS, *Re*, U.K. *v.* E.C. COMMISSION (No. 133/84) 1462
FERCOMETAL SARL *v.* MEDITERRANEAN SHIPPING CO. 3386
FERGUSON *v.* WELSH 2612
FERRAIOLI *v.* DEUTSCHE BUNDESPOST (No. 153/84) 1643
FERRIERE SAN CARLO SpA *v.* E.C.COMMISSION (No. 235/82 Rev) 1543
FILIATRA LEGACY, THE 3393
FILMS ROVER INTERNATIONAL *v.* CANNON FILM SALES 3022
FINEGAN *v.* GENERAL MEDICAL COUNCIL .. 2417
FIORAVANTI *v.* AMMISTRAZIONE DELLE FINANZE DELLO STATO (No. 99/83) 1514
FIRMA KARL-HEINZ NEUMANN *v.* BUNDESANSTALT FÜR LANDWIRTSCHAFTLICHE MARKTORDNUNG (No. 299/84) 1457
FIRST NATIONAL SECURITIES *v.* WILEMAN. 2919
FISHER (DONALD) (EALING) *v.* SPENCER (INSPECTOR OF TAXES) 552
FITZGERALD *v.* LANE 2566
FITZPATRICK *v.* NORTHERN IRELAND HOUSING EXECUTIVE 2712
FLACK *v.* BALDRY 1797
FLOCKTON (IAN) *v.* CUSTOMS AND EXCISE COMMISSIONERS 3815
FLYNN *v.* VANGE SCAFFOLDING & ENGINEERING 2598
FOLLETT (CHARLES) *v.* CABTELL INVESTMENTS 2135
FOO LOKE YING *v.* TELEVISION BROADCASTS 528
FOOD CORP. OF INDIA *v.* ANTCLIZO SHIPPING CORP.; ANTCLIZO, THE 133
FOOD CORP. OF INDIA *v.* MARASTRO CIA NAVIERA S.A.; TRADE FORTITUDE, THE .. 143
FOOD CORP. OF INDIA *v.* MOSVOLDS REDERI A/S; ARRAS, THE AND HOEGH ROVER, THE 3440
FOOT *v.* FOOT 2508
FOOT *v.* LONDON BOROUGH OF WANDSWORTH 3106

PARA.

FORD *v.* FORD 1770
FORD *v.* STAKIS HOTELS AND INNS 1385
FORD (CHARLES E.) *v.* AFEC INC 3331
FORD MOTOR CO. *v.* NAWAZ 1340
FOREX NEPTUNE (OVERSEAS) *v.* MILLER 1376
FORSIKRINGSAKTIELSKAPET VESTA *v.* BUTCHER 2567
FORTE & CO. *v.* GENERAL ACCIDENT LIFE ASSURANCE 2221
FOSTER *v.* BRITISH GAS 1370
FOWLER *v.* MINCHIN 2182
FOX (JOHN) *v.* BANNISTER KING & RIGBEYS 3560
FRAMPTON (TRUSTEES OF WORTHING RUGBY FOOTBALL CLUB) *v.* I.R.C. *See* WORTHING RUGBY FOOTBALL CLUB TRUSTEES *v.* I.R.C.
FRANCHISE AGREEMENTS OF COMPUTERLAND EUROPE S.A., *Re* (No. IV/32.034) 1495
FRANCIS *v.* TOWER HAMLETS BOROUGH COUNCIL 1373
FRANKLAND AND MOORE *v.* R. 802
FREEHOLD MANAGEMENT (TRADERS) *v.* PLUMLEY (LRA/4/1986) 2152
FRENCH'S (WINE BAR), *Re* 384
FROGLEY *v.* ALGAR 1183
FRONTIER DISPUTE (BURKINA FASO/MALI). 2094
FRY *v.* JACKSON (ROBERT A.) (BUILDER AND CONTRACTOR) 241
FRYDMAN PROPERTIES *v.* BEJAM GROUP .. 1841
FULLER *v.* SECRETARY OF STATE FOR THE ENVIRONMENT 3617

G. (A MINOR), (CHILD ABUSE: STANDARD OF PROOF), *Re* 2474
G. (A MINOR) (ROLE OF THE APPELLATE COURT), *Re* 2527
G. (MINORS) (CHILD ABUSE: EVIDENCE), *Re* 2470
G. *v.* CHIEF SUPERINTENDENT OF POLICE, STROUD, GLOUCESTERSHIRE 819
G. P. & P. *v.* BULCRAIG & DAVIS 1129
GADHOK *v.* CHIEF ADJUDICATION OFFICER 3489
GAFTA SOYA BEAN MEAL FUTURES ASSOCIATION, *Re* (No. IV/29.036) 1507
GALE (JOHN) *v.* CUSTOMS AND EXCISE COMMISSIONERS 3829
GALLAGHER *v.* MORGAN (BT/118/1986) 2690
GALLAGHER *v.* PATTERSON 900
GARDEX *v.* SORATA 2798
GASPET (FORMERLY SAGA PETROLEUM (U.K.)) *v.* ELLISS (INSPECTOR OF TAXES) 544
GATEWAY FOOD MARKETS *v.* SIMMONDS . 1815
GAUNT *v.* NELSON 3308
GAZ FOUNTAIN, THE 2332
GEE *v.* GENERAL MEDICAL COUNCIL. *See* R. *v.* GENERAL MEDICAL COUNCIL, *ex p.* GEE
GEERS GROSS, *Re* 367
GENERAL ACCIDENT FIRE AND LIFE ASSURANCE CORP. *v.* ELECTRONIC DATA PROCESSING CO. 2198
GENERAL MOTORS ACCEPTANCE CORP. (U.K.) *v.* I.R.C. 555
GENERICS (U.K.), *Re* 2811
GEORGE *v.* GEORGE 2924
GEORGE *v.* THORNBORROW 1198

TABLE OF CASES

PARA.

GEORGE S., THE. *See* AMOCO OIL CO. *v.* PARPADA SHIPPING CO., GEORGE S., THE
GIAMETTI *v.* HAIGH 1204
GILES *v.* ADLEY 2121
GILES *v.* FOX 618
GILL *v.* CHIPMAN 2795
GIMBLETT *v.* McGLASHAN 174
GIRLS' PUBLIC DAY SCHOOL TRUST *v.* KHANNA 1300
GLAVERBEL'S PATENT 2805
GLENEAGLES HOTEL *v.* CUSTOMS AND EXCISE COMMISSIONERS 3844
GLOVER *v.* KUONI TRAVEL 1151
GOLD *v.* HARINGEY HEALTH AUTHORITY 2601
GOLDEN BEAR, THE. *See* EXCOMM *v.* GUAN GUAN SHIPPING (PTE); GOLDEN BEAR, THE
GOLDENGLOW NUT FOOD CO. *v.* COMMODIN (PRODUCE) 3124
GOLDMAN *v.* HESPER 1710
GOLDSMITH *v.* BURROW CONSTRUCTION CO. 1232
GOLDSWORTHY *v.* BRICKELL 456
GOMBA HOLDINGS U.K. *v.* MINORIES FINANCE 355
GOOD HERALD, THE 3370
GOODFELLOW (R. W.) *v.* CUSTOMS AND EXCISE COMMISSIONERS 3838
GORING, THE 3428
GORING *v.* BRITISH ACTORS EQUITY ASSOCIATION 3767
GOVERNMENT OF BELGIUM *v.* POSTLETHWAITE 1703
GOVERNORS OF THE PEABODY DONATION FUND *v.* HAY 1904
GOVERNORS OF THE PEABODY DONATION FUND *v.* LONDON RESIDUARY BODY 463
GRACE SHIPPING INC. AND HAI NGUAN & CO. *v.* C. F. SHARP & CO. (MALAYA) PTE. 427
GRAHAM *v.* GRAHAM 1742
GRAHAM *v.* NORTHERN IRELAND HOUSING EXECUTIVE 2710
GRANSDEN (E.C.) AND CO. AND FALKBRIDGE *v.* SECRETARY OF STATE FOR THE ENVIRONMENT AND GILLINGHAM BOROUGH COUNCIL 3691
GRATTON-STOREY *v.* LEWIS 2166
GRAY *v.* GRAY 3061
GREAT YARMOUTH BOROUGH COUNCIL AND FIELDS (G.W.) & SONS (GREAT YARMOUTH) 3609
GREATER LONDON COUNCIL *v.* CLEVELAND BRIDGE AND ENGINEERING CO. 245
GREATER LONDON COUNCIL *v.* PORT OF LONDON AUTHORITY 2394
GREATER LONDON COUNCIL *v.* SECRETARY OF STATE FOR THE ENVIRONMENT AND LONDON DOCKLANDS DEVELOPMENT CORP. AND CABLECROSS PROJECTS; LONDON BOROUGH OF TOWER HAMLETS *v.* SAME 3657
GREEN *v.* FINE SPINNERS AND DOUBLERS. 1193
GREENMAST SHIPPING CO. S.A. *v.* JEAN LION ET CIE S.A.; SARONIKOS, THE 3446
GREENSTONE SHIPPING CO. *v.* INDIAN OIL CORP 3417
GREENWICH LONDON BOROUGH COUNCIL *v.* MILLCROFT CONSTRUCTION 3778

PARA.

GREY *v.* DURHAM COUNTY COUNCIL 3109
GRIFFITHS *v.* BIRMINGHAM CITY DISTRICT COUNCIL 2172
GRIFFITHS *v.* KINGSLEY-STUBBS 1227
GRIX *v.* CHIEF CONSTABLE OF KENT 3230
GROUP OF THE EUROPEAN RIGHT AND THE NATIONAL FRONT PARTY *v.* EUROPEAN PARLIAMENT (No. 221/86R) 1557
GROVESIDE HOMES *v.* ELMBRIDGE BOROUGH COUNCIL 3725
GRUNWICK PROCESSING LABORATORIES *v.* CUSTOMS AND EXCISE COMMISSIONERS 3799
GUESS ? INC. *v.* LEE SECK MON 2884
GUEVARA *v.* HOUNSLOW LONDON BOROUGH COUNCIL 3052
GUILDFORD BOROUGH COUNCIL AND 3H MOTORS 3693
GUINNESS *v.* SAUNDERS 317
GUINNESS *v.* SAUNDERS (No. 2) 335
GUINNESS PEAT PROPERTIES *v.* FITZROY ROBINSON PARTNERSHIP 3060
GÜL *v.* REGIERUNGSPRÄSIDENT DÜSSELDORF (No. 131/85) 1629
GULF OIL (GREAT BRITAIN) *v.* PAGE 2298
GULL *v.* SCARBOROUGH (NOTE) 3232
GUMBLEY *v.* CUNNINGHAM; GOULD *v.* CASTLE 3269
GURSAN 1976
GUYLL *v.* BRIGHT 3274
GWYNEDD COUNTY COUNCIL *v.* JONES 1353

H. (MINORS), *Re* 2481
H. (MINORS) (CHILD ABUSE: EVIDENCE), *Re* 2476
H. *v.* B. (FORMERLY H.) 1732
H. *v.* H. 1751
H.H. PROPERTY *v.* RAHIM 2113
HABIB BANK A.G. ZURICH *v.* MINDI INVESTMENTS 3112
HADJILOUCAS *v.* CREAN 2162
HAFTON PROPERTIES *v.* McHUGH (INSPECTOR OF TAXES) 2004
HAGHIGAT-KHOU *v.* CHAMBERS 3279
HAIL RISK FOR DUTCH FRUIT FARMERS, *Re* 1648
HALL *v.* KING 2178
HALVANON INSURANCE *v.* JEWETT DUCHESNE (INTERNATIONAL) 2946
HAMBLETT *v.* GODFREY (INSPECTOR OF TAXES) 2034
HAMBRO LIFE ASSURANCE *v.* WHITE YOUNG & PARTNERS 2584
HAMILTON *v.* WHITELOCK (No. 79/86) 3307
HAMLET *v.* GENERAL MUNICIPAL BOILERMAKERS AND ALLIED TRADES UNION 3763
HANCOCK *v.* SECRETARY OF STATE FOR THE ENVIRONMENT AND TORRIDGE DISTRICT COUNCIL 3616
HANDGATE, THE *See* ETS SOULES ET COMPAGNIE *v.* HANDGATE CO. S.A.; HANDGATE, THE
HANIEL HANDEL GmbH, *Re* 1508
HANNA *v.* CHIEF CONSTABLE OF THE ROYAL ULSTER CONSTABULARY 2647
HANNIBAL (E.) & CO. *v.* FROST 320
HANSON *v.* LORENZ AND JONES 3552
HARFORD *v.* SWIFTRIM 1394

TABLE OF CASES

PARA.

HARINGEY LONDON BOROUGH COUNCIL *v.* SANDHU 2312
HARNETT *v.* ASSOCIATED OCTEL 3072
HARRIS *v.* HARRIS 2283
HARRIS *v.* SHEFFIELD UNITED FOOTBALL CLUB 2869
HARRIS *v.* WYRE FOREST DISTRICT COUNCIL 2586
HARRISON *v.* PROJECT & DESIGN CO. (REDCAR) 2792
HARRISON *v.* TEW 2957
HARROGATE BOROUGH COUNCIL *v.* SECRETARY OF STATE FOR THE ENVIRONMENT AND PROCTOR 3624
HARROW LONDON BOROUGH COUNCIL AND SMITH & BARON 3679
HART (S.W.) & CO. PTY. *v.* EDWARDS HOT WATER SYSTEMS 502
HARTLAND *v.* ALDEN 3247
HARTLEY *v.* INTASUN HOLIDAYS 1149
HARTNELL *v.* CHELMSFORD DISTRICT COUNCIL (Ref/8/1986) 392
HARVEY *v.* HARVEY 1787
HARVEY *v.* SOUTH WEST THAMES REGIONAL HEALTH AUTHORITY 1172
HAUGHIAN *v.* PAINE 2603
HAUGHIAN *v.* UNIVERSITY HOSPITAL BOARD, UNIVERSITY OF SASKATCHEWAN 2995
HAUPTZOLLAMT SCHWEINFURT *v.* MAINFRUCHT OBSTVERWERTUNG GmbH (No. 290/84) 1213
HAW *v.* HAMPSHIRE COUNTY COUNCIL 1213
HAWKINS 1173
HAWKINS *v.* CROWN PROSECUTION SERVICE 724
HAWKINS *v.* DHAWAN AND MISHIKU 2609
HAWKINS (FRANCIS), *Re* 1704
HAWTHORNE *v.* ULSTER FLYING CLUB (1961) 2638
HAYIM *v.* CITIBANK N.A. 1425
HAYMAN *v.* GRIFFITHS; WALKER *v.* HANBY 3834
HAYWARD *v.* CAMMELL LAIRD SHIPBUILDERS 1328
HAYWARD *v.* CAMMELL LAIRD SHIPBUILDERS (No. 2) 1321
HEASMANS (A FIRM) *v.* CLARITY CLEANING CO. 1316
HEINEMANN *v.* COOPER 1163
HELLYER BROTHERS *v.* McLEOD; BOSTON DEEP SEA FISHERIES *v.* WILSON 1354
HEMENS (V.O.) *v.* WHITSBURY FARM AND STUD 3192
HEMSTED *v.* LEES AND NORWICH CITY COUNCIL 1866
HENRY BOOT BUILDING *v.* CROYDON HOTEL AND LEISURE CO. *See* BOOT (HENRY) BUILDING *v.* CROYDON HOTEL AND LEISURE CO.
HENTHORN *v.* SCOTT ROBERTSON 3096
HERROE AND ASKOE, THE. *See* REDERIAKTIEBOLAGET GUSTAV ERIKSON *v.* DR. FAWZI AHMED ABOU ISMAIL, HERROE AND ASKOE, THE
HERTFORDSHIRE COUNTY COUNCIL *v.* BOLDEN 3779
HERTFORDSHIRE COUNTY COUNCIL *v.* RETIREMENT LEASE HOUSING ASSOCIATION 2819
HI-FI EQUIPMENT (CABINETS), *Re* 356

PARA.

HIGHGATE WAREHOUSE (TEXTILES) *v.* CUSTOMS AND EXCISE COMMISSIONERS 3805
HIGHLANDS INSURANCE CO. *v.* CONTINENTAL INSURANCE CO. 2077
HILL *v.* CHIEF CONSTABLE OF WEST YORKSHIRE 2857
HILL *v.* GRIFFIN 2131
HILL (WILLIAM) (SOUTHERN) *v.* CABRAS 1231
HILLEGOM MUNICIPALITY *v.* HILLENIUS (CORNELIS) (No. 110/84) 1472
HILLGATE HOUSE *v.* EXPERT CLOSING SERVICE AND SALES 2146
HILLS *v.* CRAIG AND GUBBER 1205
HINDES *v.* EDWARDS 2887
HIRSCHLER *v.* BIRCH 848
HIRST AND AGU *v.* CHIEF CONSTABLE OF WEST YORKSHIRE 805
HITACHI SALES (U.K.) *v.* MITSUI OSK LINES 3045
HIZZETT *v.* HARGREAVES 1164
HODGES *v.* BLEE 2188
HODGSON *v.* TRAPP 1137
HOGAN'S APPLICATION, *Re* 2720
HOLDEN *v.* CHIEF CONSTABLE OF LANCASHIRE 1144
HOLLAND HANNEN & CUBITTS (NORTHERN) *v.* WELSH HEALTH TECHNICAL SERVICES ORGANISATION 233
HOLLINS *v.* CLARKE 1200
HOLMAN (JOHN MALCOLM) *v.* EVERARD (F.T.) & SONS; JACK WHARTON, THE 2613
HOLMES *v.* BANGLADESH BIMAN CORP. 286
HOLMES *v.* CHECKLAND 3089
HOLTHAM *v.* COMMISSIONER OF POLICE OF THE METROPOLIS 1154
HOME BREWERY CO. *v.* DAVIS (WILLIAM) & CO. (LEICESTER) 2752
HONE AND McCARTAN'S APPLICATION, *Re* 2725
HOOK *v.* HAIR 1192a
HOTSON *v.* EAST BERKSHIRE HEALTH AUTHORITY, *sub nom.* HOTSON *v.* FITZGERALD 2604
HOUGHTON *v.* CHIEF CONSTABLE OF GREATER MANCHESTER 811
HOUSE OF FRASER *v.* A.C.G.E. INVESTMENTS 359
HOWMAN (V.O.) *v.* VOGT (LVC/88/1986) 3169
HUA CHIAO COMMERCIAL BANK *v.* CHIAPHUA INDUSTRIES 2154
HUDDLESTON *v.* CONTROL RISKS INFORMATION SERVICES 2988
HUDSON (A.) PTY. *v.* LEGAL AND GENERAL LIFE OF AUSTRALIA 2210
HUGHES *v.* HOLLEY 600
HUGHES' APPLICATION, *Re* 2724
HUNT *v.* DOUGLAS (R. M.) (ROOFING) 2947
HUNTER & PARTNERS *v.* WELLINGS & PARTNERS 3074
HURST *v.* WAKEFIELD METROPOLITAN DISTRICT COUNCIL 53
HUSSAIN *v.* NEW TAPLOW PAPER MILLS 1161
HUTCHINGS (P.H.V.) *v.* CUSTOMS AND EXCISE COMMISSIONERS 3823

I. (A MINOR), *Re* 2510
I.C.I. & I.C.I. FRANCE S.A. *v.* MAT TRANSPORT 2325
I.P.H. *v.* CHIEF CONSTABLE OF SOUTH WALES 766

TABLE OF CASES

PARA.

IAN FLOCKTON DEVELOPMENTS *v.* CUSTOMS AND EXCISE COMMISSIONERS. *See* FLOCKTON (IAN) DEVELOPMENTS *v.* CUSTOMS AND EXCISE COMMISSIONERS
IBSTOCK BUILDING PRODUCTS *v.* CUSTOMS AND EXCISE COMMISSIONERS 3816
IDRISH (MUHAMMED) *v.* SECRETARY OF STATE FOR THE HOME DEPARTMENT..... 1946
IMMIGRATION APPEAL TRIBUNAL *v.* CHELLIAH. *See* CHELLIAH *v.* IMMIGRATION APPEAL TRIBUNAL
IMPERIAL CHEMICAL INDUSTRIES *v.* E.C. COMMISSION (No. 212/86).......... 1492
IMPERIAL COLLEGE OF SCIENCE AND TECHNOLOGY *v.* EBDON (V.O.) AND WESTMINSTER CITY COUNCIL.......... 3193
IMPERIAL COLLEGE OF SCIENCE AND TECHNOLOGY *v.* NORMAN AND DAWBARN (A FIRM).......... 223
IMPORTATION OF A CROCODILE-SKIN BRIEFCASE, *Re*.......... 1584
IMPULSE DISPLAY CENTRE *v.* STEELE (BT/100/1986).......... 2691
INDIAN OIL CORP. *v.* GREENSTONE SHIPPING CO. S.A. (PANAMA).......... 443
INDUSTRIE CHIMICHE ITALIA CENTRALE *v.* TSAVLIRIS (ALEXANDER G.) & SONS MARITIME CO.; PANCRISTO SHIPPING CO. S.A. AND BULA SHIPPING CORP.; CHOKO STAR, THE.......... 3367
INFABRICS *v.* JAYTEX.......... 2943
INGERSOLL (V.O.) *v.* Mc SORLEY (LVC/133/1986).......... 3170
INGLIS *v.* CANT.......... 1132
INGRAMS *v.* SYKES.......... 2956
I.R.C. *v.* BRACKETT.......... 2039
I.R.C. *v.* CHALLENGE CORP.......... 2036
I.R.C. *v.* CRAWLEY.......... 2011
I.R.C. *v.* FRAMPTON (TRUSTEES OF WORTHING RUGBY FOOTBALL CLUB). *See* WORTHING RUGBY FOOTBALL CLUB TRUSTEES *v.* I.R.C.
I.R.C. *v.* MOBIL NORTH SEA.......... 3226
INQUIRY UNDER THE COMPANY SECURITIES (INSIDER DEALING) ACT 1985, AN, *Re*.......... 2934
INSOLVENCY COURT USERS' COMMITTEE.. 211
INSTITUTE OF LEISURE AND AMENITY MANAGEMENT *v.* CUSTOMS AND EXCISE COMMISSIONERS.......... 1661
INSTITUTION OF PROFESSIONAL CIVIL SERVANTS *v.* SECRETARY OF STATE FOR DEFENCE.......... 1527
INSURANCE SERVICES, *Re*: E.C. COMMISSION (NETHERLANDS AND U.K. INTERVENING) *v.* DENMARK (BELGIUM AND IRELAND INTERVENING) (No. 252/83)....... 1572
INSURANCE SERVICES, *Re*: E.C. COMMISSION *v.* GERMANY (No. 205/84).......... 1632
INTERA CORP.'s APPLICATION.......... 2782
INTERFOTO PICTURE LIBRARY *v.* STILETTO VISUAL PROGRAMMES.......... 445
INTERLEGO A.G. *v.* FOLLEY (ALEX) (VIC) PTY.......... 515
INTERLEGO A.G. *v.* TYCO INDUSTRIES......... 511
INTERNATIONAL TIN COUNCIL, *Re*.......... 310

PARA.

INTERNATIONAL WESTMINSTER BANK *v.* OKEANOS MARITIME CORP. *See* COMPANY, A (No. 00359 of 1987), *Re*
INTERPOOL *v.* GALANI.......... 402
INVESTMENT & FREEHOLD ENGLISH ESTATES *v.* CASEMENT.......... 2174
INZE *v.* AUSTRIA (No. 15/1986/113/161)......... 1915
IORIO (PAOLO) *v.* AZIENDA AUTONOMA DELLE FERROVIE DELLO STATO (ITALIAN STATE RAILWAYS) (No 298/84).......... 1567
IOS 1, THE.......... 127
IPSWICH BOROUGH COUNCIL AND LADBROKE RACING.......... 3664
IRISH AGRICULTURAL WHOLESALE SOCIETY *v.* PARTENREEDEREI: M.S. EUROTRADER; EUROTRADER, THE......... 128
IRISH GRAIN BOARD (TRADING) *v.* MINISTER FOR AGRICULTURE (No. 254/85).......... 1586
IRVING AND IRVING *v.* POST OFFICE.......... 1349
ISHIHARA SANGYO KAISHA *v.* DOW CHEMICAL CO.......... 2796
ISLAMIC ARAB INSURANCE CO. *v.* SAUDI EGYPTIAN AMERICAN REINSURANCE CO. 3133
ISLAMIC REPUBLIC OF IRAN SHIPPING LINES *v.* DENBY (PETER JONATHAN)........ 3553
ISLAMIC REPUBLIC OF IRAN SHIPPING LINES *v.* ROYAL BANK OF SCOTLAND; ANNA CH., THE.......... 3438
ISLINGTON LONDON BOROUGH COUNCIL AND JETSPAN.......... 3680
ITALY II, THE.......... 3363

J., *Re*.......... 2452
J. (A MINOR) (ADOPTION APPLICATION), *Re* 2526
J. S. C. AND C. H. C. *v.* WREN.......... 2483
JACK WHARTON, THE. *See* HOLMAN (JOHN MALCOLM) *v.* EVERARD (F. T.) & SONS; JACK WHARTON, THE
JACKMAN *v.* CORBETT.......... 1160
JACKSON *v.* INVICTA PLASTICS.......... 1379
JACKSON *v.* SECRETARY OF STATE FOR THE ENVIRONMENT AND BROMLEY LONDON BOROUGH COUNCIL.......... 3688
JACQUES *v.* AMALGAMATED UNION OF ENGINEERING WORKERS (ENGINEERING SECTION).......... 3768
JAGENDORF AND TROTT *v.* SECRETARY OF STATE AND KRASUCKI.......... 3687
JALAMATSYA, THE.......... 3362
JAMES *v.* BRITISH CRAFT CENTRE.......... 2207
JAMES *v.* CLIFFE.......... 2936
JAMES INDUSTRIES' PATENT.......... 2814
JAMES INVESTMENTS (IOM) *v.* PHILLIPS CUTLER PHILLIPS TROY.......... 2985
JAMESON *v.* MANLEY.......... 2963
JANE *v.* BROOME.......... 999
JANRED PROPERTIES *v.* ENTE NAZIONALE PER IL TURISMO (No. 2).......... 1442
JARVIS (JOHN) *v.* ROCKDALE HOUSING ASSOCIATION.......... 235
JIT SINGH MATTO *v.* D.P.P. *See* MATTO (JIT SINGH) *v.* D.P.P.
JOHN FOX (A FIRM) *v.* BANNISTER KING & RIGBEYS (A FIRM). *See* FOX (JOHN) (A FIRM) *v.* BANNISTER KING & RIGBEYS (A FIRM)
JOHN GUEST (SOUTHERN)'S PATENT.......... 2813

PARA.

JOHN JARVIS *v.* ROCKDALE HOUSING ASSOCIATION *See* JARVIS (JOHN) *v.* ROCKDALE HOUSING ASSOCIATION
JOHN LAING CONSTRUCTION *v,* DASTUR. *See* LAING (JOHN) CONSTRUCTION *v.* DASTUR
JOHN MICHAEL DESIGN *v.* COOKE 431
JOHN MICHALOS, THE. *See* PRESIDENT OF INDIA *v.* N.G. LIVANOS MARITIME CO.; JOHN MICHALOS, THE
JOHNSON & BLOY (HOLDINGS) *v.* WOLSTENHOLME RINK 1295
JOHNSON (PAUL ANTHONY) DEC'D., *Re*...... 3882
JOHNSTON *v.* IRELAND (No. 6/1985/92/139) 1912
JOHNSTON'S ESTATE, *Re,* MORGAN *v.* McCAUGHEY 2755
JOINT OWNERSHIP OF HARGREAVES (ANTWERP) N.V., *Re* 1497
JOINT RECEIVERS AND MANAGERS OF NILTAN CARSON *v.* HAWTHORNE 372
JONES *v.* CHIEF CONSTABLE OF BEDFORDSHIRE 2065
JONES *v.* DEPARTMENT OF EMPLOYMENT. 3466
JONES *v.* KELSEY 587
JONES *v.* THOMAS (JOHN BARRIE) 3278
JORDAN *v.* MID-GLAMORGAN COUNTY COUNCIL 1217
JOYCE *v.* KING 2873

K. (MINORS), *Re* 746
K., *Re*; F., *Re* 58
K. *v.* DEVON COUNTY COUNCIL 2455
K. *v.* K. 1717
K/S A/S BANI *v.* KOREA SHIPBUILDING AND ENGINEERING CORP 2081
KADEER *v.* KADEER 1775
KANSA GENERAL INSURANCE CO. *v.* BISHOPSGATE INSURANCE 145
KAPETAN GEORGIS, THE; *sub nom.* VIRGO STEAMSHIP CO. S.A. *v.* SKAARUP SHIPPING CORP 3587
KARIM *v.* SUNBLEST BAKERIES 1319
KARIN VATIS, THE *See* VAGRES COMPANIA MARITIMA *v.* NISSHO-IWAI AMERICAN CORP.; KARIN VATIS, THE
KAY *v.* AYRSHIRE AND ARRAN HEALTH BOARD 2564
KAYE *v.* INTASUN HOLIDAYS 1150
KELSALL *v.* ALLSTATE INSURANCE CO. 2079
KEMP *v.* CHIEF CONSTABLE OF KENT 3231
KEMP *v.* INTASUN HOLIDAYS 1130
KEMPF *v.* STAATSSECRETARIS VAN JUSTITIE (No. 139/85) 1565
KENNISON *v.* DAIRE 791
KENT FREE PRESS *v.* NATIONAL GRAPHICAL ASSOCIATION 2938
KENYA RAILWAYS *v.* ANTARES CO. PTE.; ANTARES, THE (Nos. 1 and 2) 3380
KENYON SWANSEA, *Re* 371
KERRUTT (HANS-DIETER) AND KERRUTT (UTE) *v.* FINANZAMT (TAX OFFICE) MÖNCHENGLADBACH-MITTE (No. 73/85). 1663
KESTONGATE *v.* MILLER 1393
KETTEMAN *v.* HANSEL PROPERTIES 2330
KEY TERRAIN *v.* GERDES (V.O.) (LVC/289/1985) 3171
KEYPAK HOMECARE, *Re* 373
KHAN *v.* KHAN 1713

PARA.

KHAN *v.* SECRETARY OF STATE FOR THE HOME DEPARTMENT; DEEN *v.* SAME...... 1922
KHAN (AMANULLAH), *Re* 1948
KIELY *v.* KIELY 1738
KIMBELL *v.* HART DISTRICT COUNCIL 242
KING *v.* COMMISSIONER OF VALUATION FOR NORTHERN IRELAND (VR/8/1987) 2729a
KING *v.* REDLICH 2571
KINGSLEY *v.* I.R.C. (Det/2/1982) 1692
KINGSTON-UPON-THAMES LONDON BOROUGH COUNCIL AND QUICK HAMBURGER RESTAURANTS (WHITBREAD) AND PIZZA HUT 3670
KININMOUTH *v.* CHIEF ADJUDICATION OFFICER 2502
KIRBY (INSPECTOR OF TAXES) *v.* THORN E.M.I. 277
KIRKLAND *v.* ROBINSON 117
KLEINWORT BENSON *v.* BARBRAK; SAME *v.* CHOITHRAM (T.) & SONS (LONDON): SAME *v.* CHEMICAL IMPORTATION AND DISTRIBUTION STATE ENTERPRISES: SAME *v.* SHELL MARKETS (M.E.); MYRTO, THE (No. 3) 3125
KNIBB *v.* KNIBB 1785
KNIBB *v.* NATIONAL COAL BOARD 2429
KODIAK TRADE MARK 3754
KROHN & CO. IMPORT-EXPORT GmbH & CO. KG *v.* E.C. COMMISSION (No. 175/84) 1451
KUMAR *v.* DUNNING 2147
KUMAR (RAMESH) *v.* ENTRY CLEARANCE OFFICER, NEW DELHI 1953
KURKJIAN (S.N.) (COMMODITY BROKERS) *v.* MARKETING EXCHANGE FOR AFRICA (FORMERLY MOTIRAM (T.M.) (U.K.) (No. 1) 3336
KURKJIAN (S.N.) (COMMODITY BROKERS) *v.* MARKETING EXCHANGE FOR AFRICA (FORMERLY MOTIRAM (T.M.) (U.K.) (No. 2) 124
KYNASTON *v.* D.P.P.; HERON (JOSEPH) *v.* D.P.P.; HERON (TRACEY) *v.* D.P.P. 706
KYTE *v.* KYTE 1754
KYZIKOS, THE. *See* BULK TRANSPORT GROUP SHIPPING CO. *v.* SEACRYSTAL SHIPPING; KYZIKOS, THE

L. (A MINOR), *Re* 3077
L. (A MINOR) (ADOPTION: PARENTAL AGREEMENT), *Re* 2446
L. H. (A MINOR) (WARDSHIP: JURISDICTION), *Re* 2522
LA POINTE, THE. *See* C.C.R. FISHING *v.* TOMENSON INC.: LA POINTE, THE
LABOUR PARTY *v.* OAKLEY 1414
LADBROKE ENTERTAINMENTS *v.* CLARK..... 1313
LADBROKE GROUP *v.* BRISTOL CITY COUNCIL 2222
LAING (JOHN) CONSTRUCTION *v.* DASTUR.. 2967
LAMBETH BOROUGH COUNCIL AND WESTMINSTER MOTOR SUPPLIES 3660
LANCASHIRE COUNTY COUNCIL *v.* LORD (V.O.) (LVC/962/1984) 3172
LANCER TRADE MARK 3741
LANCER U.K. *v.* CUSTOMS AND EXCISE COMMISSIONERS 3864
LANG *v.* DEVON GENERAL 1389

TABLE OF CASES

PARA.

LANSON HOMES *v.* DEPARTMENT OF THE ENVIRONMENT FOR NORTHERN IRELAND (R./26/1985) 2634
LANTON LEISURE *v.* WHITE AND GIBSON ... 1390
LARKINS *v.* NATIONAL UNION OF MINEWORKERS 409
LASH ATLANTICO, THE 3390
LATHIA *v.* DRONSFIELD BROS. 357
LATIMER (E.) *v.* HUGHES (R.A.) (V.O.) 3173
LAURA ASHLEY *v.* COLOROLL 3751
LAW SOCIETY *v.* SHANKS 3065
LAWRIE-BLUM *v.* LAND BADEN-WÜRTTEMBERG (No. 66/85) 1569
LAWSON *v.* BRITFISH 1329
LAWTON *v.* B.O.C. TRANSHIELD 2579
LEAKEY *v.* TAYLOR 1181
LEANDER *v.* SWEDEN 1919
LEARY *v.* LEARY 2948
LEBENSMITTELWERKE (WALTER RAU) *v.* E.E.C. (REPRESENTED BY THE E.C. COMMISSION) (JOINED CASES NOS. 279, 280, 285 and 286/84) 1453
LEE *v.* GOVERNOR OF PENTONVILLE PRISON AND THE GOVERNMENT OF THE U.S.A. 1705
LEE *v.* HEATON 81
LEEGAS, THE. *See* BARLEE MARINE CORP. *v.* TREVOR REX MOUNTAIN; LEEGAS, THE
LEE-STEERE *v.* JENNINGS 2180
LEICESTER CITY COUNCIL AND UNIVERSITY OF LEICESTER 3709
LEMENDA TRADING CO. *v.* AFRICAN MIDDLE EAST PETROLEUM CO. 421
LEOMINSTER DISTRICT COUNCIL *v.* BRITISH HISTORIC BUILDINGS AND S.P.S. SHIPPING 3633
LES CROUPIERS CASINO CLUB *v.* PATTINSON (INSPECTOR OF TAXES) 2003
LESLIE AND GODWIN INVESTMENTS *v.* PRUDENTIAL ASSURANCE CO. 2136
LETTS *v.* LETTS 2880
LEVERTON *v.* CLWYD COUNTY COUNCIL ... 1332
LEVY (A.) & SON *v.* MARTIN BRENT DEVELOPMENTS 2132
LEWIS 1178
LEWIS *v.* GRATTON-STOREY. *See* GRATTON-STOREY *v.* LEWIS
LEWIS *v.* LETHBRIDGE 841
LEWIS *v.* SURREY COUNTY COUNCIL 1391
LEWISHAM LONDON BOROUGH *v.* W. & P. 2926
LIBYAN ARAB FOREIGN BANK *v.* BANKERS TRUST CO. 201
LILO BLUM *v.* SECRETARY OF STATE FOR THE ENVIRONMENT AND THE LONDON BOROUGH OF RICHMOND UPON THAMES 3620
LINDON PRINT *v.* WEST MIDLANDS COUNTY COUNCIL (Ref./110/1982) 393
LINKLETER *v.* LINKLETER 2932
LIPMAN BRAY (A FIRM) *v.* HILLHOUSE 3556
LIPS MARITIME CORP. *v.* NATIONAL MARITIME AGENCIES CO.; STAR OF KUWAIT, THE 3425
LIPS MARITIME CORP. *v.* PRESIDENT OF INDIA; LIPS, THE 3399
LIPS, THE. *See* LIPS MARITIME CORP. *v.* PRESIDENT OF INDIA; LIPS, THE

PARA.

LIQUIDATOR OF WEST MERCIA SAFETYWEAR *v.* DODD 328
LIVERPOOL ROMAN CATHOLIC ARCHDIOCESAN TRUSTEES INC. *v.* GIBBERD 2882
LLOYD *v.* McMAHON 3162
LLOYD CHEYHAM & CO. *v.* LITTLEJOHN & CO. 318
LLOYD (J. J.) INSTRUMENTS *v.* NORTHERN STAR INSURANCE CO.; MISS JAY JAY, THE 3409
LLOYDS BANK *v.* DUKER 1689
LLOYDS BANK *v.* GUARDIAN ASSURANCE AND TROLLOPE & COLLS 2756
LLOYDS BOWMAKER *v.* BRITANNIA ARROW HOLDINGS 3067
LOAT *v.* ANDREWS *sub nom.* LOAT *v.* JAMES 814
LODGE *v.* MAGNET JOINERY 1206
LOMBARD NORTH CENTRAL *v.* BUTTERWORTH 419
LONDON AND ASSOCIATED INVESTMENT TRUST *v.* CALOW 2163
LONDON CONGREGATIONAL UNION INC. *v.* HARRISS AND HARRISS 229
LONDON GRAIN FUTURES MARKET, *Re* (No. IV/29.688) 1499
LONDON MEAT FUTURES EXCHANGE, *Re* (No. IV/31.614) 1500
LONDON MERCHANT SECURITIES *v.* ISLINGTON LONDON BOROUGH COUNCIL 3194
LONDON PARACHUTING AND RECTORY FARM (PAMPISFORD) *v.* SECRETARY OF STATE FOR THE ENVIRONMENT AND SOUTH CAMBRIDGESHIRE DISTRICT COUNCIL 3606
LONDON POTATO FUTURES ASSOCIATION, *Re* (No. IV/30.176) 1501
LONDON REGIONAL TRANSPORT *v.* WIMPEY GROUP SERVICES 2223
LONGLEY *v.* NATIONAL UNION OF JOURNALISTS 3760
LONSLOW *v.* HENNIG (FORMERLY LONSLOW) 2487
LOPINOT LIMESTONE *v.* ATT.-GEN. OF TRINIDAD AND TOBAGO 3678
LORNE STEWART *v.* SINDALL (WILLIAM) AND N.W. THAMES REGIONAL HEALTH AUTHORITY. *See* STEWART (LORNE) *v.* SINDALL (WILLIAM) AND N.W. THAMES REGIONAL HEALTH AUTHORITY
LOTHIAN REGIONAL ASSESSOR *v.* HOOD ... 3157
LOWE v. LESTER 3268
LUIS MARBURG & SÖHNE GmbH *v.* SOCIETÁ ORI MARTIN SpA 1549
LUSOGRAIN COMERCIO INTERNACIONAL DE CEREAS *v.* BUNGE A.G. 3325
LUTTON *v.* SAVILLE TRACTORS (BELFAST) .. 2740
LYNCH *v.* SUBJIC 187
LYONS *v.* EAST SUSSEX COUNTY COUNCIL 2414

M. (A MINOR) (CHILD ABUSE: EVIDENCE), *Re*, (Note) 2473
M. (A MINOR) (CUSTODIANSHIP: JURISDICTION), *Re* 2449
M. AND H. (MINORS) (LOCAL AUTHORITY: PARENTAL RIGHTS), *Re* 2485
M. (MINORS) (CONFIDENTIAL DOCUMENTS), *Re* 2922

TABLE OF CASES

PARA.

M. *v.* LAMBETH BOROUGH COUNCIL (No. 3) 2523
M. *v.* M 2493
M. *v.* M 1764
M. *v.* M. (FINANCIAL PROVISION) 1749
M. *v.* M. (MINOR: CUSTODY APPEAL) 2494
M.R.A. ENGINEERING *v.* TRIMSTER CO. 458
M/S ASWAN ENGINEERING ESTABLISHMENT CO. *v.* LUPDINE 3337
MABANAFT GmbH *v.* HAUPTZOLLAMT EMMERICH (No. 36/83) 1475
McALEER *v.* COMMODORE CINEMAS (NORTHERN IRELAND) (BT/120/1986); McCALLION *v.* COMMODORE CINEMAS (NORTHERN IRELAND) (BT/121/1986); McGUIGAN *v.* COMMODORE CINEMAS (NORTHERN IRELAND) (BT/125/1986) 2692
MACAULAY *v.* SCREENKARN 518
McBRIDE *v.* DEPARTMENT OF THE ENVIRONMENT FOR NORTHERN IRELAND (R/15/1986) 2642a
McCANDLESS (ENGINEERS) *v.* SECRETARY OF STATE FOR NORTHERN IRELAND 2651
McCANN *v.* CANAGAN 3029
McCARTNEY'S APPLICATION, *Re* 2726
McCLEAN *v.* LIVERPOOL CITY COUNCIL 2238
McCLELLAND *v.* MONTAGU (R/18/1985) 2697a
McCORMICK *v.* McCORMICK 1426
McDERMID *v.* NASH DREDGING AND RECLAMATION CO. 2615
McDERMOTT *v.* DEPARTMENT OF AGRICULTURE FOR NORTHERN IRELAND AND H.M. TREASURY (R/11/1986) 2666
McDERMOTT AND COTTER *v.* MINISTER FOR SOCIAL WELFARE AND THE ATT.-GEN. (No. 286/85) 1636
MACDONALD *v.* TRUSTEES OF HENRY SMITH'S CHARITY 2164
McDONALD'S HAMBURGERS *v.* BURGER-KING (U.K.) 2944
McDONALD'S HAMBURGERS *v.* WINDLE 1818
McDOWELL *v.* McKIBBIN; BRANNON *v.* GUTHRIE 2697
MacFARQUHAR *v.* PHILLIMORE; MARKS *v.* PHILLIMORE 2169
McGARRY (E.) (ELECTRICAL) *v.* BURROUGHS MACHINES 3030
McGOLDRICK *v.* BRENT LONDON BOROUGH COUNCIL 1308
McGRATH *v.* FIELD 3270
McGRATH *v.* SHAH 465
McGREGOR *v.* GENERAL MUNICIPAL BOILERMAKERS AND ALLIED TRADES UNION 1331
McGROTHER *v.* POLICE AUTHORITY FOR NORTHERN IRELAND (R/20/1985) 2635, 2636
McINTOSH *v.* McGOWAN 306
MACKAY *v.* JACKSON 1128
MACKINLAY (INSPECTOR OF TAXES) *v.* ARTHUR YOUNG McCLELLAND MOORES & CO. 2040
McKOEN *v.* ELLIS 3291
MACLAINE WATSON & CO. *v.* DEPARTMENT OF TRADE AND INDUSTRY 312
MACLAINE WATSON & CO. *v.* INTERNATIONAL TIN COUNCIL 2989
MACLAINE WATSON & CO. *v.* INTERNATIONAL TIN COUNCIL 2093
McLAREN *v.* NATIONAL COAL BOARD 1407

PARA.

McLEAN ENTERPRISES *v.* ECCLESIASTICAL INSURANCE OFFICE 2055
McLELLAN *v.* FLETCHER 3559
McLEOD *v.* HUNTER (JOHN) 1162
McMANUS & SON *v.* BURROWS, GILBERT AND POTTIE (BT/81/1986) 2693
McMILLAN *v.* CROSSEY (BT/21/1985) 2694
McNEIL *v.* LONDON ELECTRICITY BOARD 1185
McNICHOLL (ANTHONY) *v.* MINISTER FOR AGRICULTURE 1456
MacPHERSON *v.* I.R.C. 284
McSORLEY *v.* MacNEILE-DICKSON (R/30/1986; R/31/1986) 2696a
McV. *v.* B 1708
MACEY *v.* QAZI 425
MAFRACHT *v.* PARNES SHIPPING CO. S.A. APOLLONIUS, THE 125
MAIL NEWSPAPERS *v.* EXPRESS NEWSPAPERS 510
MALINOWSKI, *Re* 747
MALONE'S APPLICATION, *Re* 2623
MAMMOTH PINE, THE *See* NETHERLANDS INSURANCE CO. EST. 1845 *v.* LJUNGBERG (KARL) & CO. AB; MAMMOTH PINE, THE
MANCHESTER CITY COUNCIL *v.* SECRETARY OF STATE FOR THE ENVIRONMENT 2352
MANCHESTER STEEL *v.* E.C. COMMISSION (No. 46/85) 1652
MANICKAVASAGAR *v.* COMMISSIONER OF METROPOLITAN POLICE 1967
MANKU *v.* SEEHRA 2902
MANSOURI *v.* BLOOMSBURY HEALTH AUTHORITY 2920
MAPLES (FORMERLY MELAMUD) *v.* MAPLES; MAPLES (FORMERLY MELAMUD) *v.* MELAMUD 405
MARC RICH & CO. *v.* TOURLOTI COMPANIA NAVIERA S.A. *See* RICH (MARC) & CO. *v.* TOURLOTI COMPANIA NAVIERA S.A.
MARGRIE HOLDINGS *v.* CUSTOMS AND EXCISE COMMISSIONERS 3852
MARIANA ISLANDS STEAMSHIP CORP. *v.* MARIMPEX MINERALOEL-HANDELSGESELLSCHAFT m.b.H. & Co. K.G.; MEDUSA, THE 3384
MARKEY (INSPECTOR OF TAXES) *v.* SANDERS 279
MARKOU *v.* DA SILVAESA; CRANCOUR *v.* MEROLA 2246
MARLEY *v.* FORWARD TRUST GROUP 1297
MARS G.B. *v.* CADBURY 3749
MARSH *v.* CHIEF CONSTABLE OF AVON AND SOMERSET CONSTABULARY 1795
MARSON (INSPECTOR OF TAXES) *v.* MORTON 2022
MARTIN *v.* MARTIN 494
MARTIN'S APPLICATION, *Re* (No. LP/40/1985) 3713
MARZELL INVESTMENT *v.* TRANS TELEX 3099
MASEFIELD *v.* TAYLOR 3635
MASI A.G. *v.* COLOROLL 2797
MASUDA'S APPLICATION 2775
MATHEW *v.* MAUGHOLD LIFE ASSURANCE CO. 2563
MATTHEWS *v.* WICKS 115
MATTISON *v.* BEVERLEY BOROUGH COUNCIL 3154
MATTO (JIT SINGH) *v.* D.P.P. 572

TABLE OF CASES

PARA.

MAULDON *v.* BRITISH TELECOMMUNICATIONS ... 1415
MAWSON *v.* OXFORD ... 3306
MAWYER (A.W.) & CO. *v.* CUSTOMS AND EXCISE COMMISSIONERS ... 3800
MAXWELL *v.* PRESSDRAM ... 1678
MAYCLOSE *v.* CENTRAL ELECTRICITY GENERATING BOARD ... 1288
MAYOR AND BURGESSES OF CAMDEN LONDON BOROUGH *v.* PERSONS UNKNOWN ... 2183
MAYOR AND BURGESSES OF WANDSWORTH LONDON BOROUGH *v.* ORAKPO ... 1865
MEAH *v.* MAYOR AND BURGESSES OF THE LONDON BOROUGH OF TOWER HAMLETS ... 1127
MECHAM *v.* SADDINGTON ... 1207
MEDUSA, THE. *See* MARIANA ISLANDS STEAMSHIP CORP. *v.* MARIMPEX MINERALOEL-HANDELSGESELLSCHAFT m.b.H. & CO. K.G.; MEDUSA, THE
MEEK *v.* CITY OF BIRMINGHAM DISTRICT COUNCIL ... 1399
MELLOR *v.* SECRETARY OF STATE FOR THE ENVIRONMENT ... 3665
MERCANTILE CREDIT CO. *v.* ELLIS; SAME *v.* JAMES; SAME *v.* CARRINGTON; SAME *v.* HUXTABLE; SAME *v.* STANGER ... 2917
MERRIMAN *v.* HARDY ... 2488
MERSEY DOCKS AND HARBOUR CO. *v.* MERSEYSIDE DEVELOPMENT CORPORATION (Ref./12/1983) ... 394
MERVYN ... 1187
METAALHANDEL JA MAGNUS B.V. *v.* ARDFIELDS TRANSPORT ... 184
METAL BOX *v.* CURRYS ... 1157
METAL FABRICATIONS (VIC) PTY *v.* KELCEY 415
METRO-SB-GROßMÄRKTE GmbH & CO. K.G. (U.K. INTERVENING) *v.* E.C. COMMISSION (SABA GmbH AND GERMANY INTERVENING) (No. 2) (No. 75/84) ... 1494
METROLAND INVESTMENTS *v.* DEWHURST (J.H.) ... 2202
MEWIS *v.* WOOLF ... 1155
MEWIS *v.* WOOLF ... 1175
MICHAEL *v.* MICHAEL ... 1734
MIDLAND BANK *v.* SHEPHARD ... 457
MIDLOTHIAN DISTRICT COUNCIL *v.* STEVENSON ... 3629
MILES *v.* WAKEFIELD DISTRICT COUNCIL ... 1380
MILK MARKETING BOARDS, *Re*: E.C. COMMISSION (SUPPORTED BY FRANCE, INTERVENER) *v.* U.K. (No. 23/84) ... 1459
MILLER *v.* HAMWORTHY ENGINEERING ... 1377
MILLER *v.* I.R.C. ... 285
MINCHBURN *v.* FERNANDEZ ... 2184
MINERALS AND METALS TRADING CORP. OF INDIA *v.* ENCOUNTER BAY SHIPPING CO.; SAMOS GLORY, THE ... 3442
MINISTÈRE PUBLIC *v.* MÜLLER AND KAMPFMEYER-FRANCE SÀRL (No. 304/84) 1580
MINISTRY OF AGRICULTURE, FISHERIES AND FOOD *v.* PORTER ... 1458
MINOR *v.* CROWN PROSECUTION SERVICE 839
MIRO B.V. (No. 182/84) ... 1576
MIRROR NEWSPAPER *v.* JOOLS ... 1140

PARA.

MISS JAY JAY, THE. *See* LLOYD (J.J.) INSTRUMENTS *v.* NORTHERN STAR INSURANCE CO.; THE MISS JAY JAY
MISSET *v.* E.C. COUNCIL (No. 152/85) ... 1540
MITO, THE. *See* COMMODITY OCEAN TRANSPORT CORP. *v.* BASFORD UNICORN INDUSTRIES; MITO, THE
MITSUBISHI *v.* FIAT ... 3758
MITSUBISHI *v.* ALAFONZOS ... 432
MOBIL NORTH SEA *v.* I.R.C. *See* I.R.C. *v.* MOBIL NORTH SEA
MOBIL SHIPPING AND TRANSPORTATION *v.* SHELL EASTERN PETROLEUM (PTE) ... 3382
MONNELL AND MORRIS *v.* U.K. (No. 7/1985/93/140–141) ... 1917
MONSANTO *v.* TRANSPORT AND GENERAL WORKERS' UNION ... 3770
MONTAGU'S SETTLEMENTS, *Re*; DUKE OF MANCHESTER *v.* NATIONAL WESTMINSTER BANK ... 1432
MOORE *v.* DURHAM CITY COUNCIL ... 3181
MOORE *v.* JOHNSTON ... 1202
MOORE (D.W.) AND CO. *v.* FERRIER ... 2333
MORAN *v.* SECRETARY OF STATE FOR SOCIAL SERVICES ... 3453
MORDAUNT, *Re* ... 1182
MORGAN *v.* COMMISSIONER OF VALUATION FOR NORTHERN IRELAND (VR/3/1986) ... 2730
MORGAN GUARANTY TRUST CO. OF NEW YORK *v.* HADJANTONAKIS (DEMETRE) ... 3101
MORGAN GUARANTY TRUST CO. OF NEW YORK *v.* HADJANTONAKIS (DEMETRE) ... 3113
MORRIS *v.* AMBER FILM SALES ... 2899
MORRIS *v.* LONDON IRON & STEEL CO. ... 1337
MORRIS *v.* MURPHY (J.) CABLE CONTRACTORS & CIVIL ENGINEERS ... 2959
MORRIS *v.* PATEL ... 2133
MORRIS-THOMAS *v.* PETTICOAT LANE RENTALS ... 441
MORTIMER *v.* MORTIMER-GRIFFIN ... 1788
MOSSMAIN, *Re* ... 349
MOTHERCARE U.K. *v.* PENGUIN BOOKS ... 530
MOTT, *Re, ex p.*, TRUSTEE OF THE PROPERTY OF THE BANKRUPT *v.* MOTT AND McQUITTY ... 212
MOWBRAY (KEVIN) *v.* CUSTOMS AND EXCISE COMMISSIONERS ... 3863
MOYES *v.* HYLTON CASTLE WORKING MEN'S SOCIAL CLUB AND INSTITUTE ... 1386
MUFFETT (S.H.) *v.* HEAD ... 1387
MUIR, *Re* ... 1696
MULHOLLAND *v.* McKENNA (BT/7/1987) ... 2695
MULTI GUARANTEE CO., *Re* ... 1427
MUNIR *v.* JANG PUBLICATIONS ... 1342
MURCO PETROLEUM *v.* FORGE ... 1412
MURPHY (MARY) *v.* BORD TELECOM EIREANN ... 1574
MURPHY *v.* COMMISSIONER OF VALUATION FOR NORTHERN IRELAND (VR/20/1986) ... 2731
MURRAY *v.* BIRMINGHAM CITY COUNCIL ... 2236
MURRAY *v.* CHICKEN CABINS ... 1186
MURRI FRÈRES *v.* EUROPEAN COMMISSION (No. 33/82) ... 1476
MUSA *v.* LE MAITRE ... 500

TABLE OF CASES

PARA.

MUSISI, *Re. See* BUGDAYCAY *v.* SECRETARY OF STATE FOR THE HOME DEPARTMENT; NELIDOW SANTIS *v.* SAME; NORMAN *v.* SAME; MUSISI, *Re*

MYLES J. CALLAGHAN (IN RECEIVERSHIP) *v.* CITY OF GLASGOW DISTRICT COUNCIL. *See* CALLAGHAN (MYLES J.) (IN RECEIVERSHIP) *v.* CITY OF GLASGOW DISTRICT COUNCIL

MYRTO, THE (No. 3). *See* KLEINWORT BENSON *v.* BARBRAK; SAME *v.* CHOITHRAM (T.) & SONS (LONDON); SAME *v.* CHEMICAL IMPORTATION AND DISTRIBUTION STATE ENTERPRISES; SAME *v.* SHELL MARKETS (M.E.) MYRTO, THE (No. 3)

N. (MINORS) (CHILD ABUSE: EVIDENCE), *Re* 2472

N. (MINORS) (WARDSHIP: EVIDENCE), *Re* 2517

N. AND L. (MINORS) (ADOPTION PROCEEDINGS: VENUE), *Re* 3117

N.R.D.C.'s IRISH APPLICATION 2779

NAPIER BROWN AND CO. *v.* BRITISH SUGAR 1493

NASH *v.* SECRETARY OF STATE FOR THE ENVIRONMENT AND EPPING FOREST DISTRICT COUNCIL 3623

NASIM (TRADING AS YASMINE RESTAURANT) *v.* CUSTOMS AND EXCISE COMMISSIONERS 3840

NATIONAL BANK OF GREECE *v.* CONSTANTINOS DIMITRIOU 3070

NATIONAL COAL BOARD v. McGINTY 1402

NATIONAL COAL BOARD *v.* NATIONAL UNION OF MINEWORKERS 3762

NATIONAL COAL BOARD *v.* RIDGWAY AND FAIRBROTHER. *See* RIDGWAY AND FAIRBROTHER *v.* NATIONAL COAL BOARD

NATIONAL DOCK LABOUR BOARD *v.* SABAH TIMBER CO. 3038

NATIONAL EMPLOYERS MUTUAL GENERAL INSURANCE ASSOCIATION *v.* JONES 3345

NATIONAL TRUST FOR PLACES OF HISTORIC INTEREST OR NATURAL BEAUTY *v.* WHITE 1233

NATIONWIDE BUILDING SOCIETY *v.* NATIONWIDE ESTATE AGENTS 531

NATURALLY YOURS COSMETICS *v.* CUSTOMS AND EXCISE COMMISSIONERS 3856

NAVIERA AMAZONICA PERUANA *v.* COMPANIA INTERNACIONAL DE SEGUROS DE PERU 135

NAVIERA MOGOR S.A. *v.* SOCIETE METALLURGIQUE DE NORMANDIE 3372

NAYLOR *v.* PRESTON AREA HEALTH AUTHORITY; FOSTER *v.* MERTON AND SUTTON HEALTH AUTHORITY; THOMAS *v.* NORTH WEST SURREY HEALTH AUTHORITY; IKUMELO *v.* NEWHAM HEALTH AUTHORITY 3006

NAYLOR *v.* WROTHAM PARK SETTLED ESTATES 2984

NAZ *v.* RAJA 469

NEAL *v.* CUSTOMS AND EXCISE COMMISSIONERS 3821

NEELY *v.* ROURKE (INSPECTOR OF TAXES) . 272

PARA.

NEESON'S APPLICATION, *Re* 2705

NEGUS *v.* ALLEN 3047

NEPTUNE C, THE. *See* STANDARD OCEAN CARRIERS S.A. *v.* UNION DE REMORQUAGE ET DE SAUVETAGE S.A.; NEPTUNE C, THE

NEPTUNE NAVIGATION CORP *v.* ISHIKAWAJIMA—HARIMA HEAVY INDUSTRIES CO. 3424

NETHERLANDS *v.* FEDERATIE NEDERLANDSE VAKBEWEGING (No. 71/85) 1575

NETHERLANDS, THE *v.* REED (ANN FLORENCE) (No. 59/85) 1568

NETHERLANDS INSURANCE CO. EST. 1845 *v.* LJUNGBERG (KARL) & CO. AB; MAMMOTH PINE, THE 3371

NEVINS 1177

NEVINS *v.* LAW 208

NEW PINEHURST RESIDENCE ASSOCIATION (CAMBRIDGE) *v.* SILOW 2173

NEWA LINE *v.* ERECTHION SHIPPING CO. S.A. 3431

NEWBURY DISTRICT COUNCIL *v.* SECRETARY OF STATE FOR THE ENVIRONMENT 3596

NEWHAM LONDON BOROUGH *v.* SECRETARY OF STATE FOR THE ENVIRONMENT 3690

NEWHAM LONDON BOROUGH COUNCIL AND PIZZA HUT (U.K.) 3672

NEWHAM LONDON BOROUGH COUNCIL *v.* SINGH 845

NEWMAN *v.* BENESCH 2933

NEWS GROUP NEWSPAPERS *v.* SOCIETY OF GRAPHICAL AND ALLIED TRADES 1982 3759

NEWS GROUP NEWSPAPERS *v.* SOCIETY OF GRAPHICAL AND ALLIED TRADES '82 (No. 2) 3771

NEWTON *v.* WOODS 3280

NG (ALIAS WONG) *v.* THE QUEEN 1821

NICHIMEN CORP. *v.* GATOIL OVERSEAS INC. 3330

NICHOLAS *v.* PARSONAGE 588

NIPPON PISTON RING CO.'S APPLICATIONS 2777

NIPPON SEIKO *v.* COUNCIL OF THE EUROPEAN COMMUNITIES (No. 258/84) 1468

NIXON *v.* WOOD 2768

NORBROOK LABORATORIES *v.* SMYTH 2668

NORDGLIMT, THE 3361

NORSK HYDRO POLYMERS *v.* PLASTICS PROCESSING INDUSTRY TRAINING BOARD 3732

NORTH DOWN BOROUGH COUNCIL'S APPLICATION, *Re* 2704

NORTH EASTERN CO-OPERATIVE SOCIETY *v.* NEWCASTLE-UPON-TYNE CITY COUNCIL 2209

NORTH WEST GAS *v.* HYMANSON 1145

NORTHAMPTONSHIRE COUNTY COUNCIL *v.* H. 2458

NORTHERN COUNTIES CO-OPERATIVE ENTERPRISES *v.* CUSTOMS AND EXCISE COMMISSIONERS 3814

NORTHUMBERLAND COUNTY COUNCIL AND CRAKE SCAR OPENCAST 3695

NORWICH UNION LIFE INSURANCE SOCIETY *v.* BRITISH RAILWAYS BOARD 2225

NOTIFICATION OF THE BELGISCHE VERENIGING DER BANKEN/ASSOCIATION BELGE DES BANQUES, *Re* (No. IV 261-A) 1488

TABLE OF CASES

PARA.

NOTOS, THE. *See* SOCIÉTÉ ANONYME MAROCAINE DE L'INDUSTRIE DU RAFFINAGE *v.* NOTOS MARITIME CORP. OF MONROVIA: NOTOS THE
NOTTINGHAMSHIRE COUNTY COUNCIL *v.* NOTTINGHAM CITY COUNCIL 3187
NOZARI-ZADEH *v.* PEARL ASSURANCE 2126
NUGENT *v.* RIDLEY 3311
NURIT BAR *v.* PATHWOOD INVESTMENTS 2127
NURSING DIRECTIVES, *Re*: E.C. COMMISSION *v.* GERMANY (No. 29/84) 1521
NYE SAUNDERS (A FIRM) *v.* BRISTOW 2573

O. *v.* U.K.; H. *v.* SAME; W. *v.* SAME; B. *v.* SAME; R. *v.* SAME (Nos. 2/1986/100/148 to 6/1986/104/152) 1916
OAKLEY *v.* LABOUR PARTY *See* LABOUR PARTY *v.* OAKLEY
OBESTAIN INC. *v.* NATIONAL MINERAL DEVELOPMENT CORP.; SANIX ACE, THE. 3376
OFFSHORE VENTILATION, *Re* 354
OGWO *v.* TAYLOR 2614
O'HAGAN *v.* DEPARTMENT OF THE ENVIRONMENT FOR NORTHERN IRELAND (R/27/1985; R/33/1985) 2752a
OJELAY *v.* NEOSALE 62
OLD *v.* SAMPSON 1215
OLD CHIGWELLIANS' CLUB *v.* CUSTOMS AND EXCISE COMMISSIONERS 3845
O'MAHONY *v.* GAFFNEY 3092
OMEGA LEROS, THE. *See* EURICO S.p.A. *v.* LEROS SHIPPING CO. AND SEABOARD MARITIME INC.; OMEGA LEROS, THE
ORCHARD *v.* SOUTH EASTERN ELECTRICITY BOARD 3547
ORDER 14 APPEALS 3075
ORESUNDSVARVET AKTIEBOGAG *v.* LEMOS 448
ORIANI *v.* DORITA PROPERTIES 2177
O'SULLIVAN *v.* HERDMANS 2721
OTTER *v.* NORMAN 2186
OURO FINO, THE 3394
OUTHWAITE (RICHARD) *v.* COMMERCIAL BANK OF GREECE S.A.; SEA BREEZE, THE 3412
OVERSEAS CONTAINERS (FINANCE) *v.* STOKER (INSPECTOR OF TAXES) 546
OVERSEAS FORTUNE SHIPPING PTE. *v.* GREAT EASTERN SHIPPING CO.; SINGAPORE FORTUNE, THE 119
OWEN *v.* JONES 3260
OWUSU-SEKYERE'S APPLICATION, *Re* 1944
OXFORD *v.* BAXENDALE 3233

P. (A MINOR) (WARDSHIP), *Re* 2512
P. (MINORS), *Re* 2445
P. (MINORS) (SURROGACY), *Re* 2513
P., *Re*; LINCOLNSHIRE COUNTY COUNCIL *v.* P. 2529
PLM TRADING CO. (INTERNATIONAL) *v.* GEORGIOU 430
P.X. NUCLEAR, *Re* 2641
PADMORE *v.* I.R.C. 2021
PADOVANI *v.* AMMINISTRAZIONE DELLE FINANZE DELLO STATO (No. 69/84) 1577
PAGNAN (R) & FRATELLI *v.* FINAGRAIN COMPAGNIE COMMERCIALE AGRICOLE ET FINANCIERE S.A.; ADOLF LEONHARDT, THE 3423

PARA.

PAGNAN SpA *v.* GRANARIA B.V. 444
PAGNAN SpA *v.* TRADAX OCEAN TRANSPORTATION S.A. 3326
PALMER *v.* SANDWELL METROPOLITAN BOROUGH 1901a
PANAGHIA TINNOU, THE. *See* C.H.Z. "ROLIMPEX" *v.* EFTAVRYSSES COMPANIA NAVIERA S.A.; PANAGHIA TINNOU, THE
PANTHER SHOP INVESTMENTS *v.* KEITH POPLE 2208
PARKINSON (PATRICK) *v.* CUSTOMS AND EXCISE COMMISSIONERS 3830
PARRY *v.* BOYLE 744
PARRY *v.* ROBINSON-WYLLIE 2114
PARSONS *v.* EAST SURREY HEALTH AUTHORITY 1371
PARTIE ECOLOGISTE "LES VERTS" *v.* EUROPEAN PARLIAMENT (No. 294/83) 1555
PASSEE *v.* PASSEE 459
PASSMORE *v.* GILL AND GILL 1756
PATEL *v.* BLAKEY 671
PATEL *v.* PATEL 3590
PATEL *v.* SMITH (W. H.) (EZIOT) 3039
PATEL *v.* WRIGHT 2314
PATERSON *v.* AGGIO 2235
PATERSON ZOCHONIS & CO. *v.* MERFARKEN PACKAGING 523
PATTERSON *v.* MINISTRY OF DEFENCE 1194
PATTNI (PURSHOTAM M.) & SONS *v.* CUSTOMS AND EXCISE COMMISSIONERS 3837
PAUL *v.* NATIONAL ASSOCIATION OF LOCAL GOVERNMENT OFFICERS 1283
PAULS MALT *v.* GRAMPIAN ASSESSOR 3184
PEABODY INTERNATIONAL'S APPLICATION 2783
PEAK PARK JOINT PLANNING BOARD AND TARMAC ROADSTONE (WESTERN) 3682
PEAKE, *Re* 215
PEARCE *v.* SECRETARY OF STATE FOR DEFENCE 2569
PEARCY (JOHN) TRANSPORT *v.* SECRETARY OF STATE FOR THE ENVIRONMENT 3615
PEARSON *v.* COMMISSIONER OF POLICE OF THE METROPOLIS 3252
PEOPLE, THE (ATT.GEN.) *v.* GILLILAND 1694
PEREZ-ADAMSON *v.* PEREZ-RIVAS 1782
PERGO, THE. *See* FAIRBAIRN (DAVID JAMES) *v.* VENNOOTSCHAP G VER VRIES ZN; PERGO, THE
PERRIN (V.O.) *v.* LEICESTER (LVC/91/1986) ... 3174
PERRY *v.* MERCER 1216
PERRY *v.* MIDLAND BANK 2544
PERRYLEASE *v.* IMECAR AG 1670
PESCA VALENTIA *v.* MINISTER FOR FISHERIES AND FORESTRY 1562
PETER MILLETT & SONS *v.* SALISBURY HANDBAGS 2125
PETROSHIP B, THE 3388
PFEIFFER WEINKELLEREI-WEINEINKAUF (E.) *v.* ARBUTHNOT FACTORS 3325
PHILIPS ELECTRONIC AND ASSOCIATED INDUSTRIES PATENT 2770
PHILLIPS (A. B. W.) AND STRATTON (ALBERT) *v.* DORINTAL INSURANCE 2076
PHILLIPS (JOHN) *v.* INTEGRITY Asbl 1645
PHILLIPS PRODUCTS *v.* HYLAND (NOTE) 423
PHIPPS-FAIRE *v.* MALBERN CONSTRUCTION 2200

PARA.

PHOENIX GENERAL INSURANCE CO. OF GREECE S.A. *v.* HALVANON INSURANCE CO.: SAME *v.* ADMINISTRATIA ASIGURARILOR de STAT 2050
PHOTO-SCAN TRADE MARK 3744
PICKSTONE *v.* FREEMANS 1322
PILLAR P.G. *v.* HIGGINS (D.J.) CONSTRUCTION 239
PIMBLETT (JOHN) & SONS *v.* COMMISSIONERS OF CUSTOMS AND EXCISE 3839
PINE *v.* McMILLAN 2296
PINE TOP INSURANCE CO. *v.* UNIONE ITALIANA ANGLO SAXON REINSURANCE CO. 2074
PIVER (L.T.) S.a.r.l. *v.* S. & J. PERFUME CO. 2883
PLAUMANN *v.* MACHINEFABRIEK A. VAN DER LINDEN B.V. 1551
PLEASANTS *v.* ATKINSON (INSPECTOR OF TAXES) 2002
PLIX PRODUCTS *v.* WINSTONE (FRANK M.) (MERCHANTS) 508
PLUMMER *v.* I.R.C. 401
PLYMOUTH CITY COUNCIL *v.* QUIETLYNN; PORTSMOUTH CITY COUNCIL *v.* QUIETLYNN; QUIETLYNN *v.* OLDHAM BOROUGH COUNCIL 2319
POLIVETTE *v.* COMMERCIAL UNION ASSURANCE CO. 2057
POLKEY *v.* DAYTON (A.E) SERVICES 1398
POLKEY *v.* EDMUND WALKER (HOLDINGS). *See* POLKEY *v.* DAYTON (A.E.) SERVICES
POLO PICTURES *v.* TRAFFORD METROPOLITAN BOROUGH COUNCIL 3191
POPES LANE PET FOOD SUPPLIES *v.* CUSTOMS AND EXCISE COMMISSIONERS 3857
PORTMAN REGISTRARS & NOMINEES *v.* MOHAMMED LATIF 2239
PORZELACK KG *v.* PORZELACK (U.K.) 2954
POST OFFICE *v.* AQUARIUS PROPERTIES 2141
POST OFFICE *v.* ORKNEY AND SHETLAND ASSESSOR 3158
POSTGATE & DENBY (AGENCIES), *Re* 336
POULTON'S WILL TRUSTS, *Re* 3878
POWER *v.* POWER 2889
POWER SECURITIES (MANCHESTER) *v.* PRUDENTIAL ASSURANCE CO. 2206
POWLSON (INSPECTOR OF TAXES) *v.* WELBECK SECURITIES 278
PRACTICE DIRECTION (ADMIRALTY) (REMUNERATION OF NAUTICAL AND OTHER ASSESSORS) 2877
PRACTICE DIRECTION (CHANCERY: SHORT SUMMONS LIST) (No. 2 of 1987) 2916
PRACTICE DIRECTION (CH.D.) (COMPANIES COURT: COMPULSORY WINDING UP) 324
PRACTICE DIRECTION (CH.D.) (PROCEDURE: APPLICATIONS UNDER S.48 OF THE ADMINISTRATION OF JUSTICE ACT 1985) (No. 1 of 1987) 2906
PRACTICE DIRECTION (CH.D.) (PROCEDURE: APPLICATIONS UNDER THE VARIATION OF TRUSTS ACT 1958) (No. 3 of 1987) 2907
PRACTICE DIRECTION (C.A.) (APPEALS: DOCUMENTATION) 2900
PRACTICE DIRECTION (C.A.) (APPEALS FROM REPORTED JUDGMENTS) 3048

PARA.

PRACTICE DIRECTION (C.A.) (CROWN COURT BUSINESS: CLASSIFICATION) 639
PRACTICE DIRECTION (EVIDENCE: WRITTEN STATEMENTS) 750
PRACTICE DIRECTION (FAM.D.) (AFFIDAVITS: FILING) 288
PRACTICE DIRECTION (FAM.D.) (BUSINESS: TRANSFER) 3118
PRACTICE DIRECTION (FAM.D.) (PERIODICAL PAYMENTS: CHILDREN) 3008
PRACTICE DIRECTION (FAM.D.) (WARDS: CRIMINAL INJURIES COMPENSATION BOARD) 653
PRACTICE DIRECTION (FAM.D.) (WARDS: DISCLOSURE OF EVIDENCE) 3009
PRACTICE DIRECTION (FAM.D.) (WARDS WITNESS IN CRIMINAL PROCEEDINGS) 654
PRACTICE DIRECTION (LORD CHANCELLOR) (COUNTY COURT PRACTICE: SUMMONSES: FORMS) 2972
PRACTICE DIRECTION (Q.B.D.) (BAIL: FAILURE TO SURRENDER TO CUSTODY) 2910
PRACTICE DIRECTION (Q.B.D.) (NEW ADMIRALTY AND COMMERCIAL COURT REGISTRY) 2875
PRACTICE DIRECTION (Q.B.D.) (SERVICE OUT OF THE JURISDICTION) 3134
PRACTICE DIRECTION (Q.B.D.) (TRIAL OUT OF LONDON) 3120
PRACTICE NOTE (BANKRUPTCY) (No. 2 of 1987) 2914
PRACTICE NOTE (CH.D.) (BANKRUPTCY: STATUTORY DEMAND) (No. 5 of 1986) 2912
PRACTICE NOTE (CH.D.) (BANKRUPTCY: STATUTORY DEMAND: SETTING ASIDE) (No. 1 of 1987) 2913
PRACTICE NOTE (COMMERCIAL COURT) (LIMITATION OF TIME FOR INTERLOCUTORY HEARINGS) 2921
PRACTICE NOTE (C.A.) (LIST OF FORTHCOMING APPEALS) 2976
PRACTICE NOTE (C.A.) (LONG VACATION) 2977
PRACTICE NOTE (COURT OF PROTECTION) (SOLICITORS' FIXED COSTS) 2978
PRACTICE NOTE (Q.B.D.) (CROWN OFFICE LIST) 2979
PRACTICE NOTE (Q.B.D.) (CROWN OFFICE LIST) 2980
PRACTICE NOTE: REIMBURSEMENT OF ANTI-DUMPING DUTIES 1469
PRAGER *v.* TIMES NEWSPAPERS 2302
PRASAD *v.* GENERAL MEDICAL COUNCIL 2409
PRESIDENT OF INDIA *v.* DAVENPORT MARINE PANAMA S.A. 3401
PRESIDENT OF INDIA *v.* LIPS MARITIME CORP.; LIPS, THE. *See* LIPS MARITIME CORP. *v.* PRESIDENT OF INDIA; LIPS THE
PRESIDENT OF INDIA *v.* N.G. LIVANOS MARITIME CO.; JOHN MICHALOS, THE 3439
PRESIDENT OF INDIA *v.* SLOBODONA PLIVIDBA S YUGOSLAVIA 3400
PRESMAN (BULLION) *v.* CUSTOMS AND EXCISE COMMISSIONERS 3825
PRESS CONSTRUCTION *v.* PILKINGTON BROTHERS 3129
PRICE *v.* BOUCH 3654
PRICE *v.* STEINBERG 2908

TABLE OF CASES

PARA.

PRICE CONTROLS AND REIMBURSEMENT OF MEDICINAL PRODUCTS (POLICY STATEMENT) (No. 86/C 310/08) 1585
PRINCIPALITY BUILDING SOCIETY *v.* LLEWELLYN 2940
PRIOR *v.* HASTIE (BERNARD) AND CO 1219
PRITCHARD *v.* COBDEN (J.H.) 1168
PRITCHETT *v.* McINTYRE 1395
PROCEEDINGS IN TWO FORA, *Re* 1554
PROCURATORE DELLA REPUBBLICA *v.* MIGLIORINI (No. 199/84) 1597
PROCUREUR DE LA REPUBLIQUE *v.* GERARD TISSIER (No. 35/85) 1623
PRODUCTION AND MARKETING OF FRENCH NEW POTATOES, *Re* 1484
PROMEDIA S.A. *v.* BORGHT 525
PRONTAPRINT *v.* LANDON LITHO 3737
PRUDENTIAL ASSURANCE CO. *v.* GRAY 2213
PUBLIC WORKS CONTRACTS, *Re*: E.C. COMMISSION *v.* ITALY (No. 274/83) 1523
PUDAS *v.* SWEDEN (No. 12/1986/110/158); BODEN *v.* SWEDEN (No. 18/1986/116/164) 1908
PUGH *v.* PIDGEN; SAME *v.* POWLEY 804
PURCELL *v.* KHAYAT 3012
PYE (J. A.) (OXFORD) ESTATES *v.* SECRETARY OF STATE FOR THE ENVIRONMENT AND WYCHAVON DISTRICT COUNCIL 3689

QUIETLYNN *v.* PLYMOUTH CITY COUNCIL. *See* PLYMOUTH CITY COUNCIL *v.* QUIETLYNN

R. (A MINOR), *Re* 2439
R. (A MINOR) (ADOPTION), *Re* 2453
R. (A MINOR) (ADOPTION OR CUSTODIANSHIP), *Re* 2448
R.M. AND L.M. (MINORS) (WARDSHIP: JURISDICTION), *Re* 2524
R.T.Z. OIL AND GAS *v.* ELLISS (INSPECTOR OF TAXES) 550a
R. *v.* A.I. INDUSTRIAL PRODUCTS 1852
R. *v.* AGRICULTURAL DWELLING-HOUSE ADVISORY COMMITTEE FOR BEDFORDSHIRE, CAMBRIDGESHIRE AND NORTHAMPTONSHIRE, *ex p.* BROUGH 3
R. *v.* AHMAD (ZAFAR) 2192
R. *v.* ALFARO 894
R. *v.* ALI 704
R. *v.* ALLEN 1020
R. *v.* ANDERSON, BEE AND HODGKINS 1085
R. *v.* ANDREWS (D.J.) 659
R. *v.* ASHFORD AND TENTERDEN MAGISTRATES' COURT, *ex p.* WOOD 3249
R. *v.* ASHLEY 694
R. *v.* ASKEW 946
R. *v.* ATT.-GEN., *ex p.* I.C.I. 3222
R. *v.* AVON MAGISTRATES' COURT COMMITTEE, *ex p.* BATH LAW SOCIETY 686
R. *v.* AYTON 873
R. *v.* BADHAM 707
R. *v.* BAINES 749
R. *v.* BANKS 1087
R. *v.* BANNERJEE 996
R. *v.* BARNETT 1028
R. *v.* BARTHOLOMEW 1072
R. *v.* BARTON 637
R. *v.* BASILDON DISTRICT COUNCIL, *ex p.* MARTIN GRANT HOMES 3681

PARA.

R. *v.* BATESON 2646
R. *v.* BEACONSFIELD JUSTICES, *ex p.* STUBBINGS. *See* STUBBINGS *v.* BEACONSFIELD JUSTICES
R. *v.* BEARD 668
R. *v.* BEDFORDSHIRE COUNTY COUNCIL, *ex p.* C.; R. *v.* HERTFORDSHIRE COUNTY COUNCIL, *ex p.* B. 2460
R. *v.* BELLMAN 666
R. *v.* BENT 937
R. *v.* BEST 826
R. *v.* BEVAN 808
R. *v.* BEVANS (RONALD) 761
R. *v.* BEVERIDGE 664
R. *v.* BICKENHILL PARISH COUNCIL, *ex p.* SECRETARY OF STATE FOR THE ENVIRONMENT AND SOLIHULL METROPOLITAN BOROUGH COUNCIL AND THE TRUSTEES OF WINGFIELD DIGBY ESTATES AND ARLINGTON SECURITIES 3706
R. *v.* BILINSKI 926
R. *v.* BIRD 915
R. *v.* BIRMINGHAM CITY JUVENILE COURT, *ex p.* BIRMINGHAM CITY COUNCIL 2459
R. *v.* BIRMINGHAM CITY COUNCIL, *ex p.* EQUAL OPPORTUNITIES COMMISSION 2388
R. *v.* BIRMINGHAM JUSTICES, *ex p.* GUPPY 2757
R. *v.* BLAND 816
R. *v.* BLISS 2101
R. *v.* BLYTH VALLEY JUSTICES, *ex p.* DOBSON 589
R. *v.* BLYTH VALLEY JUVENILE COURT, *ex p.* S. 674
R. *v.* BOARD OF VISITORS OF THORP ARCH PRISON, *ex p.* DE HOUGHTON 3139
R. *v.* BOARDMAN 892
R. *v.* BOLDEN 888
R. *v.* BOND (EDWARD) 885
R. *v.* BOOTHE 943
R. *v.* BOSWELL; R. *v.* HALLIWELL 3010
R. *v.* BOURNEMOUTH JUSTICES, *ex p.* GREY; R. *v.* SAME, *ex p.* RODD 1688
R. *v.* BOW STREET STIPENDIARY MAGISTRATE, *ex p.* ROCHE; SAME *v.* SAME, *ex p.* RILEY 689
R. *v.* BOWDEN 1067
R. *v.* BOWEN (T.J.) 3262
R. *v.* BOYLE (G.) AND BOYLE (J.) 758
R. *v.* BRADEN 685
R. *v.* BRENT LONDON BOROUGH COUNCIL, *ex p.* ASSEGAI 36
R. *v.* BRENTFORD MAGISTRATES' COURT, *ex p.* CLARKE 3242
R. *v.* BRINKLEY 1060
R. *v.* BRISTOL CROWN COURT, *ex p.* BRISTOL PRESS AND PICTURE AGENCY 708
R. *v.* BRISTOL JUSTICE, *ex p.* BROOME 2500
R. *v.* BRISTOL RENT ASSESSMENT COMMITTEE, *ex p.* DUNWORTH 2145
R. *v.* BRITISH RAILWAYS BOARD, *ex p.* BRADFORD METROPOLITAN CITY COUNCIL 3785
R. *v.* BRITTON 578
R. *v.* BROUGHTON 890
R. *v.* BROWN (R. B.); R. *v.* DALEY 715
R. *v.* BROWNSWORD 869
R. *v.* BURKE 803
R. *v.* BURNETT (LEROY) 1018
R. *v.* BURY JUSTICES, *ex p.* ANDERTON 691

	PARA.
R. *v.* BUTLER (DENNIS)	728
R. *v.* BUTT	891
R. *v.* CALLAGHAN; R. *v.* HILL; R. *v.* HUNTER; R. *v.* McILKENNY; R. *v.* POWER; R. *v.* WALKER	720
R. *v.* CAMDEN LONDON BOROUGH COUNCIL, *ex p.* CHRISTEY	1899
R. *v.* CAMDEN LONDON BOROUGH, *ex p.* WAIT	1878
R. *v.* CAMPBELL	698
R. *v.* CANTERBURY CITY COUNCIL, *ex p.* GILLESPIE	1907
R. *v.* CARDIFF MAGISTRATES' COURT, *ex p.* CARDIFF CITY COUNCIL	649
R. *v.* CARTER	1022
R. *v.* CATTELL	880
R. *v.* CENTRAL CRIMINAL COURT, *ex p.* CARR	729
R. *v.* CENTRAL CRIMINAL COURT, *ex p.* GARNIER	652
R. *v.* CHESTER CROWN COURT, *ex p.* PASCOE AND JONES	2309
R. *v.* CHIEF CONSTABLE OF SOUTH WALES, *ex p.* THORNHILL	34
R. *v.* CHIEF CONSTABLE OF THAMES VALLEY POLICE, *ex p.* STEVENSON	40
R. *v.* CHRISTCHURCH BOROUGH COUNCIL, *ex p.* CONWAY	1877
R. *v.* CHURCHER	655
R. *v.* CIVIL AVIATION AUTHORITY, *ex p.* AIRWAYS INTERNATIONAL CYMRU	173
R. *v.* CIVIL SERVICE APPEAL BOARD, *ex p.* BRUCE	10
R. *v.* CLACTON JUSTICES, *ex p.* CUSTOMS AND EXCISE COMMISSIONERS	680
R. *v.* CLERKENWELL MAGISTRATES' COURT, *ex p.* D.P.P.	682
R. *v.* CLERKENWELL MAGISTRATES' COURT, *ex p.* EWING; EWING *v.* CLERK	2935
R. *v.* CLEWS	975
R. *v.* CLITHEROE	1051
R. *v.* CLOUDEN	823
R. *v.* COFFEY	810
R. *v.* COLEMAN	556
R. *v.* COLLINS	1109
R. *v.* COMMISSIONER FOR THE SPECIAL PURPOSES OF THE INCOME TAX ACTS, *ex p.* R. W. FORSYTH	3221
R. *v.* COMMISSIONERS OF CUSTOMS AND EXCISE, *ex p.* STRANGEWOOD *See* R. *v.* CUSTOMS AND EXCISE COMMISSIONERS, *ex p.* STRANGEWOOD	
R. *v.* COMMITTEE ACTING FOR THE VISITOR OF THE UNIVERSITY OF LONDON, *ex p.* VIJAYATUNGA. *See* R. *v.* UNIVERSITY OF LONDON, *ex p.* VIJAYATUNGA	
R. *v.* CONNOLLY	1066
R. *v.* COOK (CHRISTOPHER)	571
R. *v.* COOKE	932
R. *v.* COOKE (GARY)	557
R. *v.* CORBY JUVENILE COURT, *ex p.* M	2477
R. *v.* CORCORAN	985
R. *v.* CORONER FOR THE CITY OF PORTSMOUTH, *ex p.* ANDERSON	532
R. *v.* COURT	665
R. *v.* COVENTRY CITY JUSTICES, *ex p.* FARRAND	847
R. *v.* COX	944
R. *v.* COX (DAVID)	638
R. *v.* CRAIG	982
R. *v.* CRESSWELL	1025
R. *v.* CRESSWELL (JEANINE MICHELLE)	1052
R. *v.* CRIMINAL INJURIES COMPENSATION BOARD, *ex p.* BRADY	633
R. *v.* CRISTINI	737
R. *v.* CROSS	1122
R. *v.* CROWN COURT, *ex p.* BAINES AND WHITE	712
R. *v.* CROYDON JUVENILE COURT, *ex p.* N.	2462
R. *v.* CROYDON LONDON BOROUGH COUNCIL, *ex p.* LENEY	2369
R. *v.* CROYDON LONDON BOROUGH, *ex p.* TOTH	1901
R. *v.* CRUMLEY	2645
R. *v.* CUMMINS	970
R. *v.* CUMMINS; R. *v.* PERKS	717
R. *v.* CURTIS	1041
R. *v.* CUSTOMS AND EXCISE COMMISSIONERS, *ex p.* NISSAN (U.K.)	3254
R. *v.* CUSTOMS AND EXCISE COMMISSIONERS, *ex p.* STRANGEWOOD	3832
R. *v.* CUTTS	949
R. *v.* DAIRY PRODUCE QUOTA TRIBUNAL, *ex p.* WYNN JONES	91
R. *v.* DAIRY PRODUCE QUOTA TRIBUNAL FOR ENGLAND AND WALES, *ex p.* DAVIES	92
R. *v.* DANIELS	883
R. *v.* DARBY	1076
R. *v.* DARBY (MARTIN DAVID)	954
R. *v.* DARTEY	656
R. *v.* DAVIES (COLIN STUART)	722
R. *v.* DAVIES (DAVID WILLIAM)	1077
R. *v.* DAVIES (T.J.)	1056
R. *v.* DAVIS (JASON MICHAEL)	980
R. *v.* DAVIS (SEATON ROY)	617
R. *v.* DEACON	611
R. *v.* DEMPSTER	1035
R. *v.* DENTON	3303
R. *v.* DEVON COUNTY COUNCIL, *ex p.* C.	1274
R. *v.* DHUNAY	1055
R. *v.* DILLON (R.W.) (Note)	573
R. *v.* DOHERTY	1043
R. *v.* DONCASTER CROWN COURT, *ex p.* CROWN PROSECUTION SERVICE	609
R. *v.* DONCASTER METROPOLITAN BOROUGH COUNCIL, *ex p.* BRAIM	316
R. *v.* DONCASTER METROPOLITAN DISTRICT COUNCIL, *ex p.* BRITISH RAILWAYS BOARD	3700
R. *v.* DONOGHUE	736
R. *v.* DOUGHTY	799
R. *v.* DOWNEY	865
R. *v.* EALAND AND STANDING	1080
R. *v.* EALING LONDON BOROUGH COUNCIL, *ex p.* TIMES NEWSPAPERS; R. *v.* HAMMERSMITH AND FULHAM LONDON BOROUGH COUNCIL, *ex p.* SAME; R. *v.* CAMDEN LONDON BOROUGH COUNCIL, *ex p.* SAME	29
R. *v.* EALING LONDON BOROUGH COUNCIL HOUSING BENEFIT REVIEW BOARD, *ex p.* SAVILLE	1888
R. *v.* EAST HERTFORDSHIRE DISTRICT COUNCIL, *ex p.* BANNON	1871
R. *v.* EDE AND SIDDONS	905
R. *v.* EDWARDS; R. *v.* LARTER	1012
R. *v.* EL-GAZZAR	994
R. *v.* ELLIS	2655

TABLE OF CASES

	PARA.
R. *v.* ELLIS, STREET AND SMITH	1113
R. *v.* EPPING AND ONGAR JUSTICES, *ex p.* BREACH; R. *v.* SAME, *ex p.* SHIPPAM (C.)	657
R. *v.* EPPING AND ONGAR JUSTICES, *ex p.* SHIPPAM (C.); R. *v.* SAME, *ex p.* BREACH. *See* R. *v.* EPPING AND ONGAR JUSTICES, *ex p.* BREACH; R. *v.* SAME, *ex p.* SHIPPAM (C.)	
R. *v.* EPSOM JUVENILE COURT, *ex p.* G.	2465
R. *v.* ESSEX COUNTY COUNCIL, *ex p.* WASHINGTON	2478
R. *v.* ETHICAL COMMITTEE OF ST. MARY'S HOSPITAL, *ex p.* HARRIOT	2415
R. *v.* EVANS	972
R. *v.* EVANS (DAVID JOHN)	861
R. *v.* EVANS (NIGEL STEPHEN)	973
R. *v.* EVERETT	981
R. *v.* FAIRHURST	1079
R. *v.* FELIXSTOWE JUSTICES, *ex p.* LEIGH	679
R. *v.* FISH	1019
R. *v.* FISHER	794
R. *v.* FLEET	1000
R. *v.* FORD (TREVOR RAYMOND)	1014
R. *v.* FOWLER	710
R. *v.* FOX	942
R. *v.* FRANCIS	714
R. *v.* FRANCIS (ANNE)	911
R. *v.* FRAZER	2105
R. *v.* FRENCH	1090
R. *v.* FULLING	559
R. *v.* FUNNELL	860
R. *v.* FYFIELD EQUIPMENT	3619
R. *v.* GALVIN	815
R. *v.* GARCIA	779
R. *v.* GARWOOD	762
R. *v.* GAUTAM	643
R. *v.* GAVIN	962
R. *v.* GENERAL MEDICAL COUNCIL, *ex p.* GEE	2399
R. *v.* GHANDI	940
R. *v.* GIBBONS	919
R. *v.* GIBSON	1034
R. *v.* GILLIGAN	580
R. *v.* GODBER	1086
R. *v.* GOLD; R. *v.* SCHIFREEN	780
R. *v.* GORDON	700
R. *v.* GORING	1013
R. *v.* GORMAN	2099
R. *v.* GOVERNOR OF ASHFORD REMAND CENTRE, *ex p.* POSTLETHWAITE. *See* GOVERNMENT OF BELGIUM *v.* POSTLETHWAITE	
R. *v.* GOVERNOR OF LATCHMERE HOUSE REMAND CENTRE, *ex p.* KAIKANEL	1960
R. *v.* GOVERNOR OF PENTONVILLE PRISON, *ex p.* HERBAGE (No. 2) *sub nom.* R. *v.* SECRETARY OF STATE FOR THE HOME DEPARTMENT, *ex p.* HERBAGE (No. 2)	28
R. *v.* GOVERNOR OF PENTONVILLE PRISON, *ex p.* HERBAGE, (No. 3)	807
R. *v.* GOVERNOR OF PENTONVILLE PRISON, *ex p.* LEE. *See* LEE *v.* GOVERNOR OF PENTONVILLE PRISON AND THE GOVERNMENT OF THE U.S.A.	
R. *v.* GOVERNOR OF PENTONVILLE PRISON, *ex p.* OSCAR	1700
R. *v.* GOVERNOR OF PENTONVILLE PRISON, *ex p.* SYAL	1695
R. *v.* GOVERNOR OF SPRING HILL PRISON, *ex p.* SOHI; SAME *v.* SAME, *ex p.* DHILLON	640
R. *v.* GOY	1071
R. *v.* GRANT	1058
R. *v.* GRANT (LANGFORD)	875
R. *v.* GREAT YARMOUTH BOROUGH COUNCIL, *ex p.* BOTTON BROTHERS ARCADES	3694
R. *v.* GREAT YARMOUTH BOROUGH COUNCIL, *ex p.* SAWYER	3789
R. *v.* GREATER LONDON COUNCIL, *ex p.* LONDON RESIDUARY BODY	2357
R. *v.* GREATER MANCHESTER CORONER, *ex p.* WORCH	539
R. *v.* GREATER MANCHESTER COUNCIL, *ex p.* GREATER MANCHESTER RESIDUARY BODY	2373
R. *v.* GREAVES	646
R. *v.* GREENHILL	1075
R. *v.* GRIFFITHS (WILLIAM HENRY)	906
R. *v.* GUILDFORD CROWN COURT, *ex p.* BREWER	583
R. *v.* GUINEY	950
R. *v.* GULLEFER	759
R. *v.* H.	740
R. *v.* HACKNEY LONDON BOROUGH COUNCIL, *ex p,* EVENBRAY	2358
R. *v.* HACKNEY LONDON BOROUGH COUNCIL, *ex p.* FLEMING	3159
R. *v.* HACKNEY LONDON BOROUGH COUNCIL, *ex p.* THRASYVOULOU	1879
R. *v.* HADDOCK	1021
R. *v.* HADIGATE	956
R. *v.* HALL (JOHN HAMILTON)	2421
R. *v.* HAMMERSMITH AND FULHAM LONDON BOROUGH COUNCIL, *ex p.* BEDDOWES	1867
R. *v.* HAMMERSMITH JUVENILE COURT, *ex p.* O. (A MINOR)	684
R. *v.* HANCOCK	960
R. *v.* HARDCASTLE	955
R. *v.* HARRIS (MARTIN)	785
R. *v.* HARRY	568
R. *v.* HARWOOD	1002
R. *v.* HAWKINS	872
R. *v.* HAWKINS (THOMAS JOHN)	1032
R. *v.* HAYLES	3283
R. *v.* HAYWARD AND STACEY	862
R. *v.* HEGARTY	2654
R. *v.* HENMAN	790
R. *v.* HENRY	968
R. *v.* H.M. CORONER FOR NORTH NORTHUMBERLAND, *ex p.* ARMSTRONG	536
R. *v.* H.M. CORONER FOR SOUTH GLAMORGAN, *ex p.* B.P. CHEMICALS	535
R. *v.* H.M. TREASURY, *ex p.* DAILY MAIL AND GENERAL TRUST	1479
R. *v.* HERBERT	929
R. *v.* HEREFORD AND WORCESTER COUNTY COUNCIL, *ex p.* LASHFORD	1270
R. *v.* HEWSON	959
R. *v.* HIGHBURY CORNER STIPENDIARY MAGISTRATE, *ex p.* D.H.S.S.	3493
R. *v.* HILL (FREDERICK)	751
R. *v.* HILLINGDON LONDON BOROUGH, *ex p.* THOMAS	1873
R. *v.* HILLS	620
R. *v.* HILLS (PENELOPE ANNE)	889
R. *v.* HOPKINS	939

PARA.

R. *v.* HOPWOOD 903
R. *v.* HORROCKS 974
R. *v.* HORSCROFT 1007
R. *v.* HORSEFERRY ROAD MAGISTRATES' COURT, *ex p.* BERNSTEIN 1758
R. *v.* HORSEFERRY ROAD STIPENDIARY MAGISTRATE, *ex p.* WILSON 658
R. *v.* HOUGHTON 963
R. *v.* HOUSING BENEFIT REVIEW BOARD OF SOUTH HEREFORDSHIRE DISTRICT COUNCIL, *ex p.* SMITH 1885
R. *v.* HOWE; R. *v.* BANNISTER; R. *v.* BURKE; R. *v.* CLARKSON 800
R. *v.* HOWELL (SEYMOUR JOSEPH) 913
R. *v.* HUISH 886
R. *v.* HUNT (RICHARD) 796
R. *v.* HUNTINGDON MAGISTRATES' COURT, *ex p.* YAPP 2292
R. *v.* IBBITSON 931
R. *v.* IMMIGRATION APPEAL TRIBUNAL, *ex p.* ALI (CHERAG) 1964
R. *v.* IMMIGRATION APPEAL TRIBUNAL, *ex p.* A. 1966
R. *v.* IMMIGRATION APPEAL TRIBUNAL, *ex p.* ALSAWAF; R. *v.* SECRETARY OF STATE FOR THE HOME OFFICE, *ex p.* THANANSYA 1983
R. *v.* IMMIGRATION APPEAL TRIBUNAL, *ex p.* ATWAL 1987
R. *v.* IMMIGRATION APPEAL TRIBUNAL, *ex p.* BASHIR (MOHAMMED) 1925
R. *v.* IMMIGRATION APPEAL TRIBUNAL, *ex p.* BEGUM 1935
R. *v.* IMMIGRATION APPEAL TRIBUNAL, *ex p.* BIBI (FARIDA) 1985
R. *v.* IMMIGRATION APPEAL TRIBUNAL, *ex p.* BIBI (ZAINIB) 1934
R. *v.* IMMIGRATION APPEAL TRIBUNAL, *ex p.* BIBI AND PURVEZ 1952
R. *v.* IMMIGRATION APPEAL TRIBUNAL, *ex p.* HAQUE; SAME *v.* SAME, *ex p.* RUHUL; SAME *v.* SAME, *ex p.* RAHMAN 1963
R. *v.* IMMIGRATION APPEAL TRIBUNAL, *ex p.* HASSANIN, KANDEMIR AND FAROOQ 1937
R. *v.* IMMIGRATION APPEAL TRIBUNAL, *ex p.* JONES (ROSS) 1923
R. *v.* IMMIGRATION APPEAL TRIBUNAL, *ex p.* KARIM 1941
R. *v.* IMMIGRATION APPEAL TRIBUNAL, *ex p.* KOBIR 1951
R. *v.* IMMIGRATION APPEAL TRIBUNAL, *ex p.* KUMAR 1957
R. *v.* IMMIGRATION APPEAL TRIBUNAL, *ex p.* MENDIS (VIRAJ) 1988
R. *v.* IMMIGRATION APPEAL TRIBUNAL, *ex p.* MILLER 1981
R. *v.* IMMIGRATION APPEAL TRIBUNAL, *ex p.* MUKITH 1931
R. *v.* IMMIGRATION APPEAL TRIBUNAL, *ex p.* MURUGANANDARAJAH AND SURESHKUMAR 1996
R. *v.* IMMIGRATION APPEAL TRIBUNAL, *ex p.* NG 1979
R. *v.* IMMIGRATION APPEAL TRIBUNAL, *ex p.* PATEL 1945
R. *v.* IMMIGRATION APPEAL TRIBUNAL, *ex p.* RAHMAN 1965
R. *v.* IMMIGRATION APPEAL TRIBUNAL *ex p.* SAFFIULLAH 1993

PARA.

R. *v.* IMMIGRATION APPEAL TRIBUNAL *ex p.* SHEIKH 1936
R. *v.* IMMIGRATION APPEAL TRIBUNAL, *ex p.* SHEK AND SHEK 1942
R. *v.* IMMIGRATION APPEAL TRIBUNAL, *ex p.* SINGH 1978
R. *v.* IMMIGRATION APPEAL TRIBUNAL, *ex p.* SWARAN SINGH 1950
R. *v.* IMMIGRATION APPEAL TRIBUNAL, *ex p.* TAMDJID-NEZHAD 1938
R. *v.* IMMIGRATION APPEAL TRIBUNAL, *ex p.* UDDIN AND UDDIN 1930
R. *v.* IMMIGRATION APPEAL TRIBUNAL AND SECRETARY OF STATE FOR THE HOME DEPARTMENT, *ex p.* ALGHALI 1947
R. *v.* IMMIGRATION OFFICER, GATWICK AIRPORT, *ex p.* HARJENDAR SINGH 1971
R. *v.* I.R.C., *ex p.* COOK 2032
R. *v.* I.R.C., *ex p.* FULFORD-DOBSON 274
R. *v.* I.R.C., *ex p.* ROTHSCHILD (J.) HOLDINGS 24
R. *v.* I.R.C., *ex p.* SIMS 2014
R. *v.* I.R.C., *ex p.* WOOLWICH EQUITABLE BUILDING SOCIETY 2006
R. *v.* INNER LONDON CROWN COURT, *ex p.* BAINES AND BAINES 730
R. *v.* INNER LONDON CROWN COURT, *ex p.* BENJAMIN 599
R. *v.* INNER LONDON CROWN COURT, *ex p.* SPRINGHALL AND SMITH 595
R. *v.* IRWIN 597
R. *v.* JAGODZINSKI 1054
R. *v.* JAGWANI AND JAYES 896
R. *v.* JAIN 630
R. *v.* JAMES (SIMON PETER) 976
R. *v.* JANAWAY 961
R. *v.* JAUNCEY 917
R. *v.* JEARY 916
R. *v.* JEFFERSON 1074
R. *v.* JEFFORD 3612
R. *v.* JOHN (CLIFFORD LEONARD) 877
R. *v.* JONES; R. *v.* CAMPBELL: R. *v.* SMITH; R. *v.* NICHOLAS; R. *v.* BLACKWOOD; R. *v.* MUIR 754
R. *v.* JONES (KEITH DESMOND) 812
R. *v.* JONES (PETER) 718
R. *v.* JUHASZ 1023
R. *v.* KEEYS 3626
R. *v.* KELLY 1078
R. *v.* KEMPSTER 958
R. *v.* KENSINGTON AND CHELSEA LONDON BOROUGH COUNCIL, *ex p.* WOOLRICH 1889
R. *v.* KEYS AND SWEEN; R. *v.* McMINN 858
R. *v.* KHAN (JUNAID) 748
R. *v.* KING AND STOCKWELL 809
R. *v.* KIRKLEES METROPOLITAN BOROUGH COUNCIL, *ex p.* MOLLOY 1255
R. *v.* KNIGHTSBRIDGE CROWN COURT, *ex p.* JOHNSON 673
R. *v.* KNUTSFORD CROWN COURT, *ex p.* JONES 863
R. *v.* KOWALSKI 1757
R. *v.* LACK 778
R. *v.* LAKE 922
R. *v.* LAMBETH LONDON BOROUGH, *ex p.* CLAYHOPE PROPERTIES 1905
R. *v.* LAMBETH LONDON BOROUGH, *ex p.* LY 1875

PARA.
R. *v.* LAMBETH LONDON BOROUGH COUNCIL, *ex p.* CARROLL 1896
R. *v.* LAMBETH LONDON BOROUGH COUNCIL, *ex p.* SHARP 3699
R. *v.* LATIMER 2648
R. *v.* LEICESTER CROWN COURT, *ex p.* D.P.P. 731
R. *v.* LEVY (NORMAN) 605
R. *v.* LEWES MAGISTRATES' COURT, *ex p.* OLDFIELD 645
R. *v.* LIMA 879
R. *v.* LING 2104
R. *v.* LIVERPOOL COTTON ASSOCIATION, *ex p.* COTTON CORP. OF INDIA 121
R. *v.* LIVERPOOL CROWN COURT, *ex p.* BRAY 667
R. *v.* LIVERPOOL JUVENILE COURT, *ex p.* R. 560
R. *v.* LIVERPOOL STIPENDIARY MAGISTRATE, *ex p.* ATKINSON 1027
R. *v.* LLEWELLYN (KEVIN ANTHONY) 945
R. *v.* LOCAL COMMISSIONER FOR ADMINISTRATION FOR THE SOUTH, THE WEST, THE WEST MIDLANDS, LEICESTERSHIRE, LINCOLNSHIRE AND CAMBRIDGESHIRE, *ex p.* EASTLEIGH BOROUGH COUNCIL 17
R. *v.* LONDON RENT ASSESSMENT PANEL, *ex p.* TRUSTEES OF HENRY SMITH'S CHARITY KENSINGTON ESTATE 2248
R. *v.* LONDON RESIDUARY BODY, *ex p.* INNER LONDON EDUCATION AUTHORITY 31
R. *v.* LUNT 727
R. *v.* LYDON (SEAN) 569
R. *v.* MABBOTT 2119
R. *v.* MacCAIG 918
R. *v.* McALENY 1011
R. *v.* McAUSLANE 1095
R. *v.* McCUE 1033
R. *v.* McDONALD 602
R. *v.* McGRATH 893
R. *v.* McIVOR 613
R. *v.* McKENNA 966
R. *v.* MacKENZIE 933
R. *v.* McKINNEY 856
R. *v.* McKINNON (WILLIAM HAROLD) 1016
R. *v.* McMURRAY 855
R. *v.* McNAMEE 1093
R. *v.* McVEY 585
R. *v.* MADDEN 681
R. *v.* MAGINNIS 797
R. *v.* MAHOOD 868
R. *v.* MAINWARING AND HULME 1009
R. *v.* MALCOLM 1036
R. *v.* MALONEY 902
R. *v.* MALTBY 1092
R. *v.* MALVERN JUSTICES, *ex p.* EVANS; R. *v.* EVESHAM JUSTICES, *ex p.* McDONAGH 675
R. *v.* MARA 1861
R. *v.* MARYLEBONE METROPOLITAN STIPENDIARY MAGISTRATE, *ex p.* OKUNNU 683
R. *v.* MASON (CARL) 561
R. *v.* MASON (COLIN ARTHUR) 1062
R. *v.* MATHIESON 887
R. *v.* MATTAN 987
R. *v.* MATTHEWS 920
R. *v.* MATTHEWS (TERENCE ROY PERCIVAL) 1063
R. *v.* MAVJI 764
R. *v.* MBATHA 992
R. *v.* MENDAY 628
R. *v.* MENTAL HEALTH REVIEW TRIBUNAL, *ex p.* SECRETARY OF STATE FOR THE HOME DEPARTMENT 48
R. *v.* MERSEY MENTAL HEALTH REVIEW TRIBUNAL, *ex p.* D. 2420
R. *v.* MERSEYSIDE PASSENGER TRANSPORT AUTHORITY, *ex p.* CROSVILE MOTOR SERVICES 3777
R. *v.* METCALFE 971
R. *v.* MIDLANDS ELECTRICITY BOARD, *ex p.* BUSBY; SAME *v.* SAME, *ex p.* WILLIAMSON 1286
R. *v.* MIDYA 1030
R. *v.* MILLARD 614
R. *v.* MILLARD AND VERNON 757
R. *v.* MILLER (MARTIN JOHN) 1061
R. *v.* MILLS 1045
R. *v.* MILLWARD 1031
R. *v.* MINISTER FOR THE CIVIL SERVICE, *ex p.* PETCH 2821
R. *v.* MITCHELL 1046
R. *v.* MOIED 988
R. *v.* MONMOUTH DISTRICT COUNCIL, *ex p.* JONES 3697
R. *v.* MONOPOLIES AND MERGERS COMMISSION, *ex p.* BROWN (MATTHEW) 3736
R. *v.* MONOPOLIES AND MERGERS COMMISSION, *ex p.* ELDERS IXL 3735
R. *v.* MOORE 864
R. *v.* MORE 777
R. *v.* MORGAN 897
R. *v.* MORGAN 991
R. *v.* MOSS 936
R. *v.* MOSS (LINDA) 1059
R. *v.* MOSSOP 948
R. *v.* MOUSIR 765
R. *v.* MULLERVY 1029
R. *v.* MUNDAY 1100
R. *v.* MURANYI 1039
R. *v.* MURPHY AND DUKE 998
R. *v.* MURRAY 1083
R. *v.* NALTY 990
R. *v.* NANAYAKKARA; R. *v.* KHOR; R. *v.* TAN 837
R. *v.* NATIONAL COAL BOARD, *ex p.* NATIONAL UNION OF MINEWORKERS 12
R. *v.* NATIONAL COAL BOARD, *ex p.* THE UNION OF DEMOCRATIC MINEWORKERS 2430
R. *v.* NEVE 899
R. *v.* NEVILLE 947
R. *v.* NEWCASTLE-UNDER-LYME JUSTICES, *ex p.* HEMMINGS 670
R. *v.* NEWCASTLE UPON TYNE JUSTICES, *ex p.* SKINNER 604
R. *v.* NEWHAM LONDON BOROUGH COUNCIL, *ex p.* HAGGERTY 2389
R. *v.* NEWHAM LONDON BOROUGH COUNCIL, *ex p.* McL 9
R. *v.* NEWLAND 927
R. *v.* NOBLE 859
R. *v.* NORWICH JUSTICES, *ex p.* TIGGER (FORMERLY LILLY) 721
R. *v.* NOTTINGHAM JUSTICES, *ex p.* FOHMANN 627
R. *v.* O'CONNOR 619
R. *v.* O'DRISCOLL 1042
R. *v.* OFFORD 1065
R. *v.* O'GRADY 824
R. *v.* OKAI 709

PARA.
R. *v.* O'LAUGHLIN AND McLAUGHLIN 563
R. *v.* O'NEALE 577
R. *v.* OULESS AND OULESS 1044
R. *v.* OWEN 789
R. *v.* OXFORD CITY JUSTICES, *ex p.* BERRY. 608
R. *v.* OXFORD CITY JUSTICES, *ex p.* CHIEF CONSTABLE OF THAMES VALLEY POLICE 629
R. *v.* OXFORD REGIONAL MENTAL HEALTH REVIEW TRIBUNAL, *ex p.* SECRETARY OF STATE FOR THE HOME DEPARTMENT 2425
R. *v.* OXFORDSHIRE COUNTY COUNCIL, *ex p.* W 1269
R. *v.* OXFORDSHIRE EDUCATION AUTHORITY, *ex p.* W 2962
R. *v.* OZDEMIR 904
R. *v.* PADWICK AND NEW 969
R. *v.* PALMA 1006
R. *v.* PANAYI; R. *v.* KARTE 756
R. *v.* PANEL ON TAKE-OVERS AND MERGERS, *ex p.* DATAFIN 21
R. *v.* PARKER (KEITH ROBERT) 930
R. *v.* PARKINSON, ROBERTS AND MULLINER 1081
R. *v.* PASSMORE 1050
R. *v.* PATEL (HARIVADAN) 1057
R. *v.* PAWAR 965
R. *v.* PEGRUM 924
R. *v.* PERRY 1068
R. *v.* PETERBOROUGH CITY COUNCIL, *ex p.* QUIETLYNN 2317
R. *v.* PETERBOROUGH MAGISTRATES' COURT, *ex p.* WILLIS 690
R. *v.* PHARMACEUTICAL SOCIETY OF GREAT BRITAIN, *ex p.* ASSOCIATION OF PHARMACEUTICAL IMPORTERS; R. *v.* SECRETARY OF STATE FOR SOCIAL SERVICES, *ex p.* ASSOCIATION OF PHARMACEUTICAL IMPORTERS 2412
R. *v.* PHILLIPS 725
R. *v.* PHILLIPS (KEITH) 1005
R. *v.* PICKARD 907
R. *v.* PITTENDRIGH 901
R. *v.* PITTS AND DAVIES 989
R. *v.* PLYMOUTH CITY COUNCIL AND CORNWALL CITY COUNCIL, *ex p.* FREEMAN 2227
R. *v.* PLYMOUTH JUVENILE COURT, *ex p.* F. AND F 2463
R. *v.* POULTER 1064
R. *v.* POWELL (MARK) 1010
R. *v.* POWER 949
R. *v.* POWIS AND PRITCHARD 1040
R. *v.* PREFAS AND PRYCE 662
R. *v.* PRESLEY 1094
R. *v.* PROCTOR 1098
R. *v.* R. AND H. (HARROW LONDON BOROUGH COUNCIL INTERVENING) 2891
R. *v.* RADFORD 878
R. *v.* RAMPLING 739
R. *v.* RANDALL 601
R. *v.* RANDALL 742
R. *v.* RAPHAEL 986
R. *v.* RAVIRAJ; R. *v.* KANSAL; R. *v.* GUPTA .. 2103
R. *v.* READER 592
R. *v.* READING BOROUGH COUNCIL, *ex p.* EGAN, SAME *v.* SAME, *ex p.* SULLMAN ... 3790
R. *v.* READING CROWN COURT, *ex p.* HUTCHINSON, SAME *v.* DEVIZES JUSTICES, *ex p.* LEE; SAME *v.* SAME, *ex p.* D.P.P. 678

PARA.
R. *v.* REED 874
R. *v.* REIGATE AND BANSTEAD BOROUGH COUNCIL, *ex p.* DI DOMENICO 1906
R. *v.* RENNES 857
R. *v.* REYNOLDS 1097
R. *v.* RHODES 957
R. *v.* RHOOMS 983
R. *v.* RICHARDS (LENNOX TIMOTHY) 1091
R. *v.* ROBERTS 1084
R. *v.* ROBERTS (PHILEMON) 909
R. *v.* ROBERTS (WILLIAM) 783
R. *v.* ROBERTSON; R. *v.* GOLDER 562
R. *v.* ROSS AND VISZKOK 997
R. *v.* RUBY 870
R. *v.* RUNNYMEDE BOROUGH COUNCIL, *ex p.* SARVAN SINGH SEEHRA 3721
R. *v.* RUSHMOOR BOROUGH COUNCIL, *ex p.* BARRETT 1772
R. *v.* RUSSELL AND RUSSELL 695
R. *v.* RUSSELL AND RUSSELL 995
R. *v.* RYAN 952
R. *v.* ST. HELENS JUSTICES, *ex p.* CRITCHLEY 692
R. *v.* SALFORD HEALTH AUTHORITY, *ex p.* JANAWAY 1312
R. *v.* SALISBURY MAGISTRATES' COURT, *ex p.* MASTIN 632
R. *v.* SAUNDERS 699
R. *v.* SCALISE AND RACHEL 1070
R. *v.* SECRETARY OF STATE AND BROMLEY LONDON BOROUGH COUNCIL, *ex p.* JACKSON 3605
R. *v.* SECRETARY OF STATE FOR EDUCATION, *ex p.* SCHAFFTER 1259
R. *v.* SECRETARY OF STATE FOR EDUCATION AND SCIENCE, *ex p.* L 1250
R. *v.* SECRETARY OF STATE FOR THE ENVIRONMENT, *ex p.* BIRMINGHAM CITY COUNCIL 3190
R. *v.* SECRETARY OF STATE FOR THE ENVIRONMENT, *ex p.* BOURNEMOUTH BOROUGH COUNCIL 3598
R. *v.* SECRETARY OF STATE FOR THE ENVIRONMENT, *ex p.* CAMDEN LONDON BOROUGH COUNCIL 2387
R. *v.* SECRETARY OF STATE FOR THE ENVIRONMENT, *ex p.* GREAT GRIMSBY BOROUGH COUNCIL 3651
R. *v.* SECRETARY OF STATE FOR THE ENVIRONMENT, *ex p.* GREENWICH LONDON BOROUGH COUNCIL 3189
R. *v.* SECRETARY OF STATE FOR THE ENVIRONMENT, *ex p.* KENSINGTON AND CHELSEA ROYAL BOROUGH COUNCIL 1863
R. *v.* SECRETARY OF STATE FOR THE ENVIRONMENT, *ex p.* LEICESTER CITY COUNCIL 389
R. *v.* SECRETARY OF STATE FOR THE ENVIRONMENT, *ex p.* MANCHESTER CITY COUNCIL. *See* MANCHESTER CITY COUNCIL AND SECRETARY OF STATE FOR THE ENVIRONMENT
R. *v.* SECRETARY OF STATE FOR THE ENVIRONMENT, *ex p.* MELTON BOROUGH COUNCIL 390
R. *v.* SECRETARY OF STATE FOR THE ENVIRONMENT, *ex p.* NEWHAM LONDON BOROUGH COUNCIL 2361

TABLE OF CASES

PARA.

R. *v.* SECRETARY OF STATE FOR THE ENVIRONMENT, *ex p.* SOUTHWARK LONDON BOROUGH COUNCIL 3650
R. *v.* SECRETARY OF STATE FOR FOREIGN AND COMMONWEALTH AFFAIRS, *ex p.* EVERETT 47
R. *v.* SECRETARY OF STATE FOR THE HOME DEPARTMENT, *ex p.* ADEMUYIWA 1991
R. *v.* SECRETARY OF STATE FOR THE HOME DEPARTMENT, *ex p.* ALI 1920
R. *v.* SECRETARY OF STATE FOR THE HOME DEPARTMENT, *ex p.* ALI; SAME *v.* SAME, *ex p.* ULLAH; SAME *v.* SAME, *ex p.* UDDIN. *See* R. *v.* SECRETARY OF STATE FOR THE HOME DEPARTMENT, *ex p.* ROFATHULLAH
R. *v.* SECRETARY OF STATE FOR THE HOME DEPARTMENT, *ex p.* ALP 1992
R. *v.* SECRETARY OF STATE FOR THE HOME DEPARTMENT, *ex p.* BOTTA (JACQUELINE) 1564
R. *v.* SECRETARY OF STATE FOR THE HOME DEPARTMENT, *ex p.* BUGDAYCAY; R. *v.* SAME, *ex p.* NELIDOW SANTIS; R. *v.* SAME, *ex p.* NORMAN. *See* BUGDAYCAY *v.* SECRETARY OF STATE FOR THE HOME DEPARTMENT; NELIDOW SANTIS *v.* SAME; NORMAN *v.* SAME; MUSISI, *Re.*
R. *v.* SECRETARY OF STATE FOR THE HOME DEPARTMENT, *ex p.* COONHYE 1977
R. *v.* SECRETARY OF STATE FOR THE HOME DEPARTMENT, *ex p.* DEVON AND CORNWALL POLICE AUTHORITY 2853
R. *v.* SECRETARY OF STATE FOR THE HOME DEPARTMENT, *ex p.* DEW 6
R. *v.* SECRETARY OF STATE FOR THE HOME DEPARTMENT, *ex p.* H. 1969
R. *v.* SECRETARY OF STATE FOR THE HOME DEPARTMENT, *ex p.* HANDSCOMBE 993
R. *v.* SECRETARY OF STATE FOR THE HOME DEPARTMENT, *ex p.* HERBAGE (No. 2). *See* R. *v.* GOVERNOR OF PENTONVILLE PRISON, *ex p.* HERBAGE (No. 2) ....
R. *v.* SECRETARY OF STATE FOR THE HOME DEPARTMENT, *ex p.* HUSEYIN (ZALIHE) ... 1939
R. *v.* SECRETARY OF STATE FOR THE HOME DEPARTMENT, *ex p.* KAUR 1998
R. *v.* SECRETARY OF STATE FOR THE HOME DEPARTMENT, *ex p.* KIRKLEES BOROUGH COUNCIL 3577
R. *v.* SECRETARY OF STATE FOR THE HOME DEPARTMENT, *ex p.* MAHAL 1949
R. *v.* SECRETARY OF STATE FOR THE HOME DEPARTMENT, *ex p.* MALIK 1955
R. *v.* SECRETARY OF STATE FOR THE HOME DEPARTMENT, *ex p.* MEYER-WULFF 1940
R. *v.* SECRETARY OF STATE FOR THE HOME DEPARTMENT, *ex p.* NORTHUMBRIA POLICE AUTHORITY 2868
R. *v.* SECRETARY OF STATE FOR THE HOME DEPARTMENT, *ex p.* OLASEBIKAN 1958
R. *v.* SECRETARY OF STATE FOR THE HOME DEPARTMENT, *ex p.* OZKURTULUS 1997
R. *v.* SECRETARY OF STATE FOR THE HOME DEPARTMENT, *ex p.* PATEL (DHIRUBHAI GORDHANBHAI) 1933
R. *v.* SECRETARY OF STATE FOR THE HOME DEPARTMENT, *ex p.* RAJU 1980

PARA.

R. *v.* SECRETARY OF STATE FOR THE HOME DEPARTMENT, *ex p.* RAZAK 1961
R. *v.* SECRETARY OF STATE FOR THE HOME DEPARTMENT, *ex p.* READ (GARY JOHN). 1038
R. *v.* SECRETARY OF STATE FOR THE HOME DEPARTMENT, *ex p.* ROFATHULLAH 1995
R. *v.* SECRETARY OF STATE FOR THE HOME DEPARTMENT, *ex p.* RUDDOCK 20
R. *v.* SECRETARY OF STATE FOR THE HOME DEPARTMENT, *ex p.* SINGH 1982
R. *v.* SECRETARY OF STATE FOR THE HOME DEPARTMENT, *ex p.* SIVAKUMARAN 23
R. *v.* SECRETARY OF STATE FOR THE HOME DEPARTMENT, *ex p.* SIVAKUMARAN 1926
R. *v.* SECRETARY OF STATE FOR THE HOME DEPARTMENT, *ex p.* SURESHKUMAR 1968
R. *v.* SECRETARY OF STATE FOR THE HOME DEPARTMENT, *ex p.* TURKOGLU 2909
R. *v.* SECRETARY OF STATE FOR THE HOME DEPARTMENT, *ex p.* ULLAH. *See* R. *v.* SECRETARY OF STATE FOR THE HOME DEPARTMENT, *ex p.* ROFATHULLAH
R. *v.* SECRETARY OF STATE FOR THE HOME DEPARTMENT, *ex p.* YAKUB 1921
R. *v.* SECRETARY OF STATE FOR THE HOME DEPARTMENT, *ex p.* YEBOAH, R. *v.* SAME, *ex p.* DRAZ 1943
R. *v.* SECRETARY OF STATE FOR THE HOME OFFICE, *ex p.* ATTIVOR 1990
R. *v.* SECRETARY OF STATE FOR THE HOME OFFICE, *ex p.* AWUKU; SAME *v.* SAME, *ex p.* OTCHERE; SAME *v.* SAME, *ex p.* DZIVENU 1970
R. *v.* SECRETARY OF STATE FOR THE HOME OFFICE, *ex p.* BETANCOURT; R. *v.* IMMIGRATION APPEAL TRIBUNAL, *ex p.* ACQUAH; SAME *v.* SAME, *ex p.* RAHMAN; SAME *v.* SAME, *ex p.* GONZALES-ROJAS; R. *v.* SECRETARY OF STATE FOR THE HOME OFFICE, *ex p.* TOLBA; SAME *v.* SAME, *ex p.* ALCINSANMI 1972
R. *v.* SECRETARY OF STATE FOR THE HOME OFFICE, *ex p.* CHUBB 672
R. *v.* SECRETARY OF STATE FOR THE HOME OFFICE, *ex p.* DEW. *See* R. *v.* SECRETARY OF STATE FOR THE HOME DEPARTMENT, *ex p.* DEW
R. *v.* SECRETARY OF STATE FOR THE HOME OFFICE, *ex p.* STITT 817
R. *v.* SECRETARY OF STATE FOR SOCIAL SERVICES, *ex p.* CAMDEN LONDON BOROUGH COUNCIL 3567
R. *v.* SECRETARY OF STATE FOR SOCIAL SERVICES, *ex p.* CLARK 1326
R. *v.* SECRETARY OF STATE FOR SOCIAL SERVICES, *ex p.* CYNON VALLEY BOROUGH COUNCIL; R. *v.* KENSINGTON AND CHELSEA ROYAL LONDON BOROUGH COUNCIL, *ex p.* GOODSON 1887
R. *v.* SECRETARY OF STATE FOR SOCIAL SERVICES, *ex p.* SCHERING CHEMICALS. 1591
R. *v.* SECRETARY OF STATE FOR SOCIAL SERVICES, *ex p.* WALTHAM FOREST LONDON BOROUGH COUNCIL; SAME *v.* SAME, *ex p.* WORCESTER CITY COUNCIL 2344
R. *v.* SECRETARY OF STATE FOR SOCIAL SERVICES, *ex p.* WELLCOME FOUNDATION 3750

TABLE OF CASES

	PARA.
R. *v.* SECRETARY OF STATE FOR TRANSPORT, *ex p.* GWENT COUNTY COUNCIL	35
R. *v.* SECRETARY OF STATE FOR TRANSPORT, *ex p.* SHERRIF & SONS	3784
R. *v.* SECRETARY OF STATE FOR WALES AND A. B. HUTTON (SECRETARY TO THE MAES GERDDI RESIDENTS ASSOCIATION)	3867
R. *v.* SEKHON	574
R. *v.* SHAH (MUZAFFAR ALI)	866
R. *v.* SHARP	732
R. *v.* SHARP (DAVID)	774
R. *v.* SHAW	898
R. *v.* SHELTON	842
R. *v.* SHEPHERD	648
R. *v.* SHERIDAN	871
R. *v.* SHREWSBURY CORONERS COURT, *ex p.* BRITISH PARACHUTE ASSOCIATION	538
R. *v.* SILVERMAN	806
R. *v.* SIMMONS	626
R. *v.* SKINNER	895
R. *v.* SLACK	884
R. *v.* SLOUGH JUSTICES, *ex p.* STIRLING	687
R. *v.* SMITH AND DOE	663
R. *v.* SMITH AND ROBERTS	978
R. *v.* SMITH (ERIC)	565
R. *v.* SMITH (IVOR)	984
R. *v.* SMITH (PASCOE DONALD)	912
R. *v.* SMITH (PHILLIP ANDREW)	934
R. *v.* SOUTHWARK CORONER, *ex p.* HICKS	533
R. *v.* SOUTHWOOD	846
R. *v.* SPECIAL COMMISSIONER, *ex p.* FORSYTH (R.W.)	549
R. *v.* SPECIAL COMMISSIONER, *ex p.* NAPIER	2026
R. *v.* SPICER	581
R. *v.* SPIGHT	590
R. *v.* STANLEY	1096
R. *v.* STEADMAN	979
R. *v.* STEER	770
R. *v.* STEVENS	925
R. *v.* STEVENS	935
R. *v.* STEWART	625
R. *v.* STEWART (LIVINGSTONE)	1015
R. *v.* STOKE	703
R. *v.* STOREY	1088
R. *v.* SUNDERLAND JUVENILE COURT, *ex p.* G. (A MINOR)	2466
R. *v.* SURREY COUNTY COUNCIL, *ex p.* MONK,	3701
R. *v.* SWAYSLAND	2915
R. *v.* TAYLOR	1003
R. *v.* TAYLOR	977
R. *v.* TAYLOR (ANDREW); R. *v.* TAYLOR (BRIAN),	923
R. *v.* TELFORD JUSTICES, *ex p.* DARLINGTON	693
R. *v.* THOMAS (HORATIO GERALD)	696
R. *v.* THOMAS (MICHAEL STEPHEN)	1008
R. *v.* THOMPSON (PETER ROBERT)	1073
R. *v.* THORPE	1794
R. *v.* TOMINEY	1001
R. *v.* TOOR	784
R. *v.* TOWER BRIDGE METROPOLITAN STIPENDIARY MAGISTRATE, *ex p.* D.P.P.	3282
R. *v.* TOWER HAMLETS LONDON BOROUGH COUNCIL, *ex p.* CHETNIK DEVELOPMENTS	3188
R. *v.* TOWER HAMLETS LONDON BOROUGH COUNCIL, *ex p.* MONAF, ALI AND MIAH	1874
R. *v.* TOWERS	1069
R. *v.* TOWNSEND	570
R. *v.* TREVITHICK	928
R. *v.* TURTON (MARK JOHN)	1099
R. *v.* TYLER	1089
R. *v.* TYNESIDE JUSTICES, *ex p.* NORTH TYNESIDE BOROUGH COUNCIL	2316
R. *v.* UMOH	711
R. *v.* UNIVERSITY OF LONDON, *ex p.* VIJAYATUNGA	1275
R. *v.* UTTING	781
R. *v.* VALUATION OFFICER, *ex p.* HIGH PARK INVESTMENTS	3183
R. *v.* VAN HUBBARD	953
R. *v.* VINCENT AND THE DEPARTMENT OF TRANSPORT, *ex p.* TURNER	3653
R. *v.* VOLENHOLVEN	1082
R. *v.* WAINFOR	1004
R. *v.* WALKER	798
R. *v.* WALMSLEY	867
R. *v.* WALTHAM FOREST LONDON BOROUGH COUNCIL, *ex p.* BAXTER	5
R. *v.* WALTHAM FOREST LONDON BOROUGH COUNCIL, *ex p.* WALTHAM FOREST RATEPAYERS ACTION GROUP	2381
R. *v.* WANDSWORTH BOROUGH COUNCIL, *ex p.* BANBURY	1876
R. *v.* WANDSWORTH LONDON BOROUGH, *ex p.* HENDERSON AND HAYES	1872
R. *v.* WANDSWORTH LONDON BOROUGH, *ex p.* LINDSAY	1880
R. *v.* WALTON	938
R. *v.* WARD (J.D.)	801
R. *v.* WARWICK	967
R. *v.* WARWICK CROWN COURT, *ex p.* SMALLEY	596
R. *v.* WAYNE	908
R. *v.* WEBBER (JACK JOHN)	623
R. *v.* WEBBER (MARTIN FREDERICK)	624
R. *v.* WEBSTER	1024
R. *v.* WELLS	1053
R. *v.* WELLS STREET MAGISTRATES, *ex p.* WESTMINSTER CITY COUNCIL	3647
R. *v.* WEST (ALAN RICHARD)	921
R. *v.* WEST (WILLIAM JOHN)	876
R. *v.* WEST DORSET DISTRICT COUNCIL, *ex p.* POUPARD	1886
R. *v.* WEST LONDON CORONERS' COURT, *ex p.* GRAY; SAME *v.* SAME, *ex p.* DUNCAN	534
R. *v.* WEST LONDON STIPENDIARY MAGISTRATE, *ex p.* WATTS	914
R. *v.* WEST MALLING JUVENILE COURT, *ex p.* K.	2461
R. *v.* WESTERN	854
R. *v.* WESTMINSTER CITY COUNCIL, *ex p.* COSTI	3037
R. *v.* WESTMINSTER CITY COUNCIL, *ex p.* HAZAN	2359
R. *v.* WESTMINSTER CITY COUNCIL, *ex p.* SIERBENS	3035
R. *v.* WESTMINSTER VALUATION OFFICER, *ex p.* RENDALL	14
R. *v.* WESTON	1017
R. *v.* WESTON-SUPER-MARE JUSTICES, *ex p.* SHAW	677
R. *v.* WHITE	738

TABLE OF CASES

	PARA.
R. *v.* WHITING	763
R. *v.* WHITTINGHAM	882
R. *v.* WHYTE	853
R. *v.* WILKINSON	1037
R. *v.* WILLESDEN JUSTICES, *ex p.* CLEMMINGS	591
R. *v.* WILLIAMS (ALAN)	2102
R. *v.* WILLIAMS (CLARENCE)	576
R. *v.* WILLIAMS (GERALD)	881
R. *v.* WOOD (WILLIAM)	567
R. *v.* WOODS (MARKS RONALD)	2100
R. *v.* WOOLWICH JUSTICES, *ex p.* ARNOLD	2315
R. *v.* YORK CROWN COURT, *ex p.* COLEMAN	593
R. *v.* ZOABIR	910
RAE *v.* YORKSHIRE BANK	193
RAFIDAIN BANK *v.* AGOM UNIVERSAL SUGAR TRADING CO.	3001
RAFIDAIN BANK *v.* AGOM UNIVERSAL SUGAR TRADING CO.	3016
RAHMAN *v.* SECRETARY OF STATE FOR THE HOME DEPARTMENT	1974
RAI	1209
RAINEY *v.* GREATER GLASGOW HEALTH BOARD	1325
RAJ (REWAL) *v.* ENTRY CLEARANCE OFFICER, NEW DELHI	1973
RAJABALLY *v.* RAJABALLY	3880
RAMWADE *v.* EMSON (W. J.) & CO.	2064
RANSOM *v.* RANSOM	1739
RAWLINS *v.* BROWN	3240
RAYCHEM'S APPLICATIONS	2772
RAYNER (J.H.) (MINCING LANE) *v.* DEPARTMENT OF TRADE AND INDUSTRY,	2092
RAYNHAM FARM CO. *v.* SYMBOL MOTOR CORP.	447
RAZZAQ *v.* RAZZAQ	2528
READER *v.* BUNYARD	3289
READING BOROUGH COUNCIL *v.* SECRETARY OF STATE FOR THE ENVIRONMENT AND COMMERCIAL UNION PROPERTIES (INVESTMENTS)	3658
RECKITT AND COLMAN PRODUCTS *v.* BORDEN INC.	3041
RECKITT AND COLMAN PRODUCTS *v.* BORDEN INC. (No. 2)	1680
RECKITT AND COLMAN PRODUCTS *v.* BORDEN INC. (No. 3)	2807
REDBRIDGE LONDON BOROUGH COUNCIL AND ASSOCIATED DAIRIES; BRITISH RAILWAYS BOARD AND TESCO STORES	3675
REDERIAKTIEBOLAGET GUSTAV ERIKSON *v.* DR. FAWZI AHMED ABOU ISMAIL; HERROE AND ASKOE, THE	3443
REDMOND *v.* ALLIED IRISH BANKS	198
REES *v.* U.K.	1914
REEVES (V.O.) *v.* MARSH (LVC/108/1987)	3175
REGENT INDEMNITY CO. *v.* FISHLEY AND FISHLEY	471
REID *v.* BRITISH TELECOMMUNICATIONS	2618
REID AND REID *v.* ANDREOU	2250
REISS ENGINEERING *v.* HARRIS	2960
REMIA B.V. AND VERENIGDE BEDRIJVEN NUTRICIA *v.* E.C. COMMISSION (No. 42/84)	1503
RENDALL *v.* DUKE OF WESTMINSTER	3180
REYNOLDS' APPLICATION, *Re* (Ref. LP/44/1985)	3714
RHODES (JOHN T.), *Re*	323
RHODES (JOHN T.), *Re*	3116
RICCI *v.* CHOW	2992
RICH (MARC) & CO. *v.* TOURLOTI COMPANIA NAVIERA S.A.	3436
RICHARDS *v.* CRESSWELL	1685
RICHMOND-UPON-THAMES LONDON BOROUGH COUNCIL *v.* SECRETARY OF STATE FOR THE ENVIRONMENT AND BEECHGOLD	3636
RICKARDS *v.* KERRIER DISTRICT COUNCIL	228
RICKETT (WIDOW AND ADMINISTRATRIX OF THE ESTATE OF THOMAS RICKETT, DEC'D.) *v.* ROADCRAFT (CRANE & PLANT HIRE)	2994
RICKLESS *v.* UNITED ARTISTS CORP.	516
RIDGEWAY *v.* RIDGEWAY	2496
RIDGWAY *v.* RIDGWAY	2890
RIDGWAY AND FAIRBROTHER *v.* NATIONAL COAL BOARD	3766
RIGBY *v.* FERODO	1305
RIGG *v.* ELLIOTT	1184
RIGNALL DEVELOPMENTS *v.* HALIL	2108
RILEY *v.* RILEY	2489
RILEY *v.* WEBB	3321
RIO CLARO, THE. *See* TRANSWORLD OIL *v.* NORTHBAY SHIPPING CORP., RIO CLARO, THE	
RIVER RIMA, THE	3360
ROBERT *v.* SOCIETE CREHALLET-FOLLIOT-RECHERCHE ET PUBLICITE	496
ROBERT BRUCE & PARTNERS *v.* WINYARD DEVELOPMENTS. *See* BRUCE (ROBERT) & PARTNERS *v.* WINYARD DEVELOPMENTS	
ROBERTS *v.* MACILWRAITH CHRISTIE	2244
ROBERTSON (BELFAST) *v.* McLEAN (BT/110/1986)	2696
ROBINSON *v.* HUGHES	118
ROCHE *v.* ROCHE	2495
ROCKWELL INTERNATIONAL *v.* SERCK INDUSTRIES	2810
RODGERS *v.* TAYLOR	3298
ROE *v.* ROE	1753
ROELSTRAETE (HENRI), CRIMINAL PROCEEDINGS AGAINST (No. 116/84)	1588
ROGER BULLIVANT *v.* ELLIS. *See* BULLIVANT (ROGER) *v.* ELLIS	
ROGERS *v.* PARISH (SCARBOROUGH)	3333
ROLLS-ROYCE *v.* DOUGHTY	1315
ROOKER *v.* ROOKER	1730
ROOTS *v.* ROOTS	1726
ROSE *v.* INFORMATION SERVICES	520
ROSEMARY SIMMONS MEMORIAL HOUSING ASSOCIATION *v.* UNITED DOMINIONS TRUST; BATES & PARTNERS (A FIRM) (THIRD PARTY)	321
ROSEMARY WINE MARKETS *v.* COMMISSIONER OF VALUATION FOR NORTHERN IRELAND (VR/52/1985)	2732
ROSLING *v.* PINNEGAR	1235
ROUSSEAU WILMOT S.A. *v.* CAISSE DE COMPENSATION DE L'ORGANISATION AUTONOME NATIONALE DE L'INDUSTRIE ET DU COMMERCE (COMPENSATION FUND OF THE NATIONAL INDEPENDENT ORGANISATION FOR TRADE AND INDUSTRY-ORGANIC) (No. 295/84)	1664
ROUSSEL-UCLAF (CLEMENCE & LE MARTRET'S) PATENT	2800

PARA.

ROVER INTERNATIONAL *v.* CANNON FILMS SALES ... 446
ROWE *v.* WALT DISNEY PRODUCTIONS ... 406
ROYAL BANK TRUST CO. (TRINIDAD) *v.* PAMPELLONNE (J. N.) ... 2576
ROYAL BOROUGH OF WINDSOR AND MAIDENHEAD AND WOOTEN ... 3632
ROYAN, ABUKIRK, BRETAGNE AND AUBERNE, THE. *See* CO-OPERATIVE CENTRALE RAIFFEISEN- BOERELEENBANK B.A. *v.* SUMITOMO BANK, THE; ROYAN, ABUKIRK, BRETAGNE AND AUBERNE, THE
RUBYCLIFF *v.* PLASTIC ENGINEERS ... 512
RUDD *v.* SECRETARY OF STATE FOR TRADE AND INDUSTRY ... 3579
RULE *v.* ATLAS STONE CO. ... 2335
RULES OF THE BALTIC INTERNATIONAL FREIGHT FUTURES EXCHANGE (BIFFEX), *Re* (No. IV/31.764) ... 1485
RUMMLER *v.* DATO-DRUCK GmbH ... 1529
RUNNYMEDE BOROUGH COUNCIL *v.* SMITH 3720
RUSHMOOR BOROUGH COUNCIL *v.* GOUCHER AND RICHMOND ... 2201
RYAN (INSPECTOR OF TAXES) *v.* CRABTREE DENIMS ... 553

S. ... 1210
S. (A MINOR) (ADOPTION), *Re* ... 2451
S. (A MINOR) (ADOPTION OR CUSTODIANSHIP), *Re* ... 2443
S. (A MINOR) (CARE PROCEEDINGS: WARDSHIP SUMMONS), *Re* ... 2457
S. (MINORS) (WARDSHIP: POLICE INVESTIGATION), *Re* ... 2530
S. *v.* S. ... 1725
S. *v.* S. ... 2432
S.A. DES POMPES FUNÈBRES GÉNÉRALES *v.* LECLERC ... 1502
S.A. MAGNIVISION N.V. *v.* GENERAL OPTICAL COUNCIL ... 1595
S.A. MAGNIVISION N.V. *v.* GENERAL OPTICAL COUNCIL (No. 2) ... 1619
S.C.F. FINANCE CO. *v.* MASRI (No. 2) ... 195
S.C.F. FINANCE CO. *v.* MASRI (No. 3) ... 3014
SABTINA *v.* MOUNTAFIAN COMMODITIES ... 130
ST. ANDREW'S NORTH WEALD BASSETT, *Re* ... 1240
ST. MARY'S, BANBURY, *Re* ... 1242
ST. MARY'S, BARTON-UPON-HUMBER, *Re* ... 1241
ST. STEPHEN'S WALBROOK, *Re* ... 1238
SALVATION ARMY TRUSTEE CO. *v.* DEPARTMENT OF THE ENVIRONMENT FOR NORTHERN IRELAND (R/4/1987) ... 2746
SAMOS GLORY, THE. *See* MINERALS AND METALS TRADING CORP. OF INDIA *v.* ENCOUNTER BAY SHIPPING CO.; SAMOS GLORY, THE
SAMPSON, *Re* ... 2282
SAMUELSON *v.* NATIONAL INSURANCE AND GUARANTEE CORP. ... 2068
SAN SEBASTIAN PTY. *v.* MINISTER ADMINISTERING THE ENVIRONMENTAL PLANNING LAND ASSESSMENT ACT 1979 ... 2588
SANIX ACE, THE. *See* OBESTAIN INC. *v.* NATIONAL MINERAL DEVELOPMENT CORP., SANIX ACE, THE

PARA.

SANKO IRIS AND SANKO VENUS, THE. *See* SANKO STEAMSHIP CO. *v.* EACOM TIMBER SALES; SANKO IRIS AND SAMKO VENUS, THE
SANKO STEAMSHIP CO. *v.* EACOM TIMBER SALES; SANKO IRIS AND SANKO VENUS, THE ... 428
SARONIKOS, THE. *See* GREENMAST SHIPPING CO. S.A. *v.* JEAN LION ET CIE S.A.; SARONIKOS, THE
SARWAN SINGH DEU *v.* DUDLEY METROPOLITAN BOROUGH COUNCIL ... 836
SATURNIA, THE. *See* SUPERFOS CHARTERING A/S *v.* N.B.R. (LONDON); SATURNIA, THE
SAUDI EAGLE, THE. *See* ALPINE BULK TRANSPORT CO. INC. *v.* SAUDI EAGLE SHIPPING CO. INC.; SAUDI EAGLE, THE
SAUNDERS *v.* EDWARDS ... 1826
SAUTER AUTOMATION *v.* GOODMAN (MECHANICAL SERVICES) (IN LIQUIDATION) ... 451
SAVINGS & INVESTMENT BANK *v.* GASCO INVESTMENTS (NETHERLANDS) B.V. (No. 2) ... 2931
SCANDINAVIAN BANK GROUP, *Re* ... 365
SCHERING AGROCHEMICALS *v.* ABM CHEMICALS ... 2986
SCHIFFSHYPOTHEKENBANK ZU LUEBECK A.G. *v.* COMPTON (NORMAN PHILIP); ALEXION HOPE, THE ... 3411
SCHLOH (BERNARD) *v.* AUTO CONTROLE TECHNIQUE (No. 50/85) ... 1593
SCHLUMBERGER INLAND SERVICES INC. *v.* CUSTOMS AND EXCISE COMMISSIONERS ... 3798
SCHOTT SOHNE *v.* RADFORD ... 3585
SCOTT *v.* MARTIN ... 1236
SCOTT *v.* SCOTT ... 2499
SCOTT-WHITEHEAD *v.* NATIONAL COAL BOARD ... 3866
SEA BREEZE, THE. *See* OUTHWAITE (RICHARD) *v.* COMMERCIAL BANK OF GREECE S.A.; SEA BREEZE, THE
SEA CALM SHIPPING CO. S.A. *v.* CHANTIERS NAVALS DE L'ESTEREL S.A.; UHENBELS, THE ... 3374
SEA TRIUMPH SHIPPING CO. S.A. *v.* SAUDI EUROPE LINES ... 141
SEACRYSTAL SHIPPING *v.* BULK TRANSPORT GROUP SHIPPING CO.; KYZIKOS, THE. *See* BULK TRANSPORT GROUP SHIPPING CO. *v.* SEACRYSTAL SHIPPING, KYZIKOS, THE
SEASPEED DORA, THE. *See* SLAZENGERS *v.* SEASPEED FERRIES INTERNATIONAL; SEASPEED DORA, THE
SEATON *v.* SEATON ... 1735
SECOND W.R.V.S. HOUSING SOCIETY *v.* BLAIR ... 1902
SECRETARY OF STATE FOR EMPLOYMENT *v.* COHEN ... 1355
SECRETARY OF STATE FOR EMPLOYMENT *v.* FORD (A.) & SON (SACKS) ... 1345
SECRETARY OF STATE FOR EMPLOYMENT *v.* MILK & GENERAL HAULAGE (NOTTINGHAM) ... 1363
SECRETARY OF STATE FOR THE ENVIRONMENT *v.* ESSEX, GOODMAN & SUGGITT ... 2321

TABLE OF CASES

PARA.

SECRETARY OF STATE FOR SOCIAL SERVICES *v.* ELKINGTON ... 3511
SEFTON HOLDINGS *v.* CAIRNS ... 2241
SEGERS (D.H.M.) *v.* BESTUUR VAN DE BEDRIJFSVERENIGING VOOR BANK -EN VERZEKERINGSWEZEN, GROOTHANDEL EN VRIJE BEROEPEN (No. 79/85) ... 1535
SEKTKELLEREI C.A. KUPFERBERG & CIE K.G. a.A. *v.* HAUPTZOLLAMT MAINZ (No. 253/83) ... 1598
SELBY *v.* CHIEF CONSTABLE OF AVON AND SOMERSET ... 3275
SELWYN (L.) *v.* CUSTOMS AND EXCISE COMMISSIONERS ... 3822
SERAY-WURIE *v.* SERAY-WURIE ... 1778
SETHIA *v.* STERN ... 1668
SEVERN TRENT WATER AUTHORITY *v.* CARDSHOPS ... 3198
SEVERN TRENT WATER AUTHORITY *v.* CROSS ... 2368
SHAMSHER JUTE MILLS *v.* SETHIA (LONDON) ... 3328
SHAPER *v.* ROBINSON ... 755
SHARNEYFORD SUPPLIES *v.* EDGE; BARRINGTON BLACK & CO. (THIRD PARTY) ... 1225
SHARP *v.* McARTHUR AND SHARP ... 2160
SHARP *v.* SPENCER ... 3244
SHARPE *v.* DUKE STREET SECURITIES N.V. ... 2168
SHAW *v.* COMMISSIONER OF POLICE FOR THE METROPOLIS ... 3312
SHAW *v.* NATALEGAWA. *See* SHAW *v.* COMMISSIONER OF POLICE OF THE METROPOLIS
SHEARS *v.* SHEARS ... 3114
SHEARS COURT (WEST MERSEA) MANAGEMENT CO. *v.* ESSEX COUNTY COUNCIL ... 3097
SHEARSON LEHMAN BROTHERS INC. *v.* MACLAINE, WATSON & CO. ... 2982
SHEARSON LEHMAN BROTHERS INC. *v.* MACLAINE WATSON & CO., INTERNATIONAL TIN COUNCIL INTERVENING ... 1676
SHEFFIELD UNITED FOOTBALL CLUB *v.* SOUTH YORKSHIRE POLICE AUTHORITY. *See* HARRIS *v.* SHEFFIELD UNITED FOOTBALL CLUB
SHELL INTERNATIONAL PETROLEUM CO. *v.* TRANSNOR (BERMUDA) ... 3000
SHENAVAI *v.* KREISCHER (No. 266/85) ... 1548
SHEPHARD *v.* MIDLAND BANK ... 1828
SHEPHERD ... 1190
SHEPTONHURST *v.* CITY OF WAKEFIELD METROPOLITAN DISTRICT COUNCIL ... 2318
SHERDLEY *v.* SHERDLEY ... 2504
SHIELD PROPERTIES *v.* ANGLO OVERSEAS TRANSPORT ... 2214
SHINE *v.* GENERAL GUARANTEE CORP. ... 3338
SHREWSBURY AND ATCHAM BOROUGH COUNCIL AND BUTTERY ... 3718
SIAM VENTURE AND DARFUR, THE ... 3447
SIDEY *v.* PHILLIPS (INSPECTOR OF TAXES) ... 2033
SIDI BISHR, THE ... 3365
SILVER ATHENS, THE (No. 1) ... 3369
SILVER ATHENS, THE (No. 2) ... 3368
SIMAAN GENERAL CONTRACTING CO. *v.* PILKINGTON GLASS ... 1686
SIMISTER *v.* SIMISTER ... 1750
SIMISTER *v.* SIMISTER (No. 2) ... 1743
SIMMS *v.* DEPARTMENT OF AGRICULTURE (R/34/1984) ... 2636a
SIMON *v.* BRIMHAM ASSOCIATES ... 1351
SIMON-CARVES *v.* COSTAIN CONSTRUCTION ... 2264
SIMPSON *v.* THE LAW SOCIETY ... 2295
SINGAPORE FORTUNE, THE. *See* OVERSEAS FORTUNE SHIPPING PTE. *v.* GREAT EASTERN SHIPPING CO.; SINGAPORE FORTUNE, THE
SINGH *v.* RATHOUR ... 2063
SINGH *v.* THAPER ... 2320
SIP HENG WONG NG *v.* THE QUEEN. *See* NG (ALIAS WONG) *v.* THE QUEEN
SIPOREX TRADE S.A. *v.* COMDEL COMMODITIES ... 137
SIVYER *v.* PARKER ... 3239
SIX ARLINGTON STREET INVESTMENTS *v.* PERSONS UNKNOWN ... 3005
SLATER *v.* UNITED KINGDOM CENTRAL COUNCIL FOR NURSING MIDWIFERY AND HEALTH VISITORS ... 38
SLAZENGERS *v.* SEASPEED FERRIES INTERNATIONAL; SEASPEED DORA, THE ... 2951
SLOUGH INDUSTRIAL ESTATES *v.* SECRETARY OF STATE FOR THE ENVIRONMENT ... 3656
SMITH *v.* BAILEY (V.O.) (LVC/55/1985) ... 3176
SMITH *v.* BUSH (ERIC S.) (A FIRM) ... 2620
SMITH *v.* CITY OF GLASGOW DISTRICT COUNCIL ... 1408
SMITH *v.* CROFT ... 370
SMITH *v.* CROFT (No. 2) ... 327
SMITH *v.* LITTLEWOODS ORGANISATION; MALOCO *v.* SAME ... 2597
SMITH *v.* MELLORS AND SOAR ... 752
SMITH *v.* NORTHSIDE DEVELOPMENTS ... 2161
SMITH *v.* SCOT BOWYERS ... 2595
SMITH *v.* SECRETARY OF STATE FOR THE ENVIRONMENT ... 3108
SMITH *v.* SMITH ... 2929
SMITH *v.* SPRINGER ... 2966
SMITH (M. H.) (PLANT HIRE) *v.* MAINWARING (D. L.) (t/a INSHORE) ... 2904
SMITHS INDUSTRIES AEROSPACE AND DEFENCE SYSTEMS *v.* BROOKES ... 1311
SNOWBALL *v.* GARDNER MERCHANT ... 1336
SOCIAL SECURITY DECISION No. R(A) 3/86 ... 3454
SOCIAL SECURITY DECISION No. R(FIS) 1/87 ... 3470
SOCIAL SECURITY DECISION No. R(FIS) 2/87 ... 3471
SOCIAL SECURITY DECISION No. R(G) 1/86 ... 3485
SOCIAL SECURITY DECISION No. R(G) 2/86 ... 3480
SOCIAL SECURITY DECISION No. R(I) 2/86 ... 3479
SOCIAL SECURITY DECISION No. R(I) 6/85 ... 3476
SOCIAL SECURITY DECISION No. R(I) 1/87 ... 3477
SOCIAL SECURITY DECISION No. R(M) 3/86 ... 3490
SOCIAL SECURITY DECISION No. R(M) 4/86 ... 3488
SOCIAL SECURITY DECISION No. R(M) 5/86 ... 3491
SOCIAL SECURITY DECISION No. R(S) 3/86 ... 3481
SOCIAL SECURITY DECISION No. R(S) 5/86 ... 3483
SOCIAL SECURITY DECISION No. R(S) 6/86 ... 3499
SOCIAL SECURITY DECISION No. R(S) 1/87 ... 3482
SOCIAL SECURITY DECISION No. R(SB) 9/86 ... 3523
SOCIAL SECURITY DECISION No. R(SB) 13/86 ... 3517
SOCIAL SECURITY DECISION No. R(SB) 16/86 ... 3525
SOCIAL SECURITY DECISION No. R(SB) 17/86 ... 3524
SOCIAL SECURITY DECISION No. R(SB) 18/86 ... 3510

PARA.
SOCIAL SECURITY DECISION No. R(SB) 19/86 3504
SOCIAL SECURITY DECISION No. R(SB) 20/86 3505
SOCIAL SECURITY DECISION No. R(SB) 21/86 3521
SOCIAL SECURITY DECISION No. R(SB) 22/86 3529
SOCIAL SECURITY DECISION No. R(SB) 23/86 3526
SOCIAL SECURITY DECISION No. R(SB) 24/86 3527
SOCIAL SECURITY DECISION No. R(SB) 25/86 3522
SOCIAL SECURITY DECISION No. R(SB) 26/86 3519
SOCIAL SECURITY DECISION No. R(SB) 27/86 3531
SOCIAL SECURITY DECISION No. R(SB) 28/86 3520
SOCIAL SECURITY DECISION No. R(SB) 1/87 3502
SOCIAL SECURITY DECISION No. R(SB) 2/87 3512
SOCIAL SECURITY DECISION No. R(SB) 3/87 3509
SOCIAL SECURITY DECISION No. R(SB) 4/87 3516
SOCIAL SECURITY DECISION No. R(SB) 7/87 3518
SOCIAL SECURITY DECISION No. R(U) 1/86. 3533
SOCIAL SECURITY DECISION No. R(U) 3/86. 3536
SOCIAL SECURITY DECISION No. R(U) 5/86. 3540
SOCIAL SECURITY DECISION No. R(U) 6/86. 3535
SOCIAL SECURITY DECISION No. R(U) 7/86. 3534
SOCIAL SECURITY DECISION No. R(U) 1/87. 3539
SOCIAL SECURITY DECISION No. R(U) 2/87. 3538
SOCIÉTÉ ANONYME MAROCAINE DE L'INDUSTRIE DU RAFFINAGE *v.* NOTOS MARITIME CORP. OF MONROVIA; NOTOS, THE 3383
SOCIÉTÉ CO-OPERATIVE DES LABORATOIRES DE PHARMACIE LEGIA *v.* MINISTER FOR HEALTH (LUXEMBOURG) (Nos. 87–88/85) 1592
SOCIETE MICROFOR *v.* Sàrl LE MONDE 504
SOCIÉTÉ NATIONALE INDUSTRIELLE AEROSPATIALE *v.* LEE KUI JAK 3024
SOLICITOR, A, *Re*. 3550
SOLICITOR, A, *Re*. 3558
SOLIHULL BOROUGH COUNCIL *v.* SECRETARY OF STATE FOR THE ENVIRONMENT 3702
SOMAK TRAVEL *v.* SECRETARY OF STATE FOR THE ENVIRONMENT AND BRENT LONDON BOROUGH 3621
SOMMER ALLIBERT (U.K.) *v.* FLAIR PLASTICS 2786
SONIC TAPE'S PATENT 2781
SOPHOCLEOUS *v.* RINGER 558
SORGE (A. V.) & CO., *Re*. 374
SOUNION, THE. *See* SUMMIT INVESTMENT INC. *v.* BRITISH STEEL CORP.; SOUNION, THE
SOUTH BEDFORDSHIRE DISTRICT COUNCIL *v.* SECRETARY OF STATE FOR THE ENVIRONMENT AND BOYLE 3708
SOUTH BRITISH INSURANCE CO. AND NEW ZEALAND SOUTH BRITISH INSURANCE *v.* MEDITERRANEAN INSURANCE & REINSUR ANCE CO. AND WRIGHT (F. E.) (U.K.) 2990
SOUTH DERBYSHIRE DISTRICT COUNCIL AND COOK 3712
SOUTH HOLLAND DISTRICT COUNCIL *v.* KEYTE 1881
SOUTH OXFORDSHIRE DISTRICT COUNCIL AND DUKE 3716
SOUTH STAFFORDSHIRE DISTRICT COUNCIL *v.* SECRETARY OF STATE FOR THE ENVIRONMENT AND BICKFORD 3614
SOUTHWARK LONDON BOROUGH COUNCIL *v.* SECRETARY OF STATE FOR THE ENVIRONMENT AND WATERHOUSE 3645
SOUTHWELL *v.* CHADWICK 813
SPECIALIST PLANT SERVICES *v.* BRAITHWAITE 369
SPILIADA MARITIME CORP. *v.* CANSULEX; SPILIADA, THE 3135
SPILIADA, THE. *See* SPILIADA MARITIME CORP. *v.* CANSULEX; SPILIADA, THE
SPOONER, *ex p.*; DE ROHAN, *ex p*. 793
SPORT INTERNATIONAL BUSSUM *v.* HI-TEC SPORTS 3748
STAATSANWALT FREIBURG *v.* KELLER (No. 234/85) 1573
STAFFORDSHIRE COUNTY COUNCIL *v.* SECRETARY OF STATE FOR EMPLOYMENT 1364
STAGE CLUB *v.* MILLERS HOTELS PROPRIETARY 2329
STAINES WAREHOUSING CO. *v.* MONTAGUE EXECUTOR & TRUSTEE CO. 2199
STANDARD LIFE ASSURANCE CO. *v.* OXOID; OXOID *v.* STANDARD LIFE ASSURANCE CO. 2219
STANDARD OCEAN CARRIERS S.A. *v.* UNION DE REMORQUAGE ET DE SAUVETAGE S.A.: NEPTUNE C, THE 152
STANDARD PROPERTY INVESTMENT *v.* BRITISH PLASTICS FEDERATION 2542
STANFORD *v.* KOBAYASHI 2968
STANFORD SERVICES, *Re* 333
STANÑARD *v.* ISSA 485
STAR CINEMAS (LONDON) *v.* BARNETT 2892
STAR OF KUWAIT, THE. *See* LIPS MARITIME CORP. *v.* NATIONAL MARITIME AGENCIES CO.; STAR OF KUWAIT, THE
STATE *v.* MOTTE (No. 247/84) 1590
STATE AIDS TO EXPORTS, *Re*: GREECE *v.* E.C. COMMISSION (No. 57/86R) 1648
STATE AIDS TO THE STEEL INDUSTRY, *Re*: GERMANY *v.* EUROPEAN COMMISSION (No. 214/83) 1651
STATE EQUITY HOLDING, *Re*: E.C. COMMISSION *v.* BELGIUM (No. 52/84) 1649
STATE OF HIMACHAL PRADESH THE 3396
STEAMSHIP MUTUAL UNDERWRITING ASSOCIATION (BERMUDA) *v.* THAKUR SHIPPING CO. (NOTE) 3066
STEEL *v.* WELLCOME CUSTODIAN TRUSTEES 295
STEEL REDUNDANCY BENEFIT, *Re* (No. C.114/85) 1530
STEFF *v.* BECK 3302
STENT *v.* MONMOUTH DISTRICT COUNCIL. 2140
STEPHENS *v.* ANGLIAN WATER AUTHORITY 3593
STEPHENSON 1174
STEPHENSON *v.* CLIFT 3237
STEVENS *v.* BRODRIBB SAWMILLING CO. PTY. 2621
STEVENS *v.* CHRISTY 792
STEVENSON (INSPECTOR OF TAXES) *v.* WISHART 2035
STEWART *v.* THE LAW SOCIETY 2294

TABLE OF CASES

PARA.

STEWART *v.* QUIGLEY (R/18/1986)................ 2658
STEWART (LORNE) *v.* SINDALL (WILLIAM) AND N.W. THAMES REGIONAL HEALTH AUTHORITY 144
STIELLER *v.* PORIRUA CITY COUNCIL.......... 2585
STINNES A.G. *v.* HAUPTZOLLAMT KASSEL (No. 214/84).. 1578
STOCKPORT METROPOLITAN BOROUGH COUNCIL *v.* ALWIYAH DEVELOPMENTS .. 3715
STOCKTON-ON-TEES BOROUGH COUNCIL *v.* BROWN.. 1358
STOCKTON PLANT AND EQUIPMENT *v.* CUSTOMS AND EXCISE COMMISSIONERS 3810
STOCKPORT METROPOLITAN BOROUGH COUNCIL AND HALL............................ 3671
STOKES *v.* SAYERS 3253
STRAUDLEY INVESTMENTS *v.* BARPRESS.... 2153
STROUD *v.* WEIR ASSOCIATES.................... 1893
STUBBES *v.* TROWER, STILL & KEELING...... 1301
STUBBINGS *v.* BEACONSFIELD JUSTICES.... 3641
STUDWELL *v.* WHITE.................................. 1208
SUBSIDY FOR ITALIAN MOTOR VEHICLES, *Re*; E.C. COMMISSION *v.* ITALY 1596
SUGAR TAX, *Re*; E.C.COMMISSION *v.* GERMANY (No. 303/84)............................. 1463
SUGARWHITE *v.* BUDD (INSPECTOR OF TAXES) 2037
SULLIVAN *v.* BROXTOWE BOROUGH COUNCIL (Ref/205/1984) 396
SUMMERS *v.* SUMMERS................................ 1776
SUMMIT INVESTMENT INC. *v.* BRITISH STEEL CORP.; SOUNION, THE................. 3429
SUN TAI CHEUNG CREDITS *v.* ATT.-GEN. OF HONG KONG 361
SUNNYSIDE NURSING HOME *v.* BUILDERS CONTRACT MANAGEMENT 231
SUPERFOS CHARTERING A/S *v.* N.B.R. (LONDON); SATURNIA, THE...................... 3437
SURREY COUNTY COUNCIL *v.* LEWIS. *See* LEWIS *v.* SURREY COUNTY COUNCIL
SURREY HEATH BOROUGH COUNCIL *v.* SECRETARY OF STATE FOR THE ENVIRONMENT AND ELLIOT DEVELOPMENTS 3696
SUTCH *v.* CROWN PROSECUTION SERVICE. 3261
SUTCLIFFE *v.* SAYER..................................... 2596
SUTER *v.* SUTER AND JONES....................... 1727
SUTHERLAND.. 1180
SWANBRAE *v.* ELLIOTT 2240
SYNTEX CORPORATION'S PATENT 2806

T. (A MINOR: WARDSHIP), *Re*; T. *v.* T. (OUSTER ORDER)... 1773
T. H. KNITWEAR (WHOLESALE), *Re* 3806
T. *v.* T. (MINORS: CUSTODY APPEAL)........... 2490
T., *Re*; T. *v.* T.. 2426
T. *v.* T. 1747
T.B.A. INDUSTRIAL PRODUCTS *v.* LAINÉ...... 1854
T.C.B. *v.* GRAY.. 1844
T. & D. TRANSPORT (PORTSMOUTH) *v.* LIMBURN 1341
TADDALE INVESTMENTS *v.* BANQUE HYPOTHECAIRE DU CANTON DE GENEVE......... 3100
TADDALE PROPERTIES *v.* I.R.C.................... 3602
TANDRIDGE DISTRICT COUNCIL AND HOMEWOOD AND THE HONEY FARM............... 3717
TAX CREDITS, *Re*: E.C. COMMISSION *v.* FRANCE (No. 270/83) 1533

PARA.

TAXATION OF WINE, *Re*: E.C. COMMISSION *v.* DENMARK (No. 106/84); WALKER (JOHN) & SONS *v.* MINISTERIET FOR SKATTER OG AFGIFTER (243/84) 1659
TAY BOK CHOON *v.* TAHANSAN SDN BHD.. 377
TAYLOR *v.* CHIEF CONSTABLE OF CHESHIRE.. 743
TAYLOR *v.* CHIEF CONSTABLE, ROYAL ULSTER CONSTABULARY 2718
TAYLOR *v.* COMMISSIONER OF POLICE OF THE METROPOLIS 3259
TAYLOR *v.* MASEFIELD.................................. 2374
TAYLOR *v.* TAYLOR.. 1786
TECHNOINTORG *v.* E.C. COMMISSION (No. 294/86R).. 1602
TEJANI *v.* SUPERINTENDENT REGISTRAR FOR THE DISTRICT OF PETERBOROUGH. 3203
TELEPHONE RENTALS *v.* BURGESS SALMON 450
TEM LOC *v.* ERRILL PROPERTIES................. 240
TEPPER'S WILL TRUSTS, *Re*; KRAMER *v.* RUDA 3877
TEZI TEXTIEL B.V. *v.* E.C. COMMISSION (NETHERLANDS AND U.K. INTERVENING) (No. 59/84); TEZI TEXTIEL B.V. *v.* MINISTER FOR ECONOMIC AFFAIRS (No. 242/84)..... 1581
THAHA *v.* THAHA 1748
THANET DISTRICT COUNCIL AND HOST GROUP.. 3628
THETFORD CORPORATION *v.* FIAMMA SpA 2791
THORMAN *v.* NEW HAMPSHIRE INSURANCE CO. (U.K.) 2069
THOMAS *v.* NATIONAL COAL BOARD; BARKER *v.* NATIONAL COAL BOARD........ 1324
THOMAS *v.* UNIVERSITY OF BRADFORD...... 1276
THOMAS *v.* WIGNALL.................................... 1226
THOMAS (INSPECTOR OF TAXES) *v.* REYNOLDS 2009
THOMPSON *v.* BRADFORD HEALTH AUTHORITY.. 1218
THOMPSON *v.* ELMBRIDGE BOROUGH COUNCIL.. 1903
THOMPSON *v.* LOHAN (T.) (PLANT HIRE) 424
THOMPSON *v.* THOMPSON 2491
THORNTON (J. W.) *v.* BLACKS LEISURE GROUP... 2124
THURROCK BOROUGH COUNCIL AND MOBIL OIL CO. 3684
TILCON *v.* LAND AND REAL ESTATE INVESTMENTS.. 3082
TILLEY AND NOAD *v.* DOMINION INSURANCE CO. 2072
TIME FOR SERVICE OF BELGIAN DEFAULT PROCEEDINGS, *Re*.................................... 1547
TINEY ENGINEERING *v.* AMODS KNITTING MACHINERY 412
TIRUNA AND PELORUS, THE. *See* BAREMEDA ENTERPRISES PTY. *v.* O'CONNOR (RONALD PATRICK) AND K.F.V. FISHERIES (QLD) PTY.; TIRUNA AND PELORUS, THE
TITTERRELL *v.* TOZER (V.O.) (LVC/334/1986). 3177
TOBI *v.* NICHOLAS 647
TODD (INSPECTOR OF TAXES) *v.* MUDD 271
TOM'S SETTLEMENT, *Re*, ROSE *v.* EVANS... 1437
TOPPING *v.* WARNE SURGICAL PRODUCTS. 2672
TOWER HAMLETS LONDON BOROUGH COUNCIL *v.* QAYYUM.............................. 1350

PARA.
TRADE FORTITUDE, THE. *See* FORD CORP. OF INDIA *v.* MARASTRO CIA NAVIERA S.A.; TRADE FORTITUDE, THE
TRAMWAY BUILDING AND CONSTRUCTION CO., *Re* 380
TRANSCONTAINER EXPRESS *v.* CUSTODIAN SECURITY 290
TRANSCONTINENTAL UNDERWRITING AGENCY *v.* GRAND UNION INSURANCE CO. 2075
TRANSOCEAN TOWAGE CO. *v.* HYUNDAI CONSTRUCTION CO. 1552
TRANSOCEANICA FRANCESCA AND NICOS V, THE 3391
TRANSPORT AND GENERAL WORKERS' UNION *v.* LEDBURY PRESERVES (1928) 1359
TRANSWORLD OIL *v.* NORTH BAY SHIPPING CORP.; RIO CLARO, THE 3435
TREMAYNE *v.* HILL 2589
TRENDWORTHY TWO *v.* ISLINGTON LONDON BOROUGH COUNCIL 3196
TRIUMPH SECURITIES *v.* REID FURNITURE CO. 150
TROUGHTON *v.* METROPOLITAN POLICE 840
TRUSTHOUSE FORTE HOTELS *v.* SECRETARY OF STATE FOR THE ENVIRONMENT 3711
TUCKER (A BANKRUPT), *ex p.* TUCKER, *Re* .. 209
TUCKER *v.* HUTCHINSON 2111
TUDOR *v.* ELLESMERE PORT AND NESTON BOROUGH COUNCIL 32
TUDOR *v.* HAMID 480
TUKAN TIMBER *v.* BARCLAYS BANK 203
TURKOGLU, *Re* 1924
TURNER *v.* CHEEK (V.O.) (LVC/281/1985) 3178
TURNER *v.* LABOUR PARTY AND THE LABOUR PARTY SUPERANNUATION SOCIETY 1374
TURNER (P.) (WILSDEN), *Re* 344
TURTON *v.* TURTON 1439
29 EQUITIES *v.* BANK LEUMI (U.K.) 477
TWM BARLWN COMMON, RICSA AND ROGERSTONE, *Re*, (Ref. No. 273/D/106–107) 315

U.C.B. LEASING *v.* HOLTOM 434
UDALL *v.* CAPRI LIGHTING, (IN LIQUIDATION) 3562
UDDINS APPLICATION, *Re* 1975
UHENBELS, THE. *See* SEA CALM SHIPPING CO. S.A. *v.* CHANTIERS NAVALS DE L'ESTEREL S.A.; UHENBELS, THE
UNICORN SHIPPING *v.* DEMET NAVY SHIPPING CO 3069
UNILEVER'S (STRIPED TOOTHPASTE NO. 2) TRADE MARKS 3742
UNION CARBIDE CORP. *v.* NATURIN 1669
UNION NATIONALE DES ENTRAINEURS ET CADRES TECHNIQUES PROFESSIONELS DU FOOTBALL (UNECTEF) *v.* HEYLENS (No. 222/86) 1566
UNITED BANK OF KUWAIT *v.* HAMMOUD 3561
UNITED CO-OPERATIVES *v.* SUN ALLIANCE AND LONDON ASSURANCE CO. 2218
U.K. *v.* E.C. COMMISSION (No. 84/85) 1639
UNITED KINGDOM NIREX *v.* BARTON 3121
U.S. LITIGATION BETWEEN DUPONT DE NEMOURS (E.I.) & CO. AND AKZO N.V., *Re* 1559

PARA.
UNIVERSAL CO. *v.* YIP 1845
UNIVERSAL PETROLEUM CO. *v.* HANDELS UND TRANSPORT GESELLSCHAFT MBH .. 146
USHER *v.* INTASUN HOLIDAYS 418
USINOR *v.* E.C. COMMISSION (No. 62/84R) .. 1608

VAGRES COMPANIA MARITIMA *v.* NISSHO-IWAI AMERICAN CORP.; KARIN VATIS, THE 3385
VALE OF GLAMORGAN BOROUGH COUNCIL *v.* SECRETARY OF STATE FOR WALES AND SIR BRANDON RHYS-WILLIAMS 3707
VAN DER LELY'S APPLICATION 2774
VAN GESTEL *v.* CANN 454
VARGAS PENA APEZ TEGUIA Y CIA SAIC *v.* PETER CREMER GmbH 3329
VASS *v.* G.R.E. INSURANCE 2056
VAUGHAN *v.* SOCIAL SECURITY ADJUDICATION OFFICER 3506
VAUSE *v.* BRAY 2997
VEL *v.* OWEN *sub nom.* VEL (KEVIN) *v.* CHIEF CONSTABLE OF NORTH WALES 575
VEL (KEVIN) *v.* CHIEF CONSTABLE OF NORTH WALES. *See* VEL *v.* OWEN
VENNER *v.* NORTH EAST ESSEX AREA HEALTH AUTHORITY 2606
VERBAND DER SACHVERSICHERER eV (SUPPORTED BY GESAMTVERBAND DER DEUTSCHEN VERSICHERUNGSWIRTSCHAFT eV, INTERVENER) *v.* E.C. COMMISSION (No. 45/85) 1496
VERDEGAAL (G.A.) & ZONEN EXPORT B.V. *v.* PULLEN 3093
VERENIGING SLACHTPLUIMVEE-EXPORT eV *v.* REWE-ZENTRAL A.G. (No. 96/84) 1616
VIDEO ARTS *v.* PAGET INDUSTRIES 509
VIKOMA INTERNATIONAL *v.* SECRETARY OF STATE FOR THE ENVIRONMENT AND WOKING BOROUGH COUNCIL 3652
VILVARAJAH, *Re* 1927
VINEYARD REDUCTIONS, *Re*: E.C. COMMISSION *v.* ITALY (No. 309/84) 1465
VIRGO STEAMSHIP CO. S.A. *v.* SKAARUP SHIPPING CORP. *See* KAPETAN GEORGIS, THE; *sub nom.* VIRGO STEAMSHIP CO. S.A. *v.* SKARRUP SHIPPING CORP.
VISCOUNT DE L'ISLE *v.* TIMES NEWSPAPERS 3119

W. (A MINOR), *Re* 2441
W. (MINORS) (CHILD ABUSE: EVIDENCE), *Re* 2475
W. AND L. (MINORS) (INTERIM CUSTODY), *Re* 2497
W. *v.* K. (PROOF OF PATERNITY) 2509
W. *v.* P. 2498
WADDINGTON'S PATENT 2769
WADHAM STRINGER (FAREHAM) *v.* FAREHAM BOROUGH COUNCIL 3595
WAKELEY *v.* HYAMS 3241
WALES TOURIST BOARD *v.* ROBERTS 2895
WALKER, *ex p.* 2546
WALKER *v.* WALKER 1716
WALLS *v.* SINNETT (INSPECTOR OF TAXES) 2015
WALSALL METROPOLITAN BOROUGH COUNCIL AND CASSIDY REPRODUCTIONS AND J. AND L. K. CASSIDY 3625

	PARA.
WALSH *v.* CROYDON GENERAL COMMISSIONERS	2023
WALTER L. JACOB & CO., *Re*	379
WALTERS, *Re*	564
WALTHAM FOREST LONDON BOROUGH COUNCIL AND MULTI-TILE	3618
WANDSWORTH LONDON BOROUGH COUNCIL *v.* FADAYOMI	2230
WANDSWORTH LONDON BOROUGH COUNCIL *v.* SPARLING	1882
WANDSWORTH LONDON BOROUGH COUNCIL *v.* WINDER (No. 2)	2385
WANSBECK DISTRICT COUNCIL *v.* MARLEY	2229
WARD *v.* CHIEF CONSTABLE OF AVON AND SOMERSET CONSTABULARY	3555
WARD (S.) (COINS) *v.* CUSTOMS AND EXCISE COMMISSIONERS	3826
WARD'S APPLICATIONS	2780
WARD-STEMP *v.* GRIFFIN (INSPECTOR OF TAXES)	2017
WARNED LIST EXERCISE	3122
WARREN *v.* KILROE (T.) & SONS	3057
WARRINGTON AND RUNCORN DEVELOPMENT CORP. *v.* GREGGS	2216
WARRINGTON INC'S APPLICATION, *Re*	3755
WATSON, *ex p.*	3053
WATTS *v.* YEEND	75
WAVERLEY BOROUGH COUNCIL *v.* HILDEN	3609a
WAVERLEY BOROUGH COUNCIL *v.* SECRETARY OF STATE FOR THE ENVIRONMENT AND CLARKE HOMES (SOUTHERN) AND CLARKE HOMES (SOUTH EASTERN)	3705
WEALDEN DISTRICT COUNCIL AND BENN	3666
WEBB *v.* CRANE	3305
WEBSTER *v.* BRITISH RAILWAYS BOARD	1196
WEDDELL *v.* PEARCE (J.A.) AND MAJOR	206
WEEKS *v.* U.K. (No. 3/1985/89/136)	1918
WELBECK SECURITIES *v.* POWLSON (INSPECTOR OF TAXES). *See* POWLSON (INSPECTOR OF TAXES) *v.* WELBECK SECURITIES	
WEST *v.* KNEELS	1381
WEST CUMBERLAND BY PRODUCTS *v.* D.P.P.	716
WEST MIDLANDS PASSENGER TRANSPORT EXECUTIVE *v.* SINGH	1352
WEST YORKSHIRE INDEPENDENT HOSPITAL (CONTRACT SERVICES) *v.* CUSTOMS AND EXCISE COMMISSIONERS	3861
WESTCOTT (INSPECTOR OF TAXES) *v.* WOOLCOMBERS	281
WESTERN FRONT *v.* VESTRON INC	499
WESTLAKE v. BRACKNELL DISTRICT COUNCIL	2587
WESTMINSTER CITY COUNCIL *v.* CLIFFORD CULPIN AND PARTNERS	2903
WESTMINSTER CITY COUNCIL AND RADIO LUXEMBOURG (LONDON)	3703
WESTON *v.* BRIAR	3115
WHEELER *v.* PATEL	1416
WHELAN ASSOCIATES *v.* JASLOW DENTAL LABORATORY	505
WHITBREAD & CO. *v.* THOMAS	1400
WHITBY (V.O.) *v.* COLE (LVC/243/1985)	3179
WHITTY *v.* HACKNEY BOROUGH COUNCIL	1211
WIGAN METROPOLITAN BOROUGH COUNCIL *v.* SECRETARY OF STATE FOR THE ENVIRONMENT AND BROSELEY ESTATES	3698
WILDE *v.* WILDE	1777
WILKINS *v.* BOWER	1133
WILKINSON *v.* ANCLIFF (B. L. T.)	2336
WILLAIRE SYSTEMS, *Re*	363
WILLCOX *v.* HASTINGS	1360
WILLIAM HILL (SOUTHERN) *v.* CABRAS. *See* HILL (WILLIAM) (SOUTHERN) *v.* CABRAS	
WILLIAMS *v.* ATT.-GEN.	2998
WILLIAMS *v.* BARCLAYS BANK. *See* WILLIAMS *v.* WILLIAMS: TUCKER *v.* WILLIAMS	
WILLIAMS *v.* BOWATER CONTAINERS	1199
WILLIAMS *v.* CO-OPERATIVE RETAIL SERVICES	610
WILLIAMS *v.* JORDAN	2961
WILLIAMS *v.* WILLIAMS; TUCKER *v.* WILLIAMS	1674
WILLIAMS (INSPECTOR OF TAXES) *v.* MERRYLEES	280
WILLIAMSON *v.* MOLDLINE	2794
WILLIAMSON MUSIC *v.* PEARSON PARTNERSHIP	513
WILSHER *v.* ESSEX AREA HEALTH AUTHORITY	2605
WILSON *v.* COMMISSIONER OF VALUATION FOR NORTHERN IRELAND (VR/49/1985)	2733
WIMPEY GROUP SERVICES *v.* CUSTOMS AND EXCISE COMMISSIONERS	3859
WIMPEY INTERNATIONAL *v.* WARLAND (INSPECTOR OF TAXES); ASSOCIATED RESTAURANTS *v.* SAME	542
WINCH *v.* AMPLETT & CO. (A FIRM)	3127
WINDSOR AND MAIDENHEAD BOROUGH COUNCIL AND ARNOLD	3683
WINDSURFING INTERNATIONAL INC. *v.* E.C. COMMISSION (No. 193/83)	1504
WINE VINEGAR (No. 2), *Re*: E.C. COMMISSION *v.* ITALY (No. 281/83)	1579
WINKWORTH *v.* BARON (EDWARD) DEVELOPMENT CO.	2109
WIRTSCHAFSVEREINIGUNG EISEN-UND STAHLINDUSTRIE *v.* E.C. COMMISSION (No. 27/84)	1538
WISEMAN *v.* SIMPSON	1780
WOKING BOROUGH COUNCIL AND CREST HOMES	3685
WOLFF *v.* ENFIELD LONDON BOROUGH	2224
WOLKIND AND NORTHCOTT *v.* PURA FOODS	1817
WOOD *v.* MILNE	3258
WOOD (JOHN D.) & CO. *v.* DANTATA	63
WOODBRIDGE *v.* WESTMINSTER PRESS	2123
WOODCOCK *v.* COMMITTEE FOR THE TIME BEING OF THE FRIENDS SCHOOL, WIGTON AND GENWISE	1417
WOOLF PROJECT MANAGEMENT *v.* WOODTREK	481
WOOLWORTHS *v.* CHARLWOOD ALLIANCE PROPERTIES	2116
WORBOYS *v.* CARTER	1445
WORKMAN (GEORGE GROSVENOR) *v.* BLAENAU FFESTINIOG MAGISTRATES' COURT	2311
WORLD STAR, THE	123
WORLD STAR, THE	3364
WORMELL *v.* R.H.M. AGRICULTURE (EAST).	3327
WORSTER *v.* CITY AND HACKNEY HEALTH AUTHORITY	2619

TABLE OF CASES

	PARA.
WORTHING RUGBY FOOTBALL CLUB TRUSTEES *v.* I.R.C.	307
WRAY *v.* GREATER LONDON COUNCIL	2560
WREATH *v.* DEPARTMENT OF THE ENVIRONMENT FOR NORTHERN IRELAND (R/7/1986)	2747
WRIGHT *v.* JESS	2930
WYBOT *v.* FAURE (No. 149/85)	1556
WYCHAVON DISTRICT COUNCIL *v.* MIDLAND ENTERPRISES (SPECIAL EVENTS)	3449
X., *Re*	2397
XYZ, *Re*	348
X. *v.* Y	3020
YASIN *v.* RASHID	1141
YELIC *v.* TOWN OF GIMLI	2610
YOUNG *v.* DALGETY	2155
YOUNG *v.* G.L.C. AND MASSEY	2328
YUEN KUN-YEU *v.* ATT.-GEN. OF HONG KONG	2580
ZAKHEM INTERNATIONAL CONSTRUCTION *v.* NIPPON KOKKAN KK	3110
ZAKHEM INTERNATIONAL CONSTRUCTION *v.* NIPPON KOKKAN KK	3111
ZAMBIA STEEL & BUILDING SUPPLIES *v.* CLARK (JAMES) & EATON	155
ZAVERI (S.) *v.* CUSTOMS AND EXCISE COMMISSIONERS	3820
ZUHAL K., THE	3373

QUANTUM OF DAMAGES
PERSONAL INJURIES OR DEATH

The table below is a cumulative guide to quantum of damages cases reported in Current Law in 1987.

Injury	*Case*	*Award* General	Total	*Reference*
		£	£	
Maximum severity	*Charalambous* v. *Islington Health Authority*	360,387		[1987] C.L.Y. 1171
	Harvey v. *South West Thames Regional Health Authority*		350,000	[1987] C.L.Y. 1172
Multiple injuries	*Hawkins*	40,000		[1987] C.L.Y. 1173
	Stephenson	6,000		[1987] C.L.Y. 1174
	Mewis v. *Woolf*	5,500	13,242·48	[1987] C.L.Y. 1175
	Dawson v. *Thompson*	5,500		[1987] C.L.Y. 1176
Brain and skull	*Nevins*	46,250		[1987] C.L.Y. 1177
	Lewis	29,824	32,000	[1987] C.L.Y. 1178
	Ellis v. *Biggins*	27,000	30,108	[1987] C.L.Y. 1179
	Sutherland	10,000		[1987] C.L.Y. 1180
Face, lip, ear, nose	*Leakey* v. *Taylor*	2,000		[1987] C.L.Y. 1181
	Mordaunt, Re	10,000		[1987] C.L.Y. 1182
	Frogley v. *Algar*	2,000		[1987] C.L.Y. 1183
Skin	*Rigg* v. *Elliott*	40,000	80,076	[1987] C.L.Y. 1184
Burns and scars	*McNeil* v. *London Electricity Board*	7,000		[1987] C.L.Y. 1185
	Murray v. *Chicken Cabins*	1,800	1,810	[1987] C.L.Y. 1186
Sight	*Mervyn*	18,000		[1987] C.L.Y. 1187
	Adams v. *Rowcliffe*	14,000	14,873·13	[1987] C.L.Y. 1188
	Cole	15,000	15,305	[1987] C.L.Y. 1189
	Shepherd	12,500	28,222	[1987] C.L.Y. 1190
Hearing	*Drake*	7,500		[1987] C.L.Y. 1191
Neck	*Bennet* v. *Gower-Smith*	10,000	13,000	[1987] C.L.Y. 1192
	Hook v. *Hair*	1,100		[1987] C.L.Y. 1192a
Respiratory organs	*Green* v. *Fine Spinners and Doublers*	18,810		[1987] C.L.Y. 1193
	Patterson v. *Ministry of Defence*	1,250 (provisional)		[1987] C.L.Y. 1194
Internal organs	*Cookson* v. *Leyland Vehicles*	4,750		[1987] C.L.Y. 1195

Injury	*Case*	*Award* General	Total	*Reference*
		£	£	
Spleen	*Webster* v. *British Railway Board*	4,000		[1987] C.L.Y. 1196
Pelvis and hip	*Charlton* v. *Tyne Ship Repairers*	25,094		[1987] C.L.Y. 1197
Shoulder	*George* v. *Thornborrow*	2,000	2,733·66	[1987] C.L.Y. 1198
Arm	*Williams* v. *Bowater Containers*	17,500	21,020·56	[1987] C.L.Y. 1199
	Hollins v. *Clarke*	2,000		[1987] C.L.Y. 1200
Fingers	*Batty* v. *Southern Counties Storage*	12,500		[1987] C.L.Y. 1201
	Moore v. *Johnston*	2,300	2,598·44	[1987] C.L.Y. 1202
Leg	*Churms* v. *Grayston Plant*	93,395		[1987] C.L.Y. 1203
Ankle	*Giametti* v. *Haigh*	5,500		[1987] C.L.Y. 1204
	Hills v. *Craig and Gubber*	4,500		[1987] C.L.Y. 1205
	Lodge v. *Magnet Joinery*	2,000		[1987] C.L.Y. 1206
Foot	*Mecham* v. *Saddington*	20,327		[1987] C.L.Y. 1207
	Studwell v. *White*	3,500		[1987] C.L.Y. 1208
Traumatic neurosis	*Rai*	72,500		[1987] C.L.Y. 1209
	S.	12,000	12,887	[1987] C.L.Y. 1210
	Whitty v. *Hackney Borough Council*	4,500		[1987] C.L.Y. 1211
	Coddington v. *Hern*	6,500		[1987] C.L.Y. 1212
Pre-existing condition: osteo arthritis	*Haw* v. *Hampshire County Council*	5,350		[1987] C.L.Y. 1213
Minor injuries	*Old* v. *Sampson*	2,250		[1987] C.L.Y. 1215
	Perry v. *Mercer*	1,800		[1987] C.L.Y. 1216
	Jordan v. *Mid-Glamorgan County Council*	850		[1987] C.L.Y. 1217
	Thompson v. *Bradford Health Authority*	650		[1987] C.L.Y. 1218
Fatal accidents	*Prior* v. *Hastie (Bernard) and Co.*	73,737		[1987] C.L.Y. 1219

The table below is a cumulative guide to quantum of damages cases reported in Scottish Current Law in [1987].

Injury	*Case*	*Award* *Solatium*	*Total*	*Reference*
		£	£	
Maximum severity	*Degan*	80,000	111,000	[1987] C.L.Y. 1170
Paraplegia	*MacIntosh* v. *National Coal Board*	30,000	162,068 (special needs 107,468)	[1987] C.L.Y. 4317
Brain and skull	*Forsyth's Curator Bonis* v. *Govan Shipbuilders*	60,000	214,877	[1987] C.L.Y. 4342
Head	*Cunliffe* v. *Chief Constable, Central Scotland Police*	3,000		[1987] C.L.Y. 4328
	Stephen v. *British Railways Board*	1,200	1,575	[1987] C.L.Y. 4318
Burns	*Bruce* v. *Ailsa Vacuum Extraction*	6,000	15,290	[1987] C.L.Y. 4326
Soft tissue injuries	*Goldie* v *National Coal Board*	4,000	5,200	[1987] C.L.Y. 4321
Eye	*McKinlay* v. *British Steel Corporation*	32,000	91,890	[1987] C.L.Y. 4755
	Buchan v. *J. Marr (Aberdeen)*	3,500	6,300	[1987] C.L.Y. 4327
Whiplash	*Quinn* v. *Bowie (No. 1)*	700		[1987] C.L.Y. 4334/5
Heart attack	*Power* v. *Greater Glasgow Health Board*	2,000		[1987] C.L.Y. 4332
Lungs	*Howard* v. *Comex Houlder Diving*	3,500		[1987] C.L.Y. 4324
Asbestosis	*Bateman* v. *Newalls Insulation Co.*	14,000		[1987] C.L.Y. 4341
Back	*McGrath* v. *City of Glasgow District Council*	5,000	7,250	[1987] C.L.Y. 4315
	Shepherd v. *Lothian Health Board*	4,000		[1987] C.L.Y. 4333
Hip, knee, wrist	*MacKinnon* v. *R. & W. Scott*	15,000	19,800	[1987] C.L.Y. 4325
Arm	*Faith* v. *CBI Constructors*	4,750	38,004	[1987] C.L.Y. 4319
Fingers	*Clews* v. *B.A. Chemicals*	4,500	7,000	[1987] C.L.Y. 4340

Injury	*Case*	*Award* Solatium	Total	*Reference*
		£	£	
Thumb	*Anderson* v. *Thames Case*	4,000	4,200	[1987] C.L.Y. 4331
	Starkey v. *National Coal Board*	3,750		[1987] C.L.Y. 4316
Legs	*Kirkpatrick* v. *Scott Lithgow*	35,000	37,585	[1987] C.L.Y. 4336
	Hewson v. *Secretary of State for Scotland*	25,000		[1987] C.L.Y. 4337
Knee	*White* v. *Inveresk Paper Co. (No. 2)*	3,000	4,250	[1987] C.L.Y. 4339
	McClafferty v. *British Telecommunications*	4,000	4,175	[1987] C.L.Y. 4746
	Poole v. *John Laing*	4,000		[1987] C.L.Y. 4323
Death	*Worf* v. *Western S.M.T. Co.*	Loss of society 9,000 (widow) 4,750, £5,500, 6,500 (children)		[1987] C.L.Y. 4322
	Rafferty v. *J. & C. M. Smith (Whiteinch)*	Loss of society 6,500, 7,800 (children)		[1987] C.L.Y. 4329

ALPHABETICAL TABLE OF STATUTORY INSTRUMENTS 1987

ADMINISTRATIVE LAW

C.L.Y.

Parliamentary Commissioner Order 1987 (No. 661) 45

AGENCY

Enduring Powers of Attorney (Prescribed Form) Regulations 1987 (No. 1612) 59
Restriction on Agreements and Conduct (Tour Operators) Order 1987 (No. 1131) 70

AGRICULTURE

Aberdeen and District Marketing Scheme (Amendment) Approval Order 1987 (No. 740) 3924
Agricultural Holdings (Arbitration on Notices) Order 1987 (No. 710) 73
Agricultural Holdings (Forms of Notice to Pay Rent or to Remedy) Regulations 1987 (No. 711) 77
Agricultural Holdings (Units of Production) Order 1987 (No. 1465) 72
Agricultural Improvement (Amendment) Regulations 1987 (No. 1950) 87
Agricultural or Forestry Tractors and Tractor Components (Type Approval) (Amendment) Regulations 1987 (No. 1771) 100
Cereal Seeds (Amendment) Regulations 1987 (No. 1091) 98
Environmentally Sensitive Areas (Breadalbane) Designation Order 1987 (No. 653) 3929
Environmentally Sensitive Areas (Breakland) Designation Order 1987 (No. 2029) 83
Environmentally Sensitive Areas (Cambrian Mountains—Extension) Designation Order 1987 (No. 2026) 83
Environmentally Sensitive Areas (Lleyn Peninsula) Designation Order 1987 (No. 2027) 83
Environmentally Sensitive Areas (Loch Lomond) Designation Order 1987 (No. 654) 3929
Environmentally Sensitive Areas (North Peak) Designation Order 1987 (No. 2030) 83
Environmentally Sensitive Areas (Shropshire Borders) Designation Order 1987 (No. 2031) 83
Environmentally Sensitive Areas (South Downs—Western Extension) Designation Order 1987 (No. 2032) 83
Environmentally Sensitive Areas (Suffolk River Valleys) Designation Order 1987 (No. 2033) 83
Environmentally Sensitive Areas (Test Valley) Designation Order 1987 (No. 2034) 83
Farm Business Specification Order 1987 (No. 1948) 84
Farm Diversification Grant Scheme 1987 (No. 1949) 84
Fodder Plant Seeds (Amendment) Regulations 1987 (No. 1092) 98
Heather and Grass etc. (Burning) (Amendment) Regulations 1987 (No. 1208) 85
Hill Livestock (Compensatory Allowances) (Amendment) Regulations 1987 (No. 2129) 86
Home-Grown Cereals Authority Levy Scheme (Approval) Order 1987 (No. 671) 80
Home-Grown Cereals Authority (Rate of Levy) Order 1987 (No. 1194) 80
Import and Export (Plant Health) (Great Britain) (Amendment) Order 1987 (No. 428) 96
Import and Export (Plant Health) (Great Britain) (Amendment) (No. 2) Order 1987 (No. 1679) 96
Import and Export (Plant Health Fees) (England and Wales) Order 1987 (No. 340) 96
Import and Export (Plant Health Fees) (Scotland) Order 1987 (No. 880) 3935
Meat and Livestock Commission Levy Scheme (Confirmation) Order 1987 (No. 1303) 89
Milk Quota (Calculation of Standard Quota) (Amendment) Order 1987 (No. 626) 90
Oil and Fibre Plant Seeds (Amendment) Regulations 1987 (No. 1097) 98
Olive Oil (Marketing Standards) Regulations 1987 (No. 1783) 93
Plant Health (Great Britain) Order 1987 (No. 1758) 96
Plant Varieties and Seeds (Isle of Man) Order 1987 (No. 2210) 95
Potato Marketing Scheme (Amendment) Order 1987 (No. 282) 97
Potatoes (Prohibition on Landing) (Great Britain) Order 1987 (No. 19) 97
Seed Potatoes (Amendment) Regulations 1987 (No. 547) 97
Seed Potatoes (Fees) Regulations 1987 (No. 649) 97
Seed Potatoes (Fees) (Scotland) Regulations 1987 (No. 498) 3936
Seeds (Fees) (Amendment) Regulations 1987 (No. 1148) 98
Seeds (National Lists of Varieties) (Fees) Regulations 1987 (No. 188) 98
Seeds (Registration, Licensing and Enforcement) (Amendment) Regulations 1987 (No. 1098) 98
Sheep and Goats (Removal to Northern Ireland) (Amendment) Regulations 1987 (No. 949) 99
Vegetable Seeds (Amendment) Regulations 1987 (No. 1093) 98

ALPHABETICAL TABLE OF STATUTORY INSTRUMENTS 1987

ANIMALS

Artificial Insemination (Cattle and Pigs) (Fees) Regulations 1987 (No. 390) 104
Artificial Insemination of Cattle (Advertising Controls etc.) (Great Britain) Regulations 1987 (No. 904) 104
Brucellosis (Scotland) Amendment Order 1987 (No. 135) 3944
Coypus (Keeping) (Revocation) Regulations 1987 (No. 2224) 106
Coypus (Prohibition on Keeping) Order 1987 (No. 2195) 106
Designation of Local Authority (Portsmouth Port Health District) Order 1987 (No. 709) 110
Diseases of Animals (Approved Disinfectants) (Amendment) Order 1987 (No. 74) 109
Diseases of Animals (Approved Disinfectants) (Amendment) (No. 2) Order 1987 (No. 1447) 109
Diseases of Animals (Waste Food) (Amendment) Order 1987 (No. 232) 109
Diseases of Animals (Waste Food) (Fees for Licences) Order 1987 (No. 361) 109
Easington Lagoons (Area of Special Protection) Order 1987 (No. 1163) 103
Export of Sheep (Prohibition) Order 1987 (No. 211) 109
Export of Sheep (Prohibition) (Amendment) Order 1987 (No. 248) 114
Export of Sheep (Prohibition) (No. 2) Order 1987 (No. 1808) 114
Importation of Bees (Amendment) Order 1987 (No. 867) 105
Infectious Diseases of Horses Order 1987 (No. 790) 109
Marek's Disease (Restriction on Vaccination) Order 1987 (No. 905) 109
Mink (Keeping) Order 1987 (No. 2196) 111
Mink (Keeping) (Amendment) Regulations 1987 (No. 2225) 111
Movement and Sale of Pigs (Amendment) Order 1987 (No. 233) 112
Sheep and Goats (Removal to Northern Ireland) (Amendment) Regulations 1987 (No. 949) 99
Sheep Scab (Amendment) Order 1987 (No. 836) 114
Slaughterhouse Hygiene (Scotland) Amendment Regulations 1987 (No. 1957) 3948
Warble Fly (England and Wales) (Amendment) Order 1987 (No. 1601) 116
Welfare of Battery Hens Regulations 1987 (No. 2020) 107
Welfare of Calves Regulations 1987 (No. 2021) 107
Welfare of Livestock (Prohibited Operations) (Amendment) Regulations 1987 (No. 114) 107

ARBITRATION

Arbitration (Foreign Awards) Order 1987 (No. 1029) 134

ARMED FORCES

Armed Forces Act 1986 (Commencement No. 3) Order 1987 (No. 1998) (c. 60) 159
Army, Air Force and Naval Discipline Acts (Continuation) Order 1987 (No. 1262) 160
Courts Martial and Standing Civilian Courts (Additional Powers on Trial of Civilians) (Amendment) Regulations 1987 (No. 1999) 167
Injuries in War (Shore Employments) Compensation (Amendment) Scheme 1987 (No. 529) 162
Protection of Military Remains Act 1986 (Guernsey) Order 1987 (No. 1281) 164
Rules of Procedure (Air Force) (Amendment) Rules 1987 (No. 2000) 158
Rules of Procedure (Air Force) (Amendment No. 2) Rules 1987 (No. 2172) 158a
Standing Civilian Courts (Amendment) Order 1987 (No. 2001) 167
Standing Civilian Courts (Amendment No. 2) Order 1987 (No. 2173) 167

ATOMIC ENERGY

British Nuclear Fuels plc (Financial Limit) Order 1987 (No. 875) 168
Nuclear Installations (Isle of Man) (Variation) Order 1987 (No. 668) 169
Nuclear Installations (Jersey) (Variation) Order 1987 (No. 2207) 169

AVIATION

Aerodromes (Designation) (Detention and Sale of Aircraft) Order 1987 (No. 1377) 171
Aerodromes (Designation) (Detention and Sale of Aircraft) (No. 2) Order 1987 (No. 2229) 171
Air Navigation (General) (Second Amendment) Regulations 1987 (No. 2078) 172
Air Navigation (Noise Certification) Order 1987 (No. 2212) 172
Air Navigation (Restriction of Flying) (Molesworth Aerodrome) Regulations 1987 (No. 1885) 172
Air Navigation (Second Amendment) Order 1987 (No. 2062) 172
Airports Act 1986 (Government Shareholding) Order 1987 (No. 2232) 181
Airports Byelaws (Designation) Order 1987 (No. 380) 179
Airports Byelaws (Designation) (No. 2) Order 1987 (No. 2246) 180
Aviation Security (Anguilla) Order 1987 (No. 451) 178
Civil Aviation Act 1980 (Government Shareholding) Order 1987 (No. 747) 178
Civil Aviation Authority (Amendment) Regulations 1987 (No. 379) 178
Civil Aviation (Joint Financing) (Fifth Amendment) Regulations 1987 (No. 2100) 179
Civil Aviation (Navigation Services Charges) (Second Amendment) Regulations 1987 (No. 269) 179

AVIATION—*cont.*

C.L.Y.
Civil Aviation (Route Charges for Navigation Services) (Fourth Amendment) Regulations 1987 (No. 2083) 179
London City Airport Byelaws (Designation) Order 1987 (No. 1132) 180
Rules of the Air and Air Traffic Control (Third Amendment) Regulations 1987 (No. 1145) 172
Rules of the Air and Air Traffic Control (Fourth Amendment) Regulations 1987 (No. 1812) 172
Stansted Airport Aircraft Movement Limit Order 1987 (No. 874) 175
Tokyo Convention (Anguilla) Order 1987 (No. 456) 179

BANKING

Asian Development Bank (Fourth Replenishment of the Asian Development Fund) Order 1987 (No. 1252) 186
Banking Act 1979 (Advertisements) (Amendment) Regulations 1987 (No. 64) 185
Banking Act 1979 (Exempt Transactions) (Amendment) Regulations 1987 (No. 65) 200
Banking Act 1987 (Commencement No. 1) Order 1987 (No. 1189) (c. 32) 191
Banking Act 1987 (Commencement No. 2) Order 1987 (No. 1664) (c. 50) 191
Banking Act 1987 (Disclosure of Information) (Specified Persons) Order 1987 (No. 1292) 196
Banking Appeal Tribunal (Scottish Appeals) Regulations 1987 (No. 1336) 3960
National Savings Bank (Interest on Ordinary Deposits) Order 1987 (No. 2096) 204
National Savings Bank (Investment Deposits) (Limits) (Amendment) Order 1987 (No. 329) 204
Savings Banks (Ordinary Deposits) (Limits) (Amendment) Order 1987 (No. 330) 205

BANKRUPTCY

Insolvency (Amendment of Subordinate Legislation) Order 1987 (No. 1398) 214

BRITISH COMMONWEALTH

Alderney (Transfer of Property etc.) Order 1987 (No. 1273) 216
Bermuda (Evidence) Order 1987 (No. 662) 217
Cayman Islands (Constitution) (Amendment) Order 1987 (No. 2199) 218
Commonwealth Development Corporation (Additional Enterprises) Order 1987 (No. 1253) 219
Evidence (Proceedings in Other Jurisdictions) (Turks and Caicos Islands) Order 1987 (No. 1266) 221
St. Helena (Constitution) (Amendment) Order 1987 (No. 1268) 220
Turks and Caicos Islands (Constitution) (Interim Amendment) Order 1987 (No. 934) 221
Turks and Caicos Islands (Constitution) (Interim Amendment) (No. 2) Order 1987 (No. 1271) 221
Turks and Caicos Islands (Constitution) (Interim Amendment) (No. 3) Order 1987 (No. 1829) 221

BUILDING AND CONSTRUCTION

Building (Disabled People) Regulations 1987 (No. 1445) 232
Building (Inner London) Regulations 1987 (No. 798) 227
Building (Procedure) (Scotland) Amendment Regulations 1987 (No. 1232) 3972
Building Standards (Scotland) Amendment Regulations 1987 (No. 1231) 3973

BUILDING SOCIETIES

Building Societies (Accounts and Related Provisions) Regulations 1987 (No. 2072) 247
Building Societies Act 1986 (Accounts and Related Transitional Provisions) Order 1987 (No. 395) 250
Building Societies Act 1986 (Meetings) (Transitional Provision) Order 1987 (No. 426) 251
Building Societies (Aggregation) Rules 1987 (No. 2133) 246
Building Societies Appeal Tribunal Regulations 1987 (No. 891) 248
Building Societies (Banking Institutions) Order 1987 (No. 1670) 249
Building Societies (Business Premises) Order 1987 (No. 1942) 252
Building Societies (Designation of Pension Companies) Order 1987 (No. 1871) 255
Building Societies (Designation of Qualifying Bodies) (Amendment) Order 1987 (No. 2018) 266
Building Societies (General Charge and Fees) Regulations 1987 (No. 391) 253
Building Societies Investor Protection Scheme (Maximum Protected Investment) Order 1987 (No. 1349) 258
Building Societies (Isle of Man) Order 1987 (No. 1498) 259
Building Societies (Jersey) Order 1987 (No. 1872) 260
Building Societies (Limit on Non-Retail Funds and Deposits) Order 1987 (No. 2131) 263
Building Societies (Limited Credit Facilities) Order 1987 (No. 1975) 254
Building Societies (Liquid Asset) Regulations 1987 (No. 1499) 261
Building Societies (Mergers) Regulations 1987 (No. 2005) 262
Building Societies (Non-Retail Funds and Deposits) Order 1987 (No. 378) 263
Building Societies (Prescribed Bands for Disclosure) Order 1987 (No. 723) 256
Building Societies (Prescribed Contracts) (Amendment) Order 1987 (No. 1500) 264
Building Societies (Provision of Services) Order 1987 (No. 172) 265
Building Societies (Provision of Services) (No. 2) Order 1987 (No. 1848) 265
Building Societies (Provision of Services) (No. 3) Order 1987 (No. 1976) 265
Building Societies (Provision of Services) (No. 4) Order 1987 (No. 2019) 265
Building Societies (Residential Use) Order 1987 (No. 1671) 267

ALPHABETICAL TABLE OF STATUTORY INSTRUMENTS 1987

CAPITAL GAINS TAX

Capital Gains Tax (Annual Exempt Amount) Order 1987 (No. 436) 269
Capital Gains Tax (Gilt-edged Securities) Order 1987 (No. 259) 275

CAPITAL TAXATION (SCOTLAND ONLY)

Inheritance Tax (Delivery of Accounts) (Scotland) Regulations 1987 (No. 1128) 3982

CHARITIES

Exempt Charities Order 1987 (No. 1823) 294

CHILDREN AND YOUNG PERSONS (SCOTLAND ONLY)

Social Work (Residential Establishments—Child Care) (Scotland) Regulations 1987 (No. 2233) 4027

CIVIL DEFENCE

Civil Defence (Grant) (Amendment) Regulations 1987 (No. 622) 302
Civil Defence (Grant) (Scotland) Amendment Regulations 1987 (No. 677) 4032
International Headquarters and Defence Organisations (Designation and Privileges) (Amendment) Order 1987 (No. 927) 301
Visiting Forces and International Headquarters (Application of Law) (Amendment) Order 1987 (No. 928) 303

COMPANY LAW

Companies (Forms) (Amendment) Regulations 1987 (No. 752) 339
Companies (Mergers and Divisions) Regulations 1987 (No. 1991) 346
Insolvency (Amendment) Regulations 1987 (No. 1959) 343
Insolvency (Amendment) Rules 1987 (No. 1919) 343
Insolvency (Scotland) Amendment Rules 1987 (No. 1921) 4049
Insolvent Companies (Disqualification of Unfit Directors) Proceedings Rules 1987 (No. 2023) 331

COMPULSORY PURCHASE

Acquisition of Land (Rate of Interest after Entry) Regulations 1987 (No. 405) 395
Acquisition of Land (Rate of Interest after Entry) (No. 2) Regulations 1987 (No. 889) 395
Acquisition of Land (Rate of Interest after Entry) (Scotland) Regulations 1987 (No. 397) 4060
Acquisition of Land (Rate of Interest after Entry) (Scotland) (No. 2) Regulations 1987 (No. 890) 4060
Acquisition of Land (Rate of Interest after Entry) (Scotland) (No. 3) Regulations 1987 (No. 1842) 4060

CONFLICT OF LAWS

Reciprocal Enforcement of Maintenance Orders (Hague Convention Countries) (Variation) Order 1987 (No. 1282) 407

CONSTITUTIONAL LAW

Transfer of Functions (Minister for the Civil Service and Treasury) Order 1987 (No. 2039) 410

CONSUMER CREDIT

Consumer Credit (Exempt Agreements) (No. 2) (Amendment) Order 1987 (No. 1578) 411

CONVEYANCING

Land Registration (District Registries) Order 1987 (No. 360) 472
Land Registration (District Registries) (No. 2) Order 1987 (No. 2213) 472
Land Registration Rules 1987 (No. 2214) 475
Licensed Conveyancers' Discipline and Appeals Committee (Legal Assessor) Rules 1987 (No. 788) 478
Licensed Conveyancers' Discipline and Appeals Committee (Procedure) Rules Approval Order 1987 (No. 789) 478
Registration of Title Order 1987 (No. 939) 483

COPYRIGHT

Copyright (Computer Software) (Extension to Territories) Order 1987 (No. 2200) 497
Copyright (International Conventions) (Amendment) Order 1987 (No. 2060) 524
Copyright (Singapore) Order 1987 (No. 940) 526
Copyright (Singapore) (Amendment) Order 1987 (No. 1030) 526
Copyright (Taiwan) (Extension to Territories) Order 1987 (No. 1826) 529
Copyright (Taiwan Order) (Isle of Man Extension) Order 1987 (No. 1833) 529

ALPHABETICAL TABLE OF STATUTORY INSTRUMENTS 1987

CRIMINAL EVIDENCE AND PROCEDURE

Act of Adjournal (Criminal Legal Aid Rules) 1987 (No. 430) 4137
Act of Adjournal (Service of Documents on Accused Persons) 1987 (No. 1328) 4157
Advice and Assistance (Assistance By Way of Representation) (Scotland) Regulations 1987 (No. 642) .. 4137
Combined Probation Areas (Cornwall) Order 1987 (No. 2140) 713
Combined Probation Areas (Cumbria) Order 1987 (No. 2222) 713
Combined Probation Areas (Dorset) Order 1987 (No. 2135) 713
Combined Probation Areas (Gloucestershire) Order 1987 (No. 2181) 713
Combined Probation Areas (Hereford and Worcester) Order 1987 (No. 2223) 713
Combined Probation Areas (Lancashire) Order 1987 (No. 1855) 713
Combined Probation Areas (Northamptonshire) Order 1987 (No. 356) 713
Combined Probation Areas (Nottinghamshire) Order 1987 (No. 2136) 713
Combined Probation Areas (West Yorkshire) Order 1987 (No. 2141) 713
Criminal Appeal (Amendment) Rules 1987 (No. 1977) (L. 9) 584
Criminal Justice Act 1987 (Commencement No. 1) Order 1987 (No. 1061) (C. 27) 635
Criminal Justice (Scotland) Act 1987 (Commencement No. 1) Order 1987 (No. 1468) (C.45) 4094
Criminal Justice (Scotland) Act 1987 (Commencement No. 2) Order 1987 (No. 1594) (C.48) 4094
Criminal Justice (Scotland) Act 1987 (Commencement No. 3) Order 1987 (No. 2119) (C.62) 4094
Criminal Legal Aid (Scotland) (Fees) Regulations 1987 (No. 365) 4137
Criminal Legal Aid (Scotland) (Fees) Amendment Regulations 1987 (No. 824) 4137
Criminal Legal Aid (Scotland) (Fees) Amendment (No. 2) Regulations 1987 (No. 1358) 4137
Criminal Legal Aid (Scotland) Regulations 1987 (No. 307) 4137
Crown Court (Advance Notice of Expert Evidence) Rules 1987 (No. 716) (L. 2) 650
Crown Prosecution Service (Witnesses' Allowances) (Amendment No. 4) Regulations 1987 (No. 902) .. 641
Crown Prosecution Service (Witnesses' Allowances) (Amendment No. 5) Regulations 1987 (No. 1636) 641
Crown Prosecution Service (Witnesses' Allowances) (Amendment No. 6) Regulations 1987 (No. 1851) 641
Justices of the Peace (Size and Chairmanship of Bench) (Amendment) Rules 1987 (No. 1137) (L. 5) 676
Legal Aid (Scotland) (Fees in Criminal Proceedings) Amendment Regulations 1987 (No. 826) 4137
Legal Aid (Scotland) (Fees in Criminal Proceedings) Amendment (No. 2) Regulations 1987 (No. 1357) .. 4137
Petty Sessional Divisions (Cornwall) Order 1987 (No. 1796) 705
Petty Sessional Divisions (Cumbria) Order 1987 (No. 1925) 705
Petty Sessional Divisions (Dorset) Order 1987 (No. 1739) 705
Petty Sessional Divisions (Gloucestershire) Order 1987 (No. 1912) 705
Petty Sessional Divisions (Gwynedd) Order 1987 (No. 1201) 705
Petty Sessional Divisions (Hereford and Worcester) Order 1987 (No. 1913) 705
Petty Sessional Divisions (Kirklees) Order 1987 (No. 1786) 705
Petty Sessional Divisions (Lancashire) Order 1987 (No. 1688) 705
Petty Sessional Divisions (Northamptonshire) Order 1987 (No. 184) 705
Petty Sessional Divisions (Northamptonshire) (Amendment) Order 1987 (No. 519) 705
Petty Sessional Divisions (Northumberland) Order 1987 (No. 1962) 705
Petty Sessional Divisions (Nottinghamshire) Order 1987 (No. 1797) 705
Prosecution of Offences (Custody Time Limits) Regulations 1987 (No. 299) 642

CRIMINAL LAW

Misuse of Drugs (Licence Fees) (Amendment) Regulations 1987 (No. 298) 795
Public Order Act 1986 (Commencement No. 2) Order 1987 (No. 198) (C. 4) 820
Public Order Act 1986 (Commencement No. 3) Order 1987 (No. 852) (C. 23) 820
Public Order (Football Exclusion) Order 1987 (No. 853) 818
Repatriation of Prisoners (Overseas Territories) (Amendment) Order 1987 (No. 1828) 821
Video Recordings Act 1984 (Commencement No. 4) Order 1987 (No. 123 (C. 1)) 850
Video Recordings Act 1984 (Commencement No. 5) Order 1987 (No. 1142) (C. 29) 850
Video Recordings Act 1984 (Commencement No. 6) Order 1987 (No. 2155) (C. 64) 850
Video Recordings Act 1984 (Scotland) (Commencement No. 4) Order 1987 (No. 160) (C.2) 4248
Video Recordings Act 1984 (Scotland) (Commencement No. 5) Order 1987 (No. 1249) (C. 37) 4248
Video Recordings Act 1984 (Scotland) (Commencement No. 6) Order 1987 (No. 2273) (C.70) 4248

ALPHABETICAL TABLE OF STATUTORY INSTRUMENTS 1987

CUSTOMS AND EXCISE

Agricultural Levy Reliefs (Frozen Beef and Veal) Order 1987 (No. 134) ... 1101
Counterfeit Goods (Customs) Regulations 1987 (No. 2097) ... 1105
Customs and Excise (Community Transit) Regulations 1987 (No. 763) ... 1104
Customs and Excise (Community Transit) (No. 2) Regulations 1987 (No. 2105) ... 1104
Customs Duties (ECSC) Order 1987 (No. 2184) ... 1106
Customs Duties (ECSC) (No. 2) (Amendment No. 6) Order 1987 (No. 973) ... 1106
Customs Duties (ECSC) (No. 2) (Amendment No. 7) Order 1987 (No. 1053) ... 1106
Customs Duties (ECSC) (No. 2) (Amendment No.8) Order 1987 (No. 1125) ... 1106
Customs Duties (ECSC) (No. 2) (Amendment No. 9) Order 1987 (No. 1218) ... 1106
Customs Duties (ECSC) (No. 2) (Amendment No. 10) Order 1987 (No. 1804) ... 1106
Customs Duties (ECSC) (No. 2) (Amendment No. 11) Order 1987 (No. 1902) ... 1106
Customs Duties (ECSC) (Quota and Other Reliefs) Order 1987 (No. 2126) ... 1121
Customs Duties (Portugual) (Transitional Measures) Order 1986 (No. 2182) ... 1120
Customs Duties (Quota Relief) Order 1987 (No. 1122) ... 1121
Customs Duties (Repeals) (Revocation of Savings) Order 1987 (No. 2106) ... 1107
Customs Duties (Spain) (Transitional Measures) Order 1986 (No. 2178) ... 1123
Customs Duties (Temporary Importation) (Revocation) Regulations 1987 (No. 1781) ... 1108
Excise Duties (Small Non-Commercial Consignments) Relief (Amendment) Regulations 1987 (No. 149) 1116
Export of Goods (Control) Order 1987 (No. 2070) ... 1110
Export of Goods (Control) (Amendment No. 8) Order 1987 (No. 215) ... 1110
Export of Goods (Control) (Amendment No. 9) Order 1987 (No. 271) ... 1110
Export of Goods (Control) (Amendment No. 10) Order 1987 (No. 1350) ... 1110
General Betting Duty Regulations 1987 (No. 1963) ... 1102
General Betting Duty (Amendment) Regulations 1987 (No. 312) ... 1102
Import Duty Reliefs (Revocation) Order 1987 (No. 1785) ... 1112
Methylated Spirits Regulations 1987 (No. 2009) ... 1115
Northern Ireland (Prescribed Area) Regulations 1987 (No. 2114) ... 1117
Origin of Goods (Petroleum Products) Regulations 1987 (No. 2107) ... 1118
Police and Criminal Evidence Act 1984 (Application to Customs and Excise) Order 1987 (No. 439) ... 1119
Spoilt Beer (Remission and Repayment of Duty) Regulations 1987 (No. 314) ... 1124

ECCLESIASTICAL LAW

Ecclesiastical Judges and Legal Officers (Fees) Order 1987 (No. 1297) ... 1244
Faculty Jurisdiction (Amendment) Rules 1987 (No. 2266) ... 1243
Legal Officers (Annual Fees) Order 1987 (No. 1296) ... 1244
Methodist Church Act 1976 (Guernsey) Order 1987 (No. 1279) ... 1245
Patronage (Benefices) Rules 1987 (No. 773) ... 1239
United Reformed Church Act 1981 (Guernsey) Order 1987 (No. 2051) ... 1246

EDUCATION

Colleges of Education (Allowances to Governors: Prescribed Bodies) (Scotland) Regulations 1987 (No. 308) ... 4404
Colleges of Education (Scotland) Regulations 1987 (No. 309) ... 4404
Direct Grant Schools (Amendment) Regulations 1987 (No. 1182) ... 1251
Education (Abolition of Corporal Punishment) (Independent Schools) Regulations 1987 (No. 1183) ... 1247
Education (Abolition of Corporal Punishment: Prescription of Schools) (Scotland) Order 1987 (No. 1140) 4396
Education (Assisted Places) (Amendment) Regulations 1987 (No. 1312) ... 1248
Education (Assisted Places) (Incidental Expenses) (Amendment) Regulations 1987 (No. 1313) ... 1248
Education (Assisted Places) (Scotland) Amendment Regulations 1987 (No. 1147) ... 4399
Education Authority Bursaries (Scotland) Amendment Regulations 1987 (No. 1366) ... 4399
Education (Bursaries for Teacher Training) (Amendment) Regulations 1987 (No. 499) ... 1271
Education (Bursaries for Teacher Training) (Amendment) (No. 2) Regulations 1987 (No. 1393) ... 1271
Education (Fees and Awards) (Amendment) Regulations 1987 (No. 1364) ... 1257
Education (Fees and Awards) (Scotland) Amendment Regulations 1987 (No. 1383) ... 4399
Education (Governing Bodies of Institutions of Further Education) Regulations 1987 (No. 1160) ... 1260
Education (Grant) (Amendment) Regulations 1987 (No. 1126) ... 1258
Education (Grants) (City Technology Colleges) Regulations 1987 (No. 1138) ... 1258
Education (Grants) (Music and Ballet Schools) (Amendment) Regulations 1987 (No. 1314) ... 1258
Education (Grants for Further Training of Teachers and Educational Psychologists) (Scotland) Regulations 1987 (No. 291) ... 4399
Education (Grants for Further Training of Teachers and Educational Psychologists) (Scotland) (No. 2) Regulations 1987 (No. 644) ... 4399
Education (Grants for Further Training of Teachers and Educational Psychologists (Scotland) Amendment Regulations 1987 (No. 1801) ... 4399

EDUCATION—*cont.*

C.L.Y.

Education (Grants for Training of Teachers and Community Education Workers) (Scotland) Amendment Regulations 1987 (No. 208) 4399
Education (Mandatory Awards) Regulations 1987 (No. 1261) 1249
Education (No. 2) Act 1986 (Commencement No. 2) Order 1987 (No. 344 (C. 8)) 1256
Education (No. 2) Act 1986 (Commencement No. 3) Order 1987 (No. 1159) (C.30) 1256
Education (Publication and Consultation etc.) (Scotland) Amendment Regulations 1987 (No. 2076) 4401
Education (Publication of Proposals to Change Status of a Controlled School) Regulations 1987 (No. 34) 1268
Education (School Government) Regulations 1987 (No. 1359) 1266
Education (School Teachers' Pay and Conditions) Order 1987 (No. 1433) 1272
Education (School Teachers' Pay and Conditions of Employment) Order 1987 (No. 650) 1272
Education (Schools and Further Education) (Amendment) Regulations 1987 (No. 879) 1253
Education Support Grants (Amendment) Regulations 1987 (No. 1960) 1258
Education (Training Grants) Regulations 1987 (No. 96) 1258
Further Education Act 1985 (Commencement No. 2) (Scotland) Order 1987 (No. 1335) (C. 44) 4398
Pupils' Registration (Amendment) Regulations 1987 (No. 1285) 1262
Remuneration of Teachers (Primary and Secondary Education) (Amendment) Order 1987 (No. 137) 1263
Remuneration of Teachers (Primary and Secondary Education) (Amendment) (No. 2) Order 1987 (No. 236) 1263
Remuneration of Teachers (Primary and Secondary Education) (Amendment) (No. 3) Order 1987 (No. 398) 1263
St. Mary's Music School (Aided Places) Amendment Regulations 1987 (No. 1146) 4399
Schools (General) (Scotland) Amendment Regulations 1987 (No. 290) 4394
State Awards (Amendment) Regulations 1987 (No. 1365) 1249
Students' Allowances (Scotland) Regulations 1987 (No. 864) 4399

ELECTION LAW

Local Elections (Communities) (Welsh Forms) Order 1987 (No. 561) 1278
Local Elections (Parishes and Communities) (Amendment) Rules 1987 (No. 260) 1278
Local Elections (Principal Areas) (Amendment) Rules 1987 (No. 261) 1278
Local Elections (Principal Areas) (Welsh Forms) Order 1987 (No. 562) 1278
Parish and Community Meetings (Polls) Rules 1987 (No. 1) 1279
Parish and Community Meetings (Polls) (Amendment) Rules 1987 (No. 262) 1279
Parliamentary Constituencies (England) (Miscellaneous Changes) Order 1987 (No. 462) 1280
Parliamentary Constituencies (England) (Miscellaneous Changes) (No. 2) Order 1987 (No. 937) 1280
Parliamentary Constituencies (England) (Miscellaneous Changes) (No. 3) Order 1987 (No. 2208) 1280
Parliamentary Constituencies (England) (Miscellaneous Changes) (No. 4) Order 1987 (No. 2209) 1280
Parliamentary Constituencies (Scotland) (Miscellaneous Changes) Order 1987 (No. 469) 4406
Parliamentary Constituencies (Wales) (Miscellaneous Changes) Order 1987 (No. 2050) 1280
Representation of the People Act 1985 (Commencement No. 4) Order 1987 (No. 207 (C.5)) 1282
Representation of the People (Variation of Limits of Candidates' Election Expenses) Order 1987 (No. 903) 1277
Returning Officers' Expenses Regulations 1987 (No. 899) 1277

ELECTRICITY

Electricity Generating Stations and Overhead Lines (Inquiries Procedure) Rules 1987 (No. 2182) 1285
Electricity Generating Stations (Fuel Control) Order 1987 (No. 2175) 1284
Meters (Certification) Order 1987 (No. 730) 1287
Meters (Determination of Questions) (Expenses) Regulations 1987 (No. 901) 1287

EMERGENCY LAWS

Suppression of Terrorism Act 1978 (Designation of Countries) Order 1987 (No. 2137) 1290
Suppression of Terrorism Act 1978 (Hong Kong) Order 1987 (No. 2045) 1292
Prevention of Terrorism (Supplemental Temporary Provisions) (Amendment) Order 1987 (No. 119) 1289
Prevention of Terrorism (Supplemental Temporary Provisions) (Amendment No. 2) Order 1987 (No. 1209) 1289
Prevention of Terrorism (Temporary Provisions) Act 1984 (Continuance) Order 1987 (No. 273) 1291

EMPLOYMENT

Employment Subsidies Act 1978 (Renewal) (Great Britain) Order 1987 (No. 1124) 1320
Guarantee Payments (Exemption) (No. 23) Order 1987 (No. 1757) 1334
Job Release Act 1977 (Continuation) Order 1987 (No. 1339) 1343
Maternity Pay and Maternity Allowance (Transitional) Regulations 1987 (No. 406) 1346
Race Relations (Offshore Employment) Order 1987 (No. 929) 1347
Sex Discrimination and Equal Pay (Offshore Employment) Order 1987 (No. 930) 1368
Social Security (Maternity Allowance) Regulations 1987 (No. 416) 1346

EMPLOYMENT—*cont.*

Social Security (Maternity Allowance) (Work Abroad) Regulations 1987 (No. 417) 1346
Statutory Maternity Pay (Medical Evidence) Regulations 1987 (No. 235) 1346
Statutory Maternity Pay (Persons Abroad and Mariners) Regulations 1987 (No. 418) 1346
Statutory Six Pay (Additional Compensation of Employers) Amendment Regulations 1987 (No. 92) 1378
Statutory Sick Pay (General) Amendment Regulations 1987 (No. 372) 1378
Statutory Sick Pay (General) Amendment (No. 2) Regulations 1987 (No. 868) 1378
Statutory Sick Pay (Rate of Payment) Regulations 1987 No. 33) 1378
Transfer of Undertakings (Protection of Employment) (Amendment) Regulations 1987 (No. 442) 1384
Unlicensed Place of Refreshment Wages Council (Variation) Order 1987 (No. 801) 1418
Wages Councils (Meetings and Procedure) Regulations 1987 (No. 862) 1418
Wages Councils (Notices) Regulations 1987 (No. 863) 1418
Wages Councils (Notices) (No. 2) Regulations 1987 (No. 1852) 1418

EQUITY AND TRUSTS

Chevening Estate Act 1987 (Commencement) Order 1987 (No. 1254) (C.38) 1422
Irish Sailors and Soldiers Land Trust Act 1987 (Commencement) Order 1987 (No. 1909 (C.57)) 1429
Public Trustee (Amendment) Rules 1987 (No. 2249) 1431
Public Trustee (Custodian Trustee) Rules 1987 (No. 1891) 1431
Public Trustee (Fees) (Amendment) Order 1987 (No. 403) 1431
Recognition of Trusts Act 1987 (Commencement) Order 1987 (No. 1177) (C.31) 1434
Reverter of Sites Act 1987 (Commencement) Order 1987 (No. 1260 (C.39)) 1436

EUROPEAN COMMUNITIES

Architects' Qualifications (EEC Recognition) Order 1987 (No. 1824) 1471
Common Agricultural Policy (Wine) Regulations 1987 (No. 1843) 1466
European Assembly Elections (Day of By-Elections) (Midlands West Constitutency) Order 1987 (No. 20) 1536
European Assembly Elections Regulations 1986 (No. 2209) 1536
European Communities (Definition of Treaties) (International Convention on the Harmonised Commodity Description and Coding System) Order 1987 (No. 2040) 1517
European Communities (Designation) Order 1987 (No. 448) 1518
European Communities (Designation) (No. 2) Order 1987 (No. 926) 1518
Semiconductor Products (Protection of Topography) Regulations 1987 (No. 1497) 1630
Veterinary Surgeons Qualifications (EEC Recognition) (Spanish and Portuguese Qualifications) Order 1987 (No. 447) 1667

EVIDENCE (CIVIL)

Blood Tests (Evidence of Paternity) (Amendment) Regulations 1987 (No. 1199) 1675

EXPENSES (SCOTLAND ONLY)

Act of Sederunt (Fees of Solicitors in the Sheriff Court) (Amendment) 1987 (No. 865) 4452
Act of Sederunt (Legal Aid Rules) (Children) 1987 (No. 427) 4444
Act of Sederunt (Rules of Court Amendment No. 2) (Solicitors' Fees) 1987 (No. 871) 4433
Act of Sederunt (Rules of Court Amendment No. 3) (Shorthand Writers' Fees) 1987 (No. 1079) 4433
Act of Sederunt (Shorthand Writers' Fees) 1987 (No. 1078) 4453
Advice and Assistance (Scotland) Amendment Regulations 1987 (No. 883) 4441
Advice and Assistance (Scotland) Amendment (No. 2) Regulations 1987 (No. 1356) 4441
Civil Legal Aid (Scotland) (Fees) Regulations 1987 (No. 366) 4441
Civil Legal Aid (Scotland) (Fees) Amendment Regulations 1987 (No. 823) 4441
Civil Legal Aid (Scotland) (Fees) Amendment (No. 2) Regulations 1987 (No. 895) 4441
Court of Session etc. Fees Amendment Order 1987 (No. 38) 4433
Court of Session etc. Fees Amendment (No. 2) Order 1987 (No. 771) 4433
High Court of Justiciary Fees Amendment Order 1987 (No. 772) 4437
Lands Tribunal for Scotland (Amendment) (Fees) Rules 1987 (No. 1139) 4440
Legal Advice and Assistance (Scotland) Amendment Regulations 1987 (No. 1355) 4441
Legal Aid (Scotland) (Fees in Civil Proceedings) Amendment Regulations 1987 (No. 825) 4441
Legal Aid (Scotland) (Fees in Civil Proceedings) Amendment (No. 2) Regulations 1987 (No. 894) 4441
Scottish Land Court (Fees) Amendment Rules 1987 (No. 643) 4439
Sheriff Court Fees Amendment Order 1987 (No. 39) 4452

EXTRADITION

Extradition (Hijacking) (Amendment) Order 1987 (No. 2041) 1697
Extradition (Internationally Protected Persons) (Amendment) Order 1987 (No. 2042) 1699
Extradition (Protection of Aircraft) (Amendment) Order 1987 (No. 2043) 1693
Extradition (Suppression of Terrorism) (Amendment) Order 1987 (No. 2206) 1701
Extradition (Taking of Hostages) (Amendment) Order 1987 (No. 2044) 1702

EXTRADITION—*cont.*

Fugitive Offenders (Anguilla) Order 1987 (No. 452) 1698
United States of America (Extradition) (Amendment) Order 1987 (No. 2046) 1697

FIRE SERVICE

Firemen's Pension Scheme (Amendment) Order 1987 (No. 1302) 1793

FISH AND FISHERIES

Cod (Specified Sea Areas) (Prohibition of Fishing) Order 1987 (No. 2192) 1803
Fish Farming (Financial Assistance) Scheme 1987 (No. 1134) 1799
Fishing Vessels (Acquisition and Improvement) (Grants) Scheme 1987 (No. 1135) 1800
Fishing Vessels (Financial Assistance) Scheme 1987 (No. 1136) 1800
Herring and White Fish (Specified Manx Waters) Licensing (Variation) Order 1987 (No. 1564) 1803
North West Water Authority (Returns of Eels Taken) Order 1986 (No. 745) 1798
North West Water Authority (Solway Firth) Trout Close Season Order 1985 1987 (No. 99) 1802
Northumbrian Water Authority (T Nets) (Northern Area) Order 1987 (No. 612) 1805
Northumbrian Water Authority (T Nets) (Southern Area) Order 1987 (No. 1054) 1805
Plaice (Specified Sea Areas) (Prohibition of Fishing) Order 1987 (No. 2011) 1803
Plaice and Saithe (Specified Sea Areas) (Prohibition of Fishing) Order 1987 (No. 1227) 1801
Saithe (Specified Sea Areas) (Prohibition of Fishing) Order 1987 (No. 718) 1803
Saithe (Specified Sea Areas) (Prohibition of Fishing) (Revocation) Order 1987 (No. 1900) 1803
Sea Fish Licensing (Variation) Order 1987 (No. 1565) 1803
Sea Fishing (Enforcement of Community Control Measures) (Amendment) Order 1987 (No. 1536) 1803
Sea Fishing (Enforcement of Community Quota Measures) Order 1987 (No. 2234) 1803
Sea Fishing (Specified Western Waters) (Restrictions on Landing) Order 1987 (No. 1566) 1803
Several and Regulated Fisheries (Form of Application) Regulations 1987 (No. 217) 1804
Shellfish (Specification of Molluscs) Regulations 1987 (No. 218) 1804
Sole (North Sea) (Enforcement of Community Conservation Measures) Order 1987 (No. 213) 1803
Third Country Fishing (Enforcement) Order 1987 (No. 292) 1803

FOOD AND DRUGS

Authorised Officers (Meat Inspection) Regulations 1987 (No. 133) 1812
Coffee and Coffee Products (Amendment) Regulations 1987 (No. 1986) 1806
Coffee and Coffee Products (Scotland) Amendment Regulations 1987 (No. 2014) 4468
Colouring Matter in Food (Amendment) Regulations 1987 (No. 1987) 1807
Colouring Matter in Food (Scotland) Amendment Regulations 1987 (No. 1985) 4469
Condensed Milk and Dried Milk (Scotland) Amendment Regulations 1987 (No. 26) 4476
Food Protection (Emergency Prohibitions) Amendment Order 1987 (No. 1567) 1808
Food Protection (Emergency Prohibitions) Amendment No. 2 Order 1987 (No. 1696) 1808
Food Protection (Emergency Prohibitions) (England) Order 1987 (No. 1893) 1808
Food Protection (Emergency Prohibitions) (England) (No. 2) Amendment Order 1987 (No. 153) 1808
Food Protection (Emergency Prohibitions) (England) (No. 2) Amendment No. 2 Order 1987 (No. 249) 1808
Food Protection (Emergency Prohibitions) (England) (No. 2) Amendment No. 3 Order 1987 (No. 906) 1808
Food Protection (Emergency Prohibitions) (England) (No. 2) Amendment No. 4 Order 1987 (No. 1555) 1808
Food Protection (Emergency Prohibitions) (England) (No. 2) Amendment No. 5 Order 1987 (No. 1687) 1808
Food Protection (Emergency Prohibitions) (No. 2) Order 1987 (No. 1450) 1808
Food Protection (Emergency Prohibitions) (No. 2) Amendment Order 1987 (No. 1568) 1808
Food Protection (Emergency Prohibitions) (No. 2) Amendment No. 2 Order 1987 (No. 1697) 1808
Food Protection (Emergency Prohibitions) (No. 3) Order 1987 (No. 1837) 1808
Food Protection (Emergency Prohibitions) (No. 4) Order 1987 (No. 1888) 1808
Food Protection (Emergency Prohibitions) (No. 10) Revocation Order 1987 (No. 270) 1808
Food Protection (Emergency Prohibitions) Order 1987 (No. 1165) 4470
Food Protection (Emergency Prohibitions) Amendment Order 1987 (No. 1567) 4470
Food Protection (Emergency Prohibitions) (No. 2) Amendment Order 1987 (No. 1568) 4470
Food Protection (Emergency Prohibitions) (No. 4) Order 1987 (No. 1888) 4470
Food Protection (Emergency Prohibitions) (Wales) Order 1987 (No. 1181) 1808
Food Protection (Emergency Prohibitions) (Wales) (No. 2) Order 1987 (No. 1436) 1808
Food Protection (Emergency Prohibitions) (Wales) (No. 2) Amendment Order 1987 (No. 182) 1808
Food Protection (Emergency Prohibitions) (Wales) (No. 2) Amendment No. 2 Order 1987 (No. 263) 1808
Food Protection (Emergency Prohibitions) (Wales) (No. 2) Amendment No. 3 Order 1987 (No. 885) 1808
Food Protection (Emergency Prohibitions) (Wales) (No. 3) Order 1987 (No. 1515) 1808
Food Protection (Emergency Prohibitions) (Wales) (No. 4) Order 1987 (No. 1638) 1808
Food Protection (Emergency Prohibitions) (Wales) (No. 4) Amendment Order 1987 (No. 1682) 1808
Food Protection (Emergency Prohibitions) (Wales) (No. 4) Amendment No. 2 Order 1987 (No. 1802) 1808
Food Protection (Emergency Prohibitions) (Wales) (No. 5) Order 1987 (No. 1894) 1808
Fresh Meat Export (Hygiene and Inspection) Regulations 1987 (No. 2237) 1812
Fresh Meat Export (Hygiene and Inspection) (Scotland) Regulations 1987 (No. 800) 4475
Materials and Articles in Contact with Food Regulations 1987 (No. 1523) 1811

FOOD AND DRUGS—*cont.*

	C.L.Y.
Meat Inspection Regulations 1987 (No. 2236)	1812
Milk and Dairies and Milk (Special Designation) (Charges) Regulations 1987 (No. 212)	1813
Milk (Cessation of Production) (England and Wales) Scheme 1987 (No. 908)	1813
Milk (Cessation of Production) (Scotland) Scheme 1987 (No. 882)	4477
Milk (Community Outgoers' Scheme) (England and Wales) (Amendment) Regulations 1987 (No. 410)	1813
Milk (Community Outgoers' Scheme) (England and Wales) (Amendment) (No. 2) Regulations 1987 (No. 909)	1813
Milk (Community Outgoers' Scheme) (Scotland) Amendment Regulations 1987 (No. 425)	4477
Milk (Community Outgoers' Scheme) (Scotland) Amendment (No. 2) Regulations 1987 (No. 881)	4477
Milk Marketing Scheme (Amendment) Regulations 1987 (No. 735)	1813
Milk Quota (Calculation of Standard Quota) (Scotland) Amendment (No. 2) Order 1987 (No. 870)	4476
Slaughterhouses (Hygiene) (Amendment) Regulations 1987 (No. 2235)	1812
Sugar Beet (Research and Education) Order 1987 (No. 310)	1816

FORESTRY

Forestry (Felling of Trees) (Amendment) Regulations 1987 (No. 632)	1823

GAMING AND WAGERING

Betting, Gaming and Lotteries Act 1963 (Variation of Fees) Order 1987 (No. 95)	1833
Betting, Gaming and Lotteries Act 1963 (Variation of Fees) (Scotland) Order 1987 (No. 93)	4489
Gaming Act (Variation of Fees) Order 1987 (No. 242)	1833
Gaming Act (Variation of Fees) (Scotland) Order 1987 (No. 255)	4489
Gaming Act (Variation of Monetary Limits) Order 1987 (No. 608)	1838
Gaming Act (Variation of Monetary Limits) (Scotland) Order 1987 (No. 630)	4489
Gaming (Amendment) Act 1987 (Commencement) Order 1987 (No. 1200) (C.33)	1835
Gaming Clubs (Hours and Charges) (Amendment) Regulations 1987 (No. 609)	1836
Gaming Clubs (Hours and Charges) (Scotland) Amendments Regulations 1987 (No. 631)	4485
Lotteries (Gaming Board Fees) Order 1987 (No. 243)	1837

GAS

Gas Act 1986 (Government Shareholding) Order 1987 (No. 866)	1839

HEALTH AND SAFETY AT WORK

Control of Asbestos at Work Regulations 1987 (No. 2115)	1848
Control of Industrial Air Pollution (Transfer of Powers of Enforcement) Regulations 1987 (No. 180)	1856
Dangerous Substances in Harbour Areas Regulations 1987 (No. 37)	1849
Gas Cylinders (Pattern Approval) Regulations 1987 (No. 116)	1855
Health and Safety (Explosives and Petroleum Fees) (Modification) Regulations 1987 (No. 52)	1851
Health and Safety (Fees) Regulations 1987 (No. 605)	1853

HOUSING

Common Parts Grant (Eligible Expense Limits) Order 1987 (No. 2276)	1862
Grants by Local Housing Authorities (Appropriate Percentage and Exchequer Contributions) Order 1987 (No. 1379)	1868
Home Purchase Assistance (Price-limits) Order 1987 (No. 268)	1870
Home Purchase Assistance (Recognised Lending Institutions) Order 1987 (No. 1202)	1870
Home Purchase Assistance (Recognised Lending Institutions) (No. 2) Order 1987 (No. 1809)	1870
Homes Insulation Grants Order 1987 (No. 2185)	1869
Housing and Planning Act 1986 (Commencement No. 2) Order 1987 (No. 178 (C.3))	1883
Housing and Planning Act 1986 (Commencement No. 3) Order 1987 (No. 304 (C.7))	1883
Housing and Planning Act 1986 (Commencement No. 4) Order 1987 (No. 348 (C.9))	1883
Housing and Planning Act 1986 (Commencement No. 5) Order 1987 (No. 754) (C. 20)	1883
Housing and Planning Act 1986 (Commencement No. 6) Order 1987 (No. 1554 (C.47))	1883
Housing and Planning Act 1986 (Commencement No. 7) (Scotland) Order 1987 (No. 1607) (C.53)	5193
Housing and Planning Act 1986 (Commencement No. 8) Order 1987 (No. 1759) (C.53)	1883
Housing and Planning Act 1986 (Commencement No. 9) Order 1987 (No. 1939) (C.58)	1883
Housing and Planning Act 1986 (Commencement No. 10) Order 1987 (No. 2277 (C.71))	1883
Housing Benefit (General) Regulations 1987 (No. 1971)	1884
Housing Benefit (Implementation Subsidy) Order 1987 (No. 1910)	1884
Housing Benefit (Transitional) Regulations 1987 (No. 1972)	1884
Housing Benefits (Amendment) Regulations 1987 (No. 1440)	1884
Housing Benefits (Subsidy) Order 1987 (No. 1805)	1884
Housing Corporation (Recognised Bodies for Heritable Securities Indemnities) (Scotland) Order 1987 (No. 1389)	4557
Housing (Extension of Right to Buy) Order 1987 (No. 1732)	1900

HOUSING—*cont.*

C.L.Y.
Housing (Improvement and Repairs Grants) (Approved Expenses Maxima) (Scotland) Order 1987 (No. 2269) 4561
Housing Revenue Account Rate Fund Contribution Limits (Scotland) Order 1987 (No. 11) 4559
Housing (Right to Buy) (Priority of Charges) Order 1987 (No. 1203) 1900
Housing (Right to Buy) (Priority of Charges) (No. 2) Order 1987 (No. 1810) 1900
Housing Support Grant (Scotland) Order 1987 (No. 332) 4567
Housing Support Grant (Scotland) Variation Order 1987 (No. 331) 4567
Local Authorities (Recognised Bodies for Heritable Securities Indemnities) (Scotland) Order 1987 (No. 1388) 4566
Mortgage Indemnities (Recognised Bodies) (No. 2) Order 1987 (No. 1811) 1894

HUMAN RIGHTS

Data Protection (Fees) Regulations 1987 (No. 272) 1910
Data Protection (Fees) (No. 2) Regulations 1987 (No. 1304) 1910
Data Protection (Functions of Designated Authority) Order 1987 (No. 2028) 1910
Data Protection (Miscellaneous Subject Access Exemptions) Order 1987 (No. 1906) 1910
Data Protection (Regulations of Financial Services etc.) (Subject Access Exemption) Order 1987 (No. 1905) 1910
Data Protection (Subject Access) (Fees) Regulations 1987 (No. 1507) 1910
Data Protection (Subject Access Modification) (Health) Order 1987 (No. 1903) 1910
Data Protection (Subject Access Modification) (Social Work) Order 1987 (No. 1904) 1910

IMMIGRATION

British Citizenship (Designated Service) (Amendment) Order 1987 (No. 611) 1929
Immigration (Control of Entry through Republic of Ireland) (Amendment) Order 1987 (No. 2092) 1932
Immigration (Ports of Entry) Order 1987 (No. 177) 1984
Transfer of Functions (Immigration Appeals) Order 1987 (No. 465) 1999

INCOME TAX

Capital Allowances (Corresponding Northern Ireland Grants) Order 1987 (No. 362) 2008
Double Taxation Relief (Taxes on Income) (Belgium) Order 1987 (No. 2053) 2013
Double Taxation Relief (Taxes on Income) (Bulgaria) Order 1987 (No. 2054) 2013
Double Taxation Relief (Taxes on Income) (Canadian Dividends and Interests) (Amendment) Regulations 1987 (No. 2071) 2013
Double Taxation Relief (Taxes on Income) (France) Order 1987 (No. 466) 2013
Double Taxation Relief (Taxes on Income) (France) (No. 2) Order 1987 (No. 2055) 2013
Double Taxation Relief (Taxes on Income) (Ivory Coast) Order 1987 (No. 169) 2013
Double Taxation Relief (Taxes on Income) (Malaysia) Order 1987 (No. 2056) 2013
Double Taxation Relief (Taxes on Income) (Mauritius) Order 1987 (No. 467) 2013
Double Taxation Relief (Taxes on Income) (Nigeria) Order 1987 (No. 2057) 2013
Double Taxation Relief (Taxes on Income) (Pakistan) Order 1987 (No. 2058) 2013
Income Tax (Building Societies) (Amendment) Regulations 1987 (No. 844) 2007
Income Tax (Cash Equivalents of Car Benefits) Order 1987 (No. 1897) 2010
Income Tax (Entertainers and Sportsmen) Regulations 1987 (No. 530) 2016
Income Tax (Indexation) Order 1987 (No. 434) 2018
Income Tax (Interest on Unpaid Tax and Repayment Supplement) Order 1987 (No. 513) 2019
Income Tax (Interest on Unpaid Tax and Repayment Supplement) (No. 2) Order 1987 (No. 898) 2019
Income Tax (Interest on Unpaid Tax and Repayment Supplement) (No. 3) Order 1987 (No. 1492) 2019
Income Tax (Interest on Unpaid Tax and Repayment Supplement) (No. 4) Order 1987 (No. 1988) 2019
Income Tax (Interest Relief) (Housing Associations) (No. 3) Regulations 1987 (No. 404) 2020
Income Tax (Interest Relief) (Qualifying Lenders) Order 1987 (No. 1224) 2020
Income Tax (Interest Relief) (Qualifying Lenders) (No. 2) Order 1987 (No. 2127) 2020
Income Tax (Official Rate of Interest on Beneficial Loans) Order 1987 (No. 512) 2005
Income Tax (Official Rate of Interest on Beneficial Loans) (No. 2) Order 1987 (No. 886) 2005
Income Tax (Official Rate of Interest on Beneficial Loans) (No. 3) Order 1987 (No. 1493) 2005
Income Tax (Official Rate of Interest on Beneficial Loans) (No. 4) Order 1987 (No. 1989) 2005
Income Tax (Reduced and Composite Rate) Order 1987 (No. 2075) 2027
Pension Scheme Surpluses (Administration) Regulations 1987 (No. 352) 2024
Pension Scheme Surpluses (Valuation) Regulations 1987 (No. 412) 2024
Personal Equity Plan (Amendment) Regulations 1987 (No. 2128) 2025
Revenue Appeals Order 1987 (No. 1422) 2000

INDUSTRIAL AND FRIENDLY SOCIETIES

Financial Services (Transfer of Functions Relating to Friendly Societies) Order 1987 (No. 925) 2044

INDUSTRIAL AND FRIENDLY SOCIETIES—*cont.*

C.L.Y.
Financial Services Act 1986 (Transfer of Functions Relating to Friendly Societies) (Transitional Provisions) Order 1987 (No. 2069) 2044
Friendly Societies Act 1984 (Jersey) Order 1987 (No. 1276) 2042
Friendly Societies (Fees) Regulations 1987 (No. 392) 2041
Friendly Societies (Long Term Insurance Business Regulations 1987 (No. 2132) 2043
Industrial and Provident Societies (Amendment of Fees) Regulations 1987 (No. 394) 2041
Industrial and Provident Societies (Credit Unions) (Amendment of Fees) Regulations 1987 (No. 393) 2041

INHERITANCE TAX

Estate Duty (Interest on Unpaid Duty) Order 1987 (No. 892) 2047
Inheritance Tax and Capital Transfer Tax (Interest on Unpaid Tax) Order 1987 (No. 887) 2049
Inheritance Tax (Delivery of Accounts) Regulations 1987 (No. 1127) 2045
Inheritance Tax (Delivery of Accounts) (Scotland) Regulations 1987 (No. 1128) 2045
Inheritance Tax (Double Charges Relief) Regulations 1987 (No. 1130) 2046
Inheritance Tax (Indexation) Order 1987 (No. 435) 2048

INSURANCE

Insurance Brokers Registration Council (Indemnity Insurance and Grants Scheme) Rules Approval Order 1987 (No. 1496) 2059
Insurance Companies (Assistance) Regulations 1987 (No. 2130) 2060
Insurance Companies (Mergers and Divisions) Regulations 1987 (No. 2118) 2061
Insurance (Fees) Regulations 1987 (No. 350) 2053
Motor Vehicles (Compulsory Insurance) Regulations 1987 (No. 2171) 2062

INTERNATIONAL LAW

Anguilla (Public Seal) Order 1987 (No. 450) 2080
Consular Fees Order 1987 (No. 1264) 2082
Diplomatic and Consular Premises Act 1987 (Commencement No. 1) Order 1987 (No. 1022) (C.26) 2085
Diplomatic and Consular Premises Act 1987 (Commencement No. 2) Order 1987 (No. 2248) (C.68) 2085
Foreign Compensation Commission (Union of Soviet Socialist Republics) Rules Approval Instrument 1987 (No. 143) 2086
Foreign Compensation (Financial Provisions) Order 1987 (No. 164) 2086
Foreign Compensation (Financial Provisions) (No. 2) Order 1987 (No. 1028) 2086
Foreign Compensation (People's Republic of China) Order 1987 (No. 2201) 2086
Foreign Compensation (Union of Soviet Socialist Republics) (Distribution) Order 1987 (No. 663) 2086
Genocide (Anguilla) Order 1987 (No. 453) 2087
Internationally Protected Persons (Anguilla) Order 1987 (No. 454) 2097
Taking of Hostages (Anguilla) Order 1987 (No. 455) 2088
Treaty of Peace (Bulgaria) Vesting Order 1948 Revocation Order 1987 (No. 856) 2096
Treaty of Peace (Hungary) Vesting Order 1948 Revocation Order 1987 (No. 857) 2096
Treaty of Peace (Roumania) Vesting Order 1948 Revocation Order 1987 (No. 858) 2096

INTOXICATING LIQUORS (SCOTLAND ONLY)

Sumburgh Airport Licensing (Liquor) Order 1987 (No. 838) 4585

LAND CHARGES

Local Land Charges (Amendment) Rules 1987 (No. 389) 2107

LANDLORD AND TENANT

Assured Tenancies (Approved Bodies) (No. 1) Order 1987 (No. 737) 2118
Assured Tenancies (Approved Bodies) (No. 2) Order 1987 (No. 822) 2118
Assured Tenancies (Approved Bodies) (No. 3) Order 1987 (No. 1164) 2118
Assured Tenancies (Approved Bodies) (No. 4) Order 1987 (No. 1525) 2118
Assured Tenancies (Prescribed Amount) Order 1987 (No. 122) 2118
Housing Association Shared Ownership Leases (Exclusion from Leasehold Reform Act 1967 and Rent Act 1977) Regulations 1987 (No. 1940) 2234
Landlord and Tenant Act 1987 (Commencement No. 1) Order 1987 (No. 2177 (C.66)) 2151
Protected Shorthold Tenancies (Rent Registration) Order 1987 (No. 265) 2185
Rent Act 1977 (Forms etc.) (Amendment) Regulations 1987 (No. 266) 2196
Rent Assessment Committee (England and Wales) (Leasehold Valuation Tribunal) (Amendment) Regulations 1987 (No. 2178) 2197
Rent (Relief from Phasing) Order 1987 (No. 264) 2195
Secure Tenancies (Notices) Regulations 1987 (No. 755) 2228

ALPHABETICAL TABLE OF STATUTORY INSTRUMENTS 1987

LEGAL AID

Legal Advice and Assistance at Police Stations (Remuneration) (Amendment) Regulations 1987 (No. 388) 2280
Legal Advice and Assistance (Financial Conditions) Regulations 1987 (No. 627) 2279
Legal Advice and Assistance (Financial Conditions) (No. 2) Regulations 1987 (No. 396) 2279
Legal Advice and Representation (Duty Solicitor) (Remuneration) Regulations 1987 (No. 443) 2293
Legal Aid Act 1974 (Deduction from Taxed Costs) Regulations 1987 (No. 2098) 2286
Legal Aid (Financial Conditions) Regulations 1987 (No. 628) 2288
Legal Aid in Criminal Proceedings (Costs) (Amendment) Regulations 1987 (No. 369) 2285
Legal Aid in Criminal Proceedings (General) (Amendment) Regulations 1987 (No. 422) 2285

LICENSING

London City Airport Licensing (Liquor) Order 1987 (No. 1982) 2308
Sumburgh Airport Licensing (Liquor) Order 1987 (No. 838) 2308

LITERARY AND SCIENTIFIC INSTITUTIONS

Armed Forces Museums (Designation of Institutions) Order 1987 (No. 1945) 2341
National Library of Wales (Delivery of Books) (Amendment) Regulations 1987 (No. 918) 2342
Public Lending Right Scheme 1982 (Amendment) Order 1987 (No. 1908) 2338

LOCAL GOVERNMENT

Block Grant (Education Adjustments) (England) Regulations 1987 (No. 347) 2347
Block Grant (Education Adjustments) (Wales) Regulations 1987 (No. 359) 2347
Borough of Chelmsford (Electoral Arrangements) Order 1987 (No. 483) 2354
Borough of Dinefwr (Electoral Arrangements Order 1987 (No. 300) 2354
Borough of Oadby and Wigston (Electoral Arrangements) Order 1987 (No. 1625) 2354
Borough of South Ribble (Electoral Arrangements) Order 1987 (No. 484) 2354
Borough of Torbay (Electoral Arrangements) Order 1987 (No. 1626) 2354
Buckinghamshire (District Boundaries) Order 1987 (No. 339) 2348
Definition of Capital Expenses (Scotland) Order 1987 (No. 943) 4665
Devon (District Boundaries) Order 1987 (No. 1576) 2348
Disabled Persons (Services, Consultation and Representation) Act 1986 (Commencement No. 1) Order 1987 (No. 564) (C.13) 2353
Disabled Persons (Services, Consultation and Representation) Act 1986 (Commencement No. 2) Order 1987 (No. 729) (C.19) 2353
Disabled Persons (Services, Consultation and Representation) Act 1986 (Commencement No. 3) (Scotland) Order 1987 (No. 911 (C. 25)) 4662
District of Carmarthen (Electoral Arrangements) Order 1987 (No. 176) 2354
District of Kingswood (Electoral Arrangements) Order 1987 (No. 485) 2354
District of Montgomeryshire (Electoral Arrangements) Order 1987 (No. 486) 2354
District of Preseli (Electoral Arrangements) Order 1987 (No. 301) 2354
Dorset (District Boundaries) Order 1987 (No. 2228) 2348
Essex (District Boundaries) Order 1987 (No. 1598) 2348
Hereford and Worcester (District Boundaries) Order 1987 (No. 338) 2348
Inner Urban Areas (Designated Districts) (Wales) Order 1987 (No. 115) 2362
Kent (District Boundaries) Order 1987 (No. 305) 2348
Leicestershire (District Boundaries) Order 1987 (No. 2247) 2348
Liquor Licensing (Fees) (Scotland) Order 1987 (No. 1738) 4675
Local Authorities (Allowances) (Scotland) Amendment Regulations 1987 (No. 1381) 4677
Local Authorities (Armorial Bearings) Order 1987 (No. 162) 2346
Local Authorities (Publicity Account) (Exemption) Order 1987 (No. 2004) 2379
Local Government Act 1986 (Commencement) Order 1987 (No. 2003) (C.62) 2370
Local Government (Allowances) (Amendment) Regulations 1987 (No. 1483) 2345
Local Government (Direct Labour Organisations) (Competition) (Amendment) Regulations 1987 (No. 181) 2351
Local Government (Prescribed Expenditure) (Amendment) Regulations 1987 (No. 351) 2377
Local Government (Prescribed Expenditure) (Consolidation and Amendment) Regulations 1987 (No. 2186) 2377
Local Government (Prescribed Expenditure) (Works) Regulations 1987 (No. 1583) 2377
Local Government Reorganisation (Capital Money) (Greater London) Order 1987 (No. 118) 2386
Local Government Reorganisation (Housing Association Mortgages) Order 1987 (No. 117) 2393

LOCAL GOVERNMENT—*cont.*

C.L.Y.

Local Government Reorganisation (Pensions etc.) (Greater Manchester and Merseyside) Order 1987 (No. 1579) 2386
Local Government Reorganisation (Pensions etc.) (South Yorkshire) Order 1987 (No. 2110) 2386
Local Government Reorganisation (Property) (Greater Manchester) Order 1987 (No. 1446) 2386
Local Government Reorganisation (Property) (South Yorkshire) Order 1987 (No. 651) 2386
Local Government Reorganisation (Property) (Tyne and Wear) Order 1987 (No. 1288) 2386
Local Government Reorganisation (Property) (West Midlands) Order 1987 (No. 1077) 2386
Local Government Reorganisation (Property) (West Yorkshire) Order 1987 (No. 15) 2386
Local Government Reorganisation (Property) (West Yorkshire) (No. 2) Order 1987 (No. 1451) 2386
Local Government Reorganisation (Property, etc.) (Merseyside) Order 1987 (No. 1463) 2386
Local Statutory Provisions (Postponement of Repeal) (Scotland) Order 1987 (No. 2090) 4676
London Government Reorganisation (Housing Association Mortgages) Order 1987 (No. 117) 2393
London Government Reorganisation (Housing Association Mortgages) (No. 2) Order 1987 (No. 2219) ... 2393
Nottinghamshire (District Boundaries) Order 1987 (No. 221) 2348
Preseli (Communities) Order 1987 (No. 124) 2350
Recreation Grounds (Revocation of Parish Council Byelaws) Order 1987 (No. 1533) 2382
Shropshire (District Boundaries) Order 1987 (No. 1737) 2348

LONDON

London (British Rail) Taxi Sharing Scheme Order 1987 (No. 839) 2395
London Cab Order 1987 (No. 999) 2395
London Regional Transport (Levy) Order 1987 (No. 125) 2396
London Taxi Sharing Scheme Order 1987 (No. 1535) 2395

MEDICINE

General Medical Council (Constitution) Amendment Order 1987 (No. 457) 2406
General Medical Council (Constitution of Fitness to Practise Committees) (Amendment) Rules Order of Council 1987 (No. 1120) 2406
General Medical Council Health Committee (Procedure) Rules Order of Council 1987 (No. 2174) 2406
General Medical Council (Registration (Fees) (Amendment) Regulations) Order of Council 1987 (No. 102) 2406
General Medical Council (Registration (Fees) (Amendment) Regulations) (No. 2) Order of Council 1987 (No. 2166) 2406
General Optical Council (Registration and Enrolment (Amendment) Rules) Order of Council 1987 (No. 1887) 2410
Irish Republic (Termination of 1927 Agreement) Order 1987 (No. 2047) 2401
Medicines (Carbadox Prohibition) (Revocation) Order 1987 (No. 2216) 2404
Medicines (Child Safety) Amendment Regulations 1987 (No. 877) 2416
Medicines (Exemptions from Licences) (Carbadox and Olaquindox) Order 1987 (No. 2217) 2408
Medicines (Exemptions from Restrictions on the Retail Sale or Supply of Veterinary Drugs) (Amendment) Order 1987 (No. 1123) 2418
Medicines (Exemptions from Restrictions on the Retail Sale or Supply of Veterinary Drugs) (Amendment) (No. 2) Order 1987 (No. 1980) 2418
Medicines (Fees) Amendment Regulations 1987 (No. 1439) 2405
Medicines (Pharmacies) (Application for Registration and Fees) Amendment Regulations 1987 (No. 2099) 2413
Medicines (Products Other Than Veterinary Drugs) (General Sale List) Amendment Order 1987 (No. 910) 2407
Medicines (Products Other Than Veterinary Drugs) (Prescription Only) Amendment Order 1987 (No. 674) 2404
Medicines (Products Other Than Veterinary Drugs) (Prescription Only) Amendment (No. 2) Order 1987 (No. 1250) 2404
Pharmaceutical Qualifications (EEC Recognition) Order 1987 (No. 2202) 2411

MINING LAW

Coal Industry (Restructuring Grants) Order 1987 (No. 770) 2427
Opencast Coal (Compulsory Rights and Rights of Way) (Forms) Regulations 1987 (No. 1915) 2431
Opencast Coal (Rate of Interest on Compensation) Order 1987 (No. 700) 2431
Redundant Mineworkers and Concessionary Coal (Payments Schemes) (Amendment) Order 1987 (No. 1258) 2427

MINORS

Child Abduction and Custody (Parties to Conventions) (Amendment) Order 1987 (No. 163) 2469
Child Abduction and Custody (Parties to Conventions) (Amendment) (No. 2) Order 1987 (No. 1825) 2469
Children Act 1975 and the Adoption Act 1976 (Commencement No. 2) Order 1987 (No. 1242) (C.36) ... 2479

ALPHABETICAL TABLE OF STATUTORY INSTRUMENTS 1987

NATIONAL HEALTH

Disablement Services Authority (Establishment and Constitution) Order 1987 (No. 808) 2548
Disablement Services Authority Regulations 1987 (No. 809) 2548
Health Education Authority (Establishment and Constitution) Order 1987 (No. 6) 2550
Health Education Authority Regulations 1987 (No. 7) 2550
Health Service Commissioner for England (Disablement Services Authority) Order 1987 (No. 1272) 2548
National Health Service (Amendment) Act 1986 (Commencement No. 1) Order 1987 (No. 399 (C.11)) .. 2553
National Health Service (Charges for Drugs and Appliances) Amendment Regulations 1987 (No. 368) ... 2552
National Health Service (Charges for Drugs and Appliances) (Scotland) Amendment Regulations 1987 (No. 367) 4719
National Health Service (Charges to Overseas Visitors) Amendment Regulations 1987 (No. 371) 2552
National Health Service (Charges to Overseas Visitors) (Scotland) Amendment Regulations 1987 (No. 387) 4719
National Health Service (Food Premises) Regulations 1987 (No. 18) 2552
National Health Service (Food Premises) (Scotland) Regulations 1987 (No. 2) 4723
National Health Service Functions (Amendment of Directions to Authorities) Regulations 1987 (No. 245) 2552
National Health Service (General Dental Services) Amendment Regulations 1987 (No. 736) 2547
National Health Service (General Dental Services) Amendment (No. 2) Regulations 1987 (No. 1512) 2547
National Health Service (General Dental Services) Amendment (No. 3) Regulations 1987 (No. 1965) 2547
National Health Service (General Dental Services) (Scotland) Amendment Regulations 1987 (No. 1634) 4720
National Health Service (General Medical and Pharmaceutical Services) Amendment Regulations 1987 (No. 5) 2551
National Health Service (General Medical and Pharmaceutical Services) Amendment (No. 2) Regulations 1987 (No. 401) 2551
National Health Service (General Medical and Pharmaceutical Services) Amendment (No. 3) Regulations 1987 (No. 407) 2551
National Health Service (General Medical and Pharmaceutical Services) Amendment (No. 4) Regulations 1987 (No. 1425) 2551
National Health Service (General Medical and Pharmaceutical Services) (Scotland) Amendment Regulations 1987 (No. 385) 4721
National Health Service (General Medical and Pharmaceutical Services) (Scotland) Amendment (No. 2) Regulations 1987 (No. 386) 4721
National Health Service (General Medical and Pharmaceutical Services) (Scotland) Amendment (No. 3) Regulations 1987 (No. 1382) 4721
National Health Service (Service Committees and Tribunal) Amendment Regulations 1987 (No. 445) 2552
National Health Service (Transferred Staff—Appeals Amendment) Order 1987 (No. 1428) 2559
Nurses, Midwives and Health Visitors (Entry to Training Requirements) Amendment Rules Approval Order 1987 (No. 446) 2554
Nurses, Midwives and Health Visitors (Professional Conduct) Rules 1987 Approval Order 1987 (No. 2156) 2554
Nurses, Midwives and Health Visitors (Temporary Registration) Amendment Rules Approval Order 1987 (No. 944) 2554
Special Hospital Boards (Amendment of Constitution) Order 1987 (No. 192) 2557
Welsh Health Promotion Authority (Establishment and Constitution) Order 1987 (No. 151) 2549
Welsh Health Promotion Authority Regulations 1987 (No. 152) 2549

NORTHERN IRELAND

ADMINISTRATIVE LAW

Audit (Northern Ireland) Order 1987 (No. 460 (N.I. 5)) 2622a

AGENCY

Enduring Powers of Attorney (Northern Ireland) Order 1987 (No. 1627 (N.I.16)) 2627

AGRICULTURE

Agriculture (Environmental Areas) (Northern Ireland) Order 1987 (No. 458 (N.I.3)) 2629a
Agriculture and Fisheries (Financial Assistance) (Northern Ireland) Order 1987 (No. 166 (N.I.1)) 2629

CHARITIES

Charities (Northern Ireland) Order 1987 (No. 2048 (N.I.19)) 2637

CLUBS AND ASSOCIATIONS

Registration of Clubs (Northern Ireland) Order 1987 (No. 1278 (N.I.14)) 2639

CRIMINAL LAW

Public Order (Northern Ireland) Order 1987 (No. 463 (N.I.7)) 2652a

NORTHERN IRELAND—*cont.*

C.L.Y.

EDUCATION

Education (Corporal Punishment) (Northern Ireland) Order 1987 (No. 461 (N.I.6)) 2660
Education (Northern Ireland) Order 1987 (No. 167 (N.I.2)) 2661

ELECTRICITY

Electricity Supply (Amendment) (Northern Ireland) Order 1987 (No. 1275 (N.I.12)) 2664

EMPLOYMENT

Industrial Relations (Northern Ireland) Order 1987 (No. 936 (N.I.9)) 2669

LICENSING

Licensing (Northern Ireland) Order 1987 (No. 1277 (N.I.13)) 2700

LIMITATION OF ACTIONS

Limitation (Amendment) (Northern Ireland) Order 1987 (No. 1629 (N.I.17)) 2701

MEDICINE

AIDS (Control) (Northern Ireland) Order 1987 (No. 1832 (N.I.18)) 2707

MINORS

Adoption (Northern Ireland) Order 1987 (No. 2203 (N.I.22)) 2708

POLICE

Police (Northern Ireland) Order 1987 (No. 938 (N.I.10)) 2717

REVENUE AND FINANCE

Appropriation (Northern Ireland) Order 1987 (No. 459 (N.I.4)) 2735
Appropriation (No. 2) (Northern Ireland) Order 1987 (No. 1274 (N.I.11)) 2736
Appropriation (No. 3) (Northern Ireland) Order 1987 (No. 2204 (N.I.23)) 2737

SOCIAL SECURITY

Social Fund (Maternity and Funeral Expenses) (Northern Ireland) Order 1987 (No. 464 (N.I.8)) 2741a

TORT

Consumer Protection (Northern Ireland) Order 1987 (S.I. 1987 No. 2049 (N.I.20)) 2743
Occupiers' Liability (Northern Ireland) Order 1987 (No. 1280 (N.I.15)) 2744

WATER AND WATERWORKS

Water (Fluoridation) (Northern Ireland) Order 1987 (S.I. 1987 No. 2052 (N.I.21)) 2753

PARLIAMENT

House of Commons Disqualification Order 1987 (No. 449) 2760
Lord Chancellor's Salary Order 1987 (No. 941) 2762
Ministerial and other Salaries Order 1987 (No. 1836) 2766
Parliamentary and other Pensions Act 1987 (Commencement No. 1) Order 1987 (No. 1311 (C.42)) 2765
Resolution of the House of Commons, dated March 20, 1987, passed in pursuance of the House of Commons Members' Fund Act 1948, s.3 (11 and 12 Geo. 6 c.36) and the House of Commons Members' Fund and Parliamentary Pensions Act 1981, s.2 (1981 c.7) (No. 511) 2761

PATENTS AND DESIGNS

Designs (Amendment) Rules 1987 (No. 287) 2787
Patents (Amendment) Rules 1987 (No. 288) 2809
Patents (Fees) Rules 1987 (No. 610) 2789
Patents (Fees) (Amendment) Rules 1987 (No. 753) 2789

PENSIONS AND SUPERANNUATION

British Council and Commonwealth Institute Superannuation Act 1986 (Commencement No. 2) Order 1987 (No. 588 (C.14)) 2818
Contracting-out (Transfer) Amendment Regulations 1987 (No. 1099) 2824
Contracting-out (Widowers' Guaranteed Minimum Pensions) Regulations 1987 (No. 1100) 2824
Judicial Pensions (Preservation of Benefits) Order 1987 (No. 374) 2828
Judicial Pensions (Requisite Benefits) Order 1987 (No. 373) 2828
Judicial Pensions (Widows' and Children's Benefits) Regulations 1987 (No. 375) 2828
Local Government Superannuation (Miscellaneous Provisions) Regulations 1987 (No. 293) 2829
Local Government Superannuation (Scotland) Regulations 1987 (No. 1850) 4787
Money Purchase Contracted-out Schemes Regulations 1987 (No. 1101) 2824
National Health Service (Superannuation) Amendment Regulations 1987 (No. 2218) 2831
Naval, Military and Air Forces etc. (Disablement and Death) Service Pensions Amendment Order 1987 (No. 165) 2817
Occupational Pension Schemes (Additional Voluntary Contributions) Regulations 1987 (No. 1749) 2832
Occupational Pension Schemes (Auditors) Regulations 1987 (No. 1102) 2832
Occupational Pension Schemes (Contracted-out Protected Rights Premiums) Regulations 1987 (No. 1103) 2832
Occupational Pension Schemes (Contracting-out) Amendment Regulations 1987 (No. 1104) 2832
Occupational Pension Schemes (Disclosure of Information) (Amendment) Regulations 1987 (No. 1105) 2832
Occupational Pension Schemes (Maximum Rate Lump Sum) Regulations 1987 (No. 1513) 2832
Occupational Pension Schemes (Qualifying Service—Consequential and Other Provisions) Regulations 1987 (No. 1106) 2832
Occupational Pension Schemes (Transfer Values) Amendment Regulations 1987 (No. 1107) 2832
Occupational Pensions (Revaluation) Order 1987 (No. 1981) 2832
Pension Schemes (Voluntary Contributions Requirements and Voluntary and Compulsory Membership) Regulations 1987 (No. 1108) 2844
Pensions Increase (Review) Order 1987 (No. 130) 2834
Personal and Occupational Pension Schemes (Abatement of Benefit) Regulations 1987 (No. 1113) 2816
Personal and Occupational Pension Schemes (Consequential Provisions) Regulations 1987 (No. 1114) . 2823
Personal and Occupational Pension Schemes (Incentive Payments) Regulations 1987 (No. 1115) 2826
Personal and Occupational Pension Schemes (Modification of Enactments) Regulations 1987 (No. 1116) 2830
Personal and Occupational Pension Schemes (Protected Rights) Regulations 1987 (No. 1117) 2839
Personal Injuries (Civilians) Amendment Scheme 1987 (No. 191) 2835
Personal Pension Schemes (Appropriate Schemes) Regulations 1987 (No. 1109) 2836
Personal Pension Schemes (Deferment of Commencement) Regulations 1987 (No. 1933) 2836
Personal Pension Schemes (Disclosure of Information) Regulations 1987 (No. 1110) 2836
Personal Pension Schemes (Personal Pension Protected Rights Premiums) Regulations 1987 (No. 1111) 2836
Personal Pension Schemes (Provisional Approval) Regulations 1987 (No. 1765) 2836
Personal Pension Schemes (Transfer Values) Regulations 1987 (No. 1112) 2836
Police Cadets (Pensions) (Scotland) Amendment Regulations 1987 (No. 1699) 4788
Police Pensions (Lump Sum Payments to Widows) Regulations 1987 (No. 1462) 2838
Police Pensions (Purchase of Increased Benefits) Regulations 1987 (No. 2215) 2838
Police Pensions Regulations 1987 (No. 257) 2838
Police Pensions (Supplementary Provisions) Regulations 1987 (No. 256) 2838
Police Pensions (War Service) (Transferees) (Amendment) Regulations 1987 (No. 1907) 2838
Protected Rights (Transfer Payment) Regulations 1987 (No. 1118) 2839
Royal Irish Constabulary (Lump Sum Payments to Widows) Regulations 1987 (No. 1461) 2838
Social Security (Class 1 Contributions—Contracted-out Percentages) Order 1987 (No. 656) 2840
State Scheme Premiums (Actuarial Tables) Regulations 1987 (No. 657) 2841
State Scheme Premiums (Actuarial Tables—Transitional Provisions) Regulations 1987 (No. 658) 2841
Superannuation (Children's Pensions) (Earnings Limit) Order 1987 (No. 209) 2820
Superannuation (Judicial Offices) (Aggregation of Service) Rules 1987 (No. 376) 2827
War Pensions (Mercantile Marine) (Amendment) Scheme 1987 (No. 585) 2845

PETROLEUM

Foreign Fields (Specification) (No. 1) Order 1987 (No. 545) 2846
Petroleum Act 1987 (Commencement No. 1) Order 1987 (No. 820) (C.22) 2849
Petroleum Act 1987 (Commencement No. 2) Order 1987 (No. 1330) (C.43) 2849

POLICE

Police (Amendment) Regulations 1987 (No. 1753) 2861
Police Cadets (Amendment) Regulations 1987 (No. 1754) 2854
Police Cadets (Injury Benefit) Regulations 1987 (No. 158) 2859
Police Cadets (Injury Benefit) (Amendment) Regulations 1987 (No. 342) 2859
Police Cadets (Injury Benefit) (Scotland) Regulations 1987 (No. 1700) 4794
Police Cadets (Pensions) (Amendment) Regulations 1987 (No. 157) 2854
Police Cadets (Scotland) Amendment Regulations 1987 (No. 424) 4793
Police Cadets (Scotland) Amendment (No. 2) Regulations 1987 (No. 1878) 4793
Police (Common Services) (Scotland) Order 1987 (No. 1537) 4790
Police (Discipline) (Scotland) Amendment Regulations 1987 (No. 2226) 4791
Police Federation (Amendment) Regulations 1987 (No. 1062) 2863
Police (Injury Benefit) Regulations 1987 (No. 156) 2859
Police (Injury Benefit) (Amendment) Regulations 1987 (No. 341) 2859
Police Regulations 1987 (No. 851) 2867
Police (Scotland) Amendment Regulations 1987 (No. 423) 4795
Police (Scotland) Amendment (No. 2) Regulations 1987 (No. 1914) 4795
Special Constables (Injury Benefit) Regulations 1987 (No. 159) 2859
Special Constables (Injury Benefit) (Amendment) Regulations 1987 (No. 343) 2859
Special Constables (Injury Benefit) (Scotland) Regulations 1987 (No. 1698) 4797

PRACTICE

Act of Sederunt (Civil Legal Aid Rules) 1987 (No. 492) 4872
Act of Sederunt (Rules of Court Amendment No. 1) (Drug Trafficking) 1987 (No. 12) 4818
Act of Sederunt (Rules of Court Amendment No. 4) (Miscellaneous) 1987 (No. 1206) 4818
Act of Sederunt (Rules of Court Amendment No. 5) (Miscellaneous) 1987 (No. 2160) 4818
Act of Sederunt (Sessions of Court and Sederunt Days) 1987 (No. 40) 4819
Administration of Justice Act 1985 (Commencement No. 4) Order 1987 (No. 787) (C.21) 2874
Advice and Assistance (Financial Conditions) (Scotland) Regulations 1987 (No. 704) 4873
Advice and Assistance (Scotland) Regulations 1987 (No. 382) 4872
Civil Legal Aid (Financial Conditions) (Scotland) Regulations 1987 (No. 705) 4873
Civil Legal Aid (Scotland) Regulations 1987 (No. 381) 4872
Civil Legal Aid (Scotland) Amendment Regulations 1987 (No. 431) 4872
County Court (Amendment) Rules 1987 (No. 493) (L.1) 2971
County Court (Amendment No. 2) Rules 1987 (No. 1397) (L.7) 2971
County Court (Forms) (Amendment) Rules 1987 (No. 1119) (L.4) 2969
Court Funds Rules 1987 (No. 821) (L.3) 2970
Crown Office Fees Order 1987 (No. 1464) 2981
Legal Aid (Scotland) Act 1986 (Commencement No. 2) Order 1987 (No. 289) (C. 6) 4878
Legal Aid (Scotland) (Children) Regulations 1987 (No. 384) 4874
Maximum Number of Judges Order 1987 (No. 2059) 3043
Non-Contentious Probate Rules 1987 (No. 2024) (L.10) 3087
Reciprocal Enforcement of Foreign Judgments (Canada) Order 1987 (No. 468) 3011
Reciprocal Enforcement of Foreign Judgments (Canada) (Amendment) Order 1987 (No. 2211) 3011
Rules of the Supreme Court (Amendment) 1987 (No. 1423) (L.8) 3090

PRISONS

Prison (Amendment) Rules 1987 (No. 1256) 3143
Prison (Amendment No. 2) Rules 1987 (No. 2176) 3143
Prison (Scotland) Amendment Rules 1987 (No. 2231) 4925

PUBLIC ENTERTAINMENTS AND RECREATION

Fire Safety and Safety of Places of Sport Act 1987 (Commencement No. 1) Order 1987 (No. 1762 (C.54)) 3146
Safety of Sports Grounds (Designation) Order 1987 (No. 1689) 3147
Safety of Sports Grounds Regulations 1987 (No. 1941) 3147
Sports Grounds and Sporting Events (Designation) (Amendment) Order 1987 (No. 1520) 3147

PUBLIC HEALTH

Control of Noise (Code of Practice for Construction and Open Sites) Order 1987 (No. 1730) 3151
Control of Pollution (Anti-Fouling Paints and Treatments) Regulations 1987 (No. 783) 3150
Control of Pollution (Exemption of Certain Discharges from Control) (Variation) Order 1987 (No. 1782) . 3150
Lawnmowers (Harmonization of Noise Emission Standards) (Amendment) Regulations 1987 (No. 876) . 3152
Smoke Control Areas (Authorised Fuels) Regulations 1987 (No. 625) 3149
Smoke Control Areas (Authorised Fuels) (No. 2) Regulations 1987 (No. 2159) 3149
Smoke Control Areas (Exempted Fireplaces) Order 1987 (No. 1394) 3149
Smoke Control Areas (Exempted Fireplaces) (Scotland) Order 1987 (No. 383) 4929

ALPHABETICAL TABLE OF STATUTORY INSTRUMENTS 1987

RATING AND VALUATION

Abolition of Domestic Rates (Domestic and Part Residential Subjects) (Scotland) Regulations 1987 (No. 2179) ... 4938
Abolition of Domestic Rates Etc. (Scotland) Act 1987 Commencement Order 1987 (No. 1489) (C. 46) .. 4940
Non-domestic Rates and Community Charges (Timetable) (Scotland) Regulations 1987 (No. 2167) ... 4945
New Valuation Lists Order 1987 (No. 921) ... 3197
New Valuation Lists (Time and Class of Hereditaments) Order 1987 (No. 604) ... 3197
Rate Limitation (Designation of Authorities) (Exemption) Order 1987 (No. 785) ... 3186
Rate Limitation (Designation of Authorities) (Exemption) (Wales) Order 1987 (No. 786) ... 3186
Rate Limitation (Designation of Authorities) (Exemption) (Wales) (No. 2) Order 1987 (No. 1251) ... 3186
Rate Support Grant (Scotland) Order 1987 (No. 275) ... 4943
Rate Support Grant (Scotland) (No. 2) Order 1987 (No. 1329) ... 4943
Rate Support Grant (Scotland) (No. 3) Order 1987 (No. 2279) ... 4943
Revaluation Rate Rebates (Scotland) Order 1986 (No. 345) ... 4944
Valuation Timetable (Scotland) Amendment Order 1987 (No. 432) ... 4947
Valuation Timetable (Scotland) Amendment (No. 2) Order 1987 (No. 794) ... 4947

REGISTRATION OF BIRTHS, DEATHS AND MARRIAGES

Public Record Office (Fees) Regulations 1987 (No. 444) ... 3200
Registration of Births, Deaths and Marriages (Fees) Order 1987 (No. 50) ... 3199
Registration of BIrths and Deaths Regulations 1987 (No. 2088) ... 3202
Registration of Births and Deaths (Welsh Language) Regulations 1987 (No. 2089) ... 3204

REVENUE AND FINANCE

Financial Services Act 1986 (Applications for Authorisation) (Appointed Day) Order 1987 (No. 2157) 3216
Financial Services Act 1986 (Commencement) (No. 4) Order 1987 (No. 623) (C.15) ... 3217
Financial Services Act 1986 (Commencement) (No. 5) Order 1987 (No. 907) (C.24) ... 3217
Financial Services Act 1986 (Commencement) (No. 6) Order 1987 (No. 1997) (C.59) ... 3217
Financial Services Act 1986 (Commencement) (No. 7) Order 1987 (No. 2158) (C.65) ... 3217
Financial Services Act 1986 (Delegation) Order 1987 (No. 942) ... 3218
Financial Services Act 1986 (Delegation) (Transitional Provisions) Order 1987 (No. 2035) ... 3219
Financial Services Act 1986 (Overseas Investment Exchanges and Overseas Clearing Houses) (Notification) Regulations 1987 (No. 2142) ... 3214
Financial Services Act 1986 (Overseas Investment Exchange and Overseas Clearing Houses) (Periodical Fees) Regulations 1987 (No. 2143) ... 3214
Financial Services (Disclosure of Information) (Designated Authorities No. 2) Order 1987 (No. 859) 3213
Financial Services (Disclosure of Information) (Designated Authorities No. 3) Order 1987 (No. 1141) 3213
National Savings Stock Register (Amendment) Regulations 1987 (No. 1635) ... 3223
Petroleum Revenue Tax (Nomination Scheme for Disposals and Appropriations) Regulations 1987 (No. 1338) ... 3225

ROAD TRAFFIC

Community Drivers' Hours and Recording Equipment (Exemptions and Supplementary Provisions) (Amendment) Regulations 1987 (No. 805) ... 3264
Community Drivers' Hours (Passenger and Goods Vehicles) (Temporary Exception) Regulations 1987 (No. 27) ... 3264
Community Drivers' Hours (Passenger and Goods Vehicles) (Temporary Exception) (Revocation) Regulations 1987 (No. 97) ... 3264
Criminal Justice (Scotland) Act 1987 Fixed Penalty Order 1987 (No. 2025) ... 5028
Crown Roads (Royal Parks) (Application of Road Traffic Enactments) Order 1987 (No. 363) ... 3257
Drivers' Hours (Goods Vehicles) (Keeping of Records) Regulations 1987 (No. 1421) ... 3264
Drivers' Hours (Passenger and Goods Vehicles) (Exemption) Regulations 1987 (No. 28) ... 3264
Drivers' Hours (Passenger and Goods Vehicles) (Exemption) (Revocation) Regulations 1987 (No. 98) 3264
Goods Vehicles (Authorisation of International Journeys) (Fees) (Amendment) Regulations 1987 (No. 2012) ... 3276
Goods Vehicles (Operators' Licences, Qualifications and Fees) (Amendment) Regulations 1987 (No. 841) ... 3276
Goods Vehicles (Operators' Licences, Qualifications and Fees) (Amendment) (No. 2) Regulation 1987 (No. 2170) ... 3276
Goods Vehicles (Prohibitions) (Exemptions and Appeals) Regulations 1987 (No. 1149) ... 3276
Greenwich (Prescribed Routes) (No. 5) Traffic Order 1973 (Variation) Order 1987 (No. 897) ... 3300
International Carriage of Perishable Foodstuffs (Amendment) Regulations 1987 (No. 1066) ... 3255

ROAD TRAFFIC—*cont.*

C.L.Y.
International Carriage of Perishable Foodstuffs (Vehicles With Thin Side Walls) Regulations 1987 (No. 869) ... 3255
Islington (Prescribed Routes) (No. 4) Traffic Order 1985 (Variation) Order 1987 (No. 2168) ... 3300
Local Roads Authorities' Traffic Orders (Procedure) (Scotland) Regulations 1987 (No. 2245) ... 5037
Motor Cycles (Eye Protectors) (Amendment) Regulations 1987 (No. 675) ... 3293
Motor Vehicles (Authorisation of Special Types) (Amendment) Order 1987 (No. 1327) ... 3296
Motor Vehicles (Authorisation of Special Types) (Amendment) (No. 2) Order 1987 (No. 2161) ... 3296
Motor Vehicles (Competitions and Trials) (Scotland) Amendment Regulations 1987 (No. 346) ... 4982
Motor Vehicles (Driving Licences) Regulations 1987 (No. 1378) ... 3265
Motor Vehicles (Driving Licences) (Amendment) Regulations 1987 (No. 560) ... 3265
Motor Vehicles (Tests) (Amendment) Regulations 1987 (No. 1144) ... 3297
Motor Vehicles (Type Approval) (Amendment) Regulations 1987 (No. 524) ... 3310
Motor Vehicles (Type Approval and Approval Marks) (Fees) (Amendment) Regulations 1987 (No. 315) .. 3310
Motor Vehicles (Type Approval and Approval Marks) (Fees) (Amendment) (No. 2) Regulations 1987 (No. 1556) ... 3310
Motor Vehicles (Type Approval for Goods Vehicles) (Great Britain) (Amendment) Regulations 1987 (No. 1508) ... 3310
Motor Vehicles (Type Approval) (Great Britain) (Amendment) Regulations 1987 (No. 1509) ... 3310
"Pelican" Pedestrian Crossings Regulations and General Directions 1987 (No. 16) ... 3299
Public Passenger Vehicles (Exemptions, and Appeals Against Refusals to Issue Certificates or Remove Prohibitions) Regulations 1987 (No. 1150) ... 3301
Recovery Vehicles (Prescribed Purposes) Regulations 1987 (No. 2120) ... 3304
Road Traffic Accidents (Payments for Treatment) Order 1987 (No. 353) ... 3227
Road Vehicles (Construction and Use) (Amendment) Regulations 1987 (No. 676) ... 3256
Road Vehicles (Construction and Use) (Amendment) (No. 2) Regulations 1987 (No. 1133) ... 3256
Road Vehicles (Excise) (Prescribed Particulars) (Amendment) Regulations 1987 (No. 2122) ... 3272
Road Vehicles Lighting (Amendment) Regulations 1987 (No. 1315) ... 3287
Road Vehicles (Marking of Special Weights) (Amendment) Regulations 1987 (No. 1326) ... 3288
Road Vehicles (Prescribed Regulations for the Purposes of Increased Penalties) Regulations 1987 (No. 2085) ... 3277
Road Vehicles (Prescribed Regulations for the Purposes of Increased Penalties) Regulations (Northern Ireland) 1987 (No. 2086) ... 2738
Road Vehicles (Registration and Licensing) (Amendment) Regulations 1987 (No. 2123) ... 3272
Secretary of State's Traffic Orders (Procedure) (Scotland) Regulations 1987 (No. 2244) ... 5037
Traffic Signs General (Amendment) Directions 1987 (No. 1706) ... 3309

SALE OF GOODS

Approval of Safety Standards Regulations 1987 (No. 1911) ... 3319
Asbestos Products (Safety) (Amendment) Regulations 1987 (No. 1979) ... 3313
Benzene in Toys (Safety) Regulations 1987 (No. 2116) ... 3320
Bunk Beds (Entrapment Hazards) (Safety) Regulations 1987 (No. 1337) ... 3314
Consumer Protection (Cancellation of Contracts Concluded away from Business Premises) Regulations 1987 (No. 2117) ... 3315
Consumer Safety Act 1978 (Commencement No. 3) Order 1987 (No. 1681) (C.52) ... 3323
Cosmetic Products (Safety) (Amendment) Regulations 1987 (No. 1920) ... 3316
Nightwear (Safety) (Amendment) Regulations 1987 (No. 286) ... 3317
Plugs and Sockets etc. (Safety) Regulations 1987 (No. 603) ... 3318
Price Marking (Petrol) (Amendment) Order 1987 (No. 8) ... 3340
Uniform Laws on International Sales Order 1987 (No. 2061) ... 3334

SEA AND SEASHORE

Civil Jurisdiction (Offshore Activities) Order 1987 (No. 2197) ... 3349
Continental Shelf (Designated Areas) (Extended Territorial Sea) Order 1987 (No. 1265) ... 3347
Criminal Jurisdiction (Offshore Activities) Order 1987 (No. 2198) ... 3350
Food and Environment Protection Act 1985 (Guernsey) Order 1987 (No. 665) ... 3348
Food and Environment Protection Act 1985 (Isle of Man) Order 1987 (No. 666) ... 3348
Food and Environment Protection Act 1985 (Jersey) Order 1987 (No. 667) ... 3348
Offshore Installations (Life-saving Appliances and Fire-fighting Equipment) (Amendment) Regulations 1987 (No. 129) ... 3353
Offshore Installations (Safety Zones) Regulations 1987 (No. 1331) ... 3351
Offshore Installations (Safety Zones) Orders made under the Oil and Gas (Enterprise) Act 1982 (c.23), s.21(1) to (3):

SEA AND SEASHORE—*cont.*

	C.L.Y.
Offshore Installations (Safety Zones) (Amendment) Order 1987 (No. 4)	3351
Offshore Installations (Safety Zones) Order 1987 (No. 54)	3351
Offshore Installations (Safety Zones) (No. 2) Order 1987 (No. 55)	3351
Offshore Installations (Safety Zones) (No. 3) Order 1987 (No. 56)	3351
Offshore Installations (Safety Zones) (No. 4) Order 1987 (No. 57)	3351
Offshore Installations (Safety Zones) (No. 5) Order 1987 (No. 58)	3351
Offshore Installations (Safety Zones) (No. 6) Order 1987 (No. 59)	3351
Offshore Installations (Safety Zones) (No. 7) Order 1987 (No. 61)	3351
Offshore Installations (Safety Zones) (No. 8) Order 1987 (No. 62)	3351
Offshore Installations (Safety Zones) (No. 9) Order 1987 (No. 66)	3351
Offshore Installations (Safety Zones) (No. 10) Order 1987 (No. 67)	3351
Offshore Installations (Safety Zones) (No. 11) Order 1987 (No. 68)	3351
Offshore Installations (Safety Zones) (No. 12) Order 1987 (No. 69)	3351
Offshore Installations (Safety Zones) (No. 13) Order 1987 (No. 70)	3351
Offshore Installations (Safety Zones) (No. 14) Order 1987 (No. 71)	3351
Offshore Installations (Safety Zones) (No. 15) Order 1987 (No. 72)	3351
Offshore Installations (Safety Zones) (No. 16) Order 1987 (No. 200)	3351
Offshore Installations (Safety Zones) (No. 17) Order 1987 (No. 201)	3351
Offshore Installations (Safety Zones) (No. 18) Order 1987 (No. 202)	3351
Offshore Installations (Safety Zones) (No. 19) Order 1987 (No. 203)	3351
Offshore Installations (Safety Zones) (No. 20) Order 1987 (No. 204)	3351
Offshore Installations (Safety Zones) (No. 21) Order 1987 (No. 205)	3351
Offshore Installations (Safety Zones) (No. 22) Order 1987 (No. 206)	3351
Offshore Installations (Safety Zones) (No. 23) Order 1987 (No. 591)	3351
Offshore Installations (Safety Zones) (No. 24) Order 1987 (No. 592)	3351
Offshore Installations (Safety Zones) (No. 25) Order 1987 (No. 593)	3351
Offshore Installations (Safety Zones) (No. 26) Order 1987 (No. 594)	3351
Offshore Installations (Safety Zones) (No. 27) Order 1987 (No. 713)	3351
Offshore Installations (Safety Zones) (No. 28) Order 1987 (No. 812)	3351
Offshore Installations (Safety Zones) (No. 29) Order 1987 (No. 813)	3351
Offshore Installations (Safety Zones) (No. 30) Order 1987 (No. 814)	3351
Offshore Installations (Safety Zones) (No. 31) Order 1987 (No. 974)	3351
Offshore Installations (Safety Zones) (No. 32) Order 1987 (No. 975)	3351
Offshore Installations (Safety Zones) (No. 33) Order 1987 (No. 976)	3351
Offshore Installations (Safety Zones) (No. 34) Order 1987 (No. 977)	3351
Offshore Installations (Safety Zones) (No. 35) Order 1987 (No. 978)	3351
Offshore Installations (Safety Zones) (No. 36) Order 1987 (No. 979)	3351
Offshore Installations (Safety Zones) (No. 37) Order 1987 (No. 980)	3351
Offshore Installations (Safety Zones) (No. 38) Order 1987 (No. 981)	3351
Offshore Installations (Safety Zones) (No. 39) Order 1987 (No. 982)	3351
Offshore Installations (Safety Zones) (No. 40) Order 1987 (No. 983)	3351
Offshore Installations (Safety Zones) (No. 41) Order 1987 (No. 984)	3351
Offshore Installations (Safety Zones) (No. 42) Order 1987 (No. 985)	3351
Offshore Installations (Safety Zones) (No. 43) Order 1987 (No. 986)	3351
Offshore Installations (Safety Zones) (No. 44) Order 1987 (No. 987)	3351
Offshore Installations (Safety Zones) (No. 45) Order 1987 (No. 988)	3351
Offshore Installations (Safety Zones) (No. 46) Order 1987 (No. 1094)	3351
Offshore Installations (Safety Zones) (No. 47) Order 1987 (No. 1095)	3351
Offshore Installations (Safety Zones) (No. 49) Order 1987 (No. 1400)	3351
Offshore Installations (Safety Zones) (No. 50) Order 1987 (No. 1401)	3351
Offshore Installations (Safety Zones) (No. 51) Order 1987 (No. 1402)	3351
Offshore Installations (Safety Zones) (No. 52) Order 1987 (No. 1403)	3351
Offshore Installations (Safety Zones) (No. 53) Order 1987 (No. 1404)	3351
Offshore Installations (Safety Zones) (No. 54) Order 1987 (No. 1405)	3351
Offshore Installations (Safety Zones) (No. 55) Order 1987 (No. 1406)	3351
Offshore Installations (Safety Zones) (No. 56) Order 1987 (No. 1407)	3351
Offshore Installations (Safety Zones) (No. 57) Order 1987 (No. 1408)	3351
Offshore Installations (Safety Zones) (No. 58) Order 1987 (No. 1409)	3351
Offshore Installations (Safety Zones) (No. 59) Order 1987 (No. 1410)	3351
Offshore Installations (Safety Zones) (No. 60) Order 1987 (No. 1411)	3351
Offshore Installations (Safety Zones) (No. 61) Order 1987 (No. 1412)	3351
Offshore Installations (Safety Zones) (No. 62) Order 1987 (No. 1413)	3351
Offshore Installations (Safety Zones) (No. 63) Order 1987 (No. 1414)	3351
Offshore Installations (Safety Zones) (No. 64) Order 1987 (No. 1415)	3351
Offshore Installations (Safety Zones) (No. 65) Order 1987 (No. 1416)	3351
Offshore Installations (Safety Zones) (No. 67) Order 1987 (No. 1418)	3351
Offshore Installations (Safety Zones) (No. 68) Order 1987 (No. 1419)	3351
Offshore Installations (Safety Zones) (No. 69) Order 1987 (No. 1420)	3351
Offshore Installations (Safety Zones) Orders made under the Petroleum Act 1987 (c.12), s.22(1)(2):	
Offshore Installations (Safety Zones) (No. 48) Order 1987 (No. 1332)	3351

SEA AND SEASHORE—*cont.*

C.L.Y.
Offshore Installations (Safety Zones) (No. 70) Order 1987 (No. 2016) 3351
Offshore Installations (Safety Zones) (No. 71) Order 1987 (No. 2017) 3351
Offshore Installations (Safety Zones) (Revocation) Orders made under the Oil and Gas (Enterprise) Act 1982 (c.23), s.21(1):
Offshore Installations (Safety Zones) (Revocation) Order 1987 (No. 53) 3352
Offshore Installations (Safety Zones) (Revocation) (No. 2) Order 1987 (No. 199) 3352
Offshore Installations (Safety Zones) (Revocation) (No. 3) Order 1987 (No. 595) 3352
Offshore Installations (Safety Zones) (Revocation) (No. 4) Order 1987 (No. 989) 3352
Offshore Installations (Safety Zones) (Revocation) (No. 5) Order 1987 (No. 1399) 3352
Oil and Gas (Enterprise) Act 1982 (Commencement No. 4) Order 1987 (No. 2272 (c.69)) 3354
Territorial Sea Act 1987 (Commencement) Order 1987 (No. 1270 (c.40)) 3357
Territorial Sea (Limits) Order 1987 (No. 1269) 3355

SHERIFF COURT PRACTICE (SCOTLAND ONLY)

Debtors (Scotland) Act 1987 (Commencement No. 1) Order 1987 (No. 1838) (C. 55) 5014

SHIPPING AND MARINE INSURANCE

Admiralty Jurisdiction (Gibraltar) Order 1987 (No. 1263) 3359
Carriage of Passengers and their Luggage by Sea (Domestic Carriage) Order 1987 (No. 670) 3377
Carriage of Passengers and their Luggage by Sea (Notice) Order 1987 (No. 703) 3377
Carriage of Passengers and their Luggage by Sea (Parties to Convention) Order 1987 (No. 931) 3377
Carriage of Passengers and their Luggage by Sea (United Kingdom Carriers) Order 1987 (No. 855) 3377
Control of Pollution (Landed Ships' Waste) Regulations 1987 (No. 402) 3398
Harbour Authorities (Teignmouth) (Constitution) Order 1987 (No. 222) 3403
Hovercraft (Civil Liability) (Amendment) Order 1987 (No. 1835) 3404
Hovercraft (Fees) Regulations 1987 (No. 1637) 3404
Hovercraft (Fees) (Amendment) Regulations 1987 (No. 136) 3404
Jersey (Navigator Hyperbolic System) Order 1987 (No. 171) 3418
London Pilotage (Amendment) Order 1987 (No. 1143) 3419
Lowestoft Pilotage (Amendment) Order 1987 (No. 1484) 3419
Manchester Ship Canal Revision Order 1987 (No. 1790) 3403
Merchant Shipping Act 1979 (Commencement No. 11) Order 1987 (No. 635 (C.16)) 3416
Merchant Shipping Act 1979 (Commencement No. 12) Order 1987 (No. 719 (C.18)) 3416
Merchant Shipping (BCH Code) Regulations 1987 (No. 550) 3414
Merchant Shipping (Certification of Deck and Marine Engineer Officers and Licensing of Marine Engine Operators) (Amendment) Regulations 1987 (No. 884) 3414
Merchant Shipping (Closing of Openings in Hulls and in Watertight Bulkheads) Regulations 1987 (No. 1298) 3414
Merchant Shipping (Confirmation of Legislation) (Anguilla) Order 1987 (No. 932) 3414
Merchant Shipping (Confirmation of Legislation) (Cayman Islands) Order 1987 (No. 1267) 3414
Merchant Shipping (Confirmation of Legislation) (Falkland Islands) Order 1987 (No. 1827) 3414
Merchant Shipping (Confirmation of Legislation) (Gibraltar) Order 1987 (No. 933) 3414
Merchant Shipping (Control of Pollution by Noxious Liquid Substances in Bulk) Regulations 1987 (No. 551) 3414
Merchant Shipping (Fees) Regulations 1987 (No. 63) 3402
Merchant Shipping (Fees) (Amendment) Regulations 1987 (No. 548) 3414
Merchant Shipping (Fees) (Amendment) (No. 2) Regulations 1987 (No. 854) 3414
Merchant Shipping (Fees) (Amendment) (No. 3) Regulations 1987 (No. 2113) 3414
Merchant Shipping (Fishing Boats Registry) (Amendment) Order 1987 (No. 1284) 3414
Merchant Shipping (IBC Code) Regulations 1987 (No. 549) 3414
Merchant Shipping (Indemnification of Shipowners) Order 1987 (No. 220) 3414
Merchant Shipping (Light Dues) (Amendment) Regulations 1987 (No. 244) 3414
Merchant Shipping (Light Dues) (Amendment No. 2) Regulations 1987 (No. 746) 3414
Merchant Shipping (Passenger Ship Construction) (Amendment) Regulations 1987 (No. 1886) 3414
Merchant Shipping (Pilot Ladders and Hoists) Regulations 1987 (No. 1961) 3414
Merchant Shipping (Prevention and Control of Pollution) Order 1987 (No. 470) 3414
Merchant Shipping (Prevention and Control of Pollution) (Hong Kong) Order 1987 (No. 664) 3415
Merchant Shipping (Reporting of Pollution Incidents) Regulations 1987 (No. 586) 3414
Merchant Shipping (Seamen's Documents) Regulations 1987 (No. 408) 3414
Merchant Shipping (Smooth and Partially Smooth Waters) Regulations 1987 (No. 1591) 3414
Merchant Shipping (Submersible Craft) (Amendment) Regulations 1987 (No. 306) 3414
Merchant Shipping (Submersible Craft Operations) Regulations 1987 (No. 311) 3414
Merchant Shipping (Submersible Craft Operations) (Amendment) Regulations 1987 (No. 1603) 3414
Newlyn Pier and Harbour Revision Order 1987 (No. 2095) 3403
Padstow Harbour Revision Order 1987 (No. 420) 3403
Pilotage Act 1987 (Commencement No. 1) Order 1987 (No. 1306) (c.41) 3421
Pilotage Act 1987 (Commencement No. 2) Order 1987 (No. 2138 (c.63)) 3421
Pilotage Act 1987 (Pilots' National Pension Fund) Order 1987 (No. 2139) 3419
Pilotage Commission Provision of Funds Scheme 1987 (Confirmation) Order 1987 (No. 295) 3419

SHIPPING AND MARINE INSURANCE—*cont.*

C.L.Y.
Scalloway, Shetland, Pilotage Order 1987 (No. 1756) 3419, 5136
Scottish Transport Group (Scalasaig Pier) Harbour Revision Order 1987 (No. 1016) 5139
Sullom Voe, Shetland, Pilotage (Amendment) Order 1987 (No. 843) 3419, 5136
Warkworth Harbour Revision Order 1987 (No. 1514) 3403

SHOPS, MARKETS AND FAIRS

London City Airport Shops Order 1987 (No. 1983) 3448
Sumburgh Airport Shops Order 1987 (No. 837) 3448, 5141

SOCIAL SECURITY

Child Benefit (General) Amendment Regulations 1987 (No. 357) 3459
Family Credit (General) Regulations 1987 (No. 1973) 3468
Family Credit (Transitional) Regulations 1987 (No. 1974) 3468
Family Income Supplements (Computation) Regulations 1987 (No. 32) 3469
Family Income Supplements (General) Amendment Regulations 1987 (No. 281) 3469
Income Support (General) Regulations 1987 (No. 1967) 3475
Income Support (Transitional) Regulations 1987 (No. 1969) 3475
National Assistance (Charges for Accommodation) Regulations 1987 (No. 370) 3493
National Assistance (Charges for Accommodation) (Scotland) Regulations 1987 (No. 364) 5151
Pensioners' Lump Sum Payments Order 1987 (No. 1305) 3496
Pneumoconiosis, Byssinosis and Miscellaneous Diseases Benefit (Amendment) Scheme 1987 (No. 400) 3478
Social Fund (Maternity and Funeral Expenses) (General) Regulations 1987 (No. 481) 3484
Social Fund (Maternity and Funeral Expenses) (Northern Ireland) Order 1987 (No. 464) (N.I.8) 2741a
Social Security Act 1986 (Commencement No. 5) Order 1987 (No. 354) 3561
Social Security Act 1986 (Commencement No. 6) Order 1987 (No. 543) (c.12) 3501
Social Security Act 1986 (Commencement No. 7) Order 1987 (No. 1096 (c.28)) 3501
Social Security Act 1986 (Commencement No. 8) Order 1987 (No. 1853 (c.56)) 3501
Social Security (Adjudication) Amendment Regulations 1987 (No. 1424) 3451
Social Security (Adjudication) Amendment (No. 2) Regulations 1987 (No. 1970) 3451
Social Security (Attendance Allowance) Amendment Regulations 1987 (No. 1426) 3452
Social Security (Australia) Order 1987 (No. 935) 3455
Social Security (Austria) Order 1987 (No. 1830) 3456
Social Security Benefit (Computation of Earnings) Amendment Regulations 1987 (No. 606) 3462
Social Security Benefit (Dependency) Amendment Regulations 1987 (No. 355) 3465
Social Security Benefits Up-rating Order 1987 (No. 45) 3452
Social Security Benefits Up-rating (No. 2) Order 1987 (No. 1978) 3542
Social Security Benefits Up-rating Regulations 1987 (No. 327) 3542
Social Security (Claims and Payments) Regulations 1987 (No. 1968) 3460
Social Security (Claims and Payments) Amendment Regulations 1987 (No. 878) 3460
Social Security Commissioners Procedure Regulations 1987 (No. 214) 3461
Social Security (Contributions) Amendment Regulations 1987 (No. 106) 3463
Social Security (Contributions) Amendment (No. 2) Regulations 1987 (No. 413) 3463
Social Security (Contributions) Amendment (No. 3) Regulations 1987 (No. 1590) 3463
Social Security (Contributions) Amendment (No. 4) Regulations 1987 (No. 2111) 3463
Social Security (Contributions, Re-rating) Order 1987 (No. 46) 3463
Social Security (Credits) Amendment Regulations 1987 (No. 414) 3464
Social Security (Credits) Amendment (No. 2) Regulations 1987 (No. 687) 3464
Social Security (Earnings Factor) Amendment Regulations 1987 (No. 316) 3467
Social Security (Earnings Factor) Amendment (No. 2) Regulations 1987 (No. 411) 3467
Social Security (Hospital In-Patients) Amendment Regulations 1987 (No. 31) 3472
Social Security (Hospital In-Patients) Amendment (No. 2) Regulations 1987 (No. 1683) 3472
Social Security (Industrial Injuries) (Prescribed Diseases) Amendment Regulations 1987 (No. 335) 3478
Social Security (Industrial Injuries) (Prescribed Diseases) Amendment (No. 2) Regulations 1987 (No. 2112) 3478
Social Security (Industrial Injuries) (Reduced Earnings Allowance and Transitional) Regulations 1987 (No. 415) 3478
Social Security (Medical Evidence) Amendment Regulations 1987 (No. 409) 3487
Social Security (Notification of Deaths) Regulations 1987 (No. 250) 3494
Social Security (Payments on Account, Overpayments and Recovery) Regulations 1987 (No. 491) 3495
Social Security (Portugal) Order 1987 (No. 1831) 3498
Social Security Revaluation of Earnings Factors Order 1987 (No. 861) 3467
Social Security (Treasury Supplement to and Allocation of Contributions) (Re-rating) Order 1987 (No. 48) 3532
Social Security (Unemployment, Sickness and Invalidity Benefit) Amendment Regulations 1987 (No. 317) 3541

SOCIAL SECURITY—*cont.*

C.L.Y.
Social Security (Unemployment, Sickness and Invalidity Benefit) Amendment (No. 2) Regulations 1987 (No. 688) 3541
Social Security (Widow's Benefit) Transitional Regulations 1987 (No. 1692) 3543
Social Security (Widow's Benefit and Retirement Pensions) Amendment Regulations 1987 (No. 1854) . 3543
Supplementary Benefit (Conditions of Entitlement) Amendment Regulations 1987 (No. 358) 3507
Supplementary Benefit (Housing Requirements and Resources) Amendment Regulations 1987 (No. 17) 3508
Supplementary Benefit (Requirements) Amendment Regulations 1987 (No. 2193) 3513
Supplementary Benefit (Requirements and Resources) Amendment and Uprating Regulations 1987 (No. 659) 3514
Supplementary Benefit (Requirements and Resources) Amendment Regulations 1987 (No. 1325) 3514
Supplementary Benefit (Resources) Amendment Regulations 1987) (No. 660) 3515
Supplementary Benefit (Single Payments) Amendment Regulations 1987 (No. 36) 3528
Supplementary Benefit (Single Payments) Amendment (No. 2) Regulations 1987 (No. 2010) 3528
Supplementary Benefit Up-rating Regulations 1987 (No. 49) 3530
Workmen's Compensation (Supplementation) Amendment Scheme 1987 (No. 419) 3544
Workmen's Compensation (Supplementation) Amendment (No. 2) Scheme 1987 (No. 429) 3544

SOLICITORS

Scottish Solicitors' Discipline Tribunal (Increase of Maximum Fine) Order 1987 (No. 333) 5157

STAMP DUTIES

Stamp Duty (Exempt Instruments) Regulations 1987 (No. 516) 3564
Stamp Duty Reserve Tax (Interest on Tax Repaid) Order 1987 (No. 514) 3565
Stamp Duty Reserve Tax (Interest on Tax Repaid) (No. 2) Order 1987 (No. 888) 3565
Stamp Duty Reserve Tax (Interest on Tax Repaid) (No. 3) Order 1987 (No. 1494) 3565
Stamp Duty Reserve Tax (Interest on Tax Repaid) (No. 4) Order 1987 (No. 1990) 3565

STOCK EXCHANGE

Stock Transfer (Gilt-edged Securities) (CGO Service) (Amendment) Regulations 1987 (No. 1293) 3569
Stock Transfer (Gilt-edged Securities) (Exempt Transfer) Regulations 1987 (No. 1294) 3569

TELECOMMUNICATIONS

Broadcasting Act 1981 (Channel Islands) Order 1987 (No. 2205) 3571
Broadcasting (Extension of Duration of IBA's Function) Order 1987 (No. 673) 3573
Cable and Broadcasting Act 1984 (Commencement No. 3) Order 1987 (No. 672 (C.17)) 3574
Public Telecommunication System Designation (British Cable Services Limited) Order 1987 (No. 827) .. 3575
Public Telecommunications System Designation (Kingston upon Hull City Council and Kingston Communications (Hull) PLC) Order 1987 (No. 2094) 3575
Public Telecommunication System Designation (Swindon Cable Limited) Order 1987 (No. 3) 3575
Wireless Telegraphy (Cordless Telephone Apparatus) (Restriction) Order 1987 (No. 774) 3578
Wireless Telegraphy (Exemption) (Amendment) (Cordless Telephone Apparatus) Regulations 1987 (No. 775) 3578
Wireless Telegraphy (Exemption) (Amendment) (Model Control Apparatus) Regulations 1987 (No. 776) 3578

TORT

Consumer Protection Act 1987 (Commencement No. 1) Order 1987 (No. 1680) (C.51) 3584

TOWN AND COUNTRY PLANNING

Black Country Development Corporation (Area and Constitution) Order 1987 (No. 922) 3726
Black Country Development Corporation (Planning Functions) Order 1987 (No. 1340) 3661
Cardiff Bay Development Corporation (Area and Constitution) Order 1987 (No. 646) 3726
Gipsy Encampments (Borough of Great Yarmouth) Order 1987 (No. 1709) 3642
Gipsy Encampments (Borough of Kettering) Order 1987 (No. 1639) 3642
Gipsy Encampments (City of Lancaster) Order 1987 (No. 556) 3642
Gipsy Encampments (County of Northumberland) Order 1987 (No. 1640) 3642
Gipsy Encampments (Designation of the Borough of Maidstone) Order 1987 (No. 73) 3642
Gipsy Encampments (District of Cherwell) Order 1987 (No. 1641) 3642
Peterborough New Town (Exclusion of Land) Order 1987 (No. 104) 3655
Teesside Development Corporation (Area and Constitution) Order 1987 (No. 923) 3661
Town and Country Planning Appeals (Determination by Appointed Person) (Inquiries Procedure) (Scotland) Amendment Rules 1987 (No. 1522) 5195
Town and Country Planning (Appeals) (Written Representations Procedure) Regulations 1987 (No. 701) 3597

TOWN AND COUNTRY PLANNING—*cont.*

C.L.Y.
Town and Country Planning (Black Country Urban Development Area) Special Development Order 1987 (No. 1343) 3726
Town and Country Planning (British Coal Corporation) (Amendment) Regulations 1987 (No. 1936) 3599
Town and Country Planning (British Coal Corporation) (Scotland) Amendment Regulation 1987 (No. 1937) 5197
Town and Country Planning (Control of Advertisements) (Amendment) Regulations 1987 (No. 804) 3594
Town and Country Planning (Control of Advertisements) (Amendment No. 2) Regulations 1987 (No. 2227) 3594
Town and Country Planning (Determination of Appeals by Appointed Persons) (Prescribed Classes) (Scotland) Regulations 1987 (No. 1531) 5191
Town and Country Planning (Fees for Applications and Deemed Applications) (Amendment) Regulations 1987 (No. 101) 3639
Town and Country Planning General Development (Amendment) Order 1987 (No. 702) 3640
Town and Country Planning General Development (Amendment) (No. 2) Order 1987 (No. 765) 3640
Town and Country Planning (Listed Buildings and Buildings in Conservation Areas) Regulations 1987 (No. 349) 3648
Town and Country Planning (Listed Buildings and Buildings in Conservation Areas) (Scotland) Regulations 1987 (No. 1529) 5196
Town and Country Planning (Minerals) Act 1981 (Commencement No. 4) (Scotland) Order 1987 (No. 2002) 5203
Town and Country Planning (Simplified Planning Zones) (Excluded Development) Order 1987 (No. 1849) 3719
Town and Country Planning (Simplified Planning Zones) Regulations 1987 (No. 1750) 3719
Town and Country Planning (Simplified Planning Zones) (Scotland) Regulations 1987 (No. 1532) 5202
Town and Country Planning (Structure and Local Plans) (Amendment) Regulations 1987 (No. 1760) 3722
Town and Country Planning (Teesside Urban Development Area) Special Development Order 1987 (No. 1344) 3726
Town and Country Planning (Trafford Park Urban Development Area) Special Development Order 1987 (No. 738) 3723
Town and Country Planning (Tyne and Wear Urban Development Area) Special Development Order 1987 (No. 1345) 3726
Town and Country Planning (Use Classes) Order 1987 (No. 764) 3728
Trafford Park Development Corporation (Area and Constitution) Order 1987 (No. 179) 3601
Trafford Park Development Corporation (Planning Functions) Order 1987 (No. 739) 3723
Tyne and Wear Development Corporation (Area and Constitution) Order 1987 (No. 924) 3726
Tyne and Wear Development Corporation (Planning Functions) Order 1987 (No. 1342) 3661
Wakefield (Derelict Land Clearance Area) Order 1987 (No. 1653) 3600

TRADE AND INDUSTRY

Industrial Assurance (Fees) Regulations 1987 (No. 377) 3730
Industrial Training Levy (Clothing and Allied Products) Order 1987 (No. 1534) 3731
Industrial Training Levy (Construction Board) Order 1987 (No. 29) 3731
Industrial Training Levy (Engineering Board) Order 1987 (No. 607) 3731
Industrial Training Levy (Hotel and Catering) Order 1987 (No. 896) 3731
Industrial Training Levy (Plastics Processing) Order 1987 (No. 717) 3731
Industrial Training Levy (Road Transport) Order 1987) (No. 1964) 3731
Industry Act 1972 (Amendment) Regulations 1987 (No. 1807) 3733
Industry Act 1980 (Increase of Limit) Order 1987 (No. 520) 3734
Statistics of Trade Act 1947 (Amendment of Schedule) Order 1987 (No. 669) 3739

TRADE MARKS AND TRADE NAMES

Counterfeit Goods (Consequential Provisions) Regulations 1987 (No. 1521) 3745
Hallmarking (International Convention) (Amendment) Order 1987 (No. 1892) 3747
Trade Marks and Service Marks (Fees) Rules 1987 (No. 751) 3746
Trade Marks and Service Marks (Fees) (Amendment) Rules 1987 (No. 964) 3757
Trade Marks and Service Marks (Relevant Countries) (Amendment) Order 1987 (No. 170) 3757

TRADE UNIONS

Certification Officer (Amendment of Fees) Regulations 1987 (No. 258) 3761

TRANSPORT

Bridges

Bedfordshire County Council (Leighton-Linslade Southern Bypass Yttingaford Bridge) Number Two Scheme 1985 Confirmation Instrument 1987 (No. 1954) 3773
Buckinghamshire County Council H8 Standing Way (Canal Bridge) Scheme 1987 Confirmation Instrument 1987 (No.2241) 3773

TRANSPORT—*cont.*

Cheshire County Council (Forrest Way Bridge, Warrington) Scheme 1986 Confirmation Instrument 1987 (No. 544) 3773
County Council of Humberside (Stoneferry Bridge, Kingston Upon Hull) Scheme 1987 Confirmation Instrument 1987 (No. 2084) 3773
County Council of West Midlands (Black Country Route) (Bridge over Birmingham Canal (Wolverhampton Level) Scheme 1985 Confirmation Instrument 1987 (No. 251) 3773
Devon County Council (Exeter, River Exe Bridge) Scheme 1985 Confirmation Instrument 1987 (No. 791) 3773
Essex County Council (Maldon Bypass) (Blackwater Canal Bridge) Scheme 1986 Confirmation Instrument 1987 (No. 945) 3773
Essex County Council (Maldon Bypass) (Chelmer Viaduct) Scheme 1986 Confirmation Instrument 1987 (No. 946) 3773
Essex County Council (Maldon Bypass) (Whiteladies Canal Bridge) Scheme 1986 Confirmation Instrument 1987 (No. 947) 3773

Bus companies

Bus Companies (Dissolution) Order 1987 (No. 1613) 3774

Channel Tunnel

Channel Tunnel Act (Competition) Order 1987 (No. 2068) 3775

International passenger services

Road Transport (International Passenger Services) (Amendment) Regulations 1987 (No. 1755) 3780

Light railways

Derwent Valley Railway (Transfer) Light Railway Order 1987 (No. 75) 3781
North Norfolk (Extension and Amendment) Light Railway Order 1987 (No. 950) 3781
South Tynedale Railway (Light Railway) Order 1987 (No. 1984) 3781
Swanage Light Railway Order 1987 (No. 1443) 3781
Yorkshire Dales Light Railway Order 1987 (No. 1088) 3781

Special roads

A41 (M) Watford-Tring Motorway and Connecting Roads (Tring Bypass Section) (Partial Revocation) Scheme 1987 (No. 1070) 3787
A423 (M) Motorway (Maidenhead Thicket Section) and Connecting Roads Scheme 1987 (No. 1867) 3787
County Council of West Midlands (M6 Motorway Junction 10) (Connecting Road) Scheme 1985 Confirmation Instrument 1987 (No. 252) 3787
Knowsley Metropolitan Borough Council (M57 Motorway Associated Special Roads) (Huyton Spur) Revocation Scheme 1987 Confirmation Instrument 1987 (No. 1441) 3787
M1 Motorway (Catthorpe Interchange) Connecting Roads Scheme 1987 (No. 2253) 3787
M3 Motorway (Compton-Bassett Section) Connecting Roads Scheme 1987 (No. 1368) 3787
M3 Motorway (Compton-Bassett Section (Revocation) Scheme 1987 (No. 1369) 3787
M3 Motorway (Compton-Bassett Section) (Revocation) (No. 2) Scheme 1987 (No. 1370) 3787
M3 Motorway (Compton-Bassett Section) Scheme 1987 (No. 1367) 3787
M3 Motorway (Hockley-Compton Section) (Revocation) Scheme 1987 (No. 1371) 3787
M3 Motorway (Popham-Hockley Section) (Variation) Scheme 1987 (No. 1372) 3787
M6 Motorway (Catthorpe Interchange) Connecting Roads Scheme 1987 (No. 2254) 3787
M20 Motorway (Maidstone East Interchange) Connecting Roads Scheme 1987 (No. 1429) 3783
M40 London–Oxford–Birmingham Motorway (Waterstock to Warwick Section) and Connecting Roads (No. 1) Scheme 1984 Variation Scheme 1987 (No. 1057) 3787

Taxis

Heathrow Taxi Sharing Scheme Order 1987 (No. 784) 3788

Transport Act 1985

Transport Act 1985 (Commencement No. 7) Order 1987 (No. 1228) (C.34) 3792
Transport Act 1985 (Modifications in Schedule 4 to the Transport Act 1968) (Amendment) Order 1987 (No. 337) 3791

Trunk roads

A4 Trunk Road (Great West Road, Hounslow) (Prescribed Routes) Order 1987 (No. 1432) 3793
A6 London–Inverness Trunk Road (Kettering Southern Bypass) Order 1987 (No. 1693) 3793
A6 London–Inverness Trunk Road (Rothwell Interchange) Order 1987 (No. 2257) 3793
A10 Trunk Road (Great Cambridge Road, Enfield) (Prohibition of Cycling and of Horse Riding in Subways) Order 1987 (No. 2134) 3793
A11 London–Norwich Trunk Road (Thetford Bypass) Order 1987 (No. 1731) 3793
A13 Trunk Road (Ripple Road, Barking and Dagenham) (Prohibition of Use of Gaps in Central Reservation) Order 1987 (No. 13) 3793

TRANSPORT—*cont.*

Trunk roads—cont.

(A16) Norman Cross–Grimsby Trunk Road (Diversion between London Road, Boston and Algarkirk) (Variation) Order 1987 (No. 546) 3793
A17–King's Lynn–Sleaford–Newark Trunk Road (Long Sutton–Sutton Bridge Bypass) Order 1987 (No. 326) 3793
A17–King's Lynn–Sleaford–Newark Trunk Road (Long Sutton–Sutton Bridge Bypass Detrunking) Order 1987 (No. 328) 3793
(A19) East of Snaith–Sunderland Trunk Road (A19/A1290 Downhill Junction and Slip Roads) Order 1987 (No. 2148) 3793
A19–East of Snaith–York–Thirsk–Stockton-on-Tees–Sunderland Trunk Road (Burnhope Way Roundabout Grade Separated Junction) Order 1987 (No. 699) 3793
A20 Trunk Road (Sidcup Bypass, Bexley and Bromley) (Prescribed Routes) Order 1987 (No. 1542) 3793
A34 Winchester–Preston Trunk Road (Peartree Hill Slip Roads) Order 1987 (No. 146) 3793
A40 London–Fishguard Trunk Road (Swakeleys Road Junction Improvement Trunk Road and Slip Roads) Order 1987 (No. 490) 3793
A41 London–Birmingham Trunk Road (Bicester Bypass) Order 1987 (No. 1931) 3793
A41 London–Birmingham Trunk Road (North Street to Graven Hill, Bicester) (Detrunking) Order 1987 (No. 1930) 3793
A41 Trunk Road (Edgware Way, Barnet) (Prescribed Routes) Order 1987 (No. 998) 3793
A41 Trunk Road (Watford Way, Barnet) (Prescribed Routes) Order 1987 (No. 1048) 3793
A43 Oxford–Market Deeping Trunk Road (Kettering Northern Bypass) Order 1987 (No. 1694) 3793
A49–Shrewsbury–Whitchurch–Warrington Trunk Road (Prees By-Pass) Order 1987 (No. 707) 3793
A52 Nottingham–West of Grantham Trunk Road (Bottesford Bypass) Order 1987 (No. 1025) 3793
A52 Nottingham–West of Grantham Trunk Toad (Bottesford Bypass) Detrunking Order 1987 (No. 1026) 3793
(A64) Leeds–York–Scarborough Trunk Road (Copmanthorpe Grade Separated Junction) (Trunking) Order 1987 (No. 2274) 3793
(A65) Liverpool–Preston–Leeds Trunk Road (Addingham Bypass) Order 1987 (No. 1333) 3793
(A65) Liverpool–Preston–Leeds Trunk Road (Heathness Gill to Lumb Gill Lane) (Detrunking) Order 1987 (No. 1334) 3793
A65 Skipton–Kendal Trunk Road (Whoop Hall Diversion) Order 1987 (No. 1491) 3793
(A168) Boroughbridge–Thirsk Trunk Road (Dishforth Interchange, Slip Roads and Link Roads) Order 1987 (No. 1353) 3793
A316–(County of Surrey Boundary to M3 Trunking) Order 1987 (No. 720) 3793
A316 Trunk Road (Twickenham Road, Richmond Upon Thames) (Prescribed Routes) Order 1987 (No. 105) 3793
A404 Burchetts Green to M40 (Trunking and Slip Roads) Order 1987 (No. 1866) 3793
A406 Trunk Road (Angel Road, Enfield) (Prescribed Routes) Order 1987 (No. 1380) 3793
A406 Trunk Road (Hanger Lane, Ealing) (Prohibition of Left Turn) Order 1987 (No. 617) 3793
A421 (Wendlebury to Bicester Section, Trunking) Order 1987 (No. 1582) 3793
A423 West of Maidenhead–Oxford Trunk Road (Burchetts Green to A4142 Heyford Hill Roundabout) Detrunking Order 1987 (No. 1868) 3793
A423 West of Maidenhead–Oxford Trunk Road (Maidenhead Thicket–Burchetts Green Section) Detrunking Order 1987 (No. 1865) 3793
A423 West of Maidenhead–Oxford Trunk Road (Maidenhead Thicket–Burchetts Green Section) and Slip Roads Order 1987 (No. 1864) 3793
A452–London–Holyhead Trunk Road (Detrunking from Streetly to Erdington) Order 1987 (No. 531) 3793
A453–North East of Birmingham–Nottingham Trunk Road (Appleby Magna to Asbhy-de-la-Zouch) Detrunking Order 1987 (No. 523) 3793
A604 Catthorpe–Harwich Trunk Road (Catthorpe to Rothwell Section and Slip Roads) Order 1987 (No. 2256) 3793
A604 Catthorpe–Harwich Trunk Road (Kettering to Thrapston Section and Slip Roads) Order 1987 (No. 1695) 3793
A604–Catthorpe–Harwich Trunk Road (Thrapston to Brampton Section and Slip Roads) Order (No. 2) 1987 (No. 840) 3793
Bath–Lincoln Trunk Road (Alcester Bypasses A435/A422) Order 1987 (No. 2261) 3793
Bath–Lincoln Trunk Road A46 (Upper Swainswick to A420 Cold Ashton Roundabout) Order 1987 (No. 1799) 3793
Bath–Lincoln Trunk Road A46 (Upper Swainswick to A420 Cold Ashton Roundabout) (Detrunking) Order 1987 (No. 1800) 3793
Bath–Lincoln Trunk Road (A439) (Norton to Stratford-upon-Avon) Detrunking Order 1987 (No. 2262) 3793
Bath to West of Southampton Trunk Road A36 (Beckington Bypass) Order 1987 (No. 2101) 3793
Bath to West of Southampton Trunk Road A36 (Beckington Bypass) (Detrunking) Order 1987 (No. 2102) 3793
Birmingham–Great Yarmouth Trunk Road (High House and Other Diversions) (Amendment) Order 1987 (No. 100) 3793
Carlisle–Sunderland Trunk Road (A69) (Brampton Bypass) Order 1987 (No. 1205) 3793

TRANSPORT—*cont.*

Trunk roads—cont.

County Council of Hampshire (M275 Rudmore Flyover Portsmouth) Motorway Scheme 1987 Confirmation Instrument 1987 (No. 2147) 3793
Evesham–Birmingham Principal Road (A435) (Alcester to Portway) Trunking Order 1987 (No. 2264) 3793
Evesham–Birmingham Principal Road (A435) (Norton to Arrow) Trunking Order 1987 (No. 2265) 3793
Exeter–Launceston–Bodmin Trunk Road (A30) (Alder Quarry Realignment) Order 1987 (No. 1570) 3793
Exeter–Launceston–Bodmin Trunk Road A30 (Launceston to Plusha Improvement and Slip Roads) Order 1987 (No. 1701) 3793
Fishguard–Bangor (Menai Suspension Bridge) Trunk Road (Cardigan Bypass) Order 1987 (No. 2194) 3793
Folkestone–Honiton Trunk Road (A27 Pevensey Bypass and Slip Road) Order 1987 (No. 1431) 3793
Folkestone–Honiton Trunk Road A35 (Axminster Bypass and Slip Road) Order 1987 (No. 2267) 3793
Folkestone–Honiton Trunk Road A35 (Axminster Bypass and Slip Road) (Detrunking) Order 1987 (No. 2268) 3793
Folkestone–Honiton Trunk Road (Dittons–Pevensey Section DeTrunking) Order 1987 (No. 1430) 3793
Hungerford–Hereford Trunk Road (A419) (Stratton St. Margaret Bypass Slip Roads) Order 1987 (No. 1435) 3793
Leicester–Great Yarmouth Trunk Road (A47) (Guyhirn Diversion) Order 1987 (No. 2036) 3793
Leicester–Great Yarmouth Trunk Road (A47) (Detrunking at Guyhirn) Order 1987 (No. 2037) 3793
Leicester–Great Yarmouth Trunk Road (A47) (Guyhirn Diversion) (River Nene Bridge) Order 1987 (No. 2038) 3793
London–Brighton Trunk Road (A23 Albourne (B2116)–Muddleswood) Order 1987 (No. 1861) 3793
London–Brighton Trunk Road (A23 Hickstead) Order 1987 (No. 472) 3793
London–Brighton Trunk Road (A23 Hickstead Slip Roads) Order 1987 (No. 473) 3793
London–Brighton Trunk Road (A23 Muddleswood Slip Roads) Order 1987 (No. 1862) 3793
London–Brighton Trunk Road (A23 Warninglid Flyover–South of Bolney) Order 1987 (No. 474) 3793
London–Brighton Trunk Road (Sayers Common–Muddleswood DeTrunking) Order 1987 (No. 1863) 3793
London–Fishguard Trunk Road (A48) and Newhouse–High Beech Principal Road (A466) (County of Gwent) Order 1987 (No. 322) 3793
London–Fishguard Trunk Road (A48) (County of Mid Glamorgan) Detrunking Order 1987 (No. 321) 3793
London–Fishguard Trunk Road (A48) (County of South Glamorgan) and Cardiff–Glan Conwy Trunk Road (A470) (County of South Glamorgan) Detrunking Order 1987 (No. 320) 3793
London–Fishguard Trunk Road (A48) (County of West Glamorgan) and Swansea–Manchester Trunk Road (A483) (Penllergaer Roundabout, M4 to A483/A4070 Ivorites Junction) Detrunking Order 1987 (No. 319) 3793
London–Fishguard Trunk Road (Flether Hill–Southleys Improvement) Order 1987 (No. 1784) 3793
London–Fishguard Trunk Road (Nant-Y-Caws-Coed-Hirion Bypass) Order 1987 (No. 1932) 3793
London–Great Yarmouth Trunk Road A12 (Saxmundham Bypass, Suffolk) Order 1987 (No. 1013) 3793
London–Holyhead Trunk Road A5 (Chirk Bypass) Order 1987 (No. 1037) 3793
London–Holyhead Trunk Road A5 (Rhoswiel–Whitehurst Detrunking) Order 1987 (No. 1038) 3793
London–Penzance Trunk Road A303 (Ilchester–South Petherton and Slip Roads) Order 1987 (No. 1632) 3793
London–Penzance Trunk Road A303 (Ilchester–South Petherton and Slip Roads) (Detrunking) Order 1987 (No. 1633) 3793
London–Penzance Trunk Toad A303 (Sparkford Bypass) Order 1987 (No. 792) 3793
London–Penzance Trunk Road A303 (Sparkford Bypass) (Detrunking) Order 1987 (No. 793) 3793
London–Portsmouth Trunk Road A3 (Ham Barn–Petersfield Section) Order 1987 (No. 1580) 3793
London–Portsmouth Trunk Road A3 (Ham Barn–Petersfield Section Slip Roads) Order 1987 (No. 1581) 3793
North East of Birmingham–Nottingham Trunk Road–Birmingham–Nottingham Route (Appleby Magna to Kegworth Section and Slip Roads) (Variation) Order 1987 (No. 522) 3793
North East of Birmingham–Nottingham Trunk Road–Birmingham–Nottingham Route (Ashby-de-la-Zouch Slip Roads) Order 1987 (No. 521) 3793
North of Newcastle-under-Lyme–Tarvin Trunk Road (A51 Diversion North of Hurleston) Order 1987 (No. 990) 3793
Queensferry–South of Birkenhead Trunk Road (A550–Ledsham Station Diversion) Order 1987 (No. 2074) 3793
Swansea–Manchester Trunk Road A483 (Improvement at Boundary Terrace Llandrindod Wells) Order 1987 (No. 1470) 3793
Swansea–Manchester Trunk Road (Newbridge, Ruabon and Johnstown Bypass and Slip Roads) Order 1982 (Variation) Order 1987 (No. 285) 3793
West of Southampton–Bath Trunk Road A36 (Steeple Langford Bypass) Order 1987 (No. 1442) 3793
Worcester–Banbury Principal Road (A422) (South and East of Alcester) Trunking Order 1987 (No. 2263) 3793

VALUE ADDED TAX

Value Added Tax (Betting, Gaming and Lotteries) Order 1987 (No. 517) 3801
Value Added Tax (Cash Accounting) Regulations 1987 (No. 1427) 3802
Value Added Tax (Charities) Order 1987 (No. 437) 3803
Value Added Tax (Construction of Buildings) Order 1987 (No. 781) 3804

VALUE ADDED TAX—*cont.*

Value Added Tax (Construction of Buildings) (No. 2) Order 1987 (No. 1072) 3804
Value Added Tax (Education) Order 1987 (No. 1259) 3809
Value Added Tax (Finance) Order 1987 (No. 860) 3812
Value Added Tax (General) (Amendment) Regulations 1987 (No. 150) 3811
Value Added Tax (General) (Amendment) (No. 2) Regulations 1987 (No. 510) 3797
Value Added Tax (General) (Amendment) (No. 3) Regulations 1987 (No. 1916) 3797
Value Added Tax (Imported Goods) Relief (Amendment) Order 1987 (No. 155) 3813
Value Added Tax (Imported Goods) Relief (Amendment) (No. 2) Order 1987 (No. 2108) 3813
Value Added Tax (Increase of Registration Limits) Order 1987 (No. 438) 3831
Value Added Tax (International Services) Order 1987 (No. 518) 3818
Value Added Tax (Repayments to Third Country Traders) Regulations 1987 (No. 2015) 3851
Value Added Tax (Small Non-Commercial Consignments) Relief (Amendment) Order 1987 (No. 154) 3813
Value Added Tax (Supplies by Retailers) (Amendment) Regulations 1987 (No. 1712) 3836
Value Added Tax (Terminal Markets) (Amendment) Order 1987 (No. 806) 3850
Value Added Tax (Tour Operators) Order 1987 (No. 1806) 3853

WATER AND WATERWORKS

Anglian Water Authority (Littleport and Downham Internal Drainage District) Order 1987 (No. 815) 3868
Anglian Water Authority (Moor Farm Heighington) Order 1987 (No. 1602) 3869
Anglian Water Authority (Tunstead) Order 1987 (No. 1839) 3869
Bristol Waterworks Order 1987 (No. 842) 3868
Cambridge Water (Hinxton Borehole) Order 1987 (No. 2006) 3869
Cambridge Water Order 1987 (No. 750) 3869
East Surrey Water Order 1987 (No. 1434) 3869
General Drainage Charge (Anglian Water Authority) (Ascertainment) Order 1987 (No. 318) 3865
Hartlepools Water (Red Barns Borehole) Order 1987 (No. 1597) 3869
Mid Southern Water Order 1987 (No. 613) 3869
Severn–Trent Water Authority (Abolition of the Elford Internal Drainage District) Order 1987 (No. 2230) 3868
Severn–Trent Water Authority (Reconstitution of the Corporation of the Level of Hatfield Chase) Order 1987 (No. 1928) 3868
Severn–Trent Water Authority (Reconstitution of the Rivers Idle and Ryton Internal Drainage Board) Order 1987 (No. 1929) 3868
Severn–Trent Water Authority (Shelton Borehole) Order 1987 (No. 2271) 3869
Severn–Trent Water Authority (Wallgrange Boreholes) Order 1987 (No. 1322) 3869
Southern Water Authority (Romney Marsh Levels Internal Drainage District) Order 1987 (No. 555) 3868
Sunderland and South Shields Water Order 1987 (No. 2073) 3869
Tendring Hundred Water Order 1987 (No. 234) 3869
Thames Water Authority (Gatehampton Farm Boreholes) Order 1987 (No. 2007) 3869
Thames Water Authority (Leckhampstead Borehole) Order 1987 (No. 2008) 3869
Thames Water Authority (Transfer of Property of Dartford and Crayford Navigation Commissioners) Order 1987 (No. 1360) 3868
Water Authorities (Return on Assets) Order 1987 (No. 2022) 3868
Welsh Water Authority (Llwyn Isaf Boreholes) (Discharge) Order 1987 (No. 107) 3868
Welsh Water Authority (Moreton-on-Lugg) (Acquisition of Mains) Order 1987 (No. 1599) 3869
Wessex Water Authority (Blashford Lakes Discharge) Order 1987 (No. 1354) 3868
Yorkshire Water Authority (Catterick Boreholes) Order 1987 (No. 1235) 3869
Yorkshire Water Authority (Cayton Borehole) Order 1987 (No. 1236) 3869
Yorkshire Water Authority (Howe Bridge Boreholes) Order 1987 (No. 1234) 3869
Yorkshire Water Authority (Studforth Boreholes) Order 1987 (No. 1237) 3869

WEIGHTS AND MEASURES

Measuring Instruments (EEC Initial Verification Requirements) (Fees) (Amendment) Regulations 1987 (No. 802) 3873
Measuring Instruments (EEC Pattern Approval Requirements) (Fees) Regulations 1987 (No. 803) 3873
National Metrological Co-ordinating Unit (Transfer of Functions and Abolition) Order 1987 (No. 2187) ... 3874
Weights and Measures (Carriage of Solid Fuel by Rail) Order 1987 (No. 216) 3871
Weights and Measures (Local and Working Standard Capacity Measures and Testing Equipment) Regulations 1987 (No. 51) 3872
Weights and Measures (Quantity Marking and Abbreviations of Units) Regulations 1987 (No. 1538) 3875

WILLS AND SUCCESSION

Family Provision (Intestate Succession) Order 1987 (No. 799) 3879

NUMERICAL TABLE OF STATUTORY INSTRUMENTS 1987

Note: References to paragraph numbers exceeding 3886 are to the Scottish edition of the Current Law Year Book 1987.

1986	C.L.Y.
2178	1123
2182	1120
2209	1536

1987	C.L.Y.
1	1279
2 (S. 1)	4723
3	3575
4	3351
5	2551
6	2550
7	2550
8	3340
11 (S. 2)	4559
12 (S. 3)	4818
13	3793
15	2386
16	3299
17	3508
18	2552
19	97
20	1536
26 (S. 4)	4476
27	3264
28	3264
29	3731
31	3472
32	3469
33	1378
34	1268
36	3528
37	1849
38 (S. 5)	4433
39 (S. 6)	4452
40 (S. 7)	4819
45	3542
46	3463
48	3532
49	3530
50	3199
51	3872
52	1851
53	3352
54	3351
55	3351
56	3351
57	3351
58	3351
59	3351
61	3351
62	3351
63	3402
64	185
65	200
66	3351
67	3351
68	3351
69	3351

1987	C.L.Y.
70	3351
71	3351
72	3351
73	3642
74	109
75	3781
92	1378
93 (S. 8)	4489
95	1833
96	1258
97	3264
98	3264
99	1802
100	3793
101	3639
102	2406
104	3655
105	3793
106	3463
107	3868
112 (S. 9)	4655
114	107
115	2362
116	1855
117	2393
118	2386
119	1289
122	2118
123 (C. 1)	850
124	2350
125	2396
129	3353
130	2834
133	1812
134	1101
135 (S. 10)	3944
136	3404
137	1263
143	2086
146	3793
149	1116
150	3811
151	2549
152	2549
153	1808
154	3813
155	3813
156	2859
157	2854
158	2859
159	2859
160 (C. 2) (S. 11)	4248
162	2346
163	2469
164	2086
165	2817
166 (N.I 1)	2629
167 (N.I. 2)	2661
169	2013
170	3757

1987	C.L.Y.
171	3418
172	265
176	2354
177	1984
178 (C. 3)	1883
179	3601
180	1856
181	2351
182	1808
184	705
188	98
191	2835
192	2557
198 (C. 4)	820
199	3352
200	3351
201	3351
202	3351
203	3351
204	3351
205	3351
206	3351
207 (C. 5)	1282
208 (S. 12)	4399
209	2820
211	109
212	1813
213	1803
214	3461
215	1110
216	3871
217	1804
218	1804
220	3414
221	2348
222	3403
232	109
233	112
234	3869
235	1346
236	1263
242	1833
243	1837
244	3414
245	2552
248	114
249	1808
250	3494
251	3773
252	3787
255 (S. 13)	4489
256	2838
257	2838
258	3761
259	275
260	1278
261	1278
262	1279
263	1808
264	2195
265	2185
266	2196
268	1870
269	179
270	1808
271	1110
272	1910
273	1291
275 (S. 14)	4943
281	3469
282	97
285	3793
286	3317
287	2787
288	2809
289 (C. 6) (S. 15)	4878
290 (S. 16)	4394
291 (S. 17)	4399
292	1803
293	2829
295	3419
298	795
299	642
300	2354
301	2354
304 (C. 7)	1883
305	2348
306	3414
307 (S. 18)	4137
308 (S. 19)	4404
309 (S. 20)	4404
310	1816
311	3414
312	1102
314	1124
315	3310
316	3467
317	3541
318	3865
319	3793
320	3793
321	3793
322	3793
326	3793
327	3542
328	3793
329	204
330	205
331 (S. 21)	4567
332 (S. 22)	4567
333 (S. 23)	5157
334 (S. 24)	4655
335	3478
337	3791
338	2348
339	2348
340	96
341	2859
342	2859
343	2859
344 (C. 8)	1256
345 (S. 25)	4944
346 (S. 26)	4982
347	2347
348 (C. 9)	1883
349	3648
350	2053
351	2377
352	2024
353	3227
354	3561
355	3465
356	713
357	3459
358	3507
359	2347
360	472
361	109

1987	C.L.Y.
362	2008
363	3257
364 (S. 27)	5151
365 (S. 28)	4137
366 (S. 29)	4441
367 (S. 30)	4719
368	2552
369	2285
370	3493
371	2552
372	1378
373	2828
374	2828
375	2828
376	2827
377	3730
378	263
379	178
380	179
381 (S. 31)	4872
382 (S. 32)	4872
383 (S. 33)	4929
384 (S. 34)	4874
385 (S. 35)	4721
386 (S. 36)	4721
387 (S. 37)	4719
388	2280
389	2107
390	104
391	253
392	2041
393	2041
394	2041
395	250
396	2279
397	4060
398	1263
399 (C. 11)	2553
400	3478
401	2551
402	3398
403	1431
404	2020
405	395
406	1346
407	2551
408	3414
409	3487
410	1813
411	3467
412	2024
413	3463
414	3464
415	3478
416	1346
417	1346
418	1346
419	3544
420	3403
422	2285
423 (S. 38)	4795
424 (S. 39)	4793
425 (S. 40)	4477
426	251
427 (S. 41)	4444
428	96
429	3544
430 (S. 42)	4137
431 (S. 43)	4872

1987	C.L.Y.
432 (S. 44)	4947
434	2018
435	2048
436	269
437	3803
438	3831
439	1119
442	1384
443	2293
444	3200
445	2552
446	2554
447	1667
448	1518
449	2760
450	2080
451	178
452	1698
453	2087
454	2097
455	2088
456	179
457	2406
458 (N.I. 3)	2629a
459 (N.I. 4)	2735
460 (N.I. 5)	2622a
461 (N.I. 6)	2660
462	1280
463 (N.I. 7)	2652a
464 (N.I. 8)	2741a
465	1999
466	2013
467	2013
468	3011
469	4406
470	3414
472	3793
473	3793
474	3793
481	3484
483	2354
484	2354
485	2354
486	2354
490	3793
491	3495
492 (S. 46)	4872
493 (L. 1)	2971
498 (S. 47)	3936
499	1271
510	3797
511	2761
512	2005
513	2019
514	3565
516	3564
517	3801
518	3818
519	705
520	3734
521	3793
522	3793
523	3793
524	3310
529	162
530	2016
531	3793
543 (C. 12)	3501
544	3773

1987	C.L.Y.
545	2846
546	3793
547	97
548	3414
549	3414
550	3414
551	3414
555	3868
556	3642
560	3265
561	1278
562	1278
564 (C. 13)	2353
585	2845
586	3414
588 (C. 14)	2818
591	3351
592	3351
593	3351
594	3351
595	3352
603	3318
604	3197
605	1853
606	3462
607	3731
608	1838
609	1836
610	2789
611	1929
612	1805
613	3869
617	3793
622	302
623 (C. 15)	3217
625	3149
626	90
627	2279
628	2288
630 (S. 48)	4489
631 (S. 49)	4485
632	1823
635 (C. 16)	3416
642 (S. 50)	4137
643 (S. 51)	4439
644 (S. 52)	4399
646	3726
649	97
650	1272
651	2386
653 (S. 53)	3929
654 (S. 54)	3929
656	2840
657	2841
658	2841
659	3514
660	3515
661	45
662	217
663	2086
664	3415
665	3348
666	3348
667	3348
668	169
669	3739
670	3377
671	80
672 (C. 17)	3574

1987	C.L.Y.
673	3573
674	2404
675	3293
676	3256
677 (S. 55)	4032
687	3464
688	3541
699	3793
700	2431
701	3597
702	3640
703	3377
704 (S. 56)	4873
705 (S. 57)	4873
707	3793
709	110
710	73
711	77
713	3351
716 (L. 2)	650
717	3731
718	1803
719 (C. 18)	3416
720	3793
723	256
729 (C. 19)	2353
730	1287
735	1813
736	2547
737	2118
738	3723
739	3723
740 (S. 59)	3924
745	1798
746	3414
747	178
750	3869
751	3746
752	339
753	2789
754 (C. 20)	1883
755	2228
763	1104
764	3728
765	3640
770	2427
771 (S. 60)	4433
772 (S. 61)	4437
773	1239
774	3578
775	3578
776	3578
781	3804
783	3150
784	3788
785	3186
786	3186
787 (C. 21)	2874
788	478
789	478
790	109
791	3773
792	3793
793	3793
794 (S. 62)	4947
798	227
799	3879
800 (S. 63)	4475
801	1418

1987	C.L.Y.
802	3873
803	3873
804	3594
805	3264
806	3850
808	2548
809	2548
812	3351
813	3351
814	3351
815	3868
820 (C. 22)	2849
821 (L. 3)	2970
822	2118
823 (S. 64)	4441
824 (S. 65)	4137
825 (S. 66)	4441
826 (S. 67)	4137
827	3575
836	114
837	3448, 5141
838	2308, 4585
839	2395
840	3793
841	3276
842	3868
843	3419, 5136
844	2007
851	2867
852 (C. 23)	820
853	818
854	3414
855	3377
856	2096
857	2096
858	2096
859	3213
860	3812
861	3467
862	1418
863	1418
864 (S. 68)	4399
865 (S. 69)	4452
866	1839
867	105
868	1378
869	3255
870 (S. 70)	4476
871 (S. 71)	4433
874	175
875	168
876	3152
877	2416
878	3460
879	1253
880 (S. 72)	3935
881 (S. 73)	4477
882 (S. 74)	4477
883 (S. 75)	4441
884	3414
885	1808
886	2005
887	2049
888	3565
889	395
890	4060
891	248
892	2047
894 (S. 76)	4441

1987	C.L.Y.
895 (S. 77)	4441
896	3731
897	3300
898	2019
899	1277
901	1287
902	641
903	1277
904	104
905	109
906	1808
907 (C. 24)	3217
908	1813
909	1813
910	2407
911 (C. 25) (S. 78)	4662
918	2342
921	3197
922	3726
923	3661
924	3726
925	2044
926	1518
927	301
928	303
929	1347
930	1368
931	3377
932	3414
933	3414
934	221
935	3455
936 (N.I. 9)	2669
937	1280
938 (N.I. 10)	2717
939	483
940	526
941	2762
942	3218
943 (S. 79)	4665
944	2554
945	3773
946	3773
947	3773
949	99
950	3781
964	3757
973	1106
974	3351
975	3351
976	3351
977	3351
978	3351
979	3351
980	3351
981	3351
982	3351
983	3351
984	3351
985	3351
986	3351
987	3351
988	3351
989	3352
990	3793
998	3793
999	2395
1013	3793
1016 (S. 80)	5139

1987	C.L.Y.
1022 (C. 26)	2085
1025	3793
1026	3793
1028	2086
1029	134
1030	526
1032 (S. 81)	5218
1037	3793
1038	3793
1048	3793
1053	1106
1054	1805
1057	3787
1061 (C. 27)	635
1062	2863
1066	3255
1070	3787
1072	3804
1077	2386
1078 (S. 82)	4453
1079 (S. 83)	4433
1088	3781
1091	98
1092	98
1093	98
1094	3351
1095	3351
1096 (C. 28)	3501
1097	98
1098	98
1099	2824
1100	2824
1101	2824
1102	2832
1103	2832
1104	2832
1105	2832
1106	2832
1107	2832
1108	2844
1109	2836
1110	2836
1111	2836
1112	2836
1113	2816
1114	2823
1115	2826
1116	2830
1117	2839
1118	2839
1119 (L. 4)	2969
1120	2406
1122	1121
1123	2418
1124	1320
1125	1106
1126	1258
1127	2045
1128	2045, 3982
1130	2046
1131	70
1132	180
1133	3256
1134	1799
1135	1800
1136	1800
1137 (L. 5)	676
1138	1258
1139 (S. 84)	4440

1987	C.L.Y.
1140 (S. 85)	4396
1141	3213
1142 (C. 29)	850
1143	3419
1144	3297
1145	172
1146 (S. 86)	4399
1147 (S. 87)	4399
1148	98
1149	3276
1150	3301
1159 (C. 30)	1256
1160	1260
1163	103
1164	2118
1165	4470
1177 (C. 31)	1434
1181	1808
1182	1251
1183	1247
1189 (C. 32)	191
1194	80
1199	1675
1200 (C. 33)	1835
1201	705
1202	1870
1203	1900
1205	3793
1206 (S. 88)	4818
1208	85
1209	1289
1218	1106
1224	2020
1227	1801
1228 (C. 34)	3792
1231 (S. 89)	3973
1232 (S. 90)	3972
1234	3869
1235	3869
1236	3869
1237	3869
1242 (C. 36)	2479
1249 (C. 37) (S. 91)	4248
1250	2404
1251	3186
1252	186
1253	219
1254 (C. 38)	1422
1256	3143
1258	2427
1259	3809
1260 (C. 39)	1436
1261	1249
1262	160
1263	3359
1264	2082
1265	3347
1266	221
1267	3414
1268	220
1269	3355
1270 (C. 40)	3357
1271	221
1272	2548
1273	216
1274 (N.I. 11)	2736
1275 (N.I. 12)	2664
1276	2042
1277 (N.I. 13)	2700

1987	C.L.Y.	1987	C.L.Y.
1278 (N.I. 14)	2639	1381 (S. 101)	4677
1279	1245	1382 (S. 102)	4721
1280 (N.I. 15)	2744	1383 (S. 103)	4399
1281	164	1388 (S. 104)	4566
1282	407	1389 (S. 105)	4557
1284	3414	1390 (S. 106)	5218
1285	1262	1391 (S. 107)	5218
1288	2386	1392 (S. 108)	5218
1292	196	1393	1271
1293	3569	1394	3149
1294	3569	1397 (L. 7)	2971
1296	1244	1398	214
1297	1244	1399	3352
1298	3414	1400	3351
1302	1793	1401	3351
1303	89	1402	3351
1304	1910	1403	3351
1305	3496	1404	3351
1306 (C. 41)	3421	1405	3351
1311 (C. 42)	2765	1406	3351
1312	1248	1407	3351
1313	1248	1408	3351
1314	1258	1409	3351
1315	3287	1410	3351
1322	3869	1411	3351
1325	3514	1412	3351
1326	3288	1413	3351
1327	3296	1414	3351
1328 (S. 92)	4157	1415	3351
1329 (S. 93)	4943	1416	3351
1330 (C. 43)	2849	1418	3351
1331	3351	1419	3351
1332	3351	1420	3351
1333	3793	1421	3264
1334	3793	1422	2000
1335 (C. 44) (S. 94)	4398	1423 (L. 8)	3090
1336 (S. 95)	3960	1424	3451
1337	1341	1425	2551
1338	3225	1426	3452
1339	1343	1427	3802
1340	3661	1428	2559
1341	1258	1429	3783
1342	3661	1430	3793
1343	3726	1431	3793
1344	3726	1432	3793
1345	3726	1433	1272
1349	258	1434	3869
1350	1110	1435	3793
1353	3793	1436	1808
1354	3868	1439	2405
1355 (S. 96)	4441	1440	1884
1356 (S. 97)	4441	1441	3787
1357 (S. 98)	4137	1442	3793
1358 (S. 99)	4137	1443	3781
1359	1266	1445	232
1360	3868	1446	2386
1364	1257	1447	109
1365	1249	1450	1808
1366 (S. 100)	4399	1451	2386
1367	3787	1461	2838
1368	3787	1463	2386
1369	3787	1464	2981
1370	3787	1465	72
1371	3787	1468 (S. 109)	4094
1372	3787	1470	3793
1377	171	1483	2345
1378	3265	1484	3419
1379	1868	1489 (C. 46) (S. 110)	4940
1380	3793	1491	3793

1987	C.L.Y.
1492	2019
1493	2005
1494	3565
1496	2059
1497	1630
1498	259
1499	261
1500	264
1507	1910
1508	3310
1509	3310
1512	2547
1513	2832
1514	3403
1515	1808
1520	3147
1521	3745
1522 (S. 111)	5195
1523	1811
1525	2118
1529 (S. 112)	5196
1530 (S. 113)	4655
1531 (S. 114)	5191
1532 (S. 115)	5202
1533	2382
1534	3731
1535	2395
1536	1803
1537 (S. 116)	4790
1538	3875
1542	3793
1554 (C. 47)	1883
1555	1808
1556	3310
1564	1803
1565	1803
1566	1803
1567	1808, 4470
1568	1808, 4470
1570	3793
1576	2348
1578	411
1579	2386
1580	3793
1581	3793
1582	3793
1583	2377
1590	3463
1591	3414
1594 (C. 48) (S. 117)	4094
1597	3869
1598	2348
1599	3869
1601	116
1602	3869
1603	3414
1607 (C. 49) (S. 118)	5193
1612	59
1613	3774
1625	2354
1626	2354
1627 (N.I. 16)	2627
1629 (N.I. 17)	2701
1632	3793
1633	3793
1634 (S. 119)	4720
1635	3223
1636	641
1637	3404

1987	C.L.Y.
1638	1808
1639	3642
1640	3642
1641	3642
1653	3600
1664 (C. 50)	191
1670	249
1671	267
1679	96
1680 (C. 51)	3584
1681 (C. 52)	3323
1682	1808
1683	3472
1687	1808
1688	705
1689	3147
1692	3543
1693	3793
1694	3793
1695	3793
1696	1808
1697	1808
1698 (S. 120)	4797
1699 (S. 121)	4788
1700 (S. 122)	4794
1701	3793
1706	3309
1709	3642
1712	3836
1730	3151
1731	3793
1732	1900
1737	2348
1738 (S. 123)	4675
1739	705
1749	2832
1750	3719
1753	2861
1754	2854
1755	3780
1756	3419, 5136
1757	1334
1758	96
1759 (C. 53)	1883
1760	3722
1762 (C. 54)	3146
1763 (S. 124)	5218
1764 (S. 125)	5218
1765	2836
1771	100
1781	1108
1782	3150
1783	93
1784	3793
1785	1112
1786	705
1790	3403
1796	705
1797	705
1799	3793
1800	3793
1801 (S. 126)	4399
1802	1808
1804	1106
1805	1884
1806	3853
1807	3733
1808	114
1809	1870

NUMERICAL TABLE OF STATUTORY INSTRUMENTS 1987

1987	C.L.Y.
1810	1900
1811	1894
1812	172
1823	294
1824	1471
1825	2469
1826	529
1827	3414
1828	821
1829	221
1830	3456
1831	3498
1832 (N.I. 18)	2707
1833	529
1835	3404
1836	2766
1837	1808
1838 (C. 55) (S.127)	5014
1839	3869
1842	4060
1843	1466
1848	265
1849	3719
1850 (S. 128)	4787
1851	641
1852	1418
1853 (C. 56)	3501
1854	3543
1855	713
1861	3793
1862	3793
1863	3793
1864	3793
1865	3793
1866	3793
1867	3787
1868	3793
1871	255
1872	260
1878 (S. 129)	4793
1879 (S. 130)	5218
1885	172
1886	3414
1887	2410
1888	1808, 4470
1891	1431
1892	3747
1893	1808
1894	1808
1897	2010
1900	1803
1902	1106
1903	1910
1904	1910
1905	1910
1906	1910
1907	2838
1908	2338
1909 (C. 57)	1429
1910	1884
1911	3319
1912	705
1913	705
1914 (S. 131)	4795
1915	2431
1916	3797
1919	343
1920	3316
1921 (S. 132)	4049

1987	C.L.Y.
1925	705
1928	3868
1929	3868
1930	3793
1931	3793
1932	3793
1933	2836
1936	3599
1937 (S. 133)	5197
1939 (C. 58)	1883
1940	2234
1941	3147
1942	252
1943 (S. 134)	4655
1945	2341
1948	84
1949	84
1950	87
1954	3773
1957 (S. 135)	3948
1959	343
1960	1258
1961	3414
1962	705
1963	1102
1964	3731
1965	2547
1967	3475
1968	3460
1969	3475
1970	3451
1971	1884
1972	1884
1973	3468
1974	3468
1975	254
1976	265
1977 (L. 9)	584
1978	3542
1979	3313
1980	2418
1981	2832
1982	2308
1983	3448
1984	3781
1985 (S. 136)	4469
1986	1806
1987	1807
1988	2019
1989	2005
1990	3565
1991	346
1997 (C. 59)	3217
1998 (C. 60)	159
1999	167
2000	158
2001	167
2002 (C. 61) (S. 137)	5203
2003 (C. 62)	2370
2004	2379
2005	262
2006	3869
2007	3869
2008	3869
2009	1115
2010	3528
2011	1803
2012	3276
2014 (S. 138)	4468

1987	C.L.Y.
2015	3851
2016	3351
2017	3351
2018	266
2019	265
2020	107
2021	107
2022	3868
2023	331
2024 (L. 10)	3087
2025 (S. 139)	5028
2026	83
2027	83
2028	1910
2029	83
2030	83
2031	83
2032	83
2033	83
2034	83
2035	3219
2036	3793
2037	3793
2038	3793
2039	410
2040	1517
2041	1697
2042	1699
2043	1693
2044	1702
2045	1292
2046	1697
2047	2401
2048 (N.I. 19)	2637
2049 (N.I. 20)	2743
2050	1280
2051	1246
2052 (N.I. 21)	2753
2053	2013
2054	2013
2055	2013
2056	2013
2057	2013
2058	2013
2059	3043
2060	524
2061	3334
2062	172
2068	3775
2069	2044
2070	1110
2071	2013
2072	247
2073	3869
2074	3793
2075	2027
2076 (S. 140)	4401
2077 (S. 141)	4655
2078	172
2083	179
2084	3773
2085	3277
2086	2738
2088	3202
2089	3204
2090 (S. 142)	4676
2092	1932
2094	3575
2095	3403

1987	C.L.Y.
2096	204
2097	1105
2098	2286
2099	2413
2100	179
2101	3793
2102	3793
2105	1104
2106	1107
2107	1118
2108	3813
2110	2386
2111	3463
2112	3478
2113	3414
2114	1117
2115	1848
2116	3320
2117	3315
2118	2061
2119 (S. 143)	4094
2120	3304
2122	3272
2123	3272
2126	1121
2127	2020
2128	2025
2129	86
2130	2060
2131	263
2132	2043
2133	246
2134	3793
2135	713
2136	713
2137	1290
2138 (C. 63)	3421
2139	3419
2140	713
2141	713
2142	3214
2143	3214
2147	3793
2148	3793
2155 (C. 64)	850
2156	2554
2157	3216
2158 (C. 65)	3217
2159	3149
2160 (S. 144)	4818
2161	3296
2166	2406
2167 (S. 145)	4945
2168	3300
2170	3276
2171	2062
2172	158a
2173	167
2174	2406
2175	1284
2176	3143
2177 (C. 66)	2151
2178	2197
2179 (S. 146)	4938
2181	713
2182	1285
2184	1106
2185	1869
2186	2377

NUMERICAL TABLE OF STATUTORY INSTRUMENTS 1987

1987	C.L.Y.
2187	3874
2188 (S. 147)	4655
2192	1803
2193	3513
2194	3793
2195	106
2196	111
2197	3349
2198	3350
2199	218
2200	497
2201	2086
2202	2411
2203 (N.I. 22)	2708
2204 (N.I. 23)	2737
2205	3571
2206	1701
2207	169
2208	1280
2209	1280
2210	95
2211	3011
2212	172
2213	472
2214	475
2215	2838
2216	2404
2217	2408
2218	2831
2219	2393
2222	713
2223	713
2224	106
2225	111
2226 (S. 148)	4791
2227	3594

1987	C.L.Y.
2228	2348
2229	171
2230	3868
2231 (S. 149)	4925
2232	181
2233 (S. 150)	4027
2234	1803
2235	1812
2236	1812
2237	1812
2241	3773
2244 (S. 151)	5037
2245 (S. 152)	5037
2246	180
2247	2348
2248 (C. 68)	2085
2249	1431
2253	3787
2254	3787
2256	3793
2257	3793
2261	3793
2262	3793
2263	3793
2264	3793
2265	3793
2266	1243
2267	3793
2268	3793
2269 (S. 153)	4561
2271	3869
2272 (C. 69)	3354
2273 (S. 154)	4248
2274	3793
2276	1862
2277 (C. 71)	1883
2279 (S. 155)	4943

TABLE OF S.R. & O. and S.I.
AFFECTED BY
STATUTORY INSTRUMENTS OF 1987

This Table describes the effect on existing Statutory Rules and Orders and Statutory Instruments of Statutory Instruments of 1987. The first entry, for example, shows that Statutory Instrument No. 348 of 1912 was amended by Statutory Instrument 1891 of 1987, and that the 1987 Instrument is digested at paragraph 1431. For the effect on post 1946 Statutory Instruments of all subsequent Statutory Instruments see the Table of Statutory Instruments Affected in the *Current Law Legislation Citator*.

Note: References to paragraph Numbers exceeding 3886 are to the Scottish edition of the Current Law Year Book.

1912
348 amended No. 1891 § 1431
348 amended No. 2249 § 1431

1922
112 revoked No. 1758 § 96

1924
400 revoked No. 918 § 2342

1925
1093 amended No. 2214 § 475

1926
357 revoked No. 773 § 1239

1931
413 amended No. 2070 § 1110

1933
789 amended No. 735 § 1813
830 revoked No. 1758 § 96
838 revoked No. 1758 § 96
878 amended No. 180 § 1856
1148 revoked No. 773 § 1239

1934
1346 amended No. 999 § 2395

1935
488 amended No. 1078 § 4453
1328 revoked No. 1758 § 96

1936
120 revoked No. 1758 § 96

1937
525 amended No. 2070 § 1110
1122 amended No. 1143 § 3419

1938
193 revoked No. 790 § 109
228 revoked No. 790 § 109

1944
1399 amended No. 801 § 1418

1946
743 revoked No. 801 § 1418

1947
1065 revoked No. 1758 § 96
1731 revoked No. 801 § 1418
2304 revoked No. 1758 § 96

1948
2092 revoked No. 856 § 2096
2093 revoked No. 857 § 2096
2094 revoked No. 858 § 2096

1949
889 revoked No. 1333 § 3793
1544 amended No. 100 § 3793

1950
411 revoked No. 1758 § 96
838 revoked No. 1273 § 216
839 amended No. 1273 § 216
964 revoked No. 1758 § 96

1952
225 revoked No. 1758 § 96

1953
1531 revoked No. 2114 § 1117
1777 amended No. 622 § 302
1804 amended No. 677 § 4032

1954
796 revoked No. 2024 § 3087

1955
690 amended No. 282 § 97
814 revoked No. 1781 § 1108
1346 revoked No. 1781 § 1108

1956
357 amended No. 1285 § 1262
1978 revoked No. 918 § 2342

1957
753 revoked No. 1758 § 96
2208 amended No. 180 § 1856
2233 amended No. 613 § 3869

1958
136 revoked No. 52 § 1851
1061 revoked No. 730 § 1287
1814 revoked No. 1758 § 96
1872 revoked No. 492 § 4872
2141 revoked No. 1781 § 1108

1959
1131 amended No. 750 § 3869
1832 amended No. 1182 § 1251

1960
1557 revoked No. 1758 § 96
2195 revoked No. 381 § 4872
2269 revoked No. 492 § 4872

1961
72 revoked No. 2024 § 3087
1549 revoked No. 492 § 4872
2031 revoked No. 1263 § 3359
2192 amended No. 750 § 3869

1962
761 amended No. 234 § 3869
918 revoked No. 1781 § 1108
1586 revoked No. 1135 § 1800
1616 revoked No. 1135 § 1800
1869 amended No. 935 § 3455
2158 revoked No. 217 § 1804
2653 revoked No. 2024 § 3087

1963
1 revoked No. 1781 § 1108
2 revoked No. 1781 § 1108
1229 revoked No. 2236 § 1812

1964
321 revoked No. 1135 § 1800
388 amended No. 1256 § 3143
388 amended No. 2176 § 3143
1173 revoked No. 1135 § 1800
1409 revoked No. 430 § 4137
1410 revoked No. 430 § 4137
1513 revoked No. 381 § 4872
1622 revoked No. 492 § 4872
1848 amended No. 1986 § 1806
2058 amended No. 585 § 2845

1965
321 amended No. 871 § 4433
321 amended No. 1079 § 4433
321 amended No. 1206 § 4818
1497 revoked No. 2236 § 1812
1500 revoked No. 821 § 2970
1535 amended No. 927 § 301
1536 amended No. 928 § 1347
1776 amended No. 1423 § 3090
1788 revoked No. 430 § 4137
1839 amended No. 1984 § 3781
1995 amended No. 394 § 2041
2041 revoked No. 1781 § 1108

1966
162 revoked No. 1758 § 96
915 revoked No. 2236 § 1812
1458 amended No. 1268 § 220

1967
29 revoked No. 309 § 4404
372 revoked No. 1135 § 1800
748 revoked No. 2024 § 3087
940 revoked No. 1781 § 1108
1002 amended No. 2266 § 1243
1131 revoked No. 1135 § 1800
1310 amended No. 394 § 2041
1873 revoked No. 2224 § 106

1968
208 amended No. 424 § 4793
208 amended No. 1878 § 4793
1231 amended No. 422 § 2285
1262 amended No. 1977 § 584
1363 revoked No. 376 § 178
1675 revoked No. 2024 § 3087
1869 amended No. 466 § 2013
1869 amended No. 2055 § 2013
1933 revoked No. 430 § 4137
2006 revoked No. 2224 § 106
2049 amended No. 2088 § 3202
2050 revoked No. 2088 § 3202
2071 revoked No. 376 § 2828

1969
203 revoked No. 2089 § 3204
690 revoked No. 2115 § 1848
888 revoked No. 16 § 3299
939 amended No. 330 § 205
955 revoked No. 381 § 4872
1547 revoked No. 821 § 2970
1689 revoked No. 2024 § 3087
1787 amended No. 1062 § 2863
1829 amended No. 2210 § 95

1970
147 amended No. 453 § 2087
148 amended No. 453 § 2087
380 revoked No. 1785 § 1112
423 revoked No. 1781 § 1108
1021 revoked No. 376 § 2827
1287 revoked No. 1758 § 96
1710 amended No. 51 § 3872
1714 amended No. 51 § 3872

1971
124 revoked No. 864 § 4399
174 revoked No. 492 § 4872
194 revoked No. 381 § 4872
218 amended No. 1139 § 4440
219 revoked No. 492 § 4872
232 amended No. 256 § 2838
260 revoked No. 821 § 2970
287 revoked No. 427 § 4444
288 revoked No. 384 § 4874
317 revoked No. 381 § 4872
374 amended No. 2107 § 1118
450 amended No. 2085 § 3277
450 amended No. 2123 § 3272
554 revoked No. 384 § 4874
797 revoked No. 1135 § 1800
926 revoked No. 430 § 4137
968 revoked No. 613 § 3869
1065 amended No. 2178 § 2197
1356 revoked No. 1781 § 1108
1795 revoked No. 427 § 4444
1796 revoked No. 492 § 4872
1861 amended No. 1199 § 1675
1912 revoked No. 381 § 4872
1914 revoked No. 381 § 4872
1977 revoked No. 2024 § 3087
2020 revoked No. 1149 § 3276
2070 revoked No. 2224 § 106
2102 amended No. 451 § 178
2102 amended No. 2041 § 1697
2103 amended No. 456 § 179

1972
334 revoked No. 821 § 2970
419 amended No. 2000 § 158

1972—*cont.*
878 amended No. 613 § 3869
973 amended No. 2070 § 1110
1101 amended No. 2199 § 218
1148 amended No. 1712 § 3836
1295 revoked No. 408 § 3414
1385 revoked No. 764 § 3728
1610 amended No. 2092 § 1932
1668 revoked No. 177 § 1984
1876 amended No. 884 § 3414
1891 revoked No. 309 § 4404

1973
116 revoked No. 1135 § 1800
123 amended No. 1372 § 3787
173 amended No. 806 § 3850
268 amended No. 897 § 1253
390 revoked No. 382 § 4872
390 amended No. 1355 § 4441
428 amended No. 156 § 2859
428 revoked No. 256 § 2838
429 revoked No. 256 § 2838
430 amended No. 157 § 2859
434 amended No. 1699 § 4788
434 amended No. 1700 § 4794
467 amended No. 1070 § 3787
673 revoked No. 430 § 4137
966 amended No. 1302 § 1793
1059 revoked No. 1758 § 96
1060 revoked No. 1758 § 96
1145 revoked No. 430 § 4137
1268 amended No. 1258 § 2427
1330 amended No. 2056 § 3043
1340 amended No. 1987 § 1807
1468 amended No. 736 § 2574
1468 amended No. 1512 § 2547
1468 amended No. 1965 § 2547
1736 revoked No. 1371 § 3787
1756 amended No. 451 § 178
1756 amended No. 2043 § 1693
1774 revoked No. 492 § 4872
1776 amended No. 1114 § 2823
1822 amended No. 2099 § 2413
1911 revoked No. 1 § 1279
1936 amended No. 232 § 109
2125 revoked No. 381 § 4872
2143 amended No. 2171 § 2062

1974
44 revoked No. 375 § 2828
82 revoked No. 2213 § 472
160 amended No. 1425 § 2551
160 amended No. 5 § 2551
160 amended No. 401 § 2551
160 amended No. 407 § 2551
194 revoked No. 1135 § 1800
229 revoked No. 375 § 2828
455 amended No. 445 § 2552
505 amended No. 1634 § 4720
506 amended No. 385 § 4721
506 amended No. 386 § 4721
506 amended No. 1382 § 4399
572 revoked No. 2089 § 3204
597 revoked No. 2024 § 3087
812 revoked No. 1850 § 4787
1006 amended No. 1936 § 3599
1152 revoked No. 1758 § 96
1159 revoked No. 1758 § 96
1187 revoked No. 864 § 4399
1533 amended No. 256 § 2838

1974—*cont.*
1673 revoked No. 256 § 2838
1734 revoked No. 408 § 3414
1796 amended No. 256 § 2838
1846 revoked No. 1369 § 3787
1847 revoked No. 1370 § 3787
2083 revoked No. 671 § 80
2170 amended No. 180 § 1856
2227 amended No. 1032 § 5218

1975
135 revoked No. 2266 § 1243
203 amended No. 233 § 112
205 amended No. 392 § 2041
360 revoked No. 1135 § 1800
536 amended No. 258 § 3761
553 amended No. 416 § 1346
555 amended No. 31 § 3472
555 amended No. 1683 § 3472
556 amended No. 414 § 3464
556 amended No. 687 § 3464
598 amended No. 1426 § 3452
638 revoked No. 1850 § 4787
640 revoked No. 309 § 4404
686 amended No. 1381 § 4677
717 revoked No. 307 § 4137
719 revoked No. 401 § 2551
812 amended No. 935 § 3455
835 revoked No. 430 § 4137
836 revoked No. 430 § 4137
888 revoked No. 790 § 109
889 revoked No. 790 § 109
1135 amended No. 290 § 4394
1183 revoked No. 376 § 2827
1254 revoked No. 1537 § 4790
1280 amended No. 1937 § 5197
1319 revoked No. 1538 § 3875
1366 revoked No. 603 § 3318
1573 amended No. 491 § 3495
1573 amended No. 1968 § 3460
1718 amended No. 256 § 2838
1803 revoked No. 821 § 2970
1842 revoked No. 1758 § 96
2000 amended No. 897 § 3300
2054 revoked No. 1915 § 2431
2069 revoked No. 1529 § 5196
2136 revoked No. 862 § 1418
2137 revoked No. 862 § 1418
2138 revoked No. 863 § 1418
2221 revoked No. 177 § 1984
2222 revoked No. 2224 § 106
2223 amended No. 2225 § 111
2225 revoked No. 1758 § 96

1976
60 revoked No. 492 § 4872
185 amended No. 1114 § 2823
304 revoked No. 1135 § 1800
306 revoked No. 256 § 2838
333 revoked No. 381 § 4872
339 revoked No. 430 § 4137
371 revoked No. 430 § 4137
373 revoked No. 492 § 4872
512 revoked No. 381 § 4872
615 amended No. 409 § 3487
702 amended No. 950 § 3781
730 amended No. 1892 § 3747
882 revoked No. 2236 § 1812
940 amended No. 306 § 3414
963 amended No. 491 § 3495

1976—*cont.*

965 amended No. 357 § 3459
965 amended No. 491 § 3495
974 revoked No. 234 § 3869
1073 amended No. 423 § 4795
1073 amended No. 1914 § 4795
1099 revoked No. 1781 § 1108
1142 amended No. 2073 § 3869
1156 amended No. 1271 § 221
1156 amended No. 1829 § 221
1208 revoked No. 603 § 3318
1263 revoked No. 1941 § 3147
1267 amended No. 1978 § 3542
1300 revoked No. 1941 § 3147
1362 revoked No. 2024 § 3087
1447 revoked No. 1421 § 3264
1541 amended No. 843 § 3419, 5136
1707 amended No. 256 § 2838
1758 amended No. 491 § 3495
1885 amended No. 546 § 3793
2003 amended No. 37 § 1849
2012 amended No. 1635 § 3223
2019 amended No. 346 § 4982
2067 revoked No. 1 § 1279
2080 revoked No. 2088 § 3202
2081 revoked No. 2088 § 3202
2092 revoked No. 2089 § 3204
2136 revoked No. 1135 § 1800
2234 revoked No. 821 § 2970
2235 revoked No. 821 § 2970

1977

87 amended No. 1999 § 167
88 amended No. 2001 § 167
120 revoked No. 2213 § 472
176 amended No. 1887 § 2410
208 revoked No. 1757 § 1334
228 revoked No. 349 § 3648
252 revoked No. 1591 § 3414
255 revoked No. 1529 § 5196
289 amended No. 702 § 3640
289 amended No. 765 § 3640
343 amended No. 355 § 3465
429 amended No. 668 § 169
486 amended No. 129 § 3353
548 revoked No. 363 § 2008
632 revoked No. 1591 § 3414
634 revoked No. 309 § 3414
717 revoked No. 374 § 2828
744 revoked No. 613 § 3869
890 revoked No. 37 § 1849
972 revoked No. 2107 § 1118
985 amended No. 389 § 2107
988 revoked No. 1758 § 96
1027 amended No. 26 § 4476
1085 revoked No. 1738 § 4675
1181 revoked No. 408 § 3414
1210 amended No. 329 § 204
1509 amended No. 416 § 1346
1683 revoked No. 1538 § 3875
1705 amended No. 256 § 2838
1762 revoked No. 382 § 4872
1805 amended No. 2235 § 1812
1858 revoked No. 373 § 2828
1912 revoked No. 2088 § 3202
2102 revoked No. 374 § 2828
2121 revoked No. 2224 § 106
2136 revoked No. 1135 § 1800
2173 revoked No. 256 § 2838
2185 revoked No. 374 § 2828
2628 revoked No. 2106 § 1107

1978

32 amended No. 74 § 109
32 amended No. 1447 § 109
107 revoked No. 408 § 3414
134 revoked No. 657 § 2841
257 revoked No. 710 § 73
375 revoked No. 256 § 2838
407 revoked No. 374 § 2828
408 revoked No. 373 § 2828
415 amended No. 1258 § 2427
475 revoked No. 1850 § 4787
505 revoked No. 1758 § 96
528 revoked No. 1914 § 4795
611 amended No. 129 § 3353
622 revoked No. 381 § 302
750 revoked No. 821 § 3351
801 revoked No. 1591 § 3414
881 revoked No. 750 § 3869
884 revoked No. 133 § 1812
979 revoked No. 408 § 3414
986 amended No. 750 § 3869
1096 amended No. 1365 § 1249
1106 amended No. 2206 § 1701
1121 amended No. 1439 § 2405
1131 revoked No. 1968 § 3460
1273 amended No. 1957 § 3948
1348 revoked No. 256 § 2838
1368 revoked No. 373 § 2828
1378 revoked No. 1850 § 4787
1420 amended No. 1986 § 1806
1482 amended No. 1434 § 3869
1565 revoked No. 382 § 4872
1578 amended No. 256 § 2838
1698 amended No. 606 § 3462
1723 amended No. 605 § 1853
1758 revoked No. 408 § 3414
1794 revoked No. 1850 § 4787
1800 amended No. 2020 § 107
1820 revoked No. 1135 § 1800
1926 revoked No. 1850 § 4787
1927 revoked No. 1523 § 1811

1979

95 revoked No. 430 § 4137
106 revoked No. 821 § 2970
112 amended No. 457 § 2406
210 revoked No. 375 § 2828
221 amended No. 1771 § 100
379 amended No. 643 § 4439
393 revoked No. 1303 § 89
401 revoked No. 16 § 3299
406 revoked No. 256 § 2838
408 revoked No. 1496 § 2059
453 amended No. 454 § 2097
453 amended No. 2042 § 1699
591 amended No. 106 § 3463
591 amended No. 413 § 3463
591 amended No. 417 § 1346
591 amended No. 1590 § 3463
591 amended No. 2111 § 3463
628 amended No. 416 § 1346
628 amended No. 878 § 3460
628 amended No. 1968 § 3460
642 amended No. 1854 § 3543
656 revoked No. 2213 § 472
668 revoked No. 376 § 2827
676 amended No. 316 § 3467
676 amended No. 411 § 3467
791 amended No. 632 § 1823
921 amended No. 1831 § 3498

1979—*cont.*

937 amended No. 393 § 2041
1168 amended No. 842 § 3868
1198 amended No. 1327 § 3296
1198 amended No. 2161 § 3296
1259 amended No. 256 § 3809
1287 amended No. 256 § 2838
1317 amended No. 1282 § 407
1436 amended No. 51 § 3872
1457 amended No. 2073 § 3869
1470 revoked No. 851 § 2867
1470 amended No. 1753 § 2861
1596 amended No. 135 § 3944
1620 revoked No. 821 § 2970
1635 revoked No. 177 § 1984
1668 revoked No. 2224 § 106
1692 revoked No. 1135 § 1800
1715 amended No. 2060 § 524
1719 amended No. 51 § 3872
1727 amended No. 1754 § 2854

1980

8 revoked No. 1538 § 3875
82 revoked No. 256 § 2838
111 revoked No. 353 § 3227
180 revoked No. 1850 § 4787
272 revoked No. 256 § 2838
295 revoked No. 353 § 3227
330 revoked No. 188 § 98
335 revoked No. 1566 § 1803
342 revoked No. 1850 § 4787
362 amended No. 2218 § 2831
405 revoked No. 851 § 2867
420 amended No. 428 § 96
420 amended No. 1679 § 96
420 revoked No. 1758 § 96
499 revoked No. 1758 § 96
535 amended No. 1886 § 3414
540 revoked No. 1298 § 3414
543 revoked No. 1961 § 3414
762 revoked No. 763 § 1104
780 amended No. 2071 § 2013
792 amended No. 867 § 105
803 revoked No. 851 § 2867
958 amended No. 2116 § 3320
1050 amended No. 1914 § 4795
1058 amended No. 803 § 3873
1121 amended No. 8 § 3340
1182 amended No. 524 § 3310
1339 revoked No. 755 § 2228
1437 amended No. 281 § 3469
1437 amended No. 491 § 3495
1438 revoked No. 1968 § 3460
1455 revoked No. 851 § 2867
1503 amended No. 368 § 2552
1527 amended No. 2207 § 169
1580 revoked No. 491 § 3495
1616 amended No. 256 § 2838
1641 amended No. 481 § 3484
1643 amended No. 491 § 3495
1643 amended No. 1972 § 1884
1674 amended No. 367 § 4719
1675 revoked No. 1531 § 5191
1677 amended No. 1522 § 5195
1697 amended No. 266 § 2196
1709 amended No. 402 § 3398
1735 revoked No. 1379 § 1868
1791 revoked No. 381 § 4872
1792 revoked No. 382 § 4872

1980—*cont.*

1793 revoked No. 381 § 4872
1838 revoked No. 1523 § 1811
1848 amended No. 776 § 3578
1858 revoked No. 821 § 2970
1885 revoked No. 1850 § 4787
1898 amended No. 396 § 2279
1973 revoked No. 1135 § 1800

1981

41 revoked No. 851 § 2867
57 amended No. 2078 § 172
67 amended No. 1914 § 4795
257 amended No. 1150 § 3301
262 revoked No. 1150 § 3301
271 amended No. 2178 § 2197
313 revoked No. 408 § 3414
342 revoked No. 188 § 98
354 amended No. 244 § 3414
354 amended No. 746 § 3414
387 revoked No. 430 § 4137
388 revoked No. 430 § 4137
454 revoked No. 2237 § 1812
501 revoked No. 368 § 2552
581 revoked No. 1961 § 3414
605 amended No. 1830 § 3456
740 amended No. 1284 § 3414
809 revoked No. 1359 § 1266
815 amended No. 491 § 3495
859 amended No. 1706 § 3309
880 amended No. 1127 § 2045
881 amended No. 1128 § 2045, 3982
929 revoked No. 353 § 3227
952 amended No. 560 § 3265
952 revoked No. 1378 § 3265
976 revoked No. 353 § 3227
1017 revoked No. 309 § 4404
1034 revoked No. 800 § 4475
1066 revoked No. 1303 § 89
1086 amended No. 879 § 1253
1098 amended No. 306 § 3414
1121 amended No. 467 § 2013
1170 revoked No. 1758 § 96
1180 revoked No. 1359 § 1266
1371 revoked No. 851 § 2867
1441 amended No. 1129 § 2682
1443 revoked No. 430 § 4137
1499 amended No. 1232 § 3972
1525 revoked No. 1968 § 3460
1525 amended No. 1972 § 1884
1526 amended No. 358 § 3507
1527 amended No. 17 § 3508
1527 amended No. 659 § 3514
1527 amended No. 660 § 3515
1527 amended No. 1325 § 3514
1528 amended No. 36 § 3528
1528 amended No. 481 § 3484
1528 amended No. 2010 § 3528
1529 amended No. 481 § 3484
1578 revoked No. 265 § 2185
1589 revoked No. 821 § 2970
1596 amended No. 1231 § 3973
1654 amended No. 2130 § 2060
1687 amended No. 493 § 2971
1687 amended No. 1397 § 2971
1694 amended No. 1144 § 3297
1712 revoked No. 1378 § 3265
1741 amended No. 781 § 3804
1741 amended No. 1072 § 3804
1794 amended No. 442 § 1384

1981—*cont.*
1825 revoked No. 803 § 3873
1841 revoked No. 2182 § 1285
1892 revoked No. 1850 § 4787

1982
99 revoked No. 1378 § 3265
121 revoked No. 430 § 4137
123 revoked No. 821 § 2970
203 amended No. 1428 § 2559
230 revoked No. 1378 § 3265
234 amended No. 1601 § 116
265 revoked No. 2088 § 3202
266 revoked No. 2089 § 3204
271 revoked No. 851 § 2867
287 amended No. 245 § 2552
289 revoked No. 368 § 2552
334 amended No. 450 § 2080
385 revoked No. 1850 § 4787
423 revoked No. 1378 § 3265
446 revoked No. 2024 § 3087
468 revoked No. 430 § 4137
492 revoked No. 657 § 2841
493 revoked No. 656 § 2840
555 amended No. 1760 § 3722
578 revoked No. 1843 § 1466
586 amended No. 1119 § 2969
599 revoked No. 1758 § 96
717 amended No. 288 § 2809
719 amended No. 1908 § 2338
786 revoked No. 821 § 2970
811 amended No. 802 § 3873
844 amended No. 188 § 98
863 amended No. 371 § 2552
894 amended No. 372 § 1378
894 amended No. 868 § 1378
898 amended No. 387 § 4719
937 revoked No. 1378 § 3265
955 revoked No. 2088 § 3202
1004 amended No. 611 § 1929
1151 revoked No. 256 § 2838
1161 revoked No. 292 § 1803
1194 revoked No. 353 § 3227
1197 amended No. 369 § 2285
1241 amended No. 491 § 3495
1252 revoked No. 353 § 3227
1271 amended No. 1508 § 3310
1303 revoked No. 1850 § 4787
1400 revoked No. 214 § 3461
1408 amended No. 327 § 3542
1408 amended No. 491 § 3495
1408 amended No. 1968 § 3460
1442 revoked No. 730 § 1287
1486 revoked No. 851 § 2867
1489 amended No. 419 § 3544
1489 amended No. 429 § 3544
1540 amended No. 455 § 2088
1697 amended No. 775 § 3578
1701 revoked No. 1523 § 1811
1727 amended No. 2237 § 1812
1784 amended No. 2100 § 179
1882 revoked No. 2224 § 106
1884 amended No. 114 § 107
1877 revoked No. 381 § 4872

1983
74 amended No. 1126 § 1258
104 amended No. 491 § 3495
126 revoked No. 243 § 1837
136 amended No. 400 § 3478

1983—*cont.*
160 revoked No. 851 § 2867
173 revoked No. 2237 § 1812
174 revoked No. 2236 § 1812
217 revoked No. 363 § 3257
252 revoked No. 2009 § 1115
258 revoked No. 292 § 1803
290 revoked No. 821 § 2970
291 revoked No. 821 § 2970
293 revoked No. 188 § 98
296 amended No. 351 § 2377
296 revoked No. 2186 § 2377
306 amended No. 368 § 2552
313 revoked No. 401 § 2551
368 amended No. 404 § 2020
422 amended No. 469 § 4406
506 amended No. 1258 § 2427
550 amended No. 379 § 178
623 revoked No. 2024 § 3217
685 amended No. 177 § 1984
686 amended No. 191 § 2835
720 revoked No. 292 § 1803
787 revoked No. 821 § 2970
793 revoked No. 800 § 4475
798 revoked No. 864 § 4399
873 amended No. 446 § 2554
873 amended No. 944 § 2554
883 amended No. 165 § 2817
887 revoked No. 2156 § 2554
910 amended No. 1326 § 3288
972 revoked No. 430 § 4137
973 amended No. 1364 § 1257
996 revoked No. 256 § 2838
1000 amended No. 491 § 3495
1042 revoked No. 1843 § 1466
1058 revoked No. 643 § 4439
1128 revoked No. 1836 § 2766
1140 amended No. 605 § 1853
1151 revoked No. 1 § 1279
1158 amended No. 949 § 99
1185 revoked No. 1261 § 1249
1191 revoked No. 2186 § 2377
1204 amended No. 1564 § 1803
1205 revoked No. 1566 § 1803
1206 amended No. 1565 § 1803
1212 amended No. 674 § 2404
1212 amended No. 1250 § 2404
1215 amended No. 1383 § 4399
1349 revoked No. 851 § 2867
1389 revoked No. 1892 § 3747
1398 amended No. 470 § 3414
1399 amended No. 17 § 3508
1399 amended No. 49 § 3530
1399 amended No. 659 § 3514
1399 amended No. 1325 § 3514
1399 amended No. 1972 § 1884
1399 amended No. 2193 § 3513
1421 revoked No. 1850 § 4787
1428 revoked No. 1139 § 4440
1450 revoked No. 52 § 1851
1451 revoked No. 443 § 2293
1485 revoked No. 1758 § 96
1500 revoked No. 188 § 98
1518 revoked No. 1264 § 2082
1536 revoked No. 864 § 4399
1598 amended No. 317 § 3541
1598 amended No. 327 § 3542
1598 amended No. 688 § 3541
1614 revoked No. 764 § 3728
1640 revoked No. 52 § 1851

1983—*cont.*
1649 amended No. 2115 § 1848
1654 amended No. 51 § 3872
1662 revoked No. 1378 § 3265
1674 amended No. 101 § 3639
1811 amended No. 2130 § 2060
1812 revoked No. 851 § 2867
1831 amended No. 2012 § 3276
1916 revoked No. 1464 § 2981
1954 revoked No. 2035 § 3219

1984
92 revoked No. 1566 § 1803
166 revoked No. 242 § 1833
176 amended No. 841 § 3276
176 amended No. 2170 § 3276
210 revoked No. 382 § 4872
223 revoked No. 2186 § 2377
243 revoked No. 188 § 98
247 amended No. 608 § 1838
248 amended No. 609 § 1836
252 amended No. 772 § 4437
254 revoked No. 1850 § 4787
256 amended No. 38 § 4433
256 amended No. 771 § 4433
274 revoked No. 1378 § 3265
285 revoked No. 821 § 2970
298 amended No. 368 § 2552
306 revoked No. 1758 § 96
338 revoked No. 255 § 4489
341 amended No. 1134 § 1799
352 revoked No. 2213 § 472
380 amended No. 657 § 2841
380 amended No. 1100 § 2824
380 amended No. 1103 § 2832
380 amended No. 1104 § 2832
380 amended No. 1106 § 2832
380 amended No. 1114 § 2823
380 amended No. 1117 § 2839
412 amended No. 547 § 97
415 revoked No. 214 § 3461
416 revoked No. 1758 § 96
418 amended No. 119 § 1289
418 amended No. 1209 § 1289
421 amended No. 804 § 3594
421 amended No. 2227 § 3594
432 revoked No. 291 § 4399
451 amended No. 335 § 3478
451 amended No. 491 § 3495
451 amended No. 1968 § 3460
457 amended No. 1258 § 2427
458 amended No. 491 § 3495
464 amended No. 740 § 3924
468 amended No. 630 § 4489
470 amended No. 631 § 4485
516 revoked No. 292 § 1803
519 revoked No. 366 § 4441
519 amended No. 825 § 4441
520 revoked No. 365 § 4137
520 amended No. 826 § 4137
520 amended No. 1357 § 4137
613 revoked No. 214 § 3461
614 amended No. 1106 § 2832
720 revoked No. 899 § 1277
721 revoked No. 899 § 1277
722 revoked No. 900 § 2662
737 revoked No. 1378 § 2118
746 amended No. 155 § 3813
746 amended No. 2108 § 3813
748 amended No. 1755 § 3780

1984—*cont.*
769 amended No. 910 § 2407
812 amended No. 1315 § 3287
839 revoked No. 1758 § 96
856 revoked No. 2094 § 3575
938 amended No. 491 § 3495
955 revoked No. 1591 § 3414
981 amended No. 1509 § 3310
996 amended No. 1529 § 5196
1005 revoked No. 2138 § 3421
1015 amended No. 349 § 3648
1098 amended No. 1960 § 1258
1155 revoked No. 1264 § 2082
1179 revoked No. 1261 § 1249
1216 amended No. 1886 § 3414
1224 revoked No. 755 § 2228
1232 revoked No. 1850 § 4787
1260 amended No. 1920 § 3316
1300 revoked No. 710 § 73
1305 amended No. 1986 § 1806
1308 revoked No. 711 § 77
1404 amended No. 315 § 3310
1404 amended No. 1556 § 3310
1504 amended No. 432 § 4947
1504 amended No. 794 § 4947
1519 amended No. 26 § 4476
1579 revoked No. 360 § 472
1590 revoked No. 851 § 2867
1685 amended No. 1806 § 3853
1802 amended No. 1979 § 3313
1808 revoked No. 851 § 2867
1819 revoked No. 1264 § 2082
1871 revoked No. 1758 § 96
1885 revoked No. 800 § 4475
1920 amended No. 2083 § 179
1921 amended No. 1114 § 2823
1934 amended No. 1057 § 3787
1960 amended No. 491 § 3495
1960 amended No. 1968 § 3460
1979 revoked No. 1264 § 2082
1989 amended No. 287 § 2787
1991 revoked No. 214 § 3461
2011 revoked No. 53 § 3352
2024 amended No. 2129 § 86

1985
67 amended No. 2237 § 1812
111 amended No. 1914 § 4795
130 revoked No. 851 § 2867
156 revoked No. 256 § 2838
202 revoked No. 353 § 3227
216 revoked No. 2237 § 1812
220 amended No. 64 § 185
257 amended No. 351 § 2377
257 revoked No. 2186 § 2377
263 amended No. 2168 § 3300
281 revoked No. 353 § 3227
313 revoked No. 292 § 1803
326 amended No. 368 § 2552
337 revoked No. 382 § 4872
356 revoked No. 188 § 98
373 amended No. 403 § 1431
383 amended No. 387 § 4719
385 revoked No. 498 § 3936
397 revoked No. 890 § 4060
438 revoked No. 649 § 97
487 amended No. 1536 § 1803
554 revoked No. 365 § 4137
557 revoked No. 366 § 4441
568 revoked No. 2088 § 3202

1985—*cont.*
569 revoked No. 2089 § 3204
575 amended No. 608 § 1838
637 revoked No. 1758 § 96
641 amended No. 630 § 4489
660 amended No. 1886 § 3414
661 amended No. 1886 § 3414
677 amended No. 1440 § 1884
684 amended No. 1314 § 1258
685 amended No. 1312 § 1248
716 amended No. 1434 § 3869
751 amended No. 455 § 2088
751 amended No. 2044 § 1702
757 amended No. 1578 § 411
823 revoked No. 786 § 3186
827 amended No. 39 § 4452
830 amended No. 1313 § 1248
849 amended No. 215 § 1110
849 amended No. 271 § 1110
849 amended No. 1350 § 1110
849 revoked No. 2070 § 1110
852 revoked No. 803 § 3873
854 amended No. 752 § 339
885 revoked No. 851 § 2867
886 amended No. 150 § 3811
886 amended No. 510 § 3797
967 amended No. 335 § 3478
967 amended No. 2112 § 3478
975 amended No. 1092 § 98
976 amended No. 1091 § 98
977 amended No. 1097 § 98
979 amended No. 1093 § 98
980 amended No. 1098 § 98
981 amended No. 1148 § 98
995 revoked No. 401 § 2551
1045 revoked No. 851 § 2867
1065 amended No. 1445 § 232
1066 amended No. 798 § 227
1067 amended No. 798 § 227
1068 amended No. 800 § 4475
1071 amended No. 1066 § 3255
1108 revoked No. 52 § 1851
1130 revoked No. 700 § 2431
1131 revoked No. 405 § 395
1133 amended No. 2088 § 3202
1134 revoked No. 2089 § 3204
1144 amended No. 1293 § 3569
1151 amended No. 1520 § 3147
1160 revoked No. 1261 § 1249
1161 revoked No. 1378 § 3265
1213 revoked No. 2233 § 4027
1230 revoked No. 1758 § 96
1232 revoked No. 2024 § 3087
1266 amended No. 1950 § 87
1293 revoked No. 2070 § 1110
1294 revoked No. 2070 § 1110
1306 amended No. 884 § 3414
1323 amended No. 1099 § 2824
1323 amended No. 1114 § 2823
1411 amended No. 92 § 1378
1465 amended No. 1304 § 1910
1576 amended No. 798 § 227
1577 revoked No. 851 § 2867
1593 amended No. 675 § 3293
1596 revoked No. 3 § 3575
1605 amended No. 136 § 3404
1605 revoked No. 1637 § 3404
1607 revoked No. 63 § 3402
1627 amended No. 314 § 1124
1630 amended No. 973 § 1106

1985—*cont.*
1630 amended No. 1053 § 1106
1630 amended No. 1125 § 1106
1630 amended No. 1218 § 1106
1630 amended No. 1804 § 1106
1630 amended No. 1902 § 1106
1630 revoked No. 2184 § 1106
1643 amended No. 1812 § 172
1643 revoked No. 2062 § 172
1650 amended No. 1916 § 3797
1665 revoked No. 220 § 3414
1712 revoked No. 1425 § 2551
1713 amended No. 1382 § 4721
1714 amended No. 1145 § 172
1727 revoked No. 63 § 3402
1733 amended No. 423 § 4795
1777 amended No. 1826 § 529
1777 amended No. 1833 § 529
1800 amended No. 439 § 1119
1823 amended No. 1123 § 2418
1823 amended No. 1980 § 2418
1857 amended No. 904 § 104
1858 revoked No. 904 § 104
1862 revoked No. 904 § 104
1880 amended No. 388 § 2280
1883 revoked No. 96 § 1258
1890 revoked No. 2256 § 3793
1903 amended No. 337 § 3791
1928 amended No. 657 § 2841
1929 amended No. 1106 § 3832
1929 amended No. 1114 § 2823
1930 amended No. 1106 § 2832
1931 amended No. 1107 § 2832
1931 amended No. 1114 § 2823
1936 amended No. 798 § 227
1960 revoked No. 50 § 3199
1975 revoked No. 373 § 2828
1984 revoked No. 1264 § 2082
2005 revoked No. 2256 § 3793
2011 revoked No. 783 § 3150
2029 amended No. 256 § 2838
2029 amended No. 1907 § 2838
2030 amended No. 347 § 2347
2042 amended No. 1979 § 3313
2043 amended No. 286 § 3317

1986
5 revoked No. 74 § 109
24 amended No. 293 § 2829
24 amended No. 1579 § 2386
67 revoked No. 45 § 3542
71 amended No. 1916 § 3797
82 revoked No. 2070 § 1110
121 amended No. 424 § 4793
126 revoked No. 1612 § 59
140 amended No. 275 § 4943
149 amended No. 102 § 2406
149 amended No. 2166 § 2406
194 revoked No. 1758 § 96
195 revoked No. 1758 § 96
214 revoked No. 1850 § 4787
215 revoked No. 2070 § 1110
254 revoked No. 382 § 4872
296 revoked No. 220 § 3414
334 revoked No. 244 § 3414
338 revoked No. 188 § 98
344 revoked No. 785 § 3186
383 revoked No. 889 § 395
386 amended No. 1224 § 2020
388 amended No. 331 § 2280

1986—*cont.*

392 revoked No. 605 § 1853
400 amended No. 312 § 1102
400 revoked No. 1963 § 1102
402 revoked No. 295 § 3419
403 amended No. 269 § 179
405 amended No. 884 § 3414
405 amended No. 902 § 641
405 amended No. 1636 § 641
405 amended No. 1851 § 641
416 amended No. 298 § 795
424 revoked No. 389 § 2107
428 amended No. 1208 § 85
432 revoked No. 368 § 2552
443 amended No. 349 § 3648
446 revoked No. 350 § 2053
449 revoked No. 772 § 4437
450 revoked No. 771 § 4433
459 amended No. 371 § 2552
482 amended No. 844 § 2007
510 amended No. 208 § 4399
540 revoked No. 2070 § 1110
576 amended No. 423 § 4795
583 amended No. 288 § 2809
583 amended No. 610 § 2789
588 revoked No. 1381 § 4677
608 revoked No. 377 § 3730
612 revoked No. 2023 § 331
620 revoked No. 392 § 2041
621 revoked No. 394 § 2041
622 revoked No. 393 § 2041
625 amended No. 1258 § 2427
669 revoked No. 605 § 1853
673 revoked No. 382 § 4872
674 revoked No. 365 § 4137
680 revoked No. 63 § 3402
681 revoked No. 366 § 4441
697 revoked No. 444 § 3200
724 amended No. 1483 § 2345
748 revoked No. 1378 § 3265
779 revoked No. 292 § 1803
784 revoked No. 851 § 2867
814 revoked No. 209 § 2820
831 revoked No. 803 § 3873
837 revoked No. 63 § 3402
859 revoked No. 2174 § 2406
861 revoked No. 370 § 3493
862 amended No. 836 § 114
938 amended No. 149 § 1116
939 amended No. 154 § 3813
946 revoked No. 374 § 2828
963 amended No. 192 § 2557
978 amended No. 865 § 4452
1032 amended No. 942 § 3218
1043 revoked No. 802 § 3873
1045 revoked No. 1941 § 3147
1046 amended No. 1105 § 2832
1050 revoked No. 364 § 5151
1078 amended No. 676 § 3256
1078 amended No. 1133 § 3256
1103 amended No. 1146 § 4399
1104 amended No. 1147 § 4399
1117 revoked No. 45 § 3542
1118 revoked No. 327 § 3542
1120 revoked No. 32 § 3469
1132 revoked No. 989 § 3352
1135 revoked No. 1758 § 96
1142 revoked No. 821 § 2970
1144 amended No. 1296 § 1244
1144 amended No. 1297 § 1244
1154 revoked No. 381 § 4872

1986—*cont.*

1157 amended No. 934 § 221
1159 amended No. 163 § 2469
1159 amended No. 1825 § 2469
1169 revoked No. 941 § 2762
1199 amended No. 4 § 3351
1224 revoked No. 363 § 3257
1227 amended No. 1366 § 4399
1250 revoked No. 902 § 641
1256 revoked No. 1465 § 72
1290 revoked No. 74 § 109
1303 amended No. 170 § 3757
1304 revoked No. 2212 § 172
1305 amended No. 1835 § 3404
1306 revoked No. 1261 § 1249
1324 amended No. 499 § 1271
1324 amended No. 1393 § 1271
1325 revoked No. 1261 § 1249
1353 revoked No. 309 § 4404
1357 revoked No. 1199 § 1675
1358 revoked No. 381 § 4872
1359 revoked No. 382 § 4872
1368 revoked No. 2216 § 2404
1369 revoked No. 1378 § 3265
1379 revoked No. 256 § 2838
1390 amended No. 1120 § 2406
1397 revoked No. 1261 § 1249
1437 revoked No. 1566 § 1803
1442 amended No. 2088 § 3202
1446 revoked No. 2070 § 1110
1447 revoked No. 751 § 3746
1449 revoked No. 1850 § 4787
1456 amended No. 805 § 3264
1464 revoked No. 199 § 3352
1475 amended No. 870 § 4476
1493 revoked No. 1421 § 3264
1511 revoked No. 268 § 1870
1530 amended No. 626 § 90
1611 amended No. 410 § 1813
1611 amended No. 909 § 1813
1612 revoked No. 908 § 1813
1613 amended No. 425 § 4477
1613 amended No. 881 § 4477
1614 revoked No. 882 § 4477
1623 amended No. 1782 § 3150
1627 revoked No. 901 § 1287
1681 amended No. 182 § 1808
1681 amended No. 263 § 1808
1681 amended No. 885 § 1808
1681 revoked No. 1181 § 1808
1689 amended No. 153 § 1808
1689 amended No. 249 § 1808
1689 amended No. 906 § 1808
1689 amended No. 1555 § 1808
1689 amended No. 1687 § 1808
1689 revoked No. 1893 § 1808
1707 revoked No. 1181 § 1808
1712 amended No. 65 § 200
1713 amended No. 356 § 713
1713 amended No. 1855 § 713
1713 amended No. 2222 § 713
1713 amended No. 2223 § 713
1715 amended No. 2018 § 266
1734 revoked No. 211 § 109
1741 revoked No. 199 § 3352
1746 revoked No. 595 § 3352
1756 revoked No. 1181 § 1808
1775 revoked No. 1181 § 1808
1777 amended No. 855 § 3377
1795 amended No. 876 § 3152

1986—*cont.*

1818 amended No. 1851 § 641
1839 revoked No. 199 § 3352
1841 revoked No. 53 § 3352
1842 revoked No. 53 § 3352
1844 revoked No. 989 § 3352
1849 revoked No. 1181 § 1808
1877 amended No. 1670 § 249
1881 revoked No. 1264 § 2082
1915 amended No. 1921 § 4049
1925 amended No. 1919 § 343
1934 revoked No. 2070 § 1110
1948 amended No. 2128 § 2025
1960 amended No. 1978 § 3542
1965 amended No. 275 § 4943
1993 revoked No. 2248 § 2085
1994 amended No. 1959 § 343
2001 amended No. 1398 § 214
2004 amended No. 192 § 2557
2006 amended No. 192 § 2557
2020 amended No. 2046 § 1697
2027 revoked No. 468 § 3011
2032 revoked No. 851 § 2867
2049 amended No. 1538 § 3875
2052 revoked No. 199 § 3352
2057 revoked No. 595 § 3352
2058 revoked No. 595 § 3352
2059 revoked No. 595 § 3352
2098 amended No. 1500 § 264
2103 revoked No. 1908 § 2338
2115 revoked No. 821 § 2970
2152 revoked No. 2005 § 262
2155 revoked No. 391 § 253
2161 revoked No. 2096 § 204
2172 revoked No. 1968 § 3460
2173 revoked No. 481 § 3484
2180 revoked No. 122 § 2118
2208 revoked No. 1893 § 1808
2214 amended No. 261 § 1278
2215 amended No. 260 § 1278
2218 amended No. 335 § 3478
2218 amended No. 1424 § 3451
2218 amended No. 1970 § 3451
2226 amended No. 1828 § 821
2241 revoked No. 851 § 2867
2242 revoked No. 1181 § 1808
2248 revoked No. 270 § 1808
2300 revoked No. 783 § 3150

1987

1 amended No. 262 § 1279
19 revoked No. 1758 § 96
27 revoked No. 97 § 3264
28 revoked No. 98 § 3264
38 revoked No. 771 § 4433
45 revoked No. 1978 § 3542
52 amended No. 605 § 1853
63 amended No. 548 § 3414
63 amended No. 854 § 3414
63 amended No. 2113 § 3414
67 revoked No. 199 § 3352
69 revoked No. 1399 § 3352
70 revoked No. 989 § 3352
71 revoked No. 199 § 3352
102 revoked No. 2166 § 2406
136 revoked No. 1637 § 3404
153 revoked No. 1893 § 1808
156 amended No. 256 § 2838
156 amended No. 341 § 2859
158 amended No. 342 § 2859

1987—*cont.*

159 amended No. 343 § 2859
163 revoked No. 1825 § 2469
178 revoked No. 304 § 1883
182 revoked No. 1181 § 1808
184 amended No. 519 § 705
202 revoked No. 989 § 3352
211 amended No. 248 § 114
211 revoked No. 1808 § 114
215 revoked No. 2070 § 1110
248 revoked No. 1808 § 114
249 revoked No. 1893 § 1808
256 amended No. 341 § 2859
257 amended No. 341 § 2859
257 amended No. 2215 § 2838
263 revoked No. 1181 § 1808
271 revoked No. 2070 § 1110
272 revoked No. 1304 § 1910
275 amended No. 1329 § 4943
288 amended No. 610 § 2789
291 revoked No. 644 § 4399
311 amended No. 1603 § 3414
312 revoked No. 1963 § 1102
351 revoked No. 2186 § 2377
365 amended No. 824 § 4137
365 amended No. 1358 § 4137
366 amended No. 823 § 4441
366 amended No. 895 § 4441
381 amended No. 431 § 4872
382 amended No. 883 § 4441
382 amended No. 1356 § 4441
405 revoked No. 889 § 395
423 amended No. 1914 § 4795
424 revoked No. 1878 § 4793
428 revoked No. 1758 § 96
468 amended No. 2211 § 3011
519 amended No. 894 § 4441
548 revoked No. 854 § 3414
560 revoked No. 1378 § 3265
610 amended No. 753 § 2789
644 amended No. 1801 § 4399
650 revoked No. 1433 § 1272
670 amended No. 855 § 3377
718 revoked No. 1978 § 3542
734 revoked No. 870 § 4476
751 amended No. 964 § 3757
763 revoked No. 2105 § 1104
784 revoked No. 1535 § 2395
786 revoked No. 1251 § 3186
839 revoked No. 1535 § 2395
851 amended No. 1753 § 2861
885 revoked No. 1181 § 1808
890 revoked No. 1842 § 4060
906 revoked No. 1893 § 1808
940 amended No. 1030 § 526
974 revoked No. 1399 § 3352
979 revoked No. 1399 § 3352
981 revoked No. 1399 § 3352
982 revoked No. 1399 § 3352
985 revoked No. 1399 § 3352
986 revoked No. 1399 § 3352
987 revoked No. 1399 § 3352
1096 amended No. 1853 § 3501
1108 amended No. 1933 § 2836
1109 revoked No. 1933 § 2836
1115 amended No. 1933 § 2836
1165 amended No. 1567 § 1808, 4470
1165 amended No. 1696 § 1808
1165 revoked No. 1837 § 1808
1181 revoked No. 1436 § 1808

1987—*cont.*
1350 revoked No. 2070 § 1110
1436 revoked No. 1515 § 1808
1450 amended No. 1568 § 1808, 4470
1450 amended No. 1697 § 1808
1450 revoked No. 1888 § 1808, 4470
1515 revoked No. 1638 § 1808
1553 revoked No. 1638 § 1808
1555 revoked No. 1893 § 1808
1567 revoked No. 1837 § 1808
1568 revoked No. 1888 § 1808, 4470
1583 revoked No. 2186 § 2377
1638 amended No. 1682 § 1808

1978—*cont.*
1638 amended No. 1802 § 1808
1638 revoked No. 1894 § 1808
1679 revoked No. 1758 § 96
1682 revoked No. 1894 § 1808
1687 revoked No. 1893 § 1808
1696 revoked No. 1837 § 1808
1697 revoked No. 1888 § 1808, 4470
1802 revoked No. 1894 § 1808
1803 revoked No. 1893 § 1808
2000 amended No. 2172 § 158a
2001 amended No. 2173 § 167

ALPHABETICAL TABLE OF NORTHERN IRELAND STATUTORY RULES AND ORDERS 1987

ADMINISTRATIVE LAW

Audit (1987 Order) (Commencement) Order (Northern Ireland) 1987 (No. 137 (C.5)) 2622
Lands Tribunal (Salaries) Order (Northern Ireland) 1987 (No. 359) 2622
Public Use of Records (Amendment) Rules (Northern Ireland) 1987 (No. 98) 2622
Salaries (Comptroller and Auditor General and Others) Order (Northern Ireland) 1987 (No. 41) 2622
Salaries (Parliamentary Commissioner and Commissioner for Complaints) Order (Northern Ireland) 1987 (No. 360) 2622

AGENCY

Enduring Powers of Attorney (Northern Ireland Consequential Amendment) Order 1987 (No. 1628) 2626

AGRICULTURE

Agricultural and Horticultural Co-operation Scheme (Northern Ireland) 1987 (No. 63) 2628
Agricultural Products Processing and Marketing (Improvement Grant) Regulations (Northern Ireland) 1987 (No. 78) 2628
Agriculture and Horticulture Development Regulations (Northern Ireland) 1987 (No. 154) 2628
Agriculture and Horticulture Grant Scheme (Northern Ireland) 1987 (No. 158) 2628
Agriculture Improvement Regulations (Northern Ireland) 1987 (No. 156) 2628
Agriculture Improvement (Amendment) Regulations (Northern Ireland) 1987 (No. 452) 2628
Calf Premium (Protection of Payments) Regulations (Northern Ireland) 1987 (No. 317) 2628
Control of Pesticides Regulations (Northern Ireland) 1987 (No. 414) 2628
Eggs (Marketing Standards) Regulations (Northern Ireland) 1987 (No. 407) 2628
Farm and Horticulture Development Regulations (Northern Ireland) 1987 (No. 155) 2628
Farm Business Specification Order (Northern Ireland) 1987 (No. 448) 2628
Farm Diversification Grant Scheme (Northern Ireland) 1987 (No. 451) 2628
Farm Structure (Payments to Outgoers) (Continuation) Scheme (Northern Ireland) 1987 (No. 94) 2628
Grassland Scheme (Northern Ireland) 1987 (No. 197) 2628
Hill Livestock (Compensatory Allowances) Regulations (Northern Ireland) 1987 (No. 92) 2628
Hill Livestock (Compensatory Allowances) (Amendment) Regulations (Northern Ireland) 1987 (No. 445). 2628
Import and Export (Plants and Plant Products) (Plant Health) (Amendment) Order (Northern Ireland) 1987 (No. 120) 2628
Milk (Cessation of Production) Scheme (Northern Ireland) 1987 (No. 357) 2628
Milk (Community Outgoers Scheme) (Amendment) Regulations (Northern Ireland) 1987 (No. 114) 2628
Milk (Community Outgoers Scheme) (Amendment No. 2) Regulations (Northern Ireland) 1987 (No. 225) 2628
Milk (Partial Cessation of Production) (Amendment) Scheme (Northern Ireland) 1987 (No. 64) 2628
Milk Regulations (Northern Ireland) 1987 (No. 229) 2628
Pigs (Carcase Classification Scheme) (Amendment) Order (Northern Ireland) 1987 (No. 235) 2628
Pig Improvement Scheme (Northern Ireland) 1987 (No. 381) 2628
Potatoes (Assured Markets) Order (Northern Ireland) 1987 (No. 83) 2628
Potatoes (Prohibition on Landing) Order (Northern Ireland) 1987 (No. 9) 2628
Potatoes (Protection of Guarantees) Order (Northern Ireland) 1987 (No. 84) 2628
Seeds (Fees) Regulations (Northern Ireland) 1987 (No. 321) 2628
Seed Potatoes (Crop Fees) Regulations (Northern Ireland) 1987 (No. 96) 2628
Seed Potatoes (Levy) (Amendment) Order (Northern Ireland) 1987 (No. 89) 2628
Seed Potatoes (Tuber and Label Fees) (Amendment) Regulations (Northern Ireland) 1987 (No. 312) 2628
Suckler Cow Premium Regulations (Northern Ireland) 1987 (No. 85) 2628

ANIMALS

Animals (Scientific Procedures) (Procedure for Representations) Rules (Northern Ireland) 1987 (No. 2)... 2631
Canada Geese Order (Northern Ireland) 1987 (No. 403) 2631
Export of Sheep (Prohibition) Order (Northern Ireland) 1987 (No. 119) 2631
Export of Sheep (Prohibition) (No. 2) Order (Northern Ireland) 1987 (No. 372) 2631
Game Birds Preservation Order (Northern Ireland) 1987 (No. 262) 2631
Importation of Bees (Amendment) Order (Northern Ireland) 1987 (No. 320) 2631

Sheep Scab (Amendment) Order (Northern Ireland) 1987 (No. 223) 2631
Welfare of Battery Hens Regulations (Northern Ireland) 1987 (No. 425) 2631
Welfare of Livestock (Prohibited Operations) Regulations (Northern Ireland) 1987 (No. 415) 2631

BANKRUPTCY

Bankruptcy (Fees and Deposit) Regulations (Northern Ireland) 1987 (No. 419) 2632

BUILDING AND CONSTRUCTION

Building (Amendment) Regulations (Northern Ireland) 1987 (No. 268) 2633

COMPANY LAW

Companies (Accounting Thresholds) (Modification) Regulations (Northern Ireland) 1987 (No. 37) 2640
Companies (Consolidation of Fees) Regulations (Northern Ireland) 1987 (No. 258) 2640
Companies (Disclosure of Directors' Interests) (Exceptions) Regulations (Northern Ireland) 1987 (No. 208) 2640
Companies (Mergers and Divisions) Regulations (Northern Ireland) 1987 (No. 442) 2640
Companies (Winding-Up) Fees Regulations (Northern Ireland) 1987 (No. 418) 2640

COMPULSORY PURCHASE

Compulsory Acquisition (Interest) Order (Northern Ireland) 1987 (No. 147) 2642
Compulsory Acquisition (Interest) (No. 2) Order (Northern Ireland) 1987 (No. 232) 2642
Compulsory Acquisition (Interest) (No. 3) Order (Northern Ireland) 1987 (No. 400) 2642

CRIMINAL LAW

Misuse of Drugs (Amendment) Regulations (Northern Ireland) 1987 (No. 68) 2652
Misuse of Drugs (Designation) Order (Northern Ireland) 1987 (No. 66) 2652
Misuse of Drugs (Safe Custody) (Amendment) (Northern Ireland) Regulations 1987 (No. 67) 2652
Public Order (Exceptions) Order (Northern Ireland) 1987 (No. 126) 2648a
Rehabilitation of Offenders (Exceptions) (Amendment) Order (Northern Ireland) 1987 (No. 393) 2653

CUSTOMS AND EXCISE

General Betting Duty (Northern Ireland) (Amendment) Regulations 1987 (No. 313) 2656

EDUCATION

Education (Corporal Punishment) (1987 Order) (Commencement) Order (Northern Ireland) 1987 (No. 271 (C.10)) 2659
Payment of Teachers' Salaries and Allowances Regulations (Northern Ireland) 1987 (No. 127) 2659
Students Awards Regulations (Northern Ireland) 1987 (No. 420) 2659
Teachers' (Eligibility) Regulations (Northern Ireland) 1987 (No. 266) 2659
Teachers' Salaries (Amendment) Regulations (Northern Ireland) 1987 (No. 252) 2659
Teachers' Salaries (Maternity Absence) Regulations (Northern Ireland) 1987 (No. 206) 2659
Teachers' Salaries Regulations (Northern Ireland) 1987 (No. 384) 2659
Teachers' Salaries (Reorganisation Allowances) Regulations (Northern Ireland) 1987 (No. 385) 2659
Teachers' (Terms and Conditions of Employment) Regulations (Northern Ireland) 1987 (No. 267) 2659

ELECTION LAW

Local Elections (Northern Ireland) (Amendment) Order 1987 (No. 168) 2662
Returning Officers' Expenses (Northern Ireland) Regulations 1987 (No. 900) 2662

EMERGENCY LAWS

Northern Ireland (Emergency Provisions) Act 1978 (Continuance) Order 1987 (No. 30) 2665
Northern Ireland (Emergency Provisions) Act 1987 (Commencement No. 1) Order (No. 1241 (C.35)) 2665

ELECTRICITY

Electricity (Permitted Supply) Order (Northern Ireland) 1987 (No. 456) 2663

EMPLOYMENT

Employment Subsidies (Renewal) Order (Northern Ireland) 1987 (No. 215) 2667
Industrial Relations (1987 Order) (Commencement) Order (Northern Ireland) 1987 (No. 308 (C.12)) 2667
Industrial Relations (Variation of Limits) Order (Northern Ireland) 1987 (No. 73) 2667
Redundancy Payments (Local Government Etc.) (Modification) (Amendment) Order (Northern Ireland) 1987 (No. 28) 2667
Sex Discrimination (Training Designations) Order (Northern Ireland) 1987 (No. 319) 2667

Unfair Dismissal (Increase of Compensation Limit) Order (Northern Ireland) 1987 (No. 74) 2667
Unfair Dismissal (Increase of Limits of Basic and Special Awards) Order (Northern Ireland) 1987 (No. 318) 2667

EVIDENCE (CIVIL)

Blood Tests (Evidence of Paternity) (Amendment) Regulations (Northern Ireland) 1987 (No. 375) 2673

EXECUTORS AND ADMINISTRATORS

Administration of Estates (Rights of Surviving Spouse) Order (Northern Ireland) 1987 (No. 378) 2674

FIRE SERVICE

Fire Services (Betting, Gaming and Amusement Premises) Order (Northern Ireland) 1987 (No. 334) 2675

FISH AND FISHERIES

Eel Fishing (Licence Duties) Regulations (Northern Ireland) 1987 (No. 423) 2676
Fisheries (Licence Duties) Byelaws (Northern Ireland) 1987 (No. 436) 2676
Fishing Vessels (Financial Assistance) Scheme (Northern Ireland 1987 (No. 113) 2676
Foyle Area (Angling) (Amendment) Regulations 1987 (No. 31) 2676
Foyle Area (Close Seasons for Angling) Regulations 1987 (No. 344) 2676
Foyle Area (Control of Netting) (Amendment) Regulations 1987 (No. 219) 2676
Foyle Area (Licensing of Fishing Engines) (Amendment) Regulations 1987 (No. 32) 2676
Foyle Area (Licensing of Fishing Engines) (Amendment No. 2) Regulations 1987 (No. 467) 2676
Rainbow Trout Waters Byelaws (Northern Ireland) 1987 (No. 18) 2676
Rainbow Trout Waters (No. 2) Byelaws (Northern Ireland) 1987 (No. 422) 2676
Sea Fisheries (Amendment) Regulations (Northern Ireland) 1987 (No. 69) 2676

FOOD AND DRUGS

Authorised Officers (Meat Inspection) Regulations (Northern Ireland) 1987 (No. 141) 2677
Colouring Matter in Food (Amendment) Regulations (Northern Ireland) 1987 (No. 471) 2677
Condensed Milk and Dried Milk (Amendment) Regulations (Northern Ireland) 1987 (No. 65) 2677
Control of Pesticides (Advisory Committee) Order (Northern Ireland) 1987 (No. 341) 2677
Control of Pesticides (Advisory Committee) (Terms of Office) Regulations (Northern Ireland) 1987 (No. 342) 2677
Food Protection (Emergency Prohibitions) Order (Northern Ireland) 1987 (No. 367) 2677
Food Protection (Emergency Prohibitions) (Amendment) Order (Northern Ireland) 1987 (No. 395) 2677
Food (Revision of Penalties and Mode of Trial) Regulations (Northern Ireland) 1987 (No. 38) 2677
Materials and Articles in Contact with Food Regulations (Northern Ireland) 1987 (No. 432) 2677
Olive Oil (Marketing Standards) Regulations (Northern Ireland) 1987 (No. 431) 2677

GAMING AND WAGERING

Amusements with Prizes (Form of Pleasure Permit) Regulations (Northern Ireland) 1987 (No. 195) 2678
Betting and Gaming (Fees and Variation of Monetary Limits) Order (Northern Ireland) 1987 (No. 186) 2678
Betting, Gaming, Lotteries and Amusements (1985 Order) (Commencement No. 2) Order (Northern Ireland) 1987 (No. 6 (C.1)) 2678
Betting, Gaming, Lotteries and Amusements (1985 Order) (Commencement No. 3) Order (Northern Ireland) 1987 (No. 185 (C.8)) 2678
Bookmaking (Conduct of Licensed Offices) Order (Northern Ireland) 1987 (No. 396) 2678
Bookmaking (Licensed Offices) Regulations (Northern Ireland) 1987 (No. 192) 2678
Gaming (Bingo) Regulations (Northern Ireland) 1987 (No. 8) 2678
Gaming (Bingo) (Amendment) Regulations (Northern Ireland) 1987 (No. 398) 2678
Gaming (Form of Bingo Club Licence) Regulations (Northern Ireland) 1987 (No. 7) 2678
Gaming (Variation of Monetary Limit and Charges) Order (Northern Ireland) 1987 (No. 397) 2678
Horse Racing and Betting (Amendment) Order (Northern Ireland) 1987 (No. 265) 2678
Lotteries Regulations (Northern Ireland) 1987 (No. 193) 2678
Lottery (Form of Certificate) Regulations (Northern Ireland) 1987 (No. 194) 2678

HEALTH AND SAFETY AT WORK

Agriculture (Poisonous Substances) Regulations (Northern Ireland) 1987 (No. 364) 2680
Agriculture (Tractor Cabs) (Amendment) Regulations (Northern Ireland) 1987 (No. 376) 2680
Asbestos (Licensing) (Medical Fees Revocation) Regulations (Northern Ireland) 1987 (No. 430) 2679
Dry Cleaning (Metrication) Regulations (Northern Ireland) 1987 (No. 33) 2679
Health and Safety (Medical Fees) Regulations (Northern Ireland) 1987 (No. 427) 2679
Ionising Radiations (Medical Fees Revocation) Regulations (Northern Ireland) 1987 (No. 429) 2679
Medical Examinations (Fees) (Revocation) Regulations (Northern Ireland) 1987 (No. 428) 2679

HOUSING

Home Purchase Assistance (Price Limit) Order (Northern Ireland) 1987 (No. 298) 2681
Housing Benefit (Transitional) Regulations (Northern Ireland) 1987 (No. 462) 2681
Housing Benefits (Amendment) Regulations (Northern Ireland) 1987 (No. 77) 2681
Housing Benefits (Amendment No. 2) Regulations (Northern Ireland) 1987 (No. 95) 2681
Housing Benefits (Amendment No. 3) Regulations (Northern Ireland) 1987 (No. 332) 2681
Housing (Houses in Multiple Occupation) (Prescribed Forms) Regulations (Northern Ireland) 1987 (No. 132) 2681
Housing (Right to Equity-Sharing Lease) (Rent and Service Charge Adjustment) Order (Northern Ireland) 1987 (No. 162) 2681
Housing (Unoccupied Premises—Continuance of Powers) Order (Northern Ireland) 1987 (No. 340) 2681

INHERITANCE TAX

Estate Duty (Northern Ireland) (Interest on Unpaid Duty) Order 1987 (No. 893) 2682
Inheritance Tax (Delivery of Accounts) (Northern Ireland) Regulations 1987 (No. 1129) 2682

JURIES

Jury Trial (Amendment) (Northern Ireland) Order 1987 (No. 1283) 2683

LANDLORD AND TENANT

Registered Rents (Increase) Order (Northern Ireland) 1987 (No. 42) 2684

LEGAL AID

Legal Advice and Assistance (Amendment) Regulations (Northern Ireland) 1987 (No. 102) 2698
Legal Advice and Assistance (Financial Conditions) Regulations (Northern Ireland) 1987 (No. 103) 2698
Legal Aid (Financial Conditions) Regulations (Northern Ireland) 1987 (No. 104) 2698

LICENSING

Licensing (1987 Order) (Commencement No. 1) Order (Northern Ireland) 1987 No. 365 (C.13)) 2699

LOCAL GOVERNMENT

Chief Building Control Officers (Qualifications) Regulations (Northern Ireland) 1987 (No. 300) 2702
Cinematograph and Petroleum-Spirit Licences (Fees) (Increase) Order (Northern Ireland) 1987 (No. 408) 2702
District Councils (Goods, Services and Staff) (Specified Bodies) Regulations (Northern Ireland) 1987 (No. 269) 2702
Local Government (General Grant) Order (Northern Ireland) 1987 (No. 48) 2702

MEDICINE

Pharmaceutical Qualifications (EEC Recognition) Regulations (Northern Ireland) 1987 (No. 457) 2706
Poisons (Amendment) Regulations (Northern Ireland) 1987 (No. 240) 2706
Poisons List (Amendment) Order (Northern Ireland) 1987 (No. 239) 2706

NATIONAL HEALTH

Charges for Drugs and Appliances (Amendment) Regulations (Northern Ireland) 1987 (No. 108) 2709
General Dental Services (Amendment) Regulations (Northern Ireland) 1987 (No. 190) 2709
General Dental Services (Amendment No. 2) Regulations (Northern Ireland) 1987 (No. 346) 2709
General Medical and Pharmaceutical Services (Amendment) Regulations (Northern Ireland) 1987 (No. 1) 2709
General Medical and Pharmaceutical Services (Amendment No. 3) Regulations (Northern Ireland) 1987 (No. 323) 2709
Health and Personal Social Services (Amendment) (1986 Order) (Commencement) Order (Northern Ireland) 1987 (No. 200 (C.9)) 2709
Nurses, Midwives and Health Visitors (Professional Conduct) Rules 1987, Approval Order (Northern Ireland) 1987 (No. 473) 2709
Welfare Foods (Amendment) Regulations (Northern Ireland) 1987 (No. 373) 2709

NORTHERN IRELAND ACT 1974

Northern Ireland Act 1974 (Interim Period Extension) Order 1987 (No. 1207) 2713

PENSIONS AND SUPERANNUATION

Contracting-Out (Transfer) (Amendment) Regulations (Northern Ireland) 1987 (No. 277) 2714
Contracting-Out (Widowers' Guaranteed Minimum Pensions) Regulations (Northern Ireland) 1987 (No. 278) 2714
Firemen's Pension Scheme (Amendment) Order (Northern Ireland) 1987 (No. 424) 2714

Judicial Pensions (Northern Ireland) (Widows' and Children's Benefits) Regulations 1987 (No. 101)........ 2714
Judicial Pensions (Northern Ireland) (Widows' and Children's Benefits) (Amendment) Regulations 1987 (No. 160)........ 2714
Money Purchase Contracted-Out Schemes Regulations (Northern Ireland) 1987 (No. 279)........ 2714
Occupational Pension Schemes (Auditors) Regulations (Northern Ireland) 1987 (No. 280)........ 2714
Occupational Pension Schemes (Contracting-Out) (Amendment) Regulations (Northern Ireland) 1987 (No. 282)........ 2714
Occupational Pension Schemes (Contracted-Out Protected Rights Premiums) Regulations (Northern Ireland) 1987 (No. 281)........ 2714
Occupational Pension Schemes (Disclosure of Information) (Amendment) Regulations (Northern Ireland) 1987 (No. 283)........ 2714
Occupational Pension Schemes (Qualifying Service—Consequential and Other Provisions) Regulations (Northern Ireland) 1987 (No. 284)........ 2714
Occupational Pension Schemes (Transfer Values) (Amendment) Regulations (Northern Ireland) 1987 (No. 285)........ 2714
Occupational Pensions (Revaluation) Order (Northern Ireland) 1987 (No. 434)........ 2714
Pensions Increase (Review) Order (Northern Ireland) 1987 (No. 70)........ 2714
Pension Schemes (Voluntary Contributions Requirements and Voluntary and Compulsory Membership) Regulations (Northern Ireland) 1987 (No. 286)........ 2714
Personal and Occupational Pension Schemes (Abatement of Benefit) Regulations (Northern Ireland) 1987 (No. 291)........ 2714
Personal and Occupational Pension Schemes (Consequential Provisions) Regulations (Northern Ireland) 1987 (No. 292)........ 2714
Personal and Occupational Pension Schemes (Incentive Payments) Regulations (Northern Ireland) 1987 (No. 293)........ 2714
Personal and Occupational Pension Schemes (Modification of Enactments) Regulations (Northern Ireland) 1987 (No. 294)........ 2714
Personal and Occupational Pension Schemes (Protected Rights) Regulations (Northern Ireland) 1987 (No. 295)........ 2714
Personal Pension Schemes (Appropriate Schemes) Regulations (Northern Ireland) 1987 (No. 287)........ 2714
Personal Pension Schemes (Deferment of Commencement) Regulations (Northern Ireland) 1987 (No. 433)........ 2714
Personal Pension Schemes (Disclosure of Information) Regulations (Northern Ireland) 1987 (No. 288)........ 2714
Personal Pension Schemes (Personal Pension Protected Rights Premiums) Regulations (Northern Ireland) 1987 (No. 289)........ 2714
Personal Pension Schemes (Transfer Values) Regulations (Northern Ireland) 1987 (No. 290)........ 2714
Protected Rights (Transfer Payment) Regulations (Northern Ireland) 1987 (No. 296)........ 2714
Royal Ulster Constabulary Pensions (Lump Sum Payments to Widows) Regulations 1987 (No. 379)........ 2714
Teachers' Superannuation (Amendment) Regulations (Northern Ireland) 1987 (No. 76)........ 2714
Teachers' Superannuation (Amendment No. 2) Regulations (Northern Ireland) 1987 (No. 86)........ 2714
Teachers' Superannuation (Amendment No. 3) Regulations (Northern Ireland) 1987 (No. 315)........ 2714
Ulster Special Constabulary Pensions (Lump Sum Payments to Widows) Regulations 1987 (No. 380)........ 2714

PETROLEUM

Petroleum Production Regulations (Northern Ireland) 1987 (No. 196)........ 2715

POLICE

Royal Ulster Constabulary (Amendment) Regulations 1987 (No. 205)........ 2716
Royal Ulster Constabulary (Amendment No. 2) Regulations 1987 (No. 441)........ 2716

PRACTICE

County Court (Amendment) Rules (Northern Ireland) 1987 (No. 124)........ 2719
Magistrates' Courts (Betting, Gaming, Lotteries and Amusements) Rules (Northern Ireland) 1987 (No. 24)........ 2719
Magistrates' Courts (Betting, Gaming, Lotteries and Amusements) (No. 2) Rules (Northern Ireland) 1987 (No. 234)........ 2719
Magistrates' Courts (Bingo Club Licence) Fees Order (Northern Ireland) 1987 (No. 34)........ 2719
Magistrates' Courts (Blood Tests) (Amendment) Rules (Northern Ireland) 1987 (No. 417)........ 2719
Magistrates' Courts (Bookmaker's Licence, Bookmaking Office Licence and Lottery Certificate) Fees Order (Northern Ireland) 1987 (No. 270)........ 2719
Rules of the Supreme Court (Northern Ireland) (Amendment) 1987 (No. 304)........ 2719
Supreme Court (Non-Contentious Probate) Fees (Amendment) Order (Northern Ireland) 1987 (No. 412) 2719

PUBLIC HEALTH

Alkali, &c. Works Order (Northern Ireland) 1987 (No. 123)........ 2727
Construction Plant and Equipment (Noise Emission) Regulations (Northern Ireland) 1987 (No. 328)........ 2727

Interest on Recoverable Sanitation Expenses Order (Northern Ireland) 1987 (No. 148) 2727
Interest on Recoverable Sanitation Expenses (No. 2) Order (Northern Ireland) 1987 (No. 233) 2727
Interest on Recoverable Sanitation Expenses (No. 3) Order (Northern Ireland) 1987 (No. 401) 2727

RATING AND VALUATION

Rates (Regional Rate) Order (Northern Ireland) 1987 (No. 75) 2728

REVENUE AND FINANCE

Financial Services Act 1986 (Transfer of Functions Relating to Friendly Societies) (Transitional Provisions) Order (Northern Ireland) 1987 (No. 440) 2734
Financial Services (Transfer of Functions Relating to Friendly Societies) Order (Northern Ireland) 1987 (No. 228) 2734
Ulster Savings Certificates (Index Linked) (Supplement) Regulations 1987 (No. 139) 2734
Ulster Savings Certificates (Thirty-third Issue) Regulations 1987 (No. 209) 2734

ROAD TRAFFIC

Community Drivers' Hours and Recording Equipment (Exemptions and Supplementary Provisions) Regulations (Northern Ireland) 1987 (No. 218) 2738
Goods Vehicles (Certification) (Amendment) Regulations (Northern Ireland) 1987 (No. 352) 2738
Large Private Passenger Vehicles (Certification) (Amendment) Regulations (Northern Ireland) 1987 (No. 351) 2738
Motor Vehicle Testing (Extension) Order (Northern Ireland) 1987 (No. 366) 2738
Motor Vehicle Testing (Fees) (Amendment) Regulations (Northern Ireland) 1987 (No. 350) 2738
Motor Vehicles (Construction and Use) (Amendment) Regulations (Northern Ireland) 1987 (No. 227) 2738
Motor Vehicles (Driving Licences) (Amendment) Regulations (Northern Ireland) 1987 (No. 211) 2738
Motor Vehicles (Type Approval) (Amendment) Regulations (Northern Ireland) 1987 (No. 389) 2738
Motor Vehicles (Type Approval and Approval Marks) (Fees) (Amendment No. 2) Regulations (Northern Ireland) 1987 (No. 390) 2738
Motor Vehicles (Type Approval) (EEC) Regulations (Northern Ireland) 1987 (No. 306) 2738
Passenger and Goods Vehicles (Recording Equipment) (Amendment) Regulations (Northern Ireland) 1987 (No. 217) 2738
Public Service Vehicles (Licence Fees) (Amendment) Regulations (Northern Ireland) 1987 (No. 349) 2738
Road Traffic (Prescribed Regulations for the Purposes of Increased Penalties) Regulations (Northern Ireland) 1987 (No. 2086) 2738
Orders made under S.I. 1981 No. 154 (N.I.1): Art. 21(1):
Belfast Order 1987 (No. 16) 2738
Belfast Order 1987 (No. 40) 2738
Belfast Order 1987 (No. 159) 2738
Belfast Order 1987 (No. 214) 2738
Belfast Order 1987 (No. 237) 2738
Belfast Order 1987 (No. 242) 2738
Belfast Order 1987 (No. 314) 2738
Belfast Order 1987 (No. 371) 2738
Belfast Order 1987 (No. 386) 2738
Coleraine Order 1987 (No. 46) 2738
Coleraine Order 1987 (No. 353) 2738
Coleraine Order 1987 (No. 358) 2738
Dromore, Co. Down Order 1987 (No. 17) 2738
Enniskillen Order 1987 (No. 236) 2738
Fivemiletown Order 1987 (No. 416) 2738
Galgorm Road, Ballymena Order 1987 (No. 189) 2738
Londonderry Order 1987 (No. 426) 2738
Newry Order 1987 (No. 35) 2738
Newtownards Order 1987 (No. 207) 2738
Short Strand, Belfast Order 1987 (No. 411) 2738
Tynan Order 1987 (No. 435) 2738
Art. 22(1):
Belfast Order 1987 (No. 238) 2738
Donegall Place, Belfast Order 1987 (No. 4) 2738
Larne Order 1987 (No. 110) 2738
Larne Order 1987 (No. 347) 2738
Whitehead Order 1987 (No. 388) 2738
Art. 50(4):
Speed Limits Order 1987 (No. 164) 2738
Speed Limits Order 1987 (No. 165) 2738
Art. 65(1):
Londonderry Order 1987 (No. 307) 2738

Art. 105(1):
Antrim, Ballymena Order 1987 (No. 241) 2738
Enniskillen Order 1987 (No. 324) 2738
Off-Street Parking Order 1987 (No. 49) 2738
Off-Street Parking Order 1987 (No. 62) 2738
Off-Street Parking Order 1987 (No. 109) 2738
Off-Street Parking Order 1987 (No. 133) 2738
Off-Street Parking Charges Order 1987 (No. 181) 2738
Off-Street Parking in Ballymoney Order 1987 (No. 45) 2738
Arts. 107(1), 109(2), 110, 111(1)(2):
On-Street Parking Order 1987 (No. 410) 2738
On-Street Parking Order 1987 (No. 444) 2738

SALE OF GOODS

Electrical Equipment (Safety) Regulations (Northern Ireland) 1987 (No. 337) 2739

SOCIAL SECURITY

Child Benefit (General) (Amendment) Regulations (Northern Ireland) 1987 (No. 130) 2741
Family Credit (General) Regulations (Northern Ireland) 1987 (No. 463) 2741
Family Credit (Transitional) Regulations (Northern Ireland) 1987 (No. 464) 2741
Family Income Supplements (Computation) Regulations (Northern Ireland) 1987 (No. 14) 2741
Family Income Supplements (General) (Amendment) Regulations (Northern Ireland) 1987 (No. 97) 2741
Income Support (Transitional) Regulations (Northern Ireland) 1987 (No. 460) 2741
Maternity Pay and Maternity Allowance (Transitional) Regulations (Northern Ireland) 1987 (No. 163) 2741
Social Fund (Maternity and Funeral Expenses) (Claims and Payments) Regulations (Northern Ireland) 1987 (No. 100) 2741
Social Security (Adjudication) Regulations (Northern Ireland) 1987 (No. 82) 2741
Social Security (Adjudication) (Amendment) Regulations (Northern Ireland) 1987 (No. 325) 2741
Social Security (Adjudication) (Amendment No. 2) Regulations (Northern Ireland) 1987 (No. 466) 2741
Social Security (Attendance Allowance) Regulations (Northern Ireland) 1987 (No. 413) 2741
Social Security (Attendance Allowance) (Amendment) Regulations (Northern Ireland) 1987 (No. 322) 2741
Social Security (Australia) Order (Northern Ireland) 1987 (No. 231) 2741
Social Security (Austria) Order (Northern Ireland) 1987 (No. 402) 2741
Social Security Benefit (Computation of Earnings) (Amendment) Regulations (Northern Ireland) 1987 (No. 201) 2741
Social Security Benefit (Dependency) (Amendment) Regulations (Northern Ireland) 1987 (No. 129) 2741
Social Security Benefits Up-Rating Order (Northern Ireland) 1987 (No. 22) 2741
Social Security Benefits Up-Rating (No. 2) Order (Northern Ireland) 1987 (No. 458) 2741
Social Security Benefits Up-Rating (Amendment) Order (Northern Ireland) 1987 (No. 111) 2741
Social Security Benefits Up-Rating Regulations (Northern Ireland) 1987 (No. 128) 2741
Social Security (Claims and Payments) Regulations (Northern Ireland) 1987 (No. 465) 2741
Social Security (Class 1 Contributions—Contracted-Out Percentages) Order (Northern Ireland) 1987 (No. 174) 2741
Social Security Commissioners (Pensionable Service) Regulations (Northern Ireland) 1987 (No. 61) 2741
Social Security Commissioners Procedure Regulations (Northern Ireland) 1987 (No. 112) 2741
Social Security (Consolidated Fund of Northern Ireland Supplement to, and Allocation of, Contributions) (Re-Rating) Order (Northern Ireland) 1987 (No. 25) 2741
Social Security (Contributions) (Amendment) Regulations (Northern Ireland) 1987 (No. 29) 2741
Social Security (Contributions) (Amendment No. 2) Regulations (Northern Ireland) 1987 (No. 143) 2741
Social Security (Contributions) (Amendment No. 3) Regulations (Northern Ireland) 1987 (No. 348) 2741
Social Security (Contributions) (Amendment No. 4) Regulations (Northern Ireland) 1987 (No. 468) 2741
Social Security (Contributions, Re-Rating) Order (Northern Ireland) 1987 (No. 26) 2741
Social Security (Credits) (Amendment No. 2) Regulations (Northern Ireland) 1987 (No. 220) 2741
Social Security (Earnings Factor) (Amendment) Regulations (Northern Ireland) 1987 (No. 115) 2741
Social Security (Earnings Factor) (Amendment No. 2) Regulations (Northern Ireland) 1987 (No. 138) 2741
Social Security (Hospital In-Patients) (Amendment) Regulations (Northern Ireland) 1987 (No. 12) 2741
Social Security (Hospital In-Patients) (Amendment No. 2) Regulations (Northern Ireland) 1987 (No. 391) 2741
Social Security (Industrial Injuries) (Prescribed Diseases) (Amendment) Regulations (Northern Ireland) 1987 (No. 116) 2741
Social Security (Industrial Injuries) (Prescribed Diseases) (Amendment No. 2) Regulations (Northern Ireland) 1987 (No. 454) 2741
Social Security (Industrial Injuries) (Reduced Earnings Allowance and Transitional) Regulations (Northern Ireland) 1987 (No. 142) 2741
Social Security (Maternity Allowance) Regulations (Northern Ireland) 1987 (No. 170) 2741
Social Security (Maternity Allowance) (Work Abroad) Regulations (Northern Ireland) 1987 (No. 151) 2741
Social Security (Medical Evidence) (Amendment) Regulations (Northern Ireland) 1987 (No. 117) 2741

Social Security (1986 Order) (Commencement No. 2) Order (Northern Ireland) 1987 (No. 20 (C.2)) 2741
Social Security (1986 Order) (Commencement No. 3) Order (Northern Ireland) 1987 (No. 21 (C.3)) 2741
Social Security (1986 Order) (Commencement No. 4) Order (Northern Ireland) 1987 (No. 121 (C.4)) 2741
Social Security (1986 Order) (Commencement No. 4) (Amendment) Order (Northern Ireland) 1987 (No. 184 (C.7)) 2741
Social Security (1986 Order) (Commencement No. 5) Order (Northern Ireland) 1987 (No. 161 (C.6)) 2741
Social Security (1986 Order) (Commencement No. 6) Order (Northern Ireland) 1987 (No. 299 (C.11)) 2741
Social Security (1986 Order) (Commencement No. 7) Order (Northern Ireland) 1987 (No. 449 (C.14)) 2741
Social Security (Notification of Deaths) Regulations (Northern Ireland) 1987 (No. 81) 2741
Social Security (Payments on Account, Over-Payments and Recovery) Regulations (Northern Ireland) 1987 (No. 122) 2741
Social Security (Portugal) Order (Northern Ireland) 1987 (No. 399) 2741
Social Security Revaluation of Earnings Factors Order (Northern Ireland) 1987 (No. 230) 2741
Social Security (Unemployment, Sickness and Invalidity Benefit) (Amendment) Regulations (Northern Ireland) 1987 (No. 90) 2741
Social Security (Unemployment, Sickness and Invalidity Benefit) (Amendment No. 2) Regulations (Northern Ireland) 1987 (No. 221) 2741
Social Security (Widow's Benefit and Retirement Pensions) (Amendment) Regulations (Northern Ireland) 1987 (No. 404) 2741
Social Security (Widow's Benefit) (Transitional) Regulations (Northern Ireland) 1987 (No. 387) 2741
State Scheme Premiums (Actuarial Tables) Regulations (Northern Ireland) 1987 (No. 175) 2741
State Scheme Premiums (Actuarial Tables—Transitional Provisions) Regulations (Northern Ireland) 1987 (No. 176) 2741
Statutory Maternity Pay (Compensation of Employers) Regulations (Northern Ireland) 1987 (No. 80) 2741
Statutory Maternity Pay (Medical Evidence) Regulations (Northern Ireland) 1987 (No. 99) 2741
Statutory Maternity Pay (Persons Abroad and Mariners) Regulations (Northern Ireland) 1987 (No. 171) 2741
Statutory Sick Pay (Additional Compensation of Employers) (Amendment) Regulations (Northern Ireland) 1987 (No. 79) 2741
Statutory Sick Pay (General) (Amendment) Regulations (Northern Ireland) 1987 (No. 131) 2741
Statutory Sick Pay (General) (Amendment No. 2) Regulations (Northern Ireland) 1987 (No. 248) 2741
Statutory Sick Pay (Rate of Payment) Regulations (Northern Ireland) 1987 (No. 23) 2741
Supplementary Benefit (Conditions of Entitlement) (Amendment) Regulations (Northern Ireland) 1987 (No. 149) 2741
Supplementary Benefit (Requirements) (Amendment) and Up-Rating Regulations (Northern Ireland) 1987 (No. 173) 2741
Supplementary Benefit (Requirements and Resources) (Amendment No. 2) Regulations (Northern Ireland) 1987 (No. 311) 2741
Supplementary Benefit (Resources) (Amendment) Regulations (Northern Ireland) 1987 (No. 172) 2741
Supplementary Benefit (Single Payments) (Amendment) Regulations (Northern Ireland) 1987 (No. 13) 2741
Supplementary Benefit (Single Payments) (Amendment No. 2) Regulations (Northern Ireland) 1987 (No. 439) 2741
Supplementary Benefit Up-Rating Regulations (Northern Ireland) 1987 (No. 15) 2741
Workmen's Compensation (Supplementation) (Amendment) Regulations (Northern Ireland) 1987 (No. 118) 2741
Workmen's Compensation (Supplementation) (Amendment No. 2) Regulations (Northern Ireland) 1987 (No. 152) 2741

TOWN AND COUNTRY PLANNING

Certificates of Alternative Development Value Regulations (Northern Ireland) 1987 (No. 437) 2745
Planning (Fees) Regulations (Northern Ireland) 1987 (No. 335) 2745
Planning (Fees) (Amendment) Regulations (Northern Ireland) 1987 (No. 27) 2745
Planning (General Development) (Amendment) Order (Northern Ireland) 1987 (No. 36) 2745
Planning (General Development) (Amendment No. 2) Order (Northern Ireland) 1987 (No. 438) 2745

TRADE AND INDUSTRY

Industrial Development (Date of Application) Order (Northern Ireland) 1987 (No. 125) 2748
Industrial Development (Exclusions from Grant) Order (Northern Ireland) 1987 (No. 204) 2748
Industrial Development (Variation of Rate of General Assistance Grants) Order (Northern Ireland) 1987 (No. 374) 2748
Industrial Development (Variation of Rate of General Assistance Grants) (No. 2) Order (Northern Ireland) 1987 (No. 394) 2748
Industrial Development (Variation of Rate of General Assistance Grants) (Revocation) Order (Northern Ireland) 1987 (No. 382) 2748
Orders made under S.I. 1984 No. 1159 (N.I. 9), Art. 23(1):
Distributive Industry Order 1987 (No. 177) 2749
Food and Drink Industry Order 1987 (No. 179) 2749
Textiles Industry Order 1987 (No. 178) 2749

Arts. 23, 24:
Catering Industry Order 1987 (No. 260) 2749
Clothing Industry Order 1987 (No. 327) 2749
Construction Industry Order 1987 (No. 257) 2749
Engineering Industry Order 1987 (No. 259) 2749
Road Transport Industry Order 1987 (No. 272) 2749

TRANSPORT

European Communities (International Passenger Services) Regulations (Northern Ireland) 1987 (No. 383) 2750
Level Crossing (Lurgan (Bells Row)) Revocation Order (Northern Ireland) 1987 (No. 345) 2751
Road Transport (Great Britain Passenger Services) (Fee) Regulations (Northern Ireland) 1987 (No. 188) 2750
Road Transport (Great Britain Passenger Services) Regulations (Northern Ireland) 1987 (No. 187) 2750
Road Transport Licensing (Fees) (Amendment) Regulations (Northern Ireland) 1987 (No. 47) 2750

WEIGHTS AND MEASURES

Weights and Measures (Testing and Adjustment Fees) Regulations (Northern Ireland) 1987 (No. 309) 2754
Weights and Measures (Weights) Regulations (Northern Ireland) 1987 (No. 310) .... 2754.

NORTHERN IRELAND

NUMERICAL TABLE OF STATUTORY RULES AND ORDERS 1987

1987	C.L.Y.
1	2709
2	2631
4	2738
6 (C. 1)	2678
7	2678
8	2678
9	2628
12	2741
13	2741
14	2741
15	2741
16	2738
17	2738
18	2676
20 (C. 2)	2741
21 (C. 3)	2741
22	2741
23	2741
24	2719
25	2741
26	2741
27	2745
28	2667
29	2741
30	2665
31	2676
32	2676
33	2679
34	2719
35	2738
36	2745
37	2640
38	2677
40	2738
41	2622
42	2684
45	2738
46	2738
47	2750
48	2702
49	2738
61	2741
62	2738
63	2628
64	2628
65	2677
66	2652
67	2652
68	2652
69	2676
70	2714
73	2667
74	2667
75	2728
76	2714
77	2681
78	2628
79	2741
80	2741

1987	C.L.Y.
81	2741
82	2741
83	2628
84	2628
85	2628
86	2714
89	2628
90	2741
92	2628
94	2628
95	2681
96	2628
97	2741
98	2622
99	2741
100	2741
101	2714
102	2698
103	2698
104	2698
108	2709
109	2738
110	2738
111	2741
112	2741
113	2676
114	2628
115	2741
116	2741
117	2741
118	2741
119	2631
120	2628
121 (C. 4)	2744
122	2741
123	2727
124	2719
125	2748
126	2648a
127	2659
128	2741
129	2741
130	2741
131	2741
132	2681
133	2738
137 (C. 5)	2622
138	2741
139	2734
141	2677
142	2741
143	2741
147	2642
148	2727
149	2741
151	2741
152	2741
154	2628
155	2628

NUMERICAL TABLE OF NORTHERN IRELAND S.R. & O.1987

1987	C.L.Y.
156	2628
158	2628
159	2738
160	2714
161 (C. 6)	2741
162	2681
163	2741
164	2738
165	2738
168	2662
170	2741
171	2741
172	2741
173	2741
174	2741
175	2741
176	2741
177	2749
178	2749
179	2749
181	2738
184 (C. 7)	2741
185 (C. 8)	2678
186	2678
187	2750
188	2750
189	2738
190	2709
192	2678
193	2678
194	2678
195	2678
196	2715
197	2628
200 (C. 9)	2709
201	2741
204	2748
205	2716
206	2659
207	2738
208	2640
209	2734
211	2738
214	2738
215	2667
217	2738
218	2738
219	2676
220	2741
221	2741
223	2631
225	2628
227	2738
228	2734
229	2628
230	2741
231	2741
232	2642
233	2727
234	2719
235	2628
236	2738
237	2738
238	2738
239	2706
240	2706
241	2738
242	2738
248	2741
1987	C.L.Y.
252	2659
257	2749
258	2640
259	2749
260	2749
262	2631
265	2678
266	2659
267	2659
268	2633
269	2702
270	2719
271 (C. 10)	2659
272	2749
277	2714
278	2714
279	2714
280	2714
281	2714
282	2714
283	2714
284	2714
285	2714
286	2714
287	2714
288	2714
289	2714
290	2714
291	2714
292	2714
293	2714
294	2714
295	2714
296	2714
298	2681
299 (C. 11)	2741
300	2702
304	2719
306	2738
307	2738
308 (C. 12)	2667
309	2754
310	2754
311	2741
312	2628
313	2656
314	2738
315	2714
317	2628
318	2667
319	2667
320	2631
321	2628
322	2741
323	2709
324	2738
325	2741
327	2749
328	2727
332	2681
334	2675
335	2745
337	2739
340	2681
341	2677
342	2677
344	2676
345	2751
346	2709

NUMERICAL TABLE OF NORTHERN IRELAND S.R. & O. 1987

1987	C.L.Y.
347	2738
348	2741
349	2738
350	2738
351	2738
352	2738
353	2738
357	2628
358	2738
359	2622
360	2622
364	2680
365 (C. 13)	2699
366	2738
367	2677
371	2738
372	2631
373	2709
374	2748
375	2673
376	2680
378	2674
379	2714
380	2714
381	2628
382	2748
383	2750
384	2659
385	2659
386	2738
387	2741
388	2738
389	2738
390	2738
391	2741
393	2653
394	2748
395	2677
396	2678
397	2678
398	2678
399	2741
400	2642
401	2727
402	2741
403	2631
404	2741
407	2628
408	2702
410	2738
411	2738
412	2719
413	2741
414	2628

1987	C.L.Y.
415	2631
416	2738
417	2719
418	2640
419	2632
420	2659
422	2676
423	2676
424	2714
425	2631
426	2738
427	2679
428	2679
429	2679
430	2679
431	2677
432	2677
433	2714
434	2714
435	2738
436	2676
437	2745
438	2745
439	2741
440	2734
441	2716
442	2640
444	2738
445	2628
448	2628
449 (C. 14)	2741
451	2628
452	2628
454	2741
456	2663
457	2706
458	2741
460	2741
462	2681
463	2741
464	2741
465	2741
466	2741
467	2676
468	2741
471	2677
473	2709
893	2682
900	2662
1129	2682
1207	2713
1241 (C. 35)	2665
1283	2683
1628	2626
2086	2738

TABLE OF ABBREVIATIONS

A.B.L.R. = Australian Business Law Review.
A.C. = Appeal Cases (Law Reports).
A.J.I.L. = American Journal of International Law.
A.L.J. = Australian Law Journal.
A.L.J.R. = Australian Law Journal Reports.
A.L.M.D. = Australian Legal Monthly Digest.
A.L.Q. = Arab Law Quarterly.
A.L.R. = Australian Law Reports.
A.R. = Alberta Reports 1977–
A.T.R. = Australian Tax Review.
Acct. = Accountant.
Acct.Rec. = Accountants Record.
Accty. = Accountancy.
Admin. = Administrator.
All E.R. = All England Law Reports.
Anglo-Am. = Anglo-American Law Review.
Art. = Article.
Aus. = Australia.

BCC = British Company Law Cases.
BCLC = Butterworths Company Law Cases.
B.C.L.R. = British Columbia Law Reports.
B.L.R. = Business Law Review.
B.T.R. = British Tax Review.
Brit.J.Criminol. = British Journal of Criminology.
Build.L.R. = Building Law Reports.
Bull.E.C. = Bulletin of the European Communities.
Bull.J.S.B. = Bulletin of Judicial Studies Board.

c. = Chapter (of Act of Parliament).
C.A. = Court of Appeal.
C.A.T. = Court of Appeal Transcript.
C. & S.L.J. = Company and Securities Law Journal.
C.C.A. = Court of Criminal Appeal.
C.C.L.T. = Canadian cases on the Law of Torts 1976–
C.I.L.J.S.A. = Comparative and International Law Journal of Southern Africa.
C.I.L.L. = Construction Industry Law Letter.
C.I.P.A. = The Journal of the Chartered Institute of Patent Agents.
C.J.Q. = Civil Justice Quarterly.
C.L. = Current Law.
C.L.B. = Commonwealth Law Bulletin.
C.L.C. = Current Law Consolidation.
C.L.J. = Cambridge Law Journal.
C.L.L.R. = City of London Law Review.
C.L.P. = Current Legal Problems.
C.L.R. = Commonwealth Law Reports.
C.L.Y. = Current Law Year Book.
C.M.L.R. = Common Market Law Reports.
C.M.L.Rev. = Common Market Law Review.
C.Q.S. = Chartered Quantity Surveyor.
C.S.W. = Chartered Surveyor Weekly.
Can. = Canada.
Can. Bar J. = Canadian Bar Journal.
Can.B.R. *or* Canadian B.R. = Canadian Bar Review.
Can.C.L. = Canadian Current Law.
Ch. = Chancery (Law Reports).
Co.Law. = Company Lawyer.
Co. Law Dig. = Company Law Digest.
Com.Cas. = Commercial Cases.
Commercial Acct. = Commercial Accountant.
Comp.L. & P. = Computer Law & Practice.
ConLR = Construction Law Reports.
Const.L.J. = Construction Law Journal.
Conv.(n.s.) (*or* Conv. *or* Conveyancer) = Conveyancer and Property Lawyer (New Series).
Cox C.C. = Cox's Criminal Cases.
Cr.App.R. = Criminal Appeal Reports.
Cr.App.R.(S.) = Criminal Appeal Reports (Sentencing).
Crim.L.R. = Criminal Law Review.
Cts.-Martial App.Ct. = Courts-Martial Appeal Court.

D.C. = Divisional Court.
D.L.R. = Dominion Law Reports.

E. = England.
E.A.T. = Employment Appeal Tribunal.
E.C.C. = European Commercial Cases.
E.C.L.R. = European Competition Law Review.
E.C.R. = European Court Reports.
E.C.S.C. = European Coal and Steel Community.
E.E.C. = European Economic Community.
E.G. = Estates Gazette.
E.G.L.R. = Estates Gazette Law Reports.
E.I.P.R. = European Intellectual Property Review.
E.H.R.R. = European Human Rights Reports.
E.L.Rev. = European Law Review.
E.O.R. = Equal Opportunities Review.
E.P.L. Leaflet = Excess Profits Levy Leaflet.
E.P.T. Leaflet = Excess Profits Tax Leaflet.

F.L.R. = Federal Law Reports.
F.L.R. = Family Law Reports.
FLR = Financial Law Reports.
F.S.R. = Fleet Street Reports.
FTLR = Financial Times Law Reports.
Fam. = Family Division (Law Reports).
Fam.Law = Family Law.

G.W.D. = Green's Weekly Digest.

H.L. = House of Lords.
H.L.R. = Housing Law Reports.
Harv.L.R. *or* Harvard L.R. = Harvard Law Review.

I.B.F.L. = Butterworths Journal of International Banking and Financial Law
I.B.L. = International Business Lawyer.
I.C.L.Q. = International and Comparative Law Quarterly.
I.C.L.R. = International Construction Law Review.
I.C.R. = Industrial Cases Reports.
IFL Rev = International Financial Law Review.
I.L.J. = Industrial Law Journal.
I.L.P. = International Legal Practitioner.
I.L.R.M. = Irish Law Reports Monthly.
I.L.T. *or* Ir.L.T. = Irish Law Times.
I.L.T.R. = Irish Law Times Reports.
Imm.A.R. = Immigration Appeals Reports.

Imm. and Nat.L. & P. = Immigration and Nationality Law and Practice.
Ins.L. & P. = Insolvency Law & Practice.
I.R. *or* Ir.R. = Irish Reports (Eire).
I.R.L.R. = Industrial Relations Law Reports.
Ir.Jur. = Irish Jurist.
Ir.Jur.(N.S.) = Irish Jurist (New Series).
Ir.Jur.Rep. = Irish Jurist Reports.
I.T.R. = Industrial Tribunal Reports.

J. *and* JJ. = Justice, Justices.
J.A.L. = Journal of African Law.
J.B.L. = Journal of Business Law.
J.C. = Justiciary Cases.
J.C.L. = Journal of Criminal Law.
J.C.L. & Crim. = Journal of Criminal Law and Criminology.
J.Crim.L., C. & P.S. = Journal of Criminal Law, Criminology and Police Science.
J.E.R.L. = Journal of Energy and Natural Resources Law.
J.I.B. = Journal of the Institute of Bankers.
J.I.B.L. = Journal of International Banking Law.
J.L.A. = Jewish Law Annual.
J.L.H. = Journal of Legal History.
J.L.S. = Journal of the Law Society of Scotland.
J.P. = Justice of the Peace Reports.
J.P.L. = Journal of Planning and Environment Law.
J.P.N. = Justice of the Peace Journal.
J.R. = Juridical Review.
J.S.W.L. = Journal of Social Welfare Law.
Jam. = Jamaica.

K.B. = King's Bench (Law Reports).
K.I.R. = Knight's Industrial Reports.

L.C. = Lord Chancellor.
L.C.J. *or* C.J. = Lord Chief Justice.
L.Exec. = Legal Executive.
L.G.C. = Local Government Chronicle.
L.G.R. = Local Government Reports.
L.G.Rev. = Local Government Review.
L.J. = Law Journal Newspaper.
L.J. *and* L.JJ. = Lord Justice, Lords Justices.
L.J.A.C.R. = Law Journal Annual Charities Review.
L.J.N.C.C.R. = Law Journal Newspaper County Court Reports.
L.J.R. = Law Journal Reports.
L.M.C.L.Q. = Lloyd's Maritime and Commercial Law Quarterly.
L.P. = Reference to denote Lands Tribunal decisions (transcripts available from the Lands Tribunal).
L.Q.R. = Law Quarterly Review.
L.R. = Law Reports.
L.R.R.P. = Reports of Restrictive Practices Cases.
L.S. = Legal Studies.
L.S.Gaz. = Law Society's Gazette.
L.T. = Law Times.
L.Teach. = Law Teacher.
L.T.J. = Law Times Journal.
L.V.App.Ct. = Lands Valuation Appeal Court (Scotland).
L.V.C. = Reference to denote Lands Tribunal decisions (transcripts available from the Lands Tribunal).
L. & J. = Law and Justice.

Ll.L.Rep. = Lloyd's List Reports (before 1951).
Ll.P.C. = Lloyd's Prize Cases.
Law M. = Law Magazine
Lit. = Litigation.
Liverpool L.R. = Liverpool Law Review.
Lloyd's Rep. = Lloyd's List Reports (1951 onwards).

M.L.J. = Malayan Law Journal.
M.L.R. = Modern Law Review.
M.R. = Master of the Rolls.
McGill L.J. = McGill Law Journal.
Mag.Ct. = Magistrates' Court.
Mal. = Malaya.
Mal.L.R. = Malaya Law Review.
Man.Law = Managerial Law.
Med.Sci. & Law = Medicine, Science and the Law.
Melbourne Univ.L.R. = Melbourne University Law Review.
Mel.L.J. = Melanesian Law Journal.

NATO R. = NATO Review.
N.I. = Northern Ireland; Northern Ireland Reports.
N.I.J.B. = Northern Ireland Judgment Bulletin.
N.I.L.Q. = Northern Ireland Legal Quarterly.
N.I.L.R. = Northern Ireland Law Reports.
N.Z.L.R. = New Zealand Law Reports.
N.Z.U.L.R. = New Zealand Universities Law Review.
New L.J. = New Law Journal.
New L.R. = New Law Reports, Ceylon.
Nig.L.J. = Nigerian Law Journal.

O.H. = Outer House of Court of Session.
O.J. = Official Journal of the European Communities.
O.J.L.S. = Oxford Journal of Legal Studies.
Oklahoma L.R. = Oklahoma Law Review.
Ord. = Order.
Osgoode Hall L.J. = Osgoode Hall Law Journal.

P. = Probate, Divorce and Admiralty (Law Reports).
P.A.D. = Planning Appeal Decisions.
P. & C.R. = Property and Compensation Reports.
P.C. = Privy Council.
PCC = Palmer's Company Cases.
P.L. = Public Law.
P.N. = Professional Negligence.
P.S. = Petty Sessions.
P.T. = Profits Tax Leaflet.
Pr.A.S.I.L. = Proceedings of the American Society of International Law.

Q.B. = Queen's Bench (Law Reports).
Q.J.P.R. = Queensland Justice of the Peace Reports.
Q.L.R. = Queensland Law Reporter.
Q.S. = Quarter Sessions.
Q.S.R. = Queensland State Reports.

r. = Rule.
R.A. = Rating Appeals.
R. & I.T. = Rating and Income Tax.
R. & V. = Rating and Valuation.

R.C.N. = Rating Case Notes.
R.F.L. = Reports of Family Law (Canadian).
R.I.C.S. = Royal Institution of Chartered Surveyors, Scottish Lands Valuation Appeal Reports.
R.P.C. = Reports of Patent, Design and Trade Mark Cases.
R.P.Ct. = Restrictive Practices Court.
R.P.R. = Real Property Reports (Canada).
R.R.C. = Ryde's Rating Cases.
R.T.R. = Road Traffic Reports.
R.V.R. = Rating and Valuation Reporter.
reg. = Regulation.
Reg.Acct. = Registered Accountant.
Rep. of Ir. = Republic of Ireland.

s. = Section (of Act of Parliament).
S. *or* Scot. = Scotland.
S.A. = South Africa.
S.A.L.J. = South African Law Journal.
S.A.L.R. = South African Law Reports.
S.A.S.R. = South Australian State Reports.
S.C. = Session Cases.
S.C.C.R. = Scottish Criminal Case Reports.
S.C.(H.L.) = Session Cases (House of Lords).
S.C.(J.) = Session Cases (High Court of Justiciary).
S.C.L.R. = Scottish Civil Law Reports.
SCOLAG = Journal of the Scottish Legal Action Group.
S.I. = Statutory Instrument.
S.J. = Solicitors' Journal.
S.J.Suppl. = Supplement to the Solicitors' Journal.
S.L.C.R. = Scottish Land Court Reports.
S.L.C.R.App. = Scottish Land Court Reports (appendix).
S.L.G. = Scottish Law Gazette.
S.L.R. = Scottish Law Reporter (Reports 1865–1925).
S.L.R. = Scottish Law Review (Articles 1912–63).
S.L.R. = Scottish Law Review (Sheriff Court Reports 1885–1963).
S.L.R. (and date) = Statute Law Reform Act (Statute Citator only).
S.L.R. = Statute Law Revision.
S.L.T. = Scots Law Times.
S.L.T.(Land Ct.) = Scots Law Times Land Court Reports.
S.L.T.(Lands Tr.) = Scots Law Times Lands Tribunal Reports.
S.L.T.(Lyon Ct.) = Scots Law Times Lyon Court Reports.
S.L.T.(News) = Scots Law Times, News section.
S.L.T.(Notes) = Scots Law Times Notes of Recent Decisions (1946–1981).
S.L.T.(Sh.Ct.) = Scots Law Times Sheriff Court Reports.
S.N. = Session Notes.
S.P.L.P. = Scottish Planning Law and Practice.
S.R. & O. = Statutory Rules and Orders.
S.T.C. = Simon's Tax Cases.
Sc.Jur. = Scottish Jurist.
Sh.Ct.Rep. = Sheriff Court Reports (Scottish Law Review) (1885–1963).
Sol. = Solicitor.
Stat.L.R. = Statute Law Review.
Sydney L.R. = Sydney Law Review.

T.C. *or* Tax Cas. = Tax Cases.
T.C. Leaflet = Tax Case Leaflet.
T.L.R. = Times Law Reports.
T.P.G. = Town Planning and Local Government Guide.
T.U.L.B. = Trade Union Law Bulletin.
Tas.S.R. = Tasmanian State Reports.
Tax. = Taxation.
Tr.L. = Trading Law.
Traff.Cas. = Railway, Canal and Road Traffic Cases.
Trial = Trial.
Trib. = Tribunal.
Trust L. & P. = Trust Law and Practice.
Tulane L.R. = Tulane Law Review.

U.G.L.J. = University of Ghana Law Journal.
U.S. = United States Reports.
U.T.L.J. = University of Toronto Law Journal.

V.A.T.T.R. = Value Added Tax Tribunal Reports.
V.L.R. = Victorian Law Reports.

W.A.L.R. = West Australian Law Reports.
W.I.A.S. = West Indies Associated States.
W.I.R. = West Indian Reports.
W.L.R. = Weekly Law Reports.
W.N. = Weekly Notes (Law Reports).
W.W.R. = Western Weekly Reports.
Washington L.Q. = Washington Law Quarterly.

Yale L.J. = Yale Law Journal.

DATES OF COMMENCEMENT

STATUTES

This Table contains all statutory dates of commencement during 1987. Where an Act or part of an Act is brought into force by a statutory instrument the instrument's number and the *Current Law* paragraph reference are given. Where the commencement provisions are contained in the Act inself, the section number containing those provisions is given. Where the Act is silent, as to part or whole, that part or whole comes into force on the date of the Royal Assent by virtue of s.4 of the Interpretation Act 1978 (this is indicated by the words "Royal Assent" in the Authority column). For further information on statutes see the *Current Law Statute Citators* (subscribers to *Current Law Statutes Annotated* should also consult the latest Citator part issued therewith).

References to paragraph numbers exceeding 3886 are to the *Scottish Current Law Year Book 1987.* For a complete guide to the commencement, amendment, judicial consideration, repeal, etc. of Statutes since 1947 see the *Current Law Statute Citators.*

Statute	*Commencement*	*Authority*
Abolition of Domestic Rates Etc. (Scotland) Act 1987 (c.47)		
ss.1–5, 6–8 (in part), 9, 10–11 (in part), 12–17, 21–25(1), 25(2)–(3) (in part), 26(1), 26(2) (in part), 27–33, 34 (in part), 35, Scheds. 1 (in part), 2–4, 5–6 (in part)	September 14, 1987	S.I. 1987/1489 [1987] C.L.Y. 4940
ss.6–8 (remainder), 10–11 (remainder), 25(2)–(3) (remainder), 26(2) (remainder), 34 (in part), Scheds. 1 (remainder), 5 (remainder) and 6 (in part)	April 1, 1989	S.I. 1987 No. 1489 [1987] C.L.Y 4940
ss.18–20	October 1, 1988	S.I.1987/1489 [1987] C.L.Y. 4940
s.34 (remainder) and Sched. 6 (remainder)	April 1, 1994	S.I. 1987 No. 1489 [1987] C.L.Y. 4940
Access to Personal Files Act 1987 (c.37)		
All provisions	May 15, 1987	Royal Assent
Administration of Justice Act 1985 (c.61)		
ss.6(1)–(3), 11, 14–21, 23–33, 34(1)(2), 35–37, 39	May 11, 1987	S.I. 1987/787 [1987] C.L.Y. 2874
s.6(4)	December 1, 1987	S.I. 1987/787 [1987] C.L.Y. 2874
Adoption Act 1976 (c.36)		
All sections except ss.58A, 73(2)(3) (part), 74. Scheds. 3 (in part), 4 (in part)	January 1, 1988	S.I. 1987/1242 [1987] C.L.Y. 2479
Agricultural Training Board Act 1987 (c.29)		
All provisions	July 15, 1987	s.2
AIDS (Control) Act 1987 (c.33)		
All provisions	May 15, 1987	Royal Assent

Statute	*Commencement*	*Authority*
Animals (Scotland) Act 1987 (c.9)		
All provisions	June 9, 1987	s.9
Appropriation Act 1987 (c.17)		
All provisions	May 15, 1987	Royal Assent
Appropriation (No. 2) Act 1987 (c.50)		
All provisions	July 23, 1987	Royal Assent
Armed Forces Act 1986 (c.21)		
All remaining provisions	December 31, 1987	S.I. 1987/1998 [1987] C.L.Y. 159
Banking Act 1987 (c.22)		
ss.82–87, 102, 106, 107 (in part), 108(1) (in part) (2) (in part), 109, 110, Scheds. 5, para. 14, 6, para. 26(5), 7 (in part)	July 15, 1987	S.I. 1987/1189 [1987] C.L.Y. 191
s.91	May 15, 1987	s.110
All remaining provisions except s.38 and Sched. 7, Pt. I (in part)	October 1, 1987	S.I. 1987 No. 1664 [1987] C.L.Y. 191
Billiards (Abolition of Restrictions) Act 1987 (c.19)		
All provisions	May 15, 1987	Royal Assent
British Council and Commonwealth Institute Superannuation Act 1986 (c.51)		
All remaining provisions	April 1, 1987	S.I. 1987/588 [1987] C.L.Y. 2818
British Shipbuilders (Borrowing Powers) Act 1987 (c.52)		
All provisions	July 23, 1987	Royal Assent
Broadcasting Act 1987 (c.10)		
All provisions	April 9, 1987	Royal Assent
Cable and Broadcasting Act 1984 (c.46)		
ss. 45, 46	April 6, 1987	S.I.1987/672 [1987] C.L.Y. 3574
Channel Tunnel Act 1987 (c.53)		
All provisions	July 23, 1987	Royal Assent
Chevening Estate Act 1987 (c.20)		
All provisions	September 1, 1987	S.I. 1987/1254 [1987] C.L.Y. 1422
Children Act 1975 (c.72)		
ss.1, 2, Sched. 3, para. 74(b) (in part)	January 1, 1988	S.I. 1987/1242 [1987] C.L.Y. 2479
Coal Industry Act 1987 (c.3)		
ss. 1–5, 9, 10	March 5, 1987	Royal Assent
ss.6–8	May 5, 1987	s.10
Consolidated Fund Act 1987 (c.8)		
All provisions	March 25, 1987	Royal Assent
Consolidated Fund (No. 2) Act 1987 (c.54)		
All provisions	November 17, 1987	Royal Assent

Statute	Commencement	Authority
Consolidated Fund (No. 3) Act 1987 (c.55)		
All provisions	December 10, 1987	Royal Assent
Consumer Protection Act 1987 (c.43)		
Pt. I, s.36, s.41(2) (in part), s.45 (in part), s.46 (in part), s.48(1) (in part), s.48(3) (in part), Scheds. 1, 3, Sched. 4, paras. 5, 8, 12, Sched. 5 (part)	March 1, 1988	S.I. 1987/1680 [1987] C.L.Y. 3584
Pt. II, Pt. IV (in part), ss.37–47 (in part), s.48(1) (in part) (2)(3) (in part), ss.49, 50, Sched. 2, Sched. 4, paras. 1,2, 4, 6, 7, 9–11, 13, Sched. 5 (in part)	October 1, 1987	S.I. 1987/1680 [1987] C.L.Y. 3584
Consumer Safety Act 1978 (c.38)		
s.10(1) (remaining part), Sched. 3 (remaining part)	October 1, 1987	S.I. 1987/1681 [1987] C.L.Y. 3323
Criminal Justice Act 1987 (c.38)		
ss.1 (in part), 12, 14, Sched. 1 (in part)	July 20, 1987	S.I. 1987/1061 [1987] C.L.Y. 635
ss.13, 16-18	May 15, 1987	s.16
Criminal Justice (Scotland) Act 1987 (c.41)		
ss.48, 49, 60, 64, 69, Sched. 1, paras. 3, 10(b), 11–14, 16–19, Sched. 2 (in part)	October 1, 1987	S.I. 1987 No. 1594 [1987] C.L.Y. 4094
ss.51–56, 58, 61–63, 65, 68, 70 (in part), Sched. 1, paras. 7–9 and 10(a) and Sched. 2 (in part)·	January 1, 1988	S.I. 1987 No. 2119 [1987] C.L.Y. 4094
ss.57, 70 (in part), Sched. 1, paras. 1, 2, 4–6 and Sched. 2 (in part)	September 1, 1987	S.I. 1987/1468 [1987] C.L.Y. 4094
Crossbows Act 1987 (c.32)		
ss.1–6	July 15, 1987	s.8
ss.7, 8	May 15, 1987	Royal Assent
Crown Proceedings (Armed Forces) Act 1987 (c.25)		
All provisions	May 15, 1987	Royal Assent
Debtors (Scotland) Act 1987 (c.18)		
ss.75, 76, 97	November 2, 1987	S.I. 1987 No. 1838 [1987] C.L.Y. 5014
Deer Act 1987 (c.28)		
All provisions	July 15, 1987	s.2
Diplomatic and Consular Premises Act 1987 (c.46)		
ss.1–5, 8, Sched. 1	January 1, 1988	S.I. 1987/2248 [1987] C.L.Y. 2085
ss.6, 7, Sched. 2	June 11, 1987	S.I. 1987/1022 [1987] C.L.Y. 2085

Statute	*Commencement*	*Authority*
Disabled Persons (Services, Consultation and Representation) Act 1986 (c.33)		
ss.4 (in part), 8(1), 9, 10	April 1, 1987	S.I. 1987/564 [1987] C.L.Y. 2353
ss.4 (except para. (*b*)), 8(1) (Scotland)	October 1, 1987	S.I. 1987/911 [1987] C.L.Y. 4662
ss.9–12, 14, 16–18 (Scotland)	June 1, 1987	S.I. 1987/911 [1987] C.L.Y. 4662
ss.16–18	April 17, 1987	S.I. 1987/729 [1987] C.L.Y. 2353
Education (No. 2) Act 1986 (c.61)		
ss.1–16, 18–29, 32, 34–43, 57, 58, 61, 62, 67(4) (remaining part), 67(5), 67(6) (in part), Scheds. 1–3, 4 (remaining part), 5, 6 (in part)	September 1, 1987	S.I. 1987/344 [1987] C.L.Y. 1256
ss.47, 48	August 15, 1987	S.I. 1987/344 [1987] C.L.Y. 1256
s.67(6) (in part), Sched. 6 (in part)	September 1, 1987	S.I. 1987/1159 [1987] C.L.Y. 1256
Financial Services Act 1986 (c.60)		
ss.1 (in relation to Sched. 1, para. 23), 12, 20, 96, 140 (in relation to Sched. 11, para. 6), 189, Sched. 1, para. 23, Sched. 6, Sched. 11, para. 6, Sched. 14 (in part)	December 1, 1987	S.I. 1987/1997 [1987] C.L.Y. 3127
s.1 (remaining part), Sched. 1 (remaining part)	January 18, 1988	S.I. 1987/2158 [1987] C.L.Y. 3217
ss.8–11, 13, 14, 15 (in part), 16–19, 21, 36(2)(3), 37 (in part), 38(2)(3), 39 (in part), 41, 46, 48–52, 54, 55, 56 (in part), 102, 103, 104(2)(3), 107, 110, 112(1)–(4), 113(1), 119, 120, 122, 125(1)–(7), 127, 129, 138(1)(2)(6), 140 (in part), 187 (in part), 190, 191, 198(3)(*b*), 200(1)(*a*)(*b*) (in part) (3)(4)(5)–(8) (in part), 206(1)–(3), 211(3) (in part), 212(2) (in part), Scheds. 2, 3, 4	June 4, 1987	S.I. 1987/907 [1987] C.L.Y. 3217
ss.26, 27, 28, 29, 30, 31(4) (in part), 112(5) (in part), 140 (in part), s.189 (in part), 200(1)(*a*) (in part) (*b*) (in part), (5) (in part), Sched. 5, Sched. 14 (in part)	January 1, 1988	S.I. 1987/2158 [1987] C.L.Y. 3217
ss.37 (in part), 39 (in part), 40	November 23, 1987	S.I. 1987/1997 [1987] C.L.Y. 3217
ss. 63, 183 (in part), 184(1)–(3) (in part), 184(5)(7), 185, 186(1)–(5)(7) (in part), 201(3)	April 23, 1987	S.I. 1987/623 [1987] C.L.Y. 3217

Statute	Commencement	Authority
Financial Services Act 1986—*cont.*		
s.140, Sched. 11, para. 22(4) (for certain purposes)	October 3, 1988	S.I. 1987/1997 [1987] C.L.Y. 3217
s.211(3) (in part), Sched. 15, para. 1(1)–(3), (5), para. 16 (in part)	February 27, 1988	S.I. 1987/2158 [1987] C.L.Y. 3217
Fire Safety and Safety of Places of Sport Act 1987 (c.27)		
ss. 3, 4, 8, 9, 11–14, s.16(1) (in part) (2) (in part), s.17, s.18(1) (in part) (2) (in part) (3) (in part), Pt. II, s.46, s.49 (in part), s.50(1)(2)(3)(4) (in part) (5) (in part) (6) (in part), (7) (in part), Sched. 1 (in part), Sched. 2, Sched. 4 (in part), Sched. 5, paras. 1, 3, 4, 5, 6, 7, 9	January 1, 1988	S.I. 1987/1762 [1987] C.L.Y. 3146
Gaming (Amendment) Act 1987 (c11)		
All provisions	August 1, 1987	S.I. 1987/1200 [1987] C.L.Y. 1835
Housing and Planning Act 1986 (c.63)		
s.9	May 13, 1987	S.I. 1987/754 [1987] C.L.Y. 1883
s.15, Sched. 5, para. 9	February 17, 1988	S.I. 1987/2277 [1987] C.L.Y. 1883
s.18 (in part), s.24(3) (in part)	December 11, 1987	S.I. 1987/1939 [1987] C.L.Y 1883
s.24(1) (in part)	September 22, 1987	S.I. 1987/1554 [1987] C.L.Y. 1883
ss.25, 41(1)(2)(3), 49(1) (in part), (2) (in part)	November 2, 1987	S.I. 1987/1759 [1987] C.L.Y. 1883
ss.26, 50, 51, Sched. 6, Pts. III and IV, Sched. 9, Pt. II	October 1, 1987	S.I. 1987 No. 1607 [1987] C.L.Y. 5193
ss.40, 49(2) (in part), Sched. 9, Pt. I	April 1, 1987	S.I. 1987/348 [1987] C.L.Y. 1883
s.49 (in so far as it relates to Sched. 11, para. 8)	March 2, 1987	S.I. 1987/304 [1987] C.L.Y. 1883
Sched. 11, para. 8	March 2, 1987	S.I. 1987/178 [1987] C.L.Y. 1883
Housing (Scotland) Act 1987 (c.26)		
All provisions	August 15, 1987	s.340
Immigration (Carriers' Liability) Act 1987 (c.24)		
All provisions	March 4, 1987	s.2
Irish Sailors and Soldiers Land Trust Act 1987 (c.48)		
All provisions	November 4, 1987	S.I. 1987/1909 [1987] C.L.Y 1429
Landlord and Tenant Act 1987 (c.31)		
ss.1–20, 45–60, 61(1), 62	February 1, 1988	S.I. 1987/2177 [1987] C.L.Y. 2151

Statute	Commencement	Authority
Legal Aid (Scotland) Act 1986 (c.47)		
All remaining provisions except Pt. V and s.30	April 1, 1987	S.I. 1987/289 [1987] C.L.Y. 4878
Licensing (Restaurant Meals) Act 1987 (c.2)		
All provisions	May 2, 1987	s.3
Local Government Act 1986 (c.10)		
s.5	April 1, 1988	S.I. 1987/2003 [1987] C.L.Y. 2370
Local Government Act 1987 (c.44)		
All provisions	May 15, 1987	Royal Assent
Local Government Finance Act 1987 (c.6)		
All provisions	March 12, 1987	Royal Assent
Merchant Shipping Act 1979 (c.39)		
ss.14(1)(2)(4)(5)(6), 15(2) (in part), Sched. 3, (Pts. I–II)	April 30, 1987	S.I. 1987/635 [1987] C.L.Y. 3416
s.35(2) (in part)	April 30, 1987	S.I. 1987/719 [1987] C.L.Y. 3416
Ministry of Defence Police Act 1987 (c.4)		
All provisions	May 5, 1987	s.8
Minor's Contracts Act 1987 (c.13)		
All provisions	June 9, 1987	s.5
National Health Service (Amendment) Act 1986 (c.66)		
s.3	April 1, 1987	S.I. 1987/399 [1987] C.L.Y. 2553
Northern Ireland (Emergency Provisions) Act 1987		
ss.1–11, 13–16, 25–27, Scheds. 1, 2	June 15, 1987	s.26
Oil and Gas (Enterprise) Act 1982 (c.23)		
ss.22, 23 (in part), 27(1)(*a*), 37 (in part), Sched. 3, paras. 2, 3, 34, 42, 43, Sched. 4 (in part)	February 1, 1988	S.I. 1987/2272 [1987] C.L.Y. 3354
Parliamentary and Health Service Commissioners Act 1987 (c.39)		
All provisions	July 15, 1987	s.10
Parliamentary and other Pensions Act 1987 (c.45)		
s.4(1)(3)	July 23, 1987	S.I. 1987/1311 [1987] C.L.Y. 2765
Petroleum Act 1987 (c.12)		
ss.1–16, 19, 20, 25–32, Sched. 3 (in part)	June 9, 1987	s.31
ss.17, 18, Scheds. 1, 2	June 30, 1987	S.I. 1987/820 [1987] C.L.Y. 2849
ss.21–24, Sched. 3 (part)	September 1, 1987	S.I. 1987/1330 [1987] C.L.Y. 2849

Statute	*Commencement*	*Authority*
Pilotage Act 1987 (c.21)		
ss.24, 25, 28, 30, 31, 32(1)–(3), 33, Sched. 1 (part)	September 1, 1987	S.I. 1987/1306 [1987] C.L.Y. 3421
s.27	May 15, 1987	Royal Assent
s.32(5) (in part)	February 1, 1988	S.I. 1987/2138 [1987] C.L.Y. 3421
Prescription (Scotland) Act 1987 (c.36)		
All provisions	May 15, 1987	Royal Assent
Protection of Animals (Penalties) Act 1987 (c.35)		
All provisions	July 15, 1987	s.2
Public Order Act 1986 (c.64)		
ss.1–10, 12–15, 17–29, 39, 40 (in part), Scheds. 2 (in part), 3 (in part)	April 1, 1987	S.I. 1987/198 [1987] C.L.Y. 820
ss.30–37	August 1, 1987	S.I. 1987/852 [1987] C.L.Y. 820
Recognition of Trusts Act 1987 (c.14)		
All provisions	August 1, 1987	S.I. 1987/1177 [1987] C.L.Y. 1434
Register of Sasines (Scotland) Act 1987 (c.23)		
All provisions	July 15, 1987	s.3
Representation of the People Act 1985 (c.50)		
Sched. 4, para. 34	March 30, 1987	S.I. 1987/207 [1987] C.L.Y. 1282
Reverter of Sites Act 1987 (c.15)		
All provisions	August 17, 1987	S.I. 1987/1260 [1987] C.L.Y. 1436
Scottish Development Agency Act 1987 (c.56)		
All provisions	December 17, 1987	Royal Assent
Social Fund (Maternity and Funeral Expenses) Act 1987 (c.7)		
All provisions	March 17, 1987	Royal Assent
Social Security Act 1986 (c.50)		
ss.1, 3, 4, 5, 12 (in part), 15 (in part), Sched. 10 (para. 31) (and s.86(1) in so far as it relates to para. 31), Sched. 11 (in part) (and s.86(2) in so far as it relates to those parts)	January 4, 1988	S.I. 1987/543 [1987] C.L.Y. 3501
ss.2, 13, 14, 17, 79(1)(2), 80 (in part), Sched. 1, 10 (in part) (and s.86(2) in so far as it relates to those parts)	May 1, 1987	S.I. 1987/543 [1987] C.L.Y. 3501
ss.6, 7, 9, 10, 12 (in part), 15 (in part), 18(2)–(6), 19, Scheds. 2, 10 (in part), Sched. 11 (in part) (and s.86(2) in so far as it relates to those parts)	April 6, 1988	S.I. 1987/543 [1987] C.L.Y. 3501

Statute	Commencement	Authority
Social Security Act 1986—*cont.*		
ss.18(1), 39 (in part), 86(1)(2) (in part), Sched. 3, paras. 4, 5(1) (in part) (3), 6, 7, 16, Sched. 10, paras. 1, 10, 11, 67 (in part), 73, Sched. 11 (in part)	April 6, 1987	S.I. 1987/354 [1987] C.L.Y. 3501
ss.20(1)(7)(8)(9)(11)(12), 24(4)–(7), 22, 28, 29, 31(1)–(3)(5)–(7), 31, 86(1) (in part) (2) (in part), Sched. 10, paras. 44, 48, 49, 52, 58–60, Sched. 11 (in part) (all according to circumstances)	April 1, 1988	S.I. 1987/1853 [1987] C.L.Y. 3501
ss.20(1)(7)(8)(9)(11)(12), 24(4)–(7), 22, 28, 29, 31(1)–(3)(5)–(7), 31, 86(1) (in part) (2) (in part), Sched. 10, paras. 44, 48, 49, 52, 58–60, Sched. 11 (in part) (all according to circumstances)	April 4, 1988	S.I. 1987/1853 [1987] C.L.Y. 3501
ss.20, 21, 22 (all in part), 23, 24, 25, 26, 27 (in part), 32, 33–35, 39, 65(4), 67(2)(*b*), 73, 77, 79(3), 86(1) (in part) (2) (in part), Sched. 3, para. 8, Sched. 7, para. 3, Sched. 10, paras. 32–43, 45–47, 48, 50–51, 54–57, 61, Sched. 11 (in part)	April 11, 1988	S.I. 1987/1853 [1987] C.L.Y. 3501
ss.36, 39 (in part), 51 (remaining part), 65(1) to (3), 66, 78, 86(1) (in part), 86(2) (in part), Scheds. 10 (in part), 11 (in part)	April 11, 1988	S.I. 1987/1096 [1987] C.L.Y. 3501
s.39 (in part), Sched. 3 (in part)	April 10, 1988	S.I. 1987/1096 [1987] C.L.Y. 3501
s.86(1) (in part) (2) (in part), Scheds. 10 (in part), 11 (in part)	June 26, 1987	S.I. 1987/1096 [1987] C.L.Y. 3501
s.86(1) (in part), Sched. 10 (in part)	April 6, 1988	S.I. 1987/1096 [1987] C.L.Y. 3501
Teachers' Pay and Conditions Act 1987 (c.1)		
All provisions	March 2, 1987	Royal Assent
Territorial Sea Act 1987 (c.49)		
All provisions	October 1, 1987	S.I. 1987/1270 [1987] C.L.Y. 3357
Transport Act 1985 (c.67)		
All remaining provisions except s.139(3) (part), Sched. 8 (part)	August 13, 1987	S.I. 1987/1228 [1987] C.L.Y. 3792
Urban Development Corporations (Financial Limits) Act 1987 (c.57)		
All provisions	February 17, 1987	s.2

Statute	*Commencement*	*Authority*
Video Recordings Act 1984 (c.39)		
ss.9, 10 (for certain purposes)	March 1, 1987	S.I. 1987/123 [1987] C.L.Y. 850
ss. 9, 10 (Scotland: further purposes)	March 2, 1987	S.I. 1987/160 [1987] C.L.Y. 4248
ss.9, 10 (for certain other purposes)	September 1, 1987	S.I. 1987/1142 [1987] C.L.Y. 850
ss. 9, 10 (Scotland: for certain further purposes)	September 1, 1987	S.I. 1987/1249 [1987] C.L.Y. 4248
ss.9, 10 (for certain other purposes)	March 1, 1988	S.I. 1987/2155 [1987] C.L.Y. 850
ss. 9, 10 (Scotland: for certain further purposes)	March 1, 1988	S.I. 1987/2273 [1987] C.L.Y. 4248

CURRENT LAW YEAR BOOK

1987

ADMINISTRATIVE LAW

1. Costs—legal aid contribution order—judicial review. See SAMPSON, *Re*, §2282.

2. Housing—control order—appropriate form of challenge. See MAYOR AND BURGESSES OF WANDSWORTH LONDON BOROUGH *v.* ORAKPO, §1865.

3. Judicial review—agricultural dwelling-house advisory committee—procedural unfairness—jurisdiction to quash decision

[Rent (Agriculture) Act 1976 (c.80), ss.27, 28, 29.]

The applicant was the owner of forestry land, and employed a forester who occupied a small cottage on the land. In 1984 the forester was dismissed and the applicant wished him to move. As he refused to do so, the applicant applied to the relevant housing authority for a finding that suitable alternative accommodation should be provided by the authority. At his instigation, the agricultural dwelling house advisory committee for the area was asked to consider the matter of agricultural need. The committee saw the parties separately. They first saw the applicant and then the worker who made allegations which threw doubt on the bona fides of the application. No opportunity was given to the applicant to rebut these allegations. The committee concluded that there was no need to provide suitable alternative accommodation principally on the grounds that the presence of a forester on the estate was not needed. The applicant sought judicial review to quash the decision.

Held, allowing the application, that in view of the overwhelming expert evidence before the committee, the reasons given were wholly inadequate; (2) the way the proceedings had been conducted amounted to a procedural irregularity and were unfair; (3) certiorari would go to quash the decision of the committee even though it was only an advisory committee because the determining authority were obliged by statute to take full account of its view and because there was some evidence that in practice they would.

R. *v.* AGRICULTURAL DWELLING-HOUSE ADVISORY COMMITTEE FOR BEDFORDSHIRE, CAMBRIDGESHIRE AND NORTHAMPTONSHIRE, *ex p.* BROUGH (1987) 19 H.L.R. 367, Hodgson J.

4. Judicial review—alternative avenue of appeal—abandonment. See R. *v.* SECRETARY OF STATE FOR THE HOME OFFICE, *ex p.* ATTIVOR, §1990.

5. Judicial review—application—considerations

When deciding an application for judicial review, the Court should consider how any grievance could be remedied in terms of the speed and economy of the proceedings. It should not allow judicial review to be used to punish respondents to the application, whether in costs or in any other way.

R. *v.* WALTHAM FOREST LONDON BOROUGH COUNCIL, *ex p.* BAXTER, *The Times,* July 1, 1987, C.A.

6. Judicial review—availability of remedy—circumstances in which order for proceedings to continue as if begun by writ should be made

[Supreme Court Act 1981 (c.54), s.31, R.S.C., Ord. 53, r.9(5).]

An order under R.S.C., Ord. 53, r.9(5) for proceedings for judicial review to continue as if begun by writ could only be made where the proceedings sought a declaration, an injunction or damages and that relief was derived from or ancillary to a claim in the field of public law in respect of which relief by prerogative units could have been granted.

D was arrested and remanded in custody in March 1984. In July 1985 he was tried and sentenced to 18 years' imprisonment. At the time of his arrest D was suffering from a bullet wound in his right arm. In June 1984 and April 1985 doctors advised that D be treated by way of a bone graft and plate. All the while D's arm was useless and painful and held by a plastic support and sling. D applied for judicial review alleging breaches of the Prison Act 1952 and the Prison Rules 1964 in connection with the medical attention he received. The application was dated November 1, 1985 and sought orders for mandamus and injunctions to secure proper medical care, an order for certiorari to quash the preceding decisions made in connection with D's medical care and damages. In December 1985 D was operated on. At the time the case came before the court D's counsel conceded that the appropriate treatment had been obtained so that relief by way of mandamus, injunction and certiorari could no longer be pursued. By a notice of motion dated March 21, 1986, the Secretary of State sought an order for the proceedings to be struck out and the application for judicial review to be dismissed on the grounds that there was no reasonable claim in public law and the proceedings amounted to an abuse of the process of the court. D contended that an order should be made for the proceedings to contine as if begun by writ pursuant to R.S.C., Ord. 53, r.9(5).

Held, that an order under R.S.C., Ord. 53 r.9(5) could only be made where the relief sought in the proceedings included a declaration, on injunction or damages. If none of these were sought no order could be made for the proceedings to continue as if begun by writ. D's cases involved no arguable public law complaint. At best D had a private law claim for damages at common law for negligence. The terms of s.31 of the Supreme Court Act 1981 made it clear that relief by way of a declaration, an injunction or damages was only available in cases where relief by way of prerogative writ would have been available. A claim for damages under s.31(4) of the Act was derivative or ancillary to such relief. Given that there was no claim to damages of a nature envisaged by s.31 and Ord. 53, r.9(5) no order could be made for the proceedings to continue as if begun by writ. In any event, as D had no arguable complaint in public law the proceedings were liable to be struck out as an abuse of the process of the court. In that event there were no proceedings in which an order under Ord. 53 r.9(5) could be made (*R.* v. *British Broadcasting Corp., ex. p. Lavelle* [1983] C.L.Y. 15, *R.* v. *Deputy Governor of Camphill Prison, ex. p. King* [1985] C.L.Y. 2752, *R.* v. *Bromley London Borough Council, ex. p. Lambeth London Borough Council* [1984] C.L.Y. 11, *R.* v. *East Berkshire Health Authority, ex. p. Walsh* [1984] C.L.Y. 14, *R.* v. *South Glamorgan Health Authority, ex. p. Phillips* [1986] C.L.Y. 28, *R.* v. *Governor of Pentonville Prison, ex. p. Herbage (No. 2)* [1987] C.L.Y. 28 considered).

R. *v.* SECRETARY OF STATE FOR THE HOME DEPARTMENT, *ex p.* DEW [1987] 2 All E.R. 1049, McNeill J.

7. Judicial review—binding over to keep the peace—jurisdiction of Divisional Court. See R. *v.* INNER LONDON CROWN COURT, *ex p.* BENJAMIN, §599.

8. Judicial review—care proceedings—decision not to rehabilitate—unproven allegations against parents. See R. *v.* BEDFORDSHIRE COUNTY COUNCIL, *ex p.* C.; R. *v.* HERTFORDSHIRE COUNTY COUNCIL, *ex p.* B., §2460.

9. Judicial review—care proceedings—whether appropriate remedy

Although the remedy of judicial review is available to challenge the decisions of local authorities in child care cases, it is frequently inappropriate, and does not meet the needs of parents wishing to complain about the authorities' decisions. On such an application for judicial review, the judge, when granting leave to apply, may recommend that wardship proceedings be started.

R. *v.* NEWHAM LONDON BOROUGH COUNCIL, *ex p.* McL. *The Times,* July 25, Latey J.

10. Judicial review—civil servant—dismissal—review of Appeal Board's decision

Although the court had jurisdiction to review the board's decision since an issue of public law was involved, its discretion to do so would not be exercised since the applicant has sufficient avenues open to him in proceedings before an industrial tribunal which had already been instituted (*Council of Civil Service Unions* v. *Minister for the Civil Service* [1985] C.L.Y. 12, *Dunn* v. *The Queen* [1896] 1 Q.B. 116, *Rederiaktiebolaget Amphitrite* v. *The King* [1921] 3 K.B. 500, *R.* v. *East Berkshire Health Authority, ex p. Walsh,* [1984] C.L.Y 14 considered).

R. *v.* CIVIL SERVICE APPEAL BOARD, *ex p.* BRUCE, *The Times,* June 22, 1987, D.C.

11. Judicial review—claim in public law—claim linked to private law rights—claim begun by writ. See GUEVARA *v.* HOUNSLOW LONDON BOROUGH COUNCIL, §3052.

12. Judicial review—decision by National Coal Board to close colliery—whether susceptible to judicial review

A decision by the National Coal Board to shut a colliery was not a decision in the field of public law and thus not susceptible to judicial review. The National Coal Board decided to close Bates Colliery in Northumberland notwithstanding that the Independent Review Body had recommended that the colliery be kept open. Four unions representing employees at the colliery applied for judicial review of the decision to close the colliery.

Held, that the decision was only open to judicial review if it was made by a public body acting as such and that the applicants' public law rights had been infringed. The decision of the Board was an executive, or business or management decision. Although the decision had public interest and dealt with public money it was not a decision in the field of public law. In any event the Board was not bound to accept the Independent Review Body's recommendation and the consideration it gave to the recommendation was not open to criticism (*Council of Civil Service Unions* v. *Minister for the Civil Service* [1985] C.L.Y. 12, *O'Reilly* v. *Mackman* [1982] C.L.Y. 2603, *R.* v. *Manners* [1977] C.L.Y. 480 considered).

R. *v.* NATIONAL COAL BOARD, *ex p.* NATIONAL UNION OF MINEWORKERS [1986] I.C.R. 791, Macpherson J.

13. Judicial review—effect of undue delay in applying for judicial review. See R. *v.* IMMIGRATION APPEAL TRIBUNAL, *ex p.* KOBIR, §1951.

14. Judicial review—enfranchisement of lease—reduction of rateable value to level below statutory limit—valuation officer's method of valuation

[Housing Act 1974 (c.44), Sched. 8, para. 3(2).]

A decision by the valuation officer is only reviewable by way of judicial review if it has made illegally, is wholly irrational, or has been made by a procedural impropriety. Although in the instant case the valuation officer had not sought a potentially relevant file it had been found during the hearing and could be seen to contain nothing helpful. The applicant had failed to satisfy the tests, and the appeal was dismissed. (*Council of Civil Service Unions* v. *Minister for the Civil Service* [1985] C.L.Y. 12 followed).

R. *v.* WESTMINSTER VALUATION OFFICER, *ex p.* RENDALL (1986) 26 R.V.R. 220, C.A.

15. Judicial review—housing—waiting list application—whether discretion fettered. See R. *v.* CANTERBURY CITY COUNCIL, *ex p.* GILLESPIE, §1907.

16. Judicial review—inquest—delay. See R. *v.* H.M. CORONER FOR NORTH NORTHUMBERLAND, *ex p.* ARMSTRONG, §536.

17. Judicial review—local ombudsman—critical report

[Local Government Act 1974 (c.7), s.34(3).]

Although there was power in the court to review the decision of a local ombudsman, in the absence of impropriety the court should decline to provide an avenue of appeal where statute had not provided for any machinery of appeal.

R. *v.* LOCAL COMMISSIONER FOR ADMINISTRATION FOR THE SOUTH, THE WEST, THE WEST MIDLANDS, LEICESTERSHIRE, LINCOLNSHIRE AND CAMBRIDGESHIRE, *ex p.* EASTLEIGH BOROUGH COUNCIL, *The Times,* July 14, 1987, Nolan J.

18. Judicial review—milk quotas—base year review claim—application to quash decision of local panel. See R. *v.* DAIRY PRODUCE QUOTA TRIBUNAL, *ex p.* WYNN-JONES, §91.

19. Judicial review—N.H.S.—allocation of resources. See WALKER, *ex p.*, §2546.

20. Judicial review—national security—phone tapping—warrant of Secretary of State—legitimate expectation

The court would not decline to exercise its supervisory jurisdiction over the Home Office merely because a claim of national security was raised in answer to a claim of telephone interception. Since the Home Secretary had published the criteria governing interception warrants, this established a legitimate expectation that the criteria would be followed, and the exercise of his powers was subject to review by the courts.

The applicant claimed that his telephone calls had been intercepted pursuant to a warrant signed by the Home Secretary in August 1983. He applied for judicial review to quash the warrant claiming that it was unlawful as not complying with the published criteria governing such interceptions and because he had been deprived of his legitimate expectation that the Secretary of State would follow the published criteria. The Secretary of State declined to confirm or deny the existence of a warrant but contended that the court ought to decline jurisdiction on the grounds of national security and that the doctrine of legitimate expectation did not apply.

Held, that it would not decline to exercise its supervisory jurisdiction merely because a minister claimed that national security was at risk. In all cases, cogent evidence of potential damage to national security had to be adduced, whether in open court or *in camera,* to justify any modification of the court's normal procedure. On the facts, the evidence did not suggest that it would be harmful to the national security to consider the application. (*The Zamora* [1916] 2 A.C. 77 and *Council of Civil Service Unions* v. *Minister for the Civil Service* [1985] C.L.Y. 12 considered). The doctrine of legitimate expectation imposed a duty to act fairly and was not restricted, as the Home Secretary contended, to cases where the expectation was to be consulted or to be given the opportunity to make representations before a decision was made. Where *ex hypothesi* there was no right to be heard it could be more important to fair dealing that an undertaking by a minister as to how he should proceed should be kept. Since the criteria governing the issuing of interception warrants had been published six times between 1952 and 1982 and had been expressly adopted by the Secretary of State, that clearly established a legitimate expectation that he would follow the criteria. However, although the evidence showed that a warrant had been issued, it did not support the claim that the Home Secretary had acted with an improper motive or had deliberately flouted the criteria. He was not guilty of misfeasance in a public office. Nor could it be said that his attitude was one that no reasonable Secretary of State could have taken. Accordingly, the application was dismissed (Dicta of Lord Diplock in *O'Reilly* v. *Mackman* [1982] C.L.Y. 2603, of Lord Scarman in *Findlay* v. *Secretary of State for the Home Department* [1984] C.L.Y. 2756, *Council of Civil Service Unions* v. *Minister for the Civil Service* [1985] C.L.Y. 12, dictum of Dunn L.J. in *R.* v. *Secretary of State for the Home Department, ex p. Khan* [1985] C.L.Y. 1702 and *Bourgoin S.A.* v. *Ministry of Agriculture, Fisheries and Food* [1986] C.L.Y. 1437 considered).

R. *v.* SECRETARY OF STATE FOR THE HOME DEPARTMENT, *ex p.* RUDDOCK [1987] All E.R. 518, (Crown Office List), Taylor J.

21. Judicial review—panel on take-overs and mergers

Decisions of the Panel on Take-overs and Mergers are susceptible to judicial review.

A Co., who were bidding against B Co. to take over X Co., complained to the Panel on Take-overs and Mergers that B Co. were acting in breach of the City Code. A Co. sought orders of mandamus and certiorari but the High Court refused on the ground of lack of jurisdiction.

Held, that the High Court had supervisory jurisdiction over any body performing public law duties, supported by public law sanctions, and under a duty to act judicially, whose power was not simply by consent of those over whom it was exercised. On the facts, the panel operated as an integral part of a governmental framework for the regulation of the City with statutory powers and penalties, and did not exist simply by consent of those whom it controlled; accordingly, the courts had power to interfere (*R.* v. *Criminal Injuries Compensation Board, ex p. Lain* [1967] C.L.Y. 724 applied).

R. *v.* PANEL ON TAKE-OVERS AND MERGERS, *ex p.* DATAFIN [1987] 2 W.L.R. 699, C.A.

22. Judicial review—proceedings before commissioners—whether taxpayer entitled to judicial review of commissioner's determination. See R *v.* SPECIAL COMMISSIONER, *ex p.* NAPIER, §2026.

23. Judicial review—refusal to grant asylum—review on usual principles

A decision of the Secretary of State's not to grant asylum is subject to judicial review on the usual *Wednesbury* principles. When an immigrant seeks asylum, it is arguable that the way in which he arrived in the U.K. is irrelevant (although the Divisional Court, in giving leave to apply for judicial review, did not adjudicate on this point) (*Bugdaycay* v. *Secretary of State for the Home Department* [1987] C.L.Y. 1989 applied).

R. *v.* SECRETARY OF STATE FOR THE HOME DEPARTMENT, *ex p.* SIVAKUMARAN, *The Independent*, February 25, 1987, D.C.

24. Judicial review—Revenue documents—discovery

The applicants in judicial review proceedings sought discovery of documents relating to the practice of the Inland Revenue in applying F.A. 1973, Sched. 19, para. 10, in relation to share exchanges. In the High Court it was held that the Revenue's practice in operating the relevant provisions of the 1973 Act was likely to illuminate the issues of fact, and discovery should be ordered, but should be confined to the internal documents of the Revenue of a general character, excluding documents, indicating how particular individual cases had been dealt with. The Revenue appealed. The applicants cross-appealed, contending that the order should be varied to include copies of Form PUC3 where the applications had been successful and the letters to the Revenue accompanying those Forms.

Held, dismissing both the appeal and the cross appeal, that (1) there were no grounds for saying that in making the order for discovery the judge had erred in the exercise of his discretion, and (2) the Court was not satisfied that the Order ought to be extended to include Forms PUC3.

R. *v.* I.R.C., *ex p.* ROTHSCHILD (J.) HOLDINGS [1987] S.T.C. 163, C.A.

25. Judicial review—undue delay in application. See CRIMINAL EVIDENCE AND PROCEDURE, §605.

26. Judicial review—validity of local authority's procedure—licensing—sex establishment. See PLYMOUTH CITY COUNCIL *v.* QUIETLYNN, §2319.

27. Judicial review—wardship—children in care—challenge to exercise of local authority's statutory powers—whether wardship jurisdiction could be exercised—whether judicial review appropriate remedy. See R.M. AND L.M. (MINORS) (WARDSHIP JURISDICTION), *Re,* §2524.

28. Judicial review—whether available—detention in breach of Bill of Rights

Although judicial review was not generally available in respect of an alleged breach of the Prison Rules until a complaint had been adjudicated upon by the board of visitors, conduct which was a breach of the provisions of the Bill of Rights was subject to judicial review.

Pending his extradition, the applicant, who suffered from physical disabilitites, but was not of unsound mind, was detained in the hospital wing of a prison in close proximity to mentally disturbed inmates. He complained that he was subjected to "cruel and unusual punishment" contrary to the Bill of Rights 1688. He sought by way of an order of judicial review an order of mandamus directing the Secretary of State and the prison governor to detain him according to law. The judge granted the application and he applied for an order for discovery of medical reports concerning himself. That was granted. The respondents appealed on the ground that leave to apply was not justified, and therefore, the order for discovery was unjustified.

Held, dismissing the appeal, by a majority that although judicial review was not generally available inrespect of an alleged breach of the Prison Rules until the governor had considered a complaint and his adjudication had been considered by the board of visitors, conduct which was a breach of the provisions of the Bill of Rights raised issues beyond the ambit of the Prison Rules and was subject to judicial review. The judge was on the facts entitled to grant leave to apply for judicial review and to order discovery (dicta of Lord Denning M.R. and Roskill L.J. in *Congreve* v. *Home Office* [1976] C.L.Y. 22 applied; *R.* v. *Deputy Governor of Camphill Prison, ex p. King* [1985] C.L.Y. 2752 distinguished; *R.* v. *Board of Visitors of Hull Prison, ex p. St. Germain* [1979] C.L.Y. 2195 and *W.E.A. Records* v. *Visions Channel 4* [1983] C.L.Y. 2947 considered). On an appeal against an order for discovery made in proceedings for judicial review, it was not open to the court to consider whether it was wrong to have granted leave to apply for the judicial review.

R. *v.* GOVERNOR OF PENTONVILLE PRISON, *ex p.* HERBAGE (No. 2) [1987] 2 W.L.R. 226, C.A.

29. Library authority—ban on publications—weapon in industrial dispute—whether valid

[Public Libraries and Museums Act 1964 (c.75), ss.7(1)(2), 10(1)(2).]

Local authorities are in breach of their statutory duty to provide a proper library service as defined in s.7 of the 1964 Act there they ban certain publications to assist parties involved in an industrial dispute.

Certain newspaper publishers were involved in an industrial dispute with their former employees. Three borough councils, in response to a trade union request, banned the group's newspapers from public libraries. The applicants contended that the councils were in breach of their statutory duties to provide a proper library service.

Held, granting the applications, the councils' reasons for the ban was to use it as a weapon in the dispute, which was not within their powers under s.7 of the 1964 Act

(*Padfield* v. *Minister of Agriculture, Fisheries and Food* [1968] C.L.Y. 1667 and dicta in *Wheeler* v. *Leicester City Council* [1985] C.L.Y. 17 applied).

R. *v.* EALING LONDON BOROUGH COUNCIL, *ex p.* TIMES NEWSPAPERS: R. *v.* HAMMERSMITH AND FULHAM LONDON BOROUGH COUNCIL, *ex p.* SAME: R. *v.* CAMDEN LONDON BOROUGH COUNCIL, *ex p.* SAME (1987) 85 L.G.R. 316, D.C.

30. Ministerial undertaking—payment of grant for rail freight facilities—withdrawal—necessity for reasons. See R. *v.* SECRETARY OF STATE FOR TRANSPORT, *ex p.* SHERRIF & SONS, §3784.

31. Mistake of fact—challenge to executive decision—relevance of facts

[Local Government Reorganization (Property etc.) Order 1986 (S.I. 1986 No. 148), Art. 11(3).]

A mistake of fact could only be a ground for challenge of a decision if the mistaken fact was a condition precedent of the decision, was the only evidential basis for it, or was a matter which expressly or impliedly had to be taken into account (*Secretary of State for Education and Science* v. *Tameside Metropolitan Borough Council* [1976] C.L.Y. 829; *Daganayasi* v. *Minister of Immigration* [1980] 2 N.Z.L.R. 130 considered).

R. *v.* LONDON RESIDUARY BODY, *ex p.* INNER LONDON EDUCATION AUTHORITY, *The Times*, July 24, 1987, D.C.

32. Natural justice—allegation made in closing speech

[Town Police Clauses Act 1847 (c.89), s.37; Transport Act 1985 (c.67), s.16.]

T sought a hackney carriage licence. The local authority refused it. At the conclusion of the hearing of the appeal the authority made an allegation that she was not a fit and proper person. The allegation had not been made before and evidence was not led in support of it. T had no opportunity to deal with the allegation. T's appeal was dismissed on the ground, inter alia, that she was not a fit and proper person.

Held, allowing T's appeal, that there had been a breach of the requirements of natural justice (*R.* v. *Barnsley Metropolitan Borough Council, ex p. Hook* [1976] C.L.Y. 24 considered).

TUDOR *v.* ELLESMERE PORT AND NESTON BOROUGH COUNCIL, *The Times,* May 8, 1987, D.C.

33. Natural justice—care proceedings—order that parents not to be treated as representing the child—parents not given opportunity to make representations prior to making of order—parents not notified of order. See R. *v.* PLYMOUTH JUVENILE COURT, *ex p.* F. AND F., §2463.

34. Natural justice—disciplinary procedure—police officer

[Police Act 1964 (c.48), s.33(*b*); Police (Discipline) Regulations 1977 (S.I. 1977 No. 580).]

T, a police sergeant, was charged with misconduct under the Police Regulations and disciplinary steps were taken. The Regulations provided that in such cases an investigating officer reports to a chief officer who makes a decision as to whether charges should be brought, without any further input from the investigating officer. Following the disciplinary meeting, the chief officer retired to his room to consider the decision and during that time the investigating officer entered his room. The chief officer subsequently found T guilty and dismissed him. T brought an action for judicial review claiming breach of natural justice. The Divisional Court found that the chief officer had explained after the hearing that the investigating officer had entered his room in order to discuss another urgent matter which was in no way connected with T's case and they therefore refused the motion for judicial review. T appealed.

Held, dismissing the appeal, that the Divisional Court had correctly held that there had not been a denial of natural justice. The application of the principles of natural justice depended on the circumstances of each case and where a tribunal was exercising a "quasi-judicial" function then the court's approach must be flexible when reviewing its decision. Unlike a court of law, the police force is obliged to continue its other functions at all times, in addition to considering its findings in order to reach a decision in disciplinary proceedings. The chief officer's explanation as to the presence of the investigating officer was sufficient to dispel the apparent breach of natural justice in view of the imperative requirements of the chief officer's other responsibilities.

R. *v.* CHIEF CONSTABLE OF SOUTH WALES, *ex p.* THORNHILL [1987] I.R.L.R. 313, C.A.

35. Natural justice—duty to hear parties at public inquiry

[Severn Bridge Tolls Act 1965, ss.1(1), 3(3), 4, Sched. 2; Severn Bridge Tolls Order 1985.]

The crucial issue in considering whether to grant judicial review of a decision was not whether there had been procedural impropriety, but whether those entitled to consideration had been treated fairly.

The 1965 Act empowered the Secretary of State to levy a toll on users of the bridge subject to holding an inquiry to consider any objections to the proposed toll. In 1981 the Secretary of State proposed to increase the tolls by 150 per cent., and six local authorities objected. An inquiry was held but the inspector refused to evaluate or comment on the objections on the grounds that they fell within matters of government policy upon which he was not permitted to express an opinion. The 1985 Order increased the tolls as originally proposed. The applicant authority sought judicial review on the grounds that the inquiry was invalidated. The judge declared the order invalid.

Held, on appeal, that the proper criterion was not whether there was procedural impropriety and whether it had been cured, but whether the objectors had been treated fairly, looking at the whole of the procedure. There had been no procedural impropriety because the inspector had a discretion whether or not to express his views, and looking at the whole procedure the objectors had not been treated unfairly (*Bushell* v. *Secretary of State for the Environment* [1980] C.L.Y. 1337 considered).

R. *v.* SECRETARY OF STATE FOR TRANSPORT, *ex p.* GWENT COUNTY COUNCIL [1987] 1 All E.R. 161, C.A.

36. Natural justice—exclusion from local authority premises—right to make representations

A local authority is bound, by the rules of natural justice, to accord an individual the right to make representations before it excludes him from its premises on the ground of his conduct.

R. *v.* BRENT LONDON BOROUGH COUNCIL, *ex p.* ASSEGAI, *The Independent,* June 12, 1987, D.C.

37. Natural justice—inquiry —whether Inspector in breach of rules. See TOWN AND COUNTRY PLANNING, § 3645.

38. Natural justice—nurse—removal of name from register—appeal

[Nurses, Midwives and Health Visitors Act 1979 (c.36), s.13.]

The Court can determine an appeal by a nurse against a decision to remove his name from the register of nurses by allowing it or directing a retrial.

SLATER *v.* UNITED KINGDOM CENTRAL COUNCIL FOR NURSING MIDWIFERY AND HEALTH VISITORS, *The Independent,* June 9, 1987, D.C.

39. Natural justice—planning permission—plans for proposed development amended—objectors unable to make representations on alleged inaccuracy of plans. See TOWN AND COUNTRY PLANNING, § 3697.

40. Natural justice—police probationer—dismissal

The rules of natural justice require a Chief Officer of Police, who is considering discharging a probationer from the force, to show him a report from a delegated officer setting out judgments and opinions and making a recommendation.

R. *v.* CHIEF CONSTABLE OF THAMES VALLEY POLICE, *ex p.* STEVENSON, *The Times,* April 22, 1987, Mann J.

41. Natural justice—refugees refused leave to enter—no opportunity to comment on grounds—whether contrary to natural justice. See R. *v.* SECRETARY OF STATE FOR THE HOME OFFICE, *ex p.* AWUKU, §1970.

42. Natural justice—selection for sports team—whether rules of natural justice applicable

The rules of natural justice may not be invoked in the courts in support of a sportsman not selected to play in an amateur team.

CURRIE *v.* BARTON, *The Times,* March 27, 1987, Scott J.

43. Natural justice—unfair dismissal—whether witnesses of an alleged misdemeanour resulting in dismissal should be involved in the decision to dismiss. See MOYES *v.* HYLTON CASTLE WORKING MEN'S SOCIAL CLUB AND INSTITUTE, §1386.

44. Parliamentary and Health Service Commissioners Act 1987 (c.39)

This Act makes further provision in relation to the Parliamentary Commissioner for Administration and the Health Service Commissioners for England, Wales and Scotland, and provides for the appointment of persons for a limited period to act as the

Parliamentary Commissioner, or as a Health Service Commissioner. The Act extends the period within which complaints may be referred to the Health Service Commissioner for England or Wales by a body subject to investigation, and makes fresh provision in relation to references of complaints to the Health Service Commissioner for Scotland.

The Act received the Royal Assent on May 15, 1987, and comes into force two months from that date.

The Act only extends to Northern Ireland in so far as it relates to the Parliamentary Commissioner Act 1967 (c.13) and to the repeal of any enactment amending that Act.

45. Parliamentary Commissioner

PARLIAMENTARY COMMISSIONER ORDER 1987 (No. 661) [45p], made under the Parliamentary Commissioner Act 1967 (c.13), s.5(4); operative on May 6, 1987; amends Sched. 3 to the 1967 Act so as to exclude from the provisions of that Sched. any action taken on behalf of the Secretary of State by the Broadmoor Hospital Board and the Moss Side and Park Lane Hospitals Board.

46. Parole system—new policy in respect of discretionary and mandatory life sentences—effect. See R. *v.* SECRETARY OF STATE FOR THE HOME DEPARTMENT, *ex p.* HANDSCOMB, §993.

47. Passport—refusal to issue passport—whether reviewable decision

The decision not to issue a passport was subject to review in suitable cases notwithstanding that it was an exercise of the Royal Prerogative (*Council of Civil Service Unions* v. *Minister for the Civil Service* [1985] C.L.Y. 12 considered).

R. *v.* SECRETARY OF STATE FOR FOREIGN AND COMMONWEALTH AFFAIRS, *ex p.* EVERETT, *The Times,* December 10, 1987, Mann J.

48. Powers of mental health tribunal—patient detained in hospital—application for discharge

[Mental Health Act 1983 (c.20), s.70.]

A tribunal to whom application is made for the discharge of a patient detained in a hospital has no power to adjourn the proceedings so as to monitor the patients progress.

R. *v.* MENTAL HEALTH REVIEW TRIBUNAL, *ex p.* SECRETARY OF STATE FOR THE HOME DEPARTMENT, *The Times,* March 25, 1987, Farquharson J.

49. Public meetings—right to use suitable room on school premises—whether private law right or public law right. See ETTRIDGE *v.* MORRELL, §2378.

50. Refugee—asylum—considerations. See BUGDAYCAY *v.* SECRETARY OF STATE FOR THE HOME DEPARTMENT, §1989.

51. Refugee—letter from High Commissioner of applicant's home state—whether relevant in considering refugee status. See IMMIGRATION, §1988.

52. Regulations—lawfulness—whether directory part of regulations laid before Parliament. See R. *v.* SECRETARY OF STATE FOR SOCIAL SERVICES, *ex p.* CAMDEN LONDON BOROUGH COUNCIL, §3567.

53. Sex shop—licence—whether objectors allowed to address hearing. See SHEPTONHURST *v.* WAKEFIELD METROPOLITAN DISTRICT COUNCIL, §2318.

54. Surcharge for wilful misconduct—failure to make rate—district auditor's failure to offer oral hearing. See LLOYD *v.* McMAHON, § 3162.

AGENCY

55. Air travel agency—licensing—disclosure of status See GIMBLETT *v.* McGLASHAN, §174.

56. Authority of agent—reinsurance—retrocession agreement. See TRANSCONTINENTAL UNDERWRITING AGENCY *v.* GRAND UNION INSURANCE CO., §2075.

57. Contract of affreightment—concluded contract—whether broker had authority to conclude agreement. See GRACE SHIPPING INC. AND HAI NGUAN & CO. *v.* C. F. SHARP & CO. (MALAYA) PTE., §427.

58. Enduring power of attorney—donor incapable of management of own affairs at time of execution

[Enduring Powers of Attorney Act 1985 (c.29), ss.1(1), 4, 6(5).]

An enduring power of attorney is created where the donor is not capable of managing his affairs at the time of execution but is capable of understanding the nature and effect of the deed (*Drew* v. *Nunn* (1879) 4 Q.B.D. 661 considered).

K., *Re*; F., *Re, The Independent*, November 3, 1987, Hoffmann J.

59. Enduring powers of attorney—prescribed form

ENDURING POWERS OF ATTORNEY (PRESCRIBED FORM) REGULATIONS 1987 (No. 1612) [£1·60], made under the Enduring Powers of Attorney Act 1985 (c.29), s.2(2); operative on November 1, 1987; prescribe a revised form of an enduring power of attorney.

60. Estate agency—commission contract—construction—whether requirement of "effective cause"

D, a property company who were seeking a tenant for new office premises, circularised estate agents in the following terms: "We . . . offer a full-scale letting fee to your company should you introduce a tenant by whom you are unable to be retained, and with whom we have not been in previous communication, and who subsequently completes a lease". A subsequent circular letter offered double commission on otherwise similar terms. In April 1982 P introduced M, who were seeking new premises, and subsequently "chased" them, but M decided later that year that they would not move for the time being. In 1983 M's interest in a move revived and R, another agent, purported to reintroduce M to D. R were ineligible for commission from D, since they were retained by M and since M had been in previous communication with D. When M eventually completed a lease, P claimed that they had satisfied all D's requirements and were accordingly entitled to double commission. D objected, claiming that P had not been the effective cause of the letting: they conceded that the requirements of the commission clause had in other respects been satisfied. The judge held that the effective cause of the letting was not P but R, but that on the true construction of the commission clause P were nonetheless entitled to double commission, as being the party who had first introduced the eventual lessee.

Held, dismissing D's appeal, that the commission clause worked quite satisfactorily without the implication of an "effective cause" requirement, since commission was not payable unless a lease was completed, and since the words "with whom we have not been in previous communication" ensured that only one valid claim for commission could be made (*Luxor (Eastbourne)* v. *Cooper* [1941] A.C. 108 considered).

COOPER (BRIAN) & CO. *v.* FAIRVIEW ESTATES (INVESTMENTS) (1987) 282 E.G. 1131, C.A.

61. Estate agency—commission contract—whether applicable to prior introduction through sub-agent

A, a firm of estate agents acting as sub-agents, for P, another such firm, introduced U, a prospective purchaser, to a property which D wished to sell. At the time of the original introduction, P had not yet been appointed as D's agents, but at a subsequent meeting D, who knew that U had been introduced to the building but did not know U's name, agreed to pay commission to P should the sale to P's applicant go through. D made this agreement in the knowledge that P were acting through a sub-agent. Subsequently, P arranged for U to meet with D and inspect the property and the sale was duly completed. D, however, refused to pay P's commission arguing that the agreement to pay P commission did not extend to antecedent introductions, nor to introductions effected through a sub-agent; and that in any event, on the complicated facts of the case, P had not been the effective cause of the sale.

Held, giving judgment for P, that (1) P had not been the effective cause of the sale; (2) D had expressly agreed that the contract for commission extended to the antecedent introduction of U; (3) D had likewise agreed to and authorised the antecedent appointment of P as sub-agents; (4) D were accordingly liable to P for commission (*Samuel & Co.* v. *Saunders Brothers* (1886) 3 T.L.R. 145, *Mccann (John) & Co. (a firm) v. Pow* [1975] C.L.Y. 30 and *Wyld* v. *Sparg* [1977] 2 S.A.L.R. 75 considered).

BRUCE (ROBERT) & PARTNERS *v.* WINYARD DEVELOPMENT (1987) 282 E.G. 1255, Stewart Q.C.

62. Estate agency—deposit paid to vendor's agent—insolvency of agent—effect

P exchanged contracts with D for the purchase of D's house after paying £10,000 to D's estate agent S by way of deposit. When S subsequently failed to pay over the

£10,000 to D and went backrupt, D refused to complete and P obtained a decree of specific performance. On appeal D contended that the deposit had been paid to S conditionally upon its payment over by S to D, and that it was an implied term of the contract of sale that such a payment should be made.

Held, dismissing D's appeal, that where a deposit has been paid to a stakeholder and contracts have been exchanged, it is well established that, if the stakeholder defaults, the loss falls on the vendor and not on the purchaser. That is the case *a fortiori* where the person who receives the stake does so as the vendor's agent. Furthermore, there is a presumption unless the contrary is made clear that an estate agent receives such a deposit not as a stakeholder but as the vendor's agent.

OJELAY *v.* NEOSALE (1987) 283 E.G. 1391, C.A.

63. Estate agency—two estate agents—whether each "effective cause" of sale—whether commission payable twice

D wished to sell a house in Hampstead, and instructed two firms of estate agents. Upon the sale of the property to O, both agents sought commission from D, and claimed to have been the effective cause of the sale. The judge found that P2 had been responsible for the original introduction of O and for his initial offer of £650,000; that P1 had subsequently persuaded O to raise his offer to £750,000; and that P2 had then been responsible for persuading him to raise it further to £800,000 which D accepted. The judge held that P2's introduction had been the effective cause of the sale.

Held, dismissing appeals by D and P1, that (1) on the judge's findings of fact it could not be said that both agents had been the effective cause of the sale; (2) the effective cause had been P2.

WOOD (JOHN D.) & CO. *v.* DANTATA (1987) 283 E.G. 314, C.A.

64. Estate agency—undisclosed principal—whether election not to enforce rights against agent

P, a firm of estate agents, accepted instructions from D, a solicitor, to find a purchaser for a leasehold property in Chelsea, and stipulated that their commission would be 3 per cent. of the sale price. It subsequently transpired that D was acting for an undisclosed foreign principal R Co, on whose behalf P duly agreed to act, and upon successfully introducing a purchaser P addressed their commission account to R Co via D's firm. When a dispute arose as to whether P were entitled to their full commission, P sued D, whereupon D claimed that P had exercised an election to enforce the contract for payment of commission against R Co., and that they were therefore precluded from enforcing it against D. The assistant recorder found that there had been such an election or alternatively a novation, and gave judgment for T.

Held, allowing P's appeal, that a party who has contracted with an agent for an undisclosed principal is entitled to enforce his rights against both agent and principal, unless he had made an unequivocal election to look to one party only and to abandon his rights against the other (*Clarkson Booker* v. *Andjel* [1964] C.L.Y. 23 applied). In this case there was no evidence of such an election and abandonment by P; nor was there evidence of a novation whereby P clearly gave up their rights against D in return for a consensual right against R Co. alone.

Per curiam: the clearest evidence of the exercise of an election is at least the commencement of proceedings by the plaintiff against one or other of the two relevant parties.

CHESTERTONS (A FIRM) *v.* BARONE (1987) 282 E.G. 87, C.A.

65. Liquidator's liability for conversion—liquidator acting as agent for liquidated company. See TORT, §3585.

66. Non-existent principal—measure of damages against agent. See FARLEY HEALTH PRODUCTS *v.* BABYLON TRADING CO., §1126.

67. Power of attorney—extent of power—verifying affidavit

[Powers of Attorney Act 1971 (c.27), s.7.]

In the course of a probate action the master ordered Pir to verify certain documents by affidavit. The affidavit was sworn by his wife to whom he had granted a power of attorney. C applied for judgment on the grounds that Pir was debarred from defending the action by reason of non-compliance with the master's order.

Held, that a party could not do by an attorney an act which he was only competent to do by virtue of some duty of a personal nature requiring skill or discretion for its exercise. S.7 of the 1971 Act did not enlarge the powers of an attorney and was purely procedural.

CLAUSS *v.* PIR [1987] 2 All E.R. 752, Francis Ferrie Q.C.

68. Shipbrokers—drilling supply contract—whether agents ever agreed with suppliers that they would be entitled to commission

This Hong Kong case, which was decided purely upon its own facts, concerned an allegation by P, shipping brokers, that D, a Hong Kong company of shiprepairers agreed to pay (whether expressly or by custom) P a commission in respect of a contract for the supply of a drillship.

Held, on the facts and the evidence, that no agreement was ever entered into or contemplated for the payment of commissions by D to P. Nor was there any custom or trade usage that required the payment of such commissions.

EGGAR FORRESTER OFFSHORE *v.* HONG KONG UNITED DOCKYARDS; ENERGY SEARCHER, THE [1987] 1 Lloyd's Rep. 493, Supreme Ct. of Hong Kong, Rhind J.

69. Soil survey—vendors refusal to bear costs—whether vendor's agent authorised to give instructions for work to be done

S, who were potential purchasers of a site in Salford owned by D, insisted on a soil survey involving the drilling of boreholes. D pressed its architects to arrange for the boreholes to be sunk, but made it clear on several occasions that it did not expect to pay for the work. The architects in due course instructed P to perform the drilling work. When S decided not to purchase, P sued D for the price of the work, but D denied liability on the grounds that A had not had authority to instruct P, in view of D's expressed intention not to pay for the work. The judge held D liable.

Held, dismissing D's appeal, that having regard to D's clear instructions to the architects to arrange the drilling work, the only possible conclusion was that the architects had D's authority to instruct P, and that D were liable for the price.

ADVANCE DRILLING & GROUTING *v.* BRIAN HAULAGE (1987) 283 E.G. 555, C.A.

70. Tour operators—restriction on agreements and conduct

RESTRICTION ON AGREEMENTS AND CONDUCT (TOUR OPERATORS) ORDER 1987 (No. 1131) [85p], made under the Fair Trading Act 1973 (c.41), ss.56(2), 90(2)(4), Sched. 8, Pt I, paras. 1, 2, 4, 7; operative on July 31, 1987 save for Art. 4 which is operative on October 7, 1987; makes it unlawful for a tour operator to make or carry out an agreement for agency services with a travel agent which prohibits or intends to prohibit the agent from offering inducements to the public to purchase the operator's foreign package holidays through him.

AGRICULTURE

71. Agricultural de-rating—agricultural building—whether "contiguous" to agricultural land. See LOTHIAN REGIONAL ASSESSOR *v.* HOOD, §3157.

72. Agricultural holdings

AGRICULTURAL HOLDINGS (UNITS OF PRODUCTION) ORDER 1987 (No. 1465) [£1·30], made under the Agricultural Holdings Act 1986 (c.5), Sched. 6, para. 4; operative on September 12, 1987; prescribes units of production for various enterprises relating to agricultural land.

73. Agricultural holdings—arbitration

AGRICULTURAL HOLDINGS (ARBITRATION ON NOTICES) ORDER 1987 (No. 710) [£1·60], made under the Agricultural Holdings Act 1986 (c.5), Sched. 4, paras. 1–6, 8–13, Sched. 5, para. 5; operative on May 12, 1987; consolidates S.I. 1978 No. 257 as amended and makes provision in relation to arbitrations under the 1986 Act.

74. Agricultural holdings—assignment of tenancy by agent—made without T's authority—estoppel. See WORBOYS *v.* CARTER, §1445.

75. Agricultural holdings—grazing agreement—whether "during some specified part of the year"

[Agricultural Holdings Act 1948 (c.63), s.2(1).]

Rights to land granted in contemplation that it should be used for grazing create a seasonal grazing licence which comes within the proviso to s.2(1) of the Act.

In 1968 A granted to Y certain rights for an indefinite term over part of A's land, which Y then used for grazing. On A's death, her personal representative claimed possession on the grounds that Y had been granted a grazing licence "during some specified period of the year", within the proviso to s.2(1) of the 1948 Act which had been revoked on A's death. Y claimed to have an agricultural tenancy.

Held, that where a landowner granted a licence in contemplation that the land would be used for grazing, that created a seasonal grazing licence well understood in agricultural circles as referring to a period of less than a year, and that this came within the proviso to s.2(1) of the Act, as properly construed. (*Mackenzie* v. *Laird* [1959] C.L.Y. 26 applied).

WATTS *v.* YEEND [1987] 1 W.L.R. 323, C.A.

76. Agricultural holdings—landlord's undertaking to complete works—whether condition precedent to tenant's agreement to pay new rent

[Agricultural Holdings Act 1948 (c.63), Sched. 6 paras. 25(2) and 25A(2); Agricultural Holdings (Notices to Quit) Act 1977 (c.12), s.2(3) Case D.]

A dispute between the parties over a proposed increase in the rent payable in respect of an agricultural holding let to T was resolved by an agreement contained in two documents. This agreement specified the new rent and also contained undertakings by L to carry out certain works on the land and buildings. When in due course T failed to pay the new rent, L served a notice to pay rent and subsequently served a notice to quit under Case D of s.2(3) of the Agricultural Holdings (Notices to Quit) Act 1977. T sought arbitration in respect of the notice to quit, and argued before the arbitrator that the rent specified in the notice to pay had been incorrectly stated, since it was a condition precedent of T's liability to pay the new rent that the works should have been completed by the agreed date, and this had not been done. The arbitrator found that completion of the work was indeed a condition precedent of T's liability for the new rent, and that in consequence the notice to pay had not correctly specified the rent payable and the notice to quit had been invalid. On L's application under paras. 25(2) and 25A(2) of Sched. 6 to the Agricultural Holdings Act 1948, the judge found that there was one error of law on the face of the award and varied it by substituting a finding that the notice to quit was good.

Held, dismissing T's appeal, that the judge's construction of the agreement was correct, especially having regard to the practical difficulties consequent upon the construction contended for by T. (*Yorkbrook Investments* v. *Batten* [1985] C.L.Y. 1867 and *Graves* v. *Legg* (1854) 9 Exch. 709 considered).

BURTON *v.* TIMMIS (1987) 281 E.G. 795, C.A.

77. Agricultural holdings—payment of rent

AGRICULTURAL HOLDINGS (FORMS OF NOTICE TO PAY RENT OR TO REMEDY) REGULATIONS 1987 (No. 711) [£1·60], made under the Agricultural Holdings Act 1986 (c.5), Sched. 3, Pt. II, para. 10(1)(*a*)(2); operative on May 12, 1987; revoke and replace S.I. 1984, No. 1308.

78. Agricultural Training Board Act 1987 (c.29)

This Act makes further provision with respect to the functions of the Agricultural Training Board.

The Act received the Royal Assent on May 15, 1987, and comes into force two months from that date.

The Act does not extend to Northern Ireland.

79. Butter—reduced price of butter in intervention stores. See EUROPEAN COMMUNITIES, §1453.

80. Cereals

HOME-GROWN CEREALS AUTHORITY LEVY SCHEME (APPROVAL) ORDER 1987 (No. 671) [£1·30], made under the Cereals Marketing Act 1965 (c.14), ss.16(4), 23(1); operative on August 1, 1987; approves a scheme for financing the said Authority.

HOME-GROWN CEREALS AUTHORITY (RATE OF LEVY) ORDER 1987 (No. 1194) [45p], made under the Cereals Marketing Act 1965 (c.14), ss.13(3) and 23(1); operative on August 1, 1987, specifies the rates of dealer levy, grower levy and processor levy which appear to Ministers to be sufficient to meet the amounts apportioned to certain cereals grown in the U.K. namely, wheat (including durum wheat), barley, oats, rye, maize, triticale or any two or more of such cereals grown as one crop.

81. Dairy Produce Quota Tribunal decision

T was tenant of an agricultural holding, and had covenanted to L, ". . . not to dispose of the whole or any part of any basic quota under a marketing scheme allotted to the holding." In October 1986 T applied under the Milk (Community Outgoers Scheme) (England and Wales) Regulations 1986 (S.I. 1986 No. 1611), claiming compensation for an undertaking to discontinue milk production on the holding, and also applied for L's consent to his giving up milk production and surrendering his entire quota under the 1986 Regulations. L withheld consent in reliance upon Regulations 9(1)(*a*) and 9(1)(*b*)(ii) and upon the terms of T's covenant; and the arbitrator held that L's refusal of consent was not unreasonable. The tribunal took the view that the quota allotted to T under the Dairy Produce Quota Regulations was not "basic quota under a marketing scheme" within the meaning of the covenant, since those regulations were made to give effect to the common agricultural policy of the EEC, which did not seek to establish a scheme for regulating the marketing of milk, but rather to impose a levy on disposals of milk production within the Community with a view to curtailing the growth in milk production. Furthermore, the true construction of the covenant was a point of law, and could be taken before the tribunal on appeal under Reg. 17 of the Regulations, notwithstanding that it had not been raised before the arbitrator, provided that no injustice resulted to L. The award was thus set aside and remitted to the arbitrator.

LEE *v.* HEATON (1987) 283 E.G. 1076.

82. Eggs—labelling. See MINISTRY OF AGRICULTURE, FISHERIES AND FOOD *v.* PORTER, §1458.

83. Environmental sensitive areas

ENVIRONMENTALLY SENSITIVE AREAS (BRECKLAND) DESIGNATION ORDER 1987 (No. 2029) [£1·60]:

ENVIRONMENTALLY SENSITIVE AREAS (CAMBRIAN MOUNTAINS-EXTENSION) DESIGNATION ORDER 1987 (No. 2026) [£1·30]:

ENVIRONMENTALLY SENSITIVE AREAS (LLEYN PENINSULA) DESIGNATION ORDER 1987 (No. 2027) [£1·30]:

ENVIRONMENTALLY SENSITIVE AREAS (NORTH PEAK) DESIGNATION ORDER 1987 (No. 2030) [£1·30]:

ENVIRONMENTALLY SENSITIVE AREAS (SHROPSHIRE BORDERS) DESIGNATION ORDER 1987 (No. 2031) [£1·30]:

ENVIRONMENTALLY SENSITIVE AREAS (SOUTH DOWNS–WESTERN EXTENSION) DESIGNATION ORDER 1987 (No. 2032) [85p]:

ENVIRONMENTALLY SENSITIVE AREAS (SUFFOLK RIVER VALLEY'S) DESIGNATION ORDERS 1987 (No. 2033) [£1·30]:

ENVIRONMENTALLY SENSITIVE AREAS (TEST VALLEY) DESIGNATION ORDER 1987 (No. 2034) [85p]:

All the above orders were made under the Agriculture Act 1986 c.49), s.18(1)(4)(11); all are operative on January 1, 1988; designates areas specified as being areas which are environmentally sensitive.

84. Farms

FARM BUSINESS SPECIFICATION ORDER 1987 (No. 1948) [85p], made under the Agriculture Act 1970 (c.40), s.28(1); operative on January 1, 1988; specifies certain businesses which, when carried on by a person also carrying on a business consisting in the pursuit of agriculture on the same or adjacent land, are included in the definition of "agricultural business" in s.28(1).

FARM DIVERSIFICATION GRANT SCHEME 1987 (No. 1949) [£2·20], made under the Agriculture Act 1970, ss.28 and 29; operative on January 1, 1988; provides for aid for the diversification of agricultural businesses in the form of grants in respect of expenditure incurred in connection with the establishment or carrying on of ancillary farm businesses.

85. Heather and grass burning

HEATHER AND GRASS etc. (BURNING) (AMENDMENT) REGULATIONS 1987 (No. 1208) [45p], made under the Hill Farming Act 1946 (c.73), s.20(1); operative on August 14, 1987; amend S.I. 1986 No. 428.

86. Hill farming

HILL LIVESTOCK (COMPENSATORY ALLOWANCES) (AMENDMENT) REGULATIONS 1987 (No. 2129) [85p], made under the European Communities Act 1972 (c.68), s.2(2); operative on January 1, 1988; further amend S.I. 1984 No. 2024.

87. Improvement regulations

AGRICULTURAL IMPROVEMENT (AMENDMENT) REGULATIONS 1987 (No. 1950) [45p], made under the European Communities Act 1972 (c.68), s.2(2); operative on January 1, 1988; further amend S.I. 1985 No. 1266 in relation to expenditure on on-farm craft and tourism.

88. Levy reliefs—frozen beef and veal. See CUSTOMS AND EXCISE, §1101.

89. Meat and Livestock Commission

MEAT AND LIVESTOCK COMMISSION LEVY SCHEME (CONFIRMATION) ORDER 1987 (No. 1303) [£1·30], made under the Agriculture Act 1967 (c.22), s.13A; operative July 24, 1987; the Meat and Livestock Commission Levy Scheme, which revokes and replaces that confirmed by the Meat and Livestock Commission Levy Scheme (Confirmation) Order 1979 as varied, is confirmed.

90. Milk—quota

MILK QUOTA (CALCULATION OF STANDARD QUOTA) (AMENDMENT) ORDER 1987 (No. 626) [85p], made under the Agriculture Act 1986 (c.49), Sched. 1, para. 6; operative on April 5, 1987; amends S.I. 1986 No. 1530 by substituting a new schedule prescribing new milk quotas for the purpose of determining payments to a tenant in respect of milk quotas on the termination of the tenancy.

91. Milk quota—base year review claim—application to quash decision of local panel—judicial review

[Dairy Produce Quota Regulations 1984 (S.I. 1984 No. 1047) and Dairy Produce Quota (Determination of Base Year Review Claims) Regulations 1984 (S.I. 1984 No. 1048).]

A applied under the 1984 Regulations for his milk quota to be based not on his production for 1984, as envisaged under the quota scheme, but upon his 1981 production, on the grounds that his production in 1983 had been substantially reduced by bad weather and flooding. His application also revealed that there had been problems with leptospirosis and mastitis. The Minister rejected the claim on the grounds that A had failed to demonstrate separately the amount of milk production lost through bad weather and that lost through disease, and could not therefore show that the bad weather had caused a milk yield loss of at least 15 per cent., as required by the Regulations. The local panel dismissed A's appeal in October 1984, and A applied for judicial review to quash that decision in November 1986. In granting leave for the application, the judge left the question of delay over to the Divisional Court, but R chose not to rely on it at the hearing. The Divisional Court nonetheless pointed out that this did not debar them from considering the question of delay, and that the swift prosecution of judicial review proceedings and their determination is essential to the efficient and proper exercise of the judicial review jurisdiction. However, in all the circumstances it would not raise the point in the present case.

Held, dismissing the application, that (1) the various criticisms of the panel's decision advanced by A could not be sustained, and that the panel had been fully entitled to say that A's case had not been proved; (2) even if those criticisms had been sustained, the court would have exercised its discretion against granting judicial review, since the abolition of local panels by the 1986 Regulations meant that the Minister's decision would still stand.

R. *v.* DAIRY PRODUCE QUOTA TRIBUNAL, *ex p.* WYNN-JONES (1987) 283 E.G. 643, D.C.

92. Milk quota—special case claim—whether expected increased annual yield properly calculated

[Dairy Produce Quota Regulations 1984 (S.I. 1984 no. 1047) Sched. 2, paras. 2(1), 7, 9(2)(3) and (6), 10(1) and 11(1); Sched. 5, para. 8.]

A applied under the Dairy Produce Quota Regulations 1984 for a primary milk quota based on an annualised quantity of 238,686 litres of milk, and also made a special case development claim under para. 7 of Sched. 2 to the Regulations in respect of capital investment on his holding, which was represented by an increased number of cows and was calculated to achieve a substantially higher average monthly quantity of milk production. The claim was rejected by the minister and referred to a local panel, whose task in summary was to establish the increased number of milking cows that A could reasonably expect to have in his herd as a result of the investment, and to establish the expected annual yield from those extra milking cows. The tribunal, to which an appeal lay from the local panel, had issued general guidance that local panels "may assume in default of satisfactory evidence to the contrary a standard yield per cow of 5,000 litres." It was agreed that, as a result of the investment, A's herd numbered 60 cows, and A's evidence was that beforehand there had been 34 cows. The panel however estimated the increase in quota at 41,132 litres, based on the standard yield of 5,000 litres for an increase of 13 cows only. Neither the panel nor the tribunal, who rejected A's appeal, gave any indication as to how the figure of 13 additional cows had been arrived at. A applied to quash the tribunal's findings on the basis that its reasons were inadequate, and that it must have estimated the number of cows before the investment by dividing the annualised figure of 238,686 by the standard yield figure of 5,000: this in A's contention was an improper use of the standard figure. The judge found that there was a real risk that the tribunal had incorrectly thought that it was bound so to use the standard figure if it distrusted the evidence as to the original number of cows.

Held, granting the application and remitting the matter for reconsideration by another tribunal, that (1) the tribunal's reasons were inadequate; (2) it was possible that adequate reasons would have exposed an error of law.

R. *v.* DAIRY PRODUCE QUOTA TRIBUNAL FOR ENGLAND AND WALES *ex p.* DAVIES (1987) 283 E.G. 463, Schiemann J.

93/4. Olive oil

OLIVE OIL (MARKETING STANDARDS) REGULATIONS 1987 (No. 1783) [85p], made under the European Communities Act 1972 (c.68), s.2(2); operative on November 1, 1987; make provision for the enforcement of Art. 35 of Regulation No. 136/66/EEC.

95. Plant breeders

PLANT VARIETIES AND SEEDS (ISLE OF MAN) ORDER 1987 (No. 2210) [45p], made under the Plant Varieties and Seeds Act 1964 (c.14), s.40; operative on February 1, 1988; extends the Plant Varieties Act 1983 to the Isle of Man.

96. Plant health

IMPORT AND EXPORT (PLANT HEALTH FEES) (ENGLAND AND WALES) ORDER 1987 (No. 340) [£1·40], made under the Plant Health Act 1967 (c.8), ss.2, 3(1), 4A; operative on April 1, 1987; prescribes fees for specified services in relation to the importation and exportation of plants.

IMPORT AND EXPORT (PLANT HEALTH) (GREAT BRITAIN) (AMENDMENT) ORDER 1987 (No. 428) [45p], made under the Plant Health Act 1967, ss.1(2)(*b*), 2, 3(1)(2); operative on March 18, 1987; further amends S.I. 1980 No. 420.

IMPORT AND EXPORT (PLANT HEALTH) (GREAT BRITAIN) (AMENDMENT) (No. 2) ORDER 1987 (No. 1679) [45p], made under the Plant Health Act 1967, ss.2, 3(1)(2); operative on October 3, 1987; amends S.I. 1980 No. 420 so as to prohibit the importation of consignments of certain vegetables if they contain more than a specified percentage of soil.

PLANT HEALTH (GREAT BRITAIN) ORDER 1987 (No. 1758) [£7·50], made under the Plant Health Act, ss.2–4(1); operative on November 1, 1987; contains protective measures against the introduction into member States of organisms harmful to plants or plant products.

97. Potatoes

POTATO MARKETING SCHEME (AMENDMENT) ORDER 1987 (No. 282) [45p], made under the Agricultural Marketing Act 1958 (c.47), s.2, Sched. 1; operative on March 1, 1987; further amends S.I. 1955 No. 690.

POTATOES (PROHIBITION ON LANDING) (GREAT BRITAIN) ORDER 1987 (No. 19) [45p], made under the Plant Health Act 1967 (c.8), ss.2, 3(1)(2); operative on February 6, 1987; prohibits the landing in Great Britain of potatoes grown in or consigned from West Germany.

SEED POTATOES (AMENDMENT) REGULATIONS 1987 (No. 547) [80p], made under the Plant Varieties and Seeds Act 1964 (c.14), ss.16(1)–(3), (8) and 36; operative on April 23, 1987, as to arts. 1–3, 5, 7, and 8, and on March 1, 1988, as to arts. 2, 4, 6; amend S.I. 1984 No. 412.

SEED POTATOES (FEES) REGULATIONS 1987 (No. 649) [80p], made under the Plant Varieties and Seeds Act 1964, s.16(1)(1A); operative on April 28, 1987; prescribe fees payable in respect of certain matters arising under S.I. 1984 No. 412.

98. Seeds

CEREAL SEEDS (AMENDMENT) REGULATIONS 1987 (No. 1091) [45p], made under the Plant Varieties and Seeds Act 1964 (c.14), ss.16(1)(1A)(2)–(5)(8), 17(1)–(4), 36; operative on July 27, 1987 save for reg. 2(3)(*b*)(ii) which is operative on July 1, 1988; amend S.I. 1985 No. 976 so as to implement art. 3 of Council Directive 87/120/EEC.

FODDER PLANT SEEDS (AMENDMENT) REGULATIONS 1987 (No. 1092) [£1·30], made under the Plant Varieties and Seeds Act 1964, ss.16(1)(1A)(2)-(5)(8), 17(1)–(4), 36; operative on July 27, 1987; implement art. 2 of Commission Directive 87/120/EEC.

OIL AND FIBRE PLANT SEEDS (AMENDMENT) REGULATIONS 1987 (No. 1097) [85p], made under the Plant Varieties and Seeds Act 1964, ss.16(1)(1A)(2)–(5)(8), 17(1)–(4), 36; operative on July 27, 1987; amend S.I. 1985 No. 977 so as to implement art. 4 of Council Directive 87/120/EEC.

SEEDS (FEES) (AMENDMENT) REGULATIONS 1987 (No. 1148) [£1·90], made under the Plant Varieties and Seeds Act 1964, s.16(1)(1A)(*e*)(5)(*a*)(5A)(8); operative on August 1,

1987; amend S.I. 1985 No. 981 by prescribing new fees in relation to the matters contained therein.

SEEDS (NATIONAL LISTS OF VARIETIES) (FEES) REGULATIONS 1987 (No. 188) [£1·40] made under the Plant Varieties and Seeds Act 1964, s.16(1)(1A)(*e*)(8); operative on April 1, 1987; prescribe fees in respect of various matters arising under S.I. 1982 No. 844.

SEEDS (REGISTRATION, LICENSING AND ENFORCEMENT) (AMENDMENT) REGULATIONS 1987 (No. 1098) [85p], made under the Plant Varieties and Seeds Act 1964, ss.16(1)(1A)(3)(4)(8), 24(5), 26(2), 36; operative on July 27, 1987; amend S.I. 1985 No. 980.

VEGETABLE SEEDS (AMENDMENT) REGULATIONS 1987 (No. 1093) [45p], made under the Plant Varieties and Seeds act 1964, ss.16(1)(1A)(2)–(5)(8), 17(1)–(4), 36; operative on July 27, 1987; amend S.I. 1985 No. 979 so as to implement art. 5 of Commission Directive 87/120/EEC.

99. Sheep and goats

SHEEP AND GOATS (REMOVAL TO NORTHERN IRELAND) (AMENDMENT) REGULATIONS 1987 (No. 949) [85p], made under the European Communities Act 1972 (c.68), s.2(2); operative on May 20, 1987; amend S.I. 1983 No. 1158.

100. Tractors

AGRICULTURAL OR FORESTRY TRACTORS AND TRACTOR COMPONENTS (TYPE APPROVAL) (AMENDMENT) REGULATIONS 1987 (No. 1771) [£1·30], made under the European Communities Act 1972 (c.68), s.2(2); operative on November 5, 1987; amend S.I. 1979 No. 221.

101. Wine—common agricultural policy. See EUROPEAN COMMUNITIES, §1466.

ANIMALS

102. Animals (Scotland) Act 1987 (c.9)

This Act makes provision for Scotland with respect to civil liability for injury or damage caused by animals, the detention of straying animals, and the protection of persons or livestock from animals.

The Act received the Royal Assent on April 9, 1987, and comes into force two months from that date.

The Act extends to Scotland only.

103. Areas of special protection

EASINGTON LAGOONS (AREA OF SPECIAL PROTECTION) ORDER 1987 (No. 1163) [45p], made under the Wildlife and Countryside Act 1981 (c.69), s.3(1); operative on July 27, 1987; establishes land owned by the Yorkshire Water Authority at Easington Lagoons in Humberside as an area of special protection for the Little Tern.

104. Artificial insemination

ARTIFICIAL INSEMINATION (CATTLE AND PIGS) (FEES) REGULATIONS 1987 (No. 390) [80p], made under the Animal Health and Welfare Act 1984 (c.40), ss.10(1), (3)(*c*) and 11(3); operative on April 1, 1987; provide for the payment of fees in connection with the issue of licences and approvals under regulations relating to the artificial insemination of pigs and cattle.

ARTIFICIAL INSEMINATION OF CATTLE (ADVERTISING CONTROLS ETC.) (GREAT BRITAIN) REGULATIONS 1987 (No. 904) [£1·30], made under the Animal Health and Welfare Act 1984, s.10; operative on June 30, 1987; impose controls on the advertisement in Great Britain of semen from bulls of dairy breeds.

105. Bees

IMPORTATION OF BEES (AMENDMENT) ORDER 1987 (No. 867) [45p], made under the Bees Act 1980 (c.12), s.1(1)(2); operative on June 4, 1987; prohibits the importation of bee pests except under a licence.

106. Coypus

COYPUS (KEEPING) (REVOCATION) REGULATIONS 1987 (No. 2224) [45p], made under the Destructive Imported Animals Act 1932 (c.12), s.2; operative on January 1, 1988; revoke S.I. 1967 No. 1873.

COYPUS (PROHIBITION ON KEEPING) ORDER 1987 (No. 2195) [45p], made under Destructive Imported Animals Act 1932, s.10(1); operative on January 1, 1988; prohibits the keeping of coypus in Great Britain.

107. Cruelty

WELFARE OF BATTERY HENS REGULATIONS 1987 (No. 2020) [85p], made under the Agriculture (Miscellaneous Provisions) Act 1968 (c.34), s.2; operative on January 1, 1988; lay down minimum standards for the protection of laying hens kept in battery cages.

WELFARE OF CALVES REGULATIONS 1987 (No. 2021) [45p], made under the Agriculture (Miscellaneous Provisions) Act 1968, s.2; operative on January 1, 1990; prohibit a person from keeping a single calf in a pen or stall on agricultural land unless certain requirements are complied with.

WELFARE OF LIVESTOCK (PROHIBITED OPERATIONS) (AMENDMENT) REGULATIONS 1987 (No. 114) [45p], made under the Agriculture (Miscellaneous Provisions) Act 1968, s.2; operative on February 1, 1987; amend S.I. 1982 No. 1884 by prohibiting tooth grinding of sheep.

108. Deer Act 1987 (c.28)

This Act makes it lawful for deer kept on farms in England and Wales to be killed during a close season.

The Act received the Royal Assent on May 15, 1987, and comes into force two months from that date.

The Act extends to England and Wales only.

109. Diseases

DISEASES OF ANIMALS (APPROVED DISINFECTANTS) (AMENDMENT) ORDER 1987 (No. 74) [£1·90], made under the Animal Health Act 1981 (c.22), ss.1, 7(1)(*a*)(*b*)(*c*)(2), 23(*f*)(*g*); operative on January 31, 1987; amends S.I. 1978 No. 32 by substituting new Scheds. 1 and 2.

DISEASES OF ANIMALS (APPROVED DISINFECTANTS) (AMENDMENT) (No. 2) ORDER 1987 (No. 1447) [85p], made under the Animal Health Act 1981, ss.1, 7(1)(*a*)–(*c*), 23(*f*) and (*g*), operative on August 27, 1987; amends S.I. 1978 No. 32.

DISEASES OF ANIMALS (WASTE FOOD) (AMENDMENT) ORDER 1987 (No. 232) [45p], made under the Animal Health Act 1981, ss.1, 8(1); operative on March 10, 1987; amends S.I. 1973 No. 1936 removes exemptions from the prohibition on the processing of waste food without a licence.

DISEASES OF ANIMALS (WASTE FOOD) (FEES FOR LICENCES) ORDER 1987 (No. 361) [80p], made under the Animal Health Act 1981, s.84(1); operative on April 1, 1987; specifies fees payable for the grant or renewal of licences under S.I. 1973 No. 1936.

EXPORT OF SHEEP (PROHIBITION) ORDER 1987 (No. 211) [45p], made under the Animal Health Act 1981 s.11; operative on February 17, 1987; prohibits the export of sheep which originate in a designated area.

INFECTIOUS DISEASES OF HORSES ORDER 1987 (No. 790) [£2·60], made under the Animal Health Act 1981, ss.1, 7(1), 8(1), 15(4), 17(1)(2), 23, 28, 35(3), 72, 87(2), 88(2); operative on May 20, 1987; consolidate with amendments S.R.C.O. 1938 No. 193, as amended, relating to the diseases of horses.

MAREK'S DISEASE (RESTRICTION ON VACCINATION) ORDER 1987 (No. 905) [45p], made under the Animal Heath Act 1981, ss. 1, 72, 88(4); operative on May 31, 1987; prohibits the use of a specified type of vaccine in the vaccination of poultry against Marek's disease.

110. Importation of animals

DESIGNATION OF LOCAL AUTHORITY (PORTSMOUTH PORT HEALTH DISTRICT) ORDER 1987 (No. 709) [45p], made under the Animal Health Act 1981 (c.22), s.50(4); operative on April 24, 1987; makes the Portsmouth Port Health Authority the local authority for the District for the purposes of the 1981 Act which relate to imported animals.

111. Mink

MINK (KEEPING) ORDER 1987 (No. 2196) [45p], made under the Destructive Imported Animals Act 1932 (c.12), s.10(1); operative on January 1, 1988; prohibits the keeping of mink on certain off-shore islands of Great Britain and in certain parts of the Highland Region of Scotland and prohibits the keeping in the rest of Great Britain except under a licence.

MINK (KEEPING) (AMENDMENT) REGULATIONS 1987 (No. 2225) [45p], made under the Destructive Imported Animals Act 1932, s.2; operative on January 1, 1988; increase the fee for a licence to keep mink from £58 to £115.

112. Pigs—movement and sale

MOVEMENT AND SALE OF PIGS (AMENDMENT) ORDER 1987 (No. 233) [80p], made under the Animal Health Act 1981 (c.22), ss.1,7(1), 8(1), 25; operative on March 10, 1987; amends S.I. 1975 No. 203 in relation to the movement of pigs from premises.

113. Protection of Animals (Penalties) Act 1987 (c.35)

The Act amends the Protection of Animals Act 1911 (c.27) to increase penalties for offences against animals under s.1(1) of that Act.

The Act received the Royal Assent on May 15, 1987, and comes into force two months from that date.

The Act does not extend to Scotland or Northern Ireland.

114. Sheep

EXPORT OF SHEEP (PROHIBITION) (AMENDMENT) ORDER 1987 (No. 248) [45p], made under the Animal Health Act 1981 (c.22), s.11; operative on February 27, 1987; amends S.I. No. 211.

EXPORT OF SHEEP (PROHIBITION) (No. 2) ORDER 1987 (No. 1808) [85p], made under the Animal Health Act 1981, s.11; operative on October 19, 1987; prohibits the export of sheep from designated areas to member states of the EEC.

SHEEP SCAB (AMENDMENT) ORDER 1987 (No. 836) [85p], made under the Animal Health Act 1981, ss.1, 7(1), 8(1), 14(1)(2), 15(4), 17(1), 23, 25; operative on May 27, 1987; amends S.I. 1986 No. 862.

115. Tort—trespass—grazing

[Animals Act 1971 (c.22), ss.4, 5(5).]

The right to graze animals on common land does not include the right to let them wander at will on to and along the highways adjoining that land as they pass from one piece of grazing to another. The grazing right therefore provides no defence under s.5(5) of the Animals Act 1971 to a claim for trespass under s.4 of that Act.

MATTHEWS *v.* WICKS, *The Times*, May 25, 1987 C.A.

116. Warble fly

WARBLE FLY (ENGLAND AND WALES) (AMENDMENT) ORDER 1987 (No. 1601) [85p], made under the Animal Health Act 1981 (c.22), ss.1, 8(1), 86(1); operative on September 11, 1987; amends S.I. 1982 No. 234.

117. Wildlife—possessing wild live birds—whether strict liability

[Wildlife and Countryside Act 1981 (c.69), s.1(2)(a).]

K appealed against conviction of possession of live wild birds, contrary to s.1(2)(*a*) of the 1981 Act.

Held, dismissing his appeal, that the justices had correctly held that the offence was one of strict liability and that it was not necessary to prove that the accused knew that the birds were wild birds within the Act (*Warner* v. *Metropolitan Police Commissioner* [1968] C.L.Y. 2439, *Sweet* v. *Parsley* [1969] C.L.Y. 2210, *Sherras* v. *De Rutzen* [1895] 1 Q.B. 918, *Alphacell* v. *Woodward* [1972] C.L.Y. 3549, *Chilvers* v. *Rayner* [1984] C.L.Y. 631/2, *Lim Chin Aik* v. *R.* [1963] C.L.Y. 771 and *Gammon (Hong Kong)* v. *Att.-Gen. of Hong Kong* [1984] C.L.Y. 951 considered).

KIRKLAND *v.* ROBINSON [1987] Crim.L.R. 643, D.C.

118. Wildlife—setting poisoned substance to injure wild bird

[Wildlife and Countryside Act 1981 (c.69), s.5(1)(*a*).]

H laid down eggs containing Alpha-chloralose.

Held, dismissing the prosecutor's appeal against H's acquittal of setting in position a poisoned substance calculated to cause bodily injury to any wild bird coming into contact therewith, contrary to s.5(1)(*a*) of the 1981 Act, that the justices had correctly acceded to a submission of no case to answer, since there was no evidence that Alpha-chloralose was a "poisoned substance." An analytical chemist had described it as a "narcotic." S.5 distinguishes between substances which are "poisonous," "poisoned" and "stupefying." The section creates separate offences. Where there is doubt as to the category which the substance is in, separate informations should be laid. H's admission that he knew it was illegal to put down poison but that Alpha-chloralose was "very mild", was not evidence that the substance was in fact stupefying or poisonous or poisoned, since there was no evidence that H had any specialist chemical knowledge (*R.* v. *Cramp* (1880) 5 Q.B. 307 distinguished; *Bird* v. *Adams* [1972] C.L.Y. 558 and *R.* v. *Chatwood* [1980] C.L.Y. 531 applied).

ROBINSON *v.* HUGHES [1987] Crim.L.R. 644, D.C.

ARBITRATION

119. Alleged misconduct—procedural mishap—whether material

In this matter, arbitrators proceeded to an interim award upon the basis of written submissions. The respondents submitted that they had not been given a fair opportunity to reply to all of the submissions of the claimants, and that the arbitrators should have granted them an extension of time to deal with the claimants' submissions. They sought to set aside the award for misconduct or to have it remitted.

Held, that on the facts and the evidence there was no misconduct, and any such procedural mishaps as there had been did not result in injustice to the respondents.

OVERSEAS FORTUNE SHIPPING PTE. *v.* GREAT EASTERN SHIPPING CO.; SINGAPORE FORTUNE, THE [1987] 1 Lloyd's Rep. 270, Evans J.

120. Alleged misconduct—reference to "without prejudice" discussion—whether arbitrator should consider without prejudice issue

During the course of a construction arbitration, a dispute arose over the admissibility of allegedly "without prejudice" correspondence that had been introduced by the claimant (C) at the hearing. The arbitrator adjourned the hearing so as to enable the respondent (R) to apply to the High Court for an injunction to restrain the arbitrator from proceeding. Objection was taken to the court, and R invited the arbitrator either to withdraw from the reference or give his consent under s.2 of the Arbitration Act 1979 to the matter being referred to the Court. There followed various correspondence, and the arbitrator ultimately refused his consent. R applied to have the arbitrator removed on the grounds of misconduct, in that he was aware of "without prejudice" discussions, and had failed adequately to consider the submissions made by R in inviting him to refer the matter to the Court.

Held, that (1) although reference had been made during the course of the reference to "without prejudice" discussions the arbitrator was entitled to continue with the reference and ignore those discussions; (2) the arbitrator was obliged to carefully consider whether he should act and hear submissions on behalf of R as to why he should not. The matter would be remitted accordingly.

BROWN (IAN KEITH) *v.* C.B.S. (CONTRACTORS) [1987] 1 Lloyd's Rep. 279, Hawser Q.C., Deputy Judge.

121. Appeal—power to grant extension of time for appeal

Where the rules of the arbitral body in question, and the provisions of the contract giving rise to the arbitiration, failed to provide for an extension of time for appealing, there was no power to grant such an extension of time (*Amalgamated Metal Corp.* v. *Khoon Seng Co.* [1977] C.L.Y. 115 considered.)

R *v.* LIVERPOOL COTTON ASSOCIATION, *ex p.* COTTON CORP. OF INDIA, *The Times*, February 13, 1987, Taylor J.

122. Application for rescission of reference to arbitration—principles. See PRACTICE (CIVIL), §2908.

123. Arbitration argument—arrest of vessel—stay of action—whether arrest should be maintained.

[Arbitration Act 1975 (c.3), s.1; Civil Jurisdiction and Judgments Act 1982 (c.27).]

P agreed to carry a number of cargoes for F from Australia to Europe. P chartered D's vessel to perform a voyage, the charterparty containing a London arbitration clause. The vessel was lost with all her cargo and F claimed damages from P in arbitration. P commenced an action against D, the sole purpose thereof being to obtain security for any award obtained in the arbitration. D applied for a stay of the action under S.1 of the Arbitration Act 1975 and for the release of a vessel which had been arrested.

Held, that (1) the action would be stayed pursuant to the 1975 Act; (2) However, the Court had a power under s.26 of the Civil Jurisdiction and Judgments Act 1982 to order that the property arrested be retained as security for the satisfaction of an award; (3) this was an appropriate case for the imposition of such an order.

WORLD STAR, THE [1986] 2 Lloyd's Rep. 274, Sheen J.

124. Arbitrator's fees—whether reasonable

In determining a commodity dispute, the Board of Appeal of the Cocoa Association charged over £25,000 in fees, some £8,000 of which had been expended on legal fees. The losing party contended that the fees were unreasonable.

Held, that (1) as to the Board of Appeal member's fees, these could not be said to be unreasonable; (2) as to the fees of the legal adviser, it was plain that these were excessive and that the Board of Appeal had never taxed or questioned those fees. The award would be set aside in relation to these fees.

KURKJIAN (S. N.) (COMMODITY BROKERS) *v.* MARKETING EXCHANGE FOR AFRICA (FORMERLY MOTIRAM (T. M.) (U.K.) (No. 2)) [1986] 2 Lloyds Rep. 618, Staughton J.

125. Award—alleged misconduct—remission

O let their vessel to C for a time charter. The charter went badly after a while and C obtained a report condemning the condition of the vessel. C put the vessel off-hire, and O, when C had failed to pay two hire instalments, placed C in repudiatory breach of charter. Arbitrators found in favour of O. C contended that they had misconducted themselves in relying upon prior unpunctual hire payments as evidence of repudiatory breach, and applied for a remission under s.22 of the Arbitration Act 1950. They had further failed to annex telex exchanges to the award which C contended was misconduct.

Held, that (1) C was not entitled to remission, there being no evidence that the arbitrators were wrong, or that anything had gone wrong which caused C injury; (2) it was not misconduct not to annex the telex exchanges despite C's request that they be annexed.

MAFRACHT *v.* PARNES SHIPPING CO. S.A.: APOLLONIUS, THE [1986] 2 Lloyd's Rep. 405, Bingham J.

126. Award—enforcement—Mareva injunction

Where a party to an arbitration agreement which contains a choice of law clause in favour of non-English law obtains an award he will be entitled to leave to enforce the award here as a judgment provided (a) the parties intended to create legally enforceable rights and obligations, (b) the agreement was sufficiently certain to constitute enforcement, and (c) there are no public policy objections to enforcement.

If a debt is enforceable within the jurisdiction it constitutes an asset to which a Mareva injunction can attach.

D.S.T. and R entered into an agreement to explore for oil, which included a term providing for arbitration in Geneva according to a proper law adopted by the arbitrators. Later D.S.T. referred a claim to arbitration and received a substantial award, while R obtained recission of the agreement and damages from a court in a Gulf State. Neither party took part in the proceedings instituted by the other. D.S.T. later discovered that an English company, S, had bought oil from R and obtained leave to enforce the arbitration award in England as a judgment, and a Mareva injunction. R obtained leave to serve a writ out of the jurisdiction on D.S.T. claiming enforcement of its judgment.

Held, on appeal, that D.S.T.'s Mareva injunction and leave should not be discharged, while R's leave should be. The choice of law clause was effective because the parties had intended to create legally-enforceable rights and obligations, the agreement was sufficiently certain as to constitute a contract and enforcement would not be contrary to public policy. Further the Mareva injunction was valid despite the fact that S's indebtedness to R would normally be settled in U.S. dollars in New York, since in default it could be enforced within the jurisdiction (*Czarnikow* v. *Roth Schmidt* [1922] 2 K.B. 478, *Orion* v. *Belfort Maatschappij* [1962] C.L.Y. 87 and *Eagle Star Insurance Co.* v. *Yuval Insurance Co.* [1978] C.L.Y. 1710 considered).

DEUTSCHE SCHACHTBAU-UND TIEFBOHRGESELLSCHAFT mbH *v.* RAS AL KHAIMAH NATIONAL OIL CO. [1987] 2 All E.R. 769, C.A.

127. Award—misconduct—failure to give effect to sealed offer in award of costs

Before the hearing of a Lloyd's salvage arbitration P, the respondent cargo owners, made a sealed offer. D, the contractors, appealed the award of the original arbitrator. Although the award was increased, it still did not "beat" the sealed offer made by P. The appeal arbitrator made no special order as to costs. He gave no reasons as to why he had acted thus. P asked for the award to be set aside or remitted to the arbitrator on the grounds that the award or order for costs was erroneous.

Held, (1) that it was usual, when a successful sealed offer had been made, for the offeror to be awarded his costs after the date when the offer was made; (2) there was nothing which justified the appeal arbitrator in not awarding P the costs of the arbitration from the date of their offer and the award would be remitted with a direction to that effect.

IOS 1, THE [1987] 1 Lloyd's Rep. 321, Leggatt J.

128. "Centrocon" arbitration clause—no arbitrator appointed within time limit—application for extension of time—leave to appeal

[Arbitration Act 1950 (c.27), s.27.]

O and C entered into a voyage charter on the Gencon form: this incorporated a Centrocon arbitration clause (amended to six months) which provided that claims and arbitration proceedings were to be commenced within that period or they would "be deemed to be waived and absolutely barred." Cargo was discharged in a damaged condition and the master of the vessel was notified thereof. No arbitrator was appointed in time by C, and two months after the expiry of the time bar period C's solicitors asked O to appoint arbitrators or accept the claim. O rejected the claim as being out of time. C waited three months to appoint an arbitrator, and then asked for an extension of time. Steyn J. refused such an extension, holding that although O has suffered no material prejudice, the delay of C in commencing arbitration proceedings *after* the time bar point had been taken was sufficiently culpable to deprive them of an exercise of the court's discretion in their favour. C sought leave to appeal.

Held, refusing leave to appeal, that the judge did not err in principle in any way and the Court of Appeal would not be justified in interfering with the exercise by him of his discretion.

IRISH AGRICULTURAL WHOLESALE SOCIETY *v.* PARTENREEDEREI: M.S. EUROTRADER; EUROTRADER, THE [1987] 1 Lloyd's Rep. 418, C.A.

129. Charterparty—demurrage claim—limitation of time—oral agreement to pay—jurisdiction to extend time. See MARIANA ISLANDS STEAMSHIP CORP. *v.* MARIMPEX MINERALOEL-HANDELSGESELLSCHAFT mbH, §3384.

130. Coffee—European contract—notification requirements for arbitration

[European Contract for Coffee Terms, Art. 40.]

Art. 40 of the European Contract for Coffee Terms requires the formal decision to initiate arbitration proceedings to be notified within 45 days of its having been taken. The article requires no more than that an unequivocal decision to initiate arbitration proceedings should have been taken and notified by one party to the other within 45 days of the first claim.

SABTINA *v.* MOUNTAFIAN COMMODITIES, *The Times,* May 25, 1987, Saville J.

131. Contract—arbitration clause—allegations of fraud. See CONTRACT, §414.

132. Contract entered into as a result of alleged negligence—whether arbitration clause applied.

Where it was alleged that a defendant's negligence caused the plaintiff to enter into a contract, this was not a claim arising "out of the contract or the carrying out of works", or "in connection with the contract". The dispute could not, therefore, be the subject of an arbitration clause contained in the contract.

BLUE CIRCLE INDUSTRIES *v.* HOLLAND DREDGING CO. (U.K.), *The Times,* March 23, 1987

133. Delay in prosecution—whether arbitration agreement abandoned by mutual consent

Arbitration proceedings had been commenced by P against D in 1975. The cause of action arose in 1974. Nothing was done, and the arbitrators closed their files in 1978. There was no further communication until 1983, when D's solicitors wrote a letter setting forth their claim. P applied for a declaration that the arbitration had been abandoned by mutual consent. Evans J. rejected their claim, finding that there was no evidence that there had been a mutual abandonment. P appealed.

Held, that (1) the Judge could not be criticised for the result which he had reached. There had been mention of the dispute from time to time; (2) P were not entitled to claim a declaration merely on the grounds of excessive delay; (3) the court was bound by, but doubted the appropriateness of, the decisions of the House of Lords in *Bremer Vulkan* v. *South India Shipping Corp.* [1981] C.L.Y. 119 and *The Hannah Blumenthal* [1982] C.L.Y. 139.

FOOD CORP. OF INDIA *v.* ANTCLIZO SHIPPING CORP.; ANTCLIZO, THE [1987] 2 Lloyd's Rep. 130, C.A.

134. Foreign arbitration awards

ARBITRATION (FOREIGN AWARDS) ORDER 1987 (No. 1029) [45p], made under the Arbitration Act 1975 (c.3), s.7(2); operative on July 1, 1987; specifies that China and Singapore are parties to the 1958 New York Convention on the Recognition and Enforcement of Foreign Arbitral Awards (Cmnd. 6419).

135. Forum for proceedings—arbitration clause providing that the law of a certain country should govern procedure

Where an arbitration clause in a contract provides that the arbitration procedure shall be that of a particular country, the presumption is that the forum for such proceedings will also be that country.

NAVIERA AMAZONICA PERUANA *v.* COMPANIA INTERNACIONAL DE SEGUROS DE PERU, *The Independent*, November 11, 1987, C.A.

136. GAFTA 100—claim time-barred—whether arbitration should proceed—injunction

By a contract made in 1972, on the GAFTA 100 form, S sold soya bean meal to B c.i.f. Rotterdam. The export of the soya from the U.S.A. became the subject of an embargo in June 1973. It was not until 1983 that B sought to make a claim under the contract and claim arbitration. S sought a declaration that B's claim was time-barred and an injunction restraining the arbitration. B contended that the GAFTA rules were the only rules relating to time, and that the *Scott* v. *Avery* clause provided that no court proceedings were to be heard until all matters had been determined by the arbitrators.

Held, granting the injunction, that (1) the Arbitration Rules did not give the arbitrators a discretion to override the limitation acts; (2) S was seeking to restrain B from breaching the arbitration agreement.

COMPAGNIE EUROPEENE DE CEREALS S.A. *v.* TRADAX EXPORT S.A. [1986] 2 Lloyd's Rep. 301, Hobhouse J.

137. Injunction to restrain arbitration on grounds of estoppel *per res judicatum*—Mareva injunction—discharge

By this originating summons, P sought (a) to restrain an arbitration from proceeding on the grounds that the claims made by D in it had already been adjudicated in a separate arbitration; (b) to have a Mareva injunction obtained by D in support of that second arbitration discharged.

Held, that (1) there was no estoppel *per res judicatum*, and the arbitration would not be restained; (2) the Mareva would be discharged, as when it had been obtained D had no existing legal or equitable right to such relief, their only cause of action having been for a declaration.

SIPOREX TRADE S.A. *v.* COMDEL COMMODITIES [1986] 2 Lloyd's Rep. 428, Bingham J.

138. International arbitration—security for costs. See INTERNATIONAL LAW, §2081.

139. JCT Minor Works contract—arbitration clause—whether arbitration clause effective after completion of contract

The arbitration clause in the contract was effective even when the architect had issued a final certificate.

CRESTAR *v.* CARR, *The Times*, May 6, 1987, C.A.

140. JCT standard form—dispute at date of contract—whether dispute fell within the scope of the arbitration clause

A dispute based upon mistake at the date of contract, or alleged negligence as to misrepresentation or mis-statement at that date was one arising in connection with the contract, and so fell within the arbitration clause that it contained.

ASHVILLE INVESTMENTS *v.* ELMER CONTRACTORS, *The Times*, May 29, 1987, C.A.

141. Judgment—amendment—misnomer of party

An award was made in arbitration proceedings in favour of P who thereafter applied under s.26 of the Arbitration Act 1950 for an order that the award might be enforced in the same manner as an order of the court to the same effect. The application was granted and P signed judgment. P encountered certain difficulties in enforcing the judgment against the defendant Saudi Europe Lines because there was no legal *persona* of that name. The judge directed that the judgment be amended by the substitution of a Mr. Orri "trading as Saudi Europe Lines" for the name "Saudi Europe Lines." Mr. Orri contended that (i) there was no jurisdiction to make any such alteration in the present case because there had been an arbitration and the power of the court under s.26 of the 1950 Act could only be to make an order or another judgment in the same terms as the arbitration award, and (ii) the court only had power to alter a name where the name used failed to give effect to the true intention of the court making the original order when the original judgment was entered and the intention throughout the proceedings was to proceed against Saudi Europe Lines.

Held, refusing Mr. Orri's application for leave to appeal, that (i) the award merged in the judgment when judgment was entered and the court had the same inherent powers to correct that judgment as it would have had if the proceedings had been in the court throughout; (ii) the intention was throughout to obtain redress and make an award against the person carrying on business as Saudi Europe Lines, whom the court now knew to be Mr. Orri. (*Pearlman (Veneers) SA (Pty)* v. *Bernhard Bartels* [1954] C.L.Y. 2607 followed).

SEA TRIUMPH SHIPPING CO. S.A. *v.* SAUDI EUROPE LINES. Appeal from Leggatt J. April 28, 1986. (C.A.T. No. 380).

142. Limitation—extension of time—whether Court had jurisdiction to extend the time in which to commence arbitration proceedings in circumstances where the Hague-Visby Rules were incorporated. See SHIPPING AND MARINE INSURANCE, §3380.

143. Money paid prior to award—power to award interest on such sum

[Arbitration Act 1950 (c.27), s.19A.]

It is an implied term of an arbitration agreement that the arbitrator should conduct the reference in accordance with the law in force at the time of the hearing, and accordingly in respect of an arbitration agreement made prior to April 1, 1983 the arbitrator has jurisdiction to award interest on sums paid prior to the award.

Following a dispute over demurrage arising under a voyage charterparty made in1974 the arbitrator, in 1985, found in favour of the owners, and included interest on a payment on account made by the charterers in 1982.

Held, that the charterers had failed to establish to the requisite degree (a strong prima facie case) that the arbitrator had slipped accidentally, so remission would be refused; it was an implied term of any arbitration agreement that the hearing should be conducted in accordance with the law then in force, which the arbitrator had done here. Interest on the payment on account had been properly allowed.

FOOD CORP. OF INDIA *v.* MARASTRO CIA NAVIERA S.A.; TRADE FORTITUDE, THE [1986] 3 All E.R. 500, C.A.

144. Name—borrowing—status and effect of name-borrowing in arbitration—NFBTE/FASS nominated sub—contract

S engaged L as their sub-contractors in executing work for N. The main contract was in the JCT 1963 standard form. The sub-contract was in the NFBTE/FASS nominated form. Disputes arose between S and N and between L and S, in which L attempted, pursuant to the provisions of its sub-contract to "borrow" S's name and claim against N.

Three arbitrations were started, one settled but questions arose on the surviving arbitrations as to the status of L and S, which lead to both L and S issuing originating summonses.

Held, that (1) there was an implied term of the sub-contract that S should provide necessary co-operation to enable L to pursue its right to use the main contractors' name; (2) the name-borrowing arbitration was in effect a tripartite arbitration and the arbitrators' orders as to discovery, *etc.* bound all three parties. In particular, L were entitled to discovery against S including documents in respect of which privilege might have been claimed in the main arbitration. Equally, S had to disclose in the name-borrowing arbitration non-privileged documents which had been disclosed in the sub-contract arbitration; (3) L could use the documents disclosed by S in the sub-contract arbitration in the name-borrowing arbitration and vice versa.

STEWART (LORNE) *v.* SINDALL (WILLIAM) AND N.W. THAMES REGIONAL HEALTH AUTHORITY (1987) 35 Build.L.R. 109, Judge Hawser Q.C., O.R.

145. Reasoned award—further reasons

Where an arbitrator gives reasons at a party's request, and on appeal it is claimed that he dealt so inadequately with Counsel's submissions as to give rise to a point of law, the Court can look at Counsel's submissions in order to decide whether to order further reasons (*C.T.I.* v. *Oceanus* [1984] C.L.Y. 3193 and *Universal Petroleum Co.* v. *Handels und Transport Gesellschaft mbH* [1987] C.L.Y. 146 applied).

KANSA GENERAL INSURANCE CO. *v.* BISHOPSGATE INSURANCE, *Financial Times,* November 18, 1987, Hirst J.

146. Reasoned award—request for further reasons—circumvention of primary findings—jurisdiction

[Arbitration Act 1979, (c.42), s.1.]

The court cannot order an arbitrator to give reasons for his primary findings in a reasoned award which is otherwise unappealable.

In a dispute about the terms of a contract for the sale of cargo oil, the arbitrator made a reasoned award. The buyers sought leave to remit the award for reconsideration and further reasons. The judge granted their application.

Held, allowing the appeal, that the court cannot order an arbitrator to give reasons for his primary findings in a reasoned award which is otherwise unappealable (*Barenbels,*

The [1985] C.L.Y. 3224, *Mondial Trading GmbH* v. *Gill & Duffus Zuckerhandelsgesellschaft* mbH [1980] C.L.Y. 75 and *Nema, The* [1981] C.L.Y. 76 referred to).

UNIVERSAL PETROLEUM CO. *v.* HANDELS UND TRANSPORT GESELLSCHAFT MBH [1987] 1 FTLR 429, C.A.

147. Reference—want of prosecution—whether reference abandoned or rescinded

In this case, D had commenced arbitration proceedings against P in 1975 in respect of cargo claims arising out of damage to cargo carried on P's vessel. A further arbitration was commenced in respect of demurrage claims. That dispute was resolved in arbitration. In 1985 D commenced proceedings, seeking a declaration that the arbitration agreement had been abandoned.

Held, (1) that on the facts and the evidence D's conduct was such as to entitle P to assume that the reference had been abandoned. P's conduct and inactivity constituted acceptance; (2) D would not have been precluded from proceeding with the cargo claim, however, on the ground that the demurrage claim had been separately decided; (3) the arbitration had been abandoned and/or rescinded.

EXCOMM *v.* GUAN GUAN SHIPPING (PTE); GOLDEN BEAR, THE [1987] 1 Lloyd's Rep. 330, Staughton J.

148. Reinsurance—arbitration clause—retrocession agreement—whether arbitration agreement incorporated into retrocession agreement. See INSURANCE, §2074.

149. Rent review—arbitrator's decision—inter-related break clause. See METROLANDS INVESTMENTS *v.* DEWHURST, §2202.

150. Rent review—whether error of law on face of award

[Arbitration Act 1979 (c.42), s.1.]

A applied under s.1 of the Arbitration Act 1979 for leave to appeal against the award of an arbitrator assessing the revised rent due under a rent review clause, and argued that the arbitrator had on the face of the award erroneously concluded that the Lands Tribunal had laid down a general rule of law that a discount of 14 per cent. for frontage to a depth should always be made.

Held, refusing leave, that the arbitrator had done no such thing, and that there was no error of law of any sort disclosed on the face of the award.

TRIUMPH SECURITIES *v.* REID FURNITURE CO. (1987) 283 E.G. 1071, Harman J.

151. Salvage arbitration—interlocutory injunction to restrain arbitration. See SHIPPING AND MARINE INSURANCE, §3367.

152. Scope of those matters referred to arbitration—private "*ad hoc*" submission

D claimed to have rendered salvage services to P's vessel and it was agreed that the question of whether such services had been rendered would be referred to arbitration in London. In support of their claim D had obtained security in Antwerp by arresting the vessel. P claimed that such arrest was wrongful. It was contended by D that the question of whether the arrest was wrongful had also been referred to arbitration in London.

Held, on the facts and the evidence that the parties had never agreed to refer the question of wrongful arrest to London arbitration.

STANDARD OCEAN CARRIERS S.A. *v.* UNION DE REMORQUAGE ET DE SAUVETAGE S.A.; NEPTUNE C, The [1986] 2 Lloyd's Rep. 609, Bingham J.

153. Security in arbitration proceedings—admiralty practice—retention of property—stay of action. See SILVER ATHENS, THE (No. 2), §3368.

154. Stay of action—commencement of action seeking declaration of right as to time bar in arbitration agreement—whether a dispute to be referred to arbitrators

P and D entered into two sale contracts on FOSFA terms, each containing a FOSFA arbitration clause that made provision for the appointment of arbitrators within specific time periods. P also established performance bonds in D's favour. D had to make a call on the bonds, and obtained judgment against the banks which had issued them. P then commenced arbitration proceedings against D. D indicated that they were going to take a time bar defence, and P applied to the court for (i) an extention of time under s.27 of the Arbitration Act 1950, and (ii) a declaration that the claims were not time-barred. D applied for a stay of action under s.1 of the Arbitration Act 1975.

Held, (1) the time bar point depended upon a dispute over the construction of the FOSFA rules, which was within the jurisdiction of the arbitrators; (2) the court would accordingly stay the action.

COMDEL SECURITIES *v.* SIPOREX TRADE S.A. [1987] 1 Lloyd's Rep. 325, Steyn J.

155. Stay of action—whether written agreement to arbitrate

[Arbitration Act 1975 (c.3), S.I.]

P made an enquiry about the purchase of glass from D, and D produced a written quotation providing that it was subject to their terms of business which included, *inter alia,* an arbitration clause. A contract was thereafter negotiated and concluded and the goods were delivered. Some glass was damaged in transit, and P issued High Court proceedings. D moved to stay the proceedings on the ground that there was a binding arbitration agreement that the Court was bound to stay the proceedings under s.1 of the Arbitration Act 1975.

Held, allowing D's appeal, that the contract was partly made in writing and that it did contain a written argument to arbitrate. The proceedings would therefore, be stayed.

ZAMBIA STEEL & BUILDING SUPPLIES *v.* CLARK (JAMES) & EATON [1986] 2 Lloyd's Rep. 225, C.A.

156. Stay of proceedings—discretion to order—ability or willingness to arbitrate

[Can.] D contracted with M to supply supervisory services for a construction project in Iran. The contract provided for the arbitration of disputes in accordance with the Rules of the I.C.C. and stipulated that it was to be governed by the laws of Iran. M deposited $2 million in British Columbia by way of security for payment and the Bank of Montreal issued a letter of credit to it on behalf of D. A dispute arose in 1980 about D's payment and an action was begun, in which it was alleged that M fraudulently attempted to obtain the proceeds of the letter of credit. The bank also sued D and M in respect of the letter of credit and the two actions were due to be heard together. In 1981, D served a notice to arbitrate upon M, who did nothing. In 1984, M applied for a stay of D's action pending arbitration. At first instance it was held that M had failed to establish that it was, when the proceedings were begun, and remained ready and willing to do all things necessary to the conduct of the arbitration.

Held, dismissing M's appeal, that the curial law established by the contract required the application of the law of Iran. The Constitution of Iran requires the approval by the council of ministers of the settlement of disputes involving a foreigner. There was no evidence that such approval had been granted, nor that M had pressed forward the arbitration since the commencement of the action. M's bare assertion of its willingness to take all necessary steps to proceed therewith was insufficient to establish its willingness and ability to arbitrate. *Hiller* (*James*) *& Partners* v. *Whitworth Street Estates* (*Manchester*) [1970] C.L.Y. 326 and *Dalmia Cement* v. *National Bank of Pakistan* [1974] C.L.Y. 108 considered.)

DILLINGHAM CANADA INTERNATIONAL *v.* MANA CONSTRUCTION, (1985) 69 B.C.L.R. 133, British Columbia C.A.

157. Stay of proceedings—refusal—joinder of party

[Arbitration Act 1975 (c.3), s.1.]

Entitlement to apply for a stay pursuant to s.1 of the 1975 Act only extended to parties involved in the dispute which it was intended should be referred to arbitration.

M. Co. and K. Co. manufactured fans under licence from a French company. The licence agreement provided that disputes should be referred to arbitration in the country of the defending party. The French company's sister company E. Co. sued NMB, a subsidiary of M. Co. and K. Co., alleging breach of copyright in respect of the fans. NMB served a defence and was thus prevented by s.1 of the 1975 Act from having proceedings stayed while the matter was referred to arbitration. M. Co. & K. Co. sought to be joined to the action so that they could obtain such a stay.

Held, (1) the right to seek a stay under s.1 only extended to parties to the dispute which was to be referred to arbitration so even if M. Co. and K. Co. were joined, they would not be entitled to a stay; (2) the general jurisdiction to order a stay would only rarely be exercised on a subject covered by statute, and would not be exercised here.

ETRI FANS CO. *v.* NMB (U.K.) [1987] 2 All E.R. 763, C.A.

ARMED FORCES

158. Air force—rules of procedure

RULES OF PROCEDURE (AIR FORCE) (AMENDMENT) RULES 1987 (No. 2000) [85p], made under the Air Force Act 1955 (c.19), ss.103 and 209; operative on January 1, 1988; amend S.I. 1972 No. 419.

RULES OF PROCEDURE (AIR FORCE) (AMENDMENT No. 2) RULES 1987 (No. 2172) [45p], made under the Air Force Act 1955, ss.103 and 209; operative on January 1, 1988; correct an error in S.I. 1987 No. 2000.

159. Armed Forces Act 1986—commencement

ARMED FORCES ACT 1986 (COMMENCEMENT No. 3) ORDER 1987 (No. 1998 (c.60)) [45p], made under the Armed Forces Act 1986 (c.21), s.17; brings all remaining provisions of the 1986 Act into force on December 31, 1987.

160. Army, Air Force and Naval Discipline Acts—continuation

ARMY, AIR FORCE AND NAVAL DISCIPLINE ACTS (CONTINUATION) ORDER 1987 (No. 1262) [45p], made under the Armed Forces Act 1986 (c.21), s.1(2); continues in force for 12 months beyond August 31, 1987 the Army Act 1955, the Air Force Act 1955 and the Naval Discipline Act 1957.

161. Crown Proceedings (Armed Forces) Act 1987 (c.25)

This Act repeals s.10 of the Crown Proceedings Act 1947 (c.44) and provides for the revival of that section in certain circumstances.
The Act received the Royal Assent on May 15, 1987.
The Act extends to Northern Ireland.

162. Injuries in war—compensation

INJURIES IN WAR (SHORE EMPLOYMENTS) COMPENSATION (AMENDMENT) SCHEME 1987 (No. 529) [45p], made under the Injuries in War Compensation Act 1914 (c.18), s.1; increases the maximum weekly allowance payable to former members of the Women's Auxiliary Forces who suffered disablement during service overseas in 1914–18 to £64·50.

163. Irish Sailors and Soldiers Land Trust Act 1987 (c.48). See EQUITY AND TRUSTS, §1428.

164. Protection of Military Remains Act 1986—Guernsey

PROTECTION OF MILITARY REMAINS ACT 1986 (GUERNSEY) ORDER 1987 (No. 1281) [85p], made under the Protection of Military Remains Act 1986 (c.35), s.10(4); operative on August 21, 1987; extends the 1986 Act to Guernsey.

165. Royal Marines Museum. See LITERARY AND SCIENTIFIC INSTITUTIONS, §2341.

166. Service pensions. See PENSIONS AND SUPERANNUATION, §2817.

167. Standing civilian courts

COURTS MARTIAL AND STANDING CIVILIAN COURTS (ADDITIONAL POWERS ON TRIAL OF CIVILIANS) (AMENDMENT) REGULATIONS 1987 (No. 1999) [45p], made under the Army Act 1955 (c.18), Sched. 5A, para. 17, the Air Force Act 1955 (c.19), Sched. 5A, para. 17, and the Naval Discipline Act 1957 (c.53), Sched. 4A, para. 17; operative on January 1, 1988; amend S.I. 1977 No. 87.

STANDING CIVILIAN COURTS (AMENDMENT) ORDER 1987 (No. 2001) [85p], made under the Armed Forces Act 1976 (c.52), Sched. 3, para. 12; operative on January 1, 1988; amends S.I. 1977 No. 88.

STANDING CIVILIAN COURTS (AMENDMENT No. 2) ORDER 1987 (No. 2173) [45p], made under the Armed Forces 1976, s.22(4) and Sched. 3, para. 12; operative on January 1, 1988; corrects errors in S.I. 1987 No. 2001.

ATOMIC ENERGY

168. British Nuclear Fuels—financial limit

BRITISH NUCLEAR FUELS PLC (FINANCIAL LIMIT) ORDER 1987 (No. 875) [45p], made under the Nuclear Industry (Finance) Act 1977 (c.7), s.2(1)(*a*); operative on May 15, 1987; extends to £1,500 million the limit contained in s.1 of the 1977 Act.

169. Nuclear installations

NUCLEAR INSTALLATIONS (ISLE OF MAN) (VARIATION) ORDER 1987 (No. 668) [80p], made under the Nuclear Installations Act 1965 (c.57), s.28 as extended by the Congenital Disabilities (Civil Liability) Act 1976 (c.28), s.4(6) and the Energy Act 1983 (c.25), s.33; operative on May 7, 1987; amends S.I. 1977 No. 429 so as to extend to the Isle of Man the amendments to the 1965 Act effected by the 1976 and the 1983 Acts.

NUCLEAR INSTALLATIONS (JERSEY) (VARIATION) ORDER 1987 (No. 2207) [85p], made under the Nuclear Installations Act 1965, s.28 as extended by the Congenital Disabilities (Civil Liability) Act 1976, s.4(6) and the Energy Act, s.33; operative on January

18, 1988; amends S.I. 1980 No. 1527 so as to extend to Jersey the amendments of the 1965 Act effected by the 1976 and 1983 Acts.

170. Nuclear weapons testing—Crown immunity—negligence. See PEARCE *v.* SECRETARY OF STATE FOR DEFENCE, §2569.

AVIATION

171. Aerodromes

AERODROMES (DESIGNATION) (DETENTION AND SALE OF AIRCRAFT) ORDER 1987 (No. 1377) [45p], made under the Civil Aviation Act 1982 (c.16), s.88(10); operative on September 2, 1987; permits the detention and sale of aircraft by specified aerodrome operators for the non-payment of airport charges.

AERODROMES (DESIGNATION) (DETENTION AND SALE OF AIRCRAFT) (No. 2) ORDER 1987 (No. 2229) [45p], made under the Civil Aviation Act 1982 (c.16), s.88(10); operative on January 20, 1988; designates specified aerodromes as aerodromes to which s.88 applies.

172. Air navigation

AIR NAVIGATION (GENERAL) (SECOND AMENDMENT) REGULATIONS 1987 (No. 2078) [85p], made under S.I. 1985 No. 1643; operative on January 1, 1988; amend S.I. 1981 No. 57.

AIR NAVIGATION (NOISE CERTIFICATION) ORDER 1987 (No. 2212) [£2·60], made under the Civil Aviation Act 1982 (c.16), ss.60, 61, 101, 102; operative on January 1, 1988; revokes and replaces S.I. 1986 No. 1304.

AIR NAVIGATION (RESTRICTION OF FLYING) (MOLESWORTH AERODROME) REGULATIONS 1987 (No. 1885) [45p], made under S.I. 1985 No. 1643; operative on January 14, 1988; restricts flying in the area of Molesworth Aerodrome.

AIR NAVIGATION (SECOND AMENDMENT) ORDER 1987 (No. 2062) [£2·90], made under the Civil Aviation Act 1982, ss.60, 61, 102; operative on June 1, 1988 for the purposes of Art. 2(36)–(46), operative on July 1, 1989 for the purposes of Art. 2(13)(30) and operative on January 1, 1988 for all other purposes; amend S.I. 1985 No. 1643.

RULES OF THE AIR AND AIR TRAFFIC CONTROL (THIRD AMENDMENT) REGULATIONS 1987 (No. 1145) [45p], made under S.I. 1985 No. 1643; operative on October 1, 1987; further amends S.I. 1985 No. 1714.

RULES OF THE AIR AND AIR TRAFFIC CONTROL (FOURTH AMENDMENT) REGULATIONS 1987 (No. 1812) [85p], made under S.I. 1985 No. 1643; operative on December 17, 1987; amend S.I. 1985 No. 1714.

173. Air transport licence—temporary exemption—considerations in granting exemption

The C.A.A. could take the potential damage caused by a refusal to grant a licence into consideration in deciding to grant a temporary exemption so as to permit certain limited operations (*R.* v. *Hillingdon London Borough Council ex p. Pulhofer* [1985] C.L.Y. 1615 considered).

R. *v.* CIVIL AVIATION AUTHORITY *ex p.* AIRWAYS INTERNATIONAL CYMRU, *The Times,* June 10, 1987, Roch J.

174. Air travel agency—licence—disclosure of status

[Civil Aviation (Air Travel Organisers Licensing) Regulations (S.I. 1972 No. 223), reg. 2.]

An air travel agent who relies on the exemption from holding a licence because his principal holds a licence is required to disclose that he is an agent in any transaction involving the provision of flight accommodation.

GIMBLETT *v.* McGLASHAN. *The Times,* December 22, 1986, D.C.

175. Aircraft—movement

STANSTED AIRPORT AIRCRAFT MOVEMENT LIMIT ORDER 1987 (No. 874) [45p], made under the Airports Act 1986 (c.31), ss.32, 79; operative on June 1, 1987; sets a limit of 78,000 aircraft movements per annum for Stansted Airport.

176. Airport licensing—liquor. See LICENSING, §2308.

177. Airport shops. See SHOPS, MARKETS AND FAIRS, §3448.

178. Carriage by air. See CARRIERS, §286.

179. Civil aviation

AIRPORTS BYELAWS (DESIGNATION) ORDER 1987 (No. 380) [45p], made under the Airports Act 1986 (c.31), s.63(1); operative on April 10, 1987; designates airports listed in the Schedule, for the purposes of s.63 of the 1986 Act.

AVIATION SECURITY (ANGUILLA) ORDER 1987 (No. 451) [£1·40], made under the Aviation Security Act 1982 (c.36), ss.9(2) and 39, the Extradition Act 1870 (c.52), ss.2, 17, and 21, and the Fugitive Offenders Act 1967 (c.68), s.17; operative on April 17, 1987; extends to Anguilla certain provisions of the 1982 Act.

CIVIL AVIATION ACT 1980 (GOVERNMENT SHAREHOLDING) ORDER 1987 (No. 747) [45p], made under the Civil Aviation Act 1980 (c.60), s.7; operative on June 1, 1987; sets the target investment limit for Government shareholding in British Airways at 2·5 per cent. of voting stock.

CIVIL AVIATION AUTHORITY (AMENDMENT) REGULATIONS 1987 (No. 379) [80p], made under the Civil Aviation Act 1982 (c.16), s.7(2); operative on April 13, 1987; amend S.I. 1983 No. 550.

CIVIL AVIATION (JOINT FINANCING) (FIFTH AMENDMENT) REGULATIONS 1987 (No. 2100) [45p], made under the Civil Aviation Act; 1982 (c.16), ss.73, 74; operative on January 1, 1988; further amend S.I. 1982 No. 1784 by increasing certain charges.

CIVIL AVIATION (NAVIGATION SERVICES CHARGES) (SECOND AMENDMENT) REGULATIONS 1987 (No. 269) [80p], made under the Civil Aviation Act 1982 (c.16), ss.73, 74; operative on April 1, 1987; increase charges for navigation services provided by the Civil Aviation Authority at specified aerodromes.

CIVIL AVIATION (ROUTE CHARGES FOR NAVIGATION SERVICES) (FOURTH AMENDMENT) REGULATIONS 1987 (No. 2083) [£1·30], made under the Civil Aviation Act 1982, ss.73, 74; operative on January 1, 1988; amend S.I. 1984 No. 1920 so as to increase certain charges.

TOKYO CONVENTION (ANGUILLA) ORDER 1987 (No. 456) [£1·60], made under the Tokyo Convention Act 1967 (c.52), s.8, the Civil Aviation Act 1982 s.108, the Aviation Security Act 1982 (c.36), s.39 and the Extradition Act 1870 (c.52), ss.2, 17 and 21; operative on April 17, 1987; extends to Anguilla certain provisions of the 1982 Act.

180. Designation

AIRPORT BYELAWS (DESIGNATION) (No. 2) ORDER 1987 (No. 2246) [45p] made under the Airports Act 1986 (c.31), s.62(1); operative on February 3, 1988; designates the airports listed in the Schedule for the purposes of s.63 of the 1986 Act.

LONDON CITY AIRPORT BYELAWS (DESIGNATION) ORDER 1987 (No. 1132) [45p], made under the Airports Act 1986 (c.31), s.63(1); operative on July 30, 1987; designates the London City Airport for the purposes of s.63 of the 1986 Act.

181. Government shareholding

AIRPORTS ACT 1986 (GOVERNMENT SHAREHOLDING) ORDER 1987 (No. 2232) [45p], made under the Airports Act 1986 (c.31), s.7; operative on January 28, 1988; sets the target investment limit for the Government shareholding in BAA plc at 4·548 per cent. of the voting stock.

182. Protection of aircraft. See EXTRADITION, §1693.

BAILMENT

183. Car park—nature of parking—delivery

Where a vehicle was parked on D's land for a fee, but there was no barrier, the land was open, no keys to the vehicle were given to D, and the vehicle owner locked the vehicle and retained the keys himself, no bailment of the vehicle took place (*B. G. Transport Services* v. *Marston Motor Co.* [1971] C.L.Y. 526 considered).

CHAPPELL (FRED) *v.* NATIONAL CAR PARKS, *The Times,* May 22, 1987, Hamilton Q.C.

184. Sub-bailment—quasi—bailee—duty of care—damages—foreign currency

[Supply of Goods and Services Act 1982 (c.29), s.13.]

Where a contract of bailment for reward is entered into and the potential bailee never actually takes possession of the goods but sub-contracts the storage of them to another, he is in the position of a quasi-bailee. He can sub-contract the performance of his contract but not its responsibilities, and therefore he is liable for his sub-contractors' negligence in respect of the goods.

The fact that a foreign plaintiff kept his books and accounts and principally his business in a foreign currency would not automatically lead to an award of damages in that currency (*Folias, The* [1978] C.L.Y. 710 considered).

METAALHANDEL JA MAGNUS BV. *v.* ARDFIELDS TRANSPORT, *Financial Times*, July 21, 1987, Gatehouse J.

BANKING

185. Advertising

BANKING ACT 1979 (ADVERTISEMENTS) (AMENDMENT) REGULATIONS 1987 (No. 64) [45p], made under the Banking Act 1979 (c.37), s.34(1)(2); operative on February 16, 1987; amends S.I. 1985 No. 220.

186. Asian Development Bank

ASIAN DEVELOPMENT BANK (FOURTH REPLENISHMENT OF THE ASIAN DEVELOPMENT FUND) ORDER 1987 (No. 1252) [45p], made under the Overseas Development and Co-operation Act 1980 (c.63), s.4; operative on July 7, 1987; provides for a payment of £95,082,840 to the said Fund as the U.K.'s contribution to the fourth replenishment.

187. Assignment of cheque—dentist—whether assignment of public funds

The assignment of a cheque by an associate dentist to the senior practitioner of the dental practice is not tainted with illegality as being an assignment of public funds.

LYNCH *v.* SUBJIC, *The Times*, May 18, 1987, Hirst J.

188. Bank security—artificial transaction—constructive trust. See BARCLAYS BANK *v.* WILLOWBROOK INTERNATIONAL, §1423.

189. Bankers' books—right to inspect and take copies as evidence—cheques and credit slips—whether "other records". See WILLIAMS *v.* WILLIAMS: TUCKER *v.* WILLIAMS, §1674.

190. Banking Act 1987 (c.22)

This Act makes new provision for regulating the acceptance of deposits in the course of a business, for protecting depositors and for regulating the use of banking names and descriptions. S.187 of the Consumer Credit Act 1974 (c.39) is amended in relation to arrangements for the electronic transfer of funds. The powers conferred by s.183 of the Financial Services Act 1986 (c.60) are clarified.

The Act received the Royal Assent on May 15, 1987. S.91 will come into force immediately. The remaining provisions will come into force on days to be appointed by the Treasury.

The Act extends to Northern Ireland.

191. Banking Act 1987—commencement

BANKING ACT 1987 (COMMENCEMENT No. 1) ORDER 1987 (No. 1189 (c.32)) [45p], made under the Banking Act 1987, s.110(2); brings into force on July 15, 1987 Pt. V, ss.102, 106, 107 (in part), 108(1) (in part), 109, 110, Sched. 5, para. 14, Sched. 6, para. 26(5) and Sched. 7 (in part).

BANKING ACT 1987 (COMMENCEMENT No. 2) ORDER 1987 (No. 1664 (C.50)) [45p], made under the Banking Act 1987, s.110(2); brings the 1987 Act into force on October 1, 1987 save for s.38 and Sched. 7, Pt. I (in part).

192. Bills of Exchange—promisory note—option to repay before certain date

[Bills of Exchange Act 1882 (c.61), s.26(1), 83(1).]

Where a document expresses a loan to be repayable "by" a certain date, that imports an option to pay earlier which prevents there being an unconditional promise to pay at a fixed or determinable time, such promise being necessary for s.83(1) of the 1882 Act.

C lent £7,600 to a company of which B was the major shareholder. B signed a document headed with the company's name and address stating that it was to be repaid "by July 1, 1983". The company went into liquidation and C sought to recover from B personally on the grounds that this was a promissory note within s.83(1) of the 1882 Act and that B was personally liable on it under s.26(1). B appealed against the county court judgment against him.

Held, allowing the appeal, that the expression "by July 1, 1983" imported an option to pay earlier and thus created an uncertainty or contingency which prevented there being an unconditional promise to pay at a fixed or determinable future time, as required for s.83. Further the document was primarily a receipt and was not intended to be negotiable or capable of being enforced by a holder in due course. (*Williamson* v. *Rider* [1962] C.L.Y 187 and *Akbar Khan* v. *Attar Singh* [1936] 2 All E.R. 545 applied).

CLAYDON *v.* BRADLEY [1987] 1 All E.R. 522, C.A.

193. Cheque—dishonoured cheque—bank's breach of contract—damages

An individual who was not a trader was only entitled to nominal damages in respect of the bank's wrongful dishonour of his cheques without proof of special damage.

RAE *v.* YORKSHIRE BANK, *The Times,* October 12, 1987, C.A.

194. Cheque—whether triable issue raised

Where a cheque in payment for goods has been procured on the innocent misrepresentation that the payee would supply further goods in the future it is very doubtful whether leave would be given to the drawer to defend an action on the cheque.

FAMOUS *v.* GE IM EX ITALIA SRL, *The Times,* August 3, 1987, C.A.

195. Commodity brokers—acceptance of deposit from clients interest charged—whether deposit-taking business.

[Banking Act 1979 (c.37), s.1.]

A broker who takes deposits from his clients to secure trading on the clients' behalf is not precluded by the Banking Act 1979 from suing to claim reimbursement of the clients' trading losses.

D opened an account with P, commodity brokers, for the purpose of dealing in financial and commodity futures. He made an initial deposit of $50,000 but his trading deficit soon increased to substantially in excess of that sum. P agreed to allow him to run a deficit of $400,000; from time to time D reduced his liability to P but his account was never cleared. During the time when the account was in deficit P charged interest on the account outstanding. Eventually P liquidated D's position when the deficit stood at $910,000 and sued to recover that sum. D argued that P had been carrying on a deposit-taking business in contravention of s.1 the Banking Act 1979. The judge held that the Act did not apply to such a transaction.

Held, dismissing this appeal by D, that moneys accepted by a person in the course of his business as security for payment for property or services supplied by his business were excluded from the provisions of the Act by s.1(6); P were not holding themselves out as willing to accept deposits on a day to day basis within s.1(3)(*a*); and in any event, even if P had unlawfully accepted a deposit, their contractual rights would have remained unaffected. (*St. John Shipping Corp.* v. *Joseph Rank* [1956] C.L.Y. 8303 applied).

S.C.F. FINANCE CO. *v.* MASRI (No. 2) [1987] 2 W.L.R. 58, C.A.

196. Disclosure of information

BANKING ACT 1987 (DISCLOSURE OF INFORMATION) (SPECIFIED PERSONS) ORDER 1987 (No. 1292) [45p], made under the Banking Act 1987 (c.22), s.84(2); operative on August 13, 1987; specifies the Panel on Take-overs and Mergers for the purposes of s.84 of the 1987 Act.

197. Duty of care—bank—advice sought as to investments. See ROYAL BANK TRUST CO. (TRINIDAD) *v.* PAMPELLONNE (J. N.), §2576.

198. Duty of care—cheques crossed "not negotiable"—cheques endorsed by payee and paid by customer into account—whether bank obliged to warn customer of risk of defective title to cheques

A bank was not under a duty to advise a customer of the risks involved in cashing through his bank account a cheque crossed "not negotiable—account payee only" which appeared to have been endorsed by the payee.

P wished to cash a number of cheques for his friend G. The cheques were crossed "not nogotiable—account payee only" and were made out to individual payees. The cheques appeared to have been generally endorsed by the payees. P assumed G obtained the cheques from persons to whom he had sold motor cars in the course of his business. The cheques were drawn by Wagon Finance Ltd. The cheques were paid into P's account by D and P then received cash from D. In fact the cheques had been obtained by fraud and none of the holders of the cheques ever had good title. Wagon Finance Ltd. sued D for conversion. Subsequently, D paid Wagon Finance Ltd. and debited P's account with the value of the cheques. P sued D in negligence claiming that D owed him a duty of care to warn him of the consequences of dealing with the cheques in the manner he did in that he might find himself liable if a previous holder did not have good title to the cheques.

Held, that the relationship between a bank and its customer gave rise to a duty to take reasonable care in interpreting, ascertaining and acting in accordance with the customer's instructions. The duty imposed on the bank did not require it to warn against or advise on any risks inherent in pursuing the customer's instructions or attendant upon something the customer wishes to do. Accordingly, P was not entitled to recover from D the sums debited to his account in respect of the cheques.

REDMOND *v.* ALLIED IRISH BANKS [1987] FLR 307. Saville J.

199. Equitable set-off—customers' accounts—allegation that customers mere nominees

Where a bank alleged that one nominee of several was overdrawn and that other alleged nominees were in credit, the bank had no entitlement to set off the sums in the latter accounts against the former unless it was clear and indisputable that the monies were in truth all part of the same fund (*Aries Tanker Corp.* v. *Total Transport* [1977] C.L.Y. 2741, *Morier, ex p.* (1879) 12 Ch.D. 491 considered).

BHOGAL *v.* PUNJAB NATIONAL BANK, *The Independent,* November 25, 1987, C.A.

200. Exempt transactions

BANKING ACT 1979 (EXEMPT TRANSACTIONS) (AMENDMENT) REGULATIONS 1987 (No. 65) [45p], made under the Banking Act 1979 (c.37), s.2(1)(5); operative on February 16, 1987; amend S.I. 1986 No. 1712 as a consequence of the commencement of Pt. IV of the Financial Services Act 1986.

201. Freezing of Libyan assets by U.S. banking law—U.S. bank in England—Libyan customer's demand for its funds in England

P had funds in D bank, both in a current account in New York and a deposit account in London. A U.S. executive order froze all Libyan assets under U.S. control. P sought to withdraw the funds in London.

Held, that since it was possible for the London funds to be transferred to P by a method involving no U.S. transaction, and since the operation of the London deposit account was governed by English law, D was obliged to pay out the deposit account to P (*Toprak Mahsulleri Ofisi* v. *Finagrain Compagnie Commerciale Agricole et Financiere S.A.* [1979] C.L.Y. 2391, *Regazzoni* v. *Sethia (K.C.) (1944)* [1957] C.L.Y. 585 considered).

LIBYAN ARAB FOREIGN BANK *v.* BANKERS TRUST CO., *The Times,* September 19, 1987, Staughton J.

202. Letters of credit—discrepant documents—failure to accept or return documents by confirming bank—whether confirming bank could raise interest charges due to late acceptance

A bank's late acceptance of discrepant documents under a letter of credit constitutes waiver of the discrepancies, rendering them as though they did not exist.

B purchased butter oil from S. B's bank opened a letter of credit ("L/C") and telexed D, the confirming bank, with details of the L/C, which provided for payment of 90 per cent. of the consignment value against presentation of shipping documents complying with the L/C, and the balance within 60 days after discharge of the cargo. The L/C was subject to the Uniform Customs and Practice for Documentary Credits 1974 ("UCP"). D passed on the terms to P1 the beneficiary bank. Documents were presented to P, and did not conform with the L/C. P confirmed to D that they would assume full responsibility for the discrepancies, and D accordingly paid P the 90 per cent. instalment. D later claimed repayment of that sum, which had been paid under reserve, although D retained the documents that had been tendered. A full and correct set of documents was eventually obtained, and D paid over the final 10 per cent. having deducted therefrom the interest on the original 90 per cent. which they had paid under reserve. P brought an action claiming that D was not entitled to set off that loss, and seeking recovery of that sum.

Held, that (1) D had had a reasonable time in which to choose whether to accept or reject discrepant documents. In this case they did neither but merely sat on the documents and failed to lift the reserve; (2) in those circumstances the discrepancies were waived as though they had never existed, and D was not entitled to set off the interest charges incurred by them.

CO-OPERATIVE CENTRALE RAIFFEISEN-BOERENLEENBANK B.A. *v.* SUMITOMO BANK, THE [1987] 1 FTLR 233, Gatehouse J.

203. Letters of credit—fraud—injunction to restrain bank paying beneficiaries

Plaintiffs were not entitled to an injunction to restrain a bank making payments under an irrecoverable letter of credit on the ground of fraud where they could not show that a further fraudulent demand would be made notwithstanding that fraudulent demands had already been made.

P were engaged in the timber trade with a Brazilian company. At P's request D issued a letter of credit in favour of the Brazilian company that included provision for advance payment upon receipt by D of a simple receipt from the Brazilian company countersigned by a director of P. The letter of credit was issued in substitution for earlier letters of credit. The Brazilian company had threatened to issue receipts to obtain advance payments using signatures of P's directors supplied previously for other purposes. The new letter of credit provided for different signatures from the directors of P. After the issue of the letter, on two occasions the Brazilian company sought advance payments using receipts countersigned by a director of P in its original as opposed to new form. D refused to pay the Brazilian company. P commenced proceedings against D and sought an interlocutory injunction to restrain D from making any advance payments under the letter of credit.

Held, that there was a heavy burden of proof on P to show that there was fraud on the part of the Brazilian company. The second attempt to obtain an advance payment was only consistent with fraud. Notwithstanding that, the relief sought would not be granted because P had failed to show that a further fraudulent demand for advance payment would be made using signatures in the new form. In any event, it would not be a proper case in which to grant an interlocutory injunction because the damage D might sustain to its reputation could not be properly compensated by P if the injunction should not have been granted (*United Trading Corp. S.A.* v. *Allied Arab Bank* [1984] C.L.Y. 175 applied).

TUKAN TIMBER *v.* BARCLAYS BANK [1987] 1 FTLR 154, Hirst J.

204. National Savings Bank

NATIONAL SAVINGS BANK (INTEREST ON ORDINARY DEPOSITS) ORDER 1987 (No. 2096) [45p], made under the National Savings Bank Act 1971 (c.29), s.5(5); operative on January 1, 1988; continues the two-tier interest rate structure for ordinary deposits in the N.S.B. but reduces the rates of interest from January 1, 1988.

NATIONAL SAVINGS BANK (INVESTMENT DEPOSITS) (LIMITS) (AMENDMENT) ORDER 1987 (No. 329) [45p], made under the National Savings Bank Act 1971, s.4; operative on March 3, 1987; further amends S.I. 1977 No. 1210 so deposits in excess of the limit may be treated as lawful if at the time of the deposit it was not known that the limit had been exceeded.

205. Savings banks

SAVINGS BANKS (ORDINARY DEPOSITS) (LIMITS) (AMENDMENT) ORDER 1987 (No. 330) [45p], made under the National Savings Bank Act 1971 (c.29), s.4; operative on March 3, 1987; further amends S.I. 1969 No. 939 so that deposits in excess of the limit may be treated as lawful if at the time of the deposit it was not known that the limit had been exceeded.

BANKRUPTCY

206. Action in negligence by bankrupt—cause of action assigned back to bankrupt by trustee—required permission for assignment not given—whether writ a nullity

[Bankruptcy Act 1914 (c.59), ss.55(1), 56(4).]

On his bankruptcy, any cause of action then vested in a bankrupt becomes vested in his trustee by operation of law and no notice thereof is required to be given to those subject to the chose in action. Although the permission of the Department of Trade would be required for the assignment of the cause of action back to the bankrupt by his trustee, the failure to obtain that consent did not make a subsequent action brought by the bankrupt a nullity because he was an equitable assignee.

In 1980 W obtained legal advice from solicitors and counsel concerning the question whether a contract for sale was enforceable against him. In 1984 he was declared bankrupt. In 1986 the trustee in bankruptcy assigned to W any legal rights of action he might have against the solicitors and counsel arising out of that advice; a writ was subsequently issued alleging professional negligence. The defendants sought to strike out the action on the ground that W had no *locus standi.*

Held, that (i) the vesting of the cause of action in the trustee occurred by operation of law on W's bankruptcy, and no notice was required to be given to the potential defendants; (ii) the permission of the Department of Trade was necessary to the assignment back to W of the cause of action; (iii) the failure to obtain that consent did not make the writ a nullity: W simply became an equitable assignee, with the right to sue, the effect of his being merely an equitable assignee being that he could not recover damages or a permanent injunction until joined in the action by the legal assignee; (iv) the defect could be, and was, subsequently cured when W became legal assignee of the cause of action (*Ramsey* v. *Hartley* [1977] C.L.Y. 185 applied).

WEDDELL *v.* PEARCE (J.A.) AND MAJOR [1987] 3 W.L.R. 592, Scott J.

207. Authorised insolvency practitioners—annual directory

The Department of Trade and Industry has published the first ever annual Directory of Authorised Insolvency Practitioners. The Directory is available from H.M.S.O. (ISBN 0 11 513996 6) [£13·50].

208. Bankruptcy notice—language should be understood by plain debtors

L, the petitioning creditor, had a judgment debt against N. A bankruptcy notice was issued on May 1, 1986. On June 3 the time for service was extended to September 15. The debtor was evading service. On August 1, application was made for substituted service of a bankruptcy notice. On August 11 the order was made in the following terms: "it is ordered on August 11, 1986, that the sending of a sealed copy of the above mentioned bankruptcy notice together with a sealed copy of this order by ordinary 1st class post addressed to John Bernard Nevis c/o his solicitors . . . shall be deemed to be good and sufficient service of the said bankruptcy notice on the said John Bernard Nevins within seven days of completing such a posting as aforesaid."

Held, that the language of the order must be capable of being understood by ordinary plain debtors. An ordinary debtor would be very confused as to what was meant by "within." The test is not was the debtor confused but was he possibly capable of being confused.

NEVINS *v.* LAW, January 28, 1987; D.C. [*Ex rel. Leathers Prior, Solicitors.*]

209. Inquiry as to debtor's dealings and property—summons to "any person" capable of giving information—British subject resident abroad

[Bankruptcy Act 1914 (c.59), s.25(1); Bankruptcy Rules 1952, r.86.]

S.25(1) of the Bankruptcy Act 1914 empowers the court to summon before it "any person" who is capable of giving evidence without any qualification as to residence or nationality, and covers at least a British citizen resident outside the jurisdiction.

The trustee in bankruptcy of D the debtor believed that certain Channel Island companies were controlled by A, the applicant, D's brother, who was a British citizen resident in Belgium. The trustees believed that D was the beneficial owner of the assets through A. The trustee summonsed A under s.25 of the Bankruptcy Act 1914 to attend the Court for examination, and obtained authorisation for services out of the jurisdiction under r.86 of the Bankruptcy Rules 1952.

Held, dismissing A's application for rescission of the order, that (1) s.25(1) empowered the court to summon before it "any person" without any qualification as to residence or nationality and (2) the court accordingly had jurisdiction to order service out of the jurisdiction under r.86 (*Sawers, ex p. Blain, Re* [1874–80] All E.R.Rep. 708, dicta of Fry L.J. in *Pearson, ex p. Pearson, Re* [1891–4] All E.R.Rep. at 1068, of Lord Porter in *Theophile* v. *Solicitor General* (1947–1950) C.L.C. 640 of Lord Scarman in *Clark (Inspector of Taxes)* v. *Oceanic Contractors Inc.* [1983] C.L.Y. 1968 and of Hoffmann J. in *MacKinnon* v. *Donaldson Lufkin & Jenrette Securities Corp.* [1986] C.L.Y. 1501 applied; *Anglo-African Steamship Co., Re* (1886) 32 Ch.D. 348, *ex p. O'Loghlen; O'Loghlen, Re* (1871) L.R. 6 Ch.App. 406 and *Att.-Gen.* v. *Power* [1938] 3 All E.R. 32 considered).

TUCKER (A BANKRUPT), *ex p.* TUCKER, *Re* [1987] 2 All E.R. 23, Scott J.

210. Insolvency proceedings. See COMPANY LAW, §343.

211. New legislation—monitoring effect

An Insolvency Court Users' Committee has been set up. The Secretary is Dominic Hartley, Chancery Chambers, Royal Courts of Justice.

INSOLVENCY COURT USERS' COMMITTEE, *The Independent*, April 8, 1987, Browne-Wilkinson V.-C.

212. Order for sale—case of hardship

[Law of Property Act 1925 (c.20), s.30.]

Q had lived in a house for over 40 years with both her late husbands. She was 70. The house was full of memories and she had done a lot of work on it. She was in poor health which the doctor said would deteriorate if she was forced to move. She and her son, M, had purchased the freehold in 1980 from the local authority. M's creditors were largely the State in the form of the Inland Revenue and the D.H.S.S. M had left home in 1986 and disappeared. In a claim by M's trustee in bankruptcy under s.30 for an order for sale of the house, Q sought postponement of sale until after her death.

Held, the trustee's claim would be dismissed. It was necessary to balance the legal and moral claims of the creditors and the mother and to take into account the hardship which the latter would suffer. It would be difficult to imagine a more extreme case of hardship than this one. The creditors should wait until after Q's death (*Holliday, Re* [1980] C.L.Y. 1406 and *Thames Guaranty* v. *Campbell* [1984] C.L.Y. 1323 applied).

MOTT, *Re, ex p.* TRUSTEE OF THE PROPERTY OF THE BANKRUPT *v.* MOTT AND QUITTY, March 30, 1987, Hoffmann J. [ex rel. Anthony Radevsky, Barrister.]

213. Practice notes. See PRACTICE, §§2912–2914.

214. Subordinate legislation

INSOLVENCY (AMENDMENT OF SUBORDINATE LEGISLATION) ORDER 1987 (No. 1398) [45p], made under the Insolvency Act 1986 (c.45), ss.439 and 441(1); operative on September 1, 1987; clarifies the effect of S.I. 1986 No. 2001 in relation to bankruptcy proceedings where a petition was presented before the commencement date of the 1986 Act.

215. Voluntary arrangement—possession taken of entire stock—application for release of goods

[Insolvency Act 1986 (c.45), s.253.]

P was the owner and occupier of small shop premises from which he ran a man's outfitters. He applied for a voluntary arrangement. At the behest of two judgment creditors the sheriff took possession of his entire stock, effectively prohibiting him from continuing to trade. An immediate application was made for an interim order under s.253 and after the creditors had approved the arrangement, an application was made to the court for further directions to secure the release of the goods retained by the sheriff.

Held, that goods already seized are liable to be returned to the supervisor of the arrangement for disposal by him for the general benefit of the creditors. He will not suffer financial penalty for such application and the burden of the cost will fall upon the judgment creditor seeking to enforce his judgment.

PEAKE, *Re,* July 15, 1987; Mr. Registrar Ashworth, Blackburn County Ct. [*Ex rel. Haworth, Nuttall and Warburton, Solicitors.*]

BRITISH COMMONWEALTH

216. Alderney

ALDERNEY (TRANSFER OF PROPERTY ETC.) ORDER 1987 (No. 1273) [45p], made under the Alderney (Transfer of Property etc.) Act 1923 (c.15) s.1(1)(2); operative on August 21, 1987; provides for the transfer of certain property to the States of Guernsey as appointees of the States of Alderney and transfers other specified property to the States of Alderney.

217. Bermuda

BERMUDA (EVIDENCE) ORDER 1987 (No. 662) [45p], made under the Evidence (Proceedings in Other Jurisdictions) Act 1975 (c.34), s.10(3); operative on July 1, 1987; extends to Bermuda the provisions of the 1975 Act.

218. Cayman Islands

CAYMAN ISLANDS (CONSTITUTION) (AMENDMENT) ORDER 1987 (No. 2199) [85p], made under the West Indies Act 1962 (c.19), ss.5, 7; operative on January 30, 1988, save for Arts. 2–5 which come into force on a date to be appointed; amends the Constitution of the Cayman Islands.

219. Commonwealth development corporation

COMMONWEALTH DEVELOPMENT CORPORATION (ADDITIONAL ENTERPRISES) ORDER 1987 (No. 1253) [45p], made under the Commonwealth Development Corporation Act 1978 (c.2), s.3(3); operative on August 15; adds to the classes of enterprises to which the powers of the said Corporation relate.

220. St. Helena

ST. HELENA (CONSTITUTION) (AMENDMENT) ORDER 1987 (No. 1268) [45p], made under the Government of India Act 1833 (c.85), s.112 and the British Settlement Acts 1887 (c.54) and 1945 (c.7); operative on a day to be appointed; amends the Constitution of St. Helena contained in S.I. 1966 No. 1458 so as to change the title of the office of Treasurer of St. Helena to that of Financial Secretary.

221. Turks and Caicos Islands

EVIDENCE (PROCEEDINGS IN OTHER JURISDICTIONS) (TURKS AND CAICOS ISLANDS) ORDER 1987 (No. 1266) [£1·30], made under the Evidence (Proceedings in Other Jurisdictions) Act 1975 (c.34), s.10(3); operative on August 19, 1987; extends the provisions of the Evidence (Proceedings in Other Jurisdictions) Act 1975, which sets out a comprehensive code for the taking of evidence by courts on behalf of other courts, to the Turks and Caicos Islands, with exceptions, adaptations and modifications.

TURKS AND CAICOS ISLANDS (CONSTITUTION) (INTERIM AMENDMENT) ORDER 1987 (No. 934) [45p], made under the West Indies Act 1962 (c.19), s.5; operative on a date to be published; increases to six the number of persons who may be appointed by the governor as nominated members of the Executive Council for the Islands.

TURKS AND CAICOS ISLANDS (CONSTITUTION) (INTERIM AMENDMENT) (No. 2) ORDER 1987 (No. 1271) [£1·30], made under the West Indies Act 1962, s.5; operative on August 20, 1987; amends the Constitution of the Turks and Caicos Islands relating to disqualifications of candidates for elections, and provides for the establishment of a Public Service Commission and an Ombudsman for the Islands.

TURKS AND CAICOS ISLANDS (CONSTITUTION) (INTERIM AMENDMENT) (No. 3) ORDER 1987 (No. 1829) [85p], made under the West Indies Act 1962, s.5; operative on November 20, 1987; establishes new electoral districts for the purposes of elections to the legislative council of the Turks and Caicos Islands.

BUILDING AND CONSTRUCTION

222. Architect—duty of care—estimate for building project. See NYE SAUNDERS (A FIRM) *v.* BRISTOW, §2573.

223. Architects—negligence—limitation—requirement of occurrence of relevant and significant damage

P engaged D as architects in 1956 to design a 12-storey building. The outside of the building was clad with ceramic tiles as recommended by D. Practical completion occurred in 1962 and a final certificate was issued in 1968. In 1976 a survey of the building took place in which hollow tiles were recorded. In October 1977 tiles fell off the building and in consequence remedial works were adopted consisting of re-cladding the building with curtain walling. P commenced proceedings against D.

Held, that (1) damage had been caused by D's negligent failure to take reasonable steps to protect adequately against excessive water penetration and to supervise properly the workmanship of the tilers; (2) the action was not statute-barred since hollowness of the tiles did not constitute relevant and significant damage and D had not rebutted the inference that relevant and significant damage first occurred in October 1977 when the tiles first fell off; (3) D had not been negligent in recommending the use of ceramic tiles to clad the building and if they had been then P's loss was economic loss and irrecoverable in tort; (4) the fact that P would receive wholly new cladding in substitution for the tiles which were to be replaced as part of the remedial works should be ignored and no credit given for betterment since P had no alternative but to replace the external cladding of the building.

IMPERIAL COLLEGE OF SCIENCE AND TECHNOLOGY *v.* NORMAN AND DAWBARN (A FIRM) (1986) 2 Const.L.J. 280, H.H. Judge Smout Q.C., O.R.

224. Architects—qualifications—EEC recognition. See EUROPEAN COMMUNITIES, §1471.

225. Building contract—whether implied term to nominate new sub-contractor—default—cost of delay

[Aus.] A mechanical services sub-contractor failed financially. Upon the architect's instructions, the main contractor terminated the sub-contract and arranged for others to complete the work. When delay occurred, the architect gave contractual notice to the main contractor to complete the works. The employer arranged for the works to be carried out independently and sued the main contractor for the cost. The main contractor contended that only a nominated sub-contractor could carry out the work and that the employer was in breach of an implied term that, upon the failure of the first such sub-contractor, the architect was obliged to nominate another.

Held, that the contract imposed on the main contractor responsibility for the execution and completion of the whole of the work. The contract conditions and the circumstances of the case precluded the implication of the term for which the main contractor contended. The architect's notice was validly given and binding (*North West Metropolitan*

Regional Hospital Board v. *Bickerton (J. A.) and Son* [1970] C.L.Y. 241 and *Bilton (Percy)* v. *Greater London Council* [1982] C.L.Y. 236 distinguished).

CORPORATION OF THE CITY OF ADELAIDE *v.* JENNINGS INDUSTRIES [1984–85] 156 C.L.R. 274, High Ct. of Australia.

226. Building contractor—duty to supervise sub-contractor—liability in tort. See D. & F. ESTATES *v.* CHURCH COMMISSIONERS FOR ENGLAND, §3582.

227. Building regulations

BUILDING (INNER LONDON) REGULATIONS 1987 (No. 798) [£1·60], made under the Building Act 1984 (c.55), ss.1(1), 3, 8(2), 16(9)(10), 17(1)(6), 35, 47(1)–(5), 49(1)(5), 50(1)(3)(4)(6)(7), 51(1)(2), 52(1)–(3)(5), 53(2)(4), 54(1)–(3)(5), 56(1)(2), Sched. 1, paras. 1–3, 5, 7, 8, 10, 11, Sched. 3, paras. 2, 3 and Sched. 4, paras. 1, 2(1)(2)(4)(5), 3(1)(2), 4(2)(4), 5; operative on July 1, 1987; completes the application of the national system of building control to inner London.

228. Building regulations—burden of proof

[Building Act 1984 (c.55), s.36.]

A local authority who have served a notice for non-compliance with building regulations bear the burden of showing that the offending work does not comply with the approved document. Thereafter, the appellant against the notice bears the burden of showing that the regulations have been complied with.

RICKARDS *v.* KERRIER DISTRICT COUNCIL, *The Times,* April 7, 1987, Schiemann J.

229. Defective drains—architects' negligence—whether claim statute-barred

D, a firm of architects, designed and supervised the construction of a new church and hall for P, the church being constructed on top of the hall. Practical completion and handover of the building occurred in January 1970. P subsequently complained that, following heavy rain in August 1971, the drains had "surcharged," causing severe flooding to the building, and that there had been several subsequent instances of flooding. They also complained that there had been penetration from damp, owing to the lack of a damp-proof course between the staircases and the outside brickwork. Proceedings for negligence were brought by writ dated February 18, 1977, in which D admitted liability in repect of the damp-proofing and were held to have been negligent in respect of the drains, but argued that P's claims were statute-barred by the Limitation Act 1939. The judge held that they were not so barred, and gave judgment for P.

Held, dismissing D's appeal as to the drains, but allowing it as to the damp-proofing, that (1) the cause of action in tort arose when physical damage occurred to the building. (*Pirelli General Cable Works* v. *Faber (Oscar) and Partners* [1983] C.L.Y. 2216 applied); (2) by a majority, the damage had occurred within the meaning of *Pirelli's* case not when the building was handed over with defective drains in January 1970, but when the first flooding occurred in August 1971; the building could not be described as "doomed from the start"; and the claim in respect of the drains could not be described as one for economic loss dating from the date of handover (*Tozer Kemsley and Millbourn (Holdings)* v. *Jarvis (J.) & Sons* [1985] C.L.Y. 209 and *Ketteman* v. *Hansel Properties* [1984] C.L.Y. 2675 considered; *Forster* v. *Outred* [1982] C.L.Y. 1849, *Howell* v. *Young* (1826) 5 B. & C. 259 and *Junior Books* v. *Veitchi Co.* [1982] C.L.Y. 766 distinguished); (3) the burden of proof was on P to show that the damage caused by the failure to damp-proof had occurred within the period of six years previous to the issue of the writ, and this they had failed to do (*Cartledge* v. *Jopling (E.) & Sons* [1963] C.L.Y. 2023 applied).

LONDON CONGREGATIONAL UNION INC. *v.* HARRISS AND HARRISS (1986) 280 E.G. 1342, C.A.

230. Defective foundations—negligent inspection—whether duty of care owed to owner who had never been in occupation. See HAMBRO LIFE ASSURANCE *v.* WHITE YOUNG & PARTNERS, §2584.

231. Design defects—liability of building contractor

P invited tenders from contractors for the construction of flats. The tender documents were prepared by architects and engineers and these professionals also prepared detailed drawings based upon a structural system chosen by the successful tenderer. Defects appeared in the works and proceedings were commenced. During the course of the proceedings the issue arose as to what, if any, liability P had for the design of the works.

Held, that since D had not undertaken to carry out work that would perform a certain function and since P had not in fact relied upon D but had engaged architects and engineers, the usual rule applied that the contractor was not liable for defects in design

(*Brunswick Construction* v. *Nowlan* [1975] C.L.Y. 247 and *Thorn* v. *London Corporation* (1876) 1 App.Cas. 120 considered).

SUNNYSIDE NURSING HOME *v.* BUILDERS CONTRACT MANAGEMENT (1986) 2 Const. L.J. 240, Saskatchewan Ct. of Q.B..

232. Disabled people

BUILDING (DISABLED PEOPLE) REGULATIONS 1987 (No. 1445) [85p], made under the Building Act 1984 (c.55), ss.1(1), 3(1) and 8(2), and Sched. 1, paras. 1, 2, 7, 8 and 10; operative on December 14, 1987; deal with access and facilities to be provided for disabled people.

233. Duties of structural consultant engineers—whether extend to visual appearance

W determined to build a hospital. They engaged PTP as architects, WEP as structural engineers and C as main contractors. CED were the nominated flooring sub-contractors. AMP were consulting engineers who from time to time advised CED in connection with projects undertaken by them, and who advised them on this particular project. The design of the hospital floor provided for the use of pre-cast concrete slabs and these were installed in 1972 by CED. The floors when installed sagged; the deflection was such that C could not erect partitions upon the floor until further instructions were given. C incurred losses due to the associated delay and issued proceedings against W, and CED, W issued third party proceedings against CED, PTP and WEP; CED sought an indemnity from AMP. C's claim was settled by a joint payment by CED, PTP and WEP of £396,681. The third party proceedings were pursued and the trial judge held that CED had been negligent in their design and AMP in their advice to CED. Liability was apportioned as to PTP and WEP at one-third and as to CED two thirds and as between PTP and WEP one-half each. AMP appealed.

Held, (1) CED had been in breach of their collateral warranty to W and so had been correctly held liable to W; (2) AMP had undertaken to advise CED as their consultant structural engineers; their responsibilities for this purpose extended to questions of safety and fitness for purpose but not to appearance. The justified complaint in this case was merely a complaint about appearance and AMP were not therefore liable to CED; (3) PTP's failure to act properly in respect of the problem was irrelevant and so the proper apportionment would be two-thirds PTP and WEP and one-third CED.

HOLLAND HANNEN & CUBITTS (NORTHERN) *v.* WELSH HEALTH TECHNICAL SERVICES ORGANISATION (1987) 7 Con.L.R. 14, C.A.

234. JCT Minor Works contract—arbitration clause—whether arbitration clause effective after completion of contract. See CRESTAR *v.* CARR, §139.

235. JCT 1980 Form—cl. 28.1.3.4—whether determination unreasonable or vexatious

D engaged P to construct 50 flats and ancillary accommodation upon the terms of the JCT standard form of building contract 1980 Edition. Sub-contractors were nominated to carry out the piling work. In July 1983, the piling sub-contractors withdrew from the site. The architect thereupon instructed P to stop work. This instruction was conceded to be an instruction issued under cl. 23.2. In September 1983, P purported to give notice determining their engagement pursuant to cl. 28.1.3.4. and commmenced proceedings for the work done. Preliminary issues were tried, D contending that P's determination had been unlawful.

Held, that (1) the phrase "negligence or default of the contractor" in cl. 28.1.3.4. referred to the main contractor his servant or agents but not to his nominated sub-contractors; (2) the word "unreasonably" in cl. 28.1.3.4. was a general term and connoted something outside the band of possible reasonable decisions with which opposite conclusions were possible. "Vexatiously" in the same clause connoted an ulterior motive to oppress, harass or annoy.

JARVIS (JOHN) *v.* ROCKDALE HOUSING ASSOCIATION (1987) 3 Const.L.J. 24, C.A.

236. JCT standard form—dispute at date of contract—whether dispute fell within the scope of the arbitration clause. See ASHVILLE INVESTMENTS *v.* ELMER CONTRACTORS, §140.

237. JCT standard form—final certificate signed but not issued—effect

In 1969, P employed D to construct a housing development; the contract was substantially in the JCT standard form 1963 Edition (July 1968 Revision). The works included a 20-storey block clad in brickwork. Practical Completion took place in stages up to December 1973. In 1977, a Final Certificate was prepared and signed by P's in house architect but it was not issued to D. In 1983 P commenced proceedings against D claiming damages for breach of contract and negligence for defective workmanship in connection with the brickwork. D contended that they were protected from any liability by the Final Certificate and consequently a preliminary issue was tried.

Held, that since the Final Certificate had not been issued nor had it ever been intended that it should be issued the final certificate had no effect.

CAMDEN LONDON BOROUGH COUNCIL *v.* McINERNEY (THOMAS) AND SONS (1986) 2 Const.L.J. 293, H.H. Judge Esyr Lewis Q.C., O.R.

238. JCT standard form—retention monies—whether necessary to set aside separate trust fund. See BOOT (HENRY) BUILDING *v.* CROYDON HOTEL AND LEISURE CO., §438.

239. JCT standard form—set-off—whether notice necessary when set-off of disruption claim.

A were sub-contractors to R; the sub-contract was in the JCT 1980 NSC/4a form. A became entitled to approximately £7,000 in respect of measured work but R refused to pay them this sum contending that they were entitled to set-off against it a claim by them for disruption costs caused to them by A. A commenced proceedings for summary judgment. It was conceded by R that notice of intent to set-off had not been given pursuant to clause 23.2.3. of the sub-contract but argued that summary judgment should not be given because the issue whether such a notice was a precondition of the right to set-off was an arguable issue and/or that such a notice was not a precondition where the set-off was for the costs of disruption.

Held, that the point raised was one which turned upon the plain meaning of the words of the clause which did not restrict the character of the set-off in respect of which the notice had to be given. Therefore summary judgment would be ordered.

PILLAR P. G. *v.* HIGGINS (D. J.) CONSTRUCTION (1986) 2 Const. L.J. 223 C.A.

240. JCT standard form contract—interpretation—clause 24

Where clause 24 was part of the agreement, but the rate at which the liquidated damages (as provided for by clause 24) were to be calculated was agreed to be nil, there was no scope for any claim for damages for late completion of the works.

TEMLOC *v.* ERRILL PROPERTIES, *The Times,* August 22, 1987, C.A.

241. Liability of builder—liability of local authority—negligence—breach of statutory duty

P were the owners of two houses built in 1976 by D1, builders. D2, the local authority, passed plans and made inspections during the course of the works. The deposited plans had shown concrete strip foundations below the load-bearing walls and had been approved subject to a note prohibiting variations. Despite this a building inspector agreed with D1 that foundations of a thickened oversite reinforced with mesh could be substituted. In 1978 and 1979 cracks and other defects appeared due to the inadequacy of the foundations provided. P commenced proceedings for the cost of the remedial works.

Held, (1) D1 were liable in negligence to P1 and P2 and in contract to P2 who had bought their house from D1 whilst the works were in progress; (2) D2 were not negligent in passing the plans but by their building inspector had failed to exercise skill and care when permitting a departure from the plans. In consequence there had been a breach of Regulation D3 of the Building Regulations 1972 which had resulted in a danger to the health and safety of the P's (*Anns* v. *Merton* [1977] C.L.Y. 2030, *Investors in Industrial Commercial Properties* v. *South Bedfordshire District Council* [1986] C.L.Y. 2259 applied).

FRY *v.* JACKSON (ROBERT A.) (BUILDER AND CONTRACTOR) (1987) 7 Con.L.R. 97, Q.B.D., H.H. Judge Newey Q.C., O.R.

242. Local authority—negligence—whether present or imminent danger to the health or safety of the occupiers

P purchased a house in 1975 which had been built in 1964. In 1978 they noticed a gap between floor and skirting boards and after a survey they had extensive remedial works executed to rectify the discrepancy in the levels across the ground floor slab. Proceedings were started against D, the local authority, claiming damages for negligence and breach of statutory duty; D brought in the builders as third parties but P did not sue them directly.

Held, that substantial settlement of the ground floor slab had occurred but there was no evidence that the damage was such as to have given rise to any present or imminent danger to the health or safety of persons present on the premises, or such as was likely to arise soon but for the execution of remedial works. Therefore the claim was dismissed

(*Anns* v. *Merton London Borough Council* [1977] C.L.Y. 2030 and *Jones* v. *Stroud District Council* [1986] C.L.Y. 1993 applied).

KIMBELL *v.* HART DISTRICT COUNCIL (1986) 2 Const.L.J. 288, H.H. Judge Smout Q.C., O.R.

243. NFBTE/FASS nominated sub-contract—status and effect of name-borrowing in arbitration. See STEWART (LORNE) *v.* SINDALL (WILLIAM) AND N.W. THAMES REGIONAL HEALTH AUTHORITY, §144.

244. NFBTE/FASS non-nominated sub-contract—clause 15(2)—set off

[Arbitration Act 1950 (c.27), s.4; R.S.C., Ord. 14.]

D were main contractors who engaged P as their sub-contractors upon the terms of the NFBTE/FASS non-nominated form of sub-contract. D contended that P had delayed the completion of the main contract works and in March 1985, one year before the then current date for completion of the main contract works, set off and deducted from sums otherwise due to P an assessment of the costs which D contended they would incur. D purported to do this pursuant to clause 15(2) of the sub-contract. P issued proceedings under Ord. 14. D applied to stay the proceedings pursuant to s.4 of the Arbitration Act 1950. The official referee gave judgment to P. D appealed.

Held, dismissing the appeal, that (1) since D's costs had not actually been incurred at the date of the notice of set off, clause 15(2) did not apply; (2) where, on the hearing of an application under Ord. 14, the court concludes that the defence is bad in law then, notwithstanding the arbitration clause, judgment will be given for the plaintiffs.

CHATBROWN *v.* ALFRED McALPINE CONSTRUCTION (SOUTHERN) (1987) 35 Build.L.R. 44, C.A.

245. Price adjustment clause—due diligence—implied term

P engaged D to manufacture, deliver to site and erect gates and gate arms for the Thames Barrier. Clause 51 of the contract was substantially the same as the then BEAMA contract price adjustment clause used in conjunction with the I Mech.E/IEE Conditions of Contract. By clause 51, D might be entitled to an increase in their contract price provided that such increase was not caused by their default. The contract provided that D should perform their contract by certain key dates and D in fact met these dates. P however contended that there was an implied term of the contract that D should carry out their work with due diligence and expedition and alternatively that clause 19 (which provided P with a right to determine the contract if D failed to perform with due diligence) of the contract expressly required them to do this and that breach of these terms deprived D of the benefits otherwise available to them under the terms of the contract price adjustment clause. Still further P contended that lack of due diligence was a default within the meaning of the proviso. These disputes were referred to arbitration and the arbitrator having found against P, D appealed.

Held, that (1) although neglect by D to execute the works with due diligence and expedition would entitle P to determine the contract pursuant to clause 19, failure by D to exercise due diligence would not constitute a breach of clause 19; D's express obligations were to complete by the due dates; (2) the implied term contended for was not necessary to give business efficacy to the contract and because the effect of a failure to use due diligence could have radically different financial consequences dependent upon the movement of the indices upon which the contract price adjustment clause was based, no certain purpose could be attributed to such an implied term; (3) any lack of due diligence by D could not deprive them of the benefit of the contract price adjustment clause by operation of the proviso to clause 51 if they met the key dates.

GREATER LONDON COUNCIL *v.* CLEVELAND BRIDGE AND ENGINEERING CO. (1986) 34 Build.L.R. 50, C.A.

BUILDING SOCIETIES

246. Aggregation rules

BUILDING SOCIETIES (AGGREGATION) RULES 1987 (No. 2133) [85p], made under The Building Societies Act 1986 (c.53), ss.7(10), 8(3) and 20(9);operative on December 31, 1987; provide for aggregation of assets and liabilities of associated bodies of a building society with those of the society for a specified purpose.

247. Annual accounts

BUILDING SOCIETIES (ACCOUNTS AND RELATED PROVISIONS) REGULATIONS 1987 (No. 2072) [£5·00], made under the Building Societies Act 1986 (c.53), ss.73, 74(3)(6),

75(1), 76(3); operative on December 31, 1987; prescribe the format of building society annual accounts.

248. Appeals

BUILDING SOCIETIES APPEAL TRIBUNAL REGULATIONS 1987 (No. 891) [£1·60], made under the Building Societies Act 1986 (c.53), s.48(3); operative on June 8, 1987; makes provision with respect to appeals under s.46 of the 1986 Act.

249. Banking institutions

BUILDING SOCIETIES (BANKING INSTITUTIONS) ORDER 1987 (No. 1670) [45p], made under the Building Societies Act 1986 (c.53), ss.7(9), 15(2), 34(2); operative on October 1, 1987; amends provisions of the 1986 Act and S.I. 1986 No. 1877 by replacing references to recognised banks and licensed institutions with references to authorised institutions under the Banking Act 1987.

250. Building Societies Act 1986—accounts and related transitional provisions

BUILDING SOCIETIES ACT 1986 (ACCOUNTS AND RELATED TRANSITIONAL PROVISIONS) ORDER 1987 (No. 395) [£2·70], made under the Building Societies Act 1986 (c.53), s.121; operative on April 1, 1987; provides for changes in accounts, directors' reports and annual returns of building societies.

251. Building Societies Act 1986—meetings

BUILDING SOCIETIES ACT 1986 (MEETINGS) (TRANSITIONAL PROVISIONS) ORDER 1987 (No. 426) [45p], made under the Building Societies Act 1986 (c.53), s.121; operative on March 18, 1987; makes provision in relation to transitional meetings of a building society.

252. Business premises

BUILDING SOCIETIES (BUSINESS PREMISES) ORDER 1987 (No. 1942) [85p], made under the Building Societies Act 1986 (c.53), s.17(7); operative on December 31, 1987; provides that where less than 30 per cent. of the area of premises occupied by a building society is used for the business of the society then those premises are treated as held under s.17 of the 1986 Act and are thus class three assets.

253. Charges and fees

BUILDING SOCIETIES (GENERAL CHARGES AND FEES) REGULATIONS 1987 (No. 391) [£1·40], made under the Building Societies Act 1986 (c.53), ss.2(2) and 116(2); operative on April 1, 1987; provide for a general charge to be paid by authorised building societies towards the expenses of the Building Societies Commission.

254. Credit facilities

BUILDING SOCIETIES (LIMITED CREDIT FACILITIES) ORDER 1987 (No. 1975) [85p], made under the Building Societies Act 1986 (c.53), s.19; operative on November 19, 1987; provides that certain building societies can operate accounts with overdraft facilities and may make advances of up to £10,000 for the purchase of mobile homes.

255. Designation—pension companies

BUILDING SOCIETIES (DESIGNATION OF PENSION COMPANIES) ORDER 1987 (No. 1871) [45p], made under the Building Societies Act 1986 (c.53), s.18(2)(*c*); operative on November 20, 1987; designates companies acting as trustees in respect of pension schemes as bodies corporate which building societies may invest in and for which they may provide supporting services.

256. Disclosure—prescribed bands

BUILDING SOCIETIES (PRESCRIBED BANDS FOR DISCLOSURE) ORDER 1987 (No. 723) [45p], made under the Building Societies Act 1986 (c.53), Sched. 10, para. 9; operative on June 2, 1987; prescribes bands for the disclosure by a building society of the number of cases in which a business associate has acted for the society and the aggregate amount of money paid in such cases.

257. Income tax—dividends and other payments—scope of enabling legislation. See R. *v.* I.R.C., *ex p.* WOOLWICH EQUITABLE BUILDING SOCIETY, §2006.

258. Investor protection scheme

BUILDING SOCIETIES INVESTOR PROTECTION SCHEME (MAXIMUM PROTECTED INVESTMENT) ORDER 1987 (No. 1349) [45p], made under the Building Societies Act 1986 (c.53), s.27(6); operative on October 1, 1987; amends s.27(5)(*b*) of the 1986 Act so as to substitute for the sum of £10,000 the sum of £20,000.

259. Isle of Man

BUILDING SOCIETIES (ISLE OF MAN) ORDER 1987 (No. 1498) [85p], made under the Building Societies Act 1986 (c.53), s.14; operative on November 15, 1987; empowers societies with assets of at least £100 million to make advances on the security of land in the Isle of Man.

260. Jersey

BUILDING SOCIETIES (JERSEY) ORDER 1987 (No. 1872) [85p], made under the Building Societies 1987; empowers certain building societies to make advances on the security of land in Jersey.

261. Liquid assets

BUILDING SOCIETIES (LIQUID ASSET) REGULATIONS 1987 (No. 1499) [£1·60], made under the Building Societies Act 1986 (c.53), s.21(7); operative on October 1, 1987; set out the liquid assets which a building society may hold under s.21 for the purposes of meeting its liabilities as they arise.

262. Mergers

BUILDING SOCIETIES (MERGERS) REGULATIONS 1987 (No. 2005) [45p], made under the Building Societies Act 1986 (c.53), s.96(5); operative on December 31, 1987; replace S.I. 1986 No. 2152 and prescribe a limit in relation to any bonus distribution by a building society in consideration of a merger.

263. Non-retail funds and deposits

BUILDING SOCIETIES (LIMIT ON NON-RETAIL FUNDS AND DEPOSITS) ORDER 1987 (No. 2131) [45p], made under the Building Societies Act 1986 (c.53), s.7(15); operative on January 1, 1988; prescribes 40 per cent. as the maximum percentage of a building society's share and deposit liabilities which may be represented by non-retail funds and deposits.

BUILDING SOCIETIES (NON-RETAIL FUNDS AND DEPOSITS) ORDER 1987 (No. 378) [£1·40], made under the Building Societies Act 1986 (c.53), s.7(9); operative on April 1, 1987; amends s.7 of the 1986 Act which empowers a building society to raise funds and borrow money and places a limit on non-retail funds and borrowing. It changes the coverage of that limited category.

264. Prescribed contracts

BUILDING SOCIETIES (PRESCRIBED CONTRACTS) (AMENDMENT) ORDER 1987 (No. 1500) [45p], made under the Building Societies Act 1986 (c.53), s.23(2); operative on October 1, 1987; amends S.I. 1986 No. 2098.

265. Provision of services

BUILDING SOCIETIES (PROVISION OF SERVICES) ORDER 1987 (No. 172) [80p], made under the Building Societies Act 1986 (c.53), s.34(2); operative on March 5, 1987; varies Sched. 8 of the 1986 Act.

BUILDING SOCIETIES (PROVISION OF SERVICES) (No. 2) ORDER 1987 (No. 1848) [45p], made under the Building Societies Act 1986 s.34(2), (8); operative on November 15, 1987; varies Sched. 8 of the 1986 Act in relation to the power of building societies to manage the mortgage investments of others and arrange for the provision of credit by others.

BUILDING SOCIETIES (PROVISION OF SERVICES) (No. 3) ORDER 1987 (No. 1976) [45p], made under the Building Societies Act 1986, s.34(2)(8); operative on November 19, 1987; varies Sched. 8 of the 1986 Act so as to include the provision of investment advice to individuals and arranging for customers to acquire units in a unit trust.

BUILDING SOCIETIES (PROVISION OF SERVICES) (No. 4) ORDER 1987 (No. 2019) [45p], made under the Building Societies Act 1986, s.34(2)(8); operative on December 18, 1987; varies Sched. 8 of the 1986 Act in relation to pensions schemes.

266. Qualifying bodies

BUILDING SOCIETIES (DESIGNATION OF QUALIFYING BODIES) (AMENDMENT) ORDER 1987 (No. 2018) [85p], made under the Building Societies Act 1986 (c.53), s.18(2)(*c*); operative on December 18, 1987; amends S.I. 1986 No. 1715.

267. Residential use

BUILDING SOCIETIES (RESIDENTIAL USE) ORDER 1987 (No. 1671) [85p], made under the Building Societies Act 1986 (c.53), s.12(1)(2); operative on April 1, 1988; specifies circumstances in which land is for a person's residential use for the purposes of s.11(2) of the 1986 Act.

BURIAL AND CREMATION

268. Protection of Military Remains Act 1986—Guernsey. See ARMED FORCES, §164.

CAPITAL GAINS TAX

269. Annual exempt amount

CAPITAL GAINS TAX (ANNUAL EXEMPT AMOUNT) ORDER 1987 (No. 436) [45p], made under the Capital Gains Tax Act 1979 (c.14), s.5(1C); specifies £6,600 as the amount which, under s.5 of the 1979 Act, is the exempt amount for 1987–88 unless Parliament otherwise determines.

270. Assessment—error as to year—validity

[Taxes Management Act 1970 (c.9), s.114.]

The taxpayers, as trustees, were assessed to capital gains tax. By a typing error, the assessment was stated to be for 1974/75, whereas it should have been for 1975/76. The taxpayers failed to notice the error, and by the time the Inspector became aware of it the time limit for raising an assessment for 1975/76 had expired. Without notifying the taxpayers, the Inspector then "vacated" the assessment in the assessment book.

Held, allowing the taxpayers' appeal, that (1) the assessment for 1974/75 could not be vacated by unilateral act of the Inspector, and (2) T.M.A. 1970, s.114(1), was not in terms wide enough to justify treating an assessment for one fiscal year as an assessment for another.

BAYLIS (INSPECTOR OF TAXES) *v.* GREGORY, *The Times,* April 2, 1987, C.A.

271. Business assets—replacement—relief—partnership

[Capital Gains Tax Act 1979 (c.14), s.115.]

In April 1982 the taxpayer disposed of a business asset realising a chargeable gain of £155,688. In June he and his wife entered into a partnership deed to carry on business as hoteliers from a property which they were in the process of purchasing. The deed provided that the property would be purchased in joint names and would belong as to 75 per cent. to the taxpayer and 25 per cent. to his wife. The deed also provided that the property was to be used as to 75 per cent. for business purposes and as to 25 per cent. for personal purposes. The property was purchased at a cost of £209,093. The taxpayer claimed to roll-over his chargeable gain under s.115, Capital Gains Tax Act 1979, against his 75 per cent. share of the cost of £209,093 (i.e., £156,820).

Held, allowing the Crown's appeal, that relief under s.115 was to be determined by reference to the taxpayer's 75 per cent. undivided share of 75 per cent. of the property to be used for business purposes.

TODD (INSPECTOR OF TAXES) *v.* MUDD [1987] S.T.C. 141, Vinelott J.

272. Disposal of shares—attribution of consideration—Commissioners' determination

T carried on business in partnership with two others. In 1974 the partnership business was transferred to a company in exchange for the issue of shares. In 1976 T sold his shares to one of his former partners; he received a payment of £30,000, and was assessed to capital gains tax accordingly. T appealed against the assessments, contending that the sum of £30,000 included unpaid remuneration for work done for the company by him and his wife and repayments of a loan which he had made to the company. The General Commissioners determined that the sum of £30,000 included remuneration of £5,750 due to T, of £6,000 due to his wife, and repayment of a loan of £7,000. They reduced the assessement accordingly. T was dissatisfied with the quantum of the determination and appealed.

Held, dismissing the appeal, that T was not able to show that in arriving at their determination the Commissioners had erred in law, or that their determination was contrary to the only true and reasonable conclusion open to them on the facts.

NEELY *v.* ROURKE (INSPECTOR OF TAXES) [1987] S.T.C. 30, Vinelott J.

273. Disposal of shares—loss—"reorganisation"

[Finance Act 1965 (c.25), Sched. 7, para. 4.]

In 1977 the taxpayer company acquired for £16,!00 all of the 1000 £1 issued shares in J Ltd. The affairs of J Ltd. led to that company becoming indebted to the taxpayer company in the sum of £200,911. In June 1979, J Ltd. increased its share capital by the creation of 200,000 new ordinary shares of £1 each which it issued to the taxpayer company at par. Out of the moneys received, J Ltd. then repaid its indebtedness to the taxpayer company. The taxpayer company then sold all of its shares in J Ltd. for £38,000, and claimed that on that disposal it sustained an allowable loss for corporation tax purposes. The essential question was whether the base cost to the taxpayer company of the new 200,000 ordinary shares was their market value when issued or, by reason of the "reorganisation" provisions of F.A. 1965, Sched. 7, para. 4, the sum of £200,000 actually subscribed.

Held, dismissing the taxpayer company's appeal, that the expression "reorganisation" in F.A. 1965, Sched. 7, para. 4, was not apt to cover the transaction whereby the taxpayer company had acquired the 200,000 new ordinary shares in J Ltd.

DUNSTAN (INSPECTOR OF TAXES) *v.* YOUNG, AUSTEN & YOUNG, *The Times,* October 21, 1987, Warner J.

274. Extra-statutory concession—whether attempt to use it amounted to tax avoidance—whether concession *ultra vires*

In 1977 F's wife inherited a farm. In 1980, she decided to sell it, and at about the same time F entered an agreement whereby he would live and work in Germany. In order to take advantage of extra-statutory concession D2, which granted substantial relief from capital gains tax on disposal made after a taxpayer ceased to be ordinarily resident in the U.K., F's wife then transferred the farm to him by deed of gift. F then left for Germany, the house was sold at auction and the proceeds invested outside the U.K. The inspector assessed F to tax on the full amount, relying on the rubric to the concession which it would not be applied where an attempt was made to use it for tax avoidance purposes.

Held, dismissing F's application for judicial review that (1) the concession and the restriction upon it were *intra vires,* being neither secret nor discriminatory and coming within the concept of good management and administrative common sense; (2) the transaction had not involved F suffering a reduction in income nor an increase in expenditure such as to justify a reduction in tax and was thus an arrangement for tax avoidance; (3) although there was no appeal against the revenue's decision to withhold the concession, F had had the opportunity to make submissions and thus the assessment could not be criticised (*Vestey* v. *I.R.C. (Nos. 1 & 2)* [1980] C.L.Y. 1489 distinguished; *R.* v. *I.R.C., ex p. National Federation of Self-Employed and Small Businesses* [1981] C.L.Y. 1433, *I.R.C.* v. *Duke of Westminster* [1936] A.C. 1. *Ramsay (W.T.)* v. *I.R.C.* [1981] C.L.Y. 1385 and *I.R.C.* v. *Challenge Corp.* [1987] C.L.Y. 2036 considered).

R. *v.* I.R.C., *ex p.* FULFORD-DOBSON [1987] 3 W.L.R. 277, McNeill J.

275. Gilt-edged securities

CAPITAL GAINS TAX (GILT-EDGED SECURITIES) ORDER 1987 (No. 259) [£1·40], made under the Capital Gains Tax Act 1979 (c.14), Sched. 2, para. 1; specifies gilt-edged securities which are exempt from C.G.T. if held for more than 12 months.

276. Machinery and plant—whether wasting assets—capital allowances

[Finance Act 1968 (c.44), Sched. 12, para.1.]

In 1973 the Taxpayer Company acquired a printing press at a cost of approximately £1m. In the four succeeding years it obtained capital allowances in respect of that cost. In 1978 it sold the press at a price showing a realised gain of approximately £650,000. As the press had never in fact been used for the purposes of the Taxpayer Company's trade, the capital allowances which it had obtained were withdrawn under F.A. 1971, s.41(2). In these circumstances, the Taxpayer Company contended that the gain on the disposal of the press was not a chargeable gain, para.1(2) of Sched. 12 to the F.A. 1968 not applying to exclude para. 1(1) of that Schedule (tangible movable property being a wasting asset).

Held, dismissing the Crown's appeal, that in circumstances where entitlement to capital allowances had been withdrawn, it was correct to regard para. 1(2) of Sched. 12 as not applying.

BURMAN (INSPECTOR OF TAXES) *v.* WESTMINSTER PRESS [1987] S.T.C. 669, Knox J.

277. Non-competition covenant—asset—disposal

[Finance Act 1965 (c.25), s.22(3).]

In 1977, Thorn and MI, a wholly owned subsidiary, entered into an agreement whereunder MI sold shares in three companies to GE and, in consideration of £575,000, Thorn entered into a covenant with GE that for a period of five years neither it nor any of its subsidiaries would engage in any of the businesses carried on by the three companies. Thorn claimed that the sum of £575,000 did not accrue to it from the disposal of any asset and so did not represent a taxable, chargeable gain.

Held, allowing the Crown's appeal, that the gain was derived from Thorn's reputation (goodwill) and arose on a disposal within F.A. 1965, s.22(3). The case should be remitted to the Commissioners so that evidence could be adduced as to computation, and evidence and arguments as to the existence of such goodwill.

KIRBY (INSPECTOR OF TAXES) *v.* THORN E.M.I. [1987] S.T.C. 621, C.A.

278. Option—abandonment—disposal—capital sum

[Finance Act 1965 (c.25), s.22(3), and Sched. 7, para. 14(3).]

T Co. owned an option to participate in a property development. Subsequently, by way of settlement of litigation, it consented to an order whereunder in consideration of £2m. it released and abandoned its option. T Co. claimed that, as under F.A. 1965, Sched. 7, para. 14(3), the abandonment of an option was not the disposal of an asset, it was not liable for corporation tax in respect of the receipt of £2m.

Held, dismissing T Co.'s appeal, that Sched. 7, para. 14(3) did not exclude a disposal, and a consequent charge, under F.A. 1965, s.22(3), where a capital sum was received (*Golding* v. *Kaufman* [1985] C.L.Y. 241, followed).

WELBECK SECURITIES *v.* POWLSON (INSPECTOR OF TAXES) [1987] S.T.C. 468, C.A.

279. Private residence—separate buildings—exemption

[Capital Gains Tax Act 1979 (c.14), ss.101, 102.]

A separate dwelling may only form part of a private residence for the purposes of exemption from tax if it is very closely adjacent.

T, the taxpayer, sold in a single transaction, her country house, and the staff bungalow which she had built 130 metres away. The bungalow and its own garden were separated by trees. The tax inspector refused her claim for exemption on the ground that the bungalow was too far away to form part of a single dwelling-house. The commissioners upheld the appeal by T.

Held, allowing the appeal by the Crown, that although a separate dwelling could form part of a private residence for the purposes of exemption from tax if it was very closely adjacent, so that the group of buildings as a whole could be regarded as a single dwelling-house, in the present case it was impossible to come to such a conclusion (*Batey* v. *Wakefield* [1982] C.L.Y. 1588 distinguished).

MARKEY (INSPECTOR OF TAXES) *v.* SANDERS [1987] 1 W.L.R. 864, Walton J.

280. Private residence—separate buildings—exemption

[Capital Gains Tax Act 1979 (c.14), ss.101, 102.]

The taxpayer owned and occupied as his principal residence a country house situated in some four acres of land. In the grounds, about 200 metres from the house, was a single storey lodge that was at all material times occupied by the taxpayer's domestic help. In 1975, the taxpayer sold the house and most of the land, but retained the lodge and less than one acre of garden. In 1979, he sold the lodge and the remaining land for £33,860. He claimed that for the period from 1956 to 1975, the lodge formed part of his private residence, and that on the sale of the lodge in 1979 he was entitled to exemption from capital gains tax accordingly.

Held, dismissing the Crown's appeal, that the Commissioners' determination that the lodge had formed part of the residence ought not to be disturbed.

WILLIAMS (INSPECTOR OF TAXES) *v.* MERRYLEES, *The Times,* June 30, 1987, Vinelott J.

281. Share exchange within group of companies—disposal

[Finance Act 1965 (c.25), Sched. 7, paras. 4 and 6, and Sched. 13, para. 2.]

In 1965, W Ltd. acquired shares in three companies at a cost of £1.2m. In 1966, when the shares in the three companies were taken to be worth £600,000 (approximately), W Ltd. transferred the shares to a subsidiary T Ltd., in exchange for shares issued to it by T Ltd. The "share exchange" provisions of paras. 4 and 6 of Sched. 7 to the F.A. 1965 applied to that transaction to treat W Ltd. as not disposing of the shares in the three companies. Subsequently, T Ltd. transferred the shares in the three companies intra-group to the taxpayer company, para. 2 of Sched. 13 to the F.A. 1965 applying to that transaction to transmit to the taxpayer company the base cost of those shares to T Ltd. The three companies were wound up, the taxpayer company receiving in the course of the liquidation approximately £600,000. The issue was what was the base cost of the shares to the taxpayer company. The answer to that question depended upon whether para. 2 of Sched. 13 to the F.A. 1965 applied to the transaction in 1966 whereby, by way of share exchange, T Ltd. had acquired the shares in the three companies from W Ltd.

Held, dismissing the Crown's appeal, that paras. 4 and 6 of Sched. 7 to the F.A. 1965 did not prevent there being a disposal of the shares in the three companies by W Ltd. to

T Ltd. for the purposes of para 2 of Sched. 13 to the F.A. 1965. Accordingly, the base cost of the shares to T Ltd. (and, subsequently, to the taxpayer company) must be taken as their actual cost to W Ltd. (£1.2m), with the consequence that on the subsequent liquidations allowable losses were to be taken as having accrued to the taxpayer company.

WESTCOTT (INSPECTOR OF TAXES) *v.* WOOLCOMBERS [1987] S.T.C. 600, C.A.

282. Tax avoidance scheme—composite transaction

[Finance Act 1965 (c.25), s.19.]

Consecutive transfers of the same assets are not taxable as one composite transaction for the purposes of capital gains tax if, when the first took place, the transferor intended to avoid tax but has not yet planned the second or did not have the firm intention or practical ability to complete it.

In the case of three appeals before the Court of Appeal, in each case the taxpayer had disposed of assets to a company, followed by a disposition by the company to an ultimate purchaser. The first disposition had no commercial purpose save tax avoidance. In none of the cases was there a contractual obligation to effect the second disposition when the first was made. The Crown asserted that for fiscal reasons, applying *Ramsay (W.T.)* v. *I.R.C.* the two transactions should be treated as a single composite transaction under which there was a "disposal" by the taxpayer in favour of the ultimate purchaser, pursuant to s.19 of the Finance Act 1965. They relied on the decisions of the Lords in *Furniss* v. *Dawson* on composite transactions giving rise to a disposal for capital gains tax purposes.

Held, dismissing the appeals, that two transactions, each with legal effect, could not be described as a single composite transaction, unless all essential features of the second had already been determined by a person who had the firm intention and practical ability to procure its implementation. A transfer by A to B, followed by a sale by B to C, could not be described as one single transaction of a preordained series unless at the time of the first transfer C had been identified as a prospective purchaser and all the main terms of the sale to him had been agreed in principle. If that were not so, they were independent transactions. If they were not independent it would be difficult in practice to determine the date of disposal and the base value of the assets and the date of their ascertainment. In Craven, the taxpayer did not have the practical ability to ensure the second transaction; in Bowater the judge had correctly decided that the second transaction was independent; in Baylis the initial transfer was made solely by way of strategic tax planning and at that time no sale was contemplated (*Ramsay (W.T.)* v. *I.R.C.* [1981] C.L.Y. 1385, *Furniss* v. *Dawson* [1984] C.L.Y. 270 distinguished).

CRAVEN *v.* WHITE; I.R.C *v.* BOWATER PROPERTY DEVELOPMENTS; BAYLIS *v.* GREGORY; BAYLIS *v.* GREGORY AND WEARE [1987] 1 FTLR 551, C.A.

CAPITAL TRANSFER TAX

283. Interest on unpaid tax. See INHERITANCE TAX, §2049.

284. Settlement—appointment of life interest—associated operations

[Finance Act 1975 (c.7), s.20(4), and Sched. 5, para. 6(3).]

The trust fund of a discretionary settlement comprised a number of valuable paintings. In 1977 the trustees entered into an agreement with a connected person whereunder for a period of fourteen years he was to have custody of the paintings in consideration of payment of an annual sum of £40 and undertaking certain obligations in relation to insurance and loss. After entering into the agreement, the trustees appointed a life interest in the paintings to a beneficiary. The Inland Revenue claimed that the agreement depreciated the value of the paintings and that a capital distribution charge arose under F.A. 1975, Sched. 5, para. 6(3). The trustees claimed that para. 6(3) was excluded by F.A. 1975, s.20(4). The Inland Revenue contended that the agreement and the appointment were "associated operations," and that the gratuitous element in the resulting "disposition" prevented s.20(4) from applying.

Held (Sir Roger Ormrod dissenting), allowing the Crown's appeal, that it was correct to regard the agreement and the subsequent appointment as "associated operations," with the consequence that the trustees were not able to rely upon s.20(4) to exclude the operation of para. 6(3).

MacPHERSON *v.* I.R.C. [1987] S.T.C. 73, C.A.

285. Settlement—power to appropriate revenue to meet depreciation of capital value—beneficiary entitled to whole free annual income—whether power administrative or dispositive—whether interest in possession

[Finance Act 1975 (c.7), ss.22, 23.]

Under the terms of a trust deed Mrs. R. was entitled to receive for the whole of her life the whole free annual income or produce of the trust fund, but the trust deed granted power for the trustees, before stocking the free income or produce for any year, to appropriate such portion of the revenue as they might think proper for meeting depreciation of the capital value of any of the assets of the trust. The trustees contended that since under the power given to them in the trust deed they were capable of applying the whole of the net income for purposes other than making payments to Mrs. R, her enjoyment of the trust funds was at their discretion so that she did not have an interest in possession in the trust funds for capital transfer tax purposes.

Held, dismissing the trustees' appeal, that the trustees' powers were not dispositive, but only administrative, and since they were exercisable prior to the ascertainment of the free annual income, Mrs. R was entitled to receive the whole free annual income and, accordingly, had an interest in possession in the whole of the trust funds for capital transfer tax purposes.

MILLER *v.* I.R.C. [1987] S.T.C. 108, Ct. of Session.

CARRIERS

286. Carriage by air—jurisdiction—deceased on internal Bangladesh flight—aircraft crashed—whether plaintiff could invoke jurisdiction of English court in relation to non-international carriage

P was killed on D's aircraft in Pakistan. P's estate brought an action against D, claiming that they were entitled to D's limit under the Carriage by Air Acts (Application of Provisions) Order 1967. D contended that they were entitled to limit their liability to £913 either by contract or under the Bangladesh Carriage by Air Act 1934. D contended that the 1967 Order did not apply to "non-international" carriage, P had been killed on an internal domestic flight.

Held, that (1) P's right to claim depended upon whether they could properly issue proceedings and serve them out of the jurisdiction on D; (2) P was entitled to sue D in England, and consequently entitled to the English limits of liability.

HOLMES *v.* BANGLADESH BIMAN CORP. [1987] 2 Lloyd's Rep. 192, Leggatt J.

287. Carriage by road. See ROAD TRAFFIC, §3255.

288. Carriage by road—C.M.R. Convention—limitation period. See I.C.I. FIBRES *v.* M.A.T. TRANSPORT, §2325.

289. Carriage by sea. See SHIPPING AND MARINE INSURANCE, §§3377–3380.

290. Subcontract for carriage—subcontracting carrier did not have actual or legal possession—whether carrier could sue third party for loss of goods

A carrier who sub-contracts the carriage of goods and never has actual or legal possession of them, cannot sue a third party in negligence for the loss of the goods, unless he can establish possessory title (*Leigh & Sillvan* v. *Aliakmon Shipping Co.* [1986] C.L.Y. 2252 applied).

TRANSCONTAINER EXPRESS *v.* CUSTODIAN SECURITY, *The Independent,* October 20, 1987, C.A.

291. Time bar—through-carriers claiming indemnity from on-carriers—dismissal for want of prosecution—whether proper exercise of discretion

[Carriage of Goods by Sea (Hong Kong) Order (S.I. 1980 No. 1508), art. 2, Sched.; Carriage of Goods by Sea Act 1971 (c.19), Sched., art. III, paras. 6, 6 *bis*; Limitation Ordinance (Laws of Hong Kong, 1976 rev., c.347), s.4(1)(*a*).]

In order for a claim to an indemnity to fall within para. 6 *bis* of Art. III of the Hague-Visby Rules, there is no requirement that the initial liability of the party claiming the indemnity should have been under a contract to which those Rules applied; in any event the period of three months mentioned in that paragraph was the minimum time limit, not the maximum, so that where a fresh action could be started it would be wrong to strike out the original claim.

A cargo of clothing was originally shipped under a contract to which the Hague-Visby Rules did not apply. After transhipment (to which contract the Rules did apply) and eventual delivery, some of the goods were found to be damaged. The shippers claimed damages against both sets of owners; the first owners also issued proceedings against the second, claiming an indemnity. they did not, however, serve a statement of claim, and their action was struck out.

Held, allowing the appeal, that no action would be struck out where it was still open to the plaintiffs to issue fresh proceedings. In the present case the indemnity claim was subject to a six-year limitation period, that being the appropriate time limit under the Limitation Ordinance. In order for para. 6 *bis* to apply, it was not necessary that the original contract should have been subject to the Hague-Visby Rules.

CHINA OCEAN SHIPPING CO. (OWNERS OF XINGCHENG) *v.* ANDROS (OWNERS OF THE ANDROS) [1987] 1 W.L.R. 1213, P.C.

CHARITIES

292. Annual Report

The Charity Commissioners have published their Annual Report for 1986. Copies of the Report are available from H.M.S.O. [£5.]

293. Enforcement of charitable trust—executors of estate of deceased founder of trust—covenant by executors not to challenge performance of trust—whether executors able to institute proceedings

[Charities Act 1960 (c.58), s.28(1).]

The executors of the estate of the deceased founder of a charitable trust were not persons within the definition of "any person interested in the charity" for the purposes of s.28 Charities Act 1960 and thus not entitled to institute proceedings seeking to enforce the trust.

In 1976 the deceased conveyed certain farmland to the University College of Wales, Aberystwyth on charitable trusts. Disputes arose between the deceased and the college that were continued by the executors of the deceased's estate. In August 1982 the executors executed a deed of comprise wherein they covenanted not to instigate any proceedings to enforce or challenge the performance of the trusts created by the 1976 conveyance. In September 1986 the executors commenced proceedings by way of originating summons challenging the performance of the trusts by the college and seeking their enforcement. The college applied to strike out the originating summons on the ground that the executors had no *locus standi* to bring the proceedings.

Held, allowing the application, by s.28 of the Charities Act 1960 proceedings may be brought under the court's jurisdiction with respect to trusts in relation to the administration of a trust for charitable purposes by any person interested in the charity. The executors could not be described as persons interested in the charity. The deceased did not fall within that description and even if she did her interest could not have passed to the executors. The deed of compromise was binding on the executors, its execution not being contrary to public policy. The public interest in the enforcement of the trusts was guarded by the Attorney General (*Haslemere Estates* v. *Baker* [1982] C.L.Y. 281 considered).

BRADSHAW *v.* UNIVERSITY COLLEGE OF WALES, ABERYSTWYTH [1987] 3 All E.R. 200, Hoffmann J.

294. Exemptions

EXEMPT CHARITIES ORDER 1987 (No. 1823) [45p], made under the Charities Act 1960 (c.58), Sched. 2; declares the Institute of Education, University of London to be an exempt charity within the meaning of the 1960 Act.

295. Managing of trustees—powers of investment—new scheme

A new scheme giving the trustees of a charity established in 1932 a discretion in choosing proper investments was approved bearing in mind the statutory protection afforded and the range and quality of advice available.

STEEL *v.* WELLCOME CUSTODIAN TRUSTEES (1987) 131 S.J. 1589, Hoffmann J.

296. Public charitable trust—action by Attorney General—whether trustees entitled to rely on Limitation Act. See ATT.-GEN. *v.* COCKE, §2323.

297. Reverter of Sites Act 1987 (c.15) See EQUITY AND TRUSTS, §1435.

298. Supervision of charities

A report has been published which examines the supervision of charities and makes recommendations for reform. Copies of *Efficiency Scrutiny of the Supervision of Charities* are available from H.M.S.O. (ISBN 0 11 340856 0) [£5·50].

299. Tax benefits

A revised edition of *Tax Benefits for Charities*, an explanatory booklet for use by charities and donors has been published recently by the Home Office.

300. Tax reliefs

The Inland Revenue has published a leaflet explaining the tax reliefs to which charities are entitled. Copies of the leaflet can be obtained free of charge from any tax office or from the Inland Revenue, Public Enquiry Room, West Wing, Somerset House, London WC2R 1LB.

CIVIL DEFENCE

301. International headquarters and defence organisations

INTERNATIONAL HEADQUARTERS AND DEFENCE ORGANISATIONS (DESIGNATION AND PRIVILEGES) (AMENDMENT) ORDER 1987 (No. 927) [45p], made under the International Headquarters and Defence Organisations Act 1964 (c.5), s.1(4); operative on June 17, 1987; amend S.I. 1965 NO. 1535 so as to add to it COMSUBEASTLANT and CINCUITAIR.

302. Reimbursement of expenses

CIVIL DEFENCE (GRANT) (AMENDMENT) REGULATIONS 1987 (No. 622) [45p], made under the Civil Defence Act 1948 (c.5), ss.3, 8; operative on April 14, 1987; makes provision in connection with the reimbursement of expenses incurred by local and police authorities in the discharge of their civil defence functions.

303. Visiting forces

VISITING FORCES AND INTERNATIONAL HEADQUARTERS (APPLICATION OF LAW) (AMENDMENT) ORDER 1987 (No. 928) [45p], made under the Visiting Forces Act 1952 (c.67), s.8(6); operative on June 17, 1987; amends S.I 1965 No. 1536 so as to add to it COMSUBEASTLAND and CINCUKAIR.

CIVIL LIBERTIES

304. Access to Personal Files Act 1987 (c.37)

This Act provides access for individuals to information relating to themselves maintained by certain authorities, and allows individuals to obatain copies of, and require amendments to, such information.

The Act received the Royal Assent on May 15, 1987.

The Act does not extend to Northern Ireland.

305. Data protection. See HUMAN RIGHTS.

CLUBS AND ASSOCIATIONS

306. Standing orders—Labour Group constitution—disciplinary proceedings

The Corby District Council Labour Group was allowed to proceed with disciplinary proceedings against P for matters concerning a time when he had had the Labour whip withdrawn since there did not appear to be any reason in the poorly drafted constitution to prevent it.

McINTOSH *v.* McGOWAN, *The Times,* January 21, 1987, C.A.

307. Unincorporated association—development land tax—property vested in trustees—liability to tax—club or trustees

[Development Land Tax Act 1976 (c.24), s.28(1), (3).]

A club, founded as in unincorporated association, is a 'person' for the purposes of assessment for development land tax.

A club was founded as an unincorporated association. In 1926 it acquired six acres of land for use as sports grounds. The club's property was vested in trustees. In the late seventies the land was sold in two separate transactions. The club was assessed, *inter alia,* for development land tax. The question arose as to who was liable to pay the tax, the club, the trustees or the individual members.

Held, dismissing the trustees' appeal, that by virtue of s.19 of the Interpretation Act "person" included an unincorporated association unless the contrary intention appeared; since no such contrary intent appeared in s.28(1) of the 1976 Act the club was to be regarded as an entity for the purpose of assessment for development land tax.

WORTHING RUGBY FOOTBALL CLUB TRUSTEES *v.* I.R.C. [1987] 1 W.L.R. 1057, C.A.

308. Unincorporated association—International Tin Council—confidential documents—protection. See SHEARSON LEHMAN BROTHERS INC. *v.* MACLAINE WATSON & CO., INTERNATIONAL TIN COUNCIL INTERVENING, §1676.

309. Unincorporated association—International Tin Council— discovery—disclosure of assets of judgment debtor. See PRACTICE, §2989.

310. Unincorporated associated—International Tin Council—established by treaty—winding up—jurisdiction of court

[Companies Act 1985 (c.6), s.665; International Tin Council (Immunities and Privileges) order 1972, para. 6(1).]

The court does not have jurisdiction to wind up the International Tin Council, an organisation established by treaty between sovereign states.

The International Tin Council was establihsed by treaty between independent sovereign states, with its headquarters in London. In 1985 the I.T.C. ran out of funds and collapsed. The petitioning creditor sought to have the council wound up on the grounds that it was an unregistered company within s.665. The I.T.C. applied to strike out the petition on the grounds that it was not subject to the jurisdiction of the court.

Held, that on its true construction s.665 did not confer on the court jurisdiction to wind up the council, an international body established by treaty between sovereign states.

INTERNATIONAL TIN COUNCIL, *Re* [1987] 1 All E.R. 890, Millet J.

311. Unincorporated association—International Tin Council—failure to meet commercial obligations—whether creditors entitled to claim from members of organisation personally. See RAYNER (J. H.) (MINCING LANE) *v.* DEPARTMENT OF TRADE AND INDUSTRY, §2092.

312. Unincorporated association—International Tin Council—whether a legal entity distinct from its members

Although the International Tin Council is not a body corporate, Parliament has endowed it with the legal capacities of such a body, and it has sufficient legal personality to enable it to incur liabilities on its own account, independent of its component members.

MACLAINE WATSON & CO. *v.* DEPARTMENT OF TRADE AND INDUSTRY, *The Times,* September 7, 1987, Millett J.

313. Unincorporated association—*locus standi*—whether an unincorporated association could be classified as a trade union

[Trade Union and Labour Relations Act 1974 (c.52), ss.2(1), 28(1)(*a*).]

BAALPE issued a writ against the National Union of Teachers and other unions claiming an injunction, a declaration and damages in respect of an alleged breach of contract. The action was struck out by the High Court on the grounds that BAALPE was an unincorporated association rather than a trade union within the meanings of s.28 of the 1974 Act and therefore had no right to bring proceedings. BAALPE appealed to the Court of Appeal.

Held, allowing the appeal, that the definition of "trade union" as "an organisation whose principal purposes include the regulation of relations between workers . . . and employers or employers' associations" contained in s.28(1)(*a*) covered a body whose constitutional aim was to "be concerned with the professional interests of its members". The term "professional interests" included the interests of the members in relation to their employers and BAALPE had established that they had taken an active part in the negotiation of salaries and conditions for their members. Therefore BAALPE satisfied the requirements of the Act to qualify as a trade union regardless of its size, and was thus entitled to bring an action.

BRITISH ASSOCIATION OF ADVISERS AND LECTURERS IN PHYSICAL EDUCATION *v.* NATIONAL UNION OF TEACHERS [1986] I.R.L.R. 497, C.A.

314. Unincorporated associations—conflict of interest amongst members—whether appropriate to proceed against individuals. See UNITED KINGDOM NIREX *v.* BARTON, §3121.

COMMONS

315. Definition of waste land—whether land was occupied—whether fact land was let is conclusive, or only a relevant factor—relevance of fencing

Since 1926 the land was let by the owners to a series of tenants, all of whom were permitted to license others to graze there, and did so.

Held, that (1) the mere fact that the land was let does not, of itself, prevent the land from being common land; (2) the question remains whether as a matter of fact the land is shown to be "unoccupied"; (3) the fact that land is let merely gives a right to occupy; if the tenant never goes to the land, it may remain unoccupied; (4) the fact that the land is not fully fenced cannot be conclusive that it is unoccupied, otherwise no sense can be given to the term "open" in Watson Bs's definition of waste land (*Att.-Gen.* v. *Hanmer* (1858) 27 L.J.Ch. 837, *Box Hill Common, Re* [1979] C.L.Y. 253 applied).

TWM BARLWM COMMON, RISCA AND ROGERSTONE, *Re* (Ref. No. 273/D/106–107), Chief Commons Commissioner.

316. Land used by members of public for recreation—whether user as of right—whether "open space" requiring advertisement

[Local Government Act 1972 (c.70), s.123(2A) (as amended by the Local Government, Planning and Land Act 1980 (c.65), s.118, Sched. 23, paras. 14, 15.]

Where land had been used by the public since 1860, the court was entitled to presume a grant to the public of the right to use it. Even if the use by the public depended on the existence of a bare licence, the landowner had to give reasonable notice of termination of the licence.

A common was used by the public for recreation, who had so used it continuously since 1860. The Council owned it and part of it was used as a racecourse and as a golf course. The Council intended to grant a lease of part of the common to a golf club which wanted to build a club house. Members of the public had right of air and access over the land pursuant to s.193 of the Law of Property Act 1925, but the common was not registered under the Commons Registration Act 1965. The applicant sought by judicial review a declaration that the land constituted "open space" within the meaning of s.123(2A) of the Local Government Act 1972 as amended and an injunction restraining the council from disposing of any part of the common until they had complied with the Act.

Held, that the court was entitled to presume from the evidence of user that a grant to the public of the right now claimed had been made before 1860, and so the public's right to make use of it was not only lawful but as of right. Further, user by the public did not have to be as of right for the purposes of s.123(2A) of the Local Government Act 1972 provided that it was lawful. Even if the public had not held a right to use it, but user had been dependent on the existence of a bare licence, the council still had to give reasonable notice of termination: since no such notice had been given, the applicant was in any event entitled to the declaration sought (*Hadden, Re* [1932] 1 Ch. 133 applied; *Mounsey* v. *Ismay* (1865) 3 H. & C. 486, *Ellenborough Park, Re* [1955] C.L.Y. 882, *Tyne Improvements Commissioners* v. *Imrie; Att.-Gen.* v. *Tyne Improvements Commissioners* (1899) 81 L.T. 174, *Goodman* v. *Mayor of Saltash* (1882) 7 App. Cas. 633 and *Att.-Gen* v. *Antrobus* [1905] 2 Ch. 188 considered).

R. *v.* DONCASTER METROPOLITAN BOROUGH COUNCIL *ex p.* BRAIM (1987) 85 L.G.R. 233, McCullough J.

COMPANY LAW

317. Agreement that director be paid—agreement not known to other directors—disclosure of agreement

[Companies Act 1985 (c.6), s.317.]

A director of Guinness plc., one Ward, had the benefit of a secret agreement that he would be paid by Guinness. It was alleged that S, also a director, was party to the agreement.

Held, that (1) since W did not appear at first sight to have a defence to an allegation of breach of fiduciary duty the court would order Mareva injunctions in relation to funds under his control; (2) since S worked in Switzerland, had said that his home was there, and was domiciled there, the court would make Mareva orders preventing him disposing of any of his assets in this country.

GUINNESS *v.* SAUNDERS, *The Independent,* April 16, 1987, Browne-Wilkinson V.-C.

318. Auditors—auditors negligence—duty of care to investors

The company's business was letting trailers. The company ran into difficulties and approached P. P agreed to inject cash having studied the audited accounts. This was known to D, the auditors. The accounts made no separate provision for tyre repair and replacement which was a major item of expenditure. P made no independent investigation into the matter, relying on the management's assurance that that item would continue at the same rate as before. P then found that the immediate cost of new tyres would be so great as to prevent the company from becoming profitable. P sued D on the basis of their auditing of the accounts.

Held, dismissing the action, that although in the circumstances D owed P a duty of care in the preparation of accounts, there was no evidence that they were in breach of it. Whilst it would have been possible to arrive at a separate figure for tyre replacements, it would have been uncertain, and D was entitled to take the view that this criterion for accruing costs under the accruals concept could not be met. Further, D's duty of care did not free P from the need to take care to protect themselves, and P had failed to made the usual inquiries to obtain the usual warranties.

LLOYD CHEYHAM AND CO. *v.* LITTLEJOHN AND CO. 1986 PCC 389, Woolf J.

319. Authorised insolvency practitioners—annual directory. See BANKRUPTCY, §207.

320. Bribery to secure business for company—whether *ultra vires*

Bribery using a company's money is *ultra vires* the power of its officers.

HANNIBAL (E.) & CO. *v.* FROST, *The Times,* October 8, 1987, C.A.

321. Charitable company—objects—implied process

A power gratuitously to guarantee the obligations of a non-charitable company with which it has no legal connection is not easily to be implied into the objects of a charitable association.

R.S. Co. needed a loan to finance a housing development which it was undertaking in pursuance of its objects. The work was to be done by R. Co., which had no legal connection with R.S. Co., but which was controlled by virtually the same body of persons. U.D.T. Co. agreed to provide the loan direct to R. Co., in return for R.S. Co. guaranteeing the loan and executing certain mortgages. R.S. Co. later contended that the loan guarantee and mortgage were *ultra vires* and void.

Held, that it was not within R.S. Co.'s corporate capacity gratuitously to guarantee the obligations of a non-charitable company with which it had no legal connection. Thus the transactions were *ultra vires* and void (*Baldry* v. *Feintuck* [1972] C.L.Y. 340 and *Rolled Steel Products (Holdings)* v. *British Steel Corp.* [1985] C.L.Y. 306 considered.

ROSEMARY SIMMONS MEMORIAL HOUSING ASSOCIATION *v.* UNITED DOMINIONS TRUST. BATES & PARTNERS (A FIRM) (THIRD PARTY) [1986] 1 W.L.R. 1440, Mervyn Davis J.

322. Company resident in U.K.—transfer of residence within EEC—whether Treasury consent necessary. See R. *v.* H.M. TREASURY, *ex p.* DAILY MAIL AND GENERAL TRUST, §1479.

323. Compulsory winding up—examination before Registrar—whether oppressive, vexatious or unfair.

[Companies Act 1948 (c.38), s.268.]

A, the applicant, held a majority shareholding in the company, and acted as a director without having been appointed as such. A controlled four other associated companies. A instructed the sale of the company's principal assets to one of the other companies and the company became insolvent and unable to pay its debts to the other companies. A obtained a debenture over all the company's assets for the repayment of a loan from him, used the loan money to pay the debts to the other companies then claimed under the debenture. On A's presenting a winding up petition the liquidator began proceedings to set the debenture aside. Before those proceedings were finally compromised, the liquidator obtained information from A through discovery, and further and better particulars of the defences, and was reimbursed by A as to costs. After the compromise and repayment of all moneys that had come with the hands of the receiver, the receiver sought, and was granted, an order from the Registrar for the examination of A in relation to other aspects of the company's affairs and A's role in its arrangement. A applied to strike out the order as oppressive.

Held, dismissing the application, that anyone involved in the affairs of an insolvent company had a duty to help the liquidator. The liquidator had no source of information other than A, he could not have applied for examination earlier when he had resolved to take proceedings over the debenture, and at this stage he was not seeking to sue A again, merely to obtain information. Accordingly, the examination would not be oppressive, vexatious or unfair (*Spiraflite, Re* [1979] C.L.Y. 283 applied).

RHODES (JOHN T.), *Re* 1986 PCC 366, Hoffmann J.

324. Compulsory winding up—hearing—opposed and unopposed hearing—unopposed petitions and related applications—other petitions and motions

With effect from the commencement of the Hilary Sittings 1987, the list of winding-up petitions, as present heard by the Judge acting as Companies Court judge of the term on a Monday, will be heard by the Companies Court Registrar on a Wednesday. The Registrar will sit in court on a Wednesday each week of the term, when he will hear all unopposed petitions and related applications other than those for relief under s.522 of the Companies Act 1985 or for the restraint of advertisement of a petition. In accordance with the Practice Direction of the Lord Chief Justice of May 9th, 1986 ([1986] C.L.Y. 2694, solicitors, properly robed, will be permitted rights of audience before the Registrar.

The Companies Court Judge of the term will continue to sit on a Monday each week of the term, when he will deal with (1) petitions to confirm reductions of capital and/or share premium account, (2) petitions to sanction schemes of arrangement, (3) motions and (4) opposed winding-up petitions which have been adjourned to him by the Registrar.

PRACTICE DIRECTION (CH.D) (COMPANIES COURT: COMPULSORY WINDING UP) 1987 PCC 35.

325. Contributory's petition to wind up—application to pay money from bank account—doubts as to solvency

[Companies Act 1985 (c.6), s.522; Insolvency Act 1986 (c.45), s.127.]

The purpose of granting an order under s.522 of the Companies Act 1985 is to enable the company to carry on trading, notwithstanding that a winding-up petition may be pending, where that trading will be of benefit to those interested in the assets of the company, so that where there was a serious doubt as to the company's solvency, and continued trading would deplete the assets of the company, such an order would be refused.

P, a shareholder and formerly managing director of the company, complained that he had been unfairly excluded from its management and that it was, therefore, just and equitable that the company be wound up. The company sought to restrain advertisement of the petition, and also an order under s.522 of the 1985 Act.

Held, whilst great weight should be accorded to the views of the directors on an application for an order under s.522, the overriding purpose underlying s.522 was that the company should be enabled to carry on trading, unhampered by the pending petition, where that trading would be to the advantage of those interested in the company's assets. Since, on the facts, there were serious doubts as to the company's solvency and it appeared that continued trading would deplete the company's assets, the order would be refused.

COMPANY, A (No. 007523 of 1986), *Re* [1987] BCLC 200, Mervyn Davies J.

326. Debenture—demand made—whether amount needed to be specified—reasonable time

A notice demanding repayment of moneys secured by a debenture did not have to specify the amount due. Once demand had been made the debtor company was entitled to reasonable time to transfer the money but not to raise the money, if not at hand.

On September 22, 1981, two associated companies executed a debenture in favour of a bank in respect of moneys owed. It provided for repayment "on demand" of all moneys thereby secured, and in default for the bank to appoint a receiver. The following day the three shareholders in the companies and their wives executed guarantees to the bank in support of the debenture. In November 1983 the bank acted under the debenture and served a notice on the companies demanding all moneys due to them. About an hour later the bank appointed a receiver who took control of the companies. Later the bank brought an action against the shareholders and their wives under the guarantees. They contended that the appointment of receiver was invalid since the demand for repayment did not specify the moneys due, and that the companies had not been given reasonable time to arrange to pay the due sums from an alternative source of finance of which the bank were aware.

Held, that the bank were entitled to judgment under the guarantees. (1) A notice demanding repayment of moneys secured by a debenture did not have to specify the amount due, and the demand by the bank was valid (*Bunbury Foods Pty* v. *National Bank of Australasia* (1984) 51 A.L.R. 609 followed); (2) if money due was payable on demand, the debtor company was entitled once demand had been made to reasonable time to implement the mechanics of payment, *e.g.* to deliver a cheque by return or to transfer the necessary funds from one bank account to another, but it was not entitled to any time to raise the money if it was not at hand (*Cripps (Pharmaceutical)* v. *Wickenden* [1973] C.L.Y. 337 applied; *Massey* v. *Sladen* (1869) L.R. 4 Exch. 13 considered; *ANZ Banking Group (N.Z.)* v. *Gibson* [1981] 2 N.Z.L.R. 513; *Lister (Ronald Elwyn)* v. *Dunlop Canada* (1982) 135 D.L.R. (3d) 1, *Mister Broadloom Corp. (1968)* v. *Bank of Montreal* (1984) 4 D.L.R. (4th) 74 and *Bunbury Foods Pty.* v. *National Bank of Australasia* (1984) 51 A.L.R. 609 not followed).

BANK OF BARODA *v.* PANESSAR [1986] 3 All E.R. 751, Walton J.

327. Derivative action by minority shareholder—application to strike out—principles to be applied

[R.S.C., Ord. 18, r.19; Ord. 33, r.3.]

A minority shareholder bringing a derivative action must establish a prima facie case that the company is entitled to the relief claimed, and that the action falls within the rule in *Foss* v. *Harbottle.*

P, as minority shareholders, brought an action claiming that various payments from the company's funds had been made improperly, and should be repaid to the company. D applied to strike out the action, on the ground that it was an abuse of process, or frivolous or vexatious.

Held, on the contention by P that procedure was inappropriate, that either Ord. 18, r.19, or Ord. 33, r.3, were appropriate measures by which to determine whether P could commence a derivative action. D had shown substantial doubts over the propriety of P's action, which, if resolved one way, would be decisive of the matter; further the issues of fact were within a narrow area. There were accordingly no grounds for dismissing D's application at this stage.

SMITH *v.* CROFT (No. 2) [1987] BCLC 206, Knox J.

328. Director—fraudulent preference—transfer of monies

A company controlled by D and in respect of which he had guaranteed personally its debts was owed money by WMS, of which he was also a director. Both companies were insolvent and banked at the same bank, which had given instructions that their respective accounts should not be operated. D caused £4,000 to be transfered from the account of WMS to the company controlled by him.

Held, that the transfer was a clear fraudulent preference and D was guilty of misfeasance and breach of trust, and was in breach of his fiduciary duty to WMS and to its shareholders. (*Washington Diamond Mining, Re* [1893] 3 Ch. 95 considered; *Multinational Gas and Petrochemical Co.* v. *Multinational Gas and Petrochemical Services* [1983] C.L.Y. 383 distinguished).

LIQUIDATOR OF WEST MERCIA SAFETYWEAR *v.* DODD, *The Times,* November 24, 1987, C.A.

329. Director—theft—sale in fraud of company. See ATT.-GEN. OF HONG KONG *v.* CHAN NAI-KEUNG (DANIEL), §838.

330. Directors—disqualification

[Companies Act 1985 (c.6), ss.300, 741(1).]

Powers under s.300 extend to persons "occupying the position of director" within s.741(1) or who are *de facto* directors.

Per curiam: the section applies in respect of directors of any company being wound up in England whether or not it was incorporated here.

The Official Receiver sought an order pursuant to s.300 to disqualify S from holding further posts as director of any company. S was associated with seven companies, three of which were incorporated in Liberia and the other four in England. All were being wound up in England. S was not a *de jure* director of any of them but was actively concerned in their management.

Held, that the fact that S was not a *de jure* director was immaterial since s.300 should be read as applying to persons" occupying the position of director" within s.741(1) of the Act, or who were *de facto* directors. The order sought should thus be granted.

EUROSTEM MARITIME, *Re* 1987 PCC 190, Mervyn Davies J.

331. Directors—disqualification—insolvent companies

INSOLVENT COMPANIES (DISQUALIFICATION OF UNFIT DIRECTORS) PROCEEDINGS RULES 1987 (No. 2023) [£1·80], made under the Insolvency Act 1986 (c.45), s.411 and the Company Directors Disqualification Act 1986 (c.46), s.21; operative on January 11, 1988; set out the procedure for applications by the Secretary of State or the official receiver for the disqualification of directors by a court ss.7 and 8 of the Disqualification Act.

332. Directors—disqualification—owing debts to Crown

[Companies Act 1985 (c.6), s.300 (now Company Directors (Disqualification) Act 1986 (c.46), ss.6–9.]

Before a director could be disqualified from so acting on the application of the official receiver, there had to be conduct in breach of standards of commercial morality or gross incompetence which meant that he was a danger to the public. Failure to pay debts to the Crown was not enough.

The official receiver applied under s.300 of the Companies Act 1985 for an order disqualifying D from acting as a director or being concerned in the management of a company. He was a director of two companies which had been compulsorily wound up owing large amounts of debts in unpaid PAYE, NIC, VAT and rates. The official receiver alleged that the companies had paid very little of what was owed and that the money was not the company's to be spent on its business but quasi-trust money.

Held, dismissing the application, that the evidence did not show that D was unfit. There had to be conduct in breach of the standards of commercial morality or gross incompetence which persuaded the court that D would be a danger to the public if he continued to be involved in company management. Failure to pay debts to the Revenue or the Commissioners of Customs and Excise in itself did not render a director unfit. They had appointed traders as tax collectors on their behalf and must take the attendant risk. There was no obligation on traders to keep such moneys in a separate account, as they would have to if they were really trust moneys. They were simply a debt owed by the company.

DAWSON PRINT GROUP, *Re* (1987) 3 BCC 322, Hoffmann J.

333. Directors—disqualification—owing debts to Crown

[Companies Act 1985 (c.6), s.300 (now Company Directors (Disqualification) Act 1986 (c.46), ss.6–9.]

Where a director of a company which owed large debts by way of PAYE, NIC and VAT continued to trade where he ought to have known that the company was unable to meet its liabilities, he was acting recklessly and improperly and could be disqualified.

The official receiver applied under s.300 of the Companies Act 1985 for an order to disqualify I from acting as a director or being concerned in the management of a company. He was a director of three companies which owed large amounts in PAYE, NIC and VAT. The disqualification order was made.

Held, that the evidence showed that the business of one company was acquired and the business of another commenced, and that they were continued when the respondent ought to have known that they were insolvent. Although such moneys were not trust moneys, and the failure to set sums aside for them were not in itself a breach of commercial morality, there was a difference between those Crown debts and debts due to ordinary trade creditors. The Crown was an involuntary creditor, and traders were under a statutory obligation to keep a record of and to account for PAYE, NIC and VAT. If they were overdue and irrecoverable on a winding up, the court might draw the inference that the directors were continuing to trade when they ought to have known that the company was insolvent. Such a director was either in breach of his duty to keep himself properly informed about the company's financial situation or was acting improperly in continuing to trade at the expense of moneys which ought not to be used to finance the company's current trade (*Dawson Print Group, Re* [1987] C.L.Y. 332 distinguished).

STANFORD SERVICES, *Re* (1987) 3 BCC 326, Vinelott J.

334. Directors' fiduciary duty—alleged improper exercise of power to allot shares—indemnity as to costs

[Companies Act 1985 (c.6), s.459.]

Where a shareholder alleges that directors are in breach of their fiduciary duty by allotting shares for an improper purpose, he is not entitled to an order for indemnity as to costs.

A large country house had been converted into 30 flats; the freehold of these was owned by a management company, in which each flat owner owned one share. The company proposed a new scheme for shares to be allotted in proportion to contributions to the service charge. The petitioning shareholder alleged that the proposed issue of shares was a misuse by the directors of their fiduciary powers as it concealed the real and more sinister motive. The petitioner sought an advance order indemnifying him for costs.

Held, he was not entitled to such an indemnity under the principle of *Wallersteiner* v. *Moir* (*Wallersteiner* v. *Moir* (No. 2) [1975] C.L.Y. 2606 considered).

COMPANY, A (No. 005136 of 1986), *Re* [1987] BCLC 82, Hoffmann J.

335. Director's remuneration—failure to disclose interest in contracts—secret profit—whether company entitled to reclaim benefit

[Companies Act 1985 (c.6), s.317(1).]

A director who fails to disclose his interest in a contract to a directors' meeting holds his "secret profit" on trust for the company.

W was a director of Guinness when it launched a take-over bid for Distillers. After the bid had succeeded, W received £5·2 million as additional remuneration in return for services in connection with the bid. Guinness argued that any agreement made by W was in breach of his fiduciary duty and was not disclosed at a directors' meeting as required by s.317. They pursued their claim in Ord. 14 proceedings.

Held, giving judgment for Guinness, that W by failing to make the required statutory disclosure was in breach of duty; the director, W, held the money on trust for the company who were entitled to recover it in summary proceedings.

GUINNESS *v.* SAUNDERS (No. 2) (1987) 3 BCC 520, Browne-Wilkinson V.-C.

336. Directors selling company business—unfair prejudice to non-voting shareholders

[Companies Act 1985 (c.6), s.459.]

Where a shareholder claimed that he was likely to be unfairly prejudiced by the directors' legitimate action, he had to show special circumstances which gave rise to a legitimate expectation they would act in an unfair manner.

The share capital of a company consisted of 100 voting shares and 25,000 non-voting equity shares. Due to events that transpired the directors proposed a series of management buyouts. This gave rise to a conflict of interest as the purchases were to be made by concerns in which the company directors were interested. The necessary formalities were complied with but P, an equity shareholder, began proceedings under s.459 of the 1985 Act, seeking an order restraining sale unless the agreements were approved by the equity shareholders.

Held, refusing to grant the relief, there were no special circumstances here to show that the shareholder was likely to suffer unfair prejudice as a result of the directors' actions.

POSTGATE & DENBY (AGENCIES), *Re* [1987] BCLC 8, Hoffmann J.

337. Disposition of company's assets—reorganisation—whether disposition of half assets *ultra vires*

[Companies Act 1985 (c.6), ss.151, 153.]

A trading company's disposition of half its assets for the benefit of one of its two major shareholders may be invalid.

The company carried on a family business and the two major shareholders were brothers. They were in dispute, and a scheme was devised to divide the assets in two while keeping the company in being.

Held, that the memorandum could not authorise the giving away of so much of the company's assets, and a scheme which required the company to give financial assistance for the purchase of its own shares was not in the interests of the company.

BRADY *v.* BRADY (1987) 3 BCC 535, C.A.

338. Dissolution of Company—accrual of debt after dissolution

[Companies Act 1948 (c.38), s.353.]

P, the petitioner, sought restoration of the company to the register and its compulsory winding up on the grounds of insolvency P having been deceived into making an advance to a bank on the company's behalf some time after the dissolution of the company. There were still sufficient assets to cover P's claim.

Held, that P had no *locus standi* to present the petition. It could not be said that P was a person who "felt aggrieved" by the striking off within section 353(6) of the Companies Act 1948 when the debt was incurred afterwards. (*New Timbiqui Gold Mines, Re* [1961] C.L.Y. 1167 and dicta of Megarry J. in *Lindsay Bowman, Re* [1969] C.L.Y. 396 followed; *Bayswater Trading Co, Re* [1970] C.L.Y. 289, *Morris* v. *Harris* [1927] A.C. 252 and *Tymans* v. *Craven* [1952] C.L.Y. 480 distinguished).

A.G.A. ESTATE AGENCIES, *Re* 1986 PCC 358 Harman J.

339. Forms

COMPANIES (FORMS) (AMENDMENT) REGULATIONS 1987 (No. 752) [£2·60], made under the Companies Act 1985 (c.6), ss.6(1)(*b*)(i), 54(4), 88(2)(*a*)(3), 122(1), 123(2), 128(1)(3)(4), 129(1))2)(3), 157(3), 169(1), 176(3))*a*), 190(5), 224(2), 225(1)(2), 266(1)(3), 287(2), 288(2), 318(4), 325(5), 353(2), 362(3), 386(2), 400(2), 403(1), 416(1), 419(1), 428(2), 429(2)(3)(4), Sched. 13, para. 27, Sched. 14, para. 1(1), the Companies Consolidation (Consequential Provisions) Act 1985 (c.9), s.4(1), the Insolvency Act 1986 (c.45), s.109 and the Financial Services Act 1986 (c.60), s.172; operative on April 30, 1987; further amend S.I. 1985 No. 854 so as to prescribe new forms.

340. Insolvency—administration orders—notice—whether court can reduce period of notice to person entitled to appoint an administrative receiver

[Insolvency Act 1986 (c.45), Pt. II; Insolvency Rules 1986 (S.I. 1986 No. 1925), rr.2, 12.]

Where it is proposed that an administrator should be appointed, the person with the power to appoint an administrative receiver should have an adequate opportunity to exercise his power before it was extinguished by the appointment of an administrator.

The directors of a company applied under Part II of the Insolvency Act 1986 for an administration order. The order was opposed by the company's bankers who had a fixed and floating charge with power to appoint a receiver. Shortly before the hearing, the bank appointed an administrative receiver.

Held, that under the Insolvency Rules 1986, r.27(1) a person entitled to appoint an administrative receiver had to be given five clear days' notice before the date fixed for the hearing of an application for the appointment of an administrator. The court might abridge this period of notice under r.12.9 where the affairs of the company were parlous and the person entitled to appoint an administrative receiver was aware of the intention to petition for the appointment of an administrator. The court had no power to appoint an interim administrator but under r.9(4) could appoint a suitable person to take control of the company and to manage its affairs if the proceedings for the appointment of an administrator were adjourned so as to allow a person entitled to appoint an administrative receiver to consider whether he wished to do so. Once an administrative receiver was appointed, the court was required by s.9(3) to dismiss the petition for an administration order and it could not continue the appointment of a person to manage the affairs of the company pending the hearing of the petition.

COMPANY A (No. 00175 of 1987), *Re* [1987] BCLC 467, Vinelott J.

341. Insolvency—administration orders—purpose achieved—winding up petitions presented—whether court should exercise discretion to discharge order

[Insolvency Act 1986 (c.45), ss.8(3)(*a*)(*d*), 23, 27, 140, Sched. 1, para. 21.]

The court may be prepared to discharge administrative orders once their purpose has been achieved notwithstanding non-compliance with s.23 of the 1986 Act.

Administration orders were made in respect of a number of companies when they became insolvent. The purpose of the orders were (a) the survival if possible of the companies, and (b) the more advantageous realisation of assets than would occur in a winding up. The administrator, satisfied that (a) could not be achieved, went ahead with (b) without making a report to the Registrar of his proposals. The companies then presented winding up petitions in respect of themselves. An application was then made to discharge the administration orders.

Held, allowing the application, that the orders would be discharged as their purpose had been achieved, notwithstanding there had been a failure to comply with s.23.

CHARNLEY DAVIES BUSINESS SERVICES, *Re* (1987) 3 BCC 408, Harman J.

342. Insolvency—administration orders—rival airline applying for revocation of licences—whether consent of administrators or court required

[Insolvency Act 1986 (c.45), s.11(3)(*d*).]

A competitor airline is not prevented from applying for revocation of air transport licences because the other company is subject to an administration order.

An airline which held air transport licences was the subject of an administration order; a rival airline applied for revocation of the licences and the company sought to have the hearings adjourned. The argument was that the licensing authority had no jurisdiction to hear the application while the administration order was in force. The adjournment was refused and the company applied for judicial review.

Held, that the only activities prohibited were activities of creditors. Other activities by for example, competitors, were not barred.

AIR ECOSSE *v.* CIVIL AVIATION AUTHORITY (1987) 3 BCC 492, Ct. of Session.

343. Insolvency proceedings

INSOLVENCY (AMENDMENT) REGULATIONS 1987 (No. 1959) [85p], made under S.I. 1986 No. 1925; operative on January 11, 1988; amend S.I. 1986 No. 1994 which regulates matters of an administrative character in the conduct of company and individual insolvency proceedings.

INSOLVENCY (AMENDMENT) RULES 1987 (No. 1919) [£9·20], made under the Insolvency Act 1986 (c.45), ss.411, 412; operative on January 11, 1988; makes detailed amendments to S.I. 1986 No. 1925.

344. Liquidator acting for two companies—conflict—appointment of provisional liquidator—application to set aside—costs

[Companies (Winding Up) Rules 1949, r.226.]

Where the affairs of two companies, both in liquidation, are inextricably intertwined, an order appointing a separate (provisional) liquidator of one of them will not be interfered with as it will be necessary in order to ensure that no conflict arises.

The business affairs of two companies, both controlled by a man and his wife, were completely intertwined; one of the companies was hopelessly insolvent and went into creditors' voluntary liquidation; the other company went into members' voluntary liquidation on the same day. E, a chartered accountant, was appointed liquidator of both companies, notwithstanding objections from some creditors that there would be a conflict of interest between the two liquidations. On application to the Court the registrar appointed a provisional liquidator of one of the companies. E brought proceedings to set aside the appointment of the provisional liquidator.

Held, that the appointment of the second liquidator had been perfectly proper and necessary to avoid a possible conflict of interest. That being so, E's application failed. Since the appointment of the second liquidator was a reasonable course, the judge's order that E pay the costs on an indemnity basis would stand, although he would not be ordered to pay the costs of an *ex parte* application of which he had no knowledge, and which he did not attend.

TURNER (P.) (WILSDEN), *Re* [1987] BCLC 149, C.A.

345. Loan to company—receiver appointed—whether loan held on resulting trust for lender

Where money had been loaned to a company for a specific purpose which had not been carried through, and the company's bankers had appointed receivers under a debenture, the money was subject to a resulting trust in favour of the lender and were not assets of the company.

The appellant loaned £60,000 to a company run by a friend which was in financial difficulties. The loan was for the lease of equipment. The company ordered the equipment but before it was delivered the company's bankers appointed receivers under a debenture secured by a floating charge on the assets of the company. The receivers claimed to be entitled to retain the balance of the sum loaned (part of which had been spent on temporary equipment) as assets of the company. The judge at first instance held that no trust attached to it and they were assets of the company.

Held, allowing the appeal, that the purpose of the loan was for the company to acquire the equipment and not just enter into an abortive contract for its purchase. The purpose of the provision had failed, and the money was subject to a resulting trust in favour of the appellant.

EVTR, *Re* (1987) 3 BCC 389, C.A.

346. Mergers and divisions

COMPANIES (MERGERS AND DIVISIONS) REGULATIONS 1987 (No. 1991) [£1·90], made under the European Communities Act 1972 (c.68), s.2(2); operative on January 1, 1988; provide for mergers of public limited liability companies and the division of such companies.

347. Minority interest—prejudicial conduct—whether relating to manner in which company run—motion to strike out petition

[Companies Act 1985 (c.6), s.459.]

Relief under s.459 of the Companies Act 1985 is available only where unfair prejudice arises from the manner in which the affairs of the company are being conducted, or from some act or omission by the company, and is not available where the conduct complained of is that of a shareholder, acting in his personal capacity.

P asserted that R was acting in an unfairly prejudicial manner by paying off a loan due from the company to the bank, and taking a transfer of the bank's security. P petitioned the Court for an order that R sell her shares to P. R moved to strike out the petition, as disclosing no cause of action, or alternatively as being an abuse of process.

Held, granting the motion and striking out the petition, that s.459 of the 1985 Act was available only in respect of matters arising in the course of the management of the affairs of the company. It was of no application to anything done by a shareholder in her private capacity, outside the course of the company's business. The allegation relating to the paying off of the bank loan could not constitute a ground for relief under s.459, and nor, on the facts, did any of the other allegations made, so that the petition would be struck out.

COMPANY, A (No. 001761 of 1986), *Re* [1987] BCLC 141, Harman J.

348. Minority shareholders—unfair prejudice—exclusion from management—leaving terms and compensation

[Companies Act 1985 (c.6), s.459.]

Where a corporate quasi-partnership breaks down resulting in the exclusion of one party, the fairness of that exclusion needs to be judged in the light of the reasonableness of requiring him to leave and the compensation offered.

The petitioner formed a company with finance provided by the respondent who took 61 per cent. of the shares. Eventually their relationship deteriorated and the petitioner was dismissed from his post. His shares were valued at an unacceptably low figure, at which point the company sought to enforce their right to purchase. The petitioner sought to prevent the sale or to wind-up the company; the respondent moved to strike out the petitions.

Held, granting the motion to strike out, that whether the petitioner's exclusion was unfair would depend in part on the terms he is offered for his shares or in compensation for his loss of employment.

XYZ, *Re* 1987 PCC 92, Hoffmann J.

349. Minority shareholders—unfair prejudice—*locus standi* to petition

[Companies Act 1985 (c.6), s.459(2).]

A transferee of shares has locus standi under s.459(2) of the 1985 Act only if shares have been transferred by proper instrument duly executed and delivered.

The company was formed by the petitioner and three respondents. The petitioner's wife was later made a director and shareholder in his place. Disagreements ensued, and following unsuccessful negotiations to purchase the wife's shares, both the petitioner and his wife were excluded from the management of the company. The petitions sought orders for the purchase of the shares or for winding-up. The respondents moved to strike out the petitioner's name on the grounds that he had no *locus standi* to present the petition.

Held, granting the motion, that the petitioner had no *locus standi* because *inter alia,* the shares held by his wife had not been transferred to him by instrument of transfer properly executed and delivered; and agreement to transfer shares was not sufficient.

MOSSMAIN, *Re* 1987 PCC 104, Hoffmann J.

350. Minority shareholders—unfairly prejudicial conduct towards—whether striking out of petition

[Companies Act 1985 (c.6), s.459.]

H was managing director and H and W held all the shares in A Co. which was trading profitably. H and W were led to believe by X and Y who controlled B plc that if they sold their shares to B plc, substantial sums would be invested in A Co., H and W would continue as directors, and H would be managing director, and be invited on to the board of B plc. After the exchange of shares in B plc, B plc turned out not to have the necessary funds, A Co. was run down and ceased to be a going concern, and H was removed as managing director of A Co. and asked to resign from the board of B plc. H and W petitioned under s.459 of the Companies Act 1985 that X and Y be ordered to buy their shares in B plc at a price equivalent to the value of the A Co. shares at the time of sale. X and Y moved to strike out the petition.

Held, that although generally s.459 was limited to conduct unfairly prejudicial to the interests of members as members, the court could have regard to wider equitable considerations, and it could not be said that there was no evidence that H's employment as managing director of A Co. was not part of his legitimate expectations as a member of B plc (dicta of Lord Wilberforce in *Ebrahimi* v. *Westbourne Galleries* [1972] C.L.Y. 393 applied).

COMPANY A, (No. 00477 of 1986), *Re* 1986 PCC 372, Hoffmann J.

351. Oppression of minority—appointment of receiver—principles to be adopted

[Supreme Court Act 1981 (c.54), s.37, Companies Act 1985 (c.6), s.459.]

Where there is a dispute between the majority and the minority in a company which is effectively a quasi-partnership, as to the manner in which the company is being run, and the Court is asked to appoint a receiver at an early stage, the Court will act upon principles similar to those which would be applied in a partnership dispute.

The shareholding in the company was divided equally between P and S. S was the chairman, and consequently held a casting vote in many matters. A dispute arose between them as to the management of the company. P presented a contributory's petition seeking that she be entitled to purchase the shares held by S, alternatively that the company be wound up on the just and equitable ground. Pending hearing of the petition, and a cross-petition presented by S, P applied for the appointment of a receiver under s.37 of the Act of 1981.

Held, that the company being in this case a quasi-partnership, the Court would apply principles similar to those applied in a partnership dispute, in which it would normally be the practice to appoint a receiver at an early stage. Such a course implied no judgment on the merits of the position, but was taken to preserve the status quo. Since there was evidence that S was not managing the affairs of the company in the interests of all, a receiver would be appointed.

COMPANY, A (No. 00596 of 1986), *Re* [1987] BCLC 133, Harman J.

352. Prescription (Scotland) Act 1987 (c.36)

This Act amends Pt. I of the Prescription and Limitation (Scotland) Act 1973 (c.52).

The Act received the Royal Assent on May 15, 1987.

The Act extends to Scotland only.

353. Quasi-partnership private company—director excluded—petition—whether jurisdiction to make interim order for payment

[Companies Act 1985 (c.6), ss.459(1), 461(1); R.S.C., Ord. 27, r.3.]

Where a petition is brought under s.459(1), the Court has no jurisdiction to make an interim payment order.

The company was established with an issued share capital of £100,000. The petitioner holding 30 per cent., the balance being held by two others. The company was run as a quasi-partnership, and there came a time when the petitioner was told he was no longer wanted. An offer was made to purchase the petitioners' shareholding for £45,000. The offer was rejected, the petitioner having had the company independently valued at about £600,000. The petitioner moved for an interim payment order of £40,000.

Held, dismissing the application, that the Court had no jurisdiction on a petition brought under s.459(1) to make an interim payment order.

COMPANY, A (No. 004175 of 1986), *Re* [1987] 1 W.L.R. 585, Scott J.

354. Receivership—company lessee of property part of which sublet—payments of rent by underlessees—statutory assignment to landlord—equitable assignment to mortgagee—priority of assignments

[Law of Distress Amendment Act 1908 (c.53), ss.1, 3, 6.]

An equitable assignment of a sub-lessee's rent has priority over a statutory assignment to the landlords where the landlords have prior notice of the equitable assignment.

The receivers issued a summons to the landlords of premises occupied by the company. The company had sublet part of the premises. A debenture was held by a bank, the effect being that the payments of rent by the underlessees were assigned in equity. The landlords served notices which created in effect a statutory assignment of the rent to them. The receivers argued that the statutory assignment could not affect the equitable assignment which was first in time and of which the landlords had notice.

Held, declaring that the receivers were entitled to the money, that the deeming provisions applied only between landlord and tenant and did not affect the mortgagee.

OFFSHORE VENTILATION, *Re* (1987) 3 BCC 486, Harman J.

355. Receivership—documents brought into being by receiver—receiver appointee of debenture holder

The ownership of documents brought into being during a receivership depended upon the capacity in which the receiver was acting at the time. Where the documents in question were brought into being in order for the receiver, as appointee, to make his report to the debenture holder, the company could not claim those documents, which were the property of the debenture holder.

GOMBA HOLDINGS U.K. *v.* MINORIES FINANCE, *Financial Times,* November 11, 1987, Hoffmann J.

356. Receivership—"fixed plant and machinery"—machinery sold—whether within fixed or floating charge

Woodworking machinery not firmly attached to premises does not come within the definition of "fixed plant and machinery."

A company became insolvent and a bank which held a debenture appointed receivers. The receivers sold the company's woodworking machines at auction. A summons was issued on the question of whether the machines fell within the fixed charge as "fixed plant and machinery" or were caught only by the floating charge. If the latter, the proceeds would be subject to preferential charges which would rank first.

Held, that the phrase fixed plant and machinery was a composite phrase, it referred to machinery in some way firmly attached to the premises; the machines in question were not so fixed and fell within the floating charge.

HI-FI EQUIPMENT (CABINETS), *Re* (1987) 3 BCC 478, Harman J.

357. Receivership—liability of receiver—procuring breach of contract by company

Receivers appointed under a debenture can be liable for a breach of contract by the company only where they have failed to act bona fide, or have acted outside the scope of their authority.

D1 contracted to supply P with certain equipment which it failed to deliver; P sued D1 and joined D2 and D3 as receivers and managers, alleging that they had induced D1's breach of contract. *Held,* allowing the appeal by D2 and D3 that the claim against them should be struck out, that D2 and D3 were the agents of D1, and as such were immune from any claim for breach of contact by D1, unless they had not acted bona fide or acted outside the scope of their authority. Further, they owed their duty not to the company's creditors, but to the debenture holder, and the company.

LATHIA *v.* DRONSFIELD BROS. [1987] BCLC 321, Sir Neil Lawson.

358. Receivership—powers and liability of receiver—set-off and counterclaim

[Companies Act 1985 (c.6), s.469(7), 471, 473(4).]

[Scot.] It was clear from s.473(4) of the Companies Act 1985 that the company remained the debtor and creditor in relation to obligations under a contract entered into before the appointment of a receiver. The company and not the receiver was the proper person to seek payment of a debt arising out of such a pre-existing contract. But the receiver had authority to raise an action under s.471(1)(*f*).

In 1974 or early 1975 the Council entered a contract with the company to do renovation works in Glasgow. Before the works were finished, the company was wound up and a receiver appointed. The Council contracted with another firm to finish the work and the new firm used plant and equipment left by the company which deteriorated. The company, as pursuers, sought the cost of this equipment while the Council counterclaimed for the increased cost of the contract. The pursuers moved for the counterclaim to be dismissed, but this plea was repelled. The pursuers argued that the counterclaim was incompetent as being directed against both the company and the receiver which was an attempt to involve the receiver in personal liability for a contractual obligation on pre-dating his appointment. The Council submitted that the pursuer was simply the company.

Held, that it was clear from s.473(4) of the Companies Act 1985 that the company remained the debtor and creditor in relations to contracts made before the appointment of a receiver, and it was for the company to vindicate its rights: authority to raise such an action was vested in the receiver under s.471(1)(*f*). The receiver had power to bring the action in the name and on behalf of the company, and the counterclaim was against the company.

The pursuers argued that compensation or set-off could not be used to defeat the security which the holder of a floating charge obtained through the appointment of a receiver, which attached on appointment under s.469(7) of the Companies Act. It was held that under the terms of s.469(7) that attachment "has effect as if the charge was a fixed security over the property to which it has attached" did not imply an actual assignation with all the effects that that would have on title. The provision was concerned with the effect of a security as a security. Title remained in the company (as it would not on assignation and intimation) but all the security effects of an assignation were available to the receiver. However, this was not a case of a security holder ingathering an asset over which he had some security right. The only relevant asset in relation to the security was the company's *jus crediti.* There was no reason why, by having acquired the company's interest in a *jus crediti* for security purposes, the receiver should also have acquired some right when suing in the company's name to deny the ordinary defences available to third parties against the company. The *jus crediti* remained subject to extinction by set-off as well as by payment. The pursuer's claim for return of their property or payment was open to a defence of set-off, subject to rights vested in them pending the date for return or payment. It seemed that the pursuer's claim arose and existed in the requisite sense prior to liquidation.

CALLAGHAN (MYLES J.) (IN RECEIVERSHIP) *v.* CITY OF GLASGOW DISTRICT COUNCIL (1987) 3 BCC 337, Ct. of Session.

359. Reduction of capital—cancellation of preferred shares—whether variation or abrogation

[Companies Act 1985 (c.6), s.136(1).]

[Scot.] The cancellation of preference shares is not a variation or abrogation of the rights of the preference shareholders.

The company by special resolution at an extraordinary general meeting resolved to reduce its capital by paying off and cancelling the preference shares. No class meeting of preference shareholders was held to approve the resolution. By article 12 such a meeting was to be held if the shares were "modified, commuted, affected or dealt with."

Held, that the preference shareholders had by contract the right to prior repayment on a winding-up, and the liability to prior repayment on a reduction of capital. The article had no application since the prior return of capital was merely part of the fulfilment of the preference shareholders' contracts and no variation or abrogation of their rights was involved (*Saltdean Estate, Re* [1968] C.L.Y. 401 approved).

HOUSE OF FRASER *v.* A.C.G.E. INVESTMENTS [1987] 2 W.L.R. 1083 H.L.(Sc).

360. Register of members—rectification

When a company's register of members had been physically lost, it was appropriate to seek an order from the Court for rectification to enable the names of members to be entered in the new, empty register.

DATA EXPRESS, *Re, The Times,* April 27, 1987, Vinelott J.

361. Registration of charges—company in liquidation—particulars of charges

[Companies Ordinance (Hong Kong), ss.80, 83; Companies (Forms) Regulations (Hong Kong), para. 2.]

[H.K.] A mortgagee was only entitled to registration of his charges if the prescribed particulars were given to the registrar on time and in the relevant form.

A Hong Kong company agreed to repay on demand advances made by a bank. The company deposited with the bank the title deeds of certain properties to prepare a sub-mortgage. The deposit automatically charged the company's interest to the bank as equitable sub-mortgagee to secure repayment. Shortly after the company went into liquidation, the bank applied to register the charges created by the deposits. They submitted the relevant form to the registrar on time, but the registrar did not register the charges because the form did not specify the date of or describe the charge sought to be registered. The bank failed to amend the form within the time limit. The Court of Appeal of Hong Kong refused an order to register the charge; the assignees of the bank's appeal was dismissed.

Held, that a mortgagee was only entitled to registration if the prescribed particulars were delivered to the registrar on time. He had to prove his right by dating the charge. The bank had not done this. Further, the charge had to indicate the particulars required to be registered, and this had not been done.

SUN TAI CHEUNG CREDITS *v.* ATT.-GEN. OF HONG KONG (1987) 3 BCC 357, P.C.

362. Representation by company—fictitious profits—whether liquidator estopped from denying profits ever made

A liquidator is not bound by representations as to its profits made by the company of which he is liquidator.

The two companies were commodity speculators. During the course of their activities they published, to certain investors, fictitious claims to profit, allegedly made for those persons.

Held, on the question whether the liquidator was estopped from denying that those fictitious profits had been made, that it was not the liquidator, but the company, which had made the representations said to give rise to the estoppel, so he was not bound. Further, and in any event, for the liquidator to acknowledge the estoppel would be to defeat the statutory scheme, which obliged the liquidator to distribute the assets of the company among the true creditors.

EXCHANGE SECURITIES AND COMMODITIES (IN LIQUIDATION) *Re;* EXCHANGE SECURITIES FINANCIAL SERVICES (IN LIQUIDATION), *Re* [1987] 2 W.L.R. 893, Harman J.

363. Rights issue—reduction of capital—minor inaccuracies in special resolution—whether resolution invalid

[Companies Act 1985 (c.6), ss.135, 137, 359.]

Where a resolution for reduction of a company's capital contains minor inaccuracies the court has jurisdiction to confirm the reduction on terms that correct the error.

The company summoned an E.G.M. to authorise a rights issue and to effect a reduction of capital. The circular set out the special resolution to be voted on; it was duly approved. W received shares which he renounced and which were eventually registered in the name of S. It was subsequently discovered that there were a number of minor inaccuracies in the special resolution. W sought to have the register rectified, contending that the resolution was rendered ineffective due to the inaccuracies. Mervyn Davies J. refused to make the order. W appealed.

Held, dismissing the appeal, where the errors were so small that no one could be prejudiced by their correction, the court had statutory (s.137) or inherent jurisdiction to confirm the reduction on terms which corrected the error.

WILLAIRE SYSTEMS, *Re* [1987] BCLC 67, C.A.

364. Settlement of an action—liability—effect of decree of court

[Law Reform (Miscellaneous Provisions) (Scotland) Act 1940 (c.42), s.3(2).]

A company is "found liable" within the meaning of s.3(2) of the Law Reform (Miscellaneous Provisions) (Scotland) Act 1940 where there has been a formal decree of the court giving effect to an agreed settlement by the company: a judicial ruling on liability and quantum, after a contested hearing, is not necessary.

COMEX HOULDER DIVING *v.* COLNE FISHING CO., *The Times,* March 20, 1987, H.L.

365. Share capital—multi-currency share capital

[Companies Act 1985 (c.6), ss.2(5)(*a*), 18(1), 45(2)(*a*), 121(2)(*a*), 738(2), (4).]

A company is entitled to have multi-currency share capital where any share can be identified as being of a particular currency.

The company wished to reorganise its share capital into fixed amounts in various foreign currencies plus the minimum issued capital for a public company of £50,000.

Held, approving the company's minute, that there was no requirement under s.2(5)(*a*) of the Companies Act 1985 that the "amount" of the share capital to be stated in monetary sums need be stated in a single aggregate sum, and provided the company had the minimum issued capital of £50,000, it could also have amounts of share capital expressed in other currencies (*Miliangos* v. *Frank (George) (Textiles)* [1975] C.L.Y. 2657 applied; *Adelaide Electric Supply Co.* v. *Prudential Assurance Co.* [1934] A.C. 122 distinguished; dicta of Dillon L.J. and Sir John Donaldson M.R. in *Pattison* v. *Marine Midland* [1984] C.L.Y. 456 considered).

SCANDINAVIAN BANK GROUP, *Re* [1987] 2 W.L.R. 752, Harman J.

366. Shares—pre-emption provision—valuation procedure

[Companies Act 1985 (c.6), s.459]

Where a company's articles of association lay down a machinery for valuing a member's shares, the member should use that machinery, and will not ordinarily be entitled to complain of unfairness unless he has done so.

In 1981 the petitioner held 39 out of 100 shares in a company" The remaining 61 were held by T, his family, and a business associate. Articles of association were adopted which provided that a member who was employed by the company or a director was bound to give a transfer notice in respect of all his shares within 14 days of his ceasing to be an employee or director. There was machinery for the valuation of the shares by the company's auditor in the event of disagreement as to the value, the vendor then being bound to transfer them. In 1983 the petitioner sold 9 of his shares at a price of £5,000 per share, which the auditors advised was an approximate value. On May 31, 1985 the petitioner was summarily dismissed and on July 26, 1985 he was removed as a director. The company's solicitors required him to give a transfer notice and offered him £900 a share for his 30 shares. He rejected the offer, and the auditors then valued his shares at £800 a share. He presented a petition for relief under s.459 of the Companies Act 1985 to restrain the compulsory acquisition of his shares. The respondents moved to strike out the petition, and succeeded.

Held, that where there was an irretrievable breakdown in relations between members of a corporate quasi-partnership, the exclusion of one quasi-partner from management and employment did not *ipso facto* entitle him to petition under s.459. In any event the articles provided for what was to happen if the majority shareholders having exercised their statutory right to exclude a minority shareholder as director exercised their right to purchase his shares at a fair price as determined by the auditors. The petitioner was bound to sell his shares at their valuation. *Company (No. 007623 of 1984), Re* [1986] BCLC 362 and *Postgate & Denby (Agencies), Re* [1987] C.L.Y. 336 considered.

Per curiam: If a company's articles of association provide a method for determining the fair value of a party's shares, a member seeking to sell his shares on a breakdown of relations with other shareholders should not ordinarily be entitled to complain of unfair conduct if he has made no attempt to use the machinery provided by the articles.

COMPANY, A (No. 004377 of 1986), *Re* [1987] 1 W.L.R. 102, Hoffmann J.

367. Shares in public company—investigation of share acquisitions—failure to provide information—restrictions on shares—application to lift restrictions to permit sale

[Companies Act 1985 (c.6), ss.212, 216, 454, 456.]

Shares "frozen" because of the holder's refusal to give information about them, may not have the restrictions lifted merely because the holder intends to sell them.

Shares were held by a Swiss bank for its clients through a nominee company. The shares were ordered to be "frozen" when the bank refused to disclose its clients names. The bank applied for the restrictions to be lifted because it intended to sell the shares.

Held, dismissing the bank's appeal, that the court had jurisdiction to lift the restrictions, but would not do so here as it considered the failure to disclose provided an objection to the court exercising its discretion to lift the restrictions.

GEERS GROSS, *Re* (1987) 3 BCC 528, C.A.

368. Summary dismissal of chief executive—dismissal allegedly for misconduct and incompetence as a director and employee. See JACKSON *v.* INVICTA PLASTICS, §1379.

369. Title reservation—repair to goods involving supply of parts—whether charge void for non-registration

[Companies Act 1985 (c.6), ss.395, 396.]

Where a contract for repair provided for ownership by the repairer of any article for which it had supplied parts pending payment, it created a charge which was void if not registered.

SPS carried on the business of repair of machinery. A standard term of its contract was that SPS were to retain ownership of machinery for which it had supplied parts, as surety for the debt. The defendant company's bank appointed receivers at a time when SPS had not been paid. SPS claimed a proprietary interest in the machinery and obtained an injunction preventing the receivers selling the machinery before action.

Held, discharging the injunction, the contract created a charge which was void for non-registration under s.395.

SPECIALIST PLANT SERVICES *v.* BRAITHWAITE [1987] BCLC 1, C.A.

370. *Ultra vires*—effect of view of majority shareholders

Where minority shareholders claim that transactions by directors were *ultra vires,* their action will be struck out if it can be shown that, had a meeting of independent shareholders been called, the majority of their votes, having regard to the benefit of the company, would have opposed the continuation of the minority shareholders' action (*Allen* v. *Gold Reefs,* (1900)) 1 Ch. 656, and *Prudential Assurance Co.* v. *Newman Industries (No. 2)* [1982] C.L.Y. 331 applied).

SMITH *v.* CROFT, *The Financial Times,* February 11, 1987, Knox J.

371. Unfair prejudice—protection of company's members—requirements for petition

[Companies Act 1985 (c.6), s.459.]

A member of a company can petition under s.459 of the Companies Act 1985 on the ground that any actual or proposed act or omission of the company is or will be unfairly prejudicial to the interests of some part of the members, so long as at the date of the petition there is an immediate danger of such an act taking place. It is sufficient to found such a petition that an act has been proposed that if carried out or completed will be prejudicial to the petitioner.

KENYON SWANSEA, *Re, The Times,* April 29, 1987, Vinelott J.

372. Winding up—agreement to lease premises to a director to run business for personal profit—whether agreement illegal

[Companies Act 1980 (c.22), s.48 (now Companies Act 1985 (c.6), s.320).]

The party that alleges a breach of s.48 of the Companies Act 1980 as to non-cash assets exceeding the requisite value, must prove the fact with relevant evidence.

The company agreed to lease one of its hotel premises to one of its directors to carry on a business for personal profit. The agreement was made with the approval of another director. The managing director was subsequently made a receiver in winding up proceedings and claimed that the agreement was contrary to s.48, which prevented a director acquiring non-cash assets of the requisite value without the sanction of a general meeting.

Held, that the party that alleged that the non-cash asset exceeded the requisite value, had to prove that fact by evidence. In the absence of such evidence, it was impossible to hold that the agreement contravened s.48.

JOINT RECEIVERS AND MANAGERS OF NILTAN CARSON *v.* HAWTHORNE (1987) 3 BCC 454, Hodgson J.

373. Winding up—creditors' voluntary winding up—replacement of liquidator—basis on which court will exercise its discretion

[Insolvency Act 1986 (c.45), s.108(2).]

Under s.108(2) of the Insolvency Act 1986, a court can only remove a liquidator "on cause shown" by the applicant, but it was not necessary to show personal misconduct or unfitness. Failure to carry out his duties with sufficient vigour was enough.

E agreed to act as liquidator in the winding up of a company. He had considerable experience in this role. His appointment was opposed at a creditor's meeting but he was appointed with the support of the managing director of the company who held a large number of proxies. H was favoured by other creditors but not supported. An application was made under s.108(2) of the Insolvency Act 1986 to replace E as liquidator. It was ordered that he be replaced and H appointed in his stead.

Held, that although there were no allegations against the personal propriety of E, there was adequate grounds justifying the court in removing him from office. He had failed to display sufficient vigour in carrying out his duties: he had made no examination of the sales and purchase ledgers and not investigated whether stock was missing. He had made no enquiries of the company, NB Ltd., now operating from the same premises with substantially the same staff, vehicles and stock, and had not interviewed the employees of the company to determine exactly what had happened before the company ceased to trade. He had been in office almost three months but was not in a position to explain the figures as to the stock of the company nor had he taken up the question or sought legal advice. He had appeared to assume improperly that the directors could close down the business and carry it on through another company from the same premises and with the same staff, and that all the creditors could expect was the forced sale price for the stock. The value of the stock would have covered the cost of a preliminary investigation, and he could have sought the authorisation of the creditors for this. He had failed to carry out his duties with sufficient vigour and had displayed a relaxed and complacent attitude to the possibility of wrongdoing on the part of directors, and therefore ought to be replaced.

KEYPAK HOMECARE, *Re* [1987] BCLC 409, Millett J.

374. Winding up—expenses incurred "previously" to compulsory winding up—voluntary liquidator

[Companies (Winding-Up) Rules 1949 (S.I. 1949 No. 330 (L. 4), r.195.]

The company was in financial difficulties and went into voluntary liquidation. The voluntary liquidator took a number of steps in the liquidation. Then a compulsory order was made and the voluntary liquidator was displaced by the new liquidator under the compulsory order. The voluntary liquidator issued a summons seeking an order fixing his remuneration and allowing his disbursements. The order was granted, and the new liquidator moved to have it discharged.

Held, dismissing the motion, that r.195 of the Companies (Winding-Up) Rules 1949 entitled a voluntary liquidator to have his remuneration fixed by the court if his liquidation was "previously cancelled" at any time before the making of the compulsory order, and he was entitled to claim priority for his legitimate expenses before and after the compulsory order (*Waterloo Mfg Co. (Burnley), Re* (1936) 3 C.C.R. 281 disapproved; *Adler (William) & Co., Re* [1935] Ch. 138 considered.)

SORGE (A.V.) & CO., *Re* 1986 PCC 380, Hoffmann J.

375. Winding up—foreign corporation—no assets in jurisdiction—loan on security of ship—court's jurisdiction to make order.

[Insolvency Act 1986 (c.45), s.221(1)(5).]

The court has jurisdiction to make a winding up order on a foreign company even though it has no assets here, provided a sufficient connection can be established.

A Liberian company operated through ship agents in London. It borrowed $13·5 million from the petitioning bank on the security of the vessel. In 1986 the company defaulted on interest payments, and the plaintiff having obtained judgment for the debt, petitioned for the winding up of the company.

Held, the court had jurisdiction to make the order; it was not necessary to show the company had assets here, but a sufficiently close contact had to be established. The court made the order (*Companies Merabello San Nicholas S.A., Re* [1972] C.L.Y. 388, *Eloc Electro-Optieck and Communicatie BV, Re* [1981] C.L.Y. 265 applied).

COMPANY, A (No. 00359 of 1987), *Re* [1987] 3 W.L.R. 339, Gibson J.

376. Winding up—injunction—powers of court to order examination of officers

[Supreme Court Act 1981 (c.54), s.37; Companies Act 1985 (c.6), s.561; Insolvency Act 1986 (c.46), s.236.]

Despite the fact that there is no cause of action in the liquidator, the court has the power on their application to order that an officer of a company who is the subject of an order under s.561 of the 1985 Act shall attend the examination.

G was the director of and driving force behind, O.C. Co., which was a licensed deposit-taker, and left the jurisdiction shortly before it went into liquidation. The liquidators learnt he was to return for a short time and obtained an order for his examination under s.561 of the 1985 Act. On the liquidators further application, *ex parte,* the court made an order by way of injunction requiring him to attend the examination. G applied for this order to be discharged.

Held, that the order would not be discharged. Though the liquidators had no cause of action, the court had the power to make the order, being anticipatory of their powers of arrest for failure to attend, granted by s.561(4) (*Siskina, The* [1977] C.L.Y. 2344 considered; dictum of Cumming-Bruce L.J. in *House of Spring Gardens* v. *Waite* [1985] C.L.Y. 2674 applied).

COMPANY, A (No. 003318 of 1987), *Re* [1987] 3 BCC 564, Harman J.

377. Winding up—parties relying on affidavit evidence—whether court has power to examine deponents

[Mal.] [Companies Act 1965 (Laws of Malaysia Act 125, rev. 1973), s.218(1); R.S.C. Ord. 38, r.2(3).]

In a company winding-up where all the evidence is presented by affidavit, the judge has no power to give directions regarding the cross-examination of deponents.

The company was incorporated in Malaysia with four equal shareholders as directors. The petitioner acquired the shares of one of the four and became a director, and subsequently chairman. The other shareholders, against his wishes, transferred all executive powers to a managing director and removed him. He presented a petition for winding up, and all parties swore affidavits, but neither called oral evidence or applied to cross-examine. The judge made a winding-up order. The Court of Appeal allowed the appeal, indicating that the court should have examined the litigant. The petitioner appealed.

Held, allowing the appeal; in the absence of an application by a litigant, a trial judge had no power to give directions as to the evidence to be presented.

TAY BOK CHOON *v.* TAHANSAN SDN BHD. [1987] 1 W.L.R. 313, P.C.

378. Winding up—procedure

[Companies Act 1985 (c.6), s.459.]

All members of the company should be joined to a winding-up petition under s.459.

COMPANY, A (No. 007281 of 1981), *Re, The Times,* April 13, 1987, Vinelott J.

379. Winding up—provisional liquidator—special manager—costs and remuneration—petition dismissed—who to bear costs

[Insolvency Rules 1986 (S.I. 1986 No. 1925), r.4.27, 4.31.]

The Insolvency Rules contemplate that a company the subject of a winding up petition bear the costs even of an unsuccessful petition.

The Secretary of State for Trade and Industry presented a petition for the winding up of a company on the ground of public interest. A provisional liquidator and a special manager were appointed; the petition was dismissed. The question arose as to who would bear the costs and the remuneration of the appointees.

Held, that the costs were subject to the rules, and r.4.28 and 4.30 plainly provided that the company bear the costs even where the petition failed. The court had a discretion which it was not prepared to exercise to make a contrary order.

WALTER L. JACOB & CO., *Re* (1987) 3 BCC 532, Harman J.

380. Winding up—transfer of land by company in liquidation—validation after commencement of winding up—jurisdiction

[Companies Act 1948 (c.38), s.227 (now Insolvency Act 1986 (c.45), s.127).]

The Court may be prepared in certain circumstances retrospectively to validate a disposition made after the commencement of winding up.

The company had charged its main asset, a building site, to the bank. The bank was prepared to finance development of the site but could not do so after a winding up petition was served. The company then sold the site to another company to pay off the indebtedness; the bank would then finance the new company's development. The question was whether the court would validate the transfer retrospectively.

Held, validating the transfer, that the order would have been authorised if it had been made earlier, and the transfer would not then or now reduce assets available to unsecured creditors.

TRAMWAY BUILDING AND CONSTRUCTION CO., *Re* (1987) 3 BCC 443, Scott J.

381. Winding up—voluntary winding up—disclaimer of lease—effect of vesting order where onerous property disclaimed

[Companies Act 1985 (c.6), ss.618, 619; Insolvency Act 1986 (c.45), ss.178, 179.]

S.619(6) of the Companies Act 1985 enables an underlessee to apply for a vesting order with respect to property which a company in liquidation has been allowed to disclaim. The court dealt in this case with the effect on the disclaimer on the underlease, and on other parties entitled to apply under s.619(6).

In 1982 Bell granted a lease to A.E. Realisations (the company) for 25 years. Gold Case joined in the lease as surety for payment of the rent and also covenanted that if the lease was disclaimed by the company it would if required by Bell take a lease of the unexpired term of the lease.

In 1984 the company leased the premises to W for ten years, and W deposited with the company's solicitors £25,000 as security for the performance by W of the covenants in the underlease. The freehold was transferred to English National. In June 1985 the company went into liquidation and the liquidator successfully applied to disclaim the lease entered into with Bell. English National thereon called on Gold Case to take a lease under its covenant. Gold Case then applied in the present proceedings under ss.618 and 619 of the Companies Act 1985 for an order that the lease along with the underlease between the company and W be vested in it together with the benefit of the agreement whereby W had deposited £25,000 as security for performance of the covenants.

Held, that s.619(6) of the 1985 Act enabled an underlessee to apply for a vesting order in respect of property disclaimed by a company in liquidation. If the underlessee did not apply but other parties entitled to apply under the section did apply for a vesting order, the underlessee would be put to his election either himself to apply for a vesting order or to be excluded from all interest in the property. If the vesting order was made in favour of someone other than the underlessee, it would destroy the underlessee's interest in the property so that he would no longer have any rights of occupation or be obliged to pay the rent or perform any other covenants. As W had indicated that he did not wish the lease to be vested in him, an order of the court vesting the property in Gold Case would have no different effect than if the present lessor were to grant a new lease to Gold Case and so the application of Gold Case for a vesting order would be dismissed.

A. E. REALISATIONS (1985), *Re* [1987] BCLC 486, Vinelott J.

382. Winding up—voluntary winding up—insurance premiums paid by customers—whether premiums formed part of company's property. See MULTI GUARANTEE CO., *Re* §1427.

383. Winding up—voluntary winding up in progress—whether compulsory order for winding up should be made

In deciding whether or not to make a winding up order where there was a voluntary winding up in progress, the court was not obliged to give equal weight to all debts of an equal amount but must also consider the quality of the debts and to have regard to other interests that may influence the views of the creditors and in addition should take into account the general principles of fairness and morality that underlie the details of insolvency law.

F Ltd., held almost the whole of the share capital of the compamy. J was the controlling shareholder in F Ltd. and also in V Ltd. J claimed that the company owed him £58,000, owed F Ltd. £17,600 and V Ltd. £1,500. J and his wife, as directors of the company, convened an extraordinary general meeting of the company and a meeting of its creditors to consider a resolution to wind it up. Shortly after the notice was sent out, a petition to wind up the company was presented. A resolution to wind up the company was passed and H was appointed liquidator against the wishes of one creditor who wanted B appointed. This proposal was voted down by J. The petition was supported by 43 creditors and opposed by 12, including J. Conflicting evidence was given as to the debts owed to the supporting and opposing creditors.

Held, on the facts, taking into account the principles given above, that a winding up order should be made. The debts owed to J and his associated companies should not be taken into account and made determinative of the issue. The reason J wanted a voluntary winding up order was that he was willing to postpone the debts owed to him and his associated companies to the claims of other creditors so as to minimise the damage to his commercial reputation. This consideration of personal advantage should not be allowed to prevail over the views of the majority of other creditors. That majority would be left with a legitimate sense of grievance if against their wishes the winding up was left in the hands of a liquidator chosen by those in control of the company and who were prima facie responsible for its insolvency.

FALCON (R. J.) DEVELOPMENTS, *Re* [1987] BCLC 437, Vinelott J.

384. Winding up—whether transfer of lease pursuant to agreement constitutes a disposition

[Companies Act 1985 (c.6), s.522; Insolvency Act 1986 (c.45), s.127.]

Where, before the presentation of a winding up petition, a company has entered into an unconditional contract for the sale of property which is specifically enforceable, the completion of the contract in accordance with its terms after the presentation of the petition does not constitute a disposition within the meaning of s.522 of the Companies Act 1985.

The company entered into a contract in October 1985 for the sale of its leasehold premises, goodwill, fixtures and fittings, and its stock in trade. The contract provided that the company could rescind if it could not obtain the necessary consent from the landlord to the assignment. The completion date was January 31, 1986 but the purchaser was allowed into possession on paying a deposit in October 1985. A petition was presented to wind it up on December 5, 1985 and a compulsory winding up order was made on January 20, 1986. On January 17, 1986, the contract was completed and the lease transferred to the purchaser and the proceeds of sale given to the company's bank. An application was made for an order that the completion should not be avoided by s.522 of the Companies Act.

Held, that the order should be made. Where the contract entered into before the presentation of the petition was unconditional and specifically enforceable, the completion of the contract after presentation of the petition would not constitute a disposal. It might be otherwise where the contract was conditional or voidable. Although the company might have had the right to rescind if the lessor had refused his consent to the assignment, in practice it could not have been since the company had no money to repay the deposit and the company had been operating the business for a period of time. On the facts, in so far as the completion of the contract and the distribution of the assets were void as disposition under s.522, an order would be made that they should be treated as valid and effective as there would have been no conceivable benefit to the creditors in refusing consent.

Per curiam: Unless a contract entered into by a company in liquidation is quite plainly specifically enforceable and there is no possible defence, it would be prudent to seek the approval of the court for the completion of the contract.

FRENCH'S (WINE BAR), *Re* [1987] BCLC 499, Vinelott J.

385. Winding up petition—respondent—striking out

[Companies Act 1985 (c.6), s.459; Companies (Unfair Prejudice Applications) Proceedings Rules 1986 (S.I. 1986 No. 2000).]

All members of a small private company ought to be joined in a winding-up petition.

In 1979, the petitioner and three others set up in business, and took equal shares in a company of which all four were directors. Later one of them left the company and the other three bought his shares equally. In 1983, the company obtained capital from an investment company which agreed to provide it in return for preference shares and pre-emption provisions. A reorganisation took place, and then the petitioner was voted off the board. He presented his petition after finding, he alleged, that the directors had set up rival companies and stripped the company of its assets so that it was insolvent. There was no allegation that the investment company had been guilty of prejudicial acts. The investment company was a respondent to the petition but submitted that it ought not to be joined under s.459 unless some relief was sought against it.

Held, that the respondent company should not be struck out as a respondent. In the case of a small private company, every member ought to be joined. If the relief sought was the purchase of the petitioner's shares by the respondents against whom allegations of unfairly prejudicial conduct had been made, or the purchase by the petitioner of their shares, other shareholders would be affected if the articles contained pre-emption provisions which would be overridden by the purchase, or if the balance of voting rights would be affected, as it almost inevitably would. If an order for winding-up or regulation of the future conduct of the company was sought, those entitled to vote on a resolution for winding-up or for the appointment of directors should be heard. The investment company was clearly affected by the relief sought in the petition and was properly made a respondent. It would be unnecessary to join all the members where the articles contained no pre-emption provisions and some members were investors who took no part in the formation and management of the company, *e.g.* where there was a public limited company controlled *de facto* by a small group of shareholders. In such a case it might be sufficient merely to give notice of the petition. Under the Companies (Unfair Prejudice Applications) Proceedings Rules 1986, the court was required on the first hearing to give directions as to service of the petition on anyone not then a respondent. Any doubt could be resolved then.

COMPANY, A (No. 007281 of 1986), *Re* (1987) 3 BCC 375, Vinelott J.

COMPULSORY PURCHASE

386. Compensation—land—use restricted—valuation—whether to take account of restriction

A developers' agreement with the council restricting the use of land, operated as a restrictive covenant affecting the land for the purposes of valuation for compensation after compulsory purchase.

A development company bought 13 hectares of agricultural land near Towcester, and made an agreement under s.52 of the 1971 Act for outline planning permission for residential development and a site for a primary school. In 1983 the council compulsorily purchased 1.3 hectares for use as a primary school, and granted development permission for its erection. The developer applied for an order that the restriction imposed by the agreement should be discharged. The tribunal held that the agreement did not create a restrictive covenant and the 1.23 hectares should be valued without reference to the restriction for school purposes.

Held, allowing the appeal, that the agreement did operate as a *Tulk* v. *Moxhay* restrictive covenant, and it was not obsolete. The compensation must be determined on the basis that the land was affected by a restrictive covenant.

ABBEY HOMESTEADS (DEVELOPMENTS) *v.* NORTHAMPTONSHIRE COUNTY COUNCIL (1987) 53 P & C.R. 1, C.A.

387. Compensation for disturbance—single notice of entry physical possession taken in stages—date for assessment of compensation

[New Towns Act 1965 (c.59), sched. 6, para. 4(1)(2).]

When a single notice of entry upon land compulsorily acquired is served under para. 4(2) of sched. 6 of the New Towns Act 1965 the first entry on to any part of the land constitutes entry on to the whole of the land described in the notice for the purposes of calculating compensation.

Following a compulsory purchase order under s.7 of the New Towns Act 1965, the authority served on P a statutory notice of entry in accordance with para. 4(2) of sched. 6, describing the whole of the land. The authority then took possession of the land in eight separate parcels, P remaining in occupation until giving up actual possession. The lands tribunal held that P's compensation should be assessed by reference to the dates when actual possession was given up.

Held, allowing the appeal, that the first entry on to any part of the land described in a single notice constituted entry on to the whole of the laws for the purposes of calculating compensation.

Per curiam: an acquiring authority can, if it wishes, serve instead a series of notices.

CHILTON *v.* TELFORD DEVELOPMENT CORP. [1987] 1 W.L.R. 872, C.A.

388. Compulsory purchase order—confirmation by Secretary of State—discretion

The Secretary of State's power to confirm a compulsory purchase order is discretionary, and not subject to any special rule.

EVELYN DE ROTHSCHILD AND ERANDA HERDS *v.* SECRETARY OF STATE FOR TRANSPORT, *The Times,* November 16, 1987, D.C.

389. Compulsory purchase order—confirmation by Secretary of State—refusal to confirm—council's motives for making order

[Town and Country Planning Act 1971 (c.78), s.112(1).]

The Council applied for judicial review of a decision of the Secretary of State not to confirm Leicester City Council's compulsory purchase order.

Held, dismissing the application, that the Council's purpose in making the order was to encourage owners to make financial contributions towards a cost which would otherwise have to be borne by the ratepayers. That was not a proper reason. The Secretary of State had rightly refused to confirm the order.

R. *v.* SECRETARY OF STATE FOR THE ENVIRONMENT, *ex p.* LEICESTER CITY COUNCIL [1987] J.P.L. 787, McCullough J.

390. Compulsory purchase order—confirmation by Secretary of State—whether duty to obtain all necessary information—whether refusal to confirm order reasonable

The Secretary of State was not obliged to obtain all necessary information before refusing to confirm a compulsory purchase order; it was for the acquiring authority to lay all the necessary information before the Secretary of State to convince him to confirm the order.

The council decided to build a rear service road to shops on the main shopping street in Melton Mowbray. There were two viable routes for the road, scheme B involved the use of land belonging to shops to be served by the road and part of a public carpark. Scheme C involved the use of part of land held by the Council under the Open Spaces Act 1906 and a disused graveyard. The Council adopted scheme B and made a compulsory purchase order to acquire the necessary land. Objections were raised and a public inquiry was held in October 1982. One objector's written objections suggested scheme C should be followed. At the inquiry evidence was given that scheme C was to be preferred in highway engineering terms. The Council did not adopt scheme C on planning and legal grounds. The most detailed evidence was in the form of an extract of a planning committee meeting held in July 1980. The Council did not elaborate or explain what planning and legal difficulties prevented the adoption of scheme C. The Secretary of State refused to confirm the compulsory purchase order. The Council sought judicial review of that decision contending that there was ample evidence that scheme C was not viable, the council should have had an opportunity to call further evidence on scheme C and that the reasons for the Secretary of State's decision were incomprehensible.

Held, dismissing the application, that on the information put before him the Secretary of State was entirely justified in refusing to confirm the order on the ground that the non-viability of scheme C had not be made out. The Secretary of State was not under any duty to gather information showing that scheme C was viable. The Council, as the authority seeking the confirmation of the order, were under a duty to put all the necessary information before the Secretary of State to convince him to confirm the order. The Council had ample opportunity to present evidence that scheme C was not viable and ample notice that the viability of scheme C was a matter of importance. The Secretary of State's reasons for his decision could not be described as incomprehensible (*Prest* v. *Secretary of State for Wales* [1982] C.L.Y. 359, *Sabey (H.) & Co.* v. *Secretary of State for the Environment* [1978] C.L.Y. 22 considered).

R. *v.* SECRETARY OF STATE FOR THE ENVIRONMENT *ex p.* MELTON BOROUGH COUNCIL (1986) 52 P. & C.R. 318, Forbes J.

391. Lands Tribunal decisions

This was a reference to determine the compensation payable following the compulsory acquisition of premises in Derby, which were originally a dwelling-house but were last used as a printing workshop with ancillary offices and storerooms. Planning permission had been granted for use falling within Class III of the Town and Country Planning (Use Classes) Order 1972, and the authority stated that an application for planning permission for retail use under Class I of the Order was unlikely to have been refused. The tribunal found that there would be little or no advantage to a prospective developer in expending money on a conversion to such use, and accordingly valued the premises on the basis of availability for light industrial use. A rental value of £4,350 at eight years purchase gave a capital value of £34,000, from which £10,000 was deducted as representing the cost of necessary repairs, giving a final award of £24,800.

CLOWES (C. W.) (INVESTMENTS) *v.* DERBY CITY COUNCIL (Ref./197/1985) (1987) 283 E.G. 835.

392. This was a reference to determine the amount of compensation payable following the compulsory acquisition of an end-of-terrace building on three floors in a prominent position at the junction of two busy main roads in Chelmsford. The premises were let by the claimants on a 15-year lease from March 1982 at a rent of £5,000 for the first five years and £6,500 for the next five, the rent for the last five years being subject to review. On the ground floor of the building the lessee operated a Chinese takeaway restaurant, whilst the upper floors consisted of flats which were occupied by the lessee and his family. Attached to one of the flank walls of the building was an advertising hoarding, which had the benefit of a deemed consent under reg. 11 of the Town and Country Planning (Control of Advertising) Regulations 1984, and was at the valuation date let to an advertiser at £650 p.a. The tribunal found that the rent review clause would have given rise to a rent for the final five years of the term of at least £6,500, and treated the rent as available in perpetuity deferred for one year nine months, and as being reasonably secure. It accepted the claimant's evidence that the rental value of the hoarding would have been £900 p.a. after 1985, but treated the rental value as being slightly less secure than the rent payable under the lease. Total compensation was assessed at £70,072.

HARTNELL *v.* CHELMSFORD DISTRICT COUNCIL (Ref./8/1986) (1987) 284 E.G. 71.

393. This was a reference to determine the amount of compensation payable following the compulsory acquisition of a single-storey building and premises consisting of a workshop, offices, dark-room, store rooms and ancillary accommodation in Aston, Birmingham. The freehold premises had been owned and occupied for many years by L Ltd., a printing company producing commercial stationery and jobbing printing, whilst part of the premises were also occupied by an associated company CM Ltd., which had no staff and was a selling organisation for L Ltd's products. The premises had been included in a compulsory purchase order made in 1969, but no valid notice to treat or notice of entry had been served on either company. In October 1980, a further compulsory purchase order was made, which eventually took effect on November 30, 1981. L Ltd., received notices to treat and of entry on October 23, 1981, and bailiffs evicted both companies on December 23, 1981. L Ltd. thereupon ceased to trade, but CM moved first to temporary accomodation and then, in March 1983, to permanent premises. In assessing compensation for interest acquired payable to L Ltd., the tribunal assumed that necessary works had been carried out and then deducted their cost and a management fee, arriving at a net figure of £36,000. The authority argued that no compensation for disturbance was payable, on the grounds that both companies had failed to mitigate their loss, in particular by their failure to complete on a contract to acquire alternative premises entered into in January 1981. The tribunal however accepted evidence on behalf of L Ltd. and CM Ltd. that honest and strenuous efforts had been made to find suitable alternative accommodation, but that they had not had sufficient funds to purchase, lease or adapt alternative accommodation once found, especially in view of the making of the compulsory purchase order and the speed of its enforcement. The authority had accordingly failed to discharge the onus of proving that they had failed to mitigate their loss, and L Ltd.'s losses were to be assessed on the basis of total extinguishment of business. L Ltd. was thus awarded an agreed sum of £26,700 for losses on forced sale of plant and machinery, £125,000 for loss of goodwill, £2,310 for direct costs of eviction, and £11,400 for directors' and other expenses incurred in preparation of the claims. Total compensation payable to L Ltd. thus came to £201,410 plus surveyors' fees, whilst CM Ltd. were awarded removal costs totalling £5,065.86.

LINDON PRINT *v.* WEST MIDLANDS COUNTY COUNCIL (Ref./110/1982) (1987) 283 E.G. 70.

394. [Local Government, Planning and Land Act 1980 (c.65), s.141, Sched. 27.]

P claimed compensation for the land and for disturbance from D in respect of D's compulsory acquisition of considerable areas of land, buildings and docks in Liverpool.

Held, that (1) with reference to compensation for the loss of the properties (a) a possible lease that had never been entered into and which was not specifically enforceable was irrelevant (b) poor access to some of them had to be taken into account as did (c) P's liabilities to maintain river dock walls, etc. together with P's other statutory liabilities; (2) with reference to compensation for disturbance, P was not entitled to sums equivalent to redundancy payments or pension fund contributions in respect of staff made redundant by the compulsory acquisition since the Secretary of State had already made payments to P by way of grant which comprehended such losses, and P was not entitled to the claimed loss of rents because, *inter alia,* it was not shown that such loss was the natural and reasonable consequence of the acquisition. Nor was P entitled to compensation for loss of economy of scale since no such loss had been proved (*Bird* v. *Wakefield Metropolitan District Council* [1979] C.L.Y. 303, *Chapman Lowry & Puttick* v. *Chichester District Council* [1984] C.L.Y. 341, *Palatine Graphic Arts Co.* v. *Liverpool City Council* [1986] C.L.Y. 350, *Parry* v. *Cleaver* [1969] C.L.Y. 906, *Pointe Gourde Quarrying and Transport Co.* v. *Superintendent of Crown Lands* (1947–51) C.L.C. 1433, *Treml* v.

Gibson (E. W.) & Partners [1984] C.L.Y. 242, *Trocette Property Co.* v. *Greater London Council* [1984] R.V.R. 306 considered).

MERSEY DOCKS AND HARBOUR CO. *v.* MERSEYSIDE DEVELOPMENT CORPORATION (Ref./12/1983) (1987) 27 R.V.R. 97.

395. Rate of interest after entry

ACQUISITION OF LAND (RATE OF INTEREST AFTER ENTRY) REGULATIONS 1987 (No. 405) [45p], made under the Land Compensation Act 1961 (c.33), s.32(1); operative on April 3, 1987; reduces to $11\frac{1}{4}$ per cent per annum the rate of interest payable where entry is made onto land before the payment of compensation.

ACQUISITION OF LAND (RATE OF INTEREST AFTER ENTRY) (No. 2) REGULATIONS 1987 (No. 889) [45p], made under the Land Compensation Act 1961 s.32(1); operative on June 4, 1987; reduce to 10 per cent. per annum the rate of interest payable where entry is made on land before the payment of compensation.

396. Valuation of property—ten isolated houses

For valuation purposes a group of ten cottages in an isolated position and in poor repair were dealt with as a unit but in order to assess the value of the unit it was necessary to examine the values of the individual properties.

Held, that in so doing, where there was some doubt as to the correct valuation, the benefit of that doubt would be given to the claimant; the purchasing authority had wrongly failed to allow for the provision of improvement grants and regard should have been given to the likelihood of s.60 Housing Act 1974 certificates being given by a prospective purchaser. Otherwise the matter was dealt with on the facts.

SULLIVAN *v.* BROXTOWE BOROUGH COUNCIL (Ref/205/1984), (1986) 26 R.V.R. 243, Lands Tribunal.

CONFLICT OF LAWS

397. Choice of law rules—marriage—proposals for reform. See LAW REFORM, §2275.

398. Divorce—stay of proceedings—balance of fairness and convenience—juridical advantage. See K. *v.* K., §1717.

399. Divorce—stay of proceedings—foreign petition

[Domicile and Matrimonial Proceedings Act 1973 (c.45), Sched. 1, para. 9(1).]

In determining whether properly constituted matrimonial proceedings should be stayed under para. 9(1) and (2) of Sched. 1 to the Domicile and Matrimonial Proceedings Act 1973, the court should not in general be deterred from granting a stay merely because the plaintiff in this country would be deprived of a legitimate advantage, provided the court was satisfied that substantial justice would be done in the overseas forum.

The parties were French nationals who married there in 1977. H's family owned an estate there producing cognac. In 1979 they moved to London, and their child was born there in 1982. In 1984 W opened a business in New York and in March 1985 she took the child to New York and in April refused to move back to London at H's request. He started divorce proceedings in France and later W filed a petition in London for divorce. H applied to stay W's petition under s.5(6) and para. 9(1) of the Sched. 1 to the 1973 Act. The President refused the stay on the ground that under the French proceedings she might receive less favourable financial provision if she were to be found to be solely responsible for the breakdown of the marriage. The Court of Appeal dismissed H's appeal. H's further appeal to the House of Lords was allowed.

Held, that when considering the balance of fairness and convenience to determine whether the proceedings should be stayed, the court should adopt the same approach as that adopted at common law in cases of *forum non conveniens* where there was a *lis alibi pendens.* Accordingly the court should not, as a general rule, be deterred from granting a stay merely because the plaintiff in this country would be deprived of a legitimate personal or juridical advantage, provided that the court was satisfied that substantial justice would be done in the forum overseas. In the particular case, it was impossible to conclude that, objectively considered, justice would not be done if W was compelled to pursue her remedy for financial provision in France, which, most plainly, provided the natural forum for the dispute (dicta of Lord Diplock in *MacShannon* v. *Rockware Glass* [1978] C.L.Y. 2390, and *Abidin Daver, The* [1984] C.L.Y. 3151) considered; *Spiliada Maritime Corporation* v. *Cansulex* [1987] C.L.Y. 3135 applied).

DE DAMPIERRE *v.* DE DAMPIERRE [1987] 2 W.L.R. 1006, H.L.

400. Domicile—recommendations for reform of the rules for determining a person's domicile. See LAW REFORM, §2266.

401. Domicile—two residences—displacement of domicile of origin

The taxpayer was born in London of English parents. In 1979 her grandmother bought a house in Guernsey; in 1980, when the taxpayer was fifteen, her mother and younger sister took up residence with the grandmother. Her father continued to maintain a house in London. Throughout this time and through until 1984/85 the taxpayer continued in education in England, spending weekends and holiday periods in Guernsey. The taxpayer claimed to be domiciled in Guernsey for the years of assessment 1983/84 and 1984/85.

Held, dismissing the taxpayer's appeal, that in the circumstances that the taxpayer had not established her chief place of residence in Guernsey, she continued to enjoy her English domicile of origin.

PLUMMER *v.* I.R.C., *The Times,* October 24, 1987, Hoffmann J.

402. Enforcement of foreign judgment—examination of judgment debtor—whether jurisdiction to order answers relating to property outside jurisdiction

[Foreign Judgments (Reciprocal Enforcement) Act 1933 (c.13); R.S.C., Ord. 48, r.1(1).]

A judgment debtor may be required to answer questions relating to assets outside the jurisdiction.

I Ltd. obtained a judgment in France against G in the sum of $8,196,000, which was subsequently registered under the 1933 Act in the High Court in England. During his examination under R.S.C., Ord. 48, G refused to answer questions relating to assets held outside the jurisdiction. The judge ordered him to do so.

Held, that the judge was correct. The 1933 Act did not purport to confer any jurisdiction over assets held abroad, from which it followed that G could be compelled to disclose details of his extra-jurisdictional assets (*MacKinnon* v. *Donaldson, Lufkin and Jenrette Securities Corp.* [1986] C.L.Y. 1501 distinguished).

INTERPOOL *v.* GALANI [1987] 2 All E.R. 981, C.A.

403. *Forum conveniens*—civil action—whether conviction abroad relevant. See PURCELL *v.* KHAYAT, §3012.

404. *Forum conveniens*—restraint of foreign proceedings—injunction—jurisdiction. See PRACTICE, §3024.

405. Marital status—enforceability of foreign judgments

[Foreign Judgments (Reciprocal Enforcement) Act 1933 (c.13), s.8(1)(2); Domicile and Matrimonial Proceedings Act 1973 (c.45), s.16(1).]

Section 8 of the Foreign Judgments (Reciprocal Enforcement) Act 1933 does not apply to judgments affecting marital status.

H and W were married in Israel. The family later came to England where the marriage broke down. After formalities at the Beth Din in London H granted and W accepted a get acknowledging the dissolution of the marriage according to Jewish law. The district court of Haifa issued a judgment confirming the get. The question of the validity of the divorce arose. Since the proceeding, involving the Beth Din, was an extrajudicial proceeding, s.16(1) of the Domicile and Matrimonial Proceedings Act 1973 did not validate the divorce in English law. However, H argued that the get was valid in English law by virtue of s.8 of the Foreign Judgments (Reciprocal Enforcement) Act 1933.

Held, looking at the provisions of the Act as a whole, that the Act did not apply to judgments as to marital status and the divorce was invalid (dicta of Lord Reid in *Black-Clawson International* v. *Papierwerke Waldhof-Aschaffenburg Aktiengesellschaft A.G.* [1975] C.L.Y. 361 and of Sir John Arnold in *Vervaeke* v. *Smith; Messina and Att.-Gen Intervening* [1982] C.L.Y. 946 considered).

MAPLES (FORMERLY MELAMUD) *v.* MAPLES; MAPLES (FORMERLY MELAMUD) *v.* MELAMUD [1987] 3 W.L.R. 487, Latey J.

406. Moral rights—whether French laws applicable in France to English law contracts—copyright infringement

M suggested to P the idea for a film which R wrote. P informally assigned the rights in the film "The Aristocats" to M who assigned the rights to Disney, who some five years later made an animated cartoon entitled "The Aristocats". Six years later P brought an action in France against Disney, seeking to set aside the original assignments. The trial court in Paris found that it had jurisdiction but that since laches under English law was established the assignments were valid. It further found a breach of P's droit moral in D's failure to acknowledge paternity and awarded him 250,000 French francs.

Held, on appeal, that (1) English law does not recognise droit moral; (2) since the contracts were all governed by English law he could not rely on droit moral, even though he was a U.S. citizen resident in France. Defendants appeal allowed.

ROWE *v.* WALT DISNEY PRODUCTIONS [1987] F.S.R. 36 Cour d'Appel, Paris.

407. Reciprocal enforcement—maintenance orders

RECIPROCAL ENFORCEMENT OF MAINTENANCE ORDERS (HAGUE CONVENTION COUNTRIES) (VARIATION) ORDER 1987 (No. 1282) [45p], made under the Maintenance Orders (Reciprocal Enforcement) Act 1972 (c.18), ss.40, 45(1); operative on August 20, 1987; amends S.I. 1979 No. 1317 by adding the Federal Republic of Germany to the list of Hague Convention Countries.

408. Reinsurance contract—reinsurance in country other than that of original contract of insurance. See FORSIKRINGSAKTIELSKAPET VESTA *v.* BUTCHER, §2567.

409. Sequestration—trade union fined for civil contempt—union funds transferred to bank in Republic of Ireland

[Rep. of Ire.] The National Union of Mineworkers failed to comply with an order of the High Court in England restraining it from doing certain acts and was fined £200,000 for contempt. When it failed to pay the fine, sequestrators were appointed by the High Court and they were authorised to bring proceedings in the Republic of Ireland for the recovery of N.U.M. funds which were on current account with D2, a bank in the Republic. The High Court in the Republic, on application by the sequestrators, granted an interim injunction restraining the N.U.M. and the bank from dealing with the funds and ordering the bank to produce books for inspection by the sequestrators. The High Court in England, by interlocutory order, removed the trustees of the N.U.M.'s assets and appointed a receiver to recover those assets. The receiver was added as a fifth plaintiff to the action brought in the High Court in the Republic by the sequestrators.

Held, that (1) the contempt of which the N.U.M. was convicted was contumacious civil contempt, the proceedings by the sequestrators were penal in effect and, accordingly, the claims by the sequestrators must be dismissed as the High Court would not entertain a suit brought for the purpose of enforcing within the Republic a penal law or process of a foreign State; (2) the receivership was not simply an indirect method of enforcing the sequestration and, accordingly, was not an indirect attempt to enforce the penal law of a foreign State but, as the order appointing the receiver was interlocutory in nature, the funds should stay with D2, the bank, until permanent trustees of the N.U.M.'s funds were appointed in accordance with English law.

LARKINS *v.* NATIONAL UNION OF MINEWORKERS [1985] I.R. 671, Barrington J.

CONSTITUTIONAL LAW

410. Ministers—transfer of functions

TRANSFER OF FUNCTIONS (MINISTER FOR THE CIVIL SERVICE AND TREASURY) ORDER 1987 (No. 2039) [85p], made under the Ministers of the Crown Act 1975 (c.26), s.1; operative on December 25, 1987; transfers to the Treasury some of the functions of the Minister for the Civil Service.

CONSUMER CREDIT

411. Exempt agreements

CONSUMER CREDIT (EXEMPT AGREEMENTS) (No. 2) (AMENDMENT) ORDER 1987 (No. 1578) [45p], made under the Consumer Credit Act 1974 (c.39), ss.16(1)(4), 182(2)(4); operative on October 1, 1987; further amends S.I. 1985 No. 757 so as to exempt credit agreements secured on land where creditor is specified in the Order.

CONTRACT

412. Accord and satisfaction—acceptance of lesser sum—consideration

P claimed that it was agreed that D would pay them a commission of 10 per cent. of the price on sale of a certain knitting machine. D said that a commission of 5 per cent.

only was agreed to be paid. P rendered an invoice for 10 per cent. There was no reply to it. P then made attempts to recover the 10 per cent. commission. A meeting then took place. At that meeting the invoice for the 10 per cent. commission was amended so as to claim on a basis of 5 per cent. and P's representative initialed the amended invoice underneath the words "accepted in full and final settlement." D then immediately paid the 5 per cent. commission (£3,000). P thereafter claimed the remaining 5 per cent. commission on the basis that the commission payable was 10 per cent. The judge found that the original agreement between the parties was that a 10 per cent. commission was to be paid and that there had been no consideration for the agreement to accept £3,000 in full and final settlement. The judge accordingly gave judgment in favour of P. D appealed.

Held, dismissing the appeal, that the judge was entitled on the evidence to hold that there was no consideration for the agreement (*D. & C. Builders* v. *Rees* [1966] C.L.Y. 1739 considered).

TINEY ENGINEERING *v.* AMODS KNITTING MACHINERY, May 15, 1986 (C.A.T. No. 440).

413. Accord and satisfaction—acceptance of lesser sum—extent of compromise

P suffered damages in a road accident for which D admitted liability. P were paid part of the damages directly from their insurers and they entered into correspondence with D's solicitors in respect of their uninsured losses which amounted to £166·57 plus V.A.T. They eventually accepted a sum of £100 plus V.A.T. signing a receipt that the sum of £115 was being accepted "in full and final settlement of all our claims" arising out of the accident. In proceedings brought against D by P's insurers in respect of the moneys paid by them to P, D contended, *inter alia*, that he had a complete defence to the claim by virtue of the form of receipt signed by P.

Held, that the contract of compromise between P and D was constituted by several documents and not just the form of receipt. The court could look at the covering with which the form of receipt was enclosed for the purpose of construing the form of receipt. On its true construction the compromise was in respect of P's uninsured losses only and not all their claim against D. (*Neuchatel Asphalte Co.* v. *Barnett* [1957] C.L.Y. 235 applied).

CAPON *v.* EVANS, April 11, 1986 (C.A.T. No. 413).

414. Arbitration clause—allegations of fraud

[Arbitration Act 1950 (c.27), ss.4 and 24.]

Where a party to an agreement containing an arbitration clause is suing the other party alleging fraud, the court will normally, on the application of the party against whom fraud is alleged, stay the action to enable the matter to be arbitrated (*Russell* v. *Russell* (1880) 14 Ch.D. 417 considered).

CUNNINGHAM-REID *v.* BUCHANAN-JARDINE, *The Times,* June 27, 1987, C.A.

415. Breach—damages—mitigation—onus of proof

[Aus.] Where, in an action for damages for breach of contract, the defendant alleges that the plaintiff failed to mitigate its loss, the onus rests upon the former to prove a failure to take reasonable steps to mitigate loss (*Selvanayagau* v. *University of the West Indies* [1983] C.L.Y. 1064 not followed and *Temple Bar (Owners)* v. *Guildford (Owners); The Guildford* [1956] C.L.Y. 8249 considered).

METAL FABRICATIONS (VIC.) PTY. *v.* KELCEY [1986] V.R. 507, Supreme Ct. of Victoria.

416. Breach—oral contract—whether contract existed—whether exclusive jurisdiction clause incorporated. See COCOA MERCHANTS *v.* NORTH BORNEO PLANTATIONS SDN BHD, §3132.

417. Breach—tour operator—extent of liability. See KEMP *v.* INTASUN HOLIDAYS, §1130.

418. Breach—tour operator—honeymoon

The plaintiffs booked their honeymoon in Tenerife with the defendant tour operator. As a result of industrial action and technical problems, their flight was late, stopped for several hours in Madrid, and they arrived over a day late in Tenerife. This was a bitterly upsetting start to their honeymoon. Furthermore, no-one from the defendants was able to put the minds of the plaintiffs at rest as to what was going on or why.

Held, that a tour operator is not liable for the acts of a properly chosen sub-contracting airline. This is just common sense as they have no control over the airline. Furthermore, even if that were wrong, the defendants could rely on their exclusion clauses as these were not unfair contract terms in a field where the plaintiffs had plenty of choice from a large number of tour operators. The defendants should, however, have done more to reassure the plaintiffs and for their breach of contract in failing to do so, there would be a total award of £50.

USHER *v.* INTASUN HOLIDAYS, May 18, 1987; Mr. Registrar H. D. H. Jones, Cardiff County Ct. [*Ex rel. Mason-Bond, Solicitors.*]

419. Breach of condition—repudiation—penalty

A clause making time of the essence and thus prompt performance a condition of a contract is not to be struck down merely because a breach of the obligation would not be sufficient on its own to constitute a repudiation.

D hired a computer from P. By clause 2(*a*) of the hire agreement prompt payment of the quarterly rental was to be of the essence of the contract. By clause 5 P was entitled to repossess in the event of failure to pay punctually and by clause 6(*a*) in the event of repossession D was to pay all arrears, damages for breach and all further rentals which would have fallen due. D failed to pay punctually.

Held, (1) D had not repudiated the agreement, and clause 6(*a*) was a penalty in so far as it related to rental instalments which had not accrued, but (2), a clause making time of the essence and thus prompt performance a condition was not to be struck down merely because breach would not have been sufficient on its own to constitute repudiation. Accordingly P were entitled to their full damages. (*Steedman* v. *Drinkle* [1916] A.C. 275, *Capital Finance Co.* v. *Donati* [1977] C.L.Y. 1504, C.A. and *Financings* v. *Baldock* [1963] C.L.Y. 1639, C.A. applied).

LOMBARD NORTH CENTRAL *v.* BUTTERWORTH [1987] 2 W.L.R. 7 C.A.

420. Building contract—whether implied term to nominate new sub-contractor—default—cost of delay. See BUILDING AND CONSTRUCTION, §225.

421. Commission paid for personal influence—enforceability of such a contract—public policy

P paid D a commission to use his influence with a foreign government minister to secure benefits for P.

Held, that this contract was unenforceable as being contrary to English public policy on moral grounds, as well as being contrary to public policy in the country of performance (*Montefiore* [1918] 2 K.B. 241 applied).

LEMENDA TRADING CO. *v.* AFRICAN MIDDLE EAST PETROLEUM CO., *Financial Times,* December 2, 1987, Phillips J.

422. Construction—joint venture agreement—strike—whether *force majeure* clause applicable

P and D had been operating in competition in and about the provision of ferry services from the U.K. to the Channel Islands. In 1986 they entered into discussions designed to merge their operations and provide a single profitable operation. A Joint Venture Agreement (JVA) was concluded, which provided that P should provide one vessel, and D two vessels to be demise chartered to a new company. The crews of D's vessels promptly took industrial action and organised sit-ins. D offered to time charter the vessels to the company set up by the JVA, although this would have prevented them from using offshore crews. P commenced proceedings, claiming that D was in breach.

Held, that (1) upon its true construction the JVA did not permit the time chartering of vessels to the JVA company; (2) although D sought to rely upon the strikes as *force majeure* under the JVA, D were unable to show that the strikes had come about for reasons beyond their control, or that they had taken reasonable steps to mitigate its effects. There would be judgment for P.

CHANNEL ISLAND FERRIES *v.* SEALINK U.K. [1987] 1 Lloyd's Rep. 559, Hirst J.

423. Construction of clause—liability for claims—whether an exclusion clause

[Unfair Contract Terms Act 1977 (c.50), ss.2(2), 11(1)].

A clause in a plant hire contract providing for the hirer to be liable for negligence upon the part of the owners employee operating the plant was an exclusion clause in that the owner sought to place reliance on it to exclude his liability to the hirer.

D was engaged in the plant hire business. P hired an excavator and a driver from D. The hire agreement was on the Construction Plant Association's standard terms and conditions. Clause 8 provided that operators should for all purposes be regarded as the servants of the hirer who alone should be responsible for all claims arising in connection with the operation of the plant. The driver of the excavator negligently caused over £3,000 worth of damage to P's premises. D conceded that in the normal course of events they would be liable for the negligence of the driver but contended that clause 8 of the contract provided them with a complete defence. P contended that clause 8 on its wording did not exclude D's liability and that if it did, D was precluded from relying on it by virtue of the provisions of the Unfair Contract Terms Act 1977. The trial judge upheld P's second contention and found against D.

Held, dismissing D's appeal, that it could not be argued that there was no negligence on the part of D within the meaning of s.1(1) of the Act where the contract specifically excluded any duty to take care. In considering whether there was a breach of a duty or obligation of the nature referred to in s.1(1) of the Act, the court had to leave out of account the term relied on by D to defeat P's claim. Clause 8 was a term that excluded or restricted liability within the meaning of s.2(2) of the Act. The court had to consider the effect of the term. The effect of clause 8 was to exclude D's liability for the acts of their employee. On the evidence adduced at the trial it was not possible to say that the judge erred in the circumstances of this particular case in holding that clause 8 did not satisfy the requirement of reasonableness set out in the Act (*Mitchell (George) (Chesterhall)* v. *Finney Lock Seeds* [1983] C.L.Y. 3314 applied).

PHILLIPS PRODUCTS *v.* HYLAND (NOTE) [1987] 1 W.L.R. 659, C.A.

424. Construction of clause—liability for claims—whether an exclusion clause

A clause in a plant hire contract providing for the hirer to be liable for negligence upon the part of the owner's employee operating the plant was not an exclusion clause in that it did not purport to exclude liability to a person injured by the employee's negligence.

D was engaged in the business of hiring out plant and machinery with operators if required. P and H were both operators employed by D. Plant and machinery was hired together with P and H as operators by TP. P was killed due to H's negligence. P's estate sued D and TP and obtained judgment against D. D claimed to be indemnified by TP under the terms of the hire agreement. The hire agreement was on the Construction Plant Association's standard terms and conditions clause 8 of which provided that operators should for all purposes be regarded as the servants of the hirer who alone should be responsible for all claims arising in connection with the operation of the plant or machinery. D succeeded against TP. TP appealed arguing that clause 8 was not sufficiently well worded to absolve D of liability for the negligence of their employees or alternatively it was an exclusion clause and thus invalidated by s.2(1) Unfair Contract Terms Act 1977.

Held, dismissing TP's appeal, that (1) the clause was effective to pass liability for H's negligence from D to TP at common law (*Spalding* v. *Tarmac Civil Engineering* [1967] C.L.Y. 361 applied); (2) clause 8 was not a clause seeking to restrict or exclude liability for negligence within the meaning of s.2(1) Unfair Contract Terms Act 1977. S.2(1) was concerned to protect the victim of negligence, *i.e.* P. clause 8 did not purport to restrict or exclude the liability owed to P. By clause 8, D and TP merely decided between themselves which of them was to bear that liability (*Phillips Products* v. *Hyland (Note)* [1987] C.L.Y. 423 distinguished).

THOMPSON *v.* LOHAN (T.) (PLANT HIRE) [1987] 1 W.L.R. 649, C.A.

425. Construction of document—*contra proferentem* rule

The rule that a document is to be construed *contra proferentem* should only be used as a last resort, and where the document is open to more than one interpretation. The rule does not impose on the party who drew up the agreement the burden of establishing what it means, nor that it is not only capable of being enforced but also intelligible to the other side.

MACEY *v.* QAZI, *The Times,* January 13, 1987, C.A.

426. Consumer Protection Act 1987 (c.43). See TORT, §3583.

427. Contract of affreightment—concluded contract—whether broker had authority to conclude agreement

A agreed to sell a quantity of Romanian fertiliser to B, on f.o.b. terms. Brokers were instructed to find tonnage to lift the cargo. P instructed two firms of brokers, H and S, and H in their turn instructed D. D entered into negotiations with P, a shipowner and agreement was reached. B refused to ratify the agreement having agreed, through S, to place the cargo with other owners. P commenced proceedings in Singapore against B and D, although it soon transpired that D had no authority to act on behalf of B. D then added H as third party, claiming indemnity. The Court of Appeal in Singapore held that there was no concluded contract reached with P, but had there been such a contract, then D had been authorised by H to enter into the contract. P and H appealed to the Privy Council.

Held, that (1) on the facts and the evidence a binding contract of affreightment had been reached between P and D, and D were liable to damages for breach of warranty of authority; (2) H had authorised D to conclude the contract, and D was entitled to be indemnified by H.

GRACE SHIPPING INC. AND HAI NGLAN CO. *v.* C. F. SHARP & CO. (MALAYA) PTE. [1987] 1 Lloyd's Rep. 207, P.C.

428. Contract of affreightment—insolvency of shipowners leading to unreliability in performance—whether breach going to root of contract

This Canadian case concerned a contract of affreightment between P and D for the carriage by P of D's lumber products. During the currency of the contract, P made an application to the Japanese Courts, thereby indicating it was or might be insolvent. P's vessel, which had D's cargo on board, was arrested by stevedores and U.S. ports refused to handle the vessel unless part expenses were put up in advance. Similar problems occurred with another vessel, and D sought an assurance that their vessel would not be delayed. P could not give such an assurance, and D purported to accept P's conduct as being a repudiation of the contract. P claimed that such repudiation was wrongful.

Held, that (1) D was entitled to doubt P's future ability to perform the C.O.A., provided that D's decision to accept an alleged repudiation was reasonably based upon such a doubt; (2) D was entitled to rely upon repudiation by conduct rather than upon bare future impossibility of performance by P; (3) the apparent loss of reliability by P was a breach going to the root of the contract that amounted to a renunciation of the contract.

SANKO STEAMSHIP CO. *v.* EACOM TIMBER SALES; SANKO IRIS AND SANKO VENUS, THE [1987] 1 Lloyd's Rep. 487, Supreme Ct. of British Columbia, Macdonald J.

429. Contract of employment—breach—terms of contract—remedies. See STUBBES *v.* TROWER STILL & KEELING, §1301.

430. Course of dealings between parties—implied terms

P claimed against D as surety £5,533 the price of goods sold and delivered to D's company. There had been a number of transactions between the parties. The goods supplied by P would be sent with their "Order/Confirmation of Order" form which was brought back after having been signed by D on delivery of the goods. The form contained on the front (amongst other things) two boxes for signatures, one for "The Buyer" and one for "The Surety". The reverse side of the form set out the surety clause. On the first and second occasions D signed both The Buyer box and The Surety box. On the third and fourth occasions D did not sign The Buyer but signed The Surety box only. On the fifth occasion (the subject matter of the present action) the two boxes were signed upon delivery of the goods by Mr. Harris D's employee as D was busy elsewhere. However as Mr. Harris was not known to P, P later brought back the form to be signed by D and D then signed the form himself. The question was whether there was a sufficient course of dealing between the parties to show that D had knowledge of the terms of the suretyship contained on the back of the form or to understand what he was doing when he filled in the surety box on the front of the order form and signed it. It was contended that the contract in the case had been made on the telephone, that it had been executed by delivery of the goods and thereafter the fact that D signed the form at the request of P did not mean that he should be fixed with knowledge, or that in doing so, he was making himself responsible for the price of £5,533.

Held, dismissing D's appeal, that there was here such a course of dealing as would lead to the inference that (i) D knew that if he gave the order over the telephone, when the goods were delivered there would also be not merely the delivery note but the confirmation of order document with it and that a signature would be required by him to be taken back by the van driver; (ii) looking at the documents which had been signed in the past where D had on two occasions signed both The Buyer box and The Surety box, that D was well aware that it was a term of his contract with P that the goods would only be supplied to his company on the understanding that D would make himself the surety for the company for the payment of the price of the goods (*McCutcheon* v. *MacBrayne (David)* [1964] C.L.Y. 568 distinguished).

PLM TRADING CO. (INTERNATIONAL) *v.* GEORGIOU, June 6, 1986 (C.A.T. No. 538).

431. Covenant against competition—enforcement—injunction–scope

Where a contract of employment contained a covenant against an employee competing with his former employers, that can be enforced by injunction, and the injunction should cover dealing with all customers of the employers, even those who have stated that they have no desire to trade with the employer in the future.

In 1985 the defendants, an associate director and a senior designer employed by the plaintiffs, left to set up business on their own. Their contracts of employment contained a covenant not to canvass, solicit, or accept from any client of the plaintiffs any business for two years from the termination of their contracts. In December 1986, the plaintiff learned that clients of theirs were about to place a contract with the defendants and sought an injunction to restrain the defendants from acting in breach of their covenants. The clients were not in any event going to place further business with the plaintiffs. The judge found that the covenants were enforceable but excluded the particular contract from the scope of an interlocutory injunction on the balance of convenience.

Held, allowing the appeal, that although a covenant restraining competition would always be looked at closely, if the court decided that it would be just to grant an interlocutory injunction, the plaintiff was entitled prima facie to protection in respect of all his customers, and it was wrong in principle to exclude some. The fact that a particular customer would not do any further business with the plaintiff was not *per se* a reason for excluding him from the scope of the injunction since such an eventuality was the very thing against which the covenant was designed to give protection.

Per curiam: since the decision to grant or withhold an injunction is usually decisive because of the short time limits involved, the court must decide if the covenant is prima facie good: if so, in the ordinary course of events, an offending defendant should be restrained. (Dictum of Lord Denning M.R. in *Office Overload* v. *Gunn* [1976] C.L.Y. 2160 applied).

JOHN MICHAEL DESIGN *v.* COOKE [1987] 2 All E.R. 332, C.A.

432. Enforcement—contracts designed to deceive third parties—public policy

English courts have, as a matter of public policy, always refused to allow claims based on contracts drafted or structured so as to mislead third parties. On this head of public policy, however, the courts should always proceed with great caution, on the particular facts of the case. The court gave leave to argue the point of whether a party could rely on a contract that was lawful but intended to deceive (*Alexander* v. *Rayson* [1936] 1 K.B. 169 and *Saunders* v. *Edwards* [1987] C.L.Y. 1826 applied).

MITSUBISHI CORP. *v.* ALAFONZOS, *Financial Times,* October 28, 1987, Steyn J.

433. Enforcement of agreement by party in default—construction of contract

The question whether a party in default on an agreement can enforce a clause thereof is a question of construction of the agreement (*New Zealand Shipping Co.* v. *Société des Ateliers et Chantiers de France* [1919] A.C. 1, *Quesnel Forks Gold Mining Co.* v. *Ward* [1920] A.C. 222 considered).

ALGHUSSEIN ESTABLISHMENT *v.* ETON COLLEGE, *The Times,* February 16, 1987, C.A.

434. Hire—defective goods—measure of damages

Where a hirer of defective goods has lost his right to repudiate the agreement through delay in communicating his intention to, he is nonetheless entitled to damages which would amount to an equivalent sum to that outstanding under the agreement subject to a deduction for any use of the goods.

U.C.B. LEASING *v.* HOLTOM, *The Independent,* June 24, 1987, C.A.

435. Illegality—evasion of stamp duty by false apportionment of value between house and chattels—effect of illegality. See SAUNDERS *v.* EDWARDS, §1826.

436. International body—action against individual members—liability. See RAYNER (J.H.) (MINCING LANE) *v.* DEPARTMENT OF TRADE AND INDUSTRY, §2092.

437. JCT standard form—dispute at date of contract—whether dispute was one arising in connection with the contract—whether dispute fell within the scope of the arbitration clause. See ASHVILLE INVESTMENTS *v.* ELMER CONTRACTORS, §140.

438. JCT standard form—retention monies—whether necessary to set aside separate trust fund

P undertook to construct an hotel for D. The contract was in the JCT standard form 1963 edition 1977 revision. Disputes arose between the parties which were referred to arbitration. The accumulated retention fund was in excess of £350,000 and P applied for a mandatory injunction ordering D to pay the sum into a separate bank account to be applied in accordance with clause 30(4)(*a*) of the conditions. D resisted the application on the ground that the architect had issued a clause 22 certificate and that the liquidated and ascertained damages which D were entitled to deduct in reliance upon that certificate exceeded the aggregate of the retained monies.

Held, that on the true construction of clauses 22 and 30(4)(*a*) of the conditions, where there was a subsisting right of the employer to deduct liquidated and ascertained damages there was no obligation to set aside equivalent retained funds.

BOOT (HENRY) BUILDING *v.* CROYDON HOTEL AND LEISURE CO. (1986) 2 Const. L.J. 183 C.A.

439. Leasing agreement for chattels—non-payment of instalments of rent—lessee not repudiating—measure of damages— penalty clause

[Aus.] A was sued on guarantees in relation to two lease agreements made with AFL as lessor. The extent of A's liability was measured by that of the principal debtor, the lessee. In breach of each agreement but without repudiation, the lessee failed to pay instalments when they became due and AFL exercised its right to determine each hiring. It was conceded that a provision requiring the lessee to pay the full balance of the unpaid rent to AFL was, in the circumstances, a penalty. It was held that AFL was entitled to recover only the sum of unpaid instalments of rent at the date of termination or repossession with interest.

Held, by a majority, that AFL's appeal should be dismissed. (1) *Per* Gibbs C.J.: AFL was entitled to recover its actual damage which flowed from the breach. The additional damage claimed resulted not from the breach but from the determination of the hiring, which AFL chose to bring about; (2) *per* Mason and Wilson JJ.: when a lessor terminates pursuant to a contractual right for breach by the lessee, the loss which he can recover for non-fundamental breach is limited to the loss flowing from the lessee's breach. The loss flowing from the termination is not recoverable, being attributable to the lessor's act, not the lessee's conduct (*Financings* v. *Baldock* [1963] C.L.Y. 1639 approved and *Bridge* v. *Campbell Discount Co.* [1962] C.L.Y. 1307 distinguished).

AMEV- UDC FINANCE *v.* AUSTIN, 68 A.L.R. 185, High Ct. of Australia.

440. Letter of comfort—offer to take over liabilities of subsidiary—whether offer accepted—time limit for acceptance

Where a company offered to take over the liabilities of its subsidiary in the event that it disposed of the subsidiary, the offer lapsed if it was not accepted within a reasonable time of the disposal of the subsidiary.

P agreed to lease computer equipment to CMC Italy under three separate leases for five year periods in 1979, 1980 and 1981. The equipment was valued at approximately two billion Italian Lire. CMC Italy was a wholly owned subsidiary of D. Prior to the lease agreements, D provided P with a letter of comfort. In the letter, D undertook to notify P prior to the disposal of their interest in CMC Italy during the life of the leases. D also undertook to take over the liabilities of CMC Italy to P in the event that the new shareholders were unacceptable to P. In December 1981, D disposed of its interest in CMC Italy. CMC Italy notified P of the disposal on December 14, 1981.

P received confirmation in January 1982 that D had disposed of its interest in CMC Italy. On July 23, 1982, CMC Italy went into liquidation. By letter dated September 3, 1982, P called upon D to discharge CMC Italy's liabilities to P stating that P did not find the new shareholders acceptable. D refused to do so on the ground that it was too late for P to claim under the letters of comfort. P issued proceedings against D relying upon D's failure to give prior notification of the disposal of CMC Italy and D's failure to take over CMC Italy's liabilities after September 3, 1982. The trial judge held that the undertaking to take over CMC Italy's liabilities was an offer that required acceptance by P within a reasonable time. He found four months from January 1982 to be a reasonable time and that P had not accepted the offer within that time.

Held, dismissing P's appeals, that the letter of comfort conferred an option on P exercisable in the event that D disposed of CMC Italy and its new shareholders were unacceptable to P. D could not be under any liability to P until their offer to take over the liabilities of CMC Italy had been accepted. As the offer was not limited in time expressly, it lapsed after a reasonable time for acceptance had passed. It was not possible to impugn the judge's conclusion that four months from January 1982 was a reasonable time. D's offer was not accepted within that time and thereafter lapsed. D's failure to give notice of the disposal could only affect the time from which a reasonable time to accept the offer might start to run. The failure to give notice could not turn the offer or option into an everlasting one.

CHEMCO LEASING S.p.A. *v.* REDIFFUSION [1987] 1 FTLR 201, C.A.

441. Licence of property—no express term as to fitness—whether term to be implied

When considering whether a term must necessarily be implied into a licence to give it efficacy, the Court will consider the nature of the premises and the use to which they are being put.

P used an oven, which had formerly been part of a bacon curing factory, for the storage and sale of antiques. Her use was on the basis of a licence from D, which could be determined on non-payment of the licence fee. D determined the licence for non-payment, and P contended that D was in breach of an implied term that the oven should at all times be fit for the sale and storage of antiques. Appealed.

Held, that, (i) the nature of the premises was to be considered when considering whether such a term had to be implied into the licence; having regard to the fact that this was a bacon curing oven built over 100 years ago, there was no need to imply such a term in order to give efficacy to the licence; (ii) in any event, P's occupation of the oven had been the subject of litigation which had been compromised in 1969; that was the occasion on which any such term as was now alleged should have been incorporated into the licence, and expressly so.

MORRIS-THOMAS *v.* PETTICOAT LANE RENTALS (1987) 53 P. & C.R. 238, C.A.

442. Minors' Contracts Act 1987 (c.13)

This Act amends the law relating to minors' contracts.

The Act received the Royal Assent on April 9, 1987, and comes into force two months from that date.

The Act extends to England and Wales only.

443. Mixing of goods—same nature and quality—entitlement

Where A mixes up his foods with those of B which are substantially of the same nature and quality, his entitlement is to receive such proportion as represents his food with any doubt resolved against him. If his action has caused B loss he is liable in damages.

INDIAN OIL CORP. *v.* GREENSTONE SHIPPING CO. S.A. (PANAMA), *The Times,* April 23, 1987, Staughton J.

444. Negotiations—whether final contract ever concluded.

P and D negotiated for the sale by the former to the latter of 21,000 MT of Chinese manioc and by the latter to the former of a like quantity of Thai tapioca. D contended that a concluded contract had been reached, but although many of the terms had been agreed, P maintained that no final contract had been arrived at. Hirst J. held on the evidence that the contract was never finally concluded. P appealed.

Held, dismissing the appeal, that on the facts and the evidence it was clear that the parties were still negotiating at the time when P contended the contract had been concluded.

PAGNAN SpA *v.* GRANARIA BV [1986] 2 Lloyd's Rep. 547, C.A.

445. Onerous condition—standard terms and conditions—whether part of contract

An unusually onerous condition in a form of standard terms and conditions must be specifically drawn to the attention of the contracting party before it becomes part of the contract (*Parker* v. *South Eastern Railway* (1877) 2 C.P.D. 416, *Spurling* v. *Bradshaw* [1956] C.L.Y. 525, *Thornton* v. *Shoe Lane Parking* [1971] C.L.Y. 1741 considered).

INTERFOTO PICTURE LIBRARY *v.* STILETTO VISUAL PROGRAMMES, *The Times,* November 14, 1987, C.A.

446. Pre-incorporation contract—validity—estoppel

[Companies Act 1985 (c.6), s.36(4), 735.]

A contract did not exist where it had been made between a company and another before the formation of the company: nor could an estoppel arise in those circumstances.

The first plaintiff claimed on a contract alleged to have been made in December 1985. In fact the plaintiff was only incorporated in Guernsey in February 1986. The plaintiff argued that there was a valid contract signed for the plaintiff in January 1986 and the defendant had signed after the plaintiff was incorporated, constituting acceptance by the defendant of an offer in writing extant at the time of the acceptance. The plaintiff also argued that the defendant was estopped from denying the validity of the contract because the parties subsequently acted on a common belief that there was such a contract. Thirdly, the plaintiff argued that the fourth plaintiff, Mr. de Rossi, was the contracting party with the defendant under s.36(4) of the Companies Act 1985 which provides: "where a contract purports to be made by a company, or by a person as agent for a company, at a time when the company has not been formed, then . . . the contract has effect as one entered into by the person purporting to act for the company or as agent for it." The plaintiffs also claimed in the alternative on a *quantum meruit* as for moneys had and received.

Held, giving judgment for the defendant, that, (1) There was no evidence that the defendant had signed the contract after the date of incorporation of the plaintiff. It was signed by both parties before the incorporation. There was no contract since if someone did not exist, they could not contract. (2) There was no estoppel on the basis of a common mistake. Where one party did not exist at the time of the supposed assumption of agreed facts, it could not make an assumption of agreed facts. (3) "Company" in s.36(4) was restricted to U.K. companies: see s.735(1). As the first plaintiff was a Guernsey company, the fourth party was not a contracting party. (4) There was no basis for a claim for *quantum meruit*. It was impossible to make out where both parties acted on the basis of a contract. Likewise there was no claim for moneys had and received since the consideration, if there had been a contract, had not failed at all.

ROVER INTERNATIONAL *v.* CANNON FILM SALES (1987) 3 BCC 369, Harman J.

447. Recission—meaning of "new"—effect of damage

Where a vehicle has been damaged to the point that it cannot be restored to a new condition it cannot properly be described in a contract of sale as "new" (*Hill (Christopher)* v. *Ashington Piggeries* [1971] C.L.Y. 10517 considered).

RAYNHAM FARM CO. *v.* SYMBOL MOTOR CORP., *The Times*, January 27, 1987, Michael Wright Q.C.

448. Repayment term—default—whether term constituted a penalty clause

A shipbuilding contract contained a provision that if repayment instalments were not kept up, the whole sum owed, "together with all other monies due to the lenders" would fall due.

Held, that the words "all other monies due to the lenders" meant "all other monies due at the time of default", not "under the contract as a whole, were it to have been completed". Accordingly the clause was not a penalty clause, and was enforceable.

ORESUNDSVARVET AKTIEBOGAG *v.* LEMOS, *The Independent*, November 12, 1987, C.A.

449. Repudiation—innocent party refusing to accept—charterparty. See SHIPPING AND MARINE INSURANCE, §3386.

450. Repudiation—refusal to accept—continuing performance made impossible by repudiating party

If X repudiates his contract with Y, who does not accept the repudiation, Y is not absolved from continuing to perform the contract. If X makes it impossible for Y to continue to perform his side of the bargain, Y cannot earn his payments under the contract, and has no choice but to treat it as at an end and claim damages.

TELEPHONE RENTALS *v.* BURGESS SALMON, *The Independent*, April 22, 1987, C.A.

451. Retention of title clause—whether incorporated

P were sub-contractors to D for the supply, delivery and commissioning of equipment required as part of a boiler installation. P sent to D their quotation which included a clause which, they contended, provided that title in the goods should remain with P until payment. D then sent to P an Order incorporating terms inconsistent with the terms of P's quotation. P supplied the equipment. Before payment D went into liquidation. P issued a writ claiming declarations that the equipment was their property and an order for its delivery, alternatively for the price at which D had sold it to the employer and issued a notice of motion seeking appropriate interlocutory injunctive relief.

Held, that D's order was a counter-offer which killed P's offer by their quotation and which had been accepted by P by conduct in executing the works. Accordingly the retention of title clause had not been incorporated.

SAUTER AUTOMATION *v.* GOODMAN (MECHANICAL SERVICES) (IN LIQUIDATION) (1986) 34 Build.L.R. 81, Mervyn Davies J.

452. Sale of land—damages—breach of covenant to carry out remedial work prior to sale

A sold a house to D and covenanted to carry out work to prevent the "leaking of water from the patio" into the cellar. This was not done, but would anyway have not kept the cellar dry. It would have only kept out about 70 per cent. of the water; the rest would have come in from the surrounding soil. In an action for breach of contract, D was awarded only nominal damages.

Held, that D had suffered damage since if A had performed his contractual obligations, the cellar would have been substantially less wet. He was therefore entitled to substantial damages (*Radford* v. *De Froberville* [1978] C.L.Y. 2484 applied; *Wigsell* v. *School for Indigent Bind* (1882) 8 Q.B.D. 357 and *James* v. *Hutton* [1950] C.L.Y. 5416 considered).

DEAN *v.* AINLEY [1987] 3 All E.R. 748, C.A.

453. Sale of ship—Norwegian sale form—whether ship in deliverable state—whether cancellation wrongful—proper parties to the contract—novation. See SHIPPING AND MARINE INSURANCE, §3426.

454. Secret profit—duty to disclose

A positive duty to disclose fraud or secret profit before entering a contract only arises where the contract is one of *uberrimae fidei* or a financing or similar special relationship exists between the parties.

VAN GESTEL *v.* CANN, *The Times,* August 7, 1987, C.A.

455. Terms—agreement on terms—term requiring one party to do the impossible

Parties to a contract are entitled to agree any terms they please, including a term requiring one of them to do the impossible, although the courts will be cautious before holding that they have so contracted.

EURICO *v.* PHILIPP BROTHERS, *The Times,* May 18, 1987, C.A.

456. Undue influence—presumption—circumstances

The presumption of undue influence would be raised where the gift or transaction was so large or the transaction so improvident that it could not reasonably be accounted for on the ground of friendship, relationship, charity, or other motives on which ordinary people acted, and if the person effecting it had reposed in the other such a degree of trust and confidence as to place the other in a position to influence him into effecting it.

In 1977 the plaintiff, a widower then aged 85, granted a tenancy of his 436 acre farm to the first defendant at an annual rental of £500, and made an agreement whereby they became equal partners. The farm was in poor condition and was making a loss: he had run it since 1970 with the help of his son from whom he was partially estranged. The plaintiff was in good health but had come to rely on the first defendant implicitly. The tenancy agreement granted the first defendant an option to buy the farm on very favourable terms. In 1979 the partnership was determined by agreement, the first defendant buying out the plaintiff's half interest. In 1982 the plaintiff was reconciled to his son in favour of whom he executed a general power of attorney, and received advice for the first time on the validity of the tenancy agreement. In 1983 he claimed against the first defendant that the agreement had been procured by his undue influence, and alternatively against his former solicitors for damages for negligence in failing to advise him of his right to have the agreement rescinded. The judge dismissed his claims, and he appealed.

Held, that the presumption of undue influence would be raised where the gift was so large or the transaction so improvident that it could not reasonably be accounted for on the ground of friendship, relationship, charity or other motives on which ordinary men acted and if the person effecting it had reposed in the other such a degree of trust and confidence as to place the other into a position to influence him into effecting it. It was not necessary to show that the other had assumed a role of dominating influence. The judge was right to conclude that the presumption applied in this case and that the agreement had not been entered into by the plaintiff after full, free, and informed thought, and that its execution had been manifestly and unfairly disadvantageous to the plaintiff, and was so improvident that it could not reasonably be accounted for by ordinary motives. *Allcard* v. *Skinner* (1887) 36 Ch.D. 145 and *Tufton* v. *Sperni* [1952] C.L.Y. 1485 applied. *National Westminster Bank* v. *Morgan* [1985] C.L.Y. 413 and *Poosathurai* v. *Kannappa Chettiar* (1919) L.R. 47 I.A. 1 P.C. considered.

The judge had found in favour of the first defendant on the ground of promissory estoppel. The appeal against this finding was allowed. The presumption of undue influence having been found, the agreement would be set aside unless the plaintiff had subsequently affirmed it by words or conduct so as to render it inequitable to set it aside. Since the evidence had not established such a clear representation by the plaintiff that he would not exercise his right to set the agreement aside, or any act by the first defendant in reliance on such a representation, either to his detriment or at all, the plaintiff had not affirmed the agreement, and the defence of promissory estoppel could not succeed. Accordingly the agreement was rescinded. *Quaere:* Whether a plaintiff's ignorance of his right to seek rescission is necessarily a bar to the defence of acquiescence. The court made an order that the plaintiff recover his costs against the first defendant, including those incurred as a result of joining the solicitors as a party (even though the claim against the solicitors was dismissed). The order provided for the solicitors to recover their costs against the first defendant. The plaintiff had properly joined the solicitors even though the cause of action against them was different. *Per curiam:* There is no rule that a Bullock order requiring a party to pay another party's costs, but entitling him to recover such costs from yet another party, will not be made where the cause of action against the different defendants are separate and distinct or based on separate and distinct sets of facts. Note 62/2/46 in the White Book which suggests that a Bullock order will not be made when there are different causes of action is not sustained by authority.

GOLDSWORTHY *v.* BRICKELL [1987] 2 W.L.R. 133, C.A.

457. Undue influence—presumption—review

The Court of Appeal reviewed the authorities on the presumption of undue influence, concluding: (1) the relationship of husband and wife does not give rise to the presumption; (2) if a relationship does give rise to the presumption, the transaction will not be set aside unless it is to the manifest disadvantage of one of the parties; (3) if it was to the disadvantage of a party, the Court should consider all the facts to decide whether it would be unfair to let it stand; and (4) the Court would not enforce a debt when the creditor had entrusted the procurement of the debtor's signature to a person with whom the debtor stood in a relationship giving rise to the presumption (*National Westminster Bank* v. *Morgan* [1985] C.L.Y. 413 and *Kings North Trust* v. *Bell* [1986] C.L.Y. 2227 applied).

MIDLAND BANK *v.* SHEPHARD, *The Times,* February 2, 1987, C.A.

CONVEYANCING

458. Access rights—whether preserved

[Law of Property Act 1925 (c.20), s.62.]

Rights of access granted to an existing tenant do not pass on a sale of land after the surrender of the lease unless expressly reserved in the conveyance.

M.R.A. ENGINEERING *v.* TRIMSTER CO., *The Times,* October 22, 1987, C.A.

459/60. Beneficial interest—contributions—respective shares

A court must take into account all relevant factors, including contribution to mortgage repayment and the cost of capital improvement, in determining the respective shares in beneficial interest in property.

PASSEE *v.* PASSEE, *The Independent,* July 9, 1987, C.A.

461. "Commonhold"—freehold flats. See LAW REFORM, §2257.

462. Consumer protection for home buyers—proposals for reform. See LAW REFORM, §2259.

463. Covenants—whether covenants can be validated by statute

Covenants unenforceable under common law may be validated by statute when (i) the conveyance containing them is entered into pursuant to statutory powers; and (ii) making the covenants so enforceable clearly gives effect to Parliament's intentions.

GOVERNORS OF THE PEABODY DONATION FUND *v.* LONDON RESIDUARY BODY, *The Times,* July 25, Browne-Wilkinson V.-C.

464. Delays—consultation paper. See LAW REFORM, §2260.

465. Deposit—forfeiture

Forfeiture of deposit cannot be escaped by a purchaser of land where he has failed to complete by maintaining that at the time of the service of the notice he claims to have been in a position to rescind for misrepresentation.

McGRATH *v.* SHAH, *The Times,* October 22, 1987. Mr. John Chadwick, Q.C.

466. Documents—privilege. See R. *v.* CROWN COURT, *ex p.* BAINES AND WHITE, §712.

467. Duty of solicitor—purchase—insurance policy as security. See SOLICITORS, §3559.

468. Estate agent—deposit paid to vendor's agent—insolvency of agent—effect. See OJELAY *v.* NEOSALE, §62.

469. Failure of vendor to furnish his authority to inspect register—whether notice to complete valid

[Land registration Act 1925 (c.21), s.110(1).]

A vendor's failure to furnish his authority to inspect the register under s.110(1) of the Land Registration Act 1925 does not invalidate his notice to complete, so long as he is ready and willing to fulfil his own outstanding obligations.

NAZ *v.* RAJA, *The Times,* April 11, 1987, C.A.

470. Joint tenants—contract for sale—husband forged wife's signature—whether wife bound

A wife who owns property jointly with her husband is not bound by a contract for the sale of that property that her husband fraudulently enters into on her behalf (*Williams & Glyn's Bank* v. *Boland*, [1980] C.L.Y. 1847 applied; *Cedar Holdings* v. *Green*, [1979] C.L.Y. 1827 not followed).

AHMED *v.* KENDRICK, *The Times*, November 12, 1987, C.A.

471. Joint tenants—divorce—fraudulent legal charge—application for property adjustment order

[Land Registration Act, s.70(1)(*g*).]

H and W purchased a house in 1979. The were joint owners of the legal estate. W issued a divorce petition in 1982. In 1984 a mortgage was entered into purportedly between H and W and the plaintiffs, P. In fact, H had forged W's signature. In 1986 W applied for a property adjustment order within the divorce procedings. No pending land action was registered by W. P sought a declaration that the legal charge executed by H in 1984 had created an equitable charge in favour of P of H's beneficial interest in the house.

Held, granting the declaration sought, (1) that the fraudulent legal charge severed the joint tenancy and granted P an equitable charge over H's beneficial interest,)2) until an order of the court transferring H's interest in the property had taken place, W had no claim over H's interests, and therefore any charge over those interests will take free of W's claim unless the pending action has been registered before the legal charge took place. S.70(1)(*g*) protects only W's own rights as they were at the time of the fraudulent land charge and does not give her any rights in H's beneficial interest (*First National Securities* v. *Hegerty* [1984] C.L.Y. 1691 applied).

REGENT INDEMNITY CO. *v.* FISHLEY AND FISHLEY, July 21, 1987; Mr. Recorder Walton; Birmingham County Ct. [*Ex rel. David di Mambro, Barrister*.]

472. Land registration

LAND REGISTRATION (DISTRICT REGISTRIES) ORDER 1987 (No. 360) [80p], made under the Land Registration Act 1925 (c.21), ss.132, 133; operative on June 1, 1987; replaces S.I. 1984 No. 1579 and transfers responsibility for the registration of titles in certain areas.

LAND REGISTRATION (DISTRICT REGISTRIES) (No. 2) ORDER 1987 (No. 2213) [85p], made under the Land Registration Act 1925 s.132; operative on April 1, 1988; replaces S.I. 1987 No. 360.

473. Land registration—implied covenant of good title—interest of another title number

[Land Registration Rules (S.R. & O. 1925 No. 1093 (L.28), rr.76, 77(1)(*a*)).]

"The register" in rule 77 of the Land Registration Rules does not mean the global register of all registered land but refers only to the register of the individual title in question, so that on a conveyance of registered land, an implied covenant of good title takes effect only subject to any other interest in the land protected on the register under that title number.

D as beneficial owners transferred to P land described as "all that freehold property edged with red on the plan annexed hereto being . . . part of the freehold property registered at H.M. Land Registry under title number P7608." The annexed plan appeared to include within the red edging a piece of land to which D no longer had title. P claimed damages for breach of the covenants of title implied in the transfer under s.76 of and Sched. 2 to the Law of Property Act 1925 and rules 76 and 77 of the Land Registration Act 1925. The judge found that the transfer had purported to include land to which D had no title, but held that by virtue of rule 77(1)(*a*) of the Rules of 1925, D implied covenants of title took effect subject to the registered title of the true owners of that part of the land which was not the defendants', and that they were not liable.

Held, allowing P's appeal, that by using the coloured edging as a primary description, the transfer did include land to which the defendants had no title. The purpose of rule 77 of the Rules of 1925 was to limit the scope of covenants of title implied into the transfer by making them subject to existing interests appearing on "the register." In the context of rule 77(1)(*a*) "the register" meant only the register of land under the particular title number, not the global register of all land or even the property register of adjoining land which contracting purchasers could inspect under rule 288. Therefore the title of the true owners of the land purportedly conveyed was not an interest subject to which D's covenants of good title took effect. They were liable for the breach of covenant and the case was remitted for an inquiry as to the damages.

DUNNING (A. J.) & SONS (SHOPFITTERS) *v.* SYKES & SON (POOLE) [1987] 2 W.L.R. 167, C.A.

474. Land registration—overriding interest—execution of charge by two trustees for sale—whether interest overreached. See CITY OF LONDON BUILDING SOCIETY *v.* FLEGG, §2540.

475. Land registration—rules

LAND REGISTRATION RULES 1987 (No. 2214) [£1·30], made under the Land Registration Act 1925 (c.21), s.144; operative on February 1, 1988; amend S.R. & O. 1925 No. 1093 rule 288.

476. Leasehold conveyancing—law reform. See LAW REFORM, §2274.

477. Leasehold property—landlord's consent to assign—delay by purchaser—whether right to rescind

Where a right of rescission of a contract of sale depends on the fact that a licence "cannot be obtained," a purported exercise of that right is ineffective unless it is certain that the licence cannot be obtained.

A lease contained a covenant by the lessees not to assign without the landlords' written permission, not to be unreasonably withheld. The vendor contracted to sell the residence to T. Co. The contract incorporated the National Conditions of Sale, which included a term that if a licence to assign "cannot be obtained" the vendors might rescind. The landlords required guarantors of T. Co. as a condition of the licence. By the date of completion, T. Co. had proposed guarantors but no response was received. The vendors gave notice of rescission.

Held, that on a true construction "cannot be obtained" does not mean "is not forthcoming," and it was impossible to say at the date of completion whether the licence could be obtained. Thus the vendors' notice was ineffective to bring an end to the contract.

29 EQUITIES *v.* BANK LEUMI (U.K.) [1986] 1 W.L.R. 1490, C.A.

478. Licensed conveyancers

LICENSED CONVEYANCERS' DISCIPLINE AND APPEALS COMMITTEE (LEGAL ASSESSOR) RULES 1987 (No. 788) [45p], made under the Administration of Justice Act 1985 (c.61), Sched. 4, para. 3(2); operative on May 26, 1987; regulates the functions of the assessor appointed under para. 3(1) of Sched. 4 to the 1985 Act.

LICENSED CONVEYANCERS' DISCIPLINE AND APPEALS COMMITTEE (PROCEDURE) RULES APPROVAL ORDER 1987 (No. 789) [£1·90], made under the Administration of Justice Act 1985, Sched. 4, para. 1; operative on May 26, 1987; provides for the procedure for hearing disciplinary cases against licensed conveyancers.

479. Misrepresentation—central heating working when representation given—water later froze

[Misrepresentation Act 1967 (c.7), s.2(1).]

D had vacated the house before P became interested in buying it. In September P made an acceptable offer for the house. P's solicitor sent inquiries before contract. D represented that the central heating was in good order. This was true but before exchange of contracts three months later the water in the radiators froze, causing damage. D was unaware of this. No further representation was sought or given.

Held, D liable for damages under s.2(1) on the grounds that the representation given was a continuing one. If, at the date of the contract, the representation was no longer true then D was liable unless he could prove a statutory defence under the section.

CORNER *v.* MUNDY, January 7, 1987, Judge Hewitt Middlesbrough County Ct. [*Ex rel. Richard Merrit, Barrister.*]

480. Monies received from purchaser—status of solicitor

Unless the contrary is agreed between the parties, a vendor's solicitor receives money paid by a purchaser as an agent and not as a stakeholder. When the vendor has fully performed the obligation to assign the property he is at liberty to release the monies to him.

TUDOR *v.* HAMID, (1987) 137 New L.J. 79, C.A.

481. Purchase price—whether caution can protect additional sum

Where a contract for the sale of land provides for an extra payment in the event that the purchaser develops the land, this is not part of the purchase price and cannot be protected by registering a caution.

WOOLF PROJECT MANAGEMENT *v.* WOODTREK, *The Times,* October 22, 1987, Mervyn Davies J.

482. Register of Sasines (Scotland) Act 1987 (c.23)

The Act makes provision as to the methods of keeping the Register of Sasines.

The Act received the Royal Assent on May 15, 1987, and comes into force two months from that date.

The act extends to Scotland only.

483. Registration of title

REGISTRATION OF TITLE ORDER 1987 (No. 939) [85p], made under the Land Registration Act 1925 (c.21), s.120(1) and (6), and the London Government Act 1963 (c.33), ss.80(2) and 90; operative on December 1, 1987; extends the system of compulsory registration of title on sale of land to the districts mentioned in art. 2(1)(*a*) and (*b*).

484. Report on land registration—greater protection for property buyers. See LAW REFORM, §2270.

485. Restrictive covenants—discharge or modification—restriction against sub-division

[Restrictive Covenants (Discharge and Modification) Act (No. 2 of 1960, s.3(1)(*b*), (*d*)).]

Where land was subject to restrictive covenants, an applicant wishing to modify them under the law of Jamaica had to show that the covenants without modification hindered the reasonable use of the land to a sensible degree, and not merely that some reasonable use of the land was impeded to a sensible degree.

A plot of land on the coast of Jamaica was sub-divided into 11 lots. The applicant purchased two which together with six others was subject to covenants not to sub-divide the land, not to erect a building other than one costing not less than £2,000 to erect, and not to carry on trade or business or any commercial activity. They were intended to preserve the privacy of the land and its quality. By 1982 seven of the lots had a single dwelling house, and they constituted a peaceful seaside enclave. The applicant wished to develop her land by erecting 6 blocks of three storey buildings comprising 40 apartments and two swimming pools. She applied to a judge of the Supreme Court of Jamaica in Equity for modification of the covenants under subss. 3(1)(*b*) and (*d*) of the Restrictive Covenants (Discharge and Modification) Act 1960. The other owners objected. The applicant was later granted planning permission. The judge dismissed the application but his decision was reversed by the Court of Appeal of Jamaica which ordered modification of the covenants. The objectors' appeal to the Judicial Committee was allowed.

Held, that in order to establish that the continued existence of the restrictions without modification would impede the reasonable user of the applicant's land within s.3(1)(*b*) the applicant had to establish that the covenants without modification to a real or sensible extent hindered the reasonable use of that land and not merely that some reasonable use of the land was impeded to a sensible degree. Since despite the restrictions, reasonable use of the land was still possible and it could without difficulty be developed or disposed of for development, the applicant had failed to satisfy the first limb of para. (*b*) and the application was properly dismissed. *Ghey and Galton's Application, Re* [1957] C.L.Y. 3009 applied. It was a clear benefit for the objectors to preserve the peaceful character of their neighbourhood by restricting the number of dwellings. The judge was correct to hold this and in being unpersuaded that the requirements in para. (*d*) that the modification proposed would not injure the objectors had been satisfied.

STANNARD *v.* ISSA [1987] 2 W.L.R. 188, P.C.

486. Reverter of Sites Act 1987 (c.15). See EQUITY AND TRUSTS, §1435.

487. Sale of house and chattels—false apportionment of value of house and chattels to avoid stamp duty—effect of illegality. See SAUNDERS *v.* EDWARDS, §1826.

488. Sale of land—damages—breach of covenant to carry out remedial work prior to sale. See DEAN *v.* AINLEY, §452.

489. Sale of land—time to be of essence only after completion notice—extension after purchaser's failure to complete—whether time of the essence—whether vendor entitled to rescind

When extending time for completion, the failure by a vendor to specify that time was to be regarded as of the essence from that date and the fact that he receives recompense for any delay, will mean that he fails to rebut the presumption that time is to be of the essence.

The vendor sold land under a contract which provided that time should not be of the essence unless a completion notice was served. The purchaser failed to complete by the due date, and the vendor served a notice; the purchaser again failed to complete by that date. A fresh written agreement was reached whereby a third date was substituted; again the purchaser failed to complete. The vendor purported to rescind the contract, and sued for damages, entering a caution against the property. The purchaser sought to vacate the caution on the ground that time had not become of the essence under the second agreement, and the vendor had not, therefore, been entitled to rescind.

Held, allowing the purchaser's appeal, that time had not become of the essence. A reasonable person would have expected that the second agreement would have provided expressly that time was to be of the essence, if that was the parties' intention. There was no injustice to the vendor because he had been adequately compensated.

CHANCERY LAND DEVELOPMENTS *v.* WADES DEPARTMENTAL STORES (1987) 53 P. & C.R. 306, C.A.

490. Sale of land part of settlement of action—absence of note or memorandum—whether original action discharged. See O'MAHONY *v.* GAFFNEY, §3092.

491. Scottish system of buying and selling houses—availability in England and Wales

The Conveyancing Standing Committee has published a report entitled *House Selling the Scottish Way for England and Wales.* Copies of the report are available free from The Law Commission, Conquest House, 37/38 John Street, Theobalds Road, London WC1N 2BQ.

492. Transfer of land—title—damages

The Law Commission has published a report entitled *Transfer of land—The Rule in Bain* v. *Fothergill.* Copies of the report are available from H.M.S.O. (Law Com. No. 166, Cmnd. 192) [£4·10].

493. Transfer of land—title on death. See LAW REFORM, §2261.

494. Trust for sale—beneficial interest—contradictory expressions in conveyance—whether beneficial joint tenancy or tenancy in common

The phrase "beneficial joint tenants in common in equal shares" in a conveyance constituted words of severance and so created a tenancy in common and not a joint tenancy.

The plaintiffs were the son and daughter-in-law of the late Mrs. Martin, and the defendant was the elder brother of the first plaintiff. In 1980, the plaintiffs and the deceased bought a property where they could live together which was conveyed to them and Mrs. Martin as purchasers. Under clause 2, the purchasers declared that the property was held "upon trust for sale for themselves as beneficial joint tenants in common in equal shares". On Mrs. Martin's death it was necessary to decide whether the conveyance created a beneficial joint tenancy to which the plaintiffs were solely entitled by survivorship or whether it created a beneficial tenancy in common in which case the equitable share formed part of her estate on death.

Held, that the words "in equal shares" constituted words of severance or provided a controlling context for the word "joint" and so created a tenancy in common and not a joint tenancy. If the court applied the rule that where there were two inconsistent provisions that cannot be reconciled, the first in time prevails, the first provision in the present case created a beneficial joint tenancy. However the second inconsistent phrase then constituted a severance of the equitable joint tenancy and the creation of a beneficial tenancy in common.

MARTIN *v.* MARTIN (1987) 54 P. & C.R. 238, Millett J.

495. Vacant possession—landlord agreeing to sell with vacant possession—enforceability against protected tenant. See APPLETON *v.* ASPIN, §2189.

COPYRIGHT

496. Collective works—individual author's rights—editor's rights

[France.] The author of a contribution to a collective work has the personal rights defined in the Copyright Act 1957, s.6.

The editor of a collective work owns the copyright. Under s.6 both (a) intellectual and personal attributes, and (b) material attributes are protectable.

ROBERT *v.* SOCIETE CREHALLET-FOLLIOT-RECHERCHE ET PUBLICITE [1987] F.S.R. 537, Cour de Cassation, France.

497. Computer software

COPYRIGHT (COMPUTER SOFTWARE) (EXTENSION TO TERRITORIES) ORDER 1987 (No. 2200) [45p], made under the Copyright Act 1956 (c.74), s.31; operative on February 1, 1988; extends the Copyright (Computer Software) Amendment Act 1985 to specified territories subject to certain exceptions and modifications.

498. Copyright owner's rights—foreign owner

[Germany.] The creator of an artistic work who is a foreign plaintiff has the same enforceable exclusive rights as a national copyright holder. The court granted an injunction to restrain the Green Party from plagiarising the French *Asterix* comic strip.

COPYRIGHT AND TRADE MARK RIGHTS IN "ASTERIX," *Re* (2 U 115/84) [1987] F.S.R. 534, Court of Appeal, Bremen.

499. Film—licence agreement—unlawful interference with contractual relations—duty of care

[Copyright Act 1956 (c.74), ss.19, 36; Copyright Act 1968, s.196, R.S.C., Ord. 14.]

W owned copyright in a cinematograph film of which H was the producer. V and H agreed orally that V should have video rights. After the film was completed, V sued H and W sued V because V and W contended that there was no agreement. V sought to strike out W's allegations of wrongful interference with contractual relations. He was successful. W alleged that V had acted negligently and without taking sufficient care to ascertain whether there was any valid agreement.

Held, that the allegation should be struck out. W's application for summary judgment declaring that there was no concluded agreement would be dismissed because V's case was arguable and could be determined only on the evidence.

WESTERN FRONT *v.* VESTRON INC. [1987] F.S.R. 66, Gibson J.

500. Film—whether publication occurred—whether copies infringing copies

[Copyright Act 1956 (c.74), ss.13, 18, 21, 49; Copyright (International Conventions) Order 1979.]

D was convicted by magistrates under the Copyright Act 1956, s.21(4A). D appealed contending that the prosecution had not proved that the video cassettes were infringing copies and further that D knew this to be so. When asked if he claimed to be the owner of copyright or had authority to copy the films he had said "No."

Held, (1) the ingredients of the offence had not been proved in respect of the film made in the U.S.A. The appeal would therefore be allowed in respect of these items; (2) substence of copyright could be proved by showing that first publication occurred in a country to which s.13 applied; (3) expert evidence could establish whether copies were infringing. There was no need to have evidence from the maker of the film or the current owner of the copyright.

MUSA *v.* LE MAITRE [1987] F.S.R. 212, D.C.

501. Incitement to commit offence—injunction—whether claim sustainable

[Copyright Act 1956 (c.74), s.21(3).]

The alleged incitement to commit an offence under s.21(3) of the Copyright Act 1956 does not give rise to an equitable right for injunctive relief to prevent such alleged incitement.

In 1984 Amstrad introduced models of tape to tape machines onto the market and they were advertised in terms likely to encourage home copying of tapes. The British Phonographic Industry (B.P.I.) wrote to Amstrad and its principal trade outlets asserting that Amstrad was encouraging the public to break the law. Amstrad then sought a declaration against B.P.I. that they had not acted unlawfully: in this action the plaintiffs sued on behalf of themselves and members of the Mechanical Rights Society (M.R.S.) and B.P.I. alleging that Amstrad and Dixons had incited others to infringe copyright. They claimed injunctive relief. They alleged that the advertising material might be capable of amounting to incitement to commit a crime under s.21(3) of the Copyright Act 1956.

Held, that the plaintiff had no right in equity to enforce the observance of the criminal law where the statute did not give rise to a claim in tort. Only the Attorney General had standing to enforce the observance of the criminal law through a civil court (*Emperor of Austria* v. *Day and Kossuth* (1861) 3 de G.F. & J. 216, *Gouriet* v. *Att.-Gen.* [1977] C.L.Y. 690, *R.C.A. Corp.* v. *Pollard* [1982] C.L.Y. 436, *Lonrho* v. *Shell Petroleum Co.* [1981] C.L.Y. 2649 considered).

C.B.S. SONGS *v.* AMSTRAD CONSUMER ELECTRONICS [1987] 1 FTLR 488, C.A.

502. Infringement—artistic works—substantial part

[Aus.] [Copyright Act 1968 (Cth.), ss.14, 21, 71, 74, 77.]

P claimed that D infringed his artistic copyright in engineering drawings relating to a solar hot water system. D admitted access to P's drawings when manufacturing its similar system. The trial judge found that D had substantially reproduced P's work and that D could not rely on a defence under s.71 (which corresponded to Copyright Act 1956, s.9(8)).

Held, on appeal, that (1) the onus is on D to establish the defence; (2) the notional non-expert is an observant person of reasonable intelligence with at least sufficient ability to interpret drawings to enable him to perform his notional function intelligently. The appeal was dismissed.

HART (S. W.) & CO. PTY *v.* EDWARDS HOT WATER SYSTEMS [1986] F.S.R. 575, High Ct. of Australia.

503. Infringement—boat hulls—whether hulls registrable as designs

[Can.] P owned the copyright in drawings for the hulls of two sorts of boats. In an action for infringement, P succeeded at first instance in relation to one boat hull drawing. On appeal, D contended that the plans were not protected by copyright since the designs were registrable, and not excluded from the operation of the Copyright Act 1970, s.46(1) by the Industrial Design Rules 1978, r.11(1).

Held, allowing the appeal, that the contention of D was correct.

BAYLINER MARINE CORP. *v.* DORAL BOATS [1987] F.S.R. 497, Fed. C.A., Canada.

504. Infringement—collective works

[Fra.] (1) The copyright in collective works such as newspapers is vested in the owner who could seek an injunction prohibiting the infringement of its property right by the partial reproduction of the collective works as a whole. (2) The reproduction without the consent of the newspaper proprietor of the headings of articles is illegal. (3) Where an index to copyright works contains descriptive summaries which are mere abridgements, they are not a press review within the Copyright Act 1957, s.41. The Court held that the Canadian index of extracts from *Le Monde* and *Le Monde Diplomatique* entitled *France Actualités* contained no original intellectual input, it must therefore be an infringement of the copyright of the newspaper proprietor.

SOCIETE MICROFOR *v.* Sàrl LE MONDE [1987] F.S.R. 206, Cour D'Appel, Paris.

505. Infringement—computer programs—copying of structure—substantial similarity

[U.S.A.] [17 United States Code, ss.101,102,103; Federal Rules of Evidence, rr.401,403,702.]

D1 made dental prosthetics and devices. J, an officer and shareholder in D, hired S to write a program for an IBM computer. W, an employee of S, wrote Dentalab in EDL language. W left S and formed the P company, which acquired S's interest. J formed D2 in order to market a program in BASIC language written by him. The district court found that this language (Dentcom) was substantially similar to Dentalab, and that the D's sales infringed P's copyright in the Dentalab program. The D's appealed on the question of infringement, arguing that copyright protected only the literal code and not its overall structure.

Held, that (1) the proper test of substantial similarity had been applied; (2) the structure of the Dentalab program was part of the expression and not the mere idea of the program. Infringement had taken place.

WHELAN ASSOCIATES *v.* JASLOW DENTAL LABORATORY [1987] F.S.R. 1, U.S. Ct. of Appeals.

506. Infringement—defence of fair dealing—interlocutory injunction

[Copyright Act 1956 (c.74), s.6(2)(3).]

P obtained exclusive rights to letters between the Duke and Duchess of Windsor. They printed these in the Daily Mail. D published one letter in the Sun, and part of another. P sought and obtained an injunction to restrain breach of copyright and sought in addition an injunction which would protect their interest until their exclusive rights expired.

Held, that (1) there was no interference with freedom of speech; (2) D's motive, which was relevant to the defence of fair dealing, was simply to boost its readership; (3) the publication was not a criticism or review within s.6(2); (4) D was not reporting a current event within s.6(3). Injunction granted for two weeks when their rights expired.

ASSOCIATED NEWSPAPERS GROUP *v.* NEWS GROUP NEWSPAPERS [1986] R.P.C. 515, Walton J.

507. Infringement—indirect copying—joint tortfeasors

[N.Z.] [Copyright Act 1962 (N.Z.), ss.6, 7, 9, 25.]

The High Court issued an injunction preventing D1 from manufacturing, distributing or selling caravan windows constructed with extrusions which infringed P's copyright in drawings. P recovered conversion damages against D1 amounting to one-third of the gross value of the windows. Judgment was entered in favour of D2 and D3. P and D appealed. D1 had borrowed one of P's windows, dismantled it, took measurements and drew it, and used the drawings to make die drawings and dies from which the new windows were made.

Held, that D1's product was similar to P's as a result of the copying of an extrusion made by P and derived from P's drawings. D2, which sold glass to the manufacturer of the infringing windows, was a party to the copying and liable as joint tortfeasor. P's appeal allowed.

CRYSTAL GLASS INDUSTRIES *v.* ALWINCO PRODUCTS [1986] R.P.C. 259, C.A. of N.Z.

508. Infringement—indirect copying—passing off

[N.Z.] [Copyright Act (N.Z.) 1962, ss.5, 7, 9; Copyright Act 1956 (c.74), s.4; Kiwifruit Licensing Regulations (N.Z.) 1977 (S.R. 281/77).]

P were the sole manufacturers of "pocket packs" for packaging kiwifruit. D designed packs by reference only to the specification of the kiwifruit authority regulations, exporters' packing instructions and samples of kiwifruit. D's packs looked almost identical to P's. P alleged infringement of copyright in lost drawings, the models and their packs, and passing off.

Held that, (1) P's copyright was infringed by copying from verbal description; (2) P was entitled to copyright protection of the lost drawings.

PLIX PRODUCTS *v.* WINSTONE (FRANK M.) (MERCHANTS) [1986] F.S.R. 608, N.Z. C.A.

509. Infringement—interlocutory injunction

In an interlocutory application in an action for infringement of copyright P sought an injunction to restrain infringement in respect of named films and "otherwise infringing a copyright in any cinematograph film the copyright in which belongs to or under the copyright in which P are exclusive licensees."

Held, that there was insufficient evidence of prospective probable infringement to warrant the court making an order in wider terms than the proved activities of D.

VIDEO ARTS *v.* PAGET INDUSTRIES [1986] F.S.R. 623, Knox J.

510. Infringement—interlocutory injunction—wedding photographs

Mrs. B was kept on a life-support system in order to allow her baby to be born alive. Mr. B entered into an agreement with P for exclusive rights to his photographs and undertaking to pose exclusively for P with his baby. P obtained *ex parte* injunctions restraining D from publishing wedding photographs.

Held, that (1) Mr. and Mrs. B were joint tenants of the copyright in their wedding photographs; (2) it was not clear whether Mrs. B was legally dead; (3) the balance of convenience lay in favour of granting the injunction.

MAIL NEWSPAPERS *v.* EXPRESS NEWSPAPERS [1987] F.S.R. 90, Millett J.

511. Infringement—LEGO toys—designs

[H.K.] [Copyright Act 1956 (c.74), ss.9, 10, 17, 48, Sched. 7, para. 8(2); Copyright Act 1911 (c.46), s.22; Design Copyright Act 1968 (c.68); Registered Designs Act 1949 (c.88), s.1: Copyright (Hong Kong) Orders 1972 and 1979; United Kingdom Designs (Protection) Ordinance, Cap. 44.]

P manufactured moulded interlocking plastic LEGO toys. D decided to manufacture in Hong Kong similar plastic blocks. In an action for infringement, P argued that their blocks made before 1973 were not "capable of registration" as they were not novel. As to articles made after 1972, D claimed *inter alia* that Lego was estopped having obtained registered designs which had expired and had abandoned their copyright in drawings equivalent to those in the expired patents. The trial judge decided that infringement had occurred and that P was entitled to relief. D appealed.

Held, that (1) the pre-1973 Lego works were capable of registration and copyright therefore did not subsist (*Amp Inc.* v. *Utilux Pty.* [1972] C.L.Y. 2593 applied); (2) post-1972 Lego drawings were sufficiently original to attract copyright, even if ultimately derived from other drawings; (3) consequently there could be no public estoppel preventing P from seeking remedy; (4) P had not abandoned copyright.

INTERLEGO A.G. *v.* TYCO INDUSTRIES [1987] F.S.R. 409, C.A. of H.K.

512. Infringement—mould—balance of convenience—damages

[Copyright Act 1956 (c.74), ss.9, 18; Torts (Interference with Goods) Act 1977 (c.32), s.3.]

P manufactured boxes for the storage of floppy disks, according to drawings. They agreed to sell their rights to PCL to manufacture and sell. During the short operation of this agreement, B and C were involved as employees of PCL. P ascertained that D was intending to ship a mould of a box similar to P's box to the U.S.A. D contracted with A for the sale of the patent and design rights of their box which they claimed was new. A and L promoted the box in the U.S.A. Evidence showed that C was the moving spirit behind A, and that L used the address of a company owned by B. A and L applied to intervene.

Held, (1) leave to intervene granted; (2) the balance of convenience lay in favour of an injunction. Once the mould had left the U.K. it was unlikely any order for delivery up would be enforceable. P could compensate D adequately if P were ultimately unsuccessful at trial; (3) where there was an order for delivery up, there could be in addition an order for consequential damages.

RUBYCLIFF *v.* PLASTIC ENGINEERS [1986] R.P.C. 573, Browne-Wilkinson V.C.

513. Infringement—parody of song used as advertisement—injunction

[Copyright Act 1956 (c.74), ss.2, 49.]

P were exclusive licencees of copyright in the musical "South Pacific". D was an advertising agency with a bus company as clients. P alleged that D's song which was a parody of P's, was infringing their lyrics and music.

Held, granting the injunction, that (1) the proper test was whether the parody made use of a substantial part of the expression of literary copyright; (2) D's song could not be said to infringe P's words, but there was a serious question to be tried as to whether the music constituted an infringement; (3) the balance of convenience favoured P.

WILLIAMSON MUSIC *v.* PEARSON PARTNERSHIP [1987] F.S.R. 97, Judge Paul Baker Q.C.

514. Infringement—practice—delay in prosecution

P obtained an *Anton Piller* order against D whom they alleged had infringed dress designs. They obtained another five months later and issued a writ. Seven months later leave to defend was given to D with order for a speedy trial. After nearly six years D issued a summons to dismiss for want of prosecution.

Held, that (1) P's delay was inordinate in that the time which had elapsed was materially longer than that regarded by the court and profession as acceptable; (2) the staleness of the action would make a fair trial difficult; (3) P's delay was inexcusable.

BESTWORTH *v.* WEARWELL [1986] R.P.C. 527, Falconer J.

515. Infringement—registered design—LEGO toy

[Copyright Act 1956 (c.74), s.10, Sched. 7, para. 8; Registered Designs Act 1949 (c.88), ss.1, 4.]

P claimed copyright in drawings which when moulded were sold as LEGO or DUPLO. P's patent had expired. He had registered designs for many of the drawings. P argued that none of the drawings were capable of registration and that he was therefore entitled to claim infringement of copyright.

Held, dismissing P's claim, that (1) P's registration had been rightly accepted by the Registry of Designs; (2) P's objection on grounds of novelty were to be ignored for the purpose of the Registered Designs Act 1949, s.1(3), (*Amp Inc.* v. *Utilux Pty.* [1972] C.L.Y. 2593 applied).

INTERLEGO A.G. *v.* FOLLEY (ALEX) (VIC) PTY. [1987] F.S.R. 283, Whitford J.

516. Infringement—right of action—clips from films of deceased actor—whether cause of action enforceable after death

(Dramatic and Musical Performers' Protection Act 1958 (c.44) s.2.)

S.2 of the Dramatic and Musical Performers' Protection Act 1958 conferred a right of civil remedy at the suit of a performer whose performance was exploited by others without his consent, and the right vested in his personal representative when he died.

The defendants made five films starring Peter Sellers in which he played Inspector Clouseau. After his death they made a new film using out-takes from the previous films without obtaining the consent of the plaintiffs, his personal representatives. They brought an action for damages for breach of s.2 of the Dramatic and Musical Performers' Act 1958. They were awarded damages of one million U.S. dollars plus an account of the profits. The defendants appealed.

Held, dismissing the appeal, that s.2, as well as imposing a criminal penalty of a fine for a breach, imposed an obligation or prohibition for performers, and conferred on them a right to civil remedies against those who exploited their work without written consent. This right was not personal but vested in their personal representatives when they died, (Dictum of Lord Diplock in *Lonrho* v. *Shell Petroleum Co.* (1981) C.L.Y. 2649 applied; *Ex parte Island Records* [1978] C.L.Y. 2377 and *R.C.A. Corp.* v. *Pollard* [1982] C.L.Y. 436 considered). The defendants were held to have expressly or impliedly contracted that his performance would be used only for the purposes of the particular film, and the right to enforce that negative covenant passed to his personal representatives on his death. The defendants were liable for inducing a breach of a purely negative condition obligation under the agreements notwithstanding that in other respects they had been since performed, (*British Motor Trade Association* v. *Salvadori* (1949) C.L.C. 1721).

RICKLESS *v.* UNITED ARTISTS CORP. [1987] 1 All E.R. 679, C.A.

517. Infringement—service outside jurisdiction—application to set aside

[Copyright Act 1956 (c.74), ss.1, 5, 12, 16; R.S.C., Ord. 11, r.4.]

P alleged that D had pirated their copyright in a tape recording. Leave to serve D6 and D8 outside the jurisdiction had been obtained. They applied to set aside the order on the ground that the acts complained of had been done outside the U.K.

Held, that under the Copyright Act 1956 only acts in the U.K. and countries to which the Act applied could be regulated.

DEF-LEPP MUSIC *v.* STUART-BROWN [1986] R.P.C. 273, V.-C.

518. Infringement—settlement—whether claim in conversion extinguished

[Torts (Interference with Goods) Act 1977 (c.32), s.5.]

P alleged that D's 1, 2, 3 and 5 had infringed his copyright in original artistic work made in advertisements by D5. P's case against D5 was settled during the hearing, upon terms that P accepted a sum in full and final settlement of his claim against D5 and without prejudice to P's claims against the other D's. D3 argued that P's claim in conversion was therefore extinguished.

Held, the burden was on P to show that the settlement had not compensated him for the whole of his interest in the goods. Since in this case P had not done so, P's claim in conversion was extinguished.

MACAULAY *v.* SCREENKARN [1987] F.S.R. 257, Falconer J.

519. Infringement—tape recordings—representative action—striking out

[Copyright Act 1956 (c.74), ss.12, 13; R.S.C., Ord. 15, r.12(1).]

[Hong Kong] P alleged infringement of sound recordings. They sued on behalf of themselves and all of the members of the International Federation of Phonogram and Videogram Producers (IFPI). D, a television station, sought to strike out those parts of the claim relating to P's entitlement to sue in a representative capacity. They alleged that P had an ulterior motive and further that there was no common interest between P and members of IFPI.

Held, (1) P had failed to establish that the representative action was appropriate. (*EMI Records* v. *Riley* [1981] C.L.Y. 1175 distinguished; *Prudential Assurance* v. *Newman Industries* [1979] C.L.Y. 2175 applied); (2) there was prima facie evidence that P had an ulterior motive; (3) representantive action disallowed.

CBS/SONY HONG KONG *v.* TELEVISION BROADCASTS [1987] F.S.R. 262, Supreme Ct. Hong Kong.

520. Infringement—title and format of diary

P published The Lawyer's Diary 1986. He claimed literary copyright in these words and artistic copyright in the cover decoration and typeface. He alleged that the publishers of Butterworth's Law Diary 1986 infringed his rights.

Held, dismissing the action, that copyright did not subsist in P's diary.

ROSE *v.* INFORMATION SERVICES [1987] F.S.R. 254, Hoffmann J.

521. Infringement—video games—whether intellectual works

[Fra.] The Court held that (1) P's three video games were protected from breach of copyright by the Copyright Act 1957; (2) drawings, images and sounds and animations, if recorded in writing, are considered as intellectual works provided that they are original. Video games are original intellectual works, even if not aesthetically a work of art.

ATARI IRELAND AND ATARI INC. *v.* VALADON (ALAIN) [1987] F.S.R. 208, Cour de Cassation, France.

522. Infringement—whether droit moral recognised in English law contracts. See ROWE *v.* WALT DISNEY PRODUCTIONS, §406.

523. Infringement aiding passing off by third party—damages—whether to include damages resulting from the passing off

[Copyright Act 1956 (c.74), s.17.]

Damages may be awarded under s.17 of the Copyright Act 1956 in respect of the damage to the value of the copyright alone, and may not be awarded in respect of damage resulting from improper use made of the material by a third party. There is no duty on a printer to take reasonable care to prevent infringement of copyright.

A third party decided fraudulently to copy P's product and the designs for their packaging. Orders were placed with D, who were printers, for such packaging. P sued D alleging infringement of copyright, and alleging negligence in that D should have made inquiry to confirm that the work was authorised, and ought reasonably to have foreseen that damage would flow from the use to which the packaging was to be put.

Held, that the jurisdiction under s.17 of the 1956 Act was in respect of depreciation of the copyright as a chose in action; since there was no claim by P to that effect the judge had correctly struck out the copyright element of the claim. Further, there was no duty on a printer to enquire into the purpose for which an article is being manufactured, and the use to which it was to be put. (*Sutherland Publishing Co.* v. *Caxton Publishing Co.* [1936] 1 All E.R. 180 applied).

PATERSON ZOCHONIS & CO. *v.* MERFARKEN PACKAGING [1986] 3 All E.R. 522, C.A.

524. International conventions

COPYRIGHT (INTERNATIONAL CONVENTIONS) (AMENDMENT) ORDER 1987 (No. 2060) [45p], made under the Copyright Act 1956 (c.74), ss.31, 32 and 47; operative on December 25, 1987; restores copyright protection in the U.K. to works originating in the Bahamas, Barbados, Cyprus, Fiji, Malta and Zimbabwe, which were first published between June 1, 1957, and September 26, 1957, and which depended for their copyright protection of the time of first publication solely upon the author's being domiciled or resident in one of those countries.

525. Registered designs—Benelux Uniform Law

[Belgium.] The Benelux Uniform Law applies in addition to copyright protection provided that the criteria are fulfilled. Advertising work cannot be a design or model protected by the Benelux Uniform Law. It can, however, be protected by copyright because it is original artistic work.

PROMEDIA S.A. *v.* BORGHT [1987] F.S.R. 536, Cour d'Appel, Brussels.

526. Singapore

COPYRIGHT (SINGAPORE) ORDER 1987 (No. 940) [45p], made under the Copyright Act 1956 (c.74), ss.31, 32, 47; operative on June 18, 1987; provides for the copyright protection in the U.K. of works and other subject-matter originating in Singapore.

COPYRIGHT (SINGAPORE) (AMENDMENT) ORDER 1987 (No. 1030) [45p], made under the Copyright Act 1956, ss.31, 32, 47; operative on July 9, 1987; extends S.I. 1987 No. 940 to Gibraltar.

527. Singapore—whether Copyright Act 1911 applies

[Copyright Act 1911 (c.46).]

The Copyright Act 1911 applies to Singapore for works published between July 1, 1912, and June 1, 1957, and between January 27, 1959, and the present day.

BUTTERWORTH & CO. *v.* NG SUI NAM, *The Financial Times,* May 1, 1987, High Court of the Republic of Singapore.

528. Subsistence of copyright—statutory construction

[Malaysia] [Copyright Act 1969 (Malaysia), ss.2, 3, 4, 5, 6, 7, 12, 20.]

R1 was the maker of videos and owned Hong Kong copyrights therein. R2 and R3 were licensees. The videos were published in Hong Kong and then in Malaysia within 30 days. A sought a declaration that R1 was not entitled to copyright in Malaysia.

Held, on appeal, that video recordings were "cinematograph film" within the Act. Upon a proper construction of the Act copyright in the films vested in R1.
FOO LOKE YING *v.* TELEVISION BROADCASTS [1987] F.S.R. 57, Supreme Ct. of Malaysia.

529. Taiwan—extension
COPYRIGHT (TAIWAN) (EXTENSION TO TERRITORIES) ORDER 1987 (No. 1826) [45p], made under the Copyright Act 1956 (c.74), ss.31, 47; operative on November 20, 1987; provides for the extension of S.I. 1985 No. 1777 to specified dependant territories.
COPYRIGHT (TAIWAN ORDER) (ISLE OF MAN) EXTENSION ORDER 1987 (No. 1833) [45p], made under the Copyright Act 1956, s.31; operative on November 21, 1987; extends to the Isle of Man the provisions of S.I. 1985 No. 1777.

530. Trade name—book title—passing off—infringement
The use of the words "Mother Care" in the title of a book *Mother Care/Other Care* was not passing off nor an infringement of a trade mark.
MOTHERCARE U.K. *v.* PENGUIN BOOKS, *The Times,* July 8, 1987, C.A.

531. Use of "Nationwide" in business name—lack of goodwill in name—interlocutory injunction
P was planning a national chain of estate agents after the de-regulation of building society business on January 1, 1987. D set up business in October 1986. Although P had established an arguable case and although damages would not be an adequate remedy an interlocutory injunction would not be granted since at the date of the start of the action P had no goodwill to protect in the same commercial field as D.
NATIONWIDE BUILDING SOCIETY *v.* NATIONWIDE ESTATE AGENTS, *The Times,* June 22, 1987, Browne-Wilkinson V.-C.

CORONERS

532. Death by misadventure and accidental death—whether valid distinction
There is no valid distinction between the verdicts of "death by misadventure" and "accidental death."
R. *v.* CORONER FOR THE CITY OF PORTSMOUTH, *ex p.* ANDERSON, *The Times,* August 6, 1987, D.C.

533. Directions to jury—lack of care—circumstances in which verdict of "lack of care" appropriate
A verdict of "lack of care" at an inquest is appropriate only to indicate the physical condition of the deceased which was a cause of death, not to attribute blame or fault.
After the death of Keith Hicks in Brixton prison, an inquest was held. The jury returned a verdict of "misadventure". The Coroner refused to admit evidence or leave to the jury the question whether death was caused by "lack of care".
Held, on an application for judicial review to quash the verdict, allowing the application and ordering a new inquest; that the issue of "lack of care" should have been investigated and left to the jury with appropriate careful directions.
R. *v.* SOUTHWARK CORONER, *ex p.* HICKS [1987] 2 All E.R. 140, D.C.

534. Directions to jury—unlawful killing
[Coroners Act 1887 (c.71) ss.4(3), 6; Coroners Rules 1984 (S.I. 1984 No. 552), r.42.]
A Coroner should direct a jury that they should only reach a verdict of unlawful killing if they are satisfied beyond reasonable doubt that the death was the result of the acts or omissions of a particular person.
D, the deceased, was arrested and detained in a police station. Shortly afterwards, he became ill, was taken to a hospital, and died. At the inquest the coroner, in the absence of counsel, handed his notes on the law to the jury whilst they were in retirement. The jury returned a verdict of unlawful killing, adding "as a result of the degree of care given to him after he was overpowered". Those words were not recorded on the face of the inquisition.
Held, quashing the verdict and inquisition, (1) that the coroner should have directed the jury that they must be satisfied that the act or omission of a particular person amounted to unlawful conduct which was a substantial cause of death, that it was reckless, and that mere neglect was not enough; (2) that the standard of proof was proof beyond reasonable doubt; (3) that in the circumstances, the coroner's handing over of his notes

was a material irregularity; and (4) that the added words were part of the jury's verdict and should have been recorded on the face of the inquisition.

R. *v.* WEST LONDON CORONER, *ex p.* GRAY; R. *v.* WEST LONDON CORONER, *ex p.* DUNCAN, [1987] 2 W.L.R. 1020 D.C.

535. Inquest—form of verdict—"industrial disease"

[Coroners Act 1887 (c.71), s.6; Coroners (Amendment) Act 1926 (c.59), s.19; Births and Deaths Registration Act 1953 (c.20), ss.23, 29; Coroners Rules 1953 (S.I. 1953 No. 205), r.43.]

The court has jurisdiction to quash an inquest verdict where the jury has been misdirected or there is no evidence to support the verdict. The verdict need not be in any particular form, and a verdict of "industrial disease" is acceptable where there is evidence to support it.

R. *v.* H.M. CORONER FOR SOUTH GLAMORGAN, *ex p.* B.P. CHEMICALS (1987) 151 J.P.N. 808, D.C.

536. Inquest—judicial review of inquest—delay

[R.S.C., Ord. 53, r.4(1); Supreme Court Act 1981 (c.54), s.31(6), (7).]

Leave was granted for the making of an application for judicial review of an inquest where the delay of 14 months was largely explicable, no third party would be prejudiced and it would not be substantially more difficult to investigate the facts by reason of the delay. Since there was insufficient evidence before the coroner for him to reach the verdict that he in fact reached, a fresh inquest would be ordered.

Per Curiam; an application or action which merely requires the *fiat* of the Attorney-General is not a relator action (*R.* v. *Stratford-on-Avon District Council, ex p. Jackson* [1986] C.L.Y. 2662, *R.* v. *Cardiff City Coroner, ex p. Thomas* [1970] C.L.Y. 389 considered).

R. *v.* H.M. CORONER FOR NORTH NORTHUMBERLAND, *ex p.* ARMSTRONG, (1987) 151 J.P. 773, D.C.

537. Inquest—pathologist's opinion revised after inquest—rectification of register of deaths

[Coroners Act 1887 (c.71), s.6; Coroners (Amendment) Act 1926 (c.59), s.19; Births and Deaths Registration Act 1953 (c.20), ss.23, 29.]

Where an inquest has decided the cause of death, which subsequently turns out to have been incorrect, the register of births and deaths can only be rectified by quashing the original inquisition.

ATT.-GEN. *v.* HARTE (J.D) (1987) 151 J.P.N. 750, Taylor J.

538. Jury—recommendation by jury

[Coroners Rules (S.I. 1984 No. 552), r.36(2).]

R.36(2) of the 1984 Coroners Rules forbids Coroners' juries to make recommendations.

R. *v.* SHREWSBURY CORONERS COURT, *ex. p.* BRITISH PARACHUTE ASSOCIATION, *The Times,* September 21, 1987, D.C.

539. Post-mortem examination—order for examination before inquest

[Coroners Act 1887 (c.71), s.3(1); Coroners (Amendment) Act 1926 (c.59), s.21(1), (3).]

A coroner may order an examination before an inquest where there has been a sudden death the cause of which is unknown. If it transpired that death was due to natural causes the coroner may then be satisfied that an inquest is unnecessary.

R. *v.* GREATER MANCHESTER CORONER, *ex p.* WORCH, *The Times,* August 1, 1987, C.A.

540. Statistics of deaths

The Home Office has published statistics of deaths reported to coroners in England and Wales during 1986. Copies are available from the Home Office, Statistical Department, Lunar House, Croydon, Surrey CR0 9YD. Tel: 01–760 2850. [£1·50.]

CORPORATION TAX

541. Assessment—burden of proof—false evidence—remittance to commissioners

General Commissioners discharged two alternative assessments to corporation tax on the basis that, there being no evidence that the payments, in relation to which the assessments were raised, had been made to the Company, the Inland Revenue would seem to be alleging that there had been fraud, and that it was incumbent on the Inland Revenue to prove fraud. The case put to the Commissioners was materially false, and this to the knowledge of the managing director of the Company. Browne-Wilkinson V.-C.

directed that the case be remitted to the Commissioners for re-hearing with a direction that fresh evidence be admitted.

Held, dismissing the Company's appeal, that (1) the Commissioners having misdirected themselves in law as to onus of proof, the case should be remitted to them for re-hearing, and (2) (Mustill L.J. dissenting) in the circumstances, the Inland Revenue should be permitted to adduce new evidence.

BRADY (INSPECTOR OF TAXES) *v.* GROUP LOTUS CAR COMPANIES [1987] S.T.C. 635, C.A.

542. Capital allowances—machinery and plant—decor

The Taxpayer Company operated fast food restuarants. In 1976 it embarked upon a major programme of refurbishment involving the installation of plate-glass shop fronts, floor and wall tiles, new electrical lighting, suspended ceilings and raised floors. It claimed that the expenditure on these items qualified for capital allowances as expenditure on the provision of machinery and plant.

Held, dismissing the Taxpayer Company's appeal (save to the items of electrical lighting) that the expenditure was on items being part of the "place" or "premises" in which the business was carried on, and so was not on the provision of machinery or plant attracting capital allowances (*I.R.C.* v. *Scottish & Newcastle Breweries* [1982] C.L.Y. 475 distinguished).

WIMPEY INTERNATIONAL *v.* WARLAND (INSPECTOR OF TAXES); ASSOCIATED RESTAURANTS *v.* SAME, *The Times,* November 30, 1987, Hoffmann J.

543. Capital allowances—whether allowances mandatory

[Finance Act 1965 (c.25), s.56.]

A company may waive its right to claim capital allowances against corporation tax, and if it chooses to do so the allowances are not automatically deductible by the revenue.

B.P. Tyne and B.P. Oil incurred capital expenditure on the provision of machinery and plant for trading purposes prior to the end of 1972. S.2 of the Finance Act (No. 2) of 1975 prevented them from carrying forward losses incurred before the end of 1972. The companies therefore decided not to claim allowances in respect of the expenditure for the periods before the end of 1972, giving them increased allowances for 1973 and subsequent years. The Inland Revenue contended that the companies were obliged to take the allowances in the periods in which the expenditure was incurred.

Held, dismissing the Crown's appeals, that the legislation did not oblige the companies to take the allowances in the periods in which the expenditure was incurred; they were free to renounce the allowances for those periods.

ELLIS (INSPECTOR OF TAXES) *v.* B.P. NORTHERN IRELAND REFINERY; ELLIS (INSPECTOR OF TAXES) *v.* B.P. TYNE TANKER CO. [1987] 1 FTLR 253, C.A.

544. Capital allowances—whether oil exploration directly undertaken on behalf of tax payer.

[Capital Allowances Act 1968 (c.3), s.91(1)(*a*).]

S.91(1)(*a*) of the Capital Allowances Act 1968 requires some close and direct link between the claimant and person undertaking research, akin to agency.

The taxpayer company and S were subsidiaries of a Norwegian partnership. S was a member of two syndicates engaged in oil exploration of Ireland, but in neither syndicate was S the operator (the actual exploring company). By an "illustrative agreement" the taxpayer company agreed to bear S's share of exploration costs in return for any accruing benefits. The shares of expenditure incurred by the operators for which S was responsible were charged by the partnership (equivalent amounts) to the taxpayer's loan account with the partnership. The taxpayer appealed against an assessment to corporation tax claiming entitlement to capital allowances on those amounts as they were capital incurred on scientific research directly undertaken on its behalf. The commissioners dismissed their appeal.

Held, dismissing the taxpayer's further appeal, that s.9(1)(*a*) was restrictive in effect and denoted a close relationship akin to agency between the claimant and the person doing the research.

GASPET *v.* ELLISS (INSPECTOR OF TAXES), [1987] 1 W.L.R. 769, C.A.

545. Double taxation relief—set-off for advance corporation tax

[Income and Corporation Taxes Act 1970 (c.10), ss.497, 501, 505; Finance Act 1972 (c.41), ss.84, 85, 100.]

In its accounting period to June 1980, the Taxpayer Company was entitled to relief under I.C.T.A. 1970, s.497, from double taxation by way of credit for foreign withholding tax and foreign underlying tax in respect of dividends which it had received. For the same accounting period, the Taxpayer Company had available for relief under F.A. 1972, s.85, advance corporation tax attributable to dividends of £2.2m paid by it. The Inland Revenue claimed that the relief for the advance corporation tax must be taken before double taxation relief was given under I.C.T.A. 1970, s.497.

Held, dismissing the Crown's appeal, that the Taxpayer Company was entitled to take credit for double taxation relief before setting-off advance corporation tax.

COLLARD *v.* MINING AND INDUSTRIAL HOLDINGS, *Financial Times*, December 1, 1987, C.A.

546/7. Foreign exchange losses—trading

O.C.L. Co. obtained substantial deutschmark loans, initially to finance the construction of container ships in German shipyards. In expectation of the devaluation of sterling against the deutschmark, O.C.L. (Finance) Co. was formed. By novation it took over the loans and lent equivalent sums in sterling to O.C.L. at two per cent. over U.K. base rate. It thus assumed the risk of depreciation in return for the interest differential. When depreciation took place, it incurred substantial losses which it claimed were deductible in assessing the corporation tax of the O.C.L. group.

Held, that this arrangement was designed solely to transmute losses on foreign loans on capital account into trading losses for fiscal purposes. Thus the losses were not trading losses and were not deductible.

OVERSEAS CONTAINERS (FINANCE) *v.* STOKER (INSPECTOR OF TAXES) [1987] 1 W.L.R. 1521, Vinelott J.

548. Schedule D, Case I—exchange losses—loans—whether capital or revenue

[Income and Corporation Taxes Act 1970 (c.10), s.130(f).]

In 1971 and 1972, T Co. raised loans, each being in the sum of 50M. Swiss francs and each being for a period of five years. It converted the francs into sterling. Subsequently, it bought Swiss francs to repay the loans, incurring a loss of £11·4M. by reason of the depreciation of sterling against the Swiss franc. T Co. claimed that the loss was on revenue account, and no deductible in its Schedule D, base I, computation.

Held, allowing the Crown's appeal, that loans for a period as long as five years had the character of capital, regardless of the purpose for which the money was borrowed. Accordingly, the loss on repayment was on capital account and was precluded from deduction by I.C.T.A. 1970, s.130(*f*).

BEAUCHAMP (INSPECTOR OF TAXES) *v.* WOOLWORTH (F. W.) [1987] S.T.C. 279, Hoffmann J.

549. Scottish company—judicial review—jurisdiction

T Co., a Scottish company, appealed against two assessments to corporation tax and applied for postponement of payment of tax. All proceedings were taken in Scotland, except for the postponement application which, at the request of T Co., was heard in London. The postponement application having been refused, T Co. applied for leave to apply for judicial review. Leave was granted on November 8, 1985 and a stay of proceedings was ordered until determination of the application. However, the Crown sought to recover the tax not postponed, and on October 10, 1986 the Court of Session pronounced a decree in favour of the Crown. The basis of the decision was that the English court had no jurisdiction in the matter. The Crown then applied to strike out the judicial review proceedings.

Held (1) the English courts had jurisdiction to grant leave to apply for judicial review in a tax case notwithstanding that it concerned a Scottish company, but (2) in the circumstances, and having regard to the fact that such proceedings did not affect recovery of the tax not postponed, the proceedings should be stayed.

R. *v.* SPECIAL COMMISSIONER, *ex p.* FORSYTH (R. W.) [1986] S.T.C. 565, MacPherson J.

550. Tax avoidance—transactions in securities—tax advantage. See BIRD *v.* I.R.C., §2038.

550a. Trade—deduction in computing profits—capital expenditure

[Income and Corporation Taxes Act 1970 (c.10), s.130(*f*).]

R.T.Z. Co. joined an oil exploration consortium which was obliged to cap all oil wells when the reserves it was exploiting ran dry. It also chartered a rig and two tankers and was obliged by the charterparties to return them to their original condition. For the two years before the projected closure date of the oilfield, it included in its accounts provisions for the expenditure necessary to fulfill these obligations. It claimed these provisions were deductible in computing corporation tax.

Held, that the equipment in question and the proposed expenditure was of a capital nature and not deductible.

R.T.Z. OIL AND GAS *v.* ELLISS (INSPECTOR OF TAXES) [1987] 1 W.L.R. 1442, Vinelott J.

551. Trade—payments to employees' trust—profits—deduction of payments

[Income and Corporation Taxes Act 1970 (c.10), s.130.]

T. Co. traded as fishmongers; its shares were held by two elderly directors and their wives. The employees were concerned that on the deaths of the directors the company would be unable to continue in its original form. Accordingly, on advice of accountants, a trust was constituted for the benefit of T. Co's employees with a view to acquiring the share capital of T. Co. The company made an initial payments to the trustees of £2,500 and two further payments of £2,224 and £1,000. The Inspector refused to allow deduction of these payments in computing the company's Sched. D, Case I, profits.

Held, allowing T. Co's appeal, that the payments were made wholly and exclusively for its trade within I.C.T.A. 1970, s.130(*a*), and deduction should have been allowed.

BOTT (E.) *v.* PRICE (INSPECTOR OF TAXES) [1987] S.T.C. 100, Hoffmann J.

552. Trade—profits—damages

As a result of the negligence of estate agents, T Co., a trading company, found itself paying higher than expected rent for business premises which it occupied. It recovered £14,000 by way of damages from the estate agents.

Held, dismissing T Co.'s appeal, that, for corporation tax purposes, the sum of £14,000 fell to be brought into account as a trading receipt (*Gray* v. *Lord Penrhyn* [1937] 3 All E.R. 468 and *Rolfe* v. *Nagel* [1982] C.L.Y. 1616 applied).

FISHER (DONALD) (EALING) *v.* SPENCER (INSPECTOR OF TAXES) [1987] S.T.C. 423, Walton J.

553. Trade—profits—Government grant—whether a capital or a revenue receipt

[Industry Act 1972 (c.63), s.7.]

In March 1973 the Department of Trade and Industry made a grant of £47,000 to the taxpayer company under s.7 of the Industry Act 1972; it was described as an "interest relief grant". The grant was not linked to any specific purpose, and was found by the General Commissioners to have been made "to keep the business alive and thus maintain employment."

Held, allowing the Crown's appeal, that the payment fell to be treated as a revenue receipt of the taxpayer company's trade.

RYAN (INSPECTOR OF TAXES) *v.* CRABTREE DENIMS [1987] S.T.C. 402, Hoffmann J.

554. Trade—profits—stock relief—trading stock

[Finance Act 1976 (c.40), Sched. 5, paras. 29, 30.]

The taxpayer company carried on the business of the delivery of motor vehicles by road. For this purpose, it had a specialised fleet of lorries, and it maintained a stock of spare parts and diesel fuel. As at March 31, 1980, the spare parts and diesel fuel stood at a value of £63,140. The taxpayer company claimed entitlement to stock relief in respect of this sum.

Held, dismissing the Crown's appeal, that the spare parts and diesel fuel were "such material as is used" in the performance of its services by the taxpayer company, and so were "trading stock" within F.A. 1976, Sched. 5, para. 30.

ASHWORTH (INSPECTOR OF TAXES) *v.* MAINLAND CAR DELIVERIES [1987] S.T.C. 481, Knox J.

555. Trade—profits—stock relief—trading stock

[Finance Act 1976 (c.40), Sched. 5, para 29.]

T Co. was a finance company within the General Motors Group. It purchased cars from Vauxhall Motors and, in consideration of a handling charge, supplied them to dealers on a "sale or return" basis. Dealers would then purchase the cars as they negotiated sales to customers. Two issues arose; (1) were the cars "trading stock" of T Co. within F.A. 1976, Sched 5, para. 29, and (2) if so, were they "let on hire" by T Co. and so prevented from being treated as trading stock.

Held, dismissing the Crown's appeal, that (1) the cars were "trading stock" of T Co. within the definition in para. 29, and (2) since any element of hiring was only incidental to the business, they were not excluded from that definition.

GENERAL MOTORS ACCEPTANCE CORP. (U.K.) *v.* I.R.C. [1987] S.T.C.122, C.A.

CRIMINAL EVIDENCE AND PROCEDURE

556. Adjournment—whether wrong to refuse—rebuttal evidence

A recorder who called a police witness after the prosecution had closed its case was wrong to refuse the defence an adjournment to enable rebuttal evidence to be called.

R. *v.* COLEMAN, *The Times,* November 21, 1987, C.A.

557. Admissibility—admissions by several defendants to one officer—rejection of officer's evidence—whether rejection admissible in subsequent trials of other defendants

Where the jury acquit one of a number of accused, charged with one of a series of offences, and the essential evidence against that accused was one of a series of interviews, all conducted by the same police officer, in which it was said that the accused had admitted the offence, the remaining accused are entitled, in the trials, to cross-examine the officer and put before their respective juries evidence that that officer had had his evidence rejected in the earlier trial.

Five defendants were charged with a number of offences of conspiracy, two of them with robbery. All were arrested on the same day, and interviewed that day and the next. The two who were charged with robbery, and C, were all interviewed by the same officer, and all complained, long before their trials, that the interviews never took place. At the robbery trial, the only real evidence was the alleged admissions. Those two defendants were acquitted, from which it followed that the jury had rejected the officer's evidence of the interviews. At the trial of C his counsel was not allowed to cross-examine the officer on the previous rejection of his evidence on the interviews.

Held, that the judge had been wrong to prevent the cross-examination, which went so clearly to the officer's credibility, and was such a vital issue in the case. It was always a matter of degree, but here justice demanded that the defence be allowed to explore the matter. Appeal allowed.

R. *v.* COOKE (GARY) (1987) 84 Cr.App.R. 286, C.A.

558. Admissibility—computer evidence—excess alcohol in blood

[Police and Criminal Evidence Act 1984, (c.60), s.69.]

At D's trial for driving with excess alcohol, a laboratory scientist gave evidence of analyses of blood samples by gas chromatography carried out by a computer which printed out results in graph and tabulated form.

Held, dismissing D's appeal, that s.69 of the 1984 Act was not apt when the scientist who had used the computer as a tool gave evidence. It was right that the scientist should be able to refresh her memory from the computer's figures. Evidence as to the operation and accuracy of the computer was not necessary before evidence as to the computer's results was admissible (*R.* v. *Wood* [1983] C.L.Y. 636 considered).

SOPHOCLEUS *v.* RINGER [1987] Crim.L.R. 422, D.C.

559. Admissibility—confession—what is meant by oppression—whether some impropriety required

[Police and Criminal Evidence Act 1984 (c.60), s.76(2)(*a*)(*b*).]

The word "oppression" in s.76(2)(*a*) of the Police and Criminal Evidence Act 1984 should be given its natural and ordinary meaning, which imports some harsh, wrongful, cruel or unjust treatment of a suspect.

Per curiam: a confession may be invalid under the provisions of s.76(2)(*b*) of the 1984 Act even where there is no suspicion of improper behaviour.

F made a full confession when interviewed by police, but appealed on the ground that the confession had been extracted from her by oppressive conduct on the part of the police.

Held, dismissing the appeal, that the word "oppression" in s.76(2) necessarily imported some impropriety of conduct by the interrogator. It had to be harsh, cruel, or unjust conduct—conduct which was in some way wrongful before the section came into play.

R. *v.* FULLING [1987] 2 W.L.R. 923, C.A.

560. Admissibility—confession—whether admissibility should be determined as a preliminary issue

[Police and Criminal Evidence Act 1984 (c.60), s.76(2).]

Where representations were made to justices as to the admissibility of a confession that the prosecution proposed to tender in evidence, the justices were bound by s.76(2) of the Police and Criminal Evidence Act 1984 to conduct a *voir dire* to resolve the issue of admissibility.

D appeared before the juvenile court charged with burglary. The only evidence the prosecution had was a confession by D. Both prosecution and defence solicitors advised the justices that the admissibility of the confession was challenged on the grounds that it was improperly obtained. The justices were invited to resolve the issue of admissibility as a preliminary issue by holding a *voir dire.* On the advice of their clerk they refused to do so. D applied for judicial review seeking an order of mandamus directing the justices to hold a *voir dire.* The advantage to D was that in a *voir dire,* the truth of the confession was irrelevant and if the confession were inadmissible D would be able to avoid giving evidence in his own defence within the substantive trial.

Held, allowing D's application, that where representations were made to the justices in a summary trial that a confession had been improperly obtained they were bound to hold a *voir dire* to determine the issue of admissibility by virtue of the provisions of s.76(2) of the Police and Criminal Evidence Act 1984. D was entitled to a ruling on the admissibility of his confession at the end of the prosecution case. It was within D's discretion at what stage in the proceedings on attack was mounted on the admissibility of a confession. Questions on admissibility put in cross-examination were not representations giving rise to a requirement to hold a *voir dire.* It should never be necessary for the prosecution to call evidence twice in connection with the obtaining of the confession (*S. J. F. (An Infant)* v. *Chief Constable of Kent, ex p. Margate Juvenile Court* [1982] C.L.Y. 1974 considered).

R. *v.* LIVERPOOL JUVENILE COURT, *ex p.* R. [1987] 2 All E.R. 668, D.C.

561. Admissibility—confession—whether "evidence" put forward by prosecution—whether confession can be excluded even though not obtained by oppression nor likely to be unreliable

[Police and Criminal Evidence Act 1984 (c.60), ss.76, 78(1).]

For the purposes of s.78 of the Police and Criminal Evidence Act 1984 "evidence" included a confession and accordingly a judge had a discretion to exclude such evidence even though it had not been obtained by oppression not likely to be unreliable.

The police, although they had no direct evidence against M, told him that they had whereupon he confessed. At trial, he challenged the admissibility of the confession. The trial judge, considering s.78(1) of the 1984 Act decided that it would not be unfair to admit the evidence. M appealed. The Crown contended that a confession, being expressly dealt with by s.76 of the Act did not fall within the meaning of "evidence" for the purposes of s.78(1).

Held, that for the purposes of s.78 "evidence" included all evidence that might be introduced by the prosecution. The trial judge could exclude a confession under s.78 if it would have an adverse affect on the fairness of the trial even though it had not been obtained by oppression nor was likely to be unreliable. On the facts, that discretion had been wrongly exercised and the appeal would be allowed. The confession, because of the deceit practised on M, would be excluded and as that was the only evidence against him, the prosecution would be quashed.

R. *v.* MASON (CARL) [1987] 3 All E.R. 481, C.A.

562. Admissibility—convictions of other persons—relevance to an "issue"—meaning of "conviction"

[Police and Criminal Evidence Act 1984 (c.60), ss.74(1), 78(1).]

In relation to a trial, "issue", in s.74(1) of the 1984 Act, is to be given a wider meaning, to include an "evidential issue" arising in the course of the proceedings.

Two appeals were heard together; in both evidence of the conviction of co-defendants was adduced under s.74(1) of the 1984 Act. In one case although the co-defendant had pleaded guilty he had not yet been sentenced.

Held, dismissing both appeals, "issue" had an extended meaning in this context, to include "evidential" issue arising in the trial; it was not limited to proof of convictions of offences in which the defendant played no part. "Conviction" was to be construed as a finding of guilt on a plea, it did not include the passing of sentence (dicta in *S. (An Infant)* v. *Recorder of Manchester* [1969] C.L.Y. 2189 applied).

Per curiam: S.74 should be sparingly used.

R. *v.* ROBERTSON; R. *v.* GOLDER [1987] 3 W.L.R. 327, C.A.

563. Admissibility—depositions—whether "compiled by a person acting under a duty"

[Criminal Justice Act 1925 (c.86), s.13(3); Police and Criminal Evidence Act 1984 (c.60), ss.68 and 78.]

The evidence against O and M was in depositions of two women cross-examined in detail at committal proceedings and of a man who had made a statement to police officers. A police officer testified that the women were living in the Republic of Ireland

and had told the police they were too frightened to give evidence, having received threats. The man had disappeared.

Held, that (1) the women's depositions were not admissible under s.13(3) of the 1925 Act. For them to be admissible, it had to be proved beyond reasonable doubt and by admissible evidence (not hearsay) that there had been procurement; (2) the threats had to be made "on behalf" of the accused. This did not mean merely "for his benefit" or "with his interests at heart"; (3) in any event, the evidence would have been excluded under s.78 of the 1984 Act; (4) the depositions were not admissible under s.68 of the 1984 Act as documentary records compiled by persons acting under a duty from information supplied by persons with personal knowledge. They were not information supplied by a witness to the Magistrates' Clerk; (5) the police statement was not a record of information supplied to the police officer by the witness within s.68. The record was made by the witness himself (*Gaspet* v. *Ellis* [1985] C.L.Y. 454 and *Barkway* v. *South Wales Transport Co.* (1947–51) C.L.C. 7470 applied).

R. *v.* O'LAUGHLIN AND McLAUGHLIN [1987] Crim.L.R. 632, Central Criminal Ct.

564. Admissibility—detention without access to solicitor—authorisation—extradition

[Police and Criminal Evidence Act 1984 (c.60), ss.58 and 66.]

W was committed for extradition on a charge of conspiracy. Evidence of an interview with police officers was admitted though the police had delayed W's access to a solicitor for two to three hours, during which time the interview took place.

Held, dismissing W's application for habeas corpus, that the evidence was properly admitted. Only the provisions of s.58 of the 1984 Act and the detailed Codes of Practice issued by the Home Secretary pursuant to s.66 were relevant in determining the obligations of police officers when suspects were in police stations. The magistrate was entitled to find the superintendant's decision to authorise delay in access to a solicitor reasonable on the facts of this case.

WALTERS, *Re* [1987] Crim.L.R. 577, D.C.

565. Admissibility—detention without access to solicitor—whether justified

[Police and Criminal Evidence Act 1984 (c.60), ss.58(8), 78 and 116 and Sched. 5.]

Three men committed a robbery at knife-point at a retail store and used S's car to make their escape with two video recorders and £116 cash. S was interviewed following his arrest, a superintendent having authorised withholding of access to a solicitor on the grounds of serious arrestable offence and likelihood that other suspects would be alerted. S denied that his car would have been in the vicinity at the relevant time. S was released but rearrested about a month later after another, B, had implicated him in the robbery. S was again refused access to a solicitor on the grounds that other suspects would be alerted and recovery of stolen property would be hindered. By the next day, all persons implicated by B had been arrested. S was interviewed further, having still been refused access to a solicitor.

Held, that (1) it was doubtful whether the robbery was a serious arrestable offence under s.116 of and Sched. 5 to the 1984 Act; (2). The Learned Recorder was not satisfied that reasonable grounds existed entitling authorisation to withhold access to a solicitor in relation to the initial interviews; (3) no such grounds existed in relation to the later interviews; (4) evidence of the interviews would therefore be excluded under s.78.

R. *v.* SMITH (ERIC) [1987] Crim.L.R. 579, Stafford Crown Ct.

566. Admissibility—fresh evidence—remission of tax appeal to Commissioners. See BRADY (INSPECTOR OF TAXES) *v.* GROUP LOTUS CAR COMPANIES, §541.

567. Admissibility—handling—evidence of previous possession—statement made on other occasion

[Theft Act 1968 (c.60), s.27(3).]

S.27(3) of the Theft Act does not allow for the admission of evidence of earlier circumstances of possession of stolen goods, nor of earlier explanations.

The appellant was charged with handling; he had previous convictions for the same and prosecuting counsel sought to adduce evidence under s.27(3) of a statement made by the defendant on an earlier occasion about other stolen goods found at his lodgings. The defence objected on the ground that the bare fact of earlier possession only could be proved, not the surrounding circumstances. The judge admitted the statement in an edited form, and the appellant was convicted.

Held, dismissing the appeal, that the section did not authorise evidence to be admitted concerning the circumstances of an earlier possession, nor of a previous explanation, but where the judge admitted an edited statement, purged of irrelevancies and designed only to prove prior possession, there was no irregularity (*R.* v. *Bradley* [1981] C.L.Y. 525 applied; *R.* v. *Smith* [1918] 2 K.B. 415 not followed).

R. *v.* WOOD (WILLIAM) 1987 1 W.L.R. 779, C.A.

568. Admissibility—hearsay

P and H were alleged to have used a flat for drug dealing. H's case was that only P so used the flat. Following their arrest, a police officer remained at the flat and received many telephone calls from persons asking for P and asking whether there were any drugs for sale. The trial judge allowed H's counsel to ask the police whether there had been a number of calls and whether any callers had asked to speak to H. Upon objection by prosecution counsel and P's counsel, H's counsel was not allowed to cross-examine as to the contents of the calls. P was acquitted.

Held, dismissing H's appeal against conviction, that the excluded evidence was hearsay and inadmissible (*R.* v. *Ratten* (1972) 56 Cr.App.R. 18 applied; *Woodhouse* v. *Hall* [1981] C.L.Y. 427 considered).

R. *v.* HARRY [1987] Crim.L.R. 325, C.A.

569. Admissibility—hearsay—document connecting defendant with offence

There was substantial evidence of identification against L, who was charged with robbery of a post office. He put forward an alibi defence. The judge allowed evidence to be called that a gun had been found on a grass verge about a mile from the post office on the road where the car used in the robbery was found and that nearby were found two pieces of paper bearing the writing "Sean rules" and "Sean rules 85". L's name was Sean. Ink of similar appearance and dye was found on the gun barrel.

Held, dismissing L's appeal against conviction, that the reference to Sean involved no assertion as to the truth of the contents of the documents. If the jury were satisfied that the gun was used in the robbery and that the pieces of paper were linked with the gun, the reference to Sean could fit in with L having committed the offence. But the most important issue for the jury was the accuracy of the identification evidence. The probative value of the evidence was not great but it was not hearsay and the judge had not erred in the exercise of his discretion (*R.* v. *Romeo* (1982) 30 S.A.S.R. 243 applied).

R. *v.* LYDON (SEAN) [1987] Crim.L.R. 407, C.A.

570. Admissibility—hearsay—expert copy of note of car number made by witness—whether admissible as exhibit or only as document from which witness could refresh memory

Following an attempted robbery, the victim, N, tried to write the registration number of the culprit's car on a piece of paper. The ink ran out. A fingerprint officer examined the paper with specialist equipment which revealed the indented writing as showing the number OBL 804. The result was produced at court but the original piece of paper had been lost.

Held, that (1) the reproduction of the note was inadmissible but (2) it could be looked at by N to refresh her memory (*R.* v. *Smith* [1976] C.L.Y. 449, *R.* v. *McLean* [1968] C.L.Y. 699, *R.* v. *Kelsey* [1982] C.L.Y. 598 and *Topham* v. *McGregor* (1844) 1 C. & K. 320 considered).

R. *v.* TOWNSEND [1987] Crim.L.R. 411, Lewes Crown Ct.

571. Admissibility—photofit picture—whether previous consistent statement—whether hearsay

A photofit picture is admissible in evidence at a criminal trial, since it is neither hearsay nor a previous consistent statement.

C was charged with robbery and indecent assault. A photofit picture compiled by a policeman from the victim's description was admitted in evidence. C appealed against conviction on the grounds that such a picture was inadmissible as hearsay and a previous consistent statement of the victim.

Held, dismissing the appeal, that a photofit was not a statement in writing so as to come within the rule against hearsay, and thus could not be a previous consistent statement (*R.* v. *Tolson* (1864) 4 F. & F. 103 applied).

R. *v.* COOK (CHRISTOPHER) [1987] 2 W.L.R. 775, C.A.

572. Admissibility—police acting *mala fide*—effect on evidence of subsequent analysis of breath

[Police and Criminal Evidence Act 1984 (c.60), s.78.]

Police saw M driving too fast and later momentarily losing control of his car before driving into his driveway. They noticed drink on his breath and that he had glazed eyes. Despite M's protest that they were on his private property, the police persisted with a request that he provide a breath sample.

Held, allowing M's appeal against conviction of driving with excess alcohol, that although the procedure under s.8 of the Road Traffic Act 1972 had been properly carried out at the police station, the evidence of what happened after M's arrest should have been ruled inadmissible in view of the unfairness of the procedure at his property and the Crown Court's finding that the police had acted *mala fide,* knowing that their licence to remain on M's property had been terminated. The Crown Court's finding that M gave the first sample voluntarily was inconsistent with the finding of *mala fides.* S.78 of the 1984 Act required the court to consider the way the evidence was obtained (*Fox* v. *Chief Constable of Gwent* [1985] C.L.Y. 2986 distinguished).

MATTO (JIT SINGH) *v.* D.P.P. [1987] Crim.L.R. 641, D.C.

573. Admissibility—police notes of interview—not signed by defendant—whether notes should be shown to jury as *aide memoire*

D, on trial for burglary, objected to the jury being shown transcripts of interviews. He disputed the authenticity of both sets of notes and he had not signed or initialled them. The judge held that, after cross-examination as to the authenticity of the notes, they should be shown to the jury. D was convicted and appealed.

Held, that an unsigned contemporaneous note of an interview between the defendant and the police, the authenticity of which is disputed, should not be shown to the jury to jog their memories where there was nothing they could decide as to whether the document was bogus or not by looking at it. On the authorities, a jury cannot see an unsigned contemporaneous note for the purpose of jogging their memories (*R.* v. *Fenlon* [1980] C.L.Y. 466 applied).

R. *v.* DILLON (R.W.) (NOTE) (1987) 85 Cr.App.R. 29, C.A.

574. Admissibility—police observation log—signed and verified by officers

S was charged with offering to supply a controlled drug. Part of the evidence against him was a police observation log compiled by an officer summarising his observations and those of other officers. The other officers signed and verified the log. At trial the officers were closely examined as to their notes and the log from which they had refreshed their memory. The jury asked to see the log. The recorder ruled that the log should be made an exhibit to assist the jury to decide whether it was an honest or dishonest document. S was convicted and appealed.

Held, that notes can be referred to by witnesses to refresh their memory on the usual basis and these should be available to the other parties for inspection and cross-examination. Where cross-examination suggests that the evidence is concocted, the notes are admissible to rebut that suggestion. The record is admissible as evidence of inconsistency where the witness's evidence is not consistent with it. The notes can be used as an *aide memoire* by the jury. The record is not evidence of the truth of its contents. Had the jury not raised the matter, the Crown would have introduced the log, otherwise the cross-examination of the officers could not have been assessed by the jury. However, they should have been told of its precise status. That had not been done but having regard to the summing-up as a whole, that was not a material irregularity and the conviction was not unsafe (*R.* v. *Fenlon* [1980] C.L..Y 466 and *R.* v. *Dillon* [1984] C.L.Y. 749 distinguished).

R. *v.* SEKHON (1987) 85 Cr.App.R. 19, C.A.

575. Admissibility—procedure in magistrates' court

[Police and Criminal Evidence Act 1984 (c.60), s.78.]

Counsel for V invited justices to exclude evidence of V's interview with police under s.78 of the 1984 Act and to call V as on a trial within a trial. The application was declined.

Held, dismissing V's appeal, that no general rule could be laid down. S.78 was discretionary. S.76 was not. Under s.78, there was no burden on the Crown to disprove unfairness. Where an application to exclude evidence was made under s.78 and not s.76, the procedure in the magistrates' court should be precisely as it had always been (*A.D.C.* v. *Chief Constable of Greater Manchester* (unrep. March 15, 1983) and *S. F. J. (An Infant)* v. *Chief Constable of Kent, ex p. Margate Juvenile Court* [1982] C.L.Y. 1974 applied).

VEL *v.* OWEN *sub nom.* VEL (KEVIN) *v.* CHIEF CONSTABLE OF NORTH WALES [1987] Crim.L.R. 496, D.C.

576. Admissibility—threatening to kill—admissibility of previous assault

[Offences against the Person Act 1861 (c.100), s.16.]

On a charge of threatening to kill, evidence of a previous assault is admissible as tending to prove that the accused intended his victim to take the threat seriously.

W was charged with threatening to kill, contrary to s.16 of the 1861 Act. The judge admitted evidence that W had previously assaulted the same intended victim. After conviction W appealed.

Held, that the judge had a discretion to admit the evidence, and that W had been rightly convicted. Such evidence was admissible because it went to the seriousness of the threat, and that he meant it to be taken seriously.

R. *v.* WILLIAMS (CLARENCE) (1987) 84 Cr.App.R. 299, C.A.

577. Admissibility—unsupervised L-driver—charged with causing death by reckless driving

The fact that a defendant charged with causing death by reckless driving was at the time of the accident an unsupervised learner-driver is irrelevant *per se,* unless it can be shown to be causally connected with the accident.

R. *v.* O'NEALE, *The Times,* November 12, 1987, C.A.

578. *Aide memoire*—production to jury—circumstances

When a witness refers to an aide-memoire in the course of his evidence-in-chief, it can be produced as an exhibit if cross-examination on it goes beyond the parts of it that were used for refreshing memory.

D was arrested for assault during the printing dispute at Wapping. On his release he made a note of what had happened. At his trial he was allowed to use the note as an aide-memoire during examination-in-chief. In the course of cross-examination he was asked about other matters contained in the note. He applied for the note to be exhibited. The application was refused.

Held, allowing the appeal, that since cross-examination had gone beyond the parts used for refreshing memory, D could insist on its becoming an exhibit. There had been a material irregularity and the conviction was unsafe and unsatisfactory (*Gregory* v. *Tavernor* (1833) 6 C. &. P. 280 and *Senat* v. *Senat* [1965] C.L.Y. 1586 applied).

R. *v.* BRITTON [1987] 1 W.L.R. 539, C.A.

579. Alternative verdicts—standard of proof

Where a jury is entitled to bring in an alternative verdict, it must be satisfied beyond reasonable doubt that the defendant has committed the offence of which it is convicting him. It is therefore a misdirection, for example, for a judge to tell a jury that provided they are satisfied that a defendant has committed either theft or robbery, they should convict him of whichever they think it is more probable that he committed.

ATT.-GEN. OF HONG KONG *v.* YIP KAI-FOON, *The Times,* December 9, 1987, P.C.

580. Anonymity of victim—attempted rape—murder

[Sexual Offences (Amendment) Act 1976 (c.82), s.4.]

G pleaded guilty to murder of a 15-year-old girl and his plea of attempted rape of the girl was accepted. A newspaper applied for leave to report the girl's name under s.4(3) of the 1976 Act. Neither Crown nor the Defence opposed the application. In a sworn affidavit, the victim's mother said she had no objection.

Held, that it was in the public interest for the girl's name to be published in relation to both the murder and the attempted rape. S.4 was designed to avoid the likelihood of embarrassing the victim. The mother's affidavit removed any other possible fear of embarrassment. The murder could not practically be reported without identifying the victim of the attempted rape.

R. *v.* GILLIGAN [1987] Crim.L.R. 501, Nottingham Crown Ct., Boreham J.

581. Appeal—abandonment—leave of court

An appellant does not need the leave of the Court of Appeal to abandon his appeal before he or his counsel has opened it, but leave for abandonment is needed thereafter (*R.* v. *De Courcy* [1964] C.L.Y. 683 applied).

R. *v.* SPICER, *The Times,* October 29, 1987, C.A.

582. Appeal—divisional court—case stated—jurisdiction

Justices committed the appellants for trial, having rejected their submissions that certain enforcement notices of which they were alleged to have been in breach could not have been effective pending appeals against them.

Held, dismissing appeals against the justices' decision, that the Divisional Court had no jurisdiction to entertain such appeals and examining justices had no power to state a case for consideration by the Divisional Court (*Card* v. *Salmon* [1953] C.L.Y. 2108 applied; *Streames* v. *Copping* [1985] C.L.Y. 2128 considered).

CRAGG *v.* LEWES DISTRICT COUNCIL [1986] Crim.L.R. 800, D.C.

583. Appeal—from Magistrates' Court—absence of appellant

The Crown Court can hear an appeal from the Magistrates' Court where the prosecution attend, even in the absence of the defence, if the notice of appeal has neither been withdrawn nor an application made to do so.

R. *v.* GUILDFORD CROWN COURT, *ex p.* BREWER, *The Independent,* October 14, 1987, D.C.

584. Appeal—rules

CRIMINAL APPEAL (AMENDMENT) RULES 1987 (No. 1977 (L.9)) [£2·20], made under the Supreme Court Act 1981 (c.54), ss.84(1), (2), 86 and 87(4); operative on January 1, 1988; amend S.I. 1968 No. 1262.

585/6. Appeal—summing-up defective—proviso

[Criminal Appeal Act 1968 (c.19), s.2(1).]

Where the judge omitted any definition of the offence charged in his summing-up to the jury, the defect was so fundamental that the proviso could not be applied. The prosecutor for the Crown could and should remind a judge of a fundamental omission.

R. *v.* McVEY, *The Times,* October 24, 1987, C.A.

587. Arrest—breach of community service order—whether necessary for warrant to be in possession of arresting officer

[Powers of Criminal Courts Act 1973 (c.62), s.16(1); Magistrates' Courts' Act 1980 (c.43), s.125.]

D assaulted X, a policewoman, as she was attempting to arrest another for breach of a community service order. A warrant had been issued pursuant to s.16(1) of the 1973 Act but was not in the possession of X.

Held, allowing the prosecutor's appeal, that X had been acting in the execution of her duty. S.125(3) of the 1980 Act applied to the warrant. Accordingly, it was not required to be in X's possession at the time of arrest. The s.16(1) proceedings were proceedings "in connection with an offence" within s.125(4) of the 1980 Act, as added by the Police and Criminal Evidence Act 1984.

JONES *v.* KELSEY [1987] Crim.L.R. 392, D.C.

588. Arrest—validity—request for name and address

[Road Traffic Act 1972 (c.20), s.18; Police Act 1964 (c.48), s.51(1); Police and Criminal Evidence Act 1984 (c.60), ss.25, 28.]

N was stopped by the police for riding a cycle in a dangerous manner. Neither constable involved knew N's name and address. N was asked for his name as he was riding his cycle in a dangerous manner. He refused, was warned that he could be arrested under the 1984 Act and was asked for his name and address. N refused and one constable informed him that he was being arrested for failing to give his name and address. N tried to ride away, the constable tried to stop him, and N assaulted him. N was convicted of riding a bicycle without due care and attention and assaulting a policeman in the execution of his duty.

Held, dismissing the appeal, that the requirements of s.25(1) and (3) were satisfied by these circumstances. That the requirements in s.28(3) were fulfilled if, a short but reasonable time before the arrest, it was indicated the nature of an offence in respect of which the name and address were required. Whether such words were spoken at the time of arrest or not was a matter of fact for the justices.

NICHOLAS *v.* PARSONAGE [1987] R.T.R. 199, D.C.

589. Assault—private prosecution—whether triable on indictment

[Offences against the Person Act 1861 (c.100), ss.42, 46, 47.]

D is not entitled to elect trial by jury in a case of privately prosecuted common assault.

R. *v.* BLYTH VALLEY JUSTICES, *ex p.* DOBSON, *The Times,* November 7, 1987, D.C.

590. Attempting to procure act of gross indecency—indictment—evidential burden

[Sexual Offences Act 1956 (c.69), s.13; Sexual Offences Act 1967 (c.60), ss.1 and 4.]

Two police officers gave evidence of an approach by S near a public lavatory.

Held, dismissing his appeal against conviction of attempting to procure an act of gross indecency, that (1) such an attempt should be charged under s.13 of the 1956 Act and S.I. of the 1967 Act; (2) identification of the place was unnecessary (but the Court expressed no view on whether the indictment need include the words "in a public place"). Ss.1(1), (6) and (7) and s.4(3) of the 1967 Act read with s.13 of the 1956 Act meant that there was an evidential burden on S to raise the defences of privacy, consent or exempted age. As no evidence raised these issues in this case, the judge had no duty to leave them to the jury.

R. *v.* SPIGHT [1986] Crim.L.R. 817, C.A.

591. *Autrefois acquit*—action previously dismissed for want of prosecution

The defence of *autrefois acquit* is not available when an action has previously been dismissed for want of prosecution, because there has been no trial on the merits. Following such a dismissal, recommencement of the proceedings will be lawful unless it is clearly an abuse of the process of the Court.

R. *v.* WILLESDEN JUSTICES, *ex p.* CLEMMINGS, *The Times,* October 21, 1987, D.C.

592. Bail—absconding—whether "escape"—whether contempt of court

[Bail Act 1976 (c.63), ss.3(1), 6(1)(5)(7); Contempt of Court Act 1981 (c.49), s.14.]

Although punishable as if it were a contempt of court, absconding from bail is not contempt and may only be punished under the provisions of the Bail Act.

R was on unconditional bail during his trial for offences of burglary. He absconded. In due course the breach of bail came to be dealt with, R admitting to the judge that he was thereby in contempt of court. The judge sentenced him to two years on the basis that he had escaped from lawful custody, and that that was a contempt of court.

Held, on appeal, that the judge had misdirected himself in holding that R had escaped from lawful custody. When he absconded he was not in custody, but on unconditional bail. Absconding from bail had never been a contempt of court. But it was a bad case of absconding, and within the language of s.6(5) of the 1976 Act, so that the sentence would be varied to the maximum allowed thereunder, namely 12 months.

R. *v.* READER (1987) 84 Cr.App.R. 294, C.A.

593. Bail—estreatment

A judge erred in ordering the estreatment of the whole of recognisances of two sureties in circumstances where the defendant attended court on the day of his trial but absconded over the luncheon adjournment.

R. *v.* YORK CROWN COURT, *ex p.* COLEMAN, *The Times,* May 12, 1987, D.C.

594. Bail—failure to surrender to custody—practice direction. See PRACTICE, § 2910.

595. Bail—recognisance—forfeiture

N, who was charged with involvement in a serious drugs conspiracy, absconded to Spain. X and Y, sureties in the sum of £15,000 each, reported N's disappearance within two days and asked to withdraw from their sureties. At the hearing, there was great confusion as to the facts, in particular as to when a twice-daily reporting condition had been lifted and when N had absconded.

Held, quashing an order of forfeiture of the recognisances with liberty to apply for the order to be varied if N attended for his trial, that (1) the judge had failed to have regard to the conduct of X and Y, how far they had taken reasonable measures to ensure N's attendance for trial and how promptly they had notified the police; (2) the judge had also erred in failing to take into account the muddle over the reporting condition. In this case the change would have affected the minds of the sureties; (3) no forfeiture order should have been made until N had failed to attend for trial; (4) an order of mandamus would be quoted directing another judge to rehear the question of whether the recognisances should be estreated (*R.* v. *Southampton Justices, ex p. Green* [1975] C.L.Y. 2038, *R.* v. *Waltham Forest Justices, ex p. Parfrey* [1980] C.L.Y. 436, *R.* v. *Wells Street Magistrates' Court* [1982] C.L.Y. 516 considered).

R. *v.* INNER LONDON CROWN COURT, *ex p.* SPRINGHALL AND SMITH [1987] Crim.L.R. 252, D.C.

596. Bail—recognisance—forfeiture

[Bail Act 1976 (c.63), s.8(4); Crown Court Rules 1982 (S.I. 1982 No. 1109), s.21(1).]

Where a recognisance has been entered into before a justice of the peace, it can properly be forfeited by the Crown Court despite the fact that a High Court judge has at some stage varied conditions of bail.

The defendant was bailed by the justices, his brother standing surety in the sum of £100,000. Later bail conditions were varied by the High Court to allow him to go to the USA; the surety gave his consent. The defendant failed to attend his trial and a Crown Court judge estreated the £100,000 recognisance

Held, on an application for judicial review on whether the Crown Court had jurisdiction, that the order for recognisance having originally been made by a justice, was unaffected by the High Courts variation; it was therefore appropriate for the Crown Court judge to order estreatment rather than the High Court (*R.* v. *Uxbridge Justices, ex p. Heward-Mills* [1983] C.L.Y. 920 followed).

R. *v.* WARWICK CROWN COURT, *ex p.* SMALLEY (1987) 84 Cr.App.R. 51, D.C.

597. Barrister—alibi witness—duty to obtain instructions from defendant before omitting to call witness

Where in the course of a re-trial defence counsel proposed not to call alibi witnesses who had given evidence in the first trial, he was under a duty to obtain his client's instructions before adopting that course.

D was tried on two counts of causing criminal damage. D's defence was that he was not the person who committed the crimes. D's wife and daughter were called as alibi witnesses. The jury failed to agree on a verdict. At the re-trial, D's counsel did not call the alibi witnesses to give evidence. D was convicted. The reasons for not calling the witnesses were that their evidence did not provide D with a complete alibi, the evidence had failed to secure a not guilty verdict at the first trial and their credibility might be destroyed if they attempted to "improve" on their evidence the second time round. D's counsel failed to obtain D's instructions before following that course of action. D appealed.

Held, allowing the appeal, that D's counsel was under a duty to obtain D's instructions before proceeding not to call the alibi witnesses at the re-trial. Having regard to the differing verdicts obtained at the two trials, D's conviction was unsatisfactory. There was a material irregularity in the re-trial.

R. *v.* IRWIN [1987] 1 W.L.R. 902, C.A.

598. Binding over—court's powers. See LAW REFORM, §2254.

599. Binding over—jurisdiction of Divisional Court—judicial review

B was acquitted of assaulting a police officer. He refused to be bound over and the judge committed him to prison for seven days or until he agreed to be bound over.

Held, dismissing B's application for judicial review, that (1) the Divisional Court had jurisdiction to entertain the application but (2) there was ample evidence before the judge to justify the order (*Smalley, Re* [1985] C.L.Y. 555 and *R.* v. *Maidstone Crown Court, ex p. Gill* [1986] C.L.Y. 604 applied).

R. *v.* INNER LONDON CROWN COURT, *ex p.* BENJAMIN [1987] Crim.L.R. 417, D.C.

600. Binding over—soliciting a policewoman for prostitution

[Justices of the Peace Act 1361 (c.1).]

Justices found that, in a "red light" district, D stopped his car and accosted and solicited for immoral purposes a policewoman in plain clothes. Evidence of the accosting of respectable women in the district was admitted as relevant to the propriety of binding D over.

Held, dismissing D's appeal from an order under the 1361 act binding him over, that (1) whether D's conduct was *contra bonos mores* was for the justices to decide. The phrase meant contrary to a good way of life; (2) although there could be no bind over unless D might otherwise repeat his conduct and although the Crown Court felt it unlikely that he would, in view of the justices' finding and publicity, the justices' order was proper, since D might have repeated his conduct had he not been brought before the justices; (3) evidence as to other events in the locality was admissible, though it would have been better to adduce such evidence after the court had decided whether the facts were proved (*Lansbury* v. *Riley* [1914] 3 K.B. 229; *Crook* v. *Edmondson,* [1966] C.L.Y. 12325, *R.* v. *Sandbach Justices, ex p. Williams* (1935) 99 J.P. 51 and *R.* v. *Aubrey-Fletcher, ex p. Thompson* [1969] C.L.Y. 2157 considered).

HUGHES *v.* HOLLEY [1987] Crim.L.R. 253, D.C.

601. Binding over—whether conditions could be imposed—whether binding over valid

[Justices of the Peace Act 1361.]

When R was brought before the Crown Court for alleged breach of a probation order, it was conceded that his conduct did not constitute a breach. The judge nevertheless purported to bind him over to keep the peace and be of good behaviour for three years and not to teach or try to teach anyone under 18 for three years. He later admitted a breach of that order and the Crown Court estreated £250 for the breach.

Held, that (1) the order binding R over was a nullity, since no conditions could be attached to such an order under the 1361 Act, (2) the Court of Appeal had no jurisdiction to entertain R's appeal, since R had not been dealt with "for an offence" within s.10 of the Criminal Appeal Act 1968 when the bind over was imposed. Nevertheless, the Court would reconstitute itself as a Divisional Court and grant certiorarii to quash the orders (*R.* v. *Ayu* [1958] C.L.Y. 979 considered).

R. *v.* RANDALL [1987] Crim.L.R. 254, C.A. and D.C.

602. Burden of proof—judge's comments

Nothing must be said that in any way detracts from the fundamental principle that the burden of proof rests with the prosecution.

R. *v.* McDONALD, *The Times,* March 27, 1987, C.A.

603. Byelaws—validity of military byelaws—presumption

[Military Lands Act 1892 (c.43), Part II; R.A.F. Mildenhall Byelaws 1986, No. 2(*a*).]

B climbed through a perimeter fence which had been cut and was charged with contravention of byelaw 2(*a*) of the 1986 Mildenhall Byelaws.

Held, allowing the prosecutor's appeal, that justices had erred in acquitting B on the basis that the byelaws had not been proved beyond reasonable doubt to be valid. Once proved, byelaws are presumed valid unless and until the defendant shows otherwise. The courts were not concerned with whether or not a requirement of either House of Parliament's standing orders had been met. The fact that these byelaws prohibited all use of the relevant lands, subject to exercise of a dispensing power under byelaw 7, did not invalidate the byelaws.

D.P.P. *v.* BUGG [1987] Crim.L.R. 625, D.C.

604. Case stated—recognisance—means of applicant—consideration by justices

[Magistrates' Courts Act 1980 (c.43), s.114.]

If Magistrates are considering requiring a recognisance before stating a case under s.114 of the Magistrates' Courts Act 1980 they must consider the applicants' means before fixing the amount, and in deciding whether or not to require a recognisance at all.

D was convicted by magistrates of burglary. He requested the court to state a case for the opinion of the High Court. He was required to enter into a recognisance of £500 under s.114 of the Magistrates' Courts Act to cover the work involved. D had no money and was in receipt of supplementary benefit. He sought an order of mandamus requiring the justices' to state a case without a recognisance.

Held, granting the order sought, that while magistrates were perfectly entitled to require a recognisance to ensure that the applicant genuinely intended to pursue the appeal, they must have regard to his means in fixing the amount, and in deciding whether or not to require a recognisance at all.

R. *v.* NEWCASTLE UPON TYNE JUSTICES, *ex p.* SKINNER [1987] 1 All E.R. 349, D.C.

605. Character—relevance of good character—direction to jury

The prosecution alleged a long-term fraud committed through X Co., of which D and L were the only directors. D alleged that the things done wrong were done by L without D's knowledge. L had a previous conviction for handling stolen goods.

Held, dismissing D's appeal against conviction, that the trial judge had not erred in directing the jury that possession of a good character went to the issue of D's credibility. Where there was an issue between defendants, one of whom had a good character and the other of whom did not, it would be wrong of the judge to direct as to the second advantage of good character (*i.e.* to show a lack of propensity to commit offences of the kind in question) (*R.* v. *Bryant and Oxley* [1978] C.L.Y. 652 and *R.* v. *Stannard* (1837) 7 C. & P. 673, 675 distinguished).

R. *v.* LEVY (NORMAN) [1987] Crim.L.R. 48, C.A.

606. Child abuse—interview technique—hypothetical and unclear questions—use of sexually explicit dolls—evidential status. See MINORS.

607. Child abuse—standard of proof—whether on balance of probabilities. See G. (A MINOR) (CHILD ABUSE: STANDARD OF PROOF), *Re,* §2474.

608. Committal proceedings—failure to inquire into circumstances in which confession obtained—whether committal would be quashed

[Police and Criminal Evidence Act 1984 (c.60), s.76(2).]

Although it is open to the divisional court to quash a committal on the ground that the magistrates refused to conduct an inquiry into the circumstances in which a confession had been obtained, it would be a wholly exceptional course to pursue on that ground alone.

The applicant moved to quash a committal for trial on five charges of burglary by the magistrates' court. He appeared in person at the committal hearing, and indicated that he wished to challenge the admissibility of his alleged confessions, which were the only evidence against him. The court refused to let him do so, holding that it was a matter for the judge at the Crown Court. The grounds of the application were that s.76(2) of the Police and Criminal Evidence Act 1984 required the prosecution to prove a confession reliable beyond reasonable doubt, and that by declining to hear this evidence, the justices declined jurisdiction and thus their decision could be challenged by certiorari.

Held, that since judicial review was a discretionary remedy, the court would not, save in exceptional circumstances quash committal proceedings on the ground of omission to inquiry into a confession alone, since the inquiry could be made by the judge at the trial (*R.* v. *Carden* (1878) 5 Q.B.D. 1, *R.* v. *Marsham* [1892] 1 Q.B. 371 considered).

R. *v.* OXFORD CITY JUSTICES, *ex p.* BERRY [1987] 1 All E.R. 1244, D.C.

609. Committal proceedings—joint committal of adult and juvenile

[Magistrates' Courts Act 1980 (c.43), s.24(1)(*b*).]

A juvenile and several adults appeared before justices jointly charged with burglary. The magistrates declined jurisdiction in relation to the trial of the adults and decided that it was necessary to commit the juvenile to trial at the Crown Court. An order was made committing the adults to trial at the Crown Court and a similar order was made in respect of the juvenile on the following day by a different bench. The Crown Court judge declined to deal with the juvenile as the committal was not valid under s.24(1)(*b*) of the Magistrates' Courts Act 1980 because the joint committal should not have been split. The prosecutor sought judicial review of the judge's decision.

Held, allowing the application, that there was nothing in s.24(1)(*b*) to show that an order to commit for trial had to be made on the same occasion for an adult and a juvenile, but there should have been consideration of s.24(1)(*b*) when both the adults and the juvenile were before the court. That had been done here. The magistrates had acted properly.

R. *v.* CROWN COURT AT DONCASTER, *ex p.* SOUTH YORKSHIRE PROSECUTION SERVICE *sub nom.* R. *v.* DONCASTER CROWN COURT, *ex p.* CROWN PROSECUTION SERVICE (1987) 85 Cr.App.R. 1, D.C.

610. Comparative sentences—information—procedure

Information as to comparative sentences should be obtained from the clerk of the court, not by the issue of a witness summons against the borough solicitor.

WILLIAMS *v.* CO-OPERATIVE RETAIL SERVICES, *The Times,* March 28, 1987, D.C.

611/2. Confession—access to solicitor refused—breach of code of conduct

[Police and Criminal Evidence Act 1984 (c.60), s.78.]

At D's trial, the prosecution relied on admissions made by D at a police station after declining to take part in a contemporaneously recorded interview. When taken into custody at 2.53 a.m., D had said that he wanted a solicitor in the morning. He was interviewed at 10.10 a.m. after the Acting Superintendent had signed the custody record to the effect that D's rights under s.58(6) of the 1984 Act were to be withheld because the offences (two residential burglaries) were serious arrestable offences and "notification would hinder recovery" of a considerable amount of unrecovered property.

Held, excluding evidence of the confessions under s.78, that the police erred in refusing D access to a solicitor and allowing the evidence would have an adverse effect upon the fairness of the trial. Technical breaches of the police code of conduct were to be taken into account.

R. *v.* DEACON [1987] Crim.L.R. 404, Guildford Crown Ct.

613. Confession—solicitor wrongfully refused—effect on admissibility

[Police and Criminal Evidence Act 1984 (c.60), ss.56, 76 and 116.]

M, an animal rights activist, was charged with conspiracy to steal dogs from certain kennels. 28 dogs, worth £880, were stolen. When brought into the police station, M asked to see a solicitor. The request was denied (a) on the basis that the offence was a serious arrestable offence and (b) because access to a solicitor might prejudice enquiries. He subsequently made admissions.

Held, that (1) the offence was not a serious arrestable offence within s.116 of the 1984 Act. 28 dogs owned collectively by Ecclesfield Beagles' hunt was not a serious financial loss; (2) in any event, the conditions in s.58(8) for delaying access to a solicitor were not satisfied; (3) it was improper to refuse access to a solicitor because the defendant would be advised to remain silent; (4) accordingly, the confession should be excluded under s.76.

R. *v.* McIVOR [1987] Crim.L.R. 409, Sheffield Crown Ct.

614. Confession—whether *voire dire* required—procedure

[Police and Criminal Evidence Act 1984 (c.60), s.76(2).]

Defence counsel informed the judge that there would be an issue as to the admissibility of two confessions and whether they had been obtained in consequence of anything done or said which was likely to render them unreliable, under s.76(2) of the 1984 Act.

The defence wished the matter to be dealt with by a single cross-examination before the jury with a defence submission on the issue of admissibility at the close of its case.

Held, that (1) the court was bound to hold a *voire dire* but (2) defence counsel was not bound to put his case to witnesses in the *voire dire* and was entitled to raise the question of admissibility at any later stage (*Ajodha* v. *The State* [1981] C.L.Y. 415 not followed).

R. *v.* MILLARD [1987] Crim.L.R. 196, Central Criminal Ct.

615. Contempt—arrest of person who was at police station to inspect civil litigation documents—whether breach of time limit. See PRACTICE (CIVIL), §2935.

616. Contempt—committal proceedings—whether civil proceedings—standard of proof. See SAVINGS & INVESTMENT BANK *v.* GASCO INVESTMENTS (NETHERLANDS) B.V. (No. 2) §2931.

617. Contempt—failure to surrender to bail—appropriate procedure

A court that decides of its own motion to deal with a failure to answer bail as a contempt of court should give the defendant an opportunity to provide an explanation and invite his counsel to make submissions before sentencing him.

D pleaded guilty to charges of burglary. He had been committed for trial on bail and failed to surrender to the Crown Court. One year later he was arrested and was sentenced to 30 months' imprisonment for the burglaries and six months' consecutive for the failure to surrender.

Held, that the court would not interfere with the sentences for the burglaries and would not have interfered with the sentence for the failure to surrender had the correct procedure been followed. Unfortunately, the judge did not seek any explanation from the appellant nor did he invite counsel to make submissions. The sentence for the bail offence would be quashed.

R. *v.* DAVIS (SEATON ROY) (1986) 8 Cr.App.R.(S.) 64, C.A.

618. Contempt—intimidation of witness

P was a station officer employed by the London Fire and Civil Defence authority. P had given evidence on their behalf in a personal injury action brought by a fireman, W. Later P was interviewed by D, a divisional officer, who cautioned P and handed him a letter saying he was the subject of disciplinary proceedings on the grounds that "it is alleged that whilst you were giving evidence . . . with regard to a fireman's compensation claim you did not give that evidence as you had agreed it with the solicitor . . ."

Held it is a contempt of court to intimidate or put in fear a witness who has given evidence in a court of law because it is likely that intimidation will inhibit all witnesses in all actions who are liable to disciplinary proceedings from coming forward and giving free, truthful and uninhibited evidence in any future proceedings (*Roebuck* v. *National Union of Mineworkers (Yorkshire Area)* [1978] C.L.Y. 2997 followed).

GILES *v.* FOX, April 10, 1987; Drake J. [*Ex rel. Robin Thompson & Partners, Solicitors.*]

619. Conviction of co-accused—conspiracy—whether guilty plea of appellant's co-accused should have been admitted

[Police and Criminal Evidence Act 1984, ss.74, 75 and 78.]

At O's trial for conspiracy to obtain property by deception, by taking part with X in a scheme to defraud an insurance company, evidence was admitted, under s.74(1) of the 1984 Act, of X's plea of guilty to the conspiracy.

Held, that once the details of the indictment against X went before the jury, it was unrealistic to say they were not entitled to infer that O had conspired with X. The evidence should have been excluded under the discretion given by s.78.

R. *v.* O'CONNOR [1987] Crim.L.R. 260, C.A.

620/1. Corroboration—accumulation of circumstances

B, an accomplice, gave evidence for the prosecution against H. The judge directed the jury that certain facts and circumstances (listed by the judge) were not individually capable of corroborating B's evidence but that it was for the jury to decide whether they did so collectively.

Held, allowing H's appeal against conviction, that (1) some of the matters listed by the judge were dependent themselves on B's evidence; (2) it could not be said which items the jury selected as potential corroboration; (3) Corroboration can be provided by a combination of pieces of evidence, each innocuous on its own, which together tend to show that the defendant committed the crime.

R. *v.* HILLS [1987] Crim.L.R. 567, C.A.

622. Corroboration—direction to jury

A judge who has provided the normal directions on evidence and corroboration need not tell the jury that the evidence of a suspect witness has to be credible before it can be corroborated.

D was charged with importing opium into Hong Kong. The prosecution relied on accomplice evidence together with D's confession. D did not give evidence. The judge warned the jury strongly of the danger of convicting on the uncorroborated evidence of accomplices, and he explained the meaning of corroboration. He directed the jury that they could convict on uncorroborated evidence if they were satisfied that it was true. D appealed against his conviction on the ground that the judge should have directed a two-stage test: (1) whether the evidence was credible, then (2) whether it was corroborated.

Held, that the judge was under no duty to give such a direction (Dicta of Lord Hailsham of St. Marylebone L.C. and Lord Reid in *D.P.P.* v. *Kilbourne* [1973] C.L.Y 524 applied; dicta of Lord Morris of Borth-y-Gest in *D.P.P.* v. *Hester* [1972] C.L.Y. 631 considered).

ATT.-GEN. OF HONG KONG *v.* WONG MUK PING [1987] 2 W.L.R. 1033, P.C.

623. Corroboration—direction to jury—whether correct

W and I were tried on a charge of robbery of a post office. M pleaded guilty to handling the proceeds and gave evidence against W and I. The judge directed the jury that evidence of post office staff who identified I as one of the robbers could amount to corroboration of M's evidence. In relation to W, there was no evidence capable of corroborating M's evidence. The judge warned of the dangers of convicting on uncorroborated evidence of an accomplice, but went on the suggest that if the jury considered the case against I first and found that M's evidence against him was right, they should ask themselves whether that would affect the amount of credit and weight which they would attach to her evidence against W.

Held, dismissing W's appeal against conviction, that the judge's direction was unwise, since lay jurors may not see that the direction to consider the cases against I and W was not being blurred. There was a danger of the jury bring misled into regarding something which was not corroboration as corroboration or something near to it. There was, however, in this case no lurking doubt about the conviction.

R. *v.* WEBBER (JACK JOHN) [1987] Crim.L.R. 413, C.A.

624. Corroboration—judge's duty to assist the jury

W appealed against conviction of drug offences on the basis that the judge had failed to direct the jury as to what evidence could amount to corroboration of evidence given against W by an accomplice who had pleaded guilty to similar offences.

Held, dismissing W's appeal, that (1) the summing up was defective, as suggested on W's behalf, but (2) properly directed, the jury would inevitably have reached the same verdict in this case. (*R.* v. *Cullinane* [1984] C.L.Y. 595 applied).

R. *v.* WEBBER (MARTIN FREDERICK) [1987] Crim.L.R. 412, C.A.

625. Corroboration—lack of warning—proviso—living on earnings of prostitution

[Sexual Offences Act 1956 (c.69), s.30; Criminal Appeal Act 1968 (c.19), s.2(1).]

On a charge of living on the earnings of prostitutes by charging them exorbitant rents, directions emphasising knowledge of the purpose of the letting, and saying that it was immaterial that the letting was at a higher than normal rent, are correct in law and otherwise unexceptionable. Where the main evidence on a charge is that of an accomplice the corroboration warning must be clear and decisive. S was charged with living off the earnings of prostitution contrary to the 1956 Act, by charging exorbitant rents for flats knowing they were to be used by prostitutes. The main prosecution witness was A, a prostitute who gave evidence of having used one of the flats for prostitution and of having collected rents for S from other prostitutes. The jury was unable to reach a verdict on three counts and a re-trial was ordered. In the first trial the judge directed the jury that if the letting was referable to prostitution it was immaterial whether or not it was at a higher than normal rent. In the second trial the judge's direction dealt with the joint venture by which the women earnt money from prostitution and the man to take a share, sometimes in the guise of inflated rents. S was convicted on a number of counts at both trials and appealed on the basis of these directions and also on the basis that at the second trial the judge, though he had warned the jury to treat A as an accomplice, had failed to direct on the danger of convicting on her evidence without corroboration and that there was no corroboration.

Held, that there was nothing in the directions on the law to which exception could be taken. Further, as to corroboration, that the proper direction was a decisive warning to the jury that if they convicted on A's evidence alone they were in danger of convicting an innocent man. Accordingly the appeals would be allowed on the two counts where A's evidence was fundamental, there being no grounds for applying the proviso to s.2(1) of the 1968 Act, but as to the count where there was other evidence to support the conviction, that would stand (*R.* v. *Silver* [1956] C.L.Y. 8988 disapproved; *R.* v. *Beck* [1982] C.L.Y. 563 considered).

R. *v.* STEWART (1986) 83 Cr.App.R. 327, C.A.

626. Corroboration—whether warning as to danger of convicting on uncorroborated evidence should have been given—whether the three categories in which such a warning is required should be extended

S was alleged to have refused to allow X to leave S's home following a session with S as a professional tarot reader. S was alleged to have told X that the cards said they were to be lovers. X ran and locked herself in a bathroom and believed S to be masturbating outside the bathroom door.

Held, dismissing S's appeal against conviction of false imprisonment, that the trial judge had correctly decided not to warn the jury about the danger of acting on uncorroborated evidence of X. The charge was not of a sexual offence. If the unlawful imprisonment was accompanied by any sexual activity by S, it was not such that it justified extending the usual three categories in which such a warning was to be given (*R.* v. *Kilbourne* [1973] C.L.Y. 524, *R.* v. *Hester* [1972] C.L.Y. 631 and *R.* v. *Spencer*; *R.* v. *Smails* [1986] C.L.Y. 561 considered).

R. *v.* SIMMONS [1987] Crim.L.R. 630, C.A.

627. Costs—defendant on supplementary benefit—fine—order to pay prosecution costs in addition

[Costs in Criminal Cases Act 1973 (c.14), s.2(2).]

Where Justices order that a defendant pay the whole or any part of the prosecution costs the order should be kept to a reasonable level having regard to any fine imposed at the same time, and should be such, having regard to the defendant's means, that he could pay it off within a reasonable time. If a defendant has any grievance against such an order it can be challenged only by certiorari.

F pleaded guilty to obtaining property by deception and was fined £400, and was also ordered to pay prosecution costs of £600, the whole at £10 per week. His only income was supplementary benefit.

Held, quashing the order for costs and remitting it to a fresh bench, that an order for costs, like a fine, should be kept in line with the means of the offender. Only such amount as the defendant could pay off within a reasonable time, such as 12 months, should be ordered. Here the amount was so grossly excessive that the court was bound to intervene. (*R.* v. *Tottenham Justices, ex p. Joshi* [1982] C.L.Y. 1944 and *R.* v. *Holden* [1986] C.L.Y. 807 applied).

R. *v.* NOTTINGHAM JUSTICES, *ex p.* FOHMANN (1987) 84 Cr.App.R. 316, D.C.

628. Costs—judges discretion—consideration

Before making an order as to costs at the end of a criminal trial a judge should bear in mind that the Court of Appeal cannot interfere with an order to contribute to a legal aid certificate and that the overall effect of a number of orders may be excessive.

R. *v.* MENDAY, *The Times*, February 17, 1987, C.A.

629. Costs—legally-aided defendant—whether justices erred

It was wrong of justices to order the prosecutor, where the proceedings had been properly brought, to pay the costs on a private client basis of legally-aided defendants.

R. *v.* OXFORD CITY JUSTICES, *ex p.* CHIEF CONSTABLE OF THAMES VALLEY POLICE, *The Times,* April 24, 1987, D.C.

630. Costs—order for costs from central funds—order for payment to person other than defendant

[Prosecution of Offences Act 1985 (c.23), s.16.]

The court has the power to order costs to be paid from central funds directly to a person other than the defendant where appropriate, as in the instant case where D's mother had funded his defence and he had in the meantime been adjudicated bankrupt.

R. *v.* JAIN, *The Times,* December 10, 1987, C.A.

631. Court of Appeal—jurisdiction—order to produce documents to police during course of investigation—whether "criminal cause or matter"

[Police and Criminal Evidence Act 1984 (c.60), s.9, Sched. 1, para. 4; Supreme Court Act 1981 (c.54), s.18(1)(*a*).]

An order made by a circuit judge that documents be produced to the police in order to further an investigation is made in the context of a "criminal cause or matter" notwithstanding that no proceedings have yet begun, so that an appeal from the Divisional Court's refusal to quash the decision lies direct to the House of Lords and not to the Court of Appeal.

A circuit judge ordered the production to the police of certain accounts relating to the affairs of a youth association. C applied for judicial review to quash the decision; the Divisional Court refused the order sought, and determined, as a matter of law, that the application was made in a "criminal cause or matter," so that any appeal lay direct to the House of Lords. C appealed to the Court of Appeal.

Held, that the Court of Appeal had no jurisdiction to hear the appeal. The order had been made in the context of aiding a criminal investigation, so that it was made in a criminal cause or matter" within s.18 of the 1981 Act. The fact that no criminal proceedings had yet begun made no difference (*R.* v. *Southampton Justices ex p. Green* [1975] C.L.Y. 2038 doubted).

CARR *v.* ATKINS [1987] 3 W.L.R. 529, C.A.

632. Criminal damage—ascertainment of value of damage—whether prosecution entitled to proceed on basis that defendant caused less than £400 damage when he might have caused more than £400 worth—whether prosecution bound to charge jointly persons concerned in a joint enterprise

The prosecution were not bound to charge jointly persons involved in a joint enterprise nor bound to undertake to prove damage to a value in excess that which they could definitely prove on a charge of criminal damage notwithstanding that in consequence the defendant was deprived of the right to elect for a trial in the Crown Court.

M was the driver of one of 30 vehicles that were driven into and around a beanfield. In consequence the whole crop of beans to the value of £5,800 was destroyed. Each of the drivers was individually charged with causing criminal damage notwithstanding the fact that there was some evidence of a joint enterprise. The summonses did not state the value of the property each was alleged to have damaged. At the hearing the justices were obliged to consider the value of the property damaged. If it were less than £400 M would not be entitled to elect for trial in the Crown Court as the charge would only be triable summarily. The prosecution had a video showing the path taken through the field by some of the vehicles. At the hearing the prosecution stated that the minimum damage caused by M's vehicle was that caused by taking a straight line between where the vehicle entered the field and came to rest in it. The value of that damage was between £16 and £117. The prosecution undertook to prove damage to that value. The magistrates in consequence decided that M's charge was only triable summarily on the basis that the value involved did not exceed £400. M applied for judicial review of that decision.

Held, dismissing M's application, that although there was evidence to support the suggestion that M was involved in a joint enterprise the prosecution were not bound to take on an additional burden of proving a joint enterprise by jointly charging M and the other drivers. Given the difficulty the prosecution would have in proving the value of the damage actually caused by M in the course of driving through the beanfield, the prosecution were entitled to take the course they did and undertake to prove only the minimum damage caused by M's vehicle. The justices were entitled to adopt the course they did in the absence of any evidence to indicate M had caused damage in excess of £400 value. The summonses did not have to state the value of the goods allegedly criminally damaged.

R. *v.* SALISBURY MAGISTRATES' COURT, *ex p.* MASTIN (1987) 84 Cr.App.R. 248, D.C.

633. Criminal Injuries Compensation Board—witness statements received from police—whether duty to show applicant

The Criminal Injuries Compensation Board is under no duty to show an applicant any witness statements it has received from police authorities.

R. *v.* CRIMINAL INJURIES COMPENSATION BOARD, *ex p.* BRADY, *The Times,* March 11, 1987, D.C.

634. Criminal Justice Act 1987 (c.38)

This Act makes further provision for the investigation of and trials for fraud.

The Act received the Royal Assent on May 15, 1987, and comes into force on days to be appointed by the Secretary of State.

The whole Act extends to England and Wales only. Parts of the Act extend to Scotland and Northern Ireland. (See s.17 of the Act.)

635. Criminal Justice Act 1987—commencement

CRIMINAL JUSTICE ACT 1987 (COMMENCEMENT NO. 1) ORDER 1987 (No. 1061 (c.27)) [45p], made under the Criminal Justice Act 1987 (c.38), s.16; brings into force on July 20, 1987 ss.1 (for a specified purpose), 12, 14, Sched. 1 of the 1987 Act.

636. Criminal Justice (Scotland) Act 1987 (c.41)

This Act makes provision for Scotland as regards the recovery of the proceeds of drug trafficking, and makes further provision as regards criminal justice in Scotland.

The Act received the Royal Assent on May 15, 1987, and comes into force on days to be appointed by the Secretary of State.

The Act as a whole extends to Scotland only. Some sections extend to England and Wales. (see s.72(4) of the Act.)

637. Cross-examination—rape complainant—defence of consent—genuine but mistaken belief

[Sexual Offences (Amendment) Act 1976 (c.82), ss.1 and 2.]

B was charged with the rape of a woman who it was said would scream, bang her feet and head and kick during intercourse. The only issue at trial was consent in both its forms, (actual consent or genuine but mistaken belief in consent). The appellant sought to cross-examine the complainant about her sexual past. The judge refused. The appellant was convicted and appealed on the ground that s.1(2) of the Sexual Offences (Amendment) Act 1976 allowed the jury to consider the reasonableness of the appellant's genuine belief in consent but they had been prevented from so doing because the appellant had not been allowed to give reasons for his belief.

Held, that the reasonableness had to be considered in conjunction with "any other relevant matters" which must mean relevant matters before the jury. The 1976 Act did not permit the circumvention of s.2 by s.1(2) as s.2 controlled what matters could go before the jury. The relevance of the complainant's past promiscuity or the appellant's belief and the admissibility of such evidence was a question for the judge on the facts before him. The judge had been correct (*R.* v. *Lawrence* [1977] C.L.Y. 659 and *R.* v. *Viola* [1982] C.L..Y 596 considered).

R. *v.* BARTON (1987) 85 Cr.App.R. 5, C.A.

638. Cross-examination—rape complainant—previous sexual experience

[Sexual Offences (Amendment) Act 1976 (c.82), s.2.]

The trial judge erred in law in refusing to allow cross-examination of a complainant in a rape case about a previous incident in which the complainant alleged she had been raped and subsequently admitted she had not.

D was charged with rape. His defence was that the complainant consented to have intercourse with him. He claimed that she subsequently accused him of rape because she feared her boyfriend might leave her if he thought she had consented to sexual intercourse with D. D sought leave to cross-examine the complainant about an earlier occasion when she had sexual intercourse with another man in similar circumstances and afterwards falsely accused him of rape. The trial judge refused to allow the cross-examination. D was convicted and appealed.

Held, allowing the appeal, that to stop D cross-examining about the previous incident was unfair to D (*R.* v. *Viola* [1982] C.L.Y. 596 considered).

R. *v.* COX (DAVID) (1987) 84 Cr.App.R. 132, C.A.

639. Crown Court—distribution of business—classification and allocation to Crown Court centres—practice direction

[Supreme Court Act 1981 (c.54), s.75(1)(2).]

The following practice direction was issued by the Lord Chief Justice with the concurrence of the Lord Chancellor on November 2, 1987.

With the concurrence of the Lord Chancellor and pursuant to ss.75(1) and (2) of the Supreme Court Act 1981 I direct that, with effect from January 1, 1988, the following directions shall supersede those given on October 14, 1971 in *Practice Direction* (*Crime: Crown Court Business*) [1971] C.L.Y. 9159, as amended:

CLASSIFICATION

1. For the purposes of trial in the Crown Court, offences are to be classified as follows:

Class 1:

(1) Any offences for which a person may be sentenced to death.
(2) Misprision of treason and treason felony.

(3) Murder.
(4) Genocide.
(5) An offence under s.1 of the Official Secrets Act 1911.
(6) Incitement, attempt or conspiracy to commit any of the above offences.

Class 2:

(1) Manslaughter.
(2) Infanticide.
(3) Child destruction.
(4) Abortion (s.58 of the Offences against the Person Act 1861).
(5) Rape.
(6) Sexual intercourse with a girl under 13.
(7) Incest with a girl under 13.
(8) Sedition.
(9) An offence under s.1 of the Geneva Conventions Act 1957.
(10) Mutiny.
(11) Piracy.
(12) Incitement, attempt or conspiracy to commit any of the above.

Class 3:

All offences triable only on indictment other than those in Classes 1, 2 and 4.

Class 4:

(1) Wounding or causing grievous bodily harm with intent (s.18 of the Offences against the Person Act 1861).
(2) Robbery or assault with intent to rob (s.8 of the Theft Act 1968).
(3) Incitment or attempt to commit any of the above offences.
(4) Conspiracy at common law, or conspiracy to commit any offence other than those included in Classes 1 and 2.
(5) All offences which are triable either way.

Committals for trial

2. A magistrates' court on committing a person for trial under s.6 of the Magistrates' Courts Act 1980 shall, if the offence or any of the offences is included in Classes 1 to 3, specify the most convenient location of the Crown Court where a High Court judge regularly sits, and if the offence is in Class 4 shall specify the most convenient location of the Crown Court.

3. In selecting the most convenient location of the Crown Court, the justices shall have regard to the considerations referred to in s.7 of the Magistrates' Courts Act 1980, and to the location or locations of the Crown Court designated by a presiding judge as the location to which cases should normally be committed from their petty sessions area.

4. Where on one occasion a person is committed in respect of a number of offences, all the committals shall be to the same location of the Crown Court and that location shall be the one where a High Court judge regularly sits if such a location is appropriate for any of the offences.

Committals for sentence or to be dealt with

5. Where a probation order, order for conditional discharge or a community service order has been made, or suspended sentence passed, and the offender is committed to be dealt with for the original offence or in respect of the suspended sentence, he shall be committed in accordance with the paragraphs below.

6. If the order was made or the sentence was passed by the Crown Court, he shall be committed to the location of the Crown Court where the order was made or suspended sentence was passed, unless it is inconvenient or impracticable to do so.

7. If he is not so committed and the order was made by a High Court judge he shall be committed to the most convenient location of the Crown Court where a High Court judge regularly sits.

8. In all other cases where a person is committed for sentence or to be dealt with he shall be committed to the most convenient location of the Crown Court.

9. In selecting the most convenient location of the Crown Court the justices shall have regard to the location or locations of the Crown Court designated by a presiding judge as the locations to which cases should normally be committed from their petty sessions area.

Appeals and proceedings under the Crown Court's original civil jurisdiction

10. The hearing of an appeal or of proceedings under the civil jurisdiction of the Crown Court shall take place at the location of the Crown Court designated by a presiding judge as the appropriate location for such proceedings originating in the area concerned.

Application for removal of a driving disqualification

11. Application should be made to the location of the Crown Court where the order of disqualification was made.

Transfer of proceedings between locations of the Crown Court

12. Without prejudice to the provisions of s.76 of the Supreme Court Act 1981 (committal for trial: alteration of place of trial) directions may be given for the transfer from one location of the Crown Court to another of:

(i) appeals;
(ii) proceedings on committal for sentence, or to be dealt with;
(iii) proceedings under the original civil jurisdiction of the Crown Court where this appears desirable for expediting the hearing, or for the convenience of the parties.

13. Such directions may be given in a particular case by an officer of the Crown court, or generally, in relation to a class or classes of case, by the presiding judge or a judge acting on his behalf.

14. If dissatisfied with such directions given by an officer of the Crown Court, any party to the proceedings may apply to a judge of the Crown Court who may hear the application in chambers.

ALLOCATION OF BUSINESS WITHIN THE CROWN COURT

General

1. Cases in Class 1 are to be tried by a High Court judge. A case of murder, or incitement, attempt or conspiracy to commit murder may be released, by or on the authority of a presiding judge, for trial by a circuit judge approved for the purpose by the Lord Chief Justice.

2. Cases in Class 2 are to be tried by a High Court judge unless a particular case is released by or on the authority of a presiding judge for trial by a circuit judge. A case of rape, or of a serious sexual offence against a child of any Class, may be released by a presiding judge for trial only by a circuit judge approved for the purpose by the Lord Chief Justice.

3. Cases in Class 3 may be tried by a High Court judge or, in accordance with general or particular directions given by a presiding judge, by a circuit judge or a recorder.

4. Cases in Class 4 may be tried by a High Court judge, a circuit judge, a recorder or an assistant recorder. A case in Class 4 shall not be listed for trial by a High Court judge except with the consent of that judge or of a presiding judge.

5. Appeals from decisions of magistrates and committals to the Crown Court for sentence shall be heard by:

(i) a resident or designated judge, or
(ii) a circuit judge, nominated by the resident or designated judge, who regularly sits at the Crown Court centre, or
(iii) an experienced recorder specifically approved by the presiding judges for the purpose, or
(iv) where no circuit judge or recorder satisfying the requirements above is available and it is not practicable to obtain the approval of the presiding judges, by a circuit judge or recorder selected by the resident or designated judge to hear a specific case or cases.

6. Applications or matters arising before trial (including those relating to bail) should be listed where possible before the judge by whom the case is expected to be tried. Where a case is to be tried by a High Court judge who is not available, the application or matter should be listed before any other High Court judge then sitting at the Crown Court centre at which the matter has arisen; before a presiding judge; before the resident or designated judge for the centre; or, with the consent of the presiding judge, before a circuit judge nominated for the purpose. In other cases, if the circuit judge, recorder or assistant recorder who is expected to try the case is not available, the matter shall be referred to the resident or designated judge or, if he is not available, to any judge or recorder then sitting at the centre.

7. Matters to be dealt with (*e.g.,* in which a probation order has been made or suspended sentence passed) should, where possible, be listed before the judge who originally dealt with the matter, or, if not, before a judge of the same or higher status.

Allocation of proceedings to a court comprising lay justices

8. In addition to the classes of case specified in s.74 of the Supreme Court Act 1981 (appeals and proceedings on committals for sentence) any other proceedings apart from cases listed for pleas of not guilty which in accordance with these directions are listed for hearing by a circuit judge or recorder are suitable for allocation to a court comprising justices of the peace.

Transfer of cases between circuits

9. An application that a case be transferred from one circuit to another should not be granted unless the judge is satisfied that:—

(i) the approval of the presiding judges and circuit administrator for each circuit has been obtained, or

(ii) the case may be transferred under general arrangements approved by the presiding judges and circuit administrators.

10. When a resident or designated judge is absent from his centre, the presiding judges may authorise another judge who sits regularly at the same centre to exercise his responsibility.

Presiding judges' directions

11. For the just, speedy and economical disposal of the business of a circuit, presiding judges shall with the approval of the senior presiding judge issue directions as to the need where appropriate to reserve a case for trial by a High Court judge and as to the allocation of work between circuit judges, recorders and assistant recorders and where necessary the devolved responsibility of resident or designated judges for such allocation. In such directions specific provision should be made for cases in the following categories:—

(a) Cases where death or serious risk to life, or the infliction of grave injury are involved, including motoring cases of this category arising from reckless driving and/or excess alcohol.

(b) Cases where loaded firearms are alleged to have been used.

(c) Cases of arson or criminal damage with intent to endanger life.

(d) Cases of defrauding government departments or local authorities or other public bodies of amounts in excess of £25,000.

(e) Offences under the Forgery and Counterfeiting Act 1981 where the amount of money or the value of goods exceeds £10,000.

(f) Offences involving violence to a police officer which result in the officer being unfit for duty for more than 28 days.

(g) Any offence involving loss to any person or body of a sum in excess of £100,000.

(h) Cases where there is a risk of substantial political or racial feeling being excited by the offence or the trial.

(i) Cases which have given rise to widespread public concern.

(j) Cases of robbery or assault with intent to rob where gross violence was used, or serious injury was caused, or where the accused was armed with a dangerous weapon for the purpose of the robbery, or where the theft was intended to be from a bank, a building society or a post office.

(k) Cases involving the manufacture or distribution of substantial quantities of drugs.

(l) Cases the trial of which is likely to last more than 10 days.

(m) Cases involving the trial of more than five defendants.

(n) Cases in which the accused holds a senior public office, or is a member of a profession or other person carrying a special duty or responsibility to the public, including a police officer when acting as such.

(o) Cases where a difficult issue of law is likely to be involved, or a prosecution for the offence is rare or novel.

12. With the approval of the senior presiding judge, general directions may be given by the presiding judges of the South Eastern Circuit concerning the distribution and allocation of business of all Classes at the Central Criminal Court.

PRACTICE DIRECTION (C.A.) (CROWN COURT BUSINESS: CLASSIFICATION) [1987] 1 W.L.R. 1671.

640. Crown Court trial—time limit—effect

The provision requiring that the trial of a defendant committed to the Crown Court commence not later than the expiration of the prescribed period is directory and not mandatory.

R. *v.* GOVERNOR OF SPRING HILL PRISON, *ex p.* SOHI; SAME *v.* SAME, *ex p.* DHILLON, *The Independent*, July 29, 1987, D.C.

641. Crown prosecution service

CROWN PROSECUTION SERVICE (WITNESSES' ALLOWANCES) (AMENDMENT No. 4) REGULATIONS 1987 (No. 902) [45p], made under the Prosecution of Offences Act 1985 (c.23), s.14(1)(*b*)(2); operative on June 22, 1987; increases maximum witness allowances.

CROWN PROSECUTION SERVICE (WITNESSES' ALLOWANCES) (AMENDMENT No. 5) REGULATIONS 1987 (No. 1636) [45p], made under the Prosecution of Offences Act 1985, s.14(1)(*b*)(2); operative on October 7, 1987; increase witnesses' allowances.

CROWN PROSECUTION SERVICE (WITNESSES' ALLOWANCES) (AMENDMENT No. 6) REGULATIONS 1987 (No. 1851) [45p], made under the Prosecution of Offences Act 1985, s.14(1)(*b*)(2); operative on November 16, 1987; increase witnesses' subsistence allowances.

642. Custody time limits

PROSECUTION OF OFFENCES (CUSTODY TIME LIMITS) REGULATIONS 1987 (No. 299) [£1·40], made under the Prosecution of Offences Act 1985 (c.23), ss.22(1)(2), 29(2); operative on April 1, 1987; prescribe the maximum period a person accused of an indictable offence in Avon, Kent, Somerset and the West Midlands may be remanded in custody while waiting for committal for trial or for trial.

643/4. Defence—counsel taking a particular course—whether ground of appeal

The taking by counsel of a particular course while conducting his client's defence will very rarely afford a ground of appeal;

R. *v.* GAUTAM, *The Times*, March 4, 1987, C.A.

645. Dismissal of proceedings for want of prosecution at a hearing to fix date for trial—judicial review

O brought proceedings before justices alleging various offences under the Town and Country Planning Act 1971, mainly involving trees. The alleged offences took place in August 1985, and the informations were laid in October 1985. Subsequently further informations were laid, but then nothing happened. The court listed the matter of its own motion for April 30, 1986 in order to fix a date for trial, but on that date the justices dismissed the informations for want of prosecution. O brought proceedings for judicial review eight days before the three-month period therefore expired.

Held, the justices may have been wrong to dismiss the informations after indicating that the hearing was merely a holding date, but O had taken an unduly long time about the judicial review proceedings, and his application would be refused.

R. *v.* LEWES MAGISTRATES COURT, *ex p.* OLDFIELD, *The Times,* May 6, 1987, D.C.

646. Doctrine of recent possession—evidence—inference

The doctrine of recent possession is a rule of evidence in that it is an inference to be drawn with the proper degree of certainty from the evidence (*R.* v. *Smythe* [1981] C.L.Y. 459 considered).

R. *v.* GREAVES, *The Times,* July 11, 1987, C.A.

647. Drink/drive offence—late service of certificate of level of alcohol—admissibility—*res gestae*

[Road Traffic Act 1972 (c.20), s.10(5).]

Where the Prosecution serve the relevant certificate showing the level of alcohol in D's blood on the morning of the hearing, the certificate is inadmissible notwithstanding any purported waiver of the inadmissibility. The *res gestae* does not extend to a visit 20 minutes after the event of an accident to the premises of one of the alleged drivers involved (*R.* v. *Andrews* [1987] C.L.Y. 659, *R.* v. *Chandler* [1976] C.L.Y. 459 considered).

TOBI *v.* NICHOLAS, *The Independent,* July 3, 1987, D.C.

648. Duress—whether defence could be relied upon—whether a matter for the jury

Where a defendant advances the defence of duress to burglary it was a matter for the jury to decide whether the fact he had voluntarily joined a gang to commit an initial offence meant that he had freely accepted the risk of duress and therefore could not rely on the defence.

R. *v.* SHEPHERD, *The Times,* May 16, 1987, C.A.

649. Election for trial—election not put—whether subsequent trial a nullity

A magistrates court trial and acquittal of D was a nullity where the offence was triable either way and D had not been put to his election (*R.* v. *Tottenham Justices, ex p. Arthur's Transport Services* [1981] C.L.Y. 1714 considered).

R. *v.* CARDIFF MAGISTRATES COURT, *ex p.* CARDIFF CITY COUNCIL, *The Times,* February 24, 1987, D.C.

650. Expert evidence

CROWN COURT (ADVANCE NOTICE OF EXPERT EVIDENCE) RULES 1987 (No. 716 (L.2)) [45p], made under the Supreme Court Act 1981 (c.54), ss.84(1), 86 and the Police and Criminal Evidence Act 1984 (c.60), s.81; operative on July 15, 1987; provides for the disclosure of expert evidence between the parties to criminal proceedings in the Crown Court.

651. Factual basis for sentence—offender seeking to establish mitigating factor—offender's story implausible—whether court bound to hear evidence. See R. *v.* WALTON, §938.

652. Failure of prosecution to prove case—adjournment—whether adjournment to be granted

Where D made a submission of no case to answer because the prosecution had failed to adduce evidence that went to a central point in their case the court should not grant an adjournment to allow the prosecution to attempt to gather such evidence. (*R.* v. *Pilcher* [1975] C.L.Y. 737, *Royal* v. *Prescott-Clarke* [1966] C.L.Y. 2402 considered).

R. *v.* CENTRAL CRIMINAL COURT, *ex p.* GARNIER, *The Times,* March 16, 1987, D.C.

653. Family Division—wards—Criminal Injuries Compensation Board—practice direction

The following practice direction was issued by the Senior Registrar of the Family Division with the approval of the President and the Concurrence of the Lord Chancellor on December 10, 1987.

Where a ward of court has a right to make a claim for compensation to the Criminal Injuries Compensation Board, application must be made by the *guardian ad litem* of the child for leave to apply and to disclose to the Board such documents on the wardship proceedings file as are considered necessary to establish eligibility and quantum. If leave has not been given by the Judge at the wardship hearing, the application may be made *ex parte* to a Registrar by the child's *guardian ad litem* or, if no guardian has been appointed, by the Director of Social Services of the local authority having care of the child or the person or persons having care and control of the child.

Any order giving leave should state that any award made by the Board be paid into Court immediately on receipt and application made forthwith thereafter to the Court as to its management and administration unless the Judge or Registrar otherwise directs.

PRACTICE DIRECTION (FAM. D.) (WARDS: CRIMINAL INJURIES COMPENSATION BOARD) December 10, 1987.

654. Family Division—wards—witness in criminal proceedings—practice direction

The following practice direction was issued by the Senior Registrar of the Family Division with the concurrence of the Lord Chancellor on November 11, 1987.

In the case of *K. (Minors), Re* [1987] 9 C.L. 134, the court held that where a child has been interviewed by the police in connection with contemplated criminal proceedings and the child subsequently becomes a ward of court, no leave of the wardship court is required for the child to be called as a witness in those proceedings. Where the police desire to interview a child who is already a ward of court application must be made for leave for the police to do so. Where leave is given the order should, unless there is some special reason which requires the contrary, give leave for any number of interviews which may be required by the prosecution or the police. If it is desired to conduct any interview beyond what is permitted by the order further application should be made for this purpose.

No evidence or documents in the wardship proceedings or information about wardship proceedings should be disclosed in the criminal proceedings without the prior leave of the wardship court.

The President directs that all of the above applictions be made to a Judge on summons on notice to all parties.

PRACTICE DIRECTION (FAM.D.) (WARDS: WITNESS IN CRIMINAL PROCEEDINGS) November 11, 1987.

655. Forfeiture—dispute of relationship between thing and offence—whether evidence should be taken before determination thereof

[Misuse of Drugs Act 1971 (c.38), s.27.]

C pleaded guilty to various charges including supplying and possessing with intent to supply controlled drugs, namely amphetamine and cannabis. Sentenced to two years' imprisonment and forfeiture orders made in respect of two sums of money, £610 and £577, found in his possession at the time of his apprehension. The forfeiture order was made without allowing the appellant to call evidence to show that the two sums of money were not related to the offences under the Misuse of Drugs Act 1971.

Held, that proper investigations had not been made to ensure that the provisions of the statute were fulfilled and the court was concerned that the appellant had not had a proper opportunity to establish that the court should be satisfied that the money was not related to the offence. The forfeiture orders would be quashed.

R. *v.* CHURCHER (1986) 8 Cr.App.R.(S.) 94, C.A.

656. Further evidence—introduction by prosecution after close of case—practice to be followed

Where the prosecution desire to adduce further evidence after closing their case, and this is not in rebuttal or because a new point has arisen, the proper course is to serve a notice of additional evidence, but the failure to do so will not be a material irregularity unless some serious prejudice results.

D was charged with conspiracy to make false statements in regard to marriages. Whilst he was giving evidence at his re-trial the prosecution cross-examined him on certain documents which had not formed part of the evidence led for the prosecution. D was convicted and appealed.

Held, that although generally the Crown should have served a notice of additional evidence with regard to these documents, the fact was that the defence were well aware of their existence, and no prejudice had been suffered through their being admitted. Appeal dismissed.

R. *v.* DARTEY (1987) 84 Cr.App.R. 352, C.A.

657. Guilty plea by post—mitigating factors for, sentence in letter not read out in court—whether convictions and sentences a nullity

[Magistrates' Courts Act 1980 (c.43), s.12.]

B and S Co. were driver and owner of an overloaded vehicle and pleaded guilty by post to a charge of using it on a road. At the proceedings, the mitigation in the letter was not read out. B & S Co. applied for certiorari to quash their convictions for lack of compliance with s.12 of the Act.

Held, that the proceedings were defective and the proper remedy was to grant the applications and make declarations that the proceedings were a nullity (*R.* v. *Oldham Justices, ex p. Morrissey* [1958] C.L.Y. 1988 considered).

R. *v.* EPPING AND ONGAR JUSTICES, *ex p.* BREACH; R. *v.* SAME, *ex p.* SHIPPHAM (C.) [1987] R.T.R. 233, D.C.

658. Hearing by stipendiary—adjournment

Where a stipendiary has indicated that a case should be heard after an adjournment, a second stipendiary is not fettered by that observation and may in turn adjourn the case.

R. *v.* HORSEFERRY ROAD STIPENDIARY MAGISTRATES, *ex p.* WILSON, *The Times,* February 3, 1987, D.C.

659. Hearsay evidence—whether evidence of conversation admissible under *res gestae* doctrine

Hearsay evidence of a conversation in which a deceased victim identified the defendant as his attacker was admissible as evidence of the truth of the facts stated under the doctrine of *res gestae* where the conversation took place in such circumstances that the possibility of concoction or distortion by the victim could be disregarded.

M was attacked and stabbed by two men in his flat and robbed. Within minutes of the attack and bleeding profusely from a deep stomach wound he went to the downstairs flat for assistance. Within a couple of minutes of the neighbour's call to the police P.C. W and P.C. H arrived. P.C. W asked M how he received his injuries. M stated he had been attacked by two men, one called Peter O'Neill and the other he knew as Donald. P.C. H, making a note of what was said, recorded "Donovan" rather than "Donald". M died 2 months after the attack as a result of his injuries. Peter O'Neill and Donald Andrews were charged with murder. Andrews pleaded not guilty. At his trial the prosecution sought leave to adduce evidence of the conversation between M and P.C. W as evidence of the truth of what M had said under the *res gestae* exception to the rule against the admissibility of hearsay evidence. The conversation was not admissible as a dying declaration on account of the fact that there was no evidence that M thought he was dying at the time the conversation took place. The trial judge granted the application and Andrews was convicted of murder. His appeal to the Court of Appeal was unsuccessful.

Held, dismissing Andrews's appeal, that hearsay evidence of a conversation was admissible in evidence with a view to establishing the truth of facts stated in the conversation under the *res gestae* doctrine where the possibility of concoction or distortion can be disregarded. The trial judge must consider whether the circumstances in which the statement was made were so unusual, startling or dramatic as to dominate the thoughts of the declarant so that his utterance was an instinctive reaction to the event rather than reasoned reflection. The trial judge could conclude that the possibility of concoction or distortion could be excluded where the statement was made in conditions of approximate but not exact contemporaneity where the declarant's mind was still dominated by the event. The statement must be closely associated with the event. Once the trial judge was satisfied that there was no possibility of concoction or distortion by the declarant to his own advantage the evidence was admissible. The possibility of error in the facts stated went to the weight to be attached to the evidence and was thus a matter for the jury to consider. The evidence was rightly admitted at Andrews's trial (*Ratten* v. *The Queen* [1971] C.L.Y. 4587 applied; *R.* v. *Bedingfield* (1879) 14 Cox C.C. 341 overruled; *Myers* v. *D.P.P.* [1965] C.L.Y. 1461 considered).

R. *v.* ANDREWS (D.J.) [1987] 2 W.L.R. 413, H.L.(E.).

660. Home Office Research and Planning Unit Research Bulletin. See CRIMINAL SENTENCING, §951.

661. Home Office research programme. See CRIMINAL LAW, §786.

662. Hostile witness—previous inconsistent statement

An essential issue at a trial was whether a prosecution witness, K, had supplied certain containers to P1. The judge allowed the prosecution to cross-examine K as hostile on the basis that he was deliberately refraining from telling the truth. He was alleged to have told the police officer, shortly before the trial, that he had recognised P1 on an identification parade but had not said so, out of fear for the safety of himself and his family. The cross-examination was unsuccessful. The judge then allowed evidence about the alleged previous inconsistent statement.

Held, dismissing appeals against conviction, that (1) there was foundation for treating K as hostile—that the previous statement was oral did not affect the principle; (2) the judge acted within the area of his proper discretion in admitting the evidence of the previous statement.

R. *v.* PREFAS AND PRYCE [1987] Crim.L.R. 327, C.A.

663. Identification—videotape—admissibility

An elderly lady identified S's car as having been used in burglary of a neighbour's house. Later she identified D when S and D were brought down an escalator at a shopping precinct. She later claimed to have recognised S but to have been too frightened to say so. Her evidence in court was extremely confused. Evidence of a videotape of the events at the shopping precinct and of a police officer as to what happened when the lady was shown it before the trial was admitted in evidence.

Held, allowing appeals against conviction, that (1) the judge should have directed the jury to acquit; (2) use of the videotape was not permissible to improve the quality of the lady's evidence as to identification at the precinct.

R. *v.* SMITH AND DOE [1987] Crim.L.R. 267, C.A.

664. Identification parades—trial within trial

[Police and Criminal Evidence Act 1984 (c.60), s.78(1).]

At B's trial for robbery and assault with intent to rob, the judge refused to hold a trial within a trial in relation to the identification of B at an identification parade.

Held, dismissing B's appeal against conviction, that s.78(1) of the 1984 Act required the judge to consider the depositions and the statements and counsel's submissions when a point was taken on an identification parade. The cases would be rare, however, in which the judge would consider it desirable to hold a trial within a trial to determine his course of action (*R.* v. *Walshe* [1982] C.L.Y. 586 considered).

R. *v.* BEVERIDGE [1987] Crim.L.R. 401, C.A.

665. Indecent assault—evidence of secret motive—whether admissible

[Sexual Offences Act 1956 (c.69), s.14(1).]

Evidence of an indecent motive is not irrelevant to a charge under s.14(1) of the 1956 Act.

C, a shop assistant, for no apparent reason struck a 12-year-old girl customer on the buttocks some 12 times. When asked by the police why he had done this he replied. "I don't know—buttock fetish." He was charged with indecent assault contrary to s.14(1) of the 1956 Act. He pleaded guilty to assault but denied that it was indecent, and submitted that the statement should be excluded as evidence of secret uncommunicated motive which could not make the assault indecent. The judge refused to exclude the evidence and C was convicted.

Held, dismissing the appeal, that although an indecent motive was not a necessary element of the offence, evidence of such a motive does not have to be excluded as irrelevant (*R.* v. *Pratt* [1984] C.L.Y. 634 disapproved).

R. *v.* COURT [1986] 3 W.L.R. 1029, C.A.

666. Indictment—mutually exclusive counts—election

The prosecution must make an election as to which counts they seek to proceed on where the counts are mutually exclusive.

R. *v.* BELLMAN, *The Times*, May 29, 1987, C.A.

667. Indictment—voluntary bill—validity

[Administration of Justice (Miscellaneous Provisions) Act 1933 (c.36), s.2(2); Indictment (Procedure) Rules 1971 (S.I. 1971 No. 1253), r.8; Prosecution of Offences Act 1985 (c.23), s.1(6).]

An application for a voluntary bill of indictment was made before a High Court judge under s.2(2) of the 1933 Act. R.8 of the 1971 Rules required an affidavit unless the application was by or on behalf of the D.P.P. There was no affidavit. The Crown Prosecutor for Manchester made the application.

Held, dismissing an application for a declaration that the bill was granted without jurisdiction, that (1) s.1(6) of the 1985 Act gave every Crown Prosecutor the equivalent power of the D.P.P. to initiate prosecutions; (2) since the application related to trial on indictment it was doubtful whether the Divisional Court had jurisdiction to entertain the application.

R. *v.* LIVERPOOOL CROWN COURT, *ex p.* BRAY [1987] Crim.L.R. 51, D.C.

668. Indictment—wording—burden on prosecutor—cruelty to child

[Children and Young Persons Act 1933 (as amended) (c.12), s.1(1).]

The prosecutor should take care to ensure that the correct allegation in the particular circumstances is chosen from the possibilities for which the Act provides (*R.* v. *Hayles* [1968] C.L.Y. 1947 considered).

R. *v.* BEARD, *The Times,* May 22, 1987, C.A.

669. Information—breach of regulation charged—whether bad for duplicity

[Public Service Vehicles (Conduct of Drivers, Conductors, and Passengers) Regulations 1936 (S.R. & O. 1936 No. 619), reg. 4, as amended by S.I. 1980 No. 915).]

Reg. 4 of the Public Service Vehicles (Conduct of Drivers, Conductors, and Passengers) Regulations 1936 creates six separate offences, and an information which merely charges a breach of the regulation will be bad for duplicity.

AMOS *v.* D.P.P., *The Times,* December 9, 1987, D.C.

670. Information—duplicity of charge

[Magistrates' Courts Act 1980 (c.43), s.6.]

H was charged with unlawful possession of "cannabis and cannabis resin."

Held, refusing leave to apply for judicial review of the justices' order committing H for trial, that (1) by s.6 of the 1980 Act, justices were permitted to commit for indictable offences disclosed by the material put before them; (2) that they commit on charge which is duplicitous as it stands would not entitle the Divisional Court to quash the committal; (3) it was doubtful whether, once the matter had proceeded to the Crown Court, the Divisional Court had power to act under the Supreme Court Act 1981; (4) a charge framed as alleging possession of cannabis as cannabis resin is not *ipso facto* duplicitous (*Hargreaves* v. *Alderson* [1963] C.L.Y. 2135 distinguished; *R.* v. *Lamb* [1968] C.L.Y. 670 and *R.* v. *Best* [1980] C.L.Y. 529 considered).

R. *v.* NEWCASTLE-UNDER-LYME JUSTICES, *ex p.* HEMMINGS [1987] Crim.L.R. 416, D.C.

671. Information laid out of time—costs—whether jurisdiction to award to defendant

[Costs in Criminal Cases Act 1973 (c.14), s.12(3).]

A magistrates' court has jurisdiction to award costs to a defendant where there is no jurisdiction to try him because the information was laid out of time.

PATEL *v.* BLAKEY, *The Times,* February 26, 1987, D.C.

672. Judicial review—ex gratia payment to wrongly convicted person—refusal by Secretary of State

The Secretary of State for the Home Office refused to make an ex gratia payment to C, who had had his conviction of a criminal offence quashed as a result of a defective summing-up after he had served 15 months in prison.

Held, refusing C's application for judicial review, that the Secretary of State had a complete discretion in the matter which was not subject to judicial review (*R.* v. *Criminal Injuries Compensation Board, ex p. Lain* [1967] C.L.Y. 724 distinguished).

R. *v.* SECRETARY OF STATE FOR THE HOME OFFICE, *ex p.* CHUBB [1986] Crim.L.R. 809, D.C.

673. Judicial review—order made in absence of party

Owing to a misunderstanding between J and his solicitors, he failed to appear at the hearing of his appeal against a conviction by magistrates. The Crown Court refused an adjournment and dismissed the appeal.

Held, granting J's application for judicial review and remitting the case for determination on its merits, that it would have been proper to grant an adjournment (*R.* v. *Diggines, ex p. Rahmani* [1985] C.L.Y. 1734 considered).

R. *v.* KNIGHTSBRIDGE CROWN COURT, *ex p.* JOHNSON [1986] Crim.L.R. 803, D.C.

674. Justices—awareness of applicant's previous convictions—bench included a justice who had convicted applicant on previous occasion—whether justices erred

S applied for Legal Aid to a bench of magistrates. In the course of the application, they were told of his previous convictions. The bench included a justice who had convicted S of an offence on a previous occasion. They rejected S's application, and proceeded to try the charge, to which he had pleaded not guilty. They convicted him.

Held, that the justices erred (1) in trying the case when they knew of the convictions, especially as the Legal Aid application form expressly stated that if an applicant pleaded not guilty, the information on the form would not be made known to the justices who tried the case; and (2) in including among their number a justice who had previously convicted S.

R. *v.* BLYTH VALLEY JUVENILE COURT, *ex p.* S, *The Times,* April 11, 1987, D.C.

675. Justices—proceeding *in camera*—whether lawful—justices taking the address of a defendant in written form—whether lawful

[Magistrates' Courts Act 1980 (c.43), s.121(4); Contempt of Court Act 1981 (c.49), s.11.]

There is power in a magistrates court to exclude press and public, but only when it has become necessary to the administration of justice. Such cases will be extremely rare.

The prohibition of publication of a defendant's address, where motivated by sympathy for the defendant's well-being, was not a matter with which the administration of justice was concerned and the prohibition was a misuse of s.11 of the Contempt of Court Act 1981 (*Scott* v. *Scott* [1913] A.C. 417, *Att.-Gen.* v. *The Leveller* [1979] C.L.Y. 2120, *R.* v. *Governor of Lewes Prison, ex p. Doyle,* [1917] 2 K.B. 254, *Simms* v. *Moore* [1970] C.L.Y. 1658, *R.* v. *Ealing Justices, ex p. Weafer* [1982] C.L.Y. 1960, *R.* v. *Reigate Justices, ex p. Argus Newspapers* [1984] C.L.Y. 866 considered).

R. *v.* MALVERN JUSTICES, *ex p.* EVANS; R. *v.* EVESHAM JUSTICES, *ex p.* McDONAGH, *The Times,* August 1, 1987, D.C.

676. Justices—size and chairmanship of bench

JUSTICES OF THE PEACE (SIZE AND CHAIRMANSHIP OF BENCH) (AMENDMENT) RULES 1987 (No. 1137) (L.5)) [45p], made under the Justice of the Peace Act 1979 (c.55), s.18; operative on August 1, 1987; amend S.I. 1986 No. 923 in relation to the eligibility of a Justice to be elected chairman.

677. Justices—unrelated charges list—whether creating bias

The proper test for justices to apply in dealing with a possibility of bias was whether a reasonable and fair-minded person sitting in court with knowledge of the facts would have a reasonable suspicion that a fair trial would not be possible.

S appeared before justices on seven charges, the first of which stemmed from an incident entirely separate from that which gave rise to the other six. His solicitor applied to the justices not to try the other six, since they had seen a copy of the list, with all seven thereon, and this might give rise to suspicions of bias. The justices retired to consider the matter, took advice from their clerk and concluded that no suspicion would arise. S was convicted and received a custodial sentence. He applied for judicial review.

Held, that the proper test for the justices to apply was whether a reasonable and fair-minded person sitting in court and knowing all the relevant facts would have a reasonable suspicion that a fair trial would not be possible. In the circumstances this test was applied and the justices exercised their discretion correctly. Further that the publication of a full charge sheet was not unlawful, and there was nothing improper in placing it before the magistrates.

R. *v.* WESTON-SUPER-MARE JUSTICES, *ex p.* SHAW [1987] 2 W.L.R. 305, D.C.

678. Justices—validity of by-laws—whether justices have jurisdiction to determine the issue of validity

Justices have jurisdiction to look into the validity of by-laws, and are bound to do so when a defendant relies on their invalidity as a defence.

R. *v.* READING CROWN COURT, *ex p.* HUTCHINSON; SAME *v.* DEVIZES JUSTICES, *ex p.* LEE; SAME *v.* SAME, *ex p.* D.P.P., *The Independent,* August 5, 1987, D.C.

679. Justices—withholding of justices' names—whether lawful

Justices should not depart from the general rule of open justice any more than they consider to be necessary in order properly to dispense justice, and may not therefore refuse to disclose their names if requested so to do by any bona fide inquirer, including the press, parties and their advisers.

Justices were hearing a case of gross indecency with a very young child. The chairman of the bench refused to divulge the names of the justices hearing the case for "security reasons". L, a journalist, was refused the names of the justices of the basis that it was their policy to refuse to be identified.

Held, that L's application for judicial review would be granted. (1) Justices could not withhold their names from the parties, their advisers, and bona fide inquirers (which included the press), because they should only depart from the general rule that justice should be done in public and openly where satisfied that to do so was necessary to serve the ends of justice. (2) L did not, strictly, have *locus standi* to seek judicial review because he was not a journalist present in court at the time of the refusal, but as a guardian of the public interest L, or perhaps the press in general, had an interest sufficient to give him *locus standi* (*Att.-Gen.* v. *Leveller Magazine* [1979] C.L.Y. 2120 and *R.* v. *I.R.C., ex p. National Federation of Self-Employed and Small Businesses* [1981] C.L.Y. 1433 applied).

R. *v.* FELIXSTOWE JUSTICES, *ex p.* LEIGH [1987] 2 W.L.R. 380, D.C.

680. Justices' warrant of commitment—consideration of means—interest of Customs and Excise

[Customs and Excise Management Act 1979 (c.2), s.151.]

Where justices were asked to deal with a sum held by the prosecutor by warrant of commitment the prosecutor must be notified, and the justices must consider the defendant's means.

R. *v.* CLACTON JUSTICES, *ex p.* CUSTOMS AND EXCISE COMMISSIONERS, *The Times*, October 5, 1987, D.C.

681. Letters—admissibility against recipient

Letters from the father of M's children, written to M at least one year previously, were found at her home. M admitted that she knew the letters referred to cannabis and its importation. Her home had been searched following delivery to it of a trunk containing cannabis.

Held, dismissing M's appeal against conviction of being knowingly concerned in the fraudulent evasion of the prohibition on importation of a controlled drug, that the trial judge had correctly ruled the letters admissible against M to rebut her defence that her receipt of the trunk was unsolicited and without knowledge of its contents.

R. *v.* MADDEN [1986] Crim.L.R. 804, C.A.

682. Magisterial law—adjournment—prosecution's application—whether prosecution treated unfairly

The stipendiary magistrate should have allowed a prosecution application for an adjournment after allowing the defendant to change his election to one for summary trial.

R. *v.* CLERKENWELL MAGISTRATES' COURT, *ex p.* D.P.P., *The Times*, May 20, 1987, D.C.

683. Magisterial law—binding over—grounds

Notwithstanding the consent of the defendant, a magistrate should not bind over someone unless there is evidence to make the court apprehensive of a breach of the peace.

R. *v.* MARYLEBONE METROPOLITAN STIPENDIARY MAGISTRATE, *ex p.* OKUNNU, *The Times*, November 4, 1987, D.C.

684. Magisterial law—change of mode of trial after beginning of trial

O pleaded not guilty to two burglaries. Justices accepted jurisdiction to try O summarily and fixed a date for trial. By the time O could be produced for trial, he faced also a charge of attempted robbery.

Held, quashing the justices decision to remand O for committal proceedings regarding the burglary charges, that (1) O's trial began when he entered his plea; (2) the justices had no jurisdiction to commit O for trial save under s.25(5) of the 1980 Act; (3) the justices had also erred in taking into account O's criminal record when deciding whether or not to accept jurisdiction to try the attempted robbery charge (*R.* v. *Colchester Justices, ex p. North Essex Building Co.* [1977] C.L.Y. 1849 and *R.* v. *South Hackney*

Juvenile Court, ex p. R. G. and C. B. [1984] C.L.Y. 2117 applied; dicta in *R.* v. *Newham Juvenile Court, ex p. F.* [1986] C.L.Y. 2091 not followed).

R. *v.* HAMMERSMITH JUVENILE COURT, *ex p.* O. [1987] Crim.L.R. 639, D.C.

685. Magisterial law—criminal damage—amount

[Magistrates' Courts Act 1980 (c.43), s.22(1) and Sched. 2.]

Magistrates should not commit a defendant for trial on a single charge of criminal damage where the damage is less than £400.

R. *v.* BRADEN, *The Times,* October 14, 1987, C.A.

686. Magisterial law—"cross-remanding"—whether lawful

[Magistrates' Court Act 1980 (c.43).]

Nothing prevents a court which first hears a case on a bank holiday or Saturday from remanding the case to another court within the same county.

R. *v.* AVON MAGISTRATES' COURT COMMITTEE, *ex p.* BATH LAW SOCIETY, *The Independent,* July 16, 1987, D.C.

687. Magisterial law—detention without charge—magistrates' authorisation—time-limit for application

[Police and Criminal Evidence Act 1984 (c.60), s.43.]

Magistrates authorised further detention of S under s.43 of the 1984 Act, although the application had been made two hours later than 36 hours after the start of S's detention.

Held, quashing the magistrates' order, that magistrates have no discretion not to dismiss an application for authority to detain further if it is out of time and they decide that the police acted unreasonably in not bringing the matter before the court within the relevant period.

R. *v.* SLOUGH JUSTICES, *ex p.* STIRLING [1987] Crim.L.R. 576, D.C.

688. Magisterial law—jurisdiction of resident magistrate—whether resident magistrate has jurisdiction to hear case already part-heard before a different resident magistrate

[Jamaica] Where an adjourned hearing of a part heard trial before a resident magistrate took place before a different resident magistrate the second resident magistrate had jurisdiction to accept a change of plea to guilty from the defendant and sentence him.

B appeared before a resident magistrate charged with a motoring offence. B pleaded not guilty and the magistrate proceeded to hear the evidence. The trial was adjourned part heard. At the resumed hearing the original magistrate was unavailable so the case was heard by a second resident magistrate. At the resumed hearing B changed his plea to guilty and was fined $20. Thereafter the second magistrate changed his mind about the propriety of accepting B's guilty plea and ordered the summons to be reissued and his previous order to be vacated. B subsequently reappeared before the court and relied upon a plea of *autrefois convict.* The plea was not accepted, B was duly convicted and fined $40. His appeal to the Court of Appeal was dismissed on the basis that the second magistrate had no jurisdiction to hear a case begun before another magistrate.

Held, allowing B's appeal, that the second magistrate had jurisdiction to accept a guilty plea from B. Had the second magistrate continued the trial, hearing evidence and convicted B the verdict would be liable to be quashed on account of the fact that he had not heard all the evidence himself. There was nothing unfair in the second magistrate accepting a change of plea to guilty and hearing from the prosecution as to the facts of the case. It was in the public interest to do so, thereby avoiding the expense of a further unnecessary hearing before the original magistrate (*R.* v. *Ebanks* (1944) 4 J.L.R. 158 distinguished).

BESWICK *v.* THE QUEEN [1987] 1 W.L.R. 1346, P.C.

689. Magisterial law—plea—leave to change

D was unrepresented when he pleaded guilty to an offence before a magistrate. At a later hearing, when legally represented, D asked leave to change his plea. The magistrate, believing that D's real reason for wanting to change his plea was fear of a custodial sentence, refused.

Held, that this was a proper exercise of the magistrate's discretion.

R. *v.* BOW STREET STIPENDIARY MAGISTRATE, *ex p.* ROCHE AND RILEY, *The Times,* February 5, 1987, D.C.

690. Magisterial law—potential witness—whether likely to be able to give material evidence

[Magistrates' Courts Act 1980 (c.43), s.97(1).]

When justices have to consider, on an application for a witness summons under s.97(1) of the Magistrates' Courts Act 1980, whether a potential witness "is likely to be able to give material evidence," they must enquire into the nature of the evidence that the witness will be called on to give, and whether it is material. It is not enough to apply for a summons in order to find out what evidence, if any, the witness will be able to give.

R. *v.* PETERBOROUGH MAGISTRATES' COURT, *ex p.* WILLIS, *The Times,* June 23, 1987, D.C.

691. Magisterial law—summons—whether abuse of process

Summonses were issued on behalf of R Co. against A, the Chief Constable of Greater Manchester, and others alleging conspiracy to pervert the course of justice by procuring and causing one of their number to lay a false and improper sworn information in reliance upon which the Recorder of Manchester had made bank access orders and a stipendiary magistrate had issued search warrants.

Held, quashing the summonses and consequential orders, that their issue was an abuse of the court's process and the allegations contained in them were vexatious and oppressive. The application for them was one day before Chancery proceedings for an order against A and the Police Authority for an order that disclosure be made of documents leading to the issue of the orders and warrants. The High Court Judge in the Chancery proceedings refused to make that order. The main aim of the summonses was to secure discovery of the same documents. Neither R Co. nor its directors or advisers had any idea of what the contents of the informations before the Recorder and Stipendiary Magistrate had been and there was no other evidence of the alleged conspiracy save for inferences (*R.* v. *West London Metropolitan Stipendiary Magistrate, ex p. Klahn* [1979] C.L.Y. 1713 considered).

R. *v.* BURY JUSTICES, *ex p.* ANDERTON [1987] Crim.L.R. 638, D.C.

692. Magisterial law—triable either way—election

Where magistrates have consented to a defendant's election of summary trial on his plea of not guilty, they cannot later commit him for trial without having at least started to hear the evidence.

R. *v.* ST. HELENS JUSTICES, *ex p.* CRITCHLEY, *The Times,* October 22, 1987, D.C.

693. Magisterial law—whether justices obliged to accept guilty plea

Justices are obliged to accept an equivocal plea of guilty. If the defendant, having entered a proper plea of guilty, disputes facts on which the prosecution relies, the justices should if necessary hear evidence and resolve the issue before passing sentence (*R.* v. *Newton* [1983] C.L.Y. 815 and *R.* v. *Dudley Justices, ex p. Gillard* [1984] C.L.Y. 2105 applied).

R. *v.* TELFORD JUSTICES, *ex p.* DARLINGTON, *The Times,* November 23, 1987, D.C.

694. Majority verdicts—usual direction to jury not given—whether material irregularity

A direction such as that given in *R.* v. *Walhein* is not to be given unless the jury have been out for a considerable length of time, certainly longer than two and a half hours.

A was charged with wounding with intent. At his trial a number of difficult issues were raised. After the jury had been considering their verdict for two and a half hours, they were directed to reach unanimous agreement by adjusting their individual views, following *R.* v. *Walhein* [1953] C.L.Y. 804. Within 20 minutes, they returned with a verdict of guilty, by a majority of 10 to 2.

Held, allowing A's appeal, that the direction was not appropriate unless the retirement of the jury had been for a lengthy period, given the complexity of the issues involved. The judge's words might have brought improper pressure to bear on the jury, with the result that their verdict had to be quashed (*R.* v. *Walhein* [1953] C.L.Y. 804 considered; *R.* v. *Isequilla* [1975] C.L.Y. 554 distinguished).

R. *v.* ASHLEY [1987] 1 W.L.R. 712, C.A.

695. Manslaughter—joint defendants—parents—no evidence implicating one rather than the other

Registered heroin addicts lived with their 15-month-old daughter who died from a huge overdose of methadone. Each denied giving the child methadone, save in insignificant amounts to placate her when teething. Both were convicted of manslaughter, the jury indicating that the verdict was based on deliberate administration.

Held, dismissing appeals, that the Crown had to prove that the defendant at least aided, abetted, conselled or procured the commission of the crime by the other. A parent may have a duty to intervene where a stranger had no such duty. In the absence of any explanation from the defendants, the jury could infer from the admissions of each of being a party to administering tiny doses, that administration of the drug on the day of

death was a joint enterprise (*R.* v. *Gibson and Gibson* [1985] C.L.Y. 584 and *R.* v. *Lane and Lane* [1986] C.L.Y. 637 considered).
R. *v.* RUSSELL AND RUSSELL [1987] Crim.L.R. 494, C.A.

696. Material irregularity—map requested by jury—proviso

Whilst it was a material irregularity to comply with a jury's request for a map which was not admitted in evidence without consulting counsel, the court would apply the proviso.
R. *v.* THOMAS (HORATIO GERALD), *The Times*, February 9, 1987, C.A.

697. Mauritius—defendant convicted by magistrate who had not heard the evidence and submissions made—whether trial fair under Mauritian constitution. See NG (ALIAS WONG) *v.* THE QUEEN, §1821.

698. Murder—defence of diminished responsibility—defence not relied on—duty of judge where evidence to support defence

It was for the defendant to raise the defence of diminished responsibility on a murder charge so that the judge should not direct a jury to consider that defence unless the issue had been raised by the defendant.

C was convicted of murder having pleaded guilty to manslaughter by reason of provocation, that plea being unacceptable to the prosecution. The jury heard evidence from a psychiatrist on C's state of mind. Neither C nor the judge raised the issue of diminished responsibility under s.2 Homicide Act 1957. C appealed contending that the defence of diminished responsibility should have been put before the jury for their consideration in the light of the psychiatrist's evidence.

Held, dismissing C's appeal, that the evidence of the psychiatrist did not indicate any substantial impairment of responsibility on C's part sufficient to found the defence. Under s.2 of the Act the burden of proving the defence of diminished responsibility lay on the defendant, it was the defendant's decision whether the issue should be raised at all. If the trial judge detected evidence sufficient to support that defence he should bring that matter to the notice of the defendant's counsel in the absence of the jury so that the defendant could decide whether or not to raise the issue.
R. *v.* CAMPBELL (1987) 84 Cr.App.R. 255, C.A.

699. Murder—jury not able to agree—manslaughter verdict without prior murder acquittal

[Criminal Law Act 1967 (c.58), s.6(2).]

S.6(2) of the Criminal Law Act 1967 does not apply to a situation where a jury has been unable to reach a verdict at all.

The appellant was tried on a single count of murder. The jury were having difficulty with the question of intent and the prosecution agreed to accept a verdict of manslaughter. The judge discharged the jury from a verdict of murder and they returned a verdict of manslaughter. The appellant appealed submitting that the jury could not validly return a guilty verdict on manslaughter without first acquitting of murder.

Held, dismissing the appeal, s.6(2) did not apply where a jury had never been able to reach a verdict at all, the judge was entitled to discharge them and to accept the lesser verdict (*Winsor* v. *The Queen* (1866) L.R. 1 Q.B. 289 applied).
R. *v.* SAUNDERS [1987] 3 W.L.R. 355, H.L.

700. Not guilty plea—direction by trial judge to convict

When a defendant pleads not guilty and clearly wishes to hear the verdict of a jury, the judge should not direct the jury to return a verdict of guilty, even if all the evidence (including the defendant's own) makes a conviction inevitable (*D.P.P.* v. *Stonehouse,* [1977] C.L.Y. 1450, *R.* v. *Thompson,* [1984] C.L.Y. 965 and *R.* v. *Challinor,* [1985] C.L.Y. 896 applied).
R. *v.* GORDON, *The Times*, May 11, 1987, C.A.

701. Obtaining property by deception—false claims for unemployment benefit—evidence of receipt of benefit

D was found to have obtained girocheques which he had cashed by false representation that he was unemployed. Evidence was given that claims for benefit were accorded a commencement date and that, unless there was a break exceeding two weeks in subsequent claims, girocheques were produced by a computer ready for posting. As cleared girocheques were destroyed after one year, none alleged to have been cashed were available.

Held, quashing D's convictions, that evidence of the system did not of itself prove that D's claim had gone through the system.
BOGDAL *v.* HALL [1987] Crim.L.R. 500, D.C.

702. Offshore activities—jurisdiction. See SEA AND SEASHORE, §3350.

703. Oral admission of judgment—whether valid evidence of judgment

Oral admission of a civil judgment is valid evidence of that judgment.
R. *v.* STOKE, *The Times,* August 6, 1987, C.A.

704. Part-heard case—resumption after delay—justices' discretion

[Magistrates' Courts Act 1980 (c.43), s.10(1).]
Whether or not it is unfair that a part-heard case should proceed after a delay of five months since the previous hearing is a matter within the justices' discretion under s.10(1) of the Magistrates' Courts Act 1980.
R. *v.* ALI, *The Times,* July 6, 1987, D.C.

705. Petty sessional divisions

PETTY SESSIONAL DIVISIONS (CORNWALL) ORDER 1987 (No. 1796) [85p], made under the Justices of the Peace Act 1979 (c.55), s.23(3)(5); operative on January 1, 1988; provides for the combination of the divisions of Falmouth and Penryn to form the new petty sessional division of Falmouth—Penryn, and provides for the combination of the divisions of Truro, West Powder and South Powder to form the new petty sessional division of Truro and South Powder.

PETTY SESSIONAL DIVISIONS (CUMBRIA) ORDER 1987 (No. 1925) [85p], made under the Justices of the Peace Act 1979, s.23(3) and (5); provides for the reorganisation of petty sessional divisions within Cumbria.

PETTY SESSIONAL DIVISIONS (DORSET) ORDER 1987 (No. 1739) [£1·30], made under the Justices of the Peace Act 1979 s.23(3)(5); operative on January 1, 1988 provides for the abolition of the petty sessional divisions of Blandford, Shaftesbury and Sturminster and the creation of two new petty sessions of Blandford and Sturminster, and Shaftesbury.

PETTY SESSIONAL DIVISIONS (GLOUCESTERSHIRE) ORDER 1987 (No. 1912) [85p], made under the Justices of the Peace Act 1979, s.23(3)(5); operative on January 1, 1988; provides for the combination of the petty sessional divisions of Coleford, Lydney and Newnham to form the new division of Forest of Dean.

PETTY SESSIONAL DIVISIONS (GWYNEDD) ORDER 1987 (No. 1201) [85p], made under the Justices of the Peace Act 1979, s.23(3)(5); operative on July 1, 1987; gives effect to a draft Order submitted by the magistrates' courts committee for the county of Gwynedd and provides for the transfer to the Conwy and Llandudno division of the community of Llanfairfechan.

PETTY SESSIONAL DIVISIONS (HEREFORD AND WORCESTER) ORDER 1987 (No. 1913) [£1·30], made under the Justices of the Peace Act 1979, s.23(3)(5); operative on January 1, 1988; provides for the formation of seven new petty sessional divisions—North Herefordshire, South Herefordshire, Malvern Hills, Bewdley and Stourport, Mid-Worcestershire, Vale of Evesham and City of Worcester.

PETTY SESSIONAL DIVISIONS (KIRKLEES) ORDER 1987 (No. 1786) [85p], made under the Justices of the Peace Act 1979, s.23(3)(5); operative on January 1, 1988; provides for the combination of the divisions of Batley and Dewsbury to form a new petty sessional division of Batley and Dewsbury.

PETTY SESSIONAL DIVISIONS (LANCASHIRE) ORDER 1987 (No. 1688) [85p] made under the Justices of the Peace Act 1979, s.23(3)(5); operative on January 1, 1988; provides for the combination of the divisions of Accrington and Church to form the new petty sessional division of Hyndburn.

PETTY SESSIONAL DIVISIONS (NORTHAMPTONSHIRE) ORDER 1987 (No. 184) [£1·40], made under the Justice of the Peace Act 1979, s.23(2)(5); operative on April 1, 1987; provides for the amalgamation of the petty sessional divisions of Brackley, Mid-Northants and Oundle and Thrapston with other divisions in the county.

PETTY SESSIONAL DIVISIONS (NORTHAMPTONSHIRE) (AMENDMENT) ORDER 1987 (No. 519) [45p], made under Justice of the Peace Act 1979, s.23(3)(5); operative on April 1, 1987; corrects certain errors in S.I. 1987 No. 184.

PETTY SESSIONAL DIVISIONS (NORTHUMBERLAND) ORDER 1987 (No. 1962) [85p], made under the Justices of the Peace Act 1979, s.23(3)(5); operative on April 1, 1988; provides for the combination of the petty sessional divisions of Glendale Ward and Berwick-upon-Tweed to form the new division of Berwick-upon-Tweed.

PETTY SESSIONAL DIVISIONS (NOTTINGHAMSHIRE) ORDER 1987 (No. 1797) [£1·30], made under the Justices of the Peace Act 1979, s.23(3)(5); operative on January 1, 1988; provides for the reorganisation of the petty sessional divisions in Nottinghamshire.

706. Police powers—entry and search of premises

[Police and Criminal Evidence Act 1984 (c.60), s.17.]

Where a police officer has reasonable grounds to suspect that a person, who is suspected of having committed an arrestable offence, is on certain premises, he is empowered to enter, search for and arrest that person.

KYNASTON *v.* D.P.P.; HERON (JOSEPH) *v.* D.P.P.; HERON (TRACEY) *v.* D.P.P., *The Times,* November 4, 1987, D.C.

707. Police powers—search of premises—whether inspector's authorisation "in writing"—whether search "upon arrest"

[Police and Criminal Evidence Act 1984 (c.60), ss.18 and 32(2)(*b*).]

B's sons were arrested. The arresting officer later obtained authorisation from a police inspector for a seach of B's house. The inspector made an entry in his notebook that authorisation had been given. B refused police officers entry and demanded to see the authority for the search.

Held, allowing B's appeal against conviction of obstructing a police officer in the execution of his duty, that (1) the authorisation given by the inspector had not been given "in writing" as required by s.18(4) of the 1984 Act and (2) the officers were not entitled to enter the house to search pursuant to s.32(2)(*b*) since that section applied only to search "upon arrest" and did not give an open-ended right to return to the premises.

R. *v.* BADHAM [1987] Crim.L.R. 202, Wood Green Crown Court.

708. Press photographs of riot—application under s.9 of 1984 Act—judicial review of order

[Police and Criminal Evidence Act 1984 (c.60), s.9) and Sched. 1.]

Following a riot, police obtained an order under s.9 of the 1984 Act, that BPPA Co. produce photographs of the riot taken by their photographers.

Held, that (1) the decision of the Crown Court was to be regarded as a criminal cause or matter as the photographs were required for investigation of criminal offences and the decision was amenable to judicial review but; (2) although no particular photograph could be identified as relating to any particular incident of violence or criminal offence, the judge was entitled to conclude that there were reasonable grounds (within the 1984 Act, Sched. 1, para. 2(*a*)(iii) and (iv)) for believing that the material was likely to be of substantial value to the investigation. The judge had properly weighed the balance of public interest in the conviction of offenders and elimination of the innocent from the criminal process and the importance of ensuring independence and safety of the press.

R. *v.* BRISTOL CROWN COURT, *ex p.* BRISTOL PRESS AND PICTURE AGENCY [1987] Crim.L.R. 329, D.C.

709. Previous consistent statement—admissibility

The trial judge refused to allow re-examination of O by putting in evidence O's written statement given to his solicitor at the magistrates' court which was consistent with the defence run by him at the Crown Court.

Held, dismissing O's appeal, that a self-serving statement does not become admissible merely because the prosecution suggests that the defence version is false and cross-examines on that basis (*Nominal Defendant* v. *Clements* (1961) 104 C.L.R. 476 considered).

R. *v.* OKAI [1987] Crim.L.R. 259, C.A.

710. Previous convictions—leave to adduce evidence—extent

[Theft Act 1968 (c.60), s.27(3).]

When the prosecution is given leave under s.27(3) of the Theft Act 1968 to adduce evidence of a defendant's previous convictions for handling, the jury may only be told the facts, dates and places of the convictions. They may not be told any of the details of the offences.

R. *v.* FOWLER, *The Independent,* July 21, 1987, C.A.

711. Privilege—conversations with prison officer concerning legal aid application by defendant—admission made by defendant—whether conversation privileged

Admissions made by a defendant in the course of receiving advice from a prison officer about the substance of making an application for legal aid should be privileged against disclosure in court on the ground of public interest.

D was convicted by a jury of conspiracy to supply heroin. Part of the evidence against D adduced at trial was evidence of a principal prison officer about admissions made to him by D whilst D was in prison awaiting trial. D appealed against his conviction. D claimed that the admissions were made in the course of a conversation with the prison officer to which privilege attached. D claimed the conversation was privileged because it concerned D's application for legal aid. D contended that the trial judge erred in refusing his application to exclude the evidence of the prison officer.

Held, dismissing D's appeal, that on the facts the admissions were not made in the course of a discussion about an application for legal aid or as a result of D asking for advice or assistance on the substance of his legal aid application. Given that prison rules provide the facility of assistance from a legal aid officer it was desirable in the public interest that conversations between a defendant and a legal aid officer about the substance of the defendant's legal aid application should be privileged. Discussions and disclosures on other occasions when a defendant was not being advised by the legal aid officer on the substance of his application should not be privileged.

R. *v.* UMOH (1987) 84 Cr.App.R. 138, C.A.

712. Privilege—conveyancing documents

[Police and Criminal Evidence Act 1984 (c.60), s.10 and Sched. 1, para. 1.]

On an application for production under the Act, a solicitor may be compelled to produce the records of a conveyancing transaction transacted on behalf of a client, as these documents are not privileged from production.

R. *v.* CROWN COURT, *ex p.* BAINES AND WHITE, (1987) 137 New L.J. 945, D.C.

713. Probation areas

COMBINED PROBATION AREAS (CORNWALL) ORDER 1987 (No. 2140) [45p], made under the Powers of Criminal Courts Act 1973 (c.62), s.54(4) and Sched. 3, para. 1; operative on January 1, 1988; amends S.I. 1986 No. 1713.

COMBINED PROBATION AREAS (CUMBRIA) ORDER 1987 (No. 2222) [45p], made under the Powers of Criminal Courts Act 1973, s.54(4) and Sched. 3, para. 1; amends S.I. 1986 No. 1713 to the account of the reorganisation of petty sessional divisions within Cumbria.

COMBINED PROBATION AREAS (DORSET) ORDER 1987) (No. 2135) [45p], made under the Powers of Criminal Courts Act 1973, s.54(4) and Sched. 3. para. 1 ; operative on January 1, 1988; amends S.I. 1986 No. 1713.

COMBINED PROBATION AREAS (GLOUCESTERSHIRE) ORDER 1987 (No. 2181) [45p], made under the Powers of Criminal Courts Act 1973, s.54(4) and Sched. 3 para. 1; operative on January 1, 1988; amends S.I. 1986 No. 1713.

COMBINED PROBATION AREAS (HEREFORD AND WORCESTER) ORDER 1987 (No. 2223) [45p], made under the Powers of Criminal Courts Act 1973, s.54(4) and Sched. 3, para. 1; amends S.I. 1986 No. 1713 to the account of the reorganisation of a number of petty sessional divisions in Hereford and Worcester.

COMBINED PROBATION AREAS (LANCASHIRE) ORDER 1987 (No. 1855) [45p], made under the Powers of Criminal Courts Act 1973, s.54(4), Sched. 3, para. 1; operative on January 1, 1988; amends S.I. 1986 No. 1713 to take account in changes to the Lancashire petty sessional divisions.

COMBINED PROBATION AREAS (NORTHAMPTONSHIRE) ORDER 1987 (No. 356) [45p], made under the Powers of Criminal Courts Act 1973, s.54(4), Sched. 3, para. 1; operative on April 1, 1987; amend S.I. 1986 No. 1713 to take account of the reorganisation of certain petty sessional divisions in Northamptonshire.

COMBINED PROBATION AREAS (NOTTINGHAMSHIRE) ORDER 1987 (No. 2136) [45p], made underthe Powers of Criminal Courts Act 1973, s.54(4), Sched. 3, para. 1; operative on January 1, 1988; amends S.I. 1986 No. 1713 to take account of the new petty sessional division of Nottingham.

COMBINED PROBATION AREAS (WEST YORKSHIRE) ORDER 1987 (No. 2141) [45p], made under the Powers of Criminal Courts Act 1973, s.54(4) and Sched. 3, para. 1; operative on January 1, 1988; amends S.I. 1986 No. 1713.

714. Prosecution counsel—second address to jury

If it is necessary to make a second speech to the jury, prosecuting counsel should only make a short speech (*R.* v. *Bryant and Oxley* [1978] C.L.Y. 652 considered).

R. *v.* FRANCIS, *The Times,* October 28, 1987, C.A.

715. Prosecution evidence—police seeking to withhold evidence of surveillance vehicle

The police were not entitled to withhold evidence that was disputed about a vehicle used in a surveillance operation.

R. *v.* BROWN (R. B.); R. *v.* DALEY, *The Times,* November 24, 1987, C.A.

716. Prosecution under one section of an Act—whether possible to convict under another section

[Health and Safety at Work etc. Act 1974 (c.37), ss.33, 36; Dangerous Substances (Conveyance by Road in Road Tankers and Tank Containers) Regulations (S.I. 1981 No. 1059), reg. 10(1), (2).]

Reg. 10(1) of the Dangerous Substances (Conveyance by Road in Road Tankers and Tank Containers) Regulations applies to the operators of vehicles, and reg. 10(2) to drivers. Where a company is prosecuted under reg. 10(2) and s.33 of the Health and Safety at Work Act 1974, it cannot be convicted of an offence under s.36.

WEST CUMBERLAND BY PRODUCTS *v.* D.P.P., *The Times,* November 12, 1987, D.C.

717. Prosecution witness subsequently convicted of perjury—whether conviction unsafe

A conviction is not necessarily unsafe when a prosecution witness is subsequently convicted of perjury in relation to evidence given at the trial, if the evidence is peripheral to the main issue.

C was convicted *inter alia* of reckless driving. At the trial there was an issue as to who was the driver of the car, C or a co-defendant, P. The prosecution's case was that it was C and there was strong independant identification to support it. There was a conflict of evidence between P and a Police officer, A, on a peripheral issue. Sometime after the trial A was convicted of perjury in relation to this evidence. Both defendants appealed on the basis that their convictions were unsafe.

Held, dismissing the appeal, that the identification evidence was not contaminated by the perjured evidence which was on a peripheral issue.

R. *v.* CUMMINS; R. *v.* PERKS (1987) 84 Cr.App.R. 71, C.A.

718. Provocation—summing up—direction to jury

In a long and complex case where provocation was raised as a defence to a charge of murder, the judge should always draw the jury's attention to the facts relied upon in that defence.

R. *v.* JONES (PETER), *The Times,* April 16, 1987, C.A.

719. Recent possession—right to silence—exception—direction to jury. See R. *v.* RAVIRAJ; R. *v.* KANSAZ: R. *v.* GUPTA, §2103.

720. Reference by Home Secretary to Court of Appeal—evidence on reference

On a reference, the court is entitled to examine any relevant material including a report brought into being in civil proceedings.

R. *v.* CALLAGHAN; R. *v.* HILL; R. *v.* HUNTER; R. *v.* McILKENNY; R. *v.* POWER; R. *v.* WALKER, *The Times,* October 17, 1987, C.A.

721. Refusal to pay fine—committal to prison—consideration of other methods of enforcement

[Magistrates' Courts Act 1980 (c.43), s.82(4)(*b*).]

Where D refused to pay a fine on moral grounds, it was incumbent upon the justices to consider all other methods of enforcing the fine before committing him to prison.

R. *v.* NORWICH JUSTICES, *ex p.* TIGGER (FORMERLY LILLY), *The Times,* June 26, 1987, D.C.

722. Request to change counsel—effect of refusal

When D appeared in court at the beginning of his trial, he told the judge that he wished to change his counsel. The judge presented D with the choice of continuing with his present counsel, or with no counsel at all. D refused to take any further part in the trial, retired to the cells, and was eventually convicted. He appealed.

Held, that in the circumstances, the judge acted improperly in presenting D with this choice, and, in the regrettable absence of any power of the Court of Appeal to order a retrial, D's appeal would be allowed (*R.* v. *Kingston (Mary),* (1948) 32 Cr.App.R. 183, 190 applied).

R. *v.* DAVIES (COLIN STUART), *The Times,* February 11, 1987, C.A.

723. Restraint or charging order—discovery—full disclosure by prosecution—whether privilege against self-incrimination a protection

[Drug Trafficking Offences Act 1986 (c.32), ss.8, 9; R.S.C. Ord. 115, r.3(4).]

Ss.8 and 9 of the Drug Trafficking Offences Act 1986 allow a Court to make a restraint order or a charging order against a defendant's property when it is satisfied that the defendant has benefited from drug trafficking. When in the course of the case the prosecutor seeks an order for discovery against a defendant, the situation is analogous to an application for a *Mareva* injunction, and full and frank disclosure of the prosecution evidence is required. Where the evidence sought to be obtained from the defendant might lead to his prosecution on further serious charges, the privilege against self-incrimination will not protect him, if the prosecutor is willing to undertake to make no future use of that information except in the instant case (*Rank Film Distributors* v. *Video Information Centre* [1981] C.L.Y. 2148 distinguished).

DEFENDANT, A, *Re The Independent,* April 2, 1987, Webster J.

724. Service of documents—certificate

[Magistrates' Court Rules (S.I. 1981 No. 552), r.67(2).]

The rule is satisfied by the production of a certificate from a person who has effected service of a document to the proper address, showing the place, date and time.

HAWKINS *v.* CROWN PROSECUTION SERVICE, *The Times,* August 24, 1987, D.C.

725. Severance of counts on indictment—conspiracy—direction to jury

[Criminal Evidence Act 1898 (c.36), s.1; Indictments Act 1915 (c.90), s.5(3).]

(1) The trial judge has a discretion whether to sever the counts on an indictment, and may take into account not only the possibility that D's evidence on one count might incriminate him on another, but also the expense and inconvenience to witnesses of separate trials. (2) It is unnecessary, where only one conspiracy is alleged and other defendants had pleaded guilty to it, and the court also included persons unknown, to direct the jury that they must each be satisfied that D conspired with the same person or persons. (3) In the instant case the appeal would be allowed since evidence of confessions obtained by inducement should have been treated as inadmissible (*R.* v. *Brown* [1984] C.L.Y. 624, *R.* v. *Moore* (unrep. February 28, 1986, C.A.) considered).

R. *v.* PHILLIPS, *The Times,* January 31, 1987, C.A.

726. Sex shop—operating without a licence—whether council's reasons for refusing licence relevant. See PLYMOUTH CITY COUNCIL *v.* QUIETLYNN; PORTSMOUTH CITY COUNCIL *v.* QUIETLYNN; QUIETLYNN *v.* OLDHAM BOROUGH COUNCIL, §2319

727. Similar fact—evidence of accomplice—guidelines

L was alleged to have admitted buying a stolen cheque book and cheque card for two women to use in return for being given some of the goods to be obtained by the women. He was charged with handling the cheque book and card, forging a cheque and using a cheque with the intention of it being accepted as genuine.

Held, dismissing his appeal against conviction, that the trial judge had not erred in allowing evidence of one of the women dealing not only with the occasion referred to in the indictment but also other occasions when 24 cheques were used to obtain goods and services. Such evidence was probative as to the part played by L, whose case was that he accompanied the women but did not participate in the use of cheques. There was no rule requiring a judge to exercise his discretion to exclude such evidence automatically where it is to be provided by an accomplice, though care should be taken.

R. *v.* LUNT [1987] Crim.L.R. 405, C.A.

728. Similar fact—rape—evidence of consensual sexual practices with another woman—whether admissable

In sexual cases, evidence of a former girlfriend of consensual sexual practices are admissable if of a strikingly similar character and of positive probative value.

The appellant was charged with rape and indecent assault on two young women. Both had been picked up at bus stops, asked to perform similar sex acts, and raped. Forensic evidence supported their stories. A former girlfriend was called to give evidence of similar consensual sexual practices with the appellant, and identified the scenes of the rapes as places she had been for sexual purposes with him.

Held, on appeal on the question of the admissability of the similar fact evidence that the evidence showed a striking similarity and was probative; it was properly admitted.

R. *v.* BUTLER (DENNIS) (1987) 84 Cr.App.R. 12, C.A.

729. Special procedure material—disclosure material at more than one place and in the control of more than one person

[Police and Criminal Evidence Act 1984 (c.60), ss.9, 14(2), Sched. 1 paras. 2(*a*)(ii), 4, 12.]

An order for production or disclosure of special procedure material may properly be made against a number of people and in respect of a number of premises if the court is satisfied that there are grounds for belief that the material is on the premises (*R.* v. *Central Criminal Court, ex p. Adegbesan* [1986] C.L.Y. 912 considered).

R. *v.* CENTRAL CRIMINAL COURT, *ex p.* CARR, *The Independent,* March 5, 1987, D.C.

730. Special procedure material—legal privilege—admissibility of prejudicial evidence

[Police and Criminal Evidence Act 1984 (c.60), ss.9(1), (2), 10(1)], Sched. 1.]

S.9(1) of the Police and Criminal Evidence Act 1984 allows the Police access to certain documents, by applying to the courts under Sched. 1. S.9(2) exempts from production, *inter alia,* items subject to legal privilege, which are defined in s.10(1), but which do not include documents relating to conveyancing. When the Police make an application, they are not strictly bound by the rules of evidence, but they may not rely on unsubstantiated and purely prejudicial statements. Whatever evidence is served on the court must also be served on the party required to produce the documents, although the Police are not required to produce information in advance of the hearing (*R.* v. *Central Criminal Court, ex p. Adegbesan* [1986] C.L.Y. 912 considered).

R. *v.* INNER LONDON CROWN COURT, *ex p.* BAINES AND BAINES (A FIRM), *The Times,* September 8, 1987, D.C.

731. Special procedure material—whether duty to notify accused

[Police and Criminal Evidence Act 1984 (c.60), s.9(1), Sched. 1, para. 7.]

There is no requirement to notify the accused on an application for the production of special procedure material, but only the custodian of the material.

The police applied to the Crown Court for an order granting access to F's bank and building society accounts under s.9(1) of the Police and Criminal Evidence Act 1984 in order to further an investigation. The judge ruled that para. 7 of Sched. 1 to the Act made the application *inter partes,* and that it was necessary for the person whose activities were under investigation to be a party to the proceedings and that before the order could be made F had to be served with notice of the application. The D.P.P. applied for judicial review of the ruling.

Held, granting the application, that para. 7 of Sched. 1 did not require a suspect in a criminal investigation to be given notice, as it was inconceivable that Parliament could have contemplated that a suspect should be made aware of the intention of the police to seek an order under s.9(1). The only parties referred to were the police who made the yapplication and the person or institution in whose custody the material to which access was sought was thought to be.

R. *v.* LEICESTER CROWN COURT, *ex p.* D.P.P. [1987] 1 W.L.R. 1371 D.C.

732. Statement out of court—mixed statement—evidential value—direction to jury

When a defendant makes a statement to a police officer that contains both self-incriminating and self-exculpatory material, the jury should be directed to consider the document as a whole, and not to consider only the self-incriminatory passages (*R.* v. *Duncan* [1981] C.L.Y. 437 and *R.* v. *Hamand* [1986] C.L.Y. 553 applied).

R. *v.* SHARP, *The Times,* January 22, 1987, C.A.

733. Statistics—cautions, court proceedings and sentencing

The Home Office has published a statistical bulletin which provides summary information on offenders dealt with in 1986 by formal police cautions or criminal court proceedings in England and Wales. The bulletin, Issue 21/87, is available from the Statistical Department, Home Office, Lunar House, Croydon, Surrey CR0 9YD. Tel. 01-760 2850 [£2·50].

734. Statistics—operation of police powers under the Police and Criminal Evidence Act 1984. See CRIMINAL LAW, §833.

735. Statistics—time taken to process criminal cases in magistrates' courts

The Home Office has published statistics of the time taken to process criminal cases in magistrates' courts between June 1985 and June 1986. Copies of the bulletin are available from the Home Office, Statistical Department, Lunar House, Croydon, Surrey CRO 9YD. Tel. 01–760 2850. [£2·50].

736. Summing-up-directions to jury—judge omitting essential direction

It is the duty of prosecuting counsel to ensure, preferably by means of a check-list, that the judge gives adequate directions to the jury by drawing any omission to his attention.

R. *v.* DONOGHUE, *The Times,* August 29, 1987, C.A.

737. Summing-up—issue raised by judge not previously canvassed in trial—duty to give prior warning to counsel

C sold a car, the odometer in which recorded 24,000 miles and was alleged to have assured the purchasers that it was a genuine mileage. He gave the purchasers a receipt on which he had written "sold as seen." He subsequently told them he had changed the odometer, which he said had been faulty (but had not "clocked" it) and had not told them because they would not have purchased the car. The receipt was not referred to in evidence or by counsel in closing speeches but the judge, without notice to counsel, directed the jury that they could infer from the words on it that that was a representation they could take note of as emanating from the appearance of the odometer as being an accurate record of the distance travelled by the car.

Held, allowing C's appeal against conviction of obtaining property by deception, that a judge should give ample warning to counsel in the absence of the jury, before counsel's speeches began, if he intended to introduce in a summing-up an issue which had not been actively canvassed during the trial.

R. *v.* CRISTINI [1987] Crim.L.R. 504, C.A.

738. Summing-up—issue raised by judge not previously canvassed in trial—duty to give prior warning to counsel

W was convicted of theft of a pouch of letters from a bicycle left unattended by a postman. The prosecution alleged that W was one of two men seen running to a motor car which belonged to W. In his summing-up, the judge, without having consulted counsel, referred for the first time to the possibility that there were three men at the scene, one remaining in the car as driver.

Held, allowing W's appeal, that the judge's failure to inform defence counsel of his intention to raise this point so that he would have an opportunity of dealing with it was a material irregularity.

R. *v.* WHITE [1987] Crim.L.R. 505, C.A.

739. Tape recorded interview—transcript of recording—use at trial

The court gave guidance about the use of both tape recordings and the transcripts of them at trial.

R. *v.* RAMPLING, *The Times,* August 29, 1987, C.A.

740. Tape recordings—obtained by trap—admissibility

[Police and Criminal Evidence Act 1984 (c.60), s.78.]

At D's trial for rape, evidence of tape recordings of telephone conversations between D and his alleged victim, X, was excluded under s.78 of the 1984 Act. Following D's release pending further enquiries, X had instigated the conversations, the police having installed the recording equipment with her consent. In all the circumstances, including the way in which the recordings were obtained the court held that they would have an adverse effect on the proceedings.

R. *v.* H. [1987] Crim.L.R. 47, Winchester Crown Court, Gatehouse J.

741. Theft—dishonesty—proof required

Where, because of the required standard of proof, it was not possible to say which of two jointly indicted defendants had committed the offence, both should be acquitted.

COLLINS *v.* D.P.P., *The Times,* October 20, 1987, D.C.

742. Unanimity direction—whether appropriate

A *Walhein* direction (urging a jury to deliberate further and try to reach a unanimous verdict) is inappropriate in most cases, and certainly where the jury has not been given (i) enough time to consider a verdict, and (ii) a majority direction (*R.* v. *Walhein* [1953] C.L.Y. 804 considered; *R.* v. *Wright (Shirley)* October 13, 1987 applied).

R. *v.* RANDALL, *The Times,* November 18, 1987, C.A.

743. Video-recording—admissibility of viewers' evidence—whether hearsay

Evidence of witnesses who have seen a video recording of the incidents alleged to constitute an offence is not hearsay.

T was charged with theft of some batteries from a shop. The prosecution evidence came from witnesses who had seen a video recording of events alleged to constitute the offence, the recording itself having later been inadvertently erased. The justices ruled the evidence admissible and T was convicted.

Held, dismissing the appeal, that such evidence was not rendered inadmissible by the hearsay rule.

TAYLOR *v.* CHIEF CONSTABLE OF CHESHIRE [1986] 1 W.L.R. 1479, D.C.

744. View of alleged scene of crimes—whether justices should be accompanied by parties

It is desirable that a visit by magistrates to the scene of an alleged offence should be made in the presence of both parties.

B was involved in a multiple collision when negotiating a junction of a minor road and a dual carriageway road. She was charged with driving without due care and attention. At the conclusion of the prosecution case the defendants gave no evidence and the justices stated that they would view the scene. Neither party attended the view, after which the justices dismissed the information on the grounds of the inadequacy of the road signs. The prosecutor appealed, seeking guidance on visits by magistrates to scenes of alleged offences.

Held, that there had been an implied invitation to the parties to attend the view, but it was undesirable in this case for the justices to make a view without the parties, since the parties should have a chance to evaluate matters which the justices noticed. However as the justices had directed themselves correctly on the law, and as it could not be said that they were not entitled to come to the conclusion they did on the facts, the appeal would be dismissed (*Goold* v. *Evans & Co.* [1951] C.L.Y. 3714 and *Salsbury* v. *Woodland* [1969] C.L.Y. 2432 approved).

PARRY *v.* BOYLE (1986) 83 Cr.App.R. 310, D.C.

745. Ward of court—child in care of local authority—police investigating whether wards subjected to criminal offence—police seeking disclosure of medical and local authority records—whether leave of court required. See S. (MINORS) (WARDSHIP: POLICE INVESTIGATION) *Re,* §2530.

746. Ward of court—whether necessary to seek leave before calling a ward to give evidence

It is not necessary to seek leave of the Hight Court before calling a ward to give evidence

K. (MINORS), *Re, The Times,* September 10, 1987, Waterhouse J.

747. Warrants—backing—verification

[Backing of Warrants (Republic of Ireland) Act 1965 (c.45), s.1(3); Magistrates' Courts (Backing of Warrants) Rules 1965 (S.I. 1965 No. 1906), r.5(3).]

The applicants were convicted in County Cork of offences and were sentenced to imprisonment. They were Polish nationals resident in West Germany. They were released on bail pending appeals. They came to England and were later detained in reliance on endorsements under s.1 of the 1965 Act. The purpose of the Irish warrant was said to be to secure the production of the applicants before the Circuit Court in Cork to enable that court to hear their appeals.

Held, granting writs of habeas corpus and ordering the applicants' release, that to secure the hearing of an appeal was not a proper purpose within s.1(3) of the 1965 Act, which precluded endorsement of a warrant unless the purpose of arrest was to bring before a court for sentence or delivery to prison to serve a sentence. Furthermore, r.5(3) of the 1965 Rules required verification of an affidavit by a certificate purporting to be sworn by the person before whom it was sworn and certifying that it was so sworn. The jurats of the affidavits were not sufficient verification.

MALINOWSKI, *Re* [1987] Crim.L.R. 324, D.C.

748. Wife of polygamous marriage—competence as prosecution witness

A woman who has gone through a polygamous ceremony of marriage is a competent witness for the Crown against her "husband".

The appellant and A were charged with the importation of heroin. At the trial a woman gave evidence for the prosecution and it became known that she had gone through a Moslem form of marriage with A when his wife was still alive. The Judge ruled that she was not A's wife under English law and was a competent witness for the prosecution.

Held, dismissing the appeal, that the woman was a competent witness for the Crown (*R.* v. *Yacoob* [1981] C.L.Y. 410 applied).

R. *v.* KHAN (JUNAID) (1987) 84 Cr.App.R. 44, C.A.

749. Witness—ability of witness affected by drugs to give evidence—stopping of trial

At B's trial for robbery the victim, X, felt unwell during cross-examination and took tranquillisers exceeding the recommended dose. X was thereafter unable to give comprehensible evidence. The judge adjourned the case over the weekend, refusing to discharge the jury.

Held, refusing leave to appeal against conviction, that the judge had properly exercised his discretion and directed the jury carefully.

R. *v.* BAINES [1987] Crim.L.R. 508, C.A.

750. Written statements—practice direction

The following practice direction was issued by the Lord Chief Justice on June 3, 1986.

1. This Practice Direction is in substitution for that given by the Lord Chief Justice on October 17, 1969 (54 Cr.App.R. 29; [1969] 1 W.L.R. 1862).

2. Where the prosecution proposes to tender written statements in evidence under either section 102 of the Magistrates' Courts Act 1980 or section 9 of the Criminal Justice Act 1967 it will frequently be not only proper, but also necessary for the orderly presentation of the evidence, for certain statements to be edited. This will occur either because a witness has made more than one statement whose contents should conveniently be reduced into a single, comprehensive statement or where a statement contains inadmissible, prejudicial or irrelevant material. Editing of statements should in all circumstances be done by a Crown prosecutor (or by a legal representative, if any, of the prosecutor if the case is not being conducted by the Crown Prosecution Service) and not by a police officer.

3. *Composite Statements*

A composite statement giving the combined effect of two or more earlier statements or settled by a person referred to in paragraph 2 above must be prepared in compliance with the requirements of section 102 of the 1980 Act or section 9 of the 1967 Act as appropriate and must then be signed by the witness.

4. *Editing Single Statements*

(1) By marking *copies* of the statement in a way which indicates the passages on which the prosecution will not rely. This merely indicates that the prosecution will not seek to adduce the evidence so marked. The *original signed statement* to be tendered to the Court is not marked in any way. The marking on the copy statement is done by lightly striking out the passages to be edited so that what appears beneath can still be read, or by bracketing, or by a combination of both.
It is not permissible to produce a photocopy with the deleted material obliterated, since this would be contrary to the requirement that the defence and the court should be served with copies of the signed original statement.
Whenever the striking out/bracketing method is used, it will assist if the following words appear at the foot of the frontispiece or index to any bundle of copy statements to be tendered.;
"The prosecution does not propose to adduce evidence of those passages of the attached copy statements which have been struck out and/or bracketed. (Nor will it seek to do so at the trial unless a Notice of Further Evidence is served)."

(2) By obtaining a fresh statement, signed by the witness, which omits the offending material, applying the procedure in paragraph 3 above.

5. In most cases where a single statement is to be edited, the striking out/bracketing method will be the more appropriate, but the taking of a fresh statement is preferable in the following circumstances.

(a) When a police (or other investigating) officer's statement contains details of interviews with more suspects than are eventually charged, a fresh statement should be prepared and signed omitting all details of interviews with those not charged except, insofar as it is relevant, for the bald fact that a certain named person was interviewed at a particular time, date and place.

(b) When a suspect is interviewed about more offences than are eventually made the subject of committal charges, a fresh statement should be prepared and signed omitting all questions and answers about the uncharged offences unless either they might appropriately be taken into consideration or evidence about those offences is admissible upon the charges preferred, such as evidence of system. It may however be desirable to replace the omitted questions and answers with a phrase such as:
"After referring to some other matters, I then said . . ." so as to make it clear that part of the interview has been omitted.

(c) A fresh statement should normally be prepared and signed if the only part of the original on which the prosecution are relying is only a small proportion of the whole although it remains desirable to use the alternative method if there is reason to believe that the defence might themselves wish to rely, in mitigation or for any other purpose, on at least some of those parts which the prosecution do not propose to adduce.

(d) When the passages contain material which the prosecution is entitled to withhold from disclosure to the defence.

6. Prosecutors should also be aware that, where statements are to be tendered under section 9 of the 1967 Act in the course of *summary* proceedings, there will be a greater need to prepare fresh statements excluding inadmissible or prejudicial material rather than using the striking out or bracketing method.

7. None of the above principles applies, in respect of committal proceedings, to documents which are exhibited (including statements under caution and signed contemporaneous notes). Nor do they apply to oral statements of a defendant which are recorded in the witness statements of interviewing police officers, except in the circumstances referred to in paragraph 5(b) above. All this material should remain in its original state in the committal bundles, any editing being left to prosecuting counsel at the Crown Court (after discussion with defence counsel and, if appropriate, the trial judge).

8. Whenever a fresh statement is taken from a witness, a copy of the earlier, unedited statement(s) of that witness will be given to the defence in accordance with the Attorney General's Guidelines (1982) 74 Cr.App.R. 302 on the disclosure of unused material unless there are grounds under paragraph 6 of the Guidelines for withholding such disclosure.

PRACTICE DIRECTION (EVIDENCE: WRITTEN STATEMENTS) (1986) 83 Cr.App.R. 212.

CRIMINAL LAW

751. Administering noxious thing—intent to injure—test to apply

[Offences against the Person Act 1861 (c.100), s.24.]

At trial for an offence under s.24 of the 1861 Act, the test to be applied was whether the defendant intended to cause harm to the health of the victim.

H obtained some slimming tablets available on prescription, of which the normal dose was one per day. He induced two boys aged 11 and 13 to take three of the tablets by saying they were stimulants and would make them feel cheerful and happy. At 11.30 p.m. the same night the younger boy returned to H's flat and was induced to take another tablet. H on arrest admitted to a homosexual interest in young boys. The boys suffered from vomiting and diarrhoea for two days. At H's trial for administering a noxious thing contrary to s.24 of the 1861 Act, the judge directed that causing injury included any harm to the body, and this could include administering drugs with the intention of keeping someone awake for an unnatural period of time. The Court of Appeal quashed the conviction.

Held, on the prosecutor's appeal to the House of Lords, that the test was whether the defendant intended to cause harm to the health of the victim. The judge's direction was correct and the conviction should be restored.

R. *v.* HILL (FREDERICK) (1986) 83 Cr.App.R. 386, H.L.

752. Aiding and abetting—excess alcohol—two occupants of car charged as principals—whether necessary to identify driver of car

[Road Traffic Act 1972 (c.20), s.691 (as substituted by Transport Act 1982 (c.56), s.25(3), Sched. 8); Magistrates' Courts Act 1980 (c.43), s.44.]

Where one of two persons must have been the driver of a car, and the other a passenger, it is open to justices to convict each person, as a principal, of driving with excess alcohol, provided each knew that the other was unfit to drive, and the passenger could therefore be said to be aiding and abetting the offence.

Per curiam: Where the circumstances of an alleged offence are such that the Court is compelled to the view that each of two persons, driver and passenger, is equally guilty of driving with excess alcohol, it is open to the Court to convict both, irrespective of which actually was the driver.

D1 and D2 were arrested after running away from a car stationary on a building site, access to which could only have been by road. Both were above the breath/alcohol limit. Each claimed the other had been driving. Each was charged as a principal, on the basis that either he was, in fact, driving or he was aiding and abetting the other to drive. The justices dismissed the charges.

Held, on appeal, that the appeal had to be dismissed as there was no direct evidence of the states of mind of the respective defendants, and it would be unreasonable to infer that each was aware of the other's unfitness to drive. The precise identity of the driver was irrelevant only if it could be shown that there was a joint enterprise, with each being aware that the other should not be driving.

SMITH *v.* MELLORS AND SOAR (1987) 84 Cr.App.R. 279, D.C.

753. Assault—assaulting police officer—mens rea—relevance of belief by defendant that under attack—self defence

A police officer, X, laid his hand on A's arm, believing a breach of the peace to be about to take place. A, thinking that he was under attack, hit X.

Held, that self-defence could be a defence to a charge of assault on a police officer (*Kenlin* v. *Gardner* [1967] C.L.Y. 3041 not followed; *Albert* v. *Lavin* [1982] C.L.Y. 683 applied).

ANSELL *v.* SWIFT [1987] Crim.L.R. 194, Lewes Crown Court.

754. Assault—defence—consent—right to have defence considered by jury

Genuinely held belief in consent to rough and undisciplined play is a defence to assault, and is a matter to be left to a jury.

The defendants were pupils at a school and indulged in a game whereby two other boys were thrown in the air, and received serious injury on landing. Their defence was that they had not foreseen that such serious injury would result. The trial judge declined to give a direction that if the jury thought the defendants had indulged in "rough and undisciplined" play with no intent to injure, and in the genuine belief that the victims consented, they should be acquitted. The defendants then changed their pleas to guilty.

Held, that the appeals should be allowed because such a defence should be left to the jury, even if far-fetched, and they had only changed their pleas because of the judge's ruling (*R.* v. *Kimber* [1983] C.L.Y. 693 and *R.* v. *Williams* [1984] C.L.Y. 502/503 applied; *Att.-Gen.'s Reference (No. 6 of 1980)* [1981] C.L.Y. 362 considered).

R. *v.* JONES; R. *v.* CAMPBELL; R. *v.* SMITH; R. *v.* NICHOLAS; R. *v.* BLACKWOOD; R. *v.* MUIR (1986) 83 Cr.App.R. 375, C.A.

755. Assault—wrongful imprisonment—burden of proof

P is a barrister and D a police constable. On the evening of November 30, 1983, P and another lawyer friend met at a wine bar and drank two bottles of wine. Afterwards, while looking for their car, P was arrested for being drunk in a public place. The charge was later dismissed by magistrates. P then brought an action against D for assault, wrongful arrest and wrongful imprisonment. The matter was heard in December 1984 and the judge directed the jury that ". . . reasonable grounds do not have to be proved by the police. It is for the plaintiff to prove that he was not drunk or that there were no reasonable grounds for the arrest." P appealed to the Court of Appeal, which held that in actions for false imprisonment, proof of the existence of reasonable cause is upon the defendant since arrest is prima facie a tort and demands justification. A retrial was ordered and at the retrial the jury returned a verdict in P's favour. No award was made for the assault (the placing of the officer's hands on P during the arrest). He was awarded £500 for the arrest and £1,000 for the imprisonment.

SHAPER *v.* ROBINSON, February 2, 1987; H.H. Judge Martin, Q.C.; Bloomsbury and Marylebone County Ct. [*Ex. rel. Lincoln Crawford, Barrister.*]

756. Assisting commission of offence—offence to be committed outside U.K.—offence never taking place

[Misuse of Drugs Act 1971 (c.38), s.20.]

It is not an offence known to law to assist in acts preparatory to the commission of an offence if the offence is not in fact committed.

R. *v.* PANAYI; R. *v.* KARTE, *The Times,* July 24, 1987, C.A.

757. Attempt—criminal damage—whether recklessness sufficient

[Criminal Attempts Act 1981 (c.47), s.1(1).]

The appellants were alleged to have pushed repeatedly against a wooden wall at a football ground, intending to break the line of planking. They denied intending to damage the wall.

Held, allowing appeals against conviction of attempting to damage property, contrary to s.1(1) of the 1981 Act, that the judge had erred in directing the jury that recklessness was an alternative to intention as an element of the substantive offence. Recklessness was incompatible in this case with the intent required by s.1(1) for the offence of attempt.

R. *v.* MILLARD AND VERNON [1987] Crim.L.R. 393, C.A.

758. Attempt—test to be applied

[Criminal Attempts Act 1981 (c.47), s.1.]

If the question is raised as to whether an act is more than merely preparatory for the offence, the Court is entitled to look at the law as it stood before the Criminal Attempts Act 1981, and the tests then applied.

B(G) and B(J) were alleged to have damaged the door of a flat so that they could enter the flat and steal therefrom. They were convicted and appealed contending that there was no sufficient evidence of *actus reus.*

Held, that there was more than enough evidence that they had intended to enter the flat and commit theft. When considering the question of whether a particular act was or was not any more than mere preparation, the Court was entitled to look at the tests that were applied prior to the passing of the 1981 Act. Appeals dismissed.

R. *v.* BOYLE (G.) AND BOYLE (J.) (1987) 84 Cr.App.R. 270, C.A.

759. Attempt—theft—whether act more than merely preparatory

[Criminal Attempts Act 1981 (c.47), s.1.]

G backed a greyhound. When it seemed to be losing, G jumped on to the track to distract the dogs, hoping that a "no race" would be declared so that he could demand the return of his stake.

Held, quashing G's conviction of attempted theft, that G's acts had not gone beyond mere preparation within s.1 of the 1981 Act.

R. *v.* GULLEFER [1987] Crim.L.R. 195, C.A.

760. Attempt to procure an act of gross indecency—whether offence

[Sexual Offences Act 1956 (c.69), s.13; Criminal Attempts Act 1981 (c.47), s.1(4)(*b*).]

S.1(4)(*b*) of the Criminal Attempts Act 1981 does not preclude the charging of an attempt to procure an act of gross indecency.

The defendant was charged with attempting to procure the commission of an act of gross indecency. The justices dismissed the charge concluding that by virtue of s.1(4)(*b*) of the 1981 Act, no such offence could be committed.

Held, allowing the appeal that the section did not preclude the charge because procuring the act of gross indecency was itself a substantive charge.

CHIEF CONSTABLE OF HAMPSHIRE *v.* MACE (1987) 84 Cr.App.R. 40, D.C.

761. Blackmail—demand for medicine—patient in pain

[Theft Act 1968 (c.60), s.21.]

D was in severe pain from an arthritic hip. He threatened to shoot V, a doctor, unless V injected him with morphine.

Held, that D was guilty of blackmail under s.21 of the Theft Act 1968.

R. *v.* BEVANS (RONALD), *The Times,* December 1, 1987, C.A.

762. Blackmail—"menaces"—direction to jury

Theft 1968 (c.60), s.21(1); Criminal Appeal Act 1968 (c.19), s.2(1).]

On a charge under s.21(1) of the Theft Act 1968, the existence of menaces were established when threats which would not have affected a person of normal stability affected the victim, provided the accused realised their likely effect.

Per curiam: The meaning of "menaces" is clear to any jury, and only rarely with a judge need to define it.

G was charged with blackmail contrary to s.21(1) of the Theft Act. After a short retirement by the jury and in response to a question from them as to the definition of "menaces", the judge repeated his earlier definition and added words suggesting that menaces had been proved to exist even though a person of normal stability would not have been influenced by G's behaviour, and G was unaware that the victim was unduly susceptible to threats.

Held, on appeal against conviction, that menaces were shown where threats which would not have affected a person of normal stability affected the victim's mind, provided G was aware of the likely effect of his actions on the victim. The jury had been misdirected but the appeal would be dismissed on the grounds that the case was eminently suitable for the application of the proviso to s.2(1) of the Criminal Appeal Act 1968.

R. *v.* GARWOOD [1987] 1 W.L.R. 319, C.A.

763. Burglary—alternative verdict—charge of entering and stealing—conviction of entering with intent to steal

[Theft Act 1968 (c.60), ss.9(1)(*a*), (*b*) Criminal Law Act 1967 (c.58), s.6(3).]

W was charged with entering as a trespasser and stealing contrary to s.9(1)(*b*) of the Theft Act 1968. The jury, whilst satisfied that he had entered the premises with intent to steal, could not be satisfied that he stole anything W was convicted of entering a building as a trespasser with intent to steal under s.9(1)(*a*).

Held, that the critical question under s.9(1)(*b*) impliedly included an allegation of such entry with the relevant intent. Although s.9(1)(*b*) did not require intent to steal when entry was made, in very many cases that was the position. The trial judge was correct in

allowing the alternative verdict (*R.* v. *Wilson and Jenkins* [1983] C.L.Y. 686 applied; *R.* v. *Hollis* [1971] C.L.Y. 2108 disapproved).
R. *v.* WHITING (1987) 85 Cr.App.R. 78, C.A.

764. Cheating the public revenue—ingredients—whether positive deception necessary

Deception is not a necessary ingredient of the offence of cheating the Public Revenue.

The appellant had traded in gold in such a way as to have made an inevitable loss but for the adding of V.A.T., for which he had not accounted to customs. He was convicted of the common law offence of "cheating the revenue". He appealed on the basis that prosecution had failed to prove a positive deception.

Held, dismissing the appeal, that the offence did not require a false representation by words or conduct; any form of conduct which resulted in diverting money from the Revenue sufficed (*R.* v. *Hudson* [1956] C.L.Y. 1885 applied).
R. *v.* MAVJI (1987) 84 Cr.App.R. 34, C.A.

765. Child abduction—attempt—meaning of "lawful control"

[Child Abduction Act 1984 (c.37).]

M offered X, a 14-year-old boy on his way home from school, money to go home with him. The boy carried on walking but M followed him home, squeezing X's buttocks and putting his hand inside X's trousers.

Held, dismissing M's appeal against conviction of attempted abduction, that if X had been persuaded to go to M's flat, he would have been detained so as to keep him out of his mother's "lawful control" if, apart from M's persuasion, he would have returned to his mother's home and control (*Hewer* v. *Bryant* [1969] C.L.Y. 2101 distinguished).
R. *v.* MOUSIR [1987] Crim.L.R. 561, C.A.

766. Children—presumption of innocence—rebuttal

H, aged 11, and others were convicted of criminal damage to a van. The van's windows were smashed, its paint was scratched and it was pushed into a post. H had admitted pushing the van and that his action would cause damage. He gave no evidence.

Held, allowing his appeal, that since H was aged between 10 and 14, he could not be convicted unless there was evidence that he knew that what was done was seriously wrong and was more than naughtiness or childish mischief. There was no such evidence (*J. B. H. and J. H.* v. *O'Connell* [1981] Crim.L.R. 632 and *B.* v. *R.* [1959] C.L.Y. 725 considered; *J. M. (A Minor)* v. *Runeckles* [1985] C.L.Y. 586 affirmed).
I.P.H. *v.* CHIEF CONSTABLE OF SOUTH WALES [1987] Crim.L.R. 42, D.C.

767. Conspiracy to defraud—review of the law. See LAW REFORM, §2258.

768. Crime prevention—home security

The Home Office has recently published the results of research into home security undertaken on its behalf by NOP. The results can be read in the latest edition of the quarterly *Crime Prevention News* (Issue 3/1987 Home Office). For further information contact Barry Richardson on 01–213 5321.

769. Crime prevention—robbery—prevention at sub-post offices

The Home Office has published a report entitled *Preventing Robberies at Sub-Post Offices: an Evaluation of a Security Initiative.* Home Office Crime Prevention Unit Paper 9, by Dr. Paul Ekblom, is available free of charge from Room 583A, Home Office, 50 Queen Anne's Gate, London SW1H 9AT.

770. Criminal damage—intention to endanger life

[Criminal Damage Act 1971 (c.48), s.1(2)(*b*).]

Intention or recklessness in s.1(2) of the 1971 Act is directed to dangers to life caused by the damaged property and not by the way in which it is damaged.

S, after a disagreement with his business partner, went to his partner's bungalow and fired shots from a rifle at two windows and the door. No injuries were caused. S was charged with damaging property with intent, being reckless as to whether life would be endangered, contrary to s.1(2) of the 1971 Act. The trial judge rejected a submission of no case whereupon S pleaded guilty and appealed against conviction. The Court of Appeal upheld the appeal and the Crown appealed.

Held, dismissing the Crown's appeal, that the section was directed at danger to life caused by the damaged property not by the way in which it was damaged (dictum of Parker L.J. in *R.* v. *Hardie* [1985] C.L.Y. 692 distinguished).
R. *v.* STEER [1987] 3 W.L.R. 205, H.L.

771. Criminal damage—recklessness—defendant recognising risk and taking precautions to minimise it

[Criminal Damage Act 1971 (c.48), s.1(1).]

A defendant who recognises the risk involved in some action of his, but thinks that due to some expertise he possesses he has minimised it, may nevertheless be 'reckless' if damage results.

The defendant and friends were larking about outside a shop one evening. The defendant went to demonstrate his prowess and control by making as if to strike the glass window with his foot, intending to come close but make no contact. He broke the window and was charged with criminal damage. The justices acquitted him on the basis that he had perceived the risk and assessed it as minimal in view of his skill in the martial arts.

Held, allowing the appeal, that the appellant had recognised the risk, and was reckless.

CHIEF CONSTABLE OF AVON AND SOMERSET CONSTABULARY *v.* SHIMMEN (1987) 84 Cr.App.R. 7, D.C.

772. Criminal Injuries Compensation Board

The Criminal Injuries Compensation Board has published its Twenty-Third Annual Report. Copies of the Report are available from H.M.S.O. (Cm. 265) [£4·50].

773. Crossbows Act 1987 (c.32)

This Act creates offences relating to the sale and letting on hire of crossbows to, and the purchase, hiring and possession of crossbows by, persons under the age of seventeen.

The Act received the Royal Assent on May 15, 1987. Ss.1–6 of the Act will come into force two months from that date.

Ss.1–6 of the Act do not extend to Northern Ireland.

774. Duress—person voluntarily joining gang of armed robbers—reluctant participation in robbery when victim shot and killed—whether defence of duress available

Duress is not available as a defence to a man who voluntarily joins a gang, when he knows he might be put under some pressure to commit an offence.

S joined a gang knowing that they used firearms. Whilst taking part in a robbery, one of the gang shot and killed the victim. On his trial for murder S was convicted of manslaughter, the judge having rejected the defence that he was under duress.

Held, that the judge was quite right, and the appeal would be dismissed. S knew of the nature of the gang when he joined, and knew he might come under pressure to commit some offence. He had been an active member when the pressure was applied and the defence was not available.

R. *v.* SHARP (DAVID) [1987] 3 W.L.R. 1, C.A.

775. Evasion of customs duty—declaration of gift. See R. *v.* COLLINS, §1109.

776. Forged cheque—whether theft of chose in action

A person who draws, presents and negotiates a forged cheque commits theft of a chose in action, *i.e.* the debt owed by the bank to its customer. This is so even if the bank is not entitled to debit the customer's account with the amount (*Tai Hing Cotton Mill* v. *Liu Chong Hing Bank* [1985] C.L.Y. 150 applied).

CHAN MAN-SIN *v.* THE QUEEN, *The Times,* December 1, 1987, P.C.

777. Forgery—account in false name

[Forgery and Counterfeiting Act 1981 (c.45), s.9(1).]

The opening of an account in a false name, and the subsequent withdrawal of monies therein by the same person using the same false name does not amount to the offence of forgery. (*R.* v. *Brown (Kevin)* [1984] C.L.Y. 624 considered).

R. *v.* MORE, *The Times,* November 9, 1987, H.L.

778. Forgery—company documents made after liquidation—whether forgery

[Forgery and Counterfeiting Act 1981 (c.45), s.9(1)(*a*).]

Documents created after the liquidation of a company, but which purport to have been made by the company before that liquidation are forgeries.

L and K had an interest in a company which began to suffer financial difficulties. In order to try and save something from the wreck of its liquidation, they created various documents which were used to claim in the liquidation. All the documents purported to have been made whilst the company was in existence, but were in fact created afterwards.

Held, that the documents were clearly false, and were forgeries within the 1981 Act.
R. *v.* LACK (1987) 84 Cr.App.R. 342, C.A.

779. Forgery—false instrument—intent

[Forgery and Counterfeiting Act 1981 (c.45), ss.3 and 10.]

The sections show that the offence of using a false instrument requires a double intent upon which a jury must be directed. A potential prejudice to a person is insufficient as the offence requires that prejudice will result.

R. *v.* GARCIA, *The Times*, November 3, 1987, C.A.

780. Forgery—gaining access to a computer data bank—whether forgery

[Forgery and Counterfeiting Act 1981 (c.45), ss.1, 8(1)(*d*).]

Dishonestly gaining access to a computer data bank electronically ("hacking") is not an offence under the Forgery and Counterfeiting Act 1981.

The appellants dishonestly gained access to a computer network electronically. They were indicted under s.1 of the 1981 Act, and submitted at the close of the prosecution case that there was no case to answer. The submission was rejected and they were convicted.

Held, allowing the appeal, that as the electronic impulses used to enter the system were not *ejusdem generis* with disc tape or sound track and were not the device on which information was recorded or stored, they could not be a device within s.8(1)(*d*) of the Act. Since forgery involved both a message about the document itself (*e.g.* that it is a cheque) and a message in its words that it was to be accepted and acted upon (*e.g.* that a banker was to pay £x), and since the user segment (which cleared the password) did not carry such a message it was not brought within the ambit of forgery.

Per curiam: The 1981 Act does not seek to deal with information that is held for a moment while automatic checking takes place and is then expunged. The process is not one to which the words "recorded or stored" can be properly applied suggesting as they do a degree of continuance.

R. *v.* GOLD; R. *v.* SCHIFREEN [1987] 3 W.L.R. 803, C.A.

781/2. Forgery—intent—"other person" acting to their prejudice

[Forgery and Counterfeiting Act 1981 (c.45), s.1.]

A person who makes a false instrument with the intention that the police should accept it as genuine and therefore not prosecute him does not commit forgery.

A solicitor received moneys from insurers to settle a client's claim and paid £45,000 of it into his own account. When asked by the police about this, the solicitor showed them a photocopy of a document which purported to be an agreement between the solicitor and the client that the client would lend him £45,000. He was charged, *inter alia*, with forgery, contrary to s.1 of the Forgery and Counterfeiting Act 1981, the particulars being that he had made a false instrument to induce someone to accept it as genuine and by reason of accepting it not to do some act to the prejudice of the solicitor. The prosecution case was that the photocopy was produced by the solicitor with the intention that the police would accept it as genuine and not prosecute him. The judge, in summing up, gave a direction to the jury on the basis that the false instrument was the original document and not the photocopy.

Held, allowing the appeal against conviction that (1) the direction to the jury that it was the original document and not the photocopy that was the purported false instrument was a sufficient misdirection to require that the conviction be quashed since the defence would have answered the prosecution's case differently if the original document was the alleged forgery; (2) for an offence to be committed under s.1. there had to be an intention that the victim or some other person would accept the instrument as genuine and thereby induce somebody to act or refrain from acting to his or "any other person's" prejudice. The forger could not be that "other person" within the meaning of the section, and therefore, even if the document was false, the solicitor could not have committed an offence by producing it so that he would not be prejudiced by the police prosecuting him for an offence.

R. *v.* UTTING [1987] 1 W.L.R. 1375, C.A.

783. Handling—dishonesty—offer to return goods

[Theft Act 1968 (c.60), s.22(1).]

The prosecution do not have to prove that dishonesty in s.22(1) of the Theft Act is *vis-à-vis* the loser.

Two valuable paintings were stolen in a burglary. Loss adjusters offered a reward. Some time later the appellant telephoned the loss adjusters and offered to get them back for a reward. The appellant was arrested and charged with handling. The appellant was convicted and appealed on the basis (i) that 'dishonest' meant *vis-à-vis* the loser and (ii) that a full *Ghosh* direction should have been given.

Held, that there was no authority to support ground (i); the full *Ghosh* direction was unnecessary since the appellant had never contended that his conduct was honest, or raised the problem (*R.* v. *Ghosh* [1982] C.L.Y. 659 considered).

R. *v.* ROBERTS (WILLIAM) (1987) 84 Cr.App.R. 117, C.A.

784. Handling—knowing or believing goods to be stolen—belief

T owned a grocery store and bought a number of goods from C that had been stolen and were intended for use on an airline. T paid a very low price for them and never received a receipt. T appealed against conviction on the basis that the judge had misdirected on the issue of knowledge or belief that the goods were stolen.

Held, that although it may be prudent in a number of cases, particularly those where much reference is made to "suspicion", to provide the jury with the guidance outlined in *R.* v. *Hall* it is not necessary to do so in every case where the issue resolves around "belief". It is sufficient to direct the jury that they are entitled to infer that the defendant believed the goods were stolen if it was the only inference to be drawn from the facts (*R.* v. *Hall* [1986] C.L.Y. discussed; *R.* v. *Harris* [1987] C.L.Y. 785 applied).

R. *v.* TOOR (1987) 85 Cr.App.R. 116, C.A.

785. Handling—summing up—meaning of belief—whether direction required

In most cases of 'handling' it is not necessary for the judge to define the meaning of 'belief' in s.22.

The appellant was charged with handling a copying machine, stolen from office premises. The defendant did not give evidence and was convicted. He appealed on the basis, *inter alia,* that the judge did not define the meaning of 'belief'.

Held, dismissing the appeal, that 'knowledge or belief' were ordinary English words; in most cases all that was necessary was to tell the jury that they had to be satisfied that the defendant received the goods, knowing or believing them to be stolen.

R. *v.* HARRIS (MARTIN) (1987) 84 Cr.App.R. 75, C.A.

786. Home Office research programme

The Home Office Research and Planning Unit has published its Research Programme for 1987–88. Projects are listed in the following categories: Criminal Justice System and Process; Crime Prevention; Police; Prisons; Immigration, Nationality and Equal Opportunities; British Crime Survey. The Research Programme booklet can be obtained from The Information Section, Research and Planning Unit, 50 Queen Anne's Gate, London SW1H 9AT.

787. Importing prohibited goods—*mens rea.* See R. *v.* ELLIS, STREET AND SMITH, §1113.

788. Indecent or obscene articles—prohibition on importation—goods which can lawfully be made and sold within U.K. See CONEGATE *v.* H.M. CUSTOMS AND EXCISE, §1114.

789. Indecent photograph—photograph of child—whether age of child relevant in determining whether photograph indecent

[Protection of Children Act 1978 (c.37), s.1(1)(*a*).]

The age of the person photographed is relevant to the issue of indecency in a charge of taking an indecent photograph of a child contrary to s.1(1)(*a*) of the Protection of Children Act 1978. If the photograph is not intrinsically indecent apart from the age of the subject, but is indecent when the age is taken into consideration, the offence has been committed.

R. *v.* OWEN, *The Times,* October 10, 1987, C.A.

790. Kidnapping—lawful excuse—motive of defendant to save victim from spiritual harm

H tried forcefully to take an acquaintance he believed to be in moral and spiritual danger away from a religious sect which she had joined.

Held, dismissing H's appeal, that the judge had correctly ruled that H had no lawful excuse. A lawful excuse for kidnapping is not recognised by the law unless it can properly be said that a necessity has arisen, recognised by the law as such, causing the kidnapper's conduct (*R.* v. *D.* [1984] C.L.Y. 651 considered).

R. *v.* HENMAN [1987] Crim.L.R. 333, C.A.

791. Larceny—consent of victim—automatic bank teller machine—customer closing account and then withdrawing money—whether bank consented

[Aus.] The holder of a magnetised card, which allowed him to use an automatic bank teller machine to withdraw money from his account, closed his account and then withdrew money from the machine by using the card. This was possible because the machine was unable to tell whether the card-holder had any current account or whether the account was in credit. A condition of using the card was that the account could only be drawn against up to the extent it was in funds.

Held, that the bank had not consented to the withdrawal of the money and the card-holder was guilty of the local offence of larceny.

KENNISON *v.* DAIRE (1985–1986) 160 C.L.R. 129, High Ct. of Aus.

792. Management of brothel—meaning of brothel

[Sexual Offences Act 1956 (c.69), s.33.]

The appellants worked on different days as receptionists at premises used by different prostitutes for prostitution. No more than one prostitute each day used the premises. The appellants outlined the available services to a stream of men and secured the premises in the evening.

Held, dismissing their appeals against conviction of assisting in the management of a brothel, contrary to s.33 of the 1956 Act, that whether premises constituted a brothel was a question of fact and degree. There was evidence of heavy regular use by a team of prostitutes and the appellants for large scale sexual activity (*Singleton* v. *Ellison* [1895] 1 Q.B. 607, *Gorman* v. *Standen* [1963] C.L.Y. 636 and *Caldwell* v. *Leech* (1913) 109 L.T. 188 considered).

STEVENS AND STEVENS *v.* CHRISTY [1987] Crim.L.R. 503, D.C.

793. Manslaughter—corporate body

A corporate body can be guilty of manslaughter but only if both the *mens rea* and the *actus reus* of the offence can be established against those identified as the embodiment of the corporate body itself.

SPOONER, *ex p.;* DE ROHAN, *ex p., The Times,* October 10, 1987, D.C.

794. Manslaughter—self-defence—circumstances as defendant perceived them to be

F, a night-club doorman, intervened in a fight between X and Y. He grabbed X around the neck. The evidence suggested that X bit F, who punched him at least once, rendering X unconscious. F claimed that he knew X to have been homosexual and that F was scared of catching AIDS. F said nothing in evidence about self-defence, as opposed to instinctive and angry response to the bite. F then took X to the exit and pushed him down a flight of stairs. He then carried X down another flight, bumping X's head on the way. The judge directed the jury that if they were satisfied that X's death was caused by any of F's acts or a combination of them the only possible verdicts were manslaughter or murder.

Held, allowing F's appeal, that, *inter alia,* (1) a ruling that self-defence did not arise in law was not justified; (2) whether F was shown not to be acting in self-defence was to be considered by reference to what F believed the circumstances to be. The questions were questions of reasonableness for the jury (*R.* v. *Shannon* (1960) 71 Cr.App.R. 223 and *R.* v. *Cousins* [1982] C.L.Y. 730 applied).

R. *v.* FISHER [1987] Crim.L.R. 334, C.A.

795. Misuse of drugs

MISUSE OF DRUGS (LICENCE FEES) (AMENDMENT) REGULATIONS 1987 (No. 298) [45p], made under the Misuse of Drugs Act 1971 (c.38), ss.30, 31, 37(1); operative on April 1, 1987; increase fees imposed under S.I. 1986 no. 416 for a licence issued under the 1971 Act or subordinate regulations.

796. Misuse of drugs—exceptions to prohibition against possession—burden of proof

[Misuse of Drugs Act 1971 (c.38), s.5(1)(2); Misuse of Drugs Regulations 1973 (S.I. 1973 No. 797), reg. 4(1); Sched. 1, para. 3 (as amended by Misuse of Drugs (Amendment) Regulations 1983 (S.I. 1983 No. 788), reg. 2).]

It was for the prosecution to prove that the defendant possessed morphine in a proscribed form, and not for him to prove that he did not.

Under reg. 4(1) and para. 3 of Sched. 1 to the Misuse of Drugs Regulations 1973 the following is an exception to the prohibition against possession of drugs:

> "Any preparation of medicinal opium or of morphine containing not more than 0·2 per cent of morphine . . . being a preparation compounded with one or more other active or inert ingredients in such a way that the opium or . . . the morphine cannot be recovered by readily applicable means or in a yield which would constitute a risk to health."

Police officers found in the appellant's home a paper fold containing 154 milligrams of a white powder which was found to be morphine mixed with caffeine and atropine. He was charged under s.5(2) of the Misuse of Drugs Act 1971 with unlawful possession of a controlled drug, morphine. The prosecution called no evidence as to the proportion of morphine in the powder and the defence submitted there was not case to answer.

The judge ruled that there was a case to answer, and the appellant changed his plea to guilty. His appeal against conviction to the Court of Appeal was dismissed. He further appealed to the House of Lords.

Held, allowing the appeal, that the burden of proving guilt was on the prosecution save in the defence of insanity and any statutory exception. Such exception might be express or implied, either in the same instrument or in a subsequent proviso, and whether it was an indictable or summary offence. The defendant would discharge it on a balance of probabilities. Where a linguistic construction did not indicate clearly on whom the burden of proof should lie, the court might look to other considerations to determine the intention of Parliament, such as the mischief at which the provision was aimed and practical considerations such as the ease or difficulty for the respective parties of discharging the burden of proof (*Woolmington* v. *D.P.P.* (1935) A.C. 1, *Mancini* v. *D.P.P.* [1942] A.C. 1; *Nimmo* v. *Cowan (Alexander) & Sons* [1967] C.L.Y. 1653 and *R.* v. *Edwards* [1974] C.L.Y. 600 considered). On its true construction, reg. 4(1) dealt not with exceptions to what would otherwise be unlawful but with the definitions of the essential ingredients of an offence. As it was an offence to possess morphine in one form and not another, it was for the prosecution to prove that the morphine in the appellant's possession had been in the prohibited form, which it had not done. No burden fell on the defendant.

Per Lord Mackay of Clashfern: This case emphasises the need for absolute clarity in the terms of the analyst's certificate founded on by the prosecution in cases of this sort.

R. *v.* HUNT (RICHARD) [1986] 3 W.L.R. 1115, H.L.

797. Misuse of drugs—intention to supply—bailee

[Misuse of Drugs Act 1971, ss.4(1)(*b*), 5(3).]

Where a bailee of drugs intends to return them to the bailor in order that the bailor may use them for his own purposes, that constitutes "intention to supply" for the purposes of s.5(3) of the 1971 Act.

M pleaded guilty to possession of cannabis contrary to s.5(2) of the 1971 Act, but not guilty to possession with intent to supply contrary to s.5(3). His evidence was that the cannabis under his car seat belonged to a friend and he expected the friend to come round and pick it up. The judge ruled that this constituted intention to supply and M changed his plea to guilty.

Held, allowing the appeal, that "supply" did not necessarily involve supplying from the suppliers own resources, and if the drugs were to be returned with the intention that the friend use them for his own purposes, that constituted "intention to supply" (*Donnelly* v. *H.M. Advocate* [1985] S.L.T. 243 approved; *R.* v. *Delgado* [1984] C.L.Y. 663 and *R.* v. *Dempsey* [1986] C.L.Y. 646 considered).

R. *v.* MAGINNIS [1987] 2 W.L.R. 765, H.L.

798. Misuse of drugs—possessing preparation of class A drug—meaning of "preparation"

[Misuse of Drugs Act 1971 (c.38), s.5(2), Sched. II, Part 1.]

1,000 to 2,000 dried psilocybin mushrooms were found in a small container in W's van. W claimed that they must have dried naturally after he had picked them. A forensic scientist testified that they must have been dried out deliberately by laying them out.

Held, allowing W's appeal against conviction of possessing a "preparation". of psilocybin (a class A drug), contrary to s.5(2) and Schedule II, Part I of the 1971 Act, that the judge had failed to direct the jury adequately that before they could convict they had to be satisfied that there was a preparation containing the drug. "Preparation" had to be given its ordinary and natural meaning (*R.* v. *Stevens* [1981] C.L.Y. 483 and *R.* v. *Cunliffe* [1986] C.L.Y. 641 applied).

R. *v.* WALKER [1987] Crim.L.R. 565, C.A.

799. Murder—defence—provocation

[Homicide Act 1957 (c.11), s.3.]

Where there is evidence at a murder trial of a causal link between provocation and the defendants response, s.3 of 1957 Act was mandatory and required the issue of the objective test of provocation to be left to the jury.

D's baby cried persistently for several hours, and D finally lost his temper and tried to silence the child by putting cushions over his head and kneeling on them. The baby died. At D's trial for murder the judge refused to allow the defence of provocation to be left to the jury as required by s.3 of the 1957 Act.

Held, that since there was evidence of a causal link between the crying of the baby and D's response, s.3 of the 1957 Act was mandatory. The conviction would be quashed and one of manslaughter substituted (*D.P.P.* v. *Camplin* [1978] C.L.Y. 558 applied).

R. *v.* DOUGHTY (1986) 83 Cr.App.R. 319, C.A.

800. Murder—duress—whether a defence—incitement to commit murder—killer convicted of manslaughter

Duress cannot be a defence to murder.

When one incites another to commit murder and that other is convicted of manslaughter, the inciter may nevertheless be convicted of murder.

In the first appeal, A and B were taken to a desolate place by X, together with the victim. A, B and X assaulted the victim, and X killed him. On another occasion, A and B strangled their victim. On a further occasion, their victim escaped. A and B were charged on two counts of murder and one count of conspiracy to murder. Their defence was duress in that they feared for their own lives from X. The judge left that defence on the first murder, and the conspiracy, but not on the second.

In the second appeal, C and D were charged with murder. C had killed the victim, but his defence was that he had agreed with D to kill through fear that he himself would be killed by D, and that the gun had gone off accidentally. The judge directed the jury that duress was no defence to murder, but that it could be relevant in deciding whether C's act was unintentional, or whether C was guilty of manslaughter. He directed the jury that if they convicted C of manslaughter, they could not convict D of murder. C and D were convicted of murder. Appeals to the Court of Appeal were dismissed.

Held, dismissing the appeals that duress was no defence to a charge of murder. Further, the judge had erred in the second appeal, and D could have been convicted of murder, even if C had been acquitted, and convicted of manslaughter.

Per curiam: when the defence of duress is raised the test is whether the threat was of such gravity that it might well have caused a reasonable man placed in the same situation to act in the same way (*R.* v. *Dudley and Stephens* (1884) 14 Q.B.D. 273 and *Abbott* v. *R.* [1976] C.L.Y. 513 applied; *R.* v. *Graham (Paul)* [1982] C.L.Y. 556 approved; *D.P.P. for Northern Ireland* v. *Lynch* [1975] C.L.Y. 622 overruled).

R. *v.* HOWE; R. *v.* BANNISTER; R. *v.* BURKE; R. *v.* CLARKSON [1987] 2 W.L.R. 568, H.L.

801. Murder—foresight of consequences of defendant's actions—intent—joint enterprise—direction of jury

The appellant and P got into a fight with A and others during which A was knocked to the ground and received two fatal stab wounds with a pair of scissors and a knife owned by the appellant and P respectively. The appellant admitted stabbing but denied any intention to cause injury and knowledge that P had a knife. Both were convicted of murder. The appeal was on the basis of a misdirection to the jury because the judge had stated that (1) intention means a desire to bring about a particular consequence or foresight that killing or harm would result and if such foresight was proved the defendant was taken to have intended the killing or harm; (2) a person was responsible for the acts of another if he contemplates and foresees those acts as a possible part or result of a planned joint enterprise.

Held, that only rarely is it necessary to go beyond the simple direction on intent—that the jury must feel sure that the defendent intended to kill or do serious harm. That would have been sufficient here. The direction on foresight was wrong as it did not make clear that foresight was only evidence of intent. There was no misdirection on the question of joint enterprise—the law was still that laid down by *R.* v. *Anderson and Morris.* As the direction on foresight was unnecessary, the misdirection could not have caused a miscarriage of justice and the proviso would be applied (*R. Moloney* [1985] C.L.Y. 642, *R.* v. *Hancock and Shankland* [1986] C.L.Y. 652 and *R.* v. *Anderson and Morris* [1986] C.L.Y. 2603 applied).

R. *v.* WARD (J.D.) (1987) 85 Cr.App.R. 71, C.A.

802. Murder—intent—whether test objective or subjective

The test of intent in murder at common law was not an objective test but a subjective test.

F was charged with murder in the Isle of Man. F had bound and gagged the deceased and tied him to his bed in an effort to prevent the deceased from communicating information about F to F's girlfriend, designed to sabotage the relationship between F and his girlfriend. The deceased was a 67-year-old man who suffered from chronic bronchitis, a degenerative condition of the lungs and hardening of the coronary arteries. 48 hours later and before F returned to free him, the deceased died. F said he thought the deceased was a healthy man and that no serious harm would come to him; he did not intend to kill him but just to keep him away from his girlfriend. The trial judge directed the jury in accordance with *D.P.P.* v. *Smith* on the issue of intent, stating that the relevant intention would be established if the jury were satisfied that F intended to do something unlawful to the deceased knowing the circumstances, whether he realised or not, which would render the act likely to cause death or serious injury. F was convicted and his subsequent appeal dismissed. F appealed to the Privy Council.

Held, allowing his appeal, that the *mens rea* for the offence of murder was the same at common law and the law of the Isle of Man. The Isle of Man courts are not bound to follow English decisions although they should generally do so unless there was contrary provision to be found in Manx legislation or case law or some local condition gave good reason not to follow the English decision in question. The trial judge erred in directing the jury in accordance with *D.P.P.* v. *Smith.* The decision, in so far as it laid down an objective test of intent in the crime of murder, did not accurately represent the English common law. At common law, there was a rebuttable presumption of fact that a man intended the natural and probable consequences of his acts. The direction given to the jury, in so far as it invited them to ignore F's state of mind, improperly raised that rebuttable presumption to an irrebuttable rule of law (*D.P.P.* v. *Smith* [1960] C.L.Y. 739 disapproved; *R.* v. *Hyam* [1974] C.L.Y. 657, *R.* v. *Moloney* [1985] C.L.Y. 642, *R.* v. *Hancock* [1986] C.L.Y. 652 considered).

FRANKLAND AND MOORE *v.* R. [1987] 2 W.L.R. 1251, P.C.

803. Murder—provocation—direction to jury

B was convicted of murder. She appealed on the basis that the judge's summing-up on the issue of provocation was wrong.

Held, dismissing B's appeal, that it was not necessary to rehearse the exact words used by Lord Diplock in the *Camplin* case. On a fair reading of the whole summing-up the jury could not have been in doubt that the "ordinary" girl whom they were to consider was an ordinary girl with the characteristics of B who had undergone what she had undergone in the past (in considering the effects of the matters alleged to constitute provocation). (*D.P.P.* v. *Camplin* [1978] C.L.Y. 558 considered).

R. *v.* BURKE [1987] Crim.L.R. 336, C.A.

804. Obstruction of the highway—stall—effect of payment of rates

[Highways Act 1980 (c.66), s.137(1).]

The operation of a stall in the same position for several years and the payment of rates do not impliedly constitute lawful authority within the meaning of s.137(1) of the Highways Act 1980. Nor would the fact that the stallholder tried to ensure that his customers queued around the stall onto private land and not on the pavement of itself amount to a defence.

PUGH *v.* PIDGEN: SAME *v.* POWLEY, *The Times,* April 2, 1987, D.C.

805. Obstruction of the highway—wilful obstruction—reasonable user—burden of proof

[Highways Act 1980 (c. 66), s.137.]

The appellants protested outside and in the doorway of a shop and thereby attracted attention from passers-by who gathered together and blocked the street. The appellants handed out leaflets and held banners.

Held, allowing appeals against convictions of wilful obstruction of free passage along the street without lawful authority or excuse, that it was for the prosecution to prove that the defendant was obstructing the highway without lawful excuse. The test was whether the defendant's activity was reasonable user of the highway. The Crown Court had erred in deciding that it was bound to find that to stand in the highway offering and distributing leaflets or holding a banner was not incidental to its lawful user (*Waite* v. *Taylor* [1985] C.L.Y. 1600 not followed; *Nagy* v. *Weston* [1965] C.L.Y. 1778 followed).

HIRST AND AGU *v.* CHIEF CONSTABLE OF WEST YORKSHIRE [1987] Crim.L.R. 330, D.C.

806. Obtaining by deception—implied representation—builder's excessive quotation

S charged two elderly sisters grossly excessive prices for work done on their property. He had worked for their family previously.

Held, allowing S's appeal against conviction of obtaining property by deception, that (1) in circumstances of mutual trust where one party depends on the other for fair and reasonable conduct, a criminal offence may be committed if one takes dishonest advantage of the other by representing as fair a charge which he, but not the other, knows is dishonestly excessive; (2) the judge had not, however, dealt with the defence adequately and had wrongly directed the jury that S's explanation in his police interview was of no evidential value.

R. *v.* SILVERMAN [1987] Crim.L.R. 574, C.A.

807. Obtaining cheques by deception through post—whether cheques obtained within jurisdiction—evidence of substantive law of foreign country—whether accused properly committed to prison to await extradition

Where cheques were obtained by deception through the post it was a question of fact for the jury as to where the cheques were obtained.

H allegedly operated a fraud whereby American investors were persuaded to invest in H's companies. The investors posted cheques to one of H's companies in Amsterdam. H used the money invested for his own purposes and rendered false statements to the investors showing how their investments were prospering. He was charged with 25 offences in the U.S.A. The English equivalent offences were obtaining by deception, false accounting and handling stolen goods contrary to ss.15, 17 and 22 of the Theft Act 1968. The U.S. Government requested the extradition of H. H was subsequently committed to prison by a stipendiary magistrate to await extradition. H applied for a writ of habeas corpus.

Held, that obtaining property by deception, false accounting and handling stolen goods were extradition crimes for the purposes of the Extradition Act 1870. A duly authenticated foreign warrant authorising H's arrest having been produced, the magistrate was bound to decide whether the evidence produced would be sufficient to justify H's committal for trial for the offences in question. H's submission that the cheques were obtained in Amsterdam so that no offence contrary to s.15, Theft Act 1968, was disclosed failed. It was a question of fact for a jury to decide whether the cheques were obtained in Amsterdam or when posted in the U.S.A. There was sufficient evidence that H had obtained the cheques within the U.S.A. that would justify committing him for trial for offences contrary to s.15, Theft Act 1968. H's contention that false accounts were not produced in the U.S.A. but were produced in England so that there was no jurisdiction to entertain those charges failed. Production occurred when the false accounts were communicated to the investors, not when they were "uttered". There was prima facie evidence that H undertook or assisted in the retention, removal, disposal or realisation of cheques. H's was not an exceptional accusation case. The magistrate was not obliged to consider whether the U.S. courts had jurisdiction according to U.S. law to try H. By virtue of the Extradition Treaty provisions having application, the magistrate was bound only to consider whether or not the offences were punishable by imprisonment for more than one year or were time-barred. H was properly committed to prison to await extradition (*R.* v. *Harden* [1962] C.L.Y. 644; *R.* v. *Tirado* [1974] C.L.Y. 662; *Government of Denmark* v. *Nielson* [1984] C.L.Y. 1543 considered).

R. *v.* GOVERNOR OF PENTONVILLE PRISON, *ex p.* HERBAGE (No. 3) (1987) 84 Cr.App.R. 149, D.C.

808. Obtaining pecuniary advantage by deception—bank account debited by cash drawn by cheque supported by cheque card—whether allowed to borrow by way of overdraft—cheque card used abroad—jurisdiction

[Theft Act 1968 (c.60), s.16.]

A bank customer was allowed to borrow by way of overdraft when his account became overdrawn upon presentation of cheques supported by a cheque guarantee card notwithstanding the fact that no overdraft limit had been agreed and the customer had been told specifically not to overdraw the account.

D was convicted of four offences of obtaining a pecuniary advantage by deception contrary to s.16, Theft Act 1968. D opened a bank account in London. He was told that the cheque guarantee card provided did not permit him to overdraw the account. No overdraft was agreed. D cashed cheques supported by the cheque card at other banks, three of which were in Belgium. When the cheques arrived at D's bank, the bank honoured them and debited D's account, which consequently became overdrawn. The prosecution alleged D obtained a pecuniary advantage in that he was allowed to borrow by way of overdraft. D appealed contending (1) in the absence of any agreement by the bank to his overdrawing the account it could not be said that he was allowed to borrow by way of overdraft within the meaning of s.16(2)(*b*), Theft Act 1968; and (2) the court had no jurisdiction to try the charges relating to cheques cashed in Belgium.

Held, dismissing D's appeal, that (1) when D cashed the cheques there was an implied request by D for an overdraft. When D's bank met the cheques upon presentation and debited D's account it willingly albeit reluctantly agreed to grant D an overdraft. Accordingly D was allowed to borrow by way of overdraft; (2) D's conduct abroad resulted in him obtaining a pecuniary advantage in England. In those circumstances the courts had jurisdiction to try the offences. (*R.* v. *Waites* [1982] C.L.Y. 657 followed; *R.* v. *Kovacs* [1974] C.L.Y. 660, *Metropolitan Police Commissioner* v. *Charles* [1976] C.L.Y. 529 considered).

R. *v.* BEVAN (1987) 84 Cr.App.R. 143, C.A.

809. Obtaining property by deception—false oral representation to obtain work—subsequent carrying out of work—whether a criminal offence

[Theft Act 1968 (c.60) s.16.]

Where there is a false oral representation to obtain work, and the work is then done for pay there is a criminal deception if the deception was an operative cause of the obtaining of the payment.

A and B went to a house falsely claiming to be from a firm of tree surgeons, saying that essential work was necessary to remove trees to prevent damage to the gas supply and house foundations. The householder went in a distressed state to a building society to get the money, and the cashier called the police. A and B were charged with attempting to obtain property by deception. The judge rejected a motion to quash and a submission of no case.

Held, dismissing the appeals, that had the attempt succeeded it would have been a question for the jury whether or not the deception had been an operative cause of A and B obtaining the money, and the motion and submission had been rightly rejected (*R.* v. *Martin* (1867) L.R. I.C.C.R. 56 and *R.* v. *Moreton* (1913) 8 Cr.App.R. 214 applied; *R.* v. *Lewis* (unreported) Russell on Crime 12th ed., vol. 2, p.1186, n.66 considered).

R. *v.* KING (DAVID); R. *v.* STOCKWELL [1987] 2 W.L.R. 746, C.A.

810. Obtaining property by deception—intention permanently to deprive

[Theft Act 1968 (c.60), s.6.]

By using a worthless cheque, C obtained machinery from X in order to exert pressure on X (with whom C was in dispute) until C achieved what he wanted.

Held, allowing C's appeal against conviction of obtaining the machinery by deception, that the judge's summing up in relation to the element of intention permanently to deprive was defective. The culpability of C's act depended on the quality of intended detention in all its aspects, including C's assessment at the time of the likelihood of X coming to terms and the period for which the machinery would have to be kept. It was right for s.6(1) of the 1968 Act to be brought to the jury's attention. The expression "equivalent to an outright disposal" was a useful illustration. S.6(1) was expository of ss.1(1) and 15(1) rather than an enlargement of their scope but attributed a wider significance to those sections. Deprivation would not always be confined to the tangible object itself. "Deprivation" can be "permanent" even if meant to be temporary (*R.* v. *Warner* [1971] C.L.Y. 2826, *R.* v. *Cocks* [1976] C.L.Y. 410, *R.* v. *Lloyd, Buhee and Ali* [1985] C.L.Y. 888, *R.* v. *Downes* [1984] C.L.Y. 963, *R.* v. *Duru and Asghar* [1973] C.L.Y. 581 and *R.* v. *Easom* [1971] C.L.Y. 2816 considered).

R. *v.* COFFEY [1987] Crim.L.R. 498, C.A.

811. Offensive weapon—possession of police truncheon as part of fancy dress costume—whether reasonable excuse—whether offensive weapon *per se*

[Prevention of Crime Act 1953 (c.14), s.1(1)(3).]

A police truncheon is an offensive weapon *per se,* but when worn as part of a fancy dress costume the wearer may have a reasonable excuse for having it in his possession.

H was walking home after attending a fancy dress party dressed as a police officer; to add authenticity to the costume he was carrying a police truncheon. He was stopped by police officers, and arrested for being in possession of an offensive weapon, subsequently being charged with that offence. At his trial, however, the police offered no evidence; he was acquitted with costs. H claimed for unlawful arrest, false imprisonment and malicious prosecution.

Held, allowing H's appeal in part, that (1) there was insufficient evidence of malice on the part of the officers, so that part of the claim failed; (2) a police truncheon is an offensive weapon *per se*; (3) its use as a prop to add authenticity to his costume afforded H a reasonable excuse for having it in his possession; (4) there was no suggestion that H had refused to give his name and address, so the officers had had, in fact, no power to arrest him.

HOUGHTON *v.* CHIEF CONSTABLE OF GREATER MANCHESTER (1987) 84 Cr.App.R. 320, C.A.

812. Offensive weapon—smuggler in possession of pistols—whether "armed"

[Customs and Excise Management Act 1979 (c.2) s.86.]

A smuggler is "armed with an offensive weapon within the meaning of s.86 of the Customs and Excise Management Act 1979 simply if he is carrying the weapon, or if he has it readily available, without there being any need to prove that he intended to, or would have, used the weapon.

When Customs boarded a boat they found on board a very large amount of cannabis; they also found, in a locker in the wheelhouse, two pistols. The guns were not loaded, but their ammunition clips were next to them.

Held, that the offence of being armed with an offensive weapon when smuggling was not limited to cases where the weapon was actually being carried by the accused, but extended to cases where the weapon was easily and readily available. Furthermore, the offence did not require it to be proved that the accused intended to, or would have, used the weapon if the need had arisen (*R.* v. *Kelt* [1978] C.L.Y. 1474 applied).

R. *v.* JONES (KEITH DESMOND) [1987] 1 W.L.R. 692, C.A.

813. Offensive weapons—whether offensive *per se*

[Prevention of Crime Act 1953 (c.14), s.1(4).]

Neither a machete in a scabbard nor an especially powerful catapult is "made or adapted for use for causing injury to the person" within s.1(4) of the Prevention of Crime Act 1953. They are therefore not offensive *per se.* Even if they had been, it would have been a reasonable excuse for the possession of the latter that the owner was going to shoot squirrels, and of the former that he was going to use it to cut from a tree a branch on which to string and carry away the squirrels so killed.

SOUTHWELL *v.* CHADWICK, *The Times,* January 8, 1987, D.C.

814. Official secrets—civilian employed by county council in police station—whether "employed under" a person who held an office under Her Majesty

A civilian working in a police station under the supervision of a police inspector was a person employed under a person who held an office under Her Majesty for the purposes of the Official Secrets Acts notwithstanding that his employer was a county council.

D was employed by West Midlands County Council to work as a computer operator at Dudley Police Station. D was not a police officer but worked under the supervision of a police inspector and took instructions from police officers. D was convicted of two offences under the Official Secrets Acts being a person who was employed under a person who held an office under Her Majesty. D appealed unsuccessfully to the Crown Court. D appealed to the Divisional Court by way of case stated contending that he was not employed under a person who held an office under Her Majesty.

Held, dismissing D's appeal, that the words "employed under" did not mean "employed by" in a contractual sense. D was employed exclusively at the police station to carry out police work with police officers from whom he took instructions. In the circumstances D was employed under a police officer. A police officer was a person holding an office under Her Majesty (*Lewis* v. *Cattle* [1938] 2 K.B. 454 applied, *R.* v. *Reason* (1853) 17 J.P. 743 considered).

LOAT *v.* ANDREWS [1986] J.C.R. 679, D.C.

815. Official secrets—defence of implied authorisation—whether a matter for the jury

[Official Secrets Act 1911 (c.28), s.2(2).]

On a charge of unlawful reception of a document contrary to s.2(2) of the Official Secrets Act 1911, the defence of implied authorisation is a question of fact for the jury.

D, a dealer in spare parts for naval vessels, wanted to supply spare parts for Rolls-Royce Olympus marine engines. Through an associate, he secured the loan of the manufacturer's manual for the aero engine from a service man. The Ministry of Defence had classified the manual as "restricted" but had disseminated it without restriction as to its further use. D was charged with the unlawful reception of the documents contrary to s.2(2) of the Official Secrets Act 1911. The judge directed the jury that the essential question was to what extent the service man had restricted or permitted the dissemination. D was convicted.

Held, allowing the appeal, that that was not the real issue. The defence of implied consent was a question of fact for the jury and they should have been directed to consider whether the Ministry of Defence, by disseminating the manual without restriction as to its further use, had given implied consent for anyone who came into possession of it to make such use of it as he saw fit. Accordingly, the conviction would be quashed. (*R.* v. *Crisp and Homewood* (1919) 83 J.P. 121 approved; *Boyer* v. *The King* (1948) 94 C.C.C. 195 considered).

R. *v.* GALVIN [1987] 3 W.L.R. 93, C.A.

816. Passive assistance—criteria

To be convicted of "passive assistance" in the commission of an offence, an offender must be shown either to have encouraged the offence or to have failed to exercise control where he had a right or duty so to do.

R. *v.* BLAND, *The Times,* August 25, 1987, C.A.

817. Prevention of terrorism—exclusion order

[Prevention of Terrorism (Temporary Provisions) Acts 1976 (c.8) and 1984 (c.8).]

The Secretary of State for the Home Department need not give reasons for excluding a person from entry into Great Britain.

R. *v.* SECRETARY OF STATE FOR THE HOME OFFICE, *ex p.* STITT, *The Times,* February 3, 1987, D.C.

818. Public order

PUBLIC ORDER (FOOTBALL EXCLUSION) ORDER 1987 (No. 853) [45p], made under the Public Order Act 1986 (c.64), ss.34(4), 36(1); operative on August 1, 1987; prescribes the General Secretary of The Football Association Ltd. for the purposes of s.34 of the 1986 Act.

819. Public order—abusive words or behaviour whereby breach of peace likely to occur

[Public Order Act 1936, s.5; Police Act 1964, s.51(1).]

Police officers A and B attended the scene of an altercation involving D. D's mother told him to go home. As he walked away, he made a rude gesture towards A and shouted "fuck off". When A told D to stop and followed, D repeated the gesture and words. A held D's arm, saying D was under arrest for his behaviour. D punched A in the face. B attempted to restrain D in the ensuing struggle.

Held, dismissing D's appeal against convictions of using abusive words and behaviour whereby a breach of the peace was likely to be occasioned contrary to s.5 of the 1936 Act, and assaulting A in the execution of his duty contrary to s.51(1) of the 1964 Act, that it sufficed if A reasonably believed that a breach of the peace was likely to be occasioned, even if that breach was likely to be by D himself rather than any other person. D's behaviour justified A's belief. Police officers had to act on the spur of the moment and full allowance had to be made for the circumstances in emergencies (*Parkin* v. *Norman; Valentine* v. *Lilley* [1982] C.L.Y. 632, *R.* v. *Oakwell* [1978] C.L.Y. 585 considered).

G. *v.* CHIEF SUPERINTENDENT OF POLICE, STROUD, GLOUCESTERSHIRE [1987] Crim.L.R. 269, D.C.

820. Public Order Act 1986—commencement

PUBLIC ORDER ACT 1986 (COMMENCEMENT No. 2) ORDER 1987 (No. 198 (C.4)) [80p], made under the Public Order Act 1986 (c.64), s.41; brings into force on April 1, 1987 ss.1–10, 12–15, 17–29, 39, 40 (in part), Scheds. 2 (in part), 3 (in part).

PUBLIC ORDER ACT 1986 (COMMENCEMENT No. 3) ORDER 1987 (No. 852 (C.23)) [45p], made under the Public Order Act 1986, s.41; brings into force on August 1, 1987 ss.30–37 of the 1986 Act.

821. Repatriation of prisoners

REPATRIATION OF PRISONERS (OVERSEAS TERRITORIES) (AMENDMENT) ORDER 1987 (No. 1828) [45p], made under the Repatriation of Prisoners Act 1984 (c.47), s.9(4); operative on November 16, 1987; extends the provisions of the 1984 Act to Hong Kong subject to certain modifications.

822. Research study

The Home Office has published a Research Study entitled *The Validity of the Reconviction Prediction Score.* Copies of Home Office Research Study No. 94 are available from H.M.S.O. (ISBN 0 11 340882 X) [£4·50].

823. Robbery—force—whether force on actual person necessary

C approached X from behind and wrenched her basket down from her hands and made off with it.

Held, dismissing C's appeal against conviction of robbery, that the old distinction between force on the actual person and force on property causing force on the person had gone. Whether force was used on any person in order to steal was an issue for the jury (*R.* v. *Dawson and James* [1979] C.L.Y. 545 applied).

R. *v.* CLOUDEN [1987] Crim.L.R. 56, C.A.

824. Self-defence—homicide—mistake of fact induced by intoxication

A mistake of fact induced by voluntary intoxication cannot be relied upon for self-defence.

The appellant, who was intoxicated, killed a man and raised the issue of self-defence. He was tried on a count of murder. The jury were directed that if he mistakenly believed he was under attack he was entitled to defend himself, but not beyond what was reasonable. He was convicted of manslaughter. The defendant appealed on the question as to whether the direction should have included the possibility of mistake as to the severity of the attack.

Held, as far as self-defence was concerned reliance could not be placed on a mistake of fact induced by voluntary intoxication (*R.* v. *Majewski* [1976] C.L.Y. 487, *R.* v. *Williams (Gladstone)* [1984] C.L.Y. 504 considered).

R. *v.* O'GRADY [1987] 3 W.L.R. 321, C.A.

825. Self-defence—whether belief of accused to be reasonable—whether honest belief sufficient

An honest belief in circumstances which, if true, would entitle a defendant to use force to defend himself, is sufficient for the defence of self-defence to succeed on a charge of murder. The reasonableness, or otherwise, of his belief is relevant, but only on the question of whether the belief was in fact honestly held.

At his trial for murder, B. who was a police officer, claimed that he believed that the deceased had been shooting at him, and another officer; and that he had returned fire in self-defence. The trial judge's direction on self-defence referred to B having "reasonably believed" that his life was in danger. The jury convicted, and B was sentenced to death.

Held, allowing the appeal and quashing the conviction, that the correct test to be applied was whether B honestly believed the facts which, if true, would have entitled him to use reasonable force to protect himself. The reasonableness or otherwise of his belief was relevant only in so far as it went to support, or detract from, the honesty of his belief. Since it could not be certain that the jury would have reached the same verdict if properly directed, the proviso could not be applied and the conviction would be quashed.

BECKFORD *v.* THE QUEEN [1987] 3 W.L.R. 611, P.C.

826. Share applications—cheating

Persons who cheat on the Stock Market by making multiple applications are on notice that both their assets and their liberty are at risk.

R. *v.* BEST, *The Times,* October 6, 1987, C.A.

827. Statistics—annual volume

The annual volume *Criminal Statistics, England and Wales, 1986* has been published. Copies are available from H.M.S.O. (Cm. 233) [£15·80].

828. Statistics—criminal careers of those born in 1953—persistent offenders and desistance

The Home Office has published a statistical bulletin (Issue 35/87) which gives some further results from a study of the convictions, in England and Wales, of a sample of persons born in 1953. Earlier results were published in Home Office Statistical Bulletin 7/85 [1985] C.L.Y. 869. Copies of the latest Bulletin are available from the Statistical Department, Home Office, Lunar House, Croydon, Surrey CRO 9YD. Tel.: 01–760 2850 [£2·50].

829. Statistics—criminal cases committed for trial in the Crown Court

The Lord Chancellor's Department has published figures of the number of criminal cases committed for trial in the Crown Court during 1986. Copies of *Judicial Statistics 1986* are available from H.M.S.O. (Cm. 173) [£9·10].

830. Statistics—criminal cases in magistrates' courts

The Home Office has published a statistical bulletin which gives details of *Statistics of the Time Taken to Process Criminal Cases in Magistrates' Courts during June 1985, October 1985 and February 1986.* Issue 1/87 is available from the Statistical Department, Home Office, Lunar House, Croydon, Surrey CR0 9YD. Tel.: 01-760-2850. [£2·50.]

The Home Office has published a statistical bulletin which gives details of statistics of the times taken to process criminal cases in magistrates' courts during June 1985, October 1985, February 1986, June 1986 and October 1986. Issue 20/87 is available from the Statistical Department, Home Office, Lunar House, Croydon, Surrey CR0 9YD. Tel.: 01-760-2850. [£2·50.]

The Home Office has published a statistical bulletin which gives details of statistics of the times taken to process criminal cases in magistrates' courts (June 1985 to February 1987). Issue 33/87 is available from the Statistical Department, Home Office, Lunar House, Croydon, Surrey CR0 9YD. Tel.: 01-760 2850. [£2·50].

831. Statistics—domestic proceedings in magistrates' courts

The Home Office has published a statistical bulletin which gives details of statistics of domestic proceedings in magistrates' courts in England and Wales during 1986. Copies of the bulletin (Issue 17/87) are available from the Statistical Department, Home Office, Lunar House, Croydon, Surrey CR0 9YD. Tel.: 01-760-2850 [£2·50].

832. Statistics—notifiable offences

The Home Office has published a statistical bulletin which sets out details of notifiable offences recorded by the police in England and Wales during 1986. The bulletin, Issue 4/87, is available from Statistical Department, Home Office, Lunar House, Croydon, Surrey CR0 9YD. Tel. 01–760–2850. [£1·50].

The Home Office has published a statistical bulletin which sets out details of notifiable offences recorded by the police in England and Wales during the first quarter of 1987. It also sets out details of notifiable offences in which firearms were used during 1986. The bulletin, Issue 16/87, is available from the Statistical Department, Home Office, Lunar House, Croydon, Surrey CR0 9YD. Tel.: 01-760-2850 [£1·50].

The Home Office has published a statistical bulletin which sets out details of notifiable offences recorded by the police in England and Wales during the second quarter of 1987. The bulletin, Issue 27/87, is available from the Statistical Department, Home Office, Lunar House, Croydon, Surrey CR0 9YD. Tel.: 01-760 2850 [£1·50].

The Home Office has published a statistical bulletin which sets out details of notifiable offences recorded by the police in England and Wales during the third quarter of 1987. The bulletin, Issue 38/87, is available from the Statistical Department, Home Office, Lunar House, Croydon, Surrey CR0 9YD. Tel.: 01-760 2850 [£1·50].

833. Statistics—operation of police powers under the Police and Criminal Evidence Act 1984

The Home Office has published a statistical bulletin (Issue 12/87) containing statistics on the first year of operation of certain powers under the Police and Criminal Evidence Act 1984, which were implemented on January 1, 1986. The statistics cover: stops and searches; persons detained for more than 24 hours without charge; and intimate searches. The bulletin is available from the Statistical Department, Home Office, Lunar House, Croydon, Surrey CR0 9YD [£2·50].

The Home Office has published a statistical bulletin containing statistics on the operation of certain police powers under the Police and Criminal Evidence Act 1984, which were implemented on January 1, 1986. The statistics cover: stops and searches, road checks, persons detained for more than 24 hours without charge, and intimate searches. The bulletin, issue 23/87, is available from the Statistical Department, Lunar House, Croydon, Surrey CR0 9YD. Tel. 01–760 2850. [£2·50].

The Home Office has published a statistical bulletin containing statistics of certain police powers under the Police and Criminal Evidence Act 1984 during the second quarter of 1987. The bulletin, Issue 32/87, is available from the Statistical Department, Home Office, Lunar House, Croydon, Surrey CR0 9YD. Tel.: 01-760 2850. [£2·50].

834. Statistics—prevention of terrorism

The Home Office has published statistics on the operation of the prevention of terrorism legislation during the fourth quarter of 1986. Copies of the Bulletin (Issue 2/87) are available from the Statistical Department, Home Office, Lunar House, Croydon, Surrey CR0 9YD. Tel.: 01-760-2850. [£2·50].

The Home Office has published a statistical bulletin on the operation of the prevention of terrorism legislation during the first quarter of 1987 (Issue 11/87). The bulletin is available from the Statistical Department, Home Office, Lunar House, Croydon, Surrey, CR0 9YD. [£2·50].

The Home Office has published a statistical bulletin on the operation of the prevention of terrorism legislation during the second quarter of 1987. The bulletin (Issue 25/87) is available from the Statistical Department, Home Office, Lunar House, Croydon, Surrey CR0 9YD. Tel.: 01-760-2850 [£2·50].

The Home Office has published a statistical bulletin on the operation of the prevention of terrorism legislation during the third quarter of 1987. The bulletin (Issue 34/87) is available from the Statistical Department, Home Office, Lunar House, Croydon, Surrey CR0 9YD. Tel.: 01-760 2850 [£2·50].

835. Statistics—reconvictions and recalls of life licensees

The Home Office has published a statistical bulletin giving details of the reconviction and/or recall of those released on licence up to the end of 1985. Copies of the bulletin (Issue 18/87) are available from the Statistical Department, Home Office, Lunar House, Croydon, Surrey CR0 9YD. Tel.: 01-760-2850. [£2·50].

836. Supply of fireworks—"apparently" under age of 16

[Consumer Safety Act 1978 (c.38); S.I. 1986 No. 1323, reg. 2.]

On October 29, 1986, A sold a box of fireworks to a child aged 13. The appeal against conviction and sentence of an offence contrary to reg. 2 (made under the 1978 Act) concerned the proper interpretation of the words "no person shall supply . . . fireworks to any person apparently under the age of sixteen years."

Held, that the prosecution must satisfy the court that the child was apparently under 16 at the time of the offence, and if the prosecution so satisfied the court, it was open to the appellant to show that it was not apparent to him but the child was under 16.

SARWAN SINGH DEU *v.* DUDLEY METROPOLITAN BOROUGH COUNCIL, July 10, 1987; Sedgley Crown Ct. [*Ex rel. Jeremy Cahill, Barrister.*]

837. Theft—"acceptance" of valuable security—meaning

[Theft Act 1968 (c.60), s.20(2).]

"Acceptance" in 20(2) of the Theft Act 1968 is used in the technical sense of acceptance of a bill of exchange: mere receipt of a stolen security is not acceptance.

United States social security orders for payment of money drawn on the United States Treasury and payable only in America were stolen in California. The first appellant accompanied S to a bank in London where S indorsed a number of them to be credited to his bank account in America. The police were told, and the appellants were charged with conspiracy to procure the execution of valuable securities by deception, the particulars alleging that they had conspired to procure the execution of the securities by the acceptance of the orders. The judge ruled that the offence had been committed within the jurisdiction and that "acceptance" within s.20(2) of the Theft Act 1968 meant "taking into possession" and was not restricted to its technical meaning as used in the Bills of Exchange Act 1882. Two appellants were convicted and the third pleaded guilty.

Held, allowing their appeals against conviction, that "acceptance" in s.20(2) was used in the technical sense of acceptance of a bill of exchange. Therefore, the handing over of the indorsed orders to a London bank was not an acceptance within s.20(2). Since the execution of the valuable securities could only have taken place in America, the court had no jurisdiction to try the offence charged (*R.* v. *Beck (Brian)* [1985] C.L.Y 892 distinguished).

R. *v.* NANAYAKKARA; R. *v.* KHOR; R. *v.* TAN [1987] 1 W.L.R. 265, C.A.

838. Theft—director of company—sale in fraud of company

[H.K.] A director of a company who had general authority to sell the company's property was guilty of theft if he dishonestly sold the company's property at an undervalue and assumed the rights of an owner over it.

The respondent was the minority shareholder in a company in Hong Kong which exported textiles and held quotas registered with the Hong Kong Department of Trade and Industry. These quotas were saleable subject to the approval of the Department. The respondent had a general authority to deal in these quotas on the company's behalf. While his co-director was away, he sold a large number of quotas at a gross undervalue. He was charged with theft and the court convicted him. The Court of Appeal of Hong Kong quashed the conviction on the ground that the respondent was the alter ego of the company and never appropriated the quotas or assumed the rights of an owner.

Held, allowing the Attorney-General's appeal and restoring the conviction, that the quotas, since they were freely bought and sold, were property within the meaning of the English Theft Act and the Hong Kong Theft Ordinance. Although not "things in action" they were a form of "other intangible property" within the statutory definition. An agent authorised to sell could have no authority to sell dishonestly against the interests of the owner. The respondent had dishonestly sold his principal's property at an undervalue and exceeded his authority. He had thereby assumed the right of an owner in a way which amounted to an appropriation under the English and Hong Kong legislation.

ATT.-GEN. OF HONG KONG *v.* CHAN NAI-KEUNG (DANIEL) (1987) 3 BCC 403, P.C.

839. Theft—going equipped for theft-attempted theft or theft—whether proper to charge both offences

[Theft Act 1968 (c.60), s.25(1).]

There is no reason why a person cannot be charged with going equipped as well as theft or attempted theft.

MINOR *v.* CROWN PROSECUTION SERVICE, *The Times*, August 28, 1987, D.C.

840. Theft—making off without paying taxi-fare—whether liable to pay

[Theft Act 1978 (c.31), s.3.]

X, a taxi-driver, agreed to drive T home. During the journey, X stopped to obtain directions from T, who was drunk and had not given his address. Following an argument in which T accused X of making an unnecessary diversion and in which X could not obtain an address from T, X drove to a police station. There was conflicting evidence as to what happened there.

Held, allowing T's appeal against conviction of making off without payment, contrary to s.3 of the 1978 Act, that as the journey had not been completed, X was in breach of contract in leaving the route to T's home instead of resolving the argument and could not lawfully demand the fare (*R.* v. *Brooks and Brooks* [1983] C.L.Y. 710 considered).

TROUGHTON *v.* METROPOLITAN POLICE [1987] Crim.L.R. 138, D.C.

841. Theft—proceeds of money collected for charity—whether property belonging to another

[Theft Act 1968 (c.60), s.5(3).]

L obtained sponsorship for X, who entered the London Marathon. The charity's rules did not require L to hand over the very notes and coins collected. He received £54 which he failed to hand over.

Held, allowing L's appeal against conviction of theft from the charity, that the debt owed by L to the charity was not "proceeds" of the property received by L within s.5(3) of the 1968 Act with which he was under an obligation to deal in a particular way. He had no obligation to keep in existence a fund equivalent to the property he had received.

LEWIS *v.* LETHBRIDGE [1987] Crim.L.R. 59, D.C.

842. Theft and handling—alternative offence—guidelines

[Theft Act 1968 (c.60), ss.1(1), 22(1).]

The following guidelines should govern whether theft and handling should be charged in the alternative; (1) the practice of charging theft and handling as alternatives should be followed wherever there is a real possibility that the evidence might support one rather than the other; (2) there is a danger of confusion arising from reference to second and subsequent appropriations. How the appropriation happened is irrelevant provided it happened in the course of theft; (3) a jury should be told that a handler can be a thief, but he cannot be convicted of both; (4) handling is the more serious offence; (5) in the unlikely event of the jury not agreeing whether theft or handling has been proved they should be discharged; (6) judges and counsel should avoid confusing intellectual subtleties when addressing juries.

S was charged with theft of a cheque book and of obtaining property by deception by means of three of the cheques, two of which carried S's palm print. The cheque book had been stolen from the owner's office between 9.00 a.m. and 3.30 p.m., and the cheques were presented and paid between 1 p.m. and 3 p.m. on the same day. The recorder left only the first count to the jury and directed them about the possibility of a second appropriation and directed that if S dishonestly took the cheque book into his possession on that day, the other elements also being proved, he was guilty of theft.

Held, that the judge was quite entitled to give the direction he did on the facts (*R.* v. *Loughlin* [1957] C.L.Y. 2281, *Stapylton* v. *O'Callaghan* [1973] C.L.Y. 654 and *R.* v. *Devall* [1984] C.L.Y. 960 considered).

R. *v.* SHELTON (1986) 83 Cr.App.R. 379, C.A.

843. Trade descriptions—holiday brochure—representation

[Trade Descriptions Act 1968 (c.29), s.14(1).]

A false description of an hotel made in 1983, acted upon by the consumer in January 1984, and still inaccurate when the holiday took place in September 1984 was made recklessly in view of the lapse of time during which no enquiries were made and the silence surrounding the situation.

BEST TRAVEL CO. *v.* PATTERSON, (1987) 151 J.P.N. 348, D.C.

844. Trade descriptions—mileage reading on motor car—disclaimer

[Trade Descriptions Act 1968 (c.29), s.1(1).]

A notice in a showroom was not an effective disclaimer where negotiations took place on the garage forecourt. (*Waltham Forest London Borough Council* v. *Wheatley (T.G.) (Central Garage)* [1978] C.L.Y. 2653 considered).

BLUNDEN *v.* GRAVELLE, (1987) 151 J.P.N. 348, D.C.

845. Trade descriptions—mileage reading on motor car—disclaimer

[Trade Descriptions Act 1968 (c.29), S.I. 1(*a*), (*b*).]

The words of the disclaimer were sufficient to establish that D desired to prevent any purchaser associating the mileage reading of the odometer with the actual mileage done by the car in question, thus preventing the odometer reading becoming a trade description.

NEWHAM LONDON BOROUGH COUNCIL *v.* SINGH, *The Times,* December 10, 1987, D.C.

846. Trade descriptions—mileage reading on motor car—disclaimer

[Trade Descriptions Act 1968 (c.29), ss.1(1)(*a*), 24.]

If a dealer falsifies the mileometer reading of a car that he is selling, he applies a false trade description to it under s.1(1)(*a*) of the Trade Descriptions Act 1968, and the defence allowed by s.24 is not available to him. Nor can he rely on a disclaimer to avoid criminal liability (*R.* v. *Hammerton Cars* [1976] C.L.Y. 2470 distinguished).

R. *v.* SOUTHWOOD, *The Times,* July 1, 1987, C.A.

847. Trade descriptions—MOT certificate

[Trade Descriptions Act 1968 (c.29) ss.1, 2.]

P bought a car from G, a garage, who told him that it had been made in about 1971. A new MOT certificate supplied with the car confirmed this date. In fact, the car had been made in 1962, and G was prosecuted under the Trade Descriptions Act 1968.

Held, that the prosecution was entitled to rely on the MOT certificate for its representation that the car's year of manufacture was 1971 (*Wycombe Marsh Garages* v. *Fowler* [1972] C.L.Y. 3107 distinguished.)

R. *v.* COVENTRY CITY JUSTICES, *ex p.* FARRAND, (1987) 151 J.P.N. 702, D.C.

848. Trade descriptions—neglect—delegation of duty

[Trade Descriptions Act 1968 (c.29), ss.1(1)(*b*), 20(1), 23, 24(1)(*a*).]

When delegation of duty is relied on it is necessary to look at the facts of the particular case; one director may not simply accept the assurance of another.

D and X, co-directors, who had no knowledge of marketing car parts, bought several thousand rear window brake lights. Prior to doing so, D had told X to make inquiries, and X had assured D that they were legal in the U.K. They were in fact illegal, because they were too bright. D was prosecuted under s.1(1)(*b*) and s.20 of the Trade Descriptions Act 1968. On conviction, he appealed on the ground that he was entitled to rely on the inquiry which he had delegated to X.

Held, dismissing the appeal, that the facts of each particular case must be looked at, and the justices were entitled to find that the offence was attributable to D's neglect (*Huckerby* v. *Elliott* [1969] C.L.Y. 850, D.C. and *City Equitable Fire Insurance Co., Re* [1925] Ch. 407, C.A. distinguished).

HIRSCHLER *v.* BIRCH [1987] R.T.R. 13, D.C.

849. Trade descriptions—reasonable diligence—test

[Trade Descriptions Act 1968 (c.29), s.24(3).]

The respondent offered to supply audio cassette tapes. They were in fact pirate tapes which had a description of the company by whose authority the tapes were said to have been produced. The respondent was an itinerant market trader, almost illiterate in English, who normally dealt in clothing and had paid a similar price to that which he had paid for tapes of Indian music for his own use.

Held, allowing the prosecutor's appeal but giving the respondent an absolute discharge, that the justices had erred in finding that the respondent had established a defence under s.24(3) of the 1968 Act and that he could not be expected to have exercised any further diligence. The standard of reasonable diligence was to be set by reference to the nature of the establishment of sale, the sort of articles or goods sold and generally the extent to which a reasonable person would think it right to take precautions. Personal attributes such as those taken into consideration by the justices in this case were irrelevant.

DENARD *v.* ABBAS [1987] Crim.L.R. 424, D.C.

850. Video Recordings Act 1984—commencement

VIDEO RECORDINGS ACT 1984 (COMMENCEMENT No. 4) ORDER 1987 (No. 123 (c.1)) [45p], made under the Video Recordings Act 1984 (c.39), s.23(2); brings into force on March 1, 1987, ss.9 and 10 of the 1984 Act.

VIDEO RECORDINGS ACT 1984 (COMMENCEMENT No. 5) ORDER 1987 (No. 1142 (c.29)) [45p], made under the Video Recordings Act 1984, s.23(2); brings ss.9 and 10 of the Act into force on September 1, 1987, subject to specified limitations.

VIDEO RECORDINGS ACT (COMMENCEMENT No. 6) ORDER 1987 (No. 2155 (c.64)) [45p], made under the Video Recordings Act 1984, s.23(2); brings ss.9 and 10 of the Act into force on March 1, 1988, for specified purposes.

851. Wildlife—possession of live birds—whether strict liability. See KIRKLAND *v.* ROBINSON, §117.

852. Wildlife—setting poisoned substance to injure wild bird. See ROBINSON *v.* HUGHES, §118.

853. Wounding—self-defence

W stabbed K with a lock-knife, which was already opened, when K punched him in the face. At W's trial for wounding with intent the judge directed the jury that it was for them to decide whether W had used the knife in self-defence and whether its use was reasonable. W was convicted and appealed on the basis that the judge ought to have directed the jury that they ought to acquit if they thought W had only done what he honestly thought was necessary in a moment of unexpected anguish.

Held, dismissing the appeal, that since W had used a knife in circumstances when it could not possibly be reasonable, the absence of a direction about acting in the agony of the moment was irrelevant (dictum of Lord Morris in *Palmer* v. *R.*; *Irving* v. *R.* [1971] C.L.Y. 2509 considered).

R. *v.* WHYTE [1987] 3 All E.R. 416, C.A.

CRIMINAL SENTENCING

854. Abstracting electricity—attaching "black box" to meter—whether sentence of immediate imprisonment justified

Age: 40. Pleaded guilty. Woman living alone. Meter readings suggested only one unit consumed in a month, despite various electrical appliances in house, including radiator in use. Marks on cables suggested a "black box" had been fitted and used. No previous convictions. W was responsible for 14-year-old son. One months' imprisonment and £50 fine to he paid at £5 per month held not wrong in principle. Appeal allowed so that W, having been released on bail, not required to return to serve few remaining days of sentence.

R. *v.* WESTERN [1987] Crim.L.R. 350, C.A.

855. Adjournment for assessment of offender for non-custodial measure—custodial sentence passed following favourable assessment

Sentence was adjourned to enable M to attend a Day Assessment Centre, a social inquiry report suggesting M might respond to non-custodial sentence. Later sentenced to 12 months' imprisonment despite favourable report.

Held, that a sense of grievance may have arisen. M had reasonable expectation of non-custodial sentence if he complied with expectations and purpose of the adjournment. Sentence reduced to allow immediate release (*R.* v. *Gillam* (1980) 2 Cr.App.R.(S.) 267 applied; *R.* v. *Horton and Alexander* [1986] C.L.Y. 703 considered).

R. *v.* McMURRAY [1987] Crim.L.R. 515, C.A.

856. Adjournment for report on suitability for non-custodial sentence

Aged. 29. Pleaded guilty to burglary, handling, theft and possessing heroin. Granted bail during adjournment for reports on suitability for treatment programme. Given warning that could not rely on getting non-custodial sentence. Another judge adjourned sentence again with bail conditional on M residing where required by organisation running residential training course. Third judge sentenced M to 18 months' imprisonment despite favourable report.

Held, that M had clear expectation after second adjournment that if he continued satisfactorily he would be placed on probation. Sentence unfair. Probation order substituted (*R.* v. *Gillam* (1980) 2 Cr.Appr.R.(S.) 267 applied).

R. *v.* McKINNEY [1987] Crim.L.R. 142, C.A.

857. Adjournment for reports by Magistrates' Court—favourable community service assessment—committed for sentence to Crown Court—principle in Gillam.

Where a magistrates' court adjourns for reports in circumstances in which a reasonable expectation of a non-custodial sentence is created and a favourable report is received, if the magistrates' court commits the offender for sentencing, the Crown Court should not impose a custodial sentence.

R was convicted at the magistrates' court on a number of offences relating to a stolen cheque book and driving licence and to quantities of cannabis. The magistrate adjourned for reports. The community service assessment was favourable but R was committed to the Crown Court for sentence. Sentenced to 12 months' imprisonment.

Held, that if D's legitimate expectations were defeated he would suffer a sense of injustice. In the present case no warning had been given to R at the time the court ordered the reports that would have avoided such an expectation by the defendant. The fact that the reports had been ordered by the magistrates' court but that it was the Crown Court that passed sentence made no difference—the defendant's legitimate expectations of a non-custodial sentence should not be defeated. Everything depended on what the defendant had been led to expect—there was no absolute rule. (*R.* v. *Gillam* (1980) 2 Cr.App.R.(S.) 267 applied; *R.* v. *Stokes* [1984] C.L.Y. 723 considered).

R. *v.* RENNES (1985) 7 Cr.App.R.(S.) 343, C.A.

858. Affray—guidelines

In cases of very serious affray involving preparation, organisation and direction of participants the ringleaders can expect to be sentenced to imprisonment for a term in excess of seven years.

K, S and M were involved in the Broadwater Farm Estate riots in October 1986. The riots lasted many hours involving great disorder, barricades were formed with burning vehicles, police were attacked and bombarded with bricks, stones, bottles and petrol bombs, houses were set on fire and firemen were attacked. Over 200 policemen were injured and one was murdered. The riots were organised and directed and planned beforehand. All were charged with affray. K and S pleaded guilty, M was convicted by a jury. K was 21 at the time and spent three hours on the estate at the height of the riot. He threw bottles and stones at the police and witnessed the murder. S was 17 at the time and involved in setting up a barricade of burning motor cars and part of a crowd throwing missiles at the police. He spent one and a half hours on the estate. M was involved in three separate attacks on the police and threw more than 50 missiles at the police. He played a more active part than K and S. K and S had previous convictions for offences of dishonesty and violence, K had previously served a custodial sentence. Both came from an unsettled background and had some redeeming features in their characters. M was 18 at the time of the offence. He was married with a young child and described as neither disruptive nor aggressive. K and S were sentenced to five years' youth custody. M was sentenced to seven years youth custody.

Held, allowing their appeals against sentence, that in cases of very serious affray involving some measure of preparation, organisation and direction the ring leaders could expect to receive sentences of imprisonment in the range of seven years and upwards. In a concerted major affray involving prolonged and vicious attacks on the police participants, however slight their involvement, could expect a sentence of at least 18 months' to two years' imprisonment. In the present case the proper sentence for K and S was three and a half years' youth custody and for M was four and a half years' youth custody.

R. *v.* KEYS, SWEEN AND MACMINN (1987) 84 Cr.App.R. 204, C.A.

859. Affray—violent behaviour in club

N pleaded guilty to affray. Together with three others he had gone to a private club and attacked a man, knocking him to the ground and rendering him unconscious. In the resulting violence 10 people were injured. Sentenced to three years' imprisonment.

Held, that the judge was quite correct in imposing a deterrent sentence. It was the least N would reasonably have expected and a longer sentence might have been upheld.

R. *v.* NOBLE (1985) 7 Cr.App.R.(S.) 233, C.A.

860. Aggravated burglary—home of old person—victim tied up

F and another pleaded guilty to aggravated burglary and a third pleaded guilty to conspiracy to burgle. The third remained outside in a car when the other two entered the home of a man of 84 carrying an imitation firearm and blank cartridges. They tied the man to a chair loosely but did not commit any other act of violence. When they left, the victim freed himself and telephoned the police who were able to apprehend them. The two intruders were sentenced to nine years' imprisonment and the third to four years' imprisonment, being unaware of the victim's age or that a weapon was carried.

Held, that this case was not as serious as *O'Driscoll* where the victim was subject to grave violence. The court must heed the observations in *O'Driscoll* about the need to protect old people by such steps as they can. The sentences were too severe and sentences of six years were substituted for those of nine years and a sentence of three years for the sentence of four years (*R.* v. *O'Driscoll* [1987] C.L.Y. 1042 considered).

R. *v.* FUNNELL (1986) 8 Cr.App.R.(S.) 143, C.A.

861. Allegations against police officer—whether relevant to sentence

E was convicted of possessing cannabis resin. He was in a public house which was raided by police officers and when he was searched a half-burnt "reefer" containing 63 milligrammes of cannabis was found in his pocket. At his trial E claimed that the reefer had been planted on him. Sentenced to three months' imprisonment, suspended for one year. In sentencing, the sentencer commented that he would normally have imposed a fine but he took into account E's attitude to society and to the police as indicated by his allegations against one officer.

Held, that it was established that the fact that an offender attacked the police should not add to his sentence. Applying that principle the appeal was allowed and a fine of £25 substituted for the suspended sentence (*R.* v. *Skone* [1967] C.L.Y. 868 considered).

R. *v.* EVANS (DAVID JOHN) (1986) 8 Cr.App.R.(S.) 197, C.A.

862. Appeal from magistrates—severity of sentence—forum

Unless it is alleged that the sentence passed is unlawful, the severity of a sentence is not a matter of law for the Divisional Court.

R. *v.* HAYWARD AND STACEY, *The Times,* March 27, 1987, D.C.

863. Appeal to Crown Court against sentence passed by magistrates—correct approach in Crown Court

J and two others pleaded guilty before the magistrates to assaulting a constable and were sentenced to a detention centre order of four months. They appealed to the Crown Court. The judge stated that the Crown Court would have imposed a lesser sentence but that the sentences imposed by the magistrates were not so out of proportion to the offences that the Crown Court would be justified in interfering.

Held by the Divisional Court that an appeal against sentence from a magistrates' court to a Crown Court was a rehearing. The Crown Court should first of all go through the sentencing procedure without regard to the magistrates' order and should decide how the offender ought to be sentenced. If that sentence differed from the magistrates' order to a significant degree the appeal should be allowed. Here the Crown Court must have been contemplating a reduction of at least one month—a significant difference to the magistrates' order. The sentences would be quashed and sentences of three months imposed (*Dyson* v. *Ellison* [1975] C.L.Y. 2920 applied; *R.* v. *St. Albans Crown Court ex p. Cinnamond* [1981] C.L.Y. 396 referred to).

R. *v.* KNUTSFORD CROWN COURT *ex p.* JONES (1985) 7 Cr.App.R.(S.) 448, D.C.

864. Arson—arson of residential premises by person suffering from personality disorder

M, aged 56 and suffering from long-term personality disorder, barricaded herself in flat in nine-storey block and threatened to set it on fire. When firemen attempted entry, M set fire to sofa. Neighbours evacuated; front door of M's flat damaged to value £650. Medical prognosis poor: distinct risk of further offences. 19 previous convictions, including two arson in distant past. 10 years' imprisonment reduced to seven since fire was suicidal gesture, danger to others minimised, damage modest, M was aging prematurely and 10 years crushed any hope for future.

R. *v.* MOORE [1987] Crim.L.R. 145, C.A.

865. Arson—dutch barn and contents

D pleaded guilty to arson. After drinking, he set fire to a dutch barn and its contents, which included various items of agricultural equipment. The total extent of the loss was £53,000. D had a grudge against the owner of the farm. Sentenced to three years' imprisonment.

Held, that there was no ground to interfere with the sentence.

R. *v.* DOWNEY (1986) 8 Cr.App.R.(S.) 168, C.A.

866. Arson—of shop—intent to defraud insurers

S pleaded guilty to counts of arson and attempting to obtain property by deception. He had bought a fish and chip business in rented premises, taken out insurance giving a false figure for the annual profit of the business and then set fire to the shop, causing £14,000 worth of damage. Sentenced to four years' imprisonment for conspiracy to commit arson and 12 months' consecutive for the attempt to obtain by deception.

Held, that the two offences were separate and the sentence of five years was not excessive.

R. *v.* SHAH (MUZAFFAR ALI) (1985) 7 Cr.App.R.(S.) 456, C.A.

867. Arson—of unoccupied premises

W, aged 43 and of previous good character, pleaded guilty to three counts of arson. He set fire to a church, the premises of a community welfare organisation and a tax office. Damage was estimated at £17,500 in all. The buildings were all unoccupied at the time. All three fires were started on the same morning and he immediately surrendered to the police. He claimed that he started the fires to draw attention to the grievances of the poor and the old. Sentenced to three years' imprisonment.

Held, that this was not a case of a man suffering from a mental condition. He knew what he was doing and thought himself justified. The offences called for an immediate sentence of imprisonment but three years was too long and the appropriate term was two years.

R. *v.* WALMSLEY (1986) 8 Cr.App.R.(S.) 130, C.A.

868. Arson—throwing a petrol bomb at bar staff

M pleaded guilty to inflicting grievous bodily harm and was convicted of arson and throwing an explosive substance with intent to do bodily injury. Following an incident outside a cocktail bar, he struck a member of the staff of the bar with a wheel brace, causing a fractured jaw and extensive bruising. Some months later, late at night, he threw a petrol bomb at the owner and some of the staff standing in the doorway of the bar. The bomb exploded but no serious injury or damage was done. Sentenced to 10 years' imprisonment concurrent for arson and throwing an explosive substance with 30 months' concurrent for inflicting grievous bodily harm.

Held, that the present case was more serious than *Meade* to which the court was referred. M had previous convictions for offences involving petrol bombs and had returned to the scene of his previous act. However, sentences of 10 years were excessive and could be reduced to seven years (*R.* v. *Meade* [1983] C.L.Y. 766 cited).

R. *v.* MAHOOD (1986) 8 Cr.App.R.(S.) 188, C.A.

869. Arson—whether appropriate for judge to refer to the danger to other people inherent in the offence during sentencing

B pleaded guilty to one offence of criminal damage and one of arson. He threw paint over the motor caravan of a man with whom he was in dispute then went in to the man's house when the other was away and started a fire. The total damage was £11,600. Sentenced to 30 months' youth custody for arson with three months' concurrent for criminal damage. In passing sentence the sentencer referred to the fact that the house next door to the house set on fire was occupied.

Held, that the sentencer was in error in referring to the family next door. However, on the basis of sentencing for the offence he had committed alone, the sentence was perfectly correct.

R. *v.* BROWNSWORD (1986) 8 Cr.App.R.(S.) 139, C.A.

870. Assault—death

Where an unlawful blow leads to death, the sentence should contain an element to reflect that fact rather than as though the offence was a simple unlawful wounding.

R. *v.* RUBY, *The Times,* July 29, 1987, C.A.

871. Attempted buggery of 13 year-old boy—no consent.

S was convicted of indecent assault and attempted buggery. He had taken a 13 year-old boy into a shed and committed various acts of indecency with the boy's consent. He then attempted buggery with the boy against his will. S later threatened to kill the boy if he told anyone what had occurred. Sentenced to five years' imprisonment for attempted buggery and six months' concurrent for indecent assault.

Held, that although there were reported decisions that indicated that sentences as low as two years' or 30 months' imprisonment may be appropriate, this was a very different case. S had destroyed any mitigation available to him by his failure to show any contrition and forcing the boy to give evidence. The sentence was appropriate.

R. *v.* SHERIDAN (1986) 8 Cr.App.R.(S.) 10, C.A.

872. Basis for sentence—plea tendered on particular basis—facts incapable of belief

Where a guilty plea is tendered on the basis of facts that are manifestly false the sentencer may sentence on the basis of the natural inference from the evidence without requiring the prosecution to call evidence.

H pleaded guilty to burglary. He had been the driver of a car that had deposited two men who burgled a house and H returned to collect them some two hours later. He claimed that he did not know that a burglary had been planned until he came back to collect the men. He pleaded guilty because the theft was a continuing offence.

Held, that this was not a *Newton* type case as the story put forward by H was so manifestly false the judge was entitled to reject it without the need for the prosecution to call evidence (*R.* v. *Newton* [1983] C.L.Y. 815 distinguished).

R. *v.* HAWKINS (1985) 7 Cr.App.R.(S.) 351, C.A.

873. Bomb hoax—demanding money from bank

A pleaded guilty to demanding money with menaces, possessing an imitation bomb and possessing an imitation firearm when committing an offence. She went into a bank with her face concealed and pushed a note at a cashier which demanded cash and stated that she had a limpet mine under the counter. She then showed the cashier the imitation bomb. The cashier handed over £1,600 but A was detained by another customer. A claimed that she was trying to draw attention to the plight of the starving but the sentencer heard evidence and declined to accept the story. Sentenced to five years' imprisonment on each count concurrent.

Held, that the offence was a terrifying one and the sentences took the mitigating circumstances of A's good character and plea of guilty into account.

R. *v.* AYTON (1986) 8 Cr.App.R.(S.) 232, C.A.

874. Burglary—with intent to rape

R was convicted of burglary with intent to rape and indecent assault. He pleaded guilty to burglary with intent to steal. He broke into a first floor flat occupied by a man, his pregnant wife and their young daughter. The husband left to get help in which time R entered, threatened the woman and her daughter to keep quiet and went round the flat looking for things to steal. He then returned and indecently assaulted the wife by touching her thigh before the police arrived and arrested him after a struggle. He had an appalling record with several previous convictions for sexual offences including rape. Sentenced to eight years' imprisonment for burglary with intent to rape with concurrent sentences for other offences.

Held, that the sentence was not wrong in principle nor excessive.

R. *v.* REED (1986) 8 Cr.App.R.(S.) 152, C.A.

875. Casting corrosive fluid

G pleaded guilty to possessing an offensive weapon (a machete) and casting corrosive fluid with intent. After an argument at a pool club, G went home and returned with the machete and a bottle containing nitric and sulphuric acid. He threw some of the acid into the man's face, causing superficial burns over a large part of the face and neck and some damage to an eye. G then ran off to hide in a police station. Sentenced to five years' imprisonment.

Held, that the sentence was appropriate for offences of this sort.

R. *v.* GRANT (LANGFORD) (1986) 8 Cr.App.R.(S.) 4, C.A.

876. Causing death by reckless driving—driver subject to epileptic fits—warned not to drive

W was convicted of causing death by reckless driving. He was aged 60 and suffered from epilepsy. He had been warned in 1974 and 1975 not to drive. He continued to drive, being unwilling to accept he was unfit to do so. His car mounted the pavement and killed a 13-year-old girl. Sentenced to 12 months' immediate imprisonment and disqualified until he passed a driving test.

Held, that in the circumstances, W. was wicked to continue to drive. He saw the risk but nevertheless took a chance on avoiding disaster. He came within one of the categories of reckless driving that deserved severe punishment. Although an immediate custodial sentence was necessary, six months' imprisonment would be sufficient (*R.* v. *Boswell* [1984] C.L.Y. 831 considered).

R. *v.* WEST (WILLIAM JOHN) 8 Cr.App.R.(S.) 5, C.A.

877. Causing death by reckless driving—excessive speed—driving while affected by alcohol

J pleaded guilty to causing death by reckless driving and taking a conveyance without consent. He had taken a parked car and, having been drinking, took his girlfriend out in the car. He took a bend at excessive speed and lost control of the car. His girlfriend, who was pregnant by him was killed. Sentenced to four years' youth custody.

Held, several of the aggravating factors set out in *R.* v. *Boswell* [1984] C.L.Y. 831 were present—driving a stolen car without a valid driving licence, driving after drinking and at an excessive speed. However, given the mitigating factors—J's plea and his remorse—the sentence was too severe and would be reduced to two years' youth custody (*R.* v. *Boswell* [1984] C.L.Y. 831 discussed).

R. *v.* JOHN (CLIFFORD LEONARD) (1985) 7 Cr.App.R.(S.) 208, C.A.

878. Causing grievous bodily harm with intent—squirting corrosive fluid into the face

R pleaded guilty to causing grievous bodily harm with intent. He and another had gone to the house of a man suspected of having an affair with R's wife. When the man answered the door R squirted ammonia into his face. The man had lost the use of one eye and would require out-patient treatment indefinitely. Sentenced to five years' imprisonment.

Held, that this was a cowardly attack. It also involved deliberation and no immediate provocation by the victim. The sentence was appropriate (*R.* v. *Cole* [1984] C.L.Y. 930 and *R.* v. *Ali* [1984] C.L.Y. 925 considered).

R. *v.* RADFORD (1986) 8 Cr.App.R.(S.) 60, C.A.

879. Cheque fraud—possession of stolen travellers' cheques

L pleaded guilty to having custody of a false instrument with intent to use it, and of going equipped to cheat. He had been found to be in possession of nine false passports which he intended to use to encash £20,000 worth of stolen travellers' cheques. Sentenced to five years' imprisonment.

Held, dismissing *R.* v. *Copeland* [1983] C.L.Y. 787 and *R.* v. *Silverman* [1983] C.L.Y. 834, that insufficient allowance had been made for L's guilty plea. The sentence would be reduced to a total of three and a half years (*R.* v. *Copeland* [1983] C.L.Y. 787 and *R.* v. *Silverman* [1983] C.L.Y. 834 discussed).

R. *v.* LIMA (1985) 7 Cr.App.R.(S.) 330, C.A.

880. Committal for sentence in respect of summary offences—necessity for Crown Court to observe the limitations on the aggregate sentence available to the magistrates court

C was subject to a suspended sentence imposed by the Crown Court. He pleaded guilty in the magistrates' court to four offences of driving with excess alcohol: offences which made him liable to the activation of the suspended sentence. He was committed to the Crown Court under the Powers of Criminal Courts Act 1973, s.24(2) to be dealt with in respect of the suspended sentence and under the Criminal Justice Act 1967, s.56 for sentence on the excess alcohol offences. Sentenced to three months' imprisonment for each excess alcohol offence all consecutive, and the suspended sentence was activated as to three months, consecutive, making a total of 15 months in all.

Held, that on a committal under s.56, the Crown Court was empowered to impose only the same sentence as would have been within the jurisdiction of the magistrates' court. The Magistrates' Court Act 1980, s.133(1) limited the aggregate sentence to six months (where all the offences were summary). It was unfortunate that 20 years later courts were still falling into the same trap. The sentences were quashed and the Court substituted consecutive sentences of three months on the first two charges and concurrent terms on the second two charges making a total of six months with the suspended sentence consecutive.

R. *v.* CATTELL (1986) Cr.App.R.(S) 268, C.A.

881. Community service order—failure to comply with order—suspended sentence imposed—whether length of sentence should allow for the part of the original order which was completed

W pleaded guilty to handling stolen property. He assisted a burglar to remove stolen property from one address to another and was sentenced to 180 hours community service. After completing 141 hours, he was arrested and remanded in custody for several months on another matter on which the prosecution offered no evidence. He did not resume the community service order and was brought before the magistrates' court for breach of the order. These proceedings were adjourned and he again failed to resume. He then came before the Crown Court where the order was revoked and he was sentenced to 12 months' imprisonment suspended for two years for the original offence.

Held, that the sentencer had erred because he knew that the sentence was going to be suspended. The fact that W had completed 80 per cent. of the community service order made the sentence of 12 months' excessive and a sentence of three months suspended for two years was substituted (*R.* v. *Paisley* (1979) 1 Cr.App.R.(S.) 196 considered).

R. *v.* WILLIAMS (GERALD) (1986) 8 Cr.App.R.(S.) 230, C.A.

882. Community service order—failure to comply with order—whether custodial sentence should be reduced to allow for completed hours of service

W, of previous good character, pleaded guilty to assault occasioning actual bodily harm. He was seeking shelter, with colleagues, from the rain in a hut on the site where he was working. There was an electric wire with a bare end in the hut which he connected to the door handle so that when a workmate tried to enter he received an electric shock but was not seriously or permanently injured. He was sentenced to 180 hours community service but completed only 68½ hours and failed to attend regularly thereafter despite warnings. Sentenced in the Crown Court to two months' imprisonment with no credit given for completing one third of the order satisfactorily.

Held, that the revocation of the order and imposition of a term of imprisonment could not be criticised. However, some credit ought to have been given for the satisfactory completion of one third of the community service order. The period of imprisonment served (about two and a half weeks) was sufficient and the sentence was varied to allow for his immediate release.

R. *v.* WHITTINGHAM (1986) 8 Cr.App.R.(S.) 116, C.A.

883. Community service order—whether magistrates' court has power to commit offender for sentence on failure to comply with order

D pleaded guilty before the Crown Court to an indictment charging aggravated burglary and criminal damage. He was sentenced for these offences to a total of two years' imprisonment. Two suspended sentences of six months were activated consecutively. A further term, of 18 months' imprisonment was imposed in respect of an offence of burglary for which he had been ordered by a magistrates' court to perform 200 hours community service. The magistrates' court which made the order had revoked the order on the grounds that the appellant had failed to comply with its requirements and committed him to the Crown Court for sentence, purporting to act under the Powers of Criminal Courts Act 1973, s.16(3)(*a*) and the Magistrates' Courts Act 1980, s.37.

Held, that it had been held in *R.* v. *Worcester Crown Court and Birmingham Magistrates' Court, ex p. Lamb* [1986] C.L.Y. 782 that where an offender, who has been ordered to perform community service by a magistrates' court appears before the court for non-compliance with the order, the provisions of s.16(3)(*a*) allowing the court to revoke the order and deal with the offender for the original offence in any manner in which it could have dealt with him if the community service order had not been made, did not extend to allow a committal for sentence: the magistrates' court must pass sentence itself. The sentence imposed by the Crown Court in respect of the offence for which the community service order had been made was quashed. Having regard to the circumstances of the other matters for which D was before the Crown Court, the Court reduced the total sentence by six months.

R. *v.* DANIELS (1986) 8 Cr.App.R.(S.) 257, C.A.

884. Compensation order—basis of ability to pay compensation disappearing by time of appeal—whether compensation order to be quashed on appeal

Offences of dishonesty. 18 months' imprisonment and ordered to pay £1,200 compensation. Had offered to pay compensation from proceeds of business he was about to start. Gave specific instructions to counsel as to instalments he could pay, building up from £10 per week to £25 per week. Business failed as a result of adverse publicity following the hearing. Appeal dismissed: sentencer entitled to rely upon what counsel told court. Subsequent events may justify variation or recission of order if justice so required but this was not such a case.

R. *v.* SLACK [1987] Crim.L.R. 428, C.A.

885. Compensation order—duty to verify information as to means of offender before mitigating on basis that means to pay compensation are available

B pleaded guilty to theft on seven counts, with 83 similar offences taken into consideration. He had stolen property worth £8,192 from his employers over a period of two years. Sentenced to six months' imprisonment suspended and ordered to pay £3,200 compensation. That was in the basis of information provided by B's counsel that his employers still retained £3,000 of his wages. In fact, only £604 of wages were owing, all of which had been paid over to B. The employers received no compensation. B, on supplementary benefit, had no money to pay them with.

Held, that instructions had been taken orally on the day of the trial but nothing had been done to verify that information. Counsel should be wary of accepting instructions of that kind. The court should be careful to ensure there was in fact a proper financial basis for payment of compensation. There was no alternative but to quash the compensation order.

R. *v.* BOND (EDWARD) (1986) 8 Cr.App.R.(S.) 11, C.A.

886. Compensation order—examination of means

Before a compensation order may be made a careful examination of the defendant's means is required. Evidence should be given orally or on affidavit.

H pleaded guilty to fraudulent evasion of VAT. It was indicated to the judge that H would be able to pay a compensation order in the full amount. The judge then sentenced

H to 12 months' imprisonment, suspended and order him to pay compensation of £22,900, In fact H was in no position to pay, his liabilities far exceeding his assets. He knew this at the time of sentence but was afraid to say so.

Held, on appeal, that insufficient care had been taken to determine H's means. The court should have had evidence as to his means. If necessary the proceedings should have been adjourned. There was no alternative but to quash the order.

R. *v.* HUISH (1985) 7 Cr.App.R.(S.) 272, C.A.

887. Compensation order—imposed with suspended sentence—whether should be quashed when suspended sentence later activated

Sentenced in 1985 to 12 months' imprisonment, suspended for two years, for theft in 1984 and ordered to pay £2,500 compensation. Failed to pay. Failed to attend means enquiry in proceedings to enforce compensation order. Then lost job and committed further offences leading to a six-months' prison sentence with suspended sentence being activated so he had 12 months to serve with remainder suspended. Leave granted to appeal out of time against compensation order. Order quashed (*R.* v. *Wallis* [1979] C.L.Y. 548 considered).

R. *v.* MATHIESON [1987] Crim.L.R. 511, C.A.

888. Compensation order—offender apparently in possesion of substantial means but no precise evidence available to court—whether compensation order properly made

Offences of dishonesty. Sentence: two years' imprisonment: four months to serve and balance suspended; fines £4,000; compensation £9,000. Evidence at Crown Court showed (a) £1,950 found at B's address; (b) paying-in books showing £31,000 paid into B's account over 18 months; (c) building society books showing total balance over £5,000; (d) B and his wife drove expensive cars. B put no evidence regarding means before Crown Court and his evidence before Court of Appeal lacked completeness and particularity. Appeal dismissed (*R.* v. *Inwood* [1975] C.L.Y. 699 considered).

R. *v.* BOLDEN [1987] Crim.L.R. 431, C.A.

889. Compensation order—payment by instalments—length of repayment period

H pleaded guilty to two offences of theft. She was a bookmaker and over a period of time she stole a total of £6,058 in a sophisticated manner. Sentenced to 100 hours community service and ordered to pay £5,000 compensation at a rate of £200 per month.

Held, that H was fortunate to have received a community service order as opposed to a sentence of imprisonment. The order for payment of £5,000 by instalments of £200 per month was not in accordance with the principles laid down by the Court, as the repayments were larger than H's means justified and would have taken more than two years to repay. The usual maximum period for the payment of compensation was twelve months and counsel for H had indicated that she could afford £120 per month. Accordingly, the compensation order was reduced to £1,440 payable by instalments of £120 per month.

R. *v.* HILLS (PENELOPE ANNE) (1986) 8 Cr.App.R.(S.) 199, C.A.

890. Compensation order—personal injuries

B assaulted X, breaking his nose and causing abrasions, scratches and bruises. Conditional discharge, £475 compensation and £125 prosecution costs to be paid at £25 per month. Compensation reduced to £250: judge not wrong to start by taking Criminal Injuries Compensation Board figures but erred in consideration of B's capacity to pay. Normally, a period of about 12 months should be considered for instalments. Costs and £250 compensation would take B about 15 months.

R. *v.* BROUGHTON [1987] Crim.L.R. 140, C.A.

891. Compensation order—substantial amount—made in assumption that matrimonial home can be sold to realise amount required—whether correct in principle

B pleaded guilty to two counts of obtaining by deception and asked for 44 similar offences to be considered. He claimed supplementary benefit over a period of nearly two years on the basis that he was unemployed and had no other source of income. In fact he was receiving various amounts from tenants of rooms at various houses. Sentenced to 18 months' imprisonment and ordered to pay £6,540.56 compensation with 12 months' imprisonment in default.

Held, that the compensation order had been made on the basis that B had a house which could be sold so that he could satisfy the order but it was not clear that this was the case. The Court had indicated in previous cases that if the matrimonial home was the only asset available to satisfy a compensation order then such an order would be inappropriate. If the sale of the house would result in B's family becoming homeless as the proceeds would be inadequate to provide alternative accommodation, this was a consideration which militated against the making of a compensation order. The order was quashed (*R.* v. *Harrison* (1980) 2 Cr.App.R.(S.) 313 considered).

R. *v.* BUTT (1986) 8 Cr.App.R.(S.) 216, C.A.

892. Compensation order—theft—property recovered intact—whether order appropriate

Agreed to buy houseboat and paid deposit. Agreed property to pass only when balance paid. Before whole balance paid, removed boat. Pleaded guilty to theft. Compensation order in amount of balance owing quashed: vendor did not lose the balance as result of the theft. He still owned the boat and could enforce the contract if he wished (authorities including *R.* v. *Cadamarteri* [1976] C.L.Y. 573 considered).

R. *v.* BOARDMAN [1987] Crim.L.R. 430, C.A.

893. Consecutive sentences—firearms

[Firearms Act 1968 (c.27), s.17(2) and Sched. 6, para. 6.]

M used stolen rifle and pistol to fire at shop windows, a car and an office. Sentence: 12 months' imprisonment for handling and criminal damage, all concurrent; 12 months consecutive for possessing firearm whilst committing a scheduled offence, contrary to s.17(2) of 1968 Act.

Held, that the judge had wrongly construed s.17(2) and para. 6 of Sched. 6 to the Act as obliging him to pass consecutive sentences. Sentences varied to make all concurrent (*R.* v. *Bottomley* [1986] C.L.Y. 877 applied).

R. *v.* McGRATH [1987] Crim.L.R. 143, C.A.

894. Consecutive sentences—pickpocket

D was a central member of a highly professional gang of Chilean pickpockets operating on the Underground. Having escaped arrest for picking a pocket, he was caught attempting to do the same thing again two days later. He was sentenced to three years' imprisonment for conspiracy to steal, with a further consecutive year for the attempt.

Held, that the consecutive sentence was justified by (1) the serious nature of the offence; (2) D's audacity in continuing to offend after his initial near escape; and (3) by D's involvement in and importance to the gang.

R. *v.* ALFARO, *The Times,* January 30, 1987, C.A.

895. Consecutive sentencing—reckless driving and driving while disqualified on same occasion

S pleaded guilty to reckless driving and driving while disqualified. He had been disqualified from driving for six months when seen by police officers driving at excess speed, veering across the road and driving along a footpath at 50 to 60 m.p.h. before driving down a high street on the wrong side of the road. Sentenced to nine months' imprisonment for reckless driving with three months consecutive for driving while disqualified and a suspended sentence of three months activated consecutively.

Held, that concurrent sentences were often appropriate where driving on a single occasion gave rise to more than one offence. Although there are exceptional cases where consecutive sentences were appropriate such as *Wheatley* and *Dillon* this case was not so exceptional and S did not have a very bad driving record. The sentences were ordered to run concurrently (*R.* v. *Jones* [1981] C.L.Y. 525, *R.* v. *Wheatley* [1984] C.L.Y. 750 and *R.* v. *Dillon* [1984] C.L.Y. 749 considered).

R. *v.* SKINNER (1986) 8 Cr.App.R.(S.) 166, C.A.

896. Conspiracy to contravene Copyright Act—making film available for copying by "video pirates"—custodial sentence

Both appellants were convicted of conspiracy to contravene s.21(1)(*a*) of the Copyright Act 1956. The first appellant managed a cinema and arranged for a film to be removed for copying. The second appellant was transporting the film from the cinema to premises where copying equipment was available. Sentenced to nine months' imprisonment.

Held, that a custodial sentence was appropriate but given that both appellants were "fairly low cogs in the machine which arranged for copying and pirating" the sentence was too severe. A short sharp shock was necessary. The sentences would be reduced to enable both men to be released (both having been in custody for three months).

R. *v.* JAGWANI AND JAYES (1985) 7 Cr.App.R.(S.) 281, C.A.

897. Conspiracy to manufacture amphetamine on large scale

M pleaded guilty and B and A were convicted of conspiracy to manufacture amphetamine sulphate. They and others had planned to produce two kilos of the drug per week. The conspiracy had lasted about three months and about two and a half kilos had been marketed. M was sentenced to six years' imprisonment, B and A receiving eight and seven years' imprisonment respectively.

Held, R. v. *Aramah* [1983] C.L.Y. 764 discussed guidelines for class B drugs generally. *R.* v. *Rubinstein* [1982] C.L.Y. 684 was a wholly exceptional case and would not be applicable to these offenders. Although it was accepted that the production of a class B drug was analogous to importing the drug, in this case the offenders were involved in producing the drug as a criminal enterprise. Eight years' was appropriate as the highest sentence and, as the sentencer had seen each of the offenders roles. The sentences would not be altered (*R.* v. *Aramah* [1983] C.L.Y. 764 referred to; *R.* v. *Rubinstein* [1982] C.L.Y. 684 distinguished).

R. *v.* MORGAN (1985) 7 Cr.App.R.(S.) 443, C.A.

898. Conspiracy to manufacture amphetamine on large scale

S was convicted of conspiracy to manufacture a controlled drug. He was arrested, having purchased substantial quantitites of chemicals necessary to manufacture amphetamine. A list of chemicals needed for that purpose was also found. Sentenced to 10 years' imprisonment.

Held, that in *R.* v. *Aramah* [1983] C.L.Y. 764, which dealt with the wholesale importation of Class B drugs, sentences of 10 years' were said to be appropriate for those playing other than a subordinate role. Manufacture was analogous to importing the drug. The value of the drugs which would have been manufactured was between £2 to £7 million. There was sufficient evidence to infer that S was one of the ringleaders. The sentence of 10 years' imprisonment was entirely appropriate—there was not one single mitigating factor (*R.* v. *Aramah* [1983] C.L.Y. 764 considered).

R. *v.* SHAW (1986) 8 Cr.App.R.(S.) 16, C.A.

899. Contempt of court-failure to surrender to bail-subsequent acquittal of drugs offences for which bailed—false documents obtained—whether custodial sentence appropriate

N was convicted summarily by the Crown Court of contempt of court, in the form of a failure to surrender to bail. He had been committed for trial on bail on charges of conspiracy to supply and to possess controlled drugs. Following his release on bail, he went abroad and obtained false documents of identity. He did not attend to take his trial, but returned to England some time after the trial of his co-defendants was concluded. He was tried and acquitted of the charges in respect of which he had been committed for trial on bail. Sentenced to six months' imprisonment and ordered to forfeit £10,000 deposited as security.

Held, that it was necessary to deter other accused persons from leaving the country with which there was no extradition treaty. The sentence could not be criticised

R. *v.* NEVE (1986) 8 Cr.App.R.(S.) 270, C.A.

900. Contempt of court—immediate custodial sentence—exercise of discretion

D, who was subject to a non-molestation injunction, was given an immediate custodial sentence of one month for carrying out a serious assault on P in breach of the order. D appealed contending that in all the circumstances and in reliance upon dicta of the court in the case of *Ansah* v. *Ansah* [1977] C.L.Y. 1567, it was inappropriate to make an order providing for an immediate custodial sentence or if that order was appropriate, that it should be for a much lesser period than one month. *Held,* in allowing D's appeal and reducing the sentence to seven days imprisonment, the court stated that it deprecated references to *Ansah's* case or indeed to any other case as laying down rules which were applicable in all circumstances. Judges who were faced with applications to commit had to exercise their discretion in the light of all the circumstances of the particular case. Whilst the court would accept everything that was said in *Ansah* about the undesirability of a committal order except as a remedy of last resort, it by no means followed that on the first occasion upon which there was an allegation of a breach of an injunction a judge should not make an immediate committal order if the circumstances would otherwise justify it. Furthermore, *Ansah* was a case which was considered by the court before the passing of the Domestic Violence and Matrimonial Proceedings Act 1976 and what was there contemplated was that when that Act came into force, the intermediate stage between making an injunction and committing somebody to prison for contempt of an injunction would be the giving of a power of arrest under that Act by way of reinforcement of the seriousness with which the court regarded any breach of its orders.

GALLAGHER *v.* PATTERSON, October 9, 1986 (C.A.T. No. 855).

901. Contempt of court—threatening a witness

P was found guilty of contempt of court. At his son's trial he had threatened a witness who had already given evidence. Sentenced to 18 months' imprisonment.

Held, that it was a grave contempt of court for which a custodial sentence was inevitable. As the meeting was accidental and there was only one isolated act of contempt the sentence would be reduced to nine months' imprisonment.

R. *v.* PITTENDRIGH (1985) 7 Cr.App.R.(S.) 221, C.A.

902. Contempt of court—threatening witness about to give evidence

M was adjudged guilty of contempt of court when he walked past a witness waiting to give evidence at the trial of his brother for burglary and said "You're in for a seeing to." Sentenced to six months' detention under the Criminal Justice Act 1982, s.9.

Held, that the sentence could not be criticised. People who were required to come to court to give evidence must be able to do so without fear of violence or threat of violence and interference with witnesses would be regarded seriously by the courts.

R. *v.* MALONEY (1986) 8 Cr.App.R.(S.) 123, C.A.

903. Corruption—corruption in private employment—bribes

H, a director of a company, pleaded guilty to one count of corruption and was convicted on four others. He placed an order with a company who supplied inferior quality steel in return for the rewiring of his house. Later on he accepted sums totalling £200,000 for failing to disclose a fraud carried out against his employers by a third party that cost the employers £1¾ million over several years. Sentenced to six months', 12 months', and 2 years' imprisonment to run consecutively.

Held, that it is an oddity that the maximum sentence for this kind of corruption is two years' imprisonment. Having regard to the length of time and number of incidents involved it was right to impose a number of consecutive sentences. (*per* Lawton L.J.: H was lucky that his sentence was no longer than three-and-a-half years.)

R. *v.* HOPWOOD (1985) 7 Cr.App.R.(S.) 402, C.A.

904. Corruption—offering bribe to police officer

O was convicted of corruption. He had been stopped whilst in the passenger seat of a car driven by his 14-year-old son. When the police officer indicated that the boy would be reported for driving without a licence O offered him £50 for a free meal at O's restaurant not to do so. Sentenced to 12 months' imprisonment with six months' suspended.

Held, that in *R* v. *McGovern* (1980) 2 Cr.App.R.(S.) 389 it was said that the maximum term for offences of this sort was two years imprisonment. This case was not as serious as *McGovern's* case. O was a man of good character, the bribe involved only a small sum and the offence O was seeking to avoid by offering the bribe related to his son, not directly to O. Although a custodial sentence is almost inevitable for this sort of offence, the present sentence was too severe and would be reduced to three months' imprisonment to be served immediately.

R. *v.* OZDEMIR (1985) 7 Cr.App.R.(S.) 382, C.A.

905. Counterfeiting—dealing on a substantial scale

E and S pleaded guilty to possessing counterfeit currency with intent to pass or tender. S was found by police in possession of counterfeit notes with a face value of £19,000. He had undertaken to dispose of the notes which had been obtained by E, who was in possession of notes with a face value of £250. A further batch of notes with a face value of £30,000 was to be obtained. S pleaded guilty on another indictment to stealing four cars which he had obtained on a rental agreement and sold. Sentenced to five years' imprisonment and four and a half years' imprisonment respectively.

Held, that counterfeiting offences were always regarded seriously. Apart from the loss and stress to individuals to whom the notes were ultimately passed, they posed a threat to the commercial community. Deterrence was an important factor in sentencing anyone convicted of offences of this kind and personal mitigation must be a matter of secondary importance. The sentences could not be considered excessive (*R.* v. *Howard* [1986] C.L.Y. 859 considered).

R. *v.* EDE and SIDDONS (1986) 8 Cr.App.R.(S.) 246, C.A.

906. Counterfeiting—middle man

G pleaded guilty to counts of dealing with forged currency. He had been found to have about 1,500 forged £5 notes and was arrested when attempting to deliver 500 of them. G claimed that he was not the printer or principal in the operation but merely a middle man or "runner." Sentenced to four years' imprisonment.

Held, that the sentence was too severe given G's role in the counterfeiting operation and should be reduced to two-and-a-half years' imprisonment.

R. *v.* GRIFFITHS (WILLIAM HENRY) (1985) Cr.App.R.(S.) 251, C.A.

907. Counterfeiting—passing single note

P pleaded guilty to tendering counterfeit currency. He made three attempts to pass a counterfeit £20 note. He was not the prime mover in putting the notes into circulation. Sentenced to nine months' imprisonment.

Held, that it would be just to vary the sentence to one of six months' imprisonment with the additional three month's suspended (*R.* v. *Carter* [1984] C.L.Y. 846 referred to).

R. *v.* PICKARD (1985) 7 Cr.App.R.(S.) 279, C.A.

908. Counterfeiting—possessing and uttering counterfeit currency

W, and others, pleaded guilty to having custody or control of counterfeit notes, tendering a counterfeit note and passing a counterfeit note. They were found in possession of notes with a face value of £2,350 after visiting a number of shops where forged notes were tendered. Sentenced in each case to 30 months' imprisonment and order to pay compensation and an order was made for the forfeiture of a car belonging to one of them.

Held, that the present case was not as serious as *Huntingdon* and the sentence was reduced to 21 months, partly suspended in the case of the appellant of previous good character so as to allow his immediate release (*R.* v. *Horrigan* [1986] C.L.Y. 809 and *R.* v. *Huntingdon* [1986] C.L.Y. 860 considered).

R. *v.* WAYNE (1986) 8 Cr.App.R.(S.) 141, C.A.

909. Counterfeiting—possession of substantial quantity of counterfeit notes

R pleaded guilty to having control of counterfeit currency. He had been found in possession of 460 forged £50 notes (face value £23,350). He was looking after the notes for his brother. Sentenced to 30 months' imprisonment.

Held, that there has been a tendency for offences of this sort to increase and so there may soon be a need for change in sentencing policy. Comparing this case with *R.* v. *Howard* , R was not concerned in uttering the notes but a far greater quantity of notes was involved. The sentence was not excessive (*R.* v. *Howard* [1986] C.L.Y. 859 considered).

R. *v.* ROBERTS (PHILEMON) (1986) 8 Cr.App.R.(S.) 2, C.A.

910. Counterfeiting—tendering small number of counterfeit notes

Z pleaded guilty to two charges of tendering counterfeit notes, two of deception and one of possessing a class B drug. A further offence of tendering a counterfeit note was taken into consideration. He had tendered the counterfeit notes in public houses on the same evening in payment for drinks. When arrested he was found in possession of a small amount of cannabis. He claimed that he had bought the two £50 notes for £40. Sentenced to three and a half years' imprisonment on each count of tendering and deception, all concurrent, with three months' concurrent for possession of cannabis. In addition, a suspended sentence of six months was activated to run consecutively and he was sentenced to three months consecutive for an offence for which he was on probation.

Held, that tendering counterfeit notes was always a serious offence but the total sentence in the present case of four years and three months was too long. The sentences of three and a half years were reduced to two and a half years so that the total was three years and three months (*R.* v. *Horrigan* [1986] C.L.Y. 809, R. v. *Huntingdon* [1986] C.L.Y. 860 and *R.* v. *Howard* [1986] C.L.Y. 859 considered).

R. *v.* ZOABIR (1986) 8 Cr.App.R.(S.) 206, C.A.

911. Criminal damage—causing criminal damage in course of political demonstration—previous convictions for similar offences

Those who insist on persistently breaking the law must expect to be punished even if acting out of honestly held beliefs.

F was convicted of criminal damage. Together with other women she had cut the fence of the R.A.F. station at Greenham Common as part of a protest. She had a number of previous convictions for similar offences although she had not been sentenced to imprisonment. She indicated that she would continue to offend whatever the Court did. Sentenced to 12 months' imprisonment.

Held, that F was a persistent offender and must expect to be punished. She had forfeited any mitigating features by contesting the case at the Crown Court to air her views. An immediate custodial sentence was appropriate but that imposed was too long. The sentence would be varied so that six months of the sentence would be suspended.

R. *v.* FRANCIS (ANNE) (1985) 7 Cr.App.R.(S.) 222, C.A.

912. Custodial sentence—judge's comments

It is not part of a judge's function when passing a sentence of imprisonment to make known his views on the conditions under which the sentence should be served.

R. *v.* SMITH (PASCOE DONALD), *The Times,* October 6, 1987, C.A.

913. Dangerous offender with personality disorder—life imprisonment—whether proper course

Where it is clear that an offender suffers from personality disorder and a bed is available in a secure hospital for him then the proper course is to impose a hospital order together with an indefinite restriction.

H was convicted of two counts of rape. He had raped two women in their homes using violence and threats to kill. He was diagnosed as suffering from schizophrenia and a severe personality disorder. Although a bed was available for him at a secure hospital the judge elected to pass a sentence of life imprisonment.

Held, that that was not the proper course to take. In circumstances such as these a hospital order should be made together with a restriction order without limit of time under the provisions of sections 37 and 41 of the Mental Health Act 1983.

R. *v.* HOWELL (SEYMOUR JOSEPH) (1985) 7 Cr.App.R.(S.) 360, C.A.

914. Deferred sentence—sentencing outside six-month limit

[Powers of the Criminal Courts Act 1973 (c.62), s.1(2).]

A magistrate erred in sentencing a defendant on a deferred sentence four days after the expiry of the six-month time limit in s.1(2) of the Powers of the Criminal Courts Act 1973.

R. *v.* WEST LONDON STIPENDIARY MAGISTRATE, *ex p.* WATTS, *The Times,* May 30, 1987, D.C.

915. Delay in dealing with offender—substantial delay caused by offender's absconding—whether relevant to sentence

Pleaded guilty to robbery in 1976. Had absconded in 1976 whilst on bail. Two accomplices were sentenced in 1976 to five years' imprisonment. Sentence: five years' imprisonment with 12 months concurrent for failing to surrender to bail. Reduced on appeal to two years and 12 months consecutive. Correct sentence in 1976 would have been four years as B played smaller role; would have pleaded guilty then if thought it safe to do so; two years should be deducted to give credit for having changed to law-abiding life since offence. In exceptional circumstances of this case, sentencer was wrong not to take into account period of 10 years since offence, even though delay resulted from B's absconding.

R. *v.* BIRD [1987] Crim.L.R. 517, C.A.

916. Detention centre—taking conveyances without authority.

Age: 18. With others, took cars and drove them fast around a city, colliding several times with each other. Two collided head-on and one car was a write-off. They then drove off in the remaining car which mounted a verge and hit a tree. One previous conviction: attendance centre order and fine.

Held, it was counsel's duty to ask for a social inquiry report to be obtained if he wanted one. Counsel did not do so. The sentencer was entitled to proceed without a report. Total of four months' detention centre upheld. The offences were so serious that a non-custodial sentence could not be justified.

R. *v.* JEARY [1987] Crim.L.R. 283, C.A.

917. Discount for guilty plea—where defendant disputes prosecution version of facts

Wounding with intent to do grievous bodily harm charged. Plea of guilty to unlawful wounding. Caused wound to wife with knife extending from mouth to ear. Had previously collected the knife from his home. Reported his offence to police immediately. One previous conviction for minor offence. After trial of issues judge rejected J's claim that wounding was reckless rather than intentional but accepted J had not collected the knife from home intending to injure his wife. Three years' imprisonment reduced to two in view of provocation and fact that maximum sentence five years. Little (though some) credit for guilty plea appropriate since J did little or nothing to assist in detection of the case by his plea, as conviction would have been inevitable.

R. *v.* JAUNCEY [1987] Crim.L.R. 215, C.A.

918. Disqualification from driving—careless driving—whether resulting death relevant to period of disqualification

M, aged 19 and of previous good character, was acquitted of causing death by dangerous driving but pleaded guilty to careless driving. He was driving with three other students in his father's car when he lost control of the car and collided with a stone wall. One of the passengers was killed. Fined £150 and disqualified from driving for two years. The Judge observed that the disqualification was the real punishment and that he could not ignore the death of the passenger.

Held, that the Judge erred in taking into account the death of the passenger. The disqualification could not be removed altogether, but would be reduced to six months (*R.* v. *Krawec* [1985] C.L.Y. 3001 considered).

R. *v.* MacCAIG (1986) 8 Cr.App.R.(S.) 77, C.A.

919. Disqualification from driving—disqualification imposed in conjunction with imprisonment—whether appropriate for disqualification to extend beyond expected period of custody under sentence

Under 21 years of age. Whilst disqualified, took car from car park, obtained petrol from garage without paying, drove dangerously for 18 miles, chased by police cars and collided with other cars. Various previous convictions including attempted robbery and reckless driving. 12 months' youth custody and four years' disqualification upheld, though G was keen on and made his living in connection with cars. Safety of public had to be considered.

R. *v.* GIBBONS [1987] Crim.L.R. 349, C.A.

920. Disqualification from driving—disqualification imposed in conjunction with imprisonment—whether appropriate for disqualification to extend beyond expected period of custody under sentence

Convicted of driving whilst disqualified. Pleaded guilty to theft. 12 months' imprisonment for theft upheld. Six year disqualification reduced to three. 17 previous convictions, including six for driving whilst disqualified. Three years marked gravity of the driving whilst disqualified.

R. *v.* MATTHEWS [1987] Crim.L.R. 348, C.A.

921. Disqualification from driving—extending for substantial period beyond expected date of release from custodial sentence—whether appropriate

W was convicted of driving while disqualified. He had five previous convictions in respect of eight similar offences. Sentenced to 12 months' imprisonment and disqualified from driving for five years.

Held, that in view of W's change in attitude since the commission of the offence, the sentence of imprisonment was too long and six months of the sentence was suspended. In light of *Hansel*, it was clear that the overhang of the disqualification was too long. It would not be for the benefit of the public or W that there should be so long a period of disqualification which would handicap him in his attempts to rehabilitate himself and lead an honest life. The disqualification was reduced to two years (*R.* v. *Hansel* [1983] C.L.Y. 817 cited).

R. *v.* WEST (ALAN RICHARD) (1986) 8 Cr.App.R.(S.) 266, C.A.

922. Disqualification from driving—vehicle used in commission of crime—sentencer's duty to raise matter

Before disqualifying an offender under the Powers of Criminal Courts Act 1973 (c.62), s.44, the sentencer should give an indication to counsel to enable him to indicate why such a course would be inappropriate.

L and others pleaded guilty to burglary, criminal damage and handling stolen goods. They had driven into a town in four cars, smashed a shop window causing £2,000 worth of damage and stole £80 worth of goods. Sentenced to detention centre orders of two or three months, all were disqualified from driving and two were ordered to pay compensation of £150 and £300.

Held, that the custodial sentences were appropriate. Although there was a power to disqualify the offenders from driving and, in principle the order to disqualify them was not wrong, the sentencer had failed to indicate to counsel that he was considering such a course. Counsel was not allowed to bring to the court's attention matters that may have made the disqualification orders inappropriate. The court should always be anxious to know the affect of disqualification on the offender's prospects of employment. The appellants might reasonably feel a sense of grievance and so the disqualification orders would be quashed. Compensation orders should only be made where the offender had adequate means to pay within a reasonable time. There was no material here on which compensation orders could be based; the two offenders had received custodial sentences. The compensation orders would be quashed.

R. *v.* LAKE (1986) 8 Cr.App.R.(S.) 69, C.A.

923. Divergence between prosecution and defence on facts—guilty plea

Where there was a divergence between the facts put forward by the prosecution and defence on a guilty plea the prosecution was under a duty to bring that divergence to the attention of the judge and remind the judge of the manner in which to resolve such divergence.

A.T. and his brother B.T. pleaded guilty to robbery. The prosecution opened the case on the basis that A.T. and B.T. had both dragged a taxi driver from his taxi and proceeded to beat and kick him. A.T. claimed to have played a peripheral part in the incident that could only have merited a short sentence of imprisonment at worst. B.T. claimed that only punches had been exchanged with the taxi driver. A.T. and B.T. were sentenced to 33 months youth custody the judge having accepted the prosecution version of the events.

Held, allowing A.T. and B.T.'s appeals against sentence, that where there was a divergence between the facts put forward by the prosecution and the defence it was the duty of the prosecution to bring that divergence to the attention of the judge and remind the judge of the methods set out in *R.* v. *Newton* [1983] C.L.Y. 815 for resolving such divergence. The judge, having not taken any steps to resolve the divergence on the facts, was bound to sentence A.T. and B.T. on their version of the events.

R. *v.* TAYLOR (ANDREW); R. *v.* TAYLOR (BRIAN) (1987) 84 Cr.App.R. 202, C.A.

924. Driving whilst disqualified—maximum penalty

P was convicted of driving whilst disqualified. He had a bad criminal record and had a number of convictions for driving whilst disqualified, having been disqualified on several occasions. Sentenced to the maximum of 12 months' imprisonment.

Held, that this was one of the worst cases of its sort. The sentence was entirely appropriate.

R. *v.* PEGRUM (1986) 8 Cr.App.R.(S.) 27, C.A.

925. Driving without due care and attention—maximum penalty imposed

S was convicted of careless driving on an indictment for reckless driving. He and a friend had raced their cars at speeds in excess of 70 m.p.h. for 4½ miles, partly through built up areas, The other car was in a collision and the driver and passenger in that car were killed. S was fined £500 (the maximum) and disqualified for three years.

Held, that this was a bad case of careless driving. The maximum fine was appropriate but the period of disqualification could be reduced to six months.

R. *v.* STEVENS (1985) 7 Cr.App.R.(S.) 346, C.A.

926. Drug importation—belief of importer

An importer who genuinely believed that he was smuggling cannabis, not heroin as was in fact the case, was entitled to some reduction in sentence therefor (*R.* v. *Aramah* [1983] C.L.Y. 764 considered).

R. *v.* BILINSKI, *The Times,* October 19, 1987, C.A.

927. Enforcement notice—prosecution for failure to comply—subsequent application for planning permission—whether sentence should be deferred until decision on planning permission known

Where a defendant pleaded guilty to failing to comply with an enforcement notice but had appealed against refusal of planning permission, the court should defer sentence if the result of the appeal was expected in a matter of weeks.

In September 1983, the appellant erected a mobile home on her field together with a concrete access road. Enforcement notices were served on her and an appeal was unsuccessful. The appellant did not comply with them and summonses were issued. Meanwhile she applied for planning permission which was refused, but appealed against the refusal. The appeal was heard on September 30, 1985 and the decision of the inspector allowing her appeal was given on November 5, 1986. On October 17, 1986, she pleaded guilty to failing to comply with the enforcement notices and the judge refused to adjourn sentence until the outcome of the planning application was known. She was fined £3,000 in total.

Held, that the trial judge erred in refusing to defer the sentence where the result of the appeal was expected within a matter of weeks. The appeal was successful and planning permission was granted and that had an important bearing on the penalty to be applied for the failure to comply with the enforcement notice. In addition, the fine of £3,000 was grossly excessive and more than she could pay. A fine of £100 on each of the two counts was substituted.

R. *v.* NEWLAND (1987) 54 P. & C.R. 222, C.A.

928. Evasion of income tax—substantial sums

T, with previous convictions for dishonesty, pleaded guilty to seven counts of making false statements with intent to prejudice the Revenue. T was a property dealer and over four years had concealed profits from the Revenue, resulting in evasion of liability to pay £48,000 income tax. Before the trial, T had repaid all of the income tax with interest. Sentenced to two years' imprisonment and ordered to pay £2,000 towards prosecution costs.

Held, that those who perpetrate frauds of this nature and to this extent must expect substantial sentences. The sentence of two years' imprisonment was appropriate.

R. *v.* TREVITHICK (1986) 8 Cr.App.R.(S.) 31, C.A.

929. Exportation of prohibited goods—computers to Eastern Bloc

H and another, together with a limited company pleaded guilty to counts of conspiracy to contravene the Customs and Excise Management Act 1979 by exporting to the Soviet Union and other Eastern Bloc countries computer equipment without licences. They expected a profit of about £245,000. H was sentenced to 12 months' imprisonment whilst the company was fined £10,000.

Held, that other countries permitted the export of such goods was irrelevant. The government had decided that it was against the public interest, and H had decided to make a large profit by breaking the law. The sentences were not too severe.

R. *v.* HERBERT (1985) 7 Cr.App.R.(S.) 399, C.A.

930. Extended sentence

P pleaded guilty to burglary. He had broken into dwelling houses and stolen £600 worth of property. P had nine previous convictions, mostly for burglary but had gone without conviction for 13 months following his release from his last sentence. Sentenced to five years' imprisonment certified as an extended sentence.

Held, that the authorities were clear that an extended sentence was only appropriate where the offender made no attempt to rehabilitate himself but had commenced committing offences almost immediately after his release. This was not a case for an extended sentence but, given P's record, the normal sentence for these offences would be a substantial one. The sentence would be quashed and a sentence of four years' imprisonment would be substituted for it (*R.* v. *Bourton* [1985] C.L.Y. 791 applied).

R. *v.* PARKER (KEITH ROBERT) (1985) Cr.App.R.(S.) 242, C.A.

931. Extended sentence—whether appropriate for persistent offender with significant gap in his record between his last release and the beginning of the latest series of offences

Age: 38. Pleaded guilty. Many burglaries over six month period, mostly dwellings. Numerous previous convictions, longest previous sentence 10 years. Had appeared in 1983 for offences in 1979 and was bound over for two years on condition that he returned to Ireland for two years. No further offences during that period but began re-offending after return to England immediately after the two years. Eight years' imprisonment, certified as extended sentence, reduced to five years not certified as extended with nine months consecutive for a Bail Act offence. Extended sentence inappropriate where defendant had tried to go straight for something more than a minimal period.

R. *v.* IBBITSON [1987] Crim.L.R. 352, C.A.

932. Factual basis for sentence—affray—whether appropriate to sentence on basis that offender responsible for individual acts of violence not charged separately in the indictment

Convicted of affray. Sentenced on basis that C had, during the affray, hit two people with a hammer.

Held, that the judge fully entitled to sentence on such basis, though no specific count alleging the assaults with the hammer. Sentence reduced on other grounds (*R.* v. *Solomon and Triumph* [1985] C.L.Y. 863 distinguished).

R. *v.* COOKE [1987] Crim.L.R. 514, C.A.

933. Factual basis for sentence—disputed facts—guilty plea.

M pleaded guilty to assault occasioning actual bodily harm. The prosecution case was that M had waited in a ladies' lavatory and attacked a lady, striking her on the mouth and attempting to put a bicycle tyre around her arms, to rob her. M's version was that he went into the lavatory because he was drunk, there was no motive of theft and he did not use the bicycle tyre in the manner alleged. The sentencer did not resolve this conflict before sentencing M to three years' imprisonment.

Held, that although M's version of the facts was absurd the sentencer should not have proceeded on the prosecution's version alone. He would have heard M's evidence and then, if M's evidence had any credibility heard the evidence of the victim. Alternatively he could have indicated to M that any credit for a guilty plea would be lost if it became necessary for the victim to give evidence. As it was M now had to be sentenced on his version of events. The sentence would be reduced to two years' imprisonment. (*R.* v. *Newton* [1983] C.L.Y. 815 discussed).

R. *v.* MACKENZIE (1985) 7 Cr.App.R.(S.) 441, C.A.

934. Factual basis for sentence—disputed facts—hearing to determine facts—whether hearing necessary where not requested by counsel

S, who was mentally handicapped, pleaded guilty to using a firearm with intent to resist arrest. Armed with an air pistol, he ran into the street pursued by a police officer when the latter came to investigate a complaint. S fell over a verge and the pistol pointed at the officer as he got to his feet. The pistol was discharged at some stage. The officer claimed that S tried to shoot him whereas S claimed that the gun was discharged accidentally.

Held, that if the court was not prepared to sentence on the basis of the defendant's version of the facts then it should proceed to hear evidence as established in *Newton* and extended in *Williams* v. *Another.* The hearing does not depend on consent from counsel for the defendant. The sentencer had erred in not following *Williams* v. *Another* and on the evidence before the court the sentence was reduced from three years to two years. A psychiatric probation order was not appropriate (*R.* v. *Newton* [1983] C.L.Y. 815 and *Williams* v. *Another* (1983) 5 Cr.App.R.(S.) 134 referred to).

R. *v.* SMITH (PHILLIP ANDREW) (1986) 8 Cr.App.R.(S.) 169, C.A.

935. Factual basis for sentence—effect on discount for guilty plea

S pleaded guilty to malicious wounding of X. After hearing evidence on the issue of whether X had consented to the assault, the judge decided that there had been consent to sexual activity but not to force. The judge said that full credit for a guilty plea would not be allowed as S had required the victim to give evidence. Two years' imprisonment upheld: judge's comments were correct.

R. *v.* STEVENS [1987] Crim.L.R. 139, C.A.

936. Factual basis for sentence—importation of cocaine

Concerned in importation of cocaine (street value £2 million). Appellant claimed to be acting as a courier who was paid £3,000 in the belief that the drugs were class B drugs and not cocaine. Evidence showed he had bought a farm for £162,000 and made flights to and from Brazil. Offer by sentencer to defence to have prosecution witnesses called and for defendant to give evidence declined on basis that the sentencer had all necessary evidence before him. 12 years' imprisonment. Appeal dismissed: no duty on sentencer to take more active role in securing a hearing of the evidence. Court could not see what more sentencer could have done, having indicated that he drew the inference from material before him that M was not a mere courier and that he knew he was importing cocaine. (*R.* v. *Williams* [1984] C.L.Y. 727 and *R.* v. *Smith* [1987] C.L.Y. 934 considered).

R. *v.* MOSS [1987] Crim.L.R. 426, C.A.

937. Factual basis for sentence—minor dispute as to facts not affecting sentence—procedures in Newton

B pleaded guilty to theft and common assault. The prosecution alleged he had punched a security officer in the face and struck him with a stick. B claimed that he had merely punched the security officer and threatened him with a stick. The judge referred to B striking the security guard with the stick. It was argued that the issue should have been determined in accordance with *R.* v. *Newton* [1983] C.L.Y. 815.

Held, that the gravamen of the charge was that B had resisted arrest, whether he had actually struck the blows or simply waved his fist and the stick would not affect his sentence. *R.* v. *Newton* dealt with cases where there was a substantial conflict affecting sentence—there should not be a slavish following of its procedures for minor disputes of this sort. Here it was not necessary for the judge to follow the procedure in *Newton* particularly as it was not requested by the defence (*R.* v. *Newton* [1983] C.L.Y. 815 considered).

R. *v.* BENT (1986) 8 Cr.App.R.(S.) 19, C.A.

938. Factual basis for sentence—mitigation—whether court bound to hear evidence

Pleaded guilty to two offences of driving whilst disqualified. In mitigation, gave implausible story that he had been told by D.V.L.C. centre in Swansea that he was free to drive.

Held, reducing W's sentence from maximum to give credit for guilty pleas, that the sentencer had not been bound to allow W to give evidence or to indicate that he was not disposed to believe W's story (*R.* v. *Newton* [1983] C.L.Y. 815 distinguished).

R. *v.* WALTON [1987] Crim.L.R. 512, C.A.

939. Factual basis for sentence—when trial of issues necessary

H pleaded guilty to arson. He had set fire to a boatyard. It was claimed he had been present when the fire was put out, in possession of an extinguisher and covered in powder from it. His counsel declined the judge's offer to try the issue of whether H had helped extinguish the fire, preferring to mitigate simply on the basis that H had been present with an extinguisher when the fire was put out. Three years' imprisonment upheld. The judge had clearly accepted the facts put forward in mitigation but not that H had helped put the fire out.

R. *v.* HOPKINS [1987] Crim.L.R. 204, C.A.

940. Factual basis for sentence—where defendant pleads guilty on certain basis and then gives evidence for prosecution against co-accused

G pleaded guilty to possessing heroin with intent to supply on the basis that he had believed the drug to be cannabis. G then gave evidence for the prosecution against a co-accused, N. When the jury were considering their verdict against N, the judge tried the issue of whether G had believed the drug was cannabis. Counsel for the prosecution outlined the facts against G but called no evidence. G gave evidence in line with that which he had given in N's trial and was not cross-examined. The defence called a customs officer who confirmed that G had never admitted knowing the drug was heroin. The judge found that he was sure G had known the drug was heroin, *inter alia* because of the amount that he was to be paid. Eight years' imprisonment with recommendation for deportation: upheld save that imprisonment reduced to seven years. Judge entitled to try the issue and reach conclusion he did. Where Crown called one defendant as a witness against another, an issue such as that in the present case should be tried after conclusion of co-defendant's trial. Even if Crown felt unable to challenge by evidence defendant's version, he should consider extent to which he could assist court by exploring in cross-examination any feature of defendant's story which required cross-examination.

R. *v.* GHANDI [1987] Crim.L.R. 205, C.A.

941. Fine payable by instalments—term of imprisonment in default—whether term to be expressed as in default of payment of the fine rather than of any one instalment

P pleaded guilty to counts of obtaining £983·50 in benefit by deception with four other offences taken into consideration. Fined £800 payable by weekly instalments of £15 with seven days' imprisonment in default of any one instalment.

Held, that the sentence was justified but where payment by instalments was ordered, the default term should be expressed as in default of the whole sum, not of each instalment. If the offender failed to pay one instalment, he would be liable to serve the whole default term scaled down according to how much of the fine he had paid. The sentence would be varied by substituting a default term of 60 days.

R. *v.* POWER (1986) 8 Cr.App.R.(S.) 8, C.A.

942. Fines—imposed in conjunction with sentences of imprisonment

Police found 253.9 grammes of cannabis resin and £23,000 in cash in and about F's home. F subsequently made admissions of supplying probably about £9,000 worth of cannabis. Sentence: five years' imprisonment, £16,000 fine and £1,800 costs.

Held, having concluded that F came by the money through unlawful dealing, that the judge had not erred in imposing the £16,000 fine (*R.* v. *Ayensu* [1983] C.L.Y. 822 and *R.* v. *Aramah* [1983] C.L.Y. 764 considered).

R. *v.* FOX [1987] Crim.L.R. 518, C.A.

943. Forfeiture—car used to transport drugs—money in offender's possession

[Powers of Criminal Courts Act 1973 (c.62), s.43; Misuse of Drugs Act 1971 (c.38), s.27.]

B had in his car a quantity of cocaine. There was evidence that it had been taped to the underside of one of the car seats. Five years' imprisonment, for possessing a controlled drug with intent to supply and possessing a controlled drug, reduced to four as sentencer wrongly took view B was a "regular full-time dealer". Order of forfeiture of the car under s.43 of the 1973 Act upheld. Order of forfeiture of £1,489 found in B's possession under s.27 of 1971 Act quashed: since, if the money was the proceeds of dealing in drugs, it must have been the proceeds of dealing with drugs other than those found in the car, there was no power to order its forfeiture under s.27.

R. *v.* BOOTHE [1987] Crim.L.R. 347, C.A.

944. Forfeiture—forfeiture of money found in possession of offender—convicted of possession with intent to supply

[Misuse of Drugs Act 1971 (c.38), s.27.]

Admitted supplying small amounts of cannabis to friend over period of months, possessing 2,867 grammes cannabis with intent to supply, offering to supply cannabis to someone who was carrying £1,600 to buy cannabis from C. Sentence: four years' imprisonment; ordered to forfeit £2,520 cash found at C's home, under s.27 of the 1971 Act.

Held, that the forfeiture orders were quashed, since there was no evidence that the cash found related to the offences for which C was being sentenced; imprisonment reduced to three years (*R.* v. *Llewellyn* [1987] C.L.Y. 945 applied).

R. *v.* COX [1987] Crim.L.R. 141, C.A.

945. Forfeiture—money found in possession of drug dealer.

[Misuse of Drugs Act 1971 (c.38), s.27.]

The power to order forfeiture under s.27 of the Misuse of Drugs Act 1971 applies only to property shown to be connected to the offence of which the offender is convicted—not to property that may be used to facilitate the commission of further offences.

L pleaded guilty to possession of cannabis with intent to supply. The police had found quantities of drugs at his home as well as £400 in cash. The trial judge found that L was dealing commercially in the sale of the drugs and that the £400 was to be used to finance purchases of more drugs for resale. Sentenced to nine months' imprisonment and a forfeiture order on the £400 under the Misuse of Drugs Act 1971.

Held, that the forfeiture order could only relate to property shown to be connected with the commission of the offence of which L had been convicted. The £400 was to be used to facilitate further offences but was not related to the cannabis he had in his possession and intended to sell. It could not therefore be the subject of a forfeiture order and that order would be quashed (*R.* v. *Morgan* [1977] C.L.Y. 643, *R.* v. *Ribeyre* [1982] C.L.Y. 826 and *R.* v. *Cuthbertson* [1980] C.L.Y. 526 applied).

R. *v.* LLEWELLYN (KEVIN ANTHONY) (1985) 7 Cr.App.R.(S.) 225, C.A.

946. Forfeiture and deprivation—cash found in possession of drug dealer

[Misuse of Drugs Act 1971 (c.38), s.27.]

Found in flat in possession of cannabis resin and other equipment, such as scales and knife bearing traces of resin. Pleaded guilty to supplying cannabis for £210. Later found in possession of amphetamine. Forfeiture orders made under s.27 of 1971 Act in relation to £1,065 found in baby's changing box and £250 in A's jacket quashed as the sums were not shown to be related to offence of which A was convicted. Accordingly, orders beyond sentencer's powers (*R.* v. *Morgan* [1977] C.L.Y. 643 applied).

R. *v.* ASKEW [1987] Crim.L.R. 584, C.A.

947. Forfeiture and deprivation—cash found in possession of drug dealer

[Powers of Criminal Courts Act 1973 (c.62), s.43.]

Drugs, scales and £9,800 in a plastic bag found in N's flat. Convicted of two counts of possession of controlled drug with intent to supply. Order under s.43 of 1973 Act depriving N of rights in the £9,800 quashed. If the sentencer thought the money was result of past drug trading, he did not have power to make deprivation order (*R.* v. *Slater* [1986] C.L.Y. 603 applied).

R. *v.* NEVILLE [1987] Crim.L.R. 585, C.A.

948. Fraud in breach of trust by professional man—guidelines in *Barrick*

M pleaded guilty to counts of obtaining property by deception. As a dentist he had submitted false remission claims to the National Health Service for patients allegedly exempt from charges, as well as false claims for emergency treatment and inventing a false patient. The total amount obtained was between £6,800 to £10,000 over nine months'. Sentenced to nine months' imprisonment.

Held, that in *R.* v. *Barrick* [1985] C.L.Y. 765 it was said that where professional men betrayed the trust placed in them and stole under £10,000 the appropriate sentence was up to 18 months' imprisonment. Having regard to the gravity of M's offences and the relatively long period of time involved in their commission the sentence of nine months' imprisonment was not too severe (*R.* v. *Barrick* [1985] C.L.Y. 765 discussed).

R. *v.* MOSSOP (1985) 7 Cr.App.R.(S.) 283, C.A.

949. Grievous bodily harm—injuries inflicted by husband on wife—whether occurrence of the assault in a domestic context a mitigation

The husband and wife were separated and living apart. The husband, in a drunken and abusive state visited the wife and seriously assaulted her. He pleaded guilty to inflicting grievous bodily harm. The judge found that the wife's injuries were extremely serious and sentenced the husband to 18 months' imprisonment. The husband appealed.

Held, that the fact that a serious assault occurred in a domestic scene was no mitigation and was no reason for proceedings not to be taken. The idea that serious assaults were rendered trivial because of a relationship of marriage was outdated. The sentence was not too long—the husband was lucky that he did not receive a longer sentence.

R. *v.* CUTTS (1987) 17 Fam.Law 311, C.A.

950. Heroin—small scale dealing

G pleaded guilty to counts of supply and of possessing heroin. He had been arrested with 20 paper wraps of heroin and £375 in cash on his person. He admitted selling heroin to friends and existing addicts. Sentenced to six years' imprisonment.

Held, that in R. v. *Gee* the offender fell somewhere between the small scale social supplier and the small scale professional middle man. So too did the appellant. In the interests of consistency the appellants' sentence should be the same as that in *Gee* although should the menace of heroin continue to increase and should Parliament increase the maximum sentence the court would raise the penalties in cases of this sort. Sentence reduced to four years' imprisonment (*R.* v. *Gee* [1985] C.L.Y. 800 applied).

R. *v.* GUINEY (1985) 7 Cr.App.R.(S.) 200, C.A.

951. Home Office Research Bulletin

The Home Office has published a number of research studies in the *Home Office Research and Planning Unit Research Bulletin No. 23.* The topics covered are: female offenders and social enquiry reports; managing the prisons; Home Office Statistical Department; use of video in court proceedings; compensation by the magistrates' courts for injury; residential aspects of theft of, and damage to, cars; child molestation; senior attendance centres and day centres; burglary, comparison between the U.S.A. and Canada; international comparisons of prison populations. Copies of the bulletin are available from the Information Section, Research and Planning Unit, Queen Anne's Gate, London SW1H 9AT.

952. Importing cocaine

R was convicted of being concerned in the importation of cocaine. He landed from a ship and boarded a train before being arrested in connection with another matter. He subsequently attempted to collect a holdall which he had left on the train, and which had been found to contain 881 grammes of cocaine worth £140,000. Sentenced to nine years' imprisonment.

Held, that the guidelines indicated that for a class A drug, including cocaine, sentence of seven years and upwards were appropriate. There was nothing in this case to take it outside the guidelines and R had not pleaded guilty. The sentence was not wrong in principle or manifestly excessive and the appeal was dismissed (*R.* v. *Aramah* [1983] C.L.Y. 764 and *R.* v. *Martinez* [1986] C.L.Y. 833 considered).

R. *v.* RYAN (1986) 8 Cr.App.R.(S.) 213, C.A.

953. Importing cocaine

V pleaded guilty to importing a controlled drug. He landed at a channel port and went through the green customs channel. He was searched and found to have 177 grammes of cocaine in the sleeve of his jacket which had a value of £26,000. He admitted that he bought the cocaine for £5,000 and that he intended to sell at least part of it. Sentenced to six years' imprisonment.

Held, that this was not the case of a courier, as in *Aramah,* but of a man who was an experienced traveller who had been warned by a previous conviction for a minor offence of importing and who disguised his travelling arrangements. The sentence was not out of line with the guidelines and the appeal was dismissed (*R.* v. *Aramah* [1983] C.L.Y. 764 and *R.* v. *Parada and Rodriguez* [1984] C.L.Y. 767 considered).

R. *v.* VAN HUBBARD (1986) 8 Cr.App.R.(S.) 228, C.A.

954. Importing substantial quantity of cocaine

D pleaded guilty to being concerned with the importation of cocaine. He had been arrested carrying almost three kilogrammes of 80 per cent. pure cocaine, valued at about £475,000. Sentenced to 10 years' imprisonment.

Held, that this was large scale importation of a class A drug. The sentence of 10 years' imprisonment fell within the guidelines set by *R.* v. *Aramah* and was appropriate (*R.* v. *Aramah* [1983] C.L.Y. 764 applied).

R. *v.* DARBY (MARTIN DAVID) (1986) 8 Cr.App.R.(S.) 33, C.A.

955. Incest—grandfather with granddaughter—previous offences

H pleaded guilty to incest and indecent assault. He admitted having sexual intercourse and committing acts of indecency and indecent assault with his granddaughter (aged between 10 and 11) on a number of occasions. He made the girl swear on her mother's life not to tell anyone what had been done. H had been sentenced to four years' imprisonment for incest with his daughter in 1966. Sentenced to seven years' imprisonment.

Held, that the sentence was appropriate and took account of the few mitigating factors in the case, including H's plea of guilty.

R. *v.* HARDCASTLE (1985) Cr.App.R.(S.) 270, C.A.

956. Incest carried on over long period of years—appropriate sentence

H, a man of 57, pleaded guilty to two counts of incest. Over a period of 18 years, he regularly had intercourse with his daughter beginning when she was 16. He and his wife separated when the daughter was three and the daughter lived with him. There was no violence or threats but the daughter claimed that she feared that she would be beaten if she refused. She had sexual intercourse with another person before this time. At a later stage, father and daughter lived together as man and wife but eventually the daughter decided to marry another man and H threatened to kill her. The matter was reported to police by his daughter's daughter. Sentenced to three years' imprisonment on each count concurrent.

Held, that the real gravity of the offence was when the association started. The Court could not take the view that the sentence should be mitigated by the fact that the girl had some sexual experience before the association began. She should have had the guidance that she was entitled to expect as a child. Taking all matters into account, the element of corruption during the later period was less serious. The sentence on the first count was reduced to two years and the sentence on the second count, which reflected the end of the period, was reduced to six months to run concurrently (*R.* v. *Moores* (1980) 2 Cr.App.R.(S.) 317 and *R.* v. *Darby* (1981) 3 Cr.App.R.(S.) 219 cited).

R. *v.* HADIGATE (1986) 8 Cr.App.R.(S.) 273, C.A.

957. Indecent assault—choirmaster on choirboy

R pleaded guilty to two counts of indecent assault. R was a choirmaster providing choirboys with a corduroy uniform. R had a fetish for corduroy. He invited one of the choirboys to his home to try on a uniform in front of a video camera. R then assaulted him by stroking him through the clothing and seizing the boy's genitals. Sentenced to 12 months' imprisonment, with six to serve and the balance suspended.

Held, that the sentence was correct and appropriate. Children must be protected and R had grossly abused his position of trust.

R. *v.* RHODES (1985) 7 Cr.App.R.(S.) 341, C.A.

958. Indecent assault—man of previous good character—nine-year-old girl

K, a 47-year-old man of previous good character, pleaded guilty to two counts of indecent assault on a girl aged nine. Each offence involved touching the girl's vagina whilst masturbating. The girl was a daughter of a friend of K. There was no use of force or penetration. Sentenced to three years' imprisonment.

Held, that although this was a serious case as K was in a position of trust and the offences had occurred over a long period, there were mitigating features, the most important of which was K's guilty plea. The sentence was too harsh and would be reduced to two years' imprisonment.

R. *v.* KEMPSTER (1986) 8 Cr.App.R.(S.) 74, C.A.

959. Indecent assault—on boy—preventive sentence

Aged 22. Convicted of indecently assaulting boy aged eight. Accosted the boy returning home from errand, pulled boy's clothes down and sucked his penis. boy screamed and mother came to find him. Several previous convictions, some similar. H had deep-rooted personality disorder, put own gratification first, did not learn and did not consider others' well-being. Nine years' imprisonment upheld. Court could not pass preventive sentence on persistent offender save by using statutory extended sentence powers. Nevertheless, court have regard to protection of public in passing non-extended sentence on sexual offender (*R.* v. *Gooden* [1980] C.L.Y. 571 and *R.* v. *Houghton* [1987] C.L.Y. 963 considered).

R. *v.* HEWSON [1987] Crim.L.R. 146, C.A.

960. Indecent assault—on young boy by woman—whether custodial sentence appropriate

H, a young woman, pleaded guilty to indecent assault and four counts of indecency with children. H indecently assaulted the three-year-old son of a neighbour by masturbating him, biting his penis and inserting a finger into his anal passage. She also invited him to fondle her indecently. Sentenced to 12 months' youth custody for the indecent assault.

Held, that H was not in need of psychiatric treatment. Whilst a probation order would be in her best interests, the court had a duty to ensure that the public interest was considered. Sexual abuse of young children is a matter of public concern and in a serious case such as this the court had no alternative to imposing a custodial sentence. The sentence was upheld. The court did not approve of the practice of imposing no separate penalty on other counts in the indictment.

R. *v.* HANCOCK (1986) 8 Cr.App.R.(S.) 159, C.A.

961. Indecent assault—on young boys

J pleaded guilty to three counts of indecently assaulting a male person and one of indecency with a child. He committed acts of indecency against four boys aged respectively three, five, 10 and 11, which included acts of masturbating them and sucking the penis of two of them on a number of occasions. He had previous convictions for similar offences. Sentenced to five years' imprisonment.

Held, that the sentence was on the high side but not so high as to be the subject of criticism (*R.* v. *Willis* [1975] C.L.Y. 714 considered).

R. *v.* JANAWAY (1986) 8 Cr.App.R.(S.) C.A.

962. Indecent assault on young boys by man of 50 of previous good character—whether imprisonment appropriate

G, of previous good character, pleaded guilty to two counts of taking indecent photographs and two of indecent assaults on a male person. He took a number of indecent photographs of a boy aged eight with whose family he had brcome friendly and indecently assaulted a number of boys aged about 10 when he was helping at a Cub group camp. The assaults were not of the gravest nature. Sentenced to 12 months' imprisonment on each count of indecent assault and four months on each count of taking an indecent photograph, all concurrent.

Held, that the public expected that courts would impose an immediate sentence of imprisonment, notwithstanding the good character of the offender, for offences of this kind save in the most exceptional case. The sentences were not manifestly excessive individually or in total and the appeal was dismissed.

R. *v.* GAVIN (1986) 8 Cr.App.R.(S.) 211, C.A.

963. Indecent assault—on young boys by man with record of persistent offending

H, aged 27, pleaded guilty to two offences of indecent assault. He established a friendship with a woman through use of his CB radio and later went to stay in her home. He indecently assaulted her nine-year-old son and an eight-year-old son of one of her friends. Each of the assaults consisted of touching the boy's penis, ceasing when the boy objected. He had previous convictions for similar offences including one buggery and had received sentences of up to 30 months imprisonment. A social inquiry report indicated that although he recognised it was illegal, he did not feel it was morally wrong and he was likely to repeat the offences. Sentenced to six years' imprisonment concurrent on each count with six months consecutive for an offence for which he was on probation.

Held, that the total sentence could be said to be too severe for the offences although there was a need to protect the public. Sentence reduced to four years' imprisonment with six months consecutive. An extended sentence imposed under the statutory procedure would not be interfered with if he offended again (*R.* v. *Gooden* [1980] C.L.Y. 571 considered).

R. *v.* HOUGHTON (1986) 8 Cr.App.R.(S.) 80, C.A.

964. Juvenile—appeal to Crown Court—adjournment—juvenile becoming adult during adjournment and while appeal pending—whether lawful to impose "adult" sentence

[Magistrates' Courts Act 1980 (c.43), s.10(1)(3); Supreme Court Act 1981 (c.54), s.48(2)(4).]

It is an abuse and unlawful for a Crown Court to adjourn an appeal against sentence so that by the time the appeal comes on for hearing a juvenile has become an adult.

D, aged 20, pleaded guilty, *inter alia,* to two charges of assault and was sentenced by the magistrates to four months' detention. He appealed. The Crown Court took the view that custodial sentences were appropriate, but that they could be suspended. In order to circumvent the fact that D was still a juvenile the Crown Court adjourned sentence until D was 21, and then passed a suspended sentence. The prosecutor appealed, supported by counsel for D.

Held, that the Crown Court had acted unlawfully. The power to adjourn may only be exercised judicially, which was not the case here. Appeal allowed (*R.* v. *St. Albans Crown Court, ex p. Cinnamond* [1981] C.L.Y. 396 not followed).

ARTHUR *v.* STRINGER (1987) 84 Cr.App.R. 361, C.A.

965. Juvenile—detention—robbery

Aged 15, P followed girl and attacked her with a piece of concrete causing cuts and bruises to her head. Had previously burgled the petrol station where the girl worked. No significant previous convictions. Two and a half years' detention under s.53(2) of the Children and Young Persons Act 1933 for robbery upheld. 6 months' youth custody concurrent for burglary quashed with no separate penalty imposed (*R.* v. *Fairhurst* [1987] C.L.Y. 1079 applied).

R. *v.* PAWAR [1987] Crim.L.R. 279, C.A.

966. Juvenile—detention—whether power to impose

[Children and Young Persons Act 1933 (c.12), s.53(2).]

The power to order detention of a juvenile under the Children and Young Persons Act 1933, s.53(2) is not available where the juvenile has been committed for sentence under the Magistrates' Court Act 1980, s.37.

M, aged 16 was convicted on indictment of rape and indecent assault. He was committed to the care of a local authority for preparation of a social enquiry report. During that period he robbed a woman. He admitted the offence before a juvenile court who committed him for sentence to the Crown Court. Sentenced to two years' detention under the Children and Young Persons Act 1933, s.53(2) for the rape and 12 months' detention consecutive for the robbery.

Held, that there was no power to impose a detention under the Children and Young Persons Act 1933 on a committal for sentence. In those circumstances the Court could vary the sentence to one of 12 months' youth custody but that was not a desirable step as the methods of release on licence differ. Alternatively the Court could quash the 12 months' detention and the two-year detention and pass a term of three years' detention in respect of the rape. This would mean that the appellant would not be dealt with more severely than in the court below and so the Court could adopt this course under the Criminal Appeal Act 1968, s.11(3). Accordingly the sentence for rape would be varied to three years' detention with no separate sentence for the robbery. (*R.* v. *Gaskin* [1985] C.L.Y. 755 dismissed).

R. *v.* McKENNA (1985) 7 Cr.App.R.(S.) 348, C.A.

967. Juvenile—detention—wounding with intent

W, aged 16, was convicted of wounding with intent. He had stabbed a man in the abdomen causing a near-fatal wound. He had a poor history, including offences involving violence. He was sentenced to eight years' detention under the Children and Young Persons Act 1933.

Held, that eight years' amounted to half of W's age and was too long a time having regard to his age. The sentence would be reduced to six years' detention. No further reduction was possible.

R. *v.* WARWICK (1985) 7 Cr.App.R.(S.) 354, C.A.

968. Juvenile—long-term detention

Where the court is dealing with an offender who is a danger only in the sense that he will not refrain from committing offences (rather than in the sense of being violent) the sentence of detention should be no greater than that which would have been imposed had he qualified for youth custody of over 12 months.

H (aged 16) pleaded guilty to two counts of burglary. He and others stole some £180 from the homes of old people. He had previously served 12 months' youth custody and other sentences for similar offences. Sentenced to five years' detention under Children and Young Persons Act 1933, s.53(2).

Held, that the term of detention was an upper limit. There was power to release him at any time during the course of the sentence. As H was not a violent person but was a danger because he was a persistent offender he should be dealt with as if he could be sentenced to greater than 12 months' youth custody. The jump from 12 months' youth custody to five years' detention was too great—four years' would be the appropriate upper limit.

R. *v.* HENRY (1985) 7 Cr.App.R.(S.) 434, C.A.

969. Juvenile—long-term detention—arson

[Children and Young Persons Act1933 (c.12), s.53(2).]

P and N, both aged 14 pleaded guilty to arson, burglary and criminal damage with other offences taken into consideration. They had broken into their school, stolen sweets and a stop watch, sprayed graffiti over walls and a computer and had set fire to a room causing £70,000 worth of damage. Sentenced to two years detention under the Children and Young Persons Act 1933 s.53(2).

Held, that the purposes of any order for detention under the 1933 Act included both punishment and rehabilitation of the offenders. The reports on the boys' progress since the order confirmed that the sentences imposed were in their best interests and would not be altered.

R. *v.* PADWICK AND NEW (1985) 7 Cr.App.R.(S.) 452, C.A.

970. Juvenile—long-term detention—arson causing extensive damage.

C aged 16 pleaded guilty to arson with six other offences taken into consideration, including entering schools and causing damage. He broke into a youth club having consumed a quantity of alcohol and set fire to the premises. The building had to be demolished and replaced at a cost of £235,000. Sentenced to five years' detention under the Children and Young Persons Act 1933.

Held, that although five years would seem a very long time at the age of 16, if C behaved and got good reports, the Secretary of State would bear that in mind when exercising his statutory discretion. There was nothing wrong with the sentence.

R. *v.* CUMMINS (1986) 8 Cr.App.R.(S) 7, C.A.

971. Juvenile—long-term detention—attempted robbery

M, aged 16, pleaded guilty to two counts of burglary and one count of attempted robbery. In the attempted robbery, M, wearing a hood and carrying an axe, broke into the house of a man aged 69 but ran away when the victim blew a whistle. Several previous convictions for which he had received sentences including two custodial sentences. Sentenced to four years' detention under s.53(2) of the Children and Young Persons Act 1933 for attempted robbery with two years' concurrent for the burglaries.

Held, that it was correct to operate s.53(2) but in deciding the length of sentence the judge might have erred in assessing the severity of the offence and misled himself in scaling down the sentence in accordance with s.53(2) considerations. Sentence reduced to three years' detention (*R.* v. *Storey* [1985] C.L.Y. 810 considered).

R. *v.* METCALFE (1986) 8 Cr.App.R.(S.) 110 C.A.

972. Juvenile—long-term detention—buggery

Aged 15, pleaded guilty—buggery on nephew aged five; sexual acts with another boy nearer own age—very disturbed background—four years' detention under Children and Young Persons Act 1933, s.53(2) reduced to three as sentences under s.53(2) should not be such that far end would seem completely out of sight.

R. *v.* EVANS [1986] Crim.L.R. 821, C.A.

973. Juvenile—long-term detention—buggery of young boys

E, aged 15, pleaded guilty to two counts of buggery. He had committed buggery on a boy of 5, who was his nephew and had committed sexual acts with another boy nearer his own age. Sentenced to four years' detention under the Children and Young Persons Act 1933 (c.12), s.53(2).

Held, that it had been stated in *Storey* that when using the powers under the 1933 Act it was important that courts should not impose a sentence of which the far end would seem completely out of sight. The Court considered that there was great force in that thinking and would adopt it. E deserved to be punished but a period of three years would be appropriate instead of four years (*R.* v. *Storey* [1985] C.L.Y. 810 cited).

R. *v.* EVANS (1986) 8 Cr.App.R.(S.) 253, C.A.

974. Juvenile—long-term detention—detention for 18 months—whether appropriate use of power

H, aged 16, pleaded guilty to counts of burglary, attempted burglary and handling stolen goods, Together with another had broken into a house stolen several hundreds of pounds' worth of goods and done £2,400 worth of damage. Sentenced to 18 months detention under s.53 of the Children and Young Persons Act 1933 for the burglary with

12 months' youth custody for the attempted burglary and six months' youth custody for the handling charge, both concurrent.

Held, that the power to order detention was used as a deterrent in cases of really serious crime or for the public's protection. Generally sentences of detention were for substantial terms. In this case detention had been used to add six months' on to what would otherwise have been a maximum of 12 months' youth custody. S.53 had been used inappropriately. Even though this was an unpleasant burglary it did not merit the use of s.53. The proper sentence, one of 12 months' youth custody, would be substituted for the term of detention (*R.* v. *Gaskin* [1985] C.L.Y. 755 referred to).

R. *v.* HORROCKS (1986) 8 Cr.App.R.(S.) 23, C.A.

975. Juvenile—long-term detention—detention of juvenile aged under 15

Aged 14. Pleaded guilty to burglary of flat in daytime and handling stolen watch. Four previous findings of guilt. Co-defendant, aged 17, sentenced to two years' youth custody. Two years' detention under Children and Young Persons Act 1933, s.53(2) reduced to 12 months. Normal minimum of two years not always applicable with offenders under 15 (*R.* v. *Fairhurst* [1987] C.L.Y. 1079 applied).

R. *v.* CLEWS [1987] Crim.L.R. 586, C.A.

976. Juvenile—long-term detention—manslaughter—in course of fight between schoolboys

J, aged 15, pleaded guilty to manslaughter. He and some friends threw snowballs at the house of another boy and pushed snow through the letter box. The boy reported the matter to the police and J was cautioned as a result. The following day J and others attacked the boy who fell to the ground and was kicked on a number of occasions. J started the fight and played a leading part. The victim died as a result of ventricular dysrhythymia caused by one of the blows or kicks. Sentenced to four years' detention under the Children and Young Persons Act 1933, s.53(2).

Held, that the Court had to decide what was the proper level of sentence for a young man who kicked a man in the chest to teach him a lesson, which resulted in death which was unexpected or unforeseen. The sentencer had pitched the sentence too high and the proper sentence under s.53(2) would have been 30 months. J. had served one month in care and the Court reduced the sentence to 29 months as this would not be deducted from a sentence under s.53(2).

R. *v.* JAMES (SIMON PETER) (1986) 8 Cr.App.R.(S.) 281, C.A.

977. Juvenile—long-term detention—multiple rapes

Age: 16. Pleaded guilty. Entered beauty clinic with knife and mask, threatened proprietress, demanded money, tore out telephone, raped proprietress and customer at knifepoint several times and subjected them to other indignities. No previous sexual offences but various others, mostly dishonesty. Said by psychiatrist to be emotionally immature. Offences attributed to glue sniffing and pornography. Nine years detention upheld.

R. *v.* TAYLOR [1987] Crim.L.R. 649, C.A.

978. Juvenile—long-term detention—robbery

Ages: S; 19; R; 16. Pleaded guilty to robbery. Robbed two men in street, threatening them with violence including stabbing with screwdrivers and took watch, ring and small amount of cash. S had several previous appearances for minor offences; R had various, including taking vehicles and attempted robbery. Sentence: initially 15 months' youth custody each. Sentencer substituted 15 month's detention under s.53(2) of Children and Young Persons Act 1933 in case of R when told sentence unlawful in his case. R's sentence varied on appeal to 12 months' youth custody, since detention under s.53(2) should not normally be for less than two years. S's sentence also reduced to 12 months as his culpability no greater than that of R. (*R.* v. *Fairhurst* [1987] C.L.Y. 1079 applied).

R. *v.* SMITH AND ROBERTS [1987] Crim.L.R. 425, C.A.

979. Juvenile—long-term detention—robbery

S. pleaded guilty to robbery. He had gone to the home of a disabled youth, punched and threatened the youth, stolen £16 and left the youth handcuffed to a door. S. had numerous court appearances behind him and had served periods of detention and youth custody before. Sentenced to 4 years' detention under the Children and Young Persons Act 1953.

Held, that the sentence was no longer then was necessary.

R. *v.* STEADMAN (1985) 7 Cr.App.R.(S.) 431, C.A.

980. Juvenile—long-term detention—robbery and conspiracy to rob

D and others pleaded guilty to conspiracy to rob and to robbery. They planned to rob a petrol station with a loaded air pistol. The first attempt was abandoned but at the second garage £100 was taken. Sentenced to 30 months' and 21 months' detention under the Children and Young Persons Act 1933 s.53(2) on each count of robbery and conspiracy to rob concurrent. It was argued that the Children and Young Persons Act should not have been used.

Held, that the decided cases indicated that the power to order detention should not be for cases within the general run of adolescent crime and should generally not be a period of detention less than three years. Robbery with a loaded air pistol was not a normal adolescent crime—it was a serious offence from which the public should be protected. The sentence of 30 months' detention could not be criticised—the sentencer could have imposed three years' detention. The sentence of 21 months' detention, only nine months' more than the maximum period of youth custody, would be altered to 12 months' youth custody, in accordance with the decided cases (*R.* v. *Jenkins-Smith* (November 29, 1985) and *R.* v. *Horrocks* [1987] C.L.Y. 974 followed).

R. *v.* DAVIS (JASON MICHAEL) (1986) 8 Cr.App.R.(S.) 35, C.A.

981. Juvenile—long-term detention—robbery of shopkeeper

E, aged 16 pleaded guilty to robbery and burglary with four other offences taken into consideration. Together with another youth he held up a shopkeeper taking £50. E's role was that of lookout. He made no threats. E was subsequently involved in the burglary of a public house. He was sentenced to three years' detention under s.53(2) of the Children and Young Persons Act 1933.

Held, that as E's role was a minor one in the robbery and as his accomplice had received three years' detention also E's sentence should be reduced to reflect his lesser part in the robbery. The sentence was also too severe having regard to E's age and would be reduced to two years' detention.

R. *v.* EVERETT (1985) 7 Cr.App.R.(S.) 339, C.A.

982. Juvenile—long-term detention—series of burglaries

C, aged 16, pleaded guilty to five counts of burglary and asked for 10 other offences to be taken into consideration. He burgled the homes of old people, gaining access by pretending to be a police officer or similar pretext. Various small sums were stolen. Many previous convictions with sentences including two periods of detention and supervision orders. Sentenced to five years' detention under the Children and Young Persons Act 1933.

Held, that the offences were petty, mean and distressing. The period of five years' detention was not too long and it was always possible for the Home Secretary to release him on licence.

R. *v.* CRAIG (1986) 8 Cr.App.R.(S.) 135, C.A.

983. Juvenile—long-term detention—use of knife in course of affray

R. aged 16, was convicted of affray and unlawful wounding. Together with a number of others, R attacked two men in the street, striking one of them with a knife cutting his lip, and threatening the other. A psychiatrist report described R as having a character disorder. Sentenced to six years' detention under s.53(2) of the Children and Young Persons Act 1933 for affray with no separate penalty for unlawful wounding. R considered to be a danger to the public.

Held, that an order for detention was appropriate but having regard to the extent of the injuries and the use made of the knife the sentence was longer than was necessary. Sentence reduced to four years' detention (*R.* v. *Butler* [1985] C.L.Y. 815, *R.* v. *Bosomworth* [1973] C.L.Y. 633 referred to).

R. *v.* RHOOMS (1986) 8 Cr.App.R.(S.) 99, C.A.

984. Juvenile—long-term detention—whether appropriate to impose detention for less than two years

S aged under 17 pleaded guilty to assault and was convicted on counts of assault and blackmail. S and his brother had assaulted a man whom they believed had informed on them. The victim spent several days in hospital and when he came out S demanded £200 from him, threatening a further assault. S subsequently attacked a police officer. Sentenced to six months' and 12 months' youth custody for the assaults and 18 months' detention under the Children and Young Persons Act 1933 for the blackmail.

Held, that detention under the Children and Young Persons Act 1933 was not reserved for exceptionally grave cases. The sentence could be used if the court considered that no other sentence was appropriate. Although detention may have been a proper sentence as the term of detention was 18 months the difference between that and the maximum available term of youth custody (12 months) was not sufficiently great to make youth custody unsuitable. Accordingly the detention order would be varied to a term of 12 months' youth custody. (*R.* v. *Dewberry and Stone* [1986] C.L.Y. 772 and *R.* v. *Butler* [1985] C.L.Y. 815 applied).

R. *v.* SMITH (IVOR) (1985) 7 Cr.App.R.(S.) 462, C.A.

985. Juvenile—restrictions on sentencing in Crown Court after committal for sentence from magistrates' court—necessity for magistrates' courts to refrain from accepting jurisdiction in serious cases

C pleaded guilty before a juvenile court to two charges of robbery, 13 of burglary, two of taking a vehicle, one of going equipped and two of failing to surrender to bail. He asked for 52 other offences, including four attempted robberies, to be taken into consideration. 12 of the burglaries were of dwellings where cash and property from £3 to £3,000 in value was taken. On a later occasion, he and another took a car without authority and robbed two old ladies, one of whom was kicked in the stomach by his accomplice. In all, the value of property stolen exceeded £20,000. Sentenced in the Crown Court to three years' detention on the charges of robbery and burglary, all concurrent with one day's detention for taking a conveyance after being committed for sentence under the Magistrates' Courts Act 1980, s.37.

Held, that the sentence imposed, although deserved, was unlawful. Powers under the Children and Young Persons Act 1933 s.53(2) were only available after conviction on indictment, and where a juvenile is committed for sentence under the Magistrates' Courts Act 1980, s.37, the powers of the Crown Court were those provided by the Powers of Criminal Courts Act 1973, s.42(2) which allows for the imposition of a term of youth custody not exceeding twelve months or any sentence which was open to the magistrates' court. Accordingly, the sentence was quashed and a period of 12 months' youth custody substituted. If the justices had taken the view that their powers of sentence were inadequate, then they should have committed C for trial so that the Crown Court would have a wider range of sentencing powers. In cases of this degree of gravity, justices should not accept jurisdiction.

R. *v.* CORCORAN (1986) 8 Cr.App.R.(S.) 118, C.A.

986. Kidnapping—arising out of family dispute

R was convicted of kidnapping and assault. The woman with whom R was living and by whom he had had a child, left him to stay with friends. He went to the house, forced his way in when refused entry, struck the woman on the thigh with a hammer, dragged her into his car and drove her back to his flat where she remained until the police arrived and arrested R. Sentenced to 18 months' imprisonment.

Held, R. v. *Spence and Thomas* [1984] C.L.Y. 876 set out guidelines for kidnapping cases. Sentences of 18 months' would be adequate for kidnapping arising out of family or lovers' disputes. As there was violence in this case the sentence was not wrong in principle or excessive (*R.* v. *Spence and Thomas* [1984] C.L.Y. 876 considered).

R. *v.* RAPHAEL (1985) 7 Cr.App.R.(S.) 275, C.A.

987. Kidnapping—driver of motor vehicle

M and another pleaded guilty to kidnapping, common assault and taking a vehicle without consent. They had been given a lift in a van in the early hours of the morning. When the driver refused to go any further they pushed him into the back of his van, hit him with a wheel brace, threatened him with violence and drove off. They detained the driver for one hour and damaged the van extensively. Sentenced to two years' imprisonment (the co-defendant received 15 months' imprisonment).

Held, that the judge was entitled to differentiate between the two defendants on the basis of the previous record. M had a record of offences of violence, his co-defendant did not. There was no ground upon which an appeal could be allowed.

R. *v.* MATTAN (1985) 7 Cr.App.R.(S.) 415, C.A.

988. Kidnapping—kidnap of daughter on father's instructions

The appellants were convicted of kidnapping. A was the father of a girl who had moved away from home. With the help of M, A hired a private detective who, by pretending to be the police, persuaded the girl to go with them. The girl was blindfolded for seven hours, kept at A's house and then taken by the private detective to the house of A's nephew. A eventually admitted the offence to the police and disclosed the whereabouts of his daughter. Sentenced: A 18 months' imprisonment, M two years' imprisonment, the nephew six months' imprisonment and the private detective three years' imprisonment.

Held, that the appellants had not pleaded guilty. There must be an element of deterrence in the sentences. This could not be described as a lover's tiff or family quarrel. The sentences were not excessive and could have been longer (*R.* v. *Spence and Thomas* [1984] C.L.Y. 876 considered).

R. *v.* MOIED (1986) 8 Cr.App.R.(S.) 44, C.A.

989. Kidnapping—woman detained for ransom

P was convicted of kidnapping, robbery, blackmail, and false imprisonment. D was convicted of the same offences and also of possessing a firearm without a certificate. Together with others they had kidnapped a woman from her home whilst her husband was in prison. They transported her in a van and the boot of a car to a chalet where she was kept blindfolded. She was threatened by various men and a ransom of £50,000 was demanded of her family. After six days she was released. P assisted in the organisation and was held more culpable than D. P was sentenced to 18 years concurrent for kidnapping and false imprisonment with concurrent terms of 10 years for robbery and blackmail. D was sentenced to 14 years concurrent for kidnapping and false imprisonment with concurrent terms of 10, 9 and 3 years for robbery, blackmail and possessing firearms without a certificate respectively.

Held, that it was right to distinguish between P and D but there was some room for reduction in both cases. P's sentence of 18 years was reduced to 15 years and D's sentence of 14 years was reduced to 11 years.

R. *v.* PITTS and DAVIES (1986) 8 Cr.App.R.(S.) 84, C.A.

990. Length of sentence—administering a noxious substance

[Offences against the Person Act 1861 (c.100), s.24.]

N pleaded guilty to one count of administering a noxious substance contrary to s.24. He admitted one committal for sentence for shoplifting. He had visited a probation office to discuss with his ex-girlfriend access to his young child. He lost his temper with the probation officer and as he left the building he let off a small glass capsule, bought in Spain. The gas released caused the occupants of the building to suffer running of the eyes, burning in the throat and choking sensations. The building was evacuated and the occupants taken to hospital. Most of the symptoms passed off within a matter of minutes. There were nine previous convictions for burglary, theft and assaults. N was sentenced to 18 months' imprisonment and three months concurrent for committal for sentence.

Held, that the sentence for the substantive offence be reduced to six months after consideration of overall effects of gas on occupants but committal for sentence ordered to be consecutive. Total nine months.

R. *v.* NALTY, June 16, 1987, C.A., [*Ex rel. Richard Martin, Barrister.*]

991. Life imprisonment—imposition of discretionary life sentence

The sentencing judge should always inform counsel when he is considering the imposition of a discretionary life sentence so that representations concerning such a sentence can be made (*R.* v. *O'Dwyer* (Unrep.) May 6, 1986 considered).

R. *v.* MORGAN, *The Times,* May 21, 1987, C.A.

992. Life imprisonment—mental disorder—bed available—special hospital

Where the medical evidence clearly indicates that the offender suffers from a mental disorder and where a bed is available at a special hospital it is appropriate to make a hospital order under the Mental Health Act 1983, s.37 without limit as to time than to impose a sentence of life imprisonment.

M pleaded guilty to counts of rape, buggery, attempted rape, attempted buggery and burglary with intent to rape. He had a history of sexual offences and was diagnosed as suffering from a manic depressive psychosis. A bed was available for him in a special hospital. Sentenced to life imprisonment.

Held, that the Court fully understood the judge's desire to protect the public. In this sort of case the more appropriate course was to impose a hospital order together with a restriction order without limit of time under sections 37 and 41 of the Mental Health Act 1983 (*R.* v. *Howell* [1987] C.L.Y. 913 discussed).

R. *v.* MBATHA (1985) 7 Cr.App.R.(S.) 373, C.A.

993. Life sentences—discretionary and mandatory—parole system—new policy—effect

[Criminal Justice Act 1967 (c.80), s.61(1).]

In November 1983 the Home Secretary announced a new policy in the administration of the parole system, and in April 1985 it was made clear that this policy applied to discretionary as well as mandatory life sentences. With very few exceptions, this meant that no consultation about parole took place until a prisoner had been detained for three to four years.

Held, that this policy was an improper exercise of the Home Secretary's powers under s.61(1) of the Criminal Justice Act 1967. By not obtaining a judicial review until three or four years had gone by, a life prisoner served the equivalent of a nine-year fixed sentence (three years before request to the judges, three years review process, three years notional remission), This removed flexibility, and meant that in some cases time spent in custody might be excessive and beyond the contemplation of the sentencer.

R. *v.* SECRETARY OF STATE FOR THE HOME DEPARTMENT, *ex p.* HANDSCOMB, *The Times*, March 4, 1987, D.C.

994. Living on earnings of prostitution—managing an agency supplying prostitutes—whether imprisonment appropriate

E was convicted of living on the earnings of prostitution. He organised and operated an escort agency which arranged for prostitutes to visit clients in hotels or other premises. The prostitutes collected an agency fee of about £30 from each client and made their own arrangements for a fee for sexual intercourse. E was fully aware of the activities but there was no suggestion that he procured women to become prostitutes or induced women to work for the agency by threats of violence. Sentenced to 12 months' imprisonment and a fine of £2,000 with 90 days' imprisonment in default.

Held, that as between the decisions of the court in *Colton* and *Farrugia*, the court would apply the principles set out in *Farrugia*. It seemed that in *Colton* the court did not take into account the public interest nor was reference made to *Farrugia* and the court decided that *Colton* must be regarded as decided *per incuriam*. Following the principles established in *Young* v. *Bristol Aeroplane Co.*, the court was entitled to disregard *Colton*, and in future *Colton* should not be relied on when courts consider this kind of case, referring instead to *Farrugia*. There was nothing wrong with the sentence of 12 months' imprisonment (*R.* v. *Farrugia* [1979] C.L.Y. 540, *R.* v. *Colton* [1981] C.L.Y. 525 and *Young* v. *Bristol Aeroplane Co.* [1944] K.B. 718 cited).

R. *v.* EL-GAZZAR (1986) 8 Cr.App.R.(S.) 182, C.A.

995. Living on earnings of prostitution—operating "massage parlour"

Father and son were convicted of living on the earnings of prostitution by running a massage parlour where women provided sexual services for payment. There was no suggestion that the women or their clients had been coerced or corrupted by the appellants. The father, who played a lesser role than that of the son, was sentenced to 12 months' imprisonment, the son to two years' imprisonment.

Held, that the basis for the court to approach such cases was plainly established by decided cases. Short immediate sentences of imprisonment would be appropriate. The sentences would be quashed and replaced by sentences of three months' and four months' respectively (*R.* v. *Hilton* [1983] C.L.Y. 843, *R.* v. *Jackson and Sullivan* [1983] C.L.Y. 844 and *R.* v. *Robinson* [1985] C.L.Y. 814 applied).

R. *v.* RUSSELL AND RUSSELL (1985) 7 Cr.App.R.(S.) 257, C.A.

996. Living on earnings of prostitution—organising agency supplying prostitutes in form of visiting massage service

B, a man of previously good character, pleaded guilty to living on the earnings of prostitution. He had been concerned in the management of a company which advertised a visiting massage service: the girls who provided the massage also offered sexual services. The company received a proportion of the fee charged for the massage but not for the sexual services. Sentenced to nine months' imprisonment.

Held, that there was no question of coercion or corruption of the girls employed by the company and no profit had been made out of the business. A sentence of immediate imprisonment was correct but the appropriate period was four months.

R. *v.* BANNERJEE (1986) 8 Cr.App.R.(S.) 102, C.A.

997. Living on earnings of prostitution—organising "escort agency" providing prostitutes—whether custodial sentence appropriate

R and V were convicted respectively of exercising control over prostitutes and living on the earnings of female prostitution, and of living on the earnings of male prostitution. Over a period of three months they were concerned in running two escort agencies which advertised in various publications. Clients who telephoned the agency were charged an agency fee of £30 or £50 and put in touch with a prostitute, male or female. About 70 prostitutes were available and a set of cards recording details and the various services which particular prostitutes were willing to provide was found at their premises. It was estimated that the agencies would have received £150,000 in a full year.

Sentenced to 15 months' imprisonment in each case and ordered to pay £2,000 towards the costs of the prosecution.

Held, that the principle was well established in the light of *El-Gazzar* that in escort agency cases it was not only appropriate but usually necessary to pass custodial sentences and in some instances to pass very severe sentences of imprisonment. After considering *El-Gazzar* and *Farrugia* and the scale of the punishment which Parliament had allowed courts to inflict, the Court did not doubt that an immediate custodial sentence was right but the right sentence would have been nine months in each case and the sentences were reduced accordingly (*R.* v. *Colton* [1981] C.L.Y. 525, *R.* v. *El-Gazzar* [1987] C.L.Y. 994 and *R.* v. *Farrugia* [1979] C.L.Y. 540 considered).

R. *v.* ROSS AND VISZKOK (1986) 8 Cr.App.R.(S.) 249, C.A.

998. Long term detention of juvenile and youth custody—remand to care of local authority pending trial—credit to be given when determining sentence

When juvenile offenders are committed for trial in the care of a local authority in secure accommodation, that time does not count towards sentence, but when sentencing the courts should make some allowance for it.

M and D pleaded guilty to burglary and conspiracy to rob. They broke into a house and a garage and planned to rob a shop. While awaiting trial, each had spent six months in secure accommodation in the care of the local authority. Sentenced to four years' detention under the Children and Young Persons Act 1933.

Held, that whilst the sentences of four years' detention were not to be criticised, the judge had erred in failing to make any allowance for the period spent in secure accommodation. The sentences would be reduced by six months to take account of that period.

R. *v.* MURPHY AND DUKE (1986) 8 Cr.App.R.(S.) 72, C.A.

999. Magisterial law—increase in sentence—reconvened court

[Magistrates Courts Act 1980 (c.43), s.142.]

The Act entitles magistrates to reconvene a sentencing court so that a sentence improperly passed can be altered for a proper sentence, even if it is more severe.

JANE *v.* BROOME, *The Times,* November 2, 1987, D.C.

1000. Malicious wounding—use of a glass—facial injuries

Offences involving the use of a glass, even if used impetuously and without premeditation are serious and will almost invariably result in immediate imprisonment.

F was convicted of unlawful wounding on an indictment charging him with wounding with intent to do grievous bodily harm. There had been an incident at a party in a private house where serious facial injuries were sustained from the use of a glass by F. F claimed they were caused accidentally whilst the victim said that they were deliberate. Sentenced to three years' imprisonment.

Held, that although the offence required an immediate custodial sentence the court was bound to give effect to the jury's verdict and to do so the sentence would be reduced to two years' imprisonment (*R.* v. *Singh Ajit* (1981) 3 Cr.App.R.(S.) 180 discussed).

R. *v.* FLEET (1985) 7 Cr.App.R.(S.) 245, C.A.

1001. Manslaughter—accidental discharge of a firearm in the course of robbery

T and others were convicted or pleaded guilty to manslaughter and attempted robbery. They formed a plan to rob a security van after several hours of drinking. In the course of attempting to execute this plan, a sawn-off shotgun was accidentally discharged whilst held at the head of a security guard who died of his injuries. Sentences were passed of 22 years, 18 and 17 years for manslaughter; and for attempted robbery, 12 years on those who pleaded guilty and 15 years on one who pleaded not guilty.

Held, that the sentences were higher than they need have been notwithstanding the serious nature of the offences. It was argued, relying on *McNamara* that the sentence for manslaughter should not exceed that for the substantive offence by any great amount. The starting point for robbery of a security van where no injury was caused would be 15 years as indicated in *Turner.* Sentences of 22 years were reduced to 18 years and of 18 and 17 years to 14 and 13 years respectively (*R.* v. *McNamara* [1986] C.L.Y. 849, *R.* v. *Turner* [1975] C.L.Y. 559 and *R.* v. *O'Brien and Noonan* [1975] C.L.Y. 613 referred to).

R. *v.* TOMINEY (1986) 8 Cr.App.R.(S.) 161, C.A.

1002. Manslaughter—blows to head with brick

H was convicted of manslaughter on an indictment for murder. He was a drug addict. He had gone to his grandmother's house to discuss his addiction with her but when she refused to do so he struck her over the head five times with a brick. The 96-year-old woman was killed. H then ransacked her home for money and drugs. Sentenced to 10 years' imprisonment.

Held, that the sentences for manslaughter may vary considerably, the court had to look at what the appellant did. If, as in this case, there had been a brutal killing, the sentence must be severe. The appeal would be dismissed.

R. *v.* HARWOOD (1985) 7 Cr.App.R.(S.) 362, C.A.

1003. Manslaughter—death caused by kicking in course of fight

Age: 20. Convicted of manslaughter on charge of murder. After a night drinking, T and X quarrelled. T tried to leave by taxi but X got in and travelled to T's house. X there attacked T. When X fell to the ground in the ensuing fight, T kicked him 3 times on the head, causing his death. Many previous convictions, including 2 for assault occasioning actual bodily harm, but none in recent past. Six years' youth custody upheld (*R.* v. *McNamara* (1984) 6 Cr.App.R.(S.) 356 distinguished).

R. *v.* TAYLOR [1987] Crim.L.R 282, C.A.

1004. Manslaughter—diminished responsibility—single incident of violence to child

W pleaded guilty to manslaughter by reason of diminished responsibility. He was intellectually and educationally subnormal. His wife, having spent most of their money on gambling machines, left him in charge of their 3-year-old son. When the son refused to eat W took out his anger on the boy, hitting him several times and banging his head on the floor. The boy died. There was no evidence of previous violence. Sentenced to five years' imprisonment.

Held, that as this was an isolated incident and bearing in mind W's subnormality three years' imprisonment was an appropriate sentence.

R. *v.* WAINFOR (1985) 7 Cr.App.R.(S.) 231, C.A.

1005. Manslaughter—head striking pavement after blows with fist

P pleaded guilty to manslaughter. He had a dispute with a drinking companion and hit him in the face a number of times. The victim fell to the ground, hit his head on the pavement and suffered cerebral injury from which he later died. Sentenced to seven years' imprisonment.

Held, that manslaughter embraced a wide variety of circumstances and the court had to pay heed to those circumstances. In cases where death resulted after a fall to the pavement caused by blows to the victim the usual sentence was 12 month's imprisonment. This was a more serious case because there was no reason for the assault which was carried out with some ferocity and because of P's history of violent behaviour seven years' was too harsh a sentence for this offence—two years' imprisonment was more appropriate.

R. *v.* PHILLIPS (KEITH) (1985) 7 Cr.App.R.(S.) 235, C.A.

1006. Manslaughter—setting fire to occupied premises

P pleaded guilty to manslaughter, arson, being reckless as to whether life was endangered, conspiracy and theft. He had been dismissed from his employment for stealing as a result of information provided by S. He went to S's house in the early hours of the morning, poured petrol through the letterbox and set light to it. S was at work but his wife and son were in the house: the son died in the fire. Sentenced to 12 years' imprisonment.

Held, that this was as bad a case of manslaughter as it was possible to have short of murder. The court could see nothing wrong with the sentence.

R. *v.* PALMA (1986) 8 Cr.App.R.(S.) 148, C.A.

1007. Manslaughter—young child by father

H pleaded guilty to manslaughter of his three-year-old son. H was raising both of his children alone since his wife left him. H shook his son and inflicted fatal head injuries. Sentenced to five years' imprisonment.

Held, that although no violence had been used in the past and this was not a case of death after a long period of cruelty it was not a case where death had occurred by mischance. It was a case of a single act of violence in a fit of temper resulting in death. Five years' imprisonment was an appropriate sentence.

R. *v.* HORSCROFT (1985) Cr.App.R.(S.) 254, C.A.

1008. Manslaughter—young child by friend of mother—violence over several days

T, aged 20, pleaded guilty to manslaughter. He had gone to live with a women and her two young children. While the woman was taking the older child to school, T struck the other, a three-year-old boy, on the head for soiling his trousers. The child was taken to hospital where he died from a severe head injury. There was medical evidence of previous assaults over a period of four days. Sentence of seven years' youth custody upheld.

R. *v.* THOMAS (MICHAEL STEPHEN) (1986) 8 Cr.App.R.(S.) 75, C.A.

1009. Manslaughter—youth custody

M and H, both aged 18, pleaded guilty to manslaughter. They had stretched a rope across the road and secured it at both ends. A passing motor cyclist driving along the road was killed. Sentenced to 30 months' youth custody.

Held, that the sentence must reflect society's abhorrence at the loss of life caused by criminal folly and the reckless disregard for the life of others. The sentences were appropriate.

R. *v.* MAINWARING AND HULME (1985) 7 Cr.App.R.(S.) 418, C.A.

1010. Misconduct in the face of the court—increasing sentence for original offence

P was convicted of possessing an offensive weapon and sentenced to three month's detention. When the sentence was announced there was swearing and shouting from the dock. The defendant was brought back into the dock and the judge reviewed the sentence and substituted a sentence of six months' youth custody.

Held, that the judge was wrong. The correct procedure was to deal with P for a contempt of court separately from the initial offence and a separate sentence should be passed. The sentence of youth custody would be quashed and a sentence of 3 months' detention would be substituted.

R. *v.* POWELL (MARK) (1985) 7 Cr.App.R.(S.) 247, C.A.

1011. Mitigation—disclosure of information relating to offences committed by other persons—whether a mitigating factor where offender not a "supergrass"

Robbery of post office during which employee suffered serious facial injuries. Gave information to police relating to whereabouts of stolen blank traveller's cheques and sawn-off shot-gun. 10 years' imprisonment upheld: Information given to police was unconnected with the crime of which M was convicted. Accordingly, it was not mitigation to be taken into account by the sentencer. Case distinguished from "supergrass" cases.

R. *v.* McALENY [1987] Crim.L.R. 587, C.A.

1012. Mugging—attack on woman at night

Sentences of five years' imprisonment on the attackers of a female bus conductor at night in a mugging would remain undisturbed, even though great violence was not used, nor was a very substantial sum obtained (*R.* v. *O'Brien* [1986] C.L.Y. 700 considered).

R. *v.* EDWARDS; R. *v.* LARTER, *The Times*, February 3, 1987, C.A.

1013. Obtaining by deception—director obtaining £110,000 from company—early confession accompanied by voluntary reparation

G pleaded guilty to two counts of obtaining by deception. He was a director of a company with responsibility for a budget of more than £3 million. He wrote two cheques on the company's account in favour of his wife's company for a total of £110,858. When he came under suspeicion he admitted what had been done at an early stage and repaid the whole of the amount of which the company had been defrauded. Sentenced to a total of three years' imprisonment.

Held, that the appellant had confessed to his crimes at an early stage and had made full reparation. He had done irreparable damage to his own future and jeopardised his marriage. The Court had considered a number of similar cases and had reached the conclusion that a sentence of three years in a case involving £100,000 was usually passed on persons who initially showed no contrition and made no reparation. In the present case there was a very considerable amount of mitigation which had not been reflected in the sentence which was reduced to 12 months on each count concurrent (*R.* v. *Barrick* [1985] C.L.Y. 765 considered).

R. *v.* GORING (1986) 8 Cr.App.R.(S.) 243, C.A.

1014. Obtaining by deception—fraudulent supplementary benefit claims over substantial period.

F pleaded guilty to five counts of obtaining by deception with 68 minor offences taken into consideration. He had obtained supplementary benefit over a period of six years when he and his wife and later just his wife had been working. The total overpayment was over £7,200. Sentenced to 12 months' imprisonment.

Held, that there were a number of authorities that suggested that sentences of six months' imprisonment were appropriate for this type of offence. Regrettably those sentences did not deter those who would defraud the D.H.S.S. and the time had come to make it clear that such people would be dealt with by custodial sentences of greater

length than those that had been passed in previous years. The sentence was appropriate.
R. *v.* FORD (TREVOR RAYMOND) (1986) 8 Cr.App.R.(S.) 1, C.A.

1015. Obtaining property by deception—social security fraud—guidelines

The Court of Appeal on hearing nine appeals against sentence for social security fraud laid down the following guidelines:

(a) the element of deterrence should not play a large part in sentencing; (b) immediate custodial sentences of two and a half years and upwards would be appropriate for carefully organised frauds by professionals involving considerable sums of money. Sentence would depend on the scope of the fraud, and there should be appropriate discount. Such cases would be rare; (c) as to the remainder, the court should inquire, with the assistance of the Crown, as to what steps the appropriate department was taking against the offender; (d) other considerations would be: (1) a guilty plea; (2) the amount involved and the length of time the fraud was persisted in; (3) the circumstances where the offence began (e.g. whether it began as a legitimate claim); (4) the use to which the money was put; (5) previous character; (6) matters special to the offender (e.g. illness; family difficulties); (7) any voluntary repayment; (e) in many cases the ideal form of punishment would be a suspended sentence or community service order; (f) if immediate imprisonment was necessary, a short term of up to about 9 or 12 months would usually suffice in a contested case involving up to £10,000; (g) a partially suspended sentence might well be appropriate where a short immediate sentence was insufficient; and (h) when the offender was in work, no immediate custodial sentence was imposed and a sum of less than £1,000 was involved, the court should consider a compensation order (*R.* v. *Barrick* [1985] C.L.Y. 765 considered).

R. *v.* STEWART (LIVINGSTONE) [1987] 1 W.L.R. 559, C.A.

1016. Parole—further conviction—effect

[Criminal Justice Act 1967 (c.80), ss.60 and 62(7) and (10).]

Where a person is sentenced to imprisonment during the currency of a parole licence in respect of a previous sentence and the court elects to revoke that licence, the defendant cannot become entitled within one year from the revocation to be considered for parole in repsect of any sentence.

The appellant was convicted in September 1985 for an offence committed in December 1984, and was released on licence under s.60 of the Criminal Justice Act 1967 in March 1986. The licence was due to expire in August 1986. On April 30, 1986 he was sentenced to 12 months' imprisonment for an offence committed between May 1984 and January 1985. The judge exercised his discretion to revoke his licence under s.62(7) of the Act. He appealed against the revocation of the licence on the ground that he had not been in breach of the licence.

Held, allowing the appeal that under s.62(10) of the Act of 1967 a person who was released on licence and was subsequently convicted and sentenced to a term of imprisonment and whose licence was revoked was ineligible for release on licence in respect of any sentence imposed on him for a period of one year from the date of the revocation. In deciding whether to revoke a licence the court should consider the consequences of revocation in the light of s.62(10) and whether they were justified. Accordingly, since the appellant had committed no offence while released on licence it would be unjust that he should be ineligible for release on parole during the currency of his second term of imprisonment, and the revocation of his licence should be quashed.

R. *v.* McKINNON (WILLIAM HAROLD) (1987) 1 W.L.R. 234, C.A.

1017. Persistent burglaries by juvenile—whether long term detention appropriate

W pleaded guilty to burglary (five counts) and possessing a firearm. A number of other offences—including burglaries—were taken into consideration. W had broken into a number of houses and stolen £9,000 worth of property. A sawn-off shotgun was found at his home. Sentenced to four years' detention under the Children and Young Persons Act 1933.

Held, that W was a professional burglar equipped with a lethal weapon. The sentence was an upper limit within which he could be released. The Secretary of State is entitled to recommend his release at an earlier date but the upper limit must be fixed at such a period as to avoid the risk of releasing him into society when he is still a menace. The sentence was entirely proper.

R. *v.* WESTON (1985) 7 Cr.App.R.(S.) 420, C.A.

1018. Perverting justice—threatening witness with violence

B pleaded guilty to doing an act tending to pervert the course of public justice. He was present in a flat belonging to a woman friend when his companion broke into her electricity meter and stole £24. After warrants for the arrest of B and his companion had been issued, he went to the woman's flat, threatened to throw acid over her and to burn down the flat. The woman attempted to withdraw the accusation. Sentenced to three years' youth custody.

Held, that this was a serious offence in two senses: attempting to pervert the course of justice was always a serious matter and the nature of the threat was serious. Three years was longer than was necessary to show public disapproval and the sentence was reduced to two years' youth custody.

R. *v.* BURNETT (LEROY) (1986) 8 Cr.App.R.(S.) 220, C.A.

1019. Possessing firearm with intent to endanger life—firing weapon

F pleaded guilty to possessing a firearm and ammunition with intent to endanger life. He had been ejected from a house by the man who shared the house with F's former mistress. F, who was heavily intoxicated went home and fetched a shotgun and some cartridges. He returned to the house, fired into the eaves and told the woman to send the man down. Having fired a second shot into the front door he left. He gave himself up to the police shortly afterwards. Sentenced to four years' imprisonment.

Held, that although it was necessary to mark the offence with a severe sentence it is not to be supposed that F would have shot the man. He was acting out of jealousy and bravado whilst drunk. The sentence was too severe and should be reduced to two years' imprisonment.

R. *v.* FISH (1985) 7 Cr.App.R.(S.) 310, C.A.

1020. Possessing firearm with intent to endanger life—life imprisonment

Age: 53. Pleaded guilty. A's relationship with X ended in 1981 when A hit her. He was fined and bound over. Later he kidnapped X, threatened to kill her and was sentenced to three years' imprisonment. When released, A formed a relationship with Y but when that broke down he sprinkled petrol on Y's flat, set fire to it and was sentenced to four years' imprisonment. Following release went to public house where X lived with another man, left when X called police but was found in his car with a sawn-off shotgun loaded with a cartridge inscribed with X's name and a scalpel taped to his leg. Medical evidence; no mental disorder. Life imprisonment upheld. Overriding duty to protect public where there was danger such as in present case. A's "mental state" made him dangerous to the public. "Mental state" included uncontrollable strong feelings of passion and jealously leading to A's conduct (*R.* v. *Wilkinson* [1984] C.L.Y. 880 considered).

R. *v.* ALLEN [1987] Crim.L.R. 645 C.A.

1021. Possessing firearm with intent to endanger life—threats to police

H pleaded guilty to possessing a firearm with intent to endanger life, wounding and assaults occasioning actual bodily harm. He had been told by his wife that she was going to leave him. He fetched a shotgun and threatened to shoot her when she insisted on leaving him whereupon she called for the police. Upon the arrival of the police H pointed the shotgun through the front door, only inches away from the officers and threatened to shoot them. When they eventually seized the gun he violently resisted arrest assaulting and wounding the officers. Sentenced to a total of three years' imprisonment.

Held, that the sentence was entirely appropriate. The judge had taken into account all of the mitigating factors such as the previous good character, the background of domestic difficulties and the fact that H had been drinking, which he did not normally do.

R. *v.* HADDOCK (1985) 7 Cr.App.R.(S.) 306, C.A.

1022. Possession of heroin with intent to supply—supplying heroin

Age: 33. Admitted selling heroin in small quantities to about eight people for profit sufficient to enable C to buy heroin for his own use. No previous convictions. Total of six years' imprisonment reduced to five to reflect guilty plea (though C had little option but to plead guilty). (Guidelines in *R.* v. *Aramah* [1983] C.L.Y. 764, *R.* v. *Gee* [1985] C.L.Y. 800, *R.* v. *Guiney* [1987] C.L.Y. 950 and *R.* v. *Hyam* [1984] C.L.Y. 868 reconsidered and not followed, in light of increase in drug abuse and in maximum penalty for the relevant offences.)

R. *v.* CARTER [1987] Crim.L.R. 212, C.A.

1023. Possession of heroin with intent to supply—supplying heroin

Age: 40. Convicted of two counts of supplying heroin and one of possessing with intent to supply; pleaded guilty to one count of possessing. J's flat contained a quantity of plastic bags, some scales and squares of paper. J had about 10 to 12 customers. One previous conviction for possessing heroin and LSD: two months' imprisonment suspended. Total: six years' imprisonment with suspended sentence activated consecutively reduced to five years with suspended sentence activated consecutively (*R.* v. *Gee* [1985] C.L.Y. 800, *R.* v. *France* [1985] C.L.Y. 801 and *R.* v. *Guiney* [1987] C.L.Y. 950 considered).

R. *v.* JUHASZ [1987] Crim.L.R. 212, C.A.

1024. Possession of offensive weapon—Stanley knife—record of violence

W was convicted of possessing an offensive weapon. He had been arrested for insulting behaviour and found to be carrying a Stanley knife in his jacket which, he said, was in case he was attacked. He had a record of offences of violence. Sentenced to 12 months' imprisonment.

Held, that W could not call on his previous record in mitigation. Nor had he shown remorse by pleading guilty. The sentence was a proper one.

R. *v.* WEBSTER (1985) 7 Cr.App.R.(S.) 359, C.A.

1025. Possession of sawn-off shotgun—intent to commit indictable offence

C pleaded guilty to possessing a firearm with intent to commit an indictable offence, possessing a firearm in a public place and possessing a firearm following release from custody. He was found in possession of a sawn-off shotgun and ammunition. He had a lengthy criminal record and had served terms of imprisonment. He said he had received threats and needed the gun as protection. He had reported the threats to the police. Sentenced to four years' imprisonment.

Held, that the carrying of weapons of this sort for use in public cannot be tolerated. The sentence adequately reflected C's guilty plea, the threats that had been made and the assistance he had given the police.

R. *v.* CRESSWELL (1986) 8 Cr.App.R.(S.) 29, C.A.

1026. Prison rules—remission—sentences for a term of 12 months or less. See PRISONS, §3143.

1027. Probation—breach of order—role of probation officer

Where a probation officer causes a defendant who is subject to a probation or community service order to be brought back to court for breach of that order, the officer's role is analogous to that of a prosecutor. He is, however, entitled to suggest an appropriate sentence to the court, and this does not breach the fundamental rule that a prosecutor should not advocate the type or magnitude of a sentence.

R. *v.* LIVERPOOL STIPENDIARY MAGISTRATE, *ex p.* ATKINSON, *The Times,* May 30, 1987, D.C.

1028. Probation order—consent—whether obtained by duress

[Powers of the Criminal Courts Act 1973 (c.62), s.2(6).]

Consent for the purposes of s.2(6) of the 1973 Act is not vitiated by making the defendant aware of the realistic, but unpleasant alternative sentences.

B. was charged with theft and convicted. The medical report suggested some psychological difficulty. The judge considered probation appropriate and asked B. if he consented, pointing out that the alternative was a short spell of imprisonment. B. said he preferred probation to imprisonment and consented, but made clear that he regarded probation as onerous.

Held, that to satisfy s.2(6) of the 1973 Act the defendant should know the realistic alternative and imprisonment was a realistic alternative, so knowledge of it did not vitiate consent.

R. *v.* BARNETT (1986) 86 Cr.App.R. 365, C.A.

1029. Probation order—whether appropriate to extend a probation order when imposing a custodial sentence

It is wrong in principle to make a probation order at the same time as imposing a custodial sentence.

M was convicted of robbery. M was a prostitute who robbed a client of £50 when she was subject to a conditional discharge and a probation order. She also pleaded guilty to theft. Sentenced to four months' and one day youth custody for the robbery, one month concurrent youth custody for the theft, fined £10 in respect of the conditional discharge and the probation order was extended.

Held, that it had been clearly stated that it was wrong in principle to impose a period of custody together with a probation order. It was also wrong to avoid this by extending an existing probation order. The extension would be quashed but the sentence of youth custody was entirely appropriate and would remain (*R.* v. *Emmett* [1969] C.L.Y. 753 considered).

R. *v.* MULLERVY (1986) 8 Cr.App.R.(S.) 41, C.A.

1030. Procuring passport by false statement—doctor signing applications for passports by persons not known to him—whether custodial sentence appropriate

M pleaded guilty to 11 counts of making a false statement to procure a passport. He was a doctor in general practice who signed applications for passports, and accompanying photographs, which were then used fraudulently to obtain passports for persons who were not entitled to them. He claimed that he acted in good faith and it was not alleged that he had acted with a view to obtaining large sums of money. Sentenced to 12 months' imprisonment.

Held, that although the appellant had not made a substantial gain from dealing with passports, he had broken his trust by signing application forms without knowing the truth of what was certified and that was a serious offence justifying a deterrent sentence even on a person of previous good character. The sentence was not wrong in principle or excessive.

R. *v.* MIDYA (1986) 8 Cr.App.R.(S.) 264, C.A.

1031. Public nuisance—persistently telephoning police station

M pleaded guilty to two counts of public nuisance. He had, over a period of two years, made numerous telephone calls to a young woman police officer with whom he had become infatuated at the police station where she worked. On one day, he made 636 such calls. M had been brought before the court on six occasions and had been put on probation three times, sentenced to terms of imprisonment, suspended, and to a term of immediate imprisonment; the latest offences were committed following his release after serving part of a partly suspended sentence of imprisonment. Sentenced to 30 months' imprisonment, with the balance (six months) of the partly suspended sentence activated consecutively.

Held, that there was no alternative to the sentence passed.

R. *v.* MILLWARD (1986) 8 Cr.App.R.(S.) 209, C.A.

1032. Rape-by intruder

H pleaded guilty to rape. He broke into the house of woman who lived with her children at 5.00 a.m. and threatened her with a knife, forcing her to have oral sex with him and then raped her. On a previous occasion he had been sentenced to 10 years' imprisonment for offences involving violence towards a woman. Sentenced to 15 years' imprisonment.

Held, that the offence was of the utmost gravity but not at the very top of the scale. A sentence of 12 years' imprisonment was substituted for the sentence of 15 years (*R.* v. *Billam* [1986] C.L.Y. 868 considered).

R. *v.* HAWKINS (THOMAS JOHN) (1986) 8 Cr.App.R.(S.) 181, C.A.

1033. Rape—by stranger of girl aged 16

Aged 28. Pleaded guilty. Rape of 16-year-old girl, whom he did not know, on way home. Pushed her over fence and into field, punched her, slapped her, took most of her clothes off, forced oral sex before and after the rape and then left her—no previous convictions—had been drinking; gave himself up to police within 24 hours—seven years' imprisonment reduced to five to reflect guilty plea.

R. *v.* McCUE [1987] Crim.L.R. 345, C.A.

1034. Rape—series of rapes on different women

Aged 26. Shortly after release from prison took a woman out and attacked her on way home. After knocking her to ground, forced her to woods and after struggles raped her. Then committed burglaries. Whilst on bail for the rape, committed several more burglaries and twice raped another woman at knife-point (having previously had intercourse with her with her consent). Weeks later, entered a house, threatened a woman with a knife and raped her four times. Numerous previous convictions for burglary, theft and wounding. 15 years' imprisonment for each rape reduced to 12. Three years for burglaries consecutive upheld. Total reduced from 18 to 15 years to reflect guilty pleas.

R. *v.* GIBSON [1987] Crim.L.R. 346, C.A.

1035. Rape—series of rapes on different women—life imprisonment

Age 34. Pleaded guilty. Entered house at night and raped X several times at knifepoint, threatening to kill, tying X to bed and gagging her. Days later accosted Y, walking home, at knifepoint, raped her in underground garage, took her elsewhere and raped her again. Threatened to kill Y if she reported the matter. Many previous convictions including violence but no sexual offences. Medical evidence: psychopathic but no mental illness. Life imprisonment upheld: normally court required medical evidence that offender unstable and likely to commit such offences in future. Probably facts of the two offences would not alone justify life imprisonment but with the medical evidence sentence was correct (*R.* v. *Hodgson* [1968] C.L.Y. 848, *R.* v. *de Havilland* [1984] C.L.Y. 883, *R.* v. *O'Dwyer* (unrep.) May 6, 1986, *R.* v. *Blackburn* [1981] C.L.Y. 525 and *R.* v. *Owen* [1981] C.L.Y. 525 considered).

R. *v.* DEMPSTER [1987] Crim.L.R. 647, C.A.

1036. Rape—victim's fear of AIDS

A woman's fear that she might have contracted AIDS as a result of having been raped is not an aggravating factor meriting an increased sentence, unless she has a particular reason for this fear (*R.* v. *Billam* [1986] C.L.Y. 868 considered).

R. *v.* MALCOLM, *The Times,* November 28, 1987, C.A.

1037. Remand for report with view to probation order and hostel residence—favourable report—subsequent custodial sentence

The handing down of a custodial sentence on the grounds of public opinion, and by a judge other than the judge who remanded D on bail for his assessment, and following a favourable report on that assessment, was unjust and wrong (*R.* v. *Gillam* (1980) 2 Cr.App.R.(S.) 267 followed).

R. *v.* WILKINSON, *The Times,* November 28, 1987, C.A.

1038. Repatriation of prisoner—period of detention in U.K.—relationship to foreign sentence

[Repatriation of Prisoners Act 1984 (c.47), ss.1, 3(3), 10(2).]

The Home Secretary has the power to reduce the sentence to be served by a person repatriated in order to serve his sentence in U.K. to a sentence in accordance with U.K. sentencing principles. He is not confined to reducing the foreign sentence to the maximum allowed by U.K. law.

R. *v.* SECRETARY OF STATE FOR THE HOME DEPARTMENT, *ex p.* READ (GARY JOHN), *The Times,* November 2, 1987, D.C.

1039. Riot—instigator of premeditated attacks on football supporters

M pleaded guilty to riot. He was concerned in planning and instigating a number of attacks by between 30 and 150 people on visiting football supporters, a number of whom suffered serious injuries (including one stabbed in the neck with a bottle which severed an artery). In this activity he attracted the nickname "The General". Sentenced to five years' imprisonment.

Held, that a deterrent sentence was called for and the sentence was upheld.

R. *v.* MURANYI (1986) 8 Cr.App.R.(S.) 176, C.A.

1040. Robbery—elderly man in own home—guilty plea

P1 and P2 (both under 21) entered a farmhouse occupied by X, aged 73. One carrried a shotgun and the other a pickhandle. X was manhandled and struck from behind with one of the weapons. The house was ransacked, the telephone disconnected and a safe containing £5,000 taken. Both had five previous convictions or findings of guilt and had served at least one custodial sentence. Plea: guilty. 10 years' youth custody reduced to eight (*R.* v. *Wood* [1985] C.L.Y. 817, *R.* v. *O'Driscoll* [1987] C.L.Y. 1042, *R.* v. *Funnell* [1987] C.L.Y. 860 considered).

R. *v.* POWIS AND PRITCHARD [1987] Crim.L.R. 280, C.A.

1041. Robbery—juvenile

Aged 16, pleaded guilty. With two older youths robbed a man working in a car park and stole his wage packet containing £65. C kicked him when he was on the ground and had £25 of the £65. Nine months' youth custody reduced to five since no weapon involved, no serious injury and C had no previous conviction. Court had no duty to tailor sentence to allow offenders to continue education at a particular date. Offence too serious for non-custodial sentence or detention centre.

R. *v.* CURTIS [1987] Crim.L.R. 66, C.A.

1042. Robbery—of elderly householder with grave violence

O was convicted of attempted burglary, robbery and causing grievous bodily harm with intent. With another, he gained entry to the house of a man aged 80 and hit him several times with a hammer on the head, shoulders and leg. He took the victim's wallet and then held a lighted gas poker to his face. He and his accomplice then bound the victim with wire and gagged him. Sentenced to 15 years' imprisonment.

Held, that in cases such as this when old people were selected as victims and tortured in their own homes to try to make them hand over their valuables, this sort of sentence should be expected.

R. *v.* O'DRISCOLL (1986) Cr.App.R.(S.) 121, C.A.

1043. Robbery—of householders by armed intruders—sentence appeals

Masked and with a loaded shotgun, an iron bar and a pickhandle, the three appellants broke into a dwelling-house at 4.30 a.m. Violence was offered to one occupier but no serious injury was inflicted. The other occupier took the appellants to a safe, which was rifled.

Held, that the sentences imposed began at the wrong level. Twelve years' youth custody, 13 years' imprisonment and 15 years' imprisonment reduced to 10 years' youth custody, 11 years' imprisonment and 12 years' imprisonment respectively.

R. *v.* DOHERTY [1987] Crim.L.R. 284, C.A.

1044. Robbery—series of robberies—firearms carried—whether appropriate for court to take account of possibility of remission in determining sentence—whether appropriate to take account of separation of child and mother in determining sentence

Mr. O, aged 26, pleaded guilty to 23 counts of robbery, attempted robbery, possessing a firearm with intent and converting a weapon. He had committed a series of robberies of banks, post offices and a shop. In most a sawn-off shotgun was carried and in some cases shots were fired to frighten customers and staff. A total of £61,000 was stolen. Sentenced to 15 years' imprisonment.

Held, that the sentence was correct (*R.* v. *Turner* [1975] C.L.Y. 559).

Mrs. O, the wife of Mr. O, pleaded guilty to five counts of robbery or attempted robbery. She assisted in planning the robberies and had waited for him in a car when he was committing them but had not participated further. Sentenced to five years' youth custody. At the time of the trial, she was pregnant and it was argued that the sentence should be reduced to such a term that (with remission) the child could remain with her.

Held, that a court should not take account of remission when sentencing and that the treatment of the child was a matter for the Home Office. The function of the court was to assess the proper sentence for the offence and the offender. The fact that Mrs. O had a young child could not be ignored but the Court came to the conclusion that the sentence passed was right (*R.* v. *Maguire* [1956] C.L.Y. 2130 considered).

R. *v.* OULESS AND OULESS [1986] 8 Cr.App.R.(S.) 124, C.A.

1045. Social security fraud—obtaining supplementary benefit while in employment

Aged 47. Pleaded guilty. Obtained supplementary benefit over period of two years and three months whilst in full-time employment earning £60 per week. Obtained £6,000. Nine previous convictions, including two on same occassion of similar nature. Living with four children of own aged between 12 and 22, one being mentally handicapped, and two foster children aged seven and four. Began offences when threatened with cut-off of electricity supply for non-payment of £1,000 electricity bill. If son had to continue to look after family, he would lose his job and the younger children would go into care. 12 months' imprisonment reduced to six with all but 28 days suspended.

R. *v.* MILLS [1987] Crim.L.R. 351, C.A.

1046. Social security fraud—obtaining unemployment benefit by deception

M pleaded guilty to counts of deception and attempted deception, with 62 similar offences taken into consideration. He obtained unemployment benefit to which he was not entitled drawing up to £5,000, drawing some of it under a false name. M had been on probation at the time of the offences. Sentenced to 18 months' imprisonment.

Held, that in *R.* v. *Burns* it had been observed that custodial sentences for this type of fraud were inevitable. Usually sentences in the order of six months' were appropriate. Here the offender had been on probation at the time of the offences and had used a false name. Even so the sentence passed was out of line with what had been suggested as an appropriate sentence. The sentence would be reduced to nine months' imprisonment. (*R.* v. *Burns* [1984] C.L.Y. 894 dismissed).

R. *v.* MITCHELL (1985) 7 Cr.App.R.(S.) 368, C.A.

1047. Statistics—cautions, court proceedings and sentencing. See CRIMINAL EVIDENCE AND PROCEDURE, §733.

1048. Statistics—offenders sentenced to immediate custody 1979–1985

The Home Office has published a statistical bulletin (Issue 9/87) analysing the large increase in the number of offenders sentenced to immediate custody between 1979 and 1985 and examining the contributory factors in this change. Copies of the bulletin are available from Statistical Department, Home Office, Lunar House, Croydon, Surrey CR0 9YD [£2·50].

1049. Statistics—probation

The Home Office has published a statistical bulletin which provides statistics about the work of the probation service in 1986 together with corresponding information for earlier years. The bulletin, issue 22/87, is available from the Statistical Department, Lunar House, Croydon, Surrey CRO 9YD. Tel. 01–760 2850. [£2·50].

1050. Statutory criteria for custodial sentence—obligation to have regard to criteria

[Criminal Justice Act 1982 (c.48), s.1(4).]

When dealing with an offender who had not previously been the subject of a custodial sentence the court should refer to the provisions of the Criminal Justice Act 1982 s.1(4) whether or not counsel does so.

P was convicted of assault and theft. He had been involved in a disturbance in a restaurant, had punched a waiter and stolen a salt cellar. The sentencer did not obtain a social inquiry report nor did he refer to the criteria set out in s.1(4) but sentenced P to three months' detention for the assault and one month concurrent for the theft.

Held, that the Court should refer itself, without being asked to the provision of the Act before taking away an offender's liberty. P's conduct was the sort that should be met with a short custodial sentence or a community service order. The sentence of three months' detention was longer than necessary. The sentence for the theft was wrong in principle. The sentence would be varied to allow P's immediate release (*R.* v. *Bradbourn* [1986] C.L.Y. 897 referred to).

R. *v.* PASSMORE (1985) 7 Cr.App.R.(S.) 377, C.A.

1051. Suspended sentence—activation—following conviction for offence of different character

Stabbed police officer in chest with wall-paper stripping knife, in anger. Four years' imprisonment with six month suspended sentence for handling, activated consecutively. Upheld: mere fact subsequent offence differed widely in character from original offence was no proper ground for not ordering suspended sentence to take effect in full. Fact offence committed in anger did not necessarily make any difference (*R.* v. *O'Connell* [1983] C.L.Y. 760 and *R.* v. *Prince* [1982] C.L.Y. 684 not followed; *R.* v. *Saunders* [1970] C.L.Y. 519, *R.* v. *Craine* [1981] C.L.Y. 525, *R.* v. *Vanston* [1972] C.L.Y. 712, *R.* v. *Barton* [1974] C.L.Y. 711 and *R.* v. *Wootton* (October 28, 1974) applied).

R. *v.* CLITHEROE [1987] Crim.L.R. 583, C.A.

1052. Suspended sentence—activation—whether appropriate in Crown Court following conviction and imposition of community service order in magistrates' court

C admitted a number of offences of theft before the Crown Court after being caught stealing in a shop, with other stolen items in her possession and was sentenced to six months' imprisonment, suspended for two years. Three months later, she pleaded guilty before a magistrates' court to a theft committed during the operational period of the suspended sentence where she stole a door lock and some soap claiming that the lock was to replace a broken lock on her door. Sentenced to 240 hours community service by the magistrates' court although they were informed about the suspended sentence. She subsequently appeared before the Crown Court where the suspended sentence was activated and the community service order revoked.

Held, that the right order in the view of the court would have been to make no order with respect to the suspended sentence. The instant offence was not of great importance and a credible explanation was given to the court. Furthermore, she had brought the matter of the suspended sentence to the attention of the magistrates' court herself as it did not appear on her antecedents and she had received an offer of employment in the meantime. The order activating the suspended sentence was quashed and the community service order reinstated.

R. *v.* CRESSWELL (JEANINE MICHELLE) (1986) 8 Cr.App.R.(S.) 113, C.A.

1053. Suspended sentence—further offence of different character—whether unjust to activate suspended sentence

Drove van towing vehicle driven another whom W knew to be disqualified. Many previous convictions, including three for driving whilst disqualified. Sentence: six months' imprisonment for aiding and abetting driving whilst disqualified; two suspended sentences for handling stolen goods activated concurrently with each other but consecutive to new sentence (total: 12 months). Appeal dismissed: sentencer entitled not to take view that new offence relatively trivial, although of difference character.

R. *v.* WELLS [1987] Crim.L.R. 429, C.A.

1054. Suspended sentence—whether activation is necessary when a subsequent offence not warranting imprisonment is committed

In October 1985, J pleaded guilty to stabbing his wife after matrimonial difficulties and was sentenced to 12 months' imprisonment, suspended for two years with a supervision order. In January 1986 he pleaded guilty to possessing a small quantity of cannabis before a magistrates' court and was fined £75. He then appeared before the Crown Court where the suspended sentence was activated with the term reduced to eight months. It was argued on principle and on the basis of *Aramah, Aldred, McElhorne* and *Stewart* that it was inappropriate to activate the suspended sentence.

Held, that the judge was wrong in activating the suspended sentence: the order activating the suspended sentence was quashed and the suspended sentence continued in effect (*R.* v. *Aramah* [1983] C.L.Y. 764, *R.* v. *Aldred* [1984] C.L.Y. 904, *R.* v. *McElhorne* [1984] C.L.Y. 742 and *R.* v. *Stewart* [1985] C.L.Y. 841 referred to).

R. *v.* JAGODZINSKI (1986) 8 Cr.App.R.(S.) 150, C.A.

1055. Theft—baggage handlers at Heathrow airport—persistent stealing over period of time

D and others pleaded guilty to specimen charges of theft. They were all baggage handlers at Heathrow airport and had been detected stealing from luggage passing through one of the airport terminals. Sentenced to terms varying between three and four years' imprisonment.

Held, that for persistent pilfering from luggage at airports, three years imprisonment was a starting point. The guilty pleas were the only mitigating factor and as the offences were recorded by video cameras, this could not reduce their sentences as much as would otherwise be the case. Sentences in each case reduced to 30 months' imprisonment (*R.* v. *Barrick* [1985] C.L.Y. 765 referred to).

R. *v.* DHUNAY (1986) 8 Cr.App.R.(S.) 107, C.A.

1056. Theft—breach of trust—sum in excess of £10,000

D pleaded guilty to counts of forgery, false accounting and using a false instrument. Whilst working as a bank clerk he opened accounts in false names, withdrew £15,669 against overdraft facilities and transferred money from the bank's house account to the accounts to close them. Once dismissed from his post he obtained a job in another bank by writing his own reference. The amount he had stolen as well as his mortgage was repaid to the bank by his mother. Sentenced to two years' imprisonment.

Held, that repayment by someone other than the offender was not a ground for mitigation. The sentence imposed was unexceptional (*R* v. *Barrick* [1985] C.L.Y. 765 and *R.* v. *Carr* [1985] C.L.Y. 849 considered).

R. *v.* DAVIES (T. J.) (1986) 8 Cr.App.R.(S.) 25, C.A.

1057. Theft—breach of trust—theft by accounts clerk

P was convicted on nine counts of theft. As an accounts clerk he has stolen about £9,000. Sentenced to 12 months' imprisonment.

Held, that the sentence was consistent with the guidelines in *Barrick*. The fact that the employer had taken civil proceedings to recover his loss was not a mitigating factor; P had failed to repay the loss himself (*R.* v. *Barrick* [1985] C.L.Y. 765 considered).

R. *v.* PATEL (HARIVADAN) (1986) 8 Cr.App.R.(S.) 67, C.A.

1058. Theft—fraudulent conveyancer—guidelines

The guidelines in *R.* v. *Barrick* do not apply in cases where the offender has a record of dishonesty.

G pleaded guilty to counts of theft and obtaining by deception. He had set up in business as a conveyancer. He withdrew large sums of money from the accounts of two clients, representing their life savings, and gambled the money away. G also had previous convictions for robbery and blackmail to get money for gambling. Sentenced to four years' imprisonment.

Held, that *Barrick* applied in cases where people of good character ruin their lives by making off with other people's money. It does not apply to this case. G was thoroughly dishonest and had inflicted a great deal of suffering on private individuals by depriving them of their life savings. The sentence was entirely appropriate (*R.* v. *Barrick* [1985] C.L.Y. 765 distinguished).

R. *v.* GRANT (1985) 7 Cr.App.R.(S.) 322, C.A.

1059. Theft—from shop by young woman of previous good character—committed in company with younger people—whether custody appropriate

M, a woman of 24 of previous good character was convicted of two counts of theft. She had gone with her sister and half sister, aged 15 and 14, and with her own children aged eight and two, into two large shops, and stolen items worth £12 from one and £20 from the other. Sentenced to two months' immediate imprisonment.

Held, that the most disturbing feature of the case was the involvement of the girls aged 15 and 14. A sentence of three months had been upheld in *Oakley* where a woman of previous good character took her seven-year-old son to assist in stealing from shops. In the present case the sentencer was justified in describing the incident as a shoplifting expedition and the sentence was not wrong in principle (*R.* v. *Oakley* (1979) 1 Cr.App.R.(S.) 366 cited).

R. *v.* MOSS (LINDA) (1986) 8 Cr.App.R.(S.) 276, C.A.

1060. Theft—sums totalling £6,000 from employer by foreman

B pleaded guilty to eight counts of theft. He was a despatch foreman for a printing company. Over a period of eighteen months he obtained sums totalling £6,000 by claiming reimbursement of sums which he purported to have spent on behalf of the company on postage. Sentenced to two years' imprisonment.

Held, that the sentence was excessive and a sentence of twelve months' imprisonment was substituted.

R. *v.* BRINKLEY (1986) 8 Cr.App.R.(S.) 105, C.A.

1061. Theft—theft by accountant from company—more than £300,000

M pleaded guilty to counts of theft and false accounting. As assistant chief accountant he took large sums of money from his employers by manipulating accounts entries. The total taken was over £500,000, some of which was paid back, leaving a deficiency of more than £300,000. Sentenced to four years' imprisonment.

Held, that in *R.* v. *Barrick* it was said that for thefts in breach of trust in excess of £100,000 a term of three and a half to four years' imprisonment may be appropriate, subject to a discount for a guilty plea. Given that decision a reduction in sentence here was appropriate in the light of M's guilty plea. The sentence would be reduced to three years' imprisonment. (*R.* v. *Barrick* [1985] C.L.Y. 765 and *R.* v. *Strubell* [1983] C.L.Y. 897 discussed).

R. *v.* MILLER (MARTIN JOHN) (1985) 7 Cr.App.R.(S.) 318, C.A.

1062. Theft—theft by employee—£10,000

M pleaded guilty to one count of theft and two of obtaining by deception. He stole a cheque book from his employers, and cashed two cheques for a total of £10,000. Sentenced to 18 months' imprisonment.

Held, that the guidelines suggested that where the sum involved in such a case did not exceed £10,000, a sentence of 18 months' would be appropriate on the basis that the accused did not plead guilty. In the present case a proper discount had not been given for M's plea and the sentence was reduced to 12 months (*R.* v. *Barrick* [1985] C.L.Y. 765 considered).

R. *v.* MASON (COLIN ARTHUR) (1986) 8 Cr.App.R.(S.) 226, C.A.

1063. Theft and obtaining by deception—mortgage broker fraudulently accepting deposits and using them for own purposes

M was convicted of two counts of obtaining by deception and one of theft. He started a business as a mortgage broker after being made redundant. He received deposits from two women with a view to arranging mortgages and applied them for his own purposes including the purchase of a car. The total amount lost was £5,348. Sentenced to 18 months' imprisonment for obtaining £3,000 by deception, 12 months' consecutive for theft of £1,348 and 12 months' concurrent for obtaining £1,000 by deception.

Held, that in *Barrick* the guidelines laid down that a sentence of 18 months was appropriate for cases involving sums up to £10,000. Although in this case M had defrauded victims who could ill afford to lose the money and had used it extravagantly, there was nothing to justify a departure from the guidelines and the sentences were made concurrent to bring them into line (*R.* v. *Barrick* [1985] C.L.Y. 765 considered).

R. *v.* MATTHEWS (TERENCE ROY PERCIVAL) (1986) 8 Cr.App.R.(S.) 204, C.A.

1064. Theft by postman—breach of trust

P, a postman, pleaded guilty to theft. He had opened letters containing small amounts of cash and on one occasion stole a bathroom cabinet from the post. The total involved was about £100. Sentenced to 18 months' imprisonment.

Held, that it was a serious offence causing distress to the public and undermining their confidence in the postal system. Although the amounts were small, that did not outweigh the gravity of tampering with the mail. However in view of P's plea of guilty and his remorse the sentence would be reduced to 12 months' imprisonment (*R.* v. *Barrick* [1985] C.L.Y. 765 referred to).

R. *v.* POULTER (1985) 7 Cr.App.R.(S.) 260, C.A.

1065. Theft of large sums by solicitor

O pleaded guilty to counts of theft, evading liability by deception and acting as a solicitor whilst unqualified. Over a period of 18 months he had defrauded clients of £242,000. Sentenced to five years' imprisonment.

Held, that the courts had to deal sternly with those who abused trust placed in them—the greater the abuse of trust the greater the need to punish severely. It was no credit to O that those who were defrauded would be compensated by the Law Society at the expense of solicitors generally. However, it was no longer necessary for very long sentences to be passed on professional men in these circumstances—more moderate sentences would assuage the sense of public outrage. A sentence of three years' imprisonment would have been enough.

R. *v.* OFFORD (1985) 7 Cr.App.R.(S.) 327, C.A.

1066. Thefts from students

Those convicted of "walk in" thefts from students' rooms should expect very severe sentences.

R. *v.* CONNOLLY, *The Times,* December 11, 1986, C.A.

1067. Threatening to kill—common assault

B, aged 37, pleaded guilty to threatening to kill and common assault. He had lived with a woman and her three children for some time, then entered hospital for treatment for alcoholism. When he said that he was about to return she told him that she did not want to see him again. He knocked on her door late at night, entered, took a sword off the wall and threatened her with it. He subsequently barricaded himself and the woman in a bedroom for two hours before the police forced entry and arrested him. Sentenced to five years' imprisonment.

Held, that the sentence made by the judge was a proper one. There was no material on which a hospital order could be made and the safety of the public must be considered.

R. *v.* BOWDEN (1986) 8 Cr.App.R.(S.) 155, C.A.

1068. Threatening to kill ex-wife following divorce

P, aged 50, pleaded guilty to threatening to kill. He and his wife were divorced after 25 years of marriage. After two injunctions had been granted to restrain P from communicating with or approaching his ex-wife, he broke into her house and shot her with a shotgun then shot himself. He was convicted of causing grievous bodily harm and sentenced to imprisonment. After release from prison and a chance meeting he made a series of telephone calls to his ex-wife in which he threatened to kill her. Sentenced to four years' imprisonment.

Held, that there was some doubt whether his former wife was actually put in fear and in view of P's age and poor health the sentence was reduced to two years' imprisonment.

R. *v.* PERRY (1986) 8 Cr.App.R.(S) 132, C.A.

1069. Time in custody before sentence—offence taken into consideration—sentence passed in respect of different offence

[Criminal Justice Act 1967 (c.80), s.67 (as amended).]

Time spent in custody in respect of an offence taken into consideration but in respect of which no separate sentence was passed was relevant to the overall length of sentence and should be given due weight in sentencing (*R.* v. *Webb* [1953] C.L.Y. 863 considered).

R. *v.* TOWERS, *The Times,* July 24, 1987, C.A.

1070. Time spent in custody abroad pending extradition—whether appropriate to reduce sentence—offenders resisted and prolonged extradition proceedings

S and R were convicted of robbery. They had robbed a jewellers and fled to the United States where they were arrested on arrival. They remained in custody in the U.S.A. for three years resisting and prolonging extradition proceedings by every possible means. Sentenced to 15 years' imprisonment.

Held, that although time spent in custody overseas would normally be taken into account—this was not a "normal" case. Their behaviour had considerably extended the time they spent in custody in the U.S.A. It would not be right to interfere with the sentences imposed because of what happened in the U.S.A.

R. *v.* SCALISE AND RACHEL (1985) 7 Cr.App.R.(S.) 395, C.A.

1071. Unlawful sexual intercourse—with step-daughter aged 15

G pleaded guilty to two counts of unlawful sexual intercourse with two others taken into consideration. He had had sexual intercourse with his 15-year-old step-daughter four times following the breakdown of relations with his wife. Sentenced to two years' imprisonment.

Held, that the sentence was appropriate taking into account his guilty plea and the effect the sentence had on G and his other children.

R. *v.* GOY (1986) 8 Cr.App.R.(S.) 40, C.A.

1072. Unlawful sexual intercourse—with step-daughter under 13

B, aged 35, pleaded guilty to indecent assault, unlawful sexual intercourse with a girl under the age of 13 and to unlawful sexual intercourse with a girl between the ages of 13 and 16. He had committed various sexual acts with his stepdaughter over a period of about three years when she was aged between 11 and 13. Sentenced to four years imprisonment for unlawful sexual intercourse with a girl under the age of 13 with concurrent sentences of 18 months on the other charges.

Held, that although this was not a case of incest, B was in the position of the child's father and the sentence was thoroughly deserved.

R. *v.* BARTHOLOMEW (1986) 8 Cr.App.R.(S.) 92, C.A.

1073. Violence by father towards child—series of incidents

T pleaded guilty to counts of inflicting grievous bodily harm and assault with seven other offences taken into consideration. Over a period of two years he had used violence on his young son, breaking a rib and an arm on separate occasions. Most of the offences were committed when T was looking after the son on his own, his wife having left him. Sentenced to four years' imprisonment.

Held, that the judge's overriding duty was to maintain the standards of parental responsibility. The sentence was appropriate.

R. *v.* THOMPSON (PETER ROBERT) (1985) 7 Cr.App.R.(S.) 240, C.A.

1074. Violence to children

J pleaded guilty to assault occasioning actual bodily harm. He was left in charge of his daughter aged two and a half and lost his temper when she wet the bed. He bit her on the cheek leaving teeth marks but not breaking the skin and no significant or lasting injury was caused. He had previous convictions for twice assaulting the same child when she was 13 weeks old breaking her right arm and striking her face and stomach, for which he was sentenced to 12 months' youth custody. After being into care, the child was returned to the mother on condition that she did not resume cohabitation with J. However, shortly after they did resume cohabitation without informing the social services. Sentenced to three years' imprisonment.

Held, that this was a case where the explanation was to be found in social inadequacy or momentary loss of temper and the injuries were relatively minor rather than one of brutality. In the judgment of the Court, the sentence was manifestly excessive and was reduced to 18 months.

R. *v.* JEFFERSON (1986) 8 Cr.App.R.(S.) 278, C.A.

1075. Violence to young children

G, aged 24, pleaded guilty to inflicting grevious bodily harm. She was living in a home with her son, aged four weeks. Following an argument with the father of the child, she returned and when the baby would not stop crying, she lost her temper and threw him towards the crib. When the baby continued to scream she hit him on the head with her hand about six times. The baby sustained fractures of the skull and the lower leg. There was a suspected healing fracture of the right clavicle, apparently 10 days old, but G did not admit causing that injury and the Court dealt with the case on the basis of a single unpremeditated assault. Sentenced to three years' imprisonment.

Held, that there was evidence in social inquiry and psychiatric reports that a probation order was desirable if the case was looked at solely from G's point of view, but the court found it impossible to say that a sentence of immediate imprisonment was unjustified. The court endorsed the view in *Boswell* that the only protection which could be afforded to a child of a few weeks old was for the law to step in and make it plain that such cases would be met with severe sentences. However, in all the circumstances a sentence of three years was unnecessarily long and a term of 12 months was substituted (*R.* v. *Boswell* [1983] C.L.Y. 850 referred to).

R. *v.* GREENHILL (1986) 8 Cr.App.R.(S.) 261, C.A.

1076. Wounding—victim attacking rapist after release from prison

D, a young woman who had been raped by X, went with three men to X's house, after he had been released on licence from an 18–month sentence after serving six months and punched and kicked him and hit him with sticks. X had returned to live near D and had taunted her whenever they met. D's boyfriend had suggested punishing X.

Held, in view of D's personal circumstances, the fact that X's sentence was much lower than now would be passed and the fact that he was released after only six months, D's sentence of six months' youth custody altered to probation, D having served two months' imprisonment. D had been separated from her 12-month-old child. But for the mitigating factors, 30 months might have been appropriate for this attack (*R.* v. *Billam* [1986] C.L.Y. 868 considered).

R. *v.* DARBY [1987] Crim.L.R. 281, C.A.

1077. Wounding with intent—attacking wife with hammer, causing grave injuries

D pleaded guilty to wounding his wife and with intent. He attacked her with a hammer following an argument over their baby and struck several blows causing fractures of the skull, nose, jaw and the bony cavity of an eye resulting in the loss of the eye. Sentenced to seven years' imprisonment.

Held, that the attack would have merited a longer sentence and the judge had given credit for all the mitigating factors. The sentence was proper in the circumstances.

R. *v.* DAVIES (DAVID WILLIAM) (1986) 8 Cr.App.R.(S.) 97, C.A.

1078. Wounding with intent—isolated offence of violence—conflicting medical evidence—whether custody for life appropriate

Under 21. Pleaded guilty. K was an assistant at a late-night hamburger stall, saw X, whom he believed to have caused trouble at the stall. K struck X with a heavy hammer, causing depressed skull fracture and injuries leading to removal of eye. Two previous findings of guilt as juvenile: burglary and making off. Medical evidence: no mental illness but psychopathic disorder. Further report on appeal suggested no personality disorder. Custody for life altered to five years youth custody (*R.* v. *de Havilland* [1984] C.L.Y. 883 considered).

R. *v.* KELLY [1987] Crim.L.R. 648, C.A.

1079. Young offenders—detention—guidelines

[Children and Young Persons Act 1933 (c.12), s.53(2) (as amended by Criminal Justice Act 1961 (c.39), s.2(1); Criminal Justice Act 1982 (c.48), s.7(8).]

A balance has to be struck when sentencing young offenders between keeping youths under 17 years of age from long terms in custody, and on the other hand providing appropriate punishment and deterrent in cases of serious crime.

F and others had received custodial sentences for a number of offences such as burglary, rape, arson, etc.

Held, on their appeals, that it was necessary to balance the principle of keeping young persons out of long jail terms, but at the same time consideration had to be given to meting out proper punishment, deterrence and sometimes protection of the public (*R.* v. *Oakes* [1984] C.L.Y. 875, and *R.* v. *Butler* [1985] C.L.Y. 815 not followed).

R. *v.* FAIRHURST [1986] 1 W.L.R. 1374, C.A.

1080. Young offenders—offence not of utmost gravity but meriting substantial sentence—whether sentence of detention appropriate

[Children and Young Persons Act 1933 (c.12), s.53(2); Criminal Justice Act 1982 (c.48), s.7(8)(9).]

Where a juvenile commits an offence which does not make him dangerous for the future, but which is of sufficient gravity that the maximum term of youth custody is inadequate the court should use its powers under s.53(2) of the 1933 Act to deal with the matter.

S. aged 16 and E. aged 18, who had criminal records, pleaded guilty to two counts of burglary. E also pleaded guilty to two counts of theft, and S. asked for 13, and E. for four similar cases to be taken into consideration. S. was sentenced to two years detention under the 1933 Act, and E to two years youth custody. Both appealed against sentence, S. contending that his sentence was wrong in principle in the light of the provisions of the 1982 Act.

Held, that both sentences were entirely appropriate (*R.* v. *Butler* [1985] C.L.Y. 815 applied; *R.* v. *Bosomworth* [1973] C.L.Y. 633, *R.* v. *Oakes* [1984] C.L.Y. 875 and *R.* v. *Nightingale* [1985] C.L.Y. 805 considered).

R. *v.* EALAND AND STANDING (1986) 83 Cr.App.R. 241, C.A.

1081. Youth custody—arson

Ages: P and M 17, R 16. Pleaded guilty to arson. Sentences; P and R 12 months' youth custody, M nine months. Sentencer said that he gave R credit for plea.

Held, that where sentencer considers appropriate sentence is more than 12 months' youth custody but reduces it to 12 months to reflect plea of guilty, no duty to reduce sentence further to reflect plea because 12 months was maximum youth custody for offender under 17. (Sentences reduced for other reasons) (*R.* v. *Murphy and Duke* [1986] C.L.Y. 724 considered).

R. *v.* PARKINSON, ROBERTS AND MULLINER [1987] Crim. L.R. 519, C.A.

1082. Youth custody—buggery by youth under 21 in private with man of 50—whether youth custody appropriate

V pleaded guilty to buggery. He had committed buggery on numerous occasions with a man of 50 with whom he had lived for several months. Sentenced to six months' youth custody for buggery consecutive to sentences totalling 30 months' youth custody for burglary and other offences.

Held, that the sentence was warranted by the offence.

R. *v.* VOLENHOLVEN (1986) 8 Cr.App.R.(S.) 260, C.A.

1083. Youth custody—burglary—whether offence so serious that non-custodial sentence not justified

Age: 19. Pleaded guilty to burglary of doctor's surgery, whose he stole fan heater, typewriter and £2. Six burglaries taken into consideration, including three of unoccupied council houses. Much of stolen property recovered. No previous convictions. Nine months' youth custody varied to community service order, since offence not "so serious that a non-custodial sentence cannot be justified" and none of other statutory criteria for youth custody were satisfied.

R. *v.* MURRAY [1987] Crim.L.R. 213, C.A.

1084. Youth custody—burglary—whether offence so serious that non-custodial sentence not justified—multiple offences

[Criminal Justice Act 1982 (c.48), s.1(4).]

Age: 18. Pleaded guilty. Three burglaries; 12 more taken into consideration. Included unoccupied dwelling-houses. No offences at night. Mostly within two-month period. No previous convictions. Social inquiry report recommended non-custodial sentence. 18 months' youth custody reduced on appeal to nine. Sentencer wrong in deciding offences so serious that non-custodial sentence could not be justified: in applying that test under s.1(4) of the 1982 Act, each offence should be considered individually. In considering under s.1(4) whether custodial sentence necessary for protection of public, however, broader approach justified and number of offences was relevant. Youth custody therefore justified.

R. *v.* ROBERTS [1987] Crim.L.R. 581, C.A.

1085. Youth custody—criminal damage—mitigating circumstances—length of sentence

The three defendants, aged 18, 18 and 17, pleaded guilty to one count of criminal damage. All three young men had been drinking in a public house and then a disco. On their way home they went into a cemetery to urinate. They then began to knock over gravestones in an area set aside for the Commonwealth Graves Commission. Sixty gravestones were damaged. Forty were damaged beyond repair and the total repair bill was estimated at £6,000. None had previous convictions and all were described as being of excellent character and from respectable homes. They were each sentenced to 12 months' youth custody. It was argued that once the trial judge had decided that a custodial sentence was inevitable to mark public outrage at the offence he could take into account the exellent mitigating circumstances and order a period at a detention centre.

Held, that the nature of the case was such as to cause outrage amongst the public and punishment was a proper element in the sentence. The sentence was right in principle and amount.

R. *v.* ANDERSON, BEE AND HODGKINS, June 23, 1987, C.A. [*Ex rel. Richard Martin, Barrister.*]

1086. Youth custody—discount for plea

Robbery, two burglaries and one theft. Thirteen offences taken into consideration. Sentence of 12 months' youth custody (maximum youth custody) upheld despite guilty plea, since a 2-year term of detention under s.53(2) of the Children and Young Persons Act 1933 would have been a proper sentence for the robbery (*R.* v. *Pilford* [1985] C.L.Y.

754, *R.* v. *Stewart* [1984] C.L.Y. 936, *R.* v. *Fleming* [1985] C.L.Y. 809 and *R.* v. *Reynolds* [1987] C.L.Y. 1097 considered).

R. *v.* GODBER [1987] Crim.L.R. 278, C.A.

1087. Youth custody—endangering safety of railway passengers by placing concrete slab on railway line

B, aged 20, was convicted of endangering the safety of railway passengers and obstructing the railway and also pleaded guilty to burglary and obtaining by deception. He placed one or more slabs of concrete on a railway line which was struck by a passenger train travelling at high speed, almost derailing it. Sentenced to 10 years' youth custody.

Held, that the sentencer's reasoning was correct in that there was nothing wrong mentally with B and the sentence reflected the need for deterrence and punishment, and provided protection for the public whilst he matured.

R. *v.* BANKS (1986) 8 Cr.App.R.(S.) 157, C.A.

1088. Youth custody—guilty plea—whether maximum 12 months appropriate

Age: 16—wounding with intent—stabbing. If S had been 17 or older, at least two years' imprisonment would have been appropriate. Nevertheless, 12 months' youth custody (maximum) reduced to 10 to reflect guilty plea. Importance of giving credit for guilty pleas emphasised.

R. *v.* STOREY [1987] Crim.L.R. 209, C.A.

1089. Youth custody—manslaughter of father by daughter

T, aged 18, was convicted of manslaughter on an indictment for murder. After a series of incidents in which her father behaved aggressively and provocatively towards her, she stabbed him with a kitchen knife which she had picked up some time earlier. Sentenced to four years' youth custody.

Held, that it was necessary to tailor the punishment to the degree of provocation which existed in the individual case, and to the individual circumstances of the offender. The sentence was reduced to two years' youth custody.

R. *v.* TYLER (1986) 8 Cr.App.R.(S.) 254, C.A.

1090. Youth custody—manslaughter of father by son

F, aged 17, pleaded guilty to manslaughter on an indictment for murder. He had shot his father with a shotgun after finding him in a violent argument with his mother. There was a long history of violent episodes in which the mother had been the victim. Sentenced to two years' youth custody.

Held, that the sentence was right. It was necessary to make clear that weapons of this type must not be resorted to in these sort of circumstances, and it was necessary that F should expiate his crime.

R. *v.* FRENCH (1986) 8 Cr.App.R.(S.) 147, C.A.

1091. Youth custody—planned robbery—violence used

R pleaded guilty to robbery and two counts of burglary. R, aged 16, was associating with a girl who in turn associated with a man of 53 who gambled. It was arranged for the girl to go with the man to a casino. R approached him knocked him unconscious and kicked him dislocating his shoulder. R stole the man's wallet with £620 in cash. The burglaries were sneak thefts of handbags or wallets from shops. Sentenced to three years' youth custody for the robbery and six months' consecutive for the burglaries.

Held, that the robbery was so serious that a non-custodial sentence could not be justified. It was a carefully planned and vicious street attack. The sentence was entirely appropriate. Had it not been for R's guilty plea, a sentence of four an a half years' youth custody would have been justified.

R. *v.* RICHARDS (LENNOX TIMOTHY) (1986) 8 Cr.App.R. (S.) 14, C.A.

1092. Youth custody—robbery of shop

M, aged 17 and of previous good character pleaded guilty to robbery. He entered a newsagent's shop and stole £270 from the woman assistant who was alone. When chased, M threw the money away. Sentenced to 18 months' youth custody.

Held, that anyone committing this sort of offence, however young and however good his character, should expect a custodial sentence. The offence was pre-calculated and was of a sort that caused alarm to the public. The sentence was appropriate.

R. *v.* MALTBY (1986) 8 Cr.App.R.(S.) 62, C.A.

1093. Youth custody—robbery of shop by youth carrying firearm

M was convicted of robbery. He had threatened a shop assistant in a grocer's shop with a firearm and stolen £50. Sentenced to six years' youth custody.

Held, that a custodial sentence was the only appropriate way of dealing with M and the sentence must be one to deter others M. had not pleaded guilty and so forced the shop assistant to give evidence. The sentence was an appropriate one.

R. *v.* McNAMEE (1985) 7 Cr.App.R.(S.) 384, C.A.

1094. Youth custody—series of rapes

P was convicted of rape and indecent assault. He had raped a 14 year old and a 15 year old girl and indecently assaulted a 13 year old. The offences happened over a period of 16 months. In each case the victims were threatened with a knife. Sentenced to nine years' youth custody.

Held, that P was prepared to use violence if necessary. This was a course of violent conduct over a long period against young women. Some of the aggravating features set out in *R.* v. *Roberts* [1982] C.L.Y. 703 were present. The sentence was correct (*R.* v. *Roberts* [1982] C.L.Y. 703 referred to).

R. *v.* PRESLEY (1985) 7 Cr.App.R.(S.) 267, C.A.

1095. Youth custody—stabbing in course of robbery

M, aged 19, pleaded guilty to robbery, wounding and attempted theft. He had tried to snatch a young girl's handbag in a car park late at night. When she resisted he stabbed her in the back, causing grave injuries. Sentenced to six years' youth custody.

Held, that this was an extremely grave form of robbery. It is necessary to deter others from carrying knives and using them when robbing people. The sentence was neither wrong in principle nor excessive. (*R.* v. *Paton* [1982] C.L.Y. 684 referred to).

R. *v.* McAUSLANE (1985) 7 Cr.App.R.(S.) 316, C.A.

1096. Youth custody—theft—whether offence so serious that non-custodial sentence not justified

Age: 16. Pleaded guilty to six counts of theft. 24 taken into consideration. Assistant in jewellers' shop stole jewellery worth over £5,000 over six month period. No previous convictions. Youth custody upheld but reduced from nine to six months. Custodial sentence was only appropriate sentence since offences so serious.

R. *v.* STANLEY [1987] Crim.L.R. 214, C.A.

1097. Youth custody—12 months' youth custody imposed on juvenille after guilty plea

R, aged 16, pleaded guilty to robbery and attempted robbery. He pushed a 72 year-old lady to the ground and stole £38 in cash. Later with an accomplice he attempted to rob a shop armed with an air rifle but ran off. Sentenced to 12 months' youth custody. R appealed arguing that insufficient credit had been given to his guilty plea.

Held, that the sentencer had considered a term of detention but had decided against that, partly because R had already been in custody for three months. Any discount on the youth custody sentence would have made the sentence inadequate. The judge had taken account of the mitigating factors and the sentence was correct.

R. *v.* REYNOLDS (1985) 7 Cr.App.R.(S.) 335, C.A.

1098. Youth custody—wounding with intent after provocation.

P aged 18 and of good character, pleaded guilty to wounding with intent. His girlfriend was pregnant by him. He met with her to discuss the child and was armed with a knife to protect himself against the girl's brother. She taunted P and he stabbed her six times. Sentenced to three years' youth custody.

Held, that where an offence had been committed under great emotional pressure a sentence would have no deterrent affect on others in a similar position. There was no need to pass a deterrent sentence on P but it was necessary for the court to express its disapproval of P's conduct, punish him for his wrongdoing and pass a sentence which would allow him to expiate his guilt. A sentence of two years' youth custody would be appropriate (*R.* v. *Black* [1983] C.L.Y. 911, *R.* v. *Hayley* [1983] C.L.Y. 764, *R.* v. *Cole* [1984] C.L.Y. 930 considered).

R *v.* PROCTOR (1985) 7 Cr.App.R.(S.) 237, C.A.

1099. Youth custody for life—observations on criteria for use

T, aged 17, pleaded guilty to burglary, attempted robbery and wounding with intent. He broke into a school and caused extensive damage. Then a few days later, wearing a balaclava mask, he accosted another youth in the street at night, threatening him with a breadknife and demanded money. The youth ran away but T caught up with him in a nearby house and lunged at him with the knife causing wounds to his face and hand. T asked for five other offences to be considered including an assault on a youth with a beer glass. He had several previous convictions for dishonesty and violence. Sentenced to custody for life for attempted robbery and wounding with intent, with 12 months youth custody concurrent for burglary.

Held, that the sentencer had taken the view that a sentence of custody for life was appropriate so that the situation could be reviewed from time to time and did not have in mind the criteria for life imprisonment mentioned in *Pither*. The offences were clearly very serious and revealed that T was disturbed although not mentally ill but a determinate sentence was appropriate. Eight years' youth custody substituted (*R.* v. *Pither* (1979) 1 Cr.App.R.(S.) 209 cited).

R. *v.* TURTON (MARK JOHN) (1986) 8 Cr.App.R.(S.) 174, C.A.

1100. Youth custody sentence—statutory criteria

[Criminal Justice Act 1982 (c.48), s.1(4).]

M aged 17 pleaded guilty to six counts of theft. Togther with another he had stolen property from a number of shops in the course of a single afternoon to a value of £168. M had one previous conviction for theft with a fine of £40. Sentenced to six months' youth custody.

Held, that the protection of the public from M was not an issue, the offence was not so serious that a non-custodial sentence could not be justified and, although M had a few months earlier been fined for a similar offence that was not sufficient ground for saying that he was unwilling to respond to non-custodial sentences. As the provisions of the Criminal Justice Act 1982 s.1(4) had not been complied with, the Court would substitute a fine for the sentence of youth custody but as M had already served two months' in custody the fine would only be £2 on each count.

R. *v.* MUNDAY (1985) 7 Cr.App.R.(S.) 216, C.A.

CUSTOMS AND EXCISE

1101. Agricultural levies

AGRICULTURAL LEVY RELIEFS (FROZEN BEEF AND VEAL) ORDER 1987 (No. 134) [80p], made under the Customs and Excise Duties (General Reliefs) Act 1979 (c.3), s.4; operative on February 27, 1987; provides for the allocation of a levy free importation of frozen beef and veal.

1102. Betting duty

GENERAL BETTING DUTY REGULATIONS 1987 (No. 1963) [£1·60], made under the Betting and Gaming Duties Act 1981 (c.63), s.12(2) and Sched. 1, para. 2; operative on December 20, 1987; replace S.I. 1986 No. 400 with modifications which reflect the abolition of the on-course rate of general betting duty by s.3 of the Finance Act 1987.

GENERAL BETTING DUTY (AMENDMENT) REGULATIONS 1987 (No. 312) [45p], made under the Betting and Gaming Duties Act 1981 (c.63), s.12(2), Sched. 1, para. 2; operative on March 29, 1987; simplify the accounting procedures of off-course bookmakers.

1103. Cheating the public revenue—whether positive deception necessary. See R. *v.* MAVJI, §764.

1104. Community transit

CUSTOMS AND EXCISE (COMMUNITY TRANSIT) REGULATIONS 1987 (No. 763) [£1·30], made under the European Communities Act 1972 (c.68), s.2(2); operative on June 1, 1987; replace S.I. 1980 No. 762 and provide for penalties and forfeiture of goods in relation to breaches of certain Community transit of goods regulations.

CUSTOMS AND EXCISE (COMMUNITY TRANSIT) (No. 2) REGULATIONS 1987 (no. 2105) [85p], made under the European Communities Act 1972 s.2(2); operative on January 1, 1988; replace S.I. 1987 No. 763 and provide for a penalty and forfeiture for breaches of certain Community transit regulations.

1105. Counterfeit goods

COUNTERFEIT GOODS (CUSTOMS) REGULATIONS 1987 (No. 2097) [85p], made under the European Communities Act 1972 (c.68, s.2(2); operative on January 1, 1988; makes provision consequential upon Council Regulations (EEC) No. 3842/86 so as to provide for measures to prohibit the release for free circulation of counterfeit goods.

1106. Customs duties

CUSTOMS DUTIES (ECSC) ORDER 1987 (No. 2184) [85p], made under the European Communities Act 1972 (c.68), s.5(1) and (3); operative on January 1, 1988; replaces S.I. 1985 No. 1630.

CUSTOMS DUTIES (ECSC) (No. 2) (AMENDMENT No. 6) ORDER 1987 (No. 973) [45p], made under the European Communities Act 1972 (c.68), s.2(2); operative on May 26, 1987; amends S.I. 1985 No. 1630.

CUSTOMS DUTIES (ECSC) (No. 2) (AMENDMENT No. 7) ORDER 1987 (No. 1053) [45p], made under the European Communities Act 1972, s.5(1)(3), Sched. 2, para. 4; operative on June 17, 1987; amends S.I. 1985 No. 1630.

CUSTOMS DUTIES (ECSC) (No. 2) (AMENDMENT No. 8) ORDER 1987 (No. 1125) [45p], made under the European Communities Act 1972, s.5(1)(3), Sched. 2, para. 4; operative on July 3, 1987; amends S.I. 1985 No. 1630 so as to reintroduce duties on certain importations from Yugoslavia.

CUSTOMS DUTIES (ECSC) (No. 2) (AMENDMENT No. 9) ORDER 1987 (No. 1218) [45p], made under the European Communities Act 1972, s.5(1)(3); operative on July 15, 1987; continues in effect the provisions formerly contained in S.I. 1987 Nos. 973 and 1053.

CUSTOMS DUTIES (ECSC) (No. 2) (AMENDMENT No. 10) Order 1987 (No. 1804) [45p], made under the European Communities Act 1972, s.5(1)(3), Sched. 2, para. 4; operative on October 25, 1987; continues in effect provisions formerly contained in S.I. 1987 No. 1125 relating to goods falling within heading 73.13 originating in Yugoslavia.

CUSTOMS DUTIES (ECSC) (No. 2) (AMENDMENT No. 11) ORDER 1987 (No. 1902) [45p], made under the European Communities Act 1972, s.5(1)(3), Sched. 2, para 4; operative on November 6, 1987; reimposes duties on goods falling with headings 73.08, 73.11A1 AIV a) 1 and 73.11B originating in Yugoslavia.

1107. Customs duties—revocation of savings

CUSTOMS DUTIES (REPEALS) (REVOCATION OF SAVINGS) ORDER 1987 (No. 2106) [45p], made under the European Communities Act 1972 (c.68), s.4, Sched. 3, Pt. 1; operative on January 1, 1988; revokes S.I. 1977 No. 2028.

1108. Customs duties—temporary importation—revocation

CUSTOMS DUTIES (TEMPORARY IMPORTATION) (REVOCATION) REGULATIONS 1987 (No. 1781) [45p], made under the Customs and Excise Management Act 1979 (c.2), s.48; operative on November 10, 1987; provides for the revocation of a number of statutory instruments which relate to relief from duty on goods temporarily imported as that is now subject to Council Regulation (EEC) No. 3599/82.

1109. Evasion of duty—importer

[Customs and Excise Management Act 1979, s.170(2).]

C, a minibus operator and driver brought back from Heidelberg to England wines, etc., and tobacco to the maximum duty free allowance for the number of passengers he was carrying. He purported to give the items to the passengers but did not intend genuine gifts.

Held, dismissing C's appeal against conviction, that there was no relief from duty unless the articles were carried with or in the accompanying baggage of the person importing them. "Importer", at any time between importation and delivery of the goods out of charge, included, by s.1 of the 1979 Act, any person for the time being possessed of or beneficially interested in the goods. The jury were entitled to find C to have been the owner and possessor and beneficially interested in these goods to the passengers' exclusion.

R. *v.* COLLINS [1979] Crim.L.R. 256, C.A.

1110. Export controls

EXPORTS OF GOODS (CONTROL) ORDER 1987 (No. 2070) [£7·90], made under the Import, Export and Customs Powers (Defence) Act 1939 (c.69), s.1; operative on January 1, 1988; replaces S.I. 1985 No. 849.

EXPORT OF GOODS (CONTROL) (AMENDMENT No. 8) ORDER 1987 (No. 215) [45p], made under the Import, Export and Customs Powers (Defence) Act 1939 (c.69), Ss.1; operative on January 24, 1987; Further amends S.I. 1985 No. 849.

EXPORT OF GOODS (CONTROL) (AMENDMENT No. 9) ORDER 1987 (No. 271) [45p], made under the Import, Export and Customs Powers (Defence) Act 1939, s.1; operative on March 10, 1987; further amends S.I. 1985 No. 849.

EXPORT OF GOODS (CONTROL) (AMENDMENT No. 10) ORDER 1987 (No. 1350) [45p], made under the Import, Export and Customs Powers (Defence) Act 1939 (c.69), s.1; operative on August 17, 1987; amends S.I. 1985 No. 849 in relation to the exportation of helicopters and aircraft to Libya, South Africa or Namibia.

1111. Goods declared voluntarily in green channel—whether an offence

[Customs and Excise Management Act 1979 (c.2), s.78(1), (3).]

A person who declared goods voluntarily in the green "nothing to declare" channel rather than in the red "goods to declare" channel was guilty of an offence, since s.78(1) of the Customs and Excise Management Act created an absolute offence.

CUSTOMS AND EXCISE COMMISSIONERS *v.* CLAUS, *The Times*, July 6, 1987, D.C.

1112. Import duty reliefs—revocation

IMPORT DUTY RELIEFS (REVOCATION) ORDER 1987 (No. 1785) [45p], made under the Customs and Excise Duties (General Reliefs) Act 1979 (c.3), ss.1, 4; operative on November 10, 1987; revokes S.I. 1970 No. 380.

1113. Importation of drugs—belief that goods were pornographic films—both prohibited goods—whether "knowingly concerned" in importation of drugs

[Customs and Excise Management Act 1979 (c.2), s.170(2).]

A person was guilty of being knowingly concerned in the fraudulent evasion of the prohibition against the importation of a controlled drug where he mistakenly believed the goods to be pornographic films subject to a prohibition against importation.

E was concerned in the importation of cannabis into England concealed in a secret compartment in a motor car. E was indicted with being knowingly concerned in the fraudulent evasion of the prohibition against the importation of a controlled drug contrary to s.170(2) of the Customs and Excise Management Act 1979. E pleaded not guilty. The trial judge ruled that even if E's defence were accepted he would still be guilty of the offence whereupon E changed his plea to guilty and appealed. E's defence was that he believed the cannabis to be pornographic films subject to a prohibition against importation. The importation of such goods was in fact prohibited. E contended that the provisions of the Misuse of Drugs of Act 1971 created separate offences of being knowingly concerned in the fraudulent evasion of the prohibition against the importation of controlled drugs of Class A, B and C respectively. Consequently it could not be said that knowingly importing prohibited pornographic films constituted a sufficient *actus reus* and *mens rea* for the commission of an offence concerning controlled drugs.

Held, dismissing E's appeal, that "knowingly" in s.170(2) Customs and Excise Management Act 1979 was concerned with knowing that a fraudulent evasion of a prohibition against importing goods was taking place. It did not matter what goods E thought he was importing provided he thought those goods were subject to a prohibition against importation and the goods he thought he was importing as well as the actual goods he was importing were subject to such a prohibition. There was no separate offence purely confined to the importation of drugs nor separate offences for each class of controlled drugs (*R.* v. *Hussain* [1969] C.L.Y. 854, *R.* v. *Hennessey* [1979] C.L.Y. 472 applied; *R.* v. *Taaffe* [1984] C.L.Y. 581, *R.* v. Courtie [1984] C.L.Y. 523, *R.* v. *Shivpuri* [1986] C.L.Y. 482 considered).

R. *v.* ELLIS, STREET AND SMITH (1987) 84 Cr.App.R. 235, C.A.

1114. Indecent or obscene articles—prohibition on importation—goods which can lawfully be made and sold within U.K.

[Customs Consolidation Act 1876 (c.36), s.42; EEC Treaty (Cmnd. 5179–11) arts. 30, 36, 234.]

A prohibition on the importation of articles of an indecent nature cannot be justified when the articles may be lawfully bought and sold within the boundaries of the U.K.

D imported rubber female dolls of an erotic nature. They were impounded by the Customs and Excise. The justices decided that their importation was prohibited by s.42 of the Customs Consolidation Act 1876 as being indecent and obscene, and ordered forfeiture. An appeal to Judge Anwyl-Davies in the Crown Court was dismissed. The Divisional Court referred the matter to the European Court of Justice.

Held, allowing the appeal and quashing the order for forfeiture that the prohibition was not justified on the grounds of public morality and constituted an arbitrary discrimination on trade between Member States (*R.* v. *Henn* [1980] C.L.Y. 1195 applied).

CONEGATE *v.* H.M. CUSTOMS AND EXCISE [1987] 2 W.L.R. 39, Kennedy J.

1115. Methylated spirits

METHYLATED SPIRITS REGULATIONS 1987 (No. 2009) [£2·20], made under the Alcoholic Liquor Duties Act 1979 (c.4), s.77; operative on December 29, 1987; revoke and replace S.I. 1983 No. 252.

1116. Non-commercial consignments relief

EXCISE DUTIES (SMALL NON-COMMERCIAL CONSIGNMENTS) RELIEF (AMENDMENT) REGULATIONS 1987 (No. 149) [45p], made under the European Communities Act 1972 (c.68), s.2(2); operative on March 9, 1987; increases the level of relief from excise duty on imports on certain small consignments of a non-commercial nature.

1117. Northern Ireland

NORTHERN IRELAND (PRESCRIBED AREA) REGULATIONS 1987 (No. 2114) [45p], made under the Customs and Excise Management Act 1979 (c.2), s.1(1); operative on January 5, 1988; revokes S.I. 1953 No. 1531 and prescribes a strip of land 20 miles wide on the land boundary as the prescribed area.

1118. Petroleum products

ORIGIN OF GOODS (PETROLEUM PRODUCTS) REGULATIONS 1987 (no. 2107) [85p], made under the Customs and Excise Management Act 1979 (c.2), s.120(1) and (2); operative on January 1, 1988; lay down the conditions under which certain petroleum products are to be treated as originating in a country for the purposes of preferential rates of customs duties.

1119. Police and Criminal Evidence Act 1984—application

POLICE AND CRIMINAL EVIDENCE ACT 1984 (APPLICATION TO CUSTOMS AND EXCISE) ORDER 1987 (No. 439) [45p], made under the Police and Criminal Evidence Act 1984 (c.60), s.114(2); operative on April 7, 1987; amends S.I. 1985 No. 1800 by adding a reference to s.107 of the 1984 Act in Sched. 1 to that Order.

1120. Portugal

CUSTOMS DUTIES (PORTUGAL) (TRANSITIONAL MEASURES) ORDER 1986 (No. 2182) [£6·00], made under the European Communities Act 1972 (c.68), s.5(2)(3); operative on January 1, 1987; implements obligations of the U.K. in relation to the accession of Portugal to the eec.

1121. Quota relief

CUSTOMS DUTIES (ECSC) (QUOTA AND OTHER RELIEFS) ORDER 1987 (No. 2126) [£1·90], made under the Customs and Excise Duties (General Reliefs) Act 1979 (c.3), ss.1, 4; operative on January 1, 1988; provides for reliefs from customs duties on certain iron and steel products originating in a specified developing country.

CUSTOMS DUTIES (QUOTA RELIEF) ORDER 1987 (No. 1122) [45p], made under the Customs and Excise Duties (General Reliefs) Act 1979, s.4; operative on July 1, 1987; provides exemptions on the importation of rum, arrack and tafia from the ACP countries.

1122. Reckless completion of false document—construction of document

[Customs and Excise Management Act 1979 (c.2), s.167(1).]

C provided certificates of export which gave as the export dates, dates several days after the date of signature. The defence suggested that the documents should be construed as certifying that goods would be exported. The prosecution submitted that either the documents must be regarded as certifying that goods had been exported prior to the date of signature as the documents, if nonsense, were false in a material particular.

Held, quashing C's conviction of recklessly completing a document false in a material particular, contrary to s.167(1) of the 1979 Act, that the judge had erred in ruling that construction of the documents was a matter for the jury. They could not be construed to mean that the goods had already been exported at the date of signature.

R. *v.* CROSS [1987] Crim.L.R. 43, C.A.

1123. Spain

CUSTOMS DUTIES (SPAIN) (TRANSITIONAL MEASURES) ORDER 1986 (No. 2178) [£12·50] made under the European Communities Act 1972 (c.68), s.5(2)(3), Sched. 2, para. 4; operative on January 1, 1987; implements obligations of the U.K. in relation to the accession of Spain to the EEC.

1124. Spoilt beer

SPOILT BEER (REMISSION AND REPAYMENT OF DUTY) REGULATIONS 1987 (No. 314) [£1·40], made under the Alcoholic Liquor Duties Act 1979 (c.4), ss.2, 3, 36; operative on April 1, 1987; specify conditions to be complied with in claiming relief on spoilt beer after it has been delivered from a brewery.

DAMAGES

1125. Admiralty practice—collision—currency of claim. See SHIPPING AND MARINE INSURANCE, §3390, 3391.

1126. Agent—non-existent principal—assessment of damages

When an agent has held himself out as acting for a principal which has ceased to exist, the measure of damages against the agent is the expenditure wasted in (a) the manufacturing, packing and shipping of goods not paid for, and (b) costs thrown away in claiming against the non-existent principal.

FARLEY HEALTH PRODUCTS *v.* BABYLON TRADING CO., *The Times,* July 29, 1987, Sir Neil Lawson.

1127. Assessment—loss of enjoyment of flat due to damp and infestation

P occupied a flat for three-and-a-half years with her three children as tenants of the local authority. The premises were damp. A leaking roof had caused cracks and staining to the ceilings. The dampness was aggravated by condensation and caused black mould on the window frames. The kitchen was infested by black beetles. The family retreated into one bedroom as the other rooms were so cold. Damages were assessed at £3,284—(1) speical damages were awarded to compensate P for her loss of enjoyment caused by the landlord's breaches of the repairing obligations; (2) special damages in respect of damage to clothing and furniture caused by the dampness was assessed at 75 per cent. of the acquisition cost; (3) general damages of £1,750 were awarded for the inconvenience and ill-health suffered by P and her children; (4) interest at 15 per cent. was awarded on items of special damage, and 2 per cent. on items of general damages.

MEAH *v.* MAYOR AND BURGESSES OF THE LONDON BOROUGH OF TOWER HAMLETS, August 14, 1986, Bow County Ct. [*Ex rel. Robert Latham, Barrister.*]

1128. Assessment—loss of use of car after traffic accident

P was involved in a road traffic accident. Her car was so badly damaged that it was beyond economical repair. P was without use of the car for nine weeks. She worked as a laboratory assistant, six miles from home. She had used the car to travel to work, to attend church services twice a week and other social activities. P claimed damages for loss of use of her vehicle in addition to the pre-accident value of the car, the petrol within the car, the loss of her radio, storage and recovery charges. Special damages of £1,229·50 were awarded and £540 general damages (for the nine-week loss of use at £60 p.w.)

MACKAY *v.* JACKSON, January 2, 1987, H.H. Judge J. R. Arthur, Birkenhead County Ct. [*Ex rel. Fanshaw, Porter & Hazlehurst, Solicitors.*]

1129. Beneficial occupation of premises—method of valuation

In quantifying damages, the correct method of valuing beneficial occupation of premises for set-off against the final award is to take the rental value of the refurbished premises and deduct from it the rent actually paid under the lease.

G. P. & P. *v.* BULCRAIG & DAVIS, *The Times,* October 30, 1987, C.A.

1130. Breach of contract—tour operator—extent of liability

A tour operator is liable for consequences which flow naturally from his breach of contract, and for any additional consequences which should reasonably have been within his contemplation when contracting.

W, P's wife, booked a holiday with D for herself and P. At the time of booking, W told D that P was asthmatic, could not be there because he was ill, and needed health insurance. The first two days of the holiday were sufficiently disastrous to bring on an asthmatic attack lasting several days, which ruined the holiday, and for which (*inter alia*) P sought damages against D. The judge found that asthma was not sufficiently common for P's attack to be reasonably foreseeable or to bring it within D's contemplation, but held that in view of W's remarks about P's health, D was put on notice. He allowed £800 damages for P's asthmatic attack, D appealed.

Held, allowing the appeal, that W's remarks about P's health had been merely conversational and not part of the booking arrangements, and therefore D was not liable for damages for the attack (*Koufos* v. *Czarnikow* [1967] C.L.Y. 3623 applied).

KEMP *v.* INTASUN HOLIDAYS, *Financial Times,* July 1, 1987, C.A.

1131. Breach of contract—tour operator—honeymoon. See USHER *v.* INTASUN HOLIDAYS, §418.

1132. Building contract—breach—damages for distress and inconvenience

P sued D for breach of a building contract whereby D had agreed to carry out renovation works to P's house. Time was not of the essence but three months was contemplated as time to completion. D was dismissed finally after seven months, the works being either unfinished or done in a defective manner. During the works, P and her three children were forced to live in a house with no central heating and were without running water for seven weeks. P had to take a second job to pay for the work. The alternative was to forfeit all moneys paid to her under a local authority grant. P suffered considerable distress and anxiety. On the assessment of damages, in addition to damages for the cost of remedial work, £750 was awarded for distress and inconvenience (*Mattia* v. *Amato* [1983] C.L.Y. 963 and *Franks* v. *Gates* [1984] C.L.Y. 1011 considered).

INGLIS *v.* CANT, February 19, 1987, Mr. Recorder Baker, Newport, Isle of Wight, County Ct. [*Ex rel. Philip Glen, Barrister.*]

1133. Building contract—breach—damages for inconvenience

P sued D for breach of a building contract whereby D had agreed to carry out conversion work to P's house. The work was carried out in late 1979. P suffered rainwater coming through the roof during the weekend during the works, then continual entry of rainwater into most of the bedrooms. This continued until February 1981. P put up with a collapsed ceiling and a pigeon flying in her bedroom on one occasion. The standard of workmanship was described as appalling by surveyors. The roof sealant was permitted to run down the side of the house. There was fungus and dry rot in the house. Window catches were too high for P to reach. P had to put down towels on the window-ledge to mop up the water. On one occasion P filled two buckets with this water from one window. In addition to damages for the cost of remedial work, general damages of £1,500 were awarded for inconvenience, vexation and loss of amenity of the home.

WILKINS *v.* BOWER, H.H. Judge J. A. Stannard, Official Referee. [*Ex rel. John Pugh, Barrister.*]

1134. Cargo damage—whether owners of cargo could claim substantial damages from shipowners. See SHIPPING AND MARINE INSURANCE, §3376.

1135. Charterparty—demurrage—calculation in dollars and payment in sterling—depreciation of sterling—whether currency exchange loss recoverable as special damages. See PRESIDENT OF INDIA *v.* LIPS MARITIME CORP., §3399.

1136. Commencement of action—offer of payment before action without costs—whether action an abuse. See SMITH *v.* SPRINGER, §2966.

1137. Consortium—damages for impairment

P's wife received such severe brain damage in an accident that she was reduced to the mental level of a small child, and she was so badly physically incapacitated that she was totally dependent on others.

Held, that P was entitled to damages for impairment, as opposed to total loss, of consortium. In this case the impairment of the bundle of rights associated with consortium was so gross that P had been left with a helpless child to look after. Damages of £20,000 were awarded.

HODGSON *v.* TRAPP, *The Times,* May 9, 1987, Taylor J.

1138. Contract of employment—repudiatory breach—unilateral variation of terms—reduction in pay—whether damages limited to notice period. See RIGBY *v.* FERODO, §1305.

1139. Contract of employment—repudiatory breach—whether permissible to award damages for injured feelings. See BLISS *v.* SOUTH EAST THAMES REGIONAL HEALTH AUTHORITY, §1303.

1140. Defamation—loss of reputation—distress—loss of income—reduction on account of similar publications

[Aus.] The appellant appealed against the damages awarded to a medical practitioner in respect of whom evidence before a coronial inquiry had been misreported.

Held, dismissing the appeal, that (1) damages for loss of reputation were not limited to pecuniary loss suffered by the respondent, the respondent being entitled to be compensated under this head of damage for loss of professional standing, injury to his feelings and effects on his health; (2) although local statute precluded the recovery of exemplary damages, the inadequacy of a published correction and the failure to publish an apology were relevant to assessment of damages for loss of reputation and distress; (3) the conduct of a defendant to a defamation action up to and including the hearing was relevant to the assessment of damages for loss of reputation and distress (*Cassell and Co.* v. *Broome* [1972] C.L.Y. 2745 applied); (4) although the trial judge had properly reduced the claim for economic loss on account of similar publications in other newspapers, it had not been shown that the award of damages for loss of reputation and distress was excessive (*Lewis* v. *Daily Telegraph* [1964] C.L.Y. 2130 referred to).

MIRROR NEWSPAPERS *v.* JOOLS (1986) 65 A.L.R. 174, Federal Ct. of Australia.

1141. Distress and inconvenience—breach of domestic building contract

P sued D for breach of a building contract whereby D had agreed to carry out works at P's home including the construction of a new bathroom and kitchen and the conversion of the existing bathroom into a bedroom. It was an express term of the contract that the work would take five weeks. After four months D abandoned the works in an incomplete state. P could not afford the £1,380 required by other builders to finish the work. For 18 months P had to share his bedroom with his son. A surveyor described the kitchen as "appalling . . . unfit for use" and the bathroom as "serviceable but very old-fashioned and unpleasant." The garden was strewn with rubble and unsuitable as a play area for P's infant daughter. In addition to damages based on the additional cost needed to finish the work, there was an award of £1,000 general damages for inconvenience and distress.

YASIN *v.* RASHID, April 22, 1987, H.H. Judge Wootton, Birmingham County Ct. [*Ex rel. Jonathan Perkins, Barrister.*]

1142. Effect of collateral funding arrangements—whether D prevented from recovering damages counterclaimed

P were architects who sued D a registered housing association for their fees. D counterclaimed for damages for alleged negligence in or about P's design, supervision and administration of certain housing development schemes. P contended that in no event had D suffered damage since the arrangements between D and their funding authority, the Housing Corporation, and the Department of the Environment included undertakings by these bodies to pay to D the actual cost of the projects. P further contended that since these undertakings remained unaffected by any negligence by P, D had suffered no loss. The issue was tried as a preliminary issue.

Held, that neither the approval of the projects by the Secretary of State for the Environment nor the fact that grants had actually been made whether pursuant to an entitlement in D or otherwise, operated to prevent D from recovering from P any of the damages counterclaimed (dicta of Donovan L.J. in *Browning* v. *War Office* [1963] C.L.Y. 951 considered and applied).

DESIGN 5 *v.* KENISTON HOUSING ASSOCIATION (1986) 34 B.L.R. 92, H.H. Judge Smout Q.C., O.R.

1143. Exemplary damages—landlord convicted of malicious wounding

P had been a tenant since 1977 and D the landlord since July 1983. D had threatened P, had pushed a door into his face in March 1984 thereby breaking his glasses, and had pushed P in the face with his hand in May 1984. In November 1984 D had assaulted P with a hammer and knife causing a number of injuries including lacerations to the head, and had stabbed P through the right chest puncturing his lung. P was in hospital for five days but eventually made a full recovery. D was convicted of malicious wounding in respect of this last assault. In June 1984 P had agreed to move temporarily from his room to another room in the house to enable repairs to be carried out. D refused subsequently to allow P back into his room.

Held, that this was an appropriate case for an award of exemplary damages. P was awarded £3,000 (*Drane* v. *Evangelon* [1978] C.L.Y. 1822, *Asghan* v. *Ahmed* [1985] C.L.Y. 1652 and *Hodgson* v. *Jacobs* [1984] C.L.Y. 1002 referred to).

COLLIER *v.* BURKE, February 17, 1987, H.H. Judge Babington, Wandsworth County Ct. [*Ex rel. Mark George, Barrister.*]

1144. Exemplary damages—wrongful arrest—misdirection of jury

Wrongful arrest by a police officer fell within the category of oppressive, arbitrary or unconstitutional action by the servants of the government for which exemplary damages would be awarded, regardless of whether there was oppressive behaviour in addition.

P, who had a criminal record, was arrested and detained for 20 minutes by a member of D's police force. He brought an action for damages for wrongful arrest, and the judge ruled that the arrest and detention were wrongful. He withdrew from the jury consideration of the question of exemplary damages on the ground that there was no suggestion of oppressive behaviour on the part of the police. He directed the jury that if they thought that the wrongful arrest arose out of a mistake by the officer, "ample compensation" was not called for. The jury awarded P £5.

Held, allowing P's appeal and ordering a retrial, that wrongful arrest by a police officer fell within the category of "oppressive, arbitrary or unconstitutional action by the servants of the government" for which exemplary damages could be awarded, regardless of whether there was, additionally, oppressive behaviour. The question of exemplary damages ought to have been left to the jury (dictum of Lord Devlin in *Rookes* v. *Barnard* [1964] C.L.Y. 3703 applied). The direction to the jury as to the case not calling for ample compensation was confusing, if not misleading, in that it might have indicated to the jury that they should reduce the amount of compensation they might otherwise have awarded because the arrest arose out of a mistake by the police, and so influenced them in coming to the low figure of £5. It was not safe to allow the verdict to stand and the case would be remitted to the county court for a new trial.

HOLDEN *v.* CHIEF CONSTABLE OF LANCASHIRE [1986] 3 W.L.R. 1107, C.A.

1145. Explosion and fire—loss of use of home for six months—building works in process of being carried out—surveyors' fees—claims assessors' fees

P's claim arose as the result of an explosion, caused by an employee of North West Gas, resulting in a fire in May 1984. P was having building work done at the time of the fire. P instructed another firm to have a look at the work done and see what had not been done on the date of the fire. When news of the explosion reached the Press, a firm of insurance claims assessors called and their services were retained. P instructed a surveyor in respect of work put right after the fire damage and to inspect the completed works. P claimed for personal injury inconvenience, loss and damage.

Held, (1) that the claim for personal injury failed as a reasonable person, although they would accept it as very bad news, would not react as P had done being that she was miles away at the time; (2) the claim for inconvenience was successful in that P was unable to move into her home for six months—£750 awarded; (3) it is always open to a plaintiff to instruct loss assessors in a claim such as this and their fees were allowed as being payable by D; (4) with regard to the surveyors' fees, there had been no duplication of the loss assessors' fees. P employed a separate firm of builders after the fire and was entitled to be advised in the matter. P was also awarded further sums in relation to cattery fees and Norweb re-connection fees and moneys paid to a neighbour for the supply of electricity. The total award for damages was £3,704·23.

NORTH WEST GAS *v.* HYMANSON, March 11 1987, Eastham J. [*Ex rel. Foysters, Solicitors.*]

1146. Foreign currency—whether foreign plaintiff who principally conducts his business in a foreign currency automatically receives damages in that currency. See BAILMENT, §184.

1147. Hire agreement—defective goods—measure of damages. See U.C.B LEASING *v.* HOLTOM, §434.

1148. Holiday—flight

P booked a flight to Teneriffe for himself, two other adults and three children. P had assured his children the flight would be on a Tristar aircraft. P considered the Tristar superior to the Boeing 727. On March 20, 1985, P duly booked the seats at a total cost of £1,161. The booking form referred to the flight being with British Airtours. A few days before departure P received the tickets and discovered they were in respect of a Dan Air Boeing 727. Furthermore the departure time was now 7.30 a.m. (instead of 10.10 a.m.). P gave evidence that with young children this caused considerable inconvenience. P boarded the aircraft but found his family was split up in the seating arrangements. P sued for special damages of £147, being his loss caused by being given a flight he could have obtained for £147 cheaper from another travel agent. He claimed further general damages for inconvenience. The judge found that as the booking-form referred to a British Airtours aircraft and P was put on a Dan Air Boeing, this was in breach of contract. P was awarded £147 in special damages and £150 in general damages for stress and inconvenience.

BALDWIN *v.* TAMESIDE TRAVEL, February 2, 1987, H. H. Judge Hardy; Manchester County Ct. [*Ex rel. Edmund G. Farrell, Barrister.*]

1149. Holiday—flight missed—failure to supply booked accommodation

P booked a holiday with D in Majorca. He became confused as to his departure date and arrived at the airport a day late. D's representative said there would be room on a later flight to Ibiza from where he could fly to Majorca. She would telex the resort to keep his hotel room available. On arrival, P found his room re-let and he was accommodated in inferior accommodation in a different resort. P sued D, claiming that they had failed to supply the accommodation he had booked.

Held, in accordance with the booking conditions of D (standard trade conditions within the ABTA code of conduct), change of departure date by P constituted a cancellation by him of his holiday which attracted 100 per cent. cancellation charges. D were entitled to retain the whole purchase price and do nothing to make alternative arrangements for P. They should not be penalised in damages for attempting to patch up some sort of holiday for P. Claim dismissed.

HARTLEY *v.* INTASUN HOLIDAYS, August 12, 1987; Mr. Registrar O. T. Williams, Ellesmere Port County Ct. [*Ex rel. Mason Bond, Solicitors.*]

1150. Holiday—loss of enjoyment—duty of tour operator

P booked a holiday with D to stay at a hotel in Spain for 14 nights at a price of £798 for a family of four. The hotel was a four-star hotel. During the first three nights the rooms were invaded by a large number of cockroaches, which disappeared during the day. P's daughter was extremely upset. P got no sleep and the holiday was spoilt. The hotel fumigated the room and their clothes which smelt awful for the rest of the holiday. The food was "abysmal" and the entertainment disappointing.

Held, that the duty of the tour operator was to use skill and care in the choice of hotels and to take reasonable steps to monitor the state of repair thereafter, the evidence was that no other cockroaches had been found before or after. D had taken all reasonable steps. P contended that the mere existence of cockroaches meant they were not able to enjoy the standards of a four-star hotel. This was not a correct approach to the law. The other complaints were too trivial to merit an award. Judgment for D.

KAYE *v.* INTASUN HOLIDAYS, July 23, 1987; H.H. Judge Gerrard; Salford County Ct. [*Ex rel. Mason Bond, Solicitors.*]

1151. Holiday—loss of enjoyment—quantum

P1 and P2 were keen on watersports and underwater photography. They paid £2,290.81 for a 21-day family holiday in the Maldive Islands. The brochure described the islands as a haven for water sports, and stated that the facilities included a well-equipped scuba diving shop with a professional instructor. The plaintiffs' luggage (all their clothes, personal effects and diving equipment) went to Madras where it remained until after their return to England. D's representative was unhelpful, unsympathetic and rude. The diving shop was ill-equipped and the instructor useless. The islands had no shops and the plaintiffs had to borrow clothes from fellow-guests at the hotel. P2 felt degraded and embarrassed. If D had not been in breach of the representation to take all reasonable steps to assist wherever possible, the luggage would have been recovered by the fifth day of the holiday.

Held, P1 and P2 were entitled to the following damages: (1) £2,290·81 being the full price of the holiday; (2) £1,600 compensation for stress, anxiety and disappointment at £100 per day; (3) special damages of £508; (4) interest of £1,266.

GLOVER *v.* KUONI TRAVEL, March 2, 1987; Judge Mark Smith, Reigate County Ct. [*Ex rel. Kenneth Hamer, Barrister.*]

1152. Industrial action—trade union ballot—unlawful interference with contract—whether trade union liable in damages to P who suffered loss as a result of a strike called without a ballot. See FALCONER *v.* A.S.L.E.F. and N.U.R., §3765.

1153. Interest—damages for inconvenience and disappointment—whether interest should be awarded. See SAUNDERS *v.* EDWARDS, §1826.

1154. Interest—non-economic loss—wrongful arrest and false imprisonment

[Criminal Law Act 1967 (c.58), s.4(1).]

No interest will be awarded on damages for non-economic loss such as damages for wrongful arrest and false imprisonment.

HOLTHAM *v.* COMMISSIONER OF POLICE FOR THE METROPOLIS, *The Independent,* November 26, 1987, C.A.

1155. Interest—special damages—rate of interest

[Supreme Court Act 1981 (c.54), s.35A.]

P claimed against D damages for assault, including damages for loss of earnings and other special damage, the majority of which was sustained within three and a half months of the tort occurring. P normally worked overseas.

Held, on P's claim for interest on the special damages, that (1) the fact that the tort in question involved intention and that P was not liable to U.K. income tax did not take the case outside the ordinary rule or practice as to the rate at which interest on special damages should be awarded; (2) interest should, therefore, be awarded at one half of the relevant short-term investment rate from the date of the tort until trial (*Dexter* v. *Courtaulds* [1984] C.L.Y. 1044 applied).

MEWIS *v.* WOOLF, September 12, 1986, Sir Hugh Park sitting as a Deputy High Court Judge at Exeter. [*Ex rel. Nicholas Davidson, Barrister.*]

1156. Interim payment—procedural rules. See PRACTICE, §2982.

1157. Loss of chattel—non-profit making—interest—entitlement

When a plaintiff recovers damages for the loss of a non-profit making chattel, he is entitled to interest on those damages.

METAL BOX *v.* CURRYS, *The Times,* March 9, 1987, McNeill J.

1158. Loss of dependency—quantum—approach by a court

In a case where a disabled person claimed damages for loss of dependency including loss of care and attention, the right approach was to assess damages broadly.

ABRAMS *v.* COOK, *The Times,* November 26, 1987, C.A.

1159. Loss of earning capacity—loss of education

P was a cyclist and 14½. She was injured by a car in November 1981. She sustained leg and wrist fractures and a hip wound which kept her away from school until September 1982. She had been expected to get three Grade 1 C.S.E.'s in the summer 1983 examinations but because of the accident she only got one Grade 1 and Grades 4 and 5 in the other two. Her chances of entry to a two-year secretarial course at Canterbury College were diminished by the accident and instead she had to take a year's course at a technical college, providing a lesser qualification. By the trial in February 1986 she was earning about £1,200 per annum net less than a friend at school who was roughly comparable with her prior to the accident. The judge took into account the disadvantage to P of not having such good exam results, the earlier start at work than her friend and the chances of marriage limiting her working life, of her not achieving a place at Canterbury College anyway or of not surviving the course. Damages for loss of earning capacity/disadvantage on the labour market: £4,000. Appeal dismissed.

COMER *v.* BOLTON, March 23, 1987; C.A. [*Ex rel. Jeremy Gordon, Barrister.*]

1160. Loss of earnings—credit for social security benefits received—whether benefits received more than five years after cause of action accrued deductible

[Law Reform (Personal Injuries) Act 1948 (c.41), s.2(1).]

Social security benefits received by a plaintiff more than five years after his cause of action accrued were not deductible from an award of damages for loss of earnings consequent upon a personal injury.

P was injured in a road accident in 1980. He had not worked since that date nor was he likely to gain employment. P had received and was continuing to receive invalidity benefit. At the date of trial he was receiving £46·35 per week. His loss of earnings was £83·75 per week. In awarding damages for loss of earnings, the trial judge took into account one half of the state benefits received by P in the five years after his accident. The trial judge made no deduction in respect of benefits received after the expiry of that period. D appealed.

Held, dismissing the appeal, that s.2(1) of the Law Reform (Personal Injuries) Act provided a complete and exhaustive code to apply in the deduction of social security benefits from damages for loss of earnings. No deduction fell to be made on account of such benefits received more than five years after the plaintiff's cause of action accrued (*Denman* v. *Essex Area Health Authority* [1984] C.L.Y. 1033, *Haste* v. *Sandell Perkins* [1984] C.L.Y. 1033 approved; *Hultquist* v. *Universal Pattern and Precision Engineering Co.* [1960] C.L.Y. 880 considered).

JACKMAN *v.* CORBETT [1987] 2 All E.R. 699, C.A.

1161. Loss of earnings—employee in receipt of sick pay—sick pay funded by permanent health insurance scheme—scheme set up and premiums paid by employer—whether sick pay to be taken into account in calculating loss of earnings

An employee was required to give credit for sick pay received under his contract of employment against his claim for loss of earnings against his employer where the sick pay was funded by payments from a permanent health insurance scheme set up and paid for by the employer of which the employee was a member.

P was employed by D. P's contract of employment provided for the payment of injury pay for the first 13 weeks from the date of injury and thereafter sick pay. Long-term sickness was covered by a permanent health insurance scheme run by the employer. As an employee P was a member of the scheme. The scheme paid benefit in respect of employees after a 13-week deferment period at the rate of 50 per cent. of the employee's salary in the previous year. The policy was issued in favour of D and the benefits were payable to D to hold on trust for "the employer" *i.e.* itself or other employers covered by the scheme. The costs of the scheme were borne by D. P was injured at work and successfully sued D for negligence and breach of statutory duty. The trial judge assessed loss of future earnings in the sum of £59,250. The trial judge refused to take into account the sums P had and would receive as sick pay through the permanent health insurance scheme on account of the fact that they were insurance moneys belonging to P. D appealed.

Held, allowing the appeal, that P had no equitable interest in the benefits payable under the policy. The scheme did not insure P but rather D's liability to pay P sick pay under his contract of employment. P did not pay any of the premiums through receiving less in wages nor did the provision of the insurance scheme form part of his wage structure. P received sick pay under his contract of employment and not benefits under the insurance scheme. The sick pay paid to P was in the nature of wages and therefore P had not lost earnings to the extent of the sick pay paid. As a matter of public policy if employers made *ex gratia* payments to employees in such circumstances those payments ought to be taken into account to reduce any damages ultimately payable by the employer (*Parry v. Cleaver* [1969] C.L.Y. 906; *Palfrey* v. *Greater London Council* [1985] C.L.Y. 949 considered).

HUSSAIN *v.* NEW TAPLOW PAPER MILLS [1987] I.C.R. 28, C.A.

1162. Loss of holiday—loss of enjoyment—measure of damages

P booked a holiday with D, in May 1986, for a luxury villa in St. Jean Cap Ferrat. He paid £1,030 for the accommodation for the week commencing August 2. The villa was described as being "a quality villa" with spectacular views. It had an elegant interior with accommodation for eight. P intended the stay as the highpoint and rest-over after a touring holiday with his wife and three children. Immediately before the family set off, D cancelled the booked accommodation and P agreed to take an alternative which D assured him would be found. This turned out to be sub-standard. It was an apartment rather than a house; it was cramped and very uncomfortable. It did not provide the luxurious rest which P had bargained for. On arrival, it was too late to change elsewhere.

Held, that (1) for diminution in value of the holiday provided: £439; (2) general damages for inconvenience and disappointment: £500; (3) interest at $12\frac{1}{2}$ per cent. from August 9, 1986, to January 8, 1987.

McLEOD *v.* HUNTER (JOHN), January 8, 1987; H.H. Judge Harris, Q.C.; Westminster County Ct. [*Ex rel. Daniel Janner, Barrister.*]

1163. Misrepresentation—service charge on flat—quantum

The plaintiff wished to purchase a flat but was concerned as to the level of the service charge. The defendant did not know what the level was but agreed that it would be ascertained and subsequently stated that it would not exceed £250. Contracts were exchanged and completed at a price of £77,500. The plaintiff then received an account for the first year's service charge amounting to £800. The plaintiff sued alleging misrepresentation. At the trial it was not disputed that the contract was induced by a misrepresentation as to the amount of service charge. The issue was the measure of damages. The plaintiff's expert stated that by reason of the service charges, the capital value fell to be reduced by £3,000. The defendant's expert stated that the disclosure of the higher level of service charge would have reduced the price below £77,500. The judge accepted the view of the plaintiff's expert and gave judgment for the plaintiff for the sum of £3,000. The defendant appealed.

Held, dismissing the appeal, that the measure of damages in an action in tort for misrepresentation is the difference between the price actually paid and the market value of the property at the time of the sale; the judge had preferred the evidence of the plaintiff's expert as she was fully entitled to do.

HEINEMANN *v.* COOPER (1987) 19 H.L.R. 262, C.A.

1164. Negligent misrepresentation—loss attributable—use and occupation of premises.

As a result of the negligent misrepresentation by D that he was the landlord of and legally in a position to let certain premises, T was induced to enter into an agreement for a lease of the premises for a term of three years at a weekly rent of £25. D appealed against the award of damages for P for the negligent misrepresentation contending, *inter alia,* that although he could not claim "rent" because the agreement was not valid, nevertheless he should be entitled to something for "use and occupation" of the premises for the nineteen weeks that P had occupied the premises.

Held, dismissing D's appeal, that since there was no lease there could be no rent and nothing had ever been agreed upon on an alternative basis. It would be wrong to say that D should be entitled to anything for the use of the premises during the period that P had mistakenly believed he was entitled to be there.

HIZZETT *v.* HARGREAVES, April 28, 1986 (C.A.T. No. 419).

1165. Negligent survey—defective house—measure of damages. See WESTLAKE *v.* BRACKNELL DISTRICT COUNCIL, §2587.

1166. Nervous shock—injunction

P discovered a three-foot snake in the cylinder cupboard of her terraced house, causing her nervous shock. The snake had escaped from her neighbour's house (D). D kept 24 snakes and tarantulas in his attic. P and her family moved out, believing at least one snake was still at large. P developed a phobia about snakes. D admitted negligence and nuisance although none of the animals he kept had been classified as belonging to a dangerous species or were listed in the Sched. to the Dangerous Wild Animals Act 1976. D accepted that the court had the power to grant an injunction restraining him from keeping the snakes in his house, but argued that an injunction should not be granted since he had improved security. Expert evidence confirmed that even in the best regulated circumstances, snakes tended to escape.

Held, that an injunction would be granted restraining D from keeping snakes and monitor lizards. There was evidence of negligence on D's part causing P to develop a neurosis which would not improve whilst there was a continuing risk of escape. £1,000 was awarded for nervous shock, and £600 for the inconvenience of removal from the family home for four months.

CLARKSON *v.* BRANSFORD, January 2, 1987; H.H. Judge Walker; Huddersfield County Ct. [*Ex rel. J. M. Bradshaw, Barrister.*].

1167. Personal injuries—loss of an eye—future earnings

An award of £20,000 for pain and suffering and loss of amenity for the loss of an eye by a 15-year-old, whilst on the high side, did not warrant interference. However, £10,000 for loss of earning capacity was too high and was reduced to £4,000.

CRONIN *v.* REDBRIDGE LONDON BOROUGH COUNCIL, *The Independent,* May 20, 1987, C.A.

1168. Personal injuries—loss of future earnings—date of calculations—loss arising from divorce caused by injury

In personal injury cases the date of trial is the appropriate date on which to determine actual loss of earnings and future loss of earnings.

The financial consequences of a divorce caused by the injury are not recoverable.

P, aged 30, suffered serious injuries in a car accident for which D were liable. As a result, P's marriage broke down and a decree nisi of divorce followed. P claimed damages, *inter alia,* for the cost of the divorce and financial provision. The wife's claim for financial provision and P's action against D were heard together. The judge awarded P £381,126 under the usual heads of damage, and financial provision for the wife, which he added on to the damages against D, of £53,000, making a total of £434,126. D appealed on the ground that assessment of damages as at the date of trial led to excessive awards for future loss of earnings, and that the award for the expense of divorce was unlawful.

Held, allowing the appeal in part, that (1) the date of trial was the appropriate date for calculating actual loss of earnings and future loss of earnings. There was no good reason for reducing the multiplier by the time elapsed since the accident; (2) but the expenditure in the divorce was not recoverable; it was a redistribution of assets not a loss, it was too remote, and would in any event be excluded as contrary to public policy.

PRITCHARD *v.* COBDEN (J.H.) [1987] 1 All E.R. 300 C.A.

1169. Personal injuries or death—quantum

Details have been received of the following cases in which damages for personal injuries or death were awarded. The classification and sequence of the classified awards follows that adopted in Kemp and Kemp, *The Quantum of Damages,* Vol. 2. Unless there is some statement to the contrary the age of the applicant is his age at the time of the court hearing. The damages are stated on the basis of full liability, *i.e.* ignoring any deduction made for contributory negligence. The sum is the total amount of the damages awarded unless otherwise stated. Interest is excluded in all cases.

Injuries of maximum severity

1170. DEGAN (December 2, 1986; Criminal Injuries Compensation Board; Glasgow). Male, aged 40 at date of injury and 47 at date of hearing. Unemployed for some eight months before injury. Previously employed in various capacities ranging from farm worker to semi-skilled welder's mate and more often in than out of work. Mugged. Major head injury resulting in cerebellar atrophy, total loss of sense of smell and substantial impairment of sense of taste and gross tremor affecting all four limbs, head and trunk. Mental capacity initially that of a "lame brain", but later returned wholly to normal. Unable to walk even with assistance and could, therefore, no longer benefit from physiotherapy. Confined to wheelchair. Unable to feed himself. Required permanent institutional care and would remain in hospital where he was a patient at present. Aware of his situation and future prospects. Damages for *solatium* assessed at £80,000 and for loss of earnings at £31,000, consisting of £13,000 for the loss to date of hearing and £18,000 for the future loss (based on multiplier of nine and multiplicand of £2,000). *Total Damages:* £111,000. [*Ex rel. Anne Smith of the Scottish Bar*].

1171. CHARALAMBOUS *v.* ISLINGTON HEALTH AUTHORITY (July 17, 1987; Leonard J.). Male, aged 16 at date of accident and 23 at trial. Vulnerable personality with easy loss of temper, who had obtained 5 "CSE" levels and one "O" level and was capable of improving on those results if, as planned, he resumed school. Fracture of first lumbar vertebra resulting in paraplegia; fractures of both wrists, left tibia and right os calcis; severe reactive depression. In hospital one year initially, then further year in rehabilitation centre. Developed equinus deformity in both feet; pressure sore on buttock, which necessitated further hospital admissions each year between 1982 and 1985, when surgical closure effected; and occasional urinary infections. Some residual sensation, limited anal sphincter control and partial urinary incontinence. Depression caused reduced I.Q. performance, difficulties in social relationships and inability to find or retain employment. Had achieved some independence. Lived in flat near his parents, which was not wholly suitable to his needs. Would be likely to require domestic assistance in future and more full-time care in later life. Risk of recurrence of primary infections unless personal care scrupulous. Life expectancy reduced by about 10 years. General damages were assessed as follows: (1) for pain and suffering and loss of amenities: £60,000; (2) for future loss of earnings: £127,732 (based on multiplier of 14 after discount of 2 to take account of particular uncertainties); (3) for future care: £69,138 (based on multiplier of 13 for domestic assistance only and multiplier of 3 for living-in care); (4) for future equipment needs: £30,000; (5) for additional cost of acquiring new house: £22,000; (6) for cost of adapting house to plaintiffs special needs: £19,250; (7) for future additional motor car costs: £15,400; (8) for future help with home maintenance: £6,239; (9) for future additional holiday costs: £5,100; (10) for future physiotherapy: £2,808; (11) for future additional heating costs: £2,720. Special Damages were assessed as follows: (12) for past loss of earnings: £20,000; (13) for past care by plaintiff's family: £12,298 (including £2,444 for mother's loss of earnings); (14) for past additional travel and motoring costs: £2,255; (15) for past holiday costs: £420; (16) for additional clothing: £300; (17) for equipment £230. *Total Special Damages:* £35,503. *Total General Damages:* £360,387. *Per curiam.* The award for past care and attendance by members of the plaintiff's family was, as a matter of principle, special damage rather than general damage and so attracted interest at half the Short Term Investment Account rate under s.35A of the Supreme Court Act, 1981 (*Jefford* v. *Gee* [1970] C.L.Y. 603 applied; *Roberts* v. *Johnstone,* July 25, 1986 (unreported) (Alliott J.) not followed). [*Ex rel. Duncan Pratt, Barrister*].

1172. HARVEY *v.* SOUTH WEST THAMES REGIONAL HEALTH AUTHORITY (April 25, 1986; Butler Sloss J.; Lewes). Boy aged 8. In course of birth sustained fractured skull and severe brain damage. Had mental age of 6 to 12 month old baby. Vision and speech impaired and had negligible speech recognition. Severely handicapped physically by cerebral palsy: unable to walk, sit or stand without support and had to be carried everywhere. Double incontinence. No significant improvement in condition anticipated. Would require constant care and attention for rest of life, specially adapted accommodation and gadgets to keep him occupied and amused. Life expectancy 20 to 30 years. Pre-trial special damages estimated at £27,701 with interest of £14,958. General damages made up as follows: (1) for pain and suffering and loss of amenities: £60,000; (2) for loss of expectation of life: £1,750; (3) for loss of future earnings: £12,000 (based on multiplicand of £6,000, representing average net industrial wage for men, and multiplier of 2); (4) for costs in connection with provision of specially adapted accommodation £52,560 (consisting of £34,560 in respect of cost of purchase of £48,000, £15,000 for cost of alterations and £3,000 for removal expenses); (5) for cost of special aids: £23,375 (consisting of initial capital outlay of £9,025, maintenance costs of £9,360 (based on multiplicand of £1,040 and multiplier of 9) and replacement costs of £4,990 (based on multiplicand of £2,495 and multiplier of 2)); (6) for cost of future nursing care: £90,698 (consisting of (a) £53,550 in respect of loss of earnings of woman who had given up her job to look after plaintiff from November 1982 in place of his mother (based on multiplicand of £5,950 and multiplier of 9); and (b) £25,770 for cost of additional help during school holidays on assumption plaintiff left school in 1995 (based on multiplicand of £4,295 and multiplier of 6); and (c) £11,378 for cost of additional help after he left school (based on multiplicand of £5,869 and multiplier of 2)); (7) for cost of future holidays: £4,862; (8) for cost of adapted vehicles: £24,682 (consisting of £8,815 for first such vehicle and £15,867 for replacement vehicles, based on multiplicand of £1,763 and multiplier of 9 and assuming replacement required every 5 years); (9) for additional costs of nursing home: £4,375 (based on multiplicand of £486·13 and multiplier of 9); (10) for future cost of extra clothing and nappies: £4,329 (based on multiplicand of £481 and multiplier of 9); (11) for fees of special school: £28,884 (based on annual fees for day boys of £7,221 and multiplier of 4); (12) for Court of Protection costs: £9,000 (based on multiplicand of £1,000 and multiplier of 9). The judge approved an award of *Agreed Total Damages* and interest of £350,000. [*Ex rel. Frank R. Moat, Barrister.*]

Multiple injuries

1173. HAWKINS (November 25, 1986; Criminal Injuries Compensation Board (Sir Denis Marshall, Chairman)). Female, aged 39 at date of offence and 44 at hearing. Former assistant cook. Shot in back at close range by 12 bore shotgun. Permanent damage to left kidney, which was riddled with pellet wounds and ceased to function initially; damage to diaphragm, spleen and descending colon; permanent damage to nerves supplying left leg; multiple pellet wounds over lumbar spine and left loin. In hospital six weeks. Under intensive care five days and had three operations. Off work nine months. Left with obvious scars on lower back and scars on thigh, burning sensations in lumbar region and left buttock, discomfort in back and abdomen, weakness and muscle wasting in left leg, stiffness and cramping pains, abnormal sensations in left foot, depression and headaches and constipation. Walked with slight limp and had difficulty sleeping. Unable to resume pre-accident work and now a domestic. Permanent risk of hypertension. Small risk of toxic effects from lead shot still in body, some of which might later require removal. Agreed future loss of earnings of £1,304. *Agreed Special Damages:* £3,560. *Total General Damages:* £40,000. [*Ex rel. Glen Tyrell, Barrister*].

1174. STEPHENSON (November 21, 1986; Criminal Injuries Compensation Board (Chairman Beryl Cooper Q.C.); Leeds). Married woman, aged 60 at date of injury and 61 at date of hearing. Pensioner.

Violent assault: threatened with imitation gun and beaten with it about head neck and shoulders. Fractures of two ribs, three lacerations of scalp, two requiring sutures, with traumatic neuritis; bruising to head and shoulders; aggravation of pre-existing spondylosis. Developed slight depression and marked phobic anxiety state causing grave limitation of activities, in particular preventing her from going out alone for several months, and considerable distress. Left with visible scar in hair line, sensitivity and discomfort at site of two scalp wounds and continuing intermittent symptoms in neck, necessitating frequent use of cervical collar. Psychological symptoms gradually resolving, but feelings of apprehension easily aroused by stimuli related to offence and would remain liable to occasional emotional upsets, possibly of some severity, in such circumstances. *General Damages:* £6,000. [*Ex rel. Irwin Mitchell, Solicitors*].

1175. MEWIS *v.* WOOLF (September 12, 1986; Sir Hugh Park, sitting as a Deputy High Court Judge Exeter.) Male, aged 56 at date of assault and 58 at date of trial. Lost consciousness in savage attack; stabbed 3 times close to heart; a deep vertical wound, 1.5–2 cms. long, to left of sternum; a superficial 1 cm. wound, between sternum and left nipple, and a jagged oblique 3 cm. wound just below and medial to the left nipple, a 4th stab wound, deep to the dorso-lateral surface of the left hand, divided the extensor tendon of the small finger and the dorsal (sensory) branch of the ulna nerve. Pneumothorax. In intensive care 3 days. Wounds suffered; plaster slab applied to hand. Transferred to convalescent home for week. Apprehensive about going home as neighbour had assaulted him. 4 months' after attack, chest wound became swollen and began to discharge. Eventually required an excision of the sinne tract, granuloma and underlying costal cartilage. Suffered symptoms of tiring easily, shortness of breath and minor aches and pains in chest as result of anxiety over episode. By date of trial, left little finger had settled to a permanent reduction of extension and flexion, back of hand had tight sensation and an area of numbness; residual scarring consisted of one slightly depressed scar of 6 cms. long about the left 4th costal cartilage, and 2 other scars in the chest. Left hand had 3 scars. *Special damages*: £7742·48. *General damages* (pain, suffering and loss of amenity): £5,500. [*Ex rel. Nicholas Davidson, Barrister.*]

1176. DAWSON *v.* THOMPSON (December 12, 1986; Deputy Judge Johnson; Q.B.D.; Newcastle-upon-Tyne). Male, aged 55 at date of accident and 58 at trial. Storeman. Right-handed. Horrifying road accident. Whiplash injury to neck accelerating by four years symptoms from pre-existing condition; deep lacerated wound of left knee with fracture of upper end of tibial spine accelerating by four years symptoms from pre-existing condition; bruising of right shoulder; lacerated wound over back of left ankle; momentary unconciousness, bruising to front of chest and two small lacerated wounds to right knee, from all of which made full recovery. In hospital 11 days, resumed clerical work after three months and pre-accident work after five months. Left with significant, but not extreme, disability in neck, right shoulder, left knee and ankle, all of which would have developed in time in any event. 25 per cent. loss of mobility in neck, restriction of movements in right shoulder so that unable to work with arm above shoulder height and slight laxity of cruciate ligaments of left knee. Gardening and home do-it-yourself work restricted and unable to continue dancing and golf. No future loss of earnings or handicap on labour market. *Agreed Special Damages:* £834·30. *General Damages:* £5,500. [*Ex rel. Roger Thorn, Barrister*].

Brain and Skull

1177. NEVINS (March 27, 1987; Criminal Injuries Compensation Board; Newcastle-upon-Tyne). Male, aged about 23 at date of offence and 27 at date of award. Former butcher. Fracture of parieto-temporal area of skull, facial lacerations and significant concussion with post-traumatic amnesia. In hospital initially six days. Shortly after discharge suffered two attacks of "grand mal" epilepsy and re-admitted for four days. Despite anti-convulsant drugs, suffered six further "grand mal" seizures, last being six months before hearing. Occasional blurring of right eye had largely resolved by date of hearing. Left with permanent, total loss of senses of taste and smell, notable scarring under right eye, feelings of lethargy and fatigue and had no enthusiasm for former hobbies and sporting activities. Reasonable prospects that epilepsy would be well controlled provided anti-convulsant drugs taken daily. Now unemployed and work prospects severely restricted by possibility of further seizures. General damages for pain and suffering and loss of amenities assessed at £34,000 and for future loss of earnings or handicap on labour market at £12,250. *Special Damages:* £3,307.85. *Total General Damages:* £46,250. [*Ex rel. Jeremy Freedman, Barrister*].

1178. LEWIS (June 16, 1986; Criminal Injuries Compensation Board; London). Male, aged 23 at date of accident and 27 at date of hearing. Before accident had 3 'A' levels, was taking 'A' level Chemistry and Biology with view to career in medical profession and had motivation, determination and mental agility to achieve his ambition. Beaten about head with glass. Depressed fracture of skull, contusion of brain and large haematoma. Dura mater intact. In hospital 8 days. Underwent lateral craniotomy to elevate fracture. Severely dysphasic initially, but this improved slowly. Continuing impairment of short term memory and speech difficulty. Had become aggressive, belligerent and unable to cope with stress. Considerable insight into his condition, which was source of much distress. Would be unable to achieve his pre-accident potentialities. Had attempted degree course in surveying, but was unable to cope and failed his 2nd year exams. *Special damages*: £2,176. *Total damages*: £32,000. [Ex rel. *Andrew W. Lewis, Barrister*].

1179. ELLIS *v.* BIGGINS (July 14, 1986; Mr. Recorder Peter Crawford Q.C.; Nottingham). Male, aged 18 at date of accident and 21 at date of trial. Former police cadet. But for accident could have become police constable within 6 months. Sociable, energetic person who enjoyed sports, including golf and table tennis, and chess and had good prospects of successful career as police officer. Fracture of right temporal region of skull; post-concussional syndrome; bruises and lacerations. In hospital 2½ days. Off work 2 months. Severe headaches for 2 or 3 months, then gradual recovery. Developed severe vertigo, which forced him to abandon police career, but no longer caused him any significant disability by time of trial and would resolve within 18 months. Marked personality change. Now rather slow in his reactions, with impaired concentration and flat emotional responses, and easily fatigued; was depressed; had lost much of his pleasure and enthusiasm for sports; was less good at chess; and had become quieter and more serious person. No significant improvement likely. Now a civilian employed in police control room with agreed continuing loss of earnings of £500 p.a. General damages for pain and suffering and loss of amenities and loss of chosen career assessed at £19,000; and for loss of future earnings at £8,000 (based on multiplier of 16). *Agreed special* damages: £3,108. *Total general damages*: £27,000. *Per curiam.* The fact that police officers normally retired at age of 55 did not justify a reduction in the multiplier to be applied in assessing the loss of future earnings. [*Ex rel. Robert P. Glancy, Barrister*].

1180. SUTHERLAND (January 8, 1987; Criminal Injuries Compensation Board). Male, aged 26 at date of injury and 29 at date of hearing by full Board. Self-employed painter and decorator. Blow to head. Very severe head injury; cortical contusion; laceration to right fronto-parietal region. No fracture. In hospital 19 days. Fully unconscious 15 hours; partly unconscious one or two days. Resumed part-time work after one year and full-time work six months later. Initial giddiness and loss of memory and concentration had gradually improved. Intense numbness of inner left side of mouth persisted for 18 months. Left with some permanent loss of memory and concentration, though these functions were "good enough"; quite marked dysarthria in form of slurring and stumbling of speech; left-sided sensory and motor deficit resulting in slowness and clumsiness in movements of left upper and lower limbs, residual numbness from forehead to jaw and some numbness in left fingertips and leg; 2" diameter scar on forehead, which was not significant cosmetic defect. Would continue to improve, but would never achieve complete physical normality. One per cent. risk of epilepsy. No future loss of earnings or loss of earning capacity. *Special Damages:* £1,020. *General Damages:* £10,000. [*Ex rel. Stephen Monkcom, Barrister*].

Face, lip, ear, nose

1181. LEAKEY *v.* TAYLOR (January 9, 1987; Mr. Registrar Richardson; Luton County Ct.). Boy, aged 8 at date of accident and 10 at date of hearing of application for approval of settlement. Rear seat passenger in car involved in collision. Projected through front windscreen and landed on bonnet. Multiple facial lacerations requiring 36 stitches. Did not lose consciousness. Not detained in hospital. Off school a few days. Left with $2\frac{1}{2}$" scar on right cheek, which was clearly visible at close range; faint curved 1"scar on right side of forehead; faint $1\frac{1}{4}$" long 'V' shaped scar on bridge of nose; faint $\frac{1}{4}$" long scar below mouth. No psychological damage. *Agreed General Damages:* £2,000. [*Ex rel. Knowles Cave and Co., Solicitors*].

1182. MORDAUNT, *Re* (January 28, 1987; Criminal Injuries Compensation Board). Male, aged 21 at date of offence and 27 at date of hearing. Right ear completely bitten off and hearing impaired. Over three years underwent four operations involving skin grafting and attempted reconstruction of ear. Left with poor and useless replica, which was insufficient to hold in place right limb of sunglasses, but which he was able to conceal from casual view by wearing his hair long. Right-sided loss of hearing of 60 db.(A.) at 4KHz. No loss of earning capacity *General Damages:* £10,000. [*Ex rel. R. E. Thorn, Barrister*].

1183. FROGLEY *v.* ALGAR (February 17, 1987; Mr. Registrar Bailey Cox; Portsmouth County Ct.). Male aged 44. Knocked off bicycle by car. Laceration to right eyebrow and right upper lip, cracking of two incisors and bruising to right cheek. Damaged teeth removed and replaced with porcelain crowns, involving six visits to dentist over three month period. Left with permanent scarring to right eyebrow and upper lip, which caused discomfort, but barely visible. *Special Damages*: £489. *General Damages*: £2,000. [*Ex rel. Hubert Way and Barker, Solicitors*].

Skin

1184. RIGG *v.* ELLIOTT (February 13, 1987; Deputy Judge Philip Cox Q.C.; Q.B.D.; Birmingham). Boy, aged 9 at date of accident and 15 at trial. Methylated spirits spilt over him and ignited. Severe burns to jaw, neck, back, chest, left arm and, to lesser extent, legs. 34 per cent. of total body area affected, excluding most of face. In hospital about 11 months in all, during which time underwent eight skin grafts and five other operations. Grafts repeatedly failed due to infections. On three occasions placed in cruciform cast, to prevent grafts shearing, for periods totalling about two months. Treatment excruciatingly painful; needed sedation, counselling and hypnotherapy to withstand daily changes of dressings. After discharge from hospital wore pressure garments for a year. Missed year at school. On return was teased and lost confidence. Sent to boarding school to enable him to rehabilitate with other boys and catch up on schooling. After two years went to public school to complete rehabilitation. By date of trial had caught up scholastically and was well integrated at school. Left with extensive scarring, but now well healed with only moderate discolouration, though texture irregular and drawn. Risk of further psychological damage if rejected by girl friends or suppressed memories of hospital treatment were triggered by some other misfortune. General damages for pain and suffering and loss of amenities assessed at £40,000. *Total award* (including school fees until 18 and interest): £80,076. [*Ex rel. Frank Chapman, Barrister*].

Burns and scars

1185. McNEIL *v.* LONDON ELECTRICITY BOARD (October 17, 1986; Ian Kennedy J.). Male, aged 24 at date of accident and 27 at date of trial. Labourer. Electrocuted when struck with spade underground live mains cable, causing explosion which threw him to ground. Very painful deep and superficial flash burns to 20 per cent. of total body area, involving left arm and hand, left side of trunk, buttock and thigh; depression. In hospital 5 weeks. In intensive care 2 days, then received conservative treatment, narrowly avoiding skin grafting. Returned to work after 6 months. Left with "orange peel" skin in affected areas and genuine phobia of working anywhere near electrical cables or apparatus. Cosmetic effect obvious if one looked for it and when plaintiff raised arm, so stretching skin, but not distressing to look at nor so striking as to provoke stares. Skin now sensitive to extremes of temperature and susceptible to cracking if struck or stressed, following which would take longer to heal than normal. Had had to give up football. Because of phobia duties at work had been changed, with result no longer pulling his weight and prospects of promotion slightly reduced. General damages for pain and suffering and loss of amenities assessed at £6,000 and for loss of chance of promotion at £1,000. Total General Damages: £7,000. [*Ex rel. Simon S. Brown, Barrister.*]

1186. MURRAY *v.* CHICKEN CABINS (September 16, 1986; Judge Cotton; Sheffield County Court). Married woman, aged 28. Kitchen worker. Right arm scalded by boiling water. Wound healed within about 1 month. Left with 9 cm. by 3 cm. elliptical-shaped scar on medial aspect of arm, which was fairly well concealed when arm in normal position, and impaired sensation in that area. *Agreed Special Damages:* £10·00. *General Damages:* £1,800. [*Ex rel. Irwin Mitchell, Solicitors.*]

Sight

1187. MERVYN (October 30, 1986; Criminal Injuries Compensation Board; London). Male, aged 23 at date of offence and 26 at date of hearing. Struck in face with beer mug. Rupture of left eye globe, partial avulsion of left eye lids, severe, multiple lacerations to face, split lip and bruising. In hospital 19 days initially. Underwent unsuccessful operation to repair left eye and required 100 stitches. After 15 days underwent second operation involving removal of eye, fitting of prosthesis and plastic surgery to socket and lid, including insertion of dermofat graft in socket. About 10 months later re-admitted to hospital for 5 days for third operation to reshape left eye. After further 18 months underwent fourth operation involving implant to improve appearance of eye. Left with permanent disfigurement of and around left eye with scarring extending from inner corner of eye to left cheek. Due to extensive damage to eyelids, movement of prosthesis only 10 per cent. of normal range and so at once obvious to any observer. Eye painful and often watered. Suffered frequent headaches. Lacked social confidence and constantly wore dark glasses to avoid embarrassment. Had obtained work as a carpenter after 2 years. No special damages. *General Damages:* £18,000. [*Ex rel. Nicholas Hamblin, Barrister*].

1188. ADAMS *v.* ROWCLIFFE (December 3, 1986; MacPherson J.; Preston). Female, aged 32 at date of accident and 36 at date of trial. Before accident suffered from myopia in left eye and less serious myopia and "cobble-stone" retinal degeneration in right eye. But for accident would probably have suffered traumatic retinal detachment in left eye at some time in future, though probably not for 20 years. Left side of head struck car windscreen resulting in retinal detachment in left eye. To all intents and purposes now blind in that eye. No prospects of recovery of sight. General damages for pain and suffering assessed at £14,000 on the footing that: (1) in the case of a person of the plaintiff's age the current conventional award for loss of sight in one, normal eye was £15,000; (2) an addition of £5,000 was required to take account of the fact that she was in a worse position than a plaintiff whose remaining eye was good; (3) £6,000 should be deducted to take account of the fact that she was at risk of losing her sight in the injured eye in the future in any event. *Special Damages*: £873·13. *General Damages*: £14,000. [*Ex rel. Philip A. Butler, Barrister*].

1189. COLE (November 12, 1986; Criminal Injuries Compensation Board (Chairman James Black Q.C.); Manchester). Female, aged 14 at date of offence and 16 at date of hearing. Had intended to join Army. Wooden projectile struck right eye causing 4 mm laceration of cornea, which sealed itself, and severe damage to crystalline lens, which resulted in formation of cateract requiring operative removal. Now effectively blind in right eye unless wore contact lens, had to wear glasses for reading and eye felt tired after normal reading and homework. No cosmetic disability. Unless particular contact lens lotion used, suffered great irritation in eye. Usual sporting activities curtailed. Small but significant risk of future problems, such as posterior capsule spacification, glaucoma or retinal detachment. Career in Army now impossible. Considering nursing. General damages for pain and suffering and loss of amenities assessed at £10,000 and for handicap on labour market at £5,000. *Special Damages:* £305. *Total General Damages:* £15,000. [*Ex rel. Barrie Searle, Barrister*].

1190. SHEPHERD (April 7, 1987; Criminal Injuries Compensation Board; Birmingham). Male, aged 39 at date of offence and 43 at date of award. Former taxi driver. Hit in eye with blunt instrument and stabbed in back and throat. Blow out fracture of left orbital floor. In hospital five days. Sialastic implant inserted to support orbital contents. Out-patient five months. No loss of visual acuity, but left with restricted movement of left eye and consequent diplopia, which would be permanent and would not improve, but for which he compensated well by turning his head. Superficial scars to back and scar to throat hidden by beard. Because of diplopia, could not concentrate for more than about two hours when driving and unable to resume pre-accident occupation and had to give up hobby of angling as he found difficulty in following float. Unemployed. Hoped to be able to take advantage of "Enterprise Allowance" scheme to set up business dealing in taxi-cabs. General damages for pain and suffering and loss amenities assessed at £12,500. Loss of earnings assessed at £15,722. *Total Damages:* £28,222. [*Ex rel. K. N. Bladon, Barrister*].

Hearing

1191. DRAKE (June 3, 1986; Criminal Injuries Compensation Board; Manchester). Male, aged 19 at date of assault and 23 at date of hearing. Chef. Clinical fracture of skull with bleeding from right ear. Unconscious 2 days. Post-traumatic amnesia for one week. In hospital two weeks. Off work one month. Suffered intermittent rotary vertigo for 12 months and right-sided deafness for two years, after which underwent successful operation to restore hearing. Following operation suffered headaches daily lasting three to four hours and of moderate severity, which were expected to resolve completely within about a year. Left with slightly impaired memory, poor concentration, fairly severe right-sided tinnitus, which would be permanent, and slight hearing loss, which tended to enhance tinnitus. In quiet environment became depressed and irritable. Had to play background music to get to sleep. *General damages*: £7,500. [*Ex rel. John Barrett, Barrister*].

Neck

1192. BENNET *v.* GOWER-SMITH (December 3, 1986; Peter Pain J.). Male, aged 24 at date of accident and 29 at date of hearing. Chartered accountant. Former athlete and "fitness fanatic". Pre-existing Klippel-Feil syndrome, which made him more vulnerable to trauma than person with normal cervical spine. Thrown off motorcycle. Injury to spinal cord, resulting in quadriplegia from below neck for a few days. In hospital 19 days. Able to walk within a week. Resumed pre-accident work after 14 weeks. No continuing pain. Left with minor loss of sensitivity and fine co-ordination of fingers, now able to run and swim at only below-average standard, vulnerability to trauma increased and effects of ageing would be experienced at earlier stage than before accident (though not possible to say when). No loss of earning capacity. *Agreed Special Damages*: £3,000. *General Damages* (for pain and suffering and loss of amenities): £10,000. [*Ex rel. Jonathan Sofer, Barrister*].

1192a. HOOK *v.* HAIR (September 18, 1986; H.H. Judge Clarke; Exeter County Court). Female, aged 20 at date of accident and 23 at date of trial. Whiplash injury to cervical spine with sprain of soft tissues. Following day neck stiff and painful. Pain and discomfort for following month. Continued to suffer occasional aches in neck lasting ½–1 hour. Off work 3 days. *General damages*: £1,100. [*Ex rel. Christopher Naish, Barrister.*]

Respiratory organs

1193. GREEN *v.* FINE SPINNERS AND DOUBLERS (May 14, 1986; Macpherson J.; Manchester). Male, aged 57. Supervisor in card room of cotton mill. Former cigarette smoker. Had worked in cotton industry for 34 years. As result of exposure to cotton dust, by 1963 had developed early byssinosis, though symptoms insufficient to entitle him to benefit on that account. Condition remained relatively stable until 1981 or 1982, when it deteriorated. There was little or no change between 1982 and date of trial when position was as follows: (1) He suffered from shortness of breath and a sensation of restricted breathing, which was particularly marked on Mondays and Tuesdays. His chest was worse after a long break from work and was then "very wheezy". Sometimes he had some tightness of the chest in bed at night. (2) He was restricted in walking and gardening and avoided heavy exertion. He had a regular morning cough. He did not look fit, but was not "in a really bad way". (3) His overall disability was assessed at 10 per cent. or slight with a weighting towards slight to moderate. Despite medical advice to the contrary, he intended to go on working in the cotton industry. (The defendants did not contend that he should leave it.) There was a reasonable prospect that he would be kept on in his present job and he would probably continue working for 4 or 5 years. His condition would probably worsen slowly, but not drastically so, at worst resulting in an overall disability of 20 per cent. to 30 per cent. When he stopped working in the industry, his condition would probably not worsen and, owing to the fact that he was an ex-smoker, would probably not improve significantly. It was conceded that one half of the plaintiff's overall disability was attributable to emphysema caused by cigarette smoking. On this basis: (a) general damages for pain and suffering and loss of amenities were assessed at £7,000 (the Judge having concluded that, if the plaintiff's disability was wholly attributable to the defendant's breaches of duty, the appropriate award would be between £10,000 and £18,000); (b) general damages for loss of future earnings were assessed at £11,300 based on a multiplier of $1\frac{1}{2}$ (after taking into account accelerated payments and the causative effect of smoking); (c) general damages for loss of earning capacity or handicap on the labour markets were assessed at £500 (after taking into account the plaintiff's probable working life and prospects). *Total General Damages:* £18,810. [*Ex rel. John Pickering, Solicitors*].

1194. PATTERSON *v.* MINISTRY OF DEFENCE (July 29, 1986; Simon Brown J.). Male, aged 59, who had worked in naval dockyards for 40 years until made redundant at age of 56. Had developed and continued to suffer from productive coughing, chest tightness and shortness of breath, which were agreed to be constitutional in origin. In 1980 he was diagnosed as suffering from asymptomatic pleural changes in the form of pleural plaques and thickening, which were caused by exposure to asbestos in his former work, and was told of this. Although reassured that the chances of his developing serious asbestos-related illness were slim, he suffered anxiety and concern for his future health and welfare. There was a 2 per cent. to 3 per cent. risk of his developing malignant mesothelioma, which would be fatal, and a 5 per cent. risk of increased pleural thickening with an associated increase in breathlessness. On an application under s.32A of the Supreme Court Act, 1981, and R.S.C. Ord. 37, r.8, for an award of provisional damages the judge assessed general damages in respect of the plaintiff's present pleural changes, anxiety and risk of future worsening of pleural thickening at £1,250, and directed that he should be entitled to apply for further damages, without limit as to time, if he developed mesothelioma in the future. No special damages. *Provisional General Damages*: £1,250. *Per Curiam.* Asymptomatic physical changes of the kind suffered by the plaintiff and anxiety falling short of nervous shock amounted to "actionable damage" for the purposes of s.32A of the Act (decision of Rose J. in *Morrison* v. *Central Electricity Generating Board,* March 1985 (unreported) not followed). [*Ex rel. Allan Gore, Barrister*].

Internal organs

1195. COOKSON *v.* LEYLAND VEHICLES (June 10, 1986; Mars-Jones J.; Preston). Married man, aged 46 at date of accident and 49 at date of trial. Formerly enjoyed full social and married life. Employed as vertical borer. Right inguinal hernia. Following accident continued pre-accident work wearing truss, which was uncomfortable, inconvenient and chafed skin; at end of shift felt exhausted, took off truss and could then do very little due to aching in groin; sexual intercourse ceased due to pain; Social life virtually ended; unable to do decorating, swimming or dancing. After 15 months admitted to hospital for four days for operative repair of hernia. Wound infection prolonged convalescence by some two weeks. Made gradual recovery, aided by daily swimming for three to four weeks, before returning to work 21 months after accident. Since then had coped with pre-accident job, which was quite strenuous, had occasional twinges of pain, had not resumed sexual intercourse, but no reason why should not continue as before. *General Damages:* £4,750. [*Ex rel. Janet Smith, Barrister*].

Spleen

1196. WEBSTER *v.* BRITISH RAILWAYS BOARD (November 24, 1986; Judge Cotton; Sheffield County Court). Male, aged 30. Struck by timber. Tear of spleen; lengthwise laceration of tongue, which was almost divided; bruising of right arm between elbow and wrist. Required 17 stitches in tongue, had to take food through straw for 2 days and off work a week. After 4 days admitted to hospital due to abdominal pain, laparotomy revealed injury to spleen, which was removed. Full recovery within 3½ months. Tongue well healed. Left with 4" post-operative scar on abdomen, of which he was self-conscious. Slightly increased susceptibility to infection, immunological disorders and abdominal adhesions. General damages for injury to spleen assessed at £3,000 and for other injuries at £1,000. *Total General Damages*: £4,000. [*Ex rel. Christopher D. Mills, Barrister*].

Pelvis and Hip

1197. CHARLTON *v.* TYNE SHIP REPAIRERS (December 17, 1986; Deputy Judge J. Johnson; Q.B.D.: Newcastle-upon-Tyne). Married man, aged 62 at date of accident and 64 at date of trial. Former chargehand shot blaster, who had not been unemployed in 20 years. Before accident very easy going, gentle man, who enjoyed normal sex life, gardening, walking, dancing and watching football. Run over by fork-lift truck. Fracture dislocation of pelvis, involving both ischial and pubic rami, right sacro-iliac joint and symphysis pubis; contusion and abrasions of both shoulders and lower back. In hospital 2½ months. Fractures reduced and symphysis pubis closed by manipulation under general anaesthetic, then underwent skeletal traction. On discharge walking slowly with two sticks. In constant discomfort, which frequently became pain. Took pain killing drugs every day and had to wear corset to relieve pain at least 1 day a week. Had not enjoyed full night's sleep since accident: slept for 4 hours at most, then woken by pain and discomfort. Unable to sit without discomfort for more than ½ hour. Acute limp. With aid of stick could walk 200 yards. Unable to garden, perform do-it-yourself tasks in home, travel to football matches or go out dancing with wife. Permanently impotent. Combination of pain, immobility, deprivation of recreational activities and impotence had caused change of personality: now short-tempered and flared into anger at least provocation. Unemployable. General damages for pain and suffering and loss of amenities assessed at £21,000 consisting, in broad terms, of £16,000 for the pelvic injuries and £5,000 for the impotence. Agreed future loss of earnings of £4,094. *Agreed Special Damages*: £9,620. *Total General Damages*: (£25,094. [*Ex rel. D. J. B. Trotter, Barrister*].

Shoulder

1198. GEORGE *v.* THORNBORROW (August 27, 1986; Judge G. Baker Q.C., Todmorden County Court, sitting at Halifax). Male, aged 17 at date of accident and 21 at date of hearing. Apprentice foundryman. Right handed. Crack fracture to neck of left humorus and scapula. Head and chest injuries. Nasty abrasion to right iliac cast. Minor abrasions to knees. Briefly unconscious. Coughing blood. In hospital 5 days. Left shoulder immobilised in bandage 4 weeks and rested in collar and cuff further 4 weeks. Headaches and chest pains for several months. Abrasion slow to heal leaving scar. Full recovery except for minor shoulder pain in cold weather and on sudden movement, persisting for 4–6 years. Off work 3 months, then resumed light duties. Full work resumed within 7 months. *Agreed special damages*: £733·66. *General damages*: £2,000. [*Ex rel. Andrew T. A. Dallas, Barrister.*]

Arm

1199. WILLIAMS *v.* BOWATER CONTAINERS (February 28, 1986; Wood J., Chester). Female, aged 26. Right-handed. Severe crushing injury to right hand and forearm. Substantial skin loss on arm and muscle damage. Median nerve supply to thumb muscles damaged. Five operations. Skin grafting carried out to injuries on forearm. Web space between thumb and index finger released. Scar tissue was excised; thumb stabilised in the abducted position. Left with impaired grip and manual dexterity. Wrist and thumb stiff. Also left with severe scarring which was extensive and obvious. Misshapen thumb. Psychological difficulties. Had problems with caring for her baby and with housework. She has left job to have baby. Wanted further child so likely to be out of employment 10 years. Real risk that employment after that would be unavailable. *Special damages*: £3,530.56; *Smith* v. *Manchester* award £4,000: *General damages*: £17,500. [*Ex rel. Brian Thompson & Partners, Solicitors.*]

1200. HOLLINS *v.* CLARKE (December 2, 1986; Judge Blomefield; Newbury County Ct.). Housewife, aged about 30 at date of accident and 33 at trial. Right-handed. Struck by broken glass. Three inch long scoop laceration to lateral side of right upper arm with removal of strip of skin over one and a half inches wide, which remained attached at upper end; loss of one and a half inch diameter circular patch of skin from ulnar border of right forearm, exposing muscle, tendon and bone; jagged square laceration on inner side of right fifth finger with attached skin flap; several small cuts on right palm. Wounds healed well leaving only minor scarring. Continuing aching in little finger in cold weather and "pins and needles" sensation if it was knocked, washing-up and sewing restricted, could only shake hands with left hand and unable to use little finger when carrying shopping bag, which had to be suspended from three fingers. *General Damages:* £2,000. [*Ex rel. M. F. Ollerenshaw, Barrister*].

Fingers

1201. BATTY *v.* SOUTHERN COUNTIES STORAGE (July 1987; Judge Dillon Q.C.; Birmingham County Ct.). Male, aged 18 at date of accident and nearly 21 at trial. Right-handed. Warehouseman, who possessed typing qualification and had hoped to obtain office work. Traumatic amputation of left middle, ring and little fingers. Courageously resumed light work after a month. Left with significant reduction in grip, unable to lift heavy weights, ability to type impaired, stumps tender, especially in cold weather, and occasionally embarassed by appearance of hand. Pre-accident hobbies of cricket, rowing and horse riding adversely affected. Present job in some doubt and would be at real disadvantage on open labour market. General damages for pain and suffering and loss of amenities assessed at £7,500 and for loss of earning capacity at £5,000. *Total General Damages:* £12,500. [*Ex rel. Ralph Lewis, Barrister*].

1202. MOORE *v.* JOHNSTON (September 4, 1986; H.H. Judge McKinnay; Portsmouth County Court). Male, aged 41 at the date of accident and 42 at date of trial. Engineering worker. Right-handed. Fracture of interphalangeal joint of left thumb. Mild concussion, slight cut to head. Fracture in plaster 3 weeks; 3 weeks' physiotherapy. Left with slight loss of grip in left hand. Small amount of discomfort experienced when practising hobby of archery. Off work 9 weeks. Able to carry on work though found difficulty in picking up small components with left hand and with operating certain types of lathes. *Agreed special damages*: £298·44. *General damages*: £2,300. [*Ex rel. Stephen J. Murray, Barrister.*]

Leg

1203. CHURMS *v.* GRAYSTON PLANT (February 16, 1987; Deputy Judge Wilson Mellor Q.C.; Q.B.D.; Birmingham). Male, aged 37 at date of accident and 44 at trial. Former foreman steel erector. Metal girder fell across left leg resulting in most disabling combination of injuries comprising (1) fracture of tibia in two places, lower fracture being compound and comminuted; (2) fracture of fibula; (3) severe soft tissue injuries to left foot; (4) fracture separation of first and second metatarsals. Regular hospital attendances for three and a half years, by which time fractures of leg had united. Left with 20° "bow leg" deformity and 15° restriction of plantar flexion in ankle. Appearance of leg unsightly and it was vulnerable to breakdown in event of even slight injury, necessitating wearing of gaiter about lower leg as protective measure. Now walked with stick and marked limp and range could cover without pain was measured in hundreds of yards. Unable to resume pre-accident work. Now fit only for work involving no lifting or carrying, little walking and no prolonged standing. General damages for pain and suffering and loss of amenities assessed at £20,000, for future loss of earnings at £70,595 (based on multiplier of 11) and for additional cost of car with automatic gearbox at £2,800 (based on multiplier of 14). *Special Damages:* £34,070. *Total General Damages:* £93,395. [*Ex rel. Robin Thompson and Partners (Cardiff Office), Solicitors*].

Ankle

1204. GIAMETTI *v.* HAIGH (January 23, 1987; Deputy Judge Michael Wright Q.C.; Q.B.D.). Male, aged 17 at date of accident and 20 at trial. Trainee hairdresser in father's business. Very keen on physical fitness and Kung Fu, which he had begun at 14½ and was a very significant part of his life. Before accident had achieved Blue Sash status and would probably have attained Black Sash and become instructor. Severe lacerations to left ankle requiring 17 stitches; bruising and grazing. Off work five months. Confidence and general outlook on life affected for a time. Left with sensitive scar on back of ankle, which was clearly visible when exposed, but not seriously disfiguring, although he was conscious of it; and stiffness, swelling and "pins and needles" sensation in ankle at end of a busy day, which would be a "permanent nuisance". Unable to continue Kung Fu, though still did some training and running. Employment prospects unaffected. *Agreed Special Damages:* £1,205. *General Damages:* £5,500. [*Ex rel. David Foskett, Barrister*].

1205. HILLS *v.* CRAIG AND GUBBER (December 22, 1986; Judge Hunter; Wandsworth County Ct.). Female, aged 70 at date of accident and 72 at date of hearing. Before accident enjoyed good health and full mobility. As result of fall suffered sprain of right ankle and multiple injuries to left ankle comprising: (1) comminuted fracture of lateral malleolus; (2) Avulsion of tibial attachment of anterior part of tibio-fibular syndesmosis; (3) rupture of anterior capsule of ankle joint; (4) comminuted fracture of medial malleolus; (5) damage to articular surface of talus. In hospital three months. Underwent operation to fix fractures with plate and screws and left leg put in below-knee plaster. After two weeks further operation under general anaethetic revealed infection. After six weeks skin graft performed, followed three weeks later by further operation under general anesthetic to treat infection of donor site. Below knee plaster then re-applied. Non-weight bearing for two months. Continued physiotherapy at home. Showed positive attitude throughout.

Remarkable recovery within nine months. 10 per cent. reduction of dorsiflexion of left ankle. Otherwise full range of movements and no loss of power. Continuing loss of confidence and fear of going out. Minimal risk of degenerative osteo-arthritis. No special damages. *General Damages:* £4,500. [*Ex rel. Janet Waddicor, Barrister*].

1206. LODGE *v.* MAGNET JOINERY (March 25, 1987; Judge Pickles; Keighley County Ct.). Male, aged about 28 at date of accident and 31 at trial. Heavy goods vehicle fitter. Undisplaced fracture of medial malleolus and lower one inch of fibula involving left ankle. Fractures manipulated under general anaesthetic. In plaster eight weeks and off work nine weeks. Had regained full range of painless movements in ankle, but continued to suffer ache in cold weather and "twinge" of pain when jumping down from vehicles. Further deterioration unlikely. *Agreed Special Damages:* £395.51. *General Damages:* £2,000. [*Ex rel. James Goss, Barrister*].

Foot

1207. MECHAM *v.* SADDINGTON (December 18, 1986; Leonard J.). Married woman, aged 47 at date of accident and 50 at date of trial. Pre-accident employment guaranteed until 65. Her husband and she were enthusiastic cyclists and had never learned to drive. Owing to negligence of defendant in failing to hold, or stand close to handrail, of moving escalator he lost his balance and fell against plaintiff, knocking her to bottom of escalator. Fracture dislocation of left foot involving mid-tarsal joints. In hospital two weeks initially, when fracture pinned. After two months re-admitted for two days for further operation to remove pin. Walked with aid of crutches or stick for about a year. Permanent restriction of movement and pain in ankle and foot. Now needed help with housework. Could no longer cycle. Had learned to drive and bought car (which but for accident would not have done) to enable her to get about and shop. Unable to resume pre-accident work. Limited earning capacity until 60 in some form of clerical work. Had already developed early osteo-arthritis and prognosis poor. Prospects of successful arthrodesis in dispute. But agreed that ultimately for patient to decide whether to undergo operation and that there was 50 per cent. chance that plaintiff would choose to do so. General damages for pain and suffering and loss of amenities assessed at £8,500; (2) for cost of future domestic help for one hour each weekday at £6,500 (based on multiplier of 10 and multiplicand of £650); (3) for loss of future earnings at £3,952 consisting of (a) partial loss to age 60 of £1,326 (based on multiplier of 6 and multiplicand of £221) and (b) total loss between 60 and 65 of £2,626 (based on multiplier of 2 and multiplicand of £1,313); (4) for chance of future operation (50 per cent. of present cost) £1,375. Cost of driving lessons and purchase of car assessed at £1,250, net loss of earnings to trial agreed at £3,120 and other special damage at £161.70. *Total Special Damages:* £4,531.70. *Total General Damages:* £20,327 [*Ex rel. Allan Gore, Barrister*].

1208. STUDWELL *v.* WHITE (September 8, 1986; Mr. District Registrar Bailey Cox; Portsmouth County Ct.). Female, aged 43 at date of accident and 45 at date of hearing. Unmarried. Right foot trapped under pedals in car accident. Avulsion fracture of navicular bone with severe discomfort. Leg in plaster three weeks; off work five weeks. Pain in ankle gradually resolved and had ceased by date of hearing. No suggestion of any real future discomfort. No scarring. Unable to wear thin high heeled shoes. *Special Damages:* £659·04. *General Damages:* £3,500. [*Ex rel. Blake Lapthorn, Solicitors*].

Traumatic neurosis

1209. RAI (January 20, 1987; Criminal Injuries Compensation Board; Birmingham). Married man, aged 41 at date of offence and 46 at date of hearing. Sikh. Former bus driver.

Attacked by gang of youths. Minor physical injuries, but developed severe depressive anxiety state. Underwent electro-convulsive therapy without success. Suffered recurrent nightmares, headaches and loss of libido and had lost interest in his family life and religion. Still taking medication. Prognosis poor. Had not worked since accident, would never again be able to drive public service vehicle and was unlikely to work again in any capacity. Agreed continuing loss of earnings of £6,101 p.a. General damages for pain and suffering and loss of amenities assessed at £12,500 and for future loss of earnings, pension and free bus travel at £60,000. *Special Damages:* £20,700. *Total General Damages:* £72,500. [*Ex rel. Ralph Lewis, Barrister*].

1210. S. (October 21, 1986; Criminal Injuries Compensation Board.) Female, aged 31 at date of offence and 33 at date of hearing. Attractive, well balanced person. Married with 3 children, but separated from husband. Subjected to various sexual assault, involving rape; no weapon used. Full recovery from physical injuries within a month, but developed depression, anxiety state, phobia, personality change and skin problems. Attempted suicide on 5 occasions. Admitted to hospital for 5 days for treatment in mental ward. Condition very much improved by date of hearing. But had continuing nightmares and was still unable to lead normal life. Slept with axe under pillow, panicked in company of men and afraid to be alone. More likely to make suicide attempts or gestures and to be dependent on alcohol than would otherwise have been the case. Risk of psychiatric breakdown if she experienced other traumas in her life, whether or not involving men. Unlikely to be capable of forming normal relationship with a man and possibility of reconciliation with husband and chances of remarriage remote. Skin problems likely to persist for up to 4 years and might become established. Agreed loss of earnings £887. General damages for pain and suffering and loss of amenities assessed at £12,000. *Total award*: £12,887. [*Ex rel. Stamp Jackson and Procter, Solicitors*].

1211. WHITTY *v.* HACKNEY BOROUGH COUNCIL (February 5, 1987; MacNeill J.). Married woman, aged about 25 at date of accident and 31 at date of trial. When only son aged 21 months he touched broken illuminated sign, to which power supply had not been turned off, and was electrocuted. Plaintiff heard sound of explosion and shriek from son, saw him lying prostrate in pall of smoke and at first thought he was dead. Suffered severe nervous shock, probable reoccurrence of depressive conditions and nightmares. Required tranquilisers and sleeping tablets and received psychiatric counselling. Condition aggravated by fact that defendants did not remove sign for over a year, despite repeated requests and numerous promises to do so. For about two years lost normal maternal affection for son and became alienated from him. Full recovery after about two and a half years. *General Damages:* £4,500. [*Ex rel;. John Reide, Barrister*].

1212. CODDINGTON *v.* HERN (August 28, 1986; Mr. Deputy District Registrar Hamilton; Boston County Court). Female, aged 46. Former nanny and helper for handicapped children; at date of accident worked as pre-packer. Involved in head-on collision. Anxiety state, bruising and shock. Principal symptoms were overwhelming fear of being involved in accident every time a vehicle approached her and hence of driving, palpitations, sweating and fear of passing out. Was using public transport or walking. General damages for pain and suffering and loss of amenities assessed at £6,000 and for loss of earning capacity at £500. *Special Damages*: £347·14. *Total General Damages*: £6,500. [*Ex rel. Ringrose and Co., Solicitors*].

Pre-existing condition: osteo arthritis

1213. HAW *v.* HAMPSHIRE COUNTY COUNCIL (January 21, 1987; Master Trench). Female, aged 41 at date of accident and 45 at date of hearing. Six children. Pre-existing, but symptomless, osteo arthritis in left knee. Before accident had booked one month holiday in Africa. Tripped in hole in road and fell heavily on left knee. Laceration of knee; considerable pain, restriction of movements and swelling; acceleration by four years of inevitable onset of symptoms from pre-existing condition and aggravation of severity of symptoms. On crutches three months. Due to pain unable to get good night's sleep for six months. After about a year there was some improvement. Underwent arthroscopy under general anaesthetic. At date of hearing still suffered pain, restriction of movement and swelling and took pain killers twice a month on average. Unable to sit for any length of time and hence to enjoy theatre-going or dinner parties. Could not garden, do heavy housework or participate in teenage activities of children. General damages for pain and suffering and loss of amenities assessed at £4,850 and for loss of enjoyment of holiday at £500. *Special Damages:* £3,375·57. *Total General Damages:* £5,350. [*Ex rel. Richard Dening and Simon Coltart, Barristers*].

Pain and suffering

1214. PRIOR *v.* HASTIE (BERNARD) AND CO. See *Fatal accidents* below.

Minor injuries

1215. OLD *v.* SAMPSON (January 13, 1987; Judge Paynter Reece; Romford County Ct.). Male, aged 59 at date of accident and 60 at date of trial. Knocked off bicycle. Acute strain of left trapezius muscle, extensive bruising to left leg, soft tissue injury to left calf and small laceration of left ankle. Confined to bed one week, left arm in sling four weeks, unable to walk properly for six weeks and off work eight weeks. Left with pains in shoulder when subjected to stress or when he lay on it in bed, which disturbed his sleep; thickening of tissues of left calf, which ached in cold weather; tender scar on left ankle and pain which affected hobby of horse riding. Some improvement likely, but complete recovery uncertain. *Agreed Special Damages:* £618·79. *General Damages:* £2,250. [*Ex rel. Roger Hiorns, Barrister*].

1216. PERRY *v.* MERCER (October 28, 1986; Judge Butter; Bow County Court). Female, aged 20. Secretary. Whiplash injury to neck and back. Off work 2 weeks. In cervical collar 4 weeks. Thereafter suffered some pain and stiffness on rotation of neck, some mild low backache and headaches once or twice a week. Symptoms resolved after about 13 months. Slightly increased risk of degenerative changes in neck in middle age. (*Bowen* v. *O'Neill* [1986] C.L.Y. 1042 followed). *General Damages*: £1,800. [*Ex rel. E. Edwards, Son and Noice, Solicitors*].

1217. JORDAN *v.* MID-GLAMORGAN COUNTY COUNCIL (October 9, 1986; Judge ap Robert; Pontypridd County Court). Boy, aged 9 at date of accident. Right arm then in plaster after previous accident. Tripped and fell on left shoulder. Fracture of left clavicle. Not detained in hospital. Left arm and shoulder immobilised in figure-of-eight strapping. For 3 weeks had use of neither arm and had to be fed, washed, dressed and everything else done for him by his parents. Then began to mobilise left arm. Off school 6 weeks. Pain and stiffness gradually diminished. Left with small, detached bony spicule at fracture site, which would be absorbed as he grew. Otherwise full recovery within 8 months. *General Damages:* £850. [*Ex rel. Keith Bush, Barrister.*]

1218. THOMPSON *v.* BRADFORD HEALTH AUTHORITY (July 7, 1986; Mr. Recorder F. W. Williamson Q.C., Bradford County Court). Female, aged 55 at date of accident. State enrolled nurse. Fire extinguisher fell onto left thigh and calf, causing bruising and severe swelling. Leg in bandage 2 weeks and unable to move comfortably for first week. Reasonably off work 4 to 5 weeks. *General Damages:* £650. [*Ex rel. Basil Garratt, Barrister.*]

Fatal accidents

1219. PRIOR *v.* HASTIE (BERNARD) AND CO. (December 12, 1986; Deceased, male, aged 46 at date of death. Former lagger. Developed malignant peritoneal mesothelioma. In February 1985 first symptoms experienced: suprapubic pain during micturition and defaecation and loss of weight. By mid-March 1985 abdomen swollen, began to suffer central abdominal pain and aching in both flanks radiating into loins, could not sit or lie still in bed, suffering increasing discomfort, but still struggled to work. On April 4, 1985 admitted to hospital, where he remained until his death. Fluid drained from peritoneum. Bowel became matted, there was difficulty in continuing drainage from peritoneum and he became increasingly ill and in pain. On April 24, 1985 laparotomy performed and massive tumour involving whole omentum found. Then deteriorated rapidly and died on May 1. After death found to have mild asbestosis of both lungs, but this had not caused symptoms. General damages for 11 weeks' pain and suffering and loss of amenities assessed at £7,000. Dependency assessed at £63,237, consisting of £50,737 in respect of deceased's future earnings (based on multiplier of 12 and agreed multiplicand of £4,850) and £12,500 in respect of value to widow of deceased's painting, decorating, gardening and use of company car. Bereavement award: £3,500 (on which interest awarded at full short-term investment rate from date of death). *Agreed Special Damages:* £7,982. *Total General Damages:* £73,737. [*Ex rel. Field, Fisher and Martineau, Solicitors*].

1220. Personal injuries pension scheme—whether damages to include pension contributions

A plaintiff who takes time off work as the result of an accident, and therefore cannot make obligatory pension contributions, is not entitled to any sum in damages in respect of those contributions where his pension rights have not been affected.

The plaintiff was required to belong to the Mineworkers Pension Scheme; he was obliged to make a weekly contribution to it, matched by the Coal Board. The plaintiff was off work for 31 weeks as the result of an accident, and for some of that period received no pay and therefore made no contributions. He suffered no loss of pension rights. He was awarded damages and claimed in addition an amount equal to the gross contributions (of his and the Board's) which would have been made. The judge allowed him an amount equivalent to his own contributions; the Board appealed successfully.

Held, dismissing the plaintiff's appeal, damages were compensatory in nature, and as the plaintiff had suffered no loss of pension rights, the plaintiff was not entitled to recover any sum in respect of these lost contributions (*British Transport Commission* v. *Gourley* [1955] C.L.Y. 724, *Parry* v. *Cleaver* [1969] C.L.Y. 906 applied).

DEWS *v.* NATIONAL COAL BOARD [1987] 3 W.L.R. 38, H.L.

1221/2. Provisional Damages—Supreme Court Act 1981, s.32A. See PATTERSON *v.* MINISTRY OF DEFENCE.

1223. Retraction of libel—made without apology—mitigation of damages. See PINE *v.* McMILLAN, §2296.

1224. Sale of land—breach of covenant to carry out remedial work prior to sale. See DEAN *v.* AINLEY, §452.

1225. Sale of land with vacant possession—vendor unable to give possession and complete—measure of damages

An unwillingness on the part of a vendor to use his best endeavours to fulfill his contractual obligations is sufficient to amount to the bad faith necessary in order to exclude the rule in *Bain* v. *Fothergill,* so that a failure by a vendor to serve a notice to quit on the occupiers of his land amounts to sufficient bad faith to exclude the rule.

P bought land from D, stressing throughout that vacant possession was required. The occupants of the land refused to vacate claiming a business tenancy; following counsel's advice that proceedings for possession would be unlikely to succeed, D did not serve a notice to quit on the occupiers.

Held, on the preliminary issue of whether D's damages were to be limited under the rule in *Bain* v. *Fothergill,* that the failure to serve a notice to quit amounted to a failure on the part of D to use its best endeavours to secure possession. Such a failure was to be treated as sufficient to show the bad faith necessary to avoid the rule in *Bain* v. *Fothergill.* Damages were accordingly recoverable under the general law. (*Day* v. *Singleton* [1899] 2 Ch. 320 and *Malhotra* v. *Choudhury* [1978] C.L.Y. 3058 applied).

SHARNEYFORD SUPPLIES *v.* EDGE, BARRINGTON BLACK & CO. (THIRD PARTY) [1987] 2 W.L.R. 363, C.A.

1226. Tax element in assessment—whether higher taxation on large award to be considered—future loss of earnings

The effect of higher rate tax on the income from a large award of damages is a proper factor to take into account when assessing damages for future care, and future loss of earnings.

In the course of routine surgery T. sustained severe permanent brain damage due to the admitted negligence of the anaesthetist and his employers. The trial judge awarded £679,264 damages, which included £435,000 for the cost of future care; having started with a multiplier of 14 he increased that to 15 to compensate for the effect of higher rate taxation.

Held, dismissing the appeal that the incidence of such tax was properly to be taken into account. The judge had been entitled to increase the multiplier from 14 to 15 in the circumstances of the case.

THOMAS *v.* WIGNALL [1987] 2 W.L.R. 930, C.A.

1227. Trespass to land—inconvenience to development planning—amount

D built a bathroom extension, the footings of which extended a maximum of one and a half inches into P's next door land which had outline planning permission for the erection of a single house. The encroachment did not affect the development potential of P's land. The judge decided it was not an appropriate case for granting an injunction and awarded damages in lieu in the sum of £1,250. D appealed contending that the damages should be merely nominal.

Held, that this was not an ordinary trespass case where the trespass was temporary and would be at an end when matters had been made good. It was a question of an award of damages in lieu of the grant of an injunction, and the effect of witholding the injunction was that the trespass became permanent. It was not a case for a mere nominal award. D was getting the benefit of the footings remaining in P's land and that reduced a fairly narrow site from the point of view of development, and though it did not affect the development potential it was to some extent an inconvenience in the planning for development. That was a factor which could be compensated by a reasonable award of damages. The appropriate sum to award was £400. Accordingly the appeal would be allowed and the award of damages reduced from £1,250 to £400 (*Wrotham Park Estate Co.* v. *Parkside Homes* [1974] C.L.Y. 3130 and *Bracewell* v. *Appleby* [1975] C.L.Y. 1017 considered).

GRIFFITHS *v.* KINGSLEY-STUBBS, June 3, 1986 (C.A.T. No. 506).

1228. Unlawful eviction—assault. See REID AND REID *v.* ANDREOU, §2250.

1229. Unlawful eviction—sexual harassment. See AMUSAN *v.* TAUSSIG, §2251.

1230. Value added tax—whether the amount of value added tax should be added to the damages assessed

In *Elite Investments* v. *T. I. Bainbridge Silencers* [1986] C.L.Y. 1854, the judge gave judgment against T in the sum of £84,364 for the cost of repairs under a repairing covenant to the roof of an industrial building in Blackpool. L subsequently brought a further action contending that the judgment sum should bear VAT at 15 per cent. The judge found that the damages had been paid almost immediately after judgment was given on May 9, 1986, that no attempt had been made in the meantime to repair the roof, and that L, who had acquired the original landlord's claim by assignment during the course of the proceedings, were not registered for VAT. In the lack of any evidence as to L's intention with regard to the building, the judge was left with the impression that L had no intention of doing any sort of work on the premises.

Held, that in the circumstances, VAT was not recoverable (*Drummonds* v. *S. & U. Stores* [1981] C.L.Y. 1522 distinguished).

ELITE INVESTMENTS *v.* T. I. BAINBRIDGE SILENCERS (No. 2) (1987) 283 E.G. 747, H.H. Judge Paul Baker Q.C.

EASEMENTS AND PRESCRIPTION

1231. Illuminated signs—whether continuing use permitted under lease—whether license or easement—whether "appurtenances"

Where premises are permitted to be used as a betting shop, the demise of the "appurtenances" to the shop will generally include any signs advertising the shop's presence and the tenant will be allowed to maintain such signs.

C's predecessors in title had let the first floor of certain premises to WH for use as a betting shop. There were already in position two signs advertising the shop's existence; with the express consent of the then landlord, WH replaced one of the signs. On C acquiring the reversion, it was asserted by C that the signs existed subject to a licence revocable on reasonable notice.

Held, dismissing C's appeal, that although there was no grant of the right to exhibit the signs, on a proper construction, the right to maintain the signs was granted by the demise of the appurtenances to the demised premises. Bearing in mind the permitted user of the premises and the practical and commercial considerations, it was to be supposed that the appurtenances included the right to maintain the signs.

HILL (WILLIAM) (SOUTHERN) *v.* CABRAS (1987) 54 P. & C.R. 42, C.A.

1232. Pathway—use of path—gate periodically locked

[Prescription Act 1832 (c.71), s.4.]

Where the use of a pathway was periodically blocked by locking a gate no easement could arise since the user was not, on the facts, capable of amounting to an easement and it was not necessary to consider whether the interruptions were to be disregarded by virtue of the Act.

GOLDSMITH *v.* BURROW CONSTRUCTION CO., *The Times,* July 31, 1987, C.A.

1233. Right of way—access to archaeological site—way used to gain access to car park en route to site—whether permissible use

A right of way granted for the purpose of obtaining access to an archaeological site could be used to obtain access to a car park provided for the use of visitors to the site.

The National Trust were the owners of Figsbury Ring, an Iron Age hill fort. Access to the Ring was provided by a track from the main road. The track ran along land belonging to D. In 1970, the county council built a one and a half acre car park on land belonging to the Ministry of Defence adjoining the track and opposite D's land. Thereafter, visitors to the Ring were able to park their cars in the car park and proceed along the track on foot. The right of way granted over the track was for the owners for the time being of the Ring and all other persons authorised by them to pass and repass over the road or track of a width of 20 feet. The right of way was granted in 1921. D purchased his land in 1973. D objected to the level of traffic passing along the track to the car park. He placed a gate across the track and purported to prevent visitors passing along the track. The National Trust sought a declaration that all persons authorised by them were entitled to pass over the track whether in a vehicle or otherwise for the purposes of visiting the Ring and gaining access to the car park in connection with visiting the Ring and injunctive relief.

Held, that a servient owner was not permitted to derogate from the grant of a right of way nor was the dominant owner permitted to make unreasonable demands upon it. Whether there was a derogation or unreasonable demand was to be judged against the construction to be placed on the grant and the factual circumstances. The creation of the car park could not properly be described as an enlargement of the dominant tenement. D's argument that the extent to which the track was currently used was beyond anything contemplated at the time the right was granted could not suceed. The right granted was ". . . at all times and for all purposes . . ." and not restricted in any way (*Harris* v. *Flower* (1904) 74 L.J. Ch. 127, *White* v. *Grand Hotel, Eastbourne* [1913] 1 Ch. 113, *Pettey* v. *Parsons* [1914] 2 Ch. 653, *Jelbert* v. *Davis* [1968] C.L.Y. 1315 considered).

NATIONAL TRUST FOR PLACES OF HISTORIC INTEREST OR NATURAL BEAUTY *v.* WHITE [1987] 1 W.L.R. 907, Warner J.

1234. Right of way—disputed public footpath—statutory procedure for resolution of dispute—civil proceedings by landowner—whether strike out or stay civil proceedings. See SHEARS COURT (WEST MERSEA) MANAGEMENT CO. *v.* ESSEX COUNTY COUNCIL, §3097.

1235. Right of way—excessive and unreasonable use—injunction

A court may, by injunction, control the detailed use of a right of way in order to prevent excessive and unreasonable use and possible nuisance.

In 1982 the appellant P acquired a house and enjoyed a right of way under the conveyance in common with 25 residents of the hamlet. He restored the house and opened it to the public. The respondents contended that the invitation to the public to use the right of way constituted an excessive and wrongful user of the right of way and that the extra traffic generated excessive noise and invasion of privacy. The county court judge granted an injunction restraining the appellant from interfering unreasonably with the use of the right of way by the respondents and specifying in detail the numbers of people permitted to use the right of way and dates when the public could use it. He appealed against the judgment, and the respondents sought to vary the injunction to prevent the appellant inviting the public to use it.

Held, that the grant of the right of way was expressed to be "for all purposes". The mere fact that there had been a change of use and the house made open to the public which attracted traffic was not itself a breach of the terms of the grant, and no injunction would be granted to prevent the appellant opening the house to the public. However, the grant was expressed to be in "common with the Purchaser and all persons deriving under him" which required that the use of the right of way must not be such as to interfere unreasonably with the use by other persons entitled to use the right of way. On the facts, the evidence was that the user was excessive. An injunction was an appropriate remedy. The appeal was dismissed, and the order for an injunction upheld with minor modifications.

ROSLING *v.* PINNEGAR (1987) 54 P. & C.R. 124, C.A.

1236. Right of way plan annexed to conveyance—planning permission—whether admissible for purposes of construction.

An annexed plan is admissible to explain unclear terms in a conveyance; planning permission is also admissible as to the background to the conveyance.

P's house was served by a private road over which he had a right of way. The road was not defined in the conveyance but was depicted on the annexed plan as being accompanied by three-foot wide verges. This accorded with the original grant of planning permission. The verges subsequently disappeared. On conveyance of the adjoining land, P sought a declaration that the right of way included the verges. The declaration was refused.

Held, allowing the appeal, that the plan was admissible to explain unclear terms in the conveyance, and the planning permission was admissible as to the background to the conveyance. By reference to those, the right of way included the three-foot verges.

Per curiam: the burden of proof on a question of construction does not lie on the plaintiff; a question of construction is a question of law in respect of which no burden lies on either side (*Wigginton and Milner* v. *Winster Engineering* [1978] C.L.Y. 2500 applied; *Wilson* v. *Greene* [1971] C.L.Y. 9887 distinguished).

SCOTT *v.* MARTIN [1987] 1 W.L.R. 841, C.A.

1237. Rights of access—whether preserved on sale of land. See M.R.A. ENGINEERING *v.* TRIMSTER CO., §458.

ECCLESIASTICAL LAW

1238. Altar—whether holy table—whether faculty should be granted for installation of sculpture into church—church listed building—effect on alterations

An altar fell within the definition of a holy table for the purposes of Holy Communion in a Church of England church.

The parochial church council for the parish of St. Stephen Walbrook and the rector of the church petitioned for a faculty permitting the introduction of a large stone alter carved by Henry Moore into the church. The church was designed by Christopher Wren and acknowledged as one of his masterpieces. It was a listed building. It was proposed to place the altar in the centre of the church below its dome. The altar was circular, eight feet in diameter and three feet five inches high. It was recognised to be a work of art of exceptional excellence. The chancellor held he could not grant the faculty as a matter of law on the ground that an altar could not be a holy table used for the purposes of Holy Communion and if that were wrong he would not have granted it in the exercise of his discretion on the ground that the petitioners had failed to disprove the respondent's evidence that the altar was wholly inappropriate having regard to the geometry of the church. The petitioners appealed.

Held, allowing the appeal, that an altar can lawfully and properly be called a holy table for the purposes of celebrating Holy Communion. The approach adopted by the chancellor in posing the question of whether the petitioners had succeeded in proving that the evidence that the altar was architectually inappropriate was wrong in law. The burden of proof lay upon the petitioners. They were required to show clearly and manifestly the benefits to be derived from the alteration or satisfy the court that the general desire of the parishioners was in favour of the change. It was not a question of considering if witnesses were wrong but considering the evidence as a whole as to the effect of the alteration. In the present case the evidence as a whole on the issue of architectural congruity was evenly balanced and did not warrant the dismissal of the petition. The wishes of the rector and parishoners were in favour of granting the faculty. The chancellor had not given sufficient weight to some of the evidence adduced. Accordingly, the court was entitled to exercise its own discretion to grant the faculty in substitution for the discretion exercised by the chancellor. The fact that the church was a listed building was a relevant consideration in deciding whether or not to grant a faculty but it did not have effect so as to require that a faculty should only be granted in cases of clearly proved necessity (*Peek* v. *Trower* (1881) 7 P.D. 21, *St. Michael and All Angels, Great Torrington, Re* [1985] C.L.Y. 1089 applied; *Faulkner* v. *Litchfield and Stearn* (1845) 1 Rob. Eccl. 184, *Liddell* v. *Westerton* (1857) 29 L.T.O.S 54, *Nickalls* v. *Briscoe* [1892] P. 269, *St Mary's, Banbury,* [1987] C.L.Y. 1242 considered).

ST. STEPHEN'S WALBROOK, *Re* [1987] 2 All E.R. 578, Ct. of Ecclesiastical Causes Reserved.

1239. Benefices

PATRONAGE (BENEFICES) RULES 1987 (No. 773) [£3·40], made under the Patronage (Benefices) Measure 1986 (No. 3), s.38; operative on Janurary 1, 1989 save for rules 1–10, 14, 15, and 17 which are operative on October 1, 1987; provides for notification of interests in relation to benefices.

1240. Churchyard—adjacent cemetery—proposal for access via churchyard

The churchyard of a parish church was consecrated ground used for burials, but no further space was available. The parish council purchased adjacent land for a cemetery, and planning permission was granted subject to access being through the churchyard. The council petitioned for a faculty to provide a licence to pass and repass for access purposes.

Held, that the jurisdiction of the consistory court was not limited by the incumbent's proprietary interest in the churchyard. The function of the church was as a focus for the worshipping congregation, and the proposed arrangement might give the impression that the church existed as a cemetery chapel, and the licence would thus not be granted.

ST. ANDREW'S, NORTH WEALD BASSETT, *Re* [1987] 1 W.L.R. 1503, Chelmsford Consistory Ct.

1241. Coat of arms and chest sold without faculty—value enhanced by restoration work—whether title passed in absence of faculty

Title does not pass in respect of ecclesiastical property sold without a faculty, and although a confirmatory faculty might subsequently be granted. that would require some good and sufficient reason.

Per curiam: antique dealers, who should be very well aware of the existence of the faculty jurisdiction, should take steps to satisfy themselves of the lawfulness of proposed sale of church property.

In 1977 a medieval chest was sold by a churchwarden for £85, and in 1980 a coat of arms for £50. After restoration the coat of arms was valued in a London sale room at £9,000. The vicar and churchwardens sought a faculty confirming the sale.

Held, refusing the faculty, that disposal of such articles without a faculty was ineffective to pass title, which remained therefore in the churchwardens. A confirmatory faculty would only be granted for some good and sufficient reason, which had not been demonstrated here. Both the churchwardens and the dealers (who should be taken to be very well aware of the existence of the faculty jurisdiction) had repeatedly failed to comply with the jurisdiction and the faculty would be denied (*St. Gregory's, Tredington. Re* [1971] C.L.Y. 3773 applied; *St. Mary's Balham, Re* [1978] C.L.Y. 849 and *St. Agnes's, Toxteth Park, Re* [1985] C.L.Y. 1092 considered)

ST. MARY'S, BARTON-UPON-HUMBER *Re* [1986] 3 W.L.R. 906, Const. Ct.

1242. Faculty—removal of pews allotted to parishioners

[1790 (30 Geo. 3, c.72).]

In 1790 an Act was passed allowing a church to be pulled down and rebuilt. The freehold remained vested in the rector but trustees were empowered to "allot and appoint" pews to anyone who subscribed £10 or more towards the rebuilding, and to "sell and dispose" of any of the remaining to purchasers as the trustees saw fit. In 1983 the rector and churchwardens petitioned for a faculty to remove the pews and replace them with chairs. The petition was opposed by three persons who proved title to numbered pews.

Held, on appeal from the Oxford Consistory Court that the wording of the statute was consistent only with a perpetual right, and the pews could not be removed without the consent of the owners. No faculty could remove the statutory right and to remove all but three pews would be absurd. There was accordingly no jurisdiction to grant the faculty sought, and the petitioners appeal would be dismissed.

ST. MARY'S, BANBURY, *Re* [1987] 1 All E.R. 247, Arches Court of Canterbury.

1243. Faculty jurisdiction

FACULTY JURISDICTION (AMENDMENT) RULES 1987 (No. 2266) [£2·20], made under the Faculty Jurisdiction Measure 1964 (No. 5), s.14; operative on April 1, 1988; amend S.I. 1967 No. 1002.

1244. Fees

ECCLESIASTICAL JUDGES AND LEGAL OFFICERS (FEES) ORDER 1987 (No. 1297) [85p], made under the Ecclesiastical Fees Measure 1986 (No. 2), s.4; operative on January 1, 1988; increases certain fees.

LEGAL OFFICERS (ANNUAL FEES) ORDER 1987 (No. 1296) [£1·60], made under the Ecclesiastical Fees Measure 1986 (No. 2), s.4; operative on January 1, 1988; increases certain fees.

1245. Methodist Church Act 1976—Guernsey

METHODIST CHURCH ACT 1976 (GUERNSEY) ORDER 1987 (No. 1279) [85p], made under the Methodist Church Act 1976 (c.xxx), ss.28, 30; provides that the Methodist Church Union Act 1929 shall cease to apply to Guernsey and extends the Methodist Church Act 1976 to Guernsey.

1246. United Reformed Church Act 1981—Guernsey

UNITED REFORMED CHURCH ACT 1981 (GUERNSEY) ORDER 1987 (No. 2051) [45p], made under The United Reformed Church Act 1981 (c.xxiv), s.31; operative on December 26, 1987; extends to Guernsey certain provisions of the 1981 Act.

EDUCATION

1247. Abolition of corporal punishment—independent schools

EDUCATION (ABOLITION OF CORPORAL PUNISHMENT) (INDEPENDENT SCHOOLS) REGULATIONS 1987 (No. 1183) [45p], made under the Education (No. 2) Act 1986 (c.61), s.47(5)(*a*)(iii); operative on August 15, 1987; prescribe the classes of independent schools where corporal punishment may not be lawfully administered.

1248. Assisted places

EDUCATION (ASSISTED PLACES) (AMENDMENT) REGULATIONS 1987 (No. 1312) [85p], made under the Education Act 1980 (c.20), ss.17(6), 35(4); reg. 1 operative on August 1, 1987, regs. 2–4 (for the purposes specified in reg. 1(2)(*a*)(*b*)) operative on August 1, 1987, regs. 2–4 for all other purposes operative on September 1, 1987; amend S.I. 1985 No. 685.

EDUCATION (ASSISTED PLACES) (INCIDENTAL EXPENSES) (AMENDMENT) REGULATIONS 1987 (No. 1313) [45p], made under the Education Act 1980, ss.18, 35(4); operative on August 15, 1987; further amend S.I. 1985 No. 830.

1249. Awards

EDUCATION (MANDATORY AWARDS) REGULATIONS 1987 (No. 1261) [£4·00], made under the Education Act 1962 (c.12), ss.1, 4(2), Sched. 1, paras. 3, 4 and the Education Act 1973 (c.16), s.3(1)(3); operative on September 1, 1987; make provision in relation to the payment of mandatory awards for further education.

STATE AWARDS (AMENDMENT) REGULATIONS 1987 (No. 1365) [45p], made under the Education Act 1962, ss.3(*b*) and (*c*) and 4; operative on September 1, 1987; make European Community nationals, resident in the community for three years (other than for education), eligible for an award consisting of payments towards fees.

1250. Child with "special educational needs"—criteria for decision

[Education Act 1981 (c.60), ss.1, 2(2)(3), 4(1), 5(1), 7(1), 9.]

The courts will not interfere with an authority's decision on a child's special educational needs where the correct criteria, set out in the judgment, are applied.

The parents of a girl of 13, thought, as the result of reports received, that she might be dyslexic; the local authority did not accept that she was. The authority decided that her needs could be met in the remedial class of an ordinary school and that no statement of "special educational needs" was necessary. The parents applied for judicial review.

Held, dismissing the application, that in reaching their decision the authority had applied the right criteria and reached decisions to which they were entitled to come.

R. *v.* SECRETARY OF STATE FOR EDUCATION AND SCIENCE, *ex p.* L. (1987) 85 L.G.R. 333 D.C.

1251. Direct grant schools

DIRECT GRANT SCHOOLS (AMENDMENT) REGULATIONS 1987 (No. 1182) [45p], made under the Education Act 1944 (c.31), s.100(1)(3); operative on August 15, 1987; amend S.I. 1959 No. 1832.

1252. Disciplinary procedure—investigation by governors—whether authority's disciplinary sub-committee bound by the findings of fact made by the governors. See McGOLDRICK *v.* BRENT LONDON BOROUGH COUNCIL, §1308.

1253. Duration of school year

EDUCATION (SCHOOLS AND FURTHER EDUCATION) (AMENDMENT) REGULATIONS 1987 (No. 879) [45p], made under the Education Act 1980 (c.20), ss.27(1)(*e*)(7), 35(4); operative on August 1, 1987 save for regs. 1 and 2 which are operative on June 8, 1987; amends S.I. 1981 No. 1086 so that the duration of the school year is a minimum of 380 sessions.

1254. Education committee—requirement to include "persons of experience in education"—whether limited to teachers. See R. *v.* CROYDON LONDON BOROUGH COUNCIL, *ex p.* LENEY, §2369.

1255. Education committee—whether a bare recommendation can amount to "a report"

[Education Act 1944 (c.31), Sched. 1, Part II, para. 7.]

A bare recommendation from an education committee cannot amount to "a report" for the purposes of para. 7 of Sched. 1, Part II, of the Education Act 1944. A proper report should contain the committee's reasons for reaching its conclusions, although the exact contents of a proper report will vary from case to case.

R. *v.* KIRKLEES METROPOLITAN BOROUGH COUNCIL, *ex p.* MOLLOY, *The Independent,* July 28, 1987, C.A.

1256. Education (No. 2) Act 1986—commencement

EDUCATION (No. 2) ACT 1986 (COMMENCEMENT No. 2) ORDER 1987 (No. 344 (C.8)) [£1·60], made under the Education (No. 2) Act 1986 (c.61), s.66; brings into force on August 15, 1987, ss.47 and 48 and brings into force on September 1, 1987, ss.1–16, 18–29, 32, 34–43, 57, 58, 61, 62, 67(4) (in part) (5) (6), Scheds. 1, 2, 3, 4 (in part), 5, 6 (in part).

EDUCATION (No. 2) ACT 1986 (COMMENCEMENT No. 3) ORDER 1987 (No. 1159 (C.30)) [45p], made under the Education (No. 2) Act 1986, s.66; brings into force on September 1, 1987, s.67(6) and Sched. 6, both of which are concerned with repeals.

1257. Fees and awards

EDUCATION (FEES AND AWARDS) (AMENDMENT) REGULATIONS 1987 (No. 1364) [85p], made under the Education (Fees and Awards) Act 1983 (c.40), ss.1, 2; operative on September 1, 1987; amends S.I. 1983 No. 973 by making it unlawful to adopt rules of eligibility which exclude EEC nationals from eligibility for awards of fees when they satisfy the condition of residence within the EEC.

1258. Grants

EDUCATION (GRANT) (AMENDMENT) REGULATIONS 1987 (No. 1126) [45p], made under the Education Act 1944 (c.31), s.100(1)(3); operative on July 31, 1987; amend S.I. 1983 No. 74 by adding a reference to the Cranfield Information Technology Institute.

EDUCATION (GRANTS) (CITY TECHNOLOGY COLLEGES) REGULATIONS 1987 (No. 1138) [45p], made under the Education Act 1944, s.100(1)(*b*)(3); operative on August 10, 1987; authorise the payment of grants in connection with the establishment and maintenance of city technology colleges.

EDUCATION (GRANTS) (MUSIC AND BALLET SCHOOLS) (AMENDMENT) REGULATIONS 1987 (No. 1314) [85p], made under the Education Act 1944 (c.31), s.100(1)(*b*)(3); operative on August 15, 1987; further amend S.I. 1985 No. 684.

EDUCATION SUPPORT GRANTS (AMENDMENT) REGULATIONS 1987 (No. 1960) [85p], made under the Education (Grants and Awards) Act 1984 (c.11), ss.1(2)–(4), (7) and 3(4); operative on December 1, 1987; amend S.I. 1984 No. 1098.

EDUCATION (TRAINING GRANTS) REGULATIONS 1987 (No. 96) [£1·40], made under the Education (No. 2) Act 1986 (c.61), ss.50, 63 and the Education Act 1962 (c.12), ss.3(*a*), 4; operative on March 1, 1987; provide for the payment of training grants by the Secretary of State to local authorities.

1259. Grants—sex discrimination—indirect discrimination—consideration of appropriate class of people—effect of European Community law

[EEC Equal Treatment Directive, Arts. 1, 2(1), 4; Sex Discrimination Act 1975 (c.65), ss.1(1)(*b*), 51; Education (Mandatory Awards) Regulations, reg. 5(3), Sched. 2, para. 18; Education (Students' Dependants' Allowances) Regulations, Sched. 4.]

By virtue of the Education (Mandatory Awards) Regulations and the Education (Students' Dependants' Allowances) Regulations, parents who have once been married but lost their spouse receive an additional hardship grant which is not awarded to lone parents who have never been married. Ms. S alleged under the EEC Equal Treatment Directive that this was a form of indirect sex discrimination, in that it affected more women than men since statistics indicated that there were a greater number of female lone parents than male lone parents. The first issue was whether indirect discrimination could be established by showing a disproportionate effect of a practice on women. If so, the second issue was whether the practice was justifiable in this instance.

Held, that there was a prima facie case of indirect discrimination in contravention of the EEC Equal Treatment Directive, since it had been proved that the practice, although apparently sexually mutual, actually had a greater effect upon members of one sex. The appropriate class to consider was all students with dependent children who claimed grants and, on this basis, it had been established that four times as many women as men were affected by the provisions. No objective justification had been proved and the applicant was therefore granted the relief sought.

R. *v.* SECRETARY OF STATE FOR EDUCATION, *ex p.* SCHAFFTER [1987] I.R.L.R. 53, Schiemann J.

1260. Institutions of further education—governing bodies

EDUCATION (GOVERNING BODIES OF INSTITUTIONS OF FURTHER EDUCATION) REGULATIONS 1987 (No. 1160) [85p], made under the Education (No. 2) Act 1986 (c.61), ss.61(2), 62, 63(3); operative on September 1, 1987; make provision with respect to the governing bodies of those institutions of further education which are both maintained by local education authorities and required, by virtue of s.1 of the Education (No. 2) Act 1968 (c.37), to have instruments of government.

1261. Registered Establishments (Scotland) Act 1987 (c.40). See LOCAL GOVERNMENT, §2384.

1262. Registration of pupils

PUPILS' REGISTRATION (AMENDMENT) REGULATIONS 1987 (No. 1285) [45p], made under the Education Act 1944 (c.31), s.80; operative on September 1, 1987; amend S.I. 1956 No. 357 in the light of the new right of appeal in cases of expulsion introduced by the Education (No. 2) Act 1986 (c.61).

1263. Remuneration of teachers

REMUNERATION OF TEACHERS (PRIMARY AND SECONDARY EDUCATION) (AMENDMENT) ORDER 1987 (No. 137) [£1·60], made under the Remuneration of Teachers Act 1965 (c.3), ss.2(6), 7(3); operative on February 17, 1987; prescribes salary scales for teachers in primary and secondary schools maintained by local authorities.

REMUNERATION OF TEACHERS (PRIMARY AND SECONDARY EDUCATION) (AMENDMENT) (No. 2) ORDER 1987 (No. 236) [80p], made under the Remuneration of Teachers Act 1965, ss.2(6), 7(3); operative on February 25, 1987: amends S.I. 1983 No. 1463.

REMUNERATION OF TEACHERS (PRIMARY AND SECONDARY EDUCATION) (AMENDMENT) (No. 3) ORDER 1987 (No. 398) [£1·90], made under the Remuneration of Teachers Act 1965, s.2(6), 7(3); operative on February 28, 1987; makes provision in relation to the remuneration of teachers in primary and secondary schools maintained by local authorities.

1264. School—non-attendance—prosecution of parents

[Education Act 1944 (c.31), ss.36, 37.]

Only one prosecution is possible under s.37(5) of the Act in respect of a simple school attendance order.

The local authority served a school attendance order upon parents requiring them to cause their son to receive efficient full-time education within s.36 of the 1944 Act. The parents failed to comply, and later pleaded guilty to informations charging them with offences under ss.37(5) and 40(1) of the Act. Later the authority formed the view that they were still failing to comply and they were again charged under s.37(5) and convicted.

Held, on appeal, that although this was a continuing offence, the section created only one offence, so no second prosecution was possible in respect of the same school attendance order.

ENFIELD LONDON BOROUGH COUNCIL *v.* F. (1987) 85 L.G.R. 526, D.C.

1265. School—special school for children having "special educational needs"—rate rebate. See RATING AND VALUATION, §3187.

1266. School government

EDUCATION (SCHOOL GOVERNMENT) REGULATIONS 1987 (No. 1359) [£2·60], made under the Education (No. 2) Act 1986 (c.61), ss.8(6)(7)(10), 16(2), 36(2), 62, 63, Sched. 2, paras. 10(4), 12(3), 22(5); operative on September 1, 1987; make provision as to the meetings and proceedings of the governing bodies of all county, voluntary and maintained special schools.

1267. School places—whether local council in breach of statutory duty—sex discrimination. See R. *v.* BIRMINGHAM CITY COUNCIL, EQUAL OPPORTUNITIES COMMISSION, §2388.

1268. Schools

EDUCATION (PUBLICATION OF PROPOSALS TO CHANGE STATUS OF A CONTROLLED SCHOOL) REGULATIONS 1987 (No. 34) [45p], made under the Education (No. 2) Act 1986 (c.61), s.54(3); operative on April 1, 1987; prescribe the manner of publication.

1269. Special educational needs—speech therapy—whether non-educational need

A boy needed a substantial amount of speech therapy because of a chromosome disorder. He attended a special nursery school run by the local authority for the physically handicapped where he received speech therapy. A full assessment of his educational needs was made by the local authority and speech therapy was placed under the heading "additional non-educational provision" not "special educational needs". The parents challenged that by way of judicial review and also argued that the authority had failed to consider any power to make a grant for private speech therapy.

Held, that if speech therapy would be described as "special educational provision" it would be listed in s.7(2) of the Education Act 1981 (c.60). It was not. Instead the provision of speech therapy in an educational setting was part of the N.H.S. and was part of the powers conferred by the National Health Service Act 1977 (c.49). The authority's decision was not irrational or so unreasonable that no reasonable authority would have reached that decision. The local authority had no power to provide a grant for the speech therapy under either the Scholarships and Other Benefits Regulations 1977 (S.I. 1977 No. 1443) or the Local Government Act 1972 (c.70).

R. *v.* OXFORDSHIRE COUNTY COUNCIL, *ex p.* W. [1987] 2 F.L.R. 193, D.C.

1270. Special educational needs—statement—discretion of education authority

[Education Act 1981 (c.60), s.7.]

A local education authority has a discretion whether to make and maintain a statement in respect of children for whom it is responsible and who have special educational needs, but is not obliged so to do.

R. *v.* HEREFORD AND WORCESTER COUNTY COUNCIL, *ex p.* LASHFORD, *The Times,* May 13, 1987, C.A.

1271. Teacher training—bursaries

EDUCATION (BURSARIES FOR TEACHER TRAINING) (AMENDMENT) REGULATIONS 1987 (No. 499) [45p], made under the Education Act 1962 (c.12), ss.3(*a*), 4; operative on April 24, 1987; amend S.I. 1986 No. 1324 in relation to those persons undergoing training to teach mathematics, physics, design and technology.

EDUCATION (BURSARIES FOR TEACHER TRAINING) (AMENDMENT) (No. 2) REGULATIONS 1987 (No. 1393) [45p], made under the Education Act 1962, ss.3(*a*), 4; operative on September 1, 1987; amend S.I. 1986 No. 1324 so as to increase bursaries to £1,250.

1272. Teachers' pay and conditions

EDUCATION (SCHOOL TEACHERS' PAY AND CONDITIONS) ORDER 1987 (No. 1433) [45p], made under the Teachers' Pay and Conditions Act 1987 (c.1), s.3(3)(4)(5)(7)(8); operative October 1, 1987; directs that provisions in a specified H.M.S.O. document shall have effect for determining teachers' pay and conditions.

EDUCATION (SCHOOL TEACHERS' PAY AND CONDITIONS OF EMPLOYMENT) ORDER 1987 (No. 650) [£2·70], made under the Teachers' Pay and Conditions Act 1987 (c.1), s.3(3)–(5)(7)–(9); operative on April 30, 1987; makes provision with respect to the remuneration and other conditions of employment of school teachers in England and Wales.

1273. Teachers' Pay and Conditions Act 1987 (c.1)

This Act repeals the Remuneration of Teachers Act 1965. It makes temporary provision with respect to the remuneration and other conditions of employment of school teachers and certain arrangements for settling the remuneration and other conditions of employment of teachers in further education.

The Act received the Royal Assent on March 2, 1987.

1274. Transport to school—free transport—provision of transport

[Education Act 1944 (c.31), ss.39(2)(*c*), (5), 55(1), (3).]

Where a child was within walking distance of his school as defined by the Act but an application was made for free transport the local authority should take into account in determining the application the age of the child, the nature of any route he could reasonably be expected to take, whether or not he should be accompanied and whether or not he could reasonably be so accompanied (*Rogers* v. *Essex County Council* [1986] C.L.Y. 1145 considered).

R. *v.* DEVON COUNTY COUNCIL, *ex p.* C., *The Independent,* April 29, 1987, Mann J.

1275. University—visitor—jurisdiction—complaint that examiners not properly qualified—nature of investigation visitor required to undertake

The decision of the visitor of a university that two examiners were properly qualified to act as examiners of a PhD thesis was not open to attack on the ground that the visitor had failed to carry out his own factual inquiry into the qualifications of the examiners.

The applicant was a student of Bedford College of the University of London studying for a PhD degree in zoology. The course required the submission of a thesis for examination. Two examiners were appointed by the University to examine the applicants thesis. The applicant did not think either examiner was properly qualified to examine her thesis. She advised the registrar of Bedford College of her apprehensions. Subsequently, the applicant was not awarded a PhD. She complained to the visitor of the university that the examiners had not been properly qualified to examine her thesis. Prior thereto, the thesis was re-examined by five examiners including the two original examiners and was not found to be of the required standard. The applicant's petition to the visitor set out her complaints as to the examiners' qualification. In answer, the university set out the qualifications of the examiners, the manner in which they were appointed and the grounds upon which they were considered suitable to examine the applicant's thesis. The visitor's decision stated that it was not part of the visitor's duty to interfere in matters of scientific or technical judgment and that it would not be proper to express their own view as to the choice of examiners or interfere in any way with the decision of the examiners unless it was apparent from the facts that the examiners were plainly not qualified to perform their task. The visitor declined to grant any relief to the applicant. The applicant applied for judicial review of the visitor's decision.

Held, dismissing the application, that the court's powers to supervise the visitor's exercise of his functions by way of judicial review was not limited in any way. The court had power to make orders of prohibition, mandamus and certiorari against the visitor if it thought fit. The visitor's powers fell to be exercised in an almost infinite variety of situations and the exercise must be left to the discretion of the visitor provided he acts judicially. In some circumstances the powers might require exercise in a supervisory manner similar to judicial review and in others in an appellate manner. In the present case the visitor was not bound to investigate the applicant's grievances to the extent of satisfying himself directly that the appointment of the examiners was not unreasonable in the circumstances or that they were suitable to be appointed. There was no error of law or other complaint on which judicial review of the visitor's decision could be founded (*Thomas* v. *University of Bradford* [1987] C.L.Y. 1276 applied).

R. *v.* UNIVERSITY OF LONDON, *ex p.* VIJAYATUNGA [1987] 3 All E.R. 204, D.C.

1276. University—visitor—jurisdiction—dismissal of lecturer

Where a dispute relates to the correct interpretation of a university's domestic laws even if its resolution affects a party's contract of employment, the matter will fall within the jurisdiction of the visitor and not the courts of law.

P was a lecturer at Bradford University which was a corporation by Royal Charter and within the jurisdiction of a visitor. The university dismissed P. She claimed that her dismissal was *ultra vires* because the rules under the university's charter and statutes which were part of her contract of employment had not been complied with. The university sought but was refused an order to stay the proceedings, and that refusal was upheld on appeal. The university appealed to the House of Lords.

Held, allowing the appeal, that the dispute related to the correct interpretation and the fair administration of other domestic laws of the university, and it fell within the jurisdiction of the visitor and not the courts of law. P's action accordingly should be struck out (*Patel* v. *University of Bradford Senate* [1979] C.L.Y. 2736, *Wislang's Application, Re* [1984] C.L.Y. 2462 and *Hines* v. *Birkbeck College* [1985] C.L.Y. 3552 applied; *Carson* v. *University of Aston in Birmingham* [1983] C.L.Y. 3827 considered).

THOMAS *v.* UNIVERSITY OF BRADFORD [1987] 2 W.L.R. 677, H.L.

ELECTION LAW

1277. Election expenses

REPRESENTATION OF THE PEOPLE (VARIATION OF LIMITS OF CANDIDATES' ELECTION EXPENSES) ORDER 1987 (No. 903) [85p], made under the Representation of the People Act 1983 (c.2), ss.76A(1), 197(3); operative on May 14, 1987; increases maximum amounts of candidates election expenses at parliamentary and local government elections.

RETURNING OFFICERS' EXPENSES REGULATIONS 1987 (No. 899) [£1·30], made under the Representation of the People Act 1983, s29(3); operative on May 20, 1987; increase maximum fees payable in respect of returning officers' expenses.

1278. Local elections

LOCAL ELECTIONS (COMMUNITIES) (WELSH FORMS) ORDER 1987 (No. 561) [£1·90], made under the Welsh Language Act 1967 (c.66), s.2(1); operation on April 6, 1987;

prescribes the Welsh version of certain forms to be used in connection with community elections in Wales.

LOCAL ELECTIONS (PARISHES AND COMMUNITIES) (AMENDMENT) RULES 1987 (No. 260) [45p], made under the Representation of the People Act 1983 (c.2), s.36(2); operative on March 11, 1987; amends S.I. 1986 No. 2215.

LOCAL ELECTIONS (PRINCIPAL AREAS) (AMENDMENT) RULES 1987 (No. 261) [45p], made under the Representation of the People Act 1983, s.36(2); operative on March 11, 1987; amends S.I. 1986 No. 2214.

LOCAL ELECTIONS (PRINCIPAL AREAS (WELSH FORMS)) ORDER 1987 (No. 562) [£1·60], made under the Welsh Language Act 1967, s.2(1); operative on April 6, 1987; prescribe the Welsh version of certain forms to be used in connection with county and district elections in Wales.

1279. Parish and community meetings

PARISH AND COMMUNITY MEETINGS (POLLS) RULES 1987 (No. 1) [£2·90], made under the Local Government Act 1972 (c.70), Sched. 12, Pt. III, para. 18(5) Pt. I, para. 34(5) and the Representation of the People Act 1983 (c.2), s.36; operative on February 16, 1987; replace S.I. 1973 No. 1911, as amended, and provide for the conduct of a poll consequential upon a parish or community meeting.

PARISH AND COMMUNITY MEETINGS (POLLS) (AMENDMENT) RULES 1987 (No. 262) [45p], made under the Local Government Act 1972, Sched. 12, Pt. III, para. 18(5), Pt. V, para. 34(5); operative on March 11, 1987; amend S.I. 1987 No. 1.

1280. Parliamentary constituencies

PARLIAMENTARY CONSTITUENCIES (ENGLAND) (MISCELLANEOUS CHANGES) ORDER 1987 (No. 462) [£1·90], made under the Parliamentary Constituencies Act 1986 (c.56), s.4; operative on April 1, 1987; gives effect to recommendations of the Boundary Commission for England of February 9, 1987.

PARLIAMENTARY CONSTITUENCIES (ENGLAND) (MISCELLANEOUS CHANGES) (No. 2) ORDER 1987 (No. 937) [45p], made under the Parliamentary Constituencies Act 1986, s.4; operative on May 18, 1987; amends the constituencies of Reading East and Wokingham.

PARLIAMENTARY CONSTITUENCIES (ENGLAND) (MISCELLANEOUS CHANGES) (No. 3) ORDER 1987 (No. 2208) [£2·20], made under the Parliamentary Constituencies Act 1986, s.4; operative on December 18, 1987; amends S.I. 1983 No. 417.

PARLIAMENTARY CONSTITUENCIES (ENGLAND) (MISCELLANEOUS CHANGES) (No. 4) ORDER 1987 (No. 2209) [45p], made under the Parliamentary Constituencies Act 1986, s.4; operative on December 18, 1987; amends S.I. 1983 No. 417.

PARLIAMENTARY CONSTITUENCIES (WALES) (MISCELLANEOUS CHANGES) ORDER 1987 (No. 2050) [£1·30], made under the Parliamentary Constituencies Act 1986, s.4; operative on November 26, 1987; alters the boundaries of certain parliamentary constituencies in Wales.

1281. Public meetings—local government election—right to use suitable room on school premises—whether private law right or public law right. See ETTRIDGE *v.* MORRELL, §2378.

1282. Representation of the People Act 1985—commencement

REPRESENTATION OF THE PEOPLE ACT 1985 (COMMENCEMENT No. 4) ORDER 1987 (No. 207 (C.5)) [45p], made under the Representation of the People Act 1985 (c.50), s.29(2); brings into force on March 30, 1987, Sched. 4, para. 34 to the 1985 Act.

1283. Trade unions—expenditure

[Trade Union Act 1913 (c.30), s.3(1).]

The Court held that the expenditure during the election campaign of money on the distribution of literature which had as its main aim persuading people not to vote Conservative was unlawful.

PAUL *v.* NATIONAL ASSOCIATION OF LOCAL GOVERNMENT OFFICERS, *The Times*, June 4, 1987, Sir Nicolas Browne-Wilkinson.

ELECTRICITY

1284. Generating stations

ELECTRICITY GENERATING STATIONS (FUEL CONTROL) ORDER 1987 (No. 2175) [45p], made under the Energy Act 1976 (c.76), s.14(4)(5); operative on January 27, 1988;

limits the requirements of s.14(1) of the 1976 Act so that it will not apply to generating stations with a capacity of less than 10 megawatts.

1285. Inquiries procedure

ELECTRICITY GENERATING STATIONS AND OVEREHAD LINES (INQUIRIES PROCEDURE) RULES 1987 (No. 2182) [£1·90], made under the Tribunals and Inquiries Act 1971 (c.62), s.11; operative on January 14, 1988; prescribe the procedure to be followed at public inquiries held under the Electricity Act 1957, s.34.

1286. Meter burgled—subscribers' liability for replacement

[Electric Lighting (Clauses) Act 1899 (c.19); Electrical Lighting Acts 1882 (c.56), 1909 (c.34); Electricity Acts 1947 (c.54), 1957 (c.48).]

It is not *ultra vires* the powers of an electricity board to require a subscriber whose electricity meter has been burgled and damaged to pay for the replacement meter and to pay the debt that would otherwise have been paid by the coins in the meter. Moreover, such a requirement was not one so unreasonable that it fell within the *Wednesbury* principles (*Associated Provincial Picture Houses* v. *Wednesbury Corporation* (1948) C.L.C. 8107 considered).

R. *v.* MIDLANDS ELECTRICITY BOARD, *ex p.* BUSBY: SAME *v.* SAME, *ex p.* WILLIAMSON, *The Times*, October 28, 1987, Schiemann J.

1287. Meters

METERS (CERTIFICATION) ORDER 1987 (No. 730) [85p], made under the Electricity Act 1957 (c.48), s.30(1)(2); operative on June 1, 1987; prescribes periods after which the certification of electricity meters ceases to have effect.

METERS (DETERMINATION OF QUESTIONS) (EXPENSES) REGULATIONS 1987 (No. 901) [45p], made under the Electric Lighting (Clauses) Act 1899 (c.19), s.57(5); operative on June 15, 1987; re-enacts S.I. 1986 No. 1627 by altering the amounts of monthly payments to the Secretary of State by the Electricity Boards in respect of his expenses for determining the correctness of electricity meters.

1288. Siting of power lines—whether statutory right to compensation excluded by terms of deed of grant.

[Electric Lighting Act 1882 (c.56), s.17.]

P. Ltd. owned land on which they proposed to build houses, and over which the C.E.G.B. wished to site power lines. In 1965, after lengthy negotiations, P Ltd. entered into a deed of grant under which it sold to the C.E.G.B. the necessary rights, and which provided *inter alia* that the C.E.G.B. would pay compensation if planning permission were granted for the land, but it proved to be of reduced value for development because of the existence of the power lines. In 1971, P Ltd. conveyed the land to M Ltd., whose subsequent application for planning permission was refused outright. When M Ltd. sought compensation from the C.E.G.B. under s.17 of the Electric Lighting Act 1882, arguing that the refusal of permission was the result of the electricity lines, the Lands Tribunal held on a preliminary point of law that the rights of the parties were governed exclusively by the deed of grant, so that any claim by M Ltd. for compensation under the 1882 Act was excluded. On appeal, M Ltd. contended that a refusal of permission because of the power lines, as opposed to a mere reduction in development value, was not covered by the deed of grant.

Held, dismissing M Ltd.'s appeal, that the deed of grant encompassed the whole of the relationship between the parties, and excluded any potential right to compensation under the 1882 Act.

MAYCLOSE *v.* CENTRAL ELECTRICITY GENERATING BOARD (1987) 283 E.G. 192, C.A.

EMERGENCY LAWS

1289. Prevention of terrorism

PREVENTION OF TERRORISM (SUPPLEMENTAL TEMPORARY PROVISIONS) (AMENDMENT) ORDER 1987 (No. 119) [45p], made under the Prevention of Terrorism (Temporary Provisions) Act 1984 (c.8), ss.13, 14(7), Sched. 3, para. 1(6); operative on April 1, 1987; amends S.I. 1984 No. 418 by adding Poole Harbour to the list of ports designated for the purposes of that Order.

PREVENTION OF TERRORISM (SUPPLEMENTAL TEMPORARY PROVISIONS) (AMENDMENT No. 2) ORDER 1987 (No. 1209) [45p], made under the Prevention of Terrorism

(Temporary Provisions) Act 1984 (c.8), ss.13, 14(7), Sched. 3, para. 1(6); operative on October 1, 1987; amends S.I. 1984 No. 418 by adding London City Airport to the list of airports which are designated ports for the purposes of art. 11 of the 1984 Order.

1290. Prevention of terrorism—statistics. See CRIMINAL LAW, §834.

1291. Prevention of Terrorism (Temporary Provisions) Act 1984—continuance

PREVENTION OF TERRORISM (TEMPORARY PROVISIONS) ACT 1984 (CONTINUANCE) ORDER 1987 (No. 273) [45p], made under the Prevention of Terrorism (Temporary Provisions) Act 1984 (c.8), s.17(2)(*a*); operative on March 22, 1987; continues in force the temporary provisions of the 1984 Act for a further 12 months.

1292. Suppression of terrorism

SUPPRESSION OF TERRORISM ACT 1978 (DESIGNATION OF COUNTRIES) ORDER 1987 (No. 2137) [45p], made under the Suppression of Terrorism Act 1978 (c.26), s.8;operative on February 1, 1988; designates France for the purposes of the 1978 Act so that it becomes a convention country within the meaning of the Act.

SUPPRESSION OF TERRORISM ACT 1978 (HONG KONG) ORDER 1987 (No. 2045) [£1·30], made under the Suppression of Terrorism Act 1978, s.7(3); operative on January 1, 1988; extends ss.1–5, 8 and 9 of the 1978 Act to Hong Kong.

EMPLOYMENT

1293. Breach of confidence—ex-employee setting up competing business and soliciting custom from employers' customers while still employed—whether breach of duty to set up business while still employed

D2 gave notice of termination of his contract of employment and set up a competing business and solicited custom from a customer of his employer during the period when he was still employed, but not attending work. P sought interlocutory relief.

Held, that (1) D was entitled to set up a business when still employed; (2) D might be found to have been in breach of contract in soliciting custom when still employed but no injunction was proper at this state; (3) it was arguable that P was entitled to restrain D from using confidential information concerning P's products and methods on the ground that these were trade secrets but they could not prevent him from using his knowledge and experience.

Upon D's undertaking in appropriate terms, injunction refused.

BALSTON *v.* HEADLINE FILTERS [1987] F.S.R. 330, Scott J.

1294. Breach of confidence—springboard doctrine—injunction

When the court makes an order restricting a defendant's freedom to do business so as to prevent him from acquiring an unfair advantage in starting up in competition with the plaintiff through misuse of the plaintiff's confidential information, it should limit the order to the period that the advantage might reasonably have been expected to last.

P who specialised in underpinning buildings employed D as managing director under a contract of employment which restrained him for 12 months after termination doing business with any person who had done business with P during a period of 12 months before termination. D resigned, taking P's business secrets and card index of clients, and started up in business on his own. P brought proceedings for breach of contract and infringement of patent, and was granted an interlocutory injunction restraining D until judgment or further order from contracting with persons named in the card index who had been contacted by D while the index was in their possession.

Held, allowing the appeal, that since the contract contemplated that any benefit from the confidential information would have ceased by 12 months after termination, the injunction should have been limited to that period.

BULLIVANT (ROGER) *v.* ELLIS [1987] I.C.R. 464, C.A.

1295. Breach of confidence—whether ex-employee could use employer's confidential information pending trial

The Court of Appeal considered the circumstances in which an injunction will be granted to prevent an ex-employee from using his former employer's confidential information pending trial. It must be shown that there is an arguable case that the information is confidential or a trade secret. The fact that the employer suffers no possibility of competition pending trial is irrelevant (*Bullivant (Roger)* v. *Ellis* [1987] C.L.Y. 1294 applied).

JOHNSON & BLOY (HOLDINGS) *v.* WOLSTENHOLME RINK, *Financial Times,* October 9, 1987, C.A.

1296. Breach of contract—failure to give proper notice—whether employer entitled to restrain employee from working for rival during contractual notice period

An interlocutory injunction could properly be granted to restrain an employee from working for one of his employers' rivals in breach of his contract of employment where the contract was not at an end and the employers undertook to honour it.

H was employed as a production manager by the plaintiffs under a contract of employment terminable upon either side by one year's previous notice in writing. The contract contained a term prohibiting H from working for anyone else without the plaintiffs' permission. In September 1986 H wrote to the plaintiffs stating that he wished to terminate his employment on November 7, 1986. H intended to leave the plaintiffs to work in a similar capacity on the "London Daily News" newspaper in competition with the plaintiffs. The plaintiffs did not accept H's repudiation of his contract of employment but applied to the court for an interlocutory injunction in reliance on the terms of H's contract to restrain him from working for anyone else until the date 12 months after his letter purporting to terminate his employment on November 7. The judge refused to grant the relief sought notwithstanding the plaintiffs undertaking to continue paying H until the contract of employment terminated at the end of the 12-month period.

Held, allowing the plaintiffs' appeal, that if H was permitted to work for a rival newspaper in breach of his contract of employment, damage would be caused to the plaintiffs that would be extremely difficult if not impossible to quantify. In the circumstances it was proper to grant the relief sought upon the plaintiffs undertaking to (1) honour H's contract of employment, (2) permit H to continue working for them if he so wished and (3) forgo any claim for damages against H in the event that he chose not to work out his notice period (*American Cyanamid Co.* v. *Ethicon* [1985] C.L.Y. 2640 applied; *Warner Brothers Pictures Inc.* v. *Nelson* [1937] 1 K.B. 209 considered).

EVENING STANDARD CO. *v.* HENDERSON [1987] I.C.R. 588, C.A.

1297. Collective agreement incorporated into contract of employment—binding in honour only—whether enforceable

A collective agreement, expressed to be binding in honour only, incorporated into an employee's contract is enforceable at the suit of the employee.

The employees' contract of employment incorporated the terms of a collective agreement with the trade union. The agreement contained a provision, binding in honour only, giving an employee who was redeployed due to redundancy, six months in which to assess its suitability. The employers decided to close a regional office and moved the employee to London; within two months he informed his employers that the position was unsuitable. The employers treated him as having been moved under a mobility clause and as having resigned. The employee complained to an industrial tribunal of unfair dismissal. The application was dismissed there and on appeal to the E.A.T.

Held, allowing the appeal, that the terms of the collective agreement were enforceable; if a redundancy situation arose the employers could not rely on the mobility clause. (*Robertson* v. *British Gas Corp.* [1983] C.L.Y. 1213 considered.)

MARLEY *v.* FORWARD TRUST GROUP [1986] I.C.R. 891, C.A.

1298. Compensation award—supplementary benefit—treatment of compensation award made by an Industrial Tribunal. See SOCIAL SECURITY, §3521.

1299. Constructive dismissal—contract of employment—job grading—meaning of "appointed"

[Employment Protection (Consolidation) Act 1978 (c.44), s.55(2)(*c.*)]

The appellant commenced employment with the respondent in September 1980 as a Tutor Organiser on a Lecturer Grade I salary. Sometime after she had commenced employment the amount of work expanded, to a level of 75 units as provided in the Burnham Agreement which applied to her contract. The Agreement further provided "where a teacher is appointed . . . to take charge . . . where the unit total is 75, teachers shall be graded not less than Lecturer Grade II". The Appellant asked that her post be upgraded and in May 1982 she was informed that this would take effect from January 1983. She subsequently asked to be upgraded to a Senior Lecturer. This was refused and she resigned. The appellant claimed she had been constructively dismissed as a result of her employers failing to implement the upgrading immediately the workload reached the level of 75 units. The Industrial Tribunal held that no constructive dismissal had occurred and this decision was upheld by the Employment Appeal Tribunal. The appellant appealed.

Held, dismissing the appeal, that the employers had not committed a breach of contract by failing to upgrade as soon as the workload expanded to a level which would have merited the Grade II scale if a new person were to have been appointed to the post. The Burnham agreement provided the scale in relation to a new appointment and the fact that the workload subsequently increased to the relevant level did not amount to such a new appointment. Obiter, *per* Sir John Donaldson M.R., a party does not commit a repudiatory breach merely by adopting a view as to the construction of the contract which subsequently transpires to be incorrect. It must be shown that the party did not intend to be bound by the contract as properly construed.

BRIDGEN *v.* LANCASHIRE COUNTY COUNCIL [1987] I.R.L.R. 58, C.A.

1300. Continuous employment—teaching periods—short breaks—whether part of working hours

[Employment Protection (Consolidation) Act 1978 (c.44), Sched. 13, paras. 3, 4 (as amended by Employment Act 1982 (c.46), Sched. 2, para. 7(2)).]

A part time teacher had the right to bring a complaint of unfair dismissal as being normally employed for 16 hours a week, since she could have been required to perform duties during break periods which were correctly included in her hours of employment, as were regular meetings with her department head. The employee was employed as a part time teacher and by her letter of appointment was required to share in supervisory duties and assist the head in providing a proper educational and pastoral programme. She complained of unfair dismissal, and sought to include in addition to an undisputed 14 hours and 50 minutes teaching and supervision per week, three hours preparation work at home, two 20-minute morning breaks, periods of 10 minutes between morning assembly and before afternoon lessons, and a 30-minute discussion period with her department head that took place most weeks. On a preliminary issue of law as to whether her weekly hours of employment were fewer than 16 so that they had no jurisdiction to hear the complaint, the industrial tribunal held that they did have jurisdiction since the mid-morning break and the weekly discussions with her head of department should be included in her normal weekly hours of employment so that she was normally employed for 16 hours a week.

Held, dismissing the employers' appeal, that (1) she could not include the preparatory work outside school hours in order to fulfil her contractual duties. Sufficient time was allocated within the 14 hours, 50 minutes (*Lake* v. *Essex County Council* [1979] C.L.Y. 1064 applied); (2) since the employee could have been required by her contract to undertake supervisory or pastoral duties during her breaks, these were correctly included in her hours of employment; (3) she was not bound to be present before morning assembly and afternoon leasons, and these periods were not to be included; (4) the 30-minute periods with her head of department were necessary and should be included in her total weekly hours of employment.

Since her total working week exceeded 16 hours she was entitled to bring a complaint within Sched. 13 of the Employment Protection (Consolidation) Act 1978 as amended.

GIRLS PUBLIC DAY SCHOOL TRUST *v.* KHANNA [1987] I.C.R. 339, E.A.T.

1301. Contract of employment—breach—terms of contract—remedies

S who intended to sit the Solicitors Final Examination in July 1983 applied for articles of clerkship with the respondent solicitors in 1982. The respondents offered him articles to commence in September 1984 at a certain salary, although the letter stated that the salary would be slightly lower if he commenced employment before the results of the finals exam were known. S accepted the offer. In July 1983 S sat the exam and failed, although the respondents were unaware of this. In May 1984 they wrote a standard letter to S setting out the terms of the articles. S entered into correspondence and revealed that he had failed to pass the exam in 1983 and did not intend to resit it in 1984. The respondents informed S that as he had no definite plans to resit the exam they would not accept him into articles. The High Court dismissed S's claim for damages for breach of contract and he appealed.

Held, allowing the appeal, that the High Court had erred in its finding that no breach of contract had occurred and in finding an implied term in the contract that at the commencement of articles S would either have passed the exam or be awaiting the results. To establish such an implied term, the respondents would have had to show that such a term was necessary in order to give the contract any sense and that it was omitted merely because it was so obvious that there was no need to make it explicit. There was no such finding in this case. The judge had also erred in holding an implied term that articles were offered on standard terms, since these terms were not contained in the original offer letter. Further, the award of damages in respect of loss of future employment prospects would be comparatively small, as in personal injury cases, since such a loss was purely speculative.

STUBBES *v.* TROWER STILL & KEELING [1987] I.R.L.R. 321, C.A.

1302. Contract of employment—covenant against competition—injunction—scope of enforcement. See JOHN MICHAEL DESIGN *v.* COOKE, §431.

1303/4. Contract of employment—repudiatory breach—damages

No damages for injured feelings are to be awarded for breach of an employment contract.

B was employed by the defendants as a consultant. He was involved in a dispute with a colleague and accepted a six-month appointment abroad. While abroad, he wrote a number of angry and offensive letters to hospital staff. The defendants considered that these did not establish pathological behaviour, but required B on his return to undergo a psychiatric examination. B refused and was suspended and later dismissed for his earlier conduct. The defendants then lifted the requirement and B was given time to decide on his future and was paid his salary. B's solicitors then wrote to the defendants alleging repudiation of the contract of employment, and accepting it.

Held, that it was an implied term of B's contract of employment that the defendants would not, without reasonable cause, act in a manner likely to damage the relationship of confidence and trust between the contracting parties, and the requirement for psychiatric examination was a repudiatory breach of that term. B's action in continuing to receive his salary did not amount to affirmation. Further, that in an action in contract, no damages could be awarded for injured feelings (*Addis* v. *Gramophone Co.* [1909] A.C. 488 applied; *Jarvis* v. *Swan Tours* [1973] C.L.Y. 723 and *Heywood* v. *Wellers* [1976] C.L.Y. 2637 distinguished; *Cox* v. *Philips Industries* [1976] C.L.Y. 875 overruled).

BLISS *v.* SOUTH EAST THAMES REGIONAL HEALTH AUTHORITY [1987] I.C.R. 700, C.A.

1305. Contract of employment—unilateral variation of terms—reduction in pay—effect

A cut in wages, unilaterally imposed on an employee but never accepted, does not terminate his contract and he can continue to work and claim the difference in wages.

RIGBY *v.* FERODO, *The Daily Telegraph,* October 23, 1987, H.L.

1306. Deductions from wages—whether "fines"

[Truck Act 1896 (c.44), ss.1(1)(2), 2, 4.]

Deductions from an employee's wages pursuant to an agreement to make good losses whether or not caused by his acts or omissions are "fines" within the meaning of the Truck Act 1896.

E was a cashier at D's petrol station. In his contract of employment he undertook to make good his share of any cash or stock losses on his shifts whether or not caused by his acts or omissions. Deductions were made every week for five weeks. E preferred five informations against D for making deductions in respect of "fines" contrary to ss.1 and 4 of the Truck Act 1896.

Held, E's contract did not specify any act or omission in respect of which the deduction might be imposed, nor was liability restricted to acts or omissions likely to cause damage or loss or interruption to D's business and such deductions were not permissible under s.1(1)(*b*) or (*c*); they were also unfair under s.1(*d*). The word "fine" in s.1 was not restricted to deductions of a punitive nature, and the deductions were unlawful. (*Sealand Petroleum Co.* v. *Barratt* [1986] C.L.Y. 1292 approved).

BRISTOW *v.* CITY PETROLEUM [1987] 1 W.L.R. 529, H.L.

1307. Defective equipment—liability of ship's master—whether "equipment" includes ship

[Employer's Liability (Defective Equipment) Act 1969 (c.37), s.1(1)(3).]

The word "equipment" within the meaning of s.1 of the Employer's Liability (Defective Equipment) Act 1969 is not apt to include the workplace provided by an employer, so that a ship cannot be regarded as equipment.

In 1980 a ship owned by D sank with all hands off the coast of Japan. P, as personal representatives of one of the deceased crew members, sued D as his employer, contending that the ship had been unseaworthy, and that D had, therefore, been in breach of its duty under s.1 of the 1969 Act.

Held, allowing D's appeal, that a ship is not "equipment" within the ordinary meaning of that word. Equipment is usually ancillary to something, and would not apply to the workplace. Nor could ships come within the meaning of "plant" within s.1(3).

COLTMAN *v.* BIBBY TANKERS, DERBYSHIRE, THE [1987] 1 All E.R. 932, C.A.

1308. Disciplinary procedure—construction of provisions—racial discrimination

[Education Act 1944 (c.31), s.24(1).]

Miss M was suspended from her position as headmistress of Sudbury Infants' School, after being accused by a member of the Council's education staff of making a racist remark. The matter was referred to the school's governors who recommended immediate reinstatment after deciding that there was no evidence to substantiate the allegation, but the authority's disciplinary committee failed to accept the recommendation and decided to hear new evidence on the matter. The High Court made a declaration that the sub-committee was bound by the finding of the school's governors. The authority appealed.

Held, allowing the appeal, that the sub-committee were not bound by findings of facts of the school's governors in relation to the complaint and the disciplinary procedure. The school's articles of government provided that the authority "shall . . . be entitled to dismiss a head teacher . . . without a recommendation of the governors". The relevant part of the authority's disciplinary procedure related to a situation where the governors have made a recommendation for dismissal or other disciplinary penalty, which they had not done in this particular case. The Respondent's contract incorporated the two procedures. On a correct construction, the sub-committee was entitled to exercise its powers under the articles of government since the governors had not recommended dismissal or other disciplinary penalty.

McGOLDRICK *v.* BRENT LONDON BOROUGH COUNCIL [1987] I.R.L.R. 67, C.A.

1309. Disciplinary procedure—police officer—natural justice. *See* R. *v.* CHIEF CONSTABLE OF SOUTH WALES, *ex p.* THORNHILL, §34.

1310. Disciplinary procedure—private discussion—whether breach of natural justice

P was dismissed by E, his employer, whose disciplinary procedure allowed P to appeal. Before the hearing of the appeal, E had a private discussion with the appeal tribunal about P's case.

Held, that this was a serious breach of the rules of natural justice. Although a certain amount of informality was allowable in internal appeals, such a private discussion was an impropriety which was a matter of substance, not of form.

CAMPION *v.* HAMWORTHY ENGINEERING, *The Times,* January 30, 1987, C.A.

1311. Dismissal—on grounds of incapacity due to employee's prolonged ill health—provision in contract not restricting employer's rights

[Employment Protection (Consolidation) Act 1978 (c.44), ss.57(2)(*a*), and 57(3).]

The respondent's contract of employment provided that his employer could terminate his employment with minimum statutory notice if he had been incapacitated by virtue of ill health for an aggregate period of not less than 225 working days in the 12 months prior to termination. The respondent was dismissed after a recurrent illness had caused him to be absent from work for a period of time, although not amounting to 225 days in the previous 12 months. The Industrial Tribunal held that the employer had breached the terms of the contract and the dismissal was therefore unfair. The employer appealed.

Held, allowing the appeal, that the contract merely set out particular circumstances in which the employer could terminate the contract and these circumstances were not necessarily exhaustive. The employer was entitled to dismiss an employee on reasonable notice in other circumstances relating to sickness, even if the absence did not amount to 225 days, provided such a dismissal was reasonable in those circumstances. The dismissal was therefore not necessarily unfair.

SMITHS INDUSTRIES AEROSPACE AND DEFENCE SYSTEMS *v.* BROOKES [1986] I.R.L.R. 434, E.A.T.

1312. Dismissal—refusal to carry out duties—conscientious objection—participation in treatment—typing of letters of referral for abortion

The applicant was a medical receptionist employed by the health authority and part of her duties included typing letters of referral of patients to specialists for abortion. She refused to type such letters and maintained that that activity amounted to "participation" in the treatment of abortion and so she was protected by s.4(1) of the Abortion Act 1967 (c.87) as a conscientious objector. The health authority decided that the secretarial duties did not amount to participation and dismissed her. She sought judicial review.

Held, that the treatment referred to recent treatment by or under control of a medical practitioner in hospital. Although the Act was concerned with amending the criminal law, it did not follow that "participation" had to be construed with reference to the criminal law. The word should be given its ordinary meaning of "taking part". It was impossible as a matter of plain English to describe the typing of a letter of referral as participating in the subsequent treatment of the patient. The applicant did not succeed.

R. *v.* SALFORD HEALTH AUTHORITY, *ex p.* JANAWAY (1987) 17 Fam. Law 345, Nolan J.

1313. Dismissal—request for written statement of reasons—not provided due to oversight—whether unreasonable refusal

[Employment Protection (Consolidation) Act 1978 (c.44), s.53(4).]

An employer did not unreasonably refuse to provide a written statement to an employee of the reasons for his dismissal where the failure to do so was due to an oversight.

C was dismissed by her employers for misconduct. The employers undertook to send her a written statement of the reasons for her dismissal. The employers failed to do so on account of an oversight. C complained to the tribunal that the employers had unreasonably refused to provide a written statement of the reasons for her dismissal in breach of s.53(4), Employment Protection (Consolidation) Act 1978. The tribunal held that the employers should reasonably be expected to provide a written statement and that by failing to do so they unreasonably refused to provide one within the meaning of s.53(4) of the Act.

Held, allowing the employers' appeal, that a mere failure to provide a written statement of the reasons for an employee's dismissal did not amount to an unreasonable refusal to do so on the part of the employers. There must be some deliberate withholding of the statement or evasion of the request to establish an unreasonable refusal to provide a statement.

LADBROKE ENTERTAINMENTS *v.* CLARK [1987] I.C.R. 585, E.A.T.

1314. Duty of care—employer giving reference for ex-employee—whether duty owed to ex-employee. See LAWTON *v.* B.O.C. TRANSHIELD, §2579.

1315. Employer—whether "the state"—test

[EEC Council Directive 76/207/EEC, art. 5(1).]

In deciding whether an employer is "the state" for the purpose of art. 5(1) of EEC Council Directive 76/207/EEC, the correct test is to ask whether the body concerned could be said to be an organ or agent of the state carrying out a state function (*Lonrho* v. *Shell Petroleum Co.* [1980] C.L.Y. 2135 considered).

ROLLS-ROYCE *v.* DOUGHTY, *The Times,* August 10, 1987, E.A.T.

1316. Employer's liability for acts of employees—contracts of services—misconduct by employees carrying out contract—implied terms of contract

An employee of Clarity, who had contracted to clean Heasmans' offices and equipment, made telephone calls at those offices to the cost of £1,400, for which Heasmans were liable. The contract between the parties provided that Clarity was strictly liable for acts of their employees while on Heasmans' premises although there was no specific clause relating to these circumstances. The County Court Judge held that Clarity were vicariously liable under the terms of the contract, or alternatively that there was an implied term to this effect which was necessary in order to give the contract business efficacy. Clarity appealed.

Held, allowing the appeal, that Clarity could not be held to be vicariously liable for tortious or criminal acts committed by an employee which were wholly outside the scope of his employment merely because the employment provided the employee with the opportunity to commit that act. In order to establish vicarious liability it was necessary to show some nexus between the circumstances of the employment and the tortious act beyond mere opportunity. The County Court Judge had also erred in his alternative finding, since the term he sought to imply was collateral and did not go to the root of the contract.

HEASMANS *v.* CLARITY CLEANING [1987] I.R.L.R. 286, C.A.

1317. Employment Appeal Tribunal—appeal to—agreed orders

Where both parties to an appeal to the Employment Appeal Tribunal were agreed on the order to be made on the appeal, the Tribunal would in future sanction such order as was agreed, upon application in correspondence by the parties.

The employers appealed against a decision of an industrial tribunal that F was an employee and entitled to bring a complaint of unfair dismissal. Before the hearing of the appeal, F and the employers reached agreement that the appeal should be allowed and that F would be paid £8,000 by the employers. F appeared in person and the employers by counsel to seek the sanction of the Employment Appeal Tribunal to the order they had agreed.

Held, that the agreed order would be made. In future the sanction of the Tribunal could be sought in correspondence. If upon looking at the correspondence the Tribunal was not satisfied that both parties understood the position or that it was a proper order to make, the parties would be called upon to appear in open court (*Comet Radiovision Services* v. *Delahunty* [1979] C.L.Y. 1033 considered).

BRITISH PUBLISHING CO. *v.* FRASER [1987] I.C.R 517, E.A.T.

1318. Employment Appeal Tribunal—application to call fresh evidence—exercise of discretion to admit further evidence

[Industrial Tribunals (Rules of Procedure) Regulations 1985 (S.I. 1985 No. 16), Sched. 1, r.10(1)(*d*).]

The Employment Appeal Tribunal should only allow an application to call fresh evidence on an appeal if the Tribunal is satisfied that the existence of the evidence in question could not have been reasonably known or reasonably foreseen.

P was dismissed for assaulting a fellow employee. When the allegation was first raised P denied it. Before dismissing P the employers obtained a medical report from a doctor that confirmed the employee had sustained injuries consistent with an assault. In his originating application claiming that he was unfairly dismissed P contended that the employee had fallen over. P had raised that new version before his dismissal but the employers did not seek a further opinion from the doctor on whether the employee's injuries were consistent with a fall. The tribunal found P had been unfairly dismissed but contributed to his dismissal by 60 per cent. The tribunal considered that a further opinion from the doctor should have been sought and that the employers acted unreasonably in failing to do so. The employers appealed and applied to call fresh evidence in the form of a second opinion from the doctor on P's second version of the incident.

Held, dismissing the application, that the tribunal could only allow fresh evidence to be called if it was satisfied that the existence of the evidence could not have been reasonably known or reasonably foreseen. That test was to be preferred to the "reasonable exploration" for not calling the evidence at the original hearing test. The intended informality of industrial tribunal procedure was a factor to be taken into account in assessing what was reasonable as was a lack of legal advice received by a litigant in preparing his case. In the present case the industrial tribunal considered it reasonable for the employers to have obtained a second report from the doctor. In the light of that finding the Appeal Tribunal could not allow fresh evidence in the form of a second report from the doctor to be admitted (*Bagga* v. *Heavy Electricals (India)* [1972] C.L.Y. 1223, *International Aviation Services (U.K.)* v. *Jones* [1979] C.L.Y. 863 considered).

BORDEN (U.K.) *v.* POTTER [1986] I.C.R. 647, E.A.T.

1319. Employment Appeal Tribunal—findings of fact—interference

[Employment Protection (Consolidation) Act 1978 (c.44), ss.54, 55, 140(1).]

The E.A.T. should not interfere with findings of fact made by the industrial tribunal where those findings have been made after proper consideration of all the facts before it (*Igbo* v. *Johnson Matthey Chemicals* [1986] C.L.Y. 1263, *West Midlands Co-operative Society* v. *Tipton* [1986] C.L.Y. 1285 considered).

KARIM *v.* SUNBLEST BAKERIES, *The Daily Telegraph,* November 2, 1987, C.A.

1320. Employment subsidies

EMPLOYMENT SUBSIDIES ACT 1978 (RENEWAL) (GREAT BRITAIN) ORDER 1987 (No. 1124) [45p], made under the Employment Subsidies Act 1978 (c.6), s.3(2)(*a*); operative on July 1, 1987; renews until December 31, 1988, the powers contained in s.1 of the 1978 Act.

1321. Equal pay—basic rates less favourable—whether other conditions relevant

Equal Pay Act 1970 (c.41), s.1(2) as amended by Sex Discrimination Act 1975 (c.65), s.8 and Equal Pay (Amendment) Regs 1983, reg. 2(1).]

S.1(2)(*c*) of the Equal Pay Act should be construed broadly to include not only basic rates of pay but all other considerations.

The applicant, a female cook in a shipyard canteen, was paid as an "unskilled" worker. She complained that male comparators were paid at a higher rate. A valuation rated her work as of equal value, but the tribunal held that it was not sufficient just to compare her basic rates and overtime, but that all the terms and conditions of employment were relevant.

Held, dismissing the appeal, that the section was ambiguous and should be construed in the light of E.E.C. law; that "pay" had a broad meaning which included other considerations than basic rates, and she was not entitled to a declaration on basic rates alone.

HAYWARD *v.* CAMMELL LAIRD SHIPBUILDERS (No. 2) [1986] I.C.R. 862, E.A.T.

1322. Equal pay—choice of comparator—effect of EEC Treaty

[Equal Pay Act 1970 (c.41), s.1(2)(*a*)(*c*); EEC Treaty, Art. 119.]

A woman can claim equal pay to that of a man doing another job of equal worth who is being paid more than her, even though a man is doing the same job as her and being paid the same as she is. The EEC Treaty, art. 119, is directly applicable and overrides the domestic legislation to the contrary.

The employers employed both men and women as warehouse operatives and as checker warehouse operatives. The applicants were female warehouse operatives and claimed that they were entitled to equal pay with a male checker warehouse operative on the basis that they were doing work of equal value within the meaning of s.1(2)(*c*) of the Equal Pay Act 1970 as amended. The employers resisted this on the basis that men were also employed as warehouse operatives within the meaning of s.1(2)(*a*) and so the applicants (were not entitled to rely on the equal value provisions. The industrial tribunal dismissed the claims on that basis. The appeal tribunal dismissed the appellants' appeal.

Held, allowing the appeal, that the express requirement in s.1(2)(*c*) that the work alleged to be of equal value was not work to which para. (*a*) or (*b*) applied was clear and unambiguous, and since the applicants were employed on like work with men under para. (*a*) their claim based on work of equal value under para. (*c*) was excluded under the Act. However, art. 119 of the EEC Treaty created personal rights directly enforceable in national courts notwithstanding any restriction on such rights imposed by national legislation. The provisions of that article, as restated in art. 1 of Council Directive (75/117/EEC) did not exlcude a claim based on work of equal value where women were employed on like work with men, so that the applicants were not debarred from claiming that they were employed on work of equal value with the male comparator.

The matter was remitted to the tribunal to determine whether their work was of equal value to that of the comparator and whether any difference in pay was due to factors unconnected with discrimination on the grounds of sex (*Defrenne* v. *Sabena* (No. 43/75) [1976] C.L.Y. 1164, *Macarthys* v. *Smith (No. 129/79)* [1980] C.L.Y. 1218 and *Worringham* v. *Lloyds Bank (No. 69/80)* [1981] C.L.Y. 849, 1052 applied).

PICKSTONE *v.* FREEMANS [1987] 3 W.L.R. 811, C.A.

1323. Equal pay—job evaluation study

[Equal Pay Act 1970, (c.41) s.1(5).]

A job evaluation study does not have to be "analytical" to comply with the Act.

BROMLEY *v.* QUICK (H. & V.), *The Times* August 24, 1987, E.A.T.

1324. Equal pay—"like work"

[Equal Pay Act 1970 (c.41), s.1.]

Female canteen assistants employed during the daytime are not engaged "in like work" to a male employed alone and at night. (*National Coal Board* v. *Sherwin* [1978] C.L.Y. 942, *Dance* v. *Dorothy Perkins* [1978] C.L.Y. 935 considered).

THOMAS *v.* NATIONAL COAL BOARD; BARKER *v.* NATIONAL COAL BOARD, *The Times,* May 20, 1987, E.A.T.

1325. Equal pay—material difference—whether justified

[Equal Pay Act 1970 (c.41), s.1(3).]

A "material difference" within s.1(3) of the 1970 Act means a significant and relevant difference, and for this all relevant circumstances, and not just personal qualifications are to be considered.

The Board was required to set up a prosthesis service within the Scottish National Health Service in place of existing arrangements with private contractors. It considered the standard pay scales might not attract enough qualified prosthetists and offered to employees coming from the private sector their previous rates of pay, but intended in general that remuneration of the new employees should be related to standard scales. The result was that R was remunerated on standard pay scales, having come directly to the National Health Service, while a similarly qualified male colleague, who had previously been employed in the private sector, was paid more.

Held, that there was here a "material difference" between the woman's case and the man's, within the terms of s.1(3) of the Act, there being sound administrative reasons for the difference in remuneration. (*Jenkins* v. *Kingsgate (Clothing Productions)* [1981] C.L.Y. 915 and *Bilka-Kaufhaus* v. *Weber von Hartz* [1986] C.L.Y. 1458 applied; Dicta in *Clay Cross (Quarry Services) v. Fletcher* [1978] C.L.Y. 945 not applied).

RAINEY *v.* GREATER GLASGOW HEALTH BOARD [1986] 3 W.L.R. 1017, H.L.

1326. Equal pay—pay fixed by statutory instrument—procedure for challenged amount of pay

[Equal Pay Act 1970 (c.41), ss.1(2)(*c*), 1(3), 2A(1)(*b*).]

Where a worker's pay was fixed by regulation by statutory instrument, the proper procedure for challenging the amount of pay was not by application for judicial review of the making of the instrument itself, but by direct application to an industrial tribunal. If the employer was not in fact bound by law to pay the amount in question because, for example, it offended against European law, the tribunal could so determine (*Hoffmann-La Roche (F.) & Co. A.G.* v. *Secretary of State for Trade and Industry* [1974] C.L.Y. 3801, *Rainey* v. *Greater Glasgow Health Board* [1986] C.L.Y. 1190 considered).

R. *v.* SECRETARY OF STATE FOR SOCIAL SERVICES, *ex p.* CLARK, *The Times*, November 13, 1987, D.C.

1327. Equal pay—physical exertion as a criterion—different treatment of men and women. See RUMMLER *v.* DATO-DRUCK GmbH, §1529.

1328. Equal pay—terms of contract—payment in cash or money's worth

[Equal Pay Act 1970 (c.41), s.1(2); EEC Treaty, art. 119.]

When considering whether the pay of an employee is equal to the pay of another employee, no distinction was to be made between payments in cash and in kind but the tribunal should look at the overall remuneration package.

The appellant was a cook in a canteen in the respondent's shipyard. A report by an independent expert stated that she was employed on work of an equal value to that of male shipyard workers who were relevant comparators, but she was not paid the same basic wage or overtime. An industrial tribunal refused to make a declaration that her pay should be equal to that of her comparators under s.1(2) of the Equal Pay Act 1970 since the term "pay" had to be construed broadly in accordance with art. 119 of the EEC Treaty so that it was right to consider the whole of her terms and conditions of employment rather than specific terms which, taken on their own, were less favourable. The Employment Appeal Tribunal agreed.

Held, dismissing the appeal, that s.1(2) required equally favourable terms in contracts of employment for men and women engaged on like or equivalent work or work of equal value. Where the term concerned pay, the court had to have regard to the whole of that term and could not take one item of the woman's remuneration and compare that in isolation to a corresponding item in the man's remuneration. The court should consider the overall remuneration package, including such variations as productivity bonuses, sickness benefits, free meals, the use of a car and so on. No distinction was to be made between payments in cash and in kind. Such an approach was supported by art. 119. The appeal was dismissed since the tribunal had adopted this approach, but the matter was referred to them to determine the question of favourability accordingly. The House of Lords later gave leave to appeal.

HAYWARD *v.* CAMMELL LAIRD SHIPBUILDERS [1987] 2 All E.R. 344, C.A.

1329. Equal pay—work of equal value—male comparator employed at same factory

[Equal Pay Act 1970 (c.41), ss.1, 8 and Sched. 1 as amended.]

The requirement for "common terms and conditions of employment" as between applicant and comparator in s.1(6) only applied where they were employed at different establishments.

L and her colleagues were food process workers who claimed equality of pay with a male general handyman working at the same factory, on the basis of s.1(2)(*c*) of the 1970 Act. The tribunal found certain differences between L's employment and that of the male comparator, but dismissed the applications on the grounds that "common terms and conditions of employment" were not observed as between L and the comparator, within s.1(6).

Held, that the phrase related to an outside establishment and was not a relevant consideration where the applicant and the comparator were employed at the same establishment. Accordingly, the tribunal had erred in law and the case would be remitted for further hearing.

LAWSON *v.* BRITFISH [1987] I.C.R. 726, E.A.T.

1330. Equal pay—work of equal value—preliminary hearing

[Equal Pay Act 1970 (c.41), s.2(A)(1)(*a*), Equal Pay (Amendment) Regulations 1983.]

D was employed as a supervisor and her job was graded as CO2 under the company's grading system. She alleged in her application to the tribunal that her job was equal to male clerical officers who were graded CO3, although she did not specify a particular comparator, which was generally necessary by virtue of the Equal Pay (Amendment)

Regulations 1983. A preliminary hearing was held under s.2A(1)(*a*) of the Act of 1970, which provides *inter alia* that a tribunal shall not determine an issue regarding equal pay unless it is "satisfied that there are no reasonable grounds for determining that the work is of equal value." At the hearing an expert witness gave evidence in D's favour. The tribunal held that the application did not establish a prima facie case of unequal pay for work of equal value and the expert's evidence could not cure this defect. D appealed.

Held, allowing the appeal, that the tribunal had misdirected themselves by dismissing the application on the basis that no prima facie case was disclosed, by virtue of the requirements of s.2A(1)(*a*). The tribunal should have considered the evidence of the applicant and the expert at the preliminary hearing in order to establish whether there were any reasonable grounds for determining at that stage that the work was of equal value.

DENNEHY *v.* SEALINK U.K. [1987] I.R.L.R. 120, E.A.T.

1331. Equal pay—work of equal value—relevant factors

[Equal Pay Act 1970 (c.41), s.1(3)(*b*) (as amended by Sex Discrimination Act 1975 (c.65)); Equal Pay (Amendment) Regulations 1983 (S.I. 1983 No. 1794), reg. 2.]

In approaching a defence to an equal value claim under s.1(3)(*b*) of the Equal Pay Act 1970 (as amended) a tribunal should ask itself (1) Is there a variation between the man's contract and the woman's contract? (2) Is there a material factor, other than the difference of sex, which is a material difference between the woman's case and the man's case, or other material difference? (3) Has the employer proved that it is more probable than not that the variation is genuinely due to that material factor (or factors)?

Three personal secretaries to the union's national industrial officers sought equal pay with a male executive assistant to an executive officer. The tribunal held that the work was of equal value but that the differential was justified by a material factor other than sex under s.1(3) of the Equal Pay Act 1970 (as amended), namely that the executive assistant had worked for the union for a long time and had exceptional experience of its affairs.

Held, dismissing the appeal, that the tribunal should ask itself (1) Was there a variation between the man's contract and the women's contracts? In this case there was, namely pay. (2) Was there a material factor, other than the difference of sex, which was a material difference between the women's case and the man's case, or other material difference? (3) Had the employer proved that it was more probable than not that the variation was genuinely due to that material factor? In this case it could not be said that the tribunal had erred in law, and the decision would be upheld.

McGREGOR *v.* GENERAL MUNICIPAL BOILERMAKERS AND ALLIED TRADES UNION [1987] I.C.R 505, E.A.T.

1332. Equal pay—work of equal value—same employment

[Equal Pay Act 1970 (c.41), s. 1(2)(*c*), (6) (as amended by Sex Discrimination Act 1975 (c.65), s.8(6) and Equal Pay (Amendment) Regulations 1983 (S.I. 1983 No. 1794), reg. 2(1).]

The expression 'terms and conditions of service' in s.(6) of the Equal Pay Act 1970 could not be restricted to terms relevant to all local authority employees, but included individual contractual obligations such as hours worked and length of holidays, so that one employee was not necessarily in the same employment as others for the purposes of the Act.

The applicant was a nursery nurse employed by the county council. She sought the inclusion in her contract of an equality clause pursuant to s.1 of the Equal Pay Act 1970, basing her claim on the disparity between her salary and that of male clerical officers employed by the council. None of the comparators worked at the same establishment as the applicant, and she enjoyed shorter working hours and longer holidays than them. The industrial tribunal found that the hours worked and holiday entitlement were so radically different that it could not be said that each were employed on common terms and conditions within s.1(6), and that the variation in pay was due to those differences which constituted a material factor other than the difference of sex. They dismissed the application. The appeal was dismissed, with leave to appeal.

Held, dismissing the appeal, that in s.1(6) 'establishments in Great Britain which include that one' should be construed as meaning establishments which did not exclude the one where the applicant worked. The comparators could accordingly all be drawn from other establishments different from that of the applicant. But, although the applicant and the comparators were employed under conditions of service relevant to all local authority employees, 'terms and conditions of service' in s.1(6) could not be restricted to those terms, but included their individual contractual obligations such as hours worked and length of holidays. Accordingly the applicant could not be considered to be in the same employment as the comparators, and the tribunal had not erred in law in dismissing her claim, under s.1(2)(*c*), that her work was of equal value to that of the comparators. But there was insufficient evidence for the finding that the employers had established under s.1(3) of the Act that the difference in pay between her contract and those of the comparators was genuinely due to a material factor.

LEVERTON *v.* CLWYD COUNTY COUNCIL [1987] 1 W.L.R. 65, E.A.T.

1333. Factories—unfenced loading bay—whether bay "opening" in floor—whether safe place to work

[Factories Act 1961 (c.34), ss.28(4), 29(1).]

A loading bay in a factory cannot properly be described as an opening in the floor that requires fencing within the provisions of s.28(4) of the Factories Act 1961.

P was employed by D at its factory as a fork-lift truck driver. At one end of the factory there were two rectangular loading bays that were four feet deep. The bays were separated by an area forming part of the factory floor that was 18 feet wide. The area was used for the storage of goods on pallets. When the area was being so used the pallets formed an effective barrier at the edge of the loading bays. The pallets were removed twice per year for stocktaking purposes. P was in the process of putting pallets back into position after a stocktaking when he drove his fork-lift truck backwards into one of the loading bays. P sustained serious injuries for which the trial judge assessed damages in the sum of £10,150. However, the trial judge found for D on the issue of liability. P appealed.

Held, that (1) the loading bay could not be described as an opening in the floor of the factory within the meaning of s.28(4) of the Factories Act 1961. P fell over the edge of the floor into the loading bay and not into an opening in the factory floor. Accordingly s.28(4) did not impose any obligation to fence the loading bays on D. (2) P's place of work was unsafe within the meaning of s.29(1) Factories Act 1961. A drop of four feet into the loading bay was a potential danger. The width of the floor area between the loading bays was limited. The danger remained a danger even though P was only exposed to it twice per year by virtue of the fact that the stored goods provided an effective barrier except during stocktaking. Given that the area was used for storage it could not be said it was not practicable to provide a permanent barrier at the edge of each loading bay and the area in question. The parties were both liable in equal shares on account of P's negligence in driving his fork-lift truck in the wrong direction into the loading bay. (*Bath* v. *British Transport Commission* [1954] C.L.Y. 885, *Street* v. *British Electricity Authority* [1952] C.L.Y. 1383, *Walker* v. *Bletchley Flettons* [1937] 1 All E.R. 170, *Edwards* v. *National Coal Board* [1949] C.L.Y. 6274 considered).

ALLEN *v.* AVON RUBBER CO. [1986] I.C.R. 695, C.A.

1334. Guarantee payments

GUARANTEE PAYMENTS (EXEMPTION) (No. 23) ORDER 1987 (No. 1757) [85p], made under the Employment Protection (Consolidation) Act 1978 (c.44), s.18(1)(5); operative on November 12, 1987; excludes from the operation of s.12 of the 1978 Act employees to whom the National Agreement of the Wire and Wire Rope Industries apply.

1335. Industrial injuries benefit. See SOCIAL SECURITY.

1336. Industrial tribunal—evidence—sex discrimination

[Sex Discrimination Act 1975 (c.65), s.6(2)(*b*); Industrial Tribunals (Rules of Procedure) Regulations 1985 (S.I. 1985 No. 16), Sched. 1, r.8(1).]

S made a complaint about sexual harassment and during the hearing was cross-examined about her attitudes to sexual matters in a manner intended to show that she had suffered no detriment within s.6(2)(*b*) of the 1970 Act. S denied the various suggestions made and her counsel objected to attempts by the employers to adduce evidence in support of the suggestions, on the basis that either the matters were collateral and the answers were binding, or they were irrelevant. The evidence was admitted and S appealed.

Held, that under r.8(1) of Sched. 1 to the 1985 Regulations, the tribunal had a wide discretion as to the admissibility of evidence. This evidence was relevant in assessing the degree of the alleged detriment suffered by the applicant, and accordingly the industrial tribunal's ruling that the evidence was relevant and admissible would be upheld.

SNOWBALL *v.* GARDNER MERCHANT [1987] I.C.R. 719, E.A.T.

1337. Industrial tribunal—findings of fact—inability to decide—finding on burden of proof

A tribunal of fact was under a duty to make findings of fact. In those very rare cases where it was unable to decide what was proved by the evidence, the principle of the burden of proof decided which party should succeed.

On a complaint alleging unfair dismissal, the industrial tribunal were unable to decide on the evidence on the balance of probabilities whether the employee had been dismissed or had resigned. They dismissed the claim on the basis that the employee had not discharged the burden of proof incumbent on him to prove that he had been dismissed.

The Employment Appeal Tribunal allowed his appeal on the ground that the tribunal was under a duty to make findings of fact and their failure to do so had left the whole matter undecided, and it remitted the case to a different tribunal for rehearing.

Held, allowing the employer's appeal, that a tribunal of fact was under a duty to make findings of fact, drawing appropriate inferences from the evidence, if it was conscientiously able to do so. However, in those very rare cases where it was unable to decide what had or had not been proved on the evidence on the balance of probabilities, the principle of the burden of proof determined which party should succeed. Since the tribunal had conscientiously considered the evidence and were unable to decide the issue, the burden of proof was on the employee, and the tribunal had been right to dismiss the claim (*Baker* v. *Market Harborough Industrial Co-operative Society* [1953] C.L.Y. 2473 and *Bray* v. *Palmer* [1953] C.L.Y. 2472 distinguished).

MORRIS *v.* LONDON IRON AND STEEL CO. [1987] 2 All E.R. 496, C.A.

1338/9. Industrial tribunal—originating application—whether document effective notwithstanding deficiencies

An originating application to a tribunal which indicates that the complaint is of discrimination on grounds of race and/or sex, but which fails to specify which or particularize the complaint, was not fatally defective and could be cured by a request for particulars.

DODD *v.* BRITISH TELECOMMUNICATIONS (1987) 84 L.S. Gaz. 1239, E.A.T.

1340. Industrial tribunal—procedure—discovery

[County Court Rules 1986, Ord. 14, r.8(1).]

Discovery in unfair dismissal proceedings is not necessarily restricted to material available to the manager who took the decision to dismiss at the time he took it.

N was consistently absent from work, ostensibly due to ill-health. He agreed to be examined by the employer's doctor, who declared him fit to return to work. When N continued to be absent, the employer's production manager dismissed him. In proceedings for unfair dismissal an order was made for discovery of the doctor's notes. The employer appealed on the grounds that these were documents which the manager himself had not seen when he took the decision to dismiss.

Held, that discovery of such documents were necessary for the fair disposal of the matter and the appeal would be dismissed.

FORD MOTOR CO. *v.* NAWAZ [1987] I.C.R. 434, E.A.T.

1341. Industrial tribunal—procedure—notice of hearing

[Interpretation Act 1978 (c.30), s.7; Industrial Tribunals (Rules of Procedure) Regulations 1985, (S.I. 1985 No. 16) Sched. 1, r.10(1)(*b*).]

The power of review in r.10(1)(*b*) of Sched. 1 to the 1985 Regulations is grounded when the conditions for service in s.7 of the 1978 Act are fulfilled.

The employers failed to attend an industrial tribunal hearing because they had not received notification of the date. The tribunal found against them in their absence. The employers application for a review under r.10(1)(*b*) of Sched. 1 to the 1985 Regulations was refused on the grounds that the notice had been posted.

Held, that s.7 of the 1978 Act applied to the receipt as well as the sending of the relevant document, and thus to an application under r.10(1)(*b*), so the appeal would be dismissed.

T. & D. TRANSPORT (PORTSMOUTH) *v.* LIMBURN [1987] I.C.R. 696, E.A.T.

1342. Industrial tribunal—second tribunal hearing similar facts—different finding—*res judicata*

[Employment Protection (Consolidation) Act 1978 (c.44), s.62.]

An industrial tribunal is not bound by the doctrine of *res judicata* in relation to facts found by another industrial tribunal on similar evidence.

MUNIR *v.* JANG PUBLICATIONS (1987) 84 L.S.Gaz. 2450, E.A.T.

1343. Job Release Act 1977—continuation

JOB RELEASE ACT 1977 (CONTINUATION) ORDER 1987 (No. 1339) [45p], made under the Job Release Act 1977 (c.8), s.1(4)(*b*); operative on September 30, 1987; continues in force until September 29, 1988, s.1 of the 1977 Act.

1344. Maternity leave—statutory rights—contractual rights—extended maternity leave

[Employment Protection (Consolidation) Act 1978 (c.44), ss.45(1), 46, 47(1), 47(3)(*b*), 47(4), 48(1), 48(2), 55, 56, Sched. 2, para. 6(2).]

D became pregnant with twins and informed her employers that she wished to take maternity leave and it was also agreed that she could take one week's holiday at the end of such leave. In the event the twins were born approximately 10 weeks early and therefore the statutory date of return to work was brought forward accordingly. Shortly prior to that date D sent a sick note postponing the date of her return by a further four weeks due to ill health. However, she continued to the unwell and did not return on the due date and her employers then refused to accept her back. The tribunal dismissed her claim of unfair dismissal, which decision was upheld by the E.A.T. D appealed.

Held, dismissing the appeal, that the E.A.T. had correctly upheld the tribunal's decision that D was not entitled to complain of unfair dismissal. D had a statutory right to return to work by reason of her pregnancy and a contractual right to return by reason of the extension of the period by one week's holiday. She was not entitled to bring a complaint of unfair dismissal under s.55 since her dismissal had effectively occurred after her attempt to return to work following maternity leave, even though this had in fact been extended by one week's holiday. Further, D was not entitled to bring a claim under s.56 since she had failed to exercise her rights under ss.47 and 48 by seeking to return to work later than she was entitled to. She had also failed to give notice of the intended date of return to work in accordance with s.47(1).

DOWUONA *v.* JOHN LEWIS [1987] I.R.L.R. 310, C.A.

1345. Maternity pay—beginning of expected week of confinement—employment for two years—whether employers entitled to rebate

[Employment Protection (Consolidation) Act 1978 (c.44), ss.33(3), 153(1) Sched. 13, para. 24.]

In order to calculate time periods for the payment of maternity pay the relevant definitions are in s.153(1) of the Act, and in para. 24 of the Sched. 13.

The employee, first employed on August 1, 1983 became pregnant, her expected confinement date being October 18, 1985. The employers considered she had been employed for two years beginning at the 11th week prior to the expected date of confinement and paid her maternity pay. A tribunal upheld the employers' application for a rebate.

Held, allowing the appeal, that applying the relevant definitions in the Act, the start of the 11th week prior to expected confinement was July 27, or four days short of two years.

SECRETARY OF STATE FOR EMPLOYMENT *v.* FORD (A) & SON (SACKS) [1986] I.C.R. 882, E.A.T.

1346. Maternity pay and allowance

MATERNITY PAY AND MATERNITY ALLOWANCE (TRANSITIONAL) REGULATIONS 1987 (No. 406) [80p], made under the Social Security Act 1986 (c.50), ss.84(1), 89(1); regs. 1 and 4 operative on April 5, 1987 and regs. 2 and 3 operative on April 6, 1987; makes transition provision relating to statutory maternity pay and allowance.

SOCIAL SECURITY (MATERNITY ALLOWANCE) REGULATIONS 1987 (No. 416) [£1·40], made under the Social Security Act 1975 (c.14), s.22(3), Sched. 20 and the Social Security Act 1986 (c.50), ss.84(1), 89(1); operative on April 6, 1987; makes provision in relation to maternity allowance.

SOCIAL SECURITY (MATERNITY ALLOWANCE) (WORK ABROAD) REGULATIONS 1987 (No. 417) [80p], made under the Social Security Act 1975, s.131, Sched. 20; operative on April 6, 1987; enables women ordinarily resident in Great Britain to qualify in certain circumstances for maternity allowance despite having worked abroad in the 12 months preceding the expected 14th week before the expected week of confinement.

STATUTORY MATERNITY PAY (MEDICAL EVIDENCE) REGULATIONS 1987 (No. 235) [80p], made under the Social Security Act 1986, ss.49, 84(1), Sched. 4, para. 6; operative on March 15, 1987; prescribe the form in which evidence of a woman's pregnancy or her expected date of confinement is to be provided by her to her employers liable to pay statutory maternity pay.

STATUTORY MATERNITY PAY (PERSONS ABROAD AND MARINERS) REGULATIONS 1987 (No. 418) [80p], made under the Social Security Act 1986, ss.80, 84(1); operative on April 6, 1987; provide for statutory maternity pay in relation to persons abroad, women who work as mariners or women who work on the continental shelf.

1347. Race relations

RACE RELATIONS (OFFSHORE EMPLOYMENT) ORDER 1987 (No. 929) [85p], made under the Race Relations Act 1976 (c.74), ss.8(5), 74(3); operative on November 1, 1987; brings within the scope of Pt. II of the 1976 Act employment in relation to offshore installations.

1348. Race relations—breach of trust and confidence—dismissal

[Race Relations Act 1976 (c.74), ss.2(1), 3(3), 11(1), 11(3)(*b*), 78(1).]

The appellant was expelled from the respondent company, after having revealed in Industrial Tribunal proceedings that he had secretly taped conversations between other members of the company, on the grounds that this amounted to a serious breach of trust and confidence. The appellant brought another claim maintaining he had been victimised by virtue of s.2 Race Relations Act 1976. The Industrial Tribunal dismissed his application, finding that any other member of the company would have been treated in the same way if it had been revealed that they had secretly taped conversations.

Held, dismissing the appeal to the Employment Appeal Tribunal, that the appellant had failed to establish that the reason for his expulsion fell within any of the grounds set out in s.2(1)(*a*) to (*d*). The fact that the reason for loss of trust and confidence in the appellant flowed from one of the circumstances set out in grounds (*a*) to (*d*) did not preclude the company from expelling the appellant for this reason. The mere fact that one of the circumstances in (*a*) to (*d*) can be shown to exist does not prevent the company from establishing another reason for the expulsion.

AZIZ *v.* TRINITY STREET TAXIS [1986] I.R.L.R. 435, E.A.T.

1349. Race relations—employer's liability for acts of employees—acting in course of employment—misconduct by employees

[Race Relations Act 1976 (c.74), ss.1(1)(*a*), 32(1).]

E was employed by the Post Office and was authorised to write on mail to ensure that it was properly dealt with, but for no other purpose. E did not get on with the P's who were his neighbours and of Jamaican origin. While sorting mail, E wrote on an envelope addressed to the P's "Go back to Jamaica, Sambo". The P's brought an action against the Post Office under the Race Relations Act seeking a declaration and injunction against the Post Office and requesting damages. The County Court dismissed the claim on the grounds that E was not acting in the course of his employment when he wrote the abusive words. The P's appealed.

Held, dismissing the appeal, that an employer's vicarious liability for the unauthorised act of his employees depended on whether that act was merely unauthorised or whether it was entirely outside the scope of the employee's employment. In this case, E's actions could not be regarded as merely a prohibited mode of carrying out his obligations. The actions formed no part of the performance of E's duties, even though his employment gave him the opportunity to carry them out.

IRVING & IRVING *v.* THE POST OFFICE [1987] I.R.L.R. 289, C.A.

1350. Racial discrimination—application for employment

[Race Relations Act 1976 (c.74), s.1(1)(*b*).]

Q. a Bengali employed as a local authority social worker, applied for a job as team leader. No non-white candidates were shortlisted and Q complained of discrimination contrary to s.1(1)(*b*) of the 1976 Act. The industrial tribunal found that a condition of shortlisting had been three years' experience at a certain level, which P lacked, and which Bengali candidates were less likely to be able to fulfil, and upheld the claim of indirect discrimination.

Held, that the tribunal had failed sufficiently to identify Q's racial group, by which the proportional inability to comply with a condition had to be assessed, by virtue of s.1(1)(*b*). Further, that the tribunal had failed to take account of all the evidence for Q not being shortlisted, and the case would be remitted for reconsideration.

TOWER HAMLETS LONDON BOROUGH COUNCIL *v.* QAYYUM [1987] I.C.R. 729, E.A.T.

1351. Racial discrimination—refusal by applicant for employment to state religion—applicant informed that religion might preclude selection for employment—interview terminated by applicant—whether discrimination

Acts designed to discourage an applicant from continuing with an application for employment based on grounds of race or religion were capable of amounting to unlawful discrimination under the Race Relations Act 1976.

In response to a newspaper advertisement, S attended an interview with J, the respondents' chief executive. The respondents were an employment agency seeking to fill a position on behalf of their client. J stated the client was based in the Middle East and asked S how he would feel about working for Arabs who might interfere in the performance of the job. J asked S to state his religion. When S refused, J attempted to explain the purpose of the question by saying: "If for instance you were of the Jewish faith it might preclude your selection for the job." S was of the Jewish faith. He believed he was being discriminated against on racial grounds and terminated the interview, effectively withdrawing his application. The question about religion was one question on a standard checklist of questions. S complained to the industrial tribunal that he had been discriminated against on the grounds of his Jewish faith. The tribunal found that J did not know of S's faith at the time of the interview and that J had not attempted to discourage S from proceeding with his application. The tribunal held that S could not have been discriminated against on account of the fact that he had withdrawn his application before disclosing he was of the Jewish faith. S's appeal to the Employment Appeal Tribunal was dismissed on the ground that the tribunal had reached an unimpeachable decision of mixed fact and law.

Held, dismissing S's appeal, that in appropriate circumstances, words or acts of discouragement on racial grounds can, in respect of the person discouraged, amount to treatment less favourable than that given to other persons: i.e. discrimination. The tribunal were entitled to find as a matter of fact that J's explanation as to the purpose for asking the question about S's religion was just that and not a discriminatory act of discouragement on racial grounds. The fact that the alleged discriminator did not know of a complainant's racial, religious, ethnic or national group could not conclusively determine that there was no discrimination against the complainant. That did not assist S in the light of the tribunal's findings of fact and the fact that his complaint was that he individually had been discriminated against as opposed to discrimination against a member of an identified class or group.

SIMON *v.* BRIMHAM ASSOCIATES [1987] I.C.R. 596, C.A.

1352. Racial discrimination—summary of applicants for job

In a claim for unlawful discrimination on grounds of race, an employer may be ordered to produce a summary showing the numbers of white and non-white applicants for jobs (*Jalota* v. *Imperial Metal Industry (Kynoch)* [1979] C.L.Y. 914 and *Chattopadhyay* v. *Headmaster of Holloway School* [1982] C.L.Y. 1063 considered).

WEST MIDLANDS PASSENGER TRANSPORT EXECUTIVE *v.* SINGH, *The Times,* June 23, 1987, E.A.T.

1353. Racial discrimination—Welsh language job—applicants English-speaking Welsh—whether members of racial group

[Race Relations Act 1976 (c.74), ss.1(1) 3(1).]

For the purposes of s.1(1)(*b*) of the 1976 Act a racial group cannot be defined by reference to the language factor alone.

The applicants applied for jobs at a local authority residential home but were refused employment on the grounds that they did not speak Welsh. On their complaint of discrimination, the tribunal found that they belonged to an "ethnic group" which had been discriminated against, and upheld their complaints.

Held, on appeal, the tribunal had erred in defining racial group by the language factor alone and by sub-dividing the Welsh ethnic group into English or Welsh-speaking groups. The authority were not in breach, but even if they were the condition would have been justifiable.

GWYNEDD COUNTY COUNCIL *v.* JONES [1986] I.C.R. 833, E.A.T.

1354. Redundancy—continuity of employment—repeated short-term contracts—whether global contracts of employment

An arrangement whereby repeated short-term contracts of employment have existed for a long time will not be sufficient to give rise to a global contract of employment unless there remain subsisting, after the termination of each of the short-term contracts, sufficient mutual contractual obligations.

M and the other applicants were trawlermen who had sailed exclusively for their respective companies for a number of years. Each voyage, however, was regarded as being subject to a separate agreement which came to an end at the conclusion of each voyage. At such a time each applicant was free to work for another employer if he chose; at no time were any of the employers bound to offer work to any of the applicants. With the contraction in the fishing industry, the employers eventually took their whole fleets out of service. The applicants claimed redundancy.

Held, dismissing their appeal against the finding that they had not been employed at that time, and therefore not dismissed, that notwithstanding the long duration of the arrangement of the short-term agreements, there was no contract in existence in between those agreements. There were no mutual contractual obligations as between the applicants and their employers, so it could not be said that they had been dismissed.

HELLYER BROTHERS *v.* McLEOD; BOSTON DEEP SEA FISHERIES *v.* WILSON [1987] 1 W.L.R. 728, C.A.

1355. Redundancy—continuity of employment—transfer of undertaking—employment by successive companies—whether presumption of continuity of employment—burden and standard of proof

[Employment Protection (Consolidation) Act 1978 (c.44), Sched. 13, paras. 1, 17.]

Where an employee was employed by successive employers there was no presumption that the employee's employment was continuous.

In 1978 C was employed by F Ltd. F Ltd went into liquidation in March 1983 and was succeeded by W Ltd as C's employer. W Ltd went into liquidation in January 1984. Thereafter C was employed by B Ltd which went into liquidation in December 1985. C contended that for the purposes of redundancy he had been continuously employed since 1978 until December 1985. C's contention could only succeed if there were a transfer of the business of F Ltd from it to W Ltd and subsequently to B Ltd. C's evidence before the tribunal was that throughout the period he had worked in the same premises using the same machines and materials with the same employees and customers and under the same management. The tribunal held that there was a presumption of continuity of employment for the purposes of para. 17 of Sched. 13 to the Employment Protection (Consolidation) Act 1978 and found in C's favour. The Secretary of State, being a respondent to C's complaint, appealed.

Held, allowing the appeal, that the presumption of continuity of employment set out in para. 1(3) of Sched. 13 to the Act did not apply to para. 17. By virtue of para. 17(1) of Sched. 13 it only applied where there was one single employer. In the present case there were three separate employers. It was incumbent on C, as the applicant for a redundancy payment, to satisfy the tribunal on the balance of probabilities that there had been a transfer of the business satisfying the provisions of para. 17(2) of the Schedule. It was not incumbent on an applicant to produce documentary evidence of the transfer. Unchallenged evidence of the nature given by C would be sufficient to justify a finding that the business had been transferred. Given that there was evidence that the Secretary of State might put before the tribunal on the question of whether or not there had been a transfer, the case would be remitted to the tribunal (*Secretary of State for Employment* v. *Globe Elastic Thread Co.* [1979] C.L.Y. 936 applied; *Evenden* v. *Guildford City Association Football Club* [1975] C.L.Y. 1143, *Umar* v. *Pliastar* [1981] C.L.Y. 814, *Woodhouse* v. *Brotherhood (Peter)* [1972] C.L.Y. 1234 considered).

SECRETARY OF STATE FOR EMPLOYMENT *v.* COHEN [1987] I.C.R. 570, E.A.T.

1356. Redundancy—definition—whether amended by Transfer of Undertakings Regulations

[Employment Protection (Consolidation) Act 1978 (c.44), s.8(2); Transfer of Undertakings (Protection of Employment) Regulations (S.I. 1981, No. 1794) Reg. 5.]

The regulations do not amend the definition of redundancy contained in s.81(2) of the Act.

CHAPMAN *v.* CPS COMPUTER GROUP, *The Times,* June 30, 1987, C.A.

1357. Redundancy—dismissal—fixed term contract—union consultation

[Employment Protection Act 1975 (c.71), s.99(1).]

Where a university lecturer was on a fixed term contract and was dismissed thereafter, he was redundant since the requirement for him to carry out his work had ceased, and the employers were bound to consult his union within s.99(1) of the Employment Protection Act 1975.

The employee, a member of the Association of University Teachers, was engaged under a three-year fixed term contract as a temporary lecturer training teachers of the deaf. It was a condition of the contract that he would not seek compensation under the statutory redundancy or unfair dismissal provisions at the end of the term. The course could not be continued after the three-year period, for lack of funds, and the employee was dismissed. The union complained that the university had failed to carry out the necessary consultation before dismissing him as redundant, as required by s.99 of the Employment Protection Act 1975. The industrial tribunal found that he was not dismissed for redundancy since had funds been available, there was sufficient demand for the course, and the union's application failed. The union's appeal was allowed. It was held that the tribunal was wrong to consider the reason for the redundancy situation, the lack of funding, rather than whether there was in fact a redundancy situation within s.126(6)(*b*) of the Act, namely whether the non-renewal of the contract was due to the fact that the university no longer had a requirement for the work the employee had been doing. Since the requirement for the employee to carry out his work had ceased, he was redundant, and the consultation requirements in s.99(1) were applicable. The union was accordingly entitled to a declaration that the university had failed to engage in the consultation required by s.99(1) (*Delanair* v. *Mead* [1977] C.L.Y. 1068 considered).

ASSOCIATION OF UNIVERSITY TEACHERS *v.* UNIVERSITY OF NEWCASTLE-UPON-TYNE [1987] I.C.R. 317, E.A.T.

1358. Redundancy—pregnant employee—which criteria relevant in deciding whether dismissal fair

[Employment Protection (Consolidation) Act 1978 (c.44), ss.57(3), 60(1).]

An employer faced with a redundancy situation took ability as his criterion for redundancy. He chose X, who was pregnant, because of her impaired ability to attend physically at her place of work and do her job.

Held, that where the underlying reason for a dismissal is that there exists a redundancy situation, and an employee is selected for redundancy because she is pregnant, the relevant section under which to decide whether the dismissal was fair is s.57(3) of the Employment Protection (Consolidation) Act 1978, not s.60(1). S.60(1) did not apply in the present case, because X's pregnancy was neither the sole nor the principal reason for her dismissal.

STOCKTON-ON-TEES BOROUGH COUNCIL *v.* BROWN, *The Times,* March 21, 1987, C.A.

1359. Redundancy—protective award—employee dismissed before proposed date—date of protected period

[Employment Protection Act 1975 (c.71), ss.99, 101 as amended by Employment Protection (Handling of Redundancies) Variation Order 1979, art. 2.]

The protective award has to be calculated on the proposed date of the first dismissal.

Employers decided to make a number of the workforce redundant as from December 31, 1983. On October 28, 1983 one of the employees was released early because he had found alternative employment. The employers failed to consult with the union about the proposed redundancies and the union applied for a protective award. The tribunal made an award dated from October 28.

Held, allowing the appeal, that the 30 days referred to in s.99(3) had to be calculated from the proposed date of the first dismissal; the period began on December 31, 1983. (*Green (E.) & Son (Castings)* v. *Association of Scientific, Technical and Managerial Staffs* [1984] C.L.Y. 1264)

TRANSPORT & GENERAL WORKERS UNION *v.* LEDBURY PRESERVES (1928) [1986] I.C.R. 855, E.A.T.

1360. Redundancy—statutory presumption—two employees simultaneously dismissed—whether necessary to establish which employee dismissed by reason of redundancy

[Employment Protection (Consolidation) Act 1978 (c.44), ss.81(1), 81(2)(*b*), 91(2).]

W and L originally worked for W's father, who also employed one part-time worker. The business was sold to Mr. and Mrs. H who wished to work in the business themselves and also to employ their son, as well as the part-time worker. There were therefore still three full-time workers, including the proprietors, and one part-time worker.

W and L were consequently dismissed and applied to the tribunal for redundancy payments. The Tribunal dismissed their application on the grounds that they had failed to establish in relation to both of them that the requirements for employees to carry out a particular kind of work has ceased or diminished in accordance with s.81(2)(*b*). On appeal, the E.A.T. upheld the Tribunal's decision. W and L appealed.

Held, allowing the appeal, that the Tribunal had erred in holding that because two employees had been simultaneously dismissed for two different reasons they were unable to establish a redundancy. the Tribunal had failed to have regard to s.91(2) which provided a statutory presumption of redundancy unless the contrary were proved. Although it was not possible to establish which employee had been dismissed wholly or mainly by reason of redundancy, the employers had failed to rebut the presumption in the case of both employees, and therefore both employees were entitled to rely upon the presumption, not withstanding that there was only one genuine redundancy.

WILLCOX *v.* HASTINGS [1987] I.R.L.R. 298, C.A.

1361. Redundancy—steel industry—special ECSC payments. See STEEL REDUNDANCY BENEFIT, *Re* (No. C.114/85), §1530.

1362. Redundancy—whether dismissal—employees inveigled into leaving

[Employment Protection (Consolidation) Act 1978 (c.44).]

Employees who are inveigled into leaving their employment are dismissed within the meaning of s.83(2) of the 1978 Act.

C.M. Co., who undertook construction work at collieries informed their employee B, who had worked at a certain colliery for some years that there was to be a reduction in the workforce at that colliery, and suggested that he consider alternative employment. B eventually accepted an offer of employment from the National Coal Board and wrote to C.M. Co. terminating his employment. B claimed redundancy payments and C.M. Co. claimed he had left of his own accord. The industrial tribunal found that B had been inveigled into leaving and that amounted to dismissal within the meaning on s.83(2) of the 1978 Act.

Held, on appeal, that the question to be asked was who in fact terminated the employment. The effect of the tribunal's finding of fact was that the employers had done so, and accordingly B was entitled to redundancy payments (*Martin* v. *Glynwed Distribution* [1983] C.L.Y. 1226 followed).

CALEDONIAN MINING CO. *v.* BASSETT [1987] I.C.R. 425, E.A.T.

1363. Redundancy payments—rebate—eligibility for rebate

[Wages Act 1986 (c.48), s.27, Sched. 6; Employment Protection (Consolidation) Act 1978 (c.44), ss.104(5), 104A; Interpretation Act 1978 (c.30), s.7; Redundancy Rebate Regulations 1984 (S.I. 1984 No. 1066), Reg. 3(1).]

The employer's claim for a rebate had to arrive at the Department of Employment local office before the Wages Act came into force. Posting it in due time was insufficient (*R.* v. *London County Quarter Sessions Appeals Committee, ex p. Rossi* [1956] C.L.Y. 5264 considered).

SECRETARY OF STATE FOR EMPLOYMENT *v.* MILK & GENERAL HAULAGE (NOTTINGHAM) (1987) 84 L.S.Gaz. 2118, E.A.T.

1364. Redundancy payments—rebate—entitlement to rebate

[Wages Act 1986 (c.48).]

From August 1, 1986, when the Wages Act 1986 came into force, employers were no longer entitled to a redundancy rebate. Where a dismissal notice expired after that date, but the employer withdrew it, replacing it with one expiring on July 31, 1986, and paying the employee a month's salary in lieu of notice in addition to his redundancy money, the employer was entitled to the rebate.

STAFFORDSHIRE COUNTY COUNCIL *v.* SECRETARY OF STATE FOR EMPLOYMENT, *The Times,* August 19, 1987, E.A.T.

1365. Safe system of work—occupier's liability—duty to independent contractor's employees—demolition of building. See FERGUSON *v.* WELSH, §2612.

1366. Safe system of work—operation of system—ship operators. See McDERMID *v.* NASH DREDGING AND RECLAMATION CO., §2615.

1367. Safety at work—employee's misconduct—employer's vicarious liability

P was injured at work when another employee pushed an insecure washbasin against her in order to startle her. P claimed damages for personal injuries against her employers on the grounds that they had breached their duty to ensure that the washbasin was safe and that they were vicariously liable for the action of the other employee. P's claim was dismissed and she appealed.

Held, dismissing the appeal, that the High Court had correctly held that the employer was not vicariously liable for injuries sustained at work which were caused by another employee. An employer is only responsible for acts actually authorised by him and for the way an employee performs those acts. He is not responsible for unauthorised acts carried out by an employee which are beyond the scope of the employment. In this case the act committed by the other employee was independent and had no connection whatsoever with her job. Further, the High Court was correct in holding that it was not foreseeable that injury would occur from ordinary use of the washbasin, and it was therefore even less foreseeable that the washbasin would be used to cause injury deliberately.

ALDRED *v.* NACANCO [1987] I.R.L.R. 292, C.A.

1368. Sex discrimination

SEX DISCRIMINATION AND EQUAL PAY (OFFSHORE EMPLOYMENT) ORDER 1987 (No. 930) [85p], made under the Sex Discrimination Act 1975 (c.65), ss.10(5), 81(4); operative on November 1, 1987; brings within the scope of Pt. II of the 1975 Act employment in relation to offshore installations.

1369. Sex discrimination—occupational pensions—part-time workers. See BILKA-KAUFHAUS GmbH *v.* WEBER VON HARTZ (No. 170/84), §1633.

1370. Sex discrimination—retirement age—whether British Gas Corp. is a state authority for purposes of art. 5(1) Council Directive 76/207/EEC

[Sex Discrimination Act 1975 (c.65), s.6(4), Council Directive 76/207/EEC, art 5(1).]

The British Gas Corp. was not a state authority; the provisions of art. 5(1) Council Directive 76/207/EEC did not apply to it.

The applicants were all female employees of British Gas Corp. The Corporation operated a policy of compulsorily retiring female employees at 60 and male employees at 65 years of age. The applicants were all compulsorily retired upon reaching 60 pursuant to their contracts of employment. The applicants complained that they had been discriminated against on grounds of sex.

Held, that 6(2)(*b*) Sex Discrimination Act 1975 whereby discrimination on grounds of sex was made unlawful did not apply to provisions in relation to retirement by virtue of s.6(4) of the Act. The applicants were unable to rely upon the provisions of art. 5(1) Council Directive 76/207/EEC to defeat s.6(4) of the Act. Art. 5(1) provided for the equal treatment of men and women with respect to conditions governing dismissal from employment and conflicted with s.6(4) of the Act. An employee of a state authority was entitled to rely on art. 5(1) notwithstanding its conflict with s.6(4) of the Act. Although the British Gas was a public authority it could not be described as a state authority. Accordingly the applicants were not employees of a state authority and not able to rely on art. 5(1) to overcome s.6(4) of the Act. A state authority was an organ of the state in the sense that it exercised powers of state either as principal or agent. (*Marshall* v. *Southampton and South West Hampshire Area Health Authority (Teaching)* [1986] C.L.Y. 1456 considered; *Tamlin* v. *Hannaford* (1950) C.L.C. 8472 applied).

FOSTER *v.* BRITISH GAS [1987] I.C.R. 52, Industrial Tribunal.

1371. Sex discrimination—retirement age—whether retirement provisions excluded

[Sex Discrimination Act 1975 (c.65), s.6(4).]

S.6(4) of the Sex Discrimination Act 1975 does not operate so as to exclude provisions in relation to retirement from the effect of the Act.

Under the employer's retirement policy men retired at 65, women at 60. The applicant, a woman, was dismissed at 60 and complained of discrimination. The tribunal held that her complaint failed due to s.6(4) of the 1975 Act. The woman appealed on the grounds that a decision of the European Court of Justice had overruled s.6(4).

Held, allowing the appeal, that the tribunal had erred in law in their interpretation of the effect of s.6(4), and the Council Directive overruled similar provisions in the 1978 Act; the matter would be remitted for further consideration.

PARSONS *v.* EAST SURREY HEALTH AUTHORITY [1986] I.C.R. 837, E.A.T.

1372. Sex discrimination—sexual harassment—meaning of "victimisation" under Sex Discrimination Act 1975

[Sex Discrimination Act 1975 (c.65), ss.1(1)(*a*), 4(1)(*a*), 5(1), 6(1)(*a*), 6(2)(*b*).]

Mrs. C, who was a personal secretary at the College, complained of sexual harassment by a superior and as a result was transferred to another similar post on a trial basis for a period of one year. Before the year expired she requested reinstatement in the previous post and, when this was refused, issued an application in the industrial tribunal under the 1975 Act. When this was dismissed she appealed to the E.A.T. In the meantime, the year expired and she formally requested a transfer, which was refused pending the outcome of the appeal. Mrs. C. issued another application in the industrial tribunal and subsequently requested implementation of the college's grievance procedure, which was refused pending the outcome of the applications. Mrs. C. issued a further application in the industrial tribunal. She was eventually dismissed for refusing to undertake certain duties. The industrial tribunal and the E.A.T. dismissed her complaints, although the E.A.T. considered that there was a question of law as to the meaning of "victimisation" and allowed an appeal.

Held, dismissing the appeal, that the industrial tribunal had been correct in holding that no victimisation under s.4(1)(*a*) had occurred in relation to Mrs. C. bringing proceedings under the Act, even though the College had refused to exercise the grievance procedure pending the outcome of the hearings. The purpose of s.4(1)(*a*) was to protect those who brought proceedings relating to sex discrimination. Mrs. C. would have to show that in refusing her request for transfer and the right to exercise the grievance procedure pending the outcome of the proceedings, first that the College were treating her less favourably than they would any other person, and secondly that they did so because Mrs. C. had brought proceedings under the Act. This could not be clearly inferred, although the fact that Mrs. C. had brought proceedings had influenced the College's decision in that they wished to defer taking immediate action to avoid confusion since the subject matters of her complaints were allied.

CORNELIUS *v.* UNIVERSITY COLLEGE OF SWANSEA [1977] I.R.L.R. 141, C.A.

1373. Sex discrimination—sexual harassment—reinstatement of harasser alongside victim of harassment—whether victim treated less favourably on ground of her sex

[Sex Discrimination Act 1975 (c.65), ss.1(1)(*a*), 6(2)(*b*).]

The question of whether an employer has taken such steps as are reasonably practicable to prevent an act under s.6(2)(*b*) of the Sex Discrimination Act 1975 is one of fact.

F, a female employee, was sexually harassed at work by M, a male employee. She complained to E, her employer, who conducted an enquiry, found the allegations not proven, and reinstated M. F claimed that having to work alongside M was treating her less favourably on the ground of sex under s.1(1)(*a*) of the Act.

Held, that it was necessary to look at the "treatment" (*i.e.* the fact of allowing M and F to work together) and not at the consequences of the treatment (*i.e.* the possibility of sexual harassment) and that the treatment was not because of F's sex, but because of her being an employee.

FRANCIS *v.* TOWER HAMLETS BOROUGH COUNCIL (1987) L.S.Gaz. 2530, E.A.T.

1374. Sex discrimination—superannuation scheme—condition or requirement with which fewer women can comply

[Sex Discrimination Act 1975 (c.65), ss.1(1)(*b*)(i), 1(1)(*b*)(ii), 1(1)(*b*)(iii), 6(2)(*b*), 6(4), 65(1), 66(1).]

Mrs. T., a divorcee with three children, was required to join the Labour Party superannuation scheme. She brought a claim in the industrial tribunal alleging that this scheme was discriminatory because it allowed pension to be automatically payable to a spouse of a deceased member, but made only discretionary provision in relation to passing the benefit to children of a deceased member. Mrs. T. alleged that this provision mainly affected single parents, who are mostly women. The industrial tribunal dismissed the complaint on the grounds that it had no jurisdiction under s.6(4) of the 1975 Act. On appeal, the E.A.T. remitted the case to the industrial tribunal. The new industrial tribunal dismissed the complaint on a preliminary point that the provisions relating to discretionary awards to children of a deceased member was a term of the scheme, but was not a "requirement" or "condition" as specified in the 1975 Act. Mrs. T. again appealed to the E.A.T., which allowed the appeal on the basis that the requirement, properly identified, was that in order to provide a pension as of right to a survivor of a member, then that member must die leaving a spouse. The E.A.T. again remitted the case to the industrial tribunal to establish whether such a requirement contravened the Act. The Labour Party appealed.

Held, allowing the appeal, that the alleged discriminatory condition could not be held to be to Mrs. T's detriment because she "cannot comply with it" within the meaning of s.1(1)(*b*)(iii). The conditions for benefit from the pension fund have to be satisfied at a future date rather than the date at which contributions are paid, and it could not be held that Mrs. T. as a single woman "cannot" marry at a future date and therefore satisfy the conditions. It could not be said that Mrs. T. "cannot" comply with the condition of being married at a future date and thereby leaving a surviving spouse at a future date. Further it was prima facie undesirable that the case should be remitted to the industrial tribunal for a third time.

TURNER *v.* LABOUR PARTY AND THE LABOUR PARTY SUPERANNUATION SOCIETY [1987] I.R.L.R. 101, E.A.T.

1375. Sex discrimination—termination of employment upon entitlement to pension—different pensionable ages for men and women. See BEETS-PROPER *v.* F. VAN LANSCHOT BANKIERS B.V., §1637.

1376. Sex discrimination—work of equal value—pay not equal—defence of difference genuinely due to a factor other than sex—procedure

[Equal Pay Act 1970 (c.41), s.1(2)(*c*), Industrial Tribunals (Rules of Procedure) Regulations 1985 (S.I. 1985 No. 16), Sched. 2, r.7A(1).]

An industrial tribunal was not bound to obtain a job evaluation study before dismissing an application under the equal pay legislation at a preliminary stage on the ground that the difference in pay was genuinely due to a material difference unrelated to a difference in sex.

M, F and B were women employed by Forex Neptune. H was a man employed by Forex Neptune in the same capacity as B. H was paid £10,538 per annum. B was paid £8,400 per annum. F and M claimed to be doing work equivalent in value to H's work. F and M were paid £7,000 per annum. M, F and B complained to the industrial tribunal under the equal pay legislation seeking equality of pay with H. At a preliminary hearing Forex Neptune conceded B and H were doing the same job and denied M and F's work was of equivalent value to H's. Forex Neptune further claimed that the difference in pay was genuinely due to a material difference unrelated to sex in that H had been effectively demoted to the same job as B but that it was not the company's policy to reduce pay in such circumstances. Having heard evidence on that issue the tribunal found against Forex Neptune and granted B's application and ordered expert job evaluation studies on M and F's claims. Forex Neptune appealed.

Held, allowing the appeal, that the evidence clearly showed that H had been demoted albeit on his existing rate of pay. The tribunal were so involved in the intricacies and niceties of the law that they forgot a lot of the evidence and misconstrued a lot more. There was a substantial error in law in the way that the tribunal dealt with the evidence. Section 1(2)(*c*) of the Equal Pay Act 1970 and r.7A(1) of the Industrial Tribunal (Rules of Procedure) Regulations 1985 did not preclude an industrial tribunal from dismissing a claim for equal pay without first obtaining an expert job evaluation study. The tribunal were right to consider the material difference defence as a preliminary issue. If the defence succeeded there was no point in obtaining an expert job evaluation study.

FOREX NEPTUNE (OVERSEAS) *v.* MILLER [1987] I.C.R. 170, E.A.T.

1377. Short time working introduced without agreement—whether salary can be reduced pro rata

An employer, having introduced short time working, is only entitled to reduce salary *pro rata* if there is an express contractual arrangement entitling them to make the deductions.

The employee had worked for the employer for years, latterly on an annual salary paid monthly. In 1982 the employers, without the consent of the employee or his union, reduced his working week to three days. The employers reduced his salary *pro rata* without agreement. The employee sued for the difference. The judge held that there was a provision incorporated into the contract enabling the employers to vary the hours of employment, and they were not in breach.

Held, allowing the appeal, that the employers were only entitled to reduce his salary if there was an express contractual agreement entitling them to make the deductions; the documentary evidence did not establish such an agreement to a variation.

MILLER *v.* HAMWORTHY ENGINEERING [1986] I.C.R. 846, C.A.

1378. Sick pay

STATUTORY SICK PAY (ADDITIONAL COMPENSATION OF EMPLOYERS) AMENDMENT REGULATIONS 1987 (No. 92) [45p], made under the Social Security and Housing Benefits Act 1982 (c.24), ss.9(1A), 26(1), 45(2) 47; operative on April 6, 1987; amend S.I. 1985 No. 1411 by inserting a new reg. 3.

STATUTORY SICK PAY (GENERAL) AMENDMENT REGULATIONS 1987 (No. 372) [80p], made under the Social Security and Housing Benefits Act 1982 (c.24), ss.1(5), 26(1), 47 and the Social Security Act 1986 (c.50), ss.51(1)(*k*))4), 84(1), 89(1); operative on April 6, 1987; amend S.I. 1982 No. 894 so as to prescribe circumstances when the liability to pay statutory sick pay becomes that of the Secretary of State instead of that of the employer.

STATUTORY SICK PAY (GENERAL) AMENDMENT (No. 2) REGULATIONS 1987 (No. 868) [85p], made under the Social Security and Housing Benefits Act 1982, ss.3(4A)(*b*)(5), 26(1)(3), 47, Sched. 1, para. 1; operative on June 7, 1987; amends S.I. 1982 No. 894 in relation to a woman's entitlement to statutory sick pay who is not receiving either statutory maternity pay or a maternity allowance so as to prevent her receiving sick pay for a period of 18 weeks at the time of confinement.

STATUTORY SICK PAY (RATE OF PAYMENT) REGULATIONS 1987 (No. 33) [45p], made under the Social Security and Housing Benefits Act 1982, s.7(1A) and the Social Security Act 1986 (c.50), s.89(1); operative on April 6, 1987; provides for statutory sick pay to be in two rates.

1379. Summary dismissal of chief executive—where justified—misconduct and incompetence

Summary dismissal of the chief executive of a company may be justified where he is guilty of misconduct so serious that there no longer exists the confidence necessary for his continued employment, or where he is shown to be so incompetent that it is wholly impracticable for the company to retain him because of the further harm that he is likely to do.

J was a director, and the chief executive of IP; he was summarily dismissed following a boardroom conflict and claimed damages. IP alleged that he had been guilty of misconduct in supporting a move to extend directors' service contracts to three years, and that in various ways he had shown himself to be wholly incompetent.

Held, that on the facts IP had failed to make out either of its defences to J's claim, which accordingly succeeded. The allegation of misconduct failed because J had been entitled to try and hold together his management team; misconduct was sufficient summarily to terminate a director's office only where it completely undermined confidence in him. Similarly, IP had not shown J to be guilty of that degree of incompetence which would justify his summary dismissal: only if it would have been quite impracticable to keep him on, because of the damage that he would do to the company, would such a course have been justified.

JACKSON *v.* INVICTA PLASTICS [1987] B.C.L.C. 329, Peter Pain J.

1380. Superintendent registrar—Crown servant—deduction of wages—honorarium

[Registration Service Act 1953 (c.37), ss.6, 13(2) (as amended by Local Government Act 1972 (c.70), Sched. 29, para. 41.]

Although a superintendent registrar was not a servant of a local authority but the holder of an office, his position was similar to that of an employee and his salary could be deducted when he failed to do part of his work.

The plaintiff was appointed in 1974 by the defendant council as a superintendent registrar pursuant to s.6 of the Registration Service Act 1953. The local scheme made pursuant to s.13 of the Act assimilated him with an appropriate local government officer in relation to salary scales. His normal week consisted of 37 hours work, including three hours on Saturday mornings, which was the most popular time for weddings. In 1981 his trade union instructed him to refuse to conduct weddings on Saturdays as part of industrial action. He complied. He remained willing to work a 37 hour week and attend on Saturdays to do other work. The council made it clear that it did not accept this and deducted part of his salary representing the three hours. His action for damages for the lost wages was dismissed by Nicholls J. but allowed by the Court of Appeal. The council appealed to the House of Lords.

Held, allowing the appeal that although the plaintiff was not a servant of the defendant council under a contract of employment but the holder of an office, his position was similar to that of an employee, and his salary was not a mere honorarium for the mere tenure of an office. His right to remuneration depended on his being willing to do the work that he was employed to do and if he declined to do the work the employer need not pay him. His salary was therefore properly deducted.

MILES *v.* WAKEFIELD METROPOLITAN DISTRICT COUNCIL [1987] 2 W.L.R. 795, H.L.

1381. Termination of employment—oral notice—computation of time

Where an employee is given oral notice terminating his employment, time begins to run on the day after the day the notice was given.

During the afternoon of July 15, 1985 W was given seven days' notice terminating her employment. If the seven days' notice was calculated from the day upon which it was given, W would not be entitled to make a complaint alleging unfair dismissal by reason of being employed for less than one year. If notice was calculated from the next day W qualified by virtue of having been employed for exactly one year. The tribunal found against W.

Held, allowing W's appeal, that where an employee was given oral notice terminating his employment the period of notice was to be calculated from the beginning of the day after that upon which the notice was given (*Robert Cort & Son* v. *Charman* [1982] C.L.Y. 1099 considered).

WEST *v.* KNEELS [1987] I.C.R. 146, E.A.T.

1382. Transfer of undertaking—Royal dockyards—consultation. See INSTITUTION OF PROFESSIONAL CIVIL SERVANTS *v.* SECRETARY OF STATE FOR DEFENCE, §1527.

1383. Transfer of undertaking—whether redeployment of staff such a transfer—extent to which consultation with union required—whether union's complaint premature

[Transfer of Undertakings (Protection of Employment) Regulations 1981 (S.I. 1981 No. 1974), reg. 10.]

A union's complaint of failure to consult is not premature simply because a company reorganisation has not been finalised.

B bank decides to form a wholly owned subsidiary from three other subsidiary companies. Staff were transferred to the new company under new contracts of employment. Their standard contracts required them to work at any branch or department of B bank or its subsidiaries. They continued to do the same work, and no assets or goodwill were transferred. The union complained, under reg. 11 of the Transfer of Undertakings (Protection of Employment) Regulations 1981, of failure to consult. B bank argued that the application was premature since the reorganisation had not been finalised. The tribunal rejected that argument but held on the facts that there had been no transfer of an undertaking, so that the regulations did not apply.

Held, dismissing the appeal, that there had been no transfer of an undertaking.

Per curiam: the regulations were clearly designed to deal with consultation before a transfer had taken place.

BANKING INSURANCE AND FINANCE UNION *v.* BARCLAYS BANK [1987] I.C.R. 495, E.A.T

1384. Transfer of undertakings

TRANSFER OF UNDERTAKINGS (PROTECTION OF EMPLOYMENT) (AMENDMENT) REGULATIONS 1987 (No. 442) [45p], made under the European Communities Act 1972 (c.68), s.2(2); operative on April 24, 1987; amend S.I. 1981 No. 1794.

1385. Unfair dismissal—application to industrial tribunal—whether application lodged in time

The time for P to lodge an application to an industrial tribunal expired on a Bank Holiday. On the following day, P pushed his application under the door of the tribunal's office, there being no letterbox in the door.

Held, that the Bank Holiday had been a *dies non,* and time therefore expired on the next day, because as there was no letterbox P had had no proper means of presenting his complaint on the Bank Holiday (*Hetton Victory Club* v. *Swainston* [1983] C.L.Y. 1311 distinguished).

FORD *v.* STAKIS HOTELS AND INNS, *The Times,* July 1, 1987, E.A.T.

1386. Unfair dismissal—breach of natural justice—whether witnesses of an alleged misdemeanour resulting in dismissal should be involved in the decision to dismiss—contributory fault and procedural defect

[Employment Protection (Consolidation) Act 1978 (c.44), ss.57(3), 74(6).]

The appellant was dismissed on the grounds of misconduct after sexually harrassing a colleague on two occasions, the second of which was witnessed by the Chairman and Assistant Secretary of the Club. The Chairman and Assistant Secretary were members of both the sub-committee and the full committee which carried out the investigations and made a decision to dismiss. The Industrial Tribunal found that the dismissal was reasonable and adopted the view that the decision reached would have been the same in any event. The employee appealed.

Held, allowing the appeal, that there had been a breach of natural justice and that, whenever possible, witnesses of an incident should not also act as judges of that incident nor play a part in the decision to dismiss. The Employment Appeal Tribunal did not accept the appellant's contention that where a breach of natural justice has occurred, the Industrial Tribunal is subsequently precluded from considering whether there is any contributory fault on the part of the applicant.

MOYES *v.* HYLTON CASTLE WORKING MEN'S SOCIAL CLUB AND INSTITUTE [1986] I.R.L.R. 482, E.A.T.

1387. Unfair dismissal—compensation—loss of statutory rights—loss of long period of notice—assessment

The time had come to increase compensation for loss of statutory rights consequent on an unfair dismissal from a nominal £20 to a nominal £100.

H was unfairly dismissed by his employers and was awarded £1,445 compensation by an industrial tribunal including £20 for loss of statutory industrial rights. H appealed against the amount of compensation awarded.

Held, that where an employee had been unfairly dismissed he was entitled to compensation for loss of protection from unfair dismissal in the first two years of his next employment and for loss of a longer period of notice in his old employment than in his next employment. The latter head of compensation was dependent upon the double contingency of finding a new job and being dismissed from it before he had acquired the right to notice of the same length as applied to his previous employment. The industrial tribunal must use its own knowledge of local conditions and consider the remoteness of those contingencies. Given that H was a man of considerable skill and eight years' experience the double contingency was extremely unlikely. The tribunal were right to award nothing under that head. Due to the falling value of the pound, £20 was no longer adequate nominal compensation for the loss of statutory protection in the first two years of an employee's subsequent employment. The figure was not fixed and immutable. The sum should be increased to £100 and reviewed in three or four years' time (*Townson* v. *Northgate Group* [1981] I.R.L.R. 382 considered).

MUFFETT (S. H.) *v.* HEAD [1987] I.C.R. 1, E.A.T.

1388. Unfair dismissal—compensation—salary paid in lieu of notice—whether deductable from compensation for dismissal

[Employment Protection (Consolidation) Act 1978 (c.44), s.74.]

In assessing compensation for unfair dismissal an industrial tribunal should deduct any payment made in lieu of notice from the employee's total loss of earnings as calculated from the date of termination of employment.

A was unfairly dismissed in July 1984. All employees were in fact declared redundant as at September 30, 1985. At the time of his dismissal A was paid £704 in lieu of notice, a statutory redundancy payment of £703·95 and an ex gratia payment of £845 under the employer's redundancy scheme. The tribunal deducted the payments of £704 and £845 from his compensation award. That decision was overruled by the Employment Appeal Tribunal. The employer appealed against the failure to deduct the £704.

Held, allowing the appeal, that by s.74 of the Employment Protection (Consolidation) Act 1978 the tribunal was directed to assess the amount of compensatory award "having regard to the loss sustained". There was no basis under the Act for an award of the amount of wages over the period of loss in addition to the basic award and wages for that period already paid. By making the payment in lieu the employers had complied with good industrial practice. The payment made in lieu of notice should be deducted (*Norton Tool Co.* v. *Tewson* [1973] C.L.Y. 1136, *T.B.A. Industrial Products* v. *Locke* [1984] C.L.Y. 1289 followed; *Finnie* v. *Top Hat Frozen Foods* [1985] C.L.Y. 1232 not followed).

BABCOCK F.A.T.A. *v.* ADDISON [1987] 1 FTLR 505, C.A.

1389. Unfair dismissal—complaint—time limit—complaint not delivered because of arrangements between Post Office and Central Office of Industrial Tribunals—whether complaint presented in time

Where an application claiming compensation for unfair dismissal was not delivered to the Central Office of Industrial Tribunals by reason of special arrangements between the Central Office and the Post Office, the application was to be treated as delivered on the day it would have been delivered but for the special arrangements.

L was dismissed on September 17, 1985. L's application for compensation for unfair dismissal was sent by Royal Mail special delivery service to the Central Office of Industrial Tribunals on December 14, 1985. The application would have been delivered to the Central Office on December 15, 1985 but for the fact that the Central Office had requested that post for delivery on Saturdays should be held by the Post Office and delivered on Mondays. L's application was duly delivered by the Post Office to the Central Office on Monday, December 17, 1985, one day outside the time limit for applying for compensation. The industrial tribunal held that L's application was presented out of time.

Held, allowing L's appeal, that in the normal course of events L's application would have been delivered to the Central Office on Saturday, December 15. As the Post Office did not deliver the application in accordance with the request of the Central Office the Post Office held the application as a bailee for the Central Office. Accordingly his application was to be treated as delivered to the Central Office on Saturday, December 15, 1985 within the requisite time limit (*Hodgson* v. *Armstrong* [1967] C.L.Y. 2241 applied).

LANG *v.* DEVON GENERAL [1987] I.C.R. 4, E.A.T.

1390. Unfair dismissal—continuous employment—dismissal for gross misconduct—effective date of termination

[Employment Protection (Consolidation) Act 1978 (c.44), ss.49(1), 49(5), 55(4)(*b*), 55(5), 64(1)(*a*).]

W and G commenced employment with the appellant company on January 3 and 5, 1985, respectively. Both were summarily dismissed on December 28, 1985 for gross misconduct. They would only be entitled to bring claims in the industrial tribunal if s.55(5) of the Employment Protection (Consolidation) Act 1978 operated to extend the effective date of termination by one week. S.55(5) provides that "where the contract of employment is terminated by the employer and the notice required by s.49 to be given by an employer would, if duly given on the material date, expire on a date later than the effective date of termination . . . the latter date should be treated as the effective date of termination." The company argued that no notice was due as the employees had been dismissed for gross misconduct. They relied on s.49(5) of the 1978 Act which provides that where a right existed prior to the Act to dismiss without notice by reason of conduct, this right was unaffected by the passing of the Act. The tribunal rejected this argument and the company appealed.

Held, dismissing the appeal, that the tribunal were correct in holding that the fact that a dismissal was expressed to be for gross misconduct was not sufficient to exclude s.55(5). The operation of s.55(5) was not automatically excluded merely because a dismissal was without notice and expressed to be for gross misconduct as allowed by s.49(5). In order to establish whether s.49(5) applies it was necessary to ascertain initially whether there was in fact conduct which entitled the employer to dismiss without notice, otherwise an employer could always avoid s.55(5) by stating that a dismissal was for gross misconduct.

LANTON LEISURE *v.* WHITE AND GIBSON [1987] I.R.L.R. 119, E.A.T.

1391. Unfair dismissal—continuous employment—hours normally worked

[Employment Protection (Consolidation) Act 1978, (c.44), Sched. 13, paras. 4, 6, 9(1)(*b*).]

L had been employed as a part-time teacher in three separate departments under separate, short, fixed-term contracts with varying intervals in between. This had continued for 14 years but in June 1983, she was informed that she would not be offered a contract for forthcoming autumn term. She made a complaint of unfair dismissal or redundancy.

Held, that in calculating the hours of employment per week for the purposes of paras. 4 and 6 of the 1978 Act, it was not permissible to aggregate hours worked under separate concurrent contracts with the same employers (*Ford* v. *Warwickshire County Council* [1983] C.L.Y. 1230 distinguished).

LEWIS *v.* SURREY COUNTY COUNCIL [1987] 3 W.L.R. 927, H.L.

1392. Unfair dismissal—continuous employment—no reduction in quantum of work available—employer setting up labour pool leading to absence from work for employee—whether absent on account of temporary cessation of work

[Employment Protection (Consolidation) Act 1978 (c.44), Sched. 13, para. 9(1)(*b*).]

Before an employee could be treated as absent from work on account of a temporary cessation of work for the purposes of continuity of employment, his absence had to be attributable to a diminution in the quantum of work available from the employer as a whole.

B was employed as a cleansing operative on a casual basis by Birmingham City Council. His employment commenced in October 1983. Between October 1984 and March 1985, B was engaged on a fixed term contract. In March 1985 the City Council reorganised its casual labour arrangements by setting up a labour pool to distribute the available work more evenly between the city's unemployed. B applied for and was accepted as a member of the labour pool. Between March 31, 1985, and April 29, 1985, B was not in employment although he was a member of the labour pool. Thereafter B was employed by the City Council until his dismissal in July 1985. B complained that he had been unfairly dismissed. The City Council contended that the period between March 31 and April 29, 1985, could not be taken into account in calculating the period of employment required to qualify for protection under the Act. B sought to rely upon the provisions of Sched. 13, para. 9(1)(*b*), to establish continuity of employment. The tribunal and appeal tribunal found in favour of the City Council.

Held, dismissing B's appeal, that under para. 9(1)(*b*) of Sched. 13 to the Act, the period in dispute counted for the purposes of continuity of employment if B was absent from work on account of a temporary cessation of work. The expression "cessation of work" denoted that some quantum of work had for the time being ceased to exist so that it was no longer available for the employer to give to the employee. In the present case B was unemployed between March 31, and April 29, 1985, on account of the fact that the available work was redistributed to someone else under the labour pool scheme rather than the fact that there was a diminution in the work that the City Council had available to be done (*Fitzgerald* v. *Hall, Russell & Co.* [1969] C.L.Y. 1281 considered).

BYRNE *v.* BIRMINGHAM CITY DISTRICT COUNCIL [1987] I.C.R. 519, C.A.

1393. Unfair dismissal—continuous employment—sale of business—dismissal after exchange of contracts but before completion

[Transfer of Undertakings (Protection of Employment) Regulations 1981 (S.I. 1981 No. 1794), reg. 5.]

An employee who is dismissed after the exchange of contracts for the sale of the business by which he is employed but prior to completion is entitled to make a claim for unfair dismissal against the purchaser.

M was employed by R. R agreed to sell its business to K. After the exchange of contracts between R and K and prior to completion of the transaction R dismissed M at K's request. M applied to the industrial tribunal claiming that she had been unfairly dismissed and that K was liable. The industrial tribunal held that K was liable.

Held, dismissing K's appeal, that M was entitled to claim against K provided she fell within the meaning of the phrase ". . . a person so employed immediately before the transfer . . ." in reg. 5(3) of the Transfer of Undertakings (Protection of Employment) Regulations 1981. The word "transfer" referred to the period of time over which the transaction effecting the transfer was carried out, namely the period of time from exchange of contracts to completion of the sale. As M was employed by R immediately before the exchange of contracts she was entitled to claim against K (*Premier Motors (Medway)* v. *Total Oil Great Britain* [1984] C.L.Y. 1266, *Apex Leisure Hire* v. *Barratt* [1984] C.L.Y. 1316 considered).

KESTONGATE *v.* MILLER [1986] I.C.R. 672, E.A.T.

1394. Unfair dismissal—control of company—several persons

[Employment Protection (Consolidation) Act 1978 (c.44), ss.64A, 153(4).]

"Person" in s.153(4) of the Employment Protection (Consolidation) Act 1978 includes "persons", and a group of people controlling more than one company can be "a person", thus making the companies associated companies.

A Co. and B Co. were associated employers together employing less than 20 people. E, the employee, had been employed by A Co. for less than two years. C Co., which employed over 60 people, had the same shareholders as B Co. E claimed that A Co. and C Co. were associated employers within the meaning of s.153(4) of the Employment Protection (Consolidation) Act 1978 for the purposes of a complaint of unfair dismissal. The tribunal held that it had no jurisdiction to hear the complaint, since A Co. and C Co. were not companies over which a third person had control.

Held, allowing the appeal, that "person" in s.153(4) could include "persons", and a group of people controlling more than one company could be "a person", thus making the companies associated companies. Accordingly, the case would be remitted to the industrial tribunal for further consideration on that basis (*Zarb* v. *British & Brazilian Produce Co. (Sales)* [1978] C.L.Y. 1105 considered; dictum of Mustill L.J. in *South West Launderettes v. Laidler* [1986] C.L.Y. 1258 not followed).

HARFORD *v.* SWIFTRIM [1987] I.C.R. 439, E.A.T.

1395. Unfair dismissal—criminal malpractices of employees—summary dismissal—no opportunity to explain—whether dismissal fair

[Employment Protection (Consolidation) Act 1978 (c.44), s.57(1)(3) (as amended by Employment Act 1980 (c.42), s.6.)]

Although in most cases the failure of an employer to put to an employee allegations of alleged misconduct before dismissing him would make the dismissal unfair, a tribunal was entitled to conclude in particular circumstances that no purpose would have been served by it, and that a failure to do so did not make the dismissal unfair.

The applicants had been employed by a company of metal merchants. The employers discovered that stock was missing. The company investigated and concluded that the applicants had stolen scrap metal from stock and manipulated their bonus payments. They were summarily dismissed without being given any particulars of the allegations of misconduct, or the opportunity to make representations. Their claim to the industrial tribunal for unfair dismissal was dismissed. The tribunal found as a fact that had the employers put their allegations it would have made no difference since they would have been dismissed in any event. The Employment Appeal Tribunal allowed their appeal holding that it was not open to a reasonable tribunal to conclude that it would be pointless to offer an employee an opportunity of being heard before being dismissed.

Held, allowing the employers' appeal to the Court of Appeal, that although in most cases the failure of an employer to put to an employee allegations of alleged misconduct before dismissing him would make the dismissal unfair, in the particular circumstances it was open to the tribunal to conclude that no purpose would have been served by the employers' doing so. The tribunal's decision that the dismissal was not unfair was not perverse, and not one that E.A.T. were entitled to interfere with (*British Home Stores* v. *Burchell (Note)* [1980] C.L.Y. 1004 and *British Labour Pump Co.* v. *Byrne* [1979] C.L.Y. 993 considered).

PRITCHETT *v.* McINTYRE (J.) [1987] I.C.R. 359, C.A.

1396. Unfair dismissal—effective date of termination—disciplinary procedure—time limit to present application to tribunal

[Employment Protection (Consolidation) Act 1978 (c.44), ss.55(4), 67(2), 153.]

Para. 9 of the employer's disciplinary procedure provided that in cases involving exceptional gross misconduct an employee would be informed after a disciplinary hearing of the decision "which will be implemented forthwith." In other cases of misconduct, para. 5 of the procedure provided, *inter alia,* that an employee would have a right of appeal against "the punishment to be inflicted." B was charged with two minor disciplinary offences and after an internal enquiry she was informed on February 5, 1985, that she was dismissed with immediate effect. She was informed of her right to appeal, which she did. She was informed on February 25, 1985, that her appeal had failed and that the dismissal of February 5, 1985, stood. B made an application to the tribunal, which was received on May 13, 1985. The employers contended that her application was out of time. B contended that her dismissal took effect on February 25, 1985, and therefore her application was within time. The Tribunal held that since B was charged with misconduct of a relatively minor nature, para. 5 applied, which referred to an appeal against "a punishment *to be* inflicted" which contemplated an act in the future rather than in the past and therefore the dismissal was not effective until after the decision on appeal was made. The Industrial Tribunal therefore held that B's application was in time. The Employment Appeal Tribunal upheld this decision. The employers appealed.

Held, allowing the appeal, that the fact that the employer failed to follow correctly the internal disciplinary procedure did not invalidate the effect of a clear notice of dismissal. The actual date of termination of the contract was a matter of fact which could not be altered by a failure to follow the disciplinary procedure. B's dismissal had occurred on February 5, 1985, even though the employers were not entitled to dismiss summarily for the conduct in question.

BATCHELOR *v.* BRITISH RAILWAYS BOARD [1987] I.R.L.R. 136, C.A.

1397. Unfair dismissal—effective date of termination of contract

[Employment Protection (Consolidation) Act 1978 (c.44), s.55(3).]

The passing on of a copy of an originating application to employers by an industrial tribunal is not to be deemed to be notice to the employee to terminate the contract within s.55(3) of the Act.

On April 30, 1986, A was dismissed and told she need not work her three months' notice. On June 16, before the expiry of the notice period, A presented a complaint of unfair dismissal, whereupon the employers claimed she had left of her own accord. The industrial tribunal found that by presenting the complaint A had given notice to terminate her employment before the expiry of the notice period within s.55(3) of the 1978 Act, and that thus the original dismissal was effective.

Held, that the industrial tribunal had misdirected themselves in law and the case would be remitted to another tribunal for further consideration.

CARDINAL VAUGHAN MEMORIAL SCHOOL GOVERNORS *v.* ALIE [1987] I.C.R. 406, E.A.T.

1398. Unfair dismissal—failure to consult prior to dismissal for redundancy—whether making any difference—whether distinction between reason for and manner of dismissal

[Employment Protection (Consolidation) Act 1978 (c.44), s.57(3).]

There is a crucial distinction between the reason for, and the manner of, an employee's dismissal, so that an Industrial Tribunal is entitled and bound to investigate the effect of any non-compliance with procedures by the employers.

P was made redundant with no prior warning and without any consultation by the employer. He claimed that he had been unfairly dismissed. The tribunal concluded, however, that consultation would have made no difference at all to the eventual outcome, and dismissed P's claim.

Held, that what mattered was whether the employer had acted reasonably in treating redundancy as a ground for dismissal. In determining that question there was a vital distinction between the manner in which the employee was made redundant, and the real reason therefor. Thus an Industrial Tribunal was obliged to enquire into the effect of any procedural errors by the employer (*British Labour Pump Co.* v. *Byrne* [1979] C.L.Y. 993 and *Wass (W. & J.)* v. *Binns* [1982] C.L.Y. 1112 applied).

POLKEY *v.* DAYTON (A. E.) SERVICES [1987] 1 All E.R. 984, C.A.

1399. Unfair dismissal—fullness of industrial tribunal's decision—requirements

[Industrial Tribunals (Rules of Procedure) Regulations, r.9(2).]

M, who had been employed by the Council as a driver, was dismissed on the grounds that he had broken the council's rules relating to possession of building materials and using the vehicles for his own purposes. Following the tribunal's decision that he had been unfairly dismissed, the E.A.T. held that the decision was flawed since it did not make a "factual determination which would have enabled the parties to know what it was that they could or should have done". The E.A.T. remitted the case. M appealed.

Held, dismissing the appeal, that the E.A.T. had correctly held that the tribunal's decision was flawed. A tribunal's decision should outline the evidence given and indicate the tribunal's factual findings and contain a statement of the reasons leading to the tribunal's conclusion. An appellate court should be able to determine from the decision whether a question of law arose. The tribunal's decision in this instance had given no account of the evidence presented nor the reason for the decision and did not provide the basic minimum of information required.

MEEK *v.* CITY OF BIRMINGHAM DISTRICT COUNCIL [1987] I.R.L.R. 250, C.A.

1400. Unfair dismissal—group of employees—dishonestly

Where one or more or possibly all of a group of employees is being seriously dishonest or incompetent, the employer is entitled to dismiss all of them if a proper investigation has been made but no individual identification can be made, and if the act or omission justifies dismissal, and if each member of the group could have committed the act or omission.

WHITBREAD & CO. *v.* THOMAS (1987) 84 L.S.Gaz. 3500, E.A.T.

1401. Unfair dismissal—industrial tribunal procedure—joint hearing—tribunals' discretion

[Industrial Tribunals (Rules of Procedure) Regulations 1985 (S.I. 1985 No. 16), reg. 18.]

D and W, who were social workers, were both dismissed following an enquiry in the Jasmine Beckford case, in which they were involved. Both brought claims of unfair dismissal and the tribunal chairman decided to hear their cases together under reg. 15 of the 1985 Regulations. D & W contended that a joint hearing would be prejudicial because the answer one of them might give under cross examination at a joint hearing could be used against the other. The E.A.T. rejected their argument. D and W appealed.

Held, dismissing the appeal, that reg. 15 gave discretion to a tribunal chairman to decide whether two applications should be heard together. The exercise of that discretion could only be the subject of appeal if it could be established that the chairman had improperly taken some matter into account or failed to take into account a relevant matter, or that his decision was perverse. It was not accepted that a joint hearing would necessarily be prejudicial and justice would be seen to be done if the cases were heard together and blame, if any, was duly apportioned.

DIETMANN *v.* LONDON BOROUGH OF BRENT; WAHLSTROM *v.* SAME [1987] I.R.L.R. 146, C.A.

1402. Unfair dismissal—interim relief—revocation of interim order

[Employment Protection (Consolidation) Act 1978 (c.44), ss.58, 77, 79(1).]

An application to an industrial tribunal to revoke an interim relief order may be made to a different tribunal to that which made the interim order.

NATIONAL COAL BOARD *v.* McGINTY (1987) 84 L.S.Gaz., 2455, E.A.T.

1403. Unfair dismissal—liability of employer—parties settling terms of compensation—whether further award precluded

Any agreement which purports to preclude an employee from bringing proceedings for compensation is void by reason of s.140(1) of the 1978 Act.

The employee was held to have been unfairly dismissed, but the question of remedy was postponed. Prior to the adjourned hearing the parties agreed a sum in full settlement. The tribunal found the agreement void, but held that it was not equitable that the employee should receive further compensation, although his loss exceeded the settlement.

Held, dismissing the appeals, that the agreement was void by reason of s.140(1); in the circumstances it was not equitable within the meaning of s.74 to make a further award.

COURAGE TAKE HOME TRADE *v.* KEYS [1986] I.C.R. 874, E.A.T.

1404. Unfair dismissal—"lock-out"—construction of statute

[Employment Protection (Consolidation) Act 1978 (c.44), s.62, Sched. 13, para. 24; Industrial Relations Act 1971 (c.72), s.167.]

The meaning of the word "lock-out" was a matter of mixed fact and law or of fact only; construction could be assisted by other means, but a number of factors had to be considered in any given situation to ascertain whether there was a lock-out, including why the employer refused to allow his employees to work (*Att.-Gen.* v. *Lamplough* (1878) 3 Ex.D. 214 considered).

EXPRESS & STAR *v.* BUNDAY, *The Times*, July 28, 1987, C.A.

1405. Unfair dismissal—"lock-out"—relevant employees—jurisdiction of industrial tribunal

[Employment Protection (Consolidation) Act 1978 (c.44), S.62(4)(6) (as amended by Employment Act 1982 (c.46), s.9, Sched. 3, para. 18).]

The test of who were "relevant employees" within s.62(4)(*b*)(i) of the Employment Protection (Consolidation) Act 1978 was a retrospective one, and the tribunal had to consider who were the employees directly interested at the date of the lock-out.

The employers, who were haulage contractors, in an attempt to tighten working practices in relation to their drivers, unilaterally varied their employee's terms of employment. The employees objected and on October 18, 1985, the employers, believing that industrial action was due to take place, gave notice that the company would cease to operate. On October 22, they wrote to the employees telling them to return to work by October 24. Some, but not all, returned and on October 24, the employers wrote again requiring the employees, including the applicants, to return the following day or be dismissed. The applicants failed to return and were dismissed.

The applicants complained of unfair dismissal, and the industrial tribunal found that there had been no threat of industrial action and that the employers had conducted a lock-out; that "relevant employees' " as defined by s.62(4)(*b*)(i) of the 1978 Act had not been dismissed; and they had jurisdiction to hear the claims.

Held, dismissing the employers' appeal, that it was clear from the language of s.62(4)(*b*)(i) that the test of who were "relevant employees" was retrospective. The tribunal had to consider who were the employees directly interested to the dispute on October 18, the date of the lock-out. Those who had returned to work by October 25 and not been dismissed were still directly interested by reason of having been locked-out initially. Since there were "relevant employees" who had not been dismissed, the tribunal had jurisdiciton to hear the applicants' claim of unfair dismissal (*Fisher* v. *York Trailer Co.* [1979] C.L.Y. 1025 referred to).

CAMPEY (H.) & SONS *v.* BELLWOOD [1987] I.C.R. 311, E.A.T.

1406. Unfair dismissal—proposal to leave trade union—conduct—contributory fault

[Employment Protection (Consolidation) Act 1978 (c.44) (as amended), ss.58(1)(*c*), 74(6).]

The respondent was a member of the Transport and General Workers Union which effectively ran a closed shop. The respondent made it clear that he would leave the union unless certain changes occurred. He was subsequently dismissed, ostensibly under the grounds of conduct, for an offence involving the sum of 20p. The Industrial Tribunal found that he had been unfairly dismissed under s.58(1)(*c*) but reduced the damages by 15 per cent. for contributory fault.

Held, dismissing the appeal, that the words "proposed to refuse to remain a member" in s.58(1)(*c*) included a conditional proposal, as the respondent's intention was clear. The dismissal was therefore unfair. The Industrial Tribunal had erred in reducing the respondent's damages, as it had been established that the ostensible reason given for the dismissal was merely a sham.

CROSVILLE MOTOR SERVICES *v.* ASHFIELD [1986] I.R.L.R. 475, E.A.T.

1407. Unfair dismissal—reasonableness—duty to make reasonable enquiries

The duty to make reasonable enquiries before dismissing is not abrogated by the circumstances of a widespread strike.

In the course of a disagreement during a miners' strike M assaulted another miner. The colliery manager decided that M should be dismissed if he were convicted of assault but not if he were acquitted. M pleaded guilty and was dismissed. On M's complaint of unfair dismissal, the industrial tribunal found that the general principle that an employer ought to make reasonable enquiries before dismissing did not apply to this case in the special circumstances of the miners' strike.

Held, on appeal, that the employers were not entitled to rely on the circumstances of a widespread strike to enable them to omit to enquire into the case before dismissing. Accordingly the case would be remitted for further consideration (*West Midlands Co-operative Society* v. *Tipton* [1986] C.L.Y. 1285 applied).

McLAREN *v.* NATIONAL COAL BOARD [1987] I.C.R. 410, E.A.T.

1408. Unfair dismissal—reasons for dismissal—one reason not established—whether dismissal unfair

[Employment Protection (Consolidation) Act 1978 (c.44), ss.57(1)(*a*), 57(2)(*a*), 57(3).]

S was dismissed by the council following the recommendation of a special committee who had considered the various complaints against him. The conclusions reached by the committee were unanimous and were set out in a letter of dismissal, although the recommendation to dismiss was a majority one. The tribunal dismissed S's claim for unfair dismissal, although they found that one reason contained in the dismissal letter had not been established. The E.A.T. dismissed an appeal. The Court of Session allowed an appeal on the grounds that the committee had wrongly taken into consideration the reason which was found not to have been sufficiently established and that if they had not done so, their decision may have been different. The council appealed.

Held, dismissing the appeal, that the Court of Session had correctly held that the tribunal had erred in law by finding that the dismissal was fair in circumstances where one of the grounds for dismissal was found not to have been established in evidence. If it is found that an apparent reason for dismissal has not been established, it is not possible as a matter of law for such a reason to be found to be a sufficient reason for dismissal. The Council had not shown that the unestablished allegation had not formed part of their reason for dismissal, and therefore the tribunal had erred in law in finding the dismissal to be fair.

SMITH *v.* CITY OF GLASGOW DISTRICT COUNCIL [1987] I.R.L.R. 326, H.L.

1409. Unfair dismissal—redundancy—pregnancy—selection for redundancy—reasonableness of basis of selection

[Employment Protection (Consolidation) Act 1978 (c.44), ss.57(1), 57(2)(c), 59, 61.]

B was employed as a supervisor of the youth training scheme. Following the withdrawal of funding for all existing posts, the council informed B that her employment would be terminated. At the same time three vacancies had arisen under a revised scheme which was to last for one year. B who was pregnant applied for the vacant positions but the Council's personnel officer did not offer her a position on the basis that she would require maternity leave and would be unable to fulfil the contract. B was dismissed by reason of redundancy. The tribunal held that the dismissal was unfair. The E.A.T. allowed an appeal, holding that the council had followed their selection criteria for redundancy and the dismissal was therefore fair. B appealed.

Held, dismissing the appeal, that the E.A.T. had been correct in holding that B had not been dismissed contrary to s.60 because of her pregnancy or a reason connected with it, merely because she had not been offered the alternative post. If an employee is selected for redundancy because she is pregnant where there is a genuine redundancy situation and this is in accordance with the selection criteria, then redundancy is the principal reason for dismissal. In order to determine whether the dismissal is fair, the provisions of s.57 rather than s.60 should therefore be applied.

BROWN *v.* STOCKTON-ON-TEES BOROUGH COUNCIL [1987] I.R.L.R. 230, C.A.

1410. Unfair dismissal—redundancy—refusal of employer to permit employee to work for a trial period in alternative employment offered

It was unreasonable for an employer to refuse to allow a redundant employee to work for a trial period in the alternative employment offered to him.

E was employed as a cutting room manager by the employers at one of their two factories. The employers decided to close that factory, thereby making E redundant. E had been employed by the employers for some 30 years. The cutting room manager in the remaining factory was less senior than E. E was offered alternative employment at the remaining factory under that cutting room manager at the same salary but without the benefit of a company car. E asked the employers to allow him to work in the new job for a four-week trial period. The employers refused to allow E a trial period. E complained that he had been unfairly dismissed. Pursuant to s.84(3) of the Employment Protection (Consolidation) Act 1978 the employers were legally bound to allow E a four-week trial period. The tribunal held that both parties acted under a mutual mistake of law in presuming that E was not entitled to a trial period. The tribunal decided that the dismissal was not unfair given that E must be presumed to know the law, *viz.* that he was entitled to a trial period notwithstanding the employers' purported refusal.

Held, allowing E's appeal, that the tribunal misdirected itself in law. It was senseless to presume that employees were familiar with complex legislation. The tribunal were bound to consider whether the terms of employment offered to E were reasonable without regard to the questions of whether each and every term was binding in law. The tribunal failed so to do. The refusal to allow E a trial period was unreasonable having regard to the fact that he would be required to work under the supervision of a more junior employee. The acceptability of the alternative employment was very much dependent on the relationship established between E and the other cutting room manager. In addition the refusal to allow E a trial period was likely to lead to confusion in E's mind as to his rights under the legislation.

ELLIOT *v.* STUMP (RICHARD) [1987] I.C.R. 579, E.A.T

1411. Unfair dismissal—reinstatement—practicability—contribution towards dismissal

[Employment Protection (Consolidation) Act 1978 (c.44), s.69(5)(*c*).]

Section 69(5)(*c*) of the Employment Protection (Consolidation) Act 1978 providing that the tribunal must consider whether it is just to order reinstatement where the complainant caused or contributed to some extent to his dismissal is to be applied in the same way as s.74(6) of the Act which provides for a reduction of compensation in similar circumstances.

L was employed as a shift chemist in a relatively senior and responsible position by B. A was L's immediate superior. A's superior was Dr. P, director of chemical productions. L was dismissed for misconduct involving the theft of a packet of Sweetex. L complained to an industrial tribunal alleging unfair dismissal and seeking reinstatement. L contended that he had absent-mindedly put the Sweetex in his pocket. The tribunal found L had been unfairly dismissed. B objected to reinstatement on the ground that other employees were convinced of L's guilt and his position would therefore be untenable. The tribunal found that Dr. P was convinced that L was guilty and nothing would persuade him otherwise and that he did not think B should deal with the matter so as to ensure that no stigma attached to L. Whilst not expressly referring to s.69(5) of the Act the tribunal held there was no convincing evidence of impracticability and ordered L's reinstatement.

Held, dismissing B's appeal, that the case was heard by an experienced tribunal and it was clear from their decision that they had the requirements of s.69(5) in mind although the section was not expressly referred to. Dr. P's contact with L was very limited. The tribunal's finding was in effect that notwithstanding Dr. P's views of L which might give rise to difficulties Dr P's views did not make it impracticable for L to be reinstated. That finding was not open to criticism. The requirement to consider whether reinstatement was just where the complainant caused or contributed to some extent to his dismissal set out in s.69(5)(*c*) was to be construed and applied in the same way as s.74(6) which provides for a reduction in compensation where the complainant has caused or contributed to his dismissal. The fact that forgetfulness or stress was the cause of L putting the Sweetex in his pocket was not something that fell to be considered as a cause or contribution by L to his dismissal.

BOOTS CO. *v.* LEES-COLLIER [1986] I.C.R. 728, E.A.T.

1412. Unfair dismissal—repudiatory conduct—entitlement to annual pay rise—implied term

There is no general principle that there is an implied obligation on an employer to pay regular pay increases.

In May 1985 the employee resigned because she failed to receive a pay increase having received one for each of the previous 10 years. Her complaint of unfair dismissal was upheld by an industrial tribunal on the ground that the employers were in breach of their contract of employment by excluding her from a general pay increase without previous warning. They held that there was an implied term that she would be given an annual increase, and that the employers had repudiated her contract of employment, so that she was entitled to treat herself as constructively dismissed, and that her dismissal was unfair.

Held, allowing the employers' appeal, that there was no general principle that an implied term to provide regular pay increases should be read into a contract of employment. The tribunal had erred in law in so holding. Even if there was an implied term that an employer would not treat an employee arbitrarily, capriciously, or inequitably in matters of pay, the tribunal had failed to consider the matter. If they had they would have concluded that the employers had not so acted. She had not been unfairly dismissed. (*Robinson* v. *Crompton Parkinson* [1978] C.L.Y. 892 and *Gardner (F.C.)* v. *Beresford* [1978] C.L.Y. 897 considered).

MURCO PETROLEUM *v.* FORGE [1987] I.C.R. 282, E.A.T.

1413. Unfair dismissal—repudiatory conduct—transfer of employee—refusal to belong to trade union—no closed shop

On a complaint of unfair dismissal an industrial tribunal had to consider whether an employer's conduct was unreasonable and whether it amounted to repudiatory breach of an employee's contract of employment. Whether a term could be implied that an employee might be transferred to another place of work was a question of fact in each case.

In July 1985 the employee who had worked at a transport depot for 12 years, eased to be a member of the T.G.W.U. As a result the rest of the workforce threatened industrial action. There was no closed shop. The employers asked him to move to another depot a mile away but he refused and resigned. He complained of unfair dismissal. The tribunal found that there was no union membership agreement and he was not obliged to belong to a union. It held that it would be unreasonable in the circumstances to require him to move elsewhere and that he was entitled to refuse to go. It held that the employers were in fundamental breach of the contract of employment, that he was constructively dismissed, and that the dismissal was unfair.

Held, dismissing the employers' appeal by a majority, that the reasonableness or otherwise of an employer's behaviour could indicate either the presence or absence of a repudiatory breach. Unreasonable behaviour did not necessarily result in a breach of a fundamental contractual term but the tribunal had correctly directed themselves both whether the employers' conduct was unreasonable and whether it amounted to a repudiatory breach of the employee's contract of employment. Whether a term was to be implied in a contract empowering the employer to transfer the employee to a different place of work was a question of fact in each case. The tribunal had applied the correct test that there was no implied term in this case (*O'Brien* v. *Associated Fire Alarms* [1969] C.L.Y. 1424 considered).

COURTAULDS NORTHERN SPINNING *v.* SIBSON [1987] I.C.R., 329, E.A.T.

1414. Unfair dismissal—restructuring

[Employment Protection (Consolidation) Act 1978 (c.44), s.57(1), (3).]

When a tribunal has decided that an employer has fulfilled the requirement of s.57(1) of the Employment Protection (Consolidation) Act 1978 that there was a substantial reason to justify dismissal, it then has to ascertain whether, under subs. (3), the dismissal was fair or unfair. Where the employer has decided to get rid of an employee, and makes restructuring the pretext for this, the dismissal will be unfair.

LABOUR PARTY *v.* OAKLEY, *The Daily Telegraph,* October 30, 1987, C.A.

1415. Unfair dismissal—retirement—"normal retiring age"—statistical approach

[Employment Protection (Consolidation) Act 1978 (c.44), s.64(1)(*b*).]

Athough retention may be a matter of discretion for the employers, the tribunal should assess an employee's reasonable expectation objectively having regard to both the contractual and statistical situation.

E, the employee, was employed by D Co. under a contract of employment which provided for retirement at the age of 60. D Co., who normally retained employees beyond that age, dismissed E when he was 63 on the grounds of health. When E complained of unfair dismissal the tribunal held that it had no jurisdiction since E had reached normal retiring age under s.64(1)(*b*) of the Employment Protection (Consolidation) Act 1978. In reaching that decision the tribunal declined to adopt the statistical approach to the fact that a considerable proportion of employees were retained until 65, on the ground that retention was in the discretion of D Co.

Held, allowing the appeal, that nevertheless, in conjunction with considering the contractual situation, the tribunal was bound also to consider the statistical situation. The correct conclusion was that the normal retiring age was 65, and the complaint of unfair dismissal would be remitted for consideration (*Waite* v. *Government Communications Headquarters* [1983] C.L.Y. 1327 applied; dictum of Lawton L.J. in *Post Office* v. *Wallser* [1981] C.L.Y. 965 not applied).

MAULDON *v.* BRITISH TELECOMMUNICATIONS [1987] I.C.R. 450, E.A.T.

1416. Unfair dismissal—transfer of trade or business

[Transfer of Undertakings (Protection of Employment) Regulations 1981 (S.I. 1981 No. 1794), regs. 5, 8.]

W was given a month's notice of her dismissal from employment in a shop, which was being sold. The date of dismissal was after exchange of contracts but before completion.

Held, on her complaint of unfair dismissal, allowing the appeal, that reg.5(3) of the 1981 Regulations applied where the contract was subsisting at the date of the transfer, which was the date of completion. The achievement of the agreement for sale was not an "economic" reason for dismissal within reg. 8(2) so reg. 8(1) applied to make the dismissal unfair (*Secretary of State for Employment* v. *Spence* [1986] C.L.Y. 1237 applied; *Kestongate* v. *Miller* [1986] C.L.Y. 1287 considered; *Anderson* v. *Dalkeith Engineering* [1985] C.L.Y. 1263 not followed).

WHEELER *v.* PATEL [1987] I.C.R. 631, E.A.T.

1417. Unfair dismissal—Transfer of Undertaking Regulations—construction of "commercial venture"—charitable status of school

[Transfer of Undertaking (Protection of Employment) Regulations 1981 (S.I. 1981 No. 1974), reg. 2(1).]

The appellants were teachers at the Friends School which had charitable status and was run by a religious denomination with the aim of breaking even rather than making a profit. It was decided to close the school and the appellants were given notice. An agreement was subsequently made to sell the school to the second respondents. The tribunal held as a preliminary point that the proper respondents were the vendors of the school rather than the purchasers as the transfer did not fall within the 1981 Regulations. The E.A.T. upheld the decision and the appellants appealed to the Court of Appeal.

Held, dismissing the appeal, that the tribunal and the E.A.T. had correctly held that the school was not an undertaking to which the Transfer of Undertaking Regulations applied, as it was not "within the nature of a commercial venture." It was not possible to provide a conclusive list of operations which could be described as "commercial ventures" but the dictionary definition of "commercial" as being "interested in financial return rather than artistry" gave an indication of its meaning. Furthermore, the question of whether an operation was a commercial venture was one of fact. Therefore a tribunal's finding on this point could only be the subject of an appeal if it could be established that such a finding was one which no reasonable tribunal would reach.

WOODCOCK *v.* COMMITTEE FOR THE TIME BEING OF THE FRIENDS SCHOOL, WIGTON AND GENWISE [1987] I.R.L.R. 98, C.A.

1418. Wages councils

UNLICENSED PLACE OF REFRESHMENT WAGES COUNCIL (VARIATION) ORDER 1987 (No. 801) [85p], made under the Wages Act 1986 (c.48), s.13(1); operative on June 13, 1987; excludes from the scope of the said Wages Council workers employed in a central catering establishment, employed by a local authority, and employed in an industrial or staff canteen.

WAGES COUNCILS (MEETINGS AND PROCEDURE) REGULATIONS 1987 (No. 862) [45p], made under the Wages Act 1986, s.25, Sched. 2, para. 7; operative on June 4, 1987; prescribes procedures which are to apply to meetings of wages councils.

WAGES COUNCILS (NOTICES) REGULATIONS 1987 (No. 863) [85p], made under the Wages Act 1986, ss.19(2)(3), 25, Sched. 3, paras. 1, 2; operative on June 4, 1987; require a wages council proposing to make an order under the 1986 Act to publish notice of their proposals.

WAGES COUNCILS (NOTICES) (No. 2) REGULATIONS 1987 (No. 1852) [85p], made under the Wages Act 1986, ss.19(2)(3), 25, Sched. 3, paras. 1, 2; operative on November 25, 1987; require wages councils proposing to make an order under the 1986 Act to publish a notice of those proposals and prescribes the matters which must be contained in such a notice.

1419. Wrongful dismissal—breach of contract—summary dismissal

A panel of inquiry reported to the defendant council gross negligence on the part of D, one of their social workers. D's contract of employment provided for instant dismissal for gross misconduct, which was defined in terms of various criminal and quasi-criminal acts. D was summarily dismissed, and claimed damages for wrongful dismissal, a declaration that the dismissal was void and an injunction restraining the council from acting upon it.

Held, that (1) D's conduct did not constitute gross misconduct within the terms of the contract. She was entitled to a fair hearing, and the summary dismissal was a repudiatory breach; (2) D was not entitled to an injunction since she had accepted the repudiation; (3) D was entitled to damages for wrongful dismissal from repudiation until the date when the contract could lawfully have been terminated, plus a reasonable period for a disciplinary hearing. (Dicta in *Marshall (Thomas) (Exports)* v. *Guinle* [1978] C.L.Y. 916, *Gunton* v. *Richmond-upon-Thames London Borough Council* [1980] C.L.Y. 895 and *London Transport Executive* v. *Clarke* [1981] C.L.Y. 941 applied).

DIETMAN *v.* BRENT LONDON BOROUGH COUNCIL [1987] I.C.R. 737, Hodgson J.

EQUITY AND TRUSTS

1420. Charging order—real property—claim that resulting trust defeated charging order.
See BARCLAYS BANK *v.* FORRESTER, §2537.

1421. Chevening Estate Act 1987 (c.20)

This Act establishes an incorporated board of trustees of the trusts contained in the trust instrument set out in the Schedule to the Chevening Estate Act 1959. The 1987 Act confers functions on, and transfers property, rights and liabilities to, the board. The trust instrument is amended.

The Act received the Royal Assent on May 15, 1987, and comes into force on a day to be appointed.

1422. Chevening Estate Act 1987—commencement

CHEVENING ESTATE ACT 1987 (COMMENCEMENT) ORDER 1987 (No. 1254 (C.38)) [45p], made under the Chevening Estate Act 1987 (c.20), s.5(2); brings the 1987 Act into force on September 1, 1987.

1423. Constructive trust—bank security—artificial transaction

Debts charged by a creditor as security for an overdraft are held on constructive trust for the bank when paid into an account elsewhere.

In 1982 a number of companies controlled by one individual entered into a group debenture in favour of Barclays to secure their indebtedness. Some of them, the "farm companies" executed mortgages in favour of "International", another of that same individual's companies. On the same day, International executed sub-mortgages under those mortgages in favour of Barclays. Also in existence was a complicated scheme for the transfer of funds from a Ghana company also controlled by the same person; the purpose of which was to use money's from the Ghana company, already charged to Barclays, to redeem International's sub-mortgages of the farm companies' land and stock. The question arose as to whether the farm companies who received the money from International held the money on constructive trust for the bank.

Held, allowing the appeal, that debts charged by a creditor to his bank as security for an overdraft are held on constructive trust for the bank when paid into his account elsewhere and cannot be used (artificially) to redeem sub-mortgages executed by him as additional security.

BARCLAYS BANK *v.* WILLOWBROOK INTERNATIONAL [1987] 1 FTLR 386, C.A.

1424. Discretionary trust—appointment of capital—whether income. See STEVENSON (INSPECTOR OF TAXES) *v.* WISHART, §2035.

1425. Duty of trustee—whether beneficiaries under a trust have a right of action for breach of trust against secondary trustees

Beneficiaries under a trust have no right of action for breach of trust against secondary trustees holding property in trust for the trustees of the primary trust.

T made a will in Hong Kong of which the Hong Kong bank was executor and trustee, by which the residue of his property outside the U.S. was to be held on trust for sale with power to postpone sale for Citibank to hold upon the trusts of T's American will. The American will, of which Citibank was trustee and executor, applied to all T's American estate and all property which thereafter should become added. The U.S. will provided that Citibank should be relieved of any responsibility to the U.S. beneficiaries in respect of a house in Hong Kong included in the residuary Hong Kong estate. Citibank instructed the Hong Kong bank to postpone sale even though that was against the interests of the U.S. beneficiaries. Sale was postponed and the value of the house fell. The U.S. beneficiaries claimed against the Hong Kong bank for breach of trust.

Held, that the Hong Kong bank held the house on trust not for the U.S. beneficiaries but for Citibank. Citibank were entitled under the will to disregard the interests of the U.S. beneficiaries, and there had been no breach of trust.

HAYIM *v.* CITIBANK N.A. [1987] 3 W.L.R. 83, P.C.

1426. Gifts—perfection of incomplete gifts—verbal gift of land—whether improvement by donee

[Can.] The parties were brothers. Their father purchased under an agreement for sale some land, which he offered to give to the plaintiff on condition that he paid the taxes. P moved onto the property, farmed the land, paid the taxes and broke and cleared some 30 to 40 acres. His father moved off the land, indicated to others that he had given it to P and stated in his will that P had already received his equal share of the estate. During his lifetime the father was unable to obtain title to the land and, after his death, title was transferred to D, as executor. It was found that P's substantial improvements had perfected the verbal gift.

Held, that the gift was binding and should be enforced (*Dillwyn* v. *Llewelyn* [1861–73] All E.R. Rep. 384 and *Ramsden* v. *Dyson* (1866) L.R. 1. H.L. 129 referred to).

McCORMICK *v.* McCORMICK [1987] 3 W.W.R. 286, Saskatchewan C.A.

1427. Insurance premiums paid by customers and banked—creditors' voluntary winding up—whether trust of the premiums created

Certainty of words is required before a company can be said to constitute itself a trustee of monies for the benefit of one class of creditor, to the exclusion of the general body of creditors.

MG operated a scheme providing insurance cover after the end of manufacturers' warranties on domestic appliances. V Ltd. collected the premiums for the scheme from its customers, and paid them over to MG. After V became concerned at the level of insurance cover MG had obtained, the monies representing the premiums paid were held in a special bank account. Subsequently it was agreed between MG and V that the monies in this account should be repaid to V; before this was done MG went into creditors' voluntary liquidation. V claimed that the payment of the premiums into a separate account meant that MG had constituted itself a trustee of them, for V's customers, alternatively that it would be dishonest or shabby for the liquidator to claim that they formed part of the company's property.

Held, dismissing the appeal, that (1) there was insufficient certainty of words to demonstrate that MG had constituted itself a trustee of the monies in the special bank account; (ii) there was no basis for asserting that the liquidator was acting dishonestly in claiming the monies for the general body of creditors.

MULTI GUARANTEE CO., *Re* [1987] BCLC 257, C.A.

1428. Irish Sailors and Soldiers Land Trust Act 1987 (c.48)

This Act provides for the distribution of the surplus funds of the Irish Sailors and Soldiers Land Trust, and makes provision for the winding up and dissolution of the trust.

The Act received the Royal Assent on May 15, 1987 and will come into force on a day to be appointed by the Secretary of State.

The Act extends to Northern Ireland.

1429. Irish Sailor and Soldiers Land Trust Act 1987—commencement

IRISH SAILORS AND SOLDIERS LAND TRUST ACT 1987 (COMMENCEMENT) ORDER 1987 (No. 1909 (c.57), [45p], made under the Irish Sailors and Soldiers Land Trust Act 1987 (c.48), s.3(2); brings the said Act into force on November 4, 1987.

1430. Loan to company—receiver appointed—whether loan held on resulting trust for lender. See EVTR, *Re,* §345.

1431. Public Trustee

PUBLIC TRUSTEE (AMENDMENT) RULES 1987 (No. 2249) [45p], made under the Public Trustee Act 1906 (c.55), s.14(1); operative on February 1, 1988; enable the Public Trustee to pay trust monies into court, for investment in an authorised manner.

PUBLIC TRUSTEE (CUSTODIAN TRUSTEE) RULES 1987 (No. 1891) [45p], made under the Public Trustee Act 1906, s.14(1); operative on January 1, 1988; amend S.R. & O. 1912 No. 348.

PUBLIC TRUSTEE (FEES) (AMENDMENT) ORDER 1987 (No. 403) [45p], made under the Public Trustee Act 1906, s.9; operative on April 1, 1987; amends S.I. 1985 No. 373.

1432. Recipient of trust property—whether recipient is a constructive trustee of trust property

It is unlikely that there could ever be imputed knowledge in relation to imposing a constructive trust.

In 1923 the future tenth Duke of Manchester assigned to trustees chattels to which he was absolutely entitled in remainder expectant on the death of his father, the ninth Duke, on trusts that the trustees should make inventories of such chattels as in their absolute discretion they should consider suitable for inclusion in the settlement and to hold the residue in trust for the tenth Duke absolutely. After the death of the ninth Duke, no inventory was made, and the trustees delivered certain of the chattels to the tenth Duke and many were sold. After the death of the tenth Duke the eleventh Duke claimed that the trustees had acted in breach of trust, and that as constructive trustee, so had the tenth Duke with the result that the Dowager Duchess now held the chattels as constructive trustee or as a volunteer.

Held, it was unlikely that knowledge could ever be imputed in relation to imposing a constructive trust. There was no reason why the Duke's solicitor's knowledge of the meaning of the clause allowing release of the chattels should be imputed to the Duke. Even if he had understood the clause, there was no evidence that he remembered it at the time of receiving the chattels. It could not be said that his conscience was affected and that there was a duty on him to make inquiry. Accordingly, although the trustees had transferred the chattels in breach of trust, the Duke had not received them as constructive trustee. (*Carl Zeiss Stiftung* v. *Smith (Herbert) & Co. (No. 2)* [1969] C.L.Y. 3367 applied; *Baden, Delvaux and Lecuit* v. *Société General pour Favoriser le Développement du Commerce et de l'Industrie en France S.A.* [1983] BCLC 325 considered).

MONTAGU'S SETTLEMENT TRUSTS, *Re;* DUKE OF MANCHESTER *v.* NATIONAL WESTMINSTER BANK [1987] 2 W.L.R. 1192, Sir Robert Megarry V.-C.

1433. Recognition of Trusts Act 1987 (c.14)

This Act enables the United Kingdom to ratify the Convention on the law applicable to trusts and on their recognition which was signed on behalf of United Kingdom on January 10, 1986.

The Act received the Royal Assent on April 9, 1987, and will come into force on such date as the Lord Chancellor and the Lord Advocate may appoint.

The Act extends to Northern Ireland.

1434. Recognition of Trusts Act 1987—commencement

RECOGNITION OF TRUSTS ACT 1987 (COMMENCEMENT) ORDER 1987 (No. 1177 (C.31)) [45p], made under the Recognition of Trusts Act 1987 (c.14), s.3(2); brings all provisions of the Act into force on August 1, 1987.

1435. Reverter of Sites Act 1987 (c.15)

This Act amends the law with respect to the reverter of sites that have ceased to be used for particular purposes.

The Act received the Royal Assent on April 9, 1987, and will come into force on such day as the Lord Chancellor shall appoint.

The Act extends to England and Wales only.

1436. Reverter of Sites Act—commencement

REVERTER OF SITES ACT 1987 (COMMENCEMENT) ORDER 1987 (No. 1260 (C.39)) [45p], made under the Reverter of Sites Act 1987 (c.15), s.9(2); brings the 1987 Act into force on August 17, 1987.

1437. Settlement—construction—class closing rules

The trustees of a settlement exercised a power of appointment by executing a deed by which they held the funds on trust for such of the settler's great-grandchildren as had attained the age of 18 by, or were alive on, the vesting day. The deed also provided that on "the closing date" those of the beneficiaries then alive would acquire an interest in possession in the fund. It was not unlikely that other great-grandchildren would be born but E, the oldest then alive, attained the age of 18 in 1986, well before either the vesting day or the closing date.

Held, on the trustees' summons for directions that the rule that the class closed on E's 18th birthday was rebutted if the terms of the trust instrument were inconsistent with the rule, which here it was (*Re Edmondson's Will Trusts* [1972] C.L.Y. 3159 applied; *Andrews* v. *Partington* (1791) 3 Bro. C.C. 401 distinguished).

TOM'S SETTLEMENT, *Re;* ROSE *v.* EVANS [1987] 1 W.L.R. 1021 Browne-Wilkinson V.-C.

1438. Settlement—power to appropriate revenue to meet depreciation of capital value—beneficiary entitled to whole free annual income—whether power administrative or dispositive—whether interest in possession. See MILLER *v.* I.R.C., §285.

1439. Trust for sale—property in joint names—express declaration of trust—valuation of interests—whether discretion as to date of valuation

The courts had no discretion to value the interests of beneficiaries under a trust for sale at any date other than the date upon which their interests were realised.

T and T lived together as man and wife although they were not in fact married. In 1972 they purchased a property in their joint names. The conveyance declared that they held the property on a trust for sale in trust for themselves as joint tenants beneficially. Mr. T provided £3,000 of the purchase price, the remainder being raised on a mortgage of the property. All mortgage payments were made by Mr. T. Their relationship broke down in August 1975 when Ms. T left the property. The mortgage was redeemed in December 1981. Notice of severance of the beneficial joint tenancy was served by Ms. T in September 1982. In August 1983 Ms T. issued on originating application in the Southampton County Court seeking an declaration that the property was held in trust for themselves as beneficial tenants in common in equal shares and an order for sale. The judge found for Ms. T and made an order for the sale of the property. The judge also held that the purpose of the trust ended when the parties separated in August 1975 and that Ms. T's half share was to be valued as at that date. On that basis, Ms. T's half share was worth about £2,750. If valued as at the date of the judgment, it was worth about £15,000. Ms. T appealed.

Held, allowing the appeal, that the interest of a beneficiary under a trust for sale gave rise to an absolute and indefeasible right to share in the proceeds of the sale. The beneficiary's interest could only be valued at the date it was realised. The court had no discretion to substitute any other date for that date. Accordingly, the judge erred in holding that Ms. T's interest was to be valued as at the date of the parties' separation. In any event, where there was an express declaration of their interests under the trust for sale, that declaration fixed their respective rights. The substitution of a date other than the date of sale for the purposes of valuing their shares could only operate in derogation of what was expressed in the conveyance. This could not be done (*Goodman* v. Gallant [1986] C.L.Y. 2037, *Walker* v. *Hall* [1984] C.L.Y. 1675 followed; *Hall* v. *Hall* [1981] C.L.Y. 996 disapproved).

TURTON *v.* TURTON [1987] 2 All E.R. 641, C.A.

1440. Trust income from abroad for non-resident beneficiaries—whether trustee liable to pay income tax. See DAWSON *v.* I.R.C., §2029.

ESTOPPEL

1441. Action estoppel—whether English proceedings stayed after foreign judgment

A foreign judgment is capable of giving rise to a cause of action estoppel, but only where the foreign judgment is a final judgment in which the matter has been finally disposed of in the foreign country.

C Co. was a Liberian company. K was a Greek shipowner who owned K Co. P, another Greek shipowner, controlled T group. K also controlled J Co. another Liberian company. K sought to restrain an action in England whereby C Co. sought to sue him as first defendant and X to enforce C Co.'s alleged rights to 75 shares in J Co. as assignee of the rights of X under a "trust deed" made between K and X. C Co. had taken proceedings in Greece against K seeking delivery of the shares. There was no law of trusts in Greek law. C Co. could have pleaded that the proper law was English law. C Co.'s Greek claim was dismissed on procedural grounds, and subsequent appeals were dismissed. K alleged that the Greek action could be revived; C Co. alleges that it could not. The English judge dismissed K's application for a stay.

Held, dismissing the appeal, that the evidence before the court did not establish that C Co. was no longer free to litigate its claim in Greece, and no abuse of the process had been established. The English court was the more convenient forum for determining questions of English trust law, and also C Co. had a legitimate juridical advantage in an English action, and there were no grounds for ordering a stay (*Carl Zeiss Stiftung* v. *Rayner & Keeler* [1966] C.L.Y. 1665 applied).

CHARM MARITIME INC. *v.* KYRIAKOU [1987] 1 FTLR 265, C.A.

1442. Agreement by foreign party—necessity for approval by foreign party's government—failure to obtain approval—whether estopped from denying the agreement

Where a foreign party fails to obtain the requisite approval of its government, but by its acts affirms an agreement that it has made, if a detriment has been suffered by the other contracting party, the foreign party is estopped from denying the agreement.

JANRED PROPERTIES *v.* ENTE NAZIONALE PER IL TURISMO (No. 2), *Financial Times,* May 22, 1987, C.A.

1443. Conduct—agreement "subject to contract"—substantial performance—formal documents not executed—whether company entitled to withdraw from agreement

An estoppel will not arise unless a party's actions are unfair, unjust or unconscionable so that where the evidence showed that one party expressly retained a right to resile from an agreement an estoppel will not arise.

An agreement in principle, "subject to contract" was reached between HK and HE to the effect that in exchange for acquiring 83 flats from HE, HK would grant a Crown lease of certain land, and a permission to develop. HK moved some civil servants into the flats, spending some money on them, and HE did some work on the land, the subject of the intended lease. HE withdrew from the agreement.

Held, on appeal, that HE were entitled to withdraw. On the evidence it was not shown by HK that HE had encouraged an expectation that it would not withdraw from the agreement. Notwithstanding that HK had acted to its detriment it had not been shown to be unjust, unconscionable, or unfair to allow HE to withdraw. Thus HE were entitled to withdraw from the agreement (*Salvation Army Trustee Co.* v. *West Yorkshire Metropolitan County Council* [1982] C.L.Y. 1149 distinguished).

ATT.-GEN. OF HONG KONG *v.* HUMPHREYS ESTATE (QUEEN'S GARDENS) [1987] 2 W.L.R. 343, P.C.

1444. Conduct—proprietary estoppel—belief in future rights

The principle of proprietary estoppel was not limited to acts done in reliance on a belief relating to an existing right but extended to acts done on a belief that future rights would be granted.

P's mother married the deceased when she was 15. P helped them run their business and was never paid, but understood that she would inherit the deceased's property when he died. In 1947 P's husband was offered a job with a tied house, but the deceased opposed that, purchasing instead for her future use a tenanted cottage with money largely provided by P's mother. She died in 1976, and the deceased moved into the cottage which had become vacant. There was a boundary dispute between the deceased and a neighbour in which P was told by the deceased to take advice from her own solicitors since the house belonged to her. P and her husband helped the deceased with the day to day running of the house, and she was told by him that she would lose nothing by it. A few days before his death he said to her that she was to have his house. He died intestate and P claimed a declaration against two of his nieces who were administrators *de bonis non* of his estate that she was absolutely and beneficially entitled to the house, the furniture, and other property. The declaration was granted. It was held that the principle of proprietary estoppel extended to acts done in reliance on a belief that future rights would be granted, and was not limited to acts done in reliance on a belief relating to an existing right. A proprietary estoppel could be raised in relation to the grant of rights over residuary estate. Accordingly, since P had established that she had acted to her detriment in reliance on her belief, encouraged by the deceased, that she would ultimately benefit by receiving his property on his death, she was absolutely and beneficially entitled to his residuary estate, including the house (*Greasley* v. *Cooke* [1980] C.L.Y. 1066; *Cleaver (decd.), Re* [1981] C.L.Y. 2889 and *Taylor Fashions* v. *Liverpool Victoria Friendly Society* [1979] C.L.Y. 1619 considered).

BASHAM (DEC'D.) *Re* [1986] 1 W.L.R. 1498, Edward Nugee Q.C. sitting as a High Court Judge.

1445. Contract to assign agricultural holding by agent—made without T's authority—whether T estopped from denying its effect

In the mistaken belief that he had the requisite authority, T's agent purported to contract with W for the assignment to W of T's agricultural holding. In fact, T had no intention of assigning the holding but, taking the view that it was for his agent to correct the mistake, he never informed W that the purported contract had been made without his authority, and W duly sold his own farm in reliance upon his expectation that completion would take place. When T failed to complete, W applied under R.S.C., Ord. 86, for summary judgment for specific performance of the contract to assign. The judge held that the contract had been made without T's authority, but that T had ratified it and was estopped from denying its existence.

Held, dismissing T's appeal, that (1) having regard to the fact that T had never wished to be bound by the contract, it was doubtful whether he could be said to have ratified it; however (2) he had represented by conduct to W that the contract was binding, and was estopped from denying that he was bound (*Spiro* v. *Lintern* [1973] C.L.Y. 399 applied).

WORBOYS *v.* CARTER (1987) 283 E.G. 307, C.A.

1446. Pre-incorporation contract—whether a valid contract—whether defendant company estopped from denying validity of contract. See ROVER INTERNATIONAL *v.* CANNON FILM SALES, §446.

1447. Property adjustment order—charge on matrimonial home—loan taken out fraudulently by wife—whether estoppel created by wife's conduct. See AINSCOUGH *v.* AINSCOUGH (CEDAR HOLDINGS INTERVENING), §1781.

1448. Proprietary estoppel—landlord and tenant—essential ingredients

The appellants had originally been tenants of the ground floor and back bedroom on the first floor of a house owned by the respondents. When the rest of the house became vacant, they moved into all of it. From that time onwards they expended some £30,000 in works of repair and improvement. The judge at first instance made an order for possession of the upper part of the house in favour of the respondent landlord.

Held, dismissing the appeal, that on the evidence the appellants could not establish that the expenditure which they had incurred had taken place in the belief that they would obtain an interest in the property, nor could it be said that the landlord had encouraged any such belief as he had no knowledge of it; accordingly the appellants had failed to establish the essential ingredients of a proprietary estoppel.

BRINNAND *v.* EWENS (1987) 19 H.L.R. 415, C.A.

1449. Representation by company—fictitious profits—whether liquidator estopped from denying profits ever made. See COMPANY LAW, §362.

1450. *Res judicata*—industrial tribunal—second tribunal hearing—similar facts—different finding. See MUNIR *v.* JANG PUBLICATIONS, §1342.

EUROPEAN COMMUNITIES

1451. Action for damages—admissibility—Commission

Krohn & Co. Import-Export GmbH & Co. KG ("Krohn") applied for import licences for manioc from Thailand in accordance with procedures under the EEC-Thailand Co-operation Agreement 1982 and the implementing Commission Regulation 2029/82, but was refused by the German intervention agency acting on the mandatory instructions of the European Commission. Krohn brought proceedings for damages against the Commission.

Held, that the action was admissible and should proceed on the merits. The Court rejected the argument that the German intervention agency should have been sued rather than the Commission, as the Court regarded the Commission as responsible for the alleged unlawful conduct which it had directed. The admissibility of the action was not dependent on the exhaustion of national remedies, nor were proceedings barred by reason of Krohn not challenging the last action of the Commission by proceedings for annulment under Art. 173(2) EEC.

KROHN & CO. IMPORT-EXPORT GmbH & CO. KG *v.* E.C. COMMISSION (No. 175/84) [1987] 1 C.M.L.R. 745, European Ct.

1452. Administrative error—withdrawal of Decision—whether valid

The European Commission made a Decision on April 7, 1982 by which it set the maximum amount of aid to the applicant Co-operative at 4,298,543,500 lira. The Commission adopted a further Decision on October 31, 1984, in identical terms, save that the maximum amount of aid was reduced to 3,343,181,208 lira. The applicant brought proceedings to annul the 1984 Decision on the basis that it purported to withdraw the 1982 Decision. The Commission explained that due to an administrative error the figure of 4,298,543,500 lira was incorrectly calculated and was wrongly entered in the 1982 Decision. Accordingly, it argued that it was entitled to withdraw it by its Decision in 1984.

Held, that the Decision of October 31, 1984, was void. An irregular administrative act was presumed to be valid until it had been annulled or properly withdrawn by the institution which had made it. As the internal rules relating to the calculation of such aid had not been published, no one, apart from Commission officials, could have known that the rules had been infringed and that annulment proceedings could have been brought. The purported withdrawal by the 1984 Decision was not valid, as withdrawal had to occur within a reasonable time and the Commission had to pay sufficient regard to the extent to which the applicant might have been led to rely on the lawfulness of the measure concerned. A delay of over two years before taking the 1984 Decision could not be regarded as reasonable, as the error could have been detected by the Commission within a couple of days of the notification of the 1982 Decision.

CONSORZIO COOPERATIVE D'ABBRUZZO *v.* E.C. COMMISSION (No. 15/85) *The Times,* March 23, 1987, European Ct.

1453. Agriculture—butter—reduced price of butter in intervention stores

The applicants, West German margarine manufacturers, brought proceedings for compensation in respect of damage which they allegedly suffered as a result of the "Christmas butter" scheme adopted and made subject to the rules fixed by European Commission Reg. 2956/84 on the disposal of butter at a reduced price. The Reg. established a "Christmas butter" scheme with the object of selling 200,000 tonnes of butter from EEC stores with a reduction in price of 1.6 ECU per kilogram.

The applicants argued that the "Christmas butter" scheme had led to market distortions which, contrary to Art. 39(1)(*c*) EEC, had disturbed the equilibrium between the two markets for butter and for margarine. They argued that they had thereby suffered damage as a result of the fact that the intervention butter was preferred, not only to fresh butter which had then to be taken into intervention, but also to margarine, a competing and substitutable product whose sales went down markedly during and after the "Christmas butter" campaign.

Held, dismissing the application, that the Commission had acted within its powers in adopting a scheme for the disposal at a reduced price of butter held in intervention stores and that scheme did not discriminate against producers of margarine.

LEBENSMITTELWERKE (WALTER RAU) *v.* EEC (REPRESENTED BY THE E.C. COMMISSION) (Joined Cases Nos. 279, 280, 285 and 286/84), *The Times,* March 23, 1987. European Ct.

1454. Agriculture—directives, decisions and regulations

Commission Regulation (EEC) No. 471/87 of February 16, 1987, amending Regulation (EEC) No. 798/80 laying down detailed rules on the advance payments of export refunds and positive monetary compensatory amounts in respect of agricultural products. (O.J. 1987 L48/10.)

Commission Regulation (EEC) No. 1302/87 of May 11, 1987 amending Regulation (EEC) No. 4129/86 as regards the amounts expressed in ECU. (O.J. 1987 L123/5.)

Commission Regulation (EEC) No. 2390/87 of August 3, 1987 amending Regulation (EEC) No. 3153/85 laying down detailed rules for the calculation of monetary compensatory amounts. (O.J. 1987 L218/22.)

Council Regulation (EEC) No. 822/87 of March 16, 1987 on the common organization of the market in wine. (O.J. 1987 L84/1.)

Council Regulation (EEC) No. 1889/87 of July 2, 1987 amending Regulation (EEC) No. 1677/85 as regards the rules for calculating monetary compensatory amounts in agriculture. July 2, 1987 (O.J. 1987 L182/1.)

Council Regulation (EEC) No. 3146/87 of October 19, 1987 amending Regulation (EEC) No. 822/87 on the common organization of the market in wine. (O.J. 1987 L300/4.)

1455. Agriculture—discrimination—milk powder

By various Regs., the European Commission allowed the intervention agencies to sell skimmed milk powder at reduced prices for feeding to pigs and poultry. Biovilac S.A. ("Biovilac") made feedingstuffs for piglets and poultry from whey, a waste product from cheese. Biovilac brought proceedings against the Commission claiming that the cut-price sale of milk powder was unfair competition and entitled it to damages under Art. 215(2) EEC.

Held, dismissing the action, that there was no discrimination against Biovilac under Arts. 39 and 40 EEC. In any event, Biovilac was facing ordinary commercial risks which it should have foreseen. EEC measures taken under the common organisation of an agricultural market did not deprive Biovilac of its property or of its freedom to use it in commerce.

BIOVILAC S.A. *v.* E.C. COMMISSION (No. 59/83) [1987] 2 C.M.L.R. 881, European Ct.

1456. Agriculture—exports—forfeiture of deposits

The plaintiffs had agreed to export to Sweden beef, which had been sold to them out of Irish intervention stocks. Some of that beef was stolen in England whilst it was awaiting trasportation to Sweden. The Irish Minister for Agriculture informed the plaintiffs that he would forfeit the export deposits in accordance with European Commission Reg. 2173/79 in proportion to the quantity not exported to Sweden. The plaintiffs sued for a declaration and to annul the Minister's decision. The Irish High Court asked the European Court under Art. 177 EEC for a preliminary ruling on the interpretation of Reg. 2173/79, on the defence of *force majeure* and on the principles of proportionality.

McNICHOLL (ANTHONY) *v.* MINISTER FOR AGRICULTURE [1987] 1 C.M.L.R. 847, Irish High Court.

1457. Agriculture—forfeiture of security—unfairness

On March 27, 1981, the German plaintiff made a purchase application under Commission Reg. 713/81 for some beef and veal held by intervention agencies and the plaintiff lodged its security. Adjustments to the central rates of the Community currencies came into effect within the E.M.S. as from March 23, 1981. The Council did not change the "green rates" (the representative rates to be applied in agriculture) for beef until April 6, 1981. This adjustment meant that the meat purchased by the plaintiff cost 349.67 D.M. per tonne more than if the plaintiff had made a purchase application after April 6, 1981. The plaintiff revoked its purchase application. The defendant forfeited the security on the ground that the plaintiff had not paid the monies it was obliged to pay as a result of its purchase application. The plaintiff brought proceedings in the Verwaltungsgericht to recover the security. That Court asked the European Court under Art. 177 EEC for a preliminary ruling.

Held, that (1) Council Reg. 850/81 amending Reg. 878/77 on the exchange rates applicable in agriculture did not imply that the Council intended to avoid a situation in which a purchaser, who before the adjustment of the green rates made an application to buy meat held in intervention whose price was set in advance in ECUs, had to pay a higher price in national currency than competitors who made their applications after the green rates were adjusted; (2) There was no general principle of EEC law that an EEC provision may not be applied by a national authority if it causes someone hardship which the EEC legislature would have tried to avoid if it had thought of that possibility when it adopted that provision. A national court which considers that there is such a case of hardship may ask the European Court under Art. 177 EEC for an interpretation of the EEC Provision in question or for a declaration that it is invalid, if it considers it necessary to give judgment; (3) Forfeiture of the security was not a disproportionate measure in the circumstances. EEC regulations gave the purchaser a choice. He could either lodge his purchase application and security, on the basis of the prevailing green rate, and run the risk that the rate would be adjusted to the advantage of those who submitted their applications after it was adjusted, or he could wait for it to be adjusted and run the risk that the stock might be exhausted by then. If, having made his choice, the purchaser refuses to accept the goods on the set terms of sale, it cannot be regarded as disproportionate to forfeit the security, when the purpose of the security was to ensure that those terms were met.

FIRMA KARL-HEINZ NEUMANN *v.* BUNDESANSTALT FÜR LANDWIRTSCHAFTLICHE MARKTORDNUNG (No. 299/84) [1987] 3 C.M.L.R. 4, European Ct.

1458. Agriculture—labelling—eggs

Mrs. Porter, an egg packer, was prosecuted by the Ministry of Agriculture for marketing one large pack of eggs whose labelling failed to comply with the provisions of Arts. 2(1) and 17 of Council Reg. 2772/75 contrary to Reg. 9(*d*) of the Eggs (Marketing Standards) Regs. 1973 (S.I. 1973 No. 15), as amended and s.2(2) of the European Communities Act 1972. The pack bore one label indicating that the week of packing was No. 37 and another label indicating the week of packing was No. 40. The magistrates dismissed the information against Mrs. Porter and the Ministry appealed.

Held, allowing the appeal, that Art. 17 required a packer to place a band or lable, which was clearly visible and legible indicating the correct packing week number. Art. 17 was infringed where a pack bore one correct label and another incorrect label, which indicated the wrong packing week.

MINISTRY OF AGRICULTURE, FISHERIES AND FOOD *v.* PORTER [1987] 3 C.M.L.R. 57, D.C.

1459. Agriculture—milk—pricing

The European Commission brought proceedings under Art. 169 EEC against the U.K. for authorising the Milk Marketing Boards to operate a certain dual pricing system and differential pricing system for whole milk. The European Commission maintained that such systems infringed Council Reg. 1422/78 and Commission Reg. 1565/79.

Held, that the U.K. had failed to fulfil the obligations under Art. 10 of Reg. 1422/78 and Art. 6 of Reg. 1565/79 by authorising the Milk Marketing Boards to operate: (i) a system of dual pricing for whole milk used for the manufacture of butter depending on whether it was to be sold as intervention or bulk butter or as package butter on the retail market; and (ii) differential pricing for whole milk used for the manufacture of butter and cream depending on whether the skimmed milk obtained in such manufacture was used as animal feed or processed into skimmed milk powder. This reduced the effectiveness of the EEC's scheme of aid for liquid skimmed milk used for animal feed.

MILK MARKETING BOARDS, *Re;* E.C. COMMISSION (SUPPORTED BY FRANCE, INTERVENER) *v.* U.K. (No. 23/84) [1987] 1 C.M.L.R. 607, European Ct.

1460. Agriculture—monetary compensatory amounts—*force majeure*

In January 1977, Denkavit France Sàrl ("Denkavit"), a French firm, exported to the U.K. animal feedingstuffs which entitled it to monetary compensatory amounts on importation into the U.K. A T5 form was completed. In April 1977 Denkavit informed the defendant French intervention agency that the original of the T5 control copy had not been returned to it. In November 1977 Denkavit sent the documents in its possession, including a letter from the U.K. customs authorities, stating that the T5 control copy had been lost, to the defendant with a view to being paid the monetary compensation amounts. In August 1978 Denkavit lodged equivalent British documents with the defendant together with an application for payment of monetary compensation amounts. The defendant refused payment stating that the application was out of time, being well after July 1977. The defendant relied on Art. 15 of Commission Reg. 1380/75 regarding the application of monetary compensation amounts. Art. 15 provided that "except in cases of *force majeure,* no claim for payment of a monetary compensation amounts shall be entertained unless the relevant documents are submitted within the six months following the day on which customs formalities were completed." Denkavit argued, *inter alia,* that (a) to bar its application on the ground that it had been submitted out of time was a penalty disproportionate to the objective pursued and Art. 15 of Reg. 1380/75 was thus invalid; (b) the application could not be regarded as having been submitted out of time since the loss of the T5 document by the customs authorities amounted to *force majeure*. The Tribunal Administratif Rouen, asked the European Court under Art. 177 EEC for a preliminary ruling on the validity and interpretation of Art. 15 of Reg. 1380/75.

Held, that (1) Art. 15 of Reg. 1380/75 was valid; (2) where a T5 control copy has not been returned, the person concerned may not raise *force majeure* if he failed to make an application before the expiry of the six-month period, for other documents to be regarded as equivalent pursuant to Art. 11(5) of Reg. 1380/75.

DENKAVIT FRANCE Sàrl *v.* FONDS D'ORIENTATION ET DE RÉGULARISATION DES MARCHÉS AGRICOLES (No. 266/84) [1987] 3 C.M.L.R. 202, European Ct.

1461. Agriculture—producer group—implementation of Regulation

The European Commission brought proceedings against Italy under Art. 169 EEC for a declaration that Italy had failed to fulfil its EEC obligations by not properly implementing Council Reg. 1360/78 of June 19, 1978 on agricultural producer groups and associations.

Held, that Italy had failed to meet its obligations under the EEC Treaty by (i) including among the conditions for granting and withdrawing recognition of producer groups covered by Reg. 1360/78 the requirement that such groups must carry on their commercial activities as representatives of their members; (ii) not adopting in some of its regions and in two of its provinces the measures necessary to fully comply with the Reg.

AGRICULTURAL PRODUCER GROUPS, *Re:* E.C. COMMISSION *v.* ITALY (No. 272/83) [1987] 2 C.M.L.R. 426, European Ct.

1462. Agriculture—production aids—money

U.K. brought proceedings under Art. 173(1) EEC for the annulment of European Commission Decisions 84/212/EEC and 84/213/EEC of February 8, 1984 on the clearance of the accounts presented by the U.K. in respect of the European Agricultural Guidance and Guarantee Fund (FEOGA). The Commission had refused to allow the U.K. to recover certain payment in respect of seed production aid for peas and field beans and skimmed-milk powder and butter.

Held, that (1) Decision 84/212/EEC and 84/213/EEC were void, in so far as the European Commission refused to charge to FEOGA, as expenditure arising from certain sales of skimmed-milk powder at reduced prices, the amount of £1,662 for the 1978 financial year and the amount of £71,946·92 for the 1979 year and, as regards sales of butter the amount of £586,571·56 for the 1979 financial year; (2) if the seed crop was used for animal feedingstuffs it could not qualify for production aid as seed and the U.K. was not entitled to recover such payments from FEOGA.

FEOGA ACCOUNTS, *Re:* U.K. *v.* E.C. COMMISSION (No.133/84) [1987] 1 C.M.L.R. 294, European Ct.

1463. Agriculture—sugar production levies—payment

EEC States were required by Regs. 700/73 and 2891/77 to collect from each sugar producer annually a production levy and to pay the proceeds to the EEC as part of the EEC's revenue by the 20th day of the 2nd month following the month in which the entitlement (i.e. assessment) had been established; entitlements were to be determined by December 31, 1981. Germany missed that date in 1980–81 and did not assess the entitlements until February 1, 1982; it subsequently paid the proceeds to the EEC by April 20. The European Commission brought proceedings against West Germany under Art. 169 EEC for failing to fulfil its obligations under the EEC Treaty.

Held, that West Germany had failed to meet its obligations under the EEC Treaty by failing to determine within the set period certain sugar production levies for the 1980–81 year, by failing to pay the proceeds to the E.C. Commission within the set period, and by refusing to pay interest on those arrears.

SUGAR TAX, *Re;* E.C. COMMISSION *v.* GERMANY (No. 303/84) [1987] 2 C.M.L.R. 867, European Ct.

1464. Agriculture—tenderers—*locus standi*—regulations

By Reg. 71/81 the European Commission required the Italian intervention agency (AIMA) to put up for sale by tender six lots of olive oil which had been in store for over two years. Sale by tender took place in accordance with the Reg. Successful tenderers were chosen on June 1, 1981. On August 3, 1981 the Commission sought to cancel the sale by means of two further Regs. (2238 and 2239/81) because the current olive oil season had been less productive than anticipated and the Commission was concerned that unfair profits might be made by the successful tenderers and that they might corner a share of the market to which they were not entitled. The successful tenderers sought annulment of Regs. 2238 and 2239/81.

Held, that (1) the tenderers had *locus standi* to sue as being directly and individually concerned by the Regs; (2) Regs. 2238 and 2239/81 were void on the basis that the only ground relied upon by the Commission to justify the repeal of Reg. 71/81 was vitiated by errors of fact.

AGRICOLA COMMERCIALE OLIO Srl *v.* E.C. COMMISSION (No. 232/81) [1987] 1 C.M.L.R. 363, European Ct.

1465. Agriculture—vines—premiums for abandonment of viticulture

Council Reg. 456/80 established a special scheme under which premiums are provided for the temporary or permanent abandonment of wine growing in certain areas. From 1982 many Italian wine growers, who had grubbed up their vines in order to get the premiums, complained to the European Commission about the delay in Italy paying the premiums. The Commission took proceedings against Italy in respect of this delay. The Italian Government maintained that it had agreed to the financing of the premiums, but that the various legislative procedures had not been completed due to the dissolution of Parliament.

Held, that Italy had failed to meet its obligations under Reg. 456/80 by delaying the payment of premiums due under that Regulation.

VINEYARD REDUCTIONS, *Re:* E.C. COMMISSION *v.* ITALY (No. 309/84) [1987] 2 C.M.L.R. 657, European Ct.

1466. Agriculture—wine

COMMON AGRICULTURE POLICY (WINE) REGULATIONS 1987 (No. 1843) [£2·60], made under the European Communities Act 1972 (c.68), s.2(2); operative on November 20, 1987; provide for the enforcement of specified EEC regulations concerned with the production and marketing of wine and related products.

1467. Anti-dumping duties—assessment

Allied Corps. and others (the applicants) brought annulment proceedings in respect of Council Regulation 101/83 of January 17, 1983 which imposed a definitive anti-dumping duty on certain chemical fertilisers originating in the USA.

Held, Reg. 101/83 was annulled as the Council had failed to take into account Art. 13 of Council Reg. 3017/79 in fixing the amount of the anti-dumping duties. According to Art. 13(3) of Reg. 3017/79, the amount of anti-dumping duties may not exceed the dumping margin and should be less if such lesser duty would be sufficient to remove the injury. It had not been shown that the anti-dumping duties imposed on the applicants were the minimum necessary to remove the injury.

ALLIED CORP. *v.* E.C. COUNCIL (No. 53/83) [1986] 3 C.M.L.R. 605, European Ct.

1468. Anti-dumping duties—calculation

Nippon Seiko ("Nippon") sought a declaration that Council Reg. 2089/84 of July 19, 1984, which imposed a definitive anti-dumping duty on imports of ball bearings with a maximum external diameter of not more than 30 millimetres originating in Japan and Singapore, was void in so far as it affected Nippon. Nippon argued, *inter alia,* that the method used thereunder for calculating the dumping margin was incompatible with Council Reg. 3017/79 of December 20, 1979, on protection against dumping from non-EEC countries.

Held, application dismissed. Arts. 2(13)(b) and (c) of Reg. 3017/79 set out various possible ways in which the dumping margin might be calculated, but did not impose any obligation that the methods chosen for calculating the normal value and the export price should be similar or identical. Contrary to Nippon's argument, Art. 2(9) of Reg. 3017/79 did not require the normal value and the export price to be calculated according to the same method.

NIPPON SEIKO *v.* COUNCIL OF THE EUROPEAN COMMUNITIES (No. 258/84), *The Times,* May 8, 1987, European Ct.

1469. Anti-dumping duties—reimbursement—procedure

The European Commission issued a Practice Note setting out guidelines regarding the application of Art. 16 of Council Regulation 2176/84 on the reimbursement of anti-dumping duties. These guidelines are also applicable to Art. 16 of Commission Decision 2177/84/ECSC.

PRACTICE NOTE: REIMBURSEMENT OF ANTI-DUMPING DUTIES [1986] 3 C.M.L.R. 633, E.C. Commission.

1470. Approximation—directives, decisions and regulations

86/609/EEC

Council Directive of November 24, 1986 on the approximation of laws, regulations and administrative provisions of the Member States regarding the protection of animals used for experimental and other scientific purposes. (O.J. 1986 L358/1.)

87/94/EEC:

Commission Directive of December 8, 1986 on the approximation of the laws of the Member States relating to procedures for the control of characteristics of, limits for and resistance to detonation of straight ammonium nitrate fertilizers of high nitrogen content. (O.J. 1987 L38/1.)

87/143/EEC:

Commission Directive of February 10, 1987 amending the first Directive 80/1335/EEC on the approximation of the laws of the Member States relating to methods of analysis necessary for checking the composition of cosmetic products. (O.J. 1987 L57/56.)

87/184/EEC:

Commission Directive of February 6, 1987 amending Annex II to Council Directive 72/276/EEC on the approximation of the laws of the Member States relating to certain methods for the quantitative analysis of binary textile fibre mixtures. (O.J. 1987 L75/21.)

87/252/EEC:

Commission Directive of April 7, 1987 adapting to technical progress Council Directive 84/538/EEC on the approximation of the laws of the Member States relating to the permissible sound power level of lawnmowers. (O.J. 1987 L117/22.)

87/308/EEC:

Commission Directive of June 2, 1987 adapting to technical progress Council Directive 76/889/EEC on the approximation of the laws of the Member States relating to radio interference caused by electrical household appliances, portable tools and similar equipment. (O.J. 1987 L155/24.)

87/310/EEC:

Commission Directive of June 3, 1987 adapting to technical progress Council Directive 76/890/EEC on the approximation of the laws of the Member States relating to the suppression of radio interference with regard to fluorescent lighting luminaries fitted with starters. (O.J. 1987 L155/27.)

87/566/EEC

Commission Directive amending Directive 77/535/EEC on the approximation of the laws of the Member States relating to methods of sampling and analysis for fertilizers. (O.J. 1987 L342/32.)

87/19/EEC:

Council Directive of December 22, 1986 amending Directive 75/318/EEC on the approximation of the laws of the Member States relating to analytical, pharmaco-toxicological and clinical standards and protocols in respect of the testing of proprietary medicinal products. (O.J. 1987 L15/31.)

87/20/EEC:

Council Directive of December 22, 1986 amending Directive 81/852/EEC on the approximation of the laws of the Member States relating to analytical, pharmaco-toxicological and clinical standards and protocols in respect of the testing of veterinary medicinal products. (O.J. 1987 L15/34.)

87/21/EEC:

Council Directive of December 22, 1986 amending Directive 65/65/EEC on the approximation of provisions laid down by law, regulation or administrative action relating to proprietary medicinal products. (O.J. 1987 L15/36.)

87/22/EEC:

Council Directive of December 22, 1986 on the approximation of national measures relating to the placing on the market of high-technology medicinal products, particularly those derived from biotechnology. (O.J. 1987 L15/38.)

87/55/EEC:

Council Directive of December 18, 1986 amending for the fourth time Directive 70/357/EEC on the approximation of the laws of the Member States concerning the antioxidants authorised for use in foodstuffs intended for human consumption. (O.J. 1987 L24/41.)

87/102/EEC:

Council Directive of December 22, 1986 for the approximation of the laws, regulations and administrative provisions of the Member States concerning consumer credit. (O.J. 1987 L42/48.)

87/164/EEC:
Council Directive of March 2, 1987 amending, on account of the accession of Spain, Directive 80/987/EEC on the approximation of the laws of the Member States relating to the protection of employees in the event of the insolvency of their employer. (O.J. 1987 L66/11.)

87/219/EEC:
Council Directive of March 30, 1987 amending Directive 75/716/EEC on the approximation of the laws of the Member States relating to the sulphur content of certain liquid fuels. (O.J. 1987 L91/19.)

87/354/EEC:
Council Directive of June 25, 1987 amending certain directives on the approximation of the laws of the Member States relating to industrial products with respect to the distinctive numbers and letters indicating the Member States. (O.J. 1987 L192/43.)

87/355/EEC:
Council Directive of June 25, 1987 amending Directives 71/316/EEC on the approximation of the laws of the Member States relating to common provisions for both measuring instruments and methods of meteorological control. (O.J. 1987 L192/46.)

87/356/EEC:
Council Directive of June 25, 1987 amending Directive 80/232/EEC on the approximation of the laws of the Member States relating to the ranges of nominal quantities and nominal capacities permitted for certain pre-packaged products. (O.J. 1987 L192/48.)

87/357/EEC:
Council Directive of June 25, 1987 on the approximation of the laws of the Member States concerning products which, appearing to be other than they are, endanger the health or safety of consumers. (O.J. 1987 L192/49.)

87/358/EEC:
Council Directive of June 25, 1987 amending Directive 70/156/EEC on the approximation of the laws of the Member States relating to the type-approval of motor vehicles and their trailers. (O.J. 1987 L192/51.)

87/403/EEC:
Council Directive of June 25, 1987 supplementing Annex I to Directive 70/156/EEC on the approximation of the laws of the Member States relating to the type-approval of motor vehicles and their trailers. (O.J. 1987 L220/44.)

87/405/EEC:
Council Directive of June 25, 1987 amending Directive 84/534/EEC on the approximation of the laws of the Member States relating to the permissible sound power level of tower cranes. (O.J. 1987 L220/60.)

87/416/EEC:
Council Directive of July 21, 1987 amending Directive 85/210/EEC on the approximation of the laws of the Member States concerning the lead content of petrol. (O.J. 1987 L225/33.)

87/432/EEC:
Council Directive of August 3, 1987 on the eighth adaptation to technical progress of Directive 67/548/EEC on the approximation of laws, regulations and administrative provisions relating to the classification, packaging and labelling of dangerous substances. (O.J. 1987 L239/1.)

87/137/EEC:
Ninth Commission Directive of February 2, 1987 adapting to technical progress Annexes II, III, IV, V and VI to Council Directive 76/768/EEC on the approximation of the laws of the Member States relating to cosmetic products. (O.J. 1987 L56/20.)

1471. Architects' qualifications

ARCHITECTS' QUALIFICATIONS (EEC RECOGNITION) ORDER 1987 (No. 1824) [£1·60], made under the European Communities Act 1972 (c.68), s.2(2); operative on November 19, 1987; recognises certain European qualifications of architects.

1472. Banking—confidentiality—evidence

Hillegom Municipality (Hillegom) deposited money with the Amsterdam American Bank N.V. (AAB), which became insolvent. Hillegom subpoenaed Mr. Hillenius, to give evidence in a provisional examination of witnesses. Mr. Hillenius was head of the accountancy division of the Dutch Central Bank, which is the supervisory authority for banks in Holland. Mr. Hillenius refused to answer various questions on the grounds that they were covered by banking secrecy. The questions were directed at showing that the Dutch Central Bank had failed properly to supervise the activities of AAB. The Supreme Court of the Netherlands asked the European Court under Art. 177 EEC for a preliminary ruling on the interpretation of Art. 12 of Council Directive 77/780 (on the co-ordination of the laws, regulations and administrative provision relating to the taking up and pursuit of the business of credit institutions) and of Dutch legislation implementing the Directive. Art. 12 provided for an obligation of professional secrecy.

Held, That (1) Art. 12(1) of Directive 77/780 means that confidential information received by persons employed by competent authorities may not be disclosed to anyone except by provisions laid down by law. This applied to the giving of evidence by such persons in civil proceedings; (2) the provisions laid down by law permitting confidential information to be disclosed, as envisaged by Art. 12(1), were not restricted to specific derogating legislation but could be made by general laws, including the rules of evidence in civil proceedings. It was for the national court, who was dealing with the action to try and balance the competing interests of justice and the maintenance of the confidentiality of banking information, when deciding whether to allow such evidence to be given.

HILLEGOM MUNICIPALITY *v.* HILLENIUS (CORNELIS) (No. 110/84) [1986] 3 C.M.L.R. 422, European Ct.

1473. Breach of European Community law—whether Crown liable in damages

The Crown cannot be held liable in damages for breaches of European Community law. This includes the Crown's legislative and quasi-legislative ministerial action, as well as executive acts and omissions dependent on the exercise of judgment (*Bourgoin S.A.* v. *Ministry for Agriculture, Fisheries and Food* [1986] C.L.Y. 1437 applied).

AN BORD BAINNE CO-OPERATIVE *v.* MILK MARKETING BOARD, *The Independent,* November 19, 1987, C.A.

1474. Coal and steel—directives, decisions and regulations

86/642/ECSC:

Decision of the representatives of the governments of the Member States of the European Coal and Steel Community, meeting within the Council of December 22, 1986 establishing ceilings and Community supervision for imports of certain goods falling under the ECSC Treaty originating in Yugoslavia (1987). (O.J. 1987 L380/59.)

86/643/ECSC:

Decision of the representatives of the governments of the Member States of the European Coal and Steel Community, meeting within the Council of December 22, 1986 extending the provisional arrangements for trade between Spain and Portugal on the one hand and the African, Caribbean and Pacific States (ACP States) on the other in products falling within the ECSC Treaty. (O.J. 1987 L380/64.)

86/644/ECSC:

Decision of the representatives of the governments of the Member States of the European Coal and Steel Community, meeting within the Council of December 22, 1986 extending the arrangements for trade between Spain and Portugal on the one hand and the overseas countries (OCT) on the other in products covered by the ECSC Treaty. (O.J. 1987 L380/65.)

86/660/ECSC:

Decision of the Representatives of the Governments of the Member States of the European Coal and Steel Community, meeting within the Council, of December 22, 1986 establishing the arrangements to be applied to imports into Spain and Portugal of products covered by the ECSC Treaty originating in Austria, Finland, Norway, Sweden or Switzerland and covered by Agreements between the Community and those countries. (O.J. 1987 L382/42.)

87/239/ECSC:

Commission Decision of April 7, 1987 approving aid from Belgium to the coal industry during 1987. (O.J. 1987 L110/27.)

87/240/ECSC:

Commission Decision of April 7, 1987 approving aid from France to the coalmining industry during 1987. (O.J. 1987 L110/29.)

87/364/ECSC:

Commission Decision of June 18, 1987 derogating from High Authority Recommendation No. 1–64 concerning an increase in the protective duty on iron and steel products at the external frontiers of the Community (127th derogation). (O.J. 1987 L195/36.)

87/376/ECSC:

Commission Decision of June 24, 1987 authorising the Member States to institute intra-Community surveillance of the importation for home use of certain iron and steel products originating in certain third countries and covered by the Treaty establishing the European Coal and Steel Community and in free circulation in the Community. (O.J. 1987 L201/29.)

87/437/ECSC:
Commission Decision of July 29, 1987 derogating from High Authority recommendation No. 1-64 concerning an increase in the protective duty on iron and steel products at the external frontiers of the Community. (O.J. 1987 L238/34.)

87/438/ECSC:
Commission Decision of July 29, 1987 derogating from High Authority recommendation No. 1-64 concerning an increase in the protective duty on iron and steel products at the external frontiers of the Community (129th derogation). (O.J. 1987 L238/37.)

87/439/ECSC:
Commission Decision at July 29, 1987 derogating from High Authority recommendation No. 1-64 on tariff protection in order to enable the generalized tariff preferences to be applied to certain iron and steel products originating in the developing countries (130th derogation). (O.J. 1987 L238/38.)

87/451/ECSC:
Commission Decision of July 31, 1987 approving aid from the Federal Republic of Germany to the coal industry during 1987. (O.J. 1987 L241/10.)

87/452/ECSC:
Commission Decision of July 31, 1987 approving aid from the U.K. to the coal industry in the 1987 financial year (1987/88). (O.J. 1987 L241/13.)

87/453/ECSC:
Commission Decision of July 31, 1987 approving aid from Portugal to the coal industry during 1987. (O.J. 1987 L241/15.)

87/454/ECSC:
Commission Decision of July 31, 1987 approving aid from Spain to the coal industry during 1987. (O.J. 1987 L241/16.)

87/508/Euratom, ECSC, EEC:
Amendment of the Council's Rules of Procedure adopted by the Council on July 20, 1987, on the basis of Article 5 of the Treaty of April 8, 1965 establishing a Single Council and a Single Commission of the European Communities. (O.J. 1987 L291/27.)

87/542/ECSC:
Commission Decision of November 9, 1987 establishing the delivery levels of ECSC steel products of Spanish origin onto the rest of the Community market, excluding Portugal. (O.J. 1987 L324/39.)

87/543/ECSC:
Commission Decision of November 9, 1987 establishing the delivery levels of ECSC steel products of Portuguese origin onto the rest of the Community market, excluding Spain. (O.J. 1987 L324/40.)

Commission Decision No. 533/87/ECSC of February 23, 1987 fixing the rates of abatement for the second quarter of 1987 in accordance with Decision No. 3485/85/ECSC on the extension of the system of monitoring and production quota for certain products of undertakings in the steel industry. (O.J. 1987 L54/9.)

Commission Decision No. 1251/87/ECSC of May 5, 1987 fixing the amended rates of abatement for the second quarter of 1987 in accordance with Decision No. 3485/85/ECSC on the extensions of the system of monitoring and production quotas for certain products of undertakings in the steel industry. (O.J. 1987 L118/9.)

Commission Decision No. 1434/87/ECSC of May 20, 1987 repealing Decision No. 3524/86/ECSC amending Decision No. 3485/85/ECSC on the extension of the system of monitoring and production quotas for certain products of undertakings in the steel industry. (O.J. 1987 L136/39.)

Commission Decision No. 1435/87/ECSC of May 25, 1987 fixing the rates of abatement for the third quarter of 1987 in accordance with Decision No. 3485/85/ECSC on the extension of the system of monitoring and production quotas for certain products of undertakings in the steel industry. (O.J. 1987 L136/40.)

Commission Decision No. 2819/87/ECSC of September 21, 1987 fixing the rates of abatement for the fourth quarter of 1987 in accordance with Decision No. 3485/85/ECSC on the extension of the system of monitoring and production quotas for certain products of undertakings in the steel industry. (O.J. 1987 L269/21.)

Commission Decision No. 3309/87/ECSC of November 3, 1987 fixing the amended rates of abatement for the fourth quarter of 1987 in accordance with Decision No. 3485/85/ECSC on the extension of the system of monitoring and production quotas for certain products of undertakings in the steel industry. (O.J. 1987 L313/19.)

Commission Recommendation No. 1160/87/ECSC of April 27, 1987 on Community surveillance of imports of certain iron and steel products covered by the ECSC Treaty and originating in non-member countries. (O.J. 1987 L112/13.)

1475. Coal and steel—imports—free circulation

German customs authorities sought differential customs duties from Mabanaft GmbH ("Mabanaft") in respect of coal imported into Germany in 1977 and 1978. The coal had been imported into Germany free of customs duties as being coal of Dutch origin. It later transpired that, although the coal had been in free circulation in Holland, it had in fact come from non-EEC States. The Finance Court, Düsseldorf, asked under Art. 41 ECSC a preliminary question concerning the validity of the recommendations of the High Authority of 28th January 1959 and 30th October 1962.

Held, the recommendations of the High Authority of 28th January 1959 and 30th October 1962 were compatible with Art. 4(*a*) ECSC. These recommendations could, for the period in question, be used as a legal basis for national rules providing for the charging of a differential customs duty on coal originating in a non-EEC State and imported after its release into free circulation in another EEC State.

MABANAFT GmbH *v.* HAUPTZOLLAMT EMMERICH (No. 36/83) [1987] 1 C.M.L.R. 473, European Ct.

1476. Commission's liability—European Development Fund—public works

Murri Frères ("Murri") brought proceedings against the European Commission under Arts. 178 EEC and 215(2) EEC for damages by reason of the European Commission's liability for the unlawful conduct of its officials in connection with the implementation of public works contract 6907/EDF/72 between Murri and Madagascar and financed by the European Development Fund ("the Fund"). Murri had contracted to build a road in Madagascar. Problems arose because of the sudden rise in the cost of asphalt in 1973/74 following an oil crisis. Murri sought reimbursement of these substantial unforeseen costs.

Held, dismissing the application, that Murri had failed to establish non-contractual liability on the part of the Commission. Murri was unable to establish that action by the Commission had caused it to suffer damage distinct from the damage in respect of which it ought to have sought compensation from Madagascar, and ought still to do so if it considered that it had a valid claim, in accordance with the appropriate procedure.

MURRI FRÈRES *v.* EUROPEAN COMMISSION (No. 33/82) [1987] 1 C.M.L.R. 520, European Ct.

1477. Communities own resources—Budget—advance payment

Council Regulation 2891/77 provided that each EEC State was to credit amounts collected in respect of the Communities' own resources, such as agricultural levies, to a particular account by the second month following the month during which the entitlement was established. Art. 10(2) of Reg. 2891/77 provided that, if necessary, the European Commission might invite EEC States to bring forward by one month the crediting of such resources. If such crediting was not made as requested, interest was to be charged, until payment was made. In April, 1983, the Commission asked EEC States to credit such resources a month earlier, as agricultural expenditure had reached a very high level. The U.K. did not pay such resources until a month later, as it argued that Art. 10(2) did not impose an obligation to pay earlier. The Commission brought proceedings against the U.K. under Art. 169 EEC for failing to fulfil its obligations.

Held, that the U.K. had failed to fulfil its obligations under Art. 10(2) and Art. 11 of Reg. 2891/77, by not complying with the Commission's invitation sent to it pursuant to Art. 10(2) and by refusing to pay the interest provided for in Art. 11 in respect of the delay with which it credited the resources.

ADVANCE PAYMENT OF BUDGET CONTRIBUTIONS, *Re*: E.C. COMMISSION *v.* U.K. (No. 93/85) [1987] 1 C.M.L.R. 895, European Ct.

1478. Community drivers' hours—regulations. See ROAD TRAFFIC, §3264.

1479. Company resident in U.K.—transfer of residence within EEC—whether Treasury consent necessary

[EEC Treaty, art. 52; European Communities Act 1972 (c.68), s.2(1); Income and Corporation Taxes Act 1970 (c.10), s.482(1).]

The question of whether a U.K. company can transfer residence to an EEC country without Treasury consent must be clarified and answered by the European Court.

In 1984 a U.K. company submitted to the Treasury an application to cease to be resident in the U.K. Its motives were entirely fiscal. The Revenue was minded to reject the application. The company applied for judicial review of the Treasury's refusal to acknowledge its right to charge residence without consent.

Held, that since a serious point of EEC law arose, and there was no definitive authority on the subject, the case should be referred to the European Court.

R. *v.* H.M. TREASURY, *ex p.* DAILY MAIL AND GENERAL TRUST [1987] 1 FTLR 394, Macpherson J.

1480. Competition—abuse of dominant market position—cars

[European Communities Act 1972 (c.68), ss.1(2), 2(1) and Sched. 1; E.E.C. Treaty, art. 86; Road Traffic Act 1972 (c.20), s.47.]

B.L. Co. marketed their cars, including the Metro model, through selective distributors in Britain. Outside that network a trade developed in the reimportation of the cars in left-hand drive form from continental member states, due to lower prices being charged there. The Commission decided that B.L. Co. had infringed art. 86 of the E.E.C. treaty by refusing to issue certificates of conformity for left-hand drive models under s.47(5) of the 1972 Act when a type approval certificate was in force, by deciding no longer to seek type approval, and at other times by charging £150 to dealers and £100 to others for certificates of conformity. B.L. Co. was fined 350,000 ECU, and applied for a declaration that the Commission's decision was void.

Held, that (1) B.L. occupied a dominant position and had abused it; (2) their conduct could only be construed as deliberately creating barriers to reimportation; (3) the Commission was entitled to conclude that the fees were fixed at a level disproportionate to the economic value of the service provided and that the practice was an abuse of B.L. Co.'s monopoly position. No principles of law had been breached by the Commission. The application would be dismissed and the claim for reduction of the fine rejected.

BRITISH LEYLAND *v.* E.C. COMMISSION (MERSON INTERVENING) (No. 226/84) [1987] R.T.R. 136, European Ct.

1481. Competition—agreement—vehicle parts

Austin Rover Group ("ARG") and Unipart Group ("Unipart") notified an agreement between them. Under the agreement Unipart was to continue to be responsible for operating ARG's parts business in so far as it related to supplying parts to the parts aftermarket for fitment to ARG vehicles. The agreement contained various restrictions, including provisions that ARG will not obtain the services provided by Unipart from any other party and that the whole range of ARG fit parts had to be made available by and through Unipart. The European Commission issued a Notice stating that it intended either to take a decision granting an exemption under Art. 85(3) EEC or to issue a comfort letter. It invited interested third parties to send their observations.

AGREEMENT BETWEEN AUSTIN ROVER GROUP & UNIPART GROUP, *Re* AN [1987] 1 C.M.L.R. 446, European Commission Notice.

1482. Competition—agreement between manufacturers—pasta

The Federation of German Pasta Manufacturers notified to the Commission an outline agreement between pasta manufacturers, for which it sought negative clearance or an exemption under Art. 85(3) EEC. The agreement included undertakings to use only egg products meeting certain standards, in particular hygiene standards. The majority of the signatories came from Baden-Württemberg, but the agreement was open to other manufacturers within the EEC to sign. The European Commission issued a Notice stating that it intended to take a favourable decision towards the agreement and invited interested third parties to send their comments within a month.

AGREEMENT BETWEEN GERMAN PASTA MANUFACTURERS, *Re* (No. IV/31.682) [1986] 3 C.M.L.R. 639, E.C. Commission Notice.

1483. Competition—agreements—chemicals

ENI, The Italian State Holding Company for the energy sector, and Montedison, an Italian group involved in the chemical and pharmaceutical industries, notified agreements to the European Commission. By the agreements they, *inter alia*, transferred to one another parts of their chemicals businesses. The European Commission issued a Notice stating that it proposed to take a favourable decision on the agreements and invited interested third parties to send their observations within four weeks.

AGREEMENTS OF ENTE NAZIONALE IDROCARBURI (ENI) AND MONTEDISON SpA, *Re* THE [1987] 1 C.M.L.R. 495, European Commission Notice.

1484. Competition—agriculture—new potatoes

The French authorities requested the European Commission to apply Art. 2 of Reg. 26 to rules and decisions regarding the production and marketing of new potatoes taken by seven French regional economic committees.

The Commission issued a Notice stating that it proposed finding, pursuant to Art. 2 of Reg. 26, that these rules and decisions formed an integral part of the national market organisation in France for new potatoes and that Art. 85(1) EEC was not applicable. However, before taking such a decision, the Commission invited comments within a month from interested third parties.

PRODUCTION AND MARKETING OF FRENCH NEW POTATOES, *Re* [1987] 3 C.M.L.R. 169, E.C. Commission Notice.

1485. Competition—Baltic Exchange—freight futures

The Baltic International Freight Futures Exchange (BIFFEX) notified its articles of association and rules and regulations to the European Commission and applied for negative clearance under Council Reg. 17.

The Commission issued a Notice stating that it proposed to take a favourable decision in relation to BIFFEX's articles, rules and regulations. Prior to making such a decision, the Commission invited interested third parties to make their comments within 28 days.

RULES OF THE BALTIC INTERNATIONAL FREIGHT FUTURES EXCHANGE (BIFFEX), *Re* (No. IV/31.764) [1987] 2 C.M.L.R. 445, E.C. Commission Notice.

1486. Competition—banking—hours—clearing rules and direct debiting

The Irish Banks' Standing Committee ("IBSC") acting on behalf of its members, notified the European Commission of various agreements between its bank members. The IBSC asked for negative clearance under Art. 2 of Reg. 17 of agreements regarding bank operating hours and the operation of clearing rules and a direct debiting scheme.

Held, that negative clearance would be given. So far as the agreement regarding banking hours was concerned, any prevention, restriction or distortion of competition resulting therefrom was not appreciable. The other agreements did not have any terms which had as their object or effect the prevention, restriction or distortion of competition within the EEC. There were no grounds for taking action under Art. 85 EEC.

APPLICATIONS OF THE IRISH BANKS' STANDING COMMITTEE, *Re* (No. IV/31.362) [1987] 2 C.M.L.R. 601, E.C. Commission.

1487. Competition—banking—negative clearance—exemption

The Associazione Bancaria Italiana, a non profit-making association of banks and financial and credit institutions, notified the European Commission of various agreements relating to banking activities. The Commission issued a Notice stating that it proposed to grant negative clearance to the majority of the agreements and to grant an exemption, possibly subject to obligations for three agreements. The Commission invited interested third parties to send their comments within a month.

ASSOCIAZIONE BANCARIA ITALIANA, *Re* (No. IV/31.356) [1986] 3 C.M.L.R. 413, European Commission Notice.

1488. Competition—banking—negative clearance—exemption

The Belgische Vereniging der Banken/Association Belges des Banques, (BVB/ABB) an association comprising most banks in Belgium, notified the European Commission of various agreements relating to banking activities. The Commission sent a statement of objections concerning certain agreements. Following discussions with the Commission, the BVB/ABB abrogated these agreements. The Commission issued a Notice that in the case of three other agreements, it proposed to grant an exemption, possibly subject to obligations. The Commission invited interested third parties to send their comments within a month.

NOTIFICATION OF THE BELGISCHE VERENIGING DER BANKEN/ASSOCIATION BELGE DES BANQUES, *Re* (No. IV/261–A [1986] 3 C.M.L.R. 419, E.C. Commission Notices.

1489. Competition—broadcasting—joint rates and conditions

Various members of the European Broadcasting Union (EBU) planned to fix joint rates and conditions for supplying television news items to third parties. The European Commission advised that this would restrict competition contrary to EEC competition rules as intending purchasers would no longer be able to deal separately with individual broadcasters, but would have to deal with the group. As a result of that advice, the plans were dropped.

EUROPEAN BROADCASTING UNION, *Re* [1987] 1 C.M.L.R. 390, E.C. Commission.

1490. Competition—business secrets—discovery

R. J. Reynolds Industries Inc. ("Reynolds") and British American Tobacco Co. ("BATs") complained to the European Commission under Art. 3 of Reg. 17 that certain agreements made in 1981 between Philip Morris Inc. ("Philip Morris") and Rembrandt Group ("Rembrandt") violated Arts. 85 and 86 EEC. The Commission considered that the 1981 agreements violated Arts. 85 and 86 and served statements of objections on Philip Morris and Rembrandt. It copied the statement of objections to Reynolds and BATs but with certain parts deleted, which were regarded as relating to business secrets. Following discussions, Philip Morris and Rembrandt altered the agreements to the Commission's satisfaction so as not to infringe Arts. 85 and 86. The Commission decided to close its file and dismissed the complaints. Reynolds and BATs brought proceedings for annulment of that Decision and both applied to the Court for discovery of (i) parts of the 1981 agreements, of the statements of objections, of the replies given by Philip Morris and Rembrandt to those statements and of the minutes of the hearing, which the Commission regarded as qualifying for protection as business secrets. Reynolds applied to the Court for discovery of (ii) all documents in the Commission's possession which might reveal the reasons for which the Commission proposed to prohibit formally the 1981 agreements and for which it came to the conclusion that the altered agreements did not violate Art. 85 EEC.

Held, that the applications for discovery would be dismissed; as far as the documents in category (i) were concerned, these related to the original 1981 agreements which were not the subject of the final Decision and were therefore irrelevant to the present dispute; as far as the documents in category (ii) were concerned they could only be relevant to an allegation of inconsistency founded on improper and hidden reasons if misuse of power had been alleged, which it had not. Further, the statement of objections had no status *vis-à-vis* the complainants and could not found a finding of inconsistency. When the Commission forwards such statements to complainants, that does not commit it in any way *vis-à-vis* the complainants to maintaining the factual or legal assessments set out therein—the assessments therein are of a provisional nature.

BRITISH AMERICAN TOBACCO CO. AND REYNOLDS (R.J.) INDUSTRIES INC. *v.* E.C. COMMISSION (PHILIP MORRIS INC. AND REMBRANDT GROUP INTERVENING) (Nos. 142/84 and 156/84) [1987] 2 C.M.L.R. 551, European Ct.

1491. Competition—directives, decisions and regulations

87/1/EEC:

Commission Decision of December 2, 1986 relating to a proceeding under Article 85 of the EEC Treaty (IV/31.128—Fatty Acids). (O.J. 1987 L3/17.)

87/2/EEC:

Commission Decision of December 4, 1986 relating to a proceeding under Article 85 of the EEC Treaty (IV/30.439—Petroleum Exchange of London Limited). (O.J. 1987 L3/27.)

87/3/EEC:

Commission Decision of December 4, 1986 in proceedings under Article 85 of the EEC Treaty (IV/31.055—ENI/Montedison). (O.J. 1987 L5/13.)

87/16/EEC:

Commission Decision of April 23, 1986 on a proposal by the Italian Government to grant aid to a firm in the chemical industry (producing industrial auxiliaries, intermediates and pesticides). (O.J. 1987 L12/27.)

87/17/EEC:

Commission Decision of December 17, 1986 in proceedings under Article 85 of the EEC Treaty (IV/30937—Pronuptia). (O.J. 1987 L13/39.)

87/44/EEC:

Commission Decision of December 10, 1986 relating to a proceeding under Article 85 of the EEC Treaty (IV/29.036—The GAFTA Soya Bean Meal Futures Association). (O.J. 1987 L19/18.)

87/45/EEC:

Commission Decision of December 10, 1986 relating to a proceeding under Article 85 of the EEC Treaty (IV/29.688—The London Grain Futures Market). (O.J. 1987 L19/22.)

87/46/EEC:

Commission Decision of December 10, 1986 relating to a proceeding under Article 85 of the EEC Treaty (IV/30.176—The London Potato Futures Association Limited). (O.J. 1987 L19/26.)

87/47/EEC:

Commission Decision of December 10, 1986 relating to a proceeding under Article 85 of the EEC Treaty (IV/31.614—The London Meat Futures Exchange Limited). (O.J. 1987 L19/30.)

87/48/EEC:

Commission Decision of October 22, 1986 concerning aid in Belgium in favour of the brewery equipment industry. (O.J. 1987 L20/30.)

87/100/EEC:

Commission Decision of December 17, 1986 relating to a proceeding under Article 85 of the EEC Treaty (IV/31.340—Mitchell Cotts/Sofiltra). (O.J. 1987 L41/31.)

87/103/EEC:
Commission Decision of December 12, 1986 relating to a proceeding under Article 85 of the EEC Treaty (IV/31.356—ABI). (O.J. 1987 L43/51.)
87/135/EEC:
Commission Decision of February 23, 1987 accepting an undertaking given by Kyocera Corporation in connection with the anit-dumping proceeding concerning imports of plain paper photocopiers originating in Japan and terminating the investigation. (O.J. 1987 L54/36.)
87/210/EEC:
Commission Decision of March 23, 1987 accepting undertakings given in connection with the anti-dumping proceeding concerning imports of outboard motors originating in Japan and terminating the investigation. (O.J. 1987 L82/36.)
87/104/EEC:
Council Decision of February 9, 1987 accepting an undertaking given in connection with the anti-dumping proceeding concerning imports of paint, distemper, varnish and similar brushes originating in the Peopls's Republic of China, and terminating the investigation. (O.J. 1987 L46/45.)

Commission Decision No. 1532/87/ECSC of June 2, 1987 suspending the application of the definitive anti-dumping duty on imports of certain iron or steel coils for re-rolling originating in Venezuela. (O.J. 1987 L143/16.)

Commission Regulation (EEC) No. 1289/87 of May 8, 1987 imposing a provisional anti-dumping duty on imports of urea originating in Czechoslovakia, the German Democratic Republic, Kuwait, Libya, Saudi Arabia, the USSR, Trinidad and Tobago and Yugoslavia. (O.J. 1987 L121/11.)

Commission Regulation (EEC) No. 1361/87 of May 18, 1987 imposing a provisional anti-dumping duty on imports of ferro-silico-calcium/calcium silicide originating in Brazil. (O.J. 1987 L129/5

Council Regulation (EEC) No. 3857/86 of December 16, 1986 extending the provisional anti-dumping duty on imports of plain paper photocopiers originating in Japan. (O.J. 1986 L359/9.)

Council Regulation (EEC) No. 4056/86 of December 22, 1986 laying down detailed rules for the application of Articles 85 and 86 of the Treaty to maritime transport. (O.J. 1987 L378/4.)

Council Regulation (EEC) No. 29/87 of December 22, 1986 imposing a definitive anti-dumping duty on imports of certain deep freezers originating in the Soviet Union. (O.J. 1987 L6/1.)

Council Regulation (EEC) No. 254/87 of January 26, 1987 extending the provisional anti-dumping duty on imports of standardised multi-phase electric motors having an output of more than 0,75 kW but not more than 75 kW, originating in Bulgaria, Czechoslovakia, the German Democratic Republic, Hungary, Poland, Romania and the Soviet Union. (O.J. 1987 L26/1.)

Council Regulation (EEC) No. 374/87 of February 5, 1987 definitively collecting the provisional anti-dumping duty and imposing a definitive anti-dumping duty on imports of housed bearing units originating in Japan. (O.J. 1987 L35/32.)

Council Regulation (EEC) No. 535/87 of February 23, 1987 imposing a definitive anti-dumping duty on imports of plain paper photocopiers originating in Japan. (O.J. 1987 L54/12.)

Council Regulation (EEC) No. 1305/87 of May 11, 1987 imposing a definitive anti-dumping duty on certain imports of outboard motors originating in Japan. (O.J. 1987 L124/1.)

1492. Competition—discovery—Commission documents

ICI brought proceedings before the European Court for the annulment of the European Commission's Decision that ICI had violated Art. 85 EEC or for a reduction of the fine imposed by the Commission. ICI also applied to the Court for discovery of (i) the report of the Hearing Officer, and (ii) documents relating to press releases which appeared to reveal real reasons different from those set out in the preamble to the Decision.

Held, that discovery of those documents was refused as (i) the report of the Hearing Officer did not bind the Commission; it was an opinion in an internal document and disclosure would put the Commission in a difficult position, as its officers should be able to express their views freely during the decision-making process. The report did not constitute a decisive factor which had to be taken into account by the Court for the purpose of performing its judicial review; (ii) press releases were not to be regarded as an authoritative reflection of the Commission's position. In any event, it had not been established that statements in the press releases regarding the reasons for the contested decisions were different from those given in the preamble to the Decision.

IMPERIAL CHEMICAL INDUSTRIES *v.* E.C. COMMISSION (No. 212/86) [1987] 2 C.M.L.R. 500, European Ct.

1493. Competition—dominant position—abuse

Napier Brown & Co. ("Napier") complained to the European Commission that British Sugar had engaged in various practices designed to drive Napier out of the retail sugar market in Great Britain. The Commission sent to British Sugar a Statement of Objections, stating that British Sugar had, prima facie abused its dominant position contrary to Art. 86 EEC and had made agreements contrary to Art. 85(1) EEC. The Commission suspended interim measures and proceedings after receiving certain undertakings from British Sugar, such as an undertaking to supply sugar to Napier on terms and conditions acceptable to the Commission and an undertaking not to engage in predatory pricing practices.

NAPIER BROWN AND CO. *v.* BRITISH SUGAR [1986] 3 C.M.L.R. 594, E.C. Commission.

1494. Competition—exemption—selective distribution

METRO brought proceedings for annulment of the European Commission's Decision 83/672. By that Decision the Commission granted exemption under Art. 85(3) EEC of certain agreements forming part of SABA's selective distribution system for distributing its consumer electronics equipment in the EEC. METRO, a German low-price cash-and-carry distributor, had been refused admission to SABA's distribution system, which it regarded as anti-competitive.

Held, that (1) METRO's application was admissible as it was directly and individually concerned: (2) METRO's application was dismissed as, *inter alia*, there had been no elimination of competition, and SABA, itself, did not occupy a dominant position on the German market and there was no evidence that an increase in the degree of concentration on the market had affected the structure of competition.

METRO-SB-GROßMÄRKTE GmbH & CO. K.G. (U.K. INTERVENING) *v.* E.C. COMMISSION (SABA GmbH AND GERMANY INTERVENING) (No. 2) (No. 75/84) [1987] 1 C.M.L.R. 118, European Ct.

1495. Competition—franchise agreement—computer stores

Computerland Europe S.A. ("CLE") notified to the European Commission its standard form franchise agreement for its network of franchised retail stores in the EEC. The agreement contained certain restrictions on competition. CLE asked that the agreement be given negative clearance or, alternatively, exemption under Art. 85(3) EEC. After discussions with the Commission, CLE made some modifications to its agreement. The Commission issued a Notice stating that it proposed to adopt a favourable decision on the agreement, but before doing so, it invited interested third parties to submit any comments they might have within a month.

FRANCHISE AGREEMENTS OF COMPUTERLAND EUROPE S.A., *Re* (No. IV/32.034) [1987] 2 C.M.L.R. 389, E.C. Commission Notice.

1496. Competition—insurance—premium recommendation

Vds, an Association of property insurers authorised to transact insurance business within West Germany, applied to the European Commission for negative clearance or exemption under Art. 85/3/EEC of various matters, including an insurance premium recommendation. The European Commission issued a Decision on December 5, 1984, stating that the recommendation was contrary to Art. 85/1/EEC and refused negative clearance or to exempt it under Art. 85/3/EEC. Vds brought proceedings to annul that Decision, arguing that Art. 85 EEC was not applicable until the Council adopted special implementing measures for insurance and that trade between EEC States had not been affected.

Held, that the application was rejected because (a) EEC Competition rules were fully applicable to the insurance sector, and (b) trade between EEC States might be affected by the recommendation.

VERBAND DER SACHVERSICHERER eV (SUPPORTED BY GESAMTVERBAND DER DEUTSCHEN VERSICHERUNGSWIRTSCHAFT eV, INTERVENER.) *v.* E.C. COMMISSION (No. 45/85), *The Times*, February 7, 1987, European Ct.

1497. Competition—joint ventures—coal

The European Commission authorised the Australian company Ulan Coal Mines to acquire a 50 per cent. shareholding in a Belgian wholly-owned subsidiary called Hargreaves (Antwerp) NV. The Commission was of the opinion that the setting up of the joint venture was consistent with the requirements for authorisation under Art. 66(2) ECSC.

Each of the parent companies would control less than 5 per cent. of the Community market in steam coal for industrial use.

JOINT OWNERSHIP OF HARGREAVES (ANTWERP) N.V., *Re* [1987] 1 C.M.L.R. 389, E.C. Commission

1498. Competition—know-how licences—exemption

The European Commission published a draft Commission regulation on the application of Art. 85(3) EEC to certain categories of know-how licensing agreements.

DRAFT REGULATION ON KNOW-HOW LICENCES [1987] 3 C.M.L.R. 144, E.C. Commission.

1499. Competition—London Grain Futures—negative clearance

The London Grain Futures Market ("LGFM") notified its articles of association and regulations to the European Commission and applied for negative clearance under Council Regulation 17.

The Commission issued a Notice stating that it proposed to take a favourable decision in relation to LGFM's articles of association and regulations. Prior to taking such a decision, the Commission invited interested third parties to make their comments within a month.

LONDON GRAIN FUTURES MARKET, *Re* (No. IV/29.688) [1986] 3 C.M.L.R. 709, E.C. Commission Notice.

1500. Competition—London Meat Futures—negative clearance

The London Meat Futures Exchange ("LMFE") notified its articles of association and rules and regulations to the European Commission and applied for negative clearance under Council Regulation 17.

The Commission issued a Notice stating that it proposed to take a favourable decision in relation to LMFE's articles of association and rules and regulations. Prior to taking such a decision, the Commission invited interested third parties to make their comments within a month.

LONDON MEAT FUTURES EXCHANGE, *Re* (No. IV/31.614) [1986] 3 C.M.L.R. 701, E.C. Commission Notice.

1501. Competition—London Potato Futures—negative clearance

The London Potato Futures Association ("LPFA") notified its articles of association and rules and regulations to the European Commission and applied for negative clearance under Council Regulation 17.

The Commission issued a Notice stating that it proposed to take a favourable decision in relation to LPFA's articles of association and rules and regulations. Prior to taking such a decision, the Commission invited interested third parties to make their comments within a month.

LONDON POTATO FUTURES ASSOCIATION, *Re* (No. IV/30.176) [1986] 3 C.M.L.R. 705, E.C. Commission Notice.

1502. Competition—monopoly—anti-competitive practices

The plaintiff funeral services company brought proceedings for commercial libel against those who had conducted a newspaper campaign against its alleged monopoly practices in France.

Held, that the plaintiff company's practices could be contrary to EEC competition law, but such practices would be referred to the French Competition Commission for an opinion before there was any question of asking the European Court for a preliminary ruling under Art. 177 EEC.

S.A. DES POMPES FUNÈBRES GÉNÉRALES *v.* LECLERC [1987] E.C.C. 500, Ct. of Appeal, Paris.

1503. Competition—non-competition clause—exemption

The applicants brought proceedings for annulment of the European Commission's Decision of December 12, 1983. By that Decision the Commission took the view that a 10-year non-competition clause contained in the applicants' agreements was void as infringing Art. 85(1) EEC and refused exemption under Art. 85(3) EEC. The clauses were contained in agreements whereby a Dutch business was transferred to another Dutch undertaking.

Held, dismissing the application, that the non-competitive clause was contrary to Art 85(1) EEC, as it was excessive. The applicants had failed to show that the continuance of the non-competition clause beyond a four-year period was justified under Art. 85(3) EEC.

It had not been established that the Commission Decision was based on an inaccurate statement of reasons or an erroneous appraisal.

REMIA B.V. AND VERENIGDE BEDRIJVEN NUTRICIA N.V. *v.* E.C. COMMISSION (No. 42/84) [1987] 1 C.M.L.R. 1, European Ct.

1504. Competition—patent licensing—windsurfing boards

Windsurfing International Inc. ("Windsurfing") made certain patent licensing agreements in relation to its windsurfing sailboards. The scope of the patent granted to Windsurfing in Germany was a matter of dispute. The European Commission in its Decision of July 11 1983 found that clauses in certain patent licensing agreements infringed Art. 85(1) EEC and fined Windsurfing 50,000 ECUs. Windsurfing brought proceedings for annulment of that decision and of the fine imposed.

Held, that (1) all the clauses in the licensing agreements referred to in Art. 1 of the decision were contrary to Art. 85(1) EEC, with the exception of the clause imposing the obligation to pay royalties on components on the net selling price of the product, in so far as it applied to rigs. The Art. 1 of the decision was declared void only in relation to certain findings connected to that exception; (2) the fine was reduced to 25,000 ECUs; (3) the Court may review the European Commission's findings on the validity and extent of a patent claim under national patent law. In doing so, it was confined to deciding whether, in the light of the legal position existing in the EEC State which granted the patent, the Commission had made a reasonable assessment of the scope of the patent. Where there was no binding decision of the relevant national courts, the scope of the patent had to be decided only on the basis of the wording of the patent claim accepted by the national patent office and of the interpretative rulings given by the national courts and authorities.

WINDSURFING INTERNATIONAL INC. *v.* E.C. COMMISSION (No. 193/83) [1986] 3 C.M.L.R. 489, European Ct.

1505. Competition—performance rights—royalties

SACEM (society of authors, composers and editors of music), a French copyright-management society, brought proceedings in France against Mr. Basset. SACEM claimed that works in its repertoire were being played in Mr. Basset's discothèque in Fréjus without payment of any royalties to SACEM. Mr. Basset argued that the agreements on which such royalties were based were contrary to EEC competition law. The Court of Appeal, Versailles, asked the European Court under Art. 177 EEC for a preliminary ruling on the interpretation of Arts. 30, 36, 86 EEC.

Held, that (1) Arts. 30 and 36 EEC did not prevent national law permitting a national copyright-managing society to charge a royalty called a "supplementary mechanical reproduction fee," in addition to performance royalty on the public performance of sound recordings, even where such a supplementary fee was not provided for in the EEC State where those sound recordings were lawfully placed on the market; (2) the prohibitions contained in Art. 86 EEC did not apply to the conduct of a national copyright—management society just because it charged a royalty called a "supplementary mechanical reproduction fee", in addition to performance royalty, on the public performance of sound recordings, even where such a supplementary fee was not provided for in the EEC State where those sound recordings were lawfully placed on the market.

BASSET *v.* SACEM (No. 402/85) [1987] 3 C.M.L.R. 173, European Ct.

1506. Competition—resale ban—coffee

The European Commission asked the Instituto Brasileiro do Café (IBC) to delete clauses in contracts with coffee roasters, which prohibited the latter from re-selling green unprocessed coffee in the EEC, on the basis that such clauses were contrary to Art. 85 EEC. IBC is a non-EEC supplier of 26 per cent. of the EEC market of unprocessed coffee. IBC agreed to delete such clauses.

EUROPEAN FEDERATION OF ASSOCIATIONS OF COFFEE ROASTERS *v.* INSTITUTO BRASILEIRO DO CAFÉ [1987] 1 C.M.L.R. 763, European Commission Notice.

1507. Competition—soya bean meal futures—negative clearance

The GAFTA Soya Bean Meal Futures Association ("SOMFA") notified its articles of association and rules and regulations to the European Commission and applied for negative clearance under Council Regulation 17.

The Commission issued a Notice stating that it proposed to take a favourable decision in relation to SOMFA's articles of association and rules and regulations. Prior to taking such a decision, the Commission invited interested third parties to make their comments within a month.

GAFTA SOYA BEAN MEAL FUTURES ASSOCIATION, *Re* (No. IV/29.036) [1986] 3 C.M.L.R. 698, E.C. Commission Notice.

1508. Competition—take-over—coal

The European Commission issued a Notice stating that it had authorised under Art. 66(2) ECSC the take-over by the second biggest coal producer in the EEC of the wholesale solid fuels businesses in four German towns from a group which was withdrawing from the solid fuels sector, where the acquiring company's market share in the two sectors concerned (power stations and industry) would be increased only marginally.

HANIEL HANDEL GmbH, *Re* [1987] 1 C.M.L.R. 445, European Commission Notice.

1509. Confidentiality—duty of European Commission—business secrets

Engineering & Chemical Supplies (Epsom & Gloucester) ("ECS") complained to the European Commission that the AKZO Group had infringed EEC competition law. The European Commission carried out an investigation into the alleged infringements under Council Reg. 17. The Commission sent ECS a copy of its statement of objections alleging infringements of Art. 86 EEC. The copy of its statement of objections listed numerous annexes. Some of the annexes contained confidential information concerning AKZO. On December 14, 1984 the commission decided to send some of the annexes to ECS at ECS's request. On December 18, 1984 the Commission informed AKZO that it had sent the annexes to ECS. AKZO applied to the European Court for annulment of the Commission's decision to provide ECS with certain confidential documents.

Held, that (1) the obligation of professional secrecy set out in Art. 20(2) of Reg. 17 was qualified in respect of those to whom Art. 19(2) gave the right to be heard, such as the complainant. Commission could supply the latter with information covered by the obligation to professional secrecy to the extent that such disclosure was necessary to the smooth conduct of the investigation. However, documents containing business secrets were not to be disclosed to a complainant;

(2) it was for the Commission to determine whether a document contained business secrets. After giving the undertaking concerned an opportunity to give its views, the Commission should take a properly reasoned decision and notify it to the undertaking so that the latter has the chance to challenge the decision in the European Court;

(3) the Commission's decision to provide ECS with certain confidential information was annulled as the Commission had decided to do so before notifying its view to AKZO. Thus, it had denied AKZO the possibility of using Arts. 173 and 185 EEC to prevent the implementation of the decision. In the circumstances the decision was annulled without it being necessary to decide whether the documents actually contained business secrets.

AKZO CHEMIE BV *v.* E.C. COMMISSION (ENGINEERING & CHEMICAL SUPPLIES (EPSOM & GLOUCESTER) intervening) (No. 53/85) [1987] 1 C.M.L.R. 231, European Ct.

1510. Constitutional law—community privileges and immunities—liability

Five Brussels municipalities passed by-laws which imposed tax on people not registered in their population registers, but who had a secondary residence in such municipalities. Since, under Art. 12(*b*) of the Protocol on Privileges and Immunities of the European Communities (the "Protocol"), non-Belgian EEC officials resident in Belgium are not required (or even allowed) to put themselves on the register, they were required to pay the secondary residence tax even in respect of their primary residence. The European Commission informed the Belgian Government that it regarded the by-laws as incompatible with the Protocol. The Commission commenced Art. 169 EEC procedure against Belgium which failed to respond. The Commission brought proceedings against Belgium for failing to fulfil its obligations.

Held, that by imposing, through the tax by-laws of the five municipalities, an indirect constraint to register in the population registers on EEC officials and their families, who are exempt from the requirement of registration in those registers and who have their principal residence in those municipalities, Belgium had failed to fulfil its obligations under Art. 5 EEC and Art. 12(*b*) of the Protocol.

BELGIAN PROPERTY TAX ON COMMUNITY OFFICIALS, *Re*: E.C. COMMISSION *v.* BELGIUM (No. 85/85) [1987] 1 C.M.L.R. 787, European Ct.

1511. Constitutional law—Germany—human rights

The German appellant was refused a licence to import 1,000 tonnes of preserved mushrooms from Taiwan, on the basis of, *inter alia*, Council Reg. 865/68 on the common organisation of the market in fruit and vegetables, Council Reg. 1427/71 on protective measures and the Commission Reg. 2107/74 laying down protective measures regarding imports of preserved mushrooms. The appellant challenged the validity of Commission Reg. 2107/74 in the German Courts. The Federal Supreme Administrative Court referred certain questions to the European Court, which upheld, *inter alia*, the validity of the Reg. The Federal Supreme Court dismissed the appeal and refused to make a further reference to the European Court. The appellant then brought an individual constitutionality action to the German Federal Constitutional Court.

Held, dismissing the appeal that (1) the Federal Supreme Court was correct in not making a further reference to the European Court. Art. 19(4) of the German Constitution did not give German courts a power of judicial review over judgments of the European Court, nor did it prohibit a Supreme Federal Court from considering itself bound by a preliminary ruling of the European Court addressed to it; (2) so long as the European Communities, and in particular the European Court's case law, generally accorded effective protection of fundamental rights, the Federal Constitutional Court would no longer exercise its jurisdiction to decide on the applicability of secondary Community legislation or to review such legislation by the standard of the fundamental rights contained in the Constitution.

APPLICATION OF WÜNSCHE HANDELSGESELLSCHAFT, *Re* [1987] 3 C.M.L.R. 225, German Federal Constitutional Ct.

1512. Constitutional law—Single European Act

All the EEC States, apart from Ireland, had ratified the Single European Act ("S.E.A.") by the end of 1986. The Irish ratification Bill was passed in December 1986, but before it could be acted upon, Mr. Crotty brought an action in the Irish High Court for an order prohibiting the Irish Government from proceeding with the ratification. Proceedings reached the Irish Supreme Court and two separate judgments were given.

Held, that (1) in the first judgment the attack on the constitutionality of the European (Amendment) Act 1986, which authorised ratification, was rejected; (2) in the second judgment it was held that Title III of the S.E.A. required EEC States to co-ordinate their foreign relations to such an extent as to restrict the freedom imposed by the Irish Constitution on the Irish Government. Ratification of Part III of the S.E.A. could not occur unless a referendum of the people were held to rule in favour of amending the Constitution to permit ratification of the S.E.A.

CROTTY *v.* AN TAOISEACH [1987] 2 C.M.L.R. 666, Irish Supreme Ct.

1513. Court of Appeal decision—made without reference to EEC Council Directive—whether *per incuriam*. See DUKE *v.* RELIANCE SYSTEMS, §3084.

1514. Customs—transit—duties

Some Australian butter was imported into Belgium. The butter went from Belgium to Switzerland. The Swiss customs authorities treated the butter as being of Belgian origin and erroneously endorsed T2 (internal Community transit) on a consignment note to Italy. The butter was cleared into Italy without duty being paid. The Italian customs authorities subsequently discovered that the butter came from Australia and the transit should have been "external Community" and sought to raise duties thereon. Mr. Fioravanti refused to pay, claiming that the Italian authorities had no power to require payment of the duties since, under Art. 36 of Council Reg. 542/69, the recovery ought to be effected by the Belgian authorities, being the authorities in the EEC State in which the offence occurred. The Corte di Appello asked the European Court under Art. 177 EEC for a preliminary ruling on the interpretation of Art. 36(1) of Reg. 542/69 and on the Agreement between the EEC and the Swiss Confederation on the application of the rules on Community transit contained in Council Reg. 2812/42.

Held, that (1) where goods go from Belgium to a specified consignee in the free port of La Praille, Geneva, (Switzerland), and are reconsigned from there to Italy, this should be viewed as Community transit; (2) where goods coming from an EEC State have a consignment note on which "T2" has been entered or on which "T1" is not entered in space No. 25, the Swiss authorities are authorised, in the case of reconsignment to another EEC State, to issue a new consignment note bearing the symbol "T2" in space No. 25. If copy No. 3 of the consignment note is missing or of it bears the symbol "T1", the Swiss authorities are not authorised to issue a consignment note bearing the symbol "T2"; (3) it was for the State where the offence or irregularity was made with regard to a Community transit transaction, to recover the unpaid duties and charges.

FIORAVANTI *v.* AMMINISTRAZIONE DELLE FINANZE DELLO STATO (No.99/83) [1987] 1 C.M.L.R. 424, European Ct.

1515. Customs duties—Portugal—transitional measures. See CUSTOMS AND EXCISE, §1120.

1516. Customs duties—Spain—transitional measures. See CUSTOMS AND EXCISE, §1123.

1517. Definition of Treaties

EUROPEAN COMMUNITIES (DEFINITION OF TREATIES) (INTERNATIONAL CONVENTION ON THE HARMONISED COMMODITY DESCRIPTION AND CODING SYSTEM)

ORDER 1987 (No. 2040) [45p], made under the European Communities Act 1972 (c.68), s.1(3); declares the said system and its associated Protocol of Amendment to be Community Treaties.

1518. Designation of Ministers

EUROPEAN COMMUNITIES (DESIGNATION) ORDER 1987 (No. 448) [45p], made under the European Communities Act 1972 (c.68), s.2(2); operation on April 16, 1987; designates the Minister who may exercise powers to make regulations conferred by s.2(2) of the 1972 Act.

EUROPEAN COMMUNITIES (DESIGNATION) (No. 2) ORDER 1987 (No. 926) [45p], made under the European Communities Act 1972, s.2(2); operative on July 8, 1987; designates Ministers and Departments for specified matters.

1519. Directives—co-ordinated rules—combatting insider trading

The European Commission submitted a proposal to the Council for a Council Directive on co-ordinating regulations on insider trading.

DRAFT INSIDER TRADING DIRECTIVE [1987] 2 C.M.L.R. 765, E.C. Council.

1520. Directives—implementation—employment

The European Commission brought proceedings against Italy under Art. 169 EEC for failing to adopt within the requisite period all the measures necessary for the implementation of Council Directive 77/187 of February 14, 1977 on the approximation of the laws of the EEC States relating to the safeguarding of employees' rights in the event of transfers of undertakings, businesses or parts of businesses.

Held, that (1) the Commission had not proved that Italian law did not provide the full degree of protection required by the second subparagraph of Art. 3(3) of Directive 77/187. The Commission's complaint in relation thereto was rejected; (2) Italy had failed to meet its obligations under the EEC Treaty by failing to adopt within the requisite period all the measures required to comply fully with Art. 6(1) and 6(2) of Directive 77/187.

BUSINESS TRANSFER LEGISLATION, *Re:* E.C. COMMISSION *v.* ITALY (No. 235/84) [1987] 3 C.M.L.R. 115, European Ct.

1521. Directives—implementation—nursing

The European Commission brought proceedings against Germany under Art. 169 EEC for failing to adopt the necessary measures, within the prescribed period, to implement Council Directive 77/452 concerning the mutual recognition of diplomas, certificates and other evidence of the formal qualifications of nurses for general care and Council directive 77/453 concerning the co-ordination of provisions laid down by law, regulation or administrative action in respect of the activities of nurses responsible for general care.

Held, that Germany had failed to fulfil its obligations under the EEC Treaty by failing to take the necessary measures to implement Directives 77/452 and 77/453. Germany's argument that the recognition of diplomas under Directive 77/452 from other EEC States was sufficiently guaranteed by existing German laws was rejected, as these laws were too general; Directive 77/452 had laid down provisions of a precise and detailed nature which had to be implemented. Further, the adoption by Germany of the Council of Europe Convention on the training of nurses did not fully cover all the requirements of Directive 77/453 and could not be relied upon as amounting to sufficient implementation of Directive 77/453.

NURSING DIRECTIVES, *Re:* E.C. COMMISSION *v.* GERMANY (No. 29/84) [1986] 3 C.M.L.R. 579 European Ct.

1522. Directives—implementing legislation—verbatim wording not necessary

The Commission sought a declaration that Italy had failed to meet its obligations under the EEC Treaty by not adopting within the set period the provisions necessary to comply with Council Directive 80/502/EEC of May 6, 1980, amending Directive 74/63/EEC on the fixing of maximum permitted levels for undesirable substances and products in feedingstuffs.

Held, application refused as the Commission had failed to show that the scope of the Italian legislation differed from that of the EEC rules in Directive 80/502. The implementation of a Directive in national law did not necessarily require the verbatim adoption of its provisions by specific legislation.

E.C. COMMISSION *v.* ITALY (No. 363/85), *The Times,* May 5, 1987, European Ct.

1523. Directives—public works contracts—notification of legislation

The European Commission brought proceedings against Italy under Art. 169 EEC for a declaration that, by adopting certain provisions concerning the award of public works contracts and by failing to inform the Commission of the main provisions of national law which it took in the area covered by Council Directive 71/305 of July 26, 1971 regarding the co-ordination of procedures for the award of public works contracts, Italy had failed to fulfil its EEC obligations.

Held, that Italy had failed to fulfil (1) its obligations under Directive 71/305 by adopting the first, third and fifth paragraphs of s.10 and s.13 of Act 741; (2) its obligations under Art. 33 of Directive 71/305 by failing to inform the Commission officially of the text of Act 741. The Directive required EEC States to inform the Commission of the text of the national legislation implementing the Directive. Failure to inform was not rectified by the Commission getting to know of the text by some other means.

PUBLIC WORKS CONTRACTS, *Re*: E.C. COMMISSION *v.* ITALY (No. 274/83) [1987] 1 C.M.L.R. 345, European Ct.

1524. Economic Affairs—directives, decisions and regulations

87/108/EEC:

Commission Decision of December 22, 1986 on applications for assistance from the European Communities concerning exceptional financial support for Greece in the social field, submitted by Greece (1986). (O.J. 1987 L45/21.)

87/178/EEC:

Council Decision of March 9, 1987 giving a discharge to the Commission in respect of the implementation of the operations of the European Development Fund (1969) (Third EDF) for the financial year 1985. (O.J. 1987 L71/30.)

87/179/EEC:

Council recommendation of March 9, 1987 concerning the discharge to be given to the Commission in respect of the implementation of the operations of the European Development Fund (1975) (Fourth EDF) for the financial year 1985. (O.J. 1987 L71/31.)

87/180/EEC:

Council recommendation of March 9, 1987 concerning the discharge to be given to the Commission in respect of the implementation of the operations of the European Development Fund (1979) (Fifth EDF) for the financial year 1985. (O.J. 1987 L71/32.)

87/186/Euratom, ECSC, EEC:

Final adoption of the general budget of the European Communities for the financial year 1987. (O.J. 1987 L86/1.)

87/281/EEC:

Decision of the European Parliament of April 7, 1987 granting a discharge to the Commission in respect of the financial management of the third European Development Fund in the financial year 1985. (O.J. 1987 L13/23.)

87/282/EEC:

Decision of the European Parliament of April 7, 1987 granting a discharge to the Commission in respect of the financial management of the fourth European Development Fund in the financial year 1985. (O.J. 1987 L137/24.)

87/283/EEC:

Decision of the European Parliament of April 7, 1987 granting a discharge to the Commission in respect of the financial management of the fifth European Development Fund in the financial year 1985. (O.J. 1987 L137/25.)

87/284/EEC:

Decision of the European Parliament of April 7, 1987 granting a discharge to the Administrative Board of the European Centre for the Development of Vocational Training in respect of the implementation of its appropriations for the 1985 financial year. (O.J. 1987 L137/28.)

87/285/EEC:

Decision of the European Parliament of April 7, 1987 granting a discharge to the Administrative Board of the European Foundation for the Improvement of Living and Working Conditions in respect of the implementation of its appropriations for the 1985 financial year. (O.J. 1987 L137/29.)

87/398/Euratom, ECSC, EEC:

Final adoption of amending and supplementary budget No. 1 of the European Communities for the financial year 1987. (O.J. 1987 L211/1.)

1525. Education—grants—sex discrimination—effect of European Community law. See R. *v.* SECRETARY OF STATE FOR EDUCATION *ex p.* SCHAFFTER, §1259.

1526. Employer—whether "the state"—test. See ROLLS-ROYCE *v.* DOUGHTY, §1315.

1527. Employment—business transfer—consultation

Two Royal dockyards were placed under commercial management and the yards' employees were transferred into the employment of companies set up to run them. The plaintiffs, trade unions, brought proceedings in which they claimed that the Defence Secretary had not consulted them in accordance with his duty under the Dockyard Services Act 1986 (c.52), which regulated the transfer. That Act re-enacted certain provisions of the Transfer of Undertakings (Protection of Employment) Regulations 1981 (S.I. 1981 No. 1794) (the "1981 Regulations") which were introduced in Britain in pursuance of the EEC Business Transfer Directive 77/187.

Held, dismissing the action, that the Minister had fulfilled his statutory duties; he had taken all reasonable steps to inform the workforce and their representatives and to consult the unions on the introduction of commercial management into the dockyards. In case of ambiguity, the 1981 Regulations should be interpreted, if possible, in conformity with Directive 77/187.

INSTITUTION OF PROFESSIONAL CIVIL SERVANTS *v.* SECRETARY OF STATE FOR DEFENCE [1987] 3 C.M.L.R. 35, Millett J.

1528. Employment—business transfer—employee's rights

Mr. Abels was employed by "X Ltd.". X Ltd. was granted judicial leave to suspend payment of debts, before being put into liquidation on June 9, 1982. On June 10, 1982 the liquidator transferred X Ltd's business to "Y Ltd.", which continued to operate the undertaking and took over most of its employees, including Mr. Abels. Mr. Abels had not received wages for the period from June 1 to 9, 1982 from X Ltd. or Y Ltd. nor certain accrued holiday pay; he sued the Bedrijfsvereniging for those sums, as he claimed that the latter was subsidiarily liable to pay them under Dutch law. The Raad van Beroep, Zwolle, asked the European Court under Art. 177 EEC for a preliminary ruling on the interpretation of Arts. 1(1) and 3(1) of Council Directive 77/187 of February 14, 1977, on the approximation of the laws of the EEC States relating to the safeguarding of employees' rights in the event of transfers of undertakings, businesses or parts of businesses.

Held, that (1) Art. 1(1) of Directive 77/187 does not apply to the transfer of a business or part of a business where the transferor has been declared insolvent and the business in question forms part of the assets of the insolvent transferor, although EEC States are free to apply the principles of the Directive to such a transfer if they wish to do so. However, the Directive does apply where a business or part thereof is transferred to another employer in the course of a procedure such as judicial leave to suspend payment of debts; (2) Art. 3(1) of Directive 77/187 covers obligations of the transferor resulting from employment and arising before the date of the transfer, subject only to the exceptions provided for in Art. 3(3). The second sub-paragraph of Art. 3(1) indicates that it is the transferee who is primarily liable for meeting the liabilities resulting from employees' rights existing at the time of the transfer, but EEC States may provide that the transferor is to bear concurrent liability therefor after the transfer.

ABELS *v.* ADMINISTRATIVE BOARD OF THE BEDRIJFSVERENIGING VOOR DE METAALINDUSTRIE EN DE ELECTROTECHNISCHE INDUSTRIE (No. 135/83) [1987] 2 C.M.L.R. 406, European Ct.

1529. Employment—equal pay—physical exertion as a criterion—different treatment of men and women

[EEC Directive 75/117, Art. 1(1), 1(2).]

Art. 1(2) of the EEC Equal Pay Directive provides that a job classification system "must be based on the same cirterion for both men and women and so drawn up as to exclude any discrimination on the grounds of sex." The respondents, a German printing firm, had a job grading system based on experience, effort and exertion, and responsibility. The applicant contended that she should have been placed in a higher grade than that which the respondents wished, as the physical exertion involved in lifting heavy parcels for her as a woman satisfied the criteria of that higher grade, even though it may not have done so for a man. The Oldenburg Labour Court sought assistance on whether the Directive permitted the use of physical effort as a job evaluation factor and, if so, whether it should be applied in a different way for men and women.

Held, that Art. 1(2) does not preclude the use of physical effort or exertion as a criterion for grading employment if the job does actually require a level of physical strength, provided the system in its entirety precludes discrimination because it takes other criteria into account. A grading system is not discriminatory merely because one of its criteria relates to a characteristic more commonly associated with men, although to preclude discrimination it should permit other criteria to be considered, for which women may show a special aptitude. The EEC Directive does not permit job classification criteria to be applied in a different way to men and women. Work performed must be remunerated according to its nature, regardless of whether it is carried out by men or women.

RUMMLER *v.* DATO-DRUCK GmbH [1987] I.R.L.R. 32, European Ct.

1530. Employment—redundancy—special ECSC payments—steel industry

An employee of British Steel was made redundant. She claimed special "scheme benefit" under the European Communities (Iron & Steel Employees Re-adaptation Benefits Scheme) Regulations 1979–1982, a scheme funded by the ECSC and U.K. Government. She gave all the requisite information in sufficient time in accordance with U.K. Government leaflets. However, she had been given an out of date leaflet. She had taken on part-time work, which although permissible according to the outdated information, disqualified her from receiving scheme benefit. The matter was investigated by the British Ombudsman who found that the Agency Office administering the scheme failed to make proper use of the information which she supplied. The Agency Office were at fault. The Department of Trade and Industry made an exgratia payment to compensate her for being disqualified from such benefit.

STEEL REDUNDANCY BENEFIT, *Re* (No. C114/85) [1987] 1 C.M.L.R. 261, The British Ombudsman.

1531. Environment—directives, decisions and regulations

87/56/EEC:

Council Directive of December 18, 1986 amending Directive 78/1015/EEC on the approximation of the laws of the Member States relating to the permissible sound level and exhaust system of motorcycles. (O.J. 1987 L24/42.)

87/217/EEC:

Council Directive of March 19, 1987 on the prevention and reduction of environmental pollution by asbestos. (O.J. 1987 L85/40.)

Commission Regulation (EEC) No. 526/87 of February 20, 1987 laying down certain detailed rules for the application of Council Regulation (EEC) No. 3528/86 on the protection of the Community's forests against atmospheric pollution. (O.J. 1987 L53/14.)

1532. Equal pay—choice of comparator—effect of EEC Treaty on domestic legislation. See PICKSTONE *v.* FREEMANS, §1322.

1533. Establishment—insurance companies—discrimination

French tax legislation granted shareholder tax credits on the taxable profits of French companies. It gave such credits to French insurance companies and French subsidiaries of foreign insurance companies which held qualifying shares, but not unincorporated French branches of foreign insurance companies. The Commission brought proceedings against France under Art. 169 EEC on the basis that such legislation discriminated against branches and agencies of insurance companies whose registered office was in another EEC State and amounted to an indirect restriction on the freedom to set up a secondary establishment contrary to EEC law and, in particular, Art. 52 EEC.

Held, that France had failed to fulfil its obligations under Art. 52 EEC by not granting to the branches and agencies in France of insurance companies whose registered office is in another EEC State on the same terms as apply to insurance companies whose registered office is in France the benefit of shareholders' tax credits in respect of dividends paid to such branches or agencies by French companies.

TAX CREDITS, *Re*: E.C. COMMISSION *v.* FRANCE (No. 270/83) [1987] 1 C.M.L.R. 401, European Ct.

1534. Establishment—professions—*numerus clausus*

Italian surgeons (the plaintiffs) sued their employers in respect of the unilateral termination of their employment contracts. The plaintiffs argued that their contracts were terminated as a result of the excessive number of young doctors arriving on the market in Italy owing to the absence of a *numerus clausus* for medical students. The plaintiffs alleged that the absence of a *numerus clausus* for medical students was contrary to EEC law. The Preture di Roma asked the European Court for a preliminary ruling under Art. 177 EEC on the interpretation of Arts. 3(*c*) and 57(3) EEC and of the Community Directives on freedom of movement for doctors, in order to ascertain whether those provisions require EEC States to limit the number of students admitted to medical faculties by introducing a *numerus clausus* system.

Held, that EEC law did not require EEC States to limit the number of students admitted to medical faculties by introducing a *numerus clausus* system.

BERTINI *v.* REGIONE LAZIO (No. 98/85, 162/85 and 258/85) [1987] 1 C.M.L.R. 774, European Ct.

1535. Establishment—social security—sickness benefit

Mr. Segers, a Dutch national, was a director of Slenderose Ltd., a company incorporated according to English law. In practice, all its business was conducted by its subsidiary, solely in Holland. Mr. Segers sought sickness insurance benefits under the Ziektewet (the Dutch Act establishing a general sickness insurance scheme). Such benefits were refused on the grounds that he had no employment contract with Slenderose and consequently was not subordinate to an employer. The Ziektewet states that any person in a subordinate position in relation to another person (an employer) is insured. Dutch case law established that a director of a Dutch company was in a subordinate position to it, but it was argued that this did not apply to a company incorporated under foreign law. Mr. Segers claimed that such benefits should be available to directors of foreign companies doing business in Holland. The Centrale Raad van Beroep asked the European Court under Art. 177 EEC for a preliminary ruling on the interpretation of Arts. 52, 58, 60 and 66 EEC and Art. 3 of Council Reg. 1408/71.

Held, that Arts. 52 and 58 EEC prevented EEC States from excluding a director of a company from a national sickness insurance benefit scheme solely on the ground that the company was incorporated according to the law of another EEC State, where it also has its registered office, even though it does not do any business there.

SEGERS (D. H. M.) *v.* BESTUUR VAN DE BEDRIJFSVERENIGING VOOR BANK- EN VERZEKERINGSWEZEN, GROOTHANDEL EN VRIJE BEROEPEN (No. 79/85) [1987] 2 C.M.L.R. 247, European Ct.

1536. European Assembly—elections

EUROPEAN ASSEMBLY ELECTIONS (DAY OF BY-ELECTIONS) (MIDLANDS WEST CONSTITUENCY) ORDER 1987 (No. 20) [45p], made under the European Assembly Elections Act 1978 (c.10), Sched. 1, para. 3(3); operative on January 23, 1987; appoints March 5, 1987 as the date for the Midlands West European Assembly constituency by-election.

EUROPEAN ASSEMBLY ELECTIONS REGULATIONS 1986 (No. 2209) [£4·90], made under the European Assembly Elections Act 1978 (c.10), Sched. 1, para. 2; provide for the conduct of the election of representatives to the European Assembly in England, Wales and Scotland.

1537. Euratom—directives, decisions and regulations

87/183/Euratom:

Commission Decision of March 9, 1987 concerning the final conclusion on behalf of the European Atomic Energy Community, of the Framework Agreements for scientific and technical cooperation between the European Communities and the Kingdom of Sweden, the Swiss Confederation, the Republic of Finland, the Kingdom of Norway and the Republic of Austria. (O.J. 1987 L71/36.)

1538. ECSC—steel production quota figures—disclosure

The applicant, a German iron and steel association, brought an action under Art. 33(2) ECSC asking the Court to annul the Commission's Decision contained in a letter, dated January 13, 1984, to the applicant, whereby it refused to disclose the figures for each steel undertaking (including those which were not members of the applicant) resulting from the fixing and adjustment of steel production quotas under the system introduced pursuant to Art. 58 ECSC. The applicant argued that it wished to secure the complete transparency of the system of the production quotas introduced by the Commission. The Commission argued that Art 47 ECSC on the protection of business secrets obliged it not to disclose such information without agreement of the firms concerned.

Held, that the Decision was void in so far as it refused to disclose figures concerning the quota adjustments granted, pursuant to Arts. 10 to 14c of Decisions 2177/83 and 234/84, to each of the undertakings not belonging to the Eurofer confederation. One had to balance the need for transparency of the common market in steel products against the need to protect the business secrecy of individual undertakings by looking at the circumstances of the particular undertakings involved. In certain instances the need to protect business secrecy would prevail and justify the non-disclosure of figures.

WIRTSCHAFTSVEREINIGUNG EISEN-UND STAHLINDUSTRIE *v.* E.C. COMMISSION (No. 27/84) [1987] 1 C.M.L.R. 171, European Ct.

1539. European Convention on Human Rights—The European School. See HUMAN RIGHTS, §1913.

1540. European Court—annulment proceedings—time-limit

Mr. Misset brought proceedings to annul a decision of the Secretary General of the Council, which was made and notified to him on February 18, 1985. The Council objected to the admissibility of the action as Mr. Misset's application for annulment was lodged on May 21, 1985, which was outside the three months time-limit provided for such an application.

Held, the action was dismissed as inadmissible due to it having been brought outside the requisite three months time-limit. The three months time-limit was expressed in calendar months. Accordingly, the time-limit expired at the end of the day of the relevant month bearing the same number as the day from which time began to run, namely the day of notification.

MISSET *v.* E.C. COUNCIL (No. 152/85), *The Times*, March 23, 1987, European Ct.

1541. European Court—procedure—discovery

Four Greek companies (the "applicants") brought proceedings to annul Decision 86/59 whereby the Council terminated the anti-dumping proceedings regarding imports of dead-burned natural magnesite from the People's Republic of China and North Korea. In order to pursue their action the applicants obtained access to the European Commission's non-confidential file concerning the discontinued anti-dumping proceedings. However, the Commission was continually adding new documents to the file which caused procedural delays as the applicants then required more time to submit comments on the fresh evidence. The applicants applied in summary proceedings under Art. 83 of the Rules of Procedure for an interim order that December 31, 1986 be fixed as the final day for completion of the Commission's file or that any documents not then there should be ignored or that they be given an opportunity to consult and refute the new documents without the danger of over-running the procedural time limits.

Held, that the application would be dismissed as the summary procedure was not a suitable procedure for obtaining measures such as those requested by the applicants. It was indicated that a similar application might have been made under either Art. 45 or Art. 91 of the Rules of Procedure

EPIKHIRISEON METALLEFTIKON VIOMIKHANIKON KAI NAFTILIAKON A.E. *v.* E.C. COUNCIL AND E.C. COMMISSION (No. 2) (Nos. 121–122/86R) [1987] 2 C.M.L.R. 558, European Ct.

1542. European Court—procedure—reference for a preliminary ruling

An Italian magistrate brought criminal proceedings against persons unknown under legal provisions relating to the protection of water supplies. The magistrate took such proceedings after receiving complaints about the high rate of dead fish in an Italian river. The magistrate asked the European Court under Art. 177 EEC for a preliminary ruling on the interpretation of Council Directive 78/659/EEC of July 18, 1978 on the quality of fresh waters needing protection or improvement to support fish life.

Held, that (1) the application was admissible. It was for the national court, and not the European Court to determine at what stage it was appropriate to ask for a preliminary ruling. The decision as to when to make a reference was dictated by considerations of procedural organisation and efficiency. A national court could always make a further reference to the European Court if it thought fit to do so, for example, if a defendant was identified; (2) Council Directive 78/659 could not have the effect, by itself and independently of the internal law of an EEC State adopted for its implementation, of determining or aggravating the criminal liability of persons who acted contrary to its provisions.

CRIMINAL PROCEEDINGS AGAINST A PERSON OR PERSONS UNKNOWN (No. 14/86) *The Times*, June 20, 1987, European Ct.

1543. European Court—procedure—revision of judgment—inadmissibility

Ferriere San Carlo Sp.A ("Ferriere") brought an action for revision of a judgment given by the European Court in Case 235/82 [1983] E.C.R. 3949. That judgment upheld fines imposed by the European Commission on Ferriere for exceeding its steel production quota. While negotiating with the Commission for a longer period of payment for the fine and interest. Ferriere discovered that the Commission applied different interest rates in different EEC States. Ferriere argued that this was contrary to provisions of the European Convention for the Protection of Human Rights, the EEC and ECSC Treaties, and that this discovery entitled it to apply for revision of the judgment.

Held, dismissing the application for revision as inadmissible, that the application was not directed at the judgment but at the means adopted by the Commission for its implementation.

FERRIERE SAN CARLO SpA *v.* E.C. COMMISSION (No. 235/82–Rev) [1987] 3 C.M.L.R. 1, European Ct.

1544. European Court—procedure—service—time limit

Cockerill-Sambre S.A. (the applicant) sought the annulment of Commission Decision C(84)1958/1 of October 19, 1984 which imposed a fine on the applicant for exceeding fixed steel quotas. The Decision was addressed to the applicant's registered office by a letter, dated January 8, 1985. The applicant then sent it to its head office where it was received on January 11, 1985. The applicant's notice of appeal reached the European Court on the very last day if time ran from receipt at head office, but out of time if time ran from receipt at the registered office. The applicant had told the Commission on several occasions to send communications to its head office. The Commission argued that the application was inadmissible as being out of time.

Held, that the application was inadmissible as being out of time; service on the registered office was sufficient and valid. Companies had no right to require communications to be delivered to another place or to a particular person other than the company itself.

COCKERILL-SAMBRE S.A. *v.* E.C. COMMISSION (No. 42/85) [1987] 1 C.M.L.R. 325, European Ct.

1545. EEC Judgments Convention—enforcement—address for service

Mr. Carron sought to set aside the enforcement of a German judgment against him. He argued that the proceedings were void on the ground that in the application initiating the proceedings Germany had failed to give an address for service. An address for service had been given in the document notifying Mr. Carron of the order for enforcement. The Hof van Cassatie, Belgium, asked the European Court to give a preliminary ruling on the interpretation of Art. 33 of the European Judgments Convention.

Held, (1) Art. 33 meant that the obligation to give an address for service had to be done in accordance with the rules set by the law of the State in which enforcement is sought. If that law makes no provision as to the time at which that formality must be met, it should not be done later than the date on which the decision authorising enforcement is served; (2) Art. 33 leaves it to the State in which enforcement is sought, to determine, in accordance with the aims of the Convention, the consequences of a failure to comply with the rules regarding an address for service.

CARRON *v.* GERMANY (No. 198/85) [1987] 1 C.M.L.R. 838, European Ct.

1546. EEC Judgments Convention—enforcement—place of residence

The defendant brought proceedings to challenge leave to register in the Netherlands a default judgment of a Belgian court on the grounds that he was not served with the writ. The defendant had lived and had been registered as living within the jurisdiction of the Belgian court. Prior to proceedings being commenced against him in Belgium, he moved to Holland and registered himself as resident there, but failed to cancel his Belgian registration. The process server could not serve him with the Belgian proceedings at his registered Belgian address, so proceedings were served in accordance with Belgian law on the authority assigned for the case when no person is found on whom the writ can be served. A default judgment was obtained in Belgium.

Held, that the defendant had been properly served under Belgian law and the judgment could be registered for execution in Holland. The Court sought and received advice from the Belgian Minister of Justice as a Belgian law on registration, domicile and service of proceedings.

DONHUYSEN *v.* Pvba BUILDING MATERIALS VAN DEN BROECK [1987] E.C.C. 429, District Ct. 's-Hertogenbosch.

1547. EEC Judgments Convention—enforcement—service

The plaintiff sought to enforce a Belgian Commercial Court judgment against a defendant in Germany.

Held, that enforcement would be refused because the period of time between the date of serving proceedings and the first hearing date in Belgium was only 13 days, which was less than the two week period set by German law and was regarded as insufficient time to prepare a defence in German law. Under Art. 27(2) of the EEC Judgments Convention it was for the "executing" court to decide whether a defendant had been given sufficient time to prepare his defence.

TIME FOR SERVICE OF BELGIAN DEFAULT PROCEEDINGS, *Re* [1987] E.C.C. 276, German Federal Supreme Ct.

1548. EEC Judgments Convention—jurisdiction—contract

P, an architect in Rockenhausen, West Germany, brought proceedings for payment of fees in respect of plans for buildings to be built for D within the Rockenhausen district. Proceedings were brought in the local court of Rockenhausen. D disputed jurisdiction on the basis that he was resident and domiciled in Holland, and Art. 2 of the EEC Judgments Convention laid down the general rule that jurisdiction was based on the place of domicile of D. The Regional Court asked the Court for a preliminary ruling on the interpretation of Art. 5(1) of the EEC Judgments Convention, which provided that in matters of contract D might also be brought before the courts for "the place of performance of the obligation in question".

Held, that in order to determine the place of performance in Art. 5(1) of the EEC Judgments Convention, the obligation to be taken into account in proceedings for recovery of fees brought by an architect instructed to draw up plans for buildings, was the contractual obligation upon which proceedings were founded.

SHENAVAI *v.* KREISCHER (No. 266/85) *The Times,* January 16, 1987, European Ct.

1549. EEC Judgments Convention—jurisdiction—counterclaim

Luis Marburg ("Marburg"), a German company, ordered goods from Ori Martin ("Martin") an Italian company. The order was written in German in a standard printed form, the front of which referred to conditions on the back, which, *inter alia,* contained a jurisdiction clause giving jurisdiction to the German courts. Martin sued Marburg in Italy. Marburg filed defences, both as to jurisdiction and the merits, and counterclaimed.

Held, that the forum clause was valid and binding under Art. 17 of the EEC Judgments Convention. The fact that Marburg had counterclaimed did not prevent it from relying on Art. 18 of the Convention, as Italian procedure required a defendant to file a defence in order to obtain a right of audience before a court so as to have its jurisdictional objections heard. Marburg's position in taking the jurisdiction point was not prejudiced by filing a counterclaim.

LUIS MARBURG & SÖHNE GmbH *v.* SOCIETÀ ORI MARTIN SpA [1987] E.C.C. 424, Italian Supreme Ct.

1550. EEC Judgments Convention—jurisdiction—forum clause

Mr. Anterist acted as a guarantor of a firm's debts *vis-à-vis* the Crédit Lyonnais, a French bank. He signed a guarantee which stated that the court within whose jurisdiction (the relevant branch of the bank) is situated shall have exclusive jurisdiction to adjudicate upon all matters concerning the performance of the agreement. As a result of the firm's failure to pay its debt, the bank brought proceedings in Germany against the guarantor. Mr. Anterist challenged the jurisdiction of the German Courts arguing that a French court should have exclusive jurisdiction under the terms of the agreement contained in the guarantee. The Bundesgerichtshof asked the European Court for a preliminary ruling on the interpretation of Art. 17 of the EEC Judgments Convention.

Held, that (1) Art. 17 of the EEC Judgments Convention permitted the parties to select, by agreement, the court(s) which were to have jurisdiction in relation to any disputes between them. Para. 1 of Art. 17 conferred exclusive jurisdiction on the court(s) referred to in the clause, while para. 3 preserved the right of the party for whose benefit the clause had been included to bring proceedings before any other court which had jurisdiction by virtue of the Convention; (2) para. 3 of Art. 17 was to be interpreted so as to give effect to the joint intention of the parties on the conclusion of the agreement; (3) an agreement conferring jurisdiction was not to be regarded as having been concluded for the benefit of only one of the parties within the meaning of para. 3 of Art. 17 when it was established only that the parties had agreed that jurisdiction was to be conferred upon the court(s) of the contracting State in which that party was domiciled.

ANTERIST *v.* CRÉDIT LYONNAIS (No. 22/83) [1987] 1 C.M.L.R. 333, European Ct.

1551. EEC Judgments Convention—jurisdiction—forum clause—default judgment

Mr Plaumann, a German, sought to set aside a default judgment obtained against him by the Dutch firm of Machinefabriek A. Van der Linden B.V. ("Linden") in the Arrondissementsrechtbank, Middelburg. Mr Plaumann argued that that Court did not have jurisdiction, but the German Courts had jurisdiction. The Dutch plaintiff had relied on a forum clause contained in a letter confirming the parties' agreement which referred in English to its conditions and a reference to the jurisdiction of the Rechtbank, Middelburg.

Held, that the judgment was set aside. Linden could not rely on the forum clause as it had not been raised in the oral agreements between the parties and it was only mentioned in English as one of its conditions printed on the back of its standard notepaper which it used to confirm the agreements reached. The clause could not be regarded as freely agreed by both parties. Thus, the forum clause did not form part of the agreement between the parties and it did not comply with Art. 17 of the EEC Judgments Convention. Accordingly Linden's claim was inadmissible.

PLAUMANN *v.* MACHINEFABRIEK A. VAN DER LINDEN B.V. [1987] E.C.C. 20, District Ct. Middelburg.

1552. EEC Judgments Convention—jurisdiction—forum clause—sufficient connection

Transocean Towage Co., a Maltese company, issued a writ against Hyundai Construction Co., a Korean company, in a Dutch court. The writ related to a dispute about the performance of a contract concluded in Bahrain. The contract contained a forum clause in favour of Dutch courts.

Held, that jurisdiction would be refused. Art. 17 of the EEC Judgments Convention requires that before a court of an EEC State can assume jurisdiction under a forum clause in a contract, at least one of the contracting parties has to be domiciled in one of the EEC States. Neither contracting party had sufficient connection with Holland to found jurisdiction in a Dutch Court.

TRANSOCEAN TOWAGE CO. *v.* HYUNDAI CONSTRUCTION CO. [1987] E.C.C. 282, Supreme Ct. of the Netherlands.

1553. EEC Judgments Convention—jurisdiction—tort—contract

A German company brought proceedings to recover from a German bank the amount of guarantees wrongly enforced against it by the bank after its successful completion of an agreement with a Belgian firm, now in liquidation, for the construction of water-filtering and fuel storage plant for a factory in Libya. The bank disputed the jurisdiction of the German courts.

Held, that the German courts had jurisdiction (1) in tort in light of the broad interpretation given by the European Court to the concept of 'a tort, delict or quasi-delict' contained in Art. 5(3) of the EEC Judgments Convention; and (2) in contract since the place of performance of the contract of gurarantee for the purposes of Art. 5(1) of the Convention was Germany.

BANK GUARANTEE, A, *Re* [1987] E.C.C. 26, German Federal Supreme Ct.

1554. EEC Judgments Convention—jurisdiction—two fora

The plaintiff brought proceedings in Italy and then in Germany based on the same cause of action and against the same defendant. He wished to go ahead with his action in Germany as proceedings were going too slowly in Italy.

Held, that that proceedings would be stayed in Germany; the slowness of proceedings in Italy was not sufficient reason for ousting Art. 21 of the EEC Judgments Convention. Under Art. 21(1) it was the duty of the second Court to decline jurisdiction in favour of the first Court.

PROCEEDINGS IN TWO FORA, *Re* [1987] E.C.C. 273, German Federal Supreme Ct.

1555. European Parliament—elections—campaign costs

The general budget of the EEC included item 3708 which provided for appropriations intended as a "contribution to the costs of preparations" for the next European elections. On October 12, 1982, the Bureau of the European Parliament adopted a decision establishing the distribution of the appropriations allocated to item 3708. That decision was elaborated upon by rules adopted on September 29, 1983. The rules provided that 31 per cent. of the appropriations allocated to item 3708 were to be distributed to political groupings which took part in the 1983 elections while the remaining 69 per cent. were to be divided among the parties represented in the European Parliament elected in 1979. The French Ecologist Party, "Les Verts", sought the annulment of the 1982 decision and the 1983 rules on the ground, *inter alia,* that in accordance with Art. 138 EEC and Art. 7(2) of the Act concerning the election of the representatives of the assembly by direct universal suffrage of September 20, 1976, that financial scheme was to be governed by the national legislation of the EEC States and that parties already represented in the 1979 Parliament were able to draw on both the 69 per cent. and the reserve fund of 31 per cent. and were thereby given a considerable advantage by comparison with political grouping which had no representatives in the assembly elected in 1979.

Held, that (1) an action for annulment might be brought against acts of the European Parliament which were intended to have legal force with regard to third parties; (2) "Les Verts" was an association which was individually concerned by the disputed acts; (3) at the present state of EEC law, the establishment of a system of reimbursement of election campaign costs and the determination of its detailed implementation remained within the competence of the Member States pursuant to Art. 7(2) of the Act. Thus, the European Parliament had infringed Art. 7(2) of the Act by adoption of the decision of October 12, 1982 and the 1983 rules. Accordingly, the decision and rules were void.

PARTIE ECOLOGISTE "LES VERTS" *v.* EUROPEAN PARLIAMENT (No. 294/83) [1987] 2 C.M.L.R. 343, European Ct.

1556. European Parliament—Member of European Parliament—legal immunity

Mr. Faure, a Member of the European Parliament (a "MEP") was summoned to appear in the Tribunal Correctionel, Paris, to answer a charge of being an accessory to the public defamation of a civil servant. It was argued on Mr. Faure's behalf that he enjoyed, during the session of the Parliament, the immunities, including legal immunity, conferred by Art. 10 of the Protocol on Privileges and Immunities of the European Communities ("the Protocol"). The Parliament had been in session from March 5, 1982 to March 7, 1983, although not actually sitting on the date of the summons, January 27, 1983. The Cour d'Appel asked the European Court under Art. 177 EEC for the preliminary ruling on the interpretation of Art. 10 of the Protocol.

Held, that Art. 10 of the Protocol which granted MEPs immunity "during the sessions of the Assembly," was to be interpreted as meaning that the European Parliament was to be regarded as being in session, even if it was not actually sitting, up to the time of the closure of the annual or extraordinary sessions. An interpretation of "sessions" as being merely times when the Parliament was actually sitting would jeopardise the achievement of the various activities of the Parliament.

WYBOT *v.* FAURE (No. 149/85) [1987] 1 C.M.L.R. 819, European Ct.

1557. European Parliament—payments to political parties—interim measures

The Bureau of the European Parliament made a decision, dated July 10 1986, on the distribution of funds of political parties with regard to direct elections in Spain and Portugal, which was disadvantageous to the European Right Group and National Front Party ("the applicant"). The applicant brought an action for annulment of that decision. On September 11, 1986 the applicant applied for interim suspension of the decision. Despite being informed of this decision, the Parliament had distributed most of the ECUs to political parties in accordance with the decision.

Held, that in order to ensure that the interlocutory proceedings were not deprived of their substance and their effect, the following interim measures were ordered: (1) operation of the decision suspended until an order is made terminating these interlocutory proceedings; (2) the European Parliament was directed that (i) it should not pay out the remaining sums which had been designated for distribution until an order is made terminating these interlocutory proceedings; (ii) it must take all necessary steps to ensure that the political groups within the Parliament did not use the sums paid to them by Parliament pursuant to the decision; (iii) it should notify the President of the European Court by September 22, 1986 of steps it had taken to comply with the Court order.

GROUP OF THE EUROPEAN RIGHT and THE NATIONAL FRONT PARTY *v.* EUROPEAN PARLIAMENT (No. 221/86R [1986] 3 C.M.L.R. 462, President of the European Ct.

1558. Export—butter—buying cruises—monetary compensatory amounts

The plaintiff was a supplier of butter for sale on "butter-buying cruises". These cruises left Holland and sailed for a short time outside territorial waters so passengers could purchase goods, including butter, free of duties and other charges. The plaintiff asked the Produktschap (the Dutch body responsible for organising the Dutch market in milk products) whether butter supplied for "butter-buying cruises" qualified for monetary compensatory amounts ("m.c.a.s."). The Produktschap said they did qualify for m.c.a.s. and paid the plaintiff m.c.a.s. for some months. Later the European Commission informed the Dutch Government that m.c.a.s. should not be paid in respect of supplies to such butter-buying cruises. The Dutch Government instructed Produktschap to reject such applications for m.c.a.s. Produktschap informed the plaintiff that m.c.a.s. would no longer be granted. The plaintiff challenged that decision before the College van Beroep. The latter asked the European Court for a preliminary ruling under Art. 177 EEC on the interpretation of Commission Regs. 2730/79 and 1371/81.

Held, that Arts. 1 and 2 of Reg. 1371/81 and Art. 5 of Reg. 2730/79 meant that no m.c.a.s. may be granted in respect of butter supplied for sale to passengers during cruises at sea which begin from, and return to, one and the same EEC State. There was no exportation of the butter, nor was it being supplied to victual the ship.

COÖPERATIEVE MELKPRODUCTENBEDRIJVEN "NOORD- NEDERLAND" BA *v.* PRODUKTSCHAP VOOR ZUIVEL (No. 275/84) [1987] 1 C.M.L.R. 809, European Ct.

1559. Exports—unfair commercial practices—GATT

AKZO complained to the European Commission that the application of s.337 of the U.S. Tariff Act 1930 in the matter of "certain aramid fibres", an action instigated by Dupont, amounted to an illicit commercial practice of the U.S. Government, and that the resulting order by the U.S. International Trade Commission to exclude from the U.S. market unlicensed imports of certain types of aramid fibre manufactured outside the U.S. by AKZO, an EEC producer, was causing or threatening to cause injury to an EEC industry. AKZO was the sole producer of aramid fibres in the EEC. The European Commission regarded the complaint as justifying it opening an investigation procedure under Reg. 2641/84. The Commission completed the examination procedure under Art. 6 of Reg. 2641/84.

Held, that (1) the application of s.337 of the U.S. Tariff Act 1930 in the case of "certain aramid fibres" showed sufficient evidence of an illicit commercial practice and resultant threat of injury as defined by Reg. 2641/84 to warrant further action; (2) the procedure for consultation and dispute settlement referred to in Art. XXIII of GATT is to be initiated with regard to the application of s.337 of the U.S. Tariff Act 1930 in respect of certain types of aramid fibre manufactured by AKZO.

U.S. LITIGATION BETWEEN E.I. DUPONT DE NEMOURS & CO. AND AKZO N.V., *Re* [1987] 2 C.M.L.R. 545, E.C. Commission.

1560. External affairs—directives, decisions and regulations

86/658/EEC:

Council Decision of December 22, 1986 on the conclusion of an Agreement in the form of an exchange of letters concerning the provisional application of the Protocol establishing the fishing rights and financial compensation provided for in the Agreement between the European Economic Community and the Government of the Republic of Senegal on fishing off the coast of Senegal for the period October 1, 1986 to February 28, 1988. (O.J. 1987 L382/30.)

86/661/EEC:

Council Decision of December 22, 1986 on the conclusions of an Agreement in the form of an Exchange of Letters between the European Economic Community and the Republic of Finland concerning trade in certain wines and spirituous beverages. (O.J. 1987 L383/46.)

87/114/EEC:

Commission Decision of December 12, 1986 authorising the U.K. to introduce intra-Community surveillance of imports of certain television receivers originating in the People's Republic of China which have been put into free circulation in the other Member States. (O.J. 1987 L49/28.)

87/121/EEC:

Commission Decision of January 16, 1987 authorising the Portuguese Republic to introduce intra-Community surveillance of imports of motorcycles originating in Japan which have been put into free circulation in one of the Member States. (O.J. 1987 L49/44.)

87/443/EEC:

Commission Decision of July 30, 1987 amending an undertaking and accepting an undertaking given in connection with the anti-dumping review investigation concerning imports of copper sulphate originating in Poland and the U.S.S.R. respectively, and terminating the investigation as it concerns these countries. (O.J. 1987 L235/22.)

87/267/EEC:

Council Decision of April 28, 1987 concerning the conclusion of a Convention between the European Economic Community and the Republic of Austria, the Republic of Finland, the Republic of Iceland, the Kingdom of Norway, the Kingdom of Sweden and the Swiss Confederation on the simplification of formalities in trade in goods. (O.J. 1987 L134/1.)

87/370/EEC:

Council Decision of May 26, 1987 concerning the conclusion of the Agreement in the form of an Exchange of Letters amending the Agreement of July 14, 1986 adjusting the Agreement between the European Economic Community and the Kingdom of Norway, concerning mutual trade in cheese (O.J. 1987 L196/77.)

87/415/EWG:

Council Decision of June 15, 1987 concerning the conclusion of a Convention between the European Community, the Republic of Austria, the Republic of Finland, the Republic of Iceland, the Kingdom of Norway, the Kingdom of Sweden and the Swiss Confederation on a common transit procedure. (O.J. 1987L226/1.)

87/474/EEC:

Council Decision of September 17, 1987 concerning the conclusion of an Agreement in the form of an Exchange of Letters concerning the provisional application of the Agreement between the European Economic Community and the Government of the People's Republic of Angola on fishing off Angola. (O.J. 1987 L268/64.).

87/518/EEC:

Council Decision of October 19, 1987 on the conclusion of an Agreement in the form of an Exchange of Letters concerning the provisional application, from June 1, 1987, of the Agreement amending the Agreement between the European Economic Community and the Government of the Democratic Republic of São Tomé and Principe on fishing off São Tomé and Principe, signed at Brussels on February 1, 1984, with effect from June 1, 1987. (O.J. 1987 L300/31.)

87/531/EEC:
Council Decision of October 20, 1987 on the conclusion of the Agreement in the form of an exchange of letters between the European Economic Community and the Government of the German Democratic Republic on trade in sheep and goats and sheepmeat and goatmeat. (O.J. 1987 L309/107.)

Commission Decision No. 1822/87/ECSC of June 29, 1987 concerning the application of Decision No. 2/87 of the ACP—EEC Council of Ministers on the advance implementation of the Protocol to the Third ACP—EEC Convention, consequent on the Accession of the Kingdom of Spain and the Portuguese Republic to the European Communities, with regard to products covered by the ECSC Treaty. (O.J. 1987 L172/105.)

Commission Regulation (EEC) No. 4131/86 of December 23, 1986 amending the Annexes to Council Regulation (EEC) No. 182/86 and Regulation (EEC) No. 3714/85 in so far as concerns imports of certain textile products originating in the People's Republic of China. (O.J. 1987 L383/10.)

Commission Regulation (EEC) No. 4132/86 of December 23, 1986 concerning Annexes III and VII to Council Regulation (EEC) No. 2072/84 on common rules for imports of certain textile products originating in the People's Republic of China. (O.R. 1987 L383/20.)

Commission Regulation (EEC) No. 2409/87 of August 6, 1987 imposing a provisional anti-dumping duty on imports of ferro-silicon originating in Brazil and accepting undertakings offered by Italmagnesio S.A. of Brazil and from Promsyrio-Import of the U.S.S.R. (O.J. 1987 L219/24.)

Council Regulation (EEC) No. 3973/86 of December 22, 1986 concerning the application of the Protocols on financial and technical cooperation concluded between the Community and Algeria, Morocco, Tunisia, Egypt, Lebanon, Jordan, Syria, Malta and Cyprus. (O.J. 1986 L370/5.)

Council Regulation (EEC) No. 4130/86 of December 22, 1986 amending Regulation (EEC) No. 2072/84 on common rules for imports of certain textile products originating in the People's Republic of China. (O.J. 1987 L383/1.)

Council Regulation (EEC) No. 252/87 of January 19, 1987 on the conclusion of the Agreement amending the Agreement between the European Economic Community and the Government of the Republic of Equatorial Guinea on fishing off the coast of Equatorial Guinea, signed at Malabo on June 15, 1984. (O.J. 1987 L29/1.)

Council Regulation (EEC) No. 253/87 of January 19, 1987 on the conclusion of the Agreement between the European Economic Community and the Government of the Republic of Guinea amending the Agreement between the European Economic Community and the Government of the Revolutionary People's Republic of Guinea on fishing off the coast of Guinea, signed at Conakry on February 7, 1983. (O.J. 1987 L2959.)

Council Regulation (EEC) No. 428/87 of February 9, 1987 setting up a system of compensation for loss of export earnings for least-developed countries not signatory to the Third ACP—EEC Convention. (O.J. 1987 L43/1.)

Council Regulation (EEC) No. 429/87 of February 9, 1987 laying down detailed rules for the implementation of Regulation (EEC) No. 428/87 setting up a system of compensation for loss of export earnings for least-developed countries not signatory to the Third ACP—EEC Convention. (O.J. 1987 L43/3.)

Council Regulation (EEC) No. 1316/87 of May 11, 1987 on the safeguard measures provided for in the Third ACP-EEC Convention. (O.J. 1987 L125/1.)

Council Regulation (EEC) No. 1820/87 of June 25, 1987 concerning the application of Decision No. 2/87 of the ACP—EEC Council of Ministers on the advance implementation of the Protocol to the Third ACP—EEC Convention consequent on the Accession of the Kingdom of Spain and the Portuguese Republic to the European Communities. (O.J. 1987 L172/1.)

Council Regulation (EEC) No. 2512/87 of August 18, 1987 amending Regulation (EEC) No. 2786/83 imposing a definitive anti-dumping duty on imports of copper sulphate originating in Czechoslovakia and the U.S.S.R. (O.J. 1987 L235/18.)

Council Regulation (EEC) No. 3442/87, of October 19, 1987, concerning the conclusion of an Agreement in the form of an exchange of letters on the amendment of the Agreement between the European Economic Community and the Republic of Austria on the application of the rules on Community transit and concerning the application in the Community of Decision No. 1/87 of the EEC-Austria Joint Committee on Community transit amending the Agreement between the European Economic Community and the Republic of Austria on the application of the rules on Community transit, and the Appendices thereto. (O.J. 1987 L332/1.)

Council Regulation (EEC) No. 3442/87, of October 19, 1987, concerning the conclusion of an Agreement in the form of an exchange of letters on the amendment of the Agreement between the European Economic Community and the Swiss Confederation on the application of the rules on Community transit and concerning the application in the Community of Decision No. 1/87 of the EEC-Switzerland Joint Committee on Community transit amending the Agreement between the European Economic Community and the Swiss Confederation on the application of the rules on Community transit, and the Appendices thereto. (O.J. 1987 L332/108.)

Council Regulation (EEC) No. 3544/87 of November 23, 1987 relating to the conclusion of the Agreement amending the Agreement between the European Economic Community and the Government of the Democratic Republic of São Tomé and Principe on fishing off São Tomé and Principe, signed at Brussels on February 1, 1984. (O.J. 1987 L337/1.)

Council Regulation (EEC) No. 3620/87 of November 30, 1987 concerning the conclusion of the Agreement between the European Economic Community and the Government of the People's Republic of Angola on fishing off Angola. (O.J. 1987 L341/1.)

Information on the date of entry into force of the Additional Protocol to the Cooperation Agreement between the European Economic Community and the Republic of Tunisia, signed in Brussels on May 26, 1987. (O.J. 1987 L309/113.)

Information on the date of entry into force of the Agreement amending the Agreement between the European Economic Community and the Government of the Democratic Republic of Madagascar on fishing off the coast of Madagascar, signed at Antananarivo on January 28, 1986. (O.J. 1987 L342/31.)

Information on the date of entry into force of the Agreement between the European Economic Community and the Republic of Seychelles on fishing off Seychelles. (O.J. 1987 L309/106.)

Notice of the date of entry into force of the Agreement amending the Agreement between the European Economic Community and the Government of the Republic of Equatorial Guinea on fishing off the coast of Equatorial Guinea, signed at Malabo on June 15, 1984. (O.J. 1987 L326/30.)

1561. Fisheries—directives, decisions and regulations

87/37/EEC:

Commission Decision of December 15, 1986 on the extension of the multiannual guidance programme for 1986 in respect of the fishing fleet submitted by the Federal Republic of Germany pursuant to Council Regulation (EEC) No. 2908/83. (O.J. 1987 L17/25.)

87/38/EEC:

Commission Decision of December 15, 1986 on the extension of the multiannual guidance programme for 1986 in respect of the fishing fleet submitted by Belgium pursuant to Council Regulation (EEC) No. 2908/83. (O.J. 1987 L17/28.)

87/278/EEC:

Council Decision of May 18, 1987 on Community financial contribution to the development of the monitoring and supervision facilities necessary for applying the Community arrangements for the conservation of fishery resources. (O.J. 1987 L135/31.)

87/446/EEC:

Commission Decision of July 31, 1987 amending Decision 74/441/EEC relating to the setting up of a Joint Committee on Social Problems in Sea Fishing. (O.J. 1987 L240/35.)

Commission Regulation (EEC) No. 3771/86 of December 10, 1986 concerning the stopping of fishing for haddock by vessels flying the flag of Belgium. (O.J. 1986 L349/26.)

Commission Regulation (EEC) No. 3946/86 of December 22, 1986 concerning the stopping of fishing for haddock by vessels flying the flag of the Netherlands. (O.J. 1987 L365/37.)

Commission Regulation (EEC) No. 3947/86 of December 22, 1986 modifying Regulation (EEC) No. 3582/86 concerning the stopping of fishing for herring by vessels flying the flag of Ireland. (O.J. 1987 L365/38.)

Commission Regulation (EEC) No. 3948/86 of December 22, 1986 concerning the stopping of fishing for sprat by vessels flying the flag of Denmark. (O.J. 1987 L365/39.)

Commission Regulation (EEC) No. 3958/86 of December 23, 1986 concerning the stopping of fishing for horse mackerel by vessels flying the flag of a Member State apart from Spain and Portugal. (O.J. 1987 L365/59.)

Commission Regulation (EEC) No. 3988/86 of December 23, 1986 suspending for the 1987 fishing year the duties applicable to fresh fishery products originating in Morocco and coming from joint fishery ventures set up between natural or legal persons from Portugal and Morocco, on the direct landing of such products in Portugal. (O.J. 1986 L370/47.)

Commission Regulation (EEC) No. 3989/86 of December 23, 1986 opening tariff quotas for the 1987 fishing year for fishery products coming from joint ventures set up between natural or legal persons from Spain and from other countries. (O.J. 1986 L370/48.)

Commission Regulation (EEC) No. 4099/86 of December 23, 1986 fixing, for the 1987 fishing year, the withdrawal and selling prices for fishery products listed in Annex I (A), (D) and (E) of Regulation (EEC) No. 3796/81. (O.J. 1986 L379/1.)

Commission Regulation (EEC) No. 4100/86 of December 23, 1986 fixing the standard values to be used in calculating the financial compensation and the advance pertaining thereto in respect of fishery products withdrawn from the market during the 1987 fishing year. (O.J. 1986 L379/9.)

Commission Regulation (EEC) No. 4101/86 of December 23, 1986 amending Regulation (EEC) No. 3321/82 as regards the sizes of sardine and anchovy eligible for the carry-over premium. (O.J. 1986 L379/11.)

Commission Regulation (EEC) No. 4102/86 of December 23, 1986 fixing the amount of the carry-over premium for certain fishery products for the 1987 fishing year. (O.J. 1986 L379/13.)

Commission Regulation (EEC) No. 4103/86 of December 23, 1986 fixing the storage premium for certain fishery products for the 1987 fishing year. (O.J. 1986 L379/15.)

Commission Regulation (EEC) No. 4104/86 of December 23, 1986 modifying Regulation (EEC) No. 3611/84 fixing the conversion factors for frozen squid. (O.J. 1986 L379/17.)

Commission Regulation (EEC) No. 4105/86 of December 23, 1986 fixing the reference prices for fishery products for the 1987 fishing year. (O.J. 1986 L379/19.)

Commission Regulation (EEC) No. 4106/86 of December 23, 1986 fixing the guaranteed minimum price for Atlantic sardines. (O.J. 1986 L379/25.)

Commission Regulation (EEC) No. 4107/86 of December 23, 1986 fixing the compensatory allowance for Mediterranean sardines. (O.J. 1986 L379/26.)

Commission Regulation (EEC) No. 4108/86 of December 23, 1986 fixing the reference prices for intra-Community trade in anchovies and Atlantic sardines for the 1987 fishing year. (O.J. 1986 L379/27.)

Commission Regulation (EEC) No. 4109/86 of December 23, 1986 fixing, for the 1987 fishing year, the annual import quotas for the products subject to the rules for the application by Spain and Portugal of quantitative restrictions on fishery products. (O.J. 1986 L379/28.)

Commission Regulation (EEC) No. 4110/86 of December 23, 1986 fixing, for the 1987 fishing year, the overall foreseeable level of imports for the products subject to the supplementary trade mechanism in the fisheries sector. (O.J. 1986 L379/30.)

Commission Regulation (EEC) No. 209/87 of January 23, 1987 on the financing of transport costs resulting from the free distribution of fishery products withdrawn from the market. (O.J. 1987 L22/28.)

Commission Regulation (EEC) No. 237/87 of January 27, 1987 amending Regulation (EEC) No. 546/86 laying down detailed rules for applying the supplementary trade mechanism to fishery products. (O.J. 1987 L25/13.)

Commission Regulation (EEC) No. 362/87 of February 4, 1987 concerning the stopping of fishing for cod, whiting, plaice, sole and hake by vessels flying the flag of the Netherlands. (O.J. 1987 L35/8.)

Commission Regulation (EEC) No. 659/87 of March 4, 1987 concerning the stopping of fishing for salmon by vessels flying the flag of Denmark. (O.J. 1987 L63/16.)

Commission Regulation (EEC) No. 735/87 of March 13, 1987 concerning the stopping of fishing for cod by vessels flying the flag of France. (O.J. 1987 L71/23.)

Commission Regulation (EEC) No. 742/87 of March 16, 1987 concerning the stopping of fishing for cod by vessels flying the flag of Germany. (O.J. 1987 L75/5.)

Commission Regulation (EEC) No. 894/87 of March 27, 1987 laying down transitional provisions and detailed rules for the application, as regards measures for the modernisation of the fishing fleet, of Council Regulation (EEC) No. 4028/86. (O.J. 1987 L88/1.)

Commission Regulation (EEC) No. 970/87 of March 26, 1987 laying down transitional measures and detailed rules for the application of Council Regulation (EEC) No. 4028/86 with regard to the renewal and restructuring of the fishing fleet, the development of aquaculture and structural works in coastal waters. (O.J. 1987 L96/1.)

Commission Regulation (EEC) No. 1075/87 of April 15, 1987 concerning the stopping of fishing for saithe by vessels flying the flag of the United Kingdom. (O.J. 1987 L104/23.)

Commission Regulation (EEC) No. 1381/87 of May 20, 1987 establishing detailed rules concerning the marking and documentation of fishing vessels. (O.J. 1987 L132/9)

Commission Regulation (EEC) No. 1382/87 of May 20, 1987 establishing detailed rules concerning the inspection of fishing vessels. (O.J. 1987 L132/11.)

Commission Regulation (EEC) No. 1425/87 of May 25, 1987 concerning the stopping of fishing for cod by vessels flying the flag of the Netherlands. (O.J. 1987 L136/12.)

Commission Regulation (EEC) No. 1629/87 of June 10, 1987 concerning the stopping of fishing for cod by vessels flying the flag of Germany. (O.J. 1987 L152/14).

Commission Regulations (EEC) No. 1766/87 of June 24, 1987 concerning the stopping of fishing for horse mackerel by vessels flying the flag of a Member State apart from Spain and Portugal. (O.J. 1987 L167/19.)

Commission Regulation (EEC) No. 1791/87 of June 26, 1987 amending Regulation (EEC) No. 1677/87 concerning the stopping of fishing for cod by vessels flying the flag of Belgium. (O.J. L168/30.)

Commission Regulation (EEC) No. 1880/87 of June 30, 1987 amending Regulation (EEC) No. 4034/86 fixing, for certain fish stocks and groups of fish stocks, the total allowable catches for 1987 and certain conditions under which they may be fished. (O.J. 1987 L179/4.)

Commission Regulation (EEC) No. 2066/87 of July 14, 1987 concerning the stopping of fishing for sand eel by vessels flying the flag of a Member State. (O.J. 1987 L194/6.)

Commission Regulation (EEC) No. 2067/87 of July 14, 1987 concerning the stopping of fishing for shrimps by vessels flying the flag of Denmark. (O.J. 1987 L194/7.)

Commission Regulation (EEC) No. 2149/87 of July 20, 1987 concerning the stopping of fishing for plaice and saithe by vessels flying the flag of the U.K. (O.J. 1987 L201/28.)

Commission Regulation (EEC) No. 2177/87 of July 20, 1987 amending Regulations (EEC) No. 4043/86, (EEC) No. 4022/86 and (EEC) No. 3513/86 opening, allocating and providing for the administration of community tariff quotas for fish and fish fillets originating in Norway or Sweden. (O.J. 1987 L203/1.)

Commission Regulation (EEC) No. 2186/87 of July 23, 1987 fixing for the 1987/88 marketing year the reference prices for carp. (O.J. 1987 L203/22.)

Commission Regulation (EEC) No. 2228/87 of July 27, 1987 concerning the stopping of fishing for cod by vessels flying the flag of Spain. (O.J. 1987 L206/7.)

Commission Regulation (EEC) No. 2248/87 of July 28, 1987 amending Regulation (EEC) No. 4109/86 fixing, for the 1987 fishing year, the annual import quotas for the products subject to the rules for the application by Spain and Portugal of quantitative restrictions on fishery products. (O.J. 1987 L207/25.)

Commission Regulation (EEC) No. 2389/87 of August 6, 1987 concerning the stopping of fishing for saithe by vessels flying the flag of Ireland. (O.J. 1987 L218/21.)

Commission Regulation (EEC) No. 2452/87 of August 13, 1987 concerning the stopping of fishing for haddock by vessels flying the flag of the Netherlands. (O.J. 1987 L227/14.)

Commission Regulation (EEC) No. 2489/87 of August 17, 1987 concerning the stopping of fishing for plaice by vessels flying the flag of Belgium. (O.J. 1987 L231/6.)

Commission Regulation (EEC) No. 2490/87 of August 17, 1987 concerning the stopping of fishing for plaice by vessels flying the flag of Belgium. (O.J. 1987 L231/7.)

Commission Regulation (EEC) No. 2538/87 of August 21, 1987 concerning the stopping of fishing for Norway pout by vessels flying the flag of a Member State. (O.J. 1987 L241/5.)

Commission Regulation (EEC) No. 2623/87 of August 31, 1987 concerning the stopping of fishing for herring by vessels flying the flag of the Netherlands. (O.J. 1987 L248/24.)

Commission Regulation (EEC) No. 2624/87 of August 31, 1987 concerning the stopping of fishing for pollack by vessels flying the flag of Ireland. (O.J. 1987 L248/25.)

Commission Regulation (EEC) No. 2625/87 of August 31, 1987 concerning the stopping of fishing for plaice by vessels flying the flag of the Netherlands. (O.J. 1987 L248/26.)

Commission Regulation (EEC) No. 2626/87 of August 31, 1987 concerning the stopping of fishing for cod by vessels flying the flag of Germany. (O.J. 1987 L248/27.)

Commission Regulation (EEC) No. 2848/87 of September 23, 1987 concerning the stopping of fishing for sole by vessels flying the flag of the U.K. (O.J. 1987 L272/13.)

Commission Regulation (EEC) No. 2899/87 of September 29, 1987 concerning the stopping of fishing for sole by vessels flying the flag of the Netherlands. (O.J. 1987 L277/5.)

Commission Regulation (EEC) No. 2977/87 of October 2, 1987 repealing Regulation

(EEC) No. 1836/87 concerning the stopping of fishing for whiting by vessels flying the flag of Belgium. (O.J. 1987 L280/18.)

Commission Regulation (EEC) No. 2978/87 of October 2, 1987 concerning the stopping of fishing for plaice by vessels flying the flag of Belgium. (O.J. 1987 L280/19.)

Commission Regulation (EEC) No. 3067/87 of October 12, 1987 concerning the stopping of fishing for cod by vessels flying the flag of Belgium. (O.J. 1987 L290/19.)

Commission Regulation (EEC) No. 3132/87 of October 20, 1987 repealing Regulation (EEC) No. 2685/87 concerning the stopping of fishing for pollack by vessels flying the flag of Spain. (O.J. 1987 L296/17.)

Commission Regulation (EEC) No. 3137/87 of October 20, 1987 repealing Regulation (EEC) No. 1677/87 concerning the stopping of fishing for cod by vessels flying the flag of Belgium. (O.J. 1987 L298/5.)

Commission Regulation (EEC) No. 3138/87 of October 20, 1987 repealing Regulation (EEC) No. 2624/87 copncerning the stopping of fishing for pollack by vessels flying the flag of Ireland. (O.J. 1987 L298/6.)

Commission Regulation (EEC) No. 3151/87 of October 22, 1987 concerning the catch declarations of vessels flying the flag of a Member State and operating in the fishing zone of certain developing countries. (O.J. 1987 L300/15.)

Commission Regulation (EEC) No. 3165/87 of October 22, 1987 repealing Regulation (EEC) No. 3041/87 concerning the stopping of fishing for horse mackerel by vessels flying the flag of a Member State apart from Spain and Portugal. (O.J. 1987 L301/17.)

Commission Regulation (EEC) No. 3166/87 of October 22, 1987 concerning the stopping of fishing for cod by vessels flying the flag of Denmark. (O.J. 1987 L301/18.)

Commission Regulation (EEC) No. 3167/87 of October 22, 1987 concerning the stopping of fishing for sprat by vessels flying the flag of Denmark. (O.J. 1987 L301/19.)

Commission Regulation (EEC) No. 3288/87 of October 30, 1987 repealing Regulation (EEC) No. 3166/87 concerning the stopping of fishing for cod by vessels flying the flag of Denmark. (O.J. 1987 L309/82.)

Commission Regulation (EEC) No. 3314/87 of November 3, 1987 ordering the stopping of fishing for mackerel by vessels flying the flag of the Netherlands. (O.J. 1987 L315/22.)

Commission Regulation (EEC) No. 3315/87 of November 3, 1987 concerning the stopping of fishing for mackerel by vessels flying the flag of the United Kingdom. (O.J. 1987 L315/23.)

Commission Regulation (EEC) No. 3333/87 of November 4, 1987 concerning the stopping of fishing for mackerel by vessels flying the flag of a Member State. (O.J. 1987 L316/22.)

Commission Regulation (EEC) No. 3363/87 of November 9, 1987 concerning the stopping of fishing for plaice by vessels flying the flag of the Netherlands. (O.J. 1987 L320/8.)

Commission Regulation (EEC) No. 3456/87 of November 18, 1987 concerning the stopping of fishing for mackerel by vessels flying the flag of Denmark. (O.J. 1987 L328/33.)

Commission Regulation (EEC) No. 3457/87 of November 18, 1987 repealing Regulation (EEC) No. 1075/87 concerning the stopping of fishing for saithe by vessels flying the flag of the United Kingdom. (O.J. 1987 L328/34.)

Commission Regulation (EEC) No. 3472/87 of November 19, 1987 concerning the stopping of fishing for saithe by vessels flying the flag of Germany. (O.J. 1987 L329/19.)

Commission Regulation (EEC) No. 3520/87 of November 23, 1987 concerning the stopping of fishing for cod by vessels flying the flag of Belgium. (O.J. 1987 L335/7.)

Commission Regulation (EEC) No. 3570/87 of November 26, 1987 concerning the stopping of fishing for whiting by vessels flying the flag of the Netherlands. (O.J. 1987 L338/17.)

Commission Regulation (EEC) No. 3616/87 of December 1, 1987 concerning the stopping of fishing for sprat by vessels flying the flag of a Member State. (O.J. 1987 L340/24.)

Commission Regulation (EEC) No. 3624/87 of December 2, 1987 concerning the stopping of fishing for sole, hake and megrim by vessels flying the flag of the United Kingdom. (O.J. 1987 L341/20.)

Commission Regulation (EEC) No. 3626/87 of December 1, 1987 concerning the stopping of fishing for plaice by vessels flying the flag of Denmark. (O.J. 1987 L341/23.)

Commission Regulation (EEC) No. 3640/87 of December 2, 1987 concerning the stopping of fishing for herring by vessels flying the flag of France. (O.J. 1987 L342/8.)

Commission Regulation (EEC) No. 3645/87 of December 3, 1987 concerning the stopping of fishing for plaice by vessels flying the flag of the United Kingdom. (O.J. 1987 L342/20.)

Commission Regulation (EEC) No. 3669/87 of December 8, 1987 concerning the stopping of fishing for mackerel by vessels flying the flag of Ireland. (O.J. 1987 L345/16.)

Council Regulation (EEC) No. 3930/86 of December 18, 1986 fixing the guide prices for the fishery products listed in Annex 1(A), (D) and (E) of Regulation (EEC) No. 3796/81 for the 1987 fishing year. (O.J. 1987 L365/5.)

Council Regulation (EEC) No. 3931/86 of December 18, 1986 fixing the guide prices for the fishery products listed in Annex II to Regulation (EEC) No. 3796/81 for the 1987 fishing year. (O.J. 1987 L365/8.)

Council Regulation (EEC) No. 3932/86 of December 18, 1986 fixing the Community producer price for tuna intended for the canning industry for the 1987 fishing year. (O.J. 1987 L365/10.)

Council Regulation (EEC) No. 4026/86 of December 18, 1986 amending Regulation (EEC) No. 3094/86 laying down certain technical measures for the conservation of fishery resources. (O.J. 1987 L376/1.)

Council Regulation (EEC) No. 4027/86 of December 18, 1986 amending Regulation (EEC) No. 2057/82 establishing certain control measures for fishing activities by vessels of the Member States. (O.J. 1987 L376/4.)

Council Regulation (EEC) No. 4028/86 of December 18, 1986 on Community measures to improve and adapt structures in the fisheries and aquaculture sector. (O.J. 1987 L376/7.)

Council Regulation (EEC) No. 4035/86 of December 22, 1986 allocating certain catch quotas between Member States for vessels fishing in the Norwegian economic zone and the fishery zone around Jan Mayen. (O.J. 1987 L376/80.)

Council Regulation (EEC) No. 4036/86 of December 22, 1986 allocating catch quotas between Member States for vessels fishing in Swedish waters. (O.J. 1987 L376/83.)

Council Regulation (EEC) No. 4038/86 of December 22, 1986 allocating catch quotas between Member States for vessels fishing in Faroese waters. (O.J. 1987 L376/92.)

Council Regulation (EEC) No. 1171/87 of April 28, 1987 on the conclusion of the Agreement amending for the second time the Agreement between the European Economic Community and the Government of the Republic of Guinea-Bissau on fishing off the coast of Guinea-Bissau. (O.J. 1987 L110/1.)

Council Regulation (EEC) No. 1172/87 of April 28, 1987 allocating additional catch quotas among Member States for vessels fishing in Swedish waters. (O.J. 1987 L113/11.)

Council Regulation (EEC) No. 1392/87 of May 18, 1987 amending Regulation (EEC) No. 500/87 fixing catch possibilities for 1987 for certain fish stocks and groups of fish stocks in the Regulatory Area as defined in the NAFO Convention. (O.J. 1987 L133/11.)

Council Regulation (EEC) No. 1365/87 of May 18, 1987 amending Regulation (EEC) No. 4034/86 fixing, for certain fish stocks and groups of fish stocks, the total allowable catches for 1987 and certain conditions under which they may be fished. (O.J. 1987 L129/15.)

Council Regulation (EEC) No. 1638/87 of June 9, 1987 fixing the minimum mesh size of pelagic trawls used in fishing for blue whiting in that part of the area covered by the Convention on Future Multilateral Cooperation in the North-East Atlantic Fisheries which extends beyond the maritime waters falling within the fisheries jurisdiction of Contracting Parties to the Convention. (O.J. 1987 L153/7.)

Council Regulation (EEC) No. 3545/87 of November 23, 1987 amending for the fourth time Regulation (EEC) No. 4034/86 fixing, for certain fish stocks and groups of fish stocks, the total allowable catches for 1987 and certain conditions under which they may be fished. (O.J. 1987 L337/7.)

1562. Fishing—crews—nationality

Irish legislation was passed in 1983 requiring that three-quarters of crew members on fishing boats registered in Eire or the U.K. and fishing within Irish exclusive fishery limits should be EEC nationals. The plaintiff, an Irish-Spanish joint-venture company, fished in Irish waters. The plaintiff's crews were Spanish nationals and were not EEC nationals as Spain had not yet become a member of the EEC. The plaintiff argued that the legislation was contrary to EEC law. The Irish High Court asked the European Court under Art. 177 EEC for a preliminary ruling on the interpretation of Arts. 100 and 102 of the Act of Accession 1972, Arts. 1 and 2(1) of Reg. 101/76 and Art. 6 of Reg. 170/83, and on whether the legislation was discriminatory on grounds of nationality contrary to Art. 7 EEC.

PESCA VALENTIA *v.* MINISTER FOR FISHERIES & FORESTRY [1987] 1 C.M.L.R. 856, Irish High Court.

1563. Food regulations—materials and articles in contact with food. See FOOD AND DRUGS, §1811.

1564. Free movement of workers—aliens—deportation—residence

Mrs. Botta, a Mauritian national, married a German national. She and her husband lived for some years in England and were convicted of criminal offences. Deportation orders were issued against them both. Mr. Botta was deported. Mrs. Botta's appeal against her deportation order was allowed. She then went to Germany for two months and on her return was refused entry to the U.K. She applied for judicial review of the decision to refuse entry.

Held, that the application for judicial review was refused as (1) Mrs. Botta had no right of entry as the wife of an EEC national as her husband was no longer resident in the U.K.; (2) she was not a "returning resident" as she could not show the five years continuous residence required for registration as a British subject. Once the deporation order against Mr. Botta took effect, Mrs. Botta lost the privilege of living with him in the U.K. as the spouse of an EEC worker.

R. *v.* SECRETARY OF STATE FOR THE HOME DEPARTMENT, *ex p.* BOTTA (JACQUELINE) [1987] 2 C.M.L.R. 189, Russell J.

1565. Free movement of workers—part-time worker—claiming social security benefits

Mr. Kempf, a German, came to Holland and worked as a part-time music teacher. He received social security payments from Dutch public funds. He applied for a residence permit in order "to pursue an activity as an employed person" in Holland. It was refused because, *inter alia,* he did not qualify as a favoured EEC citizen within the meaning of Dutch immigration legislation as he had had recourse to public funds in Holland and was therefore unable to meet his needs out of the income received from his employment. The Raad van State asked the European Court under Art. 177 EEC for a preliminary ruling on the interpretation of EEC law on the free movement of workers.

Held, that an EEC national who pursues within another EEC State work, which is effective and genuine part-time employment, cannot be excluded from the provisions of EEC law on the freedom of movement of workers merely because his income therefrom is below the level of the minimum means of subsistence and he seeks to supplement it by other lawful means of subsistence. It is irrelevant whether the supplementary income comes from property or from the employment of a relative or from public funds. Such a person is a "worker" within the broad interpretation given to that word by EEC law.

KEMPF *v.* STAATSSECRETARIS VAN JUSTITIE (No. 139/85) [1987] 1 C.M.L.R. 764, European Ct.

1566. Free movement of workers—qualifications—recognition

Mr. Heylens, a Belgian national, held a Belgian football trainer's diploma and was a professional trainer at a French Club. His application for recognition of his Belgian diploma was rejected after an adverse decision by a French Committee, which gave no reasons for its decision. Criminal proceedings were taken against him (and his club) for working as a football trainer without the French diploma or a recognised foreign qualification. The Regional Court, Lille, asked the European Court under Art. 177 EEC for a preliminary ruling.

Held, that where in an EEC State, access to a profession was subject to the possession of a national qualification or of a foreign qualification recognised as its equivalent the principle of the free movement of workers set by Art. 48 EEC required that a decision which refused a worker recognition of a qualification issued by an EEC State of which he was a national, should be subject to legal remedy. Such legal redress would enable the legality of that decision to be established with regard to EEC law. Further, the person involved should be told the reasons upon which the decision was based.

UNION NATIONALE DES ENTRAINEURS ET CADRES TECHNIQUES PROFESSIONELS DU FOOTBALL (UNECTEF) *v.* HEYLENS (No. 222/86) *The Times,* October 26, 1987, European Ct.

1567. Free movement of workers—rail travel—discrimination

Mr. Iorio, an Italian lawyer, boarded at Rome station a "rapido" express train, which was going to Palermo and Syracuse. Second-class passengers were only allowed to board that train if they had tickets for journeys longer than 400 km. Mr. Iorio had a second-class ticket for a shorter distance. Mr. Iorio refused to pay the fine set for such an infringement. As a result the railway administration, acting under rules provided by Italian legislation, issued an order for him to pay 30,000 lire in respect of the infringement. Mr. Iorio lodged an objection against that order, claiming that Italian rules limiting access to certain trains were contrary to EEC principles on the freedom of movement for workers and, in particular, Art. 48(3)(*b*) EEC. The Deputy Magistrate of Latina asked the European Court under Art. 177 EEC for a preliminary ruling on the interpretation of Art. 48 EEC.

Held, that Art. 48(3)(*b*) EEC and the measures adopted thereunder, do not apply to matters which are purely internal to an EEC State, such as those involving a national of an EEC State, who has never resided or worked in another EEC State. EEC law and, in particular, Art. 48 EEC, does not prevent the imposition of national rules restricting access to public transport, provided such restrictions are applied without discrimination and justified on objective and general grounds.

IORIO *v.* AZIENDA AUTONOMA DELLE FERROVIE DELLO STATO (No. 298/84) [1986] 3 C.M.L.R. 665, European Ct.

1568. Free movement of workers—residence permits—non-married partners

Miss Reed, a U.K. national went to the Netherlands. She applied for a resident permit in order to be able to live there with Mr. W., a U.K. national, who was working in the Netherlands. Miss Reed and Mr. W. had had a stable relationship for about five years. Miss Reed's application for a residence permit was rejected. She applied to the Dutch Courts for an order to restrain the Netherlands from taking any measure which might result in her deportation. She was granted such an order, but the State appealed. The Supreme Court of the Netherlands asked the European Court for a preliminary ruling under Art. 177.

Held, that the right granted by an EEC State to its own nationals to enable them to obtain permission for their non-married partners, who were not nationals of that EEC State, to reside on its territory, was a social advantage within Art. 7(2) of Council Regulation 1612/68. Therefore, an EEC State which granted such an advantage to its national workers could not refuse it to workers who were nationals of other EEC States without discriminating on the ground of nationality contrary to Arts. 7 and 48 EEC.

NETHERLANDS, THE *v.* REED (ANN FLORENCE) (No. 59/85) [1987] 2 C.M.L.R. 448, European Ct.

1569. Free movement of workers—status of trainee teacher

[EEC Treaty (Cmnd. 5179-11) Art. 48(1)(4).]

A trainee teacher is a worker for the purposes of Art. 48(1) of the EEC Treaty and has freedom of movement within the EEC; the exception as to employees in the public service under Art. 48(4) does not apply.

P, a British subject, was a trainee teacher in West Germany. Her application for admission to the preparatory service at a teachers' training college was refused on the ground that entrants were temporary civil servants, and posts in the civil service were only open to German nationals. The German courts held that a trainee teacher was not a "worker" within art. 48(1) of the EEC Treaty, and that even if he was, the exemption of public servants in art. 48(4) applied.

Held, on the reference of the case to the European Court of Justice by the federal administrative court, that, (1) "worker" in art. 48(1) should be interpreted broadly, *i.e.* one person performing services and under the direction of another person for remuneration, which included a trainee teacher, and (2); art. 48(4) should be narrowly construed as including only what was necessary to safeguard the interests of the state, *i.e.,* not a trainee teacher (*Sotgiu* v. *Deutsche Bundespost* (No. 152/73) [1975] C.L.Y. 1276, *Walrave and Koch* v. *Association Union Cycliste Internationale* (No. 36/74) [1975] C.L.Y. 1253 and *Levin* v. *Staatssecretaris van Justitie* (No. 53/81) [1982] C.L.Y. 1235 applied).

LAWRIE-BLUM *v.* LAND BADEN-WÜRTTEMBERG (No. 66/85) [1987] I.C.R. 483, European Ct.

1570. Freedom to provide services—insurance—co-insurance

The European Commission brought proceedings against Ireland under Art. 169 EEC for a declaration that Ireland had failed to fulfil its obligations under Arts. 59 and 60 EEC and Council Directive 78/473 of May 30, 1978 on the co-ordination of laws, regulations and administrative provisions relating to EEC co-insurance by (i) adopting s.4 of the European Communities (Co-Insurance) Regulations 1984, which requires EEC insurance undertakings, which wish to offer co-insurance services in Ireland as lead insurers, either to be authorised and therefore established in Ireland or to give notice to the relevant Irish Minister and obtain his consent; (ii) adopting para. 3 of the Schedule to the said regulations which prevent EEC insurers from providing co-insurance services in Ireland for contracts for sums below that set out in para. 3. The Commission further claimed that by applying the legislation referred to in (i) and (ii), instead of Arts. 59 and 60 EEC, Ireland had failed to meet the obligations imposed on it arising from the direct effect of those Articles and the primacy of EEC law.

Held, that Ireland had failed to meet its obligations under Arts. 59 and 60 EEC and Directive 78/473 by obliging EEC insurance undertakings which wished to offer co-insurance services in Ireland as lead insurers either to be authorised and therefore established in Ireland or, alternatively, to give notice to the relevant Irish Minister and obtain his consent. The remainder of the applicaiton was dismissed.

CO-INSURANCE SERVICES, *Re:* E.C. COMMISSION (NETHERLANDS AND U.K. INTERVENING) *v.* IRELAND (BELGIUM, DENMARK AND FRANCE INTERVENING) (No. 206/84) [1987] 2 C.M.L.R. 150, European Ct.

1571. Freedom to provide services—insurance—co-insurance

The European Commission brought proceedings against France under Art. 169 EEC for a declaration that France had failed to fulfil its obligations under Arts. 59 and 60 EEC by passing legislation which (i) required EEC insurance undertakings either to be established in France or to complete a procedure for prior authorisation in order to be able, as a leading insurer, to offer co-insurance services in France; (ii) prevented EEC insurance undertakings which are not established in France from participating in co-insurance operations for certain risks. The Commission further claimed that by applying the legislation referred to in (i) and (ii), instead of Arts. 59 and 60 EEC, France had failed to meet its obligations under Arts. 59 and 60 EEC and under the rule of the primacy of EEC law.

Held, that France had failed to fulfil its obligations under Arts. 59 and 60 EEC by obliging EEC insurance undertakings to be established in France and to complete a procedure for prior authorisation in order to be able to offer co-insurance services in France as a leading insurer. The remainder of the application was dismissed.

CO-INSURANCE SERVICES, *Re:* E.C. COMMISSION (U.K. AND NETHERLANDS INTERVENING) *v.* FRANCE (ITALY, BELIGUM, GERMANY AND IRELAND INTERVENING) (No. 220/83) [1987] 2 C.M.L.R. 113, European Ct.

1572. Freedom to provide services—insurance—co-insurance

The European Commission brought proceedings against Denmark under Art. 169 EEC for a declaration that Denmark had (i) failed to meet its obligations under Arts. 59 and 60 EEC by passing legislation which (a) required EEC insurance undertakings which wished to offer co-insurance services in Denmark as lead insurers to be established in Denmark, (b) prevented EEC insurance undertakings not established in Denmark from participating in certain co-insurance activities; (ii) failed to meet its obligations under Arts. 52, 59 and 60 EEC and Art. 6 of Directive 73/269 of July 24, 1973 by requiring special authorisation for insurance activities, including co-insurance, in other EEC States, and setting conditions for the grant of authorisation which differ according to whether the undertaking's principal place of business is in Denmark or whether it merely has branches in Denmark, but has its principal place of business elsewhere in the EEC; (iii) failed to meet its obligations under Arts. 59 and 60 EEC and to observe the primacy of EEC law by applying the legislation referred to in (i) and (ii) above.

Held, that Denmark had failed to meet its obligations under Arts. 59 and 60 EEC by obliging EEC insurance undertakings to become established in Denmark in order to be able to offer EEC co-insurance services in Denmark as lead insurers. The remainder of the application was dismissed.

INSURANCE SERVICES, *Re*: E.C. COMMISSION (NETHERLANDS AND U.K. INTERVENING) *v.* DENMARK (BELGIUM AND IRELAND INTERVENING) (No. 252/83) [1987] 2 C.M.L.R. 169, European Ct.

1573. Human rights—freedom of traders—labelling

Criminal proceedings were brought against Mr. Keller in Germany for having infringed Commission Reg. 997/81 by using the words "fully fermented" on the labels of table wine produced by him, whereas the only term authorised by the Regulation to indicate the residual content of that sort of wine was "dry." The Amtsgericht Breisach-am-Rhein asked the European Court under Art. 177 EEC for a preliminary ruling on the validity of Art. 2(2)(h) of Council Reg. 355/79 and Art. 13(6) of Commission Reg. 997/81.

Held, Art. 2(2)(h) of Reg. 355/79 and Art. 13(6) of Reg. 997/81 were valid. Whereas EEC rules on the labelling of wine place some restrictions on the activities of the traders concerned, they do not impinge on the the actual substance of the freedom of such traders to pursue their activities.

STAATSANWALT FREIBURG *v.* KELLER (No. 234/85) [1987] 1 C.M.L.R. 875, European Ct.

1574. Human rights—sex discrimination—equal pay

Mrs. Murphy and other female employees worked at Bord Telecom Eireann's factory where they dismantled, cleaned, oiled and reassembled telephones and other equipment. They claimed to be entitled to be paid at the same rate as a male employee in the factory. The Irish High Court asked the European Court under Art. 177 EEC for a preliminary ruling on whether "work of equal value" under Art. 1 of the Equal Pay Directive 75/117 and Art. 119 EEC could cover cases where the lower paid applicants' work was not of equal value, but was of superior value.

MURPHY (MARY) *v.* BORD TELECOM EIREANN [1987] 1 C.M.L.R. 559, Irish High Court.

1575. Human rights—sex discrimination—social security

The respondent sought an order requiring the Netherlands to suspend or render ineffective national legislation, which excluded married women from unemployment benefit in certain circumstances until such legislation was replaced by provisions implementing Art. 4 of Council Directive 79/7 on the progressive implementation of the principle of equal treatment for men and women in social security matters. The Regional Court of Appeal, The Hague, asked the European Court of Justice under Art. 177 EEC for a preliminary ruling on Art. 4(1).

Held, that Art. 4(1) of Directive 79/7 on the prohibition of sexual discrimination in social security matters, might, in the absence of implementation of the Directive, be relied upon with effect from December 23, 1984, before the national courts of EEC States as against the application of any provision of national law which did not comply with Art. 4(1).

THE NETHERLANDS *v.* FEDERATIE NEDERLANDSE VAKBEWEGING (No. 71/85) *The Times,* January 14, 1987. European Ct.

1576. Imports—appellation—jenever

Miro BV, sold in its Dutch off-licences, bottles of jenever imported from Belgium, which had an alcohol content of 30 per cent. The bottles had labels, which stated, *inter alia* "Jonge Jenever—Genièvre—30 per cent. volume". Miro was prosecuted under Dutch legislation which prohibited the appellation of, *inter alia,* "Jenever" (or any other similar appellation which might reasonably induce purchasers to believe that a distilled beverage is jenever) from being used in instances where the jenever had an alcohol content below 35 per cent. Belgium traditionally produced bottles of jenever with an alcohol content of 30 per cent. Miro BV was prosecuted for infringing Dutch Law in selling bottles with such labelling. The Gerechtshof, Arnhem, asked the European Court of Justice under Art. 177 EEC for a preliminary ruling on the interpretation of Art. 30 EEC in order to enable it to determine the compatibility of the Dutch legislation on the use of the appellation "jenever" with EEC law.

Held, that (1) the ban contained in Art.30 EEC on measures having an effect equivalent to quantitative restrictions prevented an EEC State from applying to goods of the same kind imported from another EEC State national legislation under which the appellation of a national beverage might be used only if that beverage had a minimum alcohol content provided (a) those imported goods are lawfully and traditionally made and sold under the same appellation in the EEC State from which the goods originated; and (b) purchasers are provided with proper information. (2) It is contrary to EEC Law, and, in particular Art. 30 EEC, for national legislation to restrict a generic term to one national variety to the disadvantage of other varieties, thus requiring suppliers of other varieties from other EEC States to use appellations which are either not known or held in less regard by consumers.

MIRO BV (No. 182/84) [1986] 3 C.M.L.R. 545, European Ct.

1577. Imports—customs—levy—free circulation

A consignment of maize came by ship from the U.S.A. The maize was cleared through customs at an Italian port, but was not unloaded. It was then shipped to Rotterdam and unloaded there. The plaintiffs argued that they should pay reduced import levy, as Art. 23(1) of Council Reg. 120/67 provided for the imposition of a levy at a reduced rate where certain feed grain, including maize, was imported by sea into Italy. Italy's Supreme Court of Cassation asked the European Court under Art. 177 EEC for a preliminary ruling on the interpretation of Art. 23(1) of Council Reg. 120/67 and Art. 1(3) of Council Reg. 542/69 on Community transit.

Held, that (1) the words "imported by sea" in Art. 23(1) of Reg. 120/67 on the common organisation of the market in cereals did not cover clearance of goods through customs on board ship where such goods were forwarded, without being unloaded, to a port in another EEC State. The particularly low levies provided for by Reg. 120/67 were designed to counteract the particularly high Italian port charges and, therefore, did not apply unless the goods were unloaded incurring port charges; (2) agricultural goods imported by sea into Italy with the benefit of a reduction of the levy were in free circulation within the EEC for the purposes of Art. 1(3) of Council Reg. 542/69.

PADOVANI *v.* AMMINISTRAZIONE DELLE FINANZE DELLO STATO (Nos. 69/84) [1987] 1 C.M.L.R. 62, European Ct.

1578. Imports—customs—post-clearance recovery of import duty

In 1981 Stinnes A.G. ("Stinnes") imported 502 consignments of wooded pallets into West Germany from Czechoslovakia. Stinnes were mistakenly undercharged import duty. On the basis of Council Reg. 1697/79, the Hauptzollamt Kassel issued four post-clearance recovery orders for each quarter of 1981 for import duty due. Stinnes contested the four recovery orders on the ground that they were contrary to Art. 8(1) of Reg. 1697, which provides that no action is to be taken for the post-clearance recovery of import duties where the amount involved "for a given action for recovery" was less than a specified minimum. Stinnes claimed that, if the Hauptzollamt Kassel has not combined the 502 import transactions in four post-clearance recovery orders, only five of those transactions would have given rise to the payment of supplementary duty attaining the minimum amount fixed in Art. 8(1). It claimed that it was contrary to Art. 8(1) to combine separate transactions in that way and that the recovery orders in question should therefore be cancelled. The Hessisches Finanzgericht asked the European Court under art. 177 EEC for a preliminary ruling on the interpretation of Art. 8.

Held, that the words "a given action for recovery" in Art. 8 of Reg. 1697/79 referred to each individual import or export transaction. That interpretation did not preclude the practice of combining several separate actions for recovery in a single recovery order, provided that the amount concerned in each action exceeded the amount specified in the first paragraph of Art. 8.

STINNES A.G. *v.* HAUPTZOLLAMT KASSEL (No. 214/84) [1987] 2 C.M.L.R. 379, European Ct.

1579. Imports—designation of name—vinegar

The European Commission brought proceedings against Italy under Art. 169 EEC as it had continued to restrict the designation "vinegar" solely to wine vinegar despite a ruling of the European Court that such a restriction was unlawful (*see E.C. Commission* v. *Italy (No. 193/80),* December 9, 1981, [1981] E.C.R. 3019). Such a restriction had the effect of creating marketing conditions which were more favourable to wine vinegar, which was produced in substantial quantities in Italy, as compared to comparable products of non-wine vinegar imported from other EEC States.

Held, Italy had failed to fulfil its obligations under Art. 171 EEC by continuing to restrict the designation "vinegar" solely to wine vinegar, although that limitation had been held to be contrary to Art. 30 EEC by the European Court in Case No. 193/80.

WINE VINEGAR (No. 2), *Re:* E.C. COMMISSION *v.* ITALY (No. 281/83) [1987] 1 C.M.L.R. 865, European Ct.

1580. Imports—foodstuffs—additives—health

Kampfmeyer—France Sàrl (hereafter referred to as "K") imported from West Germany a preparation called 'Phénix' used in the manufacture of pastry products. Phénix contained the emulsifying agent E 475, which was lawfully marketed in Germany, but which was not authorised in France. K and its manager, Mr. Müller, were prosecuted and convicted in France of offences connected with using this unauthorised agent. Mr. Müller appealed, relying on Art. 30 EEC and on the provisions of Council Directive 74/329 on the approximation of the laws of EEC States relating, *inter alia,* to emulsifiers for use in foodstuffs. The Court of Appeal Colmar, asked the European Court under Art. 177 EEC for a preliminary ruling on the interpretation of Directive 74/329 and Arts. 30 to 36 EEC.

Held, that (1) Directive 74/329 did not prevent an EEC State from banning the use of one of the substances listed in Annex I to the Directive, including E 475, providing the conditions laid down in Art. 5 (period and degree of prohibition) and Art. 8 (labelling) were met and, as regards the imports of foodstuff that Arts. 30 to 36 EEC were complied with; (2) Arts. 30 to 36 EEC did not stop an EEC State from banning the marketing of foodstuffs to which one of the substances listed in Annex I to Directive 74/329 has been added and which have been imported from other EEC States in which they were lawfully marketed. However, the marketing of such foodstuffs must be authorised, under a procedure easily accessible to manufacturers and traders, if the addition of the substance in question meets a genuine need and presents no danger to public health. It is up to the national authorities to prove in each case, in the light of national eating habits and with due regard to the results of international scientific research, that the rules are justified in order to give effective protection to the interests referred to in Art. 36 EEC.

MINISTÈRE PUBLIC *v.* MÜLLER AND KAMPFMEYER-FRANCE SÀRL (No. 304/84) [1987] 2 C.M.L.R. 469, European Ct.

1581. Imports—free circulation—textiles

Tezi Textiel BV ("Tezi") brought proceedings (No. 59/84) under Arts. 173(2) and 178 EEC for the annulment of the Commission's decision of December 14, 1983, authorising the Benelux countries not to apply Community treatment to certain clothing from Macao and in free circulation in other EEC States, and for compensation from the Commission for damage suffered by Tezi as a result of that decision. Tezi also challenged the Dutch Minister for Economic Affairs' refusal to grant Tezi licences to import certain clothing originating from Macao and in free circulation in Italy. The College van Beroep voor het Bedrijfsleven asked the European Court for a preliminary ruling on the interpretation of Arts. 113 and 115 EEC (No. 242/84).

Held, (1) dismissing the application in No. 59/84, that the Commission did not exceed the limits of its powers under Art. 115 EEC by authorising the Benelux States, in the contested decision, to adopt protective measures in relation to the goods in issue; (2) interpreting Arts. 113 and 115 EEC in No. 242/84, those Arts. meant that the Commission might still apply Art. 115 in relation to trade in textile goods that are subject to that regulation after the conclusion of the Arrangement regarding international trade in textiles ("the Multi-Fibre Arrangement") and the adoption of Council Reg. 3589/82.

TEZI TEXTIEL B.V. *v.* E.C. COMMISSION (NETHERLANDS AND U.K. INTERVENING) (No. 59/84); TEZI TEXTIEL B.V. *v.* MINISTER FOR ECONOMIC AFFAIRS (No. 242/84) [1987] 3 C.M.L.R. 64, European Ct.

1582. Imports—free of CCT duties—computers

Control Data Belgium Inc. sought the annulment of the European Commission's Decision No. 83/521 of October 12, 1983, in which the Commission stated that certain computers could not be imported free of common customs tariff (CCT) duties.

Held, the Decision was declared void; in deciding whether or not computers might be imported into the EEC free of CCT duties, the Commission should have considered whether they were primarily suitable for scientific purposes and, if they were, it should have admitted them duty free, even if they could also be used in industry.

CONTROL DATA BELGIUM INC. *v.* E.C. COMMISSION (No. 13/84) *The Times,* January 22, 1987, European Ct.

1583. Imports—goods in free circulation in EEC—internal tax

Cooperativa Co-frutta SRL ("Co-frutta") imported bananas into Italy which had originated in Colombia, but had been put into free circulation in the Benelux countries. Co-frutta brought proceedings before the District Court of Milan to recover monies Co-frutta had paid in respect of a state consumption tax upon those banana imports, on the ground that the tax constituted a charge having an effect equivalent to a customs duty contrary to Arts. 9 and 12 EEC. The District Court asked the European Court under Art. 177 EEC for a preliminary ruling of interpretation of Arts. 9, 12 and 95 EEC.

Held, (1) a charge described as a consumption tax, levied on imported and domestic products but which in practice applied almost totally to imported products because there was only an extremely limited domestic production, did not amount to a charge having an effect equivalent to a customs duty contrary to Arts. 9 and 12 EEC. Such a charge constituted an internal tax within Art. 95 EEC if it formed part of a general scheme of internal taxation imposed systematically on categories of products according to objective criteria which were applied independently of the origin of those products; (2) the second paragraph of Art. 95 EEC prohibited a consumption tax on certain imported fruit if it was likely to protect domestically grown fruit; (3) Art. 95 EEC applied to all products of EEC States including products originating in non-EEC States which were in free circulation within EEC States.

COOPERATIVA CO-FRUTTA SRL *v.* AMMINISTRAZIONE DELLE FINANZE DELLO STATO (No. 193/85), *The Times,* May 13, 1987, European Ct.

1584. Imports—import licences—listed endangered species

The complainant was sent a briefcase made of crocodile skin as a gift from Hong Kong. Under Art. 5 of EEC Council Reg. 3626/82 the import of listed endangered species, such as this crocodile skin, into the EEC required a licence, issued in Britain by the Department of the Environment ("D.O.E."). The complainant applied for an import licence but received a notice of seizure from Customs before his application for a licence had been determined. After months of delays, an import licence was granted.

The Ombudsman criticised the handling of the matter by Customs and the D.O.E. As a result of the case the D.O.E. changed its procedure for dealing with applications for such licences.

IMPORTATION OF A CROCODILE-SKIN BRIEFCASE, *Re* [1987] 2 C.M.L.R. 904, British Ombudsman.

1585. Imports—medicinal products—price controls

The European Commission issued a policy statement on the compatibility with Art. 30 EEC of measures taken by EEC States relating to price controls and reimbursement of medicinal products.

PRICE CONTROLS AND REIMBURSEMENT OF MEDICINAL PRODUCTS (POLICY STATEMENT) (No. 86/C 310/08) [1987] 1 C.M.L.R. 391, E.C. Commission.

1586. Imports—monetary compensatory amounts—refusal to pay

The plaintiff in Eire sold grain to purchasers in Northern Ireland. The intervention agency in Eire refused to pay monetary compensation amounts ("m.c.a.s") to the plaintiff as it believed that some of the grain had been clandestinely re-imported into Eire for re-exportation to the U.K. The plaintiff was not party to any such irregularity or fraud and he brought proceedings in Eire to recover the m.c.a.s. The Supreme Court of Ireland asked the European Court under Art. 177 EEC for a preliminary ruling on the obligation to pay m.c.a.s,

Held, that (1) the exporting EEC State, which had the obligation to pay the m.c.a.s, was justified in refusing to pay those m.c.a.s where the produce had not entered the importing EEC State for home use due to the purchaser's fraud, even though the necessary formalities and forms had been completed and the exporter had acted in good faith; (2) the exporting EEC State had to justify such refusal to make payment on the basis of grave suspicions formed on objective grounds which had not been dispelled by its inquiries. In such circumstances refusal to pay m.c.a.s. was justified unless proof was given that the produce had actually entered the importing EEC State for home use.

IRISH GRAIN BOARD (TRADING) *v.* MINISTER FOR AGRICULTURE (No. 254/85) [1987] 1 C.M.L.R. 727, European Ct.

1587. Imports—parallel imports—licence for parallel import of medicine from other EEC states—whether infringement of trade marks a relevant consideration in decision to issue parallel import licence. See R. *v.* SECRETARY OF STATE FOR SOCIAL SERVICES, *ex p.* WELLCOME FOUNDATION, §3750.

1588. Imports—price controls—meat

Mr. Roelstraete, a Belgian retail butcher, was prosecuted for selling meat at prices which exceeded those laid down by Belgian legislation. Mr. Roelstraete argued that the legislation was incompatible with Council Regulation 121/67 on the common organisation of the market of pigmeat and of Council Regulation 805/68 on the common organisation of the market in beef and veal. The Cour d'Appel, Brussels asked the European Court of Justice under Art. 177 EEC for a preliminary ruling on the interpretation of both Regulations.

Held, that (1) national legislation directed at controlling retail prices of beef, veal and pigmeat and which prohibited retailers from selling meat to consumers at a price exceeding the wholesale price plus a maximum gross profit margin covering, *inter alia,* any import costs which might be borne by retailers, amounts to a measure having an effect equivalent to a quantitative restriction contrary to Art. 30 EEC and to Art. 19 of Regulation 121/67 and Art. 22 of Regulation 805/68; (2) such national legislation also infringes Regulations 121/67 and 805/68 where the maximum gross profit margin incorporates the supply costs borne by retailers, and, as a consequence, in certain regions the distribution network for beef, veal and pigmeat is affected; (3) EEC Law does not prevent the fixing of a gross profit margin which incorporates, in addition to the retailer's net profit, only the marketing costs borne by retailers at the stage of sale to consumers, provided that that margin is not fixed at an arbitrary level and permits the retailers to receive fair remuneration for their activity.

ROELSTRAETE (HENRI) CRIMINAL PROCEEDINGS AGAINST (No. 116/84) [1986] 3 C.M.L.R. 562, European Ct.

1589. Imports—prices—quantitative restrictions—national courts

Mr. Chabrand, a petrol station owner, complained that a nearby petrol station owned by Aldis S.A. was undercutting his petrol prices by charging cheaper prices than the statutory minimum laid down by French law. Mr. Chabrand obtained an injunction in summary proceedings against Aldis S.A. The latter appealed.

Held, allowing the appeal, that (i) a first instance court in summary proceedings was entitled to apply EEC law directly against French law, and should give priority to EEC law; (ii) the French law on minimum petrol prices amounted to a quantitative restriction on imports and violated Art. 30 EEC.

ALDIS S.A. *v.* CHABRAND (ANDRE) [1987] 2 C.M.L.R. 396, Court of Appeal, Aix-en-Provence.

1590. Imports—quantitative restrictions—colorants—foodstuffs

Mr. Motte was prosecuted for having imported from Germany into Belgium potted black and red lumpfish roe, coloured by colorants which were not authorised by Belgian rules for that type of foodstuff. The colorants were authorised for potted roe in Germany and were authorised in Belgium for a number of other foodstuffs. The Court of Appeal, Brussels, asked the European Court for a preliminary ruling under Art. 177 EEC on the compatibility of such a prohibition on the use of colorants with EEC rules on the free movement of goods.

Held, that (1) at present EEC rules on the free movement of goods do not preclude national provisions which require (i) the use of a colorant in domestic and imported foodstuffs to be entered on a national positive list and (ii) an application for such an entry to be referred to a committee of experts to judge its harmfulness, the human body's tolerance of it and the need, value and suitability of its use; (2) If the authorities of the importing EEC State find that there is a real need to colour a certain foodstuff, in the light of the eating habits of that State, they may not without contravening EEC Law, particularly the last sentence of Art. 36 EEC, refuse authorisation merely on the ground that the imported foodstuff contains colorant. In considering the health risk posed by such a colorant, such authorities must heed international scientific research, especially the EEC's Scientific Committee for Food.

STATE *v.* MOTTE (No. 247/84) [1987] 1 C.M.L.R. 663, European Ct.

1591. Imports—quantitative restrictions—discrimination—drugs

Schering Chemicals ("Schering") distributed in the U.K. chemical and pharmaceutical goods made by its parent German company. The latter made a drug under the trade mark Noctamid. It complained that under new rules of the National Health Service "Noctamid" was excluded from the list of medicines for which the cost would be reimbursed, although the generic form lormetazepam was listed. This meant that although doctors could not prescribe Noctamid by name under the N.H.S., they could prescribe lormetazepam and chemists were entitled to supply Noctamid on the generic description. Schering argued that this was discriminatory and contrary to Art. 30 EEC.

Held, that although Schering lost sales as a result of its trade mark not being on the prescribable list, and those lost sales related back to imports from Germany, the scheme itself was proper, there was no discrimination against imports and no violation of Art. 30 EEC.

R. *v.* SECRETARY OF STATE FOR SOCIAL SERVICES, *ex p.* SCHERING CHEMICALS [1987] 1 C.M.L.R. 277, MacPherson J.

1592. Imports—quantitative restrictions—pharmaceuticals

Two Belgian companies (the plaintiffs) applied to the Luxembourg Minister for Health for authorisation to import medicinal products and sell them wholesale to pharmacists in Luxembourg. The Minister refused on the ground that, contrary to Luxembourg law, the plaintiffs' registered offices were not in Luxembourg and they did not have premises in Luxembourg for the storage of medicinal products. The plaintiffs challenged the Minister's decision as being contrary to EEC law. The Conseil d'Etat, Luxembourg asked the European Court under Art. 177 EEC for a preliminary ruling on the interpretation of Art. 30 EEC and Directive 75/309 on the approximation of provisions laid down by law, regulation or administrative action relating to proprietary medicinal products.

Held, that Arts. 30 to 36 EEC did not allow the authorities of an EEC State to insist that a company whose headquarters were in another EEC State, but who wanted to supply medicinal products directly to pharmacies in the first EEC State, had to have premises for storage and technical equipment in the first EEC State, when that company complied in that regard with the law of the EEC State where its headquarters were based.

SOCIÉTÉ CO-OPÉRATIVE DES LABORATOIRES DE PHARMACIE LEGIA *v.* MINISTER FOR HEALTH (LUXEMBOURG) (Nos. 87–88/85) [1987] 1 C.M.L.R. 646, European Ct.

1593. Imports—quantitative restrictions—testing

Mr. Schloh bought a Ford Granada estate car in Germany and brought it into Belgium. Belgium required it to undergo two roadworthiness tests within a matter of days. The first test was to establish the car's roadworthiness prior to it being registered in Belgium. The Belgian Government stated that the purpose of the second test was for the owner to submit a written declaration certifying that the use of the car was such as to exempt it from annual roadworthiness tests for the first four years. Mr. Schloh brought proceedings to recover the fees of the testing agency on the basis that the tests infringed Arts. 13 and 30 EEC. The Juge de Paix of Schaerbeek asked the European Court for a preliminary ruling under Art. 177 EEC on the interpretations of Arts. 13 and 30 EEC.

Held, (1) Art. 30 EEC meant that a national measure, which required a roadworthiness test for the purpose of registering an imported car carrying a certificate of its conformity to the vehicle types approved in the importing EEC State, amounted to a measure having an effect equivalent to a quantitative restriction on imports. However, such a measure was justified under Art. 36 EEC in so far as it related to cars put on the road before such registration and applied equally to imported vehicles and vehicles of national origin. A fee charged for such a test was compatible with the EEC Treaty provided it was not higher than the fee charged in the same circumstances for the testing of a vehicle of national origin; (2) Arts. 30 and 36 EEC meant that where the roadworthiness testing of an imported car had the purpose of seeking a written declaration from the car's owner, it amounted to a measure having an effect equivalent to a quantitative restriction on imports contrary to the EEC Treaty. A fee charged for such a test was contrary to the EEC Treaty.

SCHLOH (BERNHARD) *v.* AUTO CONTROLE TECHNIQUE (No. 50/85) [1987] 1 C.M.L.R. 450, European Ct.

1594. Imports—restraint of trade—beer free from additives

West German legislation on beer had the effect of prohibiting the use of any additives in the brewing of beer. The European Commission brought proceedings against West Germany on the basis that such legislation was contrary to Art. 30 EEC as it had the effect of creating barriers to imported beer lawfully brewed in other EEC States, but containing additives.

Held, that West Germany had failed to fulfil its obligations under Art. 30 EEC by prohibiting the marketing of beer lawfully produced and marketed in other EEC States, where such beer contained additives whose use was authorised in the other EEC States. West Germany's absolute prohibition on the use of additives in beer imported from other EEC States was contrary to the principle of proportionality and could not be justified on grounds of protection of health and life under Art. 36 EEC.

E.C. COMMISSION *v.* FEDERAL REPUBLIC OF GERMANY (No. 178/84) *The Times,* March 23, 1987, European Ct.

1595. Imports—restriction on sales without an optician or medical supervision—spectacles

S.A. Magnavision N.V., a Belgian company, ("Magnavision") marketed spectacles through a chain of concessions in British shops. Magnavision was convicted of selling spectacles without such a sale being effected by or under the supervision of a registered medical practitioner or registered optician contrary to s.21 of the Opticians Act 1958. Magnavision appealed against its conviction.

Held, appeal dismissed as the restriction on sale was neither discriminatory against imports nor protectionist and, thus, did not constitute a quantitative restriction on imports contrary to Art. 30 EEC.

S.A. MAGNAVISION N.V. *v.* GENERAL OPTICAL COUNCIL (No. 1) [1987] 1 C.M.L.R. 887, D.C.

1596. Imports—State aids—quantitative restrictions

Italian legislation, valid for two years, provided for public subsidies to the granted to municipal transport undertakings to cover 20 per cent. of the cost of purchasing electric vehicles made in Italy. The grant was subject to the condition that the vehicles be made in Italy. The European Commission objected to that condition and brought proceedings against Italy under Art. 169 EEC for failing to meet its obligations under Art. 30 EEC.

Held, that Italy failed to meet its obligations under Art. 30 EEC by requiring municipal transport undertakings to buy vehicles of national manufacture in order to qualify for the subsidies provided for by Italian leglisation.

SUBSIDY FOR ITALIAN MOTOR VEHICLES, *Re*; E.C. COMMISSION *v.* ITALY (No. 103/84) [1987] 2 C.M.L.R. 825, European Ct.

1597. Imports—tariff quotas—allocation

Mr. Migliorini was prosecuted for attempting to export to West Germany frozen beef and veal which had been imported from Czechoslovakia and which formed part of the share of an EEC tariff quota allocated to Italy for 1983. The Corte Suprema di Cassazione asked the European Court under Art. 177 EEC for a preliminary ruling on the interpretation of Council Reg. 3225/82.

Held, that Reg. 3225/82 was meant to ensure that allocation of the EEC tariff quota was done in proportion to the requirements of the EEC States and allocated fairly amongst the people concerned in each EEC State. However, Reg. 3225/82 did not authorise EEC States to take measures intended to prevent, limit or affect the re-exportation of goods which have been properly imported under that quota and which are subsequently in free circulation in an EEC State.

PROCURATORE DELLA REPUBBLICA *v.* MIGLIORINI (No. 199/84) [1987] 2 C.M.L.R. 841, European Ct.

1598. Imports—taxation—discrimination

The plaintiff, a German company, challenged the amount of monopoly equalisation duty imposed by the Principal Customs Office, Mainz, on spirits imported by the plaintiff and put into free circulation in West Germany between March 1 and March 17, 1976. The spirits were whisky from Great Britain, Geneva and liqueurs from Holland, armagnac and pruneaux from France, sherry from Spain and port from Portugal. The Finance Court, Rhineland—Palatinate asked the European Court for a preliminary ruling under Art. 117 EEC on the interpretation of Arts. 37 and 95 EEC, Art. 3 of the Agreement of June 29, 1970, between the EEC and Spain and Art 21(1) of the Agreement of July 22, 1972, between the EEC and Portugal.

Held, that a State-aided reduction in the selling price actually charged by the German Monopoly Administration during a particular period was not contrary to Arts. 95 and 37 EEC, Art. 21 of the Agreement between the EEC and Portugal and Art. 3 of the Agreement between the EEC and Spain and not discriminatory, provided that the rate of taxation actually applied to imported goods in that period did not exceed the rate of taxation actually levied on corresponding domestic goods. It was for a national court to decide whether imported spirits and corresponding domestic spirits were in fact taxed at different rates in a particular period.

SEKTKELLEREI C.A. KUPFERBERG & CIE K.G. a.A. *v.* HAUPTZOLLAMT MAINZ (No. 253/83) [1987] 1 C.M.L.R. 36, European Ct.

1599. Imports—valuation for customs purposes—freight charges

Mainfrucht Obstverwertung GmbH ("M.O.") imported consignments of fruit from Bulgaria into Germany. For each consignment the suppliers drew up two invoices; the first showed a net price per tonne for the fruit carriage paid at the German border. The second showed the cost of transport from the German border to M.O.'s premises in Bavaria. A dispute arose between M.O. and Hauptzollamt as to the value of the goods for customs purposes. The Federal Finance Court asked the European Court for a preliminary ruling under Art. 177 EEC.

Held, that where a purchaser had paid a foreign seller, in addition to the price of the goods, a specific sum in respect of freight charges for transport within the EEC, on the basis of a separate invoice, the transaction value for the purposes of Art. 3(1) of Reg. No. 1224/80 included only the first of these two sums. Thus, the value for customs purposes of goods imported into the EEC from non-Member States, did not include the cost of transporting the goods within the EEC.

HAUPTZOLLAMT SCHWEINFURT *v.* MAINFRUCHT OBSTVERWERTUNG GmbH (No. 290/84) [1987] 1 C.M.L.R. 684, European Ct.

1600. Industry Act 1972—amendment—extension of scope to any member State of the EEC. See TRADE AND INDUSTRY, §3733.

1601. Institutions—directives, decisions and regulations

87/490/Euratom, ECSC, EEC:

Decision of the representatives of the Governments of the Member States of the European Communities of September 22, 1987 appointing a Member of the Commission of the European Communities. (O.J. 1987 L279/26.)

87/523/Euratom, ECSC, EEC:

Council Decision of October 19, 1987 appointing members of the Court of Auditors. (O.J. 1987 L304/45.)

87/530/Euratom, ECSC, EEC:

Council Decision of October 20, 1987 amending the method of adjusting the remuneration of officials and other servants of the Communities. (O.J. 1987 L307/40.)

Council Regulation (EEC, Euratom, ECSC) No. 3855/86 of December 16, 1986 correcting the remuneration and pensions of officials and other servants of the European Communities and the weightings applied thereto laid down by Regulations

(ECSC, EEC, Euratom) No. 3580/85 and (EEC, Euratom, ECSC) No. 2126/86. (O.J. 1986 L359/1.)

Council Regulation (EEC, Euratom, ECSC) No. 3856/86 of December 16, 1986 adjusting the remuneration and pensions of officials and other servants of the European Communities and the weightings applied thereto. (O.J. 1986 L359/5.)

Council Regulation (Euratom, ECSC, EEC) No. 793/87 of March 16, 1987 adjusting the rates laid down in Art. 13 of Annex VII to the Staff Regulations of Officials of the European Communities for the daily subsistence allowance for officials on mission. (O.J. 1987 L79/1.)

Council Regulation (Euratom, ECSC, EEC) No. 2151/87 of July 20, 1987 adjusting the weightings applicable to the remuneration and pensions of officials and other servants of the European Communities. (O.J. 1987 L202/5.)

Council Regulation (Euratom, ECSC, EEC) No. 2274/87 of July 23, 1987 introducing special measures to terminate the service of temporary staff of the European Communities. (O.J. 1987 L209/1.)

Council Regulation (Euratom, ECSC, EEC) No. 3018/87 of October 5, 1987 introducing special transitional measures for the recruitment of overseas staff of the European Association for Cooperation as officials of the European Communities. (O.J. 1987 L286/1.)

Council Regulation (Euratom, ECSC, EEC) No. 3019/87 of October 5, 1987 laying down special and exceptional provisions applicable to officials of the European Communities serving in a third country. (O.J. 1987 L286/3.)

Council Regulation (Euratom, ECSC, EEC) No. 3212/87 of October 20, 1987 adjusting the rate of the special temporary levy provided for in Article 66a of the Staff Regulations of officials of the European Communities. (O.J. 1987 L307/1.)

1602. Interim measures—anti-dumping—serious and irreparable damage

Technointorg brought proceedings under Art. 173(2) EEC for a declaration that Commission Reg. 2800/86 of September 9, 1986, which imposed provisional anti-dumping duty on imports of certain deep freezers originating in the U.S.S.R. was void, in so far as it applied to Technointorg. Technointorg applied for the interim suspension of provisional anti-dumping duties ordered by Reg. 2800/86 in so far as they applied to the applicant, until judgment in the main proceedings. Technointorg offered to provide, in the interim, a bank guarantee in relation to paying any provisional duties that might be held to be due.

Held, that (1) the application for interim measures was refused; Technointorg had failed to show that it would suffer serious and irreparable damage; (2) the procedure laid down by Council Reg. 2176/84 meant that the Council would soon have to decide whether to impose a definitive duty and whether the provisional duty was to be definitely collected. To grant the applicant's request that payment of provisional duty should be suspended until the Court gave judgment in the main proceedings, albeit subject to providing a guarantee, would be tantamount to depriving the Council of its power to decide whether the provisional duty should be definitely collected and to depriving that decision of any practical effect. If the Council were to decide to impose a definitive duty and to order that provisional duty be collected, it would then be open to Technointorg to ask for interim measures.

TECHNOINTORG *v.* E.C. COMMISSION (No. 294/86R) [1987] 2 C.M.L.R. 239, European Ct.

1603. Interim measures—*ex parte* injunctions—tenders

Ireland had advertised for tenders for public works on the Dundalk Water Scheme. The European Commission considered that one of the specifications for the project discriminated against a tender from another EEC State. The Commission brought proceedings under Art. 169 EEC against Ireland and sought an interim injunction to prevent Ireland awarding the contract pending judgment.

Held, that an interim injunction was granted *ex parte,* which ordered Ireland to take such steps as might be required to prevent the award of the contract until the application by the Commission for interim measures had been disposed of or until further order. The injunction was granted *ex parte* so as to ensure that the application for interim measures was not prejudiced by a *fait accompli*; if the contract had been awarded before the application for interim measures had been decided, problems might have occurred as to the possibility of later cancelling it.

DUNDALK WATER SCHEME, *Re*: E.C. COMMISSION *v.* IRELAND (No. 45/87R) [1987] 2 C.M.L.R. 197, European Ct.

1604. Interim measures—injunctions—tenders—urgency

Ireland had advertised for tenders for public works on the Dundalk Water Scheme. The European Commission considered that one of the specifications for the project discriminated against a tender from another EEC State. The Commission brought proceedings against Ireland for breach of Art. 30 EEC and Directive 71/305 and obtained *ex parte* an interim injunction to prevent Ireland awarding the contract pending an *inter partes* hearing of its application for interim measures (see [1987] 8 C.L. 123). The application came before the President of the European Court at an *inter partes* hearing.

Held, that the application for an interim injunction was dismissed and the Directive 71/305 did not apply since it specifically excluded contracts for the supply of water. There was a *prima facie* case that the Irish Standard requirement did restrict EEC trade within Art. 30. In deciding whether there was sufficient urgency requiring the issue of an injunction, one had to consider the balance of interests; in weighing up the damage to the Commission as guardian of the EEC interest versus the consequences of delay in obtaining a water supply for the people in the Dundalk area, including the risks to their health and safety arising out of delay, the balance of interest favoured the Defendant.

DUNDALK WATER SCHEME (No. 2), *Re*: E.C. COMMISSION *v.* IRELAND (No. 45/87R) [1987] 2 C.M.L.R. 563, European Ct.

1605. Interim measures—interim suspension—*ex parte* applications

In August 1986, the Greek Government brought proceedings to annul European Commission Decision 86/475 of June 20, 1986 which decided that certain Greek agricultural expenditure should not be charged to the European Agricultural Guidance and Guarantee Fund. The Commission intended to deduct the disputed sum from its advance payment due in September 1986. The Greek Government applied for interim suspension of the Decision so that the September payment would be made to it in full.

Held, that as a precautionary measure the Commission's Decision was suspended even though the Commission had not yet presented its written observations. The suspension would continue until a final interim order was issued after hearing both parties' arguments.

F.E.O.G.A. ACCOUNTS, *Re*: GREECE *v.* E.C. COMMISSION (No. 214/86R) [1987] 1 C.M.L.R. 707, The President, European Ct.

1606. Interim measures—public works—tenders

Breda-Geomineraria ("Breda"), an Italian company, tendered for a research contract with the Government of Mali funded by the EEC under the 5th European Development Fund. Breda was favoured by the Mali Government, but the E.C. Commission favoured its German competitor. Breda brought proceedings for the annulment of the Commission's alleged decision refusing to recognise that Breda were the successful tenderers and applied for interim measures to stop the Commission blocking the award of the contract.

Held, dismissing the application for interim measures as (1) there was no prima facie case to answer as there was no Commission decision to annul and (2) in any event the measures sought by Breda prejudged the final decision since they would amount to awarding the contract, which was the purpose of the main proceedings.

BREDA-GEOMINERARIA *v.* E.C. COMMISSION (No 231/86R) [1987] 2 C.M.L.R. 782, European Ct.

1607. Interim measures—suspension of decision—urgency

Deufil GmbH & Co. KG ("Deufil"), a producer of polyamide and polypropylene yarn brought proceedings for annulment of European Commission Decision 85/471 of July 10, 1985. In that Decision the Commission declared that a State aid granted by Germany to Deufil was illegal as it infringed Art. 92 EEC. The Commission required Germany to recover the aid from Deufil. Deufil applied for suspension of the Decision until the Court had given its judgment in the main proceedings.

Held, that application for interim measures would be rejected as Deufil had failed to prove any urgency as (1) Germany had not taken any measure to recover the aid at issue and recovery could not be made immediately and (2) Deufil had not shown that implementation of the Decision would cause it to suffer serious and irreparable damage. There was no reason to believe that Deufil's rich parent company would not support its subsidiary financially if the aid were recovered.

DEUFIL GmbH & CO. KG *v.* E.C. COMMISSION (No. 310/85R) [1986] 3 C.M.L.R. 687, European Ct.

1608. Interim measures—suspension of fine—guarantee

Usinor brought annulment proceedings (Case No. 78/83) in respect of European Commission's Decision 1831/81 ECSC of June 24, 1981, by which it was fined for exceeding steel production quotas. By Decision C(84) 104/1 of January 26, 1984, the Commission imposed a further fine on Usinor for exceeding steel production quotas. Usinor applied for suspension of the latter Decision, and, in the alternative, any other interim measures which might be required.

Held, that the operation of Art. 2 of Commission Decision C(84)104/1 (regarding the imposition of a fine) was suspended until 30 days after delivery of the European Court's judgment in Case No. 78/83, on condition that Usinor gave a bank guarantee in advance guaranteeing payment of the fine imposed by that Decision and for any default interest.

USINOR *v.* E.C. COMMISSION (No. 62/84R) [1986] 3 C.M.L.R. 600, European Ct.

1609. Interim measures—suspsension of regulation—irreparable damage

ARPOSOL, a Spanish fishermen's association, had brought proceedings to annul Council Reg. 3781/85 which imposed a temporary ban on Spanish fishing boats convicted of illegally fishing in the waters of other EEC States, additional to any penalties imposed by the EEC State in whose waters the illegal fishing had taken place. ARPOSOL applied for interim suspension of the Regulation on the basis that it amounted to double jeopardy, causing serious financial loss to the shipowner and crew and being discriminatory.

Held, dismissing the application, that there was no ground for granting the interim measure sought as ARPOSOL had failed to show that irreparable damage would be suffered by its members if such measures were not granted. It was unnecessary to deal with the question of discrimination against Spanish boats as this would be dealt with in the main proceedings.

ASOCIACIÓN PROVINCIAL DE ARMADORES DE BUQUES DE PESCA DE GRAN SOL DE PONTEVEDRA (ARPOSOL) *v.* E.C. COUNCIL (No. 55/86R) [1987] 1 C.M.L.R. 113, European Ct.

1610. Interim measures—urgency—discovery of documents

Greek producers of dead-burned natural magnesite complained to the European Commission about such products being imported from China and North Korea in bulk. The Commission imposed provisional anti-dumping duties on such imported products. Two years later the Commission further investigated the matter and considered that the imports were no longer causing sufficient domestic injury. On its proposal, the Council ended the anti-dumping proceedings. The Greek producers and the Greek Government appealed against the Council's decision and, in order to obtain access to the Commission's and Council's documents relating to the terminated anti-dumping proceedings for the purpose of appealing, applied for interim measures asking for discovery.

Held, dismissing the application, that (1) the sole argument raised to justify urgency was the risk of alteration or concealment of relevant documents by European Institutions involved in the dispute. The Court would not permit such an argument, which cast doubt on the good faith and impartiality of the European Institutions, to be maintained in the absence of any proof in support of it. The applicants then withdrew the allegation and had no other argument in favour of urgency. (2) Unless there are exceptional circumstances, an application for the adoption of interim measures was not in principle an appropriate procedure for seeking production of documents of the type sought in this case.

EPIKHIRISEON METALLEFTIKON VIOMIKHANIKON KAI NAFTILIAKON A.E. *v.* E.C. COUNCIL AND COMMISSION (No. 121/86R) [1987] 1 C.M.L.R. 57, European Ct.

1611. Interim measures—urgency—predatory pricing

AKZO Chemie BV (AKZO) had brought proceedings for annulment of Commission Decision 85/609/EEC of December 14, 1985, whereby it found that AKZO had abused its dominant position contrary to Art. 86 EEC. By that Decision the Commission had prohibited AKZO from dropping its prices below those offered to comparable customers when competing with the complainant company. AKZO applied for an order suspending the operation of that prohibition until judgment in the main proceedings, so that AKZO would be entitled, acting in good faith, to align its price quotations and prices actually charged for flour additives on the lower quotations given by its competitors so far as its existing customers were concerned.

Held, dismissing the application, that AKZO had not established any urgency as it had not disclosed any serious and irreparable damage.

AKZO CHEMIE BV *v.* E.C. COMMISSION (No. 62/86R) [1987] 1 C.M.L.R. 225, European Ct.

1612. Invalid care allowance—whether Council Directive 79/7/EEC applies to invalid care allowance. See SOCIAL SECURITY DECISION NO. R(G) 2/86, §3480.

1613. JET—difference in staff treatment—discrimination

The Council of the European Communities set up the Joint European Torus Joint Undertaking ("JET") for a 12 year period and based it in England. JET's members were the host organisation, the U.K. Atomic Energy Authority ("UKAEA"), and 12 other research organisations of EEC States. Under art.s 8.4 and 8.5 of the statutes setting up

JET, staff made available to JET by UKAEA continued to be employed by UKAEA on UKAEA's terms and conditions, whilst staff made available by other members of JET were recruited to posts of temporary servants of the European Communities. The applicants were British nationals made available to JET by UKAEA, who sought annulment of the European Commission's decision, which refused to treat them as temporary servants of the European Communities and refused to compensate them for the fact that their salary from UKAEA was appreciably lower than that of people at JET, who had been recruited as temporary servants of the European Communities. The applicants argued, *inter alia,* that there was discrimination on the ground of nationality.

Held, that (1) there was no discrimination on the ground of nationality as there was nothing to prevent a Member State of JET from choosing to recruit persons of different nationality to that borne by nationals of its own State; (2) the special position of UKAEA, the host organisation in relation to JET, constituted an objective justification for the difference in treatment established by art.s 8.4. and 8.5 of the statutes. UKAEA was in the special position of having to manage staff having the same qualifications, working on the same site on the same type of work, but assigned to two legally separate organisations; UKAEA was concerned to prevent that situation from disturbing the functioning of its own organisation and, thus, wished staff, which it made available to JET, to be subject to its conditions of service.

AINSWORTH *v.* E.C. COMMISSION and COUNCIL OF THE EUROPEAN COMMUNITIES (Nos. 271/83: 15, 36, 113, 158, 203/84 and 13/85), *The Times,* January 16, 1987.

1614. Judgments—compliance—delay

The European Commission brought proceedings under Art. 169 EEC against Italy for failing to comply with the judgment delivered by the European Court on June 8, 1982 in *E.C. Commission* v. *Italy* (No. 91/81) [1983] C.L.Y. 1638. In that judgment the European Court held that by not adopting within the prescribed period the measures required in order to comply with Council Directive 75/129 on the approximation of the laws of the EEC States relating to collective redundancies, Italy had failed to fulfil its obligations under the Treaty. The Commission gave its opinion under Art. 169(1) EEC that Italy was in breach of Art. 171 EEC by not taking measures to implement the Court's judgment. Italy argued that it had not implemented the Directive because of social and economic conditions in its country and the need to maintain employment.

Held, that although Art. 171 EEC does not set a time limit within which a judgment must be complied with, implementation of a judgment has to start immediately and be completed as soon as possible. Italy was guilty of unreasonable delay and could not use domestic circumstances as an excuse for failing to implement the Directive. By not having complied with the judgment, Italy had failed to fulfil its obligations under Art. 171 EEC.

COLLECTIVE REDUNDANCIES (No. 2), *Re*: E.C. COMMISSION *v.* ITALY (No. 131/84) [1986] 3 C.M.L.R. 693, European Ct.

1615. Labelling—dangerous substances—preparations

Mr. Caldana was prosecuted after Italian authorities discovered that mineral oils (for vehicles) offered for sale by the company, whom he represented, contained polychlorinated biphenyls ("PCBs"), without labels revealing the presence of PCBs being attached to the oils' containers. Mr. Caldana was prosecuted under Italian legislation on the classification, packaging and labelling of dangerous substances, which was intended to give effect to Council Directive 67/548, was amended by Council Directive 79/831. Mr. Caldana argued that mineral oils for vehicles containing PCBs were not "preparations" within Directive 67/548, as amended, and, alternatively that the mere fact that a substance was to be found in a preparation, regardless of the proportion of the mixture which it represented, was not sufficient to make that preparation dangerous. The Pretore di Torino asked the European Court of Justice under Art. 177 EEC for a preliminary ruling on the interpretation of certain provisions of Directive 67/548 on the approximation of laws, regulations and administrative provisions relating to the classification, packaging and labelling of dangerous substances, as amended by Directive 79/831.

Held, that in the present state of EEC Law there were no common or harmonised general rules on the classification, packaging and labelling of dangerous preparations in general. Thus, each EEC State was entitled to take such national measures as it wished in relation thereto. Directive 67/548, as amended by Directive 79/831, required labelling only of dangerous substances as such; it did not require preparations containing one or more of those substances to be labelled.

CALDANA (GIACOMO) CRIMINAL PROCEEDINGS AGAINST (No. 187/84) [1986] 3 C.M.L.R. 476, European Ct.

1616. Labelling—weights and measures—prepackaging

Vereniging Slachtpluimvee-Export eV ("Vereniging"), a Dutch undertaking, contracted to supply boxes of chicken bearing the EEC 'e' sign to REWE-Central A.G. ("REWE"), a German company. Vereniging could not deliver boxes with the 'e' sign because it had not got formal authorisation from the Dutch Weights and Measures to affix the sign to its goods as required by Dutch legislation. In court proceedings in Germany concerning the contract REWE argued that performance of the contract was not impossible because Council Directive 76/211 gave the manufacturers the unreserved right to use the EEC 'e' sign. The Amtsgericht, Cologne asked the European Court of Justice under Art. 177 EEC for a preliminary ruling on the interpretation of Directive 76/211 on the approximation of the laws of the EEC States relating to the making-up by weight or by volume of certain prepackaged products.

Held, that (1) under section 4 of Annex I to Directive 76/211 a packer who measures the quantity in each prepackage is entitled to affix the EEC 'e' sign without prior authorisation from the national weights and measures authorities, but a packer who only checks the quantity of the product contained in each prepackage must, in order to be able to use the EEC 'e' sign, operate checking procedures which have been recognised by the national weights and measures authorities either by means of general provisions or by means of particular decisions; (2) a packer who shows that he is operating checking procedures which ensure that the quantity of the contents of his prepackages actually corresponds to their stated contents may rely on the provision of Directive 76/211 and Annex I thereof, against competent national authorities who decline to recognise those procedures.

VERENIGING SLACHTPLUIMVEE-EXPORT eV *v.* REWE-ZENTRAL A.G. (No. 96/84) [1986] 3 C.M.L.R. 467, European Ct.

1617. Maternity grant—effect of EEC Regulations on a claim to maternity grant based on periods of insurance or employment elsewhere within the European Community—Commissioner's decision. See SOCIAL SECURITY, §3485.

1618. Migrant workers—discrimination—income for elderly

Mrs. Castelli, an elderly Italian, was entitled in Italy to a partial survivor's pension. Since 1957 she lived in Belgium with her son. Mrs. Castelli contested the decision of the Belgian National Pensions Office whereby it refused to allow Mrs. Castelli the income guaranteed to old people under the Belgian Act of April 1, 1969, on the ground that she did not fulfil the conditions set out in that Act, since she was not a Belgian, or a national of a country with which Belgium had concluded a reciprocal agreement, and she was not entitled to a retirement pension or a survivor's pension in Belgium. The Cour du Travail, Liège, asked the European Court under Art. 177 EEC for a preliminary ruling on the interpretation of Reg. 1612/68 of 15th October 1968 on freedom of movement for workers within the EEC.

Held, Art. 7(2) of Reg. 1612/68 meant that the grant of a social advantage, such as the income guaranteed to elderly people by the legislation of an EEC State, to a dependent relative in the ascending line of a worker cannot be conditional on there being a reciprocal agreement between that EEC State and the EEC State of which such a relative is a national. Art. 7(2) is designed to prevent discrimination in cases, such as this one.

CASTELLI *v.* OFFICE NATIONAL DES PENSIONS POUR TRAVAILLEURS SALARIES (No. 261/83) [1987] 1 C.M.L.R. 465, European Ct.

1619. National Courts—referral for preliminary ruling—*acte clair*

The English Divisional Court had rejected S.A. Magnavision's ("Magnavision") appeal against conviction. During the course of the hearing of the appeal Magnavision's counsel had asked the Court to seek a preliminary ruling under Art. 177 EEC from the European Court, but this was refused as the English Court considered this unnecessary as the meaning of the legislation was clear to the judges. After judgment was given, but before the order had been drawn up, Magnavision's counsel applied for, but was refused leave to appeal to the House of Lords. Since leave to appeal had been refused, the Divisional Court was the final national appeal court and Magnavision's counsel asked the Divisional Court to seek a preliminary ruling pursuant to Art. 177(3) EEC.

Held, that referral for a preliminary ruling was refused because (i) even if the Divisional Court were to be regarded as covered by Art. 177(3) EEC it was not obliged, under the *acte clair* doctrine, to make a reference, and (ii) once judgment had been given, it was no longer possible to make an Art. 177 EEC referral.

S.A. MAGNAVISION N.V. *v.* GENERAL OPTICAL COUNCIL (No. 2) [1987] 2 C.M.L.R. 262, D.C.

1620. Patent—infringement—defence based on breach of EEC Treaty on quantitative restrictions on imports. See THETFORD CORPORATION *v.* FIAMMA S.p.A., §2791.

1621. Pharmaceutical qualifications—EEC recognition. *See* MEDICINE, §2411.

1621a. Pharmaceutical qualifications—EEC recognition—Northern Ireland regulations. See NORTHERN IRELAND, §2706.

1622. Pharmaceutical rules—code of ethics dispensing parallel import—reference to European Court of Justice. See MEDICINE, §2412.

1623. Pharmaceuticals—medicinal product—interpretation

Mr. Tissier was prosecuted in France for manufacturing and marketing products which were described as "reagents," but met the definition of "medicinal products" laid down by the French Public Health Code without having obtained the necessary authorisation of the Ministry of Health or having complied with the provisions of that Code. Mr. Tissier denied that the products were medicinal products and argued that they were not treated as medicinal products in other European countries. The Regional Court, Libourne asked the Court under Art. 177 EEC for a preliminary ruling on the interpretation of the words "medical product" and its definition in EEC law.

Held, a substance which is not used for treating or preventing diseases in humans or animals, but which is used for making medical diagnoses on them must be regarded as a medicinal product within the meaning of Art. 1 of Council Directive 65/65 of January 26, 1965, in so far as it is intended to be administered to humans or animals either by itself or mixed with other substances.

PROCUREUR DE LA REPUBLIQUE *v.* GERARD TISSIER (No. 35/85) [1987] 1 C.M.L.R. 551, European Ct.

1624. Public contracts—equipment—leasing

A German company (the "applicant") signed a contract with the E.C. Commission under Reg. 2935/79 to carry out research in respect of milk. The project budget provided for "non-durable equipment" which was to be reimbursed by the Commission at 75 per cent. of cost. The contract also provided that apparatus and other capital equipment, which might have to be obtained to perform the contract, would be reimbursed at 20 per cent. of the purchase price. The applicant leased some measuring instruments and sought 75 per cent. of the leasing cost since they were not kept at the end of the contract and so were non-durable. The applicant claimed such costs from the Commission, but the Commission refused as it did not regard those instruments as "non-durables". The applicant brought an action pursuant to Art. 181 EEC by virtue of the arbitration clause in the contract.

Held, dismissing the application, that in the absence of any contractual provisions dealing specifically with leasing, the instruments were to be classified according to their nature (durable) and not according to their method of acquisition (temporary).

CENTRALE MARKETINGGESELLSCHAFT DER DEUTSCHEN AGRARWIRTSCHAFT mbH *v.* EEC (represented by the E.C. COMMISSION (No. 251/84) [1987] 2 C.M.L.R. 788, European Ct.

1625. Quantitative restrictions—directives, decisions and regulations

Commission Regulation (EEC) No. 3914/86 of December 22, 1986 amending Regulation (EEC) No. 635/86 on the quantitative restrictions applicable to trade in certain fruit and vegetables between Spain and Portugal. (O.J. 1986 L364/33.)

Commission Regulation (EEC) No. 2044/87 of July 10, 1987 amending quantitative limits fixed for imports of certain textile products originating in Thailand (category 5). (O.J. 1987 L192/15.)

Council Regulation (EEC) No. 3976/86 of December 22, 1986 amending Regulation (EEC) No. 483/86 fixing the level of quantitative restrictions in Spain for certain fruit and vegetables coming from the Community as constituted on 31 December 1985. (O.J. 1986 L370/11.)

1626. Regional affairs—directives, decisions and regulations

86/655/EEC:

Council Directive of December 18, 1986 concerning the Community list of less-favoured farming areas within the meaning of Directive 75/268/EEC (France). (O.J. 1987 L382/23.)

87/348/EEC:

Commission Decision of June 11, 1987 amending the limits of the less-favoured areas in France within the meaning of Council Directive 75/268/EEC. (O.J. 1987 L189/35.)

Council Regulation (EEC) No. 3156/87 of October 19, 1987 amending Regulation (EEC) No. 1942/81 for the stimulation of agricultural development in the less-favoured areas of Northern Ireland. (O.J. 1987 L301/1.)

Council Regulation (EEC) No. 3157/87 of October 19, 1987 amending Regulation (EEC) No. 1975/82 on the acceleration of agricultural development in certain regions of Greece. (O.J. 1987 L301/3.)

1627. Regulations—legal basis for—annulment

The European Commission sought a declaration that Council Regs. (EEC) Nos. 3599/85 and 3600/85 of December 17, 1985 applying generalised tariff preferences for 1986 in respect of certain industrial and textile goods originating in third world countries were void on the ground of failure to state the precise legal basis upon which they were adopted.

Held, (1) Regs. 3599/85 and 3600/85 did not comply with the requirements of Art. 190 EEC and had not adopted on the correct legal basis. The Council should have adopted them by a qualified majority pursuant to Art. 113 EEC and could not rely on Art. 235 EEC, as it had purported to do. Accordingly, those Regs. were void; (2) the effect produced by those Regs. were to be considered as definitive.

E.C. COMMISSION *v.* COUNCIL OF THE EUROPEAN COMMUNITIES (No. 45/86) *The Times,* April 25, 1987, European Ct.

1628. Research and development—directives, decisions and regulations

87/551/EEC:

Council Decision of November 17, 1987 adopting a research and development coordination programme of the European Economic Community in the field of medical and health research (1987 to 1991). (O.J. 1987 L334/20.)

Council Regulation (EEC) No. 3252/87 of October 19, 1987 on the coordination and promotion of research in the fisheries sector. (O.J. 1987 L314/17.)

1629. Right to work—professions—medicine—spouse of EEC national

Mr. Gül, a Cypriot national, was married to a British national working in Germany. He obtained a degree in medicine from the University of Istanbul. He obtained temporary authorisation to practise medicine in Germany in order to permit him to specialise in anaesthesiology. That authorisation, which was renewed several times, was granted on condition that Mr. Gül undertook to return to his country or to another developing country after completing or discontinuing his training as a specialist in Germany. Mr. Gül's application for further renewal of his authorisation was rejected. Mr. Gül brought proceedings against the rejection of his application before the Verwaltungsgericht, Gelsenkirchen, relying on the right to take up employment provided for spouses of EEC workers and on the principle of non-discrimination. The Verwaltungsgericht asked the European Court for a preliminary ruling on the interpretation of Council Reg. 1612/68 of 15th October 1968 on freedom of movement for workers within the EEC.

Held, (1) Art. 11 of Reg. 1612/68 meant that the right of the spouse of a worker entitled to move freely within the EEC to take up any activity as an employed person carries with it the right to follow occupations subject to a system of administrative authorisation and to special legal rules governing their exercise, such as the medical profession, if the spouse shows that he has the professional qualifications and diplomas required by the host EEC State for the exercise of the occupation at issue; (2) a spouse of a worker who is a national of an EEC State to whom Art. 11 of Reg. 1612/68 applies is entitled to be treated in the same manner as a national of the host State with regard to access, as an employed person, to the medical profession and the practice of that profession whether his qualifications are recognised under the legislation of the host EEC State alone or pursuant to Directive 75/363. Discriminatory treatment on grounds of nationality is contrary to Art. 3(1) of Reg. 1612/68.

GÜL *v.* REGIERUNGSPRÄSIDENT DÜSSELDORF (No. 131/85) [1987] 1 C.M.L.R. 501, European Ct.

1630. Semiconductor products

SEMICONDUCTOR PRODUCTS (PROTECTION OF TOPOGRAPHY) REGULATIONS 1987 (No. 1497) [£1·60], made under the European Communities Act 1972 (c.68), s.2(2); operative on November 7, 1987; implement Council Directive 87/54/EEC on the legal protection of topographies of semiconductor products.

1631. Services—insurance—establishment

The European Commission brought proceedings under Art. 169 EEC against Germany for failing to fulfil its obligations under Arts. 59 and 60 EEC, in relation to the freedom to provide services in the field of insurance and under Council Directive 78/473 on the co-ordination of laws, regulations and administrative provisions relating to co-insurance.

Held, that (1) Germany had failed to fulfil its obligations under Arts. 59 and 60 EEC by requiring insurance undertakings, who wished to provide services in Germany in relation to insurance business (other than transport insurance, Community co-insurance and compulsory insurance), through salesmen, representatives, agents and other intermediaries, to be "established" in Germany; (2) Germany had failed to fulfil its obligations under Arts. 59 and 60 EEC and under Council Directive 78/473 by requiring that, for services provided in connection with Community co-insurance, where the risk was situated in Germany, the lead insurer be "established and authorised" in Germany.

E.C COMMISSION (SUPPORTED BY THE NETHERLANDS AND THE U.K., INTERVENERS) *v.* FEDERAL REPUBLIC OF GERMANY (SUPPORTED BY BELGIUM, DENMARK, FRANCE, IRELAND AND ITALY, INTERVENERS) (No. 205/84) *The Times,* January 13, 1987, European Ct.

1632. Services—insurance—establishment

The European Commission brought proceedings under Art. 169 EEC against Germany for failing to fulfil its obligations under Arts. 59 and 60 EEC, in relation to the freedom to provide services in the field of insurance and under Council Directive 78/473 on the co-ordination of laws, regulations and administrative provisions relating to co-insurance.

Held, that (1) Germany had failed to fulfil its obligations under Arts. 59 and 60 EEC by requiring insurance undertakings, who wished to provide services in Germany in relation to insurance business (other than transport insurance, Community co-insurance and compulsory insurance), through salesman, representatives, agents and other intermediaries, to be "established" in Germany; (2) Germany had failed to fulfil its obligations under Arts. 59 and 60 EEC and under Council Directive 78/473 by requiring that, for services provided in connection with Community co-insurance, where the risk was situated in Germany, the lead insurer be "established and authorised" in Germany.

INSURANCE SERVICES, *Re*: E.C. COMMISSION *v.* GERMANY (No. 205/84) [1987] 1 C.M.L.R. 69, European Ct.

1633. Sex discrimination—occupational pensions—part-time workers

[E.E.C. Treaty Art. 119.]

An entitlement to benefits under an occupational pension scheme fell to be considered as "pay" for the purposes of Art. 119 E.E.C. Treaty.

W was employed as a part-time worker by B, a department store. B operated an occupational pension scheme which provided certain pension benefits for employees who had been employed full-time for at least 15 years. W was employed full-time for $11\frac{1}{2}$ years and thereafter $3\frac{1}{2}$ years part-time at her own request. W was refused benefits under the scheme on account of the fact that she had not worked full-time for 15 years. W claimed that B's policy infringed art. 119 E.E.C. Treaty in that it indirectly discriminated against women as women were predominant amongst part-time workers on account of family commitments.

Held, that the scheme formed an integral part of the contracts of employment between B and its employees. As such the benefits payable under the scheme were consideration received by a worker from his employer in respect of his employment within art. 119, para. 2 E.E.C. Treaty. B would be in breach of art. 119 if the exclusion of part-time employees from its pension scheme affected a far greater number of women than men unless B was able to show that the exclusion was based on objectively justified factors unrelated to any discrimination on grounds of sex. The need to discourage part-time employment was capable of being such a factor. The limitation of benefits under the scheme to full-time employees would be justified if it were found to be an appropriate means and necessary to achieve that objective. Art. 119 does not require an employer to organise its occupational pension scheme so as to take into account its employee's family responsibilities in fixing their entitlement to benefits under the scheme (*Jenkins* v. *Kingsgate (Clothing Productions)* [1981] C.L.Y. 915 applied).

BILKA-KAUFHAUS GmbH *v.* WEBER VON HARTZ (No. 170/84) [1987] I.C.R. 110, European Ct.

1634. Sex discrimination—retirement age—whether British Gas Corp. is a State authority for purposes of Art 5(1) Council Directive 76/207/EEC. See FOSTER *v.* BRITISH GAS, §1370.

1635. Sex discrimination—social security benefits

In 1983 Mrs. Clarke's application for a non-contributory invalidity pension was refused on the basis of a condition concerning her ability to perform normal household duties which was imposed only on married women. In November 1984 that pension was abolished and replaced by a severe disablement allowance which was available to claimants of either sex from November 1985. Transitional provisions from November 1984 to November 1985 contained the above restriction regarding married women. Mrs. Clarke appealed to the Social Security Commissioner on the basis that that was discriminatory. The latter asked the European Court under Art. 177 EEC for a preliminary ruling on the interpretation of Art. 4(1) of Council Directive 79/7/EEC of December 19, 1978 on the progressive implementation of the principle of equal treatment for men and women in matters of social security.

Held, that (1) Art. 4(1) of Council Directive 79/7 could be relied upon as from December 22, 1984 in order to prevent the extension beyond that date of the effects of an earlier national provision inconsistent with Art. 4(1); (2) in the absence of appropriate measures for the implementation of Art. 4(1), women were entitled to be treated in the same way and to have the same rules applied to them as men who were in the same situation, since, where the Directive had not been implemented, those rules remained the only valid reference point.

CLARKE *v.* CHIEF ADJUDICATION OFFICER (No. 384/85), *The Times*, June 25, 1987, European Ct.

1636. Sex discrimination—social security benefits

Mrs. McDermott and Mrs. Cotter brought proceedings to quash decisions made on behalf of the Irish Minister for Social Welfare which terminated the payment of unemployment benefit to them after a shorter period than if they had been men or single women. They argued before the Irish High Court that those decisions infringed their rights under Art. 4(1) of Council Directive 79/7 on the progressive implementation of the principle of equal treatment for men and women in matters of social security. Art 4(1) prohibits all discrimination on grounds of sex in social security matters. The Irish High Court asked the European Court under Art. 177 EEC for a preliminary ruling on the interpretation of Directive 79/7.

Held, that (1) where Directive 79/7 has not been implemented, Art. 4(1) of the Directive could be relied on by individuals before national courts as from December 23, 1984, in order to prevent the application of any national provision which was contrary to Art. 4(1); (2) where there are no measures implementing Art. 4(1), women are entitled to have identical rules applied to them as are applied to men who are in the same position, in accordance with the provisions of the Directive.

McDERMOTT AND COTTER *v.* MINISTER FOR SOCIAL WELFARE AND THE ATT.-GEN. (No. 286/85) [1987] 2 C.M.L.R. 607, European Ct.

1637. Sex discrimination—termination of employment upon entitlement to pension—different pensionable ages for men and women

[Council Directive 76/207/EEC, art. 5(1).]

An employer unlawfully discriminates between male and female employees where those employees' contracts of employment terminate when aged 60 in the case of women and 65 in the case of men by reason of the fact that they became entitled to an old-age pension under the employer's pension scheme.

F.V.L. employed Mrs. B as a secretary. Mrs. B was a member of F.V.L.'s pension scheme which provided her with an entitlement to an old-age pension as from the pensionable date. The pensionable date under the scheme was 60 years of age for women and 65 for men. F.V.L. took the view that when Mrs. B reached 60 years of age in August 1982 her contract of employment automatically terminated. F.V.L. refused to admit her to work from that date. Mrs. B applied in the Netherlands courts for an order requiring F.V.L. to allow her to resume work. The Netherlands Civil Code provided by Article 1637ij that an employer may not make any distinction between men and women as regards terms of employment and the termination of contracts of employment, and that terms of employment did not include benefits or entitlements under pension schemes. Article 1637ij was introduced to comply with Council Directive 76/207/EEC dealing with the equal treatment of men and women in the field of employment. In the course of the proceedings the Netherlands courts referred to the European Court of Justice the question whether Member States were free to include among the conditions of employment in respect of which equal treatment for men and women must be laid down pursuant to Council Directive 76/207/EEC an express or implied condition concerning the termination of a contract of employment on the ground of an employee's age where that condition related to the age at which the employee became entitled to a pension.

Held, that Member States were not free to exempt from the application of the principle of equality of treatment embodied in Council Directive 76/207/EEC, art. 5(1) a condition providing for the termination of employment on the ground that an employee had reached pensionable age where the pensionable age for men and women was different. The preliminary question must be answered in the negative (*Burton* v. *British Railways Board* [1982] C.L.Y. 1220 considered).

BEETS-PROPER *v.* F. VAN LANSCHOT BANKIERS N.V. [1986] I.C.R. 706, European Ct.

1638. Social affairs—directives, decisions and regulations

87/171/EEC:

Commission Decision of February 27, 1987 amending Decision 86/221/EEC on the Guidelines for the Management of the European Social Fund in the financial years 1987 to 1989 in respect of the list of areas of high and long-term unemployment and/or industrial and sectoral restructuring. (O.J. 1987 L68/34.)

87/436/EEC:

Commission Decision of July 29, 1987 on the rates of assistance from the European Social Fund towards expenditure on recruitment, setting up and employment premiums. (O.J. 1987 L238/33.)

87/445/EEC:

Commission Decision of July 31, 1987 amending Decision 74/442/EEC relating to the setting up of a Joint Committee on Social Problems of Agricultural Workers. (O.J. 1987 L240/34.)

87/569/EEC:

Council Decision of December 1, 1987 concerning an action programme for the vocational training of young people and their preparation for adult and working life. (O.J. 1987 L346/32.)

Council Regulation (EEC) No. 2095/87 of July 13, 1987 amending Regulation (EEC) No. 1883/78 laying down general rules for the financing of interventions by the Guarantee Section of the European Agricultural Guidance and Guarantee Fund. (O.J. 1987 L196/3.)

1639. Social policy—European Social Fund—grants—legitimate expectation

In 1984 the U.K. applied to the European Commission for financial support from the European Social Fund ("E.S.F.") in respect of the "Community programme" established by the U.K. Manpower Services Commission. By Decision 83/621 of November 30, 1983 the European Commission had determined the financial rate of assistance to be provided to the U.K. for the 1984 financial year at £19·50 per person per week. By Decision No. C (84) 1941 of December 1984 the European Commission stated that for the 1984 financial year the relevant rate only applied to a full-time job, and only half that rate was payable for half-time work. The U.K. brought proceedings for the annulment of Decision No. C (84) 1941.

Held, that Decision No. C (84) 1941 was void in so far as it sought to make reductions of £13,083,004 to grants from the E.S.F.; the U.K. had a legitimate expectation that the European Commission's practice regarding the levels of grants from the E.S.F. in cases of part-time work, would not be altered during the course of a financial year in such a way as to take effect in the same year.

U.K. *v.* E.C. COMMISSION (No. 84/85), *The Times,* October 7, 1987, European Ct.

1640. Social policy—migrants—employees

The U.K., Denmark, France, Germany and Holland brought proceedings for the annulment of the European Commission's Decision 85/381 of July 8, 1985, which set up a prior communication and consultation procedure on migration policies in relation to non-EEC States.

Held, that (1) Decision 85/381 was void in so far as the European Commission lacked competence (i) to enlarge by means of Art. 1, the scope of the communication and consultation procedure to cover issues regarding the cultural integration of employees from non-EEC States and members of their families, and (ii) to provide, in the second indent of Art. 3, that the aim of the consultation was to ensure that the draft national measures and agreements complied with EEC policies and actions; (2) migration policies regarding non-EEC States were capable of coming within the EEC's social field within the meaning of Art. 118 EEC in so far as it related to the position of employees from non-EEC States as regards their impact on the EEC employment market and on working conditions.

FEDERAL REPUBLIC OF GERMANY, FRANCE, THE NETHERLANDS, DENMARK AND U.K. *v.* E.C. COMMISSION (SUPPORTED BY THE EUROPEAN PARLIAMENT, INTERVENER) (Nos. 281, 283, 284, 285 and 287/85), *The Times,* September 17, 1987, European Ct.

1641. Social security—benefits—national law

Mrs. Burchell, an unemployed divorcee, lived in the U.K. with her children, while her ex-husband worked in Holland. Her ex-husband received family allowances under Dutch Law in Holland in respect of the children. Mrs. Burchell's application for child benefit in the U.K. was refused by an insurance officer on the basis of Art. 73 of Council Reg. 1408/71 on the application of social security schemes to employed persons and their families moving within the EEC and Art. 10(1)(2) of Council Reg. 574/72, which lay down the procedure for implementing Reg. 1408/71. Mrs. Burchell appealed against such refusal and the Social Security Commissioner asked the European Court under Art. 177 EEC for a preliminary ruling on the interpretation of Art. 10(1)(*a*) of Reg. 574/72.

Held, that EEC rules against overlapping benefits did not apply where a family benefit was due under national legislation and without reference to any entitlement under EEC law. The first sentence of Art. 10(1)(*a*) of Reg. 574/72 did not apply where a benefit was due under national law alone and not in pursuance of Art. 73 of Reg. 1408/71.

BURCHELL *v.* ADJUDICATION OFFICER (No. 377/85), *The Times*, September 9, 1987.

1642. Social security—dependants—equality of treatment

Mrs. Lebon, a French national in her late twenties, lived in Belgium with her French father, who was in receipt of a Belgian pension. She brought proceedings regarding the Belgian authorities' refusal to pay her "minimex", a form of social security, whilst she was sick and unemployed. In the course of such proceedings the Labour Court, Mons, asked the European Court under Art. 177 EEC for a preliminary ruling on the interpretation of Council Reg. 1612/68 of October 15, 1968 on freedom of movement of workers.

Held, that (1) descendants who lived with an employee who was a national of an EEC State and who had been employed in another EEC State and then stayed on there, after having obtained a retirement pension, did not have the right to equality of treatment with regard to social security benefits provided by the legislation of the host EEC State, when they were over 21 years of age, were no longer dependent on the employee and were not themselves workers; (2) the status of a dependent family member within the meaning of Art. 10(1) and (2) of Reg. 1612/68, arose from a factual situation where support was given by the employee, without it being necessary to decide the reasons for which that support was required; (3) the equality of treatment with regard to social and tax advantages set by Art. 7(2) of Reg. 1612/68, was for the benefit of workers alone and not nationals of EEC States who sought employment in another EEC State.

CENTRE PUBLIC D'AIDE SOCIALE DE COURCELLES *v.* LEBON (No. 316/85), *The Times*, September 9, 1987, European Ct.

1643. Social security—family allowances—overlapping

Mr, Ferraioli, an Italian working in West Germany, received German family allowances for his children. His wife lived with their children in Italy, where she worked and received some Italian family allowances. A dispute arose as to Mr. Ferraioli's entitlement to claim German family allowances. The Bundesozialgericht asked the European Court under Art. 177 EEC for a preliminary ruling on the interpretation of Arts. 73 and 76 of Council Reg. 1408/71 on the application of social security schemes to employed persons and their families moving within the EEC.

Held, that Arts. 73 and 76 of Reg. 1408/71 meant that in so far as the wife was not receiving Italian family allowances because she had not applied for them, the husband was entitled to payment of German family allowances in full. In so far as the wife was receiving Italian family allowances, which were lower than the German ones, he was entitled to payment of the German allowances up to the difference between the two sums.

FERRAIOLI *v.* DEUTSCHE BUNDESPOST (No. 153/84) [1987] 2 C.M.L.R. 911, European Ct.

1644. Social security—unemployment—benefits

Mrs. Guyot had been living and working in Germany. She resigned from that work and registered with the German authorities as unemployed. She then went to France to rejoin her husband. She received German unemployment benefits for three months. The French Caisse Primaire d'Assurance Maladie ("the Fund") refused to reimburse her for medical expenses on the grounds that Art. 25 of Council Regulation 1408/71 gave unemployed migrant workers the right to sickness and maternity benefits only if they were also entitled to unemployment benefits. The Fund stated that she was not entitled to French unemployment benefits because she had not worked in France before becoming unemployed. The Cour d'Appel, Rouen, asked the European Court under Art. 177 for a preliminary ruling on Art. 71 of Regulation 1408/71.

Held, that under Regulation 1408/71 an unemployed worker who leaves her country of last employment is only entitled to receive unemployment benefit from that EEC State for a further three months, whereupon she must return if she wishes to continue to qualify. Art. 71 provides an exception to the three months rule for workers who while employed did not live in the same EEC State as that in which they worked. Art. 71 does not apply to someone who, during her last employment, was residing in the EEC State in which she was employed.

CAISSE PRIMAIRE D'ASSURANCE MALADIE DE ROUEN *v.* GUYOT (ANTJE) (No. 128/83) [1986] 1 C.M.L.R. 454, European Ct.

1645. Social security contributions—self-employed person

Mr. Philips, a British resident, carried on business in Britain and in Belgium as an antique dealer. He was assessed to British income tax and social security contributions based on his total income, wherever earned, including his Belgian income. Mr. Philips was also required to pay in Belgium social security contributions based on his business income earned in Belgium. There was no relevant double taxation agreement in force between Belgium and the U.K. Mr. Philips appealed against an order that he should pay the Belgian contributions, arguing that this was discriminatory as he was already paying social security contributions in Britain.

Held, that no discrimination was found to exist; a Belgian national working as a self-employed person in Britain and in Belgium, who paid social security contributions in Britain would be liable to pay social security contributions in Belgium. Hence, Arts. 52 and 53 EEC were not applicable and no reference would be made to the European Court for a preliminary ruling.

PHILIPS (JOHN) *v.* INTEGRITY Asbl [1986] 3 C.M.L.R. 673, Belgian Supreme Ct.

1646. State aids—domestic fiscal measures—misapplication of statute—distortion of completion. See R. *v.* ATT.-GEN., *ex p.* I.C.I., §3222.

1647. State aids—fruit farmers—protection against risk of hail damage

The European Commission issued a Notice stating that it regarded the Dutch authorities' draft aid scheme (intended to compensate Dutch farmers whose orchards had been damaged by hail) as incompatible with Art. 92(1) EEC. Accordingly, it had begun the procedure provided for in Art. 93(2) in respect of that draft aid measure and invited comments from interested third parties (other than EEC States) within four weeks.

HAIL RISK FOR DUTCH FRUIT FARMERS, *Re* [1987] 3 C.M.L.R. 113, E.C. Commission Notice.

1648. State aids—interim measures—prima facie case

Greece brought proceedings under Art. 173 EEC for annulment of the European Commission's Decision C(85)2087 of November 13, 1985 that certain interest rebates granted by Greece to Greek exporters infringed Art. 92 EEC. Greece applied for interim suspension of the operation of the Decision.

Held, that the application for interim suspension of the Decision was rejected as Greece had failed to establish a prima facie case for such suspension and no cogent arguments had been put forward with regard to urgency.

STATE AIDS TO EXPORTS, *Re:* GREECE *v.* E.C. COMMISSION (No. 57/86R) [1986] 3 C.M.L.R. 596, European Ct.

1649. State aids—state shareholding—withdrawal of aid

By Decision 83/130 of February 16, 1983, the European Commission found that the acquisition by a public regional holding company of a holding worth 475 million Belgian francs in the capital of a Belgian company manufacturing ceramic ware amounted to aid incompatible with Art. 92 EEC and should therefore be withdrawn. Belgium did not bring any action to annul the Decision within the requisite time-limit. The Commission brought proceedings against Belgium for failing to comply with the Decision. Belgium contested the accuracy of the statement of reasons given in the Decision. It argued that it was impossible to redeem the capital holding on account of Belgian provisions, which would require the winding up of the company. It also asked the Commission to explain the meaning of "withdrawal of the aid."

Held, that Belgium had failed to fulfil its obligations under the EEC Treaty by not complying within the set period with Commission Decision 83/130 on aid granted by Belgium to a company manufacturing ceramic ware. The implementation of the Decision was not impossible as it was possible to wind up the company. If implementation had been impossible due to unforeseen difficulties or events, Belgium should have submitted them to the Commission in a genuine attempt to find a solution.

STATE EQUITY HOLDING, *Re*: E.C. COMMISSION *v.* BELGIUM (No. 52/84) [1987] 1 C.M.L.R. 710, European Ct.

1650. State monopolies—directives, decisions and regulations

87/388/EEC:
Commission Recommendation of July 3, 1987 to the French Republic concerning the adjustment of the State monopoly of a commercial character in potassic fertilizers *vis-à-vis* the new Member States. (O.J. 1987 L203/53.)

87/389/EEC:
Commission Recommendation of July 3, 1987 to the French Republic concerning the adjustment of the State monopoly of a commercial character in matches *vis-à-vis* the new Member States. (O.J. 1987 L203/56.)

87/390/EEC:
Commission Recommendation of July 3, 1987 to the French Republic concerning the adjustment of the State monopoly of a commercial character in manufactured tobacco *vis-à-vis* the new Member States. (O.J. 1987 L203/58.)

1651. Steel—aids—discrimination

Germany brought proceedings under Art. 33(1) ECSC in which it sought a declaration that Commission Decisions 83/391, 83/393, 83/399 of June 29, 1983 on aid which the Belgian, French, Italian and U.K. Governments proposed to grant to the steel industry were partially void. Germany claimed that by these Decisions the Commission had authorised aids substantially higher and required reductions in capacity substantially lower than those needed in order to bring about an expeditious and adequate adjustment in the production capacity of the European steel industry. It argued that, as a result, the European Commission breached, *inter alia,* the principle of equality to the detriment of the German steel industry. It also claimed that the Commission had acted contrary to various provisions of the Second Aids Code.

Held, dismissing the proceedings, that there was no discrimination against the German steel industry as it had not borne a disproportionate share of the burden of restructuring. Under the Second Aids Code the Commission was not entitled to authorise aid if the plans to grant or alter the aid had not been notified to it by September 30, 1982, but such plans did not mean precise amounts of money so long as the actual sums authorised later were not such as to alter the character of the aid. The fact that Belgium, France, Italy and the U.K. had later asked, and been authorised, to grant larger sums, than were in their notified plans did not invalidate the authorisations.

STATE AIDS TO THE STEEL INDUSTRY, *Re*: GERMANY *v.* EUROPEAN COMMISSION (No. 214/83) [1987] 1 C.M.L.R. 566, European Ct.

1652. Steel—production quotas—fines

Manchester Steel Ltd. ("Manchester") brought annulment proceedings of the Commission's decision imposing a fine for it exceeding its production quota by less than 3 per cent. Manchester, which produced one category of steel, claimed that it should have enjoyed the benefit of the 3 per cent. tolerance granted by Art. 11 of Decision 1831/81.

Held, dismissing the action, that (i) since single-category producers only enjoyed the tolerance on their distribution quota, but always within the limit of their production quota and (ii) since the tolerance enjoyed by multi-category producers per category had to be contained within the sum total of their overall production quotas for all categories combined, there was no discrimination between the two kinds of producer, both having to remain within the overall limit of their total assigned quota.

MANCHESTER STEEL *v.* E.C. COMMISSION (No. 46/85) [1987] 2 C.M.L.R. 857, European Ct.

1653. Steel—quotas exceeded—fines

The European Commission imposed fines on five steel undertakings for violating Art. 58 ECSC and Decisions thereunder by exceeding set production quotas.

COMMUNITY, THE *v.* ACCIAIERIE E FERRIERA DEL CALEOTTO S.p.A. [1987] 2 C.M.L.R. 277, E.C. Commission.

1654. Stock Exchanges—mutual recognition—listing particulars

The European Commission submitted to the Council a proposal for a Council Directive amending Council Directive 80/390 co-ordinating the requirements for the drawing-up, scrutiny and distribution of the listing particulars to be published for the admission of securities to official stock exchange listing.

DRAFT STOCK EXCHANGE LISTING PARTICULARS (MUTUAL RECOGNITION) DIRECTIVE [1987] 2 C.M.L.R. 486, E.C. Council.

1655. Subsidiary bodies—directives, decisions and regulations

87/144/EEC:

Commission Decision of February 13, 1987 amending Decision 80/686/EEC setting up an Advisory Committee on the Control and Reduction of Pollution Caused by Hydrocarbons Discharged at Sea. (O.J. 1987 L57/57.)

87/305/EEC:

Commission Decision of May 26, 1987 setting up an advisory committee on the opening-up of public procurement. (O.J. 1987 L152/32.)

1656. Sunday trading—ban—whether lawful—EEC Treaty. See WYCHAVON DISTRICT COUNCIL *v.* MIDLAND ENTERPRISES (SPECIAL EVENTS), §3449.

1657. Tachograph—exemption—breakdown vehicle. See HAMILTON *v.* WHITELOCK (No. 79/86), §3307.

1658. Taxation—directives, decisions and regulations

Application of Article 27 of the sixth Council Directive of May 17, 1977 on value-added tax. (O.J. 1987 L132/22.)

1659. Taxation—drink—differentiation

In Case No. 106/84, the European Commission brought proceedings against Denmark under Art. 169 EEC for a declaration that, by taxing wine made from grapes at a higher rate than that made from other fruit, Denmark had failed to fulfil its obligations under Art. 95 EEC. Denmark imposed excise duty on grape wine at 10.725 D.kr per litre (table wine) and 19.93 D.Kr (fortified wine up to 23 per cent. alcohol by volume); on fruit wine other than grape at 6.92 D.Kr (table wine up to 14 per cent.) and 11.02 D.Kr (fortified wine up to 20 per cent.); on spirits above those alcohol limits at a much higher rate calculated on the basis of different criteria.

In Case No. 243/84, the Ostre Landsret asked the European Court under Art. 177 EEC for a preliminary ruling on the interpretation of Art. 95 EEC, in order to enable it to assess the compatibility of the system of differential taxation applied in Denmark to Scotch and fruit wine of the liqueur type.

Held, that in Case No. 106/84, Denmark failed to fulfil its obligations under Art. 95 EEC by taxing wine made from grapes at a higher rate than wine made from other fruit.

Held, that in Case No. 243/84, Art. 95 EEC meant that goods such as Scotch whisky and fruit wine of the liqueur type might not be treated as similar products; in view of the present state of EEC law, particularly para. 2 of Art. 95 EEC, an EEC State was not prohibited from imposing taxation which differentiated between certain drinks on the basis of objective criteria. Such a taxation system did not favour domestic producers where a significant proportion of domestic production of alcohol drinks fell within each of the different tax categories.

TAXATION OF WINE, *Re*: E.C. COMMISSION *v.* DENMARK (No. 106/84); WALKER (JOHN) & SONS LTD. *v.* MINISTERIET FOR SKATTER OG AFGIFTER (No. 243/84) [1987] 2 C.M.L.R. 278, European Ct.

1660. Transport—directives, decisions and regulations

86/646/EEC:

Council Decision of December 16, 1986 extending the collection of information concerning the activities of carriers participating in cargo liner traffic in certain areas of operation. (O.J. 1987 L382/1.)

86/647/EEC:

Council Decision of December 16, 1986 fixing the allocation to Member States of the extra Community authorisations for 1987 resulting from the annual and additional increase in the Community quota for the carriage of goods by road. (O.J. 1987 L382/2.)

87/467/EEC:

Commission Decision of July 31, 1987 setting up a Joint Committee on Maritime Transport. (O.J. 1987 L253/20.)

87/475/EEC:

Council Decision of September 17, 1987 relating to maritime transport between Italy and Algeria. (O.J. 1987 L272/37.)

87/540/EEC:
Council Directive of November 9, 1987 on access to the occupation of carrier of goods by waterway in national and international transport and on the mutual recognition of diplomas, certificates and other evidence of formal qualifications for this occupation. (O.J. 1987 L322/20.)
Council Decision of May 26, 1987 on the application between the Community and Switzerland of the provisions laid down in Sections II and III of the Agreement on the International Carriage of Passengers by Road by means of Occasional Coach and Bus Services (ASOR). (O.J. 1987 L143/32.)
Council Regulation (EEC) No. 4055/86 of December 22, 1986 applying the principle of freedom to provide services to maritime transport between Member States and between Member States and third countries. (O.J. 1987 L378/1.)
Council Regulation (EEC) No. 4056/86 of December 22, 1986 laying down detailed rules for the application of Articles 85 and 86 of the Treaty to maritime transport. (O.J. 1987 L378/4.)
Council Regulation (EEC) No. 4057/86 of December 22, 1986 on unfair pricing practices in maritime transport. (O.J. 1987 L378/14.)
Council Regulation (EEC) No. 4058/86 of December 22, 1986 concerning coordinated action to safeguard free access to cargoes in ocean trades. (O.J. 1987 L378/21.)
Council Regulation (EEC) No. 4059/86 of December 22, 1986 on the granting of financial support to transport infrastructure projects. (O.J. 1987 L378/24.)
Council Regulation (EEC) No. 1879/87 of June 30, 1987 amending Regulation (EEC) No. 3164/76 on the Community quota for the carriage of goods by road between Member States. (O.J. L179/3.)

1661. VAT—sixth VAT Directive—aims of a civic nature

The Institute of Leisure and Amenity Management (the "Institute") claimed that the services, which it supplied its members in consideration of their subscriptions, should be exempt from VAT under Art. 13A1(1) of the 6th VAT Directive. The Institute was set up to encourage management skills with regard to leisure and skills with regard to leisure and recreation establishments, such as parks, theatres and conference centres. Most of its membership were employed by local authorities although such a requirement was not mandatory.

Held, the Institute's services were not exempt from VAT as the Institute's aims were not of "a civic nature" within the meaning of Art. 13 A1(1).

INSTITUTE OF LEISURE AND AMENITY MANAGEMENT *v.* CUSTOMS AND EXCISE COMMISSIONERS [1987] 2 C.M.L.R. 60, VAT Tribunal.

1662. VAT—sixth VAT Directive—bad debt relief

[Value Added Tax Act, 1983 (c.55), s.22.]

Euro-Academy Limited ("Euro-Academy") provided English tuition for Greek students which was to be paid for by Mr. Sophiades in Greece. Mr. Sophiades was made bankrupt in Greece and never paid the cost of the tuition. Euro-Academy claimed that it did not have to pay VAT on the unpaid bill as s.22 of the Value Added Tax Act 1983 provided for exemption if the debtor became bankrupt.

Held, the 1983 Act was only applicable to bankruptcies within the U.K. and not to bankruptcies in other EEC States. The 6th VAT Directive did not require EEC States to give bad debt relief and, thus, no such relief could be granted.

EURO-ACADEMY *v.* CUSTOMS AND EXCISE COMMISSIONERS [1987] 2 C.M.L.R. 29, VAT Tribunal.

1663. VAT—sixth VAT Directive—building—transfer tax

The German tax authorities sought from Mr. and Mrs. Kerrutt real property transfer tax on a co-proprietors' building scheme called "Bauherrenmodell". The Kerrutts and other people commissioned trustees to buy building land and contractors to build homes thereon. The Kerrutts also made various contracts on their own behalf in relation to the building and financing of their house purchase. Mr. and Mrs. Kerrutt disputed the tax demands in so far as the transfer tax was calculated on the basis of the consideration for all the various transactions. The Finance Court, Düsseldorf, asked the European Court under Art. 177 EEC for a preliminary ruling on the interpretation of the 6th VAT Directive.

Held, that (1) under a transaction such as the "Bauherrenmodell", the supply of goods and services under a parcel of contracts for work and services in connection with the construction of a building—but not the supply of the building—are subject to VAT by reason of Art. 2(1) of the 6th VAT Directive; (2) EEC law does not prevent an EEC State from levying on a transaction, which is subject to VAT under the 6th VAT Directive, other taxes on transfers and transactions, provided that such taxes cannot be regarded as turnover taxes.

KERRUTT (HANS-DIETER) AND KERRUTT (UTE) *v.* FINANZAMT (TAX OFFICE) MÖNCHENGLADBACH-MITTE (No. 73/85) [1987] 2 C.M.L.R. 221, European Ct.

1664. VAT—sixth VAT Directive—social security tax

Rousseau Wilmot S.A. and its receiver ("the objectors") objected to paying solidarity levies and mutual assistance charges to ORGANIC, a French body responsible for collecting such levies and charges. The objectors argued that the solidarity levy was calcuated at 0.1 per cent. of turnover whereas EEC rules, in particular Art. 33 of the 6th VAT Directive, regarding the harmonisation of laws relating to turnover taxes limited the powers of EEC States to introduce or maintain such taxes. ORGANIC argued that the solidarity levy and mutual assistance charges were intended to provide additional sums for the old-age and sickness benefit schemes for traders and self-employed craftsmen and, thus, the levies were in the nature of social security contributions whereas Art. 33 of the 6th VAT Directive related only to fiscal matters. The Cour d'Appel, Douai, asked the European Court under Art. 177 EEC for a preliminary ruling on the interpretation of Art. 33 of the 6th VAT Directive.

Held, that the prohibition in Art. 33 of the 6th VAT Directive, which bans EEC States from introducing any taxes or levies which can be characterised as turnover taxes, seeks to prevent competing national fiscal measures operating in a way comparable to VAT. The purpose of Art. 33 is not to prevent EEC States from maintaining or introducing duties or charges which are not fiscal, but which have been introduced in order to finance social funds and which are based on the activity of undertakings or certain types of undertakings and calculated on the basis of the undertakings' total annual turnover.

ROUSSEAU WILMOT S.A. *v.* ORGANIC (No. 295/84) [1986] 3 C.M.L.R. 677, European Ct.

1665. VAT—6th VAT Directive—value of supply—consideration—party plan sales. See VALUE ADDED TAX, §3856.

1666. VAT—8th Council Directive—refund of tax within the EEC—place of supply of services. See VALUE ADDED TAX, §3827.

1667. Veterinary surgeons qualifications—recognition

VETERINARY SURGEONS QUALIFICATIONS (EEC REGULATIONS) (SPANISH AND PORTUGUESE QUALIFICATIONS) ORDER 1987 (No. 447) [45p], made under the European Communities Act 1972 (c.68), s.2(2); operative on April 16, 1987; provides for recognition of Spanish and Portuguese veterinary surgeon qualifications.

EVIDENCE (CIVIL)

1668. Admissibility—certificate of public interest immunity—admissibility of contents of certificate

The Secretary of State for Defence issued a certificate claiming public interest immunity in respect of S's diaries. S did not challenge this certificate.

Held, that this did not imply S's acceptance of the truth of the contents of the certificate.

SETHIA *v.* STERN, *The Independent,* October 30, 1987, C.A.

1669. Admissibility—foreign conviction—whether admissible in U.K. Court

[Civil Evidence Act 1968 (c.64), s.11.]

P manufactured sausage skins in Spain. P alleged infringement of patent and breach of confidence. Five employees of D2 were convicted in the French court for theft of P's confidential information from P's factory in France. P pleaded this under the Civil Evidence Act 1968 s.11 as evidence. D sought to strike out this and, in addition, the allegation against D1 who had imported and sold sausage skins in the U.K.

Held, that (1) P could not rely upon the convictions pursuant to the Civil Evidence Act 1968, s.11; (2) P had an arguable case against the importer. The scope of the law was not entirely clear.

UNION CARBIDE CORP. *v.* NATURIN [1987] F.S.R. 538, C.A.

1670. Admissibility—guarantees in respect of vehicle leasing—whether extrinsic evidence admissible to identify leasing agreements

[Statute of Frauds 1677 (c.3), s.4.]

There is no difference between the rules governing admissibility of evidence to construe written contracts in general, and those written contracts which are subject to the Statute of Frauds.

The defendants, a Swiss car rental group, set up a car rental business in the U.K. to be operated by S. They wished to lease a large number of cars from the plaintiff for that purpose. The plaintiff entered into leasing agreements in May 1979 and the defendants in July signed formal guarantees in "respect of the proposed leasing." Thereafter further leasing agreements were entered into. In August 1980 S ceased trading and was wound up. The plaintiff repossessed the vehicles but was still owed £65,224 which it sought to recover from the guarantors. The defendants contended that extrinsic evidence to identify the relevant leasing agreements was not admissible.

Held, objective extrinsic evidence was admissible to construe the guarantees, which covered, therefore, leasing agreements entered into after the guarantees were signed (*Holmes* v. *Mitchell* (1859) C.B.N.S. 361 distinguished; *Sheers* v. *Thimbleby* (1897) 76 L.T. 709 considered).

PERRYLEASE *v.* IMECAR A.G. [1987] 2 All E.R. 373, Scott J.

1671. Admissibility—hearsay evidence—wardship proceedings. See N. (MINORS) (WARDSHIP: EVIDENCE), *Re* §2517.

1672. Admissibility—woman subjected to sexual harassment at work—evidence of woman's attitude to sexual matters—whether evidence admissible to show lack of detriment. See SNOWBALL *v.* GARDNER MERCHANT, §1336.

1673. Affidavit—anonymous letter exhibited to affidavit—admissibility

An anonymous letter exhibited to an affidavit was not admissible, and consequently there was no evidence of any arguable case that could be raised by D on P's application for summary judgment. In any event, such a letter was evidence showing how D had come to be suspicious of the matters alleged in it, but more suspicion did not found an arguable case.

BARCLAYS BANK *v.* ANDERSON, *The Times,* March 10, 1987, C.A.

1674. Bankers' books—cheques and credit slips—whether "other records used in the ordinary business of the bank"—whether order of inspection to be made

[Bankers' Books Evidence Act 1879 (c.11), ss.7, 9.]

Cleared cheques and credit slips are not entries in a banker's book or other records used in the ordinary business of the bank and thus not amenable to an order for inspection and the taking of copies under s.7 Bankers' Books Evidence Act 1879.

In proceedings for judicial separation, W sought ancillary relief against her husband. The husband failed to co-operate in disclosing his means. Their matrimonial home was owned by trustees of an unregistered charity. In consolidated proceedings the trustees sought an order for possession. W contended that her husband had used his position as chairman or director of the charity to hide his wealth in the charity's bank accounts and that his money purchased the matrimonial home. On an *ex parte* application, W obtained an order under s.7 of the Bankers' Books Evidence Act 1879 permitting her to inspect and take copies of all entries in the books of Barclays Bank plc at Orpington, Kent including all cleared cheques and credit slips relating to the accounts of the charity and the husband. On the bank's appeal the judge deleted the references to cleared cheques and credit slips.

Held, dismissing W's appeal, that under s.7 of the Bankers' Books Evidence Act 1879 the court had power to permit the inspection and taking of copies of entries in bankers books. Pursuant to s.9 of the Act bankers books included "other records used in the ordinary business of the bank". That phrase was to be construed *ejusdem generis* with ledgers, day books, cash books and account books. Bundles of unsorted cheques and paying in slips were not other records within the meaning of the Act. In the circumstances of the case, it was proper for the cheques and paying in and credit slips to be discovered by making an order for specific discovery against the husband and the charity which the bank could be ordered to comply with as their agent. Alternatively a *subpoena duces tecum* could be issued against an officer of the bank returnable on a date set aside for production of the relevant documents with the remainder of the hearing adjourned to a date to be fixed.

WILLIAMS *v.* WILLIAMS; TUCKER *v.* WILLIAMS [1987] 3 W.L.R. 790, C.A.

1675. Blood tests

BLOOD TESTS (EVIDENCE OF PATERNITY) (AMENDMENT) REGULATIONS 1987 (No. 1199) [45p], made under the Family Law Reform Act 1969 (c.46), s.22; operative on August 17, 1987; increase the charges which may be made in respect of blood tests carried out for the purposes of determining paternity in civil proceedings.

1676. Confidential documents—International Tin Council—protection

Whilst statute conferred inviolability on documents in the possession of the Council protecting them against use as Evidence in Court, the same does not apply to documents not in their possession unless the possessor has secured them unlawfully or in breach of confidence.

SHEARSON LEHMAN BROTHERS INC. *v.* MACLAINE WATSON & CO., INTERNATIONAL TIN COUNCIL INTERVENING, *Financial Times,* August 5, 1987, C.A.

1677. Disclosure—information sought by patient—extent of hospital's obligation to disclose

Where a patient seeks information on a drug that had been recommended for her condition, the hospital is not bound to give her all the information that it has in its possession but rather a reasonable amount depending on all the circumstances.

BLYTH *v.* BLOOMSBURY HEALTH AUTHORITY, *The Times,* February 11, 1987, C.A.

1678. Disclosure—sources—whether in "interests of justice"

[Contempt of Court Act 1981 (c.49), s.10.]

A journalist will only be required to disclose his source if it is necessary in the technical sense in the administration of justice rather than merely relevant or expedient.

Maxwell sued *Private Eye* for libel, and sought exemplary damages. PE pleaded justification and fair comment but could not call evidence of the truth of their articles. M applied under s.10 of the Contempt of Court Act 1981 for an order that PE disclose their sources. The judge ruled that although such evidence went to recklessness and exemplary damages the public interest in the protection of sources outweighed the interest of justice.

Held, dismissing the appeal, that the words "in the interests of justice" were used in a technical sense of disclosure being necessary, rather than merely relevant or expedient. The judge had indicated that he would deal with the matter in his summing-up and was entitled to find that disclosure was not necessary. (Dicta of Lord Diplock in *Secretary of State for Defence* v. *Guardian Newspapers* [1984] C.L.Y. 2596 applied).

MAXWELL *v.* PRESSDRAM [1987] 1 W.L.R. 298, C.A.

1679. Disclosure—wards—practice direction. See PRACTICE, §3009.

1680. Expert evidence—passing off action—whether market research witness an expert

Objection was taken to the calling of a witness for the plaintiff who was a market researcher who had conducted for the plaintiff studies of public response to the plaintiff's goods.

Held, that the market researcher would present to the court only the information which he had collated. He would not be expressing any opinion. He was therefore not acting as an expert witness.

RECKITT & COLMAN PRODUCTS *v.* BORDEN INC. (No. 2) [1987] F.S.R. 407, Walton J.

1681. Expert evidence—time limits—variation of directions—courts

[C.C.R., Ord. 38, r.44.]

P was in breach of a direction requiring exchange of expert evidence 28 days prior to a county court hearing. D had complied. P disclosed five days late, having first sent D's report to his expert prior to preparation of his own. P relied on Ord. 38, r.44 to vary the direction and permit expert evidence at the trial. The registrar granting the application awarded P costs in any event stating D had taken a false point. D appealed.

Held, that D were entitled to stand by their rights accrued by virtue of the first direction which was a hard and fast rule to be observed and not varied lightly. They had not taken a false point. Justice however required that P be allowed to adduce some expert evidence at trial but D were entitled to the costs of the hearing before the registrar and the costs of the appeal. P, in breach of a time limit, had come before the court asking for its indulgence and it was not correct to penalise D in costs. The correct procedure for P's solicitors would have been to inform D's solicitors immediately they anticipated they were likely to be in breach of the direction and ask for an extension of time at that stage.

BRADLEY *v.* PORTAS, March 23, 1987; H.H. Judge Hutchinson; Lincoln County Ct. [*Ex rel. Langleys, Solicitors.*]

1682. Expert evidence—whether a person was a mental defective—whether opinion of medical expert relevant or admissible. See R. *v.* HALL (JOHN HAMILTON), §2421.

1683. Expert witness—meaning of ordinary English words—no custom or practice alleged—costs. See HALVANON INSURANCE CO. *v.* JEWETT DUCHESNE (INTERNATIONAL), §2946.

1684. Personal injuries—disclosure of expert evidence

The Lord Chancellor's Department has issued a consultation paper which suggests that medical experts reports in all personal injury cases should normally be disclosed to the other side in the proceedings. Copies of the paper, *Expert Evidence in Actions for Personal Injuries,* are available free from N. Hodgson Esq., Lord Chancellor's Department, Trevelyan House, 30 Great Peter Street, London, SW1P 2BY. Tel. 01-210-8720.

1685. Privilege—planning inquiry—letter sent to Inspector

An inquiry into an appeal against an enforcement notice is an administrative rather than judicial proceeding and letters sent to the inspector do not attract absolute privilege.

RICHARDS *v.* CRESSWELL, *The Times,* April 24, 1987, Turner J.

1686/7. Security for costs—without prejudice negotiations

[R.S.C., Ord. 23, r.1(1)(*a*).]

Evidence of without prejudice negotiations is not admissible on a summons for security for costs.

P a company incorporated in Abu Dhabi were claiming damages against D, an English company, for negligence in the supply of coated glass units. D denied liability and issued a summons under R.S.C., Ord. 23, r.1(1)(*a*) seeking security for costs. P submitted that the court could take into account 'without prejudice' offers of settlement by D in order to assess P's likely chances of success, and whether it would be just to require security.

Held, that such evidence was not admissible.

SIMAAN CENTRAL CONTRACTING CO. *v.* PILKINGTON GLASS [1987] 1 All E.R. 345; John Newey Q.C., Official Referee.

1688. Witness summons—affiliation proceedings—evidence from adoption agency—public interest immunity

The mother brought affiliation proceedings against W who denied paternity. The mother had to have corroborative evidence. She alleged that she and W had discussed the child's adoption and W had signed a form as father of the unborn child. The social worker at the adoption agency involved refused to provide the evidence on the basis that it was confidential information protected by public interest immunity. The mother obtained a magistrates' court witness summons. The social worker sought an order of certiorari, the mother sought an order of mandamus for the justices to direct the social worker to produce the document.

Held, that where justices were satisfied that a person was likely to be able to give material evidence, as in this case, and that person would not attend court voluntarily, it was mandatory for them to issue a witness summons. The question of immunity would be considered at court. The adoption agency's claim for public interest immunity was not justified; that type of immunity (although recently extended) was a restricted one, there was no analogy between informants to the police or the N.S.P.C.C. and the father in this case. The evidence sought was precisely known and vital to the justice of the case. Therefore the social worker's application would be refused. There was no need to make an order on the wife's application (*Air Canada* v. *Secretary of State for Trade* [1981] C.L.Y. 141, *Campbell* v. *Tameside Metropolitan Council* [1982] C.L.Y. 2467, *Conway* v. *Rimmer* [1968] C.L.Y. 3099, *Crompton Amusement Machines* v. *Customs and Excise Commissioners (No. 2)* [1973] C.L.Y. 2642, *D. (Infants), Re* [1970] C.L.Y. 1359, *D.* v. *N.S.P.C.C.* [1978] C.L.Y. 2324, *Gaskin* v. *Liverpool City Council* [1980] C.L.Y. 2139, *Marks* v. *Beyfus* (1890) 25 Q.B.D. 494, *R.* v. *Greenwich Juvenile Court* [1978] C.L.Y. 1977, *R.* v. *Lewes Justices, ex p. Gaming Board for Great Britain* [1972] C.L.Y. 1610, *R.* v. *Nottingham County Justices, ex p.* Bostock [1970] C.L.Y. 140, *R.* v. *West London Justices, ex p. Klahn* [1979] C.L.Y. 1713 referred to).

R. *v.* BOURNEMOUTH JUSTICES, *ex p.* GRAY: R. *v.* SAME, *ex p.* RODD [1987] 1 F.L.R. 36, Hodgson J.

EXECUTORS AND ADMINISTRATORS

1689. Distribution of estate—company shares forming part of residuary estate—whether bound to divide and distribute shares in accordance with aliquot parts of estate

The executors of an estate were not bound to divide up and distribute the shares of a company between the various beneficiaries in accordance with their respective shares in the estate where to do so would result in one beneficiary being favoured beyond what the testator had intended.

The testator was the registered holder of 999 out of 1000 issued shares in Rowland Smith Hotels Ltd. The company was a private company that owned and operated a substantial hotel in Torquay worth between £3 million and £3·5 million. The shares formed part of the residuary estate which was to be divided as to 46/80ths to the testator's wife and the remainder among a number of other members of the family. Before the residuary estate was distributed the testator's wife died leaving her estate to D who was the managing director of the hotel. D contended that the bank as the executor of the testator's estate should transfer to him 547 shares in the company. The remaining beneficiaries contended that all the shares should be sold in the open market and the proceeds of sale distributed to the beneficiaries. On the company's asset value each share was worth approximately £3,000. D through his and the company's accountants had written to the other beneficiaries offering to pay them £403 per share which was expressed to be substantially more than the value of the shares as minority shareholdings. On the evidence it was clear that the value per share of a holding of 574 shares being part of a controlling shareholding was markedly higher than the value per share of a holding of 425 being the whole block of remaining shares. The bank applied to the court for directions as to how to distribute the estate.

Held, that the bank was bound to hold an even hand among the beneficiaries and not favour one as against another. If D were to take 574 shares he would be favoured beyond what was intended in that the value he would receive would be far in excess of 46/80ths as provided in the testators' will. If the shares were distributed they would be of little value to the remaining beneficiaries given D's stated intention not to declare dividends on account of his development plans and the inability of the minority shareholders to press for a winding up of the company. In the circumstances it was right to make an exception to the general rule that the beneficiaries were entitled to have the shares transferred to them and order them to be sold in the open market with all the beneficiaries being at liberty to purchase if they so wished (*Marshall, Re* [1914] 1 Ch. 192, *Sandeman's Will Trusts, Re* [1937] 1 All E.R. 368, *Wiener, Re* [1956] C.L.Y. 3324 considered).

LLOYDS BANK *v.* DUKER [1987] 1 W.L.R. 1324, John Mowbray Q.C. sitting as a deputy High Court judge.

1690. Duty to beneficiary—third party. See HAYIM *v.* CITIBANK N.A., §1425.

1691. Foreign executor—debt—jurisdiction

Unless he has intermeddled with an estate as executor *de son tort,* the Court has no jurisdiction to entertain a claim for debt against the foreign executor of a foreign estate where he cannot be affixed with personal liability within the jurisdiction.

DEGAZON *v.* BARCLAYS BANK INTERNATIONAL, *Financial Times,* October 14, 1987, C.A.

1692. Lands Tribunal decision

A appealed in his capacity as personal representative against an estate duty determination in relation to 22 properties in Halifax which were subject to regulated tenancies as at May 1984. When the D.V. produced a schedule of four comparable premises, A sought wide-ranging discovery including details of sales of all tenanted property in the D.V.'s district between 1973 and 1976, and of subsequent sales of those properties. This would have involved a search of some 70–80,000 separate records. At the pre-trial review A modified his request to cover instead records of all relevant transactions in the D.V.'s district and in the area covered by each party's comparables within a reasonable period before and after the material date, and limited the request to those residential properties which were subject to regulated tenancies. The tribunal took the view that it was not for the D.V. to make available his own records in order to rectify deficiencies in A's evidence or comparables, and that to order such discovery would not be in the interests of securing a just, expeditious or economical disposal of the proceedings within the meaning of r.45A(2) of the Lands Tribunal Rules. Discovery would however be ordered of the identities of the purchasers involved in transactions concerning D's comparables.

KINGSLEY *v.* I.R.C. (Det/2/1982) (1987) 283 E.G. 1518.

EXTRADITION

1693. Aircraft

EXTRADITION PROTECTION OF AIRCRAFT (AMENDMENT) ORDER 1987 (No. 2043) [45p], made under the Extradition Act 1870 (c.52), ss.2, 17, 21 and the Aviation Security Act 1982 (c.36), ss.9(2), 39(1); operative on January 1, 1988; amends S.I. 1973 No. 1756 by adding Honduras, Madagascar and Yemen Arab Republic to Sched. 3, Part I.

1694. Bail—test to be applied

[Rep. of Ire.] G was committed to prison on foot of an order for his extradition to the United States of America. His application for bail was granted by the judge who applied the test of whether it was probable or not that G would abscond. The Attorney-General appealed.

Held, dismissing the appeal, that there was no reason for applying the absconding test any differently in extradition cases as compared with ordinary criminal cases.

PEOPLE, THE (ATT.-GEN.) *v.* GILLILAND [1985] I.R. 643, Supreme Ct. of Ire.

1695. Extradition to Germany—date of apprehension—whether two month period is a limitation period

[Extradition Act 1870 (c.52), s.9; Anglo-German Extradition Treaty 1872, Art. XII.]

Art. XII of the Anglo-German Extradition Treaty 1872 provides that if sufficient evidence for the extradition of a fugitive is not provided within two months from the date of his apprehension, he shall be set free, The "date of his apprehension" is the date of his first appearance before magistrates. The two month period is not a limitation period; if extradition proceedings under the 1872 Treaty are aborted, fresh proceedings can be started outside the two-month period under s.9 of the Extradition Act 1870.

R. *v.* GOVERNOR OF PENTONVILLE PRISON, *ex p.* SYAL, *The Times,* May 18, 1987, D.C.

1696. Extradition to the U.S.—time-limit for request—time-limit for accompanying evidence

[U.K.-U.S. Extradition Treaty 1972 (1976 S.I. No. 2144), Arts. 7(3), 8(2).]

A request for a persons's extradition is made within the time limit of 60 days from the date of arrest pursuant to Art. 8(2) of the U.K.-U.S. Extradition Treaty 1972 notwithstanding that the accompanying evidence required by Art. 7(3) is in the form of an affidavit sworn outside the time-limit. The evidence must, however, accompany the request at the hearing of proceedings in the U.K. for the accused's committal to custody.

An indictment sealed by a U.S. federal magistrate in the exercise of his discretion upon its return by a grand jury is "found" when it is sealed. U.K. justices cannot review this exercise of discretion (*U.S.A.* v. *Srulowitz* 819 Fed. (2nd Series) 37 distinguished).

MUIR, *Re, The Independent,* December 9, 1987, D.C.

1697. Fugitive offenders

EXTRADITION (HIJACKING) (AMENDMENT) ORDER 1987 (No. 2041) [45p], made under the Extradition Act 1870 (c.52), ss.2, 17 and 21, and the Aviation Security Act 1982 (c.36), ss.9(2) and 39(1); operative on January 1, 1988; amends S.I. 1971 No. 2102.

UNITED STATES OF AMERICA (EXTRADITION) (AMENDMENT) ORDER 1987 (No. 2046) [45p], made under the Extradition Act 1870, ss.2, 17 and 21; operative on January 1, 1988; amends S.I. 1986 No. 2020.

1698. Fugitive offenders—Anguilla

FUGITIVE OFFENDERS (ANGUILLA) ORDER 1987 (No. 452) [£1·60], made under the Fugitive Offenders Act 1967 (c.68), ss.17 and 20; operative on April 17; extends the provisions of the 1967 Act to Anguilla.

1699. Internationally protected persons

EXTRADITION (INTERNATIONALLY PROTECTED PERSONS) (AMENDMENT) ORDER 1987 (No. 2042] [45p], made under the Internationally Protected Persons Act 1978 (c.17), ss.3(2) 4(1) and the Extradition Act 1870 (c.52), ss.2, 17, 21; operative on January 1, 1988; amends S.I. 1979 No. 453.

1700. Return of offender—indictment remaining on file after trial—authentication of witness statements

[Fugitive Offenders Act 1967 (c.68), ss.9, 11.]

Where a count or an indictment is ordered to lie on the file, it has not been disposed of and no order could be made for the return of an offender. As to authentication of statements, it was not necessary for each statement to bear a certificate, but it was sufficient for all the statements read together to be authenticated (*R.* v. *Central Criminal Court, ex p. Raymond* [1986] C.L.Y. 625 considered).

R. *v.* GOVERNOR OF PENTONVILLE PRISON, *ex p.* OSCAR, *The Times,* May 29, 1987, D.C.

1701. Suppression of terrorism

EXTRADITION (SUPPRESSION OF TERRORISM) (AMENDMENT) ORDER 1987 (No. 2206) [45p], made under the Extradition Act 1870 (c.52), ss.2, 21; operative on February 1, 1988; applies the Extradition Act 1870 to 1935 in the case of France with regard to the suppression of terrorism.

1702. Taking of hostages

EXTRADITION (TAKING OF HOSTAGES) (AMENDMENT) ORDER 1987 (No. 2044) [45p], made under the Extradition Act 1870 (c.52), ss.2, 17, 21 and the Taking of Hostages Act 1982 (c.28), s.5(1); operative on January 1, 1988; amends S.I. 1985 No. 751 by adding Austria to Sched. 2 and by adding Japan, Senegal and Togo to Sched. 3, Part I.

1703. Treaty—interpretation—evidence within two months—whether required to be legally admissible

Extradition Act 1870 (c.52), s.10; Anglo-Belgian Extradition Treaty 1901 (S.R. & O. 1902, No. 208), Art. 5.)]

For the purposes of extradition to Belgium and the two-month time limits, it is not necessary for the statements of English witnesses to be in legally admissible form, provided they comply with s.102 of the Magistrates' Courts Act 1980.

On July 3, 1986, the Belgian government issued a requisition for the surrender of 26 English football fans allegedly involved in Heysel riot. In addition to the Belgian evidence the D.P.P. submitted statements of English witnesses under s.102. The magistrates issued warrants. At the committal proceedings it was argued that the statements had not been presented within the two-month time limit, in that they had not been tendered without objection, or with oral evidence to substantiate their contents. The magistrate made the order, the Divisional Court discharged the defendants.

Held, allowing the appeal, that where the evidence was of witnesses in England, it was not necessary for it to be in legally admissable form; there was sufficient compliance with time limits by the production of s.102 evidence (*Beese* v. *Governor of Ashford Remand Centre and Federal German Republic* [1973] C.L.Y. 1434, *Government of the Federal Republic of Germany* v. *Sotiriadis* [1974] C.L.Y. 1605 applied).

GOVERNMENT OF BELGIUM *v.* POSTLETHWAITE [1987] 3 W.L.R. 365, H.L.

1704. Warrant—certificate—requirements

[Backing of Warrants (Republic of Ireland) Act 1965 (c.45), s.7(*b*).]

The only evidence required in a certificate produced under s.7(*b*) of the Backing of Warrants (Republic of Ireland) Act 1965 is a statement that the offence specified in the attached warrant is an indictable offence under Republic of Ireland law. Surplus words should be ignored, unless they materially alter the nature of the certificate.

HAWKINS (FRANCIS), *Re, The Times,* February 11, 1987, D.C.

1705. Warrant—foreign warrant—authentic copy—photocopy of authenticated copy

[Extradition Act 1870 (c.52), ss.10, 15.]

A magistrate made a committal order under s.10 of the 1870 Act, relying on an affidavit purporting to exhibit a true and authentic copy of the original warrant of arrest issued in California. The exhibit was in fact a photocopy of a copy. The photocopy was not authenticated.

Held, allowing L's application for a writ of habeas corpus, that the requirements of s.15 of the Act were not satisfied. An unauthenticated copy of an authenticated copy of a warrant was insufficient (*R.* v. *Ganz* (1882) 9 Q.B.D. 93 and *R.* v. *Bow Street Magistrates' Court, ex p. Van der Holst* [1986] C.L.Y. 1521 distinguished).

LEE *v.* GOVERNOR OF PENTONVILLE PRISON AND THE GOVERNMENT OF THE U.S.A. [1987] Crim.L.R. 635, D.C.

1706. Whether accused properly committed to prison to await extradition—extradition in respect of fraud. See R. *v.* GOVERNOR OF PENTONVILLE PRISON, *ex p.* HERBAGE (No. 3), §807.

FAMILY

1707. Affiliation proceedings—evidence from adoption agency—witness summons. See R. *v.* BOURNEMOUTH JUSTICES, *ex p.* GREY; R. *v.* SAME, *ex p.* RODD, §1688.

1708. Affiliation proceedings—refusal to have blood test—whether refusal corroborative evidence

[Affiliation Proceedings Act 1957 (c.55), s.4(1).]

The refusal of a putative father to submit to a blood test in a paternity case can be sufficient corroborative evidence to satisfy s.4(1) of the Affiliation Proceedings Act 1957 (*L., Re* [1968] C.L.Y. 1239, *B.* v. *B. & E.* [1969] C.L.Y. 1079 and *R.* v. *Smith (Robert William)* [1986] C.L.Y. 563 applied).

McV. *v.* B., *The Times,* November 28, 1987, Wood J.

1709. Assault by husband on wife—grievous bodily harm—whether occurrence of assault in a domestic context a mitigation. See R. *v.* CUTTS, §949.

1710. Costs—taxation—privileged documents—natural justice

On taxation of the defendant's bill of costs the plaintiff sought inspection of all documents including privileged ones such as instructions to counsel, correspondence between the defendant and her advisers and counsel's brief. The taxing registrar refused to allow such inspection. He looked at the documents himself and heard evidence on them.

Held, on appeal, that there appeared to be two inconsistent decisions. In *Pamplin* v. *Express Newspapers* [1985] C.L.Y. 1994 it was held that the principles of natural justice outweighed legal privilege. In *Hobbs* v. *Hobbs and Cousens* [1959] C.L.Y. 2559 there was held to be no entitlement to see privileged documents even though the litigation had been concluded. In the Family Division the latter decision prevailed and privilege would be maintained. The paying party had the advantage of knowing that the taxing master would know that the paying party had not seen the documents and hence the master or registrar would make sure that charges in respect of such documents were reasonable (*Pamplin* v. *Express Newspapers* [1985] C.L.Y. 1994 distinguished; *Hobbs* v. *Hobbs and Cousens* [1959] C.L.Y. 2559 followed).

GOLDMAN *v.* HESPER (1987) 17 Fam. Law 315, Eastham J.

1711. Divorce—behaviour—test to be applied

In determining whether the respondent had behaved in such a way that the petitioner could not reasonably be expected to live with the respondent, the correct test for the purposes of s.1(2)(*b*) of the Matrimonial Causes Act 1973 was whether a right-thinking person knowing the parties and all the circumstances would consider it reasonable to expect the petitioner to live with the respondent. It was not necessary for the petitioner to prove that the marriage breakdown had been caused by the facts relied upon for the purposes of s.1(2)(*b*).

BUFFERY *v.* BUFFERY, *The Times,* December 10, 1987, C.A.

1712. Divorce—decree absolute—appeal out of time

[Supreme Court Act 1981 (c.54), s.18(1)(*d*).]

W had filed a petition on the ground of H's unreasonable behaviour and H had cross-prayed for the marriage to be annulled on the ground of non-consummation, which W denied. At the hearing of the suit in December 1982 the judge rejected H's prayer and pronounced a decree nisi. It later appeared that there was a document in existence, purporting to be signed by H and W and a witness, confirming H's allegation of non-consummation. H had taken the decision not to mention the document at the hearing because of the extra expense that its investigation in court would have entailed. W disputed the validity of the document at all times. In March 1983 H applied for a rehearing of the divorce proceedings on the basis of the existence of the document and that W had obtained the decree nisi by giving perjured evidence. The application was dismissed and the decree was made absolute. H did not appeal because he thought that the matter of the document could be raised in the ancillary proceedings, which, in July 1984, considered and decided that the document was genuine. H then applied to the

Court of Appeal for a declaration to the effect that he was not precluded by s.18(1)(*d*) from appealing from the decree absolute.

Held, dismissing the application, that the provisions of s.18(1)(*d*) were objective and absolute, based on the obvious necessity of public policy to bring a state of finality in questions of matrimonial status. Here, H's delay coupled with his unsuccessful application in March 1983 were steps, and thereby an opportunity, which he had exercised to have the decree nisi set aside.

CROSBY *v.* CROSBY (1986) 16 Fam. Law 328, C.A.

1713. Divorce—decree absolute—appeal to Court of Appeal—listing of appeal

W applied to the Court of Appeal seeking to appeal against the decree absolute of divorce under s.18(1)(*d*) of the Supreme Court Act 1981 on the ground that she had not "had time and opportunity to appeal from the decree nisi on which that decree was founded". W filed an affidavit alleging various matters in support and H filed an affidavit denying all those allegations.

Held, on the question of how the issue thereby arising under s.18(1)(*d*) was to be resolved and having regard to two further cases listed on that day, that it was obvious that this was not a matter which could be dealt with substantially on that day. It was not clear for what purpose it had been listed that day. Counsel's intention and impressions as a result of communications with the Registrar of Civil Appeals was equally that the matter would not be dealt on its merits today. It was obvious that it could not be since both parties agreed that the contradictory allegations on affidavit must be tested by cross-examination; it was also proposed to call other witnesses whose evidence would in the first instance be on affidavit but that may also be followed by applications to cross-examine. If the matter was listed as an intended application for leave to appeal, this would have been misconceived. This action was not one which provided for any leave to appeal. The listing only made sense if it was for directions. It was clear that an application could properly be made to the Court of Appeal, as had been done in this case, under s.18(1)(*d*). As the law stood, the Court of Appeal would then have to hear the application on its merits, since it concerned the jurisdiction of the court. If for example it were held in a case such as the present one that the wife's allegations were true, and that she had been misled by her husband and had never had the opportunity of appealing against the decree nisi, then it would follow immediately that the decree absolute could not stand. Any further hearing by way of appeal from the decree absolute, which would then be permissible notwithstanding s.18(1)(*d*), would become a formality, with the result that the decree absolute would no doubt be set aside forthwith. It was clear that the substantive hearing of the issue would require the presence of the parties, of an interpreter and possibly other witnesses. Both counsel agreed that it might take two days or possibly more of the court's time as and when it was ready for hearing. This was unfortunate and it would clearly be preferable if some other procedure were available to deal with cases of this kind without involving two or possibly three Lord Justices. But it appeared that at present there was no alternative solution. That being the position, the matter could not proceed today. It should not have been listed at all and similar applications should not be listed in this way. They should only be listed as and when they were ready for the substantive hearing, with an adequate allowance of time, unless and until some better procedural means could be devised. Accordingly the application would be adjourned generally. Meanwhile the court would give directions for affidavits and notices to cross-examine, if so advised; but any necessary preliminary applications under the provision should in future be listed before the Registrar of Civil Appeals.

KHAN *v.* KHAN, October 6, 1986 (C.A.T. No. 702).

1714. Divorce—decree absolute—mandatory steps to be taken

[Matrimonial Causes Rules 1977, r.65(2).]

A decree nisi was pronounced. In ancillary relief proceedings the registrar decided that he had no jurisdiction unless the decree had been made absolute and asked the parties whether they wished him to do so. He then granted decrees absolute and ordered the wife to transfer her share in the home to the husband upon payment of a lump sum. The husband died and the wife appealed. No administrative steps had been taken by either party to apply for a decree absolute, there had been no endorsement on the decree nisi and the registrar and court officials had failed to carry out the mandatory duty to search the court minutes. The judge on the wife's appeal held as a preliminary issue that there had been no decree absolute and the marriage had been dissolved by death.

Held, that it was clear from r.66 of the Matrimonial Causes Rules 1977 that r.65 laid down mandatory requirements that had to be complied with before a decree nisi could become absolute. Those requirements were of fundamental importance and had not been met here. There had been no valid decree absolute.

DACKHAM *v.* DACKHAM (1987) 17 Fam. Law 345, C.A.

1715. Divorce—domicile—jurisdiction

The parties were both French nationals. The wife developed a relationship with an Englishman. She was sent for a year to England by her employers. Two weeks after her arrival she presented a divorce petition in the English Courts. The husband took a preliminary point on the question of jurisdiction. The judge held that the wife had established a clear domicile of choice in England because of her intention to marry an Englishman. The husband appealed.

Held, that the correct approach was whether the court was satisfied that there was a clear and settled intention to reside in England indefinitely, not whether there was a reciprocated desire to marry an English national. The wife's intention had not yet crystallised into certainty—she had left a number of relevant matters in France unresolved, such as her employment and her children's schooling. The judge had misdirected herself and the appeal would be allowed.

CRAMER *v.* CRAMER [1987] 1 F.L.R. 116, C.A.

1716. Divorce—special procedure—notice of date and place of pronouncement of decree nisi—no notice—whether decree should be set aside

A decree nisi was granted by way of special procedure while the wife was in Canada. Neither she nor her solicitors received notice of the day and place fixed for the granting of the decree as required by the Matrimonial Causes Rules 1977. The wife applied to set aside the decree nisi and for a rehearing.

Held, that there was no justification in the court granting a decree nisi without notice to the other party, regardless of the requirement of notice in the rules. To do so would be contrary to natural justice. The court had an inherent jurisdiction to set aside an order obtained without notice—accordingly the decree would be set aside and a rehearing directed.

WALKER *v.* WALKER [1987] 1 F.L.R. 31, C.A.

1717. Divorce—stay of proceedings—balance of fairness and convenience—juridical advantage

[Domicile and Matrimonial Proceedings Act 1973 (c.45), Sched. 1, paras. 9(1), (2).]

W, a German national, and H a Dutch national, had been married in Holland in 1969. Before the marriage an ante-nuptial agreement, binding in Dutch law, had been made excluding community of property between them. In 1973 the parties moved from Holland to England. In 1984 W took the one child of the marriage to Holland and subsequently informed H that she had decided to leave him and live permanently in Holland. Both parties instructed Dutch lawyers; and it was agreed that the forum for the divorce proceedings should be in Holland. Under Dutch law it was likely that the ante-nuptial agreement would be declared valid. The Dutch courts could order periodical payments but had no power to order a transfer of property or lump sum. In 1985 W filed a divorce petition in England. H then issued a writ for divorce in the Dutch court and issued a summons to stay the English proceedings under para. 9 of sched. 1 of the 1973 Act on the ground that "the balance of fairness and convenience" so required.

Held, refusing H's application that on balance W had a clear juridical advantage in the English proceedings. H's main assets were in England and, in reality, he had a much greater connection with England than Holland. From H's point of view the ante-nuptial agreement, on its face, regulated property between the parties. W and the child were living in Holland and the forum had been agreed between the Dutch lawyers. Balancing these considerations H could not show that the Dutch proceedings could do justice between the parties at substantially less convenience and expense and that a stay would not deprive W of her legitimate personal or juridical advantage available in the English proceedings but not in the Dutch proceedings. (*MacShannon* v. *Rockware Glass* [1978] C.L.Y. 2390 applied; *Gadd* v. *Gadd* [1985] C.L.Y. 1061 considered).

K. *v.* K. [1986] 2 F.L.R. 411. Hollis J.

1718. Divorce—stay of proceedings—foreign petition. See DE DAMPIERRE *v.* DE DAMPIERRE, §399.

1719. Divorce—unreasonable behaviour—financial irresponsibility

The wife petitioned for divorce on the basis of the husband's financial irresponsibility as unreasonable behaviour. The judge found that his inability to manage financial affairs had affected the family and caused stress for the wife. The judge found the petition proved.

Held, that the judge had considered the evidence carefully and had found that the husband's behaviour was having an affect on the wife and the family. Accordingly, his decision was a proper one and would not be upset.

CARTER-FEA *v.* CARTER-FEA (1987) Fam. Law 131, C.A.

1720. Divorce—validity of divorce—declaration that divorce decree invalid—whether statutory or inherent jurisdiction appropriate. See WILLIAMS *v.* ATT.-GEN., §2998.

1721. Domestic jurisdiction—research

A research team from the University of Bristol Socio-Legal Centre for Family Studies has recently completed a two-year project on the overlapping domestic jurisdiction of county courts and magistrates' courts. *The Overlapping Family Jurisdiction of County Courts and Magistrates' Courts* is available from Mervyn Murch, Socio-Legal Centre for Family Studies, University of Bristol, 21/22 Berkeley Square, Bristol BS8 1HP [£6·50].

1722. Domestic proceedings—magistrates' courts—application to vary periodical payments order—duty of clerk to take notes of evidence. See GRAY *v.* GRAY, §3061.

1723. Domestic proceedings in magistrates' courts—statistics. See CRIMINAL LAW, §831.

1724. Family Law Reform Act 1987 (c.42)

This Act reforms the law relating to the consequences of birth outside marriage. It makes further provision with respect to the rights and duties of parents and the determination of parentage.

The Act received the Royal Assent on May 15, 1987, and comes into force on days to be appointed by the Lord Chancellor.

The whole Act extends to England and Wales only. Parts of the Act extend to Scotland and Northern Ireland. (See s.34(4) of the Act).

1725. Financial provision—ancillary relief—periodical payments—backdating—commutation into lump sum

The Court of Appeal allowed an appeal against an order which backdated periodical payments by seven years.

The husband appealed from a decision of Waite J. [1986] C.L.Y. 1101 under which he ordered *inter alia* that the husband make periodical payments to the wife at the rate of £70,000 per annum subject to tax, backdated to April 5, 1979, credit being given for sums actually paid by way of maintenance, on the grounds that it was excessive and that it was wrong to backdate it to 1979.

Held, allowing the appeal, that while the figure of £70,000 was at the upper limit of the scale, there was no ground to vary it. However, it should be backdated only to April 5, 1986. There was no appeal against the judge's order that the court had jurisdiction under section 31(7) of the Matrimonial Causes Act 1973 to order that on the payment of a sum sufficient to commute the periodical payments, those payments would terminate, so giving effect to the clean break principle.

S. *v.* S. [1987] 2 W.L.R. 382, C.A.

1726. Financial provision—children—responsibility to maintain

A person having an obligation to maintain his children was under an obligation to order his financial affairs with due regard to his responsibility to pay reasonable maintenance for his children and to meet his reasonable financial obligations.

ROOTS *v.* ROOTS, April 10, 1986 (C.A.T. No. 331).

1727. Financial provision—children under 18—clean break—whether children overriding consideration

[Matrimonial Causes Act 1973 (c.18), ss.25(1), 25A(2) (as substituted by Matrimonial and Family Proceedings Act 1984 (c.42), s.3).]

Whenever the court makes a periodical payments order there is a mandatory duty upon it to consider whether it is appropriate to limit the term of the order's operation; when so doing, whilst the welfare of the children of the family was of first importance, it was not paramount or overriding.

H divorced W because of her adultery with the co-respondent. She was awarded custody, care and control of the two children, and continued to live in the matrimonial home. The co-respondent, who earned £7,000 per annum, spent most nights with W, but made no contribution to living expenses. H was ordered to transfer his entire interest in the house to W, and to make periodical payments to her of £100 per month, and to the children of £200 per month.

Held, allowing H's appeal, that (i) in every case, whether or not there were children below the age of 18, it was incumbent on the judge to consider the imposition of a time-limit on any periodical payments order; (ii) whilst the welfare of the children was of great importance, it was not the paramount or overriding consideration. In the present case it would be inequitable on the facts to disregard the financial resources available to W and the co-respondent. The periodical payments order against H would be reduced to £1 per annum.

SUTER *v.* SUTER AND JONES [1987] 3 W.L.R. 9, C.A.

1728. Financial provision—civil legal aid certificate granted for application to increase periodical payments order—order terminated and future claims surrendered on payment of fixed sum—whether statutory charge attaches to such sum. See STEWART *v.* THE LAW SOCIETY, §2294.

1729. Financial provision—consent order—appeal

The marriage was dissolved in 1981 and a consent order was made dividing the matrimonial assets on a 50–50 basis. The wife subsequently discovered in 1983 that the husband's pension entitlement was greater than she had thought. She sought to set aside the consent order on the basis of a material non-disclosure by the husband. The judge found that the wife knew of the existence of the pension (although not the full details) and there had been no material non-disclosure.

Held, that the wife was aware of the pension. There had been no material non-disclosure. The parties had intended a clean break and the consent order would not be set aside.

BARBER *v.* BARBER (1987) 17 Fam. Law 125, C.A.

1730. Financial provision—consent order—delay in implementation—variation

A consent order had been made for a lump sum payment out of the proceeds of the sale of certain property. The wife sought to vary the order on the basis that the husband had deliberately delayed the sale of the property. As a result the wife could not buy accommodation with the lump sum and sought an order for a greater sum.

Held, that for the consent order to be varied, the wife had to show that the order was vitiated by some material supervening event that falsified the assumptions upon which the consent order was based. Here the husband's delay did not amount to a supervisory event. It was a failure to comply with the terms of the order and the wife's remedy was to apply to the Court for enforcement of the order.

ROOKER *v.* ROOKER, *The Independent,* June 17, 1987, C.A.

1731. Financial provision—consent order—drawn up before decree nisi—amendment under slip rule or inherent jurisdiction

The wife petitioned for divorce and agreement was reached with regard to financial provision whereby £30,000 was to be paid to the wife in instalments. Application for a consent order was made and came before the registrar on May 17, 1983 when the registrar endorsed the application "consent order as prayed on decree nisi" and on May 23 a consent order was drawn up and signed by the registrar. The decree nisi was on June 17, 1983. The wife died and her personal representative sought to enforce the agreement. The husband applied to have it set aside. The registrar did not set aside the order but amended its date to June 17, under the slip rule of the court's inherent jurisdiction. On appeal to the judge, that was held to be wrong and the order set aside.

Held, that there are two possible situations. The first is where an order is made within the judge's jurisdiction but when drawn up, does not give effect to his expressed intention. That was an appropriate case for amendment under the slip rule or the court's inherent jurisdiction. The second case, as here, is where a judge makes an order that he has no jurisdiction to make. The slip rule or the court's inherent jurisdiction cannot be applied to remedy that situation. The order made is invalid and matters cannot be put right by way of the slip rule (*Munks* v. *Munks* [1985] C.L.Y. 2722 applied).

BOARD *v.* CHECKLAND (1987) 17 Fam. Law 236, C.A.

1732. Financial provision—consent order—subsequent questionnaire of means—whether appropriate

[Matrimonial Causes Rules 1977 (S.I. 1977 No. 344), r.77(4).]

A questionnaire under rule 77(4) is only appropriate where proceedings are pending, and not as an exploratory exercise to uncover a possible basis for starting proceedings.

In divorce proceedings the wife was granted a decree absolute in November 1977, and in ancillary relief proceedings orders were made in 1981 whereby the former matrimonial home was conveyed into the joint names of the parties on condition that the wife took no further proceedings for financial provision for herself or for property adjustment orders. In 1986 the wife's solicitors served on the husband a questionnaire under rule 77(4) relating to his financial resources, and obtained an order requiring him to answer it.

Held, on appeal, that such a questionnaire could only be used where there were proceedings pending between the parties. In the absence, therefore, of any application to set aside or appeal the 1981 orders, the court had no jurisdiction to require the husband to answer the questionnaire, which was designed to trawl for a basis upon which further financial relief could be sought from the husband.

H. *v.* B. (FORMERLY H.) [1987] 1 W.L.R. 113, Hollings J.

1733. Financial provision—foreign decree of divorce—whether retrospective power to make lump sum order

[Matrimonial and Family Proceedings Act 1984 (c.42), s.12(1).]

The court has power under s.12 of the Matrimonial and Family Proceedings Act 1984 to make an order for financial provision consequent on a foreign decree of divorce notwithstanding that that decree was pronounced before the Act came into force.

Between 1976 and 1984 H and W, who were Lebanese, lived in Cheshire. In 1985 the marriage was dissolved by a court in Lebanon, by a decree which would be recognized in the U.K. W then applied under the 1984 Act; H contended that the Act was of no application to a foreign divorce granted before September 16, 1985.

Held, that the Act was retrospective in effect and W could, accordingly, pursue her application.

CHEBARO *v.* CHEBARO [1987] 1 All E.R. 999, C.A.

1734. Financial provision—husband's application for lump sum and property adjustment order—wife's expectancy of inheriting interest in property—whether "property she was likely to have in the foreseable future"

After divorce the wife and the two children lived in the matrimonial home. The husband applied for a lump sum payment and property adjustment order. The house was owned by the wife's mother. The wife had an expectancy of inheriting the house under the mother's will. The judge, overturning the decision of the Registrar, held that the wife had a reasonable prospect of inheriting a valuable interest in the near future and adjourned the husband's application accordingly.

Held, that s.25(2)(*a*) of the Matrimonial Causes Act 1973 was to be construed broadly. It was not confined to vested or contingent interests in property or financial resources but could also include a mere expectancy in certain circumstances (such as an interest under a will). However, on the facts of this case, the uncertainties were too great to be able to conclude that there was any real possibility of the wife inheriting the house in the near future to enable her to make financial provision for the husband. Accordingly the judge should not have adjourned the husband's application and it should be dismissed (*Davies* v. *Davies* [1986] 8 C.L. 686, *Hardy* v. *Hardy* [1981] C.L.Y. 717, *Minton* v. *Minton* [1979] C.L.Y. 766, *Milne* v. *Milne* [1981] C.L.Y. 716, *Morris* v. *Morris* [1978] C.L.Y. 1600 and *Priest* v. *Priest* [1980] C.L.Y. 782 referred to).

MICHAEL *v.* MICHAEL [1986] 2 F.L.R. 389, C.A.

1735. Financial provision—husband's application for periodical payments—husband incapacitated and unlikely to improve

During the latter years of the marriage the husband was unable to keep a steady job, the wife bore the financial burdens of the marriage. The wife then left the husband who petitioned for divorce. The husband later suffered a major stroke and was severely incapacitated with no earning capacity and no significant prospect of recovery.

Held, that on the special facts of the case the wife had made a substantial contribution to the marriage over a number of years without any contribution from the husband, it would be unjust to impose any further obligation to the husband upon the wife's income which was not such as would do more than enable her to lead a reasonable life. As the husband was totally dependent on others it would be wrong to impose a continuing obligation to support him. His application should be dismissed. It was also right that the husband should not be allowed to make any further application.

SEATON *v.* SEATON [1986] 2 F.L.R. 398, C.A.

1736. Financial provision—length of marriage—relevance of children of the family

[Domestic Proceedings and Magistrates' Courts Act 1978 (c.22), s.3.]

Magistrates had ordered H to pay £15 per week to W and £5 per week to each of two children. H and W had known each other for four years before the marriage. They married on May 21, 1985, and H left six weeks' later. W had two children from a previous marriage. H had treated the children as children of the family. Before the magistrates, H admitted desertion. He contended that no order for maintenance should be made because (1) of the shortness of the marriage, and (2) W was no worse off as a result of his desertion as she began to receive social security again. The submission was rejected. H appealed against the magistrates' order.

Held, that all the factors in s.3 had been applied and the magistrates were entitled to make the order. Further, there is no rule of law that, in a short childless marriage where there are children of the family, prevents an order being made. In cases where there are no children at all it is appropriate to make no order or a short order.

DAY *v.* DAY, November 26, 1986, Wood J. [*Ex rel. John Robson, Barrister.*]

1737. Financial provision—lump sum and periodical payments—husband dies—application for financial provision out of husband's estate

In ancillary proceedings, the wife was awarded a lump sum of £50,000 and periodical payments of £5,500 per annum. Shortly after the order, the husband died in 1979. The wife received only one periodical payment and eventually used up all her capital, finally going into debt. The husband had made no provision for her in his will. The wife applied under the Inheritance (Provision for Family and Dependants) Act 1975 for financial provision out of the husband's estate.

Held, that having regard to the wife's age, the duration of the marriage, her contribution to the marriage and the factors set out at s.3 of the Act, provision ought to have been made by the husband for the wife. Having regard to her resources and those of the estate, the appropriate order was £5,000 per annum with a lump sum of £15,000 to take into account the seven years without any payments (*Crawford (Dec'd.), Re* [1983] C.L.Y. 3920, *Eyre, Re* [1968] C.L.Y. 1273, *Fullard (Dec'd.), Re* [1982] C.L.Y. 3385 considered).

FARROW (DEC'D.), *Re*]1987] 1 F.L.R. 205, Hollings J.

1738. Financial provision—lump sum order—ability to pay dependent on sale of matrimonial home in the future

The wife applied for a lump sum order. The judge ordered that the husband should make a lump sum payment of £4,000 to each of the two children when they attained 18 years of age. The judge found that the husband could not afford the payments at present but would be able to do so when the matrimonial home (which was in the wife's name with the husband having a 50 per cent. share) was sold.

Held, that the husband's ability to pay the lump sum dependend upon the realisation of his charge over the house. It was not certain that that would raise sufficient funds. In those circumstandes, he would be unable to fulfil the order and would be in contempt of court. It was an improper exercise of the court's discretion to order a lump sum payment that put the husband in that position.

KIELY *v.* KIELY, *The Times,* July 7, 1987, C.A.

1739. Financial provision—lump sum order—Air Force Act 1955 s.203—jurisdiction

The wife applied to the registrar for an order that the husband pay her a lump sum upon his discharge from the R.A.F. The registrar ordered him to pay her 20 per cent. of his terminal gratuity. The husband appealed successfully to the judge. The wife appealed.

Held, that the order made by the registrar was void by virtue of s.203 of the Air Force Act 1955 (c.19). The courts had no jurisdiction to make such an order.

RANSOM *v.* RANSOM, *The Times,* August 12, 1987, C.A.

1740. Financial provision—lump sum order—husband misleading court as to means

In proceedings for ancillary relief, the husband claimed that his only asset was a bond worth £4,000. The registrar adjourned for production of the bond and it then emerged that the husband had a number of bonds and bank accounts and had been misleading the court. In the Family Division, Judge Callman held that there was a duty on the parties to make a full disclosure of their means—the husband, having actively misled the court could not complain if the court drew unfavourable inferences. The judge, having decided that the husband had assets worth £14,000 took into account the extra weight by way of the Law Society's charge that would fall on the wife and awarded her £10,000.

Held, that the right approach was to consider each case in accordance with s.25 of the Matrimonial Causes Act 1973. The judge should not have taken into account the extra costs incurred by the wife. The appropriate order was £7,500 for the wife.

COLLINS *v.* COLLINS [1987] F.L.R. 226, C.A.

1741. Financial provision—lump sum order—one-third rule

The husband formed a company which become highly successful. The wife was employed as a director in the company at an initial salary of £8,000 rising to £50,000. The parties separated and the marriage was dissolved. The wife embarked on a course to start a market garden business, the husband continued to run the company. It was agreed that there should be a clean break with a lump sum payment to the wife and a transfer by her of her shares in the company to the husband. The paper value of the parties' assets were £1,000,000 for the husband and £60,000 for the wife.

Held, using the one-third rule as a starting point, that the wife's share would be £350,000. Having adjusted that figure, the proper award was £135,000. That figure took account of the husband's need to keep the company going, of the wife's need for capital to start a new business and it reflected the wife's contribution to the company (*Bullock* v. *Bullock* [1986] C.L.Y. 1088 and *Potter* v. *Potter* [1982] C.L.Y. 935 referred to).

DEW *v.* DEW [1986] 2 F.S.R. 341, Lincoln J.

1742. Financial provision—lump sum order—order to bring money into court—committal for breach

H was ordered to pay into court £4,068.26 to be held by the court pending the hearing of W's application for a lump sum payment under s.23 of the Matrimonial Causes Act 1973. H failed to pay the money into court and W applied for H to be committed to prison for non-payment under s.5 of the Debtors Act 1869 as amended by the Administration of Justice Act 1970. H contended that the application to commit him related to the order requiring him to bring into court £4,068.26, that the order was made under s.37 of the 1973 Act and was not within Sched. 8, para. 2A of the Administration of Justice Act 1970 and accordingly the court had no jurisdiction to commit him on W's application.

Held, dismissing H's appeal, s.37 of the 1973 Act clearly envisaged that process under that section was part and parcel of the process of obtaining an order for financial relief such as a lump sum and steps taken under s.37 (if and in so far as those steps were directly to be related to an order, or prospective order, under the provisions of ss.22, 23, or 24 of the 1973 Act) fell within para. 2 of Sched. 8. The order to bring the sum into court fell within Sched. 8 of the 1970 Act and therefore was an order in respect of which process could be taken under s.5 of the Debtors Act 1869. Further, to order a litigant to bring money into court as security for the future determination of a liability to pay was not an order for the payment of a sum of money falling within s.4 of the Debtors Act 1869 (*Bates* v. *Bates* (1888) 14 P.D. 17 and *Farrant* v. *Farrant* [1957] C.L.Y. 1086 considered).

GRAHAM *v.* GRAHAM, September 5, 1986 (C.A.T. No. 780).

1743. Financial provision—maintenance agreement—change of circumstances making agreement inequitable—variation of maintenance agreement

The parties separated and a maintenance agreement was reached whereby, *inter alia*, the wife was to receive one-third of the husband's gross income. The wife later petitioned for divorce but no application was made for ancillary relief. The husband's business career improved dramatically and his salary shot up. He came to find the agreement to pay his wife one-third of his salary burdensome and refused to co-operate with her solicitors' attempts to compute the amounts of maintenance and arrears. The wife commenced enforcement proceedings. The husband applied to vary the agreement under s.35 of the Matrimonial Causes Act 1973, he applied in ancillary proceedings for periodical payments to be made against him and he sought a property transfer order transferring the wife's rights under the agreement to him.

Held, that the intention behind the legislation was for s.35 to be applied before and after the institution of divorce proceedings. The distinction between the jurisdiction to vary ancillary relief and maintenance agreements was maintained. The husband had to establish a case under s.35 to obtain relief. That he had done as the wife was being maintained at a level in excess of her maximum needs. The change of circumstances rendered the agreement inequitable. The inequity of the requirement on the husband to pay a fixed proportion of his salary would be removed. The wife would be left with sufficient to meet her reasonable needs by periodical payments of £10,000 p.a. (*Edgar* v. *Edgar* [1980] C.L.Y. 791, *Gorman* v. *Gorman* [1964] C.L.Y. 1148, *Hyman* v. *Hyman* [1929] A.C. 601, *K.* v. *K.* [1961] C.L.Y. 2737, *Ratcliffe* v. *Ratcliffe* [1962] C.L.Y. 984 and *Sherdley* v. *Sherdley* [1987] C.L.Y. 2504 referred to).

SIMISTER *v.* SIMISTER (No. 2) [1987] 1 F.L.R. 194, Waite J.

1744. Financial provision—matrimonial home only family asset—order transferring home to husband—whether proper in all the circumstances

The wife petitioned for divorce and the husband was ordered to vacate the matrimonial home. Cross decrees were announced. Custody of the eldest daughter was given to the husband whilst custody of the two younger children was given to the wife. The matrimonial home, jointly owned, had an equitable value of £18,000. The judge ordered that the wife's interest in the home should be transferred to the husband who should pay a lump sum of £9,000 to the wife, £2,500 of it within nine months and the balance of £6,500 within five years. The judge also ordered periodical payments to the wife of 5p a year for the wife and £10 a week each for the younger children. The wife appealed on the basis that the judge was wrong to assume the husband would have to pay the mortgage and other outgoings on the house if the wife remained in it and took the wife's behaviour into account when he should not have done so. The wife also asked for an increase in the periodical payments.

Held, that (1) the judge's conclusions were based on an erroneous assumption that the husband would have to pay the outgoings on the house if the wife remained in occupation—in fact the wife would pay them in those circumstances. There was nothing in the wife's conduct of such a serious nature as to justify any reliance upon it. The judge's order would deprive the wife and the two younger children of a suitable home in exchange for a lump sum of only £2,500 as the remaining £6,500 would be taken by the Legal Aid fund. The judge's order was plainly wrong. The home would be held on a trust for sale in equal shares postponed until the wife's remarriage or cohabitation or until the youngest child attained majority with the wife to bear the outgoings on the house. There should be liberty to either party to apply for an earlier sale. The periodical payments to the two children should also be increased to £20 per week; (2) the divorce proceedings had been protracted. Both parties were legally aided and the combined costs came to about £8,000 which the Law Society could recover out of the only family asset—the matrimonial home. Therefore nearly half of that asset had been eaten up. Solicitors should explain and constantly reiterate to legally aided clients that they could not conduct litigation free of charge (*Mesher* v. *Mesher* [1980] C.L.Y. 785 considered).

ANTHONY *v.* ANTHONY [1986] 2 F.L.R. 353, C.A.

1745. Financial provision—order of court—whether jurisdiction to make further order

[Matrimonial Causes Act 1973 (c.18), ss.23, 24.]

Once the court has made an order under ss.23 or 24 of the Matrimonial Causes Act 1973 in relation to particular property, it can make no further order save in the limited circumstances prescribed by s.31.

H and W were divorced in 1979. In 1980 a consent order was made providing for periodical payments by H to W and the child, and for sale of the matrimonial home and division equally of the proceeds when the child reached 17 or ceased full-time education whichever was the later. H gave up his employment and fell into arrears. W was granted a charging order in respect of the arrears. H applied for a variation of the order for periodical payments to a nominal sum, an order remitting the arrears and for immediate sale of the matrimonial home, the child having reached 17 and no longer being in full-time education. W applied for, *inter alia,* a transfer of property order and an order further postponing sale of the matrimonial home, and that H's interest be transferred to her subject to a charge in H's favour. The judge granted H's applications, but held that he had no jurisdiction to make the orders sought by W. The Court of Appeal reversed that decision.

Held, allowing the appeal, that the consent order of 1980 had finally and conclusively determined the rights of the parties in the matrimonial home and the judge had rightly concluded that he had no jurisdiction to make any further order (*De Lasala* v. *De Lasala* [1979] C.L.Y. 2200 applied; *Carson* v. *Carson* [1983] C.L.Y. 1874 approved).

DINCH *v.* DINCH [1987] 1 W.L.R. 252, H.L.

1746. Financial provision—order that wife to have matrimonial home absolutely—death of wife and children within weeks of order—whether husband able to appeal

[Matrimonial Causes Rules 1977 (S.I. 1977 No. 344 (L.6)), rr.3(1), 125(1); County Court Rules 1981 (S.I. 1981 No. 1687 (L.20)), Ord. 13, r.4(1).]

Where following a consent order for financial provision on divorce, a fundamental assumption (such as that the wife and children would need a home for a considerable period of time) has been invalidated by a supervening event, such as the death of the wife and children, the Court may allow the other party to appeal out of time.

Per curiam: It is unlikely that it would be proper that the matter be re-opened if as much as a year had passed between the making of the order and the supervening event.

In divorce proceedings it was ordered, by consent, that H transfer his interest in the matrimonial home to W absolutely, and that he make substantial periodical payments to the children of the family. Some five weeks later, whilst the order was still executory, but after the time for appealing had elapsed, W killed the children and then committed suicide. The only beneficiary of W's estate was her mother, herself a woman of some means. The judge granted H's application for leave to appeal out of time, and allowed his appeal, setting aside the consent order on the ground that there had been a fundamental assumption that W and the children were going to need the home for some years, and that had been vitiated by subsequent events. The Court of Appeal allowed an appeal by W's mother, as intervener.

Held, on appeal by H, that the judge had been correct. The judge had had jurisdiction to hear an application for leave to appeal out of time, and had made the correct order. Albeit tacitly, it had been assumed by both sides, and their advisers, that W and the children would need a home for some years after the making of the order: that assumption had been proved totally invalid. Such an order (giving leave to appeal out of time) should only be made where the appeal, if heard, was likely to succeed, if the supervening event had happened shortly after the making of the order, and if the application was made promptly. It should not be made if to do so would prejudice innocent third parties.

BARDER *v.* CALUORI *sub nom.* BARDER *v.* BARDER (CALUORI INTERVENING) [1987] 2 W.L.R. 1350, H.L.

1747. Financial provision—periodical payments—"or further order"—construction of order

An order was made that H should pay periodical payments to W *inter alia* until his retirement . . . "or further order".

Held, that after his retirement there was no liability to pay, nor any jurisdiction in the court to vary the order. The words "or further order" meant "or further order in the meantime" (*Thompson* v. *Thompson* [1985] C.L.Y. 1076 followed).

T. *v.* T. (1987) 84 L.S.Gaz. 2690, Butler-Sloss J.

1748. Financial provision—periodical payments—recovery of arrears—writ *ne exeat regno*

Upon divorce, a periodical payments order was made. The husband returned to his native country and, although he returned to England from time to time he ceased to pay the periodical payments. In 1986, the wife discovered he was in England, issued a judgment summons for £7,132 and applied *ex parte* for leave to issue a writ *ne exeat regno.*

Held, that the issue of the writ was discretionary and the standard of proof required was "such as to convince the court." The requirements of s.6 of the Debtors Act 1869 had to be satisfied. In this case they were in that the husband would formerly have been liable to arrest at law in the action; it was an action for a sum in excess of £50, there was probable cause to believe that the husband would leave the country unless arrested and, if he did so, the wife's claim would be prejudiced materially. The court would therefore exercise its discretion and grant leave to issue the writ.

THAHA *v.* THAHA (1987) 17 Fam. Law 234, Wood J.

1749. Financial provision—periodical payments and lump sum—termination of periodical payments after five years—whether appropriate

The parties were divorced, the matrimonial home sold and the proceeds split equally between the parties. During the marriage the wife had done some part-time work but most of her married life had been spent at home so her job prospects were not good. The husband earned a substantial salary (£60,000 p.a.) and had pension rights which would have passed to the wife if he had predeceased her had it not been for the divorce. It was agreed that the wife's earning capacity was £6,000 p.a. and that her reasonable needs amounted to an extra £14,000 p.a. to be met by way of periodical payments. The husband contended that the payments should end after five years as provided by s.25A of the Matrimonial Causes Act 1973. The wife sought a lump sum payment.

Held, that the termination of the periodical payments after five years would be unjust. It was unlikely that the wife's earnings would reach the agreed figure of £6,000 p.a. for a year or so. It was unrealistic to think that she would become self-supporting within five years or any other specified period. She had also lost the chance of future security from the husband's pension rights. The termination would cause hardship to her whilst the husband was in a secure position. There were powers of variation under s.31 of the Act should the husband's position deteriorate in the future. There was an imbalance of capital in favour of the wife which should be set against her debts. It was appropriate to award her a lump sum of £7,500.

M. *v.* M. (FINANCIAL PROVISION) [1987] 2 F.L.R. 1, Heilbron J.

1750. Financial provision—periodical payments to wife—husband seeking order

Competence in law to make an application for ancillary relief is not restricted to the party who is to benefit from the relief.

S's marriage was dissolved on his wife's undefended petition, and she made no application for periodical payments since S had covenanted to pay her maintenance in the form of one-third of his income. S., wishing to be relieved of the maintenance agreement, applied for a periodical payments order to be made against him. The registrar, on the wife's application, struck out S's application on the grounds that he was not competent in law to make it.

Held, that the court had jurisdiction to hear the application (dictum of Booth J. in *Peacock* v. *Peacock* [1984] C.L.Y. 1123 applied).

SIMISTER *v.* SIMISTER [1986] 1 W.L.R. 1463, Waite J.

1751. Financial provision—Registrar's power to declare no further applications allowed

When dealing with an agreed financial order following divorce, the Registrar had power to declare that the wife should not make any further applications under ss.23 and 24 of the Matrimonial Causes Act 1973 even though there is no statutory authority for such a declaration. Each case depended upon its own facts and finances. In the present case, the declaration was appropriate.

H. *v.* H., *The Times,* November 23, 1987, Bush J.

1752. Financial provision—sale of property—discharge of creditors—jurisdiction

[Matrimonial Causes Act 1973 (c.18), s.24A.]

H and W had married in 1967 and separated in 1981. In 1982 H formed a relationship with R who, lived with him in the former matrimonial home. She lent H £10,000 to buy out W's interest in the former matrimonial home. However H frittered away the money instead. In ancillary proceedings H disclosed certain outstanding debts in his affidavit of means but made no reference to the loan of £10,000. In 1985 the registrar ordered that the former matrimonial home be sold and that the debts should be discharged out of the proceeds of sale, the balance of which should be paid to W in full and final settlement of all her financial claims against H. R applied and was granted a charging order nisi in respect of the £10,000 loan. She also applied to set aside the registrar's order.

Held, that there was no jurisdiction in the court to order one party to pay the debts of either that party or of the other party which were not connected to an interest in the matrimonial property. Equally, s.24A did not extend the powers of the court to allow for the payment of creditors unconnected with an interest in the property. Its purpose was to recognise an existing jurisdiction that the court had a power of sale. In this case the registrar, by her order, was rearranging the finances of the parties including the disposal of debts. As it was not possible to sever the good from the bad parts the only way to do justice in the circumstances was to set aside the whole order in respect of the disposition of the net proceeds of sale (*Milne* v. *Milne* [1981] C.L.Y. 716 and *Mullard* v. *Mullard* [1982] C.L.Y. 1513 followed).

BURTON *v.* BURTON (1986) 2 F.L.R. 419, Butler-Sloss J.

1753. Financial provision—solicitor acting contrary to wishes of client—whether relevant factor

A solicitor acted contrary to the express instructions of his client and by so doing entered into an agreement which was less advantageous to the client than compliance with the instructions would have provided.

Held, that this was a relevant factor to be taken into account when considering the justice of the case and deciding whether or not the agreement reached between the parties in respect of financial matters after divorce should be made an order of the court.

ROE *v.* ROE, 1986 (C.A.T. No. 356).

1754. Financial provision—whether conduct relevant

In 1980, the husband began suffering from depression and spent periods in hospital. He attempted suicide in 1982 and 1983. On one of those occasions, the wife took him alcohol and tablets. When he did not go through with the attempt, she accused him of having no guts. She formed a liaison with another man, began divorce proceedings and obtained an ouster injunction against the husband whereupon the other man moved into the house. The husband, realising that his illness was being used as a means of dissolving the marriage, cross-petitioned. The registrar found the wife had lied to him on oath about her relationship with the other man—her main objective was to set up house with him. The registrar took her behaviour into account and ordered the wife, who received the whole interest in the matrimonial home, to hand over to the husband her share of the business.

Held, that the court was entitled to look at the whole of the picture under s.25 of the Matrimonial Causes Act 1973. That included the conduct of the parties during and after the marriage which might have contributed to the breakdown or would be inequitable to ignore.

KYTE *v.* KYTE, *The Independent,* July 24, 1987, C.A.

1755. Financial provision—wife cohabiting with men of relatively insubstantial means—conduct.

Both parties to the marriage had lived like millionaires but had developed extra-marital relationships. The wife was cohabiting with another man who, in comparison to the husband, was of insubstantial means. The husband agreed that the wife was entitled to a comfortable lifestyle. Both parties agreed that conduct was not relevant. The judge, applying s.25A(1) of the Matrimonial Causes Act 1973, decided not to attach any weight to the wife's cohabitation and ordered a transfer of property and a lump sum payment. The husband appealed, as the wife's cohabitee would benefit from the lump sum payment arguing that that and the possibility of the wife's remarriage were grounds for a smaller lump sum order coupled with periodical payments where the court retained control of the situation.

Held, that the cohabitation was irrelevant—the judge had to consider the wife's reasonable needs, and the sum of money needed to meet those needs. How the money was spent was up to her. S.25 of the Matrimonial Causes Act 1973 was a financial not a moral exercise—conduct was only relevant where it would be inequitable to disregard it. The court would not interfere with the exercise of the judge's discretion in applying s.25 (*Bellenden (orse. Satterthwaite)* v. *Satterthwaite* (1948) C.L.C. 3046, *Preston* v. *Preston* [1981] C.L.Y. 714 and *Trippas* v. *Trippas* [1973] C.L.Y. 925 considered).

DUXBURY *v.* DUXBURY [1987] 1 F.L.R. 7, C.A.

1756. Financial provision—wife dying shortly after variation order—appeal against variation order out of time

In divorce proceedings, orders were made for periodical payments by the husband to the wife and child. The matrimonial home was to be sold and the proceeds were to be apportioned between the parties. On the wife's appeal to the judge, the periodical payments were increased, the order relating to the home was unaltered. Soon afterwards the wife died. The husband applied for leave to appeal against the variation out of time on the basis that the wife's death had falsified the order.

Held, allowing the appeal, that there was jurisdiction to hear an appeal out of time because if the registrar or the judge had known that under a month later the wife would die, he would have made an order less favourable to her because her needs would have been quite different from those which were contemplated. The additional equitable interest conferred by the variation order would be set aside.

PASSMORE *v.* GILL AND GILL [1987] 1 F.L.R. 441, C.A.

1757. Indecent assault within marriage—whether consent could be implied by virtue of marriage

The appellant, having burst in on the wife carrying a sharp knife, placed the knife against her throat and forced her to commit fellatio after which he had sexual intercourse with her. The wife had consented to fellatio in the past. At the trial for indecent assault, the judge ruled against the submission that a husband could not be guilty of an indecent assault on his wife. The husband appealed against conviction.

Held, that it was clear that a man could not be guilty of rape on his wife because of the implied consent to sexual intercourse arising from the state of marriage. However, consent to fellatio could not run backwards to attach to the marriage vows even if long practised. Consent had to be a particular consent. The trial judge had been correct.

R. *v.* KOWALSKI, *The Times,* October 9, 1987, C.A.

1758. Maintenance arrears—suspended committal orders—application for case to be stated—refused because of alternative method of reconsidering decision—whether appropriate

The husband, in arrears under a magistrates' court maintenance order, had a suspended committal order made against him in enforcement proceedings. The husband applied for a case to be stated by the stipendiary magistrate who declined the application on the basis that the order could be reviewed under s.18 of the Maintenance Orders Act 1958. The husband sought judicial review of that refusal.

Held, that the suspended committal order was a decision made by the magistrate. The husband at that stage was entitled to apply for the case to be stated—the existence of an alternative way of reconsidering the decision did not alter the propriety of a request for the case to be stated. An order of mandamus would issue (*Dickens* v. *Pattison* [1985] C.L.Y. 2166 discussed; *Streames* v. *Copping* [1995] C.L.Y. 2128 distinguished).

R. *v.* HORSEFERRY ROAD MAGISTRATES' COURT, *ex p.* BERNSTEIN [1987] 1 F.L.R. 504, Sir John Arnold.

1759. Maintenance order in magistrates' court—varied by wife's application—husband sought variation—no change in circumstances

A maintenance order made in the County Court was registered in the magistrates' court. The wife applied successfully to vary the level of maintenance upwards. The husband, by way of complaint, sought a downward variation. The magistrates found that there had been no change in the financial circumstances of the parties and that the proper course was for the husband to appeal but treated his application as an application to vary and made a downward variation.

Held, that as there had been no change in circumstances, the magistrates were in effect sitting as a court of appeal over the previous bench. The proper course was for the husband to appeal. The magistrates had no power to vary the order.

BROMILLEY *v.* BROMILLEY (1987) 17 Fam. Law 165, Ewbank J.

1760. Maintenance orders—reciprocal enforcement. See CONFLICT OF LAWS, §407.

1761. Marriage—choice of law rules—proposals for reform. See LAW REFORM, §2275.

1762. Matrimonial home—application by wife to re-enter—home owned and occupied jointly by husband and his father—wife excluded from home—common law right to occupy matrimonial home

After an attack on the wife by the husband's family there was a reconciliation and the wife moved in with the husband and his family in a house that had been purchased by the husband and his father. The wife was subsequently excluded from that house. She applied under the Matrimonial Homes Act 1983 for an order permitting her to enter the house. The judge found that the husband and wife were not on good terms and divorce proceedings were imminent, that any return by the wife to the house would create a miserable situation and decided that it was unrealistic to make the order sought by the wife even though there was no justification for excluding the wife from the house. The wife appealed on the basis that she had a common law right to live in the matrimonial home relying on *Gurasz* v. *Gurasz* [1969] C.L.Y. 1645.

Held, that the judge had exercised his discretion under the 1983 Act perfectly properly. *Gurasz* v. *Gurasz* did not apply as it was limited to circumstances where the matrimonial home was owned by one or other spouse (or both). It did not apply where there was some third person who was an owner-occupier—the common law right could not exist against a third party (*Gurasz* v. *Gurasz* [1969] C.L.Y. 1645 distinguished, *Jones* v. *Jones* [1971] C.L.Y. 5439 and *Hoggett* v. *Hoggett* [1980] C.L.Y. 1621 discussed).

CHAUDHRY *v.* CHAUDHRY [1987] 1 F.L.R. 347, C.A.

1763. Matrimonial home—husband not in residence—liability for rates. See MOORE *v.* DURHAM CITY COUNCIL, §3181.

1764. Matrimonial home—power to order immediate sale—husband wishing to retain property but without financial means to do so

The parties purchased a grade 2 listed building in need of considerable repair with a view to obtaining funds from the public. When the marriage broke down the indebtedness on the property was £280,000. There was an offer from one of the creditors to buy the property for £550,000 but the husband wished to retain it. The judge ordered that, upon the husband paying the wife £50,000 she should transfer her share in the property to him. The judge was of the view that the payment of £50,000 would not attract capital gains tax.

Held, on appeal, the judge had not addressed his mind as to whether the main private residence exemption would apply to the wife (who had not been in occupation of the main house since 1984). Accordingly he had misdirected himself when exercising his statutory discretion. The wife should not be deprived from benefiting from the sale of the house at £550,000. The husband could not afford to retain the property—to do so would mean that the family would be paralysed by the debt—that was not in the best interests of the children. The court would exercise the jurisdiction to order the sale of the house. The court was entitled to interfere with the judge's discretion as he had misdirected himself on the question of capital gains tax.

M. *v.* M., *The Times,* August 26, 1987, C.A.

1765. Matrimonial home—wife left in sole occupation—liability for rates

In April 1984, the husband left the matrimonial home, leaving the wife in sole occupation. She obtained a decree nisi in April 1985. The rating authority considered that as there had been no court order until April 1985 and the husband had an obligation to maintain the wife until then, he would be liable for rates until then. On an application for a distress warrant the justices found that the husband had not been in rateable occupation and was not liable to pay rates. Accordingly, they would not grant a distress warrant.

Held, that the justices had properly found that the separation had been so complete that the husband had no responsibility for the wife during the period of separation before the decree nisi. The conclusion that the husband was not in rateable occupation was one which a reasonable bench would have reached (*Cardiff Corporation* v. *Robinson* [1957] C.L.Y. 7289 discussed; *Routhan* v. *Arun District Council* [1982] C.L.Y. 2256 applied).

DONCASTER METROPOLITAN BOROUGH COUNCIL *v.* LOCKWOOD (1987) 17 Fam. Law 241, McCullough J.

1766. Non-molestation injunction—breach—contempt of court. *See* GEORGE *v.* GEORGE, §2924.

1767. Non-molestation injunction—breach—contempt of court—whether order for committal should be set aside. See BOWEN *v.* BOWEN, §2927.

1768. Non-molestation injunction—breach—*ex parte* application for committal—no notice served. *See* BENESCH *v.* NEWMAN, §2933.

1769. Non-molestation order—breach—immediate custodial sentence—discretion of court. See GALLAGHER *v.* PATTERSON, §900.

1770. Nullity—wilful refusal to consummate—respondent in prison

The parties met and had a casual relationship, which included sexual intercourse on three occasions, but they never lived together. The respondent was arrested, convicted and sentenced to five years' imprisonment. The petitioner continued to visit him and they were married in prison. They were left alone in a room on occasions but, despite the petitioner's advances the respondent refused to have sexual intercourse. He told the petitioner that he no longer desired her visits, he displayed no interest in living with her upon his release and, when granted a home visit he stayed with a former girlfriend. The petitioner sought a decree of nullity for wilful refusal to consummate.

Held, that as there was no right to conjugal visits in prison, refusal to have sexual intercourse on a prison visit could not amount to a wilful refusal. However, although there was no reasonable opportunity for consummation, the respondent's conduct showed a determination not to consummate the marriage in the future and amounted to a wilful refusal to consummate.

FORD *v.* FORD (1987) 17 Fam. Law 232, Croydon County Ct.

1771. Occupation of premises by tenant's wife—whether to be regarded as occupation of tenant where premises not matrimonial home. See HALL *v.* KING, §2178.

1772. Order for sale of property—council house—whether parties exempted from obligation to repay discount

[Matrimonial Causes Act 1973 (c.18), ss.23, 24 and 24A; Housing Act 1985 (c.68), s.160(1)(*c*).]

An order for the sale of property and distribution of proceeds is an order made under s.24A of the 1973 Act, and not ss.23 or 24, and thus it is not encompassed within s.160(1)(*c*) of the 1985 Act.

B and his then wife purchased their council home from the local authority in 1984. The price was discounted by £12,650, a portion of this discount to be repaid to the council if they resold within five years. Their marriage was dissolved in 1985 and they agreed to an order whereby the house was sold and the proceeds divided equally. The property was sold and the local authority demanded 80 per cent. of the discount.

Held, that the order for sale had been made pursuant to s.24A, and not ss.23 or 24 of the 1973 Act and thus the exemption from repayment under s.160(1)(*c*) of the 1985 Act did not apply (*Ward* v. *Ward and Greene (Note)* [1980] C.L.Y. 792 and *Thompson* v. *Thompson* [1985] C.L.Y. 1076 considered).

R. *v.* RUSHMOOR BOROUGH COUNCIL, *ex p.* BARRETT [1986] 3 W.L.R. 998, Reeve J.

1773. Ouster and wardship—proceedings heard together—criteria to be considered—exercise of discretion

The parties had two children. The mother killed the boy and later pleaded guilty to manslaughter. The girl was made the subject of a place of safety order and was made a ward of court at a later stage, interim care and control being given to the local authority with reasonable access to the father. The mother, after discharge from the hospital she had attended as part of her probation order, went back to the matrimonial home. The father filed for divorce, applied under the Guardianship and Minors Acts 1971–1973 in the wardship proceedings and also applied for an ouster order under the Matrimonial Homes Act 1983. Having considered the wardship application first, the judges went on to grant the ouster order. The wife appealed on the basis that the hearing of the first application (where the welfare of the ward was paramount) had influenced the second unfairly as the child's welfare there was only one of four criteria. The wife also contended the judge had erred in the weight attached to certain factors.

Held, that there was no difficulty involved in deciding first what was best for the child and then going on to consider the other criteria under the Matrimonial Homes Act 1983.

That did not necessarily mean the child's interests were elevated above other considerations. The order made by the judge was a proper one within the ambit of the exercise of his discretion and would not be altered (*G.* v. *G. (Minors: Custody Appeal)* [1985] C.L.Y. 2594 applied; *Associated Provincial Picture Houses* v. *Wednesbury Corporation* (1948) C.L.C. 8107, *Bellenden (orse. Satterthwaite)* v. *Satterthwaite* (1948) C.L.C. 3046, *Richards* v. *Richards* [1983] C.L.Y. 1861 and *Ward* v. *James* [1964] C.L.Y. 3023 referred to).

T. (A MINOR: WARDSHIP), *Re*; T. *v.* T. (OUSTER ORDER) [1987] 1 F.L.R. 181, C.A.

1774. Ouster order—appeal—applications under different statutes. See POWER *v.* POWER, §2889.

1775. Ouster order—conduct of parties

The parties married in January 1967. They had two children, girls now aged 19 and 13, living with them. In about March 1985, H discovered that W had had an affair with another man and their relationship thereafter started to deteriorate. In June 1986 W presented a petition for divorce and H filed an answer. W then applied for an ouster order against H pursuant to s.9 of the Matrimonial Homes Act 1983. W alleged that H made excessive sexual demands upon her causing her distress and that because of that she had left the matrimonial bedroom and now slept on the floor in the study. The judge found that there had been no physical violence and that W was in a state of tension, the cause of it being H's presence in the matrimonial home. The judge felt that a short settling down period would solve the situation between the parties and that if H vacated the matrimonial home for a short period of time, upon his return the parties should be able to occupy the house in a better atmosphere until the divorce proceedings were concluded. The judge accordingly ordered that H should vacate the matrimonial home on or before 6.00 p.m. on Monday August 18, 1986 and should not return, without leave of the court, before Saturday October 18, 1986. H appealed.

Held, allowing H's appeal, this was a case where there was no physical violence. In the circumstances, the making of an ouster order, even for a short period, was too serious a step to take to solve the problem to which the judge referred. The decision of the judge was plainly wrong.

KADEER *v.* KADEER, August 15, 1986 (C.A.T. No. 764).

1776. Ouster order—grounds for making such an order

The Court of Appeal stressed that an order excluding one party to a marriage from the matrimonial home was a drastic one to be made only in cases of real necessity. It is not a ground for such an injunction that the marriage is breaking up, and there is an atmosphere of tension in the home (*Burke* v. *Burke* [1987] C.L.Y. 1779 explained).

SUMMERS *v.* SUMMERS, *The Times,* May 19, 1987, C.A.

1777. Ouster order—marriage already dissolved—jurisdiction—interests of children

After their divorce, the parties continued to reside in the matrimonial home but maintained separate households. The situation created tension and the wife applied for an order that the husband should vacate the home pending ancillary proceedings in respect of the property. The judge decided that an order as sought would be in the best interests of the children and made an order under s.37(1) of the Supreme Court Act 1981. The husband appealed on the basis that the court had no jurisdiction to make such an order after the dissolution of the marriage.

Held, that the power under s.37(1) would only be exercised to enforce an existing legal or equitable right. After divorce there were no rights under the Matrimonial Homes Act 1967 and 1983, nor under the Domestic Violence and Matrimonial Proceedings Act 1976. However, the court had an inherent jurisdiction where the protection of the welfare of the children was involved. The court was entitled to intervene to protect the welfare of the children here (*Richards* v. *Richards* [1982] C.L.Y. 1520 considered; *Quinn* v. *Quinn* [1983] C.L.Y. 1864 applied).

WILDE *v.* WILDE, *The Independent,* December 2, 1987, C.A.

1778. Ouster order—non-molestation order—interlocutory proceedings—validity of marriage

The wife petitioned for divorce and applied for a declaration under the Matrimonial Homes Act 1983 that she had right of occupation and for an injunction that the husband should vacate the home and be restrained from molesting her. The husband argued that the marriage was invalid and presented evidence to that effect. The judge ruled that the question of the validity of the marriage should be determined at the substantive divorce hearing as a preliminary point and granted the wife the relief sought.

Held, that if the court had no jurisdiction to grant relief under the 1983 Act it could do so under the Domestic Violence and Matrimonial Proceedings Act 1976 (c.50). The husband's argument that the judge should have determined the validity of the marriage as, if there was no valid marriage there was no jurisdiction to grant relief could not succeed. The relief sought was interlocutory relief. There was a triable issue. The validity of the marriage could not be determined at an interlocutory stage. The judge had reached the right decision.

SERAY-WURIE *v.* SERAY-WURIE [1987] 17 Fam. Law 124, C.A.

1779. Ouster order—operation of order postponed for eight weeks—whether appropriate

The wife filed for divorce proceedings and sought non-molestation and ouster orders against the husband. The judge found that the wife's allegations of violence against the husband proved and made the orders sought. He found that the domestic situation was intolerable and it would be inappropriate to continue until the divorce proceedings but he postponed the operation of the ouster order for eight weeks to allow the parties to reconsider their positions. The wife appealed.

Held, that if an ouster order is justified on the facts of the case it should take effect within 7 to 14 days to allow the party to vacate the matrimonial home and make alternative arrangements. It is undesirable to postpone the operation of the order for longer than that unless there were compelling circumstances. The judge had exercised his discretion wrongly and a period of two weeks would be substituted (*Chadda* v. *Chadda* [1981] C.L.Y. 1342 applied; *Bassett* v. *Bassett* [1975] C.L.Y. 1617 and *Richards* v. *Richards* [1982] C.L.Y. 1520 discussed).

BURKE *v.* BURKE [1987] 2 F.L.R. 71, C.A.

1780. Ouster order—power to grant—criteria

[Domestic Violence and Matrimonial Proceedings Act 1976 (c.50).]

The Court of Appeal stressed that an order made under the Domestic Violence and Matrimonial Proceedings Act 1976, excluding a party from the matrimonial home, is a draconian one, and the power to grant it should be sparingly used. Once the judge has considered the statutory provisions (*e.g.* conduct, needs, financial resources, and children), he should then consider whether, in all the circumstances of the case, it is just and reasonable to make the ouster order (*Richards* v. *Richards* [1983] C.L.Y. 1861 and *Summers* v. *Summers* [1986] C.L.Y. 1657 considered).

WISEMAN *v.* SIMPSON, *The Independent*, October 6, 1987, C.A.

1781. Property adjustment order—charge on matrimonial home—loan taken out fraudulently by wife—estoppel

The matrimonial home, purchased in joint names with money provided by the husband alone had had substantial improvements carried out by the husband. He applied for the transfer of the property. The wife and her employer, without the husband's knowledge had taken out a loan purportedly in the wife and husband's name, secured by a legal charge on the home. They were convicted of deception and forgery. The finance company claimed an equitable charge on the wife's interest in the matrimonial home. The husband had received no benefit from the loan. For three and a half years he had been paying £60 per month to the wife for an endowment policy but instead of receiving the £4,000 he expected, he only received £135.

Held, that the transfer was to be free of the charge claimed. The wife had only contributed in a small way to the home and her share would have been worth only £4,000. She had already received that from her husband. The wife's conduct was an abuse of the fiduciary relationship between her and her husband and her conduct estopped her from saying she had any share in the property. The finance company could therefore have no charge.

AINSCOUGH *v.* AINSCOUGH (CEDAR HOLDINGS INTERVENING) (1987) 17 Fam. Law 347, Wigan County Ct.

1782/3. Property adjustment order—charge on matrimonial home—priority

[Land Charges Act 1972 (c.61), s.5(7).]

A claim for property adjustment is sufficient to register a *lis pendens* against specific property thus postponing later charges.

On the breakdown of the marriage, W left the matrimonial home which was wholly owned by H. In her petition, W sought a property adjustment order generally, without reference to any specific property. She registered her claim as a *lis pendens* under s.5 of the Land Charges Act 1972, thereby charging the matrimonial home. Subsequently the bank gave H a loan secured by a first legal charge on the matrimonial home, having failed to make any search at the Land Charges Registry. H then left the country. On his application, the judge set aside the bank's mortgage.

Held, dismissing the appeal, that W had made a claim for property adjustment, she had sufficiently particularised the property on registration, and her claim took priority (*Calgary and Edmonton Land Co.* v. *Dobinson* [1974] C.L.Y. 2045 and *Whittingham* v. *Whittingham (National Westminster Bank, intervener)* [1978] C.L.Y. 1748 considered).

PEREZ-ADAMSON *v.* PEREZ-RIVAS [1987] 2 W.L.R. 500, C.A.

1784. Property adjustment order—legally aided wife receiving lump sum payment—whether legal aid fund's costs payable forthwith—whether discretion in Law Society to defer payment. See SIMPSON *v.* THE LAW SOCIETY, §2295.

1785. Property adjustment order—option to redeem charge on home—application for extension of time to exercise option—jurisdiction

In ancillary proceedings, an order was made vesting the matrimonial home in the wife with a charge in favour of the husband at 40 per cent. of the value of the property. The wife was given an option to reduce the charge within four months of the date of the order by paying the husband £3,500. She failed to do so in time and applied for an extension of time. That application was dismissed but on appeal the judge allowed the wife a seven day extension under Ord. 13, r.4 of the County Court Rules. The husband appealed.

Held, that Ord. 13, r.4 was a procedural provision that related to an act in proceedings—it did not empower the court to vary the terms of a properly constituted property adjustment order particularly where the term involved was vital as to time as in this case and where to do so would subvert the clear intention of the Matrimonial Causes Act 1973, s.31. The judge had no jurisdiction to grant the extension.

KNIBB *v.* KNIBB (1987) 17 Fam. Law 346, C.A.

1786. Property adjustment order—property vested in husband—wife and children having right to exclusive occupation—effect of Matrimonial Causes Act 1973 s.24A

The parties were divorced in 1974 and a property adjustment order was made charging the house that was owned by the husband to the wife with a two-fifths share of the proceeds of any sale. The wife and children had exclusive occupation. In 1986, the husband applied under s.24A of the 1973 Act (as inserted by the Matrimonial Homes and Property Act 1981). The recorder decided that the 1974 order gave implied liberty to apply which enabled the husband to apply under s.24A and, without hearing evidence or determining the merits, the recorder made the order.

Held, that whether s.24A applied was not determined by whether or not there was liberty to apply. If s.24A was available, an application could be made under that section regardless of the question of liberty to apply. There was jurisdiction to hear the application under the section. As the recorder had not heard any evidence, the case would be remitted to the county court to be considered afresh (*Thompson* v. *Thompson* [1985] C.L.Y. 1076, *Mesher* v. *Mesher and Hall* [1980] C.L.Y. 785 and *Lewis* v. *Lewis*]1985] C.L.Y. 1692 referred to).

TAYLOR *v.* TAYLOR [1987] 1 F.L.R. 142, C.A.

1787. Property adjustment order—trust for sale—matrimonial home deteriorating—improvement grant to repair requiring joint signatures—husband refusing—appointment of receiver

The Court of Appeal varied an order and transferred the matrimonial home into joint names upon a trust for sale with the wife occupying the home with the children. The home was worth £40,000 but was in a bad state of disrepair. The wife wished to obtain a second mortgage and a home improvement grant—both of which required the husband's signature. The husband refused to sign and the wife applied for a receiver to be appointed in his place.

Held, that the purpose of appointing a receiver was to prevent a jointly held asset from deteriorating—this was clearly an appropriate case for such an appointment. The matrimonial house should not be allowed to diminish in value. A receiver would be appointed (*Levermore* v. *Levermore* [1979] C.L.Y. 1404 applied).

HARVEY *v.* HARVEY [1987] 1 F.L.R. 67, Lincoln J.

1788. Property adjustment order—wife maintaining self and child—husband unemployed

The parties had one child aged 14. The marriage broke up in 1976 and all matters had been settled apart from the matrimonial home. As at 1976 the parties had contributed equally to the marriage. The husband was made redundant in 1984 and was unemployable. The wife maintained herself and paid for the child's private education. The husband had a house worth £30,000 with a mortgage of £10,000. The wife was still in the matrimonial home, now worth £70,000 and she earned £10,000 per annum. The registrar gave the husband a 20 per cent. interest in the matrimonial home with the sale to be postponed. On the husband's appeal, he was given a 40 per cent. interest. The wife appealed.

Held, that since the marriage had broken down, the wife had shouldered a disproportionate burden and if, as was suggested, the child went on to higher education it would be an open-ended commitment. Even a 20 per cent. interest for the husband could not be justified, he should receive a lump sum of £2,500 (bearing in mind anything above that would find its way back to the legal aid fund). Mesher type orders were subject to all sorts of problems and were likely to produce harsh results (*Mesher* v. *Mesher and Hall* [1980] C.L.Y. 785 considered).

MORTIMER *v.* MORTIMER-GRIFFIN [1986] 2 F.L.R. 315, C.A.

1789. Undertaking—breach—contempt of court—standard of proof—whether civil or criminal standard. See DEAN *v.* DEAN, §2937.

1790. Undue influence—husband and wife—charge over matrimonial home in joint ownership to secure husband's indebtedness to bank—undue influence exercised by husband—whether charge valid. See PERRY *v.* MIDLAND BANK, §2544.

1791. Undue influence—husband and wife—joint bank account—overdraft—bank enforcing debt against husband and wife. See SHEPHARD *v.* MIDLAND BANK, §1828.

FIRE SERVICE

1792. Fire Safety and Safety of Places of Sport Act 1987 (c.27). See PUBLIC ENTERTAINMENTS AND RECREATION, §3145.

1793. Firemen's pension scheme

FIREMEN'S PENSION SCHEME (AMENDMENT) ORDER 1987 (No. 1302) [£1·90], made under the Fire Services Act 1947 (c.41), s.26; operative October 1, 1987; amends S.I. 1973 No. 966 so as to provide that regular firemen, where eligible, may elect to purchase increases in the personal and dependants' benefits payable by a fire authority under the scheme set out in the 1973 Order up to the limit allowed by that scheme.

FIREARMS AND EXPLOSIVES

1794. Air pistol fired by compressed carbon dioxide—whether "lethal barrelled weapon"

[Firearms Act 1968 (c.27) ss.1(3)(*b*), 57(1); Firearms (Dangerous Air Weapons) Rules 1969 (S.I. 1969 No. 47, r.2(1).]

An "air weapon" within the meaning of the Firearms Act 1968, is a weapon actuated by air, so that a weapon depending upon compressed carbon dioxide cannot be regarded as an air weapon. But a weapon which is capable, if misused, of causing injury from which death might result, is capable of being a firearm within the meaning of that Act.

T was charged with possessing a firearm without a firearms certificate; the particular weapon was a revolver which fired airgun pellets by means of carbon dioxide, stored under pressure in a cylinder in the butt. Evidence was given that a pellet so fired was capable of breaking the skin and shattering an eye, from which death might result. It was contended that the pistol was an air weapon. T was convicted.

Held, dismissing the appeal that an "air weapon" within the meaning of the 1968 Act was a weapon fired by means of air, and that compressed carbon dioxide was not within that definition, so that the pistol could not be considered as an air weapon. Under s.57(1) of the 1968 Act, a lethal weapon was one which was capable of causing an injury from which death might result.

R. *v.* THORPE [1987] 1 W.L.R. 383, C.A.

1795. Ammunition—left concealed in car—whether in actual use, or in a secure place

[Firearms Rules 1969 (S.I. 1969 No. 1219), r.11(ii).]

While driving home from a shooting range, D left live ammunition concealed in the back of his unattended car for about an hour.

Held, that while it was so left, the ammunition was neither "in actual use" nor "kept in a secure place with a view to preventing access to [it] by unauthorised persons" within the meaning of r.11(ii) of the Firearms Rules 1969.

MARSH *v.* CHIEF CONSTABLE OF AVON AND SOMERSET, *The Independent,* May 8, 1987, D.C.

1796. Control of firearms—proposals for reform. See LAW REFORM, §2268.

1797. Electric stun gun—whether within Firearms Act

[Firearms Act 1968 (c.27), s.5(1)(*b*).]

An electric stun gun does not fall within the terms of the Act.

FLACK *v.* BALDRY, *The Times*, November 7, 1987, D.C.

FISH AND FISHERIES

1798. Eels

NORTH WEST WATER AUTHORITY (RETURNS OF EELS TAKEN) ORDER 1987 (No. 745) [45p], made under the Salmon and Freshwater Fisheries Act 1975 (c.51), s.28(3)(6), Sched. 3, para. 1(*c*); operative on April 25, 1987; empowers the said Authority to make byelaws in relation to the fishing for eels other than with rod and line.

1799. Fish farming

FISH FARMING (FINANCIAL ASSISTANCE) SCHEME 1987 (No. 1134) [85p], made under the Fisheries Act 1981 (c.29), s.31(1)(3)(4)(5); operative on July 4, 1987; provides for the making of grants for fish farming projects.

1800. Fishing vessels

FISHING VESSELS (ACQUISITION AND IMPROVEMENT) (GRANTS) SCHEME 1987 (No. 1135) [£1·60], made under the Fisheries Act 1981 (c.29), ss.15(1)(2), 18(1); operative on July 4, 1987; provides for the making of grants towards expenses incurred in the acquisition or improvement of sea fishing vessels.

FISHING VESSELS (FINANCIAL ASSISTANCE) SCHEME 1987 (No. 1136) [£1·30], made under the Fisheries Act 1981, ss.15(1)(2), 18(1); operative on July 4, 1987; provides for the making of grants for the purpose of re-organising and developing the sea fish catching industry.

1801. Prohibition of fishing

PLAICE AND SAITHE (SPECIFIED SEA AREAS) (PROHIBITION OF FISHING) ORDER 1987 (No. 1227) [85p], made under the Sea Fish (Conservation) Act 1967 (c.84), ss.5(1) and 15(3); operative on July 17, 1987; prohibits fishing for plaice or saithe by any British fishing boat registered in the U.K. or the Isle of Man within any part of a sea area specified in the Schedule to the Order or by any British fishing boat registered in any of the Channel Islands or by any British-owned fishing boat within any part of such a sea area which lies inside British fishery limits.

1802. Salmon and freshwater fisheries

NORTH WEST WATER AUTHORITY (SOLWAY FIRTH) TROUT CLOSE SEASON ORDER 1987 (No. 99) [45p], made under the Salmon and Freshwater Fisheries Act 1975 (c.51), s.28(3)(6), Sched. 3, para. 1(*c*); operative on February 10, 1987, alters the close season for fishing for trout with rod and line in the Solway Firth to 168 days.

1803. Sea fishing

COD (SPECIFIED SEA AREAS) (PROHIBITION OF FISHING) ORDER 1987 (No. 2192) [£1·30], made under the Sea Fish (Conservation) Act 1967 (c.84), ss.5(1), 15(3); operative on December 19, 1987; prohibits the fishing for cod by British fishing boats in specified sea areas.

HERRING AND WHITE FISH (SPECIFIED MANX WATERS) LICENSING (VARIATION) ORDER 1987 (No. 1564) [45p], made under the Sea Fish (Conservation) Act 1967 (c.84), ss.4, 15(3), 20(1); operative on September 8, 1987; varies S.I. 1983 No. 1204.

PLAICE (SPECIFIED SEA AREAS) (PROHIBITION OF FISHING) ORDER 1987 (No. 2011) [85p], made under the Sea Fish (Conservation) Act 1967, ss.5(1), 15(3) operative on November 26, 1987; prohibits fishing for plaice by British fishing boats in specified sea areas.

SAITHE (SPECIFIED SEA AREAS) (PROHIBITION OF FISHING) ORDER 1987 (No. 718) [85p], made under the Sea Fish (Conservation) Act 1967, ss.5(1), 15(3); prohibits fishing for saithe by British registered boats in specified sea areas.

SAITHE (SPECIFIED SEA AREAS) (PROHIBITION OF FISHING) (REVOCATION) ORDER 1987 (No. 1900) [45p], made under the Sea Fish (Conservation) Act 1967, ss.5(1), 15(3) and 20(1); operative on November 9, 1987; revokes S.I. 1987 No. 718.

SEA FISH LICENSING (VARIATION) ORDER 1987 (No. 1565) [85p], made under the Sea Fish (Conservation) Act 1967, ss.4, 15(3), 20(1); operative on September 8, 1987; varies S.I. 1983 No. 1206.

SEA FISHING (ENFORCEMENT OF COMMUNITY CONTROL MEASURES) (AMENDMENT) ORDER 1987 (No. 1536) [85p], made under the Fisheries Act 1981 (c.29), s.30(2); operative on September 3, 1987; amends S.I. 1985 No. 487.

SEA FISHING (ENFORCEMENT OF COMMUNITY QUOTA MEASURES) ORDER 1987 (No. 2234) [£1·30]; made under the Fisheries Act 1981, s.30(2), operative on January 1, 1988; revokes S.I. 1986 No. 2329.

SEA FISHING (SPECIFIED WESTERN WATERS) RESTRICTIONS ON LANDING) ORDER 1987 (No. 1566) [£1·60], made under the Sea Fish (Conservation) Act 1967, ss.6(1)–(3), 15(3), 20(1); operative on September 8, 1987; consolidates S.I. 1980 No. 335, as amended.

SOLE (NORTH SEA) (ENFORCEMENT OF COMMUNITY CONSERVATION MEASURES) ORDER 1987 (No. 213) [£1·40], made under the Fisheries Act 1981, s.30(2); operative on February 18, 1987; makes provision for the enforcement of the prohibition on retaining on board or landing more than 30 per cent. of sole taken in the North Sea as a percentage of the total catch of fish.

THIRD COUNTRY FISHING (ENFORCEMENT) ORDER 1987 (No. 292) [£1·40], made under the Fisheries Act 1981, s.30(2); operative on March 30, 1987; makes breaches of specified EEC Regulations offences for the purposes of U.K. law if they occur within British fishery limits.

1804. Shellfish

SEVERAL AND REGULATED FISHERIES (FORM OF APPLICATION) REGULATIONS 1987 (No. 217) [80p], made under the Sea Fisheries (Shellfish) Act 1967 (c.83), s.1(2); operative on March 1, 1987; prescribe the form of applications for the grant of several or regulating orders in relation to shellfish fisheries under s.1 of the 1967 Act.

SHELLFISH (SPECIFICATION OF MOLLUSCS) REGULATIONS 1987 (No. 218) [45p], made under the Sea Fisheries (Shellfish) Act 1967, s.1(1); operative on March 1, 1987; adds scallops and queens to the list of shellfish in s.1 of the 1967 Act.

1805. "T" nets

NORTHUMBRIAN WATER AUTHORITY (T NETS) (NORTHERN AREA) ORDER 1987 (No. 612) [45p], made under the Salmon and Freshwater Fisheries Act 1975 (c.51), s.28(3)(5)(6, Sched. 3, para. 1(*c*); operative on March 26, 1987; replaces expired Order and makes provision for the use of "T" nets in the said area.

NORTHUMBRIAN WATER AUTHORITY (T NETS) (SOUTHERN AREA) ORDER 1987 (No. 1054) [85p], made under the Salmon and Freshwater Fisheries Act 1975, s.28(3)(5)(6), Sched. 3, para. 1(*c*); operative on September 11, 1987 save for Art. 2(1)(*b*)(*c*) which is operative on June 11, 1987; makes provision in relation to the use of T nets in the said area.

FOOD AND DRUGS

1806. Coffee

COFFEE AND COFFEE PRODUCTS (AMENDMENT) REGULATIONS 1987 (No. 1986) [£1·60], made under the Food Act 1984 (c.30), ss.4, 7, 118, 119; operative on December 21, 1988 save for regs. 1 and 4 which are operative on December 22, 1987; implement Council Directive No. 85/573/EEC.

1807. Colouring

COLOURING MATTER IN FOOD (AMENDMENT) REGULATIONS 1987 (No. 1987) [45p], made under the Food Act 1984 (c.30), ss.4, 7, 118; operative on January 2, 1988; further amend S.I. 1973 No. 1340.

1808. Contamination

FOOD PROTECTION (EMERGENCY PROHIBITIONS) AMENDMENT ORDER 1987 (No. 1567) [85p], made under the Food and Environment Protection Act 1985 (c.48), ss.1(1)(2), 24(1)(3); operative on September 7, 1987; amends S.I. 1987 No. 1165 so as to exempt certain specified sheep from the prohibitions contained in that Order.

FOOD PROTECTION (EMERGENCY PROHIBITIONS) AMENDMENT No. 2 ORDER 1987 (No. 1696) [85p], made under the Food and Environment Protection Act 1985 (c.48), ss.1(1)(2), 24(1)(3); operative on September 28, 1987, amends S.I. 1987 No. 1165 so as to exempt from the prohibitions on the movement, slaughter and supply contained in that Order certain specified sheep.

FOOD PROTECTION (EMERGENCY PROHIBITIONS) (ENGLAND) ORDER 1987 (No. 1893) [£1·30], made under the Food and Environment Protection Act 1985, ss.1(1), 24(3); operative on November 7, 1987; imposes restrictions on the supply or slaughter of sheep from a designated area of England.

FOOD PROTECTION (EMERGENCY PROHIBITIONS) (ENGLAND) (No. 2) AMENDMENT ORDER 1987 (No. 153) [45p], made under the Food and Environment Protection Act 1985 (c.48), ss.1(1), 24(3); operative on February 16, 1987; exempts from the prohibition on the slaughter and supply of sheep which have been examined and specially marked.

FOOD PROTECTION (EMERGENCY PROHIBITIONS) (ENGLAND) (No. 2) AMENDMENT No. 2 ORDER 1987 (No. 249) [45p], made under the Food and Environment Protection Act 1985 (c.48), ss.1(1), 24(3); operative on February 27, 1987; exempts from the prohibition on slaughter sheep from the designated areas which have been specially marked.

FOOD PROTECTION (EMERGENCY PROHIBITIONS) (ENGLAND) (No. 2) AMENDMENT No. 3 ORDER 1987 (No. 906) [85p], made under the Food and Environment Protection Act 1985 (c.48), ss.1(1), 24(3); operative on May 25, 1987; amend S.I. 1986 No. 1689.

FOOD PROTECTION (EMERGENCY PROHIBITIONS) (ENGLAND) (No. 2) AMENDMENT (No. 4) ORDER 1987 (No. 1555) [85p], made under the Food and Environment Protection Act 1985, ss.1(1), 24(3); operative on September 7, 1987; exempts from the prohibitions contained in S.I. 1986 No. 1689 certain specified sheep.

FOOD PROTECTION (EMERGENCY PROHIBITIONS) (ENGLAND) (No. 2) AMENDMENT No. 5 ORDER 1987 (No. 1687) [45p], made under the Food and Environment Protection Act 1985, ss.1(1), 24(3); operative on September 28, 1987; exempts from the prohibition on the slaughter and supply of sheep referred to in S.I. 1986 No. 1689 certain specified sheep.

FOOD PROTECTION (EMERGENCY PROHIBITIONS) (No. 2) ORDER 1987 (No. 1450) [£1·60], made under the Food and Environment Protection Act 1985 (c.48), ss.1(1)(2), 24(1)(3); operative on August 13, 1987; specifies areas in Scotland from which the movement and slaughter of sheep is prohibited.

FOOD PROTECTION (EMERGENCY PROHIBITIONS) (No. 2) AMENDMENT ORDER 1987 (No. 1568) [85p], made under the Food and Environment Protection Act 1985, ss.1(1)(2), 24(1)(3); operative on September 7, 1987; amends S.I. 1987 No. 1450 so as to exempt sheep from the prohibitions contained in that Order.

FOOD PROTECTION (EMERGENCY PROHIBITIONS) (No. 2) AMENDMENT No. 2 ORDER 1987 (No. 1697) [85p], made under the Food and Environment Protection Act 1985, ss.1(1)(2), 24(1)(3); operative on September 28, 1987; amends S.I. 1987 No. 1450 so as to exempt from the prohibitions on the movement, slaughter and supply contained in that Order certain specified sheep.

FOOD PROTECTION (EMERGENCY PROHIBITIONS) (No. 3) ORDER 1987 (No. 1837) [£1·30], made under the Food and Environment Protection Act 1985 (c.48), ss.1(1)(2), 24(1)(3); operative on October 22, 1987; re-enacts S.I. 1987 No. 1165, as amended and continues the prohibition on the movement and slaughter of sheep in designated areas unless exempted from that prohibition by the Order.

FOOD PROTECTION (EMERGENCY PROHIBITIONS) (No. 4) ORDER 1987 (No. 1888) [£2·20], made under the Food and Environment Protection Act 1985, ss.1(1)(2), 24(1)(3); operative on November 4, 1987; revokes and re-enacts S.I. 1987 No. 1450 and imposes restrictions on the movement and slaughter of sheep in specified areas of Scotland.

FOOD PROTECTION (EMERGENCY PROHIBITIONS) (No. 10) REVOCATION ORDER 1987 (No. 270) [45p], made under the Food and Environment Protection Act 1985 (c.48), s.1(1); operative on February 27, 1987; revokes S.I. 1986 No. 2248.

FOOD PROTECTION (EMERGENCY PROHIBITIONS) (WALES) ORDER 1987 (No. 1181) [£1·90], made under the Food and Environment Protection Act 1985, ss.1(1)(2), 24(1)(3); operative on July 10, 1987; designates two areas in Wales from which the movement of sheep is prohibited.

FOOD PROTECTION (EMERGENCY PROHIBITIONS) (WALES) (No.2) ORDER 1987 (No. 1436) [£2·20], made under the Food and Environment Protection Act 1985, ss.1(1)(2), 24(1)(3); operative on August 11, 1987; designates an area of Wales from which the movement or slaughter of sheep is prohibited.

FOOD PROTECTION (EMERGENCY PROHIBITIONS) (WALES) (No. 2) AMENDMENT ORDER 1987 (No. 182) [45p], made under the Food and Environment Protection Act 1985, ss.1(1)(2), 24(1)(3); operative on February 16, 1987; exempts from the prohibition on slaughter and supply of Welsh sheep from the designated area which have been specially marked.

FOOD PROTECTION (EMERGENCY PROHIBITIONS) (WALES) (No. 2) AMENDMENT No. 2 ORDER 1987 (No. 263) [45p], made under the Food and Environment Protection Act 1985, ss.1(1), 24(1); operative on February 27, 1987; exempts from the prohibition on slaughter sheep which have been specially marked.

FOOD PROTECTION (EMERGENCY PROHIBITIONS) (WALES) (No. 2) AMENDMENT No. 3 ORDER 1987 (No. 885) [45p], made under the Food and Environment Protection Act 1985 (c.48), ss.1(1)(2), 24(1)(3); operative on May 25, 1987; exempts from restrictions contained in S.I. 1986 No. 1681 sheep that are specially marked.

FOOD PROTECTION (EMERGENCY PROHIBITIONS) (WALES) (No. 3) ORDER 1987 (No. 1515) [£2·60], made under the Food and Environment Protection Act 1985, ss.1(1)(2), 24(1)(3); operative on August 28, 1987; replaces S.I. 1987 No. 1436 and designates an area of Wales from which the movement, and in which the slaughter, of sheep is prohibited.

FOOD PROTECTION (EMERGENCY PROHIBITIONS) (WALES) (No. 4) ORDER 1987 (No. 1638) [£2·60], made under the Food and Environment Protection Act 1985, ss.1(1)(2), 24(1)(3); operative on September 18, 1987; designates an area in Wales from which the movement of sheep, and in which the slaughter of sheep, is prohibited.

FOOD PROTECTION (EMERGENCY PROHIBITIONS) (WALES) (No. 4) AMENDMENT ORDER 1987 (No. 1682) [45p], made under the Food and Environment Protection Act 1985, ss.1(1)(2), 24(1)(3); operative on September 28, 1987; amends S.I. 1987 No. 1638 so as to exempt from the prohibition on the slaughter of sheep contained therein certain specified sheep.

FOOD PROTECTION (EMERGENCY PROHIBITIONS) (WALES) (No. 4) AMENDMENT No. 2 ORDER 1987 (No. 1802) [85p], made under the Food and Environment Protection Act 1985, ss.1(1)(2), 24(1)(3); operative on October 19, 1987; excepts from the prohibition on the slaughter of sheep contained in S.I. 1987 No. 1638 certain specified sheep.

FOOD PROTECTION (EMERGENCY PROHIBITIONS) (WALES) (No. 5) ORDER 1987 (No. 1894) [£2·60], made under the Food and Environment Protection Act 1985, s.1(1)(*a*); operative on November 7, 1987; restricts various activities in order to prevent human consumption of food rendered unsuitable for that purpose after Chernobyl.

1809. Failure to ensure food fit for human consumption—added substance causing unfitness

[Food Act 1984 (c.30), s.8(1)(*b*).]

A bottle of milk contained a dead mouse; another contained pieces of glass.

Held, allowing an appeal against justices' dismissal of informations alleging failure by Unigate Dairies to ensure that the bottles of milk were fit for human consumption, contrary to s.8(1)(*b*) of the 1984 Act, that the justices had erred in deciding that, since the unfitness was alleged to have been caused by the presence of an added substance (as opposed to natural decay or putrefaction) the prosecution had to proceed under s.2 of the Act (selling to the purchaser's prejudice food not of the nature or substance or quality demanded) (*Miller* v. *Battersea Borough Council* (1955) C.L.Y. 1115 distinguished).

BARTON *v.* UNIGATE DAIRIES [1987] Crim.L.R. 121, D.C.

1810. Food not of substance demanded—food submitted to public health inspector by customer for analysis—whether sample procured

[Food and Drugs Act 1955 (c.16), s.91, 108(1A).]

Where a purchaser of food that was not of the substance demanded submitted the food to a public analyst for analysis there was no procurement of a sample within the meaning of s.91 of the Food and Drugs Act 1955 so as to require prosecution proceedings to commence within two months pursuant to s.108(1A) of the Act.

Mrs. G purchased some cheese from Presto's Bognor Regis Supermarket. The cheese contained a piece of metal. On September 10, 1984 Mrs. G took the cheese to the local council offices. The health officer submitted the cheese for analysis by a public analyst who reported by way of a certificate dated September 19, 1984 that the cheese contained a piece of lattice-like material composed of aluminium alloy. D was prosecuted for an offence contrary to s.2 of the Food and Drugs Act 1955 of selling food not of the substance demanded. Proceedings were commenced on February 26, 1985. At the trial, D successfully argued that the proceedings should have been commenced within two months of September 10, 1984 on the basis that at that time a sample had been procured under the Act. The prosecution appealed by way of case-stated.

Held, allowing the appeal, that s.91 of the Act gave the environmental health officer of the Council the power to visit a shop and procure a sample. The two month time limit in s.108(1A) of the Act applied to a prosecution based upon such a procurement. In the present case there was no procurement by the environmental health officer nor could the cheese be described as a sample. S.108(1A) of the Act did not apply (*Manson* v. *Edwards (Louis C.) & Sons (Manufacturing)* [1977] C.L.Y. 1434 applied).

ARUN DISTRICT COUNCIL *v.* ARGYLE STORES (1987) 85 L.G.R. 59, D.C.

1811. Materials and articles in contact with food

MATERIALS AND ARTICLES IN CONTACT WITH FOOD REGULATIONS 1987 (No. 1523) [£2·90], made under the European Communities Act 1972 (c.68), s.2(2); operative on October 2, 1987; implement Council Directive No. 83/229/EEC and re-act S.I. 1978 No. 1927 which is revoked.

1812. Meat

AUTHORISED OFFICERS (MEAT INSPECTION) REGULATIONS 1987 (No. 133) [45p], made under the Food Act 1984 (c.30), s.73(2); operative on February 22, 1987; prescribe the qualifications which must be held by an officer of a council authorised under the 1984 Act in relation to the examination and seizure of meat.

FRESH MEAT EXPORT (HYGIENE AND INSPECTION) REGULATIONS 1987 (No. 2237) [£4·30], made under the Food Act 1984, ss.13, 118; operative on February 5, 1988; implement Council Directive No. 86/587/EEC.

MEAT INSPECTION REGULATIONS 1987 (No. 2236) [£2·60], made under the Food Act 1984, ss.13, 118; operative on February 5, 1988; re-enact with amendments S.I. 1963 No. 1229.

SLAUGHTERHOUSES (HYGIENE) (AMENDMENT) REGULATIONS 1987 (No. 2235) [45p], made under the Food Act 1984, ss.13, 118; operative on February 5, 1988; amend S.I. 1977 No. 1805.

1813. Milk

MILK AND DAIRIES AND MILK (SPECIAL DESIGNATION) (CHARGES) REGULATIONS 1987 (No. 212) [80p], made under the Food Act 1984 (c.30), ss.33, 38, 118; operative on March 30, 1987; introduce charges for the purposes of S.I. 1959 No. 277 and S.I. 1986 No. 723 and for services performed under those Regs.

MILK (CESSATION OF PRODUCTION) (ENGLAND AND WALES) SCHEME 1987 (No. 908) [£2·20], made under the Milk (Cessation of Production) Act 1985 (c.4), s.1; operative on June 10, 1987; provides for the payment of compensation to milk producers who either wholly or in part cease production of milk.

MILK (COMMUNITY OUTGOERS SCHEME) (ENGLAND AND WALES) (AMENDMENT) REGULATIONS 1987 (No. 410) [45p], made under the European Communities Act 1972 (c.68), s.2(2); operative on March 13, 1987; implement Commission Regulation (EEC) No.261/87.

MILK (COMMUNITY OUTGOERS SCHEME) (ENGLAND AND WALES) (AMENDMENT) (No. 2) REGULATIONS 1987 (No. 909) [45p], made under the European Communities Act 1972, s.2(2); operative on June 10, 1987; implement Council Regulation (EEC) No. 1336/86, as amended.

MILK MARKETING SCHEME (AMENDMENT) REGULATIONS 1987 (No. 735) [85p], made under the European Communities Act 1972, s.2(2); operative on May 14, 1987; further implement the U.K. obligation to supervise compliance with Council Regulation (EEC) No. 1422/78 concerning the granting of certain special rights to milk producer organisations in the U.K.

1814. Sale of food—cleanliness—smoking

[Food Hygiene (Markets, Stalls and Delivery Vehicles) Regulations 1966 (S.I. 1966 No. 791), regs. 2, 8.]

B, a market trader was observed smoking a cigarette in short intervals between serving customers at his vegetable stall. While actually serving he left the lighted cigarette on a trailer parked 10 feet behind the stall. He was charged with breach of reg. 8 of the 1966 Regulations. The justices dismissed the information.

Held, allowing the appeal, that (1) "handling" of food was not confined to actual touching of the food, but included all operations within the definition in reg. 2(2); (2) a person who smoked between serving customers, leaving the cigarette lit and at hand while serving, would be in breach of reg. 8, but in view of the lapse of time in the case it would not be remitted for re-hearing.

CUCKSON *v.* BUGG (1987) 85 L.G.R. 643, D.C.

1815. Seller of unfit food—reliance upon supplier's warranty—whether goods in same state throughout

[Food Act 1984 (c.30), ss.8(1), 102(1).]

Where a seller relied upon the supplier's warranty it always remained a question of fact and degree whether the goods were put on sale in the same state that they had been in when purchased by the retailer from the supplier. The court would not interfere unless there had been a misdirection or the conclusion reached by the justices was unreasonable.

GATEWAY FOODMARKETS *v.* SIMMONDS, *The Times*, March 26, 1987, D.C.

1816. Sugar

SUGAR BEET (RESEARCH AND EDUCATION) ORDER 1987 (No. 310) [80p], made under the Food Act 1984 (c.30), s.68(1)(2); operative on April 1, 1987; provides for the programme of education and research in the year 1987/88 in relation to the growing of home-grown beet.

1817. Trade descriptions—food labelling

[Trade Descriptions Act 1968 (c.29), s.1(1)(*b*); Food Labelling Regulations (S.I. 1980 No. 1849).]

D manufactured a substance described on its label as "vegetable lard . . . 100% vegetable oils", and was prosecuted under s.1(1)(*b*) of the Trade Descriptions Act 1968 and the Food Labelling Regulations 1980 for selling goods to which a false trade description was applied. The prosecution claimed that the description "lard" was confined to pig fat.

Held, that D was not in breach of the Act, because (1) "lard" did not only mean pig fat; (2) in any event, the description on the label was not misleading, although (3) even if it were, D had given sufficient disclaimer; and (4) so far as regulation 8 was concerned, there was no failure, by the words "vegetable lard", to inform the purchaser with sufficient precision of the true nature of the food (*Holmes* v. *Pipers* [1914] 1 K.B. 47, *Sandeman* v. *Gold* [1924] 1 K.B. 107, and *Kat* v. *Diment* (1950) C.L.C. 10305 distinguished; *R.* v. *Hammertons Cars* [1976] C.L.Y. 2470; *Norman* v. *Bennett* [1974] C.L.Y. 3448 and *Wandsworth London Borough Council* v. *Bentley* [1981] C.L.Y. 2408 applied).

WOLKIND AND NORTHCOTT *v.* PURA FOODS, *The Times*, January 30, 1987, D.C.

1818. Whether food sold of "quality" demanded in—whether offence committed

[Food Act 1984 (c.30), s.2(1)(*c*).]

McD Co. displayed at their premises a "nutrition guide" indicating that their ordinary Cola contained 96 to 187 kilocalories per serving whereas their Diet Cola contained less than one kilocalorie per serving. On two occasions a sampling officer demanded Diet Cola but was served with ordinary Cola.

Held, dismissing McD Co.'s appeal against convictions of selling food not of the quality demanded by the purchaser, contrary to s.2(1)(*c*) of the 1984 Act, that the justices were entitled to find on the facts that there was a contravention of s.2(1)(*c*) and that the food sold was not of the quality demanded. The court looked at the commercial transaction out of which the sale arose, (*Anness* v. *Grivell* [1915] 3 K.B. 685, *Hunt* v. *Richardson* [1916] 2 K.B. 446, *Goldup* v. *Manson (John)* [1981] C.L.Y. 1243, *Barber* v. *Co-operative Wholesale Society* [1983] C.L.Y. 1717, *Preston* v. *Greenclose* (1975) 139 J.P. 245 and *Shearer* v. *Rowe* [1985] C.L.Y. 1558 followed).

McDONALD'S HAMBURGERS *v.* WINDLE [1987] Crim.L.R. 200, D.C.

FOREIGN JURISDICTIONS

1819. Dominica—compulsory acquisition of land—compensation—interest on compensation

[Land Acquisition Ordinance (Laws of Dominica 1963 rev., c.170), s.21; Commonwealth of Dominica Constitution Order 1978 (S.I. 1978 No. 1027) Sched. 1, ss.6(1)(2), 16(1)(2) Sched. 2, para. 12.]

A landowner of compulsorily acquired land is entitled to simple interest on compensation at six per cent. per annum, however long the delay in payment.

The Government of Dominica compulsorily acquired P's land but failed to comply with the Land Acquisition Ordinance by assessing compensation. On P's application, the High Court assessed compensation at £250,000. When dealing with interest, the judges held that the six per cent. simple interest restriction under s.21 of the Ordinance was only mandatory if compensation was paid within a reasonable time and that otherwise there would be a conflict with s.6(1) of the Constitution which gave P the right to have adequate compensation paid within a reasonable time. He accordingly awarded interest at 10 per cent. per annum compound.

Held, the Court's power of redress was limited by s.16(2) of the Constitution to ensuring that acquisition was in accordance with the Ordinance, and P was only entitled to six per cent. per annum simple.

BLOMQUIST *v.* ATT.-GEN. OF THE COMMONWEALTH OF DOMINICA [1987] 2 W.L.R. 1185 P.C.

1820. Jamaica—jurisdiction of resident magistrate—whether resident magistrate has jurisdiction to hear case already part-heard before a different resident magistrate. See BESWICK *v.* THE QUEEN, §688.

1821. Mauritius—constitution—defendant convicted by magistrate who had not heard the evidence and submissions made—whether trial fair

[Constitution of Mauritius s.10(1), Courts Act 1945, s.124.]

A defendant who was convicted by a tribunal consisting of two magistrates of whom one had heard none of the evidence or submissions made did not receive a fair trial.

The appellant and three others appeared before the Intermediate Court of Mauritius charged with theft. The Court consisted of two magistrates, A and B. The trial commenced on December 8, 1982 and continued on April 26, June 17, August 4 and September 27, 1983. Submissions of no case to answer were heard on October 12 and 17, 1983 and judgment reserved. The submissions were rejected on March 13, 1984 by a court comprising two magistrates A and C, C had heard none of the evidence or submissions. The trial continued on April 17, 1984 when the defendants gave their evidence and closing speeches were made. The verdict of the court was given on October 15, 1984 when the court comprised two magistrates A and D. The verdict was delivered by D who had heard none of the case. The appellant and the other defendants were convicted. By 10(1) of the Mauritius Constitution any person charged with a criminal offence was to be afforded a fair hearing within a reasonable time. The appellants appeal to the Court of Appeal was dismissed.

Held, allowing the appeal, that it was a fundamental requirement of justice that those called upon to deliver a verdict must have heard all the evidence. The appellant had been denied the fair hearing guaranteed by the constitution. S.124 of the Courts Act 1945 did not entitle a magistrate to take up a part-heard case as a replacement for another magistrate. In the event that the magistrate was replaced the trial must start again from the beginning (*Syea* v. *The Queen* [1968] M.R. 100 overruled).

NG (ALIAS WONG) *v.* THE QUEEN [1987] 1 W.L.R. 1356, P.C.

1822. Trinidad and Tobago—planning permission—development of land as a quarry—whether compensation payable for refusal. See LOPINOT LIMESTONE *v.* ATT.-GEN. OF TRINIDAD AND TOBAGO, §3678.

FORESTRY

1823. Felling of trees

FORESTRY (FELLING OF TREES) (AMENDMENT) REGULATIONS 1987 (No. 632) [£1·60], made under the Forestry Act 1967 (c.10), ss.10(1), 17B(1), 24(2), 25(1), 32(1)(2); operative on May 1, 1987; amend S.I. 1979 No. 791 in relation to a number of procedural matters concerned with felling and restocking.

1824. Tractors—type approval. See AGRICULTURE, §100.

FRAUD, MISREPRESENTATION AND UNDUE INFLUENCE

1825. Criminal Justice Act 1987 (c.38). See CRIMINAL EVIDENCE AND PROCEDURE, §634.

1826. Fraudulent misrepresentation—claim arising in connection with a contract tainted by illegality—whether damages recoverable—time at which damages to be measured—*ex turpi causa non oritur actio*

The maxim *ex turpi causa non oritur actio* did not provide a good defence to a claim in tort based on fraudulent misrepresentation where the contract secured by the representation was tainted by illegality in the form of evasion of stamp duty.

D sold a flat to P. D fraudulently misrepresented to P that the flat included a roof garden. P paid £45,000 for the flat. The price was agreed in May 1983 and completion took place in November 1983. The flat included a number of fixtures, fittings and chattels. At P's instigation, the purchase price was apportioned as to £40,000 for the flat and £5,000 for the fixtures, fittings and chattels. The purpose of the apportionment was to reduce P's liability to stamp duty by £300. The fixtures, fittings and chattels were only worth between £500 and £1,000. P claimed damages and was awarded £7,000 being the difference between £45,000 and the value of the flat without a roof garden in May 1983, £500 for inconvenience and disappointment and interest at the rate of 12½ per cent. from the date of the writ.

Held, allowing D's appeal in part, that the proper date to assess P's loss was the date of completion when the flat became P's. As the value of the flat had increased between May and November 1983, the proper measure of P's loss was £4,350. With regard to damages for inconvenience and disappointment, P was entitled to a moderate award bearing some relation to the particular circumstances of the case. An award of a moderate but substantially greater amount would have been justified. Given that such damages were assessed at the date of the trial it was not appropriate to award interest on that part of the award. The contract to purchase the flat was tainted by illegality namely the fraudulent evasion of the liability to pay stamp duty. It was likely that the courts would hold contracts of that nature to be unenforceable. A solicitor who was a party to such an apportionment of value must be guilty of professional misconduct. The conduct and relative moral culpability of the parties may be relevant in determining whether the *ex turpi causa* defence is to be upheld as a matter of public policy. P had an unanswerable claim based on fraudulent misrepresentation which was not connected with the apportionment of the price in the contract. P was not seeking to enforce the contract or relief based upon it. P's claim remained the same whether the contract was tainted by illegality or not. The court should consider two questions, first had there been illegality of which the court ought to take notice and second would it be an affront to the public conscience to grant the relief sought. D's defence of *ex turpi causa* could not in the circumstances succeed (*Thackwell* v. *Barclays Bank* [1986] C.L.Y. 158 approved; *Alexander* v. *Rayson* [1936] 1 K.B. 169, *National Coal Board* v. *England* [1954] C.L.Y. 2076, *Singh* v. *Ali* [1960] C.L.Y. 3263, *Chettiar* v. *Chettiar* [1962] C.L.Y. 1205, *Shelley* v. *Paddock* [1980] C.L.Y. 1306 considered).

SAUNDERS *v.* EDWARDS [1987] 2 All E.R. 651, C.A.

1827. Husband and wife—charge over matrimonial home in joint ownership to secure husband's indebtedness to bank—undue influence exercised by husband—whether charge valid. See PERRY *v.* MIDLAND BANK, §2544.

1828. Husband and wife—joint bank account—overdraft—bank enforcing debt against husband and wife

The defendant's husband opened a bank account and had become overdrawn. By agreement with the bank that account was closed and transferred to a joint account with the defendant. The joint account mandate signed by the wife included a term making her jointly liable for any loan or overdraft. The husband obtained a £10,000 overdraft which he would not repay. The bank brought proceedings against the defendant and her husband. Her defence was that the husband, acting as the agent of the bank, had used undue influence to obtain her signature to the joint account mandate and that the transaction was manifestly disadvantageous to her. The plaintiff bank obtained summary judgment. The defendant appealed from the judge's affirmation of the Master's order.

Held, that the relationship of husband and wife did not of itself give rise to a presumption of undue influence and, even where there was such a presumption, the transaction would not be set aside unless it was manifestly disadvantageous to the person influenced. To determine this the facts of each case had to be considered. A transaction would not be enforced if it was shown that the creditor had entrusted the task of obtaining a signature on a document to a person who was, to the knowledge of the creditor, in a position to procure the signature by means of undue influence. Here there was no evidence to show that undue influence had been exerted on the wife although the transaction was arguably disadvantageous to her. There was no evidence that the bank had any knowledge that the husband would bring any influence to bear on the defendant. Accordingly there was no arguable defence to the claim (*Turnbull* v. *Duval* [1902] A.C. 429, *King's North Trust* v. *Bell* [1986] C.L.Y. 2227 and *National Westminster Bank* v. *Morgan* [1985] C.L.Y. 413 discussed).

SHEPHARD *v.* MIDLAND BANK (1987) 17 Fam.Law 309, C.A.

1829. Misrepresentation of service charges on flat—quantum. See HEINEMANN *v.* COOPER, § 1163.

1830. Property adjustment order—charge on matrimonial home—loan taken out fraudulently by wife—estoppel. See AINSCOUGH *v.* AINSCOUGH (CEDAR HOLDINGS INTERVENING), §1781.

GAMING AND WAGERING

1831. Betting duty. See CUSTOMS AND EXCISE, §1102.

1832. Billiards (Abolition of Restrictions) Act 1987 (c.19)

This Act abolishes the restrictions by way of licensing or otherwise on the public playing of billiards, bagatelle and similar games, and also abolishes the related power of entry.

The Act received the Royal Assent on May 15, 1987.

The Act extends to England and Wales only.

1833. Fees

BETTING, GAMING AND LOTTERIES ACT 1963 (VARIATION OF FEES) ORDER 1987 (No. 95) [45p], made under the Betting, Gaming and Lotteries Act 1963 (c.2), Sched. 1, para. 20(1A); operative on March 2, 1987; increases fees payable for the grant and renewal of betting agency permits and betting office licences and the renewal of bookmakers' permits.

GAMING ACT (VARIATION OF FEES) ORDER 1987 (No. 242) [45p], made under the Gaming Act 1968 (c.65), ss.48(5), 51(4); operative on April 1, 1987; increases fees chargeable under the 1968 Act.

1834. Gaming (Amendment) Act 1987 (c.11)

This Act amends s.18 of the Gaming Act 1968 with respect to the hours for gaming.

The Act received the Royal Assent on April 9, 1987, and comes into force on a day to be appointed by the Secretary of State.

The Act does not extend to Northern Ireland.

1835. Gaming (Amendment) Act 1987—commencement

GAMING (AMENDMENT) ACT 1987 (COMMENCEMENT) ORDER 1987 (No. 1200 (C.33)) [45p], made under the Gaming (Amendment) Act 1987 (c.11), s.2(2); brings all provisions of the 1987 Act into force on August 1, 1987.

1836. Hours and charges

GAMING CLUBS (HOURS AND CHARGES) (AMENDMENT) REGULATIONS 1987 (No. 609) [45p], made under the Gaming Act 1968 (c.65), ss.14(2), 51; operative on May 4, 1987; increase maximum charges for admission to gaming in bingo club premises to £4·60.

1837. Lotteries

LOTTERIES (GAMING BOARD FEES) ORDER 1987 (No. 243) [45p], made under the Lotteries and Amusements Act 1976 (c.32), ss.18(1)(*e*)(2), 24(2); operative on April 1, 1987; increases fees payable under Sched. 2, para. 7(1) of the 1976 Act.

1838. Monetary limits

GAMING ACT (VARIATION OF MONETARY LIMITS) ORDER 1987 (No. 608) [45p], made under the Gaming Act 1968 (c.65), ss.20(3)(8), 51(4); operative on May 4, 1987; increases the monetary limits specified in s.20(3)(8) of the 1968 Act.

GAS

1839. Government shareholding

GAS ACT 1986 (GOVERNMENT SHAREHOLDING) ORDER 1987 (No. 866) [45p], made under the Gas Act 1986 (c.44), s.54(1); operative on June 3, 1987; sets the target limit for the Government shareholding in British Gas p.l.c. at 2·680 of voting rights exercisable in all circumstances at general meetings of the company.

GUARANTEE AND INDEMNITY

1840. Bank guarantee—default—entitlement to summary judgment. See CONTINENTAL ILLINOIS NATIONAL BANK & TRUST CO. OF CHICAGO *v.* PAPANICOLAOU, §2911.

1841. Co-sureties—contribution—successive assignments of lease

In October 1973 P granted a lease to D. In March 1981 the lease was assigned by D to Deval with Deamer (Third Party—"TP") as surety. In January 1982 Deval assigned the lease to Dorchester with Silver (Fourth Party—"FP") as surety. The assignments and the licences to assign relating thereto contained the usual indemnity covenants between the various parties in respect of non-payment of rent to P. In September 1983 P commenced proceedings against D claiming arrears of rent and fire insurance. D had no defence to the claim by virtue of the covenants entered into and issued third party proceedings against TP claiming to be indemnified against their liability to P by virtue of the covenants contained in the assignment of March 1981. TP admitted liability to indemnify D and issued fourth party proceedings against FP reciting P's claim against D, D's claim against him and claiming a contribution from FP under the Civil Liability (Contribution) Act 1978. The judge held that the claim by TP was within the 1978 Act and held FP liable to pay a contribution to TP and the judge assessed the contribution at 100 per cent. FP appealed.

Held, allowing the appeal, that P did not make any claim against TP and D did not claim contribution under the 1978 Act from TP. TP was liable to D under the assignment of March 1981, the payment which TP had been ordered to make was in satisfaction of that claim and it was in respect of that payment that TP sought contribution from FP. The wording of s.1(1), (2) and s.6(1) of the 1978 Act made it clear that FP was not liable to D in respect of the damage for which TP had been ordered to pay compensation.

FRYDMAN PROPERTIES *v.* BEJAM GROUP, May 12, 1986 (C.A.T. No. 431).

1842. Guarantor of debt—signature

[Statute of Frauds 1677 (c.3), s.4.]

Any writing by which the guarantor of a debt can be identified in a memorandum of the guarantee, and which shows an intention to adopt the guarantee, suffices as a signature for the purposes of s.4 of the Statute of Frauds 1677.

DECOUVREUR *v.* JORDAN, *The Times,* May 25, 1987, C.A.

1843. Letter of comfort—offer to take over liabilities of subsidiary—whether offer accepted. See CHEMCO LEASING S.p.A. *v.* REDIFFUSION, §440.

1844. Money borrowed by debenture—whether issue of valid debenture condition of personal guarantee

Where a guarantor wishes to make his guarantee dependent on the giving of some collateral warranty, the onus is on him to establish that this was a condition of the guarantee.

The majority shareholder in two companies gave a personal guarantee to a bank which loaned money to one of the companies. The loan was also to be secured by a debenture issued by the other company. The companies were compulsorily wound up, and when the bank called in the money on the shareholder's personal guarantee, he claimed the debenture was itself invalid, and that his personal guarantee was conditional on the bank obtaining a valid debenture from the company.

Held, dismissing the appeal, that there was no sufficient evidence to establish that it was a term of the agreement between the shareholder and the bank that his guarantee was subject to the issue of a valid debenture.

T.C.B. *v.* GRAY (1987) 3 BCC 503, C.A.

1845. Partnership—responsibility for losses—change in constitution of firm—whether guarantee revoked

D gave a guarantee to P1, a partnership, making himself responsible, *inter alia,* for losses of money resulting from the employment by P1 of a Mr. C. P1 was later taken over by P2, a limited company. It was found that C had not properly accounted to his employers for monies he had collected from customers and it was agreed between the parties that the total amount of the losses suffered by P1 and P2 amounted to some £2,147. P1 and P2 sought to recover that sum from D under the guarantee. D contended that s.18 of the Partnership Act 1890 operated as a bar to the recovery by P1 and P2 of that sum as, in the absence of agreement to the contrary, the guarantee was revoked by the change in the constitution of the firm to which the guarantee was given.

Held, dismissing D's appeal, that since the two plaintiffs were joined in the action, and having regard to the agreement between the parties as to a global figure as to the loss sustained by the plaintiffs without differentiation as to how much loss was sustained by each plaintiff, s.18 of the Partnership Act 1890 did not prevent recovery under the guarantee.

UNIVERSAL CO. *v.* YIP, June 18, 1986 (C.A.T. No. 581).

1846. Time charterparty—whether authority to grant guarantee—whether sufficient writing

P let their vessel to X, a company that was in financial difficulties. P required that there would be a guarantee of all sums due. In previous cases, D Co. (which had a container leasing agreement with X) had provided such a guarantee. Mr. B of X indicated that D would provide the guarantee. X owed money under the charter, and P sued D under the guarantee. D contended that it had not been given with their authority, and that in any event, an oral contract of guarantee was unenforceable.

Held, that (1) on the evidence, Mr. B of X had the express or implied authority of D to give a guarantee on X's behalf; (2) there was a sufficient note or memorandum of the agreement for the purpose of the Statute of Frauds and judgment would be given for P.

CLIPPER MARITIME *v.* SHIRLSTAR CONTAINER TRANSPORT; ANEMONE, THE [1987] 1 Lloyd's Rep. 546, Staughton J.

1847. Surety in respect of performance of tenant's covenants—enforcement at suit of assignee of reversion. See KUMAR *v.* DUNNING, §2147.

HEALTH AND SAFETY AT WORK

1848. Asbestos

CONTROL OF ASBESTOS AT WORK REGULATIONS 1987 (No. 2115) [£2·20], made under the Health and Safety at Work etc. Act 1874 (c.37), ss.15(1)(2)(3)(*a*) (4)(*a*)(5)(*b*)(9), 43(2)(4)–(6), 82(3)(*a*), Sched. 3, paras. 1(1)–(4), 3(2), 6(1), 8–11, 14, 15(1), 16; operative on March 1, 1988; implement Council Directives No. 83/477/EEC and No. 76/769/EEC, the latter as amended by Council Directive No. 83/478/EEC.

1849. Dangerous substances

DANGEROUS SUBSTANCES IN HARBOUR AREAS REGULATIONS 1987 (No. 37) [£5·00], made under the Health and Safety at Work etc. Act 1974 (c.37), ss.15(1)–(3)(*a*)(*c*), 4, 5(*b*), 6(*a*)(*b*)(*g*), 43(2)(4)–(6)(9), 80(1)(4), 82(3)(*a*), Sched. 3, paras. 1(1)–(4), 2(1), 3, 4, 6, 7, 9, 11, 12, 13(2), 14, 15(1), 16, 18(*a*), 20, 21(*a*)–(*c*), 22 and the Explosives Act 1875 (c.17), s.97(5); operative on June 1, 1987; provide for the control of carriage, loading, unloading and storage of dangerous substances in harbours and harbour areas.

1850. Employers' liability—protective clothing—whether duty of care extends to instructions and checks. See SMITH *v.* SCOT BOWYERS, §2595.

1851. Explosives and petroleum fees

HEALTH AND SAFETY (EXPLOSIVES AND PETROLEUM FEES) (MODIFICATION) REGULATIONS 1987 (No. 52) [£1·60], made under the Health and Safety at Work etc. Act 1974 (c.37), ss.15(1)(3)(*a*), 43(2)(4)(5)(6)(9), 82(3)(*a*); operative on February 20, 1987; determine fees payable for licences necessary in connection with the storage of explosives and petroleum spirit.

1852. Factory—asbestos dust—protection

[Factories Act 1961 (c.34), s.155(2): Asbestos Regulations 1969, regs. 2(3), 5(1), 8(1).]

The word "process" in the 1961 Act does not encompass a single operation such as the demolition of a kiln.

Some of A.I. Co.'s employees were engaged on the demolition of a kiln at the company's factory. One of them did not use a respirator until a large cloud of dust was raised, when he searched for, and found, a respirator. The dust contained considerable amounts of asbestos fibres. A.I. Co. was charged with contravening regs. 5(1) and 8(1) of the 1969 Regulations and s.155(2) of the 1961 Act by failing to provide approved respiratory equipment. The recorder ruled that "process" meant any activity involving asbestos, and that the definition of asbestos dust did not involve any consideration of the amount of asbestos in the dust or the employee's liability to injury.

On this basis A.I. Co. changed their plea to guilty.

Held, that "process" did not include a single operation such as the demolition of a kiln and the conviction should be quashed (dicta in *Ward* v. *Coltness Iron Co.* [1944] S.C. 318 and *Joyce* v. *Boots Cash Chemists* [1951] C.L.Y. 3934).

R. *v.* A.I. INDUSTRIAL PRODUCTS [1987] I.C.R. 418, C.A.

1853. Fees

HEALTH AND SAFETY (FEES) REGULATIONS 1987 (No. 605) [£2·90], made under the Health and Safety at Work etc. Act 1974 (c.37), ss.11(2)(*d*), 43(2)(4)(5)(6)(9), 82(3)(*a*);

operative on April 29, 1987; provide for new fees chargeable in relation to certain specified industrial processes.

1854. Fencing dangerous machinery—installed machine in process of modification and development—whether obligation to fence.

[Factories Act 1961 (c.34), s.14.]

A machine that was being modified and developed for use in a company's manufacturing process was required to have its dangerous parts securely fenced pursuant to s.14 Factories Act 1961.

D was prosecuted for a contravention of s.14 of the Factories Act 1961 in that a dangerous part of a machine in D's factory was not securely fenced. The machine in question was designed to be used for breaking down rag waste for processing. At the relevant time D was in the process of modifying the machine and testing its suitability for processing glass fibre. D intended to use the machine in its manufacturing process if it proved suitable. It was accepted that the machine had dangerous parts that were not securely fenced. D contended that s.14 of the Act did not apply to the machine as the machine was undergoing development rather than being used in D's manufacturing processes. D was convicted and appealed.

Held, dismissing the appeal, that the phrase "any machinery" in s.14 of the Act was limited so as to exclude machinery that was a product of the manufacturing process and machinery in the process of installation. The machine in question did not fall within either category of machine and in consequence s.14 of the Act applied to it. The machine was in close proximity to D's other manufacturing machines and easily operable. The fact that it was in the process of modification and development for use in D's manufacturing process did not prevent it falling within the definition of "any machinery" in s.14 of the Act (*Parvin* v. *Morton Machine Co.* [1952] C.L.Y. 1378, *Irwin* v. *White, Tomkins and Courage* [1964] C.L.Y. 1512 considered).

T.B.A. INDUSTRIAL PRODUCTS *v.* LAINÉ [1987] I.C.R. 75, D.C.

1855. Gas cylinders

GAS CYLINDERS (PATTERN APPROVAL) REGULATIONS 1987 (No. 116) [80p], made under the European Communities Act 1972 (c.68), s.2(2); operative on March 3, 1987; implement Council Directives 76/767/EEC, 84/525/EEC, 84/526/EEC and 84/527/EEC which relate to the pattern approval of gas cylinders.

1856. Industrial air pollution

CONTROL OF INDUSTRIAL AIR POLLUTION (TRANSFER OF POWERS OF ENFORCEMENT) REGULATIONS 1987 (No. 180) [80p], made under the Health and Safety at Work etc. Act 1974 (c.37), ss.15(1)(3)(*a*), (*c*), 50(1), 82(3)(*a*); operative on April 1, 1987; transfers to the Secretary of State responsibility for enforcing enactments restricting emissions from certain industrial premises.

1857. Insecure washbasin—foreseeability of injury—employee's misconduct.—See ALDRED *v.* NACANCO, §1367.

1858. Prosecution under s.33 of the Health and Safety at Work etc. Act 1974—whether possible to convict under s.36. See WEST CUMBERLAND BY PRODUCTS *v.* D.P.P., §716.

1859. Safe system of work—occupiers liability—duty to independent contractor's employees—demolition of building. See FERGUSON *v.* WELSH, §2612.

1860. Safe system of work—vicarious liability—limitation of liability. *See* McDERMID *v.* NASH DREDGING AND RECLAMATION CO., §2615.

1861. Use of company equipment by others—company's liability

[Health and Safety at Work etc. Act 1974 (c.37), s.3(1).]

Where a cleaning company left their machines in the store they were contracted to clean, and permitted the stores' employees to use them, a director of the company was liable under the Health and Safety at Work Act, s.3(1), where a machine was faulty and killed an employee of the store.

A company had a contract to clean a store on Monday to Friday each week between 7.30 and 9 a.m., and by agreement electrical cleaning machines left at the store by the company could be used by employees of the store at other times. On a Saturday afternoon, an employee of the store used one of the machines which had a damaged cable, and the electric shock killed him. The appellant, a director of the company, was convicted under s.3(1) of the Health and Safety at Work Act 1974 by consenting or conniving at a breach by the company as employer to conduct the company's undertaking in such a way as to ensure that persons not in the company's employment were not thereby exposed to risk to their health and safety. He appealed against the conviction on the ground that the company did not conduct business at the store on Saturdays.

Held, dismissing the appeal, that for the purposes of s.3(1) of the Act, the conduct of the company's undertaking was held to be not confined to the hours when the company's employees were actually in the building carrying out the services of cleaning the store, but included also the manner in which the company left their machines in the store and permitted the store's employees to use them. Accordingly, the appellant had been properly convicted.

R. *v.* MARA [1987] 1 W.L.R. 87, C.A.

HOUSING

1862. Common parts grant

COMMON PARTS GRANT (ELIGIBLE EXPENSE LIMITS) ORDER 1987 (No. 2276) [45p], made under the Housing Act 1985 (c.68) s.498F; operative on February 17, 1988; prescribes the manner of ascertaining the eligible expense limits for the purpose of grants under the 1985 Act.

1863. Compulsory purchase of housing accommodation—relevance of harassment—appropriateness of judicial review during enquiry

[Housing Act 1985 (c.68), Pt. XI.]

In 1984 the housing authority imposed control orders on 5 houses in multiple occupation which were all owned directly or indirectly by the same landlord. There had been complaints of harassment, intimidation, damage, neglect, and frequent changes of ownership by L. A year later, the authority sought to purchase the properties compulsorily. At the inquiry it was stated that the justification for the making of the C.P.O. was based substantially, but not entirely, on the evidence of harassment and intimidation. An environmental health officer was called to give evidence. The evidence was excluded by the inspector as irrelevant. The authority applied for an adjournment so that the ruling could be tested in court before the inquiry continued.

Held, granting the application, that (1) if by reason of the landlord's conduct, a tenant is put in fear, or harrassed, or threatened, if essential services are not being provided it would be a callous misuse of language to say that he was being provided with proper housing accommodation; (2) while the inspector has the discretion to decide what evidence to admit, that discretion must be exercised in accordance with the law: it is not such an exercise to exclude totally evidence on whole issues which are relevant; (3) it would not normally be right for a court to intervene during an inquiry, but in the special circumstances of the case the court was entitled to hear an application for judicial review.

R. *v.* SECRETARY OF STATE FOR THE ENVIRONMENT, *ex p.* ROYAL BOROUGH OF KENSINGTON AND CHELSEA (1987) 19 H.L.R. 161, Taylor J.

1864. Consultation paper. *See* LAW REFORM, §2269.

1865. Control order—appropriate form of challenge

[Housing Act 1985 (c.68), Part XI.]

D owned a house in multiple occupation. P authority served a number of notices requiring works to be carried out, none of which had been complied with. In 1982 the P's began proceedings to restrain D from interfering with the carrying out of repairs by them and these were restored after negotiations had broken down in August 1984. D gave a number of undertakings to the Court to carry out the works, but did not do so in a full and satisfactory manner and in November 1985 the authority made a control order. D argued that this order was a nullity as the conditions of the house were not such as to justify the making of the order. This writ was struck out on the grounds that it was improper to proceed by writ rather than by judicial review. Leave to seek judicial review was refused. D then issued a summons for leave to serve a counterclaim in the 1982 action. In July 1986 this was dismissed on two grounds (1) that the relief sought would be final if granted and (2) that the relief claimed was really a matter for judicial review. D then renewed his application for judicial review, and this was again dismissed, and sought leave, which was granted, to appeal against the decision in July.

Held, dismissing both appeals, that (1) the proposed counterclaim was clearly an attack on the validity of the control order, and was therefore a matter of public law; (2) the appeal procedure for challenging a control order was still available to the defendant; (3) on the facts of the case there was no special reason for proceeding by way of judicial review rather than by statutory procedure.

MAYOR AND BURGESSES OF WANDSWORTH LONDON BOROUGH *v.* ORAKPO (1987) 19 H.L.R. 57, C.A.

1866. Determination of council housing rent—discretion of local authorities—whether reasonable

[Housing Act 1957 (c.56), Part V; Housing Finance Act 1972 (c.47), s.12 and Sched. 1; Housing Act 1985 (c.68), Part XIII and Sched. 14.]

The applicant was a ratepayer who objected to the accounts of the respondent authority for the year ending March 31, 1983. The particular objection was to a sum in the Housing Revenue Account which was described as a "contribution to social expenditure". It was contended that the authority in fixing their rents should have regard to the rent which that accommodation would be capable of producing if let on the open market, and that it was unlawful for the authority to resolve a level of subsidy from the General Rate Fund until the level of rents had been fixed. Finally, it was said that the social expenditure contribution could not be justified under the Housing Finance Act 1972.

Held, dismissing the application, that (1) three principles emerge from the cases: (a) the council have a wide discretion in fixing of rents, (b) they are entitled to approach this as a matter of social policy, (c) they are neither obliged to relate their rents to market rents or make a profit; (2) there was nothing in the documents to show that the authority made the contribution of social expenditure exclusively under para. 10(a) of Sched. 1 to the Housing Finance Act 1972 as alleged; accordingly the social expenditure was lawful.

HEMSTED *v.* LEES AND NORWICH CITY COUNCIL (1986) 18 H.L.R. 424, McCowan J.

1867. Disposal of council estate to private developers—whether sale of part of estate subject to covenants restricting the use of the remainder unlawful—whether tenants properly consulted

[Housing Act 1985 (c.68), ss.32, 105, Part II.]

The applicant was a secure tenant of Fulham Court, an estate divided into nine blocks. All the blocks were in a bad state of repair and the Council resolved first to enter into a joint venture for rehabilitation by a developer with a part buy-back, then, when it became apparent that a single non-profit making organisation could not afford to buy, that the project would have to be phased in order to facilitate rehousing and participation by separate developers. Agreement was agreed in principle for the sale of Block A with a housing association who withdrew when it was proposed that the sale should be subject to restrictive covenants in essence preventing the creation of any new lettings on the remainder of the estate save by long leases at a premium. A commercial developer then put in a bid at a higher price and was willing to be bound by the covenants. The Council resolved that this should be accepted. The applicant sought judicial review of that decision on the grounds of (1) bad faith, (2) lack of proper consultation, (3) failure to have regard to relevant considerations, (4) irrationality. The application was dismissed and the applicant appealed, abandoning the first point. The principal argument put forward was that the covenants imposed an unlawful fetter on the council's powers as a housing authority.

Held, dismissing the appeal, that (1) the Council's policy was consistent with the provision of housing accommodation; a policy which is designed to provide good accommodation for owner occupiers is not any less within the purpose of the Housing Act than the provision of rented accommodation; if the restrictive covenants are necessary for the furtherance of a statutory power then the creation of the covenants is not a fetter; (2) there was appropriate consultation in 1984 which was not "too early"; the identity of the developer is not a matter likely substantially to affect the secure tenants; (3) leave granted to appeal to the House of Lords.

R. *v.* HAMMERSMITH AND FULHAM LONDON BOROUGH, *ex p.* BEDDOWES (1986) 18 H.L.R. 458, C.A.

1868. Grants

GRANTS BY LOCAL HOUSING AUTHORITIES (APPROPRIATE PERCENTAGE AND EXCHEQUER CONTRIBUTIONS) ORDER 1987 (No. 1379) [85p], made under the Housing Act 1985 (c.68), ss.509(1)(2), 517(1)(2); operative on July 31, 1987; prescribes the "appropriate percentage" for the purposes of s.509 of the 1985 Act.

1869. Home insulation

HOMES INSULATION GRANTS ORDER 1987 (No. 2185) [45p], made under the Housing Act 1985 (c.68), s.521(3)(5) and the Housing (Scotland) Act 1987 (c.26), s.252(3)(5); operative on February 1, 1988; specifies the percentage of the cost of work eligible for a grant and the maximum money available by way of a grant under the Homes Insulation Scheme 1987.

1870. Home purchase assistance

HOME PURCHASE ASSISTANCE (PRICE-LIMITS) ORDER 1987 (No. 268) [45p], made under the Housing Act 1985 (c.68), s.445(2)(3), and the Home Purchase Assistance and Housing Corporation Guarantee Act 1978 (c.27), ss.1(2), 2(7); operative on March 27, 1987; prescribes limits on the value of property being purchased for the purposes of home purchase assistance.

HOME PURCHASE ASSISTANCE (RECOGNISED LENDING INSTITUTIONS) ORDER 1987 (No. 1202) [45p], made under the Housing Act 1985 (c.68), s.447(2); operative on July 30, 1987; specifies two additional bodies for the purposes of s.447 of the Housing Act 1985.

HOME PURCHASE ASSISTANCE (RECOGNISED LENDING INSTITUTIONS) (No. 2) ORDER 1987 (No. 1809) [45p], made under the Housing Act 1985 (c.68), s.447(2); operative on November 4, 1987; specifies two bodies for the purposes of s.447 of the 1985 Act.

1871. Homeless persons—intentional homelessness—acquiescence in another's conduct

[Housing Act 1985 (c.68), s.60.]

The applicant lived with C from 1973 onwards. They had seven children. In May 1983 they went to live at premises owned by the respondent authority. C was the tenant. In August 1984 possession proceedings were instituted against C on the grounds of, *inter alia,* arrears of rent, and nuisance and annoyance, in particular the frequent use of a CB radio which interfered with neighbour's TV sets and radios, and the breaking up of machinery in the garden. In effect the complaints were made against the family as a whole. In January 1985 the respondent authority were granted an order for possession, suspended until March 25. The applicant's relationship with C having broken down, the applicant then approached the authority who found that she was to be regarded as having acquiesced in C's behaviour and accordingly that she was homeless intentionally. The evidence before the authority at the time of the decision was that she was only directly responsible for one act of nuisance arising from a bonfire. The applicant sought judicial review of the decision.

Held, dismissing the application, that the authority was entitled to consider whether the applicant had acquiesced in the conduct of the family as a whole, either in the sense of being a party to it or in the sense of doing nothing to prevent it, on the basis of the material before them it could not be said that their decision was unreasonable.

R. *v.* EAST HERTFORDSHIRE DISTRICT COUNCIL, *ex p.* BANNON (1986) 18 H.L.R. 515, Webster J.

1872. Homeless persons—intentional homelessness—appropriate enquiries—ignorance of material fact

[Housing Act 1985 (c.68), s.60.]

The applicants were tenants of a flat. Possession proceedings were brought against them on the grounds of arrears of rent. The tenants counterclaimed alleging disrepair. By the time the claim was heard the arrears were in excess of £3,600. After hearing the solicitor for the landlord and counsel for the tenants the court ordered (1) that the landlord recover possession of the premises, (2) that there be no order on the landlord's claim for arrears and the counterclaim be dismissed and (3) there be no order as to costs. The applicant applied to the respondent authority as homeless who determined that they were homeless intentionally in that they had lost accommodation because of rent arrears and because they had consented to an order for possession. The authority stated that they had taken into account the outstanding repairs, but considered that it would have been reasonable for them to remain in occupation while they were being carried out. The applicants also stated that they were unaware of a relevant fact, namely that they could have stayed in occupation during the works.

Held, dismissing the application, that (1) if it was the case that the state of repair at the premises was relevant to the applicants leaving those premises, it was incumbent on them to make this clear to the authority so that they could investigate; (2) having regard to the size of the arrears, and the prospects of success in the counterclaim it did not appear that the factors put forward by the applicants were relevant to the deliberate decision to permit the order to be made against them; (3) the present case did not fall outside the *Wednesbury* principles.

R. *v.* LONDON BOROUGH OF WANDSWORTH, *ex p.* HENDERSON AND HAYES (1986) 18 H.L.R. 525, McNeill J.

1873. Homeless persons—intentional homelessness—delay in application

[Housing Act 1985 (c.68), Part III.]

The applicant and her daughter left a rented flat after the electricity (which powered all the services, *i.e.* lighting, hot water, heating, and cooking) was disconnected following a dispute with the electricity board. In July 1984, the applicant's husband applied to the authority as homeless and in August 1984 he left the flat. The applicant applied to the authority on three occasions, August 1984, October 1984, and again in May 1985. By a letter dated August 14, 1985 the authority informed the applicant that they considered her to be intentionally homeless because she had vacated the flat when it would have been reasonable to continue to occupy it. By a further letter in September 1985, the authority stated that they had great difficulty in accepting that the applicant had been unaware of and not a party to the husband's decision to relinquish his tenancy. The applicant challenged the decisions.

Held, dismissing the application, that (1) on the facts there were inconsistencies in the applicant's statements which the authority were entitled to take into account; (2) in any event, in view of the history of the case and the fact that the application had not been made until February 28, 1986, relief would be refused on grounds of delay.

R. *v.* HILLINGDON LONDON BOROUGH *ex p.* THOMAS (1987) 19 H.L.R. 197, Taylor J.

1874. Homeless persons—intentional homelessness—whether lifestyle a relevant factor in homelessness decision

[Housing Act 1985 (c.68); Child Care Act 1980 (c.5), s.2(1)(*b*).]

In deciding whether a Bangladeshi applicant for housing under the Housing Act 1985 is intentionally homeless, the local authority is entitled to look at the lifestyle and customs of the Bangladeshi community in this country. S.2(1)(*b*) of the Child Care Act 1980 does not impose a housing obligation on a council where the parents have made themselves intentionally homeless.

R. *v.* TOWER HAMLETS LONDON BOROUGH COUNCIL, *ex p.* MONAF, ALI AND MIAH, *The Times*, August 6, 1987, D.C.

1875. Homeless persons—persons who might reasonably be expected to reside with the applicant

[Housing Act 1985 (c.68), Part III.)]

A, a 74 year old refugee, fled with her family from Vietnam in 1978. The rest of her family, son, daughter in law, and eight grandchildren, came to England in 1980, having lost contact with her. When contact was re-established she came over in July 1985. Before her arrival the rest of her family applied to R to be rehoused, and had indicated that they would be prepared to be split into two groups with the four older children being rehoused separately. On arrival the applicant applied as homeless. In discharge of its duty, R offered her a four bedroomed flat intended for her and the four eldest grandchildren. The offer was rejected, as A contended that the authority were bound to offer accommodation for the whole of the family.

Held, dismissing the application, that (1) the question of who is to be regarded as a person who might reasonably be expected to reside with the applicant is a question of fact for the authority; (2) in determining this it is relevant to consider the nature and ambit of the family, and, in some cases appropriate to have regard to such factors as the practicability of providing accommodation for the whole family, the possibility of splitting the family into smaller groups and the willingness of the family to be so split; (3) it was impossible to brand the decision as perverse, *i.e.* a decision so unreasonable as to verge on absurdity.

R. *v.* LAMBETH LONDON BOROUGH, *ex p.* LY (1987) 19 H.L.R. 51, Simon Brown J.

1876. Homeless persons—priority need

[Housing Act 1985 (c.68), Part III.]

A was a single man of 47 suffering from grand mal epilepsy. In January 1986 having become homeless, he presented himself to the authority with a note from his G.P. stating his illness. This was supplemented by a note from his consultant neurologist. The authority held, having referred the matter to the Medical Officer, that he was not vulnerable, and refused to alter their decision in spite of further medical evidence being put before them. The applicant sought judicial review of the decision.

Held, dismissing the application, that (1) whether grand mal epilepsy makes a person vulnerable must at all times be a question of fact and degree; on the totality of the evidence the conclusion of the respondent authority was one to which a reasonable authority could come; (2) the decision must be taken by the authority and not the

Medical Officer of Health, but on the facts the inference could not be drawn that the authority had simply rubber-stamped the decision of the medical officer.

R. *v.* WANDSWORTH BOROUGH COUNCIL, *ex p.* BANBURY (1987) 19 H.L.R. 76, Russell J.

1877. Homeless persons—settled accommodation—act or omission in good faith

[Housing Act 1985 (c.68), Part III, s.60(3).]

The applicant had a protected shorthold tenancy in Dorset for a term of six months which could be extended for up to five years. Towards the end of the tenancy, the landlords wrote offering her a further year and stating that the offer for the extended tenancy would only remain open up to and including "June 10, next". The applicant misunderstood the effect of the letter believing that the extension would continue until June 10, 1986 (and not 1985). She decided to take up the offer but did so on June 17, after having ascertained that she would be eligible for housing benefit. The landlords were no longer prepared to extend the lease. The applicant applied to the respondent authority as homeless who found her intentionally homeless for knowingly allowing the use of her accommodation to come to an end by not taking up the landlord's offer. The applicant sought judicial review of the decision.

Held, granting the application, that (1) the court would not interfere with the finding that the protected shorthold tenancy was settled accommodation; (2) in addressing the issue of whether the omission to take up the offer of the extended lease was deliberate, the authority had failed to bear in mind that under the terms of the statute an act or omission in good faith on the part of a person unaware of a relevant fact was not to be regarded as deliberate; on the facts the authority's decision could not be supported.

R. *v.* CHRISTCHURCH BOROUGH COUNCIL, *ex p.* CONWAY (1987) 19 H.L.R. 238, Taylor J.

1878. Homeless persons—short life accommodation—priority need—whether discharge of duty to secure accommodation

[Housing Act 1985 (c.68), ss.65, 69.]

The applicant lived in short life accommodation, *i.e.* accommodation pending redevelopment or major improvement by the authority. The authority intended to carry out major works in or about August 1985, which works required vacant possession. In May 1985 there was a fire which made the flat uninhabitable. The authority then made available to the applicant another short life property for three months. The applicant applied to the authority as homeless after having moved into that accommodation. The authority stated that they had discharged their duty under the Act by extending the licence to occupy the second premises until November 1985. The authority did not accept that its duty was to secure that accommodation became available permanently or indefinitely. The applicant sought to challenge the decision.

Held, granting the application, that the duty under s.65(3) is a lesser duty than under s.65(2); the duties have to be contrasted; in s.65(3) specific attention is required to the period provided; no such qualification is provided in s.65(2) and the applicant was entitled to be provided with accommodation indefinite in length.

R. *v.* CAMDEN LONDON BOROUGH, *ex p.* WAIT (1986) 18 H.L.R. 434, McCowan J.

1879. Homeless persons—temporary accommodation—whether premises "occupied" by families

[Housing Act 1961 (c.65), ss.15(1), 19(1).]

Homeless families living temporarily in premises whilst awaiting rehousing are occupants of the premises for the purposes of ss.15(1) and 19(1) of the Housing Act 1961.

T owned several premises which were let out as furnished rooms on a bed and breakfast basis from day to day. Nearly all the residents at the various premises were homeless families accommodated by arrangement with principally Tower Hamlets London Borough Council. The accommodation was provided by the Tower Hamlets Council in compliance with their duties under the Housing (Homeless Persons) Act 1977. The homeless families resided at the premises temporarily whilst awaiting the provision of permanent housing. The average length of stay was six months. Hackney London Borough Council formed the view that the premises were in multiple occupation and that the condition of the various premises was not reasonably suitable for the number of persons in occupation. Hackney Council served notices on T under s.19(1) of the Housing Act 1961 to limit the number of persons occupying the premises. T applied for judicial review by way of certiorari to quash the notices. T's application was rejected and T appealed. T contended that having regard to the transitory and temporary nature of the homeless families' residence at the various premises they could not be described as occupants for the purposes of s.15(1) and s.19(1) Housing Act 1961.

Held, dismissing the appeal, that the point raised by T was unarguable. It would be a misuse of language to say that the families were not occupying the premises. The premises were the only residences of the families in question and their homes until other permanent accommodation could be made available (*Silbers* v. *Southwark London Borough Council* [1978] C.L.Y. 1569, *Simmons* v. *Pizzey* [1977] C.L.Y. 1520 considered).

R. *v.* HACKNEY LONDON BOROUGH COUNCIL, *ex p.* THRASYVOULOU (1986) 84 L.G.R. 823, C.A.

1880. Homeless persons—whether accommodation offered by local authority suitable—whether offer held open for a reasonable time

[Housing Act 1985 (c.68), s.65(2).]

The applicant was a young single mother. She applied to the authority as homeless, and was offered accommodation consisting of a two bedroomed maisonette on the eighth and ninth floors of a tower block. It was accepted that the premises required redecoration for which a £200 allowance was made. The applicant was shocked and distressed when she visited the premises, and was very concerned by what she saw as a danger to her young children. On January 23 the respondents wrote again to the applicant saying that they had re-inspected, that they remained of the view that the premises were fit for letting and that she had until January 28 to make up her mind. On January 29 the applicant contacted solicitors, who wrote to the authority on February 8, setting out her objections. The applicant sought judicial review challenging the sufficiency of the offer, or, alternatively, on the ground that she was not given an adequate opportunity to consider it.

Held, dismissing the application, that (1) premises offered by way of discharge of the authority's duty under the 1985 Act need only be premises properly so describable even if in certain respects they were unfit, inadequate or otherwise unsuitable; and (2) that while the duty to provide accommodation carries with it a duty that the accommodation should remain available for a reasonable time and that while regard should be had to all the circumstances it was not permissible to have regard to the unsuitability of the offer to determine the question; the court would only intervene on the basis that the time allowed was absurd, or perversely inadequate.

R. *v.* LONDON BOROUGH OF WANDSWORTH, *ex p.* LINDSAY (1986) 18 H.L.R. 502, Simon Brown J.

1881. Homelessness—discharge of duty—appropriate forum of challenge

[Housing Act 1985 (c.68), Pt. III; Housing Act 1980 (c.51), Sched. 3.]

D became homeless and applied to the authority under the Housing Act. Pending enquiries she was granted a licence of a flat. The authority then concluded that she was homeless, in priority need and not intentionally homeless. They gave her notice to quit in respect of the flat and offered her alternative accommodation. D refused to move from the flat and the authority issued proceedings. At trial, it was accepted that she did not have a secure tenancy of the flat, and D then sought leave to counterclaim that the accommodation offered by the authority was not suitable. The assistant recorder refused leave to introduce the counterclaim and made an order for possession. D appealed.

Held, dismissing the appeal, that (1) it was not necessary to decide whether or not D had a tenancy; (2) once the authority had reached the decision to rehouse her a private right was created which she was entitled to pursue by way of a separate action; in such an action it was simply a matter for the court to determine whether or not it had been fulfilled. In the present case the Assistant Recorder was right to reject the very late counterclaim.

SOUTH HOLLAND DISTRICT COUNCIL *v.* KEYTE (1985) 19 H.L.R. 97, C.A.

1882. Housing Act 1985, s.369(5)—two separate offences

[Housing Act 1985 (c.68), s.369(5).]

S.369(5) of the Housing Act 1985 creates two separate offences—those of (i) knowingly, and (ii) without reasonable excuse, failing to comply with a particular regulation.

WANDSWORTH LONDON BOROUGH COUNCIL *v.* SPARLING, *The Times,* November 21, 1987, D.C.

1883. Housing and Planning Act 1986—commencement

HOUSING AND PLANNING ACT 1986 (COMMENCEMENT No. 3) ORDER 1987 (No. 304 (C.7)) [45p], made under the Housing and Planning Act 1986 (c.63), s.57(2); brings into force on March 2, 1987, s.49 insofar as it relates to Sched. 11, para. 8 to the 1986 Act. (This Order supersedes S.I. 1987 No. 178 (C.3)).

HOUSING AND PLANNING ACT 1986 (COMMENCEMENT No. 4) ORDER 1987 (No. 348 (C.9)) [80p], made under the Housing and Planning Act 1986, s.57(2); brings into force on April 1, 1987 s.40 of, and Sched. 9, Pt. I, to the 1986 Act.

HOUSING AND PLANNING ACT 1986 (COMMENCEMENT No. 5) ORDER 1987 (No. 754 (C.20)) [45p], made under the Housing and Planning Act 1986, s.57(2); brings s.9 of the 1986 Act into force on May 13, 1987.

HOUSING AND PLANNING ACT 1986 (COMMENCEMENT No. 6) ORDER 1987 (No. 1554 (C.47)) [45p], made under the Housing and Planning Act 1986, s.57(2); s.24(1), as it relates to Sched. 5, para. 8 of the Act, comes into force on September 22, 1987.

HOUSING AND PLANNING ACT 1986 (COMMENCEMENT No. 8) ORDER 1987 (No. 1759 (C.53)) [85p], made under the Housing and Planning Act 1986, s.57(2); brings into force on November 2, 1987 ss.25, 41(1)(2)(3), 49(1) (in part), 49(2) (in part) of the 1986 Act.

HOUSING AND PLANNING ACT 1986 (COMMENCEMENT No. 9) ORDER 1987 (No. 1939 (C.58)) [85p], made under the Housing and Planning Act 1986, s.57(2); brings into force on December 11, 1987 ss.18 (in part) and 24(3) (in part) of the 1986 Act.

HOUSING AND PLANNING ACT 1986 (COMMENCEMENT No. 10) ORDER 1987 (No. 2277 (C.71)) [45p], made under the Housing and Planning Act 1986, s.57(2), brings into force on February 17, 1988, s.15 of and Sched. 5, para. 9 to the Housing and Planning Act 1986.

1884. Housing benefit

HOUSING BENEFIT (GENERAL) REGULATIONS 1987 (No. 1971) [£6·80], made under the Social Security Act 1986 (c.50), ss.20(1)(*c*), (8), (11) and (12), 21(5)–(7), 22, 28(2) and (5), 29, 51(1)(*a*)–(*c*), (*g*), (*k*) and (*m*), and the Social Security Act 1975 (c.14), s.166(1)–(3A); operative on April 1, 1988, and on April 4, 1988; provide for matters concerning entitlement to, the amount of and the claiming and payment of housing benefit.

HOUSING BENEFIT (IMPLEMENTATION SUBSIDY), ORDER 1987 (No. 1910) [85p], made under the Social Security Act 1986, s.30(4) and the Social Security Act 1975, s.166(1)–(3); operative on December 7, 1987; specifies the manner in which the subsidy payable to authorities implementing the housing benefit scheme under the 1986 Act is to be calculated.

HOUSING BENEFIT (TRANSITIONAL) REGULATIONS 1987 (No. 1972) [£1·30], made under the Social Security Act 1986, ss.84(1), 89(1); operative on December 31, 1987; make transitional provision in connection with the new statutory scheme for the granting of rent and rate rebates and rent allowances introduced in the 1986 Act.

HOUSING BENEFITS (AMENDMENT) REGULATIONS 1987 (No. 1440) [85p], made under the Social Security Act 1975 (c. 14), s. 166(2) and (3); operative on September 1, 1987; amend S.I. 1985 No. 677 in relation to students.

HOUSING BENEFITS (SUBSIDY) ORDER 1987 (No. 1805) [85p], made under the Social Security and Housing Benefits Act 1982 (c.24), s.32(2); operative on November 16, 1987; sets out the manner in which the subsidy payable under s.32 of the 1982 Act to authorities who grant rate and rent rebates or allowances is to be calculated for the financial year 1987/88.

1885. Housing benefit—availability of alternative cheaper accommodation

[Housing Benefit Regulations 1985 (S.I. 1985 No. 677), regs 9, 20.]

The applicant claimant was a gipsy who owned her own caravan. She found a site for the caravan at a cost of £15·00 per week. The authority at first paid the whole amount by way of housing benefit, but then reduced it to £7·00 per week. The applicant appealed to the Housing Benefit Review Board who accepted that other possible sites were not available to the applicant for a number of reasons. The Board increased the amount of benefit from £7·00 to £9·00 per week and stated that while they accepted that the applicant would have great difficulty in finding accommodation in the immediate area, she could move outside that area as she owned a caravan, and that it would not be unreasonable for her to move if necessary. The applicant sought judicial review of this decision and a declaration that there was no other place to which she could reasonably be expected to move.

Held, granting the application, that (1) it was not reasonable to expect the applicant to seek alternative cheaper accommodation having regard to the evidence of non-availability to suitable alternative accommodation; (2) it is not necessary for an authority to be able to identify specific accommodation if they are satisfied that there is such accommodation, but in the present case there was nowhere she could have gone; (3) regard was wrongly had to sites outside the authority's area; the availability of cheaper accommodation outside the area was immaterial.

R. *v.* HOUSING BENEFIT REVIEW BOARD OF SOUTH HEREFORDSHIRE DISTRICT COUNCIL, *ex p.* SMITH (1987) 19 H.L.R. 217, McCullough J.

1886. Housing benefit—meaning of income—drawings made on overdraft facility

[Housing Benefit Regulations 1985 (S.I. 1985 No. 677.]

The applicant sought housing benefit in relation to their rates for the year 1984–1985. In August 1985, the applicant moved from one house, which he sold for £39,000, to another which he purchased with £75,000 with the help of a loan of £40,000 from a bank. In 1985 the applicant had set up a business which did not make any profits, but by drawing on the overdraft facility at the bank, secured against the business property, the applicant was able to meet his day-to-day expenses. He also received rent from letting a flat over the business premises. The Housing Benefit Review Board held, following an application for housing benefit for the rates on the applicant's home, that (a) they would not accept the applicant's accounts because they were uncertified; (b) the rent from the flat was income and could not be set against the business losses and (c) they were entitled to conclude that the drawings on the overdraft facility for the day-to-day living expenses were income. The applicant sought judicial review of the decision.

Held, dismissing the application, that (1) it is a question of fact in each case whether withdrawals from an account are income: in this case money regularly drawn from a loan facility provided by a bank could properly be regarded as income; (2) the question is essentially whether as a fact the applicant can be said to have an income when he is the possessor of substantial capital and chooses to use it so that while it produces no immediate profit, it secures for him the payment of sums of money on a regular basis for day-to-day expenses.

R. *v.* WEST DORSET DISTRICT COUNCIL, *ex p.* POUPARD (1987) 19 H.L.R. 254, Macpherson J.

1887. Housing benefit—retrospective payments

[Housing Benefit Regulations 1985 (S.I. 1985 No. 677), reg. 28(2)(*b*).]

In exceptional circumstances, a local housing authority can consider retrospective payments up to 12 months prior to the date of the claim.

R. *v.* SECRETARY OF STATE FOR SOCIAL SERVICES, *ex p.* CYNON VALLEY BOROUGH COUNCIL, *The Times,* November 13, 1987, D.C.

1888. Housing benefit—strike pay received during benefit period—amount of strike pay known—assessment of income

[Housing Benefits Regulations 1982 (S.I. 1982 No. 1124), reg. 14.]

Where the actual income of an applicant for housing benefit was known the local authority were not entitled to look at his income before or after the benefit period in assessing his income during the benefit period.

S went on strike for three weeks in November and December 1986 and applied to Ealing London Borough Council for housing benefit at the beginning of the strike. During the strike S received £22·50 per week strike pay. S's total income for November and December was approximately £2,000. After the strike had finished S's application was rejected. The matter was referred to the Council's Review Board at S's request. The Council's decision was upheld on the ground that it was reasonable to take into account S's income for November and December in its assessment of income for the benefit period under reg. 14(4) of the Housing Benefits Regulations 1982. S applied for judicial review seeking to quash the Review Board's decision.

Held, quashing the decision, that reg. 14 provided for the assessment of what was likely to be the income of the applicant during the benefit period. It did not provide for the assessment of what income or resources the applicant ought to have available having regard to his past or future earnings. As the Review Board knew what S's income was for the benefit period the question of assessing his likely income did not arise. Reg. 14(4) did not give the Council or the Review Board power to have regard to the applicant's income before and after the benefit period once his actual income for the benefit period was known.

R. *v.* EALING LONDON BOROUGH COUNCIL HOUSING BENEFIT REVIEW BOARD, *ex p.* SAVILLE (1986) 84 L.G.R. 842, Kennedy J.

1889. Housing benefit—student—student not in receipt of grant

[Social Security and Housing Benefits Act 1982 (c.24), s.28(1); Housing Benefit Regulations 1985 (S.I. 1985 No. 677), Sched. 1A, para. 10; Housing Benefit Amendment (No. 3) Regulations 1986 (S.I. 1986 No. 1009), para. 10.]

The amendment made by the 1986 regulations was not made *ultra vires* the Act, and so a non grant-aided student was subject to the same constraints as a grant-aided student in obtaining housing benefit.

R. *v.* KENSINGTON AND CHELSEA LONDON BOROUGH COUNCIL *ex p.* WOOLRICH, *The Times,* September 1, 1987, Kennedy J.

1890. Housing improvement grant—satisfaction with works—date of certification. See R. *v.* WESTMINSTER CITY COUNCIL *ex p.* HAZAN, §2359.

1891. Housing (Scotland) Act 1987 (c.26)

This Act consolidates with amendments to give effect to recommendations of the Scottish Law Commission, certain enactments relting to housing in Scotland.

The Act received the Royal Assent on May 15, 1987, and comes into force three months from that date.

The Act extends to Scotland only.

1892. Loss of enjoyment of flat due to damp and infestation—damages—assessment. See DAMAGES, §1127.

1893. Mobile homes—construction of agreement—ascertainment of pitch fee

[Mobile Homes Act 1975 (c.49).]

S was the tenant of a mobile home site. In 1983 he was served with a new statement containing the express terms of the agreement between the parties, to which he did not object. The annual review of the pitch fee would be made having regard, as before to the Index of Retail Prices, and to sums expended by the owner for the benefit of the occupiers of the park and, for the first time, to any other relevant factors including the effect of legislation applicable to the operation of the park. In August 1983 WA purported to increase the pitch fee from £564 p.a. to £705·12 p.a. S applied to the county court for a declaration that the fee was excessive. The judge determined that the pitch fee should only be increased to take into account the R.P.I. increase. He refused to take into account pitch fees on other sites and held that on its true construction these were excluded by the pitch fee review clause. WA appealed.

Held, dismissing the appeal, (1) in determining a dispute over pitch fees the court is acting as an arbitrator, and can decide the figures; (2) the words 'applicable to the operation of the park' should be construed as applying to the whole phrase and are not limited only to the words 'the effect of the legislation'; (3) the exercise of putting before the court detailed evidence of rent on allegedly comparable sites does not provide evidence of relevant factors applicable to the operation of the park.

STROUD *v.* WEIR ASSOCIATES, (1987) 19 H.L.R. 151, C.A.

1894. Mortgage indemnity—recognised bodies

MORTGAGE INDEMNITY (RECOGNISED BODIES) (No. 2) ORDER 1987 (No. 1811) [45p], made under the Housing Act 1985 (c.68), s.444(1); operative on November 4, 1987; specifies three bodies for the purposes of s.444 of the 1985 Act.

1895. Order for sale of property—council house—whether exemption from repayment of discount. See R. *v.* RUSHMOOR BOROUGH COUNCIL, *ex p.* BARRETT, §1772.

1896. Priority need—vulnerability—medical officer's opinion

[Housing Act 1985 (c.68), s.59(1)(*c*)]

Priority need for rehousing due to "vulnerability" on account of age, mental illness, handicap, physical disability or other special reason must be identified by regard to all relevant factors, and not just on the basis of the opinion of a medical officer who has neither seen nor examined the applicant.

R. *v.* LAMBETH LONDON BOROUGH COUNCIL, *ex p.* CARROLL, *The Guardian,* October 8, 1987, Webster J.

1897. Property in multiple occupation—provision of means of escape from fire—notice to provide means of escape

[Housing Act 1961 (c.65), ss.17(1)(*a*), (*c*); Housing Act 1980 (c.51), s.147, Sched. 24.]

For the purpose of deciding whether the proposed works were reasonable or not, the date at which reasonableness fell to be considered was the date of the appeal hearing in the county court (*Maurice (Leslie) & Co.* v. *Willesden Corporation* [1953] C.L.Y. 1609 considered).

BERG *v.* TRAFFORD BOROUGH COUNCIL, *The Times,* July 14, 1987, C.A.

1898. Rent increase—considerations—discretion of local authority. See WANDSWORTH LONDON BOROUGH COUNCIL *v.* WINDER (NO. 2) §2385.

1899. Repairs grants—conditions—whether local authority entitled to impose conditions

[Housing Act 1985 (c.68), ss.503, 504.]

The applicant purchased the freehold of premises and applied to the authority for four mandatory repairs grants, one relating to the flat on each floor. At the time of the application, the authority insisted that he complete certificates of availability for letting in relation to each grant application. The applicant did so on a without prejudice basis, contending that he was not required to do so which contention the authority then accepted. The grants were then approved subject to conditions under ss.503 and 504 of the Housing Act 1985 that the flats should be let on regulated tenancies or restricted contracts. The applicant sought judicial review to challenge the additional conditions on the ground that they could not be imposed where no certificate of future occupation is required.

Held, dismissing the application, that ss.503 and 504 of the Housing Act 1985 contain their own complete and general code as to when the s.504 conditions may be imposed; if the exclusion of those sections in mandatory repair cases had been intended, it would have been expressly stated; accordingly the respondent authority were entitled to impose the conditions under s.504.

R. *v.* CAMDEN LONDON BOROUGH COUNCIL, *ex p.* CHRISTEY (1987) 19 H.L.R. 420, Macpherson J.

1900. Right to buy

HOUSING (EXTENSION OF RIGHT TO BUY) ORDER 1987 (No. 1732) [£2·60], made under the Housing Act 1985 (c.68), s.171; operative on October 23, 1987; extends the right to buy in specified cases by a secure tenant.

HOUSING (RIGHT TO BUY) (PRIORITY OF CHARGES) ORDER 1987 (No. 1203) [45p], made under the Housing Act 1985 (c.68), s.156(4); operative on July 30, 1987; specifies five additional bodies for the purposes of s.156(4) of the Housing Act 1985.

HOUSING (RIGHT TO BUY) (PRIORITY OF CHARGES) (No. 2) ORDER 1987 (No. 1810) [45p], made under the Housing Act 1985, s.156(4); operative on November 4, 1987; specifies two bodies for the purposes of s.156(4) of the 1985 Act.

1901. Secure tenancy—abandonment—whether applicant intentionally homeless

[Housing Act 1985 (c.68), ss.60, 79, 81, 82, 83, 84, Sched. 2.]

In August 1981 the respondent authority granted the applicant a secure tenancy. In March 1982 she married, and in August 1983 her husband left her. A few days after this, men unknown to the applicant came to the house and made threats to the effect that if her husband did not repay money owed to them, they would hurt her and her child. As a result of these threats the applicant put her furniture into store and stayed with a relative. In September 1983 the authority concluded that she had left, and changed the locks. In December 1983 the applicant applied to the authority as homeless. In answer to a question she stated that her tenancy had ceased in September 1983. In January 1984 she was advised that she was homeless intentionally. In November 1984 proceedings were instituted for judicial review seeking a declaration that she remained a secure tenant of the premises and would remain so until a possession order was made and quashing the respondent's decision that she was intentionally homeless.

Held, dismissing the application, that (1) it is not the case that a secure tenancy can only cease to be secure if a possession order is made: if a tenant ceases to occupy the dwelling house as an only or principal home the tenant condition ceases to be satisfied; (2) on the facts it was impossible to say that the respondent authority misdirected itself in law.

R. *v.* LONDON BOROUGH OF CROYDON, *ex p.* TOTH (1986) 18 H.L.R. 493, Simon Brown J.

1901a. Secure tenancy—proposed variation by local authority—whether proposal amounted to a variation

[Housing Act 1980 (c.51), ss.40, 41.]

Where a local authority made detailed draft proposals for a new tenancy agreement but no formal offer or acceptance was entered into there was no variation of the original agreement.

PALMER *v.* SANDWELL METROPOLITAN BOROUGH, *The Times,* October 12, 1987 C.A.

1902. Secure tenancy—reasonableness of possession order—offer of 'rent direct'

[Housing Act 1985 (c.68), s.84 and Sched. 2.]

D was the secure tenant of a flat. As a result of a psychiatric illness he became unable to manage his affairs, and fell into arrears. When he finally obtained benefit, he spent it on food rather than on paying the rent. At the first hearing for possession, D appeared in person. The hearing was adjourned to allow D to consult a solicitor from the Law Centre. An order for possession was made suspended on terms that D pay off the arrears within two months. D appealed. The solicitor's note of what had occurred in court stated that she had asked the judge to adjourn the case to allow medical evidence to be called, and that she had suggested that the Law Centre would pay the rent direct to the landlords.

Held, allowing the appeal, (1) it could not be said that the judge had erred in refusing to allow an adjournment for medical evidence: he had taken D's medical condition into account and was entitled to take the view that further evidence would not help him; (2) it did not appear that the judge had taken into account the fact that the Law Centre would ensure the payment of rent direct. The case would be remitted to the county court for reconsideration.

SECOND W.R.V.S. HOUSING SOCIETY *v.* BLAIR (1986) 19 H.L.R. 104 C.A.

1903. Secure tenancy—suspended possession order—non-compliance with terms

[Housing Act 1985 (c.68), s.82(2).]

Where T failed to comply with the terms of a suspended possession order, the order became effective and the tenancy was terminated from that moment (*Sheerin* v. *Brand* [1956] 1 Q.B. 403 considered.)

THOMPSON *v.* ELMBRIDGE BOROUGH COUNCIL (1987) 84 L.S.Gaz. 2456, C.A.

1904. Setting aside possession order—effect on executed warrant

[Housing Act 1985 (c.68), s.85(2), County Court Rules Ord. 37.]

An order was made for recovery forthwith of premises, together with a judgment for arrears of rent and costs amounting to some £415. It was a term of the order that the sums should be paid on or before May 12, 1986. The amount was paid in full into court on that day. On the following day a warrant for possession was issued, and was served on June 12. The tenant's solicitors were informed of this on June 11 and proposed to apply the next day to set aside judgment and to have warrant suspended. On the morning of June 12, the bailiffs entered and changed the locks. In the afternoon the assistant recorder made an order setting aside the judgment and giving the tenant leave to defend. He also set aside the warrant for possession. The landlords applied to the recorder for leave to appeal, particularly with regard to the warrant for possession. He refused and the landlords appealed.

Held, dismissing the appeal, under C.C.R., Ord. 37, r.8(3) where a judgment or order is set aside, then any extension that has been issued shall cease to have effect, unless the court otherwise orders; s.85(2) of the Housing Act 1985 was not intended to cover the situation after an order had been executed; the recorder had full power to set aside the warrant for possession.

GOVERNORS OF THE PEABODY DONATION FUND *v.* HAY (1986) 19 H.L.R. 145, C.A.

1905. Statutory repairing notice—whether properly served—whether a flat a "house"

[Housing Act 1957 (c.56), s.9(1A).]

Dover Mansions is a block of 20 flats. The block was in disrepair and substantial repairs were needed particularly to the common parts. Notices were served by the authority, one in respect of each flat. Attached to each notice was a schedule divided into two parts. Part A specified works of internal repair relating to the particular flat. Part B specified external works of repair to the whole block and internal works to the shared common parts. Applications were then made for mandatory repairs grants. The authority took fresh legal advice as to the validity of the notices as a result of which they refused to pay the grants. The applicant landlords sought judicial review to compel the authority to pay the grants. In the High Court, Hodgson J. dismissed the application. The applicants appealed.

Held, dismissing the appeal, that (1) the individual flats in the building were not each a house; a house in its ordinary sense means a separate building; (2) a notice under s.9(1A) of the Housing Act 1957 in relation to works on the roof and common parts cannot be served on the leaseholder of a flat as an individual; the premises a person can be required to repair are those included in his demise and no more; (3) accordingly, the applicants were not entitled to an order requiring the payment of the mandatory grants.

R. *v.* LAMBETH LONDON BOROUGH, *ex p.* CLAYHOPE PROPERTIES (1987) 19 H.L.R. 426, C.A.

1906. Vulnerability—whether an epileptic vulnerable

[Housing Act 1985 (c.68), s.59(1)(*c*).]

"Vulnerable" in s.59(1)(*c*) of the Housing Act 1985 means "vulnerable in a housing context". The mere fact that an applicant is an epileptic does not qualify him as vulnerable (*R.* v. *Waveney District Council, ex p. Bowers* [1982] C.L.Y. 1467 and *R.* v. *Bath City Council, ex p. Sangermano* [1985] C.L.Y. 1631 applied).

R. *v.* REIGATE AND BANSTEAD BOROUGH COUNCIL, *ex p.* DI DOMENICO, *The Independent,* October 21, 1987, Mann J.

1907. Waiting list application—duty to give reasonable preference in selection of tenants to certain categories—whether discretion fettered

[Housing Act 1985 (c.68), ss.22, 106.]

A left premises of which she was a secure joint tenant because of the breakdown of the relationship with her cohabitant. She applied to R for housing who would not place her on their waiting list until she gave up her joint secure tenancy as it was council policy not to accept anyone on the waiting list who had an interest in council accommodation elsewhere. A's solicitors wrote to R saying this was not possible since, although A had a custody order in her favour of the two children, her cohabitant had actual care of the older child. In April 1985 leave to bring proceedings for judicial review was granted to A, and following this R decided to add her name to the waiting list on receipt of a valid application. On receipt of that application R resolved that no applicant on the waiting list be given housing whilst holding a sole or joint tenancy of council accommodation unless (a) a reciprocal agreement could be reached with that other authority whereby the council may nominate its own tenant for rehousing or (b) the case is a priority need case within Part III of the Housing Act 1985 and that as neither these exceptions applied, no further consideration would be given to A's application. A proceeded with application for judicial review.

Held, granting the application, that R's policy would be quashed as it constituted a rule rather than a general approach subject to exceptions; the authority had failed to apply their minds to the particular problems which the applicant gave for not being able to relinquish her interest in the secure tenancy.

R. *v.* CANTERBURY CITY COUNCIL, *ex p.* GILLESPIE, (1987) 19 H.L.R. 7, Simon Brown J.

HUMAN RIGHTS

1908. Administrative measures—civil rights affected—judicial hearing

Mr. Pudas's transport licence was revoked by the County Administrative Board of Norrbotten, North Sweden. His appeals to the Ministry of Transport were refused. Mr. Boden was part-owner of some properties which his Swedish local Council wished to develop. The Council applied to the Government for an expropriation permit for, *inter alia*, these properties. Despite Mr. Boden's objections, the Government issued the permit. Mr. Pudas and Mr. Boden complained to the European Commission of Human Rights that Sweden had violated Art. 6 of the European Convention of Human Rights as they were not entitled to bring their disputes concerning administrative measures before a Court in Sweden.

Held, that (1) Sweden had violated Art. 6(1) of the Convention by (i) not providing Mr. Pudas with the opportunity of having the revocation of his transport licence heard by a Court; and (ii) not giving Mr. Boden the opportunity of challenging the expropriation permit before a Court. The right to a fair trial, as provided for in Art. 6 of the Convention, was violated if people were not entitled to bring before a Court disputes concerning administrative measures which directly affected their civil rights; (2) Mr. Pudas was awarded compensation, but none was considered appropriate in Mr. Boden's case as he had regained his interest in the properties in question pursuant to an agreement with the Council.

PUDAS *v.* SWEDEN (No. 12/1986/110/158); BODEN *v.* SWEDEN (No. 18/1986/116/164), *The Times*, November 13, 1987, European Ct. of Human Rights.

1909. Commission for Racial Equality—annual report

The Commission for Racial Equality has published its tenth Annual Report (ISBN 0 907920 83 7) [£1·00].

1910. Data protection

DATA PROTECTION (FEES) REGULATIONS 1987 (No. 272) [45p], made under the Data Protection Act 1984 (c.35), ss.8(5), 40(7), 41; operative on March 16, 1987; prescribe a fee of £22 for a renewal of an application for registration under the 1984 Act.

DATA PROTECTION (FEES) (No. 2) REGULATIONS 1987 (No. 1304) [45p], made under the Data Protection Act 1984, ss.6(7), 8(5), 40(7) and 41; operative on November 11, 1987; increase from £22 to £40 the fee which is to accompany an application to the Data Protection Registrar for registration or for the renewal of registration under the Data Protection Act 1984.

DATA PROTECTION (FUNCTIONS OF DESIGNATED AUTHORITY) ORDER 1987 (No. 2028) [85p], made under the Data Protection Act 1984, s.37; operative on January 1,

1988; specifies functions to be discharged by the Data Protection Registrar as the designated authority for the purposes of the Convention for the Protection of Individuals with regard to Automatic Processing of Personal Date.

DATA PROTECTION (MISCELLANEOUS SUBJECT ACCESS EXEMPTIONS) ORDER 1987 (No. 1906) [85p], made under the Data Protection Act 1984, ss.34(2), 40(2); operative on November 11, 1987; provide for the exemption from the subject access provisions of the Act of data the disclosure of which is prohibited or restricted by certain enactments and subordinate instruments.

DATA PROTECTION (REGULATION OF FINANCIAL SERVICES ETC.) (SUBJECT ACCESS EXEMPTION) ORDER 1987 (No. 1905) [£2·60], made under the Data Protection Act 1984, s.30(2) and the Financial Services Act 1986 (c.60), s.190; operative on November 11, 1987; designates functions for the purposes of s.30 of the 1984 Act thereby exempting those functions from the subject access provisions of the Act.

DATA PROTECTION (SUBJECT ACCESS) (FEES) REGULATIONS 1987 (No. 1507) [45p], made under the Data Protection Act 1984, s.21(2), 41; operative on November 11, 1987; prescribes a maximum fee of £10 for the supply of information in response to a request under s.21 of the 1984 Act.

DATA PROTECTION (SUBJECT ACCESS MODIFICATION) (HEALTH) ORDER 1987 (No. 1903) [£1·30], made under the Data Protection Act 1984, s.29(1)(3); operative on November 11, 1987; provides for the partial exemption from the provisions of the 1984 Act of data relating to the physical or mental health of the data subject.

DATA PROTECTION (SUBJECT ACCESS MODIFICATION) (SOCIAL WORK) ORDER 1987 (No. 1904) [£1·30], made under the Data Protection Act 1984, s.29(1)–(3); operative on November 11, 1987; provides for the partial exemption from the provisions of the 1984 Act of data likely to prejudice the carrying out of social work.

1911. Deprivation of liberty—deportation

Italy had requested the extradition of Mr. Bozano from France. That request received a negative ruling from the Limoges Court of Appeal. Mr. Bozano was also charged in France with offences allegedly committed in France. One evening he was served with a deportation order made several weeks earlier and was taken forcibly by the French police to the Swiss border, where he was handed over to the Swiss police. He was extradited from Switzerland to Italy.

Held, that France had violated Art. 5(1) of the European Convention of Human Rights. Mr. Bozano's deprivation of liberty was neither "lawful" within the meaning of Art. 5(1)(*f*), nor compatible with the "right to security of person". Depriving Mr. Bozano of his liberty in a forcible way without giving him the opportunity of even choosing the frontier over which he might be expelled, nor giving him the opportunity to speak to his wife or his lawyer, amounted in fact to a disguised form of extradition designed to circumvent the negative ruling of the Limoges Court of Appeal. It was not "detention" in the ordinary course of action taken with a view to deportation.

BOZANO *v.* FRANCE (No. 5/985/91/138), *The Times,* January 7, 1987, European Court of Human Rights.

1912. Divorce—respect for family life

Mr. Johnston (the first applicant) was married in Ireland in 1952. Since 1971 he had lived with the second applicant, who had borne him a daughter (the third applicant). Mr. Johnston could not get a divorce in Ireland so as to enable him to marry the second applicant because of the prohibition of divorce contained in the Irish Constitution. The applicants argued, *inter alia,* that the non-availability of divorce under Irish law violated the European Convention of Human Rights and that the illegitimate status of the third applicant under Irish law violated Art. 8 of the Convention.

Held, that (1) the non-availability of divorce under Irish law and a couple's resultant inability to marry each other did not violate Art. 8 nor Art. 12 of the Convention. As to other aspects of the couple's own unmarried status under Irish law, no violation of Art. 8 was found to exist; (2) the legal status of the third applicant under Irish law did violate Art. 8 as regards both her and her parents. The natural family ties between the first and second applicants and their daughter required that she should be placed, legally and socially, in a position akin to a legitimate child. However, Irish law placed her in a legal situation which differed markedly from that of legitimate children. This resulted in a failure by Ireland to respect the applicant's family life; (3) the claims for material and non-pecuniary loss under Art. 50 of the Convention were rejected, but the applicants were awarded a sum in respect of their costs and expenses.

JOHNSTON *v.* IRELAND (No. 6/1985/92/139), *The Times,* January 7, 1987, European Court of Human Rights.

1913. European Convention on Human Rights—the European School—EEC

D, an Italian pupil, who was in the sixth form at the European School in Brussels, was not allowed to join the upper sixth form. Since there was no provision for appealing that decision under the treaty establishing the European School, her father sued in the Belgian Conseil d'État for breach of Art. 13 of the European Convention on Human Rights and Art. 2 of its first Protocol. That action was dismissed. D applied to the European Commission of Human Rights in respect of the alleged breaches.

Held, the application was inadmissible because (1) the Commission could not consider the claim against Belgium as the European School was set up under a Treaty to which EEC States were parties. Thus, acts of the School were not within Belgium's jurisdiction and Belgium could not be held liable for such acts; (2) the Commission could not consider the claim against the European Communities as the latter were not contracting parties to the European Convention on Human Rights.

EUROPEAN SCHOOL IN BRUSSELS, *Re*: D. *v.* BELGIUM AND THE EUROPEAN COMMUNITIES [1987] 2 C.M.L.R. 57, European Commission of Human Rights.

1914. European Convention on Human Rights—transsexual—unable to change birth register—legal impediment in U.K. to marry persons of same biological sex—whether domestic law in breach of convention

R was born with all the physical and biological characteristics of a female and was recorded as a female in the register of births. Following surgical sexual conversion, R changed names, and all official documents, except for the birth certificate, recorded R as male. R made several unsuccessful attempts to have his birth certificate altered. He applied to the European Court arguing that the U.K. was in breach of Art. 8 (in failing to respect his private life and full integration into society) and Art. 12 (by not recognising marriages to people of the same biological sex) of the convention.

Held, that in the U.K. there was no uniform general decision adopted as to the status of transsexuals. There was no integrated system of civil status registration but separate registers of births, deaths, marriages and so on. All people were free to change their names at will but such persons, when required to establish their identity, would have to do so by means of a birth certificate. The U.K. had endeavoured to fulfil R's requirements to the fullest extent but to do so fully would require a system of civil status registration. The U.K. authorities were entitled in the exercise of their margin of appreciation to take account of all the factors before determining the measures to adopt. The U.K. were not obliged to alter their present system and so there had been no breach of Art. 8. Art. 12 referred to the traditional marriage between people of different biological sex. The legal impediment on marriages between people of the same biological was not therefore a breach of Art. 12.

REES *v.* U.K. (1987) 17 Fam. Law 157, European Court of Human Rights.

1915. Illegitimate son—mother dying intestate—entitlement to estate

Mr. Inze was the illegitimate son of his mother who died intestate. An Austrian Court awarded her farm to Mr. Inze's legitimate half-brother pursuant to the Carinthian Hereditary Farms Act 1903, which gave precedence to legitimate over illegitimate children.

Held, that Austria was in breach of Art. 14 of the European Convention on Human Rights, taken together with Art. 1 of its First Protocol, as a difference in treatment based on whether a child was legitimate or illegitimate was discriminatory as it could not be objectively and reasonably justified. Mr. Inze was awarded damages and costs.

INZE *v.* AUSTRIA (No. 15/1986/113/161), *The Times,* November 13, 1987, European Ct. of Human Rights.

1916. Parental rights—children in care

Five cases (namely "O.", "H.", "W.", "B." and "R.") came before the European Court of Human Rights in which parents challenged various actions by local authorities in relation to children in the authorities' care as being contrary to the European Convention on Human Rights.

Held, that (1) in the cases of W., B. and R., Art. 8 of the Convention had been breached because the local authorities had failed to involve the parents sufficiently in their decision-making processes in relation to the parents' children who were in the authorities' care; (2) in the cases of O., W., B. and R., Art. 6 of the Convention had been breached because the parents were unable, whilst their children were in the authorities' care, to have questions of their access to their children decided by a tribunal in accordance with Art. 6; (3) in the case of H., Arts. 6(1) and 8 of the Convention were breached in that the length of the proceedings concerning the parent's access to her child, who was in the care of the local authority, and the child's adoption, had exceeded a reasonable time and had resulted in a failure to respect the parent's right to family life; (4) the claims for just satisfaction under Art. 50 of the Convention were reserved.

O. *v.* U.K.; H. *v.* SAME; W. *v.* SAME; B. *v.* SAME; R. *v.* SAME (Nos. 2/1986/100/148 to 6/1986/104/152).

1917. Prisoners' appeals—time pending appeal applications—whether this time counts towards service of sentence

The applicants were convicted prisoners who persisted in unmeritorious applications for leave to appeal. The Criminal Division of the English Court of Appeal directed that time spent in prison pending the determination of these applications for leave to appeal should not count towards the period of service of the sentence. The applicants alleged that this direction was contrary to Arts. 5, 6, and 14 of the European Convention on Human Rights.

Held, that the U.K. had not violated the right to liberty under Art. 5, nor the right to a fair trial under Art. 6, nor had there been any discrimination contrary to Art. 14 of the Convention, when the English Court of Appeal had directed that time spent in custody pending unmeritorious applications for leave to appeal should not count towards service of sentence.

MONNELL AND MORRIS *v.* U.K. (No. 7/1985/93/140–141), *The Times*, March 3, 1987, European Court of Human Rights.

1918. Re-detention of prisoner released on licence—non-disclosure of matters adverse to prisoner

The applicant had been convicted and given a life sentence in 1966 when he was 17 years old. He was released on licence in 1976, but was later recalled to prison by the Home Secretary in June 1977. He alleged that his re-detention was contrary to (1) Art. 5(1)(*a*) of the European Convention on Human Rights, which provided for the lawful detention of someone after conviction by a court; and (2) Art. 5(4) of the Convention, as he was unable to challenge the lawfulness of his re-detention before a court at the time of his recall or to have periodic judicial review of his detention at reasonable intervals throughout his imprisonment.

Held, that (1) Art. 5(1) had not been violated by the U.K.; in circumstances where the applicant had shown unstable, disturbed and aggressive behaviour, there were grounds for the Home Secretary to reach the view in June 1977 that the applicant's continued liberty would constitute a danger to the public and to himself; (2) Art. 5(4) had been violated by the U.K. in two respects: (i) the recalled prisoner was not entitled to full disclosure of adverse material in the possession of the Parole Board. The procedure adopted did not, therefore, enable proper participation by the individual adversely affected by the contested decision, that being one of the principal guarantees of a judicial procedure for the purposes of the Convention. Thus, neither in relation to consideration of the applicant's recall to prison, nor in relation to periodic examination of his detention with a view to release on licence, could the Parole Board be seen as meeting the requirements of Arts. 5(4); (ii) the scope of control provided by judicial review before the English High Court was not wide enough to bear on the condition essential for the "lawfulness" of a detention, *viz.* whether it was consistent with and justified by the objectives of the indeterminate sentence imposed on the applicant. The remedy of judicial review could neither of itself provide the proceedings required by Art. 5(4), nor serve to remedy the inadequacy of the procedure before the Parole Board.

WEEKS *v.* U.K. (No. 3/1985/89/136), *The Times*, March 5, 1987, European Court of Human Rights.

1919. Security vetting—infringement of private life

Mr. Leander applied for a post in a Swedish museum, which was partly located within a naval base. Appointment to this post had to be preceded by a security check, which involved consulting information held on a secret register kept by the security police. As a result of this security vetting Mr. Leander was refused such employment. The Swedish Government rejected Mr. Leander's complaints. Mr. Leander brought proceedings against Sweden alleging (i) that the storing of information on the secret police register regarding Mr. Leander's private life, and the refusal to allow him to refer to it, amounted to an interference with his right to respect for private life in breach of Art. 8 of the European Convention of Human Rights; (ii) breach of his freedom to express opinions and of his freedom to receive information contained on the register contrary to Art. 10 of the Convention; (iii) there was no effective national remedy for his complaints contrary to Art. 13 of the Convention.

Held, (1) there was no breach of Art. 8 as Sweden's interference with Mr. Leander's life was in accordance with Swedish domestic law, and, having regard to the wide margin of appreciation available to it, Sweden was entitled to consider that the interests of security outweighed Mr. Leander's interests; (2) there was no breach of Art. 10; Art. 10 did not confer a right of access to a register containing information on a person; (3) the aggregate of available remedies, such as the Ombudsman, in Sweden, satisfied the requirements of Art. 13. Accordingly there was no breach of Art. 13.

LEANDER *v.* SWEDEN, *The Times 25,* 1987, European Court of Human Rights.

IMMIGRATION

1920. Admission—whether entitled to admission—burden of proof

[Statement of Changes in Immigration Rules (H.C. 169 of 1983), para. 56.]

The burden of proof is on the applicant to show that he is entitled to admission under this paragraph, on the balance of probabilities. Whether a decision to refuse admission is reasonable must be decided on the criteria laid down in *Associated Provincial Picture Houses* v. *Wednesbury Corporation* (1948) C.L.C. 8107.

R. *v.* SECRETARY OF STATE FOR THE HOME DEPARTMENT, *ex p.* ALI, *The Times,* May 1, 1987, Nolan J.

1921. Appeal—misconceived grounds

The Legal Aid authorities should take note of an increased incidence of appeals where irrelevant and extraneous matters were dragged into an appeal and where wrong legal advice led to a danger that such merits as there were might be obscured.

R. *v.* SECRETARY OF STATE FOR THE HOME DEPARTMENT, *ex p.* YAKUB, *The Times,* November 5, 1987, C.A.

1922. Appeal—whether validly withdrawn

[Immigration Appeals (Procedure) Rules 1972 (S.I. 1972 No. 1684), rr.6(5)(*a*), 26(2).]

Although r.6(5)(*a*) of the Immigration Appeals (Procedure) Rules 1972 requires withdrawal of an Immigration Appeal to be made by a written notice to the Home Office signed by the appellant, it can also under r.26(1) be withdrawn before the adjudicator by properly instructed counsel, even in the absence of the appellant.

KHAN *v.* SECRETARY OF STATE FOR THE HOME DEPARTMENT; DEEN *v.* SAME, *The Independent,* July 2, 1987, C.A.

1923. Appeals—oral hearing—whether oral hearing could be dispensed with

[Immigration Act 1971 (c.77); Immigration Appeals (Procedure) Rules (S.I. 1984 No. 2041), r.20.]

R.20 of the Immigration Appeals (Procedure) Rules, which allows certain appeals under the Immigration Act 1971 to proceed without the hearing of oral evidence, is not *ultra vires* the Immigration Act 1971.

R. *v.* IMMIGRATION APPEAL TRIBUNAL, *ex p.* JONES (ROSS), *The Times,* December 9, 1987, C.A.

1924. Application for judicial review—appeal—bail

In immigration cases, a High Court judge can grant immediate bail if he grants or adjourns an application for leave to apply for judicial review. He cannot grant bail if he refuses the application. The Court of Appeal can hear a direct appeal from a refusal to grant bail, and can also grant bail where an unsuccessful application for leave to apply for review is renewed before it (*Dhillon, Re* [1977] C.L.Y. 393 overruled).

TURKOGLU, *Re, The Times,* May 23, 1987, C.A.

1925. Application for permanent stay—discretion of Secretary of State—exceptional circumstances

[H.C. 241, para. 24A.]

A married his wife in the U.K., but was incapable of consummating the marriage. As a result A left his wife's home and she had no intention of continuing to live with him. The Secretary of State refused A's application for leave to remain permanently on the basis of the marriage. The Tribunal found that incompatibility between parties was not so exceptional a circumstance as itself alone to justify the extension of leave to remain in the U.K. on the basis of marriage.

Held, that (1) it was wrong to assert that any disability which had precluded the continuation of a marriage could not by itself be a reason for the exercise of the discretion embodied in the relevant rule; (2) in considering the term "not normally" the

Tribunal should consider what matters if any might justify a departure from what was normal; it was unhelpful to substitute the terms "exceptional" and "abnormal."

R. *v.* IMMIGRATION APPEAL TRIBUNAL, *ex p.* BASHIR (MOHAMMED) [1985] Imm.A.R. 231, C.A.

1926. Asylum—refugee—"well-founded fear of persecution"

A well-founded fear of persecution is a fear reasonably suffered by a person of reasonable courage, whether or not it is objectively reasonable (*Immigration and Naturalization Service* v. *Cardoza-Fonseca* (1987) 107 S.Ct. 1207 (U.S.A.))

R. *v.* SECRETARY OF STATE FOR THE HOME DEPARTMENT, *ex p.* SIVAKUMARAN, *The Times,* October 13, 1987, C.A.

1927. Bail—application—jurisdiction

When an immigrant is detained pending examination, he must apply for bail to the adjudicator having jurisdiction. When he is detained following an examination and a determination that he should not be admitted but be required to leave, bail should be sought by way of judicial review of the Secretary of State's refusal to grant bail. The Court of Appeal has jurisdiction to grant bail in the latter case.

VILVARAJAH, *Re, The Independent,* October 28, 1987, C.A.

1928. British citizenship—definition of "right of abode"—interpretation of "ordinarily resident there for the last five years or more"—whether periods as an overstayer break continuity of residence

R was a citizen of U.K. and Colonies. In May 1975 she came to U.K. as a visitor. Extensions were granted to December 31, 1976. She then became on overstayer. On February 9, 1977, she applied for further leave to remain, which was granted to December 31, 1977. She then became an overstayer again. On January 10, 1978, she again applied for further leave to remain, and was granted indefinite leave on February 2, 1978. Under section 11(1) of the British Nationality Act 1981 she qualified as a British citizen if, within the meaning of section 2(1)(*c*) of the Immigration Act 1971, she had on January 1, 1983, a right of abode in U.K. Her application for British citizenship was refused, and she appealed.

Held, that (1) periods spent in U.K. as an overstayer were periods when the respondent was in U.K. unlawfully and could not constitute periods of ordinary residence; (2) the Secretary of State had no power to grant or vary leave to remain retrospectively, *i.e.* the grant made on February 2, 1978, could not be treated as beginning on January 1, 1978; (3) the requirement of being "ordinarily resident . . . for the last five years or more" required an unbroken period, *i.e.* periods of unlawful residence could not be discounted by adding to the period earlier periods of lawful residence (*R.* v. *Secretary of State for the Home Department, ex p. Margueritte* [1982] C.L.Y. 1555; *R.* v. *Barnet London Borough, ex p. Shah* [1983] C.L.Y. 1157, 1815; *Grant* v. *Borg* [1982] C.L.Y. 1556 referred to).

CHELLIAH *v.* IMMIGRATION APPEAL TRIBUNAL [1985] Imm.A.R. 192, C.A.

1929. British citizenship—designated service

BRITISH CITIZENSHIP (DESIGNATED SERVICE) (AMENDMENT) ORDER 1987 (No. 611) [45p], made under the British Nationality Act 1981 (c.61), s.2(3); operative on April 30, 1987; designates the Agricultural and Food Research Council for the purposes of s.2 of the 1981 Act.

1930. Children—admission—one parent having "sole responsibility"—H.C. 394 para. 46(e)

The wording of H.C. 394 para. 46(*e*) simply raises the question whether the sponsor has had the sole responsibility for the upbringing of the child in question for a period of time not being an insubstantial period. As this matter was remitted, no view was expressed on the facts.

R. *v.* IMMIGRATION APPEAL TRIBUNAL *ex p.* UDDIN AND UDDIN [1986] Imm.A.R. 203, Webster J.

1931. Children over 18—discretion of entry clearance officer

There is no discretion to admit a child over 18 if he does not qualify for admission in his own right.

R. *v.* IMMIGRATION APPEAL TRIBUNAL, *ex p.* MUKITH, *The Times,* November 14, 1987, C.A.

1932. Control of entry—through Republic of Ireland

IMMIGRATION (CONTROL OF ENTRY THROUGH REPUBLIC OF IRELAND) (AMENDMENT) ORDER 1987 (No. 2092) [45p], made under the Immigration Act 1971 (c.77), ss.9(2), 32(1); operative on January 1, 1988; amends S.I. 1972 No. 1610.

1933. Deception—false passport—evidence—use of affidavits at hearing without cross-examination—practice and procedure—whether Secretary of State can switch basis of case in course of hearing of an appeal

P claimed to be the son of GP and MP. As their son, he was admitted to the U.K. The Secretary of State subsequently concluded P was not their son, and that P's birth certificate and application form for a passport contained false information. On an application for judicial review, the case was decided entirely on affidavit evidence, counsel for the Secretary of State declining an invitation from P's counsel to cross-examine P. In the course of the hearing, the Secretary of State obtained leave to extend the basis of the case from an offence under s.26(1)(*d*) to one also under s.26(1)(*c*). The factual basis of the offence was unaltered.

Held, that (1) The silent presentation of a passport known to contain false information was deception sufficient to treat P as an illegal immigrant (*ex p. Addo* not approved); (2) The Court had been justified in deciding the case on affidavit evidence. It did not follow that P's evidence should be accepted merely because it had not been challenged by cross-examination; (3) The court had not been wrong to allow a late extension to the basis of the case to include offences under s.26(1)(*c*): a short adjournment would have sufficed had it been requested.

R. *v.* SECRETARY OF STATE FOR THE HOME DEPARTMENT, *ex p.* PATEL (DHIRUBHAI GORDHANBHAI) [1986] Imm. A.R. 515, C.A.

1934. Dependent relatives—construction of rules

[Statement of Changes in Immigration Rules (H.C. 169: Feb. 1983), para. 52.]

The paragraph should be construed so as not to exclude a single parent or grandparent under the age of 65.

R. *v.* IMMIGRATION APPEAL TRIBUNAL, *ex p.* BIBI (ZAINIB), *The Times,* April 7, 1987, Kennedy J.

1935. Dependent relatives—whether the requirement in para. 52 of H.C. 169 that applicant's standard of living had to be substantially below that of his own country was reasonable

B applied for admission under para. 52 of H.C. 169. The application and subsequent appeal were refused. The Tribunal held that it was bound to take into account the support given to B by her brother in the U.K. Another unreported decision of the Tribunal in *Patel* had held that no account should be taken of remittances from the U.K. in assessing the relative standard of living.

Held, that the approach in *Patel* was wholly unsustainable; but (2) the requirement in para. 52 was unreasonable, and *ultra vires* the enabling statutory power in the Immigration Act 1971, and was accordingly invalid; (3) the case would be remitted to the Tribunal for consideration as though that requirement were not contained in para. 52.

R. *v.* IMMIGRATION APPEAL TRIBUNAL, *ex p.* BEGUM [1986] Imm.A.R. 385, Simon Brown J.

1936. Deportation—abuse of law by immigrant—whether deportation available on ground that conducive to public good

[Immigration Act 1971 (c.77), s.3(5)(*b*).]

An immigrant entered the UK legally but accelerated obtaining indefinite leave to remain by bribing an official. S.3(5)(*b*) of the Immigration Act 1971 allows for deportation of a non-patrial if deportation would be conducive to the public good.

Held, that such an abuse of the law would justify the activation of s.3(5)(*b*).

R. *v.* IMMIGRATION APPEAL TRIBUNAL, *ex p.* SHEIKH, *The Times,* April 29, 1987, D.C.

1937. Deportation—appeal—admissibility of evidence

[Immigration Act 1971 (c.77), s.19(1)(*a*)(ii).]

On appeal to an adjudicator under s.19(1)(*a*) (ii) of the 1971 Act evidence of facts in existence at the time of the exercise of the Home Secretary's discretion, but not known to him at that time, is admissible.

In each of three cases the applicant entered the U.K. as a visitor with leave to stay for a limited period and stayed longer. The Home Secretary made a decision to deport, and on appeal to an adjudicator each sought to put forward additional facts which, though in existence at the time of the Home Secretary's decision, had not been made known to him. The appeals to the adjudicator were dismissed, as were subsequent appeals to the Immigration Appeals Tribunal. Judicial review of the appeal tribunal's decisions was refused in each case.

Held, dismissing the appeal, that such evidence was admissible, and two of the cases would thus be remitted to the appeal tribunal.

R. *v.* IMMIGRATION APPEAL TRIBUNAL, *ex p.* HASSANIN, KANDEMIR AND FAROOQ, [1986] 1 W.L.R. 1448, C.A.

1938. Deportation—conducive to the public good—factors to be taken into account

T was an Iranian national. He arrived in the U.K. in 1974 as a visitor and secured extensions of leave as a student. A subsequent application for a further extension was refused. Between 1977 and 1980 he was convicted of a series of drug offences of increasing seriousness. In 1979 he harmed an Irish citizen living and working in the U.K. In 1981 he was sentenced to five years' imprisonment for smuggling heroin. The Secretary of State decided to deport him. The Appeal Tribunal allowed his appeal because the Secretary of State had not taken into account the special factors relevant to the spouse of an EEC worker. The Secretary of State reviewed the case and issued a new notice of intention to deport. That decision was appealed, and the appeal was dismissed by the Tribunal.

Held, on an application for judicial review, that (1) the Tribunal had properly applied the principles set out in *R.* v. *Bouchereau* [1978] C.L.Y. 629, and thus had not misdirected itself in law; (2) the Tribunal had given proper weight to the various compassionate circumstances in the case.

R. *v.* IMMIGRATION APPEAL TRIBUNAL, *ex p.* TAMDJID-NEZHAD [1986] Imm.A.R. 396, Taylor J.

1939. Deportation—expiry of leave to remain—marriage to Commonwealth citizen settled in U.K.

[Immigration Act 1971 (c.77), s.1(5).]

The Act does not enable the Home Secretary to deport an overstayer who subsequently marries a Commonwealth citizen who was himself settled in the U.K. on January 1, 1973 (*R.* v. *Immigration Appeal Tribunal, ex p. Haque* [1987] C.L.Y. 1963 referred to).

R. *v.* SECRETARY OF STATE FOR THE HOME DEPARTMENT, *ex p.* HUSEYIN (ZALIHE), *The Times,* October 31, 1987, C.A.

1940. Deportation—overstayer—non-service of notices if whereabouts unknown—if whereabouts subsequently known whether obligation to serve notice

M was a Ghanian who entered the U.K. as a visitor. He sought leave to remain, which was refused. His appeal failed and he disappeared. Deportation proceedings were initiated. Notice of that intention could not be served on M because his whereabouts were unknown. The Secretary of State therefore relied on reg. 3(4) of the 1972 Immigration Appeals (Notices) Regulations. However, M was discovered in 1984. No copy of the notice was served on him.

Held, that the provisions of the 1972 Regulations applied to the circumstances that obtained at the date of the Secretary of State's decision. At that date M's whereabouts were unknown.

R. *v.* SECRETARY OF STATE FOR THE HOME DEPARTMENT, *ex p.* MEYER-WULFF [1986] Imm.A.R. 258, D.C.

1941. Deportation—post-entry deception—use of passport issued to another person

When questioned by an immigration officer, A produced a passport which the Secretary of State contended had been issued to another person, and in which the photograph of A had been inserted. That passport contained the endorsement on which A relied to show he was in the U.K. with leave. The Secretary of State concluded the passport was false, and as a result there had been post-entry deception, by representation that the passport was genuine. The Secretary of State suspected, but accepted he could not prove on the test required in *Khawaja* that there had been deception on entry. However, on the basis of post-entry deception alone, he decided to initiate deportation proceedings under s.3(5)(*b*) of the 1971 Act.

Held, that (1) following *ex p. Cheema,* the Secretary of State's powers under s.3(5)(*b*) could be used in cases where post-entry deception was proved; (2) in the present case, assuming the facts could be proved, there had been a continuing post-entry deception; (3) although A had not, until questioned, made any positive claim based on the passport, his conduct could not be distinguished from that which justified deportation in *ex p. Owusu-Sekyere;* (4) a person, whose only claim to remain in the U.K. depends on a forged passport to which he has no lawful right, cannot be described as a "perfectly respectable established resident" as indicated in *Khawaja;* (5) obiter, the Secretary of State would be obliged to prove the post-entry deception to a high degree of probability (*R.* v. *Immigration Appeal Tribunal, ex p. Cheema* [1984] C.L.Y. 1750, *R.* v. *Secretary of*

State for the Home Department, ex p. Khawaja [1983] C.L.Y. 1908 and R. v. Immigration Appeal Tribunal, ex p. Owusu-Sekyere [1987] C.L.Y. 1944 referred to).

R. v. IMMIGRATION APPEAL TRIBUNAL, *ex p.* KARIM [1986] Imm. A.R. 428, Simon Brown J.

1942. Deportation—procedure—whether the Tribunal was able to take a different view from that of adjudicator without hearing witnesses

S and his wife were British Dependent Territories Citizens. S was admitted to the U.K. in 1975 for 12 months with a work permit allowing him to work at the Mayflower Restaurant in Glasgow, subject to a condition that he should not change employment without consent from the Department of Employment. In 1978, he applied for further leave to remain. The Home Department then made enquiries. It was discovered that he had worked elsewhere than at the restaurant from January to March 1978, and also from April to July 1979. He was therefore refused leave. His appeal was dismissed and he was advised to leave the U.K., but he did not do so. Deportation proceedings were therefore initiated, against which he appealed. The adjudicator allowed his appeal, considering that it would be unjust to deport S and his wife for a breach of conditions that took place long ago and the seriousness of which S did not appreciate. The Secretary of State appealed to the Tribunal, who allowed the appeal, holding that the adjudicator had wrongly exercised his discretion.

Held, on an application for judicial review, that (1) the Tribunal was empowered to hear and consider the whole matter afresh; its discretion was unfettered; (2) the Tribunal should be slow to take a different view of discretion from that of an adjudicator where its exercise depended on the impression made by a particular witness or on his credibility; (3) in such cases, the Tribunal should call evidence before it; (4) where the view of discretion did not depend on the credibility or demeanour of witnesses, no such inhibition should restrict the Tribunal (*R.* v. *Immigration Appeal Tribunal, ex p. Singh (Mahendra)* [1985] C.L.Y. 1705 applied).

R. *v.* IMMIGRATION APPEAL TRIBUNAL, *ex p.* SHEK AND SHEK [1986] Imm.A.R. 178, Mann J.

1943. Deportation—proceedings—notice of decision to deport—service

A notice of a decision to deport is adequately served by posting it recorded delivery to the applicant's last known or usual place of abode; and time begins to run from the posting of the notice not its receipt.

R. *v.* SECRETARY OF STATE FOR THE HOME DEPARTMENT, *ex p.* YEBOAH; R. *v.* SAME, *ex p.* DRAZ, *The Independent*, April 15, 1987, C.A.

1944. Deportation—whether deception after entry a ground for deportation

[Immigration Act 1971 (c.77), s.3(5)(*b*).]

Deception after entry is a ground for deportation under s.3(5)(*b*) of the Immigration Act 1971 (*R.* v. *Immigration Appeal Tribunal, ex p. Cheema* [1984] C.L.Y. 1750 and *R.* v. *Secretary of State for the Home Department, ex p. Khawaja* [1983] C.L.Y. 1908 considered).

OWUSU-SEKYERE'S APPLICATION, *Re, The Times*, April 22, 1987, C.A.

1945. Deportation—whether entry by deception justifies deportation

[Immigration Act 1971, (c.77), s.3(5)(*b*).]

The main fact that an immigrant had secured entry to the country by deception is insufficient to justify deportation as "conducive to the public good".

R. *v.* IMMIGRATION APPEAL TRIBUNAL, *ex p.* PATEL, *The Independent*, August 21, 1987, C.A.

1946. Deportation—whether protection against removal also amounts to authorisation—whether a person can be in the U.K. lawfully when without leave, but with the authorisation of the Secretary of State

A was a citizen of Bangladesh. He was granted leave to remain in U.K. until May 21, 1980. His stay was extended to January 13, 1982. His application for further leave was refused. His appeal was dismissed, and his application for leave to appeal further was refused. At that time a deportation order was made against A on the basis that he had remained in the U.K. without authority. In considering the factors relevant to the public interest, the Tribunal found that A had disappeared from view between 1977 and 1979, but since then had exercised lawful rights and had been involved in legal proceedings, acting at all times on legal advice. The Secretary of State had thus extended an indulgence to A and permitted him to remain until deportation proceedings were begun. In considering the factors set out in H.C. 169, para. 156, the Tribunal found A had been in the U.K. since 1976, that he was integrated into the community and had become a social worker with fairly unique skills.

Held, that (1) the protection against removal which is embodied in s.14(1) of the Immigration Act 1971 does not amount to "authorisation" within the meaning of para. 158 of H.C. 169; but (2) it is possible for a person who is subject to immigration control to be in the U.K. lawfully when without leave, but with the authorisation of the Secretary of State (*R.* v. *Immigration Appeal Tribunal, ex p. Subramaniam* [1976] C.L.Y. 13, *R.* v. *Immigration Appeal Adjudicator, ex p. Bhanji* [1977] Imm.A.R. 89, *R.* v. *Immigration Appeal Tribunal, ex p. Singh (Bakhtaur)* [1985] C.L.Y. 1713 referred to).

IDRISH (MUHAMMAD) *v.* SECRETARY OF STATE FOR THE HOME DEPARTMENT [1985] Imm.A.R. 155, Imm.App.Trib.

1947. Deportation—whether Secretary of States' powers of deportation were circumscribed by the provisions of the Mental Health Act 1959 (c.72)

A was a citizen of Sierra Leone. He was admitted to the U.K. as a student and became an overstayer, and disappeared. The Secretary of State later signed a deportation order against him. Six years later he was found and the notices were served on him. He was for some time detained pending removal. During his detention he spent some time in the hospital wing of the remand centre suffering from schizophrenia and epilepsy. A appealed to an adjudicator against the removal directions under s.17 of the 1971 Act. The appeal was dismissed. When the matter came before the Appeal Tribunal it was contended that the Secretary of State was not empowered to issue removal directions under the Immigration Act 1971 where the subject of those directions was a patient within the meaning of s.90 of the Mental Health Act 1959.

Held, that (1) the *vires* of removal directions could not be challenged under s.17 appeal powers, as s.17 appeals were limited to issues of alternative destination. The immigration appellate authorities had no jurisdiction to determine a conflict between the Secretary of State's powers under different Acts. that properly was an issue that could only be raised in the High Court which would apply the *Wednesbury* principles; (2) The powers of the Secretary of State to issue removal directions in deportation cases in accordance with Sched. 3 of the 1971 Act were not "suspended, superseded or otherwise necessarily replaced" by the provisions of the Mental Health Acts.

R. *v.* IMMIGRATION APPEAL TRIBUNAL AND SECRETARY OF STATE FOR THE HOME DEPARTMENT, *ex p.* ALGHALI [1986] Imm.A.R. 376, Simon Brown J.

1948. Deportation—whether the Secretary of State had power to delegate completion of notice to detain

K was a citizen of Pakistan. He was charged with offences relating to possession of explosives, but subsequently acquitted. During the trials, the Secretary of State decided to deport K. Appropriate notices were prepared, both of intention to deport, and to detain. They were not however completed as to date and time; that was done immediately after the verdict by a police officer at court. It was contended that the Secretary of State had no power to so delegate the completion of notices of this nature.

Held, that (1) the Secretary of State did have such power; (2) only when the notices had been completed by being timed and dated did the requirements of the Immigration Appeals (Notices) Regulations 1984 come into play.

KHAN (AMANULLAH), *Re* [1986] Imm.A.R. 485, Simon Brown J.

1949. Detention—whether person can be detained pending removal directions—whether person can be detained pending application for political asylum

M applied for judicial review, and sought release from detention. M was refused admission to the U.K. as a visitor on arrival on November 17, 1985. He was granted temporary admission subject to a residence condition, which he did not observe. He was arrested and detained. Removal directions were issued by an immigration officer within the statutory period, but then cancelled. Subsequently new removal directions were issued, but these were also subsequently withdrawn because, meanwhile, M sought political asylum. While that application was under consideration he remained in detention. It was submitted that in reality M was not detained pending removal directions. He was instead detained while his application for political asylum was under consideration. If that was successful, no removal directions would be given.

Held, that (1) the use of the power of detention under para. 16(2) of Sched. 2 to the Immigration Act 1931 could be used in these circumstances; the phrase in Sched. 2 "in pursuance of any directions given" predicates that in fact there may, in the end, be no directions given; (2) thus the detention while the application for political asylum was under consideration was lawful.

R. *v.* SECRETARY OF STATE FOR THE HOME DEPARTMENT, *ex p.* MAHAL [1986] Imm.A.R. 369, McCowan J.

1950. Elderly dependant parents—admission for settlement—considerations

All the surrounding circumstances fell to be considered when deciding whether elderly dependant parents were without other close relatives in their own country to turn to, having in mind that the policy of the relevant regulation was humanitarian. (*R.* v. *Immigration Appeal Tribunal, ex p. Bastiampillai* [1983] C.L.Y. 1890 considered).

R. *v.* IMMIGRATION APPEAL TRIBUNAL, *ex p.* SWARAN SINGH, *The Independent*, July 7, 1987, C.A.

1951. Entry clearance—whether application a renewal or a fresh application—effect of undue delay in applying for judicial review

K was a citizen of Bangladesh. His first application for entry clearance was refused on July 10, 1979. He made a second application on December 13, 1980. It was argued that the second application was a continuation or renewal of the first.

Held, that the relevant rules were in H.C. Paper 394 of 1980 which took effect from March 1, 1980. R.12 applied, bringing into effect r.42 *et seq.* This was a new application. In addition the Court would not have granted relief because there had been undue delay in lodging the application for judicial review. Nine months had elapsed between publication of the Tribunal's determination and the application for leave to apply for review. No good reason had been given for that delay which offended against the principles of s.31(6) of the Supreme Court Act 1981, and R.S.C., Ord. 53, r.4.

R. *v.* IMMIGRATION APPEAL TRIBUNAL, *ex p.* KOBIR [1986] Imm.A.R. 311, McNeill J.

1952. Entry clearance—wife of Commonwealth citizen—intention to settle

B and P were citizens of Pakistan, the wife and daughter of a Commonwealth citizen who was settled in the U.K. and had been since before January 1, 1973. B and P applied in Islambad for entry clearance. B told the visa officer that she did not intend to remain in the U.K. for more than a few months. The application was refused. An appeal to the adjudicator also failed, the wife being considered a "courier wife".

Held, on an application for review that (1) nothing in the 1971 Act precluded immigration rules being concerned with the purpose of entry as well as the periods for which leave was sought; (2) by H.C. 81, para. 36, a wife was only to be admitted when she intended to settle in the U.K.

R. *v.* IMMIGRATION APPEAL TRIBUNAL, *ex p.* BIBI AND PURVEZ [1986] Imm.A.R. 61, Kennedy J.

1953. Entry Clearance Officer—interview—whether acting in an administrative or judicial capacity

The Entry Clearance Officer is performing an administrative function in conducting an interview with an applicant for entry clearance, and is not acting in a judicial capacity. He has a duty to be fair. However, the term "leading question" is inappropriate in the context of such an interview.

KUMAR *v.* ENTRY CLEARANCE OFFICER, NEW DELHI [1985] Imm.A.R. 242, Imm.App.Trib.

1954. EEC citizen—dual nationality of two member states—whether can claim benefit of EEC Regulations

A was a citizen of Iran, who married D in 1984. D was born in Northern Ireland and always regarded herself as a British citizen. In fact she also acquired Irish citizenship in 1956, unknown to her until she was legally advised of that fact in 1984. She came to Great Britain in 1975 and worked in London. A contended that his wife was a EEC worker, a citizen of Eire, working in the U.K. Under the EEC Regulations she was entitled to have her husband in the U.K.

Held, that (1) there was no provision in the relevant EEC Regulations (Council Reg. 1612/68 and Arts. 48 and 7 of the Treaty of Rome applied) dealing with the concept of dual nationality; (2) applying the principles provided by the "International Convention on certain questions relating to the conflict of nationality laws 1930," the U.K. was entitled to regard D as a British citizen as would any other country except Eire; (3) in the circumstances D was not an EEC worker within the meaning of the Regulations.

ARADI *v.* IMMIGRATION OFFICER, HEATHROW [1985] Imm.A.R. 184, Imm.App.Trib.

1955. Examination of immigrant—indefinite leave to enter

[Immigration Act 1971 (c.77), Sched. 2, paras. 2(1), 6(1).]

For the purposes of para. 6(1) of Sched. 2 of the Immigration Act 1971 (so as to deem an immigrant to have been given indefinite leave to enter the U.K.), it does not matter whether an immigration officer's examination of an immigrant is conduct under para. 2(1)(*a*), (*b*), (*c*).

R. *v.* SECRETARY OF STATE FOR THE HOME DEPARTMENT, *ex p.* MALIK, *The Independent*, October 6, 1987, Kennedy J.

1956. Home Office research programme. See CRIMINAL LAW, §786.

1957. Husband—admission when married to a woman settled in the U.K.—distinction between fiancés and husbands

The question to be decided was whether a marriage celebrated in India between a husband who had lived there all his life, and a wife who was settled in the U.K., was entered into primarily to obtain the admission of the husband to the U.K.

Held, that (1) there was no substantial difference between para. 41 (fiancés) and 54 (husbands) in H.C. 169, save that under 54(*a*) the E.C.O. is obliged to look at circumstances obtaining while the marriage was entered into, whereas under 41(*a*) his assessment of the purpose of the proposed marriage relates to the time when the application was made; (2) the events which happen since a marriage can be material; (3) neither para. 41 nor 54 presume that the primary purpose of a marriage is to gain settlement in the U.K. The rules simply place a burden of proof on an applicant to satisfy an immigration officer as to the requirements of those rules (*R.* v. *Immigration Appeal Tribunal, ex p. Bhatia (Vinod)* [1986] C.L.Y. 1701 referred to).

R. *v.* IMMIGRATION APPEAL TRIBUNAL, *ex p.* KUMAR [1986] Imm. A.R. 446, C.A.

1958. Illegal entrant—deception—re-entry by overstayer after change of name—whether entry by deception

O originally entered the U.K. as a student in the name of Ayeni. He became an overstayer. He was convicted of that offence and recommended for deportation. In fact he left voluntarily. He returned to Nigeria and changed his name by deed poll, and acquired a new passport. He returned to the U.K. and sought entry as a student in his new identity. He was granted admission. When his former identity was discovered he was detained as an illegal entrant. He contended that, on re-entry, he told no untruths, nor had he presented any false documents; further he had not been asked any questions about his previous immigration history.

Held, that (1) applying the test in *Khawaja* v. *Secretary of State for the Home Department* [1983] C.L.Y. 1908, he had been guilty of deception; (2) by his conduct he was lying about himself and doing so deliberately, knowing that if the true facts were known he would have been refused re-entry; (3) he was in breach of s.26(1)(*c*) of the Immigration Act 1971.

R. *v.* SECRETARY OF STATE FOR THE HOME DEPARTMENT, *ex p.* OLASEBIKAN [1986] Imm.A.R. 337, McCowan J.

1959. Illegal entrant—false statement—statement subsequent to original entry—whether immigration officer exceeded his powers

[Immigration Act 1971 (c.77), ss.4(2), 26(1)(*c*), Sched. 2, para. 2(1).]

An immigrant is under a duty to answer the proper questions of an immigration officer at a place and time other than the port of entry, and failure to do so is an offence.

A entered the UK illegally in 1972 having been refused entry in 1971. He was later given leave to remain. He changed his name to X. In 1984 he visited the USA, then returned. The next day he was visited by an immigration officer at his home, when he claimed that he had never been refused entry to the U.K., had not travelled here before 1972, and had always used the name of X. He was convicted of making a false statement to an immigration officer contrary to s.26(1)(*c*) of the Immigration Act 1971. D appealed.

Held, dismissing the appeal, that an immigration officer was empowered to conduct an examination on a date and at a place other than the port and date of entry if he had information which caused him to inquire whether a person was entitled to enter, and, accordingly, untrue answers to such questions were an offence under s.26(1)(*c*).

BALJINDER SINGH *v.* HAMMOND [1987] 1 W.L.R. 283, D.C.

1960. Illegal entrant—whether criminality relevant

A person is an illegal entrant when in breach of the provisions laid down by statute, not merely when in breach of the provisions which create criminal offences.

R. *v.* GOVERNOR OF LATCHMERE HOUSE REMAND CENTRE, *ex p.* KAIKANEL, *The Times,* May 29, 1987, Roch J.

1961. Illegal entrant—whether person entering by deception and in breach of Act can acquire leave to remain

R was a citizen of Bangladesh. He arrived in the U.K. in 1969 with a forged passport and using a false name. On arrival he resumed his true identity and in that name he obtained new passports. He returned to the U.K. in 1975, having left in 1973, and told falsehoods to the immigration authorities. He was given indefinite leave to enter. The same pattern was repeated in 1979. However, in 1985 he was detained, and treated as an illegal entrant.

Held, that a person who was an illegal entrant before January 1, 1973 remained so; and there was no waiver in the 1971 Act to enable A to argue that his position had become regularised.

R. *v.* SECRETARY OF STATE FOR THE HOME DEPARTMENT, *ex p.* RAZAK [1986] Imm.A.R. 44, Kennedy J.

1962. Immigration (Carriers' Liability) Act 1987 (c.24)

This Act requires carriers to make payments to the Secretary of State in respect of passengers brought by them to the United Kingdom without proper documents.

The Act received the Royal Assent on May 15, 1987.

The Act extends to Northern Ireland. There is power to extend any of the Act's provisions to the Channel Islands and the Isle of Man.

1963. Immigration rules—whether comparison between pre- and post-1971 rules required

[Immigration Act 1971 (c.77), s.1(5).]

S.1(5) of the Immigration Act 1971 requires that the immigration rules laid down by the Secretary of State should not make Commonwealth citizens settled in the U.K. any less free to come into and go from the U.K. than if the Act had not been passed. The section does not, however, require a comparison between the pre- and post-1971 rules in the case of the unmarried son, aged between the ages of 18 and 20, of Commonwealth citizens settled in the U.K.

R. *v.* IMMIGRATION APPEAL TRIBUNAL, *ex p.* HAQUE; SAME *v.* SAME, *ex p.* RUHUL; SAME *v.* SAME, *ex p.* RAHMAN, *The Independent,* August 6, 1987; C.A.

1964. Impersonation—issue not raised with representative at hearing—whether implicit in issue of identity—use of word "guarantee"

The Adjudicator had not raised the issue of impersonation with A's representative at the hearing.

Held, to be immaterial, because that was a matter which was implicit once the issue of the identity of the persons seeking entry was before the adjudicator. Further, when the adjudicator had held that certain correspondence constituted "no guarantee whatsoever that the individuals presenting themselves to the E.C.O. are those persons" the phrase "no guarantee whatsoever" was unfortunate: the words "no proof" were better advised.

R. *v.* IMMIGRATION APPEAL TRIBUNAL, *ex p.* ALI (CHERAG) [1986] Imm.A.R. 270, Kennedy J.

1965. Investment in business—origin of assets of potential immigrant

The rule that a person wishing to enter the U.K. to establish himself in business had to bring in at least £100,000 to invest in it was not satisfied where the applicant inherited a business of sufficient value which was already situated in the U.K. (*R.* v. *Immigration Appeal Tribunal, ex p. Peikazadi* [1979] 80 Imm.A.R. 191 considered.)

R. *v.* IMMIGRATION APPEAL TRIBUNAL *ex p.* RAHMAN, *The Times*, February 3, 1987, C.A. (by a majority).

1966. Leave to enter—adopted son of sponsor in U.K.—whether "*de facto*" adoption necessary

The applicant was born in Bangladesh. The sponsor had been settled in the U.K. since 1970. On the death of his father the applicant had been taken into the sponsor's home. The applicant applied for entry clearance to settle in the U.K. (under r.50 of the Changes in Immigration Rules) as the dependent adopted son of the sponsor. Leave was refused on the basis that responsibility for the applicant's upbringing was a joint family matter closer to fostering than *de facto* adoption. That decision was upheld by the I.A.T.

Held, that the immigration rules were to be construed in a commonsense manner. Islamic law had no legally recognisable adoption process. "Adoptive" should be construed in its wide sense and should not be limited to some legally recognisable adoptive process. What distinguished adoption from fostering was that adoption entailed the permanent assumption of parental duties. In determining whether there had been an adoption for r.50, the degree of permanency was the crucial question. The tribunal had erred in law and the case would be remitted for reconsideration.

R. *v.* IMMIGRATION APPEAL TRIBUNAL, *ex p.* A. (1987) 17 Fam. Law 311, Hodgson J.

1967. Leave to enter—breach of condition—whether continuing offence

[Immigration Act 1971 (c.77), s.24(1)(*b*)(ii).]

M was convicted of failing to observe a condition of limited leave to enter the U.K. by engaging in employment without authority, contrary to s.24(1)(*b*)(ii) of the 1971 Act. The issue before the Divisional Court was whether the offence was committed only on the first day of the failure or whether it was a continuing offence.

Held, dismissing M's appeal, that so long as the limited permission remained, the condition remained and if the immigrant at any time broke the condition he was liable to prosecution. He had a continuing obligation to obey the condition (*Singh (Gurdev)* v. *R.* [1973] C.L.Y. 9, and *Grant* v. *Borg* [1982] C.L.Y. 1556 distinguished).

MANICKAVASAGAR *v.* COMMISSIONER OF METROPOLITAN POLICE [1987] Crim.L.R. 50, D.C.

1968. Leave to enter—Commonwealth citizens—whether Secretary of State had power to introduce rules requiring visa to be held before leave sought

S was a citizen of Sri Lanka. He travelled to the U.K. from Germany. On arrival, he asserted that he was unaware that, by an amendment to the Immigration Rules, he required a visa for entry to the U.K. He sought leave to enter as a student. He was refused admission because he did not hold a visa.

Held, that (1) the power vested in the Secretary of State by s.3(2) of the 1971 Act allowed him to make rules which distinguished between persons, including Commonwealth citizens, on the ground of their nationality or citizenship. The amendment of para. 10 of H.C. 169 so as to impose a visa requirement on citizens of Sri Lanka was *intra vires.* (2) The wording of para. 10 of H.C. 169 was clear, and its mandatory provisions over-rode the discretionary powers in para. 24 of H.C. 169.

R. *v.* SECRETARY OF STATE FOR THE HOME DEPARTMENT, *ex p.* SURESHKUMAR [1986] Imm. A.R. 420, Nolan J.

1969. Leave to enter—refusal—national security—whether evidence lawful

[Immigration Act 1971 (c.77); Geneva Convention Relating to the Status of Refugees 1951 and Protocol of 1967.]

Where the correct procedural steps have been followed, the decision of the Secretary of State to refuse permission to enter the U.K. on the ground that exclusion was conducive to the public good, in the interests of national security, cannot be challenged on the ground that the evidence before him was not, nor could be, known to the court.

R. *v.* SECRETARY OF STATE FOR THE HOME DEPARTMENT, *ex p.* H., *The Times,* August 5, 1987, D.C.

1970. Leave to enter—refusal—no opportunity for applicant to comment on grounds

A was refused leave to enter as a refugee on grounds upon which he had no opportunity to comment, and in respect of which a perfectly satisfactory explanation existed. The decision was contrary to the rules of natural justice and would be quashed.

R. *v.* SECRETARY OF STATE FOR THE HOME OFFICE, *ex p.* AWUKU; SAME *v.* SAME, *ex p.* OTCHERE; SAME *v.* SAME, *ex p.* DZIVENU, *The Times,* October 3, 1987, McCowan J.

1971. Leave to enter—refusal—refugee status

A British protected person who has been refused entry to his normal country of residence is a refugee within the terms of the Geneva Convention and Protocol, and accordingly is not subject to refusal of leave to enter the U.K.

R. *v.* IMMIGRATION OFFICER, GATWICK AIRPORT, *ex p.* HARJENDAR SINGH, *The Times*, February 26, 1987, Nolan J.

1972. Leave to enter—restricted leave—written notice

[Immigration Act 1971 (c.77), s.4.]

An illegible stamp, or a stamp that can only be interpreted by someone with knowledge of the type of stamps used, is not sufficient written notice of a restriction upon leave to enter (*R.* v. *Immigration Appeal Tribunal, ex p. Coomasaru* [1983] C.L.Y. 1932 considered).

R. *v.* SECRETARY OF STATE FOR THE HOME OFFICE, *ex p.* BETANCOURT, *The Times,* October 5, 1987, Kennedy J.

1973. Leave to enter—whether parties have met

[H.C. 169, para. 41(*c*).]

A was a citizen of India, and was the fiancé of a woman settled in the U.K. They had in fact met 19 years ago when aged 4 and 3 respectively.

Held that, in the context of the rule, for the parties to have "met" they had to have "made one another's acquaintances," and such a meeting between infants of such tender ages did not meet the requirements of the rule.

RAJ (REWAL) *v.* ENTRY CLEARANCE OFFICER, NEW DELHI [1985] Imm.A.R. 151, Imm.App.Trib.

1974. Leave to remain—man marrying citizen—requirements

On a true construction of para. 126 of H.C. 169, the Secretary of State had to be satisfied upon each of the separate conditions contained in that paragraph before granting an extension of delay or leave to remain to a man admitted into the country in a temporary capacity who married a woman settled here. The word "and" occurred between each sub-paragraph of para. 126 and accordingly each one must be satisfied.

RAHMAN *v.* SECRETARY OF STATE FOR THE HOME DEPARTMENT, May 2, 1986 (C.A.T. No. 443).

1975. Legal aid—applications—delay

In immigration cases, it is important that the authorities should make arrangements to avoid delay in dealing with applications for legal aid.

UDDIN'S APPLICATION, *Re, The Times,* November 5, 1987, C.A.

1976. Lorry driver—visitor—whether working in breach of conditions of entry

[Immigration Act 1971 (c.77), s.24(1)(*b*).]

A was a long-distance lorry-driver with his own lorry, who contracted with a U.K. based firm to take loads from the U.K. to Germany and Turkey. On one trip he was stopped by police, arrested and charged with working in breach of the conditions of entry as a visitor. A Home Office official called by the prosecution said the normal practice with long-distance lorry-drivers was to give them leave to enter as visitors; picking up a load in the U.K. was permitted by r.19 which allowed visitors to transact business in the U.K.

Held, a submission of no case to answer would be upheld. There was no evidence to suggest that A was either employed in the U.K. or was attempting to establish himself in business or self-employment (for which leave would be required).

GURSAN, April 3, 1987, H.H. Judge Phillips, Knutsford Crown Ct. [*Ex rel. F. Webber, Barrister.*]

1977. "Means" to pay for onward passage—whether means available where airline companies decline to carry

[Immigration Act 1971 (c.77), s.11.]

A person who has the monetary means to pay for onward passage from the U.K. is nonetheless not a person who has the means to do so within the Immigration Rules if airline companies decline to carry him.

R. *v.* SECRETARY OF STATE FOR THE HOME DEPARTMENT, *ex p.* COONHYE, *The Independent,* May 14, 1987, D.C.

1978. Motive for entry—underlying reason for marriage

Once it had been shown that an applicant for entry clearance qualified as the spouse of a U.K. national and it appeared that the couple were going to live together, the entry clearance officer should not too readily find that the marriage was entered into for the purpose of gaining entry (*R.* v. *Immigration Appeal Tribunal ex p. Kumar* [1986] C.L.Y. 1697 considered).

R. *v.* IMMIGRATION APPEAL TRIBUNAL *ex p.* SINGH, *The Times,* April 13, 1987, Simon Brown J.

1979. Ordinarily resident—meaning—whether residence extends to date employment ceases including any period of accrued holiday, or to date of departure from the U.K.

N was a citizen of the U.K. and Colonies. He arrived in the U.K. in 1962 and left in 1967. He had accumulated paid leave, so that although he left his place of work on August 4, 1967 he was paid up to and including August 31, 1967. He left for Hong Kong on August 24, 1967 and began new employment there on August 31, 1967. In 1983 he was refused a certificate of patriality, as he was not considered to have been ordinarily resident in the U.K. for five years or more; to qualify he had to be ordinarily resident in the U.K. on August 29, 1967.

Held, that when A left the U.K. he intended to work and reside in Hong Kong, and thus did not remain ordinarily resident in the U.K.

R. *v.* IMMIGRATION APPEAL TRIBUNAL, *ex p.* NG [1986] Imm.A.R. 23, Webster J.

1980. Passport date stamped with cross to indicate refusal—whether Immigration Officer empowered to so mark passport

R sought a declaration that the stamping of his passport by an Immigration Officer at Heathrow, so as to record that he had been refused leave to enter the U.K., was unlawful.

Held, that (1) R himself had no direct right to object to the practice. If he were to object at all, it would have to be through the medium of the Indian Government, the owners of the document in question; (2) the Secretary of State was acting within his powers in instructing Immigration officers to mark passports. It was regarded as one of the functions of a passport to provide a medium for recording information relating to immigration control.

R. *v.* SECRETARY OF STATE FOR THE HOME DEPARTMENT, *ex p.* RAJU [1986] Imm.A.R. 348, Nolan J.

1981. Political asylum—other country available—Israel available to Jews

A Jewish South African in fear of persecution in his home country would not be admitted as an asylum seeker since there was another country available to him even though he did not wish to settle there, namely Israel, whose law of Return provides that every Jew has a right to enter and settle in Israel.

R. *v.* IMMIGRATION APPEAL TRIBUNAL, *ex p.* MILLER, *The Times,* July 3, 1987, D.C.

1982. Political asylum—temporary admission—whether "lawfully" in the country

An applicant for political asylum who has been granted temporary admission to the U.K. while his refugee status is determined is not "lawfully" in the country, and is not entitled to remain here as of right. However, such an applicant should not be returned to a country where his life or freedom would be threatened for reasons of race, religion or nationality. An immigration officer can only deal with such an applicant if it is clear that there is a country to which such an applicant can safely be removed without encountering such persecution.

R. *v.* SECRETARY OF STATE FOR THE HOME DEPARTMENT, *ex p.* SINGH, *The Times,* June 8, 1987, D.C.

1983. Political asylum—U.N. report—whether necessary consideration for Secretary of State

The *Conclusions on International Protection of Refugees* is not a matter to which the Secretary of State need have regard in refusing asylum (*Bugdaycay* v. *Secretary of State for the Home Department* [1987] C.L.Y. 1989 considered).

R. *v.* IMMIGRATION APPEAL TRIBUNAL, *ex p.* ALSAWAF; R. *v.* SECRETARY OF STATE FOR THE HOME OFFICE, *ex p.* THANANSYA, *The Times,* August 29, 1987, D.C.

1984. Ports of entry

IMMIGRATION (PORTS OF ENTRY) ORDER 1987 (No. 177) [45p], made under the Immigration Act 1971 (c. 77), s.33(3); operative on March 1, 1987; makes it an offence for the owners or agents of a ship or aircraft to call at a port for the purpose of disembarking passengers other than a designated port of entry if any of the passengers have not been given leave to enter.

1985/6. Practice and procedure—obligation to give reasons—evidence—village reports

B's application for entry clearance was refused.

Held, on appeal, that (1) there had been in this case only one issue, that of relationship. The tribunal had given adequate reasons for its decision. In *ex p. Khan* there had been two issues, and there the tribunal had failed to indicate clearly its reasons for its conclusions on each issue; (2) at the hearing, the U.K.I.A.S. author of the village report had distinguished between B and the other two applicants. However, although the author of a village report might expess a view, it was for the tribunal to weight the evidence and not simply to "rubber stamp" the author's view (*R.* v. *Immigration Appeal Tribunal, ex p. Khan (Mahmud)* [1983] C.L.Y. 1919 distinguished).

R. *v.* IMMIGRATION APPEAL TRIBUNAL, *ex p.* BIBI (FARIDA) [1986] Imm. A.R. 435, Taylor J.

1987. Primary purpose—marriage a fortnight after entry to U.K.—whether settlement was primary purpose of marriage

X was given leave to enter the U.K. on condition that while here he would not marry. A fortnight later he married Y in an arranged marriage ceremony. Y was settled in the U.K.

Held, that in determining whether X had discharged the burden of proving that the primary purpose of his marriage was not to obtain settlement in the U.K., regard should be had to the "intervening devotion", which was clearly evident.

R. *v.* IMMIGRATION APPEAL TRIBUNAL, *ex p.* ATWAL, *The Times,* October 21, 1987, McCullough J.

1988. Refugee—letter from High Commissioner of applicant's home state—whether relevant in considering refugee status

The Secretary of State was not irrational, nor did he take irrelevant matters into consideration, when he gave weight to a letter from the High Commissioners of Sri Lanka in considering a claim for refugee status by a native of that country (*R.* v. *Immigration Appeal Tribunal, ex p. Singh Bakhtaur* [1986] C.L.Y. 1684 considered).

R. *v.* IMMIGRATION APPEAL TRIBUNAL, *ex p.* MENDIS (VIRAJ), *The Times,* July 28, 1987, Mann J.

1989. Refugee—refusal of leave to enter—prohibition against appeals

[Immigration Act 1971 (c.77), ss.4(1), 13(3).]

The prohibition against appeals against refusal of leave to enter by a person in the U.K. contained in s.13(3) of the Immigration Act 1971 extends to persons claiming refugee status.

There were four consolidated appeals: in the first three the immigrants sought political asylum as refugees having lied to immigration officers to gain entry to the U.K., and then remained here for a long period of time. They were treated as illegal immigrants under s.33(1) of the Immigrant Act 1971. In the fourth appeal, the immigrant appealed for asylum on the ground that on his return he would be killed and had a statement from an African Consular official in support. The Secretary of State did not attempt to verify the statement, but refused leave on the ground that he was not a genuine refugee.

Held, (1) so far as the prior three were concerned, dismissing their appeals, that whether they were entitled to asylum fell to be determined by the immigration officers and the Secretary of State, and a claim to refugee status was no exception to the prohibitions against appeals under s.13(3) of the Immigration Act 1971; (2) allowing the fourth appeal, that although the question of whether or not there was a danger was exclusively for the Secretary of State, the question had not been adequately considered, and the order to remove the immigrant would be quashed (*Associated Provincial Picture Houses* v. *Wednesbury Corporation* (1948) C.L.C. 8107 applied; *R.* v. *Secretary of State for the Home Department, ex p. Khawaja* [1983] C.L.Y. 1908 considered).

BUGDAYCAY *v.* SECRETARY OF STATE FOR THE HOME DEPARTMENT; NELIDOW SANTIS *v.* SAME; NORMAN *v.* SAME; MUSISI, *Re* [1987] 2 W.L.R. 606, H.L.

1990. Refusal of leave to remain—abandonment of appeal—judicial review

Where A applied for further leave to remain the U.K., leave was refused and an appeal lodged, and subsequently that appeal was abandoned, and then A. made a further application which was refused, he was not entitled, save in exceptional circumstances, to proceed by judicial review (*R.* v. *Secretary of State for the Home Department, ex p. Swati* [1986] C.L.Y. 1711 followed).

R. *v.* SECRETARY OF STATE FOR THE HOME OFFICE, *ex p.* ATTIVOR, *The Independent,* October 23, 1987, C.A.

1991. Returning resident—after six years absence—matters to be considered in exercising discretion to admit

A was a citizen of Nigeria, and was settled in the U.K. when the Immigration Act 1971 came into force. He was therefore entitled to protection under s.1(5). He returned to Nigeria in 1978, and in 1984 he sought to enter as a returning resident.

Held, that (1) of the pre-1973 rules were more helpful to his case than the rules in force at the date of his re-entry, the earlier rules should be applied. In fact, the later rules were at least as beneficial to him; (2) when exercising his discretion, the immigration officer should consider *inter alia* the following: (a) the length of A's earlier stay; (b) the length of time A had been away from the U.K.; (c) the reason why the absence had extended beyond two years; (d) the purpose of A returning; (e) the nature of family ties in the U.K., and the extent to which A had maintained them during his absence; (f) whether A had a house in the U.K., and whether it was A's intention to remain and live in that house.

R. *v.* SECRETARY OF STATE FOR THE HOME DEPARTMENT, *ex p.* ADEMUYIWA [1986] Imm.A.R. 1, Farquharson J.

1992. Returning resident—original indefinite leave secured by deception—grounds for refusing admission as being "conducive to the public good"—obligation of advisers

A, in his new name, presented a new passport to the Immigration Officer, effectively concealing his previous immigration history.

Held, that (1) he committed deception by concealment of an almost classic kind and dimension; (2) the phrase "conducive to the public good" in para. 85 of H.C. 169 is not restricted to the meaning given to it in s.15(3) of the Immigration Act 1971; (3) when the solicitors had studied the affidavit filed by the respondent, they should have advised strongly against the applicant proceeding with the application; (4) accordingly, costs were awarded against the solicitors.

R. *v.* SECRETARY OF STATE FOR THE HOME DEPARTMENT, *ex p.* ALP [1986] Imm.A.R. 324, Hodgson J.

1993. Returning resident—weight to be attached to length of time applicant has been away from U.K.—misdirection of tribunal on question of fact

S was a citizen of Bangladesh. He lived in the U.K. for 11 years until 1972. He then returned to Bangladesh where he took government employment. In 1977, he returned as a visitor, and while in the U.K. applied for leave to remain permanently. That was refused. He returned to Bangladesh, and while in Bangladesh applied for leave to enter as a returning resident. That was refused. He appealed; that was dismissed by the adjudicator. He appealed to the tribunal; in dismissing that appeal the tribunal incorrectly stated the period of absence from the U.K. It was argued (1) that such an error could have materially affected its assessment of the case, and (2) on the facts the decision was perverse.

Held, that (1) it was impossible to say the decision was perverse; (2) the length of absence from the U.K. was a material factor: the longer an applicant had been away, the closer the connection with the U.K. he would have to show; (3) the application for review would be granted because the miscalculation of the period of absence could have materially affected the decision by the Tribunal. The case was remitted.

R. *v.* IMMIGRATION APPEAL TRIBUNAL, *ex p.* SAFFIULLAH [1986] Imm. A.R. 424, Simon Brown J.

1994. Right of abode—certification of entitlement—error in passport

A was a British Overseas citizen. She always travelled on a U.K. passport. Her original passport had the inscription "Holder has the right of abode in the U.K." deleted, and an amendment entered "Holder is subject to control under the Immigration Act 1971." In 1982 A applied for a new passport. This time A was issued with the first inscription intact, but with the following entry added: "Holder previously travelled on (the) passport attached hereto which shows she was granted leave to remain in the U.K. for a stay of two months on July 18, 1982." When A subsequently had to send her passport to the Home Office, it was returned with the first inscription now deleted, and with the following entry added: "Holder is subject to control under the Immigration Act 1971." A then applied for a certificate of entitlement to the right of abode in U.K., which was refused.

Held, that (1) such a right is a statutory right which an applicant either has or has not; it cannot be acquired by the exercise of a discretion. In this case A did not have that right; (2) no question of estoppel arose; (3) by recommendation that when A applied for a fresh passport it should be issued without the latest deletion of the first inscription (*R.* v. *Secretary of State for the Home Department, ex p. Ram* [1979] C.L.Y. 7 referred to).

CHRISTODOULIDOU *v.* SECRETARY OF STATE FOR THE HOME DEPARTMENT [1985] Imm.A.R. 179, Imm.App.Trib.

1995. Right of abode "without let or hindrance"—wife refused entry

[Immigration Act 1971 (c.77), s.1(1).]

The right to live in the U.K. "without let or hindrance" under s.1(1) of the Immigration Act 1971 is not infringed by refusal of entry to a spouse.

H was a British citizen with the right of abode in the U.K. "without let or hindrance" under s.(1) of the Immigration Act 1971. W, the Bangladeshi wife, came is Britain without the right of entry. W was refused entry and sent back to Bangladesh to obtain an entry certificate. H applied for judicial review.

Held, refusing the application that the right to live in the U.K. "without let hindrance" under s.1(1) of the Act did not confer any right to bring a wife who required leave to enter. (*R.* v. *Secretary of State for the Home Department, ex p. Phansopkar* [1985] C.L.Y. 7 distinguished).

R. *v.* SECRETARY OF STATE FOR THE HOME DEPARTMENT, *ex p.* ULLAH [1987] 1 All E.R. 1025, Taylor J.

1996. S.17 appeal—whether limited to issue of whether there is another country to which person could be deported

S.17(1)(2) and (3) of the Immigration Act provide that there shall be an appeal as to the choice of destination, without prejudice to the issue of whether there should be a deportation at all. That latter question is dealt with by ss.13 and 15 of the 1971 Act, and sometimes, though rarely by s.16(1)(*a*) of the 1971 Act.

R. *v.* IMMIGRATION APPEAL TRIBUNAL, *ex p.* MURUGANANDARAJAH AND SURESHKUMAR [1986] Imm.A.R. 382, C.A.

1997. Student—refusal of admission—factors immigration officer should take into account

O was a Turkish Cypriot born in 1964. While abroad he enrolled for an engineering course in London. He arrived without entry clearance and sought admission. The immigration officer noticed that O spoke very little English, could give no reason why he had decided to study engineering, and did not know what he would do with the qualification if and when he obtained it. The case therefore had to be decided under H.C. 169, para. 22, and the immigration officer had to be satisfied that O was able to, and intended to, follow a full time course.

Held, that (1) applying *Wednesbury* principles, the immigration officer's approach was entirely correct; (2) she was entitled to take into account O's command of English, his educational attainments relative to the proposed course, and his future intended career (*R.* v. *Secretary of State for the Home Department, ex p. Swati* [1986] C.L.Y. 1711 applied).

R. *v.* SECRETARY OF STATE FOR THE HOME DEPARTMENT, *ex p.* OZKURTULUS [1986] Imm.A.R. 80, Farquharson J.

1998. Temporary admission—marriage to U.K. settlor—whether entitled to indefinite leave to remain

[Immigration Act 1971 (c.77), Sched. 2, para. 21.]

When a woman is allowed temporary admission to the U.K. by an immigration officer under Sched. 2, para. 21 of the Immigration Act 1971, she is not "admitted in a temporary capacity" in the terms of para. 124 of the Statement of Changes in Immigration Rules 1983 and is therefore not entitled to be given indefinite leave to remain in the U.K. upon her marriage to a man settled in the U.K.

R. *v.* SECRETARY OF STATE FOR THE HOME DEPARTMENT, *ex p.* KAUR, *The Independent*, February 27, 1987, D.C.

1999. Transfer of functions

TRANSFER OF FUNCTIONS (IMMIGRATION APPEALS) ORDER 1987 (No. 465) [45p], made under the Ministers of the Crown Act 1975 (c.26) s.1; operative on April 1, 1987; transfers to the Lord Chancellor responsibilities in relation to immigration appeals.

INCOME TAX

2000. Appeals

REVENUE APPEALS ORDER 1987 (No. 1422) [45p], made under the Taxes Management Act 1972 (c.9), s.56A; operative on October 1, 1987; enables cases stated by the special commissioners to be referred direct to the Court of Appeal instead of to the High Court in prescribed circumstances.

2001. Assessment—appeal—allegation of abuse of power

On an appeal against an assessment to income tax, the taxpayer claimed that the assessment had been raised contrary to verbal assurances previously given to him by an Inspector of Taxes and that, in those circumstances, the raising of the assessment was an abuse of power.

Held, dismissing the taxpayer's appeal, that where abuse of power was alleged, the proper procedure was by way of judicial review, the allegation not being relevant to determination of an appeal against an assessment.

ASPIN *v.* ESTILL (INSPECTOR OF TAXES), *The Times,* November 10, 1987, C.A.

2002. Assessment—time limit—wilful default—agent

[Taxes Management Act 1970 (c.9), s.36.]

The Inland Revenue raised an assessment under T.M.A. 1970, s.36, outside the normal six-year time limit on the ground of wilful default. The circumstances were that at the relevant time the taxpayer's accounts were prepared by a firm of accountants, who improperly deducted certain private expenses of the taxpayer in his business computations. In the absence of evidence or explanation from the accountants, the General Commissioners concluded that they had been guilty of wilful default. The taxpayer was wholly unaware that incorrect returns had been made.

Held, dismissing the taxpayer's appeal, that notwithstanding the taxpayer's innocence, the wilful default of the accountants acting on his behalf enabled an assessment to be raised under T.M.A. 1970, s.36.

PLEASANTS *v.* ATKINSON (INSPECTOR OF TAXES), *The Times,* November 13, 1987, Hoffmann J.

2003. Back duty—appeal—evidence

M and T were partners in a gaming club; each opened a bank account in a false name and deposited a deed box with the bank. In September 1977, after inspecting their deed boxes, M and T saw the bank manager, and in October 1977 the accounts of M and T were credited with £5,000 each. Following a police inquiry, the bank manager and accountant were convicted of theft from the branch of the bank. In the course of that inquiry, these bank note bands (each for £500) stamped with the club's stamp were found in the manager's desk, and M's chauffeur stated that M had complained that £80,000 had been stolen from the deed boxes. The Inland Revenue issued estimated assessments on the club in the sum of £80,000.

Held, dismissing M's and T's appeals, that an inference of fact which involved fraud or other criminal conduct could be justified only by primary facts having substantial probative value. Applying the test, the Commissioners' inference that the deed boxes had contained takings from the club was justified.

LES CROUPIERS CASINO CLUB *v.* PATTINSON (INSPECTOR OF TAXES) [1987] S.T.C. 594, C.A.

2004. Bank interest—deduction of tax

[Income and Corporation Taxes Act 1970 (c.10), s.54.]

T Co. was a property investment company which in 1980 borrowed £350,000 from Savings and Investment Bank Ltd., which was an Isle of Man Bank having its registered office in Douglas. T Co. made payments of interest to the bank without deducting income tax under I.C.T.A. 1970, s.54.

Held, dismissing T Co's appeal, that the bank, albeit making loans to U.K. residents, was not carrying on a bona fide Banking Business in the U.K., so that income tax should have been deducted by T Co. from the interest paid (*United Dominion Trust* v. *Kirkwood* [1966] C.L.Y. 7762, applied).

HAFTON PROPERTIES *v.* McHUGH (INSPECTOR OF TAXES) [1987] S.T.C. 16, Gibson J.

2005. Beneficial loans

INCOME TAX (OFFICIAL RATE OF INTEREST ON BENEFICIAL LOANS) ORDER 1987 (No. 512) [45p], made under the Finance Act 1986 (c.40), s.66(9); operative on April 6,

1987; prescribes 11½ per cent. per annum as the official rate of interest for the purposes of s.66 of the 1976 Act.

INCOME TAX (OFFICIAL RATE OF INTEREST ON BENEFICIAL LOANS) (No. 2) ORDER 1987 (No. 886) [45p], made under the Finance Act 1976, s.66(9); operative on June 6, 1987; 10½ per cent. per annum is prescribed as the official rate of interest for the purposes of s.66 of the said Act.

INCOME TAX (OFFICIAL RATE OF INTEREST ON BENEFICIAL LOANS) (No. 3) ORDER 1987 (No. 1493) [45p], made under the Finance Act 1976, s.66(9); operative on September 6, 1987; prescribes a rate of interest of 11½ per cent. per annum for the purposes of s.66 of the 1976 Act.

INCOME TAX (OFFICIAL RATE OF INTEREST ON BENEFICIAL LOANS) (No. 4) ORDER 1987 (No. 1989) [45p], made under the Finance Act 1976, s.66(9); operative on December 6, 1987; prescribes the official rate of interest for the purposes of s.66 as 10½ per cent. per annum on and after December 6, 1987.

2006. Building society—dividends and other payments—scope of enabling legislation

[Income and Corporation Taxes Act 1970 (c.10), s.343(1A); Income Tax (Building Societies) Regulations (S.I. 1986 No. 482), reg. 11.]

By reg. 11 of the Income Tax (Building Societies) Regulations 1986, which were made under s.343(1A) of the I.C.T.A. 1970, tax was levied on dividends and interest paid by building societies in 1985/86, which period had been the subject of special arrangements between the Societies and the Inland Revenue, and for which tax had already been paid.

Held, granting the declaration sought by the applicant Society, that the 1986 Regulations were *ultra vires* in so far as they sought to levy tax on dividends and interest paid by the Building Societies in 1985/86.

R. *v.* I.R.C., *ex p.* WOOLWICH EQUITABLE BUILDING SOCIETY [1987] S.T.C. 654, Nolan J.

2007. Building society payments

INCOME TAX (BUILDING SOCIETIES) (AMENDMENT) REGULATIONS 1987 (No. 844) [85p], made under the Income and Corporation Taxes Act 1970 (c.10), s.343(1A); operative on June 1, 1987; amend S.I. 1986 No. 482.

2008. Capital allowances

CAPITAL ALLOWANCES (CORRESPONDING NORTHERN IRELAND GRANTS) ORDER 1987 (No. 362) [45p], made under the Capital Allowances Act 1968 (c.3), ss.84(1), 95(6); operative on April 1, 1987; succeed S.I. 1986 No. 539 so as to specify certain grants payable in Northern Ireland so that the amounts are not deducted from the recipient's capital expenditure when his capital allowances are calculated.

2009. Capital allowances—trade—plant

[Finance Act 1971 (c.68), ss.41, 44.]

The taxpayers carried on business in partnership as professional tennis coaches. During the year ended March 31, 1982 they incurred expenditure on an inflatable cover of high grade polythene (together with the necessary inflating equipment and a storage hut) which could be erected over two adjacent hard courts and enable them to continue coaching during the winter months. They claimed capital allowances in respect of the expenditure. The General Commissioners found that the inflatable cover (1) enabled coaching to continue throughout the winter months; (2) protected the playing area from the weather (3) created warmer conditions on the tennis courts, and (4) increased the revenue which the partnership could earn.

Held, allowing the Crown's appeal that on the facts found by the Commissioners, the cover did not play any part in the taxpayers' business but was merely part of its "setting" or premises, so that it could not qualify as "plant" for the purposes of allowances under ss.41 and 44 of F.A. 1971 (*Dixon (Inspector of Taxes)* v. *Fitch's Garage* [1975] C.L.Y. 1637, followed).

THOMAS (INSPECTOR OF TAXES) *v.* REYNOLDS [1987] S.T.C. 135, Walton J.

2010. Cash equivalents

INCOME TAX (CASH EQUIVALENTS OF CAR BENEFITS) ORDER 1987 (No. 1897) [45p], made under the Finance Act 1976 (c.40), s.64(4); operative on April 6, 1988; specifies the cash equivalent of the benefit of a car made available for private use by reason of employment.

2011. Charity—payments due under deed of convenant—claim for repayments

[Income and Corporation Taxes Act 1970 (c.10), ss.52, 53, 528; Finance Act 1971 (c.68), s.36.]

In 1971 J. covenanted to pay £5,000 a year to a charity. The payments under the deed fell into arrears, and those due for 1974 to 1976 (inclusive) were not paid until some years later. In February 1984 the Charity made a claim for repayment of tax in respect of covenanted payments due in the year ended April 5, 1977, but not actually paid until later.

Held, allowing the Crown's appeal, that covenanted payments were income of the payee for the year in which they were due, notwithstanding that they were not paid until later. Accordingly, the claim for repayment failed as being outside the six year time-limit.

I.R.C. *v.* CRAWLEY [1987] S.T.C. 147, Vinelott J.

2012. Covenanted payments—tax reclaim—whether annual payments within Sched. D, Case III

[Income and Corporation Taxes Act 1970 (c.10), s.353.]

In 1980 the Council arranged for Mr. S's son to receive special education. An agreement was entered into under which Mr. S. became liable to reimburse the Council for the fees payable to the school. Mr. S then entered into a covenant to pay to the Council regular amounts which, together with income tax thereon, would equal the amount of the fees payable. The Council claimed repayment of income tax under T.A. 1970, s.353, on the basis that the covenanted payments were "annual payments" chargeable with tax under Case III of Sched. D within s.52 of the 1970 Act.

Held, dismissing the Council's appeal, that the covenanted payments were not "pure income profit" in the hands of the Council and so were not within T.A. 1970, s.52.

ESSEX COUNTY COUNCIL *v.* ELLAM (INSPECTOR OF TAXES), *The Times,* November 6, 1987, Hoffmann J.

2013. Double taxation

DOUBLE TAXATION RELIEF (TAXES ON INCOME) (BELGIUM) ORDER 1987 (No. 2053) [£2·90], made under the Income and Corporation Taxes Act 1970 (c.10), s.497; gives effect to a double taxation convention with Belgium replacing S.I. 1970 No. 636.

DOUBLE TAXATION RELIEF (TAXES ON INCOME) (BULGARIA) ORDER 1987 (No. 2054) [£2·60], made under the Income and Corporation Taxes Act 1970, s.497(8); contains in the schedule the Convention with Bulgaria, which provides for business profits not arising through a permanent establishment to be taxed only in the country of the taxpayer's residence.

DOUBLE TAXATION RELIEF (TAXES ON INCOME) (CANADIAN DIVIDENDS AND INTEREST) (AMENDMENT) REGULATIONS 1987 (No. 2071) [85p], made under the Income and Corporation Taxes Act 1970, s.517; operative on January 1, 1988; amend S.I. 1980 No. 780.

DOUBLE TAXATION RELIEF (TAXES ON INCOME) (FRANCE) ORDER 1987 (No. 466) [80p], made under the Income and Corporation Taxes Act 1970, s.497(8); introduces special rules in respect of income and profits from activities connected with offshore oil and gas exploration or exploitation.

DOUBLE TAXATION RELIEF (TAXES ON INCOME) (FRANCE) (No. 2) ORDER 1987 (No. 2055) [£1·90], made under the Income and Corporation Taxes Act 1970, s.497(8); contains a protocol which makes alterations to the convention set out in S.I. 1968 No. 1869.

DOUBLE TAXATION RELIEF (TAXES ON INCOME) (IVORY COAST) ORDER 1987 (No. 169) [£3·30], made under the Income and Corporation Taxes Act 1970, s.497(8); gives effect to a Convention on Double Taxation relief entered into by the governments of the U.K. and the Ivory Coast.

DOUBLE TAXATION RELIEF (TAXES ON INCOME) (MALAYSIA) ORDER 1987 (No. 2056) [£1·30], made under the Income and Corporation Taxes Act 1970, s.497(8); the protocol scheduled to the order makes certain alterations to the agreement with Malaysia signed on March 30, 1973.

DOUBLE TAXATION RELIEF (TAXES ON INCOME) (MAURITIUS) ORDER 1987 (No. 467) [80p], made under the Income and Corporation Taxes Act 1970, s.497(8); deals with the tax treatment of dividends paid by Mauritian companies to U.K. shareholders following changes made by Mauritius to its method of taxing company profits and distributions.

DOUBLE TAXATION RELIEF (TAXES ON INCOME) (NIGERIA) ORDER 1987 (No. 2057) [£2·60], made under the Income and Corporation Taxes Act 1970, s.497(8); contains in the schedule the agreement with the Federal Republic of Nigeria.

DOUBLE TAXATION RELIEF (TAXES ON INCOME) (PAKISTAN) ORDER 1987 (No. 2058) [£2·60], made under the Income and Corporation Taxes Act 1970, s.497(8); provides that arrangements specified in the convention set out in the schedule have been made with a view to affording relief from double taxation in relation to income tax, corporation tax or capital gains tax.

2014. Emoluments from office or employment—PAYE—wilful failure to deduct

[Income Tax (Employments) Regulations 1973 (S.I. 1973 No. 334), reg. 26(4).]

A company went into receivership after having failed to deduct PAYE from emoluments paid to a director who was also a substantial shareholder. The Revenue issued a discretion under Reg. 26(4) of the 1973 Regulations to recover the tax from the director.

Held, refusing an application for judicial review, that, having regard to the applicant's position, he must be taken to have received the emoluments knowing that the company had failed to deduct tax.

R. v. I.R.C., *ex p.* SIMS [1987] S.T.C. 211, Schiemann J.

2015. Emoluments from office or employment—professional singer—part-time appointment as lecturer—whether remuneration emoluments of employment

The taxpayer, a professional singer, lived and worked from his home. Apart from a number of other engagements, he held a part-time appointment as a lecturer in music at a technical college.

Held, dismissing the taxpayer's appeal, that on the evidence before them the Commissioners were justified in their conclusion that the appointment constituted an employment, the emoluments of which were taxable under Schedule E.

WALLS *v.* SINNETT (INSPECTOR OF TAXES) [1987] S.T.C. 236, Vinelott J.

2016. Entertainers and sportsmen

INCOME TAX (ENTERTAINERS AND SPORTSMEN) REGULATIONS 1987 (No. 530) [£1·60], made under the Finance Act 1986 (c.41), Sched. 11; operative on May 1, 1987; provide for a scheme of deduction of tax by payers out of payments made to non-resident entertainers and sportsmen in relation to their appearances in the U.K.

2017. Husband and wife—earnings—separate taxation

[Finance Act 1973 (c.51), s.23.]

The Taxpayer and his wife sought to maintain separate taxation of the wife's earnings, although they had failed to complete and return the form of election supplied to them by the Inland Revenue.

Held, dismissing the Taxpayer's appeal, that as the terms of F.A. 1973, s.23, had not been complied with by the Taxpayer and his wife, their claim for separate taxation necessarily failed.

WARD-STEMP *v.* GRIFFIN (INSPECTOR OF TAXES), *The Times,* December 1, 1987, Walton J.

2018. Indexation

INCOME TAX (INDEXATION) ORDER 1987 (No. 434) [45p], made under the Finance Act 1980 (c.48), s.24(9); specifies the amounts which take account of the increase in the retail prices index for the purposes of s.24 of the 1980 Act (specifying thresholds for higher rates of tax).

2019. Interest on unpaid tax

INCOME TAX (INTEREST ON UNPAID TAX AND REPAYMENT SUPPLEMENT) ORDER 1987 (No. 513) [95p], made under the Finance Act 1967 (c.54), s.40(2), the Taxes Management Act 1970 (c.9), s.89(2), and the Finance (No. 2) Act 1975 (c.45), ss.47(7) and 48(6); operative on April 6, 1987; reduces to 9 per cent. p.a. the rate of interest chargeable on unpaid income tax, surtax, capital gains tax, corporation tax, development land tax, profits tax and excess profits levy.

INCOME TAX (INTEREST ON UNPAID TAX AND REPAYMENT SUPPLEMENT) (No. 2) ORDER 1987 (No. 898) [45p], made under the Finance Act 1967, s.40(2), the Taxes Management Act 1970, s.89(2), and the Finance (No. 2) Act 1975, ss.47(7) and 48(6); operative on June 6, 1987; reduces from 9 to 8.25 per cent. the rate of interest chargeable on unpaid income tax, surtax, capital gains tax, corporation tax, development land tax, petroleum revenue tax, profits tax, excess profits tax, and overpaid development land tax.

INCOME TAX (INTEREST ON UNPAID TAX AND REPAYMENT SUPPLEMENT) (No. 3) ORDER 1987 (No. 1492) [45p], made under the Taxes Management Act 1970, s.89(2), the Finance Act 1967, s.40(2) and the Finance (No. 2) Act 1975, ss.47(7), 48(6); operative on September 6, 1987; raises to 9 per cent. per annum the rate of interest on unpaid tax.

INCOME TAX (INTEREST ON UNPAID TAX AND REPAYMENT SUPPLEMENT) (No. 4) ORDER 1987 (No. 1988) [45p], made under the Finance Act 1967, s.40(2); the Taxes Management Act 1970, s.89(2) and the Finance (No. 2) Act 1975, ss.47(7) and 48(6); operative on December 6, 1987; reduces from nine to eight-and-a-quarter per cent. per annum the rate of interest chargeable on unpaid income tax, surtax, capital gains tax, corporation tax, development land tax, petroleum revenue tax, profits tax, excess profits tax and excess profits levy.

2020. Interest relief

INCOME TAX (INTEREST RELIEF) (HOUSING ASSOCIATIONS) (No. 3) REGULATIONS 1987 (No. 404) [45p], made under the Finance Act 1982 (c.39), s.29; operative on April 6, 1987; amend S.I. 1983 No. 368, in relation to housing associations, so as to provide for the bringing into the tax deduction scheme all "limited" loans.

INCOME TAX (INTEREST RELIEF) (QUALIFYING LENDERS) ORDER 1987 (No. 1224) [85p], made under the Finance Act 1982, Sched. 7, para. 14(2); names bodies which are qualifying lenders for the purposes of mortgage interest relief.

INCOME TAX (INTEREST RELIEF) (QUALIFYING LENDERS) (No. 2) ORDER 1987 (No. 2127) [85p], made under the Finance Act 1982, Sched. 7, para. 14(2); prescribes a number of qualifying lenders for the purposes of Sched. 7, Pt. IV to the 1982 Act.

2021. Jersey partnership—U.K. resident partner—Double Taxation Convention—exemption from tax.

[Income and Corporation Taxes Act 1970 (c.10), s.497, Double Taxation Relief (Taxes on Income) (Jersey) Order (S.I. 1952 No. 1216), para. 3(2).]

T was a U.K. resident and a member of a partnership, the business of which was controlled and managed in Jersey. He claimed that, by virtue of I.C.T.A. 1970, s.497, and para. 3(2) of the Double Tax Treaty with Jersey, he was exempt from U.K. income tax in respect of his share of the partnerships profits.

Held, allowing T's appeal, (1) that the partnership was a "body of persons" and a "Jersey enterprise" for the purposes of para. 3(2) of the Treaty, and (2) that, by virtue of that paragraph, T's share of the partnership profits was exempt from U.K. income tax.

PADMORE *v.* I.R.C. [1987] S.T.C. 36, Gibson J.

2022. One-off purchase and sale of land—whether trading

[Income and Corporation Taxes Act 1970 (c.10), ss.108, 526.]

Whether a particular transaction amounts to an adventure in the nature of trade depends upon its own peculiar facts, and provided that the General Commissioners' decision is not one which no one could reasonably reach the Court will not intervene.

Per curiam: the fact that land is not producing income does not by any means, in 1986, mean that it cannot be an investment.

Taxpayers bought some land for £65,000, of which £30,000 was borrowed at a commercial rate of interest. Shortly thereafter they sold the land for £100,000. The stated reason for the purchase was to acquire an investment, neither of them having invested in land before. They were assessed to income tax under Schedule D, but the General Commissioners quashed the assessment on the basis that this was far outside their normal trading activities, and that they were not trading.

Held, dismissing the appeal by the Crown, that the question was one of fact, with which the Court would not interfere unless a wholly erroneous answer had been reached. Decided cases were of use in identifying areas and factors which could be identified with trading.

MARSON *v.* MORTON [1986] 1 W.L.R. 1343, Browne-Wilkinson V.-C.

2023. Penalty—whether commissioners had erred in law

At an interview with his tax inspector, W agreed that the accounts he had submitted for the years 1979 to 1985 had been incorrect. G, the General Commissioners, awarded a penalty of £4,250, being 65 per cent. of the maximum amount they could have awarded in the absence of a finding of fraud. W appealed.

Held, dismissing W's appeal, that G had not erred in law, and had treated W with sympathy.

WALSH *v.* CROYDON GENERAL COMMISSIONERS, *The Times,* July 10, 1987, Vinelott J.

2024. Pension scheme surpluses

PENSION SCHEME SURPLUSES (ADMINISTRATION) REGULATIONS 1987 (No. 352) [80p], made under the Finance Act 1986 (c.41), Sched. 12, Pt. I; operative on April 7, 1987; provide for the administration procedures in relation to tax payments deductible out of pension scheme surplus payments made to employers by pension scheme administrators.

PENSION SCHEME SURPLUSES (VALUATION) REGULATIONS 1987 (No. 412) [£1·60], made under the Finance Act 1986, Sched. 12, Pt. II; operative on April 6, 1987; prescribe the pension schemes to which the Regs. are to apply and prescribe principles and requirements for valuation of pension scheme excess assets and for the reduction or elimination of such excess.

2025. Personal equity plan

PERSONAL EQUITY PLAN (AMENDMENT) REGULATIONS 1987 (No. 2128) [85p], made under the Finance Act 1986 (c.41), Sched. 8; operative on January 1, 1988; amend S.I. 1986 No. 1948.

2026. Proceedings before commissioners—natural justice—judicial review

Certain estimated assessments against him having been confirmed by a Special Commissioner and a case having been stated, the taxpayer applied for judicial review to set aside the determination, alleging that the case stated did not include all the points which he wished to raise and that the principles of natural justice had not been observed during the hearing.

Held, dismissing the taxpayer's application, that there was no substance to the allegation that there had been a breach of natural justice in the proceedings and that the proper course for correction of defects in the stated case was by way of notice of motion in the Chancery Division.

R. *v.* SPECIAL COMMISSIONER, *ex p.* NAPIER [1987] S.T.C. 507, Stuart-Smith J.

2027. Reduced and composite rate

INCOME TAX (REDUCED AND COMPOSITE RATE) ORDER 1987 (No. 2075) [45p], made under the Finance Act 1984 (c.43), s.26; operative on April 6, 1988; provides that for the purposes of s.26 of the 1984 Act the reduced and composite rates shall be 23·25 per cent.

2028. Schedule D—assessments—records

The taxpayer was a taxi-cab driver; he kept a notebook of takings which regularly showed sums of £24 and £25. The Inspector of Taxes was not satisfied with the completeness or accuracy of this record and raised estimated assessments in much higher figures for a period of five years. The General Commissioners upheld the assessments.

Held, dismissing the taxpayer's appeal, that on the material before them the commissioners were entitled to confirm the estimated assessments.

COY *v.* KIME (INSPECTOR OF TAXES) [1987] S.T.C. 114, Judge John Finlay Q.C.

2029. Schedule D—trust income from abroad—trustee resident in U.K.—whether liable to tax

[Income and Corporation Taxes Act 1970 (c.10), ss.108, 114(1).]

Where the income of a discretionary trust accrues from income situated outside the U.K., and only one of three trustees is resident in the U.K., he is not liable to income tax on that part of the income of the trust.

D was one of three trustees of settlements, the greater part of which comprised overseas holdings. No part of the income from the trust was remitted to the U.K., and D was, by the terms of the settlement, prohibited from transacting trust business in the U.K. He was assessed to income tax on the entire income of the trust.

Held, allowing D's appeal, that s.108(1)(*a*)(i) of the 1970 Act extended to income from overseas trust property only where the trustees were all resident in the U.K. As D was the only trustee who was resident in the U.K., he was not liable.

DAWSON *v.* I.R.C. [1987] 1 W.L.R. 716, Vinelott J.

2030. Schedule E—agency worker—deductible expenses

[Income and Corporation Taxes Act 1970 (c.10), s.189; Finance (No. 2) Act 1975 (c.45), s.38.]

The Taxpayer worked as a locum at a hospital pursuant to agency arrangements. He sought to deduct travelling expenses between his home and the hospital in computing his taxable income.

Held, dismissing the Taxpayer's appeal, that as his earnings as a locum were taxable under Schedule E pursuant to the agency worker provisions of s.38(1), F(No. 2)A 1975, expenses sought to be deducted had to qualify under I.C.T.A. 1970, s.189, and travelling expenses between home and work did not so qualify.

BHADRA *v.* ELLAM (INSPECTOR OF TAXES), *The Times,* November 30, 1987, Knox J.

2031. Schedule E—emoluments—distribution of trust funds—cessation of source

[Income and Corporation Taxes Act 1970 (c.10), s.181.]

In 1957 and 1963 a company set up trusts for the benefit of its employees. In 1979 the company was taken over, and the taxpayer ceased to be employed by the company on April 1, 1979. It was decided to wind up the trusts and to distribute the funds. In December 1979, the trustees, exercising their discretion, decided to distribute the funds to the employees having regard to length of service and salary level. Accordingly, in 1979/80 the taxpayer received two sums totalling £18,111. The taxpayer was assessed to income tax under Schedule E in respect of those sums.

Held, allowing the taxpayer's appeal, that the sums in question were "emoluments" within Sched. E., but that, as there was no basis for attributing them to any year of assessment other than that of receipt (1979/80) and since the relevant employment had ceased prior to the commencement of that year, the sums could not be charged to income tax.

BRAY (INSPECTOR OF TAXES) *v.* BEST, *Financial Times,* November 6, 1987, C.A.

2032. Schedule E—emoluments—P.A.Y.E.—failure to deduct

[Income Tax (Employments) Regulations 1973 (S.I. 1973 No. 334), reg. 26(4).]

Between 1976/77 to 1981/82, the taxpayers, who owned all the shares in, and were the only directors of, a company, received moneys from the company without the company deducting and accounting for income tax under the P.A.Y.E. Regulations. The company subsequently went into insolvent liquidation, and the Inland Revenue, alleging that the taxpayers had received the moneys knowing that the company had wilfully failed to deduct and account for income tax, issued directions under reg. 26(4) to recover the tax from the taxpayers.

Held, dismissing the taxpayers' application for an order of certiorari, that, in the circumstances, the Commissioner's determination that there had been wilful default by the company was not unreasonable.

R *v.* I.R.C., *ex p.* COOK [1987] S.T.C. 434, Nolan J.

2033. Schedule E—employment—part-time lecturing

T was a barrister, with chambers in Lincoln's Inn, who had ceased general practice in 1960. He derived part of his income from part-time lecturing on legal subjects at the Thames Polytechnic and for the I.L.E.A. He claimed that the income derived from these sources was assessable under Schedule D, not Schedule E.

Held, dismissing T's appeal, that the income was correctly assessed under Schedule E.

SIDEY *v.* PHILLIPS (INSPECTOR OF TAXES) [1987] S.T.C. 87, Knox J.

2034. Schedule E—payment in respect of loss of rights whether taxable emolument

[Income and Corporation Taxes Act 1970 (c.10), ss.181(1), 183(1).]

A taxpayer who obtained a sum of £1,000 in respect of the loss of trade union rights had to pay income tax on the sum since it was a taxable emolument under Schedule E.

The taxpayer was employed as a civil servant at G.C.H.Q. In 1983 she lost her right to belong to a trade union and other rights under employment protection legislation. She was given the choice of moving elsewhere or if she continued at G.C.H.Q. receiving the sum of £1,000 for loss of her rights. She was assessed to tax on this sum under Schedule E under s.181 or 183(1) of the Income and Corporation Taxes Act 1970. She appealed against the assessment and the special commissioners held that it was not an emolument for the purposes of the Act but that the payment was chargeable under s.61 of the Finance Act 1976 as a benefit paid to a higher-paid employee for which no consideration has been given. The High Court held on her appeal that the payment was an emolument within Schedule E. The taxpayer's appeal was dismissed. She appealed to the Court of Appeal.

Held, dismissing the appeal, that in determining whether the payment was an emolument as defined in s.183(1) of the 1970 Act both its status and the context in which it was made had to be considered. She received the £1,000 in respect of the loss of rights that were not personal rights but which were directly connected with her employment. Accordingly the source of payment was the employment and it was made to the taxpayer because of changes in her condition of employment and for no other reason and as such it fell within Schedule E by virtue of the provisions of s.181, (*Brumby* v. *Milner* [1976] C.L.Y. 1441, *Hochstrasser* v. *Mayes* [1959] C.L.Y. 1543, *Laidler* v. *Perry* [1965] C.L.Y. 1946 and *Tyrer* v. *Smart* [1979] C.L.Y. 1475 considered).

Pur Curiam: In the circumstances it was unnecessary to consider the more complicated issues which arose under s.61 of the Finance Act 1976, namely, for instance, whether a payment in cash can be a benefit in kind.

HAMBLETT *v.* GODFREY (INSPECTOR OF TAXES) [1987] 1 W.L.R. 357, C.A.

2035. Settlement—payment under discretionary trust—capital

[Finance Act 1973 (c.51), s.17.]

Payments out of a trust fund to a beneficiary which are of a wholly capital nature do not create an income interest purely by virtue of their regular recurrence.

H was the beneficiary under a settlement the trustees of which held the funds and income thereof on such trusts for the benefit of the beneficiaries as the trustees might in their absolute discretion determine. H suffered a heart attack and over the three years between then and her death the trustees paid £109,000 out of the capital of the fund to defray nursing expenses. The Crown contended that these sums were for an income purpose and should be assessed to tax.

Held, payments such as these, of a wholly capital nature, do not create by income interest by virtue of being a regular series of payments (*Brodie's Trustees* v. *I.R.C.* [1933] 17 T.C. 432 and *Cunard's Trustees* v. *I.R.C.* [1946] 1 All E.R. 159 distinguished).

STEVENSON (INSPECTOR OF TAXES) *v.* WISHART [1987] 2 All E.R. 428, C.A.

2036. Tax avoidance—purchase by taxpayer of loss making company with view to reducing tax payer's liability—whether tax avoidance—whether arrangement void for tax purposes

[N.Z.] [Income Tax Act 1976, ss.99, 191.]

A taxpayer avoids tax when he reduces his liability to pay tax without incurring the loss on expenditure which entitles him to that benefit.

C purchased a company, P, from M for $10,000 or 22½ per cent. of the tax advantage C might secure from the purchase whichever was the greater. P had made a loss of $5·8 million which fell on M. M released the debt P owed it prior to the transaction. The purpose of the transaction was to set off P's loss against the taxable income of C so as to secure a reduction of $2·85 million in C's tax liability. By s.99 Income Tax Act 1976 any contract was absolutely void against the Commissioners of Inland Revenue if and to the extent that directly or indirectly its purpose or effect was to reduce any liability to income tax. S.191 of the Act contained provisions applying to groups of companies whereby the losses of one company in a group could be set off against the assessable income of other companies in the group. The section contained provisions seeking to prevent tax avoidance by the use of the section, principally by means of temporary share transfers, which provisions did not apply to the transaction between C and M. C contended that it was entitled under s.191 to set off P's losses against the assessable income of it and its other subsidiaries. The Commissioners contended that s.99 prevented C from dealing with P's losses in that way. In the Court of Appeal C was successful principally on the argument that s.191 provided an exhaustive code of tax avoidance provisions in relation to the operation of that section so that there was no room for the application of s.99.

Held, allowing the Commissioners appeal, that it could not be said that s.99 did not apply where the conditions for the application of s.191 had been satisfied. S.99 would be useless as a tax avoidance measure if a meticulous and mechanical compliance with the provisions granting exemptions or reliefs from tax was sufficient to oust its effect. The tax avoidance provisions contained in s.191 did not provide an exhaustive code in the application of s.191. In the light of the legislative history of s.99 and s.191 Parliament could not have intended the avoidance provisions of s.191 to apply to claims for relief under s.191 of the Act to the exclusion of s.99 of the Act. The avoidance provisions of s.191 overlapped with s.99, The third argument raised by C that if their scheme was ineffective any commercial transaction or family arrangement would be vulnerable to attack by the Commissioners under s.99 failed to recognise the material distinction between tax mitigation and tax avoidance. Tax was mitigated where the taxpayer reduced his income or incurred expenditure in circumstances that reduced his assessable income or entitled him to a reduction in his tax liability. In those circumstances s.99 could not apply as there was no "arrangement" from which the tax advantage was derived. Tax was avoided where a tax advantage was derived from an arrangement whereby the taxpayer reduced his liability to tax without involving him in the loss or expenditure entitling him to that reduction. In the present case the loss or expenditure of $5·8 million was not sustained by C but by M. The tax advantage C claimed stemmed from the arrangement with M and not from any loss sustained by C (*I.R.C.* v. *Duke of Westminster* [1936] A.C. 1, *W.T. Ramsay* v. *I.R.C.* [1981] C.L.Y. 1385 considered).

I.R.C. *v.* CHALLENGE CORP. [1987] 2 W.L.R. 24, P.C.

2037. Tax avoidance scheme—artificial transactions in land

[Income and Corporation Taxes Act 1970 (c.10), s.488.]

The taxpayer entered into arrangements with there Bahamian companies whereunder property situate in the U.K. was sold, and of the profit of £13,500, only £5,000 accrued to the taxpayer, the balance of £8,500 accruing to the Bahamian companies. No evidence was adduced to show that the Bahamian companies were anything more than passive recipients of their shares of the sale proceeds. The taxpayer was assessed to income tax under I.C.T.A. 1970, s.488, in respect of the shares of the profit to the Bahamian companies.

Held, dismissing the taxpayer's appeal, that the assessment was correctly raised there being no evidence to demonstrate that the gains accruing to the Bahamian companies were other than of a capital nature.

SUGARWHITE *v.* BUDD (INSPECTOR OF TAXES) [1987] S.T.C. 491, Vinelott J.

2038. Tax avoidance scheme—tax advantage counteraction—assessment

[Income and Corporation Taxes Act 1970 (c.10), ss.460(3), 461(*c*).]

Counteraction by the Inland Revenue to an advantage obtained under an avoidance scheme is based on the contrast between tax payable under the scheme, and that which would have been payable without it.

A property company desired to sell a valuable property in Croydon and to distribute the net proceeds. To have done that in the conventional manner would have resulted in tax absorbing most of the proceeds. A complicated tax avoidance scheme was devised. The Revenue issued notices under s.460(3) of the Act and made assessments counteracting the tax advantage. The commissioners upheld the assessments, but Vinelott J. reduced them.

Held, allowing the Revenue's cross appeals, that counteraction was based on the contrast between tax payable on the scheme and putative tax with no scheme; the assessment should not give credit for liability arising from transactions within the overall scheme, even though the overall burden on the taxpayer might finally be higher than if the scheme had not been adopted (*I.R.C.* v. *Parker* [1966] C.L.Y. 6179 referred to).

BIRD *v.* I.R.C.; BREAMS NOMINEES *v.* SAME [1987] 1 FTLR 361, C.A.

2039. Tax avoidance scheme—transfer of assets abroad—power to enjoy income

[Income and Corporation Taxes Act 1970 (c.10), s.478.]

Where a Jersey company received income in consequence of consultancy services provided by a U.K. resident within the U.K. on its behalf, the U.K. resident was liable to income tax under s.478 of the Income and Corporation Taxes Act 1970 where he had the power to enjoy that income.

B was a chartered surveyor who provided consultancy servies in his retirement. B set up a trust in Jersey for the benefit of his wife and children. The trustees formed a Jersey company called Drishane Investments Ltd. B entered into a contract of employment with Drishane to provide consultancy services on its behalf. The contract provided that he would draw no salary until he reached 70 years of age and in the meantime would be paid such sums as Drishane felt it could afford. Drishane also agreed to assist B in the realisation of his assets consisting of property holdings. Pursuant to the arrangement, clients requiring B's services entered into contracts with Drishane in Jersey. B rendered the services in England and advised Drishane now much to charge. Drishane also purchased a number of properties from B. Those transactions placed cash at B's disposal. In consequence the Revenue raised assessments to income tax for the years 1975–1979 against B under the anti-avoidance provisions of s.478 of the Income and Corporation Taxes Act 1970. B appealed successfully to the Special Commissioners against the assessments.

Held, allowing the Revenue's appeal, that B failed to show that tax avoidance was not the purpose of the transactions. There was a transfer of assets by virtue of which income became payable to persons resident out of the U.K. The contract of employment conferred on Drishane enforceable rights against B. Those rights were rights over an asset of B, namely his earning capacity, that were transferred to Drishane. "Rights of any kind" constituting assets within s.478(8) was not limited to rights *in rem.* Drishane's rights under the contract could properly be said to be created by B. The wording of s.478 requiring that income becomes payable to Drishane was wide enough to include payments in the nature of profits and gains from trade conducted by Drishane in providing B's services. B was deemed to have the power to enjoy the income in the hands of Drishane by virtue of s.478(5)(*c*) in that he received benefits out of the tax-free fund accumulated in Jersey by Drishane. The benefits were the provision of cash through the purchase of properties from B, the payments of salary to B, the provision of cash for repairs to B's properties and the discharge of B's moral obligations to his wife and children. S.478(5)(*b*) also applied (*Latilla* v. *I.R.C.* (1943) 25 T.C. 107, *O'Brien* v. *Benson's Hosiery (Holdings)* [1982] C.L.Y. 1574 considered).

I.R.C. *v.* BRACKETT [1987] 1 FTLR 8, Hoffmann J.

2040. Trade—partner's removal expenses—whether deductible

[Income and Corporation Taxes Act 1970, (c.10), s.130.]

Relocation expenses reimbursed to partners in a firm are not tax deductible as being incurred wholly and exclusively for business purposes.

A Co. were a large firm of chartered accountants which reimbursed its partners for relocation expenses incurred when they were required to move to work in an office in another part of the country. In the fiscal year 1981–82 A Co. incurred expenditure totalling £8,568 in this way, which a tax inspector refused to allow in computing the profits of the partnership.

Held, that such expenditure could not be regarded as being incurred wholly and exclusively for business purposes and was not deductible in ascertaining taxable profits.

MacKINLAY (INSPECTOR OF TAXES) *v.* ARTHUR YOUNG McCLELLAND MOORES & CO. [1986] 1 W.L.R. 1468, Vinelott J.

INDUSTRIAL AND FRIENDLY SOCIETIES

2041. Fees

FRIENDLY SOCIETIES (FEES) REGULATIONS 1987 (No. 392) [80p], made under the Friendly Societies Act 1974 (c.46), s.104(1); operative on April 1, 1987; generally increase by about four per cent. the fees to be paid for matters to be transacted and for the inspection of documents under the 1974 Act.

INDUSTRIAL AND PROVIDENT SOCIETIES (AMENDMENT OF FEES) REGULATIONS 1987 (No. 394) [80p], made under the Industrial and Provident Societies Act 1965 (c.12), ss.70(1), 71(1), as applied by the Industrial and Provident Societies Act 1967 (c.48), s.7(2); operative on April 1, 1987; amends S.I. 1965 No. 1995 so as to substitute a new Sched. 2 to those Regulations.

INDUSTRIAL AND PROVIDENT SOCIETIES (CREDIT UNIONS) (AMENDMENT OF FEES) REGULATIONS 1987 (No. 393) [80p], made under the Industrial and Provident Societies Act 1965, ss.70(1), 71(1), as applied by the Industrial and Provident Societies Act 1967 (c.48), s.7(2), and the Credit Unions Act 1979 (c.34), s.31(2); operative on April 1, 1987; supersede S.I. 1986 No. 622 and increase fees payable in respect of certain matters arising out of the said Acts.

2042. Friendly Societies Act 1984—Jersey

FRIENDLY SOCIETIES ACT 1984 (JERSEY) ORDER 1987 (No. 1276) [45p], made under the Friendly Societies Act 1984 (c.62), s.4(3); operative on August 21, 1987; extends ss.1 and 2 of that Act to Jersey.

2043. Long term insurance business

FRIENDLY SOCIETIES (LONG TERM INSURANCE BUSINESS) REGULATIONS 1987 (No. 2132) [£4·50], made under the European Communities Act 1972 (c.68), s.2(2); operative on January 1, 1988; implemented for friendly societies the relevant provisions of the First Council Directive on the co-ordination of laws, regulations and administrative provisions relating to the business of direct life assurance.

2044. Transfer of functions

FINANCIAL SERVICES ACT 1986 (TRANSFER OF FUNCTIONS RELATING TO FRIENDLY SOCIETIES) (TRANSITIONAL PROVISIONS) ORDER 1987 (No. 2069) [45p], made under the Financial Services Act 1986, s.118(2), Sched. 11, para. 31, operative on January 1, 1988; makes transitional provision in relation to the transfer of most of the functions of the Chief Registrar of Friendly Societies to the Securities and Investments Board Ltd. under the 1986 Act.

FINANCIAL SERVICES (TRANSFER OF FUNCTIONS RELATING TO FRIENDLY SOCIETIES) ORDER 1987 (No. 925) [85p], made under the Financial Services Act 1986 (c.60), Sched. 11, para. 28, Sched. 15, para. 11; operative on May 19, 1987; transfers, with two exceptions the functions of the Chief Registrar of Friendly Societies under the 1986 Act to the Securities and Investments Board Ltd.

INHERITANCE TAX

2045. Delivery of accounts

INHERITANCE TAX (DELIVERY OF ACCOUNTS) REGULATIONS 1987 (No. 1127) [45p], made under the Inheritance Tax Act 1984 (c.51), s.256(1); operative on August 1, 1987; amend S.I. 1981 No. 880 so as to dispense with the need to deliver an account where the value of the estate does not exceed £70,000 in respect of deaths after April 1, 1987.

INHERITANCE TAX (DELIVERY OF ACCOUNTS) (SCOTLAND) REGULATIONS 1987 (No. 1128) [45p], made under the Inheritance Tax Act 1984 (c.51), s.256(1); operative on August 1, 1987; exempts from the need to deliver an account where a deceased's estate is less than £70,000 in respect of deaths after April 1, 1987.

2046. Double charges relief

INHERITANCE TAX (DOUBLE CHARGES RELIEF) REGULATIONS 1987 (No. 1130) [£2·60], made under the Finance Act 1986 (c.41), s.104; operative on July 22, 1987; makes provision for avoiding in certain circumstances double charges to inheritance tax in respect of transfers of value occurring after March 18, 1986.

2047. Estate duty

ESTATE DUTY (INTEREST ON UNPAID DUTY) ORDER 1987 (No. 892) [45p], made under the Finance Act 1970 (c.24), s.30; operative on June 6, 1987; prescribes six per cent. per annum as the rate of interest chargeable on unpaid duty.

2048. Indexation

INHERITANCE TAX (INDEXATION) ORDER 1987 (No. 435) [45p], made under the Inheritance Tax Act 1984 (c.51), s.8(9); substitutes a new table of rate bands and rates for the table which was substituted by the Finance Act 1986.

2049. Interest on unpaid tax

INHERITANCE TAX AND CAPITAL TRANSFER TAX (INTEREST ON UNPAID TAX) ORDER 1987 (No. 887) [45p], made under the Inheritance Tax Act 1984 (c.51), s.233; operative on June 6, 1987; prescribes six per cent. per annum as the rate of interest on unpaid tax.

INSURANCE

2050. Contingency monetary losses—whether authorised business

[Insurance Companies Act 1974 (c.49), ss.3(1)(*a*), 83(4)(6); Insurance Companies (Classes of General Business) Regulations 1977 (S.I. 1977 No. 1552), reg. 3(1), Scheds. 1, 4, para. 2.]

If an insurer carries on authorised business within the "marine, aviation, and transport" class, he may insure contingency monetary losses arising from adjustment to aircraft insurance premiums. Such insurance contracts will be valid even though excluded by statutory reclassification from the "aviation" class.

The plaintiffs were authorised under the Insurance Companies Act 1974 s.3(1)(*a*) to carry on business as aviation insurers within the definition of marine, aviation, and transport insurance in s.83(4) of the Act. The definition included all types of insurance covering the hull of the aircraft and the various types of aviation contingency insurance covering premiums payable under the former insurances. Aviation contingency insurance was normally effected under separate policies and the plaintiffs would separately reinsure these policies with underwriters. On January 1, 1978 the Insurance Companies (Classes of General Business) Regulations 1977 which modified the Act came into force, and the revised definitions of aviation insurance did not cover the plaintiffs' contingency insurance business. They continued with the business and entered into contracts of reinsurance with both defendants. When the plaintiffs sought indemnity under these contracts, the defendants alleged that the plaintiffs were not authorised to write the aviation contingency business so that the contracts of reinsurance were illegal and void. They also alleged that the plaintiffs were contractually obliged to retain part of the risk and having failed to do so, the defendants had no liability to reinsure. The plaintiffs brought actions to enforce the contracts. The judge ruled that they could not since they were not authorised. He rejected the defendants' claim that the plaintiffs had to retain part of the risk.

Held, allowing the appeal, that the purpose of the transitional provisions in Schedule 4 to the Rules of 1977 was to authorise any insurer who had been lawfully writing business in any class before January 1, 1978 to continue with it notwithstanding the reclassification of that business. They had not sought authorisation from the Secretary of State but still could carry on until the Secretary of State, if he chose to raise the issue, required the plaintiffs to satisfy him that they had carried on aviation contingency insurance before the relevant date. The contracts of reinsurance were valid and enforceable and no criminal offence under s.11 of the Act had been committed (*Howell* v. *Falmouth Boat Construction Co.* [1951] C.L.Y. 9617 and *F. Hoffman-La Roche & Co. A.G.* v. *Inter-Continental Pharmaceuticals* [1965] C.L.Y. 2957 considered). The defendants' cross-appeal was dismissed. In the absence of evidence as to the percentage of the risk to be retained by the plaintiffs and on the basis that the reinsurance slip referred to a standard full reinsurance clause, it could not be inferred that the parties intended that some percentage of the risk was to be retained by the plaintiffs, and the indications were that the parties had followed the normal practice of incorporating the full reinsurance clause. The defendants had failed to prove that the plaintiffs were under an obligation to retain part of the risk themselves.

Per curiam: Where a statute merely prohibits one party from entering into a contract without authority and/or imposes a penalty upon him if he does so, it does not follow that the contract itself is impliedly prohibited so as to render it illegal and void. Whether the statute has that effect depends upon considerations of public policy. But the Insurance Companies Act 1974 does not merely impose a unilateral prohibition on unauthorised insurers from effecting contracts of insurance but extends the prohibition to the carrying out of contracts of insurance. The extension of the prohibition has the effect that contracts made without authorisation are illegal and void and, therefore, unenforceable (*Mahmoud and Ispahani Re* [1921] 2 K.B. 716 applied; *Bedford Insurance Co.* v. *Instituto de Resseguros do Brasil* [1984] C.L.Y. 3205 approved; *Stewart* v. *Oriental Fire and Marine Insurance Co.* [1984] C.L.Y. 1830 overruled).

Leave to appeal was given.

PHOENIX GENERAL INSURANCE CO. OF GREECE S.A. *v.* HALVANON INSURANCE CO.; SAME *v.* ADMINISTRATIA ASIGURARILOR de STAT [1987] 2 W.L.R. 512, C.A.

2051. Diamonds—warranty in policy—whether breached

[Marine Insurance Act 1906 (c.41), s.41.]

A claim for insurance is "tainted by illegality" so as to preclude recovery if either the plaintiff needs to plead or prove illegal conduct in order to establish his claim or the claim is so closely connected with the proceeds of crime as to offend the conscience of the court.

P, an English company, supplied diamonds to wholesalers abroad. P sent diamonds worth $223,000 to customers in Germany with an invoice stating their value as $131,411 to enable the customer to evade duty. The diamonds were stolen in Germany. P claimed from the insurers the standard value, which was agreed to $142,173. The insurers refused on the grounds that the claim was tainted by illegality, and that by s.41 of the Marine Insurance Act 1906 it was an implied term that the adventure would be carried out lawfully.

Held, (1) a claim was tainted by illegality so as to preclude recovery if either the plaintiff needed to plead or prove illegal conduct in order to establish his claim or his claim was so closely connected with the proceeds of crime as to offend the conscience of the court: neither was the care here; (2) s.41 has no application to a contract of non-marine insurance in respect of goods alone, rather than an "adventure"; and judgment would be given for P (dictum of Lord Atkinson in *Moore* v. *Evans* [1918] A.C. at 191 applied; *Beresford* v. *Royal Insurance Co.* [1938] 2 All E.R. 602 and *Bowmakers* v. *Barnet Instruments* [1944] 2 All E.R. 579 explained; *Geismar* v. *Sun Alliance and London Insurance* [1977] C.L.Y. 1643 and *Thackwell* v. *Barclays Bank* [1986] C.L.Y. 158 distinguished; *Mackender* v. *Feldia AG* [1967] C.L.Y. 3229 considered).

EURO DIAM *v.* BATHURST [1987] 2 All E.R. 113 Staughton J.

2052. Duty of utmost good faith—duty of care—duty of insurers to insured—whether damages payable to insured

[Law Reform (Contributory Negligence) Act 1945 (c.28), s.1(1).]

Both insured and insurers owe to each other, as a matter of law, reciprocal duties of utmost good faith, breach of which by the insurers will entitle the insured to damages.

Various banks loaned money to four companies, in respect of which credit insurance policies were taken out. The policies, which contained exemptions in case of fraud, were all arranged by reputable Lloyd's brokers. The banks had agreed not to advance any money until the security was fully in place. A manager, L, working for the brokers, falsely represented that cover was complete, when in fact it was not, and on the strength of that representation the banks advanced the money. Although aware that L had deceived the banks, and that there was a gap in their insurance cover, an underwriter working for the insurers continued, without informing the brokers or the insurers, to underwrite further loans. The borrowers defaulted, and the remaining security proved to be of little value. The banks conceded that, by virtue of the exclusion clauses in the policies, the insurers were not liable on them, but claimed damages on the basis that the insurers were in breach of the duty of utmost good faith.

Held, that the banks were entitled to damages. (1) There is positive rule of law, rather than an implied term in any contract or a collateral contract, that both insured and insurers owe to each other reciprocal duties of utmost good faith. The insurers were aware of L's deceit, which was a matter of which the banks were unaware, and which they could not discover. Accordingly, the insurers were in breach of their duty of utmost good faith. (2) On such a breach, the remedies of the insured were not limited to avoiding the contract and reclaiming the premium paid, but extended to a claim for damages, if they could prove that the failure to disclose L's dishonesty induced them to make the loans. (3) Further, since it was clear that any failure to disclose L's dishonest conduct created a serious and obvious risk for the banks, there was a sufficiently close relationship between the insurers and the insured to give rise to a duty of care, of which the insurers were also in breach. (4) Where there was a breach of the duty of utmost good faith the 1945 Act was of no application.

BANQUE KEYSER ULLMAN S.A. *v.* SKANDIA (U.K.) INSURANCE CO. [1987] 2 W.L.R. 1300, Steyn J.

2053. Fees

INSURANCE (FEES) REGULATIONS 1987 (No. 350) [80p], made under the Insurance Companies Act 1982 (c.50), ss.94A, 97; operative on April 1, 1987; replace S.I. 1986 No. 446 and set out the fees to be paid by insurance companies when they deposit their accounts and other documents as required by s.22(1) of the 1982 Act.

2054. Fire—whether started deliberately by assured

P owned a warehouse containing wholesale textiles. It was insured with D. In December 1982 it caught fire and was severely damaged. P made a claim on his policy. D contended that the fire had been deliberately caused by P and denied liability.

Held, on the facts and the evidence, D had discharged the burden of proving that P had started the fire.

BROUGHTON PARK (TEXTILES) SALFORD *v.* COMMERCIAL UNION ASSURANCE CO. [1987] 1 Lloyd's Rep. 194, Brown J.

2055. Fire—whether started deliberately by assured—entitlement to recovery

P's hotel was insured for £375,000 with D. The premises were badly burned by fire and P claimed under the policy. D refused to make any payment, contending that the fire had been started, alternatively connived at by P.

Held, that (1) on the facts and the evidence, P had not connived at the fire, which was on the balance of probabilities accidental; (2) D was entitled to recover the difference between the residual value of the hotel and land and its value before the fire.

MCLEAN ENTERPRISES *v.* ECCLESIASTICAL INSURANCE OFFICE [1986] 2 Lloyd's Rep. 416, Staughton J.

2056. Fire insurance—conditions—suspension of policy while house without an inhabitant

[Aus.] An insurance contract contained a condition that the indemnity in respect of certain events should be suspended for any period in excess of sixty days during which the insured premises were left without an inhabitant therein unless with written consent.

Held, that a person inhabits a building during any period in which he uses it for the purposes for which a dwelling is usually used: cooking and eating, shelter and sleep. In some cases, fewer than all these purposes may be enough for inhabiting.

VASS *v.* G.R.E. INSURANCE [1982] Tas.R. 77, Supreme Ct. of Tasmania.

2057. Fire insurance—factory fire—whether P entitled to recover under policy

P's premises and contents were damaged by fire. P claimed against D, the underwriters. D contended that the fire was either started deliberately by P, or that if it had commenced accidentally, P would have been aware of it before leaving the premises.

Held, on the facts and the evidence, D's contentions succeeded and P's claim failed.

POLIVETTE *v.* COMMERCIAL UNION ASSURANCE CO. [1987] 1 Lloyd's Rep. 379, Garland.

2058. Friendly societies—long term insurance business. See INDUSTRIAL AND FRIENDLY SOCIETIES, §2043.

2059. Insurance Brokers Registration Council

INSURANCE BROKERS REGISTRATION COUNCIL (INDEMNITY INSURANCE AND GRANTS SCHEME) RULES APPROVAL ORDER 1987 (No. 1496) [£2·60], made under the Insurance Brokers (Registration) Act 1977 (c.46), ss.27(1), 28(1) as amended by the Financial Services Act 1986 (c.60), s.138(3); operative on October 1, 1987; replaces S.I. 1979 No. 408 and makes provision in relation to indemnity insurance for insurance brokers.

2060. Insurance companies—assistance

INSURANCE COMPANIES (ASSISTANCE) REGULATIONS 1987 (No. 2130) [85p], made under the European Communities Act 1972 (c.68), s.2(2) and the Insurance Companies Act 1982 (c.50), ss.2(5), 5(1), 15(6), 17(2), 32(1), 33(1), 97; operative on January 1, 1988; implement Assistance Directive (84/641/EEC) by amending the 1982 Act.

2061. Insurance companies—mergers and divisions

INSURANCE COMPANIES (MERGERS AND DIVISIONS) REGULATIONS 1987 (No. 2118) [45p], made under the European Communities Act 1972 (c.68), s.2(2); operative on January 1, 1988; implement Council Directive No. 78/885 concerning mergers of public limited liability companies and Council Directive 82/891 concerning the division of public limited liability companies in so far as these directives apply to life in insurance companies.

2062. Motor Insurance

MOTOR VEHICLES (COMPULSORY INSURANCE) REGULATIONS 1987 (No. 2171) [85p], made under the European Communities Act 1972 (c.68), s.2(2); operative on December 31, 1987; deal with insurance against civil liability in respect of motor vehicles.

2063. Motor insurance—consent of owner for driving vehicle—qualified consent

Where a limitation was placed upon a driver by the owner of the vehicle and the driver exceeded that limitation, his insurance was invalidated (*Whittaker* v. *Campbell* [1983] C.L.Y. 931, *R.* v. *Peart* [1970] C.L.Y. 2587 considered).

SINGH *v.* RATHOUR, *The Times,* October 20, 1987, C.A.

2064. Motor insurance—failure to obtain—measure of damages—hire of replacement

Where an insurance broker negligently fails to obtain cover for a commercial vehicle which is then damaged in a collision, damages do not extend to charges for hire of a replacement for the period after the time when the insurance company would have paid the claim.

R Co. instructed E Co. to obtain comprehensive insurance on one of their lorries. E Co. negligently failed to do so and the lorry was damaged in a road accident. When the intended insurers refused to make payment, R Co. obtained summary judgment against E Co., with damages to be assessed. The damages R Co. were eventually awarded included charges for hire of a replacement vehicle from the time when it was held that a company would have paid under a comprehensive insurance policy, to judgment. There would have been no entitlement to hire charges under the comprehensive policy.

Held, allowing the appeal, that the hire charges flowed not from E Co.'s breach but either from R Co.'s impecuniosity or from E Co.'s failure to pay damages when they fell due. They therefore did not sound in damages.

RAMWADE *v.* EMSON (W. J.) & CO. [1987] R.T.R. 72, C.A.

2065. Motor insurance—failure to obtain—police officer using own car on duty

[Road Traffic Act 1972 (c.20), ss.143, 144.]

J, a police officer, whilst on duty, drove his own uninsured car.

Held, allowing his appeal against conviction of using the car without insurance, that s.144(2) of the 1972 Act, which exempted from s.143 a vehicle being driven for police purposes by a constable, was clear. The magistrates were not entitled to look at what they believed the intention of parliament to have been.

JONES *v.* CHIEF CONSTABLE OF BEDFORDSHIRE [1987] Crim.L.R. 502, D.C.

2066. Motor insurance—permitting uninsured use. See BARNETT *v.* FIELDHOUSE, §3285.

2067. Motor insurance—using vehicle without effective insurance policy—owner allowing another to drive his car—owner believing that policy covered other driver

B pleaded guilty to using a motor vehicle on a road when there was no effective insurance policy as required by s.143(1) of the Road Traffic Act 1972. He was the owner of a car in respect of which an insurance policy was in force. He had been severely injured and was unable to drive himself so he allowed another driver to drive the car, with himself as passenger, believing that the insurance policy covered himself and the other driver. The magistrates' court granted an absolute discharge and that there were special reasons for not endorsing his licence. The prosecutor appealed by way of case stated.

Held, dismissing the appeal, that as a general principle the fact that an offence of this kind was committed unintentionally because the motorist concerned did not know the terms of his own policy was not relevant. However, in this case there were special circumstances which justified the magistrates' court in taking this action (*Rennison* v. *Knowler* (1947) C.L.C. 9062 and *Labrum* v. *Wilkinson* (1947) C.L.C. 9064 considered).

EAST *v.* BLADEN (1986) 8 Cr.App.R.(S.) 186, D.C.

2068. Motor insurance—vehicle stolen from repairer—policy exception clause—whether owner entitled to indemnity

An insurance policy may be so construed that the insurers go on and off risk at short and recurring intervals, so that the question of whether they were on risk in respect of a particular loss depended upon the precise facts obtaining at the precise moment when the loss occurred.

S effected third party, fire and theft insurance with NIGC, the policy excluding liability in any case when the car was not being driven by S, save where it was in the custody of a member of the motor trade for the purposes of repair. The mechanic drove the car to the sole U.K. agents to buy some parts, and while he was in the shop the car was stolen. NIGC sought to escape liability by contending that the car was in the mechanics custody for the purpose of being driven, and that the exception therefore applied.

Held, allowing S's appeal, that it was perfectly possible so to construe the policy that NIGC were on and off risk at short and repeated intervals, depending on the facts. Here, while the car was being driven to the agents, the exception would apply and NIGC would be off risk, but as soon as the mechanic parked it to go and buy the parts, the exception ceased to apply, and they were back on risk.

SAMUELSON *v.* NATIONAL INSURANCE AND GUARANTEE CORP. [1986] 3 All E.R. 417, C.A.

2069. Potential claim—professional indemnity—notification of potential claim to insurer—transfer of insurance

Where an insurer was notified in general terms of the breach of professional duty alleged by the building owner against the artchitect, but the statement of claim was received after the insured had transferred his insurance to other insurers, the first insurer remained liable since he had been properly notified of the potential claim.

THORMAN *v.* NEW HAMPSHIRE INSURANCE CO. (U.K.), *The Times,* October 12, 1987, C.A.

2070. Premiums paid by customers and banked—creditors' voluntary winding up—whether trust of the premiums created. See MULTI GUARANTEE CO., *Re,* §1427.

2071. Professional indemnity policy—surveyor—whether third-party proceedings excluded

P, a firm of surveyors, were associated with M, another such firm, on whose behalf they undertook work. When M were sued for alleged negligence in the design and supervision of construction of a large building, and joined P as third-party, P duly sought to rely on its professional indemnity policy, which contained two memoranda. The first memorandum specified that, ". . . so far as concerns work carried out by the Assured for and on behalf of . . . M . . . this certificate is only to cover the liability . . . of the Assured for claims made against the Assured . . . by independent third party firms or individuals." The second memorandum excluded all claims ". . . arising from associated companies, other than work undertaken for and on behalf of . . . M . . . as referred to in Memorandum 1 above."

Held, that (1) the first memorandum excluded from cover third-party claims brought against P by M; (2) the second memorandum served to exclude direct claims in relation to work undertaken by P on behalf of associated companies other than M, and was not inconsistent with Memorandum 1; (3) P were not therefore covered in respect of the third-party claim by M.

COOKE & ARKWRIGHT (A FIRM) *v.* HAYDON (1987) 283 E.G. 1068, C.A.

2072. Professional indemnity policy—whether liability excluded by non-disclosure

By an insurance policy taken out from 1983 and renewed for 1984 and 1985, D, an insurance company, agreed to indemnify P, a firm of auctioneers, surveyors, estate agents and valuers, against loss from any claims made against them, but excluded from cover *inter alia* any claims which arose from "any circumstances or occurrence known to the insured at the inception of this policy and likely to give rise to a claim . . ." The policy also required by Condition 5 that immediate notice should be given by P of "any claim made upon them or of any occurrence of which they may become aware which may subsequently give rise to a claim". In November 1984, P's senior partner M signed a proposal form for 1985 stating *inter alia* that he was not aware of any circumstances which could give rise to a claim against his firm or any of the partners. Immediately afterwards however he discovered that HP, an elderly consultant whose valuing capability had declined since 1982, had given an unreliable valuation to W; but, he did not notify D of this before the policy was renewed on January 1, 1985. When P were subsequently sued by W in respect of two earlier valuations carried out by HP in 1982 and 1984, and by BS in respect of the 1982 valuation, D repudiated liability under the policy on the grounds that P had failed to notify them of the fact that HP had been supplying unprofessional valuations.

Held, that (1) there was no evidence before March 1984 that HP become incapable of valuing; (2) accordingly D could not rely upon the exclusion clause in respect of the claim by BS, not in respect of such part of W's claim in relation to such part of W's claim as related to the 1984 valuation since M had failed to inform O of his discovery that HP had become incapable of valuing; (4) that failure was not however a breach of Condition 5, since that condition did not come into operation until the renewal of the policy, and contemplated future not existing discoveries.

TILLEY AND NOAD *v.* DOMINION INSURANCE CO. (1987) 284 E.G. 1056, Mervyn Davies J.

2073. Reinsurance contract—reinsurance in country other than that of original contract of insurance. See FORSIKRINGSAKTIELSKAPET VESTA *v.* BUTCHER, §2567.

2074. Reinsurance—retrocession agreement—arbitration clause—whether arbitration agreement incorporated into retrocession agreement

H, insurers, underwrote certain holiday insurance. They reinsured their excess of loss with, *inter alia*, D. This provided that all terms and conditions of the reinsurance were to be as per the original cover. That cover contained a limited arbitration clause. D then retroceded their risk to P, upon terms very similar to those in the reinsurance contract. Disputes arose between P and D over the scope of the cover, as H was not licensed to do business in Ireland, although they provided insurance there. P declined to pay under the retrocession agreement, and sought a declaration that the arbitration clause in the original insurance was not incorporated into the retrocession agreement.

Held, upholding P's contention, that there was no express reference to arbitration in the slip, and upon its true construction, the arbitration clause was not incorporated into the retrocession slip.

PINE TOP INSURANCE CO. *v.* UNIONE ITALIANA ANGLO SAXON REINSURANCE CO. [1987] 1 Lloyd's Rep. 476, Gatehouse J.

2075. Reinsurance—retrocession agreement—authority of agent

Where one reinsurer has made an agreement (known as a retrocession agreement) to insure the reinsurance interests of another reinsurer, the agent who actually signed the retrocession agreement may sue on it himself, and hold the proceeds for his principal.

Following an arbitration, the Court was asked to determine whether a broker who had signed a retrocession agreement, whereby one reinsurer insured the liabilities of another reinsurer in respect of reinsurances he had entered into, could himself sue on the agreement.

Held, that unless the contrary appeared from the wording of the agreement, it was well settled that such a broker or agent could maintain the action in his own name, accounting to his principal for the proceeds thereof.

TRANSCONTINENTAL UNDERWRITING AGENCY *v.* GRAND UNION INSURANCE CO. [1987] 1 FTLR 35, Hirst J.

2076. Reinsurance—retrocession agreement—scope of retrocession—construction

T were the direct insurers of an original liability. U.S. agents B arranged for the preparation of Quota Share Reinsurance (QSR) and through M, Lloyd's underwriters were invited to subscribe to the QSR agreement. M obtained reinsurance for the QSR insurers, one of the insurers being P, who was exposed upon the first U.S.$100,000 of each and every loss. P placed retrocessions in respect of such liability. These were placed by their brokers with D, and provided "100 per cent. syndicate share: 25 per cent." A question arose for decision as to whether upon their true construction the retrocession agreements amounted to an acceptance of 25 per cent. or 100 per cent. of P's proportion of the first U.S.$100,000 of each and every loss.

Held, that (1) the 25 per cent. line referred to the $100,000 each and every loss, and not to 25 per cent. of the order; (2) on the evidence, the 25 per cent. had probably been deleted upon signing anyway, and D had agreed to accept 100 per cent. of P's proportion.

PHILLIPS (A. B. W.) AND STRATTON (ALBERT) *v.* DORINTAL INSURANCE [1987] 1 Lloyd's Rep. 482, Steyn J.

2077. Reinsurance policy—material non-disclosure—whether assured can obtain relief under s.2(2) of the Misrepresentation Act 1967

[Misrepresentation Act 1967 (c.7), s.2(2).]

Loss resulting from a fire in Israel gave rise to dispute between the reinsurer and a retrocessionaire as to the liability of the latter. The retrocessionaire sought to avoid the retrocession, on grounds that that had been a material non-disclosure in the insurance slip. The reinsurer argued, in the alternative, that they were entitled to be relieved from the consequences of any non-disclosive under s.2(2) of the Misrepresentation Act 1967.

Held, that (1) on the fact and the evidence, the retrocessionaire was able to avoid the retrocession on the grounds of material non-disclosure; (2) on the facts, the reinsurers could not bring themselves within s.2(2) of the 1967 Act. Relief under that section was not, in any event appropriate in circumstances where an underwriter had validly avoided liability under an insurance policy.

HIGHLANDS INSURANCE CO. *v.* CONTINENTAL INSURANCE CO. [1987] 1 Lloyd's Rep. 109, Steyn J.

2078. Underwriting—vested in agent—duties of agent

A member of a Lloyd's underwriting syndicate vested the power to undertake on his behalf any insurance business of a non-marine nature in his agents.

Held, that the agent was thereby to have the sole control and management of the underwriting, which was not simply the task of subscribing contracts of insurance, but all aspects of the business of being a non-marine underwriter, including if necessary the commencement of litigation.

DALY *v.* LIME STREET UNDERWRITING AGENCIES, *The Times,* June 8, 1987, Staughton J.

2079. Warranty by policyholder—test for disclosure of "adverse facts"

A warranty in an insurance contract "no known adverse facts" only requires the policyholder to disclose facts that the reasonable man would recognise as adverse, and not to disclose facts not so recognised, but which later turn out to be adverse. The test of the extent of disclosure of material facts is whether they would be treated as material by a reasonable and prudent insurer, not by the individual insurer in the particular contract (*Lambert* v. *Co-operative Insurance Society* [1975] C.L.Y. 1451 applied).

KELSALL *v.* ALLSTATE INSURANCE CO., *The Times,* March 20, 1987, C.A.

INTERNATIONAL LAW

2080. Anguilla

ANGUILLA (PUBLIC SEAL) ORDER 1987 (No. 450) [45p], made under the Anguilla Act 1980 (c.67), s.1(2); operative on March 19, 1987; enables a Government of Anguilla stamp to be used in Anguilla instead of a public seal, pending provision of a seal, and validates things done with the use of such a stamp.

2081. Arbitration—security for costs

The principles to apply in considering applications for security for costs in international arbitrations are laid down in *Bank Mellat* v. *Helliniki Techniki S.A.* [1983] C.L.Y. 144.

K/S A/S BANI *v.* KOREA SHIPBUILDING AND ENGINEERING CORP., *The Indepedent,* July 8, 1987, C.A.

2082. Consular fees

CONSULAR FEES ORDER 1987 (No. 1264) [£1·90], made under the Consular Fees Act 1980 (c.23), s.1(1); operative on September 1, 1987; replaces S.I. 1983 No. 1518, as amended, and prescribed increased fees for the provision of certain services.

2083. Copyright—international conventions. See COPYRIGHT, §524.

2084. Diplomatic and Consular Premises Act 1987 (c.46)

This Act makes provision as to what land is diplomatic or consular premises. It gives the Secretary of Stare power to vest certain land in himself and imposes on him a duty to sell land vested in him in the exercise of that power. Certain provisions of the Vienna Convention on Diplomatic Relations and the Vienna Convention on Consular Relations are given the force of law in the U.K. by amending Sched. 1 to the Diplomatic Privileges Act 1964 and Sched. 1 to the Consular Relations Act 1968. S.9(2) of the Criminal Law Act 1977 is amended.

The Act received the Royal Assent on May 15, 1987, and comes into force on days to be appointed by the Secretary of State.
The Act extends to Northern Ireland.

2085. Diplomatic and Consular Premises Act 1987—commencement

DIPLOMATIC AND CONSULAR PREMISES ACT 1987 (COMMENCEMENT No. 1) ORDER 1987 (No. 1022) (c.26)) [45p], made under the Diplomatic and Consular Premises Act 1987 (c.46), s.9; brings into force on June 11, 1987 ss.6 and 7 and Sched. 2.
DIPLOMATIC AND CONSULAR PREMISES ACT 1987 (COMMENCEMENT No. 2) ORDER 1987 (No. 2248 (c.68)) [45p], made under the Diplomatic and Consular Premises Act 1987, s.9; brings ss.1–5, 8 and Sched. 1 of the Act into force on January 1, 1988.

2086. Foreign compensation

FOREIGN COMPENSATION COMMISSION (UNION OF SOVIET SOCIALIST REPUBLICS) RULES APPROVAL INSTRUMENT 1987 (No. 143) [£2·70], made under the Foreign Compensation Act 1950 (c.12), ss.4(2)(3), 8(3); operative on March 2, 1987; prescribes the procedure to be followed in relation to applications made under S.I. 1986 No. 2222.
FOREIGN COMPENSATION (FINANCIAL PROVISIONS) ORDER 1987 (No. 164) [45pp], made under the Foreign Compensation Act 1950, s.7(2) and the Foreign Compensation Act 1962, (s.4), s.3(3); operative on March 18, 1987; directs the Foreign Compensation Commission to make certain payments into the Consolidated Fund.
FOREIGN COMPENSATION (FINANCIAL PROVISIONS) (No. 2) ORDER 1987 (No. 1028) [45p], made under the Foreign Compensation Act 1950, s.7(2); operative on July 18, 1987; directs the Foreign Compensation Commission to make specified payments into the Consolidated Fund.
FOREIGN COMPENSATION (PEOPLE'S REPUBLIC OF CHINA) ORDER 1987 (No. 2201) [£1·60], made under Foreign Compensation Act 1950, s.3; operative of March 1, 1988; provides for the determination of claims to participate in sums received from China and the distribution of those sums.
FOREIGN COMPENSATION (UNION OF SOVIET SOCIALIST REPUBLICS) (DISTRIBUTION) ORDER 1987 (No. 663) [£1·40], made under the Foreign Compensation Act 1950, s.3; operative on June 1, 1987; provides for the distribution of compensation received by H.M. Government from the USSR under an agreement between them dated July 15, 1986.

2087. Genocide—Anguilla

GENOCIDE (ANGUILLA) ORDER 1987 (No. 453) [45p], made under the Genocide Act 1969 (c.12), s.3, the Extradition Act 1870 (c.52), ss.2, 17 and 21, and the Fugitive Offenders Act 1967 (c.68), s.17; operative on April 17, 1987; extends to Anguilla certain provisions of the 1969 Act, which gave effect to the Genocide Convention.

2088. Hostages—Anguilla

TAKING OF HOSTAGES (ANGUILLA) ORDER 1987 (No. 455) [45p], made under the Taking of Hostages Act 1982 (c.28), ss.3(3) and 5, the Extradition Act 1870 (c.52), ss.2, 17 and 21, and the Fugitive Offenders Act 1967 (c.68), s.17; operative on April 17, 1987; extends to Anguilla ss.3 and 4 of the 1982 Act.

2089. International body—confidential documents—protection. See SHEARSON LEHMAN BROTHERS INC. *v.* MACLAINE WATSON & CO., INTERNATIONAL TIN COUNCIL INTERVENING, §1676.

2090/1. International body—discovery—disclosure of assets of judgment debtor. See PRACTICE, §2989.

2092. International body—failure to meet obligations—creditors obtained judgment—whether entitled to claim against members personally—legal status of organisation

[International Tin Council (Immunities and Privileges) Order 1972 (S.I. 1972 No. 120), para. 5.]

The International Tin Council has sufficient legal personality for contractual purposes to make it liable for its obligations.

An arbitration award was made against the Tin Council, an international body set up by treaty. The Council had collapsed with huge liabilities. The plaintiff sought to recover against the members personally. The question arose as to the I.T.C.'s legal status, whether it had sufficient legal personality of its own, distinct from its members, as to make it liable for its debts.

Held, that although it was not a body corporate for Companies Act purposes it did have sufficient legal personality for contractual purposes.

RAYNER (J.H.) (MINING LANE) *v.* DEPARTMENT OF TRADE AND INDUSTRY (1987) 3 BCC 413, Staughton J.

2093. International body—receiver—execution—jurisdiction

No receiver could be appointed at the request of a firm owed a judgment debt arising out of the failure of the International Tin Council, which was an international organisation.

The International Tin Council, an international organisation constituted under the Sixth International Tin Agreement (the I.T.A.) which was a treaty between states, collapsed in 1985 leaving unsatisfied creditors including the applicant. The applicant obtained at arbitration an award against the I.T.C. for £6m. The applicant sought to appoint a receiver by way of equitable execution, which, it was conceded, would fall within one of the exceptions from the immunity of the I.T.C. conferred by the International Tin Council (Immunities and Privileges) Order 1972 (S.I. 1972 No. 120).

Held, dismissing the application, that (1) There was no technical objection to the appointment since the court had jurisdiction under s.37(1) of the Supreme Court Act 1981 to appoint a receiver, but only where a receiver could have been appointed prior to the Judicature Acts. (2) The property in this case could not be reached by any process of legal execution because the only asset of the I.T.C. was its right to be indemnified by its members' states, and the I.T.C. had made no demand on them. All the indemnifying parties except the U.K. government were out of the jurisdiction. The application failed since the applicant had failed to show that it had any arguable case that the I.T.C. had a cause of action against its members which was not derived from the I.T.A. The receiver was intended not to enforce the liability of the members to the applicant but the liability of the members to the I.T.C. Since any agreement as to indemnity or contribution had to arise from the I.T.A., and it was rightly conceded that the courts could not entertain such an action (see *International Tin Council, Re* [1987] C.L.Y. 310) as it was an international treaty, the claim must be dismissed.

MACLAINE, WATSON & CO. *v.* INTERNATIONAL TIN COUNCIL (1987) 3 BCC 346, Millett J.

2094. Length of boundary—dispute—appropriate law to apply

The International Court of Justice at The Hague defined a disputed length of the boundary between the former French colonies of Mali and Burkina Faso. The chief principles governing its decision were (1) the doctrine of *uti possidetis juris,* which gives pre-eminence to legal title over effective possession, and whose primary aim is to secure respect for the territorial boundaries which existed before independence was achieved; (2) the parties not having asked for determination *ex aequo et bono,* the Court would determine the question according to equity *infra legem,* that form of equity which constitutes a method of interpretation of the law in force, and which is based on law; (3) French colonial law existing at the time of the grant of independence, which was of evidential value only.

FRONTIER DISPUTE (BURKINA FASO/MALI), *The Times,* December 23, 1986, I.C.J., The Hague.

2095. Passenger services. See TRANSPORT, §3780.

2096. Peace treaties

TREATY OF PEACE (BULGARIA) VESTING ORDER 1948 REVOCATION ORDER 1987 (No. 856) [45p], made under S.R.&O. 1948 No. 114; operative on April 22, 1987; revokes S.R.&O. 1948 No. 2092.

TREATY OF PEACE (HUNGARY) VESTING ORDER 1948 REVOCATION ORDER 1987 (No. 857) [45p], made under S.R.&O. 1948 No. 116; operative on April 22, 1987; revokes S.R.&O. 1948 No. 2093.

TREATY OF PEACE (ROUMANIA) VESTING ORDER 1948 REVOCATION ORDER 1987 (No. 858) [45p], made under S.R.&O. 1948 No. 118; operative on April 22, 1987; revokes S.R.&O. 1948 No. 2094.

2097. Protected persons—Anguilla

INTERNATIONALLY PROTECTED PERSONS (ANGUILLA) ORDER 1987 (No. 454) [80p], made under the Internationally Protected Persons Act 1978 (c.17), ss.3(2) and 4, the Extradition Act 1870 (c.52), ss.2, 17 and 21, and the Fugitive Offenders Act 1967 (c.68), s.17; operative on April 17, 1987; extends to Anguilla certain provisions of the 1978 Act.

2098. Sales—uniform laws. See SALE OF GOODS, §3334.

JURIES

2099. Communication to judge—procedure—whether judge's decision to discharge jury open to review

[Criminal Appeal Act 1968 (c.19), s.2(1) (as amended by the Criminal Law Act 1977 (c.45), s.44).]

A judge who receives a note in relation to the trial from a jury in retirement should state its nature and contents in open court, except for information which the jury should not have revealed.

The Court of Appeal has no jurisdiction to review a judge's decision to discharge a jury.

D was on trial for rape. The first jury whilst in retirement sent the judge a note saying that they were deadlocked, nine to three in favour of the accused. The judge disclosed the situation without reference to the actual figures and discharged the jury. On the retrial D was convicted. He then found out the voting on the first trial, and appealed, claiming that an irregularity arose through the judge's failure to disclose the full contents of the note so that counsel could consider it fully, and through that having discharged the jury.

Held, dismissing D's appeal, that even assuming the Court could consider an irregularity in an abortive trial it has no jurisdiction to review a judge's decision to discharge a jury.

Per curiam: a judge who receives a note in relation to the trial from a jury in retirement should state its nature and content in open court, and if he considers it helpful, seek the assistance of counsel before the jury return. If the note contains information that the jury should not have revealed that information should not be disclosed by the judge.

R. *v.* GORMAN [1987] 1 W.L.R. 545 C.A.

2100. Communication to judge—procedure to be adopted by judge

Where the judge received a note from a juror he should as a matter of course deal with it in open court and in front of the whole jury. Where this was not done it would almost always be an irregularity.

R. *v.* WOODS (MARK RONALD), *The Times,* October 13, 1987, C.A.

2101. Disqualified juror—bias against defendant—whether trial vitiated

[Juries Act 1974 (c.23), s.18(1)(*b*).]

Before a deficiency in a juror can afford grounds for quashing a conviction it must be shown to be a material irregularity or otherwise render the verdict unsafe.

The appellant and his son were charged with burglary. C was one of the jurors, and he had disclosed a previous conviction and sentence. The appellant was convicted of, and the son pleaded guilty to, the burglary, and when the son came up for sentence he recognised C as being someone with whom he had had a quarrel. The appellant appealed on the grounds that C might have been hostile to him and revealed his previous convictions to the jury.

Held, dismissing the appeal, that there was no evidence to suggest that the appellant might have been prejudiced or might not have had a fair trial.

R. *v.* BLISS (1987) 84 Cr.App.R. 1, C.A.

2102. Dissent between foreman and jurors—presence of spouse of juror in court when jury excluded—whether verdict improper

Provided that a verdict is eventually returned in a regular manner overt dissent in the jury box between the foreman and members of the jury is not ground for interfering with the verdict.

The fact that the spouse of a member of a jury may be present in Court during argument between counsel in the absence of the jury is not sufficient material to set aside the verdict, unless there is some evidence of prejudice having been suffered.

W was charged with offences of assault. On two occasions when they returned to Court during their retirement there was manifest confusion on the part of the foreman of the jury as to whether or not verdicts had been agreed. Finally, however, verdicts were returned in the proper manner, acquitting W of the more serious charge, but convicting him of the lesser. Subsequently it transpired that the spouse of one of the members of the jury had been present in court when the jury had been excluded, and whilst counsel were debating a point of law.

Held, on appeal by W, that (1) although it was matter for concern that there had been such confusion in the jury box, there was no residual feeling of injustice, and the eventual verdict, proper in every way, should not on that count be set aside; (2) in so far as the presence in court of the juror's spouse was concerned, that was not a ground for disturbing the verdict unless some prejudice could be shown, or inferred. Appeal dismissed.

R. *v.* WILLIAMS (ALAN) (1987) 84 Cr.App.R. 274, C.A.

2103. Ineligible juror—whether trial a nullity or verdict unsafe—recent possession—right to silence

R and others were directors of a company trading from a warehouse in which a lorry loaded with stolen property had been found. No reply was received to the two opportunities given to R to explain matters. All were charged with conspiracy to handle stolen goods. On the jury was a juror who nine years previously had been a policeman. During his summing-up the judge implied that where the facts indicated recent possession the right to silence was overridden and an exception existed. All defendants were convicted.

Held, that the presence of a juror who was disqualified did not render the verdict a nullity. Although there may be circumstances where the presence of a disqualified juror rendered a verdict unsafe, in the present case that was no reason to suppose that the juror was biased. Had the trial taken place 10 months' later he would no longer have been disqualified. The direction on recent possession was necessary as the appellants had failed to explain the presence of stolen goods in the warehouse when innocent men could be expected to explain willingly. Although it could have been more happily expressed, there was nothing wrong with the direction (*R.* v. *Chandler* [1976] 459 *Parkes* v. *R.* [1977] C.L..Y 439, *R.* v. *Gilbert* [1978] C.L.Y. 559 followed; *R.* v. *Chapman and Lauday* [1976] C.L.Y. 614 considered; *R.* v. *Aves* [1950] C.L.Y. 2280 approved; *R.* v. *Hall* [1971] C.L.Y. 2269 doubted).

R. *v.* RAVIRAJ; R. *v.* KANSAL; R. *v.* GUPTA (1987) 85 Cr.App.R. 93, C.A.

2104. Protection—discretion of judge

The judge ordered that the jury should be protected. He did so after hearing argument from counsel and evidence.

Held, dismissing appeals against convictions, that on making an application for the jury to be protected, prosecuting counsel should state the reasons. The judge had a discretion whether to require evidence in support of the application. The defence may cross-examine. The criminal burden and standard of proof do not apply. Protection can be authorised if the evidence justifies an inference that there is a substantially increased risk of interference. The jury need not be told the reasons. The practice of counsel agreeing a formula with the judge was proper. Otherwise, the judge must decide. Exact wording was not important provided the jury were told that the fact of protection was not to be used in any way adverse to the defendants.

R. *v.* LING [1987] Crim.L.R. 495, C.A.

2105. Racially mixed jury panel—adjournment to achieve

Six of nine accused of offences concerning cannabis were of Afro-Caribbean origin. Three were white. A police officer interviewing one defendant had asked "would you say that cannabis smoking is part of West Indian culture?" The judge and prosecution accepted that, in principle, the jury should contain black people. The jury panel contained no black person.

Held, that the case would be adjourned for seven days to see whether the panel then contained black people. If so, the peremptory challenges of the defendants should ensure a racially balanced jury.

R. *v.* FRAZER [1987] Crim.L.R. 418, Leeds Crown Court.

2106. Trial by jury—exercise of discretion as to use of jury—libel action. See VISCOUNT DE L'ISLE *v.* TIMES NEWSPAPERS, §3119.

LAND CHARGES

2107. Local land charges

LOCAL LAND CHARGES (AMENDMENT) RULES 1987 (No. 389) [45p], made under the Local Land Charges Act 1975 (c.76), s.14; operative on April 1, 1987; increase fees.

2108. Local land charges—defective title—purchaser deemed to have made searches—duty of vendor to make full disclosure

[Law of Property Act 1925 (c.20), s.198(1).]

A vendor is required by equity to make a full and frank disclosure of all defects in title of which he is aware.

The defendant was the freehold owner of a house let to a protected tenant. Her predecessor in title had applied for an improvement grant under the 1974 Housing Act. The grant was registered in the register of local land charges and the defendant's solicitors knew of the entry. The defendant intended to dispose of the property by auction and it was a condition of the contract that the purchaser was deemed to have made local searches. The plaintiff agreed to purchase without having made the searches, but refused to complete once it learned of the charge, prior to its removal from the register. The defendant served notice to complete and for interest. The plaintiff sought a declaration that the defendant was not entitled to either.

Held, equity required the vendor to make full and frank disclosure, and without it she could not rely on the deeming provisions in the contract (*Nottingham Patent Brick and Tile Co.* v. *Butler* (1885) 15 Q.B.D. 261 applied).

RIGNALL DEVELOPMENTS *v.* HALIL [1987] 3 W.L.R. 394, Millett J.

2109. Overriding interest—wife in occupation—payment referable to purchase of home

[Land Registration Act 1925 (c.21), s.70(1)(*g*).]

The payment by a wife into a limited company that she and her husband owned of the proceeds of sale of their former home in order to pay the mortgage on their new home was not a payment referable to the purchase of the home she was occupying and did not create an overriding equitable interest entitling the wife to remain in occupation.

In 1980 a freehold house was bought for £70,000 by a company under the sole control of a husband and wife. They occupied it as their matrimonial home, intending eventually to buy it from the company. When they sold their former matrimonial home which was jointly owned they paid the £8,600 proceeds of sale into the company's bank account, thereby reducing its overdraft. Thereafter the overdraft increased and in 1981 P advanced £70,000 to the company under a legal charge on the property. The husband forged the wife's signature on both the legal charge and a letter acknowledging that the husband and wife occupied only as mere licensees of the company. The company went into liquidation, and in 1984 P obtained an order for possession against the husband and the company, and an order for payment of principal and interest. P then sought possession against the wife who was sole occupier of the house. The judge granted an order for possession, but the Court of Appeal held by a majority that the wife, in consequence of the payment to the company of the proceeds of sale of the former matrimonial home had acquired an overriding interest within s.70(1)(*g*) of the Land Registration Act 1925 and discharged the order for possession.

Held, allowing P's appeal, that the payment to the company of the proceeds of sale was held not to be a payment referable to the acquisition of the company's property, and so did not create an equitable interest therein entitling the wife to remain in occupation. Notwithstanding that the husband had forged the wife's signature, the company had admitted the validity of the legal charge by submitting to the orders for possession and payment, and so the mortgagee could exercise the powers conferred by the charge so as to obtain possession.

WINKWORTH *v.* BARON (EDWARD) DEVELOPMENT CO. (1986) 1 W.L.R. 1512, H.L.

2110. Property adjustment order—charge—priority. See PEREZ-ADAMSON *v.* PEREZ-RIVAS, §1782.

2111. Registration of caution pending purchase—undertaking as to damages

It was normal in a case where there was a triable issue as to whether a contract for the purchase of land had been repudiated, for the potential purchaser to be made to give an undertaking in damages in exchange for the court permitting his caution to remain on the register, in case the potential vendor might sustain losses by being unable to deal with the property should the contract in fact have been repudiated (*Clearbrook Property Holdings* v. *Verrier* [1973] C.L.Y. 1875, *Tiverton* v. *Wearwell* [1974] C.L.Y. 3952 considered).

TUCKER *v.* HUTCHINSON, *The Times*, January 17, 1987, C.A.

LANDLORD AND TENANT

2112. Application for new tenancy—landlords' intention to carry out substantial works of reconstruction—whether "interfering to a substantial extent or for a substantial time"

[Landlord and Tenant Act 1954 (c.56), s.31A(1)(*a*).]

For the purposes of s.31A(1)(*a*) of the 1954 Act only those works that are additional to those the landlord can carry out under a power of re-entry, will constitute the "work intended," in deciding whether they are "substantial."

By a lease a ground floor shop and basement were leased to the applicants; the tenancy came with Part II of the 1954 Act. The premises contained three upper storeys; the lease reserved a right of entry for repair. The landlords served a s.25 notice stating they would oppose an application by the tenants on the grounds that they intended to carry out substantial works of reconstruction. The applicants applied for a new lease relying on s.31A(1)(*a*), contending that the works would not interfere "to a substantial extent or for a substantial time" with the use of the premises. The judge found that the works, which would take six weeks, did constitute substantial interference.

Held, allowing the appeal, that (1) where a landlord's power of entry allows him to effect repairs, only those additional works will constitute "the work intended" for the purposes of s.31A(1)(*a*); (2) in this case the "additional works" to those that could be completed under the power of re-entry would only take two weeks, which did not constitute "substantial interference for a substantial time."

CEREX JEWELS *v.* PEACHEY PROPERTY CORP. (1986) 52 P. & C.R. 127, C.A.

2113. Arrears of rent—breach of interim order—whether T's defence to be struck out

[County Courts Act 1984 (c.28), s.50; County Court Rules Ord. 13, r.12 and R.S.C. Ord. 45, r.1.]

In proceedings by L for arrears of rent, the County Court made an order in October 1984 that T should make an interim payment of £14,000 plus £80 per week. Upon T's failure to comply, the judge ordered that T's defence be struck out unless the sum was paid.

Held, allowing T's appeal and setting aside the order, that, having regard to s.50 of the County Courts Act 1984, to Ord. 13, r.12 of the County Court Rules, and to R.S.C. Ord. 45, r.1, L's remedy was not to ask for the defence to be struck out, but to use the machinery of the law to enforce the interim payments.

H.H. PROPERTY CO. *v.* RAHIM, (1987) 282 E.G. 455, C.A.

2114. Arrears payable under rent review clause—whether payable by assignee of term

[Apportionment Act 1870 (c.35), s.2.]

Where a lease contained a rent review clause and the lease was assigned, the assignor is liable for the increased rent up to the date of the assignment and not the assignee.

By a lease dated November 25, 1972, the plaintiffs leased 300 acres of farmland to the tenants for 21 years with a rent review clause every three years. The tenant encountered financial difficulties and a receiver was appointed in 1977. The original rent was paid throughout, but the rent increases from March 1978 on were not determined until November 16, 1983. On December 22, 1983, the tenant company assigned the lease to the defendant. As a result of the rent review of November 16, 1983, £19,800 rent remained unpaid in respect of the period from March 25, 1978. The plaintiff claimed that the defendant was liable for the arrears.

Held, that where a lease provided for a rent review, the tenant was liable for the increased rent from the start of the period from which rent was payable even though it was only payable when the rent was actually determined. Where the lease was assigned, the Apportionment Act 1870 applied, so that the assignor was liable for the increased rent up to the date of the assignment and not the assignee, since the rent accrued from day to day even though it was not immediately payable.

Per curiam: The point decided has no bearing on a case where the landlord is seeking to re-enter for non-payment of rent. If the right of re-entry is exercisable simply in the event of non-payment of rent, the landlord will be entitled to re-enter whether it is the assignor or assignee who is under the personal obligation to pay the arrears.

PARRY *v.* ROBINSON-WYLLIE (1987) 54 P. & C.R., 187, Browne-Wilkinson V.-C.

2115. Assessment of fair rent—effect of premiums—area to be considered in assessing scarcity

[Rent Act 1977 (c.42), s.13, Pt. IV; Housing Act 1980 (c.51), Sched. 8.]

The Crown Estate Commissioners were the lessors of a large estate in central London, including a house of which C was the tenant. The terms of the lease allowed C to assign the lease with the consent of the lessor, not to be unreasonably withheld. A fair rent was registered at £9,750 p.a. The Commissioners appealed to the Rent Assessment Committee, seeking a rent of £18,250 p.a., based on two principal arguments: firstly, the fact that C could obtain an open market premium on the assignment of the lease until the end of 1990; and secondly that the value attached to the character of the premises and their location should be taken into account and not disregarded on the grounds of scarcity, and again that the demand for this type of accommodation was not greater than the supply, there should be no deduction for scarcity. The Committee did not allow the appeal. The Commissioners sought judicial review of the decision.

Held, allowing the application, that (1) the committee were entitled to look at an area wider than Regent's Park in considering scarcity; further there was evidence before them upon which they could form the view that there was an element of scarcity in relation to the premises which fell to be disregarded; (2) the right to assign the lease could not be considered a personal circumstance within s.70(1) of the Rent Act and was a factor which should be taken into account.

CROWN ESTATE COMMISSIONERS *v.* CONNOR AND THE LONDON RENT ASSESSMENT PANEL (1986) 19 H.L.R. 35, McCowan J.

2116. Assignment—consent—whether unreasonably refused

T were underlessees of premises in the Arndale Centre, Middleton, in which they operated a "Woolco" store. The underlease contained a covenant against sub-underletting or assignment without L's consent, which was not to be unreasonably refused, and further covenants to keep the premises open as a retail store during normal shopping hours. When T sought to close the "Woolco" store and to assign the premises to E, a company with neither the intention nor the practical capacity to use them as a retail store, L refused consent. T duly sought a declaration that consent had unreasonably been withheld, arguing that it was not a necessary consequence of the proposed assignment that there would be a breach of covenant; whilst L counterclaimed for specific performance of the covenant to keep the premises open as a retail store.

Held, giving judgment for L, that, (1) having regard to the considerations (i) that the covenant concerned was a positive one, which could only be enforced against the assignee by a mandatory injunction if at all; (ii) that there would be a breach of that covenant unless the assignee took positive steps to use the premises as a retail store, which it had neither the intention nor the capacity to do; (iii) that L were entitled to take into account the likely effect of the assignment upon their ability to let and obtain appropriate rents for other parts of the Centre; (iv) that any detriment that T would suffer would be collateral only and not a consequence of the refusal of consent; and (v) that the balance of detriment was on L's side, consent had not been unreasonably refused. (*Killick* v. *Second Garden Property Co.* [1973] C.L.Y. 1890 distinguished; *Re Town Investments Underlease* [1954] C.L.Y. 802, *International Drilling Fields* v. *Louisville Investments (Uxbridge)* [1986] C.L.Y. 1824 and *Fullers Theatres & Vaudeville Co.* v. *Rofe* [1923] A.C. 435 considered; (2) the Court could not grant specific performance to require T to carry on the business of a retail store. (*Braddon Towers* v. *International Stores* (unreported) followed; *Posner* v. *Scott-Lewis* [1986] C.L.Y. 1841 distinguished).

F.W. WOOLWORTH *v.* CHARLWOOD ALLIANCE PROPERTIES (1987) 282 E.G. 585, H.H. Judge Finlay Q.C.

2117. Assignment—lease containing covenant of surety guaranteeing payment of rent by tenant—assignment of reversion by landlord—whether benefit of surety's covenant assigned with reversion

[Law of Property Act 1925 (c.20), s.189(2).]

The benefit of a covenant by a surety with a "landlord", landlord being defined as any person entitled to the reversion immediately expectant on the lease, passed with the reversion on an assignment notwithstanding that the covenant was not expressly referred to.

L granted a licence for the assignment of a lease to T. The licence was by deed and contained a covenant on the part of D to pay and make good to L on demand all damages, losses, costs and expenses arising from any failure on the part of T to comply with the terms of the lease. The licence defined L as including the person or persons for the time being entitled to the reversion immediately expectant on the determination of the term. Two and a half years later, L granted P a reversionary lease of the premises for a term of $92\frac{1}{2}$ years. T failed to pay rent in December 1985 and March 1986 to P. On April 22, 1986, L expressly assigned to P the benefit of D's covenant in the licence to assign. The court was invited to decide as a preliminary issue whether or not P was entitled to the benefit of D's covenant in the licence.

Held, that the benefit of D's covenant passed to P on the grant of the reversionary lease by L to P, being a covenant with a landlord as defined in the licence to assign. P fell within that definition. D's covenant was not a covenant that touched and concerned the land demised in that the value of the land was not affected *per se* but by a collateral circumstance. D's covenant did not impose any primary liability on D but was rather a guarantee of T's performance of his obligations. As such, the covenant was not an indemnity within the meaning of S.189(2) Law of Property Act 1925. The express assignment of April 22, 1986 was ineffective. By granting a reversionary lease to P, L discharged D from any obligation owed by D to L under the covenant so that thereafter L had nothing to transfer to P (*Griffith* v. *Pelton* [1957] C.L.Y. 1962 applied; *Vyvyan* v. *Arthur* (1823) 1 B. & C. 410 distinguished; *Pinemain* v. *Welbeck International* [1985] C.L.Y. 1882, *Distributors and Warehousing, Re* [1986] C.L.Y. 1864, *Consolidated Trust Co.* v. *Naylor* (1936) 55 C.L.R. 423 considered).

COASTPLACE *v.* HARTLEY [1987] 2 W.L.R. 1289, French J.

2118. Assured tenancies

ASSURED TENANCIES (APPROVED BODIES) (No. 1) ORDER 1987 (No. 737) [45p], made under the Housing Act 1980 (c.51), s.56(4); operative on May 21, 1987; approves 13 bodies for the purposes of s.56 of the 1980 Act.

ASSURED TENANCIES (APPROVED BODIES) (No. 2) ORDER 1987 (No. 822) [45p], made under the Housing Act 1980, s.56(4); operative on June 1, 1987; approves 41 bodies for the purposes of s.56 of the 1980 Act.

ASSURED TENANCIES (APPROVED BODIES) (No. 3) ORDER 1987 (No. 1164) [45p], made under the Housing Act 1980, s.56(4); operative on August 6, 1987; approves 21 bodies for the purposes of s.56 of the 1980 Act.

ASSURED TENANCIES (APPROVED BODIES) (No. 4) ORDER 1987 (No. 1525) [45p], made under the Housing Act 1980, s.56(4); operative on October 1, 1987; approves 35 bodies for the purposes of s.56 of the 1980 Act.

ASSURED TENANCIES (PRESCRIBED AMOUNT) ORDER 1987 (No. 122) [45p], made under the Housing Act 1980, s.56B(6); operative on February 25, 1987; increases the prescribed amount for the purposes of s.56B of the 1980 Act by £2,000 in Greater London and by £1,000 elsewhere.

2119. Boarding house—fire regulation

[Fire Precautions Act 1971 (c.40), s.7(1).]

The Court considered the appropriate discretion to be given to a jury considering whether premises were a boarding house for purposes of deciding whether an offence had been committed under the Act (*Mayflower Cambridge* v. *Secretary of State for the Environment* [1975] C.L.Y. 3367 considered).

R. *v.* MABBOTT, *The Times*, August 4, 1987, C.A.

2120. Breach of covenant—claim for damages—exemplary damages

[Landlord and Tenant Act 1954 (c.56), s.37.]

P had since 1979 been the weekly tenant of premises used by himself and his predecessor as a barber's shop. When D became the landlords they served notice to quit on P. It was accepted that the notice was invalid. P's solicitors wrote to D, warning them that the document was of no effect and that no attempt should be made to evict P. D became angry, entered the premises without warning, smashed the front windows, tore the front door off its hinges and disconnected the electricity. D warned P not to "trespass" on the premises, removed roofing tiles and P's possessions.

Held, that after awarding sums for damage to personal property and loss of earnings, D should pay damages of £500 for loss of P's opportunity to claim compensation for disturbance under s.37 (£82 r.v. x 6) and for trespass, and a further £700 by way of exemplary damages, the court having described D's behaviour as "monstrous."

BREEZE *v.* ELDEN & HYDE, December 3, 1986; Mr. Deputy Registrar Sheriff; Norwich County Ct. [*Ex rel. Graham Sinclair, Barrister.*]

2121. Breach of covenant—quiet enjoyment—damages

In a full Rent Act tenancy, the rent was £42 per week for "bed and breakfast" (not provided), paid by the D.H.S.S. T was unemployed. Three months after the tenancy began L told T he would have to move. A few days later whilst T was out, L entered his room, moved his belongings downstairs and changed the lock. When the police were called, L made it clear that T could not return. T slept rough for the rest of the night, stayed with different friends for two to three days, followed by two weeks in temporary accommodation. T claimed for breach of an implied covenant for quiet enjoyment.

Held, that (1) £500 general damages would be awarded for inconvenience—discomfort of sleeping rough, shock of being locked out of room, etc.; (2) £500 exemplary damages would be awarded even though neither trespess nor exemplary damages had been pleaded; (3) no award for loss of protected tenancy on basis that T would have left if he had obtained work (as the rent was excessive) so T did not lose anything under this head.

GILES *v.* ADLEY, December 1, 1986; Assistant Recorder Boothman, Southampton County Ct. [*Ex rel. Sherwins, Solicitors.*]

2122. Breach of covenant—waiver

In 1974 J was granted a three-year tenancy of a flat. It was a term of the tenancy that the tenant would not assign, sublet or part with possession of the premises. In 1977 the tenancy was renewed for a further three-year term and J decided to return to the United States. He asked the landlords for permission to assign which was refused. he then entered into a purported agreement with the defendant whereby she would be engaged as a caretaker. She paid J. £3,000 for unspecified items and agreed to pay £35 per month for the use and deterioration of the furniture, fittings, *etc.* J wrote to the landlord's agents stating that he was going away for a while and that she would be looking after the flat. J continued to pay rent. He subsequently again wrote to the agents making it clear that he was the tenant and that she was merely a housekeeper. In November 1980 the tenancy became statutory. In 1985 the plaintiff purchased the premises and began possession proceedings. In the county court the Assistant Recorder found that the original landlords had not waived the breach and ordered possession against the defendant. The defendant appealed.

Held, dismissing the appeal, that if a landlord, who suspects there might be a breach of covenant, receives a representation from the tenant which if true means there has been no breach and he is not sufficiently confident of the untruth of what he says, then it cannot be said that the landlord knew all the facts nor that he has waived the breach.

CHRISDELL *v.* JOHNSON AND TICKNER (1987) 19 H.L.R. 406, C.A.

2123. Business tenancy—application for new tenancy—building at end of its life—terms of new tenancy

T applied for a new business tenancy of part of an office block in Uxbridge, and L sought an interim rent. The lease had been for 21 years from June 1963 at a rent of £4,250 for the first seven years of the term and of £5,000 thereafter, and T had covenanted to pay in addition "a fair proportion" of the cost of "keeping the foundations, main walls, timber, structure and roof in good repair." The building had reached the end of its useful life, and would shortly have to be demolished. In the meantime, it had already been supported by temporary props, and required the installation of a steel frame. The judge found that this would be constructed during the continuation, under s.64 of the Landlord and Tenant Act, of the existing tenancy

Held, that (1) T should contribute one half of the cost of the strengthening works; (2) the new term would be for nine months from the s.64 date; (3) the new rent would be £25,000 p.a., assessed on the basis of an agreed comparable after an adjustment to take account of the fact that the necessary major repairs would have been done and a discount of 45 per cent. to take account of the fact that the new term would only be for nine months; (4) taking account of the factors specified in s.34 of the Act and of the state and condition of the premises at the beginning of the interim period the interim rent should be £20,500 (*English Exporters (London)* v. *Eldonwall* [1973] C.L.Y. 1902 and *Fawke* v. *Viscount Chelsea* [1979] C.L.Y. 1583 considered).

WOODBRIDGE *v.* WESTMINSTER PRESS (1987) 284 E.G. 60, Baker Q.C.

2124. Business tenancy—application for new tenancy—landlord intending to occupy for own business—whether bona fide

[(Landlord and Tenant Act 1954 (c.56), s.30(1)(*g*))]

Where landlords oppose the grant of a new tenancy on the ground that they intend to use the demised premises for their own business, the time at which that intention, which must be a firm and settled intention, must be shown is the time of the hearing, so that no substantial weight should be accorded to amendments to the landlords' original scheme. Nor is it realistic to say that they were not intending to occupy the premises, because the partitions previously delineating them were to be removed.

Tenants applied for a new lease under Part II of the 1954 Act. Landlords opposed them on the ground that the demised premises were required for the landlords' own business. A scheme was put forward for the proposed use by the landlords, but at the hearing of the application they put forward a revised scheme. In each case the partitions marking the demised premises would be removed completely. The judge refused the tenants' application. The tenants appealed.

Held, dismissing the appeal: (i) what was required of the landlords was a bona fide and settled intention to use the premises for their own business, that they may have revised their initial plans on how to do so was of little weight; (ii) it could not be argued that because the partitions setting out the demised premises were to be removed, so that their identity became lost, the landlords were not therefore occupying those premises; they were in reality occupying the whole of the ground floor, which included the premises the subject of the lease.

THORNTON (J. W.) *v.* BLACKS LEISURE GROUP (1987) 53 P. & C.R. 223, C.A.

2125. Business tenancy—application for new tenancy—length of term

T sought a new tenancy under Part II of the Landlord and Tenant Act 1954 of a ground floor and basement in Oxford St., W1. The only questions in dispute were the rent and the length of the term, L proposing six months and T fourteen years. The judge found that L's professed intention that its subsidiary S should trade from the premises had been conceived late and was supported by only sketchy evidence; but took the view that L should be given an opportunity to establish that its intention so to trade was genuine and workable.

Held, that there should be a three-year term with a landlord's break clause exercisable by six months notice, but only if a company in the same group as L intended to use the premises for the purposes of a business to be carried on by that company.

PETER MILLETT & SONS *v.* SALISBURY HANDBAGS (1987) 284 E.G. 784, Mr. John Mowbray Q.C.

2126. Business tenancy—application for new tenancy—restaurant run by T's companies—whether premises occupied for the purpose of a business carried on by T

[Landlord and Tenant Act 1954 (c.56), s.23(1).]

A business tenancy of restaurant premises in London W8 became vested for the last five years of the term in T, who paid £50,000 for goodwill. At the end of the term, L served notice under Part II of the Landlord and Tenant Act 1954, terminating the tenancy and stating that L would oppose the grant of new tenancy under grounds (*a*) and (*b*) of s.30(1) of the Act, and T duly applied for a new tenancy. The judge found that the restaurant business had in fact been carried on not by T but by a series of companies controlled by T, and struck out the application on the grounds that the premises had not been ". . . occupied by the tenant and . . . so occupied for the purposes of a business carried on by him . . ." within the meaning of s.23(1) of the Act. On appeal, T contended that the companies were his "*alter ego,*" and that occupation by them had been equivalent for the purposes of s.23(1) to occupation by T.

Held, dismissing the appeal, that the application had been properly struck out (*Cristina* v. *Seear* [1985] C.L.Y. 1857 applied; *Pegler* v. *Craven* [1952] C.L.Y. 1961 and *Tunstall* v. *Steigmann* [1962] C.L.Y. 1718 considered).

NOZARI-ZADEH *v.* PEARL ASSURANCE (1987) 283 E.G. 457, C.A.

2127/8. Business tenancy—application for new tenancy—time limit—amendment to application after expiry of time limit

[Landlord and Tenant Act 1954 (c.56), s.29(3).]

Where an application had been made for the grant of a new business tenancy within the time limit specified in s.29(3) of the Landlord and Tenant Act 1954, the court has jurisdiction to allow amendments to the application after the expiry of the time limit.

The applicant was the assignee of a lease of premises in Hampstead which included a ground floor shop and basement used for her business, a ground floor studio and first floor flat used as her home, and second and third floor flats which were let by her to others unconnected to her business. The lease was dated May 28, 1964 and was for 21 years. On November 19, 1984 the respondent landlords gave notice terminating on May 28, 1985. On March 8, 1985 the applicant applied to the county for a new tenancy stating that the premises were the ground floor premises. That application was made within the time limit set by s.29(3) of the Landlord and Tenant Act 1954, the time limit expiring on March 19, 1985. In July 1985 the applicant's solicitors realised that the application did not cover the whole of the demised premises, and purported to amend it so that it covered the whole of the basement, ground floor and first floor (but not the second and third floors which were not covered by the Act). The respondents contended that she was not entitled to amend after expiry of the time limit. The registrar and the judge on appeal held that the tenant was not entitled to amend.

Held, allowing the appeal, that the court did have jurisdiction to allow amendments to be made to an application made within the time limit where the amendments were made outside it. On the facts the court should exercise its discretion to allow the amendment since she would suffer substantial detriment if the first floor flat which was her home was not protected by the 1954 Act while the landlord was not being deprived of any vested right, since it was the court's duty to decide what was the holding that was to form the subject matter of the new tenancy, and the landlord could not resist the grant of a new tenancy as defined by the Court.

NURIT BAR *v.* PATHWOOD INVESTMENTS (1987) 54 P. & C.R. 178, C.A.

2129. Business tenancy—application for new tenancy—whether sufficient intention to reconstruct demonstrated by L

[Landlord and Tenant Act 1954 (c.56), s.30(1)(*f*).]

L opposed T's application for a new tenancy of business premises which T used as a cold store and garage for ice cream vans, on the grounds that she intended to demolish and redevelop the premises by constructing 10 residential units. The evidence was that outline planning permission had been granted, that L's bank were willing in principle to help with finance, and that a local development company, which had recently carried out a similar project hearby, was willing and able to start site clearance work immediately, and construction work as soon as detailed planning permission was obtained. T however argued that, until L had reached with the developer an agreement at least as to the basic points on which the development was to proceed, it could not be said that L had demonstrated the intention to reconstruct required by s.30(1)(*f*) of the Act. The judge found that L had demonstrated the necessary intention.

Held, dismissing T's appeal, that a reasonable man looking at the matter objectively could have reached no other conclusion (*Cunliffe* v. *Goodman* (1947–51) C.L.C. 5425, *Betty's Cafés* v. *Phillips Furnishing Stores* [1958] C.L.Y. 1818, *DAF Motoring Centre (Gosport)* v. *Hutfield and Wheeler* [1982] C.L.Y. 1722, *Gregson* v. *Lord (Cyril)* [1962] C.L.Y. 171), and *Reohorn* v. *Barry Corporation* [1956] C.L.Y. 4852 considered).

CAPOCCI *v.* GOBLE (1987) 284 E.G. 230, C.A.

2130. Business tenancy—betting office—display of illuminated signs above entrance—whether "appurtenances". See HILL (WILLIAM) (SOUTHERN) *v.* CABRAS, §1231.

2131. Business tenancy—forfeiture of head tenancy—terms upon which relief to be granted

[Law of Property Act 1925 (c.20), s.146(4); Landlord and Tenant Act 1954 (c.56), s.24(2).]

S had for many years occupied business premises as sub-tenant to T, who was responsible under the head-tenancy for repairs to the premises. In 1983 L forfeited T's tenancy on grounds of T's bankruptcy, and subsequently brought proceedings for possession against S, in which the only effective issue was whether S should be granted relief from forfeiture. The judge held that he had no jurisdiction to order the grant to S of anything more than a monthly tenancy (one month being the period which, by virtue of s.24(1) of the Landlord and Tenant Act 1954, would elapse before S's tenancy could be terminated in accordance with Part II of the Act following the expiry of the term granted by the underlease and proposed terms whereby substantial necessary repairs would be carried out by S. When S declined to undertake the responsibility for repairs on the basis of a monthly tenancy only, the judge refused to grant relief and ordered possession.

Held, dismissing S's appeal, that (1) the forfeiture of the head-tenancy had had the effect of forfeiting S's tenancy also, pursuant to s.24(2) of the 1954 Act; (2) the judge had correctly applied s.146(4) of the Law of Property Act 1925 and the decision in *Cadogan* v. *Dimovic* [1984] C.L.Y. 1967 in deciding that he had jurisdiction to order the grant of a monthly tenancy but no more; (3) the judge had not erred in his discretion in refusing relief. In particular it would have been inequitable to impose on L a person whom they had never accepted as their tenant and against whom they would have had far less extensive rights in relation to repair than against T (*Creery* v. *Summersell* [1947–51] C.L.C. 5390 and *Gray* v. *Bonsall* [1904] 1 K.B. 601 considered).

HILL *v.* GRIFFIN (1987) 282 E.G. 85, C.A.

2132. Business tenancy—landlord's intention to demolish—whether proven

[Landlord and Tenant Act 1954 (c.56), s.30(1)(*f*).]

L opposed the grant to T of a new business tenancy on the grounds specified in s.30(1)(*f*) of the Landlord and Tenant Act 1954, namely that they intended to demolish or reconstruct the premises comprised in the holding or a substantial part of those premises, or to carry out substantial works of construction on the holding or part thereof, and that they could not reasonably do so without obtaining possession of the holding. The judge found that detailed plans had been prepared, the carrying out of which would call for the total demolition of the premises, and that adequate finance was available; however, that as yet there were no contracts for demolition or building, and that no materials had been bought.

Held, that on the facts L had demonstrated the requisite intention (*Cunliffe* v. *Goodman* (1947–51) C.L.C. 5425 and *Fisher* v. *Taylors Furnishing Stores* [1956] C.L.Y. 4851 considered; *Little Park Service Station* v. *Regent Oil Co.* [1967] C.L.Y. 2242 distinguished).

LEVY (A.) & SON *v.* MARTIN BRENT DEVELOPMENTS (1987) 283 E.G. 646, Mr. Julian Jeffs Q.C.

2133. Business tenancy—notice to terminate—whether in correct form

L purported to give notice determining T's tenancy of business premises under Part II of the Landlord and Tenant Act 1954 in Form 7 in Appendix 1 to the Landlord and Tenant (Notices) Regulations 1969, not appreciating that that form had been replaced by a new Form I in Sched. 2 to the Landlord and Tenant Act Part II (Notices) Regulations 1983. The judge held that the old Form 7 was a form substantially to the like effect of the new Form 1.

Held, dismissing L's application for leave to appeal out of time, that the judge had reached the correct conclusion.

MORRIS *v.* PATEL (1987) 281 E.G. 419, C.A.

2134. Business tenancy—termination of business tenancy—compensation payable—whether tenants in "occupation"—date of occupation

[Landlord and Tenant Act 1954 (c.56), s.37(2).]

For the purposes of a claim by a tenant to compensation at the termination of a business tenancy, pursuant to s.37(2)(*a*) of the Landlord and Tenant Act 1954, at six times the rateable value of the premises, it is necessary that the tenant should have been in occupation of the premises for an entire period of 14 years, so that even if the occupation is only one day short of 14 years the tenant will not be entitled to compensation on that basis.

By a letter dated August 23, 1971, Royal, as landlords, offered to let to the Department of the Environment certain premises, subject to contract. The Department of the Environment's workmen entered the premises on August 25, and began to carry out works therein; when executed the actual lease was for a 14-year term from August 23. Pursuant to the lease, Royal terminated it on August 23, 1985, with the result that they became obliged to pay compensation to the Department of the Environment.

Held, on the question whether s.37(2)(*a*) or s.37(2)(*b*) of the 1954 Act applied (which made a practical difference between the Department of the Environment recovering as compensation £333,330 or £161,665), that it was necessary in order that the Department of the Environment might recover under s.37(2)(*a*) that it should have been in actual occupation as a business tenant for 14 years. As a fact the occupation had been less than 14 years, and it was not possible to infer a binding agreement as to the lease from the pre-lease correspondence. Nor was it possible to apply the principle of *de minimis.* The Department of the Environment had not met the conditions prescribed by s.37(2)(*a*) and compensation had to be assessed under s.37(2)(*b*).

DEPARTMENT OF THE ENVIRONMENT *v.* ROYAL INSURANCE (1987) 54 P. & C.R. 26, Falconer J.

2135. Business tenancy—terms—interim rent

[Landlord and Tenant Act 1954 (c.56), s.24A.]

T applied under Part II of the Landlord and Tenant Act 1954 for a new business tenancy of a block of flats in London NW8, requiring a term of 14 years at a rent of £13,500 p.a. with a rent review after seven years, and otherwise on the terms of the original lease. In March 1983, L issued a summons for an interim rent, and then contended for a term of 10 years at a rent of £25,000 p.a. with a five-year rent review. On being advised that the rent for such a 10 or 14-year term should be £57,000 p.a., T applied instead for a one-year term at £57,000, whilst L continued to contend for 10 years, but at £125,000 p.a. At the hearing it became clear that T's principal requirement was time to consider their position, whilst L offered to meet the difficulty by inserting a break clause exercisable on six months' notice. The judge held that the new term should be for ten years, starting in four months' time, at £106,000 p.a.; but with an option to break on six months' notice, exercisable within a month of the commencement of the new tenancy. There was no appeal against this part of the judgment. He further took the view that the s.34 rental value of the premises under a tenancy from year to year was £80,000 (a figure which the parties accepted) and that, having regard to the old rent of £13,500, that figure should be reduced by 50 per cent. to give an interim rent of £40,000. However, instead of determining the interim rent at £40,000, he accepted an undertaking from P to pay £25,000 p.a. from July 1983 until March 1984, and thereafter £40,000 p.a. until commencement of the new tenancy, the reason for this decision being that L had led T to believe that the rent during that period would not exceed £25,000. On appeal, L challenged both the reduction by 50 per cent. of the figure of £80,000 and the subsequent failure to determine the interim rent at £40,000.

Held, allowing the appeal in part, that (1) it could not be said that the judge had gone wrong in principle in applying the reduction of 50 per cent. in the exercise of his discretion under s.24A(3) of Act (*English Exporters (London)* v. *Eldonwall* [1973] C.L.Y. 1902. *Janes (Gowns)* v. *Harlow Development Corporation* [1980] C.L.Y. 1579, *Ratners*

(Jewellers) v. *Lemnoll* [1981] C.L.Y. 1505, and *Halberstam* v. *Tandalco Corp N.V.* [1985] C.L.Y. 1850 considered): (2) the judge ought then to have ordered either that the old rent of £13,500 should continue, or that it be replaced by one of £40,000, and that he had gone wrong in forcing L to accept the undertaking that T should pay £25,000. The court could therefore exercise the discretion afresh, and would determine the interim rent at £40,000 for the whole period.

FOLLETT (CHARLES) *v.* CABTELL INVESTMENTS (1987) 283 E.G. 195, C.A.

2136. Business tenancy—terms of new tenancy

T were tenants of a building in the City of London under a business lease which entitled L to give notice to terminate on the grounds that they intended to demolish and redevelop. In October 1985, L served a notice under s.25 of the Landlord and Tenant Act 1954 indicating that they would not oppose the grant of a new tenancy, whereupon T issued an originating summons proposing a five-year term, a rent of £7,150 and other terms as in the previous lease. Following negotiations which failed to reach a binding agreement, the Master gave directions for trial. On T's appeal to the judge, L, who now wished to operate the break clause, offered to consent to the terms of the originating summons, but T requested leave to amend the summons, *inter alia* so as to exclude the exercise of the break clause for five years. In response, L offered to consent to receiving no rent at all, and to relief T from any obligations as to the maintenance, repair or decoration of the building or any long-term repairs to the lifts or boilers.

Held, that L's proposals represented the maximum that T could possibly obtain by way of a new lease, and that judgment should be entered for T in those terms.

LESLIE AND GODWIN INVESTMENTS *v.* PRUDENTIAL ASSURANCE CO. (1987) 283 E.G. 1565, Hoffmann J.

2137. Company lessee of property part of which sublet—payments of rent by underlessees—statutory assignment to landlord—equitable assignment to mortgagee—priority of assignments. See OFFSHORE VENTILATION, *Re,* §354.

2138. Compensation for tenant's improvements—working paper. See LAW REFORM, §2271.

2139. Covenant for quiet enjoyment—whether breach.

A lessor is not in breach of his covenant for quiet enjoyment where the acts complained of are the exercise of rights created by his predecessor in title.

L's predecessor in title built a block of flats with garages, parking spaces, a car showroom and a petrol station. It granted the tenants a right of way over the driveway. L purchased the freehold and then demised the petrol station and car showroom to X together with part of the driveway with a covenant for quiet enjoyment that X should peaceably hold the demised premises without any interruption by any person lawfully claiming under L. X planned to build a car-wash in the driveway. The tenant prevented him by injunction, and the judges dismissed his claim against L for breach of the covenant.

Held, dismissing the appeal, that the tenants were not claiming right of way "under L", since the right at all times had priority to L's title (*Griffiths, Re* (1917) 61 S.J. 268 considered).

CELSTEEL *v.* ALTON HOUSE HOLDINGS (No. 2) [1987] 1 W.L.R. 291, C.A.

2140. Covenant to repair—defective front door—whether within covenant to repair

The plaintiff was the tenant of a house owned by the defendant local authority. By the express terms of the tenancy, the authority covenanted to "repair and maintain the structure and exterior of the dwelling-house." From the outset in 1953, the house suffered from an ingress of water under the front door due to a design defect. In 1983, the authority fitted a self-sealing aluminium door which remedied the problem. The tenant sought and was awarded damages for the period prior to 1983. The defendants appealed.

Held, dismissing the appeal, that (1) if the only defect in a door is that it does not perform the primary function of keeping out the rain, and is otherwise undamaged, this does not amount to a defect for the purpose of a repairing covenant; (2) *Quick* v. *Taff Ely Borough Council* [1985] C.L.Y. 1610 might have been decided differently if there had been some actual disrepair material to the works sought; in the present case, actual damage had occurred, accordingly the fitting of a special door was within the repairing covenant and as it was something which should have been done earlier, the tenant was entitled to damages.

STENT *v.* MONMOUTH DISTRICT COUNCIL (1987) 19 H.L.R. 269, C.A.

2141. Covenant to repair—flooding arising from defects in construction—whether covenant applies

A covenant to repair is concerned only with states of disrepair, so that where defects have existed since the construction of a building, and there has been no worsening of the situation, there is no want of repair and a tenant cannot be made liable under a covenant to repair.

PO were tenants of a building, and subject to a covenant to repair. Whenever the local water table was high the building flooded in part, due to defects in its original construction. This defect had not become worse with the passage of time, but had always existed in its present form.

Held, dismissing the landlord's appeal, that disrepair connoted a change in status so that where a particular defect had always existed in its present form, the building had not fallen into a state of disrepair, and the tenant would not be liable under a covenant to repair.

POST OFFICE *v.* AQUARIUS PROPERTIES (1987) 54 P. & C.R. 61, C.A.

2142. Covenant to repair—whether assignor of term entitled to sue for breach occurring before assignment

[Law of Property Act 1925 (c.20), s.142(1).]

On the assignment of a lease, s.142(1) of the Law of Property Act 1925 does not prevent the assignor from claiming for past breaches of covenant by the landlord including for loss of profits.

L was in serious breach of a repairing covenant under a long lease. T acquired the residue of the term, then shortly afterwards attempted to resell by auction. The property did not reach its reserve. T enforced L's covenant by claiming specific performance, then assigned the lease at a profit. T claimed for loss sustained due to disrepair.

Held, that s.142(1) of the Law of Property Act 1925 did not prevent T from claiming for past breaches prior to assignment for loss suffered during the tenancy, and there would be an order for an inquiry into damages including the question of the auction costs and loss of profits.

CITY AND METROPOLITAN PROPERTIES *v.* GREYCROFT [1987] 1 W.L.R. 1085, Mr. John Mowbray Q.C.

2143. Damages—valuation of beneficial occupation of premises. See G.P. &. P. *v.* BULCRAIG & DAVIS, §1129.

2144. Distress for rent rules 1983—revision—consultation paper. See LAW REFORM, §2265.

2145. Fair rent—whether reference to Rent Assessment Committee withdrawn

A fair rent was determined in respect of the applicant's flat at £1,068 per annum in February 1986. The landlord was happy with the determination but the applicant objected. A date was fixed for hearing and inspection by the rent assessment committee. The applicant wrote to the committee saying that she would not be able to attend and suggesting that she did not wish to continue with the objection. As the clerk was not clear whether she wished to withdraw the objection, he wrote asking for confirmation. She replied that she did wish to withdraw but the letter was not sent. She was then informed of the date of inspection and hearing which was to take place at the magistrates' court. Accompanying this letter was a reply card. The applicant indicated that she would not attend and stated "I am unable to attend as it was not my intention for this case to go as far as the magistrates' courts." In the event, the rent assessment committee went ahead, and decided to increase the rent to £2,000 per annum. The applicant sought judicial review to quash the committee's decision to proceed.

Held, dismissing the application, that (1) the question before the court was whether the decision of the committee to proceed to a determination was one which no reasonable committee could have reached; (2) it is for the tenant to indicate that it is his or her wish to withdraw and on the material before it, it was not unreasonable for the committee to have proceeded with the determination.

R. *v.* BRISTOL RENT ASSESSMENT COMMITTEE, *ex p.* DUNWORTH (1987) 19 H.L.R. 351, McCullough J.

2146. Forfeiture—subsequently reversed—whether L's entry in the meantime illegal

[R.S.C. Ord. 59, r.13(1)]

L purported to forfeit T's lease for breach of a covenant to reconstruct the premises, and the judge duly held that the lease had been properly forfeited and that relief should not be granted. When T's appeal was subsequently allowed by the Court of Appeal on the grounds that L's notice under s.146 of the Law of Property Act 1925 had been defective, T claimed damages for trespass, breach of covenant of quiet enjoyment, and derogation from grant, on the grounds that L had re-entered the premises between the judgment and appeal.

Held, on a preliminary issue, that T's claim was misconceived. So long as an order of the Court is in force it must be obeyed, and acts done under it are lawful, whether or not it is subsequently reversed on appeal. (*Isaac* v. *Robertson* [1984] C.L.Y. 2660 applied; *Official Custodian for Charities* v. *Mackay* [1984] C.L.Y. 1903 considered).

HILLGATE HOUSE *v.* EXPERT CLOTHING SERVICE & SALES (1987) 282 E.G. 715, Browne-Wilkinson V.C.

2147. Guarantee to pay rent—an obligation touching and concerning land—whether a covenant running with the land

A guarantee of obligations which touch and concern demised land is capable of being a covenant running with the land.

In 1970 lessees granted a 21-year underlease to K, and in 1978 K assigned to S Ltd. pursuant to a licence granted by the then landlords. D covenanted as surety to guarantee payment of rent by S Ltd., but S Ltd. went into liquidation in 1982 and paid no rent thereafter. The headlease was assigned to new landlords without specific assignment of the benefit of the surety covenants. The new landlords pursued K for the rent. K paid, but then sued D under the guarantee contained in the licence to assign.

Held, that a surety guaranteeing obligations which touched and concerned the land itself touches and concerns the land and K's claim succeeded (dictum of Best J. in *Vyvyan* v. *Arthur* [1814–23] All E.R. 352 applied; *Dyson* v. *Forster* [1908–10] All E.R. 212 followed; *Dewar* v. *Goodman* [1908–10] All E.R. 188 doubted).

KUMAR *v.* DUNNING [1987] 2 All E.R. 801, C.A.

2148. Housing (Scotland) Act 1987 (c.26). See HOUSING, §1891.

2149. Landlord and tenant—reform of the law. See LAW REFORM, §2272.

2150. Landlord and Tenant Act 1987 (c.31)

This Act confers on tenants of flats rights with respect to the acquisition by them of their landlord's reversion. Provision is made: for the appointment of a manager at the instance of such tenants, for the variation of long leases held by such tenants, and with respect to service charges payable by tenants of flats and other dwellings. Further provision is made with respect to permissible purposes and objects of registered housing associations as regards the management of leasehold property.

The Act received the Royal Assent on May 15, 1987 and comes into force on a day to be appointed by the Secretary of State.

The Act extends to England and Wales only.

2151. Landlord and Tenant Act 1987—commencement

LANDLORD AND TENANT ACT 1987 (COMMENCEMENT No. 1) ORDER 1987 (No. 2177 (c.66)) [45p], made under the Landlord and Tenant Act 1987 (c.31), s.62(2); brings into force on February 1, 1988 ss.1–20, 45–60, 61(1), 62 of the 1987 Act.

2152. Lands Tribunal decision

This was a reference to determine the price to be paid pursuant to s.9(1) of the Leasehold Reform Act 1967 as amended for the freehold interest of a two-storey semi-detached house with a 110′ garden in Barnet, which was held on a 99-year lease with 47 years unexpired. The parties agreed that, in the absence of relevant sales of comparable cleared sites in the area, the "standing house" approach was the method to be adopted for estimating the site value of the subject premises, and that the entirety value was £58,000. Adopting percentages of 30 per cent. in relation to the site value and of 7 per cent. in relation to the s.15 rent, the tribunal determined the overall price to be paid at £855.

FREEHOLD MANAGEMENT (TRADERS) *v.* PLUMLEY (LRA/4/1986) (1987) 284 E.G 237.

2153. Lease—construction—whether roof formed part of demise

P held premises under a lease which demised to them "all that piece or parcel of ground with the messages and buildings erected thereon situate . . . on the South Side of and numbered 67, etc., in Mortimer Street". A full repairing covenant covered ". . . all additional erections and improvements together with all windows shutters leaden gutters ridges and hips leaden and other pipes . . ." P sought summary judgment for a mandatory injunction orders D to remove a fire escape and ventilation shaft which D had erected on and against the roof of the premises on the ground that there constituted a tresspass. D's defence was that the roof of the premises did not form part of the demise to P. The judge gave leave to defend.

Held, allowing P's appeal and granting the injunction, that it was crystal clear from the terms of the lease that the roof of the premises did form part of the demise to P (*Cockburn* v. *Smith* [1924] 2 K.B. 119 and *Douglas-Scott* v. *Scorgie* [1984] C.L.Y. 1908 distinguished).

STRAUDLEY INVESTMENTS *v.* BARPRESS (1987) 282 E.G. 1124, C.A.

2154. Lease—covenant to return deposit—assignment of reversion—whether covenant touched and concerned the land

Where a lease contained a covenant by the landlord that at the end of the lease he would return a deposit to the tenant, and the landlord assigned the reversion to a third party, from whom the tenant sought the return of the deposit, it was held that the covenant was not binding on the assignee, as the covenant did not touch or concern the land.

The landlord (L) granted the tenant (T) a lease of premises in Hong Kong for five years. The lease provided that the expressions 'the landlord' and 'the tenant' should include their assigns. There was payable a security deposit by T returnable at the expiration of the term, if there were no breaches of any of the terms, but otherwise forfeited. T paid the deposit and took the lease. L assigned the reversion to a bank by way of mortgage, but no reference was made to the deposit. L defaulted, and the bank entered into possession. L went into liquidation. T at the end of the term sought the return of the deposit from the bank. The High Court of Hong Kong dismissed the claim, but the Court of Appeal of Hong Kong allowed T's appeal, holding that the obligation to return the deposit touched and concerned the land, so that the burden of paying it passed to the bank. The bank's appeal to the Judicial Committee was allowed. The obligations to pay and return the deposit were held to be merely personal obligations, between the original parties to the lease, and the right to return was not enforceable against an assignee in the absence of express agreement. Although the deposit was to secure T's obligations under the lease including those which touched and concerned the land, the landlord's covenant to return the deposit was not itself a covenant dealing with the subject matter of the lease or touching or concerning the land, and did not pass with the reversion. The bank as assignee was under no obligation to pay the amount deposited with the landlord. *Dollar Land Corp.* v. *Solomon, Re* (1963) 39 D.L.R. (2d) 221 applied. *Mansel* v. *Norton* (1883) 22 Ch.D. 769, C.A.; *Lord Howard de Walden* v. *Barber* (1903) 19 T.L.R. 183 and *Moss Empires* v. *Olympia (Liverpool)* (1939) A.C. 544, distinguished.

HUA CHIAO COMMERCIAL BANK *v.* CHIAPHUA INDUSTRIES [1987] 2 W.L.R. 179, P.C.

2155. Lease—fixtures and fittings—whether tenant's fixtures

L granted to T a 30-year lease of business premises, under which T covenanted to install light fittings and floor finishes. The lighting consisted of fluorescent tubes contained in glass boxes fixed securely to the plaster of the ceiling, whilst the floor covering was carpeting secured by gripping rods fixed to the screeded floor with pins. When it subsequently became necessary for the purposes of a rent review to ascertain the ownership to these items, L contended that the effect of the covenant was to render them landlord's fixtures, since otherwise T could have removed them as soon as they had entered into the lease, and could further have benefited at the rent review from their own breach of covenant. The judge held that the items were tenant's fixtures.

Held, dismissing L's appeal, that (1) the covenant did not affect the question of ownership (*Mowats* v. *Hudson Bros.* (1911) 105 L.T. 400 applied); (2) assuming the items to be fixtures, and having regard to the general principle that fixtures attached by a tenant for the purposes of his trade or business are tenant's fixtures, the judge had been entitled on the evidence before him to conclude that the items were tenant's fixtures (*Webb* v. *Frank Bevis* [1940] 1 All E.R. 247 and *Spyer* v. *Phillipson* [1931] 2 Ch. 183 distinguished).

YOUNG *v.* DALGETY (1987) 281 E.G. 427, C.A.

2156. Lease—option to renew—observance of covenants—breaches of covenant spent by date of option—whether past breach of negative covenant precludes exercise of option

The established conventional form of option requires as a condition precedent to its exercise simply that there is no subsisting breach of covenant at the date of the option being exercised, so that where there have been past, but now spent, breaches of covenant, it is irrelevant whether they were of positive or negative covenants.

A 15-year lease made in 1982 of premises consisting of a tied public house and hotel, contained the usual covenants. The tenants had also the option to acquire a further 125 year-lease, subject to their having performed the terms of the lease. After the tenants had breached, *inter alia,* the covenant to pay the rent and water rates the landlords applied for forfeiture; relief was granted on the basis that the tenants paid the money then outstanding, which they did. On the tenants giving notice to exercise the option, the landlords refused.

Held, allowing the tenant's appeal, that the condition precedent to the exercise of the option meant simply that there should be no outstanding breaches of covenant at the date when the option came to be exercised. As the tenants' breaches of covenant were now spent it was irrelevant to consider whether they had been positive or negative in nature (*Simons* v. *Associated Furnishers* [1930] All E.R. Rep. 427 applied).

BASS HOLDINGS *v.* MORTON MUSIC [1987] 2 All E.R. 1001, C.A.

2157. Lease—oral agreement to renew—whether repudiated

L let to T a yard and lean-to shed for a term of seven years from 1977 at a rent of £50 per week. In 1979 L proposed that the term be extended until 1991 with three-yearly rent reviews, and that T should in return pay a rent of £65 per week; but this proposal was declined. There followed lengthy correspondence between the parties' solicitors. In February 1984 L purported to serve notice under s.25 of the Landlord and Tenant Act 1954, and subsequently brought proceedings for possession. The judge found that in July 1980 there had been an oral agreement that T should occupy the property until 1991 at £50 per week, and that this agreement had been supported by acts of part performance on T's part: he therefore gave judgment for T. On appeal, L eventually conceded that there had been evidence on which the judge could find there to have been such an oral agreement, but argued that T had repudiated it by a letter written by his solicitors in July 1981.

Held, dismissing the appeal, that the letter of July 1981 had been directed towards renewed proposals by L that T should pay £65 per week, and was not a repudiation of the oral agreement of July 1980.

BUSH TRANSPORT *v.* NELSON (1987) 281 E.G. 177, C.A.

2158. Lease—service charge—landlord's legal costs

[Landlord and Tenant Act 1985 (c.70), s.19.]

A long lease of a flat entitled the landlord L to recover a service charge being a proportion of "total expenditure" which was defined to mean the cost to L of performing its covenants in clause 5(5) of the lease "and any other costs and expenses reasonably and properly incurred in connection with the building." By clause 5(5) L covenanted to employ surveyors, builders, engineers, accountants "or other professional persons as may be necessary . . . to do all such works . . . as in the absolute discretion of the lessors may be considered necessary . . . for the proper maintenance . . . of the building." L claimed by way of service charge reimbursement of the legal costs incurred against another tenant who had defaulted in paying an earlier year's service charge. T considered that the sums were not recoverable pursuant to the above provisions of the lease.

Held, that the legal costs paid by L to its solicitors were the costs of employing professional persons for the proper administration of the building and were sums expended for the proper administration of the building and were reasonably incurred. Accordingly they were recoverable by way of service charge.

DELAHAY *v.* MALTLODGE, March 9, 1987; P. st. J. Langan Q.C.; West London County Court. [*Ex rel. Paul Morgan, Barrister.*]

2159. Lease or licence—exclusive possession

The appellant was the landlord of a flat which consisted of one double bedsitting room, two single rooms, a kitchen and bathroom. The respondent agreed to take the double bedsitting room on terms that she would be a licensee and would share the flat with the other occupants. Subsequently, the respondent entered into a licence to occupy the whole of the flat, not merely the room. The terms stated that she would not have exclusive possession of the whole or any part of the premises. Possession proceedings were brought which the respondent defended on the basis that she was a Rent Act protected tenant and not a licensee. The trial judge found in favour of the respondent. The landlord appealed. At the hearing of the appeal the respondent did not appear and was not represented as she had decided to leave the premises in any event.

Held, allowing the appeal, that (1) in the absence of contested argument the court's observation and decision must not be regarded as authoritative for any other case; (2) having regard to the decision in *Street* v. *Mountford* [1985] C.L.Y. 1893, it did not follow that because the respondent was not a lodger, *ergo* she had exclusive possession and was a tenant; in *Street* exclusive possession had been conceded but each case had to be considered on its own facts; in the instant case the judge had failed to consider the nature of the possession given to the respondent and the case would be remitted to the county court for a rehearing.

BROOKER SETTLED ESTATES *v.* AYERS (1987) 19 H.L.R. 246, C.A.

2160. Lease or licence—exclusive possession—whether P had rebutted the presumption of tenancy

P refurbished a property with a view to a sale. The premises were empty and displayed a "for sale" notice board. D claimed to be in urgent need of accommodation and P agreed to let him into possession pending the sale. It was agreed that D would be given one month's notice when he had to leave. P gave D a rent book to allow him to claim housing benefit, P asked D to leave, and D refused to go saying he was a tenant of the premises. An order for possession was made against D. D appealed.

Held, dismissing the appeal, that although D had exclusive possession of the premises and a rent book, and all the indicia of a tenancy were present, the circumstances of the present case were exceptional and P had rebutted the presumption of a tenancy. On the facts D had only been granted a licence to occupy the premises.

SHARP *v.* MACARTHUR AND SHARP (1987) 19 H.L.R. 364, C.A.

2161. Lease or licence—grant of occupation of shop space

By an oral licence granted in 1982 A was permitted by R to share shop space in a unit at Camden Lock Market with a co-occupier X, each paying half the rent. When X later went out of occupation, A thereafter occupied the whole of the shop space and paid the whole of the rent. When R subsequently gave A eight days' notice to move out, A contended that he was entitled to exclusive possession of the space in question, and that the requirements for the creation of a tenancy set out in *Street* v. *Mountford* [1985] C.L.Y. 1893 had been satisfied. The judge held that A had been a licensee only, but that a month would have been a reasonable period of notice.

Held, dismissing A's appeal and R's cross-appeal, that (1) it could not be inferred from the facts and circumstances of the case that A had been granted exclusive possession, whether before or after X's departure; (2) A had at all times been a licensee only (*Street* v. *Mountford* distinguished); (3) the judge had been entitled to conclude that a month was the requisite period of notice.

SMITH *v.* NORTHSIDE DEVELOPMENTS (1987) 283 E.G. 1211, C.A.

2162. Lease or licence—joint occupation agreement

A signed an agreement described as a "licence" which permitted her to share a two-roomed furnished flat with one other person for six months, without having exclusive possession, ". . . at a calendar monthly licence rental of £260 . . . so that the total calendar monthly rent actually paid by all the licensees . . . at any one time shall not together exceed £260." A's friend B, who also signed an agreement in identical form, shared the flat with A for two months, each girl occupying one room; but B's place was then taken by another girl R for the remainder of the term. Thereupon A refused to sign a further "licence" at a higher rent, stayed in the flat, and had her rent registered by the rent officer at £130. The judge made an order for possession against her, on the basis that the agreement had not conferred exclusive possession and that accordingly, on the principles in *Street* v. *Mountford* [1985] C.L.Y. 1893, no tenancy had been created.

On appeal, A contended that the agreement had created a joint tenancy, and that *Street* v. *Mountford* had effectively abolished the status of licensees so far as multiple occupation agreements, such as those in *Somma* v. *Hazelhurst* [1978] C.L.Y. 1797, *Aldrington Garages* v. *Fielder* [1979] C.L.Y. 1616, and *Sturolson and Co.* v. *Weniz* [1984] C.L.Y. 1434 were concerned. The Court of Appeal noted that, whilst the first of those cases had clearly involved a "sham" agreement, the agreements in the latter two cases could not readily be identified as "shams".

Held, allowing the appeal and remitting the matter to the judge for reconsideration, that (1) in applying *Street* v. *Mountford,* the court (i) should establish the contractual relationship by construing the documents against the factual matrix in the usual way; (ii) should in considering the objective intentions of the parties, bear in mind the intention of Parliament in enacting the Rent Act legislation, and not be astute to find ways of circumventing it; and (iii) once having established the contractual position, should only then consider whether the occupation is to be protected under the 1977 Act, bearing in mind in relation to possible joint tenancies the judgments of Megaw L.J. in *Lloyd* v. *Sadler* [1978] C.L.Y. 1806 and *Demuren* v. *Seal Estates* [1979] C.L.Y. 1605. In the final analysis each case should be considered on its own facts; (2) that the present case could not be decided without a closer examination of the factual matrix, in order to decide whether the agreements had conferred on A and B a joint tenancy with exclusive possession against the outside world, or simply two separate licences without exclusive possession. The Court listed a number of factors which required particular attention, including the question of liability to pay rent (*Snook* v. *London and West Riding Investments* [1967] C.L.Y. 1836 considered).

HADJILOUCAS *v.* CREAN (1987) 284 E.G. 927, C.A.

2163. Lease or licence—underlease of premises—provision for sub-underletting—exclusive possession—sub-underlettings never executed

Where a defendant's occupancy of premises has all the indicia of a tenancy, a tenancy is created, not a mere licence.

The defendants and other parties sought premises together to act as consultants in corporate finance. A licence was granted to allow the premises to be prepared for occupation. The plaintiff company eventually took the underlease, with each party sub-underletting the respective parts. The underlease was executed, and draft sub-underleases were prepared. In fact the sub-underleases were never executed. The defendants were eventually in sole occupation and exclusive possession of part of the premises, when the defendant resigned and left giving no notice to quit. The plaintiff company sued for rent for the rest of the term of the tenancy.

Held, allowing their application, that the defendants were tenants, not licensees; their occupancy had all the indicia of a tenancy (*Street* v. *Mountford* [1985] C.L.Y. 1893 applied).

LONDON AND ASSOCIATED INVESTMENT TRUST *v.* CALOW (1987) 53 P. & C.R. 340, H.H. Judge Paul Baker Q.C.

2164. Leasehold enfranchisement—letting value—whether premium reflected letting value—burden of proof

[Leasehold Reform Act 1967, (c.88), s.4(4).]

The annual letting value of a property at the start of a tenancy can, prima facie, be inferred from the premium paid on assignment. If the annual value exceeded three times the rent the burden of showing that the premium did not reflect the true letting value rested on the landlord.

MACDONALD *v.* TRUSTEES OF HENRY SMITH'S CHARITY, *The Times*, July 30, 1987, C.A.

2165. Leasehold enfranchisement—property let on long lease—annual rent and premium—whether let at low rent—meaning of "letting value"

"Letting value" for the purposes of s.4 of the 1967 Leasehold Reform Act can include a calculation based on the rack rent plus the annual value of any premium charged.

The respondents were tenants of four houses let on long leases in 1948 at a rent of £200 per annum and £1,250 premium. Shortly before expiry of the leases the tenants applied to purchase the properties. The landlord resisted on the basis that they were not let at a low rent within the meaning of s.4 of the 1967 Act. The issue was as to the meaning of letting value, whether it included the premium. The judge held that letting value was rent and premium and made the orders sought by the tenants. The Court of Appeal upheld the decision.

Held, dismissing the appeal, that the "letting value" could mean the rack rent and the annual value of any premium; as on the basis of this joint figure the annual rent was not more than two-thirds, the rent was a low rent within the meaning of s.4.

DUKE OF WESTMINSTER *v.* JOHNSTON (1987) 53 P. & C.R. 36, H.L.

2166. Leasehold enfranchisement—whether owner of fee simple able to acquire intermediate lease

[Leasehold Reform Act 1967 (c.88), ss.1(1), 8.]

A property was let to P and sublet to D, who subsequently acquired the freehold and, in their capacity as underlessees, purported to give notice to P of their desire to acquire P's intermediate leasehold interest under the provisions of the Leasehold Reform Act 1967. P duly obtained a declaration that D could not so acquire her interest.

Held, dismissing D's appeal, that on the true construction of the word "freehold" in ss.8 and 1(1) of the 1967 Act, whilst the Act permits a tenant to acquire the fee simple together with any intermediate interest, it does not give the existing owner of the fee simple a separate right to acquire any such intermediate interest.

GRATTON-STORY *v.* LEWIS (1987) 283 E.G. 1562, C.A.

2167. Leasehold enfranchisement—whether reduction in rateable value capable of being back-dated. See RENDALL *v.* DUKE OF WESTMINSTER, § 3180.

2168. Leasehold reform—building comprising two maisonettes—whether "house"

[Leasehold Reform Act 1967 (c.88), s.2(1).]

A building was constructed as two maisonettes, one of which was on the ground floor and the other on the first floor, there being separate doors to the street side by side in the front porch. Access to the first floor maisonette was by a hall and staircase from ground floor level, which was divided from the ground floor flat by a wall. Each flat was let on a 99-year lease from 1904, but in due course T acquired both leases and put a door in the downstairs dividing wall. In 1984 he gave statutory notice of his desire to acquire the freehold of the entire building pursuant to the Leasehold Reform Act 1967, but died in 1985, whereupon P, his personal representatives, obtained a declaration of their entitlement to the freehold. On appeal, L contended that the building was not a "house" within s.2(1) of the 1967 Act, since it was divided vertically within the meaning of s.2(1)(*b*).

Held, dismissing the appeal, that the building was a "house" and that P were entitled to acquire the freehold. In particular, s.2(1)(*b*) was concerned with the vertical division of a building into units, as in a terrace of houses; whereas the division in this case was horizontal.

SHARPE *v.* DUKE STREET SECURITIES N.V. (1987) 283 E.G. 1558, C.A.

2169. Leasehold reform—rateable value limits—effect of retrospective alterations

[Leasehold Reform Act 1967 (c.88), ss.1, 4, 6, 37(6), Rent Act 1977 (c.42), s.25(4).]

The respondent tenants who held the unexpired term of long leases applied to the county court with a view to acquiring the freehold or an extended lease. Each contended that the rateable value limits did not exceed £1,500 on April 1, 1973. In both cases the valuation lists which came into force on that date showed a rateable value in excess of £1,500. The tenants argued that they could rely on subsequent temporary reductions in rateable values granted because of building operations on a nearby site in one case and pending reconstruction works in the other. In neither case had any objection been made to the reductions which took effect from April 1, 1973. The county court held that the tenants were entitled to rely on the retrospective reductions.

Held, dismissing the landlords' appeal, that a retrospective reduction in rateable values can be taken into account in determining rateable values.

MACFARQUHAR *v.* PHILLIMORE; MARKS *v.* PHILLIMORE (1986) 18 H.L.R. 397, C.A.

2170. Leasehold reform—test of constructive occupation

The applicant T, was a tenant of a leasehold house let on a long tenancy at a low rent which was his only residence from 1964 until January 1980 when a fire rendered the house uninhabitable. He was thus obliged to live elsewhere. In May 1982 he gave notice of his desire to acquire the freehold under the Leasehold Reform Act 1967, which the landlords opposed on the ground that he was not in occupation of the house.

Held, on T's application for declaratory relief, that the same test of constructive occupation applied as under the Rent Acts, namely did T have a real hope of returning to the house to live with the practical possibility to do so within a reasonable time, and on the facts T had succeeded in establishing this.

BOLHAH *v.* JIGWOOD SECURITIES CONTINUATION, May 29, 1986; Judge R. B. H. Pearce, Q.C.; Lambeth County Ct. [*Ex rel. D. A. McConville, Barrister.*]

2171. Leasehold reform—tenancy at low rent—date of assessment

[Leasehold Reform Act 1967 (c.88), s.4(1)(*a*), (2); Rent Act 1977 (c.42), s.25(1), (3).]

The date of assessment was to be when the property in question had first appeared in the rating list either as a single hereditament or as two or more hereditaments.

DIXON *v.* ALLGOOD, *The Times,* November 27, 1987, H.L.

2172. Leasehold reform—the "appropriate day"—change of identity

[Leasehold Reform Act 1967 (c.88), s.4; Rent Act 1977 (c.42), s.25(3).]

On an application by a tenant to purchase the freehold of his house, an issue arose whether the tenancy was one at a low rent. The question depended on what was the "appropriate day" for the ascertainment of rateable value under s.4. The house had been extensively modified and improved since 1965 so if the appropriate day was March 23, 1965, or any later date prior to the value of the house in its improved state appearing in the valuation list, the rent would have been more than two-thirds of the rateable value.

Held, that (1) the correct principle to be applied was, had there been a change of identity? There must be a substantial change between the premises in their former state and their subsequent state. Mere improvement is not sufficient. The question is one of fact and degree for the judge; (2) on the facts two uninhabitable cottages had been converted into one house of character with modern amenities—there had been a change of identity; (3) the correct date for the purposes of the Act was the first date when there appeared in the valuation list a rateable value identifiable as relating to the property in its new state (*Langford Property Co.* v. *Batten* (1947–51) C.L.C. 8484 and *Capital and Provincial Property Trust* v. *Rice* (1947–51) C.L.C. 8500 considered).

GRIFFITHS *v.* BIRMINGHAM CITY DISTRICT COUNCIL, January 26, 1987; H.H. Judge Clive Tayler, Q.C., Stafford County Ct. [*Ex rel. Roger Cooke and Robert Ham, Barristers.*]

2173. Lessor's managing agents—shareholders in lessor company—whether qualified to act

P company, a tenant's association, owned and administered certain blocks of flats in Cambridge. The lessees were shareholders in the company, each having one share per flat. D held a 99-year lease which required that the annual service charge payable by the lessee to the lessor "shall be estimated and certified by the lessor's managing agents acting as experts and not as arbitrators . . .". P company appointed six of the tenants/shareholders as managing agents. Some of them were also directors of the P company. D contended that they could not properly act as managing agents and could not therefore properly give certificates of expenditure because, *inter alia,* they were too closely connected with P company. The judge found that they had ample expertise and were people who would be expected to have independence of mind; they had a direct interest in keeping the amount of expenditure within reasonable bounds whilst at the same time not neglecting items of necessary expenditure. The judge accordingly held that the managing agents appointed were not disqualified because they were to be identified with P company themselves. D appealed.

Held, dismissing the appeal, that the managing agent had to be somebody who was distinct from the lessor himself and therefore independent in that sense. He also had to possess some degree of expertise. The six individual members were clearly separate legal persons from the lessors, the company. On the judge's finding they were persons selected on the basis that they could and would exercise an independent judgment in relation to the management of the block of flats. Further, their independence could not be challenged on the ground that they themselves were tenants (*Finchbourne* v. *Rodrigues* [1976] C.L.Y. 1521 distinguished).

NEW PINEHURST RESIDENCE ASSOCIATION (CAMBRIDGE) *v.* SILOW, October 7, 1986 (C.A.T. No. 841).

2174. Long tenancy at low rent—effect of statutory provisions relating to service charges upon provisions in the lease

[Leasehold Reform Act 1967 (c.88), s.39; Housing Act 1969 (c.33), s.80(1).]

S.39 of the Leasehold Reform Act 1967 (consolidated in the Rent Act 1968) had the effect of bringing long tenancies under Rent Act Protection, so that they could not be granted or assigned for a premium where the rent exceeded two-thirds of the rateable value. However, s.80(1) of the Housing Act 1969 (now s.5(4) of the Housing Act 1977) provided that, in considering whether the rent of a long tenancy exceeded two-thirds of the rateable value, service charges were not to be treated as part of the rent. A lease of a dwelling-house on a long tenancy granted in 1972 for a term from 1968 provided, with the obvious intention of avoiding the operation of s.39, that the aggregate of the fixed ground rent and the service charge were at no time to exceed two-thirds of the rateable value and that, if it appeared likely to do so, L would be released from any obligation which would impose upon him a liability which, when recovered from T, would take the aggregate over the two-thirds figure. The lease further provided by cl. 12 that if the law "shall have been amended at any time in the future" so that service charges were no longer treated as part of the rent for the purposes of assessing whether a premium could be charged on grant or assignment, the restriction of the aggregate to two-thirds of the rateable value "shall be of no effect and the lessor shall be at liberty to demand a full contribution from the lessee . . . notwithstanding that such a contribution together with the ground rent therefore exceeds two-thirds of the rateable value."

Held, that upon the true construction of cl. 12 considered in the light of s.80 of the 1969 Act, L was no longer restricted to recovering that part only of the service charge which, when added to the ground rent, did not exceed two-thirds of the rateable value, but could recover a full contribution.

INVESTMENT & FREEHOLD ENGLISH ESTATES *v.* CASEMENT (1987) 283 E.G. 748, H.H. Judge Paul Baker Q.C.

2175. Maintenance company—shortfall in maintenance contribution—whether to be set off against rent payable to landlord

The tenants of a block of flats covenanted to pay a maintenance contribution to D, a maintenance company, which held it on trust to keep the walls, ceilings, floors and structure in repair, and which covenanted with the tenants to apply the maintenance contribution for that purpose. D was not however a party to any repairing covenant. When a shortfall arose between the cost of repairs to the basement and the contributions paid by the tenants, D contended that it was entitled under s.19(1) of the Landlord and Tenant Act 1985 to recoup the shortfall from the rents which it had collected on L's behalf.

Held, giving judgment for L, that there was no covenant for D to do repairs at its own expense, and that D was not therefore entitled to recoup the cost of the works from the rents. Hence it was not necessary to decide whether s.19 had the effect contended for by D.

ALTON HOUSE HOLDINGS *v.* CALFLANE (MANAGEMENT) (1987) 283 E.G. 844, Mr. John Mowbray Q.C.

2176. Management agreement for exclusive use of premises—whether tenancy or licence

An agreement which confers exclusive possession at a rent, and for a term, will create a tenancy notwithstanding that it does not expressly confer a right to enter upon and use the premises, if such can reasonably be inferred as necessarily incidental to some other right conferred by the agreement.

Under what was described as a management agreement D Ltd. took over an established restaurant, running it for its own account as to profits and losses, and paying a weekly fee to the owner in respect of the use of fixtures and fittings. D sought a declaration that it was a sub-tenant.

Held, that although described as a management agreement, the reality was that D had exclusive possession, for a term, and although the weekly payment was described as being for the use of the fixtures and fittings only, there had necessarily to be inferred a right to enter the premises in order to use those fixtures and fittings. A tenancy had, therefore, been created. That was the true substance of the agreement, and the remaining clauses of the agreement, some of which were there for cosmetic purposes, could not alter that substance.

DELLNEED *v.* CHIN (1987) 53 P. & C.R. 172, Millett J.

2177. New business tenancy—computation of rent

[Landlord and Tenant Act 1954 (c.56), s.34(1).]

On an application by T for a new tenancy of a cafe-restaurant in the East Precinct of St. George's Walk, Croydon, a dispute arose as to the new rent. At trial it was agreed that the correct approach was the zone A equivalent method of evaluation, and that the relevant area was 504 s.f. As comparables, L relied *inter alia* on two open market lettings of premises in the East Precinct, and T upon eleven reviews and renewals in the more sought-after West Precinct. The judge added nine of T's figures adjusted downwards by 20 per cent. to L's two figures, divided the total by eleven, and arrived at an overall figure of £12·59 p.s.f., which she described as a "fair and reasonable rent." On appeal T criticised this finding in a number of ways, but in particular on the ground that the judge had not determined the "open market rent" within the meaning of s.34(1) of the Landlord and Tenant Act 1954.

Held, dismissing T's appeal, (1) that whilst the words "fair and reasonable" had been unfortunate, it was impossible to say that the judge had had in mind anything other than the open market rent; (2) that on the evidence the judge had been entitled to approach the matter in the way she did, save that the West Precinct figures should have been adjusted to take account of increases in market rents down to April 1986 when the case was heard.

ORIANI *v.* DORITA PROPERTIES (1987) 282 E.G. 1001, C.A.

2178. Occupation of premises by tenant's wife—whether to be regarded as occupation of tenant where premises not matrimonial home

[Rent Act 1977 (c.42), s.2(1)(*a*); Matrimonial Homes Act 1983 (c.19), ss.1(6), 1(10).]

The first and second defendants Mr and Mrs King were married in 1974. In 1978 they separated. In due course Mr king found accommodation for his wife and son which was let to him for a period of 364 days. During the first six or seven weeks, Mr King used to sleep there for four or five nights in order to help their son, who had been a ward of court, become used to living with his mother again. The son then left and lived with Mr King. The plaintiff brought proceedings for possession and possession was ordered against both defendants. Mrs King appealed.

Held, dismissing the appeal, that (1) the cottage had never been the matrimonial home and therefore the Matrimonial Homes Act 1983 did not apply; (2) in order for occupation of the wife to be deemed that of the husband, it was necessary that the premises had been the matrimonial home; in the present case the second defendant was not occupying the cottage on behalf of her husband but as his licencee.

HALL *v.* KING (1987) 19 H.L.R. 440, C.A.

2179. Possession order—reasonableness

[Rent Act 1977 (c.42), Sched. 15, Case 9.]

D was the tenant of a three-bedroomed house with no bathroom. P, the landlord, his wife and two children, one of whom was epileptic, lived in a mobile home next to a busy caravan site. P instituted proceedings against D claiming possession under Case 9. At the trial, it was common ground that the mobile home was totally unsuitable for P and his family. However, P's father had died leaving him a considerable estate, a large part of which was tied up in a farm. There were two cottages on the farm each with a protected tenant in occupation. Each cottage was worth £16,000 without vacant possession and twice that if vacant. Further, there was some possibility that the value of the farm would be increased by future industrail and/or housing development. There was also evidence that P was in debt and could not buy himself a home unless the cottages were sold. The judge found that P reasonably required the house for his occupation and that D had not eastablished that they would suffer greater hardship. He then went on to consider whether it was reasonable to make the order for possession and decided that it would not, in part because he found that P would in the reasonably near future be likely to have more money. P appealed. In the week before the hearing in the Court of Appeal, one of the cottages became vacant.

Held, allowing the appeal, that (1) it was not possible on all the evidence to deduce that any immediate benefit was likely to accrue to P from his father's estate; (2) having regard to the fact that one of the cottages was now sold, the case was remitted for rehearing.

COOMBS *v.* PARRY (1987) 19 H.L.R. 384, C.A.

2180. Possession order—reasonableness—leave to adduce further evidence

P claimed possession of premises against D, a statutory tenant, on the ground of persistent non-payment of rent. The day before the hearing for possession D paid the arrears of rent. The judge considered that it was reasonable in all the circumstances to make an order for possession. D appealed and sought leave to adduce further evidence dealing with the fact that (1) because D had not paid the rent due, he could not be considered by a council for housing under the Housing (Homeless Persons) Act 1977 as having become homeless unintentionally and (2) in the opinion of a firm of insurance advisers D would have difficulty in obtaining a mortgage having been the subject of a judgment for non-payment of rent.

Held, dismissing the appeal, that these were both matters which could have been put before the court at the time of the hearing with reasonable diligence. Further it was unlikely that they would have had an important influence on the result of the case having regard to all the facts. In any event the judge would have had very well in mind that the consequences to D would inevitably be serious if an order for possession were made.

LEE-STEERE *v.* JENNINGS, April 28, 1986 (C.A.T. No. 442).

2181. Possession order—resident landlord—whether power to suspend indefinitely

[Rent Act 1977 (c.42), s.106A.]

L, a resident landlord, sought possession under s.106A of the Rent Act 1977 of accommodation let on a restricted contract to T. The judge made an order for possession suspended upon payment of arrears of rent and of the current rent.

Held, allowing L's appeal, that the judge had exceeded his jurisdiction, since by s.106A(3) of the Act he was not permitted to postpone the giving up of possession by T to a date later than three months after the making of the possession order.

BRYANT *v.* BEST (1987) 283 E.G. 843, C.A.

2182. Possession order—written notice—tied cottage

[Rent Act 1977 (c.42), Sched. 15, Case 16.]

The respondent landlord was a farmer who let a cottage to the appellant, and subsequently began proceedings for possession under Case 16. It was not alleged in the particulars of claim that notice had been given to the tenant as required by the provisions of the case, and the tenant denied that any notice, in writing or orally, had been given. The landlord maintained that by reason of the tenant's alleged representation that he would leave if the premises were required by a farm worker, the landlord had let the premises without giving the requisite notice under Case 16 and the tenant was estopped from relying on the absence of notice. At the hearing the landlord alleged in cross-examination that there had been a written agreement which his solicitors had thrown away which stated that the tenant would vacate on 28 days notice if the plaintiff required it for a farm worker. The tenant denied that this had been put in writing. The judge accepted the evidence of the landlord and that this constituted notice for the purposes of Case 16 and made an order for possession. The tenant appealed.

Held, allowing the appeal, that (1) the facts of the case which involved a serious and fundamental change in the landlord's case at the last minute were so disquieting that the court would have to seriously consider ordering a re-trial; (2) even assuming a written agreement existed in the terms alleged, it was not capable of satisfying the requirements of Case 16; although written notice for the purpose of Case 16 did not have to be any particular form it must state clearly that possession might be recovered under the Act *i.e.* that the landlord would be entitled to go to court to require the tenant to give up possession and would do so if he required the dwelling for a farm worker.

FOWLER *v.* MINCHIN (1987) 19 H.L.R. 224, C.A.

2183. Possession order against trespasser—whether entitled to immediate order

P council applied under C.C.R. (1981), Ord. 24 for a possession order against unknown persons occupying their property. At the hearing of their application a Miss Ford appeared and admitted that she was in occupation of the property without the licence or consent of the council but said that she was on the council's housing list and had no other place to live. The judge made an order for possession but directed that the warrant for possession should not be executed until P offered Miss Ford alternative accommodation. P appealed.

Held, allowing P's appeal, that the judge had no jurisdiction to make that order. P council, the owner of the property, was seeking possession from a trespasser. In such a case the lawful owner was entitled to an immediate order for possession (*McPhail* v. *Persons Unknown* [1973] C.L.Y. 2800 and *Swordheath Properties* v. *Floydd* [1978] C.L.Y. 1803a applied).

MAYOR AND BURGESSES OF CAMDEN LONDON BOROUGH *v.* PERSONS UNKNOWN, May 14, 1986 (C.A.T. No. 433).

2184. Possession proceedings—whether reasonableness considered

[Rent Act 1977 (c.42), s.98.]

R brought proceedings for possession of one room on the grounds that suitable alternative accommodation was available. A defended the proceedings on the grounds that she had lived in the same house for 24 years and in the same room since 1969 and further that the proposed accommodation was very noisy. In giving his judgment the judge indicated that the only matters upon which he had to make a decision related to the suitability of the accommodation offered, although he did ask himself the question whether the degree of noise made it unreasonable for her to occupy the property. A appealed against the order for possession.

Held, allowing the appeal, that (1) in the ordinary case where a judge is dealing with possession proceedings under s.98 of the Rent Act, the court should readily presume that he had taken all relevant matters into consideration unless there are very good reasons for holding otherwise; (2) in the light of the judge's expression that the concept of reasonableness related only to the suitability of the alternative accommodation it was not safe to presume that the judge had the requirement of reasonableness in mind; (3) the case would be remitted to the same judge.

MINCHBURN *v.* FERNANDEZ (1987) 19 H.L.R. 29, C.A.

2185. Protected shorthold tenancies—rent registration

PROTECTED SHORTHOLD TENANCIES (RENT REGISTRATION) ORDER 1987 (No. 265) [45p], made under the Housing Act 1980 (c.51), s.52(4); operative on May 4, 1987; removes the requirement for rent registration required under s.52(1)(*c*) of the 1980 Act for a tenancy to be a protected shorthold tenancy.

2186. Protected tenancy—"board"

[Rent Act 1977 (c.42), s.7(1).]

A tenancy is not protected where the landlord lets premises at a rent which includes payment for board in the form of the daily provision of a continental breakfast.

OTTER *v.* NORMAN, *The Times*, August 3, 1987, C.A.

2187. Protected tenancy—effect of bankruptcy—whether disclaimer by trustee in bankruptcy valid—whether landlord entitled to possession

[Bankruptcy Act 1914 (c.59), Bankruptcy Rules 1925.]

The plaintiff landlord let a dwelling-house to the defendant tenants for a term of seven and a quarter years from June 28, 1978. The terms included an absolute prohibition on assignment or subletting, full repairing obligation on the tenants and a covenant to deliver up in good repair at the end of the term. In January 1985 a trustee in bankruptcy was appointed, the tenants having been adjudicated bankrupt, and in August 1985 he disclaimed the lease under the Bankruptcy Act 1914. In the county court the disclaimer was challenged on the basis that the land was not burdened with onerous covenants. The judge found that the disclaimer was void, and dismissed the claim for possession.

Held, allowing the landlord's appeal that, (1) the lease was one which was on its face onerous; (2) it was not satisfactory that there should be a ruling on the validity of the disclaimer in proceedings to which the trustee is not a party in circumstances where the question is one of fact; (3) even if the disclaimer was invalid the tenants were not entitled to the protection of the Rent Acts since the term of the lease remained vested in the trustee in bankruptcy until the lease expired by effluxion of time, and immediately before that date the protected tenant was the trustee and not the defendants.

EYRE *v.* HALL, (1986) 18 H.L.R. 509, C.A.

2188. Protected tenancy—greater hardship

[Rent Act 1977 (c.42), Sched. 15, Case 9.]

T, a man of 57, had since 1972 been the tenant of a maisonette in Brentford, where he lived with his two Alsatian dogs. His weekly income consisted of £31 per week supplementary benefit and £20 per week housing benefit. In due course L, the owner of a number of properties from which he derived his income, sought possession of the premises under Case 9 of Sched. 15 to the Rent Act 1977, on the grounds that they were reasonably required as a residence for his sons M, aged 27, and G, aged 24, each of whom lived in unsatisfactory accommodation, but who earned respectively £80 and £85 per week. T contended that he would have great difficulty in obtaining alternative accommodation, because of his dogs and the fact that landlords are reluctant to accept as a tenant someone whose rent is paid by housing allowance. The judge held that possession was reasonably required by L, and that M and G would suffer greater hardship if no order was made than T would if an order was made. He therefore ordered possession.

Held, dismissing T's appeal, that it could not be said that the judge had on the evidence reached a conclusion which no reasonable judge could reach (*Coplans* v. *King* (1947) C.L.C. 8594, *Chandler* v. *Strevett* (1947) C.L.C. 8601 and *Kelley* v. *Goodwin* (1947) C.L.C. 8626 applied).

HODGES *v.* BLEE (1987) 283 E.G. 1215, C.A.

2189. Protected tenancy—landlord selling premises with vacant possession—purchaser's rights

[Rent Act 1977 (c.42), s.98(1).]

Where a landlord has agreed to sell premises with vacant possession, and a tenant of the premises has, at the same moment, agreed with the purchaser not to seek to enforce against him any rights of possession or occupation, the court can nevertheless not grant the purchaser possession of the premises as against the tenant unless the provisions of s.98(1) of the Rent Act 1977 are satisfied. Hardship to the purchaser is irrelevant to the section (*Dudley & District Benefit Building Society* v. *Emerson* (1947–51) C.L.C. 8835 distinguished).

APPLETON *v.* ASPIN, *The Times,* December 1, 1987, C.A.

2190. Protected tenancy—possession sought by landlord—condition

[Rent Act 1977 (c.42), Case 11 to Sched. 15, Part V of Sched. 15.]

The plaintiff landlord bought a house in London in which he and his family lived before moving to the West Indies as a requirement of his work. He let the property to the defendant tenant with a Case 11 notice. In 1984, a year after letting the property, he sought possession on the ground that as his anticipated tour of duty would now be ten years or more, he wished to sell the property in order to build a house near his place of work in Trinidad. The claim was originally based on a stated intention to return to England to live in the house, but the county court judge accepted that it was always his intention to sell, and that the claim was originally framed wrongly because of a mistake in his instructions to his solicitors because of the distance between them. It was submitted on behalf of the tenant that there was no evidence that the landlord intended to use the proceeds of the sale of the property to acquire at once, or within a reasonable period of time, a dwelling house more suitable to his needs. The tenant appealed against the order for possession.

Held, that on its true construction, para. (f) of Part V of Sched. 15 to the Rent Act requires a connection between the acquisition of a dwelling house by the landlord, which could include the building of such a house, and the use of the proceeds of sale of the existing house, which latter must be within a reasonable time of the former: while it was not sufficient to say that he might want to use the money sometime in the future, on the facts of the present case there was ample evidence to justify the judge's findings.

BISSESSAR *v.* GHOSN, (1986) 18 H.L.R. 486, C.A.

2191. Protected tenancy—required by L for his daughter—effect of covenant to transfer title into their joint names

[Rent Act 1977 (c.42), Sched. 15, Case 9.]

The respondent landlord was the lessor of a flat to the appellant. The property was held on trust for himself and his daughter as joint tenants in equity in equal shares, and he undertook to transfer the property into joint names when his daughter reached 18. In fact no transfer of the property into joint names was executed then or at all. Proceedings for possession were brought under Case 9, Sched. 15 of the Rent Act 1977 on the grounds that the flat was reasonably required by him as landlord for the residence of his daughter. The appellant ceased paying rent for the flat in October 1985. She subsequently counterclaimed alleging that the boiler in the flat was defective, but it was only at an advanced stage of the proceedings that she claimed the right to set off the sums due under the counterclaim against rent. In July 1986, the registrar ordered that the claim for possession be tried separately from the counterclaim. An appeal against this order was dismissed by the judge, who also dismissed an application for an adjournment of the hearing. At the hearing, an order for possession was made and judgment given in respect of the arrears of rent. The tenant appealed.

Held, dismissing the appeal, that (1) the question of whether there should have been an adjournment was entirely one for the trial judge; (2) the case had to be dealt with on the facts as they were and not as they might have been had the transfer of the respondent's interest to his daughter been executed; there was no reason why Case 9 should not apply where possession was required by a landlord for his daughter who was the beneficial joint owner of the premises; (3) although in a normal case it might well be that any judgment given before the hearing of a counterclaim should be stayed pending the hearing of the counterclaim, in the present case the counterclaim was so nebulous and ill-drafted that the judge was entitled to give judgment on the claim.

BOSTOCK *v.* DE LA PAGERIE *sub nom.* BOSTOCK *v.* TACHER DE LA PAGERIE (1987) 19 H.L.R. 358, C.A.

2192. Protection from eviction—failure to make premises habitable—whether amounted to doing acts calculated to interfere with the tenant's peace or comfort

[Protection from Eviction Act 1977 (c.43), s.1(3).]

A landlord was not guilty of doing acts calculated to interfere with the peace or comfort of a residential occupier where he failed to take steps to complete works that were necessary to make the premises occupied by the residential occupier habitable.

A was convicted of an offence contrary to s.1(3) of the Protection from Eviction Act 1977 in that he with intent to cause the residential occupier (C) of the flat he owned to give up the occupation of the flat did acts calculated to interfere with the peace or comfort of C. The facts relied on by the prosecution were that A failed to complete works that were necessary to the bathroom of the flat to render the flat habitable. The bathroom had been rendered unusable by works carried out by A with a view to improving the flat. The improvement works were halted whilst A and C attempted to agree whether C should continue to pay rent whilst the works were carried out. No agreement was reached and the works were not proceeded with. When the works were commenced A did not intend to cause C to give up occupation of the flat. A appealed.

Held, allowing the appeal, that the words of s.1(3) of the Act did not impose a responsibility to rectify damage caused by a defendant at a time when he did not possess the requisite intention to constitute an offence under the section. A's failure to complete the improvement works was not the doing of an act or acts for the purposes of s.1(3) of the Act (*R.* v. *Miller* [1983] C.L.Y. 543 considered).

R. *v.* AHMAD (ZAFAR) (1986) 52 P. & C.R. 346, C.A.

2193. Purported forfeiture of tenancy by peaceable re-entry without determination of sub-tenancy—whether valid

A landlord who purported to peaceably re-enter premises demised to a tenant and occupied by a sub-tenant without determining the sub-tenancy failed to effectively forfeit the tenant's lease.

L granted T a lease of certain premises for a term of 80 years from 29 September 1932 at a rent of £50 per annum. T granted an underlease of the premises to C for a term of 10 years from 25 March 1976 at a rent of £3,500 per annum. On 19 October 1984 L purported to forfeit T's lease, the rent payable by T being £62·50 in arrear. L's representative attended the premises to effect a peaceable re-entry. C was assured that his underlease would not be affected and that he would remain in possession under the underlease as a direct tenant of L. With C's consent L then changed the locks of the premises. C was given a letter instructing him to pay his rent to L in future. On 20 November 1984 S purchased the freehold of the premises from L at auction at a price representing its value as subject to the underlease alone. In January 1985 C received rent demands from T and S. T was unaware of the purported forfeiture of its lease. T commenced proceedings seeking a declaration that the lease had not been forfeited or alternatively relief from forfeiture.

Held, that T's lease had not been forfeited. The changing of the locks was an idle ceremony that was not intended to interfere with C's rights under his underlease. The continuance of C's underlease was wholly inconsistent with a determination by forfeiture of T's lease. Had C and L entered into an agreement for C to occupy the premises under a new lease to be granted by L in the same terms as the underlease the position would be different. In any event T would be entitled to relief from forfeiture. The fact that S had purchased the freehold on the basis that it was unencumbered by T's lease was not a consideration of any weight in granting relief from forfeiture (*Baylis* v. *Le Gros* (1858) 4 C.B.N.S. 537, *London and County (A. & D.)* v. *Wilfred Sportsman* [1970] C.L.Y. 1552 considered).

ASHTON *v.* SOBELMAN [1987] 1 W.L.R. 177, John Chadwick Q.C.

2194. Receiver and manager—power to appoint—whether power to order payment of expenses

The Court has the power to make an interlocutory order appointing a receiver and manager before the rights of the parties have been determined at trial. It has no power to order one of the parties to pay the receiver's and manager's expenses (*Boehm* v. *Goodall* [1911] 1 Ch. 155 applied).

EVANS *v.* CLAYHOPE PROPERTIES, *The Times,* November 23, 1987, C.A.

2195. Rent—relief from phasing

RENT (RELIEF FROM PHASING) ORDER 1987 (No. 264) [80p], made under the Housing Act 1980 (c.51), ss.60(5), 151(3); operative on May 4, 1987; removes the requirements for the phasing of rent increases in respect of registered rents for regulated tenancies in the Rent Act 1977 and for statutory tenancies in the Rent (Agriculture) Act 1976.

2196. Rent Act 1977—forms

RENT ACT 1977 (FORMS ETC.) (AMENDMENT) REGULATIONS 1987 (No. 266) [£1·60], made under the Rent Act 1977 (c.42), ss.49, 60, 61; operative on May 4, 1987; amend S.I. 1980 No. 1697 as a consequence of S.I. 1987 No. 264.

2197. Rent assessment committees

RENT ASSESSMENT COMMITTEE (ENGLAND AND WALES) (LEASEHOLD VALUATION TRIBUNAL) (AMENDMENT) REGULATIONS 1987 (No. 2178) [85p], made under the Landlord and Tenant Act 1987 (c.31), s.13(2) and the Rent Act 1977 (c.42), s.74(1); operative on February 1, 1988; prescribe the procedure to be followed by rent assessment committees, when constituted as Leasehold Valuation Tribunals, when dealing with matters arising under s.13 of the 1987 Act.

2198. Rent review—absence from hypothetical future lease of further rent reviews—whether future rent reviews to be implied

Unless so to do would lead to absurd results, the Court should not construe a rent review clause which makes no mention of future rent reviews, as including such a provision.

A lease provided for rent reviews after 5, 10 and 15 years; the hypothetical lease upon which the reviews were to be based did not contain any provision as to rent reviews, nor did it say that it was to be on the same terms as the existing lease. The arbitrator fixed a rent at 15 per cent. above the current market rent. The tenants appealed.

Held, that only if the result would be absurd could the Court ignore the plain words of the lease. It should not be assumed that the revised rent was always to be the market rent. The terms of the agreement were clear and workable, and there was no basis for the Court interfering with them. Appeal dismissed.

GENERAL ACCIDENT FIRE AND LIFE ASSURANCE *v.* ELECTRONIC DATA PROCESSING (1987) 53 P. & C.R. 189, Harman J.

2199. Rent review—application to R.I.C.S.—whether properly made

A rent review clause provided that the revised rent was, in default of agreement, to be determined by an independent surveyor to be appointed failing agreement by the

President of the R.I.C.S.; and that L was to apply to the President for such an appointment within a specified time, failing which the review provisions would be void. It was agreed between the parties that time was of the essence for such an application. The R.I.C.S. guidelines state that such an application should be made ". . . in writing and preferably . . . on the form obtainable on application to the R.I.C.S. . . .", and that applications will not be processed until the application fee has been received. L's agents wrote to the President within the prescribed time stating that they were making an "in time application only" for the appointment of a surveyor. They subsequently completed the application form and submitted the fee, but by this time, the time limit prescribed by the review clause had elapsed. T, who had not been informed about the "in time only" application, contended that no valid application had been made, and that L could not invoke the review provisions. The judge held that L's agents had made a valid application. The Court of Appeal noted that the procedure invoked by L's agents would not prejudice T, who could in practice discover whether or not an application had been made.

Held, dismissing T's appeal, that the application was valid.

STAINES WAREHOUSING CO. *v.* MONTAGU EXECUTOR & TRUSTEE CO. (1987) 283 E.G. 468, C.A.

2200. Rent review—appointment of valuer—whether time of the essence

A 25-year lease of business premises contained 5 rent reviews, and provided that in certain circumstances T could ". . . after the commencement of the Relevant Period . . ." serve on L a notice proposing the amount of the revised rent, ". . . and the amount so proposed shall be the revised rent for the Relevant Period, unless the lessor shall apply to the President for determination by a valuer within 3 months after service of such a notice by the lessee." T having served such a notice, L's application to the President was not made within three months thereafter.

Held, that there were no contra-indications in the lease sufficiently compelling to displace the presumption established by *United Scientific Holdings* v. *Burnley Borough Council* [1977] C.L.Y. 1758 that time was not of the essence for L's application. (*Trustees of Henry Smith's Charity* v. *AWADA Trading and Promotion Service* [1984] C.L.Y. 1952 and *Mecca Leisure* v. *Renown (Holdings)* [1984] C.L.Y. 1950 considered).

PHIPPS—FAIRE *v.* MALBERN CONSTRUCTION (1987) 282 E.G. 460, Warner J.

2201. Rent review—arbitration—whether development potential without planning permission to be taken into account

In a rent review arbitration the arbitrator can take into account the development potential (if properly proved and not excluded) even where there is no extant planning permission.

During the course of a rent review arbitration the question arose whether the development potential of the land without extant planning permission could be taken into account. An application was made to the High Court on this question.

Held, that the arbitrator need not ignore the development potential if it was proved by professional evidence and was not excluded by the review clause, but it could well be that such potential would be of little importance.

RUSHMOOR BOROUGH COUNCIL *v.* GOUCHER AND RICHMOND (1985) 52 P. & C.R. 255, Mervyn Davies J.

2202. Rent review—arbitrator's decision—interrelated break clause

T leased a shop for 21 years from L. The rent for the first 14 years was specified; for the last seven years it was to be as agreed between the parties, or in default of agreement as determined by an arbitrator appointed by both parties. The arbitrator's determination was to be secured by a specified date, subsequent to which a break clause entitled T to terminate the lease if they did not wish to pay the rent as determined. On determination, the rent could not be reduced. Neither L nor T implemented the rent review clause prior to the specified date. L attempted to do so by serving notice two weeks after it. T claimed that L was out of time. The judge held that the interrelation between the rent review and break clauses was such that time was of the essence and L could not invoke the arbitration procedure.

Held, allowing L's appeal, that the intention to be attributed to the parties was that time was not of the essence, because: (1) L would suffer greater detriment in losing the right to a rent review than T would by its delay; (2) the clause required the obtaining of the actual decision which might be delayed through no fault of L and which L could not prevent; and (3) if T were to suffer any hardship by delay, he would have initiated the rent review himself (Dictum of Lord Diplock in *United Scientific Holdings* v. *Burnley Borough Council* [1977] C.L.Y. 1758 applied; *Coventry City Council* v. *Hepworth (J.) & Sons* [1983] C.L.Y. 2137 distinguished).

METROLANDS INVESTMENTS *v.* DEWHURST (J.H.) [1986] 3 All E.R. 659, C.A.

2203. Rent review—arbitrator's decision—whether error of law on face of award. See TRIUMPH SECURITIES *v.* REID FURNITURE CO., §150.

2204. Rent review—assessment of revised rent—assumptions to be made by arbitrator

A sublease for 26 years from 1977 of premises in Curzon St, Mayfair for use as a gaming club and casino provided for rent reviews on December 8, 1983 and every five years thereafter. The revised rent, which was to be assessed by a chartered surveyor acting as arbitrator, was to be the "... highest rent at which ... the premises might reasonably be expected to be let in the open market by a willing lessor, with vacant possession, for the residue of the term hereby granted, and upon the terms and conditions including provision for rent review of this lease ...", there being disregarded any effect on rent of the fact that T or some associate of T had been in occupation, any goodwill attaching by reason of the carrying on of business by T or T's associate, any effect on rent of any improvement carried out by T, and "any addition to the value of the demised premises attributable to the gaming or justices licence which may be held in respect of such premises if it appears that having regard to the terms of the current tenancy and any other relevant circumstances the benefit of the licence belings to the tenant or some associate of the tenant." The gaming activities at the premises were at all material times conducted by C, the holder of the gaming licence. At the first review, L's expert contended for a rent of £3,000,000 p.a. exclusive, whilst T's expert contended for £180,000 p.a. The parties therefore agreed to submit a number of questions of law to the court for determination pursuant to s.2 of the Arbitration Act 1979.

Held, that (1) the arbitrator should in summary regard the hypothetical lessor and lessee as "higgling" on the basis (i) that vacant possession could be given on December 8, 1983; (ii) that the premises were suitable for casino use but had not previously been used for that purpose; (iii) that as at December 8, 1983 there were 18 licensed gaming establishments operating in the south Westminster area; (iv) that the competition for the new lease did not include C; (v) that C had not established themselves elsewhere; either (vi) that C held a gaming licence for the premises, in which case there were 21 licences held as at December 8, 1983 in respect of premises in the area; or (vii) that C did not hold such a licence, in which case 20 licences were held in the area (the correct alternative being that which would result in the lower rental value); and (viii) that in any event no one else had had a licence in respect of the premises; (2) it was for the arbitrator having considered all the admissible evidence, both of the profit-earning capacity of the premises as well as of the available comparables, to decide what, if any, weight should be attached to the evidence of the property's profit-earning capacity (*Harewood Hotels* v. *Harris* [1958] C.L.Y. 1824, *Barton (W.J.)* v. *Long Acre Securities* [1982] C.L.Y. 1730, *Scottish & Newcastle Breweries* v. *Sir Richard Sutton's Settled Estates* [1985] C.L.Y. 1925 and *Lynall* v. *I.R.C.* [1971] C.L.Y. 3309 considered); (3) the arbitrator had misdirected himself in refusing discovery of C's trading records on the grounds that trading records would be admissible only in the absence of adequate evidence of comparables; but the Court would not remit the matter to the arbitrator for rehearing, since it was extremely unlikely that any arguable case could have been put forward that these records would have been available to prospective lessee in the hypothetical open market.

Per curiam: The correct approach to rent review provisions in this form is to be found in *Evans (F.R.) (Leeds)* v. *English Electric Co.* [1978] C.L.Y. 1814 and *Norwich Union Life Insurance Society* v. *Trustee Savings Banks Central Board* [1986] C.L.Y. 1926, and requires that the hypotheses required by the rent review provisions are strictly adhered to, but that otherwise the real circumstances of the case are to be taken into account at the expense of allegedly consequential assumptions which are argued to follow from those hypotheses.

CORNWALL COAST COUNTRY CLUB *v.* CARDGRANGE (1987) 282 E.G. 1664, Scott J.

2205. Rent review—basis of assessment of revised rent

A 30-year lease of commercial premises contained regular rent reviews, the revised rent to be calculated by whichever of four alternative methods gave the highest figure. One such method was by adding to the previous rent an addition "calculated at 10 per cent. per annum on a compound basis from the date of the immediately previous rent review." At the first review this method gave the highest figure, for which L accordingly contended. T however argued that it was so expressed as only to come into effect when there had been a previous review, and that it could not therefore operate on the first review.

Held, that (1) on the true construction of the lease, T's contention was correct; (2) the revised rent should therefore be calculated according to the method giving the next highest figure, namely by adding to the previous rent a sum based on the cost of living index.

BISSETT *v.* MARWIN SECURITIES (1987) 281 E.G. 75, Vinelott J.

2206. Rent review—computation of revised rent—whether time of the essence

The lease from August 1981 of a high-class shopping centre in Manchester provided for a number of rent reviews, the first falling due in 1986. The review clause provided that the revised rent was to be assessed by reference to a formula in which the denominator was to be the total income receivable for the demised premises, which was to be assessed once and for all as at December 25, 1986 and was to be applicable for the determination of the rent payable throughout the whole residue of the term after December 25, 1986. The lease provided that the denominator as so computed was not to exceed £275,000, and further provided that, ". . . the total income receivable for the demised premises shall be agreed between the landlord and the lessee within six months after the expiration of the second year of the said term, and if not so agreed shall be the sum of £275,000." When the time for agreement of the total income so receivable passed without any attempt having been made to agree it, L (in whose interest it was for the denominator to remain as low as possible) contended that the wording of the review provision was such as to displace the presumption in *United Scientific Holdings* v. *Burnley Borough Council* [1977] C.L.Y. 1758 that time was not of the essence for agreeing the revised rent, and that the denominator was therefore to be £225,000. The judge noted that, where the parties have not only required a step to be taken in a specified time but have expressly provided for the consequences in case of default, this provides an indication of greater or less strength that time is to be of the essence, but is not necessarily decisive. He also noted that, once the prescribed time limit had been exceeded, L could have served a notice to make time of the essence.

Held, giving judgment for T, that whilst in this case it was essential for some time limit to be specified within which T was to satisfy L of the total income receivable, this did not involve any necessity for making time of the essence; and that upon the true construction of the clause time was not of the essence for the agreement of the total income receivable.

POWER SECURITIES (MANCHESTER) *v.* PRUDENTIAL ASSURANCE CO. (1987) 281 E.G. 1327, Millett J.

2207. Rent review—hypothetical lease—whether rights of user and sub-letting restricted to actual tenant

A rent review clause provided that the revised rent was to be the equivalent of the rent at which the property could be let in the open market for a term equal to the unexpired residue of the lease "in the same terms in all other respects as these presents." The lease contained a covenant restricting the use of the premises to "the storage, sale and display of craftsman's work . . . in respect of such part of the demised premises as shall for the time being be occupied and used by the lessee (here meaning the British Craft Centre . . .)." A further covenant prohibited assignment, sub-letting and parting with possession, save that, ". . . only while the lessee is the British Craft Centre the lessee may share occupation of the demised premises . . . with a holding or subsidiary company." A dispute arose at the rent review as to whether, for the purposes of assessing the revised rent, the express references to the British Craft Centre were to be retained in the hypothetical lease, thereby severely restricting the class of potential lessees and consequently the rent obtainable under the hypothetical letting. The judge held that the nature of the user restriction was intended to grant a personal privilege to the British Craft Centre to use the premises for storage, sale and display of craftsmen's work, that it was not intended that anyone else should use the premises for the purpose, and that the hypothetical lease should accordingly contain a similar restriction; but that the privilege of sharing occupation with subsidiary or holding companies was not intended to be personal to the British Craft Centre, and that the relevant clause in the hypothetical lease ought therefore not to specify the British Craft Centre, but ought to contain simply a reference to the "lessee" with the name left blank. L appealed in relation to the user restriction, but there was no cross-appeal by T in relation to the alienation restrain.

Held, dismissing L's appeal, that the judge had reached the correct conclusion in relation to the user covenant. However, in the light of that conclusion it was doubtful whether his conclusion in relation to the alienation restriction was correct.

JAMES *v.* BRITISH CRAFT CENTRE (1987) 282 E.G. 1251 C.A.

2208. Rent review—improvements under previous lease—whether to be ignored

A rent review clause in a lease of premises in Bristol provided that there was to be disregarded in assessing the revised rent any effect on rent of any improvements carried out by T other than in pursuance of an obligation to L. Under a previous lease between the same parties T had built a back extension and a storage building without any obligation to L so to do, and these had become L's fixtures by the time of the grant of the current lease. T contended that the effect of these structures was to be disregarded in assessing the revised rent.

Held, that, (1) the structures were not improvements of the premises demised under the current lease, but were part of them; (2) the effect of these structures was not to be disregarded in assessing the revised rent. (*Brett* v. *Brett Essex Golf Club* [1986] C.L.Y. 1912 applied; *Hambro Bank Executor and Trustee Co. Ltd.* v. *Superdrug Stores* [1985] C.L.Y. 1919 distinguished).

PANTHER SHOP INVESTMENTS *v.* KEITH POPLE (1987) 282 E.G. 594, Mr. John Mowbray Q.C.

2209. Rent review—independent surveyor—whether arbitrator or valuer

A lease for 42 years of a supermarket in Newcastle-upon-Tyre reserved an initial rent for the first 14 years of £5,725 p.a., and provided for rent reviews thereafter. The revised rent was to be the "rack-rental value" of the premises and, in default of agreement, was to be determined ". . . by an independent surveyor agreed between the lessors and the lessee or (in default of agreement) by an arbitrator to be nominated by the President of the RICS . . . and this lease shall be deemed for this purpose to be a submission to arbitration within the Arbitration Act 1950 . . ." At the first review the parties agreed on the appointment of K as an independent surveyor who determined the rack-rental value at £17,865 p.a. T wished to challenge this finding, since they had for the provious three years been unable to sell the lease even at the original rent of £5,725 p.a., but the parties were in doubt as to whether or not K had been acting as an arbitrator under the Arbitration Act 1950, in which care the appropriate remedy was to obtain leave to appeal against his decision and then to appeal to the High Court, or simply as an expert valuer, in which case the only remedy would be by way of an action for negligence. T applied to the court for delaration and, if appropriate, leave to appel under the 1950 Act.

Held, that (1) on the true construction of the review clause the independent surveyor appointed by agreement between the parties was not intended to act as an arbitrator but rather as an expert (*Sutcliffe* v. *Thackrah* [1974] C.L.Y. 2552, *Arenson* v. *Casson Beckman Rutley & Co.* [1975] C.L.Y. 2318 and *Palacath* v. *Flanagan* [1985] C.L.Y. 2315 considered); (2) the court would decline on this application to decide whether K was as a valuer amenable to a suit for negligence, or whether this was precluded by public interest immunity.

NORTH EASTERN CO-OPERATIVE SOCIETY *v.* NEWCASTLE-UPON-TYNE CITY COUNCIL (1987) 282 E.G. 1409, Scott J.

2210. Rent review—independent valuer—whether error in assessing revised rent

A lease of commercial property contained a rent review clause, and provided that in default of agreement the computation of the revised rent should be determined by an independent valuer acting as an expert. In their assessment the valuers included in the rentable ground floor area an area of 314.4 sq. m., which T, with L's consent, had sacrificed in order to increase the air space of the lower ground floor.

Held, dismissing T's appeal, that there was no discernible mistake in the valuation.

Per curiam: It would be a disservice to lawyers and litigants to encourage forensic attacks on valuations by experts when these attacks are based on textual criticisms more appropriate to the measured analysis of fiscal litigation.

HUDSON (A.) PTY *v.* LEGAL AND GENERAL LIFE OF AUSTRALIA (1986) 280 E.G. 1434, P.C.

2211. Rent review—landlord's application for appointment of expert—whether out of time

A 21-year lease of business premises contained three seven-yearly rent reviews. The review clause provided that L should serve the usual "trigger" notice, that T should serve a counternotice within two months thereafter, and that if L then failed to apply within a further two months to the President of the R.I.C.S. for the appointment of an independent surveyor, the new rent would be that specified in T's counternotice. Shortly before the first review the reversion was assigned, and not long afterwards the solicitors for the new L sent a "trigger" notice to T, specifying a new rent of £30,000. On the same day, T received another notice from the old L's agents, specifying a new rent of £45,000. In response to the first notice, T duly served on April 15, 1986 a counternotice contending for a new rent of £16,000. In response to the second notice, T first wrote disputing its validity, but subsequently wrote again on April 28, explaining that they had already served a counternotice in response to the earlier "trigger" notice, and enclosing "a duplicate notice". L did not apply to the President to appoint a surveyor until June 24, so that the application was out of time and invalid unless T's duplicate notice of April 28 was valid.

Held, giving judgment for T, that (1) the old L's agents had not had authority to serve a "trigger" notice on behalf of the new L, so that the second notice had been invalid; (2) T's duplicate counternotice was plainly directed to the second "trigger" notice only, and was therefore also invalid; (3) the time limit for L's application to the President had accordingly run from April 15, being the date of service of T's earlier valid counternotice; (4) L's application had accordingly been out of time, and that the new rent would therefore be £16,000 as specified in the counternotice.

CORDON BLEU FREEZER FOOD CENTRES *v.* MARBLEACE (1987) 284 E.G. 786, H.H. Judge Paul Baker Q.C.

2212. Rent review—reference to arbitration—whether T entitled to serve notice making time of the essence

A lease of a factory provided for two rent reviews, and further stipulated that in default of agreement the assessment of the revised rent was to be referred to an independent arbitrator within four months of L's "trigger" notice. It was in effect conceded at trial that time would not be of the essence for such a reference. L having served a "trigger" notice in November 1984, T sent a letter to L in May 1985 requiring L to refer the matter to arbitration within 28 days and purporting to make time of the essence.

Held, on the question of whether the notice was effective, that (1) not every time limit in every rent review clause in which time is not of the essence can be the subject of a notice making time of the essence; (2) since in this case, as in *United Scientific Holdings* v. *Burnley Borough Council* [1977] C.L.Y. 1758, it was equally open to L and to T to apply to the President of the R.I.C.S. for an arbitrator, T was not to have the alternative remedy of serving on L a notice making time of the essence, since he did not need such a remedy.

FACTORY HOLDINGS GROUP *v.* LEBOFF INTERNATIONAL (1987) 282 E.G. 1005, Warner J.

2213. Rent review—retrospective rent review—meaning of "date of review"

The review clause in a reversionary sub-underlease for a 14-year term provided that the rent payable from the commencement of the term was to be increased retrospectively to "the commercial yearly rent," so as to be equal to "the yearly rent at which the demised premises might reasonably be expected at the date of review to be let in the open market . . ." A dispute arose as to what was the "date of review" at which the "commercial yearly rent" was to be assessed.

Held, that the words "the date of review" connoted the date of actual determination, and that the "commercial yearly rent was to be assessed as at that date."

PRUDENTIAL ASSURANCE CO. *v.* GRAY (1987) 283 E.G. 648, Mr. Donald Rattee Q.C.

2214. Rent review—revision of original award—when revised rent payable—whether interest payable

On an award being remitted to the arbitrator for further consideration, the effect of the remittance was to suspend the award; when the further award was made that had the effect of completely superseding the original award.

The arbitrator on a rent review increased the annual rent of premises from £50,000 to £251,000, but the award was remitted to him for reconsideration because of a procedural irregularity. His subsequent award was £221,000. The landlords claimed interest on the difference between the original and the new rents for a period between the date for the rent review, and the first payment of the new rent.

Held, dismissing the claim, that under the terms of the lease, the new rent (including that payable between the rent review date and determination of the new rent) had not become payable until the first quarter day after determination of the new rent, when it had been paid. Interest was only payable on sums due but unpaid, and as this amount was paid when it fell due, there was no justification for the claim.

SHIELD PROPERTIES *v.* ANGLO OVERSEAS TRANSPORT CO. (1987) 53 P. & C.R. 215, Michael Wheeler Q.C.

2215. Rent review—surrender of lease and grant of new lease—whether improvements to be disregarded

Where a lease containing a rent review provision providing for the disregard of matters contained in paragraph (c) of s.34 of the Landlord and Tenant Act 1954, namely improvements by the tenant, was surrendered and replaced by a new lease containing similar provisions, improvements made in the currency of the original tenancy did not fall to be disregarded in the application of the rent review clause in the new lease.

In 1973 P leased certain land to D for a term of 50 years. Under the lease D was obliged to construct a golf course on the land. D was also permitted but not obligated to build a club house. D built a club house during the currency of the tenancy and also a nine hole golf course on adjoining land belonging to P that was not included in the lease. The lease contained a rent review clause providing for the matters set out in paragraphs (a) (b) and (c) of s.34 of the Landlord and Tenant Act 1954 to be disregarded in calculating the reviewed rent. In 1978 the lease was surrendered and a new lease executed for a longer term. The new lease included the nine hole golf course. The new lease contained the same rent review provisions as the old lease. P sought a declaration as to the effect of the rent review provisions with regard to the clubhouse and nine hole golf course. The trial judge held that the clubhouse and nine hole course were improvements carried out by "the tenant", *i.e.* D and were to be disregarded in calculating the reviewed rent under the provisions of the new lease.

Held, allowing P's appeal, that the reference to paragraphs (a), (b) and (c) of s.34 Landlord and Tenant Act 1954 in the rent review clause was a reference to that section in its unamended form and not to the section in the form substituted by s.1 of the Law of Property Act 1969. The section in its unamended form was what the rent review clause accurately described and easily incorporated and the draftsman of the lease had referred specifically to enactments as amended in other parts of the lease. As the clubhouse and nine hole golf course formed part of the premises demised by the 1978 lease they could not be described as improvements to the premises demised by that lease. As the clubhouse and nine hole golf course were constructed before the commencement of the current tenancy they could not be described as improvements carried out by "the tenant" namely the tenant under the current tenancy. The factual matrix in which the 1978 lease was executed did not compel a different conclusion from that to be gathered from the provisions of the lease, *i.e.* that the clubhouse and nine hole golf course did not fall to be disregarded in calculating the reviewed rent under the provisions of the 1978 lease (*"Wonderland" Cleethorpes Re sub nom. East Coast Amusement Co.* v. *British Transport Board* [1963] C.L.Y. 1979 considered; *Hambros Bank Executor and Trustee Co.* v. *Superdrug Stores* [1985] C.L.Y. 1919 distinguished).

BRETT *v.* BRETT ESSEX GOLF CLUB (1986) 52 P. & C.R. 330, C.A.

2216. Rent review—treatment of comparable by arbitrator—whether leave to appeal should be granted

[Arbitration Act 1979 (c.42), s.1(3)(*b*).]

A rent review clause in a 25-year lease of a shop in a modern shopping centre in Warrington provided that the revised rent was to be the current market rental value, taking into account substantial fixtures and fittings which were listed in a Schedule to a collateral agreement. In default of agreement the matter was to be determined by an independent arbitrator. At the first review L cited as a comparable premises in the same shopping centre, in respect of which a premium of £9,000 had been paid by the lessee for the landlord's fittings on the signing of the lease. In his award, which was based on devaluation to zone A the arbitrator took the comparable into account but ignored the premium. Eleven other rent reviews for properties in the shopping centre were pending. When L sought leave to appeal under s.1(3)(*b*) of the Arbitration Act 1979, T contended that the treatment of the premium was not a point of law but a matter of valuation practice. However, the judge noted that the question of whether the arbitrator was entitled to deal with the premium as he did was the very question which, if leave to appeal were given, the judge would have to determine.

Held, granting leave to appeal, that (1) the appropriate test in deciding whether or not to grant leave to appeal was not that laid down in *The Nema* [1981] C.L.Y. 76 and *The Antaios* [1984] C.L.Y. 96 (namely whether there was a strong prima facie case that the arbitrator was wrong in law) but rather that in *Lucas Industries* v. *Welsh Development Agency* [1986] C.L.Y. 1907, namely whether the Court was left in real doubt as to whether the arbitrator was right in law; (2) there was such a doubt.

WARRINGTON AND RUNCORN DEVELOPMENT CORP. *v.* GREGGS (1987) 281 E.G. 1075, Warner J.

2217. Rent review—whether independent valuer to assume a willing lessee

A 25-year lease of business premises provided for five-yearly rent reviews, at which the revised rent was to be the "yearly rent . . . at which the property might reasonably be expected to be let on the open market . . . for a term of 25 years with vacant possession and otherwise on the same terms and conditions of this lease." The judge held that, if the valuer's examination of the appropriate open market were to reveal no willing lessee at any price, he was not required by the formula to proceed on the assumption that a willing lessee could be found.

Held, allowing L's appeal, that in order to give effect to the bargain between the parties contained in the review clause, the following assumptions had to be made: (i) that there would be an open market letting; (ii) that there was a market in which that letting was agreed; and (iii) that the hypothetical landlord would be willing to let the premises and that the hypothetical tenant would be willing to take them. However the strength of the market and the rental value of the premises in the market would be matters for the valuer's discretion, based on his own knowledge and experience of the letting value of such premises (*Law Land Co.* v. *Consumers' Association* [1980] C.L.Y. 1634 considered).

DENNIS AND ROBINSON *v.* KIOSSOS ESTABLISHMENT (1987) 282 E.G. 857, C.A.

2218. Rent review—whether power to restrain appointment of expert by R.I.C.S.

A lease of commercial premises provided for regular rent reviews, which were to be initiated by L serving a "trigger" notice not less than six months before the review date. In default of agreement between the parties ". . . within three calendar months of the expiry of such notice . . ." the matter was to be determined by an expert surveyor appointed by the president of the R.I.C.S. When L duly sought to have such an expert appointed three months before the first review date, T sought an injunction to restrain the president of the R.I.C.S. from making the appointment on the grounds that it would be premature, arguing that they wished to seek rectification of the lease, and that the appointment could not be made until three months after the review date. L contended that, on the true construction of the review provision, an appointment could be made up to three months before the review date. The president's evidence was that, on receiving an application for such an appointment, his staff would check that the lease continued a power of appointment and, if so, would proceed to make the appointment without further ado.

Held, dismissing T's motion, that (1) the Court need not resolve the construction of the review clause; (2) the president owed no duty to the parties not to make an appointment, and T therefore had no cause of action.

Per curiam: if the non-applicant party considers that the appointment is void, he can apply to the Court for a declaration to that effect in proceedings to which the president would not need to be a party.

UNITED CO-OPERATIVES *v.* SUN ALLIANCE AND LONDON ASSURANCE CO. (1987) 282 E.G. 91, Hoffmann J.

2219. Rent review clause—construction

A lease of premises situated on an industrial estate in Basingstoke provided for a rent review, at which the revised rent was to be calculated by applying mathematical formula to the rack rent (calculated on a p.s.f. basis) at which "standard accommodation" could if vacant be let at the relevant time in the open market on the terms and conditions of the lease. "Standard accommodation" was defined as "a standard single-storey industrial building in the same locality as the demised premises and of like age . . ." At the time of the grant of the lease the industrial estate had comprised the subject premises, which were of 100,000 s.f. with 49 per cent. office accommodation, plus six other units of between 10,000 and 15,000 s.f. with only 20 per cent. office accommodation. At the review L argued that "standard accommodation" for the purposes of calculating the revised rent denoted these other units, whilst T argued that there was to be implied a term that the "standard accommodation" should be the same size as the subject premises, and that the words "in the same locality" were to be construed as denoting an area of up to three-quarters of a mile from the subject premises in which comparables could be sought. The judge held that L's construction was correct.

Held, allowing T's appeal, that (1) "locality" in the review clause was not that to be construed as being confined either to the industrial estate or to adjoining or neighbouring properties. Its precise ambit could be left to the good sense of the surveyor asked to determine the revised rent; (2) likewise in restricting "standard accomodation" in effect to buildings with floor area of only 10,000 s.f. or thereabouts, the judge had construed the words too narrowly; (3) the matter came down in the end to the identification of appropriate properties in the vicinity, which would be a matter for the surveyor should a dispute arise.

STANDARD LIFE ASSURANCE CO. *v.* OXOID; OXOID *v.* STANDARD LIFE ASSURANCE CO. (1987) 283 E.G. 1219, C.A.

2220. Rent review clause—construction—actual provision for future reviews—whether to be included in terms of hypothetical lease

A 70-year lease of commercial premises provided for 14-yearly rent reviews, the revised rent in each case to be 85 per cent. of the "net rental value", which was defined as the best rent obtainable on a letting of the premises with vacant possession in the open market for the residue of the actual term "upon the terms of this lease other than as to duration and rent." At the first review the parties agreed that, for the purposes of computing the "net rental value", the hypothetical lease should include the covenant to pay rent and a proviso for re-entry for non-payment of rent, but were in dispute as to whether it should include the provision in the actual lease for the remaining reviews. The judge held that the actual provision for future reviews was to be excluded from the terms of the hypothetical lease.

Held, dismissing T's appeal, that (1) notwithstanding the valuable guidelines stated in *British Gas Corp.* v. *Universities Superannuation Scheme* [1986] C.L.Y. 1911, the Court's function was to construe the particular rent review clause in issue; (2) the judge's conclusion was correct, not as a matter of necessary implication but upon the express meaning of the definition of "net rental value".

EQUITY AND LAW LIFE ASSURANCE SOCIETY *v.* BODFIELD (1987) 281 E.G. 1448, C.A.

2221. Rent review clause—construction—guidance sought on construction of clause—failure to agree rental value

Although the court may declare in certain circumstances that a limited construction may be displaced where another construction better reflects the intentions of the parties, in general it is not for the court to instruct the valuer as to what considerations he must take into account in fixing a rental value.

On the nomination of an independent surveyor to fix a rental value, but prior to his decision, P, tenant, commenced proceedings seeking guidance on the construction of the rent review clause, the construction of which was in dispute.

Held, on the true construction of the particular lease concerned, declarations would be granted (i) that the value should be fixed according to the value of the entirety of what was demised, but subject to the rights subject to which it was held; and (ii) that a limited construction of the rent review clause could be displaced where it was right to adopt another construction as better reflecting the underlying intention of the parties. Declarations were refused on questions concerning improvements, general user, and restriction of the use of the premises to a café restaurant.

FORTE & CO. *v.* GENERAL ACCIDENT LIFE ASSURANCE (1987) 54 P. & C.R. 9, Peter Gibson J.

2222. Rent review clause—construction of provision for postponement

A building lease granted for 125 years in 1973 provided for regular rent reviews, the first falling due after seven years in 1980. The review clause further provided that, since certain road works had not been carried out by March 31, 1973, the first review was to be delayed by one year for every year or part of a year until the works were completed or L gave notice that they were not in fact to be carried out. On February 10, 1981, L duly gave such notice.

Held, on the question of how long the first review was to be delayed, that the period of delay was to be computed not from March 1973, but from the date provided in the lease for the first review, namely July 5, 1980. and that the first review was accordingly to be delayed by one year.

LADBROKE GROUP *v.* BRISTOL CITY COUNCIL (1987) 283 E.G. 1071, H.H. Judge Blackett-Ord.

2223. Rent review clause—formula for ground rent agreed orally—agreement for lease contained different formula—lease when executed contained original formula—rectification

The remedy of rectification requires a mistake about the effect of the document it is sought to rectify.

Under the terms of a lease the ground rent was agreed upon, subject to a seven-year review. A formula was stated verbally in correspondence; the agreement for the grant of the lease contained a different formula, but no one noticed and the agreement was executed. When the lease was executed both parties thought, correctly, that it gave effect to the original formula, and incorrectly, to the agreement. At the first rent review, the defendants noticed the difference and applied for rectification of the lease to make it accord with the agreement. The plaintiffs refused and claimed the higher rent (the original formula).

Held, allowing the plaintiff's application, that there was no basis for rectification here, for the lease contained the terms the parties had originally agreed to and throughout thought were the terms in effect; their only mistake was in thinking that the agreement contained the same provisions.

LONDON REGIONAL TRANSPORT *v.* WIMPEY GROUP SERVICES (1987) 53 P. & C.R. 356, Hoffmann J.

2224. Rent review clause—permitted use—construction

A rent review clause provided that the revised rent was to be the fair market rent for the premises ". . . on a letting thereof as a whole with vacant possession for use for any purpose within Class III of the Town and Country Planning (Use Classes) Order 1972, or any other class or classes of the said Order within which falls the use or uses . . . permitted by the planning authorities." Shortly before the lease was granted, planning permission was given for use of the premises as a "non-teaching Service Unit for the Middlesex Polytechnic." The question for decision was whether the permitted purpose was a composite use which did not fall into any of the use classes prescribed by the 1972 Order; or whether the wording of the permitted purpose was a shorthand phrase for listing all the various uses which the Middlesex Polytechnic might seek to make of the premises. The latter construction would enable any subsequent user (not the Middlesex Polytechnic) to develop its own activities within the use classes which comprehended those particular activities of the Middlesex Polytechnic which had notionally been listed as separate permitted activities.

Held, dismissing L's appeal, that (1) the permitted use was a composite use which did not fall within any of the prescribed use classes; (2) there was nothing in the rent review clause to permit the rent to be assessed by reference to any use authorised by a use class except use for light industrial purposes within Class III of the Use Classes Order.

WOLFF *v.* ENFIELD LONDON BOROUGH (1987) 281 E.G. 1320, C.A.

2225. Rent review clause—repairing covenant—construction of "rebuild, reconstruct or replace"

In assessing the market rent payable under a rent review clause for an office building in Sheffield, an arbitrator relied on rents derived from comparables, which he adjusted downwards by 22 per cent. because the repairing covenant in the lease placed upon T the obligation, ". . . when necessary to rebuild, reconstruct or replace" the premises. L argued that the arbitrator had made an error of law, in that the obligation "to rebuild, reconstruct or replace" was on its true construction to be confined to subsidiary parts of the building only, thus rendering the covenant much less onerous to T. The judge noted that the lease had been granted for 150 years, and that it was not inconceivable that T should have accepted an obligation to rebuild the premises at the end of their natural life.

Held, giving judgment for T, that the arbitrator had correctly construed the covenant (*Collins* v. *Flynn* [1963] C.L.Y. 1958 and *Lister* v. *Lane* [1893] 2 Q.B. 212 considered).

NORWICH UNION LIFE INSURANCE SOCIETY *v.* BRITISH RAILWAYS BOARD (1987) 283 E.G. 846, Hoffmann J.

2226. Rent review clause—whether valid counter-notice served by T—effect of "subject to contract"

A rent review clause provided that unless T, in response to L's "trigger" notice, served within a specified time a counter-notice (which would if necessary bring arbitration proceedings into being), the amount specified in L's notice would be the new rent. Shortly before the expiry of the prescribed time, T sent a letter marked "subject to contract" stating the rent which T was prepared to agree. L contended that, even if this would otherwise have been a valid counter-notice, the words "subject to contract" meant that it was no more than a negotiating step.

Held, giving judgment for T, that notwithstanding the words "subject to contract," no reasonably sensible businessman could have been left in any real doubt that this was to be a counter-notice (*Sheridan* v. *Blaircourt Investments* [1984] C.L.Y. 1948 and *Shirlcar Properties* v. *Heinitz* [1983] C.L.Y. 2136 considered).

BRITISH RAIL PENSION TRUSTEE CO. *v.* CARDSHOPS (1987) 1 E.G.L.R. 127, Vinelott J.

2227. Right to buy—whether landlord condition satisfied where only one of two joint owners fell within statutory definition—Whether premises formed part of "open space" for purposes of planning legislation

[Housing Act 1985 (c.68), Pt. II; Housing (Extension of the Right to Buy) Order 1983 (S.I. 1983 No. 672); Town and Country Planning Act 1959 (c.53) (as amended by the Local Government Planning and Land Act 1980 (c.65).]

The applicant had been the tenant of property set in parkland owned by Plymouth City Council and Cornwall County Council jointly. In 1980 he sought the right to buy the house, which was denied on the grounds that he was not a secure tenant in that (a) the premises were held jointly and (b) the premises were not held for the purposes of Pt. II of the 1985 Act (at the time Pt. V of the Housing Act 1957), which later ground the applicant accepted. In May 1983, the right to buy was extended to include houses held by an authority for other than Pt. II purposes. The applicant again applied and the authorities, anxious to prevent him from so doing, devised a scheme whereby the two councils jointly granted a lease of the property for a term of 20 years less two days to Plymouth City Council (note: the right to buy only applies where the landlord owned an interest sufficient to grant a 21-year lease). No notice of their intention to grant a lease was given, and no objections considered. The applicant sought judicial review on the ground that the lease was a sham or alternatively *ultra vires* their powers. The application was granted by Hodgson J. The respondent authority appealed against the findings that (a) the "landlord condition" is satisfied if the premises belonged to one of the bodies mentioned in the relevant section even if it belongs to a body not mentioned in them and (b) that the premises formed part of an open space for the purposes of the Town and Country Planning Act as amended, and accordingly the grant of the lease without advertisement and the consideration of objections was void.

Held, allowing the appeal in part, that (1) the lease was invalid by reason of the failure to comply with Town and Country Planning legislation; (2) there was nothing in the present facts to detract from the general principle that where there is joint ownership or a joint tenancy, a reference to "owner" or "tenant" is to be construed prima facie as a reference to all owners or tenants and that accordingly the landlord condition was not satisfied where only one of two joint owners fell within the statutory definition and the appeal would be allowed to that extent.

R. *v.* PLYMOUTH CITY COUNCIL AND CORNWALL COUNTY COUNCIL, *ex p.* FREEMAN (1987) 19 H.L.R. 328, C.A.

2228. Secure tenancy

SECURE TENANCIES (NOTICES) REGULATIONS 1987 (No. 755) [£1·30], made under the Housing Act 1985 (c.68), s.83(2)(6); operative on May 13, 1987; prescribe forms of notice which are to be served on a secure tenant for the purpose of terminating the tenancy.

2229. Secure tenancy—possession—requirements

[Housing Act 1985 (c.68), s.84(1), Sched. 2, ground 10.]

In order for a local authority landlord to regain possession of a property let on a secure tenancy where the ground relates to work to be done at the property, it is necessary for the authority to show a firm and settled intention to carry out the works and also to show that the works cannot reasonably be carried out without obtaining possession (*Poppet's (Caterers)* v. *Maidenhead Borough Council* [1970] C.L.Y. 1531, *Cunliffe* v. *Goodman* [1950] C.L.Y. 5425, *Betty's Cafe* v. *Phillips Furnishing Stores* [1958] C.L.Y. 1818 considered).

WANSBECK DISTRICT COUNCIL *v.* MARLEY, *The Times,* November 30, 1987, C.A.

2230. Secure tenancy—possession proceedings—parties—joinder of tenant's family

[Housing Act 1985 (c.68), s.84(2)(*b*), Sched. 2, Pts. II, IV.]

All members of the tenant's family living in the premises have an interest in proceedings for possession brought under Pt. II to Sched. 2 of the 1985 Act such as to entitle them to be joined as a party to the proceedings. Further, there is no jurisdiction to give judgment by consent; the matters set out in s.84 must be proved or expressly admitted.

F and his wife were secure tenants of a council flat which was in the husband's name. During divorce proceedings the council brought a claim for possession of the flat under ground 10 in Pt. II of Sched. 2 to the 1985 Act. The registrar refused the wife's application to be joined as a party and ordered possession by consent. The wife appealed.

Held, that since the court had to be satisfied that there was suitable alternative accommodation for "the tenant and his family", any member of the family had an interest in the proceedings and was entitled to be joined. Further, there was no jurisdiction to make an order simply by consent; since the matters in s.84 of the Act had to be established or expressly admitted. The possession order would be set aside.

WANDSWORTH LONDON BOROUGH COUNCIL *v.* FADAYOMI [1987] 3 All E.R. 474, C.A.

2231. Service charge—assessment according to Retail Price Index—whether Index still "published" and "available"

A lease of 61 years from 1960 provided that the service charge should be £100 p.a. plus £1 for each point by which the Retail Price Index rose above the figure of 110.4; but that if the RPI should cease to be published or available, the charge should be a fair proportion of the increase in L's costs, to be determined by an independent surveyor. L contended that the RPI had so ceased to be published or available, on the grounds that, since the start of the lease, the commodities and services on which it was based and the weightings attached to them had been changed, and that the RPI itself had twice been brought back to a base of 100.

Held, that the RPI had not ceased to be published or available. The fact that changes had been made to the "basket" of commodities and services and to their weightings in order that the index should remain accurate could not possibly justify the conclusion that the revised index was no longer the index to which the lease referred; whilst the changes to the base of the index since grant of the lease could be compensated for by a single mathematical adjustment.

CUMSHAW *v.* BOWEN (1987) 281 E.G. 68, Scott J.

2232. Service charge—whether prospective expenditure "incurred" by L

In a lease of an office building, T covenanted to pay by way of a service charge a proportion of all sums "which may . . . during the said term be expended or incurred or payable by the landlord."

Held, that T was not liable to contribute such a proportion of the cost of relevant work which L had contracted with builders to have carried out, but which had not yet been done by the end of the term. It could not be said that L had "incurred" such costs within the meaning of T's covenant.

CAPITAL & COUNTIES FREEHOLD EQUITY TRUST *v.* B.L. (1987) 283 E.G. 563, H.H. Judge Paul Baker Q.C.

2233. Service charges—construction of a lease—recovery of interest payments

[Landlord and Tenant Act 1985 (c.70).]

T were long leaseholders of a flat in a block of flats, and L the leaseholders. The lease contained provisions whereby T covenanted to pay a yearly rent of £60, together with additional sums in respect of sums expended by the lessor in insuring the block and in respect of service charges. Disputes arose between T and L. In particular L claimed the right to recover reasonable interest payments reasonably incurred as a result of reasonable borrowing to finance the provision of services under the lease. In May 1983 L issued proceedings against T. At the trial the judge made a number of declarations in favour of T. However he also held that L were entitled, subject to two qualifications, to recover sums expended by way of interest incurred before the receipt of service charges was due under the lease. No order was made as to costs. T appealed the part of the order relating to interest and to costs.

Held, allowing the appeal, (1) the onus lay on L to show that under the terms of the lease T had contracted to pay the interest claimed; on its true construction, the lease did not include payments by way of interest; (2) in the light of the court's decision on the first issue it was not necessary to determine whether the judge had erred in making no order as to costs. Appeal allowed with costs in the Court of Appeal and below.

BOLDMARK *v.* COHEN AND COHEN (1985) 19 H.L.R. 135, C.A.

2234. Shared ownership leases

HOUSING ASSOCIATION SHARED OWNERSHIP LEASES (EXCLUSION FROM LEASEHOLD REFORM ACT 1967 AND RENT ACT 1977) REGULATIONS 1987 (No. 1940) [85p], made under the Leasehold Reform Act 1967 (c.88), Sched. 4A, para. 5 and the Rent Act 1977 (c.42), s.5A(3); operative on December 11, 1987; prescribe additional requirements and circumstances whereby certain shared ownership leases granted by housing associations are excluded from the relevant provisions of the Acts of 1967 and 1977.

2235. Shorthold tenancy—provision for re-entry—whether "obligation" created—whether tenancy a protected shorthold tenancy

[Housing Act 1980 (c.51), s.52(1)(*a*).]

An agreement for a protected shorthold tenancy provided that L could re-enter if T became bankrupt, entered into a composition with his creditors, or left the premises vacant for more than 21 days. T argued that the provision did not create any obligation upon him not to do any of these things; that in consequence it provided for a right of re-entry other than for non-payment of rent or breach of obligation; that accordingly it failed to comply with one of the requirements of a protected shorthold tenancy, as stipulated in the Housing Act 1980 s.52(1)(*a*); and that upon expiry of the term he was accordingly entitled to a protected tenancy under the Rent Act 1977. The judge rejected this submission, and made an order against T for possession.

Held, dismissing T's appeal, that upon its proper construction, the provision for re-entry did impose an obligation upon T not to become bankrupt, enter into a composition with his creditors or leave the premises vacant for more than 21 days; that the tenancy accordingly complied with s.52(1)(*a*); and that the judge had correctly found it to be a protected shorthold tenancy (*Watkinson* v. *Hollington* [1944] 1 K.B. 16 considered).

PATERSON *v.* AGGIO (1987) 284 E.G. 508, C.A.

2236. Statutory repairing covenant—defective roof—whether L required to replace it

[Housing Act 1961 (c.65), s.32(1)(*a*) and (3).]

L let to T on a weekly tenancy, a dwelling-house in Birmingham, the roof of which was affected by a series of incidents of disrepair. T contended that, in view of these problems, L was required by the statutory repairing covenant implied by s.32(1)(*a*) and (3) of the Housing Act 1961 (now ss.11–16 of the Landlord and Tenant Act 1985) to replace the entire roof. The Assistant Recorder held that the relevant test was whether the point had been reached at which the only practicable way of performing the covenant was to replace the roof, and that in all the circumstances such a point had not been reached.

Held, dismissing T's appeal, that the Assistant Recorder had applied the right test, and had reached the right conclusion on the evidence before him (*Sheldon* v. *West Bromwich Corporation* [1973] C.L.Y. 1579 considered).

MURRAY *v.* BIRMINGHAM CITY COUNCIL (1987) 283 E.G. 962, C.A.

2237. Statutory repairing obligations—notice to landlord authority of disrepair

[Landlord and Tenant Act 1985 (c.70), s.11.]

T was the tenant of property belonging to the landlord authority. In connection with a right to buy application, two visits were made to the property, the first by a technical assistant from the Environmental Health Department and the second by the District Valuer. In the former case, T complained to the assistant about certain items of disrepair and was advised to list them and send them to the Architectural Services Department. Following the visit of the valuer, he reported to the Chief Executive that his valuation reflected certain specified defects. Proceedings for arrears of rent were brought and T counterclaimed for breach of s.11 of the Landlord and Tenant Act 1985. The judge held that the first inspection by the Technical Assistant and the report from the District Valuer did not constitute notice. The Tenant appealed.

Held, allowing the appeal, that (1) the Technical Assistant was a responsible officer of the local authority; once items of disrepair had been brought to his attention that was notice to the authority; (2) when the Chief Executive received a report, the fact that the report was not for the purposes of complaining about the defects did not mean that it did not constitute notice.

DINEFWR BOROUGH COUNCIL *v.* JONES (1987) 19 H.L.R. 445, C.A.

2238. Statutory repairing obligations—whether local authority in breach

[Landlord and Tenant Act 1985 (c.70), s.11.]

T sued L for alleged breach of repairing obligations under s.11 of the Landlord and Tenant Act 1985 (formerly the Housing Act 1961 s.32), claiming special damages in relation to household chattels in addition to general damages. The necessary repairs, which were listed in an agreed surveyor's report, included replacement of the roof battens, felting and tiles, repointing and rendering of the exterior in several places, damp-proofing, repairs to gutter joints and the sink wastepipe, sealing of gaps around a window and a door, repairing a dangerous balustrade rail, checking the electrical system and providing kitchen ventilation. At the trial L called no evidence. The judge held that the standard of the house had not fallen below that required by the statute, and gave judgment for L.

Held, allowing T's appeal and ordering a retrial on the question of general damages only, that (1) the judge had been entitled to reject T's evidence as to special damages; however (2) he had not fully directed himself either as to the evidence of the unchallenged surveyor's report, or as to a number of other aspects of the evidence (*Newham London Borough* v. *Patel* [1979] C.L.Y. 1381 distinguished).

McCLEAN *v.* LIVERPOOL CITY COUNCIL (1987) 283 E.G. 1395, C.A.

2239. Statutory tenancy—capacity of infants to succeed

[Rent Act 1977 (c.42), Sched. 1, para. 3.]

The plaintiffs, S, P, were the owners of residential premises let to B, the defendant's (D's) mother. B died in January 1985 when D was 16 and thus a minor. D had lived in the premises with B for 10 years prior to B's death. D claimed a succession to the statutory tenancy pursuant to para. 3. P argued that as a minor D had no capacity to succeed to a statutory tenancy.

Held, that since (1) a statutory tenancy was not a legal estate in land (which a minor would have been precluded from holding); and (2) a contract for the provision of lodgings was a contract for the provision of necessaries and succession to the statutory tenancy gave rise to enforceable obligations against D, D had the capacity to and did succeed to the statutory tenancy (*Halford's Executors* v. *Boden* [1953] C.L.Y. 3137 followed).

PORTMAN REGISTRARS & NOMINEES *v.* MOHAMMED LATIF, April 23, 1987, H.H. Judge Hill-Smith, Willesden County Ct. [*Ex rel. Stephen Shaw, Barrister.*]

2240. Statutory tenancy—succession—meaning of "residing with"

[Rent Act 1977 (c.42), Sched. 1.]

T lived in house A with her parents who were the tenants until she married. She then lived with her husband in house B, two miles away from house A. In 1981 T's father died and in 1983 T's mother became ill with cancer. T visited her mother frequently and in September 1984 she moved into house A, at least on a part time basis, to look after her mother. She retained the tenancy of house B and her son continued to live there. T's mother died in April 1985, and T claimed to be entitled to succeed to a statutory tenancy of house A. In an action for possession the judge found that T had come to live in house A with the intention of helping her mother and that at no time until after her death did T form the intention to reside in the premises, and accordingly she had not been "residing with" her mother during the relevant period. T appealed.

Held, dismissing the appeal, that (1) although the words "reside with" do not mean dwell permanently in the sense of dwell indefinitely, they do mean something more than dwell transiently; "residing with" means something more than "living at"; (2) the question was one of fact and degree, and on the present facts T could not show that she had made a home in house A or that in any true sense she had become part of her mother's household there.

SWANBRAE *v.* ELLIOTT (1987) 19 H.L.R. 87, C.A.

2241. Statutory tenancy—succession—member of family

[Rent Act 1977 (c.42), s.2 and Sched. 1, para. 7.]

For the purposes of succession to a statutory tenancy on the death of the first successor of the original statutory or protected tenancy, a person must be an actual member of the deceased's family and not just be treated as such.

SEFTON HOLDINGS *v.* CAIRNS, *The Times,* November 3, 1987, C.A.

2242. Statutory tenancy—succession—stability of relationship

[Rent Act 1977 (c.42), Sched. 1, para. 3.]

An occupant is entitled to succeed to a protected or statutory tenancy on the death of the original tenant if the facts show that their relationship had arrived at a state of sufficient permanance and stability for it to be said that he was a member of the family.

CHIOS INVESTMENT PROPERTY CO. *v.* LOPEZ, *The Times,* November 3, 1987, C.A.

2243. Statutory tenancy—whether closing order in force

[Housing Act 1985 (c.68), ss.268, 270, 276, 304.]

T was a statutory tenant of a dwelling-house in Sittingbourne, in respect of which a demolition order had been made in 1973 under the provisions of the Housing Act 1957 (now consolidated with no material difference into the Housing Act 1985). No steps had ever been taken to carry that order into effect. In 1984 the premises had been listed as a grade II listed building, with the effect that the local housing authority had become required under s.304 of the 1985 Act to determine the demolition order and replace it by a closing order properly served as required by s.268 of the Act. In fact the closing order had not been made until November 7, 1986, and was only served on T on November 11, 1986, the day of the hearing before the judge. The judge made an order for possession against T on the grounds that a closing order was in force in relation to the premises, which were in consequence excluded from Rent Act protection by virtue of s.276 of the 1985 Act.

Held, allowing T's appeal, that (1) the closing order was not in force at the date of the hearing, because by s.268 of the Act it did not become operative until 21 days after service upon T; (2) there was no evidence that the previous demolition order had ever become operative through proper service upon T, so that it was not open to L to argue that the premises were excluded from protection pursuant to s.270 of the Act; nor in any event had L purported to serve notice of an operative demolition order under s.270(2); (3) the Court would not express a concluded view on the question of whether the demolition order, had it become operative, would have remained so until the closing order came into force, notwithstanding the listing of the premises and the consequent application of s.304(2).

BEANEY *v.* BRANCHETT (1987) 283 E.G. 1063, C.A.

2244. Statutory tenancy—whether premises sublet in breach of covenant—alternative accommodation—whether suitable—whether reasonable to order possession

[Rent Act 1977 (c.42), s.98(1), Sched. 15 Case 1 and Part IV para. 5(1).]

L wished to sell their house in London W8 valued at between £850,000 and £1m. The basement had been occupied since 1958 by a statutory tenant T, and since 1968 by M, whose legal status was uncertain. T was offered alternative accommodation in Shepherd's Bush Green which was smaller but in better condition, and would be held on a protected tenancy at a very low rent, which L had undertaken not to increase during T's tenancy. T however refused to leave, and L sought an order for possession. The judge held that T's tenancy agreement had contained a covenant against subletting, that M was a subtenant with the consequence that T was in breach of covenant, that the breach had not been waived, and that L were accordingly entitled to an order for possession under Case 1 of Sched. 15 to the Rent Act 1977. He further found that the alternative accommodation satisfied the requirements of para. 5(1) of part IV of Sched. 15 to the Act, and that it was reasonable within s.98(1) of the Act to make an order for possession.

Held, dismissing T's appeal, that (1) the judge had been entitled to find on the evidence that the agreement had contained such a covenant, that M was a subtenant rather than a lodger, and that T's breach of covenant had not been waived; (2) in considering whether it was reasonable within s.98(1) to make an order for possession, all the circumstances must be taken into account; and that the judge had erred in not taking separate account for this purpose of certain matters which he had already considered in relation to the suitability of the alternative accommodation; (3) the judge had erred more seriously in taking the view without evidence that the presence of a sitting tenant would reduce the sale value of the house by up to 50 per cent.; but (4) the court could safely accept the judge's primary findings of fact and that on those findings the order for possession was in all the circumstances reasonable. (*Battlespring* v. *Gates* [1983] C.L.Y. 2119, *Cresswell* v. *Hodgson* (1947–51) C.L.C. 8440, *Hill* v. *Rochard* [1983] C.L.Y. 2060, *Metropolitan Properties Co.* v. *Cordery* [1980] C.L.Y. 1645, *Mykolyshyn* v. *Noah* [1970] C.L.Y. 1549 and *Street* v. *Mountford* [1985] C.L.Y. 1893 considered).

ROBERTS *v.* MACILWRAITH-CHRISTIE (1987) 1 E.G.L.R. 224, C.A.

2245. Statutory tenancy—whether tenant resident—whether intention to return to a dwelling-house

[Rent Act 1977 (c.42), s.2.]

T had been the tenant of a cottage since 1950. From 1975 he lived at premises elsewhere, although he visited the cottage twice daily to feed the cats and chickens and look after the garden. In 1979, at the request of L, the landlord, he sublet part of the cottage. In 1982 the contractual tenancy was determined by notice to quit, and L brought proceedings for possession on the ground that T had ceased to occupy the cottage as his residence. L failed. In his notes, the judge remarked that he believed T when he said that he wanted to go back, albeit that matters might be different if he did not in fact return. In April 1983 T evicted the sub-tenant, and began to redecorate the cottage. He did not, however, return and in February 1985 L again brought proceedings, on the grounds of cessation of residence, arrears of rent, and nuisance. T moved back in April. The judge refused possession on the second two grounds but allowed it on the first. He found that in the summer of 1984 he had camped in the garden, but no more than that. T appealed.

Held, dismissing the appeal, that (1) having found that there was an intention to return in 1982 the question now was whether T had abandoned this intention, and the judge had properly addressed his mind to this question; (2) whether there is an intention to re-occupy is a question of fact for the judge and there was evidence on which the judge could find that this had been abandoned.

DUKE AND DUKE *v.* PORTER (1987) 19 H.L.R. 1, C.A.

2246. Summary proceedings for possession—licence or lease—whether claim straightforward

[R.S.C., Ord. 113.]

R.S.C., Ord. 113 is not an appropriate procedure where the landlord's claim is not clear and straightforward; the presence of arguably sham terms is a factor to be considered in deciding whether R.S.C., Ord. 113 procedure is appropriate.

Summary proceedings were begun under R.S.C., Ord. 113 for the possession of land. The appellants had signed agreements in each of two cases that appeared to grant them licences not tenancies. The appellants argued that certain clauses were evidence that the agreement was a sham; that the real nature of the agreement was for a lease not a licence. The judge refused an order to transfer the matter for hearing and granted the orders.

Held, allowing the appeals, that it was not right to make the order where the landlord's claim was not sufficiently clear and straightforward, and the arguable presence of sham clauses must be taken into account in this regard.

MARKOU *v.* DA SILVAESA; CRANCOUR *v.* MEROLA (1986) 52 P. & C.R. 204, C.A.

2247. Tenancy—whether tenancy or licence—whether rent an essential prerequisite for a tenancy

The reservation of a rent is not necessary for the creation of a tenancy (*Radaich* v. *Smith* [1969] C.L.Y 3011 and *National Provincial Bank* v. *Hastings Car Mart* [1965] C.L.Y. 1850 applied; *Street* v. *Mountford* [1985] C.L.Y. 1893 considered).

ASHBURN ANSTALT *v.* ARNOLD & CO., *The Times,* November 9, 1987, C.A.

2248. Tenants' association—whether recognised

[Landlord and Tenant Act 1985 (c.70), s.29.]

For the purpose of s.29 of the Landlord and Tenant Act 1985, a tenants' association must relate to a single converted building or block of flats, It cannot relate to, *e.g.*, a terrace of Victorian buildings that have been converted into flats.

R. *v.* LONDON RENT ASSESSMENT PANEL, *ex p.* TRUSTEES OF HENRY SMITH's CHARITY KENSINGTON ESTATE, *The Independent,* October 30, 1987, Schiemann J.

2249. Tenants improving property—whether proprietary estoppel. See ESTOPPEL, §1448.

2250. Unlawful eviction—assault—damages

[Rent Act 1977 (c.42), Sched. 15, Case 11.]

A let Rent Act protected premises to R and R. In April 1984, A's claim that he was entitled to possession under case 11 (owner/occupier provision) failed. In May, A issued fresh proceedings based on rent arrears and case 9 saying he needed the premises for his family's use. On May 26, while the second action was pending, A attempted to evict R and R. The police were called and A was warned about the illegality of eviction without a court order. Between June 1984 and the date of trial, Mrs. R lived away from the premises nursing a relative. On July 16, 1984, the parties were due to attend at court on an application relating to the outstanding litigation. A did not attend court but in R's absence put out all their possessions and changed the locks. On R's return A prevented him from entering. R was re-housed in temporary accommodation. On August 16, 1984, two men (at A's behest) questioned R and struck him on the head with an iron pipe. One of the men pointed a handgun at R. R sustained bruising to the chest wall and a wound in the head requiring six stitches.

Held, that £3,000 general, aggravated and exemplary damages be awarded for the eviction (taking into account the fact that Mrs. R was absent when the eviction took place) and £2,000 be awarded to R for the assault on August 16, 1984.

REID AND REID *v.* ANDREOU, February 14, 1986; H.H. Judge Tibber; Edmonton County Ct. [*Ex rel. R. J. Terry, Barrister.*]

2251. Unlawful eviction—sexual harassment—damages

By a written agreement dated July 24, 1985, T granted a "licence" to A, 17, of a bedroom in a three-bedroom flat together with shared use of the kitchen and bathroom with the other occupants who occupied their bedrooms on similar terms. Occasionally, during the first six months of the agreement, T (male) indicated that he found A (female) sexually attractive. On Christmas Eve 1985, T left A a note indicating that he would waive the rent for Christmas week provided she did not tell the others and agreed to have a meal with him. He described her in the letter as his "favourite licencee." A refused the offer and on Boxing Day found a note pinned to her door giving her 24 hours' notice. A did not vacate and during the evening T attended the premises with another man and attempted to enter A's room by force. A was punched in the stomach and thrown down some stairs. T and the other man were arrested but later released without charge. On February 10, 1986, T disconnected the telephone in the flat and on February 14 moved into a vacant room in the flat. A then left the premises and found alternative accommodation. By his pleadings, T denied the allegations but on the day of the trial he submitted to judgment for agreed general, aggravated and exemplary damages for £1,350.

AMUSAN *v.* TAUSSIG, July 31, 1987; H.H. Judge Harris, Q.C.; Westminster County Ct. [*Ex rel. R. J. Terry, Barrister.*]

2252. Workshop—occupation agreement—whether licence or tenancy

P purported to grant to D a "licence" to occupy a workshop and store. The written agreement provided *inter alia* that, "this licence is personal to the licensees"; that "this licence confers no exclusive right for the licensees to use and occupy the premises, and the licensor will be entitled from time to time . . . to require the licensees to transfer their occupation to other premises within the licensor's adjoining property"; and that "the licensor may by giving the required notice to the licensees increase the licence fee to such amount as may be specified in the notice." The agreement also provided that the "licensees" should permit the "licensor with necessary workmen, contractors and equipment to enter upon the premises to carry out any work deemed necessary." D, who relied in particular upon the limited right of entry conferred by the agreement on P, contended that the effect of the agreement was to create a tenancy, and the judge so held.

Held, allowing P's appeal, that on the true construction of this unusual agreement P's entitlement to require the "licensees" to transfer to other premises was wholly inconsistent with a right to exclusive possession during the continuation of the agreement, and was therefore wholly inconsistent with a tenancy. The agreement accordingly conferred a licence only (*Street* v. *Mountford* [1985] C.L.Y. 1893, *Addiscombe Garden Estates* v. *Crabbe* [1957] C.L.Y. 1937 and *Shell-Mex and B.P.* v. *Manchester Garages* [1971] C.L.Y. 6651 considered).

Per curiam: The indicia which may make it more apparent in the case of a residential tenant or occupier that he is indeed a tenant may be less applicable or less likely to have that effect in the case of some business tenancies.

DRESDEN ESTATES *v.* COLLINSON (1987) 281 E.G. 1321, C.A.

LAW REFORM

2253. Application to strike out action—criticisms of present system. See WESTMINSTER CITY COUNCIL *v.* CLIFFORD CULPIN AND PARTNERS, §2903.

2254. Binding over—courts' powers

The Law Commission has published a consultation document reviewing courts' binding over powers. The document is entitled *Binding Over: The Issues* and is available from H.M.S.O. (Law Commission Working Paper No. 103) [£3·85].

For further information contact Mr. Michael Farmer, The Law Commission, Conquest House, 37–38 John Street, Theobalds Road, London WC1N 2BQ. Tel: 01-242 0861, ext. 231.

2255. Charities—supervision—recommendations for reform. See CHARITIES, §298.

2256. Civil justice review

A consultation paper has been published with the approval of the Lord Chancellor which makes proposals to cut the cost and the delay of civil justice in England and Wales. The proposals were prepared with the help of a Committee chaired by Sir Maurice Hodgson. The consultation paper is the final paper in a series of six which have been published as part of the Lord Chancellor's Civil Justice Review.

Responses should be sent by July 31, 1987 to Mrs. P. A. James at the Lord Chancellor's Department. Consultation Paper No. 6 is obtainable from Trevor Cook, Lord Chancellor's Department, Room 611, Trevelyan House, 30 Great Peter Street, London SW1P 2BY. [£2·00].

2257. "Commonhold"—freehold flats

A report of a Working Group set up under the auspices of the Law Commission has been published. It offers the chance to buy flats on a permanent, freehold basis which could supersede sales on long leases. Enquiries should be addressed to Trevor Aldridge, Law Commission, Conquest House 37/38 John Street, Theobalds Road, London WC1N 2BQ. Copies of *Commonhold: Freehold Flats—and Freehold Ownership of other Interdependent Buildings* are available from H.M.S.O. (Cm. 179) [£7·90].

2258. Conspiracy to defraud

The Law Commission has published a Working Paper which consideres the common law offence of conspiracy to defraud. A free summary is available from the Law Commission on request. *Conspiracy to Defraud* is available from H.M.S.O. (Working Paper No. 104) [£8·10].

2259. Consumer protection for home buyers

The Law Commission has published two reports aimed at protecting both buyers and sellers of all land and property.

Contracts for the Sale etc. of Land deals with making agreements and is available from H.M.S.O. (Law Com. No. 164) (HC2) [£4·50].

Deeds and Escrows covers the formal documents used to transfer property and is also available from H.M.S.O. (Law Com. No. 163) (HC1) [£4·50].

For further information contact Mrs. Catherine Hand, The Law Commission, Conquest House, 37/38 John Street, Theobalds Road, London WC1N 2BQ. Tel: 01–242–0861, ext. 237.

2260. Conveyancing—delays

The Conveyancing Standing Committee has published a consultation paper entitled *Local Authority Enquiries: How Can We Eliminate Delays*? Five possible options are suggested for immediate remedial action. The Committee is consulting widely to find an acceptable way to eliminate the delays, and is asking for comments by March 31, 1988. Copies of the paper are available free, while stocks last, from the Secretary of the Conveyancing Standing Committee, The Law Commission, Conquest House, 37/38 John Street, Theobalds Road, London WC1N 2BQ.

2261. Conveyancing—title on death

The Law Commission has published a Working Paper which concentrates on the conveyancing aspects that arise on the death of an owner of land. *Transfer of Land: Title on Death* is available from H.M.S.O. (Working Paper No. 105) [£3·75].

2262. Debt actions in the county courts—computerisation

A consultation paper has been published which proposes the introduction of a computer system to process the routine administrative stages of debt actions in the county courts. Copies of *Computerisation of County Court Procedures in Debt Cases—the Claims Registry* are obtainable from Paul Dawson, Lord Chancellor's Department, Room 611, Trevelyan House, 30 Great Peter Street, London SW1P 2BY. Tel.: 01-210-8513. [£1·00].

2263. Debt enforcement

The Lord Chancellor's Department has published a consultation paper as part of the Civil Justice Review which proposes ways to improve the system for recovery of debt. A new study carried out by management consultants, Touche Ross, also analyses the system for recovery of debt and concludes that the system is working well. *Consultation Paper No. 5: Enforcement of Debt* [£1·00]; *A Study of Debt Enforcement Procedures* [£2·00].

2264. Delay—call for rules to penalise delay

The Supreme Court Rule Committee should give serious consideration to making rules which would impose strict criteria for bringing actions on quickly and for providing effective sanctions where there were delays.

SIMON-CARVES *v.* COSTAIN CONSTRUCTION, *The Times*, November 13, 1987, C.A.

2265. Distress for rent rules 1983—revision—consultation paper

The Lord Chancellor's Department has issued a consultation paper to seek views on the working of the Distress for Rent Rules 1983 which govern the certification procedure under which bailiffs are empowered to levy distress for rent on behalf of landlords.

Consultees are invited to submit suggestions of their own, although these should be confined to matters which could be dealt with by administrative means or changes to the Rules, rather than primary legislation. Comments should be sent by June 1, 1987 to Mr. E. S. Adams, Lord Chancellor's Department, Trevelyan House, 30 Great Peter Street, London SW1P 2BY. Copies of the consultation paper can be obtained from Mr. Adams.

2266. Domicile

The Law Commission and the Scottish Law Commission have published a joint report which makes recommendations for reforming the rules for determining a person's domicile. For further information contact Mr. P. G. Harris, The Law Commission, Conquest House, 37/38 John Street, Theobalds Road, London WC1N 2BQ. Tel.: 01–242 0861, ext. 224. The *Report on the Law of Domicile* is available from H.M.S.O. (Law Com. No. 168; Scot Law Com. No. 107) (Cm. 200) [£6·10].

2267. Efficiency in the courts—standing commission

The Standing Commission on Efficiency in the Courts, which was set up last year by the Lord Chancellor to help bring about greater economy and efficiency in the disposal of court business, has put forward its first proposals. Bulletin No. 1 from The Standing Commission on Efficiency is obtainable from P. Dawson, Lord Chancellor's Department, Room 611, Trevelyan House, 30 Great Peter Street, London SW1P 2BY.

2268. Firearms

Proposals for tightening the law on the control of firearms are contained in a White Paper. Copies of *Firearms Act 1968 Proposals for Reform* are available from H.M.S.O. (Cm. 261) [£2·20].

2269. Housing cases—consultation paper

A consultation paper, published jointly by the Lord Chancellor's Department and the Department of the Environment, proposes new methods of dealing with housing cases which come to court. The main proposals concern "housing action," as informal small claims procedure "arrears action, for handling back claims for rent." *Civil Justice Review: Consultation Paper No. 5.* [£1·00].

2270. Land registration

The Lord Chancellor's Department has published a report on behalf of the Law Commission in which greater protection for property buyers is proposed. Copies of the *Third Report on Land Registration* are available from H.M.S.O. (Law Com. No. 158) [£7·70].

2271. Landlord and tenant—compensation for tenants' improvements

The Law Commission has published a working paper entitled "Landlord and Tenant: Compensation for Tenants Improvements" (Working Paper No. 102) which concerns the question of whether a tenant who improves the property he occupies be paid compensation by his landlord when the tenancy ends. The Paper is available from H.M.S.O. [£3·60].

2272. Landlord and tenant—reform of the law

The Law Commission has published a report surveying the present law of landlord and tenant. Being a preliminary survey, the report contains no detailed recommendations. Amongst the matters examined are the Rent Acts, the language and length of leases, Crown immunity, and commercial rents. The report is available from H.M.S.O. (Cm. 145) [£4·50].

2273. Law Commission—annual report

The twenty-first annual report of the Law Commission has been published (Cm. 342) covering the period from November 1, 1985 to October 31, 1986. It is available from H.M.S.O. [£5.00].

2274. Leasehold conveyancing

The Law Commission has published a report concerning covenants in tenancies against assigning, underletting, charging or parting with possession of premises without consent and landlord's duties with respect thereto. The report is available from H.M.S.O. (Cm. 360) [£5·00].

2275. Marriage—choice of law rules

The Law Commission and the Scottish Law Commission have published a joint report which makes recommendations for reform of the rules governing the formal validity of marriages of British subjects and members of H.M. Forces performed abroad under the Foreign Marriage Act 1892 (c.23). For further information contact Mr. A. Akbar, The Law Commission, Conquest House, 37/38 John Street, Theobalds Road, London WC1N 2BQ. Tel: 01–242–0861, ext. 213. The *Report on Choice of Law Rules in Marriage* is available from H.M.S.O. (Law Com. No. 165; Scot. Law Com. No. 105) (HC3) [£4·50].

2276. Sale and Supply of Goods—implied terms—remedies

The Law Commission and The Scottish Law Commission have published its report on the sale and supply of goods. The report examines the statutory implied terms in contracts for the sale of goods; remedies for breach of those terms and the loss of the right to reject non-conforming goods. The report is available from H.M.S.O. (Cm. 137) [£9·20].

2277. Treasure trove

The Law Commission has published a paper which concludes that national policy for preserving treasures of archaeological and historical interest should be settled before the ancient treasure trove law is reformed. It recommends a Government Committee, with outside interests represented, to consider the principles. After that, a new law to protect finds should be prepared. *Treasure Trove* is free from the Law Commission while stocks last. For further information, contact Sir Roy Beldam, The Law Commission, Conquest

House, 37/38 John Street, Theobalds Road, London WC1N 2BQ. Tel.: 01-242-0861, ext. 200.

2278. Wardship

The Law Commission has published a working paper entitled *Review of Child Law: Wards of Court*. This is the fourth and last consultative paper in the Law Commission's series about child law. It puts forward three options for reform of wardship. Requests for further information or comments should be addressed to Mr. P. G. Harris, Law Commission, Conquest House, 37/38 John Street, Theobalds Road, London WC1N 2BQ. Working Paper No. 101 is available from H.M.S.O. (ISBN 0 11 730183 3) [£3·00].

LEGAL AID

2279. Advice and assistance

LEGAL ADVICE AND ASSISTANCE (FINANCIAL CONDITIONS) REGULATIONS 1987 (No. 627) [45p], made under the Legal Aid Act 1974 (c.4), ss.1, 20; operative on April 7, 1987; increases the disposable income limit for legal advice and assistance to £118 a week and the disposable capital limit to £825.

LEGAL ADVICE AND ASSISTANCE (FINANCIAL CONDITIONS) (No. 2) REGULATIONS 1987 (No. 396) [45p], made under the Legal Aid Act 1974 ss.4, 20; operative on April 6, 1987; increases to £56 a week the disposable income above which a person receiving legal advice and assistance is required to pay a contribution.

2280. Advice and assistance at police stations

LEGAL ADVICE AND ASSISTANCE AT POLICE STATIONS (REMUNERATION) (AMENDMENT) REGULATIONS 1987 (No. 388) [45p], made under the Legal Aid Act 1974 (c.4), s.20(1) and the Legal Aid Act 1982 (c.44), s.1; operative on April 1, 1987; amend S.I. 1985 No. 1880 by increasing rates of remuneration which may be paid to solicitors who give legal advice and assistance at police stations.

2281. Child cases—factors to be taken into account. See RIDGWAY *v.* RIDGWAY, §2890.

2282. Contribution to costs of defence—whether subject to judicial review

[Courts Act 1971 (c.23), s.10(5); Legal Aid Act 1952 (c.44), ss.7(1), 8(5).]

A legal aid contribution order made at the end of the trial on indictment was an integral part of the trial process and was not subject to judicial review.

The applicant received legal aid for his trial on indictment in which he was acquitted on a direction by the judge to the jury. He was nevertheless ordered to pay £250 towards his defence pursuant to s.32 of the Legal Aid Act 1974. There was no right of appeal to the Court of Appeal (Criminal Division) and the applicant sought to challenge it by way of judicial review. The Divisional Court of the Queen's Bench Division dismissed the application on the ground that they had no jurisdiction to entertain it by virtue of s.10(5) of the Courts Act 1971. The applicant's appeal was dismissed.

Held, that a legal aid contribution order like any other order as to costs which the Crown Court might make at the end of a trial on indictment was an integral part of the trial process, and thus formed part of the court's "jurisdiction in matters relating to trial on indictment" within s.10(5) of the Courts Act 1971 and so was not subject to judicial review. (*R.* v. *Cardiff Crown Court, ex p. Jones* [1973] C.L.Y. 2674 approved; *Smalley, Re* [1985] C.L.Y. 555, considered).

Per curiam: It seems that a legal aid contribution order made under s.7(1) of the Legal Aid Act 1982 can in appropriate circumstances be subject to judicial review, but not a decision of the Crown Court at the conclusion of a trial on indictment whether or not to exercise its discretion under s.8(5) of the Act to remit or order repayment of any sums due from or paid by the defendant under any legal aid contribution order.

SAMPSON, *Re* [1987] 1 W.L.R. 194, H.L.

2283. Counsel's fees—certificate for counsel refused—whether solicitor personally liable to pay counsel

[Legal Aid Act 1974 (c.4), s.10(1); S.I. 1980 No. 1894.]

An application was made in March 1985 for maintenance pending suit and for periodical payments for a child of the family. There were several interim hearings which were not attended by the respondent, R. The case was listed for full hearing on January 31, 1986. R did not attend. There was on order for legal aid taxation of the petitioner's (P's) costs. R was ordered to pay P's costs. A certificate for counsel was refused on the bases that

(a) there was no reason to suppose that R would attend, and (b) there were no complex figures, and (c) there were no complex matters of explanation.

Held, that the registrar was incorrect in his view that the solicitor was personally liable for counsel's fees having regard to s.10(1), but that he correctly excercised his discretion on the merits in refusing the certificate. Appeal dismissed.

HARRIS *v.* HARRIS, February 11, 1987, H.H. Judge Whitley, Portsmouth County Ct. [*Ex rel. Graham Garner, Barrister.*]

2284. Criminal legal aid—fees

Following discussions with the Bar and the Law Society, the Lord Chancellor has announced increases in fees for criminal legal aid work in England and Wales by between five and six per cent. from April 1, 1987.

2285. Criminal proceedings

LEGAL AID IN CRIMINAL PROCEEDINGS (COSTS) (AMENDMENT) REGULATIONS 1987 (No. 369) [£1·40], made under the Legal Aid Act 1974 (c.4), s.39; operative on April 1, 1987; amend S.I. 1982 No. 1197 so as to increase rates of remuneration for legal aid work done in criminal cases.

LEGAL AID IN CRIMINAL PROCEEDINGS (GENERAL) (AMENDMENT) REGULATIONS 1987 (No. 422) [45p], made under the Legal Aid Act 1974 s.39 and the Legal Aid Act 1982 (c.44), s.7; operative on April 6, 1987; increase to £48 a week the disposable income above which a person receiving legal aid is required to pay a contribution.

2286. Deduction from taxed costs

LEGAL AID ACT 1974 (DEDUCTION FROM TAXED COSTS) REGULATIONS 1987 (No. 2098) [45p], made under the Legal Aid Act 1974 (c.4), s.20, Sched. 2, para. 5; operative on January 1, 1988; reduced to 5 per cent. the deduction from the remuneration of person giving legal aid which is effected by Sched. 2, paras. 1(1), 2(1) to the 1974 Act.

2287. Eligibility limits

The Lord Chancellor, Lord Hailsham of St. Marylebone, has laid before Parliament Regulations containing his proposals for increases in the financial limits for both civil and criminal legal aid, and for legal advice and assistance. These increases reflect both the July 1986 and the April 1987 increases in Supplementary benefit and average 3.1 per cent. Subject to Parliamentary approval, the Lord Chancellor intends that the new limits should come into force during the first week of April, 1987.

The proposals are set out in the following regulations:

The Legal Advice and Assistance (Financial Conditions) Regulations 1987.

The Legal Aid (Financial Conditions) Regulations 1987.

The Legal Advice and Assistance (Financial Conditions) (No. 2) Regulations 1987.

The Legal Aid in Criminal Proceedings (General) (Amendment) Regulations 1987.

The proposed new income limits (old limits in brackets) are as follows:

Civil Legal Aid	*Proposed new limit*		
Lower disposable income limit	£2325	(£2255)	) per annum
Upper disposable income limit	£5585	(£5415)	)

Criminal Legal Aid *Normal Weekly disposable income*	*Weekly Contribution*
£48 and below	Nil
More than £48 but not exceeding £54	£1
More than £54 but not exceeding £58	£2
More than £58 but not exceeding £62	£3
More than £62 but not exceeding £66	£4
More than £66 but not exceeding £70	£5
More than £70 but not exceeding £74	£6
More than £74 but not exceeding £78	£7

The weekly instalment of contribution is to be increased by £1 for each £4, or part of £4, by which average weekly disposable income exceeds £78.

Legal Advice and Assistance	*Proposed new limit*
Lower disposable income limit	£56 (£54) a week
Upper disposable income limit	£118 (£114) a week

Contribution Table for advice and assistance

Disposable weekly income between £	*Contribution* £
56–64	5
64–68	11
68–72	15
72–76	20
76–80	24
80–84	28
84–88	33
88–92	37
92–96	41
96–100	46
100–106	51
106–112	58
112–118	64

The proposed new *capital* limits (old limits in brackets) are as follows:—

Civil Legal Aid lower limit	£3,000 (no change)*
Civil Legal Aid upper limit	£4,850 (£4,710)
Criminal Legal Aid limit	£3,000 (no change)*
Advice and Assistance limit	£825 (£800)
ABWOR limit	£3,000 (no change)*

* These limits are linked to the supplementary benefit capital limit which remains at £3,000.

2288. Financial conditions

LEGAL AID (FINANCIAL CONDITIONS) REGULATIONS 1987 (No. 628) [45p], made under the Legal Aid Act 1974 (c.4), ss.6, 9(2), 20; operative on April 7, 1987; increases financial limits of disposable income for legal aid to not more than £5585 a year and the upper limit of disposable capital to £4850.

2289. Immigration cases—applications for legal aid—delay. See UDDIN'S APPLICATION, *Re*, §1975.

2290. Information bulletin

The Lord Chancellor's Department has published an Information Bulletin to supplement the information provided on legal aid in the 1986 annual statistical report. The Bulletin provides statistics on legal aid applications and results for each Petty Sessional Division and Crown Court Centre in 1986 and also applications to Criminal Legal Aid Committees.

2291. New framework—White Paper

The Government has announced in a White Paper that the administration of the legal aid scheme in England and Wales is to be transferred from the Law Society to an independent board. Powers are to be taken to enable other changes to be made to the organisation of the legal aid scheme, particularly in the field of legal advice. *Legal Aid in England and Wales: A Framework* (Cm. 118) is available from H.M.S.O. [£3·30].

2292. Order made by magistrate—to pursue appeal—purported revocation by Crown Court—validity

[Legal Aid Act 1974 (c.4), ss.28(5), 31(2); Legal Aid Act 1982 (c.44), s.9(3); Legal Aid Criminal Proceedings (General) Regulations 1968 (S.I. 1968 No. 1231), regs. 2(1)(*a*)(ii), 5, 31.]

A Crown Court has no power to revoke or interfere with a legal aid order granted by the lower court.

An applicant, convicted at the magistrates' court, wished to appeal against conviction. His solicitor applied to the magistrates for legal aid and received an order purporting to grant the said aid. The solicitor then received from the Clerk of the Crown Court an order revoking the order made by the justices, saying it had been sent in error.

Held, that the Crown Court had no power to deal with the application which had been to the lower court. As no separate application had been made it could not participate in any determination.

R. *v.* HUNTINGDON MAGISTRATES' COURT, *ex p.* YAPP (1987) 84 Cr.App.R. 90, D.C.

2293. Remuneration of duty solicitors

LEGAL ADVICE AND REPRESENTATION (DUTY SOLICITOR) (REMUNERATION) REGULATIONS 1987 (No. 443) [80p], made under the Legal Aid Act 1974 (c.4), s.20(1), and the Legal Aid Act 1982 (c.44), s.1; operative on April 10, 1987; provide for the determination by the Law Society of the remuneration payable to duty solicitors providing advice and representation at magistrates' courts under s.1 of the 1982 Act.

2294. Statutory charge—divorce settlement—whether exemption

Upon divorce, a periodical payments order was made. The wife was later granted civil legal aid to apply for an increase in the payments. The parties reached an agreement whereby the wife was paid a fixed sum in return for her surrender of all future claims to periodical payments. The Law Society purported to attach the legal aid statutory charge to that sum. The wife sought a declaration that the charge did not attach.

Held, that the statutory charge did attach—the payment was a capital payment in commutation or satisfaction of any potential obligations to the wife by way of periodical payments. This sum could not be described as a periodical payment itself as was contended.

STEWART *v.* THE LAW SOCIETY [1987] 1 F.L.R. 223, Latey J.

2295. Statutory charge—property adjustment on divorce—lump sum order—whether charge immediately enforceable

[Legal Aid Act 1974 (c.4), s.9(6); Legal Aid (General) Regulations 1980 (S.I. 1980 No. 1894), regs. 88, 91(1)(2), 93(*b*).]

The Law Society has no discretion to postpone the statutory charge on a lump sum awarded in divorce proceedings, nor to allow the charge to be transferred to a substituted security.

After contested proceedings for financial provision consequent on divorce, the judge ordered that the matrimonial home be sold, and that W receive from the proceeds of the sale a lump sum of £30,000. H was ordered to pay three-quarters of W's costs. The net equity in the home was about £40,000, of which one half was W's in her own right by virtue of her half ownership of the house. After taking account of the first £2,500 which was exempt under the Regulations, the liability of the legal aid fund exceeded the balance remaining as money recovered by W in the proceedings.

Held, on W's application for a declaration that the Law Society had discretion to postpone the enforcement of the charge, alternatively to allow it to take effect against a property she would buy, that the Law Society had no such discretion. The discretion contained in s.9(6) of the 1974 Act did not extend to an order which provided for the payment of a sum of money. Such a sum had to be paid immediately to the Law Society, which was under a duty to retain thereout sufficient to satisfy the statutory charge. Nor was there any discretion to transfer the charge to some other security (*Hanlon* v. *The Law Society* [1980] C.L.Y. 1664 distinguished; *R.* v. *The Law Society, ex p. Sexton* [1983] C.L.Y. 2183 approved).

SIMPSON *v.* THE LAW SOCIETY [1987] 2 W.L.R. 1390, H.L.

LIBEL AND SLANDER

2296. Apology—retraction of libel—mitigation of damages

The sufficiency of a retraction of a libel, made without an apology for the harm done to the plaintiff's reputation, was a matter for the jury, but was unlikely to be sufficient mitigation of damages.

PINE *v.* McMILLAN, *The Times*, November 25, 1987, C.A.

2297. Communication between officials of foreign government internal embassy document—privilege.

[Diplomatic Privilege Acts 1964 (c.81), Sched. 1, art. 24.]

An internal document of a foreign embassy attracts absolute privilege.

The defendant, an acting ambassador at the London embassy of a foreign country, was responsible for the compilation of an internal memorandum criticising the conduct of the plaintiff. The plaintiff alleged libel, the defendant claimed absolute privilege. The judge held that the document was privileged.

Held, dismissing the appeal, the court would not inquire into the merits of an internal document of a foreign embassy. (*Szalatnay-Stacho* v. *Fink* [1946] 2 All E.R. 231, *Rose* v. *R.* (1947–1951) C.L.C. 5021 considered).

FAYED *v.* TAJIR [1987] 2 All E.R. 396 C.A.

2298. Conspiring to injure—publication of information with dominant or sole intention of causing injury—interlocutory injunction

An interlocutory injunction ought properly to be granted to restrain the publication of information pursuant to a conspiracy to injure another's business where it could clearly be shown that the sole or dominant purpose of the publication was to cause injury.

P contracted to sell petrol to D for its filling stations. A dispute arose between P and D resulting in P ceasing to make deliveries to D. Scott J. held that P was in breach of contract. P's head office was in Cheltenham. P also had a hospitality tent at Cheltenham racecourse at the Gold Cup meeting. D arranged for a light aircraft to fly over the racecourse towing a banner stating "Gulf exposed in fundamental breach." P applied for an interlocutory injunction to prevent a similar occurrence on the day of the Gold Cup. P's claim was based on conspiring to injure P's business. P's application was refused at first instance.

Held, allowing P's appeal on the same day, that there was ample evidence that the sole or dominant purpose of D's actions was to injure P by way of revenge. D had no interest of their own to protect or further by publishing the information to the world at large. The rule to be applied in defamation cases that publication would not be restrained where pleas of justification or fair comment were raised did not apply to an action based upon conspiracy to injure (*Bonnard* v. *Perryman* [1891] 2 Ch. 269 distinguished).

GULF OIL (GREAT BRITAIN) *v.* PAGE [1987] 3 W.L.R. 166, C.A.

2299. Defamation—functions of judge and jury—damages

[Rep. of Ire.] P brought proceedings against D for damages in respect of defamatory words published in its newspaper. D admitted publication but claimed justification. D called no evidence at the trial and the trial judge refused to leave to the jury the question whether or not the words were defamatory but ruled that they were. The jury assessed damages at £65,000. D appealed.

Held, allowing the appeal, that where a judge ruled that words were capable of a defamatory meaning it was always a matter for the jury to decide whether the words did in fact carry that meaning and that in the circumstances of the case the jury's award was excessive. A new trial was ordered.

BARRETT *v.* INDEPENDENT NEWSPAPERS [1986] I.R. 13, Supreme Ct. of Rep. of Ire.

2300. Defamation—of member of group—member not named—whether cause of action

It is arguable whether the old authorities are good law on the question whether a member of a group can be defamed by defamatory comment on unnamed members, and in the circumstances it would not be right to strike out the statement of claim (*Jones* v. *Davers* (1596) Cro. Eliz. 496, *James* v. *Rutlech* (1599) 4 Co. Rep. 17a, *Falkner* v. *Cooper* (1666) Carter 55, *Harrison* v. *Thornborough* (1714) Gilb. Cas. 114, *Chomfey* v. *Watson* (1907) V.R. 502 considered).

FARRINGTON *v.* LEIGH, *The Times,* December 10, 1987, C.A.

2301. Defamation—settlement of action—statement in open court

Ordinarily where one defendant in a defamation action settles the plaintiff's claim, the parties to the settlement are entitled to have an agreed statement read out in open court so long as there is no real risk of prejudice or defamation to the defendant.

The first defendant in a libel action sought to postpone the making of a statement in open court pursuant to a settlement of the action between the plaintiff and the second defendant, on the grounds of the prejudice which he might suffer. The jury trial of the remainder of the action would not take place for three months. The judge refused the application.

Held, dismissing the appeal, that for the judge to prevent such a statement, there has to be a real risk of prejudice or defamation of other parties, not merely a shadowy one, and the judge's decision had been correct (dicta of Greer L.J. in *Wolseley* v. *Associated Newspapers* [1934] 1 K.B. 448 and of Lawton L.J. in *Church of Scientology of California* v. *North News* [1973] C.L.Y. 1957 considered).

BARNET *v.* CROZIER [1987] 1 W.L.R. 272, C.A.

2302/3. Defamatory meaning—more than one defamatory meaning—defendant seeking to justify defamatory meaning not pleaded by plaintiff

It is open to D to attempt to justify any defamatory meaning that a reasonable jury might find in the words complained of, but D must make his case clear to P on the pleadings (*Atkinson* v. *Fitzwalter* [1987] C.L.Y. 3081 considered).

PRAGER *v.* TIMES NEWSPAPERS, *The Independent*, July 24, 1987, C.A.

2304. Loss of reputation—loss of income—damages. See MIRROR NEWSPAPERS *v.* JOOLS, §1140

2305. Reputation—defamatory newspaper article—whether plaintiff's present reputation relevant—admissibility of evidence

In a libel trial, evidence of enhanced reputation at time of trial is not normally relevant where the issues are fair comment and malice.

The plaintiff complained of a defamatory newspaper article; the defence pleaded fair comment. At the trial evidence was admitted of reviews of plays long after publication, and oral evidence to the same efect. The jury found for the plaintiff.

Held, allowing the appeal, that although evidence as to reputation at the time of publication and reviews published fairly shortly afterwards were admissable, evidence of reputation at the time of trial was not admissable or relevant to issues of fair comment or malice.

CORNWELL *v.* MYSKOW [1987] 1 W.L.R. 630, C.A.

2306. Trial by jury—exercise of discretion as to use of jury. See VISCOUNT DE L'ISLE *v.* TIMES NEWSPAPERS, §3119.

LICENSING

2307. Air travel agency—exemption—disclosure of status. See GIMBLETT *v.* MCGLASHAN, §174.

2308. Airport licensing

LONDON CITY AIRPORT LICENSING (LIQUOR) ORDER 1987 (No. 1982) [45p], made under the Customs and Excise Management Act 1979 (c.2), s.22; operative on November 20, 1987; brings s.87 of the Licensing Act 1964 into force in relation to London City Airport.

SUMBURGH AIRPORT LICENSING (LIQUOR) ORDER 1987 (No. 838) [45p], under the Licensing (Scotland) Act 1976 (c.66), s.63(1); operative on May 7, 1987; brings s.63 of the 1976 Act into force in relation to Sumburgh Airport.

2309. Application for an off-licence—application refused—whether usual policy of justices should be deciding factor

S applied for a licence for a self-service off-licence: the police objected, saying that this would contravene the justices' policy on such applications. The justices rejected the application, and on appeal to the Crown Court the judge said that nothing had been put before the court that would justify a departure from the justices' usual policy, S appealed by way of case stated.

Held, that the courts ought to have considered the application on its merits. The policy should not be the deciding factor, and the justices ought to have decided on the evidence whether or not S's application could be an exception to the general policy.

R. *v.* CHESTER CROWN COURT, *ex p.* PASCOE AND JONES, (1987) 151 J.P.N. 574, D.C.

2310. "Cinematograph exhibition"—amusement arcade—video games—whether "exhibition of moving pictures"

[Cinematograph Act 1909 (c.30), s.1(3) (as amended by Cinematograph (Amendment) Act 1982 (c.33), Sched. 1, para. 1.]

Video games in an amusement arcade are exhibitions of moving pictures and so the arcade requires a cinema licence.

The second plaintiff, which was a member of the first plaintiff trade association, opened an amusement arcade which operated video games. The local licensing authority took the view that the use of such machines constituted a cinematograph exhibition and that a licence was required for the arcade pursuant to s.1 of the Cinematograph Act 1909. The plaintiffs brought an originating summons to determine whether the operation of a video game was an "exhibition of moving pictures" within the definition of "cinematograph exhibition" in s.1(3) of the Act. The judge held that it was.

Held, dismissing the appeal, that the moving pictures in a video game were exhibited to the view of the player and possibly others, and the fact that they were not displayed as an end in themselves but merely as a means of playing a game and the player might alter the pictures was irrelevant. The expression "exhibition of moving pictures" in s.1(3) of the 1909 Act as amended by the 1982 Act clearly included the operation of video games, even though that might not have been contemplated when the amended section was enacted. It was possible to conceive that video pictures might be offensive or harmful to children, and in so far as the mischief at which the 1909 Act was aimed was to safeguard children who might see pictures exhibited, it seems to be equally applicable to pictures exhibited in the course of a video game.

Leave to appeal was granted.

BRITISH AMUSEMENT CATERING TRADES ASSOCIATION *v.* WESTMINSTER CITY COUNCIL [1987] 1 W.L.R. 977, C.A.

2311. Extension—justices' discretion

[Licensing Act 1964 (c.26), s.74(4).]

Licensing justices had a practice of not granting exemption orders under s.74(4) of the Licensing Act 1964 for after midnight.

Held, that although it was reasonable for justices to have a general policy or practice, they were still under a duty to examine each case individually, and any such policy should be made publicly clear (*R.* v. *Torquay Licensing Justices, ex p. Brockman* (1951) C.L.C. 5181 applied).

WORKMAN GEORGE GROSVENOR *v.* BLAENAU FFESTINIOG MAGISTRATES' COURT, *The Times*, January 28, 1987, Taylor J.

2312. Justices' licence—transfer—whether suitability and condition of premises a relevant consideration

[Licensing Act 1964 (c.26), s.3.]

Where a local authority raised objections to the transfer of a liquor licence that consisted of allegations relating to the condition and suitability of the premises the licensing committee could only take account of the objections in so far as they were relevant to the question whether the applicant was a fit and proper person, since the provisions of the Act should not be utilised as a means of enforcement of other statutory provisions, such as hygiene regulations (*R.* v. *Edmonton Licensing Justices, ex p. Baker* [1983] C.L.Y. 2039 considered).

LONDON BOROUGH OF HARINGEY *v.* SANDHU, *The Times*, May 6, 1987, D.C.

2313. Licensing (Restaurant Meals) Act 1987 (c.2)

This Act relaxes the day-time restrictions concerning the hours during which intoxicating liquor may be served with meals in restaurants.

The Act received the Royal Assent on March 2, 1987.

2314. Liquor licence—discretion to hear objections

[Licensing Act 1964 (c.26), s.5(5).]

Justices have a discretion to hear anybody opposing an application for a liquor licence, whether or not the objector comes within the classes set out in s.5(5) of the Licensing Act 1964.

PATEL *v.* WRIGHT, *The Times*, November 19, 1987. D.C.

2315. Occasional licence—meaning of "occasional"—club premises

A club having failed to renew its registration under the Licensing Act 1964 (c.26), s.40, an Occasional Licence was applied for under s.180.

Held, quashing a magistrates' order refusing the application and directing the magistrates to grant the licence, that (1) the inadvertent failure to renew the registration was an occasion justifying an Occasional Licence; (2) a police objection the ground that the applicant could not be present to supervise the Occasional Licence, was not a good objection. There was no requirement for a licensee to be present to supervise at the club at all times.

R. *v.* WOOLWICH JUSTICES, *ex p.* ARNOLD [1987] Crim.L.R. 572, Roch J.

2316. Prescribed time limit—jurisdiction to extend time

[Local Government (Miscellaneous Provisions) Act 1982 (c.30), Sched. 1 para. 17(1).]

Justices have no power to extend the prescribed time limit in the Act.

R. *v.* TYNESIDE JUSTICES, *ex p.* NORTH TYNESIDE BOROUGH COUNCIL, *The Times*, November 7, 1987, Schiemann J.

2317. Sex shops—determination of "relevant locality"

[Local Government (Miscellaneous Provisions) Act 1982 (c.30), s.2, Sched. 3, paras. 12(3), 29.]

The question of what is the "relevant locality" within the meaning of the Act is a question of fact, but cannot mean a whole town or the whole of an authority's administrative area.

Various applications were made by a number of applicants to different authorities for licences for sex shops. The applications were consolidated on appeal, where one common issue that arose in most of the appeals was the differing interpretations by the various authorities of the phrase, "relevant locality."

Held, allowing some appeals and refusing others that "relevant locality" was a question of fact; it carried no connotation of precise boundaries nor did it have to be a clearly pre-defined area, but an entire town, or the whole of an administrative area were too large to be a "relevant locality" within the meaning of the Act.

R. *v.* PETERBOROUGH CITY COUNCIL, *ex p.* QUIETLYNN (1987) 85 L.G.R. 249, C.A.

2318. Sex shops—licensing proceedings—discretion of local authority

[Local Government (Miscellaneous Provisions) Act 1982 (c.30), Sched. 3, para. 10.]

The code laid down in Sched. 3, para. 10 of the Local Government (Miscellaneous Provisions) Act 1982 for the licensing of sex shops is not exhaustive, and a local authority has a discretion as to how the licensing proceedings should be conducted.

SHEPTONHURST *v.* CITY OF WAKEFIELD METROPOLITAN DISTRICT COUNCIL, *The Times,* November 18, 1987, C.A.

2319. Sex shops—objections made after 28-day period—validity of procedure—jurisdiction of justices and Crown Court

[Local Government (Miscellaneous Provisions) Act 1982 (c.30), s.2, Sched. 3, para. 10(15)(19).]

It was for a local authority to determine whether to grant a licence for a sex establishment: the validity of its determination was to be questioned on judicial review and not in a prosecution for an offence under the Local Government (Miscellaneous Provisions) Act 1982, s.2. A licensing authority could hear objections made more than 28 days after the date of application for a licence.

Three local authorities determined that sex establishments in their areas should be licensed and passed a resolution that Sched. 3 to the Local Government (Miscellaneous Provisions) Act 1982 should apply in their area. The company made applications for licenses. The authorities considered objections made within 28 days of the company's applications in accordance with para. 10(15) and (19) of Sched. 3, but also considered objections made after that period, and in one case allowed a councillor who was not a member of the licensing panel to address the meeting. All three refused licenses but the company continued to trade. The company was prosecuted and convicted in all three cases under para. 20(1) of Sched. 3, and appealed. The Crown Court in two cases on appeal allowed the appeal on the ground that the authority had failed to comply with the procedural requirements for the granting of a licence in considering objections made after the 28-day period. The third appeal was dismissed.

Held, allowing the appeal by the two local authorities, and dismissing the company's appeal, that any question of the validity of the local authority's procedure was to be determined by the High Court in proceedings for judicial review. Until it was reviewed it was presumed to be valid and on a prosecution under s.2 and Sched. 3 neither the justices nor the Crown Court had jurisdiction to consider the validity of the refusal of a licence. The two decisions of the Crown Court were therefore invalid and made without jurisdiction *D.P.P.* v. *Head* [1958] C.L.Y. 718, *London & Clydeside Estates* v. *Aberdeen District Council* [1980] C.L.Y. 315 and *R.* v. *Jenner* [1983] C.L.Y. 3743 considered). Further, although a local authority was under a duty under para. 10(15) of Sched. 3 to consider objections made within 28 days of the application, it had a discretion to hear later objections provided that the applicant was given an opportunity to deal with all the objections: there was then compliance with para. 10(19) of Sched. 3 and no breach of natural justice. In the circumstances, the decisions of the local authorities were valid (Dictum of Stephen Brown L.J. in *R.* v. *Preston Borough Council, ex p. Quietlynn* [1984] C.L.Y. 2058, applied; Dictum of Forbes L.J. in *R.* v. *Birmingham City Council ex p. Quietlynn* [1985] C.L.Y. 2044 disapproved).

PLYMOUTH CITY COUNCIL *v.* QUIETLYNN; PORTSMOUTH CITY COUNCIL *v.* QUIETLYNN; QUIETLYNN *v.* OLDHAM BOROUGH COUNCIL [1987] 3 W.L.R. 189, D.C.

LIEN

2320. Due debt—lien on papers—no invoice delivered

Where no invoice has been delivered nor particulars to enable calculation of a due debt, an accountant was not entitled to claim a lien on papers of their clients pending payments.

SINGH *v.* THAPER, *The Times*, August 7, 1987, C.A.

LIMITATION OF ACTIONS

2321. Accrual of cause of action—surveyor's report—whether statute-barred

The duties of a surveyor are not analogous to those of an engineer or architect, but are confined to exercising reasonable skill and care in reporting reasonably discoverable faults existing at the time of survey. Thus any cause of action accrues at the time of reliance upon the surveyor's report.

In February 1975 a firm of surveyors prepared a report on a new building of which the Secretary of State was considering acquiring a lease. The Secretary of State, relying on the report, had committed himself to acquiring the lease by July 1975. Defects allegedly based on faulty design, first appeared in February 1982. In January 1982 the Secretary of State issued a writ against the surveyors claiming damages in tort for alleged negligence in failing to report the faulty design. The preliminary issue was whether the claim was statute-barred.

Held, dismissing the action, that any action accrued at the time of reliance upon the report (*Philips* v. *Ward* [1956] C.L.Y. 936 applied. *Pirelli General Cable Works* v. *Faber (Oscar) & Partners* [1983] C.L.Y. 2216 distinguished).

SECRETARY OF STATE FOR THE ENVIRONMENT *v.* ESSEX, GOODMAN AND SUGGITT [1986] 1 W.L.R. 1432, Judge Lewis Hawser Q.C. sitting as Official Referee.

2322. Accrual of cause of action—voyage charter—whether good notice to charterers. See MINERALS AND METALS TRADING CORP. OF INDIA *v.* ENCOUNTER BAY SHIPPING CO.; SAMOS GLORY, THE, §3442

2323. Action by Attorney General—acting for public benefit—public charitable trust—whether trustees entitled to rely on Limitation Act

[Limitation Act 1980 (c.58), s.21(3).]

Where the Attorney General took action for the public good in respect of a public charitable trust, the trustees were not entitled to rely upon the Act since the Attorney General was not a beneficiary of the trust.

ATT.-GEN. *v.* COCKE, *The Times,* November 9, 1987, Harman J.

2324. Adverse possession—enforcement of possession order—time limit

[Limitations Act 1939 (c.21), ss.4, 10, 16; Limitations Act 1980 (c.58), s.15.]

Where the limitation period of 12 years expired during the course of proceedings the cause of action was unaffected. After judgment the plaintiff had a further 12 years within which to enforce against adverse possession.

BP PROPERTIES *v.* BUCKLER, *The Times*, August 13, 1987, C.A.

2324a. Arbitration—no arbitrator appointed within time limit—application for extension of time—leave to appeal. See ARBITRATION, §128.

2325. Carriage of goods by road—C.M.R. Convention—suspension of limitation period by written claim—whether claim must be quantified—goods not delivered—effect—damages recoverable

[Convention on the Carriage of Goods by Road, Arts. 23(4), 32(1)(*a*), (*b*), 32(2).]

A letter from the owners of goods indicating that they held the carriers liable for such loss or damage to the goods as might have occurred was a sufficient written claim to suspend the running of the limitation period under the provisions of the Convention on the Carriage of Goods by Road (C.M.R.)

D agreed to deliver a consignment of yarn from England to France for P. On October 1, 1982, D's lorry was involved in a road accident in France. The yarn was never delivered to its intended destination but impounded in France in legal proceedings commenced by D. The yarn was returned to P in January 1984. In February 1984, a joint survey of the damaged yarn was conducted by P and D's insurers. They agreed the yarn was fit only for salvage to the value of £6,515·46 and that its pre-accident value was £24,335·00. P wrote to D by letter of October 11, 1982 that they held D responsible for any losses they might incur in consequence of the accident. Proceedings were issued by P in August 1985. D claimed P's action was time-barred by the limitation period set out in Art. 32 C.M.R. Art. 32(1) provided for the period of limitation to run from (a) in the case of partial loss, damage or delay in delivery, the date of delivery and (b) in the case of a total loss, the 60th day after the goods were taken over by the carrier. Art. 32(2) provided that the limitation period should be suspended by a written claim made to the carrier until the carrier, in writing rejected the claim. D rejected P's claim for the first time by letter dated December 14, 1984.

Held, that "total loss" in Art. 32(1)(*b*) was to be equated with actual total loss and did not include the concept of constructive total loss. The yarn was damaged within the meaning of Art. 32(1)(*a*). However, the fact that the yarn had not been delivered within 60 days was conclusive evidence binding on both parties that there had been a total loss within the meaning of Art. 32(1)(*b*). Accordingly, P's action was time-barred unless the running of time was suspended by Art. 32(2). P's letter of October 11, 1982 was a sufficient written claim to suspend the limitation period. The article did not require the claim to be quantified. The letter suspended the limitation period notwithstanding that it was sent in the 60-day period prior to the commencement of the limitation period under Art. 32(1)(*b*). P was entitled to recover the cost of the joint survey as "other charges in respect of the carriage of the goods" under Art. 23(4) or by deduction from the salvage value as an expense in realizing the damaged value of the goods (*Tatton (William) & Co.* v. *Ferrymasters* [1974] C.L.Y. 293, *Moto Vespa S.A.* v. *M.A.T. (Britannia Express)* [1979] C.L.Y. 235, *Thermo Engineers* v. *Ferrymasters* [1981] C.L.Y. 215, *Worldwide Carriers* v. *Ardtran International* [1983] C.L.Y. 301 considered).

I.C.I. FIBRES *v.* M.A.T. TRANSPORT [1987] 1 FTLR 145, Staughton J.

2326. Carriage of goods by sea—damage to cargo—time limit for bringing action. See CHINA OCEAN SHIPPING CO. (OWNERS OF XINGCHENG) *v.* ANDROS (OWNERS OF THE ANDROS), §291.

2327. Carriage of goods by sea—damage to cargo—whether claim subject to one year time limit of Hague-Visby Rules—whether time should be extended. See SHIPPING AND MARINE INSURANCE, §3380.

2328. Commencement of time—date of knowledge

[Limitation Act 1980 (c.58), ss.14 and 33.]

P was involved in a road traffic accident on April 14, 1981. P sustained a whiplash injury which was considered minor at the time. At Christmas 1981 he had a severe attack and went for an X-ray. He was told he had arthritis in the neck and given a soft collar. P did not consider his job was in any way under threat. He had several days off work at irregular intervals in the years following the accident. In May 1984 P was off work for a short time and consulted his G.P., who declared him unfit for work as a fireman. P remained off work. At Christmas 1984 he was visited by his superior officer. It was then that P realised his position at work was at risk. P was advised to take advice from his union. A writ was issued on March 29, 1985. P was medically retired in June 1985.

Held, that P did not think he had any significant injury until Christmas 1984. He knew that, having suffered an injury, he could have brought an action, but did not consider it worthwhile or proper. D raised limitation. The judge was satisfied that P's date of knowledge for the purposes of s.14 was not until May 1984. P brought his action within three years from his date of knowledge.

YOUNG *v.* G.L.C. AND MASSEY, December 19, 1986; Owen J. [*Ex. rel. Robin Thompson Partners, Solicitors.*]

2329. Debt—confirmation—acknowledgment—company's balance sheets—signatures of directors

[Aus.] Local statute provided that where, after a limitation period for a cause of action commences to run, but before the expiration of that period, a person against whom the cause of action lies confirms the cause of action, the time prior to the date of confirmation does not count in calculating the limitation period. Confirmation was effective only if acknowledged to the person having the cause of action. In 1962, an unincorporated club borrowed money, paying back part of the debt in 1965. The club's accounts for the years 1970 and 1971 were signed by two directors in 1971 and 1972, certified by the club's auditors and adopted at a general meeting. The accounts showed the creditor as a secured creditor and were delivered to an officer of the creditor who had become a member of the club's board of directors to watch the creditor's interests. In 1976, the creditor brought proceedings to recover the debt.

Held, by a majority, that each of the balance sheets amounted to a sufficient acknowledgment in writing of the debt by the debtor to the creditor (*Jones* v. *Bellgrove Properties* [1949] C.L.Y. 5716, *Consolidated Agencies* v. *Bertram* [1967] C.L.Y. 2140, *Gee & Co. (Woolwich), Re* [1974] C.L.Y. 321 and *Compania de Electricidad de la Provincia de Buenos Aires, Re* [1978] C.L.Y. 254 considered).

STAGE CLUB *v.* MILLERS HOTELS PROPRIETARY [1981–1982] 150 C.L.R. 535, High Ct. of Australia.

2330. Defective buildings—joinder of parties—commencement of limitation period

A person added as a defendant does not become a party until the writ is served on him, or he waives that service, *e.g.* by serving a defence. Further, the mere fact that buildings are constructed in such a way that damage is bound to occur eventually is not sufficient to cause time to run from the date of construction. Further that amendment to plead a procedural defence such as limitation ought not to be allowed at a stage when the Court had investigated the merits of the claim and the plaintiffs had taken the strain of the litigation.

In May 1980 K and others issued a writ alleging breach of contract and negligence in the construction of five houses, against the builders. The builders issued a third-party notice against the local authority who in turn issued a fourth-party notice against the architects. In June 1982 the plaintiffs obtained leave to join the local authority and architects as defendants. The writ was re-issued in September 1982, and though it was not served, the local authority and architects thereafter conducted themselves as though they were the second and third defendants, and served defences in October 1982. During closing speeches counsel became aware of new authority raising the possibility that the limitation period might run from the date of construction. The judge allowed an amendment to plead a limitation defence but ruled that joinder took effect in July 1982. This was less than six years after the damage occurred, in August and September 1976, but more than six years after construction which took place between June 1973 and June 1975. The judge held that the claim against the architects was statute-barred. On appeal the Court of Appeal held that the actions against the local authority and the architects began at the issue of the writ and so were not statute-barred.

Held, on appeal, that a person added as a defendant did not become a party until the writ was served on him, and this had been issued by service of defences in October. These defendants were deemed to be joined at that time, and time ceased to run then (*Seabridge* v. *H. Cox and Sons (Plant Hire)* [1968] C.L.Y. 3209 overruled; *Byron* v. *Cooper* (1844) 11 Cl. & Fin 556 applied. Dictum of Brandon J. in *Liff* v. *Peasley* [1980] C.L.Y. 1679). Further that the mere fact that damage to the houses was bound to occur eventually did not render the houses doomed from the start, and thus time ran from the date of damage occurring (*Pirelli General Cable Works* v. *Oscar Faber* [1983] C.L.Y. 2216 applied). Further that limitation was a procedural defence which ought to have been pleaded; the application to amend was made too late and should not have been allowed. Thus the plaintiffs succeeded on the merits.

KETTEMAN *v.* HANSEL PROPERTIES [1987] 2 W.L.R. 312, H.L.

2331. Excise licence—use of vehicle on road without excise licence—time-limit for institution of proceedings

[Vehicles [Excise] Act 1971 (c.10), ss.8(1), 28(1), (2).]

A used a vehicle on a road without a licence contrary to s.8 of the 1971 Act, and when stopped admitted the offence. Over six months later, information came to the attention of the Secretary of State about the offence which seemed to warrant proceedings, and within six months such proceedings were begun. At those proceedings, A contended that the six months within which they had to be brought in accordance with s.28 of the Act ran from the date of his being stopped by the police, and thus the proceedings had not been timeously instituted.

Held, on appeal against conviction that since the Secretary of State was an "authorised prosecutor" within s.28, the time-limit ran from the date when the matter came to his attention, and the appeal would thus be dismissed.

ALGAR *v.* SHAW [1987] R.T.R. 229, D.C.

2332. Maritime collision action—discretion of court to extend time limit—considerations

[Maritime Conventions Act 1911 (c.57), s.8.]

The court will not further extend the time for commencement of a collision action, if previous agreed extensions have given the plaintiff ample time to issue a writ.

In 1982 a collision occurred between two vessels; negotiations for settlement were conducted. Before the expiry of the two-year limitation period, a year's extension was agreed, followed by three further shorter periods. Finally, in January 1987 a writ was issued shortly after the expiry of the last extension. The plaintiffs moved to extend the limitation period.

Held, refusing the application, that there was absolutely no excuse for the failure to issue a writ in time, and the court would not be prepared to grant a further extension unless special circumstances existed.

GAZ FOUNTAIN, THE [1987] 1 FTLR 423, Sheen J.

2333. Negligent settling document—when damage occurs

Where solicitors negligently settled a document the effect of which did not transpire for many years the victim of the negligence suffered damages at the date that the document was settled, not when the damage materialised.

MOORE (D. W.) AND CO. *v.* FERRIER, *The Times*, September 3, 1987, C.A.

2334. Pending action—new claim—facts in issue

[Limitation Act 1980 (c.58), s.35(5).]

Where a new claim is sought to be added to a pending action, it had to be material to the facts of the existing claim.

FANNON *v.* BACKHOUSE, *The Times*, August 22, 1987, C.A.

2335. Personal injuries—power to override time-limit—discretion

[Limitation Act 1980 (c.58), ss.14, 33.]

P claimed as widower and administrator of his wife's estate. P's wife worked for D for 12 months in 1954. In June 1978 she began to get short of breath and was admitted to hospital. A pleural biopsy was performed which revealed a tumour consistent with mesothelioma. P and his wife were told she had cancer, probably caused by exposure to asbestos dust. She died at 44, in 1979. P took no steps to issue proceedings as he was upset and depressed. He had to look after four children and work as a long-distance lorry driver. He consulted a solicitor in 1982. A letter before action was sent to D in August 1982. Legal aid were granted in January 1983 but discharged as P failed to maintain contributions. There were further delays on P's part. Legal aid was finally granted in August 1983. A writ was issued on October 4, 1983.

Held, that (1) P had knowledge within s.14(1) at the date of death but not before May 1978 when his wife first became ill; (2) the 18-month delay between the date of expiry of the three-year limitation period following the deceased's death and the issue of proceedings was insignificant when considering the cogency of the evidence likely to be adduced by the parties upon liability; (3) P did not act promptly but this was understandable; (4) D had not been prejudiced by the delay; (5) a letter before action had been sent to D 14 months before the issue of the writ. It was therefore equitable to allow the case to proceed.

RULE *v.* ATLAS STONE CO., December 11, 1984; Simon Brown J. [*Ex rel Field Fisher & Martineau, Solicitors.*]

2336. Personal injuries—writ within time but served after expiry and out of time—discretion to override time limits

[Limitation Act 1980 (c.58), ss.11(4)(*b*), 14(1)(*b*); R.S.C., Ord. 6, r.8(2).]

When considering whether or not to override time limits in a personal injuries action what matters is when the plaintiff became aware in general terms that he had a potential claim against the defendant, rather than the date upon which he could be said to know all the details of the alleged defaults by the defendant. In an action where the writ is issued within time, but served after expiry and out of time, the Court will only exercise its discretion to renew the writ where there are special circumstances: failing to serve within time due to an oversight is not a special circumstance.

In 1981 P was diagnosed as suffering from bronchial asthma, probably brought on by conditions at work. A writ was issued in 1984, and shortly thereafter an expert's report was received setting out the measures his employers should have taken to protect him. Because of an oversight the writ was not in fact served until about three weeks after it had expired.

Held, on the question of whether the writ should be renewed, allowing D's appeal from the judge, that the Court would only exercise its discretion to renew a writ when the effect thereof would be likely to deprive a defendant of a limitation defence where there were special circumstances. The real reason here being an oversight, that could not be said to be a special circumstance and the writ would not be renewed. Time runs from the date when a plaintiff knows that he has a possible case against the potential defendants; it is not necessary that he should have all the details available to prove his case for time to start running (*Heaven* v. *Road and Rail Wagons* [1965] C.L.Y. 3252 and *Baker* v. *Bowketts Cakes* [1966] C.L.Y. 9987 applied).

WILKINSON *v.* ANCLIFF (B.L.T.) [1986] 1 W.L.R. 1352, C.A.

2337. Time-bar—accrued right

[Limitation Acts 1939–1980.]

Nothing in the Acts retrospectively removes a time bar which had accrued under the 1939 Act to the benefit of the local authority in respect of personal injuries sustained in 1943 and not discovered until 1981.

ARNOLD *v.* CENTRAL ELECTRICITY GENERATING BOARD, *The Times*, October 23, 1987, H.L.

LITERARY AND SCIENTIFIC INSTITUTIONS

2338. Libraries

PUBLIC LENDING RIGHT SCHEME 1982 (AMENDMENT) ORDER 1987 (No. 1908) [45p], made under the Public Lending Right Act 1979 (c.10), s.3(7); operative on December 10, 1987; amends S.I. 1982, No. 719 so that the sum attributed to each loan of a book from a public library for the purposes of the calculation of amounts payable in respect of those loans is altered to 1·12p.

2339. Library authority—ban on publications—weapon in industrial dispute—whether valid. See ADMINISTRATIVE LAW, §29.

2340. Library authority—whether "Spycatcher" to be made available—interference with eventual issue at trial. See LOCAL GOVERNMENT, §2364.

2341. Museums

ARMED FORCES MUSEUMS (DESIGNATION OF INSTITUTIONS) ORDER 1987 (No. 1945) [45p], made under the National Heritage Act 1983 (c.47), s.31(1); operative on December 11, 1987; effects the necessary designation (regarding offers of employment under Sched. 2 to the 1983 Act) in the case of The Royal Marines Museum.

2342. National Library of Wales

NATIONAL LIBRARY OF WALES (DELIVERY OF BOOKS) (AMENDMENT) ORDER 1987 (No. 698) [45p], made under the Copyright Act 1911 (c.46), s.15(5); operative on May 1, 1987; revokes S.R. & O. 1924 No. 400 and S.I. 1956 No. 1978.

NATIONAL LIBRARY OF WALES (DELIVERY OF BOOKS) (AMENDMENT) REGULATIONS 1987 (No. 918) [45p], made under the Copyright Act 1911, 15(5); operative on June 8, 1987; replaces S.I. 1987 No. 698 which was defective.

LOCAL GOVERNMENT

2343. Abolition of Domestic Rates etc. (Scotland) Act 1987 (c.47). See RATING AND VALUATION, §3156.

2344. Administration of housing benefit—whether local authority can recover for increased expenditure

[Social Security and Housing Benefits Act 1982 (c.24), s.32; Housing Benefits (Subsidy) (No. 1) and (No. 2) Orders 1982 (S.I. 1982 Nos. 903 and 904).]

A local authority claiming the costs of administering housing benefits under s.32 of the Social Security and Housing Benefits Act 1982 is not entitled, under the Housing Benefits (Subsidy) (No. 1) and (No. 2) Orders 1982, when construed in the light of the 1982 Act, to recover any increased expenditure on debt charges or on rent and rate collections.

R. *v.* SECRETARY OF STATE FOR SOCIAL SERVICES, *ex p.* WALTHAM FOREST LONDON BOROUGH COUNCIL; SAME *v.* SAME, *ex p.* WORCESTER CITY COUNCIL, *The Independent*, July 9, 1987, D.C.

2345. Allowances to members

LOCAL GOVERNMENT (ALLOWANCES) (AMENDMENT) REGULATIONS 1987 (No. 1483) [85p], made under the Local Government Act 1972 (c.70), s.173, 177(1)(*f*), 177A; operative on September 15, 1987; increase attendance allowance and other allowances payable to members of local authorities and certain other bodies.

2346. Armorial bearings

LOCAL AUTHORITIES (ARMORIAL BEARINGS) ORDER 1987 (No. 162) [45p], made under the Local Government Act 1972 (c.70), s.247; operative on March 1, 1987;

authorises the Longrdige Town Council to bear and use the armorial bearings of the former Longridge UDC and Yeovil Town Council to bear and use those of the former borough council of Yeovil.

2347. Block grants

BLOCK GRANTS (EDUCATION ADJUSTMENTS) (ENGLAND) REGULATIONS 1987 (No. 347) [£1·60], made under the Local Government, Planning and Land Act 1980 (c.65), Sched. 10, paras. 2, 5—8; operative on April 1, 1987; provide for the adjustment of the block grant payable to local authorities in the year 1987/88 and subsequent years in relation to certain educational expenditure.

BLOCK GRANT (EDUCATION ADJUSTMENTS) (WALES) REGULATIONS 1987 (No. 359) [£1·60], made under the Local Government, Planning and Land Act 1980 (c.65), Sched. 10, paras. 2, 5, 6, 7; operative on April 1, 1987, provide for adjustment of the block grant payable to local authorities in Wales for the financial year 1987/88 and subsequent years in relation to certain education expenditure.

2348. Boundaries

BUCKINGHAMSHIRE (DISTRICT BOUNDARIES) ORDER 1987 (No. 339) [80p], made under the Local Government Act 1972 (c.70), ss.51(2), 67(4); operative on April 1, 1987 save for the purposes of art. 2(1) which are operative on March 30, 1987; alters some district boundaries in the county of Buckinghamshire.

DEVON (DISTRICT BOUNDARIES) ORDER 1987 (No. 1576) [£1·60], made under the Local Government Act 1972, ss.51(2), 67(4); operative on April 1, 1988 save for the purposes of art. 1(2) which are operative on October 1, 1987, alters the boundary between the City of Exeter and the districts of East Devon and Teignbridge.

DORSET (DISTRICT BOUNDARIES) ORDER 1987 (No. 2228) [85p], made under the Local Government Act 1972, ss.51(2) and 67(9); operative on April 1, 1988, except art. 1(2) which is operative on February 1, 1988; transfers areas between the districts of North Dorset and Purbeck in the county of Dorset.

ESSEX (DISTRICT BOUNDARIES) ORDER 1987 (No. 1598) [85p] made under the Local Government Act 1972, ss.51(2), 67(4); operative on April 1, 1988 save for Art. 1(2) which is operative on January 1, 1988; alters the boundary between the districts of Braintree and Maldon.

HEREFORD AND WORCESTERSHIRE (DISTRICT BOUNDARIES) ORDER 1987 (No. 338) [£1·40], made under the Local Government Act 1972, ss.51(2) 67(4); operative on April 1, 1987 save for the purposes of art. 2(1) which are operative on March 30, 1987; alters the boundaries of the city of Worcester.

KENT (DISTRICT BOUNDARIES) ORDER 1987 (No. 305) [£1·60], made under the Local Government Act 1972, ss.51(2), 67(4); operative on April 1, 1987 save for the purposes of Art. 2(1) which are operative on March 30, 1987; alters boundaries within Kent.

LEICESTERSHIRE (DISTRICT BOUNDARIES) ORDER 1987 (No. 2247) [£1·30] made under the Local Government Act 1972, ss.51(2) and 67(9); operative on April 1, 1988, except art. 1(2) which is operative on February 1, 1988; transfers areas between the district of Blaby and the City of Leicester.

NOTTINGHAMSHIRE (DISTRICT BOUNDARIES) ORDER 1987 (No. 221) [£1·40], made under the Local Government Act 1972, ss.51(2), 67(4)(5); operative on April 1, 1987 save for Art. 2(1) which is operative on March 20, 1987; alters the boundary between the borough of Gedling and the district of Newark and Sherwood in the county of Nottinghamshire.

SHROPSHIRE (DISTRICT BOUNDARIES) ORDER 1987 (No. 1737) [85p], made under the Local Government Act 1972, ss.51(2), 67(4); operative on April 1, 1988 save for the purposes of Art. 1(2) which are operative on November 1, 1987; alters the boundary between the borough of Shrewsbury and Atcham and the district of North Shropshire.

2349. Breach of statutory duty under Public Health Act 1936—collection of refuse—whether local authority liable for injury caused by its own failure to collect refuse.
See DEAR *v.* NEWHAM LONDON BOROUGH COUNCIL, §3153.

2350. Communities

PRESELI (COMMUNITIES) ORDER 1987 (No. 124) [£2·90], made under the Local Government Act 1972 (c.70), s.67(4)(5), Sched. 10, paras. 7, 9; operative on April 1, 1987, save for the purposes of Art. 2(1) which is operative on February 10, 1987; continues 20 communities and constitutes 32 new communities in the District of Preseli.

2351. Direct labour organisations

LOCAL GOVERNMENT (DIRECT LABOUR ORGANISATIONS) (COMPETITION) (AMENDMENT) REGULATIONS 1987 (No. 181) [80p], made under the Local Government, Planning and Land Act 1980 (c.65), ss.7, 9(3); operative on April 1, 1987; amend S.I. 1983 No. 685 in relation to their application to highway work.

2352. Direction to sell land—consent to disposal—duty to sell at highest price

[Local Government Act 1972 (c.70), s.123; Local Government Planning and Land Act 1980 (c.65), s.98.]

Where the Secretary of State directed a local authority to sell land, it was implied that the sale did not involve a violation of the duty of the local authority to sell at the highest price.

The Secretary of State for the Environment directed the Council under s.98 of the Local Government Planning and Land Act 1980 to sell six parcels of land within four months at an auction without reserve. The appellant council applied to quash the directions on the grounds that a sale within four months would violate s.123 of the Local Government Act 1972 to obtain the best price reasonably available on the grounds that a better price could be obtained by waiting for longer than four months. The judge dismissed the application.

Held, dismissing the appeal, that s.123 of the 1972 Act only required a local authority to obtain the best consideration reasonably available at the time of a valid decision to sell and did not require them to delay until a sale might obtain the highest price. Therefore, the Secretary of State's direction to sell within four months did not involve a violation of s.123. Nor was it a contravention of s.123 to order a sale by auction without reserve, since the policy of the 1980 Act was to obtain sales in a short period of time, whereas the effect of a reserve might be to leave the land in the ownership of the council for a long period if the reserve was not reached.

Alternatively, a direction issued under s.98 contained an implied consent which the Secretary of State had power to give under s.123(2) of the 1972 Act to a sale at less than the best consideration reasonably obtainable.

MANCHESTER CITY COUNCIL *v.* SECRETARY OF STATE FOR THE ENVIRONMENT (1987) 54 P. & C.R. 212, C.A.

2353. Disabled Persons (Services, Consultation and Representation) Act 1986—commencement

DISABLED PERSONS (SERVICES, CONSULTATION AND REPRESENTATION) ACT 1986 (COMMENCEMENT No. 1) ORDER 1987 (No. 564 (C.13)) [45p], made under the Disabled Persons (Services, Consultation and Representation) Act 1986 (c.33), s.18 (2); brings into force on April 1, 1987 ss.4 (in part), 8(1), 9, 10 of the 1986 Act.

DISABLED PERSONS (SERVICES, CONSULTATION AND REPRESENTATION) ACT 1986 (COMMENCEMENT No. 2) ORDER 1987 (No. 729 (C.19)) [45p], brings into force on April 17, 1987 ss.16–18 of the 1986 Act.

2354. Electoral divisions

S.I. 1987 Nos. 176 (District of Camarthen) [80p]; 300 (Borough of Dinefwr) [80p]; 301 (District of Preseli) [80p]; 483 (Borough of Chelmsford([£1·60]; 484 (Borough of South Ribble) [£2·20], 485 (District of Kingswood) [£1·90]; 486 (District of Montgomeryshire) [80p]; 1625 (Borough of Oadby and Wigston) [45p]; 1626 (Borough of Torbay) [45p].

2355. Exclusion from local authority premises—right to make representations. See ADMINISTRATIVE LAW, §36.

2356. Fire Safety and Safety of Places of Sport Act 1987 (c.27). See PUBLIC ENTERTAINMENTS AND RECREATION, §3145.

2357. Government finance—forward funding capital housing programme—abolition of the G.L.C.

[Local Government, Planning and Land Act 1980 (c.65), s.71 and Sched. 12.]

In March 1985, the G.L.C. entered into a master contract with Satman Developments Ltd by which Satman agreed to carry out building works for the authority on properties which had belonged to the G.L.C. but which had passed to its constituent boroughs under transfer orders. Under these orders, the G.L.C. was required to carry out certain level of works each year to the stock. As a result of financial constraints, the G.L.C. had not kept up these works. In March 1985, an initial payment of £20·7 million was made, although the estimated costs were a total of £55·5 million. Satman could, by a term of the master contract, require payment later for works done in excess of the initial payment, or alternatively the G.L.C. could opt for assignment or transfer back to themselves of the construction works. By March 1986, Satman had engaged contractors for a number of works (known as the "old works") for a total of £37·5 million. It was then proposed that a further contract should be entered into with Satman ("the new works"), and decided that the old works should be assigned back. When the G.L.C. came into certain other funds as a result of a successful challenge in relation to another matter, it was decided that the old works should be paid for, instead of handed back. Minutes before the Secretary of State's general consent under the Local Government (Interim Provisions) Act 1984 (c.53) to enter into contracts relating to transferred stock was withdrawn, the new contracts with Satman were entered into, and the following day two cheques, totalling £78 million, one for the old works and one for the new, were paid over to Satman. The London Borough of Hillingdon sought to challenge both payments, and the London Residuary Body, only that relating to the new works.

Held, dismissing both applications, that (1) neither the payments for the old works nor the new works contravened the principles laid down in *R.* v. *Greater London Council, ex p. Westminster City Council* [1986] C.L.Y. 2025; (2) the decisions did not extend the G.L.C.'s existence by proxy nor did they thereby exercise in 1985–1986 the power of decision-making for 1986–1987; (3) the money paid to Satman was "expended" during 1985–1986.

R. *v.* GREATER LONDON COUNCIL, *ex p.* LONDON RESIDUARY BODY (1987) 19 H.L.R. 175, Macpherson J.

2358. Housing homeless persons—local authority using premises for homeless persons and purporting to limit number of occupants to nil—whether reasonable

[Housing Act 1961 (c.65), ss.15, 19.]

A local authority was unreasonable in seeking both to limit the occupants of a building to nil and to use the hotel of which it was a substantial part to house homeless persons (*Reed* v. *Hastings Corporation* [1964] C.L.Y. 1710 considered).

R. *v.* HACKNEY LONDON BOROUGH COUNCIL, *ex p.* EVENBRAY, *The Times*, September 15, 1987, Kennedy J.

2359. Housing improvement grant—satisfaction with works—date of certification

[Housing Act 1974 (c.44), ss.75(6), 82(5).]

The certified date within the meaning of the Act was the date at which the relevant works ceased.

R. *v.* WESTMINSTER CITY COUNCIL *ex p.* HAZAN, *The Independent*, December 10, 1987, C.A.

2360. Housing (Scotland) Act 1987 (c.26). See HOUSING, §1891.

2361. Housing transfers—effect—capital receipts

[London Government Act 1963 (c.33), s.23; Local Government Planning and Land Act 1980 (c.65), Pt. VIII.]

The respondent (transferor) authority were the owners of housing accommodation in the area of two other (transferee) authorities. These authorities requested the transfer of the accommodation to themselves under s.23 of the London Government Act 1963. No agreement could be reached as to the terms of the transfer order, and the Minister indicated his intention to determine the terms himself. Various draft orders were before him. Of these, only one provided for any compensation to be paid to the transferor, and in relation to this draft the Minister indicated that any payments received would not be considered as prescribed capital receipt for the purposes of the 1980 Act. The respondent authority sought judicial review challenging, *inter alia*, the draft order which did not include any compensation and the view indicated regarding capital receipt. Taylor J. held that the authority were entitled to receive payment for the loss of title to their property and that the transfer qualified as a prescribed capital receipt.

Held, allowing the appeal, that (1) the Minister need only include an arbitration clause where this is necessary, *i.e.* if the question of value is to play a part in the order; (2) the presumption of "no expropriation without full compensation" was not applicable since there was no aspect of confiscation of property for the public good; (3) the statutory transfer was not a "disposal" within the meaning of the 1980 Act since the concept of disposal is alien to the general statutory purpose of the 1963 Act, namely reorganisation of local government in the Greater London area with specific reference to the carrying out by local authorities and housing associations of their functions under housing legislation.

R. *v.* SECRETARY OF STATE FOR THE ENVIRONMENT, *ex p.* NEWHAM LONDON BOROUGH COUNCIL (1987) 19 H.L.R. 298, C.A.

2362. Inner urban areas

INNER URBAN AREAS (DESIGNATED DISTRICTS) (WALES) ORDER 1987 (No. 115) [45p], made under the Inner Urban Areas Act 1978 (c.50), ss.1(1), 15; operative on March 3, 1987; designates two districts for the purposes of the 1978 Act.

2363. Library authority—ban on publications—weapon in industrial dispute—whether valid. See ADMINISTRATIVE LAW, §29.

2364. Library authority—whether "Spycatcher" to be made available—interference with eventual issue at trial

Since one of the issues at trial in the "Spycatcher" case would be whether the material contained in it was already known to the public at large, any increase in the availability of the book would or might constitute an interference with the administration of justice. Such an increase in availability included the provision of the book for the public by a library authority.

ATT-GEN *v.* OBSERVER, THE: ATT.-GEN. *v.* GUARDIAN NEWSPAPERS; APPLICATION BY DERBYSHIRE COUNTY COUNCIL, *Re*, *The Times*, October 20, 1987, Knox J.

2365. Licensing—sex shops—determination of "relevant locality." See LICENSING, §2317.

2366. Licensing—sex shops—discretion of local authority. See SHEPTONHURST *v.* CITY OF WAKEFIELD METROPOLITAN DISTRICT COUNCIL, §2318.

2367. Licensing—sex shops—validity of procedure. See LICENSING, §2319.

2368. Local authority—superannuation—concurrent employments—sequential employments

[Local Government Superannuation Regulations 1974 (S.I. 1974 No. 520), reg. D21(1).]

Regulation D21(1)(*a*) of the 1974 Regulations applies only to sequential and not to concurrent periods of employment.

C was employed full-time by various local authorities from 1932 until retirement in 1974 at the age of sixty. For the last 24 years of that time he worked part-time for a water authority. He then worked for them full-time for a further five years. He paid the appropriate superannuation contributions to the water authority. A dispute arose as to whether only five years reckonable service was attributable to C's water authority pension. The question was referred to the High Court for determination.

Held, that regulation D21 which required periods of service taken into account for retirement pension to be disregarded for the purpose of calculating superannuation pension applied only to sequential and not concurrent periods of service and thus were not applicable here.

SEVERN TRENT WATER AUTHORITY *v.* CROSS (1987) 85 L.G.R. 517, Simon Brown J.

2369. Local education authority—education committee—requirement to include "persons of experience in education"—whether limited to teachers

[Education Act 1944 (c.31), Sched. 1, Pt. 2 para. 5.]

The phrase "persons of experience in education" was not limited in meaning to teachers.

By the Education Act 1944, Sched. 1, Pt. 2, para. 5 "every education committee of a local education authority shall include persons of experience in education . . ." All but two local education authorities complied with that requirement by co-opting at least one member of the teaching profession onto their education committee. The education committee of Croydon London Borough Council was entirely composed of elected members of the council. None were teachers although most had substantial involvement in educational matters as parents, school governors, members of various education committees or sub-committees or by having been educated in the borough. The National Union of Teachers was of the view that the education committee should include co-opted teacher members. The Council disagreed. The Union, through L, applied for judicial reviews seeking a declaration that the committee was properly constituted only if it included more than one person who was or had been involved in the imparting of instruction to pupils or students or was academically qualified to do so.

Held, dismissing the application, that the words "persons of experience in education" did not import any requirement for the person to be technically qualified as a teacher nor did the phrase require the persons to have experience in educating as opposed to education. By reason of their involvement in educational matters on a longstanding basis within the borough, the members of the committee were aptly described as persons of experience in education.

R. *v.* CROYDON LONDON BOROUGH COUNCIL, *ex p.* LENEY (1987) 85 L.G.R. 466, D.C.

2370. Local Government Act 1986—commencement

LOCAL GOVERNMENT ACT 1986 (COMMENCEMENT) ORDER 1987 (No. 2003 (c.62), [45p], made under the Local Government Act 1986 (c.10), s.12(2); brings s.5 of the 1986 Act into force on April 1, 1988.

2371. Local Government Act 1987 (c.44)

The Act amends Pt. VIII of the Local Government, Planning and Land Act 1980 (c.65) and makes further provision about the adjustment of block grant in connection with education.

The Act received the Royal Assent on May 15, 1987.

The Act extends to England and Wales only.

2372. Local Government Finance Act 1987 (c.6)

This Act validates things done by the Secretary of State in connection with, and to make further provision as to, rate support grants and the limitation or reduction of rates and precepts of local authorities.

The Act received the Royal Assent on March 12, 1987.

2373. Local severance scheme—redundancy of local authority employees

Where a local severance scheme failed to provide for the payment of money in lieu of notice, any payments made in that regard were invalid, and were repayable.

R. *v.* GREATER MANCHESTER COUNCIL *ex p.* GREATER MANCHESTER RESIDUARY BODY, *The Times,* March 27, 1987, Farquharson J.

2374/5. Parish meeting—whether power in trustee to commence proceedings without direction by parish meeting

[Local Government Act 1972 (c.70), s.13(4).]

A trustee of a parish had power to commence legal proceedings without a direction from the parish meeting provided such action did not conflict with any direction given by the parish meeting.

T was a trustee of Askerswell parish. The parish did not have a parish council. S.13(4) of the Local Government Act 1972 provides that the parish trustees of a parish shall act in accordance with any directions given by the parish meeting. An action involving a boundary dispute was commenced by C, T's predecessor against the defendants, M. In the course of the action, T was substituted for C as plaintiff. The parish meeting did not at any time pass a resolution authorising the commencement of the proceedings. M claimed the proceedings were unauthorised. The trial judge found in favour of T.

Held, dismissing M's appeal, that s.13(4) of the Act did not provide that the trustees had no power to commence proceedings in the absence of a direction from the parish meeting but rather that the trustees in carrying out their duties should act in compliance with any directions of the parish meeting. The trustees had an implied power to act in any way necessary or desirable in the execution of their trust which did not conflict with a direction by the parish meeting.

TAYLOR *v.* MASEFIELD (1987) 85 L.G.R. 108, C.A.

2376. Placing of caravan on grazing land—whether land "unoccupied". See STUBBINGS *v.* BEACONSFIELD JUSTICES, §3641.

2377. Prescribed expenditure

LOCAL GOVERNMENT (PRESCRIBED EXPENDITURE) (AMENDMENT) REGULATIONS 1987 (No. 351) [80p], made under the Local Government, Planning and Land Act 1980 (c.65), ss.72(3), 75(5), 84 Sched. 12, para. 4; operative on April 1, 1987; amends S.I. 1983 No. 296 by substituting a new Sched. 1.

LOCAL GOVERNMENT (PRESCRIBED EXPENDITURE) (CONSOLIDATION AND AMENDMENT) REGULATIONS 1987 (No. 2186) [£1·90], made under the Local Government, Planning and Land Act 1980, ss.72(3), 75(5), 80A(7), 84, Sched. 12, paras. 2, 4; operative on January 13, 1988; consolidate S.I. 1983 No. 294, as amended, with certain amendments.

LOCAL GOVERNMENT (PRESCRIBED EXPENDITURE) (WORKS) REGULATIONS 1987 (No. 1583) [85p], made under the Local Government, Planning and Land Act 1980 (c.65), ss.80A(7), 84; operative on October 1, 1987; prescribes two exceptions to the limits on expenditure contained in s.72(3) of the 1980 Act.

2378. Public meetings—right to use suitable room on school premises—whether private law right or public law right

The right granted to a candidate in a local government election to use a suitable school room to hold a public meeting by s.96 of the Representation of the People Act 1983 was a private law right enforceable by a writ action claiming declaratory and injunction relief.

By s.96 of the Representation of the People Act 1983; a candidate in a local government election is entitled for the purpose of holding public meetings in furtherance of his candidature to use a suitable room in school premises. E applied to the Inner London Education Authority to use a suitable room at one of three different schools for the purposes of a public meeting in support of his candidature in local government elections to be held on May 7, 1986. E undertook to be bound by the authority's terms and conditions in connection with the use of school premises. E indicated that unless he received confirmation by April 30 that a room would be made available, proceedings would be issued. E did not receive confirmation that a room would be made available and on May 1 issued an originating summons against M, as leader of the authority, seeking a declaration that he was entitled to the use of a suitable school room for a public meeting and an injunction ordering the authority to select and make available a suitable room in one of the three schools referred to in his application to the authority. The trial judge accepted the defendant's argument that E's right to the use of a school room under s.96 of the Act was a public law right enforceable by way of judicial review and dismissed E's summons.

Held, allowing E's appeal, the right granted to a candidate in a local government election to use a suitable school room to hold a public meeting in pursuance of his candidature by s.96 of the Representation of the People Act 1983 was a private law right capable of being enforced in a writ action claiming declaratory and injunctive relief (*O'Reilly* v. *Mackman* [1982] C.L.Y. 2603, *Cocks* v. *Thanet District Council* [1982] C.L.Y. 1465, *Wandsworth London Borough Council* v. *Winder* [1985] C.L.Y. 9 considered).

ETTRIDGE *v.* MORRELL (1987) 85 L.G.R. 100, C.A.

2379. Publicity account

LOCAL AUTHORITIES (PUBLICITY ACCOUNT) (EXEMPTION) ORDER 1987 (No. 2004) [85p], made under the Local Government Act 1986 (c.10), s.5(5); operative on April 1, 1988; contains exemptions to s.5(1) of the 1986 Act which provides that a local authority is required to keep a separate account of its expenditure on publicity.

2380. Rate Support Grants Act 1987 (c.5)

This Act makes further provision as to the calculation of entitlement to block grant under Pt. VI of the Local Government, Planning and Land Act 1980.

The Act received the Royal Assent on March 12, 1987.

2381. Rates—councillors voting for increase in rates—voting along party lines—whether discretion fettered thereby

Where a councillor risked withdrawal of the party whip if he voted against party policies, even if he would otherwise have done so, but would nevertheless remain an independent councillor his choice was not sufficiently fettered for the courts to say that he had not exercised his discretion when he voted.

R. *v.* WALTHAM FOREST LONDON BOROUGH COUNCIL, *ex p.* WALTHAM FOREST RATEPAYERS ACTION GROUP, *The Times*, October 2, 1987, C.A.

2382. Recreation grounds

RECREATION GROUNDS (REVOCATION OF PARISH COUNCIL BYELAWS) ORDER 1987 (No. 1533) [45p], made under the Local Government Act 1972 (c.70), s.262(8)(*d*); operative on November 1, 1987; revokes specified parish council byelaws.

2383. Refuse collection—Highway authority also refuse collecting authority

[Litter Act 1983 (c.35), s.1.]

When a local authority is both the highway authority and the refuse collecting authority, it can authorise itself to take steps in regard to the collection of litter which would otherwise be an offence under s.1 of the Litter Act 1983.

CAMDEN LONDON BOROUGH COUNCIL *v.* SHINDER, *The Times*, July 4, 1987, C.A.

2384. Registered Establishment (Scotland) Act 1987 (c.40)

This Act makes further provision as to the registration of establishments under the Social Work (Scotland) Act 1968 (c.49) and the Nursing Homes Registration (Scotland) Act 1938 (c.73).

The Act received the Royal Assent on May 15, 1987, and will come into force on days to be appointed by the Secretary of State.

The Act applies to Scotland only.

2385. Rent increase—considerations—discretion of local authority

[Housing Act 1985 (c.68), ss.21 and 24.]

The defendant was the secure tenant of property owned by the plaintiff authority. The plaintiff issued proceedings in 1982 for arrears of rent, which the defendant defended on the basis that the increases were of no effect since (a) the authority had not considered the relative means of the ratepayers as a group and tenants as a group; (b) the increase was higher than any increase in the private sector which would have been phased and (c) the increase was grossly in excess of the rate of inflation. The defendant also counterclaimed seeking a declaration to this effect. The authority sought to strike out the defence and counterclaim on the basis that they should have been the subject of judicial review proceedings. These proceedings failed in the House of Lords (see *Wandsworth London Borough Council* v. *Winder* [1985] C.L.Y. 9). The county court proceedings were then transferred to the Chancery Division.

Held, giving judgment for the plaintiff and dismissing the counterclaim, that (1) the authority have a very wide discretion in fixing rents; the measure is reasonableness, and they are under no duty to subsidise or not to subsidise rents; (2) the authority were not obliged to take into account the relative means of the ratepayers as a group and of the tenants as a group nor were they obliged to take account of the phasing provisions which operated in the private sector; (3) the authority were not obliged to regard the rate of inflation as an overriding consideration, and an increase of 37 per cent. was not perverse.

WANDSWORTH LONDON BOROUGH COUNCIL *v.* WINDER (No. 2) (1987) 19 H.L.R. 204, Mervyn Davies J.

2386. Reorganisation

LOCAL GOVERNMENT REORGANISATION (CAPITAL MONEY) (GREATER LONDON) ORDER 1987 (No. 118) [£1·60], made under the Local Government Act 1985 (c.51), ss.49, 77, 101; operative on February 27, 1987; makes provision in relation to the distribution of capital receipts by the London Residuary Body to rating authorities in Greater London.

LOCAL GOVERNMENT REORGANISATION (PENSIONS ETC.) (GREATER MANCHESTER AND MERSEYSIDE) ORDER 1987 (No. 1579) [£1·30] made under the Local Government Act 1985, s.67(3); operative on October 1, 1987; makes provision for the transfer of functions relating to pensions from the residuary Bodies, to which the Order relates, to the Boroughs of Tameside and Wirral.

LOCAL GOVERNMENT REORGANISATION (PENSIONS ETC.) (SOUTH YORKSHIRE) ORDER 1987 (No. 2110) [£1·60], made under the Local Government Act 1985, s.67(3); operative on January 1, 1988, establishes the South Yorkshire Pensions Authority and translates responsibilities for pensions from the South Yorkshire Residuary Body to that authority.

LOCAL GOVERNMENT REORGANISATION (PROPERTY) (GREATER MANCHESTER) ORDER 1987 (No. 1446) [£2·20], made under the Local Government Act 1985, s.67(2); operative on September 8, 1987; transfers certain properties to the councils of the districts in which they are situated.

LOCAL GOVERNMENT REORGANISATION (PROPERTY) (SOUTH YORKSHIRE) ORDER 1987 (No. 651), [£1·40], made under the Local Government Act 1985, s.67(3); operative on May 5, 1987; transfers property formerly owned by the South Yorkshire Metropolitan County Council to the district councils on which it is situated.

LOCAL GOVERNMENT REORGANISATION (PROPERTY) (TYNE AND WEAR) ORDER 1987 (No. 1288) [£1·30], made under the Local Government Act 1985, s.67(3); operative on August 20, 1987; transfers property formerly owned by the County Council of Tyne and Wear to councils of the districts in which that property is situated.

LOCAL GOVERNMENT REORGANISATION (PROPERTY) (WEST MIDLANDS) ORDER 1987 (No. 1077) [85p], made under the Local Government Act 1985, s.67(3); operative on July 22, 1987; transfers certain property rights and liabilities previously vested in the West Midlands County Council to specified district councils.

LOCAL GOVERNMENT REORGANISATION (PROPERTY) (WEST YORKSHIRE) ORDER 1987 (No. 15) [45p], made under the Local Government Act 1985, s.67(2); operative on March 2, 1987; transfers properties formerly owned by the West Yorkshire Metropolitan County and used for highway purposes to the districts in which they are situated.

LOCAL GOVERNMENT REORGANISATION (PROPERTY) (WEST YORKSHIRE) (No. 2) ORDER 1987 (No. 1451) [45p], made under the Local Government Act 1985, s.67(2); operative on September 8, 1987; effects transfers of property.

LOCAL GOVERNMENT REORGANISATION (PROPERTY, ETC.) (MERSEYSIDE) ORDER 1987 (No. 1463) [45p], made under the Local Government Act 1985, ss.67(3) and 101; operative on September 9, 1987; transfers certain properties formerly rested in the Merseyside county council to the councils of the districts in which they are situated.

2387. Residuary bodies—directions to such bodies by Secretary of State—effect

[Local Government Act 1985 (c.51), s.65(1), Sched. 13, para. 7(2).]

The Secretary of State for the Environment has power to give directions to residuary bodies with which they must comply.

R. *v.* SECRETARY OF STATE FOR THE ENVIRONMENT *ex p.* CAMDEN LONDON BOROUGH COUNCIL, *The Times,* July 14, 1987, D.C.

2388. School places—whether council in breach of statutory duty—sex discrimination

Birmingham City Council was held to be in breach of its statutory duty by providing fewer places at Grammar schools for girls than for boys.

R. *v.* BIRMINGHAM CITY COUNCIL, ex p. EQUAL OPPORTUNITIES COMMISSION, *The Times,* October 15, 1987, McCullough J.

2389. Standing orders—appointment of councillor to a committee conditional upon declaration of pecuniary, personal and other interests—whether unlawful

A standing order passed by a council requiring councillors to complete a detailed questionnaire relating to their pecuniary, personal and other interests as a condition of eligibility to serve on the council's committees was not unlawful.

By a resolution passed by the Council, Newham London Borough Council amended their standing orders so as to require councillors to complete a declaration of their pecuniary and personal interests as a prerequisite to appointment to membership of the Council's committees. Failure to complete the declaration meant a councillor would be ineligible for such appointment or removed from any existing committee. The declaration was over 10 pages long and extended in the most minute detail to the pecuniary interests of the councillor and his or her spouse, personal interests and other interests. The declarations of the councillors were to provide a public register of councillors' interests. H., a member of the Council, applied for judicial review arguing that the resolution was unlawful and amounted to an invasion of privacy.

Held, dismissing H.'s application, that the Council had power to establish in standing orders the criterion for appointment to a committee. S.94(4) Local Government Act (declaration of pecuniary interests by councillors) did not set any limit as to the nature of interests a council might require its councillors to declare. It merely provided for a criminal sanction in the circumstances set out in the section. The declaration of interests was properly and lawfully adopted. The consequence of failing to make the declaration could not be described as unlawful coercion or punishment (*Wheeler* v. *Leicester City Council* [1985] C.L.Y. 17 distinguished).

R. *v.* NEWHAM LONDON BOROUGH COUNCIL *ex p.* HAGGERTY (1987) 85 L.G.R. 48, Mann J.

2390. Statutory repairing covenant—defective roof—whether L required to replace it. See MURRAY *v.* BIRMINGHAM CITY COUNCIL, §2236.

2391. Statutory repairing obligations—notice to landlord authority of disrepair. See DINEFWR BOROUGH COUNCIL *v.* JONES, §2237.

2392. Statutory repairing obligations—whether local authority in breach. See McCLEAN *v.* LIVERPOOL CITY COUNCIL, §2238.

LONDON

2393. London government reorganisation

LONDON GOVERNMENT REORGANISATION (HOUSING ASSOCIATION MORTGAGES) ORDER 1987 (No. 117) [45p], made under the Local Government Act 1985, ss.67(3), 100(2); operative on February 28, 1987; transfers to the councils of districts and London boroughs housing association mortgages which were vested in the London Residuary Body.

LONDON GOVERNMENT REORGANISATION (HOUSING ASSOCIATION MORTGAGES) (No. 2) ORDER 1987 (No. 2219) [85p], made under the Local Government Act 1985 (c.51), ss.47(3) and 100(2) and (4); operative on January 29, 1988; provides for the transfer to the councils of districts and London boroughs of the London Residuary Body's rights and liabilities in relation to mortgages by housing associations in three stages.

2394. Port of London Authority—statutory powers—construction

The purpose of s.5(3) of the Port of London Act 1968 was to require effect to be given to the ordinary construction of each of the powers conferred by the Act and not to depart from the ordinary meaning of the words. In giving words their ordinary meaning, one would in some way derogate from the exercise of other equally clear powers contained in other sections of the Act. Thus s.5(3) required that the court should give effect to the ordinary meaning of the words in s.81 of the Act which were clear and authorised the acceptance by the Port of London Authority of obligations limiting the use of their land either by themselves or by other persons over which they had control even though to give the words their ordinary meaning would derogate from the powers and duties conferred on the Port of London Authority in s.66 of the Act. Appeal from Warner J.

GREATER LONDON COUNCIL *v.* PORT OF LONDON AUTHORITY, February 20, 1986 (C.A.T. No. 347).

2395. Taxicabs

LONDON (BRITISH RAIL) TAXI SHARING SCHEME ORDER 1987 (No. 839) [45p], made under the Transport Act 1985 (c.67), s.10(4)(5)(6)(10); operative on July 1, 1987; provides for the sharing of taxis to specified destinations from Waterloo and Paddington Stations.

LONDON CAB ORDER 1987 (No. 999) [85p], made under the Metropolitan Public Carriage Act 1869 (c.115), s.8, the London Cab and Stage Carriage Act 1907 (c.55), s.1 and the London Cab Act 1968 (c.7), s.1; operative on June 21, 1987; increases taxi fares in the Metropolitan Police District and the City of London.

LONDON TAXI SHARING SCHEME ORDER 1987 (No. 1535) [£1·30], made under the Transport Act 1985 (c.67), s.10(4)(5)(6)(10); operative on September 28, 1987; provides for the sharing of hiring of taxis in London.

2396. Transport

LONDON REGIONAL TRANSPORT (LEVY) ORDER 1987 (No. 125) [80p], made under the London Regional Transport Act 1984 (c.32), s.13(4); operative on February 3, 1987; prescribes a levy of 7.77 pence in the pound for the year 1987/88.

MEDICINE

2397. Abortion—consent

The Court declared that it would not be unlawful to carry out an abortion on a woman solely by reason of her lack of capacity to give informed consent.

X., *Re*, *The Times*, June 4, 1987, Reeve J.

2398. Abortion—severely mentally handicapped woman. See T., *Re*; T. *v.* T., §2426.

2399. Charge of professional misconduct—duplicity—whether charge bad—whether amendment of charge permitted

[General Medical Council Preliminary Proceedings Committee and Professional Conduct Committee (Procedure) Rules Order of Council 1980.]

The rule against duplicity does not apply to a charge of serious professional misconduct since individual events, whilst in themselves not amounting to serious professional misconduct, might, when taken together, amount to such conduct. Provided the procedure laid down in the rules is followed, no prejudice will be suffered if further particulars of the charge are given, without reference to the preliminary proceedings committee.

G was charged with serious professional misconduct, namely that over a period of 13 months he had given various drugs to "individual patients" in circumstances amounting to serious professional misconduct. When a request for particulars was made the names of eight patients were given to G, which included four patients whose cases had not previously been put before the preliminary proceedings committee. G contended that the charge was bad for duplicity, and that he should be given further particulars of the allegation of improperly prescribing drugs.

Held, dismissing the appeal by G, that (1) that where a charge of professional misconduct was concerned the rule against duplicity was of no application. It might be that a series of events, none serious enough in itself to warrant the appellation "serious professional misconduct" might, when taken together, amount to that offence; (2) as to the complaint that the introduction of the "new" four patients, provided that there was full disclosure of the evidence to G, in good time for him to consider the matter and formulate submissions, no unfairness would result from their inclusion.

R. *v.* GENERAL MEDICAL, COUNCIL, *ex p.* GEE [1987] 2 All E.R. 193, H.L.

2400. Dentist—discipline—"serious professional misconduct"

[Dentists Act 1984 (c.24), s.27(1).]

S.27(1) of the 1984 Act is not restricted to moral turpitude but includes all professional misconduct.

D was charged before the Professional Conduct Committee of the General Dental Council under s.27(1) of the 1984 Act with serious professional misconduct, including giving inadequate, and in some cases, unnecessary treatment. The Committee found D guilty and ordered his name to be erased from the register.

Held, that "serious professional misconduct" in s.27(1) of the 1984 Act was not restricted to dishonesty or moral turpitude but included all professional misconduct, whether by omission or commission. It was wrong to include the giving of unnecessary treatment within a charge of failure to complete treatment, but no miscarriage of justice had occurred as a result of this (*Felix* v. *General Dental Council* [1980] C.L.Y. 1958 distinguished; *Sivarajah* v. *General Medical Council* [1964] C.L.Y. 2357 applied).

DOUGHTY *v.* GENERAL DENTAL COUNCIL [1987] 3 W.L.R. 769, P.C.

2401. Dentists

IRISH REPUBLIC (TERMINATION OF 1927 AGREEMENT) ORDER 1987 (No. 2047) [85p], made under the Dentists Act 1984 (c.24), s.49; operative on January 1, 1988; makes provision consequential on the termination of the reciprocal recognition of the qualifications of dentists by the Irish Republic and the U.K.

2402. Doctors—duties and liabilities—duty to inform—informed consent to surgery. See HAUGHIAN *v.* PAINE, §2603.

2403. Drugs—importation—parallel import product licences—imported drug infringing trade mark rights—whether infringement a relevant consideration in decision to issue parallel import licence. See R. *v.* SECRETARY OF STATE FOR SOCIAL SERVICES, *ex. p.* WELLCOME FOUNDATION, §3750.

2404. Drugs and medicinal products

MEDICINES CARBADOX PROHIBITION) (REVOCATION) ORDER 1987 (No. 2216) [45p], made under the Medicines Act 1968, ss.62, 129(4); operative on January 15, 1988; revokes S.I. 1986 No. 1368.

MEDICINES (PRODUCTS OTHER THAN VETERINARY DRUGS) (PRESCRIPTION ONLY) AMENDMENT ORDER 1987 (No. 674) [£1·60], made under the Medicines Act 1968 (c.67), ss.58(1)(4)(5), 129(4); operative on April 30, 1987; further amends S.I. 1983 No. 1212.

MEDICINES (PRODUCTS OTHER THAN VETERINARY DRUGS) (PRESCRIPTION ONLY) AMENDMENT (No. 2) ORDER 1987 (No. 1250) [85p], made under the Medicines Act 1968, ss.58(1)(4)(*a*), 129(4); operative on July 24, 1987; further amends S.I. 1983 No. 1212.

2405. Fees

MEDICINES (FEES) AMENDMENT REGULATIONS 1987 (No. 1439) [85p], made under the Medicines Act 1971 (c.69), s.1(1)(*a*); operative on September 1, 1987; deal with the fees payable in connection with licences granted and certificates issued under the Medicines Act 1968.

2406. General Medical Council

GENERAL MEDICAL COUNCIL (CONSTITUTION) AMENDMENT ORDER 1987 (No. 457) [45p], made under the Medical Act 1983 (c.54), s.1(2), Sched. 1, paras. 1, 4; operative on May 1, 1987; provides for 13 nominated members of the G.M.C.

GENERAL MEDICAL COUNCIL (CONSTITUTION OF FITNESS TO PRACTISE COMMITTEES) (AMENDMENT) RULES ORDER OF COUNCIL 1987 (No. 1120) [85p], made under the Medical Act 1983, Sched. 1, paras. 20–22; operative on August 1, 1987; amend S.I. 1986 No. 1390 so as to add three lay members to the Professional Conduct Committee.

GENERAL MEDICAL COUNCIL HEALTH COMMITTEE (PROCEDURE) (RULES) ORDER OF COUNCIL 1987 (No. 2174) [£2·90], made under the Medical Act 1983, Sched. 4, para. 1; operative on January 14, 1988; revoke and replace S.I. 1980 No. 859.

GENERAL MEDICAL COUNCIL (REGISTRATION (FEES) (AMENDMENT) REGULATIONS) ORDER OF COUNCIL 1987 (No. 102) [80p], made under the Medical Act 1983, s.32; operative on February 1, 1987; increase the fees payable to the General Medical Council by overseas qualified medical practitioners in respect of the scrutiny of applications from such practitioners for registration.

GENERAL MEDICAL COUNCIL (REGISTRATION (FEES) (AMENDMENT) REGULATIONS) (No. 2) ORDER OF COUNCIL 1987 (No. 2166) [85p], made under the Medical Act 1983, s.32; increase registration fees.

2407. General sale list

MEDICINES (PRODUCTS OTHER THAN VETERINARY DRUGS) (GENERAL SALE LIST) AMENDMENT ORDER 1987 (No. 910) [£1.30], made under the Medicines Act 1968 (c.67), ss.51, 129(4); operative on June 1, 1987; amends S.I. 1984 No. 769 by amending the general sale list.

2408. Licences

MEDICINES (EXEMPTIONS FROM LICENCES) (CARBADOX AND OLAQUINDOX) ORDER 1987 (No. 2217) [45p], made under the Medicines Act 1968 (c.67), s.15(3); operative on January 15, 1988; provides that in respect of medicinal products containing the specified substances, the licensing requirements of ss.7 and 8 of the 1968 Act apply.

2409. Medical practitioner—complaint by officer of family practitioner committee—whether supporting statutory declaration necessary

[General Medical Council Preliminary Proceedings Committee and Professional Conduct Committee (Procedure) Rules 1980 (S.I. 1980 No. 858), r.6(2).]

An officer of a family practitioner committee is a person acting in a public capacity, and therefore is not required by r.6(2) of the General Medical Council Preliminary Proceedings Committee and Professional Conduct Committee (Procedure) Rules 1980 to make a statutory declaration in support of a complaint made against a doctor to the General Medical Committee.

PRASAD *v.* GENERAL MEDICAL COUNCIL (1987) 131 S.J. 1456, P.C.

2410. Opticians

GENERAL OPTICAL COUNCIL (REGISTRATION AND ENROLMENT (AMENDMENT) RULES) ORDER OF COUNCIL 1987 (No. 1887) [45p], made under the Opticians Act 1958 (c.32), s.7; increases fees payable in connection with registration and enrolment.

2411. Pharmaceutical qualifications

PHARMACEUTICAL QUALIFICATIONS (EEC RECOGNITION) ORDER 1987 (No. 2202) [£1·30], made under the European Communities Act 1972 (c.68), s.2(2); operative on December 28, 1987; implements Council Directive 85/433/EEC as amended by Council Directive 85/584/EEC.

2412. Pharmaceutical rules—code of ethics—dispensing parallel import—reference to European Court of Justice

[E.E.C. Treaty, Arts. 30, 36, 177; N.H.S. (General Medical and Pharmaceutical Services) Regulations 1974 (S.I. 1974 No. 160) (as amended).]

A reference can be made without considering the merits of the case [*Rewe-Zentral A.G.* v. *Bundesmonopolverwaltung (No. 120/78)* [1979] C.L.Y. 1225, *De Kikvorsch Groothandel-Import-Export BV, Re (No. 94/82)* [1984] C.L.Y. 1456, *Officier van Justitie* v. *Koninklijke Kaasfabriek Eyssen BV (No. 53/80)* [1982] C.L.Y. 1275 considered).

R. *v.* PHARMACEUTICAL SOCIETY OF GREAT BRITAIN, *ex p.* ASSOCIATION OF PHARMACEUTICAL IMPORTERS, *The Times,* September 15, 1987, C.A.

2413. Pharmacies

MEDICINES (PHARMACIES) (APPLICATIONS FOR REGISTRATION AND FEES) AMENDMENT REGULATIONS 1987 (No. 2099) [45p], made under the Medicines Act 1968 (c.67), ss.75(1), 76(1)(2)(6), 129(2)(5), 132(1); operative on January 1, 1988; increase fees for the registration of the premises at which a retail pharmacy business is, or is to be, carried on.

2414. Registered homes—cancellation of registration—appeal from justice of the peace

[Registered Homes Act 1984 (c.23), ss.10, 11, 15(1).]

In seeking cancellation of registration the authority has to show to the civil standard of proof one or more of the grounds set out in the Act. Evidence to that effect could include matters not in the authority's written statement of reasons, and could include, on an appeal, matter arising after cancellation. Only evidence relevant to the matters set out in the Act could be adduced in support of the application.

LYONS *v.* EAST SUSSEX COUNTY COUNCIL, *The Times*, July 27, 1987, Farquharson J.

2415. Removal of patient from IVF list—considerations—ethical committee

Where a consultant took a patient's name off a list of patients waiting for artificial fertilization, it could not be suggested that no reasonable doctor would have done so, nor could the ethical committee of the hospital concerned be criticized for advising the consultant that she had to exercise her own judgment over the matters in dispute, even if such a committee's advice was susceptible to judicial review.

R. *v.* ETHICAL COMMITTEE OF ST. MARY'S HOSPITAL, *ex p.* HARRIOT, *The Times*, October 27, 1987, Schiemann J.

2416. Safety

MEDICINES (CHILD SAFETY) AMENDMENT REGULATIONS 1987 (No. 877) [45p], made under the Medicines Act 1968 (c.67), ss.87(1), 129(5); operative on June 4, 1987; further amends S.I. 1975 No. 2000 in relation to child-proof containers of aspirin and paracetamol by substituting for the existing British Standard a British Standard 6652.

2417. Serious professional misconduct—Professional Conduct Committee imposing conditions on practice—powers

[Medical Act 1983 (c.54), s.36(1)(iii), (4)(*b*).]

The Professional Conduct Committee of the General Medical Council has the power at any time to revoke or vary conditions imposed upon a practitioner's registration, and when considering such a course are entitled to have regard to the wider public interest.

Over a period of years F., a doctor, obtained large quantities of controlled drugs through the National Health Service which were used by his wife. The Professional Conduct Committee judged him guilty of serious professional misconduct, and directed that his registration should for three years be conditional upon his not prescribing or possessing any controlled drugs or prescription-only medicines. Although F was represented at the hearing by counsel the Committee did not indicate in advance that they were considering the imposition of such a condition. The chairman also indicated that the Committee would resume the hearing within the three year period, to consider whether any further action should be taken.

Held, dismissing the appeal that (i) whilst F could not compel the Committee to resume the hearing of his case he had a right to ask for it, whereupon the president of the G.M.C. would be bound to consider the request. If a resumed hearing were to be held the Committee would have full power to revoke or vary the condition; (ii) there had been no breach of natural justice in not informing F's counsel of the condition being considered. No court or tribunal was under any obligation to discuss with counsel every possible means of disposing of a case. The imposition of the condition was fully justified.

FINEGAN *v.* GENERAL MEDICAL COUNCIL [1987] 1 W.L.R. 121, P.C.

2418. Veterinary drugs

MEDICINES (EXEMPTIONS FROM RESTRICTIONS ON THE RETAIL SALE OR SUPPLY OF VETERINARY DRUGS) (AMENDMENT) ORDER 1987 (No. 1123) [£2·60], made under the Medicines Act 1968 (c.67), ss.57(1)(2)(2A), 129(4); operative on July 29, 1987; further amend S.I. 1985 No. 1823.

MEDICINES (EXEMPTIONS FROM RESTRICTIONS ON THE RETAIL SALE OR SUPPLY OF VETERINARY DRUGS) (AMENDMENT) (No. 2) ORDER 1987 (No. 1980) [£2·60], made under the Medicines Act 1968 (c.67), ss.1, 57(1)(2)(24), 129(4); operative on January 1, 1988; amends S.I. 1985 No. 1823.

MENTAL HEALTH

2419. Deportation—whether Secretary of State's powers of deportation circumscribed by the provisions of the Mental Health Act 1959. See R. *v.* IMMIGRATION APPEAL TRIBUNAL AND SECRETARY OF STATE FOR THE HOME DEPARTMENT, *ex p.* ALGHALI, §1947.

2420. Detention for treatment—compulsory detention—no suitable treatment

[Mental Health Act 1983 (c.20), ss.72, 145.]

A patient could be compulsorily detained even though no treatment was available to alleviate or cure his disorder since medical treatment included nursing and care and rehabilitation under medical supervision.

R. *v.* MERSEY MENTAL HEALTH REVIEW TRIBUNAL, *ex p.* D., *The Times*, April 13, 1987, D.C.

2421. Mental defective—test to determine whether a person was a defective—whether opinion of medical expert relevant

[Sexual Offences Act 1956 (c.69) (as substituted by s.127(*b*) Mental Health Act 1959 (c.72), and amended by s.65(1) and para. 29, Sched. 3, Mental Health (Amendment) Act 1982 (c.51)), s.45.]

In determining whether a person is a defective and thereby unable to give consent to an act which would otherwise be an assault, any "severe impairment of intelligence and social functioning" was to be measured against the standard of normal persons, and although medical expert evidence was admissible to establish the extent of a victim's intelligence, the opinion of a medical expert as to whether there was severe impairment had no real weight, if indeed it was admissible at all.

R. *v.* HALL (JOHN HAMILTON), *The Times,* July 15, 1987, C.A.

2422. Notification of parties—general rule

[Mental Health Act 1983 (c.20), s.96(1)(*k*); Court of Protection Rules 1984 (S.I. 1984 No. 2035), ss.18(1), 37.]

On an application by the receiver of a mental patient under s.96(1)(*k*) of the Mental Health Act 1983, the usual rule is that all persons who may be materially and adversely affected should be notified.

The receiver applied to the Court of Protection under s.96(1)(*k*) of the Mental Health Act 1983 for an order that a power of appointment vested in the patient should be exercised in a certain way. The receiver wished to avoid notifying the beneficiaries in order to avoid a family row.

Held, that in the absence of emergency, the normal rule was that all persons who might be materially and adversely affected should be notified: such persons would normally include beneficiaries under a previous will, or next of kin, or persons entitled in default of appointment, or any person for whom the patient might in normal circumstances be expected to make provision (*H.M.F., Re* [1975] C.L.Y. 3577 applied).

B. (COURT OF PROTECTION: NOTICE OF PROCEEDINGS), *Re* [1987] 1 W.L.R. 552, Millet J.

2423. Patient detained in hospital—application for discharge—powers of tribunal. See R. *v.* MENTAL HEALTH REVIEW TRIBUNAL, *ex p.* SECRETARY OF STATE FOR THE HOME DEPARTMENT, §48.

2424. Registered Establishments (Scotland) Act 1987 (c.40). See LOCAL GOVERNMENT, §2384.

2425. Review tribunal—discharge of patient—decision of review tribunal to defer conditional discharge—whether power to reconsider decision

[Mental Health Act 1983 (c.20), s.73(2)(7).]

Mental health tribunals have no power to reconsider their decisions: an order for the conditional discharge of a patient is a final order, the operation of which can be deferred only in order that the necessary arrangements can be made.

C applied to a mental health tribunal for the review of an order restricting his discharge from a mental hospital. In February 1985 the tribunal made the order, but deferred its operation until June 1985. The Secretary of State had not been informed of the date of the original hearing and applied for judicial review. Woolf J. refused the application on the ground that it was always open to the tribunal to review its decision. The Court of Appeal allowed an appeal by the Secretary of State.

Held, dismissing the appeal, that the Court of Appeal had correctly allowed the appeal by the Secretary of State. An order for conditional discharge under s.73(2) was a final order, the effect of which could be deferred only in order that practical arrangements could be made. A mental health tribunal had no power to review its decisions, from which it followed that the Secretary of State had had a right to be heard.

CAMPBELL *v.* SECRETARY OF STATE FOR THE HOME DEPARTMENT *sub nom.* R. *v.* OXFORD REGIONAL MENTAL HEALTH REVIEW TRIBUNAL, *ex p.* SECRETARY OF STATE FOR THE HOME DEPARTMENT [1987] 3 W.L.R. 522, H.L.

2426. Severe mental handicap—patient pregnant—abortion

[R.S.C., Ord. 15, r.16.]

The patient was 19 years of age, severely mentally handicapped and had become pregnant. It had been certified that an abortion was necessary and justified.

Held, that court had power to protect her medical advisers by granting a declaration that what would otherwise be prima facie an act of trespass was in fact lawful, and would do so (*Imperial Tobacco* v. *Att.-Gen.* [1980] C.L.Y. 1317, *Mellstrom* v. *Garner* [1970] C.L.Y. 2265, *Guaranty Trust Company of New York* v. *Hannay & Co.* [1915] 2 K.B. 536, *B. (A Minor) (Wardship: Sterilisation), Re* [1987] C.L.Y. 2533, *Wilson* v. *Pringle* [1986] C.L.Y. 3464, *Collins* v. *Wilcock* [1984] C.L.Y. 506 considered).

T., *Re;* T.v. T., *The Times,* July 11, 1987, Wood J.

MINING LAW

2427. Coal industry

COAL INDUSTRY (RESTRUCTURING GRANTS) ORDER 1987 (No. 770) [85p], made under the Coal Industry Act 1987 (c.3), s.3(2); operative on April 30, 1987; specifies eligible expenditure for the purposes of s.3 of the 1987 Act.

REDUNDANT MINEWORKERS AND CONCESSIONARY COAL (PAYMENTS SCHEMES) (AMENDMENT) ORDER 1987 (No. 1258) [85p], made under the Coal Industry Act 1977 (c.39), s.7(1), (7); operative July 27, 1987; makes consequential amendments to S.I.'s 1973 No. 1268, 1978 No. 415, 1983 No. 506, 1984 No. 457, 1986 No. 625 arising from changes to social security legislation made by the Social Security Act 1986.

2428. Coal Industry Act 1987 (c.3)

This Act changes the name of the National Coal Board to the British Coal Corporation. It makes new provision with respect to grants by the Secretary of State to the Corporation. In addition, this Act makes provision for securing further participation by organisations representing employees in the coal industry in the management of trusts and other bodies connected with that industry and in the management of superannuation schemes for such employees.

The Act received the Royal Assent on March 5, 1987.

2429. Compensation for subsidence—jurisdiction to award interest—date from which interest runs

[Coal Mining (Subsidence) Act 1957 (c.59), ss.1(2), 13(1).]

The Lands Tribunal is similar to an arbitrator and required, unless the contrary is expressed, to apply English law, from which it follows that the Tribunal may award interest on a claim for subsidence, from the date when all the damage had occurred.

K made a claim, on August 31, 1975, against the NCB in respect of subsidence. By December 31, 1975 all the damage had occurred, but the Board did not elect to pay compensation (rather than execute remedial works) until 1980.

Held, on the question of interest, that there was jurisdiction to award interest on K's claim. In essence the claim was for damages, the 1957 Act envisaging the Tribunal exercising the same powers as the county court and a consensually appointed arbitrator. Further interest would run from the date when the NCB failed to act "as soon as reasonably practicable" within s.1(2) of the 1957 Act, which on the facts was December 31, 1975.

KNIBB *v.* NATIONAL COAL BOARD [1986] 3 W.L.R. 895, C.A.

2430. Establishing negotiating machinery with union—duty to consult union—criteria

[Coal Industry Nationalisation Act 1946 (c.59), s.46(1).]

The National Coal Board is obliged by s.46(1) of the Coal Industry Nationalisation Act 1946 to set up negotiating machinery with a union if that union represents a substantial proportion of its workforce as a whole, and not only if it represents a substantial proportion of a particular class of employees;

R. *v.* NATIONAL COAL BOARD, *ex p.* THE UNION OF DEMOCRATIC MINEWORKERS, *The Independent,* April 2, 1987 D.C.

2431. Opencast coal

OPENCAST COAL (COMPULSORY RIGHTS AND RIGHTS OF WAY) (FORMS) REGULATIONS 1987 (No. 1915) [£2·60], made under the Opencast Coal Act 1958 (c.69), ss.4, 15A(1)(5)(*c*)(10), 49(1), the Acquisition of Land Act 1981 (c.67), ss.7(2), 10(2), 11(1),

12, 15, 22, 29; operative on December 11, 1987; prescribe the form of certain orders, notices and advertisements required under the 1958 Act.

OPENCAST COAL (RATE OF INTEREST ON COMPENSATION) ORDER 1987 (No. 700) [45p], made under the Opencast Coal Act 1958 (c.69), ss.35 (8), 49(4); operative on May 1, 1987; decreases the rate of interest to 10¼% payable on compensation in certain circumstances.

MINORS

2432. Access—access to two children of three—access to third child refused—desirability of order

There were three children. The mother had custody and the father applied for access. The judge found that he had sexually interfered with the eldest child. Access to that child was refused but the father was granted supervised access to the two younger children. The mother appealed.

Held, that all three children had to live together as a family unit under the mother. Obviously, the father could not be allowed access to the eldest child and any access to the younger children had to be under supervision in neutral surroundings. That would not be conducive to developing the father's relationship with the two children. Allowing access to two out of three children was undesirable—it would inevitably create tension and problems explaining the position to the children. The order for access would be discharged.

S. *v.* S., *The Times*, June 19, 1987, C.A.

2433. Access—allegation of sexual abuse of child by father—no physical evidence—interview by sexual abuse clinic—leading and hypothetical questions—use of dolls—criticism of technique

On the husband's application for access, the wife alleged that he had sexually abused the child. The child had been physically examined by a doctor but no evidence of abuse had been found. When the father heard of the allegations, he reported the matter to the police. A health visitor referred the child to a sexual abuse clinic where she attended a "diagnostic interview." Before the interview, the interviewers discussed the allegations of sexual abuse with the mother in the presence of the child. The consultant psychiatrist's report stated that the girl was able to show with sexually explicit dolls that the father had attempted to abuse her. The interview had been recorded on video but that had been erased. The interview technique involved leading and hypothetical questions put to the child.

Held, that the child made no spontaneous complaint during the interview. Hypothetical and leading questions were used extensively, after the allegations had already been discussed in front of the child. No attempt was made to seek the father's account—his conduct on hearing the allegations and the daughter's attitude to him made it unlikely that any abuse had taken place. No evidential weight was to be attached to the "diagnostic interview"—the inferences drawn were probably wrong. In this case the interview did positive damage. Access would be allowed (*E. (A Minor) (Child Abuse: Evidence), Re* [1987] C.L.Y. 2471, *G. (Minors) (Child Abuse: Evidence), Re* [1987] C.L.Y. 2470, *N. (Minors) (Child Abuse: Evidence), Re* [1987] C.L.Y. 2472 referred to).

C. *v.* C. (CHILD ABUSE: EVIDENCE) [1987] 1 F.L.R. 321, Hollis J.

2434. Access—application by parent for access order—application by local authority to free children for adoption—access application adjourned pending determination of freeing application—whether right to adjourn access proceedings

The local authority obtained care orders in respect of two children and, after a period of limited access, terminated the mother's access by a notice of termination. The mother applied by way of complaint for an access order under s.12C(1) of the Child Care Act 1980. Subsequently an application was made to the County Court for an order to free the children for adoption under the Children Act 1975, s.14. When the mother's complaint came before the magistrates, the local authority applied for an adjournment on the basis that the hearing of the application for the freeing order was imminent as was a placement with prospective adopters. The mother opposed the application for an adjournment but the magistrate, having heard submissions but no evidence adjourned the complaint *sine die*. The mother appealed.

Held, that the adoption court in reaching its decision had to consider access as well as the future relationship between mother and child. Speed was of importance. It was desirable where possible for one tribunal to hear all matters. The justices had exercised their discretion properly (*Southwark London Borough Council* v. *H.* [1985] C.L.Y. 2191 distinguished).

C. *v.* BERKSHIRE COUNTY COUNCIL (1987) 17 Fam.Law 265, D.C.

2435. Access—care order made in respect of child as older brother had died from non-accidental injuries—child remained with parents—injury inflicted on child—child removed and placed with foster-parents

The parents had two children. The second child was the subject of a place of safety order because the first child died from non-accidental injury. The second child was allowed to remain with the parents until the child was found with serious non-accidental injuries. The child was placed with foster-parents in 1981. The parents applied for access to the child after adoption proceedings had broken down. Having seen and heard the parents the magistrates stated that the parents were changed people, who needed expert counselling and that although access would be initially confusing for the child after four years away from the parents, it would eventually be in the child's best interests. The magistrates granted access. On appeal by the local authority.

Held, that having regard to the dead child and the injuries inflicted on the second child, there were no circumstances in which the parents could be considered suitable parents for the child. The magistrates had not made the child's interests their paramount consideration—it was not in the child's interests to have contact with the parents—the attitude and feelings of the parents (even if they had changed) were not relevant. They had not seen the child for four years—the child would suffer substantial disturbance by seeing them again, particularly having regard to the child's injuries four years ago. There should be no access granted to the parents.

COVENTRY CITY COUNCIL *v.* T. [1986] 2 F.L.R. 301, Ewbank J.

2436. Access—claim made for children's transport fares in respect of access—whether an "exceptional need"—Supplementary Benefit (Single Payments) Regulations 1981. See VAUGHAN *v.* SOCIAL SECURITY ADJUDICATION OFFICER, §3506.

2437. Access—local authority disregarding order to rehabilitate—whether access terminated

C was a ward of court in the care and control of L, the Local Authority. The Court of Appeal ordered that there should be a gradual rehabilitation of M with C, her mother. L deliberately disregarded this order, and as a result the relationship between M and C degenerated irretrievably. M sought access to C, and this was refused. M appealed.

Held, that despite L's flouting of the law, M should no longer be allowed access to C.

D. (A MINOR), *Re The Times,* February 17, 1987, C.A.

2438. Access—no physical access—leave to appeal—extension of time

[Supreme Court Act 1981 (c.54), s.18(1)(*h*)(ii).]

At the hearing of F's application for access to his two children, the judge had made no order except that F should be allowed to correspond with the children by letters and cards. F was refused leave to appeal. He applied for leave to appeal out of time.

Held, allowing F's application, that an order which deprived an applicant of any physical access to a minor was an order which deprived the applicant of all access. It followed that leave to appeal was not required by virtue of s.18(1)(*h*)(ii). As there was an acceptable excuse for the delay in launching the substantive appeal it was appropriate to grant an extension of time to appeal against the order. (*Palata Investments* v. *Burt and Sinfield* [1985] C.L.Y. 2590 followed).

ALLETTE *v.* ALLETTE (1986) 2 F.L.R. 427, C.A.

2439. Access—sexual molestation by father

The judge found (on a balance of probabilities) that there was sexual molestation of the child, a girl aged two and a half years, by F and that she would be exposed to unnecessary risk if she were allowed to be with F. However, the judge stated that it would not follow from that that F should not see the child and referring to aspects of the case which were to F's credit, the judge held that the case was a proper one for continued access but on much fewer occasions provided such access was always supervised. M appealed.

Held, allowing the appeal, that in a case of this nature it would be wrong to allow access to continue. The judge erred in exercising his discretion. There should be no access in favour of the father (*G.* v. *G.* [1985] C.L.Y. 2594 explained). Appeal from Lincoln J.

R. (A MINOR), *Re* May 19, 1986 (C.A.T. No. 492).

2440. Access—welfare report—"conciliation method"—parties not visited at home but seen jointly at welfare officer's office—whether suitable method of providing report

The parents, who were not married, separated. The child stayed with the mother and the father applied for access. The mother opposed his application and the magistrates' court requested a welfare report. The court welfare officer adopted a "conciliation method" that involved counselling sessions with the two parents jointly. The attempt at conciliation failed. The welfare officer did not see the parties separately. The report concluded that there were no reasons to deny the father access. The magistrates, having considered the report and evidence from both parents, found that the father was genuinely concerned for the child and that access should not be denied. The mother appealed.

Held, that the "conciliation method" was entirely unsuitable. It confused the duty to conciliate with the duty to prepare a report. The report having been ordered, the parties were placed under pressure to conciliate which should be a voluntary step. In the preparation of a report, it was proper practice for the officer to see the parties separately in their own homes, to see the child and to report on the factual situation, making recommendation where appropriate. In this case, although the welfare report was unsatisfactory, it contained all the relevant information for the magistrates, who were entitled to reach the decision that they reacted.

CLARKSON *v.* WINKLEY (1987) 151 J.P.N. 526, Butler-Sloss J.

2441/2. Adoption—access by natural parents

The court should not stand in the way of an agreement that the natural parents should have access to the adopted child if it was in the child's best interests, however unusual such an order might be.

W. (A. MINOR), *Re, The Times*, June 22, 1987, C.A.

2443. Adoption—applicants bringing up child as own—mother consenting—authority preferring custodianship—considerations

[Children Act 1975 (c.72), s.37(1).]

An adoption order should be made in preference to custodianship unless the court is satisfied that custodianship would offer greater benefit than adoption.

About six months after his birth a child was placed with the applicants for fostering. The applicants had raised the child as their own and, with the mother's consent, applied for an adoption order. The local authority recommended, and the court made a custodianship order under s.37(1) of the Act instead. The applicants appealed.

Held, allowing the appeal, that before making a custodianship order under the section, the court had to be satisfied it offered a greater benefit than an adoption order; where adoption was preferable as matters were evenly balanced an adoption order should be made.

S. (A MINOR) (ADOPTION OR CUSTODIANSHIP), *Re* [1987] 2 W.L.R. 977, C.A.

2444. Adoption—application by natural parent—exclusion of other natural parent

The parents' marriage was dissolved and custody of the child was awarded to the mother. The mother remarried and she and the stepfather (who later died) applied to adopt the child. It was argued that the child had strong negative views of the father and adoption would make the child more secure by removing the possibility of the father seeking access or custody. The *guardian ad litem* was of the view that adoption was not in the child's best interests.

Held, that s.11 of the Children Act 1975 stated that the parent who wished to adopt a natural child must show some reason justifying the exclusion of the other natural parent. Here, regardless of the adoption question, the child would remain in the mother's custody—there was no prospect of access by the father against the child's wishes in the foreseeable future. There was no compelling reason why the order should be made.

C. (A MINOR) (ADOPTION BY PARENT), *Re* (1986) 16 Fam. Law 360, Crewe County Ct.

2445. Adoption—attendance at court by minor—whether necessary

[Adoption Rules 1984 (S.I. 1984 No. 265), r.23(4), (5).]

The child need not attend personally before the judge if the evidence of the guardian ad litem clearly showed that the child understood and supported the application.

P. (MINORS), *Re, The Times*, August 1, 1987, C.A.

2446. Adoption—by foster parents—mother's agreement withheld—mother suffering from mental disorder—whether incapable of withholding—whether consent unreasonably withheld

The foster parents with whom the child had been living for four years applied for adoption. The child had come from an unstable background and had improved dramatically when placed with the foster parents. The child showed no desire to return to the natural mother. It was accepted that it would be in the child's best interest to remain with the applicants. The mother, who suffered from a mental disorder within the meaning of the Mental Health Act 1983, was incapable of understanding the meaning and implication of adoption. She would not give her consent. The applicants asked for her agreement to be dispensed with on the basis that either she was incapable of withholding her consent in that she was incapable of giving agreement or that her consent was being unreasonably withheld.

Held, that the court was required by s.12(1) of the Children Act 1975 to investigate where consent *had* been given, whether it had been fully and freely given—it was not concerned with the contrary position where agreement was being withheld. The reference in s.12(1) to withholding agreement did not relate to incapacity. There is no jurisdiction to consider whether the mother is capable of withholding her consent. In this case the child's welfare required that she remained with the foster parents—accordingly the mother's agreement would be dispensed with on the grounds that it was being unreasonably withheld.

L. (A MINOR) (ADOPTION: PARENTAL AGREEMENT), *Re* [1987] 1 F.L.R. 400, Lincoln J.

2447. Adoption—dispensing with parents' consent—agreement to custodianship order—whether unreasonable refusal to consent to adoption

[Children Act 1975 (c.72), ss.12(1), 37(1)(2).]

Where a child's natural parents refuse to consent to adoption, but would be willing to agree to a custodianship order, that could amount to an unreasonable refusal to consent to the adoption if the child's security was likely to be threatened thereby.

Per curiam: (i) the burden lies upon anyone objecting to an adoption order to show that a custodianship order would be more appropriate; (ii) because so much depends upon the discretion of the judge, it would generally be very difficult to appeal a decision on the ground that a custodianship order would be more suitable than an adoption order.

A, now aged six, had been with foster parents since she was five months old; during that time she had had no contact with her natural parents. The foster parents applied to adopt her, but the natural parents refused to consent. They indicated, however, that they would be prepared to agree to a custodianship order. The judge concluded that adoption was in the best interests of A, and made the order.

Held, on appeal that that decision could not be criticised. It was obvious that the making of a custodianship order would pose a threat to the future security of the child, so that the decision of the judge could not be attacked.

A. (A MINOR) (ADOPTION: PARENTAL CONSENT), *Re* [1987] 1 W.L.R. 153, C.A.

2448. Adoption—illegitimate child—alternative of custodianship

[Children Act 1975 (c.72), ss.12, 37(2).]

An order for custodianship may be made on an application for adoption where it is more appropriate to do so. This can only be done where the requirements of s.12 are satisfied or dispensed with. (*A (A Minor) (Adoption), Re* [1985] F.L.R. 519 considered).

R. (A MINOR) (ADOPTION OR CUSTODIANSHIP), *Re* (1987) 151 J.P.N. 175, Sheldon J.

2449. Adoption—natural parents objecting to adoption—custodianship order in favour of proposed adopters instead—whether consent unreasonably withheld

[Children Act 1975 (c.72), ss.12(1), 37(2).]

The court can only make a custodianship order once the requirements of s.12 of the Children Act 1975 are satisfied, so that where the natural parents' consent has neither been given nor dispensed with there is no jurisdiction to make the order.

M's foster parents applied for an adoption order in respect of her, but the natural parents refused their consent. The judge concluded that their refusal was not unreasonable as they had indicated agreement to a custodianship order being made.

Held, that the judge had had no jurisdiction to make a custodianship order, which could be made only where the requirements of s.12 of the 1975 Act had been satisfied. As there had been neither consent from the natural parents, nor had their consent been dispensed with, there was no jurisdiction. The judge's decision having been based upon an erroneous view of the law, the Court of Appeal could reconsider the merits of the matter. It was clear that no reasonable parent would have refused consent to the adoption, so the natural parents' consent would be dispensed with. The matter would, however, have to be remitted to the judge for the personal attendance before him of the prospective adoptive parents and the child.

M. (A MINOR) (CUSTODIANSHIP: JURISDICTION), *Re* [1987] 1 W.L.R. 162, C.A.

2450. Adoption—surrogacy agreement—payment made to mother—whether unlawful

[Adoption Act 1968 (c.5). s.50(1)(3), as amended by Children Act 1975 (c.72) s. 108(1), Sched. 3, paras. 21(2)(4), 34.]

Payments made to the mother in a surrogacy agreement may not be unlawful as being contrary to s.50(1) of the 1958 Adoption Act.

Mr. and Mrs. A made an agreement with Mrs. B that if she became pregnant following intercourse with Mr. A she would hand over the child to Mr. and Mrs. A to be brought up by them. The parties agreed that the As should pay Mrs. B a sum of money. The child was handed over two days after birth, and the As applied to adopt the child. Mrs. B consented to the adoption. The question of whether there had been a payment in consideration of the adoption arose.

Held, making the adoption order, the payments made were not payments or rewards contrary to s.50(1) of the 1958 Act, even if they had been the court had jurisdiction to authorise them retroactively.

ADOPTION APPLICATION (PAYMENT FOR ADOPTION) *Re* 1987 3 W.L.R. 31, Latey J.

2451. Adoption—test on application—foster parents

[Children Act 1975 (c.72), s.3.]

A foster parent's adamant refusal to acquaint a child, who had lived with her virtually since birth, with the fact that she was not her mother did not justify a judge in dismissing an application to adopt.

S. (A MINOR) (ADOPTION), *Re, The Times*, August 26, 1987, C.A.

2452. Adoption—whether mother unreasonably withholding consent—child with foster-parents of different ethnic origin

The child was born to a West Indian mother and placed, by private arrangement, with a white family. The mother visited the child regularly but the visits died out. The applicants suggested adopting the child, whereupon the mother decided to remove the child. The applicants instituted wardship proceedings and sought leave to institute adoption proceedings, which the mother opposed.

Held, that the mother's agreement would not be dispensed with unless it had been unreasonably withheld. Her hope that the child would eventually live with her was unrealistic and contrary to the best interests of the child. However, there were a number of other factors to consider; the child's different ethnic origin and the fact that the applicants were Jehovah's Witnesses also had to be considered. It could not be said that the mother was acting unreasonably. The application for adoption therefore failed as did the application for a custodianship order. The best course for the child would be for wardship to be preserved and an order for care and control to the applicants (with two visits per annum for the mother) would be made.

J., *Re* (1987) 17 Fam. Law 88, Sheldon J.

2453. Adoption—whether mother unreasonably withholding consent—test

The question of whether a mother is unreasonably withholding consent to the adoption of her child should be considered objectively, not subjectively.

R. (A MINOR) (ADOPTION), *Re* (1987) 151 J.P.N. 142, C.A.

2454. Adoption proceedings—transfer of business to High Court. See PRACTICE, §3117.

2455. Assumption of parental rights by local authority—application to determine resolution—application for access

After the breakdown of the marriage, the two children stayed with the father, then with neighbours and were finally placed into voluntary care with the local authority and were placed with short-term foster parents. The local authority passed a resolution under s.3 of the Child Care Act 1980 (c.5), assuring parental rights. The mother applied for that resolution to be determined and, after the authority served notice terminating access, she applied for access. On the first hearing the justices held that there were no grounds for the authority to assume parental rights but in the interests of the children, refused to determine the resolution. The application for access heard at a different court was dismissed.

Held, on appeal against both decisions, that the court had to decide whether both sets of justices were plainly wrong against the paramount consideration of the children's welfare. A choice had to be made between rehabilitation and a permanent placement.

Although the mother had been a good mother, she had not looked after them for some years. The children needed to settle down. The 1980 Act say that the justices "may" determine the resolution. Their decision not to do so could not be faulted. As access would only be beneficial if leading to rehabilitation and the children would never satisfactorily be returned to their parents, it followed that both appeals should be dismissed.

K. *v.* DEVON COUNTY COUNCIL (1987) 17 Fam. Law 348, D.C.

2456. Care proceedings—child born with drug dependency—mother's conduct during pregnancy

[Children and Young Persons Act 1969 (c.54), s.1(2)(*a*).]

The juvenile court when considering whether a child's development has been avoidably neglected or his health impaired within s.1(2) of the Children and Young Persons Act 1969 is entitled in the case of a new born baby to look at the conduct of the mother during pregnancy.

A mother who was a drug addict continued to take them during her pregnancy knowing that they could affect the foetus. The father was also an addict. The child was born prematurely and suffering from drug dependency. The local authority sought a care order pursuant to s.1 of the Act of 1969 on the grounds that the child's proper development was being avoidably prevented or her health was being avoidably impaired. The child had never been given into its parents' care. It was not disputed that the child needed care and control which she was not likely to receive unless a care order was made. The court made a care order, and her guardian ad litem appealed to the Divisional Court of the Family Division which held, allowing the appeal, that events occurring before the child's birth were irrelevant for the purposes of s.1(2)(*a*) of the Act. The Court of Appeal allowed an appeal by the local authority. The child's further appeal to the House of Lords was dismissed.

Held, that the expression "is being" avoidably prevented or avoidably impaired with regard to a child's development, health or treatment, related to a continuing situation or state of affairs. The time at which the court had to consider whether a continuing situation of one of these three kinds existed was the moment immediately before the process of protection started. In considering whether a continuing situation existed, the court had to look at the situation both as it was at that point of time, and as it had been in the past. How far back it should look depended on the facts of the case. It should also look to the future but only in conjunction with the present and past in the sense of asking whether, if the process of protection had not been started, the situation would have been likely to continue. S.1(2) had to be given a broad and liberal construction in furtherance of the legislative purpose of protecting the child. The juvenile court were therefore entitled to look back at the time before the child was born when the situations which caused the prevention of her development or the impairment of her health had been caused, and the possibility of their avoidance had existed, and to conclude that a care order should be made. (*Essex County Council* v. *T.L.R. and K.B.R.* [1979] C.L.Y. 1790; *F.* v. *Suffolk County Council* [1981] C.L.Y. 1762; and *M.* v. *Westminster City Council* [1984] C.L.Y. 2206 considered). The three situations in s.1(2)(*a*) are to be regarded as alternatives, though in many cases any two or all three may co-exist. The mere fact of a past avoidable prevention of proper development or impairment of health is not sufficient to fulfil the condition of "is being" even if there are symptoms or effects that persist or manifest themselves later. There has to be a continuum in existence at the relevant time.

D. (A MINOR) *Re* [1986] 3 W.L.R. 1080, H.L.

2457. Care proceedings—child living in grandparents' home—no notice served on grandparents—grandparents take out wardship summons—juvenile court makes care order—whether wardship should continue

The mother and child were living with the child's grandparents and later at a hostel for homeless families. The child suffered severe non-accidental injuries and the N.S.P.C.C. commenced care proceedings. Pursuant to r.14 of the Magistrates' Courts (Children and Young Persons) Rules 1970 (S.I. 1970 No. 1792), notice of the proceedings was served on the mother and local authority but not on the grandparents. Interim care orders committed the child to the care of the local authority pending the full hearing. At the full hearing the grandparents told the juvenile court that they had issued an originating summons in wardship for the child to be made a ward of court with care and control vested in themselves. The juvenile court continued with the hearing and made a full care order. The grandparents' wardship application came before the judge who ordered that the wardship should continue with interim care and control to the local authority. The local authority appealed. At the appeal the grandparents contended that the decision of the juvenile court in the care proceeding was invalid or questionable as they had not been served with proper notice of the proceedings.

Held, that (1) the care order, being made by a court of competent jurisdiction was *prima facie* valid; (2) the care order affected the status of the child, giving the local authority certain powers and duties. The child and the authority should know where they stood and should not be left in limbo depending on whether or not the care order was set aside; (3) the care order stood until quashed by a court of competent jurisdiction; (4) the general principle was that a court would not exercise its powers in wardship over a child for whom the local authority had assumed responsibility under its statutory powers.

Accordingly, where a place of safety order, an interim and a full care order had been made, the court should not exercise its wardship jurisdiction. If there had been any irregularity in the failure to serve notice of the care proceedings on the grandparents the remedy lay by way of judicial review not wardship proceedings. Notice of the proceedings were to be served upon the person who had actual custody of the child. That meant actual possession of the person of the child—which was a question of fact (*A.* v. *Liverpool City Council* [1981] C.L.Y. 1796, *W. (A Minor) (Care Proceedings: Wardship), Re* [1985] C.L.Y. 2250 and *D. M. (A Minor) (Wardship: Jurisdiction), Re* [1987] C.L.Y. 2518 applied; *E. (A Minor) (Wardship: Court's Duty), Re* [1983] C.L.Y. 2469, *F. (Infants) (Adoption Order: Validity), Re* [1977] C.L.Y. 1922, *M. (An Infant), Re* [1960] C.L.Y. 1540, *Skinner* v. *Carter* (1948) C.L.C. 4852 and *W.* v. *Shropshire County Council* [1986] C.L.Y. 2216 discussed; *D.* v. *X City Council* [1986] 2 F.L.R. 122, *L. (A. C.) (An Infant), Re* [1971] C.L.Y. 5852 not followed).

S. (A MINOR) (CARE PROCEEDINGS: WARDSHIP SUMMONS), *Re* [1987] 1 F.L.R. 479, C.A.

2458. Care proceedings—interim order—attendance at court by minor

[Children and Young Persons Act 1969 (c.54), s.22(1), (2), (3) (as amended).]

On a proper construction of the Act the three subsections should be read together so that the juvenile court has power to direct that a legally represented minor need not be brought before the court for an uncontested application for a further interim care order.

NORTHAMPTONSHIRE COUNTY COUNCIL *v.* H., *The Times,* November 7, 1987, Sheldon J.

2459. Care proceedings—interim order—right to call evidence

[Children and Young Persons Act 1969 (c.54), s.2(10); Magistrates Courts (Children and Young Persons) Rules 1970 (S.I. 1970 No. 1792) r.14B.]

The parties must be allowed to call and to cross-examine witnesses in proceedings for an interim care order. (*R.* v. *Croydon Juvenile Court, ex p. N.* [1987] C.L.Y. 2462 considered).

R. *v.* BIRMINGHAM CITY JUVENILE COURT, *ex p.* BIRMINGHAM CITY COUNCIL, *The Times,* September 3, 1987, C.A.

2460. Care proceedings—judicial review—decision not to rehabilitate—unproven allegations against parents

[Children and Young Persons Act 1969 (c.54), s.1; Child Care Act 1980 (c.5), s.10.]

The Court would quash on judicial review a decision by a local authority, which had a care order on a child, not to proceed with the rehabilitation of the child to a parent where the grounds for not proceeding were unproven allegations against the parent which had not been investigated by the local authority and where the parent had not had an opportunity to answer the allegations.

In two separate cases, heard together because of their common features, two local authorities had care orders over children made under s.1(2)(*a*) of the Children and Young Persons Act 1969. In the first, the local authority were contemplating returning the children to the father's care when the mother alleged unnatural sexual practices between the father and a young boy. Without giving the father any opportunity to refute the allegations and without further investigation, the local authority decided not to proceed with the proposed rehabilitation. In the second case, a child placed with his mother on a home trial basis was taken from her after allegations by neighbours which were alleged to be not properly investigated.

Held, that the local authority had a duty as a matter of natural justice to investigate such allegations and to give the parent the opportunity to refute them. The second application was dismissed on its facts, but in the case of the father, C, the local authority's decision not to proceed with rehabilitation was quashed on judicial review (dicta of Lord Scarman in *W. (A Minor) (Wardship: Jurisdiction), Re* [1985] C.L.Y. 2255/6, of Lord Roskill in *Council of Civil Service Unions* v. *Minister for the Civil Service* [1985]

C.L.Y. 12 and of Macpherson J. in *R.* v. *Monopolies and Mergers Commission, ex p. Brown (Matthew)* [1987] C.L.Y. 3736 applied).

R. *v.* BEDFORDSHIRE COUNTY COUNCIL, *ex p.* C.; R. *v.* HERTFORDSHIRE COUNTY COUNCIL, *ex p.* B. (1987) 85 L.G.R. 218, Ewbank J.

2461. Care proceedings—late service of welfare reports—breach of natural justice

Prior to the hearing of care proceedings concerning three children, aged 11, 10 and 7, whom F had continued to look after for about three years following the death of M, F's solicitors had tried unsuccessfully to obtain detailed particulars of the allegations made against F. On the morning of the hearing copies of the welfare and guardian ad litem's response were served. These contained serious allegations concerning F's care of the children. The justices refused an application for an adjournment and proceeded with the hearing. Care orders were made. F appealed by way of judicial review to quash the orders.

Held, allowing the application, that the importance of early delivery of reports in children's cases was particularly important where, as here, such reports contained substantial criticisms or allegations against parents or others involved in the proceedings. Applying the principles of natural justice F was entitled to know the way in which the case was made against him with sufficient particularity to enable him to present his case. It would have been quite simple for the local authority to have set out the heads of complaint in a letter or even the contents of their witness statements by prior disclosure. In the circumstances the justices had erred in refusing an adjournment and the care orders would be set aside (*Kanda* v. *Government of the Federation of Malaya* [1962] C.L.Y. 254 applied; *A.R.* v. *Avon County Council* [1985] C.L.Y. 2219 and *Edwards* v. *Edwards* [1986] C.L.Y. 2187 considered).

R. *v.* WEST MALLING JUVENILE COURT, *ex p.* K. (1986) 2 F.L.R. 405, Wood J.

2462. Care proceedings—opposed application for interim care order—whether evidence necessary

The mother formed a friendship with a man with whom she left the child on occasions. The child sustained a number of injuries which were alleged not to be accidental. The local authority commenced care proceedings. The magistrates' court made an order that the parents should not represent the child's interests appointing a *guardian ad litem.* The authority sought an adjournment and an interim care order which the mother opposed. Without hearing evidence, the magistrates made the interim care order in favour of the authority. The mother applied for judicial review on the basis that the magistrates had failed to act judicially or to consider the best interests of the child by considering all courses open to them. She also argued that she had the rights of a parent or guardian under r.14B of the Magistrates' Court (Children and Young Persons) Rules 1970 (S.I. 1970 No. 1792), as "in the course of proceedings" meant from the moment the child was brought into court.

Held, that once the application for the interim order was opposed, the magistrates were obliged to hear evidence. They could not make the order without doing so. Once an authority calls evidence, r.14B applies provided that the grounds on which the interim order is sought involve allegations against the parent (as in this case). If a parent does not oppose an interim order, it is not incumbent on magistrates to hear evidence, provided they had sufficient reliable material on which they could make the interim order but were not in a position to decide what order to make. In order to preserve the status quo in the child's interests, as the case was due to go before the magistrates again, the order would not be quashed (*H.* v. *Southwark London Borough Council* [1982] C.L.Y. 1927, *R.* v. *Birmingham Juvenile Court, ex p. P. and S.* [1984] C.L.Y. 2205, *R.* v. *Gravesham Juvenile Court, ex p. B.* [1982] C.L.Y. 1928 and *R.* v. *Milton Keynes Juvenile Court, ex p. R.* [1979] C.L.Y. 1791 referred to).

R. *v.* CROYDON JUVENILE COURT, *ex p.* N. [1987] 1 F.L.R. 252, Garland J.

2463. Care proceedings—order that parents not to be treated as representing child—solicitor appointed for child—whether *functus officio* at end of juvenile court proceedings—right of appeal by parents and child

The local authority applied for the discharge of a supervision order and the substitution of a care order. Prior to that hearing, the clerk made an order that the parents should not be treated as representing the child's interests—there being a possible conflict of interests. The order, made under s.32(4) of the Children and Young Persons Act 1969, did not appoint a *guardian ad litem* but legal aid was granted to the child and a solicitor appointed to act for her. The parents were not given an opportunity to make representations prior to the order and were not told of it until an appeal against the care order was made. That appeal went to the Crown Court where, at a preliminary hearing, the local authority argued that the parents had no right to appeal because of the clerk's order. The parents sought judicial review of the order and the appeal was adjourned generally. The basis of the parents' application for judicial review was that the order was a judicial act, they had not been given an opportunity to be heard, nor had they been notified of the making of the order and no reasonable court would have failed to appoint a *guardian ad litem* as, at the end of the juvenile court proceedings the appointed solicitor would be *functus officio* and the child would be left without any right of appeal.

Held, that there had been no breach of the *audi alteram partem* rule—the clerk had to act in the best interests of the child. There was no requirement that the parents should be notified of the making of such an order (although for the avoidance of doubt they should be notified). There was an effective avenue of appeal from the care order as the appointed solicitor would not be *functus officio*—the terms of the legal aid order obliged him to consider and lodge an appeal, if necessary. This was not an obvious case for a *guardian ad litem* and the order was not one that no reasonable court could have made (*Associated Provincial Picture Houses* v. *Wednesbury Corporation* (1948) C.L.C. 8107, *A-R* v. *Avon County Council* [1985] C.L.Y. 2219, *R.* v. *Manchester Stipendiary Magistrate, ex p. Hill* [1982] C.L.Y. 1963, *Southwark London Borough* v. *Clarke* [1982] C.L.Y. 2033 referred to).

R. *v.* PLYMOUTH JUVENILE COURT *ex p.* F. AND F. [1987] 1 F.L.R. 169, Waterhouse J.

2464. Care proceedings—primary condition in s.1(2)(*bb*) of Children and Young Persons Act 1969 treated as preliminary issue—proper procedure

A man who had convictions for indecent assault on children went to live with the mother and her children and two further children were born while he was there. He then reverted to his earlier behaviour, indecently assaulting one of the children. Subsequently he left to work abroad and, on one occasion when he returned the mother obtained an injunction barring him from her home. The local authority fearing that eventually he would return to live with the mother brought care proceedings. The primary ground alleged was s.1(2)(*bb*) of the Children and Young Persons Act 1969—that the condition specified in (*a*) of the subsection would be satisfied if a person convicted of an offence listed in Sched. 1 was or might become a member of the household. The question whether if the man were to become a member of the household it was probable that the childrens' development would be prevented or neglected and whether the children were in need of care or control they were unlikely to receive unless a care order was made, was treated as a preliminary issue by the magistrates. The social workers responsible for the social enquiry report were only asked questions relating to the preliminary issue—no questions were asked about the mother's determination not to allow the man back into her home, nor was the confidence of the guardian *ad litem* in her determination investigated. The justices decided that the man was not a member of the same household and there was no prospect that he would be and so dismissed the application. The local authority appealed.

Held, that justices have a limited jurisdiction to control their own processes so long as they did not contravene any statutory provision, regulation or rule. As there was no such prohibition in this case there was no absolute rule that they could not treat one issue as a preliminary issue. However, only rarely would such a course be justified. The procedure adopted in this case was improper and unsatisfactory and may have deprived the justices of important evidence. However, having regard to all the circumstances of the case the conclusion reached was correct. It would not be overlooked that the mother had already on one occasion obtained an injunction to keep the man out of the home. The decision would not be interfered with (*F.* v. *Suffolk County Council* [1981] C.L.Y. 1762, *R.* v. *Gravesham Juvenile Court, ex p. B.* [1982] C.L.Y. 1921 and *R.* v. *Milton Keynes Justices, ex p. R.* [1979] C.L.Y. 1791 referred to).

CROYDON LONDON BOROUGH *v.* N. [1987] 2 F.L.R. 61, Sheldon J.

2465. Care proceedings—report of guardian *ad litem*—availability

[Magistrates' Courts (Children and Young Persons) Rules 1970 (S.I. 1970 No. 1792 (L32)), rr. 14A, 21.]

The effect of rr.14A and 21 of the Magistrates' Courts (Children and Young Persons) Rules 1970 is that a guardian *ad litem* should make his report available to all parties before the hearing of care proceedings in a magistrates' court.

R. *v.* EPSOM JUVENILE COURT, *ex p.* G. *The Times*, October 29, 1987, Ewbank J.

2466. Care proceedings—resolution contested—report by *guardian ad litem*—whether independent social worker should see report

[Magistrates' Courts (Children and Young Persons) Rules (S.I. 1970 No. 1792), r.21(D)(1).]

A local authority passed a resolution assuming parental rights over C, and later sought an order that that resolution should not lapse. F, C's father, objected. He obtained permission for an independent social worker to see the report prepared for the justices by the *guardian ad litem*.

Held, that under r.21(D)(1) of the Magistrates' Courts (Children and Young Persons) Rules, F himself had the right to see the *guardian ad litem's report.* The justices had jurisdiction to control their own proceedings, and had properly exercised their discretion in allowing the independent social worker to see the report.

R. *v.* SUNDERLAND JUVENILE COURT, *ex p.* G. (A MINOR), *The Times,* June 3, 1987, Butler-Sloss J.

2467. Child abduction—Act incorporating convention—whether retrospective

[Convention on the Civil Aspects of International Child Abduction 1980, art. 4; Child Abduction and Custody Act 1985 (c.60), Sched. 1.]

Sched. 1 of the Child Abduction and Custody Act 1985 incorporates art. 4 of the 1980 Convention on the Civil Aspects of International Child Abduction into English law. It does not take effect retrospectively (*Buchanan (James) & Co.* v. *Babco Forwarding and Shipping (U.K.)* [1977] C.L.Y. 248 applied).

B. (MINORS), *Re The Times,* October 29, 1987, Waterhouse J.

2468. Child abduction—attempt—meaning of "lawful control". See R. *v.* MOUSIR, §765.

2469. Child abduction and custody

CHILD ABDUCTION AND CUSTODY (PARTIES TO CONVENTIONS) (AMENDMENT) ORDER 1987 (No. 163) [45p], made under the Child Abduction and Custody Act 1985 (c.60), s.2; amends S.I. 1986 No. 1159 by substituting a new Sched. 1 which lists the Contracting States to the Convention (Cm. 33).

CHILD ABDUCTION AND CUSTODY (PARTIES TO CONVENTIONS) (AMENDMENT) (No. 2) ORDER 1987 (No. 1825) [45p], made under the Child Abduction and Custody Act 1985 (c.60), s.2; amends S.I. 1986 No. 1159 by adding a reference to Spain.

2470. Child abuse—allegation of sexual abuse—based upon child's remarks—interview—hypothetical questions and sexually explicit dolls

The mother alleged that the father had sexually assaulted their daughter and their son. There was only one incident upon which suspicion could be raised and that was two years old. The mother informed the welfare officer of her suspicions and they urged her to go to the child sexual abuse clinic at Great Ormond Street. The interview there, conducted by a psychological social worker, involved hypothetical and leading questions and the use of sexually explicit dolls. Many of the child's answers were left unclarified. The psychological social worker concluded from the interview with the children that there had been sexual abuse of both children.

Held, that the interview took a standard form and did not deal with the facts of the case. No inquiry was made of the daughter regarding the remark that had first aroused suspicions—that remark itself was open to a number of interpretations but was not clarified. On the facts, the boy had been untruthful in the interview. The conclusion that he had been abused was totally unjustified. As for the daughter, there was no corroboration of the mother's suspicions—the conclusion of the social worker could not be accepted. There was no evidence for any finding of sexual abuse. The mother would be given care and control with fortnightly access for the father.

G. (MINORS) (CHILD ABUSE: EVIDENCE), *Re* [1987] 1 F.L.R. 310, Ewbank J.

2471. Child abuse—allegation of sexual abuse—interview—hypothetical questions—videotape—evidential status

The mother made an allegation that the father had sexually abused their daughter after an incident where the father found the mother drunk and affected by drugs and had taken her to hospital against her will. The child was sent to the child sexual abuse clinic at Great Ormond Street. There was no physical examination of the child—she refused one. The child was interviewed by a psychological social worker and was asked a large number of hypothetical questions. Most of her answers were vague and unclarified or were in the negative. The interview was recorded on videotape and, by consent, produced as evidence. The psychological social worker concluded that the child had been sexually abused.

Held, that the form of interview had built in preconceptions as to the existence of sexual abuse—it was not satisfactory for the purposes of court proceedings. On the facts of the case, the social worker's conclusions were dangerous and unjustified. The evidential standing of the videotape recording of the interview was in doubt and the value of the interview technique even more doubtful.

E. (A MINOR) (CHILD ABUSE: EVIDENCE), *Re* [1987] 1 F.L.R. 269, Ewbank J.

2472. Child abuse—allegation of sexual abuse by mother's cohabitee—interview technique—leading questions and explicit dolls—mother's drug dependency—welfare of children

The mother lived with a cohabitee and her two children. The children had been committed to the care of the local authority as a result of the mother's drug dependency. The children were placed with foster parents who came to suspect sexual abuse of the children because of the behaviour of the youngest child. A physical examination revealed no evidence to support this. The child was interviewed by a psychological social worker at the Great Ormond Street Hospital where a rigorous interview technique involving leading questions and sexually explicit dolls were used. On a number of occasions, the child volunteered that no act of indecency had taken place. The interview was videotaped. The conclusion was one of sexual abuse by the cohabitee, with a risk of further abuse if the child was returned home. There were misgivings about the interview technique expressed by two psychiatrists.

Held, that it was impossible to say with certainty whether acts of indecency had occurred. The court had to balance the risk of returning the child against the risks of keeping it away from its parent. There was no physical evidence of interference. It was important that the child had volunteered that no interference had occurred. In order to understand the interview it was very important to see the videotape and to read a transcript. The technique was still experimental. Pressure had been applied and there was a risk the child would say things that were untrue. Even so, the court was concerned about the question of drug dependency. The child would remain under the care and control of the local authority with access to the mother until she and her cohabitee had undergone tests to show that they had given up drugs.

N. (MINORS) (CHILD ABUSE: EVIDENCE), *Re* [1987] 1 F.L.R. 280, Swinton-Thomas J.

2473. Child abuse—sexual abuse—interview technique—judicial comment and direction

The interviewing techniques being used are relatively new, their main function is therapeutic—to encourage sexually abused children to unburden themselves by talking about their experiences. Those children that found this difficult had to be questioned in a persistent and suggestive manner. This therapeutic step rendered the evidence less useful forensically to a court.

Broadly speaking there are two categories of cases—those where there is definite evidence of abuse and those where there are only a combination of alerting symptoms. In the former, the therapeutic steps are clearly appropriate but in the latter, although therapy is still an important function, the court needed forensic assistance. Latey J. made the following comments:

(1) At the start of each referral there should be an assessment to see which category the case fits into.

(2) If a case is in the second category, there should always be a video; not only does this assist the court but it enables other experts to prepare reports.

(3) Techniques should be reconciled with the needs for forensic evidence as well as therapy if possible.

(4) If there was a tentative diagnosis of abuse, the interview should be aimed at disconfirming that. If the diagnosis remained after such an interview, it would be that much more valid.

M. (A MINOR) (CHILD ABUSE: EVIDENCE), *Re* (Note) [1987] 1 F.L.R. 293, Latey J.

2474. Child abuse—standard of proof—whether on balance of probabilities

G, a girl born in October 1983, was in the sole care of her father, her mother having left the matrimonial home. The mother had alternate weekend staying access, and after one such weekend failed to return G to her father. Mother and grandmother alleged that G had been sexually abused by the father. A place of safety order was obtained and eventually the local authority placed the child with foster parents and commenced wardship proceedings in which the father sought care and control.

Held, on the question of the standard of proof to be applied in determining the issue of sexual abuse, that although the standard to be applied was the balance of probabilities, a rather higher degree of probability was necessary to establish that the father was guilty of sexual abuse. Nonetheless, there was here sufficient evidence to show that it was in G's best interest to remain in the care of the local authority.

G. (A MINOR) (CHILD ABUSE: STANDARD OF PROOF) *Re* [1987] 1 W.L.R. 1461, Sheldon J.

2475. Child abuse—suspected sexual abuse—interview technique—leading questions and sexually explicit dolls

The girl, aged five, came from a closely knit family. One night, she woke up screaming, was taken to hospital where her behaviour changed considerably and was heard to scream out in her sleep "Daddy don't do that" or words to that effect. The child was referred to the child sexual abuse unit at Great Ormond Street. The child was interviewed using sexually explicit dolls and leading and hypothetical questions. A conclusion of sexual abuse was reached. The interview was recorded. A physical examination established soreness of the outer labia but no further examination was possible. The local authority commenced wardship proceedings.

Held, that the medical evidence, though important, was not conclusive. On the balance of probabilities there had been sexual interference of some sort. The parents had suppressed their recollection of it. Accordingly, the paramount interests of the children required them to remain under the care and control of the local authority.

W. (MINORS) (CHILD ABUSE: EVIDENCE) *Re* [1987] 1 F.L.R. 297, Waite J.

2476. Child abuse—suspected sexual abuse by and of young boy—interview technique

A young boy was suspected of sexually abusing his two young sisters and of being sexually abused by his father. The boy was 14 years old but with a mental age of six or seven. Medical examination of all three children did not reveal any evidence to support the suspicions. The boy was interviewed by the child sexual abuse clinic of the Great Ormond Street Hospital. Hypothetical and leading questions were asked and dolls were used. The first interview resulted in a conclusion that the boy had been abused and had abused his sisters. The same conclusion was reached after the second interview. In both interviews, the boy was inarticulate and unresponsive. After the second interview, he broke down on meeting his parents saying that his father had not done anything. The local authority commenced wardship proceedings.

Held, that the hospital interviews were evidence of abuse but not conclusive. The court had to look at the evidence as a whole. The mother was right to attribute some degree of sexual interference with the two girls to the boy but there was not sufficient evidence to justify a finding of abuse against the father. The boy would remain a ward in the care and control of the local authority with increased access to the parents.

H. (MINORS) (CHILD ABUSE: EVIDENCE), *Re* [1987] 1 F.L.R. 332, Waite J.

2477. Child in care—access—application by mother

[Children Act 1948 (c.43), s.2; Child Care Act 1980 (c.5), ss.12A, 12C(1) (as added by Health and Social Services and Social Security Adjudications Act 1983 (c.41), s.6, Sched. 1, para. 1; Interpretation Act 1978 (c.30), s.17(2)(*b*).]

A juvenile court has jurisdiction to hear an application by a mother for access to a child in respect of whom a resolution assuming parental rights and duties has been passed by a local authority under s.2 of the Children Act 1948, and Part 1A of the Child Care Act 1980.

M's two children were taken into care, and the local authority passed a resolution under s.2 of the Children Act 1948 assuming parental rights and duties. Later the authority terminated M's right of access under Part 1A of this Child Care Act 1980. M applied under s.12C for an order for access in the juvenile court. The justices held that they had no jurisdiction since s.12A(1)(*h*) of Part 1A made no reference to children in care by reason of s.2 as opposed to s.3.

Held, granting M's application for judicial review, that the omission could not have been intended by Parliament; s.17(2) of the Interpretation Act 1978 would be applied, Part 1A applied and the justices had jurisdiction to hear the application.

R. *v.* CORBY JUVENILE COURT *ex p.* M. [1987] 1 W.L.R. 55, Waite J.

2478. Child in care—no contact with mother—contribution notice—mother declining information

[Child Care Act 1980 (c.5), s.46, as substituted by Health and Social Services and Social Security Adjudications Act 1983 (c.41), s.19(3).]

Where a child was in care, a local authority was entitled to seek information as to its mother's financial circumstances and to choose not to consider other matters that might be relevant to her case before serving a contribution notice on her.

Under s.46 of the Child Care Act 1980 as substituted, a local authority is entitled to serve a contribution notice on anyone liable to make a contribution in respect of a child in their care. The applicant was a married woman with three children, the eldest of whom was D, a girl born in 1969. She had had no contact with D since 1981. D had lived with her father from 1980 and in 1984 was placed in care having run away. The local authority asked for information as to the applicant's means to enable them to assess her contribution towards the costs of D's maintenance. She did not reply. The council then served a contribution notice under s.46 requiring her to pay a specified sum each week towards D's maintenance. She objected to the notice and contended that, having regard to all the circumstances, the council should exercise their discretion not to ask her for a contribution. The council refused to consider making a discretionary nil assessment until the applicant provided the requested information as to her financial circumstances. She applied by way of certiorari to quash the contribution notice.

Held, dismissing the application, that s.46(4) conferred a power and not a duty on the council to decide not to serve a contribution notice in any case if they thought fit and that the council was not under a statutory obligation to investigate all the circumstances before making that decision. They were entitled to seek information as to the applicant's financial circumstances and to choose not to consider other matters which might be relevant to her case before serving the contribution notice. She ought to have answered the information sought. If she had provided it, then the council could have withdrawn the notice on a review of all the circumstances, including the financial ones.

R. *v.* ESSEX COUNTY COUNCIL, *ex p.* WASHINGTON (1987) 85 L.G.R. 210, McCowan J.

2479. Children Act 1975—Adoption Act 1976—commencement

CHILDREN ACT 1975 AND ADOPTION ACT 1976 (COMMENCEMENT No. 2) ORDER 1987 (No. 1242 (C.36)) [£1·30], made under the Children Act 1975 (c.72), s.108(2), and the Adoption Act 1976 (c.36) s.74(2); brings into force on January 1, 1988 ss.1, 2, Sched. 3, para. 74(*b*) (in part) of the 1975 Act, all sections of the 1976 Act (except ss. 58A, 73(2)(3), 74), and Scheds. 3 (in part), 4 (in part).

2480. Children in care—access—parental rights. See HUMAN RIGHTS, §1916.

2481. Children in care—cultural considerations—children of Vietnamese origin—welfare of children

Two children of Vietnamese origin were repeatedly neglected and ill-treated by their mother. They were made the subject of a place of safety order and placed with foster parents whereupon they improved dramatically. The local authority applied to the judge in wardship proceedings for directions.

Held, that the court had to exercise parental duties placing the welfare of the children above all else. Faced with the contention that their cultural background should be given special weight, the court had to consider the reasonable objective standards of that culture so long as they did not conflict with the minimum standards set by our society. Here, by any standards, the mother's conduct had been excessive. The priority was for the children to be cared for in a family setting and foster parents (preferably Vietnamese or Chinese) should be found with a view to adoption.

H. (MINORS), *Re* [1987] 17 Fam. Law 196, Judge Callman.

2482. Children in care—judicial review—whether appropriate remedy for parents wishing to challenge decisions of local authority. See ADMINISTRATIVE LAW, §9.

2483. Consent to medical treatment—child "fully understanding" treatment by abortion—obligation to parents

[Can.] A 16-year-old girl became pregnant. She obtained approval for a therapeutic abortion but her parents sought to prevent this by way of injunction. An injunction was refused.

Held, dismissing the parents' appeal, that the expectant mother in this case had sufficient intelligence and understanding (both of the nature of the proposed treatment and of her obligation to her parents) to make up her own mind (*Gillick* v. *West Norfolk and Wisbech Area Health Authority and the Department of Health and Social Security* [1985] C.L.Y. 2230 applied).

J. S. C. AND C. H. C. *v.* WREN [1987] 2 W.W.R. 669, Alberta C.A.

2484. Crossbows Act 1987 (c.32). See CRIMINAL LAW, §773.

2485. Custody—access—putative father's application for custody and interim access to children

[Guardianship of Minors Act 1971 (c.3), s.9; Child Care Act 1980 (c.5), s.3.]

The putative father of M and H, aged six and eight, stopped co-habiting with their mother, and went abroad. Later the mother placed M & H in the care of the local authority and refused to have them back. Later the authority passed a resolution under s.3 of the 1980 Act and rested parental rights in itself. The father returned and applied under s.9 of the 1971 Act for custody and interim access. Interim access was granted.

Held, that while the court had jurisdiction to hear the fathers' application, where the authority had statutory powers over the children it must be refused (A. v. *Liverpool City Council* [1981] C.L.Y. 1796 applied; *H. (K. and M.) (Infants), Re* [1972] C.L.Y. 2179 approved; *R.* v. *Oxford Justices, ex p. D.* [1986] C.L.Y. 2183 doubted).

M. AND H. (MINORS) (LOCAL AUTHORITY: PARENTAL RIGHTS) Re [1987] 3 W.L.R. 759. C.A.

2486. Custody—appeal—events occurring after judge's decision

Where further evidence was given in the Court of Appeal, the court could reverse the judge's decision on custody, even where his decision had been within the ambit of reasonable discretion on the evidence before him, if it was proper to do so in the light of further evidence of subsequent events.

A. *v.* A., *The Times,* May 21, 1987, C.A.

2487. Custody—application to take children out of jurisdiction having been granted custody—grounds for refusing leave

The parties were divorced. The wife was granted custody of the two children. The husband was granted access which was used successfully and the children had a good relationship with him. The mother remarried and later decided to emigrate to New Zealand. She applied to take the chidlren out of jurisdiction. The husband opposed her application. The judge found that the mother's decision to emigrate was a reasonable one but that the children's relationship with their father would be disrupted and refused to grant leave to the mother.

Held, that if the proposal of a custodial parent to move abroad was a reasonable one, the court should refuse leave only if it was clearly shown that it would be against the interests of the child. Here the mother's proposal to move was reasonable. The judge had given insufficient weight to the effect on the mother's new family of not being allowed to move which would have serious adverse effects on the family—including the two children. Refusing permission to move could lead to strain and bitterness. The judge had not directed himself properly and the appeal would be allowed subject to an undertaking that the mother should return the children to the jurisdiction if ordered to do so by the Court (*Poel* v. *Poel* [1970] C.L.Y. 777 and *Chamberlain* v. *De La Mare* [1983] C.L.Y. 2447 applied).

LONSLOW *v.* HENNIG (FORMERLY LONSLOW) [1986] 2 F.L.R. 378, C.A.

2488. Custody—application to vary custody order—welfare report—failure to make appropriate inquiries

The parents separated and the father was given custody of the children with access to the mother. Access gradually increased until the mother applied to vary the order so that she should have custody of the children. A welfare report was requested. The welfare officers, after two conciliation meetings with the parents, submitted a report stating only that the parents could not agree. The magistrates varied the order.

Held, that the report, had it reported on the homes of both of the parties, the families of the parties and how the children fitted into those environments, would have been of the utmost assistance to the magistrates. None of this information was contained in the report—that failure made the report useless and a waste of time and public money.

MERRIMAN *v.* HARDY (1987) 151 J.P.N. 526, Butler-Sloss J.

2489. Custody—arrangement for child to spend alternate weeks with each parent—application to vary order

The parties separated and arranged for the child of the marriage to spend alternate weeks with each of them. The arrangement was approved by the judge in the divorce proceedings. Five years later the mother applied to vary the order to give her sole custody of the child with reasonable access to the father. The recorder dismissed her application because of a welfare officer's report that no harm had come to the child.

Held, that an order keeping the child going backwards and forwards between the two parents was wrong. That it had existed for five years without apparent harm did not make it right. The paramount interests of the child were that she should have a settled home. Where nothing could be said against either parent, that home should be with the mother. There would be an order for joint custody with care and control to the mother and reasonable access to the father (*G.* v. *G. (Minors: Custody Appeal)* [1985] C.L.Y. 2594 applied).

RILEY *v.* RILEY [1986] 2 F.L.R. 429, C.A.

2490. Custody—borderline case—function of appellate court—immediate best interests of child

The mother and father separated. The mother went to live with another man (S) whilst the father remained in the matrimonial home. Both parties applied for custody of the only child. The mother proposed that the child should live with her and S and S's child from a previous marriage. The father proposed that the child should remain in his care in the matrimonial home, assisted by his mother and a close woman friend who lived nearby. The recorder found that S was unrealistic in relation to his association with the mother and the recorder was doubtful about whether the child would fit in with S's family. He concluded that it would be wrong to move the child from a position where she was happy to one where she may or may not be happy, although the matter may need to be reassessed in two or three year's time. He decided that the child should remain with the father. The mother appealed.

Held, that this was a borderline case that could have been decided either way. Unless the recorder had erred, the appellate court would not interfere simply because it would have decided the matter differently. The recorder had not erred in law and had considered all relevant matters. He was right to consider the immediate best interests of the child, recognising that the position may have changed greatly in two years' time. It was always open to either parent to apply to vary the order (*G.* v. *G. (Minors: Custody Appeal)* [1985] C.L.Y. 2594 applied; *W., Re* [1983] 4 F.L.R. 492 and *F. (A Minor) (Wardship: Appeal), Re* [1976] C.L.Y. 1805 referred to).

T. *v.* T. (MINORS: CUSTODY APPEAL) [1987] 1 F.L.R. 374, C.A.

2491. Custody—borderline case—short term interests of child

The parties separated and both applied for custody of the child. The child had remained in the matrimonial home with the father, who proposed to care for her with the assistance of his (the father's) mother. The wife wanted the child to live with her new family. The Recorder found that the husband's approach was unrealistic but was concerned that the child would not be happy in the mother's new family. He decided not to move the child from one place where she was happy to one where she may or may not be happy, depending on circumstances. He gave custody to the father although the mother may be reassessed later. The wife appealed.

Held, dismissing the appeal, that this was a borderline case and the Recorder's exercise of his discretion would not be criticised. It was true to say that he had decided the best interests of the child in the short term but that was consistent with his approach and with the facts of the case. In three years' time the position of the child and of the parents might be quite different.

THOMPSON *v.* THOMPSON (1987) 17 Fam. Law 89, C.A.

2492. Custody—child in joint custody—care and control with mother—marriage to New Zealander—application to take child out of jurisdiction

The mother, having care and control of the child who had been placed in joint custody (with access to the father) met and married a New Zealander. She applied to take the child out of the jurisdiction as she proposed to move to New Zealand. The judge adjourned the application to December 1988 by which time the child's links with her father and her extended family in England would be established.

Held, that the judge has omitted a crucial factor in assessing the paramount interests of the child. That was the need for stability in the child's new family. Great stress would be imposed on that union were the plans to go to New Zealand to be frustrated. The courts' approach had been clearly stated in previous cases. The judge had erred in law in granting an excessive adjournment when an immediate decision was of critical importance and in misapplying the authorities. The sooner the mother and stepfather were in a position to make their plans the better. The judge's decision would be substituted for one granting the application (*Poel* v. *Poel* [1970] C.L.Y. 777 and *Chamberlain* v. *De La Mare* [1983] C.L.Y. 2447 applied).

BELTON *v.* BELTON (1987) 17 Fam.Law 344, C.A.

2493. Custody—conflict of evidence on crucial questions—judge's duty to make specific findings of fact

The parents' evidence was in conflict on such questions as the relationship between the parents and the children, the father's caring role and the mother's relationship with another man. The judge had made no specific findings of fact but awarded custody to the mother based upon his overall impression. The father appealed.

Held, that where the evidence was in conflict over matters crucial to the future of the children, the judge had a *prima facie* duty to weigh the evidence and make specific findings of fact rather than rely on an overall impression. Without the findings of fact there was no way of knowing if the judge's impression had been right or wrong. A new trial would be ordered.

M. *v.* M., *The Times*, June 23, 1987, C.A.

2494. Custody—fresh evidence—12-year-old girl—whether her views to be considered

The views of a girl, albeit only 12 years old, could and should be taken into account where she expresses adamant opposition to living with a particular parent.

The judge ordered that two girls, aged 12 and 9, should be in the custody of their mother notwithstanding the welfare officer's recommendation that the elder child should go with the father.

Held, that the judge had plainly erred in failing to take proper account of the child's strongly expressed preference for staying with her father. In such circumstances the Court of Appeal could admit fresh evidence, and exercise an original jurisdiction of its own, but only if satisfied that the facts disclosed by the fresh evidence were such as to invalidate the judge's reasoning. On the facts, it had been wrong to attempt to compel this girl to live with her mother, and the appeal would be allowed.

M. *v.* M. (MINOR: CUSTODY APPEAL) [1987] 1 W.L.R. 404, C.A.

2495. Custody—holiday abroad—leave to take on holiday

On April 7, M, who had custody of the two children, now aged 17 and 16 years, booked a ten-day holiday for them in Yugoslavia starting towards the end of May 1986. On April 11, she asked F for his consent to take the children abroad. On May 14, F's solicitors wrote refusing his consent. On May 20, M applied to the County Court for leave to take the children abroad. The judge refused the application on the ground that it was made at the last moment and the respondent, F, having in consequence only one day's notice. M appealed.

Held, allowing the appeal and granting leave, that if this had been a normal *inter partes* litigation with no children involved, the judge's reason would have been enough in itself to entitle him to dismiss the application. But that reason could not stand with the best interest of the children. On the evidence the balance was in favour of leave being granted.

ROCHE *v.* ROCHE, May 23, 1986 (C.A.T. No. 505).

2496. Custody—interference with judge's decision

The judge of first instance granted custody of a three-year-old girl to the husband. The decision was based on the judge's finding of fact that there was a history of violence in the mother's parents' relationship coupled with a few instances of neglect.

Held, allowing the appeal and granting interim custody to the mother, that too much weight had been given to the family history and too little weight to the contemporary evidence that the respondent was a good mother. The Court of Appeal will interfere with the decision of a judge who saw and heard the witnesses when, in coming to the balancing exercise, he has, in error, placed little or no weight on some factors and wholly disproportionate weight on others.

RIDGEWAY *v.* RIDGEWAY, July 30, 1986, C.A. [*Ex rel. Stuart Trimmer, Barrister.*]

2497. Custody—interim order—no welfare reports—allegations against mother

The mother had daughters by two men. She applied for custody. The fathers opposed the application as the wife and her new boyfriend had a serious drink problem and had left the children unattended on occasions. A welfare report would take three or four months to prepare. The judge refused to *subpoena* the local authority social worker who was of the view that the children were better off with the fathers. The judge granted interim care and control to the mother upon her undertakings to keep the children away from her boyfriend and not to leave them unattended.

Held, that there were allegations that the children were at risk with the mother—but no evidence that they were at risk with the fathers. The judge could not have been satisfied that it was in the childrens' interests to go back to the mother. It was appropriate that the evidence of the social worker was available to decide the question of the children's interests on a short-term basis. Accordingly, the judge should have adjourned for further evidence. The appeal would be allowed and the children should return to the fathers' care pending the hearing.

W. AND L. (MINORS) (INTERIM CUSTODY), *Re* (1987) 17 Fam. Law 130, C.A.

2498. Custody—justices' reasons for custody decision—amplification of reasons—principles to be used

[Guardianship of Minors Act 1971 (c.3), s.1.]

Justices who gave reasons for their decision at the conclusion of a hearing should not attempt to amplify or expound them after being served with a notice of appeal. Moreover, when reaching their decision it was wrong in principle to treat the welfare of the child merely as the top of a list of items for consideration. If the welfare of a child pointed to the adoption of a particular course, then that course should be followed notwithstanding the risk of interfering with the status quo (*J. v. C.* [1969] C.L.Y. 1802 considered).

W. *v.* P., *The Times,* October 26, 1987, Ewbank J.

2499. Custody—order involving transfer of custody—functions of court welfare service

There was one child of the marriage when the parties separated. After the husband petitioned for divorce, a consent order was made giving interim custody of the child to the mother with reasonable access to the father. Attempts to exercise access were unsuccessful and the father applied for custody. The case was adjourned twice for welfare reports. At the eventual hearing, the welfare reports confined themselves to attempts at conciliation and recording the efforts at conciliation. The judge, having heard both parties and their respective cohabitees found that the mother had sought deliberately to alienate the child from its father, that the mother's cohabitee was a man with an extensive criminal record who had not changed his ways and who had committed acts of indecency against the child. The judge was impressed with the father and his cohabitee. He recognised the risk of disturbance in moving the child from its mother but that was a lesser risk than leaving the child with the mother and her cohabitee. Custody was granted to the father. The mother appealed.

Held, that the judge had reached his decision on his impression of the parties and their cohabitees and had been aware of the risks involved. His decision could not be said to be plainly wrong and would not be interfered with. There had been considerable delay by the court welfare service in producing a report. They should investigate all the circumstances of the case and not confine themselves to attempts at conciliation.

SCOTT *v.* SCOTT [1986] 2 F.L.R. 320, C.A.

2500. Detention of child involved in criminal offences—application for release

[Children and Young Persons Act 1969 (c.54), s.28(2), (5).]

For a justice properly to discharge his duty under s.28(5) of the 1969 Act, he should consider whether it was in the interests of the child further to be detained, and this necessarily involved consideration of the original reaons for detention. The police should thus attend at such a hearing and give evidence.

The police, having reason to believe that a seven-year-old child was involved in criminal offences, and being satisfied that she was in moral danger, detained her under s.28(2) of the 1969 Act. Two days later the child applied to a single justice under s.28(5) to be released. The police applied to be allowed to attend and give evidence. The justice ruled that the child's application should be *ex parte* and that the police should be excluded. The Chief Constable sought judicial review of this ruling.

Held, that in order properly to deal with the matter it was necessary to deal with the original reasons for the detention. Accordingly the police should be given notice of the hearing, attend and give evidence.

R. *v.* BRISTOL JUSTICE, *ex p.* BROOME [1987] 1 W.L.R. 352, Booth J.

2501. Foetus—whether capable of being born alive—status of unmarried father

[Infant Life (Preservation) Act 1929, (c.34), s.1(1); Abortion Act 1967 (c.87), s.1.]

A foetus of between 18 and 21 weeks was not 'a child capable of being born alive' in that it could not breathe naturally or with the aid of a ventilator. Termination of a pregnancy of that length was not an offence under s.1 of the Infant Life (Preservation) Act 1929.

The first defendant, a single woman, who was between 18 and 21 weeks pregnant, wished to terminate her pregnancy. Two medical practitioners certified in accordance with s.1(1)(*a*) of the Abortion Act 1967 that the continuance of her pregnancy would involve risk of injury to her physical or mental health greater than if the pregnancy were terminated. The father sought on his own behalf, and as next friend of the child *en ventre sa mère,* an injunction restraining the first defendant from undergoing the abortion and restraining the second defendants, the health authority, from performing it. By s.1(1) of the Infant Life (Preservation) Act 1929 it was an offence for any person with intent to destroy the life of any child capable of being born alive to cause it to die before it had an existence independent of that of its mother. The father contended that it was capable of being born alive because, if delivered, it would show real and discernible signs of life, namely a primitive circulation and movement of its limbs, and so termination would be an offence under the 1929 Act. He conceded that as father of the child he had no *locus standi* but contended that he had a sufficient personal interest because the proposed termination would be a crime concerning the life of his child. He further contended that the child was a proper party to the proceedings since it was the subject of the threatened crime. The judge refused the injunction and the father appealed to the Court of Appeal.

Held, dismissing the appeal, that although a foetus of between 18 and 21 weeks could be said to demonstrate real and discernible signs of life, the medical evidence was that such a foetus would be incapable of breathing either naturally or with the aid of a ventilator. It followed that it could not properly be described as being 'capable of being born alive' within s.1(1) of the 1929 Act and so the termination of a pregnancy of that length would not constitute an offence under the Act.

Per Heilbron J. (at first instance): A foetus has no right of action until it is subsequently born alive and therefore while it is unborn it cannot be a party to an action (dictum of Baker P. in *Paton* v. *Trustees of BPAS* [1978] C.L.Y. 1588 followed).

Per Sir John Donaldson M.R.: The Court of Appeal is the final court of appeal in circumstances of real urgency and litigants are entitled to act on its judgments in such circumstances without waiting to see whether there will be an appeal to the House of Lords.

The Appeal Committee of the House of Lords later refused leave to appeal.

C. *v*. S. [1987] 1 All E.R. 1230, C.A.

2502. Fostering scheme—whether child "boarded out"—attendance allowance

A child in the local authority's care was placed with foster parents under a scheme run by Dr. Barnardo's which selected the foster parents and made payments to them. Dr. Barnardo's themselves were in receipt of a payment from the local authority. The claimant applied for an attendance allowance under the Social Security Act 1975. An allowance was not payable if the cost of the accommodation was met wholly or party by local funds. The question was whether the claimant had been "boarded out" within the meaning of the Child Care Act 1980. The social security commissioner held that the claimant had not been boarded out as the Act referred to a direct boarding out by the authority itself.

Held, that a child in care placed with foster parents under a scheme organized by an organization such as Dr. Barnardo's could qualify as "boarded out" by the local authority, with the organization acting as agent. The claimant was entitled to an attendance allowance.

KININMOUTH *v*. CHIEF ADJUDICATION OFFICER [1987] 1 F.L.R. 498, C.A.

2503. Joint custody order—jurisdiction

On H's application under the Guardianship of Minors Act 1971 the judge ordered, *inter alia*, that the joint custody of the child should remain with the parents who were separated but not yet divorced, the divorce proceedings being contemplated.

Held, that such an order was not possible under s.11A of the Guardianship of Minors Act 1971. The court had no jurisdiction to make such an order under that Act. However, when the divorce proceedings were heard it would be possible to restore an order for the custody in substitution for the one which was possible under the 1971 Act.

DOUGLAS *v*. DOUGLAS, March 25, 1986. (C.A.T. No. 387).

2504. Maintenance—school fees—periodical payments—sole motive for order tax advantage

[Matrimonial Causes Act 1973 (c.18), s.23(1)(*d*).]

The Court will grant an order for periodical payments on application by a father who has custody, care and control even though the sole purpose of the application is to secure a tax advantage.

H was given custody, care and control of the three children. He applied to the court for periodical payments orders to be made against him to pay each child an amount equivalent to their school fees after deduction of income tax at the basic rate, so that the sums paid should become separate income of the children. They could then contract with the school for payment of the fees, and H's tax burden would be reduced, the sole purpose of the application. The judge refused the order, and the Court of Appeal upheld that refusal.

Held, allowing H's appeal, that when the children were living with the father there was no reason for not making the order normally made if they were living with the mother. H's tax advantage also affected the children's welfare, and the order would be made in the terms sought.

SHERDLEY *v*. SHERDLEY [1987] 2 W.L.R. 1071 H.L.

2505. Maintenance—variation of order—whether access a relevant factor

The husband had been ordered to pay £10 per week for each of his five children. He applied for those orders to be reduced. The registrar reduced the weekly sums to £8 because the husband had been denied access and had lost contact with the children. The wife appealed.

Held, that it was clear that the conduct of the parties should not be taken into account when assessing the maintenance to be paid to children. The registrar had erred in his approach but even so the husband had limited means and could not afford more than £8. Therefore £8 per week for each of the children had been the right order.

FOOT *v.* FOOT (1987) 17 Fam. Law 13, Hollis J.

2506. Minors' Contract Act 1987 (c.13). See CONTRACT, §442.

2507. Ouster order—marriage already dissolved—jurisdiction—interests of children. See WILDE *v.* WILDE, §1777.

2508. Paternity—blood tests. See EVIDENCE, §1675.

2509. Paternity—child born to married woman—rebuttal of presumption of legitimacy—standard of proof

The standard of proof required to rebut the presumption of legitimacy is stricter than the mere balance of probabilities, but not so strict as in criminal proceedings. Accordingly, where the putative father could, by serological evidence, be the real father, and at least 95 per cent. of men could not, and in addition the mother's husband is found to be virtually infertile, there is ample evidence to satisfy the stricter standard of proof (*Re J.S. (A Minor) (Declaration of Paternity)* [1980] C.L.Y. 139, *Serio* v. *Serio* [1984] C.L.Y. 2202 followed).

W. *v.* K. (PROOF OF PATERNITY), (1987) 151 J.P.N. 156, Latey J.

2510. Paternity—party leaving jurisdiction—injunction

[Supreme Court Act 1981 (c.54), s.37.]

The court can make an injunction preventing the mother of the ward from leaving the jurisdiction where paternity is in dispute and the necessary tests have not been carried out.

I. (A MINOR), *Re, The Times,* May 22, 1987, Sheldon J.

2511. Periodical payments—practice note. See PRACTICE, §3008.

2512. Removal of newborn child by local authority—view to long-term fostering

A local authority was justified in removing a child from its parents on the day of its birth, when the parents had an appalling record of sexual abuse of their other children. The newborn child being in considerable danger, it was proper for it to remain in the care of the authority with a view to long-term fostering.

P. (A MINOR) (WARDSHIP), *Re, The Times,* March 24, 1987, C.A.

2513. Surrogacy—care and control—welfare of children

The welfare of the children is the paramount consideration, and although surrogacy arrangements may be considered they are only part of the overall background. In the instant case the children would remain with the biological mother.

P. (MINORS) (SURROGACY), *Re* (1987) 151 J.P.N. 334, Sir John Arnold P.

2514. Wards—Criminal Injuries Compensation Board—practice direction. See CRIMINAL EVIDENCE AND PROCEDURE, §653.

2515. Wards—disclosure of evidence—practice direction. See PRACTICE, §3009.

2516. Wards—witness in criminal proceedings—practice direction. See CRIMINAL EVIDENCE AND PROCEDURE, §654.

2517. Wardship—affidavit evidence—inclusion of hearsay evidence

In wardship proceedings, the local authority sought care orders and submitted an affidavit by a social worker reciting the family history. Much of the affidavit was hearsay evidence. The mother objected to the admission of that evidence.

Held, that in cases concerning children, hearsay evidence should not be excluded but the court should carefully assess the weight to be given to such evidence. Where the hearsay evidence related to a component part of allegations against the parent and there was a serious issue raised, then the original source of the information should depose to an affidavit and be tendered for cross-examination.

N. (MINORS) (WARDSHIP: EVIDENCE), *Re* [1987] 1 F.L.R. 65, Lincoln J.

2518. Wardship—as alternative to judicial review—limitations

In adoption proceedings M objected to the foster parents as prospective adopters. The adoption panel decided that they were unsuitable but did not take into account M's objections in arriving at its decision. The foster parents commenced wardship proceedings. These were discharged on the application of the local authority. On appeal it was argued that the foster parents could invoke the wardship jurisdiction as an alternative to judicial review since the latter would merely quash the decision of the adoption panel and leave the child in care.

Held, dismissing the appeal, that judicial review was specifically designed so that the courts could supervise the proper execution of their statutory duties by bodies upon whom those duties rested. For this reason the process was protracted under R.S.C., Ord. 53 by the procedure that had to be followed. These safeguards could not be put aside in cases concerning children. Accordingly, the courts would not interfere unless it could be shown that they had behaved in such a way as to justify an application for judicial review; but even if such an application was justified the court would not allow the wardship jurisdiction to be invoked as an alternative remedy. In the instant case there was a total absence of any suggestion of impropriety or fundamental error in principle, such as would have formed the basis of an application for judicial review (*Associated Provincial Picture Houses* v. *Wednesbury Corporation* (1948) C.L.C. 8107; *M, (An Infant), Re,* [1961] C.L.Y. 4336; *A.* v. *Liverpool City Council* [1981] C.L.Y. 1796; *B (A Minor), Re,* [1981] C.L.Y. 1800, *W (A Minor) (Wardship: Jurisdiction) Re,* [1985] C.L.Y. 2255 and *W.* v. *Nottinghamshire County Council* [1986] C.L.Y. 2218 considered).

D. M. (A MINOR) (WARDSHIP: JURISDICTION), *Re,* (1986) 2 F.L.R. 122, C.A.

2519. Wardship—care and control—appeal—balancing considerations

The child had been born in 1979. M and F were not married and had separated in 1980. M had care of the child. F had access. M suffered from schizophrenia and formed relationships with unsuitable partners in consequence of which she had put the child into voluntary care as a result of the child's reactions for a period of time. F had a history of drug abuse. The maternal grandparents, with whom M had either lived or kept in close contact, were in their late fifties. In wardship proceedings the judge followed the recommendations of the welfare officer and most of the social workers involved by ordering that care and control be given to F.

Held, dismissing M's appeal, that in this case the judge had to undertake a difficult balancing act between the claims of M, the maternal grandparents and F. However, the judge's decision was one to which he was entitled to come and with which the court could not possibly interfere (*G.* v. *G.* [1985] C.L.Y. 2594 applied).

C. (A MINOR) (CARE AND CONTROL), *Re,* (1987) 151 J.P.N. 79, C.A.

2520. Wardship—care and control—paternal grandmother—importance of family circle

The child had been born when M was aged 16. At that time the child was received into the care of the local authority at the request of M as both she and her parents wished for the child to be adopted. The local authority had placed the child with short-term foster parents with the intention of seeking prospective adopters. The putative father of the child (F) objected to adoption and initiated wardship proceedings asking that care and control be given to his mother. The local authority did not oppose the wardship and, on a preliminary issue, the court held that it could exercise its wardship powers (see [1986] 5 C.L. 208d). At the substantive hearing the local authority opposed the paternal grandmother's application for care and control and sought leave to place the child with long-term foster parents. After the child was received into care M saw F regularly. She lived with her parents but visited F and his mother every day. The relationship between M and the grandmother became very close. M changed her views about the future of the child and agreed that the grandmother should bring up the child, at any rate for the time being.

Held, that the grandmother was deeply fond of and committed to the child. Although a very young grandmother at the age of 35 she could offer a secure and established home with a warm and friendly family. In these circumstances if the relationship between M and F broke down there would be no danger to the child. Similarly, the grandmother would deal appropriately with the relationship of the child with the maternal grandparents and if M wanted to take over the child's care. In the circumstances it was in the child's interests, and would promote his welfare, to remain within this family circle. Care and control would be granted to the grandmother.

A. (CHILD IN CARE: WARDSHIP), *Re,* (1987) 151 J.P.N. 79, Lincoln J.

2521. Wardship—child in care—child with special educational needs

The court could exercise its wardship jurisdiction where there was no risk of conflict with the local authority and where the court's powers would or could be of assistance, and where the local authority was not abdicating its responsibilities as set out by statute (*B. (Infants), Re* [1961] C.L.Y. 3051, *A.* v. *Liverpool City Council* [1981] C.L.Y. 1796, *W. (A Minor) (Wardship Jurisdiction), Re* [1985] C.L.Y. 2255 considered).

D. (A MINOR), *Re, The Independent*, May 22, 1987, C.A.

2522. Wardship—child in care—jurisdiction

Both parents suffered from mental disorders and the child was received into voluntary care by the local authority who assumed parental rights by a resolution that was later confirmed by the juvenile court. It was decided that there was no possibility of returning the child to his parents and he should be adopted. The authority gave notice terminating access by the parents. The parents applied for access to the juvenile court where they were granted access at times to be agreed. Having given notice of intention to appeal to the High Court, the local authority instead decided to apply in wardship for the court to determine questions relating to the child's welfare. The parents applied for the summons to be struck out or that the child should cease to be a ward of the court. The basis of the parent's application was that the High Court had no jurisdiction in wardship where the authority had a power and duty to make decisions as to the welfare of the child. Alternatively, the wardship jurisdiction should not be involved where a juvenile court has adequate powers to deal with the situation.

Held, that although the High Court would not interfere with a decision of a local authority on the merits, the authority was entitled to (and should be encouraged to) seek the assistance of the High Court in difficult or complex cases. In those circumstances, there would not be any interference with the authority's decision. The mere fact that a lower court had power to deal with a particular situation (and even if that jurisdiction had already been invoked) did not prevent the local authority referring the case to the High Court in wardship. The parents objections to wardship proceedings would be rejected and directions given to expedite the hearing. (*M.* v. *Berkshire County Council* [1985] C.L.Y. 2253 and *W. (A Minor) (Care Proceedings), Re* [1985] C.L.Y. 2250 applied; *A.* v. *Liverpool City Council* [1981] C.L.Y. 1796, *Associated Provincial Picture Houses* v. *Wednesbury Corporation* (1948) C.L.C. 8107., *C.B. (A Minor) (Wardship: Local Authority), Re* [1981] C.L.Y. 1786, *D. (A Minor) (Justices' Decision: Review) Re* [1977] C.L.Y. 1930, *Hertfordshire County Council* v. *Dolling* [1982] 3 F.L.R. 423 and *P. (A Minor), Re* [1986] 1 F.L.R. 272 considered).

L.H. (A MINOR) (WARDSHIP: JURISDICTION), *Re* [1986] 2 F.L.R. 306, Sheldon J.

2523. Wardship—child in care—secure accommodation—review panel

[Child Care Act 1980 (c.5), s.21A; Secure Accommodation (No. 2) Regulations (S.I. 1983 No. 1308).]

The child, a boy born in 1969, had had a disastrously unsettled history. In December 1983, he was committed to the care of the local authority in wardship proceedings and the judge had directed that he be kept in secure accommodation. As a result of previous hearings ([1984] C.L.Y. 2251 and [1985] C.L.Y. 2263) the juvenile court had authorised that the child be kept in secure accommodation until June 1985 which was extended, at a case conference, to his sixteenth birthday in August 1985. The review panel, however, were of the view that the boy should be released immediately. The matter was therefore referred, once again, to the High Court for directions. The judge concluded that there was overwhelming evidence for the placement to continue to the later date.

Held, dismissing the local authority's appeal, that it was not necessary for the local authority to obtain directions from the High Court before applying to the juvenile court unless they were uncertain whether to make the initial approach. It was only if the juvenile court authorised the placement that directions should be sought whether or not so to place the ward. Equally, if the local authority decided that such placement was no longer appropriate they should forthwith apply for further directions. The effect of the current statutory provisions was that the juvenile court (and the Crown Court on appeal) alone had jurisdiction to decide whether criteria existed for placing the ward in secure accommodation. Accordingly, it would be better if the High Court excluded from its order giving leave to apply any findings on the matters within the exclusive jurisdiction of the juvenile court under s.21A (*Humberside County Council* v. *R.* [1977] C.L.Y. 1855, *A.* v. *Liverpool City Council* [1981] C.L.Y. 1796, *K. (Ward: Secure Accommodation) Re* [1985] C.L.Y. 2262 and *W. (A Minor) (Wardship: Jurisdiction), Re* [1985] C.L.Y. 2255 considered.

M. *v.* LAMBETH BOROUGH COUNCIL (No. 3) [1986] 2 F.L.R. 136, C.A.

2524. Wardship—children in care—challenge to exercise of local authority's statutory powers—whether wardship jurisdiction could be exercised—whether judicial review appropriate remedy

In 1976 twins were placed in the care of the local authority and a care order was made in the magistrates' court. The twins were placed with long-term foster parents. After nine years a dispute arose between the foster parents and the local authority. The children were removed from the foster parents just seven months before an application for custodianship under s.33 of the Children's Act 1975 could be made. The foster parents challenged the action by issuing an originating summons in wardship contending that the authority had improperly and illegally exercised their statutory powers if they had done so with the intention of depriving the foster parents of the right to apply for a custodianship order. Alternatively, the decision could only have been reached by disregarding the paramount consideration—the children's welfare. The local authority applied to dismiss the summons on a preliminary point of jurisdiction.

Held, that to challenge the decision of a local authority on the basis of the *Wednesbury* principles, the plaintiffs can only proceed by way of judicial review under the provisions of R.S.C., Ord. 53. There is no way to secure such a review by an exercise of the High Court's Wardship jurisdiction—the wardship jurisdiction could not be exercised, judicial review being the appropriate remedy (*A.* v. *Liverpool City Council* [1981] C.L.Y. 1796 and *W. (A Minor) (Care Proceedings: Wardship), Re* [1985] C.L.Y. 2250 followed; *Associated Provincial Picture Houses* v. *Wednesbury Corporation* (1948) C.L.C. 8107, *M. (An Infant), Re* [1961] C.L.Y. 4336, *M.* v. *Humberside County Council* [1979] C.L.Y. 1817, *T. (A. J. J.) (An Infant), Re* [1970] C.L.Y. 1360, *Council of Civil Service Unions* v. *Minister for the Civil Service* [1985] C.L.Y. 12, *W. (Minors) (Wardship: Jurisdiction), Re* [1979] C.L.Y. 1807 referred to).

R. M. AND L. M. (MINORS) (WARDSHIP: JURISDICTION), *Re* [1986] 2 F.L.R. 205, Sheldon J.

2525. Wardship—confidential records—parents requiring information from probation service's records. See M (MINORS) (CONFIDENTIAL DOCUMENTS), *Re*, §2922.

2526. Wardship—foster parents—failure of adoption application—advantages over custodianship

[Children Act 1975 (c.72), ss.12, 33, 37.]

The child, born in 1981 was of mixed race. Two months after his birth, M, who was West Indian, placed him with a married couple under a private fostering arrangement. The local authority was notified. From this time onwards the possibility of adoption was considered. M was ambivalent in her views. The frequency of her visits diminished. Finally, in 1984 the foster parents told M that they intended to adopt the child as he was now integrated into their family. M's response was to demand the child back immediately. The foster parents instituted wardship proceedings to preserve the child's placement and applied to adopt the child. M opposed both applications which were heard together.

Held, that the adoption application would be dismissed as M could not be said to be unreasonably withholding her agreement since (a) continuing contact with M could help the child later with difficulties with his ethnic origins, and (b) the foster parents were Jehovah's Witnesses. Whilst the foster parents could not take advantage of s.37 and invite the court to treat the adoption application as one made under s.33 for a custodianship order, because the requirements of s.12 (parental agreement) were not still satisfied, nevertheless the foster parents still qualified under s.33 due to the length of time the child had been with them. Since custodianship and wardship were mutually exclusive the court would have no continuing jurisdiction to supervise access by M or give directions as to blood transfusions. It was therefore in the child's best interests that the wardship should continue (*W. (An Infant*), *Re* [1971] C.L.Y. 5831 followed).

J. (A MINOR) (ADOPTION APPLICATION), *Re* (1987) 151 J.P.N. 62, Sheldon J.

2527. Wardship—interim order for care—exercise of discretion—rôle of appellate court—expenditure of public money

The child was a ward of court. He was committed to the care of the local authority by an interim order with liberty to the mother to apply to vary the order. She made an application for interim care and control to be transferred to her. That application was refused, the judge deciding not to vary the *status quo* pending the main hearing. The mother appealed against both decisions on the basis of an incorrect exercise of discretion.

Held, that the orders were made in the exercise of the judges' discretion—the appellate court would not interfere with them unless it was shown that the decision exceeded the generous ambit within which reasonable disagreement is possible and is plainly wrong. The appeal was unarguable and would be dismissed. The parties were publicly funded. In future the courts may have to investigate why public money is spent in such cases and to make appropriate orders (*C. B. (A Minor) (Wardship: Local Authority), Re* [1981] C.L.Y. 1786 and *G.* v. *G. (Minors: Custody Appeal)* [1985] C.L.Y. 2594 applied).

G. (A MINOR) (ROLE OF THE APPELLATE COURT), *Re* [1987] 1 F.L.R. 164, C.A.

2528. Wardship—jurisdiction

N ($10\frac{1}{2}$ at trial) was a British subject. Her father was a Yemeni. Her mother was half Yemeni, half British and held a British passport. N was born in the U.K. She lived there with her parents and younger sister until 1980 when the family went to the Yemen. In 1982 the mother returned from the Yemen, leaving N behind. The father went to Saudi Arabia, leaving N with his extended family. Since 1982 the mother had had no contact with N. The father had had very limited contact (letters and telephone calls). The mother warded N shortly after her return to the U.K. She obtained orders for N's return in 1982 and 1984. The father returned to the U.K. in 1986 intending to take the mother and their other children back to the Yemen. The mother would not return to the Yemen and sought an order requiring N to be returned to the U.K. and to her care and control. The father's future plans were nebulous. It seemed that he had no plans to return to the Yemen, at least not without the mother. He wished to leave N in the care of his extended family. Save that there was evidence that N lived in a house with her grandmother in a remote part of the Yemen, was provided for by the father's family, had been brought up in a Moslem culture and spoke only Arabic, there was no evidence as to her character or the circumstances in which she lived. There was no evidence as to the effect of a return to the U.K. upon N.

Held, despite the possible disruption, it was in N's interest to have contact with her mother, and the father was ordered to bring her to the U.K. for that purpose. The mother was granted interim care and control. The matter was ordered to be listed for further directions upon N's return.

RAZZAQ *v.* RAZZAQ, December 16, 1986; H.H. Judge Toyn; Birmingham High Ct. [*Ex rel. David Worster, Barrister.*]

2529. Wardship—notice of hearing

[R.S.C., Ord. 32, r.3.]

In wardship cases where a local authority seeks leave to place a child with long-term foster parents with a view to adoption and termination of the mother's access, R.S.C., Ord. 32, r.3 requires the summons to be served on the mother giving her two clear days' notice of the hearing. The rule is mandatory in its terms, and even though the mother takes part in the hearing, that hearing should be adjourned to allow her to avail herself of legal advice.

P., *Re*; LINCOLNSHIRE COUNTY COUNCIL *v.* P., *The Times,* August 10, 1987, C.A.

2530. Wardship—police seeking disclosure of medical and local authority records—leave of court

[Administration of Justice Act 1960 (c.65), s.12(1).]

The leave of the court was needed for the disclosure of records relating to a ward of court who might have been subjected to criminal offences. Disclosure should be granted in almost all cases in order to protect other children from the perpetrators of offences.

In wardship proceedings, evidence was given that the four wards might have been sexually abused by D who was living with the wards' mother. They were committed to the care of the local authority for long term fostering with a view to adoption. The local authority were granted leave to take the children to a clinic that dealt with child abuse cases. The clinic considered that some, if not all the wards had been sexually abused, and the police began an investigation to see whether criminal offences had been committed. The Commissioner of Police applied for leave to permit disclosure to them of the records and video recordings made by the clinic, leave to interview them, to medically investigate them further if necessary, and to inspect the case records of the local authority.

Held, that leave was required and directions must be sought from the judge and not from those who had the day to day control. The court had an unfettered discretion to grant leave and had to balance the interests of the wards against the public interest which required that the police should not be obstructed in pursuing criminal investigations. In all but the most exceptional cases the public interest in protecting not only the wards but other children from the perpetrators of crime by providing evidence for use in criminal proceedings would outweigh the interests of the individual ward. The court granted leave for the police to see the medical records and video recordings made, to interview the wards, and if necessary to subject them to a further medical investigation. But the case records of the local authority kept under the Boarding-Out of Children Regulations 1955 were confidential records of the local authority and were protected from disclosure under the principle of public interest immunity. The court had no jurisdiction to order the disclosure of these unless they had become part of the evidence in the wardship and thereby subject to the provisions of the Administration of Justice Act 1960 s.12(1). The local authority did not waive its immunity by making the case records the basis of its evidence in the wardship proceedings; but where extracts had been exhibited to an affidavit, the authority had waived its immunity and the provisions of s.12(1) applied so that the leave of the court was required before the extracts could be disclosed to the police. In the exercise of its discretion, the court would grant leave for those extracts to be disclosed (*D. (Infants), Re* [1970] C.L.Y. 1359 and *R. (M. J.) (A Minor) (Publication of Transcript), Re* [1975] C.L.Y. 2143 applied).

S. (MINORS) (WARDSHIP: POLICE INVESTIGATION), *Re* [1987] 3 W.L.R. 847, Booth J.

2531. Wardship—review of child law—working paper. See LAW REFORM, §2278.

2532. Wardship—social worker—jurisdiction to allocate

The court has jurisdiction to intervene in the decision whether to allocate a social worker to a ward in the care and control of a local authority.

B. (A MINOR), *Re, The Times,* October 6, 1987, Lincoln J.

2533. Wardship—sterilisation—principles

[Children and Young Persons Act 1969 (c.54). s.1(2)(*a*).]

The Court has jurisdiction to authorise the sterilisation of a ward of court as a last resort; such consent cannot be given by the natural parents or a local authority having parental rights.

B was a girl aged 17 and mentally handicapped. She was becoming sexually aware. The council in whose care she had been placed applied to have her made a ward of court so that leave could be given for a sterilisation operation since B could not understand that intercourse caused childbirth, or the principles of contraception, could not cope with normal childbirth and could not function as a mother. Leave was given by the judge, and the official solicitor's appeal was dismissed.

Held, dismissing the appeal, that although the natural parents and the council had no such power the Court had jurisdiction over a ward of court to sanction the operation as a last resort, and in the circumstances, such sanction should be given (*Eve, Re* (1986) 31 D.L.R. (4th) 1 and *D. (A Minor) (Wardship: Sterilisation), Re* [1975] C.L.Y. 2204 distinguished).

B. (A. MINOR) (WARDSHIP: STERILISATION), *Re* [1987] 2 W.L.R. 1213, H.L.

2534. Wardship and ouster—proceedings heard together—criteria to be considered—exercise of discretion. See T. (A MINOR: WARDSHIP), *Re*; T. *v.* T. (OUSTER ORDER), §1773.

2535. Wardship proceedings—role of medical experts—role of Official Solicitor—guidance

A general practitioner suspecting child abuse referred the child to a hospital where a diagnosis of non-accidental injury was made. A second opinion was sought from a consultant who was also asked by the father to assist in the preparation of a case alleging non-accidental injury against the mother. The consultant unquestioningly supported the account put forward by father and child and advised the father to tape record his access visits to the child. When the child became aware of the tape recording the child became upset. The consultant obstructed the Official Solicitor's attempts to have the child examined by making it impossible for the child to move to the hospital of the Official Paediatrician. The consultant himself engaged in a series of investigations involving close questioning of the child—the Official Solicitor was not involved in these investigations.

Held, that it is a basic tenet of wardship jurisdiction that no major step in the child's life should be taken without leave of the court. The obtaining of evidence by tape recording access interviews was a gross intrusion of the purpose of the access visit as directed by the court and was greatly to be deprecated. Medical experts should not become involved in a case where they will be giving evidence for one side—such bias is easily apparent and impedes a judge from accepting their evidence. It is of the utmost importance that the Official Solicitor, who is the independent representative of the interests of the child, should not be impeded in his investigations—he should be actively assisted in all aspects of the investigations. The submissions of the Official Solicitor are of great importance.

C. (MINORS) (WARDSHIP: MEDICAL EVIDENCE), *Re* [1987] 1 F.L.R. 418, Butler Sloss J.

2536. Wrongful removal from jurisdiction—order for return—whether practical consequences may be taken into account

[Child Abduction and Custody Act 1985 (c.60), Sched. 1.]

The practical consequences of ordering a child's return may be taken into account by a judge.

A. *v.* A.; A (A MINOR), *Re, The Times,* June 13, 1987, C.A.

MORTGAGES

2537. Charging order—real property—claim that resulting trust defeated charging order

The plaintiff bank applied to have a charging order nisi over real property made absolute. D contended that as on the (undisputed) evidence, the deposit and mortgage repayments were made by a third-party company, D was a resulting trustee for the company, despite the property being registered in D's name, and the mortgage also being in her sole name. P contended that on the evidence the payments made by the company were by way of loan, thus precluding a trust.

Held, the registrar allowing the charging order to be made absolute, that (1) a charging order only charges the defendant debtor's interest in a property, so if a trust is later proved, the third-party company can apply for the order to be discharged; (2) the company in any case only has a resulting trust to the value of its contributions to date; (3) the fact that the debtor is the only registered proprietor is good prima facie evidence in favour of allowing a charging order against him/her; (4) all of these indicate that the correct course of action where a trust is claimed to defeat a charging order, and where the affidavit evidence is inconclusive, is to allow the order to be made absolute, and postpone argument about a trust until the almost inevitable s.30 (Law of Property Act 1925) hearing.

BARCLAYS BANK *v.* FORRESTER, July 31, 1987; Mr. Registrar Jacey; Lambeth County Ct. [*Ex rel. Marc Dalby, Barrister.*]

2538. Defective house—mortgage offer—whether local authority owes duty of care. See WESTLAKE *v.* BRACKNELL DISTRICT COUNCIL, §2587.

2539. Negligent mortgage valuation—whether duty of care owed to mortgagor. See HARRIS *v.* WYRE FOREST DISTRICT COUNCIL, §2586.

2540. Overriding interest—mortgage by two trustees for sale—beneficiaries in occupation of land—whether overriding interest—whether interest overreached

[Law of Property Act 1925 (c.20), s.14; Land Registration Act 1925 (c.21), s.70(1)(*g*).]

The interest of a beneficiary under a trust for sale of land in occupation of the land was not an overriding interest and was overreached where capital moneys were advanced to both trustees pursuant to a mortgage entered into by the trustees holding the land on trust for sale.

In October 1977, Bleak House was purchased for £34,000. Mr. and Mrs. Flegg provided £18,000 of the purchase price. The remainder was provided by their son-in-law and daughter, Mr. and Mrs. Maxwell-Brown. It was necessary for the M-Bs to mortgage the house to the Hastings and Thanet Building Society to raise their contribution. In consequence, the house was transferred to Mr. and Mrs. M-B upon trust for sale as joint tenants. The house was in fact held by Mr. and Mrs. M-B on trust for sale and to stand possessed of the net proceeds of sale and rents and profits until sale upon trust for Mr. and Mrs. M-B and Mr. and Mrs. F as tenants in common in the proportions which they had contributed to the purchase price. From that time, Mr. and Mrs. M-B and Mr. and Mrs. F occupied the property in common. In January 1982, Mr. and Mrs. M-B executed a charge of the house in favour of the City of London Building Society to secure a loan of £37,500. Mr. and Mrs. M-B used the money to discharge the existing mortgage and a number of other charges. Mr. and Mrs. M-B defaulted and the Building Society sought an order for possession of the house which was granted at first instance. On Mr. and Mrs. F's appeal, the Court of Appeal held applying *Williams & Glyn's Bank* v. *Boland*, that Mr. and Mrs. F had an overriding interest in the house so that the Building Society's charge was subject to their interest.

Held, allowing the Building Society's appeal, that Mr. and Mrs. F's interest was that of a beneficiary under a trust for sale. The advancement of capital moneys by the Building Society to Mr. and Mrs. M-B, being an advancement to two trustees, overreached Mr. and Mrs. F's interest. Their interest transferred to the capital moneys in the hands of Mr. and Mrs. M-B and the equity of redemption. The enjoyment of occupation of the property did not give rise to any separate or severable right from those enjoyed under the trust for sale. S.14 of the Law of Property Act 1925 could not enlarge or add to Mr. and Mrs. F's interest; it could not create an interest in the nature of a right to occupy the property that survived the execution of the trust for sale. Upon the execution of the trust for sale, any rights in reference to the house ceased to subsist within the meaning of s.70(1)(*g*) of the Land Registration Act 1925; there was no longer a right for the time being subsisting. Accordingly, there was nothing in s.70(1)(*g*) that had the effect of preserving any rights of Mr. and Mrs. F to occupy the house against the Building Society's. In *Williams and*

Glyn's Bank v. *Boland*, the beneficiary's rights were not overreached because payment was not made to two trustees as required by s.27 Law of Property Act 1925. The same did not apply in the present case (*Williams & Glyn's Bank* v. *Boland* [1980] C.L.Y. 1847 distinguished; *Bull* v. *Bull* [1955] C.L.Y. 2313, *National Provincial Bank* v. *Hastings Car Mart* [1965] C.L.Y. 1850, *Irani Finance* v. *Singh* [1970] C.L.Y. 2277 considered).

CITY OF LONDON BUILDING SOCIETY *v.* FLEGG [1987] 2 W.L.R. 1266, H.L.

2541. Possession order—suspension of mortgagees' possession order pending counterclaim by mortgagor—whether counterclaim affecting right to possession

[Administration of Justice Act 1970 (c.31), s.36; Administration of Justice Act 1973 (c.15), s.8.]

The rule that a counterclaim does not impinge on the mortgagees' right to possession is not to be nullified by giving weight to the possibility of the counterclaim resulting in a substantial sum becoming due to the mortgagor within a reasonable time.

A borrowed £33,000 from C for the purchase of a house, which was mortgaged to C in the usual way. Prior to completion, C had had a survey done, at A's expense, which revealed rising damp and dry rot. A was never informed of the contents of the report. After completion he had a survey done himself, which quantified remedial works in the sum of £9,099. On A falling into arrears with his repayments, C obtained an order for possession from the Master, suspended for six months provided he maintained the current payments, and A prosecuted his counterclaim for damages (arising out of the undisclosed report) diligently. C appealed.

Held, allowing the appeal, that the court was required to consider unpaid instalments that had already fallen due, and those which would fall due in the course of the "reasonable period" provided by s.36 of the 1970 Act. On its true construction, it was not intended that the rule whereby a mortgagee's right to immediate possession was unaffected by the existence of a counterclaim should be circumvented by attaching weight to the possibility of a substantial recovery in the counterclaim. In any event, there was no evidence that A, however well he did in his counterclaim, would be able to repay arrears and current instalments within a reasonable time. An order would be made in favour of C (*Western Bank* v. *Schindler* [1976] C.L.Y. 1820 applied; *Royal Trust Co. of Canada* v. *Markham* [1975] C.L.Y. 2222 considered).

CITIBANK TRUST *v.* AYIVOR [1987] 1 W.L.R. 1157, Mervyn Davies J.

2542. Priority—mortgage registered as per name on title deeds—subsequent mortgagee's search against name on birth certificate

The words "name of the estate owner" in s.3(1) of the Land Charges Act 1972 means the name as disclosed by the conveyance.

In 1980 a house was conveyed to two people named as Roger Caudrelier and Hilary Caudrelier. The couple mortgaged the property to the plaintiff who registered a charge in those names. The couple then took out another mortgage with the defendant who searched in the names of Roger Denis and Hilary Claire Caudrelier. The search did not reveal the earlier mortgage. On the sale of the property the plaintiff claimed priority.

Held, that the words "name of the estate owner" meant the name as disclosed by the conveyance. The plaintiff's mortgage was properly so registered and his mortgage had priority.

STANDARD PROPERTY INVESTMENT *v.* BRITISH PLASTICS FEDERATION (1987) 53 P. & C.R. 25, Walton J.

2543. Registration of charges—equitable sub-mortgage—whether prescribed particulars of charges delivered to registrar of companies. See SUN TAI CHEUNG CREDITS *v.* ATT.-GEN. OF HONG KONG, §361.

2544. Undue influence—husband and wife—charge over matrimonial home in joint ownership to secure husband's indebtedness to bank—undue influence exercised by husband—whether charge valid

Where a bank asked a husband to obtain his wife's consent in principal to the execution of a charge over their jointly owned property to secure the husband's indebtedness, the bank did not make the husband their agent for dealing with the wife.

P and her husband jointly-owned their matrimonial home. P's husband was a second-hand car dealer and customer of Midland Bank plc ("the Bank"). P's husband wished to expand his activities and to do so required a larger overdraft facility from the Bank. He approached the Bank in March 1983 and was advised that a second mortgage on the home would be required as security. P's husband undertook to discuss the increased overdraft and required security with P and let the Bank know the outcome. On May 31, 1983, P and her husband attended at the Bank where a charge over their home was executed. The Bank's manager failed to adequately explain to P the nature and effect of the charge and the amount secured by it and failed to advise her to get independent advice about the transaction. P's husband failed to pay the Bank. Proceedings for possession were started. P claimed that the charge was invalid having been obtained through undue influence exercised over her by her husband. The trial judge held that P's husband had exercised undue influence over her to get her to execute the charge, that the Bank was not a party to that undue influence and that the Bank had been negligent in failing to advise P adequately about the transaction. The judge made an order for possession having refused to set aside the charge and an order for P's damages in consequence of the Bank's negligence to be assessed.

Held, on P's appeal against the refusal of the judge to set aside the charge, that P's husband had neither ostensible or actual authority to act as the agent of the Bank. At best, P's husband was asked to advise the Bank if P was agreeable in principle to a loan to her husband secured on their home. There was no evidence to support a finding of agency. Accordingly the Bank was not liable in respect of the undue influence exercised by the husband. In addition, the Bank had no knowledge of the undue influence exercised by the husband. As the Bank was not a volunteer, the charge was valid (*Bainbrigge* v. *Browne* (1881) 18 Ch.D. 188 applied, *Yerkey* v. *Jones* (1940) 63 C.L.R. 649 considered).

PERRY *v.* MIDLAND BANK [1987] FLR 237, C.A.

NATIONAL HEALTH

2545. AIDS (Control) Act 1987 (c.33)

This Act makes provision in relation to Acquired Immune Deficiency Syndrome and Human Immunodeficiency Virus.

The Act received the Royal Assent on May 15, 1987.

Except for s.2, the Act does not extend to Northern Ireland.

2546. Allocation of resources—judicial review of N.H.S. decision

Although N.H.S. decisions on how to allocate resources are subject to judicial review, applications for leave will only rarely be granted since the discretion will only be exercised extremely sparingly.

WALKER, *ex p., The Independent,* November 26, 1987, C.A.

2547. Dentists

NATIONAL HEALTH SERVICE (GENERAL DENTAL SERVICES) AMENDMENT REGULATIONS 1987 (No. 736) [85p], made under the National Health Service Act 1977 (c.49), ss.35(4), 126(4); operative on May 15, 1987; provides for payments to be made to dentists whose registration is suspended by the direction or order of the Health Committee.

NATIONAL HEALTH SERVICE (GENERAL DENTAL SERVICES) AMENDMENT (No. 2) REGULATIONS 1987 (No. 1512) [45p], made under the National Health Serive Act 1977, ss.35(1)(4), 36(1), 126(4); operative on October 1, 1987; amend S.I. 1973 No. 1468.

NATIONAL HEALTH SERVICE (GENERAL DENTAL SERVICES) AMENDMENT (No. 3) REGULATIONS 1987 (No. 1965) [45p], made under the National Health Service Act 1977, ss.35(1), 36(1); operative on December 21, 1987; amend S.I. 1973 No. 1468.

2548. Disablement services authority

DISABLEMENT SERVICES AUTHORITY (ESTABLISHMENT AND CONSTITUTION) ORDER 1987 (No. 808) [45p], made under the National Health Service Act 1977 (c.49), s.11; operative on July 1, 1987; provides for the establishment and constitution of the said special health authority dealing with the artificial limb and appliance service.

DISABLEMENT SERVICES AUTHORITY REGULATIONS 1987 (No. 809) [45p], made under the National Health Service Act 1977, Sched. 5, paras. 12, 16; operative on July 1, 1981; provide for the appointment and tenure of office of members of the said Authority, and for the procedure of the Authority.

HEALTH SERVICE COMMISSIONER FOR ENGLAND (DISABLEMENT SERVICES AUTHORITY) ORDER 1987 (No. 1272) [45p], made under the National Health Service Act 1977, s.109(*d*); operative on August 20, 1987; designates the Disablement Services Authority as a "relevant body" within the meaning of s.109 of the National Health Service Act 1977 so that the Health Service Commissioner for England may investigate complaints which relate to the Authority or its officers.

2549. Health authorities

WELSH HEALTH PROMOTION AUTHORITY (ESTABLISHMENT AND CONSTITUTION) ORDER 1987 (No. 151) [45p], made under the National Health Service Act 1977 (c.49), s.11; operative on March 3, 1987; provides for the establishment and constitution of the said authority.

WELSH HEALTH PROMOTION AUTHORITY REGULATIONS 1987 (No. 152) [45p], made under the National Health Service Act 1977, Sched. 5, paras. 12, 16; operative on March 3, 1987; provide for the tenure of the members of the said authority, the procedure of it and reporting to the Secretary of State.

2550. Health education authority

HEALTH EDUCATION AUTHORITY (ESTABLISHMENT AND CONSTITUTION) ORDER 1987 (No. 6) [45p], made under the National Health Service Act 1977 (c.49), s.11; operative on February 3, 1987; provides for the establishment and constitution of the said Authority which will perform specified functions relating to health education.

HEALTH EDUCATION AUTHORITY REGULATIONS 1987 (No. 7) [45p], made under the National Health Service Act 1977, Sched. 5, paras. 12, 16; provides for the tenure of office of members of the said Authority.

2551. Medical and pharmaceutical services

NATIONAL HEALTH SERVICE (GENERAL MEDICAL AND PHARMACEUTICAL SERVICES) AMENDMENT (No. 2) REGULATIONS 1987 (No. 401) [£2·70], made under National Health Service Act 1977 (c.49), ss.16(1), 41, 42, Sched. 5, para. 12; operative on April 1, 1987; amend S.I. 1974 No. 160.

NATIONAL HEALTH SERVICE (GENERAL MEDICAL AND PHARMACEUTICAL SERVICES) AMENDMENT (No. 3) REGULATIONS 1987 (No. 407) [45p], made under the National Health Service Act 1977, s.29; operative on April 6, 1987; amend S.I. 1974 No. 160.

NATIONAL HEALTH SERVICE (GENERAL MEDICAL AND PHARMACEUTICAL SERVICES) AMENDMENT (No. 4) REGULATIONS 1987 (No. 1425) [85p], made under the National Health Service Act 1977, ss.29, 41, 42 and Sched. 5, para. 12; operative on September 1, 1987; amend S.I. 1974 No. 160.

NATIONAL HEALTH SERVICE (GENERAL MEDICAL AND PHARMACEUTICAL SERVICES) AMENDMENT REGULATIONS 1987 (No. 5) [45p], made under the National Health Service Act 1977, ss.29, 41, 42; operative on February 1, 1987 save for reg. 2(4) which is operative on August 1, 1987; amend S.I. 1974 No. 160 by varying the list of drugs which may be dispensed under the N.H.S.

2552. National Health Service

NATIONAL HEALTH SERVICE (CHARGES FOR DRUGS AND APPLIANCES) AMENDMENT REGULATIONS 1987 (No. 368) [80p], made under the National Health Service Act 1977 (c.49), s.77(1)(2), 83(*a*) operative on April 1, 1987; increase the charges payable for the supply under the N.H.S. of drugs and appliances.

NATIONAL HEALTH SERVICE (CHARGES TO OVERSEAS VISITORS) AMENDMENT REGULATIONS 1987 (No. 371) [80p], made under the National Health Service Act 1977, s.121; operative on April 1, 1987, increase charges to certain overseas visitors for services forming part of the national health service.

NATIONAL HEALTH SERVICE (FOOD PREMISES) REGULATIONS 1987 (No. 18) [45p], made under the National Health Service (Amendment) Act 1986 (c.66), s.1(2)(*a*)(3)(4)(7)(*a*); operative on February 7, 1987; provides that health authorities shall be treated as owners and occupiers of premises used by them for the purposes of the Food Act 1984.

NATIONAL HEALTH SERVICE FUNCTIONS (AMENDMENT OF DIRECTIONS TO AUTHORITIES) REGULATIONS 1987 (No. 245) [45p], made under the National Health Service Act 1977, ss.13, 18; operative on April 1, 1987; makes provision so as to extend to specified authorities the function of determining the charges to be paid for health service accommodation and services provided to private patients.

NATIONAL HEALTH SERVICE (SERVICE COMMITTEES AND TRIBUNAL) AMENDMENT REGULATIONS 1987 (No. 445) [80p], made under the National Health Service Act 1977, ss.35(1), 36(1) and 37(*a*); operative on May 1, 1987, provide for notices of appeal from divisions of the Dental Estimates Board to be given to family practitioner committees rather than to the Secretary of State.

2553. National Health Service (Amendment) Act 1986—commencement

NATIONAL HEALTH SERVICE (AMENDMENT) ACT 1986 (COMMENCEMENT No. 1) ORDER 1987 (No. 399 (C.11)) [45p], made under the National Health Service (Amendment) Act 1986 (c.66), s.8(5); brings s.3 of the 1986 Act into force on April 1, 1987.

2554. Nurses, midwives and health visitors

NURSES, MIDWIVES AND HEALTH VISITORS (ENTRY TO TRAINING REQUIREMENTS) AMENDMENT RULES APPROVAL ORDER 1987 (No. 446) [80p], made under the Nurses, Midwives and Health Visitors Act 1979 (c.36), s.22(4); operative on March 31, 1987; specify additional conditions subject to which a person may enter training without complying with minimum education requirements.

NURSES, MIDWIVES AND HEALTH VISITORS (PROFESSIONAL CONDUCT) RULES 1987 APPROVAL ORDER 1987 (No. 2156) [£3·30], made under the Nurses, Midwives and Health Visitors Act 1979, s.22(4); operative on February 1, 1988; provide for circumstances in which, and the means by which, a nurse, midwife or a health visitor may be removed from or restored to the register.

NURSES, MIDWIVES AND HEALTH VISITORS (TEMPORARY REGISTRATION) AMENDMENT RULES APPROVAL ORDER 1987 (No. 944) [85p], made under the Nurses, Midwives and Health Visitors Act 1979, s.22(4); operative on June 5, 1987; provide for the registration of person qualified outside the U.K. to act as a nurse, midwife or a health visitor.

2555. Parliamentary and Health Service Commissioners Act 1987 (c.39). See ADMINISTRATIVE LAW, §44.

2556. Registered Establishments (Scotland) Act 1987 (c.40). See LOCAL GOVERNMENT, §2384.

2557. Special hospital boards

SPECIAL HOSPITAL BOARDS (AMENDMENT OF CONSTITUTION) ORDER 1987 (No. 192) [45p], made under the National Health Service Act 1977 (c.49), s.11; operative on March 13, 1987; increases membership of three special health authorities.

2558. Superannuation regulations. See PENSIONS AND SUPERANNUATION.

2559. Transferred staff

NATIONAL HEALTH SERVICE (TRANSFERRED STAFF—APPEALS AMENDMENT) ORDER 1987 (No. 1428) [45p], made under the National Health Service Reorganisation Act 1973 (c.32), ss.19(2), 54(2), 56(3); operative on September 4, 1987; amends S.I. 1982 No. 203.

NEGLIGENCE

2560. Absolute liability—defective chair

[Offices, Shops and Railway Premises Act 1963 (c.41), s.14(2).]

P sustained injuries when the chair upon which he was sitting broke. The chair was supported on a vertical metal member which rested on four splayed-out metal legs. It was one of the legs that broke. S.14(2) provides: "a seat must be adequately and properly supported while in use." It was argued by D that there was no breach of s.14(2) because P had failed to establish that D knew of the defect.

Held, that the section imposes an absolute liability and accordingly P succeeded.

WRAY *v.* GREATER LONDON COUNCIL, January 16, 1986, Mr. M. Ogden Q.C. (sitting as a deputy High Court judge). [*Ex rel. Robin Thompson & Partners, Solicitors.*]

2561. Architects—defective drains—whether claim statute barred. See LONDON CONGREGATIONAL UNION *v.* HARRISS AND HARRISS, §229.

2562. Asbestos—exposure of employee—employers failure to take reasonable precautions—liability

[Factories Act 1937 (c.67), s.47(1); Shipbuilding and Shiprepairing Regulations (S.I. 1960 No. 1932).]

An employer who fails to take reasonable precautions against exposing his employee to asbestos dust is liable for his subsequent death.

BRYCE *v.* SWAN HUNTER GROUP, *The Times,* February 19, 1987, Phillips J.

2563. Barrister—duty to represent lay client—limit

A barrister is not under any duty to a lay client, who is advised by solicitors, to ensure that the client fully understands the implications of the barrister's advice.

MATHEW *v.* MAUGHOLD LIFE ASSURANCE CO., *The Times,* February 19, 1987, C.A.

2564. Causation—competing causes of damage

K's son was admitted to hospital with meningitis and was negligently given an overdose of penicillin. After remedial treatment he recovered, but was found to be deaf. Evidence was given that in no recorded case had an overdose of penicillin caused deafness, while deafness was often a consequence of meningitis. The judge's finding at first instance in favour of the plaintiff was reversed in the Court of Appeal. The plaintiff appealed on the grounds that since the overdose increased the risk of neurological damage and deafness was a type of such damage, therefore the defendants were liable.

Held, that where two competing causes of damage existed the law could not presume that the tortious cause was responsible if it was not proved that it was an accepted fact that the tortious cause was capable of causing or aggravating such damage (*McGhee* v. *National Coal Board* [1972] C.L.Y. 2356 distinguished).

KAY *v.* AYRSHIRE AND ARRAN HEALTH BOARD [1987] 2 All E.R. 417, H.L.

2565. Cause of accident—assumption—whether usual behaviour inferred

Where there is no clear evidence of the cause of an accident, but the Court knows of habitual careless behaviour which could have caused it, the Court may assume this to be the cause in the absence of any other explanation.

CLOWES *v.* NATIONAL COAL BOARD, *The Times*, April 23, 1987, C.A.

2566. Contributory negligence—apportionment of liability

[Law Reform (Contributory Negligence) Act 1945 (c.28), s.1(1).]

In apportioning liability between a plaintiff and several defendants under s.1(1) of the 1945 Act, the plaintiffs position should be compared with each defendant separately. Further a defendant is liable where he negligently creates or increases a risk of loss, even though his contribution to the loss cannot be precisely ascertained.

F walked across a pelican crossing when the light was showing red for pedestrians. He was hit by a car driven by L, thrown into the opposite lane and hit by a car driven by P. He suffered multiple injuries and partial tetraplegia. The judge apportioned liability equally between the three parties and ordered that judgment be entered for F against both L and P for two-thirds of F's damages. Both defendants appealed on the basis that the judge was wrong to consider both defendants together when apportioning liability. P further contended that F had failed to prove that the second collision contributed materially to his injuries.

Held, that on the basis of the finding that each party was equally liable and applying the rule that in apportioning liability under s.1(1) of 1945 Act the court should balance the fault of the plaintiff against that of each defendant separately, the plaintiff should only recover half, and not two-thirds, of the damages, each defendant contributing equally. Further, in these circumstances P was liable to F as having created or increased a risk that injury would occur, even though the extent of P's contribution to F's injury could not be ascertained (dicta in *Miraflores, The, and the Abadesa* [1967] C.L.Y. 3628 applied).

FITZGERALD *v.* LANE [1987] 2 All E.R. 455 C.A.

2567. Contributory negligence—claim in contract and tort—reinsurance in country other than that of original contract of insurance

(1) Where a claim was made both in contract and in tort a defendant could properly rely on contributory negligence by the plaintiff. (2) Where an insurance claim had been settled according to the law of the insurance contract, a reinsurance contract with a follow-settlements clause must necessarily include the law of the country of insurance notwithstanding that the reinsurance contract was made elsewhere (*Sayers* v. *Harlow Urban District Council* [1958] C.L.Y. 2220, *Insurance Co. of Africa* v. *Scor* [1983] C.L.Y. 2007 considered).

FORSIKRINGSAKTIELSKAPET VESTA *v.* BUTCHER, *Financial Times*, November 3, 1987, C.A.

2568. Contributory negligence—industrial accident

P, a 21-year old blaster, claimed damages from his employer and against scaffolding contractors, following a trip and fall on a catwalk on an oil rig. In the course of his work he had to traverse the catwalk and tripped upon a scaffold clip which had been left lying. The clip was, by implication, left by the second defendants. P contended that his employers owed him a duty of care to inspect and make safe his place of work.

Held, that the duty of care upon P in such circumstances was higher than the duty upon either defendant. Such a working place (the oil rig) was fraught with potential hazards and whilst P had 20/20 vision and could not be criticised for failing to look where he was putting his feet, his normal progress should have enabled him to see the clip and prevent him from thus falling and injuring himself. P was 100 per cent. contributory negligent.

BACON *v.* JACK TIGHE (OFFSHORE) AND CAPE SCAFFOLDING, July 2, 1987; H.H. Judge Whitehead; Lincoln County Ct. [*Ex rel.* Langleys, Solicitors].

2569. Crown immunity—nuclear weapons testing

[Crown Proceedings Act 1947 (c.44), s.10(2); Atomic Energy Authority (Weapons Group) Act 1973 (c.4).]

Where a person claims damages incurred whilst he was a member of the Armed Forces due to the negligence of employees of the Atomic Energy Authority, the action is not barred by Crown immunity notwithstanding the fact that the Secretary of State for Defence had assumed the liabilities of the authority under the 1973 Act.

PEARCE *v.* SECRETARY OF STATE FOR DEFENCE, *The Times*, August 5, 1987, C.A.

2570. Drugs recommended by hospital—patient seeking information—extent of hospital's obligation to disclose. See BLYTH *v.* BLOOMSBURY HEALTH AUTHORITY, §1677.

2571. Duty and standard of care—recreational ice-hockey—player hit by puck ricocheting off goal post during pre-game warm-up—normal part of game—foreseeability

[Can.] K was injured during the warm-up prior to a recreational ice-hockey game. As K skated from behind the goal, R took a practice shot, which hit the post, ricocheted and hit K, who was not wearing a helmet. R had delayed his shot momentarily to let K clear the goal post. K's action for damages in negligence was dismissed.

Held, dismissing K's appeal, that he should be deemed to have accepted the risk of injury, since practice shots during warm-up were a normal part of the game. Although R realised a higher risk in that he saw K, he increased his level of care by delaying his shot and could not be expected to have foreseen that the puck would ricochet.

KING *v.* REDLICH [1986] 4 W.W.R. 567, British Columbia C.A.

2572. Duty of care—adjudication officer—existence of duty of care—statutory exclusion of common law rights of action. See JONES *v.* DEPARTMENT OF EMPLOYMENT, §3466.

2573. Duty of care—architect—estimate for building project

It is negligent for an architect to fail to refer to the probable impact of inflation when he gives a client an estimate of costs for a building project, which meant that the architect could not recover his fee when the project was abandoned due to increased costs.

NYE SANDERS (A FIRM) *v.* BRISTOW, *The Times*, April 27, 1987, C.A.

2574. Duty of care—auditors—preparation of accounts. See LLOYD CHEYMAN AND CO. *v.* LITTLEJOHN AND CO., §318.

2575. Duty of care—bank—cheques crossed "not negotiable"—cheques endorsed by payee and paid by customer into account—whether bank obliged to warn customer of risk of defective title to cheques. See REDMOND *v.* ALLIED IRISH BANKS, §198.

2576. Duty of care—bank advising customer on investments

[Trinidad and Tobago]

The Court of Appeal of Trinidad and Tobago were not entitled to overturn a decision of a trial judge that a bank did not owe a duty of care to its customer in respect of certain investment advice by substituting their own views for those of the judge on questions of fact.

In November 1964, P invested £6,500 in a company called Pinnock. P made further investments in Pinnock in October and December 1965 and January and August 1966. In March 1967, Pinnock was in financial difficulties and was wound up in 1968, P being paid 5p in the £ of their investments. The initial investment was made after a visit to the Bank. The manager's evidence accepted by the trial judge was that there was a meeting in October 1964 at which P was orally given a credit report on Pinnock and given a brochure and literature about Pinnock and an application form to invest in the company. In November, P returned to the Bank with the completed application form and requested the Bank to transfer the £6,500 to Pinnock. P claimed he had been negligently advised to invest in Pinnock. The trial judge held that P had failed to establish a duty of care owed by the Bank. He found that P was not advised to invest in Pinnock but rather the Bank provided information upon which P independently arrived at a decision to invest. He also held that the Bank could not be liable for the further investments made by P without seeking further advice from the Bank. The trial judge concluded that P could not be said to have relied upon the judgment of the Bank's manager nor could the manager as a reasonable man know that P was relying on him in the circumstances. On appeal, the Court of Appeal of Trinidad and Tobago overturned the judge's decision. The Court of Appeal held that a duty of care did exist having regard to the fact that the Bank was in the business of giving investment advice and its conduct was tantamount to advising P to invest in Pinnock. The court held that the Bank failed to discharge their duty of care by failing to make adequate investigations into Pinnock and P's financial position and failing to advise P not to make further investments without further advice.

Held, allowing the Bank's appeal by a majority, that in overturning the judgment of the trial judge, the Court of Appeal wrongly substituted their own view of the facts for that of the trial judge. It was a question of fact as to whether the Bank had merely furnished information on tendered advice. The trial judge, having heard the witnesses at length, concluded the Bank furnished information. It was not open to the Court of Appeal to conclude that the judge erred in that respect. There was also no basis for interfering with the judge's decision that the subsequent investments were made entirely voluntarily by P without reference to or reliance on any advice received from the Bank. The minority upheld the judgment of the Court of Appeal of Trinidad and Tobago on the basis that a duty of care existed even though P only sought information from the Bank and that the Bank breached that duty by providing inadequate and misleading information to P. It was reasonably foreseeable that P would re-invest in Pinnock and P ought to have been warned of the dangers of so doing without reconsidering the soundness of the investment. The opinion of the majority departed from the approach laid down in *Hedley Byrne & Co.* v. *Heller & Partners* [1963] C.L.Y. 2416 and subsequent cases.

ROYAL BANK TRUST CO. (TRINIDAD) *v.* PAMPELLONNE (J. N.) [1987] 1 FTLR 90, P.C.

2577. Duty of care—building contractor—supervision of sub-contractor. See D. & F. ESTATES *v.* CHURCH COMMISSIONERS FOR ENGLAND, §3582.

2578. Duty of care—car passenger—mutual knowledge that driver unqualified—standard required—*volenti non fit injuria*

[Aus.] A car passenger was injured when the car hit a pole. The passenger knew that the driver was unqualified and inexperienced.

Held, that, in the circumstances the driver was in breach of her duty of care to her passenger. In the absence of special and exceptional facts, the standard of care required is the degree of care which could reasonably be expected of an experienced and competent driver. Facts which so alter the ordinary relationship of driver and passenger that it would be plainly unreasonable for the ordinary standard to apply constitute special and exceptional facts (*Nettleship* v. *Weston* [1971] C.L.Y. 7817 disapproved).

COOK *v.* COOK, 68 A.L.R. 353, High Ct. of Australia.

2579. Duty of care—employer giving reference for ex-employee—whether duty owed to ex-employee

An employer who gave a reference to a prospective employer of one of his ex-employees owed a duty of care to the ex-employee to exercise reasonable care to ensure that the reference was accurate.

P was employed by D for 10 years until he was made redundant in May 1979. P obtained temporary employment with C. C required P to provide two references before he could be given a permanent job. P gave D as one of his referees. D completed C's standard form of reference and stated at the end that they would not re-employ P. The form was completed by U who was D's financial and administrative manager. U was telephoned by C and confirmed that D would not re-employ P. In consequence P was sacked by C. P discovered the contents of the reference and considered them incorrect. P sued D in negligence contending that D owed him a duty of care to make sure that the reference was accurate. It was accepted by P that the opinions expressed in the reference were honestly held by D. In evidence U stated that he knew it was likely that P had applied for a job with C and that C would not employ P if the reference provided was adverse and also that he regarded it as his responsibility to exercise reasonable care to provide an accurate reference. D contended that no duty of care was owed to P as the reference was given to C at C's request.

Held, that P relied upon D to give an accurate reference and D knew or ought to have known that. There was a relationship of sufficient proximity or neighbourhood for D to owe P a duty of care. The fact that C asked D to provide the reference rather than P did not prevent a duty of care arising given the foreseeability of loss to P from any negligence on D's part. P clearly relied on D to give an accurate reference. There were no reasons of public policy that negated the existence of the duty of care. The duty of care required D to exercise reasonable care to ensure that facts stated in the reference were accurate and that opinions stated were the opinions that a reasonably prudent employer would have expressed on the basis of these facts. The reference D provided was honest, accurate and not negligently written. Claim dismissed (*Donoghue* v. *Stevenson* [1932] A.C. 562, *Ministry of Housing and Local Government* v. *Sharp* [1970] C.L.Y. 1493, *Anns* v. *Merton London Borough Council* [1977] C.L.Y. 2030 applied; *Hedley Byrne & Co.* v. *Heller & Partners* [1963] C.L.Y. 2416, *Junior Books* v. *Veitchi Co.* [1982] C.L.Y. 766, *Ross* v. *Caunters* [1979] C.L.Y. 2570 considered).

LAWTON *v.* B.O.C. TRANSHIELD [1987] I.C.R. 7, Tudor Evans J.

2580. Duty of care—existence—statutory powers

[Deposit-taking Companies Ordinance 1976 (Hong Kong).]

The ordinance charged the relevant commissioner with various regulatory functions in relation to a deposit-taking business in Hong Kong. Y deposited money with a licensed deposit-taker who went into liquidation, and he lost the money. He claimed that the deposit-taker had run his business fraudulently, that the Commissioner knew or ought to have known of this, and that he was thus negligent in granting or failing to revoke the deposit-taker's licence before Y deposited his money.

Held, on appeal against the claim being struck out as disclosing no cause of action that the requirements for duty of care were foreseeability of harm, and a close and direct relationship of proximity between the parties. Only rarely would the question of whether public policy required the conclusion of liability fall to be considered. Since the commissioner had no day-to-day control over the deposit-taker there was no proximity, and the nature of the ordinance was not such as to warrant reliance by Y on the soundness of a deposit-taker licenced under it (*Donoghue* v. *Stevenson* [1932] A.C. 562, *Smith* v. *Leurs* (1945) 70 C.L.R. 256, *Hedley Byrne* v. *Heller* [1963] C.L.Y. 2416, *Home Office* v. *Dorset Yacht Co.* [1970] C.L.Y. 1849, *Anns* v. *London Borough of Merton* [1977] C.L.Y. 2030, *Junior Books* v. *Veitchi* [1982] C.L.Y. 766, *Sutherland Shire Council* v. *Heyman* [1986] C.L.Y. 2274 and *Hill* v. *Chief Constable of West Yorkshire* [1987] C.L.Y. 2857 considered).

YUEN KUN-YEU *v.* ATT.-GEN. OF HONG KONG [1987] 2 All E.R. 705, P.C.

2581. Duty of care—insurers to insured. See BANQUE KEYSER ULLMAN S.A. *v.* SKANDIA (U.K.) INSURANCE CO., §2052.

2582. Duty of care—litigants

No duty of care is owed by one litigant to another as to the manner in which the litigation is conducted, whether in regard to service or any other step in the proceedings.

The second defendant claimed to strike out the claim of the plaintiffs on the ground that it disclosed no reasonable cause of action. The second defendant claimed to be the assignee of a debt owed by the plaintiff and in June 1986 presented a petition to wind up the plaintiff based on its failure to pay the alleged debt. The petition was served and a winding-up order made. In fact the plaintiff's registered office was not at the address shown on the petition and when the plaintiff learned of the winding-up order, it successfully applied to have it set aside. The plaintiff then sued in negligence various parties including the second defendant. The alleged negligence of the second defendant was the inclusion of an incorrect address in the petition, service at the wrong address, and advertising a petition never properly served.

Held, striking out the plaintiff's claim against the second defendant, that the plaintiff was seeking to extend the duty of care to a novel situation. It was not just and reasonable that such a duty of care should be incumbent on a defendant. There was no duty of care owed by one litigant to another as to the manner of conducting the litigation, whether in regard to service of process or any other step. The safeguards against impropriety were found in the rules and procedures which controlled the litigation and not in tort. No distinction existed for this purpose between winding-up petitions and other civil actions.

BUSINESS COMPUTERS INTERNATIONAL *v.* REGISTRAR OF COMPANIES (1987) 3 BCC 395, Scott J.

2583. Duty of care—local authority—collection of refuse—whether local authority liable for injury caused by failure to collect refuse. See DEAR *v.* NEWHAM LONDON BOROUGH COUNCIL, §3153.

2584. Duty of care—local authority—defective foundations—negligent inspection—whether duty of care owed to owner who had never been in occupation

An industrial warehouse complex was built between 1974 and 1975 with defective foundations, which eventually resulted in the buildings becoming a present or imminent danger to the health and safety of the occupants. P, who had recently purchased the freehold reversion, decided as a matter of good estate management that they would do the remedial works themselves, instead of requiring the lessees of the units to carry out the works under their repairing covenants. In P's action against *inter alia* the local authority, the authority admitted negligence in failing to ensure that the plans, foundations and construction work complied with the building regulations, but argued that they owed no duty to P. The judge accepted this submission.

Held, dismissing P's appeal, that P's action failed for two reasons. Firstly, they had been under no duty to anyone to make good the damage to the units.

Secondly, they were merely owners who had never been in occupation of the property, and had therefore never been at risk in respect of their own health or safety: hence they were not part of the section of the public to whom the duty was owed. (*Anns* v. *Merton London Borough Council* [1977] C.L.Y. 2030, *Governors of the Peabody Donation Fund* v. *Sir Lindsay Parkinson and Co.* [1984] C.L.Y. 2298, *Acrecrest* v. *Hatrell W.S. & Partners* [1982] C.L.Y. 2133, and *Curran* v. *Northern Ireland Co-ownership Housing Association* [1987] C.L.Y. 2709a considered).

HAMBRO LIFE ASSURANCE v. WHITE YOUNG & PARTNERS (1987) 284 E.G. 227, C.A.

2585. Duty of care—local authority—failure properly to inspect—defects in weather-board cladding and drainage

[N.Z.] S purchased a house under construction from the builders. At the time the agreement for sale and purchase was entered into, the house was closed in with the roof, wall cladding and windows all fixed and the builders were working on the interior linings. S had limited financial means and negotiated a reduced price on condition that there would be no maintenance clause in the agreement and that S would carry out, at his own expense, certain finishing work. S took possession in May 1977, and, soon after, applied a coat of stain to the weather-boards. In June or July 1977, significant leaks developed in various parts of the house. By Christmas 1977, and after he had applied a further coat of stain to the weather-boards, S became aware that these boards were becoming twisted and deformed to an unacceptable level, and that some nails were pulling out. In June 1978, it was discovered that flooding was being caused because a stormwater drain had not been connected to an outlet. It was also found that no gutter or spouting had been provided on the front or north face of a patio. S brought a negligence action against the Council, who had issued the building permit and whose inspectors had carried out inspections while the house was being constructed. At first instance it was held that the inspections made by the Council during construction had been negligent: the building inspector ought to have seen and recognised that the weather-boards did not meet the grading standards required by the bylaws; he should also have discovered the defects in the stormwater drainage and the guttering on the patio and ensured that they were remedied before the building was completed.

Held, that the local bylaw-making power conferred on local authorities was wide enough to cover the construction of soundly built houses and the resultant safeguarding of persons who might occupy those houses against the risk of acquiring a substandard residence. The construction of houses with good materials and in a workmanlike manner was therefore a matter within the Council's control and a council might be liable for defects in exterior cladding even though questions of safety and health did not arise. The weather-boards used in the construction of the house did not comply with the Council's building code, and the Council had been negligent in failing to ensure that its own bylaws were observed (*Brown* v. *Heathcote Council* [1986] 1 N.Z.L.R. 76 applied and *Governors of the Peabody Donation Fund* v. *Sir Lindsay Parkinson & Co.* [1984] C.L.Y. 2298 distinguished).

STIELLER *v.* PORIRUA CITY COUNCIL [1986] 1 N.Z.L.R. 84, N.Z. C.A.

2586. Duty of care—local authority—negligent mortgage valuation—whether duty of care owed to mortgagor

[Housing (Financial Provisions) Act 1958 (c.42), s.43(1).]

In 1978 P sought a mortgage from D1, the local authority, in order to purchase a house in Kidderminster. The application form stated that the authority's valuation would be confidential and was solely for the information of the authority, and that," . . . no responsibility whatever is implied or accepted by the Council for the value or condition of the property by reason of such inspection or report." The authority's valuer D2 noticed that settlement had taken place, and in particular that there was a tie bar round the house, a slope in the bedroom, and bulges in the walls. However he concluded that there would be no further settlement, and accordingly valued the house at the asking price of £9,450, recommended a 90 per cent. mortgage, and impliedly represented in his report that no structural repairs were needed. When three years later P wished to sell the house, the authority, acting on a further report from D2, refused to lend any money on the security of the house unless substantial and expensive repairs were first carried out, and it duly transpired that there was, as the judge found, "a fairly large risk of a fairly substantial disaster." The judge further found that the house was not fit for human habitation within the meaning of s.43(1) of the Housing (Financial Provisions) Act 1958, and that in 1978 the house was worth £3,500 only, being the sum that a speculative builder would have paid for it.

Held, giving judgment for P in the agreed sum of £12,000 including interest, that (1) D2's initial valuation had been negligent; (2) D1 and D2 had owed a duty of care to P in respect of that valuation, and that the exemption clause in the application form did not relieve them from liability for the breach of that duty; (3) there should be no deduction from the agreed damages for contributory negligence, notwithstanding that P had failed to commission their own survey. (*Anns* v. *Merton London Borough Council,* [1977] C.L.Y. 2030, *Curran v. Northern Ireland Co-ownership Housing Association* [1987] C.L.Y. 2709a, *Governors of the Peabody Donation Fund* v. *Sir Lindsay Parkinson & Co.* [1984] C.L.Y. 2298, *Ward* v. *McMaster* [1986] C.L.Y. 2261 and *Yianni* v. *Evans (Edwin) & Sons* [1981] C.L.Y. 1837 considered).

HARRIS *v.* WYRE FOREST DISTRICT COUNCIL (1987) 1 E.G.L.R. 231, Schiemann J.

2587. Duty of care—local authority—negligent survey—defective house—measure of damages

In 1975 the plaintiffs bought a house with the assistance of a mortgage from the defendant authority. The defendants carried out a survey and stated that the structural condition of the house was good. The Plaintiffs did not have their own survey carried out, but accepted the authority's offer. They then became aware of the existence of a 20mm gap between the skirting board and the floor of the downstairs front room. They asked the authority to send round a surveyor who duly attended and told them that there was nothing to worry about. Some five years later, the plaintiffs put the house on the market and purchased another property. After a further year another report was commissioned on the house and this stated that there was evidence of settlement or subsidence progressive over a number of years and doubted whether any building society would grant a mortgage on it. The plaintiffs were not able to sell the house and had to move back to it. They sued the defendants in negligence.

Held, giving judgment for the plaintiffs, that (1) in all the circumstances the defendants owed the plaintiffs a duty of care; (2) the authority's surveyor was negligent; (3) the plaintiffs claim was not barred by s.2 of the Limitation Act 1980 in that there had been a deliberate concealment of the facts by virtue of the second inspection, accordingly time did not begin to run until then; (4) alternatively, the conduct of the surveyor was such as to raise an estoppel against the authority; (5) the plaintiffs were entitled to damages based on the difference in price between what they paid in 1975 and its true market value at the time, and to a further £1,500 for distress and inconvenience.

WESTLAKE *v.* BRACKNELL DISTRICT COUNCIL (1987) 19 H.L.R. 375, P.J. Cox Q.C.

2588. Duty of care—misrepresentations causing economic loss—government redevelopment plans applied in town planning decisions—whether duty owed to developers—whether reasonable to rely

[Aus.] The appellants were developers who acquired land relying upon a development plan published in 1968 by the State Planning Authority ("A") and the Council of the City of Sydney ("C"). The plan encouraged developers to acquire properties, permitting high density development. C adopted and followed the plan until 1972, when it was abandoned. The appellants sued in respect of their economic loss, alleging that the plan's lack of feasibility was the result of a failure to use due care in its preparation. In the Court of Appeal of New South Wales, A and C were held not to owe a relevant duty of care.

Held, dismissing the appeal, by the majority, that if the appellants' case was to succeed they must establish at least: (i) that the alleged representation was made; and (ii) that A and C made the representation with the intention of inducing members of the class of developers to act in reliance on the misrepresentation. The appellants failed under head (i), since the documents offered no assurance about development levels or C's continuing application of proposed maximum space ratios. Brennan J. further held that the circumstances gave rise to no duty of care, since it was unreasonable for a person contemplating a course of action involving a risk of loss if a public authority did not exercise its discretion in a particular way to rely upon the feasibility of a policy affecting the discretion when that discretion was to be exercised in the public interest.

SAN SEBASTIAN PTY. *v.* MINISTER ADMINISTERING THE ENVIRONMENTAL PLANNING AND ASSESSMENT ACT 1979, 68 A.L.R. 161, High Ct. of Australia.

2589. Duty of care—pedestrian crossing junction—contributory negligence—whether duty to cross at a light-controlled crossing

Per curiam: A pedestrian has no duty in law to cross a junction at a light-controlled crossing. He is entitled to cross where he wishes provided he takes reasonable care for his own safety.

T crossed diagonally over two roads at a complex junction at night, without making use of a light-controlled crossing. He believed he was protected from traffic by a red light. H drove his car through the red light and struck T. At trial of T's claim for damages the judge found H wholly to blame. H appealed.

Held, dismissing the appeal, that T had no reason to suppose H would not stop at the light, that H was guilty of serious careless driving, and that since T owed no duty of care to H any failure of T's to keep a proper lookout could not amount to contributory negligence.

TREMAYNE *v.* HILL [1987] R.T.R. 131, C.A.

2590. Duty of care—pollution of water—whether water authority negligent in failing to warn of dangerously high levels of chemicals in river water. See SCOTT-WHITEHEAD *v.* NATIONAL COAL BOARD, §3866.

2591. Duty of care—statutory authority—flooding

A local authority drainage board was held liable to house-owners who had sustained damage to a newly-built house when it was flooded by a river, at a site which the authority knew, at the time that permission to build was granted, would flood (*Yuen Kun Yeu* v. *Att.-Gen. of Hong Kong* [1987] C.L.Y. 2580, *Anns* v. *Merton London Borough Council* [1977] C.L.Y. 2030, *Hedley Byrne & Co.* v. *Heller & Partners* [1963] C.L.Y. 2416 considered.

CHRISTCHURCH DRAINAGE BOARD *v.* BROWN, *The Daily Telegraph,* October 12, 1987, P.C.

2592. Duty of care—sub-bailment—quasi-bailee. See BAILMENT, §184.

2593. Duty of care—testator's solicitors—beneficiary. See CLARKE *v.* BRUCE LANCE & CO., §3549.

2594. Duty of police—whether duty of care owed to victims or potential victims of crime. See HILL *v.* CHIEF CONSTABLE OF WEST YORKSHIRE, §2857.

2595. Employers' liability—protective clothing—whether duty of care extends to instructions and checks

An award of damages for personal injury was granted by the High Court to an employee who had slipped and injured himself after failing to request the replacement of a pair of boots with ridged soles, even though he was aware that these would be provided by his employer upon request. The employers appealed to the Court of Appeal.

Held, allowing the appeal, that the employers had not breached their duty to take reasonable care for the safety of their employees. The employers had taken reasonable steps by providing protective boots and informing employees that replacements were available on request, and they had no greater duty to instruct employees to replace worn boots or to inspect the condition of the soles from time to time.

SMITH *v.* SCOT BOWYERS [1986] I.R.L.R. 315, C.A.

2596. Estate agent—valuation—whether negligent

P purchased a house in Southport as a retirement home in reliance upon a report by D, an estate agent. The report noted that the property had settlement on the gable and required a new damp course; that the electrical wiring would need overhaul at a future date, and that the plumbing, though old, appeared in reasonable condition. It continued, "Taking into account the shortcomings we can recommend a purchase," and valued the property at £8,650. P duly bought the house for the asking price of £8,745 but, when they wished to sell it, they were unable to do so at a price which would enable them to move to the south of England. P claimed that D had been instructed to produce a full structural survey, that his report and valuation had been negligent, and that he should have warned them about the probable difficulties of resale. The judge found that D had been instructed to provide a valuation only; that he had not misinformed P; and that the valuation had been within limits completely accurate. He therefore gave judgment for D.

Held, dismissing P's appeal, that the judge had been fully entitled to reach those conclusions on the evidence before him.

Per curiam: there is no duty on a valuer to warn a purchaser as to the difficulties of resale.

SUTCLIFFE *v.* SAYER (1987) 281 E.G. 1452, C.A.

2597. Forseeability—fire started by vandals in one building—whether duty of care owed to adjoining occupier

[Scot.] Owners of a disused cinema were not liable in negligence to the owners of adjoining premises where vandals started a fire in the cinema that damaged the adjoining premises as it was not highly probable or very likely, as opposed to a mere possibility, that vandals would set fire to the cinema.

D owned a disused cinema. P owned premises nearby. D purchased the cinema in May 1976 with the intention of demolishing it and constructing a shop. In July 1976 the cinema was destroyed by a fire that had been deliberately started by vandals. P's premises were substantially damaged. P sued D for negligently failing to secure the cinema against vandals and failing to take steps to prevent vandals setting fire to it. There was evidence at the trial that a fire had been discovered in early July 1976 but that had never been reported to D or the police. There was also evidence that D knew the cinema was subject to the attentions of vandals. The trial judge found for P but that judgment was reversed on appeal. P appealed. It was conceded at the appeal that the only effective step D could have taken to prevent the fire was to have someone on the premises 24 hours per day.

Held, dismissing P's appeal, that if it was anticipated that the cinema would be set on fire so as to cause damage to neighbouring premises the occupiers of the neighbouring premises would have informed D of that risk. No-one saw fit to warn D, therefore a fire was not to be anticipated. In the circumstances of the case no reasonable person in D's position was bound to anticipate as probable that if he took no steps to secure the premises they would be set on fire with consequent risk to neighbouring premises; it was not reasonably foreseeable that vandals would deliberately set fire to the cinema in such a manner as would be likely to engulf the building. As a matter of principle what the reasonable man is bound to foresee in a case involving injury or damage by independant human agency is the probable consequences of his acts or omissions. A clear basis will be required to assert that the injury or damage is more than a mere possibility. The judge must be satisfied that the injury or damage is highly probable or very likely. In terms of probability the risk of the injury or damage that occurs must be near the top of the scale. (*Bourhill* v. *Young* [1943] A.C. 92, *Bolton* v. *Stone* [1951] C.L.Y. 6789, 6897, *Overseas Tankship (U.K.)* v. *Miller Steamship Co. Pty.* [1967] C.L.Y. 3445, *Goldman* v. *Hargrave* [1967] C.L.Y. 8145, *Dorset Yacht Co.* v. *Home Office* [1970] C.L.Y. 1849, *Evans* v. *Glasgow District Council* [1978] C.L.Y. 1789, *Lamb* v. *Camden London Borough Council* [1981] C.L.Y. 1855, *Perl (P.) (Exporters)* v. *Camden London Borough Council* [1983] C.L.Y. 2531, *Muir* v. *Glasgow Corporation* [1943] S.C. (H.L.) 3, *King* v. *Liverpool City Council* [1986] C.L.Y. 2260 considered; *Squires* v. *Perth and Kinross District Council* [1986] S.L.T. 30 doubted).

SMITH *v.* LITTLEWOODS ORGANISATION [1987] 2 W.L.R. 480, H.L.

2598. Human error—contrasted

Human error and the legal concept of negligence are not necessarily synonymous.

FLYNN *v.* VANGE SCAFFOLDING & ENGINEERING CO., *The Times,* March 26, 1987, C.A.

2599. Liability—construction of contract—whether an exclusion clause. See CONTRACT, §423, 424.

2600. Licence agreement—unlawful interference with contractual relations—duty of care. See WESTERN FRONT *v.* VESTRON INC., §499.

2601/2. Medical negligence—advice on sterilisation—standard of care—whether statement that operation irreversible a misrepresentation

Medical advice is not negligent advice if it is advice that a substantial body of doctors would have given.

The plaintiff went to hospital for advice on what action to take to avoid getting pregnant. The hospital gave no warning of the possibility of failure of the operation and allegedly represented that the operation was "irreversible". The judge held that the defendants were negligent in not warning of the possibility of failure of the operation.

Held, allowing the appeal, that (1) the test for medical advice was whether there was a substantial body of doctors who would have given the same advice; (2) the statement that it was "irreversible" could not reasonably be construed as a "misrepresentation" (*Bolam* v. *Friern Hospital Management Committee* [1957] C.L.Y. 2431 applied).

GOLD *v.* HARINGEY HEALTH AUTHORITY [1987] 2 All E.R. 888, C.A.

2603. Medical negligence—duty to inform—failure to inform patient of possibility of conservative treatment or of risks of leaving condition untreated

[Can.] In order to enable a patient to give informed consent, a surgeon should, where the circumstances so require, advise the patient of the consequences of leaving the ailment untreated and of alternative means of treatment and their risks. This was not done in the instant case, there was no real excuse for this, and, accordingly, the patient did not give informed consent to his surgery (*Sidaway* v. *Board of Governors of the Bethlem Royal Hospital and the Maudsley Hospital* [1985] C.L.Y. 2318 not followed).

HAUGHIAN *v.* PAINE [1987] 4 W.W.R. 97, Saskatchewan C.A.

2604. Medical negligence—failure by hospital to diagnose in good time—lost chance of recovery

H, then aged 13, fell from a tree and suffered an acute traumatic fracture of the left femoral epiphysis. He was not correctly treated for five days and suffered avascular necrosis, involving disability of the hip joint and the virtual certainty of osteoarthritis. The health authority admitted negligence. The trial judge assessed at 75 per cent. the chance the avascular necrosis would have developed from the fall anyway, and awarded damages based on the loss of a 25 per cent. chance of full recovery.

Held, allowing the health authority's appeal, that it was for H to establish on a balance of probabilities that delay had materially contributed to the development of avascular necrosis and that the judge's findings of fact were contrary to this and accordingly the plaintiff failed on the issue of causation and quantification did not arise.

Per curiam: The question of whether damages can be awarded for a lost chance of avoiding personal injury is not settled.

HOTSON *v.* EAST BERKSHIRE HEALTH AUTHORITY [1987] 3 W.L.R. 232, H.L.

2605. Medical negligence—specialist hospital unit—standard of care

The standard of care required of members of a specialist hospital unit is to be determined in the context of the particular posts in the unit rather than according to general rank or status.

P was an infant, born prematurely and suffering from, *inter alia,* oxygen deficiency. He was placed in a 24 hour special baby care unit in the hospital. A junior doctor wrongly inserted a catheter in a vein rather than an artery and the baby was given too much oxygen. The junior doctor checked with a senior registrar who failed to spot the mistake and indeed repeated it. P claimed damages claiming that the excess of oxygen had caused an eye condition resulting in near blindness. P was awarded £116,199.

Held, dismissing the appeal, that the junior doctor had not been negligent because he consulted a senior, the registrar had been negligent himself and the health authority was vicariously liable (*Bolam* v. *Friern Hospital Management Committee* [1957] C.L.Y. 2431 applied).

WILSHIRE *v.* ESSEX AREA HEALTH AUTHORITY [1986] 3 All E.R. 801, C.A.

2606. Medical negligence—sterilisation—existing pregnancy

P wished to be sterilised. The gynaecologist advised P either to abstain from sex or ensure that her husband used a sheath. P failed to take either precaution. On the morning of the operation the gynaecologist, during his ward round, checked that P still wanted the operation and asked her if there was any possibility that she was pregnant. He told her that the operation would not terminate any pregnancy. P told him that she was certain that she was not pregnant. No dilation and curettage ("D and C") was performed during the operation which, if done would have made the likelihood of any continuing pregnancy remote. P later gave birth to a healthy child.

Held, dismissing P's claim, that a gynaeologist was not liable in negligence to a patient who assured him that she would not be pregnant, but who was and upon whom he performed a sterlisation operation which was incapable of affecting any existing pregnancy. It was neither necessary nor desirable for a D and C to be done as a matter of course.

VENNER *v.* NORTH EAST ESSEX HEALTH AUTHORITY, *The Times,* February 21, 1987, Tucker J.

2607. Negligent settling of document—when damage occurs. See MOORE (D.W.) AND CO. *v.* FERRIER, §2333.

2608. Nervous shock—witnessing destruction of property—whether damages recoverable

There is no reason in principle why damages for nervous shock should not be recovered after witnessing property damage.

Per curiam: Questions of far-reaching principle such as recoverability of damages on grounds of public policy are not suitable to be determined as preliminary issues on assumed facts.

A engaged B G Co. to install central heating in her home and returned to find the loft on fire. The house and contents were extensively damaged, and the property claim was settled, but A also claimed for nervous shock. A preliminary issue arose as to whether a claim lay for nervous shock caused by witnessing property damage, rather than personal injury.

Held, that recovery of damages was possible in such circumstances, provided the elements of liability were proved, and the matter ought to go to trial (*Hay (or Bourhill)* v. *Young* [1942] 2 All E.R. 396 and *McLoughlin* v. *O'Brian* [1982] C.L.Y. 2153 considered).

ATTIA *v.* BRITISH GAS [1987] 3 All E.R. 455, C.A.

2609. Occupiers' liability—blocked overflow pipe causing flood to neighbouring premises

The plaintiff was the tenant of a ground floor flat. The second defendant was the occupier of the flat above. The first defendant was the landlord. Water penetrated the ceiling of the drawing room in the plaintiff's flat, having come from the second defendant's flat above. As a result of an inspection it became clear that the cause of the ingress of water was a blocked overflow in the washhand basin in the bathroom. This was mentioned to the second defendant but not to the first. The Plaintiff sued the first and second defendants in negligence. At the trial the first defendant was dismissed from the action at the end of the first day. The judge found that while the cause was the blocked overflow pipe, the second defendant was not liable in negligence since it was a necessary ingredient of negligence that the second defendant either knew that the overflow was blocked or that he had not acted reasonably in failing to inspect it. The plaintiff appealed.

Held, dismissing the appeal, that (1) it would impose too high a duty on the occupier of the upstairs flat to check if the waste was blocked; (2) the nature and extent of the second defendant's contractual and common law obligations to his landlord were not necessarily the same as those owed to his neighbours.

HAWKINS *v.* DHAWAN AND MISHIKU (1987) 19 H.L.R. 232, C.A.

2610. Occupiers' liability—duty and standard of care—plaintiff injured in climbing over defective cemetery fence—occupier aware—no licence—no unusual danger—no breach of duty

[Can.] G were the occupiers of land used as a cemetery. Y was a visitor planning to visit a grave. Because the vehicle gates were closed, Y parked his car outside and attempted to climb over a four foot high decorative fence, consisting of two horizontal pipes fastened between concrete pillars. In doing so, Y fell when the pipe gave way, suffering severe injuries. G was aware that the section of pipe was defective. At first instance, Y succeeded.

Held, allowing G's appeal, that there was no evidence that there was any reason for Y to believe that climbing the fence was a permitted short cut. In the absence of an invitation or licence, the only duty owned by G to Y was to treat him with ordinary humanity. The failure to maintain the fence was no breach of that duty. The loose bar was no covert peril or danger.

YELIC *v.* TOWN OF GIMLI [1987] 1 W.W.R. 537, Manitoba C.A.

2611. Occupiers' liability—duty owed to invitee—liability for personal injuries

[Aus.] Z was injured when she slipped in A's supermarket on a floor which had become wet as a result of people entering from the rain. At first instance, it was found that, it being a wet day, the moisture on the floor did not constitute an "unusual danger" which would found liability (*Indermaur* v. *Dames* (1866) L.R. 1 C.P. 274 applied). On appeal, it was held that the trial judge should have considered whether a general duty of care was owed by A to Z in addition to the special duty of care owed to an invitee.

Held, on further appeal, that the duty which an occupier of land owed to an invitee was properly to be seen as the ordinary common law duty to take reasonable care (*Indermaur (supra)* explained and *London Graving Dock Co.* v. *Horton* [1951] C.L.Y. 6727 disapproved).

AUSTRALIAN SAFEWAY STORES PTY. *v.* ZALUZNA, 69 A.L.R. 615, High Ct. of Australia.

2612. Occupiers' liability—duty to independent contractor's employees—safe system of work—demolition of building.

[Occupiers' Liability Act 1957 (c.31), s.2(2).]

A council contracted with S for the demolition of a building on the site of a housing scheme. In breach of an express prohibition, S sub-contracted to W, who employed an unsafe system of work which caused injury to F, W's employee. F sued W, S and the council, but neither W nor S had public liability insurance. The case against the council was dismissed.

Held, that in the absence of special circumstances or knowledge, an occupier would not be liable for the unsafe system of work of the sub-contractor, since he could reasonably be expected to supervise it. F's injury did not arise from any "use" by him of the premises within s.2(2) of the 1957 Act, and thus the appeal would be dismissed.

FERGUSON *v.* WELSH [1987] 3 All E.R. 777, H.L.

2613. Personal injuries—suffered in consequence of bad weather when ship at anchor—liability

In an action for personal injuries, P claimed as chief officer of D's vessel. P had suffered injuries when struck by a wave when on the fo'c'sle head of the vessel. He contended that the vessel had been anchored at a time when it was unsafe so to do, and that the master had negligently required him to stay on deck.

Held, on the facts and the evidence, that the decision to anchor was unseamanlike, and the master had acted negligently.

HOLMAN (JOHN MALCOLM) *v.* EVERARD (F.T.) & SONS; JACK WHARTON, THE [1986] 2 Lloyd's Rep. 382, Sheen J.

2614. Resue principle—fire—injury to fireman

A person who negligently started a fire was liable for any injury sustained by a fireman which was a foreseeable consequence of it. A person who negligently created some peril to the life or safety of others owed a duty to a third person who, acting reasonably, came to the rescue to deal with the emergency.

The defendant negligently started a fire by using a blowlamp to burn off paint under the guttering of his house thereby causing the roof timbers to catch fire. The plaintiff, a fireman, went into the roof space, and sustained serious injuries caused by steam generated by water poured onto the fire, notwithstanding that he was wearing protective clothing. There was no suggestion that the contents of the roof space were unusually combustible or that there was any special danger from any hidden cause. The plaintiff brought an action for damages in negligence, but the judge held that although the defendant had been negligent he could not have reasonably foreseen the injury to the fireman and rejected the claim.

Held, allowing the appeal that even in the absence of special circumstances not known to the fireman, a person who negligently started a fire was liable for any injury sustained by a fireman or another person fighting the fire which was a foreseeable consequence of the negligent starting of the fire. The fireman was entitled to recover damages even though he undertook to bear the ordinary risks of his calling. The injury to the plaintiff was a predictable consequence of the defendant's negligence since the injury caused by steam was not different in kind from damage caused by the flames themselves, and the defendant could not rely on the efficiency of the fireman's protective clothing to prevent him being injured. He was liable to the plaintiff on this ground, and also on the principle that a person who by negligence created some peril to the life or safety of others owed a duty to a third person who, acting reasonably, came to the rescue to deal with the emergency (*Haynes* v. *Harwood* [1935] 1 K.B. 146 and *Hughes* v. *Lord Advocate* [1963] C.L.Y. 970 applied; Dictum of Woolf J. in *Salmon* v. *Seafarer Restaurants* [1983] C.L.Y. 2552 approved).

OGWO *v.* TAYLOR [1987] 1 All E.R. 668, C.A.

2615. Safe system of work—vicarious liability—limitation of liability

[Merchant Shipping (Liability of Shipowners and Others) Act, 1958 (c.62), s.3.]

M was employed by N. Co. as a deckhand and in the course of his employment worked on a tug owned by S. Co. under the direction of its captain who was employed by S. Co. M's job was to untie the tug from a dredger and then signal to the captain that it was safe to move away. On one occasion the captain started to move the tug away before he received the signal, with the result that M was injured by the rope.

Held, that (1) N. Co. owed M a duty to devise a safe system of work and to ensure that it was operated. They remained liable even though they had delegated the performance of the duty to the captain, whose part had been central to its operation. The captain was negligent and W. Co. was liable; (2) N. Co. had no interest in the tug within s.3(1) of the Act of 1958, and the captain had remained the servant of S. Co. under s.3(2)(*a*). Accordingly N. Co. could not limit their liability pursuant to the Act.

McDERMID *v.* NASH DREDGING AND RECLAMATION CO. [1987] 3 W.L.R. 212, H.L.

2616. Solicitor—duty to exercise reasonable skill and care—unusual clause in lease—duty to explain clause to client. See COUNTY PERSONNEL (EMPLOYMENT AGENCY) *v.* PULVER (ALAN R.) & Co. (A FIRM), §3551.

2617. Statutory duty—further and better particulars sought. See PRACTICE, §3072.

2618. Statutory undertaker—liability

A statutory undertaker is not negligent in relying on a highway authority's six monthly road inspection rather than inspecting its manhole covers itself. However, it will be taken to have the same knowledge that it would or should have had if it had inspected the cover at the time that the local authority had inspected.

REID *v.* BRITISH TELECOMMUNICATIONS, *The Times*, June 27, 1987, C.A.

2619. Sterilisation operation—signed consent form—whether assurance of success

Where P signed a consent form before a sterilisation operation which warned of not being able to have children thereafter, that form was not an assurance of success in the operation. (*Hedley Byrne* v. *Heller & Partners* [1963] C.L.Y. 2416 considered).

WORSTER *v.* CITY AND HACKNEY HEALTH AUTHORITY, *The Times*, June 22, 1987, Garland J.

2620. Surveyor—general disclaimers of liability—building society valuation and report

The plaintiff sought a mortgage from a building society and paid a fee for a report and mortgage valuation. The standard application form stated that the applicant accepted that the society disclaimed all liability in respect of the report on part both of the society and the surveyor compiling it. The chartered surveyor who inspected the house failed to check whether the brickwork of the chimneys from which the chimney breasts had been removed was adequately supported. The report stated that no essential repairs were required. Two years later, one of the chimney flues collapsed. The plaintiff brought proceedings for damages in the county court against the surveyor and was awarded £4,379·97 damages including interest. The defendants appealed on the grounds that (a) on their face, the disclaimers were wide enough to absolve them from all liability in negligence and (b) the Unfair Contract Terms Act 1977 (c.50) did not prevent them from relying on the disclaimers.

Held, dismissing the appeal, that (1) the wording of the disclaimers was such as to exclude liability for negligence on part of the defendants but (2) in accordance with the Unfair Contract Terms Act 1977, it was for the defendants to show that the requirement of reasonableness was satisfied in respect of the exclusion of liability; in determining this question all the circumstances were to be taken into account and where the surveyor knew that a purchaser was likely to rely on the report, it was not reasonable to allow the defendants to rely on the disclaimer.

SMITH *v.* BUSH (A FIRM) (1987) 19 H.L.R. 287, C.A.

2621. Vicarious liability—independent contractor—extra-hazardous activity

[Aus.] *Held*, by the majority, that the notion that a principal is liable for the negligence of an independent contractor on the basis that the activities he was engaged to perform were extra-hazardous has no place in Australian law (*Honeywill & Stein* v. *Larkin Brothers* [1934] 1 K.B. 191, *Matania* v. *National Provincial Bank* [1936] 2 All E.R. 633 and *Salsbury* v. *Woodland* [1969] C.L.Y. 2432 not followed).

STEVENS *v.* BRODRIBB SAWMILLING CO. PTY. (1985–1986) 160 C.L.R. 16, High Ct. of Aus.

NORTHERN IRELAND

2622. Administrative law

AUDIT (1987 ORDER) (COMMENCEMENT) ORDER (NORTHERN IRELAND) 1987 (No. 137 (C.5)) [45p], made under S.I. 1987 No. 460 (N.I. 5), art. 1(2), and the Northern Ireland Act 1974 (c.28), Sched. 1, para. 2(1); fixes April 1, 1987, as the appointed day for the purposes of the 1987 S.I.

LANDS TRIBUNAL (SALARIES) ORDER (NORTHERN IRELAND) 1987 (No. 359) [45p], made under the Lands Tribunal and Compensation Act (Northern Ireland) 1964 (c.29), s.2(5), and the Administrative and Financial Provisions Act (Northern Ireland) 1962 (c.7), s.18; operative on October 21, 1987; increases the salaries of members of the Lands Tribunal for Northern Ireland; revokes the 1986 (No. 291) Order.

PUBLIC USE OF RECORDS (AMENDMENT) RULES (NORTHERN IRELAND) 1987 (No. 98) [80p], made under the Public Records Act (Northern Ireland) 1923 (c.20), s.9, and the Northern Ireland Act 1974 (c.28), Sched. 1, para. 2(1); operative on April 13, 1987; specify the fees payable for the inspection, search or copying of certain public records and for the handling and certification of copies; revoke the 1980 (No. 288) and 1982 (No. 299) Rules.

SALARIES (COMPTROLLER AND AUDITOR GENERAL AND OTHERS) ORDER (NORTHERN IRELAND) 1987 (No. 41) [45p], made under S.I. 1973 No. 1086 (N.I. 14), art. 4(2); operative on March 25, 1987; increases the salaries of the Comptroller and Auditor General, the Parliamentary Commissioner and the Commissioner for Complaints; revokes the 1985 (No. 265) Order.

SALARIES (PARLIAMENTARY COMMISSIONER AND COMMISSIONER FOR COMPLAINTS) ORDER (NORTHERN IRELAND) 1987 (No. 360) [45p], made under S.I. 1973 No. 1086 (N.I. 14), art. 4(2); operative on October 21, 1987; increases the salaries of the Northern Ireland Parliamentary Commissioner for Administration and the Northern Ireland Commissioner for Complaints; revokes the 1987 (No. 41) Order.

2622a. Administrative law—Audit (Northern Ireland) Order 1987 (S.I. 1987 No. 460 (N.I. 5))

This Order establishes the Northern Ireland Audit Office and provides for the salary and pension of the Comptroller and Auditor General and for the exercise by him of his functions. The Order also empowers the Comptroller and Auditor General to conduct economy, efficiency and effectiveness examinations in relation to government departments and other authorities and bodies.

The Order came into operation on April 1, 1987, save for one repeal which does not come into operation until the end of six months from a day to be appointed.

2623. Administrative law—judicial review—decision of university—sex discrimination

M was employed by Queen's University under a contract which provided for her automatic retirement at the end of the month in which she reached her sixtieth birthday. M questioned the validity of such a provision in that it applied to women and not to men and referred to *Marshall* v. *Southampton & South-West Hampshire Area Health Authority* (No. 152/84) [1986] C.L.Y. 1456. The university replied that it was not a public body and that M was obliged to retire in accordance with her contract. M applied for judicial review.

Held, on preliminary points raised by the university, that (1) as M's rights could be fully protected by an ordinary action in contract her decision to use the judicial review procedure was misconceived; and (2) the court did not have a discretion to allow M to proceed as if she had brought an action by writ.

MALONE'S APPLICATION, *Re* [1986] 9 N.I.J.B. 74, Murray J.

2624. Administrative law—judicial review—prisons—discipline—hearings disrupted by noise—application out of time—hardship. See HUGHES' APPLICATION, *Re,* §2724.

2625. Administrative law—judicial review—prisons—whether right to legal representation—discretion. See HONE AND McCARTAN'S APPLICATION, *Re,* §2725.

2626. Agency

ENDURING POWERS OF ATTORNEY (NORTHERN IRELAND CONSEQUENTIAL AMENDMENT) ORDER 1987 (No. 1628) [45p], made under the Northern Ireland Constitution Act 1973 (c.36), s.38(2), as extended by the Northern Ireland Act 1974 (c.28), Sched. 1, para. 1(7); operative on the same date as S.I. 1987 No. 1627 (N.I. 16); extends s.7(3) of the 1985 Act to instruments registered under S.I.1987 No. 1627 (N.I. 16).

2627. Agency—Enduring Powers of Attorney (Northern Ireland) Order 1987 (S.I. 1987 No. 1627 (N.I. 16))

This Order enables powers of attorney to be created which will survive any subsequent mental incapacity of the donor, sets out the circumstances in which instruments creating such powers of attorney are to be registered in the High Court and indicates the scope of an attorney's authority under such a power.

The Order comes into operation on a day to be appointed.

2628. Agriculture

AGRICULTURAL AND HORTICULTURAL CO-OPERATION SCHEME (NORTHERN IRELAND) 1987 (No. 63) [£1·90], made under S.I. 1987 No. 166 (N.I. 1), arts. 15(1)(3)(7), 19(2); operative on April 1, 1987; re-enacts the 1985 (S.I. No. 334) Scheme with amendments which provide for the transfer of certain functions to the Department of Agriculture.

AGRICULTURE AND HORTICULTURE DEVELOPMENT REGULATIONS (NORTHERN IRELAND) 1987 (No. 154) [£3·80], made under the European Communities Act 1972 (c.68), s.2(2); operative on April 1, 1987; re-enact the 1980 (No. 1298) Regulations as amended with an amendment transferring to the Department of Agriculture for Northern Ireland functions previously exercised by the Minister of Agriculture, Fisheries and Food; revoke the 1980 (No. 1298), 1981 (No. 1708), 1983 (Nos. 508, 924, 1763), 1984 (Nos. 618 1922) and 1985 (No. 1025) Regulations as they apply in Northern Ireland.

AGRICULTURE AND HORTICULTURE GRANT SCHEME (NORTHERN IRELAND) 1987 (No. 158) [£1·90], made under S.I. 1987 No. 166 (N.I. 1), arts. 16(1)(3), 19(2); operative on April 1, 1987; re-enacts with minor amendments those parts of the 1980 (No. 1072) Scheme which dealt with grants towards expenditure of a capital nature incurred on the reseeding and regeneration of grassland, burning of heather or grass, reclamation of land and the replacement of apple and pear orchards.

AGRICULTURE IMPROVEMENT REGULATIONS (NORTHERN IRELAND) 1987 (No. 156) [£2·90], made under the European Communities Act 1972, s.2(2); operative on April 1, 1987; revoke and re-enact the 1985 (No. 1266) Regulations with an amendment transferring to the Department of Agriculture functions previously exercised by the Minister of Agriculture, Fisheries and Food.

AGRICULTURAL IMPROVEMENT (AMENDMENT) REGULATIONS (NORTHERN IRELAND) 1987 (No. 452) [85p], made under the European Communities Act 1972 (c.68), s.2(2); operative on January 1, 1988; amend the 1987 (No. 156) Regulations in relation to farm improvement plans which include proposed expenditure in connection with on-farm craft and tourism projects.

AGRICULTURAL PRODUCTS PROCESSING AND MARKETING (IMPROVEMENT GRANT) REGULATIONS (NORTHERN IRELAND) 1987 (No. 78) [£1·40], made under the European Communities Act 1972 (c.68), s.2(2); operative on April 1, 1987; supplement Council Regulation (EEC) No. 355/77, as amended, on common measures to improve the conditions under which agricultural products are processed and marketed.

CALF PREMIUM (PROTECTION OF PAYMENTS) REGULATIONS (NORTHERN IRELAND) 1987 (No. 317) [£1·60], made under the European Communities Act 1972 (c.68), s.2(2); operative on September 1, 1987; provide for the implementation in Northern Ireland of Council Regulations (EEC) Nos. 1346/86, 4049/86 and 467/87 and of Commission Regulations (EEC) Nos. 1694/86, 381/87 and 1094/87 which enable premiums to be paid for certain calves.

CONTROL OF PESTICIDES REGULATIONS (NORTHERN IRELAND) 1987 (No. 414) [£2·20], made under the Food and Environment Protection Act 1985 (c. 48), ss. 16(2), 24(3); operative on January 1, 1988; impose prohibitions on the sale, supply, storage, use and advertisement of certain pesticides unless the Department of Agriculture for Northern Ireland has given an approval in relation to a pesticide.

EGGS (MARKETING STANDARDS) REGULATIONS (NORTHERN IRELAND) 1987 (No. 407) [£1·60], made under the European Communities Act 1972 (c. 68), s. 2(2); operative on December 14, 1987; supplement specified Community Regulations which relate to marketing standards for shell eggs and to the production and marketing of eggs for hatching and of farmyard poultry chicks; revoke the 1973 (No. 23) and 1978 (No. 300) Regulations.

FARM AND HORTICULTURE DEVELOPMENT REGULATIONS (NORTHERN IRELAND) 1987 (No. 155) [£5·40], made under the European Communities Act 1972, s.2(2); operative on April 1, 1987; re-enact the 1981 (No. 1707) Regulations as amended with an amendment transferring to the Department of Agriculture functions previously exercised by the Minister of Agriculture, Fisheries and Food; revoke the 1981 (No. 1707), 1983 (Nos. 507, 925, 1762), 1984 (Nos. 620, 1924) and 1986 (No. 1295) Regulations as they apply in Northern Ireland.

FARM BUSINESS SPECIFICATION ORDER (NORTHERN IRELAND) 1987 (No. 448) [85p], made under S.I. 1987 No. 166 (N.I. 1), art. 16(10); operative on January 1, 1988; specifies certain businesses which, when carried on by a person also carrying on a business consisting in or partly in the pursuit of agriculture on the same or adjacent land, are included in the definition of "agricultural business" in art. 16(10) of the 1987 S.I.

FARM DIVERSIFICATION GRANT SCHEME (NORTHERN IRELAND) 1987 (No. 451) [£2·60], made under S.I. 1987 No. 166, art. 16(1); operative on January 1, 1988; makes provision for aid for the diversification of agricultural businesses in the form of grants in respect of expenditure of a capital nature incurred in connection with the establishment or carrying on of ancillary farm businesses.

FARM STRUCTURE (PAYMENTS TO OUTGOERS) (CONTINUATION) SCHEME (NORTHERN IRELAND) 1987 (No. 94) [80p], made under S.I. 1987 No. 166, arts. 10, 11,

19(2); operative on April 1, 1987; provides for payments of grant by way of annuity to individuals who qualified for such payments under certain schemes which were revoked and which would have been payable but for such revocation.

GRASSLAND SCHEME (NORTHERN IRELAND) 1987 (No. 197) [£1·40], made under the Agriculture Act (Northern Ireland) 1949 (c.2), s.6(1); operative on April 17, 1987; provides for the payment of grants towards expenditure incurred in the reseeding and regeneration of grassland other than heathland and moorland.

HILL LIVESTOCK (COMPENSATORY ALLOWANCES) REGULATIONS (NORTHERN IRELAND) 1987 (No. 92) [£1·90], made under the European Communities Act 1972, s.2(2); operative on April 1, 1987; implement Council Directive No. 75/268/EEC, as amended by Council Directive No. 80/666/EEC, on improving the efficiency of agricultural structures.

HILL LIVESTOCK (COMPENSATORY ALLOWANCES) (AMENDMENT) REGULATIONS (NORTHERN IRELAND) 1987 (No. 445) [85p], made under the European Communities Act 1972 (c.68), s.2(2); operative on January 1, 1988; amend the 1987 (No. 92) Regulations in relation to the calculation of compensatory allowances.

IMPORT AND EXPORT (PLANTS AND PLANT PRODUCTS) (PLANT HEALTH) (AMENDMENT) ORDER (NORTHERN IRELAND) 1987 (No. 120) [45p], made under the Plant Health Act (Northern Ireland) 1967 (c.28), s.2; operative on March 19, 1987; adds Western Flower Thrips to the list of pests which may not be landed in Northern Ireland and adds certain conditions to the conditions for the landing of rooted plants and unrooted propagating material.

MILK (CESSATION OF PRODUCTION) SCHEME (NORTHERN IRELAND) 1987 (No. 357) [£1·60], made under S.I. 1985 No. 958 (N.I. 9), art. 3(3)(4)(5)(7); operative on October 2, 1987; replaces with amendments and revokes the 1986 (No. 300) and 1987 (No. 64) Schemes.

MILK (COMMUNITY OUTGOERS SCHEME) (AMENDMENT) REGULATIONS (NORTHERN IRELAND) 1987 (No. 114) [45p], made under the European Communities Act 1972, s.2(2); operative on March 13, 1987; implement Commission Regulation (EEC) No. 261/87 as regards the submission of applications for compensation for the definitive discontinuation of milk production and increase compensation payable under Council Regulation (EEC) No. 1336/86 and the maximum amount of compensation under reg. 4 of the 1986 (No. 299) Regulations.

MILK (COMMUNITY OUTGOERS SCHEME) (AMENDMENT No. 2) REGULATIONS (NORTHERN IRELAND) 1987 (No. 225) [85p], made under the European Communities Act 1972 (c.68), s.2(2); operative on June 10, 1987; amend the 1986 (No. 299) Regulations in relation to applications for compensation and the rules for acceptance of applications.

MILK (PARTIAL CESSATION OF PRODUCTION) (AMENDMENT) SCHEME (NORTHERN IRELAND) 1987(No. 64) [45p], made under S.I. 1985 No. 958 (N.I. 9), art. 3(3)(4)(5)(7); operative on February 20, 1987; amends the 1986 (No. 300) Scheme to provide for an increase in the rate of compensation payable to producers who partially surrender a milk quota.

MILK REGULATIONS (NORTHERN IRELAND) 1987 (No. 229) [£5·30], made under S.I. 1983 No. 148 (N.I. 2), arts. 4, 5(3)(6), 6(1), 7, 9(1); operative on July 1, 1987; consolidate with amendments and revoke the 1981 (No. 234), 1983 (No. 337) and 1985 (No. 316) Regulations. The principal amendment introduces a new system whereby licences are renewable on a county basis at three year intervals.

PIG IMPROVEMENT SCHEME (NORTHERN IRELAND) 1987 (No. 381) [£1·60], made under the Agriculture Act (Northern Ireland) 1949 (c.2), s.9(1)(2); operative on November 2, 1987; re-enacts with amendments and revokes the 1976 (No. 393) Scheme.

PIGS (CARCASE CLASSIFICATION SCHEME) (AMENDMENT) ORDER (NORTHERN IRELAND) 1987 (No. 235) [45p], made under S.I. 1975 No. 1038, (N.I. 8), art. 2(1)(2)(3); operative on July 6, 1987; amends the 1980 (No. 58) Order by reducing the fees payable for the marking of carcases and providing for measurement and recording of carcase length to be optional instead of compulsory.

POTATOES (ASSURED MARKETS) ORDER (NORTHERN IRELAND) 1987 (No. 83) [80p], made under S.I. 1987 No. 166 (N.I. 1), arts. 3(1)(2), 19(1); operative on April 1, 1987; enables the Department of Agriculture to purchase potatoes from producers at certain guaranteed prices and within certain quantities and facilitates the transfer of certain functions from the Ministry of Agriculture, Fisheries and Food to the Department of Agriculture for Northern Ireland.

POTATOES (PROHIBITION ON LANDING) ORDER (NORTHERN IRELAND) 1987 (No. 9) [80p], made under the Plant Health Act (Northern Ireland) 1967 (c.28), ss.2, 3(1), 3A, 3B(1), 4(1); operative on February 16, 1987; prohibits the landing in Northern Ireland of consignments of potatoes grown in, consigned from or which have passed through the Federal Republic of Germany.

POTATOES (PROTECTION OF GUARANTEES) ORDER (NORTHERN IRELAND) 1987 (No. 84) [80p], made under S.I. 1987 No. 166, arts. 5, 19(1); operative on April 1, 1987; supports the guarantee arrangements for home-produced potatoes made under art. 3 of the 1987 S.I.

SEED POTATOES (CROP FEES) REGULATIONS (NORTHERN IRELAND) 1987 (No. 96) [80p], made under the Seeds Act (Northern Ireland) 1965 (c.22), ss.1, 2(4); operative on April 15, 1987; increase fees payable in respect of the certification of seed potato crops; revoke the 1982 (No. 84) Regulations.

SEED POTATOES (LEVY) (AMENDMENT) ORDER (NORTHERN IRELAND) 1987 (No. 89) [45p], made under S.I. 1984 No. 702 (N.I. 2), art. 3(1); operative on April 15, 1987; increases the rates of levy payable to the Department of Agriculture by persons engaged by way of business in the production and marketing of seed potatoes.

SEED POTATOES (TUBER AND LABEL FEES) (AMENDMENT) REGULATIONS (NORTHERN IRELAND) 1987 (No. 312) [45p], made under the Seeds Act (Northern Ireland) 1965 (c.22), s.1(1)(2)(2A); operative on August 31, 1987; amend the 1982 (No. 236) Regulations by substituting a new schedule of fees.

SEEDS (FEES) REGULATIONS (NORTHERN IRELAND) 1987 (No. 321) [£2·20], made under the Seeds Act (Northern Ireland) 1965, ss.1(1)(2A), 2(2)(4); operative on September 10, 1987; increase fees for seed certification and licences for seed testing and provide for the charging of fees for certain labels and for application fees for certain seed lots; revoke the 1986 (No. 261) Regulations.

SUCKLER COW PREMIUM REGULATIONS (NORTHERN IRELAND) 1987 (No. 85) [£1·40], made under the European Communities Act 1972, s.2(2); operative on April 1, 1987; provide for the administration in Northern Ireland of the EEC scheme for the payment of premiums for maintaining suckler cows.

2629. Agriculture—Agriculture and Fisheries (Financial Assistance) (Northern Ireland) Order 1987 (S.I. 1987 No. 166 (N.I. 1))

This Order re-enacts with amendments certain provisions of the Agriculture Act 1957 (c.57), the Agriculture Act 1967 (c.22), the Agriculture Act 1970 (c.40) and the Fisheries Act 1981 (c.29) as they apply in Northern Ireland. The Order provides for the transfer to the Department of Agriculture of functions under those Acts formerly exercisable in relation to Northern Ireland by the Minister of Agriculture, Fisheries and Food or by the Secretary of State and confers power on the Department in relation to the provision of financial assistance to the agriculture and sea fish industries.

The Order came into operation on April 1, 1987.

2629a. Agriculture—Agriculture (Environmental Areas) (Northern Ireland) Order 1987 (S.I. 1987 No. 458 (N.I. 3))

This Order provides for the designation and management of environmentally sensitive areas where maintaining or adopting particular agricultural methods is likely to facilitate the conservation, enhancement or protection of specified aspects of the environment.

The Order came into operation on May 19, 1987.

2630. Agriculture—health and safety at work. See §2680.

2631. Animals

ANIMALS (SCIENTIFIC PROCEDURES) (PROCEDURE FOR REPRESENTATIONS) RULES (NORTHERN IRELAND) 1987 (No. 2) [80p], made under the Animals (Scientific Procedures) Act 1986 (c.14), ss.12(7), 29; operative on February 16, 1987; prescribe the procedure to be followed in the making and consideration of representations under s.12 of the 1986 Act as adapted by s.29 of that Act.

CANADA GEESE ORDER (NORTHERN IRELAND) 1987 (No. 403) [45p], made under S.I. 1985 No. 171 (N.I. 2), art. 28(1); operative on December 4, 1987; adds Canada geese to Sched. 2, Pt. I. to the 1985 S.I.

EXPORT OF SHEEP (PROHIBITION) ORDER (NORTHERN IRELAND) 1987 (No. 119) [80p], made under S.I. 1981 No. 1115 (N.I. 22), art. 32; operative on March 19, 1987; prohibits the export from Northern Ireland to a Member State of the European Communities of sheep moved from an area designated as having been affected by the accident at the nuclear reactor at Chernobyl; revokes the 1986 (No. 325) Order.

EXPORT OF SHEEP (PROHIBITION) (No. 2) ORDER (NORTHERN IRELAND) 1987 (No. 372) [85p], made under S.I. 1981 No. 1115 (N.I. 22), art. 32; operative on September 18, 1987; prohibits the export from Northern Ireland to a Member State of the European Communities of sheep moved from a farm, holding or agricultural premises in an area designated as having been affected by the accident at the Chernobyl reactor.

GAME BIRDS PRESERVATION ORDER (NORTHERN IRELAND) 1987 (No. 262) [45p], made under the Game Preservation Act (Northern Ireland) 1928 (c.25), ss.7c(1), 7F; operative on August 11, 1987; prohibits, subject to certain exemptions, the killing or taking of partridges, red-legged partridges and hen pheasants during the open season, restricts dealings in partridges, red-legged partridges and hen pheasants and prohibits dealings in grouse.

IMPORTATION OF BEES (AMENDMENT) ORDER (NORTHERN IRELAND) 1987 (No. 320) [45p], made under S.I. 1980 No. 869 (N.I. 7), art. 3(1)(2); operative on September 9, 1987; amends the 1980 (No. 211) Order by prohibiting the importation of bee pests except under licence.

SHEEP SCAB (AMENDMENT) ORDER (NORTHERN IRELAND) 1987 (No. 223) [85p], made under the S.I. 1981 No. 1115 (N.I. 22), arts. 5(1), 19, 60(1); operative on June 14, 1987; amends the 1970 (No. 240) Order by adding further provisions for the control and prevention of sheep scab.

WELFARE OF BATTERY HENS REGULATIONS (NORTHERN IRELAND) 1987 (No. 425) [£1·60], made under the European Communities Act 1972 (c.68), s.2(2), and the Welfare of Animals Act (Northern Ireland) 1972 (c.7), s.2(1); operative on January 1, 1988; implement Council Directive 86/113/E.E.C. which lays down minimum standards for the protection of laying hens kept in battery cages.

WELFARE OF LIVESTOCK (PROHIBITED OPERATIONS) REGULATIONS (NORTHERN IRELAND) 1987 (No. 415) [85p], made under the Welfare of Animals Act (Northern Ireland) 1972 (c. 7), s. 2(1); operative on December 14, 1987; prohibit the performance of certain operations on livestock for the time being on agricultural land; revoke the 1983 (No. 308) and 1984 (No. 57) Regulations.

2632. Bankruptcy

BANKRUPTCY (FEES AND DEPOSIT) REGULATIONS (NORTHERN IRELAND) 1987 (No. 419) [£1·60], made under S.I. 1980 No. 561 (N.I. 4), art. 34(1); operative on January 1, 1988; provide for the fees to be taken and the deposits to be made under the Bankruptcy Acts in respect of the Official Assignee's services and costs; revoke with a saving the 1985 (No. 195) Regulations.

2633. Building and construction

BUILDING (AMENDMENT) REGULATIONS (NORTHERN IRELAND) 1987 (No. 268) [£2·60], made under S.I. 1979 No. 1709 (N.I.16), arts. 3, 5(1); operative on August 1, 1987; amend the 1977 (No. 149) Regulations to update references to certain British Standards and British Standard Codes of Practice and to require that the design, construction and installation of any fixed installation of liquefied petroleum gas located within the curtilage of a residential building be safe and adequate for its purpose.

2634. Building and construction—execution of public works—compensation for damage—Lands Tribunal decisions

[Mineral Development Act (Northern Ireland) 1969 (c.35), s.38(2) to (6); Water and Sewerage Services (Northern Ireland) Order 1973 (S.I. 1973 No. 70 (N.I. 2)), art. 55.]

It was agreed between the Department of the Environment and a building company that a sewage pipeline would be installed along a proposed spine road on land which the company intended to develop for housing. The Department's works consisted of the excavation of a trench, the installation of the pipeline and the back-filling of soil. When the company commenced its works the Department required it to carry out further works to form a proper base for the spine road. The company claimed compensation under art. 55 of the Water and Sewage Services (Northern Ireland) Order 1973 which required the Department to make good or pay compensation for any damage caused by or in consequence of the execution of works by the Department. The company claimed that the back-filling of the trench in which the pipeline was laid was inadequate and as a result the load-bearing capacity of the land on which the spine road was to be constructed was adversely affected.

Held, by the Lands Tribunal, on a preliminary point of law, that the compensation, if any, must be assessed in accordance with art. 55 of the 1973 Order which applies s.38 of the Mineral Development Act (Northern Ireland) 1969.

LANSON HOMES *v.* DEPARTMENT OF THE ENVIRONMENT FOR NORTHERN IRELAND (R/26/1985).

2635. [Land Compensation (Northern Ireland) Order 1982 (S.I. 1982 No. 712 (N.I. 9)), art. 18.]

As a result of the erection of a police station and a high corrugated iron fence on land compulsorily acquired by the Police Authority for Northern Ireland there was substantial interference with the natural light enjoyed by an adjoining house occupied by C as a statutory tenant.

Held, that but for the statutory provisions under which the police station and fence were erected C would have had a right of action for damages and, accordingly, was entitled to damages under art. 18 of the Land Compensation (Northern Ireland) Order 1982.

McGROTHER *v.* POLICE AUTHORITY FOR NORTHERN IRELAND (R/20/1985).

2636. A police station and a high corrugated iron fence were erected on land compulsorily acquired by the Police Authority for Northern Ireland. C, the statutory tenant of an adjoining house, claimed compensation for interference with the natural light enjoyed by the front rooms of the house. On a preliminary point the Lands Tribunal held that C had a right to compensation—see [1987] C.L.Y. 2635.

Held, that the value of C's interest as a statutory tenant before the erection of the police station and fence was £300, that there was a 13 per cent. diminution in light to the ground floor living room only and that the depreciation in value of C's interest was £15.

McGROTHER *v.* POLICE AUTHORITY FOR NORTHERN IRELAND (R/20/1985).

2636a. [Drainage (Northern Ireland) Order 1973 (S.I. 1973 No. 69 (N.I. 1)), art. 17.]

While carrying out works under a flood protection scheme a contractor employed by the Department of Agriculture drilled a series of horizontal holes under a building which caused it to subside. Compensation was claimed under art. 17 of the Drainage (Northern Ireland) Order 1973 for the damage which occurred in August 1979. Compensation was agreed at £20,000 and this sum was paid on account in December 1985.

Held, that the Lands Tribunal had no power under the 1973 Order to award interest on the compensation.

SIMMS *v.* DEPARTMENT OF AGRICULTURE (R/34/1984).

2637. Charities—Charities (Northern Ireland) Order 1987 (S.I. 1987 No. 2048 (N.I. 19))

This Order (1) gives certain charities additional powers including power to alter objects, power to transfer their whole property to another charity, and power to spend capital; (2) amends the Charities Act (Northern Ireland) 1964 (c.33) in relation to financial limits, the calculation of the value of land for the purposes of the Act and the production of annual reports; (3) restricts the power of a charity which is a body corporate to alter its instruments; and (4) transfers to the Department of Finance and Personnel certain functions under the House to House Charitable Collections Act (Northern Ireland) 1952 (c.6).

The Order came into force on January 27, 1988.

2638. Clubs and associations—expulsion of member—natural justice

A company limited by guarantee was formed in 1961 to own, maintain and conduct a flying club which had been in existence for several years. No rules of the flying club were produced. The articles of association of the new company provided for its management by a committee and for admission of applicants to membership. Every member of the flying club became a member of the new company and all members of the company were subject to annual re-election at annual general meetings. Regulations were made for the operation of the aerodrome used by the club and company. A social club was later formed which by its rules confined its membership to members of the flying club or company. The committee of this social club had power under its rules to expel a member. In May 1983 the committee of the company considered that the activities of P, one of its members, was prejudicial to the trading and good name of the company and under the power contained in the rules of the social club suspended him from membership of the company. In June 1983 P, at the committee's invitation, attended a meeting to show cause why he should not be expelled. However, the committee resolved that his membership should not be renewed and P was informed accordingly. In September 1983 P issued an originating summons seeking a declaration that his expulsion was void. In October 1983 notice of an annual general meeting of the company to be held on November 28, 1983, was given to P. Before this meeting the committee admitted that P's expulsion and the decision not to renew his membership were ineffective. A resolution was passed at the annual general meeting that all members, except P, be re-elected. P then amended his summons to seek a declaration that his purported expulsion at the annual general meeting was void and in breach of the rules of natural justice.

Held, that (1) the articles of association of the company should be treated also as rules of the flying club; (2) the resolution passed at the annual general meeting validly excluded P from re-election; and (3) it would be wrong to treat the re-election procedure as expulsion procedure but in any case the rules of natural justice do not apply to a decision of members of a company on a vote in general meeting. P elected not to pursue his claim for damages for his wrongful expulsion in June 1983.

HAWTHORNE *v.* ULSTER FLYING CLUB (1961) [1986] 6 N.I.J.B. 56, Murray J.

2639. Clubs and associations—Registration of Clubs (Northern Ireland) Order 1987 (S.I. 1987 No. 1278 (N.I. 14))

This Order provides for the registration of clubs by a county court, revises the general permitted hours in registered clubs, makes it an offence for a person under the age of 18 to be in the bar of a registered club or to be supplied with intoxicating liquor, or for a person to be drunk or to permit drunkenness in a registered club and makes new provision in respect of the rights of the police to enter and inspect club premises. Existing statutory provisions are consolidated.

The Order comes into operation on days to be appointed.

2640. Company law

COMPANIES (ACCOUNTING THRESHOLDS) (MODIFICATION) REGULATIONS (NORTHERN IRELAND) 1987 (No. 37) [80p], made under S.I. 1986 No. 1032 (N.I. 6), art. 259(1); operative on March 11, 1987; raise the thresholds for turnover and balance sheet total in respect of companies which qualify as small or medium-sized for the purposes of the 1986 S.I.

COMPANIES (CONSOLIDATION OF FEES) REGULATIONS (NORTHERN IRELAND) 1987 (No. 258) [65p], made under S.I. 1986 No. 1032 (N.I. 6), arts. 309(4), 430(3), 657(1)(4), 681(1); operative on July 27, 1987; consolidate and revoke the 1981 (No. 324), 1982 (No. 256) and 1983 (Nos. 118, 119) Regulations.

COMPANIES (DISCLOSURE OF DIRECTORS' INTERESTS) (EXCEPTIONS) REGULATIONS (NORTHERN IRELAND) 1987 (No. 208) [80p], made under S.I. 1986 No. 1032 (N.I. 6), art. 332(3); operative on June 5, 1987; provide for exceptions to the requirements in art. 332 of the 1986 S.I. for the disclosure of interests by directors.

COMPANIES (MERGERS AND DIVISIONS) REGULATIONS (NORTHERN IRELAND) 1987 (No. 442) [£2·60], made under the European Communities Act 1972 (c.68), s.2(2); operative on January 1, 1988; implement Council Directive No. 78/885/EEC concerning mergers of public limited liability companies and Council Directive No. 82/891/EEC concerning the division of such companies.

COMPANIES (WINDING-UP) FEES REGULATIONS (NORTHERN IRELAND) 1987 (No. 418) [£1·60], made under S.I. 1986 No. 1032 (N.I. 6), arts. 613(6), 681(1); operative on January 1, 1988; re-enact with amendments and revoke the 1985 (No. 196) Regulations.

2641. Company law—winding up—transfer of funds by liquidator for "advantage" of creditors

Companies (Northern Ireland) Order 1978 (S.I. No. 1040), art 75(2).]

In Northern Ireland a transfer of funds by a liquidator is permissable once a relevant advantage (including financial) to creditors is proved to exist.

The liquidation of the company raised a sum which was lodged in an Insolvency Account maintained by the Department of Economic Development. Interest at $3\frac{1}{2}$ per cent. was credited. An application was made to transfer $\frac{3}{4}$ of the sum into a separate deposit account with a commercial bank paying interest at $11\frac{1}{2}$ per cent. The department rejected the application. The applicant contended that art. 75(2) of the 1978 Order was wide enough to cover this situation.

Held, granting the orders, the Department could not withhold authorisation once a relevant advantage to creditors had been proved to exist, which (unlike English Law) included financial advantage).

P.X. NUCLEAR, *Re* 1987 PCC 82, Murray J.

2642. Compulsory purchase

COMPULSORY ACQUISITION (INTEREST) ORDER (NORTHERN IRELAND) 1987 (No. 147) [45p], made under the Public Health and Local Government (Miscellaneous Provisions) Act (Northern Ireland) 1955 (c.13), s.12, the Administrative and Financial Provisions Act (Northern Ireland) 1956 (c.17), s.14, and the Local Government Act (Northern Ireland) 1972 (c.9), Sched. 6, para. 18; operative on April 22, 1987; decreases to $11\frac{1}{4}$ per cent. per annum the rate of interest on compensation payable under specified enactments for compulsorily acquired land; revokes the 1985 (No. 313) Order.

COMPULSORY ACQUISITION (INTEREST) (No. 2) ORDER (NORTHERN IRELAND) 1987 (No. 232) [45p], made under the Public Health and Local Government (Miscellaneous Provisions) Act (Northern Ireland) 1955 (c.13), s.12, the Administrative and Financial Provisions Act (Northern Ireland) 1956 (c.17), s.14, and the Local Government Act (Northern Ireland) 1972 (c.9), Sched. 6, para. 18; operative on June 23, 1987; decreases to 10 per cent. per annum the rate of interest on compensation payable under specified enactments for compulsorily acquired land; revokes the 1987 (No. 147) Order.

COMPULSORY ACQUISITION (INTEREST) (No. 3) ORDER (NORTHERN IRELAND) 1987 (No. 400) [45p], made under the Public Health and Local Government (Miscellaneous Provisions) Act (Northern Ireland) 1955 (c.13), s.12, the Administrative and Financial Provisions Act (Northern Ireland) 1956 (c.17), s.14, and the Local Government Act (Northern Ireland) 1972 (c.9), Sched. 6, para. 18; operative on November 16, 1987; increases to 11 per cent. per annum the rate of interest on compensation payable under specified enactments for compulsorily acquired land; revokes the 1987 (No. 232) Order.

2642a. Compulsory purchase—construction of reservoir—whether interest payable on compensation

The Department of the Environment compulsorily acquired part of C's land for the construction of a reservoir. Subsequently the Department constructed the reservoir and laid a water main. During the execution of the works a gravity flow of water from a well to a tap in an outhouse owned by C was cut off. Compensation was agreed at £1,500 for the land acquired, £225 for temporary disturbance, £2,000 for the loss of the water supply and £275 for the laying of the water main.

Held, by the Lands Tribunal, that interest was payable on the compensation for the land and the temporary disturbance but not on the compensation for the loss of the water supply or the laying of the water main.

McBRIDE *v.* DEPARTMENT OF THE ENVIRONMENT FOR NORTHERN IRELAND (R/15/1986).

2643. Compulsory purchase—Lands Tribunal decision

A freehold mid-terrace house in an area blighted for about fifteen years due to proposals for a through-pass road and car parking was compulsorily acquired by the Department of the Environment in 1985. The Department certified that planning permission might reasonably have been expected to be granted to permit the house to be used as a retail shop or as offices.

Held, ignoring the blight and giving more weight to open market sales of comparable properties than to settlements of compensation for other properties compulsorily acquired, that the compensation should be £20,000.

DAVIS *v.* DEPARTMENT OF THE ENVIRONMENT FOR NORTHERN IRELAND (R/2/1986).

2644. Contract—accord and satisfaction—offer of payment—cheque cashed

The Commissioners of Inland Revenue obtained judgment against B for a sum of £13,928 and costs on foot of an assessment to tax and on September 11, 1985, issued a debtor's summons. In reply to a letter dated September 18, 1985, from B's solicitors the Commissioners granted a period of eight weeks to arrange settlement. On October 2, B's solicitors sent a letter marked "Without Prejudice" stating that B was in a position to make an offer of £7,500 in settlement of the amount due. The Commissioners replied that the offer in settlement of the amount due would be accepted without prejudice but that B's proposals for clearing the balance of the debt would be expected by December 6, 1985. On November 28, 1985, B's solicitors sent a cheque for £7,500 in full and final settlement of all monies due by B on foot of the debtor's summons. This cheque was cashed and paid into an Inland Revenue bank account and a few days later the Commissioners wrote to B's solicitors asking for B's proposals for clearance of the balance. When this balance was not paid an order adjudicating B bankrupt was made by the Master but, on B giving notice of his intention to show cause against the validity of the adjudication, the Master after a hearing annulled the order. The Commissioners appealed.

Held, allowing the appeal, that (1) the essential element for an accord and satisfaction was lacking as there was no agreement between the minds of the parties and the Commissioners had not acted in such a way as to induce B's solicitors to think that the money was taken in satisfaction of the claim, and (2) if the Commissioners agreed to accept £7,500 in settlement, there was no consideration for that agreement.

BRODERICK, *Re* [1986] 6 N.I.J.B. 36, Carswell J.

2645. Criminal evidence and procedure—accomplice—admissibility

Several accused were charged with terrorist offences largely on the evidence of Q, an accomplice. The police had interviewed Q on four occasions and furnished notes of these interviews to the defence. In his cross-examination of Q, which related only to Q's credit and not to the factual matters in issue, counsel for the defence made considerable use of the note of the fourth interview. On a preliminary point as to whether this note should be admitted in evidence the trial judge ruled that, as counsel had not used the note to contradict Q's evidence and as Q's evidence could not be corroborated by proving statements to the same effect previously made by him, the note should not be admitted.

Held, convicting some of the accused on various counts and acquitting others on various counts, that (1) there was nothing new in convicting an accused on the evidence of an accomplice; (2) Q was in a position in which he could accurately name the accused and describe the crimes which they committed; (3) Q described those crimes in the greatest detail and, with a few exceptions, with great consistency; and (4) his evidence satisfied the court beyond all reasonable doubt as to the guilt of those convicted.

R. *v.* CRUMLEY [1986] 7 N.I.J.B. 1, Crown Court of Northern Ireland.

2646. Criminal evidence and procedure—appeal—incomplete transcript of trial

B and G were charged with murder and other serious offences at a trial which lasted approximately twenty sitting days. After some evidence was heard B and G dismissed their solicitors and counsel. Verbal and written statements by B and G were held to be admissible on a *voir dire* at which both B and G were present and were given copies of all material documents. After the *voir dire* B and G re-engaged their solicitors and counsel. Both were convicted and appealed. The court granted an application for a full transcript to be made available to them. A note of the whole of the trial had been taken but one of the shorthand writers had gone abroad and her notes were lost. The notes of the trial judge, who died before the hearing of the appeals, proved to be indecipherable. The available transcript included complete copies of the trial judge's ruling on admissibility and his judgment on the *voir dire,* all the medical evidence and some of the notes of the examinations in chief and cross-examinations.

Held, dismissing the appeals, that an appellant must show that there is sufficient reason to suggest that the judge's conclusions could be shown to be at fault if the transcript were available and the point at issue must be sufficiently material to be capable of affecting the validity of his conclusions. The absence of parts of the transcripts had not made the conviction of either B or G unsafe or unsatisfactory.

R. *v.* BATESON [1986] 8 N.I.J.B. 73, C.A.

2647. Criminal evidence and procedure—arrest—reasonable suspicion—admissibility

[Prevention of Terrorism (Temporary Provisions) Act 1984 (c.8), s.12.]

P, a taxi driver, stated in evidence that when he was returning to his own car on Saturday, August 11, 1984, he was told that he was being hijacked. After sitting in a public house for about an hour and a half, as instructed by the hijacker, he reported the hijacking at a police station. In the meantime P's car was used in a terrorist operation. As P was leaving the police station, he was arrested by A, a police constable, who informed him that he was being arrested under s.12 of the Prevention of Terrorism (Temporary Provisions) Act 1984 on the ground that A reasonably suspected him of being concerned in the commission, preparation or instigation of acts of terrorism. He was detained for three days and then released without charge. P claimed damages for false imprisonment. In his closing submissions P's counsel claimed that as P had not been cross-examined about P's version of the words used by A when arresting him, P's version must be accepted as correct and A's version should not be admitted in evidence.

Held, that (1) a party should not be permitted to obtain an unfair advantage of his opponent's inadvertent omission to cover a point in cross-examination by refraining from objecting to the contrary evidence when it is given and challenging its admissibility in his closing submissions; (2) the Chief Constable had established that the formalities of arrest were validly effected; (3) in considering the existence of a reasonable suspicion it was necessary to look only at the evidence relating to the mind of A, the arresting officer, and not to evidence relating to the mind of any officer by whom he had been given instructions; and (4) as A knew that P's car was involved in the terrorist operation, knew the length of time which elapsed between the hijacking of P's car and his reporting of the incident at the police station and knew that P's car had on a previous occasion been used in an armed robbery when P claimed that he had been forced to drive it by the robbers, A genuinely suspected and had reasonable grounds for suspecting that P was or had been concerned in the commission, preparation or instigation of acts of terrorism. Accordingly, P was validly arrested and lawfully detained.

HANNA *v.* CHIEF CONSTABLE OF THE ROYAL ULSTER CONSTABULARY [1986] 13 N.I.J.B. 71, Carswell J.

2648. Criminal evidence and procedure—trial—decision by Crown not to call witness who gave evidence at preliminary enquiry—no reasons given—change of decision—whether trial judge should discharge himself

At the trial of five men charged with murder the Crown decided not to call F as a witness although she had seen the gunman who committed the murder and although she had given evidence at the preliminary enquiry. Counsel for the Crown stated that it would not be fair to the defence to state the Crown's reasons for its decision. However, after hearing submissions by the defence the Crown conceded that the submissions were well-founded and, accordingly, proposed to call F as a witness. The defence then submitted that the Crown had lodged in the mind of the trial judge a clear impression that there were reasons why F should not be regarded as a reliable witness and that the judge should discharge himself from the trial.

Held that, as the Crown had unnecessarily raised a doubt and created an atmosphere about a very important witness, the judge should discharge himself from the trial (*R.* v. *Oliva* [1965] C.L.Y. 929 and *R.* v. *Foxford* [1977] C.L.Y 2071 considered).

R. *v.* LATIMER [1986] 9 N.I.J.B. 1, Hutton J.

2648a. Criminal law

PUBLIC ORDER (EXCEPTIONS) ORDER (NORTHERN IRELAND) 1987 (No. 126) [45p], made under S.I. 1987 No. 463 (N.I. 7), art. 3(4)(*b*); operative on April 1, 1987; excepts public processions customarily held along particular routes by the Salvation Army from the requirement to give advance notice under art. 3(1) of the 1987 S.I.

2649. Criminal law—criminal injury—compensation—previous conviction

[Criminal Injuries (Compensation) (Northern Ireland) Order 1977 (S.I. 1977 No. 1248 (N.I. 15)), art. 6(3)(*b*).]

D's claim for compensation under the Criminal Injuries (Compensation) (Northern Ireland) Order 1977 was rejected by the county court judge under art. 6(3)(*b*) of the Order on the ground that D had earlier been convicted of an offence of making petrol bombs.

Held, dismissing D's appeal, that, as the petrol bombs were being made by D at a time when and near a place where serious rioting was taking place, the bombs were clearly going to be put to a violent use for the purpose of putting the public or a section of the public in fear (*Kinnear* v. *Secretary of State for Northern Ireland* [1986] C.L.Y. 2314 distinguished).

DORAN *v.* SECRETARY OF STATE FOR NORTHERN IRELAND [1986] 12 N.I.J.B. 47, Hutton J.

2650. Criminal law—criminal injury—whether injury attributable to a violent offence—compensation

[Criminal Injuries (Compensation) (Northern Ireland) Order 1977 (S.I. 1977 No. 1248 (N.I. 15)), art. 2(2).]

C and two friends at a time of great tension and violence in Belfast attacked a police landrover with missiles and then ran off. The police gave chase honestly believing that they were pursuing a gunman who was firing at them and, honestly believing that C was an escaping gunman who had failed to obey an order to halt, fired at him and wounded him. C claimed compensation under the Criminal Injuries (Compensation) (Northern Ireland) Order 1977. His claim was rejected by the county court judge and he appealed.

Held, dismissing the appeal, that (1) even if a violent offence for the purposes of art. 2(2) of the 1977 Order was committed by a gunman firing at the police when they dismounted from their landrover, C's conduct in running off severed any chain of causation between the firing by the gunman and the firing by the police at C at the end of the chase and, accordingly, the firing by the police was not directly attributable to a violent offence; and (2) on the construction of para. (*b*) of the definition of "criminal injury" in art. 2(2) of the 1977 Order "an offender" is someone different from the person who sustains the injury for which compensation is claimed. The definition was not intended to give a right to compensation to an offender against whom a police officer intends to use force in making a lawful arrest.

CLARKE *v.* SECRETARY OF STATE FOR NORTHERN IRELAND [1986] 13 N.I.J.B. 93, Hutton J.

2650a. Criminal Law—Crossbows Act 1987 (c.32). See CRIMINAL LAW, §773.

2651. Criminal law—damage to property—compensation—whether a criminal offence must be committed

[Criminal Damage (Compensation) (Northern Ireland) Order 1977 (S.I. 1977 No. 1248 (N.I. 15), art. 5(1)).]

Plant and machinery belonging to C were damaged by five young boys, three of whom were under ten years of age and C claimed compensation under art. 5 of the Criminal Damage (Compensation) (Northern Ireland) Order 1977. The claim was dismissed by the Recorder of Belfast. C appealed.

Held, dismissing the appeal, that the reference in art. 5 to three or more persons unlawfully assembled together is a reference to the crime of unlawful assembly and as only two of the boys were capable of committing or intending to commit the crime, C was not entitled to compensation under the Order.

McCANDLESS (ENGINEERS) *v.* SECRETARY OF STATE FOR NORTHERN IRELAND [1986] 9 N.I.J.B. 9, Murray J.

2652. Criminal law—misuse of drugs

MISUSE OF DRUGS (AMENDMENT) REGULATIONS (NORTHERN IRELAND) 1987 (No. 68) [80p], made under the Misuse of Drugs Act 1971, ss.7, 10, 31, 38; operative on April 1, 1987; amend the 1986 (No. 52) Regulations to add certain drugs to the list of controlled drugs.

MISUSE OF DRUGS (DESIGNATION) ORDER (NORTHERN IRELAND) 1987 (No. 66) [80p], made under the Misuse of Drugs Act 1971 (c.38), s.7(4)(5)(9); operative on April 1, 1987; designates the drugs to which s.7(4) of the 1971 Act applies and the controlled drugs which are excepted from the application of that section.

MISUSE OF DRUGS (SAFE CUSTODY) (AMENDMENT) (NORTHERN IRELAND) REGULATIONS 1987 (No. 67) [80p], made under the Misuse of Drugs Act 1971, ss.10(2)(*a*), 31, 38; operative on April 1, 1987; amend the 1973 (No. 179) Regulations to specify the drugs which are exempted from the requirements of the regulations.

2652a. Criminal law—Public Order (Northern Ireland) Order 1987 (S.I. 1987 No. 463 (N.I. 7))

This Order repeals and re-enacts with amendments the Public Order (Northern Ireland) 1981. The principal amendments require not less than seven days advance notice to be given of a public procession, add to the matters to be notified, widen the grounds on which conditions may be imposed by the police on public processions and on which the Secretary of State may prohibit public processions and open-air public meetings and confer on the police new powers to impose conditions on open-air public meetings. The Order also amends the law on incitement to hatred and repeals the Flags and Emblems (Display) Act (Northern Ireland) 1954 (c.10).

The Order came into operation on April 2, 1987.

2653. Criminal law—rehabilitation of offenders

REHABILITATION OF OFFENDERS (EXCEPTIONS) (AMENDMENT) ORDER (NORTHERN IRELAND) 1987 (No. 393) [£1·60], made under S.I. 1978 No. 1908 (N.I. 27), arts. 5(4), 8(4); operative for the purposes of certain articles on December 1, 1987, and for the purposes of the remaining articles on the day on which s.189 of and Sched. 14 to the Financial Services Act 1986 (c.60), as they apply to art. 5 of the 1978 Order, come into force; amends the 1979 (No. 195) Order in relation to the exceptions to art. 5(1)(2)(3)(*b*) of the 1978 Order.

2654. Criminal law—riot—baton round fired by policeman—whether reasonable use of force

Rioting occurred during an unlawful parade at which G, who had been refused entry into the U.K. appeared. As the police moved in to arrest G who had disappeared into the crowd, H, a policeman armed with a riot gun, saw D run with a stick or pole towards two police officers, who had their backs to him, with the clear intention of striking one or other of them from the rear. H thought that the two police officers were in danger and fired a baton round at D who was then less than twenty metres away. D died as a result of the injury sustained from the baton round and H was charged with manslaughter.

Held, finding H not guilty, that (1) the question whether the force used by H was unreasonable in the circumstances was a question of fact and in deciding that question the pressures and dangers to which H and others were then exposed had to be taken into account; (2) H had less than three seconds in which to make up his mind what action to take; and (3) in the noise and disturbance of the riot it was unrealistic to suggest that H should have warned the two police officers of the threatened attack by D.

R. *v.* HEGARTY [1986] 12 N.I.J.B. 25, Hutton J.

2655. Criminal sentencing

[Criminal Appeal (Northern Ireland) Act 1980 (c.47), s.29(2).]

The Court of Appeal has power under s.29(2) of the Criminal Appeal (Northern Ireland) Act 1980 to eliminate from consideration the time spent after sentence and pending appeal and to direct that the time spent pending appeal will not count towards sentence.

R. *v.* ELLIS [1986] 10 N.I.J.B. 117, C.A.

2656. Customs and excise—betting duty

GENERAL BETTING DUTY (NORTHERN IRELAND) (AMENDMENT) REGULATIONS 1987 (S.I. No. 313) [45p], made under the Miscellaneous Transferred Excise Duties Act (Northern Ireland) 1972 (c.11), ss.24(2), 72(1), Sched. 2, paras. 1, 7; operative on March

29, 1987; amend the 1986 (S.I. No. 404) Regulations to replace the current system of weekly returns and payments by a monthly payment system.

2657. Customs and excise—prescribed area regulations. See CUSTOMS AND EXCISE, §1117.

2658. Easements and prescription—right of way—Lands Tribunal decision

S sought a declaration that a right of way which existed over her lands was now extinct. The former owner of the dominant land had ceased to use the right of way for some years before he sold the land to Q. The right of way entered a lane which at one stage was completely overgrown. Q later ploughed up this lane and this made the exercise of the right of way impossible.

Held, granting the declaration, that by ploughing up the lane Q made a substantial change to the nature of the dominant tenement and had constructively abandoned the right of way.

STEWART *v.* QUIGLEY (R/18/1986).

2659. Education

EDUCATION (CORPORAL PUNISHMENT) (1987 ORDER) (COMMENCEMENT) ORDER (NORTHERN IRELAND) 1987 (No. 271 (C.10)) [45p], made under S.I. 1987 No. 461 (N.I.6), art. 1(2), and the Northern Ireland Act 1974 (c.28), Sched. 1, para. 2(1); brought the 1987 S.I. into operation on August 15, 1987.

PAYMENT OF TEACHERS' SALARIES AND ALLOWANCES REGULATIONS (NORTHERN IRELAND) 1987 (No. 127) [45p], made under S.I. 1986 No. 594 (N.I. 3), arts. 69(3), 134(1); operative on April 15, 1987; make provision for the payment of teachers' salaries and allowances by the Department of Education or by Education and Library Boards; revoke the 1974 (No. 11) Regulations.

STUDENTS AWARDS REGULATIONS (NORTHERN IRELAND) 1987 (No. 420) [£4·80], made under S.I. 1986 No. 594 (N.I. 3), arts. 50(1)(2), 51(2), 134(1); operative on December 11, 1987, with effect from September 1, 1987; re-enact with amendments and revoke the 1986 (No. 333) Regulations.

TEACHERS' (ELIGIBILITY) REGULATIONS (NORTHERN IRELAND) 1987 (No. 266) [£1·60], made under S.I. 1986 No 594, arts. 69(1)(4), 70(1)(2), 134(1); operative on August 1, 1987; deal with the qualifications, age and health requirements, probations, recognition and eligibility of teachers in grant-aided schools and of peripatetic and supply teachers.

TEACHERS' SALARIES (AMENDMENT) REGULATIONS (NORTHERN IRELAND) 1987 (No. 252) [£2·20], made under S.I. 1986 No. 594 (N.I. 3), arts. 69(1)(4), 70(1)(2), 134(1), and the Administrative and Financial Provisions Act (Northern Ireland) 1962 (c.7. s.18; operative on JUly 30, 1987, with effect from January 1, 1987; introduce revised scales of salaries and allowances for teachers in primary, secondary and special schools and for peripatetic and supply teachers; revoke the 1973 (no. 371) Regulations.

TEACHERS' SALARIES (MATERNITY ABSENCE) REGULATIONS (NORTHERN IRELAND) 1987 (No. 206) [£1·40], made under S.I. 1986 No. 594 (N.I. 3), arts. 69(1), 70(1), 134(1); operative on May 28, 1987; continue the arrangements for payments to certain teachers during leave of absence due to pregnancy; revoke the 1980 (No. 306) Regulations.

TEACHERS' SALARIES REGULATIONS (NORTHERN IRELAND) 1987 (No. 384) [£3·80], made under S.I. 1986 No. 594 (N.I. 3), arts. 17A, 34, 69(1)(4), 70(1), 134(1); operative on October 1, 1987; increase salaries and allowances for teachers in primary, secondary and special schools and for peripatetic and supply teachers; revoke the 1981 (Nos. 111, 112, 113), 1984 (No. 350), 1986 (Nos. 81, 165) and 1987 (No 252) Regulations.

TEACHERS' SALARIES (REORGANISATION ALLOWANCES) REGULATIONS (NORTHERN IRELAND) 1987 (No. 385) [£1·60], made under S.I. 1986 No. 594, arts. 69(1)(4), 134(1), operative on October 1, 1987; provide for the payment of reorganisation allowances to certain teachers in grant-aided schools and certain peripatetic and supply teachers; revoke the 1976 (No. 237) Regulations.

TEACHERS'(TERMS AND CONDITIONS OF EMPLOYMENT) REGULATIONS (NORTHERN IRELAND) 1987 (No. 267) [2·20], made under S.I. 1986 No. 594, arts. 70(1) 134(1); operative on August 1, 1987; made provision as to the terms and conditions of employment of teachers employed in grant-aided schools and of peripatetic teachers and supply teachers

2660. Education—Education (Corporal Punishment) (Northern Ireland) Order 1987 (S.I. 1987 No. 461 (N.I. 6))

This Order removes the right of members of staff in schools to administer corporal punishment to pupils whose education is provided at grant-aided schools or is otherwise secured by education and library boards.

The Order comes into operation on a day to be appointed.

2661. Education—Education (Northern Ireland) Order 1987 (S.I. 1987 No. 167 (N.I. 2))

This Order (1) transfers to education and library boards the responsibility for the education of mentally handicapped children; (2) imposes a duty to implement proposals as to primary and secondary schools which are approved by the Department of Education; (3) makes new provision to regulate the carrying on of grant-aided schools and the employment of teachers and certain non-teaching staff; (4) empowers boards to make available the use of spare computer capacity; and (5) makes other miscellaneous amendments to the Education and Libraries (Northern Ireland) Order 1986.

The Order came into operation on April 1, 1987.

2662. Election law

LOCAL ELECTIONS (NORTHERN IRELAND) (AMENDMENT) ORDER 1987 (S.I. 1987 No. 168) [£3·60], made under the Northern Ireland Constitution Act 1973 (c.36), s.38(1)(*a*)(4); operative on February 17, 1987, save for para. 44 of Sched. 1 which comes into operation on May 11, 1987; makes changes in the law in respect of local elections in Northern Ireland equivalent to the changes in respect of parliamentary elections made by the Representation of the People Act 1985 (c.50).

RETURNING OFFICERS' EXPENSES (NORTHERN IRELAND) REGULATIONS 1987 (No. 900) [85p], made under the Representation of the People Act 1983 (c.2), s.29(3); operative on May 20, 1987; increase maximum fees payable in respect of returning officers' expenses.

2663. Electricity

ELECTRICITY (PERMITTED SUPPLY) ORDER (NORTHERN IRELAND) 1987 (No. 456) [45p], made under S.I. 1972 No. 1072 (N.I. 9), art. 31; operative on January 15, 1988; permits named persons to be supplied with electricity from a supplier outside Northern Ireland.

2664. Electricity—Electricity Supply (Amendment) (Northern Ireland) Order 1987 (S.I. 1987 No. 1275 (N.I. 12))

This Order amends S.I. 1972 No. 1072 (N.I. 9) by (1) renaming the Northern Ireland Electricity Service as Northern Ireland Electricity; (2) facilitating the generation of electricity by other bodies; (3) extending the functions and borrowing powers of the renamed body and requiring it to support schemes for use of heat produced from the generation of electricity; (4) making new provision with respect to powers of entry; (5) requiring notice to be given of the construction of private generating stations; (6) requiring a person to remedy any electric line made unsafe by his action; and (7) increasing the time within which prosecutions for certain offences can be brought.

The Order came into operation on September 22, 1987.

2665. Emergency laws

NORTHERN IRELAND (EMERGENCY PROVISIONS) ACT 1978 (CONTINUANCE) ORDER 1987 (No. 30) [45p], made under the Northern Ireland (Emergency Provisions) Act 1978 (c.5), s.33(3)(*a*); operative on January 25, 1987; continues the temporary provisions of the 1978 Act in force for a further six months.

NORTHERN IRELAND (EMERGENCY PROVISIONS) ACT 1987 (COMMENCEMENT No. 1) ORDER 1987 (S.I. No. 1241 (C.35)) [45p], made under the Northern Ireland Emergency Provisions) Act 1987 (c.30), s.26(1)(2); brings Part III of the 1987 Act, which contains provisions for the regulation of security services, into operation. Provisions relating to certificates granted by the Secretary of State came into operation on August 1, 1987 and provisions creating offences of providing security services without a licence and making payments for security services to a person who is neither the holder, nor acting on behalf of the holder, of a certificate come into operation on January 1, 1988.

2666. Emergency laws—compensation—Lands Tribunal decision

[Compensation (Defence) Act 1939 (c.75), s.7; Land Powers (Defence) Act 1958 (c.30), s.25; Lands Tribunal and Compensation Act (Northern Ireland) 1964 (c.29), s.6.]

C claimed compensation under the Compensation (Defence) Act 1939 for loss suffered by him when the Department of Agriculture in the exercise of emergency powers under that Act diverted farm milk supplies from his creamery to another creamery. Under s.7 of that Act any dispute as to compensation was to be referred to a tribunal constituted under the Act. Under s.25 of the Land Powers (Defence) Act 1958 an official arbitrator was substituted for the tribunal under the 1939 Act and under the Lands Tribunal and Compensation Act (Northern Ireland) 1964 the Lands Tribunal for Northern Ireland was substituted for the official arbitrator.

Held, that the Lands Tribunal had jurisdiction to determine the claim for compensation under the 1939 Act as the Acquisition of Land (Assessment of Compensation) Act 1919 under which official arbitrators were appointed was an enactment which the Parliament of Northern Ireland had power to amend.

McDERMOTT *v.* DEPARTMENT OF AGRICULTURE FOR NORTHERN IRELAND AND H.M. TREASURY (R/11/1986).

2667. Employment

EMPLOYMENT SUBSIDIES (RENEWAL) ORDER (NORTHERN IRELAND) 1987 (No. 215) [45p], made under the Employment Subsidies Act 1978 (c.6) s.3(2)(*b*); operative on July 1, 1987; renews the powers of s.1 of the 1978 Act, as it applies in Northern Ireland, until December 31, 1988; revokes the 1985 (No. 324) Order.

INDUSTRIAL RELATIONS (1987 ORDER) (COMMENCEMENT) ORDER (NORTHERN IRELAND) 1987 (No. 308 (C.12)) [£1·60], made under S.I. 1987 No. 936 (N.I. 9), art. 1(2), and the Northern Ireland Act 1974 (c.28), Sched. 1, para. 2(1); brought the 1987 S.I. into operation on September 6, 1987, save for parts of arts. 6 and 7 which were brought into operation on August 3, 1987.

INDUSTRIAL RELATIONS (VARIATION OF LIMITS) ORDER (NORTHERN IRELAND) 1987 (No. 73) [80p], made under S.I. 1976 No. 1043 (N.I. 16), arts. 70, 80(3), and S.I. 1976 No. 2147 (N.I. 28), arts. 5(5), 63(4); operative on April 1, 1987; increases certain limits under those S.I.s and the Contracts of Employment and Redundancy Payments Act (Northern Ireland) 1965 (c.19); revokes the 1986 (No. 54) Order.

REDUNDANCY PAYMENTS (LOCAL GOVERNMENT ETC.) (MODIFICATION) (AMENDMENT) ORDER (NORTHERN IRELAND) 1987 (No. 28) [45p], made under the Contracts of Employment and Redundancy Payments Act (Northern Ireland) 1965 (c.19), s.26(5)(*a*)(6); operative on March 25, 1987; adds certain bodies to the list of employers to whose employees the 1986 (No. 206) Order applies.

SEX DISCRIMINATION (TRAINING DESIGNATIONS) ORDER (NORTHERN IRELAND) 1987 (No. 319) [45p], made under S.I. 1976 No. 1042 (N.I. 15), arts. 17(2)(*c*), 48(4)(*b*); operative on September 1, 1987; designates certain persons and bodies for the purposes of arts. 17 and 48 of the 1976 S.I.

UNFAIR DISMISSAL (INCREASE OF COMPENSATION LIMIT) ORDER (NORTHERN IRELAND) 1987 (No. 74) [45p], made under S.I. 1976 No. 1043, arts. 37(2), 80(3); operative on April 1, 1987; increases the limit on the compensation which can be awarded by an industrial tribunal in claims for unfair dismissal as the compensatory award or as compensation for failure to comply fully with the terms of an order for reinstatement or re-engagement; revokes the 1985 (No. 37) Order subject to a transitional provision.

UNFAIR DISMISSAL (INCREASE OF LIMITS OF BASIC AND SPECIAL AWARDS) ORDER (NORTHERN IRELAND) 1987 (No. 318) [45p], made under S.I. 1976 No. 1043 (N.I. 16) arts. 34(5B), 37A(7), 80(3); operative on September 6, 1987; increase the minimum basic award and the limits applicable to the calculation of the special award.

2668. Employment—confidentiality—information acquired in course of business—agreement

N, a company manufacturing and marketing pharmaceutical products and currently spending over one million pounds on research, employed S, a chartered chemist, from November 1982 until June 1986 when he resigned in order to take up a post as an analytical chemist with P, a multi-national group enagaged in manufacturing and marketing similar products. In November 1984 S had entered into an agreement with N under which he undertook that he would not, without N's written consent, for one year after the termination of his employment with N engage directly or indirectly in any activity in which it could reasonably be anticipated that he would be required or expected to use or disclose any confidential information obtained by him during his employment with N. N sought an injunction to restrain S from taking up employment with P within a year of terminating his employment with N.

Held, granting the injunction, that (1) S had obtained confidential information during his employment with N; (2) he would be able to carry some of that information in his head; and (3) N had shown that on the balance of probabilities P would require or expect S to use or disclose that information.

NORBROOK LABORATORIES *v.* SMYTH [1986] 12 N.I.J.B. 74, Murray J.

2669. Employment—Industrial Relations (Northern Ireland) Order 1987 (S.I. 1987 No. 936 (N.I. 9))

This Order (1) requires companies to include a statement about employee involvement in their annual report; (2) amends the law relating to unfair dismissal and action short of dismissal; (3) renders void any clause in a commercial contract which requires the use of union or non-union labour or which requires recognition of a trade union; (4) makes provision for civil proceedings by and against trade unions and employers' associations; (5) abolishes certain trade union immunities; and (6) empowers the Department of Economic Development to make certain arrangements to provide or assist employment.

The Order comes into operation on a day or days to be appointed.

2670. Employment—sex discrimination—decision of university—judicial review. See MALONE'S APPLICATION, *Re,* §2623.

2671. Employment—unfair dismissal—redundancy

B, who had twenty years' experience of steel erecting, started work with D company in March 1982 and McG, who had fourteen years' experience of steel erecting, started work in February 1982. Both were dismissed for redundancy in August 1983 although three other employees with less experience and less service with the company, who had been engaged on similar work to that remaining to be done, were retained. D, a labourer who had started work with the company in October 1979 and who had during most of his service been transferred from the labourers' pool to attend various craftsmen, was also dismissed for redundancy in August 1983. It had been agreed between the labourers' shop steward and a general superintendent of the company that a labourer who had been attending craftsmen should not be transferred back to the pool unless there was work available for him in the pool. The industrial tribunal found that all three had been unfairly dismissed.

Held, dismissing the company's appeal, that B and McG had been selected for redundancy not by reference to the company's avowed criterion of those best qualified to perform the remaining work but by means of a rule of thumb not based on that criterion and, in D's case, that the agreement between the shop steward and the superintendent was made without authority and did not amount to a customary arrangement or an agreed procedure and that D's dismissal was not in accordance with the company's "best qualified" criterion.

BRESLIN *v.* DU PONT (U.K.) [1986] 8 N.I.J.B. 27, C.A.

2672. Employment—wages—Truck Acts—payment by cheque—whether current coin of the realm—injunction

[Truck Act 1831 (c.37), s.3; Payment of Wages Act (Northern Ireland) 1970 (c.12), s.1.]

Following an attempted armed robbery, P was informed by D, his employer, that his wages would be paid by cheque. P objected and sought an injunction that D be ordered to pay his wages in current coin of the realm.

Held, refusing the injunction, that (1) payment by cheque was not payment in current coin of the realm as required by s.3 of the Truck Act 1831 and this opinion was reinforced by s.1 of the Payment of Wages Act (Northern Ireland) 1970 which authorises payment by cheque where an employee so requests; and (2) the harm done to D and its staff in the event of a further armed robbery if the injunction was granted would greatly outweigh the harm done to P by the refusal of the injunction.

TOPPING *v.* WARNE SURGICAL PRODUCTS [1986] 9 N.I.J.B. 14, Hutton J.

2673. Evidence (civil)

BLOOD TESTS (EVIDENCE OF PATERNITY) (AMENDMENT) REGULATIONS (NORTHERN IRELAND) 1987 (No. 375) [85p], made under S.I. 1977 No. 1250 (N.I. 17), art. 10; operative on November 2, 1987; amend the 1978 (No. 379) Regulations so as to enable any nominated registered medical practitioner to take blood samples in pursuance of a court direction and to increase the charges payable to blood samplers and testers.

2674. Executors and administrators

ADMINISTRATION OF ESTATES (RIGHTS OF SURVIVING SPOUSE) ORDER (NORTHERN IRELAND) 1987 (No. 378) [45p], made under the Administration of Estates Act (Northern Ireland) 1955 (c.24), s.7(4A); operative on December 1, 1987; increases the amounts by reference to which a surviving spouse's rights in relation to an intestate's estate are determined.

2675. Fire service

FIRE SERVICES (BETTING, GAMING AND AMUSEMENT PREMISES) ORDER (NORTHERN IRELAND) 1987 (No. 334) [45p], made under S.I. 1984 No. 1821 (N.I. 11), art. 22(2); operative on October 1, 1987; designates the use of premises for purposes for which a bookmaking office licence, a track betting licence, a bingo club licence, an amusement or a pleasure permit is required as a use of premises for which a fire certificate is required.

2676. Fish and fisheries

EEL FISHING (LICENCE DUTIES) REGULATIONS (NORTHERN IRELAND) 1987 (No. 423) [85p], made under the Fisheries Act (Northern Ireland) 1986, s.15; operative on January 1, 1988; increase licence duties for the use of fishing engines for the taking of eels; revoke the 1985 (No. 329) Regulations.

FISHERIES (LICENCE DUTIES) BYELAWS (NORTHERN IRELAND) 1987 (No. 436) (£1·30], made under the Fisheries Act (Northern Ireland) 1966, s.26(1); operative on January 1, 1988; increase the duties for certain fishing licences, licences for certain commercial fishing engines and licences authorising the buying and selling of salmon, trout and eels; revoke the 1985 (No. 328) Byelaws.

FISHING VESSELS (FINANCIAL ASSISTANCE) SCHEME (NORTHERN IRELAND) 1987 (No. 113) [80p], made under S.I. 1987 No. 166 (N.I. 1), arts. 17(1), 19(3); operative on April 13, 1987; provides for the making by the Department of Agriculture for Northern Ireland, instead of by the Minister of Agriculture, Fisheries and Food, of laying up grants in respect of registered fishing vessels in Northern Ireland.

FOYLE AREA (ANGLING) (AMENDMENT) REGULATIONS 1987 (No. 31) [45p], made under the Foyle Fisheries Act 1952 (Rep. of Ire. No. 5), s.13(1), and the Foyle Fisheries Act (Northern Ireland) 1952 (c.5), s.13(1); operative on March 1, 1987; add certain waters to the list of waters in Sched. 1 to the 1983 (No. 317) Regulations and to the list of waters where the use of boats for angling is prohibited.

FOYLE AREA (CLOSE SEASONS FOR ANGLING) REGULATIONS 1987 (No. 344) [85p], made under the Foyle Fisheries Act 1952 (Rep. of Ire. No. 5), ss.13(1), 28(2)(4), and the Foyle Fisheries Act (Northern Ireland) 1952 (c.5), ss.13(1), 27(2)(4); operative on October 1, 1987; specify the close seasons for angling for salmon, trout and rainbow trout in the waters of the Foyle Area; revoke the 1978 (No. 50) Regulations.

FOYLE AREA (CONTROL OF NETTING) (AMENDMENT) REGULATIONS 1987 (No. 219) [45p], made under the Foyle Fisheries Act 1952 (Rep. of Ire. No. 5), s.13(1), and the Foyle Fisheries Act (Northern Ireland) 1952 (c.5), s.13(1); operative on May 29, 1987; amend the 1983 (No. 143) Regulations in relation to the materials which may be used in the construction of commercial fishing nets for the capture of salmon or trout in the Foyle Area.

FOYLE AREA (LICENSING OF FISHING ENGINES) (AMENDMENT) REGULATIONS 1987 (No. 32) [80p], made under the Foyle Fisheries Act 1952 (Rep. of Ire. No. 5), s.13(1)(2), and the Foyle Fisheries Act (Northern Ireland) 1952 (c.5), s.13(1)(2); operative on February 28, 1987; vary the licence fees payable in 1987 in respect of each type of net used and game fishing licence issued in the Foyle Area.

FOYLE AREA (LICENSING OF FISHING ENGINES) (AMENDMENT No. 2) REGULATIONS 1987 (No. 467) [85p], made under the Foyle Fisheries Act 1952 (Rep. of Ire. No. 5), s.13 (2), and the Foyle Fisheries Act (Northern Ireland) 1952 (c.5), s.1(1)(2); operative on January 31, 1988; increase the licence fees payable in 1988 in respect of each type of net used and game fishing licence issued in the Foyle Area.

RAINBOW TROUT WATERS BYELAWS (NORTHERN IRELAND) 1987 (No. 18) [45p], made under the Fisheries Act (Northern Ireland) 1966 (c.17), s.26(1); operative on March 2, 1987; designate certain waters as rainbow trout waters for the purposes of Bye-law 51 of the 1969 (No. 91) Bye-laws; revoke the 1985 (No. 367) Byelaws.

RAINBOW TROUT WATERS (No. 2) BYELAWS (NORTHERN IRELAND) 1987 (No. 422) [45p], made under the Fisheries Act (Northern Ireland) 1966 (c.17), s.26(1); operative on January 1, 1988; designate certain waters as rainbow trout waters for the purposes of bye-law 51 of the 1969 (No. 91) Byelaws; revoke the 1987 (No. 18) Byelaws.

SEA FISHERIES (AMENDMENT) REGULATIONS (NORTHERN IRELAND) 1987 (No. 69) [45p], made under the Fisheries Act (Northern Ireland) 1966, ss.19(1), 124(1)(2); operative on April 1, 1987; amend the 1972 (No. 95) Regulations so as to limit their application to British citizens only.

2677. Food and drugs

AUTHORISED OFFICERS (MEAT INSPECTION) REGULATIONS (NORTHERN IRELAND) 1987 (No. 141) [45p], made under the Food and Drugs Act (Northern Ireland) 1958 (c.27), ss.30(4)(*b*) 68; operative on May 4, 1987; prescribe the qualifications to be held by an officer of a district council authorised under the 1958 Act to act in relation to the examination and seizure of meat; revoke the 1976 (No. 100) Regulations.

COLOURING MATTER IN FOOD (AMENDMENT) REGULATIONS (NORTHERN IRELAND) 1987 (No. 471) [85p], made under the Food and Drugs Act (Northern Ireland) 1958 (c.27), ss.4, 7, 68; operative on February 15, 1988; further amend the 1973 (No. 466) Regulations.

CONDENSED MILK AND DRIED MILK (AMENDMENT) REGULATIONS (NORTHERN IRELAND) 1987 (No. 65) [£1·40], made under the Food and Drugs Act (Northern Ireland)

1958, ss.4, 7, 68, 68A; operative as to part on March 23, 1987, and as to the remainder on February 2, 1988; implement Council Directive No. 83/635/EEC relating to certain partly or wholly dehydrated preserved milk for human consumption.

CONTROL OF PESTICIDES (ADVISORY COMMITTEE) ORDER (NORTHERN IRELAND) 1987 (No. 341) [45p], made under the Food and Environment Protection Act 1985 (c.48), s.16(7); operative on October 1, 1987; establishes the Advisory Committee on Pesticides for Northern Ireland for the purpose of advising the Department of Agriculture for Northern Ireland on matters relating to the control of pests in furthering the general purposes of Pt. III of the 1985 Act.

CONTROL OF PESTICIDES (ADVISORY COMMITTEE) (TERMS OF OFFICE) REGULATIONS (NORTHERN IRELAND) 1987 (No. 342) [45p], made under the Food and Environment Protection Act 1985, s.16(7), Sched. 5, paras. 3, 8; operative on October 1, 1987; provide for the terms on which the chairman and members of the Advisory Committee on Pesticides for Northern Ireland are to hold and vacate their offices.

FOOD PROTECTION (EMERGENCY PROHIBITIONS) ORDER (NORTHERN IRELAND) 1987 (No. 367) [£1·60], made under the Food and Environment Protection Act 1985, ss.1(1), 24(3); operative on September 15, 1987; contains emergency prohibitions on various activities in order to prevent human consumption of food which has been or may have been rendered unsuitable for that purpose in consequence of the escape of radioactive substances from the Chernobyl nuclear reactor.

FOOD PROTECTION (EMERGENCY PROHIBITIONS) (AMENDMENT) ORDER (NORTHERN IRELAND) 1987 (No. 395) [45p], made under the Food and Environment Protection Act 1985 (c.48), ss.1(1), 24(3); operative on October 22, 1987; amends the 1987 (No. 367) Order by exempting certain sheep from the prohibition on slaughter and from the prohibition on supply of meat derived from such sheep.

FOOD (REVISION OF PENALTIES AND MODE OF TRIAL) REGULATIONS (NORTHERN IRELAND) 1987 (No. 38) [£1·40], made under the Food and Drugs Act (Northern Ireland) 1958 (c.27), ss.4, 7, 13, 68 and the European Communities Act 1972 (c.68), s.2(2); operative on March 9, 1987; amend certain regulations to alter the penalties for offences against those regulations and in some cases to alter the mode of trial for such offences; revoke the 1960 (No. 71) Regulations.

MATERIALS AND ARTICLES IN CONTACT WITH FOOD REGULATIONS (NORTHERN IRELAND) (No. 432) [£3·60], made under the European Communities Act 1972 s.2(2); operative on December 31, 1987 re-enact with amendments and revoke the 1981 (No. 285), 1982 (No. 144), 1983 (No. 28) and 1987 (No. 38) Regulations.

OLIVE OIL (MARKETING STANDARDS) REGULATIONS (NORTHERN IRELAND) 1987 (No. 431) [85p], made under the European Communities Act 1972 (c.68), s.2(2); operative on December 31, 1987; make provision for the enforcement of art. 35 of Council (Regulation No. 136/66/EEC on the establishment of a common organisation of the market in oils and fats.

2678. Gaming and wagering

AMUSEMENTS WITH PRIZES (FORM OF PLEASURE PERMIT) REGULATIONS (NORTHERN IRELAND) 1987 (No. 195) [£1·40], made under S.I. 1985 No. 1204, art. 160(1); operative on June 1, 1987; prescribe the form of pleasure permits.

BETTING AND GAMING (FEES AND VARIATION OF MONETARY LIMITS) ORDER (NORTHERN IRELAND) 1987 (No. 186) [80p], made under S.I. 1985 No. 1204 (N.I. 11), arts. 37(2)(5), 76(5), 106(3), 108(16), 128(3); operative on June 1, 1987; specifies fees in relation to track betting licences and increases certain monetary limits in the S.I.

BETTING, GAMING, LOTTERIES AND AMUSEMENTS (1985 ORDER) (COMMENCEMENT No. 2) ORDER (NORTHERN IRELAND) 1987 (No. 6 (C.1)) [80p], made under S.I. 1985 No. 1204 (N.I. 11), art. 1(2) and the Northern Ireland Act 1974 (c.28), Sched. 1, para. 2(1); brought into operation on February 16, 1987, provisions of the 1985 S.I. which relate to gaming on bingo club premises.

BETTING, GAMING, LOTTERIES AND AMUSEMENTS (1985 ORDER) (COMMENCEMENT No. 3) ORDER (NORTHERN IRELAND) 1987 (No. 185 (C.8)) [45p], made under S.I. 1985 No. 1204 (N.I. 11), art. 1(2), and the Northern Ireland Act 1974 (c.28) Sched. 1, para 2(1); brought into operation on June 1, 1987, those provisions of the 1985 S.I. relating to betting, lotteries, amusements and competitions which were not then in operation.

BOOKMAKING (CONDUCT OF LICENSED OFFICES) ORDER (NORTHERN IRELAND) 1987 (No. 396) [85p], made under S.I. 1985 No. 1204 (N.I. 11), art. 32(14); operative on December 7, 1987; amends art. 32 of the 1985 S.I. in relation to the use in licensed bookmaking offices of wireless sets, television sets and visual display units.

BOOKMAKING (LICENSED OFFICES) REGULATIONS (NORTHERN IRELAND) 1987 (No. 192) [80p], made under S.I. 1985 No. 1204, art. 32(1)(12); operative on June 1,

1987; require the display of certain notices inside a licensed bookmaking office and impose restrictions on the advertising which may be published outside a licensed office.

GAMING (BINGO) (AMENDMENT) REGULATIONS (NORTHERN IRELAND) 1987 (No. 398) [45p], made under S.I. 1985 No. 1204, art. 76(2); operative on December 7, 1987; increases the maximum charge for gaming by way of bingo in bingo club premises.

GAMING (BINGO) REGULATIONS (NORTHERN IRELAND) 1987 (No. 8) [80p], made under S.I. 1985 No. 1204, art. 76(2)(8); operative on February 16, 1987; authorise the making of charges in respect of gaming by way of bingo on bingo club premises up to a maximum of £4·00 during a charging period which should be no shorter than two hours in length, and specify the information which must be prominently displayed in bingo club premises.

GAMING (FORM OF BINGO CLUB LICENCE) REGULATIONS (NORTHERN IRELAND) 1987 (No. 7) [£1·40], made under S.I. 1985 No. 1204, art. 66(1); operative on February 16, 1987; prescribe the form of bingo club licences.

GAMING (VARIATION OF MONETARY LIMIT AND CHARGES) ORDER (NORTHERN IRELAND) 1987 (No. 397) [45p], made under S.I. 1985 No. 1204, arts. 75(2), 172(2); operative on December 7, 1987; increases the maximum permitted aggregate amount of winnings in respect of games of bingo in one week and the charges payable in respect of applications for the grant, provisional grant or renewal of bingo club licences.

HORSE RACING AND BETTING (AMENDMENT) ORDER (NORTHERN IRELAND) 1987 (No. 265) [45p], made under S.I. 1976 No. 1157 (N.I. 17), art. 11(2); operative on September 1, 1987; increases certain charges payable under the 1976 S.I. by on-course and off-course bookmakers; revokes the 1986 (No. 204) Order.

LOTTERY (FORM OF CERTIFICATE) REGULATIONS (NORTHERN IRELAND) 1987 (No. 194) [80p], made under S.I. 1985 No. 1204, art. 143(1); operative on June 1, 1987; prescribe the form of lottery certificates.

LOTTERIES REGULATIONS (NORTHERN IRELAND) 1987 (No. 193) [£1·40], made under S.I. 1985 No. 1204, arts. 137(17), 138(1); operative on June 1, 1987; prescribe the form of returns and impose requirements in relation to lotteries promoted by registered societies.

2679. Health and safety at work

ASBESTOS (LICENSING) (MEDICAL FEES REVOCATION) REGULATIONS (NORTHERN IRELAND) 1987 (No. 430) [45p], made under S.I. 1978 No. 1039, art. 40(2)(4); operative on December 31, 1987; revoking 6(5) of the 1984 (No. 205) Regulations.

DRY CLEANING (METRICATION) REGULATIONS (NORTHERN IRELAND) 1987 (No. 33) [45p], made under S.I. 1978 No. 1039 (N.I. 9), arts. 17(1)(3), 45(1)(2); operative on April 1, 1987; amend the 1950 (No. 117) Regulations to substitute amounts or quantities expressed in metric units for amounts or quantities not so expressed.

HEALTH AND SAFETY (MEDICAL FEES) REGULATIONS (NORTHERN IRELAND) 1987 (No. 427) [£1·60], made under S.I. 1978 No. 1039 (N.I. 9), art. 49; operative on December 31, 1987; fix fees to be paid for work done by employment medical advisers in conducting medical examinations and surveillances under certain enactments.

IONISING RADIATIONS (MEDICAL FEES REVOCATION) REGULATIONS (NORTHERN IRELAND) 1987 (No. 429) [45p], made under S.I. 1978 No. 1939, art. 40(2)(4); operative on December 31, 1987; revoke reg. 37 of the 1985 (No. 273) Regulations.

MEDICAL EXAMINATIONS (FEES) (REVOCATION) REGULATIONS (NORTHERN IRELAND) 1987 (No. 428) [45p], made under S.I. 1978 No. 1039, arts. 17(1)(3)(a), 40(2)(4), 49; operative on December 31, 1987; revoke the 1979 (No. 171) Regulations.

2680. Health and safety at work—agriculture

AGRICULTURE (POISONOUS SUBSTANCES) REGULATIONS (NORTHERN IRELAND) 1987 (No. 364) [£3·30], made under S.I. 1978 No. 1039 (N.I. 9), art. 17(1)(2)(4)(5)(6), Sched. 3, paras. 1(1)(2)(3), 6, 7(1), 8, 9, 10, 13, 14(1), 15; operative on October 19, 1987; prescribe the precautions to be taken by employers and employees when specified substances are used in certain agricultural operations.

AGRICULTURE (TRACTOR CABS) (AMENDMENT) REGULATIONS (NORTHERN IRELAND) 1987 (No. 376) [85p], made under S.I. 1978 No. 1039 (N.I. 9), art. 17(2), Sched. 3, para. 1(1)(*a*)(*c*)(2)(3); operative on November 2, 1987; make amendments to the 1981 (No. 5) Regulations, including amendments to implement Council Directive No. 79/622/EEC which relates to the static testing of roll-over protection structures of certain tractors.

2681. Housing

HOME PURCHASE ASSISTANCE (PRICE LIMIT) ORDER (NORTHERN IRELAND) 1987 (No. 298) [45p], made under S.I. 1981 No. 156 (N.I. 3), art. 153(2); operative on September 1, 1987; increases to £29,200 the prescribed limit on the purchase price of house property for which financial assistance is available under arts. 153 and 154 of the 1981 S.I.; revokes the 1986 (No. 156) Order.

HOUSING BENEFIT (TRANSITIONAL) REGULATIONS (NORTHERN IRELAND) 1987 (No. 462) [£1·60], made under S.I. 1986 No. 1888 (N.I. 18), art. 84(1); operative on December 31, 1987; make transitional provisions in connection with the new statutory scheme for the granting of rate rebates, rent rebates and rent allowances.

HOUSING BENEFITS (AMENDMENT) REGULATIONS (NORTHERN IRELAND) 1987 (No. 77) [80p], made under S.I. 1983 No. 1121 (N.I. 14), art. 3; operative on March 30, 1987; increase certain amounts and percentages specified in the 1985 (No. 282) Regulations and amend those Regulations in relation to the amounts to be disregarded when ascertaining weekly income for any housing benefit.

HOUSING BENEFITS (AMENDMENT No. 2) REGULATIONS (NORTHERN IRELAND) 1987 (No. 95) [45p], made under S.I. 1983 No. 1121, art. 3; operative on March 30, 1987; increase the amount to be disregarded in respect of parental contributions to certain students when ascertaining weekly income for any housing benefit.

HOUSING BENEFITS (AMENDMENT No. 3) REGULATIONS (NORTHERN IRELAND) 1987 (No. 332) [85p], made under S.I. 1983 No. 1121 (N.I. 14), art. 3(2); operative on September 1, 1987; amend the 1985 (No. 282) Regulations in relation to students.

HOUSING (HOUSES IN MULTIPLE OCCUPATION) (PRESCRIBED FORMS) REGULATIONS (NORTHERN IRELAND) 1987 (No. 132) [£3·40], made under S.I. 1981 No. 156 (N.I. 3), art. 162; operative on May 18, 1987; prescribe the forms of closing order, directions, notices and other forms to be used by the Northern Ireland Housing Executive for the purposes of Pt. VI of the 1981 S.I.

HOUSING (RIGHT TO EQUITY-SHARING LEASE) (RENT AND SERVICE CHARGE ADJUSTMENT) ORDER (NORTHERN IRELAND) 1987 (No. 162) [45p], made under S.I. 1986 No. 1301 (N.I. 13), Sched. 6, para. 5(2)(5); operative on June 1, 1987; requires an adjustment to be made in certain circumstances to the rent payable, or the service charge for repairs, maintenance or insurance made, under an equity-sharing lease granted under Pt. III of the 1986 S.I.

HOUSING (UNOCCUPIED PREMISES—CONTINUANCE OF POWERS) ORDER (NORTHERN IRELAND) 1987 (No. 340) [45p], made under S.I. 1981 No. 156 (N.I. 3), art. 64; operative on November 10, 1987; continues in force until November 9, 1989, certain provisions of Chap. V of Pt. III of the 1981 S.I. which empower the Northern Ireland Housing Executive to deal with certain unoccupied premises.

2682. Inheritance tax

ESTATE DUTY (NORTHERN IRELAND) (INTEREST ON UNPAID DUTY) ORDER 1987 (No. 893) [45p], made under the Finance Act (Northern Ireland) 1970 (c.21), s.1(2); operative on June 6, 1987; provides that interest on unpaid estate duty will run at six per cent.

INHERITANCE TAX (DELIVERY OF ACCOUNTS) (NORTHERN IRELAND) REGULATIONS 1987 (No. 1129) [45p], made under the Inheritance Tax Act 1984 (c.51), s.256(1); operative on August 1, 1987; exempts from the need to deliver an account where a deceased's estate is under £70,000 in respect of deaths after April 1, 1987.

2683. Juries

JURY TRIAL (AMENDMENT) (NORTHERN IRELAND) ORDER 1987 (S.I. No. 1283) [45p], made under the Judicature (Northern Ireland) Act 1978 (c.23), s.62(6); operative on August 1, 1987; amends s.62(1) of the 1978 Act by deleting personal injury actions from the classes of High Court action, which, if any party to the action so requests, are to be tried with a jury.

2684. Landlord and tenant

REGISTERED RENTS (INCREASE) ORDER (NORTHERN IRELAND) 1987 (No. 42) [45p], made under S.I. 1978 No. 1050 (N.I. 20), art. 33(2); operative on March 9, 1987; increases by 3·75 per cent. the rents of regulated tenancies registered with the Department of the Environment.

2685. Landlord and tenant—business tenancies—Lands Tribunal decisions

T's application for a new tenancy, which was made to the Lands Tribunal within four months of L's notice to determine an existing tenancy, was not accompanied by a copy of T's notification of his unwillingness to give up possession, as required by the Lands Tribuanal Rules. This ommission, when pointed out by the Registrar to the Tribunal, was rectified by T after the expiration of the four month period. The Tribunal found that the Registrar had treated T's application as valid and, as no application was made by L for a direction, the application was valid.

BALL *v.* PICKEN (BT/65/1986).

2686. Two applications for new leases of lock-up shops in Botanic Avenue, Belfast, were referred to the Lands Tribunal to determine the rents to be paid and the length of the leases and review periods. The Tribunal decided that each lease should be for a ten-year period with a rent review at the end of the fifth year and that the rents should be assessed at £13·80 per square foot for the first 15 feet in depth, £6·90 per square foot for the remainder of each shop and £2·00 per square foot for each store. An end allowance of 7·5 per cent. was made for the irregular shape of one shop.

CUMMINGS AND SCOTT *v.* PERSONAL REPRESENTATIVES OF SHERRARD (BT/84/1985: BT/85/1985).

2687. T applied for a new tenancy of a butcher's shop in Newry which he had occupied for a considerable number of years. The Tribunal found that L had not established his grounds of opposition to the application. T contended that the new tenancy should be for nine years. L contended that it should be for one year only as he intended to carry out a major refurbishment of the premises.

Held, that the tenancy should be for nine years which was the usual period for leases of business premises in the Newry area. A one-year tenancy would, to a large extent, remove the protection given to T by the previous decision of the Tribunal.

DOWNEY *v.* LOUGHRAN (BT/87/1986).

2688. T's application for a new tenancy of a shop selling videos and electronic equipment in Cookstown was opposed by L on the ground that she intended to carry on a wool shop there. L and her husband had carried on a drapery business for over 30 years and when they gave it up in 1984 they kept a counter, cash registers and shelves for storing wool. L had arranged with two wool suppliers for a supply of wool for the intended business and was willing to give an undertaking that she would carry on the business on the premises for a reasonable time.

Held, that L had established her ground of opposition to the grant of the new tenancy.

EASTWOOD *v.* LOUGHRAN (BT/130/1986).

2689. T applied for a new tenancy of premises in Kilwaughter, Co. Antrim, used for the manufacture of pre-cast concrete products. L did not oppose the application but agreement could not be reached as to the rent to be paid and the other terms of the tenancy.. The premises were held under a lease for ten years from September 1, 1962, at an annual rent of £520 plus rates, L being responsible for insurance. The rent was increased in 1979 and again in 1986.

Held, that the new tenancy should be for a term of ten years at an annual rent of £2,360, based on a price of 22p per square foot for the better parts of the premises, the rent to be reviewed at the end of the fifth year.

FALCONER & SONS *v.* REA (BT/117/1986).

2690. [Business Tenancies Act (Northern Ireland) 1964 (c.36), s.4.]

T claimed that L's notice to determine his tenancy of 7 Hill Street, Newry, did not comply with s.4 of the Business Tenancies Act (Northern Ireland) 1964 in that L's addresses had not been entered at the bottom of the notice, the notice was not dated, the date of termination had not been entered and the premises were described as "Brenda Gallagher's."

Held, that the notice could not be treated as a valid notice.

GALLAGHER *v.* MORGAN (BT/118/1986).

2691. T's application for a new tenancy of premises, Nos. 99/101 Victoria Street, Belfast, was opposed by L on the ground that he intened to carry on his business there. L's family had carried on business since 1890 but this ceased in 1976. From 1979 L carried on a somewhat similar business in other premises but was unable to obtain a new lease of those premises in 1986. Since 1986 he carried on that business from his home. The Tribunal found that L's intention to carry on business in the Victoria Street premises was real and firmly grounded and that he had established his ground of opposition to the grant of the new tenancy.

IMPULSE DISPLAY CENTRE *v.* STEELE (BT/100/1986).

2692. L opposed the applications of three tenants for new tenancies of their premises in Strabane on the ground that L intended to demolish or rebuild the premises or to carry out substantial works of construction on them and could not reasonably do so without possession of the premises. L had consulted a building contractor and an architect about a new building to replace the three premises and a formal application was made for planning permission. The Fire Authority was consulted and L's bank had confirmed that L was in a position to meet the estimated cost of the new building.

Held, by the Lands Tribunal that L's intention had moved from an exploratory into a firm decision and that L's ground of opposition to the grant of the new tenancies had been established.

McALEER *v.* COMMODORE CINEMAS (NORTHERN IRELAND) (BT/120/1986); McCALLION *v.* COMMODORE CINEMAS (NORTHERN IRELAND) IRELAND (BT/121/1986); McGUIGAN *v.* COMMODORE CINEMAS (NORTHERN IRELAND) (BT/125/1986).

2693. T's request for a new tenancy was posted to each of three landlords on January 24, 1986, but one of the landlords who lived in Australia did not receive the request until January 31, 1986. T made his application to the Lands Tribunal on May 29, 1986.

Held, that the application was made within four months of the request.

McMANUS & SON *v.* BURROWS, GILBERT AND POTTIE (BT/81/1986).

2694. In his notice dated July 5, 1984, to determine a business tenancy, L stated that he would not oppose an application to the Lands Tribunal for the grant of a new tenancy. At that time L thought that he could not get possession on the property although he had purchased it with the intention of demolishing it. On October 7, 1986, L applied for leave to amend the notice to determine to allow him to oppose the grant of a new tenancy.

Held, refusing the application, that it was mandatory for L in his notice to determine to state whether he would or would not oppose an application for a new tenancy. Even if the Tribunal had a discretion in the matter, this was not a suitable case for its exercise.

McMILLAN *v.* CROSSEY (BT/21/1965).

2695. [Business Tenancies Act (Northern Ireland) 1964 (c.36), s.4(6).]

L in her notice to determine T's tenancy of a shop in Portadown stated that she would oppose an application for a new tenancy on the ground of non-fulfilment of an existing agreement and in particular T's "failure to comply with the obligation to repair and maintain the holding." T claimed that this did not comply with s.4(6) of the Business Tenancies Act (Northern Ireland) 1964. L's notice was dated October 22, 1986, and served personally on October 29, 1986. T's notice that he was unwilling to give up the tenancy was dated December 12, 1986, and signed and posted on that day. L claimed that it was not received until January 19, 1987, that is, outside the two-month period required under the 1964 Act.

Held, (1) that L's notice indicated with sufficient clarity the case which T had to meet and was, accordingly, valid; and (2) there was no clear evidence of the non-delivery of T's notice and on the balance of probabilities it had been delivered to L's office and went astray there. It was also valid.

MULHOLLAND *v.* McKENNA (BT/7/1987).

2696. [Business Tenancies Act (Northern Ireland) 1964 (c.36), ss.10(1), 19(1).]

L in his notice to determine T's tenancy of business premises in May Street, Belfast, indicated that he would oppose an application for a new tenancy on the ground that he intended to demolish or rebuild the premises. T informed L that he would not give up possession of the premises and applied to the Lands Tribunal for a new tenancy. T obtained new premises and informed L by telephone that he might be prepared to give up possession of the old premises if he obtained compensation under s.19(1) of the Business Tenancies Act (Northern Ireland) 1964. Following further discussions by telephone L informed T that he would not oppose the application for a new tenancy.

Held, that no compensation was payable under s.19(1) of the 1964 Act as the Tribunal was not precluded from granting a new tenancy by reason of any of the grounds specified in s.10(1)(*e*)(*f*) and (*g*) of the Act, L having, at the time of the hearing, withdrawn his opposition.

ROBERTSON (BELFAST) *v.* McLEAN (BT/110/1986).

2696a. Landlord and tenant—enlargement of leasehold interest—whereabouts of certain interested persons unknown—Lands Tribunal decision

To enable the applicant to sell premises free from all encumbrances it was agreed by the parties that the fee simple be conveyed to the applicant free from encumbrances.

Held, by the Lands Tribunal, that the agreement be approved and the Registrar of the Tribunal be authorised to execute the conveyance on behalf of certain interested persons who could not be traced.

McSORLEY *v.* MacNEILE-DICKSON (R/30/1986); (R/31/1986).

2697. Landlord and tenant—regulated tenancy—obligation to repair

[Rent Restriction Law (Amendment) Act (Northern Ireland) 1951 (c.23), s.3; Housing (Miscellaneous Provisions and Rent Restriction Law (Amendment) Act (Northern Ireland) 1956 (c.10), Pt. V; Rent (Northern Ireland) Order 1978 (S.I. 1975 No. 1050 (N.I. 20), arts. 41, 46 to 58.]

P1 and P2 as statutory tenants of dwelling-houses held under regulated tenancies claimed damages for the breach of D's statutory duty under art. 41 of the Rent (Northern Ireland) Order 1978 to repair the houses and an injunction requiring D to carry out repairs specified in certificates of disrepair issued by the local authority. Under the terms of his tenancy agreement P1 was liable for repairs but he did not have a copy of this agreement and believed that D was liable for repairs. D believed that he was liable for repairs under s.3 of the Rent Restriction Law (Amendment) Act (Northern Ireland) 1951. Under Pt. V of the Housing (Miscellaneous Provisions) and Rent Restiction Law (Amendment) Act (Northern Ireland) 1956, D had increased the rent of P1's house when it was occupied by a previous tenant and this increased rent was paid both by the previous tenant and by P1. Certificates of disrepair were served on D by the local authority requiring D to carry out specified repairs to each house.

Held, that (1) when D received from P1 payment of rent under the tenancy agreement; including the increase under the 1956 Act, D became liable for the repairs under s.3(3) of the 1951 Act; (2) as P2 was not responsible under his tenancy agreement for repairs arising from dilapidation due to fair wear and tear, D was liable for the repairs specified in the certificate of disrepair in respect of P2's house; and (3) as arts. 46 to 48 of the 1978 Order provided a scheme for the enforcement of D's duty to repair, no other remedy was available to P1 or P2 and, accordingly, they had no right of action for breach of the statutory duty under art. 41 of the Order.

McDOWELL *v.* McKIBBIN; BRANNON *v.* GUTHRIE [1986] 9 N.I.J.B. 28, Higgins J.

2697a. Landlord and tenant—restrictive covenant—extinguishment—Lands Tribunal decision

[Property (Northern Ireland) Order 1978 (S.I. 1978 No. 459 (N.I. 4)), art. 5.]

McC applied under art. 5 of the Property (Northern Ireland) Order 1978 for the extinguishment of restrictive covenants in a Fee Farm Grant dated October 8, 1892, and in a lease dated May 10, 1943.

Held, by the Lands Tribunal, refusing the application, that (1) the covenants were entered into in order to protect the views from the houses on the land; (2) there had been no change in the character of the neighbourhood; and (3) the covenants secured practical benefits to the occupiers of the houses on the land.

McCLELLAND *v.* MONTAGU (R/18/1985).

2698. Legal aid

LEGAL ADVICE AND ASSISTANCE (AMENDMENT) REGULATIONS (NORTHERN IRELAND) 1987 (No. 102) [45p], made under S.I. 1981 No. 228 (N.I. 8), arts. 7(2), 22(1); operative on April 6, 1987; amend the scale of contributions payable for legal advice and assistance under art. 7(2) of the S.I.

LEGAL ADVICE AND ASSISTANCE (FINANCIAL CONDITIONS) REGULATIONS (NORTHERN IRELAND) 1987 (No. 103) [45p], made under S.I. 1981 No. 228, arts. 3(2), 7(3), 22(1); operative on April 6, 1987; increase the financial limits of eligibility for legal advice and assistance under Pt. II of the S.I.

LEGAL AID (FINANCIAL CONDITIONS) REGULATIONS (NORTHERN IRELAND) 1987 (No. 104) [45p], made under S.I. 1981 No. 228, arts. 9(2), 12(2), 22(1); operative on April 6, 1987; increase certain of the financial limits of eligibility for legal aid under Pt. II of the S.I.

2699. Licensing

LICENSING (1987 ORDER) (COMMENCEMENT NO. 1) ORDER (NORTHERN IRELAND) 1987 (No. 365 (C.13)) [85p], made under S.I. 1987 No. 1277 (N.I. 13), art. 1(2); brought into operation on October 1, 1987, provisions of the S.I. relating to ancillary businesses, imposition of conditions on applications for licences, permitted hours, minors, inspection and rights of entry, suspension of licences and penalties.

2700. Licensing—Licensing (Northern Ireland) Order 1987 (S.I. 1987 No. 1277 (N.I. 13))

This Order amends the Licensing Act (Northern Ireland) 1971 (c.13) by (1) prohibiting the consumption of intoxicating liquor, with certain exceptions, at entertainments organised for gain; (2) providing new general permitted hours for off-sales; (3) extending the permitted hours on Sundays and Christmas Days for public houses, airport refreshment rooms and theatres; (4) providing for additional permitted hours for public houses which meet certain standards; (5) extending the places of public entertainment which may obtain a licence; (6) authorising public houses to provide accommodation for guests; (7) empowering the court to suspend the operation of certain aspects of a licence; and (8) increasing the penalties for certain offences.

The Order comes into operation on days to be appointed.

2701. Limitation of actions—Limitation (Amendment) (Northern Ireland) Order 1987 (S.I. 1987 No. 1629 (N.I. 17))

This Order amends the law of limitation of actions in negligence cases involving latent damage (other than personal injuries) and provides for the accrual, in certain circumstances, of a cause of action in negligence to successive owners in respect of latent damage to property. It also reduces the limitation period for libel actions from six years to three years and authorises the High Court to extend the limitation period for defamation actions where relevant facts become known to the potential plaintiff only after that period has expired.

The Order comes into operation on December 16, 1987.

2702. Local government

CHIEF BUILDING CONTROL OFFICERS (QUALIFICATIONS) REGULATIONS (NORTHERN IRELAND) 1987 (No. 300) [45p], made under the Local Government Act (Northern Ireland) 1972 (c.9), s.41(3); operative on September 21, 1987; prescribe the qualifications required for the post of chief building control officer; revoke the 1975 (No. 263) Regulations.

CINEMATOGRAPH AND PETROLEUM—SPIRIT LICENCES (FEES) (INCREASE) ORDER (NORTHERN IRELAND) 1987 (No. 408) [85p], made under the Financial Provisions Act (Northern Ireland) 1968 (c.25), s.1(1), Sched. 1, para. 5; operative on January 1, 1988; increases the fees payable to a district council for the grant, renewal and transfer of cinematograph and petroleum-spirit licences.

DISTRICT COUNCILS (GOODS, SERVICES AND STAFF) (SPECIFIED BODIES) REGULATIONS (NORTHERN IRELAND) 1987 (No. 269) [45p], made under the Local Government Act (Northern Ireland) 1972 (c.9), s.105(7); operative on August 24, 1987; specify descriptions of bodies with which a district council may make arrangements for the supply of goods and services or for the interchange of staff.

LOCAL GOVERNMENT (GENERAL GRANT) ORDER (NORTHERN IRELAND) 1987 (No. 48) [45p], made under S.I. 1972 No. 1999 (N.I. 22), Sched. 1, Pt. I, para. 3(1); operative on April 1, 1987; specifies the districts which are to be taken into account in calculating the standard penny rate products for the year ending on March 31, 1988, for the purpose of computing the resources element of the grant from central funds.

2703. Local government—adjournment of meetings—delegation of functions

Four borough councils resolved to adjourn their meetings as a protest against the Anglo-Irish Agreement and to delegate their functions, with certain exceptions, to their clerks. Applications were made for judicial review.

Held, granting the applications, that (1) the resolutions to adjourn the meetings were *ultra vires* and unlawful; (2) although the applications were not made within three months of the resolutions to delegate functions to the clerks, those resolutions were closely linked to the resolutions to adjourn meetings and a declaration that the delegations were invalid would not cause hardship to, or unfairly prejudice the rights of, any person; (3) the resolutions delegating functions to the clerks were void as from the dates on which they were passed; and (4) a mandamus issued against a council can be enforced against individual members of the council (*Cook's Application, Re* [1986] C.L.Y. 2381 followed).

CLOSE'S APPLICATION, *Re* [1986] 13 N.I.J.B. 54, Hutton J.

2704. Local government—delegation of Council's functions—planning appeal—adjournment

The owner of a cinema applied for planning permission to change its use to that of a general retail outlet. As no determination was made by the Department of the Environment within two months, the permission was deemed to have been refused. The owner appealed and arrangements were made for a hearing on January 28, 1986. The Borough Council was informed on December 11, 1985, of the hearing and told that it could be represented. The Council at a meeting on December 3, 1985, had delegated its functions of an emergency nature to its Town Clerk and adjourned further meetings on a month to month basis as a protest against the Anglo-Irish Agreement. On January 3, 1986, the Town Clerk instructed solicitors to act on the Council's behalf and to retain the services of a planning expert. At that date it was understood that the Department intended to recommend approval of the application but on January 21, 1986, the Council learned that the Department intended to adopt a neutral stance. At the hearing on January 28 the Council applied for an adjournment on the ground that it did not have time to prepare its case properly but this was refused. At a meeting on Feburary 18, 1986, the Council ratified all decisions and actions of the Town Clerk in relation to the appeal. The Council applied for judicial review of the refusal to adjourn the hearing.

Held, that (1) it was not necessary for the Council to resolve formally that it was expedient for a specified purpose to prosecute or defend legal proceedings as a condition precedent to its power to engage in such proceedings; (2) the ratification of the Town Clerk's actions gave them retrospectively the necessary validity; (3) there was no statutory provision requiring the Department to consult the Council before the planning appeal but in reaching its decision the Planning Appeals Commission must observe the rules of natural justice; and (4) as a consequence of the Commission's refusal to adjourn the hearing the Council was unfairly deprived of an opportunity to present its case and accordingly the Commission was in breach of the rules of natural justice. The Commission was directed to hold a further hearing.

NORTH DOWN BOROUGH COUNCIL'S APPLICATION, *Re,* [1986] 6 N.I.J.B. 1, Carswell J.

2705. Local government—failure to attend council meetings—delegation of council's functions to committees

[Local Government Act (Northern Ireland) 1972 (c.9), s.9.]

A district council resolved that all its functions, save those excepted by statutory provisions, be delegated to committees. N was left off these committees. N was present at a meeting of the full council held on September 26, 1985, but not at its next meeting held on March 7, 1986. At the following meeting held on June 26, 1986, N's office as councillor was declared vacant under s.9 of the Local Government Act (Northern Ireland) 1972 on the ground that he had failed to attend a meeting for a period of three consecutive months. On an application for judicial review the trial judge held that the period of three consecutive months commenced to run on September 26, 1985, the date on which N last attended a meeting and, accordingly, that N had ceased to be a councillor. N appealed.

Held, allowing the appeal, that the period of three consecutive months commenced to run on March 7, 1986, the date of the first meeting from which N was absent, and as the Council did not meet during that period, s.9 of the 1972 Act did not take effect. A cross appeal against the trial judge's declaration that the council's resolutions delegating its functions to committees were unlawful and void was disallowed.

NEESON'S APPLICATION, *Re* [1986] 13 N.I.J.B. 24, C.A.

2706. Medicine

PHARMACEUTICAL QUALIFICATIONS (EEC RECOGNITION) REGULATIONS (NORTHERN IRELAND) 1987 (No. 457) [£1·60], made under the European Communities Act 1972 (c.68), s.2(2); operative on January 29, 1988; implement Council Directive No. 85/433/EEC, as amended by Council Directive No. 85/584/EEC, concerning the mutual recognition of diplomas, certificates and other evidence of formal qualifications in pharmacy.

POISONS (AMENDMENT) REGULATIONS (NORTHERN IRELAND) 1987 (No. 240) [45p], made under S.I. 1976 No. 1214, art. 9; operative on July 6, 1987; amend the 1983 (No. 201) Regulations by adding magnesium phosphide to the poisons to which special restrictions apply and by including, in the special exemptions, ready for use liquid preparations containing not more than one per cent of dichlorvos.

POISONS LIST (AMENDMENT) ORDER (NORTHERN IRELAND) 1987 (No. 239) [45p], made under S.I. 1986 No. 1214 (N.I. 23), art. 4(6); operative on July 6, 1987; adds magnesium phosphide to the Poisons List.

2707. Medicine—AIDS (Control) (Northern Ireland) Order 1987 (S.I. 1987 No. 1832 (N.I. 18))

This Order requires Health and Social Services Boards in Northern Ireland to make and publish reports on specified matters relating to Aids and the Human Immunodeficiency Virus.

The Order came into force on November 22, 1987.

2708. Minors—Adoption (Northern Ireland) Order 1987 (S.I. 1987 No. 2203 (N.I. 22))

This Order (*a*) imposes on each Health and Social Services Board a duty to provide an adoption service for its area; (*b*) makes new provision relating to the registration of adoption societies; (*c*) places certain restrictions on arranging adoptions and placing children for adoption; (*d*) makes provision to enable children to be freed for adoption with or without parental agreement; (*e*) makes provision for the care and protection of children awaiting adoption; (*f*) sets out the status of adopted children; (*g*) provides for the registration of adoption orders; (*h*) makes provision for adopted adults to obtain access to their birth records; and (*i*) allows for the introduction of schemes for the payment of allowances to adopters and prospective adopters in certain circumstances.

The Order comes into operation on days to be appointed.

2709. National health

CHARGES FOR DRUGS AND APPLIANCES (AMENDMENT) REGULATIONS (NORTHERN IRELAND) 1987 (No. 108) [80p], made under S.I. 1972 No. 1265 (N.I. 14), arts. 98, 106, 107, Sched. 15; operative on April 1, 1987; increase charges for certain drugs and appliances and the sums prescribed for pre-payment certificates of exemption.

GENERAL DENTAL SERVICES (AMENDMENT) REGULATIONS (NORTHERN IRELAND) 1987 (No. 190) [80p], made under S.I. 1972 No. 1265 (N.I. 14), arts. 61, 106, 107; operative on May 25, 1987; made miscellaneous amendments to the 1975 (No. 227) Regulations.

GENERAL DENTAL SERVICES (AMENDMENT NO. 2) REGULATIONS (NORTHERN IRELAND) 1987 (No. 346) [45p], made under S.I. 1972 No. 1265 (N.I. 14), arts. 61, 106, 107; operative on October 1, 1987; amend the 1975 (No. 227) Regulations to enable dentists to provide as preventive treatment the application of fissure sealants to persons under 16.

GENERAL MEDICAL AND PHARMACEUTICAL SERVICES (AMENDMENT) REGULATIONS (NORTHERN IRELAND) 1987 (No. 1) [80p], made under S.I. 1972 No. 1265 (N.I. 14), arts. 56(2), 63(2), 106, 107(6); operative on August 1, 1987, save for reg. 2(*a*)(*b*) which came into operation on February 1, 1987; amend the list of drugs for which a doctor may not issue a prescription for supply under pharmaceutical services.

GENERAL MEDICAL AND PHARMACEUTICAL SERVICES (AMENDMENT No. 3) REGULATIONS (NORTHERN IRELAND) 1987 (No. 323) [85p], made under S.I. 1972 No. 1265 (N.I. 14), arts. 56(2), 63(2), 106, 107(6); operative on September 1, 1987; amend the list of drugs and other substances for which a doctor may not issue a prescription for supply under pharmaceutical services and which may not be dispensed under those services and amend the list of drugs which may be prescribed only in certain circumstances.

HEALTH AND PERSONAL SOCIAL SERVICES (AMENDMENT) (1986 ORDER) (COMMENCEMENT) ORDER (NORTHERN IRELAND) 1987 (No. 200 (C.9)) [45p], made under S.I. 1986 No. 2023 (N.I. 20), art. 1(4), and the Northern Ireland Act 1974 (c.28), Sched. 1, para. 2(1); brought art. 5 of the 1986 S.I. into operation on June 1, 1987.

NURSES, MIDWIVES AND HEALTH VISITORS (PROFESSIONAL CONDUCT) RULES 1987, APPROVAL ORDER (NORTHERN IRELAND) 1987 (No. 473) [£3·60], made under the Nurses, Midwives and Health Visitors Act 1979 (c.36), ss.22(4), 23(3), Sched. 6; operative on February 1, 1988; provide for the circumstances in which, and the means by which, a nurse, midwife or health visitor may be removed from the register or restored to it.

WELFARE FOODS (AMENDMENT) REGULATIONS (NORTHERN IRELAND) 1987 (No. 373) [45p], made under the Welfare Foods Act (Northern Ireland) 1968 (c.26), s.1(3)(*b*); operative on October 4, 1987; increase the amount by which a supplier of welfare milk may be reimbursed for pasteurised milk; revokes the 1986 (No. 357) Regulations.

2709a. Negligence—duty of care—whether owed to subsequent occupiers by grantors of improvement grant

[Housing (Northern Ireland) Order 1976 (S.I. 1976 No. 1780), arts. 47(2)(3), 60(5).]

The grantors of an improvement grant do not owe subsequent occupiers a duty of care to withhold payment in respect of defective work.

P bought a house in Northern Ireland under a mortgage from D, a statutory body with responsibility for housing and house improvement. A predecessor in title had bult an extension with an improvement grant from D. P claimed against D for rebuilding the extension due to defective work, arguing, *inter alia*, that D owed a duty of care to P to withhold payment of the grant until the work was carried out in a proper fashion.

Held, the purpose of creating a power to withhold the grant was to protect the public revenue, not P, and there was no such duty of care (*Anns v. Merton London Borough Council* [1978] C.L.Y. 2030 distinguished).

CURRAN *v*. NORTHERN IRELAND CO-OWNERSHIP HOUSING ASSOCIATION [1987] 2 W.L.R. 1043, H.L.

2710. Negligence—occupier's liability—licensee

[Occupiers' Liability Act (Northern Ireland) 1957 (c.25), ss.2(2), 4(6).]

P illegally went as a squatter into occupation of a house owned by D. The house was in very bad repair and due for demolition. D permitted P to remain in the house on condition that he made payments for use and occupation, such payments not to be a recognition by D of a tenancy. D knew or had means of knowing that the stairs in the house were in a dangerous condition. P was injured when a tread gave way while he was descending the stairs and brought an action for damages.

Held, awarding damages to P, that (1) P occupied the house as a lawful visitor under a bare licence revocable at will; (2) the licence did not fall within the category of contractual licences and was accordingly, outside the terms of s.4(6) of the Occupiers' Liability Act (Northern Ireland) 1957; (3) D owed P the common duty of care defined in s.2(2) of the 1957 Act; and (4) D did not take such care as in all the circumstances was reasonable.

GRAHAM *v.* NORTHERN IRELAND HOUSING EXECUTIVE [1986] 8 N.I.J.B. 93, Carswell J.

2711. Negligence—personal injuries—child's brain damaged at birth—whether failure to take reasonable care

P suffered intracranial bleeding at birth which caused severe brain damage and left him mentally retarded and physically disabled. He contended that the obstetrician and midwives were negligent and claimed damages. M, his mother, who had had four previous babies and two miscarriages and was forty-four years old, was admitted to hospital by the obstetrician who considered that she was suffering from pre-eclampsia. M commenced labour at 6.00 a.m. on December 9, 1971, and was immediately moved into the labour ward. She was given injections at 7.20 a.m. and 8.00 a.m. and P was born at 8.45 a.m. on that day by precipitate delivery. M said in evidence that the midwife had left the labour ward at 8.40 a.m. and did not return until 8.50 a.m. and that she was left unattended at the birth. She claimed that P was asphyxiated as he was born with his umbilical cord around his neck.

Held, dismissing P's claim; that (1) M's pre-eclampsia was not of such a nature as to make it probable that P had suffered asphyxia; (2) P had failed to prove on the balance of probabilities that he suffered brain damage by reason of asphyxia; (3) there was no failure on the obstetrician's part in warning the hospital staff of the risks relating to M's pregnancy; (4) P had failed to prove on the balance of probabilities that the midwife was not present at the time of the birth or that P was not properly and competently nursed in the nursery; and (5) the brain damage was not caused, as claimed in an amendment to P's statement of claim which the court permitted to be made after twenty-two days of the trial, by precipitate delivery.

BARR *v.* SOUTHERN HEALTH AND SOCIAL SERVICES BOARD [1986] 10 N.I.J.B. 1, Hutton J.

2712. Negligence—retaining wall—injury to child—standard of care

P, a girl aged 6, was injured when she fell off a retaining wall built by D when they levelled a site for the erection of houses. P claimed damages.

Held, awarding P £1000, that (1) it was D's duty to take reasonable care to prevent accidents to visitors which were reasonably foreseeable; (2) it was foreseeable that very young children would frequent the area of the wall; (3) the precise nature of the accident does not have to be foreseen; and (4) a reasonable standard of care for a public authority which alters the contour of the ground in the construction of a housing estate is also a high standard.

FITZPATRICK *v.* NORTHERN IRELAND HOUSING EXECUTIVE [1986] 13 N.I.J.B. Lord Lowry L.C.J.

2713. Northern Ireland Act 1974

NORTHERN IRELAND ACT 1974 (INTERIM PERIOD EXTENSION) ORDER 1987 (S.I. No. 1207) [45p], made under the Northern Ireland Act 1974 (c.28), s.1(4); operative on July 11, 1987; extends to July 16, 1988, the operation of the temporary provisions for the government of Northern Ireland contained in Sched. 1 to the 1974 Act.

2713a. Northern Ireland (Emergency Provisions) Act 1987 (c.30)

This Act amends the Northern Ireland (Emergency Provisions) Act 1978 (c.5) confers certain rights on persons detained in police custody in Northern Ireland under or by virtue of Pt. IV of the Prevention of Terrorism (Temporary Provisions) Act 1948, and regulates the provision of security services there.

The Act received the Royal Assent on May 15, 1987. The Act will come into force one month from that date except for s.12 and Pt. III, which will come into force on a day to be appointed by the Secretary of State.

The Act extends to Northern Ireland only.

2714. Pensions and superannuation

CONTRACTING-OUT (TRANSFER) (AMENDMENT) REGULATIONS (NORTHERN IRELAND) 1987 (No. 277) [£2·20], made under S.I. 1975 No. 1503 (N.I. 15), arts. 40(1) to (1c), 71(4); operative for purposes relating to money purchase contracted-out schemes on April 6, 1988, and for all other purposes on July 27, 1987; amend the 1985 (No. 243) Regulations in relation to the transfer of accrued rights.

CONTRACTING-OUT (WIDOWERS' GUARANTEED MINIMUM PENSIONS) REGULATIONS (NORTHERN IRELAND) 1987 (No. 278) [85p], made under S.I. 1975 No. 1503 (N.I. 15), art. 38(7A), and S.I. 1986 No. 1888 (N.I. 18), art. 11(6); operative on April 6, 1988; amend the 1985 (No. 259) Regulations to set out the circumstances in which a widower's pension is to be payable and the period for which it is to be payable.

FIREMEN'S PENSION SCHEME (AMENDMENT) ORDER (NORTHERN IRELAND) 1987 (No. 424 [85p], made under S.I. 1984 No. 1821 (N.I. 11), art. 10(1)(4); operative on January 1, 1988, with effect for certain purposes on July 13, 1978, and for other purposes on March 8, 1984; amends the 1973 Scheme set out in the 1973 (No. 393) Order principally to provide benefits for the widowers of female firefighters corresponding to those provided for widows.

JUDICIAL PENSIONS (NORTHERN IRELAND) (WIDOWS' AND CHILDREN'S BENEFITS) REGULATIONS 1987 (No. 101) [£1·90], made under the Administration of Justice Act 1973 (c.15), s.10(8), Sched. 3; operative on April 1, 1987; provide for the contributions to be made towards pensions for widows and children under the County Courts Act (Northern Ireland) 1959 (c.25) or the Resident Magistrates' Pension Act (Northern Ireland) 1960 (c.2).

JUDICIAL PENSIONS (NORTHERN IRELAND) (WIDOWS' AND CHILDREN'S BENEFITS) (AMENDMENT) REGULATIONS 1987 (No. 160) [45p], made under the Administration of Justice Act 1973 (c.15), s.10(8), Sched. 3; operative on April 1, 1987; amend the 1987 (No. 101) Regulations to make two minor corrections.

MONEY PURCHASE CONTRACTED-OUT SCHEMES REGULATIONS (NORTHERN IRELAND) 1987 (No. 279) [£1·60], made under S.I. 1975 No. 1503, arts. 32(1C), 34(2D), and S.I. 1986 No. 1888, art. 4, Sched. 1, paras, 3, 6; operative on April 6, 1988; make provision about the way in which the resources of an occupational pension scheme must be invested if it is to be a money purchase contracted-out scheme and for the making of minimum payments.

OCCUPATIONAL PENSION SCHEMES (AUDITORS) REGULATIONS (NORTHERN IRELAND) 1987 (No. 280) [£1·60], made under S.I. 1975 No. 1503, art. 58M, and S.I. 1986 No. 1888 (N.I. 18), art. 55; operative on July 27, 1987; provide for the appointment, resignation and removal of auditors, for the disclosure of information by employers, auditors and trustees, for the making of statements by auditors and for the service of documents by ordinary post.

OCCUPATIONAL PENSION SCHEMES (CONTRACTING-OUT) (AMENDMENT) REGULATIONS (NORTHERN IRELAND) 1987 (No. 282) [85p], made under S.I. 1975 No. 1503, art. 33(5), Sched. 2, para. 9; operative on July 27, 1987; amend the 1985 (No. 259) Regulations in relation to elections for the issue, variation or surrender of contracting-out certificates and in relation to the alteration of rules of contracted-out schemes.

OCCUPATIONAL PENSION SCHEMES (CONTRACTED-OUT PROTECTED RIGHTS PREMIUMS) REGULATIONS (NORTHERN IRELAND) 1987 (No. 281) [£1·60], made under S.I. 1975 No. 1503, art. 46ZA(4)(6)(7)(9)(13), 53, Sched. 2, para. 6; operative on April 6, 1988; provide for the manner in which protected rights are to be calculated and verified for the purpose of determining the amount of a contracted-out protected rights premium and make various amendments to the 1985 (No. 259) Regulations.

OCCUPATIONAL PENSION SCHEMES (DISCLOSURE OF INFORMATION) (AMENDMENT) REGULATIONS (NORTHERN IRELAND) 1987 (No. 283) [£1·60], made under S.I. 1975 No. 1503, art. 58A(1)(3); operative on July 27, 1987; amend the 1986 (No. 225) Regulations to provide for the furnishing of certain information to members of occupational pension schemes and to require the trustees of occupational pension schemes to furnish certain persons with copies of auditors' statements.

OCCUPATIONAL PENSION SCHEMES (QUALIFYING SERVICE—CONSEQUENTIAL AND OTHER PROVISIONS) REGULATIONS (NORTHERN IRELAND) 1987 (No. 284) [£1·60], made under S.I. 1975 No. 1503, arts. 45(4), 53C(4)(5), 60(1A)(*a*), Sched. 1A, para. 20, Sched. 2, para. 6, Sched. 3, paras. 9(2)(3), 21, 22, 26; operative on April 6, 1988; amend regulations which are consequential upon art. 12 of S.I. 1986 No. 1888.

OCCUPATIONAL PENSION SCHEMES (TRANSFER VALUES) (AMENDMENT) REGULATIONS (NORTHERN IRELAND) 1987 (No. 285) [85p], made under S.I. 1975 No. 1503, Sched. 1A, paras. 12(2A)(2B), 13, 14; operative for certain purposes on July 27, 1987, and for all other purposes on April 6, 1988; amend the 1985 (No 358) Regulations to extend reg. 2(1) of those Regulations to members of occupational pension schemes who opt to have their transfer values used to acquire transfer credits or rights and to limit, in certain circumstances, the rights to cash equivalents.

OCCUPATIONAL PENSIONS (REVALUATION) ORDER (NORTHERN IRELAND) 1987 (No. 434) [45p], made under S.I. 1975 No. 1503 (N.I. 15), art. 53A(1); operative on January 1, 1988; specifies the appropriate revaluation percentages for specified revaluation periods.

PENSIONS INCREASE (REVIEW) ORDER (NORTHERN IRELAND) 1987 (No. 70) [£1·40], made under S.I. 1975 No. 1503 (N.I. 15), art. 69(1)(2)(5); operative on April 6, 1987; provides for increases in the rates of public service pensions.

PENSION SCHEMES (VOLUNTARY CONTRIBUTIONS REQUIREMENTS AND VOLUNTARY AND COMPULSORY MEMBERSHIP) REGULATIONS (NORTHERN IRELAND) 1987 (No. 286) [85p], made under S.I. 1986 No. 1888, arts. 14(1), 17(1); operative for the purposes of personal pension schemes on January 4, 1988, and for the purposes of occupational pension schemes on April 6, 1988; provide that art. 14(1) of the 1986 S.I. shall not apply, to a specified extent, to the rules of occupational and personal pension schemes and that art. 17(1)(*a*) of the S.I. shall not apply during certain periods.

PERSONAL PENSION SCHEMES (APPROPRIATE SCHEMES) REGULATIONS (NORTHERN IRELAND) 1987 (No. 287) [£2·60], made under S.I. 1986 No. 1888, arts. 3(1)(2)(4)(5)(9)(10)(11), 4(1)(2)(5), 5(1)(*b*)(5), 84(1), Sched. 1, paras. 2, 6; operative as to part on July 27, 1987, and as to the remainder on January 4, 1988; provide that personal pension schemes are to be appropriate schemes only if they take certain forms, set out the procedures for applying for a certificate that a scheme is an appropriate scheme and deal with minimum contributions payable by the Department of Health and Social Services.

PERSONAL PENSION SCHEMES (DEFERMENT OF COMMENCEMENT) REGULATIONS (NORTHERN IRELAND) 1987 (No. 433) [45p], made under S.I. 1986 No. 1888 (N.I. 18), arts. 3(1)(2)(4)(5)(9)(10)(11), 4(1)(2)(5), 5(1)(*b*)(2)(5), 14(1), 84(1), Sched. 1, paras. 2, 6 operative on December 15, 1987; revoke the 1987 (No. 287) Regulations and make consequential amendments to the 1987 (Nos. 286, 293) Regulations.

PERSONAL PENSION SCHEMES (DISCLOSURE OF INFORMATION) REGULATIONS (NORTHERN IRELAND) 1987 (No. 288) [£2·20], made under S.I. 1975 No. 1503, art. 58A(1)(3); operative on July 27, 1987; specify the information that is to be made available to certain persons, in certain circumstances, by the trustees or managers of personal pension schemes.

PERSONAL PENSION SCHEMES (PERSONAL PENSION PROTECTED RIGHTS PREMIUMS) REGULATIONS (NORTHERN IRELAND) 1987 (No. 289) [£1·60], made under S.I. 1975 No. 1503, art. 53, Sched. 2, para. 6, and S.I. 1986 No. 1888, art. 7(4)(7)(8)(10)(14); operative on January 4, 1988; provide for the manner in which protected rights are to be calculated and verified for the purpose of determining the amount of a personal pension protected rights premium.

PERSONAL PENSION SCHEMES (TRANSFER VALUES) REGULATIONS (NORTHERN IRELAND) 1987 (No. 290) [85p], made under S.I. 1975 No. 1503, Sched. 1A, paras. 13, 14; operative on July 27, 1987; provide for the calculation and verification of cash equivalents in relation to personal pension schemes.

PERSONAL AND OCCUPATIONAL PENSION SCHEMES (ABATEMENT OF BENEFIT) REGULATIONS (NORTHERN IRELAND) 1987 (No 291) [£1·60], made under S.I. 1975 No. 1503, art. 31(2A)(2C), and S.I. 1986 No. 1888, art. 6; operative as to regs. 1 to 3 on January 4, 1988, and as to the remainder on April 6, 1988; prescribe the rate of a guaranteed minimum pension for an earner and the widow or widower respectively and the circumstances in which the widow or widower is to be treated as entitled to it.

PERSONAL AND OCCUPATIONAL PENSION SCHEMES (CONSEQUENTIAL PROVISIONS) REGULATIONS (NORTHERN IRELAND) 1987 (No. 292) [£2·20], made under S.I. 1975 No. 1503, arts. 2(5), 33(1)(2)(5)(7), 34(2), 40(1), 41(1)(4), 43B(3), 43C(7), 45(4), 47(1), 52, 53, 53C(4)(5), Sched. 1A, para. 14, Sched. 2, paras. 1, 6, 9, and S.I. 1977 No. 610 (N.I. 11), arts. 17(2), 18(13); operative as to specified regulations on July 27, 1987, and January 4, 1988, and as to the remainder on April 6, 1988; contain consequential provisions in relation to personal pension schemes, money purchase contracted-out schemes and guaranteed minimum pensions for widowers.

PERSONAL AND OCCUPATIONAL PENSION SCHEMES (INCENTIVE PAYMENTS) REGULATIONS (NORTHERN IRELAND) 1987 (No. 293) [£1·60], made under S.I. 1986 No. 1888, arts. 5(2), 9(1)(2)(3)(6)(7), 16; operative as to part on January 4, 1988, and as to the remainder on April 6, 1988; make further provision in relation to earners employed in contracted-out employment who voluntarily leave a relevant scheme and in relation to the additional payments to be made by the Department of Health and Social Services.

PERSONAL AND OCCUPATIONAL PENSION SCHEMES (MODIFICATION OF ENACTMENTS) REGULATIONS (NORTHERN IRELAND) 1987 (No. 294) [£2·20], made under S.I. 1986 No. 1888, art. 18(1); operative on July 27, 1987, save for reg. 3(2)(4)(5) and Sched. 6 which come into operation on April 6, 1988; apply and modify, in relation to personal pension schemes, certain provisions of the 1975 S.I. and make other modifications of that S.I.

PERSONAL AND OCCUPATIONAL PENSION SCHEMES (PROTECTED RIGHTS) REGULATIONS (NORTHERN IRELAND) 1987 (No. 295) [£2·20], made under S.I. 1986 No.

1888, art. 16, Sched. 1, paras. 6, 7(2)(4)(5), 9(1)(*a*) 2, 3, 4, 7, 8, 9, 11; operative for the purposes of personal pension schemes on July 27, 1987, and for the purposes of occupational pension schemes on April 6, 1988; make provision with respect to protected rights under an appropriate personal pension scheme or a money purchase contracted-out occupational pension scheme.

PROTECTED RIGHTS (TRANSFER PAYMENT) REGULATIONS (NORTHERN IRELAND) 1987 (No. 296) [£2·20], made under S.I. 1986 No. 1888, arts. 4, 18(1)(*b*), Sched. 1, para. 9(1)(*b*); operative for the purposes of personal pension schemes on July 27, 1987, and for all other purposes on April 6, 1988; provide for the protected rights of a member of a scheme which is or was an appropriate personal pension scheme or a money purchase contracted-out scheme to be given effect to by the making of a transfer payment.

ROYAL ULSTER CONSTABULARY PENSIONS (LUMP SUM PAYMENTS TO WIDOWS) REGULATIONS 1987 (No. 379) [45p], made under the Police Act (Northern Ireland) 1970 (c.9), s.25; provide for the payment of a gratuity of £10 to certain policemen's widows.

TEACHERS' SUPERANNUATION (AMENDMENT) REGULATIONS (NORTHERN IRELAND) 1987 (No. 76) [£2·40], made under S.I. 1972 No. 1073 (N.I. 10), arts. 11(1)(2)(3)(6), 14(1), Sched. 3, paras. 1, 6, 8, 11, 12, 13; operative on March 27, 1987, with effect from various dates; make miscellaneous amendments to the 1977 (No. 260) Regulations.

TEACHERS' SUPERANNUATION (AMENDMENT No. 2) REGULATIONS (NORTHERN IRELAND) 1987 (No. 86) [45p], made under S.I. 1972 No. 1073, art. 11(1)(2), Sched. 3, paras. 2, 12, 13; operative on March 31, 1987; provide for the abolition of the Teachers' Superannuation Fund and for the transfer of its assets to the Department of Education which will credit them to the Teachers' Superannuation Account.

TEACHERS' SUPERANNUATION (AMENDMENT No. 3) REGULATIONS (NORTHERN IRELAND) 1987 (No. 315) [£1·60], made under S.I. 1972 No. 1073 (N.I. 10), arts. 11(1)(2), 14(1), Sched. 3, paras. 1, 4, 6, 11, 12, 13; operative on September 2, 1987, with effect from earlier dates; extend the 1977 (No. 260) Regulations to cover part-time teachers serving in grant-aided schools and certain other educational establishments and amend those Regulations in relation to the pensionable service of a teacher in receipt of superannuation allowances as a temporary teacher.

ULSTER SPECIAL CONSTABULARY PENSIONS (LUMP SUM PAYMENTS TO WIDOWS) REGULATIONS 1987 (No. 380) [45p], made under the Special Constables Act 1914 (c.61), s.1, and the Constabulary (Pensions) Act (Northern Ireland) 1949 (c.9), s.4(4); operative on December 7, 1987; provide for the payment of a gratuity of £10 to certain widows of former members of the Ulster Special Constabulary.

2715. Petroleum

PETROLEUM PRODUCTION REGULATIONS (NORTHERN IRELAND) 1987 (No. 196) [£3·40], made under the Petroleum (Production) Act (Northern Ireland) 1964 (c.28), s.13(1); operative on June 1, 1987; prescribe the persons by whom and the manner in which applications for petroleum licences may be made, the fees payable on applications and the maximum size of licence areas; revoke the 1965 (No. 47) and 1978 (No.136) Regulations.

2716. Police

ROYAL ULSTER CONSTABULARY (AMENDMENT) REGULATIONS 1987 (No. 205) [45p], made under the Police Act (Northern Ireland) 1970 (c.9), s.25; operative on June 11, 1987, with effect from September 1, 1986; increase the pay of senior police officers.

ROYAL ULSTER CONSTABULARY (AMENDMENT (No. 2) REGULATIONS 1987 (No. 441) [£1·30], made under the Police Act (Northern Ireland) 1970 (c.9), s.25; operative on December 29, 1987, with effect from certain earlier dates; increase rates of pay, the dog handler's allowance, the supplementary pay allowance for university scholars, the supplementary rent allowance and the period in respect of which additional removal expenses may be paid.

2717. Police—Police (Northern Ireland) Order 1987 (S.I. 1987 No. 938 (N.I. 10))

This Order provides for the establishment of an Independent Commission for Police Complaints for Northern Ireland and for the investigation of complaints against members of the police force. It also makes miscellaneous amendments to the Police Act (Northern Ireland) 1970 (c.9) in relation to discipline and the Police Association.

The Order comes into operation on a day or days to be appointed.

2718. Police—refreshment allowance—meals voucher system introduced—whether valid

[Police Act (Northern Ireland) 1970 (c.9), s.6(2); Royal Ulster Constabulary Regulations 1984 (no. 64), reg. 48(1).]

Under reg. 48(1) of the Royal Ulster Constabulary Regulations 1984 a member of the R.U.C. who works additional hours or away from his usual place of duty and who necessarily incurs additional expense to obtain food is entitled to a refreshment allowance. Under a Force Order issued by the Chief Constable a member who would otherwise be entitled to a refreshment allowance would, if police canteen facilities were available, be issued with a voucher to enable him to obtain a meal at a police canteen. P sought a declaration that the meal voucher system was invalid in that it purported to remove a member's entitlement to a refreshment allowance under the 1984 Regulations. An argument was also advanced that the Force Order was invalid on the ground that it was made for the improper motive of saving expenditure.

Held, refusing the declaration, that (1) the Force Order did not remove the entitlement to a refreshment allowance as the entitlement only arose if it was necessary for a member to incur additional expense in obtaining food and a member who had a meal voucher did not need to incur such expense; and (2) the Force Order, even if it was made for the purpose of saving expenditure, was not invalid as s.6(2) of the Police Act (Northern Ireland) 1970, which placed the police force under the direction and control of the Chief Constable, was not restricted to operational matters.

TAYLOR *v.* CHIEF CONSTABLE, ROYAL ULSTER CONSTABULARY [1986] 11 N.I.J.B. 91, Hutton J.

2719. Practice

COUNTY COURT (AMENDMENT) RULES (NORTHERN IRELAND) 1987 (No. 124) [£2·90], made under S.I. 1980 No. 397 (N.I. 3), art. 47; amend the 1981 (No. 225) Rules in relation to the remuneration of assessors, the amounts to be paid or tendered to witnesses and costs.

MAGISTRATES' COURTS (BETTING, GAMING, LOTTERIES AND AMUSEMENTS) RULES (NORTHERN IRELAND) 1987 (No. 24) [£1·90], made under S.I. 1981 No. 1675 (N.I. 26), art. 13, and S.I. 1985 No. 1204 (N.I. 11), Sched. 7, para. 3, Sched. 9, para. 2, Sched. 10, para. 3; operative on February 16, 1987; make provision, in relation to courts of summary jurisdiction, for various matters which are to be prescribed under the 1985 S.I. in relation to applications for the grant, renewal or revocation of bingo club licences.

MAGISTRATES' COURTS (BETTING, GAMING, LOTTERIES AND AMUSEMENTS) (No.2) RULES (NORTHERN IRELAND) 1987 (Northern Ireland) 1987 (No. 234) [£3·80], made under S.I. 1981 No. 1675 (N.I. 26), art. 13, and S.I. 1985 No. 1204 (N.I. 11), Sched. 1, para. 3, Sched. 2, para. 2, Sched 3, para. 3, Sched. 4, para. 3, Sched. 5, para. 2, Sched. 6, para. 2, Sched. 7, para. 3, Sched. 16, para. 2, Sched. 17, para. 3; operative on June 1, 1987; make provision, in relation to courts of summary jurisdiction, for various procedural matters in relation to bookmakers' licences, bookmaking office licences and lottery certificates.

MAGISTRATES' COURTS (BINGO CLUB LICENCE) FEES ORDER (NORTHERN IRELAND) 1987 (No. 34) [45p], made under the Judicature (Northern Ireland) Act 1978 (c.23), s.116(1); operative on February 16, 1987; fixes the fees to be taken in magistrates' courts in respect of applications for the grant or renewal of bingo club licences.

MAGISTRATES' COURTS (BLOOD TESTS) (AMENDMENT) RULES (NORTHERN IRELAND) 1987 (No. 417) [45p], made under S.I. 1981 No. 1675 (N.I. 26), art. 13; operative on November 23, 1987; amend the definition of sampler in the 1978 (No. 376) Rules.

MAGISTRATES' COURTS (BOOKMAKER'S LICENCE, BOOKMAKING OFFICE LICENCE AND LOTTERY CERTIFICATE) FEES ORDER (NORTHERN IRELAND) 1987 (No. 270) [85p], made under the Judicature (Northern Ireland) Act 1978 (c.23), s.116(1); operative on July 3, 1987; fixes the fees to be taken in magistrates' courts in respect of applications for the grant, renewal and revocation of bookmakers' licences and lottery certificates and in respect of applications for the grant, renewal, transfer and revocation of bookmaking office licences.

RULES OF THE SUPREME COURT (NORTHERN IRELAND) (AMENDMENT) 1987 (No. 304) [45p], made under the Judicature (Northern Ireland) Act 1978 (c.23), s.55; operative as to rules 1 and 2(1) on August 1, 1987, and as to rule 2(2) on September 5, 1987; amend the 1980 (No. 346) Rules so as to provide that an action claiming damages for personal injury may not (a) be set down for trial with a jury on or after August 1, 1987, or (b) be tried with a jury on or after September 5, 1987.

SUPREME COURT (NON-CONTENTIOUS PROBATE) FEES (AMENDMENT) ORDER (NORTHERN IRELAND) 1987 (No. 412) [45p], made under the Judicature (Northern Ireland) Act 1978 (c.23), s.116(1); operative on November 16, 1987; substitutes a fixed fee of £150 for the *ad valorem* charge in respect of estates of which the assessed value exceeds £40,000 but does not exceed £70,000.

2720. Practice—contempt of court—delay in serving order requiring positive act—whether court should dispense with service

[R.S.C. (N.I.), Ord. 45, r.5.]

An application was brought to have Ballymoney Borough Council fined for contempt of court in that it neglected or refused to obey the terms of a court order made on April 15, 1986, requiring it to hold such meetings as may be necessary for the transaction of its general business. The order was not served on the Council until June 19, 1986. Although the Council was aware of the terms of the order it adjourned a meeting held on April 21, 1986, as a protest against the Anglo-Irish Agreement. A meeting was held on June 2, 1986, at which an annual meeting was arranged for June 17, 1986. A full complement of business was taken at this annual meeting.

Held, dismissing the application, that (1) an order made against a body corporate can not, by virtue of Ord. 45, r.5 of R.S.C. (N.I.), be enforced by sequestration unless a copy has been served on an officer of that body before the expiration of the time within which the body was required to act; and (2) the acts or omissions of the Council before June 19, 1986, should not be taken into account in determining whether it was in contempt of the court order.

HOGAN'S APPLICATION, *Re* [1986] 9 N.I.J.B. 45, Carswell J.

2721/2. Practice—discovery—personal injury—records of medical board and appeal tribunal—order to produce

[Administration of Justice Act 1970 (c.31), s.32(1); R.S.C.(N.I.), Ord. 24, r.12(1).]

The power given by s.32(1) of the Administration of Justice Act 1970 is unfettered and may be exercised where necessary to assist the proper administration of justice.

The plaintiff brought an action for personal injury damages for an illness contracted during her employment. The defendants denied liability and sought an order under s.32(1) that the DHSS disclose the findings of the medical board that had investigated the plaintiff's condition. The application was refused, but allowed on appeal.

Held, dismissing the plaintiff's appeal, the power given to the Court by s.32(1) was unfettered and could be exercised whenever it assisted the administration of justice (*McIvor* v. *Southern Health and Social Services Board, Northern Ireland* [1978] C.L.Y. 2356 applied; *McClelland* v. *Clyde Fuel Systems (Practice Note)* [1973] N.I. 66 disapproved).

O'SULLIVAN *v.* HERDMANS [1987] 1 W.L.R. 1047, H.L.

2723. Practice—expiration of time limit for appeal—application for extension

[Criminal Damage (Compensation) (Northern Ireland) Order 1977 (S.I. 1977 No. 426 (N.I. 4)); R.S.C. (N.I.), Ord. 3, r.5(1), Ord. 55, rr.2, 3.]

C owned licensed premises which were insured under a policy of insurance which excluded damage caused by persons acting on behalf of an unlawful association. On March 10, 1980, the premises were severely damaged by fire. C claimed compensation under the Criminal Damage (Compensation) (Northern Ireland) Order 1977 on the ground that the fire was caused maliciously by three or more persons or by persons acting on behalf of an unlawful association. The claim was rejected by the Secretary of State and, on May 8, 1981, by the county court, the county court judge having refused to admit in evidence an affidavit sworn by C's bar manager who had gone to live in U.S.A. and refused to return. C's solicitor posted a notice of appeal on June 5, 1981, which was outside the 21 day time limit specified by R.S.C. (N.I.), Ord. 55, rr.2, 3. On May 7, 1982, C brought proceedings against the insurance company and these proceedings were settled on March 20, 1985, by a payment of £25,000. On September 18, 1985, C applied under R.S.C. (N.I.), Ord. 3, r.5(1) for an extension of time to enable him to appeal against the decision of the county court on May 8, 1981, and this was granted by the Master. The Secretary of State appealed against the Master's decision.

Held, allowing the appeal, that, notwithstanding that the delay was due in part to C's solicitors and in part to C having deliberately deferred his application for the extension pending resolution of his action against the insurance company, C had not discharged the onus on him to show sufficient reason why he should obtain the extension of time (*Davis* v. *Northern Ireland Carriers* [1980] C.L.Y. 1982 considered).

COYLE *v.* SECRETARY OF STATE FOR NORTHERN IRELAND [1986] 11 N.I.J.B. 71, Carswell J.

2724. Prisons—judicial review—hearings disrupted by noise—application out of time—hardship

H, who refused to wear prison clothing or report for work while in prison, lost considerable periods of remission as a result of governor's adjudications. The adjudications, which were held in the cells, were disrupted by noise created by other prisoners. H's application for judicial review, which was made out of time, was refused by the trial judge. H appealed.

Held, dismissing the appeal, that (1) where an application for leave to apply for relief by way of judicial review is out of time, the question of hardship or unfair prejudice can be considered at any stage; (2) the court was satisfied that no one would suffer hardship or have his rights unfairly prejudiced; (3) there was no breach of the principles of natural justice; and (4) H knew at all times what was alleged against him and suffered no injustice through the adverse exercise of the trial judge's discretion.

HUGHES' APPLICATION, *Re* [1986] 13 N.I.J.B. 1, C.A.

2725. Prisons—judicial review—whether right to legal representation—discretion

[European Convention for the Protection of Human Rights and Fundamental Freedoms, art. 6(3).]

A board of visitors at a hearing refused requests made by H and McC for legal representation and found both guilty of offences against prison discipline. On an application to have the board's findings quashed, the trial judge ruled as a preliminary point of law for the purposes of appeal that a sentenced prisoner appearing before a board of visitors does not have a right to legal representation and that it was a matter for the discretion of the board. H and McC appealed.

Held, dismissing the appeals, that (1) a prisoner is not entitled as a right, either at common law or by the rules of natural justice, to be legally represented before a board of visitors; (2) art. 6(3) of the European Convention for the Protection of Human Rights and Fundamental Freedoms applies only to persons charged with criminal offences as distinct from disciplinary offences; (3) a board of visitors has a discretion to grant legal representation; (4) the board had sufficient opportunity and information to assess H and McC's abilities to present their cases fully without professional assistance; and (5) the board had exercised its discretion properly.

HONE AND McCARTAN'S APPLICATION, *Re* [1986] 11 N.I.J.B. 34, C.A.

2726. Prisons—visiting—friend of prisoner elected a councillor—permission to visit withdrawn—whether decision reasonable

[Prison Rules (Northern Ireland) 1982 (No. 170), r.58.]

The Secretary of State in exercise of his powers under r.58 of the Prison Rules (Northern Ireland) 1982 refused to allow K, who had been elected a Sinn Fein member of Belfast City Council, to visit McC in prison. McC sought an order of certiorari to quash the Secretary of State's decision.

Held, refusing the order sought, that (1) the Secretary of State's decision was not so unreasonable that no reasonable authority could ever have come to it; (2) as Sinn Fein councillors were allowed to visit prisoners who were members of their immediate families, proper regard had been had to relevant personal considerations; and (3) the fact that it might have been reasonable for the Secretary of State to impose a wider ban to include unsuccessful Sinn Fein candidates or their supporters did not make it unreasonable to impose the ban on elected representatives (*Associated Provincial Picture Houses* v. *Wednesbury Corporation* (1948) C.L.C. 8107 applied).

McCARTNEY'S APPLICATION, *Re* [1986] 13 N.I.J.B. 46, Lord Lowry L.C.J.

2727. Public health

ALKALI, &c. WORKS ORDER (NORTHERN IRELAND) 1987 (No. 123) [£2·40], made under S.I. 1981 No. 158 (N.I. 4), art. 25(9); operative on May 1, 1987 extends and amends the list of gases set out in s.27 of the Alkali, &c. Works Regulation Act 1906 and the list of works set out in Sched. 1 to that Act; revokes the 1977 (No. 152) Order.

CONSTRUCTION PLANT AND EQUIPMENT (NOISE EMISSION) REGULATIONS (NORTHERN IRELAND) 1987 (No. 328) [£2·90], made under the European Communities Act 1972 (c.68), s.2(2); operative on October 1, 1987; implement Council Directives 84/532–537/EEC, as amended, in relation to the sound power level requirements, marketing, examination and use of certain construction plant and equipment.

INTEREST ON RECOVERABLE SANITATION EXPENSES ORDER (NORTHERN IRELAND) 1987 (No. 148) [45p], made under the Public Health and Local Government (Miscellaneous Provisions) Act (Northern Ireland) 1962 (c.12), s.5; operative on April 22, 1987; decreases to 11¼ per cent. per annum the rate of interest on certain expenses recoverable from owners of premises under the Public Health (Ireland) Act 1878 (c.52); revokes the 1985 (No. 314) Order.

INTEREST ON RECOVERABLE SANITATION EXPENSES (No. 2) ORDER (NORTHERN IRELAND) 1987 (No. 233) [45p], made under the Public Health and Local Government (Miscellaneous Provisions) Act (Northern Ireland) 1962 (c.12), s.5; operative on June 23, 1987; decreases to 10 per cent. per annum the rate of interest on certain expenses recoverable from owners of premises under the Public Health (Ireland) Act 1878 (c.52); revokes the 1987 (No. 148) Order.

INTEREST ON RECOVERABLE SANITATION EXPENSES (No. 3) ORDER (NORTHERN IRELAND) 1987 (No. 401) [45p], made under the Public Health and Local Government (Miscellaneous Provisions) Act (Northern Ireland) 1962 (c.12), s.5; operative on November 16, 1987; increases to 11 per cent. per annum the rate of interest on certain expenses recoverable from owners of premises under the Public Health (Ireland) Act 1878 (c.52).

2728. Rating and valuation

RATES (REGIONAL RATE) ORDER (NORTHERN IRELAND) 1987 (No. 75) [45p], made under S.I. 1977 No. 2157 (N.I. 28), arts. 7(1), 27(4); operative on April 1, 1987; fixes for the year ending March 31, 1988, the regional rate and the amount by which it is to be reduced for dwelling-houses.

2729. Rating and valuation—Lands Tribunal decision

This was an appeal against the net annual value of a semi-detached house in Portstewart, Co. Londonderry which was in poor repair.

Held, that the best indication of the tone of the list was the adjoining semi-detached house and that having regard to its net annual value of £265 and to the poor state of repair of the house in respect of which the appeal was made, the net annual value should be reduced from £255 to £230.

CHRISTIE *v.* COMMISSIONER OF VALUATION FOR NORTHERN IRELAND (VR/4/1987).

2729a. This was an appeal against the net annual value of a modern detached bungalow, 15 Amakane Road, Camlough, which was directly opposite an open silo, cattle feeding house and farmyard area.

Held, that an allowance of £20, the same as was given for 10 Amakane Road, should be given for the existence of the farmyard and is accompanying nuisances.

KING *v.* COMMISSIONER OF VALUATION FOR NORTHERN IRELAND (VR/8/1987).

2730. This was an appeal against the net annual value of a detached house opposite a large scrapyard in which a fractionaliser had been installed. The tribunal found, dismissing the appeal, that the noise from the scrapyard had not increased in a relevant way so as to warrant an increase in the end allowance of 10 per cent. given in the 1976 General Revaluation.

1987

MORGAN *v.* COMMISSIONER OF VALUATION FOR NORTHERN IRELAND (VR/3/1986)

2731. This was an appeal against the net annual value of a house adjoining a police station. A wall nine feet high with a chain link fence on top, which affected the light to the house, had been erected between the house and the police station and two static television cameras, which affected the privacy of the house, had been installed in the police station. The tribunal increased the end allowance from 15 per cent. to 25 per cent., thus reducing the net annual value from £115 to £103.

MURPHY *v.* COMMISSIONER OF VALUATION FOR NORTHERN IRELAND (VR/20/1986)

2732. The middle of three shops in a parade in Upper Newtownards Road, Belfast, was valued at £275 in 1976. When an off-licence was granted for this shop the net annual value was increased to £2,600. On appeal it was agreed that the net annual value of the premises unlicensed was £370.

Held, that the net annual value of the premises with the benefit of the licence was £370, the same as the two adjoining shops.

ROSEMARY WINE MARKETS *v.* COMMISSIONER OF VALUATION FOR NORTHERN IRELAND (VR/52/1985).

2733. This was an appeal against the net annual value of a semi-detached house with a plain kitchen and a plain bathroom. The tribunal found, dismissing the appeal, that neither the kitchen nor the bathroom although plain was so inadequate that a hypothetical tenant would adjust the rent he offered.

WILSON *v.* COMMISSIONER OF VALUATION FOR NORTHERN IRELAND (VR/49/1985).

2734. Revenue and finance

FINANCIAL SERVICES ACT 1986 (TRANSFER OF FUNCTIONS RELATING TO FRIENDLY SOCIETIES) (TRANSITIONAL PROVISIONS) ORDER (NORTHERN IRELAND) 1987 (No. 440 [45p], made under the Financial Services Act 1986 (c.60), s.118(2), Sched. 11, para. 31; operative on January 1, 1988; makes a transitional provision in connection with the transfer of functions of the Registrar of Friendly Societies for Northern Ireland to the Securities and Investments Board Limited.

FINANCIAL SERVICES (TRANSFER OF FUNCTIONS RELATING TO FRIENDLY SOCIETIES) ORDER (NORTHERN IRELAND) 1987 (No. 228) [85p], made under the Financial Services Act 1986 (c.60), Sched. 11, para. 28, Sched. 15, para. 12; operative on May 19, 1987; with two exceptions transfers to the Securities and Investments Board Limited the functions of the Registrar of Friendly Societies for Northern Ireland under the 1986 Act which are capable of being transferred under para. 28 of Sched. 11 to that Act.

ULSTER SAVINGS CERTIFICATES (INDEX LINKED) (SUPPLEMENT) REGULATIONS 1987 (No. 139) [45p], made under the Exchequer and Financial Provisions Act (Northern Ireland) 1950 (c.3), s.15(1); operative on August 1, 1987; provide for a supplement of 4 per cent. to be added to the amount repayable on certain Ulster Savings Certificates of the Index Linked Retirement and Second Index Linked Issues.

ULSTER SAVINGS CERTIFICATES (THIRTY-THIRD ISSUE) REGULATIONS 1987 (No. 209) [85p], made under the Exchequer and Financial Provisions Act (Northern Ireland) 1950 (c.3), s.15(1); operative on May 1, 1987; prescribe the terms governing the issue of Ulster Savings Certificates of the Thirty-third Issue and the maximum number of such certifcates which a person may hold and amend the 1962 (No. 36) Regulations in relation to reinvestment certificates.

2735. Revenue and finance—Appropriation (Northern Ireland) Order 1987 (S.I. 1987 No. 459 (N.I. 4))

This Order authorises the issue out of the Consolidated Fund of Northern Ireland of a further sum for the year ended March 31, 1987, and of sums on account for the year ending March 31, 1988, and appropriates those sums for specified services. It also authorises the application of certain further sums as appropriations in aid for the year ended March 31, 1987, and reduces certain sums already authorised to be so applied.

The Order came into operation on March 18, 1987.

2736. Revenue and finance—Appropriation (No. 2) (Northern Ireland) Order 1987 (S.I. 1987 No. 1274 (N.I. 11))

This Order authorises the issue out of the Consolidated Fund of Northern Ireland of further sums for the year ended on March 31, 1986, and the year ending on March 31, 1988, and appropriates those sums for specified services; also authorises the application of certain sums as appropriations in aid for the year ending on March 31, 1988, and decreases a sum authorised to be so applied for the year ended on March 31, 1986.

The Order came into operation on July 21, 1987.

2737. Revenue and finance—Appropriation (No. 3) (Northern Ireland) Order 1987 (S.I. 1987 No. 2204 (N.I. 23))

This Order authorises the issue out of the Consolidated Fund of Northern Ireland of a further sum for the year ending March 31, 1988, and appropriates that sum for a specified service in Northern Ireland.

The Order came into operation on December 18, 1987.

2738. Road traffic

COMMUNITY DRIVERS' HOURS AND RECORDING EQUIPMENT (EXEMPTIONS AND SUPPLEMENTARY PROVISIONS) REGULATIONS (NORTHERN IRELAND) 1987 (No. 218) [£1·60], made under the European Communities Act 1972, s.2(2), and S.I. 1981 No. 154, arts. 83, 218(1); operative on June 8, 1987; grant exemptions from, and supplement provisions of, Council Regulations (EEC) Nos. 3820/85 and 3821/85.

GOODS VEHICLES (CERTIFICATION) (AMENDMENT) REGULATIONS (NORTHERN IRELAND) 1987 (No. 352) [85p], made under the European Communities Act 1972, s.2(2), and S.I. 1981 No. 154, arts. 54(1), 58(1), 218(1); operative on October 19, 1987; amend the 1982 (No. 46) Regulations by re-defining "Community Recording Equipment Regulation" and increasing certain fees payable on applications and re-applications for certificates for goods vehicles (other than trailers).

LARGE PRIVATE PASSENGER VEHICLES (CERTIFICATION) (AMENDMENT) REGULATIONS (NORTHERN IRELAND) 1987 (No. 351) [85p], made under the European Communities Act 1972 (c.68), s.2(2), and S.I. 1981 No. 154, arts. 67(3), 69, 218(1); operative on October 19, 1987; amend the 1982 (No. 383) Regulations by re-defining "Community Recording Equipment Regulation" and increasing certain fees payable on applications and re-applications for inspection of large private passenger vehicles; revoke the 1986 (No. 230) Regulations.

MOTOR VEHICLE TESTING (EXTENSION) ORDER (NORTHERN IRELAND) 1987 (No. 366) [85p], made under S.I. 1981 No. 154, art. 34(4); operative on different dates for different vehicles; requires motor vehicles, other than ambulances, to be tested if registered or manufactured more than 5 years ago.

MOTOR VEHICLE TESTING (FEES) (AMENDMENT) REGULATIONS (NORTHERN IRELAND) 1987 (No. 350) [85p], made under S.I. 1981 No. 154, arts. 33(2)(6), 35(3), 36(4), 218(1); operative on October 19, 1987; increase fees payable for motor vehicle and motor cycle tests and examinations and the fees payable on appeals; revoke the 1986 (No. 228) Regulations.

MOTOR VEHICLES (CONSTRUCTION AND USE) (AMENDMENT) REGULATIONS (NORTHERN IRELAND) 1987 (No. 227) [£2·20], made under S.I. 1981 No. 154, arts. 28(1), 218(1); operative on June 22, 1987; amend the 1976 (No. 320) Regulations in relation to seat belts, anchorage points and the plating of motor vehicles.

MOTOR VEHICLES (DRIVING LICENCES) (AMENDMENT) REGULATIONS (NORTHERN IRELAND) 1987 (No. 211) [45p], made under S.I. 1981 No. 154 (N.I. 1), arts. 11(1), 218(1); operative on June 8, 1987; increase the fee for a driving test; revoke the 1983 (No. 392) Regulations.

MOTOR VEHICLES (TYPE APPROVAL) (AMENDMENT) REGULATIONS (NORTHERN IRELAND) 1987 (No. 389) [£2·20], made under S.I. 1981 No. 154 (N.I. 1), arts. 31A(1), 31D(1)(2), 218(1); operative on November 16, 1987; amend the 1985 (No. 294) Regulations in relation to certain standards and requirements; revoke the 1986 (No. 105) Regulations.

MOTOR VEHICLES (TYPE APPROVAL AND APPROVAL MARKS) (FEES) (AMENDMENT No. 2) REGULATIONS (NORTHERN IRELAND) 1987 (No. 390) [£1·60], made under S.I. 1981 No. 154, art. 31D(1)(2), and the Finance Act 1973 (c.51), s.56(1)(2)(5); operative on November 16, 1987; amend the 1985 (No. 295) Regulations to introduce new fees and increase other fees.

MOTOR VEHICLES (TYPE APPROVAL) (EEC) REGULATIONS (NORTHERN IRELAND) 1987 (No. 306) [£4·80], made under the European Communities Act 1972 (c.68), s.2(2); operative on September 1, 1987; consolidate with amendments and revoke the 1973

PASSENGER AND GOODS VEHICLES (RECORDING EQUIPMENT) (AMENDMENT) REGULATIONS (NORTHERN IRELAND) 1987 (No. 217) [85p], made under the European Communities Act 1972 (c.68), s.2(2), the Finance Act 1973 (c.51), s.56(1)(5), and S.I. 1981 No. 154, arts. 56(5), 58(1), 63, 83; operative on June 8, 1987; amend the 1979 (No. 443) Regulations in relation to recording equipment in road transport, the production of record sheets and the approval of fitters and workshops.

PUBLIC SERVICE VEHICLES (LICENCE FEES) (AMENDMENT) REGULATIONS (NORTHERN IRELAND) 1987 (No. 349) [45p], made under S.I. 1981 No. 154 (N.I. 1), arts. 61(1), 66(1), 218(1); operative on October 19, 1987; increase fees payable in connection with applications and re-applications for licences for taxis.

ROAD VEHICLES (PRESCRIBED REGULATIONS FOR THE PURPOSES OF INCREASED PENALTIES) REGULATIONS (NORTHERN IRELAND) 1987 (S.I. No. 2086) [45p], made under the Vehicles (Excise) Act (Northern Ireland) 1972 (c.10), s.34(3)(*a*); operative on January 1, 1988; prescribe the provisions of the 1973 (No. 490) Regulations where a contravention is to attract a maximum fine not exceeding level 3 on the standard scale.

Orders made under S.I. 1981 No. 154:

Art. 21(1): S.R. 1987 Nos. 16 (Belfast) [45p]; 17 (Dromore, Co. Down) [45p]; 35 (Newry) [45p]; 40 (Belfast) [45p]; 46 (Coleraine) [45p]; 159 (Belfast) [£1·40]; 189 (Galgorm Road, Ballymena) [45p]; 207 (Newtownards) [45p]; 214 (Belfast) [45p]; 236 (Enniskillen) [45p]; 237 (Belfast) [£1·60]; 242 (Belfast) [45p]; 314 (Belfast) [45p]; 353 (Coleraine) [45p]; 358 (Coleraine) [45p]; 371 (Belfast) [45p]; 386 (Belfast) [45p]; 411 (Short Strand, Belfast) [45p]; 416 (Fivemiletown) [45p].

Art. 22(1): S.R. 1987 Nos. 4 (Donegall Place, Belfast) [80p]; 110 (Larne) [45p]; 238 (Belfast) [45p]; 347 (Larne) [45p]; 388 (Whitehead) [45p]; 435 (Tynan) [45p].

Art. 50(4): S.R. 1987 Nos. 164 (speed limits) [£2·90]; 165 (speed limits) [80p].

Art. 65(1): S.R. 1987 No. 307 (Londonderry) [45p].

Art. 105: S.R. 1987 No. 181 (off-street parking charges) [80p].

Art. 105(1): S.R. 1987 Nos. 45 (off-street parking in Ballymoney) [80p]; 49 (off-street parking) [£1·40]; 62 (off-street parking) [45p]; 109 (off-street parking) [£1·40]; 133 (off-street parking) [£1·40]; 324 (Enniskillen) [85p]; 426 (Londonderry) [45p].

Arts. 107(1), 109(2), 110, 111(1)(2): S.R. 1987 Nos. 410 (on-street parking) [1·60]; 444 (on-street parking) [45p].

2739. Sale of goods

ELECTRICAL EQUIPMENT (SAFETY) REGULATIONS (NORTHERN IRELAND) 1987 (No. 337) [45p], made under the Consumer Protection Act (Northern Ireland) 1965 (c.14), s.1; operative on September 30, 1987, save for reg. 2(*b*) which comes into operation on March 1, 1988; provide that the 1977 (No. 137) Regulations shall cease to apply to the sale or possession for the purpose of sale of certain electrical devices. The safety of such devices is covered by the 1987 (S.I. No. 603) Regulations.

2740. Sale of goods—merchantable quality—defects in car—whether entitled to rescission

[Sale of Goods Act 1979 (c.54), s.14.]

P brought a high performance second-hand car from D. The car was about three years old and at the time of the sale to P was not capable of being road-tested as the battery was flat. S, the salesman for D, assured P that the car had never sustained any accident damage. D undertook to carry out a full service on the car and to repair any defects which manifested themselves within three months of the sale. P returned the car to D several times with lists of complaints. About two months after the sale, P returned the car to D and asked for his money back. This was refused and P brought proceedings for rescission of the contract and the return of an instalment which he had paid. The car had in fact sustained accident damage before the sale but P did not discover this until after he repudiated the contract.

Held, that (1) the number and seriousness of the defects in the car were such that it was neither of merchantable quality nor reasonably fit for its purpose under s.14 of the Sale of Goods Act 1979; (2) P did not at any time so act that he must be taken to have affirmed the contract and he did not, by keeping the car for a period, lose his right to rescission. P was, accordingly, entitled to rescission of the contract and to repayment of the amount credited on trade-in of his previous car and of the instalment paid by him.

LUTTON *v.* SAVILLE TRACTORS (BELFAST) [1986] 12 N.I.J.B. 1, Carswell J.

2741. Social security

CHILD BENEFIT (GENERAL) (AMENDMENT) REGULATIONS (NORTHERN IRELAND) 1987 (No. 130) [80p], made under S.I. 1975 No. 1504 (N.I. 16), arts. 4(1B)(2)(3), 6(1); operative on April 6, 1987; amend the 1979 (No. 5) Regulations in relation to the meanings of "advanced education" and "full-time education" and in relation to the circumstances in which a person is to continue to be treated as a child.

FAMILY CREDIT (GENERAL) REGULATIONS (NORTHERN IRELAND) 1987 (No. 463) [£4·30], made under S.I. 1986 No. 1888, arts. 21(1)(5)(*c*)(6)(10)(11)(12), 22(3)(6)(*a*), 23(1)(5) to (9),52(1)(*h*), and the Social Security (Northern Ireland) Act 1975, s.104(5); operative on April 11, 1988; provide for various matters which affect entitlement to family credit.

FAMILY CREDIT (TRANSITIONAL) REGULATIONS (NORTHERN IRELAND) 1987 (No. 464) [£1·60], made under S.I. 1986 No. 1888, art. 84(1); operative on January 1, 1988; make transitional provision for awards of family credit on claims made before April 11, 1988.

FAMILY INCOME SUPPLEMENTS (COMPUTATION) REGULATIONS (NORTHERN IRELAND) 1987 (No. 14) [80p], made under the Family Income Supplements Act (Northern Ireland) 1971 (c.8), ss.2(1), 3(1)(1A), 10(1)(2B); operative on April 7, 1987; increase the amounts prescribed for the purposes of ss.2 and 3 of the 1971 Act and the maximum weekly rates of family income supplement; revoke the 1986 (No. 202) Regulations.

FAMILY INCOME SUPPLEMENTS (GENERAL) (AMENDMENT) REGULATIONS (NORTHERN IRELAND) 1987 (No. 97) [45p], made under the Family Income Supplements Act (Northern Ireland) 1971 (c.8), ss.6(3), 10(1); operative on March 24, 1987; provide for awards of family income supplements to terminate not later than April 11, 1988, the date on which the new Family Credit legislation comes into operation.

INCOME SUPPORT (TRANSITIONAL) REGULATIONS (NORTHERN IRELAND) 1987 (No. 460) [£2·90], made under S.I. 1986 No. 1888, art. 84(1); operative on December 28, 1987; make transitional provisions consequential upon the winding up of supplementary benefit and the introduction of income support.

MATERNITY PAY AND MATERNITY ALLOWANCE (TRANSITIONAL) REGULATIONS (NORTHERN IRELAND) 1987 (No. 163) [80p], made under S.I. 1986 No. 1888, art. 84(1); operative as to regs. 1 and 4 on April 5, 1987, and as to regs. 2 and 3 on April 6, 1987; contain consequential and transitional provisions and savings relating to statutory maternity pay and maternity allowance.

SOCIAL FUND (MATERNITY AND FUNERAL EXPENSES) (CLAIMS AND PAYMENTS) REGULATIONS (NORTHERN IRELAND) 1987 (No. 100) [£1·90], made under the Social Security (Northern Ireland) Act 1975 (c.15), s.114, and S.I. 1986 No. 1888 (N.I. 18), arts. 52(1)(*a*)–(*r*), 55; operative on April 6, 1987; provide for the making of claims for social fund payments for maternity or funeral expenses and for the payment of sums awarded.

SOCIAL SECURITY (ADJUDICATION) REGULATIONS (NORTHERN IRELAND) 1987 (No. 82) [£4·90], made under the National Insurance Measure (Northern Ireland) 1974 (c.4), s.5)1), the Social Security (Northern Ireland) Act 1975 (c.15), ss.98(1), 100(2)(4), 101(5A)(5B), 105(2), 106(1)(4), 108(2), 109(2)(3), 110(1B)(5), 112A(3)(5), 113(1), 114, 115, 119(3)(4), Scheds. 12, 13, S.I. 1983 No. 1524 (N.I. 17), art. 5(1), and S.I. 1986 No. 1888, arts. 53(4), 84(1), Sched. 7, para. 4(2); operative on April 6, 1987; deal with the determination of claims and questions under various provisions and reflect the further changes made in the social security adjudication system by the 1986 S.I.

SOCIAL SECURITY (ADJUDICATION) (AMENDMENT) REGULATIONS (NORTHERN IRELAND) 1987 (No. 325) [45p], made under the Social Security (Northern Ireland) Act 1975, s.104(5)(*b*); operative on September 1, 1987; amend reg. 72 of the 1987 (No. 82) Regulations by imposing limitations on the payment of arrears of benefit where a decision is reviewed in consequence of a determination made by a Social Security Commissioner or by other appellate bodies.

SOCIAL SECURITY (ADJUDICATION) (AMENDMENT No. 2) REGULATIONS (NORTHERN IRELAND) 1987 (No. 466) [£2·20], made under the Social Security (Northern Ireland) Act 1975, ss.100(2), 114, 115, 119(3)(4), Sched. 13, and S.I. 1986 No. 1888, arts. 53(4), 84(1); operative in relation to income support on December 21, 1987, in relation to family credit on January 1, 1988, and for all other purposes on April 11, 1988; make consequential and other amendments to the 1987 (No. 82) Regulations.

SOCIAL SECURITY (ATTENDANCE ALLOWANCE) REGULATIONS (NORTHERN IRELAND) 1987 (No. 413) [£2·60], made under the Social Security (Northern Ireland) Act 1975, ss.35, 85(1), and the Social Security (Consequential Provisions) Act 1975 (c.18), Sched. 3, paras. 3, 7; operative on December 14, 1987; consolidate and revoke the 1975 (No. 102) and amending Regulations.

SOCIAL SECURITY (ATTENDANCE ALLOWANCE) (AMENDMENT) REGULATIONS (NORTHERN IRELAND) 1987 (No. 322) [45p], made under the Social Security (Northern Ireland) Act 1975 (c.15), s.35(2A)(5A); operative on August 31, 1987; amend the 1975 (No. 102) Regulations in relation to persons undergoing renal dialysis as an out-patient at a health service hospital or institution.

SOCIAL SECURITY (AUSTRALIA) ORDER (NORTHERN IRELAND) 1987 (No. 231) [85p], made under the Social Security (Northern Ireland) Act 1975 (c.15), s.134; operative on May 18, 1987; modifies the 1975 Act to give effect in Northern Ireland to an Agreement between the U.K. and Australia made on December 31, 1986.

SOCIAL SECURITY (AUSTRIA) ORDER (NORTHERN IRELAND) 1987 (No. 402) [£1·60], made under the Social Security (Northern Ireland) Act 1975, s.134; operative on November 1, 1987; modifies the 1975 Act to give effect in Northern Ireland to a Supplementary Convention on social security made between the U.K. and Austria.

SOCIAL SECURITY BENEFIT (COMPUTATION OF EARNINGS) (AMENDMENT) REGULATIONS (NORTHERN IRELAND) 1987 (No. 201) [80p], made under the Social Security (Northern Ireland) Act 1975 (c.15), s.3(2)(3); operative on April 28, 1987; amend the 1978 (No. 371) Regulations in relation to payments which are to be disregarded in calculating earnings for certain purposes.

SOCIAL SECURITY BENEFIT (DEPENDENCY) (AMENDMENT) REGULATIONS (NORTHERN IRELAND) 1987 (No. 129) [£1·40], made under the Social Security (Northern Ireland) Act 1975, ss.49, 84(1), Sched. 17; operative on April 6, 1987; amend the 1977 (No. 74) Regulations in relation to child benefit, invalid care allowances and maintenance of adult dependents.

SOCIAL SECURITY BENEFITS UP-RATING ORDER (NORTHERN IRELAND) 1987 (No. 22) [£1·90], made under S.I. 1986 No. 1888, art. 64; operative on April 6, 1987, save for arts. 1(1), 8 and 10(2) which came into operation on April 1, 1987; increases the rates and amounts of certain benefits and other sums.

SOCIAL SECURITY BENEFITS UP-RATING (AMENDMENT) ORDER (NORTHERN IRELAND) 1987 (No. 111) [45p], made under S.I. 1986 No. 1888, art. 64; operative on April 6, 1987; changes the weekly rate of disablement pensions, where the degree of disablement is 30 per cent., from £19·85 to £19·35.

SOCIAL SECURITY BENEFITS UP-RATING (No. 2) ORDER (NORTHERN IRELAND) 1987 (No. 458) [£2·20], made under S.I. 1986 No. 1888, art. 64; operative for certain purposes on April 3 and 6, 1988, and for all other purposes on April 11, 1988; increases the rates and amounts of certain benefits and other sums, including statutory maternity pay and statutory sick pay.

SOCIAL SECURITY BENEFITS UP-RATING REGULATIONS (NORTHERN IRELAND) 1987 (No. 128) [80p], made under the Social Security (Northern Ireland) Act 1975, ss.17(1)(*a*), 58(3), 126 and S.I. 1986 No. 1888, art. 65(2); operative on April 6, 1987; make further provision with respect to benefits increased by the 1987 (No. 22) Order and increase certain earnings limits; revoke the 1986 (No. 212) Regulations.

SOCIAL SECURITY (CLAIMS AND PAYMENTS) REGULATIONS (NORTHERN IRELAND) 1987 (No. 465) [£5·30], made under the Social Security (Northern Ireland) Act 1975, ss.27(4), 37A(5), 154A, S.I. 1975 No. 1503 (N.I. 15), art. 24(4), S.I. 1975 No. 1504 (N.I. 16), art. 8(1), and S.I. 1986 No. 1888, arts. 22(7), 52(1)(*a*) to (*r*); operative on April 11, 1988; contain provisions about the making of claims for, and the payment of benefits under the Social Security (Northern Ireland) Acts 1975 to 1986 and the Child Benefit (Northern Ireland) Order 1975.

SOCIAL SECURITY (CLASS I CONTRIBUTIONS—CONTRACTED-OUT PERCENTAGES) ORDER (NORTHERN IRELAND) 1987 (No. 174) [45p], made under S.I. 1975 No. 1503, art. 30; operative on April 6, 1988; decreases the contracted-out rates of Class 1 contributions; revokes the 1982 (No. 109) Order.

SOCIAL SECURITY COMMISSIONERS (PENSIONABLE SERVICE) REGULATIONS (NORTHERN IRELAND) 1987 (No. 61) [45p], made under the Social Security (Northern Ireland) Act 1975 (c.15), ss.97(4), 155(2), Sched. 10, para. 6(3)(*b*); operative on April 1, 1987; provide that service as a county court judge shall in certain circumstances count for pension purposes as service as a Social Security Commissioner.

SOCIAL SECURITY COMMISSIONERS PROCEDURE REGULATIONS (NORTHERN IRELAND) 1987 (No. 112) [£2·90], made under the National Insurance Measure (Northern Ireland) 1974 (c.4), s.5, the Social Security (Northern Ireland) Act 1975, ss.101(5A)(5B), 106(2), 112A(3), 114(2B)(5), 115(1)(5), Scheds. 13, 17, the Social Security Act 1980 (c.30), s.14, and S.I. 1982 No. 1082 (N.I. 14), art. 6; operative on April 6, 1987; regulate the procedure of the Social Security Commissioners in determining claims and questions.

SOCIAL SECURITY (CONSOLIDATED FUND OF NORTHERN IRELAND SUPPLEMENT TO, AND ALLOCATION OF, CONTRIBUTIONS) (RE-RATING) ORDER (NORTHERN IRELAND) 1987 (No. 25) [80p], made under the Social Security (Northern Ireland) Act 1975 (c.15), ss.1(5A), 128(4A)(5A); operative on April 6, 1987; decreases the Consolidated Fund of Northern Ireland supplement to contributions paid under the 1975 Act, increases the percentage rates of the appropriate health service allocation and reduces the percentage rates of the appropriate employment protection allocation.

SOCIAL SECURITY (CONTRIBUTIONS) (AMENDMENT) REGULATIONS (NORTHERN IRELAND) 1987 (No. 29) [45p], made under S.I. 1975 No. 1503 (N.I. 15), art. 3; operative on April 6, 1987; amend the 1979 (No. 186) Regulations to increase the weekly lower and upper earnings limits for Class 1 contributions for the year beginning on April 6, 1987.

SOCIAL SECURITY (CONTRIBUTIONS) (AMENDMENT No. 2) REGULATIONS (NORTHERN IRELAND) 1987 (No. 143) [£1·90], made under the Social Security (Northern Ireland) Act 1975, ss.3(2)(3), 4(2)(*b*)(6)(6A)(6D), 13(4)(5B), Sched. 1, paras. 1(1C) 5(1)(*a*)(*b*), 6(1)(*b*)(*c*) and S.I. 1975 No. 1503, art. 7(1); operative on April 6, 1987 further amend the 1979 (No. 186) Regulations.

SOCIAL SECURITY (CONTRIBUTIONS) (AMENDMENT No. 3) REGULATIONS (NORTHERN IRELAND) 1987 (No. 348) [85p], made under the Social Security (Northern Ireland) Act 1975 (c.15), s.3(2)(3); operative on October 6, 1987; amend the 1979 (No. 186) Regulations to provide for the disregard, for the purposes of earnings-related contributions, of certain payments made by trustees before April 6, 1990.

SOCIAL SECURITY (CONTRIBUTIONS) (AMENDMENT No. 4) REGULATIONS (NORTHERN IRELAND) 1987 (No. 468) [85p], made under the Social Security (Northern Ireland) Act 1975, ss.3(2)(3), 4(2)(*b*)(6)(6A)(6D), 11(3), 126, Sched. 1, para. 6(1)(*b*)(*h*); operative on January 6, 1988; make miscellaneous amendments to the 1979 (No. 186) Regulations.

SOCIAL SECURITY (CONTRIBUTIONS, RE-RATING) ORDER (NORTHERN IRELAND) 1987 (No. 26) [80p], made under the Social Security (Northern Ireland) Act 1975, s.120; operative on April 6, 1987; increases the amounts of weekly earnings specified for certain purposes under the 1975 Act, increases certain contributions payable under the Act and increases the amount of earnings below which an earner may be excepted from liability for Class 2 contributions and the lower and upper limits of profits or gains between which Class 4 contributions are payable.

SOCIAL SECURITY (CREDITS) (AMENDMENT No. 2) REGULATIONS (NORTHERN IRELAND) 1987 (No. 220) [85p], made under the Social Security (Northern Ireland) Act 1975, s.13(4); operative on May 10, 1987; amend the 1975 (No. 113) Regulations in relation to contribution credits for unemployment or incapacity for work.

SOCIAL SECURITY (EARNINGS FACTOR) (AMENDMENT) REGULATIONS (NORTHERN IRELAND) 1987 (No. 115) [80p], made under the Social Security (Northern Ireland) Act 1975, s.13(5)(5A) and S.I. 1975 No. 1503 (N.I. 15), art. 8(5A); operative on March 29, 1987; apply for the tax year 1986/87 new figures to the formula used to boost the earnings factor derived from certain contributions.

SOCIAL SECURITY (EARNINGS FACTOR) (AMENDMENT No. 2) REGULATIONS (NORTHERN IRELAND) 1987 (No. 138) [80p], made under the Social Security (Northern Ireland) Act 1975, s.13(5), S.I. 1975 No. 1503 (N.I. 15), art. 37(3), and S.I. 1986 No. 1888, art. 84(1); operative on April 6, 1987; amend the 1979 (No. 193) Regulations in relation to earnings factors for the tax year 1987/88 and subsequent years.

SOCIAL SECURITY (HOSPITAL IN-PATIENTS) (AMENDMENT) REGULATIONS (NORTHERN IRELAND) 1987 (No. 12) [45p], made under the Social Security (Northern Ireland) Act 1975 (c.15), s.85(1); operative on February 13, 1987; amend the 1975 (No. 109)

Regulations to provide for equality of treatment between men and women undergoing medical or other treatment as an in-patient in a hospital or similar institution.

SOCIAL SECURITY (HOSPITAL IN-PATIENTS) (AMENDMENT No. 2) REGULATIONS (NORTHERN IRELAND) 1987 (No. 391) [£1·60], made under the Social Security (Northern Ireland) Act 1975 (c.15), ss.81(4)(*d*), 82(6)(*b*), 85(1); operative as to part on November 2, 1987 and as to the remainder on April 11, 1988; amend the 1975 (No. 109) Regulations in relation to the adjustment of benefits.

SOCIAL SECURITY (INDUSTRIAL INJURIES) (PRESCRIBED DISEASES) (AMENDMENT) REGULATIONS (NORTHERN IRELAND) 1987 (No. 116) [80p], made under the Social Security (Northern Ireland) Act 1975, ss.76, 77(2), 113(1); operative on April 1, 1987, save for reg. 5 which came into operation on April 6, 1987; provide for a further industrial disease of lung cancer to be prescribed under Chap. V of Part II of the 1975 Act.

SOCIAL SECURITY (INDUSTRIAL INJURIES) (PRESCRIBED DISEASES) (AMENDMENT No. 2) REGULATIONS (NORTHERN IRELAND) 1987 (No. 454) [85p], made under the Social Security (Northern Ireland) Act 1975 (c.15), ss.76, 77(2); operative on January 4, 1988; amend the 1986 (No. 179) Regulations in relation to the occupations for which occupational deafness is prescribed and by adding four industrial diseases to the diseases specified in Sched. 1, Pt. I to those Regulations.

SOCIAL SECURITY (INDUSTRIAL INJURIES) (REDUCED EARNINGS ALLOWANCE AND TRANSITIONAL) REGULATIONS (NORTHERN IRELAND) 1987 (No. 142) [£1·40], made under the Social Security (Northern Ireland) Act 1975, s.59A(10), and S.I. 1986 No. 1888, art. 84(1); operative on April 6, 1987; provide for the determination of the probable standard of remuneration on any award of reduced earnings allowance except the first award.

SOCIAL SECURITY (MATERNITY ALLOWANCE) REGULATIONS (NORTHERN IRELAND) 1987 (No. 170) [£1·40], made under the Social Security (Northern Ireland) Act 1975, s.22(3), and S.I. 1986, No. 1888, art. 84(1); operative on April 6, 1987; specify circumstances in which a woman is to be disqualified for receiving maternity allowance and modify s.22(2) of the 1975 Act in relation to the maternity allowance period.

SOCIAL SECURITY (MATERNITY ALLOWANCE) (WORK ABROAD) REGULATIONS (NORTHERN IRELAND) 1987 (No. 151) [80p], made under the Social Security (Northern Ireland) Act 1975, s.126; operative on April 6, 1987; enable women who are ordinarily resident in Northern Ireland but who have worked abroad in the twelve months immediately preceding the fourteenth week before the expected week of confinement to satisfy, in specified circumstances, certain of the requirements for a maternity allowance.

SOCIAL SECURITY (MEDICAL EVIDENCE) (AMEDMENT) REGULATIONS (NORTHERN IRELAND) 1987 (No. 117) [£1·40], made under the Social Security (Northern Ireland) Act 1975, s.115(1), Sched. 13, para. 2; operative on April 6, 1987; amend the 1976 (No. 175) Regulations to substitute a definition of "registered midwife" for the definition of "certified midwife" and to substitute a new form of maternity certificate.

SOCIAL SECURITY (1986 ORDER) (COMMENCEMENT No. 2) ORDER (NORTHERN IRELAND) 1987 (No. 20 (C.2)) [45p], made under S.I. 1986 No. 1888 (N.I. 18), art. 1(4), and the Northern Ireland Act 1974 (c.28), Sched. 1, para. 2(1); brought art. 53 of, and Sched. 5 to, the 1986 S.I. into operation on April 6, 1987, and provides that the bringing into operation of these provisions does not affect rights of appeal from decisions of appeal tribunals recorded in writing before that date.

SOCIAL SECURITY (1986 ORDER) (COMMENCEMENT No. 3) ORDER (NORTHERN IRELAND) 1987 (No. 21 (C.3)) [£1·90], made under S.I. 1986 No. 1888, art. 1(3), and the Northern Ireland Act 1974, Sched. 1, para. 2(1); brought specified provisions of the 1986 S.I. into operation on March 15, April 6 and 7, 1987.

SOCIAL SECURITY (1986 ORDER) (COMMENCEMENT No. 4) ORDER (NORTHERN IRELAND) 1987 (No. 121 (C.4)) [£1·40], made under S.I. 1986 No. 1888, art. 1(3), and the Northern Ireland Act 1974 (c.28), Sched. 1, para. 2(1); brought specified provisions of the 1986 S.I. into operation on April 6, 1987.

SOCIAL SECURITY (1986 ORDER) (COMMENCEMENT No. 4) (AMENDMENT) ORDER (NORTHERN IRELAND) 1987 (No. 184 (C.7)) [45p], made under S.I. 1986 No. 1888, art. 1(3), and the Northern Ireland Act 1974 (c.28), Sched. 1, para. 2(1); corrects an error in the 1987 (No.121 (C.4)) Order.

SOCIAL SECURITY (1986 ORDER) (COMMENCEMENT No. 5) ORDER (NORTHERN IRELAND) 1987 (No. 161 (C.6)) [£1·40], made under S.I. 1986 No. 1888; art. 1(3), and the Northern Ireland Act 1974 (c.28), Sched. 1, para. 2(1); bring specified provisions of the 1988 S.I. into operation on May 1, 1987, January 4, 1988, and April 6, 1988.

SOCIAL SECURITY (1986 ORDER) (COMMENCEMENT No. 6) ORDER (NORTHERN IRELAND) 1987 (No. 299 (C.11)) [£1·60], made under S.I. 1986 No. 1888 (N.I. 18), art. 1(3), and the Northern Ireland Act 1974 (c.28), Sched. 1, para. 2(1); brought provisions of the 1986 S.I. relating to attachment of earnings into operation on July 21, 1987, provisions relating to the abolition of industrial death benefit into operation on April 10, 1988, and provisions relating to widowhood, claims and payments, reciprocal arrangements, pensioners' Christmas bonus and travelling expenses into operation on April 11, 1988.

SOCIAL SECURITY (1986 ORDER) (COMMENCEMENT No. 7) ORDER (NORTHERN IRELAND) 1987 (No. 449 (c.14)) [£2·20], made under S.I. 1986 No. 1888 (N.I. 18), art. 1(3), and the Northern Ireland Act 1974 (c.28), Sched. 1, para. 2(1); brings specified provisions of the 1986 S.I. relating to housing benefit into operation for some purposes on April 1, 1988, and for all other purposes on April 4, 1988, and brings specified provisions of the S.I. relating to income support, family credit and the social fund into operation on April 11, 1988.

SOCIAL SECURITY (NOTIFICATION OF DEATHS) REGULATIONS (NORTHERN IRELAND) 1987 (No. 81) [45p], made under S.I. 1986 No. 1888, art. 61; operative on April 6, 1987; require registrars of births and deaths to provide specified particulars of deaths to the Department of Health and Social Services.

SOCIAL SECURITY (PAYMENTS ON ACCOUNT, OVER-PAYMENTS AND RECOVERY) REGULATIONS (NORTHERN IRELAND) 1987 (No. 122) [£2·90], made under S.I. 1986 No. 1888, art. 28, 52(1)(*s*)(*t*), 54, 84; operative on April 6, 1987; provide for (1) the making and recovery of payments on account of social security entitlement; (2) offsetting prior payments against subsequent awards; (3) the prevention of duplication of payments; (4) direct credit transfer overpayments; (5) the revision of determinations and calculations of amounts recoverable; and (6) the process of recovering amounts determined to be repayable or recoverable under the old law or recoverable under the new law.

SOCIAL SECURITY (PORTUGAL) ORDER (NORTHERN IRELAND) 1987 (No. 399) [85p], made under the Social Security (Northern Ireland) Act 1975 (c.15), s.134, and S.I. 1975 No. 1504 (N.I. 16), art. 17; operative on October 22, 1987; modifies the 1975 Act and Order to give effect in Northern Ireland to the agreement made on September 28, 1987, between the U.K. and Portugal.

SOCIAL SECURITY REVALUATION OF EARNINGS FACTORS ORDER (NORTHERN IRELAND) 1987 (No. 230) [85p], made under S.I. 1975 No. 1503 (N.I. 15), art. 23; operative on June 22, 1987; increases certain earnings factors for specified tax years by various percentages.

SOCIAL SECURITY (UNEMPLOYMENT, SICKNESS AND INVALIDITY BENEFIT) (AMENDMENT) REGULATIONS (NORTHERN IRELAND) 1987 (No. 90) [45p], made under the Social Security (Northern Ireland) Act 1975, s.17(2)(*a*); operative on March 4, 1987; amend the 1984 (No. 245) Regulations in relation to days which are not to be treated as days of unemployment or incapacity for work.

SOCIAL SECURITY (UNEMPLOYMENT, SICKNESS AND INVALIDITY BENEFIT) (AMENDMENT No. 2) REGULATIONS (NORTHERN IRELAND) 1987 (No. 221) [45p], made under the Social Security (Northern Ireland) Act 1975, s.17(1)(*a*); operative on May 11, 1987; amend the 1984 (No. 245) Regulations in relation to the earnings limit for persons deemed incapable of work.

SOCIAL SECURITY (WIDOW'S BENEFIT AND RETIREMENT PENSIONS) (AMENDMENT) REGULATIONS (NORTHERN IRELAND) 1987 (No. 404) [85p], made under the Social Security (Northern Ireland) Act 1975, ss.29(5)(*b*), 39(4), Sched. 17, S.I. 1975 No. 1503 (N.I. 15), Sched. 1, para. 3, and S.I. 1986 No. 1888 (N.I. 18), art. 84(1); operative on April 11, 1988; make miscellaneous amendments to the 1979 (No. 243) Regulations.

SOCIAL SECURITY (WIDOW'S BENEFIT) (TRANSITIONAL) REGULATIONS (NORTHERN IRELAND) 1987 (No. 387) [45p], made under S.I. 1986 No. 1888 (N.I. 18), art. 84(1); operative on April 11, 1988; contain savings for existing beneficiaries to both widows' allowance and widow's pension.

STATE SCHEME PREMIUMS (ACTUARIAL TABLES) REGULATIONS (NORTHERN IRELAND) 1987 (No. 175) [£2·90], made under S.I. 1975 No. 1503 (N.I. 15), arts. 46(7), 46ZA(14), 46A(3), 47(4), Sched. 2, para. 6, and S.I. 1986 No. 1888 (N.I. 18), art. 7(15); operative on April 6, 1988; prescribe the tables in accordance with which the Department of Health and Social Services is required to make calculations in relation to, and for the purpose of determining the amount of, state scheme premiums other than contributions equivalent premiums; revoke the 1978 (No. 35) and 1982 (No. 108) Regulations.

STATE SCHEME PREMIUMS (ACTUARIAL TABLES—TRANSITIONAL PROVISIONS) REGULATIONS (NORTHERN IRELAND) 1987 (No. 176) [£1·90], made under S.I. 1986 No. 1888, art. 7(15); operative on January 4, 1988 and continue in operation until April 6, 1988; prescribe the tables in accordance with which the Department is required to make calculations in relation to personal pension protected rights premiums.

STATUTORY MATERNITY PAY (COMPENSATION OF EMPLOYERS) REGULATIONS (NORTHERN IRELAND) 1987 (No. 80) [80p], made under S.I. 1986 No. 1888 (N.I. 18), Sched. 4, paras. 1, 5; operative on April 6, 1987; provide for compensation of employers who have made payments of statutory maternity pay under the 1986 S.I.

STATUTORY MATERNITY PAY (MEDICAL EVIDENCE) REGULATIONS (NORTHERN IRELAND) 1987 (No. 99) [80p], made under S.I. 1986 No. 1888, Sched. 4, para. 6(*a*); operative on March 15, 1987; prescribe the form in which evidence of a woman's pregnancy and her expected date of confinement is to be provided by her to a person who is liable to pay her statutory maternity pay.

STATUTORY MATERNITY PAY (PERSONS ABROAD AND MARINERS) REGULATIONS (NORTHERN IRELAND) 1987 (No. 171) [80p], made under S.I. 1986 No. 1888, art. 80(1); operative on April 6, 1987; provide for statutory maternity pay in relation to persons abroad and women who work as mariners.

STATUTORY SICK PAY (ADDITIONAL COMPENSATION OF EMPLOYERS) (AMENDMENT) REGULATIONS (NORTHERN IRELAND) 1987 (No. 79) [45p], made under S.I. 1982 No. 1084 (N.I. 16), art. 11(1A)(*a*); operative on April 6, 1987; increase the rate of an employer's additional compensation in respect of any payment of statutory sick pay made by him.

STATUTORY SICK PAY (GENERAL) (AMENDMENT) REGULATIONS (NORTHERN IRELAND) 1987 (No. 131) [80p], made under S.I. 1982 No. 1084 (N.I. 16), art. 3(5), and S.I. 1986 No. 1888, arts. 52(1)(*j*), 84(1); operative on April 6, 1987; amend the 1982 (No. 263) Regulations in relation to the circumstances in which the liability to pay statutory sick pay is to be that of the Department of Health and Social Services and not that of the employer.

STATUTORY SICK PAY (GENERAL) (AMENDMENT No. 2) REGULATIONS (NORTHERN IRELAND) 1987 (No. 248) [85p], made under S.I. 1982 No. 1084 (N.I. 16), arts. 5(4A)(*b*)(5), 28(3), Sched. 1, para. 1; operative on June 7, 1987; amend the 1982 (No. 263) Regulations in relation to statutory maternity pay and maternity allowances and in relation to statements required to be completed by employers in connection with payments of statutory sick pay.

STATUTORY SICK PAY (RATE OF PAYMENT) REGULATIONS (NORTHERN IRELAND) 1987 (No. 23) [45p], made under S.I. 1982 No. 1084 (N.I. 16), art. 9(1A), and S.I. 1986 No. 1888, art. 84(1); operative on April 6, 1987; replace the three rates of statutory sick pay with two rates.

SUPPLEMENTARY BENEFIT (CONDITIONS OF ENTITLEMENT) (AMENDMENT) REGULATIONS (NORTHERN IRELAND) 1987 (No. 149) [£1·40], made under S.I. 1977 No. 2156 (N.I. 27), arts. 7, 9(2)(3); operative on April 6, 1987; amend the 1981 (No. 371) Regulations in relation to persons treated as available or not available for employment and in relation to persons treated as being in full-time or relevant education.

SUPPLEMENTARY BENEFIT (REQUIREMENTS) (AMENDMENT) AND UP-RATING REGULATIONS (NORTHERN IRELAND) 1987 (No. 173) [£1·40], made under S.I. 1977 No. 2156, art. 3(3), Sched. 1, para. 2; operative as to part on April 6, 1987, and as to the remainder on April 13, 1987; amend the 1983 (No. 61) Regulations in relation to boarders.

SUPPLEMENTARY BENEFIT (REQUIREMENTS AND RESOURCES) (AMENDMENT No. 2) REGULATIONS (NORTHERN IRELAND) 1987 (No. 311) [85p], made under S.I. 1977 No. 2156 (N.I. 27), Sched. 1, paras. 1, 2; operative as to regs. 1 and 2 on July 27, 1987, and as to the remainder on September 1, 1987; amend the 1983 (No. 61) Regulations by re-defining "nursing home" and by increasing the amount of the student grant disregarded in respect of books and equipment.

SUPPLEMENTARY BENEFIT (RESOURCES) (AMENDMENT) REGULATIONS (NORTHERN IRELAND) 1987 (No. 172) [£1·40], made under S.I. 1977 No. 2156 Sched. 1, para. 1; operative on April 6, 1987; make miscellaneous amendments to the 1984 (No. 54) Regulations.

SUPPLEMENTARY BENEFIT (SINGLE PAYMENTS) (AMENDMENT) REGULATIONS (NORTHERN IRELAND) 1987 (No. 13) [45p], made under S.I. 1977 No. 2156 (N.I. 27), arts. 5, 19(2)(*a*); operative on January 21, 1987, save for reg. 2 which is operative on January 26, 1987; amend the 1981 (No. 369) Regulations in relation to single payments for exceptionally cold weather.

SUPPLEMENTARY BENEFIT (SINGLE PAYMENTS) (AMENDMENT No. 2) REGULATIONS (NORTHERN IRELAND) 1987 (No. 439) [85p], made under S.I. 1977 No. 2156 (N.I. 27), arts. 5, 19(2)(*a*); operative on December 17, 1987; amend the 1981 (No. 369) Regulations in relation to the travelling expenses of close relatives attending a funeral and in relation to fuel costs during period of exceptionally cold weather.

SUPPLEMENTARY BENEFIT UP-RATING REGULATIONS (NORTHERN IRELAND) 1987 (No. 15) [80p], made under S.I. 1977 No. 2156 (N.I. 27), Sched. 1, para. 2(1)(4); operative on April 6, 1987; alter amounts specified in the 1983 (No. 61) Regulations for the purpose of determining entitlement to supplementary benefit under the 1977 S.I.

WORKMEN'S COMPENSATION (SUPPLEMENTATION) (AMENDMENT) REGULATIONS (NORTHERN IRELAND) 1987 (No. 118) [£1·40], made under the Industrial Injuries and Diseases (Northern Ireland Old Cases) Act 1975 (c.17), ss.2, 4(1); operative on April 8,

1987; amend the 1983 (No. 101) Regulations by making adjustments to the lower rates of lesser incapacity allowance consequential upon the increase in the maximum rate of that allowance made by the 1987 (No. 22) Order; revoke the 1986 (No. 222) Regulations.

WORKMEN'S COMPENSATION (SUPPLEMENTATION) (AMENDMENT No. 2) REGULATIONS (NORTHERN IRELAND) 1987 (No. 152) [45p], made under the Industrial Injuries and Diseases (Northern Ireland Old Cases) Act 1975, ss.2, 4; operative on April 6, 1987; provide for a major incapacity allowance to be payable at the same rate as disablement pension without further deduction, except for those who have retired.

2741a. Social security—Social Fund (Maternity and Funeral Expenses) (Northern Ireland) Order 1987 (S.I. 1987 No. 464) (N.I. 8))

This Order gives the Department of Health and Social Services power to prescribe the amounts of payments in respect of maternity expenses and funeral expenses out of the social fund established under art. 33(2)(*a*) of the Social Security (Northern Ireland) Order 1986.

The Order came into operation on March 25, 1987.

2742. Tort—arrest—whether continued detention lawful—whether wrongful imprisonment—damages

D, a schoolgirl aged 17 years, committed the offence of personation at a local government election in 1983 and on the direction of the presiding officer was arrested by a police constable. A person so arrested must under election law be dealt with as having been arrested without a warrant. As a large number of people were arrested for personation at that election D was brought to a police station and, apart from three short breaks, kept in a cubicle in a prison van from 3.15 p.m. until 12.55 a.m. on the following day, although she was charged with the offence at 8.15 p.m. During that time she suffered discomfort, felt isolated and was left in a state of uncertainty about the time of her release. She claimed damages.

Held, that (1) D was wrongfully imprisoned from 8.15 p.m. when she was charged until her release; and (2) as she suffered no physical injury and was not assaulted she had no claim in negligence and the police were not guilty of any actionable wrong in detaining her in a prison van. General damages of £600 were awarded for the period of wrongful imprisonment.

DAVEY *v.* CHIEF CONSTABLE OF THE ROYAL ULSTER CONSTABULARY [1986] 12 N.I.J.B. 57, Higgins J.

2743. Tort—Consumer Protection (Northern Ireland) Order 1987 (S.I. 1987 No. 2049 (N.I. 20))

This Order (1) implements EC Directive 85/374/EEC with respect to the liability of persons for damage caused by defective products; (2) deals with misleading price indications and, in particular makes it an offence to give a misleading price indication in respect of goods, services, accommodation or facilities; (3) amends S.I. 1978 No. 1039 (N.I. 9); and (4) makes further provision with respect to the disclosure of information, the defence of due diligence, the liability of persons other than the principal offender and rights of action in civil proceedings.

Specified provisions of the Order come into operation on March 1, 1988, and the remaining provisions on days to be appointed.

2744. Tort—Occupiers' Liability (Northern Ireland) Order 1987 (S.I. 1987 No. 1280 (N.I. 15))

This Order amends the law as to the liability of an occupier for the safety of persons who are on his premises without his permission and modifies the Unfair Contract Terms Act 1977 (c.50) in relation to persons obtaining access to premises for recreational or educational purposes.

The Order came into operation on September 22, 1987.

2745. Town and country planning

CERTIFICATES OF ALTERNATIVE DEVELOPMENT VALUE REGULATIONS (NORTHERN IRELAND) 1987 (No. 437) [45p], made under S.I. 1982 No. 712 (N.I. 9), art. 17; operative on January 10, 1988; provide for the application for and isue of certificates of alternative development value under art. 15 of the S.I.

PLANNING (FEES) REGULATIONS (NORTHERN IRELAND) 1987 (No. 335) [£2·90], made under S.I. 1972 No. 1634 (N.I. 17), art. 105A; operative on September 27, 1987; consolidate with amendments, including amendments increasing fees by approximately 10 per cent., and revoke the 1983 (No. 329), 1984 (No. 224), 1985 (No. 225), 1986 (No. 296) and 1987 (No. 27) Regulations.

PLANNING (FEES) (AMENDMENT) REGULATIONS (NORTHERN IRELAND) 1987 (No. 27) [£1·40], made under S.I. 1972 No. 1634 (N.I. 17), art. 105A; operative on February 25, 1987; increase fees for planning applications and appeals.

PLANNING (GENERAL DEVELOPMENT) (AMENDMENT) ORDER (NORTHERN IRELAND) 1987 (No. 36) [80p], made under S.I. 1972 No. 1634, art. 13(1)(2)(3); operative on February 27, 1987; amends the 1973 (No. 326) Order in relation to the installation of tanks for the storage of liquefied petroleum gas within the curtilage of dwelling-houses.

PLANNING (GENERAL DEVELOPMENT) (AMENDMENT No. 2) ORDER (NORTHERN IRELAND) 1987 (No. 438) [45p], made under S.I. 1972 No. 1634 (N.I. 17), art. 13(1)(2)(3); operative on January 10, 1988; amends the 1973 (No. 326) Order in relation to developments allowed without planning permission.

2746. Town and country planning—blight notice—Lands Tribunal decision

[Planning and Land Compensation Act (Northern Ireland) 1971 (c.23); Planning Blight (Compensation) (Northern Ireland) Order 1981 (S.I. 1981 No. 608 (N.I. 16)); Interpretation Act (Northern Ireland) 1954 (c.33), s.25.]

In July 1985, C served on the Department of the Environment a blight notice purported to be given under Pt. I of the Planning and Land Compensation Act (Northern Ireland) 1971. The Department contended that this blight notice was invalid as Pt. I of the 1971 Act had been repealed in May 1981 by the Planning Blight (Compensation) (Northern Ireland) Order 1981.

Held, that the blight notice was valid as it followed the prescribed form set out in regulations made under the 1971 Act, no similar regulations having yet been made under the 1981 Order. If there was a deviation, the notice was saved by s.25 of the Interpretation Act (Northern Ireland) 1954.

SALVATION ARMY TRUSTEE CO. *v.* DEPARTMENT OF THE ENVIRONMENT FOR NORTHERN IRELAND (R/4/1987).

2747. Town and country planning—compensation—limitation of actions—Lands Tribunal decision

[Statute of Limitations (Northern Ireland) 1958 (c.10), ss.8, 56(1).]

The commercial centre of Coleraine was pedestrianised by an order made by the Department of the Environment on May 8, 1978. On May 17, 1978, W claimed compensation for the depreciation in value of an area used by his staff and customers as a car park. The Department determined compensation at nil on June 13, 1983, and this was confirmed on February 14, 1984. The matter was referred to the Lands Tribunal on March 19, 1986. The Department contended that the claim was statute-barred under s.8 of the Statute of Limitations (Northern Ireland) 1958.

Held, that the six-year term under that section commenced on May 8, 1978, or May 17, 1978, but that the proof of evidence lodged with the tribunal by the Department on November 24, 1986, constituted an acknowledgment for the purposes of s.56(1) of the Statute and, accordingly, W's claim was not statute-barred. Compensation for the depreciation of the area, which could accommodate four or at most five cars, was assessed at £2,330.

WREATH *v.* DEPARTMENT OF THE ENVIRONMENT FOR NORTHERN IRELAND (R/7/1986).

2748. Trade and industry

INDUSTRIAL DEVELOPMENT (DATE OF APPLICATION) ORDER (NORTHERN IRELAND) 1987 (No. 125) [80p], made under S.I. 1982 No. 1083 (N.I. 15), art. 22(2)(*e*); operative on May 1, 1987; reduces the time limits for certain applications to grants towards approved capital expenditure incurred in providing new machinery or plant; revokes the 1973 (No. 433) Order.

INDUSTRIAL DEVELOPMENT (EXCLUSIONS FROM GRANT) ORDER (NORTHERN IRELAND) 1987 (No. 204) [45p], made under S.I. 1982 No. 1083 (N.I. 15), art. 21(1); operative on May 1, 1987; excludes persons carrying on specified businesses from the payment of grant under Pt. IV of the 1982 S.I.

INDUSTRIAL DEVELOPMENT (VARIATION OF RATE OF GENERAL ASSISTANCE GRANTS) ORDER (NORTHERN IRELAND) 1987 (No. 374) [45p], made under S.I. 1982 No. 1083 (N.I. 15), art. 22(2)(*a*); operative on September 28, 1987; reduces the rate of grant payable under Pt. IV of the 1982 S.I. from 20 per cent. to 12½ per cent. of approved capital expenditure incurred on or after September 28, 1987.

INDUSTRIAL DEVELOPMENT (VARIATION OF RATE OF GENERAL ASSISTANCE GRANTS) (No. 2) ORDER (NORTHERN IRELAND) 1987 (No. 394) [45p], made under S.I. 1982 No. 1083, art. 22(2)(*a*); operative on October 13, 1987; reduces the rate of grant payable under Pt. IV of the 1982 S.I. from 20 per cent. to 12½ per cent. in respect of approved capital expenditure incurred on or after October 13, 1987.

INDUSTRIAL DEVELOPMENT (VARIATION OF RATE OF GENERAL ASSISTANCE GRANTS) (REVOCATION) ORDER (NORTHERN IRELAND) 1987 (No. 382 [45p], made under S.I. 1982 No. 1083, art. 22(2)(*a*); operative on September 25, 1987; revokes the 1987 (No.374) Order.

2749. Trade and industry—industrial training

Orders made under S.I. 1984 No. 1159 (N.I. 9), art. 23(1); S.R. 1987 Nos. 177 (distributive industry) [£1·40]; 178 (textiles industry) [£1·40]; 179 (food and drink industry) [£1·40].

Orders made under S.I. 1984 No. 1159 (N.I. 9), arts. 23(2)(3)(4), 24(3)(4):

S.R. 1987 No. 257 (construction industry) [£1·60]; 259 (engineering industry) [£1·60]; 260 (catering industry) [£1·60]; 272 (road transport industry) [£1·60]; 327 (clothing industry) [£1·60].

2750. Transport

EUROPEAN COMMUNITIES (INTERNATIONAL PASSENGER SERVICES) REGULATIONS (NORTHERN IRELAND) 1987 (No. 383) [£3·30], made under the European Communities Act 1972 (c.68), s.2(2), the Transport Act (Northern Ireland) 1967 (c.36), s.45(*i*)(*j*), the Finance Act 1973 (c.51), s.56(1)(5), and S.I. 1981 No. 154 (N.I. 1), art. 66(1)(2); operative on November 9, 1987; replace with amendments and revoke the 1981 (No. 199) and 1984 (No. 45) Regulations.

ROAD TRANSPORT (GREAT BRITAIN PASSENGER SERVICES) (FEE) REGULATIONS (NORTHERN IRELAND) 1987 (No. 188) [45p], made under the Transport Act (Northern Ireland) 1967, s.9(1); operative on June 1, 1987; prescribe a fee of £10 in respect of an application for a Northern Ireland (Great Britain passenger transport service) authorisation as defined in art. 5(7) of the 1987 (No. 187) Regulations.

ROAD TRANSPORT (GREAT BRITAIN PASSENGER SERVICES) REGULATIONS (NORTHERN IRELAND) 1987 (No. 187) [80p], made under the Transport Act (Northern Ireland) 1967 (c.37), s.45(*i*)(*j*), and S.I. 1981 No. 154 (N.I. 1), art. 66(2); operative on June 1, 1987; exempt vehicles authorised under the law of Great Britain to carry passengers for reward there, where used in Northern Ireland for the carriage of passengers on certain services between Great Britain and Northern Ireland, from the requirements of Pts. II and IV of the 1967 Act and arts. 59, 60 and 70 of the 1981 S.I.

ROAD TRANSPORT LICENSING (FEES) (AMENDMENT) REGULATIONS (NORTHERN IRELAND) 1987 (No. 47) [45p], made under the Transport Act (Northern Ireland) 1967 (c.37), s.9; operative on April 1, 1987; increase the fees for road service licences.

2751. Transport—railways—level crossing

Order made under the Transport Act (Northern Ireland) 1967 (c.37), s.66: S.R. 1985 No. 345 (Lurgan (Bells Row)) [45p].

2752. Water and waterworks—flooding—compensation—Lands Tribunal decision

[Water and Sewerage Services (Northern Ireland) Order 1973 (S.I. 1973 No. 70 (N.I. 2)), art. 55.]

C's house was flooded when a mains water pipe, which had been laid about eight years before the flooding, fractured. The day before the flooding the Department of the Environment had carried out a swabbing operation to clear out the pipe. The parties agreed that this swabbing operation was an execution of works. C claimed compensation for the drainage caused by or in consequence of the execution of these works.

Held, by the Lands Tribunal that on the balance of probabilities the fracture of the pipe occurred in consequence of the execution of the works.

O'HAGAN *v.* DEPARTMENT OF THE ENVIRONMENT FOR NORTHERN IRELAND (R/27/1985, R/33/1985).

2753. Water and waterworks—Water (Fluoridation) (Northern Ireland) Order 1987 (S.I. 1987 No. 2052 (N.I. 21))

This Order makes provision with respect to the fluoridation of water supplies.

The Order came into operation on January 27, 1988.

2754. Weights and measures

WEIGHTS AND MEASURES (TESTING AND ADJUSTMENT FEES) REGULATIONS (NORTHERN IRELAND) 1987 (No. 309) [£1·60], made under S.I. 1981 No. 231 (N.I. 10), arts. 2(2), 9(3), 31(12), 43; operative on September 1, 1987; prescribe the fees to be paid for the inspection, testing, retesting and certification of equipment and for the adjustment of weights and measures; revoke the 1980 (Nos. 15, 456) Regulations.

WEIGHTS AND MEASURES (WEIGHTS) REGULATIONS (NORTHERN IRELAND) 1987 (No. 310) [£2·90], made under S.I. 1981 No. 231 (N.I. 10), arts. 9(1)(3), 13(1); operative as to regs. 1(4) and 13 on September 1, 1988, and as to the remainder on September 1, 1987; make provision as to the materials and principles of construction and marking of weights, testing, prescribed limits of error, stamping and obliteration of stamps; revoke the 1971 (No. 342) and 1977 (No. 136) Regulations.

2755. Wills and succession—condition—validity

T by his will bequeathed his house and land to his trustees upon trust for S, his sister, for life with remainder to McC, his grand-nephew, provided that he came to live in the house after T's death and continued to reside in it with S until S's death. If McC failed to carry out the condition, the house and land were to be sold and the proceeds divided between two charities, the decision of the trustees as to whether McC had carried out the condition to be final. The will also declared that McC was to have no legal right to reside in the house during S's life except as licensee of S who was given power to revoke this licence at any time. On T's death McC, who was then fifteen years of age, offered to reside with S but S refused.

Held, that (1) the condition was a single obligation to take up and continue residence in the house; (2) the condition was a condition subsequent; (3) the offer to come and live in the house did not constitute performance; (4) equitable relief from failure to perform a condition cannot be granted where there is a gift over; (5) as the condition envisaged that McC, who was a minor, would cease to live with his parents and reside with S, it was void as against public policy and not merely suspended during McC's minority; and (6) the condition was also void for uncertainty as McC was unable to tell properly in advance the content of the obligation imposed on him and it was not saved by the drafting stratagem of leaving the decision to the trustees. Accordingly McC took the house and lands on S's death free of the condition.

JOHNSTON'S ESTATE, *Re*; MORGAN *v.* McCAUGHEY [1986] 11 N.I.J.B. 16, Carswell J.

NUISANCE

2756. Building operations—injunction—less restrictive notice issued by local authority

[Control of Pollution Act 1974 (c.40), Pt. 3, s.60.]

D1 engaged D2 to carry out demolition and reconstruction work at a site adjacent to P's premises, a bank. The noise of the works disturbed work at the bank. P sought and obtained an interlocutory injunction limiting the hours of working. Contemporaneously the local authority issued a notice pursuant to s.60 of the Control of Pollution Act 1974 against D2, restricting the hours of work but to a lesser extent than specified in the injunction. D2 appealed against the injunction on the facts, and further contended that the court had no jurisdiction to grant an injunction in circumstances where a s.60 notice had been or was to be issued.

Held, that (1) there was sufficient evidence of nuisance to justify the injunction; (2) the jurisdiction of the court was not affected in any way by anything in Pt. 3 of the Control of Pollution Act 1974 (*Hammersmith London Borough Council* v. *Magnum Automated Forecourts* [1978] C.L.Y. 2202 considered).

LLOYDS BANK *v.* GUARDIAN ASSURANCE AND TROLLOPE & COLLS (1987) 35 Build.L.R. 34, C.A.

2757. Prohibition on recurrence of a nuisance—whether permanent

[Control of Pollution Act 1974 (c.40), s.58.]

The requirement prohibiting the recurrence of a nuisance under s.58 of the Control of Pollution Act 1974 is permanent.

R. *v.* BIRMINGHAM JUSTICES, *ex p.* GUPPY, *The Times,* October 8, 1987, D.C.

2758. Statutory nuisance—block of flats—"person aggrieved"

[Public Health Act 1936 (c.49), ss.92, 99.]

The appellant authority were the owners of a large block of flats and maisonettes. The respondents were the tenants and they laid an information before the magistrates under s.99 of the Public Health Act 1936 alleging that the house was prejudicial to health or a nuisance. Defects were alleged to the common parts of the building and in individual flats but no particular flats were selected for special attention. At the hearing there was direct evidence relating to 16 out of the 52 flats. The magistrate found that the 16 flats were affected by condensation and mould growth, and found that this was symptomatic of the block as a whole and evidence of a common system or condition. The block as a whole was found to constitute premises within the meaning of s.92 of the 1936 Act. A nuisance order was made requiring the authority to carry out works to abate the nuisance. The authority appealed.

Held, allowing the appeal, that (1) the block as a whole and each dwelling in it was capable of being described as premises within s.92; (2) it was the condensation and mould on the walls of each flat which were prejudicial to health and not the state of the block as designed, accordingly each respondent was not a person aggrieved by the same statutory nuisance and was only a person aggrieved in relation to each flat and not the block as a whole; (3) the statutory nuisance being the condensation and mould in each flat, it was the flat which constituted the relevant premises for the tenant under s.99 of the Act.

BIRMINGHAM DISTRICT COUNCIL *v.* McMAHON (1987) 17 H.L.R. 452, D.C.

2759. Trade dispute—picketing, marches and demonstrations—abusive, threatening and violent behaviour—whether public nuisance. See NEWS GROUP NEWSPAPERS *v.* SOCIETY OF GRAPHICAL AND ALLIED TRADES '82 (No. 2), §3759.

2759a. Water—flooding lower land—occupier's preventative action—whether nuisance

An occupier of lower land was entitled to take reasonable steps to prevent water from higher land entering his land, albeit that flooding was caused on the higher land, but an action in nuisance would lie where the occupier of the lower land's user was unreasonable, and damage to the higher land reasonably foreseeable.

Water drained unchannelled by percolation through the plaintiff's land into a disused osier bed and clay pit on lower adjoining land owned by the defendants. The defendants filled in the clay pit, so as to build housing, and thereby erected a partial barrier against the drainage of water, causing it to flood on the plaintiff's land. They also filled in the osier bed, forcing the water there present back onto the plaintiff's land: that 'squeezing out' lasted about five years. Pumps already installed by the plaintiff coped with the additional subsequent flooding. They claimed damages for nuisance.

Held, that an occupier of land had no cause of action against the occupier of higher adjacent land for permitting the passage of natural, unchannelled water through his land, but neither was he under any obligation to receive the water, and could take steps consistent with the reasonable user of the land to prevent it entering thereon, albeit that damage was occasioned to the occupier of the higher land. But where the occupier of the higher land proved that the lower occupier's user of his land was unreasonable, and that the resultant damage to the higher land was reasonably foreseeable, an action in nuisance would lie. Since the use of the land for housing was a reasonable user, the plaintiffs had no cause of action against them in respect of their major claim arising out of the filling of the clay pit. But the infilling of the osier bed which caused temporary additional flooding was actionable and the damage reasonably foreseeable, and the defendants were liable either in trespass or nuisance for the additional cost of pumping and maintenance during the squeezing out period. *Smith* v. *Kenrick* (1849) 7 C.B. 515; *Rylands* v. *Fletcher* (1868) L.R. 3 H.L. 330, H.L.; *Gartner* v. *Kidman* [1962] C.L.Y. 3123 and *Leakey* v. *National Trust for Places of Historic Interest and Natural Beauty* [1980] C.L.Y. 2006 applied.

HOME BREWERY CO. *v.* WILLIAM DAVIS & CO. (LEICESTER) [1987] 2 W.L.R. 117, Q.B.D., Piers Ashworth Q.C. sitting as a deputy High Court judge.

PARLIAMENT

2760. House of Commons—membership—disqualification

HOUSE OF COMMONS DISQUALIFICATION ORDER 1987 (No. 449) [45p], made under the House of Commons Disqualification Act 1975 (c.24), s.5; operative on March 18, 1987; replaces S.I. 1986 No. 2219 which is defective.

2761. House of Commons Members' Fund

Resolution of the House of Commons, dated March 20, 1987, passed in pursuance of the House of Commons Members' Fund Act 1948 (11 and 12 Geo. 6 c.36), s.3 and the House of Commons Members' Fund and Parliamentary Pensions Act 1981 (c.7), s.2: S.I. 1987 No. 511 (periodic payments to past members and widows) [45p].

2762. Lord Chancellor's salary

LORD CHANCELLOR'S SALARY ORDER 1987 (No. 941) [45p], made under the Ministerial and Other Salaries Act 1975 (c.27), s.1(4); operative on May 18, 1987; increases the Lord Chancellor's salary.

2763. Parliamentary and Health Service Commissioners Act 1987 (c.39). See ADMINISTRATIVE LAW, §44.

2764. Parliamentary and other Pensions Act 1987 (c.45)

This Act provides for the continuance in existence of the Parliamentary Contribution Pension Fund and confers power on the Leader of the House of Commons to make regulations with respect to that Fund and with respect to the application of the assets of that Fund in or towards the provision of pensions. Mr. Speaker King's Retirement Act 1971.

The Act received the Royal Assent on May 15, 1987, and will come into force on days to be appointed by the Leader of the House of Commons.

The Act extends to Northern Ireland.

2765. Parliamentary and other Pensions Act 1987—commencement

PARLIAMENTARY AND OTHER PENSIONS ACT 1987 (COMMENCEMENT No.1) ORDER 1987 (No. 1311 (C.42)) [45p], made under the Parliamentary and other Pensions Act 1987 (c.45), s.7(2); brings into force on July 23, 1987, s.4(1), (3).

2766. Salaries

MINISTERIAL AND OTHER SALARIES ORDER 1987 (No. 1836) [85p], made under the Ministerial and other Salaries Act 1975 (c.27), s.1(4); operative on January 1, 1988; increases salaries payable under the 1975 Act.

PARTNERSHIP

2767. Dissolution—death—valuation of assets—Trinidad and Tobago

On dissolution of a partnership by death, the surviving partner is entitled to his share of the partnership assets plus intermediate profits, rather than merely interest.

W and A, her son, ran a grocery. A and B, his wife, cut W out and ran the business for themselves. Two years later A died and B carried on the business for her own benefit. Three years later W sought a declaration that she was entitled to half of the business and property and half of all profits and their proceeds since A's death.

Held, the partnership was dissolved on A's death and W had a right to one half of the partnership assets valued at the date of realisation plus intermediate profits (*Barclays Bank Trust Co.* v. *Bluff* [1981] C.L.Y. 2016 approved).

CHANDROUTIE *v.* GAJADHAR [1987] 2 W.L.R. 1, P.C.

2768. Solicitors—interlocutory injunction—balance of convenience

The partners under a single partnership deed of a firm of solicitors carried on business at three separate autonomous branches. In 1985 a change in the Law Society's rules made it permissible for solicitors to carry on the business of selling property and D, the partners of one of the branches, extended their office in order to do so, but failed to inform P, the partners at the other branches, of their plans. Upon discovering these plans, P sought an injunction to restrain D from using the firm name, property or assets in connection with the proposed property selling venture, and in due course applied for an interlocutory injunction. The judge found that there was an issue to be tried as to whether the proposed venture would be in breach of the partnership deed; that whether or not an interlocutory injunction was granted there would be a risk of damage to one or other of the parties; and that the balance of convenience favoured D. He therefore refused to grant the injunction.

Held, dismissing P's appeal, that the judge's exercise of his discretion in accordance with the principles set out in *American Cyanamid Co.* v. *Ethicon* [1978] C.L.Y. 2233 could not be faulted.

NIXON *v.* WOOD (1987) 284 E.G. 1055, C.A.

PATENTS AND DESIGNS

2769. Amendment—discretion

[Patents Act 1977 (c.37), ss.27, 76, 123; Patents Act 1949 (c.87), s.29; Patents Rules 1982 (S.I. 1982 No. 717), r.106.]

P sought to amend their patent as a result of prior act which had recently come to their notice. The examiner requested them to identify the prior act. P objected.

Held, that (1) the comptroller had a discretion and he needed all relevant information in order to be able properly to exercise it; (2) the Rules authorised him to direct that documents which he required should be furnished to him.

WADDINGTON'S PATENT [1986] R.P.C. 158, Patent Office.

2770. Amendment—European patent—whether protection extended by proposed amendment

[Patents Act 1977 (c.37), ss.27, 76, 125, 130; European Patent Convention Arts. 69, 97, 29, 51.]

Proprietors of a European patent (U.K.) applied to amend their specification to delete reference numerals and add an independent omnibus claim and delete the translations. Opponents contended that this would extend the protection conferred by the patent.

Held, that upon a proper construction of the Patents Act 1977 and the European Patents Convention the amendments sought were permissible because the scope of protection under the Act was not thereby widened.

PHILIPS ELECTRONIC AND ASSOCIATED INDUSTRIES PATENT [1987] R.P.C. 244, Patent Office.

2771. Amendment—practice

In an action for infringement P sought to amend one of the specifications in issue. The judge ordered that the amendment issues be heard contemporaneously with the infringement action. D cross-examined P's witnesses on their affidavits concerning amendment and thereafter sought to cross-examine the witnesses on the counterclaim issues in the infringement proceedings. The trial judge prevented this. D appealed.

Held, that the trial judge had correctly exercised his discretion.

DU PONT DE NEMOURS (E. I.) *v.* ENKA A.G. [1986] R.P.C. 417, C.A.

2772. Application—amendment—disclosure

[Patents Act 1977 (c.37), ss.14, 15, 76.]

A sought to amend his applications by omitting the final, cross-linking, step from the claims and description. They had been filed as divisionals from an earlier application relating to a sleeve assembly formed from a web of heat recoverable polymeric material. The Patent Office refused to allow the applications to proceed. A appealed.

Held, dismissing the appeal, that (1) the claim as amended was not supported by the description; (2) the final step was an essential part of the invention as disclosed.

RAYCHEM'S APPLICATIONS [1986] R.P.C. 547, Falconer J.

2773. Application—description—amendment—micro-organism

[Patents Act 1977 (c.37), s.14, 76; Patents Rules 1982 (S.I. 1982 No. 717), r.17.]

The hearing officer held that the requirements of s.14(3) were satisfied only in respect of certain claims in the application and not in respect of other claims and refused to allow the application. The application concerned a new micro-organism used to make an antibiotic. Objection was raised that the claims not restricted to the strain deposited contravened s.14 and were not supported by the deposit in the culture collection. The applicants had only deposited the preferred strain.

Held, that it was not necessary to deposit every strain of a new species in order to support a claim relating to that species; (2) it was not necessary to deposit the best strain known for the stated purpose of the invention; (3) the deposit of the applicants' strain was sufficient to support claims relating to strains derived from that strain but not claims relating to the whole species

CHINOIN'S APPLICATION [1986] R.P.C. 39, Falconer J.

2774. Application—divisional application—matter extending beyond that disclosed

[Patents Act 1977 (c.37), ss.15, 76, 130.]

The application in suit was filed as divisional from an earlier application. The description was identical to the parent. The hearing officer found that the application disclosed matter which extended beyond that disclosed in the parent application as filed. The applicants appealed.

Held, that the hearing officer had correctly decided that upon a proper construction of the statutory provisions the application must be refused. He had no discretion.

VAN DER LELY'S APPLICATION [1987] R.P.C. 61, Patents Ct.

2775. Application—international application—error in translation—whether power in Comptroller to correct mistake

[Patents Act 1977 (c.37) ss.89, 117; Patents Rules 1982, rr.85, 100, 113.]

The application had been filed claiming priority from a Japanese application. A translation was filed at the U.K. Patent Office, but instead of the international application the

Japanese priority document was filed. The hearing officer held that he could not correct the error and allow the proper document to be filed. The applicant appealed.

Held, dismissing the appeal, that the Comptroller had no jurisdiction to correct an error which had resulted in an application failing to meet a statutory requirement (*Antiphon A.B.'s Application* [1984] R.P.C. 1 followed).

MASUDA'S APPLICATION [1987] R.P.C. 37, Patents Ct.

2776. Application—international application—translation not filed—whether late filing would be permitted

[Patents Act 1977 (c.37), s.17(3); Patents Rules 1982 (S.I. 1982 No. 714), rr.6(6), 100; Patent Co-operation Treaty, Arts. 20, 48.]

Agents in France instructed patent agents in the U.K. to deal with an international patent application designating the U.K. Priority was claimed from a French national application. The patent agents wrongly assumed that a translation had been filed. The Patent Office did not inform them that they had failed to provide the translation. The period for filing expired. The priority date was lost. The Comptroller refused to exercise his discretion to extend.

Held, on appeal to the Patents Court, that (1) there was no obligation on the Patent Office to notify applicants of outstanding requirements in international applications; (2) the applicants' failure to file the translation stemmed from an inadequate record-keeping system at the patent agents' office; (3) the discretion to allow late filing should not be exercised in this case.

APPLICATION DES GAZ's APPLICATION [1987] R.P.C. 297, Falconer J.

2777. Application—irregularity—whether discretion to rectify irregularity—filing of statement at Patents Office

[Patents Act 1977 (c.37), ss.7(2), 13(2); Patents Rules 1982 (S.I. 1982 No. 717), r.15(1), 100; European Patent Convention, arts. 62, 81, 91(2) (5).]

The two applications were filed concurrently with a third application containing a declaration of priority based on a respective earlier convention application filed in Japan. The inventor had assigned the inventions by one document. Documents were filed but a requisite statement under s.13(2) on form 7/77 had been filed in respect of only one of them. The other two applications were therefore taken to have been withdrawn. The Comptroller refused to allow the application to proceed. The applicants appealed to the Patents Court.

Held, dismissing the appeal, that there was no discretion to rectify the irregularity.

NIPPON PISTON RING CO.s APPLICATIONS [1987] R.P.C. 120, Patents Ct.

2778. Application—irregularity—whether discretion to rectify irregularity—request for substantive examination—form allegedly delivered to Patents Office—burden of proof

[Patents rules 1982 (S.I. 1982 No. 717), r.100.]

P was informed that his application had been treated as withdrawn because no request for substantive examination had been made within the prescribed period. P adduced no evidence that the form had been delivered to the Patent Office. P appealed to the Patents Court.

Held, that (1) the burden of proof was on P to establish that the form had been delivered; (2) there was no discretion to rectify the irregularity.

AOKI's APPLICATION [1987] R.P.C. 133, Patents Ct.

2779. Application—micro organism—whether an invention

[Ire.] [Patents Act 1964 (Ireland), s.2. Convention on the Unification of Certain Points of Substantive Law on Patents for Invention, art. 2(*b*); U.S. Patent Code.]

A sought to patent an invention "Improvements in or relating to cell lines." These were articles for use produced from raw materials occurring in nature by giving to these materials new forms, qualities and properties. The examiner objected that they were not inventions.

Held, that the cell lines were "manufactures" within the Act. The relevant distinction was not between living and inanimate but between products of nature and human made inventions.

N.R.D.C.'s IRISH APPLICATION [1986] F.S.R. 620, Irish Patents Office.

2780. Application—novelty—inventive step—amendment

[Patents Act 1977 (c.37), ss.1, 2, 3, 76.]

Applications related to package of nested articles leaving the mouth unobstructed. Objection was on the ground of lack of inventive step over prior art.

Held, that (1) the cited documents would not have led a man skilled in the art to carry out the claims. Lack of novelty was not made out; (2) the applicants should not specifically refer to plant pot bases since this infringed s.76(2)(*a*). Application granted.

WARD'S APPLICATIONS [1986] R.P.C. 50, Patent Office.

2781. Application—practice—confidentiality of documents—privilege

[Patents Act 1977 (c.37), s.13, 104; Patents Rules 1982, r.94, 103.]

K made an application alleging that he had the right to be described as inventor. The proprietors requested that K's exhibited letters be treated as confidential and be removed on the ground of privilege.

Held, ordering that *inter partes* letters relating to the U.K. and European applications be removed from the file, and letters including those relevant to the U.S. application be treated as confidential, that (1) there is no privilege in foreign applications once it was beyond the stage of a Patent Co-operation Treaty—privilege does not arise from the fiduciary duty; (2) joint privilege arose in the patent agent's letter written to K concerning the naming of inventors, however one joint holder could not claim it against the other joint holder; (3) the Comptroller would exercise his power to direct that confidentiality should be maintained between the patent agent and his client in respect of letters between them.

SONIC TAPE'S PATENT [1987] R.P.C. 251, Patent Office.

2782. Application—publication—withdrawal of application

[Patents Act 1977 (c.37), ss.14, 16, 19, 101, 123, 130; Patents Rules 1982 (S.I. 1982 No. 717), rr.28, 36.]

The applicants were at risk from December 5, 1985 that the Comptroller would determine that preparations for publication would be treated as complete. On January 6, 1986 the Patent Office wrote notifying them that preparations were treated as complete. On January 7, 1986, notice of withdrawal was filed at the Patent Office. The Patents Office and trial judge refused to prevent publication of the application.

Held, allowing the appeal, that (1) the application should not be published; (2) preparations for publication were completed where the specification was ready for an allocated printing contractor; (3) Rule 28 was *ultra vires*.

INTERA CORP.'S APPLICATION [1986] R.P.C. 45a, C.A.

2783. Application—publication—withdrawal of application

[Patents Act 1977 (c.37), ss.14, 16.]

A argued that preparations for publication had not been completed, when the printer had collected the folio, until the printer started keyboarding the papers. A further argued that the Comptroller had a discretion to stop publication.

Held, that (1) preparations for publication were complete when the folio was put ready for the printer; (2) the Comptroller had no discretion.

PEABODY INTERNATIONAL'S APPLICATION [1986] R.P.C. 521, Patent Appeal.

2784. Breach of confidence—confidential information used to make sausage skins in Spain—defendant importing and selling such sausage skins in U.K. See UNION CARBIDE CORP. *v.* NATURIN, §1669.

2785. Compulsory licence—ability to work—invention

[Patents Act 1977 (c.37), ss.48, 50.]

A sought compulsory licences under P's patents on the ground that the inventions were capable of being commercially worked but were not being so worked. The patents were concerned with dispensing a product from a container by means of a propellant gas. So that propellant was not wasted it was confined within the container by a flexible bag. The inventions had been used by R in America. The patentees had not used the patents in the U.K. but intended customers to import the pouches manufactured in Belgium in due course. There were no concrete plans. A indicated that they intended to use the system as operated by R. P agreed that R's system was of such poor quality that it would deter customers, and further that A had not demonstrated their ability to work the inventions.

Held, refusing the application, that A had failed to establish that they had the resources, including technical expertise to put the invention into practice.

ENVIRO SPRAY SYSTEM INC.'S PATENTS [1986] R.P.C. 147, Patent Office.

2786. Design—infringement—how infringement to be determined

[Registered Designs Act 1949 (c.88).]

Whether a design infringes one registered under the Registered Designs Act 1949 is to be determined by the eye, but by the eye of a customer interested in design.

SOMMER ALLIBERT (U.K.) *v.* FLAIR PLASTICS, *The Times*, June 6, 1987, C.A.

2787. Designs—rules

DESIGNS (AMENDMENT) RULES 1987 (No. 287) [45p], made under the Registered Designs Act 1949 (c.88), ss.36, 39(1); operative on March 24, 1987; revises rule 69 of S.I. 1984 No. 1989 as regards excluded days.

2788. European patent (U.K.)—restoration

[Patents Act 1977 (c.37), ss.25, 28, 77; Patents Rules 1982 (S.I. 1982 No. 717), rr.30, 39, 42, 100.]

The proprietor of a European Patent (U.K.) did not furnish an address for service. The European Patent Office gave his address as Germany but he had moved to France and did not receive the letter requesting an address for service. P filed through patent agents an application for restoration and sought an extension of time alleging an omission on the part of the Patent Office.

Held, that (1) P's foreign agent had no standing in post-grant proceedings. The letter from the Patent Office had properly been sent to the address given by the European Patent Office; (2) the Patent Office had not been guilty of any omission; (3) application dismissed.

DEFOREIT'S PATENT [1986] R.P.C. 142, Patent Office.

2789. Fees

PATENTS (FEES) RULES 1987 (No. 610) [£1·60], made under the Patents Act 1977 (c.37), s.123(1)(2)(3), Sched. 4, para. 14; operative on April 27, 1987 save for rules 1(2) and 3 which are operative on May 26, 1987; revoke and replace the provision for fees in S.I. 1986 No. 583.

PATENTS (FEES) (AMENDMENT) RULES 1987 (No. 753) [45p], made under the Patents Act 1977 (c.37), s.123(1)–(3), Sched. 4, para. 14; operative on April 27, 1987; replaces S.I. 1987 No. 10 which contained errors.

2790. Infringement—application for discovery of foreign patents. See PRACTICE, §2986.

2791. Infringement—defence based on breach of EEC Treaty on quantitative restrictions on imports—striking out

An application by a plaintiff in a patent infringement action to strike out paragraphs of the defence asserting that the plaintiff's claim was a breach of the provisions of the EEC Treaty on quantitative restrictions on imports failed as it could not be said that the paragraphs disclosed no reasonable defence.

D manufactured portable toilets in Italy and imported them into the U.K. P alleged that D was infringing a U.K. patent held by them in so doing. The articles were not patentable in Italy. D's defence alleged in paras. 5 to 8 that if relief was granted to P it would amount to a quantitative restriction on imports in breach of Arts. 30 and 34 of the EEC Treaty. D claimed that the relief was not justified under Art. 36 of the Treaty on the ground that the article patented was neither new nor novel. P applied to strike out those paragraphs of the defence on the ground that they disclosed no reasonable defence. P succeeded at first instance.

Held, allowing D's appeal, that there was an arguable case that P would not be entitled to the relief sought if D proved the articles in question were not new or novel. Accordingly, it could not be said that D's defence disclosed no reasonable defence. Whether or not P would be able to rely on the exception in Art. 36 for the protection of industrial and commercial property was a question of European law on which there was no direct authority. It was a question which should be referred to the European Court (*Centrafarm B.V.* v. *Sterling Drug Inc.* [1976] C.L.Y. 1194, *Hagen* v. *Fratelli D. and G. Moretti S.N.C.* [1980] C.L.Y. 1177, *Merck & Co. Inc.* v. *Stephar B.V.* [1982] C.L.Y. 1270 considered).

THETFORD CORPORATION *v.* FIAMMA SpA [1987] 1 FTLR 162, C.A.

2792. Infringement—enquiry as to damages—*res judicata*

The court decided in 1986 that one of D's chair lifts infringed P's patent but that the other did not. In a subsequent enquiry as to damages, P's executrix contended that both chairs were infringing and that D had deceived the court. The judge decided that the issue was *res judicata.* P's executrix appealed to the Court of Appeal.

Held, dismissing the appeal, that (1) P had not established deceit; (2) P could not now raise an allegation which he could with reasonable diligence have raised in an earlier action relating to the similar subject matter which had already been decided.

HARRISON *v.* PROJECT & DESIGN CO. (REDCAR) [1987] R.P.C. 151, C.A.

2793. Infringement—High Court and European Patent Office proceedings—stay of proceedings

[Patents Act 1977 (c.37), s.77(1); European Patent Convention, Arts. 2, 64, 99, 100, 138.]

P was granted a European patent. P issued proceedings in the U.K. High Court for infringement. D1 denied infringement and alleged invalidity. D2 later lodged notice of opposition at the European Patent Office seeking revocation. D1 then sought to stay the High Court proceedings pending determination of the European matter.

Held, that the European Patent Office was not an appropriate alternative forum because it could not determine the issue of infringement. Motion dismissed.

AMERSHAM INTERNATIONAL *v.* CORNING [1987] R.P.C. 53, Patents Ct.

2794. Infringement—practice—pleadings—cost

[Patents Designs and Trade Marks Act 1883 (c.57), s.29(5); Supreme Court of Judicature (Consolidation) Act 1925 (c.49), s.50(1); Patents Rules 1968; R.S.C., Ord. 21, r.3, Ord. 104, r.7.]

P alleged infringement of his patent relating to a mould release agent. A month before the date fixed for trial, two years after the writ, D sought to re-amend to allege prior use and invalidity. Falconer J. ordered that if P elected to discontinue within six weeks, P should pay D's taxed costs up to the date of D's original defence and D should pay P's thereafter. D appealed.

Held, that such an order was correct, unless D could show that he could not by reasonable diligence have apprised himself of the facts relevant to the issue of invalidity. Appeal dismissed.

WILLIAMSON *v.* MOLDLINE [1986] R.P.C. 556, C.A.

2795. Infringement—practice—pleadings—"Earth Closet" orders

In an action for infringement and counter-claim for revocation, D sought leave to amend to add a further item of prior use. P did not object to amendment but said that it should be subject to an order in the "Earth Closet" form, whereby if P elected to discontinue, their costs after the date of the amendment should be paid by D.

Held, that (1) P could not have been expected to know about the additional item. D had not been sufficiently diligent in their enquiries; (2) Leave to amend granted subject to "Earth Closet" order.

GILL *v.* CHIPMAN [1987] R.P.C. 209, Whitford J.

2796. Infringement—practice—pleadings—fair basis—striking out

[Patents Act 1949 (c.87), ss.1, 5, 69, 101; Paris Convention for the Protection of Industrial Property, Arts. A(1), A(2), A(3), D(3).]

P on July 21, 1977, filed in Japan an application for the grant of a patent for compounds containing "636". Grounds of opposition to "636" had earlier been filed by D. P then filed two U.K. applications citing "636" as its convention application. On July 22, 1977 D filed in the U.S. an application for compounds similar to "636". D had earlier obtained a European patent based on the U.S. filing. P sought revocation of D's U.S. patent and allged infringement. P sought to strike out part of D's pleadings on the ground that they contained immaterial averments. The trial judge held that they should not, and P appealed.

Held, that (1) D's allegation that "636" was not an application for protection for any invention was a proper allegation. The averment that "636" was not equivalent to a regular national filing was not unarguable; (2) that part of D's pleading which asserted the inaccuracy of the data for "636" should be struck out; (3) the averment that P had not made an initiatory step could be relevant and would be allowed to stand.

ISHIHARA SANGYO KAISHA *v.* DOW CHEMICAL CO. [1987] F.S.R. 137, C.A.

2797. Infringement—practice—preliminary point

[Patents Act 1977 (c.37), Scheds. 1, 4; R.S.C., Ord. 18, r.11; Ord. 33, r.3; Ord. 104, r.10.]

In infringement proceedings D alleged that the patent was obtained by false suggestion and further that the transitional provisions of the Patents Act 1977 did not impose liability where none existed before. P sought an order for trial of these issues as preliminary points.

Held, that no such order would be made. The questions would not be decisive of the action. Such an order would cause further delay and costs.

MASI A.G. *v.* COLOROLL [1986] R.P.C. 483, Patents Ct.

2798. Infringement—registered design—copyright

[Registered Designs Act 1949 (c.88), s.1(3); Copyright Act 1956 (c.74), s.4(4).]

P alleged that D had infringed his copyright in a drawing for a top of a plastic shower tray, and that the under-surface was an infringement of P's registered design for the under-surface.

Held, (1) the under-surface was not merely a method of construction. It had aesthetic appeal and was properly registrable; (2) the drawings in the patent specification were not the equivalent of the drawing in which P claimed copyright; (3) breach of copyright and design registration established.

GARDEX *v.* SORATA [1986] R.P.C. 623, Falconer J.

2799. Infringement—validity—dental anchoring pin—construction

[Patents Act 1949 (c.62), s.33.]

P were proprietors of a dental anchoring pin. They alleged that D's manufactured infringing dental pins designed by D3 and sold by D4.

Held, that (1) the trial judge had correctly found the patent valid and infringed; (2) the prior publication and prior use was not sufficient to establish anticipation; (3) the fact that D's pins comprised two parts fixed together, and P's specification referred to an article made in one piece, did not preclude from infringement. Appeal dismissed.

FAIRFAX (DENTAL) EQUIPMENT *v.* FILHOL (S. J.) [1986] R.P.C. 499, C.A.

2800. Licences of right—application to Comptroller to settle terms of licence

[Patents Act 1977 (c.37), s.46; Patents Rules 1982 (S.I. 1982 No. 717), r.63(1), 100.]

Prospective licensees of a new existing patent treated as endorsed licences of right filed an application for the Comptroller to settle the terms of licence. The patentees contended that the Comptroller had no jurisdiction to entertain the applications because there had been no attempt to reach agreement and because the applicants' statements in support did not set out fully the facts upon which the applicants relied. The hearing officer upheld the objection regarding the statements but refused to extend the time for P to file their counter-statement.

Held, dismissing the appeal, that the Comptroller had decided all points correctly.

ROUSSEL-UCLAF (CLEMENCE & LE MARTRET'S) PATENT [1987] R.P.C. 109, Patents Ct.

2801. Licences of right—confidentiality of documents

[Patents Act 1977 (c.37), ss.46, 118; Patents Rules 1982 (S.I. 1982 No. 717), r.94.]

P appealed from the Comptroller's decision withdrawing directions under the Patents Rules 1982, r.94 in respect of documents filed in an application by I.C.I. for settlement of terms of a licence of right under s.46(3). The Patentees had requested the comptroller to direct that the evidence filed in the proceedings be prevented from becoming open to public inspection. The hearing officer withdrew the prohibition except in respect of certain documents where the risk of disclosure being commercially harmful to the parties overrode the need for proceedings to be public.

Held, on appeal that, (1) not all documents disclosing material of commercial interest should be excluded; (2) evidence of royalties fixed with other licensees were not part of the comptrollers decision and confidentiality should be maintained; (3) information concerning royalties and prices supplied by a third party should be treated as confidential; (4) the decision on confidentiality should be given early enough for the party to withdraw in the light of the decision if he so desired.

DIAMOND SHAMROCK TECHNOLOGIES S.A.'s PATENT [1987] R.P.C. 91, Patents Ct.

2802. Licences of right—importation—direction

[Patents Act 1977 (c.37), ss.46, 48, 50, Sched. 1, para. 4.]

C's patent was a new existing patent and was treated as endorsed licenses of right. The applicants sought a licence including a right of importation from the U.S.A. at a price considerably lower than C's U.K. price. The Hearing Officer refused to exclude the clause. *Held,* on appeal, that (1) C would be unfairly prejudiced; (2) the discretion had been wrongly exercised; (3) licence to import was set aside.

CIBA-GEIGY A.G.'s PATENT [1986] R.P.C. 403, Patents Ct.

2803. Licences of right—importation—terms—drug

[Patents Act 1977 (c.37), ss.46, 48, 50, 55, 97, 99, 108, Sched. I; Patents Act 1949 (c.87), ss.35, 41; R.S.C., Ord. 104, r.14, Ord. 55, r.7.]

Application was made to the Comptroller to settle the terms of a licence to import Salbutamol, an asthma drug. The hearing officer settled terms. Both P and A then appealed to the High Court. Whitford J. held that A should not be allowed to import. The royalty should be a fixed price per kilo. The patentees' position as manufacturers should not be ignored. He further settled the terms of a licence to manufacture, providing *inter alia* that A should not be entitled to sub-contract manufacture of the final dosage form.

Held, on appeal by A that (1) The judge was to consider an appeal from the Comptroller *de novo.* (2) A could accept terms and operate a licence granted without prejudice to any appeal by him. (3) The position of the patentee was relevant. Importation was impermissible. Sub-contracting of manufacture was impermissible.

ALLEN & HANBURYS (SALBUTAMOL) PATENT [1987] R.P.C. 327, C.A.

2804. Licence of right—importation of patented drug—powers of Comptroller

[Patents Act 1977 (c.37), ss.46, 48, 50, Scheds. 2, 4; R.S.C., Ord. 53; E.E.C. Treaty, Arts. 30, 36, 177.]

B sought a licence of right in respect of P's patent for amoxycillin, to commence on August 20, 1985 for importing the drug. G sought a licence for A H's patented drug salbutamol.

The appeals from the Court of Appeal in respect of each case were heard together by the House of Lords.

Held, that (1) a licence settled by the Comptroller could not be backdated earlier than the date of his decision; (2) proceedings before the Comptroller could be commenced before the end of the sixteenth year; (3) unless the E.E.C. Treaty forbade it, the Comptroller had power to include terms prohibiting importation. The construction of Articles 30 and 36 must be referred to the European Court of Justice, for a ruling.

ALLEN & HANBURY *v.* GENERICS (U.K.) AND GIST BROCADES, BROCADES (GREAT BRITAIN); BEECHAM GROUP; COMPTROLLER GENERAL OF PATENTS [1986] R.P.C. 203, H.L.

2805. Licences of right—opposition—*locus standi*

[Patents Act 1949 (c.87), ss.35, 36; Patents Rules 1968 (S.I. 1968 No. 1389), r.106.]

G's 1970 patent was due to expire on October 26, 1986. It was extendible for four years. In February 1974, the patent was endorsed "licences of right" upon G's application. In May 1985 G applied to cancel the endorsement. When opposed by O, G argued that O had no *locus standi.*

Held, on appeal by O from the decision of the trial judge, that O had a real interest in the matter since he was the patentee of a similar process and possibly infringing G's patent.

GLAVERBEL'S PATENT [1987] F.S.R. 153, C.A.

2806. Licences of right—royalty—construction—settlement

[Patents Act 1977 (c.37), ss.46, 48, 50; Patents Act 1949 (c.87), s.41(2).]

The applicants sought a licence for naproxen, a drug which was a new existing patent and treated as endorsed licences of right. The applicants could not agree terms with the Patentees and sought to have them settled by the Comptroller. The patentees appealed to the Patents Court from the hearing officer's decision.

Held, that (1) the court must have regard to the provisions of the Patents Act 1977, ss.48(3) and 50, when settling terms; and the court must also consider whether the patentee was being reasonably remunerated; (2) the royalty should not be fixed to the selling price in this case; (3) the cases under the Patents Act 1949 were not definitive.

SYNTEX CORPORATION'S PATENT [1986] R.P.C. 585, Whitford J.

2807. Passing-off—shape of container—plastic lemon

[Trade Marks Act 1938 (c.22), s.11.]

P sold lemon juice since 1956 called JIF in a yellow plastic lemon-shaped container. D wished to market similar but larger plastic containers of lemon juice. P produced as evidence an independent survey report showing that housewives relied upon the shape and get up of P's lemon to identify it as JIF.

Held, that (1) passing off was established. The evidence showed that shoppers would be confused; (2) D must ensure that his goods did not mislead the public. He must take the market as he found it.

RECKITT AND COLMAN PRODUCTS *v.* BORDEN INC. (No. 3) [1987] F.S.R. 505, Walton J.

2808. Patent agents—rights of audience—taxation of costs. See PRACTICE, §2960.

2809. Patents—rules

PATENTS (AMENDMENT) RULES 1987 (No. 288) [£2·70], made under the Patents Act 1977 (c.37), ss.77(9), 78(8), 120(1), 123(1)–(3); operative on September 1, 1987 save for Rules 1, 8–12 and Rules 2 and 3, as provided in Rule 1(2), which are operative on March

24, 1987; bring into force ss.77(6) and 78(7) of the 1977 Act and amend S.I. 1981 No. 717 so as to prescribe relevant forms and fees.

2810. Privilege—patent agent—discovery—advice before commencement of proceedings

[Patents Act 1977 (c.37), s.104(1)(4).]

D claimed privilege from production to P of advice given by their patent agent prior to the commencement of proceedings. P possessed relevant patents.

Held, (1) a contemplated application for a patent was included within s.104(4) as a contemplated patent proceeding; (2) it is not sufficient for one person to fear without any reason that there could possibly be proceedings. The action must be "contemplated" as it plainly means. Discovery ordered.

ROCKWELL INTERNATIONAL *v.* SERCK INDUSTRIES [1987] R.P.C. 89, Falconer J.

2811. Procedure—appeal—whether rehearing

An appeal to the Patents Court from a decision of the Patent Office is a full rehearing. GENERICS (U.K.) *Re, The Times,* April 2, 1987, C.A.

2812. Restoration—failure to pay renewal fee—whether reasonable care

[Patents Act 1977 (c.37), s.38 Patents Rules 1982 (S.I. 1982 No. 717), r.100.]

B's patent lapsed on failure to pay the renewal fee. The six months grace period expired and application for restoration was filed, after the expiry of the one year period prescribed, but was allegedly because of the error, default or omission on the part of the Patent Office. The proprietors had at the time of the grant instructed the British patent agents to pay the renewal for the fifth year and an American firm to pay the sixth and subsequent years. The British patent agent did not receive the instructions. A schedule prepared by the American firm was sent by the proprietors but the British Patent agents did not regard it as an instruction to themselves to pay the fee. The application for restoration was filed when the proprietors learned that the renewal fee for the sixth year had not been accepted. The Patent Office did not refund the fee or issue a notification until after the last date for filing an application for registration had passed.

Held, that (1) B had shown reasonable care, but at the relevant time the matter was within their control; (2) the Patent Office had not been guilty of an omission within the rule.

BORG-WARNER CORP.'S PATENT [1986] R.P.C. 137, Patent Office.

2813. Revocation—office practice—obviousness—discovery

[Patents Rules 1982, r.103(3).]

Application was made for revocation of P's patent on the ground of obviousness. The patentees filed evidence of the grant of licences and of the numbers of patented couplings sold in previous years. Application was made for discovery of, *inter alia,* all documents relating to the design and specification and marketing of the goods. The patentees offered to provide audited accounts for the relevant period setting out the numbers of couplings of each model sold. The hearing officer refused to order the further discovery sought.

Held, on appeal, that (1) the licences must be disclosed in order that their exact terms be considered; (2) documents relating to the design and specification of the couplings must be disclosed; (3) the hearing officer had correctly exercised his discretion in refusing to order discovery of documents relating to marketing.

JOHN GUEST (SOUTHERN)'S PATENT [1987] R.P.C. 259, Whitford J.

2814. Revocation—prior publication—confidentiality of document—entitlement

[Patents Act 1977 (c.37), ss.2, 7, 37, 72.]

The patent in suit concerned net beds for hospital patients with bed sores. Application was made for revocation on the ground of lack of novelty and inventive step. Further the applicants for revocation sought to be joined as joint proprietors. The patentees and applicants were commercial partners freely exchanging ideas. Documents disclosed by the patentees in such circumstances were relied upon by the applicants.

Held, that (1) the letter and sketches were disclosed in confidence and were not a publication; (2) the applicants had not established on the evidence that they had shared in devising the invention. There was no implied contractual term. Applications refused.

JAMES INDUSTRIES' PATENT [1987] R.P.C. 235, Patent Office.

2815. Semiconductor products—protection of topography. See EUROPEAN COMMUNITIES, §1630.

PENSIONS AND SUPERANNUATION

2816. Abatement of benefit

PERSONAL AND OCCUPATIONAL PENSION SCHEMES (ABATEMENT OF BENEFIT) REGULATIONS 1987 (No. 1113) [£1·30], made under the Social Security Act 1975 (c.14), s.168(1), the Social Security Pensions Act 1975 (c.60), s.29(2A) and (2c) and the Social Security Act 1986 (c.50), ss.4 and 84(1); operative on January 4, 1988, as to arts. 1–3 and on April 6, 1988, as to arts. 4 and 5; prescribe the rate of the guaranteed minimum pension for the earner and the widow/widower respectively.

2817. Armed forces

NAVAL, MILITARY AND AIR FORCES ETC. (DISABLEMENT AND DEATH) SERVICE PENSIONS AMENDMENT ORDER 1987 (No. 165) [£1·90], made under the Social Security (Miscellaneous Provisions) Act 1977 (c.5), s.12(1); operative on April 6, 1987; amends S.I. 1983 No. 883 by increasing the maximum annual earnings which may be received by a disabled person while he is deemed to be unemployable for the purpose of receiving unemployability allowances.

2818. British Council and Commonwealth Institute Superannuation Act 1986—commencement

BRITISH COUNCIL AND COMMONWEALTH INSTITUTE SUPERANNUATION ACT 1986 (COMMENCEMENT No. 2) ORDER 1987 (No. 588 (C.14)) [45p], made under the British Council and Commonwealth Institute Superannuation Act 1986 (c.51), s.3(2); brings the 1986 Act into force on April 1, 1987 in relation to the Commonwealth Institute.

2819. Charitable association—employment of local authority officer—taking on pension liability—increase in prospective pension

[Local Government Superannuation Act 1953 (c.25), s.15; Pensions (Increase) Act 1971 (c.56), s.5(2); Pensions Increase (Local Authorities etc. Pensions Regulations 1974 (S.I. 1740), reg. 4(1).]

Where a charitable housing association takes on the burden of a local authority's former employee by entering into an "admission agreement", it becomes liable to the burden of joining the public sector pension regime, including any increase therein.

HERTFORDSHIRE COUNTY COUNCIL *v.* RETIREMENT LEASE HOUSING ASSOCIATION, *The Independent*, February 19, 1987, Hoffmann J.

2820. Children's pensions

SUPERANNUATION (CHILDREN'S PENSIONS) (EARNINGS LIMIT) ORDER 1987 (No, 209) [45p], made under the Judicial Pensions Act 1981 (c.20), s.21(5); operative on April 6, 1987; increases the level for emoluments to £1,178 a year in relation to children's pensions after a child reaches 16.

2821. Civil service scheme—overwork—whether industrial injury

[Principal Civil Service Pension Scheme 1974, s.11.]

A civil servant who has fallen ill through overwork is entitled to injury benefits as having suffered an industrial injury under s.11 of the Principal Civil Service Pension Scheme 1974.

R. *v.* MINISTER FOR THE CIVIL SERVICE, *ex p.* PETCH, *The Times*, November 27, 1987, Macpherson J.

2822. Company pension scheme—variation of scheme—alteration of rules—new holding company wishing to remove surplus funds for own use

IBL operated three pension schemes for its employees, each scheme being governed by its own trust deeds and rules, which defined "the company" whose employees could belong to the scheme as I.B.L. The deeds could be varied provided this did not alter the main purpose of the Fund, which was to provide retirement pensions to members. Management of the schemes was entrusted to a committee. Two of the schemes provided for variation by the company by deed, and that committee should concur in executing any such deed, and also for the admission of the other companies to the scheme and for limited substitution of I.B.L. as "the company". In anticipation of a takeover by H, the deeds were amended to close the scheme to new entrants in that event. H did acquire I.B.L. and shortly afterwards agreed to sell it to E while retaining the surplus in the funds for itself, if possible. H thus proposed that the schemes not be sold to E, that H be substituted as "the company", that employee members be transferred to a new scheme set up by E and partly funded by H, that H would make provision for other members and retain the balance of £70m for its own use or for is own employees.

H requested the committee to execute deeds to that effect and the committee sought the determination of the court as to whether they were at liberty or bound to do this.

Held, that (1) to avoid hindering amendments required by the exigencies of commercial life, they should be tested as against the situation at the time of the alteration, and not at the time of the schemes' inception (*Thellusson* v. *Viscount Valentia* [1907] 2 Ch. 1 considered); (2) on a proper construction of the rules the committee had a discretion whether or not to execute deeds for proper amendments; (3) the power of substitution of "the company" depended on the circumstances in which it could be exercised, and the validity of its exercise depended on the purpose. Since H would have no further connection in the scheme, alteration to make H "the company" would be *ultra vires.* Further, the substition had to be necessary or expedient for preservation of the scheme, which this substiution was not; (4) however, there being no entrenchment against future amendment and since a fetter on the committee's power as fiduciaries would be ineffective the committee were at liberty, but not bound, to execute the deeds (*Will's Trust Deeds* [1963] C.L.Y. 2690 applied).

COURAGE GROUP'S PENSION SCHEMES, *Re;* RYAN *v.* IMPERIAL BREWING AND LEISURE [1987] 1 All E.R. 528, Millett J.

2823. Consequential provisions

PERSONAL AND OCCUPATIONAL PENSION SCHEMES (CONSEQUENTIAL PROVISIONS) REGULATIONS 1987 (No. 1114) [£1·60], made under the Social Security Act 1973 (c.38), ss.66(7) and 67(4), the Social Security Act 1975 (c.14), s.168(1) and the Social Security Pensions Act 1975 (c.60), ss.31(1)–(5), 32(2), 38(1), 39(1), 41B(3), 41C(7), 43(4), 45(1), 51, 52 and 66(4); operative on July 27, 1987, as to arts. 1, 2, 4(1), (14) and (24), 7(1) and (2)(*a*), on January 4, 1988, as to arts. 4(2), (6), (10), (15) and (25), and 7(2)(*b*), and on April 6, 1988, as to the remainder; make amendments to specified regulations.

2824. Contracting-out

CONTRACTING-OUT (TRANSFER) AMENDMENT REGULATIONS 1987 (No. 1099) [£1·60], made under the Social Security Act 1975 (c.14), s.168(1) and the Social Security Pensions Act 1975 (c.60), ss.38(1)–(1c) and 62(4); oprative on April 6, 1988 (in part) and on July 27, 1987 (in part); amend S.I. 1985 No. 1323.

CONTRACTING-OUT (WIDOWERS' GUARANTEED MINIMUM PENSIONS) REGULATIONS 1987 (No. 1100) [85p], made under the Social Security Act 1975, s.168(1) and Sched. 20, and the Social Security Pensions Act 1975, s.36(7A), and the Social Security Act 1986 (c.50), ss.9(6) and 84(1); operative on April 6, 1988; provide for widowers' pensions.

MONEY PURCHASE CONTRACTED-OUT SCHEMES REGULATIONS 1987 (No. 1101) [£1·30], made under the Social Security Act 1975, s.168(1) and Sched. 20, the Social Security Pensions Act 1975, ss.30(1C) and 32(2D) and the Social Security Act 1986, ss.2 and 84(1); operative on April 6, 1988; provide for the way in which the resources of a money purchase contracted-out occupational pension scheme must be invested.

2825. Firemen's pension scheme. See FIRE SERVICE, §1793.

2826. Incentive payments

PERSONAL AND OCCUPATIONAL PENSION SCHEMES (INCENTIVE PAYMENTS) REGULATIONS 1987 (No. 1115) [£1·30], made under the Social Security Act 1986 (c.50), ss.3(2), 7(1)–(3), (6), (7) and 14 and 84(1); operative on January 4, 1988, as to arts. 1 and 2, and on April 6, 1988 as to the remainder; provide for the treatment of additional payments under s.7 of the 1986 Act.

2827. Judicial offices

SUPERANNUATION (JUDICIAL OFFICES) (AGGREGATION OF SERVICE) RULES 1987 (No. 376) [80p], made under the Superannuation Act 1965 (c.74), s.38; operative on April 1, 1987; provides for the aggregation of service of persons who have held more than one judicial office for the purpose of determining superannuation benefits.

2828. Judicial pensions

JUDICIAL PENSIONS (PRESERVATION OF BENEFITS) ORDER 1987 (No. 374) [£1·40], made under the Social Security Act 1973 (c.38), s.65; operative on April 1, 1987; consolidates S.I. 1977 No. 717 as amended.

JUDICIAL PENSIONS (REQUISITE BENEFITS) ORDER 1987 (No. 373) [£1·60], made under the Social Security Act 1973, s.65; operative on April 1, 1987; makes provision for certain judicial pensions.

JUDICIAL PENSIONS (WIDOWS' AND CHILDREN'S BENEFITS) REGULATIONS 1987 (No. 375) [£1·60], made under the Judicial Pensions Act 1981 (c.20), s.23; operative on April 1, 1987; provide for the contributions to be made by men who are holders of certain judicial offices toward pensions for widows and children.

2829. Local government

LOCAL GOVERNMENT SUPERANNUATION (MISCELLANEOUS PROVISIONS) REGULATIONS 1987 (No. 293) [£2·70], operative on April 1, 1987; make provision in relation to superannuation for employees of public transport and airport companies, gratuities, and employees who work less than a full week or year.

2830. Modification of enactments

PERSONAL AND OCCUPATIONAL PENSION SCHEMES (MODIFICATION OF ENACTMENTS) REGULATIONS 1987 (No. 1116) [£1·60], made under the Social Security Act 1986 (c.50), ss.17(1) and 84(1); operative on April 6, 1988, as to art. 5 and Sched. 6, and on July 27, 1987, as to the remainder; make certain provisions of the Social Security Act 1973 and the Social Security Pensions Act 1975 apply to personal pension schemes.

2831. National Health Service

NATIONAL HEALTH SERVICE (SUPERANNUATION) AMENDMENT REGULATIONS 1987 (No. 2218) [£2·60], made under the Superannuation Act 1972 (c.11), ss.10(1)(2)(3), 12(1)(2), Sched. 3, paras. 3, 6. 8, 13; operative on January 29, 1988; amend S.I. 1980 No. 362.

2832. Occupational schemes

OCCUPATIONAL PENSION SCHEMES (ADDITIONAL VOLUNTARY CONTRIBUTIONS) REGULATIONS 1987 (No. 1749) [£1·60], made under the Finance Act 1970 (c.24), Sched. 5, para. 10; operative on October 26, 1987; makes provision in relation to relief for additional voluntary contributions by employees to occupational pension schemes.

OCCUPATIONAL PENSION SCHEMES (AUDITORS) REGULATIONS 1987 (No. 1102) [85p], made under the Social Security Act 1975 (c.14), s.168(1) and Sched. 20, the Social Security Pensions Act 1975 (c.60), s.56P and the Social Security Act 1986 (c.50), ss.54(1) and 84(1); operative on July 27, 1987; make provision concerning the auditors of occupational pension schemes.

OCCUPATIONAL PENSION SCHEMES (CONTRACTED-OUT PROTECTED RIGHTS PREMIUMS) REGULATIONS 1987 (No. 1103) [£1·30], made under the Social Security Act 1975, s.168(1) and the Social Security Pensions Act 1975, ss.44ZA(4), (6), (7), (9), and (13) and 52; operative on April 6, 1988; provides for contracted-out protected rights premiums.

OCCUPATIONAL PENSION SCHEMES (CONTRACTING-OUT) AMENDMENT REGULATIONS 1987 (No. 1104) [85p], made under the Social Security Act 1975, s.168(1) and the Social Security Pensions Act 1975, ss.31(5) and 52 and Sched. 2, para. 9; operative on July 27, 1987; amend S.I. 1984 No. 380.

OCCUPATIONAL PENSION SCHEMES (DISCLOSURE OF INFORMATION) (AMENDMENT) REGULATIONS 1987 (No. 1105) [85p], made under the Social Security Act 1975, s.168(1) and the Social Security Pensions Act 1975, s.56A(1) and (3); operative on July 27, 1987; amend S.I. 1986 No. 1046.

OCCUPATIONAL PENSION SCHEMES (MAXIMUM RATE LUMP SUM) REGULATIONS 1987 (No. 1513) [85p], made under the Finance (No. 2) Act 1987 (c.51), Sched. 3, para. 20(4); operative on August 28, 1987; provide for the determination of the amount of a "maximum rate lump sum."

OCCUPATIONAL PENSION SCHEMES (QUALIFYING SERVICE–CONSEQUENTIAL AND OTHER PROVISIONS) REGULATIONS 1987 (No. 1106) [85p], made under the Social Security Act 1973 (c.38), ss.64(1A)(*a*) and 99(1) and (3), and Sched. 16, paras. 9(2), (3), 21, 22 and 26; the Social Security Act 1975, s.168(1) and Sched. 20; and the Social Security Pensions Act 1975, ss.43(4) and 52C(4) and (5); operative on April 6, 1988; make provision concerning members of occupational pension schemes and the benefit of "preservation requirements" as set out in the 1973 Act.

OCCUPATIONAL PENSION SCHEMES (TRANSFER VALUES) AMENDMENT REGULATIONS 1987 (No. 1107) [85p], made under the Social Security Act 1975, s.168(1), and the Social Security Pensions Act 1975, Sched. 1A, paras. 12 (2A), (2B), 13 and 14; operative on July 27, 1987, as to arts. 1 and 2(5) and on April 6, 1988, as to the remainder; amend S.I. 1985 No. 1931.

OCCUPATIONAL PENSIONS (REVALUATION) ORDER 1987 (No. 1981) [45p], made under the Social Security Pensions Act 1975 (c.60), s.52A(1); operative on January 1, 1988; specifies the appropriate revaluation percentage for each of the revaluation periods set out in the Schedule.

2833. Pension scheme—strike—contributory earnings related scheme—whether period of strike affected benefits

Members of a contributory earnings related pension scheme who went on strike were not entitled to have the period when they were on strike taken into account in calculating their pensions.

Miners employed by the National Coal Board went on strike for a long period. They were members of the Mineworkers Pension Scheme which was a contributory earnings related scheme under which pensions and other benefits were calculated by reference to average earnings over a period immediately preceding termination of employment and to the member's period of contributing service. In the strike most miners ceased to work for over a year, but they were not dismissed. They remained in regular full time employment but neither performed any services nor paid any contributions to the pension scheme.

The trustees of the scheme issued a summons to determine whether or not the period of the strike and the non-contribution should be taken into account in calculating the pensions.

Held, that on the proper construction of the rules of the scheme "contributing service" was a period of "eligible employment" during which contributions were made by or on behalf of a member or were deemed to have been so made. The period of the strike should not be taken into account in calculating a striking miner's pension.

This view was reinforced by the fact that a very large sum had been lost to the fund by the failure of striking miners to pay contributions during a period when they were in breach of their contractual obligations, which could only be made up by a deficiency contribution by the board which would operate unfairly on those members who had made full contributions. In any event since a pension under a contributory scheme was a form of deferred remuneration, it was inappropriate that it should be increased in respect of a period during which a member was not performing any service under his contract of employment and was not entitled to any earnings therefor.

COWAN *v.* CHARLESWORTH [1987] I.C.R. 288, Vinelott J.

2834. Pensions increased

PENSIONS INCREASE (REVIEW) ORDER 1987 (No. 130) [80p], made under the Social Security Pensions Act 1975 (c.60), s.59(1) (2) (5); operative on April 6, 1987; provides for an increase in public service pensions.

2835. Personal injuries

PERSONAL INJURIES (CIVILIANS) AMENDMENT SCHEME 1987 (No. 191) [£1·40], made under the Personal Injuries (Emergency Provisions) Act 1939 (c.82), ss.1, 2; operative on April 6, 1987; amends S.I. 1983 No. 686 by increasing pension rates.

2836. Personal schemes

PERSONAL PENSION SCHEMES (APPROPRIATE SCHEMES) REGULATIONS 1987 (No. 1109) [£2·60], made under the Social Security Act 1986 (c.50), ss.1(1), (2), (4), (5), (9)–(11), 2(1), (2) and (5), 3(1)(*b*), 84(1) and 89(1); operative on July 27, 1987, as to arts. 1–11, 19, 20, and on January 4, 1988, as to arts. 12–18; make provision concerning "appropriate schemes."

PERSONAL PENSION SCHEMES (DISCLOSURE OF INFORMATION) REGULATIONS 1987 (No. 1110) [£1·90], made under the Social Security Act 1975 (c.15), s.168(1) and Sched. 20, and the Social Security Pensions Act 1975 (c.60), s.56A(1) and (3); operative on July 27, 1987; specify the information that is to be made available to certain persons by the trustees or managers of personal pension schemes.

PERSONAL PENSION SCHEMES (DEFERMENT OF COMMENCEMENT) REGULATIONS 1987 (No. 1933) [45p], made under the Social Security Act 1986 (c.50), ss.1(1)–(5), (9)–(11), 2(1), (2) and (5), 3(1)(*b*) and (5), 12(1) and 84(1); operative on December 15, 1987; revoke S.I. 1987 No. 1109.

PERSONAL PENSION SCHEMES (PERSONAL PENSION PROTECTED RIGHTS PREMIUMS) REGULATIONS 1987 (No. 1111) [£1·30], made under the Social Security Act 1975, s.168(1) and Sched. 20, the Social Security Pensions Act 1975, s.52 and Sched. 2, para. 6 and the Social Security Act 1986, ss.5(4), (7), (8), (10) and (14) and 84(1); operative on January 4, 1988; make provisions relating to personal pension protected rights premiums.

PERSONAL PENSION SCHEMES (PROVISIONAL APPROVAL) REGULATIONS 1987 (No. 1765) [85p], made under the Finance (No. 2) Act 1987 (c.51), s.56(2); operative on October 29, 1987; makes provision for the approval of personal pension schemes by the Commissioners of Inland Revenue.

PERSONAL PENSION SCHEMES (TRANSFER VALUES) REGULATIONS 1987 (No. 1112) [85p], made under the Social Security Act 1975, s.168(1) and Sched. 20, and the

Social Security Pensions Act 1975, Sched. 1A, paras. 13 and 14; operative on July 27, 1987; make provision in relation to personal pension schemes for the calculation and verification of cash equivalents.

2837. Pilot's national pension fund. See SHIPPING AND MARINE INSURANCE, §3419.

2838. Police

POLICE PENSIONS (LUMP SUM PAYMENTS TO WIDOWS) REGULATIONS 1987 (No. 1462) [45p], made under The Police Pensions Act 1976 (c.35), ss.1, 3 and 5; operative on December 7, 1987; provide for the payment of a gratuity of £10 in the case of a policeman's widow in receipt of a discretionary increase in her pension if she is not already so entitled.

POLICE PENSIONS (PURCHASE OF INCREASED BENEFITS) REGULATIONS 1987 (No. 2215) [£1·60], made under the Police Pensions Act 1976 (c.35), ss.1, 3, 4; operative on February 1, 1988; provides for the purchase of increased benefits.

POLICE PENSIONS REGULATIONS 1987 (No. 257) [£8·90], made under the Police Pensions Act 1976 (c.35), ss.1–8; operative on April 1, 1987; consolidate S.I. 1973 No. 428, as amended, and make provision for police pensions.

POLICE PENSIONS (SUPPLEMENTARY PROVISIONS) REGULATIONS 1987 (No. 256) [£2·20], made under the Police Pensions Act 1976, ss.1–8; operative on April 1, 1987; supplement S.I. 1987 No. 257.

POLICE PENSIONS (WAR SERVICE) (TRANSFEREES) (AMENDMENT) REGULATIONS 1987 (No. 1907) [45p], made under the Police Pensions Act 1976 (c.35), ss.1, 3, 4; operative on December 21, 1987; amend S.I. 1985 No. 2029.

ROYAL IRISH CONSTABULARY (LUMP SUM PAYMENTS TO WIDOWS) REGULATIONS 1987 (No. 1461) [45p], made under the Royal Irish Constabulary (Widows' Pensions) Act 1954 (c.17), s.1; operative on December 7, 1987; provide for the payment of £10 to a widow in receipt of an allowance on pension under S.I. 1971 No. 1469 if she is not already entitled thereto.

2839. Protected rights

PERSONAL AND OCCUPATIONAL PENSION SCHEMES (PROTECTED RIGHTS) REGULATIONS 1987 (No. 1117) [£1·90], made under the Social Security Act 1986 (c.50), ss.14, 84(1), Sched. 1, paras. 6, 7(2)–(5), 9(1)(*a*), (2)–(4), and (7)–(9); operative on July 27, 1987 (in part) and on April 6, 1988 (in part); prescribe the manner of calculation and verification of protected rights mentioned in Sched. 1, para. 7(2) of the 1986 Act.

PROTECTED RIGHTS (TRANSFER PAYMENT) REGULATIONS 1987 (No. 1118) [£1·30], made under the Social Security Act 1986, ss.2, 17(1)(*b*) and 84(1); operative on July 27, 1987 (in part) and on April 6, 1988 (in part); provide for the protected rights of a member of a scheme which is or was an appropriate personal pension scheme or a money purchase contracted-out scheme to be given effect to by the making of a transfer payment.

2840. Social Security—contributions—Class 1

SOCIAL SECURITY (CLASS 1 CONTRIBUTIONS–CONTRACTED-OUT PERCENTAGES) ORDER 1987 (No. 656) [45p], made under the Social Security Pensions Act 1975 (c.60), s.28(4)(7); operative on April 6, 1988; decreases the contracted-out percentages to be deducted from the normal percentage for both primary and secondary Class 1 contributions.

2841. State scheme premiums

STATE SCHEME PREMIUMS (ACTUARIAL TABLES) REGULATIONS 1987 (No. 657) [£2·90], made under the Social Security Act 1975 (c.14), s.168(1), Sched. 20, the Social Security Pensions Act 1975 (c.60), ss.44(7), 44ZA(14), 44A(3), 45(4), Sched. 2, para. 6 and the Social Security Act 1986 (c.50), ss.5(15), 16(1), 84(1); operative on April 6, 1988; prescribe tables in accordance with which the Secretary of State is required to make calculations in relation to, and for the purpose of determining the amount of, state scheme premiums.

STATE SCHEME PREMIUMS (ACTUARIAL TABLES—TRANSITIONAL PROVISIONS) REGULATIONS 1987 (No. 658) [£1·60], made under the Social Security Act 1986 (c.50), ss.5(15), 16(1), 84(1); operative on January 4, 1988; prescribe tables for use until April 6, 1988 in accordance with which calculations in relation to personal pension protected rights premiums must be made.

2842. Superannuation—local authority—concurrent employments—sequential employments. See SEVERN TRENT WATER AUTHORITY *v.* CROSS, §2368.

2843. Superannuation scheme—condition or requirement with which fewer women can comply—whether sex discrimination. See TURNER *v.* LABOUR PARTY AND THE LABOUR PARTY SUPERANNUATION SOCIETY, §1374.

2844. Voluntary contributions

PENSION SCHEMES (VOLUNTARY CONTRIBUTIONS REQUIREMENTS AND VOLUNTARY AND COMPULSORY MEMBERSHIP) REGULATIONS 1987 (No. 1108) [85p], made under the Social Security Act 1986 (c.50), ss.12(1), 15(1) and 84(1); operative on January 4, 1988 (for the purposes of personal pension schemes) and on April 6, 1988 (for the purposes of occupational pension schemes); provide for voluntary contributions.

2845. War pensions

WAR PENSIONS (MERCANTILE MARINE) (AMENDMENT) SCHEME 1987 (No. 585) [45p], made under the Pensions (Navy, Army, Air Force and Mercantile Marine) Act 1939 (c.83), s.7 amended by the Pensions (Mercantile Marine) Act 1942 (c.26); operative on April 6, 1987; removes provision for the payment of funeral grants from S.I. 1964 No. 2058.

PETROLEUM

2846. Foreign fields

FOREIGN FIELDS (SPECIFICATION) (No. 1) ORDER 1987 (No. 545) [80p], made under the Oil Taxation Act 1983 (c.56), ss.9(5) and 12(2); specifies parts of the continental shelf under the North Sea subject to Norwegian jurisdiction as foreign fields for the purposes of the 1983 Act.

2847. On-shore drilling—rights over land—compulsory acquisition—compensation

[Petroleum (Production) Act 1934 (c.36), s.3; Mines (Working Facilities and Support) Act 1966 (c.4), ss.1, 3(1), (2), 5(2), 8(2).]

It was unreasonable for the land-owner to demand production-related payments for the necessary acquisitions since that would amount to obtaining a share in the benefit although the land-owner had no proprietary rights in any oil and took no risk in the venture. Compensatory payments for loss and damage plus an allowance for the compulsory nature of the acquisition were the proper method.

B.P. PETROLEUM DEVELOPMENT *v.* RYDER, *The Times*, June 27, 1987, Peter Gibson J.

2848. Petroleum Act 1987 (c.12)

This Act makes provision in respect of the abandonment of offshore installations and submarine pipelines and in respect of safety zones around offshore installations. The Act amends the Petroleum (Production) Act 1934 and maker provision in respect of licences under that Act. The law relating to pipelines is amended and ss.34–39 of the Petroleum and Submarine Pipelines Act 1975 are repealed.

The Act received the Royal Assent on April 9, 1987, and comes into force two months from that date (except ss.17, 18, 21–24, Scheds. 1 and 2, and the repeals of s.21 and in s.27 of the Oil and Gas (Enterprises) Act 1982, which will come into force on a day to be appointed by the Secretary of State).

The Act extends to Northern Ireland (except ss.25–27).

2849. Petroleum Act 1987—commencement

PETROLEUM ACT 1987 (COMMENCEMENT No. 1) ORDER 1987 (No. 820 (c.22)) [45p], made under the Petroleum Act 1987 (c.12), s.31(2); brings into force on June 30, 1987, ss.17 and 18 and Scheds. 1 and 2.

PETROLEUM ACT 1987 (COMMENCEMENT No. 2) ORDER 1987 (No. 1330 (C.43)) [45p], made under the Petroleum Act 1987, s.31(2); brings into force on September 1, 1987, ss.21–24, and Sched. 3 (part—repeals of s.21 and in s.27 of the Oil and Gas (Enterprise) Act 1982 (c.23)).

2850. Petroleum revenue tax—expenditure allowance—whether taxpayer entitled to supplement. See MOBIL NORTH SEA *v.* I.R.C., §3226.

2851. Petroleum revenue tax—nomination scheme for disposals and appropriations. See REVENUE AND FINANCE, §3225.

POLICE

2852. Annual Report

The Report of Her Majesty's Chief Inspector of Constabulary for the year 1986 has been published. It is available from H.M.S.O. (ISBN 0 10 203288 2) [£8·50].

2853. Assistance to one force by another—payment for assistance

[Police Act 1964 (c.48), s.14(4).]

Interest is not payable on sums paid by one police authority to another for assistance (*Swift & Co.* v. *Board of Trade* [1925] A.C. 520, *Newport Borough Council* v. *Monmouthshire County Council* [1947] C.L.Y. 5811 considered).

R. *v.* SECRETARY OF STATE FOR THE HOME DEPARTMENT *ex p.* DEVON AND CORNWALL POLICE AUTHORITY, *The Times,* March 16, 1987, D.C.

2854. Cadets

POLICE CADETS (AMENDMENT) REGULATIONS 1987 (No. 1754) [45p], made under the Police Act 1964 (c.48), s.35; operative on November 16, 1987; amend S.I. 1979 No. 1727 so as to increase the pay for police cadets.

POLICE CADETS (PENSIONS) (AMENDMENT) REGULATIONS 1987 (No. 157) [45p], made under the Police Act 1964 s.35 as extended by the Superannuation (Miscellaneous Provisions) Act 1967 (c.28), s.13 and the Superannuation Act 1972 (c.11), ss.12, 15; operative on March 17, 1987; makes provision for the payment of a special pension to the beneficiary of a police cadet who dies in the execution of his duty.

2855. Detention of child involved in criminal offences—application for release—whether police should attend hearing and give evidence. See R. *v.* BRISTOL JUSTICE, *ex p.* BROOME, §2500.

2856. Disciplinary proceedings—whether rules of natural justice breached. See R. *v.* CHIEF CONSTABLE OF SOUTH WALES, *ex p.* THORNHILL, §34.

2857. Duty of police—duty of care owed to victims of crime—failure to apprehend criminals

[Police Act 1964 (c.48), s.48(1).]

The police do not owe a general duty of care, in respect of their failure to apprehend a violent criminal, to all possible victims, and no action can be brought against them in respect thereof.

Between 1969 and 1980 S committed 13 murders and 8 attempted murders of unaccompanied women. The plaintiff was the mother and administratrix of his last victim, and brought an action under s.48(1) of the Police Act 1964 claiming damages for negligence against the Chief Constable in whose area most of the attacks occurred. She contended that it was the duty of the police to exercise all reasonable care to catch the criminal and that they had been in breach of their duty in failing to detect him when they could and should have done in the circumstances. The Chief Constable applied to strike out the claim as disclosing no cause of action under R.S.C., Ord. 18, r.19. The judge held that the police owed no duty of care to a member of the public in respect of an attack on him made by another member of the public.

Held, dismissing the plaintiff's appeal, that in the absence of any special relationship between the police and a criminal arising out of the fact that the criminal was in police custody or had escaped from it, the general duty owed by the police to suppress crime did not give rise to a duty owed to individual members of the public in respect of damage caused to them by a criminal whom the police had failed to apprehend where it had been possible to do so. On the facts there was no special relationship between the police and S since he had neither been in police custody nor escaped from it. The claim had been properly struck out (dicta of Lord Wilberforce in *Anns* v. *Merton London Borough Council* [1977] C.L.Y. 2030, of Lord Wilberforce and of Lord Edmund-Davies in *McLoughlin* v. *O'Brian* [1982] C.L.Y. 2153, and of Lord Keith in *Governors of the Peabody Donation Fund* v. *Sir Lindsay Parkinson & Co.* [1984] C.L.Y. 2298 applied; *Home Office* v. *Dorset Yacht Co.* [1970] C.L.Y. 1849 distinguished; *Smith* v. *Leurs* (1945) 70 C.L.R. 256 and *R.* v. *Commissioner of Police for the Metropolis, ex p. Blackburn* [1968] C.L.Y. 1703 considered).

HILL *v.* CHIEF CONSTABLE OF WEST YORKSHIRE [1987] 1 All E.R. 1173, C.A.

2858. Home Office research programme. See CRIMINAL LAW, §786.

2859. Injury benefit

POLICE CADETS (INJURY BENEFIT) REGULATIONS 1987 (No. 158) [45p], made under the Police Act 1964 (c.48), s.35 as extended by the Superannuation (Miscellaneous Provisions) Act 1967 (c.28), s.13 and the Superannuation Act 1972 (c.11), ss.12, 15; operative on March 17, 1987; make provision for enhanced benefits in the case of a police cadet's death or total disablement resulting from an injury incurred in the execution of his duty.

POLICE CADETS (INJURY BENEFIT) (AMENDMENT) REGULATIONS 1987 (No. 342) [45p], made under the Police Act 1964, s.35; operative on March 17, 1987; amend S.I. 1987 No. 158 so as to correct a number of errors.

POLICE (INJURY BENEFIT), REGULATIONS 1987 (No. 156) [£1·40], made under the Police Pensions Act 1976 (c.35), ss.1, 3, 4, 6; operative on March 17, 1987; makes provision for enhanced benefits in the case of a policeman's death or total disablement resulting from an injury incurred in the execution of his duty.

POLICE (INJURY BENEFIT) (AMENDMENT) REGULATIONS 1987 (No. 341) [80p], made under the Police Pensions Act 1976, ss.1, 3, 4, 6; operative on March 17, 1987; amend S.I. 1987 No. 156 so as to correct a number of errors.

SPECIAL CONSTABLES (INJURY BENEFIT) REGULATIONS 1987 (No. 159) [45p], made under the Police Act 1964 (c.48), s.34; operative on March 17, 1987; make provision for enhanced benefits in the case of a special constable's death or total disablement arising from an injury incurred in the execution of his duty.

SPECIAL CONSTABLES (INJURY BENEFIT) (AMENDMENT) REGULATIONS 1987 (No. 343) [45p], made under the Police Act 1964, s.34; operative on March 17, 1987; amend S.I. 1987 No. 159 so as to correct a number of errors.

2860. Ministry of Defence Police Act 1987 (c.4)

This Act makes fresh provision for the Ministry of Defence Police.

The Act received the Royal Assent on March 5, 1987.

2861. Pay

POLICE (AMENDMENT) REGULATIONS 1987 (No. 1753) [85p], made under the Police Act 1964 (c.48), s.33; operative on November 16, 1987; amends S.I. 1979 No. 1470 and S.I. 1987 No. 851 in relation to police pay and conditions of employment.

2862. Police complaints procedure

The Home Office has published a study entitled *The Police Complaints Procedure: A Survey of Complainants' Views.* Home Office Research Study No. 93 is available from H.M.S.O. (ISBN 0 11 340853 6) [£6·30.]

2863. Police federation

POLICE FEDERATION (AMENDMENT) REGULATIONS 1987 (No. 1062) [45p], made under the Police Act 1964 (c.48), s.44; operative on August 1, 1987; amend S.I. 1969 No. 1787 in relation to legal expenses incurred by a member of the Federation.

2864. Police pensions. See PENSIONS AND SUPERANNUATION, §2838.

2864a. Powers—entry and search of premises. See KYNASTON *v.* D.P.P.; HERON (JOSEPH) *v.* D.P.P.; HERON (TRACEY) *v.* D.P.P., §706.

2865. Powers—search of premises—whether inspector's authorisation "in writing"—whether search "upon arrest". See R. *v.* BADHAM, §707.

2866. Probationer—dismissal—natural justice. See ADMINISTRATIVE LAW, §40.

2867. Regulations

POLICE REGULATIONS 1987 (No. 851) [£5·00] made under the Police Act 1964 (c.48), s.33; operative on June 15, 1987; consolidate with amendments S.I. 1979 No. 1470, as amended.

2868. Riot equipment—power to supply

[Police Act 1964 (c.48), s.41.]

S.41 of the Police Act 1964 empowers the Home Secretary to issue Police forces with riot equipment without the consent of Police Authorities.

R. *v.* SECRETARY OF STATE FOR THE HOME DEPARTMENT, *ex p.* NORTHUMBRIA POLICE AUTHORITY, *The Times,* November 19, 1987, C.A.

2869. Special police services—police attending inside a football ground—payment

[Police Act 1964 (c.48), s.15(1).]

The regular provision of police officers inside a club's grounds for football matches, is a "special police service" for which the police authority can properly charge.

Police officers attended the premises of Sheffield football club on many occasions during the season, and many of them were on duty inside the ground. The Chief Constable billed the club for these "special police services"; the club refused to pay contending that the police attendance did not contribute "special services." Boreham J. found that the attendances did not constitute "special services" but that the services had at all times been requested by the club and that they must pay.

Held, dismissing the appeal, that the provision of officers to attend regularly inside a club's grounds constituted the provision of "special police services" (*Glasbrook Brothers* v. *Glamorgan County Council* [1925] A.C. 270 considered).

HARRIS *v.* SHEFFIELD UNITED FOOTBALL CLUB [1987] 3 W.L.R. 305, C.A.

2870. Statistics—operation of police powers under the Police and Criminal Evidence Act 1984. See CRIMINAL LAW, §833.

2871. Using car without insurance—police officer using own car on duty. See JONES *v.* CHIEF CONSTABLE OF BEDFORDSHIRE, §2065.

PRACTICE

2872. Adjournment—pending criminal proceedings

P brought an action against D for the tort of assault and battery. Criminal proceedings were pending against D for an assault under s.47 of the Offences against the Person Act 1861 arising out of the same factual incident. D applied for an adjournment of the civil action on the grounds that the trial proceedings before the criminal trial might have an adverse effect upon the prospect of D being acquitted in the criminal trial.

Held, allowing the appeal and granting an adjournment, that once it was found that there was an element of potential prejudice to the party applying for the adjournment of the civil proceeings in relation to his forthcoming criminal trial, the court was bound to consider whether the right course was not to adjourn the civil proceedings pending the criminal trial. The court should grant the adjournment on the ground that by granting the adjournment one might avoid at least a potential unfairness to D.

FARRELL *v.* STENNING, June 17, 1986 (C.A.T. No. 550).

2873. Adjournment—whether a litigant should be granted an adjournment

Although it is a matter of pure discretion whether or not to grant an application for an adjournment, it should always be granted if it would not otherwise be possible for the litigant to obtain justice.

JOYCE *v.* KING, *The Times,* July 13, 1987, C.A.

2874. Administration of Justice Act 1985—commencement

ADMINISTRATION OF JUSTICE ACT 1985 (COMMENCEMENT No. 4) ORDER 1987 (No. 787 (C.21)) [85p], made under the Administration of Justice Act 1985 (c.61), s.69(2); brings into force on May 11, 1987, sections 6(1)(2)(3)(5), 11, 14–21, 24–33, 34(1)(2), 35–37, 39, Scheds. 4–6 and brings into force on December 1, 1987, s.6(4).

2875. Admiralty and Commercial Court Registry—administrative arrangements—practice direction

The following practice direction was issued by the Lord Chief Justice with the concurrence of the Admiralty Judge and the Judge in charge of the Commercial List on October 14, 1987.

1. The Rules of the Supreme Court (Amendment) 1987 (S.I. 1987 No. 1423), the relevant provisions of which come into force on November 2, 1987, provide for the creation of an Admiralty and Commercial Court Registry. This Direction gives details of the new administrative arrangements.

2. Administrative Structure

The new Registry will combine the Admiralty Registry and the Commercial Court Listing Office and, in addition, will take over all work on Commercial Court cases previously carried out in the Central Office. While all process will need to show whether the case is proceeding in the Admiralty Court or the Commercial Court, there will be a continuous run of numbers for all originating process, one cause book and a common court file and filing system.

3. The Court File

A court file will be maintained for each case. The documents relevant to a particular case will be kept on the file, including the originating process, acknowledgement of service, notices of change of solicitors, summonses, affidavits, pleadings and orders. The Admiralty Registry and, in some cases, the Judges may make their notes of any interlocutory matter on the file. The file will normally be kept in the Registry, but it will be sent to a Judge or the Registrar when required by him. It will be available in court on the trial of any action or interlocutory application.

4. Issue of Process

All originating process in the Admiralty Court and Commercial Court, that is writs, originating summonses and originating motions will be issued in the Registry. Fees will continue to be paid to the Supreme Court Accounts Office.

5. Filing of Documents

Documents in Commercial Court proceedings will not be accepted for filing in Room 81 after October 30, 1987. All affidavits filed in Room 81 up to and including October 30, 1987 will be retained there. On the first interlocutory application made in any Commercial Court case on or after November 2, 1987 a full set of such pleadings as have been served must be lodged in the Registry together with all affidavits in the proceedings previously filed in Room 81. These will be retained on the court file. Exhibits to affidavits will normally be returned to the parties.

6. Interlocutory Applications in Commercial Court Proceedings

There will be no change in the current procedure. Parties will continue to draw any order from the Judge's endorsement. The order should be presented to the Registry for issue and entry.

7. Interlocutory Applications in Admiralty Proceedings

Orders will be drawn by the parties and should be presented to the Registry for checking against the Registrar's or Judge's note and for issue and entry.

8. Orders, Decrees and Judgments in Admiralty and Commercial Proceedings

A certificate under Ord. 35, r.10 will be issued by the Court in appropriate cases and entered on the file.

9. Judgment by Default in Commercial Actions

All applications for judgment by default should be presented to the Registry together with the appropriate supporting documents. It is not necessary to produce a certificate of non-acknowledgment of service.

10. Applications to Masters in Commercial Court Matters

Applications in Commercial Court matters which are at present dealt with by Queen's Bench Masters, *e.g.* applications for charging orders, should be made in the Registry and dealt with where possible by the Queen's Bench Master disposing of Admiralty matters or as the Senior Master may direct.

11. Listing

Listing of Admiralty and Commercial cases will be co-ordinated in the Registry.

12. Setting Down for Trial

All Admiralty and Commercial Court matters will be set down in the Registry.

PRACTICE DIRECTION (Q.B.D.) (NEW ADMIRALTY AND COMMERCIAL COURT REGISTRY) October 14, 1987.

2876. Admiralty practice. See SHIPPING AND MARINE INSURANCE.

2877. Admiralty practice—remuneration of nautical and other assessors—practice direction

The following practice direction was issued by the direction of the Lord Chief Justice and the Master of the Rolls on September 11, 1987.

1. In the absence of special directions given in a particular case, the remuneration payable to Trinity Masters, and nautical and other assessors summoned to assist the Court of Appeal, the Admiralty Court on the trial of an action, or a Divisional Court of the Queen's Bench Division hearing an appeal under Ord. 74 of the Rules of the Supreme Court shall be:—

(i) For each day of the hearing (except where (ii) or (iii) applies £100.00

(ii)	For a day on which the hearing finishes before the midday adjournment	£ 50.00
(iii)	For a day on which the hearing commences after the midday adjournment, the assessor not having attended, or having been engaged in another case before such adjournment	£ 50.00
(iv)	For attending the Court on a day on which the case is not heard	£ 50.00
(v)	For consultation with the Court on a day on which the case is not heard	£ 50.00
(vi)	For attending to hear reserved judgment (including any consultation with the Court on the same day)	£ 50.00
(vii)	If notice of attendance is countermanded less than two days before the hearing	£ 50.00

2. Assessors other than Elder Brethren of Trinity House, London, shall in addition to the above scale be entitled to receive reasonable sums in respect of travelling expenses and subsistence.

3. Where there is a cross appeal, or where appeals are heard together, or where actions are consolidated or tried together, the proceedings shall be deemed to be one appeal or action as the case may be.

4. In the absence of special directions given in a particular case, the remuneration and expenses shall be paid by the appellant or the party setting down the action as the case may be without prejudice to any right to recover from any other party the amount so paid on taxation.

5. This Practice Direction is to apply to all actions and appeals the hearing of which begins on or after October 1, 1987.

PRACTICE DIRECTION (ADMIRALTY) (REMUNERATION OF NAUTICAL AND OTHER ASSESSORS) September 11, 1987.

2878. Admission of liability—no amendment to pleading—attempt to resile from admission

A defendant who admitted liability but who did not amend his pleadings would not be allowed to resile from the admission unless it was just to do so having regard to the interests of both parties.

BIRD *v.* BIRDS EYE WALLS, *The Times*, July 24, 1987, C.A.

2879. Adoption—transfer of business to High Court. See N. AND L. (MINORS), *Re*, §3117.

2880. Advocates—note of judgment—duty

Counsel and solicitor-advocates should take a note of judgment to assist on appeal.

LETTS *v.* LETTS, *The Times*, April 8, 1987, C.A.

2881. Affidavit—filing—late filing—effect on costs—practice direction

The following practice direction was issued by the Senior Registrar of the Family Division on February 20, 1987.

Difficulties are being experienced because of the late filing of affidavits in cases proceeding in the Principal Registry.

The President and judges of the Family Division require the attention of practitioners to be drawn to the practice set out in the Registrar's Direction of February 7, 1984 ([1984] 1 All E.R. 684, [1984] 1 W.L.R. 306). Failure to comply with this practice may result in costs being disallowed or being ordered to be paid by the solicitor personally. Affidavits which are lodged in the Principal Registry within 14 days before the hearing date instead of being lodged in the Clerk of the Rules' Department or with the clerk to the registrar may not be considered at all by the judge or the registrar as the case may be.

PRACTICE DIRECTION (FAM. D.) (AFFIDAVITS: FILING) [1987] 1 All E.R. 546.

2882. Amendment—causes of action pleaded in particulars—amendment of writ and statement of claim

[R.S.C., Ord. 20, rr.5, 8.]

P engaged D1 and D2 as architects and D3 as engineers in connection with the construction of the Roman Catholic Cathedral of Liverpool. The Cathedral was completed in 1967. Between 1969 and 1979 leaks occurred which were considered by the D's at P's request. The D's reported that the leaks were not symptoms of defects in the building. Because the problems continued P issued a writ against the D's in January 1981. In the writ and in the statement of claim P pleaded negligence and breach of contract by the D's arising out of their work of design and supervision of the construction of the Cathedral up to 1967. In their defences the D's pleaded limitation, contending that any causes of action had accrued before January 1975. In June 1983 in response to a request by the D's for further and better particulars of the Scott Schedule, P introduced for the first time allegations of breach of duty by the D's in or about their investigations between 1969 and 1979 and in particular in their failure to warn P about the defects in the building. The D's objected that these matters had not been pleaded in the writ and statement of claim and P applied to make the appropriate amendments.

Held, (1) the application for leave to amend would be considered upon the basis that it had been made in June 1983; (2) in June 1983 the cause of action in respect of the advice given in 1969–1979 had not expired and therefore the Court had an unfettered discretion pursuant to R.S.C., Ord. 20, r.5(1) to grant leave upon such terms as should be just and such terms were that the leave would be conditional upon proceedings in respect of the new cause of action being deemed to have commenced in June 1983; (3) the new causes of action did not arise out of the same or substantially the same causes of action as the original design and supervision work. Therefore R.S.C., Ord. 20 r.5(2)–(5) did not apply; (4) the raising of new causes of action by way of particulars was a defect or error in the proceedings which could be corrected by the Court and in this instance would be, pursuant to R.S.C., Ord. 20, r.8. On terms that the proceedings in respect of the new causes of action should be deemed to have commenced in June 1983.

LIVERPOOL ROMAN CATHOLIC ARCHDIOCESAN FOR TRUSTEES INC. *v.* GIBBERD (1987) 7 Con.L.R. 113, H. H. Judge Fox-Andrews Q.C. O.R.

2883. Anton Piller order—counterfeiting—injunctions

A private investigator found evidence of counterfeiting the goods of R when he was in the process of executing an Anton Piller order on behalf of P. A second Anton Piller order was obtained on behalf of R. D sought *ex parte* injunctions to restrain R or the private investigator from using the goods found while executing the Anton Piller order.

Held, that provided it was properly disclosed to the court how the evidence had been obtained the court had discretion to admit it. Relief refused.

PIVER (L.T.) S.a.r.L. *v.* S. & J. PERFUME CO. [1987] F.S.R. 159, Walton J.

2884. Anton Piller order—serious non-disclosure—discharge of order—whether "yield" from Anton Piller to be considered on application for interlocutory injunction

[Hong Kong] P obtained an Anton Piller order in an action for infringement of copyright in respect of clothing. At the *inter partes* hearing the judge found serious non-disclosure of relevant facts by P. He discharged the Anton Piller order and granted an injunction, taking into account the evidence obtained by the execution of the Anton Piller order.

Held, allowing the appeal, that (1) the judges had a discretion whether to exclude evidence obtained as a result of an order wrongfully obtained; (2) where non-disclosure was serious the court would allow use of the "yield" for compelling reasons; (3) in this case without the "yield" the evidence was flimsy.

GUESS ? INC. *v.* LEE SECK MON [1987] F.S.R. 125, C.A. of Hong Kong.

2885. Anton Piller order—use of documents—discovery of documents in second Anton Piller relevant to first such order—whether usable in contempt proceedings.

[Supreme Court Act 1981 (c.54), s.72.]

In exceptional circumstances the court can modify or release a plaintiff from his undertakings in relation to documents discovered in an action.

The plaintiff in a first action obtained an Anton Piller order in respect of certain documents. A year later they commenced another action and obtained a second order in respect of that action. On execution a number of documents were discovered that allegedly broke undertakings given in the first action and which should then have been disclosed. The plaintiffs applied for leave to use those documents in taking contempt proceedings in respect of the first order. The judge refused the application, the appeal was allowed.

Held, dismissing the defendants' appeal, that quite exceptionally the court could modify or release a plaintiff from the usual implied undertakings given on discovery, and the defendants here would suffer no injustice (*Berkhor (A.J.) & Co.* v. *Bilton* [1981] C.L.Y. 2159 considered).

CREST HOMES *v.* MARKS [1987] 3 W.L.R. 293, H.L.

2886. Appeal—academic point of law—refusal to hear

The House of Lords refused to hear an appeal where the dispute between the parties had ended and the point was of academic interest only.

The House of Lords refused to hear an appeal which was called on for hearing before them where a party had been refused an injunction requiring the other to vacate a counil house, and by the time of the hearing the tenancy of the house had been terminated. It had always been a fundamental feature of the judicial system that the courts decide disputes between the parties before them and do not pronounce on abstract questions of law where there is no dispute to be resolved, even though the issue of law raised might be one of general importance, the resolution of which may have been left in doubt by different decisions of the Court of Appeal The appeal was dismissed with no hearing on its merits (Dicta of Viscount Simon L.C. in *Sun Life Assurance Company of Canada* v. *Jervis* [1944] A.C. 111 applied).

AINSBURY *v.* MILLINGTON [1987] 1 W.L.R. 379, H.L.

2887. Appeal—appeal to Court of Appeal—criterion for review of judge's exercise of discretion

The Court of Appeal stressed that it could only review a judge's exercise of his discretion if he had misdirected himself in law in reaching his conclusion.

HINDES *v.* EDWARDS, *The Times,* October 9, 1987, C.A.

2888. Appeal—appeal to Court of Appeal—"setting down"

There is no appeal extant until the appeal is set down, which the Court of Appeal is equivalent to the issue of a writ.

COLUMBUS DIXON *v.* DINGLE BELLES (ORMSKIRK), *The Times,* June 10, 1987, C.A.

2889. Appeal—applications under different statutes—desirability of specifying statute in order

In considering H's appeal from an ouster order of the judge made pursuant to an application under s.1(3) of the Matrimonial Homes Act 1983, the order itself making no specific reference to that section or to the Domestic Violence and Matrimonial Proceedings Act 1976 under which there was also an application before the court, the court stated that it was desirable that if orders were made on summons relating to more than one statute, where there was a possibility of ambiguity, that specific reference should be made to the statute under which jurisdiction was assumed.

POWER *v.* POWER, October 22, 1986 (C.A.T. No. 923).

2890. Appeal—child cases—legal aid application—factors to be taken into account

When considering applications in appeals in children's cases, the legal aid authorities should take into account two factors. First, that the time factor in a child's life was significant and should be measured differently to that of an adult. It may be more appropriate for such matters to be dealt with in two stages—a preliminary look on the available advice as to whether there were significant prospects of an appeal and then to fund the documentation necessary for an appeal. It was undesirable that months should pass when nothing is done while the question of granting legal aid is determined. Secondly, in cases concerning children, there was unlikely to be a right or wrong answer—the question was whether the court had erred.

RIDGWAY *v.* RIDGWAY (1986) 16 Fam. Law 363, C.A.

2891. Appeal—child cases—warning to advisers—use of documents

The principles governing appeals of cases concerning custody and care and control of minors are clearly set out and advisers should consider the position very carefully before advising an appeal. Furthermore, substantial bundles of unnecessary documents should not be used at the hearing.

R. *v.* R. AND H. (HARROW LONDON BOROUGH COUNCIL INTERVENING), *The Times,* July 6, 1987, C.A.

2892. Appeal—Court of Appeal—decision on an issue not determining outcome of case

The Court of Appeal will not rule on points of law that can have no effect on the outcome of the case before it.

STAR CINEMAS (LONDON) *v.* BARNETT, *The Times,* December 9, 1987, C.A.

2893. Appeal—Employment Appeal Tribunal—agreed orders. See BRITISH PUBLISHING CO. *v.* FRASER, §1317.

2894. Appeal—*ex parte* application—whether appeal lies to Court of Appeal

The judge refused on P's appearance *ex parte* before him their application for an injunction in pursuit of a restrictive covenant in a service agreement. P appealed and sought interim relief pending the hearing of the appeal.

Held, that although this was an *ex parte* application an appeal did lie to the Court of Appeal. Appeal from Gatehouse J.

BRITISH CAR AUCTIONS *v.* JACKSON, August 8, 1986 (C.A.T. No. 723).

2895. Appeal—from registrar—fresh evidence—whether to be considered

On appeal to a judge from a registrar, fresh evidence may be called even if it was available for the earlier hearing, but not called.

WALES TOURIST BOARD *v.* ROBERTS, *The Times,* January 10, 1987, C.A.

2896. Appeal—immigration appeal—whether validly withdrawn. See KHAN *v.* SECRETARY OF STATE FOR THE HOME DEPARTMENT; DEEN *v.* SAME, §1922.

2897. Appeal—planning decision—whether whole planning decision reopened on remission. See NEWBURY DISTRICT COUNCIL *v.* SECRETARY OF STATE FOR THE ENVIRONMENT, §3596.

2898. Appeal—point of law—grounds

Where an appeal lies only on a point of law, it is not a good ground of appeal that the tribunal appealed from paid insufficient heed to certain factors, or that there was no evidence to support its findings.

ELS WHOLESALE (WOLVERHAMPTON) *v.* SECRETARY OF STATE FOR THE ENVIRONMENT, *The Times*, May 19, 1987, D.C.

2899. Appeal—time estimates—whether length of judgment to be taken into account

The Court of Appeal emphasised the importance of Counsel's giving accurate time estimates of the hearing of appeals. In giving or revising their estimates, they should allow for the length of judgment, and consider whether judgment is likely to be reserved or extempore.

MORRIS *v.* AMBER FILM SALES, *The Times*, March 24, 1987, C.A.

2900. Appeals—documentation—practice direction

The following practice direction was issued by Sir John Donaldson, M.R. on October 22, 1986.

The purpose of this statement is to consolidate and expand the practice directions issued on May 18, 1983 (*Practice Note (Appeal: Documents)* [1983] C.L.Y. 2862; [1983] 2 All E.R. 416) and March 4, 1985 (*Practice Note (Appeal: Documents)* [1985] C.L.Y. 2711; [1985] 1 All E.R. 841) and at the same time to remind all concerned that it is the duty of those acting for appellants to ensure that the bundles of documents lodged for the use of the court comply with the relevant rules and directions. It is also their duty to lodge the bundles within the time limit prescribed by R.S.C., Ord. 59, r. 9(1) (as amended). Neglect of these duties may lead to the appeal being struck out. Scrutiny of the bundles submitted has shown that there are certain errors and omissions which still occur very frequently. For that reason, attention is drawn, in particular, to the following requirements.

Transcripts

All transcripts lodged (whether of evidence or of the judgment) must be originals. Photocopies are not permitted: see *The Supreme Court Practice 1985*, paragraph 59/9/2.

Notes of judgment

In cases where there is no official transcript of the judge's judgment (*e.g.* county court cases and certain High Court hearings in chambers), either the judge's own note of his judgment must be submitted, or, where there is no such note, the counsel or solicitors who appeared in the court below must prepare an agreed note of the judge's judgment and submit it to him for his approval. A copy of the approved note of judgment must be included in each bundle. It should be noted, in the case of county court appeals, that concluding lines in the judge's notebook reading "Judgment for the defendant with costs on scale 2" or the like are not "the judge's own note of his judgment." What is required is a note of the reasons for the decision.

In the majority of cases the county court judge gives an ex tempore judgment and, pending the introduction and supply of personal dictating machines, has no full written text of it. The same applies to those cases heard in the High Court for which no official transcript of judgment is available.

In all such cases a typed version of the appellant's counsel's note of the judgment (or the solicitor's note, if he appeared for the appellant in the court below) must be prepared, agreed with the other side, and submitted to the judge for his approval. Much delay has been caused in numerous cases by failure to put this in train promptly and expeditiously. To obviate such delays in future the following procedure must be adopted.

(i) Except where the county court judge handed down his judgment in writing, or it is known for certain that he has a full text of his reasoned decision, the appellant's solicitor should make arrangements for counsel's note of judgment (or, if the solicitor appeared in the court below, his own note) to be prepared, agreed with the other side, and then submitted to the judge, as soon as the notice of appeal has been served; he should not wait until the appeal has entered the List of Forthcoming Appeals. If that system is adopted, the approved note of judgment should be ready for inclusion in the bundles within the 14-day time limit for lodging documents, and no extension should be needed.

(ii) Where both sides were represented by counsel in the court below, it saves time if counsel for the appellant submits his note of judgment directly to counsel for the respondent.

(iii) Where the note of judgment has not been received back from the judge by the time the bundles are ready to be lodged, copies of the unapproved note of judgment should be lodged with the bundles; the approved note of judgment should then be substituted as soon as it is to hand.

(iv) In those cases where the appellant is appealing in person, counsel or solicitors for the other side must make available their notes of judgment, whether or not the appellant has himself made any note of the reasoned judgment.

County court notes of evidence

In county court cases a copy of the judge's notes of evidence must be bespoken from the county court concerned and a copy of those notes must be included in each bundle. Directives (Court Business 3/85, B1351, and 4/85, B1358, para. (3)) have been sent to county courts asking them to arrange for the notes of evidence to be transcribed as soon as the notice of appeal has been served on the county court registrar. The notes should then be ready for despatch to the appellant or his solicitors as soon as they formally request them and make provision for the copying charges. A directive (Court Business 4/85, B1358, para. (4)) has also been sent to county courts to the effect that the old practice which obtained in some county courts of refusing to make the notes of evidence available until counsel's agreed note of judgment has been submitted is to be discontinued.

Core bundles

In cases where the appellant seeks to place before the court bundles of documents comprising more than 100 pages, three copies of a core bundle containing the principal documents to which reference will be made must be lodged with the court. In such circumstances, it will not usually be necessary to lodge multiple copies of the main bundle. It will be sufficient if a single set of the full trial documents is lodged so that the court may refer to it if necessary.

Pagination and indexing

Bundles must be paginated clearly and there must be an index at the front of the bundle listing all the documents and giving the page references for each one. At present, many bundles are numbered merely by document. This is incorrect. Each page should be numbered individually and consecutively.

Binding of bundles

All the documents (with the exception of the transcripts) must be bound together in some form (*e.g.* ring binder, plastic binder, or laced through holes in the top left-hand corner). Loose documents will not be accepted.

Legibility

All documents must be legible. In particular, care must be taken to ensure that the edges of pages are not cut off by the photocopying machine. If it proves impossible to produce adequate copies of individual documents, or if manuscript documents are illegible, typewritten copies of the relevant pages should also be interleaved at the appropriate place in the bundle.

Time limits

Time limits must be complied with and will be strictly enforced except where there are good grounds for granting an extension. The appellant's solicitor (or the appellant, if in person) should therefore set about preparing the bundles as soon as the notice of appeal has been lodged with the Civil Appeals Office (without waiting for the appeal to enter the List of Forthcoming Appeals); in that way, in most cases, the bundles should be ready to be lodged within the 14-day time limit prescribed by R.S.C., Ord. 59, r.9. An extension of time is unlikely to be obtained where the failure to lodge the bundles, transcripts, notes of judgment or notes of evidence within the prescribed time limit is due to failure on the part of the appellant's solicitors) or the appellant, if in person) to start soon enough on the preparation of the bundles or the obtaining of the other documents.

Responsibility of the solicitor on the record

It seems likely that the work of documentation is often delegated to very junior members of the solicitor's staff, often without referring them to the relevant rule and practice direction. Delegation is not, as such, objectionable, but (a) the member of staff must be instructed fully on what is required and be capable of ensuring that these requirements are met, and (b) the solicitor in charge of the case must personally satisfy himself that the documentation is in order before it is delivered to the court. London agents too have a responsibility. They are not just postmen. They should be prepared to answer any questions which may arise as to the sufficiency of the documentation.

PRACTICE DIRECTION (C.A.) (APPEALS: DOCUMENTATION) [1986] 1 W.L.R. 1318.

2901. Appeals—failure of appellant to provide respondent with transcripts

[R.S.C., Ord. 59, r.9.]

Although observance of R.S.C., Ord. 59, r.9 (which obliges an appellant to supply the respondent with transcripts of evidence and judgment) is important, it will rarely be appropriate to dismiss an appeal because of the appellant's failure to comply with it.

DENVER *v.* McILWAINE, *The Times,* May 30, 1987, C.A.

2902. Application for withdrawal of payment in within period when open for acceptance—effect of acceptance before hearing of application—discretion

P a builder commenced proceedings for sums allegedly due in respect of building work against D. D counterclaimed for damages for breach of contract alleging that the work was defective and incomplete. The parties both instructed experts. In the light of agreements reached between the experts D made a payment into Court on 18th November 1985, exactly 21 days before the date fixed for the trial, 9 December 1985. However D also consulted a second expert whose report dated 20 November 1985 revealed double counting in P's claim. As a result, on 25 November 1985 D issued a summons seeking to withdraw the notice of payment in. On 28 November D served this summons on P who later the same day gave notice of acceptance of the payment in.

Held, dismissing D's summons, that (1) the Court had power to give D leave to withdraw a notice of payment in even when it was still open to P to accept it; (2) this power existed even where P had given notice of acceptance after the date of issue of D's summons but before it was heard; (3) however D's reasons for applying to withdraw the notice of payment in were not sufficiently good reasons to justify the exercise of discretion in his favour since in essence it was a review of information which had always been available to D and his advisers.

MANKU *v.* SEEHRA 1987 7 Con.L.R. H.H. Judge Newey Q.C., O.R.

2903. Application to strike out—criticisms of present system

On an application to strike out an action for want of prosecution, the Court of Appeal criticised the present state of the law on the subject, saying that it was highly questionable whether plaintiffs should be allowed the benefit of the full period of limitation, with virtual impunity, where the facts are known, and there is no obstacle to the speedy institution and prosecution of a claim (*Birkett* v. *James* [1977] C.L.Y. 2410 disapproved).

WESTMINSTER CITY COUNCIL *v.* CLIFFORD CULPIN AND PARTNERS, *The Times,* June 20, 1987, C.A.

2904. Application to strike out—insurers sue in name of assured—assured had ceased to exist at time of issue of writ—whether action lies

P hired a boat from D to transport a dumper by river. The boat sank and P's underwriters paid out on P's claim. They commenced proceedings in P's name, but were unaware that P had been wound up and had ceased to exist. When they did become aware of this fact, they applied to the Court for leave to substitute themselves as plaintiffs. D applied to have the action struck out. The Swansea County Court held that the action should proceed as originally constituted.

Held, allowing D's appeal, that the action should be struck out. The underwriters' right to bring a subrogated claim did not extend to a right to bring a claim in the name of a non-existent plaintiff unless a legal assignment of the claim had been taken.

SMITH M. H. (PLANT HIRE) *v.* MAINWARING D.L. (T/A) INSHORE [1986] 2 Lloyd's Rep. 244, C.A.

2905. Application to strike out—reliance on appeal on point not considered below. See JONES *v.* DEPARTMENT OF EMPLOYMENT, §3466.

2906. Applications under s.48 of the Administration of Justice Act 1985—practice direction

[Administration of Justice Act 1985 (c.61), s.48, Ord. 93, r.21.]

The following practice direction was issued by the direction of the Vice-Chancellor on January 28, 1987.

(1) The *ex parte* originating summons shall be supported by an affidavit to which shall be exhibited:

(a) copies of all relevant documents;
(b) instructions to counsel;
(c) counsel's opinion;
(d) draft minutes of the desired order.

(2) The affidavit (or the exhibits thereto) shall state:
(a) the names of all persons who are, or may be, affected by the order sought;
(b) all surrounding circumstances admissible and relevant in construing the document;
(c) the date of call of counsel and his experience in the construction of trust documents;
(d) the approximate value of the fund or property in question;
(e) whether it is known to the applicant that a dispute exists and, if so, details of such dispute.

(3) At the first hearing of the originating summons, if the evidence is complete, the Master will refer the papers to the Judge.

(4) The Judge will consider the papers and, if necessary, direct service of notices under Ord. 15, r.13A or request such further information as he may desire. If the Judge is satisfied that the order sought is appropriate, the order will be made and sent to the applicant.

(5) If following service of notices under Ord. 15, r.13A any acknowledgment of service is received, the applicant shall apply to the Master (on notice to the parties who have so acknowledged) for directions. If the applicant desires to pursue the application to the Court, in the ordinary case the Master will direct that the case proceeds as a construction summons.

(6) If on the hearing of the construction summons the Judge is of opinion that any party who has entered an acknowledgment of service has no reasonably tenable argument contrary to counsel's opinion, in the exercise of his discretion he may order such party to pay any costs thrown away, or part thereof.

PRACTICE DIRECTION (CH.D.) (PROCEDURE: APPLICATIONS UNDER s.48 OF THE ADMINISTRATION OF JUSTICE ACT 1985) (No. 1 OF 1987), January 28, 1987.

2907. Applications under the Variation of Trusts Act 1958—practice direction

[Variation of Trusts Act 1958 (c.53).]

The following practice direction was issued by direction of the Vice-Chancellor on December 8, 1987.

Applications under the Variation of Trusts Act 1958 for hearing by a Judge may be set down for hearing in the non-witness list on the lodgment of a certificate signed by counsel for all the parties, stating:—
(i) that the evidence is complete and has been filed
(ii) that the application is ready for hearing, and
(iii) the estimated length of the hearing.

There will henceforward be no need to take a first appointment before a Master simply to procure the Master's direction that the matter be adjourned to the Judge.

The Certificate together with a copy of the Originating Summons stamped with the setting down fee should be lodged in Room 156. The Court file and the documents lodged will then be forwarded to the List Office for setting down.

PRACTICE DIRECTION (CH.D.) (PROCEDURE: APPLICATIONS UNDER THE VARIATION OF TRUSTS ACT 1958) (No. 3 of 1987), December 8, 1987.

2908. Arbitration—rescission of reference—principles

[C.C.R. 1981, Ord. 19, r.2(4); Factories Act 1961 (c.34), s.14.]

P alleged she had injured a finger when it was trapped underneath the fast moving plunger of an industrial sewing-machine. She claimed damages against her employers, S, for negligence and breach of s.14. On application by S, a reference to arbitration was made. Subsequently P applied for the rescission of the arbitration under Ord. 19. The application was refused by the registrar.

Held, dismissing P's appeal, that (1) the case was factually simple and that the application of s.14(1) of the 1961 Act to industrial sewing-machines did not give rise to a difficult question of law; (2) the fact that the trade union supporting P's claim would be unable to recover costs in excess of those allowable under Ord. 19, r.6, and that they might reconsider their support for P and other textile workers in future small claims if referred to arbitration did not make it unreasonable for the claim to proceed to arbitration.

PRICE *v.* STEINBERG, January 27, 1987, H.H. Judge Hywel Robert, Pontypridd County Ct. [*Ex rel. Edward Lewis Possart, Solicitors.*]

2909. Bail—application—judicial review proceedings—jurisdiction to grant bail

T applied for bail pending appeal against refusal of judicial review of an immigration decision.

Held, that for a court to have jurisdiction to grant bail it must be properly seised of the proceedings to which bail is ancillary. Once the High Court has refused judicial review it is no longer properly seised of these proceedings and so has no jurisdiction to grant bail.

R. *v.* SECRETARY OF STATE FOR THE HOME DEPARTMENT, *ex p.* TURKOGLU [1987] All E.R. 823, C.A.

2910. Bail—failure to surrender to custody—practice direction

The following practice direction was issued by Lord Lane C.J. on December 19, 1986.

1. This *practice direction* is issued with a view to clarifying any misunderstandings as to the effect of the decision in *Schiavo* v. *Anderton* [1986] C.L.Y. 2069 in which, *inter alia*, the Divisional Court of the Queen's Bench Division provided guidance on the procedure to be adopted in magistrates' courts when dealing with allegations of failure to surrender to custody contrary to section 6 of the Bail Act 1976.

2. *Bail granted by a magistrates' court*

Where a person has been granted bail by a court and subsequently fails to surrender to custody as contemplated by section 6(1) or 6(2) of the Bail Act 1976, on arrest that person should be brought before the court at which the proceedings in respect of which bail was granted are to be heard. It is neither necessary nor desirable to lay an information in order to commence proceedings for the failure to surrender. Having regard to the nature of the offence which is tantamount to the defiance of a court order, it is more appropriate that the court itself should initiate the proceedings by its own motion, following an express invitation by the prosecutor. The court will only be invited so to move if, having considered all the circumstances, the prosecutor considers proceedings are appropriate. Where a court complies with such an invitation, the prosecutor will naturally conduct the proceedings and, where the matter is contested, call the evidence. Any trial should normally take place immediately following the disposal of the proceedings in respect of which bail was granted.

3. *Bail granted by a police officer*

Where a person has been bailed from a police station subject to a duty to appear before a magistrates' court or to attend a police station on an appointed date and/or time, a failure so to appear or attend cannot be said to be tantamount to the defiance of a court order. There does not exist the same compelling justification for the court to act by its own motion. Where bail has been granted by a police officer, any proceedings for a failure to surrender to custody, whether at a court or a police station, should accordingly be initiated by charging the accused or by the laying of an information.

PRACTICE DIRECTION (Q.B.D.) (BAIL: FAILURE TO SURRENDER) [1987] 1 W.L.R. 79, D.C.

2911. Bank guarantee default—summary judgment—entitlement to summary judgment

In this case a bank, B, sued D as personal guarantors of the indebtedness of principal debtors pursuant to certain mortgages taken out in respect of the purchase of vessels. D was undeniably liable under the guarantees, but had cross-claims for damages against B, contending that B had acted negligently in their capacity as mortgagees. B obtained a summary judgment on the guarantees, but the judge granted a stay of execution pending the determination. of the cross-claims. Both parties appealed.

Held, that (1) the banks were entitled to summary judgment: the guarantees envisaged a quick repayment and were expressly made free of set-off or counterclaim; (2) a discretion to stay execution should only be granted in exceptional cases, and this was not one of them.

CONTINENTAL ILLINOIS NATIONAL BANK & TRUST CO. OF CHICAGO *v.* J. P. PAPANICOLAOU; SAME *v.* N. F. PAPANICOLAOU; FEDORA, TATIANA AND ERETREA II, THE [1986] 2 Lloyd's Rep. 441, C.A.

2912. Bankruptcy—service—proof of service of statutory demand—practice note

The following practice note was issued on December 31, 1986 by the Chief Bankruptcy Registrar.

[Insolvency Rules 1986 (S.I. 1986 No. 1925), r.6.11.]

1. Rule 6.11–(3) of the Insolvency Rules 1986 provides that, if the statutory demand has been served personally, the affidavit of service must be made by the person who effected that service. Rule 6.11–(4) provides that, if service of the demand (however effected) has been acknowledged in writing, the affidavit of service must be made by the creditor or by a person acting on his behalf. Rule 6.11–(5) provides that, if neither paragraphs (3) or (4) apply, the affidavit must be made by a person having direct knowledge of the means adopted for serving the demand.

2. Form 6.11 (affidavit of personal service of the statutory demand).

This form should only be used where the demand has been served personally and acknowledged in writing: rule 6.11–(4). If the demand has not been acknowledged in writing, the affidavit should be made by the process server and paragraphs 2 and 3 (part) of Form 6.11 should be omitted: rule 6.11–(3).

3. Form 6.12 (affidavit of substituted service of the statutory demand).

This form can be used whether or not service of the demand has been acknowledged in writing. Paragraphs 4 and 5 (part) provide for the alternatives. Practitioners are reminded, however, that the appropriate person to make the affidavit may not be the same in both cases. If the demand has been acknowledged in writing, the appropriate person is the creditor or a person acting on his behalf. If the demand has not been acknowledged, that person must be someone having direct knowledge of the means adopted for serving the demand.

Practitioners may find it more convenient to allow process servers to carry out the necessary investigation whilst reserving to themselves the service of the demand. In these circumstances paragraph 1 should be deleted and the following paragraph substituted: "1. Attempts have been made to serve the demand, full details of which are set out in the accompanying affidavit of . . .".

PRACTICE NOTE (CH.D.) (BANKRUPTCY: STATUTORY DEMAND) (No. 5/86) [1987] 1 W.L.R. 85.

2913. Bankruptcy—statutory demand—setting aside—practice note

The following practice note was issued on January 6, 1987 by the Chief Bankruptcy Registrar.

[Insolvency Rules 1986 (S.I. 1986 No. 1925), rr.6.4, 6.5, 7.4(1).]

Application to set aside statutory demand

1. The application (Form 6.4) and affidavit in support (Form 6.5) exhibiting a copy of the statutory demand must be filed in court within 18 days of service of the statutory demand on the debtor. Where service is effected by advertisement in a newspaper the period of 18 days is calculated from the date of the first appearance of the advertisement: see *Practice Note (Bankruptcy: Substituted Service)* [1986] C.L.Y. 2576. Three copies of each document must be lodged with the application to enable the court to serve notice of the hearing date on the applicant, the creditor and the person named in Part B of the statutory demand.

2. Where, to avoid expense, copies of the documents are not lodged with the application, any order of the registrar fixing a venue is conditional upon copies of the documents being lodged on the next business day after the registrar's order otherwise the application will be deemed to have been dismissed.

3. Where the statutory demand is based on a judgment or order, the court will not at this stage go behind the judgment or order and inquire into the validity of the debt nor, as a general rule, will it adjourn the application to await the result of an application to set aside the judgment or order.

4. When the debtor (a) claims to have a counterclaim, set off or cross demand (whether or not he could have raised it in the action in which the judgment or order was obtained) which equals or exceeds the amount of the debt or debts specified in the statutory demand or (b) disputes the debt (not being a debt subject to a judgment or order) the court will normally set aside the statutory demand if, in its opinion, on the evidence there is a genuine triable issue.

5. *Applications for an extension of time to apply to set aside a statutory demand*

Each term two judges of the Chancery Division will sit to hear insolvency cases, one of whom ("the bankruptcy judge") will be primarily concerned to hear cases affecting individual debtors.

After the expiration of 18 days from the date of service of the statutory demand, the debtor must apply for an extension of time if he wishes to apply to set aside the demand. The application for extension of time and (if necessary) to restrain the presentation of a bankruptcy petition should be made to the bankruptcy judge, but in cases of urgency and where the bankruptcy judge is not available the application may be made to the judge hearing ordinary motions. (This requirement will appear in a practice direction to be published.)

Paragraphs 1 and 2 of Form 6.5 (affidavit in support of application to set aside statutory demand) should be used in support of the application for extension of time with the following additional paragraphs:

"3. that to the best of my knowledge and belief the creditor(s) named in the demand has/have not presented a petition against me.

"4. That the reasons for my failure to apply to set aside the demand within 18 days after service are as follows: . . . .

"5. Unless restrained by injunction the creditor(s) may present a bankruptcy petition against me."

(The fee on the application will be £15.)

PRACTICE NOTE (CH.D.) (BANKRUPTCY: STATUTORY DEMAND: SETTING ASIDE) (No. 1/87) [1987] 1 W.L.R. 119.

2914. Bankruptcy petitions—interest on debt accruing after date of statutory demand—practice note

The following practice note was issued by the Chief Bankruptcy Registrar on September 30, 1987. Bankruptcy Petitions. Interest on debt accruing after date of Statutory Demand. Insolvency Act 1986 s.268(1)(*a*). Insolvency Rule 6.8–(1)(*c*). Amendment to Practice Note (Bankruptcy) No. 3/86.

Para. 3 of *Practice Note (Bankruptcy) No. 3/86* [1986] C.L.Y. 2577 should be amended by *deleting* the words "except that interest on other charges" to the end of the paragraph.

Para. 3 will now read: "3. Where the petition is based on a statutory demand, only the debt claimed in the demand may be included in the petition."

PRACTICE NOTE (BANKRUPTCY) (No. 2/87) September 30, 1987.

2915. Burden of proof—direction to jury

A jury should properly be directed as to the burden of proof in a civil case that proof on a balance of probabilities means that they must be satisfied that it is more likely than not (or more probable than not) that the relevant fact was established.

R. *v.* SWAYSLAND, *The Times*, April 15, 1987, C.A.

2916. Chancery—summons—short summons list—practice direction

The Vice-Chancellor issued the following practice direction on May 12, 1987.

(1) In order to deal more quickly with summonses that are unlikely to last for more than 5 minutes, each Master will from the week beginning 6 July 1987 hear a short summons list on the following days each week between 10.30 and 11.30 a.m.

Master Munrow	—	Tuesday
Master Cholmondeley Clarke	—	Thursday
Master Dyson	—	Thurdsay
Masters Barratt and Gowers	—	Friday

Summonses will be listed in batches of 5 at 10.30; 10.45; 11.00; and 11.15 a.m.

(2) Solicitors who wish a summons to be heard in the short summons list should mark the back sheet "short summons list" and draw the Summons Clerk's attention of this marking. The copy for service on the other parties should be similarly marked.

(3) It is essential that Solicitors make sure that all documents that will be needed at the hearing are lodged beforehand, for example notices of acting as London Agents and copy pleadings. As the time available for the hearing will be very short, failure to do this may cause an adjournment of the summons.

(4) It is hoped by the clearance of the short summonses effected by this list that each Master will be able to extend for two days a week the period for taking half-hourly summonses which will begin on those two days at 11.00 instead of 11.30 a.m.

PRACTICE DIRECTION (CHANCERY: SHORT SUMMONS LIST) (No. 2 OF 1987).

2917. Charging order—judgment debt—discretion of court

[Charging Orders Act 1979 (c.53), s.1(1); County Courts Act 1984 (c.28), s.86(1).]

A Court cannot be faulted for exercising its discretion in favour of not making a charging order against a debtors property where it is clear that he has properly complied with the terms of an order for the payment of a judgment debt by instalments.

MERCANTILE CREDIT CO. *v.* ELLIS, *The Independent*, March 17, 1987, C.A.

2918. Charging order—real property—claim that resulting trust defeated charging order. See BARCLAYS BANK *v.* FORRESTER, §2537.

2919. Charging order nisi—refusal to make absolute

The registrar refused to make a charging order nisi absolute—on the grounds that W was paying compensation by instalments pursuant to a court order. He had pleaded guilty to, *inter alia*, a charge of obtaining money by deception. The charge related to the loan in respect of which the charging order was obtained. On appeal, the judge held that the registrar was not entitled to take the compensation order into account so as to refuse to make the charging order nisi absolute. The appeal was successful (*Mercantile Credit Co.* v. *Ellis* [1987] C.L.Y. 2917 considered).

FIRST NATIONAL SECURITIES *v.* WILEMAN, September 29, 1987; H.H. Judge Farrer, Q.C., Burton-on-Trent County Ct. [*Ex rel. Davis & Co., Solicitors*]

2920. Claim for personal injuries—delay by plaintiff—striking out claim

The plaintiff was granted legal aid in August 1983 to pursue a claim for personal injuries caused by negligence. The certificate was limited to taking counsel's opinion. This was not received, for a number of reasons, until May 15, 1985. The negligence relied upon took place in June 1979.

Held, that the delay was intolerable and inordinate, and P's claim would be struck out.

MANSOURI *v.* BLOOMSBURY HEALTH AUTHORITY, *The Times,* July 20, 1987, C.A.

2921. Commercial Court—limitation of time for interlocutory hearings—practice note

[R.S.C., Ord. 14, Ord. 38, r.2A.]

The following practice direction was issued by Mr. Justice Hirst in the Commercial Court of the Queen's Bench Division on October 23, 1987.

Last term Staughton J. consulted the City of London Law Society and the London Common Law and Commercial Bar Association concerning proposals for limitation of time for interlocutory hearings, which form such an important part of the Commercial Court's work.

These were supported by the solicitors, but the Bar expressed misgivings. After further consideration the Commercial Court judges have decided to prescribe stricter control of time limits for a trial period of 12 months encompassing the legal year 1987 to 1988.

Progess will be monitored meantime and any representations will be carefully considered when it comes under review in the summer of 1988.

The efficient working of the system depends on accurate estimates of the time needed for a summons. It is therefore incumbent on counsel and solicitors to take special care in this respect. In future any summons which overruns its estimate will probably be adjourned.

Subject only to the exception specified below, the Clerk to the Commercial Court will not accept estimates exceeding the following:

1. Summons to set aside service etc.	4 hours
2. R.S.C., Ord. 14	4 hours
3. Set aside judgment in default	2 hours
4. Set aside or vary injunction	2 hours
5. Amendment of pleadings	1 hour
6. Further discovery (including interrogatories)	1 hour
7. Further and better particulars	½ hour
8. Security for costs	½ hour

These are maxima, not guidelines. Proper estimates in each category will often be much shorter, and overestimating is wasteful, not only of the court's time, but also of the opportunity for other litigants to get their summonses heard.

A longer time will only be allocated on application in writing by counsel to the judge in charge of the commercial list, or such other judges as he may nominate, specifying the extra time required and the reasons why.

In all cases, whatever their duration, written outlines of submissions (which can be in note form) should be submitted by both parties in advance. In cases estimated for two hours or more, the additional documents specified in the Guide to Commercial Court Practice (see *The Supreme Court Practice 1988* vol. 1, paras. 72/A1–72/A21) will also be required.

All estimates should be made on the assumption that the judge will have read in advance the affidavits and all written submissions, but not the exhibits.

Although a departure from previous practice, this is only a further small step towards reducing the present unacceptable delays in the Commercial Court. However it signifies a determination to continue to enhance our efficiency, though the scope for improvement, particularly in cutting waiting time for the longer trials, is limited by our present resources.

Other recent measures to improve efficiency are set out in the guide, and particular attention is drawn to section X and Annex B, dealing with the requirements for the summons for directions. Their purpose is to focus the attention both of practitioners and of the court at an early stage of the proceedings on steps designed to curtail the duration and expense of the trial, especially through mutual exchange in advance of information between the parties. This also tends to promote settlements. In future the court will be unwilling to hear summonses for directions which do not comply with these requirements, and may also impose costs penalties.

It is not always appreciated that this new regime requires not only the exchanges of experts' reports, but also, in the normal run of case, the exchange of written statements of the oral evidence of intended witnesses of fact, subject of course to all proper objections, such as in fraud cases. With this innovation, made possible under the recent enactment of R.S.C., Ord. 38, r.2A, the Commercial Court, together with the Chancery Division and the official referees' court, are breaking new ground in a procedure which should curtail the amount of oral evidence (particularly evidence-in-chief) and also reduce the number of witnesses who eventually need to be called.

PRACTICE NOTE (COMMERCIAL COURT) (LIMITATION OF TIME FOR INTERLOCUTORY HEARINGS) [1987] 3 All E.R. 799.

2922. Confidential records—privilege—writ of *subpoena*—costs—wardship proceedings

The local authority sought a care order in wardship proceedings. It was suggested that the father, who had convictions for offences against a young girl, had failed to avail himself of medical treatment. To refute that suggestion, the defendents sought evidence from the Inner London Probation Service. The probation service refused to accede to that request as the information was privileged. The defendants' solicitors then issued a writ of *subpoena* against the probation officer requiring him to attend and produce his records. At the hearing the relevant information was elicited from the probation officer without disclosing the documents—the writ of *subpoena* was then set aside unopposed. The probation service applied for their costs on the grounds that it was an improper procedure to issue a *subpoena* in respect of privileged records.

Held, that a writ of *subpoena* compelled the attendance in court of the person to whom it was addressed together with any specified documents. It did not of itself require disclosure of those documents. It was up to the court to determine whether documents were privileged, the mere production at court of those documents could not therefore prejudice the question of privilege. Since the information sought had been relevant to the issues, it was appropriate for a writ to be served. The question of whether or not the documents were privileged need not be decided but as a general rule confidential records kept by a local authority were immune from disclosure unless required in the public interest. The application for costs would be dismissed. (*D. (Infants), Re* [1970] C.L.Y. 1359, *Corbett* v. *Corbett* [1970] C.L.Y. 808, *D.* v. *N.S.P.C.C.* [1977] C.L.Y. 2324 discussed).

M. (MINORS) (CONFIDENTIAL DOCUMENTS), *Re* [1987] 1 F.L.R. 46, Booth J.

2923. Contempt—breach of injunction—publication of confidential information

The Court of Appeal held that the publication by those newspapers of material derived from Peter Wright, and obtained by him in his capacity as a member of the British Security Service, could constitute contempt of court in relation to the injunction restraining two other papers from publishing such material.

ATT.-GEN. *v.* NEWSPAPER PUBLISHING *sub nom.* ATT.-GEN. *v.* THE INDEPENDENT, *The Independent*, July 16, 1987, C.A.

2924. Contempt —breach of non-molestation injunction—application for committal adjourned—subsequent acts of contempt

The husband gave an undertaking to the Court not to assault, molest or interfere with his wife. He later sent her a letter in extremely abusive terms that was held to amount to a molestation. The wife issued a notice of committal against the husband. The judge made no findings and adjourned the application generally. The husband committed two further breaches of the undertaking by screaming obscene language at the wife in the presence of the children. That too was held to be a molestation. The husband was committed to prison for four weeks by the President. The husband appealed.

Held, that when the first application for committal was adjourned the position was similar to where sentence was deferred in a criminal case. The appellant had been given an opportunity to mend his ways but instead had committed further acts of molestation. It was a serious matter, even though the molestations were not physical. The President's decision was a correct one.

GEORGE *v.* GEORGE (1986) 2 F.L.R. 347, C.A.

2925. Contempt—breach of non-molestation injunction—immediate custodial sentence—discretion of court. See GALLAGHER *v.* PATTERSON, §900.

2926. Contempt—breach of non-molestation injunction—wardship

[Power of Criminal Courts Act 1973 (c.62), s.19(1),(2); Contempt of Court Act 1981 (c.49), s.14(3).]

On July 7, 1986, three children were made wards of court. On September 10, 1986, the children's mother (D1) applied for a non-molestation order against the father of one of the children (D2). On October 1, 1986, an injunction was granted. On October 10, 1986, D2 was fined £10 for breach of the order. On May 15, 1987, D2 admitted breaches of the order made on October 1, 1986. D2 was 20 years old. Council for D2 submitted that wardship proceedings were civil and not governed by criminal statutes. S.19(1) of the 1973 Act prohibited terms of imprisonment on persons under 17. The 1981 Act, S.14(3), expressly stated that in the exercise of its jurisdiction s.19(1) should apply. Therefore it followed that a person over 17 could be commited to prison.

Held, that the sentence on D2 would be six months' imprisonment but suspended (*Morris* v. *Crown Office* [1970] C.L.Y. 2254 applied).

Per curiam: the learned judge expressed concern at this apparent lacuna in the law between the civil and criminal jurisdictions.

LEWISHAM LONDON BOROUGH *v.* W. & P., May 15, 1987; Pearlman J. [*ex rel. Peter Paul Marsh, Barrister.*]

2927. Contempt—breach of non-molestation injunction—whether order for committal should be set aside

On July 22, 1986 the judge granted an injunction against H (1) restraining him from molesting, assaulting or otherwise interfering with W or the children of the family (2) suspending his right to exercise any right of occupation of the matrimonial home and (3) restraining him from going within 100 yards of the matrimonial home or W's place of work. The judge attached to that order a power of arrest pursuant to s.2 of the Domestic Violence and Matrimonial Proceedings Act 1976. On the evening of August 8, 1986 there was an incident in which it was alleged that H did various things including causing damage to the car of the woman with whom W was out on that occasion. A policeman was called and he arrested H pursuant to the power to arrest contained in the order under s.2(3) of the 1976 Act. The following morning, H was brought before the judge as required within 24 hours of his arrest under s.2(4) of the 1976 Act. The judge committed H to prison for six months for his contempt in breaching the injunction granted on July 22. H appealed contending that the order for committal should be set aside on the grounds that (1) the offence which the judge considered he had committed, and for which the judge sentenced him, was that of damaging the car of the lady with whom W was out on the evening in question, and that that was not violence against W or a child of the family, going to the matrimonial home or going within a prohibited area, which were the only grounds on which under s.2(3) of the 1976 Act an arrest without warrant may be carried into effect and (2) he should have been given notice of what he was being charged with or what the complaint was under the Country Court Rules 1981 Ord. 29, r.4.

Held, that the points made by H were valid. Accordingly H's appeal would be allowed and the order for committal discharged (*Williams* v. *Fawcett* [1985] C.L.Y. 471 considered).

BOWEN *v.* BOWEN, August 29, 1986 (C.A.T. No. 775).

2928. Contempt—breach of order—committal proceedings in defendant's absence—application to set aside committal order

The plaintiff obtained an order restraining the defendant from assaulting her. That order was allegedly breached and the plaintiff issued notice to show cause why the defendant should not be committed. The hearing was conducted in the defendant's absence. The judge heard evidence from the plaintiff and an independent witness. The defendant appeared before the judge on the following day. The judge heard the defendant's evidence but refused an application to recall the plaintiff and her witness. Instead the judge invited counsel to comment upon the evidence as read out from his note. The judge decided that the committal order should stand.

Held, that the evidence was in two unequal parts—the plaintiff's evidence being unchallenged by cross-examination in the absence of the defendant whilst the defendant had given his evidence and been cross-examined. This did not treat the parties equally. The judge should have started the case again. The committal order should be set aside and the matter reheard.

ASLAM *v.* SINGH [1987] 1 F.L.R. 122, C.A.

2929. Contempt—committal—imprisonment

Imprisonment is not an automatic result of breach of a court order.

SMITH *v.* SMITH, *The Times*, June 20, 1987, C.A.

2930. Contempt—committal order—notice not served—*ex parte* committal—failure to dispense with service—validity of committal.

[C.C.R. 1981, Ord. 29, r.1(4), (7).]

Failure to record dispensation with service of a committal notice on an order is an irregularity which need not invalidate the order unless prejudice or unfairness results.

A notice was issued under Ord. 29, r.1(4), of the County Court Rules calling on the contemner to show cause why he should not be committed to custody for alleged breaches of an injunction. He could not be located and served by the due date but the judge made an order *ex parte,* committing him to prison for two years. The order did not mention any dispensation with service of the notice.

Held, dismissing the appeal, that (1) the judge had been entitled in proceeding *ex parte,* and to commit for contempts particularised in the notice and those committed subsequently; (2) failure to record the dispensation was a material irregularity but one which caused no prejudice (*Linnett* v. *Coles* [1986] C.L.Y. 2597 applied; *Williams* v. *Fawcett* [1985] C.L.Y. 471 considered).

WRIGHT *v.* JESS [1987] 1 W.L.R. 1076, C.A.

2931. Contempt—committal proceedings—whether civil proceedings—standard of proof

Proceedings seeking the committal of a party of a civil action for breach of an injunction or undertaking remain civil proceedings (not criminal), and are interlocutory. The standard of proof, however, is the criminal standard.

SAVINGS & INVESTMENT BANK *v.* GASCO INVESTMENTS (NETHERLANDS) B.V. (No. 2), *The Times,* November 16, 1987, C.A.

2932. Contempt—defective committal order—power to cure

[R.S.C., Ord. 59, r.10(3).]

The Court of Appeal should only exceptionally use the power to cure a defective order for committal for contempt of court.

LINKLETER *v.* LINKLETER, *The Times,* June 13, 1987, C.A.

2933. Contempt—injunction—*ex parte* application for committal—no notice served

The judge granted injunctions restraining the husband from molesting the wife and from entering the matrimonial home. The court order was not served on the husband. The judge heard an *ex parte* application to commit the husband for breaches of the injunctions. The judge was satisfied that the husband had been made aware of the injunctions, that he was in breach, dispensed with the need for notice to show cause and committed the appellant to prison for 12 months.

Held, that given the history of violence, the judge was right to proceed with the committal in the husband's absence. The judge erred in holding that the husband was in contempt for re-entering the home as there was no evidence that the order had been served personally as was required for the order to take effect. The 12-month sentence was excessive for the only proven contempt—the assault on the wife. The appropriate sentence was 28 days.

BENESCH *v.* NEWMAN [1987] 1 F.L.R. 262, C.A.

2934. Contempt—journalist refusing to disclose source of information—refusal made to DTI inspector

[Financial Services Act 1986 (c.60), s.178; Contempt of Court Act 1981 (c.49), s.10.]

A financial journalist was protected from revealing his sources to an investigation being made by the Secretary of State for Trade and Industry, unless the inspectors could persuade the court that disclosure was necessary to help prevent crime. In the instant case it was apparent that the journalist's information was likely to reveal, or help to reveal, a Crown servant guilty of insider trading.

INQUIRY UNDER THE COMPANY SECURITIES (INSIDER DEALING) ACT 1985, AN, *Re, The Times,* May 7, 1987, C.A.

2935. Contempt—person went to police station to inspect civil litigation documents—arrest

D attended a police station to inspect documents in connection with civil litigation in which he was involved. He was arrested.

Held, that this arrest was not a contempt of court. Further, there was no breach of the six-month time limit in which to issue a summons in circumstances where proceedings were commenced but not served, and fresh summonses were issued more than six months after the laying of the original information.

R. *v.* CLERKENWELL MAGISTRATES' COURT, *ex p.* EWING; EWING *v.* CLARK, *The Times,* June 3, 1987, C.A.

2936. Contempt—purpose of committal

Where the committal of a defendant is sought for his breach of an order or undertaking, the fact that no public purpose would be served by his committal is irrelevant. One of the purposes of imprisoning a contemnor is to punish him and to demonstrate that people disobey orders of the court at their peril.

JAMES *v.* CLIFFE, *The Times,* June 16, 1987, C.A.

2937. Contempt—standard of proof—whether civil or criminal standard

The wife presented a divorce petition. The husband gave undertakings to the court not to assault, molest or interfere with the wife and to vacate the matrimonial home. The husband left the matrimonial home but returned to do considerable damage to the property and to harm the wife by peering through her windows. At the committal proceedings for contempt the assistant recorder directed himself that the civil standard of proof was applicable, found the husband guilty of three charges of contempt and sentenced him to three months' imprisonment. The husband appealed.

Held, that contempt of court was a common law misdemeanour and was criminal or quasi criminal in nature. Accordingly the criminal standard of proof applied and the assistant recorder had misdirected himself. However, his findings of fact were expressed in terms that justified the criminal standard of proof and supported his decision. The misdirection had had no effect on the eventual outcome and the appeal would be dismissed (*Bramblevale, Re* [1969] C.L.Y. 2810 applied; *C. (A Minor) (Wardship: Contempt), Re* [1986] C.L.Y. 2602, *Danchevsky* v. *Danchevsky (No. 2)* (unrep., November 10, 1977), *Deborah Building Equipment* v. *Scaffco* [1986] C.L.Y. 2643; *Hornal* v. *Neuberger Products* [1956] C.L.Y. 3686, *R.* v. *Secretary of State for the Home Department, ex p. Khawaja* [1983] C.L.Y. 1908, *West Oxfordshire District Council* v. *Beratec* [1986] C.L.Y. 2601, *Yianni* v. *Yianni* [1966] C.L.Y. 9483 referred to).

DEAN *v.* DEAN [1987] 1 F.L.R. 517, C.A.

2938. Contempt—trade union—industrial action

[R.S.C., Ord. 42, rr.2(1), 3(1); Ord. 45, rr.5, 7(2), 7(3), 7(6), 7(7).]

N.G.A. member employees of a wholly owned subsidiary of P, who are publishers of free newspapers, were dismissed following their refusal to work with other employees who were not members of the union, which was not recognised by the company. As a result the N.G.A., without calling a ballot, gave instructions to N.G.A. members at two of P's typesetters not to accept P's work and also wrote to a third typesetting company requesting them to black work from P. P obtained an injunction restraining the N.G.A. from procuring interference with the typesetting employees and also a mandatory injunction requiring the N.G.A. to withdraw the blacking order immediately. The second and third D's did not implement the contents of the mandatory injunction until approximately three days after they had received copies of the orders. The N.G.A. also subsequently sent out a circular to all chapels informing them that the subsidiary company had been removed from the N.G.A.'s list of recognised offices. P filed a contempt motion.

Held, that the second and third D's were in breach of the mandatory injunction by failing to comply with its terms as soon as they received the copies, even though they had not yet been personally served as required by the Rules of the Supreme Court, since the Court was entitled to exercise its discretion to dispense with this requirement where it deemed it just to do so. The D's had full knowledge of the contents of the order and had no good reason for a delay in compliance with its terms. The D's threat to re-impose blacking was not in breach of the order, as a threat to commit a contempt did not amount to an actual contempt. The D's were in contempt by sending the circular since this amounted to a clear instruction to black contrary to the terms of the injunction. The N.G.A., who were vicariously liable for the breaches by the second and third D's, would be fined for contempt.

KENT FREE PRESS *v.* NATIONAL GRAPHICAL ASSOCIATION [1987] I.R.L.R. 267, Henry J.

2939. Costs—appeal—local authority

[Public Health Act 1936 (c.49), s.301.]

A local authority against whom an order for costs has been made by the justices has a right of appeal to the Crown Court (*R.* v. *Surrey Quarter Sessions, ex p. Lilley* [1951] C.L.Y. 4905 considered).

COOK *v.* SOUTHEND BOROUGH COUNCIL, *The Times,* April 14, 1987, Simon Brown J.

2940/1. Costs—assessment—by registrar

[R.S.C., Ord. 38, r.19(1); C.C.R. 1981.]

The appellant mortgagee appealed against an order of the register that, in an action for possession by a mortgagee, the costs be assessed at £60 plus plaint fee and that the costs be added to the security. The court has no authority to assess costs unless requested to do so by the solicitor to whom they are payable. As a matter of contract, a mortgagee is entitled to his costs as against the mortgagor unless he has acted unreasonably. Protection for the mortgagor against unreasonable bills of costs is afforded by taxation. In this case, the mortgagee had not acted unreasonably and the registrar had not been invited to assess P's costs.

Held, that the order for assessed costs be discharged and an order for costs simpliciter be substituted.

PRINCIPALITY BUILDING SOCIETY *v.* LLEWELLYN, May 1, 1987; Judge Hywel ap Robert; Pontypridd County Ct. [*Ex rel. Jonathan Walters, Barrister.*]

2942. Costs—discretion of court—costs not yet incurred

[R.S.C., Ord. 62, r.3(3).]

A judge may in appropriate circumstances make an order as to costs not yet incurred.

About 1,500 plaintiffs of whom some 1,000 were legally aided sued D for damages for side effects of the drug "Opren". P's action was treated as representative for the purpose of giving directions. The judge held that a legally aided litigant should not be insulated from the normal costs obligation and costs risk which confronted a non-legally aided litigant, and ordered that when particular plaintiffs incurred costs pursuing lead actions every other plaintiff should contribute rateably.

Held, dismissing the appeal, that R.S.C., Ord. 62, r.3(3) referred to the manner not the times at which the judge's discretion as to costs should be exercised, and a judge might in appropriate circumstances make an order as to costs not yet incurred (*Aiden Shipping Co.* v. *Interbulk* [1986] C.L.Y. 2606 applied).

DAVIES (JOSEPH OWEN) *v.* ELI LILLY & CO. [1987] 1 W.L.R. 1136, C.A.

2943. Costs—discretionary order—whether correct exercise of discretion—jurisdiction of court to review order

[Supreme Court Act 1981 (c.54), s.18.]

In a copyright infringement action P and D each partially succeeded in the High Court, Court of Appeal and the House of Lords. Costs were reserved to the judge conducting the enquiry as to damages. Upon enquiry the judge ordered D to pay one third of P's costs before the trial judge and P's costs on the enquiry. D appealed.

Held, dismissing the appeal, that (1) the Court had limited jurisdiction to review a discretionary order as to costs; (2) the judge had taken the proper factors into account in exercising his discretion, even if his decision was open to criticism.

INFABRICS *v.* JAYTEX [1987] F.S.R. 529, C.A.

2944/5. Costs—enquiry as to damages—injunction restraining passing off—offers of undertaking made before trial

[R.S.C. Ord. 18, r.8.]

P operated a chain of fast food restaurants. One of its best known products was the "Big Mac" hamburger. D ran a smaller chain and advertised "It's Not Just Big, Mac." Before trial D offered to undertake not to use the advertisements. At trial the judge granted an injunction, but refused to order an enquiry as to damages and made no order as to costs.

Held, on appeal, that (1) P was not entitled as of right to an order for costs or an enquiry as to damages in a case such as this; (2) on the facts of this case P had an arguable case for claiming damages and the Court would order the enquiry; (3) it was unjustifiable in principle in this case to make an order as to costs. D should pay one half of P's taxed costs.

McDONALD'S HAMBURGERS *v.* BURGERKING (U.K.) [1987] F.S.R. 112, C.A.

2946. Costs—expert witness—allowance

A successful party to an action will not be allowed to recover the cost of calling an expert witness where that witness has only given evidence as to the meaning of ordinary English words.

During a claim by a defendant against the third party the issue arose whether there was authority to sign a reinsurance slip. Reference was made to a document which to some extent conferred authority but it had "excluding U.S.A." inserted in the territorial limits. The defendant had produced an expert report saying that the authority did not permit the signatory to sign contracts which did not contain words "excluding U.S.A.".

Held, that no expert evidence was required to say that and no custom or practice was alleged. It was simply the ordinary meaning of the English language. No allowance would be given for the costs of the expert witness. Too often unnecessary expert evidence was adduced which simply caused prolongation of trials and unnecessary expenses.

HALVANON INSURANCE CO. *v.* JEWETT DUCHESNE (INTERNATIONAL) [1987] 1 FTLR 503, Staughton J.

2947. Costs—"on cost"

The cost of funding a litigant's disbursements between the time when the expenses are incurred and the time when an order for costs becomes effective (the "on cost") is not an expense allowable on taxation.

HUNT *v.* DOUGLAS (R.M.) (ROOFING), *The Times,* November 23, 1987, C.A.

2948. Costs—power to award costs in lieu of taxed costs—whether formal restriction

[R.S.C., Ord. 62, r.9(4).]

A judge was entitled in the exercise of her discretion, to award a gross sum in lieu of taxed costs under R.S.C., Ord. 62, r.9(4) without warning to the other side.

In proceedings for ancillary relief following the dissolution of the marriage, the husband refused to disclose his assets, which thus necessitated a long investigation. There was a protracted hearing in which the husband still failed to co-operate, and the wife's solicitors submitted an itemised schedule of her costs. The judge, without inviting the husband to address the court on costs, or declaring her intentions, assessed the wife's costs, acting under R.S.C., Ord. 62, r.9(4) in the sum of £31,000, and ordered the husband to pay it in lieu of taxed costs. He appealed.

Held, dismissing the appeal, that the power to award a gross sum in lieu of taxed costs under R.S.C., Ord. 62, r.9(4) was not subject to any formal restriction, but was to be exercised judicially. On the facts, the judge had acted in the exercise of her discretion, and was entitled to award costs without warning the husband of her intentions (*Silva* v. *Czarnikow (C.)* [1960] C.L.Y. 2482 considered).

LEARY *v.* LEARY [1987] 1 W.L.R. 72, C.A.

2949. Costs—recovery of costs—costs from legal aid fund—hardship

[Legal Aid Act 1974 (c.4), s.13(1), (3).]

Where an application for costs was made against the legal aid fund the court should assess the sum, if any, which the successful party could afford to pay by way of costs without hardship and should order that the excess be paid by the fund.

ADAMS & ADAMS *v.* RILEY (M.G.), *The Times,* October 12, 1987, Hutchison J.

2950. Costs—security—discretion

[R.S.C., Ord. 23, r.1(1)(*a*).]

There is an absolute discretion in the court to order security for costs to enable a just result to be brought about having regard to all the circumstances. In the instant case an order for security in the sum of roughly one quarter of what was sought would be made in order not to shut out the plaintiff.

CHANDLESS *v.* WHITTOME (1987) 84 L.S.Gaz. 735, Browne-Wilkinson V.-C.

2951. Costs—security—foreign co-plaintiff

[R.S.C., Ord. 23, r.1.]

There is jurisdiction to order security for costs in an action with a foreign co-plaintiff, and there is no inflexible rule of practice preventing the court from so doing. The note at R.S.C. 23/1–3/3 is incorrect in that regard (*Winthorpe* v. *Royal Exchange Assurance Co.* (1775) 1 Dick. 282, *D'Hormusgee* v. *Grey* (1882) 10 Q.B.D. 13, *Crozat* v. *Brogden* [1894] 2 Q.B. 30 considered).

SLAZENGERS *v.* SEASPEED FERRIES INTERNATIONAL, *The Times,* November 2, 1987, C.A.

2952. Costs—security—limited company in liquidation as plaintiff—need to consider all the circumstances

[Companies Act 1985 (c.6), s.726.]

Where the plaintiff in a case was a limited company in liquidation, the court could refuse to order that it give security for costs on a review of all the circumstances of the case. Its impecuniosity was only one factor to be taken into account.

The plaintiff was a limited company in liquidation. It suffered a fire in which its factory and stock were damaged. The defendant company were its insurers. They rejected the insurance claim, alleging arson and breach of warranty by the plaintiff; these allegations were denied. The plaintiff brought an action and the defendants asked for security for costs under s.726 of the Companies Act 1985 which gave the court jurisdiction to order security for costs if there was reason to believe that a plaintiff company would be unable to pay a defendant's costs if the defence succeeded. It was unlikely that the plaintiffs could pay in that event. The registrar ordered a security for costs, but the judge on appeal reversed that decision. The judge held that the plaintiff's claim was made bona fide, and had an even chance of success. The fire had probably caused the liquidation, and the plaintiff was insured by the defendants. Although the defendant would be out of pocket if it won, to uphold the registrar's decision would be to prevent the claim being brought.

Held, dismissing the appeal, that the judge had taken into account all the circumstances, as he had to under s.726; he had not misdirected himself and was entitled to exercise his discretion as he had. The plaintiff's impecuniosity and consequent inability to raise money for security for costs were of consequence because the direction for security might have oppressive consequences. The court had given proper regard to this matter.

AQUILA DESIGN (GRP PRODUCTS) *v.* CORNHILL INSURANCE (1987) 3 BCC 364, C.A.

2953. Costs—security—Northern Ireland company in receivership and liquidation—whether jurisdiction to make order

[R.S.C., Ord. 23, r.1(1)(*a*)

The court had jurisdiction to order that a Northern Ireland company in liquidation or receivership give security for costs.

P, which was a company incorporated in Northern Ireland and was in receivership and liquidation, sued D alleging conspiracy to defraud. D sought security for costs.

Held, that the court had jurisdiction to make the order sought. The principle that the court would not order security against a plaintiff not resident in England and Wales, who was resident in another part of the U.K. was of no application to a company in liquidation (*Raeburn* v. *Andrews* (1874) L.R. 9 Q.B. 118 distinguished; *Crozat* v. *Brogden* [1894] 2 Q.B. 30 considered).

D.S.Q. PROPERTY CO. *v.* LOTUS CARS [1987] 1 W.L.R. 127, Millett J.

2954. Costs—security—plaintiff resident in EEC—enforceability of judgments

[Civil Jurisdiction and Judgments Act 1982 (c.27), s.2(1); R.S.C. Ord. 23, r.1(1)(*a*).]

The 1982 Act now offers a realistic alterative to enforcing a judgment within the jurisdiction, which the court will take into account when considering an application for security for costs.

The plaintiff, a West German organisation, started an action claiming an injunction to restrain the defendant company from passing off car care products as its own. The defendant applied for security for costs. The plaintiff resisted on the basis that since the 1982 Act a U.K. judgment was enforceable in the EEC.

Held, dismissing the application, the purposes of such an order was to bring funds without the jurisdiction; the 1982 Act now provided a realistic alternative to enforcing the order in the U.K., which, although not necessarily a decisive factor, was an important factor in the exercise of the court's discretion (*Raeburn* v. *Andrews* [1874] L.R. 9 Q.B. 118 considered.

PORZELACK K.G. *v.* PORZELACK (U.K.) [1987] 1 W.L.R. 420, Browne-Wilkinson V.-C.

2955. Costs—solicitors' delay

When the costs of litigation have been increased by delays that are the fault of the solicitors involved, they should be ordered to pay the extra costs personally.

COUNTRYSIDE PROPERTIES *v.* MOORE, *The Times*, January 30, 1987, Browne-Wilkinson V.-C.

2956. Costs—taxation—application for taxation by experienced litigants after agreement to pay costs

[Solicitors Act 1974 (c.47), s.71(1).]

As part of a settlement of a libel action, D agreed to pay P's legal costs. The settlement included "Reimbursement of P's costs in the sum of £20,000 plus VAT." D received and paid a bill for £20,000 plus VAT, and then sought taxation of P's costs.

Held, that s.71(1) of the Solicitors Act 1974 gave the Court a discretion to make an order for taxation, whether or not there was a solicitor/own client relationship between the solicitor and the party presented with the bill. However, as (i) it was clear that the sum of £20,000 plus VAT was part of an overall settlement of P's claim; (ii) D was an experienced libel litigator represented by experienced solicitors; and therefore (iii) D did not need the protection of taxation, the Court would not order taxation.

INGRAMS *v.* SYKES, *The Independent*, November 12, 1987, C.A.

2957. Costs—taxation—delay greater than twelve months

[Solicitors Act 1974 (c.47), s.70(4).]

There is no jurisdiction to order a taxation of a bill of costs at the request of the paying party more than 12 months after payment. (*Storer & Co.* v. *Johnson* [1890] 15 A.C. 203, Solicitor, *A, Re* [1961] C.L.Y. 8475, *Symbol Park Lane* v. *Steggles Palmer* [1985] C.L.Y. 3363, *Shiloh Spinners* v. *Harding* [1973] C.L.Y. 1867 considered).

HARRISON *v.* TEW, *The Independent*, July 7, 1987, C.A. (by a majority).

2958. Costs—taxation—privileged documents—natural justice. See GOLDMAN *v.* HESPER, §1710.

2959. Costs—taxation—review of taxation—time limit

[R.S.C., Ord. 62, r.33(2); Legal Aid (General; Regulations 1980 (S.I. 1980 No. 1894).]

The solicitor of an assisted person who applies for a review of a taxation must do so within 21 days of the taxing officers decision or such extended period as the officer shall fix.

MORRIS *v.* MURPHY (J.) CABLE CONTRACTORS & CIVIL ENGINEERS, *The Times*, October 23, 1987, C.A.

2960. Costs—taxation—rights of audience patent agents

[Solicitors Act 1974 (c.47), ss.20, 22, 25, 27, 39, 87; Patents Act 1977 (c.37), ss.102, 103, 104; R.S.C. Ords. 5, 104.]

At a taxation of costs hearing before the master, where it had been ordered by the Comptroller and Patents Court that R should pay H's costs, the master decided that H had been improperly represented by patent agents who had no rights of audience and that there were no legal costs capable of being taxed. H applied for review.

Held, a party to an appeal to the Patents Court from a decision of the Comptroller was entitled to instruct patent agents who were allowed to appear instead of counsel.

REISS ENGINEERING *v.* HARRIS [1987] R.P.C. 171 Patents Ct.

2961. Costs—unreasonable conduct—D filing a defence denying liability

[C.C.R. 1981, Ord. 19, r.6(*c*).]

On receipt of a summons claiming damages for negligence arising out of a road traffic accident, D filed a defence denying liability and on the same day paid into court a sum slightly greater than the amount claimed as special damages. P accepted the payment but sought costs under r.6(*c*). P relied on D's unreasonable behaviour in filing a defence denying liability in order that the matter would automatically be referred to arbitration, where legal costs other than those on the summons, are not normally recoverable.

Held, that P was entitled to costs on Scale 1. It was unreasonable conduct for D to file a defence denying liability when he clearly had no intention of disputing it. Instead D could merely have submitted to interlocutory judgment with damages to be assessed. In this case the assessment would not have been necessary because P accepted the payment in. In this way P would have been entitled to costs, and it was felt that it was for this reason that D had filed the defence—to avoid the costs liability (*Newland* v. *Boardwell* [1984] C.L.Y. 472 applied).

WILLIAMS *v.* N. P. JORDAN, September 29, 1987; Mr. Registrar Rose; Edmonton County Ct. [*Ex rel. Simon P. Williams, Barrister*].

2962. Costs—when solicitors to pay costs

[R.S.C., Ord. 62, r.11.]

When solicitors were advised by counsel to join a party to proceedings, and that advice was clearly wrong but the party was nevertheless joined in the action for a short time, the solicitors would not be ordered to pay that party's costs personally (*Davy-Chiesman* v. *Davy-Chiesman* [1984] C.L.Y. 1995 distinguished).

R. *v.* OXFORDSHIRE EDUCATION AUTHORITY, *ex p.* W., *The Times*, April 11, 1987, D.C.

2963. County court injunction—obstruction of right of way—undertaking in lieu of injunction—costs order

P sought certain declarations and injunctive relief in an action against D. The judge found that (i) a right of way as contended for by P existed, (ii) P as the persons then entitled to the property known as "RC" were entitled to exercise that right of way, (iii) the caravan placed on the property by D blocked the right of way but it did not block access entirely. Without enquiring of P whether an undertaking in lieu of an injunction would be acceptable the judge held that so long as D undertook to make a proper width available round the caravan with a hardcore base he would not grant an injunction against them. Further the judge ordered, without making any enquiry as to the estimated costs of the claim and the counterclaim before him (the counterclaim relating to certain alleged encroachments on D's land in respect of which D in some measure succeeded before the judge) that D should pay P's costs of the claim and the counterclaim limited to £600. P appealed.

Held, allowing the appeal, (i) the judge was seeking to achieve a result which would enable the right of way to be used without any necessity of removing the caravan but in doing so he imposed in effect a compromise on P about which they had not been asked and to which they objected. The judge found as a matter of fact and law that there was this right of way and that the caravan was an obstruction of that right of way. They were no grounds upon which could be founded any argument that in those circumstances injunctive relief was inappropriate. In those circumstances the judge was bound to grant P the injunction that they sought, to remove the obstruction from the right of way to which they were entitled (*Charrington* v. *Simons & Co.* [1971] C.L.Y. 9300 followed); (ii) the appeal as to costs was not the sole matter appealed against in this case and consequently leave to appeal against the judge's order for costs was not required. Further, as this was a case in which leave was not required, the approach of the court to the judge's order for costs made in the exercise of his discretion below was different from the approach which the Court of Appeal ought to adopt if costs only had been appealed against and leave had not been granted. Where an appeal was brought on costs as well as on other matters, the question for the Court of Appeal was not simply "did the learned judge exercise any discretion below at all?" but the alternative question "having exercised the discretion below, is it open on general principles to disturb the true exercise of a discretion by the learned judge at first instance?". The order made by the judge in relation to costs was plainly wrong in the circumstances. The proper order to have made in the circumstances would have been for P to have recovered their costs of the claim and for D to have recovered their costs of the counterclaim (*Brown* v. *Sparrow* [1982] C.L.Y. 491 distinguished; *Medway Oil & Storage Co.* v. *Continental Contractors* (1929) A.C. 88 considered).

JAMESON *v.* MANLEY, September 4, 1986 (C.A.T. No. 779).

2964. County courts—adjournment—unjust refusal

P, a firm of accountants, claimed £2,052 from D in respect of their professional charges and disbursements. D filed a Defence that the claim was too high. On January 21 the Registrar made a standard order for directions that there be discovery by lists of documents within seven days but discovery did not take place. A further order was made on March 7, on the pre-trial review, when neither party attended, that firstly there be mutual discovery of documents by lists within fourteen days with inspection seven days thereafter, secondly accountants reports be agreed if possible and if not agreed, the expert evidence be limited to one witness for each party and thirdly the action be set down before the judge on a date to be fixed. On March 17, the court itself fixed May 16 as the date for the hearing. On April 16, D's solicitors wrote to P's solicitors asking for their list of documents but nothing was forthcoming. On May 2, D issued an application returnable on May 8 before the judge for the action to be taken out of the list for failure to comply with the directions for discovery. The application was supported by P. The judge refused the application on the ground that D should have applied to strike the action out or for a peremptory order for delivery of documents and that any inconvenience would fall on P rather than D. On the same day, D sent his list of documents to P. P sent a list on May 13 which was received by D on May 14. There was no practical possibility of the documents being examined before the action came on for a trial and for an expert accountant to have the opportunity of considering copies of the documents so as to advise D. When the case was called on May 16, P's counsel applied for an adjournment to produce the documents. D's counsel did not oppose that application. The judge refused the application and the trial proceeded. P's bill of costs was admitted in evidence and evidence was taken from one witness, Mrs. C, a chartered accountant who had been a partner in the P firm and had been responsible for preparing the bill. The judge accepted C's evidence that the bill was reasonable and gave judgment for P accordingly. D appealed.

Held, allowing D's appeal and setting aside the judge's order, that what had happened in the case was a travesty of justice because, through the judge's refusal of adjournment, D had been denied the opportunity of testing P's case or of seeking an expert witness to comment on it or having C or any other witness who might have been called effectively cross-examined. A judge erred in law when he refused an adjournment in circumstances which constituted a miscarriage of justice. The appeal would be allowed and a new trial of the action ordered before a different judge in the county court (*Dick* v. *Piller* [1943] 1 K.B. 497 considered).

BERKELEY JACKSON *v.* STEPHENS, October 14, 1986 (C.A.T. No. 878).

2965. County courts—costs—award not exceeding £500

P, employee, issued proceedings against D, employers, for damages for an injury to his thumb incurred at work limiting his claim to a sum of £3,000. The judge awarded P £200 damages and, taking the view that the claim should have been limited to £500, accordingly referred to arbitration under C.C.R., Ord. 19, r.3 and ordered that there be no order as to costs. P appealed.

Held, that if P knew or ought to have known that he could not reasonably expect to recover more than £500 but nevertheless decided that he would make his claim in excess of that sum so that he obtained a trial and not an arbitration, that would be sufficient ground for depriving him of all his costs with the exception of the costs stated on the summons under C.C.R., Ord. 19, r.6(*a*) which dealt with the costs of automatic arbitrations. However, P had reasonable grounds for taking the view that the award in his favour might well exceed £500. Accordingly the appeal would be allowed and P given his costs below on the appropriate scale (*Hobbs* v. *Marlowe* [1977] C.L.Y. 433 considered).

CUNNINGHAM *v*. B.L. COMPONENTS, April 21, 1986 (C.A.T. No. 391).

2966. County court—costs—cost of repairs in road accident case—offer of settlement to pay repairs—refusal to pay costs—whether plaintiff entitled to commence proceedings.

A plaintiff was not debarred from starting proceedings where the defendant agreed to pay all of the plaintiff's claim except solicitors' costs before the action commenced.

In a road traffic accident, D negligently damaged P's car. P's solicitors wrote to D's insurers offering to settle P's claim on payment of £109·32 of which £23·00 was P's solicitors' costs. D's insurers sent P's solicitors a cheque for £86·32, *i.e.* the sum claimed less P's solicitors' costs indicating that they did not consider themselves liable to pay the same. P's solicitors returned the cheque and commenced proceedings. In the action, P claimed an additional sum of £12·00 by way of liquidated damages and general damages for loss of use. The latter claim had been quantified at £15·00 per day in the offer of settlement. Being an unliquidated damages claim, its quantification was at large in the proceedings. D filed a defence admitting liability and paid £86·32 into court. The defence claimed that the proceedings were an abuse of the process of the court having regard to D's attempt to pay P £86·32 before the commencement of the action. On D's application the registrar struck out the proceedings as an abuse of the process. The registrar's decision was upheld by the judge.

Held, allowing P's appeal, that it was impossible to say whether the proceedings were an abuse or not until damages had been assessed and it became clear whether or not P recovered more than £86·32. It was an abuse of the process of the court merely to commence proceedings to increase the costs payable by D's insurers with a view to persuading them to pay solicitors' costs in future. As D could not prove that at the time of the application, interlocutory judgment for P would be entered and an order for damages to be assessed.

SMITH *v*. SPRINGER [1987] 3 All E.R. 252, C.A.

2967. County courts—defence of tender—claim for repairs to motor vehicle—whether defence available—amount of claim plus interest paid into court—whether good payment in—whether amount tendered before action should include interest

[County Court Rules 1981 (S.I. 1981 No. 1087 (L.20)), Ord. 1, r.10; Ord. 9, r.12; Ord. 11, r.1(8).]

A claim for the cost of repairs to a motor car consequent upon the defendant's negligence was a claim for unliquidated damages to which a defence of tender before action was not available.

D negligently collided with P's motor car. P's solicitor wrote to D's insurers offering to settle P's claim on payment of £132·50 for the cost of repairs, £5·00 for one day's loss of use and £28·80 for costs. D's insurers replied by sending a cheque for £137·50 and stating that D was not liable to pay costs. P's solicitors did not cash the cheque but commenced proceedings claiming £137·50 plus interest pursuant to s.69 County Courts Act 1984 on October 3, 1985. On October 16, D put in a defence admitting liability, denying P's entitlement to interest and costs and seeking to set up the defence of tender before action on the basis of the cheque sent to P's solicitors. D paid into court a sum representing damages and interest. The trial judge rejected the defence of tender on account of the fact that the sum paid into court was not equal to the amount tendered as the amount tendered should have included interest. D appealed.

Held, dismissing D's appeal, that D was not obliged to tender before action any amount representing interest that the court might avoid in the exercise of its discretion under s.69 County Courts Act 1984. In so far as Ord. 11, r.1(8) provided for a cause of action to include a claim for interest, it applied only to payment into court in satisfaction of a plaintiff's cause of action under the provision of Ord. 11. It had no bearing on the question of tender before action. Ord. 9, r.12 did not preclude a payment in of a greater sum. The rule was satisfied if the sum paid into court included the amount tendered. Notwithstanding the above, D's appeal failed on account of the fact that tender before action was not a good defence to a claim for unliquidated damages. P's claim was a claim for unliquidated damages. Although Ord. 1, r.10 provided for such a claim to be treated as a liquidated demand for the purposes of the County Court Rules, it could not and did not alter the substantive law so as to make the defence of tender available.

LAING (JOHN) CONSTRUCTION *v.* DASTUR [1987] 1 W.L.R. 686, C.A.

2968. County courts—fixed date for trial—application to vacate

The learned judge should not have refused a consent application to vacate the fixed date for the trial of a possession action on the ground that the defendant whose oral evidence was vital, was unavoidably out of the country.

STANFORD *v.* KOBAYASHI, *The Times*, July 29, 1987, C.A.

2969. County courts—forms

COUNTY COURT (FORMS) (AMENDMENT) RULES 1987 (No. 1119 (L.4)) [£1·60], made under the County Courts Act 1984 (c.28), s.75; substitute a new form of warrant of execution (N.42) and thus omits forms N43, N44, N45, N54 and amends N49 and N53.

2970. County courts—funds

COURT FUNDS RULES 1987 (No. 821 (L.3)) [£3·30], made under the Administration of Justice Act 1982 (c.53), s.38(7); operative on June 1, 1987; amalgamated S.I. 1975 No. 1803, as amended, with S.I. 1965 No. 1500, as amended.

2971. County courts—rules

COUNTY COURT (AMENDMENT) RULES 1987 (No. 493 (L.1)) [£1·40], operative on April 13, 1987, save for Rule 3 which is operative on June 1, 1987; amend S.I. 1981 No. 1687.

COUNTY COURT (AMENDMENT No. 2) RULES 1987 (No. 1397 (L.7)) [45p], made under the County Courts Act 1984 (c.28), s.75; operative on September 1, 1987; amend the 1981 Rules by making minor revisions relating to fixed costs.

2972. County courts—summonses—issue—forms—practice direction

The following practice direction was issued on March 17, 1987, by Lord Hailsham, L.C. [C.C.R., Ord. 50, r.1.]

1. On January 1, 1987 two new forms of default summonses were introduced: N1 (fixed amount) and N2 (amount not fixed). The practice form Request for Default Summons (N201) was also revised on that date.

2. The new lay-out of these forms provides space for plaintiffs to include on the face of the Summons, or Request, as the case may be, their particulars of claim where these can be stated within the space provided. This is frequently the case where the claim arises out of a simple debt, such as an unpaid water rate.

3. It is necessary to ensure uniformity of practice in the application of the powers conferred upon proper officers by C.C.R., Ord. 3, r.3(1A) and Ord. 6, r.1. These powers enable a proper officer to refuse to accept forms of Summonses prepared by the plaintiffs or Requests on which the particulars of claim have been endorsed

4. In order to ensure compatibility with court office reprographic equipment, the design, lay-out, size and spacing of forms N1, N2 and N201 must be in exact alignment with the forms provided to plaintiffs by the Lord Chancellor's Department at Trevelyan House, 30 Great Peter Street, London SW1P 2BY. The proper officer may refuse to allow any forms not so conforming.

5. A document may need to be photocopied by the court. Accordingly every document presented to the court must be on paper of durable quality and:

ii(i) be completed in black ink;

i(ii) be capable of producing clear copies by a reprographic or similar process;

(iii) be produced in either printed, handwritten (which must be clear and legible) or type-written form.

For the purposes of this Practice Direction any document produced by a reprographic or similar process (including laser printing) giving a clear and permanent representation free from blemishes will be treated as if it were printed, written or type-written, as the case may be. The proper officer may refuse to allow any form which does not satisfy these requirements.

Certificate of Service

6. Where summonses are served by post by the court a variation of form N12 (Certificate of Service) is authorised so that a simplified Certificate of Service can be endorsed on forms N1, N2 and N201. The endorsement should state the date of service, the date of posting and the name of the officer serving the summons. For all forms of service other than postal service by the court, form N12 shall continue to be used.

Request

7. Where plaintiffs prepare their own summonses, there is no need for the Request for Default Summons to be in form N201. This creates unnecessary paperwork particularly where plaintiffs issue large numbers of proceedings at one time in a particular court. It is also unnecessary for plaintiffs who prepare their own summonses to lodge separate Requests for each proceeding; a single Request to the court to serve the summonses, enclosing the prescribed fees and the copy documentation required by C.C.R., Ord. 6 and C.C.R., Ord. 3, r.3(1A) will be acceptable. In these cases the request should state the plaintiff's full name and address, and if the summons is entered by a solicitor the name, address and reference number of the solicitor, and list the names of the defendants against whom the plaintiff requests the issue of default summonses.

8. Subject to the foregoing, forms of summons prepared by plaintiffs and Requests including particulars of claim will be acceptable in County Courts.

9. The Practice Direction dated March 1, 1979 is hereby revoked ([1979] C.L.Y. 386).

10. This Practice Direction takes effect from April 1, 1987.

PRACTICE DIRECTION (LORD CHANCELLOR) (COUNTY COURT PRACTICE: SUMMONSES: FORMS) (1987) 137 New L.J. 294.

2973. Court of Appeal—annual review

In his review of the Court of Appeal for the year 1986 to 1987, the Master of the Rolls considered the creation of additional Lords Justice of Appeal, as well as more courtrooms. It was not practical to increase the number of working hours in the day, but a preliminary screening process for appeals was being discussed. His Lordship stressed the need for appellants to pursue their appeals diligently.

ANNUAL REVIEW 1986–87, *The Times,* October 5, 1987, Sir John Donaldson, M.R.

2974. Court of Appeal—compliance with timetables

Both appellants and respondents are required to comply strictly with the timetables of the Court of Appeal.

A. *v.* B., *The Times*, July 10, 1987, C.A.

2975. Court of Appeal—jurisdiction—order to produce documents to police during course of investigation—whether order made in "criminal cause or matter"—whether appeal from High Court to Court of Appeal (Civil Division). See CARR *v.* ATKINS, §631.

2976. Court of Appeal—list of forthcoming appeals—abolition of warned list—practice note

The following practice note was issued by the Master of the Rolls on October 2, 1987.

In the interests of achieving a further simplification and streamlining of the progress of appeals in the Court of Appeal, Civil Division, it is proposed to abolish the warned list, which has ceased to fulfil its original purpose. Its function will be taken over by the list of forthcoming appeals, which will become the sole list of pending appeals and will be printed in the Daily Cause List in the same manner and with the same frequency as the warned list appeared in the past.

With a view to assisting appellants and their legal representatives to comply with the very strict and important timetable which is based on the date when appeals enter the list of forthcoming appeals, the Civil Appeals Office, when acknowledging the setting down of an appeal, will not only inform the parties of the number allocated to the appeal in the list in which it is entered, but will also specify the date on which it is intended to include it in the list of forcoming appeals.

This change will take effect from October 2, 1987. As from that date the significance of an appeal entering the list of forthcoming appeals will be as follows.

(i) *Bundles*

The requisite number of bundles for the use of the judges must be lodged not later than 14 days after the appeal enters the list of forthcoming appeals, or within such longer period (if any) as the registrar may allow on application for cause. Any application for an extension should be made to the registrar by letter setting out the length of extension sought and the reasons for it.

The documents required to be included are listed in R.S.C., Ord. 59, r.9 (as amended) and the bundles must comply with this court's practice statement of October 22, 1986 (see *Practice Note* [1987] C.L.Y. 2900). (For further guidance on the form and content of bundles see *The Supreme Court Practice 1988* vol. I, paras. 59/9/1–59/9/12.)

(ii) *Counsel's estimates of the length of hearing*

A written estimate signed by counsel for the appellant must be sent or delivered to the Civil Appeals Office and a photocopy sent to the respondent's counsel, either directly or through the respondent's solicitors, not later than 14 days after the appeal enters the list of forthcoming appeals or within such further period as the registrar may allow on an application for cause.

It is the duty of the respondent's counsel to consider the estimate signed by the appellant's counsel as soon as it is received by him and to notify the Civil Appeals Office in writing of his own estimate if it differs from that of the appellant's counsel. In the absence of such notification the respondent's counsel will be deemed to have adopted the estimate by the appellant's counsel as his own.

It is a further, and very important, duty of both counsel to notify the Civil Appeals Office in writing of any change in their respective estimates immediately on that change taking place, whether it arises out of new matters coming to their attention or out of a revised appreciation of the position.

Listing for hearing

Without prejudice to listing earlier in case of urgency, an appeal may be listed for hearing at any time after the expiry of a period of 14 days from its entry in the list of forthcoming appeals or such longer period as the registrar may have ordered in response to an application for an extension.

In order to avoid being taken by surprise, counsel's clerks should keep in touch with the Civil Appeals Office, which will provide them with such information as can be made available on the likely progress of appeals towards being listed for hearing.

Appellants and respondents who are not represented by solicitors and counsel will be notified of the date for hearing by the Civil Appeals Office.

Default in compliance with the timetable

Non-compliance by appellants with this timetable will result in the appeal being listed to show cause why it should not be dismissed.

PRACTICE NOTE (C.A.) (LIST OF FORTHCOMING APPEALS) [1987] 3 All E.R. 434.

2977. Court of Appeal—long vacation—sittings of civil division during long vacation—practice note

[R.S.C., Ord. 64, r.2(1).]

The following practice note was issued on March 23, 1987, by the Master of the Rolls.

Having determined that sittings are necessary for the purpose of hearing appeals and applications during vacation, in the exercise of the powers conferred on me by R.S.C., Ord. 64, r.2(1), and with the concurrence of the Lord Chancellor, I direct that the Civil Division of the Court of Appeal shall sit during August and September 1987 and in the months of August and September in future years until further notice. Details of the numbers of courts sitting in August and September will be published each year, normally before Easter.

The sittings in the Civil Division of the Court of Appeal in August and September 1987 and the number and constitution of the courts expected to sit will be as follows:

3 to 7 August	one 3-judge court and one 2-judge court
10 to 14 August	one 2-judge court
14 to 30 September	one 3-judge court and three 2-judge courts

PRACTICE NOTE (C.A) (LONG VACATION) [1987] 1 All E.R. 1067.

2978. Court of Protection—solicitors' fixed costs—practice note

The following practice note was issued by the Master of the Court of Protection on August 26, 1987.

The system of fixed costs introduced in 1983 and described in detail in The Law Society's Gazette of November 26, 1986, at page 3557, continues to be popular with solicitors.

It has been agreed with The Law Society that the amounts to be allowed will be increased as follows:—

Category I Work up to and including completion of the directions contained in the First General Order £185 (plus VAT)

(The commencement fee of £50 and fees for medical evidence and evidence of notification of the patient may be added. Please produce receipts for fees paid).

Category II (a) Preparation and lodgment of a receivership account £75 (plus VAT).

(b) Preparation and lodgment of a receivership account which has been certified by a solicitor under the provisions of the Practice Notes dated September 13, 1984 [1984] C.L.Y. 2699 and March 5, 1985 [1985] C.L.Y. 2647 £87·50 (plus VAT).

Category III General Management work in the second and subsequent years £220 (plus VAT).

(Note: Categories II and III may be claimed together).

Category IV Applications under s.36(9) of the Trustee Act 1925 for the appointment of a new trustee in the place of the patient, for the purpose of making title to land £160 (plus VAT).

The increased amounts will apply as follows:—

In Category I, to all draft First General Orders sent out on or after November 2, 1987

In Category II, to all receivership accounts lodged on or after November 2, 1987

In Category III, to all general management costs in respect of years ended on or after November 2, 1987.

In Category IV, to all orders sent out on or after November 2, 1987.

In all categories, solicitors will continue to have the option of taxing costs, rather than accepting fixed costs, if they wish. If solicitors seek an order for taxation of the costs under Category II as well as Category III, the relevant items for both categories should be included in the same bill.

PRACTICE NOTE (COURT OF PROTECTION) (SOLICITORS' FIXED COSTS) August 26, 1987.

2979. Crown office list—arrangement of list—practice note

The following practice note was issued by Lord Lane C.J. on February 3, 1987.

1. As from 2 March 1987 the following arrangements will apply to the listing of cases included in the Crown Office list.

2. The Head Clerk, under the direction of the Master of the Crown Office, will arrange the Crown Office list into the following parts.

3. *Part A: cases not ready to be heard*

Cases where leave has yet to be obtained, or the time limits for the filing or lodging of notices, affidavits or other documents have not expired and where, in consequence, a case is not yet ready to be heard.

4. *Part B: cases ready to be heard*

In cases where the time limits mentioned in Part A have expired it will be assumed that all parties are ready to be heard. When a case enters Part B the applicant or his solicitors will be informed by letter. It will be the responsibility of the applicant or his solicitors to forward a copy of that letter to (i) the clerk to counsel instructed by the applicant and (ii) any respondent to the case or his solicitor, who should inform the clerk to counsel instructed by him. It will be the responsibility of counsels' clerks to inform the Head Clerk, *in writing,* of counsel's time estimate for the case and of any alteration thereto.

5. The Head Clerk will make arrangements for hearing dates to be fixed, drawing cases from Part B in order of entry so far as is practicable. While the Head Clerk will give as much notice as possible of the date fixed for hearing he cannot undertake to accommodate the wishes of applicants, respondents, their solicitors or counsel. The occasional need to list cases at short notice may mean that parties are unable to be represented by the counsel of their first choice. In particular it should be remembered that the cases listed in the Crown Office list take precedence, so far as the attendance of counsel is concerned, over cases listed for hearing in the Crown Court unless a Divisional Court or a judge otherwise directs.

6. *Part C: cases stood out*

Where a case appears in Part B, or Part E (see post), and any party to the case is of the opinion that he is not ready to be heard he may apply to the Master of the Crown Office to have the matter stood out into Part C. Where the Master of the Crown office accedes to such an application he may do so on such terms as he thinks fit. Where he declines to direct that the matter be stood out into Part C application may be made to a Divisional Court or a judge, as the case may be, by way of notice of motion.

7. *Part D: the expedited list*

Cases entered in this list will be listed for hearing as soon as practicable. In cases other than those where a Divisional Court or a judge has directed that a case be considered for expedition, application for inclusion in Part D should be made in the first instance to the Master of the Crown Office but, where he declines to direct its inclusion in Part D, application may be made to a Divisional Court or a judge, as the case may be, by way of notice of motion.

8. *Part E: cases listed for hearing*

This part of the list will contain those cases where a date for hearing has been fixed.

9. As from 2 March 1987 the Daily Cause List will, in relation to the Crown Office list, contain only such cases as are to be heard on the next sitting day.

10. A copy of Parts B, C, D and E of the Crown Office list may be inspected in the Crown Office.

11. In this Practice Direction the expression 'applicant' includes 'appellant' where the context so requires and the expression 'judge' means a judge hearing cases in the Crown Office list.

PRACTICE NOTE (Q.B.D.) (CROWN OFFICE LIST) [1987] 1 All E.R. 368.

2980. Crown office list—estimated length of hearing—notice of estimate—duty of counsel's clerks—practice note

The following practice note was issued by Mann J. on April 3, 1987.

I make the following observations with the approval of Watkins L.J. The practice direction handed down by Lord Lane C.J. on February 3, 1987 (*Practice Note* [1987] 2 C.L. 238a) prescribed the arrangements which as from March 2, 1987 apply to the listing of cases included in the Crown Office list. Part B of that list contains cases ready to be heard. Part D is the expedited list. The pressure on both of those parts is great. Particularly is it so when the case is to be heard by the single judge. In regard to both parts it is the responsibility of counsel's clerks to inform in writing the head clerk of counsel's time estimate for a case and of any variation in an estimation previously given. Dealing with the list is critically dependant on the reasonable accuracy of estimates. Plainly precision is impossible but there have been a number of cases recently where the estimate can be described only as an ill-judged underestimate. In the interests of the dispatch of business and of those who have business in this court, close attention must be paid to the reality of an estimate. I emphasise, should there be a belief to the contrary, that underestimation now secures no advantage in the listing of a case.

PRACTICE NOTE (Q.B.D.) (CROWN OFFICE LIST) [1987] 1 All E.R. 1184.

2981. Crown practice—fees

CROWN OFFICE FEES ORDER 1987 (No. 1464) [45p], made under the Great Seal (Offices) Act 1874 (c.81), s.9; operative on October 1, 1987; increases certain fees.

2982. Damages—interim payment—procedural rules

[R.S.C., Ord. 29, rr.11, 12.]

Where a plaintiff is likely to receive damages or a substantial sum of money at the trial, but it is not clear which, the court can make an interim award either under R.S.C., Ord. 29, r.11 or r.12, taking them as a whole, and the plaintiff should make application under both heads.

The plaintiffs agreed to sell tin to the defendants under standard form contracts incorporating the rules and regulations of the London Metal Exchange. Before delivery, dealings on the tin market were suspended and the defendants refused to accept the tin when the plaintiffs tried to deliver it. The committee of the London Metal Exchange then promulgated Rule M, fixing a settlement price for all such contracts, and providing for the difference between the fixed settlement price and the contract price to be paid by a specified date. The defendants conceded that if the plaintiffs accepted the validity of Rule M, they would be required to pay them £7·2 million. But the plaintiffs denied its validity and claimed the full contract price of £23·9 million, and alternatively a minimum of £7·2 million for non-acceptance. The defendants denied liability for breach of contract but contended that if they were liable, damages would not exceed £5·2 million. The plaintiffs applied for an interim payment under R.S.C., Ord. 29. The judge was satisfied that they would recover at least £5·2 million in damages under r.11 or alternatively £7·2 million within Rule M under r.12. But since he was not satisfied that the requirements of either rule could be satisfied to the exclusion of the other, he declined to make any order at all.

Held, on appeal, that the court should read rr.11 and 12 together in considering the plaintiffs' entitlement to an interim payment. They should ask the single question whether the applicant fulfilled the requirements of the rules as a whole rather than separately. Since the judge found that the plaintiffs had satisfied the requirements of each rule separately, he should have found that they fulfilled the requirements as a whole, and therefore awarded them the lesser alternative sum of £5·2 million as an interim payment.

SHEARSON LEHMAN BROTHERS INC. *v.* MACLAINE, WATSON & CO. [1987] 1 W.L.R. 480, C.A.

2983. Debtors (Scotland) Act 1987 (c.18)

This Act makes new provision with regard to Scotland for an extension of time for payment of debts, and amends the law relating to certain diligences. Provision is made in respect of messengers-at-arms and sheriff officers.

The Act received the Royal Assent on May 15, 1987, and comes in to force on days to be appointed by the Lord Advocate.

The Act extends to Scotland only.

2984. Declaratory judgment—hypothetical problem

The court will not grant a declaratory judgment in respect of a hypothetical question (*Gouriet* v. *Union of Post Office Workers* [1977] C.L.Y. 690, *Clay, Re* [1919] 1 Ch. 66, *Midland Bank* v. *Laker Airways* [1986] C.L.Y. 364 considered).

NAYLOR *v.* WROTHAM PARK SETTLED ESTATES, *The Times,* March 6, 1987, Mervyn Davies J.

2985. Delay—striking out—time

Where the cause of action accrued in 1975 and where witnesses would have to recall events 12 or 13 years old, it was reasonable to infer that the delay was likely to cause more than minimal prejudice (*Birkett* v. *James* [1977] C.L.Y. 2410 considered).

JAMES INVESTMENTS (IOM) *v.* PHILLIPS CUTLER PHILLIPS TROY, *The Times,* September 16, 1987, C.A.

2986. Discovery—action for infringement—application for discovery of foreign patents

The validity of P's patent was attacked by D on the ground of lack of fair basis. The patent related to chemical compounds for use in agriculture, which had certain particular plant physiological activities. D sought discovery of corresponding patents in other countries.

Held, refusing the application the scope of claims in foreign patents was not relevant.

SCHERING AGROCHEMICALS *v.* ABM CHEMICALS [1987] R.P.C. 185, Patents Ct.

2987. Discovery—bankers' books—cheques and credit slips. See WILLIAMS *v.* WILLIAMS; TUCKER *v.* WILLIAMS, §1674.

2988. Discovery—before commencement of proceedings—application to inspect for defamatory material before action

[Supreme Court Act 1981 (c.54), s.33(1)(*a*) (2).]

Whilst an order may be made that a document be made available prior to action where examination of its physical characteristics is sought, no such order will be made where the intention is simply to read the document in order to ascertain whether it is defamatory.

CRI had circulated a prospectus among potential clients, offering to provide a document, which was to be kept confidential, and which contained a study of anti-apartheid groups, and their connection with terrorism. H, who was a member of a group committed to legitimately campaigning against apartheid, sought an order permitting inspection prior to action, under the provisions of s.33(1) of the 1981 Act, contending that the document was "property" within the meaning of that section.

Held, refusing the order, that the court had no jurisdiction to make the order sought. H wanted to read the message contained in the document, rather than examine the physical characteristics of the document; that could not be "inspection" of the document. In any event, even if the court had had jurisdiction, there were no grounds upon which it could properly have exercised its discretion to make the order sought.

HUDDLESTON *v.* CONTROL RISKS INFORMATION SERVICES [1987] 1 W.L.R. 701, Hoffmann J.

2989. Discovery—disclosure of assets of judgment debtor—unincorporated association—International Tin Council

[R.S.C., Ord. 48, r.1.]

There is no jurisdiction to order the officer of an unincorporated association to be orally examined as to the association's assets, but there was an inherent jurisdiction to give effect to the court's judgment by ordering discovery to be verified by affidavit.

MACLAINE WATSON & CO. *v.* INTERNATIONAL TIN COUNCIL, *The Independent,* July 10, 1987, Millett J.

2990. Discovery—further and better list of documents—whether to be provided

In this appeal, the plaintiff insurers made certain claims against the defendant reinsurers under the terms of a policy of reinsurance. P contended that D had given inadequate discovery and applied for further disclosure. Bingham J. refused such disclosure.

Held, allowing P's appeal, that the discovery sought did arise out of the pleaded case and was potentially material thereto.

SOUTH BRITISH INSURANCE CO. AND NEW ZEALAND SOUTH BRITISH INSURANCE *v.* MEDITERRANEAN INSURANCE & REINSURANCE CO. AND WRIGHT (F.E.) (U.K.) [1986] 2 Lloyd's Rep. 247, C.A.

2991. Discovery—inspection by persons unconnected with proceedings—defendant objecting to such persons—court's powers to permit inspection

[R.S.C., Ord 24, r.9.]

The court will allow inspection of documents by someone who is not directly professionally involved in a case in exceptional cases where the interests of justice demand it.

A large number of persons began actions for damages for inquiries arising out of the use of the defendants' drug. Their claims were co-ordinated by a group of solicitors who employed M, a scientific journalist and writer in a crucial role to sift and analyse all the material. A consent order was made on discovery with inspection to follow, but when the defendants learnt that M was to inspect the documents they objected. The plaintiffs undertook that M would respect the documents confidentiality. A judge upheld the objection.

Held, allowing the appeal, that in exceptional circumstances the court would allow inspection by someone like M who was not directly involved in the case, if it could be shown that his assistance was essential in the interests of justice, and the Court were satisfied there would be no breach of confidentiality.

DAVIES *v.* ELI LILLY & CO. [1987] 1 All E.R. 801, C.A.

2992. Discovery—interrogatories—no other claim

[Stamp Duties on Newspapers Act 1836, s.19; R.S.C., Ord. 26, r.2.]

A person with knowledge of the identity of the publisher and printer of an alleged libel but with no other connection could not be compelled to divulge the information. (*Norwich Pharmacal Co.* v. *Customs and Excise Commissioners* [1973] C.L.Y. 2643, *British Steel Corp.* v. *Granada Television* [1980] C.L.Y. 2132 considered.)

RICCI *v.* CHOW, *The Times*, June 19, 1987, C.A.

2993. Discovery—Lands Tribunal Decision. See KINGSLEY *v.* I.R.C. (Det/2/1982), §1692.

2994. Discovery—list of documents requested—discretion of judge

[R.S.C., Ord. 25, r.8.]

The deceased was walking in front of a mobile crane owned by D and driven by their servant. The deceased was steadying a generator/welding set which was suspended from the crane. He died when the crane ran over him. P applied for a list of documents to be served by D pursuant to ord. 25 but D contended that they were not obliged to file a list because the claim arose out of a road accident as defined by sub-para. 4.

Held, that (1) although the accident constituted a collision on land involving a vehicle, the circumstances of this accident were not those of a straightforward road traffic accident; (2) there was industrial equipment involved; (3) the victim of the accident was deceased and there was at least a possibility of some discoverable record being in existence in D's possession, whilst concluding therefore that D had died as a result of a road accident, the judge exercised his discretion and ordered that a list of documents be filed by D.

RICKETT (WIDOW AND ADMINISTRATRIX OF THE ESTATE OF THOMAS RICKETT, DECD.) *v.* ROADCRAFT (CRANE & PLANT HIRE), June 20, 1986; Russell J., Liverpool Crown Ct. [*Ex rel. Brian Thompson & Partners, Solicitors.*]

2995. Discovery—physical examination—risk to plaintiff—refusal to order independent medical examination

[Can.] H was operated upon to correct a soft disc herniation. He suffered severe post-operation depression for which he received psychiatric treatment and hospitalisation. He twice attempted suicide, once after meeting his psychiatrist. After his most recent hospitalisation, he generally refused medical help. In an action against the doctor who carried out the original operation, the latter sought an order directing H to submit to an independent medical examination.

Held, that where it is shown that such an examination would involve some risk to the plaintiff, such an order should be refused. Here, the facts presented a sufficient possibility of real risk to H and it was unlikely that the defendants would be disadvantaged by the refusal to make the order (*Aspinall* v. *Sterling Mansell* [1982] C.L.Y. 2545 applied).

HAUGHIAN *v.* UNIVERSITY HOSPITAL BOARD, UNIVERSITY OF SASKATCHEWAN [1985] 6 W.W.R. 670, Saskatchewan Queen's Bench.

2996. Discovery—use of document outside action—use by one not party to action

[R.S.C., Ord. 24, r.14A.]

Where a document had been disclosed on discovery and the action had been compromised on terms, *inter alia,* that the parties might seek leave to use or produce to third parties documents produced on discovery, such leave will require good reasons and an investigation into the intended user, its value to the third party, and what control could be maintained over that user (*Home Office* v. *Harman* [1982] C.L.Y. 2433 considered).

BIBBY BULK CARRIERS *v.* CANSULEX, *The Times*, November 2, 1987, Hirst J.

2997. Disposal of assets to frustrate judgment—Mareva injunction—whether defendant should be restrained from dealing with assets

P bought a car from D, a second-hand car dealer, which was defective. When proceedings were begun D informed P's solicitors that he would see to it that no assets were available to satisfy any judgment P obtained. He disposed of his business assets, commencing to trade elsewhere under a different name. Upon being served with an *ex parte* injunction restraining D from dealing with his assets, D violently assaulted the process server and threw him off the premises.

Held, that there was evidence from which the court could conclude that D would dispose of his assets in order to frustrate the court's judgment and D should be restrained from dealing with or disposing of his property until trial (*Mareva Compania Naviera S.A.* v. *International Bulk Carriers S.A.* [1980] C.L.Y. 2156 and *Third Chandris Shipping Corp.* v. *Unimarine S.A.* [1979] C.L.Y. 2142 considered).

VAUSE *v.* BRAY, March 25, 1987, H.H. Judge Brooks, Bedford County Ct. [*Ex rel. Batcheldors, Solicitors.*]

2998. Divorce—declaration that divorce decree invalid—whether statutory or inherent jurisdiction appropriate

The petitioner sought a decree that she had married her husband in 1945 and that a subsequent divorce decree, obtained in Ohio without notice on the wife, was invalid, and accordingly she was entitled to a Ministry of Defence pension following the husband's death. The validity of the marriage in 1945 was not in dispute. The petitioner applied under s.45 of the Matrimonial Causes Act 1973 and under the court's inherent jurisdiction. The former required the Attorney-General to be joined as a party, the latter left the joinder of parties in the discretion of the court. The Attorney-General applied for an order dismissing him from the suit.

Held, that s.45 contemplates a dispute over the validity of the marriage at the time it was entered into. That was not the nature of the dispute here which was concerned with the subsistence of the marriage. Accordingly, the appropriate jurisdiction was the courts' inherent jurisdiction. There was no reason why the Attorney General should be a party. The application would be allowed (*Aldrich* v. *Att.-Gen.* [1968] C.L.Y. 199 followed; *Collett* v. *Collett* [1967] C.L.Y. 1872 referred to).

WILLIAMS *v.* ATT.-GEN. (1987) 1 F.L.R. 501, Latey J.

2999. Divorce—decree absolute—appeal out of time. See CROSBY *v.* CROSBY, §1712.

3000. Documents—bundle of documents—preparation

The Court of Appeal said that in respect of bundles of documents, consideration must always be given to whether all of them are strictly necessary. No document should be repeated in the bundle, and, if the bundle exceeded 100 pages, a separate core bundle should be prepared.

SHELL INTERNATIONAL PETROLEUM CO. *v.* TRANSNOR (BERMUDA), *The Times*, April 24, 1987, C.A.

3001. Documents—production of documents—power to order

[R.S.C., Ord. 24, r.11.]

An order could be made for the production of documents referred to in pleadings or affidavits even if the documents were not in the possession, custody or power of the party against whom the order was made.

RAFIDAIN BANK *v.* AGOM UNIVERSAL SUGAR TRADING CO., *The Times*, July 29, 1987, C.A.

3002. Execution—stay—determination of other proceedings—review of circumstances

[R.S.C., Ord. 47, r.1(1)(*a*).]

The Court of Appeal has set out the circumstances in which a stay of execution will be granted of a plaintiff's judgment on the application of a defendant who has an unresolved claim against the plaintiff.

The plaintiff obtained judgment against the defendants, his former employers, for £49,500 for the premature termination of his contract of service. S, a company associated with the defendants, had an outstanding claim for over £2m. against the plaintiff and eight other defendants for negligence. The defendants applied for a stay of execution under R.S.C., Ord. 47, r.1(1)(*a*) of the judgment pending the outcome of S's claim. The judge refused the stay, and the defendants appealed to the Court of Appeal.

Held, dismissing the appeal, that the court had power to grant a stay of execution of the plaintiff's judgment to await the outcome of another claim if there were special circumstances and the relationship of the parties was such that a stay should be granted. Factors to be considered included (a) the nature of the claim of the plaintiff; (b) the extent of identity between the defendant and the other party; (c) the interrelationship of the claims of the plaintiff and the other party; (d) the strength of the other party's claim; (e) the size of it relative to the plaintiff's claim; (f) the likely delay in deciding on the other party's claim; (g) the extent of the prejudice to the plaintiff of depriving him of the fruits of his judgment; (h) the risk of prejudice to the other party if the defendant were to pay the plaintiff. On the facts of the present case, there were no special circumstances justifying a stay.

BURNET *v.* FRANCIS INDUSTRIES [1987] 2 All E.R. 323, C.A.

3003. Execution—stay otherwise than pending appeal—cross-claim—special circumstances

[R.S.C., Ord. 47, r.1(1)(*a*).]

The court may grant a stay of execution of judgment where cross-claims exist between parties other than the plaintiff and defendant, if those parties are for all practical purposes the same.

The defendants appealed against a decision refusing their application for a stay of execution of a summary judgment in favour of the plaintiffs. The reason for the application for the stay was that the defendants contended there were cross-claims, not by the same defendant against the same plaintiff, but between parties who might for all practical purposes be regarded as being the same. It was contended that there were "special circumstances" which gave the court jurisdiction to grant the stay.

Held, there has been a tendency for the court to "pierce the veil" in recent years; the court has a wide discretion under Ord. 47, r.1(1)(*a*) to look at all the circumstances, including who controls the companies in fact, and special circumstances existed here which made it right to grant the stay.

CANADA ENTERPRISES CORP. *v.* MACNAB DISTILLERIES [1987] 1 W.L.R. 813, C.A.

3004. Execution-writ of fieri facias—erroneous setting aside of judgment subsequently reversed—priority of writ

[Supreme Court Act 1981 (c.54), s.138.]

Where judgment was obtained and a writ of fieri facias issued and delivered to the sheriff, and subsequently the judgment was erroneously overturned, and then restored, the writ of fieri facias regained its priority over all similar writs issued and delivered to the sheriff after its original delivery.

Per curiam: Where judgment pursuant to which a writ of fieri facias has been issued is set aside, it is the duty of the creditor to inform the sheriff. The sheriff cannot proceed with the execution unless and until the judgment is restored and he has been so notified. If in the meantime he has had dealings with the goods which would have been wrongful as against the creditor had the judgment not been set aside, he is not liable to the creditor in respect of such dealings. If a creditor whose judgment has been set aside gives notice to the sheriff that the order to set aside is under appeal, and thereafter the sheriff receives for execution another writ in respect of the same goods, the sheriff should not proceed beyond possession without applying to the court for directions and giving notice to both creditors of such application.

Ps obtained judgment in default against D1 and issued and delivered to the sheriff on April 9, 1986 a writ of fieri facias against his goods. On May 9, the sheriff obtained walking possession under the writ, but D1's wife gave notice that the goods belonged to her. On June 6, before the sheriff had issued an interpleader summons, Webster J. set aside the judgment, and the sheriff, on Ps' instructions, lifted the walking possession. On June 10, the intervener bank, who had also obtained judgment, delivered a writ of fieri facias against D's goods; his wife maintained her claim, and on June 25 the sheriff issued an interpleader summons. On July 7 the Court of Appeal restored the original judgment; Ps notified the sheriff, and requested him to retake possession of the goods, giving their writ of April 9 priority over the intervener's writ. The sheriff declined to do so. Ps applied to the Court of Appeal for a declaration that their writ had priority. This declaration was granted.

Held, that although a writ of fieri facias was only valid when the sheriff had instructions to execute it, the enforced withdrawal of the instructions following an erroneous order of the court, should not affect the priority of the writ. Ps writ took priority over the intervener's writ and they had no need to issue a fresh one (*P. B. J. Davis Manufacturing*

Co. v. *Fahn, Fahn (Claimant)* [1967] C.L.Y. 3591 applied; *Hunt* v. *Hooper* (1844) 12 M. & W. 644 distinguished).

BANKERS TRUST CO. *v.* GALADARI; CHASE MANHATTAN BANK N.A. (INTERVENER) [1986] 3 W.L.R. 1099, C.A.

3005. Execution—writ of possession—time for execution

A sheriff is required to execute a writ of possession as soon as is reasonably practicable.

P owned land in Newham that was occupied by gypsies with a large number of caravans on March 14, 1986. As a matter of urgency P obtained an order for possession under R.S.C., Ord. 113 on March 19, 1986. A writ of possession was obtained the same day and forwarded to the office of the under-sheriff for execution. On March 20, 1986, the sheriff's officers attended to warn the gypsies that a writ of possession was to be executed. On the same day the police informed the sheriff that any attempt to evict the gypsies before the funeral of the Queen of the Gypsies scheduled for March 26, would be liable to cause public disorder for which there were insufficient officers available. The deputy under-sheriff wrote to P on March 21, stating it would be over a week before the writ could be executed. P issued a notice of motion seeking an order that the sheriff execute the writ of possession forthwith. The motion was heard on 25 and 26 March.

Held, that the duty on the sheriff to execute a writ of possession in common with other writs of execution is to execute as soon as is reasonably practicable. There was nothing to indicate any unreasonable delay on the part of the sheriff's officers. Execution of the writ was scheduled for 26 March. Relief sought refused (*Carlile* v. *Parkins* (1822) 3 Stark. 163, *Mason* v. *Paynter* (1841) 1 Q.B. 974 applied).

SIX ARLINGTON STREET INVESTMENTS *v.* PERSONS UNKNOWN [1987] 1 W.L.R. 188, Knox J.

3006. Expert evidence—medical negligence—disclosure of reports

[R.S.C., Ord. 38, r.38.]

In the great majority of medical negligence cases, there ought to be full disclosure of experts' reports.

The plaintiffs in separate medical negligence actions claimed damages against defendant health authorites. The plaintiffs applied to the court for mutual pre-trial disclosure of expert evidence. The applications were refused.

Held, allowing the appeals, that although the court had a wide discretion, in the great majority of cases the interests of justice would best be served by full pre-trial disclosure of expert evidence. (*Rahman* v. *Kirklees Area Health Authority* (*Practice Note*) [1980] C.L.Y. 2172 disapproved).

NAYLOR *v.* PRESTON AREA HEALTH AUTHORITY [1987] 2 All E.R. 353 C.A.

3007. Extension of time—property adjustment order—option to redeem charge on matrimonial home—whether procedural power to grant extension of time. See KNIBB *v.* KNIBB, §1785.

3008. Family Division—periodical payments—children—practice direction

The following practice direction was issued by the Senior Registrar of the Family Division with the concurrence of the Lord Chancellor on July 10, 1987.

Orders for periodical payments in respect of a child have been frequently expressed as lasting until the child attains the age of 17 years or ceases full-time education or further order. It has recently been learned that the Inland Revenue treat such orders as ceasing when the first event occurs. They would of course accept orders as lasting beyond the child's 17th birthday if the order contained wording such as "until the child attains the age of 17 years or ceases full-time eductation (whichever is the later) or further order".

Orders which are intended to run until a date determined by such alternatives should clearly indicate whether the order is to cease on the happening of the earlier or later event. The words "or until further order" do not have to be qualified in this way, because such further order will only be made where the current order has not yet ceased and will immediately supersede the provisions of that current order. Where the court has made an order in the terms of the Registrar's Direction of June 16, 1983 (*Payment of School Fees*) [1983] 1 W.L.R. 800, with the intention that the order should continue until the occurrence of the later of the two events, the reaching of a specified age or cessation of full-time education, the Revenue has indicated that they will recognise for tax purposes the correction of the order by the Court, inserting the words "whichever is the later".

At county court level, the corrected order should be noted "Corrected under C.C.R. Ord. 15, r.5". At High Court level, unless formal application is made under R.S.C., Ord. 20, r.11, the corrected order should be noted "Corrected under the Court's inherent jurisdiction". In either case, a copy of the corrected order should be supplied to the petitioner and respondent by the Court in the usual way. Where the order is currently registered in a magistrates' court, a certified copy of the corrected order, for which no fee is chargeable, should also be sent to that court.

It will normally be sufficient if the application for correction of the order is made by consent on notice or summons, without the need for attendance, subject to the Court's discretion to require otherwise. No fee is chargeable on the consent application.

The Registrar's Direction of June 16, 1983 is hereby amended by substituting for the form of order therein set out the following:—

"It is ordered that the [petitioner] [respondent] do pay or cause to be paid to the child AB as from the day of 19 until [he] [she] shall attain the age of 17 years [or until [he] [she] shall cease to receive full-time education (whichever is the [later] [earlier]) or further order periodical payment for [himself] [herself]—

(a) of an amount equivalent to such sum as after deduction of income tax at the basic rate equals the school fees [but not the extras in the school bill] [including specified extras] at the school the said child attends for each financial year [by way of three payments on and and] [payable monthly]; together with

(b) the sum of £ per annum less tax payable monthly in respect of general maintenance of the said child".

The Direction is also further amended to correct a printing error by substituting the word "to" for the word "by" in the sentence which deals with the provision of certificates of tax deduction, thus making it clear that the responsibility for doing so lies with the payer.

PRACTICE DIRECTION (FAM.D.) (PERIODICAL PAYMENTS: CHILDREN) July 10, 1987.

3009. Family Division—wards—disclosure of evidence—practice direction

The following practice direction was issued by the Senior Registrar of the Family Division with the concurrence of the Lord Chancellor on October 15, 1987.

The President and Judges of the Family Division wish to remind practitioners of the need in wardship cases proceeding in private to obtain leave to disclose evidential documents to persons who are not parties, *e.g.* psychiatrists, psychologists and medical experts or any other person. Disclosure without prior leave may be a contempt of court, and this is none the less the case where the purpose of the disclosure is only to obtain advice from the expert concerned as to whether relevant expert evidence would be forthcoming or would be helpful to the court.

PRACTICE DIRECTION (FAM. D.) (WARDS: DISCLOSURE OF EVIDENCE) October 15, 1987.

3010. Fees—barrister—review of legal aid taxation—whether fee payable

[Legal Aid Act 1974 (c.4), s.37(2); Legal Aid in Criminal Proceedings (Costs) Regulations 1982 (S.I. 1982 No. 1197), reg. 11(1)(5)(14).]

A barrister who appears on a review of taxation under a legal aid order is entitled to a reasonable fee, whether representing himself or another barrister.

Leading and Junior counsel instructed in a criminal matter before the Crown Court, in which their client was legally aided, appealed to the taxing master in respect of the fees allowed. On the initial hearing before the master, the Junior appeared both for himself and the Leader; on a subsequent hearing both were represented by another barrister.

Held, on the question whether fees (as opposed to out of pocket expenses) were payable to either barrister in respect of the appeal hearings, that since one barrister may instruct another directly to appear for him on such an appeal, the barrister who was so instructed was entitled to be paid a reasonable fee, in addition to his expenses. The position was similar where a barrister appeared on his own behalf, where, in contrast to the provisions applicable to a litigant in person, the barrister was allowed a fee to reflect proper skill and care (*London Scottish Benefit Society* v. *Chorley* (1884) 13 Q.B.D. 872 applied).

R. *v.* BOSWELL; R. *v.* HALLIWELL [1987] 1 W.L.R. 705, Leggatt J.

3011. Foreign judgments

RECIPROCAL ENFORCEMENT OF FOREIGN JUDGMENTS (CANADA) ORDER 1987 (No. 468) [£2·70], made under the Foreign Judgments (Reciprocal Enforcement) Act 1933 (c.13), ss.1 and 3, and the Civil Jurisdiction and Judgments Act 1982 (c.27), s.9(2); operative on March 18, 1987; provides for the extension of Pt. I of the 1933 Act to the judgments of designated courts in Canada.

RECIPROCAL ENFORCEMENT OF FOREIGN JUDGMENTS (CANADA) (AMENDMENT) ORDER 1987 (No. 2211) [45p], made under the Foreign Judgments (Reciprocal Enforcement) Act 1933, s.1; operative on January 1, 1988; amends S.I. 1987 No. 468.

3012. Forum—convenient forum for civil action—whether conviction abroad relevant

The fact that a party to a civil dispute has criminal convictions in a foreign country may be a relevant factor in deciding whether that country would be a convenient forum for the dispute.

PURCELL *v.* KHAYAT, *The Times*, November 23, 1987, C.A.

3013. Garnishee order—discretion of court

The Court will make a garnishee order absolute, notwithstanding a risk that the garnishee may have to pay twice, where that risk derives from a foreign judgment which English Courts could not recognize and which had been arrived at in the face of a valid arbitration agreement.

DEUTSCHE SCHACHTBAU-UND-TIEFBOHRGESELLSCHAFT mbH *v.* THE R'AS AL KHAIMAH NATIONAL OIL Co. AND SHELL INTERNATIONAL PETROLEUM Co., *Financial Times*, November 4, 1987, C.A.

3014. Garnishee order—temporary physical presence—jurisdiction

[R.S.C., Ord. 49.]

The temporary presence of the garnishee within the jurisdiction at the time is sufficient to enable the Court to make the order; even if the garnishee has left before the order nisi is made, it is enough if he has submitted to the court's jurisdiction to make the order.

P obtained a *Mareva* injunction against D. D applied to have the injunction discharged. The application was adjourned until after the decision in the substantive action. Subsequently D was in court when the application was dismissed. P applied for leave to serve a garnishee order and D instructed solicitors to accept service. The judge made the garnishee order nisi. However, some hours before his doing so, D had left the jurisdiction. The order was made absolute.

Held, dismissing the appeal by D, that a garnishee's temporary presence within the jurisdiction, or his agreement to submit to the court's jurisdiction followed by his absence when the order nisi was made, was sufficient to enable the Court to make the order. (*Swiss Bank Corp.* v. *Boehmische Industrial Bank* [1923] 1 K.B. 637; *Rothmans of Pall Mall (Overseas)* v. *Saudi Arabian Airlines Corp.* [1980] C.L.Y. 127 and *Khan* v. *Goleccha International* [1980] C.L.Y. 1069 applied; *Richardson* v. *Richardson* [1927] P228 doubted).

SCF FINANCE CO. *v.* MASRI (No. 3) [1987] 2 W.L.R. 81, C.A.

3015. Grounds for stay—mortgages—possession order. See CITIBANK TRUST *v.* AYIVOR, §2541.

3016. Improbable defence—whether leave to defend

[R.S.C. Ord. 14.]

Where a defence can be described as more than shadowy but less than probable, leave to defend should be given. The Court should bear in mind (where relevant) that events may have taken place in a country with totally different mores and laws.

RAFIDAIN BANK *v.* AGOM UNIVERSAL SUGAR TRADING CO. *The Times*, December 23, 1986, C.A.

3017. In arrears of rent—breach of interim order—whether T.'s defence to be struck out. See H.H. PROPERTY *v.* RAHIM, §2113.

3018. Industrial tribunal—costs—whether discretion properly exercised

R brought proceedings before the industrial tribunal for constructive dismissal against his employers A, a firm of estate agents, after resigning because of their proposal to transfer him from their residential to their commercial office. After protracted negotiations the claim was settled shortly before the hearing, which was concerned solely with the question of costs, which each party claimed from the other under reg. 11(1) of the Industrial Tribunal (Rules of Procedure) Regulations 1980, on the grounds of frivolous, vexatious or unreasonable conduct in the proceedings. The tribunal did not have before it any pleadings or evidence directed towards the merits of the case, but merely a bundle of correspondence. It held that A should pay R's costs on the grounds that A's offer of settlement, which had been proposed in final settlement of all causes of action relied on by R, whether statutory or common law, had been unreasonable. The Employment Appeal Tribunal criticised this decision strongly, but dismissed A's appeal on the grounds that the tribunal's finding had been one of fact with which they were unable to interfere.

Held, allowing A's appeal that (1) the industrial tribunal had erred in law in its ruling as to costs, since this had necessitated it forming a view on matters as to which it had no information whatsoever, namely the merits of R's statutory and common law claims; (2)

the industrial tribunal's ruling was not a finding of fact but a reviewable exercise of discretion, which the Employment Appeal Tribunal ought to have reviewed.
CHESTERTONS *v.* COLLINS (1986) 280 E.G. 1147, C.A.

3019. Industrial tribunals—procedure—discovery. See EMPLOYMENT, §1340.

3020. Injunction—breach of duty of confidence by employee—detriment to employer

An employee of the National Health Service ("the NHS") provided Y, a newspaper, with the names of two doctors suffering from AIDS. The NHS sought an injunction to restrain Y from publishing the names.

Held, that detriment in the use of information was not a necessary pre-condition to injunctive relief. The NHS would suffer detriment if it became known that such breaches of confidentiality took place, and this outweighed the benefits to the public of knowing the information Y sought to publish (*Secretary of State for Defence* v. *Guardian Newspapers,* [1984] C.L.Y. 2596 and *Inquiry under the Company Securities (Insider Dealing) Act 1985, An, Re* [1987] C.L.Y. 2934 applied).
X. *v.* Y., *The Times,* November 11, 1987, Rose J.

3021. Injunction—full and frank disclosure—discretion of court

Notwithstanding the rule that an injunction would be discharged where it had been obtained without full and frank disclosure of material facts, the Court had discretion to continue such an order in such circumstances where to do otherwise would be to provide a vehicle for injustice.
BRINK'S-MAT *v.* ELCOMBE, *The Independent,* June 25, 1987, C.A.

3022. Injunction—mandatory interlocutory injunction—injustice to parties

An interlocutory mandatory injunction would be granted where there was a greater risk of injustice being caused to the plaintiff than to the defendant if it were not granted.

D was an English company which distributed films. They contracted with R on behalf of P that P would distribute films in Italy. Later D wished to re-negotiate the contract on terms less favourable to P. D then claimed that P was in breach of contract and refused to send P dubbing material for certain films so that P could not exhibit them in Italy. P sought an interlocutory mandatory injunction requiring the films to be delivered to P. D contended that the injunction should not be granted since P had not established a high degree of probability that it would establish its legal right at trial. The injunction was granted.

Held, that the test was the same whether the injunction was mandatory or prohibitory. The question was whether the injustice that would be caused to D if P was granted an injunction and failed at the trial outweighed the injustice that would be caused to P if an injunction was refused and he succeeded at trial. In a normal case the court was required to feel a high degree of assurance that P would succeed at trial before an injunction would be granted, but there were exceptional cases where an injunction should be granted even if the court did not feel a high degree of assurance of P's success at trial where witholding the injunction would carry a greater risk of injustice to P. In this case there was no difficulty about formulating an enforceable order, and it was difficult to see how delivery of the films to P would cause uncompensatable loss to D. Further, failure to deliver the films would cause loss to P which it was difficult to quantify and might force them to re-negotiate the terms owing to financial pressure. In addition, the *status quo* ought to be preserved and the process of distribution not interrupted. There was therefore a much greater risk of injustice being caused if the injunction was withheld and P was right than if the injunction was granted and P did not succeed at trial (*Shepherd Homes* v. *Sandham* [1970] C.L.Y. 2293 and *Locabail International Finance* v. *Agroexport* [1986] C.L.Y. 2651 considered).
FILMS ROVER INTERNATIONAL *v.* CANNON FILMS SALES [1986] 3 All E.R. 772, Hoffmann J.

3023. Injunction—publication of confidential information by former servant of the Crown—information freely available outside U.K.—whether injunction appropriate

An injunction designed to protect an important public interest, namely the secrecy of the operations of the Security Service, may be continued on an interlocutory basis so as to prevent publication or discussion of those matters by the Press, notwithstanding that elsewhere in the world the material has been published and is freely available.

Per Lord Bridge (dissenting): the book "Spycatcher" having been published in the U.S.A., there can be no remaining public interest, and there is no merit in the maintenance of a ban on the book's serialisation and discussion in the Press of the U.K., when the rest of the world knows all about the allegations contained therein, and is at liberty to discuss them freely.

The Attorney-General sought injunctions preventing newspapers from serialising and discussing a book written by W, a former member of the Security Service, in which he alleged certain improprieties by members of that Service. No injunction could be obtained preventing its publication in the U.S.A., which duly took place. The Attorney-General nonetheless continued to press his application for injunctive relief in the U.K.

Held, (Lords Bridge and Oliver dissenting) that the Attorney-General had an arguable case for the prevention of publication, so as to maintain the secrecy surrounding the Security Service. It was therefore the duty of the House to protect the Security Service. The injunctions would be continued, and would be widened so as to restrict publication of reports of the proceedings before the Australian courts with regard to the book.

ATT.-GEN. *v.* GUARDIAN NEWSPAPERS; SAME *v.* OBSERVER; SAME *v.* TIMES NEWSPAPERS [1987] 1 W.L.R. 1248, H.L.

3024. Injunction—restraint of foreign proceedings—jurisdiction

An injunction will be granted to restrain a plaintiff from proceedings in another jurisdiction where justice requires that such a plaintiff who is amenable to the jurisdiction of this court should be restrained from proceeding elsewhere.

D, a Brunei businessman resident in Brunei was killed in a helicopter crash in Brunei. The helicopter was manufactured by FM, a French company; it was owned by EOw, an English company, and operated and serviced by M Op, a Malaysian company. P, the widow in Brunei and the estate brought proceedings in Brunei against M Op and FM, in France against FM, and in Texas against FM and M Op. There was jurisdiction in Texas over FM because FM carried on business there. The claim against M Op was settled. The proceedings against FM in France were discontinued, and FM applied to the Texas court to dismiss the action on the ground of *forum non conveniens.* The application was refused, discovery took place and a date was fixed for trial. FM applied to the Brunei court for an injunction to restrain P from continuing the Texas action. The injunction was refused by the High Court and the Court of Appeal of Brunei. If P continued the Texas proceedings, FM could not claim indemnity or contribution from M Op who would only submit to Brunei jurisdiction. FM gave undertakings to protect P's position, and accepted that the law applicable in Texas was the law of Brunei.

Held, allowing the appeal by FM, that an injunction would be granted where justice required that a plaintiff amenable to the jurisdiction of the court should be restrained from proceeding in a foreign jurisdiction; the work done in Texas was not sufficient to make Texas the natural forum, and there would be serious injustice to FM in being unable to claim indemnity or contribution from M Op. FM had given the necessary undertakings to P, Brunei was the natural forum and the injunction would be granted (*McHenry* v. *Lewis* (1882) 22 Ch.D. 397 and *Peruvian Guano Co.* v. *Bockwoldt* (1883) 23 Ch.D. 225 applied; *Castanho* v. *Brown & Root (U.K.)* [1981] C.L.Y. 2200 and *Spiliada Maritime Corp.* v. *Cansulex* [1987] C.L.Y. 3135 distinguished).

SOCIÉTÉ NATIONALE INDUSTRIELLE AEROSPATIALE *v.* LEE KUI JAK [1987] 3 W.L.R. 59, P.C.

3025. Injunction—right of way—excessive and unreasonable use. See ROSLING *v.* PINNEGAR, §1235

3026. Injunction—televised re-enactment of trial—trial still in progress

A televised re-enactment of a trial or appeal broadcast while that trial or appeal is still in progress would be likely to damage public confidence in the administration of justice and will therefore be restrained by injunction if necessary (*Att.-Gen.* v. *Times Newspapers,* [1973] C.L.Y. 2618 applied).

ATT.-GEN. *v.* CHANNEL FOUR TELEVISION CO., *The Independent,* December 9, 1987, C.A.

3026a. Injunctions—effect on persons not party to the action

An injunction to restrain a defendant from committing an act does not bind any person not a party to the action. Such a person will, however, be in contempt of court if he knowingly aids or abets the defendant to breach the injunction. Further, an injunction should not be so framed as to enjoin any person not a party to the action.

ATT.-GEN. *v.* NEWSPAPER PUBLISHING, *The Times,* June 3, 1987, Browne-Wilkinson V.-C.

3027. Injunctions—interim relief—validity of injunctions—statutory nuisance

[Public Health Act 1936 (c.49), s.222; Local Government Act 1972 (c.70).]

In March 1985, R, the local council, issued a writ against 23 named gipsies seeking an order restraining them from trespassing on the council's land, from trespassing on any land within the city, and from committing nuisance and statutory nuisance on any land within the city. In July 1985 an application for an interim injunction was sought against nine defendants. The defendants opposed these injunctions on a number of grounds. The judge granted interim injunctions against five defendants in a modified form, having decided to leave the questions of law to trial. On appeal, R relied upon further evidence not before the judge which showed that the council's solicitor had decided that the appropriate proceedings would be under s.100 of the Public Health Act and s.222 of the Local Government Act, because he did not consider that summary proceedings under the Public Health Act would afford an adequate remedy, and further abandoned their claim to the second class of injunctions.

Held, (allowing the appeal in part), that (1) the judge should have provisionally decided the question of R's authority to bring the proceedings; (2) although R had not been able to show at first instance that they were entitled to bring proceedings under s.100 of the Public Health Act, the further evidence before the Court of Appeal had remedied this deficiency; (3) s.100 could not justify the grant of an injunction to a council to restrain a statutory nuisance unless it could be shown that the defendant had been responsible for the creation of a nuisance at the particular premises and in the absence of evidence to show that it was likely that there would be recurrence of conduct on the same site the council were not entitled to injunctions restraining conduct amounting to statutory nuisance on land not owned by the Council; (4) the council were not under any duty under the Caravan Sites Act 1968 which would make it wrong to grant the council injunctive relief; (5) the council were entitled to an injunction to restrain trespass and nuisance on their own land.

BRADFORD METROPOLITAN CITY COUNCIL *v.* BROWN (1987) 19 H.L.R. 16, C.A.

3028. Interest claim—pleading

There is no requirement for a claim for interest to be included in a generally endorsed writ.

BUTLER (EDWARD) VINTNERS *v.* GRANGE SEYMOUR INTERNATIONALE, *The Times,* June 9, 1987, C.A.

3029. Interim payment—personal injury

A self-employed plaintiff of modest earnings is entitled to a reasonable proportion of the damages which, in the opinion of the court, are likely to be recovered on the basis solely of medical reports and the fact that he is unemployed, although unable as yet to produce accounts for three years preceding the accident. £10,000 ordered, being approximately one-half of anticipated general damages.

McCANN *v.* CANAGAN, April 7, 1986; Turner J. [*Ex. rel. Jonathan Sofer,* Barrister.]

3030. Interlocutory appeal to Court of Appeal—appeal in course of trial of action

It was highly undesirable that there should be appeals to the Court of Appeal in the course of the trial of actions. It was altogether better that matters of an interlocutory nature which cropped up in the course of a trial should work themselves out in the course of the same trial without interlocutory recourse to the Court of Appeal before the facts had been completely determined and the trial had been concluded. The Criminal Division of the court never heard appeals in the course of the trial. The Civil Division only did so in exceptional circumstances. The reason was not just that it interrupted the trial, although that was usually a sufficient reason. There was a further reason that if it became the practice to give leave to appeal in the course of a trial, the court would soon be overwhelmed with appeals, many of which would or might in the event prove academic.

McGARRY (E.) (ELECTRICAL) *v.* BORROUGHS MACHINES April 14, 1986 (C.A.T. No. 346).

3031. Interlocutory injunction—adjournment on undertakings—application to discharge undertakings

Where an interlocutory motion was adjourned generally on undertakings it was not disposed of so that it was open to either party to re-open the status quo without showing any significant change of circumstances.

On August 18, 1986 P obtained an *ex parte* Mareva injunction against D. The injunction was continued until September 16, 1986. On that date D gave a number of undertakings whereupon P's motion seeking the injunction was adjourned generally with liberty to apply on 48 hours notice. At the hearing D's counsel indicated that an application to discharge the undertakings was likely to be made at a later date. On November 14, 1986 D applied to discharge the undertakings. The judge upheld P's objection that the undertakings could not be discharged on account of the fact that there was no significant change in circumstances since the undertakings were given.

Held, allowing D's appeal, P's motion had been adjourned generally so that it had not been dealt with or disposed of. The same was not true of a motion that was stood over to the trial of the action. Accordingly it was open to D to apply to re-open the status quo and have the matter dealt with in some other way. In any event D's undertakings had been given on the basis that there was likely to be an application to discharge them at a later date without there being any significant change in circumstances (*Chanel* v. *Woolworth (F.W.)* [1981] C.L.Y. 2126 distinguished).

BUTT *v.* BUTT [1987] 1 W.L.R. 1351, C.A.

3032. Interlocutory injunction—balance of convenience—solicitors' partnership. See NIXON *v.* WOOD, §2768.

3033. Interlocutory injunction—breach of employment contract—whether employer entitled to restrain employee working for rival during contractual notice period. See EVENING STANDARD CO. *v.* HENDERSON, §1296.

3034. Interlocutory injunction—principles

The Court refused to vary the terms of an injunction so that the defendants could insert advertising material in the plaintiff's publications so long as they included a statement dissociating the plaintiff from the material. Nonetheless, outside recognised legal categories such as passing off and trade marks, English law does not recognise a general right in a party to ensure that his product reaches the consumer in the form he intended.

ASSOCIATED NEWSPAPERS GROUP *v.* INSERT MEDIA; EXPRESS NEWSPAPERS *v.* ARNOLD, *The Independent,* March 31, 1987, Roch J.

3035. Interlocutory injunction—public authority

The normal principles governing interlocutory injunctions must be tempered by a recognition of the interest of the public when the order is sought against a public authority carrying out its public duties.

R. *v.* WESTMINSTER CITY COUNCIL, *ex p.* SIERBENS, *The Independent,* March 26, 1987, C.A.

3036. Interlocutory injunction—public interest—Church of Scientology

In the light of the delay of the Church of Scientology in applying for an interlocutory injunction to prevent a breach of copyright and disclosure of confidential information in a book about the Church, and in the light of the public interest in disclosure, the court refused an interlocutory order.

CHURCH OF SCIENTOLOGY OF CALIFORNIA *v.* MILLER, *The Times,* October 23, 1987, C.A.

3037. Interlocutory injunction—refusal—sex establishment

The Court declined to restrain the council from taking steps to inhibit use of premises as sex establishments pending the hearing of an application for judicial review of a refusal to grant permission for such use (*American Cyanamid Co.* v. *Ethicon* [1975] C.L.Y. 2640 applied).

R. *v.* WESTMINSTER CITY COUNCIL, *ex p.* COSTI, *The Independent,* March 12, 1987, Otton J.

3038. Interlocutory injunction—restraint of unlawful acts

An interlocutory injunction will lie to prevent an act if it is justified on the balance of convenience, whether or not the act prevented would in any event, prima facie, be unlawful.

NATIONAL DOCK LABOUR BOARD *v.* SABAH TIMBER CO., *The Times,* September 3, 1987, C.A.

3039. Interlocutory injunction—rights of landowner

A landowner is prima facie entitled to an injunction to restrain trespass on his land where title is not in issue even if he suffers no harm, unless the defendant can show an arguable case that he has the right to enter.

P and D were freehold owners of adjoining properties which once had been in common ownership. There was a right of way in favour of D over P's yard, plus the right to park for the purpose of loading and unloading. For 30 years D had used the yard for general parking. P commenced proceedings to restrain that use. D claimed a prescription right by virtue of a lost modern grant or 20 years' user as of right. The judge refused an interlocutory injunction.

Held, allowing the appeal, that where title was not in issue, a landowner was prima facie entitled to an injunction to restrain a trespass even if the trespass did not harm him. Only if the defendant could show an arguable case that he had a right to do what the plaintiff sought to prevent, should the court go on to consider the balance of convenience, the preservation of the status quo and the adequacy of damages as a remedy. There was no such arguable case, and the injunction would be granted *(Woollerton and Wilson* v. *Costain (Richard)* [1970] C.L.Y. 2882 and *Trenberth (John)* v. *National Westminster Bank* [1980] C.L.Y. 2765 approved; *Behrens* v. *Richards* [1905] 2 Ch. 614 distinguished; *American Cyanamid Co.* v. *Ethicon* [1975] C.L.Y. 2640 considered).

PATEL *v.* SMITH (W.H.) (EZIOT) [1987] 1 W.L.R. 853, C.A.

3040. Interlocutory injunction—salvage arbitration—injunction to restrain arbitration. See SHIPPING AND MARINE INSURANCE, §3367.

3041. Interlocutory injunction—whether arguable case—balance of convenience—passing-off

P sold lemon juice in a plastic bottle, size, shape and colour of a lemon. Lemon juice was sold in lemon shaped containers of different size and get-up by two other traders. P alleged that D's lemons were mistaken for their lemons. P moved for interlocutory relief. The trial judge refused the relief on the ground that if, as was fairly unlikely, P succeeded at trial, damages would be an adequate remedy.

Held, allowing P's appeal, that P's case was arguable and it would be very difficult to ascertain the damage if they succeeded. The balance of convenience lay in preserving the status quo.

RECKITT AND COLMAN PRODUCTS *v.* BORDEN INC. [1987] F.S.R. 228, C.A.

3042. Joinder of parties—action for wrongful interference with goods.

[Torts (Interference with Goods) Act 1977 (c.32), s.8; R.S.C. Ord. 15, r.10A(2).]

The court has jurisdiction on an application by a defendant in an action for wrongful interference with goods to join a person as defendant to establish whether at the date of the alleged tort that person had a better right to the goods than the plaintiff.

DE FRANCO *v.* COMMISSIONER OF POLICE OF THE METROPOLIS, *The Times,* May 8, 1987, C.A.

3043. Judges

MAXIMUM NUMBER OF JUDGES ORDER 1987 (No. 2059) [45p], made under the Supreme Court Act 1981 (c.54), ss.2(4), 4(4); increases the number of ordinary judges of the Court of Appeal to 28 and increases the number of puisne judges to 85.

3044. Judgment in default—application to set aside—charterparty—whether D a party to contract

P chartered a vessel pursuant to a liner booking note made between themselves and Saudi International Shipping S.A. as managers for the owners as carrier. The booking note was made subject to the Conlinebill terms and provided that the contract was between the "Merchant and the Owner of the vessel" and, further, that the agent who executed the contract on behalf of the master was not to be liable thereunder. D refused to load the cargo and P claimed damages. No notice of intention to defend was given by D. P signed interlocutory judgment in default and their damages were later assessed. D, having at one stage deliberately decided not to defend the proceedings, recalled that security had been put up by them, and accordingly applied for leave to set aside the judgment and for leave to defend on the ground that P had sued the wrong defendants. Staughton J. refused leave, holding that although there was an arguable point that the wrong defendant had been sued, the point was not meritorious and D had deliberately allowed the judgment to go by default. D appealed.

Held, dismissing D's appeal, that on the facts and evidence D had no arguable defence that judgment had been signed against the wrong party.

ALPINE BULK TRANSPORT CO. INC. *v.* SAUDI EAGLE SHIPPING CO. INC.; SAUDI EAGLE, THE [1986] 2 Lloyd's Rep. 221, C.A.

3045. Judgment in default—whether order invalid—whether judgment should be set aside

[R.S.C., Ord. 42, r.2.]

P sought an order that, unless D should deliver further and better particulars of their defence within 14 days, the defence should be struck out. D consented to that order, it was duly made and served on them several days later. It was not complied with and judgment in default was entered. D sought to set aside the order on the grounds that it did not recite any date from which the 14 days was to run, and did not comply with

R.S.C., Ord. 42, r.2 which provides, *inter alia,* that ". . . a judgment or order which requires a person to do an act must specify the time after service of the judgment as an order, or some other time, within which the act is to be done. . . ." Hirst J. held that the order was invalid and that the default judgment should be set aside. P appealed.

Held, dismissing P's appeal, that (1) both the order and thus the judgment were irregular in that no starting date had been given; (2) the Court should, unless there was waiver or estoppel, exercise its discretion in favour of the applicant to set aside when judgment was entered upon an irregular order; (3) "unless" orders had to be unambiguous.

HITACHI SALES (U.K.) *v.* MITSUI OSK LINES [1986] 2 LLoyd's Rep. 574, C.A.

3046. Judgment in default wrongly signed—stay of proceedings with condition as to costs—whether valid

P issued and duly served a writ against D claiming arrears of rent and other ancillary relief. D served a defence and counterclaim within the time limited for service of a defence. Despite that, P wrongly signed judgment against D asserting that no defence had been filed. D applied to set aside the judgment and for security for costs on the ground of a long history of deliberate harrassment on P's part. The master took an unfavourable view of P and the way in which he had behaved over the signing of judgment in asserting that there was no defence. The master ordered that the judgment be set aside and that the costs thrown away should be paid by P, to be taxed and paid forthwith, and that the proceedings be stayed until the payment of £250 by P was made on account of costs.

Held, that the master fell into error in that he ordered the equivalent of security in the sum of £250 as a condition of P being at liberty to pursue the action. There was not sufficient material before him to enable him to say that £250 would inevitably be a sum less than the amount of the costs thrown away, which would be payable after taxation. He may well have been right. It may be a good deal more. He did not choose to assess the costs as he might have done. Accordingly P's appeal would be allowed and the part of the order which read "and that the proceedings be stayed until payment of £250 by P on account of such costs" should be deleted.

ABBAS *v.* RUDOLFER, September 23, 1986 (C.A.T. No. 804).

3047. Judgment to be available—directions of court

It was most important that where a case came before the court and a considered and reasoned judgment was given, those who had to carry out the orders of the court should have made available to them a copy of the judgment so that the reasons which impelled the judge to make the order could be read and understood. It may be that someone, having read the judgment, might come to the conclusion that it was based on a mistaken view of the facts and it may be that some further interlocutory application might then be made to correct it. It was wholly undesirable that a reasoned judgment should be ignored.

NEGUS *v.* ALLEN, May 21, 1986 (C.A.T. No. 469).

3048. Judgment under appeal—counsel wishing to argue from published report of judgment—Court of Appeal to be provided with photocopies of report—practice direction

The following practice direction was issued by Sir John Donaldson, M.R. on March 13, 1987.

If the judgment under appeal has been reported before the hearing and counsel wish to argue from the published report rather than from the official transcript, the court should be provided with photocopies of the report for the use of the judges in order that they may be able to annotate it as the argument proceeds.

PRACTICE DIRECTION (C.A.) (APPEALS FROM REPORTED JUDGMENTS) [1987] 1 W.L.R. 456.

3049. Judicial review—application—considerations. See R. *v.* WALTHAM FOREST LONDON BOROUGH COUNCIL, *ex p.* BAXTER, §5.

3050. Judicial review—availability of remedy—circumstances in which order for proceedings to continue as if begun by writ should be made. See R. *v.* SECRETARY OF STATE FOR THE HOME DEPARTMENT, *ex p.* DEW, §6.

3051. Judicial review—bail

P's application for leave to apply for judicial review of his detention order (under the Immigration Act 1971) was adjourned and the judge refused to grant him bail pending the final hearing. He applied to the Court of Appeal for bail.

Held, that (1) P could not appeal from a judge's refusal to grant him leave to apply for judicial review; (2) the Court of Appeal could, however, consider new applications for such leave; (3) the Court of Appeal could therefore only consider granting bail if it was properly seised of an application for such leave (*Lane* v. *Esdaile* [1891] A.C. 210 applied).

DHILLON, *Re, The Times,* January 28, 1987, C.A.

3052. Judicial review—claim in public law—claim linked to private law rights—claim begun by writ

[R.S.C., Ord. 53.]

Where the plaintiff began an action by writ, but his claim involved a substantial element of public law, it would be struck out since the proper course was to apply for judicial review (*A.* v. *Liverpool City Council* [1981] C.L.Y. 1796, *O'Reilly* v. *Mackman* [1982] C.L.Y. 2603, *Cocks* v. *Thanet District Council* [1982] C.L.Y. 1465, *Wandsworth London Borough Council* v. *Winder* [1985] C.L.Y. 9 considered).

GUEVARA *v.* HOUNSLOW LONDON BOROUGH COUNCIL, *The Times,* April 17, 1987, Crawford Q.C.

3053. Judicial review—judge's misconduct—whether leave will be granted

When a party is entitled to appeal against a decision, leave will not be granted to apply for judicial review on the ground of the judges misconduct of the hearing.

WATSON, *ex p. The Times,* March 18, 1987, C.A.

3054. Judicial review—jurisdiction—corporation tax—Scottish company. See R. *v.* SPECIAL COMMISSIONER, *ex p.* FORSYTH (R. W.), §549.

3055. Lands tribunal—compensation for subsidence—jurisdiction to award interest. See KNIBB *v.* NATIONAL COAL BOARD, §2429.

3056. Large and co-ordinated group of co-plaintiffs—global settlement—division of monies

Where a large and co-ordinated group of co-plaintiffs were offered a global settlement, it was entirely proper for the allocation of the monies to be proposed by the various advisors, and if necessary for an arbitration system to be set up within the scope of the litigation, if necessary with the help of the court, to deal with those co-plaintiffs who were aggrieved at being omitted from the global settlement or as to their suggested share of it. The defendants would play no part in that scheme.

DAVIES *v.* ELI LILLY & CO., *The Independent,* December 10, 1987, Hirst J.

3057. Leave to appeal—same tribunal giving leave

[Supreme Court Act 1981 (c.54), s.18(1)(*h*).]

Where leave to appeal is required from the same court or tribunal that heard the proceedings the leave may be granted by another judge of the same court or tribunal.

WARREN *v.* KILROE (T.) & SONS, *The Times,* July 3, 1987, C.A.

3058. Leave to defend—conditional leave—extension of time to comply with condition

On March 6, 1985, on an appeal against the order of the Registrar setting aside the judgment obtained by P in default of notice of intention to defend by D, the judge ordered, *inter alia,* that if D paid into court within 28 days a sum of £3,025, D would have leave to defend. D sent that money for payment into court to his solicitor on March 12, but owing to his solicitor's error the money was not paid into court until April 24. D applied for an extension of time for the payment into court.

Held, allowing D's appeal, and extending the time for payment, that it would not be in accordance with justice, or with the proper exercise of discretion, to debar D from the benefits that had been awarded to him by the judge's order of March 6 on the ground of errors on the part of his solicitor. Appeal from Taylor J.

FABIKUN *v.* AMUCHIENWA, March 25, 1986 (C.A.T. No. 324).

3059. Legal professional privilege—document allegedly brought into being to facilitate crime or fraud—effect on privilege

Where a party sought to penetrate legal professional privilege by an allegation that the documents requested were part of some form of fraud, it did not matter that the fraud alleged was not some past event but was the very conduct of the case itself; however, in such a case the risk of injustice to the party relying on the privilege was so great, if the party seeking the documents was wrong, that the case against him had to be very convincing (*O'Rourke* v. *Darbishire* [1920] A.C. 581, *R.* v. *Cox and Railton* (1884) 14 Q.B.D. 153 considered).

CHANDLER *v.* CHURCH, *The Independent,* April 30, 1987, Hoffmann J.

3060. Legal professional privilege—inadvertent disclosure of document—injunction to prevent use

[R.S.C., Ord. 24, rr.5, 9.]

In assessing, for the purpose of determining privilege in a document, the dominant purpose for which it was prepared, the court should take an objective view of the evidence as a whole. An injunction is available to restrain use by opposing parties of a privileged document disclosed in error, even after discovery.

GP Co. brought an action for breach of contract against FR, a firm of architects. FR's solicitors inadvertently included in Part I of Sched. 1 of a supplemental list of documents prepared pursuant to R.S.C., Ord. 24, r.2, a letter for which they intended to claim privilege. This had been sent by FR to their insurers notifying them of the claim and expressing opinions as to liability. GP Co.'s solicitors were invited to inspect the documents, did so, copied the letter and referred to it in their experts' report. FR sought an injunction preventing GP Co. from making further use of the document.

Held, that (1) the dominant purpose for which the letter was prepared should be assessed objectively, here in the light of the insurers reasons for requiring such a notification which included the contemplation of litigation; (2) it must have been clear to GP & Co.'s solicitors that FPs solicitors had made a mistake and thus notwithstanding the rule that it was too late to claim privilege after inspection, the injunction should be granted (*Grant* v. *Downs* [1977] C.L.Y. 1367, *Waugh* v. *British Railways Board* [1979] C.L.Y. 2172, *Buttes Gas Co.* v. *Hammer (No. 3)* [1980] C.L.Y. 2184, *Ashburton* v. *Pape* [1913] 2 Ch. 469 and *Goddard* v. *Nationwide Building Society* [1986] C.L.Y. 1516 applied; *Re Highgrade Traders* [1984] C.L.Y. 1527 considered; *Jones* v. *Great Central Railway Co.* [1910] A.C. 4 and *Re Briamore Manufacturing* [1986] C.L.Y. 2623 distinguished).

GUINNESS PEAT PROPERTIES *v.* FITZROY ROBINSON PARTNERSHIP [1987] 1 W.L.R. 1027, C.A.

3061. Magisterial law—domestic proceedings—duty of clerk to take notes of evidence

The husband had been ordered to make periodical payments of £15 per week to the two children. He applied for the order to be reduced. The magistrates heard oral evidence and dismissed the application. No notes of evidence were taken. The husband appealed.

Held, that without a note of evidence the decision could not be upheld. The failure to take notes was a serious omission. The case would be remitted for a fresh hearing.

GRAY *v.* GRAY [1987] 1 F.L.R. 16, Heilbron J.

3062. Mareva injunction—application to set aside—U.S. bankruptcy proceedings—effect upon continuance of English injunction

Various English plaintiffs obtained Mareva injunctions to prevent the withdrawal of D's assets from the jurisdiction. D was a U.S. incorporated shipping line who were also registered in England as an overseas company under s.691 of the Companies Act 1985. D found themselves in severe financial difficulty, and filed "Chapter 11" bankruptcy proceedings in the U.S.A. This had the effect that of freezing all claims against D, allowing them time to restructure under the supervision of the Court. D applied to have the Mareva injunctions set aside, on the grounds that the English court should recognise the order of the U.S. Bankruptcy Court, and allow that Court to administer D's assets.

Held, that (1) although the existence of Chapter 11 proceedings was a matter of importance to be taken into account when considering whether to exercise the equitable jurisdiction of the Court, it was not an overriding or paramount consideration. The Court had to weigh up all the assertions of all parties; (2) the Mareva injunctions did not grant priority, and the assets were in safe hands. Thus the Chapter 11 proceedings were not necessarily thwarted; (3) D had demonstrated an intention to withdraw from its European operations, and it would be wrong for funds in Europe to be repatriated as the plaintiffs would suffer irreparable prejudice.

FELIXSTOWE DOCK AND RAILWAY CO. *v.* U.S. LINES INC.; FREIGHTLINERS *v.* SAME [1987] 2 Lloyd's Rep. 76, Hirst J.

3063. Mareva injunction—discharge—whether plaintiff should provide security for cross-undertaking after discharge.

P obtained a Mareva injunction against D, upon the usual cross-undertaking in damages. The injunction was later discharged, but D sought an order that P provide security for that cross-undertaking. P contended that such security should not be given after the injunction had been discharged.

Held, dismissing D's application, that (1) P had never agreed to secure the cross-undertaking, and may well have declined to take the injunction in those circumstances;

(2) the Court would be providing security upon the potential claim on the cross-undertaking. That was not appropriate.

COMMODITY OCEAN TRANSPORT CORP. *v.* BASFORD UNICORN INDUSTRIES; MITO, THE [1987] 2 Lloyd's Rep. 197, Hirst J.

3064. Mareva injunction—*ex parte* application—duty of disclosure

In obtaining a Mareva injunction *ex parte*, P failed to mention that he had in August 1984 been arrested and charged with fraud. The judge discharged the injunction on the ground that there had been no full and frank disclosure of material facts by P. P appealed.

Held, dismissing the appeal, that a matter of prime importance concerning the exercise of the court's discretion was to determine whether the implied undertaking in damages which P was giving was an undertaking which the court could safely accept. In order to enable the court to weigh that question correctly it was necessary that the court should have been told, fully and frankly by P, that he had been arrested and a charge of fraud had been made against him. It was a matter which went directly to the exercise of discretion and the court should have been informed. It did not follow that if such information had been made available to it the court would have declined to grant an injunction, although it seemed likely that the court would have adjourned the application to be heard *inter partes*.

BLOCK *v.* NICHOLSON (T/A LIMASCUE STUD), April 17, 1986 (C.A.T. No. 409).

3065. Mareva injunction—expenses

A person who hands an asset to a party subjected to a Mareva injunction does not ordinarily assist him in dissipating it. The party bound by the order should also normally be allowed his ordinary living expenses and the means to meet his ordinary debts as they fall due.

LAW SOCIETY *v.* SHANKS, *The Times*, October 14, 1987, C.A.

3066. Mareva injunction—inappropriate where only existing cause of action is for declaratory relief

In this case the Court of Appeal held that in circumstances where a plaintiff had no existing cause of action, save for a declaration, he was not entitled to a Mareva injunction. The Mareva jurisdiction was not appropriate for the grant of security for a future cause of action that would give entitlement to monetary relief.

STEAMSHIP MUTUAL UNDERWRITING ASSOCIATION (BERMUDA) *v.* THAKUR SHIPPING CO. (NOTE) [1986] 2 Lloyd's Rep. 439, C.A.

3067. Mareva injunction—material non-disclosure—application to discharge—delay in application

Where a party to an action has obtained a Mareva injunction through material non-disclosure of facts, the party that is the subject of the injunction can apply to have it discharged, even when he has delayed his application considerably. The Court has the power to grant a second injunction after discharge, but will not do so when there has been inordinate delay in prosecuting the action by the party obtaining the original injunction.

LLOYDS BOWMAKER *v.* BRITANNIA ARROW HOLDINGS, *The Times*, March 19, 1987, Glidewell J.

3068. Mareva injunction—material non-disclosure—principal's responsibility

P obtained a Mareva injunction against D on the basis of an injunction sworn by P's own solicitor, which failed to disclose material facts.

Held, that a principal's responsibility for his agent cannot be conclusive in all cases. As P would always have been entitled to a Mareva injunction had he made full disclosure, and as the non-disclosure was solely the responsibility of his solicitor, the injunction would be granted.

EASTGLEN INTERNATIONAL CORP. *v.* MONPARE S.A.; [1986] 137 New L.J. 56, C.A.

3069. Mareva injunction—rights of third party

P obtained an injunction against D which attached to the bunkers on a vessel owned by J. T. Maritime. The vessel was consequently unable to sail from harbour in England. The owners intervened to seek the discharge of the injunction since the vessel was their only trading asset, running costs were accruing, and a further charter was imperilled by the restriction.

Held, that an innocent third party must be protected in Mareva injunction proceedings, and the order would be discharged (*Galaxia Maritime S.A.* v. *Mineralimportexport* [1982]

C.L.Y. 2504, *Clipper Maritime Co. of Monrovia* v. *Mineralimportexport* [1981] C.L.Y. 2125 followed).

UNICORN SHIPPING *v.* DEMET NAVY SHIPPING CO., *Financial Times*, April 8, 1987, Hirst J.

3070. Mareva injunction—undisclosed assets abroad

P obtained a Mareva injunction freezing D's assets in the U.K. D had undisclosed and readily available assets abroad, but sought the release of his assets in this country so that he could pay his solicitors.

Held, refusing D's application, that he had been in contempt of court in not disclosing his assets. To make the order sought would defeat the point of the Mareva injunction.

NATIONAL BANK OF GREECE *v.* CONSTANTINOS DIMITRIOU, *The Times*, November 16, 1987, C.A.

3071. Mareva injunction—variation—legitimate trading activities

In this case P obtained a Mareva injunction over the assets of D, a Swiss-based oil trading company. D applied to have the injunction set aside and failed.

Held, allowing D's appeal in part, that (1) the injunction had been properly granted and P had a good arguable case that they were entitled to the sums claimed. However, (2) the injunction had prevented D from using London bank accounts for the purposes of their trade, and to the extent that such accounts are used purely for the established course of trade, the injunction would be varied.

AVANT PETROLEUM INC. *v.* GATOIL OVERSEAS INC. [1986] 2 Lloyd's Rep. 236, C.A.

3072. Negligence—statutory duty—further and better particulars sought

[Factories Act 1961 (c.34), ss.4 and 63.]

In a case of alleged exposure to harmful welding fumes, D applied for further and better particulars of P's allegations of negligence and breach of statutory duty. P was ordered to supply particulars of what measures he would contend should have been taken by D in order to comply with their duties under ss.4 and 63, and with their common law duty to provide a suitable mask or respirator and/or to carry out a medical examination of P.

Held, allowing P's appeal, that P was not obliged to tell D what measures should have been taken. It was enough if P told D what measures he alleged they had taken which were inadequate. There was no duty to provide this information at the pleading stage.

HARNETT *v.* ASSOCIATED OCTEL, November 6, 1986, Russell J., Manchester Crown Ct. [*Ex rel. Janet Smith, Barrister.*]

3073. Offshore activities—jurisdiction. See SEA AND SEASHORE, §3349.

3074. Opposed *ex parte* motion—appeal

P were chartered surveyors who drew up specifications for repair and modernisation of BISF housing. D had been a firm of estate agents, and employing ex-employees of P carried out surveys of BISF housing. P alleged D copied P's specifications. P obtained *ex parte* injunctions, in wide terms.

Held, on D's appeal, that (1) the judge had wrongly exercised his discretion. The injunction should be limited to an order restraining D from copying P's specifications; (2) P's motion should have been stood over to the *inter partes* hearing when the evidence of both sides was before the court. Thereafter an aggrieved party might appeal to the Court of Appeal.

HUNTER & PARTNERS *v.* WELLINGS & PARTNERS [1987] F.S.R. 83, C.A.

3075. Order 14 appeals—instructions

Order 14 appeals would be heard where possible within two months of the judge's decision. It is essential for practitioners to agree a note of judgment and submit it for approval within a very short time of the judgment.

ORDER 14 APPEALS, December 20, 1986, C.A.

3076. Order 14 application—defence bad in law—Arbitration Act 1950, s.4. See BUILDING AND CONSTRUCTION, §244.

3077. Order prohibiting publication of information—nature—whether service required

An order prohibiting the publication of information is in the nature of an injunction, and must be personally served upon the party it is sought to bind, unless the court thinks it right to dispense with service.

L. (A MINOR), *Re, The Times*, July 4, 1987, Booth J.

3078. Parties to proceedings—adding person as defendant—sale of property

P bank brought proceedings against D on two mortgages seeking an order for sale of the mortgaged property. D's parents who lived at the property owing to illness and other circumstances, had nowhere else to go and applied to be joined as parties to the proceedings under R.S.C., Ord. 15, r.10(1).

Held, that the parents were there as family guests and the utmost right or interest that they could assert would be those of a licensee of the kind enjoyed by somebody occupying the premises or living in the premises as a guest of the family. Such a licence was inadequate to support an application to be joined as a party under Ord. 15. Appeal from Peter Gibson J.

CYPRUS POPULAR BANK *v.* MICHAEL, April 30, 1986 (C.A.T. No. 528).

3079. Patent infringement—pleadings—cost. See PATENTS AND DESIGNS, §2794.

3080. Patents Court—procedure—appeal—whether rehearing. See GENERICS (U.K.), *Re,* §2811.

3081. Pleadings—amendment—fraud

There is no rule of practice that allegations of fraud have to be pleaded from the outset, and an amendment to plead fraud can be allowed provided that this can be done without injustice to the other side.

The plaintiff claimed damages for libel in a television programme broadcast in June 1984. In October 1984 the defendants served a defence denying that the words complained of referred to the plaintiff or were defamatory of him. In April 1986, shortly before the action was due to be tried, the defendants applied for the case to be stood out and for leave to amend their defence to plead justification and fair comment, the effect of which would be to justify the plaintiff's complaint that the programme alleged fraud against him. The judge granted the defendants' applications, and the plaintiffs appealed.

Held, allowing the appeal, that as a general principle, a party to litigation was allowed to amend his pleadings at any stage in order that all matters in controversy should be before the court, provided that to do so would not cause injustice to other parties which could not adequately be compensated for in money. There was no rule that allegations of fraud had to be pleaded at the outset and could not be added by amendment. Accordingly, the court could in the exercise of its discretion grant a defendant leave to amend the defence to plead justification and fair comment even where the plaintiff was alleging that the meaning of the words used amounted to an allegation of fraud (*Associated Leisure (Phonographic Equipment Co.)* v. *Associated Newspapers* [1970] C.L.Y. 1574 and dictum of Bowen L.J. in *Cropper* v. *Smith* (1884) 26 Ch.D. 700, 710–11 applied; dictum of Lord Esher M.R. in *Bentley & Co.* v. *Black* (1893) 9 T.L.R. 580 not followed). However, the appeal was allowed in the circumstances since the proposed particulars of justification and fair comment did not adequately identify the matters on which the defendants intended to rely. Leave to amend was not therefore granted, but the defendants were at liberty to make a further application for leave to amend to plead justification and fair comment.

ATKINSON *v.* FITZWALTER [1987] 1 W.L.R. 201, C.A.

3082. Pleadings—amendment—new remedy or fresh cause of action

An amendment of pleadings to add a fresh remedy rather than a fresh cause of action may be permitted.

P contracted for the supply of clay from D, with P to purchase a minimum quantity annually. P refused to accept the clay on the grounds of quality, and issued a writ. D counterclaimed for the stipulated minimum payment. D later sought leave to amend the counterclaim to allege repudiatory breach of contract accepted by D on the grounds of refusal to accept delivery. Leave was granted.

Held, dismissing P's appeal, that the injured party did not have to elect as to his remedy; since the facts relied on occurred before service of the counterclaim, D was rightly allowed to amend the counterclaim so as to plead a fresh remedy (*Johnson* v. *Agnon* [1979] C.L.Y. 2733 considered; *Eshelby* v. *Federated European Bank* [1932] 1 K.B. 254 distinguished).

TILCON *v.* LAND AND REAL ESTATE INVESTMENTS [1987] 1 W.L.R. 46, C.A.

3083. Powers of attorney—extent of power—verifying affidavit. See CLAUSS *v.* PIR, §67.

3084. Precedent—decision of Court of Appeal without reference to E.E.C. directive—whether per incuriam

[Sex Discrimination Act 1975 (c.65), s.6(4); Council Directive (76/207 EEC) art. 5(1).]

A decision of the Court of Appeal made without reference to an EEC directive is not thereby rendered *per incuriam.*

The Court of Appeal construed s.6(4) of the Sex Discrimination Act in a way that took no account of an EEC directive. The applicant argued that the decision had therefore been made *per incuriam.*

Held, dismissing the appeal, that the court was bound by the decision unless it was overruled by the Lords; the fact that the decision might have been different if the court was referred to the Directive was not sufficient to make it *per incuriam* (*Roberts* v. *Cleveland Area Health Authority* [1982] C.L.Y. 1219 applied).

DUKE *v.* RELIANCE SYSTEMS [1987] 2 W.L.R. 1225, C.A.

3085. Privilege—patent agent—discovery—advice before commencement of proceedings. See PATENTS AND DESIGNS, §2810.

3086. Privileged documents—whether use of information can be restrained

Where documents to which legal professional privilege attaches accidentally comes into the hands of the other party to an action, an injunction will be granted to forbid the use of any information they contain (*Lord Ashburton* v. *Pape* ([1913] 2 Ch. 469) and *Goddard* v. *Nationwide Building Society* [1986] C.L.Y. 1516 applied).

ENGLISH AND AMERICAN INSURANCE CO. *v.* SMITH (HERBERT) & CO. (A FIRM), *The Times,* January 22, 1987, Browne-Wilkinson V.-C.

3087. Probate rules

NON-CONTENTIOUS PROBATE RULES 1987 (No. 2024 (L. 10)) [£3·30], made under the Supreme Court Act 1981 (c.54), s.127 and the Colonial Probates Act 1892 (c.6), s.2(5); operative on January 1, 1988; introduces new rules relating to non-contentious probate matters.

3088. Public Trust Office

The Public Trust Office came into being on January 2, 1987. It will deal with the management and investment of a range of privately owned assets, *e.g.* funds lodged in Court, estates of mental patients and trusts and estates administered by the former Public Trustee Office.

3089. Relator actions—procedure

Unless a private citizen can show that he has suffered damages over and above any other citizen he cannot take action in the public interest other than with the *fiat* of the Attorney General.

HOLMES *v.* CHECKLAND, *The Times,* April 15, 1987, C.A.

3090. Rules of the Supreme Court

RULES OF THE SUPREME COURT (AMENDMENT) 1987 (No. 1423 (L.8)) [£2·20], made under The Supreme Court Act 1981 (c.54), s.84; operative on October 1, 1987, as to rr.1, 32–61, 63, and on November 2, 1987 as to rr.2–31; amend the Rules of the Supreme Court.

3091. Ruling of law at trial—subsequent retrial—*res judicata*

Any ruling of law made by a trial judge ceases to be binding on a retrial.

P sued D for libel. The jury failed to agree and a retrial was ordered. Pending the retrial, amendments to the pleadings by P were allowed. D appealed, on the ground that they raised issues decided by the judge at the original trial.

Held, dismissing D's appeal, that rulings in the original trial ceased to be binding on the order of a retrial (dicta in *Carl Zeiss Stiftung* v. *Rayner & Keeler (No. 2)* [1964] C.L.Y. 532 applied; *Fidelitas Shipping Co.* v. *V/O Exportchleb* [1965] C.L.Y. 100 distinguished).

BOBOLAS *v.* ECONOMIST NEWSPAPER [1987] 1 W.L.R. 1101, C.A.

3092. Settlement of action—sale of land part of settlement—absence of note or memorandum—whether original action discharged

[Rep. of Ire.] P brought proceedings against D alleging encroachment by D on P's land. Judgment was postponed to allow negotiations to take place. As a result of the negotiations D orally agreed to purchase the land for £14,000, a figure acceptable to P. P later refused to complete the sale and as there was no note or memorandum by P, specified performance proceedings brought by D failed. P sought to reactivate his original proceedings for encroachment.

Held, that P's original cause of action was discharged by the settlement agreement for the sale of the land even though D was precluded from enforcing it. P had, accordingly, no right to proceed further with his action.

O'MAHONY *v.* GAFFNEY [1986] J.R. 36, Lynch J.

3093. Slip rule—use of rule

[R.S.C., Ord. 20, r.11.]

The slip rule does not cover all mistakes of whatever nature and does not cover the situation where a defendant fails to supply his solicitors with information material to his defence (*R.* v. *Cripps, ex p. Muldoon* [1984] C.L.Y. 2606, *Mutual Shipping Corp.* v. *Bayshore Shipping Co.* [1984] C.L.Y. 104, *Food Corp. of India* v. *Marastro Cia Naviera S.A.* [1986] C.L.Y. 100 considered).

VERDEGAAL (G.A.) & ZONEN EXPORT B.V. *v.* PULLEN, *The Times*, November 27, 1987, C.A.

3094. Solicitors—undertaking to retain funds—undertaking by one firm to another—enforcement. See FOX (JOHN) *v.* BANNISTER, KING & RIGBEYS, §3560

3095. Stay of proceedings—action in foreign jurisdiction—action then commenced in England and Wales—stay of English action requested by plaintiff

[Supreme Court Act 1981 (c.54), s.49(3).]

It is proper for a plaintiff to issue proceedings in England and Wales where there are concurrent proceedings in another jurisdiction, if it is the contention of the defendant in the foreign proceedings that proceedings should be brought only in England and Wales and where a limitation defence would otherwise accrue. The English proceedings could be stayed at the instigation of the plaintiff pending the decision of the foreign court on jurisdiction (*Spiliada Maritime Corp.* v. *Cansulex* [1987] C.L.Y. 3135, *Castanho* v. *Brown & Root* [1981] C.L.Y. 2200 considered).

ATT.-GEN. *v.* ARTHUR ANDERSEN & CO., *The Times*, October 13, 1987, Steyn J.

3096. Stay of proceedings—close nexus between two actions

Between 1981 and 1983 H had worked for R's company. H worked as a self-employed engineer doing various contracts for R. Eventually the arrangements broke down and H sued R for non-payment of fees. In a separate action R sued H on a guarantee made between the bank and H which had remained unpaid. In due course both actions were side by side in the Q.B.D. at Manchester District Registry. H issued proceedings under R.S.C., Ord. 4, r.9, for a stay of the guarantee action pending the outcome of the main business action. A stay was granted. R appealed.

Held, that although there was a close nexus between the two actions, in strict law the guarantee action arose entirely from a guarantee and subsequently to the agreement which led to the main business action. There was no reason to stay the guarantee action and such stay was therefore removed.

HENTHORN *v.* SCOTT ROBERTSON, December 12, 1986, Garland J., Manchester. [*Ex rel. Edmund G. Farrell, Barrister.*]

3097. Stay of proceedings—disputed public footpath—statutory procedure for resolution of dispute—civil proceedings by landowner—whether strike out or stay civil proceedings

Where there were contemporaneous civil proceedings and statutory proceedings under the Wildlife and Countryside Act 1981 for the resolution of a dispute about the existence of a public footpath it was proper to stay the civil proceedings pending the outcome of the statutory proceedings.

P was the owner of land over which local residents alleged there was a public footpath. The local residents made representations to the county council in consequence of which the county council set in motion the statutory process in s.53 and Sched. 15 of the Wildlife and Countryside Act 1981. After investigating the dispute, the county council resolved to make an order confirming the existence of the footpath. The matter, having reached that stage, the order was subject to confirmation by the Secretary of State for the Environment after a public inquiry. P commenced proceedings seeking a declaration that no public footpath existed. The council applied to the court for an order striking out P's action on the grounds that it was an abuse of the process of the court having regard to the existing statutory proceedings. The council's application failed.

Held, allowing the appeal in part, that P was entitled to commence his action seeking a declaration notwithstanding the fact that statutory proceedings under the Wildlife and Countryside Act were continuing. There was nothing in the legislation to take away P's right to apply to the court. Having regard to the fact that both proceedings sought to resolve the same question, it was inappropriate for both to continue. The court in the exercise of its discretion would stay P's civil proceedings. The council were obliged by their duty to maintain a definitive map under the Act to proceed with the statutory procedure to confirm their order in the event that P's claim failed. P's complaint that the inspector conducting the inquiry would not be able to deal with the complex issues of fact and law involved was unfounded. Accordingly, the statutory proceedings should continue (*Pyx Granite Co.* v. *Ministry of Housing and Local Government* [1959] C.L.Y. 3260, *Wilkes* v. *Gee* [1973] C.L.Y. 324, *R.* v. *Secretary of State for the Environment, ex p. Hood* [1975] C.L.Y. 2462, *Walwin & Partners* v. *West Sussex County Council* [1975] C.L.Y. 2463, *Wandsworth London Borough Council* v. *Winder* [1985] C.L.Y. 9 considered).

SHEARS COURT (WEST MERSEA) MANAGEMENT CO. *v.* ESSEX COUNTY COUNCIL (1986) 85 L.G.R. 479, E. J. Prosser Q.C.

3098. Stay of proceedings—indemnity—whether valid

[Civil Liability (Contribution) Act 1978 (c.47), s.1.]

One defendant can claim an indemnity against another even though the action against that other defendant has been stayed by order of the court.

BENARTY, THE, *The Times*, June 23, 1987, Hobhouse J.

3099. Stay of proceedings—refusal of stay—taking step in the proceedings

D was a tenant of P under a lease dated May 18, 1977, the terms of which contained, in relation to the calculation and ascertainment of service charges, an arbitration clause within the meaning of the Arbitration Act 1950 (c.27). D disputed the amount of the service charge, some £1,300 for the year 1982, and P issued a plaint in the county court in respect of that. D delivered a substantial defence to the claim. Those proceedings had not yet been resolved. A further dispute arose in respect of the service charge, some £6,000, claimed by P for the years 1983 to 1985. In July 1985, P issued a writ in the High court in respect of that. D returned an acknowledgment of service indicating an intention to defend and in August 1985, P delivered a statement of claim. P then took out a summons before the High Court Master to consolidate the subsisting county court proceedings with the High Court proceedings. Both P and D were represented at the hearing of the summons and D mentioned the possibility of arbitration in relation to P's claim at the time, but no formal objection was taken to the hearing of the summons and no adjournment was asked for. The Master gave an order consolidating the proceedings. D did not appeal against that order. On September 30, 1985, D took out a summons seeking an extension of time to file a defence "or to apply for a stay pending arbitration". The Master made an order extending the time for delivery of a defence for a period of 14 days. The order made no reference to the application for a stay pending arbitration. On October 10, 1985, D issued a summons seeking a stay of the proceedings under s.4(1) of the Arbitration Act 1950 and, on the very next day, issued a further summons seeking a further extension of time for delivery of a defence until after the hearing of the summons seeking a stay. P contended that D were not entitled to a stay because D's attending at the hearing which resulted in the order to consolidate the county court proceedings with the high court proceedings and D's issuing the first summons for an extension of time to file a defence constituted "taking a step" in the proceedings under the provisions of s.4 of the 1950 Act. D submitted that (1) their mere attendance at the hearing of the consolidation summons and their failure to appeal against it and (2) their issuing of the summons of September 30, 1985, having regard to the particular wording of the summons could not be construed as a step in the action.

Held, dismissing D's appeal, that the judge was correct in finding that steps in the action had been taken by D. Their attendance at the hearing of the summons for consolidation and the role which they must be deemed to have played by their failure to seek an adjournment or to seek a formal objection to the hearing proceeding necessarily involved them in having taken a step in the proceedings. Further, their summons for an extension of time constituted a further step in the action. The wording of the summons, including the words "or to apply for a stay pending arbitration" did not in fact alter the character of that summons. It was essentially a summons to extend time for delivery of a defence which amounted to a step in the action.

MARZELL INVESTMENT *v.* TRANS TELEX, June 25, 1986 (C.A.T. No. 587).

3100. Summary judgment—allegation of fraud

Where the court was required to make adverse inferences amounting to an allegation of fraudulent conspiracy it was not appropriate to do so only upon affidavit evidence in an application for summary judgment.

TADDALE INVESTMENTS *v.* BANQUE HYPOTHECAIRE DU CANTON DE GENEVE, *The Times,* February 26, 1987, C.A.

3101. Summary judgment—entitlement

[R.S.C., Ord. 14.]

Whether or not a Plaintiff has issued a summons for directions is irrelevant to whether or not he is entitled to summary judgment under Ord. 14, where the sole issue is whether or not there is a defence to his claim.

BATH PRESS *v.* ROSE, *The Times,* July 13, 1987, C.A.

3102. Summary judgment—whether incompatible with a stay of the same proceedings

Summary judgment and a stay of the same proceedings are incompatible. Where applications for both are before the Court, it should consider the application for a stay first.

MORGAN GUARANTY TRUST CO. OF NEW YORK *v.* HADJANTONAKIS (DEMETRE), *Financial Times,* July 28, 1987, C.A.

3103. Summary judgment as to part—stay as to balance pending arbitration—criteria

The court may give judgment in Ord. 14 proceedings for part of a claim and stay the balance pending arbitration.

The plaintiff succeeded in Ord. 14 proceedings in obtaining judgment on part of its claim, namely £1,541 on a total claim of £26,516, the balance of the action be to stayed pending arbitration.

Held, dismissing the plaintiff's appeal, that the court may stay the balance not only if the defence on the balance is arguable, but also if it raises mixed questions of law and fact pre-eminently suited for an arbitrator rather than the court.

ARCHITAL LUXFER *v.* DUNNING (A.J.) & SON (WEYHILL) [1987] 1 FTLR 372, C.A.

3104. Supreme Court Procedure Committee—annual report 1985/86

The Supreme Court Procedure Committee has published its Annual Report for 1985–86.

3105. Supreme Court Procedure Committee—annual report 1986/87

The fifth annual report of the Supreme Court Procedure Committee has been published. Copies of this report may be obtained from Mr. T. Cook, Room 305, Lord Chancellor's Department, Trevelyan House, Great Peter Street, London SW1P 2BY.

3106. Taxation of bill—certain charges disallowed following Notes of Guidance from the Lord Chancellor's Office

[C.C.R. 1981, Ord. 38, r.3(1). Appendix A.]

On taxation of a solicitor's bill of costs under the Legal Aid Act 1974, the registrar disallowed charges under Pt. III of Appendix A for correspondence with, and telephone attendances on, the court office, counsel and counsel's clerk. At the hearing of the taxation the registrar said this work was covered by the "mark up" which was allowed at 50 per cent. In his answer to a written objection, the registrar stated that the disallowance was made pursuant to para. 52 of "Notes for Guidance on the Taxation of Civil Costs" issued by the Lord Chancellor's Dept. (July 1984). The solicitors applied to the judge for a review.

Held, that the registrar misdirected himself and the charges should be allowed. The fact that work is of a routine nature did not necessarily mean that it should not be done by a fee-earner. The para. 52 statement was not sound in principle.

FOOT *v.* LONDON BOROUGH OF WANDSWORTH, January 27, 1987, H.H. Judge White, Wandsworth County Ct. [*Ex rel. R. W. Spon-Smith, Barrister.*]

3107. Third party claim—whether limited to liability incurred in England and Wales. See KAPETAN GEORGIS, THE, §3587.

3108. Time limits—court's discretion—requirements

[R.S.C., Ord. 3, r.5.]

The time-limits in the R.S.C. are to be observed. It is not enough, when making an application for the Court to exercise its discretion under Ord, 3, r.5, to set out a chronology of the events resulting in delay without giving any reasons which would tend to excuse it.

SMITH *v.* SECRETARY OF STATE FOR THE ENVIRONMENT, *The Times,* July 6, 1987, C.A.

3109. Transfer of action

[R.S.C., Ord. 4, r.5.]

P appealed from a district registrar's decision to transfer the action from the Newcastle District Registry (where P had begun) to Durham on D's application.

Held, allowing the appeal, that (1) the question to be decided was where the balance of convenience lay at the interlocutory stages of the action; (2) that the facts that the cause of action arose in Durham and many of the witnesses lived in the area were not relevant at the interlocutory stages but only when the venue was to be decided; (3) it followed that the whereabouts of the solicitors' offices, their convenience for the registry and the costs of travelling were important considerations; (4) in a personal injuries action P's solicitor had to make the running and the balance of convenience lay in keeping the action in the registry close to P's solicitors' office.

GREY *v.* DURHAM COUNTY COUNCIL, October 31, 1985; Taylor J. [*Ex rel. Janet Smith, Barrister.*]

3110. Transfer of action—application—commercial action

The judge declined to transfer a commercial action to the Chancery division as the only real ground for the application was that waiting time was less elsewhere.

ZAKHEM INTERNATIONAL CONSTRUCTION *v.* NIPPON KOKKAN KK, *The Times,* May 12, 1987, Staughton J.

3111. Transfer of action—application—commercial action

The judge allowed an application to transfer a commercial action to the Queen's Bench Division from the Commercial Court (*Zakhem International Construction* v. *Nippon Kokkan KK* [1987] C.L.Y. 3110 considered).

ZAKHEM INTERNATIONAL CONSTRUCTION *v.* NIPPON KOKKAN KK, *The Independent,* August 20, 1987, Staughton J.

3112. Transfer of action—application dismissed—whether subsequent application can be made

[County Courts Act 1984 (c.28), s.42(1)(*a*).]

When a judge has dismissed an application under s.42(1)(*a*) to transfer a case from the County to the High Court, a subsequent application may be made, but should only be granted if there has been a significant change in circumstances.

HABIB BANK A.G. ZURICH *v.* MINDI INVESTMENTS, *The Times,* October 9, 1987, C.A.

3113. Transfer of action—Commercial Court—criterion

[R.S.C., Ord. 72, r.1(2).]

Notwithstanding the acute congestion of the list in the Commercial Court, a transfer to another division should not be ordered solely to secure an earlier trial.

MORGAN GUARANTY TRUST CO. OF NEW YORK *v.* HADJANTONAKIS, *The Independent,* October 13, 1987, Hirst J.

3114. Transfer of action—discretion of court

The judge sitting in the Chancery Division of the High Court of Justice refused an application under R.S.C., Ord. 4, r.3 to transfer certain proceedings before him to the Family Division.

Held, that that was a matter wholly for the discretion of the judge who heard the application. The judge approached the application on a proper basis and the application for leave to appeal against the order would accordingly be refused. Appeal from Donald Rattee Q.C.

SHEARS *v.* SHEARS, July 8, 1986 (C.A.T. No. 646).

3115. Transfer of action—important question of law or fact—likelihood of cheaper or speedier trial

[County Courts Act 1984 (c.28), s.40(1)(*d*).]

W brought an action against B claiming a beneficial interest in a house in which the parties had formerly lived together and which was in B's name. The value of the house exceeded the county court equity limit and the action was commenced in the High Court. B applied for the action to be transferred to a county court under s.40(1)(*d*) of the County Courts Act 1984 *i.e.* on the ground that the proceedings were not likely to raise any important question of law or fact and were suitable for determination by a county court. The district registrar said he had no jurisdiction to order a transfer but that he would have done so if he did have the jurisdiction. B appealed. It was conceded that the District Registrar was mistaken in holding that he had no jurisdiction.

Held, allowing the appeal, that (1) The word "important" in s.40(1)(*d*) was not necessarily confined to matters of general public importance. There could be cases which raised questions of facts of such importance to a party that they could be described as important within the meaning of the section. (2) The facts of the present case were important only in the sense that most litigation is of very great importance to the parties.

The law on cases of this kind could present difficulties, but ther was no particular point of law likely to arise in the present case. The requirements of s.40(1)(*d*) were therefore satisfied and the Judge had a discretion whether or not to order a transfer. (3) It could not be assumed that the costs of a hearing in the county court would necessarily be much less than those of a hearing in the High Court. It could not even be assumed that the parties would achieve a speedier hearing in the county court. However, the fact that there might be blemishes in the organisation of business in county courts or the rules for the taxation of costs should not deter the court from saying that in principle this was just the sort of case which ought to be tried locally and with less formality than in the High Court. Not to take that view would be an admission of defeat about the functioning of the whole system of justice.

WESTON *v.* BRIAR, May 15, 1987, Hoffmann J [*ex rel. Robin Spon-Smith, Barrister.*]

3116. Transfer of action—jurisdiction

An officer of the Warwick County Court acting on behalf of the Chief Clerk purported to transfer the examination of a Mr. H to the Coventry County Court which was the county court nearest to which H now resided. It was conceded that as the power to order such transfer under the County Court Rules could only be exercised by a Judge or Registrar, the purported transfer was an irregularity.

Held, that this was a matter which went far beyond any irregularity such as might be cured under the provisions of the County Court Rules 1981, Ord. 37, r.5. It was a judicial decision made by someone or purported to be made by someone who had no jurisdiction to make it. Consequently it could not properly be described as a mere failure to comply with any of the requirements of the rules within Ord. 37, r.5.

RHODES (JOHN T.), *Re,* July 14, 1986 (C.A.T. No. 665).

3117. Transfer of business—adoption proceedings

[Matrimonial and Family Proceedings Act 1984 (c.42), s.39.]

A county court judge is empowered to retain jurisdiction over applications for adoption which are apposed on the grounds of want of jurisdiction or which would result in the acquisition by a child of British nationality if the issues are not complex, difficult or grave.

H and W were authorised by the Chilean court to remove two children from Chile whom they wished to adopt. They brought them to England with the consent of the Home Office, and applied to the county court for adoption orders. Because the adoption would result in the children's acquiring British nationality, which was one of the considerations referred to in para. 2(2)(*k*) of the *Practice Direction (Fam.D.) (Transfer of Business)* [1986] C.L.Y. 2632, the registrar held that he was bound to transfer the application to the High Court. The judge held that the issues were not complex, difficult of grave, but that nevertheless the application had to be transferred.

Held, allowing the appeal by H and W, that it was for the county court first to decide on venue, and if cases falling within para. 2(2)(*k*) were not complex, difficult or grave, para. 2(1) did not apply, and the county court was empowered to retain them (*Practice Direction (Fam.D.) (Transfer of Business)* [1986] C.L.Y. 2632 considered).

N. AND L. (MINORS) (ADOPTION PROCEEDINGS: VENUE), *Re* [1987] 1 W.L.R. 829, C.A.

3118. Transfer of business—distribution of business between High Court and County Court—factors to be considered before transferring proceedings—practice direction

The following direction was issued by the President of the Family Division on February 23, 1987.

1. These directions are given under s.37 of the Matrimonial and Family Proceedings Act 1984 by the President of the Family Division, with the concurrence of the Lord Chancellor, and apply to all family proceedings which are transferrable between the High Court and county courts under ss.38 and 39 of that Act. They supersede the directions given on April 28, 1986, *Practice Direction (Family Division: Transfer of Business)* [1986] C.L.Y. 2632. They do not apply to proceedings under the following provisions (which may be heard and determined in the High Court alone):

(a) s.45(1) of the Matrimonial Causes Act 1973 (declaration of legitimacy or validity of a marriage);
(b) the Guardianship of Minors Acts 1971 and 1973 in the circumstances provided by s.15(3) of the Guardianship of Minors Act 1971;
(c) s.14 of the Children Act 1975 where the child is not in Great Britain (freeing for adoption);
(d) s.24 of the Children Act 1975 or s.6 of the Adoption Act 1968 (Convention adoptions);
(e) Part III of the Matrimonial and Family Proceedings Act 1984;

to an application for an adoption order where the child is not in Great Britain, or to an application that a minor be made, or cease to be, a ward of court.

2.—(1) Family proceedings to which these directions apply (including interlocutory proceedings) shall be dealt with in the High Court where it appears to the court seised of the case that by reason of the complexity, difficulty or gravity of the issues they ought to be tried in the High Court. (2) Without prejudice to the generality of sub-paragraph (1), the following proceedings shall be dealt with in the High Court unless the nature of the issues of fact or law raised in the case makes them more suitable for trial in a county court than in the High Court:

(a) petitions under s.1(2)(*e*) of the Matrimonial Causes Act 1973 which are opposed pursuant to s.5 of that Act;
(b) petitions in respect of jactitation of marriage;
(c) petitions for presumption of death and dissolution of marriage under s.19 of the Matrimonial Causes Act 1973;
(d) proceedings involving a contested issue of domicile;
(e) applications under s.5(6) of the Domicile and Matrimonial Proceedings Act 1973;
(f) applications to restrain a resident from taking or continuing with foreign proceedings;
(g) proceedings for recognition of a foreign decree;
(h) suits in which the Queen's Proctor intervenes or shows cause and elects trial in the High Court;
(i) proceedings in relation to a ward of court:—(i) in which the Official Solicitor is or becomes the guardian ad litem of the ward or of a party to the proceedings; (ii) in which a local authority is or becomes a party; (iii) in which an application for blood tests is made; (iv) where any of the matters specified in (j) below are in issue;
(j) proceedings concerning children in divorce and under the Guardianship Acts where: (i) an application is opposed on the grounds of want of jurisdiction; (ii) there is a substantial foreign element; (iii) there is an opposed application for leave to take a child permanently out of the jurisdiction or where there is an application for temporary removal of a child from the jurisdiction and it is opposed on the ground that the child may not be duly returned;
(k) applications for adoption or for freeing for adoption (i) which are opposed on the grounds of want of jurisdiction; (ii) which would result in the acquisition by a child of British citizenship;
(l) interlocutory applications involving—(i) *Anton Piller* orders; (ii) *Mareva* injunctions; (iii) directions as to dealing with assets outside the jurisdiction.

3. In proceedings where periodical payments, a lump sum or property are in issue the court shall have regard in particular to the following factors when considering in accordance with paragraph 2(1) above whether the complexity, difficulty or gravity of the issues are such that they ought to be tried in the High Court—(a) the capital values of the assets involved and the extent to which they are available for, or susceptible to, distribution or adjustment; (b) any substantial allegations of fraud or deception or non-disclosure; (c) any substantial contested allegations of conduct. An appeal in such proceedings from a registrar in a county court shall be transferred to the High Court where it appears to the registrar, whether on application by a party or otherwise, that the appeal raises a difficult or important question whether of law or otherwise.

4. Subject to the foregoing, family proceedings may be dealt within a county court.

5. Proceedings in the High Court which under the foregoing criteria fall to be dealt with in a county court or a divorce county court, as the case may be, and proceedings in a county court which likewise fall to be dealt with in the High Court shall be transferred accordingly, in accordance with rules of court, unless to do so would cause undue delay or hardship to any party or other person involved.

PRACTICE DIRECTION (FAM.D.) (BUSINESS: TRANSFER) [1987] 1 W.L.R. 316.

3119. Trial by jury—exercise of discretion as to use of jury—libel action

[Supreme Court Act 1981 (c.54), s.69(1), (3).]

The decision whether a jury should try a libel action is not one of judicial discretion, and the Court of Appeal can interfere with a decision that the matter be tried by a judge alone having due regard to the judge's findings of fact. The question of "convenience" in s.69(1) of the Supreme Court Act 1981 has more to do with the efficient administration of justice than with the complexity or difficulty of the issues (*Hadmor Productions* v. *Hamilton* [1982] C.L.Y. 3280, *G.* v. *G. (Minors: Custody Appeal)* [1985] C.L.Y. 2594, *Rothermere* v. *Times Newspapers* [1973] C.L.Y. 1956, *Goldsmith* v. *Pressdram* (unrep. September 21, 1984), *Lucas-Box* v. *News Group Newspapers* [1986] C.L.Y. 1984 considered).

VISCOUNT DE L'ISLE *v.* TIMES NEWSPAPERS, *The Times,* April 16, 1987; *The Independent,* April 28, 1987, C.A.

3120. Trial out of London—practice direction

The following practice direction was issued by direction of the Lord Chief Justice on July 31, 1987:

Setting Down

1. An action to be tried elsewhere than in London shall be set down for trial at the District Registry for the place of trial ("the trial centre") within the period specified in the order for directions or, where automatic directions apply, within the period specified by Rules of Court.

Readiness for Trial

2. Every action set down shall be immediately listed as being ready for trial. The party setting the action down must lodge with the pleadings a statement containing the following particulars:—
   (i) whether the order made on the summons for directions (if any) has been complied with, and in particular (where applicable):
      (a) whether medical or experts' reports have been submitted for agreement;
      (b) if so, whether they have been agreed or agreement has been refused, and in the latter case, how many medical or expert witnesses will be called;
      (c) whether plans and photographs have been agreed;
   (ii) an up-to-date estimate of the length of trial, which shall be agreed between the parties where possible;
   (iii) the names, addresses and telephone numbers of the plaintiff's and defendant's solicitors and agents (if any), their reference number or numbers and the names, addresses and telephone numbers of the parties' intended counsel, as far as they are known.

The party setting the action down must inform every other party to the action within seven days that he has done so.

Trial Dates

3. As soon as is practicable after an action has been set down the parties will be informed of the date on, or period during which, the action is to be heard.
4. Applications for fixed dates, where these can be given, or that an action be not heard before a certain date, must be made within seven days of setting down. Such applications shall be lodged at the trial centre by the parties jointly or by one of the parties on seven days' notice to every other party and shall state fully the matters relied on.
5. It is the duty at all times of the parties' solicitors to comply with R.S.C. Ord. 34 8(2) by informing the Court immediately of any settlement or of any matter affecting the length of the trial or which is likely to lead to delay or to an application for an adjournment.

Adjournments etc.

6. The following directions shall apply to applications for adjournments, postponements and vacation of fixed dates:—
   (i) Consent applications must be made to the listing officer at the trial centre who may, if he thinks fit, refer the matter to the District Register or to the Judge.
   (ii) Opposed application must be directed to the trial centre and will considered by the District Registrar or Judge. If it is likely that the action is to come on for trial within 10 days, the application will ordinarily be considered by the Judge.
   (iii) The District Registrar may refer any application to the Judge if he thinks it desirable.
7. At any time after setting down the Court may exercise its powers under R.S.C. Ord. 34 r.5(3) to call for further information as to the readiness of the action for trial. Failure to comply with such a requirement may result in the matter being dismissed for want of prosecution.
8. In any action not specifically provided for in this direction the practice set out in the Practice Direction of July 31, 1981 (Directions for London) shall be followed as nearly as circumstances may permit and subject to any special directions by the Judge.

Commencement, Revocation and Transitional Arrangements

9. This direction comes into operation on October 1, 1987. It replaces the directions given by the Lord Chief Justice on December 10, 1971, and will apply to all cases including those which were set down before October 1, 1987.

PRACTICE DIRECTION (Q.B.D.) (TRIAL OUT OF LONDON) July 31, 1987.

3121. Unincorporated associations—conflict of interest amongst members—whether appropriate to proceed against individuals

Where there is an apparent conflict of interest amongst members of, or those associated with or affiliated to, unincorporated associations, it is inappropriate to proceed against selected individuals as representatives of the whole.

UNITED KINGDOM NIREX *v.* BARTON, *The Times*, October 14, 1986, Henry J.

3122. Warned list—consent adjournments

Whilst solicitors have the right to lodge consent applications to vacate a fixture, the Clerk of the Lists has a discretion to refuse to accept them and should normally do so.

WARNED LIST EXERCISE, *The Times*, December 11, 1986, Michael Davies J.

3123. Winding up petition—injunction restraining advertisement—continuation of injunction pending appeal

An application was made to the Court of Appeal to continue an injunction against the advertisement of a petition until the hearing of the appeal to them. No application had been made to the judge below at the end of the hearing before him.

Held, that this was a proper case to continue the injunction until the hearing of the appeal. The proper procedure would have been to have made an application to the judge below for a continuation of the injunction at the end of the hearing before him. That was not done. It was not practicable in the circumstances of the case and having regard to the nature of the issue, for an application to be made now to the judge below bearing in mind the time factor, because if an application was made and refused it may not be possible to get the matter back before the Court of Appeal in the proper time to prevent the advertisement of the petition. The jurisdiction of the Court of Appeal was concurrent. In the special circumstances of the case, it was proper for the Court of Appeal to exercise jurisdiction themselves without insisting upon an application being made to the judge below. Accordingly the injunction against the advertisement would be continued until the hearing of the appeal. Appeal from the Vice Chancellor.

COMPANY, A, *Re*, June 4, 1986 (C.A.T. No. 535).

3124. Writ—extension of writ's validity

On an application for leave to extend the validity of a writ, no more than a "good reason" need be shown. The fact that a defendant knows of a possible case against him is a relevant factor to be considered. Where leave has been given to serve a writ out of the jurisdiction, and the writ has expired although the limitation period has not, it will also be relevant to consider whether, if the writ were extended, leave would be given to serve out of the jurisdiction (*Kleinwort Benson* v. *Barbrak*; *Myrto, The (No. 3)* [1987] C.L.Y. 3125 applied; *Multinational Gas and Petrochemical Co.* v. *Multinational Gas and Petrochemical Services* [1983] C.L.Y. 383 considered).

GOLDENGLOW NUT FOOD CO. *v.* COMMODIN (PRODUCE), *The Times*, September 5, 1987, C.A.

3125. Writ—extension of writ's validity

[R.S.C., Ord. 6, r.8(2).]

Power to extend the validity of a writ is not restricted to cases where there has been difficulty effecting service; exceptional circumstances are not required, through if the writ has ceased to be valid and the limitation period expired the court will require a satisfactory explanation.

The ship was mortgaged to P bank. P arrested the ship. The judge ordered the ship to be sold pendente lite. First it was necessary to discharge a cargo belonging to many owners. There was a dispute as to whether the cargo owners were liable to the cost. P issued a writ against 164 cargo-owners, which was not served pending resolution of the dispute. P proceeded instead against the major cargo owners to establish the principle of law applicable, their intention being to save legal costs. Costs were in fact substantially saved, but it ultimately became necessary for P to apply for extension of the validity of the writ after the limitation period had expired. Five cargo owners applied for the extensions to be set aside.

Held, the power to extend the validity of the writ should only be exercised for good reason, which depended on all the circumstances of the case and the balance of hardship, and possible prejudice to the defendant. The power was not restricted to cases where there had been difficulty effecting services; exceptional circumstances were not required, though if the writ had ceased to be valid and the limitation period expired the court required a satisfactory explanation. P's plan had been to save costs without any prejudice to D, and the extensions had been properly allowed (*Jones* v. *Jones* [1970]

C.L.Y. 2350 approved; *Battersby* v. *Anglo-American Oil Co.* [1945] K.B. 23 C.A. and *Heaven* v. *Road and Rail Wagons* [1965] C.L.Y. 3252 considered).

KLEINWORT BENSON *v.* BARBRAK; SAME *v.* CHOITHRAM (T.) & SONS (LONDON); SAME *v.* CHEMICAL INPORTATION AND DISTRIBUTION STATE ENTERPRISES; SAME *v.* SHELL MARKETS (M.E.) [1987] 2 W.L.R. 1053 H.L.

3126. Writ—extension of writ's validity—application to set aside writ—conduct as election—conduct raising an estoppel

P, a housing association, wished to sue D, the architects engaged by P in a housing project completed in 1976, in which defects had appeared, also in 1976. P issued a writ in June 1982, just within the limitation period. In June 1983, on an *ex parte* application, the validity of that writ was extended by the Deputy District Registrar until December 1983. The writ was served within the extended period. The Statement of Claim was served in January 1984. In February 1984 D asked for, and was granted by P, an extension of time in which to serve a Defence. In May 1984 D issued a summons seeking an order that the order extending the validity of the writ be set aside and that service of the writ on D be set aside. H.H. Judge Smout Q.C. O.R. dismissed that application. D appealed.

Held, that (1) the Deputy District Registrar should not have extended the validity of the writ in June 1983 because there were no exceptional circumstances to justify such an order (*Portico Housing Association* v. *Moorehead* [1985] C.L.Y. 2716 considered); (2) on an application to set aside the writ, the judge was entitled to exercise his discretion on the basis of all the facts at the date of the application to set aside and was not restricted to considering the material available to the Deputy District Registrar; (3) in the light of the events subsequent to the order extending the validity of the writ, the Judge had correctly refused D's application. D's solicitors, by asking for an extension of time for service of the Defence, had impliedly represented that the extension was sought for that purpose alone and so had elected to follow that course and were disentitled from following any other because the election operated as a quasi-estoppel (dicta of Lord Diplock in *Kammins Ballrooms* v. *Zenith Investments* [1970] C.L.Y. 1525 considered). D's solicitors, when asking for an extension of time for service of the Defence, had been reticent about the possible need for the extension to consider an application to set aside the writ and this constituted an omission of a known material qualification of an absolute statement; in these circumstances the stated reason was a representation that the only purpose for the extension was the preparation of the Defence and D were estopped from taking a course of action inconsistent with that representation.

DEVON AND CORNWALL HOUSING ASSOCIATION *v.* ACLAND THORMAN AND MILLER-WILLIAMS (1986) 6 Con. L.R. 41, C.A.

3127. Writ—renewal—setting aside

The validity of the writ issued by P was extended by her on three occasions, each time by *ex parte* application. On September 16, 1983, three days before the third renewal of the writ was due to expire, the writ was served on D. On September 21, 1983, D acknowledged service of the writ and gave notice of intention to defend. On December 6, 1983, the statement of claim was served. Thereafter D's solicitors requested certain particulars of the damage claimed by P and production of certain documents prior to serving their defence, and they reached agreement with P's solicitors whereby their time for serving a defence was extended generally. The particulars of the damage were served on July 12, 1984, and copies of the documents requested posted to D on March 1, 1985, together with a request that the defence be served "as soon as possible." On March 7, 1985, D applied for an order, *inter alia,* setting aside the three orders renewing the writ under R.S.C., Ord. 12, r.8. P contended, *inter alia,* that the application was made too late because (1) it was not made within the time limit prescribed by R.S.C., Ord. 12, r.8; (2) it was not made within a reasonable time within R.S.C., Ord. 2, r.2(*i*); and (3) a fresh step in the proceedings had been taken by D within R.S.C., Ord. 2, r.2, after D had become aware of the irregularity of which they made complaint, namely by their seeking by correspondence an extension of time for service of the defence and production of documents.

Held, dismissing P's appeal, that D's application was not too late because (1) the time limited for service of a defence and accordingly applying to discharge any order extending the validity of the writ under R.S.C., Ord. 12, r.8, meant not just the 14 days provided by R.S.C., Ord. 18, r.2, but any extension of that time as agreed between the parties, and D's application was within that period of time as extended by agreement; (2) when an application to set aside a renewal is made within the time specifically provided for in R.S.C., Ord. 12, r.8, that could not be regarded as not having been made within a reasonable time within R.S.C., Ord. 2, r.2. R.S.C., Ord. 12, r.8, provided a specific time within which the application to set aside must be made, namely the time limited for service of the defence, and that specific provision overrode and prevailed over the more general provision of R.S.C., Ord. 2, r.2; (3) seeking by correspondence an extension of time for service of a defence or production of documents did not constitute taking a step within R.S.C., Ord. 2, r.2 (*Reynolds* v. *Coleman* (1887) 36 Ch.D. 345 explained).

Further the judge hearing the application under R.S.C., Ord. 12, r.8, to set aside an order extending the validity of the writ had to exercise a fresh discretion because it was only on the hearing of that application by the defendants that the matter was considered *inter partes,* the practice being for the application to extend the validity of the writ and for the order extending validity to be made *ex parte* and it then being for the defendants to apply under R.S.C., Ord. 12, r.8, to set aside the extension and the service of the writ. The judge was not fettered by the *ex parte* decision of the master or judge to grant an extension and he was not sitting on appeal from the master or judge who granted the extension on the *ex parte* application. Appeal from Sir Neil Lawson.

WINCH *v.* AMPLETT & CO. (A FIRM) April 9, 1986 (C.A.T. No. 314).

3128. Writ—renewal—whether sufficient reason shown for renewal—both parties' underwriters party to the "Gold Clause Agreement"

P had cargo claims arising out of the carriage of their rice on D's vessel. P appointed an arbitrator and issued a writ within one year so as to protect their position. The writ was neither served nor renewed. There was no arbitration agreement. It was then discovered that both P's leading underwriter and D's P & I Club were parties to the "Gold Clause Agreement". This, *inter alia,* provided a mechanism for the extension of time upon request to two years, providing that notice of the claim had been given and the claim formulated within a reasonable time. P invited D to permit an extension of time but D refused, and applied to set aside the writ which Neill J. had renewed *ex parte.* Bingham J. set the writ aside.

Held, dismissing P's appeal, that (1) P had to show something exceptional in order to justify the renewal; (2) there was nothing on the facts of this case to justify an extension. Although the existence of the Gold Clause agreement could well have been relevant, here it was used as an afterthought, not as a legitimate excuse for the late commencement of proceedings.

EURICO S.p.A. *v.* LEROS SHIPPING CO. AND SEABOARD MARITIME INC.; OMEGA LEROS, THE [1987] 1 Lloyd's Rep. 530, C.A.

3129. Writ—service by post—burden of proof

P were builders of an office block constructed during 1973–75. On December 31, 1982, they issued a writ, against certain defendants who had supplied them with windows for the building which they contended were defective. On December 22, 1983, the writ was sent to D1 by first class prepaid post. D1 contended that they had not received the writ until January 3, 1984 and that service should not be extended since to do so would deprive them of a valid limitation defence.

Held, (1) that the burden of proof lay upon D1 to prove that the writ had not been delivered to them in the usual course of post *i.e.* on the day after posting. Where special collection arrangements by D1 were in force and where D1 had failed to prove that the writ would not have been delivered on time had delivery been left to the normal processes of the post D1 had failed to discharge the burden.

Obiter: In any event, time for delivery would have been extended in the special circumstances of this case it being impossible to tell before trial of the action that D1 would in fact be deprived of a limitation defence.

PRESS CONSTRUCTION *v.* PILKINGTON BROTHERS (1987) 7 Con.L.R. 80, H.H. Judge John Davies Q.C., O.R.

3130. Writ—service out of jurisdiction—alternative forum—burden of proof

On an application for leave to serve a writ out of the jurisdiction, it was not incumbent on a plaintiff to exclude by evidence any alternative forum where there was no obvious alternative forum.

D was a Panamanian company that operated one ship called the "Handgate". P was a cargo owner that wished to sue D. The bills of lading were governed by English law. D's agent was a Hong Kong company called Samaha Company Ltd. Panamanian law required the writ to be served personally on a director of D. D's registered office was in Hong Kong. P obtained leave to serve the writ out of the jurisdiction at that address. Upon attempting to do so, P discovered the address was occupied by a firm of solicitors and was no longer D's registered office. The writ was eventually served on D's company secretary and director, after enquiries at Samaha Company Ltd. D applied to set aside the leave to serve out of the jurisdiction on the basis that P had failed to prove that Hong Kong was not a more suitable alternative forum. D was successful.

Held, allowing P's appeal, that P did not have to prove Hong Kong was not a suitable alternative forum. It was only necessary to do so if it could be said Hong Kong was an obvious alternative forum. It could not be said Hong Kong was an obvious alternative forum in the absence of any evidence of D carrying on business there, the absence of any registered office and the fact that D was not registered as a foreign company carrying on business in Hong Kong.

ETS SOULES ET COMPAGNIE *v.* HANDGATE CO. S.A.; HANDGATE, THE [1987] 1 FTLR 1, C.A.

3131. Writ—service out of the jurisdiction—evidence for leave—joinder of foreign defendant

It was unreasonable to expect a plaintiff, preparing his evidence in support, on an application for leave to serve a writ out of the jurisdiction under R.S.C., Ord. 11, r.1, to anticipate and deal with all the arguments or all the points, which might be raised against his case provided there was no deliberate intention to mislead the court. Further, the judge on appeal from the Master, in considering whether or not there was an arguable case for the plaintiff, was entitled, in the absence of any deliberate non-disclosure, to take into account the totality of the evidence, both of the plaintiff and of the defendant (*B.P. Exploration Co. (Libya)* v. *Hunt* [1976] C.L.Y. 2214 and *The Hida Maru* [1981] C.L.Y. 2197 considered). On a true construction of R.S.C., Ord. 11, r.1, leave may be given for service of the writ out of the jurisdiction in a case where a person out of the jurisdiction was a *proper* party to an action properly brought against a person duly served within the jurisdiction, even if he was not a *necessary* party. The necessity or otherwise of the joinder was only one relevant factor for the court to consider. If, however, the court took the view that service out of the jurisdiction in a particular case was likely in practice to achieve no potential advantage whatever for the plaintiff, this would ordinarily not be a proper case for service out of the jurisdiction within the meaning of R.S.C. Ord. 11, r.4(2) (*Société General de Paris* v. *Dreyfus Bros.* (1885) Ch.D. 239 and *Chaney* v. *Murphy* (1948) C.L.C. 7861 considered). However, if a plaintiff had a good cause of action for damages against two defendants, one in this country and one out of the jurisdiction, it must, at least ordinarily, be of potential advantage to him to obtain a judgment in this country against the foreign defendant as well as against the defendant in this country. This would enable him to choose against which of the defendants he would seek to enforce his judgment. Further, it was not incumbent upon the plaintiff expressly to refer to this advantage in his evidence in support of the application for leave.

ELECTRIC FURNACE CO. *v.* SELAS CORP. OF AMERICA, May 9, 1986 (C.A.T. No. 428).

3132. Writ—service out of the jurisdiction—leave

The parties had had two previous transactions which had been expressly made subject to the rules of the Cocoa Association of London Limited and on the terms of that association's standard form of contract, CAL.A4, which contained an exclusive jurisdiction clause in favour of England. P issued a writ claiming damages for breach of an oral contract allegedly made between the parties in the early hours of the morning of October 30, 1982 at an airport in Sabah Malaysia and sought leave to serve the same out of the jurisdiction under R.S.C., Ord. 11, r.(1) (*f*) (iii) and r.(2). P's case was that a firm contract was made on the same terms as the earlier transactions save for one variation. D contended that (1) there was no contract at all, (2) if there was, the proper law was not English law and in any event there was no agreement to submit to the jurisdiction in relation to the determination of any question whether there was a contract or not, and (3) in any event the terms of the rules were not incorporated in any contract which was made. The judge found that there was a strong case for the existence of an oral contract and such contract included the rules which were referred to in the earlier contracts and thus included an exclusive jurisdiction clause. The judge granted the leave sought by P. D applied to set aside firstly the writ and secondly the order granting leave. It was common ground that P had to show not only a good arguable case but also a clear balance in favour of the court exercising the jurisdiction to serve out and further that if there was an exclusive jurisdiction clause, albeit the burden remained on P to satisfy the court that it was a proper case for service out, D would ordinarily be kept to his bargain. The judge refused D's application and D appealed contending that since there was a dispute about the existence of the contract, the matter must be approached on the basis that there was no exclusive jurisdiction clause relating to the principal issue, namely, whether there was a contract or not.

Held, dismissing the appeal, that if there was no dispute that the clause was incorporated, if there was a contract, and there was a strong arguable case for the existence of the contract, it was plain that leave would be given. Equally, if there was no dispute about the existence of the contract, but a dispute about the incorporation of the clause, and there was, strong ground for the incorporation of the clause, again leave would be given. If there was a good arguable case for both the existence of the contract, and the incorporation of the clause, it followed that P would succeed in holding their order for leave to serve out, unless some good reason to the contrary was shown. There being here a strong arguable case both for the existence of the contract and for the incorporation in such contract of the exclusive jurisdiction clause, the order in favour of P was rightly made, there being no special circumstances which would prevent P from holding D to the bargain which, in all probability on the evidence as it stood before the court at the moment, was made between them (*The Parouth* [1982] C.L.Y. 379 applied). Appeal from Steyn J.

COCOA MERCHANTS *v.* NORTH BORNEO PLANTATIONS SDN BHD, October 22, 1986 (C.A.T. No. 921).

3133. Writ—service out of the jurisdiction—leave—whether contracts made in England—whether England the most suitable forum

P were incorporated in the U.A.E. and carried on business in insurance and reinsurance. D were a Panamanian insurance and reinsurance company, with their head office in the U.S.A. P entered into some reinsurance treaties with D, all of which were routed through London brokers. P sought to claim recovery of sums from D, and obtained leave to issue and serve a writ out of the jurisdiction upon D. D obtained a stay of the action. P appealed.

Held, allowing P's appeal, that (1) P had a good arguable case that the reinsurance contracts were made in England; (2) England was clearly the forum in which the case could most suitably be tried.

ISLAMIC ARAB INSURANCE CO. *v.* SAUDI EGYPTIAN AMERICAN REINSURANCE CO. [1987] 1 Lloyd's Rep. 315, C.A.

3134. Writ—service out of the jurisdiction—practice direction

The following practice direction was issued by the Senior Master of the Queen's Bench Division on December 17, 1986.

1. The Civil Jurisdiction and Judgments Act 1982 comes into force on January 1, 1987.

2. One of the purposes of the 1982 Act is to waive the need to obtain leave to serve abroad where the defendants are resident in the EEC, Scotland or Northern Ireland.

3. If the plaintiff wishes to avail of this facility the writ must be indorsed, before issue, with a statement that the High Court of England and Wales has the power under the Civil Jurisdiction and Judgments Act 1982, to hear and determine this claim and that no proceedings are pending between the parties in Scotland, Northern Ireland or another convention territory of any contracting state as defined by s.1(3) of the said Act (R.S.C., Ord. 6, r.7, Ord. 11, r.1(2)(*a*)).

4. If the writ is not so indorsed then the writ must be marked "Not for service out of the jurisdiction" unless an order giving leave to issue is produced. Leave cannot be given under Ord. 11, r.1(1) if the writ could be served without leave under Ord. 11, r.1(2).

5. The countries to which the Act currently applies are as follows:

Belgium
Denmark
France
Federal Republic of Germany (West Germany)
Italy
Luxembourg
Netherlands
United Kingdom.

6. Where the writ is to be served abroad the number of days for acknowledging service under the extra-jurisdiction table (see *The Supreme Court Practice 1985,* vol. 2, para. 902) should be stated on the writ.

Default judgments

7. Where the writ has been served out of the jurisdiction under the provisions of Ord. 11, r.1(2) above, a judgment in default of notice of intention to defend can only be entered by leave of the court (Ord. 13, r.7B). The leave may be given *ex parte,* on affidavit. The leave must be drawn up and attached to the judgment.

PRACTICE DIRECTION (Q.B.D.) (SERVICE OUT OF THE JURISDICTION) [1987] 1 All E.R. 160.

3135. Writ—service out of jurisdiction—suitable forum

[R.S.C., Ord. 11, r.4(2).]

In considering whether leave should be given for service of proceedings outside the jurisdiction under R.S.C., Ord. 11, r.4(2), it was proper to take into account the fact that an analogous action was already being tried here.

In 1980 C. Co. shipped bulk sulphur in a ship belonging to S.M. Co. from Vancouver to Indian ports. S.M. Co. alleged that the sulphur had been wet on loading and obtained leave *ex parte* to serve proceedings outside the jurisdiction on the grounds that it was an action for breach of a contract governed by English law. An application to discharge the order came before Staughton J., who had already started to hear a similar action involving another ship belonging to S.M. Co. He dismissed the application. The Court of Appeal allowed C. Co.'s appeal.

Held, by the House of Lords, allowing the appeal, that the proper test was as in an application for a stay of proceedings on the grounds of *forum non conveniens,* and advantages of bringing the action in England following the other similar action were a relevant consideration. There were no grounds for interfering with the judge's exercise of direction (*Ilyssia Compania Naviera S.A.* v. *Bamaodah* [1985] C.L.Y. 3232 approved; *MacShannon* v. *Rockware Glass* [1978] C.L.Y. 2390 considered).

SPILIADA MARITIME CORP. *v.* CANSULEX; SPILIADA, THE [1986] 3 W.L.R. 972, H.L.

3136. Writ *ne exeat regno*—application by wife to recover arrears under maintenance order—whether writ should be granted. See THAHA *v.* THAHA, §1748.

3137. Writ *ne exeat regno*—purpose—validity

A writ *ne exeat regno* is valid if its primary purpose is to assist execution of judgment in the event of a successful action.

A writ *ne exeat regno* was served on the defendant, a Jordanian citizen. He was arrested and a Mareva injunction was issued. He contested the propriety of the writ in that the fourth of the "Megarry" conditions, that it would "materially prejudice . . . the prosecution of the action" was not satisfied. The plaintiff argued that "prosecution included discovery and the Mareva injunction.

Held, discharging the writ, that the writ was invalid when its primary purpose was not to prevent prejudice but to facilitate execution should it be successful.

ALLIED ARAB BANK *v.* HAJJAR [1987] 1 FTLR 455, Leggatt J.

PRISONS

3138. Annual report

The Home Office has published the fifth Annual Report of H.M. Chief Inspector of Prisons. Copies of the report are available from H.M.S.O. (Cmnd. 123) [£3·50].

3139. False allegations—criteria

[Prison Rules (S.I. 1964 No. 388).]

Statements of opinion or insulting language do not constitute false and malicious allegations contrary to the rules unless they involve allegations of fact.

R. *v.* BOARD OF VISITORS OF THORP ARCH PRISON, *ex p.* DE HOUGHTON, *The Times,* October 22, 1987, D.C.

3140. Home Office research programme. See CRIMINAL LAW, §786.

3141. Parole Board—annual report

The Parole Board has published its Annual Report for 1986. The Report is available from H.M.S.O. (HC 5) [£5·00].

3142. Prisoners' rights—medical treatment—complaint against prison—whether claim raising matter of public law. See R. *v.* SECRETARY OF STATE FOR THE HOME OFFICE, *ex p.* DEW, §6.

3143. Rules

PRISON (AMENDMENT) RULES 1987 (No. 1256) [45p], made under the Prison Act 1952 (c.52), ss.25(1) and 47; operative on August 13, 1987; amend r.5 (remission of sentence) of S.I. 1964 No. 388 so as to increase from one-third to one-half the remission which may be granted in relation to sentences for a term of 12 months or less.

PRISON (AMENDMENT No. 2) RULES 1987 (No. 2176) [45p], made under the Prison Act 1952, s.47; operative on March 1, 1988; remove the right of an unconvicted prisoner to be supplied with food at his own expense or that of his friends.

3144. State and use

The Government Reply to the Third Report from the Home Affairs Committee Session 1986–87 (HC 35–1) State and Use of Prisons has been published. Copies are available from H.M.S.O. (Cm. 263) [£2.20].

PUBLIC ENTERTAINMENTS AND RECREATION

3145. Fire Safety and Safety of Places of Sport Act 1987 (c.27)

This Act amends the Fire Precautions Act 1971 (c.40) and other enactments relating to fire precautions. The Act also amends the Safety of Sports Grounds Act 1975 (c.52) and makes like provisions as respects stands at sports grounds. The statutory provisions regulating entertainment licenses are amended and extended, with respect to indoor sports premises.

The Act received the Royal Assent on May 15, 1987, and will come into force on days to be appointed by the Secretary of State.

The Act does not extend to Northern Ireland. Ss.42, 43, 46 and 47 extend to England and Wales only. Ss.44 and 48 extend to Scotland only. The Act does not extend to the Isles of Scilly except as provided by s.50(5).

3146. Fire Safety and Safety of Places of Sport Act 1987—commencement

FIRE SAFETY AND SAFETY OF PLACES OF SPORT ACT 1987 (COMMENCEMENT No. 1) ORDER 1987 (No. 1762) (C.54)) [85p], made under the Fire Safety and Safety of Places of Sport Act 1987, s.50(2); brings into force on January 1, 1988 ss.3, 4, 8, 9, 11, 12, 13, 14, 16(1)(2) (in part), 17, 18 (in part), Pt. II, ss.46, 49 (in part), 50 (in part), Scheds. 1 (in part), 2, 4, 5, paras. 1, 3, 4, 5, 6, 7.

3147. Sports grounds

SAFETY OF SPORTS GROUNDS (DESIGNATION) ORDER 1987 (No. 1689) [45p], made under the Safety of Sports Grounds Act 1975 (c.52), s.1(1); operative on October 31, 1987; designates the Athletic Ground, Scarborough, as requiring a safety certificate under the 1975 Act.

SAFETY OF SPORTS GROUNDS REGULATIONS 1987 (No. 1941) [£1·30], made under the Safety of Sports Grounds Act 1975, ss.6(1), (4) and 10A (1) and (2); operative on January 1, 1988; replace specified regulations dealing with the safety of sports grounds.

SPORTS GROUNDS AND SPORTING EVENTS (DESIGNATION) (AMENDMENT) ORDER 1987 (No. 1520) [45p], made under the Sporting Events (Control of Alcohol etc.) Act 1985 (c.57), s.9(3); operative on September 30, 1987; amends S.I. 1985 No. 1151.

3148. Video games—amusement arcade—whether "exhibition of moving pictures." See BRITISH AMUSEMENT CATERING TRADES ASSOCIATION *v.* WESTMINSTER CITY COUNCIL, §2310.

PUBLIC HEALTH

3149. Clean air

SMOKE CONTROL AREAS (AUTHORISED FUELS) REGULATIONS 1987 (No. 625) [80p], made under the Clean Air Act 1956 (c.52), s.34(1); operative on May 1, 1987; declare Calco Cosycoke to be an authorised fuel for the purposes of the 1956 Act.

SMOKE CONTROL AREAS (AUTHORISED FUELS) (No. 2) REGULATIONS 1987 (No. 2159) [85p], made under the Clean Air Act 1956, s.34(1)(*a*) operative on January 12, 1988; declare Sovereign Briquette and Flamelite to be authorised fuels for the purpose of s.11 of the 1956 Act.

SMOKE CONTROL AREAS (EXEMPTED FIREPLACES) ORDER 1987 (No. 1394) [45p], made under the Clean Air Act 1956, ss.11(4), 33(1); operative on September 2, 1987; exempts specified fireplaces from control under s.11 of the 1956 Act.

3150. Control of pollution

CONTROL OF POLLUTION (ANTI-FOULING PAINTS AND TREATMENTS) REGULATIONS 1987 (No. 783) [85p], made under the Control of Pollution Act 1974 (c.40), ss.100, 104(1);

operative on May 28, 1987; prohibit the retail sale or supply of anti-fouling paints or treatments which contain a tri-organotin compound.

CONTROL OF POLLUTION (EXEMPTION OF CERTAIN DISCHARGES FROM CONTROL) (VARIATION) ORDER 1987 (No. 1782) [45p], made under the Control of Pollution Act 1974, ss.32(3)(*b*), 104(1)(*a*); operative on October 15, 1987; varies S.I. 1986 No. 1623 in relation to the discharge of certain effluents.

3151. Noise—construction and open sites

CONTROL OF NOISE (CODE OF PRACTICE FOR CONSTRUCTION AND OPEN SITES) ORDER 1987 (No. 1730) [45p], made under the Control of Pollution Act 1974 (c.40), ss.71, 104(1); operative on October 28, 1987; approves a Code of Practice designed to minimise noise on construction and other open sites.

3152. Noise—lawnmowers

LAWNMOWERS (HARMONISATION OF NOISE EMISSION STANDARDS) (AMENDEMENTS) REGULATIONS 1987 (No. 876) (45p), made under the European Communities Act 1972 (c.68), s.2(2); operative on July 1, 1987; amend s.1 1986 No. 1795.

3153. Refuse—collection of refuse—whether local authority liable for injury caused by its own failure to collect refuse

[Public Health Act 1936 (c.49), s.72(2).]

The mother of the infant plaintiff had been a tenant of the defendant authority since 1979, occupying the first and second floor of a converted house. Access could be gained through the back by a flight of stairs to a balcony at first floor level. Shortly after moving in, the plaintiff's mother discovered a considerable collection of rubbish and furniture in the roof space, and moved it to the balcony. The authority were then asked to remove it, and correspondence and visits by various officers of the authority followed. In August 1981, the plaintiff who was then 20 months old was found on the ground below the balcony. The Plaintiff sued the authority for personal injury. The judge who was concerned with liability only inferred that the plaintiff had woken from her sleep and had climbed onto the rubbish on the balcony and then fallen to the ground.

Held, giving judgment for the plaintiff, that (1) the authority could not be regarded as occupying the plaintiff's premises for the purposes of the Occupiers Liability Act 1957; (2) breach of s.72(2) of the Public Health Act 1936 did not of itself give rise to a cause of action; (3) on the facts the authority owed no duty of care to the plaintiff arising out of the relationship of landlord and tenant between the authority and the plaintiff's mother; (4) Part II of the Public Health Act 1936 looked at broadly established a framework of powers, duties and discretions with the general aim of securing public health and public safety; accordingly the authority owed the plaintiff's a duty of care to remove the accumulation of refuse, and their failure to do so was the substantial cause of the injury suffered.

DEAR *v.* NEWHAM LONDON BOROUGH COUNCIL (1987) 19 H.L.R. 391, Wright Q.C.

3154. Refuse—university halls of residence—whether house refuse—test

[Public Health Act 1936 (c.49), s.72.]

The test for "house refuse" under s.72 of the Public Health Act 1936 is (i) whether refuse is produced by a house and (ii) whether the refuse is the kind expected of a house occupied as a house. Refuse from university halls of residence is not "house refuse", and therefore a local authority cannot be required to collect it free of charge (*Iron Trades Mutual Employers Insurance Association* v. *Sheffield Corporation* [1974] C.L.Y. 3078, applied).

MATTISON *v.* BEVERLEY BOROUGH COUNCIL, *The Times*, February 16, 1987, C.A.

3155. Sewers—poorly constructed sewers—vesting order—Secretary of State's decision. See R. *v.* SECRETARY OF STATE FOR WALES AND A. B. HUTTON (SECRETARY TO THE MAES GERDDI RESIDENTS ASSOCIATION), §3867.

RATING AND VALUATION

3156. Abolition of Domestic Rates Etc. (Scotland) Act 1987 (c.47)

This Act abolishes domestic rates in Scotland and provides as to the finance of local government in Scotland.

The Act received the Royal Assent on May 15, 1987, and comes into force on days to be appointed by the Secretary of State.

The Act applies to Scotland only.

3157. Agricultural de-rating—agricultural building—whether "contiguous" to agricultural land

[Rating Act 1971 (c.39), s.5(5).]

Two buildings used for agricultural purposes were separated, over a distance of 62 m., from agricultural land by two roads, a house and garden, and a school playing field.

Held, that the buildings were not contiguous to the land and were not entitled to agricultural de-rating (*Strathclyde Regional Assessor* v. *B.P. Oil Refinery (Grangemouth)* (unrep. May 6, 1982) considered).

LOTHIAN REGIONAL ASSESSOR *v.* HOOD (1987) 27 R.V.R. 132, Lands Valuation Appeal Ct.

3158. Building used for two purposes—monopoly element

One building used as the headquarters and main sorting office of the local area of the Post Office was valued using a total zone A base rate of £50 psm.

Held, that the zone A rate was too high since (i) no premium was to be applied in respect of the monopoly nature of the business and (ii) the rate was too high having regard to local comparable premises. A proper rate would be £25 psm. The fact that the building was used for two distinct purposes did not mean that two separate rates should be applied, since any relevant difference in value could be effected by reducing the base rate by an appropriate fraction.

POST OFFICE *v.* ORKNEY AND SHETLAND ASSESSOR [1987] R.A. 169, Lands Valuation Appeal Ct.

3159. Duty to make rate—duty of local authority

[General Rate Act 1967 (c.9), ss.2(1), 3(5); Local Government, Planning and Land Act 1980 (c.65), ss.59(6), 60, 61, 62, 65; Local Government Finance Act 1982 (c.32), ss.5, 8; Rates Act 1984 (c.33), ss.1, 2, 3, 6, 8; Local Government Act 1972 (c.70), s.151.]

A local authority is bound by statute to make a rate, and since it cannot do so properly without a budget, it must make a budget. The budget and the rate must be lawful (*R.* v. *Secretary of State for the Environment, ex p. Brent London Borough Council* [1983] C.L.Y. 3147; *R.* v. *Secretary of State for the Environment, ex p. Hackney London Borough Council* [1984] C.L.Y. 23; *Bromley London Borough Council* v. *Greater London Council* [1982] C.L.Y. 1910 considered).

R. *v.* HACKNEY LONDON BOROUGH COUNCIL, *ex p.* FLEMING, 26 R.V.R. 182, Woolf J.

3160. Enfranchisement of lease—reduction of rateable value to level below statutory limit—valuation officer's method of valuation—judicial review. See R. *v.* WESTMINSTER VALUATION OFFICER, *ex p.* RENDALL, §14.

3161. Evidence to support valuation—quantum reduction

A supermarket was valued on appeal at a figure of £42 psm. The assessor sought £45 psm., being more than the £35 psm sought and obtained by him for zone A in the same street in other shops.

Held, that there was no basis for a zone A figure higher for this shop than for others in the same street. Size and finish were irrelevant. However the question of a quantum reduction was one of fact, and since the appeal committee rejected the claim to such a reduction and there was evidence before them in that regard, the court would not interfere with that decision (*Drybrough & Co.* v. *Strathclyde Assessor* [1982] S.L.T. 426, *Milligan* v. *Strathclyde Assessor* [1982] S.L.T. 369 considered).

ARGYLL STORES *v.* ORKNEY AND SHETLAND ASSESSOR [1987] R.A. 182, Lands Valuation Appeal Ct.

3162. Failure to make rate—surcharge for wilful misconduct—district auditor's failure to offer oral hearing

[Local Government Finance Act 1982 (c.32), s.20(1)(2)(3).]

A district auditor issued a certificate against councillors for wilful misconduct in not setting a rate. His failure to offer them an oral hearing, when they had made full written representations, and had not requested an oral hearing, did not make his decision open to challenge at law.

The District Auditor drew the attention of the Liverpool City Councillors to their failure to make a rate, warning them of the possible consequences for them financially and by way of disqualification. The council did not make a rate until June 14, 1985, after two warnings. He notified them on June 26, 1985, that he was considering certifying the sum of £106,103 consequent on their failure to make a rate, on the ground that the loss was caused by their wilful default. They were invited to make written representations on the concerns the auditor had. The councillors made a detailed written rebuttal of the auditor's points, but did not request an oral hearing. On September 6, the auditor certified the sum of £106,103 as due from them, jointly and severally, owing to their wilful misconduct, under s.20(1) of the Local Government Finance Act 1982. They appealed against the notice under s.20(3) but their claim was dismissed at all stages.

Held, that in all the circumstances including the fact that they had not requested an oral hearing and that they had been able to make full written representations, the auditor had not acted unfairly in not affording them an oral hearing and they had not been prejudiced by his failure to do so. They had had adequate notice of the matters on which the auditor had relied in issuing his certificate, and he and the courts below had been entitled to conclude that the loss was caused by their wilful misconduct. *Per curiam*: The appeal mechanism provided by s.20(3) of the 1982 Act is apt to enable the court in its discretion, notwithstanding that it finds some procedural defect in the conduct of an audit that has resulted in a certificate based on wilful misconduct, to inquire into the merits of the case and arrive at its own decision thereon.

LLOYD *v.* McMAHON [1987] 2 W.L.R 821, H.L.

3163. Lands Tribunal decisions

A proposal which showed the ratepayer's hereditament incorrectly was invalid. A notice of appeal based on the same error was also invalid.

ALUWIHARE (V.O.) *v.* M.F.I. PROPERTIES (LVC/121/1986) [1987] R.A. 189.

3164. Where a proposal is made for revaluation and at the date of the proposal a central heating system that was formerly included has been removed, and a new system has been installed, the valuation may not include the former (since it is not present) nor may it include the latter.

APPEAL OF MAUDSLEY (V.O.) *Re* (Ref. LVC/184/1982) (1986) 26 R.V.R. 181.

3165. A warehouse in Tonbridge was purpose-built in 1982 as a high-security collection point for the sorting, storage and redistribution of notes and coin, as was assessed by the LVC at £12,000 gross value, £9,972 rateable value. The Tribunal, following the approach in *Howarth* v. *Price (V.O.)* (1965) 11 R.R.C. 196, preferred the comparative method of valuation to the contractor's basis, and took into account 11 comparables and in particular a cash centre at Witham which was closest to the appeal premises in similarity of design and size, and situated on an industrial trading estate where standard warehouses had a similar value. The assessment was reduced to £7,125 gross value, £5,909 rateable value.

BARCLAYS BANK *v.* GERDES (V.O.) (Ref./LVC/242/1985) (1987) 283 E.G. 1225.

3166. The fact that the owner of a holiday mobile home was unable to use it for four months of the year due to the provisions of the site licence would not lead to a reduction in rating valuation which was to be determined with reference to a hypothetical annual letting.

BRIDGETT *v.* GREEN (V.O.) (LVC/468/1985), 26 R.V.R. 219.

3167. A newly refurbished office building of which the new central heating system was grossly defective (and which had caused substantial damage to the hereditament) was properly valued at nil for rating purposes since the premises could not be let.

CLARK (V.O.), *Re* (LVC/307/1985) [1987] R.A. 127.

3168. The appeal premises in Cardiff were purpose-built in the 1930s as a bus garage and formerly rated as a single hereditament, but since 1981 had been used for hiring out vehicles and skips. The parties agreed that they should now be rated as two separate hereditaments. The tribunal rejected a submission by the V.O. that there was a demand in Cardiff for use of the premises as workshops, whether as part of a service depot or at all, did not accept that any of the V.O.'s comparables were in the same mode or category of use as the appeal premises, and doubted whether it was in fact correct to treat them as two separate hereditaments. The larger hereditament was assessed at £5,447 gross value, £4,511 rateable value, and the smaller at £944 and £800.

COX T/A U-HAUL VEHICLES HIRE *v.* PYRKE (V.O.) (LVC/37 & 38/1985) (1987) 284 E.G. 1068.

3169. The appeal premises in Aylesbury were sited on an extremely busy and very narrow main road in a street which was gradually losing its residential users. The gross value was reduced from £200 to £170.

HOWMAN (V.O.) *v.* VOGT (LVC/88/1986) (1986) 26 R.V.R. 231.

3170. Where the hereditament was unlettable at the date of the proposal because the adjoining semi-detached property had been turned into a club-house by Hells Angels, it was correctly assessed at a nominal value of £1·00.
INGERSOLL (V.O.) *v.* McSOREY (LVC/133/1986) (1987) 27 R.V.R. 127.

3171. This was an appeal against the assessment of a new building forming part of a larger hereditament on the Aylesford Paper Mill Site industrial estate at Maidstone, Kent, in which the LVC had found there to be a "quite separate and distinct tone of value . . . in comparison with that found outside." The tribunal found that the new building was superior to the others on the site save as to height. It accepted the LVC's valuation of £5·25 p.s.m. for the main floor area with an end allowance of 4·4 per cent., and confirmed the assessment of the entire hereditament at £116,320 rateable value.
KEY TERRAIN *v.* GERDES (VO) (LVC/289/1985)(1986) 280 E.G. 1234.

3172. The appeal premises were an information centre, house garage and premises used by and for the public and the ranger in a country park. Although not physically within the boundary of the park, the premises were entitled to exemption from rates since they had no other purpose than to serve the park, were an integral part of its attractions, and were utilised only in connection with it.
LANCASHIRE COUNTY COUNCIL *v.* LORD (V.O.) (LVC/1962/1984) [1987] R.A. 153.

3173. The annual letting value of the hereditament was not reduced by neighbouring building works which, at the date of the proposal, had six weeks further to run.
LATIMER (E.) *v.* HUGHES (R. A.) (V.O.) (1987) 151 L.G.Rev. 759.

3174. [Local Government Act 1974 (c.7), s.21.]
The appeal premises near an R.A.F. base were affected by aircraft noise, but not to such an extent that a reasonable landlord would have reduced the rent payable and consequently no reduction was allowed.
PERRIN (V.O.) *v.* LEICESTER (LVC/91/1986) (1986) 26 R.V.R. 232.

3175. An uninhabitable property is nevertheless subject to rates where the cost of repairs is such that the hypothetical landlord would carry them out.
REEVES (V.O.) *v.* MARSH (LVC/108/1987) (1987) 27 R.V.R. 188.

3176. The g.v. of a boarding house in Margate was reduced from £1,100 to £1,080 in order to make allowance for the intrusion caused by the erection of a sports hall close to the rear of the building.
SMITH *v.* BAILEY (V.O.) (Ref. LVC/55/1985) (1986) 26 R.V.R. 180.

3177. Where the owner of a caravan was still in occupation after 21 months, and the caravan was connected to water and electricity supplies, had a concrete car-port, was approached by a gravel path leading to a five-barred gate and contained the usual domestic offices, the occupation was of sufficient permanence to render it rateable.
TITTERRELL *v.* TOZER (V.O.) (LVC/334/1986) (1987) 27 R.V.R. 95.

3178. The assessment on a maisonette in Thornton Heath was reduced from £320 to £50 g.v. by reason of substantial and persistent nuisance and violence from a neighbouring property.
TURNER *v.* CHEEK (V.O.) (Ref. LVC/281/1985) (1986) 26 R.V.R. 179.

3179. The appeal premises were the site of a miniature railway in a leisure park. The miniature railway was not exempted from rates since the park was not one open to the public in perpetuity, or even if it was, the miniature railway was a separate occupation and not an ancillary part of the park.
WHITBY (V.O.) *v.* COLE (LVC/243/1985) [1987] R.A. 161.

3180. Leasehold enfranchisement—whether reduction in rateable value capable of being backdated

[Leasehold Reform Act 1967 (c.88), (as amended); General Rate Act 1967 (c.9), (as amended).]

The appellant was the leasehold owner of premises in Eaton Terrace, S.W.1. The tenancy had been granted before February 18, 1966, and was a long tenancy at a low rent within the meaning of the Leasehold Reform Act. The valuation list in force on April 1, 1973, gave the rateable value of the house as £1,597, i.e. above the Leasehold Reform Act limit (£1,500). This was reduced by £88.00 in May 1981 to take account of the tenant's improvements, but the property remained outside the limits. In January 1985, the valuation list was amended under the General Rate Act 1967, first by altering the description of the premises from "house" to "house and garage" and secondly by reducing the rateable value to £1,547. The leaseholder argued, first, that if the reduction was backdated to 1973, then the reduction of £88.00 would bring it below the limit or, alternatively, that the alteration in the description meant that the property did not appear in the list until 1985, from which £88.00 fell to be deducted. In the county court it was held that the appellant was not entitled to enfranchise.

Held, dismissing the appeal, that (1) it was not correct to say that because of the alteration in the description in 1985 the "appropriate day" was in 1985 and not 1973 and (2) the reduction in rateable value to £1,547 in January 1985 could not be backdated to April 1, 1973, but only to April 1, 1984.

RENDALL *v.* DUKE OF WESTMINSTER (1987) 19 H.L.R. 345, C.A.

3181. Matrimonial home—husband not in residence—liability for rates

The husband left the matrimonial home, leaving the wife and children behind. There was a decree nisi but no decree absolute. He was not maintaining the wife and children.

Held, that the occupation of the property by the wife and children, otherwise unmaintained by the husband, was sufficient to render him liable for rates because of his unperformed common law duty to maintain them (*Cardiff Corporation* v. *Robinson* [1957] C.L.Y. 7289, *Doncaster Metropolitan Borough Council* v. *Lockwood* [1987] C.L.Y. 1765, *Laing (John) & Son* v. *Kingswood Assessment Committee* [1949] C.L.Y. 8291, *Routhan* v. *Arun District Council* [1981] C.L.Y. 2256 considered).

MOORE *v.* DURHAM CITY COUNCIL (1987) 27 R.V.R. 129, D.C.

3182. Matrimonial home—separation of parties—whether husband in rateable occupation.
See DONCASTER METROPOLITAN BOROUGH COUNCIL *v.* LOCKWOOD, §1765.

3183. Notice of proposal to enter hereditament on valuation list not served—entry made—application for judicial review after seven years

[General Rate Act 1967 (c.9), ss.67, 70.]

The company were not served with a notice proposing an entry in the valuation list. The company denied liability from 1980 onwards after it came to their attention that the entry had been made. The company mistakenly thought that the defence could be used in the magistrates' court on an attempt to levy unpaid rates.

Held, the company's mistake as to the proper forum was not a sufficient reason to extend the time for applying for judicial review, and the application was dismissed (*County and Nimbus Estates* v. *Ealing London Borough Council* [1978] C.L.Y. 2469 considered).

R. *v.* VALUATION OFFICER *ex p.* HIGH PARK INVESTMENTS (1987) 27 R.V.R. 84, Nolan J.

3184. Plant and machinery—catwalks—rateability

[Lands Valuation (Scotland) Act 1854 (c.91), s.42 (as amended by Valuation (Plant and Machinery) (Scotland) Order 1983 (S.I. 1983 No. 120.)]

Catwalks were not to be included in the rateable value of the hereditament since they were plant (*Central Region Assessor* v. *Independent Broadcasting Corp.* (May 3, 1985 unrep.) *Dumfries and Galloway Assessor* v. *Independent Broadcasting Corp.* (May 3, 1985 unrep.), *Cole Brothers* v. *Phillips* [1982] C.L.Y. 407, *Jarrold* v. *Good (John) & Sons* [1963] C.L.Y. 1705 considered).

PAULS MALT *v.* GRAMPIAN ASSESSOR, [1987] R.A. 16, Lands Valuation Appeal Ct.

3185. Rate alteration—designation of area as enterprise zone

[General Rate Act 1967 (c.9), ss.19, 20; Local Government, Planning and Land Act 1980 (c.65), s.179, Sched. 32.)

The designation of an enterprise zone nearby does not affect the state of a locality for rating purposes.

Five industrial or commercial hereditaments were situated just outside an enterprise zone established under s.179 of and Sched. 2 to the 1980 Act. The occupiers appealed for a reduction in rates on the basis value of hereditaments had been adversely affected by the zone.

Held, that in general s.20(1)(*b*) of the 1967 Act was limited to physical factors or factors affecting physical enjoyment of a hereditament, and the designation of an enterprise zone could not be taken into account in assessing the "state" of the locality for the purposes of the subsection (dicta of Sir Patrick Browne in *K. Shoe Shops* v. *Hardy (V.O.) and Westminster City Council* [1983] C.L.Y 3148 applied; *Sheerness Steel* v. *Maudling (V.O.)* [1986] C.L.Y. 2789 considered).

ADDIS *v.* CLEMENT (V.O.) (1987) 85 L.G.R. 489, C.A.

3186. Rate limitation

RATE LIMITATION (DESIGNATION OF AUTHORITIES) (EXEMPTION) ORDER 1987 (No. 785) [45p], made under the Rates Act 1984 (c.33), s.2(3)(8); operative on May 29, 1987; substitutes £12·2 million for the amount of £11·1 million specified in s.2(2)(*a*) of the 1984 Act.

RATE LIMITATION (DESIGNATION OF AUTHORITIES) (EXEMPTION) (WALES) ORDER 1987 (No. 786) [45p], made under the Rates Act 1984, s.2(3)(8); operative on May 26, 1987; substitutes £11·1 million for the amount of £10·5 million specified in s.2(2)(*a*) of the 1984 Act.

RATE LIMITATION (DESIGNATION OF AUTHORITIES) (EXEMPTION) (WALES) (No. 2) ORDER 1987 (No. 1251) [45p], made under the Rates Act 1984, s.2(3) (8); operative on August 14, 1987; substitutes an amount of £12.1 million for the amount of £11.1 million specified for Wales in s.2(2)(*a*) of the 1984 Act.

3187. Rate rebate—school—special school for children having "special educational needs"

[Rating (Disabled Persons) Act 1978 (c.40), s.2.]

A school providing "education" in the broadest sense for children with severe hearing difficulties also provides training and so falls within the category of establishments providing training for persons suffering from illness (*Vandyk* v. *Oliver (V.O.)* [1976] C.L.Y. 2279, *Church of England Children's Society* v. *Southwark London Borough Council* [1982] R.V.R. 8 considered).

NOTTINGHAMSHIRE COUNTY COUNCIL *v.* NOTTINGHAM CITY COUNCIL (1987) 27 R.V.R. 82, Nottingham County Court.

3188. Rate refund—refusal of refund—discretion—relevance of purpose of conferring discretion

[General Rate Act 1967 (c.9), s.9(1).]

In exercising their discretion as to whether to make a rate refund, the authority is bound to have regard to the object for which the power to refund has been conferred.

When the applicants developed a site it was a condition of planning approval that the buildings should not be occupied until consent to proposed user had been obtained. Completion notices were served and the applicants thereafter paid rates. Following the approved letting of one of the units, the applicants refused to pay rates. The council's distress warrant was refused on the basis that their demand for rates was unlawful. The applicants' application for a refund was refused.

Held, allowing the appeal, that the council were bound to exercise their discretion as to refunds in a way which would not frustrate the object for which the power to refund had been conferred (Dicta in *Padfield* v. *Minister of Agriculture, Fisheries and Food* [1968] C.L.Y. 1667 applied).

R. *v.* TOWER HAMLETS LONDON BOROUGH COUNCIL, *ex p.* CHETNIK DEVELOPMENTS [1987] 1 W.L.R. 593, C.A.

3189. Rate support grant—multiplier in use for calculation of grant—multiplier itself calculated on mistaken basis

[Local Government Planning and Land Act 1980 (c.65), s.59; Rate Support Grants Act 1986 (c.54), ss.1, 2, 3, Sched. 1 para. 10.]

The multiplier in use was based on a mistaken calculation relating to highway maintenance grants in respect of each London borough. The Secretary of State proposed a redetermination of the multiplier.

Held, that (1) as a matter of construction the Secretary of State was not entitled to redetermine the multiplier as he had purported to, and (2) if the wrong principle had been chosen by the Secretary of State he was not in any event empowered to alter the calculation for that reason (*R.* v. *Secretary of State for the Environment ex p. Brent London Borough Council* [1983] C.L.Y. 3147, *R.* v. *Secretary of State for the Environment ex p. Hackney London Borough Council* [1984] C.L.Y. 23 considered).

R. *v.* SECRETARY OF STATE FOR THE ENVIRONMENT, *ex p.* GREENWICH LONDON BOROUGH COUNCIL (1987) 27 R.V.R. 48, Taylor J.

3190. Rate support grant—report not laid before parliament—making of a rate

[Local Government Planning and Land Act 1980 (c.65), s.60.]

The Secretary of State had not laid a Rate Support Grant Report before parliament for the financial year 1987/88. The authority sought to force him to do so in order to enable them to comply with their obligation to fix a rate.

Held, that the authority had sufficient information to make a rate, and in any event the court would not imply a deadline by which the report had to be laid, nor, if the Secretary of State was properly exercising a discretion, had he wrongly taken an irrelevant consideration into account, namely impending legislation (*Engineers' and Managers' Association* v. *ACAS* [1980] C.L.Y. 2742, *R.* v. *Secretary of State for the Environment ex p. Nottinghamshire County Council* [1986] C.L.Y. 27, *Westminster's Deed of Appointment, Re* [1959] C.L.Y. 101, *Willow Wren* v. *British Transport Commission* [1956] C.L.Y. 6982 considered).

R. *v.* SECRETARY OF STATE FOR THE ENVIRONMENT *ex p.* BIRMINGHAM CITY COUNCIL, (1987) 27 R.V.R. 53, D.C.

3191. Reduction or remission of rates—limited company—"poverty"

[General Rate Act 1967 (c.9), ss.7, 53.]

A limited company cannot suffer "poverty" within the meaning of the Act and accordingly is unable to obtain a reduction or remission of its rates bill on that ground (*Dodwell & Co.'s Trust Deed, Re* [1978] C.L.Y. 2665, *Investors in Industry Commercial Properties* v. *Norwich City Council* [1986] C.L.Y. 2812, *R.* v. *Liverpool City Council, ex p. Windsor Securities* [1979] R.A. 159, *Rialto Builders* v. *Barnet London Borough Council* [1986] C.L.Y. 2759, *Stepney Metropolitan Borough Council* v. *Woolf* [1943] 1 All E.R. 64 considered).

POLO PICTURES *v.* TRAFFORD METROPOLITAN BOROUGH COUNCIL (1987) 27 R.V.R. 74, Manchester Crown Court.

3192. Stud farm—agricultural land—whether agricultural operation

[General Rate Act 1967 (c.9), s.26(3)(4); Rating Act 1971 (c.39), s.2.]

"Agricultural land" in s.26 of the General Rate Act 1967 covers purposes contributing to human subsistence, and "livestock" in s.2 of the Rating Act 1971 means mammals and birds that contribute to human subsistence. The pasturing of racing stock in paddocks is not an agricultural operation within s.26(4) of the 1967 Act.

The appellants owned four separate studs for breeding racehorses. Each stud consisted of buildings, and also paddocks which were "agricultural land" within s.26(3) of the General Rate Act 1967 since they were used as pasture for the grazing of horses. The buildings were essential for the running of the studs. The appellants claimed exemption from rating on the buildings, and the local valuation court upheld their claim. The Lands Tribunal reversed it and the appellants appealed.

Held, dismissing the appeal that the stud buildings did not qualify as "agricultural buildings" within s.26(4) of the 1967 Act because they were not occupied together with land on which "agricultural operations" were carried out, since even though the paddocks were "agricultural land" the purpose for which they used them was not agricultural because the grazing of thoroughbred horses was not an "agricultural operation" (*Lord Glanely* v. *Wightman* [1933] A.C. 618 distinguished). However, if the grazing of thoroughbred stock was an "agricultural operation" within s.26(4), then although the buildings were used "in connection with" that operation, nevertheless the buildings were not used "solely" in connection with the grazing, since the buildings were used for a number of purposes connected with breeding, of which grazing was only one.

The buildings did not qualify for rating exemption on the ground that they were "used for the keeping or breeding of livestock" within s.2(1)(*a*) of the 1971 Act because horses were not "livestock" as defined by s.1(3), since they did not contribute to human subsistence and were not intended for use in the farming of land (*Belmont Farm* v. *Minister of Housing and Local Government* [1962] C.L.Y. 2964 followed).

Leave to appeal to the House of Lords was granted.

HEMENS (V.O.) *v.* WHITSBURY FARM AND STUD [1987] 1 All E.R. 430, C.A.

3193. University buildings—contractors basis—valuation—capitalisation rate

[General Rate Act 1967 (c.9), s.19(6); Lands Tribunal Act 1949 (c.42), s.3(4).]

When assessing the rateable value of university buildings by using the contractors basis it is a question of fact for the tribunal as to what capitalisation rate to apply to the hypothetically borrowed money, and similarly a question of fact as to whether to apply a discount for inflation and if so, how much. Since an appeal only lies on questions of law to the Court of Appeal from the tribunal the instant appeal, relating to the above matters, was dismissed (*Baker Britt and Co.* v. *Hampsher (V.O.)* [1974] C.L.Y. 3098; *Cardiff City Council* v. *Williams (V.O.)* [1970] C.L.Y. 2406; *Dawkins (V.O.)* v. *Ash Bros. and Heaton* [1969] C.L.Y. 3019; *Dawkins (V.O.)* v. *Royal Leamington Spa Corp.* [1961] C.L.Y. 7423; *Edwards* v. *Bairstow* [1955] C.L.Y.417; *Gilmore (V.O.)* v. *Baker-Carr* [1962] C.L.Y. 2567; *Humber* v. *Jones (V.O.)* [1960] C.L.Y. 2702; *Metropolitan Water Board* v. *Chertsey Assessment Committee* [1916] A.C. 337; *Westminster City Council* v. *American School in London and Goodwin (V.O.)* [1986] R.A. 275 considered).

IMPERIAL COLLEGE OF SCIENCE AND TECHNOLOGY *v.* EBDON (V.O.) AND WESTMINSTER CITY COUNCIL [1986] R.A. 233, C.A.

3194. Unoccupied hereditament—ascertainment of date for completion of customary works of fitting out an office block

[General Rate Act 1967 (c.9), Sched. 1, paras. 8, 9.]

The date from which the time taken to complete works of fitting out an office block in accordance with its tenants requirements was to be calculated was the date upon which the office block was completed apart from those works, for the purpose of levying rates upon an unoccupied hereditament.

L were the owners of a site upon which a speculative office development providing 174,000 sq. ft. of space was constructed. I was the local rating authority. I proposed to levy rates upon the building as an unoccupied hereditament pursuant to the provisions of s.17 of and Sched. 1 to the General Rate Act 1967. To that end, I served a completion notice on L under para. 8(1) of Sched. 1. The development was to be constructed in two stages, firstly the office building and secondly the fitting out of the building to the requirements of the proposed tenant. The architect issued his certificate of practical completion on August 31, 1983. L served its completion notice on June 1, 1983 stating September 1, 1983 as the date when the erection of the building including the second stage could reasonably be expected to be completed as provided by para. 9 of the Schedule. That date was calculated on the basis that stage one was substantially completed on March 1, 1983 and that a reasonable time to carry out the works of fitting out was six months. L appealed to the County Court under para. 8(4) of the Schedule. L contended that the time for reasonable completion of stage two was to be calculated from when stage one was completed rather than substantially completed; that the time for reasonable completion of stage two should include time spent on planning and preparing for the execution of those works; and that the works to be taken into account should include works of providing kitchens, canteens, computer facilities, executive suites and the like rather than merely fitting out as offices. L contended the stage two works ought reasonably to take 12 months. L's contentions were rejected at first instance and substantially rejected by the Court of Appeal.

Held, allowing L's appeal in part, that on the proper construction of para. 9 of Sched. 1, the period within which customary works, *i.e.* fitting out works could reasonably be completed was to be ascertained from the date upon which the building apart from those works was completed. The proper date was August 31, 1983 and not March 1, 1983 when the building was only substantially completed. The time reasonably required for carrying out the work did not include the planning and preparation stages prior to carrying out the work. The proper test was to measure the time between the contractor's starting and finishing dates, that being the period in which the works would be carried out. In ascertaining the scope of works for which a reasonable time should be allowed, the court was constrained by the words of paras. 8(1))b) and 9 to look at the works remaining to be done on the building. It was not right merely to consider those works which were necessary to permit the building to be occupied. The wording did not allow a distinction to be drawn between essential and inessential works. The scope of the works was not to be measured by reference to the word "customarily" in para. 9, in its context it had nothing to do with the extent of the works to be carried out (*Watford Borough Council* v. *Parcourt Property Investment Co.* [1971] R.A. 97, *Ravenseft Properties* v. *Newham London Borough Council* [1976] C.L.Y. 2270 distinguished).

LONDON MERCHANT SECURITIES *v.* ISLINGTON LONDON BOROUGH COUNCIL [1987] 3 W.L.R. 173, H.L.

3195. Unoccupied hereditament—part listed—whether whole entitled to relief

[General Rate Act 1967 (c.9), Sched. 1, para. 2(*c*) (as amended by Town and Country Planning Act 1971 (c.78), s.291, Sched. 23); Town and Country Planning Act 1971 (c.78), s.54(9).]

The exemption from rates afforded to buildings listed as being of special architectural or historic interest does not apply to hereditaments only part of which are listed.

Under Schedule 1, para. 2(*c*) of the General Rate Act 1967, as amended, no rates are payable in respect of an unoccupied hereditament for any period during which it is included in a list compiled or approved under s.54 of the Town and Country Planning Act 1971. By s.54(9) of the Act of 1971: "for the purposes of the provisions of this Act relating to listed buildings . . . any object or structure fixed to a building, or forming part of the land and comprised within the curtilage of a building, shall be treated as part of the building." Two buildings comprised a single hereditament for rating purposes. Both were unoccupied, and the owners contended that they were not liable to pay rates since one of the buildings was listed pursuant to s.54 of the 1971 Act. The buildings were linked by a bridge and tunnel at the relevant time. The stipendiary magistrate on the authority's summons for non-payment of rates held that as only part of the hereditament was listed there was no exception from rate liability. The judge on appeal held that the entire hereditament was included in the listing, and the Court of Appeal upheld that decision.

Held, allowing the rating authority's appeal, that although the extended definition of "listed building" in s.54(9) of the 1971 Act was prefaced by the words "for the purposes of this Act", the definition applied equally for the purposes of Sched. 1, para. 2(*c*) of the Act of 1967. On its true construction only structures ancillary to the listed building and not structures constituting some other complete building were included in s.54(9). Accordingly only the first building was listed (*Att.Gen. ex. rel Sutcliffe* v. *Calderdale Borough Council* [1984] C.L.Y. 3451 distinguished). The exemption from rates afforded to listed buildings by Schedule 1 para. 2(*c*) to the Act of 1967 did not apply to hereditaments only part of which were listed, and so the owners were liable to pay rates at the relevant time (*Providence Properties* v. *Liverpool City Council* [1980] R.A. 189, applied).

DEBENHAMS *v.* WESTMINSTER CITY COUNCIL [1986] 3 W.L.R. 1063, H.L.

3196. Unoccupied property—no entry in list—whether unoccupied rate payable

[General Rate Act 1967 (C.9), ss.6, 17, Sched. I.]

In June 1983 the rating authority served a completion notice pursuant to para. 8 of Schedule I to the General Rate Act 1967 in respect of a new office block in Islington owned by P, to the effect that the building was to be treated as completed on September 1, 1983 and the valuation office made proposals in March 1984 to enter the premises in the valuation list. P appealed against the completion notice first to the County Court and subsequently to the Court of Appeal, and pending a final decision, proceedings in the local valuation court in relation to the rating proposals were adjourned *sine die.* The building remained unoccupied until April 1985 the authority apparently being unable to claim an unoccupied rate pursuant to s.17 and Schedule I to the 1967 Act because no rateable value had as yet been entered in the list. However, it made a rate demand from December 1, 1983, based on the proposals of March 1984 rather than on established rateable values, arguing that the Act applied as if the premises were occupied, that there had therefore been a notional coming into occupation of the premises and that consequent upon the proposals it was accordingly entitled to demand rates pursuant to s.6(1) and (2) of the Act. It subsequently sought to enforce the demand by proceedings for winding-up and for distress both of which were restrained by injunction. The judge held that the provisions of Schedule I as regards unoccupied property superseded any other liability—imposing provision of the 1967 Act, including s.6 and that no liability on P's part to pay unoccupied rates could arise until the premises and their respective rateable values had been entered in the valuation list.

Held, dismissing the authority's appeal, by a majority, that (1) P's liability to pay unoccupied rates did not arise until the rateable value and thus the amount to be paid had been established; but (2) an argument by P to the effect that liability could not in any event arise until the appeal against the completion notice had finally been decided was incorrect (*Hastings Borough Council* v. *Tarmac Properties* [1984] C.L.Y. 2931 and *Bar Hill Developments* v. *South Cambridgeshire District Council* [1979] C.L.Y. 2239 distinguished).

TRENDWORTHY TWO *v.* ISLINGTON LONDON BOROUGH COUNCIL (1987) 282 E.G. 1125, C.A.

3197. Valuation lists

NEW VALUATION LISTS ORDER 1987 (No. 921) [45p], made under the General Rate Act 1967 (c.9), s.68(1); operative on May 15, 1987; specifies 1990 as a year in which new valuation lists are to come into force in rating areas in England and Wales.

NEW VALUATION LISTS (TIME AND CLASS OF HEREDITAMENTS) ORDER 1987 (No. 604) [45p], made under the General Rate Act 1967, s.19A(1)(4); operative on April 28, 1987; specifies April 1, 1988 as the time by reference to which rateable values are to be ascertained for the purposes of new valuation lists, and specifies hereditaments which are to be revalued.

3198. Water rates—charges scheme—whether discriminatory

[Water Act 1973 (c.37), ss. 29(1), 30, 31 (as amended).]

The owners of 18 small shops in various towns and cities in P's area sought to show that P's charges upon them were unlawful as being discriminatory.

Held, that (1) the shopkeepers did not form part of a class of persons within the meaning of the Act; (2) in any event the court was bound by authority to rule against the shopkeepers (*Att.-Gen.* v. *Wimbledon Corporation* [1940] 1 Ch. 180, *Daymond* v. *South West Water Authority* [1975] C.L.Y. 2788, *South of Scotland Electricity Board* v. *British Oxygen Co.* [1956] C.L.Y. 3054 considered; *South West Water Authority* v. *Rumble* [1986] C.L.Y. 2819 followed).

SEVERN TRENT WATER AUTHORITY *v.* CARDSHOPS (1987) 27 R.V.R. 133, C.A.

REGISTRATION OF BIRTHS, DEATHS AND MARRIAGES

3199. Fees

REGISTRATION OF BIRTHS, DEATHS AND MARRIAGES (FEES) ORDER 1987 (No. 50) [80p], made under the Public Expenditure and Receipts Act 1968 (c.14), s.5(1)(2), Sched. 3, para. 1, 2; operative on April 1, 1987; increases certain fees relating to the registration of births, deaths and marriages.

3200. Public record office—fees

PUBLIC RECORD OFFICE (FEES) REGULATIONS 1987 (No. 444) [80p], made under the Public Records Act 1958 (c.51), s.2(5); operative on April 1, 1987; prescribe the full range of fees to be charged for authentication of copies of records and other services provided by the Public Record Office.

3201. Rectification of register of deaths—pathologist's opinion revised after inquest. See ATT.-GEN. *v.* HARTE (J.D.), §537.

3202. Regulations

REGISTRATION OF BIRTHS AND DEATHS REGULATIONS 1987 (No. 2088) [£5·50], made under the Births and Deaths Registration Act 1926 (c.39), ss.1(1), 3(1), 12, the Industrial Assurance and Friendly Societies Act 1948 (c.39), Sched. 1, para. 4, the Births and Deaths Registration Act 1953 (c.20), ss.1(1), 3A(2)(*c*), 5, 7(1), 9(1)(12)(15), 10(*b*)(i), 10A(1), 11(1)(2), 12, 13(1), 14(1)(4), 15, 20, 21(1) 22(1)(2), 23(2)(3), 24(1)(2)(4)(5), 26(1), 29(2), 33, 39, 41, the Registration Service Act 1953 (c.37), s.20(*a*), 21(1), the Foundling Hospital Act 1953, s.5(2), the Welsh Language Act 1967 (c.66), s.2(2), the Friendly Societies Act 1974 (c.46), Sched. 5, para. 5 and the Industrial Diseases (Notification) Act 1981 (c.25), s.1; operative on January 1, 1988; prescribe forms and procedures in connection with the registration of births and deaths.

3203. Request for passport—whether racial discrimination—meaning of "national origins"

[Race Relations Act 1976 (c.74) ss.1(1)(*a*), 3(1), 3(3), 20(1)(*b*).]

The appellant was born in Uganda, but is a British National and has been resident in the U.K. since 1972. He wished to marry and, upon applying for a marriage licence, was requested by the respondent to produce his passport. This was not a legal requirement but the respondent had adopted the practice of making such request to any person who came to the U.K. from abroad. The appellant claimed that he had been discriminated against contrary to s.20 of the 1976 Act. His case was dismissed at first instance and he appealed to the Court of Appeal.

Held, dismissing the appeal, that the respondent had in fact discriminated against the appellant under the provisions of s.20 in that he had treated persons coming from abroad in a different way from those who were born in the U.K., and it was irrelevant that he treated all persons coming from abroad in the same manner, because he was providing services to all members of the public and not to different sections. However, he had not discriminated on racial grounds as set out in the Act, and therefore the discrimination was not unlawful. The term "national origins" in s.1(3) refers to race rather than citizenship or residence and, since the appellant had been asked for his passport on the ground that he came from abroad without reference to any particular place of origin, he was not discriminated against on the grounds of national or racial origin (*Ealing London Borough Council* v. *Race Relations Board* [1972] C.L.Y. 28 followed).

TEJANI *v.* SUPERINTENDENT REGISTRAR FOR THE DISTRICT OF PETERBOROUGH [1986] I.R.L.R. 502, C.A.

3204. Welsh language regulations

REGISTRATION OF BIRTHS AND DEATHS (WELSH LANGUAGE) REGULATIONS 1987 (No. 2089) [£3·60], made under the Welsh Language Act 1967 (c.66); ss.2(2), 3(2); operative on January 1, 1988; consolidate with certain minor amendments S.I. 1969 No. 203, as amended.

REVENUE AND FINANCE

3205. Appropriation Act 1987 (c.17)

This Act applies a sum out of the Consolidated Fund to the service of the year ending on March 31, 1988, and appropriates the supplies granted in this Session of Parliament.

The Act received the Royal Assent on May 15, 1987.

3206. Appropriation (No. 2) Act 1987 (c.50)

This Act applies to a sum out of the Consolidated Fund to the service of the year ending on March 31, 1988, and appropriates the supplies granted in this session of parliament.

The Act received the Royal Assent on July 23, 1987.

The Act extends to Northern Ireland.

3207. Company resident in U.K.—transfer of residence within EEC without Treasury consent—permissibility. See R. *v.* H.M. TREASURY, *ex p.* DAILY MAIL AND GENERAL TRUST, § 1479.

3208. Consolidated Fund Act 1987 (c.8)

The Act applies £392,730,629·84 and £1,277,764,000 out of the Consolidated Fund to the service of the years ending March 31, 1986 and March 31, 1987 respectively.

The Act received the Royal Assent on March 25, 1987.

3209. Consolidated Fund (No. 2) Act 1987 (c.54)

This Act applies a sum out of the Consolidated Fund to the service of the year ending March 31, 1988.

The Act received the Royal Assent on November 17, 1987.

3210. Consolidated Fund (No. 3) Act 1987 (c.55)

This Act applies certain sums out of the Consolidated Fund to the service of the years ending March 31, 1988, and March 31, 1989.

The Act received the Royal Assent on December 10, 1987.

3211. Finance Act 1987 (c.16)

This Act grants certain duties, alters other duties and amends the law relating to the National Debt and the Public Revenue, and makes further provision in connection with Finance.

The Act received the Royal Assent on May 15, 1987.

3212. Finance (No. 2) Act 1987 (c.51)

This Act grants certain duties, alters other duties, and amends the law relating to the National Debt and the Public Revenue, and makes further provision in connection with Finance.

The Act received the Royal Assent on July 23, 1987.

3213. Financial services—disclosure of information

FINANCIAL SERVICES (DISCLOSURE OF INFORMATION) (DESIGNATED AUTHORITIES No. 2) ORDER 1987 (No. 859) [45p] made under the Financial Services Act 1986 (c.60), s.180(3), (4) and the Companies Act 1985 (c.6), s.449 (1b), (1c); operative on May 13, 1987; designates authorities for the purposes of s.180 of the 1986 Act and s.449 of the 1985 Act.

FINANCIAL SERVICES (DISCLOSURE OF INFORMATION) (DESIGNATED AUTHORITIES) (No. 3) ORDER 1987 (No. 1141) [45p], made under the Financial Services Act 1986 (c.60), s.180(3), (4), and the Companies Act 1985 (c.6), s.449(1B), (1C); operative July 4, 1987; designates certain authorities as authorities for the purposes of s.180 of the Financial Services Act 1986 and s.449 of the Companies Act 1985.

3214. Financial services—overseas investment exchanges and clearing houses

FINANCIAL SERVICES ACT 1986 (OVERSEAS INVESTMENT EXCHANGES AND OVERSEAS CLEARING HOUSES) (NOTIFICATION) REGULATIONS 1987 (No. 2142) [85p], made under the Financial Services Act 1986, (c.60), s.41); operative on January 8, 1988; prescribe the information which an overseas investment exchange or clearing house must provide the Secretary of State under the 1986 Act.

FINANCIAL SERVICES ACT 1986 (OVERSEAS INVESTMENT EXCHANGES AND OVERSEAS CLEARING HOUSES) (PERIODICAL FEES) REGULATIONS 1987 (No. 2143) [45p], made under the Financial Services Act 1986, s.113; operative on January 8, 1988; prescribe that an overseas investment exchange or clearing house under the 1986 Act must pay a periodical fee of £5,000.

3215. Financial services—transfer of functions relating to friendly societies

FINANCIAL SERVICES ACT 1986 (TRANSFER OF FUNCTIONS RELATING TO FRIENDLY SOCIETIES), (TRANSITIONAL PROVISIONS) ORDER 1987 (No. 2069) [45p], made under the Financial Services Act 1986 (c.60), s.118(2), Sched. 11, para. 31; operative on January 1, 1988; makes transitional provision in relation to the transfer of most of the functions of the Chief Registrar of Friendly Societies to the Securities and Investments Board Ltd. under the 1986 Act.

3216. Financial Services Act 1986—appointed day

FINANCIAL SERVICES ACT 1986 (APPLICATIONS FOR AUTHORISATION) (APPOINTED DAY) ORDER 1987 (No. 2157) [45p], made under the Financial Services Act 1986 (c.60), Sched. 15, para. 1(1); appoints February 27, 1988 for the purposes of Sched. 15, para. 1(1) to the 1986 Act.

3217. Financial Services Act 1986—commencement

FINANCIAL SERVICES ACT 1986 (COMMENCEMENT) (No. 4) ORDER 1987 (No. 623) (C.15) [80p], made under the Financial Services Act 1986 (c.60), s.211(1); brings into force on April 23, 1987, ss.63, 183 (in part), 184(1)–(3) (in part), 184(5)(7), 185, 186(1)–(5)(7), 201(3) of the 1986 Act.

FINANCIAL SERVICES ACT 1986 (COMMENCEMENT) (No. 5) ORDER 1987 (No. 907 (C.24)) [£1·30], made under the Financial Services Act 1986 (c.60), s.211(1); brings into force on June 4, 1987 ss.8–11, 13, 14, 15 (in part), 16–19, 21, 36(2)(3), 37 (in part), 38(2)(3), 39 (in part), 41, 46, 48–52, 54, 55, 56, (in part), 102, 103, 104(2)(3), 107, 110, 112(1)–(4), 113(1), 119, 120, 122, 123, 124 5(1)–(7), 127, 129, 138(1)(2)(6), 140 (in part), 187 (in part), 190, 191, 198(3)(*b*), 200(1)(*a*) (in part) (*b*) (in part), 200(3)(4)(5)–(8) (in part), 206(1)–(3), 211(3) (in part), 212(2) (in part) Scheds. 2, 3, 4.

FINANCIAL SERVICES ACT 1986 (COMMENCEMENT) (No. 6) ORDER 1987 (No. 1997) (C.59) [£1·30], made under the Financial Services Act 1986, s.211(1); brings into force on November 23, 1987 ss.37 (in part), 39 (in part), 40 and brings into force on December 1, 1987 ss.1 (in relation to Sched. 1, para. 23, Sched. 6, Sched. 11, para. 6, Sched. 14 (in part).

FINANCIAL SERVICES ACT 1986 (COMMENCEMENT) (No. 7) ORDER 1987 (No. 2158) (C.65) [£1·30], made under the Financial Services Act 1986, s.211(1); brings into force on January 1, 1988 ss. 26–30, 31(4) (in part), 43, 112(5) (in part), 140 (in part), 189 (in part), 200(1)(*a*)(*b*)(5) (in part), Scheds. 5, 11, para. 39, Sched. 14 (in part), brings into force on January 18, 1988 s.1 (in part) and Sched. 1 (in part) and brings into force on February 27, 1988 s.112(3) (in part).

3218. Financial Services Act 1986—delegation

FINANCIAL SERVICES ACT 1986 (DELEGATION) ORDER 1987 (NO. 942) [£1.30], made under the Financial Services Act 1986 (c.60), ss.114, 118, 178(10), 199(7), 201(4) and 206(4); operative on May 19, 1987, transfers certain of the Secretary of State's functions under the 1986 Act to the body known as the Securities and Investments Board Ltd.

3219. Financial Services Act 1986—transitional provisions

FINANCIAL SERVICES ACT 1986 (DELEGATION) (TRANSITIONAL PROVISIONS) ORDER 1987 (No. 2035) [45p], made under the Financial Services Act 1986 (c.60), s.118(2); operative on December 14, 1987; makes transitional provision modifying the requirements in para. 3(1) of Scheds. 2 and 3 respectively in their application to S.I. 1987 No. 942.

3220. Judicial review—Revenue documents—discovery. See R. *v.* I.R.C., *ex p.* ROTHSCHILD (J.) HOLDINGS, §24.

3221. Jurisdiction of Special Commissioner—stay of proceedings

Tax and its assessment is a United Kingdom matter and a Special Commissioner's jurisdiction extends throughout the United Kingdom.

T, the taxpayer company, was incorporated and registered and traded in Scotland. T appealed against assessments to corporation tax and applied for postponement of the tax assessed. All the proceedings took place in Scotland except that for the convenience of T one postponement hearing took place in London before a Special Commissioner, when a small part of the tax was postponed. T obtained leave to apply for judicial review and a stay pending determination of the application. The Scottish Court of Session held that the English Court had no jurisdiction in the matter and pronounced a decree for recovery for the tax not postponed. The Crown applied to strike out or stay the English judicial review proceedings on the grounds of lack of jurisdiction, alternatively that the appropriate forum was the Scottish court.

Held, that (1) tax and its assessment was a United Kingdom matter and a Special Commissioner's jurisdiction extended throughout the whole United Kingdom; accordingly, the English proceedings would not be struck out; however (2), the stay already ordered did not alter T's liability to pay the tax not postponed, and the English proceedings would accordingly be stayed (*Las Mercedes (Owners)* v. *Abidin Daver (Owners); Abidin Daver, The* [1984] C.L.Y. 3151 applied).

R. *v.* COMMISSIONER FOR THE SPECIAL PURPOSES OF THE INCOME TAX ACTS, *ex p.* R. W. FORSYTH [1987] 1 All E.R. 1035, Macpherson J.

3222. Misapplication of Statute—distortion of competition—state aid

I.C.I. sought judicial review of the manner in which the British Government gave or proposed to give effect to s.134 and Sched. 18 of the Finance Act 1982. These provisions provided an alternative formula for valuing for tax purposes ethane feedstock used in ethylene cracker plants operated by Shell, Esso and British Petroleum ("the oil companies"). I.C.I. contended that this resulted in an undervaluation of the ethane and, thus, less tax being paid by the oil companies. I.C.I. made ethylene from naphtha, but ethylene could be produced more cheaply from ethane. I.C.I. complained that what the Government had done was to add to the natural advantage of ethane an additional advantage by providing the oil companies with an artificially favourable fiscal régime, from which I.C.I. could not benefit. I.C.I. argued, *inter alia,* that the 1982 Act resulted in an aid being conferred on the oil companies, that there should have been a submission to the European Commission under Art. 93(3) EEC and a decision of the Commission in relation thereto before the measure could be brought into effect.

Held, that (1) I.C.I. had sufficient *locus standi* to ask for judicial review; (2) the persistent erroneous misapplication of statutory provisions by the Inland Revenue which produced an advantage distorting competition in favour of certain undertakings, amounted to a state aid within Art. 93 EEC or a "plan to grant aid" or a "proposed measure"; (3) declarations were granted laying down mandatory guidelines for giving an arm's length valuation of ethane.

R. *v.* ATT.-GEN., *ex p.* I.C.I. [1987] 1 C.M.L.R. 72, C.A.

3223. National debt

NATIONAL SAVINGS STOCK REGISTER (AMENDMENT) REGULATIONS 1987 (No. 1635) [85p], made under the National Debt Act 1972 (c.65), s.3; operative on October 9, 1987; amend S.I. 1976 No. 2012.

3224. Penalty awards—whether excessive

[Taxes Management Act 1970 (c.9), ss.95, 100.]

The Taxpayer appealed against 100 per cent. penalties imposed on him by General Commissions for negligently delivering incorrect returns.

Held, allowing the taxpayer's appeal, that in the absence of any information as to the type of cases in which 100 per cent. penalties were awarded or of any special circumstances affecting the view of the Commissioners in the particular case, the penalty should be reduced.

BRODT *v.* WELLS GENERAL COMMISSIONERS AND I.R.C. [1987] S.T.C. 207, Scott J.

3225. Petroleum revenue tax

PETROLEUM REVENUE TAX (NOMINATION SCHEME FOR DISPOSALS AND APPROPRIATIONS) REGULATIONS 1987 (No. 1338) [£1·60], made under the Finance Act 1987 (c.16), s.61(8) and Sched. 10; operative on August 22, 1987; establish a nomination scheme for disposal and appropriation of crude oil.

3226. Petroleum revenue tax—expenditure allowance—whether taxpayer company entitled to supplement

[Finance Act 1981 (c.35), s.111(1)(7).]

The clear intention of Parliament in passing s.111(7) of the Finance Act 1981 was to preserve supplement for expenditure to which an operator had been contractually committed before January 1, 1981, provided the expenditure had in fact been incurred by January 1, 1983.

The taxpayer company operated an oil field in the North Sea. In 1979 the company commissioned B Ltd. to build an oil production platform. Three contracts entered into in 1981 by B Ltd. as agents for the taxpayers, involved the purchase of very expensive assets. The taxpayer claimed that the expenditure had been incurred in pursuance of the 1979 contract and that it qualified for a supplement; the revenue claimed that it had been incurred pursuant to the 1981 contracts. The special commissioners upheld the taxpayer's claim; this decision was reversed on appeal.

Held, allowing the taxpayer's appeal, that since the language of s.111(7) was ambiguous, the court was bound to resolve the ambiguity by reference to Parliament's intent; interpreting s.111(7) to give effect to that clear intent the expenditure had been incurred by the taxpayer in pursuance of the 1979 agreement.

MOBIL NORTH SEA *v.* I.R.C. [1987] 1 W.L.R. 1065, H.L.

ROAD TRAFFIC

3227. Accidents—payments for treatment

ROAD TRAFFIC ACCIDENTS (PAYMENTS FOR TREATMENT) ORDER 1987 (No. 353) [80p], made under the Public Expenditure and Receipts Act 1968 (c.14), s.5, Sched. 3; operative on April 1, 1987; varies amounts payable under the Road Traffic Act 1972, ss.154(1) and 155(1) for hospital treatment arising from road traffic accidents.

3228. Blood specimen—computer evidence—admissibility. See SOPHOCLEUS *v.* RINGER, §558.

3229. Blood specimen—failure to provide—non-availability of breath test device

[Road Traffic Act 1972 (c.20), s.8.]

On a charge under s.8 of the Act of failure to provide a blood specimen the prosecution must prove the non-availability of a breath test device according to the normal rules of evidence.

D, a motorist who was arrested and at a police station, was questioned by a constable using *pro-forma* questions, in the presence of the prosecutor. At D's trial for refusing to provide a specimen of blood, the prosecutor said that the constable read out "the approved breath test device cannot be used because it is not available" and proceeded to require a specimen of blood. No further evidence of the non-availability of a device was given and D was convicted.

Held, allowing the appeal that the prosecution had to prove the unreliability of the device, and evidence of the constable's statement proved nothing without an indication from D that he accepted it or was not prepared to contradict it. The conviction would be quashed.

DYE *v.* MANNS [1987] R.T.R. 90, D.C.

3230. Blood specimen—failure to provide—offer of urine specimen—special reasons

[Road Traffic Act 1972 (c.20), ss.8, 93.]

G was required by a policeman to provide a specimen of blood for analysis in accordance with s.8(1). G refused but offered a specimen of urine. He was convicted of failing to provide a blood specimen, and appealed.

Held, that a constable requiring a blood specimen which was refused was not under a duty to investigate whether or not the motorist desired to raise a medical reason for not providing blood. Further, that the offer of a urine specimen could not constitute a special reason for not endorsing.

GRIX *v.* CHIEF CONSTABLE OF KENT [1987] R.T.R. 193, D.C.

3231. Blood specimen—failure to provide—reasonable excuse for refusing

[Road Traffic Act 1972 (c.20), s.8 as substituted.]

Whether the circumstances which caused a motorist to refuse to give a blood specimen were capable of constituting a reasonable excuse is a question of law. Whether the circumstances of a case did constitute a reasonable excuse in a question of fact for the justices.

K was a motorist who sustained a broken pelvis in a road traffic accident and was in hospital, gave a blood sample for hospital purposes. A constable ascertained that there were no medical reasons why K should not give another sample for a laboratory test and required him to give a further sample. K refused, but when he was tried under s.8 of the 1972 Act for so refusing, he raised the defence of reasonable excuse in that he had just given a specimen. The justices took the view that K understood the requirement and that the excuse did not relate to his physical or mental capacity to supply the specimen, and so convicted him.

Held, dismissing the appeal, that whether circumstances were capable of providing an excuse was a matter of law, but whether they did provide an excuse was a question of fact. Given that there was no incapacity or medical reason preventing K giving a sample, the justices were plainly entitled to reach the conclusion they reached (*Roberts* v. *Griffiths* [1978] C.L.Y. 1912 followed).

KEMP *v.* CHIEF CONSTABLE OF KENT [1987] R.T.R. 66, D.C.

3232. Blood specimen—failure to provide—unlawful arrest

[Road Traffic Act 1972 (c.20), ss.7, 8.]

A valid arrest is not a prerequisite of conviction under s.8(7) of the 1972 Act.

S was driving a car and was followed and stopped by the police in circumstances in which the magistrates held that the police had no reasonable cause to suspect that he had been driving with excess alcohol, although when stopped he did seem to have been affected by drink. S refused to provide a breath specimen, and was arrested and taken to a police station where the breath test equipment was out of order. He was then required to give a specimen of blood and refused. He was charged with refusing a roadside breath test contrary to s.7(4) and with refusing to give a blood specimen contrary to s.8(7). The defence submission of no case to answer, on the basis that stopping the defendant had not been lawful, succeeded.

Held, on appeal, that the magistrate's decision had been correct as regards the s.7(4) charge, but a valid arrest was not a prerequisite of a charge under s.8(7), and to that extent the appeal would be allowed (*Fox* v. *Chief Constable of Gwent* [1985] C.L.Y. 2986 and *Bunyard* v. *Hayes* [1986] C.L.Y. 2887 applied).

GULL *v.* SCARBOROUGH (NOTE) [1987] R.T.R. 261, D.C.

3233. Blood specimen—failure to provide—unreliable breath test device

[Road Traffic Act 1972 (c.20), ss.8, 12.]

B was required to produce two breath specimens for analysis at a police station. The printouts disclosed excess breath alcohol and B was detained for one and a half hours pending a charge. The officer then noticed that the printout also disclosed a malfunction and required B to give a specimen of blood. B refused and was charged with failing to supply such a specimen contrary to s.8 of the Act. The justices were of the opinion that the prosecutor was obliged to adduce evidence that the breath device was malfunctioning shortly before the requirement for a blood specimen was made, and in the absence of this the information was dismissed.

Held, on appeal, that since there was evidence of a malfunction, the justices were entitled to conclude that the device still did not work one and a half hours later. The case would be remitted to the justices for the hearing to continue.

OXFORD *v.* BAXENDALE [1987] R.T.R. 247, D.C.

3234. Blood specimen—grounds to require—objective test

[Road Traffic Act 1972 (c.20), s.8(3)(*a*) as substituted by Transport Act 1981 (c.56), Sched. 8.]

When requiring a motorist to provide a specimen of blood, what had to be established was whether the constable making the requirement had reasonable cause to believe that for medical reasons a specimen of breath could not be provided or should not be required and the absence of belief on the part of the police constable was immaterial.

DAVIS *v.* D.P.P., *The Times*, October 23, 1987, D.C.

3235. Blood specimen—mixture with earlier sample—admissibility

[Road Traffic Act 1972 (c.20), s.10(6) (as substituted.]

The obtaining of a blood sample had to comply strictly with the statutory provisions, and where the portion of the sample handed to the defendant was mixed with even a minimal quantity of an earlier sample, the portion retained by the police and its analysis was inadmissible.

DEAR *v.* D.P.P., *The Times*, November 27, 1987, D.C.

3236. Blood specimen—refusal to give—fear of AIDS

[Road Traffic Act 1972 (c.20), s.9.]

Fear of AIDS is not a reasonable ground for refusing to give a specimen of blood for analysis under s.9 of the Road Traffic Act 1972.

D.P.P. *v.* FOUNTAIN, *The Times*, October 10, 1987, D.C.

3237. Blood specimen—test for alcohol—different methods of testing—finding based on one method.

[Road Traffic Act 1972 (c.20), s.6(1).]

Justices can properly prefer one method of analysis of a specimen to another in finding one method more reliable, and may convict on the results of the more reliable method.

STEPHENSON *v.* CLIFT, *The Times*, July 28, 1987, D.C.

3238. Blood specimen—test for drugs—requirement for taking specimen

[Road Traffic Act 1972 (c.20), s.8(3) (*c*).]

A doctor must give as his opinion that a possible cause of D's condition may be drugs before a specimen of blood pursuant to the section may be taken.

COLE *v.* BOON, *The Times*, June 19, 1987, D.C.

3239. Blood specimen—whether taking at police station proper

[Road Traffic Act 1972 (c.20), ss.6 and 8.]

The giving of a blood specimen pursuant to the exercise of the option contained in s.8(6) of the Act is not subject to the requirements set out in s.8(1).

S provided two specimens of breath for analysis and then claimed they should be replaced by a blood specimen pursuant to s.8(6). A blood specimen was taken at a police station and was shown to contain blood alcohol in excess of the prescribed limit. S contended that the blood sample had been given pursuant to a requirement in s.8(1) and should have been taken at a hospital. The justices rejected the contention and convicted him.

Held, dismissing the appeal, that the sample had not been given pursuant to a requirement in s8(1) but in the exercise of an option under s.8(6). Use of the word "required" in s.8(6) was a reference to s.8(4) and not to s.8(1), so there was nothing improper in the sample being taken at the police station.

SIVYER *v.* PARKER [1987] R.T.R. 169, D.C.

3240. Breath specimen—admissibility

[Road Traffic Act 1972 (c.20), ss.6, 8.]

A defendant who pursuant to s.8(6) elects to have his breath specimen replaced by a blood specimen bears the onus of convincing the doctor that he consents to the giving of the blood specimen. The breath analysis printouts remain admissible unless this onus is fulfilled.

R provided two specimens of breath for analysis as required by an officer at a police station. The readings were 40 and 42 microgrammes of alcohol in 100 ml. of breath, and R claimed the right to have the specimens replaced with blood. He told the doctor that he had in the past suffered allergic reactions to hypodermic needles, and gave an equivocal consent to the sample being taken. The doctor refused to take the sample, believing R had not consented. R submitted, when charged with driving with excess breath alcohol, that the doctor's refusal to take the sample rendered the printouts inadmissible.

Held, on appeal against conviction, that the onus was on the defendant to establish consent, and he could not complain of a doctor's reasonably held impression that no true consent had been given, even if that was mistaken. Thus the prosecutor was entitled to rely on the printout evidence and the appeal would be dismissed (*Anderton* v. *Lythgoe* [1985] C.L.Y. 2994 and *Johnson* v. *West Yorkshire Metropolitan Police* [1986] C.L.Y. 2891 distinguished).

RAWLINS *v.* BROWN [1987] R.T.R. 238, D.C.

3241. Breath specimen—admissibility

[Road Traffic Act 1972 (c.20), ss.6, 8, 10, as amended.]

Failure to inform a person who has been required to provide breath specimens for analysis of his right to have those specimens replaced by specimens of blood or urine renders evidence of the breath specimens inadmissible.

H was properly required to provide two specimens of breath for analysis. This done, the constable involved did not inform H of his right to have the specimens replaced by specimens of blood or urine, but instead, innocently but mistakenly required him to provide a specimen of blood. H did so, and was later charged with driving with excess breath alcohol, alternatively excess blood-alcohol. The justices held that evidence of all specimens were inadmissible and H had no case to answer.

Held, dismissing the appeal, that the evidence of the blood specimen was inadmissible because it had not been obtained by the correct procedure. That the mere provision of a blood specimen in these circumstances did not render the breath specimens inadmissible, but the failure to inform H of his right to have them replaced by blood or urine specimens did. The justices were thus right in concluding H had no case to answer (*Howard* v. *Hallett* [1985] C.L.Y. 2992 applied; *Fox* v. *Chief Constable of Gwent* [1985] C.L.Y. 2986 considered; *Archbold* v. *Jones* [1985] C.L.Y. 3027 distinguished; *Johnson* v. *West Yorkshire Metropolitan Police* [1986] C.L.Y. 2891 and *Anderton* v. *Lythgoe* [1985] C.L.Y. 2994 applied).

WAKELEY *v.* HYAMS [1987] R.T.R. 49, D.C.

3242. Breath specimen—admissibility—identical readings

[Road Traffic Act 1972 (c.20), ss.6(1), 8, 10(3), 12(2).]

C provided two breath specimens for analysis. The Intoximeter recorded 75 microgrammes of alcohol in 100 millilitres of breath for both specimens and C was charged with driving with excess breath alcohol. C submitted that he had no case to answer since s.8(6) provided that only the lower reading could be used in evidence, and thus neither of two identical readings could be adduced.

Held, dismissing the appeal, that the purpose of the section was to entitle the prosecutor to rely only on the reading more favourable to the motorist, and this purpose would be defeated by C's construction.

R. *v.* BRENTFORD MAGISTRATES' COURT, *ex p.* CLARKE [1987] R.T.R. 205, D.C.

3243. Breath specimen—admissibility—police acting *mala fide*—effect on evidence of subsequent analysis of breath. See MATTO (JIT SINGH) *v.* D.P.P., §572.

3244. Breath test—choice of providing blood to replace breath specimens—whether comment by police officer removed choice

[Road Traffic Act 1972 (c.20), s.816.]

Having provided specimens of breath for analysis by a Lion/Intoximeter device, D was told of her right under s.8(6) of the 1972 Act to provide a blood specimen to replace the breath specimens. The officer used the *pro forma* issued by the City of London Police. When D asked if a blood specimen would make any difference, the officer replied "probably not." She then declined to give blood.

Held, dismissing D's appeal against conviction of driving with excess alcohol in her breath, that the officer's reply had not removed D's choice (*Wakeley* v. *Hyams* [1987] C.L.Y. 3241 distinguished).

SHARP *v.* SPENCER [1987] Crim.L.R. 420, D.C.

3245. Breath test—failure to provide specimen—reasonable excuse

[Road Traffic Act 1972 (c.20), s.8.]

A desire to see a doctor and a solicitor and to make a complaint about police treatment does not constitute a reasonable excuse for refusing to provide a specimen.

O, a motorist of good character, was arrested by police who were suspicious of his driving and behaviour, and roughly treated. At the police station, O refused to provide a breath specimen until he could make a complaint and see a doctor and a solicitor. He was charged with refusing to provide a specimen. The justices took the view that O's state of mind was, as a result of his treatment, such that he could not understand the consequences of his refusal. The prosecutor appealed.

Held, that the justices had concluded that O had a reasonable excuse for his failure to provide a specimen. The refusal was not due to an agitated or confused state of mind, but due to a desire to see a doctor and solicitor, and to make a complaint, which afforded no excuse for the failure. The case would be remitted to the justices with a direction to convict.

CHIEF CONSTABLE OF AVON AND SOMERSET *v.* O'BRIEN [1987] R.T.R. 182, D.C.

3246. Breath test—failure to provide specimen—reasonable excuse

[Road Traffic Act 1972 (c.20), s.8 as amended.]

The existence of a reasonable excuse under s.8(7) of the Act is a question of fact for the justices.

C was properly required to provide a breath specimen for analysis by a Lion Intoximeter 3000. No specimen was provided and he was charged with failing to provide a specimen. The justices found C to have been co-operative, and that he had tried as hard as he could, but was unable to provide a specimen, and thus had a reasonable excuse under s.8(7) of the Act.

Held, dismissing the appeal, that the excuse was a matter of fact for the justices, and they had considered it with care and heard all the witneses, so their decision could not be assailed.

COTGROVE *v.* COONEY [1987] R.T.R. 124, D.C.

3247. Breath test—failure to provide specimen—unlawful arrest—whether reasonable excuse

[Road Traffic Act 1972 (c.20), s.8.]

An invalid or unlawful arrest does not vitiate a requirement for breath specimens under s.8; nor does it provide a reasonable excuse for refusing.

H was observed driving erratically and the police followed him and wrongfully arrested him at his home. He was taken to a police station where he refused to provde a breath specimen on the grounds that his arrest had been unlawful. When prosecuted under s.8(7) of the Act he submitted that the unlawful arrest vitiated the subsequent procedures and/or provided a reasonable excuse for refusal. He appealed against conviction.

Held, that since the requirement for a specimen was made at a police station in the course of investigation into whether offences under ss.5 and 6 of the Act had been committed, s.8 had been complied with and the specimens were lawfully required. In view of this, the unlawful arrest could not provide a reasonable excuse (*Fox* v. *Chief Constable of Gwent* [1985] C.L.Y. 2986 and *Bunyard* v. *Hayes* [1986] C.L.Y. 2887 applied; *Morris* v. *Beardmore* [1980] C.L.Y. 2310 distinguished).

HARTLAND *v.* ALDEN [1987] R.T.R. 253, D.C.

3248. Breath test—failure to provide specimen—whether offence committed

[Road Traffic Act 1972 (c.20), s.8(7).]

For a driver to commit the offence of failing to supply a specimen of breath for analysis under s.8(7) of the Road Traffic Act 1972, he must (a) have been warned of the consequences of failure; and (b) have understood that warning.

CHIEF CONSTABLE OF AVON AND SOMERSET CONSTABULARY *v.* SINGH, *The Times*, April 11, 1987, D.C.

3249. Breath test—failure to supply sample—whether special reasons

[Road Traffic Act 1972 (c.20), s.8(7) (as substituted)].

The fact that a person convicted of refusing to supply a sample of breath was a passenger, not the driver, need not necessarily amount to special reasons. (*McCormick* v. *Hitchin* [1985] C.L.Y. 3031, *Bunyard* v. *Hayes* [1984] C.L.Y. 2999 distinguished.)

R. *v.* ASHFORD AND TENTERDEN MAGISTRATES COURT *ex p.* WOOD, *The Times*, May 8, 1987, D.C.

3250. Breath test—refusal to give specimen until arrival of solicitor—whether reasonable excuse

[Road Traffic Act 1972 (c.20), s.8; Police and Criminal Evidence Act 1984 (c.60), s.58.]

The right to consult a solicitor conferred on an arrested person by s.58 of the Police and Criminal Evidence Act 1984 does not affect the law relating to breath tests under s.8 of the Road Traffic Act 1972. Accordingly, the fact that a motorist has said that he will not give such a specimen until his solicitor has arrived is not a reasonable excuse for failing to give a specimen of breath.

D.P.P. *v.* BILLINGTON, CHAPPELL, RUMBLE AND EAST, *The Independent*, July 22, 1987, D.C.

3251. Breath tests—statistics

The Home Office has published a statistical bulletin (Issue 24/87) giving details of breath tests in England and Wales during 1986. Copies of the bulletin are available from Statistical Department, Home Office, Lunar House, Croydon, Surrey CR0 9YD. Tel: 01–760 2850. [£2·50.]

3252. Breathalyser—multiple breath tests

[Road Traffic Act 1972 (c.20) ss.5, 6, 8(1), as substituted by the Transport Act 1981 (c.56), Sched. 8.]

A police officer with good reason to suspect that one of a number of suspects who having consumed alcohol has been driving may require all of them to provide a specimen of breath.

PEARSON *v.* COMMISSIONER OF POLICE OF THE METROPOLIS, *The Times*, June 29, 1987, D.C.

3253. Breathalyser provisions—developments in the law—duty of legal advisors in pending appeal

Lawyers in breathalyser cases should be alert to ensure that new legal developments had not made a pending appeal unnecessary before it came on for hearing.

STOKES *v.* SAYERS, *The Times*, March 16, 1987, D.C.

3254. Car tax—when applicable

[Car Tax Act 1983 (c.53), s.2(1)(*c*)(ii).]

A roofed space behind the driver's seat which has side windows but which is not reasonably capable of accommodating human beings is not "roofed accommodation" for the purpose of s.2(1)(*c*)(ii) of the Car Tax Act 1983.

R. *v.* CUSTOMS AND EXCISE COMMISSIONERS, *ex p.* NISSAN (U.K.), *The Times*, November 23, 1987, C.A.

3255. Carriage of perishable foodstuffs

INTERNATIONAL CARRIAGE OF PERISHABLE FOODSTUFFS (AMENDMENT) REGULATIONS 1987 (No. 1066) [45p], made under the International Carriage of Perishable Foodstuffs Act 1976 (c.58), ss.3(1), 4(1); operative on July 21, 1987; increase to £260 the fee specified in S.I. 1985 No. 1071.

INTERNATIONAL CARRIAGE OF PERISHABLE FOODSTUFFS (VEHICLES WITH THIN SIDE WALLS) REGULATIONS 1987 (No. 869) [45p], made under the Finance Act 1973 (c.51), s.56(1), (2); operative on June 4, 1987; prescribe fees payable in connection with the testing of units of transport equipment with thin side walls used for the carriage of perishable foodstuffs between the U.K. and Italy.

3256. Construction and use

ROAD VEHICLES (CONSTRUCTION AND USE) (AMENDMENT) REGULATIONS 1987 (No. 676) [£1·40], made under the Road Traffic Act 1972 (c.20), s.40(1)(3); operative on May 6, 1987, save for reg. 13 which is operative on April 1, 1988, amends S.I. 1986 No. 1078 in relation to Ministry plates, semi-trailers with driven wheels, braking systems, maximum weights and steam powered vehicles.

ROAD VEHICLES (CONSTRUCTION AND USE) (AMENDMENT) (No. 2) REGULATIONS 1987 (No. 1133) [£1·90], made under the Road Traffic Act 1972, s.40(1)(3); operative on July 31, 1987; amend S.I. 1986 No. 1078 in relation to buses and coaches.

3257. Crown roads

CROWN ROADS (ROYAL PARKS) (APPLICATION OF ROAD TRAFFIC ENACTMENTS) ORDER 1987 (No. 363) [£1·40], made under the Road Traffic Regulation Act 1984 (c.27), s.131; operative on April 1, 1987; re-enacts with amendments S.I. 1977 No. 548.

3258. Dangerous vehicle—mechanical digger in condition as manufactured

[Motor Vehicles (Construction and Use) Regulations 1978 (S.I. 1978 No. 1017), reg. 97(1).]

A digger being driven on a road in its manufactured condition with unguarded two inch spikes protruding from its lowered bucket was capable of falling within the regulation.

WOOD *v.* MILNE, *The Times,* March 27, 1987, D.C.

3259. Disqualification—appeal—effective date

[Road Traffic Act 1972 (c.20), s.94 as amended.]

In the absence of firm evidence that a successful application had been made before the justices to suspend a disqualification order pending appeal, the reduced sentence should run from the date of conviction.

T was disqualified from driving for 22 months on July 23, 1985 and appealed against sentence in accordance with s.94(1) of 1972 Act. On December 4, 1985 the Crown Court reduced the disqualification to 18 months, to run from that date. T submitted that he had made no application to suspend the disqualification, and it should run from July 23, but the recorder preferred the evidence of a computer printout produced by the prosecutor and confirmed that the disqualification should run from December 4.

Held, it having been conceded that s.182 of the Act did not make the printout conclusive, that the recorder should have concluded either that no application had been made or that there was insufficient evidence to conclude that it had, the disqualification should run from July 23, the normal point of commencement (*Kidner* v. *Daniels* (1910) 74 J.P. 127 considered).

TAYLOR *v.* COMMISSIONER OF POLICE OF THE METROPOLIS [1987] R.T.R. 118, D.C.

3260. Disqualification—exceptional hardship—whether necessary to hear sworn evidence

[Transport Act 1981 (c.56), s.19(6).]

The test for "exceptional hardship" under s.19(6) of the Transport Act 1981 is not the same as for "special reasons". Accordingly, justices do not need to hear sworn evidence in the former case, although it will usually be desirable for them to do so.

OWEN *v.* JONES, *The Times,* January 28, 1987, D.C.

3261. Disqualification—refusal to supply specimen—special reasons

[Road Traffic Act 1972 (c.29), ss.8(7), 93(4), 101(2), Sched. 4; Transport Act 1981 (c.56), s.25 and Sched. 8.]

In the early hours of the morning, S was seen by police walking towards his crashed and severely damaged car; he was arrested and conveyed to a police station. He denied having driven the car and refused to supply a specimen. H testified that he had—unknown to S—driven and crashed the car before abandoning it. S testified that he had had no intention of driving his car that night.

Held, allowing S's appeal against disqualification for 12 months under the totting-up provisions of s.93(4), that there were special reasons for not ordering the obligatory number of penalty points to be endorsed on the applicant's licence and the disqualification would be quashed.

SUTCH *v.* CROWN PROSECUTION SERVICE, January 30, 1987; H.H. Judge Compton; Wood Green Crown Ct. [*Ex rel. I.R.C. Kawaley, Barrister*].

3262. Disqualification—special reasons—triviality of offence

B was charged on two counts, namely (1) no insurance, and (2) no test certificate, and he pleaded guilty. Special reasons were adduced not to disqualify B, who already had 12 points on his driving licence, on the grounds that the offences were trivial. It was claimed that a third party had brought the car to B's house (hoping B would buy it). B was to look at the car. Thus he was in possession of it. He never drove the car however. It remained on the public highway outside his house for two days. A constable came to inspect the car and suspected bald tyres. Upon request, B was unable to produce a test certificate or the insurance so was consequently summoned. The court accepted the above as a special reason not to disqualify and fined B instead.

R. *v.* BOWEN (T.J.), November 9, 1987; Llandudno Magistrates. Ct. [*Ex. rel. D. S. Kirwan J. Co., Solicitors*].

3263. Drink/drive offence—late service of certificate of level of alcohol—admissibility—*res gestae*. See CRIMINAL EVIDENCE AND PROCEDURE, §647.

3264. Drivers' hours

COMMUNITY DRIVERS' HOURS AND RECORDING EQUIPMENT (EXEMPTIONS AND SUPPLEMENTARY PROVISIONS) (AMENDMENT) REGULATIONS 1987 (No. 805) [45p], made under the European Communities Act 1972 (c.68), s.2(2); operative on June 1, 1987; amend S.I. 1986, No. 1456 by providing for further exemptions from the provisions of Council Regulation (EEC) No. 3820/85.

COMMUNITY DRIVERS' HOURS (PASSENGER AND GOODS VEHICLES) (TEMPORARY EXCEPTION) REGULATIONS 1987 (No. 27) [45p], made under the European Communities Act 1972, s.2(2); operative on January 17, 1987; provides that Council Regulation (EEC) No. 3820/85 shall apply until February 16, 1987 to transport operations.

COMMUNITY DRIVERS' HOURS (PASSENGER AND GOODS VEHICLES) (TEMPORARY EXCEPTION) (REVOCATION) REGULATIONS 1987 (No. 97) [45p], made under the European Communities Act 1972 s.2(2); operative on February 2, 1987; revokes S.I. 1987 No. 27.

DRIVERS' HOURS (GOODS VEHICLES) (KEEPING OF RECORDS) REGULATIONS 1987 (No. 1421) [£1·90], made under the Transport Act 1968 (c.73), ss.98 and 101(2); operative on November 2, 1987; introduce a simplified record book instead of the requirements in S.I. 1976 No. 1447, which is revoked.

DRIVERS' HOURS (PASSENGER AND GOODS VEHICLES) (EXEMPTION) REGULATIONS 1987 (No. 28) [45p], made under the Transport Act 1968, s.96(10); operative on January 17, 1987; provides for a bad weather exemption from the requirements of s.96(1)–(6) of the 1968 Act.

DRIVERS' HOURS (PASSENGER AND GOODS VEHICLES) (EXEMPTION) (REVOCATION) REGULATIONS 1987 (No. 98) [45p], made under the Transport Act 1968 s.96(10); operative on February 2, 1987; revokes S.I. 1987 No. 28.

3265. Driving licences

MOTOR VEHICLES (DRIVING LICENCES) REGULATIONS 1987 (No. 1378) [£3·30], made under the Road Traffic Act 1972 (c.20), ss.84–89, 96, 107, 108; operative on September 3, 1987; make provision in relation to driving licences.

MOTOR VEHICLES (DRIVING LICENCES) (AMENDMENT) REGULATIONS 1987 (No. 560) [45p], made under the Road Traffic Act 1972, ss.85(2), 107; operative on April 27, 1987; increase fees for Pt. II of the motorcycle test and the ordinary motorcar test.

3266. Driving without due care and attention—diabetes—automatism

As D was driving home, his car was driven erratically and collided with another vehicle. The evidence suggested that D, a diabetic, was in a hypoglycaemic state. It was possible to slip into such a state without warning and then to do acts unconsciously. Justices accepted that his acts were involuntary and automatic.

Held, allowing the prosecutor's appeal against D's acquittal, that if during some of the erratic driving the actions were voluntary D should have been convicted. The doctor's opinion was that D would have reacted to gross stimuli but would have reacted imperfectly. At those stages, his mind must have been controlling his limbs and he was thus driving (*Watmore* v. *Jenkins* [1962] C.L.Y. 2657 and *Beatty* v. *Att-Gen. (Northern Ireland)* [1961] C.L.Y. 1839 considered).

BROOME *v.* PERKINS [1987] Crim.L.R. 271, D.C.

3267. Drunk in charge—failure to provide specimen—whether connection

[Road Traffic Act 1972 (c.20), ss.5(2), 8(7).]

There is no connection between the two offences; D was not in charge by reason of his location *vis-à-vis* his car and he had no reasonable excuse for refusing a breath test since an investigation was being carried on (*R.* v. *Fox* [1985] C.L..Y 2986 applied).

D.P.P. *v.* WEBB, *The Times,* October 19, 1987, D.C.

3268. Duty to supply drivers identity—time limit

[Road Traffic Regulation Act 1967 (c.76), ss.31(1)(3), 85(1)(2)(ii)(3); Transport Act 1968 (c.73), ss.127(8), 130(6)(2), Sched. 14 pt. VI—Vehicles and Driving Licences Act 1969 (c.27), s.16(6).]

A driver's identity must be supplied pursuant to s.85(2)(*a*)(ii) of the Road Traffic Regulation Act 1967 either forthwith or within a reasonable time *e.g.* 14 days.

D was the registered keeper of a vehicle which was parked in a "pay and display" car park without displaying a ticket. When the excess charge was not paid, a notice under s.85(2)(*a*) of the Road Traffic Regulations Act 1967 was served requiring him to provide the identity of the driver within 14 days. D failed to do so. When charged with an offence contrary to s.85(3) three months later, he provided the information and argued that no time limit was specified by the Act, and that therefore no offence was committed. He was convicted.

Held, dismissing the appeal, that the information has to be provided forthwith or within a reasonable time and the justices had rightly regarded 14 days as such a reasonable time.

LOWE *v.* LESTER [1987] R.T.R. 30, D.C.

3269. Excess alcohol—back calculation

[Road Traffic Act 1972 (c.20) (as substituted by s.25(3) of, and Sched. 8 to, Transport Act 1981 (c.56).]

A prosecutor may adduce evidence to show that the amount of alcohol in a defendant's body exceeded the limit notwithstanding his subsequent provision of a sample indicating an amount less than the limit.

GUMBLEY *v.* CUNNINGHAM; GOULD *v.* CASTLE, *The Independent,* July 29, 1987, D.C.

3270. Excess alcohol—intoximeter reading exceeding 50 mg per 100 ml breath—relevance of Home Office voluntary option scheme re blood specimen

[Road Traffic Act 1972, as amended, s.8(6).]

D provided intoximeter breath specimens both exceeding 50 microgrammes of alcohol per 100 millilitres of breath. He asked if he could give a specimen of blood. He was told that the option was not available since the reading exceeded 50 microgrammes. The officer honestly but mistakenly believed that the "voluntary option" introduced by the Home Office for cases where the reading exceeded 50 microgrammes had ceased.

Held, dismissing D's appeal against conviction of driving with excess alcohol, that the justices had not erred in finding that the intoximeter evidence had been obtained lawfully and was admissible and should be admitted. The voluntary scheme could not be equated with the statutory provisions of s.8(6) of the 1972 Act, although in some cases it might be right to disreguard the intoximeter evidence.

McGRATH *v.* FIELD [1987] Crim.L.R. 275, D.C.

3271. Excess alcohol—two occupants of car charged as principals—whether necessary to identify which drove and which was aider and abettor. See CRIMINAL LAW, §752.

3272. Excise licence

ROAD VEHICLES (EXCISE) (PRESCRIBED PARTICULARS) (AMENDMENT) REGULATIONS 1987 (No. 2122) [85p], made under the Vehicles (Excise) Act 1971 (c.10), ss.12(1), 16(1), 37(2); operative on January 1, 1988; further amends S.I. 1981 No. 931 in relation to recovery vehicles.

ROAD VEHICLES (REGISTRATION AND LICENSING) (AMENDMENT) REGULATIONS 1987 (No. 2123) [45p], made under the Vehicles (Excise) Act 1971, ss.16, 37; operative on January 1, 1988; further amend S.I. 1971 No. 450 in relation to recovery vehicles.

3273. Excise licence—use of vehicle on road without excise licence—time-limit for institution of proceedings. See ALGAR *v.* SHAW, §2331.

3274. Excise licence—vehicle kept on road without licence in force—onus in relation to proviso—costs

[Vehicles (Excise) Act 1971 (c.10), s.8; Magistrate Courts Act 1980 (c.43), s.101.]

Nothing in the 1971 Act altered the rule in the 1980 Act that the burden of proof on an exception or proviso, such as that in s.8(1) of the 1971 Act, lay upon the defendant.

B appeared unrepresented on a charge of keeping on a road a mechanically propelled vehicle for which no vehicle excise licence was in force. The prosecutor failed to prove that the vehicle was not licensed, the justices clerk advised the justices that B had no case to answer, and they dismissed the information. The prosecutor appealed and suggested to B that he might take legal advice, and if the appeal was not opposed it could be dealt with without attendence of counsel or solicitors for the prosecution, so saving costs. No. response was received from B and he did not appear at the appeal.

Held, that nothing in the 1971 Act transferred to the prosecutor the burden of proof in relation to provisos and exceptions which lay on the defendant under s.101 of the 1980 Act, and thus the onus was on B to prove the existence of a valid vehicle excise licence, so the case would be remitted to the justices to continue the hearing. Further, that in the circumstances B should pay the costs of the prosecution at the appeal (*John* v. *Humphreys* [1955] C.L.Y. 1632, *R.* v. *Edwards* [1974] C.L.Y. 600 and *R.* v. *Oliver* [1944] K.B. 68 applied).

GUYLL *v.* BRIGHT [1987] R.T.R. 104, D.C.

3275. Failing to report an accident—involvement in accident—presumption of knowledge

[Road Traffic Act 1972 (c.20), s.25.]

When a driver is charged under s.25 of the Road Traffic Act 1972 with failing to report an accident to the police, the fact that he was involved in an accident raises a prima facie presumption that he knew about it (*Harding* v. *Price* (1948) C.L.C. 8998 applied; *Hampson* v. *Powell* [1970] C.L.Y. 2508 not followed).

SELBY *v.* CHIEF CONSTABLE OF AVON AND SOMERSET, *The Times*, February 18, 1987, D.C.

3276. Goods vehicles

GOODS VEHICLES (AUTHORISATION OF INTERNATIONAL JOURNEYS) (FEES) (AMENDMENT) REGULATIONS 1987 (No. 2012) [45p], made under the Finance Act 1973 (c.51), s.56(1)(2); operative on December 23, 1987; amend S.I. 1983 No. 1831 so as to reduce certain specified fees.

GOODS VEHICLES (OPERATORS' LICENCES, QUALIFICATONS AND FEES) (AMENDMENT) REGULATIONS 1987 (No. 841) [85p], made under the Transport Act 1968 (c.73), ss.60(2), 85(1)(2), 89(1), 91(1); operative on July 1, 1987; further amend S.I. 1984 No. 176.

GOODS VEHICLES (OPERATOR'S LICENCES, QUALIFICATIONS AND FEES) (AMENDMENT) (No. 2) REGULATIONS 1987 (No. 2170) [45p], made under the Transport Act 1968 (c.73), s.60(2); operative on January 13, 1988; amend S.I. 1984 No. 176 to exempt from operator licensing vehicles which are licensed and taxed in the recovery vehicle class.

GOODS VEHICLES (PROHIBITIONS) (EXEMPTIONS AND APPEALS) REGULATIONS 1987 (No. 1149) [45p], made under the Road Traffic Act 1972 (c.20), ss.57(10), 58(3)(6); operative on August 5, 1987; revoke and replace S.I. 1971 No. 2020.

3277. Increased penalties—prescribed regulations

ROAD VEHICLES (PRESCRIBED REGULATIONS FOR THE PURPOSES OF INCREASED PENALTIES) REGULATIONS 1987 (No. 2085) [45p], made under the Vehicles (Excise) Act 1971 (c.10), s.37(3)(*a*), Sched. 7, Pt. I, para. 24; prescribe regulations of S.I. 1971 No. 450 where a contravention will attract a maximum penalty at level 3 on the standard scale.

3278. Information—whether defective

[Road Traffic Act 1972 (c.20), s.6 as substituted; Magistrates Courts Rules 1981, r.100.]

An information was laid against T alleging an offence contrary to s.6(1) of the Road Traffic Act 1972 "as amended." T submitted that s.6 had been substituted by the Transport Act 1981, and thus the information was defective. The prosecutor declined an invitation by the justices to apply to amend. The justices upheld T's submission and dismissed the information.

Held, that the information satisfied r.100 of the 1981 Rules since it was incapable of misleading either laymen or lawyer. The appeal would be allowed and the case remitted to the justices.

JONES *v.* THOMAS (JOHN BARRIE) [1987] R.T.R. 111, D.C.

3279. Intoximeter—reliability

[Road Traffic Act 1972 (c.20), ss.6(1) and 8(3)(*b*).]

Because he believed that the Intoximeter device was defective in that the print-out apparatus was not functioning correctly, an officer required D to give a blood specimen.

Held, dismissing D's appeal against driving with excess alcohol in his blood, contrary to s.6(1) of the 1972 Act as substituted by the Transport Act 1981, that the requirement for a blood specimen was lawful. The officer's belief that the device was unreliable was reasonable. In concluding that the device was unreliable for the purposes of s.8(3)(*b*), the officer was entitled to have regard to the malfunction of the printout. The situation was different from that where a device had satisfactorily performed an analysis of the defendant's breath but failed to produce a printout. Once the officer has obtained specimens available in evidence, hd cannot properly carry out further investigation (*Morgan* v. *Lee* [1985] C.L.Y. 3049 distinguished; *Thompson* v. *Thynne* [1986] C.L.Y. 2869 applied).

HAGHIGAT-KHOU *v.* CHAMBERS [1987] Crim.L.R. 340, D.C.

3280. Intoximeter—reliability—assessment of evidence

[Road Traffic Act 1972 (c.20), ss.6(1), 8(1)(3), 10(1)(2)(3), 12(2); Transport Act (c.56), s.25(3) Sched. 8. Breath Analysis Devices (Approval) Order 1983 Sched. Lion Intoximeter 3000.]

On a charge of excess alcohol in the breath under s.10 of the Road Traffic Act 1972, there is no requirement that this Intoximeter device should be reliable, and justices may nevertheless be satisfied that an offence has been committed.

D was required at a police station to give a specimen of breath for a Lion Intoximeter 3000 device. The printout stated that the first specimen contained 48 microgrammes of alcohol per 100 millilitres of breath; and that the second, taken one minute later contained 42. He called expert evidence that there could not be a correct variation of more than one microgramme and that therefore the machine might not be functioning properly. The justices nevertheless convicted.

Held, dismissing this appeal, that in the absence of evidence directly challenging the accuracy of the lower reading, the justices were entitled to convict. (*Lucking* v. *Forbes* [1986] C.L.Y. 2940 considered; *Hughes* v. *McConnell* [1985] C.L.Y. 3055 distinguished).

NEWTON *v.* WOODS [1987] R.T.R. 41, D.C.

3281. Intoximeter—reliability—use of blood sample

[Road Traffic Act 1972 (c.20), ss.6(1), 8(3), 10(2) (as substituted).]

Where the Intoximeter appears to the officer to be unreliable or possibly to be unreliable, and a specimen of blood is required by him, any subsequent prosecution must be based upon the blood sample (*Thompson* v. *Thynne* [1986] C.L.Y. 2869 considered).

BADKIN *v.* CHIEF CONSTABLE OF SOUTH YORKSHIRE, *The Times,* August 29, 1987, D.C.

3282. Intoximeter—whether printout required—guilty plea

[Road Traffic Act 1972 (c.20), s.6.]

There is no obligation on the prosecution to produce the original intoximeter printout where the defendant is pleading guilty to a charge of driving with excess blood alcohol.

R. *v.* TOWER BRIDGE METROPOLITAN STIPENDIARY MAGISTRATE, *ex p.* D.P.P., *The Times,* May 15, 1987, D.C.

3283. Length of disqualification from driving—whether desirable to extend period longer than prison sentence

D should not generally be sentenced to a period of disqualification extended beyond his likely release from a substantial period of imprisonment.

R. *v.* HAYLES, *The Times,* January 26, 1987, C.A.

3284. Licence—endorsement—effectiveness—sentence

[Road Traffic Act 1972 (c.20), s.101; Forgery and Counterfeiting Act 1981 (c.45), s.3.]

In passing sentence for motoring offences the justices are entitled to consider all past convictions and not just those remaining effective under s.101 of the 1972 act.

W was convicted of a motoring offence and produced a clean, but false, licence. The justices decided upon the penalty, but W later admitted that the licence had been created by him. A true licence would have revealed endorsements for offences committed more than four years previously. W was charged with producing a false instrument contrary to s.3 of the 1981 Act. He submitted he had no case to answer since the justices were only entitled to consider convictions remaining effective under s.101 of the 1972 Act. The justices agreed and dismissed the information.

Held, that the justices were entitled to consider all previous convictions when passing sentence. The case should be remitted to the justices with a direction to continue the hearing.

CHIEF CONSTABLE OF WEST MERCIA POLICE *v.* WILLIAMS [1987] R.T.R. 188, D.C.

3285. Licence—endorsement—special reasons—permitting uninsured use

[Road Traffic Act 1972 (c.20), ss.101(1), (2), 143(1); Transport Act 1981 (c.56), s.30(3), Sched. 9.]

The offence of causing or permitting uninsured use of a motor vehicle is committed on each occasion when the uninsured driving of the principal is caused or permitted. Further, the fact that consecutive offences might have been avoided had the defendant been aware of the first, constituted special reasons for not endorsing his licence for the subsequent offences.

B owned a car and permitted his son to use it from a day in June onwards, despite the fact that no insurance was in force for such use within the terms of s.143 of the 1972 Act. Between October 8 and 28, B was not in communication with his son. He was charged with permitting uninsured use on October 15, and pleaded guilty. He was later charged with permitting uninsured use on October 17, was convicted and his licence was endorsed.

Held, on appeal against conviction and endorsement, that in respect of the conviction the only question was whether the uninsured driving was caused or permitted at the material time, and accordingly the appeal would be dismissed. In respect of the endorsements, the offence might have been avoided if it had been possible to inform B of the first offence and accordingly this constituted special reasons why there should be no endorsement. Accordingly the appeal against endorsement would be allowed.

BARNETT *v.* FIELDHOUSE [1987] R.T.R. 266, D.C.

3286. Licence—endorsement—special reasons—using vehicle without effective insurance policy—owner believing policy covered another driver. See EAST *v.* BLADEN, §2067.

3287. Lighting—slow-moving vehicles

ROAD VEHICLES LIGHTING (AMENDMENT) REGULATIONS 1987 (No. 1315) [85p], made under the Road Traffic Act 1972 (c.20), ss.40(1)(2A), 41(3); operative on January 1, 1988; amend S.I. 1984 No. 812 in relation to the lighting of slow-moving vehicles.

3288. Marking of special weights

ROAD VEHICLES (MARKING OF SPECIAL WEIGHTS) (AMENDMENT) REGULATIONS 1987 (No. 1326) [45p], made under the Road Traffic Act 1972 (c.20), s.172; operative on January 1, 1988; amend S.I. 1983 No. 910.

3289. Mechanically propelled vehicle—meaning—burden of proof

A car was being controlled by D whilst it was being towed. It had no engine or gearbox.

Held, allowing D's appeal against convictions involving use of the car, that the justices had erred in finding that the burden lay on D to prove that the intended use of the car was such that it had ceased to be a mechanically propelled vehicle (*Newbury* v. *Simmonds* [1961] C.L.Y. 7908, *Floyd* v. *Bush* [1953] C.L.Y. 3224, *McEachran* v. *Hurst* [1978] C.L.Y. 2537, *Smart* v. *Allen* [1962] C.L.Y. 2723, *Chief Constable of Avon and Somerset* v. *Fleming* [1987] C.L.Y. 3295 followed).

READER *v.* BUNYARD [1987] Crim.L.R. 274, D.C.

3290. Mobile crane—articulated construction—towing of trailer

[Motor Vehicles (Authorization of Special Types) General Order 1979 (S.I. 1979 No. 1198) reg. 25(2).]

An articulated mobile crane is one vehicle, not a vehicle towing a trailer.

D.P.P. *v.* EVANS AND HEWDEN STUART HEAVY CRANES, *The Times*, November 13, 1987, D.C.

3291. Motor cycle—driving

[Road Traffic Act 1972 (c.20), s.6(1); Transport Act 1981 (c.56), s.25(3), Sched 8.]

A person controlling a motorcycle movement whilst straddling it and appropriately clad for doing so may be convicted of driving it.

D, dressed in motor cycle clothing and crash helmet pushed it with lights and ignition on across the road outside his fathers' house, with his legs astride the vehicle. He was breathalysed and convicted.

Held, dismissing the appeal, that he was controlling the vehicle's movement and direction and was appropriately dressed, and the justices were entitled to convict (*R.* v. *MacDonagh* [1974] C.L.Y. 3384 applied).

McKOEN *v.* ELLIS [1987] R.T.R. 26, D.C.

3292. Motor Cycle Noise Act 1987 (c.34)

This Act prohibits the supply of motor cycle exhaust systems and silencers likely to result in the emission of excessive noise.

The Act received the Royal Assent on May 15, 1987, and will come into force on days to be appointed by the Secretary of State.

The Act does not extend to Northern Ireland.

3293. Motor cycles

MOTOR CYCLES (EYE PROTECTORS) (AMENDMENT) REGULATIONS 1987 (No. 675) [45p], made under the Road Traffic Act 1972 (c.20), s.33AA; operative on July 1, 1987; amend S.I. 1985 No. 1593 in relation to eye protectors supplied to and worn by a member of the armed forces.

3294. Motor insurance. See INSURANCE.

3295. Motor vehicle—motor-cycle for scrambling—whether a "motor vehicle"

[Road Traffic Act 1972 (c.20), s.190.]

The test of whether a vehicle is a "motor-vehicle" for the purpose of s.190 of the Road Traffic Act 1972 is whether a reasonable person, looking at the vehicle, would say that its general use encompassed possible general road use; the actual use to which it is put is irrelevant.

D was stopped whilst pushing a motor-cycle along the road. It has been made for normal use, but had been adapted for motor-cycle scrambling, by removal of its registration number, reflectors, lights and speedometer. The justices found that it had not been proved that it was a "motor vehicle" within s.190 of the Road Traffic Act 1972.

Held, dismissing the appeal, that the test was whether a reasonable person, looking at the vehicle, would say that its general use encompassed possible general road use, and the actual use to which it was put was irrelevant. Substantial alterations could cause a vehicle originally made for use on a road to cease to be a "motor-vehicle," and the justices had been entitled to reach their finding (*Burns* v. *Currell* [1963] C.L.Y. 3038 applied).

CHIEF CONSTABLE OF AVON AND SOMERSET *v.* FLEMING [1987] 1 All E.R. 318, D.C.

3296. Motor vehicles

MOTOR VEHICLES (AUTHORISATION OF SPECIAL TYPES) (AMENDMENT) ORDER 1987 (No. 1327) [£1·90], made under the Road Traffic Act 1972 (c.20), s.42; operative on January 1, 1988; amend S.I. 1979 No. 1198 in relation to large and heavy vehicles.

MOTOR VEHICLES (AUTHORISATION OF SPECIAL TYPES) (AMENDMENT) (No. 2) ORDER 1987 (No. 2161) [85p], made under the Road Traffic Act 1972 (c.20), s.42; operative on January 1, 1988; amends S.I. 1979 No. 571.

3297. Motor vehicles—tests

MOTOR VEHICLES (TESTS) (AMENDMENT) REGULATIONS 1987 (No. 1144) [45p], made under the Road Traffic Act 1972 (c.20), s.43(2)(6); operative on August 3, 1987; increase fees payable for MOT tests.

3298. Parking—restricted street—exemption for hackney carriage at stand

[Road Traffic Regulation Act 1984 (c.27), s.5(1); City of Gloucester (Eastgate Street) (Waiting Regulations) Order 1982, arts. 3 & 5.]

R left his licensed hackney carriage locked and unattended for about one hour at a hackney carriage stand in a place subject to the 1982 Order. He was convicted of contravening the restrictions on waiting there, the justices taking the view that the exception for hackney carriages waiting at hackney carriage stands did not encompass these facts. On appeal the Crown Court held that the word "wait" in the exception was impliedly restricted to waiting for a fare at the stand.

Held, dismissing the appeal, that the justices and the Crown Court had come to the correct conclusion.

RODGERS *v.* TAYLOR [1987] R.T.R. 86, D.C.

3299. Pedestrian Crossings

"PELICAN" PEDESTRIAN CROSSINGS REGULATIONS AND GENERAL DIRECTIONS 1987 (No. 16) [£3·60], made under the Road Traffic Regulation Act 1984 (c.27), ss.25, 64, 65(1); operative on February 18, 1987; makes provision in relation to the use of "pelican" pedestrian crossings.

3300. Prescribed routes

GREENWICH (PRESCRIBED ROUTES) (No. 5) TRAFFIC ORDER 1973 (VARIATION) ORDER 1987 (No. 897) [45p], made under the Road Traffic Regulation Act 1984 (c.27), s.6, Sched. 9, para. 27; operative on May 15, 1987; amends S.I. 1973 No. 268.

ISLINGTON (PRESCRIBED ROUTES) (No. 4) TRAFFIC ORDER 1985 (VARIATION) ORDER 1987 (No. 2168) [45p], made under the Road Traffic Regulation Act 1984, s.6, Sched. 9, para. 27; operative on December 14, 1987; varies GLC 1985 No. 263.

3301. Public passenger vehicles

PUBLIC PASSENGER VEHICLES (EXEMPTIONS AND APPEALS AGAINST REFUSAL TO ISSUE CERTIFICATES OR REMOVE PROHIBITIONS) REGULATIONS 1987 (No. 1150) [35p], made under the Public Passenger Vehicles Act 1981 (c.14), ss.9(9), 51(3), 60; operative on August 5, 1987; revoke and replace S.I. 1981 No. 262 and provide for appeals against refusals to issue a certificate of initial fitness or of conformity or refusal to remove a prohibition.

3302. Public service vehicle—driver—requirement to ensure safety of passengers

[Road Traffic Act 1960 (c.16), s.146(1); Public Service Vehicles (Conduct of Drivers, Conductors & Passengers) Regulations 1936, reg. 4.]

The driver of a bus is guilty of failing to ensure the safety of his passengers contrary to s.146(2) of the 1960 Act if he fails to take all reasonable precautions for their safety.

S was the driver of a bus which he knew could not be moved off without a jerk. An old age pensioner boarded the bus, showed S her pass and walked down the aisle towards a seat. Before she reached it the bus moved off and the resulting jerk caused her to fall and hit her head. S was charged with failing to ensure the safety of his passengers contrary to s.146(2) of the 1960 Act. S was convicted by the justices and his appeal to the Crown Court failed.

Held, dismissing the appeal, that in view of S's knowledge about the bus and the passenger he had failed to take all reasonable precautions to ensure the pensioners safety (*Western Scottish Motor Traction Co.* v. *Fernie* [1943] 2 All E.R. 742 and *Wragg* v. *Grout* (unreported) April 21, 1966 considered).

STEFF *v.* BECK [1987] R.T.R 61, D.C.

3303. Reckless driving—defence of necessity—whether defence could be raised

[Road Traffic Act 1972 (c.20), s.2.]

D was charged with driving recklessly and contended that he did not take risks but drove carefully throughout. He then sought to raise a defence of necessity. The trial jury refused to leave such a defence to the jury and D was convicted.

Held, that even if necessity could be raised as a defence to reckless driving it could not be raised by D, since his assertions of not taking risks and driving carefully throughout excluded any possible defence of necessity.

R. *v.* DENTON [1987] R.T.R. 129, C.A.

3304. Recovery vehicles

RECOVERY VEHICLES (PRESCRIBED PURPOSES) REGULATIONS 1987 (No. 2120) [45p], made under the Vehicles (Excise) Act 1971 (c.10), Sched. 3, Pt. I, para. 8(3)(*c*); operative on January 1, 1988; prescribe purposes for which recovery vehicles may be used without ceasing to be recovery vehicles.

3305. Seat belts—round trip

[Road Traffic Act 1972 (c.20), s.33A.]

A newsagent operating from his home who drove daily to a point to pick up papers was not excused from wearing a seat belt on the basis of a round trip.

WEBB *v.* CRANE, *The Times,* October 14, 1987, D.C.

3306. Stopping on motorway carriage—whether endorsement mandatory

[Road Traffic Regulation Act 1984 (c.27), s.17(4); Motorway Traffic (England and Wales) Regulations 1982, Reg. 7.]

D stopped on a motorway slip-road to consult a map.

Held, dismissing D's appeal against endorsement for stopping vehicle on a motorway carriageway, contrary to s.17(4) of the 1984 Act and Rep. 7 of the 1982 Regulations, that the justices had correctly decided that the offence carried mandatory endorsement.

MAWSON *v.* OXFORD [1987] Crim.L.R. 131, D.C.

3307. Tachograph—exemption—breakdown vehicle

Mr. Whitelock, a motor repairer, drove a lorry adapted for use as a breakdown vehicle, but not fitted with recording equipment as required by EEC law. Criminal proceedings were brought against Mr. Whitelock for, *inter alia,* using a lorry adapted for use as a breakdown vehicle in which recording equipment (a "tachograph") had not been installed. he argued that the lorry was a "specialised breakdown vehicle" within EEC regs. and was therefore exempt from having a tachograph installed. The High Court of Justiciary, Edinburgh, asked the European Court under Art 177 EEC for a preliminary ruling.

Held, that the exemption for "specialised breakdown vehicle" in point 9 of Art. 4 of Reg. 543/69 meant a vehicle whose construction, fitments or other permanent characteristics were such that it would be used chiefly for removing vehicles that had recently been involved in an accident or had broken down for another reason. Such a vehicle was not subject to the requirements set by Art. 3(1) of Council Reg. 1463/70, whatever use was actually made of it by its owner.

HAMILTON *v.* WHITELOCK (No. 79/86) [1987] 3 C.M.L.R. 190 European Ct.

3308. Tachograph—exemption—burden of proof

[Transport Act 1968 (c.73), s.97(1)(7); Council Regulations (EEC) No. 543/69 art. 140(3)(*a*); No. 1463/70 art. 3(3); No. 2827/70 art. 1(8); No. 2828/77 art. 1; Community Road Transport Rules (Exemptions) Regulations 1978, regs. 1(2), 4(1)(3); Weights and Measures Act 1963 (c.31) Sched. 6 paras. 3(1), 3C(1)(2)(*a*)(*b*)(4); Weights and Measures Act 1976 (c.77), s.8, Sched. 4, para. 1; Passenger and Goods Vehicles (Recording Equipment) (Amendment) Regulations 1984, reg. 2(1)(2).]

Specialised vehicles which are exempted from tachograph requirements by reg. 4(3) of the Community Road Transport Rules (Exemptions) Regulations 1978 means vehicles designed or adapted for a special function and the purpose for which the vehicle is intended or in fact used is neither the sole nor the central consideration.

D, Coal merchants were engaged in the door-to-door selling of pre-bagged coal. D used two-axle goods vehicles with no special fitments. No tachographs were fitted. D contended that the lorries were specialised vehicles for the purposes of door-to-door selling and exempted under reg. 4(3)(*b*) of the Community Road Transport Rules (Exemptions) Regulations 1978, The charges against them were dismissed.

Held, allowing the appeal by the prosecution, that "specialised" was intended to cover vehicles whose construction, fitments or other permanent equipment guaranteed that they were held primarily for a specified occupation; the onus was on the defendants and the the case would be remitted to the justices to continue the hearing (*Oxford* v. *Thomas Scott and Sons Bakery* [1983] C.L.Y. 3808 and *Stewart* v. *Richards* 1983 S.L.T. 62 applied).

GAUNT *v.* NELSON [1987] R.T.R. 1, D.C.

3309. Traffic signs

TRAFFIC SIGNS GENERAL (AMENDMENT) DIRECTIONS 1987 (No. 1706) [45p], made under the Road Traffic Regulation Act 1984 (c.27), s.65(1); operative on October 15, 1987; amend S.I. 1981 No. 859.

3310. Type approval

MOTOR VEHICLES (TYPE APPROVAL) (AMENDMENT) REGULATIONS 1987 (No. 524) [45p], made under the European Communities Act 1972 (c.68), s.2(2); operative on April 22, 1987; amend S.I. 1980 No. 1182 in relation to rear view mirrors.

MOTOR VEHICLES (TYPE APPROVAL AND APPROVAL MARKS) (FEES) (AMENDMENT) REGULATIONS 1987 (No. 315) [£4·50], made under the Road Traffic Act 1972 (c.20), s.50(1) and the Finance Act 1973 (c.51), s.56(1); operative on April 1, 1987; amend S.I. 1984 No. 1404.

MOTOR VEHICLES (TYPE APPROVAL AND APPROVAL MARKS) (FEES) (AMENDMENT) (No. 2) REGULATIONS 1987 (No. 1556) [£1·60], made under the Road Traffic Act 1972 (c.20), s.50(1), and the Finance Act 1973 (c.51), s.56(1)(2); operative on October 1, 1987; further amend S.I. 1984 No. 1404.

MOTOR VEHICLES (TYPE APPROVAL FOR GOODS VEHICLES) (GREAT BRITAIN) (AMENDMENT) REGULATIONS 1987 (No. 1508) [£1·60], made under the Road Traffic Act 1972, ss.47(1), 50(1); operative on October 1, 1987, save for reg. 4 which is operative on January 1, 1988; further amend S.I. 1982 No. 1271.

MOTOR VEHICLES (TYPE APPROVAL) (GREAT BRITAIN) (AMENDMENT) REGULATIONS 1987 (No. 1509) [£1·30], made under the Road Traffic Act 1972, ss.47(1), 50(1); operative on October 1, 1987; further amend S.I. 1984 No. 981.

3311. Urine specimen—provision of urine specimens for doctor and police

[Road Traffic Act 1972 (c.20), s.8(5).]

At a police station a doctor, X, found it to be impracticable for N to provide specimens of breath or blood and requested N to provide a urine sample. X discarded that sample and concluded that there was no reason why N should not provide a urine specimen pursuant to s.8 of the 1972 Act. N then provided two specimens, the second of which was found to contain excess alcohol.

Held, dismissing N's appeal against conviction of driving with excess alcohol, that (1) the first specimen was not required under any statutory power; (2) s.8(5) of the Act enabled a third or even later specimen to be sent for analysis provided it was after provision of a previous specimen and within an hour of the request for a specimen of

urine under the Act (*Howard* v. *Hallett* [1985] C.L.Y. 2992 distinguished; *R.* v. *Hyams* [1972] C.L.Y. 3012 and *Gabrielson* v. *Hayes* [1975] Crim.L.R. 353 considered).
NUGENT *v.* RIDLEY [1987] Crim.L.R. 640, D.C.

SALE OF GOODS

3312. Agreement for sale—dealer obtaining car from owner to sell to client—dealer agreeing to sell to purchaser but never paid—whether property passed

[Sale of Goods Act 1979 (c.54), s.21.]

Good title could not pass to a purchaser under s.21 of the Sale of Goods Act 1979 from the original owner where the purchaser and seller merely entered into an agreement for the sale of the goods in question.

N was the owner of a Porsche motor car which he advertised for sale at a price of £17,250. He was approached by L who said he was a car dealer interested in purchasing the car on behalf of a client. N gave L possession of the car on April 16, 1984. On May 1, L agreed to sell the car to another dealer, S, for £11,500. £10,000 of the purchase price was to be paid by a bankers draft. S's representative accompanied L to the bank with the draft but the bank was unwilling to give L cash, whereupon L disappeared. L had given N a post-dated cheque for the car, in addition N had given L a document certifying that he had sold the car to L. In due course the police took possession of the car. Interpleader proceedings took place between S and N. N claimed that L had been in possession of the car as his agent to sell the same rather than as a purchaser of it. The master held that there was no sale and that L was N's agent. Accordingly N rather than S was entitled to the car.

Held, on S's appeal, there were no grounds upon which to interfere with the finding of fact that L was in possession of the car as N's agent. As L was not in possession as a buyer or pursuant to an agreement to buy the car, s.25 of the Sale of Goods Act 1979 did not operate so as to transfer a good title from L to S. There was clear evidence of a representation on N's part that L was authorised to sell the car. In the circumstances a good title would pass to S under s.21. of the Act if the car was "sold" by L to S. The words "where goods are sold" in s.21 did not include the situation where there was an uncompleted agreement to sell. In the present case as L had not purported to transfer the property in the car to S by the time he disappeared a good title did not pass to S under s.21 of the Act (*Central Newbury Car Auctions* v. *Unity Finance* [1956] C.L.Y. 7973, *Eastern Distributors* v. *Goldring* [1957] C.L.Y. 1308, *Worcester Works Finance* v. *Cooden Engineering Co.* [1971] C.L.Y. 10562 considered).

SHAW *v.* COMMISSIONER OF POLICE OF THE METROPOLIS [1987] 1 W.L.R. 1332, C.A.

3313. Consumer protection—asbestos products

ASBESTOS PRODUCTS (SAFETY) (AMENDMENT) REGULATIONS 1987 (No. 1979) [45p], made under the Consumer Protection Act 1987 (c.43), s.11(5); operative on January 1, 1988; implement Council Directive No. 85/610/EEC.

3314. Consumer protection—bunk beds

BUNK BEDS (ENTRAPMENT HAZARDS) (SAFETY) REGULATIONS 1987 (No. 1337) [£1·30], made under the Consumer Safety Act 1978 (c.38), s.1; operative on September 1, 1987; prohibits the sale or supply of bunk beds which do not conform with certain specified standards.

3315. Consumer protection—contracts concluded away from business premises

CONSUMER PROTECTION (CANCELLATION OF CONTRACTS CONCLUDED AWAY FROM BUSINESS PREMISES) REGULATIONS 1987 (No. 2117) [£1·60], made under the European Communities Act 1972 (c.68), s.2(2); operative on July 1, 1988; protect the consumer in respect of contracts made at the doorstep or otherwise concluded away from business premises.

3316. Consumer protection—cosmetic products

COSMETIC PRODUCTS (SAFETY) AMENDMENT REGULATION 1987 (No. 1920) [£3·30]. made under the Consumer Protection Act 1987 (c.43), s.11; operative on December 21. 1987; amend S.I. 1984 No. 1260.

3317. Consumer protection—nightwear

NIGHTWEAR (SAFETY) (AMENDMENT) REGULATIONS 1987 (No. 286) [45p], made under the Consumer Safety Act 1978 (c.38), s.1, Sched. 2, para. 13; operative on March

1, 1987; amends S.I. 1985 No. 2043 so that they come into force on September 1, 1987 in relation to babies' garments.

3318. Consumer protection—plugs and sockets

PLUGS AND SOCKETS ETC. (SAFETY) REGULATIONS 1987 (No. 603) [£1·90], made under the Consumer Safety Act 1978 (c.38), s.1, Sched. 2, para. 13; operative on September 1, 1987 or March 1, 1988 (according to application) and reg. 5(1) is operative on September 1, 1988; make provision for consumer safety in relation to plugs and sockets and prohibit their supply unless they conform with the requirements of the regulations.

3319. Consumer protection—safety standards

APPROVAL OF SAFETY STANDARDS REGULATIONS 1987 (No. 1911) [45p], made under the Consumer Protection Act 1987 (c.43), s.11; operative on December 7, 1987; make provision whereby the Secretary of State may approve standards of safety for the purposes of s.10(3) of the 1987 Act.

3320. Consumer protection—toys

BENZENE IN TOYS (SAFETY) REGULATIONS 1987 (No. 2216) [45p], made under the Consumer Protection Act 1987 (c.43), s.11; operative on December 31, 1987; prohibit the supply of toys which contain benzene in excess of a specified concentration.

3321. Consumer protection—whether defendants took all reasonable precautions and exercised all due diligence—whether positive act required

[Consumer Protection Act 1961 (c.40), s.3(2B); Pencils and Graphic Instruments (Safety) Regulations 1974 (S.I. 1974 No. 226).]

The respondents obtained pencils from a regular and reliable supplier. Random sampling would have been unreasonable. The order for the pencils contained a condition that they must conform with statutory safety requirements.

Held, allowing the prosecutor's appeal against acquittals of offences contrary to s.3(2A) of the 1961 Act (the pencils having contained soluble hexavalent chromium above the level permitted by the 1974 Regulations), that no reasonable magistrates could have concluded that the respondents had taken all reasonable precautions and exercised all due diligence to avoid commission of the offence. They should have obtained a positive assurance from the suppliers that the pencils conformed to the specific regulations governing their sale.

RILEY *v.* WEBB [1987] Crim.L.R. 477, D.C.

3322. Consumer Protection Act 1987 (c.43). See TORT, §3583.

3323. Consumer Safety Act 1978—commencement

CONSUMER SAFETY ACT 1978 (COMMENCEMENT No. 3) ORDER 1987 (No. 1681 (C.52)) [45p], made under the Consumer Safety Act 1978 (c.38), s.12(2); brings into force on October 1, 1987 s.10(1) of, and Sched. 3 to, the 1978 Act.

3324. Contract for sale—possession before paying—re-sale—presumption

Where B takes possession of goods under a contract for sale, but has not yet paid V for them, the ordinary rule is that he is entitled to sell them. If he does, the presumption is that he is selling on his own account, and not on behalf of V (*Aluminium Industrie Vaassen BV* v. *Romalpa Aluminium* [1976] C.L.Y. 2474 distinguished).

E. PFEIFFER WEINKELLEREI-WEINEINKAUF *v.* ARBUTHNOT FACTORS, *The Times,* March 11, 1987, Phillips J.

3325. Default by buyer—date of default for purposes of calculating damages

By an f.o.b. contract made on GAFTA 64/125 terms, B agreed to buy a parcel of Argentine wheat to be delivered in two parcels. The contract also incorporated the provisions of the Centro Exportadores contract. The latter contract contained provisions requiring 15 days notice of readiness to load to be given by B, and loading within 15 days of the last date named in the contract. GAFTA 65 provided that in the event of default, damages were to be based on the actual value of the goods on the date of default. In breach of contract B nominated four vessels to lift cargo, and then cancelled the fourth declaring themselves in default of the balance of contractual quantity. S did not accept the notice of default. There was thus a dispute as to the actual date of default.

Held, on a true construction of the various contractual provisions when read together, that (1) the date of default was the day after the last day for the performance of B's main obligations; (2) S was allowed to keep the contract open until the final date for performance by B, notwithstanding B's notice of default.

LUSOGRAIN COMERCIO INTERNACIONAL DE CEREAS *v.* BUNGE A.G. [1986] 2 Lloyd's Rep. 654, Staughton J.

3326. Duty of seller—export licence—absolute duty—force majeure

[GAFTA Form 119, cl.19.]

Even where there was an absolute duty placed upon sellers in a contract to provide for an export certificate, the sellers could be excused from that duty under the provisions of GAFTA Form 119, clause 19.

By a contract in November 1982 the sellers agreed to sell to Italian buyers 35,000 tonnes of Thai tapioca. It was a special condition of the contract that the sellers would provide for an export certificate, thereby enabling the buyers to obtain the necessary import licence to enable the tapioca to be imported into the EEC. The contract also incorporated GAFTA Form 119, which included a standard force majeure clause, providing that the contract or a part of it would be cancelled where the government of the country of origin by any executive or legislative act restricted export. Shortly before the contract, Thailand and the EEC introduced a quota system governing the export of tapioca which was enforced by regulations in Thailand. The sellers were unable to make shipments in April and May 1983 since the quotas were exhausted. The buyers claimed damages, and the claim was referred to arbitrators who found in their favour. That award was set aside by the GAFTA Board of Appeal which held that the seller were relieved of liability by clause 19 of GAFTA Form 119. The buyers appealed to the High Court. It was held that the special condition on the sellers to provide for an export certificate was on the construction of the contract an absolute obligation. They did not have a duty to use reasonable diligence only (dictum of Lloyd J. in *Coloniale Import-Export* v. *Loumidis Sons* [1979] C.L.Y. 2382 considered). On balance, however, the special condition was not inconsistent with clause 19 since although there was an absolute obligation to obtain an export certificate which gave rise to a prima facie claim for damages, the sellers were excused from liability if they showed that the case was within the scope of clause 19. Further, there was no clear intention to override cl.19. The question whether the sellers were excused by clause 19 was one of fact, which the GAFTA Board of Appeal had determined in favour of the sellers. The appeal was therefore dismissed.

PAGNAN SpA *v.* TRADAX OCEAN TRANSPORTATION S.A. [1987] 1 All E.R. 81, Steyn J.

3327. Fitness for purpose—manufacturer's instructions—reasons for instructions—whether necessary

[Sale of Goods Act 1979 (c.54), s.14.]

If a manufacturer gives instructions for the use of his product, he need not give reasons for the instructions.

P, a farmer, bought D Co.'s herbicide. On the container the instructions warned that damage might occur to crops if used after the recommended growth stage. P used the herbicide late and it proved ineffective. P claimed that D Co. were in breach of the implied terms as to merchantable quality and fitness for purpose under s.14 of the Sale of Goods Act 1979. The deputy judge gave judgment for P.

Held, allowing the appeal, that a specific warning as to possible damage did not entitle P to make any assumption as to effectiveness, and D Co. could not be expected to give reasons for their instructions.

WORMELL *v.* R.H.M. AGRICULTURE (EAST) [1987] 1 W.L.R. 1091, C.A.

3328. F.o.b. contract—buyers opened letter of credit—sellers failed to comply with terms of credit—whether sellers could recover against buyers for non-payment

In this case, P, a seller of goods f.o.b. who had contracted for payment to be made under a letter of credit to be opened by the buyer, D, failed to recover the price of the goods from B in circumstances where P had failed to comply with the terms of the contract as to the provision of documentation.

Held, that P had failed to comply with the terms of the credit. Such failure was the cause of their inability to recover the contract price and they could not recover against D personally.

SHAMSHER JUTE MILLS *v.* SETHIA (LONDON) [1987] 1 Lloyd's Rep. 388, Bingham J.

3329. F.o.b. sale—requirement for letter of credit—whether waived—whether a condition or not—time of the essence—summary judgment

This case concerned an application for summary judgment by S, who agreed to sell a quantity of oil f.o.b. Sullom Voe, to B. Payment was to be by letter of credit, opened at least 10 days before the declared layday range, and S was to provide a letter of indemnity. Notwithstanding various communications, B never opened the letter of credit.

S claimed summary judgment, but Hirst J. held that B had an arguable case that the various communications lifted obligations as to the deadline and S should have imposed a reasonable further deadline. Hirst J. gave unconditional leave to defend. S applied for leave to appeal.

Held, that (1) the requirement for the letter of credit to be opened was in the nature of a condition where time was of the essence unless waived; (2) S gave B certain extensions of time but never waived the right to treat the requirement for a L/C as a condition. There was, on the facts, no express or implied waiver. B had no arguable defence.

NICHIMEN CORP. *v.* GATOIL OVERSEAS INC. [1987] 2 Lloyd's Rep. 46, C.A.

3330. F.o.b. sale on GAFTA terms—buyer purported to reject goods whilst at the same time accepting them—goods not of contract description—whether seller could recover balance of price

By a sale contract made on GAFTA terms, S sold cottonseed f.o.b. Ascuncion to B. B contended that the contract contained a term that the goods were rejectable if fat exceeded 15 per cent. B initiated a letter of credit reflecting that requirement. B purported to reject the goods on grounds that the fat content was in excess of 15 per cent., but in the event took them up and sold them. They did not, however, pay the balance of the contract price. S sought to recover the balance. The Board of Appeal of GAFTA held they were not entitled to do so. S appealed.

Held, allowing the appeal, that although the contract did contain a term relating to the fat content of the cottonseed, B did not in fact reject the goods, taking up the documents as they had. This conduct was inconsistent with rejection and S was entitled to the balance of the price.

VARGAS PENA APEZTEGUIA Y CIA SAIC *v.* PETER CREMER GmbH [1987] 1 Lloyd's Rep. 394, Saville J.

3331. GAFTA contract—failure to take joint samples—refusal to look at result of unilateral testing—whether such results admissible

By a contract incorporating GAFTA 102 and 125 B purchased soya bean meal from S. The contract contained provisions as to quality and specification and provided that samples were to be drawn "jointly by S and B." The vessel arrived in England and B noticed that the cargo was off-colour. They drew samples of the cargo and their sub-buyers rejected it. They refused to pay S. The matter was referred to arbitration, and the GAFTA Board of Appeal refused to take into account the buyers' samples. They only looked at samples taken by GAFTA analysts. B contended that their samples were admissible.

Held, allowing B's appeal, that nothing in the contract provided that the joint sampling of cargo was to be conclusive, and that evidence should have been considered by the arbitrators.

FORD (CHARLES E.) *v.* AFEC INC. [1986] 2 Lloyd's Rep. 307, Bingham J.

3332. Hire purchase—recovery of goods—informed consent to recovery

[Hire Purchase Act 1965 (c.66), ss.33, 34.]

The re-possession of goods by an H.P. company without a court order was a contravention of s.34 unless the hirer had given an informed and unqualified consent of the re-possession (*Bridge* v. *Campbell Discount Co.* [1962] C.L.Y. 1397, *United Dominions Trust (Commercial)* v. *Ennis* [1967] C.L.Y. 1827, *Mercantile Credit Co.* v. *Cross* [1965] C.L.Y. 1815 considered).

CHARTERED TRUST *v.* PITCHER, *The Independent,* February 13, 1987, C.A.

3333. Implied terms—fitness for purpose and merchantability—motor car roadworthy but seriously defective—rejection after six months

[Sale of Goods Act 1979 (c.54), s.14(2)(6).]

Where a vehicle is sold as new, but is seriously defective, it is not to be taken as being of merchantable quality and fit for its purpose just because it is capable of being driven and the defects repaired.

P bought a new Range Rover which contained a number of serious defects on delivery. During a six month period, P drove the car about 5,500 miles while a number of (generally unsuccessful) attempts were made to rectify the defects. P then repudiated the contract and sought repayment of all sums paid under the conditional sale agreement and damages.

Held, that where goods as delivered are defective, they are not of merchantable quality and do not become so simply because they are capable of being used in some way. When a new car is bought the purchaser is entitled to get it to give the pleasure, pride and performance he expected. Defects which might be acceptable in a second hand vehicle would not be acceptable in a new car. The car was not as fit for its purpose as P expected and he was entitled to reject it.

ROGERS *v.* PARISH (SCARBOROUGH) [1987] 2 W.L.R. 353, C.A.

3334. International sales—uniform laws

UNIFORM LAWS ON INTERNATIONAL SALES ORDER 1987 (No. 2061) [45p], made under the Uniform Laws on International Sales Act 1967 (c.45), s.1(5); operative on January 1, 1988; provides a replacement schedule to S.I. 1972 No. 973.

3335. Major breakdown of new car—whether of merchantable quality—full repair—whether buyer entitled to reject—lapse of time

[Sale of Goods Act 1979 (c.54), ss.11(4), 14(2)(6), 35(1).]

When considering whether a new car is of merchantable quality the Court should consider whether the car can be driven safely, the ease or otherwise of repairing the defect, whether it *can* be completely repaired, whether there are a number of minor defects and possibly any cosmetic factors. Any rejection of the car, however, must be within a reasonable time of taking delivery.

B bought a new Nissan motor car, which about three weeks after delivery broke down on the motorway; it had done 140 miles. B advised PM that he rejected the car as not being of merchantable quality. PM repaired the car, so that it was as good as new, but B refused to have it back. B claimed rescission and damages.

Held, that B was not entitled to rescind, but could claim damages limited to his cost in getting home after the breakdown, the loss of a full tank of petrol, compensation for his ruined day out, and for his loss of use while the car was being repaired (five days). When required to determine whether a car was unmerchantable the Court should consider (i) whether the car can be driven safely, (ii) the ease or otherwise of repairing the defect, (iii) whether the defect *can* be completely repaired, (iv) whether there are a number of minor defects and possibly (v) any cosmetic factors which appear to be relevant. On that approach the car was *not* of merchantable quality. B had, however, lost his right to reject because he had had the car for three weeks and had driven it for 140 miles: he had thus had sufficient time to try the car.

BERNSTEIN *v.* PAMSON MOTORS (GOLDERS GREEN) [1987] 2 All E.R. 220, Rougier J.

3336. Merchantable quality—description of goods—right to reject

S sold to B a quantity of pure prime pressed cocoa butter. Documents were tendered by S to B which suggested that the goods would not conform with the contract and it was agreed that they would be inspected. B rejected the goods, but their claim in arbitration failed, as it was held that the goods complied with their description. B appealed, contending that the goods were not of merchantable quality.

Held, that by agreeing to an inspection of the goods solely for the purpose of ascertaining whether they were of the contractual description, B could not thereafter contend that they obtained an independent right to reject the goods for want of merchantable quality.

KURKJIAN (S.N.) (COMMODITY BROKERS) *v.* MARKETING EXCHANGE FOR AFRICA (FORMERLY MOTIRAM (T.M.) (U.K.) (No. 1)) [1986] 2 Lloyd's Rep. 614, Staughton J.

3337. Merchantable quality—fitness for purpose—foreseeability of damage

[Sale of Goods Act 1979 (c.54), s.14(2)(3)(6).]

S.14(6) of the Sale of Goods Act 1979 has not brought about any substantial change in the law; goods are merchantable if they are as fit for any of the purposes for which they are commonly bought as it is reasonable to expect having regard to their description and other relevant circumstances.

P bought waterproofing compound from D for shipment to Kuwait. D selected the plastic pails in which the compound was shipped. On arrival the pails were left out in the heat and they melted. The entire consignment was lost.

Held, that (1) section 14(6) of the Sale of Goods Act 1979 had not brought about any substantial change in the law; goods were merchantable if they were as fit for any of the purposes for which they were commonly bought as it was reasonable to expect having regard to their description and other relevant circumstances. The pails were suitable for exporting the compound, and there was no breach of the section if they collapsed under extreme climatic conditions; (2) the pails were reasonably fit for use as heavy duty pails in export shipment under s.14(3) and (3) the damage to the compound was not reasonably foreseeable and was outside D's duty of care (*Hardwick Game Farm* v. *Suffolk Agricultural Poultry Producers Association* [1968] C.L.Y. 3526 applied; *Muirhead* v. *Industrial Tank Specialities* [1986] C.L.Y. 2270 distinguished).

M/S ASWAN ENGINEERING ESTABLISHMENT CO. *v.* LUPDINE [1987] 1 W.L.R. 1 C.A.

3338. Merchantable quality—purchase of motor-car—former insurance write-off—history not disclosed

[Sale of Goods Act 1979 (c.54), s.14.]

A motor-car is not of merchantable quality where it has been an insurance write-off and the ordinary manufacturers' rust warranty has been terminated by reason of an accident whereby the car became submerged in water.

SHINE *v.* GENERAL GUARANTEE CORP., *The Times*, August 18, 1987, C.A.

3339. Non-fulfilment—FOSFA 80 contract—meaning of default clause 21

C bought crude oil from S under the terms of a FOSFA contract the "default clause" of which provided that damages awarded against the defaulter shall be limited to the difference between the contract price and the market price on the day of default. C claimed the difference between the contract price and the price at which they had agreed to re-sell the goods. The FOSFA Board of Appeal refused to accede to such a contention, and C appealed.

Held, "market price" meant that price obtainable in an available market on the day of default. The arbitrator had applied the clause correctly.

C. CZARNIKOW *v.* BUNGE & CO. SAME *v.* CARGILL B.V.; BUNGE & CO. *v.* KROHN & CO.; IMPORT-EXPORT G.M.B.H & CO. K.G. [1987] 1 Lloyd's Rep. 202, Saville J.

3340. Price marking

PRICE MARKING (PETROL) (AMENDMENT) ORDER 1987 (No. 8) [45p], made under the Prices Act 1974 (c.24), s.4(3); operative on March 1, 1987; amends S.I. 1980 No. 112 by bringing unleaded petrol within the scope of the order.

3341. Remoteness of damage—loss caused by sub-sales of unmerchantable goods

The seller of unmerchantable goods may be liable in damages for economic loss occasioned by the buyer having to pay compensation to others to whom the goods were re-sold if the re-sale of the goods was within the reasonable contemplation of the seller.

DANECROFT JERSEY MILLS *v.* CRIEGEE, *The Times,* April 14, 1987, C.A.

3342. Sale and Supply of Goods—Law Commissioners Report. See LAW REFORM, §2276.

3343. Seller of unfit food—reliance upon supplier's warranty—whether goods in same state throughout. See GATEWAY FOODMARKETS *v.* SIMMONDS, §1815.

3344. Supply of fireworks—"apparently" under age of 16. See SARWAN SINGH DEU *v.* DUDLEY METROPOLITAN BOROUGH COUNCIL, §836.

3345. Title stolen vehicle—later purchased in good faith

[Factors Act 1889 (c.45), ss.2, 9; Sale of Goods Act 1979 (c.54), ss.2, 25(1), 61(1).]

N Co. were insurers of a car which was stolen and, after two resales, was bought by A Co., who sold it to M Co., who in turn sold it to J. who bought in good faith and without notice of the original owner's rights. Having paid the original owner, N Co. claimed the car from J. J claimed he had obtained good title from M Co., under s.9 of the 1889 Act.

Held, that although the seller under s.9 did not have to be the true owner, he had at least to have general property in the goods before passing them on. Since M Co. could not have obtained this from A Co., N Co. were entitled to the car (*Pacific Motor Auctions Pty.* v. *Motor Credits* [1965] C.L.Y. 3529, *Elwin* v. *O'Regan and Maxwell* [1971] N.Z.L.R. 1124, *Brandon* v. *Leckie* [1972] 29 D.L.R. (3d) 633 and dictum of Denning L.J. in *Pearson* v. *Rose and Young* (1947–1951) C.L.C. 85 followed; *Du Jardin* v. *Beadman Bros.* [1952] C.L.Y 33 and *Newtons of Wembley* v. *Williams* [1964] C.L.Y. 3288 distinguished).

NATIONAL EMPLOYERS MUTUAL GENERAL INSURANCE ASSOCIATION *v.* JONES [1987] 3 All E.R. 385, C.A.

3346. Trade descriptions. See CRIMINAL LAW.

SEA AND SEASHORE

3347. Continental shelf—extended territorial sea

CONTINENTAL SHELF (DESIGNATED AREAS) (EXTENDED TERRITORIAL SEA) ORDER 1987 (No. 1265) [45p], made under the Continental Shelf Act 1964 (c.29), s.1(7), and the Territorial Sea Act 1987 (c.49), s.3(3); operative October 1, 1987; makes clear that Orders affecting areas designated by s.1(7) of the Continental Shelf Act 1964 shall no longer affect those parts of the designated areas which are brought within the limits of the territorial sea by the Territorial Sea Act 1987, but the Orders will continue to apply to those designated areas not brought within the limits of the territorial sea.

3348. Marine pollution—Food and Environment Protection Act 1985—extension

FOOD AND ENVIRONMENT PROTECTION ACT 1985 (GUERNSEY) ORDER 1987 (No. 665) [£1·40], made under the Food and Environment Protection Act 1985 (c.48), s.26(1)(2); operative on May 1, 1987; extends Pts. II and IV of the 1985 Act to Guernsey.

FOOD AND ENVIRONMENT PROTECTION ACT 1985 (ISLE OF MAN) ORDER 1987 (No. 666) [£1·40], made under the Food and Environment Protection Act 1985 (c.48), s.26(1)(2); operative on May 1, 1987; extends Pts. II and IV of the 1985 Act to the Isle of Man.

FOOD AND ENVIRONMENT PROTECTION ACT 1985 (JERSEY) ORDER 1987 (No. 667) [£1·40], made under the Food and Environment Protection Act 1985 (c.48), s.26(1))2); operative on May 1, 1987; extends Pts. II and IV of the 1985 Act to Jersey.

3349. Offshore activities—civil jurisdiction

CIVIL JURISDICTION (OFFSHORE ACTIVITIES) ORDER 1987 (No. 2197) [85p], made under the Oil and Gas (Enterprise) Act 1982 (c.23), s.23 and the Continental Shelf Act 1964 (c.29), ss.6, 7; operative on February 1, 1988; divides the U.K. territorial waters and the U.K. continental shelf into English, Scottish and Northern Irish parts and confers civil jurisdiction on the courts of those countries.

3350. Offshore activities—criminal jurisdiction

CRIMINAL JURISDICTION (OFFSHORE ACTIVITIES) ORDER 1987 (No. 2198) [45p], made under the Oil and Gas (Enterprise) Act 1982, s.22(1)(2); operative on February 1, 1988; applies English Scottish and Northern Irish criminal law to relevant activities taking place on under above or within 500 metres of off-shore installations situated in U.K. territorial waters and the U.K. continental shelf.

3351. Offshore installations

OFFSHORE INSTALLATIONS (SAFETY ZONES) REGULATIONS 1987 (No. 1331) [45p], made under the Petroleum Act 1987 (c.12), s.23(1)(*b*); operative on September 1, 1987; specify circumstances in which the prohibition in s.23 of the 1987 Act on vessels entering safety zones established under ss.21, 22 is not to apply.

Orders made under the Oil and Gas (Enterprise) Act 1982 (c.23), s.21(1)–(3):

S.I. 1987 Nos. 4 (amends S.I. 1986 No. 1199–22–FE—operative on January 9, 1987) [45p]; 54 (Well 16/21a–7z—operative on January 24, 1987) [45p]; 55 (Well 16/21a–16—operative on January 24, 1987) [45p]; 56 (Well 16/21b–4A—operative on January 24, 1987) [45p]; 57 (Well 16/21b–12—operative on January 24, 1987) [45p]; 58 (Well 16/21b–14—operative on January 24, 1987) [45p]; 59 (Balmoral Template—operative on January 24, 1987) [45p]; 61 (Indefatigable 49/24N—operative on January 24, 1987) [45p]; 62 (Well 30/24–24—operative on January 24, 1987) [45p]; 66 (Well 30/24–32—operative on January 24, 1987) [45p]; 67 (Bowan Gorilla II—operative on January 24, 1987) [45p]; 68 (Drillstar—operative on January 24, 1987) [45p]; 69 (M.G. Hulme Jr—operative on January 24, 1987) [45p]; 70 (Ocean Bounty—operative on January 24, 1987) [45p]; 71 (Sedco 7/4—operative on January 24, 1987) [45p]; 72 (Stadrill—operative on January 24, 1987) [45p]; 200 (Audrey Template—operative on January 14, 1987) [45p]; 201 (Benvrackie—operative on February 14, 1987) [45p]; 202 (Dan Earl—operative on February 14, 1987) [45p]; 203 (High Seas Driller—operative on February 14, 1987) [45p]; 204 (Ocean Benarnin—operative on February 14, 1987) [45p]; 205 (Sedreth 701—operative on February 14, 1987) [45p]; 206 (Treasure Seeker—operative on February 14, 1987) [45p]; 591 (Arch Rowan—operative on March 28, 1987) [45p]; 592 (Benreoch—operative on March 28, 1987) [45p], 593 (F.G. McClintock—operative on March 28, 1987) [45p]; 594 (Sea Explorer—operative on March 28, 1987) [45p]; 713 (BP Cleeton 42/29—operative on April 15, 1987) [45p]; 812 (Brae B 16/7A—operative on May 8, 1987) [45p]; 813 (Conoco Valiant 49/21 PTD—operative on May 8, 1987) [45p]; 814 (Conoco/Britoil Loggs 49/16 P—operative on May 8, 1987) [45p]; 974 (Benvrackie—operative on May 21, 1987) [45p]; 975 (Britannia—operative on May 21, 1987) [45p]; 976 (Drillstar—operative on May 21, 1987) [45p]; 977 Galveston Key—operative on May 21, 1987) [45p]; 978 (High Seas Driller—operative on May 21, 1987) [45p]; 979 (Ocean Benarmin—operative on May 21, 1987) [45p]; 980 (Rowan Gorilla II—operative on May 21, 1987) [45p]; 981 (Santa Fe 140—operative on May 21, 1987) [45p]; 982 (Sedco 703—operative on May 21, 1987) [45p]; 983 (Sedco 704—operative on May 21, 1987) [45p]; 984 (Sedco 707—operative on May 21, 1987) [45p]; 985 (Sedco 714—operative on May 21, 1987) [45p]; 986 (Sednett 701—operative on May 21, 1987) [45p]; 987 (Treasure Seeker—operative on May 21, 1987) [45p]; 988 (Western Pacesetter IV—operative on May 21, 1987) [45p]; 1094

(Vulcan I 49/21—PRD—operative on June 26, 1987) [45p]; 1095 (Vanguard 49/16—PQD—operative on June 26, 1987) [45p]; 1400 (Arch Rowan—operative on August 6, 1987) [45p]; 1401 (Benreoch—operative on August 6, 1987) [45p]; 1402 (Beryl Field WISS—operative on August 6, 1987) [45p]; 1403 (Beryl 9/13 B NESS—operative on August 6, 1987) [45p]; 1404 (Cecil Provine—operative on August 6, 1987) [45p]; 1405 (Dan Earl—operative on August 6, 1987) [45p]; 1406 (Sonat DF96—operative on August 6, 1987) [45p]; 1407 (Drillstar—operative on August 6, 1987) [45p]; 1408 (Glomar Arctic III—operative on August 6, 1987) [45p]; 1409 (Glomar Moray Firth I—operative on August 6, 1987) [45p]; 1410 (High Seas Driller—operative on August 6, 1987) [45p]; 1411 (Ocean Bounty—operative on August 6, 1987) [45p]; 1412 (Ocean Nomad—operative on August 6, 1987) [45p]; 1413 (Ocean Victory—operative on August 6, 1987) [45p]; 1414 (Penrod 92—operative on August 6, 1987) [45p]; 1415 (Rowan Gorilla II—operative on August 6, 1987) [45p]; 1416 (Rowan Halifax—operative on August 6, 1987) [45p]; 1418 (Sedco 707—operative on August 6, 1987) [45p]; 1419 (Trident XI—operative on August 6, 1987) [45p]; 1420 (Western Pacesetter IV—operative on August 6, 1987) [45p].

Orders made under the Petroleum Act 1987 (c.12), s.22(1)(2):

S.I. 1987 No. 1332 (South Cormorant Well W4, P5, South Cormorant A UML, South Cormorant Well P1, Beryl Well 9/13–15, 9/13–20B, 9/13–6A, 9/13–1, 9/13A–24, Balmoral Well 16/21b–12, 16/21a–7z, 16/21a–16, 16/21b–14, 16/21b–4A, Buchan Well 21/1–10, 21/1–8, Innes Well 30/24–32, 30/24–24, Duncan Well 30/24–19, Argyll Well 30/24–18, 30/24–15, 30/24–5, 30/24–14, Duncan Manifold, Duncan Well 30/24–22, Argyll Well, 30/24–17, Audrey Template, Thames Well 49/28–01, Hewett Well 48/30–8, Thames Well 49/28–C1, Hewett Well 48–30–9, Claymore Template T1, T3, Scapa Template, Texaco Highlander Well 14/20, Petronella Wellhead, Buchan Well 20/5a–1, Morecambe Bay Well 110/2A–8, 110/2A–7—operative on September 1, 1987) [85p]; 2016 (Beryl Field WISS—operative on November 27, 1987) [45p]; 2017 (Beryl 9/13B NESS—operative on November 27, 1987) [45p].

3352. Offshore installations—revocation

Orders made under the Oil and Gas (Enterprise) Act 1982 (c.23), s.21(1):

S.I. 1987 53 (S.I. 1986 No. 1842—Penrod 92, S.I. 1986 No. 1841—Pentagone 84, S.I. 1984 No. 2011—Transworld 58—operative on January 24, 1987) [45p]; 199 (S.I. 1986 No. 1741—Dyvi Omega, S.I. 1986 No. 1839—Dyvi Sigma, S.I. 1986 No. 2052—Penrod 80, S.I. 1986 No. 1464—Penrod 85, S.I. 1987 No. 67—Rowan Gorilla 11, S.I. 1987 No. 71—Sedco 714—operative on February 14, 1987) [45p]; 595 (S.I.) 1986 No. 1746—Neddrill Trigon, S.I. 1986 No. 2057 —Ocean Nomad, S.I. 1986 No. 2058—Safe Supporter, S.I. 1986 No. 2059—Trident X—operative on March 28, 1987) [45p]; 989 (S.I. 1986 No. 1132—Cecil Provine, S.I. 1987 No. 202 Dan Earl, S.I. 1987 No. 70—Ocean Bounty, S.I. 1986 No. 1844—Sedco 700—operative on May 21, 1987) [45p]; 1399 (S.I. 1987 Nos. 974—Benrackie; 69—M G Hulme Jr.; 979—Ocean Benarmin; 981—Santa Fe 140; 982—Sedco 703; 985—Sedco 714; 986—Sedneth 701; 987—Treasure Seeker—operative on August 6, 1987) [45p].

3353. Offshore installations—safety

OFFSHORE INSTALLATIONS (LIFE-SAVING APPLIANCES AND FIRE-FIGHTING EQUIPMENT) (AMENDMENT) REGULATIONS 1987 (No. 129) [45p], made under the Mineral Workings (Offshore Installations) Act 1971 (c.61), s.6; operative on March 1, 1987; amend S.I. 1977 No. 486 and S.I. 1978 No. 611 in relation to fees payable in respect of examiners of installations.

3354. Oil and Gas (Enterprise) Act 1982—amendment

OIL AND GAS (ENTERPRISE) ACT 1982 (COMMENCEMENT No. 4) ORDER 1987 (No. 2272 (c.69)) [45p], made under the Oil and Gas (Enterprise) Act 1982 (c.23), s.38(2); brings into force on February 1, 1988 ss.22, 23 (remaining parts), 27(1)(*a*), 37 (in part), Sched. 3, paras. 2, 3, 34, 42, 43, Sched. 4 (in part).

3355. Territorial Sea

TERRITORIAL SEA (LIMITS) ORDER 1987 (No. 1269) [45p], made under the Territorial Sea Act 1987 (c.49), s.1(2); operative October 1, 1987; establishes the seaward limit of the territorial sea adjacent to the U.K. in the narrow part of the Straits of Dover and in the vicinity of the Isle of Man.

3356. Territorial Sea Act 1987 (c.49)

This Act provides for the extent of the territorial sea adjacent to the British Islands.

The Act received the Royal Assent on May 15, 1987, and will come into force on days to be appointed by Her Majesty by Order in Council.

The Act extends to Northern Ireland. S.4(4) provides for the extension of the provisions of the Act to the Channel Islands or to the Isle of Man.

3357. Territorial Sea Act 1987—commencement

TERRITORIAL SEA ACT 1987 (COMMENCEMENT) ORDER 1987 (No. 1270 (C.40)) [45p], made under the Territorial Sea Act 1987 (c.49), s.4(2); brings the 1987 Act into force on October 1, 1987.

SHIPPING AND MARINE INSURANCE

3358. Admiralty and Commercial Court Registry—administrative arrangements—practice direction. See PRACTICE, §2875.

3359. Admiralty jurisdiction—Gibraltar

ADMIRALTY JURISDICTIONS (GIBRALTAR) ORDER 1987 (No. 1263) [85p], made under the Supreme Court Act 1981 (c.54), s.150, the Merchant Shipping (Oil Pollution) Act 1971 (c.59), s.18(1), the Merchant Shipping Act 1974 (c.43), s.20(1), and the Merchant Shipping Act 1894 (c.60), s.738(1); operative on August 19, 1987; provides that the Supreme Court of Gibraltar shall have the like Admiralty jurisdiction as that of the High Court in England.

3360. Admiralty practice—action *in rem*—jurisdiction—claim in respect of goods or materials supplied to a ship for her operation or maintenance—claim in respect of container agreement

[Supreme Court Act 1981 (c.54), ss.20(2)(*m*), 21(4).]

Under an agreement the plaintiffs leased to the defendant containers which were delivered to shippers at specified depots and used interchangeably on a number of vessels owned or chartered by the defendants. The plaintiffs brought an action *in rem* for damages for breach of agreement and one of the defendant's ships was arrested. S.20(2)(*m*) of the Supreme Court Act 1981 gives the Admiralty Court jurisdiction in any claim in respect of goods supplied to a ship for her operation and an action *in rem* could be brought against the ship in connection with which the claim arose. The defendant applied for the writ to be struck out and the ship released on the ground that the plaintiff's claim did not lie within the jurisdiction of the Admiralty Court.

Held, on appeal from the judge's dismissal of the application; that it was necessary for there to be a sufficiently direct connection between the agreement and the purpose of the ship for s.20(2)(*m*) to apply. The true purpose of the agreement was for the defendant to be able to provide packaging at the convenience of the shippers. The containers were not sufficiently closely connected with the defendant's ships to bring the plaintiff's claim within the jurisdiction of s.20(2)(*m*). It had not been established that the defendant was the beneficial owner or charterer of the ship when the cause of action arose and accordingly there was insufficient evidence to justify the ship's arrest (*Gatoil International Inc. v. Arkwright-Boston Manufacturers Mutual Insurance Co.* [1985] C.L.Y. 3204 applied; *Sonia S, The* [1983] C.L.Y. 3377 not followed).

RIVER RIMA THE, [1987] 3 All E.R. 1, C.A.

3361. Admiralty practice—action *in rem*—related proceedings *in personam* against owners in foreign court for damage to cargo on sister ship—jurisdiction

[Convention on Jurisdiction and the Enforcement of Judgments in Civil and Commercial Matters 1968, Art. 21; Hague-Visby Rules, Art. 3, r.6.]

Art. 3, r. 6, of the Hague-Visby Rules provides that a ship shall be discharged from all liability in respect of goods carried unless suit is brought within one year of delivery. Where it is sought to bring proceedings *in rem* in England more than a year after delivery, suit has been brought within the period for the purpose of the rule if an action *in personam* was started against the shipowners in a foreign court of competent jurisdiction within a year. Although the action *in rem* might be related to the foreign action *in personam*, it does not come within the definition of *lis pendens* in Art. 21 of the Convention on Jurisdiction and the Enforcement of Judgments in Civil and Commercial Matters 1968. A court cannot decline jurisdiction in an action *in rem* on the grounds that related proceedings *in personam* against her owners for damage to cargo on a sister ship have been started in a foreign court.

NORDGLIMT, THE, *Financial Times*, August 11, 1987, Hobhouse J.

3362. Admiralty practice—arrest of vessel—arbitration already commenced—whether arrest should stand

[Civil Jurisdiction and Judgments Act 1982 (c.27), s.26.]

P and D referred disputes arising out of a charterparty to arbitration in 1985. D did not provide security for P's claim, and P arrested one of D's ships. D contended that the arrest was an abuse of the process, as the parties claims had been referred to arbitration prior to the arrest

Held, that the Plaintiffs were entitled to arrest pursuant to s.26 of the Civil Jurisdiction and Judgments Act 1982.

JALAMATSYA, THE [1987] 2 Lloyd's Rep. 164, Sheen J.

3363. Admiralty practice—arrest of vessel—delay in prosecution of action—whether arrest should be lifted on application of Marshal

In this case P had arrested a vessel upon a repair claim. D acknowledged service, but although the pleadings were closed, the action proceeded no further. The vessel remained under arrest for two years until the Admiralty Registrar applied to have it released and for an order that he withdraw.

Held, that although no release would be ordered in this case, it was not the function of the Marshal to be a ship-keeper for an indefinite period, and in future where there was delay in prosecuting an action the court would order the release from arrest of the vessel.

ITALY II, THE [1987] 2 Lloyd's Rep. 162, Sheen J.

3364. Admiralty practice—arrest of vessel—plaintiffs incurred costs in arresting and preserving vessel—vessel sold and proceeds paid into Court—whether plaintiffs entitled to immediate payment out of funds in Court

D's vessel was lost and P, who had chartered the vessel, issured a writ *in rem* against a sister ship. The action was stayed (there being an arbitration clause in the charterparty) but the vessel was retained as security for any award that might be obtained against her owners. The vessel was then appraised and sold pendente lite, and P (who had paid all the costs of the arrest to date) paid off and repatriated the crew with the leave of the Court. B, a bank, had a mortgage over the arrested vessel which far exceeded the proceeds of sale thereof. B moved the Court for judgment, and P applied for an order that all the expenses of the arrest and preservation of the vessel be paid out to them forthwith. B contended that P was not entitled to recover any monies until B had obtained judgment in their action.

Held, that (1) as the Plaintiffs had given the Marshal an undertaking to pay all of the costs of the arrest, which they had honoured, there could be no injustice in them obtaining immediate payment of those sums. They had an absolute priority to those sums as arrestors in any event; (2) the insurance effected by P on the vessel whilst under arrest only benefited themselves and they did not have any priority in respect of premiums paid; (3) sums would be retained in Court pending proof by P of the actual wages due to the crew members which they had paid off.

WORLD STAR, THE [1987] 1 Lloyd's Rep. 452, Sheen J.

3365. Admiralty practice—collision action—stay of action on grounds that Egypt natural forum—filing of preliminary acts by defendants in English action

In 1981 there was a collision in Alexendria Harbour between P's vessel I and D's vessel M. I was Moroccan. M was Egyptian. P commenced proceedings in England, and arrested a sister ship of the M. Security was put up by D and they acknowledged service. Both P and D filed preliminary acts in the English proceedings, and then D applied for a stay of the action, contending that Alexandria was a more convenient and appropriate forum for the resolution of the disputes.

Held, that a stay would not be granted. Some delay could be expected if the action was stayed, and D had shown a willingness to litigate in England by filing a preliminary act. Although Alexandria was the natural forum for the resolution of the dispute, there was no genuine desire on the part of D to litigate there.

SIDI BISHR, THE [1987] 1 Lloyd's Rep. 42, Sheen J.

3366. Admiralty practice—remuneration of nautical and other assessors—practice direction. See PRACTICE, §2877.

3367. Admiralty practice—salvage arbitration—cargo owners contended that not bound by LOF—interlocutory injunction to restrain arbitration

Salvage services were ordered to a vessel and her cargo in Argentina, by a Greek salvor (who subcontracted local tugs). The services were provided on the terms of

Lloyd's Open Form ("LOF"), which provided for London arbitration. It was signed by the master of the vessel for and on behalf of her owners and the cargo owners (P). Various telexes were exchanged between salvors and P, all on the basis that there was a subsisting arbitration agreement, and the Committee of Lloyd's obtained security and appointed an arbitrator. On the day of the appointment, P raised the point that the LOF was not binding upon them, in that the master of the vessel had had no authority to conclude it on their behalf. P sought an injunction to restrain the salvors from proceeding with the arbitration. Sheen J. refused to grant the injunction, and P appealed.

Held, dismissing the appeal, that (1) all the parties had initially proceeded on the basis that there would be an injunction and that there was no sufficient reason for replacing one set of proceedings (the arbitration) with another (a court action); (2) on the balance of convenience, that arbitration should continue.

INDUSTRIE CHIMICHE ITALIA CENTRALE *v.* ALEXANDER G. TSAVLIRIS & SONS MARITIME CO.; PANCRISTO SHIPPING CO. S.A. AND BULA SHIPPING CORP.; CHOKO STAR, THE [1987] 1 Lloyd's Rep. 508, C.A.

3368. Admiralty practice—stay of action—subsequent further arrest of vessel—security in arbitration proceedings

[Civil Jurisdiction and Judgments Act 1982 (c.27) s.26.]

The Admiralty Court had, in 1984, stayed an action *in rem* against the vessel "S.A." which had been brought to obtain security in arbitration proceedings. Since that date s.26 of the Civil Jurisdiction and Judgments Act 1982 had come into force, and P applied for the stay to be lifted for the purpose of providing security in the arbitration.

Held, that (1) the second arrest which had been effeced by P was not a nullity; (2) the court had power to order the retention of property as security in arbitration proceedings, and would do so in this case.

SILVER ATHENS (No. 2), THE [1986] 2 Lloyd's Rep. 583, Sheen J.

3369. Admiralty practice—vessel arrested to provide security in arbitration—previous arrest of vessel had been set aside—whether abuse of process

[Civil Jurisdiction and Judgments Act 1982 (c.27).]

P operated a liner service and chartered D's vessel "S.A." to perform a voyage. Cargo was damaged during the course of the voyage and P claimed to be indemnified from D. The matter was referred to arbitration. P then arrested "S.A." in March 1984 to obtain security in the arbitration. D had the arrest set aside. In 1986, P again arrested the vessel in respect of the same cause of action. D contended that the second arrest was an abuse of process. P contended that the coming into force of s.26 of the Civil Jurisdiction and Judgments Act 1982 gave them a right to arrest.

Held, that (1) the writ in the 1986 action was endorsed with the same claim as in the 1984 action and that action (and therefore the cause of action) had been stayed. The change in law heralded by the coming into force of s.26 of the 1982 Act did not affect such an abuse of process by P. (2) the writ and arrest would be set aside.

SILVER ATHENS (No. 1), THE [1986] 2 Lloyd's Rep. 580, Sheen J.

3370. Admiralty practice—writ *in rem*—whether substituted service can be ordered—nature of an action *in rem*.

P had a cargo claim in respect of damage to white refined sugar that had been carried on D's vessel, the "G.T.H." P issued a writ against that vessel, and after one year had passed, renewed the writ. D also owned a vessel, the "G.T.," and seeing an opportunity to arrest her, P threatened D's Protection and Indemnity Association ("the Club") that they would do so. The Club agreed to put up security to avoid such an arrest and also to instruct solicitors to accept service of proceedings. The Club went into liquidation before instructing solicitors, and D obtained an order for leave to serve the writ by substituted service on D's solicitors. D applied for the writ and the order (which had been made by the Admiralty Registrar) to be set aside.

Held, that (1) unless a writ *in rem* was endorsed with an acceptance of service thereof by the defendant or his solicitor, or the defendant acknowledges service, it must be served on the property against which the action was brought; (2) an order for substituted service could not be made in an action *in rem* which required that service be effected on the *res* itself; (3) the action *in rem* could only continue as if it were *in personam* if the *res* had been service and service therof had been acknowledged by the owners. In these circumstances the service of the writ would be set aside.

GOOD HERALD, THE [1987] 1 Lloyd's Rep. 236, Sheen J.

3371. "Bailee" clause—sue and labour costs—whether recoverable from insurers

The consignees of goods which were damaged and whose claim against the insurers was denied were entitled to recover from the insurers the costs of suing the carriers under the "bailee" clause in the policy which provided that it was the duty of the assured to preserve all rights against carriers and bailees.

The appellants "(A)" insured the respondents' "(R)" consignment of goods for a voyage from Singapore to Esbjerg. Some of the goods were short loaded or delivered damaged. R claimed against A but A denied liability. The policy contained a sue and labour clause empowering R to bring an action to recover the goods if there was any loss and entitling them to be re-imbursed by A for their expenses in doing so, and incorporated cl. 9 of the Institute Carge Clauses (All Risks) January 1 1963 edition which imposed on R a duty to take reasonable measures to avert or minimise a loss and to ensure that all rights against the carriers, bailees or other third parties were properly preserved and exercised. A asserted that R was bound by clause 9 to preserve its claims against the carriers before it was time-barred. R claimed in Japan against the carriers and in Singapore against A. In Singapore they obtained judgment for part of the claim and then claimed from A the costs of the proceedings in Japan against the carriers. A denied liability claiming that clause 9 imposed on R the duty to preserve, at their own expense, the claim against the carriers for the benefit of A. The judge dismissed the claim but the Court of Appeal of Singapore allowed R's appeal. A appealed to the Privy Council.

Held, dismissing the appeal, that the fact that R had started proceedings in Japan against the carrier at A's request did not of itself give rise to any duty by A to indemnify R since A was merely requesting, as they were justified in doing, that R perform its duty under clause 9. However, in order to give business efficacy to the contract, a term was to be implied entitling R to recover from A the costs incurred under clause 9 because the clause was to be construed in the context of the contract as a whole; the obligation imposed on R to sue the carriers was for A's benefit, and the obligation on A to pursue the proceedings would give A a positive incentive to delay a settlement if they were not liable to reimburse R's costs.

NETHERLANDS INSURANCE CO. EST. 1845 *v.* LJUNGBERG (KARL) & CO. AB; MAMMOTH PINE, THE, (1986) 3 All E.R. 767, P.C.

3372. Bill of lading—indemnity—intervening negligence

Where a shipowner is entitled to an indemnity against the consequences of signing inaccurate bills of lading, he loses that indemnity where the loss has actually been caused by intervening negligence on the part of the master.

D chartered the vessel from P to carry wire rods, manufactured by the charterers. The ship was arrested after discharge on the ground that the rods were rusty, and the receivers had an estoppel against P because the bills of lading stated that the goods were shipped in apparent good order. The claim was settled for $86,462 with legal costs to P of £28,173. P claimed against D before arbitrators, where there was no similar estoppel, and the arbitrators found that the damage had occurred before shipment, and that the master was negligent in failing to record on the mate's receipt that the cargo was damaged before shipment, so as to ensure that the ship's agents did not issue clean bills of lading.

Held, dismissing the appeal, that it was the consequences of the request or order of the charterers which were relevant; and the chain of causation could be broken, not only by dishonesty or manifest illegality but also by carelessness. Accordingly, in the light of the arbitrators' findings as to fact, the appeal must fail.

NAVIERA MOGOR S.A. *v.* SOCIETE METALLURGIQUE DE NORMANDIE [1987] 1 FTLR 243, Staughton J.

3373. Bond guarantee—bond put up at request of P and I club by insurers—liability of ship-owners to indemnify insurers

Where a bond was given by an insurance company at the request of a ship-owners' P and I club to cargo-owners to secure a claim for damages against the ship-owners so as to facilitate the release of their ship from arrest by the cargo-owners, the bond operated as a guarantee by the insurance company of the ship-owners' liability to the cargo-owners so that the ship-owners were liable to indemnify the insurance company in respect of payments made under the bond.

D were the owners of a ship that discharged its cargo at Shoreham before proceeding to Rotterdam. The cargo was damaged and the cargo-owners arrested D's ship in Rotterdam. As a matter of urgency, D requested its P and I club to obtain the release of the ship. In order to do so, the club requested P, pursuant to a bond scheme agreement between them, to give the cargo-owners a bond to secure their claim against D. D's ship was released and a bond provided by P to the cargo-owners. The bond scheme agreement provided for the club to indemnify P in respect of payments made by P and recognised that P had a right to recover from D as principal debtors. The cargo-owners' claim was settled in the sum of £23,560 which was paid by P. The club was in financial difficulties. P sought reimbursement from D.

Held, that by the bond P guaranteed D's liability to the cargo-owners. The bond stated on its face that it was given at the request of D. It could not be said that the bond was requested by the club in the discharge of their obligations to D so that D was not a party to the arrangement. D's position was that of principal debtor and P's that of surety. As such, D was liable to indemnify P in respect of the £23,560 paid to the cargo-owners. Even if in providing the bond P was a volunteer so far as D was concerned, it was just and reasonable that D should reimburse P (*Owen* v. *Tate* [1975] C.L.Y. 1531 considered).

ZUHAL K., THE [1987] 1 FTLR 76, Sheen J.

3374. Booking note—arbitration clause—commencement of arbitration proceedings—late amendment disputing title of P—whether estopped

By a booking note "2 speedboats" were shipped on P's vessel. The booking note was typed on the notepaper of H and was signed on behalf of D by D's agents and on behalf of H. It contained an arbitration clause. The cargo was shipped and freight was paid. It was then discovered by P that the boats were gunboats and P demanded a higher freight. The dispute was referred to arbitration, but in an amended defence D alleged that they had no contract with P. P contended that D, who had agreed to submit to arbitration, was estopped from contending that they were not parties to the contract.

Held, that on the facts and the evidence D had clearly represented that they had accepted that the booking note contained a contract between themselves and P, and P had acted in reliance thereupon in expending legal costs. D was thus estopped from contending that P was not a party to the contract.

SEA CALM SHIPPING CO. S.A. *v.* CHANTIERS NAVALS DE L'ESTEREL S.A.: UHENBELS, THE [1986] 2 Lloyd's Rep. 294.

3375. British Shipbuilders (Borrowing Powers) Act 1987 (c.52). See TRADE AND INDUSTRY, §3729.

3376. Cargo damage—whether owners of cargo could claim substantial damages from shipowners

O let their vessel to C for the carriage of DIR pellets from Indonesia to India. The pellets were highly reactive with water. C had bought the cargo F.O.B. and property passed to them on shipment. C had sold the cargo to end users—those agreements provided that risk was also to pass on shipment, although property could not pass until the cargo had been appropriated to that end user. C was paid by the end users soon after shipment of the DIR. Virtually all of the cargo was delivered in a damaged condition—the hatch coamings of O's vessel had leaked. C claimed, and was awarded, substantial damages by arbitrators. O appealed, contending that C had suffered no recoverable loss.

Held, dismissing O's appeal, that C was the owner of the goods, and was entitled to sue O (having more than a bare proprietary right therein) for substantial damages. The contracts of sale which C had made with the end users, and the payment to them thereunder, were *res inter alios acta.* Such considerations were too remote.

OBESTAIN INC. *v.* NATIONAL MINERAL DEVELOPMENT CORP.; SANIX ACE, THE [1987] 1 Lloyd's Rep. 465, Hobhouse J.

3377. Carriage by sea

CARRIAGE OF PASSENGERS AND THEIR LUGGAGE BY SEA (DOMESTIC CARRIAGE) ORDER 1987 (No. 670) [80p], made under the Merchant Shipping Act 1979 (c.39), s.16(2)(5); operative on April 30, 1987; provides for the Athens Convention, contained in Sched. 3, to the 1979 Act, to apply to contracts of domestic carriage.

CARRIAGE OF PASSENGERS AND THEIR LUGGAGE BY SEA (NOTICE) ORDER 1987 (No. 703) [45p], made under the Merchant Shipping Act 1979, Sched. 3, Pt. II, para. 11; operative on April 30, 1987; requires a carrier to give passengers notice of specified provisions of the Athens Convention.

CARRIAGE OF PASSENGERS AND THEIR LUGGAGE BY SEA (PARTIES TO CONVENTION) ORDER 1987 (No. 931) [45p], made under the Merchant Shipping Act 1979, Sched. 3, Pt. II, para. 10; operative on June 17, 1987; declares states which are party to the Convention relating to the Carriage of Passengers and their Luggage by Sea.

CARRIAGE OF PASSENGERS AND THEIR LUGGAGE BY SEA (UNITED KINGDOM CARRIERS) ORDER 1987 (No. 855) [45p], made under the Merchant Shipping Act 1979, ss.14, 16, Sched. 3, Pt. II, paras. 4, 5; operative on June 1, 1987; increases the limit of liability for the death of or injury to passengers carried in U.K. vessels.

3378. Carriage by sea—bill of lading—alleged short delivery

P were the owners of a cargo of North Sea crude oil which was carried by D's vessel from Teeside to Curaçao. P claimed that there was a short delivery of cargo, relying upon the discrepancy between the shore metered loading figures and the shore metered discharging figures as evidence of loss. D contended that the vessel's loading and discharge figures were most accurate, but in any event contended that all cargo loaded had been discharged.

Held, that although the shore figures were inherently impressive, P had failed to prove that there was a shortage on delivery.

AMOCO OIL CO. *v.* PARPADA SHIPPING CO.: GEORGE S, THE [1987] 2 Lloyd's Rep. 69, Staughton J.

3379. Carriage by sea—bill of lading—failure to deliver—title to sue

By two bills of lading, D acknowledged shipment on board their vessel of two parcels of seed expellers in bulk. The bills were claused "weight unknown." They were overstowed with other parcels of identical cargo. When the vessel arrived at the final discharge port (having discharged parcels from the bulk mass en route) forwarding agents acting for P presented the bills of lading. No cargo was presented under one bill of lading, and very little under the other. P.1 & 2 claimed damages for non-delivery and short delivery.

As to P1, they claimed by virtue of having presented the bills of lading, they had not produced any contract of sale to prove ownership of the goods. As to P2, they were c.i.f. purchasers of the cargo from persons other than the shippers. D denied that the cargo had been shipped on board; alternatively contended that P1 and P2 had not established that they had title to sue.

Held, that (1) on the evidence, the cargo had been loaded on board the vessel, and most probably had been discharged in error at intermediate ports; (2) D's argument, that no implied contract could arise with P1 in circumstances where no delivery had been given against bills of lading, would be rejected. P1 had the same contractual right to claim for non-delivery as a party would for short delivery; (3) P2 who had presented their bill of lading, and obtained part delivery, were also entitled to claim damages.

ARAMIS, THE [1987] 2 Lloyd's Rep. 59, Evans J.

3380. Carriage by sea—carriage of cargo on deck—arbitration clause in bill of lading—Hague-Visby Rules—failure to commence proceedings within one year—extension of time—fundamental breach.

Cargo was carried on deck by a vessel X, and was damaged during the course of such carriage. P, the consignees, assumed that the liner operators were carriers and gave notice of claim against them. There was a demise clause in the bill of lading issued by the liner operators, and they denied liability. The bill of lading was subject to the Hague-Visby Rules, and provided for arbitration in London. P were out of time in which to bring their claim against O, the true owners of the vessel, and by two separate summonses sought (1) an extension of time within which to commence arbitration proceedings pursuant to s.27 of the Arbitration Act 1950, and (2) a declaration that O had committed a fundamental breach of contract in shipping the goods on deck and were not entitled to the benefit of the Hague Rules limitation period. Both summonses were *rejected*. P appealed against both decisions.

Held, dismissing the appeals, that (1) on the first summons, Leggatt J. was correct to hold that the Court had no jurisdiction to extend the time in which to commence arbitration proceedings in circumstances where the Hague-Visby Rules were incorporated. Art. III, r.6 had the force of law and excluded the operation of s.27 of the Arbitration Act 1950; (2) the loading of cargo on deck did not amount to a fundamental breach of contract, and did not suspend the operation of the Hague-Visby Rules time bar.

KENYA RAILWAYS *v.* ANTARES CO. PTE.; ANTARES, THE (Nos. 1 and 2) [1987] 1 Lloyd's Rep. 424, C.A.

3381. Channel Island ferry services—joint venture agreement—whether JVA permitted time chartering. See CHANNEL ISLAND FERRIES *v.* SEALINK U.K., §422.

3382. Charterparty—bill of lading—laytime—whether arose through shipowners' breach

Shipowners who are in breach of charter through their master's failure to sign an original bill of lading for carriage to consignees cannot invoke an indemnity clause requiring the charterer to indemnify them against loss caused by discharge without presentation of a signed original bill; and accordingly, delay caused by their refusal to discharge without the charterer's letter of indemnity does not count against laytime.

MOBIL SHIPPING AND TRANSPORTATION *v.* SHELL EASTERN PETROLEUM (PTE), *The Financial Times,* July 22, 1987, Adrian Hamilton Q.C.

3383. Charterparty—demurrage—delay in discharge due to swell—whether within S.T.B. V.O.Y. charterparty

A delay in discharge of a ship's cargo caused by swell preventing the use of a sea line is due to "a reason or cause over which the charters have no control" within cll. 6 and 8 of the S.T.B. V.O.Y. charterparty.

The shipowners, Notos Maritime Corporation of Monrovia, chartered their vessel, the Notos, under a tanker voyage charterparty on an S.T.B. V.O.Y. form for a voyage to one safe sea line Mohammedia. The charterers operated an oil refinery there and they also owned and controlled the sea line at which the Notos discharged her cargo. At the relevant time it was the only one in operation. When the vessel arrived, there was just over 48 hours of laytime unused. Time was to start in six hours after notice of readiness was given. Thereafter discharge was delayed because of the sea swell which rendered the line unusable. Under cll. 6 and 8 of the charterparty the charterer was not liable for delay over which they had no control.

Held, dismissing the appeal by the owners from the Court of Appeal, that there was no evidence that the sea line was unsafe, and ownership and control of the sea line did not prevent swell from being a cause over which the charterers had no control.

NOTOS, THE [1987] 1 FTLR 519, H.L.

3384. Charterparty—demurrage claim—limitation of time—oral agreement to pay—jurisdiction to extend time

[Arbitration Act 1950 (c.27), s.27.]

By a charter made on an amended BP form, O let their vessel to C. The charter provided that claims for demurrage together with supporting documents were to be received within three months of discharge "otherwise such claims are time-barred." The vessel proceeded to Sirri Island, the normal waiting place for Kharg Island, and was there substantially delayed. She then loaded at Kharg and discharged in Egypt in early April 1985. C had orally accepted responsibility for the wait at Sirri Island, but O did not present their demurrage claim until three months after final discharge. O contended that the oral agreement was binding, and in the alternative claimed an extension of time in which to bring proceedings.

Held, dismissing O's appeal, that (1) the acceptance by C of responsibility to pay demurrage did not amount to an agreement outwith the charter; (2) an oral request for payment could not be regarded as a claim within the charter requirements; (3) the claims were not received within the time limit, and on the requirement for the submission of documents was entirely separate from the arbitration clause. The court did not have jurisdiction to extend time for the making of the claim.

MARIANA ISLANDS STEAMSHIP CORP. *v.* MARIMPEX MINERALOEL-HANDELS-GESELLSCHAFT mbH & CO. K.G.; MEDUSA, THE [1986] 2 Lloyd's Rep. 328, C.A.

3385. Charterparty—payment for freight—when and how due—arbitration—quantum meruit

The words "freight deemed earned as cargo loaded" in a charterparty mean that the debt accrues to the owners when the cargo is loaded, but only becomes payable in accordance with the terms of the charterparty.

Where a *quantum meruit* is claimed in an arbitration, it is immaterial that the claimants have no information enabling them to fix the amount. What matters is that such information should be available to the arbitrator.

VAGRES COMPANIA MARITIMA *v.* NISSHO-IWAI AMERICAN CORP. KARIN VATIS, THE, *The Times,* April 20, 1987, Leggatt J.

3386. Charterparty—repudiation—innocent party refusing to accept

If an innocent party to a contract which is repudiated refuses to accept repudiation and affirms the contract, the repudiating party may rely on subsequent supervening events as excusing him from compliance.

FERCOMETAL SARL *v.* MEDITERRANEAN SHIPPING CO., *The Times,* June 1, 1987, C.A.

3387. Charterparty—safe berth warranty—extent

A charterer's warranty to nominate a safe berth cannot be broken before the obligation to nominate arises.

Shipowners chartered the APJ Trity to charterers. On the voyage, the ship was struck by a missile and towed to a port where she was discharged. The owners claimed a breach of warranty in that the port nominated was an unsafe port. The arbitrators held that the charterers gave, *inter alia,* no warranty of the safety of the approach voyage.

Held, dismissing the owner's appeal, that the warranty to nominate a safe port cannot be broken before the obligation to nominate arises; in any event it only covers movement within the port, not the approach journey.

ATKINS INTERNATIONAL *v.* ISLAMIC REPUBLIC OF IRAN SHIPPING LINES [1987] 1 FTLR 379, C.A.

3388. Collision—crossing rules—lookout—apportionment of liability

On May 2, 1982 the F and the P came into collision in the Great Bitter Lake. Both vessels had been lying at anchor on the west side of the dredged channels running in a north/south direction between the east and west anchorages. Both vessels weighed anchor and the P turned to starboard to proceed in a S.E. direction to join the southbound convoy. F proceeded in a N.E. direction to join the northbound convoy. They collided at about a right angle with the stern of the P striking the port side of the F. Each vessel had little headway on. F contended that P was a give way vessel within the meaning of r.15 of the Collision Regulations. P contended that F was not in fact on any course at the time of the collision whilst F had settled on a course. F should therefore have allowed P to pass, as the situation was a close quarters situation.

Held, that (1) P had put herself on to a crossing course and was not, therefore, allowed to rely upon the crossing rule. She had no right to cross ahead of F; (2) F, however, had not kept a sufficiently keen lookout on the port side, and had she sounded her whistle the severity of the collision may well have been avoided; (3) P was 75 per cent. to blame for the collision and F was 25 per cent. to blame.

PETROSHIP B., THE [1986] 2 Lloyd's Rep. 251, Sheen J.

3389. Collision—crossing vessels—apportionment of liability

P's vessel M collided with D's vessel F in the entrance to the port of Piraeus. M was entering the port, whilst F was leaving it. P argued that the sole cause of the collision was that the F turned to port, into M's water. D contended that F had always remained in her own water, and that M had crossed onto the wrong side of the fairway.

Held, that (1) although it was clear that F's wheel had been hard-a-port prior to the collision, there was no doubt but that this had been caused by the M crossing into her wrong water; (2) both vessels were at fault for failing to keep near to the outer limit of the fairway on their starboard side; (3) the main cause of the collision was the very substantial alteration to port that had been made by the F—it made the collision virtually inevitable. F was 75 per cent. to blame and M 25 per cent.

FAETHON, THE [1987] 1 Lloyd's Rep. 538, Sheen J.

3390. Collision—currency of claim

In 1979 that was a collision between P and D's ships. It was later agreed that D were solely to blame for the collision. P's claim was referred to the admiralty registrar for the damages to be assessed. P was a Panamanian company, although their ship was managed in Piraeus. The Registrar awarded them damages in U.S. dollars. D applied to vary the order, contending that the award should have been made in drachmas. Sheen J. varied the order, holding that on the evidence P operated in drachmas.

Held, allowing P's appeal, that P's loss was in dollars. All of their relevant operations were carried out in dollars. That was the currency with which P's investment in the vessel had its closest connection. The currency in which the annual accounts were drawn up (drachmas) was irrelevant when the whole venture was actually traded in dollars.

LASH ATLANTICO, THE [1987] 2 Lloyd's Rep 114, C.A.

3391. Collision—currency of claim

In 1974 there was a collision between P and D's vessel. The parties agreed that liability should be divided. P initially expressed their claim in Italian lire, but later amended to claim U.S. Dollars. The Admiralty Registrar awarded P their damages in lire. P appealed, contending that they had felt their loss in dollars.

Held, dismissing P's appeal, that (1) on the evidence the Admiralty Registrar was correct in awarding lire; (2) as D's claim was expressed in dollars, P's claim would be converted into dollars as at the date when the amount of P's claim was agreed.

TRANSOCEANICA FRANCESCA AND NICOS V, THE [1987] 2 Lloyd's Rep 155, Sheen J.

3392. Collision—failure to keep proper lookout—limitation of liability—whether actual fault or privity

[Aus.] In this case, a collision was caused by the running down by one vessel (T), by the other (P). The P was solely to blame, and the collision was caused by her master either falling asleep whilst on duty, or leaving the bridge. P sought to limit her liability.

Held, that P was entitled to limit her liability, in that (1) the master and crew of the vessel was apparently competent; (2) the work systems operated on board the fishing vessel were normal, and were properly left to the master by his owners.

BAREMEDA ENTERPRISES PTY. *v.* O'CONNOR (RONALD PATRICK) AND K.F.Y FISHERIES (QLD) PTY.; TIRUNA AND PELORUS, THE [1986] 2 Lloyd's Rep. 536, Supreme Court of Queensland, Australia.

3393. Collision—fog—collision near anchorage—division of liability

On March 29, 1982 the M and the F collided in the approaches to Flushing. The F was inward bound close to the centre line of the channel and was steaming at full speed ahead, making 14 knots. The M had been anchored in an anchorage near the fairway. The vessels collided in dense fog close to the line marking the southern boundary of the channel. The F had intended to anchor in the southern anchorage, and the M was manoeuvring to leave the anchorage and proceed to Antwerp.

Held, that the sole effective cause of the collision was the failure of the F to maintain a proper course in approaching the anchorage.

FILIATRA LEGACY, THE [1986] 2 Lloyd's Rep. 257, Sheen J.

3394. Collision—liability—anchored vessel—improper anchorage—failure to keep good lookout

This case concerned a collision between the barge "BGL 2", which was at anchor in the care of the tug O.F., and the R which was outward bound in the River Schelde. The judge found that the barge was at anchor in an improper position and probably in the navigable channel. She did not exhibit anchor lights and those on board the tug did not signal her presence.

Held, that (1) the collision was caused by the fault of both parties as those on board the R failed to keep a good lookout and set a course too close to the edge of the channel; (2) the R was 40 per cent. to blame and the O.F./BGL 2 60 per cent.

OURO FINO, THE [1986] 2 Lloyd's Rep. 466, Sheen J.

3395. Collision—limitation period—discretion of court to extend time limit. See GAZ FOUNTAIN, THE, §2332.

3396. Collision—vessels passing safely—D's vessel suddenly turning to starboard—liability for collision—apportionment

This appeal arose out of a collision between P's vessel *Capulonix* and D's vessel *State of Himachal Pradesh* off the port of Bombay. Sheen J. found D's vessel 85 per cent. to blame in circumstances where she had turned to starboard ahead of P's vessel at less than C-5 when the vessel's had appeared to be passing each other starboard to starboard. P was found 15 per cent. to blame for failing to react to the emergency thrust upon her. Both parties appealed.

Held, that the Court was not satisfied, in circumstances where D had made the collision inevitable, that P should be held in any way to blame for the collision, and D was found wholly to blame.

STATE OF HIMACHAL PRADESH, THE [1987] 2 Lloyd's Rep. 97, C.A.

3397. Contract of affreightment—insolvency of shipowners leading to unreliability in performance—whether breach going to root of contract. See CONTRACT, §428.

3398. Control of pollution

CONTROL OF POLLUTION (LANDED SHIPS' WASTE) REGULATIONS 1987 (No. 402) [80p], made under the Control of Pollution Act 1974 (c.40), ss.3(1), 17, 30(4)(5); operative on April 6, 1987; make provision in relation to waste from the tanks and holds of ships and waste generated by cleaning such tanks and holds.

3399. Demurrage—calculation in dollars and payment in sterling—depreciation of sterling—whether currency loss recoverable

Where a charterparty provides that demurrage is to be paid at a fixed rate per day of detention, no further term can be implied that the demurrage has to be paid within two months of the discharge of cargo, so that there is no scope for owners to claim a currency exchange loss arising from the subsequent depreciation of the currency of payment.

Under a charterparty, demurrage was to be at the rate of $6,000 per day, payable in sterling at the rate prevailing on the date of the bill of lading. Following a dispute as to the length of time that the vessel had been detained, an award was made, which reflected the decline of sterling during the intervening period, resulting in the payment of an extra sum to the owners to take account of that fall. The extra sum was awarded on the basis that demurrage should have been paid within two months of the completion of discharge of the vessel.

Held, allowing the charterers appeal, that the currency exchange loss was not recoverable as special damage. No term could be implied into the charterparty that demurrage was to be paid within a two-month period.

PRESIDENT OF INDIA *v.* LIPS MARITIME CORP. [1987] 3 W.L.R. 572, H.L.

3400. Empty hatch—whether an "available working hatch"—rate of discharge of cargo

A hatch with no cargo beneath it in the hold is not "an available working hatch" for the purpose of determining the rate of discharge of the vessel. A hatch is not unavailable or unworkable, however, simply because no gear is available to load or discharge through it.

PRESIDENT OF INDIA *v.* SLOBODONA PLIVIDBA S YUGOSLAVIA, *Financial Times,* June 24, 1987, Webster J.

3401. "Entered at customs house"—meaning

"Entered at customs house" refers to final entry, and not an application for entry.

PRESIDENT OF INDIA *v.* DAVENPORT MARINE PANAMA S.A., *Financial Times,* June 23, 1987, Webster J.

3402. Fees

MERCHANT SHIPPING (FEES) REGULATIONS 1987 (No. 63) [£2·70], made under the Merchant Shipping Act 1948 (c.44), s.5(3), the Merchant Shipping (Safety Convention) Act 1949 (c.43), s.33, the Merchant Shipping (Load Lines) Act 1967 (c.27), s.26, the Fishing Vessels (Safety Provisions) Act 1970 (c.27), s.6, the Merchant Shipping Act 1970 (c.36), s.84, the Merchant Shipping Act 1974 (c.43), s.17, Sched. 5, the Merchant Shipping Act 1979 (c.39), s.21(1)(3)(*r*), the Merchant Shipping Act 1983 (c.13), s.5(1)(8), Sched., para. 2(j) and S.I. 1983 No. 1106; operative on February 1, 1987; increase certain fees payable under the said Acts.

3403. Harbours and docks

HARBOUR AUTHORITIES (TEIGNMOUTH) (CONSTITUTION) ORDER 1987 (No. 222) [45p], made under the Harbours Act 1964 (c.40), s.15A; operative on March 20, 1987; provides that the power of appointment of members of the Teignmouth Harbour Commission shall be exercised by persons other than the Secretary of State.

MANCHESTER SHIP CANAL REVISION ORDER 1987 (No. 1790) [45p], made under the Harbours Act 1964, s.14; operative on October 19, 1987; authorises the Canal Company to abandon the greater part of Dock No. 9 in Salford.

NEWLYN PIER AND HARBOUR REVISION ORDER 1987 (No. 2985) [£1·60], made under the Harbours Act 1964, s.14; operative on December 4, 1987; enables the Newlyn Pier and Harbour Commissioners to, *inter alia,* extend the jetty authorised under S.I. 1978 No. 427.

PADSTOW HARBOUR REVISION ORDER 1987 (No. 420) [£2·90], made under the Harbours Act 1964, s.14; operative on March 8, 1987; re-constitutes the Padstow Harbour Commissioners.

WARKWORTH HARBOUR REVISION ORDER 1987 (No. 1514) [45p], made under the Harbours Act 1964, s.14; operative on August 20, 1987; increases the borrowing powers of the Warkworth Harbour Commissioners.

3404. Hovercraft

HOVERCRAFT (CIVIL LIABILITY) (AMENDMENT) ORDER 1987 (NO. 1835) [45p], made under the Hovercraft Act 1968 (c.59), s.1(1)(i), 3(*f*); operative on December 1, 1987; increases the limit of liability of carriers of passengers by hovercraft to £80,009 for loss of life or personal injury.

HOVERCRAFT (FEES) REGULATIONS 1987 (No. 1637) [£1·60], made under S.I. 1972 No. 674; operative on October 15, 1987; revoke S.I. 1985 No. 1605, as amended, and prescribe increased fees.

HOVERCRAFT (FEES) (AMENDMENT) REGULATIONS 1987 (No. 136) [45p], made under S.I. 1972 No. 674; operative on February 25, 1987; amend S.I. 1985 No. 1605 by increasing fees for operating permits and exemptions.

3405. Laytime—berth charterparty—vessel arrived in port but unable to berth due to adverse weather—charterparty providing for notice of readiness "whether in berth or not"—notice of readiness given on arrival in port—whether effective

A clause in a charterparty enabling notice of readiness to discharge cargo to be given "whether in berth or not" converted a berth charter into a port charter.

C chartered the Kyzikos on a berth charter on the Gencon Box layout form. By cl. 5, the master was entitled to tender by cable a notice of readiness to load or discharge whether in berth or not. The ship arrived at the port of Houston on December 17, 1984 but was unable to proceed to her berth by reason of fog until December 20. Throughout that period, a berth was available. The master gave notice of readiness as soon as she arrived at Houston. The owners claimed demurrage from that day. C contended that the master could not give notice of readiness until the ship was proceeding to berth at the very earliest. The arbitrator held that the words "whether in berth or not" turned the berth charter into a port charter and that time began to run on December 17, the notice of readiness being properly given. On appeal the judge took a different view and held that the words "whether in berth or not" only entitled a notice of readiness to be given when the ship was not in berth because there was not a berth available.

Held, allowing the owners' appeal, that the words "whether or not in berth" converted the charter from a berth charter into a port charter. The master was entitled to give notice of readiness as soon as the vessel arrived in port. The notice given in the present case was valid. The vessel had arrived within the commercial area of the port of Houston where she was at the immediate and effective disposition of C and she was ready in herself to discharge the cargo. The state of the weather was not a relevant factor to the question of the validity of a notice of readiness (*Oldendorff (E.L.) & Co. GmbH* v. *Tradax Export S.A.*; *Johanna Oldendorff, The* [1973] C.L.Y. 3100 applied; *Federal Commerce and Navigation Co.* v. *Tradax Export S.A.*; *Maratha Envoy, The* [1977] C.L.Y. 2728 considered).

BULK TRANSPORT GROUP SHIPPING CO. *v.* SEACRYSTAL SHIPPING; KYZIKOS, THE [1987] 3 All E.R. 222, C.A.

3406. Leading underwriter clause—whether following underwriters bound by extensions to policy agreed by the lead underwriter—summary judgment.

P insured their vessel for hull and machinery under a war risks policy. The ship contained a leading underwriter clause which provided that amendments, additions and deletions, etc. to the policy to be agreed by the leading underwriter and binding on all others thereon. There were subsequently a number of endorsements and extensions to the policy, all of which were agreed by the leading underwriters. The vessel was hit by a missile in the Persian Gulf and became a C.T.L. The leading underwriter paid under the policy, but the following underwriters denied liability. P sought summary judgment. The following underwriter contended that the extensions granted by the leading underwriters conflicted with market practice.

Held, giving judgment for P, that the evidence sought to be adduced by D was inadmissible as an aid to the true construction of the leading underwriter clause. The extensions granted by the leading underwriters were within the scope of the cover, and the following underwriters were liable.

BARLEE MARINE CORP. *v.* TREVOR REX MOUNTAIN; LEEGAS, THE [1987] 1 Lloyd's Rep. 471, Hirst J.

3407. Limitation of liability—whether operators "person interested in" the vessel for limitation of liability. See McDERMID *v.* NASH DREDGING AND RECLAMATION CO., §2615.

3408. Loss—peril of the seas—entry of seawater caused by negligent act

[Can.] The B.II was a floating module, with a hull consisting of two compartments that were watertight and others that were not. Juggling of air pressure in the various non-watertight compartments enabled the B.II to be raised or lowered in the water for the purposes of oceanographic surveying. B.II was insured under a Canadian version of the Lloyd's S.G. policy. She was lost when an employee negligently allowed her to fill up with water. Underwriters contended that the loss was not a loss "by peril of the seas."

Held, that the unintentional admission of seawater into a ship, albeit negligent, that thereby causes the ship to sink, amounts to a loss by peril of the seas.

CENTURY INSURANCE CO. OF CANADA *v.* CASE EXISTOLOGICAL LABORATORIES; BAMCELL, THE [1986] 2 Lloyd's Rep. 524, Supreme Ct. of Canada.

[*Note*: Much reliance was placed by the Supreme Court of Canada upon the reasoning of Lambert J. in the Canadian Court of Appeal. That judgment is reported as BAMCELL II, THE (NOTE) [1986] 2 Lloyd's Rep. 528].

3409. Loss—vessel not seaworthy due to design and construction defects—damage through adverse sea conditions—whether loss caused by "accidental external means"—whether loss proximately caused by a peril insured against

The insurers of a vessel were bound to indemnify the owner against loss where there were two concurrent causes of damage to his vessel of which one was an insured peril and the other was not, provided that other cause was not excluded by the policy.

P owned a vessel that was found by the trial judge to be ill-designed and ill-constructed. In the course of a journey, the vessel ran into a choppy confused sea with waves about three metres high. In consequence of the action of the waves, substantial damage was caused to the hull of the vessel. The vessel was insured by D against loss caused by "accidental external means". Loss caused by the unseaworthy condition of the vessel in consequence of its design and construction was not a peril excluded by the terms of the policy. D contended that the damage to the vessel was not caused by accidental external means and alternatively that, if it was, it was not the proximate cause of the damage to the vessel. The trial judge found for P.

Held, dismissing D's appeal, that damage was caused by frequent and violent impacts of a badly designed and constructed hull on an adverse sea. Those impacts were external. The vessel ought not in the ordinary course of events to have suffered the damage that it did. Accordingly, damage by accidental external means was established. There were two concurrent causes of the damage, namely the adverse sea conditions and the design and construction of the vessel. The trial judge was justified in finding that the adverse sea conditions were a proximate cause of the damage to the vessel. D was bound to indemnify P where one of two concurrent causes of the damage was an insured peril and other was not a peril excluded by the terms of the policy (*Dudgeon* v. *Pembroke* (1877) 2 App.Cas. 284, *Leyland Shipping Co.* v. *Norwich Union Fire Insurance Society* [1918] A.C. 350, *Wayne Tank and Pump Co.* v. *Employers' Liability Assurance Corporation* [1983] C.L.Y. 395 considered).

LLOYD (J. J.) INSTRUMENTS *v.* NORTHERN STAR INSURANCE CO.; MISS JAY JAY, THE [1987] 1 FTLR 14, C.A.

3410. Loss—whether peril of the seas or ordinary wear and tear

[Can.] The tug P was laid up in Vancouver. She sank in the harbour, and her owners claimed under the insurance policy. Underwriters contended that the vessel had sunk through ordinary wear and tear, due to leakage through a variety of different places consequent upon ordinary corrosion. P contended that the ingress was sudden, and consequent upon open valves.

Held, that the vessel sank due to leakage through an open suction valve and that the loss was therefore a loss by peril of the seas.

C.C.R. FISHING *v.* TOMENSON INC., LA POINTE, THE [1986] 2 Lloyd's Rep. 513, Supreme Ct. of British Colombia.

3411. Loss by fire—whether fire an "occurrence" within policy—where "passed" meant issued by average adjuster or accepted by hull underwriters—whether mortgagees could claim under policy

P were mortgagees of O's vessel. They had taken out a mortgagee's interest policy which provided that the policy would have to pay "if an occurrence which takes place during that period of their policy causes a total or constructive total loss . . . and after a final court judgment or average adjustment having been passed, the assured is unable to recover from hull underwriters". The vessel was badly damaged in a fire and O gave notice of abandonment to hull underwriters. They refused to accept this and P commenced proceedings. Hull underwriters contended that the vessel had been deliberately cast away by O. Prior to a final determination of those proceedings, P sought the determination by the court of certain preliminary issues against the mortgagee's interest underwriters. These were (1) whether a fire was an "occurrence" within that policy; (2) whether an average adjustment that had been "passed" within the policy had to be approved by hull underwriters; (3) whether the fact of an average adjustment coupled with a refusal by underwriters to pay was sufficient to found action under the policy.

Held, that (1) a fire, even if deliberately caused, was an occurrence within the policy, and P's claim would not be barred by s.55(2)(*a*) of the Marine Insurance Act 1906, unless P themselves had connived at the loss. (2) For the purposes of the policy, an average adjustment would have to be accepted by hull underwriters if P was to have a prima facie claim under the policy; (3) the failure by hull underwriters to accept the average adjustment coupled with their refusal to pay the claim was not even prima facie evidence that the mortgagees were unable to claim from hull underwriters.

SCHIFFSHYPOTHEKENBANK ZU LUEBECK A.G. *v.* COMPTON (NORMAN PHILIP); ALEXION HOPE, THE [1987] 1 Lloyd's Rep. 60, Staughton J.

3412. Marine insurance–policy contained a warranty as to absence of other insurance—whether other insurance effected by assured

P insured O's vessel under an "Institute Time Clauses Hulls" policy which provided, *inter alia*, by cl. 20, "warranted that no insurance on any interest enumerated in . . . sections (a) to (g) in excess of the amounts permitted therein and no other insurance . . . is or shall be expected to operate during the currency of the policy . . . ." The vessel was lost, and P paid out on the insurance with the moneys going to the mortgagees. P then discovered that the vessel had also been insured under a "managing owner's interest" policy, and claimed recovery of the sums paid out.

Held, that there was a breach of the warranty, and P was entitled to recover the sums which they had paid out.

OUTHWAITE (RICHARD) *v.* COMMERCIAL BANK OF GREECE S.A.; SEA BREEZE, THE [1987] 1 Lloyd's Rep. 372, Staughton J.

3413. Master of ship—alteration of course—inevitable collision—whether negligent. See STATE OF HIMACHAL PRADESH, THE, §3396.

3414. Merchant shipping

MERCHANT SHIPPING (BCH CODE) REGULATIONS 1987 (No. 550) [£1·90], made under S.I. 1987 No. 470; operative on April 6, 1987; require chemical tankers which carry noxious liquid substances of category A, B, or C (as defined) in bulk and which were built before July 1, 1986, to comply with the code for the construction and equipment of ships carrying dangerous chemicals in bulk which was adopted by the International Maritime Organisation on December 5, 1985.

MERCHANT SHIPPING (CERTIFICATION OF DECK AND MARINE ENGINEER OFFICERS AND LICENSING OF MARINE ENGINE OPERATORS) (AMENDMENT) REGULATIONS 1987 (No. 884) [85p], made under the Merchant Shipping Act 1970 (c.36), ss.43, 92 and the Merchant Shipping Act 1979 (c.39), s.21(1)(*a*)(3)–(6); operative on June 5, 1987; make provision in relation to the certification of merchant shipping officers.

MERCHANT SHIPPING (CLOSING OF OPENINGS IN HULLS AND IN WATERTIGHT BULKHEADS) REGULATIONS 1987 (No. 1298) [£1·30], made under the Merchant Shipping Act 1979 (c.39), s.21(1)(*a*)(3)(4)(6); operative on November 1, 1987 save for reg. 3(1)(*a*)(ii) which is operative on November 1, 1988; impose additional requirements for the control of watertight doors.

MERCHANT SHIPPING (CONFIRMATION OF LEGISLATION) (ANGUILLA) ORDER 1987 (No. 932) [45p], made under the Merchant Shipping Act 1894 (c.60), s.735(1); operative on July 8, 1987; confirms the Merchant Shipping (Registry) Ordinance 1986.

MERCHANT SHIPPING (CONFIRMATION OF LEGISLATION) (CAYMAN ISLANDS) ORDER 1987 (No. 1267) [45p], made under Merchant Shipping Act 1894 (c.60), s.735(1); operative on August 19, 1987; confirms a law enacted by the Legislature of the Cayman Islands which repeals, in relation to the registration of ships in the Cayman Islands, certain provisions of Part I of the Merchant Shipping Act 1894 regarding such registration.

MERCHANT SHIPPING (CONFIRMATION OF LEGISLATION) (FALKLAND ISLANDS) ORDER 1987 (No. 1827) [45p], made under the Merchant Shipping Act 1894 (c.60), s.735(1); operative on November 20, 1987; confirms a law enacted by the Legislature of the Falkland Islands.

MERCHANT SHIPPING (CONFIRMATION OF LEGISLATION) (GIBRALTAR) ORDER 1987 (No. 933) [45p], made under the Merchant Shipping Act 1894, s.735(1); operative on July 8, 1987; confirms the Merchant Shipping (Amendment) Ordinance 1987.

MERCHANT SHIPPING (CONTROL OF POLLUTION BY NOXIOUS LIQUID SUBSTANCES IN BULK) REGULATIONS 1987 (No. 551) [£4·10], made under S.I. 1987 No. 470; operative on April 6, 1987; prohibit the discharge into the sea of noxious liquid substances or mixtures containing them.

MERCHANT SHIPPING (FEES) (AMENDMENT) REGULATIONS 1987 (No. 548) [80p], made under the Merchant Shipping (Safety Convention) Act 1949 (c.43), s.33, the Anchors and Chain Cables Act 1967 (c.64), s.1(1)(*d*), the Fishing Vessels (Safety Provisions) Act 1970 (c.27), s.6, the Merchant Shipping Act 1970 (c.36), s.84, the Merchant Shipping Act 1974 (c.43), s.17 and Sched. 5, the Merchant Shipping Act 1979 (c.39), s.21(1), (3)(*r*) and S.I. 1987 No. 63; operative on April 6, 1987; amend S.I. 1987 No. 63 and increase fees payable in respect of the registration of ships by approximately 3·6 per cent.

MERCHANT SHIPPING (FEES) (AMENDMENT) (No. 2) REGULATIONS 1987 (No. 854) [£1·30], made under the Merchant Shipping (Safety Convention) Act 1949 (c.43), s.33, the Anchors and Chain Cables Act 1967 (c.64), s.1(1)(*d*), the Fishing Vessels (Safety Provisions) Act 1970 (c.27), s.6, the Merchant Shipping Act 1970 (c.36), s.84, the Merchant Shipping Act 1974 (c.43), s.17, Sched. 5, the Merchant Shipping Act 1979 (c.39), s.21(1)(3)(*r*) and S.I. 1987 No. 470; operative on May 16, 1987; replace S.I. 1987 No. 548 and amend S.I. 1987 No. 63 so as to increase fees payable thereunder.

MERCHANT SHIPPING (FEES) (AMENDMENT) (No. 3) REGULATIONS 1987 (No. 2113) [85p], made under the Merchant Shipping Act 1970 (c.36), s.84; operative on January 1, 1988; lay down the fees of the Department of Transport where only the practical examinations for masters and officers are conducted by the Department.

MERCHANT SHIPPING (FISHING BOATS REGISTRY) (AMENDMENT) ORDER 1987 (No. 1284) [£1·30], made under the Merchant Shipping Act 1894 (c.60), ss.373(5), 738(1); operative on August 19, 1987; amends S.I. 1981 No. 740 and provides that in most cases the Registrars for ports of registry in the U.K. shall be the officers who are Registrars of British Ships for the ports in question.

MERCHANT SHIPPING (IBC CODE) REGULATIONS 1987 (No. 549) [£1·60], made under the Merchant Shipping Act 1979, ss.21(1)(*a*), (*b*), (3), (5), (6) and 22(1); operative on April 6, 1987; require chemical tankers built on or after July 1, 1986, and carrying polluting or dangerous liquid substances in bulk to comply with the international code for the construction and equipment of ships carrying dangerous chemicals in bulk.

MERCHANT SHIPPING (INDEMNIFICATION OF SHIPOWNERS) ORDER 1987 (No. 220) [45p], made under the Merchant Shipping Act 1974 (c.43), s.5(4)(*a*)(6); operative on May 1, 1987; revokes and replaces S.I. 1985 No. 1665.

MERCHANT SHIPPING (LIGHT DUES) (AMENDMENT) REGULATIONS 1987 (No. 244) [45p], made under the Merchant Shipping (Mercantile Marine Fund) Act 1898 (c.44), s.5(2); operative on April 1, 1987; increase light dues payable under the 1898 Act.

MERCHANT SHIPPING (LIGHT DUES) (AMENDMENT No. 2) REGULATIONS 1987 (No. 746) [45p], made under the Merchant Shipping (Mercantile Fund) Act 1898 (c.44), s.5(2); operative on June 1, 1987; provides for the payment of light dues by fishing vessels of 10 metres or more in length.

MERCHANT SHIPPING (PASSENGER SHIP CONSTRUCTION) (AMENDMENT) REGULATIONS 1987 (No. 1886) [85p], made under the Merchant Shipping Act 1979 (c.39), s.22(2); operative on January 1, 1988; amends S.I. 1984 No. 1216 and S.I. 1985 No. 660 in relation to U.K. ro/ro passenger ships.

MERCHANT SHIPPING (PILOT LADDERS AND HOISTS) REGULATIONS 1987 (No. 1961) [£1·60], made under the Merchant Shipping Act 1979, ss.21(1)(*a*)(*b*)(3)–(6), 22(1); operative on January 1, 1988; revoke and re-enact with amendments S.I. 1980 No. 543.

MERCHANT SHIPPING (PREVENTION AND CONTROL OF POLLUTION) ORDER 1987 (No. 470) [80p], made under the Merchant Shipping Act 1979, s.20(1)(*a*), (*d*), (3)–(5); operative on April 6, 1987; empowers the Secretary of State to make regulations relating to pollution by noxious liquid substances.

MERCHANT SHIPPING (REPORTING OF POLLUTION INCIDENTS) REGULATIONS 1987 (No. 586) [80p], made under S.I. 1987 No. 470; operative on April 6, 1987; make provision in relation to the reporting of marine pollution incidents.

MERCHANT SHIPPING (SEAMEN'S DOCUMENTS) REGULATIONS 1987 (No. 408) [£2·20], made under the Merchant Shipping Act 1970, ss.70, 71, 99(2); operative on April 8, 1987; revoke S.I. 1972 No. 1295, as amended, and re-enact them with amendments so as to make provision in relation to British seamen's documents.

MERCHANT SHIPPING (SMOOTH AND PARTIALLY SMOOTH WATERS) REGULATIONS 1987 (No. 1591) [£1·90], made under the Merchant Shipping Act 1979 (c.39), s.21(1)*a*)(*b*), 22(3); operative on October 8, 1987; replace S.I. 1977 No. 252, as amended, and extend certain limits.

MERCHANT SHIPPING (SUBMERSIBLE CRAFT) (AMENDMENT) REGULATIONS 1987 (No. 306) [80p], made under the Merchant Shipping Act 1974, ss.16, 17, Sched. 5; operative on April 1, 1987; amend S.I. 1976 No. 940 and S.I. 1981 No. 1098 so that certain definitions and other provisions accord with S.I. 1987 No. 311.

MERCHANT SHIPPING (SUBMERSIBLE CRAFT OPERATIONS) REGULATIONS 1987 (No. 311) [£2·20], made under the Merchant Shipping Act 1974, ss.16, 17; provide for the operation of manned submersible craft in U.K. waters and U.K. registered craft elsewhere.

MERCHANT SHIPPING (SUBMERSIBLE CRAFT OPERATIONS) (AMENDMENT) REGULATIONS 1987 (No. 1603) [45p], made under the Merchant Shipping Act 1974 (c.43), s.17, Sched. 5; operative on October 12, 1987; amends S.I. 1987 No. 311.

3415. Merchant shipping—Hong Kong

MERCHANT SHIPPING (PREVENTION AND CONTROL OF POLLUTION) (HONG KONG) ORDER 1987 (No. 664) [80p], made under the Merchant Shipping Act 1979 (c.39), s.20(1)(*a*)(*d*)(2)(3)(4); operative on May 6, 1987; extends to Hong Kong certain provisions of the Merchant Shipping (Prevention and Control of Pollution) Order 1987.

3416. Merchant Shipping Act 1979—commencement

MERCHANT SHIPPING ACT 1979 (COMMENCEMENT No. 11) ORDER 1987 (No. 635 (c.16)) [80p], made under the Merchant Shipping Act 1979 (c.39), ss.16(4), 52(2); brings into force on April 30, 1987 sections 14(1)(2)(4)(5)(6), 15(2) (in part), Sched. 3, Pts. I and II.

MERCHANT SHIPPING ACT 1979 (COMMENCEMENT No. 12) ORDER 1987 (No. 719 (c.18)) [80p], made under the Merchant Shipping Act 1979, s.52(2); brings s.35(2), other than in relation to fishing boats, into force on April 30, 1979.

3417. Mixing of cargo—whether cargo owner entitled to whole mixture or to his contribution only

A shipowner carrying a cargo of oil wrongfully and inseparably mixed an unknown quantity of his own oil with the cargo.

Held, that the mixture was held in common, and the cargo owner was entitled to delivery of a quantity equal to his original contribution, any doubt being resolved in the cargo owner's favour.

GREENSTONE SHIPPING CO. *v.* INDIAN OIL CORP., *Financial Times,* March 20, 1987, Staughton J.

3418. Navigation

JERSEY (NAVIGATOR HYPERBOLIC SYSTEM) ORDER 1987 (No. 171) [45p], made under the Merchant Shipping Act 1894 (c.60), s.669; operative on March 11, 1987; gives Trinity House certain powers in Jersey in connection with operation of the Decca Navigator System.

3419. Pilotage

LONDON PILOTAGE (AMENDMENT) ORDER 1987 (No. 1143) [45p], made under the Pilotage Act 1983, s.9; operative on July 31, 1987; amends S.R. & O. 1937 No. 1122 so as to remove the prohibition on the licensing of qualified pilots to conduct ships in areas both below and above Gravesend.

LOWESTOFT PILOTAGE (AMENDMENT) ORDER 1987 (No. 1484) [45p], made under the Pilotage Act 1983, s.9; operative on September 18, 1987; amends the Lowestoft Pilotage Order, 1921.

PILOTAGE ACT 1987 (PILOTS' NATIONAL PENSION FUND) ORDER 1987 (No. 2139) [45p], made under the Pilotage Act 1987, Sched. 1, para. 4(1); operative on February 1, 1988; continues in existence pilots' benefit funds under the Pilotage Act 1983, s.15(1)(i) despite the repeal of that section.

PILOTAGE COMMISSION PROVISION OF FUNDS SCHEME 1987 (CONFIRMATION) ORDER 1987 (No. 295) [45p], made under the Pilotage Act 1983, s.3(3); operative on April 1, 1987; confirms a scheme for imposing on piltotage authorities charges to provide funds for the Commission.

SCALLOWAY, SHETLAND, PILOTAGE ORDER 1987 (No. 1756) [45p], made under the Pilotage Act 1983, s.9; operative on December 21, 1987; establishes the Scalloway Pilotage District.

SULLOM VOE, SHETLAND, PILOTAGE (AMENDMENT) ORDER 1987 (No. 843) [45p], made under the Pilotage Act 1983, s.9; operative on June 3, 1987; extends the area of the Sullom Voe, Shetland pilotage district.

3420. Pilotage Act 1987 (c.21)

This Act makes new provision in respect of pilotage.

The Act received the Royal Assent on May 15, 1987, and comes into force on days to be appointed by the Secretary of State (except s.27).

The Act extends to Northern Ireland.

3421. Pilotage Act 1987 (c.21)—commencement

PILOTAGE ACT 1987 (COMMENCEMENT No. 1) ORDER 1987 (No. 1306 (c.41)) [45p], made under the Pilotage Act 1987 (c.21), s.33(2); brings into force on September 1, 1987, ss.24, 25, 28, 30, 31, 32(1)–(3), 33, and Sched. 1, paras. 1–4.

PILOTAGE ACT 1987 (COMMENCEMENT No. 2) ORDER 1987 (No. 2138 (c.63)) [45p], made under the Pilotage Act 1987, s.33(2); brings s.3(5) of the 1987 Act into force on February 1, 1988, is so far as it relates to the repeal of the Pilotage Act 1983, s.15(1)(i).

3422. Reinsurance—premium—payment in error—whether returnable

Where premiums are paid under a policy reinsuring against loss of hire, they are returnable to the reinsured if they have been paid after a constructive total loss and by administrative error on the part of the reinsured.

Two vessels were insured on hull war-risk policies, and for loss of hire; they were reinsured at Lloyd's. Both were seriously damaged by missile attack in the Gulf. Notice treating the vessels as constructive total losses was given, but after that notice, a further payment of premium in the sum of $791,820 was made.

Held, in an action claiming repayment of that premium, on the ground that it had been paid by administrative error, that the premiums, having in fact been paid in error, were returnable to the brokers.

C. T. BOWRING REINSURANCE *v.* BAXTER [1987] 1 FTLR 7, Hirst J.

3423. Sale contract—incorporation of demurrage provisions—whether an obligation to pay demurrage—congestion

P agreed to sell D a quantity of maize f.o.b. The sale contract incorporated the GAFTA terms and provided that demurrage was payable as for Centrocon charterparty. D had in fact agreed to sell a larger quantity of maize to E, for which purpose E had nominated a time-chartered vessel to lift P's cargo. The vessel was delayed in reaching the loadport by reason of congestion there, and D claimed demurrage from P. P contended (a) that they were not liable for demurrage as the delay was caused by strikes, and (b) that in any event they should not be liable to pay D more demurrage than D had to pay under their contract with E.

Held, remitting the award to the GAFTA Board of Appeal for reconsideration, that (1) under the contract between P and D, no liability for delay was placed on the sellers, however (2) by reason of the Centrocon incorporation clause, P did have an independent obligation to pay demurrage under the standard Centrocon clause, although that obligation did not crystallise in the present case.

PAGNAN (R). & FRATELLI *v.* FINAGRAIN COMPAGNIE COMMERCIALE AGRICOLE ET FINANCIERE S.A.: ADOLF LEONHARDT, THE [1986] 2 LLoyd's Rep. 395, Staughton J.

3424. Sale of ship—buyer defaults—seller seeks to sell to third party—whether buyer can obtain injunction to prevent sale

B agreed to buy a new vessel from her builders, S. Payment was to be made in instalments and it was a term of the contract that should B default in making any payment, S could after a period of 20 days, rescind the contract. S was further required by the agreement to give B the right of first refusal to purchase the vessel should S contemplate selling the vessel to somebody else. B defaulted and after 20 days S gave notice of default. S then gave notice that they were going to sell the vessel to X. Five days after the giving of such notice, B offered the same price that X was prepared to pay, but attached certain conditions to the sale. B refused those conditions and B obtained an *ex parte* injunction restraining the sale of the ship to X. S appealed.

Held, discharging the injunction, that on all the facts and the evidence, this was not a case where B were entitled to interlocutory relief. B were not ready, willing and able to perform the contract.

NEPTUNE NAVIGATION CORP. *v.* ISHIKAWAJIMA-HARIMA INDUSTRIES CO. [1987] 1 Lloyd's Rep. 24, C.A.

3425. Sale of ship—free of average damage or defects affecting class—proper construction of sale contract

S sold four vessels to B, which were to be "free of . . . average damage or defects affecting class." The vessels were delivered, and in respect of one of them B claimed damages in arbitration for damages for proven defects affecting class. B was awarded damages, and a special case was stated for the Court. S contended that "average" governed "defects" and that B could only claim for such damages as would ordinarily be covered by insurance.

Held, that "average" did not govern defects, and that S's obligation was to deliver a vessel free of defects affecting class.

LIPS MARITIME CORP. *v.* NATIONAL MARITIME AGENCIES CO.; STAR OF KUWAIT, THE [1986] 2 Lloyd's Rep. 641, Bingham J.

3426. Sale of ship—Norwegian sale form—whether ship in deliverable state—whether cancellation wrongful—proper parties to the contract—novation

P agreed to sell their vessel to D1 pursuant to a contract made on the Norwegian sale form. The contract provided that the purchasers would be a company "to be nominated by" D1. Prior to delivery, and after the vessel had been inspected by D1's surveyor, D2 was nominated as purchasers. D3 and D6 were major shareholders in D1 and D2 who were also added as defendants. D1 then raised complaints as to the condition of the vessel. P contended that they were not material, but agreed to repair them. All but one item was repaired and P undertook to repair the final item if D1 made proper payment. D1 cancelled the contract. P claimed forfeiture of the deposit and damages, against D1 as effective parties to the contract, D2 as parties, and D3 to D6 as undisclosed principals. D said the vessel was not a contractually deliverable state and P had failed to satisfy a condition precedent as to the condition of the vessel. They contended that D1, and D3–D6 were not parties to the contract.

Held, that (1) the terms as to the condition of the vessel on delivery were not conditions precedent but innominate terms; (2) there was no defect of hull or machinery such as to effect deliverability of the vessel, and all her equipment was in satisfactory working condition; (3) D1 had cancelled the contract in their name. Accordingly, the novation to D2 never took effect; (4) D3–D6 were not parties or undisclosed principals.

AKTION MARITIME CORP. OF LIBERIA *v.* KASMAS (S.) & BROTHERS; AKTION, THE [1987] 1 Lloyd's Rep. 283, Hirst J.

3427. Salvage—derelict—award

[Scot.] P, the owners, master and crew of three fishing vessels, claimed salvage in respect of services rendered to the Dutch cargo vessel X. She had been abandoned by her crew, although her engines were left running with her automatic pilot on. She eventually grounded. P exercised great skill in refloating the vessel from the strand in East Lothian, and towed her to Leith. Salvage was conceded by D, although quantum was in issue.

Held, that (1) X was a derelict, which had a bearing on the dangers faced by P; (2) there was a risk of X becoming a total loss, from which she was salved by P; (3) the services were skilful and the award would be £60,000 on a salved value of £422,500.

FAIRBAIRN (DAVID JAMES) *v.* VENNOOTSCHAP G VEIR VRIES ZIN; PERGO, THE [1987] 1 Lloyd's Rep. 582, Scottish Ct. of Session, Outer House; Lord Davidson.

3428. Salvage—non-tidal inland waters—limit of jurisdiction

There was no right to recover a salvage award for services to vessels in non-tidal waters of England.

The Goring was a small passenger vessel. It was seen to be drifting down a non-tidal stretch of the Thames towards Reading bridge. The plaintiffs got a line aboard and hauled her to a mooring. They issued a writ *in rem* claiming salvage. The Admiralty judge refused to set aside the writ on the ground that the Admiralty court had no jurisdiction over vessels on non-tidal inland waters, holding instead that the Admiralty jurisdiction was worldwide, and there were no grounds for excluding from salvage services assistance rendered to a vessel in non-tidal waters.

Held, allowing the owners' appeal to the Court of Appeal (Sir John Donaldson M.R. dissenting), that no established right had been shown to recover a salvage award for services to vessels in non-tidal waters of England. The exercise of the Admiralty jurisdiction over non-tidal stretches of rivers had never been asserted and did not exist prior to the passing of the Admiralty Act 1840, and nothing in that Act or any subsequent Act had extended it. The Admiralty jurisdiction was limited by both subject matter and locality, and there were no grounds to justify its extension by the court. The writ should be set aside (*Nicholson* v. *Chapman* (1793) 2 H.Bl. 254 and *Falcke* v. *Scottish Imperial Insurance Co.* (1886) 34 Ch.D. 234 considered).

Sir John Donaldson considered that there was no rational basis on which to confine salvage to tidal waters.

Leave to appeal to the House of Lords was granted.

GORING, THE [1987] 2 W.L.R. 1151, C.A.

3429. Time charter—domestic consumption clause—scope of clause—N.Y.P.E. form, cl. 20

Cl. 20 of the New York Produce Exchange time charter was to be construed so as to make the shipowner liable to reimburse the charterer in respect of fuel used for all the crew's domestic purposes.

The charterers chartered *The Sounion* from its owners on a New York Produce Exchange form of time charter. Cl. 20 provided that fuel used by the vessel while off hire for cooking, condensing water or for grates and stoves should be paid for by the owners. A dispute arose between the owners and the charterers as to the extent of the clause. The dispute was referred to arbitration. The majority of the arbitrators held the effect of Cl. 20 was to make the owner liable for fuel consumed for all the crew's domestic purposes. The minority arbitrator held the owners were only liable to pay for fuel consumed for cooking and heating. On appeal, Gatehouse J. agreed with the minority. The charterers appealed.

Held, allowing the appeal, that the effect of the minority arbitrator's conclusion was that the owners would have to pay for fuel used for cooking but not for fuel used to operate deep freezers and refrigerators, and fuel for heating by air-conditioning but not for cooling by air-conditioning. There was no basis in principle, commercial justice, common sense, rhyme or reason for such a conclusion. The charterers and owners must have intended that the owners would be liable to pay for all fuel consumed for the domestic purposes of the crew.

SUMMIT INVESTMENT INC. *v.* BRITISH STEEL CORP; SOUNION, THE [1987] 1 FTLR 169, C.A.

3430. Time charter—guarantee—whether authority to grant guarantee—whether sufficient writing. See CLIPPER MARITIME *v.* SHIRLSTAR CONTAINER TRANSPORT, ANEMONE, THE, §1846.

3431. Time charter—order to unload at port—vessel proceeding to destination specified by harbour authority—whether charterer liable for damage to the vessel

Where a vessel subject to a time charter is ordered by the harbour authority to proceed to an anchorage for lightening and suffers damage, the order is an order as to employment of the vessel, and the charterers are liable to indemnify the ship owners for the damage.

On a time charter trip from Flushing to West Africa the captain, though appointed by the owner, was under charterer's orders with regard to employment and agency. The owner was still responsible for navigation and the charterer was not responsible for losses sustained through negligence of pilots or tugboats. The vessel was ordered by the charterer to discharge on the Bonny River in Nigeria, where traffic was controlled by the Port Harcourt Harbour Authority. They ordered the captain to proceed to an anchorage and the vessel was damaged en route. The arbitrators found that neither the master nor pilot was negligent. The owner claimed damages from the charterer, and the arbitrators upheld the claim. The charterers appealed, and it was accepted by counsel that there was an implied obligation to indemnify against consequences caused by compliance with the charterer's orders as to employment of the vessel.

Held, that the harbour authority's order should be considered as the charterer's order for the purpose of the implied obligation as to indemnity. The order was one as to the employment of the vessel and not as to navigation. As the obligation to indemnify was only in respect of consequences caused proximately by the charterer's order, and the award was not clear as to this point, that issue was remitted to the arbitrators for further consideration. (*Stag Line* v. *Ellerman* [1949] C.L.Y. 9498 followed; *Cosmar Compania Naviera* v. *Total Transport Corp.* [1984] C.L.Y. 3227, *Mediolanum Shipping Co.* v. *Japan Lines* [1984] C.L.Y. 3174 considered).

NEWA LINE *v.* ERECHTHION SHIPPING CO. S.A., [1987] 1 FTLR 525, Staughton J.

3432. Time charter—speed and performance clause—whether sufficiently certain

This case concerned the proper construction of a complex speed and performance clause in a five-year time charterparty on the New York Produce Exchange Form. The clause provided that there should be an equitable reduction of hire in the event that the vessel, on an average basis, failed to meet her guaranteed average speed and fuel consumption. It further provided that hire would be increased in the event that the vessel bettered the stipulated performance. O claimed hire from C on the basis that the vessel had bettered the requirements. C claimed that the clause was uncertain.

Held, that the clause was sufficiently certain to give O a right to claim, and O would be rewarded with an increase of hire in just the same way as C would have been able to claim a reduction in the appropriate circumstances.

DIDYMI CORP. *v.* ATLANTIC LINES AND NAVIGATION CO. INC. [1987] 2 Lloyd's Rep. 166, Hobhouse J.

3433. Time charter—Standtime form—speed and consumption warranty—meaning of qualification "about"—nature of warranty

O let their vessel to C for a time charter on the Standtime form. The charter provided that the vessel was capable of maintaining about 15·5 knots in moderate weather at certain levels of fuel consumption. It further provided that she would maintain a guaranteed average sea speed of about 15·5 knots over one year. C alleged that the vessel, which often proceeded at speeds considerably higher than 15·5 knots, consumed more fuel at those speeds than she would have done had she been capable of performing the warranted speed at the warranted consumption figure. Arbitrators found for C, holding that the qualification "about" had to be tailored to the requirement of the individual vessel. It was also found as a fact that the vessel's consumption had been adversely affected by a fouled bottom, the responsibility for which lay with O. O appealed to the Commercial Court. Evans J. *held* that (1) O was entitled to have his liability measured by reference to the lower end of the range imported by the qualification "about"; (2) it was for the arbitrators to determine what the qualification "about" was to have in each individual case. O appealed and C cross-appealed.

Held, dismissing both parties' appeals, that (1) the margin imparted in the word "about" could not be fixed as a matter of law. It was for the arbitrators to decide in each individual case; (2) the vessel was incapable of meeting the performance warranty for the periods specified; she was not any less incapable because during other periods she performed better than warranted, and O was not entitled to credit for fuel saved during those periods.

ARAB MARITIME PETROLEUM TRANSPORT CO. *v.* LUXOR TRADING CORP. AND GEOGAS ENTERPRISE S.A., AL BIDA, THE [1987] 1 Lloyd's Rep. 124, C.A.

3434. Total loss—whether casualty connived at or procured by owners

The vessel C.P. ran aground in the Red Sea in November 1982 and while still aground suffered a major fire. Her owners, P, claimed that the vessel was a total loss and in the alternative claimed that they were entitled to recover a partial loss in respect of each casualty. D, the underwriters, contended that the losses were procured or connived at by P.

Held, that P's claim failed, on the ground that the vessel was deliberately run aground and set afire and that P had procured or connived at this loss.

CONTINENTAL ILLINOIS NATIONAL BANK & TRUST CO. OF CHICAGO AND XENOFON MARITIME S.A. *v.* ALLIANCE ASSURANCE CO.; CAPTAIN PANAGOS D.P., THE [1986] 2 Lloyd's Rep. 470, Evans J.

3435. Voyage charter—delay—whether charterers' loss too remote in law

O let their vessel to C for a carriage of crude oil from Egypt to Europe. It was a term of the contract that the vessel would sail from Greece on November 22. The charter contained a clause excepting all loss arising without the actual fault or privity of O. The vessel sailed from Greece on November 26, in consequence whereof C had to pay an increased price for the oil which they had purchased. C claimed these damages from O. C appealed.

Held, dismissing the appeal, that (1) the loss was too remote in law and the arbitrator was correct; (2) the exceptions clause would not have assisted O.

TRANSWORLD OIL *v.* NORTH BAY SHIPPING CORP.; RIO CLARO, THE [1987] 2 Lloyd's Rep. 173, Staughton J.

3436. Voyage charter—demurrage—congestion causing delay in discharge—whether an "unavoidable hindrance"

Congestion in port which causes delay in discharging may be an "unavoidable hindrance" exempting a charterer from paying demurrage.

A charterparty required a vessel to give notice of readiness to discharge, whether in berth or not, with a damages clause for delay subject to an exemption for "unavoidable hinderances." The vessel in question was in port and gave notice of readiness to discharge. Subsequently there was a long delay due to the unavailability of a discharging berth. The charterers contended that the congestion that caused the delay brought them within the exemption.

Held, that the charterers were not liable for demurrage when congestion began during laytime, temporarily prevents the vessel reaching her discharging berth (*Amstelmolen, The* [1961] C.L.Y. 8237 referred to).

RICH (MARC) & Co. *v.* TOURLOTI COMPANIA NAVIERA S.A. [1987] 1 FTLR 399, Evans J.

3437. Voyage charter—demurrage—general strikes clause—strikes delay vessel already on demurrage

O let their vessel to C pursuant to the terms of a voyage charter on the Gencon form. The general strikes clause in the charter provided that should a strike affect the discharge of the cargo after the arrival of the vessel at the discharge port, receivers were to have the option of keeping the vessel waiting until the end of the strike against paying half demurrage after the expiration of time for discharge. The vessel arrived at Lagos and went on demurrage. Shortly after she came on demurrage, various strikes then delayed her discharge. C contended that as from the time of the first strike they were only obliged to pay half demurrage. Arbitrators upheld C's contention, but were reversed on appeal by Bingham J. C appealed.

Held, dismissing C's appeal, that there was nothing in the clause which applied to a new situation arising after the expiry of laydays. In these circumstances, the maxim "once on demurrage, always on demurrage" applied.

SUPERFOS CHARTERING A/S *v.* N.B.R. (LONDON); SATURNIA, THE [1987] 2 Lloyd's Rep. 43, C.A.

3438. Voyage charter—demurrage—Iran-Iraq war—refusal to proceed because of war—whether owners entitled to claim demurrage

During a period when hostilities between Iran and Iraq had ceased, O let their vessel to C, the Iranian national line, for a voyage from West Germany to Bandar Khomeini. The charter provided that if it appeared after departure from the loading port that the vessel would be subject to war risks, then the cargo would be discharged at a safe port in the vicinity of the port of discharge. The vessel arrived at Bandar Abbar, at which time hostilities had recommenced. She waited there a month and then C ordered her to join a convoy to Bandar Khomeini. The majority of the crew refused, and eventually discharge was ordered at Bandar Abbar. O claimed demurrage for the whole of that period. Arbitrators found that the refusal to proceed was legitimate and C was obliged to order the vessel to discharge at Bandar Abbas. They had wrongfully delayed in so doing.

Held, that (1) it was rightfully conceded by O that the arbitrators' finding that C was obliged to order the vessel to discharge at Bandar Abbas was wrong: they had an option to order the vessel to discharge at any port in the vicinity. (2) demurrage ran whilst the vessel was waiting off Bandar Abbas.

ISLAMIC REPUBLIC OF IRAN SHIPPING LINES *v.* ROYAL BANK OF SCOTLAND: ANNA CH., THE [1987] 1 Lloyd's Rep. 266, Steyn J.

3439. Voyage charter—demurrage—Pacific Coast Grain form—strike—whether exception to principle "once on demurrage, always on demurrage"

By a voyage charter in the Pacific Coast Grain form, O let their vessel to C. The charter provided that C would not be liable for any delays caused by strikes, and that the days for discharging would not count during any strike by workmen essential to discharge. The vessel came on demurrage when the vessel was at the discharge port, and was then delayed by a strike of workmen. O claimed, and arbitrators, awarded, demurrage during the strike period. C appealed.

Held, allowing C's appeal, that (1) the strike was the cause of the delay and was beyond the control of C; (2) upon a proper construction of the charterparty, both laytime and demurrage were suspended during the strike.

PRESIDENT OF INDIA *v.* N. G. LIVANOS MARITIME CO.; JOHN MICHALOS, THE [1987] 2 Lloyd's Rep. 188, Leggatt J.

3440. Voyage charter—demurrage dispute—whether compromised

Various claims arose between O and C under a voyage charter party. C claimed for damage to cargo and short delivery and O had claims for demurrage. A settlement agreement was entered into, and C contended that it embraced the demurrage claim, although most of the correspondence related to the cargo claim. C sought a declaration that the demurrage claim had been compromised.

Held, that on the facts and the documentary evidence, the demurrage claim had not been compromised and C were not entitled to their declaration.

FOOD CORP. OF INDIA *v.* MOSVOLDS REDERI A/S: ARRAS AND HOEGH ROVER, THE [1986] 2 Lloyd's Rep. 597, Staughton J.

3441. Voyage charter—freight—non-payment—whether assignee could claim freight—whether charterers entitled to right of set off

O assigned all the earnings of their vessel to the P bank. O let the vessel to C pursuant to a voyage charter in the Gencon form. P learned that O's P & I Club was about to be withdrawn and gave notice of assignment to C. Shortly thereafter the vessel was arrested by a creditor of O who had hitherto provided the vessel with bunkers. O did not put up security. C accepted O's conduct as a repudiatory breach of charter, and arranged for the transhipment of the cargo. C never paid the charterparty freight, which was "deemed to be carried on signing Bills of Lading, discountless and non-returnable, vessel and/or cargo lost or not lost" although was payable within five days of signing Bills of Lading. P, as assignee, claimed the freight from C. C contended that they had terminated the charter before freight had become payable, alternatively that they were entitled to set off their damages against the freight. Arbitrators held that C had a right of set off. P appealed.

Held, that (1) the true analysis was at the time of the arrest of the vessel there was an existing liability for freight, the time for payment of which was postponed. From the time of the signing of the Bills of Lading, freight was at C's risk; (2) the liability for freight was not terminated by O's repudiatory breach of contract and C's acceptance thereof; (3) no defence of equitable set-off could be admitted in light of the well-established exception in cases of freight. Thus although C was entitled to rely upon all the defences against the assignee P that they would have had against O, none of those defences availed them. The award would be set aside.

COLONIAL BANK *v.* EUROPEAN GRAIN & SHIPPING: DOMINIQUE, THE [1987] 1 Lloyd's Rep. 239, Hobhouse J.

3442. Voyage charter—freight—when balance payable—whether action time-barred

A voyage charter provided that 10 per cent. balance of freight was payable upon completion of discharge and settlement of demurrage "on production of a paid voucher from the charterers' broker to whom commission is due under the charter." Discharge was completed in October 1974, a statement of facts was submitted in December of that year. In November 1980 O appointed their arbitrator and in December 1980 C were requested to appoint their arbitrator. C contended that O's claim was statute-barred. The arbitrator held that the claim was not time-barred. C appealed.

Held, dismissing C's appeal that (1) O's cause of action did not accrue until they had produced a paid voucher to C. Demurrage could not be settled within the meaning of the charter, unless there was agreement between the parties, and as there had been no settlement, time still had not started to run against O; (2) even had time started to run against O, they had given sufficient notice to C of the commencement of proceedings.

MINERALS AND METALS TRADING CORP. OF INDIA *v.* ENCOUNTER BAY SHIPPING CO: SAMOS GLORY, THE [1986] 2 Lloyd's Rep. 603, Bingham J.

3443. Voyage charter—GENCON form—conclusive evidence clause—quantity of goods

By two charters O let their vessels to C for the carriage of cargoes. The charters were in the Gencon form and contained the usual "owners' responsibility" clause 2. That provided that O was only to be responsible for loss of or damage to the goods in certain specified circumstances. Cl. 28 provided that bills of lading were conclusive evidence of the quantity shipped and that O was to be responsible for the quantity of cargo signed for. O issued bills of lading in 1982 that had a section headed "Shippers description of Goods" which stated the quantity of goods said to have been shipped on board. The bill further provided, however, that the "weight . . . quantity . . . unknown." They were signed by the Master for the 1983 voyage, one bill of lading had the stamp and signature of the Master placed against the cargo quantity there set out. That bill did not contain the section rubric "Shippers description of Goods." C claimed that there were short deliveries on both voyages and the disputes were submitted to arbitration. Arbitrators found that the conclusive evidence clause overrode the caveat in the bills of lading, and that O was precluded from disputing that they had short-delivered the cargo.

Held, allowing O's appeal, that (1) except in the case of the one 1983 bill of lading, the signature of the master at the foot of the bill of lading did not amount to a signing for the cargo quantity declared by C in the shipper's section; (2) O was entitled to rely upon clause 2: the shortages did not arise by way of their actionable fault.

REDERIAKTIEBOLAGET GUSTAV ERIKSON *v.* DR. FAWZI ISMAIL: THE HERROE AND ASKOE [1986] 2 Lloyd's Rep. 281, Hobhouse J.

3444. Voyage charter—obligations upon charterer as to loading and stowage of cargo—Nuvoy form (1964)

By a charter on the Nuvoy form, O let their vessel to C. The charterers were to provide stevedores and load and stow the vessel free of expense to O and O was required to pay for all "dunnage required for the proper stowage of the cargo." C loaded the vessel with a cargo of oil cakes that required to be stowed with care. It was not, in that no ventilation channels were built into the stow, the cargo was not insulated from the hold walls or the engineroom bulkhead. The cargo was severely damaged, and C instituted arbitration proceedings against O. The arbitrator held that C was only entitled to nominal damages. He stated a special case for the Commercial Court.

Held, that (1) although C's obligation to load and stow the cargo appeared to be qualified by reference to the costs thereof, this did not in fact negative their obligation so to load and stow. Those provisions relating to dunnage did not impinge upon C's primary obligation (*Canadian Transport Co.* v. *Cout Line* [1940] A.C. 934, applied); (2) it was not established, on the facts, that O's breaches had caused anything but nominal damage.

C.H.Z. "ROLIMPEX" *v.* EFTAVRYSSES COMPANIA NAVIERA S.A.: PANAGHIA TINNOU, THE [1986] 2 Lloyd's Rep. 586, Steyn J.

3445. Voyage charter—SYNACOMEX form—cessor clause—whether charterers' liability ceased

By a charter on the SYNACOMEX form, O's vessel carried a cargo of rice from the U.S. to Basrah. The charter provided that O was to have a lien on the cargo for freight, dead freight and demurrage and that C would remain responsible for freight and demurrage incurred at discharge port. The charter contained a cessor clause. Goods were discharged in a damaged condition, and O was forced to put up a guarantee in Basrah which was enforced. O claimed an indemnity from C. C argued that because of the cessor clause, they were under no liability. They lost before arbitrators and Staighton J. and applied for leave to appeal.

Held, dismissing C's applicaiton for leave to appeal, that a long line of authority had held that the cessor clause was only applicable in circumstances where the lien of O was effective. The evidence established that O did not have an effective alternative remedy.

ACTION S.A. *v.* BRITANNIC SHIPPING CORP.; AEGIS BRITANNIC, THE [1987] 1 Lloyd's Rep. 119, C.A.

3446. Voyage charter—vessel ordered to wait off discharge port—basis of remuneration for waiting period

By a voyage charterparty O let their vessel to C for a laden voyage from Antwerp to Aqaba. C had problems relating to the sale of the cargo in Aqaba, and requested the vessel to wait off the port. She did so for nine days. C admitted that O was entitled to reasonable remuneration for waiting but contended that no time was lost, as the vessel eventually discharged before the expiry of the laytime period allowed. Arbitrators agreed, and merely awarded additional running expenses.

Held, allowing O's appeal, that (1) O was entitled to fair remuneration for having performed services *outside* the terms of the charter. The arbitrators should, therefore, have awarded loss of profit in addition to the extra running costs incurred.

GREENMAST SHIPPING CO. S.A. *v.* JEAN LION ET CIE S.A., SARONIKOS, THE [1986] 2 Lloyd's Rep. 277, Saville J.

3447. Voyage charter—whether concluded agreement as to demurrage provisions

P and D agreed to a voyage charter for the carriage of a cargo of durra, and a telex proposal from D to P contained the words "discharge rate 2,500/3,000 per day". The vessel performed the carriage and notice of readiness was given at the discharge port. P claimed demurrage at the rate of U.S. $2,000 per day. D contended that no demurrage terms had been agreed and that no legal obligations arose out of the booking note.

Held, that the telex did contain a contractual discharge rate and P was entitled to demurrage.

SIAM VENTURE AND DARFUR, THE [1987] 1 Lloyd's Rep. 147, Sheen J.

SHOPS, MARKETS AND FAIRS

3448. Airport shops

LONDON CITY AIRPORT SHOPS ORDER 1987 (No. 1983) [45p], made under the Shops (Airports) Act 1962 (c.35), s.1(2); operative on November 20, 1987; designates London City Airport for the purposes of s.1 of the 1962 Act.

SUMBURGH AIRPORT SHOPS ORDER 1987 (No. 837) [45p], made under the Shops (Airports) Act 1962 (c.35), s.1(2); operative on May 7, 1987; designates Sumburgh Airport for the purposes of s.1 of the 1962 Act.

3449. Sunday trading—ban—whether lawful—EEC Treaty

[Shops Act 1950 (c.28); Treaty of the European Economic Community (EEC), Art. 30.]

The provisions of the Shops Act 1950 are not inconsistent with Art. 30 of the EEC Treaty, and the former's ban on Sunday trading is therefore lawful.

WYCHAVON DISTRICT COUNCIL *v.* MIDLAND ENTERPRISES (SPECIAL EVENTS), *The Times,* February 28, 1987, Millett J.

3450. Sunday trading—whether guilty of an offence in respect of each sale

[Shops Act 1950 (c.28), s.47 and 59.]

The occupier of a shop who serves goods on a Sunday which are not exempted under the Act commits a single offence each day and not an offence each time he transacts a sale.

B. & Q. (RETAIL) *v.* DUDLEY METROPOLITAN BOROUGH COUNCIL, *The Times,* July 15, 1987, D.C.

SOCIAL SECURITY

3451. Adjudication

SOCIAL SECURITY (ADJUDICATION) AMENDMENT REGULATIONS 1987 (No. 1424) [45p], made under the Social Security Act 1975 (c.14), s.104(5)(*b*) and Sched. 20, operative on September 1, 1987; amend S.I. 1986 No. 2218.

SOCIAL SECURITY (ADJUDICATION) AMENDMENT (No. 2) REGULATIONS 1987 (No. 1970) [£1·60], made under the Social Security Act 1975 (c.14), ss.114, 115, 119(3) and (4), 166 and Sched. 13, and the Social Security Act 1986 (c.50), ss.52(4), 84(1)(*h*) and 89(1); operative on November 23, 1987 (part), January 1, 1988 (part) and April 11, 1988 (part); amend S.I. 1986 No. 2218.

3452. Attendance allowance

SOCIAL SECURITY (ATTENDANCE ALLOWANCE) AMENDMENT REGULATIONS 1987 (No. 1426) [45p], made under the Social Security Act 1975 (c.14), s.35(2A)(5A); operative on August 31, 1987; amend S.I. 1975 No. 598.

3453. Attendance allowance—higher allowance—degree of supervision

[Social Security Act 1975 (c.14), s.35(1).]

A person who needs continual attendance by night and day as a precautionary measure qualifies for the higher allowance.

MORAN *v.* SECRETARY OF STATE FOR SOCIAL SERVICES, *The Times,* March 14, 1987, C.A.

3454. Attendance allowance—whether attention should be medically required—Commissioner's decision

[Social Security Act 1975 (c.14), s.35(1)(*b*)(i).]

A claimant for attendance allowance was mentally handicapped and suffered from grand mal epilepsy. She was incontinent by night and received attention for 15 minutes twice per night for changing night clothes and sheets. The delegated medical practitioner (DMP) considered that, if adequate padding was used, in the absence of any tendency to skin vulnerability there was no medical need for repeated changing of the bed. He did not accept that C required prolonged or repeated attention by night in connection with her bodily functions under s.35(1)(*b*)(i) Social Security Act 1975.

Held, allowing the appeal, that the Act is concerned with whether C "reasonably requires" the relevant attention from another person see *R.* v. *Social Security Commissioner, ex p. Connolly*. It is not necessary that the attention should be "medically required" and by restricting his decision to medical considerations the DMP's decision was erroneous in law.

DECISION No. R(A) 3/86.

3455. Australia

SOCIAL SECURITY (AUSTRALIA) ORDER 1987 (No. 935) [85p], made under The Social Security Act 1975 (c.14), ss.2 and 143; operative on May 18, 1987; precludes payment of unemployment benefit to visitors from one country (either Australia or the U.K.) on holiday in the other and who are entitled to work during their stay.

3456. Austria

SOCIAL SECURITY (AUSTRIA) ORDER 1987 (No. 1830) [£1·30], made under the Social Security Act 1975 (c.14), s.143; operative on November 1, 1987; makes provision for the modification of the 1975 Act in order to give effect to a convention on social security between the U.K. and Austria.

3457. Benefits—overlapping benefits. See EUROPEAN COMMUNITIES, §1641.

3458. Benefits—sex discrimination. See EUROPEAN COMMUNITIES, §1635.

3459. Child benefit

CHILD BENEFIT (GENERAL) AMENDMENT REGULATIONS 1987 (No. 357) [80p], made under the Child Benefit Act 1975 (c.61), ss.2(1B)(2)(3), 4(1), 22(1), 24(1)(5), Sched. 1, para. 1; operative on April 6, 1987; amend S.I. 1976 No. 965 in relation the education of a dependent child.

3460. Claims and payments

SOCIAL SECURITY (CLAIMS AND PAYMENTS) REGULATIONS 1987 (No. 1968) [£4·50], made under the Social Security Act 1975 (c.14), ss.165A and 166(2), the Child Benefit Act 1975 (c.61), s.6(1), and the Social Security Act 1986 (c.50), ss.21(7), 51(1)(*a*)–(*s*) and 84(1); operative on April 11, 1988; contain provisions about the making of claims for, and the payment of, benefits under the above-mentioned Acts.

SOCIAL SECURITY (CLAIMS AND PAYMENTS) AMENDMENT REGULATIONS 1987 (No. 878) [45p], made under the Social Security Act 1975 (c.14), ss.17(1)(*a*)(ii), 79(3), 165A, 166, Sched. 20; operative on July 1, 1987; amends S.I. 1979 No. 628.

3461. Commissioners

SOCIAL SECURITY COMMISSIONERS PROCEDURE REGULATIONS 1987 (No. 214) [£2·70], made under the National Insurance Act 1974 (c.14), s.6, the Social Security Act 1975 (c.14), ss.101(5A)(5B), 106(2), 112(3), 114(2c)(5), 115(1)(5)(6), Sched. 20 (in part), the Social Security Act 1980 (c.30), ss.14, 15 and the Forfeiture Act 1982 (c.34), s.4) operative on April 6, 1987; regulate the procedure of the Social Security Commissioners in determining claims and questions.

3462. Computation of earnings

SOCIAL SECURITY BENEFIT (COMPUTATION OF EARNINGS) AMENDMENT REGULATIONS 1987 (No. 606) [45p], made under Social Security Act 1975 (c.14), ss.3(2)(3), 166, Sched. 20; operative on April 28, 1987; earnings as a member of a territorial or reserve force is to be disregarded for the purposes of reg. 7(1)(*g*) of S.I. 1983 No. 1598.

3463. Contributions

SOCIAL SECURITY (CONTRIBUTIONS) AMENDMENT REGULATIONS 1987 (No. 106) [45p], made under the Social Security Pensions Act 1975 (c.60), s.1 and the Social Security Act 1975 (c.14), s.168(1), Sched. 20; operative on April 6, 1987; further amend S.I. 1979 No. 591 by increasing the weekly lower and upper earnings limits for Class 1 contributions.

SOCIAL SECURITY (CONTRIBUTIONS) AMENDMENT (No. 2) REGULATIONS 1987 (No. 413) [£1·60], made under the Social Security Act 1975 (c.14), ss.3(2)(3), 4(2)(*b*)(6)(6A)(6D), 13(4)(5B), 168(1), Sched. 1, paras. 1(1C), 5(1)(*a*)(*b*), 6(1)(*b*)(*c*), Sched. 20, the Social Security and Housing Benefits Act 1982 (c.24), ss.9(4)(5), 47 and the Social Security Act 1986 (c.50), ss.74(5), 84(1), Sched. 4, paras. 3, 4; operative on April 6, 1987; further amend S.I. 1979 No. 591.

SOCIAL SECURITY (CONTRIBUTIONS) AMENDMENT (No. 3) REGULATIONS 1987 (No. 1590) [45p] made under the Social Security Act 1975 (c.14), ss.3(2)(3), 168(1), Sched. 20; operative on October 6, 1987; further amend S.I. 1979 No. 591.

SOCIAL SECURITY (CONTRIBUTIONS) AMENDMENT (No. 4) REGULATIONS 1987 (No. 2111) [85p], made under the Social Security Act 1975 (c.14); ss.3(2)(3), 4(2)(*b*),(6) and (6A), 11(3), 131, 166(2), 168, and Sched. 1, paras. 6(1)(*b*) and (*h*); operative on January 6, 1988; amend S.I. 1979 No. 591.

SOCIAL SECURITY (CONTRIBUTIONS, RE-RATING) ORDER 1987 (No. 46) [80p], made under the Social Security Act 1975, 120(5)(6), 121(2), 123A(1)(2); operative on April 6, 1987; prescribes weekly income for the purposes of contributions.

3464. Credits

SOCIAL SECURITY (CREDITS) AMENDMENT REGULATIONS 1987 (No. 414) [£1·40], made under the Social Security Act 1975 (c.14), ss.13(4) and 168, Sched. 20, and the Social Security Act 1986 (c.50), ss.84(1) and 89(1); operative on April 6, 1987; amend S.I. 1975 No. 556.

SOCIAL SECURITY (CREDITS) AMENDMENT (No. 2) REGULATIONS 1987 (No. 687) [45p], made under the Social Security Act 1975 (c.14), ss.13(4), 166(2), 168(1); operative on May 10, 1987; amend S.I. 1975 No. 556 so as to ensure that disabled local authority councillors do not lose their entitlement to contribution credit when their local authority allowances exceed a specified amount.

3465. Dependency

SOCIAL SECURITY BENEFIT (DEPENDENCY) AMENDMENT REGULATIONS 1987 (No. 355) [80p], made under the Social Security Act 1975 (c.14), ss.49, 84(1), 166, Sched. 20; operative on April 6, 1987; amend S.I. 1977 No. 343.

3466. Duty of care owed by adjudication officer—existence of duty of care—statutory exclusion of common law rights of action

[Crown Proceedings Act 1947 (c.44), s.2(5); Social Security Act 1975 (c.14), s.117.]

In an appeal from the refusal of an application to strike out a claim as disclosing no cause of action, an argument not advanced in the court below might be put on appeal since no question of fact or evidence arose if the opposing party had been given sufficient time to consider the point.

An adjudication officer was not exercising a judicial function in deciding whether to allow a claim. However, any challenge to the correctness of the decision other than by way of statutory appeal or judicial review necessarily involved a contravention of the 1975 Act and was not permitted. In any event the nature of the relationship between the claimant and the adjudication officer was such that no common law duty of care arose (*Smith* v. *Baker & Sons* [1891] A.C. 325, *United Dominions Trust* v. *Bycroft* [1954] C.L.Y.

640, *Oscroft* v. *Benabo* [1967] C.L.Y. 674, *R.* v. *Deputy Industrial Injuries Commissioner, ex p. Moore* [1965] C.L.Y. 13, *Curran* v. *Northern Ireland Co-ownership Housing Association* [1987] C.L.Y. 2709a, *Anns* v. *Merton London Borough Council* [1977] C.L.Y. 2030, *Yuen Kun Yen* v. *Att.-Gen. of Hong Kong* [1987] C.L.Y. 2580, *Governors of the Peabody Donation Fund* v. *Sir Lindsay Parkinson* [1984] C.L.Y. 2298 considered).

JONES *v.* DEPARTMENT OF EMPLOYMENT, *The Times,* November 27, 1987, C.A.

3467. Earnings factor

SOCIAL SECURITY (EARNINGS FACTOR) AMENDMENT REGULATIONS 1987 (No. 316) [80p], made under the Social Security Act 1975 (c.14), s.13(5)(5A), Sched. 20 and the Social Security Pensions Act 1975 (c.60), s.6(5A); operative on March 29, 1987; prescribes the earnings factor for the year 1987/88 for those who pay Class 1 contributions at a reduced rate.

SOCIAL SECURITY (EARNINGS FACTOR) AMENDMENT (No. 2) REGULATIONS 1987 (No. 411) [80p], made under the Social Security Act 1975 (c.14), ss.13(5), 168(1), Sched. 20, the Social Security Pensions Act 1975 (c.60), s.35(3) and the Social Security Act 1986 (c.50), ss.84(1), 89(1); operative on April 6, 1987; amend S.I. 1979 No. 676.

SOCIAL SECURITY REVALUATION OF EARNINGS FACTORS ORDER 1987 (No. 861) [45p], made under the Social Security Pensions Act 1975 (c.60), s.21; operative on June 3, 1987; provides for a revaluation of earnings factors.

3468. Family credit

FAMILY CREDIT (GENERAL) REGULATIONS 1987 (No. 1973) [£4·00], made under the Social Security Act 1986 (c.50), ss.20(1), (5)(*c*), (6), (10)–(12), 21(3) and (6)(*a*), 22(1) and (5)–(9), 51(1)(*h*) and 84(1), and the Social Security Act 1975 (c.14), ss.104(5) and 166(1); operative on April 11, 1988; provide for various matters which affect entitlement to family credit.

FAMILY CREDIT (TRANSITIONAL) REGULATIONS 1987 (No. 1974) [£1·30], made under the Social Security Act 1986 ss. 84(1), 89(1); operative on January 1, 1988; make transitional provision for the award of family credit in relation to claims made before April 11, 1988.

3469. Family income supplement

FAMILY INCOME SUPPLEMENTS (COMPUTATION) REGULATIONS 1987 (No. 32) [80p], made under the Family Income Supplements Act 1970 (c.55), s.2(1), 3(1)(1A), 10(1)(3a); operative on April 7, 1987; prescribes rates of family income supplements.

FAMILY INCOME SUPPLEMENTS (GENERAL) AMENDMENT REGULATIONS 1987 (No. 281) [45p], made under the Family Income Supplements Act 1970 (c.55), s.6(3); operative on March 24, 1987; amends S.I. 1980 no. 1437 so as to provide for awards of family income supplement to terminate not later than April 11, 1988.

3470. Family income supplement—normal gross income—partner on maternity leave—Commissioner's decision

The C's made a claim for family income supplement for a family consisting of themselves and one child who was born on September 4, 1984. At the date of claim, November 1, 1984, the husband was engaged and normally engaged in remunerative full-time work but the wife was on maternity leave which had started on June 2, 1984. She had received full pay for the first six weeks of absence and half pay for the next 12 weeks. The period of paid maternity leave ceased on October 7, 1984, any leave after that date being without pay. It was expected that the wife would return to work no later than March 26, 1985. The adjudication officer decided that in order to determine the family's normal gross income at the date of claim it was necessary to have regard to the wife's earnings received during a period other than the five weeks, or two months, immediately preceding the claim. On the basis of the wife's salary immediately before her maternity leave began the adjudication officer disallowed the claim. On appeal the C's contended that the wife's normal income, for the purposes of the claim, was NIL because she was at the date of the claim on unpaid leave. The social security appeal tribunal unanimously confirmed the adjudication officer's decision that family income supplement was not payable although they were of the opinion that the calculation of the wife's normal weekly gross earnings should be based upon the monies paid in the two months immediately preceding the date of claim.

Held, that (1) the decision of the tribunal was erroneous in law. Nonetheless family income supplement is not payable as, at the date of claim, the resources of the family exceeded the appropriate prescribed amount; (2) the appeal turns upon the meaning to be attached to the phrase "normal gross income" in s.4 of the Family Income Supplements Act 1970 and reg. 2(2) of the Family Income Supplement (General)

Regulations; (3) in this context "normal" means "usual"; (4) accordingly, giving the word "normal" its ordinary everyday meaning, a woman on maternity leave is not, while she is not in receipt of her usual pay, earning her "normal gross income" within the meaning of s.4(1) of the Family Income Supplements Act 1970. Therefore her average weekly wage cannot be calculated under reg. 2(2) of the Family Income Supplements (General) Regulations by reference to any period when she is on such maternity leave.

DECISION No. R(FIS) 1/87.

3471. Family income supplement—normal gross income—partner on maternity leave—Commissioner's decision

The C's originally made a claim for family income supplement, for a family consisting of themselves and one child, on November 1, 1984. Following rejection of that claim by both the adjudication officer and, later, the social security appeal tribunal, the C's made a second claim for family income supplement on March 12, 1985. The husband was engaged and normally engaged in remunerative full time work, however at that time the wife had been on unpaid maternity leave with effect from October 7, 1984 and was contracted to return to full employment on completion of maternity leave. The adjudication officer decided that in order to determine the family's normal gross income at the date of claim it was necessary to have regard to the wife's earnings received during a period other than the five weeks, or two months, immediately preceding the claim. On the basis of the wife's salary before maternity leave the adjudication officer disallowed the claim. The social security appeal tribunal unanimously confirmed the adjudication officer's decision. On appeal to the Commissioner the C's contended that the calculation of the wife's normal income, for the purpose of this claim, should be based upon the two months immediately prior to the date of claim at which time her earnings were NIL.

Held, that (1) the decision of the social security appeal tribunal was erroneous in point of law for failure to give reasons; (2) for the reasons explained in decision R(FIS) 1/87, which relates to the claim made on November 1, 1984, "normal" should be given its ordinary every day meaning of "usual"; (3) consequently a woman on maternity leave, during which she is not in receipt of her usual pay, is not earning her "normal gross income" within the meaning of s.4(1) of the Social Security Act 1970. Therefore her average weekly wage cannot be calculated under reg. 2(2) of the Family Income Supplements (General) Regulations by reference to any period when she is on such maternity leave and not in receipt of her usual pay; (4) it was correct to choose the wife's earnings for the last complete month in which she worked before she commenced maternity leave; (5) family income supplement is not payable because the resources of the family, thus calculated, exceeded the appropriate prescribed amount.

DECISION No. R(FIS) 2/87.

3472. Hospitals

SOCIAL SECURITY (HOSPITAL IN-PATIENTS) AMENDMENT REGULATIONS 1987 (No. 31) [45p], made under the Social Security Act 1975 (c.14), s.85(1), Sched. 20; operative on February 13, 1987; provide for benefits to be adjusted while the beneficiary is undergoing treatment as a hospital in-patient regardless of the sex of the beneficiary.

SOCIAL SECURITY (HOSPITAL IN-PATIENTS) AMENDMENT (No. 2) REGULATIONS 1987 (No. 1683) [£1·30], made under the Social Security Act 1975 (c.14), ss.81(4)(*d*), 82(6)(*b*), 85(1), Sched. 20; operative on April 11, 1988 save for Regs. 1, 2(1)(2)(*a*)(i)–(iii)(*b*)(13)(*c*) which are operative on November 2, 1987; amend S.I. 1975 No. 555 to provide for reductions in Social Security benefits after six weeks and 52 weeks where the recipients are receiving in-patient treatment at a hospital.

3473/4. Housing benefit. See HOUSING.

3475. Income support

INCOME SUPPORT (GENERAL) REGULATIONS 1987 (No. 1967) [£9·20], made under the Social Security Act 1986 (c.50), ss.20(1)(3)(*d*)(4)(9)(11)(12), 22(1)(2)(4)(5)–(9), 23(1)(3)(5), 51(1)(*n*), 84(1) and the Social Security Act 1975 (c.14), ss.114, 116(1)–(3A); operative on April 11, 1988; make general provision in relation to entitlement to, and amount of, income support.

INCOME SUPPORT (TRANSITIONAL) REGULATIONS 1987 (No. 1969) [£2·60], made under the Social Security Act 1986, ss.84(1) and 89(1); operative on November 23, 1987; make transitional provisions consequential on the winding-up of supplementary benefit and the introduction of income support on April 11, 1988.

3476. Industrial death benefit—prescribed disease—pneumoconiosis (asbestosis)—Commissioner's decision

The Commissioner discusses copious medical evidence on the subject of a connection between exposure to asbestos and death from gastro-intestinal cancer. After many years of employment involving exposure to asbestos the deceased had died as the result of broncho-pneumonia and metastatic carcinoma of the stomach. Post-mortem, asbestos had been found in the lung tissue and a post-mortem medical board had decided that the deceased had been disabled by pneumoconiosis (asbestosis) for a short period prior to his death.

The Commissioner re-affirms the principle that death resulting from a prescribed disease may be proved if it is shown, on balance of probability, that the disease caused or materially accelerated death or substantially contributed to or aggravated the causative condition by masking it, preventing its diagnosis or delaying its treatment. However, notwithstanding the diagnosis of asbestosis, the undisputed cause of death was not a prescribed disease and therefore none of these factors was present in this case. The appeal was dismissed.

DECISION No. R(I) 6/85.

3477. Industrial disablement benefit—prescribed disease—occupational deafness—Tribunal decision

[Social Security (Industrial Injuries) (Prescribed Disease) Regulations 1985 (S.I. 1985 No. 967).]

C was employed to operate a forming press which shaped parts for the motor industry from 1/8th inch mild steel.

Held, allowing the appeal, that (1) forging is performed upon bar metal normally, but not invariably, hot; and forming is performed upon sheet metal, invariably cold; (2) sub-para. (*d*) of para. A10 of Sched. 1 of the Prescribed Diseases Regulations relates solely to the forging industry, the terms drop-stamping or drop-hammering being included simply to accommodate the terminology used in different parts of the country; (3) metal pressing or forming is a separate branch of industry involved in shaping cold sheet metal and is recognised by the experts as being quite distinct from forging. Such pressing or forming is not included within the terms of prescription for occupational deafness; (4) the words "engaged in the shaping of metal" are to be read as qualifying both "drop-forging plant (including plant for drop-stamping or drop-hammering)" and "forging press plant".

DECISION No. R(I) 1/87.

3478. Industrial injuries benefit

PNEUMOCONIOSIS, BYSSINOSIS AND MISCELLANEOUS DISEASES BENEFIT (AMENDMENT) SCHEME 1987 (No. 400) [45p], made under the Industrial Injuries and Diseases (Old Cases) Act 1975 (c.16), s.5; operative on April 1, 1987; adds lung cancer to the list of diseases in respect of which benefit is payable under S.I. 1983 No. 136.

SOCIAL SECURITY (INDUSTRIAL INJURIES) (PRESCRIBED DISEASES) AMENDMENT REGULATIONS 1987 (No. 335) [80p], made under the Social Security Act 1975 (c.14), ss.76, 77, 113, Sched. 20; operative on April 1, 1987 save for reg. 5 which is operative on April 6, 1987; provides for a further industrial disease of lung cancer.

SOCIAL SECURITY (INDUSTRIAL INJURIES) (PRESCRIBED DISEASES) AMENDMENT (No. 2) REGULATIONS 1987 (No. 2112) [85p], made under the Social Security Act 1975 (c.14), ss.76, 77, Sched. 20; operative on January 4, 1988; amend the description of those occupations for which occupational deafness is prescribed.

SOCIAL SECURITY (INDUSTRIAL INJURIES) (REDUCED EARNINGS ALLOWANCE AND TRANSITIONAL) REGULATIONS 1987 (No. 415) [80p], made under the Social Security Act 1975, s.59A(10), Sched. 20 and the Social Security Act 1986 (c.50), ss.84(1), 89(1); make provision in relation to determining reduced earnings allowance.

3479. Industrial injuries benefit—special hardship allowance—whether permanent condition affected by C's unwillingness to undergo operative treatment—Commissioner's decision

C was discharged from his regular occupation as a fireman because of the relevant loss of faculty, an injury to his ankle. The injury was sufficient to render him permanently incapable of resuming that occupation although there was the possibility that a surgical operation would restore his capacity. However, he was unwilling to undergo such treatment.

Held, allowing the appeal, that (1) although regulations provide that C may be disqualified from receiving benefit for refusal to undergo a surgical operation of a minor character, the operation in this case was not of that character and therefore refusal could not be held against him; (2) in a case where incapacity will be permanent if there is no operation, the likelihood of incapacity being permanent has to be judged by reference among other things not only to the likelihood (or the reverse) of the operation being a success but also to the likelihood (or the reverse) of C being willing to undergo it, and (3) although it was more likely than not that an operation would be successful C was

unwilling to undergo it and therefore on balance of probabilities his incapacity was likely to be permanent.
DECISION No. R(I) 2/86.

3480. Invalid care allowance—whether Council Directive 79/7/EEC applies to invalid care allowance—Commissioner's decision

C, a married woman residing with her husband, gave up work to look after her mother who was in receipt of an attendance allowance. She claimed an invalid care allowance with effect from February 5, 1985. Her claim was referred by the adjudication officer to a social security appeal tribunal. The S.S.A.T. held that notwithstanding section 37(3)(*a*) (i) of the Social Security Act 1975 (subsequently repealed with retrospective effect from December 22, 1984, by s.37 of the Social Security Act 1986), which provided that a woman was not entitled to the allowance if she was married and residing with her husband, the claimant was entitled to an individual care allowance on the ground that section 37(3)(*a*)(i) of the Social Security Act 1975 was discriminatory on grounds of sex, contrary to Council Directive 79/7/EEC. The Directive relates to the progressive implementation of the principle of equal treatment of men and women in social security matters and required Member States to bring into force by December 22, 1984, the measures necessary for compliance.

The adjudication officer appealed to the Commissioner on the ground that the Directive did not apply to invalid care allowance. The Chief Commissioner referred certain questions for preliminary ruling to the European Court of Justice who held that (1) a benefit provided by a Member State and paid to a person caring for a disabled person forms part of a statutory scheme providing protection against invalidity which is covered by Directive 79/7/EEC pursuant to Article 3(1)(*a*) of that Directive; (2) discrimination on grounds of sex contrary to Article 4(1) of Directive 79/7/EEC arises where legislation provides that a benefit which forms part of one of the statutory schemes referred to in Article 3(1) of that Directive is not payable to a married woman who lives with or is maintained by her husband, although it is paid in corresponding circumstances to a married man. (*Drake* v. *Chief Adjudication Officer (No. 150/85)* [1986] C.L.Y. 1468).

Held by the Chief Commissioner in the light of the ruling of the European Court of Justice and dismissing the appeal that (1) the terms of Directive 79/7/EEC are of direct legal effect so as to enable its provisions to be relied upon by a private individual against the U.K. as a Member State of the Community; (2) the claimant is entitled as from February 5, 1985 to invalid care allowance pursuant to the provisions of s.37 of the Social Security Act without regard to the disentitlement previously contained in s.37(3)(*a*)(i). A further reason for dismissing the adjudication officer's appeal arose from the retrospective amendment with effect from December 22, 1984 of s.37(3) of the Social Security Act 1975 by s.37 of the Social Security Act 1986 which, *inter alia,* removed the grounds of disentitlement previously contained in s.37(3)(*a*)(i).
DECISION No. R(G) 2/86.

3481. Invalidity benefit—deeming incapacity for work

The Commissioners dismissed appeals from two claimants for invalidity benefit who had both performed some work while claiming. (It is unnecessary to set out the Commissioners' decisions). Both claimants appealed to the Court of Appeal. The appeals were heard simultaneously by the Court of Appeal as they both involved the construction of reg. 3(3) of the Social Security (Unemployment, Sickness and Invalidity Benefit) Regulations. Both decisions of the Commissioners were reversed by the Court of Appeal.

Held, by the Court of Appeal, allowing the appeals on a point of law, that (1) the words "by reason only of the fact that he has done some work while so suffering" in reg. 3(3) are not to be read as a pre-condition to be fulfilled apart from the requirements of sub-paras. (i) and (ii) of the regulation; (2) if a claimant has worked and satisfied either sub-paras. (i) or (ii) and has not exceeded the earnings limit then the regulation confers a discretion for incapacity to be deemed; (3) the activity of one claimant as a local councillor was work within the meaning of reg. 3(3).
SOCIAL SECURITY No. R(S) 3/86.

3482. Invalidity benefit—failure to attend RMO examination—findings necessary when considering whether disqualification is appropriate—Commissioner's decision

[Social Security (Unemployment, Sickness and Invalidity Benefit) Regulations 1983 (S.I. 1983 No. 1598), reg. 17.]

C who suffers from chronic-backache has been in receipt of benefit since August 16, 1980. He was requested to attend for a routine medical examination by a Divisional Medical Officer of the DHSS on August 31, 1984. He did not attend. The adjudication officer disqualified the claimant from receiving invalidity benefit from September 21 to

October 25, 1984 on the ground that he had failed without good cause to attend for examination as provided by reg. 17(1)(*b*) of the Social Security (Unemployment, Sickness and Invalidity Benefit) Regulations 1983. The claimant appealed. In the written submission to the appeal tribunal the adjudication officer submitted that the claimant had also, or alternatively, failed to observe the rule of behaviour prescribed in reg. 17(1)(*d*)(ii).

Held, that (1) the tribunal's recorded findings of the material facts and their decision did not convey the reason for the decision or on which arm of the regulation the appeal had been dismissed; (2) as it was impossible to tell what evidence had been accepted a breach of reg. 19(2)(*b*) of the Social Security (Adjudication) Regulations had occurred; (3) the decision of the appeal tribunal was set aside and the case was remitted for rehearing by an entirely differently constituted tribunal; (4) there is no rule of law to preclude a fresh tribunal from having before them the proceedings of an earlier tribunal whose decision has been set aside.

DECISION No. R(S) 1/87.

3483. Invalidity benefit reference of a claim or question by an adjudication officer to a social security appeal tribunal—Tribunal decision

C, who had been found capable of work within limits, appealed against the decision of the adjudication officer disallowing his claim to invalidity benefit for the period January 4 to February 22, 1984. The adjudication officer, in his written submission, referred for the decision of the tribunal the question of C's entitlement to invalidity benefit for a further period of claim from February 23 to February 29, 1984, under the provisions of s.99(2)(*c*) of the Social Security Act 1975. A copy of that submission was sent to C in compliance with s.99(3) which provides that notice in writing of the reference shall be given to C. C continued to submit claims to invalidity benefit up to September 25, 1984 and at an adjourned hearing of the tribunal on September 10, 1984 the adjudication officer orally asked the tribunal to determine whether C was entitled to invalidity benefit for the period March 1 to September 25, 1984. C was present at the hearing and, it is to be inferred, raised no objection. The tribunal determined that invalidity benefit was not payable for the period January 4, 1984 to September 25, 1984.

Held, that (1) although no time is specified in s.99(3) for the giving of the notice in writing to C, the notice has to be given within such time before the tribunal hearing, as is reasonable in the circumstances of the particular case; (2) the giving of notice in writing under s.99(3) is a requirement which involves a clear element of public interest and a claimant is unable to waive the necessity for such a notice; (3) although there was a breach of s.99(3) when the oral reference was made on September 10, 1984, the decision of the social security appeal tribunal had an existence and was capable of being appealed; (4) it was open to the Commissioners to set the decision aside and either to substitute their own decision or to remit the case to another tribunal for determination; (5) it was right in the circumstances of the case to adopt the former course; (6) C was entitled to invalidity pension for the period from January 4, 1984 to April 30, 1984 but was not entitled to invalidity pension for the period May 1 to September 25, 1984.

DECISION No. R(S) 5/86.

3484. Maternity and funeral expenses

SOCIAL FUND MATERNITY AND FUNERAL EXPENSES (GENERAL) REGULATIONS 1987 (No. 481) [£1·60], made under the Social Security Act 1986 (c.50), ss.32(2)(*a*), 84(1), 89(1) and the Supplementary Benefits Act 1976 (c.71), ss.3, 4, 34; operative on April 6, 1987; revoke S.I. 1986 No. 2173 and make provision for payments to be made out of the social fund in certain circumstances to meet maternity and funeral expenses.

3485. Maternity grant—effect of EEC Regulations on a claim to maternity grant based on periods of insurance or employment elsewhere within the European Community—Commissioner's decision

C, a German national, was employed and insured in West Germany for several years up to March 31, 1982. She arrived in Great Britain on April 3, 1982 to join her husband, a British national working in Scotland. She went to Switzerland on May 29, 1982 to complete certain studies and returned to Great Britain on August 1, 1982. On August 13, 1982 she made a claim to British maternity grant in respect of her confinement which was expected to occur in the week commencing September 27, 1982. The adjudication officer disallowed her claim as she did not satisfy the requirement to be present in Great Britain for more than 182 days in the aggregate in the 52 weeks immediately preceding the week in which she was expected to be confined and could not be treated as having been so present. The question was whether periods of insurance and employment in West Germany could be taken into account under the EEC Regulations for the purpose of satisfying that requirement.

Held, dismissing C's appeal that, (1) C does not satisfy the conditions of reg. 3 of the Social Security (Maternity Benefit) Regulations 1977 and the provisions of reg. 3B of those regulations are not applicable to her; (2) C is covered by Council Regulation (EEC) No. 1408/71; (3) only the competent institution of a Member State in whose territory C is or was last employed is competent to aggregate insurance periods in accordance with art. 18 of the Regulation; (4) C is unable to avail herself of Art. 18(1) (which provides for aggregation of period of insurance) and para. 4(1) of point J in Annex VI to the Regulation (which provides for period of insurance to be treated as periods of presence) because the Member State in which she was last employed was Germany and not the U.K.; (5) para. 4(2)(*b*) of point J of Annex VI to the Regulation, which provides that where the husband is or was lastly subject to U.K. legislation periods of insurance or employment completed by him under the legislation of a Member State *other than* the U.K. are to be regarded as periods of presence of the wife for the purposes of the presence tests provided that she was residing with him throughout those periods, is of no assistance to C as during her periods of absence from the U.K. her husband continued to be employed and insured there; (6) neither of the reciprocal conventions on social security matters with the Federal Republic of Germany and with Switzerland respectively are of assistance to C.
DECISION No. R(G) 1/86.

3486. Maternity pay and allowance. See EMPLOYMENT, §1346.

3487. Medical evidence

SOCIAL SECURITY (MEDICAL EVIDENCE) AMENDMENT REGULATIONS 1987 (No. 409) [80p], made under the Social Security Act 1975 (c.14), s.115(1), Scheds. 13, 20; amend S.I. 1976 No. 615 in relation to maternity certificates.

3488. Mobility allowance—claim made after C had attained the age of 66—earlier claim having failed on medical grounds—whether a claim once dismissed can continue to have an effect—Tribunal decision

[Social Security Act 1975 (c.14), s.37A.]

A claim for mobility allowance made on June 17, 1981, was disallowed as the medical conditions were not satisfied. A further claim was made on May 24, 1984, by which time C had attained the age of 66. The adjudication officer decided that mobility allowance was not payable and C appealed to the Appeal Tribunal. In allowing C's appeal the Appeal Tribunal held that the intention of the regulations was to ensure that those who made early but unsuccessful claims were to be given a later chance of this benefit after the age of 65 as their condition deteriorated. The adjudication officer appealed to the Commissioner.

Held that (1) although s.37A(5)(*b*) of the Social Security Act 1975 does not in term provide that the making of a claim is to be a condition of entitlement to mobility allowance it has that effect by virtue of the words "would have been entitled but for para. (*b*) below" in para. (*aa*)(i). The result is that a claimant who shows that he satisfied the residential and medical conditions during a period immediately preceding his 65th birthday cannot be said to have been entitled in respect of that period unless the first week of the period was the week, or was later than the week, in which a claim was received by the Secretary of State; the *McCaffrey* judgment distinguished for the purposes of mobility allowance; (2) regarding s.37A(5) it is not correct that para. (*b*) is excluded from para. (*aa*)(iv). Para. (*aa*)(ii) comes into play only in cases where para. (*b*) has taken effect and prevented a claimant from taking advantage of para. (*aa*)(i); (3) a claim once dismissed cannot continue to have an effect.
DECISION No. R(M) 4/86.

3489. Mobility allowance—entitlement—duty of commissioner on appeal

There were two conditions precedent to a claim in respect of benefit for any day under s.37A of the Social Security Act 1975: First, that the prescribed conditions were all satisfied on the day when the claim was received, and, second, that in respect of any day for which benefit was claimed the conditions were satisfied on that day. There was thus a continuing test for entitlement to a continuing benefit. A claim once made was not a continuing claim, which could be deemed to be repeated on every subsequent day. Satisfaction of the conditions in respect of any day *for which* benefit was claimed was necessary for recovery. But it was not sufficient for recovery. The conditions had also to be satisfied in respect of any day on which the claim was made (*Insurance Officer* v. *Hemmant* [1984] C.L.Y. 3272 applied. *Desai* (CM/143/1984) disapproved). Further, in determining whether the applicant was "ordinarily resident in Great Britain" under reg. 2 of the Mobility Allowance Regulations 1975 (S.I. 1975 No. 1573) the question that had to be asked was: had the applicant shown that he had habitually and usually resided in the

U.K. from choice and for a settled purpose throughout the prescribed period, apart from temporary or occasional absences. It then had to be determined as a matter of fact that the applicant had shown such residence. It was not required to determine his "real home", nor need any attempt be made to discover what his long term future intentions or expectations were. The relevant period was not the future but one which had largely or wholly elapsed (*Akbar Ali* v. *Brent London Borough Council* [1983] C.L.Y. 1157, 1815 applied). Further, on an appeal to the Social Security Commissioner, the duty of the Commissioner was to make an entirely fresh appreciation of whether the applicant was entitled to payment. The duty of the adjudication officer was to place before the commissioner all the considerations which he thought to be material. The commissioner's functions were not constrained by an adjudication made by those who had previously ruled on the matter, nor were the adjudication officer's functions constrained by any submissions by his predecessor (*R.* v. *Medical Appeal Tribunal ex p. Hubble* [1959] C.L.Y. 2147 followed).

GADHOK *v.* CHIEF ADJUDICATION OFFICER, March 24, 1986 (C.A.T. No. 278).

3490. Mobility allowance—relevance of behavioural factors in determining a person's ability to walk—Tribunal decision

[Social Security Act 1975 (c.14), s.37A.]

A child, with severe mental subnormality as a result of brain damage at birth, claimed mobility allowance. The disability was accepted by the medical appeal tribunal as being physical. While capable of the physical movements of walking his behaviour while doing so was erratic and unpredictable so that at times he needed to be physically restrained while on other occasions he refused to move. The medical appeal tribunal disregarded his behavioural problems in refusing an award. In setting aside the medical appeal tribunal's decision the Tribunal of Commissioners *held*, allowing the appeal that (1) *R(M) 2/78*, in which a child suffering from Down's Syndrome was found to be virtually unable to walk, remains unaffected by the decision in *Lees* v. *The Secretary of State for Social Services* [1985] C.L.Y. 3277; (2) Where a person suffers from behavioural problems which stem from a physical disability affecting the exercise of his walking powers, two tests must be applied to determine whether he is virtually unable to walk:—

i. is his ability to walk out of doors so restricted "as regards the distance over which or the speed at which or the length of time for which or the manner in which he can make progress on foot without severe discomfort" that he is to be treated as virtually unable to walk, and if so

ii. is his condition attributable to a physical impairment, such as brain damage, so that he cannot walk as distinct from will not walk?

If the child's refusal to walk was a matter of conscious choice there could be no question of his stopping having arisen from a physical condition over which he had no control; (3) Hyperactivism does not of itself qualify a sufferer for mobility allowance. What is relevant is whether a person suffers from "temporary paralysis" so far as walking is concerned and if so to what extent.

DECISION No. R(M) 3/86.

3491. Mobility allowance—relevance of medical reports to the power to review awards of mobility allowance—Commissioner's decision

[Mobility Allowance Regulations 1975 (S.I. 1975 No. 1573), reg. 15(2); as replaced by Social Security (Adjudications) Regulations 1985 (S.I. 1984 No. 451), reg. 55(2).]

On a claim for mobility allowance C was found to be virtually unable to walk and an award was made to the age 75. A medical report was later received by the Department of Health and Social Security from a Department medical officer expressing the opinion that the claimant was well able to walk. Reference was made to the frequent replacement of surgical boots. The Secretary of State for Social Services applied for the award to be reviewed (now see reg. 60 Social Security (Adjudication) Regulations 1984). The Medical Appeal Tribunal which finally considered the application found that the award had been made in ignorance or as a result of a mistake as to a material fact and reviewed and revised the award.

Held, (1) Following R(I) 3/75 and *R.* v. *Secretary of State for Social Services ex p. Loveday* a fresh medical opinion does not of itself establish that an original decision was given in ignorance of a material fact and does not constitute a ground for reviewing an earlier award; (2) Though the fresh medical report contained particulars of material facts there was nothing in the appeal tribunal's decision to show that these facts were accepted as evidence of the claimant's ability to walk; (3) Applying *Gadhok* v. *Chief Adjudication Officer* the Commissioner, in directing that the application for a review be considered by a fresh tribunal, indicated that they should consider whether there had been a relevant change of circumstances since the original award as at the date of the application for review. While the medical report was not itself a relevant change of circumstances (see R(S) 6/78) it might be evidence that such a change had occurred. The tribunal would be entitled to decide whether there had been such a change since the decision was given, notwithstanding section 37A(7) Social Security Act 1975 (*Insurance Officer* v. *Hemmant* [1984] C.L.Y. 3272 applied).

DECISION No. R(M) 5/86.

3492. National assistance

NATIONAL ASSISTANCE (CHARGES FOR ACCOMMODATION) REGULATIONS 1987 (No. 370) [45p], made under the National Assistance Act 1948 (c.29), s.22(3) and (4); operative on April 6, 1987; increase charges for accommodation managed by a local authority.

3493. National insurance—failure to make payments—defence

[Social Security Act 1975 (c.4), s.146.]

It is not a defence to a charge of failing to make national insurance payments on time that there was no intent to avoid payment or that the accused did not possess a card.

R. *v.* HIGHBURY CORNER STIPENDIARY MAGISTRATE, *ex p.* D.H.S.S., *The Times*, February 4, 1987, D.C.

3494. Notification of deaths

SOCIAL SECURITY (NOTIFICATION OF DEATHS) REGULATIONS 1987 (No. 250) [80p], made under the Social Security Act 1986 (c.50), ss.60, 83(1), 84(1); operative on April 6, 1987; require registrars of births and deaths to provide specified particulars of death to the Secretary of State.

3495. Overpayments

SOCIAL SECURITY (PAYMENTS ON ACCOUNT, OVERPAYMENTS AND RECOVERY) REGULATIONS 1987 (No. 491) [£2·70], made under the Social Security Act 1986 (c.50), ss.27, 51(1)(*t*), (*u*), 53, 83(1), 84(1) and 89; operative on April 6, 1987; provide for, *inter alia*, the making of payments on account of social security entitlement and the prevention of duplication of payments.

3496. Pensioners' lump sum payments

PENSIONERS' LUMP SUM PAYMENTS ORDER 1987 (No. 1305) [45p], made under the Pensioners' Payments and Social Security Act 1979 (c.48), s.4(1)(2); operative on December 7, 1987; provide for a £10 payment to persons to whom ss.1–3 of the 1979 Act apply during the week beginning December 7, 1987.

3497. Personal injuries—loss of earnings—whether social security benefits received more than five years after cause of action accrued deductible. *See* JACKMAN *v.* CORBETT, §1160.

3498. Portugal

SOCIAL SECURITY (PORTUGAL) ORDER 1987 (No. 1831) [85p], made under the Social Security Act 1975 (c.14), s.143 and the Child Benefit Act 1975 (c.61), s.15(1); operative on October 22, 1987; makes provision for the modification of the said two Acts of 1975 so as to give effect to an agreement on social security between the U.K. and Portugal.

3499. Sickness benefit—deeming incapacity for work—Councillor's earnings—Tribunal decision

[Social Security Act 1975 (c.14), ss.14 and 17; Social Security (Unemployment, Sickness and Invalidity Benefit) Regulations 1983 (S.I. 1983 No. 1598) reg. 3.]

C, an assistant divisional officer of the ambulance service, claimed sickness benefit from 23.1.84 having previously received statutory sick pay from his employer. Incapacity was diagnosed as nervous debility. Although incapable of following his normal occupation the claimant had performed the duties of a Local Authority Councillor. He provided details of prospective meetings together with evidence that he had been actively encouraged to take an interest in the affairs of the Local Authority for therapeutic reasons by his general practitioner. On 16.3.84 the adjudication officer disallowed the claim from 23.1.84 to 17.4.84 and referred the period 18.4.84 to 3.7.84 to the social security appeal tribunal for determination. The adjudication officer's decision was confirmed and C appealed to the Commissioners.

Held, that (1) because of the work he had done in attending council meetings he could not be regarded as incapable of work unless he could be deemed under reg. 3(3) of the Social Security (Unemployment, Sickness and Invalidity Benefit) Regulations 1983; (2) in the context of reg. 3(3) 'earnings' means amounts to which the claimant is entitled and is not limited to payments he actually receives; (3) for the purpose of reg. 3(3) 'ordinarily' is interpreted as 'in more than half of the weeks in which the claimant has worked'; (4) a reference period of a specific length is desirable to produce a reasonable assessment of what is ordinarily earned. The suggested period of 13 weeks is not an inflexible rule however; (5) for the purposes of the earnings test weeks in which no work has been done should be discounted; (6) as the claimant did not satisfy the earnings test the claim was disallowed except for 2 weeks when no work was performed.

DECISION No. R(S) 6/86.

3500. Social Fund (Maternity and Funeral Expenses) Act 1987 (c.7)

This Act empowers the Secretary of State to prescribe, under s.32(2)(*a*) of the Social Security Act 1986, amounts, whether in respect of prescribed items or otherwise, to meet maternity expenses and funeral expenses.

The Act received the Royal Assent on March 17, 1987.

3501. Social Security Act 1986—commencement

SOCIAL SECURITY ACT 1986 (COMMENCEMENT No. 5) ORDER 1987 (No. 354) [80p], made under the Social Security Act 1986 (c.50), s.88(1); brings into force on April 6, 1987 section 18(1), 39 (in part), 86(1)(2) (in part), Sched. 3, paras. 4, 5(1) (in part) (3), 6, 7, 16, Sched. 10, paras. 1, 10, 11, 67 (in part), 73, Sched. 11 (in part).

SOCIAL SECURITY ACT 1986 (COMMENCEMENT No. 6) ORDER 1987 (No. 543 (C.12)) [£1·40], made under the Social Security Act 1986, s.88(1); brings into force on May 1, 1987 ss.2, 13, 14, 17, 79(1)(2), 80 (in part), Scheds. 1, 10 (in part) of the 1986 Act; brings into force on January 4, 1988 ss.1, 3, 4, 5, 12 (in part), 15 (in part), Sched. 10 (in part) of the said Act and brings into force on April 6, 1988 ss.6, 7, 9, 10, 12 (in part), 15 (in part), 18(2)–(6), 19, Scheds. 2, 10 (in part) of the said Act.

SOCIAL SECURITY ACT 1986 (COMMENCEMENT No. 7) ORDER 1987 (No. 1096 (C.28)) [£1·30], made under the Social Security Act 1986, s.88(1); brings into force on June 26, 1987 s.86(1)(2) (in part), Sched. 10, paras. 94(b), 102, Sched. 11 (in part) brings into force on April 6, 1988 s.86(1) (in part), Sched. 10, para. 96; brings into force on April 10, 1988 s.39, Sched. 3, paras. 8, 9, 10; brings into force on April 11, 1988 ss.36, 39 (in part) 51 (in part), 65(1)–(3), 66, 78, 86(1) (in part), Sched. 3, paras. 11, 12, Sched. 6, Sched. 10, paras. 62–66, 67 (in part), 69, 70, 85, 96, 101(*a*) (in part), 108, Sched. 11 (in part).

SOCIAL SECURITY ACT 1986 (COMMENCEMENT No. 8) ORDER 1987 (No. 1853 (C.56)) [£1·60], made under the Social Security Act 1986, s.88(1); brings into force on either April 1, 1988 or April 4, 1988, according to circumstances, ss.20(1)(7)(8)(9)(11)(12), 21(4)–(7), 22, 28, 29, 30(1)–(3)(5)–(7), 31, 86(1) (in part) (2) (in part), Sched. 10, paras. 44, 48, 49, 52, 58–60, Sched. 11 (in part), and brings into force on April 11, 1988 sections 20, 21, 22 (so far as they are not already in force) 23, 24, 25, 26, 27 (in part), 32, 33–35, 39, 65(4), 67(2)(*b*), 73, 77, 79(3), 86(1), (2), Sched. 3, para. 8, Sched. 7, para. 3, Sched. 10, paras. 32–43, 45–47, 48, 50, 51, 54–57, 61, Sched. 11 (in part).

3502. Supplementary benefit—additional requirements—award of estate rate heating addition—Commissioner's decision

[Supplementary Benefit (Requirements) Regulations (S.I. 1983 No. 1399).]

C's home was part of a housing estate recognised by the Secretary of State as having been built with a heating system which has disproportionately high running costs. The fuel supply for the heating system had been disconnected. The adjudication officer decided that an additional requirement for heating was not applicable under para. 6 of Sched. 4 to the Requirements Regulations. On appeal the tribunal upheld the adjudication officer's decision on the grounds that it would not be reasonable to allow such an additional requirement for heating when the fuel supply to the heating system had been disconnected. The claimant appealed to a Social Security Commissioner.

Held, allowing the appeal, that (1) neither reg. 12(1) of the Requirements Regulations nor the provisions of para. 6 of Sch. 4 to those regulations entitles the adjudicating authorities to refuse a heating addition on grounds of their not considering it reasonable to make a special extra allowance; (2) in order to obtain an addition under para. 6 of Sched. 4 to the Requirements Regulations C must show that: (i) she is a householder in terms of the regulations; (ii) the home is part of an estate; (iii) the estate was built with a heating system and (iv) that particular heating system is one of which the Secretary of State has in his discretion recognised the running costs to be disproportionately high. The issues at paras. (i), (ii) and (iii) are to be decided by the adjudicating authorities (the issue of a certificate as in para. (iv) is for the Secretary of State); (3) the use of the system has nothing to do with the statutory tests. Once a certificate is issued all claimants on the estate should have the appropriate rate of additional requirement included in their requirements unless they are already receiving another heating addition of at least the same amount; (4) "Estate" is a word which should be given its ordinary and natural meaning in the context in which it occurs; (5) "The home" has the meaning assigned it in reg. 2(1) of the Requirements Regulations.

DECISION No. R(SB) 1/87.

3503. Supplementary benefit—additional requirements—whether large, healthy man suffered from a "condition" entitling him to an additional allowance

[Supplementary Benefit (Requirements) Regulations 1983 (S.I. 1983 No. 1399), Sched. 4, para. 14.]

The mere mass of a large, healthy man which requires him to eat more than an average quantity of food does not constitute a "condition" within the regulations entitling him to an additional allowance for a special diet.

ADAMSON *v.* CHIEF ADJUDICATION OFFICER, *The Independent*, June 25, 1987, C.A.

3504. Supplementary benefit—additional requirements—whether laundry includes dry-cleaning and whether laundry costs should be divided between washing and drying—Commissioner's decision

[Supplementary Benefit (Requirements) Regulations 1983 (S.I. 1983 No. 1399).]

C had requested an additional requirement for laundry on the grounds that he satisfied para. 18 of Sched. 4 to the Requirements Regulations because there were no suitable washing or drying facilities to do laundry at home. On appeal against the adjudication officer's decision the tribunal found that C had suitable washing facilities but did not have suitable facilities for drying and allowed an additional requirement for drying costs only. The tribunal also recorded that they did not feel obliged to adjudicate upon C's contention that for the purposes of the Requirements Regulations "laundry" includes dry-cleaning. C appealed to the Social Security Commissioner.

Held, allowing the appeal that (1) in ordinary, everyday parlance there is a clear distinction between laundry and dry-cleaning. The term "laundry", for the purposes of para. 18 of Sched. 4 to the Requirements Regulations, does not include dry-cleaning; (2) to satisfy the condition in column 1 of para. 18(*a*) of Sched. 4 to the Requirements Regulations it is enough for the claimant to show *either* that the washing facilities are not suitable *or* that the drying facilities are not; (3) having satisfied the condition in column (1) of para. 18(*a*) of Sched. 4 to the Requirements Regulations, the amount in column (2) is applicable. There is no warrant for fragmenting C's estimated average weekly laundry costs so that the cost of drying is separated from the cost of washing.

DECISION No. R(SB) 19/86.

3505. Supplementary benefit—additional requirements—whether washing machine rental/purchase is a laundry cost—Commissioner's decision

[Supplementary Benefit (Requirements) Regulations 1983 (S.I. 1983 No. 1399).]

C had appealed against the adjudication officer's decision as to the amount of the additional requirement applicable for laundry costs. On appeal the tribunal refused to include in the calculation of the additional requirement for laundry the rental costs of a washing machine. C appealed to a Social Security Commissioner solely on that point.

Held, dismissing the appeal, that the cost of a washing machine, whether by renting or purchase, does not come within the phrase "laundry costs" in para. 18 of Sched. 4 to the Requirements Regulations.

DECISION No. R(SB) 20/86.

3506. Supplementary benefit—claimant given access to children—claim made for children's transport fares in respect of access—whether "exceptional need"

V was divorced, his wife had custody of the children and he had reasonable access which meant visits by the children to his home at weekends. As V was prohibited by injunction from going near the wife, he sent a taxi for the children or arranged their travel by public transport. As V was on supplementary benefit, he made a claim to cover the cost of that travel. The adjudication officer decided that the fares did not constitute an "exceptional need" under the Supplementary Benefit (Single Payments) Regulations 1981 and the Supplementary Benefits Act 1976. V appealed contending that exceptional meant something that was not a normal requirement even though it was a recurring need. V went to the Court of Appeal.

Held, that the scheme of the 1976 Act and Regulations distinguished between "regular recurring" needs and "exceptional" ones. An exceptional need ended after a temporary limited period. The cost of fares was a recurring need and did not come within the Regulations.

VAUGHAN *v.* SOCIAL SECURITY ADJUDICATION OFFICER [1987] 1 F.L.R. 217, C.A.

3507. Supplementary benefit—conditions of entitlement

SUPPLEMENTARY BENEFIT (CONDITIONS OF ENTITLEMENT) AMENDMENT REGULATIONS 1987 (No. 358) [80p], made under the Supplementary Benefits Act 1976 (c.71), ss.5, 6(2)(3), 34(1) and the Social Security Act 1975 (c.14), s.166(2)(3); operative on April 6, 1987; further amend S.I. 1981 No. 1526.

3508. Supplementary benefit—housing requirements

SUPPLEMENTARY BENEFIT (HOUSING REQUIREMENTS AND RESOURCES) AMENDMENT REGULATIONS 1987 (No. 17) [£1·60], made under the Supplementary Benefits Act 1976 (c.71), ss.2(2), 34(1), Sched. 1, paras. 1(2), (2(1); operative on January 26, 1987; amend S.I. 1983 No. 1399.

3509. Supplementary benefit—housing requirements—interest on unpaid road charges—Commissioner's decision

[Supplementary Benefit (Requirements) Regulations 1983 (S.I. 1983 No. 1399).]

C was asked to pay road charges for "private street works" executed by his local authority. The demand gave him the option of paying by annual instalments, each one including an amount of interest. C accepted this option and claimed a housing requirement in respect of the interest payable. The adjudication officer refused to make an award but, on appeal, the tribunal decided that the interest charges were an identifiable housing requirement. The adjudication officer appealed to the Social Security Commissioner.

Held, dismissing the appeal, that (1) requirements reg. 17 (interest on loans for repairs and improvements) can only directly apply where sums have been borrowed for repairs and improvements to the home; (2) road charges and the interest payable thereon are charges in respect of the home; (3) interest payments, but not repayments of a capital sum for road charges, are outgoings in respect of the home; (4) such interest payments are analogous (reg. 18(1)(*g*)) to interest on money forwarded for any reason falling within reg. 17(3)(*k*) (other improvements which are undertaken with a view to improving the fitness of the home for occupation); (5) the provisions of reg. 17(2) (offset of disregarded capital in excess of £500 against amounts borrowed) will apply where a housing requirement is appropriate because of the analogy to any amount provided for by reg. 17.

DECISION No. R(SB) 3/87.

3510. Supplementary benefit—normal requirements—whether board and lodging charge include adequate heating—Tribunal decision

C was a single man living in a local authority hostel. He paid a charge for his accommodation which did not cover the cost of adequate heating. Heating could be obtained at an additional cost through a prepayment slot meter. The supplementary benefit officer (now adjudication officer) decided that an amount for an *additional* requirement was not applicable. The social security appeal tribunal upheld the decision of the benefit officer and C appealed to a Social Security Commissioner claiming, in his application for leave, entitlement as part of his *normal* requirements. The appeal was heard by a Tribunal of Commissioners.

Held, that the amounts paid by way of the slot meter in order to obtain adequate heating were not part of the charge for board and lodging and hence were not part of the claimant's normal requirements.

The Tribunal set aside the decision of the social security appeal tribunal and gave their own decision refusing the claimant's request for a weekly heating allowance.

DECISION No. R(SB) 18/86.

3511. Supplementary benefit—powers of Secretary of State—payable benefit

[Supplementary Benefits Act 1976 (c.71), s.2(1A).]

The Secretary of State does not have power to determine either generally or particularly the amount of supplementary benefit payable in respect of board and lodging. Accordingly, Regulations 3(2) and 3(3) of the Supplementary Benefits (Requirements) Amendments and Temporary Provisions Regulations 1984 (S.I. 1984 No. 2034) are *ultra vires*.

SECRETARY OF STATE FOR SOCIAL SERVICES *v.* ELKINGTON, *The Independent*, March 18, 1987, C.A.

3512. Supplementary benefit—relevant education—meaning of "person" for the purposes of reg. 11*(c)* and *(d)* of the Conditions of Entitlement Regulations—Commissioner's decision

[Supplementary Benefit (Conditions of Entitlement) Regulations 1981 (S.I. 1981 No. 1526).]

C was living away from and estranged from his parents and in the care of a local authority. He was refused supplementary benefit on the grounds that he was treated as receiving relevant education and did not satisfy any of the conditions of reg. 11 of the Conditions of Entitlement Regulations under which persons so treated are entitled to benefit. On appeal the tribunal concluded that the word "person" in reg. 11(*d*) of those regulations means an individual and not a local authority or similar organisation and decided the application of that regulation by reference only to the arrangements between C and his natural parents. The appeal was allowed. The adjudication officer appealed to a Social Security Commissioner.

Held, dismissing the appeal, that the word "person" in reg. 11(*c*) and (*d*) of the Supplementary Benefit (Conditions of Entitlement) Regulations refers only to a *natural* person and not a corporate or unincorporate body such as a local authority.

DECISION No. R(SB) 2/87.

3513. Supplementary benefit—requirements

SUPPLEMENTARY BENEFIT (REQUIREMENTS) AMENDMENT REGULATIONS 1987 (No. 2193) [45p], made under the Supplementary Benefits Act 1987 (c.71), s.34(1)(*c*); operative on December 30, 1987; amend S.I. 1983 No. 1399.

3514. Supplementary benefit—requirements and resources

SUPPLEMENTARY BENEFIT (REQUIREMENTS AND RESOURCES) AMENDMENT AND UPRATING REGULATIONS 1987 (No. 659) [£1·40], made under the Supplementary Benefits Act 1976 (c.71), ss.1(3), 2(2), 34(1), Sched. 1, paras. 1, 2, and the Social Security Act 1975 (c.14), s.166(2)(3); operative on April 13, 1987 save for regs. 1, 2(*c*), 3, 7, 8 which are operative on April 6, 1987, provide for an increase in the maximum weekly board and lodging charge which will be met by supplementary benefit in respect of certain residents in nursing or residential care homes.

SUPPLEMENTARY BENEFIT (REQUIREMENTS AND RESOURCES) AMENDMENT REGULATIONS 1987 (No. 1325) [85p], made under the Supplementary Benefits Act 1976 (c.71), ss.1(3), 2(2), 33(5), 34(1), Sched. 1, paras. 1, 2 and the Social Security Act 1975 (c.14), s.166(2)(3); operative on July 27, 1987 save for reg. 4 which is operative on September 1, 1987; further amend S.I. 1983 No. 1399 in relation to claimants resident in residential care and nursing homes.

3515. Supplementary benefit—resources

SUPPLEMENTARY BENEFIT (RESOURCES) AMENDMENT REGULATIONS 1987 (No. 660) [£1·40], made under the Supplementary Benefits Act 1976 (c.71), ss.2(2), 34(1), Sched. 1, para. 1; operative on April 6, 1987; further amend S.I. 1981 No. 1527.

3516. Supplementary benefit—resources—capital deposited in a property owned by a co-operative association—Commissioner's decision

[Supplementary Benefit (Resources) Regulations 1981 (S.I. 1981 No. 1527), reg. 6.]

In August 1983, C sold her home and moved to a property owned by a Co-operative Association. The right to occupy property owned by the Association was dependent upon the occupant's purchasing one share in the Co-operative and also taking up loan stock. C deposited £11,500 as loan stock, which was payable 12 months after she resigned from the association. In the event, she gave notice of withdrawal from the Co-operative on September 14, 1984 and moved to alternative accommodation on September 22, 1984.

On a claim for supplementary benefit on October 5, 1984 the adjudication officer decided that the loan stock of £11,500 represented an actual capital resource which precluded C from receiving supplementary benefit. On appeal the tribunal overturned the decision of the adjudication officer, considering that the £11,500 had been deposited with a Housing Association and should be disregarded under Resources Regulation 6(1)*f*). The adjudication officer appealed against this decision to the Social Security Commissioner.

Held, allowing the appeal, that (1) subscription for loan stock could properly be regarded as a deposit within Resources Regulation 6(1)(*f*); (2) if reliance was to be placed on reg. 6(1)(*f*) at the date of claim, the money had first to be deposited and the home to be occupied; as C had ceased to occupy the property concerned, no advantage could be derived from this regulation; (3) provided that a deposit in an association property could be identified with the proceeds of the former home—a disregard under Resources Regulation 6(1)(*b*) may be appropriate; (4) to be afforded a disregard under reg. 6(1)(*b*), consideration would need to be given to whether or not it was reasonable in the circumstances to extend "the six month period".

DECISION No. R(SB) 4/87.

3517. Supplementary benefit—resources—notional earnings—Commissioner's decision

[Supplementary Benefit (Resources) Regulations 1981 (S.I. 1981 No. 1527), reg. 4(3).]

C, who lived alone, was unemployed and had been in receipt of supplementary allowance since 1976. He had no other income. Following the receipt of information, the

Department made enquiries which confirmed that he was working four days a week for a total of 28 hours. In a statement made at the Unemployment Benefit Office the claimant declared earnings of £8 for two days work and his employer subsequently confirmed he was paid £4 each time he worked. The benefit officer basing his findings on information obtained from a special investigator found that a rate of £1·50 per hour was a reasonable working wage and calculated C's earnings at £42 per week which precluded the payment of supplementary allowance from February 18, 1984. On appeal the tribunal confirmed the benefit officer's decision and C appealed to a Social Security Commissioner. The Commissioner held that the tribunal's findings of fact and reasons for decision were inadequate in a number of respects. He referred the case to another tribunal and gave detailed directions as to the points on which findings should be made. The Commissioner adopted the construction of reg. 4(3) of the Resources Regulations set out in CSB 92/1984.

Held, allowing the appeal, that (1) for the application of reg. 4(3) it was necessary to establish: (i) identity of the employer; (ii) the particulars of the services provided by the member of the assessment unit for that employer; (iii) the actual payment made for the services (including payment in kind); (iv) the amount which would be paid for comparable employment and for the purposes of that regulation "person" included a limited company or other corporate employer; (2) the onus of proof throughout reg. 4(3) lay with the benefit officer. The standard of proof was that of establishing the facts on a balance of probability; (3) the discretion to treat a member as possessing notional earnings should be expressed in a judicial manner taking into account all the circumstances; (4) notional earnings should be reduced by the amount actually paid by the employer and according to the employer's ability to pay.

DECISION No. R(SB) 13/86.

3518. Supplementary benefit—resources—treatment of a capital resource—gifted to relatives—Commissioner's decision

[Supplementary Benefit (Resources) Regulations 1981 (S.I. 1981 No. 1527), reg. 6(1)(*a*)(iii).]

At the relevant time, prior to moving to a residential home, lived in a flat the owned. Because her health deteriorated she later entered a nursing home where she would received continuous care. Supplementary benefit was paid from October 27, 1983 when the value of the flat was disregarded because it was for sale. C's son incurred expenditure on redecorating the flat. It was not until March 15, 1985 that the position was reconsidered (supplementary benefit being in payment throughout the intervening period) when it was disclosed that the flat was to be gifted to C's two sons. The adjudication officer considered that the flat remained the property of C and, because it could no longer be disregarded under Resources Reg. 6(1)(*a*)(iii) and the value exceeded the capital limit, C was precluded from receiving supplementary benefit.

On appeal, the tribunal decided that the flat was no longer C's property and overturned the adjudication officer's decision. The adjudication officer appealed to a Social Security Commissioner.

Held, allowing the appeal, that (1) in the transfer of a property from one person to another the courts will not complete an incomplete gift and if no deed of gift was executed the resultant incomplete gift could be revoked at any time; (2) the tribunal erred by failing to consider the doctrine of proprietary estoppel which arises when an intended recipient of a gift (in this case the flat) expends money on its improvement in the belief that he or they already own a sufficient interest in the property; (3) in the circumstances of the case, should it be decided that the flat remained the property of C, the distribution of the proceeds of sale of the flat would need to be considered in the light of Resources Reg. 4(1).

DECISION No. R.(SB) 7/87.

3519. Supplementary benefit—resources—treatment of a dependant's interest in a trust fund—Commissioner's decision

C was a widow who lived with her two sons aged 9 and 4. Her husband died on 27.9.79 and his will was contested. A Court Order was made on 25.5.82 which created a Trust Fund and directed that the balance of the estate after legal costs and a sum awarded to C should be held on trust absolutely for the 2 children in equal shares until they reached 21 years. A solicitor was made co-trustee of the funds together with the claimant. It was established from the trust's solicitor that income from the fund had been paid to the children and that during the period in issue each child had in excess of £3,000 held on trust.

The supplementary benefit officer decided that the trust income should be taken into account as a resource and a recoverable overpayment of £444·60 had occurred for the period 18.8.82–13.3.83 because C had failed to disclose that money had been paid out of the trust fund. On appeal the tribunal confirmed the decision adding that the children should be treated as possessing their capital under the trust fund by virtue of reg. 4(6) of the Resources Regulations. C appealed to the Commissioner.

Held, allowing the appeal, that (1) the tribunal erred in law by finding that the children had notional resources. In the circumstances of the case each child had an actual resource consisting of one half of the trust fund which but for their infancy, they could call for now; they were absolutely entitled but lacked legal capacity; (2) despite the fact they had not reached the age of majority (18 years) the Court had powers to make advances out of the children's absolute interest; (3) Resources Regulation 8(1) applied to both dependants. Thus the capital resources of both children must be disregarded under this regulation—the resource of each child to be treated as producing a weekly income equal to that child's requirements; (4) as reg. 8(1) applied to the children's capital resources the failure to disclose payments of income out of the trust fund could not have caused an overpayment. The tribunal therefore erred by finding that the claimant had been overpaid supplementary benefit. Failure to disclose income paid out of the trust fund was, in the circumstances of this case, irrelevant when calculating the amount of supplementary benefit payable.

DECISION No. R(SB) 26/86.

3520. Supplementary benefit—resources—treatment of allowance paid by the Manpower Services Commission—Commissioner's decision

[Supplementary Benefit (Requirements) Regulations 1983 (S.I. 1983 No. 1399), reg. 19.]

In September 1984 C made a claim for supplementary benefit because he had ceased work in order to begin a full-time TOPS course. C was the owner-occupier of a property, but to attend the course he had to live away from home and he rented a room for £19·50 per week exclusive of meals. His wife and two children continued to live in the home. While on the course he received from MSC an allowance of £106·25 per week, made up of £38 personal allowance, £24·70 dependants' allowance, £40 for living away from home and £3·55 for mid-day meals. The adjudication officer decided that C was not entitled to supplementary benefit as his resources exceeded his requirements. On appeal the tribunal confirmed the decision and C appealed to a Social Security Commissioner.

Held, allowing the appeal, that (1) the personal, living away and mid-day meals allowances within the weekly payment made by MSC to the claimant were "for his maintenance" and fell to be taken into account under reg. 11(2)(*h*) of the Supplementary Benefit (Resources) Regulations 1981; (2) the dependants' allowance made to C was not "for his maintenance"; (3) the dependants' allowance was "other income" and was to be taken into account under Resources Regulation 11(5)(*e*) and given the appropriate disregard.

DECISION No. R(SB) 28/86.

3521. Supplementary benefit—resources—treatment of compensation award made by an Industrial Tribunal—Commissioner's decision

C's employment was terminated on 9.1.84 and she claimed Supplementary Benefit on 16.5.84. In the meantime, she had taken her case to an industrial tribunal contending that she had been unfairly dismissed and on 20.3.84 the industrial tribunal found in her favour and awarded her a total of £2,952.15. This was made up of: a basic award ($2\frac{1}{2}$ weeks at £60.50) = £151.25; compensation award (9.1.84–20.3.84) = £541.50; compensation award (36 weeks from 21.3.84) = £1,949.40; loss of statutory rights = £10; loss of employer's contributions to pension rights = £300.

On 13.6.84 the adjudication officer decided that the compensation award of £1,949.40 fell to be taken into account as earnings for 36 weeks from 21.3.84 which precluded C from receiving supplementary benefit until 26.11.84. On appeal, the social security appeal tribunal revised this decision considering that the industrial tribunal compensation award of £1,949.40 was not a payment in lieu of notice or remuneration but a lump sum award and therefore capital. The adjudication officer appealed to a Social Security Commissioner.

Held, allowing the appeal, that (1) in reg. 10(1) the words 'derived from' were wide and meant having their origin in'; (2) in the circumstances of this case the compensation had its origin in past employment and it was immaterial that the award was made through a statutory body; (3) in reg. 10(1)(*d*) the word 'remuneration' meant the remuneration which would otherwise have been payable had it not been for the termination of the claimant's employment. Accordingly, a compensatory award made by an industrial tribunal constituted a payment in lieu of remuneration within reg. 10(1)(*d*).

DECISION No. R(SB) 21/86.

3522. Supplementary benefit—resources—treatment of payment under a deed of covenant—Commissioner's decision

[Taxes Management Act 1970 (c.9), s.42(7); Supplementary Benefit (Resources) Regulations 1981 regs. 4(4), 11(5).]

C was a student who had claimed benefit during the summer vacation from her course. The Department of Health and Social Security had awarded her a bursary under which approved fees were paid and maintenance requirements were calculated as £1,904. This sum was to be made up of a contribution from her parents of £1,119 and a payment by the DHSS of £785. Her father chose to make his contribution by way of a Deed of Covenant executed August 31, 1983. He undertook to pay the gross sum of £540 each September 1, January 1, and April 1 for a period of up to 7 years. He made payments net of tax (the annual net amount exceeding £1,119). The adjudication officer decided that the difference between the gross amount paid by her father and the assessed contribution was an income resource to be taken into account at the weekly rate of £9.63, subject to a disregard of £4, and awarded a weekly allowance of £15.82. C appealed against this decision. Before the appeal was heard, the adjudication officer reviewed his decision so that the annual gross figure of £1,620 was taken into account at a weekly rate subject to a £4 disregard, thereby removing her entitlement altogether. On appeal the tribunal confirmed the decision by a majority. C appealed to the Commissioner.

Held, allowing the appeal, that (1) where a payment in respect of which tax may be payable was made net of tax, reg. 11(6)(*a*) of the Supplementary Benefit (Resources) Regulations 1981 provided that any reference in reg. 11 to such a payment was a reference to the net payment; (2) whether or not her father actually made any contribution, by virtue of reg. 4(4) of the Supplementary Benefit (Resources) Regulations 1981 she had to be treated as possessing the assessed contribution of £1,119; (3) documents which may have to be acted on by persons not party to them have to be construed by reference to what they contain in the light of the surrounding circumstances. Account could be taken of the fact that the covenant was drawn up so as to benefit from the tax law relating to such covenants, but not of what was now said to have been the intention of the covenantor; (4) the covenant provided for 3 separate annual payments of £540 each. One was payable on September 1, for 7 years from September 1, 1983, one payable on January 1, for 7 years from January 1, 1984 and one payable on April 1, for 7 years from April 1, 1984; (5) in August 1984, 1/52 of each of the net payments due on September 1, 1983, January 1, 1984 and April 1, 1984 was attributable to each week. In September 1984, the payment of September 1983 would have been exhausted but the payment due September 1, 1984 would have come into play; (6) any repayment of income tax related to a period of one year. Under s.42(7) of the Taxes Management Act 1970 it was to be treated as repayable when it was repaid. Under reg. 11(5) of the Supplementary Benefit (Resources) Regulations 1981 the weekly amounts (being 1/52 of the payment) would attract a £4 disregard unless that disregard had already been used up; (7) reg. 4(4) of the Supplementary Benefit (Resources) Regulations 1981 did not make clear the period to which the notional income was to be appropriated. That did not matter in this case because the notional income was subsumed into the contribution actually made. There would only have been a notional income if the actual payment under the Deed of Covenant had been less than the assessed contribution; (8) the covenanted income fell to be taken into account in full up to the extent of the assessed contribution. The excess including the tax recovered would have the benefit of the £4 disregard permissible under reg. 11(5) of the Supplementary Benefit (Resources) Regulations.

DECISION No. R(SB) 25/86.

3523. Supplementary benefit—single payment—fuel costs—Tribunal decision

[Supplementary Benefit (Single Payments) Regulations 1981 (S.I. 1981 No. 1528), reg. 26.]

C claimed a single payment for or towards meeting the cost of her electricity bill of £91·43 which comprised a standing charge of £9·40 and £82·03 for units consumed. The adjudication officer rejected the claim by reference to reg. 26 and 30 of the Supplementary Benefit (Single Payments) Regulations 1981. On appeal the tribunal awarded a single payment of the full amount of the bill in question, apparently under reg. 26. The adjudication officer appealed to the Social Security Commissioner.

Held, allowing the appeal, that (1) The tribunal erred in law when they awarded a single payment to meet the full amount of the bill and ignored the provisions of paragraph (2)(*a*) of reg. 26; (2) The reference to the amount set aside is an indication that reg. 26 is concerned with provision for the unforeseen and falls to be interpreted by reference to the personal circumstances of the particular assessment unit and not to the average circumstances of the population as a whole. This means that the question of whether there has been a period of exceptionally severe weather falls to be determined by reference to C's own locality; (3) The word "exceptionally" is an ordinary English word which cannot be precisely defined but when it is applied to the British climate it means nothing more than "unusually" or "abnormally"; (4) The "trigger points" method employed to determine whether there has been a period of exceptionally severe weather is unsatisfactory: the method fails to take account of the fact that what is exceptional at one time of year (thereby causing an increase in fuel consumption) may well be normal for another time of year; also, what is or is not exceptional or abnormal at one place, or at one season may or may not be exceptional at another place or season; (5) The method of determining whether the period of exceptionally severe weather has resulted in increased fuel consumption by reference only to a comparison between the degree days in the period of the fuel bill with the average number of such days in the corresponding period in previous years was also rejected; (6) The adjudicating authorities are required to make value judgments as to whether there has been a period of exceptionally severe weather and if so whether it has resulted in consumption greater than normal. In reaching their decision they can rely on their own knowledge of the weather prevailing in the area and any available records. Meteorological statistics may be looked at as evidence but it should not be considered as the only relevant evidence; (7) The period (whether of a week or more) to which the claim for the cost of increased fuel consumption relate should include some period (long or short) of exceptionally severe weather. "Period" is not defined but the length of a period of weather falls to be considered as a factor in its severity.

DECISION No. R(SB) 9/86.

3524. Supplementary benefit—single payment—fuel costs and standing charges—Commissioner's decision

[Supplementary Benefit (Single Payments) Regulations 1981 (S.I. 1981 No. 1528), regs. 26(1)(2).]

C claimed a single payment for fuel costs in respect of the period July 20, 1983 to March 10, 1984, having moved to a new home with a heating system with which he was unfamiliar. The adjudication officer awarded a single payment of £24·40, excluding the amount of the standing charges included in the fuel bill. On appeal the tribunal found in C's favour, on the grounds that the phrase "fuel costs" in reg. 26(2)(*b*) of the Single Payments Regulations encompasses the standing charge in respect of fuel. The adjudication officer appealed to a Social Security Commissioner.

Held, allowing the appeal, that (1) whatever meaning is given to "fuel costs" must be consistent throughout reg. 26. Since the amount payable "to meet fuel costs" is restricted under reg. 26(1)(*a*) by reg. 26(2), to the cost of the amount of the excess over normal consumption, that restriction confers a limited meaning on the expression "Fuel costs" in reg. 26(1) and consequently also in reg. 26(2)(*b*); (2) the use of the words "outstanding liability" in para. 18(1) of R(SB) 22/84 was not intended to embrace a standing charge; (3) a definition of "fuel costs" taken from the Housing Benefit Regulations cannot be used to assist interpretation of the phrase in the Single Payments Regulations, as these are different regulations; (4) a standing charge for gas or electricity comes within the normal requirements of reg. 4(1) of Supplementary Benefit (Requirements) Regulations 1983.

DECISION No. R(SB) 17/86.

3525. Supplementary benefit—single payment—loss of money previously awarded for the item now claimed—Commissioner's decision

[Supplementary Benefit (Single Payments) Regulations 1981 (S.I. 1981 No. 1528), reg. 6(1)(*a*).]

C was awarded a single payment for floor covering for three bedrooms. The relevant girocheque was encashed, but C's wife lost the bag in which the money had been placed. C made a further claim for a single payment in respect of floor covering for the same three bedrooms. The adjudication officer and, on appeal, the tribunal refused this claim. C appealed to a Social Security Commissioner.

Held, dismissing the appeal, that (1) the expression "the circumstances surrounding that payment" in reg. 6(1)(*a*) of the Single Payment Regulations falls to be read as "the circumstances of that payment"; (2) the loss of the payment money does not constitute a material change in "the circumstances surrounding the payment"; (3) where a further single payment is allowed the relevant change of circumstances surrounding the payment should be identified.

DECISION No. R(SB) 16/86.

3526. Supplementary benefit—single payment—meaning of "funeral"—Commissioner's decision

[Supplementary Benefit (Single Payments) Regulations 1981 (S.I. 1981 No. 1528), reg. 8(1)(*c*).]

A single payment was refused for the expenses of a funeral for C's mother-in-law who had died in the U.K. After undertakers had carried out some of the functions which would normally be attendant upon a funeral the body was flown to Rawalpindi for burial. On appeal the tribunal found that the funeral took place in the U.K. and awarded a single payment towards the funeral costs. The adjudication officer appealed to a Social Security Commissioner.

Held, that (1) the words "funeral" must be given its ordinary and natural meaning in the context of which it occurs and in reg. 8(1)(*c*) of the Supplementary Benefit (Single Payments) Regulations the context is that a funeral is given as an alternative to a cremation. "Funeral" is used in the sense of burial rather than of the ceremonial or religious services which accompany burial or cremation; (2) The funeral or cremation must take place wholly within the U.K. before any payment can be made.

The Commissioner allowed the appeal, set aside the decision of the appeal tribunal and gave his own decision that C was not entitled to a single payment for funeral costs.

DECISION No. R(SB) 23/86.

3527. Supplementary benefit—single payment—meaning of "parent"—Commissioner's decision

[Supplementary Benefit (Single Payments) Regulations 1981 (S.I. 1981 No. 1528), reg. 22(1)(*c*).]

A single payment was refused for the travelling expenses involved in collecting C's daughter from her guardian and later returning her to them. On appeal whilst a dissenting member of the tribunal decided that "other parent" referred to the child's natural father the majority of the tribunal concluded that the child's guardians had been appointed as parents and that the circumstances of C's visit were in all respects those envisaged by reg. 22(1)(*c*). They therefore allowed the claim and the adjudication officer appealed to the Social Security Commissioner.

Held, that (1) the word "parent", being derived from the Latin "parere", denotes the natural father or mother and there is nothing in the regulation in question to suggest that any unusual meaning be applied in the context in which it is used. This view is supported by the qualification that it be the "other" parent with whom the child is resident. The term may, however, include an adoptive parent who has been deemed by law to be the natural parent; (2) as C's daughter was not living with her natural father the provisions of regulation 22(1)(*c*) were not satisfied.

The Commissioner allowed the appeal, set aside the decision of the appeal tribunal and gave his own decision that C was not entitled to a single payment for travelling costs to visit her daughter.

DECISION No. R(SB) 24/86.

3528. Supplementary Benefit—single payments

SUPPLEMENTARY BENEFIT (SINGLE PAYMENTS) AMENDMENT REGULATIONS 1987 (No. 36) [45p], made under the Supplementary Benefits Act 1976 (c.71), ss.3, 14(2)(*a*), 34(1) and the Social Security Act 1975 (c.14), s.166(2)(3); operative on January 21, 1987, save for reg. 2 which is operative on January 26, 1987; make provision in relation to single payments for exceptionally cold weather.

SUPPLEMENTARY BENEFIT (SINGLE PAYMENTS) AMENDMENT (No. 2) REGULATIONS 1987 (No. 2010) [£4·00], made under the Supplementary Benefits Act 1976 (c.71), ss.3, 14(2)(*a*), 34(1); operative on December 17, 1987; amend S.I. 1981 No. 1528.

3529. Supplementary benefit—single payments—reconditioned item—Commissioners' decisions—status of unreported decisions

[Supplementary Benefits Act 1976 (c.71), s.2; Social Security (Adjudication) Regulations 1984 (S.I. 1984 No. 451), reg. 27]

C's appointee appealed to the Commissioner from a decision of the Social Security Appeal Tribunal that she was entitled to a single payment of £75 for the cost of purchasing a reconditioned cooker. C's case before the tribunal was that a sum considerably in excess of £75 was necessary to purchase a gas cooker that was truly reconditioned. The appeal was initially treated as being out of time, but the tribunal accepted jurisdiction to hear the appeal.

Held, allowing the appeal, that (1) local tribunal chairmen should be particularly careful, before refusing an extension of time, to make sure that the case presented to them is a truly out-of-time case (which this case was not); (2) all Commissioners' decisions whether or not reported, must be followed by adjudication officers and by social security appeal tribunal where they decide question of legal principle, R(1) 12/75 applied; (3) reg. 10(3)(*b*) of the Supplementary Benefits (Single Payments) Regulations drew the distinction between "a second-hand item" and "a reconditioned item", R(SB) 30/85 applied; (4) the tribunal set too low a standard by drawing an analogy with sale of goods legislation.

DECISION No. R(SB) 22/86.

3530. Supplementary benefit—uprating regulations

SUPPLEMENTARY BENEFIT UPRATING REGULATIONS 1987 (No. 49), [80p], made under the Supplementary Benefits Act 1976 (c.71), ss.2(2), 34(1), Sched. 1, para. 2(1)(4); operative on April 6, 1987; varies supplementary benefit rates.

3531. Supplementary benefit—urgent cases—recoverability of payments—Commissioner's decision

[Supplementary Benefit (Urgent Cases) Regulations 1981 (S.I. 1981 No. 1529), reg. 25(6).]

C had been awarded payments under the Urgent Cases Regulations totalling £152·91 in respect of the period June 5, 1984 to June 27, 1984. On July 4, 1986 the adjudication officer decided that the claimant was unable to avail himself of reg. 25(6) of the Urgent Cases Regulations and that those payments were recoverable under s.4(2) of the Act. On appeal the tribunal upheld the adjudication officer's decision. C appealed to a Social Security Commissioner.

Held, allowing the appeal that (1) no sum awarded under the Urgent Cases Regulations is recoverable under s.4(2) of the Act until a determination to that effect has been made under reg. 25; (2) decisions as to whether payments under the Urgent Cases Regulations are recoverable are to be made having regard solely to the facts ascertainable *at the date of each payment* under those regulations. The tribunal's decision to take account of subsequent earnings was based on a false proposition and amounted to an error in law; (3) the conditions in reg. 25(6)(*b*)(i) and 25(6)(*b*)(ii) are cumulative and not in the alternative.

DECISION No. R(SB) 27/86.

3532. Treasury Supplement

SOCIAL SECURITY (TREASURY SUPPLEMENT TO AND ALLOCATION OF CONTRIBUTIONS) (RE-RATING) ORDER 1987 (No. 48) [80p], made under the Social Security Act 1975 (c.14), s.167(1); operative on April 6, 1987; decreases the Treasury supplement to contributions paid under the 1975 Act of 7 per cent.

3533. Unemployment benefit—employed to full extent normal—part-time employment following a history of full-time employment—forward disallowance—Commissioner's decision

[Social Security (Unemployment), Sickness and Invalidity Benefit) Regulations 1975 (S.I. 1983 No. 1598), reg. 7(1)(*e*).]

C was employed full-time as an electrical engineer for many years, with the exception of a few months, until August 1982. He then obtained part-time employment as a lecturer working on 2 days a week and then 4 days a week. In the autumn of 1983 his contract as a lecturer was renewed and provided for employment on 3 days a week for the academic terms from 21.9.83 to 16.12.83, 9.1.84 to 6.4.84 and 30.4.84 to 13.7.84. He was paid unemployment benefit for the days on which he did not work until 4.11.83 when his claims were disallowed in terms of reg. 7(1)(*e*) of the Social Security (Unemployment, Sickness and Invalidity Benefit) Regulations 1975.

Held, that (1) the effect of the contract current at 4.11.83 (which was for about 9 months and provided that in all but a few weeks C would be working on 3 days only) was that it was at the time normal (and ordinary) for him to be employed on those 3 days of the week only; (2) C's contract current at 4.11.83 having been preceded in an earlier period by a similar contract, which though not identical, likewise provided for part-time employment in lecturing for the same employing authority, he was not able by 4.11.83 to escape from the consequences of the full extent normal rule by virtue of the stop-gap exception; (3) once the grounds of the original disallowance have ceased to exist, so that the forward disallowance terminates (*Decision R(U) 1/78*), the disallowance does not revive if the grounds spring into existence again.

DECISION No. R(U) 1/86.

3534. Unemployment benefit—failure to make or prosecute a claim in order to avoid if possible exhaustion of unemployment benefit and the need to requalify—Tribunal decision

C ceased to claim unemployment benefit after receiving 252 days' benefit and claimed again after nine weeks had elapsed. During the nine weeks, apart from short periods at home, C visited different parts of the country in a motor caravan, attending dog shows, visiting friends and having a holiday. He appealed against the decision of the adjudication officer, confirmed by the appeal tribunal, that he was to be treated as having been entitled to unemployment benefit pursuant to s.79(4) of the Social Security Act 1975 for two periods in the nine weeks on the basis that he was in fact available for employment and was unable to show that he did not intend, by failing to acquire or establish a right to benefit, to avoid the necessity of requalifying for benefit as provided by s.18(1) of the Social Security Act 1975.

Held, that (1) on the construction of reg. 16 of the Social Security (Unemployment, Sickness and Invalidity Benefits) Regulations 1983 and s.79(4) (now re-enacted as section 18(4) of the Social Security Act 1975), the only bar to entitlement to unemployment benefit under these provisions is the delay or failure to make or prosecute a claim. The provisions cannot apply where any other bar to entitlement exists; (2) availability for employment is not of itself a condition of entitlement in terms, but under s.17(1)(*a*)(i) of the Social Security Act 1975 is a qualification without which a day cannot be treated as a day of unemployment; (3) in this context the words "delay or failure to make or prosecute a claim" are clearly to be construed compatibly with the use of the word "claim" and the references in various ways to the making of a claim elsewhere in s.79, and cannot be construed as extending to the non-satisfaction of the condition which makes a day a day of unemployment; (4) C took himself out of the employment market place during the period and could not be said to be available for employment. Accordingly, reg. 16 and s.79(4) did not apply to him.

On the question of the construction of reg. 16 and s.79(4), the Tribunal did not approve the approach suggested in *Decision R(U) 6/83.*

DECISION No. R(U) 7/86.

3535. Unemployment benefit—full extent—Community Programme worker—Commissioner's decision

[Social Security (Unemployment, Sickness and Invalidity Benefit) Regulations 1975 (S.I. 1975 No. 564), regs. 7(1)(*e*), 7(2); Social Security (Claims and Payments) Regulations 1979 (S.I. 1979 No. 628), reg. 12(5).]

C discharged himself from the Army in March 1980. He then had a spell of sickness and unemployment until March, 23, 1983 when he commenced work under the Community Programme Scheme. His contract of employment with the Community Programme provided for a temporary part-time job as a labourer/gardener working for 23½ hours per week on Wednesdays, Thursdays and Fridays, for a maximum duration of 52 weeks. The claimant was never told that his part-time job would become a full-time job but he was advised that there would be no problem in his attending job interviews if invited to any. The claimant's claim for unemployment benefit for the days of the week on which he did not work was disallowed by an adjudication officer on the basis of the "full extent normal" provisions contained in reg. 7(1)(*e*) of the Social Security (Unemployment, Sickness and Invalidity Benefit) Regulations 1975. This decision was unanimously affirmed by a local tribunal. The Commissioner upheld the tribunal's decision on appeal (subject to modification of the forward disallowance).

Held, that (1) it was not open to the Commissioner to conclude that a long term unemployed claimant who takes a temporary job for up to 52 weeks on the Community Programme has no normal working week and to conclude that the regulation cannot apply to him; (2) in determining the pattern of work, days of sickness or unemployment are not counted (Commissioner's decisions R(U) 14/59 and R(U) 14/60).

The Commissioner set out 3 stages which should be followed in determining whether reg. 7(1)(*e*) applies to a claimant: (1) the adjudicating authority must ascertain the actual facts relevant to determining whether the claimant's pattern of work in the relevant week was the normal pattern for him at that time; (2) the adjudicating authority must look into the future to decide whether the claimant's pattern of work is likely to be permanent or transitory; (3) the adjudicating authority must look to the past and consider the claimant's past history of both work and unemployment.

Decision 255/84 was held by the Court of Appeal in *Riley* v. *Chief Adjudication Officer* [1985] C.L.Y. 3345 to be supportable only on its special facts namely that in that case the claimant was informed that his part-time employment with the Community Task Force was likely to lead to full-time employment with the Community Task Force which did, in fact, happen. The present case did not have that feature.

DECISION No. R(U) 6/86.

3536. Unemployment benefit—full extent normal—stop gap employment—Tribunal decision

[Social Security Act 1975 (c.), s.17(2)(*a*); Social Security (Unemployment, Sickness and Invalidity Benefit) Regulations 1975 (S.I. 1975 No. 564), reg. 7(1)(*e*) and (2).]

C commenced employment with the Community Task Force on April 25, 1983 after a spell of unemployment from November 8, 1980 when he had been made redundant from his full-time occupation as a machine operator. C's contract of employment with the Community Task Force provided for a temporary part-time job as a painter's labourer, working 20 hours per week on Mondays, Tuesdays and Wednesdays. The contract was to end on July 15, 1983. On starting work with the Community Task Force C was informed that the part-time employment was likely to lead to full-time employment, which did, in fact, happen on August 22, 1983. C's claim for unemployment benefit for the days of the week on which he did not work was disallowed on the basis of the "full extent normal" provisions contained in reg. 7(1)(*e*) of the Social Security (Unemployment, Sickness and Invalidity Benefit) Regulations 1975.

The Commissioners held (by a majority) that: (1) to decide whether it is reasonable to say of a particular claimant that he was "employed to the full extent normal in his case", an objective view must be taken of his past employment history, his own working abilities and skills, and the nature of his present employment (its duration, terms and conditions); (2) the duration of the part-time employment is relevant and normally on the expiry of one year such employment will, in any event. lose its stop-gap nature; (3) if and when it is clear in the case of a particular claimant that the relevant part-time employment is, in the light of his disposition and his employment history, manifestly not intended in any sense to be temporary or a stop-gap, then the "full extent normal" rule will apply; (4) regard must be had to contemporary economic and social conditions and in times where there is a high degree of unemployment, it may be more readily accepted that part-time work is undertaken as a stop-gap exercise; (5) the claimant's part-time employment with the Community Task Force was undertaken as a stop-gap measure.

The Chief Commissioner considered that the stop-gap test must be applied with caution and that it would be flying in the face of economic reality to rely on the previous working history itself as pointing to a likelihood of a return to a pattern of work established by the claimant's previous employment, which in this particular case ended about $2\frac{1}{2}$ years before he started work with the Community Task Force. The Chief Commissioner noted that the part-time work with the Community Task Force was in terms on the basis that it was likely to lead to full-time employment with the Community Task Force and he inferred that the claimant was willing from the start to accept this full-time work when it was offered. By this route he concurred in the conclusion that the claimant was to be treated as ordinarily working full-time for the Community Task Force.

DECISION No. R(U) 3/86.

3537. Unemployment benefit—part-time employment—entitlement to benefit

Social Security (Unemployment Sickness and Invalidity Benefit) Regulations 1983 (S.I. 1983 No. 1538), reg. 7(1), (2).]

An employee in regular part-time employment which is for a fixed period has no entitlement to unemployment benefit in respect of those days when he is not working during that period (*Riley* v. *Adjudication Officer* (unreported June 25, 1985, C.A.) considered).

CHIEF ADJUDICATION OFFICER *v.* BRUNT, *The Independent*, July 31, 1987, C.A.

3538. Unemployment benefit—recognised or customary holiday—supply teacher—Commissioner's decision

[Social Security (Unemployment, Sickness and Invalidity Benefit) Regulations 1983 (S.I. 1983 No 1598), reg. 7(1)(*h*).]

C was engaged as a supply teacher by an Education Authority. The school at which he was working closed for the Easter holidays on March 29, 1985 and he claimed unemployment benefit on April 1, 1985. He returned to work on April 15, 1985 and was again employed until May 24, 1985 when the school closed for the half term holiday. A further claim for unemployment benefit was made on May 28, 1985. The Education Authority stated that it was understood C's appointment would be continuous from January 1985 to July 1985 despite the fact that he was paid on a daily basis. Both benefit claims were disallowed by an adjudication officer on the basis of the "recognised or customary holiday" provisions contained in regulation 7(1)(*h*) of the Social Security (Unemployment, Sickness and Invalidity Benefit) Regulations 1983. The appeal against the first decision was supported by the adjudication officer on the grounds that it was not agreed prior to the Easter holidays that C's employment would continue thereafter. The appeal against the second decision was not so supported and was dismissed by the tribunal.

Held, allowing the appeal that (1) entitlement to unemployment benefit in these circumstances depends upon whether C's employment has terminated. Only if the employment is continuing, will it be necessary to consider whether a non-working day is a day of recognised or customary holiday; (2) the appointment letters issued to C are, at best, evidence of loose arrangements between the Education Authority and the temporary teachers in their area. They do not place on either party any legally enforceable rights or duties and do not in themselves constitute contracts of employment; (3) any contract between C and the Education Authority terminated at the end of each day's work or period of work for which he had been engaged and that after finishing work on May 24, 1985, he was not on holiday but was unemployed (*Social Security Decision No. R(U)8/68* distinguished).

DECISION No. R(U) 2/87.

3539. Unemployment benefit—trade dispute—dismissal—move in the dispute—Commissioner's decision

[Social Security Act 1975 (c.14), s.19(1).]

C, one of 28 persons employed in the fleshing department of a limited company engaged in the business of fur dressing, lost employment on May 2, 1984 when he, along with the other fleshers, withdrew his labour in pursuit of an agreement on revised rates of pay for operating a new method of fleshing certain skins. They returned to the company premises the following day but the gates were locked. Letters of dismissal dated May 2, 1984 were given to the fleshers including C on May 4, 1984.

On August 6, 1984 there was a meeting between the company management and some of the fleshers following which 13 fleshers were re-employed and commenced work on August 8, 1984. C was not invited to this meeting nor was he offered re-employment.

C was disqualified for receiving unemployment benefit from and including May 2, 1984 on the ground that the dismissals were a move in the dispute.

Held that (1) C lost employment on May 2, 1984 as a result of a stoppage of work due to a trade dispute at his place of employment; (2) applying the principle of hindsight and taking into account all the events ensuing since May 2, 1984 the dismissal of C on that date was not a manoeuvre in the dispute but was intended to be and was an end to the entire relationship between the employer and C; (3) the proviso in s.19(1) of the Act operates in favour of C to put an end to his disqualification during the stoppage of work because he ceased to participate in or have any direct interest in the dispute from the date of his dismissal (*Social Security Decision No. R(U) 5/86* [1987] C.L.Y. 3540 cited); (4) the stoppage of work ended on August 23, 1984 when 13 fleshers were re-engaged and these were the total requirement in the business; (5) C does not fall to be disqualified from May 3, 1984 to August 23, 1984.

DECISION No. R(U) 1/87.

3540. Unemployment benefit—trade dispute—participation, direct interest, duration of disqualification—Tribunal decision

[Social Security Act 1975 (c.14), s.19(1).]

C, a colliery driver, was under notice of redundancy when a stoppage of work arising out of the national miners' strike began at the colliery on 23.3.84. He did not attend work from 23.3.84 to 13.4.84. After that he lost several days employment in the period to 11.5.84 and worked from then until his redundancy on 2.6.84. He then claimed unemployment benefit. The adjudication officer decided that C was disqualified for receiving unemployment benefit from and including 23.3.84 and for so long as the stoppage of work should continue. C appealed to a social security appeal tribunal who found that disqualification ran from 23.3.84 but ended on 20.8.84. The adjudication officer, who wished to contest the conclusion that the stoppage had ended as early as 20.8.84, appealed to a Social Security Commissioner.

A Tribunal of Commissioners varied the decision of the appeal tribunal and decided that the stoppage of work ended on 21.11.84. The claimant's association (the NUM) appealed, with the leave of the Commissioners, to the Court of Appeal. That appeal was dismissed.

Held, that (1) the matters in dispute must be determined and, where there is more than one, it must be decided whether it was one particular issue or a composite trade dispute that caused the stoppage of work (Court of Appeal); (2) the stoppage of work commencing on 23.3.84 at the colliery was due to a trade dispute both as to wages and pit closures (Tribunal of Commissioners); (3) the claimant lost employment by reason of the stoppage of work when violent picketing prevented him from getting to work on some days before he became redundant and he was not participating in the dispute (Tribunal of Commissioners); (4) the claimant had a direct interest in the trade dispute throughout the stoppage of work in that wages he would receive up to his redundancy stood to be increased if a settlement was made (Tribunal of Commissioners); (5) the Court of Appeal concurred with the Tribunal of Commissioners in finding that the claimant incurred disqualification throughout the stoppage of work, even though he would have been without employment in any event by reason of redundancy (Decision R(U) 12/72 cited and approved) (Tribunal of Commissioners); (6) the Court of Appeal re-affirmed decision R(U) 12/72 and emphasised that "loss of employment" cannot be regarded as "loss of job". If a claimant has lost employment by reason of the stoppage of work due to a trade dispute it is not a valid ground for the claimant to show that he had regained that employment and is without employment for some unconnected reason. Disqualification is still appropriate for as long as the stoppage continues (Court of Appeal); (7) the Tribunal of Commissioners looked at the legislative history of what is now section 19(1) and the construction of the section in its present form. They referred particularly to decisions of the Umpire and Commissioners and Decision R(U) 4/79 by a Tribunal of Commissioners in which consideration was given to the operation of the proviso to disqualify a claimant during a stoppage. The Tribunal decided, contrary to what was decided in Decision R(U) 4/79, that the proviso can operate in favour of a claimant to put an end to disqualification during a stoppage (paragraphs 15 to 29 of the Tribunal of Commissioners' decision). (This point was not argued in the Court of Appeal); (8) if contrary to the finding at 3 above the claimant was participating in the dispute, that participation ceased when he became redundant (Tribunal of Commissioners); (9) the stoppage of work ended on 21.11.84 when 77 per cent. of the workforce were back at work compared with a normal attendance of slightly below 85 per cent. (Tribunal of Commissioners).

DECISION No. R(U) 5/86.

3541. Unemployment, sickness and invalidity benefit

SOCIAL SECURITY (UNEMPLOYMENT, SICKNESS AND INVALIDITY BENEFIT) AMENDMENT REGULATIONS 1987 (No. 317) [45p], made under the Social Security Act 1975 (c.14), ss.17(2)(*a*), 166; operative on March 4, 1987; amends S.I. 1983 No. 1598.

SOCIAL SECURITY (UNEMPLOYMENT, SICKNESS AND INVALIDITY BENEFIT) AMENDMENT (No. 2) REGULATIONS 1987 (No. 688) [45p], made under the Social Security Act 1975 (c.14), s.17(1)(*a*), Sched. 20; operative on May 11, 1987; amend S.I. 1983 No. 1598 so that a person who performs work under medical supervision or work he has a good cause for doing may be treated as incapable of work so long as his earnings do not exceed £26 per week.

3542. Up-rating regulations

SOCIAL SECURITY BENEFITS UP-RATING ORDER 1987 (No. 45) [£2·20], made under the Social Security Act 1986 (c.50), s.63; operative on April 6, 1987, save for Arts. 1(1), 8, 10(2), which are operative on April 1, 1987; alters and increases benefits.

SOCIAL SECURITY BENEFITS UP-RATING (No. 2) ORDER 1987 (No. 1978) [£1·90], made under the Social Security Act 1986, s.63; operative on April 3, 1988 (part), April 6, 1988 (part) and April 11, 1988 (part); alters the rates and amounts of certain benefits and other sums.

SOCIAL SECURITY BENEFITS UP-RATING REGULATIONS 1987 (No. 327) [80p], made under the Social Security Act 1975 (c.14), ss.17(1)(*a*), 58(3), 131, Sched. 20 and the Social Security Act 1986 (c.50), s.64(2); operative on April 6, 1987; make provision in relation to the up-rating of benefits.

3543. Widow's benefit

SOCIAL SECURITY (WIDOW'S BENEFIT AND RETIREMENT PENSIONS) AMENDMENT REGULATIONS 1987 (No. 1854) [85p], made under the Social Security Act 1975 (c.14), s.29(5)(*b*), 39(4), 166(2), 168(1), Sched. 20, the Social Security Pensions Act 1975 (c.60), s.12, Sched. 1, para. 3 and the Social Security Act 1986 (c.50), s.89(1); operative on April 11, 1988; amend S.I. 1979 No. 642.

SOCIAL SECURITY (WIDOW'S BENEFIT) TRANSITIONAL REGULATIONS 1987 (No. 1692) [45p], made under the Social Security Act 1986 (c. 50), ss.84(1), 89(1); operative on April 11, 1988; make provision consequential on the coming into force of s.36 of the 1986 Act.

3544. Workmen's compensation

WORKMEN'S COMPENSATION (SUPPLEMENTATION) AMENDMENT SCHEME 1987 (No. 419) [45p], made under the Industrial Injuries and Diseases (Old Cases) Act 1975 (c.16), ss.2, 4; operative on April 6, 1987; amends S.I. 1982 No. 1489 so as to provide for major incapacity allowance to be payable at the same rate as disablement pension without further deduction except for those who have retired.

WORKMEN'S COMPENSATION (SUPPLEMENTATION) AMENDMENT (No. 2) SCHEME 1987 (No. 429) [80p], made under the Industrial Injuries and Diseases (Old Cases) Act 1975, ss.2, 4(2); operative on April 8, 1987; amends S.I. 1982 No. 1489 by making adjustments to the lower rates of lesser incapacity allowance.

SOLICITORS

3545. Clients' money—payment on account of costs—tracing

[Solicitors' Accounts Rules 1975, r.2(1).]

M stole money from C. C began proceedings against M who consulted D, solicitors, and paid them £4,000 on account of costs which she said was her money. After substantial costs had been incurred but before D had delivered a bill, it was discovered that the £4,000 belonged to C who issued proceedings against D claiming the right to trace. D claimed to be a bona fide purchaser for value without notice. It was conceded that this defence, if proved, would defeat C's claim.

Held, that (1) When a solicitor holds money paid in advance by a client on account of costs, it is "client's money" as defined by r.2(1). The solicitor is therefore a bare trustee and has no beneficial interest in the money, at least until he has delivered a bill. Having acquired no interest in the money, D could not be purchasers; (2) On the facts D had failed to make sufficient inquiries about the source of the £4,000, and had constructive (but not actual) notice of C's rights.

CONTINENTAL ILLINOIS NATIONAL BANK AND TRUST CO. OF CHICAGO *v.* DAVIES (DANIEL) & CO., July 24, 1987; E. D. R. Stone Q.C., sitting as a deputy judge of Q.B.D. [*Ex rel. Robin Spon-Smith, Barrister.*]

3546. Contract of employment—articles of clerkship—breach—terms. See STUBBES *v.* TROWER STILL & KEELING, §1301.

3547. Costs—personal liability—whether under duty to opposing party

[R.S.C., Ord. 62, r.8(1).]

Despite a solicitor's duty to the court to conduct litigation with due propriety, it is doubtful whether they owe any such duty to the opposing party; there is no basis for the contention that barristers do.

Per curiam: a threat to invoke Ord. 62, r.8 during or prior to the hearing was not proper if made to browbeat opposing solicitors into dropping a claim or procuring the revocation of a legal aid certificate.

P, who was legally aided, sued the Electricity Board on the ground that their electricity was escaping into the earth and heating water in the earth creating steam, which penetrated P's house causing wetness, and movement of physical objects. His claim was supported by highly qualified experts; however he lost the case on the ground that those phenomena were due to the intervention of a member of his own family (a thing which he must have realised at an early stage). He was ordered to pay costs. Having earlier threatened to do so, the Electricity Board applied for an order for costs against P's solicitors under R.S.C., Ord. 62, r.8. The order was refused.

Held, dismissing the appeal, that it was doubtful whether solicitors owed any duty to the opposing party such as they owed to the court; there was no basis for the contention that barristers did. The jurisdiction under R.S.C., Ord. 62, r.8 existed only when there was clearly a serious dereliction of duty or serious misconduct and should be exercised with care. P's claim had been supported by expert evidence and the judge's decision could not be assailed *Rondell* v. *Worsley* [1968] C.L.Y. 3054 considered).

ORCHARD *v.* SOUTH EASTERN ELECTRICITY BOARD [1987] 3 W.L.R. 102, C.A.

3548. Dispute within solicitors' partnership—interlocutory injunction—balance of convenience. See NIXON *v.* WOOD, §2768.

3549. Duty of care—testator's solicitors—beneficiary

A testator's solicitors do not owe a duty of care to a potential beneficiary under the will (*Yuen Kun Yeu* v. *Att.-Gen. of Hong Kong* [1987] C.L.Y. 2580, *Ross* v. *Caunters* [1979] C.L.Y. 2570, *Gartside* v. *Sheffield Young & Ellis* [1983] N.Z.L.R. 37 considered).

CLARKE *v.* BRUCE LANCE & CO., *The Independent*, November 4, 1987, C.A.

3550. Duty to client—conflict of interests

When considering what constitutes a "conflict of interests", one has to enquire what duties a solicitor owes his clients in order to determine whether they are likely to come into conflict.

SOLICITOR, *Re A* (1987) 131 S.J. 1063, Hoffmann J.

3551. Duty to exercise reasonable skill and care—unusual clause in lease—duty to explain clause to client—assessment of damages

A solicitor in exercising reasonable professional judgment must alert his client to the existence, effect and risks involved in an unusual clause in a lease.

P was negotiating with the head lessee for a 15-year under-lease of business premises. The headlease provided for five-yearly rent reviews. The underlease provided for rent increases by the same percentage as the increases on the headleases reviews. The effect was that the more the head lessee's rent was increased, the more profit he could make from P. P.'s solicitors, D, failed to ascertain the rent payable under the headlease, or to advise P to do so, or to have the property valued or to explain the clause to P. An offer of £17,000 for the underlease and the business later fell through partly because of uncertainties about rent review. When the rent was reviewed, it was increased from £3,500 to £9,022. The open market rent would have been £2,600. P surrendered the underlease on payment of £16,000, and £2,761 increased rent. P claimed against D for the amount lost on the prospective sale, the cost of surrender, and the increased rent paid. The judge dismissed the action.

Held, allowing the appeal, that the solicitors in exercising reasonable professional judgment should have alerted their client to the existence, effect and risks involved in such an unusual clause. In assessing damages, the court was not bound to apply the diminution in value principle, nor to assess damages as at the date of breach. P was entitled to the costs of surrender and possibly also to the value of a saleable lease and goodwill. The case would be remitted for the assessment of damages (Dictum of Lord Blackburn in *Livingstone* v. *Rawyards Coal Co.* (1880) 5 App.Cas. at 39 and *Dodd Properties (Kent)* v. *Canterbury City Council* [1980] C.L.Y. 642 applied).

COUNTY PERSONNEL (EMPLOYMENT AGENCY) *v.* PULVER (ALAN R.) & CO. (A FIRM)]1987] 1 All E.R. 289, C.A.

3552. Fiduciary duty—client—joint venture

A solicitor who entered into a joint venture with his client did not breach his fiduciary duty to the client if the client was made fully aware of the nature and effect of the transaction before he entered into it.

D were a firm of solicitors that acted for P in the acquisition of a lease of a property in Cheyne Walk, London. Thereafter, P and D entered into a joint venture to repair and develop the property. D, through a company they controlled, advanced to P the sums necessary to finance the development and organised the necessary works. In return, P gave the company a 50 per cent. interest in the property and executed a legal charge over the property to secure the sums advanced. There were considerable delays in the organisation and execution of the necessary development works that resulted in claims against D and their company by P. The venture made a profit. P sued D and contended that the transactions between them should be re-opened and D ordered to account for any profit they made on account of a breach of the fiduciary duty that they, as solicitors, owed to him, as their client. The trial judge held that when P entered into the transaction, he understood the nature and substance of the agreement and its effect and that the terms of the agreement were fair. P's claim was dismissed. On appeal P contended that the fairness of the agreement could not validate it in the face of D's breach of their fiduciary duty to give adequate advice to P.

Held, dismissing P's appeal, that D was not under a duty to advise P about the business or financial prudence of the transaction. D was under a duty to advise in relation to the nature and effect of the transaction. However, the trial judge had found P was fully aware of the nature and effect of the proposed transaction. D were entitled to enter into the joint venture with P provided they discharged their fiduciary duty to him. D, in the circumstances, had fulfilled their duty to him by ensuring that he knew and understood the terms of the proposed joint venture. Moreover the terms of the agreement were fair (*Demerara Bauxite Co.* v. *Hubbard* [1923] A.C. 673, *Phipps* v. *Boardman* [1966] C.L.Y. 11052, *Regal (Hastings)* v. *Gulliver* [1967] 2 A.C. 134 considered).

HANSON *v.* LORENZ AND JONES [1987] 1 FTLR 23, C.A.

3553. Fiduciary duty—conduct of litigation on behalf of client—receipt of bribe from another party—whether solicitor liable to account to client for profits made from bribe

Where in the course of representing his client in the course of litigation a solicitor received a bribe from another party, the bribe was recoverable by the client as money had and received.

P was the defendant in an action in which the plaintiff claimed between $3 million and $5 million. D was the solicitor instructed by P to act on its behalf. The litigation was settled upon payment by P of $2·2 million. In consequence, the plaintiff paid D $200,000 commission. P sought to recover that sum from D and an account of all profits earned by D from that sum of money.

Held, that the commission was a bribe. It was recoverable by P as money had and received. The relationship between P and D was that of debtor and creditor and not trustee and *cestui que trust.* The bribe could not be described as affected by a trust. Accordingly, P was not entitled to an account of the profits D derived from the money (*Metropolitan Bank* v. *Heiron* (1880) 5 Ex.D. 319, *Lister & Co.* v. *Stubbs* (1890) 45 Ch.D. 1 applied; *Phipps* v. *Boardman* [1966] C.L.Y. 11052, *Industrial Development Consultants* v. *Cooley* [1972] C.L.Y. 361 *Mareva Compania Naviera S.A.* v. *International Bulk Carriers S.A.* [1975] C.L.Y. 3169 considered).

ISLAMIC REPUBLIC OF IRAN SHIPPING LINES *v.* DENBY, [1987] 1 FTLR 30, Leggatt J.

3554. Lay Observer—annual report

The Twelfth Annual Report of the Lay Observer has been published. It is available from H.M.S.O. (H.C. 26) [£3·50].

3555. Negligence—reliance on counsel's advice—whether any misconduct in the handing of the litigation

Although a solicitor having conduct of an action is not expected to rely blindly on counsel's advice, he is justified in relying on it where it embodies a careful and sensible assessment of the legal and factual situation (*Davy-Chiesman* v. *Davy-Chiesman* [1984] C.L.Y. 1995 and *Orchard* v. *South Eastern Electricity Board* [1987] C.L.Y. 3547 applied).

WARD v. CHIEF CONSTABLE OF AVON AND SOMERSET CONSTABULARY, *The Daily Telegraph,* September 18, 1987, C.A.

3556. Negligence—review by Law Society

If a solicitor is being sued in negligence, and the action has not yet been concluded, the Law Society can still review his conduct (*Orchard* v. *South Eastern Electricity Board* [1987] C.L.Y. 3547 applied).

LIPMAN BRAY (A FIRM) *v.* HILLHOUSE, *The Times,* January 31, 1987, C.A.

3557. Negligence—undertaking given for benefit of third party—whether duty of care owed to third party—whether breach of duty—whether damage natural and probable consequence

Where a solicitor gave an undertaking for the benefit of a third party the solicitor owed the third party a duty to take reasonable care in performing the undertaking.

D were a firm of solicitors that represented P's husband, H, in the course of matrimonial proceedings between P and H. There were 2 children of the family. H was a citizen of Kuwait. In April 1981 when the marriage was in difficulty H kidnapped the children and took them to Kuwait. P persuaded H to return having obtained certain orders in the Bristol County Court. P and H then separated, P took the children and made an application for custody. H instructed D to offer the utmost resistance to P's application and forcibly expressed his intention that the children should be brought up in Kuwait. At the hearing H did not contest P's application and was granted access upon his undertaking to deposit his Kuwaiti passport with D. In May 1981 H offered to have the children's names removed from his passport. D stated in the course of correspondence that H's passport would remain in the possession of their London agents for that purpose and that the passport would not be released to H. When D's London agents attended at the Kuwaiti embassy for the passport to be altered the alteration could not be made on account of the fact that H had failed to provide necessary documents. H had been going to attend at the embassy on that day with the documents but then telephoned D to say he would not be attending and had already sent the documents in the post. D telephoned H to discover what had happened to the documents and were told by H that he would attend the embassy the next day, June 5, 1981, with the documents. In the meantime the embassy official dealing with the London agent's representative refused to give back H's passport. The official assured the representative that the passport would not be released to H. When H. attended the next day he obtained his passport from the embassy. D instructed their London agents not to attend on that day as the passport was in the safe custody of the embassy. That weekend H kidnapped the children again. P was assaulted and imprisoned in the process. H took the children to Kuwait and P did not see them again. P claimed damages against D in negligence and breach of contract for the loss of her children, the assault, anxiety and distress and costs incurred in attempting to recover the children.

Held, that there was an implied undertaking on the part of D not to release H's passport from their custody. D owed P a duty of care in tort to take reasonable care that the passport should not leave their possession and to take all reasonable steps to prevent harm coming to her from any failure to comply with any agreed relaxation of the undertaking. No contract existed between P and D. D were in breach of that duty by failing to guard against the possibility of the embassy retaining H's passport, failing to advise P's solicitors that the passport was out of their custody and that H was to attend the embassy in the absence of any representative from D. D showed a marked measure of gullibility and ought to have been alarmed by the absence of the documents on 4 June and H's offer to attend the embassy on 5 June. It was not reasonably foreseeable that the Kuwaiti embassy would part with the passport. Although it was reasonably foreseeable that H would abduct the children given the slightest opportunity it was not reasonably foreseeable that he would have that opportunity. In the circumstances the damage P suffered was too remote and her claim failed (*Ross* v. *Caunters* [1979] C.L.Y, 2570 applied).

AL-KANDARI *v.* BROWN (J.R.) & CO. [1987] 2 W.L.R. 469, French J.

3558. Practice rules—whether office open to public

[Solicitors Act 1974 (c.47); Solicitors Practice Rules 1975, r.2(6).]

A solicitor who practises from his home but does not meet his clients at that address does not have an office open to the public.

SOLICITOR, A, *Re, The Times*, July 7, 1987, C.A.

3559. Purchase of property—insurance policy as security—duty of solicitor

When it is clear that all parties to a purchase of property envisage that an insurance policy effected by the purchaser will form part of the security for the purchase, it is the duty of the solicitor for the purchaser to ensure before completion that the policy is in force.

McLELLAN *v.* FLETCHER, *The Times*, June 3, 1987, Lincoln J.

3560. Undertaking—breach—order for compensation—summary jurisdiction over solicitors

The courts' inherent jurisdiction over solicitors though summary, may be exercised wherever the case is clearly established.

W. instructed J.F. and B.K.R., two firms of solicitors, to act for him in separate matters. B.K.R. came to hold £18,000 to W's account, while W failed to meet J.F.'s professional fees.W then signed a form of authority authorising B.K.R. to give an undertaking they would retain the sum to J.F's account. B.K.R. then wrote to J.F. saying they would hold the sum "until you have sorted everything out". Subsequently B.K.R. released the sum to W. who went bankrupt. The judge held that an undertaking had been given and breached and ordered B.K.R. to pay the sum into a deposit account to the credit of W. to remain there until further order.

Held, that the court's inherent jurisdiction over solicitors, though summary was not analogous to Ord. 14 and could be exercised whenever a case was clearly established. The statement made was a undertaking and had been breached. However, the order made was inappropriate, and J.F.'s actual loss should be determined by an inquiry (*Geoffrey Silver & Drake* v. *Baines* [1971] C.L.Y. 11170 considered).

FOX (A FIRM) (JOHN) *v.* BANNISTER KING & RIGBEYS (A FIRM) [1987] 1 All E.R. 737, C.A.

3561. Undertaking—capacity in which given—effect on partners

[Partnership Act 1890 (c.39), s.5.]

The mere fact of a solicitor's name being on the firm's notepaper does not give him ostensible authority to bind his firm: An undertaking not given in his capacity as solicitor is not given "in the usual way of business" within s.5 of the Partnership Act 1890.

UNITED BANK OF KUWAIT *v.* HAMMOUD (1987) 137 N.L.J. 921, Stuart-Smith J.

3562. Undertaking—impossibility of performance—order of court

Where a solicitor gives an undertaking which becomes impossible to perform, the court will not make an order for performance in vain, but it may use its discretion to order compensation.

P sued D Co. for money for goods supplied. D Co.'s solicitor gave P's solicitor an undertaking that the directors would provide security for the company's liabilities with charges on their homes. On P's application the judge ordered that the undertaking should be carried out. This turned out to be impossible.

Held, allowing both the appeal by the solicitor and cross-appeal by the plaintiff, that the court would not order the performance of an impossible undertaking in vain; where the solicitor's conduct merited reproof the court could use its discretion to order compensation, and the case would be remitted for consideration of that question accordingly (*New Brunswick Co.* v. *Muggeridge* (1859) 4 Drew. 686, *United Mining and Finance Corp.* v. *Becher* [1910] 2 K.B. 296, *Myers* v. *Elman* [1940] A.C. 282, *Thew (R. & T.)* v. *Reeves*

(No. 2) [1982] C.L.Y. 3088 and *Fox (John)* v. *Bannister, King & Rigbeys* [1987] C.L.Y. 3560 applied).

UDALL *v.* CAPRI LIGHTING (IN LIQUIDATION) [1987] 3 W.L.R. 465, C.A.

STAMP DUTIES

3563. Evasion of stamp duty—sale of house and chattels—false apportionment of value of house and chattels to avoid stamp duty—effect of illegality. See SAUNDERS *v.* EDWARDS, §1826.

3564. Exempt instruments

STAMP DUTY (EXEMPT INSTRUMENTS) REGULATIONS 1987 (No. 516) [80p], made under the Finance Act 1985 (c.54), s.87(2); operative on May 1, 1987; specifies the provisions under which stamp duty shall not be charged on instruments.

3565. Reserve tax

STAMP DUTY RESERVE TAX (INTEREST ON TAX REPAID) ORDER 1987 (No. 514) [45p], made under the Finance Act 1986 (c.41), s.92(4); operative on April 6, 1987; specifies 9 per cent. per annum the rate of interest applicable for the purposes of s.92 of the 1986 Act.

STAMP DUTY RESERVE TAX (INTEREST ON TAX REPAID) (No. 2) ORDER 1987 (No. 888) [45p], made under the Finance Act 1986, s.92(4); operative on June 6, 1987; prescribes 8·25 per cent. per annum for the purposes of s.92 of the said Act.

STAMP DUTY RESERVE TAX (INTEREST ON TAX REPAID) (No. 3) ORDER 1987 (No. 1494) [45p], made under the Finance Act 1986, s.92(4); operative on September 6, 1987; specified a rate of interest of 9 per cent. per annum for the purposes of s.92 of the 1986 Act.

STAMP DUTY RESERVE TAX (INTEREST ON TAX REPAID) (No. 4) ORDER 1987 (No. 1990) [45p], made under the Finance Act 1986 (c.41), s.92(4); operative on December 6, 1987; specifies that eight-and-a-quarter per cent. per annum be an appropriate rate of interest for stamp duty reserve tax under s.92 of the 1986 Act.

STATUTES AND ORDERS

3566. Dates of commencement. See DATES OF COMMENCEMENT TABLE.

3567. Regulations amending statutory instrument—reference to published document setting out financial limits—validity of regulations

[Supplementary Benefit (Requirements and Resources) Miscellaneous Provisions (No. 2) Regulations 1985, Sched. 1A, para. 5(1), Sched. 2A, para. 5(1)(2).]

Where a statutory instrument properly laid refers to an external document reference to which enables benefit limits (the subject of the statutory instrument) to be calculated, the document need not itself be regarded as part of the statutory instrument.

The Secretary of State for Social Services made amending regulations pursuant to his powers under the 1976 Supplementary Benefits Act. The regulations referred to an existing publication which specified, *inter alia*, financial limits of benefits. The publication itself had never been laid before Parliament. A London Borough Council applied for judicial review and sought declarations that the figures shown in the publication were of no legal effect. Macpherson J. dismissed the application.

Held, dismissing the appeal, the publication formed no part of the statutory instrument; the Secretary of State was however entitled to set the limits in the statutory instrument by reference to a document from which they could be calculated. This was the role of the publication in the process.

R. *v.* SECRETARY OF STATE FOR SOCIAL SERVICES, *ex p.* CAMDEN LONDON BOROUGH COUNCIL [1987] 1 W.L.R. 819, C.A.

3568. Royal Assents

The following Acts received the Royal Assent during 1987:

Abolition of Domestic Rates Etc. (Scotland) Act 1987 (c.47), §3156.
Access to Personal Files Act 1987 (c.37), §304.
Agricultural Training Board Act 1987 (c.29), §78.
AIDS Control Act 1987 (c.33), §2545.

Animals (Scotland) Act 1987 (c.9), §102.
Appropriation Act 1987 (c.17), §3205.
Appropriation (No. 2) Act 1987 (c.50), §3206.
Banking Act 1987 (c.22), §190.
Billiards (Abolition of Restrictions) Act 1987 (c.19), §1832.
British Shipbuilders (Borrowing Powers) Act 1987 (c.52), §3729.
Broadcasting Act 1987 (c.10), §3572.
Channel Tunnel Act 1987 (c.53), §3776.
Chevening Estate Act 1987 (c.20), §1421.
Coal Industry Act 1987 (c.3), §2428.
Consolidated Fund Act 1987 (c.8), §3208.
Consolidated Fund (No. 2) Act 1987 (c.54), §3209.
Consolidated Fund (No. 3) Act 1987 (c.55), §3210.
Consumer Protection Act 1987 (c.43), §3583.
Criminal Justice Act 1987 (c.38), §634.
Criminal Justice (Scotland) Act 1987 (c.41), §636.
Crossbows Act 1987 (c.32), §773.
Crown Proceedings (Armed Forces) Act 1987 (c.25), §161.
Debtors (Scotland) Act 1987 (c.18), §2983.
Deer Act 1987 (c.28), §108.
Diplomatic and Consular Premises Act 1987 (c.46), §2084.
Family Law Reform Act 1987 (c.42), §1724.
Finance Act 1987 (c.16), §3211.
Finance (No. 2) Act 1987 (c.51), §3212.
Fire Safety and Safety of Places of Sport Act 1987 (c.27), §3145.
Gaming (Amendment) Act 1987 (c.11), §1834.
Housing (Scotland) Act 1987 (c.26), §1891.
Immigration (Carriers' Liability) Act 1987 (c.24), §1962.
Irish Sailors and Soldiers Land Trust Act 1987 (c.48), §1428.
Landlord and Tenant Act 1987 (c.31), §2150.
Licensing (Restaurant Meals) Act 1987 (c.2), §2313.
Local Government Act 1987 (c.44), §2371.
Local Government Finance Act 1987 (c.6), §2372.
Ministry of Defence Police Act 1987 (c.4), §2860.
Minors' Contracts Act 1987 (c.13), §442.
Motor Cycle Noise Act 1987 (c.34), §3292.
Northern Ireland (Emergency Provisions) Act 1987 (c.30), §2713a.
Parliamentary and Health Service Commissioners Act 1987 (c.39), §44.
Parliamentary and other Pensions Act 1987 (c.45), §2764.
Petroleum Act 1987 (c.12), §2848.
Pilotage Act 1987 (c.21), §3420.
Prescription (Scotland) Act 1987 (c.36), §352.
Protection of Animals (Penalties) Act 1987 (c.35), §113.
Rate Support Grants Act 1987 (c.5), §2380.
Recognition of Trusts Act 1987 (c.14), §1433.
Register of Sasines (Scotland) Act 1987 (c.23), §482.
Registered Establishments (Scotland) Act 1987 (c.40), §2384.
Reverter of Sites Act 1987 (c.15), §1435.
Scottish Development Agency Act 1987 (c.56), §3738.
Social Fund (Maternity and Funeral Expenses) Act 1987 (c.7), §3500.
Teachers' Pay and Conditions Act 1987 (c.1), §1273.
Territorial Sea Act 1987 (c.49), §3356.
Urban Development Corporations (Financial Limits) Acts (c.57), §3727.

STOCK EXCHANGE

3569. Gilt-edged securities

STOCK TRANSFER (GILT-EDGED SECURITIES) (CGO SERVICE) (AMENDMENT) REGULATIONS 1987 (No. 1293) [45p], made under the Stock Transfer Act 1982 (c.41), s.3(1); operative on August 13, 1987; amend S.I. 1985 No. 1144.

STOCK TRANSFER (GILT-EDGED SECURITIES) (EXEMPT TRANSFER) REGULATIONS 1987 (No. 1294) [45p], made under the Stock Transfer Act 1982 s.1(1)(4); operative on

August 13, 1987; specify further gilt-edged securities which may be transferred by CGO Service members through the CGO Service.

3570. Share applications—multiple applications. See R. *v.* BEST, §826.

TELECOMMUNICATIONS

3571. Broadcasting Act 1981

BROADCASTING ACT 1981 (CHANNEL ISLANDS) ORDER 1987 (No. 2205) [85p], made under the Broadcasting Act 1981 (c.68), s.66(3); operative on February 1, 1988; extends the 1981 Act, as amended by the Cable and Broadcasting Act 1984 and the Broadcasting Act 1987, to the Channel Islands.

3572. Broadcasting Act 1987 (c.10)

This Act alters the maximum period for which programmes may be provided under contracts with the Independent Broadcasting Authority.

The Act received the Royal Assent on April 9, 1987.

The Act extends to Northern Ireland.

3573. Broadcasting—IBA

BROADCASTING (EXTENSION OF DURATION OF IBA's FUNCTION) ORDER 1987 (No. 673) [45p], made under the Broadcasting Act 1981 (c.68), s.2(5); operative on April 6, 1987; amends s.2(1) of the 1981 Act by substituting for the date set out there the date December 31, 2005.

3574. Cable and Broadcasting Act 1984—commencement

CABLE AND BROADCASTING ACT 1984 (COMMENCEMENT No. 3) ORDER 1987 (No. 672 (C.17)) [45p], made under the Cable and Broadcasting Act 1984 (c.46), s.59(4); brings ss.45 and 46 of the 1984 Act into force on April 6, 1987.

3575. Public telecommunication system

PUBLIC TELECOMMUNICATION SYSTEM DESIGNATION (BRITISH CABLE SERVICES LIMITED) ORDER 1987 (No. 827) [45p], made under the Telecommunications Act 1984 (c.12), s.7; designates systems operated by the said company as public telecommunication systems.

PUBLIC TELECOMMUNICATION SYSTEM DESIGNATION (KINGSTON UPON HULL CITY COUNCIL AND KINGSTON COMMUNICATIONS (HULL) PLC) ORDER 1987 (No. 2094) [45p], made under the Telecommunications Act 1984, s.9; operative on January 1, 1988; designates the said council and company as public telecommunications operators.

PUBLIC TELECOMMUNICATION SYSTEM DESIGNATION (SWINDON CABLE LIMITED) ORDER 1987 (No. 3) [45p], made under the Telecommunications Act 1984, ss.7, 8; operative on February 6, 1987; replaces S.I. 1985 No. 1596.

3576. Televised re-enactment of trial—trial still in progress—injunction. See ATT.-GEN. *v.* CHANNEL FOUR TELEVISION CO., §3026.

3577. Television licence—fee for pensioners in residential accommodation—whether concessionary rate available

[Wireless Telegraphy (Broadcasting Licence Charges and Exemptions) Regulations (1984), S.I. 1053, reg. 1(*b*).]

There is no requirement that the facilities provided to elderly people in residential care had to be exclusive to the individual for them to be able to apply for a television licence at the concessionary rate of 5p.

R. *v.* SECRETARY OF STATE FOR THE HOME DEPARTMENT, *ex p.* KIRKLEES BOROUGH COUNCIL, *The Times,* January 26, 1987, Taylor J.

3578. Wireless telegraphy

WIRELESS TELEGRAPHY (CORDLESS TELEPHONE APPARATUS) (RESTRICTION) ORDER 1987 (No. 774) [85p], made under the Wireless Telegraphy Act 1967 (c.72), s.7(2), and the Telecommunications Act 1984 (c.12), s.85(1); operative on May 21, 1987; restricts the importation, manufacture and supply of cordless telephones which do not comply with Performance Specification MPT 1322.

WIRELESS TELEGRAPHY (EXEMPTION) (AMENDMENT) (CORDLESS TELEPHONE APPARATUS) REGULATIONS 1987 (No. 775) [45p], made under the Wireless Telegraphy

Act 1949 (c.54), s.1(1) as extended by S.I. 1952 Nos. 1899 and 1900; operative on May 21, 1987; amends S.I. 1982 No. 1697 to reflect an amendment of Performance Specification MPT 1322.

WIRELESS TELEGRAPHY (EXEMPTION) (AMENDMENT) (MODEL CONTROL APPARATUS) REGULATIONS 1987 (No. 776) [45p], made under the Wireless Telegraphy Act 1949 (c.54), s.1(1) as extended by S.I. 1952 Nos. 1899 and 1900; amend S.I. 1980 No. 1848 so as to specify the frequency which model control apparatus may use.

3579. Wireless telegraphy—forfeiture of equipment—records and tapes—whether "apparatus"

[Wireless Telegraphy Act 1949 (c.54), ss. 1(1), 14(3), as substituted by Telecommunications Act 1984 (c.12), s.82.]

Tapes and records are not "Wireless Telegraphy apparatus" within the meaning of the Act.

The defendant, who ran an illegal radio station, pleaded guilty to using apparatus for wireless telegraphy without a licence. The magistrate made a forfeiture order including, *inter alia*, a large number of records and tapes. The defendant eventually appealed successfully to the Divisional Court. The prosecutor then appealed to the Lords.

Held, dismissing the appeal, that the "apparatus in question" for those offences meant wireless telegraphy apparatus; although records and tapes might be apparatus they were not "wireless telegraphy apparatus" within the meaning of the section and not liable to forfeiture. (*D. (A Minor)* v. *Yates* [1984] C.L.Y. 981 overruled; *Elliott* v. *Grey* [1959] C.L.Y. 2903 distinguished).

RUDD *v.* SECRETARY OF STATE FOR TRADE AND INDUSTRY [1987] 1 W.L.R. 786, H.L.

TORT

3580. Animals—trespass—grazing. See ANIMALS, §115.

3581. Apportionment of damages—two independent tortfeasors. See FITZGERALD *v.* LANE, §2566.

3582. Building contractor—duty to supervise sub-contractor—liability

A building contractor may not owe a duty in tort to supervise the work of a sub-contractor where it would be unjust or unreasonable to impose such a duty.

Under a building contract, Wates agreed to be a main contractor; it sub-contracted the interior plastering. The premises were completed in 1965 and occupied on a 98-year lease. In 1980, while some decorators were working there, half the ceiling fell in. The tenants sued the landlords and the main contractor, Wates. The Judge found that the plasterers had used incorrect plaster type contrary to architect's instructions and that Wates had a duty to supervise on such a fundamental issue.

Held, allowing the appeal, that a building contractor may have a contractual or statutory duty to supervise the work of a sub-contractor, but he has no such duty in tort if in all the circumstances the imposition of such a duty would be unjust or unreasonable (*Anns* v. *Merton London Borough Council* [1977] C.L.Y. 2030, *Batty* v. *Metropolitan Property Realisations* [1978] C.L.Y. 2067, *Candlewood Navigation Corp.* v. *Mitsui OSK Lines* [1985] C.L.Y. 2310, *Cynat Products* v. *Landbuild (Investment & Property)* [1984] C.L.Y. 2283 and *Governors of the Peabody Donation Fund* v. *Sir Lindsay Parkinson & Co.* [1984] C.L.Y. 2298 referred to).

D. & F. ESTATES *v.* CHURCH COMMISSIONERS FOR ENGLAND [1987] 1 FTLR 405, C.A.

3583. Consumer Protection Act 1987 (c.43)

This Act makes provision with respect to the liability of persons for damage caused by defective products and with respect to the giving of price indications. The Consumer Safety Act 1978 and the Consumer Safety (Amendment) Act 1986 are consolidated, with amendments. Pt. I of the Health and Safety at Work etc. Act 1974 and ss.31 and 80 of the Explosives Act 1875 are amended. The Trade Descriptions Act 1972 and the Fabrics (Misdescription) Act 1913 are repealed.

The Act received the Royal Assent on May 5, 1987, and comes into force on days to be appointed by the Secretary of State.

The Act extends to Northern Ireland, with some exceptions. (See s.49 of the Act.)

3584. Consumer Protection Act 1987—commencement

CONSUMER PROTECTION ACT 1987 (COMMENCEMENT No. 1) ORDER 1987 (No. 1680 (C.51)) [85p], made under the Consumer Protection Act 1987 (c.43), s.50(2)(4)(5); brings into force on October 1, 1987. Pts. II, IV, V, ss.48(1)(2)(*b*)(3), 49, 50, Scheds. 2, 4, paras. 1, 2, 4, 6, 7, 9, 10, 11, 13. Sched. 5 and brings into force on March 1, 1988, Pt. I, ss.36, 41(2), 48(1)(3), Scheds. 1, 3, 4, 5.

3585. Conversion—whether liquidator personally liable for conversion when acting as agent of liquidated company

P sold gramophone records to a company (TOL), subject to a retention of title clause under which title to the goods did not pass to TOL until payment had been made. Before payment had been made TOL went into voluntary liquidation and D was appointed liquidator. P put D on notice of P's claim to title to the goods. Nonetheless D sold the goods in the course of the liquidation. P sued D personally for damages for conversion. D denied liability, on the basis that he had acted merely as agent for TOL.

Held, the ordinary rule, that an agent is personally liable for conversion even if acting within the scope of his agency, applied also to liquidators. D was accordingly liable to P in damages.

SCHOTT SOHNE *v.* RADFORD, February 13, 1987, H.H. Judge Tumim, Willesden County Ct. [*Ex rel. Michael McLaren, Barrister.*]

3586. Crown immunity—nuclear weapons testing. See PEARCE *v.* SECRETARY OF STATE FOR DEFENCE, §2569.

3587. Economic loss—pure economic loss—chain originating in claim for physical damage—third party claim

[Civil Liability (Contribution) Act 1978 (c.47), s.1.]

Despite the general rule that claims in tort for pure economic loss are inadmissible, damages to compensate for such loss can be claimed where it is part of a chain which originates in a claim for physical damage (*Candlewood Navigation Corp.* v. *Mitsui OSK Lines* [1985] C.L.Y. 2310 and *Leigh & Sillivan* v. *Aliakmon Shipping Co.* [1986] C.L.Y. 2252 applied).

Claims under the Civil Liability (Contribution) Act 1978 are not limited to liabilities incurred in England and Wales.

KAPETAN GEORGIS, THE; *sub nom.* VIRGO STEAMSHIP CO. S.A. *v.* SKAARUP SHIPPING CORP., *Financial Times,* October 21, 1987, Hirst J.

3588. False imprisonment—no reasonable cause for suspicion—unlawful arrest

C was employed by a market research company until, late 1985, when she was dismissed. The weekend following her dismissal, the company premises were broken into. Nothing was stolen. Two constables called to the scene, formed the view that the break-in was an inside job and enquired whether any employees had been dismissed. W, the company's owner, mentioned C but said she did not think she was involved. That afternoon the police visited C and arrested her. She was held for three and three-quarter hours until her release without charge. During her detention the police telephoned a number of colleagues to obtain information and told them of C's arrest. There was medical evidence that following her release C suffered from a stress-related disorder.

Held, that although the officers had a prima facie suspicion, before arresting C they had a duty to try to establish whether she did have a motive. They should have questioned her at home; she was a person of previous good character and unlikely to abscond. The officers did not have reasonable cause to suspect her of the offence and the arrest was therefore unlawful. Damages of £4,500 for false imprisonment were awarded.

CASTORINA *v.* CHIEF CONSTABLE OF SURREY, September 30, 1987; H.H. Judge Lermon, Q.C.; Guildford County Ct. [*Ex rel. Stephen Grosz, Solicitor*].

3589. Fraudulent misrepresentation—claim arising in connection with a contract tainted by illegality—whether damages recoverable—*ex turpi causa non oritur actio.* See SAUNDERS *v.* EDWARDS, §1826.

3590. Harassment—power to grant injunction

There is no tort of harassment, and merely approaching premises cannot give rise to a cause of action. No injunction will lie in such circumstances unless it is to prevent an actual or reasonably anticipated tort.

PATEL *v.* PATEL, *The Times,* August 21, 1987, C.A.

3591. Interference with trade or business by unlawful means—strike action. See TRADE UNIONS, §3765.

3592. Misrepresentation—service charge on flat—measure of damages. See HEINEMANN *v.* COOPER, §1163.

3593. Water abstraction—right of landowner to do so

Whatever the consequences of a landowner abstracting water flowing in undefined channels beneath his land authorities establish his right so to do.

STEPHENS *v.* ANGLIAN WATER AUTHORITY, *The Times*, August 24, 1987, C.A.

TOWN AND COUNTRY PLANNING

3594. Advertisements

TOWN AND COUNTRY PLANNING (CONTROL OF ADVERTISEMENTS) (AMENDMENT) REGULATIONS 1987 (No. 804) [85p], made under the Town and Country Planning Act 1971 (c.78), ss.63, 109, 287; operative on July 1, 1987; amend S.I. 1984 No. 421.

TOWN AND COUNTRY PLANNING (CONTROL OF ADVERTISEMENTS) (AMENDMENT No. 2) REGULATIONS 1987 (No. 2227) [85p], made under the Town and Country Planning Act 1971, ss.63 and 287(1); operative on January 29, 1988; except art. 3 which is operative on October 28, 1988; amend S.I. 1984 No. 421.

3595. Advertising balloon—attached to vehicle on site—whether offence

[Town and Country Planning (Control of Advertisements) Regulations 1984 (S.I. 1984 No. 421).]

A balloon is "attached" to a site for the purposes of the 1984 Regulations if it is securely attached to a heavy object standing on site.

The appellants flew a red and white balloon above their premises with their name "Wadham Stringer" on it. The balloon was not attached to the premises but to a vehicle standing on the premises. They were convicted of an offence contrary to the planning regulations. They appealed by case stated on the basis that the balloon was not attached to the site.

Held, dismissing the appeal, that the balloon was "attached" if it was tied to something on the land sufficiently heavy to stop it being blown away.

WADHAM STRINGER (FAREHAM) *v.* FAREHAM BOROUGH COUNCIL (1987) 53 P. & C.R. 336, D.C.

3596. Appeal—whether whole planning decision reopened on remission

[Town and Country Planning Act 1971 (c.78), s.246; R.S.C., Ord. 94, r.12.]

When an appeal under s.246 of the Town and Country Planning Act 1971 is successful and the matter is remitted for a rehearing under Ord. 94, r.12, the whole of the decision is reopened for determination.

NEWBURY DISTRICT COUNCIL *v.* SECRETARY OF STATE FOR THE ENVIRONMENT, *The Times*, July 2, 1987, Kennedy J.

3597. Appeals

TOWN AND COUNTRY PLANNING (APPEALS) (WRITTEN REPRESENTATIONS PROCEDURE) REGULATIONS 1987 (No. 701) [80p], made under the Town and Country Planning Act 1971 (c.78), s.282B; operative on May 5, 1987; prescribe the procedure and time limits for appeals against local planning authority decisions.

3598. Blight notice—whether more than one "appropriate authority"

[Town and Country Planning Act 1971 (c.78), ss.192(1)(*b*), 205(2).]

S, the lessee of land which was affected by highway proposals and was also in an area to be redeveloped for commercial purposes, served blight notices pursuant to s.192(1)(*b*) of the Town and Country Planning Act 1971 on the County Council and Borough Council respectively. On being asked to determine pursuant to s.205(2) of the Act which recipient was the "appropriate authority", the Secretary of State determined that there were in this case two distinct sets of circumstances which had enabled notices to be served, one of which rendered the County Council liable to acquire the land, the other of which rendered the Borough Council so liable; and that each authority was, on the facts of the case, the "appropriate authority".

Held, dismissing an application for certiorari and mandamus, that, where there were two such sets of circumstances, there could indeed be two "appropriate authorities".

This would enable a claimant to obtain a disclaimer of an interest to acquire from both, whilst the selection of one only as the "appropriate authority" would leave the blight notice imposed by the other unresolved.

R. *v.* SECRETARY OF STATE FOR THE ENVIRONMENT *ex p.* BOURNEMOUTH BOROUGH COUNCIL (1987) 281 E.G. 539, Mann J.

3599. British Coal Corporation

TOWN AND COUNTRY PLANNING (BRITISH COAL CORPORATION) (AMENDMENT) REGULATIONS 1987 (No. 1936) [45p], made under the Town and Country Planning Act 1971 (c.78), s.273; operative on December 11, 1987; amend S.I. 1974 No. 1006 so as to provide that the Corporation shall not be entitled to compensation in respect of the refusal to grant planning permission for opencast coal mining.

3600. Clearance areas

WAKEFIELD (DERELICT LAND CLEARANCE AREA) ORDER 1987 (No. 1653) [45p], made under the Derelict Land Act 1982 (c.42), s.1(7)(8)(*b*); operative on October 19, 1987; specifies an area in Wakefield for the purposes of the 1982 Act.

3601. Development

TRAFFORD PARK DEVELOPMENT CORPORATION (AREA AND CONSTITUTION) ORDER 1987 (No. 179) [80p], made under the Local Government, Planning and Land Act 1980 (c.65), ss.134, 135, Sched. 26, para. 1; operative on February 16, 1987; designates as an urban development area two areas in the city of Salford and the Borough of Trafford.

3602. Development Land Tax—enhancement expenditure

[Development Land Tax Act 1976 (c.24), Sched. 3, paras. 1, 6.]

In order to obtain planning permission for certain land which it owned, the taxpayer company procured another company within the group to surrender a right to use other land for industrial purposes; to compensate that other company the taxpayer company entered into arrangement under which it purchased land from that other company at an overvalue of £80,000. When the taxpayer company sold its land with the benefit of planning permission, it claimed to deduct the sum of £80,000 as enhancement expenditure within D.L.T.A. 1976, Sched. 3, paras. 1, 6.

Held, allowing the taxpayer company's appeal, that the overvalue of £80,000 was paid with a view to getting planning permission for the taxpayer company's land, and was, accordingly, deductible as enhancement expenditure within Sched. 3, para. 1.

TADDALE PROPERTIES *v.* I.R.C. [1987] S.T.C. 411, Scott J.

3603. Development Land Tax—unincorporated association—liability to tax—club or trustees. See CLUBS AND ASSOCIATIONS, §307.

3604. Enforcement notice—ambiguity—whether notice a nullity

An enforcement notice requiring the recipient to desist from holding Sunday markets within the period of summer time in any year was a nullity on account of its ambiguity.

D were the leasehold owners of premises known as Wonderland (an amusements building) on the North Promenade in Cleethorpes and some adjoining land. D had planning permission to hold Sunday markets within Wonderland between October and February each year. In 1983 D held open air markets on Sundays throughout the summer on the adjacent land. Cleethorpes Borough Council served an enforcement notice dated August 5, 1983 on D specifying a breach of planning control by holding Sunday markets on the land adjacent to Wonderland. The notice required D "to discontinue the use of the land for the holding of markets and associated car parking on such Sundays which fall within the period of summer time in any year". D appealed against the notice which the inspector varied by interpreting summer time as defined in the Summer Time Act 1972. The inspector also held that the adjacent land formed part of the curtilage of a building within the meaning of Town and Country Planning General Development Order 1977, Art. III and Sched. I, Class 4, para. 2. The inspector also took into account as a relevant consideration the fact that D had submitted no proposals for the use of the land from Mondays to Saturdays. D appealed pursuant to s.246 of the Town and Country Planning Act 1971.

Held, allowing the appeal, that the use of the words "within the period of summer time in any year" were so ambiguous that the enforcement notice was a nullity. As such there was no notice that could be varied. Whether the land formed part of the curtilage of Wonderland was a question of fact for the inspector. There was ample evidence to support his conclusion that the land was part of the curtilage of Wonderland. Whilst it might be a relevant planning consideration that the land would be vacant for six days each week as a result of holding a Sunday market it was not a relevant planning consideration that D had put forward no proposals for the use of the land on those days. There was no obligation on an owner to use his land (*Miller-Mead* v. *Minister of Housing and Local Government* [1963] C.L.Y. 3406 applied).

BOWERS (DUDLEY) AMUSEMENTS ENTERPRISES *v.* SECRETARY OF STATE FOR THE ENVIRONMENT (1986) 52 P. & C.R. 365, David Widdicombe Q.C.

3605. Enforcement notice—appeal—procedure

[Town and Country Planning Act 1971 (c.78). ss.88, 283.]

Appeal documents in an enforcement notice appeal were lost in the post. The question arose whether the appeal was barred if it was not received by the Secretary of State before the date specified in the enforcement notice.

Held, that the time limits must be strictly complied with. The enforcement notice was therefore effective.

R. *v.* SECRETARY OF STATE AND BROMLEY LONDON BOROUGH COUNCIL, *ex p.* JACKSON [1987] J.P.L. 790, MacPherson J.

3606. Enforcement notice—appeal to High Court—powers of Court

[Town and Country Planning Act 1971 (c.78), s.246.]

On an appeal against an enforcement notice under s.246 of the Town and Country Planning Act 1971 the court had jurisdiction to stay proceedings taken by a planning authority to enforce the enforcement notice pending the determination of the appeal.

South Cambridgeshire District Council served two enforcement notices requiring the cessation of parachuting activities by L.P. on land belonging to R.F. L.P. and R.F. appealed unsuccessfully against the notices to the Secretary of State under s.88 of the Town and Country Planning Act 1971. In accordance with the Secretary of State's decision letter, the period for complying with the enforcement notices expired at the end of July 1985. On May 24, 1985 L.P. and R.F. appealed to the High Court under s.246 of the Town and Country Planning Act 1971. Parachuting activities continued after the end of July 1985 and in August 1985 the Council issued a notice of motion in the Chancery Division seeking an injunction to restrain the use of the land in question for parachuting. Scott J. was minded to grant such an injunction but accepted undertakings from L.P. and R.F. which gave two days in which to appeal. L.P. and R.F. did not appeal but issued a notice of motion before the Divisional Court of the Queen's Bench Division for an order that the enforcement notices be of no effect pending the final determination of the s.246 appeal. An order was made that the enforcement notices should be of no effect until October 1, 1985. In consequence Scott J. discharged the undertakings given by L.P. and R.F.

Held, allowing the Council's appeal, that the court has power at an interlocutory stage to make an order under R.S.C., Ord. 55, rule 3(3) that an appeal under s.246 of the Town and Country Planning Act 1971 should operate as a stay of any proceedings on an enforcement notice. The court does not have the power to order that the enforcement notices should be of no effect. The provisions of s.88(10) of the Town and Country Planning Act 1971 did not provide for enforcement notices to be of no effect pending the determination of a s.246 appeal but applied only to appeals under s.88 to the Secretary of State (*Dover District Council* v. *McKeen* [1985] C.L.Y. 3411 approved).

LONDON PARACHUTING AND RECTORY FARM (PAMPISFORD) *v.* SECRETARY OF STATE FOR THE ENVIRONMENT AND SOUTH CAMBRIDGESHIRE DISTRICT COUNCIL (1986) 52 P. & C.R. 376, C.A.

3607. Enforcement notice—breach of condition—high street market place—licence granted by Royal Charter

[Town and Country Planning Act 1971 (c.78), ss.88, 94; Town and Country Planning Act 1984 (c.10), s.4; Circular 1/85.]

The appellant argued, *inter alia,* that the appellant was a person entitled to appeal against the enforcement notices, and that the matters alleged in the notice did not constitute a breach of planning control in that the right to hold a weekly market every Tuesday was granted by Royal Charter in 1637.

Held, inter alia, that (1) the licence granted to the appellant to hold a weekly street market somewhere in Moreton-in-Marsh was sufficient to satisfy the requirements of s.4(2) of the TCPA 1984 that the appellant was entitled to appeal by virtue of his being an occupier of land under a licence; (2) the contention that the grant of the right by Royal Charter made it unnecessary for planning permission to be obtained was rejected.

COTSWOLD DISTRICT COUNCIL and SPOOK ERECTION (Ref: APP/F1610/C84/3553) (1986) 1 P.A.D. 460.

3608. Enforcement notice—breach of condition—requiring completion of development for occupation—mixed development of offices and residential

[Town and Country Planning Act 1971 (c.78), ss.44, 87, 88; Circulars: 22/80, 26/81, 1/85, 14/85, 15/85.]

Planning permission was granted for a three-storey office block and a separate three-storey residential development. Condition Number 3 required that "the development hereby approved shall be carried out and completed in all respects . . . before the buildings are occupied". The breach alleged was that the office block had been occupied before the development had been completed, the residential site remained vacant. The enforcement notice required that the residential block should be erected in accordance with the planning permission. Grounds of appeal, among others, were that planning permission ought to be granted and that what was alleged did not constitute a breach. The appellants argued that the condition did not require all development to be completed before any occupation and that it sought to compel the completion of the development, contrary to advice in Circular 1/85. The Council argued that the land was allocated for residential in the Town Map and that there was an adequate supply of office accommodation.

Held, allowing the appeal, that (1) the condition was not invalidated because it failed specifically to require that all the buildings had to be erected and completed before any building could be occupied; there was no evidence that the appellant had been misled by any lack of precision in drafting; (2) in considering the planning merits, regard should be had to the reasons for the condition, which were "to obviate any detriment to the amenities of the locality by any works remaining uncompleted"; (3) no evidence had been adduced to show that occupation of the office before erection of the residential block had had any adverse environmental affects; Circulars 22/80 and 14/85 encouraged planning to be administered constructively; (4) Condition Number 3 served no useful purpose and the condition would be discharged.

EPSOM & EWELL BOROUGH COUNCIL and JAMES LONGLEY PROPERTIES; WELLCOME FOUNDATION INVESTMENT CO. and MANUFACTURERS HANOVER FINANCE (Ref: T/APP/P3610/C/84/2922) (1986) 1 P.A.D. 442.

3609. Enforcement notice—breach of condition—warehouse—operating hours—deliveries

[Town and Country Planning Act 1971 (c.78), ss.36, 88; Circulars 22/80, 1/85, 14/85.]

The appeal was against the Council's service of an enforcement notice alleging breaches of the following conditions attached to permission for a workshop; condition 3, limiting hours of operation; condition 4, excluding storage outdoors in circulation areas; and condition 6, requiring that all loading and unloading take place within the site. The appellant argued that the conditions should be discharged as there was little harm to amenity and that condition 6 was invalid in accordance with the guidance in Circular 1/85. The premises were now used as a warehouse, and it was argued by the appellants that alternative premises would have to be found if the appeal was dismissed, putting jobs at risk.

Held, dismissing the appeal against conditions 3 and 4, allowing the appeal against condition 6, that, (1) longer working hours would result in unreasonable disturbance to amenities; (2) loading activities associated with the site had material harmful effects on traffic flows and safety, consequently parts of the forecourt should not be used for storage; (3) the appellant could not ensure compliance with condition 6 because it had no control over the public highway nor did it have direct control over all vehicles which came to the site, consequently condition 6 was invalid because it was unreasonable and unenforceable.

GREAT YARMOUTH BOROUGH COUNCIL and G. W. FIELDS & SONS (GREAT YARMOUTH) (Ref: T/APP/U2615/C/85/1601/P6) (1986) 1 P.A.D. 420.

3609a. Enforcement notice—caravan site

Persons are not justified in breaching the criminal law by failing to comply with an enforcement notice because of the alleged failure of a local authority to provide a camping site for gypsies pursuant to their statutory duty.

WAVERLEY BOROUGH COUNCIL *v.* HILDEN, *The Times*, June 9, 1987, C.A.

3610. Enforcement notice—change from residential to offices—local plan policies

[Town and Country Planning Act 1971 (c.78), ss.36, 88; Circulars: 16/84, 14/85.]

The Council served an enforcement notice requiring office use to cease in a building for which the lawful use was residential. The appeal was on the basis that planning permission should be granted. The premises were in a street in which there were buildings used for industrial and office purposes next to a shopping high street. The appeal premises had not been in residential use since 1971, and had only been in intermittent use before that time. The ground floor and basement had been used for offices, retail and storage purposes since at least 1961. The Council argued that the loss of potential residential accommodation was contrary to the policies in the adopted District Plan and the Draft Alterations. The use as offices conflicted with the Council's policy against office development outside preferred office locations. There were an important number of residential units on upper floors in the High Street and in adjoining commercial areas and the granting of permission would create a damaging precedent. The appellant argued that the Council's objections were on policy grounds alone, which were not an adequate reason for refusing permission according to Circular 16/84. It would be uneconomic to convert the premises to residential use.

Held, allowing the appeal, that (1) the appellant's evidence on costs of restoration to residential use was not seriously challenged by the Council and consequently it was unlikely that residential use would be restored if permission for offices was refused; (2) the poor residential environment was not of itself an adequate reason for permitting the loss of potential housing accommodation; (3) there were in this case exceptional circumstances which justified the loss of essential residential accommodation; (4) the circumstances were not such as to set a precedent for loss of other residential accommodation in the area.

CAMDEN LONDON BOROUGH COUNCIL and LAVERY & CO. (Ref: T/APP/X5210/C/852957/P6) (1986) 1 P.A.D. 433.

3611. Enforcement notice—change of use from smallholding to a leisure plot—economic viability not definitive test

[Town and Country Planning Act 1971 (c.78), s.88.]

An Enforcement Notice was served alleging a material change of use from an agricultural smallholding to a leisure plot. The appeal site was about 0.2 ha. and was part of an estate which had been sub-divided into small "leisure plots" against which enforcement proceedings had successully been taken. The Council argued that the character of the use of the land was comparable to the uses on neighbouring plots which the Secretary of State had found to constitute use of land for leisure purposes. The appellant argued that the land was used for the rearing of goats and that sheep, ducks and ponies were kept on the land.

Held, allowing the appeal, that the main use to which the land was put was agricultural and the matters alleged therefore did not constitute a breach of planning control. The Inspector took into account that the land was probably too small to be viable as a smallholding but concluded that this was only one factor to take into account.

CANTERBURY CITY COUNCIL AND MARTY (Ref. T/APP/5273/C/83/1129/P6) (1986) 1 P.A.D. 374.

3612. Enforcement notice—discontinuance of user

[Town and Country Planning Act 1971 (c.78), s.89(1).]

B was charged with failing to take steps required by an enforcement notice within the period allowed for compliance. The notice specified the breach of planning control as "Use of the land for the siting of a caravan or caravans for residential purposes." The step required was cesser of the use by removing the caravans.

Held, that there was no offence under s.89(1) where discontinuance of the use of land was the breach. The count must be quashed.

R. *v.* JEFFORD [1986] J.P.L. 912, Judge Rubin.

3613. Enforcement notice—duality—error corrected by Inspector on appeal—whether notice a nullity

Permission was granted in 1979 personally to the occupants of a caravan to place a caravan on land. After the occupant's death M occupied the caravan. An enforcement notice was served requiring removal of the caravan and discontinuance of the use. An appeal against the enforcement notice was dismissed by the Secretary of State. The Inspector amended the notice. The magistrates dismissed the summons for non-compliance on the ground that the notice was a nullity. The Council appealed by way of case stated.

Held, that the Inspector had validily corrected the notice which was not therefore a nullity.

EPPING FOREST DISTRICT COUNCIL *v.* MATTHEWS [1987] J.P.L. 132, D.C.

3614. Enforcement notice—established use—whether established user rights had come to an end

From 1957 the main building on a seven-acre site was used for storage of various articles. This continued until 1976. In 1978, B commenced to carry on business as commercial vehicle dealers, hirers and repairers on the site. In 1980, the Council served an enforcement notice relating to the seven-acre site, alleging change of use to warehousing including storage of timber and joinery products. An inspector required discontinuance only on the open land. In 1981 planning permission was granted to increase the warehouse area. Subsequent enforcement notice and planning appeals turned on whether the changes and conditions attached to earlier planning permissions had brought the established user rights to an end.

Held, that (1) the erection of a building on part only of a site does not terminate established user rights unless the development is inconsistent with established use; (2) the Inspector had erred in law in holding that there was an established use where an earlier enforcement notice had taken effect. Any earlier established use at that point goes.

SOUTH STAFFORDSHIRE DISTRICT COUNCIL *v.* SECRETARY OF STATE FOR THE ENVIRONMENT AND BICKFORD [1987] J.P.L. 635, D.C.

3615. Enforcement notice—existing use rights

An enforcement notice cannot extinguish existing use rights.

The appellants owned a site which had been occupied by persons connected with the haulage business since 1941. In the period 1969–1980 the use for the same purpose had increased. In 1980 an application for grant of an existing use certificate had been rejected and no appeal had been lodged. On sale the price reflected only residential use. The local authority served enforcement notices requiring the discontinuance of use for haulage purposes.

Held, allowing the appeal, that the statute did not authorise an enforcement notice to extinguish existing use rights.

PEARCY (JOHN) TRANSPORT *v.* SECRETARY OF STATE FOR THE ENVIRONMENT (1987) 53 P. & C.R. 91, Widdicombe Q.C.

3616. Enforcement notice—farm unit

[General Development Order 1977, Class VI.]

An enforcement notice was served alleging that the construction of a silage clamp on a farm was in breach of development control. The farm was divided by a road. The clamp was outside the scope of G.D.O. Class VI because it was less than 25 metres from the road. The Secretary of State held that the farmhouse and garden were incapable of being land used for agriculture. He held that the rest of the farmland could also not be used in the one acre calculation since they were separated by the road.

Held, that the Secretary of State had been wrong in following *Blackmore* v. *Butler* [1954] C.L.Y. 39. Whether the farmhouse and garden were being put to agricultural use was a matter of fact and degree; (2) it is a matter of fact and degree whether two plots of land together comprise one agricultural unit. Case remitted to Secretary of State.

HANCOCK *v.* SECRETARY OF STATE FOR THE ENVIRONMENT AND TORRIDGE DISTRICT COUNCIL [1987] J.P.L. 360, Hodgson J. *The Times*, June 9, 1987, C.A.

3617. Enforcement notice—grain silos—whether farms wrongly treated as separate planning units

A farmer farmed over 2,000 acres of land in Kent comprising several separate farms, and at two of these he had built several grain silos which were used primarily for the storage of grain under the GAFTA agreement and under the EEC intervention scheme. Both activities caused a considerable nuisance from the frequent use of large lorries over narrow country lanes, and enforcement notices were served by the local authority. Following an inquiry, the inspector found that there was a material change of use amounting to development, and the Secretary of State upheld the notices. A did not challenge these findings in relation to GAFTA or intervention storage, but argued on appeal that the Secretary of State had erred in treating the two farms concerned as being separate and different planning units, and had further precluded the normal activities of a farmer in providing storage and drying facilities for neighbouring farmers and had effectively negated A's existing rights as a corn merchant.

Held, dismissing the appeal, that (1) the question of what constitutes the planning unit is one of fact and degree, and there was material upon which the Secretary of State could conclude as he did (*Williams* v. *Minister of Housing and Local Government* [1967] C.L.Y. 3817 and *Duffy* v. *Secretary of State* (1981) 259 E.G. 1081 considered); (2) the Secretary of State had not been obliged to consider the subsidiary uses referred to by A unless invited to do so, and A had not raised these matters before the inspector (*Finlay* v. *Secretary of State for the Environment* [1984] C.L.Y. 3430, and *Mason* v. *Secretary of State for the Environment* [1984] C.L.Y. 3475 considered). In any event, if the planning authority sought to prevent these activities, which seemed unlikely, L could apply for planning permission.

FULLER *v.* SECRETARY OF STATE FOR THE ENVIRONMENT (1987) 283 E.G. 847, Stuart-Smith J.

3618. Enforcement notice—lack of precision in permission—change of use from warehouse to retail showroom and distribution depot

[Town and Country Planning Act 1971 (c.78), ss.18, 36; Town & Country Planning (Use Classes Order) 1972 (S.I. No. 1385).]

An enforcement notice had been served alleging a change of use from general industrial use to wholesale warehouse with ancillary retail sales. M appealed on the ground, *inter alia,* that the matter alleged did not constitute a breach of planning control. M also appealed against the refusal by the Local Authority to grant permission for change of use from Class X warehouse to retail showroom with distribution depot for bathroom fittings. The premises under appeal was one of a pair of units of 8,640 sq. ft. in a trading estate of some 58,000 sq. ft. which was granted outline permission in 1981 to include a mixture of Class IV industry and Class X warehouses with ancillary offices. The application plan showed the appeal premises marked only as "5B" whilst the other unit in the pair was marked "industrial". Application for approval of details was made in 1983 and included a plan which showed both units marked as "warehouses". The letter in reply from the Council stated that the plan formed part of the permission. The appellant submitted that the warehouse use became part of the original permission by virtue of the Council's letter in 1983. The council submitted that the original permission was clear that units 5A and 5B were to be industrial, and that the floorspace figures in the application supported this view. On the issue of the refusal for change of use, the appellant stated that M required a distribution depot from which to supply high street shops with bathroom fittings, with an associated showroom and retail outlet for sale of bulky goods. The Council stated that this was contrary to its policy that major shopping proposals outside principal shopping centres would only be allowed where a suitable location was not available within the centres.

Held, allowing the appeals subject to conditions that (1) the outline permission lacked precision but the Council's letter of 1983 was specific in approving the warehouse use and that the retail sales were ancillary, consequently there had been no breach of planning control; (2) there was no sound and clear cut reason for refusal of planning permission for change of use to retail showroom with distribution depot.

WALTHAM FOREST LONDON BOROUGH COUNCIL AND MULTI-TILE (Ref. T/APP./U5930/C/84/4022/P6 and A/85/36439/P6) (1986) 1 P.A.D. 350.

3619. Enforcement notice—local authority resolution authorising s.89 proceedings—whether to be acted on only within reasonable period

[Town and Country Planning Act 1971 (c.78), ss.89 and 93.]

On September 22, 1980, a local planning authority resolved that the District Secretary be authorised to take such steps as he considered necessary, including proceedings under s.89 of the 1971 Act to secure cessation of unauthorised use or of certain buildings by FE Co. A complaint was received by the Council at the end of 1985 that the unauthorised use had resumed (it having ceased some years earlier following service of an enforcement notice). A summons was issued on June 6, 1986 alleging an offence by FE Co. contrary to s.89(5).

Held, that (1) By virtue of s.93(2), the enforcement notice remained in force until there was a change in the planning status of the land. (2) The resolution remained in force for the same period. There was no ground for saying that the local authority had to bring proceedings within a reasonable time of the resolution (*Grice* v. *Dudley Corporation* [1957] C.L.Y. 478 distinguished.

R. *v.* FYFIELD EQUIPMENT [1987] Crim.L.R. 507, Snaresbrook Crown Ct.

3620. Enforcement notice—material change of use

A notice alleging material change of use of the land to use as a riding school and livery stables without planning permission was served on the appellant requiring cessation within two months. The appellant appealed and the Inspector dismissed the appeal. The site had been used as a livery stable since 1950 and the riding school use was introduced in 1980/1. The use as a riding school and livery stable was a material change of use from its former existing use solely as livery stables. The appellant appealed to the High Court.

Held, that (1) the Inspector had correctly found that the introduction of the riding instruction was a material change of use; (2) the environmental impact of the development upon the visual amenities of the surrounding land was a proper consideration.

LILO BLUM *v.* SECRETARY OF STATE FOR THE ENVIRONMENT AND THE LONDON BOROUGH OF RICHMOND UPON THAMES COUNCIL [1987] J.P.L. 278, Simon Brown J.

3621. Enforcement notice—material change of use—internal staircase

Four-storey shop premises built in 1925. The shop was used by A as a travel agency. They amalgamated the first two floors together with the ground floor and converted the first two floors into offices for the purposes of the travel agency. An enforcement notice was issued requiring the appellants to discontinue the use of the first and second floors for office purposes and further to remove an internal spiral staircase. The inspector concluded that a material change of use had occurred and required the staircase to be removed.

Held, on application to the High Court for the decision to be quashed, that the notice properly could require the staircase to be removed as it was part and parcel of the material change of use.

SOMAK TRAVEL *v.* SECRETARY OF STATE FOR THE ENVIRONMENT AND LONDON BOROUGH OF BRENT [1987] J.P.L. 630, Stuart-Smith J.

3622. Enforcement notice—material change of use—take-away service

Wimpey International had planning permission for a counter service restaurant with no condition relating to a carry out service. The local authority served an enforcement notice on them requiring the cessation of the take away service. On appeal the Secretary of State held that the provision of a counter service for the sale of hot food for carrying out did not amount to a material change of use. The local authority appealed to the Court of Session

Held, that permission for a counter service restaurant included a right to take away duly purchased food.

CITY OF ABERDEEN DISTRICT COUNCIL *v.* SECRETARY OF STATE FOR SCOTLAND [1987] J.P.L. 292 Court of Session, Scotland.

3623. Enforcement notice—no appeal—application to High Court—matters to be taken into account

The loss of existing use rights because of a failure to appeal in time is a material factor for the inspector to take into account, though he need make no actual finding on the point.

The appellant was the owner of acres of land which he had used for a haulage business and on which he had for some years parked lorries. The local authority served an enforcement notice requiring the return of the land to agricultural use. There was no appeal and he was prosecuted for breaches. He applied eventually to the High Court pursuant to s.245 of the 1971 Act for an order quashing the inspector's decision on the ground that in failing to make a finding as to existing use rights, he failed to take into account personal hardship caused by loss of existing use rights by inadvertent failure to appeal in time.

Held, dismissing the appeal, that it was clear that the inspector did take into account the question of personal hardship.

NASH *v.* SECRETARY OF STATE FOR THE ENVIRONMENT AND EPPING FOREST DISTRICT COUNCIL (1985) 52 P. & C.R. 261, C.A.

3624. Enforcement notice—notice "corrected"—whether correction or variation

An enforcement notice was served alleging the making of a material change of use by using the premiums for the storage, sale and distribution of furniture and second hand goods and of two containers. The Inspector found that these were operations. He corrected the notice, and upheld it. The local authority appealed on the ground that the alterations made were variations and not corrections.

Held, that it did not matter whether the alteration was called a correction or variation. The notice as amended was valid.

HARROGATE BOROUGH COUNCIL *v.* SECRETARY OF STATE FOR THE ENVIRONMENT AND PROCTER [1987] J.P.L. 288.

3625. Enforcement notice—planning permission—workshop and showroom

[Town and Country Planning Act 1971 (c.78), ss.23, 36, 88; Local Government and Planning (Amendment) Act 1981 (c.41); Circulars 1/85, 14/85.]

The appellant appealed against an enforcement notice in respect of a breach of a condition attached to a planning permission for the use of premises as a bungalow, workshop and showroom, namely that the showroom be used only for the sale and display of furniture manufactured in the workshop. The appellant also appealed against the refusal of planning permission for the erection of a link to adjoining industrial premises and for a change of use of the enlarged site to form a composite unit of showrooms and workshops for furniture and DIY fittings. In respect of the appeal against refusal, the appellants submitted that the link with industrial premises was needed for the manufacture of the furniture and sale in adjacent showrooms and should be considered as one unit, but he would accept a condition limiting the amount of retail showroom floor space. The development would provide an increase in employment and did not harm town centre retail functions. The Council argued that the development was contrary to the Structure Plan policy relating to the protection and enhancement of existing town centres and an exception should not be made in this case. The showroom would become the dominant use and the site should not be considered as one unit. In respect of the enforcement notice, the appellant argued that the notice was unenforceable and/or void for uncertainty and that the condition was not in accordance with the advice contained in Circular 1/85, under ground (*b*) in the grounds of appeal. The appellant also appealed on grounds (*a*), (*h*), and (*g*) of s.88(2). The Council argued that the condition was justified by the Council's policy against shops outside existing centres and it limited the applicant to what he had applied for. An application for a retail operation alone would probably have been refused.

Held, allowing the planning appeal, that (1) the appeal site should be considered as one planning unit; (2) the showroom was ancillary to the industrial use and the appellant needed a showroom adjacent to the manufacturing premises; (3) the proposal was not a significant breach of the relevant policies.

Held, dismissing the enforcement notice appeal, that (1) the condition was not invalid nor did it infringe the advice in Circular 1/85; (2) use of the workshop as a showroom took access from a residential street and was harmful to amenity.

WALSALL METROPOLITAN BOROUGH COUNCIL and CASSIDY REPRODUCTIONS and J. and L. K. CASSIDY (Ref. T/APP/V4630/C/84/1671/P6 and T/APP/V4630/A/84/024544/P6) (1986) 1 P.A.D. 386.

3626. Enforcement notice—prosecution—no change in use of land

[Town and County Planning Act 1971 (c.78), ss.89, 243.]

Where there was no change in the use of the land allegedly in contravention of the notice, D was not able to allege that that use was not a breach, otherwise he would be retrospectively challenging the validity of the notice.

R. *v.* KEEYS, *The Times*, June 17, 1987, C.A.

3627. Enforcement notice—prosecution for failure to comply—subsequent application for planning permission—whether sentence should be deferred until decision on planning permission known. See R. *v.* NEWLAND, §927.

3628. Enforcement notice—public house garden—play equipment fixed to concrete plinths

[Town and Country Planning Act 1971 (c.78), s.88.]

An enforcement notice had been served requiring the removal of garden equipment (including swings, a slide, a climbing frame and a large boot) and the concrete plinths to which they were attached, from the garden of a public house. The appellant argued that as the boot was not permanently fixed to the ground it did not require planning permission, and cited *James* v. *Brecon County Council.* Also that the notice was defective in respect of the number of concrete bases stated, but agreed that the notice could be corrected without injustice. The Council argued that installation of the equipment had resulted in a great increase in noise and disturbance to nearby residents. Further, that it was visually intrusive.

Held, quashing the enforcement notice and allowing the deemed planning appeal that (1) the boot did not require planning permission; (2) the notice relating to the other features could be corrected without injustice; (3) it appeared that the harm to residential amenity had increased in recent years but the unauthorised development in itself had not caused harmful effects; (4) no material harm was caused to visual amenities.

THANET DISTRICT COUNCIL AND HOST GROUP (Ref: T/APP/22260/C/85/1459/P6) (1986) 1 P.A.D. 364.

3629. Enforcement notice—removal of caravans—whether entitled to enter land

[Scot.] [Town and Country Planning (Scotland) Act 1972 (c.52), s.88(1).]

A notice averred breach of planning control in respect of use of land around Marisbank House for the stationing of caravans. The respondent was required to remove them within three months and permanent cessation of the use of the site for stationing of caravans. The Council then sought to enter and remove the caravans.

Held, that the Council was entitled to enter and remove the caravans notwithstanding it resulted incidentally in the discontinuance of a use.

MIDLOTHIAN DISTRICT COUNCIL *v.* STEVENSON [1986] J.P.L. 913, Court of Session.

3630. Enforcement notice—requirement that occupier solely or mainly employed in agriculture—whether compliance required with enforcement notice

Justices when considering informations for non-compliance with an enforcement order are bound to consider the terms of the enforcement notice itself.

The respondents purchased a site in the green belt and acquired permission for a building, provided the occupier was employed in agriculture. The occupier was a builder who worked on the land most days and on weekends; the land did not produce a living wage. The authority served an enforcement notice requiring discontinuance of occupation of those not solely or mainly employed in agriculture. The magistrates dismissed information for non-compliance, finding that the occupiers were required to comply with the condition in the planning permission, rather than the stricter wording of the enforcement notice.

Held, allowing the appeal, that the justices were bound to consider the terms of the enforcement notice and the mode of compliance set out therein.

EPPING FOREST DISTRICT COUNCIL *v.* SCOTT (1987) 53 P. & C.R. 79, D.C.

3631. Enforcement notice—retail warehouse—breach of condition limiting amount of retail floorspace

[Town & Country Planning Act 1971 (c.78), ss.36, 88; Circular: 14/85.]

Permission had been granted by the Secretary of State on appeal for a retail warehouse subject to a condition limiting the net retail floorspace to 2,230 sq.m. In implementing the position, the appellants used a further 400 sq.m. for retail space by deducting it from the storage area. The Council served an enforcement notice, the appellant appealed on the basis that planning permission ought to be granted. The appellant also submitted a fresh application for change of use of 400 sq.m. of storage to retail, this was refused by the Council. The Council argued that the additional space might lead to parking congestion in the future, though it conceded that the car park was only half full at peak times at present. The Council also argued that if there was a need to expand the sales area, the entire retail use should be re-located on a site adjoining the town centre, in accordance with the policies of the adopted Town Centre Local Plan. The Council was also concerned with the precedent which it would set.

Held, allowing the appeals, that (1) the Local Plan Policies indicating preferred sites were of little relevance in this instance; (2) there was no evidence that the Council's objectives would be impaired by allowing the appeal, given that it was not argued by the Council that the Town Centre as a whole would suffer harm; (3) on the issue of precedent, the circumstances of the case were unusual and subsequent cases would be dealt with on their respective merits.

CHELMSFORD BOROUGH COUNCIL and HARRIS QUEENSWAY (Ref: T/APP/W 1525/5/595/P6 and A/85/2694/2/P6) (1986) 1 P.A.D. 426.

3632. Enforcement notice—riverside moorings—commercial purposes—material change of use—established use—Green Belt—area of great landscape value

[Town and Country Planning Act 1971 (c.78), ss.36, 88; Local Government and Planning (Amendment) Act (c.41), 1981.]

The site was on the south side of the River Thames, three quarters of which was covered by the river and the land part was mainly grass riverbank. There were a number of dwelling-houses nearby and to the east of the site was a boatyard. The site had originally been within the curtilage of a dwelling-house and moorings had been laid in 1950. The Council had issued an enforcement notice against the mooring of boats for commercial purposes.

Held, allowing the appeal, that (1) mooring a vessel would not normally involve development, however regularity could invest a degree of permanence so as to amount to development by a change of use and such was the case here; (2) the use of the moorings by occupiers was incidental to the enjoyment of the dwelling within a curtilage which extended to the centre line of the river and was permitted development, however this did not apply to commercial use after the land was severed; (3) it was primarily for the appellant to establish a case that the land had been used for commercial purposes since the start of 1964 to create an established use, and the Inspector was not satisfied that he had done so; (4) the Inspector was not satisfied that the moorings would lead to an unacceptable visual impact; (5) the question of congestion on the river was a matter for control by the Thames Water Authority; (6) permission would be granted subject to conditions limiting the number and size of boats to be moored.

ROYAL BOROUGH OF WINDSOR AND MAIDENHEAD and WOOTTEN (Ref: T/APP/DO325/C/85/1101) (1986) 1 P.A.D. 502.

3633. Enforcement notice—timbers of listed building—injunction

[Town and Country Planning Act 1971 (c.78), s.54, 96, 97.]

The council served listed building enforcement notices. The persons upon whom the notices were served appealed to the Secretary of State. While the appeal was pending the notice did not take effect. The council submitted that it had an arguable case for requiring the defendants to re-erect the listed building barn. It therefore sought an injunction to prevent that power from being frustrated by the export of the timbers to the U.S.A. The purchaser of the timbers contended that the timbers were not a "building" within the Act.

Held, that a temporary injunction would be granted. It was highly arguable that timbers could be treated as a building and required to be reconstructed in its former place.

LEOMINSTER DISTRICT COUNCIL *v.* BRITISH HISTORIC BUILDINGS AND S.P.S. SHIPPING [1987] J.P.L. 350, Hoffmann J.

3634. Enforcement notice—unspecified land—whether notice a nullity

[Town and Country Planning Act 1971 (c.78), s.89.]

A supplied and erected scaffolding from two premises. An enforcement notice was served not specifying on which land the allegedly unauthorised use had taken place. The magistrates convicted A of non-compliance. A appealed to the High Court.

Held, that the notice was not a nullity because in the light of the surrounding circumstances it was clear what A had to do. There was no injustice.

COVENTRY SCAFFOLDING CO. (LONDON) *v.* PARKER (JOHN BRIAN) [1987] J.P.L. 127, D.C.

3635. Enforcement notice—varied on appeal—non-compliance—prosecution—validity

A occupied a caravan on an agricultural smallholding since they were unable to obtain planning permission for the erection of a dwelling-house on a site. In October 1982, the Council served an enforcement notice in respect of the smallholding. The appeal was dismissed. The Inspector varied the notice to read as a change of use from agriculture to the mixed use of agriculture and stationing of a caravan for residential purposes. The notice required cessation of the stationing of the caravan and its removal. A was prosecuted for non-compliance and convicted.

Held, on appeal by way of case stated that (1) an enforcement notice, if varied on appeal, did not need to be re-issued in its amended form; (2) the validity of an enforcement notice could not be impugned before the magistrate.

MASEFIELD *v.* TAYLOR [1987] J.P.L. 721, D.C.

3636. Enforcement notice—whether enforcement action could be taken against an ancillary use

An enforcement notice was issued alleging material change of use of the first floor of premises to offices. The Inspector allowed the appeal on the ground that the office use was ancillary to the use as a retail outlet for lighting units and storage of builders' material and plant.

Held, on appeal, that the Inspector had erred in law in deciding that enforcement action cannot be taken against an ancillary use.

RICHMOND-UPON-THAMES LONDON BOROUGH COUNCIL *v.* SECRETARY OF STATE FOR THE ENVIRONMENT AND BEECHGOLD [1987] J.P.L. 509, McCowan J.

3637. Enforcement proceedings—not taken against other unauthorised traders—whether relevant

The fact that a local authority has not taken enforcement proceedings against other unauthorised traders in the same position as the appellant is not a material consideration either in planning-enforcement proceedings or in a deemed planning application. The fact that others have got away with it does not put the appellant in the right.

DONOVAN *v.* SECRETARY OF STATE FOR THE ENVIRONMENT, *The Times*, July 4, 1987, D.C.

3638. Established use certificate—whether power to grant certificate for lesser use than that described in application

The Secretary of State on appeal refused to grant a certificate of established use to the effect that premises had been used in multiple occupation, housing seven households with nine occupiers. He granted a certificate in the amount of six households with six occupiers. The Council appealed.

Held, dismissing the appeal, that the Secretary of State was entitled to grant a certificate for a lesser use than that described in the application.

BRISTOL CITY COUNCIL *v.* SECRETARY OF STATE FOR THE ENVIRONMENT AND WILLIAMSON (H.M.) [1987] J.P.L. 718, Stuart-Smith J.

3639. Fees

TOWN AND COUNTRY PLANNING (FEES FOR APPLICATIONS AND DEEMED APPLICATIONS) (AMENDMENT) REGULATIONS 1987 (No. 101) [£1·60], made under the Local Government, Planning and Land Act 1980 (c.65), s.87; operative on February 25, 1987; amend S.I. 1983 No. 1674 by increasing certain fees and by introducing two new fee categories.

3640. General Development Order

TOWN AND COUNTRY PLANNING GENERAL DEVELOPMENT (AMENDMENT) ORDER 1987 (No. 702) [45p], made under the Town and Country Planning Act 1971 (c.78), ss.24, 36(2), 287(3); operative on May 5, 1987; amends S.I. 1977 No. 289 in relation to appeals to the Secretary of State against certain planning decisions of local planning authorities.

TOWN AND COUNTRY PLANNING GENERAL DEVELOPMENT (AMENDMENT) (No. 2) ORDER 1987 (No. 765) [45p], made under the Town and Country Planning Act 1971, s.24; operative on June 1, 1987; amends S.I. 1977 No. 289 by substituting a new Class III in Sched. 1.

3641. Gipsy caravan stationed on grazing land—whether land "unoccupied"

[Caravan Sites Act 1968 (c.52), s.10(1).]

S.10(1) of the Caravan Sites Act states that it is an offence for a gipsy to station a caravan for the purposes of residing for any period (a) on any land situated within the boundaries of a highway; (b) on any other unoccupied land; or (c) on any occupied land without the consent of the occupier. In May 1985 A, a gipsy, contracted to buy a plot of land from V, who had at all material times used it for grazing. Pending completion, A with V's consent entered on the land, laid hardcore and a concrete base, built a wall and fencing, and subsequently stationed his caravan there. In July 1985, the local authority lodged a complaint that A's caravan had been so stationed in contravention of s.10(1) of the Act. The magistrates subsequently found that the land had been "unoccupied" within the meaning of s.10(1)(*b*) and, purportedly pursuant to s.11 of the Act, ordered A, to whom the land had by now been conveyed, to remove his caravan. The judge held that the definition of "occupier" is s.1 of the Caravan Sites and Control of Development Act 1960 did not assist in the construction of "unoccupied" in s.10(1)(*b*) of the 1968 Act, and dismissed A's application for judicial review.

Held, allowing A's appeal and quashing the magistrates' decision, that the land had been "occupied" by V within the meaning of s.10(1)(*c*) of the Act; and since A had had the occupier's consent to station his caravan there, he had not committed an offence within s.10 of the Act (*Newcastle City Council* v. *Royal Newcastle Hospital* [1959] C.L.Y. 2760 considered).

Per Curiam: (i) s.10(1) of the 1968 act is concerned with the unauthorised stationing of caravans, and the authority which is contemplated is the consent of the occupier; (ii) the proper procedure in a case of this nature is to appeal by way of case stated.

STUBBINGS *v.* BEACONSFIELD JUSTICES (1987) 284 E.G. 223, C.A.

3642. Gipsy encampments

GIPSY ENCAMPMENTS (BOROUGH OF GREAT YARMOUTH) ORDER 1987 (No. 1709) [45p], made under the Caravan Sites Act 1968 (c.52), s.12(2); operative on October 28, 1987; designates Great Yarmouth as an area to which s.10 of the 1968 Act applies.

GIPSY ENCAMPMENTS (BOROUGH OF KETTERING) ORDER 1987 (No. 1639) [45p], made under the Caravan Sites Act 1968, s.12(2); operative on October 15, 1987; designates Kettering as an area to which s.10 of the 1968 Act applies.

GIPSY ENCAMPMENTS (CITY OF LANCASTER) ORDER 1987 (No. 556) [45p], made under the Caravan Sites Act 1968, s.12(2); operative on April 23, 1987; designates Lancaster for the purposes of s.10 of the 1968 Act.

GIPSY ENCAMPMENTS (COUNTY OF NORTHUMBERLAND) ORDER 1987 (No. 1640) [45p], made under the Caravan Sites Act 1968, s.12(2); operative on October 15, 1987; designates Northumberland as an area to which s.10 of the 1968 Act applies.

GIPSY ENCAMPMENTS (DESIGNATION OF THE BOROUGH OF MAIDSTONE) ORDER 1987 (No. 73) [45p], made under the Caravan Sites Act 1968, s.12(2); operative on February 20, 1987; designates Maidstone for the purposes of s.10 of the 1968 Act.

GIPSY ENCAMPMENTS (DISTRICT OF CHERWELL) ORDER 1987 (No. 1641) [45p], made under the Caravan Sites Act 1968, s.12(2); operative on October 15, 1987; designates Cherwell as an area to which s.10 of the 1968 Act applies.

3643. Improvement grant—whether repayable upon sale by mortgagee

[Local Authorities (Historic Buildings) Act 1962 (c.36), s.2(1).]

P made a grant to D under the Local Authorities (Historic Buildings) Act 1962 for repairs and renovations to a listed building. When the property was subsequently sold within three years of the grant by a mortgagee in exercise of the power of sale, P sought repayment of part of the grant under s.2(1) of the Act, and the judge found in P's favour.

Held, allowing D's appeal, that (1) s.2(1) is directed to a disposal by way of sale, exchange or long lease, but not by way of mortgage; (2) for s.2(1) to apply, a disposal must in event be made by the recipient of the grant.

Per curiam: it may be that the position would be different in the case of collusion between mortgagor and mortgagee.

CANTERBURY CITY COUNCIL *v.* QUINE (1987) 284 E.G. 507, C.A.

3644. Inquiry—whether inspector in breach of the rules of natural justice

Planning permission for erection of 10 dog kennels was refused. The inspector upheld the appeal. The applicants contended upon appeal to the High Court that the Inspector had been in breach of the rules of natural justice in taking into account matters which the inspector said were within his own experience.

Held, that (1) there had been no breach of the rules of natural justice; (2) even though a different inspector had on similar facts in another case reached a different decision the inspector had been entitled to reach the decision as he did (*Rockhold* v. *Secretary of State for the Environment and South Oxfordshire District Council* [1986] C.L.Y. 3327 applied).

AINLEY *v.* SECRETARY OF STATE FOR THE ENVIRONMENT AND FYLDE BOROUGH COUNCIL [1987] J.P.L. 33, Taylor J.

3645. Inquiry—whether inspector in breach of the rules of natural justice

Planning permission was refused for the continued use of premises for the repair of motor vehicles. An appeal was conducted by way of written representations. The Inspector visited the site twice without the knowledge of the parties, and subsequently paid great weight to his findings on the visit. The parties complained that they had no opportunity to comment on the results.

Held, that a breach of the rules of natural justice had occurred. Decision of Inspector quashed.

SOUTHWARK LONDON BOROUGH *v.* SECRETARY OF STATE FOR THE ENVIRONMENT AND WATERHOUSE [1987] J.P.L. 36, Nolan J.

3646. Lamp-posts—erection and installation—conservation area—area of special character

[Town and Country Planning Act 1971 (c.78), s.36.]

The Council refused permission for the erection of four cast-iron lamp-posts along the lane bounded on one side by Hampstead Heath, separated by iron railings. The site was within a Conservation Area and was subject to non-statutory policies of the Council. The lane did not form the sole access for the appellants, who argued that the railings, walls, fences and houses were urban elements of a mixed urban and rural character. The Council argued that the lane was a rural part of the heath and that security did not form a problem.

Held, dismissing the appeal, that (1) by day, the lamp-posts would not cause a change in appearance significant enough to meet the test of harm to an interest of acknowledged importance; (2) by night, the lane was visually part of the heath and views of the heath from nearby properties were important pleasures; the views were radically altered by the lamps when lit and would cause loss of amenity amounting to harm to an interest of acknowledged importance; (3) the possible security benefits to the appellants were not sufficient to justify the harm to the character of the lane which the proposal would cause.

CAMDEN LONDON BOROUGH COUNCIL and LATHYRUS INC. (Ref. T/APP/X5210/A/85/029268/P4) (1986) 1 P.A.D. 395.

3647. Listed building—removal of features of special architectural interest—removal not authorised by local authority—absence of *mens rea*—whether offence of strict liability

[Town and Country Planning Act 1971 (c.78), s.55(1).]

S.55(1) of the 1971 Town and Country Planning Act creates an absolute offence.

A company, tenants of a Grade II listed building, hired a contractor to remove furniture. The contractor also removed fixtures and fittings of value, having misinterpreted his orders to "remove everything of value." Informations were laid against a company director and the contractor. At committal proceedings, both were discharged on the basis that s.55(1) required *mens rea*.

Held, allowing the application for judicial review, that the offence created by s.55(1) was an absolute offence (*Gammon (Hong Kong)* v. *Att.-Gen. of Hong Kong* [1984] C.L.Y. 951 referred to).

R. *v.* WELLS STREET MAGISTRATES, *ex p.* WESTMINSTER CITY COUNCIL (1987) 53 P. & C.R. 421, D.C.

3648. Listed buildings

TOWN AND COUNTRY PLANNING (LISTED BUILDINGS AND BUILDINGS IN CONSERVATION AREAS) REGULATIONS 1987 (No. 349) [£2·70], made under the Town and Country Planning Act 1971 (c.78), ss.54, 56B, 91, 99, 171, 172, 173, 190, 271, 277A, 287, 290, Sched. 11 and the Town and Country Planning Act 1984 (c.10), ss.1(5), 6; operative on April 1, 1987; makes procedural provision in relation to application for consent in relation to work connected with listed buildings or buildings in conservation areas.

3649. Local plan—boundaries—Secretary of State's decision

The applicants sought permission to erect a Baptist Church, old people's sheltered and warden accommodation, a community centre, a two-practitioner health centre and related residential development on land in St. Albans. The appeal site was identified in the as yet unadopted local plan as green belt land. The Secretary of State decided that he should not determine the boundary of the green belt whilst it was under consideration within the local plan procedure.

Held, that the Minister was here entitled to decide that it was premature to fix the boundaries.

BAPTIST UNION CORP. *v.* SECRETARY OF STATE FOR THE ENVIRONMENT AND ST. ALBANS DISTRICT COUNCIL [1986] J.P.L. 906, Woolf J.

3650. Local plan—consultation—whether Secretary of State is obliged to consult the local planning authority

[Town and Country Planning Act 1971 (c.78), s.14(3)(4).]

The Secretary of State for the Environment is not obliged to consult the local planning authority before calling in a local plan for his approval under s.14(3) of the Town and Country Planning Act 1971.

The applicants, prepared a local plan which was deposited and on which a local inquiry was held. The inspector recommended a number of changes, and the local authority decided to adhere to the plan with certain amendments and so informed the Secretary of State. He issued a direction under s.14(3) of the 1971 Act that the plan was not to be given effect unless approved by him. He then rejected the plan on the grounds that it conflicted with government policy on economic regeneration. The local authority applied for judicial review of his decision alleging that he was obliged to consult them before issuing a direction under s.14(3), that he was obliged to allow them to comment on objections received before rejecting the plan under s.14(4) and that in deciding to reject it he was acting in accordance with a predetermined view of its merits.

Held, dismissing the application, that the Secretary of State was under no obligation to consult a local planning authority before issuing a direction under s.14(3) that a local plan was to have no effect unless approved by him. Nor was he under a duty to allow them to comment on objections received before issuing a direction under s.14(3). He was also not obliged to allow comments on objections received before rejecting the plan under s.14(4). He was entitled to have formed a view of the merits of the plan when he issued a direction under s.14(3) but he was under a duty to consider the plan afresh when he considered whether to approve or reject it under s.14(4). There was no evidence that he had approached the decision under s.14(4) with a closed mind; the evidence was that he did consider the matter afresh.

R. *v.* SECRETARY OF STATE FOR THE ENVIRONMENT, *ex p.* SOUTHWARK LONDON BOROUGH COUNCIL (1987) 54 P. & C.R. 226, D.C.

3651. Local plan—preservation of old style plan—minister's powers

[Town and Country Planning Act 1971 (c.78), Sched. 7, as amended by Local Government Planning and Land Act 1980 (c.65).]

The Borough Council sought to retain the provisions of the old style development plan when the new style local plan was adopted. The ministerial order bringing the new plan into effect had accidentally omitted an order to preserve it.

Held, upon application for judicial review on a construction of the Schedule, that it was permissible for the Secretary of State to make an order which was subsequent to the adoption of the new local plan whereby the old style development plan be preserved.

R. *v.* SECRETARY OF STATE FOR THE ENVIRONMENT, *ex p.* GREAT GRIMSBY BOROUGH COUNCIL [1986] J.P.L. 910, Russell J.

3652. Material change of use—offices—proper approach

The appellant occupiers sought planning permission for five years in respect of a house which they had been using as offices. The Council served an enforcement notice alleging a material change of use. The Inspector upheld the enforcement notice and refusal of planning permission.

Held, that (1) the inspector had asked the wrong question. He should have applied the "fair chance" test; (2) the Inspector should have considered whether the appeal premises were desirable for A's business, not whether it was necessary.

VIKOMA INTERNATIONAL *v.* SECRETARY OF STATE FOR THE ENVIRONMENT AND WOKING BOROUGH COUNCIL [1987] J.P.L. 38, Widdicombe Q.C.

3653. Motorway inquiry—alternative route—Inspector's decision—judicial review

Objectors to a motorway plan wanted an alternative route investigated and surveyed. They sought judicial review of the Inspector's decision not to survey elsewhere and alleged bias.

Held, that (1) the Inspector had no power to order a survey; (2) the allegation of bias was unsubstantiated; (3) relief refused.

R. *v.* VINCENT AND THE DEPARTMENT OF TRANSPORT, *ex p.* TURNER [1987] J.P.L. 511, Woolf J.

3654. Mutual covenant on estate—building plans to be approved by committee—whether consent not to be unreasonably withheld—whether committee to give reasons for decision

Where a contract requires the consent of another party thereto to be obtained, there is no rule of law that such consent may not be unreasonably withheld and such a provision will only be implied where it is necessary so to do.

A deed of mutual covenant on an estate provided that no buildings were to be erected unless first approved by a majority of a committee elected from amongst those owning sites on the estate. P wished to build a house on part of their lot, but the committee rejected the plans. P sought a declaration that the committee had unreasonably withheld its consent, and that the building could proceed without the committee's consent.

Held, that the declaration would be refused. (i) There is no rule of law that where one party under a contract is required to give his consent before another party can proceed with some step, that consent may not unreasonably be withheld. (ii) Whether such a term should be implied depends upon the circumstances. Here, the power to refuse permission had been delegated to a domestic tribunal, who were bound to act honestly and fairly, and to import the necessity of reasonableness into their decisions would amount to transferring control from the domestic committee to the Courts.

PRICE *v.* BOUCH (1987) 53 P. & C.R. 257, Millett J.

3655. New towns

PETERBOROUGH NEW TOWN (EXCLUSION OF LAND) ORDER 1987 (No. 104) [45p], made under the New Towns Act 1981 (c.64), s.2(1); operative on February 27, 1987; excludes a specified area of land from the area of the Peterborough New Town.

3656. Occupancy condition—inspector's decision—whether in error

A were granted planning permission by the authority to develop an industrial estate at Littlemore, Oxford. The development was to be subject to a local occupancy condition, which was subsequently substituted by a condition that for 10 years certain of the units were to be occupied only by occupants who had, for at least two years immediately beforehand, been occupying premises within the area of the Oxford Local Plan. The inspector dismissed A's appeal against the substituted condition. A applied under s.245 of the Town and Country Planning Act 1971 to quash the inspector's decision on the grounds that he had failed to appreciate the evidence and argument contained in A's written submissions in relation to two points, namely the effect of the substituted condition upon marketing, and the effect of local unemployment.

Held, dismissing the application, that on each of these points there had been evidence upon which the inspector had been able to reach the relevant conclusions in his report.

SLOUGH INDUSTRIAL ESTATES *v.* SECRETARY OF STATE FOR THE ENVIRONMENT (1986) 280 E.G. 1257, Simon Brown J.

3657. Office and residential development—inspector refusing applications—Secretary granting applications—sufficiency of reasons given

[Town and Country Planning Inquiries Procedure Rules 1974 (S.I. 1974 No. 419), r.13.]

Rule 13 of the Inquiries Procedure Rules 1974 requires the Secretary of State to give proper and adequate reasons for differing from an inspector's recommendations.

The respondents, a development company, applied for planning permission on a large docklands site, for office and residential units. The inspector who sat with an architectural assessor recommended refusal on the grounds, *inter alia,* that the design concept was out of harmony, and the provision of offices in that area conflicted with the G.L.D.P. The Secretary of State rejected the recommendation and granted the applications. The G.L.C. and Borough of Tower Hamlets applied to quash the decision. Lloyd J. dismissed the application.

Held, dismissing the appeal, that rule 13 of the Inquiries Procedure Rules of 1974 obliged the Secretary to give proper, adequate and intelligible reasons that dealt with the points raised, and on the facts of this case he had obviously done so.

GREATER LONDON COUNCIL *v.* SECRETARY OF STATE FOR THE ENVIRONMENT AND LONDON DOCKLANDS DEVELOPMENT CORP. AND CABLECROSS PROJECTS; LONDON BOROUGH OF TOWER HAMLETS *v.* SAME (1986) 52 P. & C.R. 158, C.A.

3658. Office development—appeal to Secretary of State—non-disclosure of correspondence—whether breach of natural justice—sufficiency of Secretary of State's reasons

Natural justice required a planning authority to be given an opportunity to deal with matters raised by an appellant in correspondence with the Secretary of State on an appeal against a refusal of planning permission if fairness required that the planning authority be given a right of reply.

C applied for planning permission for an office development in Reading. The application was refused by Reading Borough Council, C appealed against the refusal. A public inquiry was held by an inspector appointed by the Secretary of State. The Council's principal objections were that the development would provide for greater office space than allowed by the Central Reading District Plan and would not provide sufficient residential or shop units. The inspector reported that he could see no overriding need for the development of the site in question to conform strictly with the mix of uses set out in the District Plan and no overriding planning objections to C's proposed development. The Secretary of State wrote to C and the Council provisionally indicating that he intended to allow the appeal. The Council wrote to the Secretary of State pointing out that no account had been taken of the Central Berkshire Structure Plan and expressing concern about the inspector's approach to the District Plan. The Council also pointed out that to allow the appeal might set an undesirable precedent that could result in Reading having 1 million square feet of offices above those provided for by the District Plan. The Council later wrote pointing out that the District Plan required that exceptional justification and overriding need must be shown in respect of developments that would provide office space in excess of the District Plan's recommendations. The Secretary of State sent copies of the Council's letters to C. C sent replies to the Secretary of State setting out at length submissions on the evidence at the inquiry. Thereafter the Secretary of State allowed the appeal. His decision letter referred to C's letters which was the first intimation the Council had of their existence. The Council appealed under s.245 Town and Country Planning Act 1971.

Held, that the decision would be quashed. The Secretary of State's conclusion that the proposed development did not deviate from the broad principles of the District Plan was unjustifiable in the context of the Structure Plan and no reasons were given to justify such a deviation. The decision letter did not clarify what, if any, circumstances made C's proposed development an exceptional one. The Secretary of State gave no proper reasons dealing with the Council's contention that to allow the development would create an undesirable precedent. The Inquiry Procedure Rules were not an exhaustive statement of the requirements of natural justice. A party alleging a breach of the requirements of natural justice had to show substantial prejudice arising from that breach. Where the alleged breach was outside the scope of the Inquiry Procedure Rules the complainant was not under a heavier burden of proof. C's letters raised matters to which fairness required the Council to have a right of reply. There was substance in the replies the Council would have sought to give. The Council were substantially prejudiced by a breach of natural justice (*Lake District Special Planning Board* v. *Secretary of State for the Environment* [1975] C.L.Y. 20, *Fairmount Investments* v. *Secretary of State for the Environment* [1976] C.L.Y. 305; *George* v. *Secretary of State for the Environment* [1980] C.L.Y. 313 considered).

READING BOROUGH COUNCIL *v.* SECRETARY OF STATE FOR THE ENVIRONMENT AND COMMERCIAL UNION PROPERTIES (INVESTMENTS) (1986) 52 P. & C.R. 385, David Widdicombe Q.C.

3659. Open space—whether premises formed part of open space. See LANDLORD AND TENANT, §2227.

3660. Outline planning permission—appeal against deemed refusal of reserved matters—highways works

[Town and Country Planning Act 1971 (c.78), ss.36, 37.]

Outline planning permission had been granted for offices, light industrial floorspace, residential use and shops on a site with access to four streets. There were conditions reserving for subsequent approval the means of access to the buildings. The Council had failed to determine an application for approval of many reserved matters, and one of the issues was highways. The original application showed that access was to be from one road. The Council now argued that it required widening. The appellant on appeal argued that such a fundamental objection to the development should have been dealt with at the time of the outline application, and not upon submission of reserved matters.

Held, dismissing the appeal relating to the reserved matters, that (1) the proposals submitted in the reserved matters were not acceptable for a number of reasons; (2) there should be no approval in the absence of a formal agreement for the necessary road widening along the appeal site frontage.

LAMBETH BOROUGH COUNCIL and WESTMINSTER MOTOR SUPPLIES (Ref: APP/N5660/A/85/031968) (1986) 1 P.A.D. 448.

3661. Planning functions

BLACK COUNTRY DEVELOPMENT CORPORATION (PLANNING FUNCTIONS) ORDER 1987 (No. 1340) [85p], made under the Local Government, Planning and Land Act 1980 (c.65), s.149(1)(3)(ii); operative on October 19, 1987; applies provisions of the Town and Country Planning Act 1971 specified in Sched. 29, Pt. II to the 1980 Act to the said Development Corporation.

TEESSIDE DEVELOPMENT CORPORATION (PLANNING FUNCTIONS) ORDER 1987 (No. 1341) [85p], made under the Local Government, Planning and Land Act 1980, s.149(1)(3)(ii); operative on September 1, 1987; applies to the said Development Corporation provisions of the Town and Country Planning Act 1971 which are specified in Sched. 29, Pt. II to the 1980 Act.

TYNE AND WEAR DEVELOPMENT CORPORATION (PLANNING FUNCTIONS) ORDER 1987 (No. 1342) [85p], made under the Local Government, Planning and Land Act 1980, s.149(1)(3)(ii); operative on October 1, 1987; applies to the said Development Corporation provisions of the Town and Country Planning Act 1971 which are specified in Sched. 29, Pt. II to the 1980 Act.

3662. Planning inquiry—letter sent to Inspector—privilege. See RICHARDS *v.* CRESSWELL, §1685.

3663. Planning permission—appeal against planning conditions—development already implemented—DIY retail development—Circular 1/85

[Town and Country Planning Act 1971 (c.78), ss.32, 36; Circulars: 1/72, 26/82, 1/85.]

The appeal was against the decision of the Council to grant planning permission subject to certain conditions. Because the development had already been implemented, the appeals were treated as arising from an application under s.32(1)(*b*) of the 1971 Act. The contested conditions were as follows; (a) that this permission shall enure solely for the benefit of B. & Q. (Retail) Limited, (b) that the site shall be maintained in a tidy condition to the satisfaction of the local planning authority, (c) the premises shall not be used for retailing . . . on Sundays, (d) noise emanating due to the operation of any permanent noise source shall not cause any increase in the hourly background noise levels as specified (dB range given). The Council conceded that condition (b) fell outside Circular 1/85.

Held, allowing the appeal, that permission was granted for the continued use of the land without compliance with conditions (a), (c), (d); condition (a) was unnecessary and unreasonable and the omission of the condition would not justify refusal of permission, condition (b) was clearly *ultra vires* and failed to meet the test of precision, condition (c) should be discharged as there was no overriding objection to Sunday trading in planning terms on amenity grounds, condition (d) was unreasonable, however the Inspector substituted his own condition limiting the dB levels and hours of operation of loudspeakers.

ENFIELD LONDON BOROUGH COUNCIL and B. & Q. (RETAIL) (Ref: T/APP/Q5300/A/85/30867/P7) (1986) 1 P.A.D. 453.

3664. Planning permission—betting office in secondary shopping location—window frontage—presumption in favour of development

[Town and Country Planning Act 1971 (c.78), s.36; Circular: 14/85; Development Control Policy Note No. 11.]

The appellant proposed to locate a betting office in a secondary shopping area and argued that there was a local need and that there had been no objection from local traders. The Council argued that the loss of the shopping frontage would be contrary to adopted Local Plan Policy and would cause further harm to that part of the town through loss of a retail shop and dead frontage created.

Held, allowing the appeal, that (1) Circular 14/85 indicated a presumption in favour of development and emphasized the need to create a climate in which small businesses using local labour could thrive; (2) it was not considered that the proposal would cause harm to that shopping street and the proposal would bring a benefit; (3) the traffic objection was not sustained; (4) it was proper to impose a condition for the maintenance of a shop window display.

IPSWICH BOROUGH COUNCIL and LADBROKE RACING (Ref: T/APP/-R3515/A/85/33406/P7) (1986) 1 P.A.D. 476.

3665. Planning permission—change of use

A owned a turkey farm. Two dwellings were required. Outline planning permission was refused in February 1984. In March 1984 application was made to change the use of the farm to a boarding house for tourists. This was refused. On appeal the applicant contended that the turkey farm was not viable without the second dwelling and therefore the boarding house was appropriate.

Held, dismissing the appeal, that the Inspector had correctly considered that the nearby cottage which the applicant was purchasing was sufficient accommodation.

MELLOR *v.* SECRETARY OF STATE FOR THE ENVIRONMENT [1987] J.P.L. 40, Mann J.

3666. Planning permission—change of use—agricultural to craft workshops—national guidance and structure plans—personal condition

[Town and Country Planning Act 1971 (c.78), s.36; Circulars 22/80, 16/84, 14/85.]

An appeal was made against the Council's refusal of permission for change of use of farm buildings to small craft businesses. It was argued that these buildings were no longer needed for agricultural use and there was a demand for small craft premises.

The Council argued that the proposal was contrary to the presumption against non-agricultural uses in rural areas contained in the approved Structure Plan.

Held, allowing the appeal, that (1) the policies relating to small firms and to development in rural areas contained in Circulars 22/80, 16/84 and 14/85 were more relevant than the Structure Plan policies put forward; (2) the buildings were of merit and worthy of retention in the event that they would again be required for agricultural use in the future; (3) the appellant's residence in the adjacent farmhouse was an effective control on amenity; (4) the permission should be personal to the appellants and should cease in the event that the premises were no longer owned by the appellants.

WEALDON DISTRICT COUNCIL and BENN (Ref: T/APP/C1435/A/85/042086/P4) (1986) 1 P.A.D. 416.

3667. Planning permission—change of use—from cinema to retail—absence of detail—need—prematurity

[Town and Country Planning Act 1971 (c.78), s.36.]

The appellant gave no indication as to the proposed retail floorspace or number of units inside the cinema which covered the entire site. The entrance faced the access to garages of a large block of flats. There was an adjacent public car park at the rear which the Council proposed to extend by use of compulsory purchase powers at some time in the future. The Council argued that customer car parking and delivery access was inadequate and impact could not be assessed without details. A Council commissioned report on the shopping need of the town was under review.

Held, dismissing the appeal, that (1) there was no evidence that the building could withstand demolition at the front required for a lay-by to take delivery lorries; (2) it would not be appropriate to allow development to proceed until the new car parking provision proposed by the Council was in use; (3) there was no evidence of an unsatisfied need for additional shopping space; (4) the Council should take into account the commissioned report before deciding on the appellant's proposals and risking prejudice to the Council's shopping plan; (6) if subsequently the report showed shopping need and the car parking was resolved, then the appeal site could be suitable for retail use.

EAST HAMPSHIRE DISTRICT COUNCIL and NASSINGTON PROPERTIES (Ref: T/APP/M1710/A/85/038828) (1986) 1 P.A.D. 469.

3668. Planning permission—change of use—Green Belt—winter storage of caravans

[Town and Country Planning Act 1971 (c.78), s.36, Circulars 38/81, 14/84, 28/84, 1/85, 14/85.]

The Council refused planning permission to the Lee Valley Regional Park Authority for change of use of 0.5 ha. of land for the winter storage of caravans. The land had planning permission for a caravan park subject to conditions preventing storage of caravans. The site was in the Lee Valley Regional Park and lay within the Metropolitan Green Belt. The appellant argued that the Authority's Consultative Draft Lee Valley Park Plan included provision for use of caravan sites for winter store of caravans without detriment to the recreational use and that the winter storage of caravans complemented the existing use of the caravan park and was thus an appropriate use in the Green Belt.

Held, dismissing the appeal, that (1) the draft local plan should be considered as an emerging local plan in accordance with Circular 24/84 and inclusion of this site in the Green Belt would not be questioned pending determination of the Green Belt boundaries upon adoption of the plan; (2) the storage of caravans does not complement the recreational use of a touring caravan site because no recreational use or amenity derives from the storage of vehicles, therefore the use conflicts with the structural plan and emerging local plan policies; (3) this proposal would seriously undermine confidence in the Green Belt, damage the implementation of Green Belt policies and would be contrary to the general presumption against the appropriate developments within Green Belts re-affirmed in Circular 14/84.

EPPING FOREST DISTRICT COUNCIL and LEE VALLEY REGIONAL PARK AUTHORITY (Ref: T/APP/J1535/A/85/029168/P2) (1986) 1 P.A.D. 383.

3669. Planning permission—change of use—part of goods yard to skip waste transfer station—amenities—temporary permission

[Town and Country Planning Act 1971 (c.78), s.36.]

The Council refused permission for the change of use of part of a goods yard to a skip waste transfer station. The relevant issues were visual amenities and highways problems.

Held, allowing the appeal, that (1) the proposal could add marginally to the dust and visual intrusion; (2) the Council proposed other uses for the site in the long term, currently there were no other sites available for relocation of the goods yard; (3) central government is keen to promote the establishment and maintenance of small businesses such as that of the appellants; (4) for the above reasons, permission was granted for two years only; (5) it was proper to impose a condition limiting the use to the distribution of skip waste and excluding Class IV of the Schedule to the Town and Country Planning (Use Classes) Order 1972.

BRENT LONDON BOROUGH COUNCIL and ALLOYDE (ref: T/APP/T5150/A/04025/P3) (1987) 2 P.A.D. 99.

3670. Planning permission—change of use—retail shop to fast food restaurant—local plan—precedent

[Town and Country Planning Act 1971 (c.78), s.36; D.C.P.N.: No. 11: Circular 14/85.]

The Council refused permission for the change of use from a retail shop to fast food restaurants with frontage on the primary shopping street in Kingston-upon-Thames. The adopted local plan policy created a presumption against changes of use from ground floor retail use in principal shopping streets.

Held, dismissing the appeal, that (1) the local plan policy to enhance the principal shopping streets should prevail, the proposal would conflict with the policy, making the shopping centre less convenient and attractive for shoppers and traders, amounting to demonstrable harm; (2) allowing the proposal could make similar applications more difficult to refuse and that would in the end totally erode the attractiveness of Kingston Town Shopping Centre; (3) there were insufficient very special circumstances to justify setting aside the presumption against change of use.

KINGSTON-UPON-THAMES LONDON BOROUGH COUNCIL and QUICK HAMBURGER RESTAURANTS (WHITBREAD) and PIZZA HUT (Ref: T/APP/Z5630/A/85/41119/P3) (1987) 2 P.A.D. 91.

3671. Planning permission—change of use—retail shop to restaurant—listed building—conservation area

[Town and Country Planning Act 1971 (c.78), s.36; Circulars 22/77, 12/81, 14/85.]

The Council refused permission for change of use of a 17th Century former tithe barn from a shop to a restaurant.

Held, dismissing the appeal, that (1) the proposal would secure the preservation of the building and there was therefore an initial presumption in favour of development; (2) the repairs and renovation upon permission would improve the appearance of the conservation area; (3) the increased parking area would be in regular late evening use, however this would not be an unacceptable disturbance to residents; (4) 18 car spaces were necessary but only 13 could be provided on site and overflow parking on the street would harm the residential character of the conservation area to a degree which would nullify the benefits of preserving and renovating the building; (5) it would not be possible for the Council to enforce the use by the staff of car parks outside the curtilage.

STOCKPORT METROPOLITAN BOROUGH COUNCIL and HALL (Ref: T/APP/C4235/A/85/042509/P4) (1987) 2 P.A.D. 93.

3672. Planning permission—change of use—retail shop to restaurant—local plan—vitality and viability of town centre—amenities

[Town and Country Planning Act 1971 (c.78), s.36; D.C.P.N.: No. 11; Circulars 22/80, 1/85, 14/85.]

The Council refused permission for the change of use from a retail shop to a restaurant in town centre prime shopping frontage, where the adopted local plan policy aimed to prevent the loss of shopping floor space.

Held, allowing the appeal, that (1) the adopted local plan was a material consideration; however this should be measured against guidance in Circulars 14/85 and 22/80; (2) the proposed redevelopment of the town centre was not imminent and no national retailers had shown interest in the site; the proposal would not significantly harm the vitality and viability of the shops at the prime retail frontage and therefore it was acceptable to allow the appeal as an exception to the local plan policies; (3) it was not accepted that this decision created a precedent which would encourage similar projects.

NEWHAM LONDON BOROUGH COUNCIL and PIZZA HUT (U.K.) (Ref: T/APP/G5750/A/86/46653/86) (1986) 2 P.A.D. 96.

3673. Planning permission—change of use—wine bar/delicatessen—loss of residential accommodation—conditions

[Town and Country Planning Act 1971 (c.78), s.36; D.O.E. Circulars 22/80; 14/85; 38/81; 1/85.]

The appeal premises were a modern two-storey building. Subsequent to a planning permission granted in 1982 the first floor was residential accommodation and the ground floor was divided into two units comprising a wine bar and delicatessen. The appellants sought to swap over the uses as between the units on the ground floor and to use the first floor for ancillary purposes. The Council did not object to the exchange of uses on the ground floor but objected to the loss of residential accommodation, of which there was a shortage locally as shown by the Greater London Development Plan. Accordingly, the District Plan contained policies to increase the provision of such accommodation and to resist its loss.

Held, allowing the appeal, that (1) the viability of the ground floor businesses would be threatened if the ancillary uses upstairs were refused. This was a compelling material consideration in light of Circular 22/80 and particularly Circular 14/85 which stresses the importance of having regard for the special needs of small firms and the self-employed, it also stresses that development plans are only one of many material considerations and should not be taken as overriding others; (2) the appellants suggested, and the Council accepted, a condition linking the first floor use to the ground floor uses. However, such a condition would be unduly restrictive according to the tests in Circular 1/85; further the uses were already linked by public health legislation.

CAMDEN LONDON BOROUGH COUNCIL and SORACCHI (Ref. T/APP/X5210/A/85/028930/P2) (1986) 1 P.A.D. 368.

3674. Planning permission—compensation for refusal of permission—whether single building

A structure containing 38 self-contained flats divided into five separate sections was one building as a matter of fact.

The applicant had applied for planning permission to build four self-contained flats by "topping out" its existing property. The existing property was a structure containing 38 self-contained flats. The structure had a continuous aspect at the front and rear but was divided into five separate sections. Each section had its own stairway and water supply. There was no intercommunication between the sections. Planning permission was refused. The applicants applied for compensation relying on paragraph 3 of Schedule 8 to the Town and Country Planning Act 1971. The applicants' entitlement to compensation was dependant upon whether or not the property was one building. The Council contended that it was a terrace of separate blocks of flats and thus more than one building.

Held, that whether the property was one building was a question of fact. Having seen the building and observed that the brickwork of the front and rear was continuously bonded and constructed as one unit the structure was one building.

CHURCH COTTAGE INVESTMENTS *v.* HILLINGDON LONDON BOROUGH COUNCIL (1986) 52 P. & C.R. 439, Lands Tribunal, V. G. Wellings Q.C.

3675. Planning permission—competing superstore proposals—balancing advantages and disadvantages of each—effect on traffic system

[Town and Country Planning Act 1971 (c.78), ss.36 and 52.]

The Inquiry considered appeals by Asda (Appeal A) and Tesco (Appeal B) for superstores to serve the same population in Goodmayes, Essex. The appellants agreed that two new superstores would result in substantial over-provision.

Held, dismissing Appeal A and allowing Appeal B, that (1) neither development would cause demonstrable harm to any interest of acknowledged importance; (2) the policies of the adopted Local Plan and the Draft Alterations to the GLDP were of little relevance as they did not accord with Government Policy; (3) the better facilities offered by a superstore would more than off-set any adverse effects through impact; (4) only one store should be permitted because of the problems which traffic from two stores would generate; (5) on the test of a balance of advantages and disadvantages, Appeal B was allowed.

REDBRIDGE LONDON BOROUGH COUNCIL and ASSOCIATED DAIRIES; BRITISH RAILWAYS BOARD and TESCO STORES (Ref: APP/W5780/A/84/022484, A/85/031051, A/84/025588) (1986) 1 P.A.D. 465.

3676. Planning permission—condition attached to planning consent—condition discharged by Secretary of State—whether error of law

The true test of whether a condition imposed by a planning authority is lawful or not is whether it is manifestly unreasonable.

Developers made application to build a number of houses a few miles from Bradford. The Council, concerned at the inadequacy of the existing road, wished it to be widened. The developers submitted amended plans and the council granted permission subject to a condition that the roadway be widened. There was a dispute as to the putting into effect of this condition, and the Secretary of State discharged the condition on the ground it was unlawful.

Held, dismissing the appeal, that the test of whether such a condition was lawful was whether it was manifestly unreasonable; if such a condition was unreasonable it was unlawful regardless of whether the developer consented to it.

BRADFORD METROPOLITAN CITY COUNCIL *v.* SECRETARY OF STATE FOR THE ENVIRONMENT (1987) 53 P. & C.R. 55, C.A.

3677. Planning permission—design of petrol station forecourt—effect on street scene

[Town and Country Planning Act 1971 (c.78), s.36.]

The Council refused permission for the erection of a canopy, new pump stand, shopfront and petrol tanks at an existing service station on the ground that the canopy and enlarged forecourt would intrude on the predominantly residential and suburban surroundings. The appellant argued that the alterations would be an improvement and delivery tankers would no longer have to reverse onto the highway. Planning permission to extend the forecourt granted in 1984 had not been implemented.

Held, allowing the appeal, that (1) the street scene was not likely to be spoilt so as to justify overriding the presumption in favour of development; in reaching this conclusion he took into account the existing 11 m. setback from the pavement and the activity associated with the adjacent shopping parade; (2) it was appropriate to impose conditions limiting the hours of operation and the areas for sale and display of cars.

CLEETHORPES BOROUGH COUNCIL AND TOTAL OIL GREAT BRITAIN (Ref. T/APP/E2015/A/85/33623/P5) (1986) 1 P.A.D. 354.

3678. Planning permission—development of land as quarry—refusal—whether compensation payable

[Trinidad and Tobago] [Town and Country Planning Act (Laws of Trinidad and Tobago, 1980 ed., vol. 7, c.35:01), ss.2, 8, 26(1), 27(1)(*a*).]

An applicant was entitled to compensation where his application for planning permission to develop land as a quarry was refused.

The appellant owned 22 acres of land that was disused but formerly a cocoa plantation. The appellant applied for planning permission to develop the land as a limestone quarry. Permission was refused. The appellant commenced proceedings in the High Court of Justice of Trinidad and Tobago seeking declarations that the refusal was a nullity and that if permission was refused compensation was payable. On the appellant's appeal the Board were invited to decide whether compensation was payable in the event of a proper refusal of planning permission. S.8 of the Town and Country Planning Act provided that permission was required for any development of land. "Development" was defined as including mining or other operations in on over or under any land and the making of any material change in the use of any buildings or other land. S.2 of the Act defined "use" in relation to land as not including the use of land by carrying out building or other operations thereon. S.27(1)(a) of the Act provided that compensation was not payable in respect of the refusal of planning permission for a development that included the making of any material change in the use of any buildings or land.

Held, that the appellant was entitled to compensation in the event of a refusal of planning permission. The phrase "material change of use" in s.27(1)(*a*) was to be construed with regard to the broad categories of development set out in s.8 of the Act. Accordingly s.27(1)(*a*) of the Act only applied to a development that fell within the meaning of "the making of any material change in the use of any buildings or other land" in s.8 of the Act. The winning and working of materials from a quarry was a series of operations of a mining nature. Such operations were excluded from the definition of "use" of land contained in s.2 of the Act. The quarry development fell within the category of mining or other operations in, on, over or under any land in s.8 of the Act. The grant of permission subject to conditions so restrictive as to frustrate the working of the quarry would amount to a refusal of permission.

LOPINOT LIMESTONE *v.* ATT.-GEN. OF TRINIDAD AND TOBAGO [1987] 3 W.L.R. 797, P.C.

3679. Planning permission—expansion of solicitors' offices—loss of retail use in shopping centre

[Town and Country Planning Act 1971 (c.78), s.36; Town and Country Planning (Use Classes) Order 1972 (S.I. 1972 No. 1385).]

The appeal premises were a small shop of 15.8 sq.m. The appellant occupied a small office on the first floor. The appellants had been seeking alternative accommodation without success and the extension to the ground floor would allow three extra full time jobs. The appellant argued that the firm provided a community service and that the Draft Local Plan discriminated unfairly against solicitors' offices. The Council argued that no objection was made to the Council policy in the recent Local Plan Inquiry; the policy allowed for solicitors' offices to replace retail use outside the main shopping area. However, the appeal premises were within the shopping area. The appeal premises were at the southern end of the shopping centre flanked by estate agents, and an undesirable concentration of non-retail uses would result if the appeal was allowed.

Held, dismissing the appeal, that (1) it was appropriate to distinguish between non-retail uses which contributed to the street scene and those which did not. It was relevant that the exclusion of solicitors' offices from this list was not objected to at the Local Plan Inquiry; (2) the premises were likely to attract an occupier within Class I of the Use Classes Order; (3) the loss of a retail unit in this key position would result in demonstrable harm to the future of the shopping centre; (4) the benefit of gains in office employment were balanced by the gains in retail employment.

HARROW LONDON BOROUGH COUNCIL and SMITH & BARON (Ref: T/APP/M5450 A/85/036526/P3) (1986) 1 P.A.D. 439.

3680. Planning permission—expansion of solicitors' offices—vacant flats—lack of amenity

[Town and Country Planning Act 1971 (c.78), s.36; Circular: 14/85.]

The Council had refused planning permission for the change of use of the second floor of two adjoining premises from residential to offices. The premises were situated on a busy shopping street with the ground floor in retail use. The proposal was to expand the firm of solicitors occupying the first floor of the premises; the firm met a local need and six-ten jobs would be created. The appellant freeholder stated that for security reasons the appeal premises would not be let as a flat irrespective of the appeal decision. The Council argued that the proposal was contrary to the adopted Local Plan Policy to resist loss of residential accommodation because of the housing shortage. The high levels of noise and disturbance and lack of amenity were common characteristics of flats above shops on main roads.

Held, dismissing the appeal, that (1) the deficiency in amenity was common to most dwellings in these situations and did not alone justify the loss of residential accommodation; (2) the appellant's assertion that the property would not be used for residential purposes in any event was not a sufficient reason for granting planning permission; (3) the Inspector had taken into account the guidance in Circular 14/85 in support of the expansion of small firms but noted that the appellant had not investigated possible alternatives.

ISLINGTON LONDON BOROUGH COUNCIL and JETSPAN (Ref: T/APP/V5570/A/85/040768/P2) (1986) 1 P.A.D. 437.

3681. Planning permission—extent of planning permission—whether matters known to district council to be imputed to planning committee.

[Town and Country Planning Act 1971 (c.78), ss.1, 22(1), 29(1).]

The planning committee of a district council is deemed to have knowledge of all matters known to the council.

The applicant applied to the District Council for planning permission to build nine houses; the applicant also submitted an application for building regulation approval to raise the height of the road and the houses for drainage purposes. Consent was given to this application and later planning permission was granted to build the houses. The planning committee of the Council then contended that their permission did not extend to the alteration of levels, as they had not known about the proposal.

Held, that where the council delegates authority to the planning committee, all knowledge available to the council is imputed to that committee. Consequently, the committee was deemed to have knowledge of the building regulation approval.

R. *v.* BASILDON DISTRICT COUNCIL, *ex p.* MARTIN GRANT HOMES (1987) 53 P. & C.R. 397, McCowan J.

3682. Planning permission—extension to quarry—national park—site of special scientific interest

[Town and Country Planning Act 1971 (c.78), ss.36, 52; Circulars: 10/73, 4/76, 21/82.]

The extension to the quarry would prolong the period of extraction from the site, guaranteeing jobs for longer and bringing economic benefits. The appellants had offered to enter a s.52 Agreement to reclaim the existing quarry and the extension at the end of their life.

Held, dismissing the appeal, that (1) adverse effects on the environment, character and natural beauty of the park, loss of amenity to the local community and the risk to the grassland of the site of special scientific interest made a compelling case against the proposal; (2) there was no clear local or national need for the reserves to be worked; (3) these factors were not outweighed by the benefits of restoration of the quarry and economic advantages of using the plaint for a longer period.

PEAK PARK JOINT PLANNING BOARD and TARMAC ROADSTONE (WESTERN) (Ref: APP/A1001/A/84/020153) (1986) 1 P.A.D. 488.

3683. Planning permission—Green Belt—commercial and recreational development—preservation of open land between Green Belt settlements

[Town and Country Planning Act 1971 (c.78) s.36; D.O.E. Circulars 42/55; 1/85.]

The Council refused permission for the erection of a glasshouse, construction of access and parking facilities for use as a commercial butterfly and tropical plant exhibition in the garden of the appellant's house which was just inside the Green Belt and bordered by houses on one side and by farmland on the other. The appellant had objected to the site's inclusion within the Green Belt in the recently adopted Green Belt Local Plan. The appellant argued that the appeal site, adjacent public house and derelict land formed a transitional area between the residential area and open farmland and that this was not "important open land". The development would be a "rounding off" permitted by Circular 42/55. There was a presumption in favour of recreational development in the Green Belt, subject to reservations in policy 15 of the Local Plan. The Council argued that the appeal site was now part of a scatter of development and it was essential to prevent consolidation.

Held, dismissing the appeal, that (1) the proposed use was recreational with a commercial element and that all the requirements of policy 15 had to be satisfied before a presumption in favour of such development arose; (2) the proposal failed to satisfy the said policy requirements in that it would reduce the rural countryside appearance of the landscape and would prejudice the preservation of important open land between Green Belt settlements, thus it was not an appropriate recreational development.

WINDSOR AND MAIDENHEAD BOROUGH COUNCIL AND ARNOLD (Ref. T/APP/D0325/A/85/35796/P5) (1986) 1 P.A.D. 359.

3684. Planning permission—Green Belt—extension to petrol station—presumption against development—evidence to override

[Town and Country Planning Act 1971 (c.78), s.36; D.O.E. Circular 14/85.]

The Council refused permission for the installation of a car wash unit some distance from an existing petrol station within the Green Belt. The appellant argued that the car wash would be ancillary to the sale of petrol and should be treated as part of the same development. It would be small in comparison with the existing filling station. A survey carried out at the filling station had established a need for the facility. The Council argued that the service to be provided was not essential, nor did the viability of the filling station depend upon it. The survey did not show that the service was needed at that particular filling station and should be located within the built-up areas.

Held, dismissing the appeal, that (1) the development would not have a serious adverse visual effect on the Green Belt area; (2) the evidence did not show that there was an essential need for a car wash; (3) to allow the appeal would make it harder to resist applications in the future.

THURROCK BOROUGH COUNCIL AND MOBIL OIL CO. (Ref. T/APP/71565/A/85/032558/P3) (1986) 1 P.A.D. 357.

3685. Planning permission—Green Belt—pre-exemption of Draft Local Plan

[Town and Country Planning Act 1971 (c.78), s.37; Circular 15/84.

The appellant appealed against the failure of the council to determine within the required period an application in outline for residential development on 6.7 acres of land known as "Five Acres." The site was shown as white land on the Old Town Map, the Draft Local Plan of 1984 allocated the site for housing. However, following public consultation the Draft Plan now proposed to include the site in the Metropolitan Green Belt.

Held, dismissing the appeal that (1) there was not a five-year supply of housebuilding land available consequently there was a presumption in favour of releasing the appeal site unless there were clear-cut planning objections; (2) the site was not in the green belt but was part of important open space, the character and amenities of which would be harmed by development; (3) the precise definition of the green belt boundary was best left for the Local Plan to determine, the development of which was at an advanced stage and the release of the appeal site for housing at this stage would pre-empt important decisions to be taken in connection with the Local Plan and was premature.

WOKING BOROUGH COUNCIL and CREST HOMES (Ref: APP/A3655/A/85/028919) (1986) 1 P.A.D. 402.

3686. Planning permission—housing land availability—structure plan

B sought permission to develop 35 acres by building 475 houses. Permission was refused on the grounds that there was sufficient land available elsewhere to meet future housing requirements, and that the development would be contrary to the structure plan. On appeal the Secretary of State granted permission. The council appealed to the High Court.

Held, that (1) circular 15/84 had not been altered by circular 22/84. Accordingly land availability must be considered in the light of the figures contained in the structure plan even though amendments to the structure plan had been submitted; (2) having thus calculated housing land requirements, the Inspector was then entitled to take into account proposals for the alteration of the structure plan. Appeal dismissed. The Inspector had carried out the exercise correctly.

BOLTON BOROUGH COUNCIL *v.* SECRETARY OF STATE FOR THE ENVIRONMENT AND BARRATTS (MANCHESTER) [1987] J.P.L. 580, Kennedy J.

3687. Planning permission—inquiry—Inspector's report—material error of fact

K sought permission to erect a single-storey, part two-storey extension to his flat. His neighbour objected. Permission was refused by the local authority on the ground that the development would result in unreasonable overlooking and loss of privacy to adjoining owners. On appeal, the inspector reached a decision, making an error of fact as to the effect on the neighbour's outlook.

Held, that the decision must be quashed due to the material error of fact.

JAGENDORF AND TROTT *v.* SECRETARY OF STATE AND KRASUCKI [1987] J.P.L. 771, Widdicombe Q.C.

3688. Planning permission—inquiry—Inspector's report—whether Inspector had addressed himself to the proper issues

J sought permission to site a gipsy mobile home on land. On appeal, the Inspector refused permission. J. appealed to the High Court.

Held, dismissing the appeal, that J had failed to establish that the Inspector had taken into account irrelevant matters or ignored relevant material. The inspector had addressed himself to the proper issues.

JACKSON *v.* SECRETARY OF STATE FOR THE ENVIRONMENT AND BROMLEY LONDON BOROUGH COUNCIL [1987] J.P.L. 785, MacPherson J.

3689. Planning permission—Inspector's decision—Circular 22/80

Planning permission to build houses was refused in 1979 and appeal dismissed. The appellants appealed to the High Court and Glidewell J. granted the decision of the Inspector. The appellants made a fresh application which in 1984 was refused and the Inspector upheld the refusal. The appellants appealed to the High Court alleging that the Inspector had failed to interpret and apply correctly Circular 22/80, Annex A, para. 3.

Held, that the Inspector had properly taken into account emerging plans when there was a shortage of housing land.

PYE (J. A.) (OXFORD) ESTATES *v.* SECRETARY OF STATE FOR THE ENVIRONMENT AND WYCHAVON DISTRICT COUNCIL [1987] J.P.L. 363, McCowan J.

3690. Planning permission—Inspector's decision—material consideration

The consideration of sound insulation in flat conversions is a planning matter.

The respondents applied for permission to convert each of two houses into two flats. The applications were refused. On appeal the inspector, allowing the appeals, rejected the authority's contention that in allowing the appeals he should impose conditions in relation to sound insulation. He held that this was not a planning consideration.

Held, allowing the appeal, that the inspector had erred in concluding that sound insulation in flat conversions was not a planning matter.

NEWHAM LONDON BOROUGH *v.* SECRETARY OF STATE FOR THE ENVIRONMENT (1987) 53 P. & C.R. 98, Webster J.

3691. Planning permission—Inspector's decision—proper considerations—Circular 22/80

In 1982 the Council refused planning permission for a residential development in Rainham because it was contrary to the housing policies of the Structure plan. The Inspector dismissed the appeal. This decision was quashed by Woolf J. in 1983. A second local inquiry was held and in 1984 the inspector rejected the appeal. The appellants appealed to the High Court. Woolf J. upheld the decision. The appellants appealed to the Court of Appeal.

Held, that the Inspector's reliance upon the fact that land might become available was perfectly proper and in accordance with the policies set out in Circular 22/80. The Inspector had performed a proper balancing exercise.

GRANSDEN (E. C.) AND CO. AND FALKBRIDGE *v.* SECRETARY OF STATE FOR THE ENVIRONMENT AND GILLINGHAM BOROUGH COUNCIL [1987] J.P.L. 365, C.A.

3692. Planning permission—Inspector's decision—relevance of acquisition costs

The appeal site was 3.3 acres of grazing land adjacent to a church. Application was made to develop 1.3 acres and was refused. The refusal was upheld by the Inspector. A contended on appeal to the High Court that in assessing the prospects of implementation of the proposal that part would be developed and part become public open space, the Inspector had failed to take into account that the land would have to be acquired at residential values. Further, it was argued that the designation of the land in the local plan as public open space should have been treated by the inspector as peverse.

Held, quashing the decision, that the Inspector had wrongly ignored the land acquisition costs.

CHICHESTER DIOCESAN FUND AND BOARD OF FINANCE (INCORPORATED) *v.* SECRETARY OF STATE FOR THE ENVIRONMENT AND WEALDEN DISTRICT COUNCIL [1987] J.P.L. 503, Mr. Recorder Widdicombe Q.C.

3693. Planning permission—Metropolitan Green Belt—conservation area—loss of residential accommodation—effect on amenities

[Town and Country Planning Act 1971 (c.78), s.36.]

Permission had been refused for the change of use of a bungalow within the curtilage of a service station from residential to snack bar and part residential. The site lay within the Metropolitan Green Belt. It was also within a conservation area and lay at the edge of a village.

Held, dismissing the appeal, that (1) there would be a loss of residential accommodation contrary to structure plan policies; (2) the increase in site activity would affect the amenities of residents to an unacceptable degree; (3) appearance and character of that part of the conservation area would suffer considerable harm.

GUILDFORD BOROUGH COUNCIL and 3H MOTORS (Ref: T/APP/Y3615/A/85/038570/P3) (1986) 1 P.A.D. 486.

3694. Planning permission—objection to grant—policy settled and no objection made—policy overturned.

Potential objectors to an application for planning permission are entitled to a real opportunity to make representations and the authority must act fairly to ensure that opportunity (*Council of Civil Service Unions* v. *Minister for the Civil Service* [1985] C.L.Y. 12 considered).

R. *v.* GREAT YARMOUTH BOROUGH COUNCIL *ex p.* BOTTON BROTHERS ARCADES, *The Times*, July 31, 1987, Otton J.

3695. Planning permission—opencast coal—arable land—effect on new town—precedent

[Town and County Planning Act 1971 (c.78), s.36; Circular 3/84.]

The site formed about 23 hectares of arable land in the countryside which was pit fallen on the periphery of Cramlington New Town.

Held, dismissing the appeal, that (1) the site would have a strong and detrimental effect on the overall visual quality of the area, which was an important feature in the attractiveness of Cramlington New Town; it would act as a deterrent to private investment and jeopardise the long term objectives for the New Town, (2) the screening would be perceived as alien features and the increase in noise levels would be noticeable; (3) there was no shortage of coal of a similar quality in the North-East and there was no justification for overriding the impact and amenity objections, accordingly the proposal failed under the tests of Circular 3/84; (4) the site was not unique and if this proposal were allowed it would be difficult to resist others like it.

NORTHUMBERLAND COUNTY COUNCIL and CRAKE SCAR OPENCAST (Ref: A/R2900/A/85/30633) (1986) 1 P.A.D. 493.

3696. Planning permission—permission for office building refused as contrary to local policy—appeal allowed—whether Inspector misconstrued policy Circular

[Town and Country Planning Act 1971 (c.78).]

An Inspector's decision of allowing an appeal against refusal of planning permission on policy grounds was itself quashed because he had misconstrued a government policy Circular.

The respondent applied to the Surrey Heath Borough Council, the applicant, for permission to build an office building in Camberley. Permission was refused on two main policy grounds. An Inspector allowed the appeal also on policy grounds as he construed the relevant government Circular. The applicant applied for an order quashing the decision.

Held, granting the application, that the Inspector had misconstrued the relevant government Circular, and failed to have regard to another material factor; his decision would be quashed.

SURREY HEATH BOROUGH COUNCIL *v.* SECRETARY OF STATE FOR THE ENVIRONMENT (1987) 53 P. & C.R. 428, Kennedy J.

3697. Planning permission—plans for proposed development amended—objectors unable to make representations on alleged inaccuracy of plans—whether breach of natural justice

Where plans submitted in support of an application are amended, the authority is under a duty to permit objectors to make representations on the amended plans.

In 1984 an application for permission further to develop a site used for boarding dogs and cats was submitted; plans were prepared to support the application. The application was approved; the main objector however discovered that the plans approved of were not the same as those supplied for inspection. He requested a deferment of the decision, but the original permission was confirmed without one and without further reference to him.

Held, granting the applicaiton for judicial review, that the authority had departed from the standard of fairness required by the 1971 Act; they had a duty to allow the objectors to make representations on the amended plans (*R.* v. *Hillingdon London Borough Council, ex p. Royco Homes* [1974] C.L.Y. 3763).

R. *v.* MONMOUTH DISTRICT COUNCIL, *ex p.* JONES (1987) 53 P. & C.R. 108, Woolf J.

3698. Planning permission—private housing—structure plan

Application was made for planning permission for private housing, and refused on the grounds that adequate land was available to meet housing needs. On appeal the Inspector recommended grant of permission on the grounds that the proposed development was in conformity with the structure plan since, as if it had transpired, the structure plan had resulted in a shortfall in the five-year supply of housing. The council appealed to the High Court.

Held, that (1) the Inspector's decision involved a substantive departure from the structure plan; (2) insufficient reasons for such departure had been given; (3) the decision to permit 50 new houses was important and should be quashed.

WIGAN METROPOLITAN BOROUGH COUNCIL *v.* SECRETARY OF STATE FOR THE ENVIRONMENT AND BROSELEY ESTATES [1987] J.P.L. 575, Widdicombe Q.C.

3699. Planning permission—procedure—conservation area

[Town and Country Planning Act 1971 (c.78), s.270; Town and Country Planning General Regulations 1976, reg. 4(2)(*c*).]

The Council declared a parkland a conservation area. They considered a proposal to develop six acres. They passed a resolution to seek permission to carry out the proposed development. They posted a notice on a gate into the park, and inserted an advertisement in a local newspaper. In 1984, Croom-Johnson J. found that there had been a failure to comply with the requirements of reg. 4(2)(*c*) because the notice in the newspaper did not specify a period for making objections. For this and other procedural irregularities, he quashed the deemed planning permission. The council appealed.

Held, dismissing the appeal, that the breach was fundamental and fatal. The procedure was important in this case and it was proper to grant relief.

R. *v.* LAMBETH LONDON BOROUGH COUNCIL, *ex p.* SHARP [1987] J.P.L. 440, C.A.

3700. Planning permission—procedure—two rival applications for the development of retail units—local authority granting themselves planning permission—judicial review

British Railways sought permission to erect a retail unit in 1982. The Board appealed in default to the Secretary of State, who held an inquiry in July 1984. Meanwhile, the council sought permission for a retail unit on their own land. On October 26, 1984, they granted themselves the permission. British Railways applied for judicial review.

Held, that the council's resolution to seek permission should have been site-specific. The proper procedure had not been followed. Decision quashed (*R.* v. *Lambeth London Borough Council, ex p. Sharp* [1987] C.L.Y. 3699 followed).

R. *v.* DONCASTER METROPOLITAN DISTRICT COUNCIL, *ex p.* BRITISH RAILWAYS BOARD [1987] J.P.L. 444, Schiemann J.

3701. Planning permission—provision for infilling after quarrying operations—whether an application on the details to be treated as a new application for full permission

Where planning consent makes provision for infilling after quarrying operations, it is an inevitable consequence that that which is to be used to fill will be waste material of some kind; an application on the details therefore is not to be treated as a new application for full permission.

In 1952 permission was granted for quarrying operations with conditions attached. One of these concerned restoration, requiring surfaces to be covered with materials suitable for plant growth. In 1984, with the quarry exhausted, the new owners applied to refill with commercial waste, ultimately to be covered with the said suitable materials. The authority treated the application not as one of full planning permission (with rights of review) but as one for approval of details of the 1952 permission. The applicant contended that this was wrong and applied for a declaration and certiorari.

Held, dismissing the application, that the authority was correct in its approach; it was a necessary implication of the 1952 permission that waste of some sort would be used to infill (*R.* v. *Derbyshire County Council, ex p. North East Derbyshire District Council* [1980] C.L.Y. 2222 referred to).

R. *v.* SURREY COUNTY COUNCIL, *ex p.* MONK (1987) 53 P. & C.R. 410, McNeill J.

3702. Planning permission—public inquiry—Secretary of State's decision

Tesco Stores sought permission for a shopping development in Birmingham. The Secretary of State called-in the application together with 10 others. Separate public inquiries were held. The Secretary of State refused one permission and granted the others.

Held, the Secretary of State had dealt properly with the applications. He had given proper reasons. Appeal dismissed.

SOLIHULL BOROUGH COUNCIL *v.* SECRETARY OF STATE FOR THE ENVIRONMENT [1987] J.P.L. 208, McNeill J.

3703. Planning permission—refusal of renewal of temporary permission for offices—need for residential accommodation in Mayfair

[Town and Country Planning Act 1971 (c.78), s.36; Circular: 14/85.]

The premises comprised a basement and five floors which had been in use as a single dwelling house before the Second World War, but which had been granted temporary permission for use as offices in 1949, following war damage. This permission had been renewed. The adopted Local Plan contained a policy to return to residential use buildings temporarily used as offices in order to achieve the balance of supply and demand for housing, to maintain Westminster's residential role in providing homes for commuters, and maintaining Mayfair's mixed use character. The Council used two criteria in applying this policy, by asking whether the property was physically capable of reversion to residential use and whether it would result in a satisfactory environment for occupiers. The Council argued that the criteria were met in this case, and that there were no very special circumstances to justify an exception to the policy. The Council conceded that it could not demonstrate harm to an interest of acknowledged importance on the basis of this case alone, but taken with the many other similar cases which could arise, they would have an cumulative and harmful affect on the character of the area. The appellant argued that there was no longer an overall shortage of housing in London and that the conversion of this property was unlikely to result in providing homes for commuters, a point which the Council conceded. The appellant argued that the Company operated on a low profit margin and there was a risk of the Company moving abroad if the appeal was lost, resulting in a loss of jobs and other benefits.

Held, dismissing the appeal, that (1) the appellant failed to show that there was no longer a housing shortage in London; (2) although the satisfactory plan was only one material consideration as emphasized by the Circular 14/85, the housing aims had been examined in detail and accepted in the Inspector's Report at the Local Plan stage and nothing had emerged at the Inquiry to indicate that a different view should now be taken; (3) the appellant had not shown exceptional circumstances to justify a departure from policy; (4) the Inspector accepted the argument that there were numerous other properties in the same situation in Mayfair which would cumulatively have a harmful effect on the character of the area.

WESTMINSTER CITY COUNCIL and RADIO LUXEMBOURG (LONDON) (Ref: T/APP/X5990/A/85033018/P2) (1986) 1 P.A.D. 429.

3704. Planning permission—residential development on agricultural land—land availability assessments

Town and Country Planning Act 1971 (c.78), s.37; Circulars 75/76, 22/80, 15/84, 14/85.] The application for residential development next to an existing housing estate at the edge of Deal where it merged with the next village. The site was classified as grade 1 agricultural land though it was not currently in productive use. The site had not been allocated for residential development in the Draft Local Plan. The appellant argued that there was a need for sites to provide houses of the size, type and price proposed, in the immediate vicinity.

Held, dismissing the appeal, that (1) the council's approach to land availability was the correct one as it related to the overall availability of housing land by reference to an area provided for in the Structure Plan; in the context of Circular 15/84L to examine only a part of the house market was questionable; (2) there was a five-year supply of land but this alone was not a sufficient reason for refusal; however the proposal was contrary to the policies of the Structure Plan, particularly the need to discourage residential development outside the boundaries of settlements; (3) the proposal would extend the built-up area of Deal and would be readily visible and would therefore cause demonstrable harm; (4) the proposal was contrary to the nationwide policy of safeguarding top quality agricultural land and would only shift the problems of urban fringe farming to the adjoining land.

DOVER DISTRICT COUNCIL AND HUTCHINGS (Ref: APP/X2220/A/84/025746) (1986) 1 P.A.D. 407.

3705. Planning permission—Secretary of State's decision—effect of Circular 15/84—council's policy

Permission was refused for residential developments on the green belt site. The Secretary of State granted permission against the advice of the Inspector. On appeal to the High Court the effect of Circular 15/84 was considered.

Held, the Secretary of State had correctly found that the Council's policy in relation to this site was arbitrary, rationing land inconsistently with the circular.

WAVERLEY BOROUGH COUNCIL *v.* SECRETARY OF STATE FOR THE ENVIRONMENT AND CLARKE HOMES (SOUTHERN) and CLARKE HOMES (SOUTH EASTERN) [1987] J.P.L. 202, Brown J.

3706. Planning permission—Secretary of State's decision—whether entitled to take into account subsequent modifications to Structure Plan

Application was to develop a business park on 148 acres in Solihull within the Green Belt. The Inspector recommended refusal. The Secretary of State took into account his own modification of the Structure Plan which had taken place after the inquiry. The Parish Council sought judicial review. The question arose as a preliminary issue whether the Parish Council had validly resolved to apply to the court.

Held, that (1) a Parish Council meeting could probably be validly carried out on the telephone; (2) the Secretary of State had acted properly in taking into account the subsequent modifications of the Structure Plan; (3) the Parish Council were not caused substantial prejudice.

R. *v.* BICKENHILL PARISH COUNCIL, *ex p* SECRETARY OF STATE FOR THE ENVIRONMENT AND SOLIHULL METROPOLITAN BOROUGH COUNCIL AND THE TRUSTEES OF WINGFIELD DIGBY ESTATES AND ARLINGTON SECURITES [1987] J.P.L. 773, Nolan J.

3707. Planning permission—sewage treatment works—whether exceptional circumstances justifying departure from policy

The fact that the Welsh Water Authority might wish to use a site for a new sewage treatment works amounted to an exceptional circumstance justifying the grant of planning permission contrary to the applicable development policy.

There was an urgent need for a new sewage treatment works to serve Llantrisant and Tonyrefail. R.-W. applied for planning permission to construct a sewage treatment works at Gwern-y-Gedrych on land that he owned. Permission was refused and R.-W. appealed to the Secretary of State. The Welsh Water Authority had the responsibility to develop and operate the new works. No decision had at that time been taken as to where the new works should be located, although there had been much discussion on the issue. A public inquiry was held and the inspector reported that Gwern-y-Gedrych was in an area of open countryside and that the development was contrary to the approved structure plan for the area. He considered that planning permission could be granted so as to provide an alternative to the WWA's proposal to construct the works at Miskin given the uncertainty surrounding that proposal. After the inquiry had been held but before the inspector's report was available the WWA were given planning permission to develop the new works at Miskin. R.-W. made a second application for planning permission at Gwern-y-Gedrych. That application was called in by the Secretary of State and a second public inquiry held by the same inspector. On the second inquiry the inspector reported that there were negotiations going on between WWA and R.-W. with a view to constructing the new works at Gwern-y-Gedrych if planning permission were granted. The inspector declined to consider the relative merits of Gwern-y-Gedrych and Miskin for the development. The inspector reported that if agreement was reached to build the works at Gwern-y-Gedrych there would be exceptional circumstances justifying the grant of planning permission. The Secretary of State allowed R.-W.'s appeal, stating in his decision letter that he accepted the inspector's views and that the urgent need for the sewage treatment works was an exceptional circumstance justifying the development. The council applied to quash the Secretary of State's decision.

Held, that the reasoning in the Secretary of State's decision letter was not open to attack. It was not essential for the Secretary of State to consider the merits of the alternative sites unless he first came to the conclusion that the environmental impact of the development was of such a nature as to make that consideration essential. It could not be said that exceptional circumstances justifying the development ceased to exist because the WWA preferred to construct the new works at Miskin. Where a development could be carried out with an acceptable environmental impact the exceptional circumstances required to justify a departure from the applicable planning policy were less onerous.

VALE OF GLAMORGAN BOROUGH COUNCIL *v.* SECRETARY OF STATE FOR WALES and SIR BRANDON RHYS-WILLIAMS (1986) 52 P. & C.R. 418, Woolf J.

3708. Planning permission—traffic considerations—inspectors report

The council refused permission for housing development on the ground that traffic conditions would be inadequate. On appeal the Inspector allowed the permission. The council appealed to the High Court.

Held, that the informed reader of the decision letter was left uncertain as to whether the inspector thought that there was a traffic problem and if there was whether there were practicable traffic management measures which could be adopted to solve it.

SOUTH BEDFORDSHIRE DISTRICT COUNCIL *v.* SECRETARY OF STATE FOR THE ENVIRONMENT AND BOYLE [1987] J.P.L. 507, Widdicombe Q.C.

3709. Planning permission—university building—housing need—conditions

[Town and Country Planning Act 1971 (c.78), s.36.]

The Council refused permission for a new biological science building which would involve the demolition of fifteen dwellings which were boarded up and unoccupied. The appellants argued that the building was needed for important research and this was the only site adjacent to the University that was available. The Council argued there was an urgent housing need in the city, and the appeal site lay in the area of greatest demand.

Held, allowing the appeal, that (1) this was an important development and this was the only site available, consequently the need of the University was greater; (2) the value of the houses was diminished by the remoteness of shops and primary schools, in the presence of busy main roads; (3) a condition was imposed restricting to University related uses.

LEICESTER CITY COUNCIL and UNIVERSITY OF LEICESTER (Ref: T/APP/U2425A/85/036161/P7) (1986) 1 P.A.D. 393.

3710. Planning permission—use of premises as fish and chip shop—temporary use as antique shop—reversion to sale of hot food—whether earlier permission spent

Planning permission may not be required for the reversion of a shop to its pre-existing use for the sale of hot food, after temporary use as an antique shop.

In 1958 planning permission was granted for the use of premises as a fish and chip shop. It was so used until 1978 when due to the ill health of the owner it was temporarily let as an antique shop. In 1983 the premises were recovered and an application was made for their use as a Chinese takeaway. The inspector held that no permission was required as the premises had not lost the benefit of the previous permission.

Held, dismissing the appeal, that although the change of use constituted a development, and the original permission was "spent", by reason of Art. 3(1) of the 1977 General Development Order, which brought the case within s.23(8) of the 1971 Act, the reversion of use as a shop for the sale of hot food did not require permission.

CYNON VALLEY BOROUGH COUNCIL *v.* SECRETARY OF STATE FOR WALES AND OI MEE LAM (1987) 53 P. & C.R. 68, C.A.

3711. Planning permission for hotel refused—Inspector recommended that need for hotel accommodation could be met on other sites—whether Inspector entitled as a matter of law to reach that conclusion when no alternative site specified

A planning authority may, as a matter of law, reject a planning application where objections are intended to be overcome by reference to need, on the basis that that need can be met on other sites, without specifying those sites, but it would generally be desirable that they be identified.

TFH wished to build a hotel on green belt land of high agricultural quality. They had been searching for a suitable site since 1972, and had examined, and rejected as unsuitable, four alternative sites suggested by the local planning authority. Permission to build was refused on the ground that the need for additional hotel accommodation did not outweight the presumption against building on green belt land, and the deleterious effect of losing high quality agricultural land.

Held, dismissing THF's appeal, that (1) although desirable in many cases, it was not essential when rejecting an application on the ground that alternative sites existed, to specify them; (ii) the Secretary of State was entitled to form a view that if there was going to be a shortfall of hotel accommodation in the area it would be made up by the law of supply and demand.

TRUSTHOUSE FORTE HOTELS *v.* SECRETARY OF STATE FOR THE ENVIRONMENT (1987) 53 P. & C.R. 293, Simon Brown J.

3712. Private gipsy caravan site—outside limits of settlement—temporary permission for part of site—personal and other conditions

[Town and Country Planning Act 1971 (c.78), s.36 (S.I. 1984 No. 967); Circulars 28/77, 57/78, 1/85, 14/85.]

The Council refused permission for a private gipsy caravan site on fields of 1.2 ha. Part of the site was currently in use as a gipsy caravan site following a temporary permission which had been granted and which was personal to the appellant. The Council argued that further infringement into the countryside was contrary to its housing policy and the approved structure plans. There were no exceptional reasons why permission should be granted, particularly as the district had now been designated under S.I. 1984, No. 967 as an area where adequate provision had been made for the accommodation of gipsies.

Held, allowing the appeal subject to conditions, that (1) the fact that the district had been designated under S.I. 1984 No. 967 was not enough as a sole or main ground of refusal; (2) the proposals had to be considered primarily on its likely effect on the applicable planning policies in the light of Circulars 28/77, 57/78 and Development Control Policy Note Number 8, which stressed that few sites would be entirely suitable; this site was associated with adjoining development, it would not create a precedent because provisions for gipsies must always be regarded individually as special cases; (3) this gipsy site had only caused minor problems in the past and following Circular 1/85 there would have to be a major change in circumstances for the temporary permission not to be made permanent on renewal, but permission here would only be justified if conditions were imposed so as to require screening and landscaping and to limit the permission for a twelve family site; the permission was personal to the appellant.

SOUTH DERBYSHIRE DISTRICT COUNCIL and COOK (Ref. T/APP/-F1040/85/A/028430/P5) (1986) 1 P.A.D. 378.

3713. Restrictive covenant—discharge—agreement imposing restriction—effect

[Town and Country Planning Act 1971 (c.78), s.52.]

An agreement made under s.37 of the 1962 Act (now s.52) operates so as to give the covenant the validity of a normal restrictive covenant.

In 1967 the applicants' predecessor in title entered into an agreement with the council under s.37 of the 1962 Act (now s.52); the agreement was to the effect that the site would remain a private open space. In 1983 the applicants sought permission to build a house on it. The council refused, but the Minister reversed their decision. The Council insisted on their rights under the 1967 agreement, so the applicants applied to the Lands Tribunal for the restriction contained in the agreement to be modified.

Held, dismissing the application, that the agreement had the validity of a normal restrictive covenant, which was not obsolete as it was designed to protect the amenities of the area.

MARTIN'S APPLICATION, *Re* (No. LP/40/1985) (1987) 53 P. & C.R. 146, Lands Tribunal.

3714. Restrictive covenant—modification—detailed plans to be submitted to covenantee if further building proposed—no consent to rebuilding sought

Where the continued existence of a restriction would impede the reasonable use of the applicant's land, without conferring upon objectors thereto any practical advantages or benefits, the restriction may be modified.

Applicants demolished a cottage and began to erect another in its place, having first obtained planning permission, but without submitting the plans to their neighbours, who had the benefit of a covenant to that effect.

Held, that on the facts the objectors had failed to establish that they derived any practical advantage from the submission of the plans; had the plans been submitted to them, as required, they could not reasonably have withheld their consent to the re-building. The restriction would, therefore, be modified, but subject to payment by the applicants of £500 compensation, on the basis that it was just possible that some advantage might have accrued to the objectors from having the plans submitted to them.

REYNOLDS' APPLICATION, *Re* (Ref. LP/44/1985) (1987) 54 P. & C.R. 121, Lands Tribunal.

3715. Restrictive covenants—sale of land next to council estate development proposal—compensation to Council

[Law of Property Act 1925 (c.20), s.84(1)(1A).]

The kind of benefit to a covenantee contemplated by subs. (1A) of s.84 of the Law of Property Act 1925 is a practical one as opposed to a pecuniary one.

The appellants were owners of a housing estate; next to it was an area which had been sold subject to a covenant requiring it not to be used except for agriculture. Some of the houses on the estate enjoyed a good view over the land. The respondents applied to the Lands Tribunal for a modification of the restriction to allow them to build 42 houses. The appellants objected; the tribunal found that the appellants could be properly compensated for the resultant diminution in value of the houses and granted the application.

Held, dismissing the appeal, that the kind of benefit to the covenantee contemplated by the section must be practical as opposed to pecuniary; the award of £2,250 would not be disturbed.

STOCKPORT METROPOLITAN BOROUGH COUNCIL *v.* ALWIYAH DEVELOPMENTS (1983) 52 P. & C.R. 278, C.A.

3716. Section 53 determination—planning permission—abandonment of residence—area of outstanding natural beauty

[Town and Country Planning Act 1947 (c.51); Town and Country Planning Act 1971 (c.78), ss.22, 36, 53; Town and Country Planning General Development Order 1971–1985; Circulars 22/80, 14/85, 31/85.

"The Bothy" was a house for staff of Badgemore House, set in its park. It was in residential use on "the Appointed Day", but fell into disuse in 1949. In 1969 planning permission was granted for a new bungalow on the site of "the Bothy" but this was not implemented and so lapsed. Other planning permissions were granted and implemented in respect of Badgemore House. The appellant sought a s.53 determination that resumption of the residential use of "the Bothy" ancillary to Badgemore Park did not constitute development within the meaning of the 1971 Act. The appellant also sought planning permission for alterations to the dilapidated building. The Council determined that planning permission was needed but should be refused. The Council argued that "the Bothy" had a nil use and formed its own self-contained site, it was in a designated area of outstanding natural beauty and the relevant policies raised a presumption against new residential units in the open countryside.

Held, dismissing the s.53 appeal but allowing the s.36 appeal subject to conditions, that (1) "the Bothy" had a "nil use" before 1969 which remained after the 1969 permission lapsed; (2) the proposed resumption of residential use required planning permission and was not ancilliary to the uses of Badgemore House so as to be "permitted development" within the General Development Order; (3) the owner of Badgemore House established a need for the proposal and in these exceptional circumstances permission could be granted contrary to policy, subject to an occupancy condition.

SOUTH OXFORDSHIRE DISTRICT COUNCIL and DUKE (Refs: APP/Q3115/G/85/71; APP/Q3115/A/85/30615) (1986) 1 P.A.D. 398.

3717. Section 53 determination—planning permission—agriculture—forestry—ancillary uses—green belt

[Town and Country Planning Act 1971 (c.78), ss.22, 30A, 36, 53, 290; Agriculture Act 1947; (c.48); Forestry Act 1967 (c.10); 38/81.]

The appellant appealed against the council's s.53 determination that the sale of bees and manufacture and sale of bee hives constituted development requiring planning permission and against the council's refusal of permission for the same. The appeal site comprised 20 acres of commercial woodland in use as a nursery and market garden, though the site was now mainly used for leisure purposes. It lay within the Metropolitan Green Belt. The appellant argued that the manufacture of hives was ancillary to the forestry use, just as the sale of bees was ancillary to the agricultural use.

Held, allowing the s.53 appeal in part and allowing the s.36 appeal, that (1) the present uses were leisure, forestry including production and sale of logs, and agriculture; (2) the manufacture of hives in any significant number would be a manufacturing process amounting to a material change of use and was not ancillary to agriculture or to the purposes of forestry; (2) the sale, in hives, of bees bred on the site was ancillary to agriculture and was not development requiring planning permission; (3) the manufacture of hives on site for the sale of bees made the enterprise viable and should be supported to ensure that Green Belt land was maintained and worked; (4) the proposals would not cause harm to the character and amenities of the area which could be protected by conditions.

TANDRIDGE DISTRICT COUNCIL and HOMEWOOD and THE HONEY FARM (Ref: APP/M3645/G/85/17, A/85/36993) (1986) 1 P.A.D. 410.

3718. Section 53 determination—resumption of residential use—temporary change of use

[Town and Country Planning Act 1971 (c.78), ss.22, 23, 53; Town and Country Planning General Development Order 1977–1985.]

A bungalow became vacant in 1964 and was thereafter used continuously for agricultural storage. The appellant appealed against the Council's determination under s.53 that resumption of the residential use constituted development requiring planning permission. He contended that the storage use was temporary and that he had always intended to resume the residential use which had not been abandoned.

Held, dismissing the appeal, that (1) the agricultural use, though temporary, led to a distinct change in the character of the building and amounted to a material change of use in 1964; (2) any resumption of the previous residential use would constitute a further material change of use requiring planning permission.

SHREWSBURY AND ATCHAM BOROUGH COUNCIL and BUTTERY (Ref: APP/B3220/G/85/1) (1986) 1 P.A.D. 404.

3719. Simplified planning zones

TOWN AND COUNTRY PLANNING (SIMPLIFIED PLANNING ZONES) (EXCLUDED DEVELOPMENT) ORDER 1987 (No. 1849) [45p], made under the Town and Country Planning Act 1971 (c.78), s.24E(3); operative on November 20, 1987; imposes restrictions on the development which may be authorised by a simplified planning zone scheme.

TOWN AND COUNTRY PLANNING (SIMPLIFIED PLANNING ZONES) REGULATIONS 1987 (No. 1750) [£1·60], made under the Town and Country Planning Act 1971 (c.78), ss.287(1), 290(1), Sched. 8A, paras. 5(2), 6(4), 13; operative on November 2, 1987; provide for the procedure for making and altering simplified planning zone schemes.

3720. Stop notice—effect—future use of residential caravan site

[Town and Country Planning Act 1971 (c.78), s.90(2)(*b*).]

S.90(2)(*b*) of the 1971 Act cannot be construed so as to render stop notices ineffective for caravans already on a site, but effective against those subsequently brought on.

The defendants purchased a site with a view to developing it as a winter quarters for travelling showmen. A showman was permitted to move his caravan on site in breach of planning control. The plaintiff served enforcement and stop notices. The defendants appealed, suspending their operation. A further twenty caravans moved on site, and the plaintiffs sought injunctions claiming that s.90(2)(*b*) of the 1971 Act did not protect those who came onto the land since the service of the notices.

Held, dismissing the application, that there was no basis for construing the section so that it was ineffective for caravans already on the land and occupied as main residences, but effective for caravans subsequently brought on and so occupied.

RUNNYMEDE BOROUGH COUNCIL *v.* SMITH (1987) 53 P. & C.R. 132, Millett J.

3721. Stop notice—precision of stop notice—whether valid

[Town and Country Planning Act 1971 (c.78), s.87.]

A stop notice may be valid even though it may be couched in language which leaves the person on whom it is served with the problem of judging whether his proposed actions are prohibited by the notice.

S allowed a celebrated Sikh religious leader to stay at his house, in a residential area of Surrey, with the result that between 40 and 100 people regularly attended at the house, chanting prayers. RBC determined that there had been a change of use, to mixed religious and residential use and served a stop notice requiring S to refrain from using the house for religious purposes, otherwise than as incidental to the enjoyment of the house as a house. S sought to quash the notice on the ground that he was uncertain whether a particular ceremony would be within the scope of the stop notice, contending that its wording, which failed to specify what was to be regarded as a normal incidence of use of the house as a house, was too vague.

Held, that the application would be refused. The notice gave S sufficient indication of what he must not do, even though it still left him with the problem of judging whether his proposed conduct was permissible.

R. *v.* RUNNYMEDE BOROUGH COUNCIL, *ex p.* SARVAN SINGH SEEHRA (1987) 53 P. & C.R. 281, Schiemann J.

3722. Structure and local plans

TOWN AND COUNTRY PLANNING (STRUCTURE AND LOCAL PLANS) (AMENDMENT) REGULATIONS 1987 (No. 1760) [85p], made under the Town and Country Planning Act 1971 (c.78), ss.12A(4), 18, 287(1), 290(1); operative on November 2, 1987; amend S.I. 1982 No. 555 to take into account the provisions of the Housing and Planning Act 1986.

3723. Trafford Park—development—planning authority

TOWN AND COUNTRY PLANNING (TRAFFORD PARK URBAN DEVELOPMENT AREA) SPECIAL DEVELOPMENT ORDER 1987 (No. 738) [85p], made under the Town and Country Planning Act 1971 (c.78), s.24 and the Local Government, Planning and Land Act 1980 (c.65), s.148(2); operative on May 15, 1987; provides permission for the carrying out of development in the Trafford Urban Development Area in accordance with proposals approved by the Secretary of State.

TRAFFORD PARK DEVELOPMENT CORPORATION (PLANNING FUNCTIONS) ORDER 1987 (No. 739) [85p], made under the Local Government, Planning and Land Act 1980 (c.65), s.149(1)(3)(ii); operative on May 15, 1987; makes the said Development Corporation the planning authority for the urban development area.

3724. Tree preservation order—land unable to be developed as grazing land—whether entitled to compensation

[Town and Country Planning Act 1971 (c.78), s.174.]

The owner of land subject to a tree preservation order was entitled to compensation on the basis that the land could have been developed to provide grazing land but for the order.

B owned 88 acres of woodland, 50 acres of which he intended to convert to grazing land. He intended to carry out the development with the assistance of grant aid under the Agriculture and Horticulture Development Scheme. Canterbury City Council made a tree preservation order in respect of the woodland and thereafter rejected an application by B to grub out 40 acres of woodland for conversion to grazing land. B appealed unsuccessfully to the Secretary of State. B then applied for compensation under s.174 of the Town and Country Planning Act 1971. The Council contended that B was entitled to compensation only in the amount he would have received for the timber he proposed to remove.

Held, that B was entitled to compensation for loss or damage caused by the refusal of his application by the council. Loss or damage was not limited to the value of the timber B was unable to fell as there was nothing to qualify the words loss or damage in the section. It was a question of fact whether any loss or damage claimed was too remote. In B's case the prospect of converting the land to grazing land was a reality and he was entitled to compensation for the loss of that prospect. The compensation was to be valued as at the date the Council refused his application under the tree preservation order. B was entitled to compensation for the loss of grant under the Agriculture and Horticulture Development Scheme notwithstanding that the grant had not been confirmed because there was a distinct possibility of receiving the grant had the Council permitted the development.

BELL *v.* CANTERBURY CITY COUNCIL (Ref. No. 166/1985) (1986) 52 P. & C.R. 428, Lands Tribunal.

3725. Tree preservation order—tree damaged by independent contractor—whether owner liable to prosecution

[Town and Country Planning Act 1971 (c.78), s.10(1).]

A tree which was subject to a tree preservation order was situated on land being developed by a contractor, who uprooted it despite being told that it was the subject of an order and should not be touched or damaged in any way. The magistrates convicted the owner company and fined it £500 with £200 costs.

Held, allowing the owner's appeal, that strict liability under the section could only attach to the owner if it was vicariously liable for the person who actually committed the offence. This could not be the case where the tree was uprooted, contrary to express instructions, by an independent contractor.

GROVESIDE HOMES *v.* ELMBRIDGE BOROUGH COUNCIL (1987) 284 E.G. 940, D.C.

3726. Urban development areas

BLACK COUNTRY DEVELOPMENT CORPORATION (AREA AND CONSTITUTION) ORDER 1987 (No. 922) [45p], made under the Local Government, Planning and Land Act 1980 (c.65), ss.134, 135, Sched. 26, para. 1; operative on May 15, 1987; designates an area in the Black Country as an urban development area.

CARDIFF BAY DEVELOPMENT CORPORATION (AREA AND CONSTITUTION) ORDER 1987 (No. 646) [45p], made under the Local Government, Planning and Land Act 1980, ss.134, 135, Sched. 26, para. 1; operative on April 3, 1987, designates an area in Cardiff as an urban development area.

TEESSIDE DEVELOPMENT CORPORATION (AREA AND CONSTITUTION) ORDER 1987 (No. 923) [45p], made under the Local Government, Planning and Land Act 1980, ss.134, 135, Sched. 26, para. 1; operative on May 15, 1987; designates two areas on Teesside as an urban development area.

TOWN AND COUNTRY PLANNING (BLACK COUNTRY URBAN DEVELOPMENT AREA) SPECIAL DEVELOPMENT ORDER 1987 (No. 1343) [85p], made under the Town and Country Planning Act 1971 (c.78), s.24 and the Local Government, Planning and Land Act 1980, s.148(2); operative on October 19, 1987; grants permission for the carrying out of approved development work within the Black Country urban development area.

TOWN AND COUNTRY PLANNING (TEESSIDE URBAN DEVELOPMENT AREA) SPECIAL DEVELOPMENT ORDER 1987 (No. 1344) [£1·30], made under the Town and Country Planning Act 1971, s.24 and the Local Government, Planning and Land Act 1980, s.148(2); operative on September 1, 1987; grants permission for the carrying out of approved development work within the area of the Teesside urban development area.

TOWN AND COUNTRY PLANNING (TYNE AND WEAR URBAN DEVELOPMENT AREA) SPECIAL DEVELOPMENT ORDER 1987 (No. 1345) [85p], made under the Town and Country Planning Act 1971, s.24 and the Local Government, Planning and Land Act 1980, s.148(2); operative on October 1, 1987; grants permission for the carrying out of approved development work within the area of the Tyne and Wear urban development area.

TYNE AND WEAR DEVELOPMENT CORPORATION (AREA AND CONSTITUTION) ORDER 1987 (No. 924) [45p], made under the Local Government, Planning and Land Act 1980, ss.134, 135, Sched. 26, para. 1; operative on May 15, 1987; designated two areas on the rivers Tyne and Wear as urban development areas.

3727. Urban Development Corporations (Financial Limits) Act 1987 (c.57)

This Act removes the limit on the amount of grants that may be made to urban development corporations and to provide a new limit applicable only to the amounts for the time being outstanding in respect of sums borrowed by them and sums issued by the Treasury in fulfilment of guarantees of their debts.

The Act received the Royal Assent December 17, 1987, and comes into force two months from that date.

The Act does not extend to Northern Ireland.

3728. Use classes

TOWN AND COUNTRY PLANNING (USE CLASSES) ORDER 1987 (No. 764) [£1·70], made under the Town and Country Planning Act 1971 (c.78), ss.22(2)(*f*), 287(3); operative on June 1, 1987; specifies classes of use of buildings or other land for the purposes of s.22(2)(*f*) of the 1971 Act.

TRADE AND INDUSTRY

3729. British Shipbuilders (Borrowing Powers) Act 1987 (c.52)

This Act raises the limits imposed by s.11(7) of the Aircraft and Shipbuilding Industries Act 1977 in relation to the finances of British Shipbuilders and its wholly owned subsidiaries.

The Act received the Royal Assent on July 23, 1987.

The Act extends to Northern Ireland.

3730. Industrial assurance

INDUSTRIAL ASSURANCE (FEES) REGULATIONS 1987 (No. 377) [45p], made under the Industrial Assurance Act 1923 (c.8), s.93; operative on April 1, 1987; increase by about four per cent. the fees payable in connection with the exercise by the Industrial Assurance Commissioner of his functions under the 1923 Act.

3731. Industrial training

S.I. 1987 Nos. 29 (levy—construction board) [£2·20]; 607 (levy—engineering board) [£1·60]; 896 (levy—hotel and catering) [£1·30]; 717 (levy—plastics processing) [£1·30]; 1534 (clothing and allied products—levy) [£1·30]; 1964 (road transport—levy) [£1·30].

3732. Industrial training—levy—plastics

[Industrial Training (Plastics Processing Board) Order 1982 (S.I. 923), Sched., para. 2(*c*)(xviii).]

The manufacture of PVC compound from PVC resin falls within the definition of the manufacture of plastics material, and thus no levy is payable in respect of the process.

NORSK HYDRO POLYMERS *v.* PLASTICS PROCESSING INDUSTRY TRAINING BOARD, *The Times*, January 29, 1987, C.A.

3733. Industry Act 1972—amendment

INDUSTRY ACT 1972 (AMENDMENT) REGULATIONS 1987 (No. 1807) [45p], made under the European Communities Act 1972 (c.68), s.2(2); operative on November 11, 1987; amend s.10(1) of the 1972 Act by extending its scope to any member State of the EEC.

3734. Industry Act 1980—financial limit

INDUSTRY ACT 1980 (INCREASE OF LIMIT) ORDER 1987 (No. 520) [45p], made under the Industry Act 1980 (c.33), s.5(5); operative on March 20, 1987; increases the financial limit specified in s.5(3) of the 1980 Act, as substituted by the Industry Act 1981, s.1(3), to £5,250 million.

3735. Monopolies and mergers—investigation—disclosure of information

[Fair Trading Act 1973 (c.41), s.133.]

The Monopolies and Mergers Commission has a duty to investigate proposed mergers to see whether they are in the public interest. Information given to it by one party to a merger is not strictly confidential and it can therefore be disclosed to the other party if the commission considers that disclosure will help its investigations.

The applicant company made a take-over bid for the second respondent, which was hostile to the bid. It was referred to the first respondent, the Monopolies and Mergers Commission by the Secretary of State for Trade and Industry acting under the Fair Trading Act 1973. The bid lapsed automatically under its terms on the referral, but the applicant company wanted to make a new bid if the merger was eventually allowed. The Commission obtained a statement from the applicant company detailing its proposed new bid, but the company asked that it be not disclosed to the respondent company.

The Commission decided to disclose it on the grounds that the Commission had to make a full investigation and that natural justice required that the respondent company be allowed to make fully informed representations about the information provided by the applicants. The applicant applied for certiorari to quash this decision, but their application was dismissed.

Held, that (1) in performing its inquisitorial function of determining whether the prospective effects of a merger would or could be expected to be against the public interest, the Commission was under a duty to act fairly to all parties who had a substantial interest in the reference. As the concept of fairness was flexible, the court had to decide what was fair in the particular situation. The Commission had been entitled in the circumstances to decide that the perceived detriment to the applicant which disclosure would cause should be subordinated to the Commission's judgment of how best to perform its statutory function, which, in the Commission's view, entailed the disclosure of the applicant's information to the respondent (Dictum of Sachs L.J. in *Pergamon Press, Re* [1970] C.L.Y. 286 applied); (2) since s.133(2) of the Act permitted the Commission to disclose information obtained by it if the disclosure was for the purpose of facilitating the performance of its functions, the court was not required to conduct an objective examination of whether the disclosure would facilitate its performance, but merely had to determine whether the Commission had made the decision to disclose with the intention of facilitating its investigation. Since it had so decided, it was entitled to disclose the information (Dictum of Lord Diplock in *Sweet* v. *Parsley* [1969] C.L.Y. 2210 applied).

R. *v.* MONOPOLIES AND MERGERS COMMISSION, *ex p.* ELDERS IXL [1987] 1 All E.R. 451, Mann J.

3736. Monopolies Commission—hearing of reference—duty to disclose

[Fair Trading Act 1973 (c.41).]

The court will not interfere with the procedure of the hearing of a reference to the Monopolies and Mergers Commission in order to force it to disclose each piece of evidence to all parties to an inquiry.

The applicant company was the subject of a take-over bid by the second respondent company. The proposed merger was referred to the first respondent, the Monopolies and Mergers Commission for investigation and report under the Fair Trading Act 1973. During the course of the investigation the respondent company submitted certain information to the Commission which the Commission did not pass on to the applicants. The report concluded that the proposed merger was not against the public interest. The applicants applied to quash the report by way of certiorari alleging a breach of the rules of natural justice since they had had no opportunity to comment on the evidence submitted. The application was dismissed.

Held, that the Commission was under a duty to act fairly and had to establish its own procedure. The question in each case was whether the Commission had adopted a procedure so unfair that it could be said to have acted with manifest unfairness. Accordingly, the court would not lay down rules for the conduct of any particular inquiry, and would not impose on the Commission a rule that every piece of evidence had to be put to the opposing party. The further evidence submitted by the respondents was merely a clearer statement of their original case, which had already been put to the applicants for comment, and it could not be said that the Commission had acted with manifest unfairness in the preparation of its report (*Board of Education* v. *Rice* [1911–1913] All E.R. Rep. 36, *Fairmount Investments* v. *Secretary of State for the Environment* [1976] C.L.Y. 305, *Att.-Gen. of Hong Kong* v. *Ng Yuen Shiu* [1983] C.L.Y. 44, and *Mahon* v. *Air New Zealand* [1984] C.L.Y. 2706 considered).

R. *v.* MONOPOLIES AND MERGERS COMMISSION, *ex p.* BROWN (MATTHEW) [1987] 1 All E.R. 463, Macpherson J.

3737. Restraint of trade—franchise operation—whether covenant in unreasonable restraint of trade

P were the registered trade mark owners of PRONTAPRINT and granted a franchise to operate printing and copying businesses by that name. The system was established nationwide. D was a former franchisee. He continued the business with a new name. A clause in the franchise agreement provided that after termination, the franchise would not operate within a half a mile of the premises or within three miles of any other of the franchise operations for a period of three years.

Held, that at full trial the clause would be likely to be found enforceable. Injunction granted.

PRONTAPRINT *v.* LANDON LITHO [1987] F.S.R. 315, Whitford J.

3738. Scottish Development Agency Act 1987 (c.56)

This Act makes provision with respect to the limit on sums borrowed by, or paid by the Secretary of State to, the Scottish Development Agency and its subsidiaries, on sums paid by the Treasury in pursuance of guarantee of loans to the Agency and on loans guaranteed by the Agency or its subsidiaries.

The Act received the Royal Assent on December 17, 1987.

The Act extends to Scotland only.

3739. Statistics

STATISTICS OF TRADE ACT 1947 (AMENDMENT OF SCHEDULE) ORDER 1987 (No. 669) [45p], made under the Statistics of Trade Act 1947 (c.39), s.5; operative on April 8, 1987; amend the 1947 Act in relation to information required to be furnished under the Act.

3740. Unit trusts

The Department of Trade and Industry has published a guide entitled *Dealers in Securities and Authorised Unit Trust Schemes*. Copies of the guide are available from H.M.S.O. (ISBN 0 11 513980 X) [£7·10].

TRADE MARKS AND TRADE NAMES

3741. Application—opposition—phonetic confusion

[Trade Marks Act 1938 (c.22), ss.11, 12.]

Application was to register LANCER as a trade mark for motor cars. The owners of the LANCIA trade mark opposed on the ground that phonetic confusion was likely. The Registrar allowed the application. Falconer J. decided that in view of the expense, there was no real risk that an unwary purchaser would be confused.

Held, dismissing the appeal, that when buying a car, any phonetic similarity giving rise to confusion would not survive the mechanism of purchase.

LANCER TRADE MARK [1987] R.P.C. 303, C.A.

3742. Application—opposition—whether device marks were trade marks

[Trade Marks Act 1938 (c.22), ss.9, 10, 68.]

A had marketed red and white striped toothpaste since 1960, called SIGNAL. There was no other such toothpaste. In 1977 A applied to register as trade marks in Part A of the Register three device marks with red and white striped toothpaste and one mark with the word RED STRIPES. The Assistant Registrar refused the applications. A appealed.

Held, dismissing the appeal, that (1) the toothpaste was not sufficiently "adapted to distinguish" or "capable of distinguishing"; (2) The red and white stripes were a feature which other traders might legitimately desire to use.

UNILEVER'S (STRIPED TOOTHPASTE NO. 2) TRADE MARKS [1987] R.P.C. 13, Hoffmann J.

3743. Application—phonetic equivalence—relevant public

[Trade Marks Act 1938 (c.22), ss.9, 10.]

A sought to register EXXATE for a chemical, as a Part A mark in class 1. The Registrar refused on the ground that it was the phonetic equivalent of "X8". A appealed.

Held, "EXXATE" was an invented word. it did not sound exactly like "X8". The relevant public were farmers. Appeal allowed.

EXXATE TRADE MARK [1987] R.P.C. 597, Whitford J.

3744. Application—whether mark descriptive or deceptive

[Trade Marks Act 1938 (c.22), ss.9, 10, 11.]

Application was to register the mark PHOTOSCAN in respect of security and surveillance apparatus. The Registrar refused. Some of the scanning apparatus but not all used a photographic process. The applicants appealed to the Secretary of State.

Held, allowing registration in part A for a restricted specification, that (1) "PHOTO" was not deceptive since it indicated a connection with light; (2) the evidence was that the mark was adapted to distinguish the applicants' non-photographic goods; (3) the mark was not adapted to distinguish nor capable of distinguishing photographic goods which scan.

PHOTO-SCAN TRADE MARK [1987] R.P.C. 213, Board of Trade.

3745. Counterfeit goods

COUNTERFEIT GOODS (CONSEQUENTIAL PROVISIONS) REGULATIONS 1987 (No. 1521) [45p], made under the European Communities Act 1976 (c.68), s.2(2); operative on January 1, 1988; made provisions consequential upon Council Regulation (EEC) No. 3842/86 laying down measures to prohibit the release for free circulation of counterfeit goods.

3746. Fees

TRADE MARKS AND SERVICE MARKS (FEES) RULES 1987 (No. 751) [£1·30], made under the Trade Marks Act 1938 (c.22), ss.40, 41; operative on May 26, 1987; revokes and replaces S.I. 1986 No. 1447.

3747. Hallmarks

HALLMARKING (INTERNATIONAL CONVENTION) (AMENDMENT) ORDER 1987 (No. 1892) [85p], made under the Hallmarking Act 1973 (c.43), ss.2(1)(*c*)(3), 21(3), 22(1); operative on December 3, 1987; amend the entry relating to Portugal in S.I. 1976 No. 730.

3748. Infringement—acknowledgement of absolute right to use trade mark—implied term

X used a trademark. He and Y reached an agreement wherein X acknowledged that Y owned absolutely the right to those trade marks.

Held, that it was an implied term of the agreement that X would no longer use the trade marks without Y's licence (*Shell U.K.* v. *Lostock Garages* [1976] C.L.Y. 2766 applied).

SPORT INTERNATIONAL BUSSUM BV *v.* HI-TEC SPORTS, *The Times,* June 23, 1987, C.A.

3749. Infringement—confectionery—TREETS

[Trade Marks Act 1938 (c.22), ss.4, 8, 13.]

P were the registered proprietors of the trade mark TREETS in Part A for confectionery. They also manufactured Mars bars and in 1972 began to market minature versions of the Mars bars in "Fun size" bags. Application by D to register their miniatures as "Treat size" was refused. P sued for infringement and D counter-claimed for expungement of TREETS.

Held, dismissing the action and counterclaim, that (1) There was no risk of confusion and (2) D was not using the phrase TREET SIZE as a trade mark.

MARS G.B. *v.* CADBURY [1987] R.P.C. 387, Whitford J.

3750. Infringement—imported medicines infringing applicants' trade marks—whether infringement a relevant consideration in decision to issue product licence for parallel imports

Infringement of trade mark rights are not relevant considerations for the Secretary of State in the exercise of his power to issue product licences (parallel imports) in respect of drugs manufactured outside the U.K.

Wellcome manufactured and marketed in the U.K. a drug under the registered trade mark Septrin. The drug was also manufactured and marketed in several European countries under the name Septrin or Eusaprim by other Wellcome companies or their licencees. Under the provisions of the Medicines Act 1968 it was unlawful to import the drug into the U.K. without a product licence issued by the Department of Health and Social Security. In 1984, the D.H.S.S. introduced a procedure for the grant of product licences to parallel importers in compliance with recent legislation and decisions in European Community law. On the application form submitted to the D.H.S.S. under the product licence (parallel imports) PL(PI) procedure, the importer was obliged to state the name of the drug for which a licence was sought. A number of PL(PI)'s were issued for a drug identified as Septrin/Eusaprim. The importers marketed the drug under the name Septrin in the U.K. in consequence of which Wellcome commenced various proceedings for infringement of their trade mark rights. Complaints were made to the D.H.S.S. in connection with the licensing of drugs the marketing of which infringed trademark rights. Wellcome asked the D.H.S.S. to take the trade mark position into account in deciding whether to grant PL(PI)'s in respect of Septrin/Eusaprim. The D.H.S.S. advised that trademark issues were excluded from their assessment of the drug for which a PL(PI) was sought although the D.H.S.S. would do their best to ensure that applicants checked their entitlement to use the name of the drug. Wellcome applied for judicial review contending that trade mark issues were relevant considerations that the D.H.S.S. should take into account in deciding whether or not to grant a PL(PI). The application was upheld.

Held, on appeal by the D.H.S.S., that infringements of trade mark rights are not relevant considerations for the Secretary of State in the exercise of his power to issue PL(PI)s. There was nothing to indicate that proprietary rights of individuals as contrasted with considerations of public policy were relevant considerations to the issue of PL(PI)'s particularly where the individual's rights were enforceable by proceedings at the suit of the individual. It was clear from European Community Law that a licence could not be refused on trade mark grounds (*Clin-Midy S.A.* v. *Belgian State (No. 301/82)* [1985] C.L.Y. 1367 applied).

R. *v.* SECRETARY OF STATE FOR SOCIAL SERVICES, *ex p.* WELLCOME FOUNDATION [1987] 2 All E.R. 1025, C.A.

3751. Infringement—logo—absence of confusion

P alleged that D infringed P's trade mark logo. P's mark contained the words "Laura Ashley" within an oval and with a floral sprig. D's contained the words "Coloroll" and a floral sprig, and a swallow.

Held, dismissing the action, that there was no evidence of confusion, despite some similarity; (2) D's intention was irrelevant.

LAURA ASHLEY *v.* COLOROLL [1987] R.P.C. 1, Whitford J.

3752. Non-use—resumption of use to protect registration—whether bona fide

[Trade Marks Act 1938 (c.22), s.26(1).]

P owned CONCORD since 1963 in a U.S. registration. CONCORD cigarettes were marketed in the U.S. in 1985. G was the parent company of the registered users who had not used the mark since 1970. G resumed use to protect their registration in 1986. They sold two million of P's cigarettes. P sought to rectify the register on the ground of continuous non-use for five years.

Held, that the mark CONCORD should be expunged. G's use was not a genuine attempt to establish trading in CONCORD cigarettes (*Imperial Group* v. *Morris (Philip) & Co. (NERIT)* [1982] C.L.Y. 3251 applied).

CONCORD TRADE MARK [1987] F.S.R. 209, Falconer J.

3753. Passing off—menswear—whether local reputation justified grant of nationwide injunction

P began trading as CHELSEA MAN in 1973 in Coventry as men's clothing wholesalers. They subsequently sold clothing in their shops called "Nickelby" in Leicester and London. In 1967 D commenced a large-scale trading operation selling women's clothes entitled CHELSEA GIRL. In 1982 they decided to sell men's clothes entitled CHELSEA MAN. P brought an action to restrain use of the name CHELSEA MAN and D brought a cross-action alleging passing off. Whitford J. granted P a nationwide injunction. On appeal, D argued that the injunction should be restricted to the areas where their shops were located.

Held, dismissing the appeal, that (1) P's business might not necessarily in future be confined to the three proposed areas; (2) since D intended a nationwide chain, prima facie P was entitled to a nationwide injunction (*Brestian* v. *Ivy* [1958] C.L.Y. 3409 applied).

CHELSEA MAN MENSWEAR *v.* CHELSEA GIRL [1987] R.P.C. 189, C.A.

3754. Rectification—non-use—person aggrieved

[Trade Marks Act 1938 (c.22), s.26.]

The applicants, K, had a name, KODAK which was protected by registration in class 38 since 1925, in respect of all articles of clothing. The apellants, W, since 1945 used in Canada and the U.S.A. the trade mark KODIAK in relation to their boots. KODAK was cited as a bar to the progress by W to register KODIAK in the U.K. W applied to expunge K's registration for non-use. K assented bona fide use of their mark and alleged that W were not persons aggrieved because they sought total removal of K's mark whereas their own mark related only to boots. The registrar amended the register so that KODAK's registration read "All goods included in class 38 except footwear." K's contention as to *locus standi* was accepted by Whitford J.

Held, on appeal, that W did have *locus standi* despite claiming relief which might be wider than that to which he was ultimately found to be entitled.

KODIAK TRADE MARK [1987] R.P.C. 269, C.A.

3755. Rectification—person aggrieved—application

[Trade Marks Act 1938 (c.22), s.26(1).]

A "person aggrieved" may properly apply for rectification of the Register of Trade Marks notwithstanding that his application was on wider grounds than that to which he was entitled.

WARRINGTON INC.'s APPLICATION, *Re, The Times,* February 9, 1987, C.A.

3756. Rectification—registered user agreement—overseas proprietor

[India] [Trade Marks and Merchandising Act 1958 (India), ss.2, 18, 46, 48, 56; Trade Marks Act 1938 (c.22), ss.28, 29; Indian Evidence Act 1847, s.14.]

A sold the antihistamine DRISTAN. A registered the mark with a view to user in India in 1958. A and G entered into a registered user agreement in 1961 and sought to register it in 1962. R in 1960 sought to register TRISTINE. A opposed the application. In 1961 R applied for rectification by the removal of DRISTAN from the register. The Registrar refused. The High Court reversed the order. A appealed to the Supreme Court.

Held, that (1) intention to use through a registered user is adequate. This legal fiction was for any purpose for which such use is material under the Act; (2) the agreements between A and G M showed bona fides, there was no evidence of trafficking in the mark. DRISTAN should not be removed from the Register (*Pussy Galore Trade Mark* [1967] C.L.Y. 3971 distinguished).

DRISTAN TRADE MARK [1986] R.P.C. 161, Supreme Court of India.

3757. Service marks

TRADE MARKS AND SERVICE MARKS (FEES) (AMENDMENT) RULES 1987 (No. 964) [45p], made under the Trade Marks Act 1938 (c.22), ss.40, 41; operative on May 26, 1987; correct an error in S.I. 1987 No. 751.

TRADE MARKS AND SERVICE MARKS (RELEVANT COUNTRIES) (AMENDMENT) ORDER 1987 (No. 170) [45p], made under the Trade Marks Act 1938 (c.22), s.39A(7); operative on March 11, 1987; amends Sched. 2 to S.I. 1986 No. 1303.

3758. Similarity of trade marks—risk of confusion

Registration of a trade mark will not be refused on the grounds of likely confusion with a registered mark unless there is a real and not a fanciful risk of confusion amongst a substantial number of people.

Fiat, who manufactured Lancia tried to prevent Mitsubishi from registering the word "Lancer" for one of its cars, as opposed to "Colt Lancer" which it had previously used. The two marks were visually easily distinguishable. The assistant registrar and the judge dismissed the opposition.

Held, dismissing the appeal, that there must be a real, not a fanciful risk of confusion amongst a substantial number of persons, and in the present case there was not.

MITSUBISHI *v.* FIAT [1987] 1 FTLR 260, C.A.

TRADE UNIONS

3759. Assets—branch funds—whether part of union's assets

Funds belonging to a branch of a trade union held by trustees appointed by the branch subject to directions from the branch do not form part of the trade union's assets.

A writ of sequestration was issued against SOGAT 1982 for contempt of court. The commissioners named in the writ applied for directions. The London branch of the union intervened claiming that its branch funds were not the property of the union and thus not subject to sequestration. The trial judge found against the branch. The branch appealed where it became apparent that the branch funds were held by three trustees appointed under the branch's rules. The rules provided that the branch funds be used to finance the activities and benefits of the branch. The rules also provided for the trustees to comply with any directions from the branch.

Held, allowing the appeal, that the branch funds did not form part of the union's assets but belonged solely and exclusively to the branch for its own use. It could not be said that the branch funds were held on trust for the union. The branch was an unincorporated association holding its own funds. There was no trust that could be described as void for perpetuity or as a non-charitable purpose trust (*Neville Estates* v. *Madden* [1961] C.L.Y. 1002, *Grant's Will Trusts, Re* [1980] C.L.Y. 2412 considered).

NEWS GROUP NEWSPAPERS *v.* SOCIETY OF GRAPHICAL AND ALLIED TRADES 1982 [1986] I.C.R. 716, C.A.

3760. Breach of union rules—interlocutory injunction—interference with domestic tribunal

[Trade Unions Act 1984 (c.49), s.10.]

Following a move by News International of its titles, all journalists were instructed to report for work to Wapping. In accordance with legal advice, the N.U.J. chapel voted to comply with this instruction. The union's National Executive Committee ("N.E.C.") subsequently issued an instruction, which was not authorised by strike ballot under s.10 of the 1984 Act, to its members not to report for work at Wapping. A complaint was laid against the fathers of the relevant chapels, including Mr. L, for failing to comply with the N.E.C. instruction. Before the N.E.C. complaints committee met to hear the complaint, Mr. L applied for an interlocutory injunction restraining the N.U.J. from taking disciplinary action for failure to comply with the instruction. The injunction was refused and Mr. L appealed.

Held, dismissing the appeal, that Mr. L had not proved conclusively that he was bound to succeed at trial, even though he had established that there were serious questions to be determined. Therefore, the test of the balance of convenience should be applied and this weighed against granting an interlocutory injunction. The Court should not intervene to restrain adjudication by a domestic tribunal unless it had acted improperly or it was inevitable that it would do so, and there was no evidence to suggest that this was the case. It was in the union's members' interests for a domestic tribunal appointed under their rules to deal with issues relating to the rules, unless there was good reason for intervention.

LONGLEY *v.* NATIONAL UNION OF JOURNALISTS [1987] I.R.L.R. 109, C.A.

3761. Certification officer

CERTIFICATION OFFICER (AMENDMENT OF FEES) REGULATIONS 1987 (No. 258) [45p], made under the Trade Union (Amalgamations, etc.) Act 1964 (c.24), s.7 the Trade Union and Labour Relations Act 1974 (c.52), s.8(4) and the Employment Protection Act 1975 (c.71), s.8(2); operative on April 1, 1987; increase specified fees.

3762. Collective agreement—coal industry conciliation agreement—consultation—new union—whether legally enforceable

[Coal Industry Nationalisation Act 1946 (c.59), s.46.]

The coal industry conciliation agreement entered into in 1946 in pursuance of the National Coal Board's duties under s.46 of the Coal Industry Nationalisation Act 1946 under which exclusive recognition was granted to the National Union of Mineworkers is not legally binding on the Board or the Union; further s.46 of the Act imposes a continuing obligation on the Board to consult with all organisations representing substantial numbers of the Board's employees.

Section 46 of the Coal Industry Nationalisation Act 1946 imposed an obligation on the National Coal Board to consult with organisations appearing to represent substantial proportions of persons in the employment of the Board with a view to concluding agreements providing for the negotiation and settlement of issues between the Board and its employees. In 1946 the National Union of Mineworkers represented the interests of the vast majority of mineworkers. The Board and N.U.M. entered into a conciliation agreement under which the N.U.M. was granted exclusive recognition. The agreement established a Joint National Negotiating Committee and provided for any matter which the Committee were unable to agree upon to be referred to the National Reference Tribunal. Each individual mineworker's contract of employment provided that it should be regulated by and subject to such national agreements as were for the time being in force. In consequence of the 1984 coal strike the Union of Democratic Mineworkers emerged representing over 30,000 mineworkers. The U.D.M. sought recognition from the Board to negotiate on behalf of its members. The Board gave notice to terminate its agreement with the N.U.M. as from May 31, 1986 and invited the N.U.M. and the U.D.M. to negotiate a new conciliation agreement. The N.U.M. refused and sought to refer the question of changes to the existing conciliation agreement to the N.R.T. Clause 38 of the mineworkers' pension scheme provided for disputes as to amendment of the pension scheme to be referred to the N.R.T. A dispute arose between the Board and the N.U.M. in connection with the pension scheme which the N.U.M. referred to the N.R.T. The Board sought declarations as to the status of the conciliation agreement and injunctions to restrain the N.R.T. from considering the disputes referred to it.

Held, that the conciliation agreement was a collective agreement. In the absence of any provision stating that the parties intended it to be legally enforceable the agreement was not legally enforceable. Accordingly both the Board and the N.U.M. were entitled to disregard the agreement if they so wished. Section 46 of the Act imposes a continuing statutory obligation on the Board. The U.D.M. represented a substantial proportion of mineworkers. The Board was under a duty to consult the U.D.M. with a view to establishing conciliation procedures for the industry. The N.R.T. became dissolved as from May 31, 1986 when the Board indicated it would no longer be bound by the conciliation agreement notwithstanding that the N.R.T. was the forum designated for the resolution of disputes in connection with the mineworkers' pension scheme. Injunctions would be granted restraining the N.U.M. from proceeding with the references to the N.R.T. of the issues that had been referred to it. The conciliation agreement was not incorporated in individual mineworkers' contracts of employment. The agreement and its surrounding circumstances indicated that it should not be enforceable at the suit of an individual mineworker. Even if it were incorporated in individual contracts there was nothing to indicate that it was intended to be legally enforceable by individual mineworkers (*R.* v. *Industrial Disputes Tribunal, ex p. Portland Urban District Council* [1955] C.L.Y. 962, *National Coal Board* v. *Galley* [1958] C.L.Y. 868, *Ford Motor Co.* v. *Amalgamated Union of Engineering and Foundry Workers* [1969] C.L.Y. 3570, *Monterosso Shipping Co.* v. *International Transport Workers' Federation* [1982] C.L.Y. 2904, *Robertson* v. *British Gas Corp.* [1983] C.L.Y. 1213 considered).

NATIONAL COAL BOARD *v.* NATIONAL UNION OF MINEWORKERS [1986] I.C.R. 736, Scott J.

3763. Elections—irregularities investigated in accordance with Unions rule book—whether member entitled to pursue complaints before the court.

A member of the General Municipal Boilermakers and Allied Trades Union who made allegations of irregularities in an election that were dealt with in accordance with the Union's rule book was unable to pursue his allegations by way of legal proceedings before the Court.

H stood as a candidate for election to be the district delegate for the South Coast of the General Municipal Boilermakers and Allied Trades Union. H was defeated and thereafter made complaint to the Union's executive council alleging irregularities in connection with the election. The result of the election was confirmed by the executive council and H's appeal to the general council of the Union was rejected. H commenced proceedings seeking a declaration that he was duly elected to the office in question on a declaration that the election was null and void. In support of those declarations H sought to rely upon the following matters:—(a) that the election at two branches was improperly conducted; (b) that the election at those branches was conducted by officials who were not entitled to do so in consequence of which the votes recorded should not count towards the result of the election; and (c) that four members of the executive council took part in the determination of H's appeal by the general council so that the decision of the general council was vitiated by a breach of natural justice. The Union applied to strike out H's statement of claim as disclosing no cause of action.

Held, allowing the Union's application, that the election irregularities complained of by H were properly considered by the executive council and general council of the Union. There was no suggestion that the machinery set out in the Union's rule book for dealing with such complaints had not been properly implemented. H's complaints could not be heard in court by way of appeal from that process. The matters relied on under (b) were also election irregularities that fell to be dealt with by complaint to the executive council of the Union. The fact that H failed to complain of those irregularities within the required time limit did not entitle H to raise those matters before the court. As to the matters relied on under (c), there was no rule of natural justice that prevented members of the executive council who considered H's initial complaints from sitting on the general council that considered H's appeal. In any event H could not complain of a breach of natural justice when the complaints H had made were dealt with according to the rules of the Union by which he was bound in contract as a member of the Union (*Dawkins* v. *Antrobus* (1881) 17 Ch.D. 615, *Knox* v. *Gye* (1872) L.R. 5 H.L. 656 applied).

HAMLET *v.* GENERAL MUNICIPAL BOILERMAKERS AND ALLIED TRADES UNION [1987] I.C.R. 150, Harman J.

3764. Industrial action—injunction—contempt. See KENT FREE PRESS *v.* NATIONAL GRAPHICAL ASSOCIATION, §2938.

3765. Industrial action—trade union ballot—unlawful interference with contract—whether trade union liable in damages to those who suffered loss as a result of a strike called without a ballot

[Trade Union and Labour Relations Act 1974 (c.52), (as amended) s.30(1); Trade Union Act 1984 (c.49), ss.10, 11.]

P had purchased a ticket from British Rail to travel by train in order to attend a business appointment. As a result of trade union action which caused the withdrawal of labour by British Rail employees, P was unable to travel on the date he wished and consequently he was obliged to incur hotel expenses. The D's had failed to call a ballot of its members in accordance with ss.10 and 11 of the Trade Union Act 1984 before withdrawing the labour. P alleged that the D's were liable to him for damages suffered as a result of their unlawful interference with the contract he had made with British Rail.

Held, that the D's had failed to comply with the requirements of the Trade Union Act 1984 and could not therefore rely on the statutory immunity from liability in tort. The D's knew of the existence of contracts between British Rail and passengers who had already purchased tickets at the time the strike was called, and they intended to interfere with the performance of such contracts by inducing British Rail employees to withdraw their labour. The interference with the performance of the contract between P and British Rail was a necessary consequence of the D's actions and therefore they were liable to him for damages.

FALCONER *v.* A.S.L.E.F. AND N.U.R. [1986] I.R.L.R. 331, Sheffield County Ct.

3766. Membership—action short of dismissal—non-payment of wage increase—whether action taken against members as individuals

[Employment Protection (Consolidation) Act 1978 (c.44), ss.23, 153.]

The N.C.B. agreed to pay increased wages to members of one trade union, the U.D.M. but not to members of another, the N.U.M. who worked alongside them. Members of the N.U.M. complained to an industrial tribunal that this was a breach of s.23(1)(*a*) of the 1978 Act. The tribunal found in their favour, finding also that the N.C.B.'s purpose was to penalise employees for being members of the N.U.M.

Held, that the term "action" in s.23 included omission so the failure to pay equal wages came within the section. Here employees were affected otherwise than merely as members of a trade union, and so were affected "as an individual". The section should be construed so as to include penalising an employee for belonging to any particular union. The board's action thus came within the section (*Carlson* v. *Post Office* [1981] C.L.Y. 2814 approved; *Ruth* v. *Cruden Construction* [1981] C.L.Y. 1110 considered).

NATIONAL COAL BOARD *v.* RIDGWAY *sub nom.* RIDGWAY AND FAIRBROTHER *v.* NATIONAL COAL BOARD [1987] I.C.R. 641, C.A.

3767. Referendum by union members—consequent instruction by union—whether *ultra vires*

[Trade Union and Labour Relations Act 1974 (c.52) (as amended), s.2(5).]

At their 1985 Annual General Meeting, the British Actors Equity Association carried a motion demanding that the union's Council issue an instruction that any Equity member who accepted work in South Afica would be expelled from the union. The Council held a membership referendum as a result of which it was voted to pass the resolution. The Council, which was bound by decisions on referendum, consequently issued the instruction. Under the union rules, a member failing to comply with an instruction could be expelled. P sought a declaration that the instruction was *ultra vires* and void.

Held, that the instruction that no member could accept professional engagements involving work in South Africa was *ultra vires* the union's rules and was therefore void. The objects of the union were stated in the rules to be those of "a non-party political and unsectarian union." The rules also provided that the union had a duty "to acknowledge the right of individual members to hold and express their personal and political and other beliefs both in their private and professional capacities." Therefore the purpose for which an instruction was issued is decisive in determining whether it is allowed under the rules. The Court could not accept that the only question was whether the instruction was capable of achieving one of the union's objects, regardless of its underlying purpose. In the event that the primary purpose was forbidden, it was irrelevant that it may be possible to establish that an instruction could achieve one of the union's objects. Furthermore, it was not accepted that the membership referendum operated as an alteration of the rules, since such an alteration had not been brought to the attention of the members prior to the vote. P's argument that the instruction unlawfully interfered with a member's right to work was not accepted, since the member had voluntarily submitted to the rules of the union.

GORING *v.* BRITISH ACTORS EQUITY ASSOCIATION [1987] I.R.L.R. 122, Browne-Wilkinson V.-C.

3768. Rules—benefits payable to members—alteration of approval requirement by Rules Revision Meeting

A trade union rule that required the approval of 40 per cent. of affected members before any abogration of benefits payable to its members could not be removed from the union's rules without the sanction of such a vote.

The rules of the A.U.E.W. provided for their alteration at a rules revision meeting. Rule 14, clause 14 provided that no rules revision meeting should have the power to abrogate any of the principal benefits of the union *viz.,* unemployment, sickness, permanent disablement, superannuation or funeral benefits unless 40 per cent. of the affected members voted in favour of the abrogation. The rules revision committee that approved the rules was recalled in September 1979 and resolved to dispense with the 40 per cent. voting requirement. In 1980 the new quinquennial rules revision meeting resolved to abrogate sickness and unemployment benefits. The plaintiffs being dissatisfied members sought declarations that the resolutions were void.

Held, that rule 14, clause 14 could not be amended without the sanction of 40 per cent. of the union members. Although not expressly stated, such an implication was required to give effect to what the authors of the rules intended, namely that there should be no abrogation of benefits without the approval of 40 per cent. of the affected members (dicta of Lord Wilberforce in *Heatons Transport (St. Helens)* v. *Transport and General Workers' Union* [1972] C.L.Y. 3452 and Viscount Dilhorne in *British Actors' Equity Association* v. *Goring* [1978] C.L.Y. 3003 applied, *Watt* v. *MacLaughlin* [1923] 1 I.R. 112, *Edwards* v. *Halliwell* (1950) C.L.C. 10390 considered).

JACQUES *v.* AMALGAMATED UNION OF ENGINEERING WORKERS (ENGINEERING SECTION) [1986] I.C.R. 683, Warner J.

3769. Strike action—whether interference with trade or business by unlawful means—interlocutory injunction to restrain action

Strike action by fatstock officers employed by the Meat and Livestock Commission at abattoirs throughout the country was not an interference with the trade or business of the abattoir owners by unlawful means.

P were members of the Association of British Abattoir Owners and associated companies in the meat trade. The Meat and Livestock Commission (MLC) was a statutory body set up to carry out statutory duties in connection with the certification of slaughtered animals for the purposes of EEC subsidies and intervention buying to prevent the bottom falling out of the meat market. The MLC employed 630 fatstock officers to carry out its functions. The fatstock officers worked at P's abattoirs. The fatstock officers through their trade union, D, were engaged in an industrial dispute concerning pay and conditions. They voted by a substantial majority to take strike action in support of their grievances. P sought an interlocutory injunction to restrain D from interfering in their business by taking or inducing strike action on the part of their members. D's members had already carried out a one-day lightning strike that had caused great inconvenience and additional expense to P in the course of their business. P founded their claim to relief upon a tort of interfering with their trade, business or employment contracts by unlawful means. The unlawful means relied upon were the inducement or procurement of a breach of statutory duty by the MLC or alternatively the breach by individual fatstock officers of their contracts of employment with the MLC.

Held, that to establish the tort of interference with P's trade or business by unlawful means, four ingredients had to be proved; (1) interference with P's trade or businss, (2) unlawful means, (3) an intention to injure P and (4) actual injury to P. Ingredients (1) and (4) were admitted. So far as unlawful means by breach of statutory duty was concerned, it was arguable that the MLC owed P a statutory duty. The MLC's statutory duty owed was a duty to provide a system adequate to carry out its functions. It was not under a duty to provide a strike-free system. The proposed strike action would not result in a breach of that duty in as much as the system was still in existence but temporarily inoperative. In consequence, unlawful means could not be established. So far as the breach of contract by individual fatstock officers by taking strike action was concerned, it was arguable that it amounted to unlawful means. However, it could not be demonstrated that there was any intention to injure P. The desire to strike was the cause of P's injury rather than the desire to injure P being the cause of the strike. The intention of D's members was to promote the settlement of their dispute. In any event, no injunction could be granted against individual fatstock officers by virtue of s.16 of the Trade Union and Labour Relations Act 1974. Even if P had been able to establish an arguable case, the relative injustices flowing from the grant or refusal of the relief sought lay in favour of refusing interlocutory relief to P (*N.W.L.* v. *Woods* [1979] C.L.Y. 2716, *Merkur Island Shipping Corp.* v. *Laughton* [1983] C.L.Y. 3704 applied; *Rookes* v. *Barnard* [1964] C.L.Y. 3703 considered).

BARRETTS & BAIRD (WHOLESALE) *v.* INSTITUTION OF PROFESSIONAL CIVIL SERVANTS [1987] 1 FTLR 121, Henry J.

3770. Suspension of industrial action following union ballot—whether resumption in furtherance of dispute—whether new ballot required

[Trade Union Act 1984 (c.49), s.10.]

A trade union may lawfully resume industrial action begun lawfully, but which had been suspended pending negotiations, without holding a fresh ballot, provided that the dispute is the same dispute in respect of which the original ballot had been held.

On an industrial dispute arising, the TGWU held a ballot, the result of which was in favour of industrial action being taken. Negotiations began, and the industrial action was suspended while they were conducted, but always on the basis that the industrial action would be recommenced if the negotiations broke down. The negotiations did break down and the industrial action recommenced.

Held, on M's claim that a fresh ballot should have been held, that no fresh ballot was needed. Once a proper ballot had been held at the beginning of a dispute, a temporary cessation of industrial action during the currency of negotiations did not mean that a fresh ballot was required if the negotiations broke down, provided of course that the industrial action was being re-imposed in respect of the same dispute.

MONSANTO *v.* TRANSPORT AND GENERAL WORKERS' UNION [1987] 1 All E.R. 358, C.A.

3771. Trade dispute—picketing, marches and demonstrations—abusive, threatening and violent behaviour—whether public nuisance—intimidation—harassment—interference with contracts—liability of trade union—suing branch officials in representative capacity

[Trade Union and Labour Relations Act 1974 (c.52), ss.13, 15.]

Interlocutory injunctions were granted in favour of the plaintiffs in an action alleging public nuisance, intimidation, harassment and interference with contracts by reason of abusive threatening and violent picketing, marches and demonstrations held in the course of a trade dispute between the plaintiffs and their former employees.

The plaintiffs were a group of companies involved in the printing and publishing of newspapers at Grays Inn Road and Bouverie Street in London. The defendants were trade unions representing P's employees and a number of branch officials sued in a representative capacity on behalf of all the members of the branches concerned. In January 1986, after unsuccessful negotiations between P and the unions in connection with pay and working practices, P's employees went on strike. The employees were sacked and P successfully transferred production of its newspapers to new premises at Wapping. The unions concerned organised daily pickets at Bouverie Street, Grays Inn Road and Wapping confined to six official pickets and occasional mass demonstrations. In addition other ex-employees of P attended at all three sites on a daily basis to demonstrate against P. Marches and rallies also took place. P's employees working at all three sites were subjected to abusive and threatening behaviour on a daily basis, some were assaulted. Mass demonstrations attempted to prevent traffic passing to and fro from Wapping and delay the distribution of P's newspapers. These demonstrations were accompanied by acts of serious violence and public disturbance which the unions contended were not caused by their members. P employed TNT to distribute their newspapers. There were frequent attacks on TNT vehicles and employees in the vicinity of Wapping and further afield. P commenced proceedings against D and sought interlocutory injunctions against D to limit any picketing to such as was lawfully permitted and to restrain D from inciting, inducing, procuring, persuading, assisting, encouraging, financing or facilitating any marches demonstrations or picketing involving the commission of unlawful acts. P's claim was based on public nuisance, tortious intimidation and harassment and tortious interference with contracts. D claimed the torts were not made out and as they were not responsible for them they could not be liable.

Held, that the conduct of the pickets and demonstrators was an unreasonable use of the highway that caused an obstruction and was therefore unlawful. It was actionable as a public nuisance if P could show substantial particular damage in consequence thereof. P established substantial particular damage at Wapping in the need to bus employees into the premises, provide extra security and in loss of journalists who were not willing to work on the newspapers but had not established damage at Grays Inn Road or Bouverie Street. P's claim in public nuisance was established so far as Wapping was concerned. Idle abuse that was not to be taken seriously would not found an action for intimidation. The threats made by the pickets were serious threats to dissuade P's employees from working at Wapping and taken seriously by those that received them. There was a real risk that the employees would succumb to them. The case for an injunction was made out even though the tort of intimidation was not complete unless the person threatened succumbed and damage was suffered. Such relief could be granted to an employer who is at risk of losing his employees. The existence of a tort of harassment as expounded by Scott J. in *Thomas* v. *National Union of Mineworkers (South Wales Area)* was doubtful. P's claims for unlawful interference with contracts was only made out with regard to P's contract with TNT to distribute P's newspapers. D knew TNT were performing a distribution contract for P's newspapers, there was unlawful interference with the contract by the commission of the torts of nuisance and intimidation and as a necessary consequence TNT were prevented or hindered from performing their primary obligation under the contract to deliver newspapers by a stipulated time. S.13 of the Trade Union and Labour Relations Act 1974 did not confer immunity on D in respect of the torts of nuisance and intimidation. The section referred only to interference with contracts. In any event the immunity did not apply to activities at Wapping on account of the fact that Wapping could not be described as "at or near" the pickets' and demonstrating ex-employees "place of work" within the meaning of s.15 of the Act. D were not liable simply because they organised a march or picketing during which tortious acts are committed by third parties even though such acts could be foreseen. There was sufficient evidence to show that D had authorised or continued the nuisance and intimidation having regard to the number of incidents that had occurred and the period of time involved. D was able to exercise substantial control over its members. If they could not control their members they should not organise the activities in question. The branch officials could not be sued in a representative capacity. The members of each branch would likely have divergent defences to P's claims. The branches were organisations which were trade unions within the meaning of s.28(1) of the Trade Union and Labour Relations Act 1974 and liable to be sued in their own name rather than by way of representative action. The balance of convenience lay in favour of granting the interlocutory injunctions P sought, P and their employees would be protected against unlawful conduct and D would still be able to picket and demonstrate peacefully (*Att-Gen.* v. *P.Y.A. Quarries* [1957] C.L.Y. 2579, *Thomas* v. *National Union of Mineworkers (South Wales Area)* [1985] C.L.Y. 3526, *Torquay Hotel Co.* v. *Cousins* [1969] C.L.Y. 3579, *Merkur Island Shipping Corp.* v. *Laughton* [1983] C.L.Y. 3704, *Dimbleby & Sons* v. *National Union of Journalists* [1984] C.L.Y. 3553, *Plessey Co.* v. *Wilson* [1982] C.L.Y. 3281, *Prudential Assurance Co.* v. *Lorenz* [1972] C.L.Y. 1270, *Barber* v. *Penley* [1893] 2 Ch. 447, *Perl (P.) (Exporters)* v. *Camden London Borough Council* [1982] C.L.Y. 2531, *Smith* v. *Scott* [1972] C.L.Y. 2532, *Sedleigh-Denfield* v. *O'Callaghan* [1940] A.C. 880 considered).

NEWS GROUP NEWSPAPERS *v.* SOCIETY OF GRAPHICAL AND ALLIED TRADES '82 (No. 2) [1987] I.C.R. 181, Stuart-Smith J.

3772. Unincorporated association—*locus standi*—whether unincorporated association could be classified as a trade union. See CLUBS AND ASSOCIATIONS, §313.

TRANSPORT

3773. Bridges

BEDFORDSHIRE COUNTY COUNCIL (LEIGHTON—LINSLADE SOUTHERN BYPASS YTTINGAFORD BRIDGE) NUMBER TWO SCHEME 1985 CONFIRMATION INSTRUMENT 1987 (No. 1954) [85p], made under the Highways Act 1980 (c.66), ss.106(3) and 325; the said scheme is confirmed without modifications.

BUCKINGHAMSHIRE COUNTY COUNCIL H8 STANDING WAY (CANAL BRIDGE) SCHEME 1987 CONFIRMATION INSTRUMENT 1987 (No. 2241) [85p], made under the Highways Act 1980, ss.106(2) and 325; confirms a scheme for the construction of a bridge over the navigable waters of the Grand Union Canal at Tinkers Bridge, Milton Keynes.

COUNTY COUNCIL OF WEST MIDLANDS (BLACK COUNTRY ROUTE) (BRIDGE OVER BIRMINGHAM CANAL (WOLVERHAMPTON LEVEL)) SCHEME 1985 CONFIRMATION INSTRUMENT 1987 (No. 251) [£1·90], made under the Highways Act 1980 (c.66), s.106(3); confirms a scheme for the construction of a bridge over the Birmingham Canal.

S.I. 1987 Nos. 544 (Cheshire County Council—Forrest Way Bridge, Warrington) [£1·60]; 791 (Devon County Council—Exeter, River Exe Bridge) [85p]; 945 (Essex County Council—Blackwater Canal Bridge) [85p]; 946 (Essex County Council—Chelmer Viaduct) [£1·30]; 947 (Essex County Council—Whiteladies Canal Bridge) [£1·30]; 2084 (Stoneferry Bridge, Kingston upon Hull—County Council of Humberside) [85p].

3774. Bus companies

BUS COMPANIES (DISSOLUTION) ORDER 1987 (No. 1613) [45p], made under the Transport Act 1985 (c.67), s.47(12)(13); operative on October 14, 1987; dissolves a number of specified bus companies.

3775. Channel Tunnel Act—competition

CHANNEL TUNNEL ACT (COMPETITION) ORDER 1987 (No. 2068) [45p], made under the Channel Tunnel Act 1987 (c.53), s.33(2); operative on December 17, 1987; provides for the application of competition legislation to the persons ("the Concessionaires") who have the function of constructing and operating a tunnel rail link between the U.K. and France.

3776. Channel Tunnel Act 1987 (c.53)

This Act provides for the construction and operation of a railway tunnel system under the English Channel, and for connected improvements in the road network near Ashford in Kent and in the rail network in South Eastern England. The Act incorporates part of the railway tunnel system into the U.K. and provides for the application and enforcement of law in relation to, and for the regulation of, that system and matters connected with it. The Act also provides for the construction of certain highways and associated works in the vicinity of Folkestone.

The Act received the Royal Assent on July 23, 1987.

The Act extends to Northern Ireland.

3777. Fares—commercial bus services—assessment of fare scale

[Transport Act 1968 (c.73), s.9A(6)(*a*).]

The words "public transport requirements" in s.9A(6) of the Transport Act 1968 refer to requirements of the public to travel and to pay a fare that they can reasonably afford. The requirements in part depend on local social conditions. A transport authority's assessment of those requirements can only be impugned in court on the ground of irrationality. The duty not to inhibit competition in para. (*a*) of subs. 6 requires a regard to fare scales on commercial bus services comparable with a subsidised service.

R. *v.* MERSEYSIDE PASSENGER TRANSPORT AUTHORITY, *ex p.* CROSVILLE MOTOR SERVICES, *The Times*, April 4, 1987, D.C.

3778. Highways—excavation of highway without permission from highway authority—whether absence of knowledge that permission required was "lawful authority or excuse"

[Highways Act 1980 (c.66), s.131(1).]

Ignorance of the law could not amount to "lawful authority or excuse".

D's premises were linked to the road by three crossings forming part of the highway. Without seeking permission from or informing the council who were the highway authority, D started to carry out repairs to one of the crossings. The repairs involved excavation of the highway. D was charged with an offence contrary to s.131(1) of the Highways Act 1980 of making an excavation in a highway without lawful authority or excuse. D claimed that it did not know permission from the highway authority was required. The case was dismissed on the basis that D's lack of knowledge constituted a "lawful excuse".

Held, allowing the highway authority's appeal, that ignorance of the law was no defence. The fact that D did not know permission was required could not amount to a lawful excuse within the meaning of s.131(1) of the Act.

GREENWICH LONDON BOROUGH COUNCIL *v.* MILLCROFT CONSTRUCTION (1987) 85 L.G.R. 66, D.C.

3779. Highways—obstruction of highway—sale of produce from trailer on footpath

[Highways Act 1980 (c.66), s.137.]

B sold vegetables from a trailer positioned at the front boundary of his property. It projected nine feet onto the footpath, and took up half the width of the path.

Held, that such an obstruction was not *de minimis.*

HERTFORDSHIRE COUNTY COUNCIL *v.* BOLDEN, *The Times,* December 9, 1986, D.C.

3780. International passenger services

ROAD TRANSPORT (INTERNATIONAL PASSENGER SERVICES) (AMENDMENT) REGULATIONS 1987 (No. 1755) [45p], made under the European Communities Act 1972 (c.68), s.2(2), the Public Passenger Vehicles Act 1981 (c.14), s.60(1)(1A) and the Finance Act 1973 (c.51), s.56(1); operative on November 1, 1987; amend S.I. 1984 No. 748.

3781. Light railways

DERWENT VALLEY RAILWAYS (TRANSFER) LIGHT RAILWAY ORDER 1987 (No. 75) [80p], made under the Light Railways Act 1986 (c.48), ss.7, 9, 12, 24; operative on January 22, 1987; transfers a length of railway from the Derwent Valley Railway Company to the Yorkshire Museum of Farming.

NORTH NORFOLK (EXTENSION AND AMENDMENT) LIGHT RAILWAY ORDER 1987 (No. 950) [£1·30], made under the Light Railways Act 1896, ss.7, 9–12, 24; operative on May 14, 1987; make provision in relation to the operation of the said Light Railway.

SOUTH TYNEDALE RAILWAY (LIGHT RAILWAY) ORDER 1987 (No. 1984) [85p], made under the Light Railways Act 1896, ss.3, 7, 9, 12; operative on November 12, 1987; makes provision for the operation of the South Tynedale Railway.

SWANAGE LIGHT RAILWAY ORDER 1987 (No. 1443) [£1·30], made under the Light Railways Act 1896 (c.48), ss.3, 7–10, the Light Railways Act 1912 (c.19), The Railways Act 1921 (c.55), Pt. V, and the Transport Act 1968 (c.73), s.121(4); operative on August 7, 1987; provides for the operation of the said light railway.

YORKSHIRE DALES LIGHT RAILWAY ORDER 1987 (No. 1088) [£1·30], made under the Light Railways Act 1896, ss.7, 9–12 and the Railways Act 1921 (c.55), Pt. V; operative on June 24, 1987; makes provisions in relation to the operation of the said light railway.

3782. London Regional Transport—levy. See LONDON, §2396.

3783. Motorways

M20 MOTORWAY (MAIDSTONE EAST INTERCHANGE) CONNECTING ROADS SCHEME 1987 (No. 1429) [45p], made under the Highways Act 1980 (c.66), s.16; operative on August 24, 1987; provides seven special roads for the purpose of connecting the said motorway with other highways.

3784. Rail freight facilities—undertaking to pay grant—withdrawal—necessity for reasons

[Railways Act 1974 (c.48), (as amended by Transport Act 1978 (c.55), s.16.)]

Where the Secretary of State decides to withdraw his undertaking to pay a grant for the provision of said freight facilities, he should give his reasons to the applicant to enable him to make representations. Furthermore, para. 2.6 of the Transport Department's "Memorandum of Explanation" fettered his discretion and was therefore *ultra vires.*

R. *v.* SECRETARY OF STATE FOR TRANSPORT, *ex p.* SHERRIF & SONS, *The Times,* December 18, 1986, Taylor J.

3785. Railway track—direct route—whether a "line" for the purposes of discontinuation of passenger services

[Transport Act 1962 (c.46), s.56(7).]

A stretch of railway track which forms part of a direct route between two stations is a "line" for the purposes of s.56(7) of the Transport Act 1962.

R. *v.* BRITISH RAILWAYS BOARD, *ex p.* BRADFORD CITY METROPOLITAN COUNCIL, *The Times,* December 8, 1987, C.A.

3786. Regulation—safety of alighting passengers—charged with breach of regulation—whether bad for duplicity. See AMOS *v.* D.P.P., §669.

3787. Special roads

S.I. 1987 Nos. 252 (M6—Junction 10) [45p]; 1057 (M40 London—Oxford—Birmingham) [45p]; 1070 (A41 (M) Watford-Tring) [45p]; 1367 (M3—Compton—Bassett) [45p]; 1368 (M3—Compton—Bassett) [45p]; 1369 (M3—Compton—Bassett) [45p]; 1370 (M3—Compton—Bassett) [45p]; 1371 (M3—Hockley—Compton) [45p]; 1372 (M3—Popham—Hockley) [45p]; 1441 (M57—Huyton Spur) [45p]; 1867 (A423(M)—Maidenhead Thicket Section) [45p]; 2147 (M275 Rudmore Flyover Portsmouth [£1·30]; 2253 (M1—Catthorpe Interchange) [45p]; 2254 (M6—Catthorpe Interchange) [45p].

3788. Taxi sharing scheme

HEATHROW TAXI SHARING SCHEME ORDER 1987 (No. 784) [85p], made under the Transport Act 1985 (c.67), s.10(4)–(6)(10); operative on June 1, 1987; provides for a taxi sharing scheme operating from Terminal 1, Heathrow to authorised destinations.

3789. Taxis—licences—de-restriction—effect on drivers

[Transport Act 1985 (c.67), s.16.]

Even where there was material before the court to show that some individual taxi drivers might suffer hardship, that was not of itself sufficient to show that the authority had exercised its powers, irrationally, nor that it had taken into account irrelevant material.

R. *v.* GREAT YARMOUTH BOROUGH COUNCIL, *ex p.* SAWYER, *The Times,* June 18, 1987, C.A.

3790. Taxis—licences—numerical limit

[Transport Act 1985 (c.67), s.16.]

Under s.16 of the Transport Act 1985, a local authority has no right to impose any numerical limit on the issue of tax licences unless and until it has obtained evidence on which it can be satisfied that there is no significant unmet demand.

R. *v.* READING BOROUGH COUNCIL, *ex p.* EGAN; SAME *v.* SAME, *ex p.* SULLMAN, *The Times,* June 12, 1987, Nolan J.

3791. Transport Act 1985

TRANSPORT ACT 1985 (MODIFICATIONS IN SCHEDULE 4 TO THE TRANSPORT ACT 1968) (AMENDMENT) ORDER 1987 (No. 337) [45p], made under the Transport Act 1985 (c.67), s.129(5); operative on April 3, 1987; extends S.I. 1985 No. 1903 so that it applies to transfers under s.50(4) of the 1985 Act.

3792. Transport Act 1985—commencement

TRANSPORT ACT 1985 (COMMENCEMENT No. 7) ORDER 1987 (No. 1228 (C.34)) [45p], made under the Transport Act 1985 (c.67), s.140(2), (3); brings into force on August 13, 1987, all remaining provisions of the Transport Act 1985 except s.139(3) (part) and Sched. 8 (part).

3793. Trunk roads

S.I. 1987 No. 13 (A13–Ripple Road, Barking and Dagenham) [45p]; 100 (Birmingham–Great Yarmouth) [45p]; 105 (A316–Twickenham Road, Richmond Upon Thames) [45p]; 146 (Winchester–Preston) [45p]; 285 (Swansea—Manchester) [45p]; 319 (London—Fishguard and Swansea—Manchester) [45p]; 320 (London—Fishguard and Cardiff—Glan Conwy) [45p], 321 (London—Fishguard) [45p], 322 (London—Fishguard) [45p]; 326 (King's Lynn—Sleaford—Newark) [45p]; 328 (King's Lynn—Sleaford—Newark) [45p]; 472 (London—Brighton) [45p]; 473 (London—Brighton) [45p]; 474 (London—Brighton) [45p]; 490 (London—Fishguard) [45p]; 521 (Birmingham—Nottingham) [45p]; 522 (Birmingham—Nottingham) [45p]; 523 (Birmingham—Nottingham) [45p]; 531 (London—Holyhead) [45p]; 546 (Norman Cross—Grimsby) [45p]; 617 (Hanger Lane, Ealing) [45p]; 699 (Snaith—York—Thirsk—Stockton—Tees—Sunderland) [45p]; 707 (Shrewsbury—Whitchurgh—Warrington) [45p]; 720 (A316 County of Surrey Boundary—M3 Trunking) [45p]; 792 (London—Penzance) [45p]; 793 (London—Penzance) [45p]; 840 (Catthorpe—Harwich) [85p]; 990 (Newcastle-under-Lyme—Tarvin) [45p]; 998 (A41—Edgware Way, Barnet) [45p]; 1013 (London—Great Yarmouth) [45p]; 1025 (Nottingham–Grantham) [45p]; 1026 (Nottingham–Grantham) [45p]; 1037 (London–Holyhead) [45p]; 1038 (London–Holyhead) [45p]; 1048 (A41–Watford Way, Barnet) [45p]; 1205 (Carlisle–Sunderland) [85p]; 1333 (Liverpool—Preston—Leeds) [45p]; 1334 (Liverpool—Preston—Leeds) [45p]; 1353 (Boroughbridge—Thirsk) [85p]; 1380 (Angel Road, Enfield) [45p]; 1430 (Folkestone—Honiton) [45p]; 1431 (Folkestone—Honiton) [45p]; 1432 (Great West Road, Hounslow) [45p]; 1435 (Hungerford—Hereford) [45p]; 1442 (West of Southampton—Bath) [45p]; 1470 (Swansea—Manchester) [45p]; 1491 (Skipton—Kendal) [45p]; 1542 (A20—Sidcup Bypass, Bexley and Bromley) [85p]; 1570 (Exeter–Launceston–Bodmin) [45p]; 1580 (London–Portsmouth) [45p]; 1581 (London–Portsmouth) [45p]; 1582 (A421 Wendlebury–Bicester) [45p]; 1632 (London–Penzance) [45p]; 1633 (London–Penzance) [45p]; 1693 (London-Inverness) [£1·60]; 1694 (Oxford-Market Deeping) [45p]; 1695 (Catthorpe-Harwich) [85p]; 1701 (Exeter-Launceston-Bodmin) [85p]; 1731 (London-Norwich) [45p]; 1784 (London-Fishguard) [45p]; 1799 (Bath-Lincoln) [45p]; 1800 (Bath-Lincoln) [45p]; 1861 (London-Brighton) [45p]; 1862 (London-Brighton) [45p]; 1863 (London-Brighton) [45p]; 1864 (Maidenhead-Oxford) [45p]; 1865 (Maidenhead-Oxford) [45p]; 1866 (Burchetts Green-M40) [45p]; 1868 (Maidenhead-Oxford) [45p]; 1930 (London-Birmingham) [45p]; 1931 (London-Birmingham) [45p]; 1932 (London—Fishguard) [45p]; 2036 (Leicester—Great Yarmouth) [45p]; 2037 (Leicester—Great Yarmouth) [45p]; 2038 (Leicester—Great Yarmouth) [£1·90]; 2074 Queensferry—South of Birkenhead) [45p]; 2101 (Bath-Southampton) [45p]; 2102 (Bath-Southampton) [45p]; 2134 (A10)—Great Cambridge Road, Enfield [45p]; 2148 (Snaith-Sunderland) [45p]; 2194 (Fishguard-Bangor) [£1·30]; 2256 (Catthorpe-Harwich) [£1·60]; 2257 (London-Inverness) [45p]; 2261 (Bath-Lincoln) [45p]; 2262 (Bath-Lincoln) [45p]; 2263 (Worcester-Banbury) [45p]; 2264 (Evesham-Birmingham) [45p]; 2265 (Evesham-Birmingham) [45p], 2267 (Folkestone-Honiton) [45p]; 2268 (Folkestone-Honiton) [45p]; 2274 (Leeds-York-Scarborough) [45p].

TRESPASS

3794. Crane—passing over land without permission—whether trespassing

A crane that passes over land without permission is trespassing.
ANCHOR BREWHOUSE DEVELOPMENTS *v.* BERKLEY HOUSE (DOCKLANDS) DEVELOPMENT, *The Times,* April 3, 1987, Scott J.

3795. Defences of *volenti* and *ex turpi causa*—contribution—provocation

Where *volenti non fit injuria* or *ex turpi causa non oritur actio* were raised as defences, they could in principle provide a complete defence, or could reduce damages otherwise properly due; provocation ordinarily could reduce exemplary damages, but not compensatory damages. None of those defences were relevant in the instant case, where D had murdered P's wife, and summary judgment with full liability had been properly given (*Fontin* v. *Katapodis* [1963] C.L.Y. 916, *Lane* v. *Holloway* [1967] C.L.Y. 1047, *Gray* v. *Barr* [1971] C.L.Y. 6012, *Murphy* v. *Culhane* [1976] C.L.Y. 2133 considered): BARNES *v.* NAYER, *The Times,* December 19, 1986, C.A.

3796. Rights of landowner—interlocutory injunction. See PATEL *v.* SMITH (W. H.) (EZIOT), §3039.

VALUE ADDED TAX

3797. Amendment regulations

VALUE ADDED TAX (GENERAL) (AMENDMENT) (No. 2) REGULATIONS 1987 (No. 510) [£1·60], made under the Value Added Tax Act 1983 (c.55), ss.14(9), 15; operative on April 1, 1987; substitute a new Pt. V in S.I. 1985 No. 886.

VALUE ADDED TAX (GENERAL) (AMENDMENT) (No. 3) REGULATIONS 1987 (No. 1916) [£1·60], made under the Value Added Tax Act 1983, ss.14(6)(9), 16(7), 19(2), Sched. 1, para. 14, Sched. 7, paras. 2(1)(5), 6(4); operative on January 1, 1988; amend S.I. 1985 No. 886 primarily in relation to registration for VAT and de-registration.

3798. Assessment in default of returns—validity

[Value Added Tax 1983 (c.55), Sched. 7, para. 4.]

For a number of years the taxpayer company had supplied services intra-group but had failed to make V.A.T. returns, incorrectly believing that the supplies were exempt. Subsequently, an Officer of the Customs and Excise raised a number of estimated assessments, which it ultimately transpired were erroneous in a number of material respects. The taxpayer company sought to have the assessments set aside.

Held, dismissing the taxpayer company's appeal, that, on the basis of the case before it; the Tribunal was entitled to conclude that the Officer raising the assessment had acted neither dishonestly, capriciously nor vindictively, but to the best of his judgment (*Van Boeckel* v. *Customs and Excise Commissioners* [1981] C.L.Y. 2839 considered).

SCHLUMBERGER INLAND SERVICES INC. *v.* CUSTOMS AND EXCISE COMMISSIONERS [1987] S.T.C. 228, Taylor J.

3799. Assessments—notification—onus of proof

[Value Added Tax Act 1983 (c.55), Sched. 7, para. 4.]

T. Co. sold scrap silver, a by-product of its film processing business, but did not include those sales in its V.A.T. returns. The commissioners assessed V.A.T. on the basis of purchases notes which they had obtained from dealers in silver and which they alleged related to sales of silver by T Co. T Co. appealed against the assessment, contending (1) that the assessment was invalid as it had not been properly notified to them in accordance with V.A.T.A. 1983, Sched. 7, para. 4, and (2) that the burden of proving that that purchase notes related to sales by T Co. lay on the Crown. Macperson J. dismissed T Co's appeal, holding, in particular, that the tribunal had been correct in its view that it was for T Co. to show that the assessment ought to the reduced.

Held, dismissing T Co's appeal, that the judge was correct to hold that the tribunal had made no error of law as to burden of proof.

GRUNWICK PROCESSING LABORATORIES *v.* CUSTOMS AND EXCISE COMMISSIONERS [1987] S.T.C. 357, C.A.

3800. Bad debt relief—debt comprising tax only—costs in civil action

M & Co. practised as solicitors in partnership. They acted for insurers in an action which P Co. brought for negligence. Such action was settled and costs of £7,836 were paid to M & Co. but tax amounting to £709 was not paid by P Co. Subsequently P Co. went into liquidation. M & Co. claimed bad debt relief pursuant to V.A.T.A. 1983 s.22(1) in respect of such £709. S.22(1) provides that where a debtor has become insolvent the creditor shall be entitled to a refund of the amount of tax chargeable by reference to the outstanding amount.

Held, that the terms of s.22(1) only permitted the refund of three twenty-thirds of such £709. The Tribunal had no power to mitigate the unfair result here.

MAWER (A. W.) & CO. *v.* CUSTOMS AND EXCISE COMMISSIONERS (1986) V.A.T.T.R. 87, V.A.T. Tribunal.

3801. Betting, gaming and lotteries

VALUE ADDED TAX (BETTING, GAMING AND LOTTERIES) ORDER 1987 (No. 517) [45p], made under the Value Added Tax Act 1983 (c.55), ss.17, 48(6); operative on May

1, 1987; amends Sched. 6, Group 4, Notes (1)(*b*) (2) to the 1983 Act to exclude, from the scope of the exemption, charges made for participating in bingo in Northern Ireland.

3802. Cash accounting

VALUE ADDED TAX (CASH ACCOUNTING) REGULATIONS 1987 (No. 1427) [85p], made under the Value Added Tax Act 1983 (c.55), s.14(1) and Sched. 7, para. 2(3A); operative on October 1, 1987; provide for a taxable person to be authorised to account for and pay tax on the basis of cash or other consideration paid and received.

3803. Charities

VALUE ADDED TAX (CHARITIES) ORDER 1987 (No. 437) [45p], made under the Value Added Tax Act 1983 (c.55), ss.16(4) and 48(6); operative on April 1, 1987; extends zero-rating provisions to cover certain supplies to charities and other public bodies.

3804. Construction of buildings

VALUE ADDED TAX (CONSTRUCTION OF BUILDINGS) ORDER 1987 (No. 781) [45p], made under the Value Added Tax Act 1983 (c.55), ss.14(10), 16(4), 48(6); operative on May 21, 1987; amends: Note (1A) of Group 8 of Sched. 5 to the 1983 Act, denying zero-rating to any extension or annexation to an existing building if it provides for internal access to the existing building, or if separate use, letting or disposal is prevented by the terms of covenant, planning consent or similar permission; Note (2A) of Group 8, excluding from zero-rating relief carpets and carpeting material when installed in the course of construction; and Article 8 of the Value Added Tax (Special Provisions) Order 1981 (S.I. 1981 No. 1741), preventing deduction when works on an existing building are done with a view to the sale or the granting of a long lease and adding carpets and carpeting materials to the list of non-standard fixtures and fittings.

VALUE ADDED TAX (CONSTRUCTION OF BUILDINGS) (No. 2) ORDER 1987 (No. 1072) [45p], made under the Value Added Tax Act 1983, ss.14(10), 16(4), 48(6); operative on June 25, 1987; replaces S.I. 1987 No. 781 which did not get House of Commons approval in the specified time.

3805. Deemed supply—lost stock—whether theft—quantum of assessment

H Co. carried on the business of operating a cash and carry warehouse. It was run by B, assisted by others. When H Co.'s accounts were prepared it was clear that a vast amount of stock was missing, worth £219,000 at cost. H Co. was subsequently put into liquidation. There was some evidence that one of those assisting A, and who had now left the country, might have sold stock and retained the proceeds. The Commissioners assessed H Co. pursuant to V.A.T.A. 1983 s.5(1) as if it had sold the missing stock at market value, claiming that to be full retail value.

Held, that the evidence indicated that there had been some dishonest conduct but there was insufficient evidence to prove that any person had sold such stock on his own account. Accordingly H Co. had not shown that the stock had been lost and could not obtain the relief given by V.A.T.A. 1983, Sched. 7, para. 4(6). H Co. must be deemed to have supplied the stock at market value which, on the facts, was 75 per cent. of cost.

HIGHGATE WAREHOUSE (TEXTILES) *v.* CUSTOMS AND EXCISE COMMISSIONERS (1986) V.A.T.T.R. 238, V.A.T. Tribunal.

3806. Distribution of assets—surplus on liquidation—whether surplus representing VAT payable to commissioners

[Finance Act 1978 (c.42), s.12.]

Where there was an unexpected surplus on a liquidation; which included a sum representing VAT payable on goods and services supplied, but which the supplier had not proved for in the liquidation, the commissioners could not recover the sum they had paid out from the surplus.

A creditor supplied goods and services to a company under a contract in which the company was bound to pay VAT. The supplier was therefore liable to pay VAT to the Customs and Excise Commissioners and did so. The company went into voluntary liquidation apparently heavily insolvent, and the supplier limited its claim in the liquidation to the basic price of the goods and services exclusive of the VAT element. The VAT which it had paid it recovered from the commissioners under s.12 of the Finance Act 1978 and the Value Added Tribunal (Bad Debt Relief) Regulations 1978. In fact the liquidator ended up with a surplus for distribution, which included the sum which represented the VAT payable on the goods and services supplied for which the company was contractually liable to the supplier and for which the supplier would have proved in the liquidation had it known that the company was solvent but which the supplier had recovered from the commissioners. The liquidator asked for directions as to the distribution of the surplus assets representing the VAT recovered from the commissioners.

Held, that since the VAT legislation did not provide for the commissioners to require the suppliers to prove in the liquidation for the amount of the VAT or for them to recover it directly from the liquidator, the commissioners had no statutory claim to recover the sum that they had paid to the suppliers. They could not recoup the money paid out under the doctrine of subrogation, since the legislative machinery was inconsistent with their obtaining the suppliers' rights to the VAT element in the price of the goods. They did not have a quasi-contractual claim against the company since the refund of VAT had not discharged the company's liability to pay the VAT to the suppliers. Even on the assumption that a liquidator in a voluntary winding up was an officer of the court there was no mistake of fact or law by reason of which the assets available for distribution had been increased so as to justify interference by the court. Accordingly the surplus should be distributed among the contributories in accordance with the provisions of the articles of association (*James, ex p.* (1874) L.R. 9 Ch.App. 609 distinguished).

T. H. KNITWEAR (WHOLESALE), *Re* [1987] 1 W.L.R. 371, Browne-Wilkinson V.-C.

3807. Exempt supply—financial services—credit-card—whether supply to retailer

T Co. carries on the business of providing credit card services. It issues cards to cardholders for use in purchasing goods from retailers. Under such transactions, T Co. pays the retailer the price of the goods less a discount, and is later paid in full by the cardholder. T Co. makes taxable and exempt supplies, the amount of the latter affecting its ability to deduct input tax. The Commissioners considered that T Co. had understated its exempt supplies as it made exempt supplies to retailers in consideration of the payment of the discount, within VATA 1983, Sched. 6, Grp. 5, Note 4. T Co. contended that its only supply was made to cardholders.

Held, allowing the appeal, that the agreements between T Co. and the retailers were factoring arrangements, under which T Co. buys the right to payment. Accordingly, there was no supply of services by T Co. to the retailer.

DINERS CLUB *v.* CUSTOMS AND EXCISE COMMISSIONERS; CARDHOLDERS *v.* SAME (1987) V.A.T.T.R. 10, V.A.T. Tribunal.

3808. Exempt supply—land—licence to occupy—box at concert hall

[Value Added Tax Act 1983 (c.55), Sched. 6, Grp. 1, item 1.]

The taxpayer held the residues of a number of 999 year leases of boxes in the Royal Albert Hall. Such leases were granted in 1867 and gave the lessee the exclusive right of occupation for the lease period. Such leases were transferable on a prescribed form. The taxpayer assigned a lease. The Commissioners assessed him to tax on such supply. The taxpayer contended that such supply was an exempt one under V.A.T.A. 1983, Sched. 6, Grp. 1, item 1, being the grant of a licence to occupy land. A Value Added Tax Tribunal upheld the taxpayer's appeal.

Held, dismissing the appeal, that the nature of the agreement between the taxpayer and the assignee was the provision of a licence to occupy, not the provision of entertainment, which was the obligation of the corporation of the Royal Albert Hall.

CUSTOMS AND EXCISE COMMISSIONERS *v.* ZINN, *The Daily Telegraph,* November 30, 1987, Nolan J.

3809. Exemptions

VALUE ADDED TAX (EDUCATION) ORDER 1987 (No. 1259) [45p], made under the Value Added Tax Act 1983 (c.55), ss.17(2), 48(6); operative on October 1, 1987; extends the scope of exemption from VAT for goods and services supplied as incidental to the provision of education training or re-training by schools, universities and certain other bodies.

3810. Export of goods—evidence—commercial documents

S Co. carried on business as suppliers of plant. It claimed that certain supplies of plant were zero-rated pursuant to V.A.T.A. 1983, s.16 and V.A.T. (General) Regs. 1980 (S.I. 1980 No. 1536), reg. 44, being supplies ultimately made to a Libyan purchaser. The Commissioners maintained that there was insufficient evidence to show that the goods had been exported. C.E.C. Notice No. 703, para. 17 provides that an exporter must keep proof of export, including normal commercial documentation. S Co. produced a bill of lading but there was nothing thereon that related to the goods supplied. A letter of confirmation from a Libyan company, produced by S Co., certified facts which could not have come from the Libyan Company's own knowledge.

Held, that S Co. had failed to produce satisfactory evidence of export.

STOCKTON PLANT AND EQUIPMENT *v.* CUSTOMS AND EXCISE COMMISSIONERS (1986) V.A.T.T.R. 94, V.A.T. Tribunal.

3811. Exports

VALUE ADDED TAX (GENERAL) (AMENDMENT) REGULATIONS 1987 (No. 150) [45p], made under the Value Added Tax Act 1983 (c.55), s.16(7); operative on March 9, 1987; increase the value of goods that can be purchased under the retail export schemes by Community travellers.

3812. Finance order

VALUE ADDED TAX (FINANCE) ORDER 1987 (No. 860) [45p], made under the Value Added Tax Act 1983 (c.55), s.17(2); operative on May 13, 1987; deletes a reference to the Exchange Control Act 1947 in item 6, Group 5 of Sched. 6 to the 1983 Act.

3813. Imports

VALUE ADDED TAX (IMPORTED GOODS) RELIEF (AMENDMENT) ORDER 1987 (No. 155) [45p], made under the Value Added Tax Act 1983 (c.55), s.19(1); operative on March 9, 1987; amends S.I. 1984 No. 746 by increasing the limit for relief from VAT on certain goods imported into the United Kingdom.

VALUE ADDED TAX (IMPORTED GOODS) RELIEF (AMENDMENT) (No. 2) ORDER 1987 (No. 2108) [45p]; made under the Value Added Tax Act 1983, s.19(1); operative on January 1, 1988; amends S.I. 1984 No. 746.

VALUE ADDED TAX (SMALL NON-COMMERCIAL CONSIGNMENTS) RELIEF (AMENDMENT) ORDER 1987 (No. 154) [45p], made under the Value Added Tax Act 1983, s.19(1); operative on March 9, 1987; increases the level of relief from VAT on imports of certain small consignments of a non-commercial nature.

3814. Input tax—non-delivery of goods—prior payment

N Co. operated a farming business. It agreed to purchaser fertilizer with £124,000 with payment met by a Bill of Exchange which, when subsequently presented, was met by N Co.'s bankers. N Co.'s supplier was forced into liquidation when fertilizer worth £73,000 had yet to be delivered. N Co. was not supplied with a tax invoice. The Commssioners refused to allow N Co. credit for input tax on such £73,000 worth of the order.

Held, that as goods worth £73,000 were never supplied, N Co. could not deduct input tax in respect of such sum.

NORTHERN COUNTIES CO-OPERATIVE ENTERPRISES *v.* CUSTOMS AND EXCISE COMMISSIONERS (1986) V.A.T.T.R. 250, V.A.T. Tribunal.

3815. Input tax—purchase and upkeep of racehorse

[Value Added Tax Act 1983 (c.55), s.14.]

The taxpayer company manufactured plastic mouldings and storage tanks. It was anxious to find new customers and purchased and raced a horse with the idea that it might in some way advance its business. The question arose whether V.A.T. on the purchase and upkeep of the horse was incurred wholly for the purposes of the taxpayer company's business. The tribunal held that, although the taxpayer company's object was to use the horse for the purposes of its business, it ought not to have had any commercial belief that the purchase and running of a racehorse could advance its business. The tribunal disallowed the claim for V.A.T. input credit accordingly.

Held, allowing the taxpayer company's that the question to be answered was a subjective one, and, in view of the tribunal's findings the V.A.T. input credit should be allowed.

FLOCKTON (IAN) DEVELOPMENTS *v.* CUSTOMS AND EXCISE COMMISSIONERS [1987] S.T.C. 394, Stuart-Smith J.

3816. Input tax—recipient of supply—accommodation—business entertainment

[Value Added Tax (Special Provisions) Order 1981 (S.I. 1981 No. 1741), Art. 9(1).]

T Co. carried on the business of manufacturing building products. It contracted to buy and have installed a brickmaking machine, under which agreement T Co. was to pay the cost of board and lodging for the supplier's engineers. T Co. booked such accommodation in its own name and subsequently paid for it. T Co. claimed to deduct, as input tax, tax suffered on the supply of such accommodation. The Commissioners refused to allow such deduction as first, they contended, the supply was made to the engineers and secondly, the supply was of business entertainment, pursuant to VAT (Special Provisions) Order 1981, Art. 9(1), which prohibits such deduction.

Held, dismissing the appeal, that although the supply was not of business entertainment and was made to T Co., T Co. had made a taxable supply of it to the engineers.

IBSTOCK BUILDING PRODUCTS *v.* CUSTOMS AND EXCISE COMMISSIONERS (1987) V.A.T.T.R. 1, V.A.T Tribunal.

3817. Input tax—self-billing invoice—deregistration of supplier

C Co. carried on business as debt collectors. It employed persons in respect of whom the Commissioners had allowed it to use a self-billing system, so that C Co., and not the other person, issued the invoice in respect of services supplied to C Co. by such person. C Co. sought to deduct as input tax all tax paid on such supplies but the Commissioners refused to allow the deduction of all such tax since, unknown to C Co., one supplier had become deregistered at the time of some supplies. C Co. contended that it was the duty of the Commissioners to inform it of such deregistration and that, as they had not, it should be entitled to deduct such tax.

Held, that C Co. could not deduct input tax in respect of invoices issued on behalf of a deregistered person.

CREDIT ANCILLARY SERVICES *v.* CUSTOMS AND EXCISE COMMISSIONERS (1986) V.A.T.T.R. 204, V.A.T. Tribunal.

3818. International services

VALUE ADDED TAX (INTERNATIONAL SERVICES) ORDER 1987 (No. 518) [45p], made under the Value Added Tax Act 1983 (c.85), ss.16(4) and 48(6); operative on May 1, 1987; extends zero-rating to exhibition services performed in overseas venues.

3819. Partnership—husband and wife—domestic arrangement

B carried on business as a shopfitter from 1977. He worked in excess of 40 hours per week in such business and his wife spent up to 15 hours per week, being responsible for the bookkeeping. They had a joint bank account used for business and private purposes. There was no formal agreement between B and his wife but B claimed that they carried on the business in partnership.

Held, dismissing the appeal, that there was no evidence from which the Tribunal could infer that there was anything more than an informal domestic arrangement.

BRITTON (VICTOR) *v.* CUSTOMS AND EXCISE COMMISSIONERS (1986) V.A.T.T.R. 209, V.A.T. Tribunal.

3820. Penalty—failure to register—reasonable excuse—fault of Commissioners

Z commenced business on September 1, 1985. He telephoned his local office of the Commissioners and asked for a registration form to be sent but did not receive one. In December 1985 his accountant telephoned that office and a form was sent and returned correctly. The Commissioners assessed Z to a penalty under F.A. 1985, s.15(1), because he had not registered in September. Z appealed and claimed that he had a reasonable excuse for such failure, within s.15(4).

Held, that although Z's request for a registration form was not effective notification of liability to be registered, such failure was due to the non-provision of a form by the Commissioners. The appeal would be allowed.

ZAVERI (S.) *v.* CUSTOMS AND EXCISE COMMISSIONERS (1986) V.A.T.T.R. 133, V.A.T. Tribunal.

3821. Penalty—failure to register—reasonable excuse—ignorance of law

[Finance Act 1985 (c.54), s.15(4).]

The taxpayer commenced business as a freelance model in April 1985. Her business prospered such that her turnover for the quarter ended September 30, 1985 was above the registration threshold. She did not then apply for registration. The commissioners assessed her to a penalty pursuant to F.A. 1985 s.15(1) for failure to register. She claimed that she had a reasonable excuse for such failure and thus was exempted from a penalty by F.A. 1985 s.15(4), since she was at the time of default ignorant of all value added tax legislation. A Value Added Tax Tribunal confirmed the penalty.

Held, dismissing the appeal, that ignorance of tax law could not constitute a reasonable excuse within s.15(4).

NEAL *v.* CUSTOMS AND EXCISE COMMISSIONERS, November 11, 1987, *The Times,* Simon Brown J.

3822. Penalty—failure to register—reasonable excuse—non-receipt by Commissioners

S commenced business in 1984. He consulted an accountant concerning his value added tax position in March 1985 and in April he completed a registration form which he sent to such accountant. The accountant sent the form to the Commissioners but they did not receive it. Subsequently another form was completed by S which the Commissioners received in November 1985. The Commissioners considered that S had failed to notify them of liability to be registered until November 1985 and imposed a penalty pursuant to F.A. 1985 s.15(1). S appealed.

Held, that as the Commissioners had not received the first form, there was no effective notification before November 1985. As, however, S had done everything that was reasonably required to notify the Commissioners, he had a reasonable excuse for non-notification within s.15(4). The appeal would be allowed.

SELWYN (L.) *v.* CUSTOMS AND EXCISE COMMISSIONERS (1986) V.A.T.T.R. 142, V.A.T. Tribunal.

3823. Penalty—failure to register at proper time—reasonable excuse

The taxpayers owned a trading company, which was VAT registered. They intended that the company should purchase a restaurant. Difficulties arose with the funding of the purchase and, as an interim measure, they bought the restaurant as partners, in November 1985. Subsequently, loan arrangements expected to be finalised were cancelled and it proved impossible for the restaurant to be bought by the company. In January 1985, they had consulted the Commissioners and were told that unless the difficulties were quickly resolved they would have to register. They applied for registration in June 1986. The Commissioners assessed them to a penalty under F.A. 1985 s.15(1). The taxpayers contended that they had a reasonable excuse for the failure.

Held, allowing the appeal, that there was no reason in law why the taxpayers' conduct did not disclose a reasonable excuse and, in the circumstances, it did.

HUTCHINGS (P.H.V.) *v.* CUSTOMS AND EXCISE COMMISSIONERS (1987) V.A.T.T.R. 58, V.A.T. Tribunal.

3824. Penalty—late registration—reasonable excuse

The directors and shareholders of E Co. had purchased it "off the shelf" from D and received an invoice from D which ended "with compliments VAT No. 241 1563 95." They assumed that such number was E Co.'s VAT registration number and charged tax using that number. In fact the number belonged to D. Some months later the mistake was realised and the Commissioners registered E Co. and imposed a penalty of £405·51 pursuant to F.A. 1985 s.15(4) for late registration. E Co. appealed against the imposition of the penalty.

Held, that since s.15(4) allowed for a penalty to be remitted if the taxpayer had a reasonable excuse for delay and, on the facts, there was a reasonable excuse bearing in mind that no tax had been lost, the appeal would be allowed.

ELECTRIC TOOL REPAIR *v.* CUSTOMS AND EXCISE COMMISSIONERS (1986) V.A.T.T.R. 257, V.A.T. Tribunal.

3825. Procedure—evidence—witness beyond the seas

P Co. carried on business as bullion dealers. It deducted input tax in respect of a supply of gold bars. The Commissioners contended that it was not entitled to such deduction and alleged that it was party to a fraud under which the gold was smuggled into the U.K. without payment of tax. Before the Tribunal, the Commissioners sought to put in evidence a statement by P, who had been convicted of smuggling gold into the U.K. and had left for Switzerland. Such statement implicated P Co. in a fraud. The Commissioners contended that the Tribunal should admit such statement in accordance with V.A.T. Tribunals Rules 1986, Rule 28(1).

Held, that since P's statement would have been admissible in proceedings before the High Court, the Tribunal would allow its admission.

PRESMAN (BULLION) *v.* CUSTOMS AND EXCISE COMMISSIONERS (1986) V.A.T.T.R. 136, V.A.T. Tribunal.

3826. Procedure—witness—incriminating evidence

W Co. claimed to deduct input tax in respect of a supply made to it by C. The Commissioners believed that no such supply had taken place and refused to allow W Co. to deduct such input tax. W Co. appealed to a Value Added Tax Tribunal. The Commissioners called C as a witness. W Co. asked that C should be cautioned that he need not answer questions which might incriminate him.

Held, that it was the Tribunal's duty to administer such a caution to C. Further, although an adjournment would not be granted, the appeal would proceed in such manner as would allow C to consult a solicitor before giving evidence.

WARD (S.) COINS *v.* CUSTOMS AND EXCISE COMMISSIONERS (1986) V.A.T.T.R. 129, V.A.T. Tribunal.

3827. Refund of tax—Eighth Council Directive—place of supply of services

T Co. was resident in West Germany. It manufactured systems for producing floor coverings. It contracted to sell such a system to X Co., a U.K. resident, through T Co.'s U.K. representative, Z Co. Delivery was to take place "ex works" in West Germany, but no evidence was led to show that X Co. collected the system in West Germany. Z Co. provided the technical services necessary for the installation of such system. It was common ground that VATA 1983 did not implement Eighth Council Directive, Art. 2, and that such provision had direct effect. T Co. contended that it was entitled to reclaim input tax suffered by it on the supply of services to it by Z Co., since the supply was in respect of movable property supplied abroad and imported.

Held, dismissing the appeal, that there was no supply of the system until delivery, which, on the facts, occurred only when the system was installed in the U.K.

AZO-MASCHINENFABRIK ADOLF ZIMMERMAN GmbH *v.* CUSTOMS AND EXCISE COMMISSIONERS (1987) V.A.T.T.R. 25, V.A.T. Tribunal.

3828. Registration—educational trust—profit motive—charity

B Co. owned and ran a college, which was a charity. It owned substantial premises at which it provided boarding and tuition to young persons in order to prepare them for university admission. It also ran summer courses in English. Under its articles of association its profits were to be applied for charitable purposes only. It set out to make an annual surplus, to be used in maintaining and improving facilities. The Commissioners decided to register B Co., but it claimed that it made only exempt supplies within V.A.T.A. 1983 Sched. 6, Grp. 6, item 2(*a*), being the provision of education of a kind provided by a school otherwise than for profit.

Held, that B Co. made exempt supplies only. Although it budgeted to make a surplus, it did not intend to make a profit in the commercial sense.

BELL CONCORD EDUCATIONAL TRUST *v.* CUSTOMS AND EXCISE COMMISSIONERS (1986) V.A.T.T.R. 165, V.A.T. Tribunal.

3829. Registration—penalty for delay—nature of offence

G commenced carrying on the business of supervising kitchen installation. In the quarter ending June 1985 his turnover exceeded the registration threshold and he became liable to notify the Commissioners of this on July 15, 1985. He did not notify them until December. The Commissioners registered him with effect from July 15, 1985, They also imposed a penalty for late registration pursuant to F.A. 1985, s.15(1)(*a*). G contended that since the period of his failure to notify commenced before the Royal Assent to F.A. 1985 on July 25, he could not be subject to such penalty.

Held, that s.15 creates an offence which takes place continuously and G was liable to a penalty from July 25. Further, his working long hours was not a reasonable excuse for his failure.

GALE (JOHN) *v.* CUSTOMS AND EXCISE COMMISSIONERS (1986) V.A.T.T.R. 185, V.A.T. Tribunal.

3830. Registration—turnover—reasonable belief—new business

P started business as a general retailer by opening a shop on September 9, 1983 with some £2,000 capital. His takings exceeded £420 in the first week of trading rising to over £1,400 in the fourth week. During such September his purchases exceeded £4,000. On December 21, 1983 he applied for registration from January 1, 1984. The Commissioners maintained that there were reasonable grounds for believing that his turnover would exceed £18,000 p.a. on such September 9, and assessed him on the basis that he was a taxable person from such date.

Held, that since P had commenced a new business with little capital, objectively, one would not have thought on September 9, that his turnover would exceed £18,000 p.a. The appeal would be allowed.

PARKINSON (PATRICK) *v.* CUSTOMS AND EXCISE COMMISSIONERS (1986) V.A.T.T.R. 126, V.A.T. Tribunal.

3831. Registration limits

VALUE ADDED TAX (INCREASE OF REGISTRATION LIMITS) ORDER 1987 (No. 438) [45p], made under the Value Added Tax Act 1983 (c.55), Sched. 1, para. 12; operative on March 18, 1987, as to arts. 1 and 2, and on June 1, 1987, as to art. 3; increases the VAT registration limit to £21,300 p.a. and also increases the limits for cancellation of registration.

3832. Repayment of excess tax—investigation

[Value Added Tax Act 1983 (c.55), s.14(5).]

The taxpayer company made a claim for repayment of £44,864 (approximately) "input tax" in respect of certain export transactions which were under investigation by the Commissioners of Customs and Excise. Repayment being withheld, the taxpayer company applied for judicial review seeking an order of mandamus compelling the repayment.

Held, dismissing the taxpayer company's application, that the Commissioners were entitled to withhold repayment for such time as would afford them a reasonable opportunity to investigate the validity of the claim.

R. *v.* CUSTOMS AND EXCISE COMMISSIONERS, *ex p.* STRANGEWOOD [1987] S.T.C. 502, Otton J.

3833. Retrospective legislation—whether presumption against it overcome by statute

[Value Added Tax Act 1983 (c.55), Sched. 1, paras. 3, 4; Finance Act 1985 (c.21), s.15.]

The rule against retrospective legislation raises a presumption only, which may be overcome by specific legislation. S.15 of the Finance Act 1985 does not operate retrospectively, and nor does it need to, as the liability created by paras. 3 and 4 of the Value Added Tax Act 1983, to which it refers, is a continuing one (*Grice* v. *Needs* [1979] C.L.Y. 2757 applied).

CUSTOMS AND EXCISE COMMISSIONERS *v.* SHINGLETON, *The Times,* December 8, 1987, Brown J.

3834. Return—failure to furnish return—posting

[Value Added Tax (General) Regulations 1985 (S.I. 1985 No. 886), reg. 58(1).]

The taxpayer completed his value added tax return in prescribed form and posted it in the pre-addressed, pre-paid envelope supplied. The return was not received by the Commissioners.

Held, that the taxpayer could not be convicted of an offence of failure to furnish a return contrary to s.39(8)(*b*) of the Value Added Tax Act 1983 (*Aikman* v. *White* [1986] C.L.Y. 3501, followed).

HAYMAN *v.* GRIFFITHS; WALKER *v.* HANBY [1987] S.T.C. 649, D.C.

3835. Sixth VAT Directive. See EUROPEAN COMMUNITIES.

3836. Supplies by retailers

VALUE ADDED TAX (SUPPLIES BY RETAILERS) (AMENDMENT) REGULATIONS 1987 (No. 1712) [45p], made under the Value Added Tax Act 1983 (c.55), Sched. 7, para. 2(3); operative on October 30, 1987; amends S.I. 1972 No. 1148.

3837. Supply—deposits—gold coin

[Finance Act 1972 (c.41), s.7; Value Added Tax (Finance) Order 1982 (S.I. 1982 No. 476).]

The taxpayers were dealers in gold coin. On some transactions they took deposits, which were returned (subject to a penalty) if the customer changed his mind, and were treated as part of the purchase price if the sale was concluded.

Held, dismissing the taxpayer's appeal, that, by virtue of F.A. 1972, s.7(4), on the payment of the deposit there was a supply for value added tax purposes.

PATTNI (PURSHOTAM M.) & SONS *v.* CUSTOMS AND EXCISE COMMISSIONERS [1987] S.T.C. 1, Russell J.

3838. Supply—for consideration—employee—deduction in remuneration

G carried on business as a hotelier. His employees were paid wages set down as the minimum by rules made under Wages Council Act 1979. Such rules lay down two rates, a lower figure applying where an employee is given board and lodging. The Commissioners considered that where an employee received board and lodging the amount of the wage reduction was monetary consideration given by him for the supply of board and lodging and that tax was due on such consideration.

Held, that, on the evidence, an employee who opted for board and lodging was then told his remuneration which accorded with the said rules. The deduction made was simply a step in calculating such remuneration. Such deductions could not be considered consideration provided by the employee. The appeal would be allowed.

GOODFELLOW (R. W.) *v.* CUSTOMS AND EXCISE COMMISSIONERS (1986) V.A.T.T.R. 119, V.A.T. Tribunal.

3839. Supply—hot food—consumption off premises—intention of seller

[Value Added Tax Act 1983 (c.55), Sched. 5, gp.1, n.3.]

The taxpayers were manufacturers and retailers of pies. The pies were prepared at a central bakery, but the final baking was carried out in ovens at the retail shops, where the pre-cooked contents were heated and the pastry crusts were baked. The purpose of finishing the baking process on the shop premises was to create an agreeable atmosphere in the shops and to encourage customers to regard the pies as freshly baked in order to increase sales; the purpose was not to sell pies which were hot from the oven.

Held, allowing the taxpayer's appeal, that value added tax was not chargeable within Sched. 5, Group 1, note 3(b)(i), where the predominant purpose of the seller was not to supply hot food.

PIMBLETT (JOHN) & SONS *v.* CUSTOMS AND EXCISE COMMISSIONERS [1987] S.T.C. 202, Taylor J.

3840. Supply—in the course of a business—agreement with former employee—whether taxpayer continuing to carry on business

[Value Added Tax Act 1983 (c.55), s.2.]

Under written agreements with a former employee (M), the taxpayer transferred the possession of the premises, fixtures, stock and the running of the business to M. However, the taxpayer continued to be responsible for the paperwork of the business and received a varying weekly sum from M.

Held, allowing the taxpayer's appeal, that on a correct view of the facts, the taxpayer had divested herself wholly of the business and was not liable to value added tax in respect of supplies made in the course of that business.

NASIM (TRADING AS YASMINE RESTAURANT) *v.* CUSTOMS AND EXCISE COMMISSIONERS [1987] S.T.C. 387, Simon Brown J.

3841. Supply of employees—parent and subsidiary—agency

T Co. owned the shares in a subsidiary, M Co., which carried on business as insurance brokers. For convenience, all of M Co.'s employees were hired and paid by T Co. M Co. did not pay T Co. but a debit was shown in respect of the employees in the consolidated accounts of the group. The Commissioners considered that T Co. was making a taxable supply of staff to M Co. in consideration of M Co. meeting the cost. A Value Added Tax Tribunal held that there had been no taxable supply. In the High Court it was held that T Co. had supplied staff to M Co. for a consideration and so had made a taxable supply. In the Court of Appeal, T Co. contended that it had not supplied the staff to M Co., since throughout it was acting as M Co.'s agent.

Held, dismissing T Co.'s appeal, there was no evidence that M Co., and not T Co., was the employer of the staff in question. This being so, in the circumstances, T Co. supplied the staff to M Co., with the latter company being ultimately responsible for the costs, and so made taxable supplies.

CUSTOMS AND EXCISE COMMISSIONERS *v.* TARMAC ROADSTONE HOLDINGS [1987] S.T.C. 610, C.A.

3842. Supply of goods—use of chattel—value of supply

[Finance Act 1972 (c.41), Sched. 3, para. 8.]

The taxpayer company purchased a yacht for business purposes. However, it also allowed its employees, their families and guests to use the yacht for private purposes. The taxpayer company depreciated the yacht in its accounts at an annual rate of 20 per cent. on its written-down value. In the relevant tax year, the yacht was used for 60 days, 51 of which represented private use by employees. The Customs and Excise contended that private use of the yacht by employees involved a supply of goods by the taxpayer company in the course of its business, that the value of the supply was the full cost, and that the full cost included an appropriate part of the annual depreciation. A V.A.T. Tribunal held that the depreciation element was to be determined by dividing the amount of the depreciation by the number of days in the relevant tax year and multiplying the resulting figure by the total number of days on which the yacht was actually used for business and for private purposes.

Held, allowing the appeal by the Commissioners of Customs and Excise, that what constituted the full cost of a supply for the purposes of F.A. 1972, Sched. 3, para. 8, was a question of law, and that in this case it was to be ascertained by dividing the annual depreciation figure by the total number of days on which the yacht had been used and multiplying the resultant figure by the number of days on which it had been used by the employees.

CUSTOMS AND EXCISE COMMISSIONERS *v.* TEKNEQUIP [1987] S.T.C. 664, Otton J.

3843. Supply of goods and services—time of supply—double glazing installation

T Co. carried on business as installers of double glazing. Until May 30, 1984, supplies, in the course of double glazing for the first time, of services or builders' materials were zero-rated, by VATA 1983, Sched. 5, Grp. 8, Items 2 and 3. Such items were amended with effect from June 1, 1984 so that such supplies, when made after that date, were standard-rated. Before June 1, 1984, T Co. contracted to supply such services and goods to X, who paid a deposit. The windows were made before June 1, 1984 but were installed, and the balance paid, after such date. T Co. claimed that the supplies fell to be treated as made when the services were performed, so that supplies of services performed before such date were zero-rated.

Held, dismissing the appeal, that the supplies of goods, *i.e.* of the windows, took place on installation. The supplies of fitting services also took place at such time.

A.P.D. INSULATIONS (GROUP) *v.* CUSTOMS AND EXCISE COMMISSIONERS (1987) V.A.T.T.R. 36, V.A.T. Tribunal.

3844. Supply of services—lease—reverse premium—contribution

G Co. entered into an agreement for a lease of hotel premises with L, the landlord, under which G Co. agreed to repair and equip the hotel to the standard of a luxury class hotel. Such works were to cost £5·4 million. On the grant of the lease L paid to G Co. £1·4 million to assist in defraying certain of such costs. The Commissioners assessed G Co. to output tax on such sum on the grounds that it was consideration for a supply of services by G Co. G Co. contended that no supply was made by it and that the £1·4 million was simply a contribution towards expenses.

Held, dismissing the appeal, that the £1·4 million was the consideration provided by L for G Co. to provide more valuable benefits under the agreement than it would otherwise have.

GLENEAGLES HOTEL *v.* CUSTOMS AND EXCISE COMMISSIONERS (1986) V.A.T.T.R. 196, V.A.T. Tribunal.

3845. Supply of services—payment in advance—time of supply—club subscription

The Club was formed in 1980. A pupil, on leaving school, paid a life membership fee of £75 plus tax. However, a subscription scheme was set up to provide for a pupil's life subscription to be fully paid up by the time he left school, by adding an instalment of £5·75 to each term's account. The parent could refuse to pay such amount and there was provision for repayment of instalments if, subsequently, a boy did not join the Club. The Commissioners decided that each instalment payment was made in respect of a taxable supply of services by the Club.

Held, allowing the appeal, that the Club did not supply any services at the time of the receipt of the instalments.

OLD CHIGWELLIANS' CLUB *v.* CUSTOMS AND EXCISE COMMISSIONERS (1987) V.A.T.T.R. 66, V.A.T. Tribunal.

3846. Supply of services—quantum of supply—gaming machine

B Co. carried on business as general retailers but installed electronic gaming machines on its premises. These machines were hired from S under an informal agreement whereby B Co. paid S half the total takings. S took its share and issued a tax invoice to B in respect of one half of the takings, being for $7\frac{1}{2}$ per cent. of the takings shown as tax. The Commissioners assessed B to tax on the full amount of the takings.

Held, dismissing the appeal, that, on the facts, S made a supply to B and B made a supply to the public. Accordingly the quantum of that supply was of the whole takings.

BENNETTS OF SHEFFIELD *v.* CUSTOMS AND EXCISE COMMISSIONERS (1986) V.A.T.T.R. 253, V.A.T. Tribunal.

3847. Supply of services—to whom supply made—nominee company

B & C practised as solicitors. They obtained a lease of premises in part of which they practised and, for convenience, this lease was transferred into the name of a nominee company. Subsequently they acquired the leases of further floors in the same property and transferred these into the name of such nominee company. B & C remained liable for rents and other liabilities. The surveyors instructed by them in relation to the new leases submitted an invoice to B & C, who deducted the input tax thereon. The Commissioners disallowed the input tax on the grounds that the supply was made to the nominee company.

Held, that the reality of the matter was that B & C had used the company in a purely nominal way. Accordingly the supply was made to B & C.

BIRD SEMPLE & CRAWFORD HERRON *v.* CUSTOMS AND EXCISE COMMISSIONERS (1986) V.A.T.T.R. 218, V.A.T. Tribunal.

3848. Tax avoidance—artificial transactions—payment of consideration—loan to customer

In 1983 F Co. contracted with D for F Co. to carry out certain building alterations for D, for consideration of £300,000. It was announced in the Budget Speech on March 1986 that, as from June 1, 1984, such buinding alterations would cease to be zero-rated if performed after that date unless payment was made before that date. F Co. entered into arrangements with D under which D paid the £300,000 before June 1. The arrangements were that D borrowed £300,000 from a bank, paid it to F Co., F Co. lent it back to D and D repaid the bank. D repaid the loan in instalments as F Co. completed the building works. The commissioners contended that these arrangements were caught by the principle in *Furniss* v. *Dawson* [1984] C.L.Y. 270, and the payment should be treated as made when the loan was repaid in instalments after June. A Value Added Tax Tribunal upheld F Co.'s appeal.

Held, dismissing the appeal, that the steps here were all genuine and the facts were to be regarded as a simple, and not a composite transaction, thus *Furniss* v. *Dawson* did not apply.

CUSTOMS AND EXCISE COMMISSIONERS *v.* FAITH CONSTRUCTION, *The Times*, November 18, 1987, Simon Brown J.

3849. Tax return—error—overpayment of tax—deduction in later return

[V.A.T. (General) Regulations (S.I. 1985 No. 886), Reg. 58(1).]

Under V.A.T. (General) Regs. 1985, Reg. 58(1), a taxpayer is obliged to complete a quarterly return showing the amount of tax payable. The taxpayer company had overstated output tax payable by it on one return and sought to deduct an amount equal to such overpayment in a later return. The commissioners contended that such correction was only allowed at their discretion. The taxpayer company claimed that such correction was a matter of right. A Value Added Tax Tribunal dismissed its appeal.

Held, allowing the taxpayer company's appeal, that V.A.T.A. 1983 Sched. 7, para. 2(4)(*c*) gave the Commissioners power to provide for a taxpayer to correct errors when making subsequent returns and they had done so in V.A.T. (General) Regs. 1985, Reg. 64. Accordingly, under Reg. 58(1), the taxpayer company was entitled to correct its error by deducting in a later return the amount overpaid.

BETTERWARE PRODUCTS *v.* CUSTOMS AND EXCISE COMMISSIONERS, *The Times*, November 21, 1987, Simon Brown J.

3850. Terminal markets

VALUE ADDED TAX (TERMINAL MARKETS) (AMENDMENT) ORDER 1987 (No. 806) [45p], made under the Value Added Tax Act 1983 (c.55), s.34; operative on June 1, 1987; amends S.I. 1973 No. 173 by adding the London Platinum and Palladium Market to the list of markets in that Order.

3851. Third country traders

VALUE ADDED TAX (REPAYMENTS TO THIRD COUNTRY TRADERS) REGULATIONS 1987 (No. 2015) [£1·90], made under the Value Added Tax Act 1983 (c.55), s.23; operative on December 31, 1987; implement Council Directive No. 86/560/EEC.

3852. Time of supply—land—when made available

M Co. had a wholly owned subsidiary, S Co. In 1983 the directors of M Co. and S Co. reached an informal understanding to sell land to a builder. From such time the builder was allowed to store materials and keep horses on the land. Subsequently a formal agreement was entered into under which S Co. sold the land to M Co., which sold it on to the builder. Actual occupation occurred on May 15, 1984. M Co. was assessed to tax on the basis that it made a supply of the land after March 1984. M Co. contended that the supply took place when the land was made available to the builder, pursuant to V.A.T.A. 1983 s.4(*a*)(*b*) and that occurred in 1983.

Held, that the supply took place on May 15, 1984.

MARGRIE HOLDINGS *v.* CUSTOMS AND EXCISE COMMISSIONERS (1986) V.A.T.T.R. 213, V.A.T. Tribunal.

3853. Tour operators

VALUE ADDED TAX (TOUR OPERATORS) ORDER 1987 (No. 1806) [£1·30], made under the Value Added Tax Act 1983 (c.55), ss.3(3), 6(6), 16(4), 37A(1)(2), 48(6); operative on April 1, 1988; introduces a special VAT scheme for supplies by tour operators.

3854. Transfer of business—income producing assets—leasing business

M Co. carried on a motor leasing business. BL Co. managed such business. In 1982 part of such business was sold by M Co. to X Co., which company sold it on to B Co. M Co. continued to receive rental payments from assets retained. In 1983 M Co. sold to B Co. the remainder of its leasing business and computer equipment bought in 1982 for leasing. B Co. continued to carry on such leasing business which included receiving rents from assets acquired. The Commissioners maintained that the 1983 sale constituted the transfer of a business as a going concern with V.A.T. (Special Provisions) Ord. 1981, Art. 12(1), so that B Co. was not entitled to any input tax deduction in respect of such sale.

Held, that the question was, whether in substance and reality this was a transfer of a business or of income producing assets only. After 1982, M Co. still carried on a leasing business, albeit a reduced one. B Co. had stepped into M Co.'s shoes. Accordingly a business had been transferred as a going concern.

BALTIC LEASING *v.* CUSTOMS AND EXCISE COMMISSIONERS (1986) V.A.T.T.R. 98, V.A.T. Tribunal.

3855. Transfer of business—transfer as going concern—sale of goodwill

D Co. was concerned in acquiring newsagents' businesses and granting franchises to others to run such businesses. In 1982 it purchased a newsagents and operated the business for two weeks. It then granted a franchise over it to R, who ran it for his own account, paying a fee to D Co. A year later D Co. sold the goodwill to R. It claimed that such sale was a supply of a business as a going concern and not subject to tax under V.A.T. (Special Provisions) Order 1981, Art. 12(1)(*b*).

Held, dismissing the appeal, that the purpose of the sale to R was to leave R free to continue to trade with the goodwill R had built up and not to transfer any business from D Co.

DELTA NEWSAGENTS *v.* CUSTOMS AND EXCISE COMMISSIONERS (1986) V.A.T.T.R. 261, V.A.T. Tribunal.

3856. Value of supply—consideration—Sixth Directive—party plan sales

T Co. carried on the business of selling cosmetics by the "party plan" method. It sold goods to a "consultant" who found "hostesses" to give parties at which goods were sold. The consultant would normally give a "Dating Gift" to a hostess as an inducement to hold a party, in which case the consultant paid T Co. £1·50 therefor, instead of the normal wholesale price of £10·14. The Commissioners determined that such supplies should be treated as made at the wholesale price since VATA 1983, s.10(2) provides that where a supply is made for a consideration in money, its value is equal to the consideration provided. Here, this was £1·50 plus the procuring of the holding of the party, being worth the £10·14 wholesale price. T Co. argued that under Sixth Council Directive Art. 11A, which has direct effect, tax is chargeable on the "consideration" but that such term was not a matter of national law.

Held, adjourning the appeal, that the question of the meaning of "consideration" in Art. 11A would be referred to the European Court of Justice.

NATURALLY YOURS COSMETICS *v.* CUSTOMS AND EXCISE COMMISSIONERS (1987) V.A.T.T.R. 45, V.A.T. Tribunal.

3857. Zero-rating—animal feeding stuffs—pet foods

P Co. carried on the business of operating a slaughterhouse. It sold the meat therefrom in packages as animal feed stuffs to customers, including zoos, colleges, security firms with guard dogs, farmers and some with pets. Supplies of animal feedstuffs are zero-rated by V.A.T.A. 1983, Sched. 5, Grp. 1, item 2, except for canned, packaged or prepared pet foods. The Commissioners contended that all such supplies constituted supplies of prepared pet foods.

Held, that to be one of pet food, supply must be of food intended by the supplier to be given to animals kept as pets. Consequently all supplies here were zero-rated except those made to owners of pet animals. As regards the other supplies, the appeal would be allowed.

POPES LANE PET FOOD SUPPLIES *v.* CUSTOMS AND EXCISE COMMISSIONERS (1986) V.A.T.T.R. 221, V.A.T. Tribunal.

3858. Zero-rating—building works—enlargement

[Value Added Tax 1983 (c.55), Sched. 5, Group 8, item 2 (as amended by Finance Act 1984 (c.43), s.10 and Sched. 6).]

A new hall and classrooms with service areas were built at the rear of an existing church building. The two buildings were not physically separate, having communications doors and other integrating features. The tribunal considered that the correct question to be determined was whether the new building was or was not an enlargement of the existing building. The tribunal determined that it was not an enlargement and the works should be zero-rated accordingly.

Held, dismissing the Crown's appeal, that the tribunal had not misdirected itself and its decision ought not to be disturbed.

CUSTOMS AND EXCISE COMMISSIONERS *v.* GREAT SHELFORD FREE CHURCH (BAPTIST) [1987] S.T.C. 249, Kennedy J.

3859. Zero-rating—building works—reconstruction—bakery rebuilt

W Co. carried on business as a building contractor. It agreed to supply certain services to B on a site at Greenford. These consisted of the demolition of most of an existing bakery and of the building of a new bakery on the site, the erection of four silos and provision of parking space. Under V.A.T.A. 1983, Sched. 5, Grp. 8, item 2, services supplied in the course of construction of a building are zero-rated, but note (1A), inserted by F.A. 1984 s.10 excludes work of reconstruction from zero-rating. The commissioners refused to allow such works to be zero-rated. A Value Added Tax Tribunal held that according to the everyday meaning of the word "reconstruction", the works were works of reconstruction and dismissed the appeal.

Held, allowing the appeal, that, applying the dictionary meaning of "reconstruction", as "to construct anew", the construction of the new building was not capable of being regarded as reconstruction.

WIMPEY GROUP SERVICES *v.* CUSTOMS AND EXCISE COMMISSIONERS, *The Times*, November 16, 1987, Mann J.

3860. Zero-rating—building works—supply

[Value Added Tax Act 1983 (c.55), Sched. 5, Group 8, Items 2 and 3.]

The taxpayer company, which carried on business as builders, entered into a contract to build houses; it sub-contracted part of the works to N. As N did not enjoy a favourable credit-rating, the taxpayer company purchased the necessary building materials and invoiced them to N at cost plus an agreed fraction. The taxpayer company was assessed to value added tax on the basis that it had supplied materials to N and the supply was standard-rated. A value added tax tribunal held that there had been no supply.

Held, dismissing the appeal by the Commissioners of Customs and Excise, that (1) the taxpayer company had supplied materials to N, but (2) the supply was zero-rated within V.A.T.A. 1983, Sched. 5, Group 8, items 2 and 3.

CUSTOMS AND EXCISE COMMISSIONERS *v.* WILLMOTT (JOHN) HOUSING [1987] S.T.C. 692, Webster J.

3861. Zero-rating—building works—time of payment—immediate loan

Until May 1985, building alteration works were zero-rated. By virtue of amendments to V.A.T.A. 1983 Sched. 4, Grp. 8 made by F.A. 1984 s.10, such works were standard rated where the supply was made after June 1, 1983. By V.A.T.A. s.4(3), services are made when performed unless the supplier receives prior payment. Y.I.H. carried on the business of running hospitals. It wished to have extensive alteration works performed in 1984 but such works could not be performed before June 1. In order to establish a tax point before such date it caused two companies to be incorporated, one of which was W.Y.I.H. Co. Its object was to provide design and building services. The other subsidiary was a finance company. On May 25, 1984 Y.I.H. paid W.Y.I.H. Co. £1,000,000 to build the extensions needed. W.Y.I.H. Co. lent the £1,000,000 to the finance company, which lent it to Y.I.H. W.Y.I.H. took control of the works and contracted with necessary third parties. The Commissioners contended that W.Y.I.H. Co. had not received payment before June 1, 1984 but received it when the loans were repaid.

Held, allowing the appeal, that the receipt of the £1,000,000 was payment in fact and law. The requirement that such sum was lent to the finance company did not alter this.

WEST YORKSHIRE INDEPENDENT HOSPITAL (CONTRACT SERVICES) *v.* CUSTOMS AND EXCISE COMMISSIONERS (1986) V.A.T.T.R. 151, V.A.T. Tribunal.

3862. Zero-rating—confectionery

[Value Added Tax Act 1983 (c.55), Sched. 5, Group 1.]

The taxpayer company manufactured confectionery by baking cereal and nuts with a syrup and mixing them with certain unbaked ingredients. A value added tax tribunal concluded that the products were more akin to biscuits than to chocolates or sweets and so were not excepted from zero-rating as confectionery similar to chocolate or sweets within excepted item no. 2 of V.A.T.A. 1983, Sched. 5, Group 1.

Held, dismissing the Commissioners' appeal, that the tribunal, having had regard to all the relevant law and facts, had reached a decision which could not be impugned.

CUSTOMS AND EXCISE COMMISSIONERS *v.* QUAKER OATS [1987] S.T.C. 638, Kennedy J.

3863. Zero-rating—food—catering—independent contractor

M carried on business as a vendor of seafoods. He bought bulk supplies of seafoods, broke them down into small packets and provided these to salesmen. Each salesman was told to sell such packets in specified pubs and in the street and received 25 per cent. commission on sales. There was no allowance given by M in respect of unsold packets. The salesmen were self-employed for income tax purposes. The Commissioners decided that supplies were made to the public by M of food in the course of catering which, pursuant to V.A.T.A. 1983, Sched. 5, Grp. 1, item 1, note (3) includes any supply of food for consumption on the premises. Such supplies are standard-rated.

Held, that the supplies were made to the public by M and all supplies were in the course of catering except those made in the street. The latter only fell to be zero-rated.

MOWBRAY (KEVIN) *v.* CUSTOMS AND EXCISE COMMISSIONERS (1986) V.A.T.T.R. 266, V.A.T. Tribunal.

3864. Zero-rating—medical or scientific equipment—surgical washing machine

L Co. manufactured expensive washing machines specially designed to clean surgical equipment. Such machines were supplied to "eligible bodies" within V.A.T.A. 1983 Sch. 5, Grp. 16 and accordingly such supplies were zero-rated if the machines were "medical, scientific or computer equipment for use in medical research, diagnosis or treatment", within Grp. 16, Note 4(*a*). L Co. maintained that such machines were within Note 4(*a*).

Held, that the question was whether the washing machines could properly be described as scientific equipment in common parlance. On the evidence, this was not the case. The appeal would be dismissed.

LANCER U.K. *v.* CUSTOMS AND EXCISE COMMISSIONERS (1986) V.A.T.T.R. 112, V.A.T. Tribunal.

WATER AND WATERWORKS

3865. Land drainage—drainage charge

GENERAL DRAINAGE CHARGE (ANGLIAN WATER AUTHORITY) (ASCERTAINMENT) ORDER 1987 (No. 318) [45p], made under the Land Drainage Act 1976 (c.70), s.49(1)(3); operative on April 1, 1987; makes provision in relation to general drainage charges which may be raised by the said Authority in their local drainage districts for the years ending March 31, 1988, 1989 and 1990.

3866. Rights of riparian owners—pollution of water—whether owner entitled to pure water

The owner of a river bank has the right to have water in the river flow past him in its natural state, both in terms of quantity and quality, so that a water authority which fails to warn him of dangerously high levels of chemicals in the water may be liable to him in negligence.

P was a farmer and was licensed by the local water authority to take water, for irrigation purposes, from a river running through his land. N.C.B. also had an agreement with the water authority that water from a nearby mining operation, which had a high chloride content, should be discharged into the river. During a year of drought there was insufficient water in the river properly to dilute the chloride, with the result that the level exceeded that which was safe for P's crops.

Held, that (i) a riparian owner is entitled to have the river flow through his land in its ordinary and unpolluted state, so that pollution of the water might be actionable as an interference with P's proprietary rights; (ii) on the facts N.C.B. had failed to establish a prescriptive right to discharge the chloride into the river, both because there was no certainty and uniformity of their use of the river, and because time began to run only from the date of the first actual damage suffered by P; (iii) further the water authority were liable in negligence because they failed to warn P of the danger inherent in the higher livel of salinity. It was reasonable for P to have relied on the water authority, who were aware of the purpose for which water was removed from the river.

SCOTT-WHITEHEAD *v.* NATIONAL COAL BOARD (1987) 53 P. & C.R. 263, Stuart-Smith J.

3867. Sewers—poorly constructed sewers—vesting order—Secretary of State's decision

[Public Health Act 1936 (c.49), s.17.]

In the 1960's planning permission was granted for residential development and for surface and foul water sewers. The sewers were defective. In 1981, residents applied to the District Council to make a declaration vesting the sewers in the Authority under the Public Health Act 1936, s.17. The application was refused. An inspector, following an inquiry, held that the lead condition of the sewers precluded him from recommending a vesting order. In November 1984 the Secretary of State directed the Council to adopt the sewers.

Held, on appeal by the Water Authority, that the Secretary of State's letter was so unreasonable in the conclusion reached that it should be quashed. He had not made a proper analysis of firm facts. Decision quashed.

R. *v.* SECRETARY OF STATE FOR WALES AND A.B. HUTTON (SECRETARY TO THE MAES GERDDI RESIDENTS ASSOCIATION [1987] J.P.L. 711, MacPherson J.

3868. Water authorities

ANGLIAN WATER AUTHORITY (LITTLEPORT AND DOWNHAM INTERNAL DRAINAGE DISTRICT) ORDER 1987 (No. 815) [85p] made under the Land Drainage Act 1976 (c.70), ss.11(4), 109(6); operative on April 24, 1987; provides for the creation of the said drainage district from two existing districts which are abolished.

SEVERN TRENT WATER AUTHORITY (ABOLITION OF THE ELFORD INTERNAL DRAINAGE DISTRICT) ORDER 1957 (No. 2230) [85p]; made under the Land Drainage Act 1976, ss.11(4) and 109(6); operative on December 8, 1987; confirms a scheme for the abolition of the Elford Internal Drainage District.

SEVERN-TRENT WATER AUTHORITY (RECONSTRUCTION OF THE CORPORATION OF THE LEVEL OF HATFIELD CHASE) ORDER 1987 (No. 1928) [45p], made under the Land Drainage Act 1976, ss.13, 109(6); operative on November 4, 1987; provide for the reconstruction of the said Corporation as the drainage board for the said district.

SEVERN-TRENT WATER AUTHORITY (RECONSTRUCTION OF THE RIVERS IDLE AND RYTON INTERNAL DRAINAGE BOARD) ORDER 1987 (No. 1929) [45p], made under the Land Drainage Act 1976, ss.13, 109(1); operative on November 3, 1987; provides for the reconstruction of the said drainage board.

SOUTHERN WATER AUTHORITY (ROMNEY MARSH LEVELS INTERNAL DRAINAGE DISTRICT) ORDER 1987 (No. 555) [£1·40], made under the Land Drainage Act 1976, ss.11(4), 109(6); operative on March 16, 1987; provides for the amalgamation of a number of internal drainage districts to form the Romney Marsh Levels Internal Drainage District.

THAMES WATER AUTHORITY (TRANSFER OF PROPERTY OF DARTFORD AND CRAYFORD NAVIGATION COMMISSIONERS) ORDER 1987 (No. 1360) [45p], made under the Water Resources Act 1963 (c.38), ss.12(1)(*c*), 82(1)(*b*)(2)(4)(9)(10)(*a*); operative on August 17, 1987; transfers to the said authority all the property, rights and liabilities of the said Commissioners.

WATER AUTHORITIES (RETURN ON ASSETS) ORDER 1987 (No. 2022) [85p], made under the Water Act 1973 (c.37), s.29(2)(*a*); operative on December 23, 1987; gives directions to the water authorities. It specifies the rate of return on the value of their net assets which the Secretary of State considers each water authority can reasonably achieve for the financial year 1988–89.

WELSH WATER AUTHORITY (LLWYS ISAF BOREHOLES) (DISCHARGE) ORDER 1987 (No. 107) [45p], made under the Water Resources Act 1971 (c.34), s.1; operative on February 9, 1987; authorises the discharge of water from the borehole.

WESSEX WATER AUTHORITY (BLASHFORD LAKES DISCHARGE) ORDER 1987 (No. 1354) [45p], made under the Water Resources Act 1971, s.1; operative on July 28, 1987; authorises the discharge of water from the River Avon into the Blashford Lakes.

3869. Water orders

Order made under the Water Act (c.42), ss.23, 33, 50 and 59(1)(*a*):
S.I. 1987 No. 1434 (East Surrey) [85p].

Orders made under the Water Act 1945 (c.42), ss.23, 32(1), 33, 50:
S.I. 1987 Nos. 234 (Tendring Hundred Water) [80p]; 613 (Mid Southern Water) [80p]; 750 (Cambridge Water) [85p]; 842 (Bristol Waterworks) [85p]; 948 (Tendring Hundred Water) [85p]; 1234 (Yorkshire Water Authority) [45p]; 1235 (Yorkshire Water Authority) [45p]; 1236 (Yorkshire Water Authority) [45p]; 1237 (Yorkshire Water Authority) [45p]; 1322 (Severn-Trent Water Authority (Wallgrange Boreholes)) [45p]; 1597 (Hartlepools Water) [45p]; 1599 (Welsh Water Authority) [45p]; 1602 (Anglian Water Authority) [45p]; 1839 (Anglian Water Authority) [45p]; 2006 (Cambridge Water) [45]; 2007 (Thames Water Authority) [85p] 2008 (Thames Water Authority) [45p]; 2073 (Sunderland and South Shields) [85p]; 2271 (Severn-Trent Water Authority) [85p].

3870. Water rates—charges scheme—whether discriminatory. See SEVERN TRENT WATER AUTHORITY *v.* CARDSHOPS, §3198.

WEIGHTS AND MEASURES

3871. Carriage of solid fuel by rail

WEIGHTS AND MEASURES (CARRIAGE OF SOLID FUEL BY RAIL) ORDER 1987 (No. 216) [45p], made under the Weights and Measures Act 1985 (c.72), ss.22(1)(2), 24, 86(1); operative on March 1, 1987; amends the provisions of Pt. IV of Sched. 5 to the 1985 Act relating to the carriage of solid fuel by rail.

3872. Local standards

WEIGHTS AND MEASURES (LOCAL AND WORKING STANDARD CAPACITY MEASURES AND TESTING EQUIPMENT) REGULATIONS 1987 (No. 51) [£1·60], made under the Weights and Measures Act 1985 (c.72), ss. 4(5)(6), 5(9), 86(1), 94(1); operative on February 16, 1987; prescribe the methods of testing and adjusting, and the limits of error for working standard capacity measures and testing equipment.

3873. Measuring instruments

MEASURING INSTRUMENTS (EEC INITIAL VERIFICATION REQUIREMENTS) (FEES) (AMENDMENT) REGULATIONS 1987 (No. 802) [45p], made under the Finance Act 1973 (c.51), s.56(1)(2); operative on June 1, 1987; further amend S.I. 1982 No. 811 so as to increase fees payable in connection with the verification of certain measuring instruments and systems.

MEASURING INSTRUMENTS (EEC PATTERN APPROVAL REQUIREMENTS) (FEES) REGULATIONS 1987 (No. 803) [85p], made under the Finance Act 1973, s.56(1)(2); operative on June 1, 1987; increase fees payable in connection with an application for grant of EEC pattern approval.

3874. National Metrological Co-ordinating Unit

NATIONAL METROLOGICAL CO-ORDINATING UNIT (TRANSFER OF FUNCTIONS AND ABOLITION) ORDER 1987 (No. 2187) [85p], made under the Weights and Measures Act 1985 (c.72), ss.62(2)(*a*)(*c*)(3), 86(1); operative on December 17, 1987; abolishes the said unit having transferred all of its functions to the Secretary of State.

3875. Quantity marking and abbreviations of units

WEIGHTS AND MEASURES (QUANTITY MARKING AND ABBREVIATIONS OF UNITS) REGULATIONS 1987 (No. 1538) [£1·60], made under the Weights and Measures Act 1985 (c.72), ss.15(1)(*g*), 23(1)(*a*)(*d*), 48(1)(*a*)(1A), 66, 68(1)(1A)(*a*), 86(1), 94(1); operative on January 1, 1988; consolidate S.I. 1975 No. 1319, as amended.

3876. Sale by measure—use of unstamped measure by licensee—whether measure used by licensee's employers

[Weights and Measures Act 1963 (c.31), s.11(2).]

The owner of a public house could be guilty of using an unstamped measure for trade where the measure was used by his employee who was the licensee of the public house.

C owned a public house in which S was employed as the manager. S was the licensee. S used a jug for measuring purposes that did not bear a stamp indicating that it had been passed fit for use for measuring by an inspector. There was evidence that C knew S was using the jug and had not issued instructions to S not to do so. The jug was not supplied by C. C was prosecuted for an offence under s.11(2) of the Weights and Measures Act 1963 of using an article for trade as equipment for measuring that had not been stamped by an inspector as fit for such use. At the end of the prosecution case C submitted that there was no case to answer because by virtue of s.160 of the Licensing Act 1964 only the licensee was capable of selling intoxicating liquor. C's submission was upheld.

Held, allowing the prosecutor's appeal, that it could not be said that C did not use the measure through the agency of their employee, S, despite the fact that only the licensee was capable of selling intoxicating liquor under s.160 Licensing Act 1964. There was sufficient evidence that in using the measure S was acting on C's behalf to establish a prima facie case (*Goodfellow* v. *Johnson* [1965] C.L.Y. 1695 considered).

EVANS *v.* CLIFTON INNS (1987) 85 L.G.R. 119, D.C.

WILLS AND SUCCESSION

3877. Condition of defeasance—beneficiaries not to marry "outside the Jewish faith"—whether void for uncertainty

The words "the Jewish faith" are not necessarily void for uncertainty when contained in a condition of defeasance, and the court may hear extrinsic evidence of the surrounding circumstances to show the meaning attributed by the testator.

T, the testator, left certain bequests to beneficiaries provided that "they shall not marry outside the Jewish faith."

Held, whether the beneficiaries' interests were vested but liable to be divested, or were contingent interests, the proviso was a condition of defeasance. However, the words were not necessarily void for uncertainty, and the court would adjourn the question for the parties to file extrinsic evidence of the surrounding circumstances to show the meaning attributed to the words by the testator (*Clayton* v. *Ramsden* [1943] A.C. 320 H.L.(E.) and *Tuck's Settlement Trusts, Re* [1978] C.L.Y. 2666 considered).

TEPPER'S WILL TRUSTS, *Re*; KRAMER *v.* RUDA [1987] 2 W.L.R. 729, Scott J.

3878. Construction—gift to daughter for life thereafter to "relatives"—whether limited to statutory next of kin

A daughter's exercise of a power of distribution conferred by her mother's will, to her "cousin's children" who were not statutory next of kin, was perfectly valid since no uncertainty arose.

A testatrix bequeathed to her daughter her possessions for life the remainder to be "divided amongst her own relatives according to her own discretion." Her estate included two freehold houses; the daughter devised them to trustees who were required to pay the income to "my cousin during her life", then sell the houses dividing the proceeds equally between the cousin's children. The daughter had 20 statutory next of kin which included the cousin, but not her children. It was accepted that the testatrix had given the daughter a life interest in the estate with a special power of appointment in favour of the daughter's relatives. The question arose whether the daughter's "relatives" apart from next of kin were entitled to take under an exercise of that special power.

Held, the gift to the cousin's children was valid, since no uncertainty arose from the use of the word "relative" (*Gansloser's Will Trusts, Re* (1947–1951) C.L.C. 10919 considered; *Deakin, Re* [1894] 3 Ch. 565 not followed).

POULTON'S WILL TRUSTS, *Re* 1987 1 W.L.R. 795 Warner J.

3879. Family provision

FAMILY PROVISION (INTESTATE SUCCESSION) ORDER 1987 (No. 799) [45p], made under the Family Provision Act 1966 (c.35), s.1(1)(*a*), (*b*); operative on June 1, 1987; increases the fixed sum in favour of a surviving spouse charged on the estate of a person dying intestate.

3880. Family provision—assurances from other parties that strict rights under will not to be enforced—whether reasonable provision made for widow

The deceased left a widow and two sons and a son by a previous marriage. The estate was divided equally between the four of them. Before his death, the wife had maintained the household and helped pay off the mortgage. After the death she and her sons continued to live in the house. The other son suffered from mental illness that affected his prospects of work. He lived in a council flat. The widow made a claim under the Inheritance (Provision for Family and Dependants) Act 1975 (c.63). At the hearing, the judge, having heard assurances from the widow's sons that they did not intend to enforce their rights under the will and from the stepson to the effect that he would take provision under the will by being bought out at a valuation that would not require the sale of the property, then decided that the widow was able to service a loan to buy out the stepson and that a reasonable provision had been made for her under the will.

Held, that it was necessary to consider two questions—did the will make reasonable provision and, if not, what provision should the Court make. The judge had to have regard to the state of facts at the date of the hearing, but it was not permissible for a conclusion that reasonable provision had been made to be based upon unenforceable assurances given at the hearing. Accordingly, the judge had misdirected himself. In fact, the widow only had one quarter of the estate—that could not be reasonable provision for her as it gave her no security in the house. Taking into account the illness and uncertain future of the stepson as well as the need to provide the widow with a secure home, the stepson would be given a legacy of £7,500 raised by a mortgage on the estate and the house would be vested in the widow absolutely.

RAJABALLY *v.* RAJABALLY (1987) 17 Fam.Law 314, C.A.

3881. Family provision—disposition to defeat

Mr. & Mrs. C married in May 1965. He was then aged 60 and she 45. For each it was a second marriage. Mr. C had one daughter, T, by his first marriage. Mr. & Mrs. C lived together in a house bought by Mr. C in 1950. In April 1977, Mr. C made a will under which he gave Mrs. C the right to live in the house until remarriage. Subject to that he gave the house to T and divided the rest of his property between Mrs. C and T. In June 1977, Mr. C executed a deed of gift whereby in consideration of natural love and affection and in consideration of a covenant on T's part, he conveyed the house to T and she entered into a covenant to permit Mr. & Mrs. C or the survivor of them to live in the property. T was to be released from the covenant if Mrs. C remarried after Mr. C's death or if she let or shared possession of the property. In June 1983, Mr. C presented a divorce petition alleging unreasonable behaviour. On July 6, 1983 he made a new will appointing T and her husband to be his executors and leaving everything if he should die possessed of to T. On July 15, 1983 Mr. C executed a deed releasing T of her covenant to allow Mrs. C to live in the house. Mr. C died in September 1983.

Held, on the question of whether the July 15, 1983 deed of variation was a "disposition" within s.10 of the Inheritance (Provision for Family and Dependants) Act 1975, that the 1983 deed of variation was a disposition within s.10. Immediately prior to the execution of that deed the deceased was possessed of the benefit of the covenant given by his daughter under the original deed of gift. He, and after his death, his personal representatives had the right to enforce, or, if he or they chose, to release that covenant. Unless and until released, the covenant was capable of being made the subject of an order for specific performance in respect of the deceased's and Mrs. C's occupation, on the application of the deceased, or after his death, his personal representatives. That right was an asset belonging to the deceased. In the event he chose to give up that right, to release it, in favour of his daughter. S.10(7) was not a comprehensive definition of "disposition" but even if it was the deed of release was a gift of property of any description within that sub-section, although the property given in this case was of a very unusual nature. Further, the benefit of the covenant was of value. Its existence was a serious fetter on T's right in and enjoyment of the house, and it substantially depreciated the property in her hands. The release of that covenant would be of considerable value to her; prima facie she could be expected to be willing to pay for the release of her obligations under that covenant. The person to whom such payment would need to be made by her would be a person alone entitled to enforce the covenant, the deceased, or, after his death, his personal representatives. In this way he had an asset which had a realisable value. Appeal from Recorder Boothman.

CLIFFORD *v.* TANNER, June 10, 1986 (CAT. No. 616).

3882. Family provision—running of time—limited grant

[Inheritance (Provision for Family and Dependants) Act 1975 (c.63), s.4.]

A limited grant had been made in 1983 of the deceased's (D's) estate to two solicitors, limited to pursuing negligence claims in relation to the road accident in which he had died. Probate of D's will was granted in 1987. The question arose whether time ran under s.4 from the date of the grant or the full grant of probate.

Held, (1) that the limited grant was not "the first taking out of representation" required for time to begin to run under s.4 as it merely enabled a particular thing to be done in relation to the estate and did not enable distribution to take place; (2) that in any case the court would have exercised its discretion to extend time for six months from the date of grant of probate.

JOHNSON (PAUL ANTHONY) DEC'D, *Re,* May 8, 1987, Latey J. [*Ex rel. John Dagnall, Barrister.*]

3883. Probate rules. See PRACTICE, §3087.

3884. Provision for widow—estate insolvent—matrimonial home transferred to daughter for £100 prior to husband's death—whether provision for widow to be ordered

P married the deceased and went to live in his house. P spent most of her savings on day-to-day living, holidays and paying off the deceased's overdraft. The deceased made a will leaving P £8,000 from the estate and a life interest in the matrimonial home. Before his death the deceased transferred the matrimonial home to his daughter for £100. As the estate was insolvent that effectively rendered the will useless to P. The deceased and P separated shortly before the deceased's death. On his death P claimed under the inheritance (Provision for Family and Dependants) Act 1975 for payment of part of the £27,000 realised by the sale of the matrimonial home by the daughter.

Held, that if the matrimonial home had been part of the deceased's estate the court would have held that no reasonable provision had been made for P and would have ordered a lump sum payment to her out of the proceeds of the sale of the home. When the deceased sold the house to his daughter he did so with the intention of preventing an order for financial provision being made. Having regard to the circumstances of P, her conduct and financial resources togther with all the other circumstances of the case the daughter would be ordered to pay a capital sum of £10,000 to P from the proceeds of the sale of the former matrimonial home.

DAWKINS (DEC'D), *Re*; DAWKINS *v.* JUDD [1986] 2 F.L.R. 360, Bush J.

3885. Testator's solicitors—whether duty of care owed to a potential beneficiary. See CLARKE *v.* BRUCE LANCE & CO., §3549.

WORDS AND PHRASES

3886. The following words and phrases have been judicially considered in 1987:

about, §3433
acceptance of valuable security, §837
action (short of dismissal), §3766
any person, §209
armed, §812
convenience, §3119
date of (rent) review, §2213
entered at customs house, §3401
equipment, §1307
evidence, §561
exhibition of moving pictures, §2310
fines, §1306
fixed plant and machinery, §356
funeral, §3526
house, §2168
importer, §1109
issue, §562
letting value, §2165
market price, §3339
motor vehicle, §3295
national origins, §3203
new, §447
occupation, §2134
open space, §2227
oppression, §559
ordinarily resident, §1979
parent, §3527
person, §3512
persons of experience in education, §2369
process, §1852
relatives, §3878
serious professional misconduct, §2400
victimisation, §1372
vulnerable, §1906
waste land, §315
whether in berth or not, §3405
wireless telegraphy apparatus, §3579

BOOKS AND ARTICLES

INDEX OF BOOKS

The following books were published in 1987. They are listed under the appropriate Current Law heading. Books relating to Scotland are listed separately.

ADMINISTRATIVE LAW

Cripps, Y.—The Legal Implications of Disclosure in the Public Interest. Hardback: £32·50: ISBN 0 906214 40 8.

Hood Phillips Constitutional and Administrative Law by O. H. Phillips and P. Jackson. [Seventh edition]. Hardback: £25·00: ISBN 0 421 35030 X. Paperback: £16·95: ISBN 0 421 35040 7.

Taggart, M. (Editor) [New Zealand]: Judicial Review of Administrative Action in the 1980s: Problems and Prospects. Hardback: £28·00. ISBN 0 19 558151 2.

AGENCY

Long, A.—Powers of Attorney and Other Instruments Conferring Authority. Hardback: £25·00: ISBN 0 902197 50 9.

AGRICULTURE

Stanley, O.—Taxation of Farmers and Landowners. [Third edition]. Hardback: £24·95: ISBN 0 406 38310 3.

Wood, D. et. al.—Milk Quotas: Law and Practice. Paperback: £25·00.

ANIMALS

Cassell, D.—The Horse and the Law. Hardback: £10·95: ISBN 0 7153 8813 4.

ARBITRATION

Bernstein, R. et al.—Handbook of Arbitration practice. Hardback: £62.00: ISBN 0 421 31790 6.

Schwebel, S.—International Arbitration: Three Salient Problems [Hersch Lauterpacht Memorial Lectures]. Hardback: £33·00: ISBN 0 949009 02 4.

AVIATION

Pryke, R.—Competition among International Airlines. [Thames Essay; No. 46]. Paperback: £8·95: ISBN 0 566 05333 0.

BANKING

Bills of Exchange Act 1882 annotated by A. Arora. [LLP Annotated Acts]. Paperback: £18·50: ISBN 1 85044 095 6.

Chorafas, D.—Strategic Planning for Electronic Banking. Hardback: £38·00: ISBN 0 406 10087 X.

Gordon-Saker, P. and Stubbs, M.—Insolvency: Procedure Notes. Paperback: £9·95: ISBN 0 08 033089 4.

Grier, I. and Floyd, R.—Voluntary Liquidation, Receivership and Administration [Longman Practitioner Series]. Second edition. Paperback: £17·95: ISBN 0 85121 180 1.

Marsh, S. H. and Soulsby, J.—Outlines of English Law. [Fourth edition]. Paperback: £7·95: ISBN: 0 07 084980 3.

Penn, G., Shea, A., and Arora, A.—Banking Law: Vol. 1; The Law relating to Domestic Banking Paperback: £18·95: ISBN 0 421 36060 7.

Pennington, R.—Bank Finance for Companies. Paperback: £15·00: ISBN 0 421 38490 5.

Vaughan J.—Banking Act 1979 [LLP Annotated Acts] Paperback: £18·50: ISBN 1 85044 106 5.

Venedikian, H. M. and Warfield, G. A.—Export-Import Financing [Wiley Professional Banking and Finance Series]. Second edition. Hardback: £33·70: ISBN 0 471 82449 6.

Weaving's Bankruptcy Procedure.—By S. A. Frieze [Longman Practitioner Series]. Ninth edition. Paperback: £12·95: ISBN 0 85121 307 3.

BANKRUPTCY

Carney, T. and Hanks, P. [Australia]—Australian Social Security Law, Policy and Administration. Hardback: £25·00: ISBN 0 19 554754 3.

Grenville, C.—Bankruptcy: the law and practice. Hardback: £28·50: ISBN 1 85190 032 2.

BANKRUPTCY—*cont.*
Grier, I. and Floyd, R.—Personal Insolvency: a practical guide. Hardback: £19·50: ISBN 0 421 36010 0.
Ratford, W. et al.—Insolvency: Understanding the New Law. Paperback: £9·95: ISBN 1 85185 062 7.

BRITISH COMMONWEALTH
Freckelton, I. [Australia]—The Trial of the Expert. Hardback: £35·00: ISBN 0 19 554566 4.
Swinfen, D.—Imperial Appeal: the Debate on the Appeal to the Privy Council, 1833–1986. Hardback: £35·00: ISBN 0 7190 1895 1.
Taggart, M. (Editor) [New Zealand] Judicial Review of Administrative Action in the 1980s: Problems and Prospects. Hardback: £28·00: ISBN 0 19 558151 2.

BUILDING AND CONSTRUCTION
Building Law Reports, vol. 34.—Edited by H. Lloyd, C. Reese and N. Baatz. Hardback: £19·00: ISBN 0 582 49495 8.
Construction Law Reports, vol. 8—Edited by M. Furmston and V. Powell-Smith. Hardback: £18·50: ISBN 0 85139 801 4.
Construction Law Reports, vol. 9.—Edited by M. Furmston and V. Powell-Smith. Hardback: £18·50: ISBN 0 85139 802 2.
Eaglestone, F.—Supplement to Insurance under the JCT Forms. Booklet: £4·95: ISBN 0 00 383434 4.
Hibberd, P.—Sub-Contracts Under the JCT Intermediate Form. Hardback: £22·50: ISBN 0 632 01869 0.
Parris, J.—Companies for Construction Professionals. Hardback: £19·95: ISBN 0 00 383325 9.
Powell—Smith, V. and Furmston, M.—A building contract casebook. [First edition (revised)]. Hardback: £27·50: ISBN 0 632 02109 8.

CAPITAL GAINS TAX
Allied Dunbar Tax Guide 1987–88—by W. I. Sinclair. Hardback: £12·95: ISBN 0 85121 292 1.
British Tax Cases 1986. Hardback: £26·00: ISBN 0 86325 123 4.
British Tax Legislation 1987–88, vols. 1A & 1B. Paperback: £18·00: ISBN 0 86325 116 1 (Vol. 1A); 0 86325 117 X (Vol. 1B).
Butterworths U.K. Tax Guide 1987–88.—Edited by J. Tiley. [Sixth edition]. Paperback: £12·00: ISBN 0 406 50496 2.
Butterworths Yellow Tax Handbook 1987–88. Twenty-sixth edition. Paperback: £19·00: ISBN 0 406 51004 0.
Potter and Monroe's Tax Planning with precedents—Edited by A. Thornhill and K. Prosser. [Tenth edition]. Hardback: £49·00: ISBN 0 421 33420 7.
Pritchard, W.—Taxation. [Eighth edition]. Paperback: £8·95: ISBN 0 7121 2038 6.
Slevin, K.—Roll-Over Relief for Business Assets: the Capital Gains Tax Rules Explained. Booklet: £7·00: ISBN 0 86325 119 6.
Tolley's Capital Gains Tax 1987–88 by P. Noakes and J. Boulding. Paperback: £14·50: ISBN 0 85459 290 3.
Tolley's Tax Guide 1987–88—by A. Homer and R. Burrows. [Fifth edition]. Hardback: £14·95: ISBN 0 85459 293 8.
Tolley's Taxwise Taxation Workbook No. 1 1987–88 by A. Homer, R. Burrows and P. Gravestock. Paperback: £14·25: ISBN 0 85459 257 1.
Touche Ross Tax Guide for the Family 1987/88—by B. Packer and C. Sandy. [Second edition]. Paperback: £4·95: ISBN 0 333 44961 4.
Whitehouse C. and Stuart-Buttle, E.—Revenue Law: Principles and Practice. [Fifth edition]. Paperback: £20·95: ISBN 0 406 00533 8.

CAPITAL TRANSFER TAX
Allied Dunbar Tax Guide 1987–88—by W. I. Sinclair. Hardback: £12·95: ISBN 0 85121 292 1.
British Tax Cases 1986. Hardback: £26·00: ISBN 0 86325 123 4.
British Tax Legislation 1987–88, vols. 1A & 1B. Paperback: £18·00: ISBN: 0 86325 116 1 (Vol. 1A); 0 86325 117 X (Vol. 1B).
Butterworths U.K. Tax Guide 1987–88.—Edited by J. Tiley. [Sixth edition]. Paperback: £12·00: ISBN 0 406 50496 2.
Potter and Monroe's Tax Planning with precedents—Edited by A. Thornhill and K. Prosser. [Tenth edition]. Hardback: £49·00: ISBN 0 421 33420 7
Tolley's Tax Guide 1987–88—by A. Homer and R. Burrows. [Fifth edition]. Hardback: £14·95: ISBN 0 85459 293 8.
Tolley's Tax Planning 1987—edited by G. Saunders [Seventh edition.] Paperback: £29·50 ISBN 0 85459 246 6.

BOOKS

CAPITAL TRANSFER TAX—*cont.*

Touche Ross Tax Guide for the Family 1987/88—by B. Packer and C. Sandy. [Second edition]. Paperback: £4·95: ISBN 0 333 44961 4.

Whitehouse, C. and Stuart-Buttle, E.—Revenue Law: Principles and Practice. [Fifth edition]. Paperback: £20·95: ISBN 0 406 00533 8.

CARRIERS

Brown, L.—Law for the Haulier. Hardback: £16·95: ISBN 1 85091 147 9.

CHARITIES

Brooks, R. and Vincent, R.—Charity Accounting. Paperback: £18·95: ISBN 0 406 26100 8.

Cracknell, D.—Charities: Law and Practice. [Longman Practitioner Series]. Third edition. Hardback: £29·50: ISBN 0 85121 300 6.

Riddall, J.—The Law of Trusts. [Third edition]. Hardback: £24·00: ISBN 0 406 64842 5. Paperback: £15·95: ISBN 0 406 64843 3.

CIVIL LIBERTIES

Marsh N. (Editor)—Public Access to Government-held information. Paperback: £28.00: ISBN 0 420 47610 5.

CLUBS AND ASSOCIATIONS

Josling, J. and Alexander, L.—Law of Clubs. [Longman Practitioner Series]. Sixth edition. Paperback: £26·50: ISBN 0 85121 297 2.

COMPANY LAW

Anderson, H.—Administrators: Part II of the Insolvency Act 1986. Hardback: £24·50: ISBN 0 421 34820 8.

Blake, A. and Bond, H.J.—Company Law. [SWOT Success Without Tears Series]. Second edition. Paperback: £7·95: ISBN 0 85185 071 6.

Blake, J.—Company Reports and Accounts: their Significance and Uses. Paperback: £13·95: ISBN 0 273 02697 6.

Bough, J.—Company Accounts. Hardback: £19·50: ISBN 0 421 36020 8.

Boyle and Birds' Company Law.—Edited by A. J. Boyle, J. Birds and G. Penn. [Second edition]. Paperback: £20·00: ISBN 0 85308 090 9.

British Companies Legislation: Companies Act 1985, Insolvency Act 1986 and related legislation—[Third edition]. Paperback: £16·00: ISBN 0 86325 126 9.

British Company Law Cases, vol. 2, 1986. Hardback: £26·00: ISBN 0 86325 125 0.

Butterworths Company Law Cases 1986. Edited by D. D. Prentice. Hardback: £61·00: ISBN 0 406 07660 X.

Butterworths Insolvency Law Handbook—Edited by M. Crystal. Paperback: £22·95: ISBN 0 406 50006 1.

Cane, L.—Guide to Company Law. [Second edition]. Paperback: £15·00: ISBN 0 86325 095 5.

Companies Consolidation Legislation 1987.—Edited by G. Morse. [Second edition]. Paperback: £36·00: ISBN 0 421 38360 7.

Company Law Materials. [Eleventh edition]. Paperback: £12·00: ISBN 0 85308 091 7.

Ferrara, R., Brown, M. and Hall, J. [U.S.A.]. Takeovers: Attack and Survival: A Strategist's Manual. Hardback: £60·00: ISBN 0 88063 099 X.

Finney, M. J. and Dixon, J. C.—Companies Operating Overseas: UK Tax Law and Practice. [Longman Commercial Series.] Hardback: £35·00: ISBN 0 85120 877 0.

Flint, D.—A Guide to Liquidation in Scotland. Paperback: £12·50: ISBN 0 85308 092 5.

Frieze, S.—Compulsory Winding Up Procedure. [Longman Practice Notes]. Second edition. Paperback: £12·95: ISBN 0 85121 179 8.

Gammie, M.—Tax Strategy for Companies. [Fourth edition.] Paperback: £30·00: ISBN 0 85120 921 1.

Gordon-Saker, P. and Stubbs, M.—Insolvency: Procedure Notes. Paperback: £9·95: ISBN 0 08 033089 4.

Greene, J. and Fletcher, I.—The Law and Practice of Receivership in Scotland. Hardback: £48·00: ISBN 0 406 00527 3.

Gurney, R.—Share Valuation Manual. Hardback: £35·00: ISBN 0 566 02678 3.

Hahlo's Cases and Materials on Company Law—by H. Hahlo and J. Farrar. [Third edition]. Hardback: £32·00: ISBN 0 421 31730 2. Paperback: £24·00: ISBN 0 421 31740 X.

Keenan, D. and Riches, S.—Business Law. Paperback: £8·95: ISBN 0 273 02415 9.

Lawton, P., Rigby, E. and Hall, L.—Meetings: their Law and Practice. [M & E Handbooks]. Fourth edition. Paperback: £6·50: ISBN 0 7121 1300 2.

Livens, L.—Share Valuation Handbook. Paperback: £12·95: ISBN 0 906840 98 8.

Loose, P. and Yelland, J.—The Company Director. [Sixth edition]. Hardback: £15·00: ISBN 0 85308 085 2.

COMPANY LAW—*cont.*

Marsh, S. H. and Soulsby, J.—Outlines of English Law. [Fourth edition]. Paperback: £7·95: ISBN 0 07 084980 3.

Mayson, S., French, D. and Ryan, C.—A Practical Approach to Company Law. [Fourth edition]. Paperback: £17·95: ISBN 1 85185 068 6.

Montague, J.—Business Law. [Chambers Commerce Series]. Paperback: £3·95: ISBN 0 550 20702 3.

Nelson's Tables: Company Procedure—by A. M. Peck and A. Robertson. [Tenth edition]. Paperback: £13·50: ISBN 0 85121 296 4.

Northey and Leigh's Introduction to Company Law—by L. H. Leigh, V. H. Joffe and D. Goldberg. [Fourth edition]. Hardback: £25·00: ISBN 0406 63106 9. Paperback: £16·95: ISBN 0 406 63107 7.

Oliver, M. C.—Company Law—Edited by E. A. Marshall. [The M & E Handbook Series]. Tenth edition. Paperback: £6·95: ISBN 0 7121 0698 7.

Parris, J.—Companies for Construction Professionals. Hardback: £19·95: ISBN 0 00 383325 9.

Pennington, R.—Bank Finance for Companies. Paperback: £15·00: ISBN 0 421 38490 5.

Pennington, R.—Company Liquidations: the Procedure. [Insolvency Law Guide and Practice Series] Paperback: £8·50: ISBN 0 85308 125 5.

Pennington, R.—Directors' Personal Liability. Hardback: £20·00: ISBN 0 00 383294 5.

Pettet, B. G.—Company Law in Change: Current Legal Problems. [Current Legal Problems]. Paperback: £16·00: ISBN 0 420 47750 0.

Power, B. [Ireland]. Accounting Law and Practice for Limited Companies. Hardback: £30·00: ISBN 0 7171 1518 6.

Ranking and Spicer's Company Law by J. M. Gullick. [Thirteenth edition]. Paperback: £14·95: ISBN 0 406 67890 1.

Ranking, Spicer and Pegler's Business Law for Accountants—by N. Bourne. [Fifteenth edition]. Paperback: £15·95: ISBN 0 406 67830 8.

Ratford, W. et al.—Insolvency: Understanding the New Law. Paperback: £9·95: ISBN 1 85185 062 7.

Ryan, C.—Company Directors. [Second edition]. Paperback: £25·00: ISBN 0 86325 094 7.

Sabine, M.—Corporate finance. Hardback: £35·00: ISBN 0 406 25956 9.

Sealy, L.—Insolvency: Disqualification and Personal Liability of Directors. [Second edition]. Booklet: £6·00: ISBN 0 86325 130 7.

Sealy, L. and Milman, D.—Insolvency: Annotated Guide to the 1986 Insolvency Legislation. Paperback: £19.50: ISBN: 0 86325 082 3.

Seidl-Hohenveldern, I.—Corporations in and under International Law. [Hersch Lauterpacht Memorial Lectures]. Hardback: £25·00: ISBN 0 949009 09 1.

Smith and Keenan's Company Law—by D. Keenan. [Seventh edition]. Paperback: £11·95: ISBN 0 273 02792 1.

Stedman, G. and Jones, J.—Shareholders' Agreements. [Longman Commercial Series.] Hardback: £42·50: ISBN 0 85121 025 2.

Stewart, G.—Administrative Receivers and Administrators. [CCH Insolvency Books]. Paperback: £35·00: ISBN 0 86325 085 8.

Sweet & Maxwell's Companies Statutes for Students—Edited by H. Rajak. [Second edition]. Paperback: £14·50: ISBN 0 421 38340 2.

Thom, G. and Hall, L.—Company Secretarial Practice. [M & E Handbooks]. [Seventh edition]. Paperback £6·50: ISBN 0 7121 0766 5.

Tolley's Company Car Tax Guide 1987/88. Prepared by Coopers & Lybrand. Paperback: £4·25: ISBN 0 85459 304 7.

Way, P.—Maximising Opportunities under the BES. Paperback: £17·50: ISBN 0 85121 248 4.

Wright, D.—Rights and Duties of Directors. Paperback: £15·95: ISBN 0 406 50470 9.

CONFLICT OF LAWS

Dashwood, A., Hacon, R. J. and White, R. C. A.—A Guide to the Civil Jurisdiction and Judgments Convention. Hardback: £94·50: ISBN 90 6544 269 3.

Dicey and Morris on the Conflicts of Laws—Edited by L. Collins. [Eleventh edition]. Hardback: £118·00: ISBN 0 420 47130 8.

Kaye, P.—Civil Jurisdiction and Enforcement of Foreign Judgments. Hardback: £95·00: ISBN 0 86205 081 2.

Lasok, D. and Stone, P.—Conflict of Laws in the European Community. Hardback: £24·50: ISBN 0 86205 071 5.

Schmidhauser, J. (Editor)—Comparative Judicial Systems. [Advances in Political Science, no. 6]. Hardback: £25·00: ISBN 0 408 03165 4.

Yelpaala, K., Rubino-Sammartano, M. and Campbell, D. (Editors)—Drafting and Enforcing Contracts in Civil and Common Law Jurisdictions. Paperback: £28·00: ISBN 90 6544 279 0.

BOOKS

CONSTITUTIONAL LAW

Casey, J. [Ireland]—Constitutional Law in Ireland. Paperback: £22·50: ISBN 0 421 31270 X.

Hood Phillips' Constitutional and Administrative Law.—By O. H. Phillips and P. Jackson [Seventh edition]. Hardback: £25·00: ISBN 0 421 35030 X. Paperback: £16·95: ISBN 0 421 35040 7.

Munro, C.—Studies in Constitutional Law. Hardback: £14·00: ISBN 0 406 26144 X. Paperback: £8·95: ISBN 0 406 26145 8.

Ojo, A. [Nigeria]—Constitutional Law and Military Rule in Nigeria. Paperback: £20·00: ISBN 978 167 569 1.

Oliver, I.—Police, Government and Accountability. Paperback: £8·95: ISBN 0 333 43226 6.

Swinfen, D.—Imperial Appeal: the Debate on the Appeal to the Privy Council, 1833–1986. Hardback: £35·00: ISBN 0 7190 1895 1.

Thornton, G. C.—Legislative Drafting. [Third edition]. Hardback: £45·00: ISBN 0 406 39982 4.

CONSUMER CREDIT

Stephenson, G.—Consumer Credit. Hardback: £20·00: ISBN 0 00 383303 8.

CONTRACT

Atiyah, P. S.—Essays on Contract. Hardback: £30·00: ISBN 0 19 825555 1.

Burrows, A. S.—Remedies for Torts and Breach of Contract. Hardback: £24·00: ISBN 0 406 50150 5. Paperback: £16·95: ISBN 0 406 50151 3.

Clark, R. [Canada]—Inequality of bargaining power. Hardback: £24·00: ISBN 0 459 38840 1.

Downes, T.—A textbook on Contract. Paperback: £14·95: ISBN 1 85185 076 1.

Eaglestone, F. Supplement to Insurance under the J.C.T. Forms—Booklet: £4·95: ISBN 0 00 383434 4.

Hibberd, P.—Sub-Contracts Under the JCT Intermediate Form. Hardback: £22·50: ISBN 0 632 01869 0.

Payne, D. and Mackenzie, K.—Employment Contract Manual. Hardback: £40·00: ISBN 0 566 02654 6.

Rose, F.—Civil Liability Statutes. Paperback: £8·50: ISBN 1 85185 053 8.

Simpson, A.—A History of the Common Law of Contract. Paperback: £19·50: ISBN 0 19 825573 X.

Taylor, R.—Law of Contract. [SWOT Success Without Tears Series]. [Second edition]. Paperback: £7·50: ISBN 1 85185 091 0.

Treitel, G.—The Law of Contract [Seventh edition]. Hardback: £28·50: ISBN 0 420 47490 0. Paperback: £19·50: ISBN 0 420 47500 1.

Yelpaala, K., Rubino-Sammartano, M. and Campbell, D. (Editors)—Drafting and Enforcing Contracts in Civil and Common Law Jurisdictions. Paperback: £28·00: ISBN 90 6544 279 0.

CONVEYANCING

Annand, R. and Whish, R.—The Contract. [Conveyancing Solutions, vol. 2]. Hardback: £16·50: ISBN 0 421 36240 5.

Artis, D. and Houghton, J.—Land Law. [Success Without Tears Series]. Paperback: £7·50: ISBN 1 85185 046 5.

Castle, R.—Conveyancing without computers. Paperback: £25·00: ISBN 1 870 08010 6.

Conveyancing Standing Committee of the Law Commission—Preliminary Enquiries: House Purchase. A Practice Recommendation. Booklet: £4·95: ISBN 0 85121 321 9.

Estates Gazette Law Reports 1986, vol. 2—Edited by J. Muir Watt. Hardback: £25·50: ISBN 0 7282 0102 X.

Estates Gazette Law Reports 1987, vol. 1.—Edited by J. Muir Watt. Hardback: £23·50: ISBN 0 7282 0111 9.

Gray, K.—Elements of Land Law. Hardback: £35·00: ISBN 0 406 50160 2. Paperback: £22·95: ISBN 0 406 50161 0.

Gretton, G.—The Law of Inhibition and Adjunction. Paperback: £16·95: ISBN 0 406 10433 6.

Hargreaves, J.—The Home-Owner's Guide. [Woodhead-Faulkner Moneyguide]. Paperback: £4·95: ISBN 0 85941 423 X.

Law Society and H.M. Land Registry—Registered Land Practice Notes. [Second edition]. Paperback: £5·95. ISBN 0 85121 257 3.

Meadowcroft, C.—The Homeowner's Guide to the Law. Paperback: £6·95: ISBN 1 85190 023 3.

Silverman, F.—Standard Conditions of Sale: a Conveyancer's Guide. [Second edition]. Paperback: £22·50: ISBN 0 406 25511 3.

Storey, I.—Conveyancing. [Second edition]. Paperback: £14·95: ISBN 0 406 01064 1.

Walter P. and Harris. J.—Claims to the Possession of Land: the Law and Practice. Hardback: £37·50: ISBN 1 85190 000 4.

Wontner's Guide to Land Registry Practice—by P. J. Timothy. [Longman Practitioner Series]. [Sixteenth edition]. Paperback: £25·00: ISBN 0 85121 284 0.

BOOKS AND ARTICLES

COPYRIGHT

Adams, J.—Merchandising Intellectual Property. Hardback: £55·00: ISBN 0 406 10340 2.
Carr, H.—Computer Software: Legal Protection in the United Kingdom. Hardback: £32·50: ISBN 0 906214 327.
Yearbook of Law Computers & Technology, vol. 3, 1987. Hardback: £18·95: ISBN 0 406 18702 9.

CORONERS

Scraton, P. and Chadwick K.—In the Arms of the Law. Paperback: £4·95: ISBN 0 7453 0244 0.

CORPORATION TAX

Allied Dunbar Tax Guide 1987–88—by W. I. Sinclair. Hardback: £12·95: ISBN 0 85121 292 1.
British Tax Cases 1986. Hardback: £26·00: ISBN 0 86325 123 4.
British Tax Legislation 1987–88, vols. 1A & 1B. Paperback: £18·00: ISBN 0 86325 116 1 (Vol. 1A); 0 86325 117 X (Vol. 1B).
Butterworths U.K. Tax Guide 1987–88—Edited by J. Tiley. [Sixth edition]. Paperback: £12·00: ISBN 0 406 50496 2.
Butterworths Yellow Tax Handbook 1987–88. [Twenty-sixth edition]. Paperback: £19·00: ISBN 0 406 51004 0.
Cooke, P. and Fox, J. (Editors)—Effective Tax Strategies for Corporate Acquisitions. Hardback: £16·00: ISBN 90 6544 255 3.
Hardman on Tax in Business 1986–87 by J. P. Hardman. Paperback: £11·95: ISBN 0 85258 841 0.
Pritchard, W.—Taxation [Eighth edition]. Paperback: £8·95: ISBN 0 7121 2038 6.
Tolley's Corporation Tax 1987–88 by G. Saunders and J. Boulding. [Twenty-third edition]. Paperback: £13·25: ISBN 0 85459 289 X.
Tolley's Tax Guide 1987–88—by A. Homer and R. Burrows. [Fifth edition]. Hardback: £14·95: ISBN 0 85459 293 8.
Tolley's Taxwise Taxation Workbook No. 1 1987–88 by A. Homer, R. Burrows and P. Gravestock. Paperback: £14·25: ISBN 0 85459 257 1.
Whitehouse, C. and Stuart-Buttle, E.—Revenue Law: Principles and Practice. [Fifth edition]. Paperback: £20·95: ISBN 0 406 00533 8.

CRIMINAL EVIDENCE AND PROCEDURE

Andrews, J. and Hirst, M.—Criminal Evidence [The Criminal Law Library; No. 4]. Hardback: £50·00: ISBN 0 08 039237 7.
Blake, S.—A Practical Approach to Legal Advice and Drafting [Second edition]. Paperback: £14·95: ISBN 1 85185 080 5.
Calvert, F.—The Constable's Pocket Guide to Powers of Arrest and Charges [Eighth edition]. Paperback: £4·95: ISBN 0 406 84205 1.
Carter, J.—Magistrates' Court: Domestic Proceedings [Longman Practitioner Series]. Paperback: £10·50: ISBN 0 85121 319 7.
Cowsill, E. and Clegg, J.—Evidence: Law and Practice [Longman Practitioner Series]. Second edition. Paperback: £15·95: ISBN 0 85121 350 2.
Freckelton, I. [Australia].—The Trial of the Expert. Hardback: £35·00: ISBN 0 19 554566 4.
Ingman, T.—The English Legal Process. [Second edition]. Paperback: £9·95: ISBN 1 85185 061 9.
Kiralfy, A.—The Burden of Proof. Hardback: £24·50: ISBN 0 86205 215 7.
Mclean, I. Criminal Appeals: a Practical Guide to Appeals to and from the Crown Court. [Second edition]. Hardback: £26·00: ISBN 0 859 92372 X.
Morrish, P and Mclean, I.—The Crown Court. [Twelfth edition]. Hardback: £28·00: ISBN 1 870 08060 2.
Murphy, P. and Beaumont J.—Evidence: Materials for Discussion. [Second Edition.] Paperback: £18·95. ISBN 0 906322 97 9
Pain, K.—Minors: the Law and Practice. Paperback: £16·95: ISBN 1 85190 030 6.
Ralphs, E. and Norman, G.—The Magistrate as Chairman. Paperback: £7·95: ISBN 0 406 10469 7.

CRIMINAL LAW

Anthony and Berryman's Magistrates' Court Guide 1987.—Edited by A. P. Carr. Paperback: £14·95: ISBN 0 406 10840 4.
Bucknell, P. and Ghodse, H.—Misuse of Drugs. Supplement no. 1. [Criminal Law Library no. 2.] Paperback: £5·00: ISBN 0 08 033081 9.
Box, S.—Recession, Crime and Punishment. Paperback: £6·95: ISBN 0 333 43853 1.
Card, R.—Public Order: the New Law. Paperback: £12·50: ISBN 0 406 50440 7.
Cameron, D. and Frazer, E.—The Lust to Kill. Paperback: £7·95: ISBN 0 7456 0336 X.
Elias, R. [U.S.A.]—The Politics of Victimization. Hardback: £35·00: ISBN 0 19 503980 7.
Garland, D., Punishment and Welfare. Paperback; £7·95 ISBN 0 566 05431 0.

CRIMINAL LAW—*cont.*

Goldstein, J. H.—Aggression and Crimes of Violence. [Second edition.] Paperback: £9·00: ISBN 0 19 503944 0.

Levi, M.—Regulating Fraud. Hardback: £35·00: ISBN 0 422 61160 3.

Marston, J.—Public Order: a Guide to the 1986 Public Order Act. Paperback: £10·95: ISBN 1 85190 024 1.

Mednick, S., Moffitt, T. and Stack, S. (Editors).—The Causes of Crime: New Biological Approaches. Hardback: £35·00: ISBN 0 521 30402 4.

Morris, A.—Women, Crime and Criminal Justice. Paperback: £7·95: ISBN 0 631 15445 0.

Morris, A. and Giller, H.—Understanding Juvenile Justice. Hardback: £22·50: ISBN 0 7099 3832 2.

Pain, K. Minors: the Law and Practice. Paperback: £16·95: ISBN 1 85190 030 6.

Power, D. J. and Selwood, D. H. D.—Criminal Law and Psychiatry. Hardback: £50·00: ISBN 1 87008 025 4.

Rock, P., A View from the Shadows: the Ministry of the Solicitor General of Canada and the making of the Justice for Victims of Crime Initiative. [Oxford Socio-Legal Studies]. Hardback: £35·00 ISBN 0 19 825523 3.

Sachs, C.—Child Abduction [Guide and Practice Series]. Paperback: £7·50. ISBN 0 85308 104 2.

Sieber, U.—The International Handbook on Computer Crime. Hardback: £24·95: ISBN 0 471 91224 7.

Sloan, K.—Police Law Primer. [Third edition]. Paperback: £7·95: ISBN 0 406 84652 9.

Smith, A.—Offences Against Public Order. Paperback: £14·95: ISBN 0 421 36580 3.

Stone, E. and Johnson, H.—Forensic Medicine [The Criminal Law Library, no. 3]. Hardback: £30·00: ISBN 0 08 039219 9.

Temkin, J.—Rape and the Legal Process. [Modern Legal Studies]. Hardback: £19·50: ISBN 0 421 33840 7. Paperback: £9·50: ISBN 0 421 33850 4.

Ten, C.—Crime, Guilt, and Punishment. Hardback: £19·50: ISBN 0 19 875082 X. Paperback: £8·95: ISBN 0 19 875081 1.

Thornton, P.—Public Order Law Including the Public Order Act 1986. Paperback: £10·75: ISBN 1 85185 040 6.

West, D. J.—Sexual Crimes and Confrontations. [Cambridge Studies in Criminology, no. 57]. Hardback: £27·50: ISBN 0 566 05380 2.

Wilkinson's Road Traffic Offences edited by P. Halnan and P. Wallis. [Thirteenth edition]. Hardback: £168·00: ISBN 0 85121 289 1.

Windlesham, D. J. G. Hennessy, Lord—Responses to Crime. Hardback: £17·95: ISBN 0 19 825583 7.

Yearbook of Law Computers & Technology, vol. 3, 1987. Hardback: £18·95: ISBN 0 406 18702 9.

Zimring, F. and Hawkins, G.—[U.S.A.] Capital Punishment and the American Agenda. Hardback: £20·00: ISBN 0 521 33033 5.

CRIMINAL SENTENCING

Jarvis's Probation Officers' Manual by W. R. Weston. [Fourth edition]. Paperback: £13·95: ISBN 0 406 25608 X.

Stockdale, E. and Devlin, K.—Sentencing. [The Criminal Law Library, no. 5]. Hardback: £30·00: ISBN 0 08 039248 2.

Ten, C.—Crime, Guilt, and Punishment. Hardback: £19·50: ISBN 0 19 875082 X. Paperback: £8·95: ISBN 0 19 875081 1.

Wasik, M. and Pease, K. (Editors).—Sentencing Reform: Guidance or Guidelines? Hardback: £30·00: ISBN 0 7190 1890 0.

DAMAGES

Atiyah's Accidents, Compensation and the Law by P. Cane. [Law in Context]. Fourth edition. Hardback: £30·00: ISBN 0 297 79052 8. Paperback: £14·95: ISBN 0 297 79053 6.

EASEMENTS AND PRESCRIPTIONS

Gregory, M. and Parrish, M.—Essential Law for Landowners and Farmers. [Second edition]. Paperback: £9·95: ISBN 0 00 383269 4.

EDUCATION

Harpwood, V. and Alldridge, P.—GCSE Law. Paperback: £7·95: ISBN 1 85185 054 6.

Scott's English Law for GCSE—Edited by M. Giles. [Fifth edition]. Paperback: £4·95: ISBN 0 406 65307 0.

ELECTION LAW

Ewing, K.—The Funding of Political Parties in Britain. Hardback: £19·50: ISBN 0 521 33446 2.

BOOKS AND ARTICLES

EMERGENCY LAWS

Northern Ireland Emergency Legislation.—Compiled and annotated by Butterworths editorial staff. Paperback: £15·00: ISBN 0 406 10577 4.

EMPLOYMENT

Benedictus, R. and Bercusson, B.—Labour Law: Cases and Materials. Paperback: £25·00: ISBN 0 421 27870 6.

Bowers, J. and Duggan, M.—The Modern Law of Strikes. Paperback: £12·95: ISBN 1 85185 066 X.

Butler, W., Hepple, B. and Neal, A. (Editors)—Comparative Labour Law. Hardback: £22·00: ISBN 0 566 05387 X.

Butterworths Employment Law Handbook.—Edited by P. Wallington [Fourth edition]. Paperbook: £23·00: ISBN 0 406 142263 7.

Clayton R.—Practice and Procedure in Industrial Tribunals: a Guide to Unfair Dismissal and Redundancy. [LAG Law and Practice Guide, No. 13.] Paperback: £7·50: ISBN 0 905099 14 1.

Julyan, A. J.—Service Agreements. [Fifth edition]. Paperback: £19·95: ISBN 0 85121 221 2.

Leonard, A.—Judging Inequality. Paperback: £9·95: ISBN 0 900137 28 2.

Lewis, R. Compensation for Industrial Injury.—Hardback: £24·50: ISBN 0 86205 214 9.

Lord Wedderburn—The Worker and the Law. [Third edition]. Hardback: £25·00: ISBN 0 421 37060 2. Paperback: £10·00: ISBN X 990 00082 2. (Published 1986).

Mead, M.—Unfair Dismissal Handbook. [Longman Commercial Series] Third edition. Hardback: £40·00: ISBN 0 85121 252 2.

Nelson-Jones, J. and Nuttall, G.—Employee Ownership. Paperback: £14·95: ISBN 1 85190 033 0.

Palmer, C. and Poulton, K.—Sex and Race Discrimination in Employment. Paperback: £14·00: ISBN 0 905099 17 6.

Payne, D. and Mackenzie, K.—Employment Contract Manual. Hardback: £40·00: ISBN 0 566 02654 6.

Tolley's Compensation for Dismissal by A. Korn. Paperback: £13·95: ISBN 0 85459 273 3.

Waud, C.—Guide to Employment Law 1987. [Third edition]. Paperback: £4·95: ISBN 0 85144 393 1.

Whincup, M.—The Right to Dismiss. [Second edition] Hardback: £17·95: ISBN 0 632 08193 3.

Younson, F. et al.—Employment Law Handbook. Hardback: £39·50: ISBN 0 566 02583 3.

EQUITY AND TRUSTS

Keeton, G. and Sheridan, L.—Equity. [Third edition]. Hardback: £40.00: ISBN 1 870 08030 0. Paperback: £25·00: ISBN 1 870 08035 1.

Ockelton M.—Trusts for Accountants. Paperback: £9·50: ISBN 0 406 50090 8.

Riddall, J.—The Law of Trusts. [Third edition]. Hardback: £24·00: ISBN 0 406 64842 5. Paperback: £15·95: ISBN 0 406 64843 3.

Soares, P.—Trusts and Tax Planning. [Practical Tax Series]. Third edition. Paperback: £32·00: ISBN 0 85120 876 2.

Todd, P.—SWOT Equity and Trusts. [Success Without Tears Series]. Paperback: £7·95: ISBN 1 85185 045 7.

Underhill and Hayton Law Relating to Trusts and Trustees—by D. J. Hayton. [Fourteenth edition]. Hardback: £98·00: ISBN 0 406 40593 X.

Vickery's Law and Accounts of Executors, Administrators and Trustees—by J. Kimmer, G. Scriven and R. Stanfield. [Twenty-first edition]. Paperback: £16·95: ISBN 0 304 31389 0.

EUROPEAN COMMUNITIES

Bellamy, C. and Child, G. Common Market Law of Competition. [Third edition]. Hardback: £75·00. ISBN 0 421 28200 2

Bullock, G.—Euronotes and Euro-Commercial Paper. Hardback: £28·00: ISBN 0 406 10410 7.

Burrows, F.—Free Movement in European Community Law. Hardback: £35·00: ISBN 0 19 825492 X.

Butterworths Competition Law Handbook. Edited by G. Lindrup. Paperback: £25·00: ISBN 0 406 10400 X.

Capotorti, F., Hilf, M., Jacobs, F. and Jacqué, J.—The European Union Treaty. Hardback: £35·00: ISBN 0 19 825548 9.

Encyclopedia of Competition Law—Edited by R. Merkin. Looseleaf: £185.00: ISBN 0 421 36870 5.

Horner, S.—Parallel Imports. Hardback: £20·00: ISBN 0 00 383366 6.

Lasok, D. and Bridge, J.—Law and Institutions of the European Communities. [Fourth edition]. Hardback: £28·00. ISBN 0 406 26880 0. Paperback: £19·95. ISBN 0 406 26881 9.

Lasok, D. and Stone, P.—Conflict of Laws in the European Community. Hardback: £24·50: ISBN 0 86205 071 5.

Law and Practice Relating to Pollution Control in the Member States of the European Communities: Recent Developments prepared by Environmental Resources Limited. [The Law and Practice Relating to Pollution Control]. Hardback: £21·00: ISBN 0 86010 806 6.

EUROPEAN COMMUNITIES—*cont.*

Matthews, R.—EEC Anti-trust Compliance. Paperback: £36·00: ISBN 0 946262 05 5.

Rudden, B.—Basic Community Cases. Hardback: £30·00: ISBN 0 19 876212 7. Paperback: £12·50: ISBN 0 19 876211 9.

Van Caenegem, R.—Judges, Legislators and Professors: Chapters in European Legal History.—Hardback: £19·50: ISBN 0 521 34077 2.

Wood, D. et. al.—Milk Quotas: Law and Practice. Paperback: £25·00.

Wyatt, D. and Dashwood, A.—The Substantive Law of the EEC [Second edition]. Hardback: £35·00: ISBN 0 421 34870 4. Paperback: £24·00: ISBN 0 421 34880 1.

EVIDENCE (CIVIL)

Cowsill, E. and Clegg, J.—Evidence: Law and Practice [Longman Practitioner Series]. Second edition. Paperback: £15·95: ISBN 0 85121 350 2.

Freckelton, I. [Australia].—The Trial of the Expert. Hardback: £35·00: ISBN 0 19 554566 4.

Murphy, P. and Beaumont, J.—Evidence: Materials for Discussion. [Second edition]. Paperback: £18·95: ISBN 0 906322 97 9.

EXECUTORS AND ADMINISTRATORS

Holloway's Probate Handbook.—By G. Maple [Eighth edition]. Hardback: £30·00: ISBN 0 85121 260 3.

Vickery's Law and Accounts of Executors, Administrators and Trustees by J. Kimmer, G. Scriven and R. Stanfield. [Twenty-first edition]. Paperback: £16·95: ISBN 0 304 31389 0.

FAMILY

Berkin, M.—Matrimonial Suits and Property Proceedings. [Third edition]. Hardback: £35·00: ISBN 1 870 08080 7.

Bird, R.—ABC Guide to the Practice of Matrimonial Causes [Second edition]. Paperback: £12·95: ISBN 0 421 37090 4.

Bromley's Family Law—by P. M. Bromley and N. V. Lowe. [Seventh edition]. Paperback: £21·95: ISBN 0 406 56015 3.

Burrows, D.—Legal Aid and the Family Lawyer. [Guide and Practice Series]. Paperback: £7·50: ISBN 0 85308 105 0.

Carter, J.—Magistrates' Court: Domestic Proceedings [Longman Practitioner Series]. Paperback: £10·50: ISBN 0 85121 319 7.

Cretney, S. M.—Elements of Family Law. Paperback: £11·95: ISBN 0 421 35240 X.

Curzon, L.B.—Criminal Law. [M. & E. Handbooks]. Fifth edition. Paperback: £6·95: ISBN 0 7121 0768 1.

De Haas, M.—Domestic Injunctions. Hardback: £19·50: ISBN 0 421 36510 2.

Duckworth, P. Matrimonial Property and Finance. [Third edition]. Paperback: £45·00: ISBN 0 85121 2816.

Family and Child Law Statutes—compiled by P. H. Niekirk. [Second edition]. Paperback: £22·50: ISBN 0 85121 348 0.

Freeman, M.—Dealing with Domestic Violence. [Family Law for Practitioners]. Paperback: £12·50: ISBN 0 86325 110 2.

Gardner, P.—Emergency Family Remedies. [Longman Practice Notes]. Paperback: £11·95: ISBN 0 85121 114 3.

Gray, J.—Taxation on Divorce and Separation. [Family Law For Practitioners]. Paperback: £10·50: ISBN 0 86325 107 2.

Hoggett, B.—Parents and Children: the Law of Parental Responsibility. [Third edition]. Paperback: £13·50: ISBN 0 421 36050 X.

Oliver, D.—Cohabitation: the Legal Implications. [Family Law for Practitioners]. Paperback: £12·50: ISBN 0 86325 108 0.

Parker, S.—Cohabitees. [Second edition]. Paperback: £17·50: ISBN 1 870 08041 6.

Pelling, M. and Purdie, R.—Matrimonial and Domestic Injunctions. [Second edition]. Paperback: £29·95: ISBN 0 406 33441 2.

Shatter A. [Ireland]—Shatter's Family Law in the Republic of Ireland. [Third edition.] Hardback: £45·00. ISBN 0 86327 080 8.

Strachan, B.—Matrimonial Proceedings in Magistrates Courts. [Second edition]. Paperback: £18·50: ISBN 0 421 38500 6.

Sweet & Maxwell's Family Law Manual—edited by R. Bird, S. M. Cretney and A. Rutherford. Looseleaf: £75·00: ISBN 0 421 35830 0.

Thomson, J.—Family Law in Scotland. Paperback: £15·95: ISBN 0 406 26190 3.

FISH AND FISHERIES

Howarth, W.—Freshwater Fishery Law. Hardback: £17·95: ISBN 1 85185 030 9.

BOOKS AND ARTICLES

FOREIGN JURISDICTIONS

Atiyah, P. and Summers, R.—Form and Substance in Anglo-American Law. Hardback: £35·00: ISBN 0 19 825577 2.
Barrett, B., Howells, R. and Hindley, B.—Safety in the Offshore Petroleum Industry. Hardback: £40·00: ISBN 1 85091 070 7.
Campbell, D. (Editor)—Legal Aspects of Doing Business in Africa. [International Business Series, vol. 4]. Hardback: £69·75: ISBN 90 6544 268 5.
Casey, J. [Ireland]—Constitutional Law in Ireland. Paperback: £22·50: ISBN 0 421 31270 X.
El-Sayed, H. M.—Maritime Regulations in the Kingdom of Saudi Arabia. Hardback: £120·00: ISBN 0 86010 736 1.
Fluehr-Lobban, C. [Sudan]—Islamic Law and Society in the Sudan. Hardback: £27·50: ISBN 0 7146 3280 5.
International Bar Association—Tax Avoidance, Tax Evasion. [Second edition]. Paperback: £15·00: ISBN 0 948711 12 4.
Irukwu, J. [Africa]—Insurance Law in Africa: Cases, Statutes and Principles. Hardback: £35·00: ISBN 0 948691 25 5.
Nasir, J. J.—The Islamic Law of Personal Status. Hardback: £45·00: ISBN 0 86010 825 2.
Ojo, A. [Nigeria]—Constitutional Law and Military Rule in Nigeria. Paperback: £20·00: ISBN 978 167 569 1.
The Penal Code of the Federal Republic of Germany [West Germany]—Translated by J. J. Darby. [The American Series of Foreign Penal Codes, no. 28]. Hardback: £33·00: ISBN 0 8377 0048 5.
Tolley's Taxation in the Republic of Ireland 1987–88—by J. Newth and G. Saunders. Paperback: £12·95: ISBN 0 85459 294 6.
Veatch, R. [U.S.A.].—The Foundations of Justice. Hardback: £22·50: ISBN 0 19 504076 7.
Zimring, F. and Hawkins, G. [U.S.A.]—Capital Punishment and the American Agenda. Hardback: £20·00: ISBN 0 521 33033 5.
Zweigert, K. and Kotz, H.—An Introduction to Comparative Law: Vol. 1: The Framework [Second edition]. Hardback: £40·00: ISBN 0 19 825572 1.
Zweigert, K. and Kotz, H.—An Introduction to Comparative Law: Vol. 2: The Institutions of Private Law [Second edition]. Hardback: £40·00: ISBN 0 19 825606 X.

GAMING AND WAGERING

Harris, D.—HAC Guide to Taxation of the Bloodstock Industry. Hardback: £20·00: ISBN 1 870382 00 5.
Smith, C. and Monkcom, S.—Law of Betting, Gaming and Lotteries. Hardback: £75·00: ISBN 0 406 29659 6.

HEALTH AND SAFETY AT WORK

Barrett, B., Howells, R. and Hindley, B.—Safety in the Offshore Petroleum Industry. Hardback: £40·00: ISBN 1 85091 070 7.

HOUSING

Hughes, D.—Public Sector Housing Law. [Second edition]. Paperback: £14·95: ISBN 0 406 60062 7.
McGurk, P. and Raynsford, N.—Guide to Housing Benefit. Paperback: £4·95: ISBN 0 948857 16 1.

HUMAN RIGHTS

Fawcett, J. E. S.—The Application of the European Convention on Human Rights. [Second edition]. Hardback: £35·00: ISBN 0 19 825510 1. Paperback: £15·00: ISBN 0 19 825509 8.
Meron, T.—Human Rights in Internal Strife: their International Protection [Hersch Lauterpacht Memorial Lectures]. Hardback: £27·00. ISBN 0 949009 04 0.
Yearbook of Law Computers & Technology, vol. 3, 1987.—Hardback: £18·95: ISBN 0 406 18702 9.

IMMIGRATION

Legomsky, S.—Immigration and the Judiciary: Law and Politics in Britain and America. Hardback: £35·00: ISBN 0 19 825561 6.
Macdonald, I.—Immigration Law and Practice in the United Kingdom [Second edition]. Hardback: £52·00: ISBN 0 406 28314 1.
Mole, N.—Immigration: Family Entry and Settlement [Family Law Guide and Practice Series]. Paperback: £7·50: ISBN 0 85308 106 9.

INCOME TAX

Allied Dunbar Tax Guide 1987–88.—By W. I. Sinclair. Hardback: £12·95: ISBN 0 85121 292 1.
Baldwin R. and Harvey R.—Tax and Financial Planning for Sportsmen and Entertainers. Paperback: £15·95: ISBN 0 406 50220 X.

INCOME TAX—*cont.*

British Tax Cases 1986.—Hardback: £26·00: ISBN 0 86325 123 4.
British Tax Legislation 1987–88, vols. 1A & 1B.—Paperback: £18·00: ISBN 0 86325 116 1 (Vol. 1A); 0 86325 117 X (Vol. 1B).
Butterworths U.K. Tax Guide 1987–88. Edited by J. Tiley. [Sixth edition]. Paperback: £12·00: ISBN 0 406 50496 2.
Butterworths Yellow Tax Handbook 1987–88.—[Twenty-sixth edition]. Paperback: £19·00: ISBN 0 406 51004 0.
James, S., Lewis A. and Allinson F. The Comprehensibility of Taxation. Hardback: £25·00: ISBN 0 566 05348 9.
Potter and Monroe's Tax Planning with precedents. Edited by A. Thornhill and K. Prosser. [Tenth edition]. Hardback: £49·00: ISBN 0 421 33420 7.
Pritchard, W.—Income Tax [Sixteenth edition]. Paperback: £9·95: ISBN 0 7121 0976 5.
Pritchard, W.—Taxation. [Eighth edition]. Paperback: £8·95: ISBN 0 7121 2038 6.
Robinson, D.—Deeds of Covenant. [Practical Tax Series]. [Third edition]. Paperback: £9.50: ISBN 0 85121 218 2.
Tolley's Income Tax 1987–88—by E. L. Harvey and G. Saunders. [Seventy-second edition]. Paperback: £15·95: ISBN 0 85459 288 1.
Tolley's Tax Bumph 1986–87—Edited by J. Boulding and N. Bowen. [Fourth edition]. Paperback: £18·95: ISBN 0 85459 247 4
Tolley's Tax Computations 1986—87—by K. M. G. Thomson McLintock. Paperback: £19·95: ISBN 0 85459 248 2.
Tolley's Tax Guide 1987–88 by A. Homer and R. Burrows. [Fifth edition] Hardback: £14·95: ISBN 0 85459 293 8.
Tolley's Taxwise Taxation Workbook No. 1 1987–88—by A. Homer, R. Burrows and P. Gravestock. Paperback: £14·25: ISBN 0 85459 257 1.
Touche Ross Tax Guide for the Family 1987/88 by B. Packer and C. Sandy. [Second edition]. Paperback: £4·95: ISBN 0 333 44961 4.
Touche Ross Tax Guide to Pay and Perks 1987/88 by B. Packer and E. Baker. [Fourth edition]. Paperback: £4·95: ISBN 0 333 44962 2.
Whitehouse, C. and Stuart-Buttle, E.—Revenue Law: Principles and Practice. [Fifth edition]. Paperback: £20·95: ISBN 0 406 00533 8.

INHERITANCE TAX

Allied Dunbar Tax Guide 1987–88—by W. I. Sinclair. Hardback: £12·95: ISBN 0 85121 292 1.
British Tax Cases 1986. Hardback: £26·00: ISBN 0 86325 123 4.
British Tax Legislation 1987–88, vol. 2. Paperback: £16·00: ISBN 0 86325 118 8.
Butterworths Orange Tax Handbook 1987–88. [Twelfth edition]. Paperback: £17·00: ISBN 0 406 50833 X.
Butterworths U.K. Tax Guide 1987–88. Edited by J. Tiley. [Sixth edition]. Paperback: £12·00: ISBN 0 406 50496 2.
Chapman's Inheritance Tax.—Edited by T. J. Lyons [Seventh edition]. Hardback: £48·00: ISBN 0 85121 326 X.
Coombes, J. and Channon, G.—Inheritance Tax. Paperback: £25·00: ISBN 0 421 37030 0.
Potter and Monroe's Tax Planning with precedents. Edited by A. Thornhill and K. Prosser. [Tenth edition]. Hardback: £49·00: ISBN 0 421 33420 7.
Pritchard, W.—Taxation. [Eighth edition]. Paperback: £8·95: ISBN 0 7121 2038 6.
Tolley's Inheritance Tax 1987–88—by R. Wareham and J. Newth. [Second edition]. Paperback: £12·95: ISBN 0 85459 291 1.
Tolley's Tax Computations 1986–87 by K. M. G. Thomson McLintock. Paperback: £19·95: ISBN 0 85459 248 2.
Tolley's Tax Guide 1987–88 by A. Homer and R. Burrows. [Fifth edition]. Hardback: £14·95: ISBN 0 85459 293 8.
Tolley's Tax Planning 1987—edited by G. Saunders. [Seventh edition.] Paperback: £29·50: ISBN 0 85459 246 6.
Touche Ross Tax Guide for the Family 1987/88 by B. Packer and C. Sandy. [Second edition]. Paperback: £4·95: ISBN 0 333 44961 4.
Vickery's Law and Accounts of Executors, Administrators and Trustees by J. Kimmer, G. Scriven and R. Stanfield. [Twenty-first edition]. Paperback: £16·95: ISBN 0 304 31389 0.
Whitehouse, C. and Stuart-Buttle, E.—Revenue Law: Principles and Practice. [Fifth edition]. Paperback: £20·95: ISBN 0 406 00533 8.

INSURANCE

Clews, R. (Editor).—A Textbook of Insurance Broking. [Second edition]. Hardback: £25·00: ISBN 0 85941 405 1.
Eaglestone, F.—Supplement to Insurance under the JCT Forms. Booklet: £4·95: ISBN 0 00 383434 4.
Golding: the Law and Practice of Reinsurance—edited by K. V. Louw. [Fifth edition]. Hardback: £25·00: ISBN 0 948691 14 X.

INSURANCE—*cont.*

Hodgin, R.—Insurance Intermediaries and the Law. Paperback: £24·00: ISBN 1 85044 107 3.

Irukwu, J. [Africa].—Insurance Law in Africa: Cases, Statutes and Principles. Hardback: £35·00: ISBN 0 948691 25 5.

Marsh, S. H. and Soulsby, J.—Outlines of English Law. [Fourth edition]. Paperback: £7·95: ISBN 0 07 084980 3.

Rose, F. (Editor)—New Foundations for Insurance Law. [Current Legal Problems]. Paperback: £16·00: ISBN 0 420 47780 2.

Witherby's Dictionary of Insurance by H. Cockerell. [Second edition]. Hardback: £14·50: ISBN 0 948691 21 2.

INTERNATIONAL LAW

Akehurst, M.—A Modern Introduction to International Law. [Sixth edition]. Paperback: £9·95: ISBN 0 04 341037 5.

Attard, D.—The Exclusive Economic Zone in International Law. [Oxford Monographs in International Law]. Hardback: £40·00: ISBN 0 19 825541 1.

Bulajić, M.—Principles of International Development Law. Hardback: £48·50: ISBN 90 247 3304 9.

Carty, A.—The Decay of International Law? [Melland Schill Monographs in International Law]. Paperback: £8·95: ISBN 0 7190 1958 3.

Cheng, B.—General Principles of Law: as applied by International Courts and Tribunals. Hardback: £40·00: ISBN 0 949009 067.

Dugard, J.—Recognition and the United Nations. [Hersch Lauterpacht Memorial Lectures]. Hardback: £27·00: ISBN 0 949009 00 8.

Eisenschitz, T.—Patents, Trade Marks and Designs in Information Work. Hardback: £25·00: ISBN 0 7099 0958 6.

Euro-Arab Arbitration Conference (1985: Port el Kantaoui, Tunisia). Proceedings of the First Euro-Arab Arbitration Conference. Paperback £78·00: ISBN 1 85044 125 1.

Gray, C.—Judicial Remedies in International Law. [Oxford Monographs in International Law]. Hardback: £27·50: ISBN 0 19 825571 3.

Grundy's Tax Havens: a World Survey—by M. Grundy. [Fifth edition]. Paperback: £15·00: ISBN 0 421 37900 6.

Hendry, I. and Wood, M.—The Legal Status of Berlin. Hardback: £55·00: ISBN 0 949009 05 9.

Jacobs, F. and Roberts, S. (Editors)—The Effect of Treaties in Domestic Law. [United Kingdom National Committee of Comparative Law Colloquia, vol. 7]. Hardback: £30·00: ISBN 0 421 37870 0.

Mara-Brown, E. O. [Nigeria]—Nigerian Law of Torts. [Nigerian Nutshells]. Paperback: £3·95: ISBN 0 421 36150 6.

Maryan Green, N.—International Law. [Third edition]. Hardback: £25·00: ISBN 0 273 02732 8.

Meron, T.—Human Rights in Internal Strife: their International Protection. [Hersch Lauterpacht Memorial Lectures]. Hardback: £27·00: ISBN 0 949009 04 0.

Morris, A. and Quest, B.—Design: The Modern Law and Practice. Hardback: £45·00: ISBN 0 406 10320 8.

Ott, D.—Public International Law in the Modern World. Paperback: £14·95: ISBN 0 273 02815 4.

Parsons, A.—Antarctica: the Next Decade. [Studies in Polar Research]. Hardback: £25·00: ISBN 0 521 33181 1.

Rodley, N.—The Treatment of Prisoners under International Law. [New Challenges to International Law.] Paperback: £15·00: ISBN 0 19 825563 2.

Schwebel, S.—International Arbitration: Three Salient Problems. [Hersch Lauterpacht Memorial Lectures]. Hardback: £33·00: ISBN 0 949009 02 4.

Seidl-Hohenveldern, I.—Corporations in and under International Law. [Hersch Lauterpacht Memorial Lectures]. Hardback: £25·00: ISBN 0 949009 09 1.

Sinclair, Sir Ian—The International Law Commission. [Hersch Lauterpacht Memorial Lectures]. Hardback: £28·00: ISBN 0 949009 10 5.

Todd, P.—Cases and Materials on Bills of Lading. Hardback: £40·00: ISBN 0 632 01857 7.

Tunkin, G. (Editor). [U.S.S.R.]. International law: a textbook. Hardback: £5·95: ISBN not given.

Yankey, G. S-A. [Africa]—International Patents and Technology Transfer to Less Developed Countries: the Case of Ghana and Nigeria. Hardback: £25·00: ISBN 0 566 05496 5.

JURISPRUDENCE

Aarnio, A.—The Rational as Reasonable: a Treatise on Legal Justification. [Law and Philosophy Library]. Hardback: £43·00: ISBN 90 277 2276 5.

Coleman, J. and Paul, E. F.—Philosophy and Law. Paperback: £8·95: ISBN 0 631 15257 1.

Eekelaar, J. and Bell, J. (Editors)—Oxford Essays in Jurisprudence. [Third Series]. Hardback: £27·50: ISBN 0 19 825507 1.

Fitzpatrick, P. and Hunt, A. (Editors). Critical Legal Studies. Paperback: £8·95: ISBN 0 631 15718 2.

JURISPRUDENCE—*cont.*

Garland, D.—Punishment and Welfare. Paperback: £7·95: ISBN 0 566 05431 0.
Gavison, R. (Editor)—Issues in Contemporary Legal Philosophy. Hardback: £35·00: ISBN 0 19 825517 9.
Goodrich, P.—Legal Discourse (Language, Discourse, Society Series)—Hardback: £29·50: ISBN 0 333 41949 9.
Greenawalt, K.—Conflicts of Law and Morality. [Clarendon Law Series]. Hardback: £24·00: ISBN 0 19 504110 0.
Honoré, T., Making Law Bind. Hardback: £30·00: ISBN 0 19 825467 9.
Hursthouse, R.—Beginning Lives. Paperback: £8·95: ISBN 0 631 15328 4.
Jackson, B.—Semiotics and Legal Theory. Paperback: £7·95: ISBN 0 7102 1214 3.
Larmore, C.—Patterns of Moral Complexity. Paperback: £7·50: ISBN: 0 521 33891 3.
McCluskey, J., Baron—Law, Justice and Democracy. Hardback: £9·95: ISBN 0 421 37890 5. Paperback: £5·95: ISBN 0 563 20549 0.
McMurrin, S. (Editor) [U.S.A.]. Liberty, Equality, and Law: Selected Tanner Lectures on Moral Philosophy. Paperback: £7·95: ISBN 0 521 34974 5.
Moles, R.—Definition and Rule in Legal Theory. Hardback: £27·50: ISBN 0 631 15342 X.
Seldon, A.—Law and Lawyers in Perspective. Paperback: £3·95: ISBN 0 14 022735 0.
Sorell, T.—Moral Theory and Capital Punishment. Paperback: £6·95: ISBN 0 631 15322 5.
Sumner, L.—The Moral Foundation of Rights. Hardback: £22·50: ISBN 0 19 824751 6.
Ten, C.—Crime, Guilt, and Punishment. Hardback: £19·50: ISBN 0 19 875082 X. Paperback: £8·95: ISBN 0 19 875081 1.
Wacks, R.—Jurisprudence. [SWOT Success Without Tears Series]. Paperback: £7·95: ISBN 1 85185 048 1.
Walicki, A.—Legal philosophies of Russian Liberalism. Hardback: £45·00: ISBN 0 19 824930 6.
Windlesham, D. J. G., Hennessy, Lord—Responses to Crime. Hardback: £17·95: ISBN 0 19 825583 7.
Zimring, F. and Hawkins, G. (U.S.A.)—Capital Punishment and the American Agenda Hardback: £20·00: ISBN 0 521 33033 5.

LAND CHARGES

Garner, J.—Local Land Charges. [Tenth edition] Paperback: £9·95: ISBN 0 7219 0125 5.

LANDLORD AND TENANT

Colbey, R., Resident Landlords and Owner-Occupiers: Law and Practice. [Longman Practice Notes]. Paperback; £12·95: ISBN 0 85121 293 X.
Estates Gazette Law Reports 1986, vol. 2: Edited by J. Muir Watt. Hardback: £25·50. ISBN 0 7282 0102 X.
Hargreaves, J.—The Home-Owner's Guide [Woodhead-Faulkner Moneyguide] Paperback: £4·95: ISBN 0 85941 423 X.
Jenkins, C.,—Practical Timeshare and Group Ownership. Paperback: £14·95: ISBN 0 406 10328 3.
Landlord & Tenant Act 1987.—Annotated by Sir Hugh Rossi [Shaw's Annotated Acts]. Paperback: £10·95: ISBN 0 7219 1070 X.
Meadowcroft, C.—The Homeowner's Guide to the Law. Paperback: £6·95: ISBN 1 85190 023 3.
Mitchell, B.—Landlord and Tenant Law. Paperback: £15·95: ISBN 0 632 01861 5.
Tromans, S.—Commercial Leases. Hardback: £22·00: ISBN 0 421 35460 7.
Webber, G. and Davidson, R.—Residential Possession Proceedings. [Second edition]. Paperback: £21·00: ISBN 0 85121 275 1.
Williams, D.—A Casebook on Repairs. Paperback: £16·00: ISBN 0 7282 0103 8.
Yates, D and Hawkins, J.—Landlord and Tenant Law. [Second edition.] Paperback: £26·00: ISBN 0 421 35430 5.
Zeidman, M. and Whippman, C.—A Short Guide to the Landlord and Tenant Act 1987. Paperback: £8·00: ISBN 1 870800 05 2.

LAW REFORM

Carney, T. and Hanks, P. [Australia]—Australian Social Security Law, Policy and Administration. Hardback: £25·00: ISBN 0 19 554754 3.
Cooper, J. and Dhavan, R. (Editors)—Public Interest Law. Hardback: £35·00. ISBN 0 631 14299 1.
Freckelton, I. [Australia]—The Trial of the Expert. Hardback: £35·00: ISBN 0 19 554566 4.
Rent review: some problems with improvements (*J. Martin*): 282 E.G. 963.

LEGAL AID

Burrows, D.—Legal Aid and Family Lawyer [Guide and Practice Series]. Paperback: £7·50: ISBN 0 85308 105 0.

LEGAL AID—*cont.*

Herrup, C.—The Common Peace: Participation and the Criminal Law in Seventeenth-Century England. [Cambridge Studies in Early Modern British History]. Hardback: £25·00: ISBN 0 521 33313 X.

Levy, L. (Editor) [U.S.A.]—Essays on the Making of the Constitution. [Second edition]. Paperback: £7·95: ISBN 0 19 504902 0.

LEGAL HISTORY

Carty, A.—The Decay of International Law? [Melland Schill Monographs in International Law]. Paperback: £8·95: ISBN 0 7190 1958 3.

Clark, R. [Canada]—Inequality of bargaining power. Hardback: £24·00: ISBN 0 459 38840 1.

Garland, D.—Punishment and Welfare. Paperback: £7·95: ISBN 0 566 05431 0.

Pocock, J. G. A.—The Ancient Constitution and the Feudal Law. [Revised edition]. Hardback: £27·50: ISBN 0 521 30352 4. Paperback: £9·95: ISBN 0 521 31643 X.

Simpson, A.—A History of the Common Law of Contract. Paperback: £19·50: ISBN 0 19 825573 X.

Simpson, A.—Legal Theory and Legal History. Hardback: £25·00: ISBN 0 907628 83 4.

Stewart, J.—History and Practice of the Law of Mines and Minerals. Paperback: £7·80: ISBN 0 9509932 1 2.

Thomas, Ph.J.—Introduction to Roman Law. Paperback: £27·00. ISBN 90 6544 245 6.

Van Caenegem, R.—Judges, Legislators and Professors: Chapters in European Legal History. Hardback: £19·50: ISBN 0 521 34077 2.

LIBEL AND SLANDER

Salmond and Heuston on the Law of Torts by R. F. V. Heuston and R. A. Buckley [Nineteenth edition]. Hardback: £28·50: ISBN 0 421 34300 1. Paperback: £19·50: ISBN 0 421 34310 9.

LICENSING

Harrison, G.—The Licence Holder's Handy Guide [Fifty-sixth edition]. Paperback: £3·90: ISBN not given.

Kavanagh, T. and March, R.—Licensing Law. Paperback: £19·00: ISBN 1 870 08016 5.

LIMITATION OF ACTIONS

Latent Damage Act 1986.—By P. Capper [Legal Studies and Services Special Report]. Paperback: £28·50: ISBN 1 85271 008 0.

Merkin, R.—Richards Butler on Latent Damage. Hardback: £35·00: ISBN 1 85044 128 6.

LITERARY AND SCIENTIFIC INSTITUTIONS

Moys, E. (Editor)—Manual of Law Librarianship. [Second edition]. Hardback: £47·50: ISBN 0 566 03512 X.

LOCAL GOVERNMENT

Griffiths, A.—Local Government Administration. [Second edition]. Paperback: £11.95: ISBN 0 7219 0712 1.

Knowles, R.—The Law and Practice of Local Authority Meetings. [Revised edition]. Hardback: £32·50: ISBN 0 902197 51 7.

Longman Directory of Local Authorities 1987/88. Paperback: £15·50: ISBN 0 85121 295 6.

Pain, K.—Minors: the Law and Practice. Paperback: £16.95: ISBN 1 85190 030 6.

MEDICINE

Eastaway, N. and Burwood, S.—Tax & Financial Planning for Medical Practitioners. [Second edition]. Paperback: £17·50: ISBN 0 406 19005 4.

Knight, B.—Legal Aspects of Medical Practice. [Fourth edition]. Paperback: £9·95: ISBN 0 443 03781 7.

Mason, J. and McCall-Smith, R.—Butterworths Medico-legal Encyclopaedia. Hardback: £55·00: ISBN 0 407 00374 6.

Mason, J. and McCall Smith, R.—Law and Medical Ethics. [Second edition]. Hardback: £18·00: ISBN 0 406 50130 0. Paperback: £12·95: ISBN 0 406 50131 9.

Stone, E. and Johnson, H.—Forensic Medicine [The Criminal Law Library, no. 3]. Hardback: £30·00: ISBN 0 08 039219 9.

MENTAL HEALTH

Unsworth, C.—The Politics of Mental Health Legislation. Hardback: £35·00: ISBN 0 19 825512 8.

BOOKS

MINING LAW

Stewart, J.—History and Practice of the Law of Mines and Minerals. Paperback: £7·80: ISBN 0 9509932 1 2.

MINORS

Bromley's Family Law—by P. M. Bromley and N. V. Lowe. [Seventh edition]. Paperback: £21·95: ISBN 0 406 56015 3.

Family and Child Law Statutes—compiled by P. H. Niekirk. [Second edition]. Paperback: £22·50: ISBN 0 85121 348 0.

Hoggett, B.—Parents and Children: the Law of Parental Responsibility. [Third edition]. Paperback: £13·50: ISBN 0 421 36050 X.

Kearney, B.—Children's Hearings and the Sheriff Court. Hardback: £38·00: ISBN 0 406 10565 0.

Levy, A.—Wardship proceedings. [Longman Practitioner Series]. [Second edition]. Paperback: £14·95: ISBN 0 85121 143 7.

Morris, A. and Giller, H.—Understanding Juvenile Justice. Paperback: £10·95: ISBN 0 7099 3890 X.

Pain, K.—Minors: the Law and Practice. Paperback: £16.95: ISBN 1 85190 030 6.

NEGLIGENCE

Jackson, R. M. and Powell, J. L.—Professional Negligence. [Second edition]. Hardback: £36·00: ISBN 0 421 34160 2.

Latent Damage Act 1986.—By P. Capper [Legal Studies and Services Special Report]. Paperback: £28·50: ISBN 1 85271 008 0.

Salmond and Heuston on the Law of Torts—by R. F. V. Heuston and R. A. Buckley. [Nineteenth edition]. Hardback: £28·50: ISBN 0 421 34300 1. Paperback: £19·50: ISBN 0 421 34310 9.

NORTHERN IRELAND

Northern Ireland Emergency Legislation—Compiled and annotated by Butterworths editorial staff. Paperback: £15·00: ISBN 0 406 10577 4.

NUISANCE

Salmond and Heuston on the Law of Torts—by R. F. V. Heuston and R. A. Buckley. [Nineteenth edition]. Hardback: £28·50: ISBN 0 421 34300 1. Paperback: £19·50: ISBN 0 421 34310 9.

PARLIAMENT

Thornton, G. C.—Legislative Drafting. [Third edition]. Hardback: £45·00: ISBN 0 406 39982 4.

PARTNERSHIP

Keenan, D. and Riches, S.—Business Law. Paperback: £8·95: ISBN 0 273 02415 9.

Montague, J.—Business Law. [Chambers Commerce Series]. Paperback: £3·95: ISBN 0 550 20702 3.

Ray, E. and Davey, N.—Partnership Taxation. [Third edition]. Paperback: £25·00: ISBN 0 406 67820 0.

Sweet & Maxwell's Companies Statutes for Students. Edited by H. Rajak. [Second edition]. Paperback: £14·50: ISBN 0 421 38340 2.

Way. P.—Maximising Opportunities under the BES. Paperback: £17·50: ISBN 0 85121 248 4.

PATENTS AND DESIGNS

Eisenschitz, T.—Patents, Trade Marks and Designs in Information Work. Hardback: £25·00: ISBN 0 7099 0958 6.

Yankey, G. S-A. [Africa]—International Patents and Technology Transfer to Less Developed Countries: the Case of Ghana and Nigeria. Hardback: £25·00: ISBN 0 566 05496 5.

PENSIONS AND SUPERANNUATION

Mascarenhas, A.—Spicer and Pegler's Accounts and Audit of Pension Schemes. Paperback: £17·95: ISBN 0 406 67910 X.

Mozley, C.—Pension Scheme Accounts: Time for a Change. [Business Accounting Guides]. Paperback: £11·95: ISBN 0 86349 115 4.

Paterson, M.—Pensions: Agenda for Change. Hardback: £32·50: ISBN 0 85941 380 2.

Wilson, J. and Davies, B.—Your New Pension Choice. [Second edition]. Paperback: £2·95: ISBN 0 85459 286 5.

BOOKS AND ARTICLES

PETROLEUM

Barrett, B., Howells, R. and Hindley, B.—Safety in the Offshore Petroleum Industry. Hardback: £40·00: ISBN 1 85091 070 7.

POLICE

Calvert, F.—The Constable's Pocket Guide to Powers of Arrest and Charges [Eighth edition]. Paperback: £4·95: ISBN 0 406 84205 1.

Clayton, R. and Tomlinson, H.—Civil Actions Against the Police. Hardback: £42·00: ISBN 0 421 34420 2.

English, J. and Houghton R.—Summonses and Charges. [Sixth edition]. Paperback: £5·60: ISBN 0 85164 026 5.

Oliver, I.—Police, Government and Accountability. Paperback: £8·95: ISBN 0 333 43226 6.

PRACTICE

Bankowski, Z., Hutton, N. and McManus, J.—Lay Justice? Paperback: £9·95: ISBN 0 567 29139 1.

Bird, R.—ABC Guide to the Practice of Matrimonial Causes. [Second edition]. Paperback: £12·95: ISBN 0 421 37090 4.

Birts, P. and Willis, A.—Trespass: Summary Procedure for Possession of Land. Paperback: £15·95: ISBN 0 406 10481 6.

Blackford, R. and Price, D.—County Court Practice Handbook. [Longman Practitioner Series]. Eighth edition. Paperback: £16·95: ISBN 0 85121 147 X.

Blake, S.—A Practical Approach to Legal Advice and Drafting. [Second edition]. Paperback: £14·95: ISBN 1 85185 080 5.

Butterworths Costs Service—Edited by F. G. Berkeley. Looseleaf: £145·00: ISBN 0 406 10749 1.

Carter, J.—Magistrates' Court: Domestic Proceedings. [Longman Practitioner Series]. Paperback: £10·50: ISBN 0 85121 319 7.

Cripps, Y.—The Legal Implications of Disclosure in the Public Interest. Hardback: £32·50: ISBN 0 906241 40 8.

Dane, J. and Thomas, P.—How to Use a Law Library. [Second edition]. Hardback: £16·50: ISBN 0 421 36030 5. Paperback: £8·95: ISBN 0 421 36040 2.

De Haas, M.—Domestic Injunctions. Hardback: £19·50: ISBN 0 421 36510 2.

Gee, S. and Andrews, G.—Mareva Injunctions: Law and Practice. Hardback: £30·00: ISBN 0 85120 939 4.

Goldrein, I. and Wilkinson, K.—Commercial Litigation: Pre-emptive Remedies. [The Litigation Library]. Hardback: £85·00: ISBN 0 421 34800 3.

Ingman, T.—The English Legal Process. [Second edition]. Paperback: £9·95: ISBN 1 85185 061 9.

Jacob, Sir Jack, I.—The Fabric of English Civil Justice [Hamlyn Lectures, 38th series]. Hardback: £15·00: ISBN 0 420 47530 3. Paperback: £9·50: ISBN 0 420 47540 0.

Kiralfy, A.—The Burden of Proof. Hardback: £24·50: ISBN 0 86205 215 7.

Ough, R. N.—The Mareva Injunction and Anton Piller Order. Paperback: £24·95: ISBN 0 406 10290 2.

Ralphs, E. and Norman G.—The Magistrate as Chairman. Paperback: £7·95: ISBN 0 406 10469 7.

Robinson, S.—The Law of Interdict. Paperback: £15·95: ISBN 0 406 10445 X.

Supreme Court Practice 1988.—Edited by Sir Jack I. H. Jacob. Hardback: £160·00: ISBN 0 421 37100 5.

The County Court Practice 1987—Edited by R.C.L. Gregory, His Honour D. E. Peck, and D. H. C. Lowis. Hardback: £75·00: ISBN 0 406 16323 5.

Williams, E.—ABC Guide to the Practice of the Supreme Court 1987. Paperback: £14·95: ISBN 0 421 37180 3.

RATING AND VALUATION

Estates Gazette Law Reports 1986, vol. 2—Edited by J. Muir Watt. Hardback: £25·50: ISBN 0 7282 0102 X.

Estates Gazette Law Reports 1987, vol. 1. Edited by J. Muir Watt. Hardback: £23·50: ISBN 0 7282 0111 9.

Plimmer, F.—Rating Valuation: A Practical Guide. Paperback: £14·95: ISBN 0 85121 320 0.

REVENUE AND FINANCE

Allied Dunbar Tax Guide 1987–88, by W. I. Sinclair. Hardback: £12·95: ISBN 0 85121 292 1.

Beckett, L. and Sabine, B.—Revenue Investigations Manual. Paperback: £18·50: ISBN 0 406 50070 3.

REVENUE AND FINANCE—*cont.*

Beidleman, C. (Editor).—The Handbook of International Investing. Hardback: £55·00: ISBN 0 566 02745 3.

British Tax Cases 1986. Hardback: £26·00: ISBN 0 86325 123 4.

British Tax Legislation 1987–88, vols. 1A & 1B. Paperback: £18·00: ISBN 0 86325 116 1 (Vol. 1A); 0 86325 117 X (Vol. 1B).

British Tax Legislation 1987–88, vol. 2. Paperback: £16·00: ISBN 0 86325 118 8.

Butterworths Orange Tax Handbook 1987–88. [Twelfth edition]. Paperback: £17·00: ISBN 0 406 50833 X.

Butterworths U.K. Tax Guide 1987–88.—Edited by J. Tiley [Sixth edition]. Paperback: £12·00: ISBN 0 406 50496 2.

Butterworths Yellow Tax Handbook 1987–88. Twenty-sixth edition. Paperback: £19·00: ISBN 0 406 51004 0.

Campbell, J.—Personal Equity Plans [Woodhead-Faulkner Moneyguide]. Paperback: £4·95: ISBN 0 85941 419 1.

Chapman's Inheritance Tax.—Edited by T. J. Lyons [Seventh edition]. Hardback: £48·00: ISBN 0 85121 326 X.

Coombes, J. and Channon, G.—Inheritance Tax. Paperback: £25·00: ISBN 0 421 37030 0.

Crichton, S. and Ferrier, C.—Understanding Factoring and Trade Credit [Waterlow's Business Library]. Paperback: £13·50. ISBN 0 08 039204 0.

Daily Telegraph Tax Guide.—By L. Livens. Hardback: £10·95: ISBN 0 86367 179 9.

Eastaway, N. and Burwood, S.—Tax & Financial Planning for Medical Practitioners [Second edition]. Paperback: £17·50: ISBN 0 406 19005 4.

Grundy's Tax Havens: a World Survey—by M. Grundy. [Fifth edition]. Paperback: £15·00: ISBN 0 421 37900 6.

International Bar Association.—Tax Avoidance, Tax Evasion [Second edition]. Paperback: £15·00: ISBN 0 948711 12 4.

Lomax, D.—London Markets after the Financial Services Act. Hardback: £25·00: ISBN 0 406 10074 8.

Martin, D.—Revenue Law. [SWOT Success Without Tears Series]. Paperback: £8·95: ISBN 0 906322 91 X.

Martin, I.—Accounting in the Foreign Exchange Market. Hardback: £35·00: ISBN 0 406 50320 6.

Mascarenhas, A.—Current Accounting Law and Practice 1987. [Twelfth edition]. Paperback £26·50: ISBN 0 906157 10 2.

Mayson, S.—A Practical Approach to Revenue Law. [Eighth edition]. Paperback: £19·50: ISBN 1 85185 079 1.

Pennington, R.—Bank Finance for Companies. Paperback: £15·00: ISBN 0 421 38490 5.

Potter and Monroe's Tax Planning with precedents. Edited by A. Thornhill and K. Prosser. [Tenth edition]. Hardback: £49·00: ISBN 0 421 33420 7.

Pritchard, W.—Income tax. [Sixteenth edition]. Paperback: £9·95: ISBN 0 7121 0976 5.

Pritchard, W.—Taxation. [Eighth edition]. Paperback: £8·95: ISBN 0 7121 2038 6.

Ray, E. and Davey, N.—Partnership Taxation [Third edition]. Paperback: £25·00: ISBN 0 406 67820 0.

Spencer, P.—Property Tax Planning Manual. Paperback: £18·95: ISBN 0 406 13739 0.

Stafford, J.—The Share-Owner's Guide [Woodhead-Faulkner Moneyguide]. Paperback: £4·95: ISBN 0 85941 402 7.

Stanley, O.—Taxation of Farmers and Landowners [Third edition]. Hardback: £24·95: ISBN 0 406 38310 3.

Thomas, S.—Family Finance [Woodhead-Faulkner Moneyguide]. Paperback: £4·95: ISBN 0 85941 420 5.

Tolley's Capital Gains Tax 1987–88—by P. Noakes and J. Boulding. Paperback: £14·50: ISBN 0 85459 290 3.

Tolley's Corporation Tax 1987–88—by G. Saunders and J. Boulding. [Twenty-third edition]. Paperback: £13·25: ISBN 0 85459 289 X.

Tolley's Income Tax 1987–88—by E. L. Harvey and G. Saunders. [Seventy-second edition]. Paperback: £15·95: ISBN 0 85459 288 1.

Tolley's Inheritance Tax 1987–88—by R. Wareham and J. Newth. [Second edition]. Paperback: £12·95: ISBN 0 85459 291 1.

Tolley's National Insurance Contributions 1987–88.—By N. D. Booth [Fourth edition]. Paperback: £16·95: ISBN 0 85459 275 X.

Tolley's Tax Data 1987–88.—By R. Wareham, N. Bowen and D. Smailes [Finance Act 1987 edition]. Spiral bound: £7·50: ISBN 0 85459 296 2.

Tolley's Tax Guide 1987–88—by A. Homer and R. Burrows [Fifth edition]. Hardback: £14·95: ISBN 0 85459 293 8.

Tolley's Taxation in the Channel Islands and Isle of Man 1987—by J. Boulding. Paperback: £11·95: ISBN 0 85459 295 4.

Tolley's Taxation in the Republic of Ireland 1987–88—by J. Newth and G. Saunders. Paperback: £12·95: ISBN 0 85459 294 6.

REVENUE AND FINANCE—*cont.*

Tolley's Taxwise Taxation Workbook No. 1 1987–88—by A. Homer, R. Burrows and P. Gravestock. Paperback: £14·25: ISBN 0 85459 257 1.

Touche Ross Tax Guide for the Family 1987/88—by B. Packer and C. Sandy [Second edition]. Paperback: £4·95: ISBN 0 333 44961 4.

Touche Ross Tax Guide for the Self-Employed 1987/88—by B. Packer and C. Sandy [Third edition]. Paperback: £4·95: ISBN 0 333 44963 0.

Touche Ross Tax Guide to Pay and Perks 1987/88—by B. Packer and E. Baker [Fourth edition]. Paperback: £4·95: ISBN 0 333 44962 2.

Wedgwood, A. J., Pell, G. A., Leigh, L. H. and Ryan, C. L.—A Guide to the Financial Services Act 1986. Paperback: £12·95. ISBN 1 85185 050 3.

Whitehouse, C. and Stuart-Buttle, E.—Revenue Law: Principles and Practice [Fifth edition]. Paperback: £20·95: ISBN 0 406 00533 8.

Whittaker, A. and Morse, G.—The Financial Services Act 1986: a Guide to the New Law. Hardback: £25·00: ISBN 0 406 55101 4.

ROAD TRAFFIC

Brown, L.—Law for the Haulier. Hardback: £16·95: ISBN 1 85091 147 9.

Morrish, P. and McLean I.—The Trial of Breathalyser Offences [Second edition]. Paperback: £23·50: ISBN 1 870 08011 4.

Wilkinson's Road Traffic Offences—Edited by P. Halnan and P. Wallis. [Thirteenth edition]. Hardback: £168·00: ISBN 0 85121 289 1.

SALE OF GOODS

Benjamin's Sale of Goods—Edited by A. Guest. [The Common Law Library, no. 11]. [Third edition]. Hardback: £96·00: ISBN 0 421 34670 1.

Harvey, B. and Parry, D.—The Law of Consumer Protection and Fair Trading [Third edition]. Paperback: £15·95: ISBN 0 406 22263 0.

Merkin, R.—A Guide to the Consumer Protection Act 1987. Paperback: £11·95: ISBN 1 85185 078 3.

Nelson-Jones, and Stewart, P.—Product Liability. Paperback: £15·95: ISBN 1 85190 034 9.

Stephenson, G. and Clark, P.—Commercial and Consumer Law [Success Without Tears Series]. Paperback: £7·50: ISBN 1 85185 043 0.

Walker, P.—Consumer Protection Act 1987: a practical guide. Paperback: £12·95: ISBN 0 85121 349 9.

SCOTLAND

Arbitration

Hunter, R. L.—The Law of Arbitration in Scotland. Hardback: £29·95: ISBN 0 567 09480 4.

Irons and Melville on Arbitration [Reprint of 1938 ed.]. Hardback: £40·00.

Children and Young Persons

Kearney, B.—Children's Hearings and the Sheriff Court. Hardback: £38·00: ISBN 0 406 10565 0.

Company Law

Flint, D.—A Guide to Liquidations in Scotland. Paperback: £12·50: ISBN 0 85308 092 5.

Greene, J. and Fletcher, I.—The Law and Practice of Receivership in Scotland. Hardback: £48·00: ISBN 0 406 50102 5.

Contract

McBryde, W. W.—The Law of Contract in Scotland. Hardback: £55·00: ISBN 0 414 00793 X.

Woolman, S. E.—An Introduction to the Scots Law of Contract. Paperback: £14·00: ISBN 0 414 819 7.

Criminal Evidence and Procedure

Bankowski, Z., Hutton, N. and McManus, J.—Lay Justice? Paperback: £9·95: ISBN 0 567 29139 1.

Macphail, I. D.—Evidence: a revised version of a research paper on the law of evidence in Scotland. Hardback: £50·00: ISBN 0 902023 18 7. Paperback: £40·00: ISBN 0 902023 19 5.

Scots Criminal Courts Statutes 1987. Paperback: £10·00: ISBN 0 414 00828 6.

Divorce and Consistorial Causes

Bennett, S. A.—A Short Guide to Divorce in the Sheriff Court [Second Edition]. Paperback: £10·00: ISBN 0 414 00781 6.

Thomson, J. M.—Family Law in Scotland. Paperback: £15·95: ISBN 0 406 26190 3.

BOOKS

European Communities

Anton, A. E. and Beaumont, P. R.—Civil Jurisdiction in Scotland Supplement. Paperback: £14·50: ISBN 0 414 00809 X.

Evidence (Civil)

Macphail, I. D.—Evidence: a revised version of a research paper on the law of evidence in Scotland. Hardback: £50·00: ISBN 0 902023 18 7. Paperback: £40·00: ISBN 0 902023 19 5.

Heritable Property and Conveyancing

Gretton, G. L.—The Law of Inhibition and Adjudication. Paperback: £16·95: ISBN 0 406 10433 6.

Halliday, J. M.—Conveyancing Law and Practice. [Vol. III.] Hardback: £32·00: ISBN 0 414 00815 4.

Scots Conveyancing Miscellany. Hardback: £27·00: ISBN 0 414 008030.

Husband and Wife

Thomson, J. M.—Family Law in Scotland. Paperback: £15·95: ISBN 0 406 26190 3.

Jurisdiction

Civil Jurisdiction in Scotland Supplement. Paperback: £14·50: ISBN 0 414 00809 X.

Justices of the Peace

Bankowski, Z., Hutton, N. and McManus, J.—Lay Justice? Paperback: £9·95: ISBN 0 567 29139 1.

Landlord and Tenant

Halliday, J. M.—Conveyancing Law and Practice. [Vol. III.] Hardback: £32·00: ISBN 0 414 00815 4.

Miscellaneous

Cusine, D. J. and Forte, A. D. M.—Scottish Cases and Materials in Commercial Law. Paperback: £23·95: ISBN 0 406 10870 6.

Gloag and Henderson's Introduction to the Law of Scotland. [Ninth Edition.] Hardback: £45·00: ISBN 0 414 00818 9.

Laws of Scotland: Stair Memorial Encyclopedia. Vol. 1: Accountants, Accounting and Auditing; Administrative Law; Admiralty; Advertising; Agency and Mandate; Agriculture. Hardback: £88·00: ISBN 0 406 23701 8. Vol. 5: Compulsory Acquisition; Constitutional Law; Consumer Credit. Hardback: £88·00: ISBN 0 406 23705 0. Vol. 9: Employment; Energy; Entertainment; Environment. Hardback: £88·00: ISBN 0 406 23709 3. Vol. 22: Social Work; Sources of Law (Formal); Sources of Law (General and Historical); Legal Method and Reform; Time. Hardback: £88·00: ISBN 0 406 23722 0.

Scottish Current Law Yearbook 1986. Scottish Current Law Case Citator 1986. Scottish Current Law Legislation Citator 1986. Cloth: £80: ISBN 0 414 00811 1 (Yearbook); 0 414 00812 X (Case Citator); 0 414 00813 8 (Legislation Citator).

Scottish Law Directory 1987. Hardback: £21·00: ISBN 0 85279 134 8.

Parent and Child

Thomson, J. M.—Family Law in Scotland. Paperback: £15·95: ISBN 0 406 26190 3.

Practice (Civil)

Anton, A. E. and Beaumont, P. R.—Civil Jurisdiction in Scotland Supplement. Paperback: £14·50: ISBN 0 414 00809 X.

Compendium of Legal Aid 1987. Paperback: £5·00: ISBN 0 414 00830 8.

Gretton, G. L.—The Law of Inhibition and Adjudication. Paperback: £16·95: ISBN 0 406 10433 6.

Scots Civil Courts Statutes 1987. Paperback: £24·00: ISBN 0 414 00827 8.

Scott Robinson, S.—The Law of Interdict. Paperback: £15·95: ISBN 0 406 10445 X.

Rights in Security

Gloag & Irvine. Rights in Security. (Reprint) Hardback: £40·00.

Greene, J. and Fletcher, I.—The Law and Practice of Receivership in Scotland. Hardback: £48·00: ISBN 0 406 50102 5.

Gretton, G. L.—The Law of Inhibition and Adjudication. Paperback: £16·95: ISBN 0 406 10433 6.

BOOKS AND ARTICLES

Sheriff Court Practice

Bennet, S. A.—A Short Guide to Divorce in the Sheriff Court. [Second edition.] Paperback: £10·00: ISBN 0 414 00781 6.

Kearney, B.—Children's Hearings and the Sheriff Court. Hardback: £38·00: ISBN 0 406 10565 0.

Nichols, D. I.—The Debtors (Scotland) Act 1987. Paperback: £10·00: ISBN 0 414 00822 7.

The Sheriff Court Rules [Second edition]. Paperback: £4·00. ISBN 0 414 00804 9.

Solicitors

Solicitors' Compendium 1987. Paperback: £4·50: ISBN 0 414 00829 4.

SEA AND SEASHORE

Attard, D.—The Exclusive Economic Zone in International Law [Oxford Monographs in International Law]. Hardback: £40·00. ISBN 0 19 825541 1.

Clark, R.—The Waters Around the British Isles: Their Conflicting Uses. Hardback: £32.50. ISBN 0 19 828492 6.

SHIPPING AND MARINE INSURANCE

Arrest of Ships 4: People's Republic of China, Nigeria, Oman, Scotland—by K. Vun-Ping et al. Hardback: £25·50: ISBN 1 85044 101 4.

Arrest of Ships 5: Bangladesh, Finland, Saudi Arabia, South Africa.—By M. Hafizullah et al. Hardback: £25·50: ISBN 1 85044 102 2.

Arrest of Ships 6: Denmark, Greece, Hong Kong, Kuwait, Qatar.—By A. Philip et al. Hardback: £25·50: ISBN 1 805044 152 9.

Astle, W.—The Safe Port or Berth Reachable on Arrival. Paperback: £12.00: ISBN 0 905045 91 2.

Brown, R.—Marine Insurance. Volume 1: Principles and Basic Practice [Fifth edition]. Hardback: £14·50: ISBN 0 948691 19 0.

Chorley and Giles' Shipping Law—by N. J. J. Gaskell, C. Debattista and R. J. Swatton [Eighth edition]. Paperback: £19·95: ISBN 0 273 02194 X.

Davies, D.—Commencement of Laytime. Hardback: £24·50: ISBN 1 85044 147 2.

De Alba, E. [Panama].—Panama [Maritime Codes: 1]. Hardback: £26·00: ISBN 1 85044 141 3.

El-Sayed, H.—Maritime Regulations in the Kingdom of Saudi Arabia. Hardback: £120·00: ISBN 0 86010 736 1.

Ganado, M.—Arrest of Ships—3: Malta, Panama, Sweden, United Arab Emirates [Arrest of Ships Series]. Hardback: £25·50: ISBN 1 85044 100 6.

Gray, J.—Futures and Options for Shipping. Hardback: £28·00: ISBN 1 85044 137 7.

Hudson, N.G. and Allen, J.C.—The Institute Clauses Handbook. Hardback: £28·50: ISBN 1 85044 093 X.

Ivamy, E.—Casebook on Shipping Law. [Fourth edition]. Paperback: £14·50: ISBN 1 85044 130 8.

Merchant Shipping Act 1970—Annotated by E. R. Hardy Ivamy [LLP Annotated Acts]. Paperback: £25·00: ISBN 1 85044 110 3.

Merchant Shipping (Liner Conferences) Act 1982 annotated by E. R. Hardy Ivamy [LLP Annotated Acts]. Paperback: £16.50. ISBN 1 85044 103 0.

Pilotage Act 1987—annotated by R.P.A. Douglas. [LLP Annotated Acts]. Paperback: £18·75: ISBN 1 85044 139 1.

Todd, P.—Cases and Materials on Bills of Lading. Hardback: £40·00: ISBN 0 632 01857 7.

Todd, P.—Modern Bills of Lading. Hardback: £19·95: ISBN 0 00 383322 4.

U.K. Marine Oil Pollution Legislation Annotated by J. H. Bates [LLP Annotated Acts]. Paperback: £16.50: ISBN 1 85044 109 X.

Ventris, F. M.—Tanker Voyage Charter Parties. Hardback: £45·00: ISBN 0 903 39397 2.

SOCIAL SECURITY

C.P.A.G.'s Supplementary Benefit and Family Income Supplement: The Legislation. Commentary by J. Mesher [Fourth edition]. Paperback: £17·50. ISBN 0 421 38200 7.

Carney, T. and Hanks, P.—Australian Social Security Law, Policy and Administration. Hardback: £25·00. ISBN 0 19 554754 3.

Duckworth, P.—Matrimonial Property and Finance. [Third edition]. Paperback: £45·00: ISBN 0 85121 2816.

Lewis, R.—Compensation for Industrial Injury. Hardback: £24.50: ISBN 0 86205 214 9.

National Welfare Benefits Handbook by B. Lakhani and J. Read [Seventeenth edition]. Paperback: £4·50. ISBN 0 946744 00 9.

Rights Guide to Non-Means-Tested Social Security Benefits by M. Rowland and J. Luba [Tenth edition]. Paperback: £4·50. ISBN 0 946744 01 7.

Tolley's Guide to the Social Security Act 1986 by J. Matthewman and H. Calvert. Paperback: £12·50: ISBN 0 85459 264 4.

BOOKS

SOCIAL SECURITY—*cont.*

Tolley's National Insurance Contributions 1987–88 by N. D. Booth [Fourth edition]. Paperback: £16·95: ISBN 0 85459 275 X.

SOLICITORS

Dane, J. and Thomas, P.—How to Use a Law Library. [Second edition]. Hardback: £16·50: ISBN 0 421 36030 5. Paperback: £8·95: ISBN 0 421 36040 2.

Hartley, M.—Checklists For Solicitors. [Fifth edition]. Spiral-bound: £15·00: ISBN 0 85121 172 0.

Introduction to Legal Practice, vol. 2. Edited by C. Osborne [Second edition]. Paperback: £16.50: ISBN 0 421 36790 3.

STAMP DUTIES

British Tax Legislation 1987–88, vol. 2. Paperback: £16·00: ISBN 0 86325 118 8.

Butterworths Orange Tax Handbook 1987–88. [Twelfth edition]. Paperback: £17·00: ISBN 0 406 50833 X.

Pritchard, W.—Taxation [Eighth edition]. Paperback: £8·95: ISBN 0 7121 2038 6.

Richards, G. and Ball, S.—Planning for Stamp Duty Reserve Tax. Hardback: £26·00: ISBN 0 406 50102 5.

Sergeant and Sims on Stamp Duties and Capital Duty.—Fifth Cumulative Supplement to the Eighth Edition. By B. J. Sims. Paperback: £16·00: ISBN 0 406 37041 9.

STATUTES AND ORDERS

Bills of Exchange Act 1882—Annotated by A. Arora [LLP Annotated Acts]. Paperback: £18·50: ISBN 1 85044 095 6.

British Companies Legislation: Companies Act 1985, Insolvency Act 1986 and related legislation—[Third edition]. Paperback: £16·00: ISBN 0 86325 126 9.

Companies Consolidation Legislation 1987. Edited by G. Morse [Second edition]. Paperback: £36·00: ISBN 0 421 38360 7.

Cross: Statutory Interpretation—by J. Bell and G. Engle. [Second edition]. Paperback: £10·95: ISBN 0 406 57017 5.

Family and Child Law Statutes—compiled by P. H. Niekirk. [Second edition]. Paperback: £22·50: ISBN 0 85121 348 0.

Is It In Force? 1987—Prepared by Butterworths Editorial Staff. Paperback: £15·50: ISBN 0 406 07282 5.

Landlord & Tenant Act 1987.—Annotated by Sir Hugh Rossi [Shaw's Annotated Acts]. Paperback: £10·95: ISBN 0 7219 1070 X.

Latent Damage Act 1986—By P. Capper [Legal Studies and Services Special Report]. Paperback: £28·50: ISBN 1 85271 008 0.

Marston, J.—Public Order: a Guide to the 1986 Public Order Act. Paperback: £10·95: ISBN 1 85190 024 1.

Merchant Shipping Act 1970—Annotated by E. R. Hardy Ivamy [LLP Annotated Acts]. Paperback: £25·00: ISBN 1 85044 110 3.

Merchant Shipping (Liner Conferences) Act 1982—annotated by E.R. Hardy Ivamy. [LLP Annotated Acts] Paperback: £16·50: ISBN 1 85044 103 0.

Merkin, R.—A Guide to the Consumer Protection Act 1987. Paperback: £11·95: ISBN 1 85185 078 3.

Northern Ireland Emergency Legislation.—Compiled and annotated by Butterworths editorial staff. Paperback: £15·00: ISBN 0 406 10577 4.

Pilotage Act 1987.—Annotated by R. P. A. Douglas [LLP Annotated Acts]. Paperback: £18·75: ISBN 1 85044 139 1.

Rose, F.—Civil liability Statutes. Paperback: £8·50. ISBN 1 85185 053 8.

Sealy, L. and Milman, D.—Insolvency: Annotated Guide to the 1986 Insolvency Legislation. Paperback: £19·50. ISBN 0 86325 082 3.

Smith, A.—Offences Against Public Order. Paperback: £14·95: ISBN 0 421 36580 3.

Sweet & Maxwell's Companies Statutes for Students.—Edited by H. Rajak [Second edition]. Paperback: £14·50: ISBN 0 421 38340 2.

Thornton, P.—Public Order Law Including the Public Order Act 1986. Paperback: £10·75: ISBN 1 85185 040 6.

Tolley's Guide to the Social Security Act 1986—By J. Matthewman and H. Calvert. Paperback: £12·50: ISBN 0 85459 264 4.

U.K. Marine Oil Pollution Legislation—Annotated by J. H. Bates [LLP Annotated Acts]. Paperback: £16·50: ISBN 1 85044 109 X.

Vaughan, J.—Banking Act 1979 [LLP Annotated Acts]. Paperback: £18·50: ISBN 1 85044 106 5.

Walker, P.—Consumer Protection Act 1987: a practical guide. Paperback: £12·95: ISBN 0 85121 349 9.

Wedgwood, A.J., Pell, G.A., Leigh, L.H. and Ryan, C.L.—A Guide to the Financial Services Act 1986. Paperback: £12·95: ISBN 1 85185 050 3.

BOOKS AND ARTICLES

STATUTES AND ORDERS—*cont.*

Whittaker, A. and Morse, A.G.—The Financial Services Act 1986: a Guide to the new Law. Hardback: £25·00: ISBN 0 406 55101 4.

Zeidman, M. and Whippman, C.—A Short Guide to the Landlord and Tenant Act 1987. Paperback: £8·00: ISBN 1 870800 05 2.

STOCK EXCHANGE

Ranking and Spicer's Company Law by J. M. Gullick [Thirteenth edition]: Paperback: £14.95: ISBN 0 406 67890 1.

TELECOMMUNICATIONS

Bate, S. de B. (Editor)—Television by Satellite: Legal Aspects. Hardback: £32·75. ISBN 0 906214 43 2.

TORT

Birts, P. and Willis, A.—Trespass: Summary Procedure for Possession of Land. Paperback: £15·95: ISBN 0 406 10481 6.

Burrows, A. S.—Remedies for Torts and Breach of Contract. Hardback: £24·00: ISBN 0 406 50150 5. Paperback: £16·95: ISBN 0 406 50151 3.

Harvey, B. and Parry, D.—The Law of Consumer Protection and Fair Trading [Third edition]. Paperback: £15·95: ISBN 0 406 22263 0.

Jones, M.A.—A Textbook on Torts. Paperback: £13·95: ISBN 1 85185 026 0.

Mara-Brown, E. O. [Nigeria]—Nigerian Law of Torts. [Nigerian Nutshells]. Paperback: £3·95: ISBN 0 421 36150 6.

Merkin, R.—A Guide to the Consumer Protection Act 1987. Paperback: £11·95: ISBN 1 85185 078 3.

Nelson-Jones, R. and Stewart, P.—Product Liability. Paperback: £15·95: ISBN 1 85190 034 9.

Rose, F.—Civil Liability Statutes. Paperback: £8·50. ISBN 1 85185 053 8.

Salmond and Heuston on the Law of Torts by R. F. V. Heuston and R. A. Buckley [Nineteenth edition]. Hardback: £28·50: ISBN 0 421 34300 1: Paperback: £19·50: ISBN 0 421 34310 9.

Walker, P.—Consumer Protection Act 1987: a practical guide. Paperback: £12·95: ISBN 0 85121 349 9.

TOWN AND COUNTRY PLANNING

Butterworths Planning Law Handbook—Edited by K. Davies. Paperback: £21·00: ISBN 0 406 50580 2.

Estates Gazette Law Reports 1986, vol. 2.—Edited by J. Muir Watt. Hardback: £25·50: ISBN 0 7282 0102 X.

Estates Gazette Law Reports 1987, vol. 1. Edited by J. Muir Watt. Hardback: £23·50: ISBN 0 7282 0111 9.

Garner, J. and Jones, B.—Countryside Law. Paperback: £9·95: ISBN 0 7219 1060 2.

Home, R.—Planning Use Classes. Paperback: £14·95: ISBN 0 632 02125 X.

Planning Applications: the RMJM Guide—by A. Salt and H. Brown. Paperback: £19·95: ISBN 0 632 01894 1.

Planning for Growth and Decline [Journal of Planning and Environment Law Occasional Papers, No. 13]. Paperback: £25·00: ISBN 0 421 38260 0.

TRADE AND INDUSTRY

Adams, J. and Prichard Jones, K.—Franchising: Practice and Precedent in Business Format Franchising. [Second Edition]. Hardback: £45·00. ISBN 0 406 10104 3.

Allen, M. and Hodgkinson, R.—Buying a Business: a Guide to the Decisions. Hardback: £30·00: ISBN 0 86010 570 9.

Butterworths Competition Law Handbook—Edited by G. Lindrup. Paperback: £25·00. ISBN 0 406 10400 X.

Corley, R. and Reed, O. [United States]—The Legal Environment of Business—[Seventh edition]. Hardback: £29·95. ISBN 0 07 013256 9.

Cusine, D. and Forte, A.—Scottish Cases and Materials in Commercial Law. Paperback: £23·95: ISBN 0 406 10870 6.

Encyclopedia of Competition law. Edited by R. Merkin. Looseleaf: £185·00: ISBN 0 421 36870 5.

Horner, S.—Parallel Imports. Hardback: £20·00: ISBN 0 00 383366 6.

Keenan, D. and Riches, S.—Business Law. Paperback: £8·95: ISBN 0 273 02415 9.

Long, O.—Law and its Limitations in the GATT Multilateral Trade System. Paperback: £20·25: ISBN 0 86010 959 3.

Mehigan, S. and Griffiths, D.—Restraint of Trade and Business Secrets: Law and Practice. [Longman Commercial Series]. Hardback: £37·50: ISBN 0 85121 174 7.

TRADE AND INDUSTRY—*cont.*

Montague, J.—Business Law. [Chambers Commerce Series]. Paperback: £3·95: ISBN 0 550 20702 3.

Morris, A. and Quest, B.—Design: The Modern Law and Practice. Hardback: £45·00: ISBN 0 406 10320 8.

Ranking, Spicer and Pegler's Business Law for Accountants by N. Bourne [Fifteenth edition]. Paperback: £15·95: ISBN 0 406 67830 8.

Spicer and Pegler's Management Buy-outs—by M. Wright, J. Coyne and A. Mills. Hardback: £25·00. ISBN 0 85941 341 8.

Stephenson, G. and Clark, P.—Commercial and Consumer Law. [Success Without Tears Series]. Paperback: £7·50: ISBN 1 85185 043 0.

Tolley's Factoring and the Accountant in Practice.—By F. R. Salinger. Booklet: £4·95: ISBN 0 85459 285 7.

Trebilcock, M. [Canada].The Common Law of Restraint of Trade: a Legal and Economic Analysis. Hardback: £35·00: ISBN 0 459 39640 4.

Way, P.—Maximising Opportunities under the BES. Paperback: £17·50: ISBN 0 85121 248 4.

Whiting, D. P.—Finance of International Trade. [Fifth edition]. Paperback: £8·95: ISBN 0 273 02734 4.

TRADE MARKS AND TRADE NAMES

Eisenschitz, T.—Patents, Trade Marks and Designs in Information Work. Hardback: £25·00: ISBN 0 7099 0958 6.

Tierney, M. [Ireland]—Irish Trade Marks Law and Practice. Hardback: £30·00. ISBN 0 7171 1440 6.

TRADE UNIONS

Bowers J. and Duggan, M.—The Modern Law of Strikes. Paperback: £12·95: ISBN 1 85185 066 X.

Lord Wedderburn—The Worker and the Law. [Third edition]. Hardback: £25·00: ISBN 0 421 37060 2. (Published 1986). Paperback: £10.00: ISBN X 990 00082 2. (Published 1986).

TRESPASS

Salmond and Heuston on the Law of Torts by R. F. V. Heuston and R. A. Buckley. [Nineteenth edition]. Hardback: £28·50: ISBN 0 421 34300 1: Paperback: £19·50: ISBN 0 421 34310 9.

VALUE ADDED TAX

Allen, C.—VAT and New Businesses.—[VAT Planning Guides]. Paperback: £12·50: ISBN 0 86325 105 6.

Allied Dunbar Tax Guide 1987–88, by W. I. Sinclair. Hardback: £12·95: ISBN 0 85121 292 1.

British Tax Cases 1986. Hardback: £26·00: ISBN 0 86325 123 4.

British Tax Legislation 1987–88, vol. 2. Paperback: £16·00: ISBN 0 86325 118 8.

Butterworths Orange Tax Handbook 1987–88. Twelfth edition. Paperback: £17·00: ISBN 0 406 50833 X.

Butterworths UK Tax Guide 1987–88. Edited by J. Tiley. [Sixth edition]. Paperback: £12·00: ISBN 0 406 50496 2.

Potter and Monroe's Tax Planning with precedents.—Edited by A. Thornhill and K. Prosser. [Tenth edition]. Hardback: £49·00: ISBN 0 421 33420 7.

Pritchard, W.—Taxation [Eighth edition]. Paperback: £8·95: ISBN 0 7121 2038 6.

Tolley's Guide to the New Compliance and Penalty Provisions for VAT.—By C. J. M. Peters and L. Lloyd-Eley. Booklet: £6·95: ISBN 0 85459 284 9.

Tolley's Tax Guide 1987–88 by A. Homer and R. Burrows. [Fifth edition]. Hardback: £14·95: ISBN 0 85459 293 8.

Whitehouse, C. and Stewart-Buttle, E.—Revenue Law: Principles and Practice. [Fifth edition]. Paperback: £20·95: ISBN 0 406 00533 8.

WILLS AND SUCCESSION

Holloway's Probate Handbook—by G. Maple. [Eighth edition]. Hardback: £30·00: ISBN 0 85121 260 3.

Option, F.G. [U.S.A.]—Decedents' Estates, Wills and Trusts in the U.S.A. Hardback: £35·00: ISBN 90 6544 271 5.

Parker's Modern Wills Precedents.—Edited by E. Taylor [Second edition]. Hardback: £25·00: ISBN 0 406 33461 7.

Practical Will Precedents—by M. Hallam, et al. Looseleaf: £95·00: ISBN 0 85121 333 2.

INDEX OF ARTICLES

The following articles were published in 1987. They are listed under the appropriate Current Law headings.

ADMINISTRATIVE LAW

Acts of state: Lord Diplock's curious inconsistency (*P. Wesley-Smith*): (1986) 6 L.S. 325.

Applying the rules of natural justice (*C. Cross*): [1987] L.G.C. June 12, 12.

Beyond *Wednesbury*: substantive principles of administrative law (*J. Jowell and A. Lester*): [1987] P.L. 368.

Boards of visitors and judicial review: the importance of practice (*P. Morris*): 150 J.P.N. 728, 743.

"Chairman's action": the courts, the local ombudsman and the Widdicombe Committee (*M. Jones*): [1987] J.P.L. 612.

Challenging public authority decisions (*P. Rogers*): 106 *Law Notes* 24.

Councils must look closely at their schemes of delegation (*C. Cross*): [1987] L.G.C., October 16, 1987, 12.

Courting trouble (*M. Dalby*): 6 Lit. 324.

Emergence of a new labour injunction? (*K. Ewing and A. Grubb*): 16 I.L.J. 145.

Exclusivity of judicial review procedure: the growing boundary dispute (*G. Peiris*): 15 Anglo-Am. 83.

Expectations in a joyless landscape (*R. Baldwin and D. Horne*): 49 M.L.R. 685.

Fairness: writ large or small? (*M. Allars*): 11 Sydney L.R. 306.

Foreign Claims Commission—the Russian claims (*A. Leslie*): 84 L.S.Gaz. 549.

GLC swan-song—doth the House of Lords protest too much? (*C. Emery*): 136 New L.J. 1033.

Inspectors' conduct of inquiries (*J. Garner*): 131 S.J. 344.

Judicial review—a new snare for magistrates (*I. Bing*): 151 J.P.N. 3.

Judicial review: the best choice? (*A. Khan*): 131 S.J. 1338.

Judicial review: the great leap forward? (*L. Guruswamy and S. Tromans*): 137 New L.J. 597.

Judicial review and children in care (*J. Ellison*): 131 S.J. 454.

Judicial review and local government—recent examples: 151 L.G. Rev. 123.

Judicial review in taxation: a modern perspective (*R. Bartlett*): [1987] B.T.R. 10.

Judicial review of hospital admissions and treatment in the community under the Mental Health Act 1983 (*M. Gunn*): [1986] J.S.W.L. 290.

Judicial review of the take-over panel and self-regulatory organisations (*R. Falkner*): [1987] 2 J.I.B.L. 103.

Judicially reviewing the powers of coroners (*R. Gordon*): 84 L.S.Gaz 1322.

ADMINISTRATIVE LAW—*cont.*

Jurisdictional review and judicial policy: the evolving mosaic (*G. Peiris*): 103 L.Q.R. 66.

Limits of judicial review (considering *Martin* v. *Bearsden and Milngavie District Council* [1987] C.L.Y. 4063 (*P. W. Ferguson*): 1987 S.L.T.(News) 306.

Local authority contracts: public or private law? (*R. Ward*): 151 L.G.Rev. 664.

Natural justice and the enforcement notice (*P. Cooling*): 84 L.S.Gaz, 21.

New territory for the ombudsman (*C. Reid*): 1987 S.L.T.(News) 325.

No appeal without leave? (*C. Emery*): 136 New L.J. 1211.

Political broadcasting, fairness and administrative law (*A. Boyle*): [1986] P.L. 562.

"Public" and "private" in English administrative law (*J. Beatson*): 103 L.Q.R. 34.

Public inquiries and government policy: a judicial bridging on troubled waters? (*A. Mowbray*): 137 New L.J. 418.

Review of the prerogative: the remaining issues (*C. Walker*): [1987] P.L. 62.

Rules of natural justice: 282 E.G. 1657.

Sex establishments, licences and judicial review: 151 L. G.Rev. 369.

Tameside revisited: prospectively "reasonable"; retrospective "maladministration" (*D. Bull*): 50 M.L.R. 307.

Transport Act—practical difficulties for authorities (*B. Hinton*): [1987] L.G.C., August 21, 12.

Trends in the use of judicial review before and after *Swati* and *Puhlhofer (M. Sunkin)*: 137 New L.J. 731.

"Unreasonable" local authority rent increases: 151 L.G.Rev. 725.

Wednesbury unreasonableness: the expanding canvas (*G. Peiris*): [1987] C.L.J. 53.

Whither data protection? (*I. Lloyd*): 1987 S.L.T. 158.

AGENCY

Agency agreements and EEC competition law: some comfort from the EEC Commission (*S. Holmes*): 84 L.S.Gaz. 1052.

Delegation, agency and the alter ego rule (*M. Dixon*): 11 Sydney L.R. 326.

AGRICULTURE

Agricultural holdings—"specified period of the year" (*H. Wilkinson*): 137 New L.J. 656.

Agricultural Holdings Act 1986 (*C. Rodgers*): [1987] Conv. 177.

Anticipating U.K. plant variety patents (*W. Lesser*): [1987] 6 E.I.P.R. 172.

ARTICLES

AGRICULTURE—*cont.*
Farm dwellings (*M. Barrett*): 119 Tax. 337.
Fishy business (*J. Golding*): 119 Tax. 549.
Milk quotas and compensation (*E. Pinfold*): 280 E.G. 1212.
New British pesticide laws and North American perspectives (*N. Hawke*): 15 Anglo-Am. 218.
"Only": a four letter word? Statutory succession and agricultural holdings (*M. Slatter*): [1986] Conv. 320.
Review of recent cases (*J. Watt*): 280 E.G. 1318.
Valuation of agricultural property (*R. Venables*): 118 Tax. 397, 418.
What is farming? (*M. Barrett*): 118 Tax. 378.

ANIMALS
Liability for animals (*D. L. Carey Miller*): 1987 S.L.T.(News) 229.
Trusts for animals (*K. McK. Norrie*): (1987) 32 J.L.S. 386.

ARBITRATION
Arbitration (*D. Stephenson*): 83 L.S.Gaz. 3813.
Arbitration: be there dragons? (*M. Rutherford*): 84 L.S.Gaz. 2422.
Changing roles in the arbitration process (with regard to the applicable law governing the new generation of the petroleum agreements) (*A. El-Kosheri and T. Riad*): (1986) 1 A.L.Q. 475.

ARMED FORCES
Injustice finally remedied? (*I. Dickinson*): 137 New L.J. 435.
Serving a serviceman (*N. McKittrick*): 151 J.P.N. 455.

AVIATION
American deregulation experience and the use of article 90 to expedite EEC air transport liberalisation (*G. Garland*): [1986] E.C.L.R. 193.
Warsaw Convention of the Warsaw system relating to international transportation by air (*M. Thakurta*): [1986] M.L.J. ccxxx.

BAILMENT
Bailment and on-site caravans (*C. Brand*): 84 L.S.Gaz. 637.
Uncollected goods: the penalties of delay (*N. Palmer*): [1987] L.M.C.L.Q. 43.

BANKING
Administrators and banks (*J. Lingard*): (1986) Ins. L. & P. 134.
Aspects of conflict of laws in banking transactions (*J. Spender and G. Burton*): 61 A.L.J. 65.
Asset sales—an analysis of risk for buyers and sellers (*M. Allen*): [1987] 1 J.I.B.L. 13
Bankers' books (*A. Samuels*): 6 Lit. 78.
Banking agreements. Are they anti-competitive? (*J. Rosell*): (1987) 7 IFL Rev 11.

BANKING—*cont.*
Banking bill (*K. Puttick*): 136 New L.J. 1166.
Banking ombudsman (*P. Morris*): [1986] J.B.L. 131; [1987] J.B.L. 199.
Banking supervision under the proposed Banking Act (*D. Lewis*): 84 L.S.Gaz. 400.
Banks and the administrator (*J. Lewis*): (1987) 3 Ins. L. & P. 71.
Concepts of payment in relation to the expropriation or freezing of bank deposits (*R. Goode*): [1987] 2 J.I.B.L. 80.
Converting to multi-currency share capital in the U.K. (*N. Daubeny*): IFL Rev, May 1987, 7.
"Dirty" drugs money and financial and business institutions (*A. Samuels*): (1986) 7 B.L.R. 315.
Discrepancy of documents in letter of credit transactions (*C. Schmitthoff*): [1987] J.B.L. 94.
Documentation of LDC asset transfers (*C. Nicolaides*): (1987) 2 I.B.F.L. 108.
Equity lending in the mortgage market; some legal problems (*A. Hill-Smith*): [1987] J.B.L. 187.
Euro-medium term notes: a new instrument in context (*A. Taylor*): [1987] 2 J.I.B.L. 74.
Euro-notes and commercial paper: The English regulatory framework (*A. Balfour*): [1986] 3 J.I.B.L. 137.
Financial Services Act 1986: April 1987 Admin. i.
Financial Services Act 1986 (*A. J. Gordon*): (1987) 32 J.L.S. 101.
Financial Services Act and small investor (*B. Ferguson*): (1987) 124 SCOLAG 3, 125 SCOLAG 22.
International regulation of securities markets: interaction between United States and foreign laws (*W. Haseltine*): 361 C.L.Q. 307.
"Internationalisation" of sovereign loan agreements (*M Pearce*): [1986] 3 J.I.B.L. 165.
Issuing sterling Euro MTNs (*S. Revell*): (1987) 8 IFL Rev 28.
Judicial review of the take-over panel and self-regulatory organisations (*R. Falkner*): [1987] 2 J.I.B.L. 103.
On-demand bonds—primary or secondary obligations? (*G. Penn*): [1986] 1 J.I.B.L. 224.
Performance bonds—irrevocable obligations (*M. Lawson*): [1987] J.B.L. 259.
Proceeds of fraud: the Bank's liability (*K. Stanton*): (1986) 2 P.N. 190.
Regulation of financial services—an overview (*T. Ashe*): 84 L.S.Gaz. 1392.
Renegotiating or rescheduling foreign debt: IFL Rev, May 1987, 27.
Sterling commercial paper (*J. Barratt and C. Norfolk*): (1987) 2 I.B.F.L. 118.
The Convention establishing the Multilateral Investment Guarantee Agency (*S. Chatterjee*): 36 I.C.L.Q. 76.
Transferability of loans and loan participations (*M. Hughes*): [1987] 1 J.I.B.L. 5.
U.K. Banking Act 1987: a review (*F. Chronnell and P. Haslam*): (1987) 2 I.B.F.L. 129.
U.K. banking practice after the Insolvency Act 1986 (*J. Lingard*): (1987) 2 I.B.F.L. 24.

BANKING—*cont.*
U.S./U.K. proposal on capital adequacy (*A. Murray-Jones and D. Spencer*): (1987) 8 IFL Rev 20.
Wither the negative pledge (*N. Broadman and J. Crosthwait*): [1986] 3 J.I.B.L. 162.

BANKRUPTCY
Acting under orders: (*T. Richmond*): 131 S.J. 427.
Bankruptcy: assignments of causes of action by trustees (*S. Lawson*): 131 S.J. 459.
Bankruptcy and the European Convention (*J. Wollaston*): (1987) 3 Ins.L. & P. 42.
Health authorities and Crown set-off: 83 L.S.Gaz. 3829.
Helping people cope with debt (*G. Coll*): (1987) 124 SCOLAG 5.
In and out of bankruptcy (*S. Gold*): 137 New L.J. 53.
Individual insolvency—a new Act with new problems (*M. Godfrey*): 1987 *Law Notes* 50.
Insolvency Act: 136 New L.J. 1135.
Insolvency Act—preferences: April 1987 Admin. vi.
Insolvency Act 1986 and retention of title (*S. Wheeler*): [1987] J.B.L. 180.
Insolvency law reforms introduced (*J. McQueen*): 9 C.Q.S. 35.
Insolvency practitioners (*J. Williams*): (1987) 3 Ins. L. & P. 39.
Insolvency Practitioners Tribunal (*R. Clements and G. Broadbent*): (1987) 3 Ins. L. & P. 34.
Matrimonial home in bankruptcy (*E. Bailey and C. Berry*): 137 New L.J. 310.
Occupation of the family home and the Insolvency Act 1985 (*J. Miller*): [1986] Conv. 393.
Statutory set-off (*T. Shea*): [1986] 3 J.I.B.L. 152.

BUILDING AND CONSTRUCTION
Beneath the surface in Hong Kong and London (*M. Abrahamson*): (1986) 3 I.C.L.R. 431.
Building problems: investigation of causes (*J. D. Spencely*): (1987) 32 J.L.S. 186.
Building regulations—the liability of local authorities (*J. Brown*): 84 L.S.Gaz. 1633.
Building Regulations 1985: something new or more of the same? (*K. Gough*): (1986) 2 Const.L.J. 262.
Changes to insurance and related provisions (*R. Knowles*): 9 C.Q.S. 11.
Charges to the insurance provisions in the J.C.T. forms of contract (*G. Harris*): 9 C.Q.S. August, 27.
Claims clauses (*R. Knowles*): 9 C.Q.S. 7.
Construction and product liability (*V. van Houtte*): (1987) 4 I.C.L.R. 126.
Contract use 1985: 9 C.Q.S. 12.
Contributory fault in construction contracts (*D. Bristow*): (1986) 2 Const.L.J. 252.
Engineers' liability to contractors (*J. Tackaberry*): (1987) 4 I.C.L.R. 59.
Fire damage—who is liable? (*R. Knowles*): 9 C.Q.S. November 9.

BUILDING AND CONSTRUCTION—*cont.*
Interest on late certification (*R. Knowles*): 9 C.Q.S. August, 7.
Liquidated and ascertained damages; common pitfalls for the Q.S. (*A. Burns*): 9 C.Q.S. 19.
Negligent mortgage valuations again (*S. Murdoch*): 282 E.G. 93.
1986 round-up (*R. Knowles*): 9 C.Q.S. 9.
No obligation (*R. Knowles*): 10 C.Q.S. 7.
North Sea construction contracts (*A. Rettie*): (1987) 4 I.C.L.R. 132.
Protecting subsequent owners (*M. Regan*): 283 E.G. 1028.
Public utilities street works: a view from the man in the street (*A. Samuels*): 151 L.G.Rev. 288.
Question of nomination (*D. Baccarini*): 9 C.Q.S., May, 27; June, 15; July, 21; August, 18.
Recasting building regulations: DoE to issue draft proposals (*M. Bar-Hillel*): 17 C.S.W. 1005.
Recent developments in the building cases (*M. Ross*): (1987) 3 P.N. 109.
Recommendations for review of the F.I.D.I.C. conditions of contract (international) for electrical and mechanical works, second edition 1980 (*A. Pike*): (1986) 3 I.C.L.R. 461.
Repudiating a construction contract for late payments (*R. de Belder*): (1987) 4 I.C.L.R. 27.
Revisions to the F.I.D.I.C. form for civil engineering works: "the point of view of the engineer"(*H. Lloyd*): (1986) 3 I.C.L.R. 504.
Settlement of building regulation disputes (*H. Clarke*): [1987] L.G.C., May 15, 13.
Statutory undertakers: confusion no more! (*G. Harris*): 9 C.Q.S. 21.
Structural survey of negligent reports (*M. Harwood*): 50 M.L.R. 588.
Subcontract adjudication (*M. Crowter*): 9 C.Q.S. July, 17.
Surveyors' duties: two recent cases (*L. Mulcahy*): (1987) 3 P.N. 79.
UNCITRAL's work on the draft legal guide on drawing up international contracts for construction of industrial works (*K. Koh*): [1986] M.L.J. ccxx.

BUILDING SOCIETIES
Building Societies Act 1986 (*C. Jobe and C. Taylor*): (1987) 5 Co. Law Dig. 15.
New law for building societies: Building Societies Act 1986 (*A. Samuels*): [1987] Conv. 36.
Sell and be sued?—the mortgagee's duty on sale (*J. Marriott*): 84 L.S.Gaz. 2756.
Structural survey of negligent reports (*M. Harwood*): 50 M.L.R. 588.

CAPITAL GAINS TAX (NOT SCOTLAND)
Capital gains and caravan living (*C. Brand*): 131 S.J. 762.
Capital profits from land (*M. Gunn*): 119 Tax. 415.

CAPITAL GAINS TAX (NOT SCOTLAND)—*cont.*
General holdover relief for gifts into/out of trusts (and to individuals) (*R. Ray*): 137 New L.J. 303.
Income Tax, Corporation Tax and Capital Gains Tax (*N. Eastaway*): 136 New L.J. 1064.
Trustee's lot (*M. Gunn*): 120 Tax. 1.
Vested interest (*M. Gunn*): 119 Tax. 210.

CAPITAL TAXATION (SCOTLAND ONLY)
Tax effective executry administration: Legal rights and capital gains tax (*E. M. Scobbie*): (1987) 32 J.L.S. 341.

CARRIERS
Transport of goods in refrigerated containers: an Australian perspective (*R. Springall*): [1987] L.M.C.L.Q. 216.

CHARITIES
Anti-avoidance with charities (*M. Gunn*): 119 Tax. 50.
Disposals of land by charities (*J. Thurston*): (1987) 1 Trust L. & P. 138.
"Old Presbyterian persons"—a sufficient section of the public? (*N. Dawson*): [1987] Conv. 114.
Payroll donations (*A. Sellwood*): 118 Tax. 212.
Powers of investment of charity trustees (*J. Thurston*): (1987) 1 Trust L. & P. 162.
Raising money for charity by going from house to house—a different view (*R. Bragg*): [1986] J.S.W.L. 302.

CHILDREN AND YOUNG PERSONS (SCOTLAND ONLY)
Applications for parental rights (considering *A. B.* v. *M.* [1987] C.L.Y. 3992) (*J. M. Thomson*): 1987 S.L.T.(News) 165.
Detention of young adult offenders in Scotland (*B. Williams and A. Creamer*): (1987) 131 SCOLAG 122.
Law Reform (Parent and Child) (Scotland) Act 1986 (*J. M. Thomson*): 1987 S.L.T.(News) 129.
Petition by natural sister for access to two sisters (considering *A.B.* v. *M.* [1987] C.L.Y. 3992) (*E. E. Sutherland*): (1987) 32 J.L.S. 274.
Under age offender (considering *Merrin* v. *S.* [1987] C.L.Y. 4003) (*J. P. Grant*): 1987 S.L.T.(News) 337.

CIVIL LIBERTIES
Contempt of Court Act 1981 and media reporting of crime (*J. G. Logie*): (1987) 32 J.L.S. 249.
Data Protection Act 1984 (*M. Deans*): (1987) 125 SCOLAG 25.
Data Protection Act 1984—subject access provisions: (1987) 32 J.L.S. 378.
How far people can see their computerised records (*A. Dhir*): (1987) 134 SCOLAG 173.
J.P.s, sheriffs and official secrets (*R. Black*): (1987) 32 J.L.S. 138.

CIVIL LIBERTIES—*cont.*
J.P.s, sheriffs and official secrets—a reply: (1987) 32 J.L.S. 221.
J.P.s, sheriffs and official secrets—again (*R. Black*): (1987) 32 J.L.S. 253.
Whither data protection? (*I. Lloyd*): 1987 S.L.T.(News) 158.

CLUBS AND ASSOCIATIONS
Sporting decisions: should the courts participate? (*J. Warburton*): 131 S.J. 868.

COMMONS (NOT SCOTLAND)
Common Land Forum report (*A. Samuels*): [1986] Conv. 391.
Commons: law and practice: proposals for reform—Countryside Commission—Common Land Forum (*A. Samuels*): 150 L.G. Rev. 772.
Doncaster Town Moor case (*A. Samuels*): 151 L.G.Rev. 868.

COMPANY LAW
Acting on delinquent directors—a review of the Company Directors Disqualification Act 1986 (*L. Leighton-Johnston*): (1987) 3 Ins. L. & P. 75.
Acting under orders: (*T. Richmond*): 131 S.J. 427.
Administration—a viable alternative (*T. Hughes*): (1987) 3 Ins. L. & P. 66.
Administrators and banks (*J. Lingard*): (1986) Ins. L. & P. 134.
Auditor's responsibility for the detection of fraud (*D. Gwilliam*): (1987) 3 P.N. 5.
Automatic crystallisation of floating charges: a review of *re Woodroffes (Musical Instruments)* and *re Brightlife Ltd.* (*A. Wilkinson*): (1986) Ins. L. & P. 162.
Banks and the administrator (*J. Lewis*): (1987) 3 Ins. L. & P. 71.
Compulsory purchase of shares in a private company—some recent developments (*D. Fox*): [1987] J.B.L. 276.
Converting to multi-currency share capital in the U.K. (N. Daubeny): IFL Rev, May 1987, 7.
Critical appraisal of "the interests of justice" as an exception to the rule in *Foss* v. *Harbottle* (*O. Osunbor*): 361 C.L.Q. 1.
Crystallization of floating charges, subordination agreements and priority conflicts (*L. Chiaw*): [1986] L.M.C.L.Q. 519.
Dealing with insiders: powers of Department of Trade and Industry inspectors under the Financial Services Act 1986 (*M. Levi*): 137 New L.J. 530.
Death and resurrection of companies (*I. Snaith*): (1986) Ins. L. & P. 180; (1987) 3 Ins. L. & P. 4.
Disqualification and the personal liability of directors (*R. Pennington*): 130 S.J. 848.
Disqualifying company directors (*B. Hannigan*): [1987] L.M.C.L.Q. 188.
Financial assistance problems in management buy-outs (*C. Lumsden*): [1987] J.B.L. 111.
Financial Services Act 1986: April 1987 Admin. i.

COMPANY LAW—*cont.*

Fixed charge over book debts: judicial and legislative responses in Ireland (*D. Tomkin and R. Byrne*): 136 New L.J. 1213.

Fixed charges over book debts (*R. Pearce*): (1987) J.B.L. 18.

Floating charges: May 1987 Admin. i.

Great divide—a review of segmental reporting (*G. Jones*): 5 Co. Law 44.

Husband and wife ltd.—the relationship between company law and divorce (*D. Gordon*): [1986] Conv. 335.

Insolvency Act: 136 New L.J. 1135.

Insolvency Act—preferences: April 1987 Admin. vi.

Insolvency administration—new and viable alternative (*T. Hughes*): (1987) 32 J.L.S. 268.

Insolvency law reforms introduced (*J. McQueen*): 9 C.Q.S. 35.

Insolvency practitioners (*J. Williams*): (1987) 3 Ins. L. & P. 39.

Insolvency Practitioners Tribunal (*R. Clements and G. Broadbent*): (1987) 3 Ins. L. & P. 34.

"Lifting the veil" in four countries: the law of Argentina, England, France and the United States (*J. Dobson*): 35 I.C.L.Q. 839.

Management buyouts (*A. Shipwright*): 131 S.J. 152.

Minority shareholder protection and section 459 (*M. Woodley*): (1987) 5 Co. Law Dig. 13.

Non-executive directors (*E. Jacobs*): [1987] J.B.L. 269.

Partly paid shares (*D. Cohen*): 118 Tax. 265.

Pension scheme surpluses in receivership and liquidation (*R. Bethell-Jones*): (1987) 3 Ins. L. & P. 68.

Purchase orders under s.459 (*B. Hannigan*): (1987) 8 B.L.R. 21.

Ratification and the release of directors from personal liability (*R. Partridge*): [1987] C.L.J. 122.

Reform of the *ultra vires* rule (*B. Hannigan*): [1987] J.B.L. 173.

Reform of the *ultra vires* rule in company law (*A. Clark*): 1987 S.L.T.(News) 80.

Removing legal obstacles to cross border mergers: EEC proposal for a tenth directive (*P. Farmery*): (1987) B.L.R. 35.

Specific implement, interdict and pre-receivership contracts (*D. P. Sellar*): 1987 S.L.T.(News) 41.

Suing in the company's name—who decides? (*A. Blake*): (1987) 5 Co. Law Dig. 19.

Takeovers: May 1987 Admin. iii.

Taxation in insolvency (*A. Davis*): 119 Tax. 98.

Theory and policy of shareholder actions in tort (*M. Sterling*): 50 M.L.R. 468.

True spirit of *Foss* v. *Harbottle* (*C. Baxter*): 38 N.I.L.Q. 6.

Trusts and floating charges (considering *Tay Valley Joinery* v. *C.F. Financial Services* [1987] C.L.Y. 5215) (*K. C. G. Reid*): 1987 S.L.T.(News) 113.

COMPANY LAW—*cont.*

U.K. banking practice after the Insolvency Act 1986 (*J. Lingard*): (1987) 2 I.B.F.L. 24.

Voluntary liquidator and the compulsory petitioner (*A. Mithani*): 84 L.S.Gaz. 1808.

Voting at company meetings—are proxies fair to the private shareholder? (1987) Admin. September 5.

Wallersteiner v. *Moir*: a decade later (*D. Prentice*): [1987] Conv. 167.

What are the voting duties of company members? (*G. Douglas*): 131 S.J. 796.

What is a debenture? (*A. Bati*): [1986] B.T.R. 255.

COMPULSORY PURCHASE

Limits of judicial review (considering *Martin* v. *Bearsden and Milngavie District Council* [1987] C.L.Y. 4063) (*P. W. Ferguson*): 1987 S.L.T.(News) 306.

CONFLICT OF LAWS

Blocking and clawback statutes: the United Kingdom approach (*L. Collins*): [1986] J.B.L. 452.

Capacity to marry and the relevance of the *lex loci celebrationis* in Commonwealth law (*D. Bradshaw*): 15 Anglo-Am. 112.

Choice of law for trusts in Australia and the United Kingdom (*A. Wallace*): 36 I.C.L.Q. 454.

Conflicts of jurisdiction in divorce cases: *forum non conveniens* (*P. Beaumont*): 36 I.C.L.Q. 116.

Domicile: the new rules (*A. Mennie*): 1987 S.L.T.(News) 321, 329.

English law in Singapore: precedent, construction and reality or 'the reception that had to be' (*A. Leong*): [1986] 2 M.L.J. civ.

Forum non conveniens in America and England: "a rather fantastic fiction" (*D. Robertson*): 103 L.Q.R. 398.

Geographical application of the Jurisdiction and Judgments Convention (*P. Kaye*): 6 Lit. 321.

Hague Convention on the law applicable to trusts and on their recognition (*D. Hayton*): 36 I.C.L.Q. 260.

International business and choice of law (*I. Baxter*): 36 I.C.L.Q. 92.

Jurisdiction in actions concerning foreign land: 1987 S.L.T.(News) 53.

Post-formation choice of law in contract (*D. Pierce*): 50 M.L.R. 176.

Proper law in the conflict of laws (*F. Mann*): 36 I.C.L.Q. 437.

Recognition of foreign divorces—the new law (*S. Poulter*): 84 L.S.Gaz. 253.

Validity of "floating" choice of law and jurisdiction clauses (*A. Briggs*): [1986] L.M.C.L.Q. 508.

CONSTITUTIONAL LAW

Anonymity, newpaper reports and open justice (*I. S. Dickinson*): (1987) 32 J.L.S. 384.

Appointment and removal of the lower judiciary (*R. Brazier*): 15 Anglo-Am. 173.

ARTICLES

CONSTITUTIONAL LAW—*cont.*

Checks and balances in public policy making (*D. Wass*): [1987] P.L. 181.
Deluge of delegation (*C. Reid*): 137 New L.J. 682.
Entick v. *Carrington* in the 1980's (*C. Gearty*): 137 New L.J. 470.
Law and the prophets (*Lord Prosser*): (1987) 32 J.L.S. 171.
New look at entrenchment (*J. Elkind*): 50 M.L.R. 158.
Parliament, policy and delegated power (*T. Bates*): [1986] Stat.L.R. 114.
Review of the prerogative: the remaining issues (*C. Walker*): [1987] P.L. 62.
Theory of constitutional change (*P. Joseph and G. Walker*): 70 J.L.S. 155.

CONSUMER CREDIT

Enforcement of consumer credit law (*A. Painter*): (1987) 8 B.L.R. 185, 217.
Equity lending in the mortgage market; some legal problems (*A. Hill-Smith*): [1987] J.B.L. 187.
Extortionate credit bargains and the Consumer Credit Act 1974 (*R. Lawson*): (1986) 7 B.L.R. 283.
Licensing appeals under the Consumer Credit Act 1974 (*D. Williams*): 84 L.S.Gaz. 250.
Repudiation of hire-purchase and related contracts (*D. Waksman*): 6 Lit. 142.

CONTRACT

Abandonment in contract (*R. Sethu*): [1987] M.L.J. xli.
Altering contracts of employment (*N. Osborn*): 131 S.J. 310.
Civil jurisdiction and consumer contracts (*A. Mennie*): 1987 S.L.T.(News) 181.
Comment on the meaning of objectivity in contract (*J. Vorster*): 104 L.Q.R. 274.
Consumer adhesion contracts and unfair terms: a critique of current theory and a suggestion (*A. Burgess*): 15 Anglo-Am. 255.
Contract—a category under attack (*F. Reynolds*): [1987] M.L.J. ccxlvi.
Contract and benefits for third parties (*L. Wilson*): 11 Sydney L.R. 230.
Contract and *quantum meruit:* the antecedents of *Cutter* v. *Powell (J. Barton):* 8 J.L.H. 48.
Contract and tort: looking across the boundary from the side of contract (*K. Mason*): 61 A.L.J. 228.
Contract and tort: stating the recent case law (*M. Duggan*): 131 S.J. 863.
Contract, reliance and business transaction (*W. Howarth*): [1986] J.B.L. 122.
Contributory fault in construction contracts (*D. Bristow*): (1986) 2 Const.L.J. 252.
Contributory negligence in contract and tort (*J. Logie*): 131 S.J. 929.
Damages for distress (*D. Grant*): (1986) 5 Tr.L. 293.
Disclaimers and deceptive conduct (*A. Terry*): (1986) A.B.L.R. 478.

CONTRACT—*cont.*

Economic duress (*E. Jacobs*): (1986) 7 B.L.R. 304.
Employers' rights against departing executives—recent developments (*P. Carolan*): 136 New L.J. 1085.
Exchange losses in contract (*L. Anderson*): 84 L.S.Gaz. 2264.
Express covenant or implied term of confidentiality? (*M. Jefferson*): (1987) 8 B.L.R. 8.
Ideologies of contract (*J. Adams and R. Brownsword*): (1987) L.S. 205.
Interest on contractual damages (*M. Conlon*): 6 Lit. 311.
Interest on debt and the late payer (*K. Michel*): 84 L.S.Gaz. 2173.
Judicial reform of privity and consideration (*E. Jacobs*): [1986] J.B.L. 466.
Latent exemption clause problems in U.K. computer contracts (*A. Kelman*): (1987) 15 I.B.L. 211.
Legal aspects of factoring (*H. Kee*): [1986] M.L.J. ccxl.
Liability for the supply of defective software (*C. Brown*): (1986) 3 Comp.L. & P. 2.
Minors' Contracts Act 1987 (*J. Holroyd*): 84 L.S.Gaz 2266.
Mole's charter?: a review of recent public interest defence cases (*S. Bate*): 84 L.S.Gaz. 1048.
Music publishing and recording contracts in perspective (*J. Tatt*): [1987] 5 E.I.P.R. 132.
New notes on the old oats (*R. Brownsword*): 131 S.J. 384.
On-demand bonds—primary or secondary obligations? (G. Penn): [1986] 1 J.I.B.L. 224.
Oral promises, *ad hoc* implication and the sanctity of written agreements (*A. Stewart*): 61 A.L.J. 119.
Out-turn clauses in c.i.f. contracts in the oil trade (*J. Lightburn and G. Nienaber*): [1987] L.M.C.L.Q. 177.
Part exchange of goods (*E. Jacobs*): 15 Anglo-Am 234.
Payment under a letter of credit (*P. Chai*): [1987] M.L.J. lxi.
Performance bonds—irrevocable obligations (*M. Lawson*): [1987] J.B.L. 259.
Post-formation choice of law in contract (*D. Pierce*): 50 M.L.R. 176.
Prepayments (*A. Samuels*): (1987) J.B.L. 30.
Professional and contractual obligations: 150 L.G.Rev. 768.
Recovery of money paid under a mistake of fact (*K. Nicholson*): 60 A.L.J. 459.
Repudiation of a substantially performed contract for defective workmanship (*J. Fisher*): 84 L.S.Gaz. 30.
Repudiation of hire-purchase and related contracts (*D. Waksman*): 6 Lit. 142.
Sales without title (*R. Lawson*): (1987) 8 B.L.R. 196.
Security for payments under major overseas projects (*E. Herzfeld*): [1986] J.B.L. 446.
Software as 'goods': *nullum simile est idem* (*A. Scott*): [1987] 3 Comp. L. & P. 133.

CONTRACT—*cont.*

Some problems with the Unfair Contract Terms Act 1977 (*D. Tiplady*): 137 New L.J. 427.

Specific implement, interdict and pre-receivership contracts (*D. P. Sellar*): 1987 S.L.T.(News) 41.

Statutory illegality and the innocent victim (*T. Brentnall*): 84 L.S.Gaz. 343.

Ten years of fair contracts in Scotland? (*W. J. Stewart*): 1987 S.L.T.(News) 361.

Transferability and sale of goods (*I. Davies*): (1987) 7 L.S. 1.

Uberrima fides in English and American insurance law: a comparative analysis (*F. Achampong*): 36 I.C.L.Q. 329.

Unfair Contract Terms Act: points when drafting contracts (*D. Pollard*): (1987) 8 B.L.R. 131.

Unfair Contract Terms Act 1977—who deals as consumer? (*R. Kidner*): 38 N.I.L.Q. 46.

Validity of "floating" choice of law and jurisdiction clauses (*A. Briggs*): [1986] L.M.C.L.Q. 508.

Written statement of terms (*J. Bowers*): 6 Lit. 22.

CONVEYANCING (NOT SCOTLAND)

Bain v. Fothergill—a reply to Mr. Farren (*M. Thompson*): 137 New L.J. 83.

Bane of *Fothergill?* (*S. Farren*): 136 New L.J. 1205.

Beneficial co-ownership behind a resulting trust and the problems of a trust for sale (*W. Swadling*): [1986] Conv. 379.

Beneficial joint tenancies: a case for abolition? (*M. Thompson*): [1987] Conv. 29.

Beneficial joint tenancies: a reply to Professor Prichard (*M. Thompson*): [1987] Conv. 275.

Beneficial joint tenancies: a riposte (*A. Prichard*): [1987] Conv. 273.

Burden and benefit of the rules of assignment (*D. Gordon*): [1987] Conv. 103.

Circumventing property statutes: can it still be done? (*P. Freedman*): 84 L.S.Gaz. 403.

Commons: law and practice: proposals for reform—Countryside Commission—Common Land Forum (*A. Samuels*): 150 L.G.Rev. 772.

Constructive trusts and proprietary estoppel: 6 Lit. 58.

Conveyancers beware the co-habitee (*M. Sookias, J. Cole and A. Price*): 84 L.S.Gaz. 1309.

Conveyancing: a practitioner's review (*P. Rank*): 131 S.J. 798.

Conveyancing aspects of repurchase of defective dwellings—pt. xvi of and sched. 20 to the Housing Act 1985 (*M. Turnbull*): 84 L.S.Gaz. 2754.

Covenants for title by joint tenants (*M. Russell*): 130 S.J. 944.

Defective buildings: where does liability lie? (*J. Thurston*): 131 S.J. 1050.

Devil's advocate—estate conveyancing explained (*P. Palmer*): 84 L.S.Gaz. 645.

CONVEYANCING (NOT SCOTLAND)—*cont.*

Disclosure by vendors (*J. Farrand*): 280 E.G. 961.

Disclosure by vendors (*I. Oddy*): 280 E.G. 1068.

Doctrine of conversion—fact or fiction? (*J. Warburton*): [1986] Conv. 415.

Flat management by trustees: an alternative to the management company (*R. Coleman*): 84 L.S.Gaz. 1307.

High life? (*P. Rank*): 131 S.J. 1202.

How much licence do the new conveyancers have? (*P. Kenny*): 131 S.J. 958.

Informal trusts and third parties (*J. Feltham*): [1987] Conv. 246.

Into the light? The Law Commission working paper on land mortgages (*G. Griffiths*): [1987] Conv. 191.

Jurisdiction in actions concerning foreign land: 1987 S.L.T.(News) 53.

Land mortgages (*H. Wilkinson*): 281 E.G. 415.

Land registration: plans for all seasons (*E. Pryer*): 84 L.S.Gaz. 635.

Land registration reform: a third instalment (*J. Sweetman*): 131 S.J. 902.

Landlord and Tenant Act 1987—part I (*J. Israel*): 84 L.S.Gaz. 2749.

Licences and land law: an alternative view (*J. Dewar*): 49 M.L.R. 741.

Mortgagees and possession (*H. Wallace*): 37 N.I.L.Q. 336.

Occupation of the family home and the Insolvency Act 1985 (*J. Miller*): [1986] Conv. 393.

Occupiers: when do they bite? (*P. Sparkes*): [1986] Conv. 309.

Pre-contract deposits: 281 E.G. 901.

Pre-contract deposits (*J. Sweetman*): 131 S.J. 242.

Pre-contract enquiries: an appraisal of the Conveyancing Committee's recommendations (*J. Adams*): 137 New L.J. 466.

Pre-contractual notice of defects in title (*M. Thompson*): 84 L.S.Gaz. 2434.

Property law review: equity and land law (*P. Rank*): 131 S.J. 278.

Purchasers in possession (*P. Sparkes*): [1987] Conv. 278.

Question of intention? (*J. Montgomery*): [1987] Conv. 16.

Remedies in sale of land transactions (*F. Silverman*): 106 *Law Notes* 276.

Rotting away of *caveat emptor*? (*L. Gleeson and E. McKendrick*): [1987] Conv. 121.

Rule in *Bain* v. *Fothergill*—an early demise? (*R. Evans and P. Rank*): 84 L.S.Gaz. 26.

Some pitfalls for mortgagees and how to avoid them (*R. Bonehill*): 130 S.J. 847.

"Subject to contract"—a different ring (*E. Guat*): 28 Mal.L.R. 191.

Time for removal of tenant's fixtures (*G. Kodilinye*): [1987] Conv. 253.

Time-sharing—self-regulation (*J. Edmonds*): 84 L.S.Gaz. 1305.

Unitisation of properties (*N. Sinclair*): 84 L.S.Gaz. 1394.

Woman's place—a conflict between law and social values (*J. Eekelaar*): [1987] Conv. 93.

ARTICLES

COPYRIGHT

Berne Convention and the public interest (*J. Phillips*): [1987] 4 E.I.P.R. 108.

Computer software piracy (*J. Buckle*): 83 L.S.Gaz. 3810.

Containers "get up" and passing off (*M. Briffa*): 84 L.S.Gaz. 2444.

Copyright: public interest and statutory powers under the Competition Act 1980 (*R. Greaves*): [1987] 1 E.I.P.R. 3.

Copyright and industrial designs (considering development of law to *British Leyland Motor Corp.* v. *Armstrong Patents Co.* [1986] C.L.Y. 432) (*H. L. MacQueen*): 1987 S.L.T.(News) 121.

Copyright and writers (*C. Golvan*): [1987] 3 E.I.P.R. 66.

Copyright in the textile industry (*E. Eder*): [1986] 10 E.I.P.R. 312.

Copyright law—a fresh start (*T. Stocks*): 136 New L.J. 1167.

Copyright piracy and the new technology (*G. McFarlane*): 131 S.J. 1376.

Fair spares for all (*P. Thornberry*): 131 S.J. 274.

Government White Paper: intellectual property and innovation (*C. Miller and G. Kamstra*): (1986) 3 Comp.L. & P. 13.

Information, equity and entropy (information technology law in England) (J. Mawhood): (1987) 3 Comp.L. & P. 186.

Infringement of copyright and the problem of "piracy" (*P. Brazil*): 61 A.L.J. 12.

Legal protection of computer software against misuse—feasibility or fond hope? (*E. Pugh*): [1987] IX Liverpool L.R. 45.

Legal rights in patented computers—as—programmed: a conflict of principles (*J. Phillips*): (1987) 3 Comp.L. & P. 125.

Moral rights in English law—the shape of rights to come (*G. Dworkin*): [1986] 11 E.I.P.R. 329.

Music publishing and recording contracts in perspective (*J. Tatt*): [1987] 5 E.I.P.R. 132.

New intellectual property right? A hidden landmine in the Cable and Broadcasting Act 1984 (*J. Phillips*): (1987) 3 Comp. L. & P. 99.

"Payola" and the calculation of music royalties (*T. Stocks*): 137 New.L.J. 391.

Status of protection for software in the U.K. and other European countries (*C. Brown*): (1986) 3 Comp.L. & P. 46.

Towards a performers' copyright: an analysis of *Rickless* v. *United Artists* (*R. Arnold*): [1987] 4 E.I.P.R. 97.

CORONERS (NOT SCOTLAND)

Judicially reviewing the powers of coroners (*R. Gordon*): 84 L.S.Gaz. 1322.

CORPORATION TAX

Income Tax, Corporation Tax and Capital Gains Tax (*N. Eastaway*): 136 New L.J. 1064.

CRIMINAL EVIDENCE AND PROCEDURE

Admissibility of hypnotically refreshed testimony (*R. Munday*): 151 J.P.N. 404, 426.

Advance disclosure in magistrates' courts: the workings of section 48 (*J. Baldwin and A. Mulvaney*): 151 J.P.N. 409.

Anonymity of justices examined (*M. Watkins*): 150 J.P.N. 787.

Arrest, charge and prosecution (*A. Sanders*): (1986) 6 L.S. 257.

Bail proceedings in magistrates' courts: basic procedures (*P. Lydiate*): 151 J.P.N. 164, 181

Bankers' books (*A. Samuels*): 6 Lit. 78.

Bias and the court sheet (*R. Stevens*): 150 J.P.N. 788.

Causation and expert evidence (considering *Hendry* v. *H.M. Advocate* [1987] C.L.Y. 4200): (1987) 32 J.L.S. 468.

Child abuse and the criminal trial (*A. Samuels*): 151 J.P.N. 603.

Children's evidence by video (*G. Williams*): 151 J.P.N. 339.

Circumstantial corroboration (*R. Munday*): 151 J.P.N. 277.

Confessions and unfair evidence—ss.76 and 78 again (*B. Gibson*): 151 J.P.N. 387.

Continuing representations in criminal law (*S. White*): 37 N.I.L.Q. 255.

Corroboration question (*G. Williams*): 137 New L.J. 131.

Criminal Justice Act 1987 (*B. Gibson*): 151 J.P.N. 435.

Criminal trials: proof by missing witness an election issue? (*D. Wolchover*): 137 New L.J. 525.

Crown Court costs; remuneration for the big case (*S. Jonas*): 137 New L.J. 179.

Deputy clerk: "he that occupieth in another man's right" (*P. Lydiate*): 151 J.P.N. 581.

Developments in the law of evidence: 151 J.P.N. 35.

Distribution of business between the Crown Court and the magistrates' court (*A. Samuels*): 150 J.P.N. 779.

Evidence of accomplices (considering *Docherty* v. *H.M. Advocate* [1987] C.L.Y. 4119): (1987) 32 J.L.S. 425.

Evidence reforms of the Criminal Justice Bill (*B. Gibson*): 151 J.P.N. 131.

Evidential repercussions of automated teller machines (*T. Kaiser*): (1986) 3 Comp. L. & P. 57.

Excited utterances and the *res gestae* doctrine (*R. Munday*): 84 L.S.Gaz. 2350.

Fines—dying a natural death (*A. James*): 151 J.P.N. 167.

Hearsay, relevance and admissibility: declarations as to state of mind and declarations against penal interest (*P. Carter*): 103 L.Q.R. 106.

Hypnosis and the enhancement of witness recall (*R. Munday*): 151 J.P.N. 452.

Judicial procedure: fundamental reappraisal (*C. Scott-Mackenzie*): (1987) 32 J.L.S. 143.

Judicial review—a new snare for magistrates (*I. Bing*): 151 J.P.N. 3.

Justice in absence? (*S. Biggin*): 151 J.P.N. 664.

CRIMINAL EVIDENCE AND PROCEDURE—*cont.*

Justices and trials within trials—yet again (*B. Gibson*): 151 J.P.N. 275.

Justices' clerks and their magistrates' courts committees—the way ahead (*P. Brown*): 151 J.P.N. 538.

Knowing the outstanding charges on a not guilty plea: 150 J.P.N. 805.

Magistrates' court and the *voir dire* (*B. Boulter*): 151 J.P.N. 184.

More about videotaping children (*G. Williams*): 137 New L.J. 369.

Motion for separation of charges (*U. R. Vass*): 1987 S.L.T.(News) 369.

New provisions as to costs in criminal cases in magistrates' courts (*M. Dodds*): 151 J.P.N. 85.

Perils of delaying legal proceedings (*B. Nelson*): [1987] L.G.C., January 16, 14.

Photofit pictures and the law of evidence (*R. Munday*): 151 J.P.N. 149.

Precedent in the House of Lords in criminal cases (*C. Gearty*): 137 New L.J. 707.

Pre-trial reviews in magistrates' courts: recent changes brought about by the new rules on advance disclosure (*J. Baldwin*): 151 J.P.N. 611.

Previous convictions and an accused's character (*U. R. Vass*): 1987 S.L.G. 30, 68.

Production of real evidence—is it necessary? (considering *Tudhope* v. *Stewart* [1986] C.L.Y. 3759) (*P. W. Ferguson*): 1987 S.L.T.(News) 173.

Prosecuting sexual assault cases (*Scottish Rape Crisis Centres*): (1987) 32 J.L.S. 470.

Recent changes in the law affecting costs (*C. Bazell*): 150 J.P.N. 707.

Recent developments in criminal evidence (*J. Clegg*): 84 L.S.Gaz. 2920.

Reform of English criminal procedure—fact or fiction (*E. Glicksman*): 15 Anglo-Am. 1.

Refusing to ask for freedom—the person who does not seek to ask for bail (*J. Spencer*): 150 J.P.N. 724.

Refuting allegations of child sexual abuse (*S. Enright*): 137 New L.J. 633, 672.

Right to silence (considering *Upton* v. *H.M. Advocate* [1986] C.L.Y. 3875): 1987 S.L.T.(News) 17.

Role of prosecution counsel: 83 L.S.Gaz. 3599.

Question of credit (*J. Clegg*): 106 *Law Notes* 164.

Serving a serviceman (*N. McKittrick*): 151 J.P.N. 455.

Similar fact evidence—the unobservable rule (*A. Zuckerman*): 104 L.Q.R. 187.

Similar facts—*Makin* out? (*P. Mirfield*): [1987] C.L.J. 83.

Socii criminis—need to warn? (considering *Scott* v. *H.M. Advocate* [1986] C.L.Y. 3775) (*P. W. Ferguson*): 1987 S.L.T.(News) 116.

Those whom the court hath joined together: let procedure put asunder (*R. Stevens*): 150 J.P.N. 775.

Time is of the essence: applications for warrants of further detention (*R. Stevens*): 151 J.P.N. 407.

Trials within trials in the magistrates' courts: a panoramic view (*R. Stevens*): 151 J.P.N. 531.

Unsafe and unsatisfactory: lurking doubt (*A. Samuels*): 151 J.P.N. 55.

Use of videotape recordings in the law of evidence (*S. Sharpe*): 151 J.P.N. 419.

Videotaping children's evidence (*G. Williams*): 137 New L.J. 108.

When the clerk is away (*J. Davis*): 151 J.P.N. 486.

Wilder permutations of section 1(*f*) of the Criminal Evidence Act 1898 (*R. Munday*): (1987) L.S. 137.

Without prejudice in the magistrates' court (*R. Gordon*): 84 L.S.Gaz. 2349.

Witness summonses: important developments (*N. McKittrick*): 151 J.P.N. 644.

Written evidence—section 9 statements (*A. Samuels*): 151 J.P.N. 441.

CRIMINAL LAW

Advance notice of processions: s.11 of the Public Order Act 1986 (*J. Marston*): 84 L.S.Gaz. 1646.

Advising victims of crime (*R. Colbey*): 6 Lit. 14.

After *Shivpuri*—what? (*B. Duffy*): 83 L.S.Gaz. 3589.

Against using P.M.S. in criminal court cases (*N. Hitton*): 151 J.P.N. 152.

AIDS and the law (*D. Brahams*): 137 New L.J. 749.

Another new chapter in conspiracy (*G. McFarlane*): 137 New L.J. 7.

Anticipating the past: the defence of provocation in Irish law (*F. McAuley*): 50 M.L.R. 133.

Arrest, charge and prosecution (*A. Sanders*): (1986) 6 L.S. 257.

Art and part guilt and "defence" of dissociation (considering *MacNeil* v. *H.M. Advocate* [1986] C.L.Y. 3723) (*P. W. Ferguson*): 1987 J.R. 131.

Attempting the impossible and converting a completed non-criminal action into a criminal attempt (*J. Yahuda*): 151 J.P.N. 389.

Attempting the impossible: recent developments in the House of Lords (*D. Selfe*): [1987] IX Liverpool L.R. 69.

Binding over—too wide a power? (*C. Bazell*): 151 J.P.N. 456.

Breath tests, blood tests and back calculation (*J. Dossett*): 84 L.S.Gaz. 2925.

Bringing trading standards legislation nearer the local trader—*Riley* v. *Webb* (*I. Thomas*): 151 J.P.N. 631.

Centralised court hearings (*J. Spencer*): 151 J.P.N. 563.

Changing your mind in the magistrates' court—a defendant's prerogative? (*W. Donnelly*): 84 L.S. Gaz. 246.

Cheating the Revenue: no deception required (*G. MacFarlane*): 131 S.J. 338.

Child abduction: the new law (*S. Cretney*): 130 S.J. 827.

Child sexual abuse: the legal issues (*G. Douglas*): 131 S.J. 1170.

CRIMINAL LAW—*cont.*

Colour of right and offences of dishonesty (*W. Brookbanks*): (1987) 11 Crim.L.J. 153.

Confessions, cautions, experts and the subnormal after *R.* v. *Silcott* (*M. Beaumont*): 137 New L.J. 807.

Conspiracy: cheating: House of Lords: parliament (*A. Samuels*): 151 J.P.N. 232.

Contempt of Court Act 1981 and media reporting of crime (*J. G. Logie*): (1987) 32 J.L.S. 249.

Continuing representations in criminal law (*S. White*): 37 N.I.L.Q. 255.

Corporate criminal liability (considering *Purcell Meats (Scotland)* v. *McLeod* [1987] C.L.Y. 4197) (*D. Whyte*): 1987 S.L.T.(News) 348.

Crime and precedent in the House of Lords (*T. McLeod*): 84 L.S.Gaz. 660.

Crimes on the football field (*J. B. Stewart*): (1987) 32 J.L.S. 420.

Criminal behaviour and medicinal treatment—iatrogenic crime (*D. Brahams*): 84 L.S.Gaz. 2175.

Criminal Justice Act 1987 (*B. Gibson*): 151 J.P.N. 435.

Criminal Justice Bill—a selection from the proposals (*B. Gibson*): 151 J.P.N. 100.

Criminal Justice Bill: new concepts in criminal law (*G. McFarlane*): 83 L.S.Gaz. 3719.

Criminal responsibility of infants (*A. Photis*): 151 J.P.N. 263.

Dealing with insiders: powers of Department of Trade and Industry inspectors under the Financial Services Act 1986 (*M. Levi*): 137 New L.J. 530.

Defence of due diligence (*R. Lawson*): 151 J.P.N. 499.

Deputy clerk: "he that occupieth in another man's right" (*P. Lydiate*): 151 J.P.N. 581.

Detention under the Police and Criminal Evidence Act 1984 (*H. Brayne*): 84 L.S.Gaz. 28.

Developments in criminal law (*B. Gibson*): 151 J.P.N. 195.

Distracting greyhounds (*J. Matthews*): 131 S.J. 992.

Doli incapax (*T. Wilkinson*): 151 J.P.N. 377.

Domestic violence: uniform response? (*A. Mackay*): (1987) 128 SCOLAG 67.

Driving recklessly—defence of necessity strictly construed (*N. McKittrick*): 151 J.P.N. 180.

Duress: sharp shooting at criminal organisations (*N. Reville*): 131 S.J. 1302.

Enforcement of consumer credit law (*A. Painter*): (1987) 8 B.L.R. 185, 217.

Entick v. *Carrington* in the 1980s (*C. Gearty*): 137 New L.J. 470.

Examination of Part I of the Public Order Act 1986 (*K. Pain*): 151 J.P.N. 198.

Exclusion orders under the Public Order Act 1986 (*J. Marston*): 84 L.S.Gaz. 2426.

Failure to provide a breath sample for analysis in the Lion intoximeter (*J. Morris*): 151 J.P.N. 249.

Football violence: the courts' new red card (*G. Broadbent*): 131 S.J. 1136.

CRIMINAL LAW—*cont.*

Footloose and duty free (*P. Breuer*): 151 J.P.N. 535.

Forced to commit murder (*B. Hogan*): Law M., May 29, 1987, 32.

Foreign elements in crime and jurisdiction (*A. Samuels*): 150 J.P.N. 714.

Forfeiture Act: a perspective (*T. Prime*): 130 S.J. 811.

Free passage v. free public protest: obstruction of the highway re-defined (*R. Stevens*): 151 J.P.N. 39.

Freezing defendants' assets before drugs trials (*D. Feldman*): 137 New L.J. 457.

Good intentions (*A. Halpin*): 137 New L.J. 696.

Guardians ad litem and pre-hearing disclosure (*N. Leighton*): 151 J.P.N. 308.

Hackers and program copying: computer case law (*G. McFarlane*): 84 L.S.Gaz. 2424.

Hacking and the criminal law (*T. Nicholls*): (1986) 3 Comp. L. & P. 64.

Harassment and unlawful eviction (*P. Watchman*): (1987) 129 SCOLAG 92.

Heysel stadium extraditions (*D. Janner*): 84 L.S.Gaz. 2342.

Higher risk of custody in the Crown Court (*D. Bale*): 151 J.P.N. 69.

Highway obstruction, lawful excuse and the right to demonstrate (*I. Bing*): 151 J.P.N. 628.

House of Lords and precedent: a new departure (*E. Canton*): 137 New L.J. 491.

Incest and prohibited degrees of marriage (*J. M. Thomson*): 1987 S.L.G. 16.

Intended consequences and unintentional fallacies (*A. Halpin*): 7 O.J.L.S. 104.

Intoxication, mistake and self-defence (*E. Macdonald*): 137 New L.J. 914.

Investigation of crime in England and Wales (*J. Burrows and R. Tarling*): 27 Brit. J. Criminol. 229.

J.P.s, sheriffs and official secrets (*R. Black*): (1987) 32 J.L.S. 138.

J.P.s, sheriffs and official secrets—a reply: (1987) 32 J.L.S. 221.

J.P.s, sheriffs and official secrets—again (*R. Black*): (1987) 32 J.L.S. 253.

Jurisdiction and criminal law in Scotland and England (*P. W. Ferguson*): 1987 J.R. 179.

Justices' identity and the rule against bias (*J. Vickers*): 151 J.P.N. 327.

Juvenile courts—grave crimes revisited (*T. Wilkinson*): 151 J.P.N. 549.

Keeping the public order (*L.Leigh*): 131 S.J. 86, 123.

Maintaining public order in the 1980s (*I. Dickinson*): 1987 S.L.T.(News) 105.

Making up for the missing element—a sideways look at attempts (*J. Stannard*): (1987) L.S. 194.

Miscarriage of justice: how does it occur? (*A. Samuels*): 151 J.P.N. 10.

Monitoring the Public Order Act 1986 (*H. Kitchin*): (1987) *Legal Action*, August 12.

Murder: the duress defence (*G. McFarlane*): 131 S.J. 383.

CRIMINAL LAW—*cont.*

"Must I see the probation officer?" What options for defendants? (*N. Stone*): 151 J.P.N. 552.

Naked exposure (*J. Spencer*): 151 J.P.N. 279.

Naming the beak (*A. Carroll*): 151 J.P.N. 470.

Nemo iudex in sua causa? (considering *Tennant* v. *Houston* [1987] C.L.Y. 4173) (*P. W. Ferguson*): 1987 S.L.T.(News) 149.

New pitfalls in attempted crimes (*M. Jefferson*): 151 J.P.N. 662.

New statutory preventive provisions in Part II of the Public Order Act 1986 (*J. Marston*): 151 L.G.Rev. 205.

Obstruction of the highway and "lawful authority" (*G. Holgate*): 151 J.P.N. 568.

"Obvious" and "serious" difficulties (*R. Lynn*): 37 N.I.L.Q. 237.

On disclaiming liability for a false mileometer (*R. Lawson*): 84 L.S.Gaz. 2760.

Parental chastisement (*A. Samuels*): 151 L.G.Rev. 210.

Parking alongside a kerbed footway, blocking the occupier (*A. Samuels*): 151 J.P.N. 88.

Perchance to dream (*M. Weller*): 137 New L.J. 52.

Police and the substantive criminal law (*L. Lustgarten*): 27 Brit.J.Criminol 23.

Possession (*A. Samuels*): 151 J.P.N. 537.

Pre-natal injury, homicide and the draft criminal code (*J. Temkin*): [1986] C.L.J. 414.

Product contamination—the impact of the Public Order Act (*S. Watson*): 84 L.S.Gaz. 13.

Prosecution and the public interest (*A. Samuels*): 151 J.P.N. 361.

Protest and public order: the Public Order Act 1986 (*J. Driscoll*): (1987) J.S.W.L. 280.

Public Order Act 1986 (*C. Walker*): 151 L.G.Rev. 364.

Public Order Act 1986: an overview of Part I (*J. Marston*): 151 L.G.Rev. 264.

Public Order Act 1986: 1 offences (*E. Rees*): *Legal Action*, February 1987, 9.

Public Order Act 1986: processions, assemblies and sporting events (*T. Owen*): *Legal Action*, April 1987, 11.

Public Order Act 1986: steps in the wrong direction? (*D. Bonner and R. Stone*): [1987] P.L. 202.

Quitting a vehicle on private premises—a gap in the regulations? (*P. Amey*): 151 J.P.N. 169.

Raising money for charity by going from house to house—a different view (*R. Bragg*): [1986] J.S.W.L. 302.

Reckless language and *Majewski (E. Macdonald)*: (1986) 6 L.S. 239.

Recklessness—ruling out the risk (*R. Taylor*): 137 New L.J. 231.

Recklessness and murder—the facts of the case (*I. Leader-Elliott*): (1986) 10 Crim.L.J. 359.

Refusing to ask for freedom—the person who does not seek to ask for bail (*J. Spencer*): 150 J.P.N. 724.

CRIMINAL LAW—*cont.*

Refuting allegations of child sex abuse (*S. Enright*): 137 New L.J. 672.

R. v. *Howe*: duress, aiding and abetting, cannibalism and morality (*J. Spencer*): 151 J.P.N. 373.

Remands in custody (*S. Dell*): 137 New L.J. 93.

Reparation and mediation in the criminal justice system (*C. Williams*): 136 New L.J. 1106, 1141.

Riot in the Riot (Damages) Act 1886 (*J. Marston*): 84 L.S.Gaz. 1797.

Road traffic—recent developments: 83 L.S.Gaz. 3572.

Road traffic—recent developments: 84 L.S. Gaz. 2667.

Road traffic—viable or arguable defences to drunken driving (*A. Samuels*): 84 L.S.Gaz. 659.

Safekeeping, supplying and misuse of drugs (*M. Christie*): (1987) 32 J.L.S. 26.

Scots criminal law and Aids (*L. Farmer, P. Brown and J. Lloyd*): 1987 S.L.T.(News) 389.

Search under the Official Secrets Act (*G. Zellick*): 137 New L.J. 160.

S.20 of the Race Relations Act 1976: "facilities" and "services" (*J. Gardner*): 50 M.L.R. 345.

Sections 14 and 39 Public Order Act 1986 (*J. Marston*): 151 J.P.N. 601, 615.

Secure Accommodation (No. 2) (Amendment) Regulations 1986 (*C. Bazell*): 150 J.P.N. 759.

Self-defence—drunk and sober (*B. Gibson*): 151 J.P.N. 547.

Self-defence—the need for clear guide-lines (*G. McFarlane*): 84 L.S.Gaz. 1623.

Shock, fright, fear, terror, discomfort but no physical injury: can the charge be gbh (*A. Samuels*): 150 J.P.N. 807.

Should juries be abolished in fraud trials? (*B. Mitchels*): 131 S.J. 986.

Social control and the criminal law (*K. Lidstone*): 27 Brit.J.Criminol. 31.

Stick no bills (*J. Vickers*): [1987] L.G.C., March 6, 1987, 12.

Supply of controlled drugs: 1987 S.L.T.(News) 225.

Tackling serious fraud? (*G. McFarlane*): 131 S.J. 926.

Taking samples from drinking drivers—effect of the continuing "non-statutory option" (*L. Connor*): 151 J.P.N. 230.

Thoughts about development in drug abuse (*P. Bucknell*): 151 J.P.N. 119, 137.

Threat element in duress (*S. Yeo*): (1987) 11 Crim.L.J. 165.

Time limits (*B. Gibson*): 151 J.P.N. 323.

Towards implementation of the Roskill Report (*G. McFarlane*): 130 S.J. 853.

Trade Descriptions Act 1968: s.24—"due diligence", "reasonable precautions" and "personal attributes" (*G. Holgate*): 151 J.P.N. 648.

Unborn child and criminal proceedings (*I. Young*): 83 L.S.Gaz. 3808.

CRIMINAL LAW—*cont.*

Under age offender (considering *Merrin* v. *S.* [1987] C.L.Y. 4003) (*J. P. Grant*): 1987 S.L.T.(News) 337.

Unruly certificates and written reports: a clerk's riposte (*P. Lydiate*): 151 J.P.N. 228.

Unsafe and unsatisfactory: Lurking doubt (*A. Samuels*): 151 J.P.N. 55.

Values in conflict: incitement to racial hatred and the Public Order Act 1986 (*W. Wolffe*): [1987] P.L. 85.

Wasting time of police—is it a crime? (considering *Bowers* v. *Tudhope* [1987] C.L.Y. 4249): (1987) 32 J.L.S. 353.

What is an indecent assault? (*G. Williams*): 137 New L.J. 870.

What is the *mens rea* of assault (*P. Dobson*): 130 S.J. 938.

What should the Code do about omissions? (*G. Williams*): (1987) 7 L.S. 92.

Wilful obstruction—the issue of reasonableness (*P. Cooling*): 151 J.P.N. 579.

Women's imprisonment (*E. Genders and E. Player*): 26 Brit.J.Criminol. 357.

CRIMINAL SENTENCING

Abolition of custody for juvenile offenders—(*B. Gibson*): 150 J.P.N. 739.

Abolition of custody for juveniles (*B. Gibson*): 150 J.P.N. 755.

Advising victims of crime (*R. Colbey*): 6 Lit. 14.

Binding over—too wide a power? (*C. Bazell*): 151 J.P.N. 456.

Boys in prison (*A. Samuels*): 151 J.P.N. 136.

Corporal punishment—what the judges say (*E.Kahn*): 150 J.P.N. 793.

Deferment of sentence—saving a man from custody (*A. Samuels*): 151 J.P.N. 40.

Disposal of drug cases (*C. R. Sandison*): (1987) 132 SCOLAG 136.

Fines—dying a natural death (*A. James*): 151 J.P.N. 167.

Fines—payments by third party (*A. Samuels*): 151 J.P.N. 117.

Great fines anomaly (*J. Jenkins*): 151 J.P.N. 515.

Help for children in custody (*G. Stewart and D. Smith*): 27 Brit. J. Criminol. 302.

Home imprisonment—the cost-effective alternative? (*K. Russell*): 83 L.S.Gaz. 3823.

Possession of small quantity of cannabis by first offender (considering *Grundison* v. *Brown* [1987] C.L.Y. 4284): (1987) 32 J.L.S. 390.

Principle of retribution v. the utility of deterrence (*W. Hughes*): 150 J.P.N. 712.

Reparation and mediation in the criminal justice system (*C. Williams*): 136 New L.J. 1106, 1141.

Restrictions on imposing youth custody and detention centre sentences—some recent cases (*M. Dodds*): 151 J.P.N. 597.

Sentencing: a time for action (*G. McFarlane*): 137 New L.J. 781.

CRIMINAL SENTENCING—*cont.*

Sentencing guidelines: causing death by reckless driving, reckless driving and careless driving—a comment (*A. Turner*): 151 J.P.N. 291.

Sentencing the drug addict: 1987 S.L.T.(News) 340.

Sentencing the dying (*A. Samuels*): 151 J.P.N. 170.

Should young people be sentenced to "a short, sharp, shock"? (*J. Kuper*): 150 J.P.N. 792.

Social security fraud sentencing guidelines (*A. Turner*): 151 J.P.N. 355.

Social workers and young offenders—who is fit and who is vulnerable? (*A. Creamer and B. Williams*): (1987) 132 SCOLAG 140.

Some aspects of sentencing in perjury cases in England (*M. Wasik*): 15 Anglo-Am. 59.

Some suggestions for the improvement of community service (*S. Eysenck*): 150 J.P.N. 808.

Unruly certificates and written reports—the uneasy ground (*S. Walinets*): 151 J.P.N. 103.

Women's imprisonment (*E. Genders and E. Player*): 26 Brit.J.Criminol. 357.

Young adult offenders and s.33 (*M. Romanes*): 151 J.P.N. 297.

CUSTOMS AND EXCISE

Customs and excise law: seizure, forfeiture and condemnation (*G. McFarlane*): 137 New L.J. 683.

Footloose and duty free (*P. Breuer*): 151 J.P.N. 535.

DAMAGES

Athens Convention 1974 and limitation of liability (*N. Gaskell*): 137 New L.J. 322.

Athens Convention 1974—the concept of limitation (*N. Gaskell*): 137 New L.J. 383.

Calculation of damages for disrepair (*D. Williams*): 280 E.G. 708.

Damages for distress (*D. Grant*): (1986) 5 Tr.L. 293.

Damages for personal injuries (*A. Samuels*): 6 Lit. 198.

Entitlement to interest in civil litigation (*R. Foster*): 6 Lit. 222.

Exchange losses in contract (*L. Anderson*): 84 L.S. Gaz. 2264.

Industrial injury benefit and assessment of damages (*R. Lewis*): 84 L.S.Gaz. 1640.

Interest on contractual damages (*M. Conlon*): 6 Lit. 311.

Interest on industrial tribunal awards: a case for modified rapture (*S. Levinson*): 84 L.S.Gaz. 2329.

Interest on industrial tribunal awards—a pressing case for reform (*J. McMullen*): 84 L.S.Gaz. 2169.

Limits on liability to the impecunious client (*M. Jones*): (1987) 3 P.N. 76.

Liquidated and ascertained damages; common pitfalls for the Q.S. (*A. Burns*): 9 C.Q.S. 19.

DAMAGES—*cont.*
Loss without damages: the strange voyage of *The Aliakmon* (*R. Pearce and D. Tomkin*): 136 New L.J. 1169.
Personal injury interest (*R. Nelson-Jones*): 84 L.S.Gaz. 2687.
Principles governing the recovery of damages for negligently caused nervous shock (*F. Trindade*): [1986] C.L.J. 476.
Provisional damages (*A. Samuels*): 131 S.J. 187.
Quantifying extra costs of handicap (*J. Buckie*): (1987) 32 J.L.S. 153.
Taxation and damages: the rule in *Gourley's* case (*W. Bishop and J. Kay*): 104 L.Q.R. 211.
Zeebrugge disaster: application of the Athens Convention 1974 (*N. Gaskell*): 137 New L.J. 285.

DIVORCE AND CONSISTORIAL CAUSES (SCOTLAND ONLY)
Aliment and tax relief (*J. A. Russell*): 1987 S.L.T.(News) 218.
Aliment and tax relief—again (*A. R. Barr*): 1987 S.L.T.(News) 301.
Challenge of conciliation (*J. Ross*): (1987) 32 J.L.S. 457.
Divorces—styles and procedures (*A. G. Johnston*): (1987) 32 J.L.S. 49.
Family Law (Scotland) Act 1985—actuarial aspects (*A. C. Martin*): (1987) 32 J.L.S. 417.

EASEMENTS AND PRESCRIPTION (NOT SCOTLAND)
Developing the law of easements: the role of tort (*A. Waite*): [1987] Conv. 47.
Extinguishment of easements (*R. Lloyd*): 84 L.S.Gaz. 644.
Rights of light (*J. Anstey*): 84 L.S.Gaz. 2519.

EDUCATION
Children's safety and the walk to school: 150 L.G. Rev. 813.
Contractors in schools: a need for basic standards (*G. Cox*): [1986] L.G.C. 1338.
Definitive ruling on school routes (*C. Cross*): [1986] L.G.C. 1306.
Education Act 1981 in the courts (*D. Milman*): (1987) J.S.W.L. 208.
Education Act 1986 contributes to withering of councils (*M. Mason*): [1987] L.G.C., August 28, 1987, 10.
Education Act 1986 (No. 2): 151 L.G.Rev. 4.
Long, long road to school (*P. Liell*): Law M., June 26, 1987, 24.
Professional obligations and industrial action (*H. Rawlings*): (1987) 3 P.N. 92.
School attendance—recent changes in the law (*C. Bazell*): 151 J.P.N. 53.
School placing appeals—could do better (*R. Marr*): (1987) 32 J.L.S. 452.
Tameside revisited: prospectively "reasonable"; retrospective "maladministration" (*D. Bull*): 50 M.L.R. 307.

ELECTION LAW
Can local authorities ever say 'no'? (*C. Vincenzi*): 131 S.J. 614.
Electoral issues (*I. S. Dickinson*): 1987 S.L.T.(News) 373.
How not to fall foul of election law (*J. Vickers*): [1987] L.G.C., May 29, 10.
Voter who moves home "change of residence" (*A. Samuels*): 150 L.G. Rev. 727.

ELECTRICITY
Tactics in fuel cases: *Legal Action*, June 1987, 9.

EMPLOYMENT
Age discrimination in employment: legal protection in the United States and in the United Kingdom (*T. Buck and B. Fitzpartick*): 15 Anglo-Am. 192.
AIDS and employment law (*N. Fagan and D. Newall*): 137 New L.J. 752.
Altering contracts of employment (*N. Ostorn*): 131 S.J. 310.
Anti-union discrimination: practice, law and policy (*S. Evans and R. Lewis*): 16 I.L.J. 88.
Aspects of industrial action—reasons and remedies for sit-ins (*S. Croall*): 137 New L.J. 918.
Changes in employment law (*A. Knell*): 74 Accts.Rec. 11.
Constructive dismissal: contributory factors (*G. Holgate*): 131 S.J. 1014.
Contract of employment (*D. Newell*): 137 New L.J. 619.
Contracting-out and the Transfer of Undertaking Regulations 1981 (*G. Holgate*): 151 L.G.Rev. 445.
Contributory fault and industrial negligence (*J. Bowers*): 131 S.J. 41.
Crisis in EEC labour law (*B. Hepple*): 16 I.L.J. 77.
Disability rights in employment (*D. Forbes*): *Legal Action,* February 1987, 17; March 1987, 12.
Discrimination and employment (*J. Bowers*): 131 S.J. 21
Discrimination and employment law (*D. Newell*): 137 New L.J. 717.
Dismissals on transfer of a business (*H. Collins*): 15 I.L.J. 244.
Emergence of a new labour injunction? (*K. Ewing and A. Grubb*): 16 I.L.J. 145.
Employers' rights against departing executives—recent developments (*P. Carolan*): 136 New L.J. 1085.
Employment: aspects of sale (*M. Duggan*): 131 S.J. 714, 764.
Employment Bill (*F. P. Davidson*): (1987) 135 SCOLAG 189.
Employment law review (*M. Edwards*): 131 S.J. 1134.
Employment law update: 151 L.G.Rev. 525.
Employment of church minister (*A. Khan*): 131 S.J. 38.
Employment protection rights: the Wages Act 1986 (*C. Bourn*): 137 New L.J. 693.

EMPLOYMENT—*cont.*

Equal pay for work of equal value—the *Hayward* case (*G. Holgate*): 151 L.G.Rev. 566.

Express covenant or implied term of confidentiality (*M. Jefferson*): (1987) 8 B.L.R. 8.

Further effects of tax avoidance and evasion (*C. Underhill*): *Legal Action*, February 1987, 15.

Gender problems and sex discrimination: 151 J.P.N. 88.

Handling disciplinary problems (*M. Edwards*): (1987) 8 B.L.R. 203.

Handling redundancy consultation (*M. Edwards*): (1986) 7 B.L.R. 311.

Handling redundancy selection (*M. Edwards*): (1986) 7 B.L.R. 302.

Health and safety at work and third-party obligations (*G. Holgate*): (1987) 8 B.L.R. 145.

Indirect discrimination (considering *Bilka-Kaufhaus GmbH* v. *Von Hartz* [1986] C.L.Y. 1458 and *Rainey* v. *Greater Glasgow Health Board* [1987] C.L.Y. 4409) (*A. I. L. Campbell*): 1987 S.L.T.(News) 96.

Industrial action and payment of wages (*B. Napier*): 131 S.J. 1230.

Interest on industrial tribunal awards; a case for modified rapture (*S. Levinson*): 84 L.S.Gaz. 2329.

Interest on industrial tribunal awards—a pressing case for reform (*J. McMullen*): 84 L.S.Gaz. 2169.

Labour law: from here to autonomy? (*Lord Wedderburn*): 16 I.L.J. 1.

Labour Pump [1979] C.L.Y. 993 and *Devis* [1977] C.L.Y. 1160: reconciliation scorned (considering also *Polkey* v. *Edmund Walker Holdings* [1987] C.L.Y. 1398 and *Pritchett and Dyjasek* v. *J. McIntyre* [1987] C.L.Y. 1395) (*I. J. Ghosh*): 1987 S.L.T.(News) 313.

Law and the employment of disabled persons 151 L.G.Rev. 864.

"Legislating for change: review of the sex discrimination legislation"—an Equal Opportunities Commission discussion document: 150 L.G.Rev. 788.

Local authority recruitment policies and discrimination: 150 L.G.Rev. 723.

Making employers liable for discrimination by their employees (considering *Irving* v. *Post Office* [1987] C.L.Y. 1349) (*I. J. Ghosh*): (1987) 132 SCOLAG 142.

Making employers liable for discrimination by employees—postscript (considering *Balgoblin* v. *London Borough of Tower Hamlets sub nom. Francis* v. *Tower Hamlets Borough Council* [1987] C.L.Y. 1373) (*I. J. Ghosh*): (1987) 135 SCOLAG 188.

Note on statutory maternity pay: 1987 S.L.T.(News) 150.

Parental leave—time for action? (*F. Davidson*): [1986] J.S.W.L. 281.

Practical problems of the time-limit in certain areas of employment protection legislation (*G. Halgate*): 6 Lit. 113.

Pregnancy and dismissal (*L. Clarke*): 15 Anglo-Am. 310.

Private prosecutions under the Wages Act 1986 Part II (*M. Turner and T. Kibling*): (1987) *Legal Action*, October 12.

Procedure for handling redundancies—aspects of consultation (*G. Holgate*): 6 Lit. 314.

Professional and contractual obligations: 150 L.G.Rev. 768.

Professional obligations and industrial action (*H. Rawlings*): (1987) 3 P.N. 92.

Proof of discrimination in the United Kingdom and the United States (*S. Willborn*): (1986) 5 C.J.Q. 321.

Protection of workers in relation to the payment of wages (*D. Janner*): 6 Lit. 101.

Proving discrimination (*M. Duggan*): 6 Lit. 6.

Racial abuse and sexual harassment (*M. Duggan*): 131 S.J. 425.

Recent cases on equal pay and discrimination (*J. Bowers*): 6 Lit. 93.

Recent decisions on equal pay (*C. Palmer*): *Legal Action*, July 1987, 16.

Recent developments in unfair dismissal (*A. Neal*): 137 New L.J. 669.

Recent developments on the Transfer of Undertakings Regulations (the European Dimension) (*J. Bowers*): 6 Lit. 291.

Recovering termination payments on discovery of past misconduct (*G. Sullivan*): 5 Co. Law 52.

Redundancy law update (*M. Edwards*): 84 L.S.Gaz. 651.

Re-employment remedies for unfair dismissal (*M. Bennett*): 84 L.S.Gaz. 1654.

Rethinking positive action (*C. McCrudden*): 15 I.L.J. 219.

Review of employment law (*M. Edwards*): 130 S.J. 966.

Review of some new developments (*V. Craig*): 1987 S.L.G. 92.

Right to return to work after pregnancy (*J. Bowers*): 6 Lit. 150.

Robbing Mrs. Hood?—redundant female pensioners (*B. Perrins*): 137 New L.J. 273.

Role of Equal Opportunities Commission (E. Walker): (1987) 130 SCOLAG 106.

Salary during industrial action (considering *Sim* v. *Rotherham Metropolitan Borough Council* [1986] C.L.Y. 1152) (*V. Craig*): (1987) 32 J.L.S. 155.

Sex Discrimination Act 1986 (*J. Bowers and M. Duggan*): 84 L.S.Gaz. 240.

Sex Discrimination Act 1986: 151 L.G.Rev. 183, 245.

Sex Discrimination Act 1986: equality or exploitation (*S. Bailey*): 137 New L.J. 227.

Sex Discrimination Act 1986 (*V. Craig*): 1987 S.L.G. 12.

Short-term contracts and continuity of employment—introduction: 150 L.G.Rev. 739.

Statutory maternity pay (*J. Bowers*): 6 Lit. 329.

Statutory maternity pay (*D. Pollard*): 131 S.J. 1198.

EMPLOYMENT—*cont.*

Strike ballots: breaking in the Trojan horse (*S. Bloxham*): [1986] VIII Liverpool L.R. 131.

Strikes and the individual worker—reforming the law (*B. Napier*): [1987] C.L.J. 287.

Trade unions: further legislative changes (*K. Miller*): 1987 S.L.T.(News) 213.

Trade unions and their members (*F. P. Davidson*): (1987) 126 SCOLAG 41.

Transfer of business and dismissal (*M. Duggan*): 131 S.J. 1409.

Transfer of undertakings (considering *Secretary of State for Employment* v. *Spence* [1986] C.L.Y. 1232) (*B. W. Napier*): 1987 S.L.T.(News) 166.

Transfer of Undertakings Regulations: recent developments (*R. Clayton*): *Legal Action*, June 1987, 14.

Transfer of Undertakings (Protection of Employment) Regulation 1981 (*K. Cave*): (1986) 7 B.L.R. 279.

Trust, corporation and the worker (*Lord Wedderburn*): 23 Osgoode Hall L.J. 203.

Unfair dismissal: the need for guidance (*M. Edwards*): 131 S.J. 610.

Unfair dismissal and industrial jury (considering *British Labour Pump* v. *Byrne* [1979] C.L.Y. 993) (*V. Craig*): 1987 S.L.T.(News) 77.

Union rights and action short of dismissal (*V. Craig*): 1987 S.L.G. 44.

Wages Act (*K. Puttick*): 136 New L.J. 1068.

Wages Act 1986: 151 L.G.Rev. 64, 207.

What's the difference? (*J. McGlyne*): New L.J. 939.

Written statement of terms (*J. Bowers*): 6 Lit. 22.

EQUITY AND TRUSTS (NOT SCOTLAND)

Beneficial joint tenancies: a case for abolition? (*M. Thompson*): [1987] Conv. 29.

Beneficial joint tenancies: a reply to Professor Prichard (*M. Thompson*): [1987] Conv. 275.

Beneficial joint tenancies: a riposte (*A. Prichard*): [1987] Conv. 273.

Choice of law for trusts in Australia and the United Kingdom (*A. Wallace*): 36 I.C.L.Q. 454.

Constructive trusts and proprietary estoppel: 6 Lit. 58.

Courage and *Imperial* cases: the lessons (*I. Pittaway*): (1987) 1 Trust L. & P. 165.

"Discharge of trustees on retirement" revisited: the real effect of Trustee Act 1925, s.69 (*M. Jacobs*): (1986) 1 Trust L. & P. 95.

Does constructive knowledge make a constructive trustee? (*M. Brindle and R. Hooley*): (1987) 1 Trust L. & P. 130.

Does constructive knowledge make a constructive trustee? (*M. Brindle and R. Hooley*): 61 A.L.J. 281.

EPA: the new regulations (*R. Oerton*): 131 S.J. 1374.

Equity and the legal divisions (*G. Samuel*): 37 N.I.L.Q. 211, 315.

EQUITY AND TRUSTS (NOT SCOTLAND)—*cont.*

Equity, estate contracts and the Judicature Acts: *Walsh* v. *Lonsdale* revisited (*S. Gardner*): 7 O.J.L.S. 60.

Estoppel and clean hands (*M. Thompson*): [1986] Conv. 406.

"Failed purpose" trusts (*D. Fox*): 131 S.J. 1438.

Hague Convention on the law applicable to trusts and on their recognition (*D. Hayton*): 36 I.C.L.Q. 260.

Informal trusts and third parties (*J. Feltham*): [1987] Conv. 246.

Keech v. *Sandford*: the case and its ramifications (*F. Spearing*): (1987) 1 Trust L. & P. 171.

Law's fine print (*M. Jacobs*): 119 Tax. 475.

"Old Presbyterian persons"—a sufficient section of the public? (*N. Dawson*): [1987] Conv. 114.

Ownership and obligation in commercial transactions (*R. Goode*): 103 L.Q.R. 433.

Powers of investment of charity trustees (*J. Thurston*): (1987) 1 Trust L. & P. 162.

Property law review: equity and land law (*P. Rank*): 131 S.J. 278.

Question of intention? (*J. Montgomery*): [1987] Conv. 16.

Settlements for children (*A. Cockman and T. Johnson*): 118 Tax. 229.

Solicitor: constructive trustee or agent? (*B. Griffin*): (1987) 1 Trust L. & P. 176.

Sporting decisions: should the courts participate? (*J. Warburton*): 131 S.J. 868.

Trust taxation (*M. Jacobs*): 119 Tax. 505.

Trustees' tightrope (*O. Clinton*): 119 Tax. 188.

Unascertainable problem in variation of trusts (*P. Luxton*): 136 New L.J. 1057.

U.K. as a trust tax haven (*B. McCutcheon*): 84 L.S.Gaz. 2840.

Unjust enrichment and unjust sacrifice (*S. Stoljar*): 50 M.L.R. 603.

Update on wills and trusts (*R. Oerton*): 131 S.J. 649.

Who is entitled to the pension fund surplus? (*R. Nobles*): 16 I.L.J. 164.

Wills and trusts update (*D. Cracknell*): 131 S.J. 1344.

ESTOPPEL (NOT SCOTLAND)

Estoppel and clean hands (*M. Thompson*): [1986] Conv. 406.

EUROPEAN COMMUNITIES

"Acte clair" in the English courts (*S. Weatherill*): 137 New L.J. 942.

Agency agreements and EEC competition law: some comfort from the EEC Commission (*S. Holmes*): 84 L.S.Gaz. 1052.

American deregulation experience and the use of article 90 to expedite EEC air transport liberalisation (*G. Garland*): [1986] E.C.L.R. 193.

Application of Articles 3(*f*), 5 and 85 to 94 EEC (*P. Slot*): 12 E.L.Rev. 179.

Banking agreements. Are they anti-competitive? (*J. Rosell*): (1987) 7 IFL Rev 11.

EUROPEAN COMMUNITIES—*cont.*

Boussois/Interpane: the treatment of know-how licences under EEC competition law (*J. Venit*): [1987] 6 E.I.P.R. 164.

Civil jurisdiction and consumer contracts (*A. Mennie*): 1987 S.L.T.(News) 181.

Civil Jurisdiction and Judgments Act 1982 (*R. C. McKenzie*): (1987) 32 J.L.S. 260.

Commission's draft for a regulation exempting knowhow licensing agreements (*V. Korah*): (1987): 8 B.L.R. 198.

Community law (*E. Hoskin*): 119 Tax. 13.

Community Patent Convention: some progress (*P. Groves*): (1987) 8 B.L.R. 170.

Competition law: mapping the minefield (*T. Frazer*): (1987) 3 Comp. L. & P. 199.

Competition policy in the 80s: more policy less competition? (*S. Hornsby*): 12 E.L.Rev. 79.

Confidential information in antidumping proceedings before United States courts and the European Court (*H. von Heydebrand und der Lasa*): 11 E.L.Rev. 331.

Consumer protection in the EEC (*Dr. R. Lawson*): 84 L.S.Gaz. 39.

Could Article 30 impose obligations on individuals? (*M. Quinn and N. MacGowan*): 12 E.L.Rev. 163.

Crisis in EEC labour law (*B. Hepple*): 16 I.L.J. 77.

Critical comments on the Commission's recent decisions exempting joint ventures to exploit research that needs further development (*V. Korah*): 12 E.L.Rev. 18.

Defective products: successor company liability (*C. Bright*): 83 L.S.Gaz. 3423.

Directives, direct effect and the European Court: the triumph of pragmatism (*P. Morris and P. David*): (1987) 8 B.L.R. 85, 116.

Distribution franchising under EEC law (*D. Fox*): 131 S.J. 378.

Domestic tribunals and art. 177: need for reconsideration? (*O. Saunders*): 131 S.J. 486.

Environmental law—the European context (*L. Spedding*): 84 L.S. Gaz. 333.

Equality in pension schemes: the redundant directive? (*G. Keane*): 84 L.S.Gaz. 565.

Errors of omission (*E. Hoskin*): 119 Tax. 115.

Establishment and services in the E.E.C.: insurance cases (*D. A. O. Edward*): (1987) 32 J.L.S. 187.

EEC Judgments Convention—an unexpected bonus for distributorships in Belgium? (*P. Bogaert*): [1987] E.C.L.R. 47.

EEC jurisdiction and judgments: a French perspective (*A. Desmazieresde Sechelles*): (1987) 32 J.L.S. 309.

EEC law: the Official Journal (*B. Harris*): 137 New L.J. 254.

EEC law and selective distribution—recent developments (*G. Leigh*): [1986] E.C.L.R. 419.

EEC product liability directive (*T. Trumpy*): 83 L.S.Gaz. 3740.

EEC trade mark legislation (*P. Groves*): (1987) B.L.R. 51.

EUROPEAN COMMUNITIES—*cont.*

European Community law and prior treaty obligations of member states: the Spanish fishermen's cases (*R. Churchill and N. Foster*): 36 I.C.L.Q. 504.

European Court case law and civil jurisdiction in Scotland (*P. Beaumont*): 1987 S.L.T.(News) 201.

European rapporteur (*R. Wallace*): 131 S.J. 1175.

Factual merger of the European Court and Commission of Human Rights (*H. Schermers*): 11 E.L.Rev. 350.

Franchising: the Commission issues a draft block exemption regulation (*M. Mendelsohn*): 84 L.S.Gaz. 2842.

Free movement of goods and public morality (*T. Millett*): 137 New L.J. 39.

Freedom of trade under the common law and European Community law: the case of the football bans (*A. Evans*): 102 L.Q.R. 510.

How to make the action suit the case (*J. Steiner*): 12 E.L.Rev. 102.

Impact of community law on Scots law (*Lord Fraser of Tullybelton*): (1987) 32 J.L.S. 90.

Impact of directives on statutory interpretation: using the Euro-meaning? (*J. Bates*): [1986] Stat.L.R. 174.

Incoming tide: responding to *Marshall (A. Arnull)*: [1987] P.L. 383.

Indirect discrimination (considering *Bilka-Kaufhaus GmbH* v. *Von Hartz* [1986] C.L.Y. 1458 and *Rainey* v. *Greater Glasgow Health Board* [1987] C.L.Y. 4409) (*A. I. L. Campbell*): 1987 S.L.T.(News) 96.

Information in EEC competition law procedures (*J. Joshua*): (1986) 11 E.L.Rev. 409.

Is the European Court of Justice "running wild"? (*M. Cappelletti*): 12 E.L.Rev. 3.

Joint ventures—an analysis of Commission decisions (*J. M. Claydon*): [1986] E.C.L.R. 151.

Jurisdiction in actions concerning foreign land: 1987 S.L.T.(News) 53.

Maritime claims: the European Judgments Convention (*G. Brice*): [1987] L.M.C.L.Q. 281.

Merger control by the E.C. Commission (*W. Elland*): [1987] E.C.L.R. 163.

Mergers: the European dimension (*W. Elland*): 84 L.S.Gaz. 2338.

Motor vehicle distribution: the block exemption (*P. Groves*): [1987] E.C.L.R. 77.

Non-market economy rules of the European Community's anti-dumping and countervailing duties legislation (*R. Denton*): 36 I.C.L.Q. 198.

Of cameras, chemicals, cars—and salami: a fresh look at interim relief under the Rome Treaty (*J. Ferry*): [1986] 11 E.I.P.R. 337.

Opening up the internal community market in retail financial services: a case study on mortgage credit (*R. Hirst*): (1986) 7 B.L.R. 313.

Parental leave—time for action? (*F. Davidson*): [1986] J.S.W.L. 281.

Predation (*T. Sharpe*): [1987] E.C.L.R. 53.

EUROPEAN COMMUNITIES—*cont.*

Predatory pricing and entry deterring strategies: the economics of *Akzo* (*R. Rapp*): [1986] E.C.L.R. 233.

Predatory pricing or competitive pricing: establishing the truth in English and EEC law (*R. Merkin*): 7 O.J.L.S. 182.

Problems of the European Community—transatlantic parallels (*Lord Mackenzie Stuart*): 36 I.C.L.Q. 183.

Procedure in anti-dumping investigations (*K. Lasok*): [1987] E.C.L.R. 143.

Product and technical standardisation under Article 85 (*A. Vollmer*): [1986] E.C.L.R. 388.

Protection of semi-conductor product designs—the EEC directive and the WIPO draft treaty (*R. Hart*): (1987) 3 Comp.L. & P. 164.

Recent developments on the Transfer of Undertakings Regulations (the European Dimension) (*J. Bowers*): 6 Lit. 291.

Reforms in EEC's legislative process: Single European Act (*W. Brown*): (1987) 32 J.L.S. 336.

Removing legal obstacles to cross border mergers: EEC proposal for tenth directive (*P. Farmery*): (1987) B.L.R. 35.

Robbing Mrs. Hood?—redundant female pensioners (*B. Perrins*): 137 New L.J. 273.

Selective distribution agreements: renewal of exemptions (*D. Fox*): 131 S.J. 1105.

Single Act revisited (*S. Crossick*): 137 New L.J. 793.

Single European Act and free movement (*N. Forwood and M. Clough*): (1986) 11 E.L.Rev. 383.

Some problems concerning the constitutional basis for Spain's accession to the European Community (*I. Aurrecoechea*): 36 I.C.L.Q. 14.

EVIDENCE (CIVIL)

Bankers' books (*A. Samuels*): 6 Lit. 78.

Hague Evidence Convention and discovery: a serious misunderstanding? (*L. Collins*): 35 I.C.L.Q. 765.

Legal professional privilege: meaning and application in Scots law (*V. M. P. Ogston and A. L. Seager*): 1987 J.R. 38.

Legal professional privilege and inadvertent disclosure (*K. Barrett*): 84 L.S.Gaz. 2928.

Opinion evidence (*P. Gillies*): 60 A.L.J. 597.

Restraining the use of privileged documents (*J. Clegg*): 84 L.S.Gaz. 464.

'Without prejudice' explained (*D. Williams*): 84 L.S.Gaz. 244.

EXECUTORS AND ADMINISTRATORS

Tax effective executry administration: legal rights and capital gains tax (*E. M. Scobbie*): (1987) 32 J.L.S. 341.

EXPENSES (SCOTLAND ONLY)

Case for contingent fee (*D. L. Carey Miller*): (1987) 32 J.L.S. 461.

FAMILY (NOT SCOTLAND)

A family court or fundamental reform? (*C. Yates*): [1987] J.S.W.L. 300.

Access to children in care—jurisdiction (*V. Smith*): 151 J.P.N. 67.

Administration of place of safety orders (*T. Norris*): (1987) J.S.W.L. 1.

Adoption in an immigration context (*D. Webb*): *Legal Action*, January 1987, 17.

Capacity to marry and the relevance of the *lex loci celebrationis* in Commonwealth law (*D. Bradshaw*): 15 Anglo-Am. 112.

Child abduction law now (*A. Samuels*): 6 Lit. 109.

Child care and family services—the White Paper (*N. McKittrick*): 151 J.P.N. 147.

Child sexual abuse: the legal issues (*G. Douglas*): 131 S.J. 1170.

Clean break—allusions to illusions and the welfare of the child (*R. Ingleby*): [1986] J.S.W.L. 257.

Common law marriage (*J. Hall*): [1987] C.L.J. 106.

Conduct: where should it be tried? (*N. Mostyn*): 6 Lit. 3.

Conflicts of jurisdiction in divorce cases: *forum non conveniens* (*P. Beaumont*): 36 I.C.L.Q. 116.

Consideration of *Re B. (a minor) (sterilization): (D. Ogbourne):* 151 L.G.Rev. 764.

Constructive trusts and proprietary estoppel: 6 Lit. 58.

Conveyancers beware the co-habitee (*M. Sookias, J. Cole and A. Price*): 84 L.S.Gaz. 1309.

Costs in domestic proceedings (*J. Spencer*): 151 J.P.N. 440.

Critical rôle in care (*N. Watt*): 131 S.J. 574

Debate on surrogate motherhood: the current situation, some arguments and issues; questions facing law and policy (*L. Harding*): (1987) J.S.W.L. 37.

Domestic violence: housing the parties (*J. Montgomery*): 131 S.J. 678.

Dower/doweries in Bangladesh and primary purpose (*M. Imman Ali*): (1987) 1 Imm. and Nat. L. & P. 125.

Excluding a former husband or cohabitant (*M. Freeman*): 6 Lit. 158.

Family courts? (*Lord McGregor*): [1987] 6 C.J.Q. 44.

Family law: a review (*S. Cretney*): 131 S.J. 246, 898.

Family Law Act: 136 New L.J. 1090.

Family Law Act 1986 (*T. Prime*): 131 S.J. 62, 91, 118, 156.

Family Law Reform Bill (*K. Puttick*): 137 New L.J. 11.

Formalities of marriage—some patterns of English law (*P. Lucas*): 83 L.S.Gaz. 3815; 84 L.S.Gaz. 2198.

Guardian ad litem and the child's solicitor (*M. Morris*): *Legal Action*, January 1987, 15.

Guardians ad litem and pre-hearing disclosure (*N. Leighton*): 151 J.P.N. 308.

Husband and wife ltd.—the relationship between company law and divorce (*D. Gordon*): [1986] Conv. 335.

FAMILY (NOT SCOTLAND)—*cont.*

Impairment of development *in utero*—a look at *re D* (*M. Rutherford*): 84 L.S.Gaz. 15.

Incest and the prohibited degrees (*C. Barton*): 137 New L.J. 502.

Interim care orders (*A. Bean*): 84 L.S.Gaz. 1382.

Interim care orders—evidence (*C. Latham*): 151 J.P.N. 245.

Judicial review and children in care (*J. Ellison*): 131 S.J. 454.

Law Commission and custody of children: 130 S.J. 857.

Law Commission's working paper on wards of court (*M. Rutherford*): 84 L.S.Gaz. 1624.

Law relating to the consummation of marriage where one of the spouses is a post-operative transsexual (*J. Taitz*): 15 Anglo-Am. 141.

Maintenance and subsistence level revisited (*D. Chatterton*): 84 L.S.Gaz. 648.

Maintenance arrears: enforcement problems (*D. Gleeson*): 151 J.P.N. 311.

Maintenance payments and school fees as the dust settles (*C. Whitehouse*): 137 New L.J. 495.

Matrimonial home in bankruptcy (*E. Bailey and C. Berry*): 137 New L.J. 310.

Necessary breath of life (*D. Brahams*): 137 New L.J. 188.

Overlapping of family jurisdictions—a critical review (*J. Graham Hall and D. Martin*): 151 J.P.N. 659.

Parental chastisement (*A. Samuels*): 151 L.G.Rev. 210.

Parental right to possession of a child (*N. Allen*): [1986] VIII Liverpool L.R. 97.

Parents, doctors and children: the *Gillick* case and beyond (*S. de Cruz*): (1987) J.S.W.L. 93.

Part III of the MFPA 1984: a panacea for foreign divorcees? (*D. Gordon*): (1986) J.S.W.L. 329.

Pensions, dependency and divorce (*J. Masson*): (1986) J.S.W.L. 343.

Question of intention? (*J. Montgomery*): [1987] Conv. 16.

Recent developments in family law (*R. Calbey*): 6 Lit. 134.

Recognition of extra-judicial divorces in the United Kingdom (*J. Young*): (1987) 7 L.S. 78.

Recognition of foreign divorces—the new law (*S. Poulter*): 84 L.S.Gaz. 253.

Recognition of non judicial divorces: some decisions (*T. Prime*): 131 S.J. 10.

Solicitor in care cases—who gives the instructions? (*I. Weintroub*): 84 L.S.Gaz. 1318.

"Split families" and Part III of the Housing Act 1985 (*D. Hoath*): (1987) J.S.W.L. 15.

Wardship jurisdiction (*P. Gallagher*): 131 S.J. 182.

Wardship jurisdiction in the future (*N. McKittrick*): 151 J.P.N. 342.

Wardship jurisdiction remains inaccessible to parents (*M. Chambers*): [1987] L.G.C., October 9, 1987, 12.

FAMILY (NOT SCOTLAND)—*cont.*

Welfare reports and conciliation (*C. Latham*): 151 J.P.N. 518.

"When did you last see your father?"—a review of child custody law (*J. Hern*): 84 L.S.Gaz. 1647.

Woman's place—a conflict between law and social values (*J. Eekelaar*): [1987] Conv. 93.

FIRE SERVICE

Bradford football fire (*MacDonald*): 137 New L.J. 481.

FISH AND FISHERIES

European Community law and prior treaty obligations of member states: the Spanish fishermen's cases (*R. Churchill and N. Foster*): 36 I.C.L.Q. 504.

Fishy business (*J. Golding*): 119 Tax. 549.

FOOD AND DRUGS

Changing shape of food standards (*L. Hanson*): (1986) 5 Tr.L. 262.

Food law: recent developments in the courts (*R. Lawson*): 151 J.P.N. 259.

Licensing (Restaurant Meals) Act 1987 (*J. Spencer*): 151 J.P.N. 247.

FOREIGN JURISDICTIONS

Case of Robert Bork (*N. Gow*): 1987 S.L.T.(News) 364.

Hague Evidence Convention and discovery; a serious misunderstanding? (*L. Collins*): 35 I.C.L.Q. 765.

Non-judicial dispute resolution in the People's Republic of China (*R. Goossen*): (1986) 7 B.L.R. 331.

FORESTRY

Dark forest (*C. Newman*): 118 Tax. 241.

Favourable tax regime (*M. Lichten and G. Jones*): 119 Tax 170.

Schedule B (*S. Owen*): 119 Tax 164.

Tree law: judicial pronouncements (*A. Samuels*): 151 L.G.Rev. 305.

FRAUD, MISREPRESENTATION AND UNDUE INFLUENCE

Disclaimers and deceptive conduct (*A. Terry*): (1986) A.B.L.R. 478.

Doctrine of undue influence—some recent developments (*P. C. Chai*): [1987] M.L.J. cclv.

Undue influence (A. Khan): 6 Lit. 236.

GAMING AND WAGERING

Tactics in fuel cases: *Legal Action*, June 1987, 9.

HEALTH AND SAFETY AT WORK

Health and safety at work and third-party obligations (*G. Holgate*): (1987) 8 B.L.R. 145.

HERITABLE PROPERTY AND CONVEYANCING (SCOTLAND ONLY)

Conveyancers cornered: invalid descriptions by reference (*R. S. H. Girdwood*): (1987) 32 J.L.S. 308.

Endowment mortgages and law of succession (*G. L. Gretton*): (1987) 32 J.L.S. 303.

Execution of deeds (*K. G. C. Reid*): (1987) 32 J.L.S. 148.

Further thoughts on inhibitions (*D. J. Cusine*): (1987) 32 J.L.S. 66.

Insurance policies, securities and claims to legal rights (*A. M. C. Dalgleish*): (1987) 32 J.L.S. 423.

Missives, interest and tax (*R. S. H. Girdwood*): 1987 S.L.T.(News) 190.

Stamp duty warning for conveyancers (considering *Saunders* v. *Edwards* [1987] C.L.Y. 1826) (*D. C. Coull*): (1987) 32 J.L.S. 389.

Trust and executry conveyancing (*G. L. Gretton*): (1987) 32 J.L.S. 111.

Wrongs and rights of vesting (*W. M. Gordon*): (1987) 32 J.L.S. 218.

HOUSING

Allocation of council housing (*G. Holgate*): 151 L.G.Rev. 425.

Bailment and on-site caravans (*C. Brand*): 84 L.S.Gaz. 637.

Councils face legal problems on hippies (*J. Whitcutt*): [1987] L.G.C., July 3, 12.

Extensions and limitations in the Housing and Planning Act (*D. Hender*): [1987] L.G.C., January 2, 8.

General rates on residential accommodation: enforcement proceedings (*D. Forbes*): (1987) *Legal Action*, August 18.

General rates on residential accommodation: minimising or avoiding liability of rates (*D. Forbes*): *Legal Action*, April 1987, 20.

Gypsy caravan site provision: the future: 151 L.G.Rev. 784.

Gypsy sites: provision problems and statutory duties: 151 L.G.Rev. 704, 750.

Homelessness since *Puhlhofer (A. McAllister)*: *Legal Action*, May 1987, 11.

Housing and Planning Act 1986 (*R. Hamilton*): 130 S.J. 906, 941.

Housing and Planning Act 1986: 151 L.G.Rev. 44.

Immobile homes—recent cases (*H. Wilkinson*): 136 New L.J. 1203.

Mobile homes: a concrete base for protection? (*J. Passmore*): 131 S.J. 422.

New law on homelessness (*T. Mullen*): (1987) 124 SCOLAG 7.

Participation in housing cases: an examination of attendance and representation at County Court possession hearings and Rent Assessment Committees (*M. Hill and A. Mercer*): (1987) J.S.W.L. 237.

Public sector housing: allocations—new legal framework? (*M. MacEwen*): (1987) 32 J.L.S. 287.

Quality of accommodation question: local authorities and homeless persons (*G. Holgate*): 151 L.G.Rev. 385.

HOUSING—*cont.*

Radical reforms in rented housing (*J. Black*): (1987) 135 SCOLAG 184.

Recent cases affecting travellers (*D. Watkinson*): *Legal Action*, July 1987, 9; August 1987, 20.

Recent cases on homelessness (*P. Robson*): (1987) 133 SCOLAG 153.

Recent developments in housing law (*J. Luba*): *Legal Action*, September 1987, 9.

Recent developments in housing law (*J. Luba and N. Madge*): *Legal Action*, March 1987, 17.

Section 1 of the Protection from Eviction Act 1977: the meaning of "occupation" (*J. Hill*): [1987] Conv. 265.

Security of tenure: competing interests (*J. Hill*): (1987) J.S.W.L. 77.

Specialist housing court?: 151 L.G.Rev. 405.

"Split families" and Part III of the Housing Act 1985 (*D. Hoath*): (1987) J.S.W.L. 15.

Sub-tenants—problems for local authorities when properties are surrendered (*W. Birtles*): [1987] L.G.C., September 18, 1987, 12.

"Unreasonable" local authority rent increases: 151 L.G.Rev. 725.

HUMAN RIGHTS

An interdependent world (*S. S. Ramphal*): (1987) 32 J.L.S. 383.

Bankruptcy and the European Convention (*J. Wollaston*): (1987) 3 Ins.L.&P. 42.

Council of Europe—property rights and the European Convention on Human Rights (*A. Sherlock*): (1987) 8 B.L.R. 113.

Data Protection Act 1984 (*M. Deans*): (1987) 125 SCOLAG 25.

Data Protection Act 1984 (*M. Hibbs*): 84 L.S.Gaz. 2745.

Data Protection Act 1984: subject access (*M. Hibbs*): 84 L.S.Gaz. 2838.

Data Protection Act 1984: subject access provisions: (1987) 32 J.L.S. 378.

Ethnic minority customs, English law and human rights (*S. Poulter*): 36 I.C.L.Q. 589.

European Commission of Human Rights: report on the 181st and 182nd sessions (*J. Gardner and S. Dollé*): 84 L.S.Gaz. 256.

European Commission of Human Rights: report on the 186th session (*J. Gardner and S. Dollé*): 84 L.S.Gaz. 2682.

Factual merger of the European Court and Commission of Human Rights (*H. Schermers*): 11 E.L.Rev. 350.

Growing impact of the European Human Rights Convention upon national case law (*A. Drzemczewski*): 84 L.S.Gaz. 561.

Human rights—Strand and Strasbourg (*D. Simpson*): 151 J.P.N. 329.

Implicit ideology of human rights and its legal expression (*J. Lenoble*): [1986] VIII Liverpool L.R. 153.

Maintaining public order in the 1980s (*I. S. Dickinson*): 1987 S.L.T.(News) 105.

New look at entrenchment (*J. Elkind*): 50 M.L.R. 158.

No hope for transsexuals (*G. Naldi*): 137 New L.J. 129.

HUMAN RIGHTS—*cont.*

Patriarchy and the law (*C. Smart*): (1987) 129 SCOLAG 94.

Sex Discrimination Act 1986 (*V. Craig*): 1987 S.L.G. 12.

Whither data protection? (*I. Lloyd*): 1987 S.L.T.(News) 158.

Women's rights in relation to human rights: a lawyer's perspective (*R. D'Sa*): 13 C.L.B. 666.

HUSBAND AND WIFE (SCOTLAND ONLY)

Domestic violence: uniform response? (*A. Mackay*): (1987) 128 SCOLAG 76.

Forbidden degrees of matrimony—Marriage (Prohibited Degrees of Relationship) Act 1986 (*D. B. Ross*): (1987) 32 J.L.S. 20.

Incest and prohibited degrees of marriage (*J. M. Thomson*): 1987 S.L.G. 16.

IMMIGRATION

Adoption in an immigration context (*D. Webb*): *Legal Action,* January 1987, 17.

Adoption in an immigration context (*D. Webb*): *Legal Action,* July 1987, 11.

Adoption in an immigration context (*D. Webb*): *Legal Action,* October 1987, 20.

Are you a genuine visitor to the U.K.? (*H. Plews*): (1986) 1 Imm. and Nat. L. & P. 85.

Challenging work permit refusals (*G. Warr*): (1987) 1 Imm. and Nat. L. & P. 124.

Commitment and contradiction in immigration law (*D. Marrington*): (1986) 6 L.S. 272.

Diplomatic exemption (*I. Macdonald*): (1987) 1 Imm. and Nat. L. & P. 120.

Immigration and unilateral divorces (*D. Pearl*): (1986) 1 Imm. and Nat. L. & P. 81.

Immigration law and legal aid (*P. Trott*): (1987) 1 Imm. and Nat. L. & P. 122.

Immigration law reports (*S. Grant*): 130 S.J. 851.

Judicial review: stay of proceedings and bail (*A. Nicol*): (1987) 1 Imm. and Nat. L. & P. 112.

Practice and procedure in immigration appeals: notice regulations and jurisdiction, sections 18–20 (*L. Fransman*): *Legal Action,* January 1987, 12.

Practice and procedure in immigration appeals: procedure on appeal to the tribunal from an adjudicator (*L. Fransman*): (1987) *Legal Action,* October 14.

Practice and procedure in immigration appeals: procedure relating to appeals to the tribunal from an adjudicator (*L. Fransman*): *Legal Action,* September 1987, 19.

Practice and procedure in immigration appeals: procedure relating to first instance appeals (*L. Fransman*): *Legal Action,* March 1987, 15; May 1987, 13.

Recent developments in immigration law (*R. Scannell*): *Legal Action,* February 1987, 20; May 1987, 16.

Recent developments in immigration law (*R. Scannell*): *Legal Action,* August 1987, 15.

IMMIGRATION—*cont.*

Refugees, race and recent developments in the law (*E. Yaansah*): (1987) 1 Imm. and Nat. L. & P. 115.

To deport or not to deport: effect on community (*A. Khan and S. Murgatroyd*): 6 Lit. 293.

INCOME TAX

Aliment and tax relief (*J. A. Russell*): 1987 S.L.T.(News) 218.

Aliment and tax relief—again (*A. R. Barr*): 1987 S.L.T.(News) 301.

Income tax and mortgages: 282 E.G. 1136.

Income Tax, Corporation Tax and Capital Gains Tax (*N. Eastaway*): 136 New L.J. 1064.

Missives, interest and tax (*R. S. H. Girdwood*): 1987 S.L.T.(News) 190.

INDUSTRIAL AND FRIENDLY SOCIETIES

New wave self-help organisations (*I. Swinney*): (1987) 126 SCOLAG 37.

INHERITANCE TAX (NOT SCOTLAND)

Finance Act 1986: inheritance tax (*A. Shipwright*): 130 S.J. 875.

Inheritance tax (*R. Ray*): 136 New L.J. 1119.

Inheritance tax for the general practitioner (*S. Northcott*): 84 L.S.Gaz. 1389.

PETs, cumulation, and the calculation of inheritance tax (*C. Whitehouse and E. Stuart-Buttle*): 83 L.S.Gaz. 3723.

Settling shares in the family company (*R. Venables*): 120 Tax. 84.

Twenty-two ways of saving inheritance tax payable on death (*W. Lee*): 137 New L.J. 690.

Valuation of agricultural property (*R. Venables*): 118 Tax. 397.

Will to disinherit the Revenue (*D. de Pass and M. Gunn*): 120 Tax. 77.

INSURANCE

Early history of fire insurance (*R. Evans*): 8 J.L.H. 88.

Establishment and services in the E.E.C.: insurance cases (*D. A. O. Edward*): (1987) 32 J.L.S. 187.

Illegal insurance (*M. Clarke*): [1987] L.M.C.L.Q. 201.

Insurable interest (*A. Tarr*): 60 A.L.J. 613.

Statutory illegality and the innocent victim (*T. Brentnall*): 84 L.S.Gaz. 343.

Third Parties (Rights Against Insurers) Act 1930 in a modern context (*K. Michel*): [1987] L.M.C.L.Q. 228.

Uberrima fides in English and American insurance law: a comparative analysis (*F. Achampong*): 36 I.C.L.Q. 329.

INTERNATIONAL LAW

Access to the courts of last resort: a comparative overview (*E. Silvestri*): (1986) 5 C.J.Q. 304.

Act of state: Lord Diplock's curious inconsistency (*P. Wesley-Smith*): (1986) 6 L.S. 325.

INTERNATIONAL LAW—*cont.*
Attitudes and practices of the specialised agencies and U.N. organs and the interpretation of their basic constitutions (*A. Campbell*): 1986 J.R. 177.
Brussels Convention and international jurisdiction (*W. Allwood*): 131 S.J. 1234.
Case studies in the jurisdiction of the International Centre for Settlement of Investment Disputes (*W. Tupman*); 35 I.C.L.Q. 813
Concept of law in modern international law (*C. Greenwood*): 36 I.C.L.Q. 283.
Convention establishing the Multilateral Investment Guarantee Agency (*S. Chatterjee*): 36 I.C.L.Q. 76.
Forum non conveniens in America and England: "a rather fantastic fiction" (*D. Robertson*): 103 L.Q.R. 398.
International law: is it shadow or substance? (*C. Battersby*): 131 S.J. 718.
International law and the child soldier (*H. Mann*): 36 I.C.L.Q. 32.
International protection of direct foreign investments in the Third World (*A. Akinsanya*): 36 I.C.L.Q. 58.
Locus standi of unrecognised states and governments before English courts: recent developments (*G. Naldi*): (1987) 8 B.L.R. 187.
Monarchy and the prerogative in Malaysia (*A. Harding*): 28 Mal. 345.
New Hague Sales Convention and the limits of the choice of law process (*C. McLachlan*): 102 L.Q.R. 591.
Of "cut-off" dates and domination: some problematic aspects of the general reception of English law in Singapore (*A. Leong*): 28 Mal.L.R. 242.
Outer Space Act 1986 (*F. Lyall*): 1987 S.L.T.(News) 137.
Position of South African "homelands" in English law and international law (considering *G. U. R. Corpn.* v. *Trust Bank of Africa* [1986] C.L.Y. 2689) (*S. D. Sutton*): 1987 S.L.G. 61.
Succession and other pitfalls (*H. Dyson*): 281 E.G. 61.
Theory and practice of informal international instruments (*A. Aust*): 35 I.C.L.Q. 787.
Third United Nations Conference on the Law of the Sea and the Preparatory Commission: models for United Nations law-making? (*G. Plant*): 36 I.C.L.Q. 525.
United Nations Convention on Conditions for Registration of Ships (*S. Sturmey*): [1987] L.M.C.L.Q. 97.

INTOXICATING LIQUORS (SCOTLAND ONLY)
Late licensing applications (considering *Main* v. *City of Glasgow District Licensing Board* [1987] C.L.Y. 4592 and *Tait* v. *City of Glasgow District Licensing Board,* [1987] C.L.Y. 4593) (*J. C. Cummins*): 1987 S.L.T.(News) 157.

JURISDICTION (SCOTLAND ONLY)
Civil jurisdiction and consumer contracts (*A. Mennie*): 1987 S.L.T.(News) 181.

JURISDICTION (SCOTLAND ONLY)—*cont.*
Civil Jurisdiction and Judgments Act 1982: 1987 S.L.T.(News) 29.
Civil Jurisdiction and Judgments Act 1982 (*R. C. MacKenzie*): (1987) 32 J.L.S. 260.
Civil Jurisdiction and Judgments Act 1982—some questions and answers (*A. Mennie*): 1987 S.L.G. 64.
Domicile—new rules (*A. Mennie*): 1987 S.L.T.(News) 321, 329.
Enforcement of Scottish decrees outside Scotland and of non-Scottish decrees within Scotland (*R. Black*): (1987) 32 J.L.S. 10.
European Court case law and civil jurisdiction in Scotland (*P. Beaumont*): 1987 S.L.T.(News) 201.
Jurisdiction and criminal law in Scotland and England (*P. W. Ferguson*): 1987 J.R. 179.
Jurisdiction in actions concerning foreign land: 1987 S.L.T.(News) 53.
Pleading jurisdiction—negative averments (*R. Black*): 1987 S.L.T.(News) 189.
Prorogation agreements in Scotland: new law (*J. Huntley*): 1987 S.L.T.(News) 277, 289.
Styles for averring jurisdiction under Civil Jurisdiction and Judgments Act 1982 (*R. Black*): 1987 S.L.T.(News) 1.

JURISPRUDENCE
Analytical positivism mark III—where does "content-independence" leave us? (*K. A. Warner*): 1987 J.R. 136.
Critical legal studies and social theory—a response to Alan Hunt (*M. Kruygier*): 7 O.J.L.S. 26.
"Ethical fictions as ethical foundations": justifying professional ethics (*N. Firak*): 24 Osgoode Hall L.J. 35.
Foundations of property and property law (*S. Coval, J. Smith and S. Coval*): [1986] C.L.J. 457.
Hermeneutics and persistent questions in Hart's jurisprudence (*I. Duncanson*): 1987 J.R. 113.
Idea of an overlapping consensus (*J. Rawls*): 7 O.J.L.S. 1.
"It all comes out in the end": judicial rhetorics and the strategy of reassurance (*W. Sadurski*): 7 O.J.L.S. 258.
James Lorimer's common sense approach to legal philosophy (*K. A. B. MacKinnon*): 1987 J.R. 12.
Judicial obligation, precedent and the common law (*S. Perry*): 7 O.J.L.S. 215.
"*Le droit subjectif*" and English law (*G. Samuel*): [1987] C.L.J. 264.
On the beginnings of foundational legal research into legal discourse (*M. Salter*): [1987] IX Liverpool L.R. 23.
Patriarchy and the law (*C. Smart*): (1987) 129 SCOLAG 94.

JUSTICES OF THE PEACE (SCOTLAND ONLY)
J.P.s, sheriffs and official secrets (*R. Black*): (1987) 32 J.L.S. 138.
J.P.s, sheriffs and official secrets—a reply: (1987) 32 J.L.S. 221.

JUSTICES OF THE PEACE (SCOTLAND ONLY)—*cont.*
J.P.s, sheriffs and official secrets—again (*R. Black*): (1987) 32 J.L.S. 253.
View from district court bench: (1987) 131 SCOLAG 121.

LAND CHARGES (NOT SCOTLAND)
Should local land charges be computerised, and, if so, at whose expense? 150 L.G.Rev. 770.

LANDLORD AND TENANT
Agricultural holdings—"specified period of the year" (*H. Wilkinson*): 137 New L.J. 656.
Agricultural Holdings Act 1986 (*C. Rodgers*): [1987] Conv. 177.
Alternative accommodation: what is reasonable? (*W. Hanbury*): 131 S.J. 580.
Burden and benefit of the rules of assignment (*D. Gordon*): [1987] Conv. 103.
Burden of covenants: 282 E.G. 875.
Business premises: escaping protection (*H. Wilkinson*): 137 New L.J. 782.
Business tenancies, occupying the holding (*H. Wilkinson*): 137 New L.J. 71.
Circumventing property statutes: can it still be done? (*P. Freedman*): 84 L.S.Gaz. 403.
Continuing liability (*S. Bright*): 84 L.S.Gaz. 642.
Covenants against assignment or subletting: 282 E.G. 599.
Damages for dumping (*H. Wilkinson*): 137 New L.J. 166.
Defaulting landlords (*J. Goudie*): 6 Lit. 51.
Distress (*T. Ellis*): 84 L.S.Gaz. 31.
Flat management by trustees: an alternative to the management company (*R. Coleman*): 84 L.S.Gaz. 1307.
Forfeiture: time for relief? (*J. Cherryman*): 84 L.S.Gaz. 1042.
Forfeiture of leases: 281 E.G. 1335.
Harassment and unlawful eviction (*P. Watchman*): (1987) 129 SCOLAG 92.
High life? (*P. Rank*): 131 S.J. 1202.
If the covenants shall have been performed (*H. Wilkinson*): 137 New L.J. 263.
Irregular notice to terminate a business tenancy (*H. Wilkinson*): 137 New L.J. 447.
Irremediable breaches of covenant: a trap for the unwary tenant (*R. Bonehill*): 84 L.S.Gaz. 1046.
Landlord and Tenant Act 1987—part I (*J. Israel*): 84 L.S.Gaz. 2749.
Landlord and tenant law review (*P. Rank*): 131 S.J. 490.
Landlords' legal fees: who should pay? (*R. Colbey*): 131 S.J. 1074.
Leases and licences: 283 E.G. 655.
Leases and licences, again (*S. Murdoch*): 281 E.G. 1455.
Letting furnished holiday accommodation (*R. Bonehill*): 84 L.S. Gaz 2753.
Liability following assignment (*S. Murdoch*): 283 E.G. 653.
Liability to remedy an inherent defect (*R. Bonehill*): 84 L.S.Gaz. 1400.

LANDLORD AND TENANT—*cont.*
"Member of the tenant's family" (*H. Wilkinson*): 137 New L.J. 586.
New Lease terms—two cases contrasted (*D. Williams*): 84 L.S.Gaz. 1401.
Non-exclusive occupation agreements since *Street* v. *Mountford (W. Hanbury)*: 84 L.S.Gaz. 1639.
Occupation of business premises pending completion (*P. Sparkes*): 84 L.S.Gaz. 2850.
Options to renew (*S. Murdoch*): 283 E.G. 566.
Participation in housing cases: an examination of attendance and representation at County Court possession hearings and Rent Assessment Committees (*M. Hill and A. Mercer*): (1987) J.S.W.L. 237.
Pitfalls in rent review machinery (*B. Denyer-Green*): 17 C.S.W. 922.
Radical reforms in rented housing (*J. Black*): (1987) 135 SCOLAG 184.
Recent cases on business tenancies (*D. Williams*): 281 E.G. 295.
Recent developments in business tenancies (*D. Williams*): 83 L.S.Gaz. 3412.
Recent developments with the Rent Acts (*D. Williams*): 281 E.G. 996.
Rent Act grounds for possession (*N. Madge*): 84 L.S.Gaz. 1313.
Rent Act grounds for possession: reasonableness (*N. Madge*): 84 L.S.Gaz. 1637.
Rent review—1986 update (*D. Williams*): 281 E.G. 1422.
Rent review: some problems with improvements (*J. Martin*): 282 E.G. 963.
Rent review clauses: time-limits: 281 E.G. 547.
Rents and the retail price index (*H. Wilkinson*): 137 New L.J. 288.
Repair or renewal? (*D. Williams*): 84 L.S.Gaz. 2253.
"Repair" reconsidered (*D. Williams*): 282 E.G. 445.
"Residing with" the tenant (*H. Wilkinson*): 137 New L.J. 563.
Section 1 of the Protection from Eviction Act 1977: the meaning of "occupation" (*J. Hill*): [1987] Conv. 265.
Security of tenure: competing interests (*J. Hill*): (1987) J.S.W.L. 77.
Some aspects of tenants' break clauses (*R. Bond*): 283 E.G. 921.
Sources of tenants' rights to repair in domestic sector (*P. D. Brown*): (1987) 134 SCOLAG 168.
Statutory tenants and occupations as a residence (*N. Madge*): 84 L.S.Gaz. 22.
Sub-tenants—problems for local authorities when properties are surrendered (*W. Birtles*): [1987] L.G.C., September 18, 1987, 12.
Tenant's rights to compensation for improvements (*D. Williams*): 280 E.G. 1422.
Time for removal of tenant's fixtures (*G. Kodilinye*): [1987] Conv. 253.
Twenty years on, and little wiser (*J. Storr*): 283 E.G. 449.
Unravelling interim rents (*N. Eden*): 18 C.S.W. 63.

LANDLORD AND TENANT—*cont.*
"Unreasonable" local authority rent increases: 151 L.G.Rev. 725.

LAW REFORM
A family court or fundamental reform? (*C. Yates*): (1987) J.S.W.L. 300.
Access to Personal Files Bill (*K. Puttick*): 137 New L.J. 271.
Amalgamating the courts—recipe for destruction? (*L. Blom-Cooper*): Law M., June 26, 1987, 30.
Antiquity in action—*ne exeat regno* revived (*L. Anderson*): 104 L.Q.R. 246.
Banking bill (*K. Puttick*): 136 New L.J. 1166.
Case for greater public participation in the legislative process (*K. Hudson-Phillips*): [1987] Stat.L.R. 76.
Commission's draft for a regulation exempting knowhow licensing agreements (*V. Korah*): (1987): 8 B.L.R. 198.
Commons: law and practice: proposals for reform—Countryside Commission—Common Land Forum (*A. Samuels*): 150 L.G.Rev. 772.
Conspiracy: cheating: House of Lords: Parliament (*A. Samuels*): 151 J.P.N. 232.
Criminal Justice Bill—a selection from the proposals (*B. Gibson*): 151 J.P.N. 100.
Criminal Justice Bill: new concepts in criminal law (*G. McFarlane*): 83 L.S.Gaz. 3719.
Draft code of practice on local government publicity: 151 L.G. Rev. 324.
Family courts? (*Lord McGregor*): [1987] 6 C.J.Q. 44.
Family Law Reform Bill (*K. Puttick*): 137 New.L.J. 11.
Finance Bill 1987 (*N. Dickens*): (1987) 3 Ins.L. & P. 77.
Franchising—is there a need for a statutory code? (*D. Glass*): 84 L.S.Gaz. 14.
Government White Paper: intellectual property and innovation (*C. Miller and G. Kamstra*): (1986) 3 Comp.L. & P. 13.
Inheritance tax (*R. Ray*): 136 New L.J. 1119.
Injustice finally remedied? (*I. Dickinson*): 137 New L.J. 435.
Insolvency law reforms introduced (*J. McQueen*): 9 C.Q.S. 35.
Into the light? The Law Commission working paper on land mortgages (*G. Griffiths*): [1987] Conv. 191.
Justice within reach?—a review of progress in reforming small claims (*G. Applebey*): [1987] 6 C.J.Q. 214.
Keith: the unfolding saga (*B. Sabine*): 119 Tax. 447.
Keith and the Revenue (*C. Reece*): 118 Tax. 382, 402.
Land mortgages (*H. Wilkinson*): 281 E.G. 415.
Land registration reform: a third instalment (*J. Sweetman*): 131 S.J. 902.
Latent Damage Act 1986 (*J. Brown*): 280 E.G. 1426.
Law Commission and custody of children: 130 S.J. 857.

LAW REFORM—*cont.*
Law Commission: in need of support (*R. Oerton*): 136 New L.J. 1071.
Law Commission: land mortgages: 136 New L.J. 1041.
Law Commission's working paper on wards of court (*M. Rutherford*): 84 L.S.Gaz. 1624.
Legislative implementation of law reform proposals (*G. Drewry*): [1986] Stat.L.R. 161.
Local legislation since 1974—the era of s.262 (*R. Morris*): [1987] Stat. L.R. 2.
Medical injury—the fault with no-fault (*M. Jones*): (1987) 3 P.N. 83.
More protection for consumers? (*B. Harvey*): 131 S.J. 150.
Parental leave—time for action? (*F. Davidson*): [1986] J.S.W.L. 281.
Pre-natal injury, homicide and the draft criminal code (*J. Temkin*): [1986] C.L.J. 414.
Pressing for reform (*D. Newall*): 131 S.J. 1379.
Proposals to change planning inquiries (*B. Greenwood*): [1987] L.G.C., September 4, 1987, 8.
Role of research in civil justice reform: small claims in the County Court (*C. Whelan*): [1987] 6 C.J.Q. 237.
Sale and supply of goods: the Law Commission Report (*E. Jacobs*): 6 Lit. 276.
Scottish Law Commission under review (*D. Walker*): [1987] Stat.L.R. 115.
Should juries be abolished in fraud trials? (*B. Mitchels*): 131 S.J. 986.
Should local land charges be computerised, and, if so, at whose expense?: 150 L.G.Rev. 770.
Should the State provide alternative dispute resolution services? (*R. Williams*): [1987] 6 C.J.Q. 142.
Specialist housing court?: 151 L.G.Rev. 405.
Strikes and the individual worker—reforming the law (*B. Napier*): [1987] C.L.J. 287.
Trade associations: time to lift the antitrust burden (*P. Groves*): (1987) 8 B.L.R. 61.
U.K. competition law: a case for radical reform (*M. Carlisle*): (1987) 8 B.L.R. 24.
Wardship jurisdiction in the future (*N. McKittrick*): 151 J.P.N. 342.
What should the Code do about omissions? (*G. Willams*): (1987) 7 L.S. 92.

LEGAL AID (NOT SCOTLAND)
Immigration law and legal aid (*P. Trott*): (1987) 1 Imm. and Nat. L. & P. 122.
Welfare benefits and legal aid (*N. Harris*): 84 L.S.Gaz. 1642.

LEGAL HISTORY
Antiquity in action—*ne exeat regno* revived (*L. Anderson*): 104 L.Q.R. 246.
Arbitration in Scotland: an 18th century view (*W. S. Gauldie*): (1987) 32 J.L.S. 349.
Authors of the law (*C. Battersby*): 130 S.J. 970.

LEGAL HISTORY—*cont.*
Contract and *quantum meruit*: the antecedents of *Cutter* v. *Powell* (*J. Barton*): 8 J.L.H. 48.
Contractual damages and the rise of industry (*J. Barton*): 7 O.J.L.S. 40.
Crime, law and order in early modern England (*J. McMullan*): 27 Brit. J. Criminol. 252.
Derry v. Peek and negligence (*C. Reed*): 8 J.L.H. 64.
Early history of fire insurance (*R. Evans*): 8 J.L.H. 88.
Enforcement of hard bargains (*J. Barton*): 103 L.Q.R. 118.
Fair swindler of Blackheath: a case study on the importance of reputation in late eighteenth century legal and commercial affairs (*M. Servian*): 8 J.L.H. 79.
Formalities of marriage—some patterns of English law (*P. Lucas*): 83 L.S.Gaz. 3815.
History of the Lands Clauses Consolidation Act 1845–2 (*F. Sharman*): [1986] Stat.L.R. 78.
Instrument of the new constitution: the origins of the general warrant (*S. Lewis*): 7 J.L.H. 256.
Intellectual property cases in Lord Mansfield's court notebooks (*J. Adams*): 8 J.L.H. 18.
Introduction and use of the grand jury in Victoria (*E. Histed*): 8 J.L.H. 167.
Judge who answered his critics (*R. Munday*): [1987] C.L.J. 303.
Jury system in early Natal (1846–1874) (*P. Spiller*): 8 J.L.H. 129.
Justices of the Peace and the United Kingdom in the age of reform (*R. Tompson*): 7 J.L.H. 273.
Law and authority: the campaign for trial by jury in New South Wales (*D. Neal*): 8 J.L.H. 107.
Law printing in eighteenth century Ireland (*P. O'Higgins*): (1986) 17 Law Librarian 93.
Lawyers and legal argument before the Senate (*J. W. Tellegen*): 1987 J.R. 195.
Legal nature of shares in landowning joint stock companies in the nineteenth century (*C. Stebbings*): 8 J.L.H. 25.
Presumption of guilt in the history of English criminal procedure (*R. Ireland*): 7 J.L.H. 243.
Proving fifteenth century promises (*K. Teeven*): 24 Osgoode Hall L.J. 121.
Public finances and private law in rescript of Emperor Diocletian (*O. E. Tellegen-Couperus*): 1987 J.R. 100.
Reparation for pure economic loss: an historical perspective of Scots law in the seventeenth and eighteenth centuries (*A. Forte*): 8 J.L.H. 3.
Revisiting Lord Hale, misogyny, witchcraft and rape (*G. Geis*): (1986) 10 Crim.L.J. 319.
Scandal of Birmingham Borough Gaol 1853: a case for penal reform (*D. Roberts*): 7 J.L.H. 315.

LEGAL HISTORY—*cont.*
Special juries in England: nineteenth century usage and reform (*J. Oldham*): 8 J.L.H. 148.
Status of women in Roman private law (*O. F. Robinson*): 1987 J.R. 143.
Statutory railway mortgage debentures and the courts in the nineteenth century (*C. Stebbings*): 8 J.L.H. 36.
Swedish jury system in press cases: an offspring of the English trial jury? (*T. Vallinder*): 8 J.L.H. 190.
The Constitutional Association: private prosecutions in reaction to Peterloo (*T. Ford*): 7 J.L.H. 293.
The judge and the businessman (*A. Tunc*): 102 L.Q.R. 549.
Trial by jury in Canada (*G. Parker*): 8 J.L.H. 178.

LIBEL AND SLANDER
Anonymity, newspaper reports and open justice (*I. S. Dickinson*): (1987) 32 J.L.S. 384.
Clarifying the justification plea (*A. Khan*): 131 S.J. 786.
Dictation: libel or slander? (*A. Hudson*): 131 S.J. 1236.
It's all Greek to me: libel law and the freedom of the press (*C. Douzinas, S. McVeigh and R. Warrington*): 137 New L.J. 609.

LICENSING
Applying for full justices' licence (*I. Goldrein*): 131 S.J. 65.
Basic guide to liquor licensing (*R. Colbey*): 6 Lit. 332.
Better public houses: a guide to the available powers (*A. Broadley*): 151 J.P.N. 566.
Licensed to sell—complying with the legal requirements (*J. Spencer*): 151 J.P.N. 116.
Licensing (Restaurant Meals) Act 1987 (*J. Spencer*): 151 J.P.N. 247.
Planning law and the control of licensed premises (*J. Lannon*): [1987] J.P.L. 754.
"Relevant locality" for sex establishments (*C. Manchester*): 151 L.G. Rev. 126.
Role of licensing committees in objecting to renewal of justices' licences (*J. Black*): 151 J.P.N. 133.
Standards in licensed premises—provision of toilet facilities (*J. Spencer*): 151 J.P.N. 310.

LIMITATION OF ACTIONS
Falling down with the Joneses (*C. Wright*): (1986) 2 P.N. 167.
Latent damage (*J. Brown*): 280 E.G. 1335.
Latent damage (*R. Knowles*): 9 C.Q.S. 9.
Latent damage: January 1987 Admin. vii.
Latent damage—the remaining uncertainties (*J. Brown*): 137 New L.J. 191.
Latent Damage Act 1986 (*P. Capper*): (1987) P.N. 47.
Latent Damage Act 1986 (*H. Crowter*): 10 C.Q.S. 23.

BOOKS AND ARTICLES

LOCAL GOVERNMENT

Amusement centres: the need for a policy (*B. Nelson*): [1987] L.G.C., January 30, 12.

Building regulations—the liability of local authorities (*J. Brown*): 84 L.S.Gaz. 1633.

Cesser approach to dealing with unrepealed statutes (*R. Morris*): [1987] L.G.C., February 20, 14.

Councils face legal problems on hippies (*J. Whitcutt*): [1987] L.G.C. July 3, 12.

Councils must look closely at their schemes of delegation (*C. Cross*): [1987] L.G.C., October 16, 1987, 12.

Definitive ruling on school routes (*C. Cross*): [1986] L.G.C. 1306.

Delegation to local authority chairmen (*J. Matthews*): 131 S.J. 89.

Dog fouling in public places: (*J. Matthews*): 151 L.G.Rev. 168.

Doncaster Town Moor case (*A. Samuels*): 151 L.G.Rev. 868.

Draft code of practice on local government publicity: 151 L.G.Rev. 324.

Fettering local democracy by contract (*A. Carroll*): 141 L.G.Rev. 625.

Fire prevention duties of district authorities (*J. Matthews*): 151 L.G.Rev. 508.

Gypsy caravan site provision: the future: 151 L.G. Rev. 784.

Gypsy sites: provision problems and statutory duties: 151 L.G.Rev. 704, 705.

How to avoid the forward funding challenge (*J. Wilson*): [1987] L.G.C., March 13, 12.

Liability for rates and non-occupation of premises: 150 L.G.Rev. 808.

Local authorities duty of care under Public Health Act 1936: 151 L.G.Rev. 605.

Local authority contracts: public or private law? (*R. Ward*): 151 L.G.Rev. 664.

Local authority recruitment policies and discrimination: 150 L.G.Rev. 723.

Local democracy and the law (*C. Bean*): 151 L.G.Rev. 105.

Local Government Act 1986 (*H. Rawlings and C. Willmore*): 50 M.L.R. 52.

Local government and "political publicity": 151 L.G.Rev. 285.

Local legislation since 1974—the era of s.262 (*R. Morris*): [1987] Stat.L.R. 2.

New parks and liability (*M. Charlton*): 151 L.G.Rev. 685.

Phenomenon of the chairmanless meeting (*T. Harrison*): [1987] L.G.C., January 9, 11.

Planning procedures (*J. Garner*): 131 S.J. 1306.

Public utilities street works: a view from the man in the street (*A. Samuels*): 151 L.G.Rev. 288.

Reacting to poll tax: (1987) 130 SCOLAG 102.

Recent cases affecting travellers (*D. Watkinson*): *Legal Action*, July 1987, 9; August 1987, 20.

Recent developments: local authorities (*J. Holyoak and D. Allen*): 137 New L.J. 299.

"Relevant locality" for sex establishments (*C. Manchester*): 151 L.G.Rev. 126.

LOCAL GOVERNMENT—*cont.*

Residence test and personal community charge (*E. M. Scobbie*): (1987) 131 SCOLAG 125.

Review of recent case law (*P. Cooling*): 151 L.G.Rev. 545.

Secure Accommodation (No. 2) (Amendment) Regulations 1986 (*C. Bazell*): 150 J.P.N. 759.

Sex shops again (*J. Matthews*): 151 L.G.Rev. 606.

Time lapse can cause chaos (*D. Swallow*): [1987] L.G.C., February 6, 12.

"Unreasonable" local authority rent increases: 151 L.G.Rev. 725.

Vital to ensure councils' procedures allow fair play (*T. Harrison*): [1987] L.G.C., June 26, 14.

Wilful misconduct sustained (*J. Ellison*): [1986] L.G.C. 1368.

Year in review—case law in 1986 (*C. Cross*): [1987] L.G.C., February 13, 12.

MEDICINE

Against using P.M.S. in criminal court cases (*N. Hilton*): 151 J.P.N. 152.

AIDS and employment law (*N. Fagan and D. Newall*): 137 New L.J. 752.

AIDS and the law (*D. Brahams*): 137 New L.J. 749.

Anatomy of violence (*M. Weller*): 137 New L.J. 881.

Biotechnology—can the law cope? (*H. Barnett*): 15 Anglo-Am. 149.

Conditional registration—a lesser penalty (*M. Mulholland*): (1987) 3 P.N. 117.

Contemporary legal and social issues in medical practice and health care (*I. Kennedy*): 13 C.L.B. 1021.

Disclosure of medical experts' reports in medical negligence cases (*A. Buchan*): 137 New L.J. 513.

Failure of medical advice: trespass or negligence? (*T. Feng*): (1987) L.S. 149.

General Medical Council on trial (*M. Brazier*): (1986) 2 P.N. 134.

Inexperience is no defence to negligent medical treatment (*D. Brahams*): 137 New L.J. 60.

Informed consent: a German lesson (*J. Shaw*): 351 I.C.L.Q. 864

Is the "wrongful life" action really dead? (*J. Fortin*): (1987) J.S.W.L. 306.

Medical injury—the fault with no-fault (*M. Jones*): (1987) 3 P.N. 83.

Medical negligence—a question of policy? (*F. Cownie*): (1987) 3 P.N. 95.

Necessary breath of life (*D. Brahams*): 137 New L.J. 188.

Parents, doctors and children: the *Gillick* case and beyond (*S. de Cruz*): (1987) J.S.W.L. 93.

Patient autonomy and consent to treatment: the role of the law? (*M. Brazier*): (1987) L.S. 169.

Policy factors in actions for wrongful birth (*C. Symmons*): 50 M.L.R. 269.

MEDICINE—*cont.*
Problem of 'informed consent' in the 'wrongful birth' cases (*C. Symmons*): (1987) 3 P.N. 56.
Suing hospitals direct: whose tort was it anyhow? (*J. Bettle*): 137 New L.J. 573.
Wisher v. *Essex AHA*—professional negligence again (*M. James*): 84 L.S.Gaz. 248.

MENTAL HEALTH
Consideration of *Re B. (a minor) (sterilization): (D. Ogbourne*): 151 L.G.Rev. 764.
Emergency admissions under Mental Health (Scotland) Act 1984 (considering *B.* v. *F.* [1987] C.L.Y. 4703) (*C. E. Marr*): 1987 S.L.T.(News) 334.
Judicial review of hospital admissions and treatment in the community under the Mental Health Act 1983 (*M. Gunn*): [1986] J.S.W.L. 290.
Mentally disordered individuals in the prison system (*S. Eysenck*): 151 J.P.N. 265.
Powers of attorney (*D. McLoughlin*): [1987] L.G.C., July 24, 14.
Powers of the courts in respect of the mentally handicapped (*D. Chatterton*): 84 L.S.Gaz. 2441.
Revival of tutors-dative (considering *Morris, Petr,* Inner House, July 11 1986, unreported) (*A. D. Ward*): 1987 S.L.T.(News) 69.

MINORS (NOT SCOTLAND)
Abolition of custody for juvenile offenders (*B. Gibson*): 150 J.P.N. 739.
Abolition of custody for juveniles (*B. Gibson*): 150 J.P.N. 755.
Access to children in care—a review of case law (*C. Bazell*): 151 J.P.N. 422.
Adoption in an immigration context (*D. Webb*): Legal Action, July 1987, 11.
Adoption in an immigration context (*D. Webb*): (1987) *Legal Action,* October 20.
Adoption or custodianship (*M. Rutherford*): 84 L.S.Gaz. 1031.
C. v. *S.*: the arguments in the Court of Appeal (*G. Wright*): 6 Lit. 266.
Care and supervision in custody proceedings (*M. Rutherford*): 84 L.S.Gaz. 1030.
Care proceedings: the relevance of conduct during pregnancy (*D. Ogbourne*): 151 L.G.Rev. 229.
Case for rejoicing (*M. Gunn*): 119 Tax. 396.
Child abduction: the new law (*S. Cretney*): 130 S.J. 827.
Child abduction law now (*A. Samuels*): 6 Lit. 109.
Child abuse and the criminal trial (*A. Samuels*): 151 J.P.N. 603.
Child care and family services—the White Paper (*N. McKittrick*): 151 J.P.N. 147.
Child sexual abuse: the legal issues (*G. Douglas*): 131 S.J. 1170.
Consideration of *Re B (a minor) (sterilization)*: (*D. Ogbourne*): 151 L.G.Rev. 764.
Criminal responsibility of infants (*A. Photis*): 151 J.P.N. 263.
Critical rôle in care (*N. Watt*): 131 S.J. 574.
Custody of child—relevance of child's views (*C. Latham*): 151 J.P.N. 439.

MINORS (NOT SCOTLAND)—*cont.*
Discharging care orders—parents' procedural problems (*W. Miles*): 84 L.S.Gaz. 2353.
Guardian ad litem and the child's solicitor (*M. Morris*): *Legal Action,* January 1987, 15.
Impairment of development *in utero*—a look at *re D (M. Rutherford*): 84 L.S.Gaz. 15.
Interest of the child (*D. Green*): 83 L.S.Gaz. 3824.
Interim care orders—evidence (*C. Latham*): 151 J.P.N. 245.
Juvenile courts—grave crimes revisted (*T. Wilkinson*): 151 J.P.N. 549.
Law Commission and custody of children: 130 S.J. 857.
Legal steps to adulthood (*J. Vickers*): 151 J.P.N. 281.
Parents, doctors and children: the *Gillick* case and beyond (*S. de Cruz*): (1987) J.S.W.L 93.
Powers of the courts in respect of the mentally handicapped (*D. Chatterton*): 84 L.S.Gaz. 2441.
Protecting the child at risk (*J. Ellison*): [1987] L.G.C., July 31, 18.
Refuting allegations of child sexual abuse (*S. Enright*): 137 New L.J. 633, 672.
Rights of the natural parents in respect of the unborn child—a critical analysis of C. *v.* S. (*D. Chatterton*): 6 Lit. 155.
Secure Accommodation (No. 2) (Amendment) Regulations 1986 (*C. Bazell*): 150 J.P.N. 759.
Settlements for children (*A. Cockman and T. Johnson*): 118 Tax. 229.
Should young people be sentenced to "a short, sharp, shock"? (*J. Kuper*): 150 J.P.N. 792.
Treadmill of child abuse (*R. SeQueira and P. Morgan*): [1987] L.G.C., July 31, 16.
Unruly certificates and written reports: a clerk's riposte (*P. Lydiate*): 151 J.P.N. 228.
Wardship jurisdiction (*P. Gallagher*): 131 S.J. 182.
Wardship jurisdiction remains inaccessible to parents (*M. Chambers*): [1987] L.G.C., October 9, 1987, 12.

MORTGAGES (NOT SCOTLAND)
Equity lending in the mortgage market; some legal problems (*A. Hill-Smith*): [1987] J.B.L. 187.
Income tax and mortgages: 282 E.G. 1136.
Into the light? The Law Commission working paper on land mortgages (*G. Griffiths*): [1987] Conv. 191.
Land mortgages (*H. Wilkinson*): 281 E.G. 415.
Mortgagees and possession (*H. Wallace*): 37 N.I.L.Q. 336.
Mortgagor as surety and the position of the legal adviser (*P. Allery*): 84 L.S.Gaz. 2178.
Sell and be sued?—the mortgagee's duty on sale (*J. Marriott*): 84 L.S.Gaz. 2756.
Some pitfalls for mortgagees and how to avoid them (*R. Bonehill*): 130 S.J. 847.

NATIONAL HEALTH

Health authorities and Crown set-off: 83 L.S.Gaz. 3829.

Suing hospitals direct: what tort? (*J. Montgomery*): 137 New L.J. 703.

Suing hospitals direct: whose tort was it anyhow? (*J. Bettle*): 137 New L.J. 573.

NEGLIGENCE

Accounting standards: a guide to negligence? (*D. Gwilliam*) : (1986) 2 P.N. 175.

Advising a client on a rent review clause in a lease—*County Personnel (Employment Agency)* v. *Alan R. Pulver & Co.* (*D. Clarke*): (1987) 3 P.N. 40.

Auditor's responsibility for the detection of fraud (*D. Gwilliam*): (1987) 3 P.N. 5.

Bradford football fire (*A. MacDonald*): 137 New L.J. 481.

Building regulations—the liability of local authorities (*J. Brown*): 84 L.S.Gaz. 1633.

Carrier and the non-owning consignee—an inconsequential immunity (*A. Tettenborn*): [1987] J.B.L. 12.

Contributory negligence in contract and tort (*J. Logie*): 131 S.J. 929.

Curran case: a retreat from justice? (*M. Arnheim*): 131 S.J. 962.

Derry v. Peek and negligence (*C. Reed*): 8 J.L.H. 64.

Disclosure of medical experts' reports in medical negligence cases (*A. Buchan*): 137 New L.J. 513.

Duty of care in the giving of references (*R. Townshend-Smith*): (1987) 3 P.N. 73.

Economic loss from damage to others' property (*W. J. Stewart*): 1987 S.L.T.(News) 345.

Failure of medical advice: trespass or negligence? (*T. Feng*): (1987) L.S. 149.

Future of negligence in product liability (*C. Newdick*): 104 L.Q.R. 288.

Industrial Injuries Scheme benefits compared to damages at common law (*R. Lewis*): 84 L.S.Gaz. 1378.

Industrial injury benefit and assessment of damages (*R. Lewis*): 84 L.S.Gaz. 1640.

Inexperience is no defence to negligent medical treatment (*D. Brahams*): 137 New L.J. 60.

Is the "wrongful life" action really dead? (*J. Fortin*): (1987) J.S.W.L. 306.

Latent damage—the remaining uncertainties (*J. Brown*): 137 New L.J. 191.

Latent Damage Act 1986 (*J. Brown*): 280 E.G. 1426.

Liability in negligence for trespassing criminals (considering *Maloco* v. *Littlewoods Organisation* [1987] C.L.Y. 4737) (*P. W. Ferguson*): 1987 S.L.T.(News) 233.

Liability of regulatory and disciplinary bodies (*D. Feldman*): (1987) 3 P.N. 23.

Limits on liability to the impecunious client (*M. Jones*): (1987) 3 P.N. 76.

Local authorities and defective houses (*J. Garner*): 130 S.J. 814.

Local authorities' duty of care under Public Health Act 1936: 151 L.G.Rev. 605.

NEGLIGENCE—*cont.*

Loss of a chance in tort (*L. Anderson*): 131 S.J. 1258.

Loss without damages: the strange voyage of *The Aliakmon* (*R. Pearce and D. Tomkin*): 136 New L.J. 1169.

Medical negligence—a question of policy? (*F. Cownie*): (1987) 3 P.N. 95.

Negligence: liability and public safety (*T. Knowles*): 131 S.J. 388.

Negligent mortgage valuations again (*S. Murdoch*): 282 E.G. 93.

Negligent mortgage valuations yet again (*S. Murdoch*): 283 E.G. 69.

Occupiers' liability: 280 E.G. 903, 1155.

Patient autonomy and consent to treatment: the role of the law? (*M. Brazier*): (1987) L.S. 169.

Personal injury law reform: a proposed first step (*S. Sugarman*): 16 I.L.J. 30.

Policy/operational dichotomy—a cuckoo in the nest (*S. Bailey and M. Bowman*): [1986] C.L.J. 430.

Policy factors in actions for wrongful birth (*C. Symmons*): 50 M.L.R. 269.

Principles governing the recovery of damages for negligently caused nervous shock (*F. Trindade*): [1986] C.L.J. 476.

Problem of 'informed consent' in the 'wrongful birth' cases (*C. Symmons*): (1987) 3 P.N. 56.

Proceeds of fraud: the bank's liability (*K. Stanton*): (1986) 2 P.N. 190.

Professional negligence and the reasonableness test (*M. James*): J.B.L. 286.

Protecting subsequent owners (*M. Regan*): 283 E.G. 1028.

Recent developments in premises liability—I (*J. Holyoak and D. Allen*): 137 New L.J. 203.

Recent developments—II: occupiers liability (*J. Holyoak and D. Allen*): 137 New L.J. 217.

Recent developments—III: local authorities (*J. Holyoak and D. Allen*): 137 New L.J. 299.

Recovery of purely economic loss in tort: some recent Canadian decisions (*N. Rafferty*): (1987) 3 P.N. 89.

Regulatory agencies and tort liability (*G. Holgate*): 151 L.G. Rev. 744.

Remoteness of injury and negligence (considering *Nacap* v. *Moffat Plant* [1987] C.L.Y. 4767): (1987) 32 J.L.S. 235.

Rise and fall of *Anns* (*L. McGarrity*): 137 New L.J. 794.

Smith v. *Eric S. Bush*—the unanswered questions (*J. Brown*): 283 E.G. 56.

Solicitors' negligence in the preparation of wills (*A. Borkowski*): (1986) 2 P.N. 151.

Structural survey of negligent reports (*M. Harwood*): 50 M.L.R. 588.

Suing for negligent police investigations (*R. Clayton and H. Tomlinson*): 84 L.S.Gaz. 1798.

Suing hospitals direct: what tort? (*J. Montgomery*): 137 New L.J. 703.

Suing hospitals direct: whose tort was it anyhow? (*J. Bettle*): 137 New L.J. 573.

NEGLIGENCE—*cont.*
- Surveyors' duties: two recent cases (*L. Mulcahy*): (1987) 3 P.N. 79.
- Surveyors' negligence—reflections on two recent cases (*S. Tromans*): (1986) 2 P.N. 171.
- Thieves and vandals in empty buildings: whose responsibility? (*R. Youngs*): 131 S.J. 1102.
- Third party acts and the duty of care: 150 L.G.Rev. 828.
- Tort liability for *ultra vires* decisions: *Takaro Properties Ltd.* v. *Rowling* (*S. Todd*): (1986) 2 P.N. 138.
- Weather, forecasting and "the limitless seas" (*D. Millington*): 104 L.Q.R. 234.
- *Wilsher* v. *Essex AHA*—professional negligence again (*M. James*): 84 L.S.Gaz. 248.

NORTHERN IRELAND
- Internment and detention without trial in Northern Ireland 1971–75: ministerial policy and practice (*R. Spjut*): 49 M.L.R. 712.
- Small claims: the Northern Ireland experience (*A. Mulvaney and D. Greer*): [1987] 6 C.J.Q. 56.

NUISANCE
- Damage by tree roots (*D. Williams*): 84 L.S.Gaz. 638.
- Gypsies—a statutory nuisance? Consequent enforcement procedures (*G. Holgate*): 151 L.G.Rev. 485.
- Natural drainage of land (*H. Wilkinson*): 137 New L.J. 867.

PARENT AND CHILD (SCOTLAND ONLY)
- Aliment and tax relief (*J. A. Russell*): 1987 S.L.T.(News) 218.
- Aliment and tax relief—again (*A. R. Barr*): 1987 S.L.T.(News) 301.
- Applications for parental rights (*J. M. Thomson*): 1987 S.L.T.(News) 165.
- Law Reform (Parent and Child) (Scotland) Act 1986 (*J. M. Thomson*): 1987 S.L.T.(News) 129.

PARLIAMENT
- Case for greater public participation in the legislative process (*K. Hudson-Phillips*): [1987] Stat.L.R. 76.
- Electoral issues (*I. S. Dickinson*): 1987 S.L.T.(News) 373.
- Legislative process today (*G. Engle*): [1987] Stat.L.R. 71.
- New territory for ombudsman (*C. T. Reid*): 1987 S.L.T.(News) 325.
- Parliament, policy and delegated power (*T. Bates*): [1986] Stat.L.R. 114.
- Procedure Committee and Public Bills: a seamless robe? (*T. Bates*): [1987] Stat.L.R. 44.

PARTNERSHIP
- Breach of trust by partners (*J. Canagarayar*): 28 Mal.L.R. 214.

PARTNERSHIP—*cont.*
- Who owns partnership property? (*G. L. Gretton*): 1987 J.R. 163.

PATENTS AND DESIGNS
- Anticipating U.K. plant variety patents (*W. Lesser*): [1987] 6 E.I.P.R. 172.
- Balancing interests in the fee payment procedure—as exemplified by the EPO's rules relating to fees (*G. Gall*): [1987] 7 E.I.P.R. 201.
- Changing face of intellectual property (*E. Armitage*): [1987] 7 E.I.P.R. 191.
- Community Patent Convention: some progress (*P. Groves*): (1987) 8 B.L.R. 170.
- Exhaustion of intellectual property rights (*D. Gladwell*): [1986] 12 E.I.P.R. 366.
- Government White Paper: intellectual property and innovation (*C. Miller and G. Kamstra*): (1986) 3 Comp.L. & P. 13.
- High technology "reverse engineering": the dual standard (*R. Hart*): [1987] 5 E.I.P.R. 139.
- Information, equity and entropy (information technology law in England (*J. Mawhood*): (1987) 3 Comp.L. & P. 186.
- Legal protection of computer software against misuse—feasibility or fond hope? (*E. Pugh*): [1987] IX Liverpool L.R. 45.
- Problem and solution approach to the inventive step (*G. Szabo*): [1986] 10 E.I.P.R. 293.
- Procedural law and practice of the Boards of Appeal of the European Patent Office (*G. Paterson*): [1987] 8 E.I.P.R. 221.
- Protection of semi-conductor product designs—the EEC directive and the WIPO draft treaty (*R. Hart*): (1987) 3 Comp. L. & P. 164.
- Status of protection for software in the U.K. and other European countries (*C. Brown*): (1986) 3 Comp. L. & P. 46.

PENSIONS AND SUPERANNUATION
- *Courage* and *Imperial* cases: the lessons (*I. Pittaway*): (1987) 1 Trust. L. & P. 165.
- Equality in pension schemes: the redundant directive? (*G. Keane*): 84 L.S.Gaz. 565.
- Family Law (Scotland) Act 1985—actuarial aspects (*A. C. Martin*): (1987) 32 J.L.S. 417.
- Financial Services Act—how it affects pension schemes (*R. Goldman and T. Cox*): (1986) 1 Trust L. & P. 103.
- New pensions arrangements arising from the Social Security Act 1986: 84 L.S.Gaz. 2677.
- Pension scheme surpluses in receivership and liquidation (*R. Bethell-Jones*): (1987) 3 Ins. L. & P. 68.
- Pension wrinkles for wrinklies (*B. Crabbie*): (1987) 32 J.L.S. 466.
- Pensions, dependency and divorce (*J. Masson*): (1986) J.S.W.L. 343.
- Robbing Mrs. Hood?—redundant female pensioners (*B. Perrins*): 137 New L.J. 273.
- Taxation of pension funds (*R. Emerson*): 120 Tax. 13.

PENSIONS AND SUPERANNUATION—*cont.*

Voyages of discovery for pension schemes (*B. Benney and B. Page*): (1987) 1 Trust L. & P. 142.

Who is entitled to the pension fund surplus? (*R. Nobles*): 16 I.L.J. 164.

POLICE

Civil actions against the police: trespass to the person and defences (*R. Clayton and H. Tomlinson*): (1987) *Legal Action*, October 16.

Domestic violence: uniform response? (*A. Mackay*): (1987) 128 SCOLAG 76.

Police accountability: developing the local infrastructure (*R. Morgan*): 27 Brit. J. Criminol. 87.

Police and the substantive criminal law (*L. Lustgarten*): 27 Brit. J. Criminol. 23.

Police services—when are they special? (*J. Harris*): [1987] L.G.C., August 7, 1987, 12.

Policing by consent: perspicuity or paradox? (*J. Watson*): (1987) 32 J.L.S. 343.

Suing for negligence police investigations (*R. Clayton and H. Tomlinson*): 84 L.S.Gaz. 1798.

Suing the police: choosing the defendant (*J. Harrison*): *Legal Action*, May 1987, 20.

PRACTICE

Abuse of legal process (*A. Khan*): 131 S.J. 1166.

Antiquity in action—*ne exeat regno* revived (*L. Anderson*): 104 L.Q.R. 246.

Anton Piller orders—a new beginning? (*C. Bell*): (1987) 1 Trust L. & P. 146.

Appellate jurisdiction to correct errors of law (*C. Emery*): 104 L.Q.R. 264.

Available at last: the Court of Appeal transcripts (*V. Tunkel*): 136 New L.J. 1045.

Bar in fusion—experience in Australia (*N. Addison*): (1987) 32 J.L.S. 271.

Changes of solicitor: what happens to papers in counsel's hands? (*A. Tettenborn*): 137 New L.J. 59.

Civil and commercial law: a distinction worth making? (*G. Samuel*): 102 L.Q.R. 569.

Civil jurisdiction and consumer contracts (*A. Mennie*): 1987 S.L.T.(News) 181.

Civil Jurisdiction and Judgments Act 1982: 1987 S.L.T.(News) 29.

Civil Jurisdiction and Judgments Act 1982 (*R. C. McKenzie*): (1987) 32 J.L.S. 260.

Civil Jurisdiction and Judgments Act 1982—some questions and answers (*A. Mennie*): 1987 S.L.G. 64.

Civil litigation review (*M. Duggan*): 131 S.J. 188.

Court and 24-hour duty solicitor schemes: 83 L.S.Gaz. 3721.

Disclosure of medical experts' reports in medical negligence cases (*A. Buchan*): 137 New L.J. 513.

Domicile: the new rules (*A. Mennie*): 1987 S.L.T.(News) 321, 329.

PRACTICE—*cont.*

Enforcement of Scottish decrees outside Scotland and of non-Scottish decrees within Scotland (*R. Black*): (1987) 32 J.L.S. 10.

Entitlement to interest in civil litigation (*R. Foster*): 6 Lit. 222.

European Court case law and civil jurisdiction in Scotland (*P. Beaumont*): 1987 S.L.T.(News) 201.

Evaluation of the function and practice of discovery (*B. Cairns*): 61 A.L.J. 79.

Ex parte Anton Piller orders with John Doe defendants (*G. Hayhurst*): [1987] 9 E.I.P.R. 257.

Exchange losses in contract (*L. Anderson*): 84 L.S.Gaz. 2264.

Fresh evidence in the Court of Appeal (*J. Hodge*): 131 S.J. 6.

Further observations on pleading alternative cases (*J. A. Russell*): 1987 S.L.T.(News) 396.

Fusion: lessons down under (*N. Addison*): 130 S.J. 878.

Geographical application of the Jurisdiction and Judgments Convention (*P. Kaye*): 6 Lit. 321.

Hague Evidence Convention and discovery: a serious misunderstanding? (*L Collins*): 35 I.C.L.Q. 765.

Health authorities and Crown set-off: 83 L.S.Gaz. 3829.

Injunctions without damages (*A. Tettenborn*): 38 N.I.L.Q. 118.

Interest on contractual damages (*M. Conlon*): 6 Lit. 311.

Interest on industrial tribunal awards: a case for modified rapture (*S. Levinson*): 84 L.S.Gaz. 2329.

Interest on industrial tribunal awards—a pressing case for reform (*J. McMullen*): 84 L.S.Gaz. 2169.

Interlocutory injunctions having final effect (*W. Sofronoff*): 61 A.L.J. 341.

Judicial procedure—fundamental reappraisal (*C. Scott-Mackenzie*): (1987) 32 J.L.S. 105, 143.

Jurisdiction in actions concerning foreign land: 1987 S.L.T.(News) 53.

Legal professional privilege and inadvertent disclosure (*K. Barrett*): 84 L.S.Gaz. 2928.

Mareva injunction: a practical guide (*R. Ough*): 137 New L.J. 413.

Material non-disclosure on *ex parte* applications—"the golden rule" (*M. Duggan and I. Gatt*): 6 Lit. 179, 228.

Mathematical functions and legal drafting (*M. Casen and J. Steiner*): 102 L.Q.R. 585.

Ne exeat regno—a return to principle (*L. Anderson*): 137 New L.J. 584.

Open justice (*R. Pearson*): 130 S.J. 969.

Payments into court and without prejudice offers (*M. Duggan*): 6 Lit. 284.

Personal injury interest (*R. Nelson-Jones*): 84 L.S.Gaz. 2687.

Pleading alternative cases (*J. Morrison*): 1987 S.L.T.(News) 193.

Pleading jurisdiction: negative averments (*R. Black*): 1987 S.L.T. 189.

PRACTICE—*cont.*

Powers of arrest in civil law: the writ *ne exeat regno* and s.6 of the Debtors Act 1869 (*G. Mitchell*): 84 L.S.Gaz. 2345.

Prison law (*T. Owen*): *Legal Action,* January 1987, 10.

Prisoners and Board of Visitors' hearings; a right to legal representation after all? (*S. Livingstone*): 38 N.I.L.Q. 144.

Prorogation agreements in Scotland: new law (*J. Huntley*): 1987 S.L.T.(News) 277, 289.

Provisional damages (*A. Samuels*): 131 S.J. 187.

Small claims: the Northern Ireland experience (*A. Mulvaney and D. Green*): [1987] 6 C.J.Q. 56.

Solicitor's personal liability for costs—a "current" decision (*P. Brinley-Codd*): 84 L.S.Gaz. 813.

Styles for averring jurisdiction under Civil Jurisdiction and Judgments Act 1982 (*R. Black*): 1987 S.L.T.(News) 1.

Summary decree in Court of Session (*G. Maher*): 1987 S.L.T.(News) 93, 101.

To forgive is divine (*M. Beaumont*) 131 S.J. 638.

Wallersteiner v. *Moir*: a decade later (*D. Prentice*): [1987] Conv. 167.

What is an "application"?: 6 Lit. 12.

Which foreign judgments should we recognise today? (*A. Briggs*): 36 I.C.L.Q. 240.

PRESS

Pressing for reform (*D. Newall*): 131 S.J. 1379.

PRISONS

Boards of visitors and judicial review: the importance of practice (*P. Morris*): 150 J.P.N. 728, 743.

Detention of young adult offenders in Scotland (*B. Williams and A. Creamer*): (1987) 131 SCOLAG 122.

Diversion to social work assistance (*I. D. Willock*): (1987) 131 SCOLAG 124.

Mentally disordered individuals in the prison system (*S. Eysenck*): 151 J.P.N. 265.

Plight of Scottish penal system (*J. Philips*): (1987) 127 SCOLAG 55.

Prison law (*T. Owen*): *Legal Action,* March 1987, 11; May 1987, 9.

Recent court decisions relating to parole policy (*R. L. Houchin*): (1987) 129 SCOLAG 90.

RATING AND VALUATION

General rates on residential accommodation: enforcement proceedings (*D. Forbes*): *Legal Action,* August 1987, 18.

General rates on residential accommodation: minimising or avoiding liability for rates (*D. Forbes*): *Legal Action,* April 1987, 20.

General rates on residential accommodation: minimising or avoiding liability for rates (*D. Forbes*): *Legal Action,* July 1987, 18.

General rates on residential accommodation: valuation (*D. Forbes*): *Legal Action,* January 1987, 21.

RATING AND VALUATION—*cont.*

"Liability for rates and non-occupation of premises": 150 L.G.Rev. 808.

Rate fixing, politics and the law: 151 L.G.Rev. 724.

Right answer by the wrong route (*J. Sedgwick*): 281 E.G. 909.

Settled without a hearing: The disposition of rating appeals in England and Wales (*J. Baldwin and S. Hill*): [1987] P.C. 400.

Tribunal membership: the role of local politics in recruitment to local valuation panels in England and Wales (*J. Baldwin and S. Hill*): [1987] 6 C.J.Q. 130.

Valuation of agricultural property (*R. Venables*): 118 Tax. 397.

REPARATION (SCOTLAND ONLY)

Product liability—Consumer Protection Act 1987, Pt. 1 (*J. Blaikie*): (1987) 32 J.L.S. 325.

Product liability—new rules (*A. Clark*): 1987 S.L.T.(News) 257.

REVENUE AND FINANCE

Accrued income scheme—implications for trustees and personal representatives (*A. Cockman and T. Johnson*): 83 L.S.Gaz. 3399.

Anti-avoidance with charities (*M. Gunn*): 119 Tax. 50.

Artificial tax avoidance—the English and American approach (*P. Millett*): [1986] B.T.R. 327.

Beneficial company schemes (*M. Gunn*): 118 Tax. 317.

British chattel security law: a new deal? (*J. Ziegel*): 131 S.J. 209.

Budget 1987: 106 *Law Notes* 133.

Can PETS bite? (*M. Blundell*): 84 L.S.Gaz. 396.

Capital gains and caravan living (*C. Brand*): 131 S.J. 762.

Capital or income: an elusive touchstone? (*S. Foster*): (1986) 1 Trust L. & P. 99.

Capital profits from land (*M. Gunn*): 119 Tax. 415.

Case for rejoicing (*M. Gunn*): 119 Tax. 396.

Chase the lady (*H. Mainprice*): 119 Tax. 493.

Cheating the Revenue: no deception required (*G. MacFarlane*): 131 S.J. 338.

Community law (*E. Hoskins*): 119 Tax. 13.

Companies: income and charges (*R. Parker*): 120 Tax. 10.

Convention establishing the Multilateral Investment Guarantee Agency (*S. Chatterjee*): 36 I.C.L.Q. 76.

Converting to multi-currency share capital in the U.K. (N. Daubeny): IFL Rev, May 1987, 7.

Credit price: income or capital (*Y. Beer*): [1986] B.T.R. 271.

Dark forest (*C. Newman*): 118 Tax. 241.

Delaware doubles: 118 Tax. 288.

Different techniques for adjusting taxable income under inflationary conditions (*A. Alter*): [1986] B.T.R. 347.

Documentation of LDC asset transfers (*C. Nicolaides*): (1987) 2 I.B.F.L. 108.

REVENUE AND FINANCE—*cont.*

Does the tax system favour incorporation? (*R. Ashton*): [1987] B.T.R. 256.

Euro-medium term notes: a new instrument in context (*A. Taylor*): [1987] 2 J.I.B.L. 74.

Euro-notes and commercial paper: the English regulatory framework (*A. Balfour*): [1986] 3 J.I.B.L. 137.

Exceptional receipts (*G. Down*): 119 Tax. 294.

Expenses of management (*M. Lee*): 119 Tax. 524.

Farm dwellings (*M. Barrett*): 119 Tax. 337.

Favourable tax regime (*M. Lichten and G. Jones*): 119 Tax. 170.

Finance Act 1986 (*A. Shipwright*): 130 S.J. 815, 830, 854, 912.

Finance Act 1986: December 1986 Admin. iii.

Finance Act 1986: inheritance tax (*A. Shipwright*): 130 S.J. 875.

Finance Bill 1987 (*N. Dickens*): (1987) 3 Ins.L. & P. 77.

Financial services: the regulatory structure (*R. Pennington*): 131 S.J. 178.

Financial Services Act 1986: April 1987 Admin. i.

Financing school fees (*M. Barrett*): 119 Tax. 399.

Fishy business (*J. Golding*): 119 Tax. 549.

General holdover relief for gifts into/out of trusts (and to individuals) (*R. Ray*): 137 New L.J. 303.

Income tax and mortgages: 282 E.G. 1136.

Inheritance tax for the general practitioner (*S. Northcott*): 84 L.S.Gaz. 1389.

Insider dealing and the Financial Services Act 1986 (*R. Pennington*): 131 S.J. 206.

Insurance commissions (*V. Durkacz*): 119 Tax. 436.

International regulation of securities markets: interaction between United States and foreign laws (*W. Haseltine*): 36 I.C.L.Q. 307.

"Internationalisation" of sovereign loan agreements (*M. Pearce*): [1986] 3 J.I.B.L. 165.

Investor protection in the commodity and financial futures markets (*H. White*): (1987) 8 B.L.R. 103.

Issuing sterling Euro MTNs (*S. Revell*): (1987) 8 I.F.L.Rev. 28.

Judicial review in taxation: a modern perspective (*R. Bartlett*): [1987] B.T.R. 10.

Judicial review of the take-over panel and self-regulatory organisations (*R. Falkner*): [1987] 2 J.I.B.L. 103.

Keith: the unfolding saga (*B. Sabine*): 119 Tax. 447.

Keith and the Revenue (*C. Reece*): 118 Tax. 382, 402.

Maintenance payments and school fees as the dust settles (*C. Whitehouse*): 137 New L.J. 495.

New framework (*S. Carson*): 119 Tax. 526.

New investor protection regime (*C. Abrams*): (1987) B.L.R. 31.

New protection for investors (*K. Blundell*): 118 Tax. 297.

Not as you like it (*M. Truman*): 119 Tax. 413.

REVENUE AND FINANCE—*cont.*

Offshore funds (*M. Gunn*): 119 Tax. 312.

Oh, to be in England (*M. Gunn*): 119 Tax. 243.

Partial exemption revisited (*V. Duckacz*): 118 Tax. 496.

Payroll donations (*A. Sellwood*): 118 Tax. 212.

PETs, cumulation, and the calculation of inheritance tax (*C. Whitehouse and E. Stuart-Buttle*): 83 L.S.Gaz. 3723.

Profit related pay (*J. Dick*): 84 L.S.Gaz. 2509.

Rare tax break (*J. Dick*): 119 Tax. 545.

Regulation of financial services—an overview (*T. Ashe*): 84 L.S.Gaz. 1392.

Reservation of benefit—uncertainties and traps (*C. Whitehouse*): 84 L.S.Gaz. 392.

Schedule B (*S. Owen*): 119 Tax. 164.

Scope of s.54 (*M. O'Brien*): 119 Tax 28.

Section 15 of the Finance Act 1985 (*A. Humphrey*): [1986] B.T.R. 264.

Settlements for children (*A. Cockman and T. Johnson*): 118 Tax. 229.

Settling shares in the family company (*R. Venables*): 120 Tax. 84.

Silver lining (*M. Gunn*): 118 Tax. 324.

Sterling commercial paper (*J. Barratt and C. Norfolk*): (1987) 2 I.B.F.L. 118.

Strictly in confidence (*J. Gullick*): 74 Accts. Rec. 25.

Taxation: developments on the *Ramsay* doctrine (*L. Cane*): (1987) 8 B.L.R. 169.

Taxation and damages: the rule in *Gourley's* case (*W. Bishop and J. Kay*): 104 L.Q.R. 211.

Taxation in insolvency (*A. Davis*): 119 Tax. 98.

Taxation of pension funds (*R. Emerson*): 120 Tax. 13.

Thin dividing line (*D. Jeffrey*): 119 Tax. 196.

Tidying tax loose ends: 1 (*M. Truman*): 131 S.J. 960.

Tidying tax loose ends: 2 (*M. Truman*): 131 S.J. 1108.

Tidying tax loose ends: 3 (*M. Truman*): 131 S.J. 1298.

Trivial pursuits (*M. Gunn*): 120 Tax. 25.

Trust taxation (*M. Jacobs*): 119 Tax 505.

Trustee's lot (*M. Gunn*): 120 Tax. 1.

Trustee's tightrope (*O. Clinton*): 119 Tax. 188.

Twenty-two ways of saving inheritance tax payable on death (*W. Lee*): 137 New L.J. 690.

U.K. as a trust tax haven (*B. McCutcheon*): 84 L.S.Gaz. 2840.

U.K. taxation treatment of commercial paper issues (*E. Norfolk*): [1986] 1 J.I.B.L. 211.

U.S./U.K. proposal on capital adequacy (*A. Murray-Jones and D. Spencer*): (1987) 8 I.F.L.Rev. 20.

Valuation of agricultural property (*R. Venables*): 118 Tax. 397, 418.

Vested interest (*M. Gunn*): 119 Tax. 210.

Will to disinherit the Revenue (*D. de Pass and M. Gunn*): 120 Tax. 77.

What is a debenture? (*A. Bati*): [1986] B.T.R. 255.

What is farming? (*M. Barrett*): 118 Tax. 378.

REVENUE AND FINANCE—*cont.*

Who are "A" and "B"? (*R. Nock*): [1987] B.T.R. 245.

Whose profits are these? (*B. Sabine*): 118 Tax. 194.

Wither the negative pledge (*N. Broadman and J. Crosthwait*): [1986] 3 J.I.B.L. 162.

RIGHTS IN SECURITY (SCOTLAND ONLY)

Trusts and floating charges (considering *Tay Valley Joinery* v. *C.F. Financial Services* [1987] C.L.Y. 5215) (*K. C. G. Reid*): 1987 S.L.T.(News) 113.

ROAD TRAFFIC

Breath tests, blood tests and back calculation (*J. Dossett*): 84 L.S.Gaz. 2925.

Driving recklessly—defence of necessity strictly construed (*N. McKittrick*): 151 J.P.N. 180.

Failure to provide a breath sample for analysis in the Lion intoximeter (*J. Morris*): 151 J.P.N. 249.

Parking alongside a kerbed footway, blocking the occupier (*A. Samuels*): 151 J.P.N. 88.

Quitting a vehicle on private premises—a gap in the regulations? (*P. Amey*): 151 J.P.N. 169.

Road traffic—recent developments: 83 L.S.Gaz. 3572; 84 L.S.Gaz. 2667.

Road traffic—viable or arguable defences to drunken driving (*A. Samuels*): 84 L.S.Gaz. 659.

Sentencing guidelines: causing death by reckless driving, reckless driving and careless driving—a comment (*A. Turner*): 151 J.P.N. 291.

Tachograph as defence witness (*J. Buchan*): (1987) 32 J.L.S. 306.

Taking samples from drinking drivers—effect of the continuing "non-statutory option" (*L. Connor*): 151 J.P.N. 230.

Taxi law (*A. Samuels*): 151 L.G.Rev. 828.

SALE OF GOODS

Caveat the vehicle vendor and purchaser (*S. Sharpe*): 131 S.J. 341.

Civil jurisdiction and consumer contracts (*A. Mennie*): 1987 S.L.T.(News) 181.

Consumer Protection Act 1987 (*J. Bradgate and N. Savage*): 137 New L.J. 929, 953.

Consumer Protection Act 1987 (*K. Cardwell*): 50 M.L.R. 622.

Consumer Protection Act 1987 (*A. Clarke*): 50 M.L.R. 614.

Consumer Protection Act 1987 (*M. James*): 1987 S.L.G. 86.

Finding fault with new cars (*G. Howells*): 131 S.J. 682.

Implied terms in contracts for the sale of goods—recent developments (*M. James*): 137 New L.J. 144.

Insolvency Act 1986 and retention of title (*S. Wheeler*): [1987] J.B.L. 180.

Latent exemption clause problems in U.K. computer contracts (*A. Kelman*): (1987) 15 I.B.L. 211.

SALE OF GOODS—*cont.*

Loss without damages: the strange voyage of *The Aliakmon* (*R. Pearce and D. Tomkin*): 136 New L.J. 1169.

Merchantable quality, fitness for purpose and cars: 6 Lit. 61.

Misleading prices (*B. Harvey*): 131 S.J. 1076.

Motorist and Sale of Goods Act (considering *Bernstein* v. *Pamson Motors (Golders Green)* [1987] C.L.Y. 3335; *Rogers* v. *Parish (Scarborough)* [1987] C.L.Y. 3333 and *Millars of Falkirk* v. *Turpie* [1976] C.L.Y. 3419) (*I. Lloyd*): 1987 S.L.T.(News) 221.

On disclaiming liability for a false mileometer (*R. Lawson*): 84 L.S.Gaz. 2760.

Ownership and obligation in commercial transactions (*R. Goode*): 103 L.Q.R. 433.

Part exchange of goods (*E. Jacobs*): 15 Anglo-Am. 234.

Product liability and safety of goods (*B. Harvey*): 131 S.J. 1053.

Product liability—Consumer Protection Act 1987, Pt. 1 (*J. Blaikie*): (1987) 32 J.L.S. 325.

Product liability—new rules (*A. Clark*): 1987 S.L.T.(News) 257.

Property problems in sale: three footnotes (*T. B. Smith*): 1987 S.L.T.(News) 241.

Purchaser's acceptance of defective goods (*M. Whincup*): 83 L.S.Gaz. 3807.

Rationalisation of Romalpa clause in Scottish law of property and obligations (*M. Sweeney*): 1987 J.R. 62.

Rejection and implied terms: anomalies and inconsistency of approach (*E. Jacobs*): 6 Lit. 95.

Retailer's liability for misleading instructions on goods (considering *Wormell* v. *R.H.M. Agriculture (East)* [1986] C.L.Y. 3005) (*W. C. H. Ervine*): 1987 S.L.T.(News) 132.

Retention of title clauses—where are we now? (*E. Jacobs*): 6 Lit. 184.

"Romalpa" retention of title clauses (*D. Chalmers*): 60 A.L.J. 545.

S.25(1) Sale of Goods Act 1979: policy or principle? (*I. R. Davies*): 1987 S.L.G. 5, 33.

Sale and supply of goods: the Law Commission Report (*E. Jacobs*): 6 Lit. 276.

Sales without title (*R. Lawson*): (1987) 8 B.L.R. 196.

Second-hand car dealers and the Trade Descriptions Act 1968 (*A. Samuels*): (1986) 5 Tr.L. 324.

Trade Descriptions Act 1968: s.24—"due diligence," "reasonable precautions" and "personal attributes" (*G. Holgate*): 151 J.P.N. 648.

Trading fairly: would a "general duty" help? (*K. Puttick*): (1986) 7 B.L.R. 299.

Transferability and sale of goods (*I. Davies*): (1987) 7 L.S. 1.

Trouble with cars (*R. Lawson*): (1987) 8 B.L.R. 88.

Warrandice of quality at common law in Scotland (*E. E. Sutherland*): 1987 J.R. 24.

SHERIFF COURT PRACTICE (SCOTLAND ONLY)
Response to small claims consultation paper: (1987) 130 SCOLAG 111.

SHIPPING AND MARINE INSURANCE
Admiralty jurisdiction of Inner London magistrates (*G. Browne*): 151 J.P.N. 23.
Athens Convention 1974 and limitation of liability (*N. Gaskell*): 137 New L.J. 322.
Bill of lading as a receipt—missing oil in unknown quantities (*C. Debattista*): [1986] L.M.C.L.Q. 468.
Canadian maritime law decisions 1985–86 (*W. Tetley*): [1987] L.M.C.L.Q. 82.
Making of the marine insurance contract: a comparison of English and U.S. law (*D. Condon*): [1986] L.M.C.L.Q. 484.
Marine insurance law: can the lawyers be trusted? (*D. O'May*): [1987] L.M.C.L.Q. 29.
Maritime claims: the European Judgments Convention (*G. Brice*): [1987] L.M.C.L.Q. 281.
New Institute Cargo Clauses (*A. George*): [1986] L.M.C.L.Q. 438.
Out-turn clauses in c.i.f. contracts in the oil trade (*J. Lightburn and G. Nienaber*): [1987] L.M.C.L.Q. 177.
Responsibility of a carrier of goods by sea under the laws of the Arabian Gulf States: "the exceptions and the rule" (*R. Price*): (1987) 2 A.L.Q. 29.
Transport of goods in refrigerated containers: an Australian perspective (*R. Springall*): [1987] L.M.C.L.Q. 216.
United Nations Convention on Conditions for Registration of Ships (*S. Sturmey*): [1987] L.M.C.L.Q. 97.
Validity of "floating" choice of law and jurisdiction clauses (*A. Briggs*): [1986] L.M.C.L.Q. 508.
Zeebrugge: is it a good offer? (*M. Arnheim*): 131 S.J. 606.
Zeebrugge disaster: application of the Athens Convention 1974 (*N. Gaskell*): 137 New L.J. 285.

SHOPS MARKETS AND FAIRS
Never on a Sunday? (*A. Khan*): 131 S.J. 646.

SOCIAL SECURITY
Board and lodging payments for young people (*N. Harris*): (1987) J.S.W.L. 150.
Compensation for industrial injury (*R. Lewis*): 137 New L.J. 43.
Decisions of the social security commissioners (*J. Luba*): *Legal Action*, September 1987, 15.
Draft guidance and directions for social fund officers (*B. Stead*): (1987) 128 SCOLAG 77.
Good cause justifying a late claim for benefit (*R. Lewis*): *Legal Action*, June 1987, 11.
Government's philosophy towards reform of social security: the case of industrial injuries benefit (*R. Lewis*): 13 I.L.J. 256.

SOCIAL SECURITY—*cont.*
Incorrect payments of social security (*J. G. Logie*): (1987) 130 SCOLAG 105.
Industrial injuries and diseases after the Social Security Act 1986: 83 L.S.Gaz. 3582.
Industrial Injuries Scheme benefits compared to damages at common law (*R. Lewis*): 84 L.S.Gaz. 1378.
Industrial injury benefit and assessment of damages (*R. Lewis*): 84 L.S.Gaz. 1640.
New pensions arrangements arising from the Social Security Act 1986: 84 L.S.Gaz. 2677.
Note on statutory maternity pay (considering Statutory Maternity Pay (General) Regulations 1986): 1987 S.L.T.(News) 150.
Politics, organisation and environment—influences on the exercise of administrative discretion within the housing benefit scheme (*I. Loveland*): (1987) J.S.W.L. 216.
Single payments for removals, furniture and bedding (*V. Macnair*): *Legal Action*, August 1987, 9.
Social fund—transitional measures and possible alternatives (*M. Rowell*): (1987) J.S.W.L. 137.
Social fund and single payments (*S. Jones*): 84 L.S.Gaz. 2334.
Social security abuse and overpayments (*J. G. Logie*): (1987) 128 SCOLAG 73.
Social Security Act 1986 (*D. Chatterton*): 136 New L.J. 1147.
Social security adjudication: the new regulations (*N. Wikeley*): *Legal Action*, April 1987, 14.
Social security case notes (*J. G. Logie and I. D. Willcock*): (1987) 130 SCOLAG 109, 131 SCOLAG 127, 132 SCOLAG 144.
Social security fraud sentencing guidelines (*A. Turner*): 151 J.P.N. 355.
Some recent attendance allowance appeals (*C. Quinn and G. Dangerfield*): (1987) 126 SCOLAG 41.
Special diets and supplementary benefit (*N. Harris*): 137 New L.J. 745.
Statutory sick pay—recent changes: 84 L.S.Gaz. 1802.
Supplementary benefit: additional requirements (*V. Macnair*): (1987) *Legal Action*, October 9.
Supplementary benefits: exceptional need payments (*H. Dutton*): 131 S.J. 1078.
"Testing the untestable": section 50 of the Social Security Act 1975 (*G. Holgate*): (1986) J.S.W.L. 321.
Unemployment benefit: the "full-extent normal rule" (*T. Buck*): (1987) J.S.W.L. 23.
Young mothers, income support and the social fund (*N. Harris*): 137 New L.J. 324.

SOLICITORS
After the review—preparing for the 21st century (*R. Elliot*): (1987) 135 SCOLAG 187.
Aids, hepatitis B and the solicitor—government health reassurance (*R. G. Covell*): (1987) 32 J.L.S. 266.

SOLICITORS—*cont.*
Bar in fusion—experience in Australia (*N. Addison*): (1987) 32 J.L.S. 271.
Case for considering contingent fee (*D. L. Carey Miller*): (1987) 32 J.L.S. 461.
Change and multi-discipline partnership (*D. M. Little*): (1987) 32 J.L.S. 444.
Changes of solicitor: what happens to papers in counsel's hands? (*A. Tettenborn*): 137 New L.J. 59.
Changing perceptions of professionalism (*A. A. Paterson*): (1987) 32 J.L.S. 368.
Choosing a computer (*D. Jack and A. Boller*): (1987) 32 J.L.S. 180.
Court and 24-hour duty solicitor schemes: 83 L.S.Gaz. 3721.
Evaluating legal needs (*A. A. Paterson*): (1987) 127 SCOLAG 58.
Incorporation of legal practices (*W. W. McBryde*): (1987) 32 J.L.S. 133.
Is he still a client? the nature and duration of retainer (*A. Samuels*): 84 L.S.Gaz. 346.
Legal defence union (*P. Burns*): (1987) 32 J.L.S. 407.
Legal professional privilege: meaning and application in Scots law (*V. M. P. Ogston and A. L. Seager*): 1987 J.R. 38.
May you live in exciting times (*R. B. Jack*): (1987) 32 J.L.S. 272.
Multi-disciplinary partnerships in England and Wales (*G. McFarlane*): 1987 S.L.T.(News) 249.
Pension wrinkles for wrinklies (*B. Crabbie*): (1987) 32 J.L.S. 466.
Reform of the solicitors' complaints procedures: fact or fiction? (*A. Newbold and G. Zellick*): [1987] 6 C.J.Q. 25.
Review of diploma in legal practice (*R. C. Elliot*): (1987) 130 SCOLAG 106.
Solicitor: constructive trustee or agent? (*B. Griffin*): (1987) 1 Trust L. & P. 176.
Solicitor and the witness (*A. Pugh Thomas*): 6 Lit. 271.
Solicitors and shoddy work: the new powers of the Law Society (*B. Walsh*): (1987) 3 P.N. 114.
Solicitor in care cases—who gives the instructions? (*I. Weintroub*): 84 L.S.Gaz. 1318.
Solicitors' negligence in the preparation of wills (*A. Borkowski*): (1986) 2 P.N. 151.
Solicitor's personal liability for costs—a "current" decision (*P. Brinley-Codd*): 84 L.S.Gaz. 813.
Twenty five years in retrospect (*J. M. Halliday*): (1987) 32 J.L.S. 108.
Very little ado about much: review of diploma in legal practice (*J. P. Grant*): (1987) 133 SCOLAG 158.

STAMP DUTIES
Finance Act 1986 (*A. Shipwright*): 130 S.J. 912.
Stamp duty reserve tax: the nature of the beast (*L. Cane*): 137 New L.J. 49.
Stamp duty warning for conveyancers (considering *Saunders* v. *Edwards* [1987] C.L.Y. 1826) (*D. C. Coull*): (1987) 32 J.L.S. 389.

STAMP DUTIES—*cont.*
Who are "A" and "B"? (*R. Nock*): [1987] B.T.R. 245.

STATUTES AND ORDERS
Acting on delinquent directors—a review of the Company Directors Disqualification Act 1986 (*L. Leighton-Johnston*): (1987) 3 Ins. L. & P. 75.
Agricultural Holdings Act 1986 (*C. Rodgers*): [1987] Conv. 177.
Building Regulations 1985: something new or more of the same? (*K. Gough*): (1986) 2 Const.L.J. 262.
Building Societies Act 1986 (*C. Jobe and C. Taylor*): (1957) 5 Co.Law.Dig. 15.
Case for greater public participation in the legislative process (*K. Hudson-Phillips*): [1987] Stat.L.R. 76.
Cesser approach to dealing with unrepealed statutes (*R. Morris*): [1987] L.G.C., February 20, 1987, 14.
Codes of practice: an update (*P. Circus*): (1986) 7 B.L.R. 307.
Comparison of British and French legislative drafting (with particular reference to their respective nationality laws) (*T. Millett*): [1986] Stat.L.R. 130.
Consumer Protection Act 1987 (*J. Bradgate and N. Savage*): 137 New L.J. 929, 953.
Consumer Protection Act 1987 (*K. Cardwell*): 50 M.L.R. 622.
Consumer Protection Act 1987 (*A. Clarke*): 50 M.L.R. 614.
Copyright: public interest and statutory powers under the Competition Act 1980 (*R. Greaves*): [1987] 1 E.I.P.R. 3.
Criminal Justice Act 1987 (*B. Gibson*): 151 J.P.N. 435.
Data Protection Act 1984 (*M. Hibbs*): 84 L.S.Gaz. 2745.
Data Protection Act 1984: subject access (*M. Hibbs*): 84 L.S.Gaz. 2838.
Detention under the Police and Criminal Evidence Act 1984 (*H. Brayne*): 84 L.S.Gaz. 28.
Education Act 1981 in the courts (*D. Milman*): (1987) J.S.W.L. 208.
Education Act 1986 contributes to withering of councils (*M. Mason*): [1987] L.G.C., August 28, 1987, 10.
Enduring Powers of Attorney Act 1985 (*P. Lewis*): 83 L.S.Gaz. 3566.
Enduring Powers of Attorney Act 1985—twelve months on (*P. Lewis*): 84 L.S.Gaz. 1219.
Environmental protection and improvement statutes and their primacy over other statutes in Australia—a noteworthy juridical feature (*J. Kodwo Bentil*): [1987] Stat.L.R. 32.
Examination of Part I of the Public Order Act 1986 (*K. Pain*): 151 J.P.N. 198.
Extensions and limitations in the Housing and Planning Act (*D. Hender*): [1987] L.G.C., January 2, 8.
Family Law Act: 136 New L.J. 1090.
Family Law Act 1986 (*T. Prime*): 131 S.J. 62, 91, 118, 156.

STATUTES AND ORDERS—*cont.*

Finance Act 1986 (*A. Shipwright*): 130 S.J. 854, 912.

Finance Act 1986: December 1986 Admin. iii.

Finance Act 1986: inheritance tax (*A. Shipwright*): 130 S.J. 875.

Financial Services Act 1986: April 1987 Admin. i.

Forfeiture Act: a perspective (*T. Prime*): 130 S.J. 811.

History of the Lands Clauses Consolidation Act 1845—2 (*F. Sharman*): [1986] Stat.L.R. 78.

Housing and Planning Act 1986 (*R. Hamilton*): 130 S.J. 906, 941.

Housing and Planning Act 1986: 151 L.G.Rev. 44.

Impact of directives on statutory interpretation: using the Euro-meaning? (*J. Bates*): [1986] Stat.L.R. 174.

Inheritance (Provision for Family and Dependants) Act 1975—precautions and pitfalls (*J. Ross Martyn*): 83 L.S.Gaz. 3571.

Insolvency Act: 136 New L.J. 1135.

Insolvency Act—preferences: April 1987 Admin. vi.

Judicial review of hospital admissions and treatment in the community under the Mental Health Act 1983 (*M. Gunn*): [1986] J.S.W.L. 290.

Landlord and Tenant Act 1987—part I (*J. Israel*): 84 L.S.Gaz. 2749.

Latent Damage Act 1986 (*J. Brown*): 280 E.G. 1426.

Latent Damage Act 1986 (*P. Capper*): (1987) 3 P.N. 47.

Latent Damage Act 1986 (*H. Crowter*): 10 C.Q.S. 23.

Legislation, linguistic adequacy and public policy (*D. Miers*): [1986] Stat.L.R. 90.

Legislative drafting: could our statutes be simpler? (*D. Berry*): [1987] Stat.L.R. 92.

Legislative drafting: could our statutes be simpler? (*Mr. Justice Nazareth*): [1987] Stat.L.R. 81.

Legislative implementation of law reform proposals (*G. Drewry*): [1986] Stat.L.R. 161.

Legislative process today (*G. Engle*): [1987] Stat.L.R. 71.

Licensing (Restaurant Meals) Act 1987 (*J. Spencer*): 151 J.P.N. 247.

Local Government Act 1986 (*H. Rawlings and C. Willmore*): 50 M.L.R. 52.

Local legislation since 1974—the era of s.262 (*R. Morris*): [1987] Stat.L.R. 2.

Minors' Contracts Act 1987 (*J. Holroyd*): 84 L.S.Gaz. 2266.

Monitoring the Public Order Act 1986 (*H. Kitchin*): *Legal Action*, August 1987, 12.

New intellectual property right? A hidden landmine in the Cable and Broadcasting Act 1984 (*J. Phillips*): (1987) 3 Comp. L. & P. 99.

New law for building societies: Building Societies Act 1986 (*A. Samuels*): [1987] Conv. 36.

STATUTES AND ORDERS—*cont.*

New statutory preventive provisions in Part II of the Public Order Act 1986 (*J. Marston*): 151 L.G.Rev. 205.

New Use Classes Order (*M. Redman*): 282 E.G. 966.

Order in Council (*C. Horsford*): 131 S.J. 462.

Outer Space Act 1986 (*F. Lyall*): 1987 S.L.T. 137.

Parliament, policy and delegated power (*T. Bates*): [1986] Stat.L.R. 114.

Planning control in national parks: the new Special Development Order (*C. Brand*): 281 E.G. 762.

Problems of legislative drafting (*I. Turnbull*): [1986] Stat.L.R. 67.

Procedure Committee and Public Bills: a seamless robe? (*T. Bates*): [1987] Stat.L.R. 44.

Public Order Act 1986 (*C. Walker*): 151 L.G.Rev. 364.

Public Order Act 1986: an overview of Part I (*J. Marston*): 151 L.G.Rev. 264.

Public Order Act 1986: offences (*E. Rees*): (1987) *Legal Action*, February 1987, 9.

Public Order Act 1986: steps in the wrong direction? (*D. Bonner and R. Stone*): [1987] P.L. 202.

Riot in the Riot (Damages) Act 1886 (*J. Marston*): 84 L.S.Gaz.1797.

Second-hand car dealers and the Trade Descriptions Act 1968 (*A. Samuels*): (1986) 5 Tr.L. 324.

Section 15 of the Finance Act 1985 (*A. Humphrey*): [1986] B.T.R. 264.

Sections 14 and 39 Public Order Act 1986 (*J. Marston*): 151 J.P.N. 601, 615.

Sex Discrimination Act 1986 (*J. Bowers and M. Duggan*): 84 L.S.Gaz. 240.

Sex Discrimination Act 1986: 151 L.G.Rev. 183, 245.

Social Security Act 1986 (*D. Chatterton*): 136 New L.J. 1147.

Statutory interpretation (*A. Wilson*): (1987) 7 L.S. 62.

Taking civil codes less seriously (*H. Kötz*): 50 M.L.R. 1.

"Testing the untestable": section 50 of the Social Security Act 1975 (*G. Holgate*): (1986) J.S.W.L. 321.

The Education Act 1986 (No.2): 151 L.G.Rev. 4.

Third Parties (Rights Against Insurers) Act 1930 in a modern context (*K. Michel*): [1987] L.M.C.L.Q. 228.

U.K. Banking Act 1987: a review (*F. Chronnell and P. Haslam*): (1987) 2 I.B.F.L. 129.

Wages Act (*K. Puttick*): 136 New L.J. 1068.

Wages Act 1986: 151 L.G.Rev. 64, 207.

STOCK EXCHANGE

Euro-medium term notes: a new instrument in context (*A. Taylor*): [1987] 2 J.I.B.L. 74.

Financial Services Act 1986: April 1987 Admin. i.

Great divide—a review of segmental reporting (*G. Jones*): 5 Co. Law 44.

STOCK EXCHANGE—*cont.*

International regulation of securities markets: interaction between United States and foreign laws (*W. Haseltine*): 36 I.C.L.Q. 307.

Issuing sterling Euro MTNs (*S. Revell*): (1987) 8 IFL Rev. 28.

Judicial review of the take-over panel and self-regulatory organisations (*R. Falkner*): [1987] 2 J.I.B.L. 103.

New protection for investors (*K. Blundell*): 118 Tax. 297.

Regulation of financial services—an overview (*T. Ashe*): 84 L.S.Gaz. 1392.

Regulatory environment for the international equity market (*R. Britton*): (1987) 2 I.B.F.L. 125.

U.S./U.K. proposal on capital adequacy (*A. Murray-Jones and D. Spencer*): (1987) 8 IFL Rev. 20.

SUCCESSION (SCOTLAND ONLY)

Endowment mortgages and law of succession (*G. L. Gretton*): (1987) 32 J.L.S. 303.

Insurance policies, securities and claims to legal rights (*A. M. C. Dalgleish*): (1987) 32 J.L.S. 423.

Succession—rights or discretion? (*M. C. Meston*): 1987 J.R. 1.

Tax effective executry administration: legal rights and capital gains tax (*E. M. Scobbie*): (1987) 32 J.L.S. 341.

Trust and executry conveyancing (*G. L. Gretton*): (1987) 32 J.L.S. 111.

TIME (SCOTLAND ONLY)

"Not later than" defined (considering *Main* v. *City of Glasgow District Licensing Board* [1987] C.L.Y. 4592) (*D. C. Coull*): 1987 S.L.T.(News) 353.

TORT (NOT SCOTLAND)

Accounting standards: a guide to negligence? (*D. Gwilliam*): (1986) 2 P.N. 175.

Are finders keepers? One hundred years since *Elwes* v. *Brigg Gas Co.* (*M. Nash*): 137 New L.J. 118.

Bradford football fire (*A. Macdonald*): 137 New L.J. 481.

Breach of statutory duty and the economic torts (*R. Townshend-Smith*): 137 New L.J. 371.

Carrier and the non-owning consignee—an inconsequential immunity (*A. Tettenborn*): (1987) J.B.L. 12.

Civil actions against the police: trespass to the person and defences (*R. Clayton and H. Tomlinson*): (1987) *Legal Action,* October 16.

Clarifying the justification plea (*A. Khan*): 131 S.J. 786.

Construction and product liability (*V. van Houtte*): (1987) 41 C.L.R. 126.

Consumer Protection Act 1987 (*J. Bradgate and N. Savage*): 137 New L.J. 929, 953.

Consumer Protection Act 1987 (*K. Cardwell*): 50 M.L.R. 622.

Consumer Protection Act 1987 (*A. Clarke*): 50 M.L.R. 614.

TORT (NOT SCOTLAND)—*cont.*

Containers "get up" and passing off (*M. Briffa*): 84 L.S.Gaz. 2444.

Contract and tort: looking across the boundary from the side of contract (*K. Mason*): 61 A.L.J. 228.

Contract and tort: stating the recent case law (*M. Duggan*): 131 S.J. 863.

Contributory negligence in contract and tort (*J. Logie*): 131 S.J. 929.

Curran case: a retreat from justice? (M. Arnheim): 131 S.J. 962.

Damage by tree roots (*D. Williams*): 84 L.S.Gaz. 638.

Defective products: successor company liability (*C. Bright*): 83 L.S.Gaz. 3423.

Derry v. *Peek* and negligence (*C. Reed*): 8 J.L.H. 64.

Developing the law of easements: the role of tort: (*A. Waite*): [1987] Conv. 47.

Environmental law—English developments (*A. de Grandis-Harrison*): 84 L.S.Gaz. 2180.

EEC product liability directive (*T. Trumpy*): 83 L.S.Gaz. 3740.

Expanding tort law—the price of a rigid contract law (*B. Markesinis*): 103 L.Q.R. 354.

Failure of medical advice: trespass or negligence? (*T. Feng*): (1987) L.S. 149.

Future of negligence in product liability (*C. Newdick*): 104 L.Q.R. 288.

Gypsies—a statutory nuisance? Consequent enforcement procedures (*G. Holgate*): 151 L.G.Rev. 485.

Industrial Injuries Scheme benefits compared to damages at common law (*R. Lewis*): 84 L.S.Gaz. 1378.

Industrial injury benefit and assessment of damages (*R. Lewis*): 84 L.S.Gaz. 1640.

Inexperience is no defence to negligent medical treatment (*D. Brahams*): 137 New L.J. 60.

Injustice finally remedied? (*I. Dickinson*): 137 New L.J. 435.

Latent damage (*R. Knowles*): 9 C.Q.S. 9.

Latent Damage Act 1986 (*H. Crowter*): 10 C.Q.S. 23.

Liability for the supply of defective software (*C. Brown*): (1986) 3 Comp. L. & P. 2.

Liability of regulatory and disciplinary bodies (*D. Feldman*): (1987) 3 P.N. 23.

Liability to trespassers—common humanity and superadded negligence (*E. Teh*): [1986] 2 M.L.J. lxxxviii.

Local authorities and defective houses (*J. Garner*): 130 S.J. 814.

Local authorities duty of care under Public Health Act 1936: 151 L.G.Rev. 605.

Loss of a chance in tort (*L. Anderson*): 131 S.J. 1258.

Loss without damages: the strange voyage of *The Aliakmon (R. Pearce and D. Tomkin*): 136 New L.J. 1169.

Medical injury—the fault with no-fault (*M. Jones*): (1987) 3 P.N. 83.

Mole's charter?: a review of recent public interest defence cases (*S. Bate*): 84 L.S.Gaz. 1048.

Natural drainage of land (*H. Wilkinson*): 137 New L.J. 867.

TORT (NOT SCOTLAND)—*cont.*

Negligence: liability and public safety (*T. Knowles*): 131 S.J. 388.

Negligent mortgage valuations again: (*S. Murdoch*): 282 E.G. 93.

Occupiers' liability: 280 E.G. 903, 1155.

Onus of proof of consent in an action for trespass to the person (*S. Blay*): 61 A.L.J. 25.

Patient autonomy and consent to treatment: the role of the law? (*M. Brazier*):(1987) L.S. 169.

Personal injury law reform: a proposed first step (*S. Sugarman*): 16 I.L.J. 30.

Pervasive but often not explicitly characterised aspect of passing off (*A. Walton*): [1987] 6 E.I.P.R. 159.

Policy/operational dichotomy—a cuckoo in the nest (*S. Bailey and M. Bowman*): [1986] C.L.J. 430.

Policy factors in actions for wrongful birth (*C. Symmons*): 50 M.L.R. 269.

Principles governing the recovery of damages for negligently caused nervous shock (*F. Trindade*): [1986] C.L.J. 476.

Proceeds of fraud: the bank's liability (*K. Stanton*): (1986) 2 P.N. 190.

Product liability and safety of goods (*B. Harvey*): 131 S.J. 1053.

Product liability—the new rules (*A. Clark*): 1987 S.L.T 257.

Recent developments in premises liability—I: (*J. Holyoak and D. Allen*): 137 New L.J. 203.

Recent developments—II: occupiers liability (*J. Holyoak and D. Allen*): 137 New L.J. 217.

Recent developments—III: local authorities (*J. Holyoak and D. Allen*): 137 New L.J. 299.

Recovery of purely economic loss in tort: some recent Canadian decisions (*N. Rafferty*): (1987) 3 P.N. 89.

Regulatory agencies and tort liability (*G. Holgate*): 151 L.G.Rev. 744.

Rise and fall of *Anns* (*L. McGarrity*): 137 New L.J. 794.

Solicitors' negligence in the preparation of wills (*A. Borkowski*): (1986) 2 P.N. 151.

Suing for negligent police investigations (*R. Clayton and H. Tomlinson*): 84 L.S.Gaz. 1798.

Suing hospitals direct: what tort? (*J. Montgomery*): 137 New L.J. 703.

Suing hospitals direct: whose tort was it anyhow? (*J. Bettle*): 137 New L.J. 573.

Surveyors' negligence—reflections on two recent cases (*S. Tromans*): (1986) 2 P.N. 171.

Theory and policy of shareholder actions in tort (*M. Sterling*): 50 M.L.R. 468.

Thieves and vandals in empty buildings: whose responsibility? (*R. Youngs*): 131 S.J. 1102.

Third party acts and the duty of care: 150 L.G.Rev. 828.

Tort liability for *ultra vires* decisions: *Takaro Properties Ltd.* v. *Rowling* (*S. Todd*): (1986) 2 P.N. 138.

TORT (NOT SCOTLAND)—*cont.*

Vicarious liability: some points for the practitioner (*R. Colbey*): 6 Lit. 244.

Weather, forecasting and "the limitless seas" (*D. Millington*): 104 L.Q.R. 234.

Wilsher v. *Essex AHA*—professional negligence again (*M. James*): 84 L.S.Gaz. 248.

Zeebrugge: is it a good offer? (*M. Arnheim*): 131 S.J. 606.

TOWN AND COUNTRY PLANNING

"Abandonment"—the current position (*P. Cooling*): 151 L.G.Rev. 266.

Amusement centres: the need for a policy (*B. Nelson*): [1987] L.G.C., January 30, 12.

Analysis of "stop notice" use in planning enforcement (*I. Bracken and J. Kingaby*): [1987] J.P.L. 538.

Archaeology and planning: a Welsh perspective (*J. Manley*): [1987] J.P.L. 552.

Award of expenses at planning inquiries: practice (*E. Young*): (1987) 32 J.L.S. 56.

"Chairman's action": the courts, the local ombudsman and the Widdicombe Committee (*M. Jones*): [1987] J.P.L. 612.

Challenging a planning decision: policy planning, prematurity and delay (*P. Needham and R. Morgan*): [1986] J.P.L. 803.

Challenging decisions (*A. Samuels*): [1986] J.P.L. 812.

Compensation—severance (*J. T. Aitken*): (1987) 22 S.P.L.P. 95.

Coping with leisure—leisure and amusement centres and leisure parks (*H. Wilkinson*): 136 New L.J. 1130.

Cost of planning appeals (*D. Williams*): 84 L.S.Gaz. 2432.

Development plans: what role for the law? (*S. Nott and P. Morgan*): [1986] J.P.L. 875.

Double effect in planning (*A. Samuels*): 151 L.G.Rev. 346.

Drafting planning agreements (*R. Hamilton*): 131 S.J. 34.

Dwelling-house use class (*R. Midgley*): [1987] J.P.L. 620.

Environmental impact assessment—proposal for paper mill (*M. J. Wrigley*): (1987) 22 S.P.L.P. 72.

Estoppel and development control counter service (*L. Rutherford, J. Peart* and *R. Pickard*): [1986] J.P.L. 891.

Extensions and limitations in the Housing and Planning Act (*D. Hender*): [1987] L.G.C., January 2, 8.

Fish and chips, *Cynon Valley* and the planning legislation (*C. Brand*): 136 New L.J. 1157.

Future for development plans? (*M. Bruton and D. Nicholson*): [1987] J.P.L. 687.

Future of development plans in Scotland (*H. M. Begg and S. H. A. Pollock*): (1987) 21 S.P.L.P. 40.

Future of the planning system (*A. Samuels*): 150 L.G.Rev. 811.

Historic buildings and conservation areas (*F. Bourne*): 84 L.S.Gaz. 2437.

Housing and Planning Act 1986 (*R. Hamilton*): 130 S.J. 906, 941.

ARTICLES

TOWN AND COUNTRY PLANNING—*cont.*

Housing and Planning Act 1986: 151 L.G.Rev. 44.

Is the burden to be lifted further? (*P. Cooling*): 151 L.G.Rev. 147.

Listed buildings: judicial pronouncements (*A. Samuels*): 151 L.G.Rev. 449.

Local enquiries and evaluation of objections: 151 L.G. Rev. 465.

Location of major retail developments (*G. Peart and T. J. Parke*): (1987) 21 S.P.L.P. 37.

Natural justice and the enforcement notice (*P. Cooling*): 84 L.S.Gaz. 21.

Need to advertise planning applications (*M. Edwards*): 84 L.S.Gaz. 2429.

Nemo index in sua causa? (considering *Tennant* v. *Houston* [1987] C.L.Y. 4173) (*P. W. Ferguson*): 1987 S.L.T. (News) 149.

New Use Classes Order (*M. Redman*): 282 E.G. 966.

No material change in use but material change in meaning (considering *City of Aberdeen District Council* v. *Secretary of State for Scotland* [1986] C.L.Y. 4739) (*S. L. Stuart*): 1987 S.L.T.(News) 44.

Ombudsman: inconsistency and maladministration in planning (*C. Himsworth*): (1987) 21 S.P.L.P. 61.

Planning agreements: s.52 agreements law and practice (*A. Samuels*): 151 L.G.Rev. 429.

Planning appeal costs (*A. Bowhill*): 84 L.S.Gaz. 2255.

Planning appeals (*A. Bowhill*): 84 L.S.Gaz. 1316.

Planning control in national parks: the new Special Development Order (*C. Brand*): 281 E.G. 762.

Planning law and the control of licensed premises (*J. Lannon*): [1987] J.P.L. 754.

Planning procedures (*J. Garner*): 131 S.J. 1306.

Private legislation procedure: A defence (*J. J. Rankin*): (1987) 20 S.P.L.P. 9.

Proposals to change planning inquiries (*B. Greenwood*): [1987] L.G.C., September 4, 1987, 8.

Purchase notices and minister's discretion (*E. Young*): 1987 S.L.T.(News) 273.

Purchase notices in practice (*E. Young*): 1987 S.L.T.(News) 269.

Question of class in town and country (*B. Denyer-Green*): 19 C.S.W. 57.

Scottish Civic Trust (*J. Gerrard*): (1987) 20 S.P.L.P. 10.

Servicing land development—the costs (*J. Rowan-Robinson and M. G. Lloyd*): (1987) 22 S.P.L.P. 69.

Sex establishments, licences and judicial review: 151 L.G.Rev. 369.

Shopping development policies (*P. Gibson*): (1987) 22 S.P.L.P. 75.

Some recent problems with section 52 agreements (*P. Smith*): 136 New L.J. 1144.

Stick no bills (*J. Vickers*): [1987] L.G.C., March 6, 1987, 12.

Stone-cleaning (*E. Young*): 283 E.G. 540.

TOWN AND COUNTRY PLANNING—*cont.*

Strategic and development planning: Scottish implications of English innovations (*U. A. Wannop*): (1987) 20 S.P.L.P. 8.

Town and Country Planning (Compensation for Restrictions on Mineral Workings) (Scotland) Regulations 1987 (*J. Rowan-Robinson*): (1987) 21 S.P.L.P. 42.

Use Classes Order—practical points for developers and investors (*I. Campbell*): 282 E.G. 1661.

Use of injunctions to enforce planning control (*W. Parkes*): [1986] J.P.L. 798.

What is a listed building? (*H. Wilkinson*): 137 New L.J. 358.

Where ignorance is bliss? (survey of conservation areas) (*C. T. Reid*): (1987) 20 S.P.L.P. 4.

TRADE AND INDUSTRY

Agency agreements and EEC competition law: some comfort from the EEC Commission (*S. Holmes*): 84 L.S.Gaz. 1052.

Banking agreements. Are they anti-competitive? (*J. Rosell*): (1987) 7 I.F.L.Rev. 11.

Blocking and clawback statutes: the United Kingdom approach (*L. Collins*): [1986] J.B.L. 452.

Bringing trading standards legislation nearer the local trader—*Riley v. Webb* (*I. Thomas*): 151 J.P.N. 631.

Commission's draft for a regulation exempting knowhow licensing agreements (*V. Korah*): (1987): 8 B.L.R. 198.

Competition law: mapping the minefield (*T. Frazer*): (1987) 3 Comp. L. & P. 199.

Competition policy in the 80's: more policy less competition? (*S. Hornsby*): 12 E.L.Rev. 79.

Confidential information in anti-dumping proceedings before United States courts and the European Court (*M. von Heydebrand und der Lasa*): 11 E.L.Rev. 331.

Countertrade on capital projects; problems of linkage (*E. Herzfeld*): [1987] J.B.L. 196.

Critical comments on the Commission's recent decisions exempting joint ventures to exploit research that needs further development (*V. Korah*): 12 E.L.Rev. 18.

Data protection in Europe (*J. Moakes*): [1986] 3 J.I.B.L. 143.

Defence of due diligence (*R. Lawson*): 151 J.P.N. 499.

Discrepancy of documents in letter of credit transactions (*C. Schmitthoff*): [1987] J.B.L. 94.

Distribution franchising under EEC law (*D. Fox*): 131 S.J. 378.

EEC law and selective distribution—recent developments (*G. Leigh*): [1986] E.C.L.R. 419.

Express covenant or implied term of confidentiality (*M. Jefferson*): (1987) 8 B.L.R. 8.

Fair spares for all (*P. Thornberry*): 131 S.J. 274.

Franchising—is there a need for a statutory code? (*D. Glass*): 84 L.S.Gaz. 14.

TRADE AND INDUSTRY—*cont.*

Franchising: the Commission issues a draft block exemption regulation (*M. Mendelsohn*): 84 L.S.Gaz. 2842.

Freedom of trade under the common law and European Community law: the case of the football bans (*A. Evans*): 102 L.Q.R. 510.

Information in EEC competition law procedures (*J. Joshua*): (1986) 11 E.L.Rev. 409.

International business and choice of law (*I. Baxter*): 36 I.C.L.Q. 92.

Joint ventures—an analysis of commission decisions (*J. M. Claydon*): [1986] E.C.L.R. 151.

Legal aspects of factoring (*H. Kee*): [1986] M.L.J. ccxl.

Merger control by the E.C. Commission (*W. Elland*): [1987] E.C.L.R. 163.

Mergers: the European dimension (*W. Elland*): 84 L.S.Gaz. 2338.

Misleading prices (*B. Harvey*): 131 S.J. 1076.

More protection for consumers? (*B. Harvey*): 131 S.J. 150.

Motor vehicle distribution: the block exemption (*P. Groves*): [1987] E.C.L.R. 77.

Need for a business, as well as a reputation in the U.K. (*R. Mallows*): (1987) 8 B.L.R. 3.

Never on a Sunday? (*A. Khan*): 131 S.J. 646.

New wave self-help organisations (*I. Swinney*): (1987) 126 SCOLAG 37.

Non-market economy rules of the European Community's anti-dumping and countervailing duties legislation (*R. Denton*): 36 I.C.L.Q. 198.

Part III of the Fair Trading Act; consumer protection or bureaucratic red tape (*P. Circus*): (1987) 8 B.L.R. 26.

Payment under a letter of credit (*P. Chai*): [1987] M.L.J. lxi.

Performance bonds—irrevocable obligations (*M. Lawson*): [1987] J.B.L. 259.

Predation (*T. Sharpe*): [1987] E.C.L.R. 53.

Predatory pricing and entry deterring strategies: the economics of *Akzo* (*R. Rapp*): [1986] E.C.L.R. 233.

Predatory pricing or competitive pricing: establishing the truth in English and EEC law (*R. Merkin*): 7 O.J.L.S. 182.

Private sellers and the Trade Descriptions Act: 1986 S.L.T. 341.

Privatising nationalised industries: constitutional issues and new legal techniques (*C. Graham and T. Prosser*): 50 M.L.R. 16.

Procedure in anti-dumping investigations (*K. Lasok*): [1987] E.C.L.R. 143.

Product and technical standardisation under Article 85 (*A. Vollmer*): [1986] E.C.L.R. 388.

Product contamination—the commercial implications (*S. Watson*): (1987) 8 B.L.R. 142.

Protection of life and health (*R. Bragg*): [1987] L.G.C., April 24, 1987, 10.

Registration alternative (*S. Jones*): (1986) Ins.L. & P. 165.

TRADE AND INDUSTRY—*cont.*

Regulation of financial services—an overview (*T. Ashe*): 84 L.S.Gaz. 1392.

Relationships between competitors under United Kingdom competition law (*M. Howe*): [1986] E.C.L.R. 327.

Second-hand car dealers and the Trade Descriptions Act 1968 (*A. Samuels*): (1986) 5 Tr.L. 324.

Security for payments under major overseas projects (*E. Herzfeld*): [1986] J.B.L. 446.

Selective distribution agreements: renewal of exemptions (*D. Fox*): 131 S.J. 1105.

Single European Act and free movement (*N. Forwood and M. Clough*): (1986) 11 E.L.Rev. 383.

Towards a general duty to trade fairly? (*P. Circus*): 136 New L.J. 1043.

Trade associations: time to lift the antitrust burden (*P. Groves*): (1987) 8 B.L.R. 61.

Trading fairly: would a "general duty" help? (*K. Puttick*): (1986) 7 B.L.R. 299.

Trust, corporation and the worker (*Lord Wedderburn*): 23 Osgoode Hall L.J. 203.

U.K. competition law: a case for radical reform (*M. Carlisle*): (1987) 8 B.L.R. 24.

U.K. competition law: a case for radical review (*M. Carlisle*): (1987) 8 B.L.R. 24.

TRADE MARKS AND TRADE NAMES

Containers "get up" and passing off (*M. Briffa*): 84 L.S.Gaz. 2444.

EEC trade mark legislation (*P. Groves*): (1987) B.L.R. 51.

Need for a business, as well as a reputation in the U.K. (*R. Mallows*): (1987) 8 B.L.R. 3.

Parasitic use of the commercial magnetism of a trade mark on non-competing goods (*F. Mostert*): [1986] 11 E.I.P.R. 342.

Pervasive but often not explicitly characterised aspect of passing off (*A. Walton*): [1987] 6 E.I.P.R. 159.

Registration of service marks (*S. Coleman*): 83 L.S.Gaz. 3406.

Service marks—some comments on the new Registry Work Manual (*K. Hodkinson*): [1987] 3 E.I.P.R. 73.

What is a trade mark?—a challenge to the House of Lords (*M. Franzosi*): [1987] 3 E.I.P.R. 63.

TRADE UNIONS

Aspects of industrial action—reasons and remedies for sit-ins (*S. Croall*): 137 New L.J. 918.

Collective labour law (*R. Benedictus*): 137 New L.J. 741.

Emergence of a new labour injunction? (*K. Ewing and A. Grubb*): 16 I.L.J. 145.

Industrial action and payment of wages (*B. Napier*): 131 S.J. 1230.

Public sector unions and political advertising: 151 L.G.Rev. 607.

Strike ballots: breaking in the Trojan horse (*S. Bloxham*): [1986] VIII Liverpool L.R. 131.

Strikes and the individual worker—reforming the law (*B. Napier*): [1987] C.L.J. 287.

TRADE UNIONS—*cont.*
Suing a trade union (*J. Bowers*): 6 Lit. 53.
Trade union law (*R. Benedictus and D. Newell*): 137 New L.J. 771.
Trade unions: further legislative changes (*K. Miller*): 1987 S.L.T.(News) 213.
Trade unions and their members (*F. P. Davidson*): (1987) 126 SCOLAG 41.
Union rule book and the miners' strike 1984–85 (*K. Miller*): 1986 J.R. 210.

TRANSPORT
Taxi Law (*A. Samuels*): 151 L.G.Rev. 828.
Tolley's National Insurance Contributions 1987–88.—By N. D. Booth [Fourth edition]. Paperback: £16·95: ISBN 0 85459 275 X.
Transport Act—practical difficulties for authorities (*B. Hinton*): [1987] L.G.C., August 21, 12.

TRESPASS (NOT SCOTLAND)
Councils face legal problems on hippies (*J. Whitcutt*): [1987] L.G.C. July 3, 12.
Failure of medical advice: trespass or negligence? (*T. Feng*): (1987) L.S. 149.
Gypsies—a statutory nuisance? Consequent enforcement procedures (*G. Holgate*): 151 L.G.Rev. 485.

TRUSTS (SCOTLAND ONLY)
Recognition of Trusts Act 1987 (*A. E. Anton*): 1987 S.L.T.(News) 377.
Trust and executry conveyancing (*G. L. Gretton*): (1987) 32 J.L.S. 111.
Trusts and floating charges (considering *Tay Valley Joinery* v. *C. F. Financial Services* [1987] C.L.Y. 5215) (*K. G. C. Reid*): 1987 S.L.T.(News) 113.
Trusts for animals (*K. McK. Norrie*): (1987) 32 J.L.S. 386.

VALUE ADDED TAX
Are VAT tribunals fair? (*H. Mainprice*): 118 Tax. 285.
Carry on planning (*C. Tailby*): 118 Tax. 127.
Chase the lady (*H. Mainprice*): 119 Tax. 493.
Community law (*E. Hoskin*): 119 Tax. 13.
Disaggregation of businesses (*C. Tailby*): 119 Tax. 339.

VALUE ADDED TAX—*cont.*
Errors of omission (*E. Hoskin*): 119 Tax. 115.
Finance Act 1986 (*A. Shipwright*): 130 S.J. 912.
Insurance commissions (*V. Durkacz*) 119 Tax. 436.
Mergers and acquisitions (*V. Durkacz*): 120 Tax. 56.
No right of appeal? (*E. Haskin*): 118 Tax. 292.
Partial exemption revisited (*V. Duckacz*): 118 Taxation 496.
VAT comes of age (*E. Hoskin*): 119 Tax. 482.
Value Added Tax (*J. Clark*): 136 New L.J. 1063.
Value added tax investigations (*D. Kelsey*): 119 Tax. 253.

WATER AND WATERWORKS
Natural drainage of land (*H. Wilkinson*): 137 New L.J. 867.

WILLS (SCOTLAND ONLY)
Execution of deeds (*K. G. C. Reid*): (1987) 32 J.L.S. 148.
Trust and executry conveyancing (*G. L. Gretton*): (1987) 32 J.L.S. 111.

WILLS AND SUCCESSION
Inheritance (Provision for Family and Dependants) Act 1975—Precautions and pitfalls (*J. Ross Martyn*): 83 L.S. Gaz. 3571.
Providing for mentally handicapped members of the family: 2 (*G. Ashton*): *Legal Action*, April 1987, 16.
Solicitors' negligence in the preparation of wills (*A. Borkowski*): (1986) 2 P.N. 151.
Substantial compliance and the execution of wills (*J. Miller*): 36 I.C.L.Q. 559.
Update on wills and trusts (*R. Oerton*): 131 S.J. 649.
Will to disinherit the Revenue (*D. de Pass and M. Gunn*): 120 Tax. 77.
Wills and the Methodist Church Act 1976 (*S. Marples*): 84 L.S.Gaz. 2278.
Wills and trusts update (*D. Cracknell*): 131 S.J. 1344.

INDEX 1987

References are to the Year Book and then the paragraph number, e.g. 87/1122 means para. 1122 in the Current Law Year Book 1987.

For references to pre-1972 material, see the Index to the Current Law Year Book 1976. The Index for the years 1972–86 may be found in the 1986 Year Book.

Abolition of Domestic Rates Etc. (Scotland) Act 1987 (c.47), 87/3156
Access to Personal Files Act 1987 (c.37), 87/304
Administering Noxious Thing
intent to injure, 87/751
Administration of Estates. *See* **Executors and Administrators**
Administrative Law, 87/1–54
judicial review. *See* **Judicial Review**
legitimate expectation doctrine, 87/20
library authorities,
powers, 87/29
local ombudsman, 87/17
mental health tribunal, 87/48
ministerial undertaking, 87/3784
mistake of fact, 87/31
natural justice, 87/32, 34–36, 38, 40, 42, 1310, 1970, 2026, 2463, 3644, 3645, 3697
Parliamentary and Health Service Commissioners Act 1987 (c.39), 87/44
Parliamentary Commissioner, 87/45
parole system, 87/993
passport, refusal to issue, 87/47
refugee, 87/1988, 1989
Adoption
access by natural parents, 87/2441
benefit to child, 87/2443
court hearing,
attendance by minor, 87/2445
custodianship as an alternative, 87/2448
exclusion of a natural parent, 87/2444
foster parents, 87/2451
parental consent, 87/2446, 2447, 2449, 2452, 2453
surrogacy agreement, 87/2450
transfer of business, 87/3117
Agency, 87/55–70
air travel agency, 87/174
broker, 87/427
estate agents,
commission, 87/60, 61, 63
deposit, 87/62
undisclosed principal, 87/64
liquidator,
conversion, 87/3585
non-existent principal, 87/1126
powers of attorney, 87/58, 59, 67
retrocession agreement, 87/2075
shipbrokers,
commission, 87/68
soil survey, 87/69
tour operators, 87/70
Agricultural Holdings
arbitration, 87/73
assignment of tenancy by agent, 87/1445
grazing agreement, 87/75
rent, 87/76, 77
units of production, 87/72
Agricultural Training Board Act 1987 (c.29), 87/78
Agriculture, 87/71–101
agricultural de-rating, 87/3157
agricultural holdings. *See* **Agricultural Holdings**
Agricultural Training Board Act 1987 (c.29), 87/78
cereals, 87/80
dairy produce quota tribunal decisions,
milk quotas, 87/81
eggs, 87/1458
environmentally sensitive areas, 87/83
farms, 87/84
heather and grass burning, 87/85
hill farming, 87/86
improvement regulations, 87/87
levy reliefs, 87/1101
Meat and Livestock Commission, 87/89
milk. *See also* **Food and Drugs**
quotas, 87/90–92
olive oil, 87/93
plant breeders, 87/95
plant health, 87/96
potatoes, 87/97
seeds, 87/98
sheep and goats, 87/99
tractors, 87/100
wine, 87/1466
AIDS (Control) Act 1987 (c.33), 87/2545
Animals, 87/102–118
Animals (Scotland) Act 1987 (c.9), 87/102
artificial insemination, 87/104
bees, 87/105
coypus, 87/106
cruelty, 87/107
Deer Act 1987 (c.28), 87/108
diseases, 87/109
importation, 87/110
mink, 87/111
pigs,
movement and sale, 87/112
Protection of Animals (Penalties) Act 1987 (c.35), 87/113
sheep, 87/114
special protection areas, 87/103
trespass, 87/115
warble fly, 87/116
wildlife,
possession of live birds, 87/117
setting poisoned substance, 87/118
Animals (Scotland) Act 1987 (c.9), 87/102
Anton Piller
counterfeiting, 87/2883
serious non-disclosure, 87/2884
use of documents, 87/2885
Appropriation Act 1987 (c.17), 87/3205
Appropriation (No. 2) Act 1987 (c.50), 87/3206
Arbitration , 87/119–157
appeal,
extension of time, 87/121

Arbitration—*cont.*
arbitrator
fees, 87/124
award,
costs, 87/127
enforcement, 87/126
prior payment,
interest on, 87/143
remission, 87/125
"Centrocon" arbitration clause, 87/128
clause,
application, 87/132
delay in proceedings, 87/133
dispute at date of contract, 87/140
estoppel *per rem judicatum*, 87/137
European Contract for Coffee Terms, 87/130
foreign arbitration awards, 87/134
forum, 87/135
fraud alleged, 87/414
international arbitration, 87/2081
JCT Minor Works contract, 87/139
judgment, amendment to, 87/141
limitation of time, 87/3380
misconduct, 87/119, 120
name-borrowing, 87/144
procedure,
application for joinder, 87/157
reasoned award, 87/145, 146
reference, 87/147, 2908
rent review, 87/150, 2201, 2202
retrocession agreement, 87/2074
salvage arbitration, 87/3367
scope of matters referred, 87/152
stay of action, 87/123, 154–157
time bar, 87/136
Armed Forces, 87/158–167
air force,
rules of procedure, 87/158
Air Force Act 1955, 87/160
Army Act 1955, 87/160
Crown Proceedings (Armed Forces) Act 1987 (c.25), 87/161
injuries in war, 87/162
Naval Discipline Act 1957, 87/160
Protection of Military Remains Act 1986, Guernsey Order, 87/164
Royal Marines Museum, 87/2341
standing civilian courts, 87/167
Assault
consent, 87/754
self defence, 87/753
wrongful imprisonment, 87/755
Associations. *See* **Clubs and Associations**
Atomic Energy, 87/168–170
British Nuclear Fuels, 87/168
nuclear installations, 87/169
nuclear weapons testing,
Crown immunity, 87/2569
Attempt
child abduction, 87/765
criminal damage, 87/757
gross indecency, 87/760
test, 87/758
theft, 87/759
Aviation, 87/171–182
aerodromes, 87/171
air navigation, 87/172
air transport licence, 87/173
air travel agent, 87/174
aircraft movement, 87/175
airport licensing, 87/2308
airport shops, 87/3448

Aviation—*cont.*
carriage by air. *See* **Carriers**
civil aviation, 87/179
designation, 87/180
government shareholding, 87/181
protection of aircraft, 87/182

Bail
absconding, 87/592
estreatment, 87/593
failure to surrender to custody, 87/2910
recognisance, 87/595, 596
Bailment, 87/183–184
sub-bailment, 87/184
vehicle in car park, 87/183
Banking, 87/185–205
advertising, 87/185
Asian Development Bank, 87/186
Banking Act 1987 (c.22), 87/190
bills of exchange, 87/192
cheque,
assignment, 87/187
triable issue, 87/194
wrongfully dishonoured, 87/193
commodity brokers, 87/195
disclosure of information, 87/196
duty of care, 87/198, 2576
equitable set-off, 87/199
exempt transactions, 87/200
freezing of assets, 87/201
letters of credit,
discrepant documents, 87/202
fraud, 87/203
National Savings Bank, 87/204
savings banks. *See* **Savings Banks**
security, 87/1423
Banking Act 1987 (c.22), 87/190
Bankruptcy, 87/206–215
assignment of cause of action, 87/206
authorised insolvency practitioners,
annual directory, 87/207
bankruptcy notice, 87/208
debtor,
inquiry into dealings,
summons, 87/209
order for sale, 87/212
practice notes, 87/2912–2914
subordinate legislation, 87/214
voluntary arrangement, 87/215
Betting, Gaming and Lotteries. *See* **Gaming and Wagering**
Billiards (Abolition of Restrictions) Act 1987 (c.19), 87/1832
Blackmail
demand for medicine, 87/761
menaces, 87/762
Breach of the Peace
constable's belief, 87/819
British Commonwealth, 87/216–221
Alderney, 87/216
Bermuda, 87/217
Cayman Islands, 87/218
Commonwealth development corporation, 87/219
Dominica, 87/1819
Jamaica, 87/688
Mauritius, 87/1821
St. Helena, 87/220
Trinidad and Tobago, 87/3678
Turks and Caicos Islands, 87/221
British Shipbuilders (Borrowing Powers) Act 1987 (c.52), 87/3729

Broadcasting Act 1987 (c.10), 87/3572
Building and Construction, 87/222–245
architects, 87/223, 1471, 2573
builder,
negligence, 87/241
building contract, 87/225
building contractor,
duty to supervise sub-contractor, 87/3582
building regulations, 87/227, 228
consultant engineers,
duties, 87/233
defective drains, 87/229
defective foundations, 87/2584
design liabilities, 87/231
disabled people, 87/232
JCT Minor Works contract,
dispute, 87/139
JCT 1980 Form, 87/235
JCT standard form,
damages, 87/240
dispute at date of contract, 87/140
final certificate, 87/237
set-off, 87/239
local authorities,
negligence, 87/241, 242
NFBTE/FASS contract, 87/144, 244
price adjustment clause, 87/245
Building Societies, 87/246–267
aggregation rules, 87/246
annual accounts, 87/247
appeal tribunal, 87/248
banking institutions, 87/249
Building Societies Act 1986, 87/250, 251
business premises, 87/252
charges and fees, 87/253
credit facilities, 87/254
disclosure prescribed bands, 87/256
income tax, 87/2006, 2007
investor protection scheme, 87/258
Isle of Man, 87/259
Jersey, 87/260
liquid assets, 87/261
mergers, 87/262
non-retail funds and deposits, 87/263
penson companies, designation, 87/255
prescribed contracts, 87/264
qualifying bodies, 87/266
residential use, 87/267
services, provision of, 87/265
Burglary,
alternative verdict, 87/763
Burial and Cremation, 87/268
Protection of Military Remains Act 1986,
Guernsey Order, 87/164

Capital Gains Tax, 87/269–282
annual exempt amount, 87/269
assessment,
error as to year, 87/270
business assets, 87/271
disposal of shares, 87/272, 273
extra-statutory concession, 87/274
gilt-edged securities, 87/275
machinery and plant, 87/276
non-competition covenant, 87/277
option, 87/278
private residence, 87/279, 280
share exchange, 87/281
tax avoidance scheme, 87/282
Capital Taxation
capital gains tax. *See* **Capital Gains Tax**
capital transfer tax. *See* **Capital Transfer Tax**
Capital Transfer Tax, 87/283–285
associated operations, 87/284
interest on unpaid tax, 87/2049
settlement, 87/284, 285
Caravans and Mobile Homes
gipsy encampments, 87/3642
pitch fee, 87/1893
private gipsy caravan site,
renewal of temporary permission, 87/3712
rates, 87/3177
stationed on agricultural holding, 87/3635
stationed on grazing land, 87/3641
winter storage of caravans,
planning permission, 87/3668
Carriers, 87/286–291
carriage by air,
jurisdiction, 87/286
carriage by road,
limitation period, 87/2325
perishable foodstuffs, 87/3255
carriage by sea, 87/3377
bill of lading, 87/3378, 3379
limitation of time, 87/291, 3380
subcontract for carriage, 87/290
Channel Tunnel Act 1987 (c.53), 87/3776
Charities, 87/292–300
annual report of Charity Commissioners, 87/292
enforcement of trust, 87/293
exemptions, 87/294
investment powers, 87/295
public charitable trust,
action by Attorney General, 87/2323
supervision, 87/298
tax benefits, 87/299, 300, 2011, 3803
Charterparty
berth charterparty, 87/3405
bill of lading,
laytime, 87/3382
demurrage, 87/3884, 3423
currency exchange loss, 87/3399
delay due to swell, 87/3383
freight,
payment for, 87/3385
repudiation, 87/3386
safe berth warranty, 87/3387
time charter,
domestic consumption clause, 87/3429
guarantee, 87/1846
liability for damage, 87/3431
speed and performance clause, 87/3432
warranty, 87/3433
voyage charter,
cesser clause, 87/3445
delay, 87/3435
demurrage, 87/3436–3440, 3447
freight, 87/3441, 3442
remuneration, 87/3446
short delivery, 87/3443
stowage, 87/3444
Cheating the Public Revenue
ingredients of offence, 87/764
Chevening Estate Act 1987 (c.20), 87/1421
Child Abduction
"lawful control", 87/765
Civil Defence, 87/301–303
international headquarters and defence organisations, 87/301
reimbursement of expenses, 87/302
visiting forces, 87/303
Civil Liberties
Access to Personal Files Act 1987 (c.37), 87/304

Clubs and Associations, 87/306–314
standing orders, 87/306
unincorporated associations, 87/307, 310, 312, 313, 1676, 2092, 2093, 3121
Coal Industry Act 1987 (c.3), 87/2428
Commencement Orders
see dates of commencement table
Commons, 87/315–316
recreation ground, 87/316
waste land, 87/315
Company Law, 87/317–385
assets, disposition of, 87/337
auditors, 87/318
bribery, 87/320
charges, registration of, 87/361
charitable company, 87/321
debenture, 87/326
directors,
disqualification, 87/330–333
exclusion of, 87/353
fiduciary duty, 87/334
fraudulent preference, 87/328
misconduct and incompetence, 87/1379
secret agreement, 87/317
secret profit, 87/335
theft, 87/838
dissolution of company, 87/338
forms, 87/339
insolvency. *See* **Insolvency**
liability after settlement, 87/364
liquidator, 87/344, 362
loans, 87/345
mergers and divisions, 87/346
minority shareholders, 87/347–351
Prescription (Scotland) Act 1987 (c.36), 87/352
receivers. *See* **Receivers**
reduction of capital, 87/359
register of members, 87/360
rights issue, 87/363
share capital, 87/365
shares,
pre-emption, 87/366
restrictions on dealing, 87/367
title reservation, 87/369
transfer within EEC, 87/1479
ultra vires, 87/370
unfair prejudice,
exclusion from management, 87/348
locus standi to petition, 87/349
requirements for petition, 87/371
sale by directors, 87/336
shareholder's private capacity, 87/347
winding up. *See* **Insolvency**
Compulsory Purchase, 87/386–396
compensation,
assessment date, 87/387
valuation,
restrictive covenant, 87/386
confirmation of order, 87/388–390
lands tribunal decisions,
compensation, 87/391–394
rate of interest after entry, 87/395
valuation, 87/396
Conflict of Laws, 87/397–409
choice of law rules,
marriage, 87/2275
divorce,
stay of proceedings, 87/399, 1717
domicile, 87/401, 2266
droit moral, recognition of, 87/406
foreign judgment, enforcement of, 87/402
forum conveniens, 87/3012, 3024
Conflict of Laws—*cont.*
marital status, 87/405
reciprocal enforcement,
maintenance orders, 87/407
reinsurance contract, 87/2567
sequestration, 87/409
Consolidated Fund Act 1987 (c.8), 87/3208
Consolidated Fund (No. 2) Act 1987 (c.54), 87/3209
Consolidated Fund (No. 3) Act 1987 (c.55), 87/3210
Conspiracy
conspiracy to defraud, 87/2258
direction to jury, 87/725
Constitutional Law
Ministers, transfer of functions, 87/410
Construction. *See* **Building and Construction**
Consumer Credit, 87/411
exempt agreements, 87/411
Consumer Protection
asbestos products, 87/3313
bunk beds, 87/3314
Consumer Protection Act 1987 (c.43), 87/3583
contracts concluded away from business premises, 87/3315
cosmetic products, 87/3316
home buyers, 87/2259
nightwear, 87/3317
plugs and sockets, 87/3318
safety of product,
defence of all reasonable precautions, 87/3321
safety standards, 87/3319
toys, benzene in, 87/3320
Consumer Protection Act 1987 (c.43), 87/3583
Contempt
arrest, 87/2935
breach of non-molestation injunction, 87/2924, 2926, 2927, 2933
committal,
defective order, 87/2932
imprisonment, 87/2929
nature of proceedings, 87/2931
proceedings in defendant's absence, 87/2928, 2930, 2933
purpose of, 87/2936
standard of proof, 87/2931
failure to surrender to bail, 87/617
journalist,
refusal to disclose source of information, 87/2934
publication of confidential information, 87/2923
standard of proof, 87/2937
trade union, 87/2938
witness,
intimidation of, 87/618
Contract, 87/412–457
accord and satisfaction, 87/412, 413
breach,
employment contract, 87/1301
mitigation of loss, 87/415
oral contract, 87/3132
repudiation, 87/419
tour operator, 87/418, 1130
breach of confidence, 87/1293–1295
construction,
joint venture agreement, 87/422
liability for claims, 87/423, 424
Consumer Protection Act 1987 (c.43), 87/3583
contra proferentem rule, 87/425
contract of affreightment, 87/427, 428

Contract—*cont.*
course of dealings, 87/430
covenant against competition, 87/431
enforcement, 87/432, 433
fraud alleged,
arbitration clause, 87/414
hire, 87/434
illegality, 87/1826
international body, 87/2092
JCT standard form, 87/140, 438
leasing agreement, 87/439
letter of comfort, 87/440
licence of property,
implied term as to fitness, 87/441
Minors' Contracts Act 1987 (c.13), 87/442
mixing of goods, 87/443
negotiations, 87/444
onerous condition, 87/445
oral contract,
existence, 87/3132
personal influence, 87/421
pre-incorporation contract, 87/446
public policy, 87/432
repayment term, 87/448
repudiation, 87/450, 3386
rescission, 87/447
retention of title, 87/451
sale of land, 87/452
secret profit, 87/454
terms, 87/455
undue influence, 87/456, 457
Contributory Negligence. *See* **Negligence**
Conveyancing, 87/458–495
beneficial interest,
contradictory expressions in conveyance, 87/494
contributions, 87/459
"commonhold," 87/2257
consumer protection for home buyers, 87/2259
covenants,
breach,
measure of damages, 87/452
validation by statute, 87/463
delays, 87/2260
deposit,
forfeiture of, 87/465
documents,
privilege, 87/712
fraudulent misrepresentation, 87/1826
joint tenants,
fraudulent forgery of signature, 87/470
fraudulent legal charge, 87/471
leasehold property,
rescission, 87/477
licensed conveyancers, 87/478
misrepresentation, 87/479
purchase money, 87/480
purchase price, 87/481
Register of Sasines (Scotland) Act 1987 (c.23), 87/482
registration of land. *See* **Land Registration**
rights of access, 87/458
Scottish system,
availability in England and Wales, 87/491
time of the essence, 87/489
title on death, 87/2261
title to land, 87/492
vacant possession, 87/2189
Copyright, 87/496–531
business name,
goodwill, 87/531

Copyright—*cont.*
collective works,
France, 87/496, 504
computer software, 87/497
incitement to commit offence, 87/501
infringement,
artistic works, 87/502
boat hulls, 87/503
book title, 87/530
collective works, 87/504
computer programs, 87/505
damages, 87/523
delay in prosecution, 87/514
droit moral, 87/406
film, 87/500
indirect copying, 87/507, 508
interlocutory injunction, 87/506, 509, 510
LEGO toys, 87/511, 515
mould, 87/512
registered design, 87/515
representative action, 87/519
right of action, 87/516
settlement, 87/518
song parody, 87/513
title and format of diary, 87/520
video games, 87/521
international conventions, 87/524
licence agreement, 87/499
National Library of Wales, 87/2342
owner's rights, 87/498
passing off, 87/530
registered designs,
Belgium, 87/525
service outside jurisdiction, 87/517
Singapore, 87/526, 527
subsistence of, 87/528
Taiwan,
extension orders, 87/529
Coroners, 87/532–540
death by misadventure and accidental death, 87/532
inquest, 87/535–537
jury,
direction to, 87/533, 534
lack of care, 87/534
recommendation, 87/538
post mortem, 87/539
statistics of deaths, 87/540
Corporation Tax, 87/541–555
appeal remitted,
fresh evidence, 87/541
burden of proof, 87/541
capital allowances, 87/542–544
Development Land Tax, 87/307
double taxation relief, 87/545
foreign exchange losses, 87/546
jurisdiction, 87/549
Schedule D, 87/548
tax avoidance, 87/2038
trade,
employees' trusts, 87/551
profits, 87/550a–555
Costs
appeal, 87/2939
assessment by registrar, 87/2940
county court, 87/2965, 2966
criminal cases, 87/627–630, 671, 2282
discretion of court,
costs not yet incurred, 87/2942
discretionary order, 87/2943
expert witness, 87/2946
in lieu of taxed costs, 87/2948

Costs—*cont.*
industrial tribunal, 87/3018
injunction, 87/2944
legal aid fund, 87/2949
"on cost", 87/2947
security for costs, 87/2950–2954
solicitors' delay, 87/2955
solicitors' liability, 87/2962, 3547
taxation, 87/1710, 2956, 2957, 2959, 2960, 3010, 3106
unreasonable conduct, 87/2961
County Court Practice. *See* **Practice**
Criminal Damage
intention to endanger life, 87/770
recklessness, 87/771
Criminal Evidence and Procedure, 87/556–750
adjournment, 87/556, 658
admissibility,
certificate of alcohol level, 87/647
computer evidence, 87/558
confession, 87/559–561, 613, 614
convictions of others, 87/562
depositions, 87/563
detention without access to solicitor, 87/564, 565
fresh evidence, 87/541
hearsay, 87/568–570
indecent motive, 87/665
L-driver unsupervised, 87/577
letters, 87/681
photofit picture, 87/571
police acting *mala fide*, 87/572
police notes of interview, 87/573
police observation log, 87/574
previous assault, 87/576
previous convictions, 87/710
procedure in magistrates' court, 87/575
rejection of officer's evidence, 87/557
statement on previous occasion, 87/567
video recording, 87/743
aide memoire, 87/578
alibi, 87/597
alternative verdicts, 87/579
anonymity of victim, 87/580
appeals,
abandonment, 87/581
absence of appellant, 87/583
divisional court, 87/582
rules, 87/584
summing-up defective, 87/585
arrest,
procedure, 87/587
validity, 87/588
assault,
private prosecution, 87/589
autrefois acquit, 87/591
bail. *See* **Bail**
barrister,
conduct of case, 87/597
binding over, 87/599–601, 683, 2254
burden of proof, 87/602
byelaws,
validity, 87/603
case stated, 87/604
character, 87/605
charging order,
drug trafficking, 87/723
child abuse, 87/2470–2476
co-accused,
admissibility of guilty plea, 87/619
committal proceedings, 87/608, 609

Criminal Evidence and Procedure—*cont.*
comparative sentences, 87/610
confession,
breach of code of conduct, 87/611
contempt. *See* **Contempt**
conviction,
magistrate did not hear evidence, 87/1821
under section not prosecuted, 87/716
coroners. *See* **Coroners**
corroboration, 87/620–626
costs. *See* **Costs**
Court of Appeal,
Home Secretary's reference, 87/720
jurisdiction, 87/631
criminal damage assessment of value, 87/632
Criminal Injuries Compensation Board, 87/633, 654
Criminal Justice Act 1987 (c.38), 87/634
Criminal Justice (Scotland) Act 1987 (c.41), 87/636
cross-examination, 87/637, 638
Crown Court,
practice direction, 87/639
time limit, 87/640
Crown prosecution service, 87/641
custody time limits, 87/642
deception, proof of, 87/701
defence, 87/643
diminished responsibility,
duty to raise defence, 87/698
direction to convict, 87/700
disclosure of records, 87/2530
dismissal for want of prosecution,
judicial review, 87/645
duress, 87/648
election for trial, 87/649
evidential burden,
gross indecency, 87/590
expert evidence, 87/650
fine, refusal to pay, 87/721
forfeiture, 87/655
further evidence, 87/656
guilty plea by post, 87/657
identification, 87/663
identification parades, 87/664
indictment, 87/666–668
information,
duplicity of charge, 87/669, 670
laid out of time, 87/671
joint defendants, 87/695
joint enterprise, 87/632
judicial review. *See* **Judicial Review**
justices,
awareness of previous convictions, 87/674
bias, 87/677
identity of, 87/679
proceeding *in camera*, 87/675
size and chairmanship of bench, 87/676
validity of by-laws, jurisdiction to determine, 87/678
warrant of commitment, 87/680
magisterial law,
adjournment, 87/682
binding over, 87/683
costs, 87/629
criminal damage, 87/685
"cross-remanding", 87/686
detention without charge, 87/687
guilty plea, 87/693
jurisdiction, 87/688
mode of trial, change of, 87/684

Criminal Evidence and Procedure—*cont.*
magisterial law—*cont.*
plea, 87/689
potential witness,
nature of evidence, 87/690
summons, 87/691
triable either way, 87/692
majority verdicts, 87/694
material irregularity, 87/696
mixed statement, 87/732
murder trial, 87/699
offshore activities, jurisdiction, 87/702
oral admission of judgment, 87/703
part-heard case,
justices' discretion, 87/704
perjured evidence, 87/717
petty sessional divisions, 87/705
police powers, 87/706, 707
practice direction,
Crown Court business, 87/639
wards,
Criminal Injuries Commission Board, 87/653
witness in criminal proceedings, 87/654
written statements, 87/750
press and public,
exclusion of, 87/675
press photographs, 87/708
previous consistent statement, 87/709
previous convictions, 87/710
private prosecution, 87/589
privilege, 87/711
conveyancing documents, 87/712
probation areas, 87/713
prohibition on publication, 87/675
prosecution,
evidence, 87/715
failure to prove case, 87/652
second address to jury, 87/714
provocation, 87/718
rape,
cross-examination, 87/637, 638
recent possession, doctrine of, 87/646
direction to jury, 87/2103
recognisance, 87/604
request to change counsel, 87/722
res gestae, 87/647, 659
research bulletin, 87/951
research programme, 87/786
restraint order,
drug trafficking, 87/723
service of documents, 87/724
severance of counts on indictment, 87/725
similar fact, 87/727, 728
social security fraud, 87/701
special procedure material, 87/729–731
statistics,
cautions and court proceedings, 87/733
criminal cases in magistrates' courts, 87/735
summing-up, 87/585, 736–738
surveillance vehicle, 87/715
tape recordings, 87/739, 740
theft,
standard of proof, 87/741
unanimity direction, 87/742
view of scene, 87/744
warrant of commitment, 87/680
warrant to arrest, 87/587
warrants, backing of, 87/747
witness,
affected by drugs, 87/749
competence of, 87/748
hostile, 87/662

Criminal Justice Act 1987 (c.38), 87/634
Criminal Justice (Scotland) Act 1987 (c.41), 87/636
Criminal Law, 87/751–853
Individual offences are listed separately
See also **Criminal Evidence and Procedure** *and* **Criminal Sentencing**
aiding and abetting, 87/752
assisting commission of offence, 87/756
attempt. *See* **Attempt**
bail. *See* **Bail**
brothel, management of, 87/792
children, 87/766
conspiracy to defraud, 87/2258
crime prevention, 87/768, 769
Criminal Injuries Compensation Board, 87/772
Crossbows Act 1987 (c.32), 87/773
drugs. *See* **Drug Abuse**
duress, 87/774
fireworks, supply of, 87/836
indecent photograph, 87/789
larceny, 87/791
misuse of drugs. *See* **Drug Abuse**
multiple share applications, 87/826
passive assistance, 87/816
prevention of terrorism, 87/817
public order, 87/818, 819
recklessness, 87/771
repatriation of prisoners, 87/821
research bulletin, 87/951
research programme, 87/786
research study, 87/822
self-defence, 87/824, 825, 853
statistics,
annual volume, 87/827
criminal careers of those born in 1953, 87/828
criminal cases in magistrates' courts, 87/830
criminal cases in the Crown Court, 87/829
domestic proceedings in magistrates' courts, 87/831
life licensees, 87/835
notifiable offences, 87/832
Police and Criminal Evidence Act 1984, 87/833
prevention of terrorism, 87/834
research study, 87/822
trade descriptions, 87/843–849
Criminal Sentencing, 87/854–1100
abstracting electricity, 87/854
adjournment for assessment, 87/855
adjournment for reports, 87/856
administering noxious substance, 87/990
affray, 87/858, 859
amphetamine manufacture,
conspiracy to, 87/897, 898
arson, 87/864–869
assault,
leading to death, 87/870
attempt,
buggery, 87/871
to obtain by deception, 87/866
bomb hoax, 87/873
burglary,
aggravated, 87/860
with intent to rape, 87/874
causing death by reckless driving, 87/876, 877
cheque fraud, 87/879
cocaine,
importing, 87/952–954
committal to Crown Court, 87/880
community service, 87/881–883

Criminal Sentencing—*cont.*
compensation order, 87/884–892
consecutive sentences, 87/893–895
contempt of court, 87/899–902
corrosive fluid, casting, 87/875, 878
corruption, 87/903, 904
counterfeiting, 87/905–910
criminal damage, 87/911
custodial sentence,
after favourable report, 87/1037
judge's comments, 87/912
statutory criteria, 87/1050
custody abroad pending extradition, 87/1070
dangerous offender, 87/913
deferred sentence, 87/914
delay in dealing with offender, 87/915
detention centre, 87/916
disqualification from driving, 87/918–922
divergence of facts, 87/923
driving whilst disqualified, 87/924
and reckless driving, 87/895
driving without due care and attention, 87/925
drug importation, 87/926
enforcement notice, 87/927
evasion of income tax, 87/928
exportation of prohibited goods, 87/929
extended sentence, 87/930, 931
factual basis, 87/872, 932–940
fine,
in conjunction with imprisonment, 87/942
term of imprisonment in default, 87/941
firearm, possession of, 87/1019–1021, 1025
foreign sentence, 87/1038
forfeiture order, 87/943–947
fraud,
in breach of trust, 87/948
grievous bodily harm,
domestic violence, 87/949
squirting corrosive fluid, 87/878
guilty plea, 87/917
heroin,
dealing, 87/950
possession and supply, 87/1022, 1023
incest, 87/955, 956
indecent assault, 87/957–963
juvenile,
adjournment of appeal until majority, 87/964
arson, 87/969, 970
buggery, 87/972–973
burglary, 87/982, 1017
detention, 87/966
long term detention, 87/968–984, 998
manslaughter, 87/976
multiple rapes, 87/977
robbery, 87/965, 971, 978–981
sentencing powers, 87/985
wounding with intent, 87/967
kidnapping, 87/986–989
life imprisonment, 87/991–993
living on earnings of prostitution, 87/994–997
magisterial law,
reconvened court, 87/999
malicious wounding, 87/1000
manslaughter, 87/1001–1009
misconduct in court, 87/1010
mitigation,
disclosure of information, 87/1011
mugging, 87/1012
obtaining by deception, 87/1013–1015
offensive weapon, possession of, 87/1024
parole, 87/1016

Criminal Sentencing—*cont.*
passport,
procuring by false statement, 87/1030
perverting justice, 87/1018
police officer, allegation against, 87/861
probation order, 87/1027–1029
public nuisance, 87/1031
rape, 87/1032–1036
reconvened court, 87/999
research bulletin, 87/951
riot, 87/1039
robbery, 87/1040–1044
severity of sentence, 87/862
social security fraud, 87/1014, 1015, 1045, 1046
statistics,
offenders sentenced to immediate custody, 87/1048
probation, 87/1049
sentencing for indictable offences, 87/733
suspended sentence,
activation, 87/1051–1054
theft,
accountant, 87/1061
baggage handlers, 87/1055
conveyancer, 87/1058
despatch foreman, 87/1060
employee, 87/1062
from shop, 87/1059
from students, 87/1066
in breach of trust
accounts clerk, 87/1057
bank clerk, 87/1056
postman, 87/1064
solicitor, 87/1065
mortgage broker, 87/1063
threatening to kill, 87/1067, 1068
time in custody, 87/1069, 1070
unlawful sexual intercourse, 87/1071, 1072
video piracy, 87/896
violence to children, 87/1073–1075
wounding, 87/1076
with intent, 87/1077, 1078
young offenders, 87/1079, 1080
youth custody,
arson, 87/1081
buggery, 87/1082
burglary, 87/1088, 1084
discount, 87/1086
for life, 87/1099
guilty plea, 87/1088, 1097
manslaughter, 87/1089, 1090
mitigating circumstances, 87/1085
railway passengers, endangering safety of, 87/1087
rape, 87/1094
robbery, 87/1092, 1093, 1095
statutory criteria, 87/1100
theft, 87/1096
wounding with intent, 87/1098
Crossbows Act 1987 (c.32), 87/773
Crown Practice. *See* **Practice**
Crown Proceedings (Armed Forces) Act 1987 (c.25), 87/161
Customs and Excise, 87/1101–1124
agricultural levies, 87/1101
betting duty, 87/1102
community transit, 87/1104
counterfeit goods, 87/1105
customs duty,
evasion of, 87/1109
regulations, 87/1106

Customs and Excise—*cont.*
customs duty—*cont.*
revocation of savings, 87/1107
temporary importation, 87/1108
declaration of goods, 87/1111
export controls, 87/1110
import duty reliefs, 87/1112
importing prohibited goods, 87/1113
indecent and obscene articles, 87/1114
methylated spirits, 87/1115
non-commercial consignments relief, 87/1116
Northern Ireland, 87/1117
petroleum products, 87/1118
Police and Criminal Evidence Act 1984, application, 87/1119
Portugal, 87/1120
quota relief, 87/1121
reckless completion of false document, 87/1122
Spain, 87/1123
spoilt beer, 87/1124

Damages, 87/1125–1230
agent,
non-existent principal, 87/1126
apportionment, 87/2566
beneficial occupation of premises, 87/1129
building contract, 87/1132, 1133
car, loss of use, 87/1128
cargo damage, 87/3376
collateral funding arrangements, 87/1142
consortium, 87/1137
currency of claim, 87/3390, 3391
defamation, 87/1140
distress and inconvenience,
building contract, 87/1141
divorce costs, 87/1168
employment contract, 87/1303
exchange rate loss, 87/3399
exemplary damages, 87/1143, 1144
explosion causing fire, 87/1145
flat,
damp and infestation, 87/1127
foreign currency, 87/184
hire agreement,
defective goods, 87/434
holiday, 87/1148–1151, 1162
industrial action, 87/3765
interest, 87/1154, 1155, 1826
interim payment, 87/2982
libel, retraction of, 87/2296
loss of chattel, 87/1157
loss of dependency, 87/1158
loss of earning capacity, 87/1159, 1167
loss of earnings, 87/1160, 1161, 1168
loss of eye, 87/1167
misrepresentation, 87/1163
negligent misrepresentation, 87/1164
negligent survey, 87/2587
nervous shock, 87/1166
pension, 87/1220
sale of land, 87/452, 1225
taxation element, 87/1226
tour operator, 87/418, 1130
trespass to land, 87/1227
unlawful eviction, 87/2250, 2251
VAT, recovery of, 87/1230
Death Duties. *See* **Inheritance Tax**
Debtors (Scotland) Act 1987 (c.18), 87/2983
Deer Act 1987 (c.28), 87/108
Defamation. *See* **Libel and Slander**
Diplomatic and Consular Premises Act 1987 (c.46), 87/2084

Discovery and Inspection
bankers' books, 87/1674
before action, 87/2988
by persons unconnected with proceedings, 87/2991
disclosure of assets, 87/2989
foreign patents, 87/2986
further and better list of documents, 87/2990
industrial tribunal, 87/1340
interrogatories, 87/2992
lands tribunal decisions, 87/1692
list of documents requested, 87/2994
medical examination, 87/2995
use of documents, 87/2885
outside action, 87/2996
Discrimination. *See* **Race Relations, Sex Discrimination**
Divorce and Matrimonial Causes. *See* **Family**
Drug Abuse
See also **Criminal Sentencing**
Criminal Justice (Scotland) Act 1987 (c.41), 87/636
importation, 87/1113
intention to supply, 87/797
licence fees, 87/795
possession,
exception to prohibition, 87/796
"preparation", 87/798

Easements and Prescription, 87/1231–1237
pathway, 87/1232
right of way, 87/458, 1233, 1235, 1236, 3097
right to affix signs, 87/1231
Ecclesiastical Law, 87/1238–1246
altar, 87/1238
benefices, 87/1239
churchyard, 87/1240
faculty,
absence of, 87/1241
jurisdiction, 87/1243
removal of pews, 87/1242
fees, 87/1244
Methodist Church Act 1976,
Guernsey Order, 87/1245
United Reformed Church Act 1981,
Guernsey Order, 87/1246
Education, 87/1247–1276
assisted places, 87/1248
awards, 87/1249
direct grant schools, 87/1251
disciplinary procedure, 87/1308
duration of school year, 87/1253
education committee, 87/1255, 2369
fees and awards, 87/1257
further education institutions, 87/1260
grants, 87/1258
equal treatment, 87/1259
independent schools,
corporal punishment, abolition of, 87/1247
pupils, registration of, 87/1262
school,
attendance order, 87/1264
government, 87/1266
places,
sex discrimination, 87/2388
publication of change of status, 87/1268
school transport, 87/1274
special educational needs, 87/1250, 1269, 1270, 3187
special school,
rate rebate, 87/3187

Education—*cont.*
teachers,
bursaries, 87/1271
pay and conditions, 87/1272
remuneration, 87/1263
Teachers' Pay and Conditions Act 1987 (c.1), 87/1273
universities. *See* **Universities**
Election Law, 87/1277–1283
European Assembly, 87/1536
expenditure, 87/1283
expenses, 87/1277
local elections, 87/1278
public meetings, 87/2378
parish meetings, 87/1279
parliamentary constituencies, 87/1280
Electricity, 87/1284–1288
generating stations, 87/1284
inquiries procedure, 87/1285
meters, 87/1287
burglary victim, 87/1286
power lines, 87/1288
Emergency Laws, 87/1289–1292
prevention of terrorism, 87/1289–1291
statistics, 87/834
suppression of terrorism, 87/1292
Employment, 87/1293–1419
breach of confidence, 87/1293–1295
constructive dismissal. *See* **Unfair Dismissal**
continuous employment. *See* **Unfair Dismissal**
contract of employment,
breach of, 87/1296, 1301
collective agreement, 87/1297
covenant against competition, 87/431
repudiatory breach, 87/1303
unilateral variation of terms, 87/1305
deduction from wages, 87/1306
defective equipment, 87/1307
disciplinary procedure, 87/34, 1308, 1310
dismissal,
ill health, 87/1311
refusal to carry out duties, 87/1312
written reasons, 87/1313
employer,
"the state", organ or agent on, 87/1315
Employment Appeal Tribunal, 87/1317–1319
employment subsidies, 87/1320
equal pay, 87/1321–1332, 1376, 1529
factories. *See* **Factories**
guarantee payments, 87/1334
health and safety at work. *See* **Health and Safety at Work**
hours of employment, 87/1300
industrial tribunal,
discovery, 87/1340
evidence, 87/1336
findings of fact, 87/1337
notice of hearing, 87/1341
originating application, 87/1338
res judicata, 87/1342
Job Release Act 1977, 87/1343
maternity,
extended leave, 87/1344
pay, 87/1345, 1346
maternity benefits. *See also* **Social Security**
racial discrimination. *See* **Race Relations**
redundancy. *See* **Redundancy**
salary,
reduction of, 87/1377
sex discrimination. *See* **Sex Discrimination**
sick pay, 87/1378

Employment—*cont.*
summary dismissal of chief executive, 87/1379
superintendent registrar,
deduction of wages, 87/1380
system of work, 87/2612, 2615
termination,
effective date, 87/1381
trade unions. *See* **Trade Unions**
transfer of undertaking, 87/1383, 1384, 1527
unfair dismissal. *See* **Unfair Dismissal**
vicarious liability of employer, 87/1316, 1367, 2615
wages councils, 87/1418
wrongful dismissal, 87/1419
Equity and Trusts, 87/1420–1440
charging order,
resulting trust, 87/2537
Chevening Estates Act 1987 (c.20), 87/1421
class closing rules, 87/1437
constructive trusts, 87/1423, 1432
discretionary trust, 87/2035
duty of trustee, 87/1425
gifts,
perfection of incomplete gifts, 87/1426
insurance premiums, 87/1427
Irish Sailors and Soldiers Land Trust Act 1987 (c.48), 87/1428
public trustee, 87/1431
Recognition of Trusts Act 1987 (c.14), 87/1433
resulting trusts, 87/345
Reverter of Sites Act 1987 (c.15), 87/1435
settlement,
capital transfer tax, 87/284, 285
trust for sale, 87/1439
trust income from abroad, 87/2029
Estoppel, 87/1441–1450
action estoppel, 87/1441
agreement subject to contract, 87/1443
contract to assign by agent, 87/1445
copyright, abandonment, 87/511
government approval, failure to obtain, 87/1442
liquidator, 87/362
pre-incorporation contract, 87/446
property adjustment order,
loan taken out fraudulently, 87/1781
proprietary estoppel, 87/1444, 1448
res judicata, 87/1342
European Communities, 87/1451–1667
agriculture,
butter, 87/1453
directives, decisions and regulations, 87/1454
discrimination, 87/1455
eggs, 87/1458
exports, 87/1456
milk, 87/1459
monetary compensatory amounts, 87/1460
potatoes, 87/1484
producer group, 87/1461
production aids, 87/1462
security, forfeiture of, 87/1457
sugar production levies, 87/1463
tenderers, 87/1464
vines, 87/1465
wine, 87/1466
anti-dumping duties, 87/1467–1469
approximation of laws,
directives, decisions and regulations, 87/1470
architects' qualifications, 87/1471
banking, 87/1472
breach of law by Crown, 87/1473
budget contributions,
advance payment, 87/1477

European Communities—*cont.*
coal and steel,
directives, decisions and regulations, 87/1474
imports, 87/1475
Commission's liability, 87/1476
Communities' own resources, 87/1477
company resident in U.K.
transfer within EEC, 87/1479
competition,
agreement, 87/1481–1483
agriculture, 87/1484
banking, 87/1486–1488
broadcasting, 87/1489
business secrets, 87/1490
chemicals, 87/1483
commodity exchange, 87/1485
directives, decisions and regulations, 87/1491
discovery, 87/1492
dominant position, 87/1480, 1493
franchise agreement, 87/1495
insurance, 87/1496
joint ventures, 87/1497
know-how licences, 87/1498
manufacturers agreement, 87/1482
monopoly, 87/1502
negative clearance, 87/1499–1501, 1507
non-competition clause, 87/1503
patent licensing, 87/1504
performance rights, 87/1505
resale ban, 87/1506
selective distribution system, 87/1494
take-over, 87/1508
vehicle parts, 87/1481
confidentiality, 87/1509
constitutional law, 87/1510–1512
customs, 87/1514
damages, action for, 87/1451
Decision, withdrawal of, 87/1452
directives, 87/1519–1523
economic affairs,
directives, decisions and regulations, 87/1524
education,
grants, equal treatment, 87/1259
employment,
business transfer, 87/1527, 1528
employer,
"the State", organ or agent of, 87/1315
equal pay, 87/1322, 1529
redundancy, 87/1530
environment,
directives, decisions and regulations, 87/1531
establishment,
insurance companies, 87/1533
professions, 87/1534
sickness benefit, 87/1535
European Assembly, 87/1536
Euratom,
directives, decisions and regulations, 87/1537
E.C.S.C.,
steel production quota figures, 87/1538
European Court,
annulment proceedings, 87/1540
procedure, 87/1541–1544
European Parliament, 87/1555–1557
exports,
butter, 87/1558
unfair commercial practices, 87/1559
external affairs,
directives, decisions and regulations, 87/1560
fisheries,
directives, decisions and regulations, 87/1561

European Communities—*cont.*
fishing crews, 87/1562
food regulations, 87/1811
freedom of movement,
workers, 87/1564–1569
freedom of traders, 87/1573
freedom to provide services,
insurance, 87/1570–1572, 1631, 1632
human rights, 87/1573–1575
See also **Human Rights**
imports,
appellation, 87/1576
common customs tariff, 87/1582
customs, 87/1577, 1578
endangered species, 87/1584
foodstuffs, 87/1580
free circulation, 87/1581, 1583
internal tax, 87/1583
medicinal products, 87/1585, 3750
monetary compensatory amounts, 87/1586
name designation, 87/1579
optical appliances, 87/1595
price controls, 87/1588
quantitative restrictions, 87/1589–1593, 1596
restraint of trade, 87/1594
tariff quotas, 87/1597
taxation, 87/1598
textiles, 87/1581
valuation for customs, 87/1599
Industry Act 1972, 87/3733
institutions,
directives, decisions and regulations, 87/1601
interim measures,
anti-dumping, 87/1602
ex parte injunctions, 87/1603
injunctions, 87/1604
public works, 87/1606
suspension of decision, 87/1607
suspension of fine, 87/1608
suspension of regulation, 87/1609
urgency, 87/1604, 1607, 1610, 1611
JET, 87/1613
judgments,
compliance with, 87/1614
Judgments Convention, 87/1545–1554
labelling, 87/1615, 1616
maternity grant, 87/3485
Member of European Parliament,
legal immunity, 87/1556
migrant worker,
dependant's pension, 87/1618
ministers, designations of, 87/1518
National Courts, 87/1619
optical appliances, 87/1595
patent infringement, 87/2791
pharmaceutical qualifications, 87/2411, 2706
pharmaceutical rules, 87/2412
pharmaceuticals, 87/1623
public contracts, 87/1624
public works contracts, 87/1523
quantitative restrictions,
directives, 87/1625
regional affairs,
directives, decisions and regulations, 87/1626
regulations, 87/1627
research and development,
directives, decisions and regulations, 87/1628
right to work,
non-EEC national, 87/1629
semiconductor products, 87/1630

European Communities—*cont.*
sex discrimination,
occupational pensions, 87/1633
retirement, 87/1370, 1371, 1637
social security benefits, 87/1635, 1636
unemployment benefit, 87/1575
social affairs,
directives, decisions and regulations, 87/1638
social policy,
European Social Fund, 87/1639
migrants, 87/1640
social security,
dependants, 87/1642
family allowances, 87/1643
overlapping benefits, 87/1641, 1643
self-employed person, 87/1645
unemployment benefit, 87/1644
state aids,
discrimination, 87/1651
domestic fiscal measures, 87/3222
fruit farmers, 87/1647
interim measures, 87/1648
state shareholding, 87/1649
state monopolies,
directives, 87/1650
steel, 87/1651–1653
stock exchanges, 87/1654
subsidiary bodies,
directives, decisions and regulations, 87/1655
Sunday trading, 87/3449
tachograph, 87/3307
taxation,
directions, decisions and regulations, 87/1658
drink, 87/1659
transport,
directives, decisions and regulations, 87/1660
international passenger services, 87/2750, 3780
treaties, definition of, 87/1517
VAT,
6th VAT directive, 87/1661–1664, 3856
8th Council Directive, 87/3827
veterinary surgeons, 87/1667
Evidence (Civil), 87/1668–1688
admissibility,
extrinsic evidence, 87/1670
foreign conviction, 87/1669
hearsay, 87/2517
public interest immunity certificate, 87/1668
reputation at time of trial, 87/2305
sex discrimination, 87/1336
affidavit, 87/1673
bankers' books, 87/1674
blood tests, 87/1675
confidential documents, 87/1676
disclosure, 87/1677, 1678, 3009
expert evidence, 87/1680, 1681, 1684, 2421, 2946, 3006
privilege,
letter to inspector of planning inquiry, 87/1685
ward of court, 87/3009
"without prejudice", 87/1686
witness summons, 87/1688
Evidence (Criminal). *See* **Criminal Evidence and Procedure**
Executors and Administrators, 87/1689–1692
distribution of estate, 87/1689
duty to beneficiary, 87/1425
foreign executor, 87/1691
lands tribunal decisions,
discovery of documents, 87/1692

Extradition, 87/1693–1706
aircraft, protection of, 87/1693
bail, 87/1694
charge on file, 87/1700
date of apprehension, 87/1695
fugitive offenders, 87/1697, 1698
internationally protected persons, 87/1699
obtaining property by deception, 87/807
suppression of terrorism, 87/1701
taking of hostages, 87/1702
time-limit,
evidence, 87/1696
treaty,
interpretation of, 87/1703
warrant, 87/1704, 1705

Factories. *See* **Health and Safety at Work**
Family, 87/1707–1791
affiliation proceedings, 87/1688, 1708
assault by husband on wife, 87/949
costs. *See* **Costs**
divorce,
behaviour, 87/1711
decree absolute, 87/1712–1714
domicile, 87/1715
special procedure, 87/1716
stay of proceedings, 87/399, 1717
unreasonable behaviour, 87/1719
validity of marriage, 87/1778, 2998
domestic jurisdiction, 87/1721
domestic proceedings in magistrates' courts, 87/3061
statistics, 87/831
Family Law Reform Act 1987 (c.42), 87/1724
financial provision,
clean break, 87/1727
committal for breach of order, 87/1742
conduct, 87/1754, 1755
consent order, 87/1729–1732
death of one party, 87/1746, 1756
further order, 87/1745
future likely inheritance, 87/1734
invalid husband, 87/1735
legal aid statutory charge, 87/2294, 2295
lump sum order, 87/1737–1742
maintenance, 87/407, 1758, 1759
out of husband's estate, 87/1737
overseas divorce, 87/1733
periodical payments,
backdating, 87/1725
construction of order, 87/1747
husband's application, 87/1750
termination, 87/1749
writ *ne exeat regno*, 87/1748
Registrar's power, 87/1751
relevant factors, 87/1726
responsibility to children, 87/1736
sale of property, 87/1752
short marriage, 87/1736
transfer of matrimonial home, 87/1744
welfare of children, 87/1727
indecent assault within marriage, 87/1757
marriage,
choice of law rules, 87/2275
matrimonial home,
application by wife to re-enter, 87/1726
council house, sale of, 87/1772
power to order sale, 87/1764
rates, liability for, 87/1765
matrimonial injunctions. *See* **Matrimonial Injunctions**

Family—*cont.*
nullity,
wilful refusal to consummate, 87/1770
paternity, 87/1675, 2509
property adjustment order,
appointment of receiver, 87/1787
effect of Matrimonial Causes Act 1973, s.24A, 87/1786
husband unemployed, 87/1788
legal aid statutory charge, 87/2295
loan taken out fraudulently, 87/1781
priority of charge, 87/1782
time-limit, 87/1785
undue influence, 87/1828, 2544
Family Law Reform Act 1987 (c.42), 87/1724
Finance Act 1987 (c.16), 87/3211
Finance (No. 2) Act 1987 (c.51), 87/3212
Fire Safety and Safety of Places of Sport Act 1987 (c.27), 87/3145
Fire service, 87/1793
firemen's pension scheme, 87/1793
Firearms and Explosives, 87/1794–1797
air weapon, 87/1794
ammunition, 87/1795
electric stun gun, 87/1797
White Paper, 87/2268
Fish and Fisheries, 87/1798–1805
eels, 87/1798
fish farming, 87/1799
fishing vessels, 87/1800
prohibition of fishing, 87/1801
salmon and freshwater fisheries, 87/1802
sea fishing, 87/1803
shellfish, 87/1804
"T" nets, 87/1805
Food and Drugs, 87/1806–1818
coffee, 87/1806
colouring, 87/1807
contamination, 87/1808
food labelling, 87/1817
materials and articles in contact with food, 87/1811
meat, 87/1812
milk, 87/1813
milk. *See also* **Agriculture**
sale of food, 87/1814, 1815, 1818
sample, procuring of, 87/1810
sugar, 87/1816
unfit for human consumption, 87/1809
Foreign Jurisdictions, 87/1819–1822
Dominica, 87/1819
Jamaica, 87/688
Mauritius, 87/1821
Forestry, 87/1823–1824
felling of trees, 87/1823
tractors, 87/100
Forgery
account in false name, 87/777
computer,
unauthorised access, 87/780
documents made after liquidation, 87/778
intent, 87/779, 781
Fraud, Misrepresentation and Undue Influence, 1825–1830
Criminal Justice Act 1987 (c.38), 87/634
ex turpi causa non oritur actio, 87/1826
husband and wife, 87/1828, 2544
misrepresentation of flat service charges, 87/1163
property adjustment order,
loan taken out fraudulently, 87/1781
Friendly Societies. *See* **Industrial and Friendly Societies**

Gaming (Amendment) Act 1987 (c.11), 87/1834
Gaming and Wagering, 87/1831–1838
betting duty, 87/1102
Billiards (Abolition of Restrictions) Act 1987 (c.19), 87/1832
fees, 87/1833
Gaming (Amendment) Act 1987 (c.11), 87/1834
hours and charges, 87/1836
lotteries, 87/1837
monetary limits, 87/1838
value added tax, 87/3801
Gas, 87/1839
government shareholding, 87/1839
Guarantee and Indemnity, 87/1840–1847
co-sureties, 87/1841
collateral security, 87/1844
letter of comfort, 87/440
partnership, 87/1845
signature, 87/1842
summary judgment, 87/2911
time charterparty, 87/1846

Handling
as alternative to theft, 87/842
belief, 87/784, 785
dishonesty, 87/783
Health and Safety at Work, 87/1848–1861
asbestos dust,
control of, 87/1848
protection, 87/1852
conviction under section not prosecuted, 87/716
dangerous substances, 87/1849
explosives and petroleum fees, 87/1851
fees, 87/1853
fencing, 87/1333, 1854
gas cylinders, 87/1855
industrial air pollution, 87/1856
system of work, 87/2612, 2615
use of equipment by others, 87/1861
Highways and Bridges. *See* **Transport**
Hire Purchase
re-possession, 87/3332
Housing, 87/1862–1907
benefits, 87/1884–1889
common parts grant, 87/1862
compulsory purchase, 87/1863
consultation paper, 87/2269
control order, 87/1865
discount, repayment of, 87/1772
disposal of council estate, 87/1867
fire-escape, 87/1897
grants, 87/1868, 2359
home insulation, 87/1869
home purchase assistance, 87/1870
homeless persons,
accommodation, appropriateness, 87/1880
accommodation, duty to provide, 87/1878
accommodation, temporary, 87/1879
act or omission in good faith, 87/1877
discharge of duty, 87/1881
intentional homelessness, 87/1871–1874, 1901
persons residing with applicant, 87/1875
priority need, 87/1876
Housing Act 1985,
s. 369(5), 87/1882
Housing (Scotland) Act 1987 (c.26), 87/1891

Housing—*cont.*
mobile homes. *See* **Caravans and Mobile Homes**
mortgage indemnity,
recognised bodies, 87/1894
possession order, 87/1904
priority need,
vulnerability, 87/1896, 1906
rent, determination of, 87/1866
rent increase, 87/2385
repair grants, 87/1899
repairs, 87/1905
right to buy, 87/1900
secure tenancy,
abandonment, 87/1901
possession order, 87/1902
suspended possession order, 87/1903
variation, 87/1901a
waiting list application, 87/1907
Housing (Scotland) Act 1987 (c.26), 87/1891
Human Rights, 87/1908–1919
administrative measures by government, 87/1908
Commission for Racial Equality. *See* **Race Relations**
data protection, 87/1910
divorce, 87/1912
EEC,
European School, 87/1913
illegitimacy, 87/1915
liberty, deprivation of, 87/1911
parental rights,
children in care, 87/1916
prisoners, 87/1917, 1918
security vetting, 87/1919
sex discrimination. *See* **Sex Discrimination**
transsexual rights, 87/1914
Husband and Wife. *See* **Family**

Immigration, 87/1920–1999
appeal,
disposal without hearing, 87/1986
misconceived grounds, 87/1921
oral hearing, 87/1923
withdrawal of, 87/1922
asylum, 87/23, 1926, 1981–1983
bail, 87/1924, 1927
burden of proof on admission, 87/1920
children, 87/1930
over 18, 87/1931
citizenship, 87/1929
control of entry,
through Republic of Ireland, 87/1932
deception, 87/1933
dependent relatives, 87/1945, 1935
deportation,
appeal, 87/1937
authorisation, 87/1946
deception, 87/1944, 1945
marriage, 87/1939
mental health patient, 87/1947
notice, competition of, 87/1948
notice, non-service of, 87/1940
notice, service of, 87/1943
post-entry deception, 87/1941
procedure, 87/1942
public good, 87/1936, 1938
detention, 87/1949
dual nationality, 87/1954
entry clearance, 87/1951, 1952
entry clearance officer, 87/1953

Immigration—*cont.*
evidence, 87/1933
exceptional circumstances, 87/1925
false statement after entry, 87/1959
husband, 87/1957
illegal entrant, 87/1958–1961
Immigration (Carriers' Liability) Act 1987 (c.24), 87/1962
immigration rules, comparison of, 87/1963
impersonation, 87/1964
indefinite leave to enter, 87/1955
investment in business, 87/1965
leave to enter,
"adoptive", 87/1966
breach of condition, 87/1967
Commonwealth citizens, 87/1968
meeting of parties, 87/1973
refusal of, 87/1969–1971
restricted leave, 87/1972
leave to remain, 87/1974, 1990
legal aid, 87/1975
"means" to proceed, 87/1977
motive for entry, 87/1978
ordinarily resident, 87/1979
passport,
date stamped to indicate refusal, 87/1980
ports of entry, 87/1984
practice and procedure, 87/1933, 1985
primary purpose, 87/1987
refugee, 87/1988, 1989
research programme, 87/786
returning resident, 87/1991–1993
right of abode, 87/1928, 1993, 1994
s. 17 appeal, 87/1996
settlement,
elderly dependent parents, 87/1950
student, 87/1997
temporary admission, 87/1998
transfer of functions, 87/1999
visitor,
lorry driver, 87/1976
Immigration (Carriers' Liability) Act 1987 (c.24), 87/1962
Income Tax, 87/2000–2040
appeals, 87/2000
assessment,
appeal, 87/2001
time limit, 87/2002
back duty, 87/2003
bank interest, 87/2004
beneficial loans, 87/2005
building society payments, 87/2006, 2007
capital allowances, 87/2008, 2009
cash equivalents, 87/2010
charitable gifts, 87/2011
covenanted donations, 87/2011
covenanted payments, 87/2012
discretionary trust, 87/2035
double taxation, 87/2013
emoluments, 87/2014, 2015, 2032
entertainers and sportsmen, 87/2016
husband and wife, 87/2017
indexation, 87/2018
interest on unpaid tax, 87/2019
interest relief, 87/2020
Jersey partnership, 87/2021
judicial review, 87/2026
land, 87/2022
partnership, 87/2040
penalty, 87/2023
pension scheme surpluses, 87/2024

Income Tax—*cont.*
personal equity plan, 87/2025
reduced and composite rate, 87/2027
schedule D, 87/2028, 2029
schedule E, 87/2030–2034
tax avoidance, 87/2036–2039
Indemnity. *See* **Guarantee and Indemnity**
Industrial and Friendly Societies, 87/2041–2044
fees, 87/2041
Friendly Societies Act 1984,
Jersey Order, 87/2042
long term insurance business, 87/2043
transfer of functions, 87/2044
Inheritance Tax, 87/2045–2049
delivery of accounts, 87/2045
double charges relief, 87/2046
estate duty, 87/2047
indexation, 87/2048
interest on unpaid tax, 87/2049
Injunctions
See also **Anton Piller, Mareva Injunctions, Matrimonial Injunctions**
breach of duty of confidence, 87/3020
confidential information, 87/3023
continuation pending appeal, 87/3123
foreign proceedings, restraint of, 87/3024
full and frank disclosure, 87/3021
harassment, 87/3590
interim relief, 87/3027
interlocutory,
balance of convenience, 87/2768, 3041
Church of Scientology, 87/3036
conspiracy to injure, 87/2298
discharge of undertakings, 87/3031
employment contract, breach of, 87/1296
principles, 87/3034
public authority, 87/3035
refusal, 87/3037
rights of landowner, 87/3039
salvage arbitration, 87/3367
unlawful acts, 87/3038
mandatory interlocutory, 87/3022
persons not party to action, 87/3026a
right of way, 87/1235
scope, 87/431
televised re-enactment of trial, 87/3026
Insolvency
administration orders, 87/340–342
authorised insolvency practitioners,
annual directory, 87/207
bankruptcy. *See* **Bankruptcy**
directors,
disqualification, 87/331
"fixed plant and machinery", 87/356
Insolvency Court Users' Committee, 87/211
liquidator,
conflict, 87/344
practice direction,
winding up, 87/324
proceedings, 87/343
winding up,
affidavit evidence, 87/377
agreement to lease premises, 87/372
compulsory winding up, 87/383
contributory's petition, 87/325
costs and remuneration, 87/379
disclaimer of onerous property, 87/381
examination ordered by court, 87/376
foreign company, 87/375
insurance premiums, 87/1427
liquidator,
remuneration of, 87/374, 379
replacement of, 87/373
Insolvency—*cont.*
procedure, 87/378, 385
transfer of land, 87/380
transfer of lease, 87/384
Insurance, 87/2050–2079
contingency monetary losses, 87/2050
duty of utmost good faith, 87/2052
fees, 87/2053
fire, 87/2054–2057
friendly societies, 87/2043
illegality, 87/2051
Insurance Brokers Registration Council, 87/2059
insurance companies,
assistance, 87/2060
mergers and divisions, 87/2061
motor insurance,
compulsory insurance, 87/2062
failure to obtain, 87/2064, 2065
permitting uninsured use, 87/3285
offence committed unintentionally, 87/2067
police officer, 87/2065
qualified consent, 87/2063
theft, 87/2068
notification of claim, 87/2069
premiums, 87/1427
professional indemnity policy, 87/2071, 2072
reinsurance, 87/2074–2077, 2567
underwriters,
agent, 87/2078
warranty,
whether breached, 87/2051
warranty by policy holder, 87/2079
International Law, 87/2080–2098
Anguilla, 87/2080
arbitration, 87/2081
boundary dispute, 87/2094
consular fees, 87/2082
copyright, 87/524
Diplomatic and Consular Premises Act 1987 (c.46), 87/2084
foreign compensation, 87/2086
genocide, 87/2087
hostages, 87/2088
international body, 87/310, 312, 1676, 2092, 2093
international passenger services, 87/3780
peace treaties, 87/2096
protected persons, 87/2097
sale of goods, 87/3334
Intoxicating Liquors
Licensing. *See* **Licensing**
Irish Sailors and Soldiers Land Trust Act 1987 (c.48), 87/1428

Judicial Review
absence of party, 87/673
agricultural dwelling-house advisory committee, 87/3
alternative proceedings,
abandonment, 87/1990
availability of, 87/10
application,
considerations, 87/5
availability of remedy, 87/6
bail, 87/3051
binding over, 87/599
breach of Bill of Rights, 87/28
care proceedings, 87/9, 2460
claim begun by writ, 87/3052
colliery closure, 87/12

Judicial Review—*cont.*
delay in application, 87/645, 1951
ex gratia payment, 87/672
housing,
waiting list application, 87/1907
inquest, 87/536
judge's misconduct, 87/3053
legal aid, 87/2282
licensing,
sex shop, 87/2319
local ombudsman, 87/17
milk quotas, 87/91
motorway inquiry, 87/3653
N.H.S. resources, 87/2546
national security, 87/20
panel on take-overs and mergers, 87/21
rating valuation, 87/14
refusal to grant asylum, 87/23
Revenue documents, 87/24
tax assessment, 87/549, 2026
wardship, 87/2524
Juries, 87/2099–2106
bias, allegations of, 87/2101
communication to judge, 87/2099, 2100
coroner's juries. *See* **Coroners**
dissent within jury, 87/2102
exclusion of jury,
spouse of juror in court, 87/2102
ineligible juror, 87/2103
protection, 87/2104
racially balanced panel, 87/2105

Kidnapping
lawful excuse, 87/790

Land Charges, 87/2107–2111
local land charges, 87/2107
disclosure, 87/2108
overriding interest, 87/2109
property adjustment order, 87/1782
undertaking in damages, 87/2111
Land Drainage
drainage charge, 87/3865
Land Registration
caution, 87/481
district registries, 87/472
implied covenant of good title, 87/473
inspection of register,
authority, 87/469
overriding interest, 87/2540
reform, 87/2270
registration of title, 87/483
rules, 87/475
Landlord and Tenant, 87/2112–2252
agricultural holdings. *See* **Agricultural Holdings**
assignment,
arrears, liability for, 87/2114
breach of covenant before assignment, 87/2142
consent, 87/2116
covenant benefit of, 87/2117
assured tenancies, 87/2118
boarding house, 87/2119
business tenancy,
application for new tenancy, 87/2123–2129
compensation, 87/2134
forfeiture of head tenancy, 87/2131
illuminated signs, display of, 87/1231
landlord's intention to demolish, 87/2132

Landlord and Tenant—*cont.*
business tenancy—*cont.*
notice to terminate, 87/2133
rent computation of, 87/2177
terms, 87/2135, 2136
covenant,
breach, 87/2120, 2121
waiver, 87/2122
payment of rent, 87/2147
quiet enjoyment, 87/2121, 2139
return of deposit, 87/2154
surety, 87/2117, 2147
to repair, 87/2140–2142
distress for rent rules 1983, 87/2265
easements. *See* **Easements and Prescription**
eviction protection from, 87/2192
exemplary damages, 87/2120
fair rent, 87/2115, 2145
guarantee to pay rent, 87/2147
"house", 87/2168
Housing (Scotland) Act 1987 (c.26), 87/1891
Landlord and Tenant Act 1987 (c.31), 87/2150
lands tribunal decision,
freehold interest price of, 87/2152
lease,
construction of clause, 87/2153
constructive occupation, 87/2170
fixtures and fittings, 87/2155
renewal,
opposition to, 87/2112
option, 87/2156
oral agreement, 87/2157
service charge, 87/2158
lease or licence, 87/2159–2163, 2176, 2247
leasehold enfranchisement, 87/2164–2166
leasehold reform, 87/2168–2172
lessor's managing agents, 87/2173
licence of property,
implied term as to fitness, 87/441
long tenancy, 87/2174
maintenance company, 87/2175
management agreement, 87/2176
possession,
against trespasser, 87/2183
alternative accommodation, 87/2184
reasonableness, 87/2179, 2180, 2184, 2244
resident landlord, 87/2181
secure tenancy, 87/2229
summary proceedings for, 87/2246
written notice, 87/2182
proprietary estoppel, 87/1448
protected tenancy, 87/2185–2191
purchase of freehold, 87/2227
re-entry, 87/2146, 2193
receiver and manager, 87/2194
rent arrears, 87/2113
rent assessment committees, 87/2197
rent assignment, 87/354
rent increases,
phasing relief from, 87/2195
rent registration,
protected shorthold tenancies, 87/2185
rent regulations,
forms, 87/2196
rent review,
application for expert surveyor, 87/2199, 2209, 2211, 2218
appointment of valuer, 87/2200, 2210, 2217
arbitrator's decision, 87/150, 2201, 2202, 2216
assessment of revised rent, 87/2204
basis of assessment, 87/2205

Landlord and Tenant—*cont.*
rent review—*cont.*
construction of clauses, 87/2219–2222, 2224, 2225
counter-notice, 87/2226
"date of review", 87/2213
development potential, 87/2201
hypothetical lease, 87/2198, 2207, 2220
improvements by tenant, 87/2208, 2215
permitted use, 87/2224
rectification, 87/2223
revision of original award, 87/2214
time, 87/2200, 2206, 2212
willing lessee, 87/2217
repairs, 87/2236–2238
restrictive covenants. *See* **Restrictive Covenants**
secure tenancy, 87/2228–2230
separated wife, 87/2178
service charge, 87/2231–2233
shared ownership leases, 87/2234
shorthold tenancy, 87/2235
statutory repairing covenant, 87/2236
statutory tenancy, 87/2243–2245
succession, 87/2239–2242
tenancy,
rent, 87/2247
tenants' association, 87/2248
unlawful eviction, 87/2250, 2251
workshop,
occupation agreement, 87/2252
Landlord and Tenant Act 1987 (c.31), 87/2150
Law Reform, 87/2253–2278
charities, supervision of, 87/298
"commonhold, 87/2257
conspiracy to defraud, 87/2258
consultation paper,
binding over, 87/2254
civil justice review, 87/2256
conveyancing delays, 87/2260
debt actions in county courts, 87/2262
distress for rent rules 1983, 87/2265
housing, 87/2269
consumer protection,
home buyers, 87/2259
conveyancing,
title on death, 87/2261
debt enforcement, 87/2263
delay in bringing action, 87/2264
domicile, 87/2266
efficiency in the courts, 87/2267
firearms, 87/2268
land registration, 87/2270
landlord and tenant, 87/2272
compensation for tenants' improvements, 87/2271
Law Commission annual report, 87/2273
leasehold conveyancing, 87/2274
marriage,
choice of law rules, 87/2275
sale and supply of goods, 87/2276
striking out action, 87/2903
treasure trove, 87/2277
wardship, 87/2278
Legal Aid, 87/2279–2295
advice and assistance, 87/2279
charge,
discretion to postpone, 87/2295
divorce settlement, 87/2294
child cases, 87/2890
counsel's fees, 87/2283
Legal Aid—*cont.*
criminal proceedings, 87/2285
deduction from taxed costs, 87/2286
duty solicitors, 87/2293
eligibility limits, 87/2287
fees, 87/2284
financial conditions, 87/2288
immigration cases, 87/1975
information bulletin, 87/2290
judicial review, 87/2282
new framework, 87/2291
revocation, 87/2292
Libel and Slander, 87/2296–2306
absolute privilege, 87/2297
conspiracy to injure, 87/2298
defamation,
damages, 87/1140, 2299
injunction, 87/2298
judge and jury, functions of, 87/2299
member of group, 87/2300
reputation, 87/2305
statement in court, 87/2301
defamatory meaning, 87/2302
jury trial, 87/3119
retraction, 87/2296
Licensing, 87/2307–2319
air travel agency, 87/174
airport licensing, 87/2308
cinematograph exhibition, 87/2310
extension, 87/2311
Licensing (Restaurant Meals) Act 1987 (c.2), 87/2313
liquor licence,
objections, 87/2314
transfer, 87/2312
Occasional Licence, 87/2315
policy of justices, 87/2309
sex shop, 87/2317–2319
time limit, jurisdiction to extend, 87/2316
Licensing (Restaurant Meals) Act 1987 (c.2), 87/2313
Lien, 87/2320
due debt, 87/2320
Limitation of Actions, 87/2321–2337
accrual of cause of action, 87/2321, 3442
acknowledgment, 87/2329
adverse possession,
enforcement of order, 87/2324
arbitrator, failure to appoint within time, 87/128
Attorney General,
enforcement of public trust, 87/2323
carriage by road, 87/2325
carriage by sea, 87/291, 3380
commencement of time, 87/2328, 2330
excise licence, 87/2331
extension of time, 87/128, 2332, 3380
"fundamental breach" cases, 87/3380
maritime collision, 87/2332
negligent settling of document, 87/2333
new claim, 87/2334
personal injuries, 87/2335, 2336
time bar, 87/291, 2337
Literary and Scientific Institutions, 87/2338–2342
libraries, 87/2338
library authorities, 87/29, 2364
museums, 87/2341
National Library of Wales, 87/2342
Local Government, 87/2343–2392
allowances to members, 87/2345
armorial bearings, 87/2346

Local Government—*cont.*
block grants, 87/2347
boundaries, 87/2348
committee members, 87/2389
communities, 87/2350
direct labour organisations, 87/2351
education committee, 87/2369
electoral divisions, 87/2354
exclusion from premises, 87/36
finance, 87/2357
Fire Safety and Safety of Places of Sport Act 1987 (c.27), 87/3145
gipsies. *See* **Caravans and Mobile Homes**
grants,
housing improvements, 87/2359
homeless persons, 87/2358
housing benefit, administration of, 87/2344
Housing (Scotland) Act 1987 (c.26), 87/1891
housing transfers, 87/2361
inner urban areas, 87/2362
library authorities,
powers, 87/29
"Spycatcher, 87/2364
Local Government Act 1987 (c.44), 87/2371
Local Government Finance Act 1987 (c.6), 87/2372
negligent survey, 87/2587
parish trustees, 87/2374
prescribed expenditure, 87/2377
public meeting, 87/2378
publicity account, 87/2379
Rate Support Grants Act 1987 (c.5), 87/2380
rates, 87/2381
recreation grounds, 87/2382
refuse collection, 87/2383, 3153
Registered Establishments (Scotland) Act 1987 (c.40), 87/2384
rent increase, 87/2385
reorganisation, 87/2386
residuary bodies, 87/2387
sale of land,
duty of authority, 87/2352
school places, 87/2388
severance scheme, 87/2373
sex shop, 87/2317–2319
statutory repairing obligations, 87/2236–2238
superannuation, 87/2368
Local Government Act 1987 (c.44), 87/2371
Local Government Finance Act 1987 (c.6), 87/2372
London, 87/2393–2396
London government reorganisation, 87/2393
Port of London Authority, 87/2394
taxicabs, 87/2395
transport, 87/2396
Lotteries. *See* **Gaming and Wagering**

Magisterial Law *See* **Criminal Evidence and Procedure**
Manslaughter
corporate body, 87/793
self-defence, 87/794
Mareva Injunctions
application to set aside, 87/3062
discharge, 87/137, 3063, 3067
disclosure, 87/3064, 3067, 3068
disposal of assets, 87/2997
existing cause of action, 87/3066
expenses, 87/3065
jurisdiction, 87/3014
Mareva Injunctions—*cont.*
third party rights, 87/3069
undisclosed assets abroad, 87/3070
variation, 87/3071
Markets and Fairs. *See* **Shops, Markets and Fairs**
Matrimonial Injunctions
non-molestation, 87/900, 1778, 2924, 2926, 2927, 2933
ouster order, 87/1773, 1775–1780, 2889
Medicine, 87/2397–2418
abortion, 87/2397, 2426
dentists, 87/2400, 2401
drugs,
importation, 87/3750
drugs and medicinal products, 87/2404
family practitioner committee,
complaint by officer, 87/2409
fees, 87/2405
General Medical Council, 87/2406
general sale list, 87/2407
IVF treatment, 87/2415
licences, 87/2408
medical negligence. *See* **Negligence**
opticians, 87/2410
pharmaceutical qualifications, 87/2411
pharmaceutical rules, 87/2412
pharmacies, 87/2413
professional conduct committee, 87/2417
professional misconduct,
dentists, 87/2400
duplicity of charge, 87/2399
registered homes, 87/2414
safety, 87/2416
veterinary drugs, 87/2418
Mental Health, 87/2419–2426
abortion, 87/2426
deportation, Secretary of State's powers, 87/1947
mental defective, definition, 87/2421
mental health tribunal, powers of, 87/48
notification, 87/2422
review tribunal,
powers, 87/2425
treatment, 87/2420
Mining Law, 87/2427–2431
coal industry, 87/2427
Coal Industry Act 1987 (c.3), 87/2428
opencast coal, 87/2431
subsidence, compensation for, 87/2429
union,
duty to consult, 87/2430
Ministry of Defence Police Act 1987 (c.4), 87/2860
Minors, 87/2432–2536
access,
adjournment of proceedings, 87/2434
after non-accidental injuries to child, 87/2435
leave to appeal, 87/2438
mother's application, 87/2477
natural parent,
adoption, 87/2441
putative father, 87/2485
sexual molestation by father, 87/2433, 2439
termination, 87/2437
to two of three children, 87/2432
travel expenses, 87/3506
welfare report, 87/2440
adoption. *See* **Adoption**
assumption of parental rights by local authority, 87/2455

Minors—*cont.*
care proceedings,
conduct during pregnancy, 87/2456
contested by parent,
right to see report, 87/2466
interim order, 87/2458, 2459, 2462
judicial review, 87/9, 2460
procedure, 87/2464
report of guardian *ad litem*, 87/2465, 2466
right of appeal, 87/2463
wardship summons taken out, 87/2457
welfare reports, 87/2461
child abduction, 87/765, 2467
child abduction and custody, 87/2469
child abuse, 87/2470–2476
children in care,
contribution notice, 87/2478
cultural considerations, 87/2481
parental rights, 87/1916
custodianship, 87/2449
custody,
appeals, 87/2486, 2891
appellate court, function of, 87/2490
borderline case, 87/2490, 2491
conflict of evidence, 87/2493
fresh evidence, 87/2486, 2494
interim order, 87/2497
joint custody, 87/2503
judge's decision,
interference with, 87/2496
justices' reasons, 87/2498
leave to take on holiday, 87/2495
putative father, 87/2485
removal from jurisdiction, 87/2487, 2492
variation of order, 87/2488, 2489
welfare reports, 87/2488, 2497, 2499
detention by police, 87/2500
foetus, 87/2501
fostering scheme, 87/2502
juvenile court,
attendance by minor, 87/2458
maintenance, 87/2504, 2505
medical treatment, consent to, 87/2483
paternity, 87/1675, 2509, 2510
periodical payments, 87/3008
removal from jurisdiction, 87/2536
removal from parents, 87/2512
surrogacy, 87/2513
Wardship. *See* **Wardship**
Minors' Contracts Act 1987 (c.13), 87/442
Mobile Homes. *See* **Caravans and Mobile Homes**
Mortgages, 87/2537–2544
charging order, 87/2537
defective house, 87/2587
negligent mortgage valuation, 87/2586
overriding interest, 87/2540
possession order,
suspension pending counterclaim, 87/2541
priority, 87/2542
registration of charges, 87/361
undue influence, 87/2544
Motor Cycle Noise Act 1987 (c.34), 87/3292
Murder
duress, 87/800
incitement, 87/800
intent, 87/802
joint enterprise, 87/801
mens rea, 87/802
provocation, 87/799, 803
self-defence, 87/824, 825

National Health, 87/2545–2559
AIDS (Control) Act 1987 (c.33), 87/2545
dentists, 87/2547
disablement services authority, 87/2548
health authorities, 87/2549
health education authority, 87/2550
medical and pharmaceutical services, 87/2551
National Health Service, 87/2552
nurses, midwives and health visitors, 87/2554
resources,
allocation, 87/2546
special hospital boards, 87/2557
superannuation regulations, 87/2558
transferred staff, 87/2559
Natural Justice. *See* **Administrative Law**
Negligence, 87/2560–2621
asbestos exposure, 87/2562
causation, 87/2564
cause of accident,
assumption of behaviour, 87/2565
contributory negligence,
claim in contract and tort, 87/2567
industrial accident, 87/2568
liability, 87/2566
Crown immunity,
nuclear weapons testing, 87/2569
defective equipment, 87/1307
drugs recommended by hospital, 87/1677
duty of care,
adjudication officer, 87/3466
architects, 87/229, 2573
auditors, 87/318
bailee, 87/184
bankers, 87/198, 2576
barrister, 87/2563
building contractors, 87/3582
car passenger, 87/2578
economic loss, 87/2588
employer, 87/2562, 2579, 2595
estate agent, 87/2596
ice-hockey, 87/2571
insurers, 87/2052
litigants, 87/2582
local authority, 87/241, 242, 2584–2587, 3153
master of ship, 87/2613
pedestrian, 87/2589
police, 87/2857
solicitors, 87/3549, 3551
statutory authority, 87/2591
test, 87/2580
water authority, 87/3866
foreseeability, 87/2597
human error, 87/2598
liability,
absolute, 87/2560
construction of contract, 87/423, 424
disclaimers, 87/2620
medical negligence,
duty to inform, 87/2603
loss of chance of recovery, 87/2604
standard of care, 87/2601, 2605
sterilisation, 87/2601, 2606
nervous shock, 87/2608
occupiers' liability, 87/2609–2612
personal injury, 87/2613
rescue principle, 87/2614
safe system of work, 87/2615
statutory duty,
further and better particulars, 87/3072
statutory undertaker, 87/2618
sterilisation operation, 87/2619
vicarious liability, 87/2621

Northern Ireland, 87/2622–2755
administrative law, 87/2622, 2622a, 2623, 2724, 2725
agency, 87/2626, 2627
agriculture, 2628, 2629, 2629a, 2680
animals, 87/2631
bankruptcy, 87/2632
building and construction, 87/2633–2636a
charities, 87/2637
clubs and associations, 87/2638, 2639
company law, 87/2640, 2641
compulsory purchase, 87/2642–2643
contract, 87/2644
criminal evidence and procedure, 87/2645–2648
criminal law, 87/2648a–2654
criminal sentencing, 87/2655
customs and excise, 87/1117, 2656
easements and prescription, 87/2658
education, 87/2659–2661
election law, 87/2662
electricity, 87/2663, 2664
emergency laws, 87/2665, 2666
employment, 87/2623, 2667–2672
evidence (civil), 87/2673
executors and administrators, 87/2674
fire service, 87/2675
fish and fisheries, 87/2676
food and drugs, 87/2677
gaming and wagering, 87/2678
health and safety at work, 87/2679, 2680
housing, 87/2681
inheritance tax, 87/2682
juries, 87/2683
landlord and tenant, 87/2684–2697a
legal aid, 87/2698
licensing, 87/2699, 2700
limitation of actions, 87/2701
local government, 87/2702–2705
medicine, 87/2706, 2707
minors, 87/2708
national health, 87/2709
negligence, 87/2709a–2712
Northern Ireland Act 1974, 87/2713
Northern Ireland (Emergency Provisions) Act 1987 (c.30), 87/2713a
pensions and superannuation, 87/2714
petroleum, 87/2715
police, 87/2716–2718
practice, 87/2719–2723
prisons, 87/2724–2726
public health, 87/2727
rating and valuation, 87/2728–2733
revenue and finance, 87/2734–2737
road traffic, 87/2738
sale of goods, 87/2739, 2740
social security, 87/2741, 2741a
tort, 87/2742–2744
town and country planning, 87/2745–2747
trade and industry, 87/2748, 2749
transport, 87/2750, 2751
water and waterworks, 87/2752, 2753
weights and measures, 87/2754
wills and succession, 87/2755
Northern Ireland (Emergency Provisions) Act 1987 (c.30), 87/2713a
Nuisance, 87/2756–2759a
building noise, 87/2756
recurrence of nuisance,
prohibition on, 87/2757
statutory nuisance,
"person aggrieved," 87/2758
water, 87/2759a

Obstruction of Highway
reasonable user, 87/805
stall operator, 87/804
Offensive Weapon
armed, meaning of, 87/812
offensive *per se*, 87/811, 813
truncheon, 87/811
Official Secrets
employment "under", 87/814
implied authorisation, 87/815

Parliament, 87/2760–2766
disqualification, 87/2760
House of Commons Members' Fund, 87/2761
Lord Chancellor's salary, 87/2762
Parliamentary and other Pensions Act 1987 (c.45), 87/2764
salaries, 87/2766
Parliamentary and Health Service Commissioners Act 1987 (c.39), 87/44
Parliamentary and other Pensions Act 1987 (c.45), 87/2764
Partnership, 87/2767–2768
assets, 87/2767
guarantee, 87/1845
solicitors, 87/2768
Patents and Designs, 87/2769–2815
amendment, 87/2769–2771
application,
amendment, 87/2772
divisional application, 87/2774
international application, 87/2775, 2776
irregularity, 87/2777, 2778
micro-organism, 87/2773, 2779
novelty, 87/2780
privilege, 87/2781
publication of, 87/2782, 2783
breach of confidence, 87/1669
compulsory licence, 87/2785
designs,
rules, 87/2787
infringement,
discovery, 87/2986
Euro-defence, 87/2791
inquiry as to damages, 87/2792
patent validity, 87/2799
practice, 87/2794–2797
registered design, 87/2786, 2798
stay of proceedings, 87/2793
invention, 87/2779
licences of right, 87/2800–2806
micro-organism, 87/2773, 2779
novelty, 87/2780
passing-off,
shape of container, 87/2807
patent agent's privilege, 87/2810
patent agents,
costs, 87/2960
patents,
fees, 87/2789
rules, 87/2809
procedure, 87/2811
restoration, 87/2788, 2812
revocation, 87/2813, 2814
semi conductor products, 87/1630
Pensions and Superannuation, 87/2816–2845
abatement of benefit, 87/2816
armed forces, 87/2817
children's pensions, 87/2820
civil service,
overwork, 87/2821

Pensions and Superannuation—*cont.*
company pension scheme,
variation, 87/2822
consequential provisions, 87/2823
contracting-out, 87/2824
firemen's pension scheme, 87/1793
incentive payments, 87/2826
increases, 87/2834
judicial offices, 87/2827
judicial pensions, 87/2828
liability, measure of, 87/2819
local government, 87/2829
Ministry of Defence Police Act 1987 (c.4), 87/2860
modification of enactments, 87/2830
National Health Service, 87/2831
occupational schemes, 87/2832
personal injuries, 87/2835
personal schemes, 87/2836
pilots' national pension fund, 87/3419
police, 87/2838
protected rights, 87/2839
social security contributions, 87/2840
state scheme premiums, 87/2841
strike,
effect on pensions, 87/2833
superannuation,
concurrent and sequential employments, 87/2368
superannuation scheme,
sex discrimination, 87/1374
voluntary contributions, 87/2844
war pensions, 87/2845
Petroleum, 87/2846–2851
foreign fields, 87/2846
on-shore drilling, 87/2847
Petroleum Act 1987 (c.12), 87/2848
petroleum revenue tax, 87/3225, 3226
Petroleum Act 1987 (c.12), 87/2848
Pilotage Act 1987 (c.21), 87/3420
Planning Law. *See* **Town and Country Planning**
Police, 87/2852–2871
annual report, 87/2852
assistance to one force by another, 87/2853
cadets, 87/2854
complaints procedure, 87/2862
detention,
of minor, 87/2500
disciplinary proceedings, 87/34
duty of care, 87/2857
injury benefit, 87/2859
Ministry of Defence Police Act 1987 (c.4), 87/2860
motor insurance, 87/2065
pay, 87/2861
pensions, 87/2838
Police and Criminal Evidence Act 1984, 87/833
police federation, 87/2863
powers,
search of premises, 87/706, 707
probationer, 87/40
regulations, 87/2867
research programme, 87/786
riot equipment, 87/2868
special police services, 87/2869
Practice—(Civil), 87/2872–3137
adjournment, 87/2872, 2873, 2964
admiralty practice. *See* **Shipping and Marine Insurance**
admission of liability, 87/2878
affidavit,
power of attorney, 87/67

Practice—(Civil)—*cont.*
amendment, 87/2882
Anton Piller order. *See* **Anton Piller**
appeal,
academic point of law, 87/2886
applications under different statutes, 87/2889
child cases, 87/2890, 2891
ex parte application, 87/2894
fresh evidence, 87/2895
grounds, 87/2898
issue not affecting outcome, 87/2892
leave, 87/3057
legal aid applications in child cases, 87/2890
opposed ex parte motion, 87/3074
setting down, 87/2888
time estimates, 87/2899
to Court of Appeal, 87/2887, 2888
to Employment Appeal Tribunal, 87/1317
transcripts, 87/2901
arbitration,
application for rescission of, 87/2908
bail,
judicial review proceedings, 87/2909, 3051
Bullock order, 87/456
burden of proof, 87/2915
charging order, 87/2537, 2917, 2919
Commercial Court,
transfer of action, 87/3113
confidential documents, 87/2922
contempt. *See* **Contempt**
costs. *See* **Costs**
county courts,
adjournment, 87/2964
costs. *See* **Costs**
defence of tender, 87/2967
fixed date for trial, 87/2968
forms, 87/2969
funds, 87/2970
injunction, 87/2963
rules, 87/2971
transfer of proceedings, 87/3116
Court of Appeal
annual review, 87/2973
jurisdiction, 87/631
timetables, 87/2974
Court of Appeal decision
without reference to EEC directive, 87/3084
Crown practice,
fees, 87/2981
damages enquiry, 87/2944
debt enforcement, 87/2263
Debtors (Scotland) Act 1987 (c.18), 87/2983
declaratory judgment,
hypothetical question, 87/2984
delay, 87/2985
discovery. *See* **Discovery and Inspection**
divorce, validity of, 87/2998
documents,
bundle of, 87/3000
production of, 87/3001
use of, 87/2891
evidence. *See* **Evidence (Civil)**
execution, 87/3002–3005
expert evidence, 87/3006
expert witness, 87/2946
fees,
barrister, 87/3010
foreign judgments, 87/3011
forum conveniens, 87/3012
further particulars,
breach of statutory duty, 87/3072

Practice—(Civil)—*cont.*
garnishee, 87/3013, 3014
global settlement, 87/3056
injunctions. *See* **Injunctions**
interest claim, 87/3028
interim payment, 87/2982, 3029
joinder of parties, 87/3042
judges, 87/3043
judgment, availability of, 87/3047
judgment in default, 87/3044, 3045
wrongly signed, 87/3046
judicial review. *See* **Judicial Review**
jury trial, 87/3119
lands tribunal, 87/2429
leave to defend,
conditional leave, 87/3058
improbable defence, 87/3016
legal professional privilege, 87/3059, 3060
limitation period. *See* **Limitation of Actions**
magisterial law,
domestic proceedings, 87/3061
note of judgment, 87/2880
offshore activities, jurisdiction, 87/3349
parties to proceedings, 87/3078
patents court,
procedure, 87/2811
payment in,
application for withdrawal, 87/2902
pleadings, 87/3081, 3082
practice direction,
Administration of Justice Act 1985, 87/2906
Admiralty and Commercial Court Registry, 87/2875
affidavits, filing, 87/2881
appeals from reported judgments, 87/3048
bail, failure to surrender to custody, 87/2910
documentation, appeals, 87/2900
periodical payments, children, 87/3008
remuneration of nautical and other assessors, 87/2877
service out of the jurisdiction, 87/3134
summons, 87/2916, 2972
transfer of business, 87/3118
trial out of London, 87/3120
Variation of Trusts Act 1958, 87/2907
wards, disclosure of evidence, 87/3009
practice note,
bankruptcy, 87/2912–2914
Commercial Court,
interlocutory proceedings, 87/2921
Crown office list, 87/2979–2980
list of forthcoming appeals, 87/2976
long vacation, 87/2977
solicitors' fixed costs, 87/2978
privileged documents, use of, 87/3086
probate rules, 87/3087
prohibitory order, 87/3077
Public Trust Office, 87/3088
relator actions, 87/3089
Rules of the Supreme Court, 87/3090
R.S.C., Ord. 14, 87/244, 3075
R.S.C., Ord. 59, 87/2901
ruling of law,
subsequent retrial, 87/3091
settlement of action, 87/3092
slip rule, 87/3093
stay, 87/3046, 3095–3099, 3102, 3103
striking out, 87/2113, 2903, 2904, 2920, 3466
summary judgment, 87/2911, 3100–3103
Supreme Court Procedure Committee, 87/3104, 3105
third party claim, 87/3587

Practice—(Civil)—*cont.*
time limit,
court's discretions, 87/3108
property adjustment order, 87/1785
transfer of action, 87/3109–3118
unincorporated associations, 87/3121
warned list, 87/3122
writ,
extension to validity, 87/3124–3126
fieri facias, 87/3004
ne exeat regno, 87/1748, 3137
renewal, 87/3127, 3128
service by post, 87/3129
service out of the jurisdiction, 87/3130–3135
Prescription (Scotland) Act 1987 (c.36), 87/352
Prisons, 87/3138–3144
annual report, 87/3138
false allegations, 87/3139
Parole Board, 87/3141
prisoners' rights, 87/6, 28
research programme, 87/786
rules, 87/3143
state and use, 87/3144
Prostitution
brothel, management of, 87/792
Protection of Animals (Penalties) Act 1987 (c.35), 87/113
Public Entertainments and Recreation, 87/3134–3148
Fire Safety and Safety of Places of Sport Act 1987 (c.27), 87/3145
sports grounds, 87/3147
video games, 87/2310
Public Health, 87/3149–3155
clean air, 87/3149
noise,
construction and open sites, 87/3151
lawnmowers, 87/3152
pollution, 87/3150
refuse, 87/3153, 3154
sewers, 87/3867

Race Relations
application for job, 87/1350, 1351
breach of trust and confidence, 87/1348
Commission for Racial Equality, 87/1909
language, 87/1353
"national origins," meaning of, 87/3203
offshore employment, 87/1347
research programme, 87/786
summary of applicants, 87/1352
vicarious liability of employer, 87/1349
Railways. *See* **Transport**
Rate Support Grants Act 1987 (c.5), 87/2380
Rating and Valuation, 87/3156–3198
Abolition of Domestic Rates Etc. (Scotland) Act 1987 (c.47), 87/3156
agricultural de-rating, 87/3157
agricultural land, 87/3192
building used for two purposes, 87/3158
capitalisation rate, 87/3193
completion notice, 87/3194
duty to make rate, 87/3159, 3162
enterprise zone, 87/3185
lands tribunal decisions,
boarding house, 87/3176
caravan, 87/3177
central heating system, 87/3164, 3167
Hells Angels club next door, 87/3170
holiday mobile home, 87/3166
maisonette, 87/3178

Rating and Valuation—*cont.*
lands tribunal decisions—*cont.*
miniature railway, 87/3179
neighbouring building works, 87/3173
new building on existing site, 87/3171
noise nuisance, 87/3169, 3174
office block, 87/3167
proposal, validity of, 87/3163
public park premises, 87/3172
two separate hereditaments, 87/3168
uninhabitable property, 87/3175
warehouse, 87/3165
leasehold enfranchisement, 87/3180
listed building, 87/3195
matrimonial home,
rateable occupation, 87/3181
separation of parties, 87/1765
plant and machinery, 87/3184
quantum reduction, 87/3161
rate alteration, 87/3185
rate limitation, 87/3186
rate rebate,
special school, 87/3187
rate support grant, 87/3189, 3190
reduction or remission of rates, 87/3191
repayment of rates, 87/3188
unoccupied hereditament, 87/3194–3196
valuation lists, 87/3197
water rates, 87/3198
Real Property and Conveyancing. *See* **Conveyancing**
Receivers
documents, ownership of, 87/355
"fixed plant and machinery", 87/356
liability, 87/357
powers and liability, 87/358
rent,
priority of assignment, 87/354
Recognition of Trusts Act 1987 (c.14), 87/1433
Redundancy
consultation with union, 87/1357
continuous employment, 87/1354, 1355
definition, 87/1356
dismissal, 87/1357, 1362
pregnant employee, 87/1358, 1409
protective award, 87/1359
redundancy payments,
rebate, 87/1363, 1364
repeated short-term contracts, 87/1354
statutory presumption, 87/1360
Register of Sasines (Scotland) Act 1987 (c.23), 87/482
Registered Establishments (Scotland) Act 1987 (c.40), 87/2384
Registration of Births, Deaths and Marriages, 87/3199–3204
fees, 87/3199
public record office, 87/3200
rectification of register, 87/537
regulations, 87/3202
request for passport, 87/3203
Welsh language, regulations, 87/3204
Restrictive Covenants
discharge of restriction, 87/3713
modification, 87/485, 3714, 3715
Revenue and Finance, 87/3205–3226
Appropriation Act 1987 (c.17), 87/3205
Appropriation (No. 2) Act 1987 (c.50), 87/3206
company resident in U.K., 87/1479
Consolidated Fund Act 1987 (c.8), 87/3208
Consolidated Fund (No. 2) Act 1987 (c.54), 87/3209
Revenue and Finance—*cont.*
Consolidated Fund (No. 3) Act 1987 (c.55), 87/3210
Finance Act 1987 (c.16), 87/3211
Finance (No. 2) Act 1987 (c.51), 87/3212
financial services, 87/3213–3219
judicial review. *See* **Judicial Review**
jurisdiction of Special Commissioner, 87/3221
misapplication of statute, 87/3222
national debt, 87/3223
penalty awards, 87/3224
petroleum revenue tax, 87/3225, 3226
Reverter of Sites Act 1987 (c.15), 87/1435
Road Traffic, 87/3227–3311
accidents,
payments for treatment, 87/3227
alcohol level,
certificate,
admissibility, 87/647
automatism, 87/3266
blood specimen, 87/558, 3229–3239
breath test,
breath specimen,
admissibility, 87/572, 3240–3242
choice of providing blood to replace, 87/3244
failure to provide, 87/3245–3250
multiple breath test, 87/3252
statistics, 87/3251
breathalyser cases, 87/3253
car tax, 87/3254
carriage by road. *See* **Carriers**
construction and use, 87/3256
Crown roads, 87/3257
dangerous vehicle, 87/3258
disqualification,
effective date, 87/3259
exceptional hardship, 87/3260
length, 87/3283
special reasons, 87/3261, 3262
drivers,
hours, 87/3264
identity of, 87/3268
driving licences, 87/3265
drunk in charge,
and failure to provide specimen, 87/3267
endorsement, 87/3284, 3285, 3306
excess alcohol,
aiders and abettors, 87/752
back calculation, 87/3269
excise licence, 87/2331, 3272, 3274
failing to report an accident, 87/3275
goods vehicles, 87/3276
increased penalties, 87/3277
information, 87/3278
intoximeter,
printout,
guilty plea, 87/3282
reliability, 87/3279–3281
voluntary option scheme, 87/3270
lighting,
slow-moving vehicles, 87/3287
marking of special weights, 87/3288
mechanically propelled vehicle, 87/3289
mobile crane, 87/3290
Motor Cycle Noise Act 1987 (c.34), 87/3292
motor cycles, 87/3291, 3293
motor insurance. *See* **Insurance**
motor vehicle,
meaning, 87/3295
special types, authorisation of, 87/3296
tests, 87/3297

Road traffic—*cont.*
motorway inquiry, 87/3653
motorway traffic, 87/3306
parking, 87/3298
pedestrian crossings, 87/3299
prescribed routes, 87/3300
previous convictions, 87/3284
public passenger vehicles, 87/3301
public service vehicle, 87/3302
reckless driving, 87/3303
recovery vehicles, 87/3304
seat belts, 87/3305
tachograph, 87/3307, 3308
traffic signs, 87/3309
type approval, 87/3310
urine specimen, 87/3311

Sale of Goods, 87/3312–3346
agreement for sale, 87/3312
consumer protection. *See* **Consumer Protection**
contract for sale, 87/3324
damage, remoteness of, 87/3341
default by buyer, 87/3325
export certificate, 87/3326
fireworks, supply of, 87/836
food, 87/1814, 1815, 1818
f.o.b. contract, 87/3328–3330
hire purchase. *See* **Hire Purchase**
international sales, 87/3334
manufacturer's instructions, 87/3327
merchantable quality, 87/3333, 3335–3338
non-fulfilment, 87/3339
price marking, 87/3340
rejection,
purported, 87/3329
rescission,
new car, 87/3335
safety of product, 87/3321
samples, 87/3331
title, 87/3312, 3345
trade descriptions. *See* **Criminal Law**
Savings Banks
ordinary deposits, 87/205
Scottish Development Agency Act 1987 (c.56), 87/3738
Sea and Seashore, 87/3347–3357
continental shelf, 87/3347
Food and Environment Protection Act 1985, 87/3348
offshore activities,
civil jurisdiction, 87/3349
offshore activities,
criminal jurisdiction, 87/3350
offshore installations, 87/3351
revocation, 87/3352
safety, 87/3353
territorial sea, 87/3355
Territorial Sea Act 1987 (c.49), 87/3356
Sentencing. *See* **Criminal Sentencing**
Settlements. See **Equity and Trusts**
Sex Discrimination
admissibility of evidence, 87/1336
equal pay. *See* **Employment**
grants, 87/1259
occupational pensions, 87/1633
offshore employment, 87/1368
part-time worker, 87/1633
retirement age, 87/1370, 1371. 1637
school places, 87/2388
social security benefits, 87/1635, 1636

Sex Discrimination—*cont.*
superannuation scheme, 87/1374
treatment,
on ground of sex, 87/1373
victimisation, 87/1372
Shipping and Marine Insurance, 87/3358–3447
admiralty jurisdiction,
Gibraltar, 87/3359
admiralty practice,
action *in rem*, 87/3360, 3361, 3370
Admiralty and Commercial Court Registry, 87/2875
arrest of vessel, 87/3362–3364, 3368, 3369
remuneration of nautical and other assessors, 87/2877
salvage, 87/3427, 3428
salvage arbitration, 87/3367
stay of action, 87/3365, 3368
bailee clause, 87/3371
bill of lading, 87/3372
booking note, 87/3347
British Shipbuilders (Borrowing Powers) Act 1987 (c.52), 87/3729
cargo,
damage, 87/3376
inseparable mixing of, 87/3417
carriage by sea. *See* **Carriers**
Channel Island ferry services, 87/422
charterparty. *See* **Charterparty**
collision, 87/2332, 3388–3396
demurrage. *See* **Charterparty**
empty hatch, 87/3400
"entered at customs house," 87/3401
fees, 87/3402
harbours and docks, 87/3403
hovercraft, 87/3404
indemnity of shipowner, 87/3372
marine insurance,
bond guarantee, 87/3373
fire, loss by, 87/3411
leading underwriter clause, 87/3406
peril of the seas, 87/3408, 3410
procured loss, 87/3434
reinsurance premium, 87/3422
two causes of loss, 87/3409
warranty,
absence of other insurance, 87/3412
merchant shipping, 87/3414
navigation, 87/3418
notice of readiness, 87/3405
pilotage, 87/3419
Pilotage Act 1987 (c.21), 87/3420
pollution,
control of, 87/3398
sale of ship, 87/3424–3426
salvage,
derelict, 87/3427
non-tidal waters, 87/3428
ship operators,
liability, 87/2615
Shops, Markets and Fairs, 87/3448–3450
airport shops, 87/3448
sex shop, 87/2317–2319
Sunday trading, 87/3449–3450
Social Fund (Maternity and Funeral Expenses) Act 1987 (c.7), 87/3500
Social Security, 87/3451–3544
adjudication, 87/3451
adjudication officer,
duty of care, 87/3466
attendance allowance, 87/3452–3454

Social Security—*cont.*
Australia, 87/3455
Austria, 87/3456
child benefit, 87/3459
claims and payments, 87/3460
commissioners, 87/3461
contributions, 87/3463
credits, 87/3464
deaths, notification of, 87/3494
dependency, 87/3465
earnings,
computation of, 87/3462
earnings factor, 87/3467
family credit, 87/3468
family income supplement,
computation, 87/3469
partner on maternity leave, 87/3470, 3471
regulations, 87/3469
hospitals, 87/3472
housing benefit, 87/1884–1889
income support, 87/3475
industrial death benefit, 87/3476
industrial disablement benefit, 87/3477
industrial injuries benefit, 87/3478, 3479
invalid care allowance, 87/3480
invalidity benefit, 87/3481–3483
maternity and funeral expenses, 87/3484
maternity grant, 87/3485
maternity pay. *See* **Employment**
medical evidence, 87/3487
mobility allowance, 87/3488–3491
national assistance, 87/3492
national insurance, 87/3493
overlapping benefits, 87/1641
overpayment, 87/3495
pensioners' lump sum payments, 87/3496
Portugal, 87/3498
sex discrimination. *See* **Sex Discrimination**
sick pay. *See* **Employment**
sickness benefit, 87/3499
Social Fund (Maternity and Funeral Expenses) Act 1987 (c.7), 87/3500
supplementary benefit,
additional requirements, 87/3502–3505
conditions of entitlement, 87/3507
"exceptional need", 87/3506
housing requirements, 87/3508, 3509
normal requirements, 87/3510
"person", 87/3512
requirements, 87/3513
requirements and resources, 87/3514
resources, 87/3515–3522
Secretary of State, powers of, 87/3511
single payments, 87/3523–3529
uprating regulations, 87/3530
urgent cases, 87/3531
treasury supplement, 87/3532
unemployment benefit,
entitlement, 87/3537
failure to claim, 87/3534
full extent normal, 87/3533, 3535, 3536
supply teacher, 87/3538
trade dispute, 87/3539, 3540
unemployment, sickness and invalidity benefit, 87/3541
up-rating regulations, 87/3542
widow's benefit, 87/3543
workmen's compensation. *See* **Workmen's Compensation**
Solicitors, 87/3545–3562
articles of clerkship, 87/1301
clients' money, 87/3545
Solicitors—*cont.*
conflict of interests, 87/3550
costs. *See* **Costs**
dispute within partnership, 87/2768
duty of care, 87/3551
testator's solicitors, 87/3549
fiduciary duty, 87/3552, 3553
Lay Observer, 87/3554
negligence, 87/3555–3557
office open to public, 87/3558
purchase,
insurance policy, 87/3559
summary jurisdiction over solicitors, 87/3560
undertaking,
capacity in which given, 87/3561
impossibility of performance, 87/3562
negligence, 87/3557
to retain funds, 87/3560
Stamp Duties, 87/3563–3565
evasion, 87/1826
exempt instruments, 87/3564
reserve tax, 87/3565
Statutes and Orders, 87/3566–3568
regulation,
validity, 87/3567
Royal Assents, 87/3568
Stock Exchange, 87/3569–3570
gilt-edged securities, 87/3569
multiple share applications, 87/826
Succession
See **Wills and Succession**
Supplementary Benefit. *See* **Social Security**

Teachers' Pay and Conditions Act 1987 (c.1), 87/1273
Telecommunications, 87/3571–3579
broadcasting,
IBA, 87/3573
Broadcasting Act 1981, 87/3571
Broadcasting Act 1987 (c.10), 87/3572
public telecommunication system, 87/3575
radio station,
apparatus, 87/3579
television licences, 87/3577
wireless telegraphy, 87/3578, 3579
Territorial Sea Act 1987 (c.49), 87/3356
Theft
acceptance of valuable security, 87/837
as alternative to handling, 87/842
charity collection, 87/841
chose in action, 87/776
director of company, 87/838
going equipped, 87/839
making off without payment, 87/840
obtaining pecuniary advantage, 87/808
obtaining property by deception, 87/701, 806, 807, 809, 810
robbery, 87/823
standard of proof, 87/741
Tort, 87/3580–3593
building contractor,
duty to supervise sub-contractor, 87/3582
Consumer Protection Act 1987 (c.43), 87/3583
conversion,
liquidator, 87/3585
Crown immunity, 87/2569
defamation. *See* **Libel and Slander**
economic loss, 87/3587
false imprisonment, 87/3588
harassment, 87/3590
interference with trade or business, 87/3769

Tort—*cont.*
negligence. *See* **Negligence**
trespass. *See* **Trespass**
vicarious liability, 87/1316, 1367, 2615
water abstraction, 87/3593
Town and Country Planning, 87/3594–3728
advertisements, 87/3594
advertising balloon, 87/3595
appeals, 87/3596, 3597
blight notice, 87/3598
British Coal Corporation, 87/3599
clearance areas, 87/3600
development, 87/3601
Development Land Tax, 87/307, 3602
enforcement notice,
agricultural occupancy condition, 87/3630
ambiguity, 87/3604
ancillary use, 87/3636
appeal,
procedure, 87/3605, 3606
breach of condition, 87/3607–3609
caravan site, 87/3609a
caravans, removal of, 87/3629
change of use, 87/3610, 3611
correction, 87/3613, 3624
deferred sentence, 87/927
discontinuance of user, 87/3612
established use, 87/3614
existing use rights, 87/3615, 3623
farm unit, 87/3616
grain silos, 87/3617
lack of precision in permission, 87/3618
local authority resolution, 87/3619
material change of use, 87/3620–3622
prosecution, 87/3626
public house garden, 87/3628
retail warehouse, 87/3631
riverside moorings, 87/3632
timbers of listed building, 87/3633
unspecified land, 87/3634
varied on appeal, 87/3635
warehouse, 87/3609
weekly street market, 87/3607
workshop and showroom, 87/3625
enforcement proceedings, 87/3637
established use certificate, 87/3638
fees, 87/3639
General Development Order, 87/3640
gipsy encampments, *See* **Caravans and Mobile Homes**
improvement grant, 87/3643
lamp-posts, 87/3646
listed buildings, 87/3647, 3648
local plan, 87/3649–3652
motorway inquiry, 87/3653
mutual covenants, 87/3654
new towns, 87/3655
open space,
meaning, 87/2227
planning functions, 87/3661
planning permission,
acquisition costs, 87/3692
betting office, 87/3664
change of use, 87/3665–3673
Circular 22/80, 87/3689, 3691
competing proposals, 87/3675
conditions, 87/3663, 3676
council's policy, 87/3705
extent, 87/3681
green belt, 87/3668, 3683–3685, 3693
hotel, 87/3711

Town and Country Planning—*cont.*
housing, 87/3686, 3698
inquiry, 87/3644, 3645, 3687, 3688
material consideration, 87/3690
natural justice, 87/3697
objection, 87/3694
occupancy condition, 87/3656
offices, 87/3657, 3658, 3679, 3680, 3703
opencast coal extraction, 87/3695
outline permission, 87/3660
policy Circular, 87/3696
procedure, 87/3699, 3700
quarrying operations, 87/3678, 3682, 3701
re-design of forecourt lay-out, 87/3677
refusal of application,
compensation for, 87/3674, 3678
reasons, 87/3657, 3658
residential development on agricultural land, 87/3704
reversion to pre-existing use, 87/3710
Secretary of State's decision, 87/3702, 3705, 3706
sewage treatment works, 87/3707
simplified planning zones, 87/3719
structure and local plans, 87/3722
traffic considerations, 87/3708
university building, 87/3709
workshop and showroom, 87/3625
restrictive covenants. *See* **Restrictive Covenants**
s.53 determination, 87/3716–3718
stop notice, 87/3720, 3721
Trafford Park, 87/3723
tree preservation order, 87/3724, 3725
urban development areas, 87/3726
Urban Development Corporations (Financial Limits) Act 1987 (c.57), 87/3727
use classes, 87/3728
Trade and Industry, 87/3729–3740
British Shipbuilders (Borrowing Powers) Act 1987 (c.52), 87/3729
industrial assurance, 87/3730
industrial training, 87/3731, 3732
Industry Act 1972, 87/3733
Industry Act 1980, 87/3734
monopolies and mergers, 87/3735, 3736
restraint of trade, 87/3737
Scottish Development Agency Act 1987 (c.56), 87/3738
statistics, 87/3739
unit trusts, 87/3740
Trade Marks and Trade Names, 87/3741–3758
application,
device mark, 87/3742
phonetic confusion, 87/3741
phonetic equivalence, 87/3743
scanning apparatus, 87/3744
counterfeit goods, 87/3745
fees, 87/3746
hallmarks, 87/3747
infringement, 87/3748–3751
non-use, 87/3752
passing-off,
menswear, 87/3753
rectification, 87/3754–3756
service marks, 87/3757
similarity, 87/3758
Trade Unions, 87/3759–3772
assets, 87/3759
ballot, 87/3765, 3770
certification officer, 87/3761

Trade Unions—*cont.*
consultation,
new union, 87/3762
duty to consult, 87/2430
elections,
validity of, 87/3763
industrial action, 87/2938
instruction to members,
whether *ultra vires*, 87/3767
membership,
action short of dismissal, 87/3766
individual's right, 87/3766
rules,
alteration, 87/3768
breach, 87/3760
strike action, 87/3769
strike called without ballot, 87/3765
trade dispute,
picketing, marches and demonstrations, 87/3771
unincorporated associations, 87/313
Transport, 87/3773–3793
bridges, 87/3773
bus companies, 87/3774
Channel Tunnel Act 1987 (c.53), 87/3776
competition, 87/3775
fares, 87/3777
harbours and docks. *See* **Shipping and Marine Insurance**
highways,
excavation of, 87/3778
obstruction, 87/3779
international passenger services, 87/3780
light railways, 87/3781
motorways, 87/3783
rail freight facilities, 87/3784
railway track,
"line", 87/3785
safety of passengers,
regulation breach, 87/669
special roads, 87/3787
taxi sharing scheme, 87/3788
taxis,
licences, 87/3789, 3790
Transport Act 1985, 87/3791
trunk roads, 87/3793
Trespass, 87/3794–3796
crane, 87/3794
damages, 87/1227
defences, 87/3795
rights of landowner, 87/3039

Unemployment Benefit. *See* **Social Security**
Unfair Dismissal
compensation, 87/1387, 1388, 1403
constructive dismissal,
job grading, 87/1299
continuous employment, 87/1300, 1390–1393
control of company, 87/1394
effective date of termination, 87/1390, 1396, 1397
group of employees, 87/1400
hours of employment, 87/1300
interim relief, 87/1402
joint hearing, 87/1401
lock-out, 87/1404, 1405
maternity,
rights, 87/1344
natural justice, 87/1386
pregnancy, 87/1409
procedure, 87/1398

Unfair Dismissal—*cont.*
proposal to leave trade union, 87/1406
reason not established, 87/1408
reasonableness, 87/1407
refusal to carry out duties, 87/1312
reinstatement, 87/1411
repudiatory conduct, 87/1412, 1413
restructuring, 87/1414
retirement age, 87/1415
summary dismissal, 87/1395
time limit for claim, 87/1389
transfer of undertaking, 87/1416, 1417
trial period, refusal of, 87/1410
tribunal decision,
requirements, 87/1399
Unincorporated Associations. *See* **Clubs and Associations**
Universities
visitor, 87/1275, 1276
Urban Development Corporations (Financial Limits) Act 1987 (c.57), 87/3727

Value Added Tax, 87/3797–3864
assessment, 87/3798, 3799
bad debt relief, 87/3800, 3806
betting, gaming and lotteries, 87/3801
buildings, construction of, 87/3804, 3860, 3861
cash accounting, 87/3802
charities, 87/3803
evidence, 87/3825, 3826
exemptions, 87/3809
export of goods, 87/3810, 3811
finance order, 87/3812
import of goods, 87/3813
input tax, 87/3814–3817
international services, 87/3818
partnership, 87/3819
penalty, 87/3820–3824
refund, 87/3827
registration, 87/3828–3830
limits, 87/3831
regulations, 87/3797
repayment, 87/3832
retrospective legislation, 87/3833
supply,
deemed, 87/3805
deposits, 87/3837
employees, of, 87/3841
exempt, 87/3807, 3808
for consideration, 87/3838
goods and services, 87/3842, 3843
hot food, 87/3839
in the course of a business, 87/3840
retailers, 87/3836
services, of, 87/3844–3847
time of, 87/3843, 3845, 3852
value of, 87/3842, 3856
surplus assets, 87/3806
tax avoidance, 87/3848
tax return,
overpayment, 87/3849
sent by post, 87/3834
terminal markets, 87/3850
third country traders, 87/3851
tour operators, 87/3853
transfer of business, 87/3854, 3855
zero-rating, 87/3857–3864

Wardship
appellate court, role of, 87/2527
as alternative to judicial review, 87/2518

Wardship—*cont.*
care and control, 87/2519, 2520
care proceedings,
failure to give notice, 87/2457
children in care, 87/2521–2524
confidential documents, 87/2922
Criminal Injuries Compensation Board, 87/653
disclosure of evidence, 87/3009
disclosure of records, 87/2530
foster parents, 87/2526
hearsay evidence, 87/2517
jurisdiction, 87/2528
medical experts, role of, 87/2535
notice of hearing, 87/2529
ouster proceedings heard with wardship proceedings, 87/1773
reform, 87/2278
secure accommodation, 87/2523
social worker,
jurisdiction to allocate, 87/2532
sterilisation, 87/2533
witness in criminal proceedings, 87/654
Water and Waterworks, 87/3865–3870
land drainage. *See* **Land Drainage**
riparian owners, rights of, 87/3866
sewers, 87/3867
water authorities, 87/3868
Water and Waterworks—*cont.*
water orders, 87/3869
water rates, 87/3198
Weights and Measures, 87/3871–3876
carriage of solid fuel by rails, 87/3871
local standards, 87/3872
measuring instruments, 87/3873
National Metrological Co-ordinating Unit, 87/3874
quantity marking and abbreviations of units, 87/3875
unstamped measure, 87/3876
Wills and Succession, 87/3877–3885
condition,
uncertainty, 87/3877
construction,
"relatives", 87/3878
family provision, 87/3879–3882, 3884
probate rules, 87/3883
testator's solicitors,
duty of care, 87/3549
Words and Phrases, 87/3886
Workmen's Compensation
supplementation, 87/3544
Wounding
self-defence, 87/853